# ROGET'S INTERNATIONAL THESAURUS

# PETER MARK ROGET

## (1779–1869)

PETER MARK ROGET was born January 18, 1779, in Broad (now Broadwick) Street, a few blocks from Soho Square. His father, John Roget, hailed from Geneva and was pastor of a French Protestant church in Soho. His mother, Catherine, was a sister of Sir Samuel Romilly, the renowned law reformer. Peter was but five years old when his father died; his mother moved to Edinburgh in 1793 and in that year, at fourteen, Peter entered the university there. He was graduated from the medical school at the early age of nineteen, and soon distinguished himself by research on subjects such as pulmonary consumption and the effects of laughing gas. In 1802 he started out on a continental tour with two sons of a wealthy Manchester merchant, to whom he acted as tutor. When the Peace of Amiens was breached, Roget found himself at Geneva, a prisoner-on-parole of the French (Napoleon had annexed Geneva to France a few years earlier). He gained his freedom by pleading the Genevan—and thus French—citizenship of his family, and made his way back to England late in 1803.

In 1805 he joined the medical staff of the Public Infirmary at Manchester and made a name for himself in that city by giving a series of lectures on medical subjects. In 1808, to advance his career, he moved to London. There, in 1810, he helped establish a charity clinic, the Northern Dispensary, and contributed his services to it, gratis, for eighteen years. Combining in an unusual degree exact knowledge with a power of apt and vivid presentation, he gained eminence as a lecturer on medical and other subjects, a work he continued for nearly fifty years. He was an early member of the Medical and Chirurgical Society and edited its *Transactions* for twelve years. In 1815 he became a Fellow of the Royal Society and served as its secretary for more than twenty years. He was examiner in physiology in the University of London. He wrote numerous papers on physiology and health, among them *On Animal and Vegetable Physiology* (1834), a two-volume work on phrenology (1838), and articles for several editions of the *Encyclopædia Britannica*.

These activities would be more than enough for most men, but Roget's insatiable thirst for knowledge and his appetite for work led him into many other fields. He played an important role in the establishment of the University of London; he was a founder of the Society for the Diffusion of Knowledge and wrote for it a series of popular manuals; he devised a slide rule and spent much time trying to perfect a calculating machine; he showed remarkable ingenuity in inventing and solving chess problems and designed an inexpensive pocket chessboard. In 1828, as head of a commission to study the water supply of London, he issued a report that was the first of its kind; but, even though it graphically documented the simultaneous use of the Thames for sewage disposal and drinking water, the government took no action on its sound recommendations for pollution control.

Roget retired from professional life in 1840, and about 1848 he began preparing for publication the one work that was to perpetuate his memory. This was a catalog of words organized by their meanings, the compilation of which had been an avocation since 1805. Its first printed edition, in 1852, was called *Thesaurus of English Words and Phrases Classified and Arranged so as to Facilitate the Expression of Ideas and Assist in Literary Composition.* During his lifetime the work had twenty-eight printings; after his death it was revised and expanded by his son, John Lewis Roget, and later by John's son, Samuel Romilly Roget.

Peter Mark Roget died at West Malvern on September 12, 1869, at the age of ninety.

P. M. Roget

# ROGET'S INTERNATIONAL THESAURUS™

## FOURTH EDITION

REVISED BY

## ROBERT L. CHAPMAN

*1817*

**HARPER & ROW, PUBLISHERS,** New York

Cambridge, Philadelphia, San Francisco, London,
Mexico City, São Paulo, Singapore, Sydney

ROGET'S INTERNATIONAL THESAURUS (Fourth Edition). Copyright 1911, 1922, 1930, 1932, 1936, 1938, 1939, 1946, 1950, © 1958, 1960, 1962, 1964, 1966, 1974, 1977 by Harper & Row, Publishers, Inc. All rights reserved. Printed in the United States of America. No part of this book may be used or reproduced in any manner whatsoever without written permission except in the case of brief quotations embodied in critical articles and reviews. For information address Harper & Row, Publishers, Inc., 10 East 53rd Street, New York, N.Y. 10022. Published simultaneously in Canada by Fitzhenry & Whiteside Limited, Toronto, and simultaneously in Great Britain by Harper & Row, Limited, 28 Tavistock Street, London WC2E7PN, and simultaneously in Australia and New Zealand by Harper & Row (Australasia) Pty. Limited, P.O. Box 226, Artarmon, New South Wales, 2064.

Library of Congress Cataloging in Publication Data

Main entry under title:

Roget's international thesaurus.
    Based on: Thesaurus of English words and phrases/by Peter Mark Roget.
    Includes index.
    1. English language—Synonyms and antonyms. I. Roget, Peter Mark, 1779–1869. Thesaurus of English words and phrases. II. Chapman, Robert L.
PE1591.R73   1984      423′.1    84-47562
ISBN 0-690-00010-3 (U.S.A.)    84  85  86  87  88  17  16  15  14  13  12  11
ISBN 0-690-00011-1 (indexed)
ISBN 0-06-091169-7 (pbk.)      84  85  86  87  88  10  9  8  7  6  5  4  3  2  1
ISBN 0-06-337001-8 (cloth outside U.S.A. and Canada)
ISBN 0-06-337038-7 (pbk. outside U.S.A. and Canada)

# CONTENTS

# CONTENTS

# HOW TO USE THIS BOOK

The *International* is a "true" thesaurus, compiled according to the plan devised originally by Peter Mark Roget. It has a text of about 250,000 words and phrases, arranged in categories by their meanings, and a comprehensive index.

The search for a word that you need is a simple, two-step process which begins in the index. Suppose that you want a word to describe something that is without a well-defined shape:

1. In the index, look up the word **shapeless** and pick the subentry closest to the meaning you want.

2. Follow its number into the text and you will find a whole paragraph of adjectives for things "shapeless" or "formless."

shaped made 167.22
  planned 654.13
shapeless
  abnormal 85.9
  formless 247.4
  inconstant 141.7
  obscure 549.15
  ugly 899.8
  unordered 62.12
  vague 514.18
shapely
  beautiful 900.17
  well-shaped 248.5
shape up
  be formed 246.8
  be in a state 7.6
  get better 691.7
  order 59.5
shard
  *n.* piece 55.3
  refuse 669.4
  *v.* pulverize 361.9
  show fragility 360.3
share
  *n.* allotment 816.5
  amount of stock
    834.3
  part 55.1
  *v.* apportion 816.6
  communicate 554.7
  emotionally respond
    855.12

## 247. FORMLESSNESS

.1 NOUNS **formlessness, shapelessness;** amorphousness, amorphism, amorphia; **chaos,** confusion, messiness, orderlessness; **disorder** 62; entropy; anarchy 740.2; **indeterminateness, indefiniteness,** indecisiveness, vagueness, mistiness, haziness, fuzziness, blurriness, unclearness, obscurity.

.2 unlicked cub, diamond in the rough.

.3 VERBS **deform, distort** 249.5; unform, unshape; disorder, jumble, mess up, muddle, confuse; obfuscate, obscure, fog up, blur.

.4 ADJS **formless, shapeless,** featureless, characterless, nondescript, inchoate, lumpen, blobby *or* baggy [both informal], inform; amorphous, amorphic, amorph(o)–; **chaotic, orderless,** disorderly 62.13, unordered, unorganized, confused, anarchic 740.6; kaleidoscopic; **indeterminate, indefinite,** undefined, indecisive, vague, misty, hazy, fuzzy, blurred *or* blurry, unclear, obscure.

.5 **unformed, unshaped,** unshapen, unfashioned, unlicked; uncut, unhewn.

Tracking down words in this simple fashion is the most obvious and direct use of the thesaurus. The notes that follow explain some of the broader, more subtle ways in which the unique features of the *International* will help you to solve word problems.

The thesaurus is basically a tool for transforming ideas into words. A dictionary will tell you many things about a word—spelling, pronunciation, meaning, and origins. You use a thesaurus, on the other hand, when you have an idea but do not know, or cannot remember, the word or phrase that expresses it best. You use a thesaurus also when the word that comes to mind strikes you as inadequate and you want a better one, because you know that there are always more ways than one to express an idea and that some are more effective than others. A thesaurus presents you with various possibilities and you choose the one that you think is best.

The *International*, besides being an efficient word-finder, has a structure especially designed to stimulate thought and help you to organize your ideas. The backbone of this structure is the ingenious overall arrangement of the large categories. The plan is outlined in the Synopsis of Categories, which begins on page xvii. It is not necessary to memorize this grandly methodical design; to make good use of the thesaurus all you need to remember is that it contains many sequences of closely related categories. Beginning at 448, for example, you will see HEARING, DEAFNESS, SOUND, SILENCE, FAINTNESS OF SOUND, LOUDNESS, etc., a procession of similar, contrasting, and opposing concepts, all dealing with the perception and quality of sounds. So, when you are not quite satisfied with what you find in one place, glance at nearby categories too; it may be that your original intention was not the best. If you are having trouble framing a thought in a positive way, you may find that it can be more effectively expressed negatively. Seeing related terms, and antonyms, will often open up lines of thought that had not occurred to you.

You will have already noticed that the large categories of ideas are numbered in sequence; there are 1042 of them in this edition of Roget. Within each category the terms are presented in short paragraphs and these are numbered also. References from the index to the text are made with two-part numbers such as 247.4, the first part being the number of the category, the second the number of the paragraph within that category. This system, unique to the *International*, makes for quick and easy pinpointing of the area in which you will find the words you need.

The terms within a category are organized also by part of speech, in this order: nouns, verbs, adjectives, adverbs, prepositions, conjunctions, and interjections. An occasional mixed bag of expressions at the end is labeled simply "phrases." This grouping by parts of speech is another aspect of the *International*'s usefulness. When you are casting about for a way of saying something, rather than looking for a specific word, do not limit your search to the narrow area of the category suggested by the index reference, but examine the offerings in all parts of speech.

There is a further refinement of word arrangement. The sequence of terms within a paragraph, far from being random, is determined by close relationships. The words closest in meaning are offered in clusters that are set off with semicolons; the semicolon signals a slight change in sense or application. A close examination of the groupings will make you aware of the fine distinctions between synonyms, and you will soon recognize that few words are truly interchangeable. As a help in focusing on the *right* word, terms with special uses—foreign words, slang, informal words, and technical terms—are identified by labels in brackets.

Cross references are another convenience of the text. They suggest additional meanings of the words you are examining and sometimes they will save you the trouble of looking back again to the index. Notice also that the paragraphs of text are highlighted with terms in boldface type. The bold words are those most commonly used for the idea at hand.

Combining forms, prefixes such as *geo-* ("earth," "of the earth") and suffixes such as *-lith* ("stone"), are inserted among the complete words that share their meanings. These are invaluable aids to vocabulary-building (and, incidentally, common fare in crossword puzzles).

The use of an apt quotation often livens up a formal speech or an essay. Here again, the *International* can help you, for it contains thousands of quotes on scores of subjects. Another bonus of the thesaurus is its dozens of word lists. These contain the names of specific things—animals, weapons, measurements, architectural ornaments—few of which have synonyms. The lists can save you many excursions to specialized reference books.

Thus, the *International* can help you in countless ways to improve your writing and speech and to enrich your vocabulary of useful words. But you should remember the caution that very few words are true synonyms and use the thesaurus in conjunction with a good dictionary whenever necessary.

# PUBLISHER'S PREFACE

Like all great reference books *Roget's International Thesaurus* is the product of continuous improvement and recurring investment. This process has been going on for roughly a century and three quarters, ever since 1805, when Dr. Peter Mark Roget began compiling a list of useful words for his own convenience.

However, that catalogue of words and phrases was not like others. There have been glossaries and word lists since literature began. Roget himself knew about the thousand-year-old *Amarakosha* ("treasury of Amara"), which was a crude arrangement of words according to subjects, by the Sanskrit grammarian Amara Sinh. Roget also knew about a *Pasigraphie*, published in Paris in 1797, which tried to classify language so that it could be understood universally without translation. But Dr. Roget, this erudite physician with a flair for invention, developed a superb and revolutionary principle: *the grouping of words according to ideas*. That mechanism enables one to find just the right expression to fit one's thought without groping and without searching through the alphabet. When in 1852 he published the first book ever to carry out this concept with thoroughness and precision, he called it a "thesaurus" (from the Greek and Latin, meaning "treasury" or "storehouse"). And *thesaurus* it has remained to this day. Indeed, any attempt to produce a "thesaurus in dictionary form" is self-destructive, for it demolishes the very structure that makes the thesaurus so effective.

So successful was this *Thesaurus of English Words and Phrases, Classified and Arranged so as to Facilitate the Expression of Ideas and Assist in Literary Composition* that a second edition followed one year later in 1853. A third "cheaper edition enlarged and improved" followed in 1855 and by Dr. Roget's death in 1869 there had been no less than twenty-eight editions and printings. Peter Roget's son, Dr. John Lewis Roget, greatly expanded the book for still another edition, which appeared a decade later in 1879.

Mr. Thomas Y. Crowell acquired that property and published the first Crowell edition in 1886. Then in 1911, as one of the last acts in his distinguished career, he published a revised and reset edition which contained many additional words and phrases. Mr. Crowell had the sagacity to enlarge the size of the page and set the book in large, clear type. This has been one of its many valuable characteristics ever since.

Mr. Crowell's son, Mr. T. Irving Crowell, undertook another edition for publication in 1922. Again revised and reset, it was greatly expanded, most especially with Americanisms and with a generous increase in foreign expressions. It was now virtually a new book, and the title was changed to *Roget's International Thesaurus*—that is, *Roget's International Thesaurus* I.

This writer, Thomas Y. Crowell's grandson, carried the work forward with *Roget's International Thesaurus* II of 1946. Then much slang and substandard speech were added, together with useful quotations. The old parallel arrangement of synonyms against antonyms was converted into a more efficient tandem format. Paragraphs were numbered, and the book was equipped with a decimal finding system for the user's convenience.

*Roget's International Thesaurus* III appeared in 1962. In this edition some 45,000 new terms were added, together with numerous words without synonyms classified in special lists. To make the book even easier to use, all key words were set in boldface type.

Now, with a very special sense of pride, we present *Roget's International Thesaurus* IV. It has been modernized and improved throughout, to the point where there are now more than

250,000 useful words and phrases, many of them from the 1970's. Among the new features is the inclusion of combining forms such as prefixes (*cryo–*, "cold") and suffixes (*–lith*, "rock" or "stone"). The new page design with its hanging indention is a delight.

There were many and varied contributions to the excellences of the Fourth Edition; we acknowledge them here with heartfelt thanks.

Our principal debt of gratitude is to Professor Robert L. Chapman, who applied his superior lexicographic skills to every category, judiciously pruning, reorganizing, and augmenting the work of his predecessors, Lester V. Berrey and C. O. Sylvester Mawson.

The new pages owe their attractive and efficient features to Milton B. Glick; regrettably, he did not live to see his design in published form.

For the demanding work of editorial preparation we owe thanks to Tania Romero and John Alleman, who copyedited the manuscript, contributed additional textual improvements, and coded the copy for CRT composition and computer-extraction of the index.

We are especially indebted to editor-proofreader Carol Cohen for contributions at successive stages in the translation of the manuscript to printed page. She brought to bear on the work considerable expertise in the handling of computer-processed copy, troubleshooting the sometimes arcane problems and making many editorial refinements. She also headed the very able corps of index editors, Cheryl Jimerson, Rebecca MacLean, Muriel Rosenblum, Lynn Miller, Joseph Blitman, Lorna Harbus, Sheila Brantley, James Cregan, Nancy Levering, and Susan Simon; our thanks to each of them.

Our thanks also to the many users of the *International* who have written over the years suggesting additions and calling our attention to editorial slips and typographical errors. We are dedicated to the perpetual improvement of the volume—work on *Roget's International Thesaurus* V has already begun—and we always appreciate hearing from those who want to help make a great reference book even better.

Robert L. Crowell

*April 11, 1977*

# PETER ROGET'S PREFACE

## TO THE FIRST EDITION

## (1852)

It is now nearly fifty years since I first projected a system of verbal classification similar to that on which the present work is founded. Conceiving that such a compilation might help to supply my own deficiencies, I had, in the year 1805, completed a classed catalog of words on a small scale, but on the same principle, and nearly in the same form, as the Thesaurus now published. I had often during that long interval found this little collection, scanty and imperfect as it was, of much use to me in literary composition, and often contemplated its extension and improvement; but a sense of the magnitude of the task, amidst a multitude of other avocations, deterred me from the attempt. Since my retirement from the duties of Secretary of the Royal Society, however, finding myself possessed of more leisure, and believing that a repertory of which I had myself experienced the advantage might, when amplified, prove useful to others, I resolved to embark in an undertaking which, for the last three or four years, has given me incessant occupation, and has, indeed, imposed upon me an amount of labor very much greater than I had anticipated. Notwithstanding all the pains I have bestowed on its execution, I am fully aware of its numerous deficiencies and imperfections, and of its falling far short of the degree of excellence that might be attained. But, in a work of this nature, where perfection is placed at so great a distance, I have thought it best to limit my ambition to that moderate share of merit which it may claim in its present form; trusting to the indulgence of those for whose benefit it is intended, and to the candor of critics who, while they find it easy to detect faults, can at the same time duly appreciate difficulties.

P. M. ROGET

*April 29, 1852*

# FOREWORD

## BY ROBERT L. CHAPMAN

This new edition of *Roget's International Thesaurus* is published in the hope and conviction that it will be more useful than its predecessors for precisely the two classes of persons Dr. Roget had in mind when he presented his original thesaurus of 1852. He expected that the book would be very welcome, first, to "those who are . . . painfully groping their way and struggling with the difficulties of composition." That is, to writers of all sorts for whom the right word has not flashed into mind. The others who might profit from his monumental effort he called "metaphysicians engaged in the more profound investigation of the Philosophy of Language." Today we would call them linguists, semanticists, or linguistic philosophers, depending on the discipline they claim.

The success of the thesaurus as a practical aid to writers has been immense. Literally millions of persons have put Roget's work to its widest proper use as a memory-jogger for words they know but cannot recall, or as a source of words new to them which, when the sense is confirmed by looking at the dictionary, can become a part of their active vocabulary. Thousands, too, have used Roget's as a browsing book, a book that stimulates thought and exploration because it uniquely collects great semantic "domains" under large conceptual headings, and shows by the manner of organization the tracks the mind may take as it ranges about in a given territory.

This edition has been prepared along lines set down by previous *International Thesaurus* editors, who have constantly improved upon the format invented by Dr. Roget. Numbered paragraphs are used to give clearly visible distinctions among sense-groups. Boldface type highlights the terms of greatest frequency within any sense-group. Everything has been done to facilitate quick consultation, while at the same time each sense-group is developed to nearly its maximum range for those whose expressive or stylistic wishes require variation, or even strangeness. Nearly every possible point-of-entry is available in the comprehensive index—one of the hallmarks of a true thesaurus.

The editor and the publisher of this fourth edition have used resources not available to previous editors. These include the newest and best general dictionaries of English and of specialized subjects, new specialized encyclopedias, and reverse-indexes of English that make the lexicon accessible in terms of sense-forming suffixes. They have used computer technology for index making, assuring a greater precision of the index than has ever been possible.

The editing policy has been exactly the same as Dr. Roget's. First, even though one cannot hope to keep up completely with our growing and shifting vocabulary, new words and phrases were carefully collected for inclusion. Second, the broadest possible range of levels and styles ("registers," as some linguists call them) has been encompassed. Noting that some of the words he entered might be condemned as vulgarisms or slang, Roget judged that "having due regard to the uses to which this Work was to be adapted, I did not feel myself justified in excluding them solely on that ground, if they possessed an acknowledged currency in general intercourse." He properly felt that choice of style was the province of the writer, and not of the reference-book maker.

For nonformal varieties of English the labels "informal" and "slang" have been used, with some trepidation. Labeling judgments are subjective and imprecise, so the designations here can hardly be taken as solidly authoritative. Nevertheless, it was felt that some sign ought to be given of the genuine semantic distinctions inherent in differences of level and style, perhaps for no better reason than that it goes against a deep semantic grain to print formal words and slang words side by side unmarked as if they were readily interchangeable.

Ready interchangeability without change of meaning is of course what makes two or more words synonymous, and a note of caution should be uttered in every thesaurus against confusing this kind of book with a synonym book. Naive users who take all the words under any heading to mean the same as the heading, and who do not read prefaces, will no doubt continue to use the thesaurus to write very strange English. Sameness or similarity of meaning is not the primary key to compiling a thesaurus. The key is membership in the cluster of linguistic signs that go to make up some very large and general concept. Most of the terms found under a major heading will in some demonstrable and logical way represent subordinate or less general parts of the larger idea. Quite inevitably, given the fact that semantic doubling or near-doubling occurs in every natural language, many of these terms will be synonymous or nearly synonymous in various parts of their range. But this is an accident of Roget's method, and not the aim of the method itself. It cannot be doubted that most users, most of the time, are in search of synonyms, and they find them, but even near-synonymity will be seen to attenuate quite rapidly as one goes along the lines of association in one direction or another.

Roget's hope that his book would "materially assist" linguistic scholars and theoreticians was largely unrealized until quite recently, but this revision has been edited in the increasing awareness that the *Thesaurus* may at last become a productive tool of linguistic research. One strain of contemporary linguistic thought, the so-called Chomskyan Revolution, has reopened speculation about the universality of language forms and elements. Roget himself worked quite consciously in the tradition of the seventeenth-century rationalist philosophers who attempted to map the totality of concepts available to the human mind, and the relations among these concepts, regardless of what language may be used to express them. The editor and the publisher believe that the new edition of the *International* constitutes the most elaborate approach yet made to the specification of possible concepts. It is the best empirical base for research in structural semantics, an area of concern generally left aside as structural linguistics worked out its theories of grammar.

To Drew University, its library, and especially to my wife, who indulged and encouraged me during the arduous years of work on this edition, I now proffer my gratitude.

# SYNOPSIS OF CATEGORIES

## CLASS ONE: ABSTRACT RELATIONS

I. EXISTENCE

A. **Being in the Abstract**
  1. Existence
  2. Nonexistence
B. **Being in the Concrete**
  3. Substantiality
  4. Unsubstantiality
C. **Formal Existence**
  5. Intrinsicality
  6. Extrinsicality
D. **Modal Existence**
  7. State
  8. Circumstance

II. RELATION

A. **Absolute Relation**
  9. Relation
  10. Unrelatedness
  11. Relationship by Blood
  12. Relationship by Marriage
  13. Correlation
  14. Identity
  15. Contrariety
  16. Difference
  17. Uniformity
  18. Nonuniformity
  19. Multiformity
B. **Partial Relation**
  20. Similarity
  21. Dissimilarity
  22. Imitation
  23. Nonimitation
  24. Copy
  25. Model
C. **Correspondence of Relationship**
  26. Agreement
  27. Disagreement

III. QUANTITY

A. **Simple Quantity**
  28. Quantity
  29. Degree
B. **Comparative Quantity**
  30. Equality
  31. Inequality
  32. Mean

  33. Compensation
  34. Greatness
  35. Smallness
  36. Superiority
  37. Inferiority
  38. Increase
  39. Decrease
C. **Conjunctive Quantity**
  40. Addition
  41. Adjunct
  42. Subtraction
  43. Remainder
  44. Mixture
  45. Simplicity
  46. Complexity
  47. Joining
  48. Analysis
  49. Separation
  50. Cohesion
  51. Noncohesion
  52. Combination
  53. Disintegration
D. **Wholeness**
  54. Whole
  55. Part
  56. Completeness
  57. Incompleteness
  58. Composition

IV. ORDER

A. **Order in General**
  59. Order
  60. Arrangement
  61. Classification
  62. Disorder
  63. Disarrangement
B. **Consecutive Order**
  64. Precedence
  65. Sequence
  66. Precursor
  67. Sequel
  68. Beginning
  69. Middle
  70. End
  71. Continuity
  72. Discontinuity
C. **Collective Order**
  73. Accompaniment
  74. Assemblage
  75. Dispersion

D. **Distributive Order**
  76. Inclusion
  77. Exclusion
  78. Extraneousness
  79. Generality
  80. Particularity
  81. Specialty
E. **Conformity to Rule**
  82. Conformity
  83. Noncomformity
  84. Normality
  85. Abnormality

V. NUMBER

A. **Number in General**
  86. Number
  87. Numeration
  88. List
B. **Determinate Number**
  89. Unity
  90. Duality
  91. Duplication
  92. Bisection
  93. Three
  94. Triplication
  95. Trisection
  96. Four
  97. Quadruplication
  98. Quadrisection
  99. Five and Over
C. **Indeterminate Number**
  100. Plurality
  101. Numerousness
  102. Fewness
  103. Repetition
  104. Infinity

VI. TIME

A. **Absolute Time**
  105. Time
  106. Timelessness
  107. Period
  108. Spell
  109. Interim
  110. Durability
  111. Transience
  112. Perpetuity
  113. Instantaneousness
  114. Measurement of Time
  115. Anachronism

xvii

## CLASS TWO: SPACE

404. Cloud
405. Bubble

III. ORGANIC MATTER

A. **Animal and Vegetable Kingdom**
406. Organic Matter

B. **Vitality**
407. Life

408. Death
409. Killing
410. Interment

C. **Vegetable Life**
411. Plants
412. Botany
413. Agriculture

D. **Animal Life**
414. Animals, Insects

415. Zoology
416. Animal Husbandry

E. **Mankind**
417. Mankind
418. Peoples

F. **Male and Female**
419. Sex
420. Masculinity
421. Femininity

# CLASS FIVE: SENSATION

I. SENSATION IN GENERAL
422. Sensation
423. Insensibility
424. Pain

II. TOUCH
425. Touch
426. Sensations of Touch

III. TASTE
427. Taste
428. Savoriness
429. Unsavoriness
430. Insipidness
431. Sweetness
432. Sourness
433. Pungency
434. Tobacco

IV. SMELL
435. Odor
436. Fragrance
437. Stench
438. Odorlessness

V. SIGHT
439. Vision
440. Defective Vision
441. Blindness
442. Spectator
443. Optical Instruments
444. Visibility
445. Invisibility
446. Appearance
447. Disappearance

VI. HEARING

A. **Perception of Sound**
448. Hearing

449. Deafness

B. **Sound**
450. Sound
451. Silence
452. Faintness of Sound
453. Loudness

C. **Specific Sounds**
454. Resonance
455. Repeated Sounds
456. Explosive Noise
457. Sibilation
458. Stridor
459. Cry, Call
460. Animal Sounds

D. **Unmusical Sounds**
461. Discord

E. **Musical Sounds**
462. Music
463. Harmonics, Musical Elements
464. Musician
465. Musical Instruments

# CLASS SIX: INTELLECT

I. INTELLECTUAL FACULTIES AND PROCESSES

A. **Faculties**
466. Intellect
467. Intelligence, Wisdom
468. Wise Man
469. Unintelligence
470. Foolishness
471. Fool
472. Sanity
473. Insanity, Mania
474. Eccentricity

B. **Comprehension**
475. Knowledge
476. Intellectual
477. Ignorance

C. **Functions of the Mind**
478. Thought
479. Idea
480. Absence of Thought
481. Intuition

D. **Reasoning Processes**
482. Reasoning
483. Sophistry

E. **Consideration**
484. Topic
485. Inquiry
486. Answer

487. Solution
488. Discovery

F. **Assessment**
489. Experiment
490. Measurement
491. Comparison
492. Discrimination
493. Indiscrimination

G. **Conclusion**
494. Judgment
495. Prejudgment
496. Misjudgment
497. Overestimation
498. Underestimation

H. **Theory**
499. Theory, Supposition
500. Philosophy

I. **Belief**
501. Belief
502. Credulity
503. Unbelief
504. Incredulity

J. **Grounds for Belief**
505. Evidence, Proof
506. Disproof

K. **Qualifications**
507. Qualification
508. No Qualifications
509. Possibility
510. Impossibility
511. Probability

512. Improbability
513. Certainty
514. Uncertainty
515. Gamble

L. **Conformity to Fact**
516. Truth
517. Maxim
518. Error
519. Illusion
520. Disillusionment

M. **Acceptance**
521. Assent
522. Dissent
523. Affirmation
524. Negation, Denial

II. STATES OF MIND

A. **Mental Attitudes**
525. Mental Attitude
526. Broad-mindedness
527. Narrow-mindedness
528. Curiosity
529. Incuriosity
530. Attention
531. Inattention
532. Distraction, Confusion
533. Carefulness
534. Neglect

B. **Creative Thought**
535. Imagination

**CLASS SIX** (Continued)

536. Unimaginativeness
**C. Recollection**
  537. Memory
  538. Forgetfulness
**D. Anticipation**
  539. Expectation
  540. Inexpectation
  541. Disappointment
  542. Foresight
  543. Prediction
  544. Presentiment

**III. COMMUNICATION OF IDEAS**

**A. Nature of Ideas Communicated**
  545. Meaning
  546. Latent Meaningfulness
  547. Meaninglessness
  548. Intelligibility
  549. Unintelligibility
  550. Ambiguity
  551. Figure of Speech
  552. Interpretation
  553. Misinterpretation
**B. Modes of Communication**
  554. Communication
  555. Manifestation
  556. Disclosure
  557. Information
  558. News
  559. Publication
  560. Communications
  561. Messenger

**C. Education**
  562. Teaching
  563. Misteaching
  564. Learning
  565. Teacher
  566. Student
  567. School
**D. Indication**
  568. Indication
  569. Insignia
  570. Record
  571. Recorder
**E. Representation**
  572. Representation
  573. Misrepresentation
**F. Arts of Design**
  574. Art
  575. Sculpture
  576. Ceramics
  577. Photography
  578. Graphic Arts
  579. Artist
**G. Language**
  580. Language
  581. Letter
  582. Word
  583. Nomenclature
  584. Anonymity
  585. Phrase
**H. Grammar**
  586. Grammar
  587. Ungrammaticalness
**I. Style; Mode of Expression**
  588. Diction
  589. Elegance
  590. Inelegance

591. Plain Speech
592. Conciseness
593. Diffuseness
**J. Spoken Language**
  594. Speech
  595. Imperfect Speech
  596. Talkativeness
  597. Conversation
  598. Soliloquy
  599. Public Speaking
  600. Eloquence
  601. Grandiloquence
**K. Written Language**
  602. Writing
  603. Printing
  604. Correspondence
  605. Book, Periodical
  606. Treatise
  607. Abridgment
**L. Linguistic Representation**
  608. Description
  609. Poetry
  610. Prose
  611. Show Business
  612. Entertainer
**M. Uncommunicativeness; Secrecy**
  613. Uncommunicativeness
  614. Secrecy
  615. Concealment
**N. Falsehood**
  616. Falseness
  617. Exaggeration
  618. Deception
  619. Deceiver
  620. Dupe

**CLASS SEVEN: VOLITION**

**I. VOLITION IN GENERAL**

**A. Will**
  621. Will
  622. Willingness
  623. Unwillingness
**B. Resolution; Determination**
  624. Resolution
  625. Perseverance
  626. Obstinacy
**C. Irresolution; Caprice**
  627. Irresolution
  628. Change of Allegiance
  629. Caprice
  630. Impulse
**D. Evasion**
  631. Avoidance
  632. Escape
  633. Abandonment
**E. Inclination**
  634. Desire
  635. Eagerness
  636. Indifference
**F. Choice**
  637. Choice
  638. Rejection

639. Necessity
640. Predetermination
641. Prearrangement
**G. Custom**
  642. Custom, Habit
  643. Unaccustomedness
  644. Fashion
  645. Social Convention
  646. Formality
  647. Informality
**H. Motive**
  648. Motivation, Inducement
  649. Pretext
  650. Allurement
  651. Bribery
  652. Dissuasion
**I. Purpose**
  653. Intention
  654. Plan
  655. Pursuit
  656. Business, Occupation
**J. Ways and Means**
  657. Way
  658. Means
  659. Provision, Equipment
  660. Store, Supply

661. Sufficiency
662. Insufficiency
663. Excess
664. Satiety
**K. Use**
  665. Use
  666. Consumption
  667. Misuse
  668. Disuse
  669. Uselessness

**II. CONDITIONS**

**A. Adaptation to Ends**
  670. Expedience
  671. Inexpedience
  672. Importance
  673. Unimportance
  674. Goodness
  675. Badness
  676. Bane
  677. Perfection
  678. Imperfection
  679. Blemish
  680. Mediocrity
**B. Wholesomeness**
  681. Cleanness
  682. Uncleanness
  683. Healthfulness
  684. Unhealthfulness

**CLASS SEVEN** (Continued)

840. Debt
841. Payment
842. Nonpayment
843. Expenditure
844. Receipts

845. Accounts
846. Price, Fee
847. Discount
848. Expensiveness
849. Cheapness

850. Costlessness
851. Economy
852. Parsimony
853. Liberality
854. Prodigality

## CLASS EIGHT: AFFECTIONS

I. PERSONAL AFFEC-
   TIONS
A. **Emotion**
   855. Feelings
   856. Lack of Feelings
B. **Excitability**
   857. Excitement
   858. Inexcitability
   859. Nervousness
   860. Unnervousness
   861. Patience
   862. Impatience
C. **Pleasure and Pleasurableness**
   863. Pleasantness
   864. Unpleasantness
   865. Pleasure
   866. Unpleasure
   867. Dislike
   868. Contentment
   869. Discontent
   870. Cheerfulness
   871. Solemnity
   872. Sadness
   873. Regret
   874. Unregretfulness
   875. Lamentation
   876. Rejoicing
   877. Celebration
   878. Amusement
   879. Dancing
   880. Humorousness
   881. Wit, Humor
   882. Banter
   883. Dullness
   884. Tedium
   885. Aggravation
   886. Relief
   887. Comfort
D. **Anticipative Emotions**
   888. Hope
   889. Hopelessness
E. **Concern**
   890. Anxiety
   891. Fear, Frightening-
        ness
   892. Cowardice
   893. Courage
   894. Rashness
   895. Caution
F. **Discriminative Affections**
   896. Fastidiousness
   897. Taste, Tastefulness
   898. Vulgarity
   899. Ugliness
   900. Beauty
   901. Ornamentation
   902. Plainness

903. Affectation
904. Ostentation
G. **Pride**
   905. Pride
   906. Humility
   907. Servility
   908. Modesty
   909. Vanity
   910. Boasting
   911. Bluster
   912. Arrogance
   913. Insolence
H. **Esteem**
   914. Repute
   915. Disrepute
   916. Honor
   917. Title
   918. Nobility
   919. Commonalty
I. **Contemplative Emotions**
   920. Wonder
   921. Unastonishment

II. SYMPATHETIC
    AFFECTIONS

A. **Social Relations**
   922. Sociability
   923. Unsociability
   924. Seclusion
   925. Hospitality, Wel-
        come
   926. Inhospitality
B. **Social Affections**
   927. Friendship
   928. Friend
   929. Enmity
   930. Hate
   931. Love
   932. Lovemaking, En-
        dearment
   933. Marriage
   934. Celibacy
   935. Divorce, Widow-
        hood
C. **Civility**
   936. Courtesy
   937. Discourtesy
D. **Benevolence**
   938. Kindness, Benevo-
        lence
   939. Unkindness, Malev-
        olence
   940. Misanthropy
   941. Public Spirit
   942. Benefactor
   943. Evildoer
E. **Sympathy**
   944. Pity

945. Pitilessness
946. Condolence
947. Forgiveness
948. Congratulation
F. **Gratefulness**
   949. Gratitude
   950. Ingratitude
G. **Ill Humor**
   951. Ill Humor
   952. Resentment, Anger
H. **Selfish Resentment**
   953. Jealousy
   954. Envy
I. **Reprisal**
   955. Retaliation
   956. Revenge

III. MORALITY

A. **Morals**
   957. Ethics
   958. Right
   959. Wrong
B. **Moral Obligation**
   960. Dueness
   961. Undueness
   962. Duty
   963. Imposition
C. **Moral Sentiments**
   964. Respect
   965. Disrespect
   966. Contempt
   967. Ridicule
   968. Approval
   969. Disapproval
   970. Flattery
   971. Disparagement
   972. Curse
   973. Threat
D. **Moral Conditions**
   974. Probity
   975. Improbity
   976. Justice
   977. Injustice
   978. Selfishness
   979. Unselfishness
   980. Virtue
   981. Vice
   982. Wrongdoing, Sin
   983. Guilt
   984. Innocence
   985. Good Person
   986. Bad Person
E. **Moral Practice**
   987. Sensuality
   988. Chastity
   989. Unchastity
   990. Indecency
   991. Asceticism
   992. Temperance

# ROGET'S
# INTERNATIONAL
# THESAURUS

# THESAURUS OF ENGLISH WORDS AND PHRASES

## 1. EXISTENCE

.1 NOUNS **existence, being;** subsistence, entity, essence, *ens* [L], *esse* [L], *l'être* [Fr]; occurrence, presence; **materiality** 376, **substantiality** 3; **life** 407; –dom, –oma *or* –ome, onto–, –ure.

.2 **reality, actuality,** factuality, empirical *or* demonstrable *or* objective existence; historicity; **truth** 516; **authenticity** 516.5; sober *or* grim reality, not a dream, more truth than poetry; accomplished fact, *fait accompli* [Fr].

.3 **fact,** the case, the truth of the matter, not opinion, not guesswork, what's what [informal]; **matter of fact,** "plain, plump fact" [R. Browning]; **bare fact,** naked fact, bald fact, **simple fact,** sober fact; **cold fact,** hard fact, **stubborn fact, brutal fact,** the nitty-gritty [informal]; **actual fact,** positive fact, absolute fact; **self-evident fact,** axiom, postulate; **accepted fact,** conceded fact, admitted fact, fact of experience, well-known fact, established fact, inescapable fact, indisputable fact, undeniable fact; **demonstrable fact,** provable fact; empirical fact; given fact, datum, **circumstance** 8; **salient fact,** significant fact.

.4 **the facts,** the information 557, the particulars, the details, the specifics, **the data,** the dope *or* the scoop *or* the score [all slang]; the picture [informal], the gen [Brit slang]; the fact *or* facts *or* truth of the matter, the facts of the case, the whole story [informal]; "irreducible and stubborn facts" [W. James]; essentials, basic *or* essential facts, brass tacks [informal].

.5 **self-existence,** uncreated being, noncontingent existence, aseity, innascibility.

.6 **mere existence,** just being, **vegetable exis-** tence, **vegetation,** mere tropism; stagnation, inertia, torpor; indolence, sloth.

.7 (philosophy of being) ontology, metaphysics, existentialism.

.8 VERBS **exist, be,** be in existence, be extant, have being; breathe, **live** 407.7; subsist, stand, obtain, hold, prevail, be the case; **occur,** be present, be there, be found, be met with, have place, happen to be.

.9 **live on,** continue to exist, persist, last, endure 110.6.

.10 **vegetate,** merely exist, just be; stagnate, pass the time.

.11 **exist in, consist in,** subsist in, lie in, rest in, repose in, reside in, abide in, inhabit, dwell in, **inhere in,** be present in, be a quality of, be comprised in, be contained in, be constituted by, be coextensive with.

.12 **become,** come to be, go, get, get to be, turn out to be; be converted into, turn into 145.17; grow 148.5; be changed 139.5; –en, –ize *or* –ise.

.13 ADJS **existent, existing,** in existence; **subsistent,** subsisting; **being,** in being; –ic(al), –etic, –ar; **living** 407.11; **present, extant, prevalent, current,** in force *or* effect, on foot, under the sun, on the face of the earth.

.14 **self-existent,** self-existing, innascible; uncreated, increate.

.15 **real, actual,** factual, veritable, for real [slang], *de facto* [L]; historical; positive, undeniable, absolute; **true** 516.12; honest-to-God [slang], genuine, **authentic** 516.14; **substantial** 3.6.

.16 ADVS **really, actually; genuinely,** veritably, **truly** 516.17; **in reality,** in actuality, in effect, in fact, *de facto* [L]; in point of fact, as a matter of fact; positively, absolutely; no buts about it [informal]; no ifs, ands, or buts [informal]; obviously, manifestly 555.14.

## 2. NONEXISTENCE

.1 NOUNS **nonexistence,** nonsubsistence; nonentity, **nonbeing,** unbeing, not-being; **nothingness,** nullity, nihility; vacancy, deprivation, emptiness, vacuity 187.2; vacuum, void 187.3; "the intense inane" [Shelley]; negativeness, negation, negativity; nonoccurrence; **unreality,** nonreality, unactuality; absence 187.

.2 **nothing,** nil, *nihil* [L], *nichts* [Ger], nix [slang], *nada* [Sp], **naught, aught;** zero, cipher, goose egg [slang]; nothing whatever, nothing at all, zilch [slang], Sweet Fanny Adams [Brit slang], nothing on earth *or* under the sun, no such thing; thing of naught 4.2.

.3 **none,** not a one, not a blessed one [informal]; never a one, ne'er a one, nary one [dial]; **not any, not a bit,** not a whit, not a hint, not a smitch *or* smidgen [dial], not a speck, not a mite, not a particle, not an iota, not a jot, not a scrap, not a trace, not a lick [informal], not a lick or smell [informal], not a suspicion, not a shadow of a suspicion, neither hide nor hair.

.4 VERBS **not exist,** not be in existence, not be met with, not occur, not be found, be absent *or* lacking.

.5 **cease to exist** *or* **be, be annihilated,** be destroyed, **be wiped out,** be extirpated, be eradicated; **go, vanish,** be no more, leave no trace, "leave not a rack behind" [Shakespeare]; **disappear** 447.2, evaporate, fade, fade away *or* out, fly, flee, dissolve, melt away, die out *or* away, pass, pass out of the picture [informal], turn to nothing *or* naught, peter out [informal]; **perish, expire,** pass away, **die** 408.19.

.6 **annihilate** 693.13, **exterminate** 693.14, eradicate, extirpate, **wipe out, stamp out** [informal], put an end to 693.12.

.7 ADJS **nonexistent,** nonsubsistent, existless, unexisting, without being, nowhere to be found; **minus, missing,** lacking, –less; **null,** nulli–, **void,** devoid; vacuous 187.13; negative.

.8 **unreal,** unactual, not real; merely nominal; **immaterial** 377.7; **unsubstantial** 4.5; **imaginary, fanciful** 535.19–22; unrealistic; illusory 519.9.

.9 **unmade,** uncreated, unborn, unbegotten, unconceived, unproduced.

.10 **no more, extinct, defunct, dead,** expired, passed away; vanished, gone glimmering; perished, annihilated; gone, all gone; all over with, had it [slang], kaput [informal], *kaputt* [Ger], done for *or* dead and done for [both informal], down the drain [slang].

.11 ADVS **none, no,** not at all, in no way, to no extent; from scratch, from the ground up.

## 3. SUBSTANTIALITY

.1 NOUNS substantiality, substantialness; materiality 376; **substance, body,** mass; **solidity,** density, concreteness, stere(o)–; **tangibility,** palpability, ponderability; **sturdiness, stability,** soundness, firmness, steadiness, stoutness, toughness, **strength,** durability.

.2 **substance, stuff, material, matter** 376.2; building blocks, fabric; atoms, medium; tangible.

.3 **something, thing,** –ing; an existence, **being, entity,** entelechy, unit, individual, person, persona, personality, ont(o)–; creature, critter [dial]; organism; life; body; soul, monad; **object** 376.4.

.4 **embodiment,** incarnation, materialization, substantiation, concretization; reification.

.5 VERBS **embody,** incarnate, **materialize,** body forth, lend substance to, reify, entify, hypostatize, solidify, concretize.

.6 ADJS **substantial,** substantive; **solid, concrete; tangible,** sensible, appreciable, palpable, ponderable; **material** 376.9; **real** 1.15.

.7 **sturdy,** stable, **solid,** sound, firm, steady, tough, stout, **strong,** "strong as flesh and blood" [Wordsworth], rugged; **durable,** lasting, enduring; hard, dense, unyielding, adamantine; **well-made,** well-constructed, well-built; **well-founded,** well-grounded; **massive,** bulky, heavy.

.8 ADVS **substantially,** essentially 5.10.

## 4. UNSUBSTANTIALITY

.1 NOUNS unsubstantiality, insubstantiality, unsubstantialness; **immateriality** 377; bodilessness, incorporeality, unsolidity, unconcreteness; **intangibility,** impalpability, imponderability; **tenuousness,** tenuity, subtlety, subtility, airiness, mistiness, vagueness, ethereality; unreality; **flimsiness** 160.2.

.2 thing of naught, nullity, zero; **nonentity, nobody** *or* nebbish [both informal]; cipher; man of straw, jackstraw, lay figure, puppet, dummy, hollow man; flash in the pan, dud [slang]; pushover [slang]; **trifle** 673.5,6; nothing 2.2.

.3 **spirit**, shadow, air, **thin air,** "airy nothing" [Shakespeare], smoke, vapor, mist, ether, **bubble,** "such stuff as dreams are made on" [Shakespeare]; "a spume that plays upon a ghostly paradigm of things" [Yeats]; illusion 519; phantom 1017.1.

.4 VERBS spiritualize, **disembody,** dematerialize; etherealize, **attenuate,** subtilize, rarefy; weaken, enervate, sap.

.5 ADJS **unsubstantial,** insubstantial, nonsubstantial, unsubstanced; intangible, impalpable, imponderable; **immaterial** 377.7; pseudo–; **bodiless,** incorporeal, unsolid, unconcrete; weightless 353.10.

.6 tenuous, subtile, subtle; rarefied; **ethereal,** airy, windy, spirituous, vaporous, gaseous; air-built, cloud-built; **chimerical,** gossamery, shadowy, phantomlike 1017.7; dreamlike, **illusory, unreal;** fatuous, fatuitous; imaginary, fanciful 535.19–22.

.7 **flimsy,** shaky, weak, unsound, infirm 160.12–16.

.8 baseless, groundless, ungrounded, **without foundation,** not well-founded, built on sand.

## 5. INTRINSICALITY

.1 NOUNS intrinsicality, internality, innerness, **inwardness; inherence,** immanence, **inbeing,** indwelling; innateness, indigenousness; essentiality, fundamentality; **subjectivity,** nonobjectivity.

.2 essence, substance, stuff, inner essence; quid, quiddity; **quintessence,** elixir, flower; **essential,** principle, fundamental, hypostasis, postulate, axiom; **gist,** gravamen, **nub** [informal], nucleus, center, focus, kernel, **core, pith,** meat, nuts and bolts, the nitty-gritty [both informal]; sap, marrow, **heart,** soul, spirit.

.3 nature, character, quality, suchness; constitution, crasis [archaic], composition, **characteristics,** makeup, constituents; physique 246.4, physi(o)–, physic(o)–; body-build, somatotype, system [informal], diathesis; complexion [archaic], humor or humors [both archaic]; **temperament,** temper, fiber, **disposition,** spirit, ethos, genius, dharma; tenor, way, habit, frame, cast, hue, tone, grain, vein, streak, stripe, mold, brand, stamp; **kind** 61.3, **sort, type,** ilk; **property, characteristic** 80.4; **tendency** 174; the way of it, the nature of the beast [slang].

.4 **inner nature,** inside, internal or inner or esoteric reality, true being, essential nature, true inwardness, center of life, vital principle, nerve center; **spirit, soul, heart, breast, bosom, inner man;** heart of hearts, secret heart, inmost heart or soul, secret or innermost recesses of the heart, heart's core, bottom of the heart, cockles of the heart; vitals, quick, depths of one's being.

.5 VERBS **inhere,** indwell, belong to or permeate by nature; run in the blood, run in the family, be born so, be built that way [informal].

.6 ADJS **intrinsic,** internal, **inner,** inward; **inherent,** resident, implicit, immanent, indwelling; inalienable, unalienable, uninfringeable, unquestionable, unchallengeable, irreducible; **ingrained,** in the very grain; infixed, implanted, inwrought, deep-seated; **subjective,** esoteric, private, secret; self–.

.7 **innate, inborn, congenital; native, natural,** natural to, connatural, native to, indigenous; **constitutional,** bodily, physical, temperamental, organic; born; **inbred, genetic, hereditary,** inherited, incarnate, bred in the bone, in the blood, running in the blood or race or strain, etc.; connate, connatal, coeval 118.4; **instinctive,** instinctual, atavistic, primal.

.8 **essential,** of the essence, **fundamental; primary,** primitive, primal, elementary, elemental, original, ab ovo [L], radical; **basic, gut** [informal], basal, underlying; substantive, substantial, material; constitutive, constituent.

.9 ADVS **intrinsically, inherently,** innately; internally, **inwardly,** immanently; originally, primally, primitively; **naturally, congenitally,** genetically, **by birth, by nature.**

.10 essentially, fundamentally, primarily, basically; at bottom, au fond [Fr], at heart; in essence, at the core, in substance, in the main; substantially, materially; per se [L], of or in itself.

## 6. EXTRINSICALITY

.1 NOUNS **extrinsicality,** externality, outwardness, **extraneousness,** otherness, discreteness; foreignness; **objectivity,** nonsubjectivity, impersonality.

.2 **nonessential,** inessential or unessential; **accessory, extra,** collateral; other, not-self; **appendage,** appurtenance, auxiliary, **supplement,** addition, addendum, superaddition, adjunct 41; secondary, subsidiary; **contingency,** contingent, incidental, accidental, accident, happenstance, mere chance.

**.3** ADJS **extrinsic, external,** outward, outside, outlying; **extraneous,** foreign; **objective,** nonsubjective, impersonal, extraorganismal.

**.4 unessential,** inessential *or* nonessential; **accessory, extra,** collateral, auxiliary; adventitious, appurtenant, adscititious, ascititious, **additional, supplementary,** supplemental, superadded, supervenient; **secondary,** subsidiary; **incidental,** circumstantial, contingent; accidental, fortuitous, casual, superfluous.

## 7. STATE

**.1** NOUNS **state,** mode, modality; **status, situation,** position, posture, footing, location, bearings, spot [informal]; estate, **rank,** station, place, **standing; condition,** circumstance 8; –ance, –ancy, –cy, –ence, –ery, –hood, –ice, –ion, –ism, –ity, –ization *or* –isation, –ment, –ness, –or, –osis, –phoria, –ry, –ship, –th, –tude, –ty, –y; case, **lot; predicament,** plight, pass, pickle [slang], fix [slang], jam [slang].

**.2 the state of affairs,** the nature *or* shape of things, the way it shapes up [informal], the way of the world, how things stack up [slang], **how things stand,** how things are, the way of things, the way it is, like it is, where it's at, **the way things are,** the way of it, the way things go, how it goes, **how it is,** the status quo, *status in quo* [L], the size of it [informal]; how the land lies, the lay of the land [informal].

**.3 good condition, bad condition;** adjustment, fettle, form, order, repair, **shape** [informal], trim.

**.4 mode, manner, way** 657, fashion, style, form, shape, guise, complexion, tenor, tone, turn.

**.5 role, capacity, character,** part, quality, relation, status, position, condition.

**.6** VERBS be in *or* have a certain state, be such *or* so *or* thus, **fare,** go on *or* along; **enjoy** *or* occupy a certain position; **get on** *or* **along,** come on *or* along [informal]; **manage** [informal], **contrive, make out** [informal], come through, get by; **turn out,** come out, stack up [slang], shape up [informal].

**.7** ADJS conditional, modal, formal; –ate(d), –phoric; a–.

**.8 in condition** *or* **order** *or* repair, etc.; out of commission [informal], **out of kilter,** out of kelter [both informal], out of whack [informal], **out of order.**

## 8. CIRCUMSTANCE

**.1** NOUNS **circumstance, occurrence, occasion, event, incident;** juncture, conjuncture, contingency, eventuality; **condition** 7.1.

**.2 circumstances,** total situation, existing conditions *or* situation, set of conditions, **environment** 233, context, status quo; whole picture [informal], full particulars, ins and outs.

**.3 particular, instance, item, detail,** point, count, case, fact, matter, article, datum, element, factor, facet, aspect, thing; respect, regard; minutia, minutiae [pl]; incidental, minor detail.

**.4 circumstantiality,** particularity, specificity, minuteness of detail; accuracy 516.3.

**.5 circumstantiation,** itemization, particularization, specification, anatomization, atomization, analysis 48.

**.6** VERBS **circumstantiate, itemize, specify,** particularize, **detail,** go *or* enter into detail, descend to particulars, give full particulars, atomize, anatomize, spell out [informal]; instance, cite, adduce, document, quote chapter and verse; **substantiate** 505.12.

**.7** ADJS **circumstantial,** conditional, provisional; **incidental,** occasional, contingent, adventitious, accidental, casual, unessential *or* inessential *or* nonessential, aleatory.

**.8** environmental, environing, surrounding, contextual.

**.9 detailed, minute, full, particular,** meticulous, fussy, finicky, picayune, nice [archaic], precise, exact, specific, special.

**.10** ADVS **thus, thusly** [informal], in such wise, thuswise, this way, this-a-way [dial], thus and thus, thus and so, **so,** just so, like so [informal], like this, like that, just like that; similarly 20.18, precisely 516.20.

**.11 accordingly, in that case, in that event, at that rate,** that being the case, such being the case, that being so, **under the circumstances,** the condition being such, as it is, as matters stand, as the matter stands, **therefore** 155.7, **consequently** 154.9; **as the case may be,** as it may be, according to circumstances; as it may happen *or* turn out, as things may fall; **by the same token,** equally.

**.12 circumstantially,** conditionally, provisionally; provided 507.12.

**.13 fully, in full, in detail,** minutely, specifically, particularly, in particular, wholly

54.13, *in toto* [L], completely 56.14–18, **at length**, *in extenso* [L].

## 9. RELATION

.1 NOUNS **relation, relationship, connection;** relatedness, connectedness, **association** 788, assemblage 74, **affiliation,** filiation, bond, union, alliance, tie, tie-in [informal], link, linkage, linking, liaison, **addition** 40, adjunct 41, junction 47.1, **combination** 52; deduction 42.1, disjunction 49.1, contrariety 15; **affinity, rapport,** mutual attraction, sympathy, accord 794; **closeness,** propinquity, **proximity,** approximation, contiguity, nearness 200, intimacy; **relations, dealings,** affairs, intercourse; **s**ĭ**milarity,** homology.

.2 relativity, dependence, contingency; **interrelation, correlation** 13.

.3 **kinship,** common source *or* stock *or* descent *or* ancestry, consanguinity, agnation, cognation, enation, blood relationship 11; family relationship, affinity 12.1.

.4 relevance, pertinence, relatedness, materiality; **appositeness,** germaneness; application, applicability; **connection,** reference, **bearing,** concern, concernment, interest, respect, regard.

.5 VERBS **relate to,** refer to, **apply to, bear on** *or* **upon,** respect, regard, **concern, involve,** touch, affect, interest; **pertain to,** appertain to, belong to; answer to, correspond to; **have to do with,** have connection with, link with, connect, tie in with [informal], liaise with [informal], deal with, treat of, touch upon.

.6 relate, associate, connect, ally, link, wed, bind, tie, couple, bracket, equate, identify; bring into relation with, bring to bear upon, apply; parallel, parallelize, draw a parallel; **interrelate,** relativize, **correlate** 13.4.

.7 ADJS **relative,** relational; **connective,** linking, associative; **relating,** pertaining, appertaining, pertinent, referring, referable; congenial, *en rapport* [Fr], sympathetic, affinitive; **comparative,** comparable; proportional, proportionate, proportionable; correlative 13.10.

.8 **approximate,** approximating, approximative, proximate; **near, close** 200.14; comparable, relatable, **like,** homologous, **similar** 20.10.

.9 **related, connected; linked,** tied, coupled, knotted, twinned, wedded, wed, conjugate, bracketed, bound, yoked, spliced, joined 47.13; **associated, affiliated,** filiated, **allied,** associate, affiliate; inter-

locked, **interrelated,** interlinked, involved, implicated, **correlated** 13.10; in the same category, of that kind *or* sort *or* ilk; parallel, collateral; –al, –an, –ar, –ary, –ative, –atory, –ean, –ese, –etic, –ey, –ial, –ian, –ic(al), –ie, –ile, –ine, –ing, –istic(al), –itious, –ling, –orial, –ory, –ular, –y.

.10 **kindred, akin, related,** of common source *or* stock *or* descent *or* ancestry, agnate, cognate, enate, connate, connatural, congeneric, congenerous, consanguine(ous), genetically related, related by blood 11.6, affinal 12.4.

.11 **relevant, pertinent,** appertaining, **germane, apposite,** material, admissible, applicable, applying, pertaining, belonging, involving, appropriate, **apropos,** *à propos* [Fr], to the purpose, **to the point,** in point, *ad rem* [L].

.12 ADVS **relatively,** comparatively, proportionately, not absolutely, to a degree, to an extent; **relevantly,** pertinently, appositely, germanely.

.13 PREPS **with** *or* **in relation to,** with *or* in reference to, **with** *or* **in regard to,** with respect to, in respect to *or* of, relative to, relating to, **pertaining to,** pertinent to, referring to, in relation with, **in connection with,** apropos of, speaking of; **as to,** as for, as respects, as regards; in the matter of, on the subject of, in point of, on the score of; re, *in re* [L]; **about,** anent, of, on, upon, **concerning,** touching, respecting, **regarding.**

## 10. UNRELATEDNESS

.1 NOUNS **unrelatedness,** irrelation; **irrelevance,** impertinence, inappositeness, immateriality, inapplicability; inconnection *or* disconnection, inconsequence, independence; unconnectedness, separateness, discreteness, dissociation, disassociation, disjuncture, disjunction 49.1.

.2 **misconnection,** misrelation, wrong *or* invalid linking, misapplication, misapplicability, misreference; misalliance, *mésalliance* [Fr].

.3 VERBS **not concern,** not involve, not imply, not implicate, not relate to, not connect with, have nothing to do with.

.4 foist, drag in 237.6; impose on 963.7.

.5 ADJS **unrelated,** irrelative, unrelatable, **unconnected,** unallied, **unassociated,** unaffiliated *or* disaffiliated; disrelated, disconnected, dissociated, detached, discrete, disjunct, removed, separated, separate, segregate, apart, other, independent;

isolated, insular; **foreign, alien,** strange, exotic, outlandish; incommensurable, incomparable; –xene; extraneous 6.3.

.6 **irrelevant, irrelative; impertinent, inapposite,** inconsequent, inapplicable, immaterial, inappropriate, inadmissible; adrift, away from the point, *nihil ad rem* [L], **beside the point,** beside the mark, **beside the question,** off the subject, not to the purpose, **nothing to do with the case,** not at issue, out-of-the-way; **unessential,** nonessential, extraneous, extrinsic 6.3; incidental, parenthetical.

.7 **farfetched, remote,** distant, out-of-the-way, strained, forced, neither here nor there, brought in from nowhere, quite another thing, something else again; improbable 512.3.

.8 ADVS **irrelevantly,** irrelatively, impertinently, inappositely; without connection, without reference *or* regard.

## 11. RELATIONSHIP BY BLOOD

.1 NOUNS **blood relationship,** blood, ties of blood, consanguinity, common descent *or* ancestry, **kinship,** kindred, **relation, relationship,** sibship; propinquity; cognation; agnation, enation; filiation, affiliation; alliance, connection, **family connection** *or* tie; motherhood, maternity; fatherhood, paternity; patrocliny, matrocliny; patrilineage, matrilineage; patriliny, matriliny; patrisib, matrisib; brotherhood, brothership, fraternity; sisterhood, sistership; cousinhood, cousinship; **ancestry** 170.

.2 **kinsmen, kinfolk** *or* **kinsfolk, kindred,** kinnery [dial], **kin,** kith and kin, **family, relatives, relations, people,** folks [informal], connections; **blood relation** *or* **relative,** flesh, blood, flesh and blood, uterine kin, consanguinean; **cognate; agnate, enate; kinsman,** kinswoman, sib, sibling; german; near relation, distant relation; next of kin; collateral relative, collateral; distaff *or* spindle side, distaff *or* spindle kin; sword *or* spear side, sword *or* spear kin; **tribesman,** clansman; **ancestry** 170, **posterity** 171.

.3 **brother,** bub *or* bubba [both dial], bud *or* buddy [both informal], frater, adelpho–; brethren [pl] 1039.1; **sister,** sis [informal], sissy [informal]; sistern [pl dial]; kid brother *or* sister; blood brother *or* sister, uterine brother *or* sister, brother- *or* sister-german; half brother *or* sister, foster brother *or* sister, stepbrother *or* stepsister; **aunt,** auntie [informal]; **uncle,** unc *or*

uncs [both slang], nunks *or* nunky [both slang], nuncle [dial]; **nephew, niece; cousin,** cousin-german; first cousin, second cousin, etc.; cousin once removed, cousin twice removed, etc.; country cousin; **great-uncle, granduncle; great-granduncle; great-aunt, grandaunt; great-grandaunt; grandnephew, grandniece; father, mother** 170.9,10; **son, daughter** 171.3.

.4 **race, people** 418, **folk, family, house, clan, tribe, nation;** patriclan, matriclan, deme, sept, gens, phyle, phyl(o)–, phratry, totem; **lineage,** line, blood, strain, stock, stem, species, stirps, **breed,** brood, kind; plant *or* animal kingdom, class, order, etc. 61.5.

.5 **family,** brood, **house, household,** hearth, ménage, people, folks [informal], homefolks [informal]; **children,** issue, **offspring,** get.

.6 ADJS **related, kindred, akin;** consanguineous *or* consanguinean *or* consanguineal, consanguine, of the blood; cognate, uterine, agnate, enate; sib, sibling; allied, affiliated, congeneric; german, germane; collateral; foster, novercal; patrilineal, matrilineal; patroclinous, matroclinous; patrilateral, matrilateral; avuncular; intimately *or* closely related, remotely *or* distantly related.

.7 **racial, tribal, national, family,** clannish, totemic, **lineal; ethnic;** phyletic, phylogenetic, genetic; gentile, gentilic.

## 12. RELATIONSHIP BY MARRIAGE

.1 NOUNS **marriage relationship,** affinity, marital affinity; connection, family connection, marriage connection.

.2 **in-laws** [informal], **relatives-in-law;** brother-in-law, sister-in-law, father-in-law, mother-in-law, son-in-law, daughter-in-law.

.3 stepfather, stepmother; stepbrother, stepsister; stepchild, stepson, stepdaughter.

.4 ADJS **affinal,** affined, by marriage; step–, –in-law.

## 13. CORRELATION

*(reciprocal or mutual relation)*

.1 NOUNS **correlation,** corelation; correlativity, correlativism; **reciprocation,** reciprocity, reciprocality, relativity 9.2; mutuality, communion; community, commutuality; proportionality, direct *or* inverse relationship, direct *or* inverse ratio, direct *or* inverse proportion; **equilibrium, balance,** symmetry 248; **correspondence, equivalence,** equipollence, coequality.

.2 **interrelation,** interrelationship; **interconnection,** interlocking, interdigitation, intercoupling, interlinking, interlinkage, interalliance, interassociation, interaffiliation, interdependence; covariation.

.3 **interaction,** interworking, intercourse, intercommunication, **interplay;** alternation, seesaw; meshing, intermeshing, mesh, engagement; complementary distribution; **interweaving,** interlacing, intertwining 222.1; **interchange** 150, tit for tat, *quid pro quo* [L]; **concurrence** 177, coaction, **cooperation** 786.

.4 **correlate,** correlative; **correspondent,** analogue, counterpart; reciprocator, reciprocatist; each other, one another.

.5 ecology, ecosystem; symbiosis, symbiotics, parasitism, commensality.

.6 VERBS **correlate,** corelate.

.7 **interrelate, interconnect,** interassociate, interlink, intercouple, interlock, interdigitate, interally, intertie, interjoin, interdepend.

.8 **interact,** interwork, **interplay;** mesh, intermesh, engage, dovetail, mortise; **interweave,** interlace, intertwine; **interchange;** coact, **cooperate.**

.9 **reciprocate, correspond,** correspond to, respond to, answer, answer to, complement, coequal.

.10 ADJS **correlative,** corelative, correlational, corelational; **correlated,** corelated; co–.

.11 **interrelated, interconnected,** interassociated, interallied, interaffiliated, interlinked, interlocked, intercoupled, intertied, interdependent; inter–.

.12 **interacting,** interactive, interworking, interplaying; in gear, in mesh; dovetailed, mortised.

.13 **reciprocal,** reciprocative; **corresponding,** correspondent, answering, analogous, homologous, equipollent, tantamount, equivalent, coequal; **complementary,** complemental; equi–.

.14 **mutual,** commutual, **common, joint,** communal, conjoint; respective, two-way.

.15 ecological, ecotopic; symbiotic, parasitic, commensal.

.16 ADVS **reciprocally,** back and forth, backward and forward, backwards and forwards, alternately, seesaw, to and fro; vice versa, *mutatis mutandis* [L].

.17 **mutually, commonly,** communally, jointly; respectively, each to each; *entre nous* [Fr], *inter se* [L].

.18 ecologically; symbiotically, parasitically, commensally.

## 14. IDENTITY

.1 NOUNS **identity,** identicalness; **sameness,** selfsameness; indistinguishability, no difference, not a bit of difference; **coincidence,** correspondence, agreement, congruence; **equivalence, equality** 30, coequality; **synonymousness,** synonymity, synonymy; **oneness, unity,** homogeneity; selfness, selfhood, self-identity; homoousia, consubstantiality.

.2 **identification,** unification, coalescence, combination, union, fusion, merger, synthesis.

.3 **the same, selfsame,** very same, one and the same, identical same, no other, none other, very *or* actual thing, a distinction without a difference, the same difference [informal]; **equivalent** 20.3; **synonym;** homonym, homograph, homophone; ditto [informal], *idem* [L], *ipsissima verba* [L, the very words]; **duplicate,** double, *Doppelgänger* [Ger], twin, very image, dead ringer [informal], spitting image *or* spit and image [both informal] 572.3, **exact counterpart,** copy 24.1–7, replica, facsimile, carbon copy.

.4 VERBS **coincide, correspond,** agree, match, tally.

.5 **identify,** make one, **unify,** unite, join, combine, coalesce, synthesize, merge, fuse 52.3.

.6 **reproduce,** copy, replicate, **duplicate,** ditto [informal].

.7 ADJS **identical,** identic; **same, selfsame, one, one and the same,** all the same, all one, of the same kidney; undifferent, indistinguishable, without distinction, without difference; **alike, like** 20.10, just alike, exactly alike, alike as two peas in a pod; duplicate, twin; homoousian, consubstantial; aut(o)–, taut(o)–.

.8 **coinciding,** coincident, coincidental; **corresponding,** correspondent, congruent; **synonymous, equivalent,** six of one and half a dozen of the other [informal]; **equal** 30.7, coequal, coextensive, coterminous; co–, equi–, hom(o)–, is(o)–.

.9 ADVS **identically,** synonymously, **alike;** coincidentally, correspondently, correspondingly, congruently; **equally** 30.11, coequally, coextensively, coterminously; on the same footing, on all fours with; **likewise,** the same way, just the same, as is, ditto, same here [informal]; *ibid., ibidem* [both L].

## 15. CONTRARIETY

.1 NOUNS contrariety, **oppositeness, opposition** 790, opposure; **antithesis, contrast,** contraposition 239, counterposition, contradiction, contraindication, contradistinction; **antagonism,** perversity, repugnance, oppugnance, oppugnancy, **hostility,** inimicalness, antipathy, clashing, confrontation, showdown, collision, crosspurposes 795.2, conflict; polarity; discrepancy, inconsistency, **disagreement** 27.

.2 **opposite, the contrary,** contra, counter, **antithesis, reverse,** inverse, converse, obverse; the other side, the mirror *or* reverse image, the other side of the coin, the flip side [slang]; the direct *or* polar opposite, the other *or* opposite extreme; antipode, antipodes; countercheck *or* counterbalance *or* counterpoise; antipole, counterpole, counterpoint; opposite number [informal], vis-à-vis; offset, setoff, foil; **antonym,** counterterm.

.3 (contrarieties joined or coexisting) selfcontradiction, **paradox** 27.2, antinomy, oxymoron, ambivalence, irony; equivocation, **ambiguity.**

.4 VERBS **go contrary to, run counter to,** counter, **contradict,** contravene, controvert, fly in the face of, be *or* play at crosspurposes; **oppose,** be opposed to, go *or* run in opposition to; **conflict with,** come in conflict with, oppugn, conflict, clash; contrast with, **offset,** set off, countercheck *or* counterbalance, countervail; **counteract,** counterwork; counterpose *or* contrapose, counterpoise, juxtapose in opposition.

.5 **reverse,** transpose 220.5.

.6 ADJS **contrary;** contrarious, perverse, **opposite,** antithetic(al), **contradictory,** counter, contrapositive, contrasted; **converse, reverse,** obverse, inverse; con–, contra–, counter–, adverse, adversative *or* adversive, **opposing, opposed,** oppositive, oppositional; anti [informal], dead against; **antagonistic,** repugnant, oppugnant, hostile, inimical, antipathetic(al), discordant; inconsistent, discrepant, conflicting, clashing, at cross-purposes, confronting, squared off [informal], eyeball to eyeball [slang]; contradistinct; antonymous; countervailing, counterpoised, balancing, counterbalancing, compensating; mis–, un–.

.7 **diametric(al),** diametrically opposite, ant(i)– *or* anth–, de(s)–, ob–, retro–; antipodal *or* antipodean; opposite as black and white *or* light and darkness *or* day and night *or* fire and water *or* the poles, etc., "Hyperion to a satyr" [Shakespeare].

.8 self-contradictory, **paradoxical,** antinomic, oxymoronic, ambivalent, **ironic;** equivocal, **ambiguous.**

.9 ADVS contrarily, contrariously, contra, contrariwise, conversely, inversely, **vice versa,** topsy-turvy, upside down, arsy-varsy [dial], **on the other hand,** *per contra* [L], **on** *or* **to the contrary,** *tout au contraire* [Fr], in flat opposition; rather, nay rather, quite the contrary, otherwise 16.11, just the other way, just the other way around, **oppositely,** just the opposite *or* reverse; by contraries, by way of opposition; against the grain, *à rebours* [Fr].

.10 PREPS **opposite,** over against, in contrast with, contrary to, vis-à-vis.

## 16. DIFFERENCE

.1 NOUNS **difference,** otherness, separateness, discreteness, distinctness, **distinction;** unlikeness, **dissimilarity** 21; **variation,** variance, variegation, variety, **mixture** 44, heterogeneity, diversity; **deviation,** divergence *or* divergency, departure; **disparity,** inequality 31; odds; **discrepancy,** inconsistency, inconsonance, incongruity, discongruity, unconformity *or* nonconformity, disconformity, unorthodoxy 1025, incompatibility, irreconcilability; **disagreement, dissent** 522, disaccord *or* disaccordance, inaccordance, discordance, dissonance, inharmoniousness, inharmony; **contrast,** opposition, **contrariety** 15; far cry, whale of a difference [slang].

.2 **margin,** wide *or* narrow margin, **differential;** differentia, distinction, point of difference; **nicety, subtlety,** refinement, delicacy, nice *or* fine *or* delicate *or* **subtle distinction,** fine point; shade *or* particle of difference, **nuance,** hairline, a distinction without a difference.

.3 **different thing,** different story [informal], **something else,** something else again [informal], *tertium quid* [L, a third something], *autre chose* [Fr], another kettle of fish [informal], different breed of cat [informal], horse of a different color, bird of another feather; **nothing of the kind,** no such thing, **quite another thing; other, another.**

.4 **differentiation,** differencing, **discrimination,** distinguishment, **distinction;** demarcation, **separation** 49, division, atomization, anatomization, analysis, disjunction, segregation, severance, severalization; **modification, alteration, change** 139, variation, diversification; specialization, particularization, individualization, individuation, personalization; disequalization, desynonymization.

.5 VERBS **differ, vary,** diverge, stand apart, be distinguished *or* distinct; **deviate from,** diverge from, divaricate from, depart from; **disagree with,** disaccord with, conflict with, contrast with, stand over against, clash with, jar with; bear no resemblance to 21.2, not square with, not accord with, not go on all fours with.

.6 **differentiate,** difference; **distinguish, make a distinction,** mark, mark out *or* off, **discriminate; separate,** sever, severalize, segregate, divide; set off, set apart; **modify,** vary, diversify, **change** 139.5,6; specialize, particularize, individualize, individuate, personalize; atomize, analyze, anatomize, disjoin 49.9; disequalize, desynonymize; split hairs, sharpen *or* refine a distinction, chop logic.

.7 ADJS **different,** differing; unlike, **dissimilar** 21.4; **distinct,** distinguished, differentiated, discriminated, discrete, separated, separate, disjoined 49.21, widely apart; **various,** variant, varying, varied, heterogeneous, multifarious, motley, assorted, variegated, diverse, divers, **diversified** 19.4; **several,** many; **divergent,** deviative, diverging, deviating, departing; **disparate,** unequal 31.4; **discrepant,** inconsistent, inconsonant, incongruous, incongruent, unconformable, incompatible, irreconcilable; **disagreeing,** in disagreement; at variance, at odds; inaccordant, disaccordant, discordant, dissonant, inharmonious; contrasting, contrasted, poles apart, poles asunder, worlds apart; **contrary** 15.6; all-(o)–, de–, dis–, heter(o)–, xen(o)–.

.8 **other, another,** else, otherwise, other than *or* from; not the same, not the type [informal], not that sort, of another sort, of a sort *or* of sorts [both informal]; **unique,** rare, **special,** peculiar, *sui generis* [L, of its own kind], in a class by itself.

.9 **differentiative,** differential; **distinguishing,** discriminating, discriminative, characterizing, individualizing, individuating, personalizing, differencing, separative; diagnostic, diacritical; **distinctive,** contrastive, characteristic, peculiar, idiosyncratic.

.10 ADVS **differently,** diversely, variously; in a different manner, in another way, with a difference.

.11 **otherwise,** in other ways, **in other respects;** elsewise, else, or else; than; other than; **on the other hand;** contrarily 15.9; alias.

## 17. UNIFORMITY

.1 NOUNS **uniformity, evenness,** equability; **steadiness,** stability 142, steadfastness, constancy, persistence, continuity, **consistency;** consonance, correspondence, accordance; unity, **homogeneity,** monolithism; equanimity, equilibrium, unruffledness, calm.

.2 **regularity, constancy,** even tenor *or* pace, smoothness, clockwork regularity; sameness, sameliness; **monotony,** monotonousness, undifferentiation, the same old thing; daily round *or* routine, treadmill; unvariation, undeviation, orderliness, invariability; monotone, drone, dingdong, singsong, monologue.

.3 VERBS **persist, prevail,** run through; run true to form *or* type, continue the same; drag on *or* along; hum, drone.

.4 **make uniform,** uniformize; **regulate,** regularize, normalize, stabilize, damp; **even, equalize,** symmetrize, harmonize, balance, equilibrize; **level,** smooth, flatten; homogenize, standardize, stereotype, assimilate to *or* with.

.5 ADJS **uniform, equable,** equal, even; **level,** flat, smooth; **regular, constant,** steadfast, persistent, continuous; **unvaried,** unruffled, unbroken, undiversified, undifferentiated, unchanged; invariable, unchangeable, immutable; **unvarying,** undeviating, unchanging, steady, stable; **ordered,** balanced, measured; **orderly,** methodic(al), systematic(al), mechanical, robotlike, automatic; **consistent,** consonant, correspondent, accordant, homogeneous, **alike,** of a piece, monolithic; equi–, hol(o)–, hom(o)–, is(o)–, mon(o)–.

.6 **same,** samely; **monotonous, humdrum,** unrelieved, tedious 884.8, boring 884.9; repetitive, drab, gray.

.7 ADVS **uniformly,** equably, **evenly;** monotonously, in a rut *or* groove, dully, tediously, routinely, unrelievedly.

.8 **regularly; constantly, steadily,** continually; **invariably,** without exception, at every turn, never otherwise; methodically, orderly, systematically; **always** 112.11; like clockwork.

## 18. NONUNIFORMITY

.1 NOUNS **nonuniformity, unevenness, irregularity,** raggedness, choppiness, jerkiness, disorder 62; **difference** 16; inequality; **inconstancy, inconsistency,** variability, changeability or changeableness, mutability, capriciousness, mercuriality, wavering, **instability, unsteadiness; variation, deviation,** divergence, differentiation, divarication; versatility, **diversification,** nonstandardization; unconformity or unconformism, nonconformity or nonconformism, unorthodoxy, **pluralism;** variegation, variety, variousness, motleyness, dappleness.

.2 VERBS **diversify, vary,** variate, variegate 374.7; differentiate; divaricate, diverge; **differ** 16.5; dissent 522.4; break up, relieve, disunify.

.3 ADJS **nonuniform,** ununiform, **uneven, irregular,** ragged, choppy, jerky, jagged, rough, disorderly, unsystematic; **different** 16.7, unequal, unequable; **inconstant, inconsistent, variable;** varying, **changeable,** changing, mutable, capricious, impulsive, mercurial, erratic, spasmodic, sporadic, wavering, **unstable, unsteady;** deviating or deviative or deviatory, divergent, divaricate, erose; **diversified,** variform, diversiform, nonstandard; **nonconformist,** unorthodox; **pluralistic,** variegated, motley 374.9–15; various; diversi–, vari(o)–, heter(o)–.

.4 ADVS **nonuniformly,** ununiformly, unequally, **unevenly, irregularly,** inconstantly, **inconsistently,** unsteadily, erratically, spasmodically, capriciously, impulsively, sporadically; unsystematically, chaotically, helter-skelter, higgledy-piggledy; in all manner of ways, every which way [informal], all over the shop; here, there, and everywhere.

### 19. MULTIFORMITY

.1 NOUNS **multiformity,** multifariousness, **variety,** nonuniformity 18, **diversity,** diversification, variation, variegation 374, manifoldness, multiplicity, heterogeneity; omniformity, omnifariousness, everything but the kitchen sink [informal], polymorphism, heteromorphism; allotropy or allotropism [both chem]; Proteus, shapeshifting, shapeshifter; "God's plenty" [Dryden], "her infinite variety" [Shakespeare].

.2 VERBS **diversify, vary,** variate, variegate 374.7; ring changes.

.3 ADJS **multiform,** diversiform, "of every shape that was not uniform" [James Russell Lowell]; **manifold,** multifold, multiplex, multiple, multifarious, multiphase; polymorphous or polymorphic, hetero-

morphous or heteromorphic, metamorphic or metamorphotic; omniform(al), omnifarious, omnigenous; protean, proteiform; allotropic(al) [chem]; allo–, diversi–, heter(o)–, multi–, omni–, parti– or party–, poecil(o)– or poikil(o)–, poly–, vari(o)–.

.4 **diversified, varied, assorted,** heterogeneous; **various,** many and various, divers {archaic}, diverse, sundry, **several, many;** of all sorts or kinds or shapes or descriptions or types.

.5 ADVS **variously, severally,** sundrily, multifariously, diversely, manifoldly.

### 20. SIMILARITY

.1 NOUNS **similarity, likeness,** alikeness, **sameness,** similitude; **resemblance,** semblance; **analogy, correspondence,** conformity, accordance, agreement, comparability, comparison, parallelism, parity, community, alliance, consimilarity; **approximation,** approach, closeness, nearness; assimilation, likening, **simile, metaphor; simulation, imitation,** copying, aping, mimicking; identity 14.

.2 **connaturality** or connaturalness, connature, connateness, congeneracy; congeniality, affinity; **kinship,** family likeness, family favor, generic resemblance.

.3 **likeness, like,** the like of or the likes of [informal]; suchlike, such; **analogue,** analogon, **parallel;** ally, associate; cognate, congener, congenator; **counterpart, complement, correspondent,** pendant, similitude, tally; coordinate, reciprocal, obverse, equivalent; correlate, correlative; **close imitation** or reproduction or copy or facsimile or replica, near duplicate, simulacrum; **close match, fellow, mate;** soul mate, kindred spirit or soul, **companion, twin,** brother, sister; mon semblable [Fr], second self, alter ego; chip off the old block; image, picture; –aria, –ee, –ella, –o, –ode, –ops(is), –type.

.4 **close** or **striking resemblance,** startling or marked or decided resemblance; close or near likeness; **faint** or **remote resemblance,** mere hint or shadow.

.5 **set,** group, matching pair or set, couple, pair, twins, look-alikes, two of a kind, birds of a feather, peas in a pod.

.6 (of words or sounds) assonance, alliteration, rhyme, slant rhyme, near rhyme, jingle, clink; pun, paronomasia.

.7 VERBS **resemble,** be like, bear resemblance; put one in mind of [informal], remind one of, bring to mind, be reminiscent of, suggest, evoke, call up, call to mind; **look like,** favor [informal], mirror; **take after,** partake of, follow, appear like, seem like, sound like; savor *or* smack of, be redolent of; **have all the earmarks of,** have every appearance of, have all the features of, have all the signs of, have every sign *or* indication of; **approximate,** approach, near, come near, come close; **compare with,** stack up with [informal]; **correspond, match, parallel;** not tell apart, not tell one from the other; **imitate** 22.5,6, **simulate,** copy, ape, mimic, counterfeit; nearly reproduce *or* duplicate *or* replicate.

.8 **similarize,** approximate, assimilate, bring near; connaturalize; –fy, –ify.

.9 **assonate,** alliterate, rhyme, chime; pun.

.10 ADJS **similar, like, alike,** something like, not unlike; **resembling,** following, favoring [informal], savoring *or* smacking of, suggestive of, **on the order of;** consimilar; **simulated, imitated,** imitation, copied, aped, mimicked, fake *or* phony [both informal], counterfeit, **mock,** synthetic, ersatz; nearly reproduced *or* duplicated *or* replicated; uniform with, homogeneous, identical 14.7; –acean, –aceous, –an, –ar, –ean, –ed, –esque, –eous, –etic, –ey, –ful, –ian, –ic(al), –ie, –ine, –ish, –like, –ly, –oid-(al), –ular, –y; hol(o)–, hom(o)– *or* home(o)–, near–, par(a)–, pseud(o)–, quasi–, semi–, syn– *or* sym–.

.11 **analogous,** comparable; **corresponding,** correspondent, equivalent; **parallel,** paralleling; **matching,** cast in the same mold, of a kind, of a size, of a piece; duplicate, twin, of the same hue *or* stripe.

.12 **such as,** suchlike, so.

.13 **connatural,** connate, cognate, agnate, enate, conspecific, correlative; congenerous, congeneric(al); congenial, affinitive; **akin, allied, connected;** brothers *or* sisters under the skin.

.14 **approximating,** approximative, approximate; **near, close;** much the same, much at one, nearly the same, same but different, "like—but oh! how different" [Wordsworth]; quasi.

.15 **very like, mighty like,** powerful like [dial], uncommonly like, remarkably like, extraordinarily like, strikingly like, **ridiculously like, for all the world like,** as like as can be; a lot alike, pretty much the same, damned little difference [informal]; as like as two peas in a pod, "as lyke as one pease is to another" [John Lyly], "as like as eggs" [Shakespeare],

*comme deux gouttes d'eau* [Fr, like two drops of water]; faintly *or* remotely like.

.16 **lifelike,** speaking, faithful, living, breathing, to the life, **true to life** *or* nature; realistic, natural.

.17 (of words or sounds) assonant, assonantal, alliterative, alliteral; rhyming, chiming, punning.

.18 ADVS **similarly,** correspondingly, **like, likewise,** either; in the same manner, **in like manner,** in kind; in that way, like that, like this; **thus** 8.10; so; by the same token, by the same sign; identically 14.9.

.19 **so to speak,** in a manner of speaking, **as it were,** in a manner, in a way; kind of, sort of [both informal].

## 21. DISSIMILARITY

.1 NOUNS **dissimilarity,** unsimilarity; **dissimilitude,** dissemblance, **unresemblance; unlikeness,** unsameness; **disparity,** diversity, divergence, **contrast, difference** 16; nonuniformity 18; incomparability, incommensurability; dissimilation, camouflage, makeup, **disguise;** poor imitation, bad likeness *or* copy, mere caricature *or* counterfeit.

.2 VERBS **not resemble, bear no resemblance,** not look like, **not compare with; differ** 16.5; have little *or* nothing in common.

.3 **dissimilate,** camouflage, **disguise;** vary 139.6.

.4 ADJS **dissimilar,** unsimilar, unresembling; **unlike, unalike,** unsame, unidentical; **disparate,** diverse, divergent, **contrasting, different** 16.7; nonuniform 18.3; scarcely like, hardly like, a bit *or* mite different; off, a bit on the off side; unmatched, odd, counter, out; offbeat; heter(o)–, near–, off–; –ish.

.5 **nothing like,** not a bit alike, not a bit of it, **nothing of the sort,** nothing of the kind, something else, something else again [informal], quite another thing, cast in a different mold, not the same thing at all; not so you could tell it, not that you would know it, **far from it,** far other [all informal]; way off, away off, a mile off, way out, no such thing, no such a thing [informal]; "no more like than an apple to an oyster" [Sir Thomas More].

.6 **not to be compared with,** not comparable to; incomparable, incommensurable, incommensurate.

.7 ADVS **dissimilarly, differently** 16.10,11, with a difference, disparately, contrastingly.

## 22. IMITATION

.1 NOUNS **imitation, copying,** counterfeiting, repetition; emulation, the sincerest form of flattery, following, mirroring; **simulation** 616.3; fakery, forgery, plagiarism or plagiary; **imposture, impersonation** 572.2, **takeoff** or hit-off [both informal], **impression;** mimesis; parody, onomatopoeia.

.2 **mimicry, mockery,** apery, parrotry; protective coloration or mimicry, aggressive mimicry, aposematic or synaposematic mimicry, cryptic mimicry, playing possum.

.3 **reproduction, duplication, imitation** 24.1, **copy** 24.1, dummy, mock-up, **replica,** facsimile, representation, paraphrase, model, version, knockoff [informal]; –een, –ette, –type; parody, burlesque, travesty 967.6.

.4 **imitator, simulator, impersonator, impostor** 619.6, **mimic,** mimicker, mimer, mime, –mimus, **mocker;** mockingbird, cuckoo; **parrot,** polly, poll-parrot or polly-parrot, **ape,** monkey; **echo,** echoer, echoist; **copier,** copyist, **copycat** [informal]; faker, counterfeiter, forger, plagiarist; dissimulator, dissembler, hypocrite, phony [informal], poseur; conformist, sheep.

.5 VERBS **imitate, copy, repeat,** ditto [informal]; do like [informal], do [slang], act like, go like [informal], make like [informal]; **mirror, reflect; echo,** reecho, chorus; **borrow,** steal one's stuff [slang], take a leaf out of one's book; assume, **affect; simulate** 616.21; counterfeit, fake [informal], hoke or hoke up [both slang], forge, plagiarize, crib.

.6 **mimic, impersonate,** mime, **mock; ape,** copycat [informal]; parrot; take off, hit off, hit off on, take off on.

.7 **emulate, follow,** follow in the steps or footsteps of, walk in the shoes of, put oneself in another's shoes, follow in the wake of, follow the example of, follow suit, follow like sheep, jump on the bandwagon; **copy after,** model after, pattern after, take after, take a leaf out of one's book, take as a model.

.8 ADJS **imitation, mock, sham** 616.26, **fake** or phony [both informal], counterfeit, forged, plagiarized; **pseudo,** synthetic(al), ersatz, hokey [slang], quasi; mim(o)–, ne(o)–, near–, semi–.

.9 **imitative, simulative; mimic,** mimetic, **apish;** emulative; echoic, onomatopoetic, onomatopoeic; –ish, –like.

.10 **imitable,** copiable.

.11 ADVS imitatively, apishly; onomatopoetically; synthetically; quasi.

.12 PREPS **in imitation of,** after, in the semblance of, on the model of, à la [Fr].

## 23. NONIMITATION

.1 NOUNS **nonimitation, originality,** novelty, newness, innovation, freshness, uniqueness; **authenticity** 516.5; inventiveness, creativity or creativeness 535.3.

.2 **original, model** 25, archetype, prototype 25.1, pattern, pilot model; **innovation,** new departure.

.3 **autograph,** holograph, first edition.

.4 VERBS **originate, invent** 167.13; **innovate** 139.8; **create** 167.10; revolutionize.

.5 ADJS **original,** novel; unique; new, fresh 122.7; underived, **firsthand; authentic** 516.14, **imaginative, creative** 535.18; avant-garde; revolutionary.

.6 **unimitated,** uncopied, **unduplicated,** unreproduced, unprecedented, unexampled; prototypal 25.9, primary.

## 24. COPY

.1 NOUNS **copy, representation, image, likeness** 20.3, **resemblance,** semblance, similitude, picture, portrait, icon, simulacrum; ectype; pastiche, *pasticcio* [Ital]; fair copy, faithful copy; certified copy; **imitation** 22.3, **counterfeit** 616.13, forgery, fake [slang], phony [slang].

.2 **reproduction, duplication,** reduplication; reprography; transcription; tracing, rubbing; mimeography, xerography, hectography.

.3 **duplicate, duplication,** dupe [slang], ditto [informal]; **double;** clone; representation, **reproduction, replica,** replication, facsimile, model, **counterpart;** chip off the old block; triplicate, quadruplicate, etc.; repetition 103.

.4 **transcript, transcription,** apograph, tenor [law]; **transfer,** tracing, rubbing, **carbon copy,** carbon; manifold [archaic]; microcopy, microform; microfiche, fiche; recording.

.5 **print,** offprint; **impression,** impress; **reprint,** proof, second edition; photostatic copy, Photostat, stat [informal]; mimeograph copy, Ditto copy, hectograph copy, Xerox copy, Xerox [informal]; photograph, positive, negative, print, enlargement, contact print, photocopy.

.6 **cast,** casting; mold, **molding,** stamp, seal.

.7 **reflection,** reflex; **shadow,** silhouette, outline 235.2, adumbration; **echo.**

.8 VERBS **copy, reproduce,** replicate, duplicate, dupe [slang]; clone; reduplicate; transcribe; trace; double; triplicate, quadruplicate, etc.; manifold [archaic], multigraph, mimeograph, mimeo, Photostat, stat [informal], facsimile, hectograph, ditto, Xerox; microcopy, microfilm.

.9 ADVS in duplicate, in triplicate, etc.

## 25. MODEL

### (thing copied)

.1 NOUNS **model, pattern, standard, criterion,** classic example, rule, mirror, paradigm; original, urtext; **type, prototype,** antetype, archetype, genotype, biotype, type specimen, type species, antitype; **precedent,** lead; representative, **epitome;** fugler, fugleman; imitatee.

.2 **example,** exemplar; **representative,** type, symbol, emblem; exponent; **exemplification,** illustration, demonstration, explanation; **instance,** relevant instance, **case,** typical example or case, case in point; object lesson.

.3 **sample, specimen;** piece, taste, swatch.

.4 **ideal,** beau ideal, ego ideal, acme, highest or perfect or best type; cynosure, apotheosis; **shining example,** hero, mirror, paragon, "the observed of all observers" [Shakespeare].

.5 artist's model, dressmaker's model, photographer's model, mannequin; dummy, lay figure; clay model, wood model, pilot model, mock-up.

.6 **mold, form** 246, cast, template, matrix, negative; **die,** punch, stamp, intaglio, seal, mint; last, shoe last.

.7 VERBS **set an example,** set the pace, lead the way; exemplify, epitomize; fit the pattern.

.8 ADJS **model, exemplary,** precedential, typical, **paradigmatic, representative,** standard, classic; ideal; type(o)–.

.9 **prototypal,** prototypic(al), archetypal, archetypic(al), antitypic(al).

## 26. AGREEMENT

.1 NOUNS **agreement, accord** 794, accordance; **concord,** concordance; **harmony, cooperation** 786, peace 803, *rapport* [Fr], concert, consort, **consonance,** unisonance, **unison,** union, chorus, oneness; **correspondence,** coincidence, intersection, overlap, parallelism, symmetry, tally, equivalence 14.1; congeniality, compatibility, affinity; **conformity,** conformance, conformation, uniformity 17; con-

gruity, congruence or congruency; **consistency,** self-consistency, coherence; synchronism, sync [informal], timing; **assent** 521.

.2 **understanding,** entente; mutual or cordial understanding, consortium, *entente cordiale* [Fr]; **compact** 771.

.3 (general agreement) consensus, consentaneity, *consensus omnium, consensus gentium* [both L], unanimity 521.5; **like-mindedness,** meeting or intersection or confluence of minds.

.4 **adjustment, adaptation,** coaptation, **regulation, attunement, harmonization, coordination,** accommodation, squaring, integration, assimilation; reconciliation, reconcilement, synchronization, timing.

.5 **fitness** or fittedness, **suitability, appropriateness,** propriety, admissibility; **aptness,** aptitude, qualification; **relevance** 9.4, felicity, appositeness, applicability.

.6 VERBS **agree, accord** 794.2, **harmonize,** concur 521.9, **cooperate** 786.3,4, **correspond, conform,** coincide, parallel, intersect, overlap, **match,** tally, hit, register, lock, interlock, check [informal], square, dovetail, jibe [informal]; **be consistent,** cohere, stand or hold or hang together, fall in together, fit together, chime; **assent** 521.8, come to an agreement 521.10, be of one or the same or like mind, see eye to eye, sing in chorus; **go together,** go with, conform with, be uniform with, square with, sort or assort with, go on all fours with, consist with, register with, answer or respond to.

.7 (make agree) **harmonize,** coordinate, accord, make uniform 17.4, equalize 30.6, similarize, assimilate, homologize or homologate; **adjust, set,** regulate, **accommodate, reconcile,** synchronize, sync [informal]; adapt, fit, tailor, measure, proportion, adjust to, trim to, cut to, gear to, key to; fix, **rectify,** true, true up, right, set right, make plumb; **tune, attune,** put in tune.

.8 **suit,** fit, **qualify, do,** serve, answer, relate 9.6, be OK [informal], do the job [informal], fill the bill [informal].

.9 ADJS **agreeing, in agreement; in accord, concurring,** positive, affirmative, in rapport, *en rapport* [Fr], **in harmony,** in accordance, **at one,** on all fours, of one or the same or like mind, **like-minded,** consentient, consentaneous, **unanimous** 521.15, unisonous or unisonant; **harmonious,** accordant, **concordant,** consonant; **consistent,** self-consistent; uniform, coherent, conformable, of a piece, equivalent, coinciding 14.8, coincident, corresponding or correspondent; answerable, reconcilable; commensurate, proportionate; **congruous**, congruent; **agreeable**, congenial, compatible, cooperating or cooperative 786.5, coexisting or coexistent, symbiotic; synchronous, **synchronized**, in synchronization, in sync [informal]; con–, syn– or sym–, uni–.

.10 **apt, apposite, appropriate, suitable;** applicable, relevant, likely, sortable, seasonable, opportune; **fitting**, befitting, **suiting**, becoming; **fit**, fitted, qualified, **suited**, adapted, geared, tailored, dovetailing, meshing; **right**, just right, **pat**, happy, felicitous, just what the doctor ordered [informal]; to the point, to the purpose, *ad rem* [L], *à propos* [Fr], **apropos**, on the button [informal]; –ile.

.11 ADVS **in step**, in concert, **in unison**, in chorus, **in line, in keeping**, hand in glove, just right; with it [slang]; **unanimously**, **harmoniously**, concordantly, consonantly, **by consensus**; agreeably, congenially, compatibly; fittingly.

.12 PREPS in agreement with, together with, with, right with, in there with, right along there with; in line with, in keeping with; together on.

.13 PHRS that's it, that's the thing, that's just the thing, that's the very thing, that's the idea, that's the ticket [both informal]; right on [informal].

## 27. DISAGREEMENT

.1 NOUNS **disagreement, discord,** discordance or discordancy; **disaccord** 795, disaccordance, inaccordance; **disunity**, disunion; **disharmony**, unharmoniousness; dissonance, dissidence; jarring, clashing; **difference** 16, **variance**, divergence, diversity; **disparity**, discrepancy, inequality; antagonism, **opposition** 790, **conflict**, controversy, faction, oppugnancy, repugnance, dissension 795.3, argumentation 482.4; **dissent** 522, negation 524, contradiction.

.2 **inconsistency**, incongruity, asymmetry, inconsonance, incoherence; **incompatibility**, irreconcilability, incommensurability; disproportion, disproportionateness, nonconformity or unconformity, nonconformability or unconformability, heterogeneity, heterodoxy, unorthodoxy, heresy; self-contradiction, paradox, antinomy, oxymoron, **ambiguity**, ambivalence, equivocality.

.3 **unfitness, inappropriateness, unsuitability,** impropriety; **inaptness**, inaptitude, **inappositeness, irrelevance** or irrelevancy, infelicity, uncongeniality, inapplicability, inadmissibility; abnormality, anomaly; **maladjustment**, misjoining, misjoinder; mismatch, mismatchment; misalliance, *mésalliance* [Fr].

.4 **misfit, nonconformist,** individualist, inner-directed person, oddball [informal]; freak, sport, anomaly; naysayer, crosspatch; fish out of water, square peg in a round hole.

.5 VERBS **disagree, differ** 16.5, vary, be at cross-purposes, **disaccord** 795.8–14, **conflict**, clash, **jar**, jangle, jostle, collide, square off, break, break off; mismatch, mismate; **dissent** 522.4, agree to disagree, object, **negate** 524.3,4, contradict, counter; be or march out of step, "hear a different drummer" [Thoreau].

.6 ADJS **disagreeing, differing** 16.7, **discordant** 795.15,16, disaccordant; dissonant, dissident; **inharmonious**, unharmonious, disharmonious; discrepant, disproportionate; divergent, variant; at variance, **at odds**, at war, at loggerheads, at cross-purposes; hostile, antipathetic, antagonistic, repugnant; inaccordant, out of accord, out of whack [informal]; clashing, grating, jarring, jangling; **contradictory, contrary; disagreeable**, cross, cranky, negative, uncongenial, incompatible, immiscible [chem]; contra–, counter–, dis–.

.7 **inappropriate, inapt**, unapt, inapposite, **irrelevant**, malapropos, *mal à propos* [Fr]; **unsuited**, ill-suited; **unfitted**, ill-fitted; **maladjusted**, unadapted, ill-adapted; ill-sorted, ill-assorted, ill-chosen; ill-matched or -mated, mismatched or mismated, misjoined; misplaced; **unfit**, inept, unqualified; unfitting, unbefitting; **unsuitable**, improper, **unbecoming**, unseemly; infelicitous, inapplicable, inadmissible; **unseasonable**, ill-timed, untimely; **out of place**, out of line, out of keeping, out of character, out of proportion, out of joint, out of tune, out of time, out of season, out of its element; ill–, mal–, mis–.

.8 **inconsistent, incongruous, inconsonant,** inconsequent, incoherent, **incompatible,** irreconcilable; incommensurable, incommensurate; disproportionate, out of proportion, self-contradictory, paradoxical, oxymoronic, **absurd; abnormal,** anomalous.

**.9 nonconformist**, individualistic, inner-directed; **unorthodox**, heterodox, heretical.

**.10** PREPS **in disagreement with**, **against**, counter to, **contrary to**, in defiance of, in contempt of, in opposition to; out of line with, not in keeping with.

## 28. QUANTITY

**.1** NOUNS **quantity**, quantum, amount, **whole** 54; mass, **bulk**, substance, matter, magnitude, amplitude, **extent**, **sum**; **measure**, measurement; strength, force, numbers.

**.2 amount**, quantity, large amount 34.3,4, small amount 35.2, **sum**, **number**, count, **measure**, parcel, **part** 55, **portion**, group, clutch, ration, lot, deal; batch, bunch, heap [informal], pack, mess [informal], gob [slang], chunk [informal], hunk [slang], budget [archaic], dose; –ful or –full.

**.3 some**, somewhat, something; **aught**; **any**, anything.

**.4** VERBS **quantify**, quantize, **count**, **number** 87.10, rate, fix; parcel, apportion, divide 49.18; **increase** 38.4–6, **decrease** 39.6, reduce 39.7; **measure** 490.11.

**.5** ADJS **quantitative**, quantitive, quantified, quantized, measured; **some**, certain, one; a, an; **any**.

**.6** ADVS **approximately**, nearly, some, about, circa; more or less, *plus ou moins* [Fr].

**.7** PREPS **to the amount of**, to the tune of [informal]; as much as, all of [informal], no less than.

**.8 indefinite quantities**

| | |
|---|---|
| armful | kettle(ful) |
| bag(ful) | lapful |
| barrel(ful) | mouthful |
| basin(ful) | mug(ful) |
| basket(ful) | pail(ful) |
| bin(ful) | pitcher(ful) |
| bottle(ful) | plate(ful) |
| bowl(ful) | pocketful |
| box(ful) | pot(ful) |
| bucket(ful) | roomful |
| can(ful) | sack(ful) |
| capful | scoop(ful) |
| carton(ful) | shovel(ful) |
| case(ful) | skepful |
| crate(ful) | spoon(ful) |
| cup(ful) | tablespoon(ful) |
| flask(ful) | tank(ful) |
| glass(ful) | teacup(ful) |
| handful | teaspoon(ful) |
| jar(ful) | thimble(ful) |
| keg(ful) | |

## 29. DEGREE

**.1** NOUNS **degree**, grade, step, *pas* [Fr], leap; round, rung, tread, stair; point, mark, peg; **notch**, cut; plane, level, plateau; **period**, space, interval; **extent**, **measure**, amount, ratio, proportion, stint, standard, height, pitch, reach, remove, compass, range, scale, scope, caliber; **shade**, shadow, nuance.

**.2 rank**, **standing**, footing, **status**, station, stage, **position**, place, sphere, order, echelon, precedence, condition; rate, rating; class, caste; **hierarchy**, power structure; –ance, –ence.

**.3 gradation**, **graduation**, grading, shading.

**.4** VERBS **graduate**, **grade**, calibrate; shade off; differentiate; **increase** 38, **decrease** 39.6,7.

**.5** ADJS **gradual**, gradational, calibrated, graduated, scalar; regular, progressive; hierarchic(al); –escent.

**.6** ADVS **by degrees**, degreewise; **gradually**, gradatim; **step by step**, grade by grade, *di grado in grado* [Ital], **bit by bit**, **little by little**, inch by inch, drop by drop; by slow degrees, by inches, by little and little, a little at a time; –meal, **inchmeal**, by inchmeal; slowly 270.13.

**.7 to a degree**, to some extent, in a way, in a measure, in some measure; somewhat, kind of [informal], sort of [informal], rather, pretty, quite, fairly; a little, a bit; slightly, scarcely, to a small degree 35.9,10; very, extremely, to a great degree 34.15–23.

## 30. EQUALITY

**.1** NOUNS **equality**, **parity**, par, equation, **identity** 14; equivalence or equivalency, **correspondence**, parallelism, equipollence, coequality; likeness, levelness, evenness, coextension; **balance**, poise, equipoise, **equilibrium**, equiponderance; symmetry, proportion; **justice**, equity.

**.2 equating** or **equation**; **equalizing** or **equalization**, equilibration, evening, evening up; coordination, integration, accommodation, adjustment.

**.3 the same** 14.3; **tie**, **draw**, **standoff** [informal], stalemate, deadlock, dead heat, neck-and-neck race, photo finish; tied or knotted score; a distinction without a difference, six of one and half a dozen of the other, Tweedledum and Tweedledee; even break [slang], fair shake [slang].

**.4 equal**, **match**, mate, twin, fellow, **like**, **equivalent**, opposite number, counterpart, equipollent, coequal, parallel, ditto [informal]; **peer**, compeer, **rival**.

**.5** VERBS **equal**, **match**, **rival**, **correspond**, reach, touch; keep pace with, keep step with, run abreast; **amount to,** come to, run to; **measure up to,** come up to, stack up with [slang], match up with; lie on a level with, **balance, parallel,** ditto [informal]; even, even off, break even [slang]; **tie, draw, knot.**

.6 **equalize; equate; even,** even up, square, level; **balance,** strike a balance, poise; compensate, counterpoise; countervail, counterbalance, cancel; coordinate, integrate, proportion; fit, accommodate, adjust.

.7 ADJS **equal, equalized,** like, **alike, even,** level, par, **on a par,** at par, au pair, commensurate, proportionate; on the same level, on the same plane, on the same footing; on terms of equality, **on even** or **equal terms,** on even ground; on a level, on a footing, in the same boat; **square,** quits, even stephen [informal]; half-and-half, **fifty-fifty;** nip and tuck, **drawn, tied,** deadlocked, stalemated, knotted; co–, equi– or aequi–, homal(o)–, is(o)–, pari–.

.8 **equivalent, tantamount,** equiparant, equipollent, coequal, coordinate; **identical** 14.7; corresponding or correspondent; convertible, much the same, as broad as long, neither more nor less; **all one,** all the same.

.9 **balanced, poised,** apoise, **on an even keel;** equibalanced, equiponderant or equiponderous; symmetric(al); stato–, sym–.

.10 **equisized,** equidimensional, equiproportional, equispaced; equiangular, isogonic, isometric; equilateral, equisided.

.11 ADVS **equally, correspondingly, proportionately,** equivalently, **evenly; identically** 14.9; without distinction, indifferently; to the same degree, *ad eundem* [L]; as, so; as well; to all intents and purposes, other things being equal, *ceteris paribus* [L]; as much as to say.

.12 **to a standoff** [informal], to a tie or draw.

## 31. INEQUALITY

.1 NOUNS **inequality, disparity, unevenness, contrariety** 15, **difference** 16, odds; **irregularity,** nonuniformity 18, heterogeneity; disproportion, asymmetry; **unbalance,** imbalance, disequilibrium, overbalance, inclination of the balance; **inadequacy,** insufficiency, shortcoming; **injustice,** inequity, unfair discrimination.

.2 VERBS **unequalize,** disproportion.

.3 **unbalance,** disbalance, disequilibrate, overbalance, **throw off balance,** upset, skew.

.4 ADJS **unequal,** disparate, **uneven; irregular**

18.3; disproportionate, **out of proportion,** skew, skewed, asymmetric(al); mismatched or ill-matched, ill-sorted; **inadequate,** insufficient; odd; aniso–.

.5 **unbalanced, ill-balanced,** overbalanced, off-balance, listing, heeling, leaning, canted, top-heavy; lopsided; unstable, unsteady.

.6 ADVS **unequally,** disparately, disproportionately, variously, **unevenly;** nonuniformly 18.4.

## 32. MEAN

.1 NOUNS **mean, median, middle** 69; **golden mean,** *juste-milieu* [Fr]; **medium,** happy medium; middle-of-the-road, middle course, *via media* [L]; middle state or ground or position or point, midpoint; **average,** balance, par, normal, norm, rule, run, generality; mediocrity; **center** 226.2.

.2 VERBS **average,** average out, **split the difference,** take the average, strike a balance, pair off; do on an average; keep to the middle, avoid extremes.

.3 ADJS **medium, mean, intermediate,** intermediary, median, medial; **average,** normal, standard; middle-of-the-road, moderate; **middling, ordinary,** usual, routine, common, mediocre, banal; **central** 226.11; medi(o)–, mes(o)–, mezzo–, semi–.

.4 ADVS **mediumly,** medianly; medially, midway 69.5, intermediately, in the mean; **centrally** 226.15.

.5 **on the average, in the long run; taking one thing with another,** taking all things together, **all in all, on the whole,** all things considered, on balance; **generally** 79.17; in round numbers.

## 33. COMPENSATION

.1 NOUNS **compensation, recompense,** repayment, indemnity, indemnification, measure for measure, rectification, restitution, **reparation, amends,** expiation, atonement; **redress,** satisfaction; commutation, substitution; **offsetting,** balancing, **counterbalancing,** counteraction; **retaliation** 955, revenge, *lex talionis* [L].

.2 **offset,** setoff; **counterbalance,** counterpoise, equipoise, counterweight, make-weight; **balance,** ballast; equivalent, consideration, something of value, *quid pro quo* [L, something for something], tit for tat, give-and-take 150.1.

.3 **counterclaim,** counterdemand.

.4 VERBS **compensate,** make compensation, make good, set right, rectify, **make up for,** make amends; do penance, atone, expiate; **recompense**, pay back, repay, indemnify; cover, fill up; give and take, retaliate.

.5 **offset** 15.4, set off, **counteract**, countervail, **counterbalance**, counterweigh, counterpoise, **balance**, equiponderate; square, square up.

.6 ADJS **compensating**, **compensatory**; recompensive, amendatory, indemnificatory, reparative, rectifying; **offsetting**, counteracting *or* counteractive, countervailing, balancing, **counterbalancing**; expiatory, penitential; retaliatory; counter–.

.7 ADVS **in compensation**, in return, back; in consideration, for a consideration.

.8 ADVS, CONJS **notwithstanding**, but, all the same [informal], still, yet, even; **however, nevertheless**, nonetheless; **although**, when, though; howbeit, albeit; **at all events**, in any event, **in any case**, at any rate; **be that as it may**, for all that, even so, **on the other hand**, rather, again, at the same time, just the same, **however that may be**; after all, after all is said and done.

.9 ADVS, PREPS **in spite of**, spite of [informal], **despite**, in despite of, with, even with; **regardless of**, regardless, irregardless [informal], irrespective of, without respect *or* regard to; cost what it may, regardless of cost, at any cost, at all costs.

## 34. GREATNESS

.1 NOUNS **greatness**, **magnitude**, muchness; **amplitude**, ampleness, fullness, plenitude, great scope *or* compass *or* reach; **grandeur**, grandness; **immensity**, enormousness *or* enormity, **vastness**, tremendousness, expanse, boundlessness, infinity 104; stupendousness, formidableness, prodigiousness; might, mightiness, strength, power, intensity; **largeness** 195.6, **hugeness**, gigantism, bulk.

.2 **eminence**, loftiness, prominence, distinction, consequence, notability, nobility, sublimity, **magnanimity**, majesty; fame, renown, **glory**; heroism.

.3 **quantity** 28, **quantities**, **much**, **abundance**, copiousness, superabundance, superfluity, profusion, plenty, plenitude; **volume**, **mass**, mountain, load; peck, bushel; bags, barrels, tons; world, worlds, acres, ocean, oceans, sea; flood, spate; **multitude** 101.3, numerousness, countlessness 104.1.

.4 **lot**, **lots**, deal, **good** *or* **great deal**, **considerable**, sight, **heap**, heaps, pile, piles, **stack**, stacks, loads, **raft**, rafts, slew, slews,

whole slew, spate, wad, wads, **batch**, mess, mint, peck, pack, pot, **tidy sum**, quite a little; **oodles, gobs, scads**, lashings [Brit].

.5 VERBS **loom, bulk**, loom large, bulk large, stand out; **tower**, rear, soar, outsoar; tower above, rise above, overtop; **exceed**, transcend, outstrip.

.6 ADJS **great**, **grand**, **considerable**, consequential; powerful, **mighty**, strong, irresistible, intense; main, maximum, **total**, **full**, plenary, comprehensive, exhaustive; grave, **serious**, heavy, deep; –ulent.

.7 **large** 195.16, **immense**, **enormous**, **huge** 195.20; **gigantic**, mountainous, titanic, colossal, mammoth, Gargantuan, monster, monstrous, outsize, sizable, overgrown, king-size, monumental; **massive**, massy, weighty, bulky, voluminous; **vast**, boundless, **infinite** 104.3, immeasurable, cosmic, astronomical, galactic; **spacious**, amplitudinous, extensive; **tremendous**, stupendous, awesome, prodigious; meg(a)–, multi–, super–.

.8 **much**, **many**, ample, **abundant**, copious, generous, overflowing, superabundant, multitudinous, plentiful, **numerous** 101.6, countless 104.3.

.9 **eminent**, **prominent**, high, elevated, towering, soaring, exalted, **lofty**, sublime; august, majestic, noble, distinguished; **magnificent**, magnanimous, heroic, godlike, superb; famous, renowned, lauded, glorious.

.10 **remarkable**, **outstanding**, extraordinary, superior, **marked**, of mark, signal, conspicuous, **striking**; **notable**, noticeable, noteworthy; **marvelous**, wonderful, formidable, exceptional, uncommon, astonishing, appalling, fabulous, fantastic, incredible, egregious.

.11 [informal terms] **terrific**, terrible, horrible, **dreadful**, **awful**, fearful, frightful, deadly; **whacking, thumping, rousing**, howling.

.12 **downright, outright, out-and-out**; **absolute, utter, perfect, consummate**, superlative, surpassing, the veriest, positive, definitive, classical, pronounced, decided, regular [informal], proper [Brit informal], precious, profound, stark; **thorough**, thoroughgoing, **complete**, total; **unmitigated**, unqualified, unrelieved, unspoiled, undeniable, unequivocal; **flagrant**, arrant, shocking, shattering, egregious, intolerable, unbearable, unconscionable, glaring, stark-staring, **rank**, crass, gross.

.13 **extreme**, **radical**, out of this world, way

*or* far out [informal], too much [slang]; **greatest, furthest, most, utmost,** uttermost; **ultra,** ultra-ultra; at the height *or* peak *or* limit *or* summit *or* zenith.

.14 **undiminished,** unabated, unreduced, unrestricted, unretarded, unmitigated.

.15 ADVS **greatly, largely,** to a large *or* great extent, in great measure, on a large scale; **much,** muchly [informal], pretty much, very much, so, so very much, ever so much, ever so, never so; **considerably,** considerable [dial]; abundantly, plenty [informal], no end of, no end [informal], not a little, galore [informal], **a lot,** a deal [informal], **a great deal,** *beaucoup* [Fr]; **highly,** to the skies; like *or* as all creation [informal], like *or* as all get-out [slang].

.16 **vastly, immensely, enormously, hugely, tremendously,** gigantically, colossally, titanically, prodigiously, stupendously.

.17 **by far, far and away,** far, far and wide, by a long way, by a great deal, by a long shot *or* long chalk [informal], out and away.

.18 **very, exceedingly;** awfully *or* terribly *or* terrifically [all informal], **quite,** just, so, **really,** real [informal], right [dial], **pretty,** only too, mightily, **mighty** [informal], almighty [dial], powerfully [dial], powerful [dial].

.19 (in a positive degree) **positively, decidedly, clearly,** manifestly, unambiguously, patently, **obviously,** visibly, unmistakably, observably, **noticeably,** demonstrably, sensibly, quite; **certainly,** actually, **really, truly,** verily, **undeniably,** indubitably, without doubt, assuredly, **indeed,** for a certainty, for real [slang], seriously, in all conscience.

.20 (in a marked degree) **intensely, acutely,** exquisitely, **exceptionally,** surpassingly, superlatively, eminently, preeminently; **remarkably, markedly, notably, strikingly,** signally, emphatically, pointedly, prominently, conspicuously, pronouncedly, impressively, famously, glaringly; **particularly, singularly,** peculiarly; uncommonly, extraordinarily, **unusually; wonderfully,** wondrous, amazingly, magically, surprisingly, astonishingly, marvelously, exuberantly, incredibly, awesomely; **abundantly,** richly, profusely, amply, **generously,** copiously; **magnificently,** splendidly, nobly, worthily, magnanimously.

.21 (in a distressing degree) **distressingly, sadly, sorely, bitterly,** piteously, grievously, miserably, **cruelly,** woefully, lamen-tably, balefully, dolorously, shockingly; **terribly, awfully, dreadfully, frightfully, horribly,** abominably, **painfully,** excruciatingly, torturously, **agonizingly,** deathly, deadly, something awful *or* fierce *or* terrible [informal], in the worst way [informal]; shatteringly, staggeringly; **excessively,** exorbitantly, extravagantly, **inordinately,** preposterously; **unduly,** improperly, intolerably, unbearably; **inexcusably,** unpardonably, unconscionably; **flagrantly,** blatantly, egregiously; **unashamedly,** baldly, nakedly, brashly, openly; **cursedly,** confoundedly, **damnably,** deucedly [informal], infernally, hellishly.

.22 (in an extreme degree) **extremely, utterly,** in the extreme, **most,** *à outrance* [Fr, to the utmost]; **immeasurably,** incalculably, indefinitely, **infinitely;** beyond compare *or* comparison, **beyond measure,** beyond all bounds, all out [informal], flat out [Brit informal]; **perfectly, absolutely,** essentially, fundamentally, radically; **purely, totally,** completely; unconditionally, unequivocally, downright, dead; with a vengeance.

.23 (in a violent degree) **violently,** furiously, hotly, fiercely, severely, **desperately,** madly, **like mad** [informal]; **wildly,** demonically, like one possessed, **frantically,** frenetically, fanatically, uncontrollably.

## 35. SMALLNESS

.1 NOUNS **smallness,** exiguity *or* exiguousness; **insignificance,** inconsiderableness, unimportance, pettiness, triviality, inconsequentiality; **slightness,** moderateness, scantiness, puniness, picayunishness, meanness, meagerness; daintiness, delicacy; tininess, diminutiveness, minuteness; **littleness** 196; **fewness** 102; insufficiency 662.

.2 **modicum,** minim; **minimum; little,** bit, little *or* wee *or* tiny bit [informal], **particle,** fragment, spot, **speck,** flyspeck, fleck, point, dot, jot, tittle, **iota,** ounce, **dab** [informal], mote, **mite** [informal] 196.7; whit, ace, **hair,** scruple, groat, farthing, pittance, dole, trifling amount, **smidgen** [informal], smitch [informal], pinch, gobbet, dribble, driblet, dram; grain, granule, pebble; molecule, **atom;** thimbleful, spoonful, handful, nutshell; trivia, minutiae; dwarf 196.6.

.3 **scrap,** tatter, smithereen [informal], patch, **stitch, shred,** tag; snip, **snippet,** snick, chip, nip; splinter, sliver, shiver; **morsel,** *morceau* [Fr], **crumb.**

.4 **hint**, *soupçon* [Fr], suspicion, suggestion, intimation; **trace, touch, dash**, cast, **smattering**, sprinkling; tinge, tincture; **taste, lick, smack**, sip, sup, **smell**; look, thought, idea; **shade**, shadow; gleam, spark, scintilla.

.5 **hardly anything, mere nothing**, next to nothing, **trifle**, bagatelle, **a drop in the bucket** *or* **ocean**; the shadow of a shade, the suspicion of a suspicion.

.6 ADJS **small, insignificant, inconsiderable, inconsequential**, negligible, trifling, petty, trivial, **no great shakes**, footling, picayune *or* picayunish; shallow, depthless, cursory, superficial, skin-deep; **little** 196.10, **tiny** 196.11, **miniature** 196.12, **meager** 662.10, **few** 102.4; **short** 203.8; **low** 208.7; mei(o)– *or* mi(o)–, sub–.

.7 **dainty**, delicate; **subtle**, subtile, tenuous, thin 205.16, rarefied 355.4.

.8 **mere, sheer**, stark, **bare**, plain, simple, unadorned, unenhanced; psil(o)–.

.9 ADVS (in a small degree) **scarcely, hardly**, not hardly [informal], **barely**, only just, by a hair, by an ace *or* jot *or* whit *or* iota, **slightly**, lightly, exiguously, scantily, **inconsequentially, insignificantly**, negligibly, imperfectly, minimally, inappreciably, **little; minutely**, meagerly, triflingly, faintly, weakly, feebly; **a little, a bit**, just a bit, to a small extent, on a small scale; ever so little, *tant soit peu* [Fr], as little as may be.

.10 (in a certain or limited degree) **to a degree, to a certain extent**, to some degree, in some measure, to such an extent, *pro tanto* [L]; **moderately**, mildly, **somewhat**, detectably, modestly, appreciably, visibly, **fairly**, tolerably, **partially**, partly, part, in part, incompletely, not exhaustively, not comprehensively; **comparatively**, relatively; **merely**, simply, purely, only; **at least**, at the least, leastwise, at worst, at any rate; **at most**, at the most, at best, at the outside [informal]; in a manner, in a manner of speaking, **in a way**, after a fashion; so far, thus far.

.11 (in no degree) **noway**, noways, **nowise**, in no wise, in no case, in no respect, **by no means**, by no manner of means, **on no account, under no circumstances**, at no hand, nohow [informal], **not in the least**, not much, **not at all**, never, not by a damn sight [slang], not by a long shot [informal]; not nearly, **nowhere near; not a bit**, not a bit of it, not a whit, not a speck, not a jot, not an iota.

## 36. SUPERIORITY

.1 NOUNS **superiority, preeminence, greatness** 34, **lead**, transcendence *or* transcendency, ascendancy, prestige, favor, prepotence *or* prepotency, preponderance; **predominance** *or* **predomination**; precedence 64, **priority**, prerogative, privilege, right-of-way; **excellence** 674.1, virtuosity, inimitability, incomparability; majority, **seniority**, deanship; one-upmanship; **success** 724, accomplishment 722, **skill** 733.

.2 **advantage**, vantage, odds, inside track [informal]; **upper hand**, whip hand; start, head *or* flying *or* running start; **edge**, bulge, jump, drop [all informal]; **card up one's sleeve** [informal], ace in the hole [informal], something extra *or* in reserve; vantage ground *or* point, coign of vantage.

.3 **supremacy, primacy**, paramountcy, **first place**, height, acme, zenith, be-all and end-all, top spot [informal]; **sovereignty, rule, control** 739.5; kingship, **dominion** 739.6; lordship, **command**, imperium, sway, hegemony, directorship, management, mastery, mastership 739.7; **headship**, presidency, **leadership; authority** 739, jurisdiction, power, say [informal], authorization; influence 172; effectiveness; maximum, highest, most, *ne plus ultra* [L, no more beyond]; **championship**, palms, first prize, blue ribbon, new high, record.

.4 **superior, chief**, head, boss [informal], commander, **ruler, leader**, dean, *primus inter pares* [L, first among equals], **master** 749; higher-up [informal], senior, principal; superman, **genius** 733.12; prodigy, nonpareil, paragon, virtuoso, ace, **star**, superstar, champion, top dog [slang], laureate, fugleman, A per se, A1, A number 1, the greatest, the most [slang].

.5 **the best** 674.8, the best people, nobility 918; **aristocracy**, barons, top people [informal], **elite**, cream, upper crust, upper class, one's betters; **the brass** [informal], the VIP's [informal], lords of creation, ruling circles, **establishment**, power elite, power structure, **ruling class**, bigwigs [informal].

.6 VERBS **excel, surpass, exceed, transcend, overcome**, overpass, best, **better**, improve on, perfect, go one better [informal]; **cap**, trump; top, tower above *or* over, overtop; **predominate**, prevail, preponderate; **outweigh**, overbalance, overbear.

.7 **best, beat, defeat** 727.6; beat all hollow [informal], **trounce**, clobber [slang], **worst**, lick [informal], skin [slang], have it all over [informal]; bear the palm, take the cake [informal], bring home the bacon [informal]; **triumph** 726.3; **win** 726.4.

.8 **overshadow, eclipse, throw into the shade**, extinguish, take the shine out of [informal]; put to shame, show up [informal], put one's nose out of joint, put down [slang], fake out [slang].

.9 **outdo, outrival**, outvie, **outclass, outshine**, overmatch; **outstrip**, outgo, outrange, outreach, outpoint, **outperform**; outplay, overplay, outmaneuver, outwit; outrun, outstep, outpace, outmarch, run rings or circles around [informal]; outride, override; outjump, overjump; outleap, overleap.

.10 **outdistance, distance;** pass, surpass, overpass; **get ahead of,** shoot ahead of; leave behind, leave in the lurch; come to the front, have a healthy lead [informal], hold the field; steal a march.

.11 **take precedence, precede** 64.2; **come** or **rank first, outrank**, rank, rank out [slang]; come to the front, **lead** 292.2; play first fiddle, star.

.12 ADJS **superior, greater**, better, finer, major, **higher**, upper, over, super, above; ascendant, in the ascendant, in ascendancy; eminent, outstanding, rare, distinguished, marked, of choice, chosen; **surpassing, exceeding, excellent** 674.12, **excelling, rivaling, eclipsing**, capping, topping, **transcending**, transcendent or transcendental; ahead, a cut or stroke above, one up on [slang]; more than a match for; ano–, meta–, out–, pre–, preter–, super–, supra–, sur–, trans–, ultra–.

.13 **superlative, supreme, greatest, best, highest,** maximal, maximum, most, utmost; top, topmost, **uppermost**, tip-top, topnotch [informal], **first-rate** 674.15, first-class, of the first water, of the highest type, A1, A number 1; –est or –st, –most.

.14 **chief, main, principal**, paramount, foremost, headmost, **leading, dominant**, crowning, capital, **cardinal;** great, arch, banner, master, magisterial; central, focal, prime, **primary**, primal, first; **preeminent, supereminent; predominant**, preponderant, prevailing, hegemonic(al); ruling, overruling; **sovereign** 739.17; topflight, ranking; star, stellar; **champion;** arch–, prot(o)–.

.15 **peerless, matchless; unmatched**, unmatchable, unrivaled, unparagoned, unparal-

leled, immortal, **unequaled,** never-to-be-equaled, unpeered, unexampled, unapproached, unapproachable, **unsurpassed, unexcelled;** unsurpassable; inimitable, **incomparable**, beyond compare or comparison, **unique;** without equal or parallel, *sans pareil* [Fr], in a class by itself, *sui generis* [L], easily first, *facile princeps* [L]; second to none, *nulli secundus* [L]; **unbeatable**, invincible.

.16 ADVS **superlatively, exceedingly, surpassingly;** eminently, egregiously, prominently; supremely, paramountly, preeminently, **the most,** transcendently, to crown all, *par excellence* [Fr]; inimitably, incomparably, to or in the highest degree, far and away.

.17 **chiefly, mainly, in the main,** in chief; dominantly, **predominantly; mostly, for the most part; principally, especially, particularly,** peculiarly; **primarily, in the first place,** first of all, **above all;** indeed, even, yea, still more, more than ever, all the more, *a fortiori* [L]; ever so, never so, no end.

.18 **peerlessly, matchlessly,** unmatchably; unsurpassedly, unsurpassably; inimitably, **incomparably; uniquely,** second to none, *nulli secundus* [L]; **unbeatably**, invincibly.

.19 **advantageously,** to or with advantage, favorably; melioratively, amelioratively, improvingly.

## 37. INFERIORITY

.1 NOUNS **inferiority, subordinacy,** subordination, secondariness; **juniority**, minority; **subservience, subjection,** servility, lowliness, humbleness, humility; back seat [informal], second fiddle [informal], second or third string [informal].

.2 **inferior, underling,** understrapper, **subordinate,** subaltern, **junior;** secondary, second fiddle [informal], second or third stringer [informal], low man on the totem pole [informal]; lightweight, follower, pawn, cog, flunky, yes-man, creature; –ling; lower class or orders or ranks, commonalty or commonality, *hoi polloi* [Gk], masses.

.3 **inadequacy, mediocrity** 680, deficiency, imperfection, insufficiency 662; **incompetence**, maladroitness, unskillfulness 734; **failure** 725; smallness 35; littleness 196; meanness, baseness, pettiness, triviality, shabbiness, vulgarity 898; **fewness** 102; subnormality.

.4 VERBS **be inferior, not come up to, not**

measure up, fall *or* come short, fail 725.8, not make *or* hack it [slang]; want, be found wanting; **not compare,** have nothing on [slang], **not hold a candle to** [informal], not approach, not come near; serve, subserve, rank under *or* beneath, follow, play second fiddle [informal], take a back seat [informal].

.5 **bow to, hand it to** [slang], tip the hat to [informal], yield the palm; retire into the shade; give in [informal], lose face.

.6 ADJS **inferior, subordinate,** subaltern, sub, **secondary; junior, minor;** co–, par(a)–, sub–; second *or* third string, second *or* third rank, low in the pecking order; **subservient,** subject, servile, low, **lowly,** humble, modest; **lesser,** less, lower; in the shade, thrown into the shade; **common,** vulgar, **ordinary;** underprivileged, disadvantaged; **beneath one's dignity** *or* station, infra dig, demeaning.

.7 **inadequate, mediocre,** deficient, imperfect, **insufficient; incompetent,** unskillful, maladroit; small, little, mean, base, petty, trivial, shabby; **not to be compared, not comparable, not a patch on** [informal]; not in it, not in the same street with, out of it, out of the picture, **out of the running,** left a mile behind [all informal].

.8 **least, smallest,** littlest, slightest, **lowest,** shortest; minimum, minimal, minim; few 102.4.

.9 ADVS **least, less,** least of all; **under, below,** short of; under par, below the mark, at a low ebb; at the bottom of the scale, at the nadir, at the bottom of the heap [informal], in the gutter [slang]; at a disadvantage.

## 38. INCREASE

.1 NOUNS **increase, gain,** augmentation, greatening, **enlargement, amplification, growth,** development, widening, spread, broadening, elevation, **extension,** aggrandizement, access, accession, **increment,** accretion; **addition** 40; **expansion** 197; **inflation,** swelling, ballooning, edema, tumescence, bloating; **multiplication, proliferation,** productiveness 165; accruement, accrual, accumulation; **advance,** appreciation, ascent, mounting, crescendo, waxing, snowballing, **rise** *or* raise, boost [informal], hike [slang], **up** *or* upping [both informal], buildup; **upturn,** uptrend, upsurge, upswing; leap, jump; boom; **flood,** surge, gush.

.2 **intensification, heightening, deepening,** tightening, turn of the screw; **strengthening,** beefing-up [informal], enhancement, **magnification,** blowup, blowing up, exaggeration; aggravation, exacerbation, heating-up; **concentration,** condensation, consolidation; **reinforcement,** redoubling; pickup, step-up, **acceleration,** speedup, accelerando; explosion, population explosion, information explosion.

.3 **gains,** winnings, increase [archaic], **profits** 811.3.

.4 VERBS **increase, enlarge,** aggrandize, **amplify, augment, extend,** maximize, **add to; expand** 197.4, **inflate;** lengthen, broaden, fatten, fill out, thicken; **raise,** exalt, boost [informal], hike *or* hike up [both slang], jack up [informal], jump up [informal], put up, up [informal]; **build, build up;** pyramid, parlay.

.5 **intensify, heighten, deepen,** enhance, **strengthen,** beef up [informal], aggravate, exacerbate; exaggerate, blow up, **magnify;** whet, sharpen; **reinforce,** double, redouble, triple; **concentrate,** condense, consolidate; **complicate,** ramify, make complex; give a boost to, **step up** [informal], accelerate; key up, hop up [slang], soup up [slang], jazz up [slang]; add fuel to the flame, heat *or* hot up [informal].

.6 **increase, advance,** appreciate; **spread, widen,** broaden; **gain,** get ahead; grow, develop, wax, swell, balloon, bloat, mount, **rise,** go up, crescendo, snowball; **intensify,** gain strength, strengthen; accrue, accumulate; **multiply, proliferate,** breed; run *or* shoot up, boom.

.7 ADJS **increased, heightened,** raised, elevated; **intensified,** deepened, reinforced, strengthened, beefed-up [informal], tightened, stiffened; **enlarged, extended,** augmented, aggrandized, amplified, **enhanced,** boosted, hiked [slang]; broadened, widened, spread; **magnified, inflated, expanded,** swollen, bloated; **multiplied,** proliferated; **accelerated,** jazzed up [slang].

.8 **increasing,** crescent, **growing,** waxing, swelling, lengthening, **multiplying,** proliferating; spreading, spreading like a cancer *or* like wildfire, expanding; tightening, intensifying; incremental; **on the increase,** crescendoing, snowballing, growing like a mushroom; –er.

.9 ADVS **increasingly,** growingly, more, **more and more,** on and on, greater and greater, ever more; in a crescendo.

## 39. DECREASE

.1 NOUNS **decrease**, decrescence, decrement, **diminishment**, diminution, **reduction**, lessening, lowering, scaling down, miniaturization; depression, damping, dampening; **letup** [informal], abatement; alleviation, relaxation, mitigation; attenuation, extenuation, weakening, sagging, dying, dying off or away, fade-out, languishment; depreciation, **deflation**; **deduction** 42.1; subtraction, **abridgment** 203.3; **contraction** 198; simplicity 45.

.2 **decline**, declension, **subsidence**, slump [informal], lapse, **drop**, collapse, crash; dwindling, wane, ebb; downturn, downtrend, retreat, remission; fall, plunge, dive, decline and fall; decrescendo, diminuendo; catabasis, deceleration, slowdown.

.3 decrement, **waste**, **loss**, dissipation, wear and tear, erosion, ablation, depletion, corrosion, attrition, consumption, shrinkage, exhaustion; deliquescence, dissolution.

.4 curtailment, retrenchment, cut, cutback, rollback [informal], pullback.

.5 **minimization**, minification, **belittling**, belittlement, detraction; qualification 507.

.6 VERBS **decrease, diminish, lessen**; let up, bate, abate; **decline, subside**, shrink, wane, ebb, dwindle, languish, sink, sag, die away, tail off [informal]; **drop**, drop off, dive, plummet, plunge, fall, fall off, fall away, fall to a low ebb, run low; **waste**, wear, waste or wear away, crumble, erode, ablate, corrode, consume, consume away, be eaten away; melt away, deliquesce.

.7 reduce, decrease, diminish, lessen, take from; **lower, depress**, damp, dampen, **step down** [informal], tune down [informal], scale down [informal]; **downgrade**; depreciate, **deflate**; **curtail**, retrench; **cut**, cut down, cut back, pare, roll back [informal]; deduct 42.9; **shorten** 203.6, abridge; **compress** 198.7; **simplify** 45.4.

.8 **abate**, bate, ease; **weaken**, dilute, water down, attenuate, extenuate; alleviate, mitigate, slacken, remit.

.9 **minimize**, minify, **belittle**, detract from; dwarf, bedwarf; play down, underplay, downplay, de-emphasize.

.10 ADJS **reduced, decreased, diminished**, lowered, dropped, fallen; bated, **abated**; deflated, contracted, shrunk, shrunken; dissipated, **eroded**, consumed, ablated, worn; curtailed, shorn, retrenched, cut-back; weakened, attenuated, watered-down; scaled-down, miniaturized; minimized, belittled; **lower**, less, lesser, smaller, shorter.

.11 **decreasing, diminishing, lessening, subsiding, declining**, languishing, dwindling, waning, on the wane; decrescent, reductive, deliquescent, **contractive**; diminuendo, decrescendo.

.12 ADVS **decreasingly, diminishingly**, less, **less and less**, ever less; decrescendo, diminuendo; on a declining scale, at a declining rate; de–.

## 40. ADDITION

.1 NOUNS **addition**, accession, annexation, affixation, suffixation, prefixation, agglutination, attachment, junction, joining 47, adjunction, uniting; **increase** 38; **augmentation, supplementation**, reinforcement; superaddition, superposition, superjunction, superfetation, suppletion; juxtaposition 200.3; adjunct 41.

.2 [math terms] plus sign, plus; addend; sum, summation, total; subtotal.

.3 **adding**, computation 87.3; **adding machine**, calculator 87.19.

.4 VERBS **add**, plus [informal], put with, **join** or **unite with, affix, attach**, annex, adjoin, append, conjoin, subjoin, prefix, suffix, infix, postfix, tag, tag on, **tack on** [informal], slap on [informal], hitch on [informal]; glue on, paste on, agglutinate; superpose, superadd; burden, encumber, saddle with; **complicate**, ornament, decorate.

.5 **add to**, augment, supplement; **increase** 38.4; **reinforce**, strengthen, fortify; recruit, swell the ranks of.

.6 **compute**, add up 87.11,12; sum, total, total up, tot or tot up [both informal], tote or tote up [both informal], tally.

.7 be added, advene, supervene.

.8 ADJS **additive**, additional, additory; **cumulative**, accumulative; summative or summational.

.9 **added**, affixed, **attached**, annexed, appended, appendant; adjoined, adjunct, conjoined, subjoined; superadded, superposed, superjoined; super–, pleo– or pleio–.

.10 **additional, supplementary, supplemental; extra**, plus, further, farther, fresh, **more**, new, **other**, another, ulterior; **auxiliary**, ancillary, supernumerary, contributory, **accessory**, collateral; **surplus**, spare.

.11 ADVS **additionally, in addition**, also, **and** also, and all [informal], and so, **as well**, too, else, beside, **besides, to boot, into the bargain; on top of, over, above; beyond, plus; extra,** on the side [informal], for lagniappe; **more, moreover,** *au reste* [Fr], *en plus* [Fr], farther, further, **furthermore,** at the same time, then, again, yet; similarly, likewise, by the same token, by the same sign; item; therewith; all included, altogether; among other things, *inter alia* [L].

.12 PREPS **with, plus, including,** inclusive of, along *or* **together with,** coupled with, **in conjunction with; as well as,** to say nothing of, not to mention, let alone; over and above, **in addition to,** added to, linked to; with the addition of, attended by.

.13 CONJS **and, also,** and also.

.14 PHRS **et cetera, etc., and so forth, and so on,** *und so weiter* [Ger]; **et al.,** *et alii* [L], and all [informal], and others, and other things, *cum multis aliis* [L, with many others]; and everything else, **and more of the same, and the rest, and the like;** and suchlike *or* and all that sort of thing *or* and all that [all informal], and all like that *or* and stuff like that [both slang]; **and what not, and what have you,** and I don't know what, and God knows what, and then some [all informal]; and the following, *et sequens* [L], et seq.

## 41. ADJUNCT

### *(thing added)*

.1 NOUNS **adjunct, addition,** increase, **increment,** *additum* [L], additament, additory, addendum, addenda [pl], accession, fixture; **annex,** annexation; **appendage,** appendant, pendant, appanage, tailpiece, coda; augment, augmentation, undergirding, reinforcement; appurtenance, appurtenant; **accessory,** attachment; **supplement,** complement, continuation, extrapolation, extension; offshoot, side issue, corollary, side effect, **concomitant, accompaniment** 73, **additive,** adjuvant.

.2 (written text) **postscript, appendix;** rider, allonge, codicil; **epilogue,** envoi, coda, tail; note, marginalia, scholia, commentary; **interpolation,** interlineation; affix, prefix, suffix, infix; enclitic, proclitic.

.3 (building) wing, **addition, annex,** extension, ell *or* L.

.4 **extra, bonus, premium,** something extra, extra dash, extra added attraction, lagniappe, something for good measure; **padding,** stuffing, filling; trimming, **frill,** flourish, filigree, decoration, ornament; superaddition; fillip, wrinkle, twist.

## 42. SUBTRACTION

.1 NOUNS **subtraction, deduction,** subduction, **removal,** taking away; abstraction, ablation, sublation; erosion, abrasion; refinement, purification.

.2 **reduction, diminution,** decrease, decrement, impairment, **cut** *or* **cutting,** curtailment, shortening, truncation; dip, lessening; **shrinkage,** depletion, **attrition,** remission; **depreciation,** detraction, disparagement, derogation; retraction, retrenchment; **extraction.**

.3 **excision,** abscission, rescission, extirpation; **elimination,** exclusion, extinction, eradication, destruction, annihilation; **amputation,** mutilation.

.4 **castration,** gelding, emasculation, deballing [slang], altering, fixing [both informal]; spaying.

.5 (written text) **deletion,** erasure, cancellation, omission; editing, blue-penciling, striking *or* striking out; expurgation, bowdlerization, censoring *or* censorship; abridgment, abbreviation.

.6 [math terms] subtrahend, minuend; negative; minus sign, minus.

.7 (thing subtracted) **deduction,** decrement, minus.

.8 (result) **difference, remainder** 43, epact [astron], discrepancy, net, balance, surplus 663.5, deficit, credit.

.9 VERBS **subtract, deduct,** subduct, take away, take from, **remove,** withdraw, abstract; **reduce,** shorten, curtail, retrench, lessen, **diminish, decrease,** impair, bate, abate; **depreciate,** disparage, detract, derogate; erode, abrade, eat *or* wear *or* rub *or* shave *or* file away; **extract,** leach, drain; thin, thin out, weed; **refine,** purify.

.10 **excise,** cut out, cut, extirpate, enucleate; **eradicate,** root out, wipe *or* stamp out, **eliminate,** annihilate, extinguish; **exclude,** except, take out, rule out, bar, ban; set aside *or* apart, isolate, pick out, cull; **cut off** *or* **away,** take *or* strike *or* knock off, truncate; **amputate,** mutilate, abscind; **prune,** pare, peel, clip, crop, bob, dock, lop, nip, shear, shave, strip, strip off *or* away.

.11 **castrate,** geld, emasculate, eunuchize, spay, fix *or* alter [both informal], unsex, deball [slang].

.12 (written text) **delete,** erase, expunge, cancel, omit; **edit,** edit out, blue-pencil; strike, strike out *or* off, rub *or* blot out, cross out or off, kill, cut; void, rescind; **censor,** bowdlerize, expurgate; abridge, abbreviate.

.13 ADJS **subtractive, reductive,** deductive; ablative, erosive.

.14 PREPS **off, from; minus,** less, without, excluding, except or excepting, with the exception of, save, leaving out or aside, barring, exclusive of, not counting, exception taken of, discounting.

## 43. REMAINDER

.1 NOUNS **remainder, remains, remnant, residue,** residuum, rest, **balance;** holdover; **leavings, leftovers; refuse,** odds and ends, scraps, rags, **rubbish, waste,** orts, candle ends; scourings, offscourings; parings, sweepings, filings, shavings, sawdust; chaff, straw, stubble, husks; **debris,** detritus, ruins; end, fag end; stump, butt or butt end, roach [slang], rump; survival, vestige, trace, shadow, afterimage, afterglow; **fossil,** relics.

.2 **dregs, grounds, lees,** dross, slag, draff, scoria, feces; **sediment, settlings, deposits,** deposition; precipitate, precipitation, sublimate [chem]; alluvium, alluvion, diluvium; silt, loess, moraine; scum, offscum, froth; ash, ember, cinder, sinter, clinker; soot, smut.

.3 **survivor,** heir, successor; **widow,** widower, relict, **orphan.**

.4 **excess** 663, **surplus,** surplusage, overplus, overage; superfluity, redundancy.

.5 VERBS **remain, be left** or **left over, survive,** subsist, rest.

.6 **leave,** leave over, leave behind.

.7 ADJS **remaining, surviving,** over, left, **leftover,** remanent, odd; **spare,** to spare; unused, unconsumed; **surplus,** superfluous; outstanding, net.

.8 **residual,** residuary; sedimental, sedimentary.

## 44. MIXTURE

.1 NOUNS **mixture,** mixing, blending; **admixture,** composition, commixture, immixture, intermixture, **mingling,** minglement, commingling or comminglement, intermingling or interminglement, interlarding or interlardment; syncretism, eclecticism; **pluralism; fusion,** interfusion; amalgamation, **integration,** alloyage, coalescence; **merger, combination** 52; –mixis.

.2 **imbuement, impregnation, infusion,** suffusion, decoction, infiltration, instillment, instillation, permeation, pervasion,

interpenetration, penetration; saturation, steeping, soaking, marination.

.3 **adulteration, corruption,** contamination, denaturalization, **pollution, doctoring** [informal]; fortifying, lacing, spiking [informal]; **dilution,** cutting [informal]; watering; debasement, bastardizing.

.4 **crossbreeding,** crossing, **interbreeding,** miscegenation; **hybridism,** hybridization, mongrelism, mongrelization.

.5 **compound, mixture, admixture,** intermixture, immixture, commixture, **composite, blend,** composition, confection, concoction, **combination,** combo [slang], ensemble; amalgam, alloy; paste, magma.

.6 **hodgepodge,** hotchpotch, hotchpot; **medley, miscellany,** mélange, pastiche, pasticcio [Ital], **conglomeration, assortment,** assemblage, mixed bag, olio, olla podrida [Sp], **scramble, jumble,** mingle-mangle, **mix,** mishmash, magpie, **mess,** mash, hash, patchwork, salad, gallimaufry, salmagundi, **potpourri,** stew, sauce, omnium-gatherum, Noah's ark, **odds and ends,** all sorts, everything but the kitchen sink [slang], "God's plenty" [Dryden], broad spectrum, what you will.

.7 (slight admixture) **tinge, tincture, touch, dash, smack,** taint, tinct, tint, **trace,** vestige, hint, inkling, intimation, soupçon, suspicion, suggestion, thought, shade, tempering; sprinkling, seasoning, sauce, spice, infusion.

.8 **mosaic,** chimera; pomato, potomato, topato.

.9 **hybrid, crossbreed,** cross, mixed-blood, mixblood, **half-breed,** half-bred, half blood, half-caste; **mongrel;** ladino [Sp]; mustee or mestee, mestizo [Sp], mestiza [Sp fem], métis [Fr], métisse [Fr fem]; Eurasian; **mulatto,** high yellow [slang], quadroon, quintroon, octoroon; sambo, zambo, cafuso [Brazil Pg], Cape Colored [S Africa], griqua [S Africa]; griffe; zebrule, zebrass, cattalo, mule, hinny, liger, tigon; tangelo, citrange, plumcot.

.10 **mixer, blender,** beater, agitator; cement mixer, eggbeater, churn; homogenizer, colloid mill, emulsifier; crucible, melting pot.

.11 VERBS **mix,** admix, commix, immix, **intermix, mingle,** bemingle, commingle, immingle, **intermingle,** interlace, interweave, intertwine, interlard; syncretize; **blend,** interblend; **amalgamate, integrate,** alloy, coalesce, **fuse, merge,** compound, compose, concoct; **combine** 52.3; mix up, hash, stir up, **scramble,** conglomerate, shuffle, **jumble**, mingle-mangle, throw or toss together; knead, work; homogenize, emulsify.

.12 **imbue**, imbrue, **infuse**, suffuse, transfuse, breathe, **instill**, infiltrate, **impregnate**, **permeate**, pervade, penetrate, leaven; **tinge, tincture**, entincture, temper, color, dye, flavor, season; saturate, steep, decoct, brew, dredge, besprinkle.

.13 **adulterate, corrupt**, contaminate, **debase**, denaturalize, pollute, denature, bastardize, **tamper with, doctor** or doctor up [both informal]; **fortify**, spike [slang], lace; **dilute**, cut [informal], water, water down [informal].

.14 **hybridize, crossbreed, cross, interbreed**, miscegenate, mongrelize.

.15 ADJS **mixed, mingled**, blended, compounded, amalgamated; **combined** 52.5; **composite**, compound, **complex**, many-sided, multifaceted, intricate; **conglomerate**, pluralistic, multiracial, multinational, heterogeneous, varied, **miscellaneous**, medley, motley, dappled, patchy; promiscuous, indiscriminate, **scrambled, jumbled**, thrown together; half-and-half, fifty-fifty [informal]; amphibious; equivocal, **ambiguous**, ambivalent, ironic; syncretic, eclectic; mixo–.

.16 **hybrid, mongrel**, interbred, **crossbred**, crossed, cross; **half-breed**, half-bred, half-blooded, half-caste; demi–.

.17 miscible, mixable.

.18 PREPS **among**, amongst, 'mongst; **amid**, mid or 'mid, amidst, midst or 'midst, **in the midst of, in the thick of; with**, together with.

## 45. SIMPLICITY

*(freedom from mixture or complexity)*

.1 NOUNS **simplicity, purity**, simpleness, **plainness**, starkness, severity; unmixedness, monism; **unadulteration**, unsophistication, fundamentality, elementarity; **singleness**, oneness, unity, integrity, homogeneity, uniformity 17.

.2 **simplification**, streamlining, refinement, purification, distillation; **disentanglement**, disinvolvement; uncluttering, unscrambling, unsnarling; stripping, stripping down, narrowing.

.3 **oversimplification, oversimplicity**, oversimplifying; **simplism**, reductivism; intellectual childishness or immaturity, conceptual crudity.

.4 VERBS **simplify**, streamline, **reduce**, reduce to elements or essentials; purify, refine, distill; strip down; narrow; oversimplify.

.5 **disinvolve**, disintricate, unmix, disembroil, **disentangle**, untangle, **unscramble**, **unsnarl**, unknot, untwist, unbraid, unweave, untwine, unwind, uncoil, unthread, **unravel**, ravel; unclutter, clarify, clear up, sort out, get to the core or nub or essence.

.6 ADJS **simple, plain**, bare, mere; hapl(o)–; **single**, uniform, homogeneous, of a piece; **pure**, simon-pure, pure and simple; **essential**, elementary, indivisible, **primary**, primal, **irreducible, fundamental**, basic, undifferentiable or undifferentiated, undifferenced, monolithic; **austere**, chaste, unadorned, uncluttered, spare, stark, severe; homely, homespun.

.7 **unmixed, unmingled**, unblended, **uncombined**, uncompounded; unleavened; **unadulterated**, uncorrupted, unsophisticated, unalloyed, untinged, undiluted, unfortified; **clear**, clarified, purified, **distilled**, rectified; **neat, straight**, absolute, sheer, naked, bare.

.8 **uncomplicated, uninvolved**, incomplex, straightforward.

.9 **simplified**, streamlined, stripped down.

.10 **oversimplified, oversimple; simplistic**, reductive; intellectually childish or immature, conceptually crude.

.11 ADVS **simply, plainly, purely**; merely, barely; **singly, solely**, only, **alone**, exclusively, just, simply and solely.

## 46. COMPLEXITY

.1 NOUNS **complexity, complication, involvement**, involution, convolution, tanglement, **entanglement**, perplexity, **intricacy**, intricateness, ramification, complexness, crabbedness, technicality, subtlety.

.2 **complex**, perplex [informal], **tangle**, tangled skein, **mess** [informal], snafu [slang], ravel, snarl; knot, Gordian knot; **maze**, meander, Chinese puzzle, **labyrinth**; webwork, mesh; wilderness, **jungle**; Rube Goldberg contraption, wheels within wheels; rat's nest, can of worms [informal], snake pit.

.3 VERBS **complicate, involve, perplex**, ramify; **confound, confuse, muddle, mix up**, ball or screw or louse up [slang], foul or mess or muck up [informal], snarl up, implicate; **tangle**, entangle, embrangle, **snarl**, ravel, knot.

.4 ADJS **complex, complicated**, many-faceted, multifarious, ramified, perplexed, **confused**, confounded, **involved**, implicated, crabbed, **intricate**, elaborate, involuted, convoluted; **mixed up**, balled or screwed or loused up [slang], fouled or messed or mucked up [informal]; **tangled**, entangled, tangly, embrangled, **snarled**, knotted, matted, twisted, raveled; mazy, daedal, **labyrinthine**, labyrinthian, meandering; **devious**, roundabout, Byzantine, subtle.

.5 **inextricable**, irreducible, unsolvable.

## 47. JOINING

.1 NOUNS **joining, junction**, joinder, jointure, **connection, union**, unification, bond, bonding, conjunction, conjoining, conjugation, liaison, marriage, hookup [informal], splice, tie, tie-up or tie-in [both informal], knotting; merger, merging; symbiosis; **combination** 52; conglomeration, **aggregation**, agglomeration, congeries; **coupling**, copulation, accouplement, **bracketing**, yoking, pairing; **linking**, interlinking, linkage, concatenation, articulation, agglutination; **meeting**, confluence, convergence, concurrence, concourse, gathering, massing, clustering; communication, intercommunication, intercourse.

.2 **interconnection**, interjoinder, **interlinking**, interlocking, interdigitation; **interassociation**, interaffiliation.

.3 **fastening, attachment, affixation**, annexation; ligation; **binding**, bonding, gluing, sticking, tieing, lashing, trussing, girding, hooking, clasping, zipping, buckling, buttoning; knot 47.21; adhesive 50.4; splice, bond, fastener 47.20; –desis; hel(o)–, perono–.

.4 **joint**, join, joining, **juncture, union, connection**, link, connecting link, **coupling**; clinch, embrace; articulation [anat & bot], symphysis [anat]; **pivot, hinge; knee; elbow**, cubito–; **wrist**, carp(o)–; **ankle**, tars(o)–; **knuckle; hip**, ischi(o)–; **shoulder**, om(o)–; **neck**, cervix, trachel(o)–; ball-and-socket joint, pivot joint, hinged joint, gliding joint; toggle, toggle joint; connecting rod, tie rod; seam, suture, stitch, closure, mortise, miter, butt, scarf, dovetail, rabbet, weld; boundary, interface; arthr(o)–.

.5 VERBS (put together) **join**, conjoin, **unite**, unify, bond, **connect**, associate, league, band, merge, **assemble**, accumulate; **gather**, mobilize, marshal, mass, amass, **collect**, conglobulate; **combine** 52.3; **couple**, pair, accouple, copulate, conjugate, marry, **link**, yoke, knot, splice, tie, chain,

bracket; articulate, concatenate, agglutinate; glue, tape, cement, solder, weld; **put together**, fix together, lay together, piece together, clap together, tack together, stick together, lump together, roll into one; **bridge**, bridge over or between, span; **include**, encompass, take in, cover, embrace, comprise.

.6 **interconnect, interjoin**, intertie, interassociate, interaffiliate, **interlink**, interlock, interdigitate.

.7 **fasten, fix, attach, affix**, annex, put to, set to; graft, engraft; **secure**, anchor, moor; cement, knit, set, grapple, belay, **make fast**; clinch, clamp, cramp; tighten, trim, trice up, screw up; cinch or cinch up.

.8 **hook**, hitch; **clasp**, hasp, clip, snap; **button**, buckle, zipper; lock, latch; **pin**, skewer, peg, nail, tack, staple, toggle, screw, bolt, rivet; **sew**, stitch; **wedge**, jam, stick; rabbet, butt, scarf, mortise, miter, dovetail; batten, batten down; cleat; **hinge**, joint, articulate.

.9 **bind, tie**, brace, truss, **lash**, leash, rope, strap, lace, wire, chain; **splice**, bend; **gird**, girt, belt, girth, girdle, band, cinch; **tie up**, bind up, do up; **wrap**, wrap up, bundle; **bandage**, swathe, swaddle.

.10 **yoke, hitch up**, hook up; harness, harness up; halter, bridle; saddle; tether, fetter.

.11 (be joined) **join, connect, unite, meet**, merge, converge, **come together**; communicate, intercommunicate; knit, grow together; cohere, adhere, hang or hold together, clinch, embrace.

.12 ADJS **joint**, joined, **conjoint**, conjunct, conjugate, corporate, compact; concurrent, coincident; inclusive, comprehensive.

.13 **joined, united, connected**, copulate, **coupled**, linked, bracketed, associated, conjoined, incorporated, integrated, **merged**, gathered, assembled, **collected**, allied, leagued, banded together; hand-in-hand, hand-in-glove, intimate; unseparated, undivided; **wedded**, matched, paired, yoked, mated; **tied, bound**, knotted, spliced; ankyl(o)–, gam(o)–; –zygous, –stylic.

.14 **fast, fastened, fixed**, secure, firm, close, tight, set; **bonded**, glued, cemented, taped; **jammed**, wedged, stuck.

.15 **inseparable**, impartible, **indivisible**, undividable, indissoluble, inalienable, inseverable, bound up in or with.

.16 **joining, connecting**, meeting; **communicating**, intercommunicating; **connective**, connectional; conjunctive, combinative, copulative, linking, binding.

.17 jointed, articulate.

.18 ADVS **jointly,** conjointly, corporately, **together; in common,** in partnership, mutually, in concord; **all together,** as one, in unison, in agreement, in harmony; concurrently, at once.

.19 **securely, firmly, fast,** tight; **inseparably,** indissolubly.

.20 **fasteners**

| | |
|---|---|
| anchor | hasp |
| band | hawser |
| bandage | haywire |
| bar | hitch |
| barrette | hitching post |
| bellyband | holdfast |
| belt | hook |
| bind | hook and eye |
| binding | inkle |
| binding stone | interlocker |
| binding twine | kevel [naut] |
| bobby pin | kingbolt |
| bollard | kingpin |
| bolt | lace |
| bonder | lacing |
| bondstone | lariat |
| box hook | latch |
| brace | latchet |
| braces [Brit] | leader |
| brad | ligament |
| braid | line |
| buckle | lock |
| button | loop |
| cable | moorings |
| carpet tack | nail |
| catch | noose |
| chain | nut |
| cinch | padlock |
| cincture | paper clip |
| clamp | pawl |
| clasp | peg |
| cleat | pin |
| clevis | pintle |
| click | *reata* [Sp, lariat] |
| clinch | ring |
| clip | rivet |
| clothespin | roller |
| corking pin [dial] | rope |
| cotter | safety pin |
| cotter pin | screw |
| detent | seal |
| dowel | sennit [naut] |
| drawing pin [Brit] | setscrew |
| fibula | skewer |
| fillet | snap |
| fishhook | snubbing post |
| funiculus | spike |
| garter | splice |
| girdle | staple |
| girth | strap |
| grab | string |
| grapnel | strop |
| grappler | stub tenon |
| grappling iron *or* hook | suspenders |
| guy | tack |
| guy rope | tag |
| hairpin | tendon |
| hank [naut] | terret |

| | |
|---|---|
| thole | tug |
| tholepin | twine |
| thong | vise |
| thumbtack | whang [Scot] |
| tie | wire |
| tie beam | withy |
| toggle | wrist pin |
| towline | zipper, slide fastener |
| treenail | |

.21 **knots**

| | |
|---|---|
| anchor knot | marling hitch |
| becket knot | Matthew Walker knot |
| Blackwall hitch | mesh knot |
| bow | midshipman's hitch |
| bowknot | netting knot |
| bowline | open hand knot |
| bowline knot | outside clinch |
| builder's knot | prolonge knot |
| carrick bend | reef knot |
| cat's-paw | reeving-line bend |
| clinch | rolling hitches |
| clove hitch | rope-yarn knot |
| cuckold's neck | round seizing |
| diamond knot | round turn and half |
| double hitch | hitch |
| Englishman's tie | running bowline |
| figure-of-eight knot | running knot |
| fisherman's bend | sheepshank |
| flat knot | shroud knot |
| Flemish knot | single knot |
| French shroud knot | slide knot |
| German knot | slipknot |
| granny knot | square knot |
| half crown | stevedore's knot |
| half hitch | stopper's knot |
| harness hitch | studding-sail halyard |
| hawser bend | bend |
| hawser fastening | stunner hitch |
| heaving-line bend | surgeon's knot |
| inside clinch | tack bend |
| lanyard knot | timber knot *or* hitch |
| loop knot | truckman's knot |
| magnus hitch | wall knot |
| manrope knot | weaver's knot *or* hitch |
| marlinespike hitch | Windsor knot |

## 48. ANALYSIS

.1 NOUNS **analysis,** analyzation, **breakdown,** breaking down, breakup, breaking up; anatomy, anatomizing, dissection; separation, **division, subdivision,** segmentation, reduction to elements *or* parts; chemical analysis, **assay** *or* assaying, resolution, titration, docimasy [archaic], qualitative analysis, quantitative analysis, volumetric analysis, gravimetric analysis; ultimate analysis, proximate analysis; microanalysis, semimicroanalysis.

.2 **itemization,** enumeration, detailing; outlining, schematization, blocking, blocking out; resolution; scansion, parsing.

.3 **classification, categorization, sorting,** sorting out, sifting, sifting out, grouping, factoring, winnowing; **weighing, evaluation,** gauging, assessment, appraisal; **identification.**

**.4 outline,** structural outline, **plan,** scheme, schema, chart, graph; table, table of contents; **diagram,** block diagram, exploded view, **blueprint; catalog,** *catalogue raisonné* [Fr].

**.5 analyst, analyzer,** examiner 485.16.

**.6** VERBS **analyze, break down,** break up, anatomize, dissect; **divide, subdivide,** segment; assay, titrate; separate, reduce, reduce to elements, resolve.

**.7 itemize,** enumerate, number, detail; **outline,** schematize, block out; resolve; scan, parse.

**.8 classify,** class, **categorize,** catalog, sort, sort out, sift, group, factor, winnow, thrash out; weigh, **evaluate,** gauge, assess, appraise; identify.

**.9** ADJS **analytical,** analytic; segmental; classificatory, enumerative; schematic.

**.10** ADVS **analytically,** by parts *or* divisions *or* sections; by categories *or* types.

## 49. SEPARATION

**.1** NOUNS **separation, disjunction,** disjointure, disjointing, disarticulation, **disconnection,** disconnectedness, discontinuity, incoherence, **disengagement,** disunion, nonunion, disassociation; **parting,** alienation, **removal,** withdrawal, isolation, detachment, abstraction; **subtraction** 42; divorce, divorcement; **division,** subdivision, partition, segmentation; districting, zoning; **dislocation** 185, luxation; separability, partibility; separatism; dis–.

**.2 severance,** disseverment *or* disseverance, **sunderance,** scission, fission, cleavage, dichotomy; **cutting, slitting,** slashing, **splitting,** slicing; **rending, tearing,** ripping, laceration, hacking, chopping, butchering, mutilation; section, resection; **surgery,** amputation, excision, abscission, enucleation; –schisis, –rrhexis.

**.3 disruption, dissolution,** abruption, cataclasm; revolution 147; **disintegration** 53, breakup, **crack-up,** shattering, fragmentation; **scattering,** dispersal, diffusion; scaling, splintering, exfoliation.

**.4 break,** breakage, **breach,** burst, **rupture, fracture; crack,** cleft, **fissure, cut, split,** slit; slash, slice; **gap, rift,** rent, rip, tear; chip, splinter, scale.

**.5 dissection, analysis** 48, resolution, breakdown, diaeresis; anatomy.

**.6 disassembly, dismantlement,** taking down *or* apart, dismemberment, dismounting; undoing, unbuilding; stripping, divestiture, deprivation.

**.7 separator,** sieve, centrifuge, ultracentrifuge; creamer, cream separator; breaker, stripper; slicer, cutter, microtome; analyzer.

**.8** VERBS **come apart,** spring apart, fly apart, come unstuck, come undone, come apart at the seams, **come** *or* **drop** *or* **fall to pieces,** go to pieces, crack up, disintegrate, unravel; come *or* fall off, peel off, carry away; get loose, give way, start.

**.9 separate, divide, disjoin, disunite,** dissociate, **disjoint,** disengage, disarticulate, **disconnect;** uncouple, unyoke; **part,** abrupt, cut the knot, **divorce,** estrange; **alienate, segregate,** sequester, isolate, shut off, set apart *or* aside, cut off *or* out *or* adrift; **withdraw, leave, depart,** split [slang]; pull out *or* away *or* back, stand apart *or* aside *or* aloof, step aside; subtract 42.9; delete 42.12; **expel,** eject, throw off *or* out, cast off *or* out.

**.10 detach, remove,** disengage, take *or* lift off, doff; **unfasten, undo,** unattach, unfix; **free, release,** liberate, loose, unloose, unleash, unfetter; **unloosen,** loosen; cast off, weigh anchor; **unhook,** unhitch, unclasp, unclinch, unbuckle, unbutton, unsnap, unscrew, unpin; unbolt, unbar; unlock, unlatch, **untie,** unbind, unbandage, unlace, unstrap, unchain; unstick, unglue.

**.11 sever, dissever,** cut off *or* away, ax, amputate; **cleave, split,** fissure; sunder, cut in two, dichotomize, halve, bisect; **cut,** incise, carve, **slice,** pare, prune, resect, excise 42.10; slit, snip, lance, scissor; **chop, hew,** hack, **slash;** gash, whittle, butcher; saw, jigsaw; **tear, rend,** rive, rend asunder.

**.12 break, burst, bust** [dial *or* slang], breach; **fracture, rupture; crack,** split, check, fissure; snap; chip, scale, exfoliate.

**.13 shatter, splinter,** shiver, break to *or* into pieces, break to *or* into smithereens [informal]; **smash,** crash, crush, crunch, squash, squish [informal]; **disrupt,** demolish, break up, smash up; **scatter,** disperse, diffuse; **fragment,** fission, atomize; **pulverize** 361.9, grind, cut to pieces, mince, make mincemeat of.

**.14 tear** *or* **rip apart,** take *or* pull apart, **pick** *or* **rip** *or* **tear to pieces,** tear to rags *or* tatters, **shred; dismember,** tear limb from limb, draw and quarter; **mangle,** lacerate, mutilate, maim; skin, flay, strip, peel, denude; defoliate.

**.15 disassemble,** take apart *or* down, tear down; **dismantle, demolish,** dismount, unrig [naut].

**.16 disjoint,** unjoint, **unhinge,** disarticulate,

dislocate, luxate, throw out of joint, unseat.

.17 **dissect, analyze** 48.6, anatomize, break down.

.18 **apportion, portion,** section, partition, compartmentalize, segment; **divide,** divide up, divvy *or* divvy up [both slang], **parcel,** parcel out, **split,** split up, cut up, subdivide; district, zone.

.19 **part company, part, separate,** split up, dispel, disband, scatter, **disperse,** break up, break it up [slang], **go separate ways,** diverge.

.20 ADJS **separate, distinct, discrete; unjoined, unconnected, unattached,** unattended, unassociated; **apart,** asunder, **in two;** discontinuous, noncontiguous, divergent; insular; noncohesive, incoherent 51.4; bipartite, dichotomous, multipartite, multisegmental; subdivided, partitioned; compartmentalized; ap(o)– *or* aph–, chori–, fissi–, par(a)–, schisto–, schiz(o)–, sub–.

.21 **separated,** disjoined, disjoint, disjointed, disjunct, **disconnected,** disengaged, detached, **disunited, divided,** removed, divorced, **alienated,** estranged, **segregated,** sequestered, shut off; scattered, dispersed, isolated, disarticulated, dislocated.

.22 **unfastened,** uncaught, unfixed, **undone, loose, clear, free;** unstuck, **shaky,** rickety; untied, unbound; unanchored, adrift, afloat, floating.

.23 **severed, cut,** cleft, cloven, riven, shivered, splintered, cracked, **split,** slit, reft; **rent, torn;** lacerated, lacerate, mangled, mutilated, ragged, tattered, shredded, in shreds; quartered, **dismembered,** in pieces; –clase, –fid(ate), –sect.

.24 **broken,** busted [dial or slang], **burst, ruptured;** sprung; shattered, in smithereens [informal].

.25 **separating, dividing,** parting; separative, disjunctive.

.26 **separable,** severable, **divisible,** alienable, cleavable, partible; **fissionable,** fissile, scissile; dissoluble, dissolvable.

.27 ADVS **disjointedly,** unconnectedly, sporadically, spasmodically, discontinuously, by bits and pieces, by fits and starts.

.28 **separately,** severally, piecemeal, one by one; **apart,** adrift, asunder, **in two,** in twain; apart from, away from, aside from; abstractly, in the abstract.

.29 **to pieces,** all to pieces, **to bits, to smithereens** [informal], to splinters, to shards, to tatters, to shreds.

## 50. COHESION

.1 NOUNS **cohesion,** cohesiveness, **coherence, adherence, adhesion,** junction 47.1, 4, sticking, cling, clinging, inseparability; cementation, conglutination, agglutination; concretion, condensation, accretion, solidification, set, congelation, congealment, clotting, coagulation; conglomeration, conglobation, compaction, agglomeration, consolidation; clustering, massing, bunching, nodality.

.2 **consistency** 26.1, connection, **connectedness;** continuity, **seriality,** sequence 65, sequentialness, **consecutiveness** 71.1, orderliness.

.3 **tenacity,** tenaciousness, **adhesiveness,** cohesiveness, retention; **tightness,** snugness; stickiness, **tackiness,** gluiness, gumminess, **viscidity,** consistency, viscosity, glutinosity; persistence *or* persistency, **stick-to-itiveness** [informal], toughness, **stubbornness, obstinacy,** bulldoggedness *or* bulldoggishness, bullheadedness.

.4 (something adhesive or tenacious) adherent, adherer, **adhesive** 50.13; **bulldog,** barnacle, leech, limpet, remora; burr, cocklebur, clotbur, bramble, brier, prickle, thorn; sticker, bumper sticker, decalcomania, decal; **glue, cement,** mucilage, epoxy resin, paste, stickum *or* gunk [both slang]; coll(o)–, gli(o)–; plaster, adhesive plaster; syrup, molasses.

.5 **conglomeration, conglomerate,** breccia [geol], agglomerate, agglomeration, cluster, bunch, mass, clot; concrete, concretion.

.6 VERBS **cohere, adhere, stick, cling,** cleave, hold, persist, stay, stay put [informal]; cling to, freeze to [informal]; hang on, hold on; take hold of, clasp, grasp, hug, embrace, clinch; **stick together, hang** *or* **hold together;** grow to, grow together; **solidify, set,** conglomerate, agglomerate, conglobate; **congeal,** coagulate, **clot; cluster,** mass, bunch.

.7 **be consistent** 26.6, **connect,** connect with, follow; **join** 47.11, link up.

.8 **hold fast, stick close,** stick like glue, stick like a wet shirt, stick closer than a brother, stick like a barnacle *or* limpet *or* leech, cling like ivy *or* a burr, hold on like a bulldog.

.9 **stick together, cement, bind, paste, glue,** agglutinate, conglutinate, gum; **weld, fuse, solder,** braze.

.10 ADJS **cohesive, coherent;** cohering, adhering, **sticking, clinging,** cleaving, holding together; stuck, agglutinate.

.11 **consistent** 26.9, **connected;** continuous 71.8, **serial,** uninterrupted, sequential, sequent, **consecutive** 71.9; orderly, tight; **joined** 47.13.

.12 **adhesive, adherent,** stickable, self-adhesive; **tenacious,** clingy; **sticky, tacky,** gluey, gummy, **viscid,** glutinous; **persistent,** tough, **stubborn, obstinate,** bulldoggish *or* bulldogged *or* bulldoggy, bullheaded.

.13 **adhesives**

| | |
|---|---|
| birdlime | mucilage |
| cement | paste |
| fish glue | putty |
| epoxy resin | rabbitskin glue |
| glue | rubber cement |
| gluten | sealing wax |
| gum | size |
| library paste | solder |
| lime | viscin |
| lute | viscum |
| mastic | wafer |

## 51. NONCOHESION

.1 NOUNS **noncohesion,** uncohesiveness, incoherence, inconsistency, discontinuity 72, nonadhesion, unadhesiveness, unadherence, untenacity; **separateness,** discreteness, aloofness; **disjunction** 49.1; **dislocation** 185; **dissolution, chaos,** anarchy, **disorder,** confusion, entropy; scattering, dispersion *or* dispersal; diffusion.

.2 **looseness, slackness,** bagginess, **laxness,** laxity, relaxation; sloppiness, shakiness, ricketiness.

.3 VERBS **loosen, slacken, relax;** slack, slack off; ease, ease off, let up; **loose, free,** let go, unleash; **disjoin** 49.9; unstick, unglue; scatter, disperse, diffuse.

.4 ADJS **incoherent,** uncoherent, noncoherent, **inconsistent, uncohesive, unadhesive,** nonadhesive, noncohesive, nonadherent, **untenacious, unconsolidated,** tenuous, lyo–; unjoined 49.20, disconnected, unconnected, gapped, open, **discontinuous** 72.4, broken, detached, discrete, aloof; like grains of sand.

.5 **loose, slack, lax, relaxed,** easy, sloppy; shaky, rickety; flapping, streaming; hanging, drooping, dangling; bagging, baggy.

## 52. COMBINATION

.1 NOUNS **combination,** combine, combo [slang], composition; hapt(o)–, zyg(o)–; **union, unification,** marriage, wedding, incorporation, embodiment, aggregation, agglomeration, conglomeration, conge-

ries; **amalgamation, consolidation,** assimilation, **integration,** solidification, **encompassment,** inclusion, ecumenism; **junction** 47.1,4; conjunction, conjugation; **alliance,** affiliation, **association** 788, merger, league, hookup [slang], tie-up [slang]; federation, confederation, confederacy, federalization, centralization, cartel; **fusion,** blend, blending, meld, melding; coalescence, coalition; synthesis, syncretism, syneresis; syndication; **conspiracy,** cabal, junta; *enosis* [Gk], *Anschluss* [Ger]; package, package deal; **agreement** 26; **addition** 40.

.2 **mixture** 44, **compound** 44.5.

.3 VERBS **combine, unite, unify,** incorporate, embody, **amalgamate, consolidate,** assimilate, **integrate,** solidify, coalesce, compound, put *or* lump together, roll into one, come together, make one; **connect, join** 47.5; **mix** 44.11; **add** 40.4; **merge,** meld, **blend,** shade into, **fuse,** flux, melt into one; interfuse, interblend; **encompass,** include, comprise; **synthesize,** syncretize; syndicate; reembody.

.4 **league, ally, affiliate, associate,** consociate; unionize, organize, cement a union; federate, confederate, federalize, centralize; **join forces,** join *or* unite with, join *or* come together [informal], join up with [informal], hook up with [slang], tie up *or* in with [slang], **throw in with** [slang], stand up with, go *or* be in cahoots [slang], **pool one's interests, join fortunes with,** stand together, make common cause with; marry, wed; **band together,** club together, bunch, bunch up [informal], gang up [informal], gang, club; team with, **team up with** [informal], couple, pair, pair off, partner; go in partnership, go in partners [informal]; **conspire,** cabal.

.5 ADJS **combined, united, amalgamated, incorporated, consolidated, integrated,** assimilated, one, **joined** 47.13, **joint** 47.12, conjoint; **conjunctive, combinative** *or* combinatory, connective, conjugate; **merged,** blended, fused; **mixed** 44.15; **synthesized,** syncretized, syncretistic, eclectic.

.6 **leagued,** enleagued, **allied, affiliated,** affiliate, **associated,** associate, corporate; federated, confederated, federate, confederate; **in league,** in cahoots [slang], in with; **conspiratorial,** cabalistic; partners with, in partnership; teamed, coupled, paired, married, wed, wedded.

.7 **combining, uniting,** incorporating; merging, blending, fusing; combinative, combinatory; associative; federative, federal; corporative, incorporative, corporational.

## 53. DISINTEGRATION

.1 NOUNS disintegration, decomposition, dissolution, decay, resolution, disorganization, degradation, breakup, atomization; erosion, corrosion, crumbling, dilapidation, wear, wear and tear, ablation, ravages of time; disjunction 49.1; incoherence 51.1; –diastasis, –lysis; lys(o)– or lysi–; –lyte.

.2 dissociation; catalysis, dialysis, hydrolysis, proteolysis, thermolysis, photolysis [all chem]; catalyst, hydrolyst [chem]; hydrolyte [chem]; decay, fission [phys], splitting.

.3 VERBS disintegrate, decompose, decay, dissolve, come apart 49.8, disorganize, break up, crack up, disjoin 49.9, split, fission, atomize, come or fall to pieces; erode, corrode, ablate, consume, wear or waste away, molder, crumble, crumble into dust; –lyze or –lyse.

.4 [chem terms] dissociate; catalyze, dialyze, hydrolyze, electrolyze, photolyze.

.5 ADJS disintegrative, decomposing, disintegrating, disruptive, disjunctive; erosive, corrosive, ablative; resolvent, solvent, separative; dilapidated, disintegrated, ruinous, moldering, ravaged, worn; disintegrable, decomposable, degradable, biodegradable.

.6 [chem terms] dissociative; catalytic, dialytic, hydrolytic, proteolytic, thermolytic, electrolytic, photolytic.

## 54. WHOLE

.1 NOUNS whole, totality, entirety, collectivity; complex; integration, embodiment; unity 89, integrity, organic unity, oneness; integer.

.2 total, sum, sum total, sum and substance, the amount, whole or gross amount, grand total.

.3 all, the whole, the entirety, everything, aggregate, assemblage, one and all, all and sundry, each and every [informal]; package, set, complement, package deal; the lot, the corpus, the ensemble; be-all, be-all and end-all, beginning and end, "alpha and omega" [Bible], A to Z, A to izzard, the whole range or spectrum, length and breadth; everything but the kitchen sink [informal].

.4 [slang terms] whole bunch, whole mess, whole caboodle, whole kit and caboodle, whole bit or shtick, whole megillah, whole shooting match, whole hog, whole deal, whole schmear, whole shebang, whole works, the works, whole ball of wax, whole show.

.5 wholeness, totality, completeness 56, unity 89, fullness, inclusiveness, exhaustiveness, comprehensiveness; holism, holistic or total approach; universality.

.6 major part, best part, better part, most; majority, generality, plurality; bulk, mass, body, main body; lion's share; substance, gist, meat, essence, thrust, gravamen.

.7 VERBS form or make a whole, constitute a whole; integrate, unite, form a unity.

.8 total, amount to, come to, run to or into, mount up to, add up to, tot or tot up to [informal], tote or tote up to [informal], reckon up to [informal], aggregate to; aggregate, unitize; number, comprise, contain.

.9 ADJS (not partial) whole, total, entire, aggregate, gross, all; integral, integrated; one, one and indivisible; inclusive, all-inclusive, exhaustive, comprehensive, omnibus, all-embracing; holistic; universal; pan(o)– or pam– or pant(o)– or panta–, coen(o)–.

.10 intact, undamaged 677.8, unimpaired.

.11 undivided, uncut, unsevered, unclipped, uncropped, unshorn; undiminished, unreduced, complete.

.12 unabridged, uncondensed, unexpurgated.

.13 ADVS (not partially) wholly, entirely, all; totally, in toto [L], from A to Z, from A to izzard, across the board; altogether, all put together, in its entirety, tout ensemble [Fr]; in all, on all counts, in all respects, at large; as a whole, in the aggregate, in the lump, in the gross, in bulk, in the mass, en masse [Fr], en bloc [Fr]; collectively, corporately, bodily, in a body, as a body; lock, stock, and barrel; hook, line, and sinker.

.14 on the whole, in the long run, all in all, to all intents and purposes, on balance, by and large, in the main, mainly, mostly, chiefly, substantially, essentially, effectually, for the most part, almost entirely, for all practical purposes, virtually; approximately, nearly.

## 55. PART

.1 NOUNS part, portion, fraction; –ile, –ite, –mere, –tome; percentage; division 49.1; share, parcel, dole, quota; section, sector, segment; quarter, quadrant; item, detail, particular; installment; subdivision, subgroup, subspecies; detachment, contingent; cross section, sample, random sample, sampling; **component** 58.2; **adjunct** 41; **remainder** 43.

.2 (part of writing) section, front *or* back matter, text, chapter, verse, article; sentence, clause, phrase, paragraph, passage; number, book, fascicle; sheet, folio, page, signature, gathering.

.3 **piece, particle, bit, scrap** 35.3, fragment, morsel, **crumb,** shard, snatch, snack; cut, cutting, clip, clipping, paring, shaving, rasher, snip, snippet, chip, slice, collop, dollop, scoop; **tatter, shred,** stitch; **splinter,** sliver; **shiver, smithereen** [informal]; **lump,** gob [informal], gobbet, **hunk, chunk; stump,** butt, end; modicum 35.2, moiety.

.4 **member, organ,** organo–; appendage; **limb,** mel–; **branch,** imp, bough, twig, sprig, spray, switch; runner, tendril; **offshoot,** ramification, scion, spur; **arm** 287.5, **leg** 273.16, tail; hand 813.4, chir(o)–; **wing,** pinion, ali–, pter(o)–, –pterus, pteryg(o)–; lobe, lobule; joint, link.

.5 **dose, portion;** slug *or* shot *or* nip *or* dram [all informal].

.6 VERBS **separate** 49.9, apportion, divide 49.18.

.7 ADJS **partial,** part; **fractional,** sectional; segmentary, segmental; **fragmentary; incomplete** 57.4; –meric, –merous, –tomus; semi–.

.8 ADVS **partly, partially,** part, **in part.**

.9 **piece by piece, bit by bit, part by part, little by little,** inch by inch, foot by foot, drop by drop; –meal, **piecemeal,** inchmeal, by inchmeal; **by degrees,** by inches; **by** *or* **in snatches,** by *or* in installments, in lots, in small doses, in driblets, in dribs and drabs; in detail.

## 56. COMPLETENESS

.1 NOUNS **completeness, totality; wholeness** 54.5, entireness, **entirety; unity, integrity,** integrality, intactness; solidity, solidarity; **thoroughness,** exhaustiveness, inclusiveness, comprehensiveness, universality; pervasiveness, ubiquity, omnipresence.

.2 **fullness,** full; **amplitude, plenitude;** impletion, **repletion,** plethora; saturation, saturation point, satiety, congestion; overfullness 663.3, surfeit; high water, high tide, flood tide, spring tide.

.3 **full measure, fill,** full house, "good measure, pressed down, and shaken together, and running over" [Bible]; **load, capacity, complement,** lading, **charge;** the

whole bit [slang]; bumper, brimmer; bellyful *or* snootful [both slang], skinful *or* mouthful [both informal]; **crush,** cram [informal], jam up [informal].

.4 **completion, fulfillment, consummation,** culmination, perfection, realization, **accomplishment** 722, topping-off, closure.

.5 **limit, end** 70, **extremity,** extreme, **acme,** apogee, climax, **maximum,** ceiling, **peak,** summit, **pinnacle,** crown, top; **utmost,** uttermost, utmost extent, highest degree, nth degree *or* power, *ne plus ultra* [L]; **all, the whole** 54.3,4.

.6 VERBS (make whole) **complete, fulfill, accomplish** 722.4; bring to completion *or* fruition, mature; fill in, **fill out,** piece out, top off, eke out, round out; **make up,** make good, replenish, refill.

.7 **fill, charge, load,** lade, freight, weight; **stuff, wad,** pad, **pack,** crowd, **cram,** jam, jam-pack, ram in, chock; **fill up,** fill to the brim, brim, top off, fill to overflowing, fill the measure of; supercharge, saturate, satiate, congest; overfill 663.15, surfeit.

.8 (be thorough) **go all lengths, go all out,** go the limit [informal], go the whole way, **go the whole hog** [slang], make a federal case, **see it through** [informal], follow out *or* up, follow *or* prosecute to a conclusion; leave nothing undone, not overlook a bet [informal]; **move heaven and earth, leave no stone unturned.**

.9 ADJS **complete, whole, total, global, entire,** intact, solid; eu–, hol(o)–, integri–, pan(o)–, per–, tel(o)– *or* tele(o)–, teleut(o)–; **full, full-fledged,** full-dress, **full-scale;** full-grown, mature, matured, ripe, developed; **uncut,** unabbreviated, undiminished, unexpurgated.

.10 **thorough, thoroughgoing,** thorough-paced, exhaustive, intensive, broad-based, comprehensive, all-embracing, all-encompassing, omnibus, radical, sweeping; **pervasive,** all-pervading, ubiquitous, omnipresent, **universal; unmitigated, unqualified, unconditional,** unrestricted, unreserved, **all-out,** wholesale, wholehog [slang]; out-and-out, **through-and-through,** outright, downright, straight; congenital, born, **consummate,** perfect, veritable, egregious, deep-dyed, dyed-in-the-wool; **utter, absolute, total; sheer,** clear, clean, **pure,** plumb [informal], plain, regular [informal].

.11 **full,** filled, **replete,** plenary, capacity, flush, round; **brimful,** brimming; **chockfull,** chuck-full, **cram-full,** topful; **jam-**

full, jam-packed; stuffed, overstuffed, packed, crammed, *farci* [Fr]; swollen 197.13, bulging 256.14, bursting, ready to burst, full to bursting, fit to bust [slang]; as full as a tick, packed like sardines *or* herrings; standing room only, SRO; **saturated,** satiated, soaked; congested; overfull 663.20, surfeited; –ful.

.12 **fraught,** freighted, **laden, loaded, charged,** burdened; heavy-laden; fullladen, full-fraught, full-charged, supercharged.

.13 **completing, fulfilling,** filling; completive *or* completory, consummative *or* consummatory, culminative, perfective; **complementary,** complemental.

.14 ADVS **completely, totally,** globally, **entirely, wholly, fully,** integrally, roundly, **altogether,** hundred per cent, **exhaustively,** inclusively, comprehensively, largely; **unconditionally,** unrestrictedly, unreservedly; **one and all;** outright, *tout à fait* [Fr]; **thoroughly,** inside out [informal]; in full, in full measure; to the hilt.

.15 **absolutely, perfectly, quite,** right, stark, clean, sheer, plumb [informal], plain; irretrievably, unrelievedly, irrevocably.

.16 **utterly, to the utmost,** all the way, **all out,** flat out [Brit], *à outrance* [Fr], *à toute outrance* [Fr], **to the full, to the limit,** to the backbone, to the marrow, to the nth degree *or* power, to the sky *or* skies, to the top of one's bent, **to a farethee-well,** to a fare-you-well *or* fare-yewell, with a vengeance, all hollow [informal].

.17 **throughout, all over,** overall, **inside and out, through and through;** through thick and thin, down to the ground [informal], **from the ground up,** from the word 'go' [informal]; **to the end** *or* **bitter end,** to the death; **at full length,** *in extenso* [L], *ad infinitum* [L]; every inch, every whit, every bit; root and branch, head and shoulders, heart and soul; to the brim, to the hilt, neck deep, up to the ears, up to the eyes; **in every respect,** in all respects, you name it [informal]; **on all counts,** at all points, for good and all; lock, stock, and barrel [informal].

.18 **from beginning to end,** from end to end, **from first to last, from A to Z,** from A to izzard, from hell to breakfast [slang], from cover to cover; **from top to bottom,** *de fond en comble* [Fr]; from top to toe, **from head to foot,** *a capite ad calcem* [L], cap-a-pie; **from stem to stern,** from clew to earing, fore and aft; from soup to

nuts [slang], *"ab ovo usque ad mala"* [L, from egg to apples; Horace].

## 57. INCOMPLETENESS

.1 NOUNS **incompleteness,** incompletion; **deficiency,** defectiveness, **inadequacy;** underdevelopment, hypoplasia, **immaturity,** callowness, arrestment; sketchiness, scrappiness, patchiness; short measure *or* weight.

.2 (part lacking) **deficiency,** want, **lack, need, deficit,** defect, **shortage;** wantage, outage, ullage; defalcation, arrearage; omission, gap, hiatus, break, lacuna, discontinuity, interval; missing link.

.3 VERBS lack 662.7; fall short 314.2.

.4 ADJS **incomplete, deficient,** defective, **inadequate;** semi–; **undeveloped,** underdeveloped, hypoplastic, **immature,** callow, infant, arrested, embryonic, **wanting, lacking,** needing, missing, **partial,** part, failing; in default, in arrear *or* arrears; **in short supply,** scanty; **short,** scant, shy [informal]; sketchy, patchy, scrappy.

.5 **mutilated,** garbled, hashed, **mangled, butchered,** docked, lopped, truncated, castrated, cut short.

.6 ADVS **incompletely, partially,** by halves, by *or* in half measures, in installments, in *or* by bits and pieces; **deficiently,** inadequately.

## 58. COMPOSITION

*(manner of being composed)*

.1 NOUNS **composition, constitution,** construction, **formation,** fabrication, fashioning, shaping, organization; embodiment, incorporation; make, **makeup,** getup *or* setup [both informal]; building, buildup, structure, structuring; **assembly,** assemblage, putting *or* piecing together; synthesis, syneresis; **combination** 52; **compound** 44.5; **junction** 47.1,4; **mixture** 44.

.2 **component, constituent, ingredient,** integrant, **element, factor, part** 55, part and parcel; appurtenance, adjunct 41; feature, aspect, specialty, circumstance, detail, item; contents, makings *or* fixings [both informal].

.3 VERBS **compose, constitute,** construct, fabricate; incorporate, embody; **form, organize,** structure; **enter into,** go into; make, **make up,** build, **build up, assemble,** put *or* piece together; **consist of,** be a feature of, form a part of, combine *or* unite in, merge in; **synthesize; combine** 52.3; **join** 47.5; **mix** 44.11.

**.4** ADJS **composed of,** formed of, **made of,** made up of, made out of, compact of, consisting of; composing, comprising, constituting, including, inclusive of, containing, embodying, subsuming; contained in, embodied in; di(a)–; –en *or* –n, –ine.

**.5** **component,** constituent, integrant, integral; **formative,** elementary.

## 59. ORDER

**.1** NOUNS **order, arrangement** 60; **organization** 60.2; **disposition,** disposal, deployment, marshaling; **formation, structure,** array, lineup, setup, layout; system; routine, even tenor; **peace,** quiet, quietude, tranquillity; regularity, uniformity 17; symmetry, proportion, concord, **harmony,** order, the music of the spheres; "the eternal fitness of things" [Samuel Clarke], "Heav'n's first law" [Pope].

**.2** **continuity,** logical order, serial order; **degree** 29; **hierarchy, gradation,** subordination, rank, place; **sequence** 65.

**.3** **orderliness, trimness, tidiness, neatness,** anality; good shape [informal], good condition, fine fettle, good trim, apple-pie order [informal], a place for everything and everything in its place; **discipline,** method, methodology, methodicalness, system, systematicness.

**.4** VERBS **order, arrange** 60.8, **organize, regulate;** dispose, deploy, marshal; **form,** structure, array, line up, set up, lay out; **pacify,** quiet, cool off *or* down [informal], **tranquilize; regularize,** harmonize; **systematize,** methodize, normalize, standardize, routinize; hierarchize, grade, rank.

**.5** **form, take form, take order, take shape,** crystallize, **shape up;** arrange *or* range itself, place itself, take its place, fall in, **fall into place,** fall into line *or* order *or* series, fall into rank, take rank; come together, draw up, gather around, rally round.

**.6** ADJS **orderly,** ordered, **regular, well-regulated, well-ordered, methodical, formal,** uniform 17.5, **systematic,** symmetrical, **harmonious;** businesslike, routine, steady, normal, habitual, usual, *en règle* [Fr], in hand; **arranged** 60.14.

**.7** **in order, in trim,** to rights [informal], in apple-pie order [informal]; **in condition,** in good condition, in kilter *or* kelter [informal], **in shape,** in good shape [informal], **in good form,** in fine fettle, in good trim, in the pink [informal], in the pink of condition; **in repair,** in commission, in

adjustment, in working order, fixed; up to scratch *or* snuff [slang].

**.8** **tidy, trim, neat,** anal, spruce, sleek, slick [informal], smart, trig, dinky [Brit informal], snug, tight, **shipshape,** shipshape and Bristol fashion; **well-kept,** wellkempt, well-cared-for, well-groomed; neat as a button *or* pin [informal].

**.9** ADVS **methodically, systematically, regularly,** uniformly, harmoniously, like clockwork.

**.10** **in order, in turn, in sequence, in succession,** hierarchically, in series, *seriatim* [L]; step by step, by stages.

## 60. ARRANGEMENT

*(putting in order)*

**.1** NOUNS **arrangement, ordering,** structuring, constitution; **disposition, disposal,** deployment, placement, marshaling, **arraying; distribution,** collation, collocation, allocation, allotment, apportionment; **formation,** formulation, form, array; regimentation; syntax; **order** 59; tax(o)– *or* taxi–, –taxia *or* –taxis.

**.2** **organization, methodization,** planning, charting, codification, regulation, regularization, routinization, normalization, rationalization; **adjustment,** harmonization, **systematization,** ordination, coordination.

**.3** **grouping,** categorization, taxonomy; **gradation,** subordination, **ranking,** placement; **sorting,** sorting out, assortment, sifting, screening, triage, culling, selection.

**.4** **table,** code, digest, **index, inventory,** census; table of organization.

**.5** **sorter,** sifter, **sieve,** riddle, **screen,** bolter, colander, grate, grating.

**.6** (act of making neat) **cleanup,** red-up [dial]; tidy-up, trim-up, police-up [informal].

**.7** **rearrangement, reorganization,** reconstitution, **reordering, restructuring,** shakeup; redisposition, redistribution, realignment.

**.8** VERBS **arrange,** order 59.4, reduce to order, **put** *or* **set in order,** right, **put** *or* **set to rights,** put in *or* into shape, whip into shape [informal], unsnarl.

**.9** **dispose, distribute, fix, place,** set out, collocate, allocate, **compose,** space, **marshal,** rally, array; align, line, **line up,** range; regiment; **allot, apportion,** parcel out, deal, **deal out.**

**.10** **organize,** methodize, **systematize,** rationalize; **harmonize,** synchronize, **tune,** tune up; **regularize,** routinize, normalize, standardize; **regulate,** adjust, coordinate, fix, settle; **plan,** chart, codify.

.11 **classify** 61.6, **group,** categorize; **grade,** gradate, rank, subordinate; **sort,** sort out, assort; **separate,** divide; collate; **sift,** size, sieve, **screen,** bolt, riddle.

.12 tidy, **tidy up,** neaten, trim, **put in trim,** trim up, trig up, **straighten up,** fix up [informal], **clean up,** police or police up [both informal], groom, spruce or spruce up [both informal], **clear up,** clear the decks.

.13 **rearrange, reorganize,** reconstitute, **reorder, restructure,** shake up; redispose, redistribute, realign.

.14 ADJS **arranged, ordered, disposed,** composed, constituted, fixed, placed, aligned, ranged, arrayed, marshaled, grouped, ranked, **graded;** organized, methodized, **regularized,** routinized, normalized, standardized, **systematized;** regulated, harmonized, synchronized; **classified** 61.8, categorized, **sorted,** assorted; **orderly** 59.6; –tactic.

.15 **organizational,** formational.

## 61. CLASSIFICATION

.1 NOUNS **classification, categorization, placement,** ranging, **pigeonholing, sorting, grouping; grading,** stratification, ranking, rating; division, subdivision; **cataloging,** codification, tabulation, indexing, filing; **taxonomy,** typology; analysis 48, **arrangement** 60.

.2 **class, category, head, order, division, branch, set, group,** grouping, bracket, pigeonhole; **section,** heading, rubric, **label,** title; **grade,** rank, rating, status, estate, stratum, level, station, position; –age, –ate, –cy, –dom, –hood; predicament [logic]; caste, clan, race, strain, blood, kin, sept; **subdivision,** subgroup, suborder.

.3 **kind, sort, ilk, type,** lot [informal], variety, **species,** speci(o)– or specie–, **genus,** genre [Fr], gen(o)–, phylum, phyl(o)–, denomination, designation, number [informal], description, style, manner, **nature, character,** persuasion, the like or likes of [informal]; **stamp, brand,** feather, color, stripe, line, grain, kidney; **make,** mark, label, shape, cast, form, mold; tribe, clan, race, strain, blood, kin, breed.

.4 **hierarchy,** class structure, power structure, pyramid, establishment, pecking order; natural hierarchy, order or chain of being; domain, realm, **kingdom,** animal kingdom, vegetable kingdom, mineral kingdom.

.5 (botanical and zoological classifications, in descending order) **kingdom;** subkingdom, **phylum** [zool], branch [bot]; superclass, **class,** subclass, superorder, **order,** suborder, superfamily, **family,** subfamily, tribe, subtribe, **genus,** subgenus, series, section, superspecies, **species;** subspecies, **variety;** biotype, genotype.

.6 VERBS **classify,** class; **categorize,** type, **pigeonhole,** place, **group, arrange** 60.8, range; **order** 59.4, rank, rate, **grade; sort,** assort; **divide, analyze** 48.6, subdivide, break down; **catalog,** list, file, tabulate, **index,** alphabetize, digest, codify.

.7 ADJS **classificational,** classificatory; **categorical, taxonomic(al),** typologic(al), ordinal; **divisional,** divisionary, subdivisional; **typical,** typal; **special,** specific, characteristic, particular, peculiar, denominative, differential, distinctive, defining.

.8 **classified, cataloged, pigeonholed,** indexed, sorted, assorted, **graded, grouped,** ranked, rated, stratified, hierarchic, pyramidal; placed; filed, on file; tabular.

.9 ADVS of any kind or sort, **of any description, at all,** whatever, soever, whatsoever.

## 62. DISORDER

.1 NOUNS **disorder, disorderliness, disarrangement,** derangement, disarticulation, disjunction 49.1, **disorganization;** discomposure, **dishevelment, disarray,** upset, disturbance, discomfiture, disconcertedness; **irregularity,** randomness, turbulence, perturbation, ununiformity or nonuniformity, unsymmetry or nonsymmetry, **disproportion, disharmony;** indiscriminateness, promiscuity, promiscuousness, haphazardness; entropy; **disruption** 49.3; **incoherence** 51.1; disintegration 53; "most admired disorder" [Shakespeare], "inharmonious harmony" [Horace].

.2 **confusion, chaos,** anarchy, misrule, license; **muddle,** morass, **mix-up** [informal], foul-up [informal], snafu [slang], screw-up [slang], hassle [informal]; pretty kettle of fish, pretty piece of business, nice piece of work; "Chaos and old Night" [Milton], "the seed of Chaos, and of Night" [Pope], "mere anarchy is loosed upon the world", "fabulous formless darkness" [both Yeats].

.3 **jumble, scramble, tumble, mess,** bloody or holy or unholy mess [slang], **turmoil,** welter, mishmash, hash, helter-skelter, farrago, higgledy-piggledy; **clutter, litter, hodgepodge** 44.6, rat's nest; topsy-turviness *or* topsy-turvydom, arsy-varsiness, hysteron proteron.

.4 **commotion, hubbub, tumult,** turmoil, **uproar, racket, riot, disturbance, rumpus** [informal], ruckus *or* ruction [both informal], **fracas, hassle,** shemozzle [Brit slang], shindy [slang], rampage; **ado,** to-do [informal], trouble, bother, pother, dustup [Brit informal], stir [informal], **fuss,** *brouhaha* [Fr], foofaraw [informal]; **row** [informal], **brawl, free-for-all** [informal], donnybrook *or* donnybrook fair, broil, embroilment, melee, scramble; helter-skelter, pell-mell, **roughhouse, rough-and-tumble.**

.5 **pandemonium,** "confusion worse confounded" [Milton], **hell, bedlam,** witches' Sabbath, Babel, confusion of tongues; **cacophony,** noise, static, racket.

.6 **slovenliness** *or* slovenry, **slipshodness,** carelessness, negligence; **untidiness,** unneatness, looseness, **messiness** [informal], **sloppiness,** dowdiness, seediness, **shabbiness,** tawdriness, chintziness [informal], shoddiness, tackiness [informal], grubbiness [informal], frowziness, blowziness; **slatternliness,** frumpishness [informal], sluttishness; **squalor,** squalidness, sordidness.

.7 **slob** [informal], **slattern, sloven,** frump [informal], sloppy Joe, schlep, schlump; drab, **slut, trollop; pig,** swine; **litterbug.**

.8 VERBS lapse into disorder, come apart 49.8, dissolve into chaos, slacken 51.3, disintegrate 53.3, degenerate, untune.

.9 **disorder, disarrange** 63.2, **disorganize,** dishevel; **confuse** 63.3, **muddle,** jumble; **discompose** 63.4, **upset,** unsettle, **disturb,** perturb; knock galley-west [slang].

.10 **riot,** roister, roil, carouse; **create a disturbance, make a commotion,** make trouble, make an ado *or* to-do [informal], raise a rumpus [informal], raise a storm [informal], raise a ruckus [informal], create a riot, **cut loose,** run wild, **run riot,** run amok, go on a rampage, go berserk.

.11 [slang or informal terms] **kick up a row,** kick up a shindy, **raise the devil,** raise the deuce *or* dickens, raise Cain, **raise hell,** raise sand, raise the roof, whoop it up, hell around, horse around; **carry on, go on,** maffick [Brit]; **cut up,** cut up rough, **roughhouse.**

.12 ADJS **unordered, orderless, disordered, unorganized, unarranged,** ungraded, unsorted, unclassified; **unmethodical,** immethodical; **unsystematic,** systemless, nonsystematic; disjunct, unjoined 49.20; **disarticulated, incoherent** 51.4; discontinuous; **formless,** amorphous, inchoate, shapeless; ununiform *or* nonuniform, unsymmetrical *or* nonsymmetrical, disproportionate, misshapen; **irregular, haphazard,** desultory, **erratic,** sporadic, spasmodic, fitful, promiscuous, indiscriminate, casual, frivolous, capricious, random, hit-or-miss, vague, dispersed, wandering, planless, undirected, **aimless,** straggling, straggly; senseless, meaningless, gratuitous; dis–.

.13 **disorderly, in disorder,** disordered, **disorganized, disarranged, discomposed,** dislocated, deranged, convulsed; **upset, disturbed,** perturbed, unsettled, discomfited, disconcerted; **turbulent,** turbid, roily; **out of order,** out of place, misplaced, shuffled; **out of kilter** *or* kelter [informal], **out of whack** [informal], out of gear, out of joint, out of tune, on the fritz [slang]; **cockeyed** [slang], awry, amiss, askew, haywire [informal].

.14 **disheveled, mussed up** [informal], messed up [informal], **rumpled,** tumbled, ruffled, snarled, snaggy; **tousled,** tously; uncombed, shaggy, matted.

.15 **slovenly, slipshod, careless, loose, slack,** informal, negligent; **untidy, unsightly,** unneat, **unkempt; messy** [informal], mussy [informal], **sloppy** [informal], scraggly, poky, seedy [informal], **shabby,** shoddy, lumpen, chintzy, grubby [informal], **frowzy, blowzy,** tacky [informal]; **slatternly, sluttish, frumpish,** frumpy, draggletailed, drabbletailed, draggled, bedraggled; down at the heel, out at the heels, out at the elbows, in rags, ragged, raggedy, tattered; **squalid,** sordid; dilapidated, ruinous, **beat-up** [slang].

.16 **confused, chaotic, anarchic, muddled, jumbled,** scattered, helter-skelter [informal], higgledy-piggledy, hugger-mugger, skimble-skamble, in a mess; **topsy-turvy,** arsy-varsy, upside-down, ass-backwards [slang]; **mixed up, balled** *or* **bollixed up** [slang], **screwed up** [slang], mucked up [informal], **fouled up** [informal], snafu [slang], galley-west [slang].

.17 ADVS **in disorder, in disarray, in confusion, in a jumble, in a tumble, in a muddle, in a mess;** higgledy-piggledy, helter-skelter [informal], hugger-mugger, skimble-skamble, harum-scarum [informal], willy-nilly [informal], every which way [informal]; all over, all over hell [slang], all over the place, all over the shop [informal].

.18 **haphazardly, unsystematically,** unmethodically, irregularly, desultorily, **erratically,** capriciously, promiscuously, indiscriminately, **sloppily** [informal], **carelessly,** randomly, **fitfully;** by *or* at intervals, sporadically, spasmodically, by fits, **by fits and starts,** by *or* in snatches, in spots [informal]; every now and then, every once in a while [both informal]; **at random,** at haphazard, **by chance, hit or miss.**

.19 **chaotically, anarchically,** turbulently, riotously; **confusedly,** dispersedly, vaguely, wanderingly, **aimlessly,** planlessly, senselessly.

### 63. DISARRANGEMENT

*(bringing into disorder)*

.1 NOUNS **disarrangement, derangement,** misarrangement, convulsion, dislocation; **disorganization,** shuffling; **discomposure,** disturbance, perturbation; **disorder** 62; insanity 473.

.2 VERBS **disarrange, derange,** misarrange; **disorder, disorganize,** throw out of order, put out of gear, dislocate, **disarray; dishevel,** rumple, ruffle; tousle [informal], muss *or* **muss up** [both informal], mess *or* **mess up** [both informal]; **litter, clutter,** scatter.

.3 **confuse, muddle, jumble,** confound, garble, tumble, scramble, fumble, pi; **shuffle,** riffle; **mix up,** snarl up, **ball** *or* **bollix up** [slang], **foul up** [informal], **screw up** [slang], muck up [informal], snafu [slang]; make a hash *or* mess of [slang], play hob with [informal].

.4 **discompose,** throw into confusion, **upset, unsettle, disturb,** perturb, trouble, distract, throw [informal], throw into a tizzy *or* snit *or* stew [informal], agitate, convulse, embroil; psych *or* spook *or* bug [all slang].

.5 ADJS **disarranged** 62.13, **confused** 62.16, **disordered** 62.12.

### 64. PRECEDENCE

*(in order)*

.1 NOUNS precedence *or* precedency, antecedence *or* antecedency, anteposition, anteriority, precession; the lead, front position; **priority,** preference, urgency; top priority; prefixation, prothesis; **superiority**

36; **dominion** 739.6; **precursor** 66; **prelude** 66.2; preceding 292.1.

.2 VERBS **precede,** antecede, **come first,** come *or* go before 66.3, **go ahead of, go in advance,** stand first, stand at the head, **head,** head up [informal], front, **lead** 292.2, take precedence, have priority; lead off, kick off, usher in; head the table *or* board, sit on the dais; rank, outrank, rate.

.3 (place before) **prefix, preface,** premise, prelude, prologize, preamble, introduce.

.4 ADJS **preceding,** precedent, **prior,** antecedent, anterior, precessional, **leading** 292.3; **preliminary,** precursory, prevenient, prefatory, exordial, prelusive, preludial, proemial, preparatory, initiatory, propaedeutic, inaugural; **first, foremost,** headmost, **chief** 36.14.

.5 **former,** foregoing; aforesaid, aforementioned, beforementioned, above-mentioned, aforenamed, forenamed, forementioned, said, named, same.

.6 ADVS **before** 240.12; above, hereinbefore, hereinabove, *supra* [L], *ante* [L].

### 65. SEQUENCE

.1 NOUNS **sequence,** logical sequence, **succession,** successiveness, consecution, consecutiveness, following, coming after; descent, lineage, line; **series** 71.2; **order,** order of succession; **progression,** procession, rotation; **continuity** 71; **continuation,** prolongation, extension, posteriority; suffixation, subjunction, postposition.

.2 VERBS **succeed, follow, ensue,** come *or* go after, **come next,** come on, **inherit,** take the mantle of, step into the shoes *or* place of.

.3 (place after) **suffix, append,** subjoin.

.4 ADJS **succeeding, successive, following, ensuing,** sequent, sequential, sequacious, posterior, **subsequent,** consequent; eka–, rere–; proximate, **next;** appendant, suffixed, postpositive, postpositional.

### 66. PRECURSOR

.1 NOUNS **precursor, forerunner,** foregoer, *voorlooper* [Du], vaunt-courier, avant-courier, front *or* lead runner; pioneer, *voortrekker* [Du], frontiersman, bushwhacker; scout, pathfinder, explorer, point, trailblazer *or* trailbreaker, guide; **leader** 748.6, bellwether, fugleman; **herald,** announcer, *buccinator* [L], messenger, harbinger, stormy petrel; **predecessor,** forebear, precedent, antecedent, **ancestor; vanguard, avant-garde,** innovator, groundbreaker.

.2 prelude, preamble, preface, prologue, foreword, introduction, *avant-propos* [Fr], protasis, proem, proemium, prolegomenon *or* prolegomena, exordium; **prefix**, prefixture; frontispiece; **preliminary**, front matter; overture, voluntary, verse; premise, presupposition, postulate, prolepsis; **innovation** 139.3, **breakthrough** [informal], leap.

.3 VERBS **go before, pioneer,** blaze *or* break the trail, be in the van *or* vanguard; guide; **lead** 292.2; **precede** 64.2; herald, forerun, usher in, introduce.

.4 ADJS **preceding** 64.4; preliminary, exploratory, inaugural; **advanced,** avant-garde, original 23.5.

## 67. SEQUEL

.1 NOUNS **sequel,** sequela *or* sequelae [pl], sequelant, sequent, sequitur, **consequence** 154.1; **continuation,** continuance, **follow-up** *or* **-through** [informal]; **supplement,** addendum, appendix, back matter; postfix, suffix; postscript, PS, subscript, postface, postlude, epilogue, conclusion, peroration, codicil; refrain, chorus, coda; envoi, colophon, tag; afterthought, second thought, double take [informal], *arrière-pensée* [Fr], *esprit d'escalier* [Fr]; parting *or* Parthian shot; last words, swan song, dying words.

.2 **afterpart,** afterpiece; wake, trail, train, queue; **tail,** tailpiece; tab, tag, trailer.

.3 **aftermath, afterclap,** afterglow, afterimage, aftereffect, side effect, by-product, aftertaste; **aftergrowth,** aftercrop; **afterbirth,** placenta, secundines, maz(o)–; afterpain.

.4 **successor, replacement,** backup man; **descendant,** posterity, **heir,** inheritor.

## 68. BEGINNING

.1 NOUNS **beginning, commencement, start,** running *or* flying start, starting point, square one [slang], **outset, outbreak, onset,** oncoming; dawn; **creation, foundation, institution, origin,** origination, establishment, setting-up, setting in motion; alpha, A; **opening,** rising of the curtain; first crack out of the box [informal], kick-off *or* jump-off *or* send-off *or* start-off *or* take-off *or* blast-off [all informal], the word 'go' [informal]; fresh start, new departure; edge, leading edge, cutting edge, thin end of the wedge.

.2 **beginner, neophyte, tyro;** newcomer 78.4; entrant, **novice,** novitiate, probationer, catechumen; recruit, raw recruit; rookie

[informal]; trainee, learner, apprentice; baby, infant; nestling, fledgling; freshman 566.6; tenderfoot, greenhorn, greeny [informal]; debutant, deb [informal].

.3 **first, prime, initial,** alpha, primitiveness *or* primitivity, **initiative,** first move, **first step,** *le premier pas* [Fr], first lap, first round, first inning, first stage; breaking-in, warming-up; opening move, gambit; first blush, first glance, first sight, first impression.

.4 **origin,** origination, **genesis, inception,** incipience *or* incipiency, inchoation; –geny, –escence; **birth,** parturition, pregnancy, nascency *or* nascence, nativity; **infancy,** babyhood, childhood, youth; freshman year; incunabula, beginnings, cradle.

.5 **inauguration,** installation *or* installment, induction, **introduction,** initiation; embarkation *or* embarkment, **launching,** floating, flotation, unveiling; debut, first appearance, coming out [informal]; opener [informal], preliminary, curtain raiser *or* lifter; maiden speech, inaugural address.

.6 **basics, rudiments, elements, principles,** principia, **outlines, primer,** hornbook, grammar, alphabet, **ABC's;** first principles, first steps; induction.

.7 VERBS **begin, commence, start; start in, start off, start out, set out,** set sail, set in, set to *or* about, get to, **turn to,** fall to, pitch in [informal], dive in [slang], plunge into, head into [informal], **go ahead,** fire *or* blast away [informal], take off *or* jump off *or* kick off *or* blast off *or* send off [all informal], get the show on the road [informal].

.8 **make a beginning,** make a move [informal], **start up,** get going [informal], get off, **get under way,** get in there [slang]; set a course, **get squared away** [informal]; make an auspicious beginning, **get off to a good start;** get in on the ground floor [informal]; **break in, warm up,** get one's feet wet [slang], cut one's teeth.

.9 enter, **enter on** *or* **upon, embark in** *or* **on** *or* **upon,** take up, go into; make one's debut, come out [informal].

.10 **initiate, originate, create,** invent; **precede** 64.2, **take the initiative, take the first step,** take the lead, pioneer 66.3; **lead,** lead off, lead the way; **head,** head up [informal], stand at the head, stand first; **break the ice,** take the plunge, break ground, cut the first turf, lay the first stone.

.11 **inaugurate, institute, found, establish,** set

up [informal]; **install,** initiate, induct; **introduce,** broach, bring up, lift up, raise; **launch,** float; christen [informal]; **usher in,** ring in [informal]; **set on foot,** set abroach, set agoing, turn on, start up, start going, start the ball rolling [informal].

.12 **open,** open up, breach, open the door to; open fire.

.13 **originate, take** or **have origin,** be born, take birth, come into the world, **become,** come to be, get to be [informal], see the light of day, rise, **arise,** take rise, take its rise, **come forth, issue,** issue forth, come out, spring or crop up; burst forth, break out, erupt, irrupt.

.14 **engender, beget,** procreate 169.8; **give birth to, bear,** birth [dial], bring to birth; father, mother, sire.

.15 ADJS **beginning, initial,** initiatory or initiative; **incipient,** inceptive, **introductory,** inchoative, inchoate; inaugural or inauguratory; **prime,** primal, **primary,** primitive, primeval; acro–, arche–, eo–, ne(o)–, proto–, ur– [Ger]; primogenial; **original,** aboriginal, autochthonous; **elementary,** elemental, **fundamental,** foundational; **rudimentary,** rudimental, abecedarian; **formative, creative,** procreative, inventive; embryonic, in embryo, in the bud, budding, fetal, gestatory, parturient, pregnant, in its infancy; infant, infantile, incunabular; **natal,** nascent, prenatal, antenatal; postnatal; –escent.

.16 **preliminary, prefatory,** preludial, proemial; prepositive, prefixed.

.17 **first, foremost,** front, **head, chief, principal,** premier, **leading, main;** maiden.

.18 ADVS **first, firstly, at first, first** off, first thing, **in the first place,** first and foremost, before everything, *primo* [L]; **principally,** mainly, chiefly; **primarily,** initially; **originally, in the beginning,** *in limine* [L], **at the start,** at the first go-off [informal], from the ground up, from the foundations, from the beginning, from the first, **from the word 'go'** [informal], *ab origine* [L], *ab initio* [L]; *ab ovo* [L].

## 69. MIDDLE

.1 NOUNS **middle,** median, midmost, **midst;** thick, thick of things; **center** 226.2; **heart, core,** nucleus, kernel; **mean** 32; interior 225.2; midriff, diaphragm; waist, waistline, zone; equator; diameter.

.2 **mid-distance,** middle distance; **equidistance; half,** moiety, mediety; halfway

point or place, midway, midcourse, halfway house; bisection.

.3 VERBS **middle,** bisect; average 32.2; **double,** fold.

.4 ADJS **middle, medial,** median, mesial, middling, mediocre, average, **medium** 32.3, mezzo [mus], **mean,** mid; **midmost,** middlemost; mid–, medi(o)–, mes(o)–, mesio–; **central** 226.11, core, nuclear; interior 225.8; **intermediate,** intermediary, intermedi(o)–; equidistant, halfway, midway, equatorial; midland, mediterranean; midships, amidships.

.5 ADVS **midway, halfway, in the middle,** betwixt and between [informal], halfway in the middle [informal]; plump or smack or slap or smack-dab in the middle [informal]; half-and-half, neither here nor there, *mezzo-mezzo* [Ital]; medially, mediumly; in the mean; *in medias res* [L]; in **the midst of,** in the thick of; midships, amidships.

## 70. END

.1 NOUNS **end,** end point, ending, **termination, terminus, terminal,** term, period, apodosis, **expiration,** cessation 144, ceasing, consummation, culmination, **conclusion, finish, finis, finale,** finality, quietus, stoppage, windup [informal], payoff [slang], curtain, curtains [slang], fall of the curtain, end of the line [informal]; decease, **death** 408; **last,** "latter end" [Bible], last gasp or breath, final twitch; omega, Ω, izzard, Z; **goal,** destination, stopping place, resting place; denouement, catastrophe, final solution, resolution; last or final words, peroration, swan song, envoi, coda, epilogue; **fate, destiny,** last things, eschatology, last trumpet, crack of doom, doom; effect 154.

.2 **extremity, extreme;** acr(o)–, tel(o)– or tele–; **limit** 56.5, **boundary,** farthest bound, jumping-off place, Thule, *Ultima Thule* [L], **pole; tip,** point, nib; **tail, tail end,** butt end, tag, tag end, fag end; bitter end; stub, stump, butt; bottom dollar [informal], bottom of the barrel [informal].

.3 **close,** closing; cessation; decline, lapse; **homestretch, last lap** or **round** or **inning** [informal], last stage; beginning of the end.

.4 **finishing stroke,** ender, **end-all,** quietus, stopper, **deathblow,** death stroke, *coup de grâce* [Fr]; **finisher,** clincher, equalizer, crusher, **settler;** knockout or knockout blow [both informal]; sockdolager,

KO *or* kayo *or* kayo punch [all slang]; final stroke, finishing *or* perfecting *or* crowning touch, last dab *or* lick [slang].

.5 VERBS **end, terminate,** determine, close, **finish, conclude,** resolve, finish *or* wind up [informal]; **stop, cease** 144.6; perorate; abort; scrap, scratch [both informal].

.6 **come to an end, draw to a close, expire, die** 408.19; lapse, become void *or* extinct *or* defunct, run out, run its course, have its time *or* have it [both informal], pass, **pass away,** die away, wear off *or* away, go out, blow over, be all over, be no more.

.7 **complete** 56.6, perfect, finish, finalize [informal]; **put an end to,** put a period to, put paid to [Brit], **make an end of,** bring to an end, end off [informal]; **get it over,** get over with *or* through with [informal]; ring down *or* drop the curtain; put the lid on [slang], fold up [informal]; call off [informal], call all bets off [informal]; **dispose of,** polish off [informal]; kibosh *or* put the kibosh on [both slang]; **kill** 409.13, extinguish, scrag [slang], zap [slang], **give the quietus,** put the finisher *or* settler on [informal], knock on *or* in the head, knock out [informal], kayo *or* KO [both slang], shoot down *or* shoot down in flames [both slang], wipe out [slang]; **cancel, delete,** expunge.

.8 ADJS **ended, at an end, terminated, concluded, finished, complete** 56.9, perfected, settled, decided, set at rest; **over, all over,** all up [slang]; all off [informal], all bets off [slang]; **done,** done with, through *or* through with [both informal]; wound up [informal], washed up [slang]; all over but the shouting [informal]; **dead** 408.30, **defunct,** extinct; fini, kaput, shot, done for, SOL, zapped [all slang], wiped out [slang]; **canceled, deleted,** expunged.

.9 **ending, closing, concluding, finishing,** culminating *or* culminative, consummative *or* consummatory, perfecting *or* perfective, terminating, crowning, capping.

.10 **final, terminal,** terminating *or* terminative, determinative, definitive, **conclusive; last,** eventual, farthest, extreme, boundary, limiting, polar, **endmost, ultimate;** caudal, tail.

.11 ADVS **finally,** in fine; **ultimately, eventually; lastly,** last, **at last,** at the last *or* end *or* conclusion, at length, at long last; **in conclusion;** conclusively, once for all.

.12 **to the end, to the bitter end, all the way,** to the last gasp, the last extremity, **to a finish,** *à outrance* [Fr], till hell freezes over [informal], "to the edge of doom", "to the last syllable of recorded time" [both Shakespeare].

.13 PHRS **that's final, that's that,** that buttons it up [informal], that's the end of the matter, so much for that, enough said; the subject is closed, the matter is ended, the deal is off [informal]; "the rest is silence" [Shakespeare].

## 71. CONTINUITY

### *(uninterrupted sequence)*

.1 NOUNS **continuity, uninterruption, uninterruptedness,** featurelessness, unrelievedness, monotony, unintermittedness, unbrokenness, **uniformity** 17, undifferentiation; fullness, plenitude; seamlessness, jointlessness, gaplessness, smoothness; **consecutiveness,** successiveness; continuousness, **endlessness, ceaselessness, incessancy; constancy** 135.2, continualness, constant flow; steadiness, steady state, equilibrium, stability 142.

.2 **series, succession,** run, **sequence,** consecution, progression, course, gradation; **continuum,** plenum; lineage, descent, filiation; **connection, concatenation,** catenation, catena, **chain,** chaining, articulation, reticulation, nexus; chain reaction, powder train; **train,** range, rank, **file, line, string,** thread, queue, **row,** bank, tier; windrow, swath; single file, Indian file; array; **round, cycle,** rotation, routine, recurrence, periodicity, flywheel effect, pendulum; endless belt *or* chain, Möbius band *or* strip, *la ronde* [Fr], endless round; gamut, spectrum, scale; drone, monotone, hum, buzz.

.3 **procession, train, column, line, string, cortege;** stream, steady stream; –cade, cavalcade, caravan, motorcade; **parade,** pomp; dress parade; promenade, review, march past, flyover [US], flypast [Brit], funeral; skimmington [Brit dial]; mule train, pack train.

.4 VERBS **continue,** be continuous, **connect, connect up, concatenate,** continuate, catenate, **join** 47.5, link, **string together,** string, thread, chain, follow in *or* form a series, run on, maintain continuity.

.5 **align, line, line up,** string out, rank, array, range; **row,** bank.

.6 **line up, get in line,** form a line, get in formation, **fall in,** fall in *or* into line, fall into rank, take rank, take one's place; queue, **queue up.**

.7 **file,** defile, file off; **parade,** go on parade, promenade, march past.

.8 ADJS **continuous**, continued, **continual**, continuing; **uninterrupted, unintermittent**, unintermitted, featureless, unrelieved, monotonous; **connected**, joined 47.13, linked, concatenated, catenated, articulated; **unbroken**, serried, **uniform** 17.5, undifferentiated, seamless, jointless, gapless, smooth, unstopped; unintermitting, unremitting; **incessant, constant**, steady, stable, **ceaseless**, unceasing, **endless**, unending, never-ending, **interminable**, perennial; **cyclical**, repetitive, **recurrent**, periodic; straight, running, **nonstop; round-the-clock**, twenty-four-hour; immediate, direct.

.9 **consecutive, successive**, successional, progressive; **serial**, ordinal, seriate, catenary; sequent, **sequential**; linear, lineal.

.10 ADVS **continuously, continually; uninterruptedly, unintermittently; without cease**, without a break, without stopping, **unbrokenly, connectedly, together**, cumulatively, on end; **incessantly, constantly, ceaselessly**, unceasingly, **endlessly**, *ad infinitum* [L], perennially, **interminably**, again and again, repetitively, cyclically, monotonously, unrelievedly, on and on, at *or* on a stretch; round the clock.

.11 **consecutively, progressively**, sequentially, successively, **in succession**, one after the other, **in turn**, turn about, turn and turn about; step by step; running, hand running [informal]; **serially**, in a series, *seriatim* [L]; **in a line**, in a row, in column, in file, in a chain, in single file, in Indian file.

## 72. DISCONTINUITY

*(interrupted sequence)*

.1 NOUNS **discontinuity**, discontinuousness, discontinuation, discontinuance, noncontinuance; **incoherence** 51.1, **disconnectedness**, disconnection, discreteness, **disjunction** 49.1; **nonuniformity** 18; irregularity, **intermittence**, fitfulness 138.1; **brokenness**; nonseriality, nonlinearity, non sequitur; incompleteness 57; episode, parenthesis; broken thread.

.2 **interruption, suspension, break**, fissure, breach, gap, hiatus, lacuna, caesura; **interval, pause**, interim 109, lull, cessation, letup [informal], **intermission**.

.3 VERBS **discontinue, interrupt** 144.6,10, **break**, break off, disjoin 49.9; **disarrange** 63.2.

.4 ADJS **discontinuous**, noncontinuous, un-successive, **incoherent** 51.4, nonserial, nonlinear, nonsequential, discontinued, **disconnected**, unconnected, unjoined 49.20, *décousu* [Fr], **broken**; nonuniform 18.3, irregular; broken off, **interrupted**, suspended; disjunctive, discrete, discretive; **intermittent, fitful** 138.3; scrappy, snatchy, spotty, patchy, jagged; choppy, chopped-off, herky-jerky [slang], jerky, spasmodic; episodic, parenthetic.

.5 ADVS **discontinuously, disconnectedly**, brokenly; at intervals; **haphazardly** 62.18, randomly, occasionally, infrequently, **by fits and starts**, by fits, by snatches, by catches, by jerks, by skips, skippingly, *per saltum* [L]; willy-nilly, **here and there, in spots; intermittently, fitfully** 138.4.

## 73. ACCOMPANIMENT

.1 NOUNS **accompaniment**, concomitance *or* concomitancy, withness *or* togetherness [both informal]; synchronism, **simultaneity** 118; coincidence, co-occurrence, **concurrence**; parallelism.

.2 **company, association**, consociation, society, community; **companionship, fellowship**, consortship, partnership.

.3 **attendant, concomitant**, corollary, **accessory**, appendage; **adjunct** 41.

.4 **accompanier, accompanist** *or* accompanyist; **attendant, companion, fellow, mate**, comate, consort, **partner**; companion piece.

.5 **escort, conductor, usher**, shepherd; **squire**, esquire, swain, cavalier; **chaperon**, duenna; **bodyguard**, guard, safe-conduct, **convoy**; companion, fellow traveler.

.6 **attendance, following, cortege, retinue, entourage**, suite, follower, attendant, satellite, rout, train, body of retainers; **court, cohort**; parasite 907.3–5.

.7 VERBS **accompany**, bear one company, **keep company with**, companion, companionize [informal], go *or* travel *or* run with, **go along with, attend**, wait on *or* upon; **associate with**, assort with, sort with, **consort with**, couple with, hang around with [informal], go hand in hand with; **combine** 52.3,4, associate, consociate, confederate, flock *or* band *or* herd together.

.8 **escort, conduct**, marshal, **usher**, shepherd, guide, lead; **convoy**, guard; **squire**, esquire, **attend**, wait on *or* upon, take out [informal]; **chaperon**.

.9 ADJS **accompanying, attending, attendant, concomitant**, accessory, collateral; **combined** 52.5,6, **associated**, coupled,

paired; **fellow, twin, joint, joined** 47.13,
conjoint, mutual; **simultaneous** 118.4,
**concurrent,** coincident; correlative 13.10;
parallel; co–, con– or col– or com– or
cor–, meta–, syn– or sym–.

.10 ADVS **hand in hand** or glove, arm in arm,
side by side, cheek by jowl, shoulder to
shoulder; therewith, therewithal, herewith.

.11 **together, collectively, mutually,** jointly,
unitedly, in conjunction, conjointly, *en
masse* [Fr], communally, corporately, **in a
body,** all at once, *ensemble* [Fr], in association, in company.

.12 PREPS **with, in company with, along with,
together with,** in association with, coupled or paired or partnered with, in conjunction with.

## 74. ASSEMBLAGE

.1 NOUNS **assemblage, assembly, collection,
gathering,** ingathering, **congregation,** col-
ligation; concourse, concurrence, conflux,
confluence, convergence; collocation, juxtaposition, junction 47.1,4; **combination**
52; mobilization, call-up, muster, *at-
troupement* [Fr]; roundup, rodeo, corral-
ling; **comparison** 491; canvass, census,
data-gathering, survey, inventory; –age,
–ana or –iana, –ery or –ry, –et(te), –oma
or –ome, –some.

.2 **assembly** (of persons), *assemblée* [Fr],
**gathering, forgathering, congregation,**
congress, convocation, concourse, **meeting,** meet, **get-together** [informal], turnout [informal]; convention, conventicle,
synod, council, diet, **conclave,** levee; caucus; mass meeting, **rally,** sit-in; **session,**
séance, sitting; panel, forum, symposium,
colloquium; committee, commission; *eisteddfod* [Welsh]; plenum, quorum;
**party, festivity** 878.4, fete, at home,
housewarming, soiree, reception, **dance,**
ball, prom, shindig or brawl [both slang];
rendezvous, date, assignation; –fest.

.3 **company, group,** grouping, groupment,
**party, band, gang, crew,** complement,
cast, outfit, pack, cohort, troop, troupe,
tribe, **body,** corps, stable, bunch [infor-
mal], mob [slang], crowd [informal];
squad, platoon, battalion, regiment, brigade, division, fleet; **team,** string; covey,
bevy; posse, detachment, contingent, detail, *posse comitatus* [L]; phalanx; **party,
faction,** movement, wing; in-group, out-
group, peer group, age group; coterie, salon, clique, **set;** junta, cabal.

.4 **throng, multitude, horde,** host, heap [in-

formal], army, panoply, legion; flock,
cluster, galaxy; **crowd,** press, crush, flood,
spate, deluge, mass; **mob,** rabble, rout,
ruck, jam, *cohue* [Fr], everybody and his
uncle [informal].

.5 (animals) **flock, bunch, pack,** colony,
host, troop, army, **herd, drove,** drive,
drift, trip; **pride** (of lions), sloth (of
bears), skulk (of foxes), gang (of elk), kennel (of dogs), clowder (of cats), pod (of
seals), gam (of whales), **school** or shoal
(of fish); (animal young) **litter** 171.2.

.6 (birds, insects) **flock,** flight, **swarm,** cloud;
covey (of partridges), bevy (of quail),
skein (of geese in flight), gaggle (of geese
on water), watch (of nightingales), charm
(of finches), murmuration (of starlings),
spring (of teal); hive (of bees), plague (of
locusts).

.7 **bunch, group,** grouping, groupment,
crop, **cluster, clump,** knot; grove, copse,
thicket; **batch, lot,** slew [slang], mess [in-
formal]; tuft, wisp; tussock, hassock;
shock, stook; botry(o)–, cym(o)– or kym-
(o)–, staphyl(o)–.

.8 **bundle,** bindle [slang], **pack, package,**
packet, deck, budget, **parcel,** fardel [dial],
bale, truss, **roll,** rouleau, bolt; fagot, fas-
cine, fasces; quiver, sheaf; bouquet, nosegay, posy.

.9 **accumulation,** cumulation, gathering,
**amassment,** congeries, acervation; agglomeration, conglomeration, glomeration, conglomerate, agglomerate; aggregation, aggregate; conglobation; **mass,
lump,** gob [slang], chunk or hunk [both
informal], wad; snowball; stockpile, stock-
piling.

.10 **pile, heap, stack; mound, hill;** molehill,
anthill; **bank,** embankment, dune; haystack, hayrick, haymow, haycock, cock,
mow, rick; drift, snowdrift; pyramid.

.11 **collection,** fund, treasure, holdings; corpus, **body,** data, raw data; compilation,
collectanea; ana; anthology, florilegium;
*Festschrift* [Ger]; chrestomathy; **museum,
library,** zoo, menagerie, aquarium.

.12 **set, suit, suite, series,** outfit or kit [both
informal]; pack, block, battery.

.13 **miscellany,** miscellanea, collectanea; **assortment, medley, variety, mixture** 44;
hodgepodge, conglomerate, **conglomeration,** omnium-gatherum [informal]; **sundries,** oddments, **odds and ends.**

.14 (a putting together) **assembly,** assemblage; assembly line, production line; assembly-line production.

.15 **collector,** gatherer, accumulator; collection agent, bill collector, dunner; tax collector, farmer, exciseman [Brit], *douanier* [Fr]; pack rat, magpie, miser; connoisseur.

.16 VERBS **come together, assemble, congregate, collect,** league 52.4; **unite** 47.5; muster, **meet, gather, forgather,** gang up [informal], mass; **merge,** converge, flow together, fuse; flock together; herd together; **throng, crowd,** swarm, hive, surge, seethe, mill, stream, horde; **cluster,** bunch, bunch up, clot; gather around, gang around [slang]; rally, rally around; **huddle,** go into a huddle; rendezvous, date; **couple,** copulate, link.

.17 **convene, meet,** hold a meeting *or* session, sit; **convoke,** summon, call together.

.18 (bring *or* gather together) **assemble, gather;** muster, rally, **mobilize; collect,** raise, take up; **accumulate,** cumulate, **amass,** mass, bulk, batch; **agglomerate,** conglomerate, aggregate; **combine** 52.3, join 47.5, **bring together,** get together, **gather together,** draw *or* lump *or* batch *or* bunch together; **bunch,** bunch up; **cluster,** clump; **group,** aggroup; **gather in,** get *or* whip in; scrape together, rake *or* dredge *or* dig up; round up, corral, drive together; **put together,** make up, compile, colligate; collocate, juxtapose, pair, match, partner; **compare** 491.4.

.19 **pile, heap, stack,** heap *or* pile *or* stack up; mound, hill, bank, bank up; rick; pyramid; drift.

.20 **bundle,** bundle up, **package,** parcel, **pack,** truss, truss up; bale; wrap, **wrap up,** do *or* tie *or* bind up; roll up.

.21 ADJS **assembled, collected, gathered;** congregate, congregated; meeting, in session; **combined** 52.5; **joined** 47.13; joint, leagued 52.6; **accumulated,** cumulate, massed, **amassed;** heaped, stacked, piled; glomerate, agglomerate, conglomerate, aggregate; **clustered,** bunched, lumped, clumped, knotted; bundled, packaged, wrapped up; fascicled, fasciculated.

.22 **crowded, packed, crammed;** jam-packed [informal]; **compact,** firm, solid, dense, close, serried; **teeming, swarming, crawling,** bristling, populous, full 56.11.

.23 **cumulative,** accumulative, total, overall.

## 75. DISPERSION

.1 NOUNS **dispersion** *or* **dispersal,** scattering, scatterment, diffraction; **distribution, spreading,** strewing, sowing, broadcasting, **broadcast, spread,** publication 559, **dissemination,** propagation, dispensation;

**radiation,** divergence 299; expansion, splay; diffusion, attenuation, dilution, volatilization, evaporation, dissipation; circumfusion; fragmentation; sprinkling, spattering; peppering, buckshot *or* shotgun pattern.

.2 **decentralization,** deconcentration.

.3 **disbandment,** dispersion *or* dispersal, diaspora, separation, parting; breakup, split-up [informal]; **demobilization,** deactivation, **release,** detachment; dismissal 310.5; dissolution, disorganization, disintegration 53.

.4 VERBS **disperse, scatter,** diffract; **distribute, broadcast, sow,** disseminate, propagate, publish 559.10; diffuse, **spread,** dispread, strew, bestrew; **radiate,** diverge 299.5; splay, branch *or* fan *or* spread out; **issue, deal out,** retail, utter, dispense; sow broadcast, scatter to the winds; overscatter, overspread, oversow; circumfuse.

.5 **dissipate, dispel,** dissolve, attenuate, dilute, thin, thin out, evaporate, volatilize; drive away, clear away, cast forth, blow off.

.6 **sprinkle,** besprinkle, **spatter,** splatter; **dot,** spot, speck, speckle, stud; **pepper,** powder, dust; flour, crumb, bread; dredge.

.7 **decentralize,** deconcentrate.

.8 **disband, disperse, scatter, separate, part,** break up, split up; part company, go separate ways; **demobilize,** demob [slang], deactivate, muster out, debrief, **release,** detach, discharge, let go; dismiss 310.18; **dissolve,** disorganize, disintegrate 53.3.

.9 ADJS **dispersed, scattered, distributed,** dissipated, disseminated, strown, strewn, broadcast, **spread,** dispread; **widespread,** diffuse, discrete, sparse, **sporadic;** straggling, straggly; all over the lot *or* place [informal], from hell to breakfast [slang].

.10 **sprinkled,** spattered, splattered, **peppered,** spotted, dotted, powdered, dusted, specked, speckled, **studded.**

.11 **dispersive, scattering, spreading,** diffractive *or* diffractional, **distributive,** disseminative, diffusive, dissipative, attenuative.

.12 ADVS **scatteringly, dispersedly,** diffusely, sparsely, **sporadically,** *sparsim* [L], **here and there;** in places, in spots [informal]; *passim* [L], at large, everywhere, throughout, wherever you look *or* turn [informal], in all quarters.

## 76. INCLUSION

.1 NOUNS **inclusion, comprisal, comprehension,** envisagement, embracement, encompassment, coverage, incorporation, embodiment, assimilation, reception; **membership**, participation, admission, admissibility, eligibility; **completeness** 56, **inclusiveness, comprehensiveness,** exhaustiveness; **whole** 54; openness, toleration *or* tolerance.

.2 **entailment, involvement, implication;** assumption, presumption, subsumption.

.3 VERBS **include, comprise, contain, comprehend, hold, take in; cover,** occupy, take up, fill; fill in *or* out, **complete** 56.6; **embrace,** encompass, enclose, encircle, incorporate, assimilate, embody, admit, receive, envisage; **reckon in,** reckon with, reckon among, count in, **number among,** take into account *or* consideration.

.4 (include as a necessary circumstance or consequence) **entail, involve, implicate,** imply, assume, presume, presuppose, subsume, affect, take in, contain, comprise, **call for, require,** take, bring, lead to.

.5 ADJS **included, comprised,** comprehended, envisaged, embraced, encompassed, covered; bound up with, forming *or* making a part of; **involved** 176.3.

.6 **inclusive, including, containing, comprising, covering, embracing,** encompassing, enclosing, encircling, assimilating, incorporating, envisaging; counting, numbering; **super–.**

.7 **comprehensive, sweeping, complete** 56.9; **whole** 54.9; **all-comprehensive,** all-inclusive 79.14; without omission *or* exception, **over-all,** universal, global, **total,** blanket, omnibus, across-the-board; encyclopedic, compendious; synoptic; bird's-eye, panoramic.

## 77. EXCLUSION

.1 NOUNS **exclusion, barring,** debarring, debarment, preclusion, exception, omission, nonadmission; **restriction, circumscription,** narrowing, demarcation; **rejection,** repudiation; **ban,** bar, taboo, injunction; relegation; prohibition, embargo, blockade; boycott, lockout; inadmissibility.

.2 **elimination, riddance,** severance 49.2; withdrawal, **removal,** detachment, disjunction 49.1; discard, eradication, clearance, **ejection,** expulsion, suspension; **deportation, exile,** expatriation, ostracism, outlawing *or* outlawry; disposal, disposition; **liquidation, purge.**

.3 **exclusiveness, narrowness,** tightness; **insularity,** snobbishness, parochialism, ethnocentrism, xenophobia, know-nothingism; **segregation, separation,** division; **isolation,** insulation, seclusion; quarantine; racial segregation, apartheid, color bar, Jim Crow, race hatred; **out-group; outsider, stranger; foreigner, alien** 78.3, outcast 926.4, *persona non grata* [L].

.4 VERBS **exclude, bar,** debar, bar out, lock out, **shut out, keep out,** count out [informal], cut off, preclude; reject, turn thumbs down on [informal], ease *or* freeze out [informal], close the door on, send to Coventry [Brit], ostracize; repudiate, **ban,** prohibit, taboo, **leave out,** omit, pass over, ignore; relegate; blockade, embargo.

.5 **eliminate, get rid of,** rid oneself of, **get quit of,** get shut of [dial], **dispose of, remove,** abstract, eject, expel, cast off *or* out, chuck [slang], throw over *or* overboard [informal]; **deport, exile,** outlaw, expatriate; clear, clear out, clear away, clear the decks; **weed out,** pick out; **cut out,** strike off *or* out, elide; eradicate, root up *or* out; **purge, liquidate.**

.6 **segregate, separate,** divide, cordon, cordon off; **isolate,** insulate, seclude; **set apart,** keep apart; quarantine, put beyond the pale, ghettoize; **set aside,** lay aside, put aside, keep aside; **sort** *or* **pick out,** cull out, sift, screen, sieve, bolt, riddle, winnow; thresh, thrash, gin.

.7 ADJS **excluded, barred,** debarred, precluded, **shut out, left out,** left out in the cold [informal]; not included, not in it, not in the picture [informal]; **banned,** prohibited, tabooed; **expelled,** ejected, **purged,** liquidated; deported, exiled.

.8 **exclusive, excluding,** exclusory; seclusive, preclusive, exceptional, inadmissible, prohibitive, preventive, prescriptive, restrictive; separative, segregative; select, selective; narrow, insular, parochial, ethnocentric, xenophobic, snobbish.

.9 PREPS **excluding, barring,** bar, exclusive of, precluding, omitting, **leaving out; excepting,** except, **except for,** with the exception of, outside of [informal], **save,** saving, save and except, let alone; **besides,** beside, **aside from,** than; unless, without, ex.

## 78. EXTRANEOUSNESS

.1 NOUNS **extraneousness, foreignness;** alienism, alienage; **extrinsicality** 6; **exteriority** 224; nonassimilation, nonconformity; intrusion.

.2 **intruder,** foreign body *or* element, foreign intruder *or* intrusion; **impurity,** blemish 679; stone, speck 196.7; mote, splinter *or* sliver, **weed,** misfit 27.4; odd-ball 85.4; black sheep; monkey wrench.

.3 **alien, stranger, foreigner, outsider,** out-lander, *Uitlander* [Afrikaans], tramon-tane, ultramontane, barbarian, foreign devil [China], *gringo* [Sp Amer]; **exile,** outlaw, wanderer, refugee, emigré, *émigré* [Fr], displaced person, D.P., *déraciné* [Fr]; the Wandering Jew.

.4 **newcomer, new arrival,** *novus homo* [L], upstart, parvenu, arriviste, Johnny-come-lately [informal], new boy [Brit]; **tender-foot,** greenhorn; settler, emigrant, immi-grant; recruit, rookie [slang]; **intruder, squatter,** gate-crasher, stowaway.

.5 ADJS **extraneous, foreign, alien,** strange, exotic; unearthly, extraterrestrial 375.26; exterior, external 224.6; extrinsic 6.3; ulte-rior, outside, outland, outlandish; barbar-ian, barbarous, barbaric; foreign-born; in-trusive; ep(i)– *or* eph–, ex(o)– *or* ef–, xen-(o)–.

.6 ADVS **abroad,** in foreign parts; oversea, **overseas,** beyond seas; on one's travels.

## 79. GENERALITY

.1 NOUNS **generality, universality,** inclusive-ness 76.1; worldwideness, globality *or* globalism, ecumenicity *or* ecumenicalism; catholicity; internationalism, cosmopoli-tanism; generalization.

.2 **prevalence, commonness,** commonality, usualness; **currency,** reign, run; **extensive-ness,** widespreadness, sweepingness, rife-ness, rampantness; **normality,** average-ness, ordinariness, routineness, habitual-ness, standardness.

.3 **generality, average,** ruck, **run,** general *or* common *or* average *or* ordinary run, **run of the mill;** any Tom, Dick, or Harry, Ev-eryman; common *or* average man, the man in the street, John Q. Public, ordi-nary Joe; girl next door; everyman, every-woman; *homme moyen sensuel* [Fr].

.4 **all, everyone, everybody, each and every one, one and all,** all hands [informal], ev-ery man Jack [informal], every mother's son [informal], **all the world,** *tout le monde* [Fr], the devil and all [informal], **whole, totality** 54.1.

.5 **any, anything,** any one, aught, either; **anybody, anyone.**

.6 **whatever,** whate'er, **whatsoever,** what-soe'er, **what, whichever,** anything soever which, no matter what *or* which.

.7 **whoever,** whoso, **whosoever, whomever,** whomso, **whomsoever,** anyone, no matter who.

.8 (idea or expression) **generalization,** gen-eral idea, **abstraction,** generalized propo-sition; glittering generality, sweeping statement; **truism, platitude,** common-place, *lieu commun* [Fr], *locus commu-nis* [L]; **cliché,** tired cliché, bromide, trite *or* hackneyed expression.

.9 VERBS **generalize, universalize,** catholi-cize, ecumenicize, globalize; **broaden, widen, expand,** extend, spread; make a generalization, deal in generalities *or* ab-stractions.

.10 **prevail, predominate, obtain,** dominate, reign, rule; be in force *or* effect; be the rule *or* fashion, be the rage *or* thing [slang], be in [slang].

.11 ADJS **general, generalized, nonspecific,** ge-neric, **indefinite,** indeterminate, vague, abstract, nebulous, unspecified, undiffer-entiated, featureless, uncharacterized, bland, neutral; **broad, wide;** collective.

.12 **prevalent, prevailing, common,** popular, **current,** running; regnant, reigning, **rul-ing, predominant,** predominating, **domi-nant; rife, rampant,** pandemic, epidemic, besetting; **ordinary, normal, average, usual,** routine, standard, stereotyped.

.13 **extensive, broad, wide,** liberal, diffuse, large-scale, **sweeping; widespread,** far-spread, far-stretched, **far-reaching,** far-go-ing, far-embracing, far-extending, far-spreading, far-flying, far-ranging, **far-flung,** wide-flung, wide-reaching, wide-ex-tending, wide-extended, wide-ranging, wide-stretching; **wholesale, indiscrimi-nate.**

.14 **universal,** heaven-wide, galactic, plane-tary, **world-wide, global; total, allover;** catholic, **all-inclusive,** all-including, **all-embracing,** all-encompassing, all-compre-hensive, all-comprehending, all-filling, all-pervading, all-covering; glob(o)–, omn-(i)–, pan(o)– *or* pam– *or* pant(o)– *or* pan-ta–; nonsectarian, nondenominational, ecumenic(al); cosmopolitan, interna-tional; national, country-wide, state-wide.

.15 **every, all,** any; **each,** each one; every one, each and every, each and all, **one and all, all and sundry,** all and some.

.16 **trite, commonplace,** hackneyed, platitu-dinous, truistic, overworked, stereotyped.

.17 ADVS **generally, in general; generally speaking,** speaking generally, **broadly,** broadly speaking, **roughly,** roughly speak-ing, as an approximation; **usually** 84.9, **as a rule, ordinarily, commonly, normally,** routinely, as a matter of course, in the usual course; **by and large,** at large, altogether, overall, **all things considered,** taking one thing with another, taking all things together, on balance, **all in all,** taking all in all, taking it for all in all, **on the whole,** as a whole, **in the long run,** for the most part, for better or for worse; prevailingly, predominantly, mostly, chiefly, mainly.

.18 universally, galactically, cosmically; **everywhere, all over,** the world over, internationally; in every instance, without exception, **invariably, always,** never otherwise.

## 80. PARTICULARITY

.1 NOUNS **particularity, individuality, singularity, differentiation,** differentness, distinctiveness, uniqueness; identity, individual or separate or concrete identity; **personality,** personship, personal identity; soul; **selfness,** selfhood, **egohood,** selfidentity, "a single separate person" [Whitman]; oneness 89.1, wholeness, integrity; personal equation, human factor; **nonconformity** 83; **individualism,** particularism; nominalism.

.2 speciality, specialness, specialty, specificality, **specificness,** definiteness; special case.

.3 the specific, the special, **the particular,** the concrete, the individual, the unique; "all things counter, original, spare, strange" [G. M. Hopkins].

.4 characteristic, peculiarity, singularity, particularity, specialty, individualism, **character,** nature, **trait,** quirk, mannerism, keynote, trick, **feature,** distinctive feature, lineaments; **mark,** marking, **earmark,** hallmark, index; badge, token; **brand,** cast, stamp, cachet, seal, mold, cut, figure, shape, configuration; impress, impression; differential, differentia; **idiosyncrasy,** idiocrasy; **quality, property, attribute;** savor, flavor, taste, gust, aroma, odor, smack, tang, taint.

.5 self, ego; **oneself,** I, I myself, me, myself, my humble self, number one [informal], yours truly [informal]; yourself, himself, herself, itself; ourselves, yourselves; themselves; you; he, she; him, her; they, them; it; inner self, inner man; subliminal or subconscious self; superego, better self, ethical self; other self, alter ego, *alter, alterum* [both L].

.6 specification, designation, stipulation, signification, determination, denomination; allocation, attribution, fixing, selection, assignment, pinning down, precision.

.7 **particularization, specialization;** individualization, peculiarization, personalization; localization; itemization 8.5.

.8 **characterization,** distinction, **differentiation;** definition, description.

.9 VERBS **particularize, specialize; individualize,** peculiarize, personalize; **descend to particulars,** precise, get down to brass tacks [informal], get down to cases [slang], come to the point; **itemize** 8.6, detail, spell out.

.10 **characterize, distinguish, differentiate, define, describe; mark, earmark,** mark off, mark out, demarcate, **set apart,** make special or unique; keynote [informal], sound the keynote, set the tone or mood, set the pace; be characteristic, **be a feature or trait of.**

.11 **specify,** specialize, **designate, stipulate,** determine, **fix,** set, assign, pin down; **name,** denominate, state, mention, select, pick out, mark, **indicate, signify,** point out, put or lay one's finger on.

.12 ADJS **particular, special, especial, specific, express,** precise, **concrete; singular, individual,** individualist(ic); aut(o)–, idio–, self–; **personal,** private, intimate, inner, solipsistic, esoteric; respective, several; **fixed, definite,** defined, distinct, different, determinate, certain, absolute; **distinguished,** noteworthy, **exceptional, extraordinary;** minute, detailed.

.13 **characteristic, peculiar, singular,** single, quintessential, intrinsic, unique, **distinctive,** marked, distinguished; appropriate, proper; idiosyncratic, idiocratic, **in character,** true to form; –acean or –aceous, –ey or –y, –ious or –ous, –ish, –ist or –istic(al), –itious, –itic, –ose, –some.

.14 **this,** this and no other, this one, this single; **these; that,** that one; those.

.15 ADVS **particularly, specially, especially, specifically, expressly,** concretely, exactly, precisely, **in particular,** to be specific; **definitely, distinctly; minutely,** in detail, item by item, singly, separately.

.16 **personally,** privately, idiosyncratically, **individually; in person,** in the flesh, *in propria persona* [L]; for all me, **for my part, as far as I am concerned.**

.17 **characteristically, peculiarly,** singularly, intrinsically, **uniquely,** markedly, **distinctively,** in its own way, like no other.

.18 **namely,** nominally, **that is to say,** *videlicet* [L], viz., *scilicet* [L], scil., sc., **to wit.**

.19 **each, apiece;** severally, respectively, one by one, each to each; *per annum, per diem, per capita* [all L].

**.20 PREPS** per, for each.

## 81. SPECIALTY

*(object of special attention or preference)*

**.1 NOUNS specialty,** speciality, **line, pursuit, pet subject, field,** area, main interest; **vocation** 656.6; **forte, métier, strong point, long suit;** specialism, specialization; technicality; **way,** manner, **style, type;** cup of tea [informal], **bag** or **thing** [both slang], weakness [informal].

**.2 special, feature,** main feature; **leader, lead item, leading card.**

**.3 specialist,** specializer, **expert, authority,** savant, scholar, connoisseur; technical expert, technician; pundit, critic; amateur, dilettante; fan, buff, freak or nut [both slang], aficionado.

**.4 VERBS specialize, feature; narrow, restrict,** limit, confine; **specialize in, go in for,** be into [slang], have a weakness or taste for, be strong in, follow, pursue, **make one's business;** major in, minor in; do one's thing [slang].

**.5 ADJS specialized,** specialist, specialistic; technical; **restricted, limited,** confined; **featured,** feature; **expert, authoritative,** knowledgeable.

## 82. CONFORMITY

**.1 NOUNS conformity; conformance,** conformation other-direction; **compliance,** acquiescence, obedience, observance, traditionalism, **orthodoxy;** strictness; **accordance,** accord, **correspondence,** harmony, agreement, **uniformity** 17; **consistency,** congruity; **line, keeping; accommodation,** adaptation, adaption, pliancy, malleability, flexibility, adjustment; reconciliation, reconcilement; **conventionality** 645.1.

**.2 conformist,** conformer, sheep, trimmer, parrot, yes-man, organization man; **conventionalist,** Mrs. Grundy [Tom Morton], Babbitt [Sinclair Lewis], Philistine, middle-class type, **bourgeois,** burgher, Middle American, plastic person or square [both informal]; model child; teenybopper [informal]; **formalist,** methodologist, perfectionist, precisianist, precisian; anal character, compulsive character; pedant.

**.3 VERBS conform, comply, correspond,** accord, harmonize; **adapt,** adjust, **accommodate,** meet, suit, fit, shape; **comply with,** agree with, tally with, chime or fall in with, go by, be guided or regulated by, observe, follow, bend, yield, take the shape of; **adapt to,** adjust to, gear to, assimilate to, **accommodate to** or **with; reconcile,** settle, compose; rub off corners; **make conform,** mold, force into a mold; straighten, rectify, correct, **discipline.**

**.4 follow the rule,** do it according to Hoyle or by the book [informal], play the game [informal]; go through channels; **fit in, follow the crowd,** follow the fashion, swim or go with the stream or tide or current, trim one's sails to the breeze, follow the beaten path, **do as others do, get** or **stay in line,** fall into line, fall in with; **keep in step, toe the mark;** keep up to standard, pass muster, come up to scratch [informal].

**.5 ADJS conformable, adaptable,** adaptive, adjustable; **compliant,** pliant, complaisant, malleable, flexible, plastic, acquiescent, other-directed, submissive, tractable, obedient.

**.6 conformist, conventional** 645.5, square or straight [both informal]; orthodox, kosher, traditionalist(ic); **bourgeois,** plastic [informal]; **formalistic,** precisianistic, anal, compulsive; pedantic, stuffy [informal], uptight [informal]; in accord, in keeping, in line, in step; **corresponding,** accordant, concordant, harmonious.

**.7 ADVS conformably,** conformingly, **obediently, pliantly,** flexibly, malleably, complaisantly, yieldingly, **compliantly,** submissively; **conventionally,** traditionally; anally, **compulsively;** pedantically.

**.8 according to rule,** *en règle* [Fr], according to regulations; **according to Hoyle, by the book,** by the numbers [all informal].

**.9 PREPS conformable to, in conformity with,** in compliance with; **according to, in accordance with, consistent with, in harmony with,** in agreement with, in correspondence to; adapted to, adjusted to, accommodated to; proper to, suitable for, agreeable to, agreeably to; answerable to, in obedience to; congruent with, uniform with, in uniformity with; **in line with,** in step with, in lock-step with, **in keeping with; after, by, per.**

**.10 PHRS don't rock the boat, don't make waves;** when in Rome do as the Romans do.

## 83. NONCONFORMITY

**.1 NOUNS nonconformity,** unconformity, nonconformism, **inconsistency,** incongruity; **inaccordance,** disaccord, disaccordance; **originality** 23.1; **nonconformance,**

disconformity; **nonobservance, noncompliance,** nonconcurrence, **dissent** 522, **protest** 522.2, disagreement, contrariety, recalcitrance, refractoriness, recusance *or* recusancy; **deviation.**

.2 **unconventionality, unorthodoxy** 1025, revisionism, heterodoxy, heresy, originality, fringiness, Bohemianism, beatnikism, hippiedom.

.3 **nonconformist,** unconformist, **original,** deviant, maverick [informal], swinger [informal], dropout, Bohemian, beatnik, hippie, freak [informal], flower child, street people, yippie; **misfit,** square peg in a round hole, ugly duckling, fish out of water; **dissenter** 522.3; **heretic** 1025.5; sectary, sectarian; nonjuror.

.4 VERBS **not conform,** nonconform, not comply; **get out of line** [informal], **rock the boat,** make waves, **leave the beaten path,** go out of bounds, break step, break bounds; drop out, opt out; **dissent** 522.4, **protest** 522.5; *"épater le bourgeois"* [Fr; Baudelaire], "hear a different drummer" [Thoreau].

.5 ADJS **nonconforming,** unconforming, nonconformable, unadaptable, unadjustable; **uncompliant,** unsubmissive; **nonobservant;** contrary, recalcitrant, refractory, recusant; **deviant; dissenting** 522.6, **dissident.**

.6 **unconventional, unorthodox,** heterodox, heretical; unfashionable, not done, not kosher, not cricket [Brit informal]; offbeat [informal], way out, far out, kinky, out in left field [informal], fringy, breakaway, **out of the way; original,** maverick, Bohemian, beat, hippie; **informal,** free and easy [informal], "at ease and lighthearted" [Whitman].

.7 **out of line, out of keeping,** out of order *or* place, misplaced, **out of step,** out of turn [informal], out of tune.

## 84. NORMALITY

.1 NOUNS **normality,** normalcy, **normalness, naturalness;** health, wholesomeness, propriety, **regularity;** naturalism, naturism, realism; **order** 59.

.2 **usualness, ordinariness, commonness,** commonplaceness, averageness; **generality** 79, **prevalence,** currency.

.3 **the normal, the usual, the ordinary, the common,** the commonplace, the way things are, the normal order of things; common *or* garden variety.

.4 **rule, law, principle, standard,** criterion, canon, code, maxim, prescription, guideline, regulation; **norm,** norma; **rule** *or* **law** *or* **order of nature,** natural *or* universal law; **form, formula,** formulary, formality, prescribed *or* set form; standing order; **hard and fast rule,** Procrustean law.

.5 normalization, standardization, regularization; codification, formalization.

.6 VERBS normalize, standardize, regularize; codify, formalize.

.7 ADJS **normal,** norm(o)–, **natural; general** 79.11; typical, unexceptional; naturalistic, naturistic, realistic; **orderly** 59.6.

.8 **usual, regular; customary,** habitual, accustomed, wonted, **normative,** prescriptive, standard, regulation, conventional; **common, commonplace, ordinary, average, everyday,** familiar, household, vernacular, stock; **prevailing, predominating,** current, popular; **universal.**

.9 ADVS **normally, naturally; normatively,** prescriptively, **regularly; usually,** commonly, ordinarily, customarily, habitually, **generally;** mostly, chiefly, mainly, for the most part, most often *or* frequently; **as a rule,** as a matter of course; **as usual,** as per usual [informal]; **as may be expected,** to be expected, as things go.

## 85. ABNORMALITY

.1 NOUNS **abnormality,** abnormity; **unnaturalness,** unnaturalism; **anomaly,** anomalousness, anomalism; **aberration,** aberrance, aberrancy; **irregularity, deviation,** divergence, **difference** 16; **eccentricity,** erraticism; teratism, monstrosity, amorphism, heteromorphism; **subnormality; inferiority** 37; **superiority** 36; **derangement** 63.1.

.2 **unusualness, uncommonness,** unordinariness, unwontedness, exceptionality; **rarity,** rareness, **uniqueness; extraordinariness, prodigiousness,** marvelousness, fabulousness, mythicalness, remarkableness, stupendousness; **incredibility** 503.3; increditability, inconceivability, **impossibility** 510.

.3 **oddity, queerness,** curiousness, quaintness, **peculiarity, absurdity** 510.1, singularity; **strangeness,** outlandishness; bizarreness, *bizarrerie* [Fr]; fantasticality, anticness; **freakishness, grotesqueness,** grotesquerie, weirdness, monstrousness, monstrosity, malformation, deformity, teratism.

.4 (odd person) oddity, **character** [informal], *type* [Fr], **case** [slang], natural, original, odd fellow, queer specimen; **oddball,** odd *or* queer fish, queer duck, rum one [Brit slang]; rare bird, *rara avis* [L]; eccentric 474.3; *meshuggenah* [Yid]; **screwball** *or* **crackpot** *or* **kook** *or* **nut** [all informal]; **fanatic, crank,** zealot; outsider, alien, pariah, loner, lone wolf, solitary, hermit; hobo, tramp; maverick; **nonconformist** 83.3.

.5 (odd thing) **oddity, curiosity,** funny *or* peculiar *or* strange thing; **abnormality, anomaly;** nonesuch, **rarity,** improbability, exception, one in a thousand *or* million; prodigy, prodigiosity; curio, conversation piece; museum piece.

.6 **monstrosity, monster,** miscreation, abortion, teratism, terat(o)–; **freak,** freak of nature, *lusus naturae* [L]; medus(i)–, –pagus.

.7 **supernaturalism,** supernaturalness *or* supernaturality, supranaturalism, supernormalness, **preternaturalism,** supersensibleness, superphysicalness, superhumanity; numinousness; **unearthliness,** unworldliness, **otherworldliness,** eeriness; transcendentalism; the supernatural, **the occult,** the supersensible; supernature, supranature; **mystery,** mysteriousness, miraculousness; faerie, witchery, elfdom.

.8 **miracle, sign, prodigy, wonder,** wonderwork, ferlie [Scot]; fantasy, enchantment.

.9 ADJS **abnormal, unnatural; anomalous,** anomalistic; **irregular,** eccentric, erratic, deviative, divergent, **different** 16.7; **aberrant,** stray, straying, wandering; heteroclite, heteromorphic; formless, shapeless, amorphous; **subnormal;** anom(o)–, anomal(o)– *or* anomali–, dys– *or* dis–, mal–, ne(o)–, par(a)–, poly–, pseud(o)–.

.10 **unusual,** unordinary, **uncustomary,** unwonted, **uncommon, unfamiliar,** unheard-of, *recherché* [Fr]; **rare, unique,** *sui generis* [L, of its own kind]; **out of the ordinary,** out of this world, out of the way, out of the common, out of the pale, **off the beaten track,** offbeat, breakaway; unexpected, not to be expected, unthought-of, undreamed-of.

.11 **odd, queer, peculiar, absurd** 510.7, **singular, curious, oddball,** kooky [informal], freaky *or* freaked out [both slang], **quaint, eccentric,** funny, rum [Brit slang]; **strange, outlandish,** off the wall [informal], passing strange, "wondrous strange" [Shakespeare]; **weird,** unearthly; off, out.

.12 **fantastic,** fantastical, fanciful, antic; **unbelievable** 503.10, **impossible, incredible,** incomprehensible, unimaginable, unexpected, unaccountable, inconceivable.

.13 **freakish,** freak [informal]; **monstrous,** deformed, malformed, misshapen, **misbegotten,** teratogenic, teratoid; **grotesque,** bizarre, baroque, rococo.

.14 **extraordinary, exceptional, remarkable,** noteworthy, **wonderful, marvelous,** fabulous, mythical, legendary; **stupendous,** stupefying, prodigious, portentous, phenomenal; unprecedented, unexampled, unparalleled, not within the memory of man; indescribable, unspeakable, ineffable.

.15 **supernatural,** supranatural, **preternatural; supernormal,** hypernormal, preternormal; **superphysical,** hyperphysical; numinous; **supersensible,** supersensual, pretersensual; **superhuman,** preterhuman, unhuman, nonhuman; **supramundane,** extramundane, transmundane, extraterrestrial; **unearthly, otherworldly,** eerie; fey; psychic(al), **spiritual, occult;** transcendental; **mysterious,** arcane, esoteric.

.16 **miraculous, wondrous,** wonder-working, thaumaturgic(al), necromantic, **prodigious; magical,** enchanted, bewitched.

.17 ADVS **unusually, uncommonly, incredibly, unnaturally,** abnormally, unordinarily, **uncustomarily,** unexpectedly; **rarely, seldom,** seldom if ever, once in a thousand years, hardly, hardly ever.

.18 **extraordinarily, exceptionally, remarkably, wonderfully, marvelously,** prodigiously, fabulously, unspeakably, ineffably, phenomenally, stupendously.

.19 **oddly, queerly, peculiarly, singularly, curiously,** quaintly, **strangely,** outlandishly, **fantastically,** fancifully; **grotesquely, monstrously; eerily, mysteriously,** supernaturally.

.20 **mythical monsters**

| | |
|---|---|
| Argus | hippocampus |
| basilisk | hippocentaur |
| Briareus | hippocerf |
| bucentur | hippogriff |
| Cacus | hircocervus |
| Caliban | Hydra |
| centaur | Kraken |
| Cerberus | Ladon |
| Ceto | Loch Ness monster |
| Charybdis | manticore |
| chimera | Medusa |
| cockatrice | mermaid |
| Cyclops | merman |
| dipsas | Midgard serpent |
| dragon | Minotaur |
| drake [archaic] | nixie |
| Echidna | ogre |
| Geryon | ogress |
| Gigantes | opinicus |
| Gorgon | Orthos *or* Orthros |
| Grendel | Pegasus |
| griffin | Python |
| Harpy | roc |

| | |
|---|---|
| Sagittary | troll |
| salamander | Typhoeus |
| satyr | Typhon |
| Scylla | unicorn |
| sea horse | vampire |
| sea serpent | werewolf |
| simurgh | windigo |
| siren | wivern |
| Sphinx | xiphopagus |
| Talos | zombie |

## 86. NUMBER

.1 NOUNS **number, numeral,** *numero* [Sp], no. *or* n., **figure, digit,** binary digit *or* bit, **cipher,** character, symbol, sign, notation.

.2 (number systems) **Arabic numerals,** algorism *or* algorithm, Roman numerals; **decimal system,** binary system, octal system, duodecimal system, hexadecimal system.

.3 (numbers) finite number; infinity 104; transfinite number; **real number,** real; imaginary number *or* pure imaginary; **complex number,** complex *or* Gaussian integer; **rational number,** rational; **irrational number,** irrational; algebraic number, surd; transcendental number; **integer,** whole number; **fraction** 86.6; mixed number; round number, abbreviated number; perfect number; imperfect number, deficient *or* defective number; abundant number; prime *or* rectilinear number; Fermat number, Mersenne number; composite *or* rectangular number; figurate number, polygonal number, pyramidal number; even number, pair; odd number, impair; cardinal number, cardinal; ordinal number, ordinal, –st, –nd, –rd, –th *or* –eth; serial number.

.4 large number, astronomical number, zillion *or* jillion [both informal]; googol, googolplex; infinity, infinitude 104.1; billion, trillion, etc. 99.12,13.

.5 sum, summation, difference, product, **number, count,** x number, n number; account, cast, **score, reckoning, tally,** tale, the story *or* whole story [both informal], the bottom line [informal], **aggregate, amount,** quantity 28; **whole** 54, **total** 54.2; box score [informal].

.6 ratio, rate, proportion; **quota,** quotum; percentage, percent; **fraction,** proper fraction, improper fraction, compound fraction, continued fraction; geometric ratio *or* proportion, arithmetical proportion, harmonic proportion; rule of three.

.7 series, progression; arithmetical progression, geometrical progression, harmonic progression; Fibonacci numbers.

.8 ADJS **numeric(al),** numeral, numerary, numerative; **odd,** impair, **even,** pair; arithmetical, algorismic *or* algorithmic; **cardinal, ordinal;** figural, **figurate,** figurative, **digital;** aliquot, submultiple, **reciprocal,** prime, fractional, decimal, exponential, **logarithmic,** logometric, differential, integral; positive, negative; rational, irrational, transcendental; surd, radical; real, imaginary; possible, impossible, finite, infinite, transfinite.

.9 **mathematical elements**

| | |
|---|---|
| addend | index |
| aliquot part | integral |
| antilogarithm | Laplace transform |
| argument | least common denominator, LCD |
| base | |
| Bessel function | least common multiple, LCM |
| binomial | |
| characteristic | logarithm |
| coefficient | mantissa |
| combination | matrix |
| common divisor *or* measure | minuend |
| | mixed decimal |
| complement | modulus |
| congruence | monomial |
| constant | multiple |
| cosecant | multiplicand |
| cosine | multiplicator |
| cotangent | multiplier |
| cube | norm |
| cube root | numerator |
| decimal | parameter |
| denominator | permutation |
| derivative | pi ($\pi$) |
| determinant | polynomial |
| difference, remainder | power |
| differential | quaternion |
| discriminate | quotient |
| dividend | radical |
| divisor | radix |
| e | reciprocal |
| elliptical function | repeating *or* circulating decimal |
| equation | |
| exponent | root |
| exponential | secant |
| factor | sine |
| factorial | square root |
| formula | submultiple |
| function | subtrahend |
| greatest common divisor, GCD | summand |
| | tangent |
| haversine | tensor |
| hyperbolic function | variable |
| i | vector |
| increment | versine |

## 87. NUMERATION

.1 NOUNS **numeration, enumeration, numbering, counting,** accounting, census, inventorying, telling, tallying; page numbering, pagination, foliation; counting on the fingers, dactylonomy; **measurement** 490; quantification, quantization.

.2 **mathematics** 87.18, math [US informal], maths [Brit informal], mathematic, **numbers, figures;** pure mathematics, abstract mathematics, applied mathematics, higher mathematics, elementary mathematics; new mathematics, new math [informal]; algorism *or* algorithm.

**.3 calculation, computation, estimation, reckoning,** calculus; adding, footing, casting, ciphering, totaling, toting *or* totting [informal].

**.4** (mathematical operations) notation, **addition** 40, **subtraction** 42, **multiplication, division,** proportion, practice, equation, extraction of roots, inversion, reduction, involution, evolution, approximation, interpolation, extrapolation, transformation, differentiation, integration.

**.5 summation, summary, summing, summing up,** recount, recounting, rehearsal, capitulation, **recapitulation,** statement, **reckoning, count,** repertory, census, inventory, head count, nose count, body count; account, accounts.

**.6 account of, count of,** a reckoning of, **tab** *or* **tabs of** [informal], tally of, check of, track of.

**.7 figures, statistics,** indexes *or* indices; vital statistics.

**.8 calculator, computer,** estimator, figurer, reckoner, abacist; statistician, actuary; accountant, bookkeeper 845.7.

**.9 mathematician, arithmetician;** geometer, geometrician; algebraist, trigonometrician, statistician, geodesist, mathematical physicist.

**.10** VERBS **number,** numerate, **enumerate, count, tell, tally,** give a figure to, put a figure on, call off, name *or* call over, run over; **count noses** *or* **heads** [informal], call the roll; census, poll; page, paginate, foliate; **measure** 490.11; quantify, quantize.

**.11 calculate, compute, estimate, reckon, figure, cipher, cast, tally, score; figure out,** work out, dope out [slang]; take account of, figure in [informal]; **add, subtract, multiply, divide,** algebraize, extract roots; **measure** 490.11.

**.12 sum up,** sum, summate; **figure up,** cipher up, reckon up, **count up, add up,** foot up, cast up, score up, **tally up;** total, total up, tote *or* tot up [informal]; **summarize, recapitulate, recap** [informal], **recount,** rehearse, recite, relate; detail, itemize, inventory.

**.13 keep account of,** keep count of, **keep track of, keep tab** *or* **tabs** [informal], keep tally, keep a check on *or* of.

**.14 check, verify** 513.12, double-check, check out; **prove,** demonstrate; balance, balance the books; **audit,** overhaul; take stock, inventory.

**.15** ADJS **numerative, enumerative; calculative,** computative, estimative; **calculating,** computing, computational, estimating; statistical; quantifying, quantizing.

**.16 calculable,** computable, **reckonable,** estimable, countable, numberable, numerable; **measurable** 490.15, mensurable, quantifiable.

**.17 mathematical,** numeric(al), arithmetic(al), algebraic(al), geometric(al), trigonometric(al), analytic(al).

**.18 mathematics**

| | |
|---|---|
| algebra | inverse geometry |
| algebraic geometry | Lagrangian function |
| analysis | Laplace's equation |
| analytic geometry | linear algebra |
| arithmetic | line geometry |
| associative algebra | mathematical physics |
| binary arithmetic | matrix algebra |
| Boolean algebra | metageometry |
| calculus | modular arithmetic |
| calculus of differences | multiple algebra |
| circle geometry | natural geometry |
| combinatorial mathematics | nilpotent algebra |
| combinatorial topology | noncommutative algebra |
| commutative algebra | non-Euclidean geometry |
| complex *or* double algebra | n-tuple linear algebra |
| denumerative geometry | number theory |
| descriptive geometry | plane trigonometry |
| differential calculus | point-set topology |
| division algebra | political arithmetic |
| elementary arithmetic | projective geometry |
| elementary *or* ordinary algebra | proper subalgebra |
| equivalent algebras | quadratics |
| Euclidean geometry | quaternion algebra |
| Fourier analysis | reducible algebra |
| game theory | Riemannian geometry |
| geodesic geometry | semisimple algebra |
| geodesy | set theory |
| geometry | simple algebra |
| Gödel's proof | solid geometry |
| graphic algebra | speculative geometry |
| group theory | spherical trigonometry |
| higher algebra | statistics |
| higher arithmetic | subalgebra |
| hyperalgebra | systems analysis |
| hyperbolic geometry | topology |
| infinitesimal calculus | trigonometry, trig [informal] |
| integral calculus | universal algebra |
| intuitional geometry | universal geometry |
| invariant subalgebra | vector algebra |
| | zero algebra |

**.19 calculators**

| | |
|---|---|
| abacus | electronic computer 349.16 |
| adding machine | listing machine |
| analog computer | Napier's bones *or* rods |
| arithmograph | pari-mutuel machine |
| arithmometer | quipu |
| calculating machine | rule |
| cash register | slide rule, sliding scale |
| Comptometer | *suan pan* [Chin] |
| counter | tabulator |
| difference engine | totalizator |
| digital computer | |

## 88. LIST

.1 NOUNS **list, enumeration, itemization,** items, **schedule, register,** registry; **inventory,** repertory, tally; **checklist;** tally sheet; active list, civil list [Brit], retired list, sick list; waiting list; blacklist.

.2 **table,** contents, table of contents; **chart; index,** thumb index, card index.

.3 **catalog;** classified catalog, *catalogue raisonné* [Fr]; **card catalog, bibliography,** finding list, handlist; publisher's catalog *or* list; **file,** filing system, letter file, pigeonholes.

.4 **dictionary,** word list, **lexicon, glossary, thesaurus, vocabulary,** terminology, nomenclator; promptorium, gradus; **gazetteer.**

.5 **bill,** statement, account, ledger, books; **bill of fare, menu,** carte; **bill of lading,** manifest, waybill, invoice.

.6 **roll, roster,** scroll, rota; **roll call,** muster, **census,** nose *or* head count [informal], **poll,** questionnaire, returns, census report *or* returns; property roll, tax roll, cadastre; muster roll, checkroll, checklist; jury list *or* panel; **calendar,** docket, **agenda,** order of business; **program,** dramatis personae, lineup, beadroll; honor roll, dean's list.

.7 **listing,** tabulation; **cataloging, itemization,** filing, indexing; **registration,** registry, enrollment.

.8 VERBS **list, enumerate, itemize, tabulate, catalog,** tally; **register,** post, enter, **enroll, book;** impanel; **file,** pigeonhole; **index;** inventory; calendar; score, keep score; **schedule,** program.

.9 ADJS **listed, enumerated, entered, itemized, cataloged,** tallied, inventoried; filed, **indexed, tabulated; scheduled,** programmed; inventorial, cadastral.

## 89. UNITY

*(state of being one)*

.1 NOUNS **unity, oneness, singleness,** singularity, **individuality,** identity, selfsameness; **particularity** 80; uniqueness; intactness, inviolability, purity, simplicity 45, irreducibility, **integrity,** integrality, integration, unification, fusion, combination 52; solidification, solidity, solidarity, indivisibility, undividedness, **wholeness** 54.5; univocity, organic unity; uniformity 17; "the sacredness of private integrity" [Emerson].

.2 **aloneness,** loneness, **loneliness, lonesomeness;** privacy, solitariness, **solitude;** separateness, aloofness, detachment, seclusion, sequestration, **withdrawal, alienation,** standing *or* moving *or* keeping apart, **isolation,** "splendid isolation" [Sir William Goschen]; celibacy, single blessedness.

.3 **one,** I, **unit,** ace, atom; monad; –on, –eme; one and only, none else, no other, nothing else, nought beside.

.4 **individual,** single, unit, **integer, entity,** singleton, **item,** article, point, module; person, persona, soul.

.5 VERBS **unify,** reduce to unity, make one; **integrate, unite** 52.3.

.6 **stand alone,** stand *or* move *or* keep apart, withdraw, alienate *or* seclude *or* sequester *or* isolate oneself; become an individual.

.7 ADJS **one, single, singular, individual, sole, unique,** a certain, **solitary, lone;** exclusive; **integral,** indivisible, irreducible, monadic, monistic, unanalyzable, noncompound, atomic, unitary, undivided, solid, uniform 17.5, simple 45.6, whole 54.9; an, any, any one, either.

.8 **alone, solitary,** solo, soli–, *solus* [L]; **isolated,** insular, apart, separate, separated, alienated, withdrawn, aloof, detached, removed; **lone, lonely, lonesome;** friendless, kithless, homeless, rootless, companionless, **unaccompanied,** unescorted, unattended; **unaided,** unassisted, unabetted, unsupported, unseconded; **single-handed;** self–.

.9 **sole, unique, singular,** absolute, unrepeated, **alone,** lone, **only,** only-begotten, **one and only,** first and last; odd, impair, unpaired, azygous, azygo–; celibate.

.10 **unitary, integrated,** integral, integrant; **unified,** united, rolled into one, composite.

.11 **unipartite,** unipart, **one-piece;** monadic *or* monadal; uni–, **unilateral, one-sided;** uniangulate, unibivalent, unibranchiate, unicameral, unicellular, unicuspid, unidentate, unidigitate; **unidimensional, unidirectional;** uniflorous, unifoliate, unifoliolate, unigenital, uniglobular, unilinear, uniliteral, unilobed, unilobular, unilocular, unimodular, unimolecular, uninuclear, uniocular; unipolar, **univalent, univocal.**

.12 **unifying, uniting,** unific; **combining,** combinative 52.5,7, combinatory; connective, connecting, connectional; conjunctive 47.16, conjunctival; coalescing, coalescent.

.13 ADVS **singly, individually,** particularly, severally, one by one, one at a time; singularly, in the singular; **alone,** by itself, *per se* [L]; **by oneself,** on one's own, singlehandedly; separately, apart; once 136.6.

.14 **solely, exclusively, only,** merely, **purely,** simply; **entirely,** wholly, totally; **integrally, indivisibly,** irreducibly, unanalyzably, undividedly.

## 90. DUALITY

.1 NOUNS **duality, dualism, doubleness,** duplexity, **twoness;** biformity; polarity; conjugation, pairing; doubling, duplication, twinning, **bifurcation,** halving; **duplicity,** two-facedness, doublethink; **irony,** ambiguity, equivocality, **ambivalence;** Janus.

.2 **two, twain** [archaic]; **couple, pair, twosome,** set of two, duo, duet, brace, team, span, yoke, double harness; match, mates; **couplet,** distich, doublet; duad, dyad; **the two, both.**

.3 **deuce;** pair, doubleton; **craps** *or* snake eyes [both dice slang].

.4 **twins,** pair of twins [informal], identical twins, fraternal twins, exact mates; Tweedledum and Tweedledee, Siamese twins; Twin Stars, Castor and Pollux, Gemini.

.5 VERBS **pair, couple, bracket,** team, **yoke,** span, double-team, double-harness; **mate, match,** conjugate; **pair off,** couple up, team up.

.6 ADJS **two, twain** [archaic]; **dual, double,** duplex; **dualistic;** dyadic; duadic; biform; bipartite, bipartisan, bilateral, two-sided, double-sided; dichotomous; bifurcated; twin, identical, matched, twinned, duplicated; ambi– *or* amph(i)–, bi– *or* bin–, bis–, deut(o)– *or* deuter(o)–, di– *or* dis–, didym(o)–, duo–, dyo–, dvi–, gem–, twi–, zyg(o)–.

.7 **both,** the two, either; for two, tête-à-tête, *à deux* [Fr].

.8 **coupled, paired,** yoked, matched, mated, **bracketed;** conjugate, conjugated; biconjugate, bigeminate; bijugate.

## 91. DUPLICATION

.1 NOUNS **duplication, reduplication,** replication, conduplication; **reproduction, doubling;** twinning, gemination, ingemination; **repetition** 103, iteration, reiteration; **imitation** 22, parroting; **copying** 22.1; duplicate 24.3.

.2 **repeat, encore,** repeat performance; echo.

.3 VERBS **duplicate, dupe** [slang], ditto [informal]; **double;** multiply by two; twin, geminate, ingeminate; **reduplicate, repro-**

duce, replicate, redouble; **repeat** 103.7; copy.

.4 ADJS **double, duplicate, duple, dual,** duplex, **twofold,** bifold, binary, binate; twinned, geminate, geminated; **second, secondary; twin,** biparous; biform, disomatous; bivalent; ambidextrous; two-sided, bilateral; two-faced, double-faced, bifacial, Janus-like; two-ply, two-story, two-level, conduplicate; bi–, bis–, deuter(o)–, di– *or* dis–, diphy(o)–, dipl(o)–, diss(o)–, twi–.

.5 ADVS **doubly,** dually, **twofold,** as much again, twice as much; twice, two times.

.6 **secondly,** second, secondarily, **in the second place** *or* instance.

.7 **again,** another time, **once more,** once again, over again, yet again, *encore, bis* [both Fr]; **anew, afresh,** new, freshly, newly; re–.

## 92. BISECTION

.1 NOUNS **bisection, bipartition,** bifidity, dimidiation; **dichotomy, halving, division, in half** *or* **by two,** splitting *or* cutting in two; subdivision; **bifurcation,** forking, ramification, branching.

.2 **half,** moiety, mediety; hemisphere, semisphere, semicircle, **fifty percent;** half-and-half *or* fifty-fifty [both informal].

.3 **bisector,** diameter, equator, halfway mark, divider, partition 237.5, line of demarcation, boundary 235.3.

.4 VERBS **bisect, halve, divide, in half** *or* **by two,** transect, subdivide; cleave, fission, **split** *or* **cut in two,** dimidiate, **dichotomize;** bifurcate, fork, ramify, branch.

.5 ADJS **half,** part, **partly, partial,** halfway, bi–, demi–, dich(o)–, hemi–, semi–, sam– [dial]; **one-and-a-half,** sesqui–.

.6 **halved, bisected, divided,** dimidiate; dichotomous; bifurcated, forked *or* forking, ramified, branched, branching; riven, split, cloven, cleft.

.7 **bipartite,** bifid, biform, bicuspid, biaxial, bicameral, binocular, binomial, binominal, biped, bipetalous, bipinnate, bisexual, bivalent, unibivalent.

.8 ADVS **in half,** in halves, **in two,** in twain, by two; half-and-half, fifty-fifty [both informal]; apart, asunder.

## 93. THREE

.1 NOUNS **three, trio, threesome,** trialogue, set of three, tierce [cards], leash, troika; **triad, trilogy, trine, trinity,** triunity, ternary, ternion; **triplet,** tercet, terzetto; trefoil, shamrock, clover; tripod, trivet; **tri-**

**angle,** tricorn, trihedron, trident, trisul; triennium, trimester, trinomial, trionym, triphthong, triptych, triplopy, trireme, triseme, triskelion, triumvirate; **triple crown,** triple threat; trey, threespot [both cards], deuce-ace [dice].

.2 **threeness,** triplicity, triality, tripleness; triunity, trinity.

.3 ADJS **three, triple,** triplex, trinal, trine, trial; triadic(al); triune, three-in-one, *tria juncta in uno* [L]; triform; **triangular,** deltoid, fan-shaped; tri–, ter–, ternati–.

## 94. TRIPLICATION

.1 NOUNS **triplication,** triplicity, trebleness, **threefoldness;** triplicate, second carbon.

.2 VERBS **triplicate, triple, treble, multiply by three,** threefold; cube.

.3 ADJS **triple,** triplicate, **treble, threefold,** triplex, trinal, trine, tern, ternary, ternal, ternate; three-ply; trilogic(al); cub(o)– *or* cubi–; ter–, tri–, tripl(o)–, tris–.

.4 **third,** tertiary, tert–, trit(o)–.

.5 ADVS **triply, trebly,** trinely; **threefold; thrice,** three times, again and yet again.

.6 **thirdly,** in the third place.

## 95. TRISECTION

.1 NOUNS **trisection,** tripartition, trichotomy.

.2 **third,** tierce, third part, one-third; *tertium quid* [L, a third something].

.3 VERBS **trisect, divide in thirds** *or* **three,** third, trichotomize; trifurcate.

.4 ADJS **tripartite,** trisected, triparted, **three-parted,** trichotomous; three-sided, trihedral, trilateral; **three-dimensional;** three-forked, three-pronged, trifurcate; trident, tridental, tridentate(d), trifid; tricuspid; three-footed, tripodic, tripedal; trifoliate, trifloral, triflorate, triflorous, tripetalous, triadelphous, triarch; trimerous, 3-merous; three-cornered, tricornered, tricorn; trigonal, trigonoid; triquetrous, triquetral; trigrammatic, triliteral; **triangular,** triangulate, deltoid; tri–.

## 96. FOUR

.1 NOUNS **four,** tetrad, quatern, quaternion, quaternary, quaternity, **quartet, quadruplet, foursome;** Little Joe [dice slang]; quadrennium; tetralogy; tetrapody; tetraphony, four-part diaphony; quadrille, square dance; quatrefoil *or* quadrifoil, four-leaf clover; tetragram, tetragrammaton; quadrangle, quad [informal], rectangle; tetrahedron; tetragon, square; bi-

quadrate; quadrinomial; quadrature, squaring; quadrilateral 251.13.

.2 **fourness,** quaternity, quadruplicity.

.3 VERBS **square, quadrate,** form *or* make four; form fours *or* squares; **cube, dice.**

.4 ADJS **four;** foursquare; quaternary, quartile, quartic, quadric, quadratic; tetrad, tetradic; quadrinomial, biquadratic; tetractinal, four-rayed, **quadruped,** four-legged; quadrivalent, tetravalent; quadrilateral 251.9; quadr(i)– *or* quadru–, tetr(a)–, tessar(a)–.

## 97. QUADRUPLICATION

.1 NOUNS **quadruplication,** quadruplicature.

.2 VERBS **quadruple, quadruplicate,** fourfold, form *or* make four, multiply by four; biquadrate, quadruplex.

.3 ADJS **quadruplicate, quadruple,** quadrable, **quadruplex, fourfold,** tetraploid, quadrigeminal, biquadratic; quadr(i)– *or* quadru–, quater–, tetr(a)–, tetrakis–.

## 98. QUADRISECTION

.1 NOUNS **quadrisection,** quadripartition, **quartering.**

.2 **fourth,** one-fourth, **quarter,** one-quarter, fourth part, twenty-five percent, twenty-five cents, two bits [archaic *or* slang]; quartern; quart; farthing; quarto *or* 4 to.

.3 VERBS **divide by four** *or* **into four; quadrisect, quarter.**

.4 ADJS **quadrisected, quartered,** quartercut; quadripartite, quadrifid, quadriform; quadrifoliate, quadrigeminal, quadripinnate, quadriplanar, quadriserial, quadrivial, quadrifurcate, quadrumanal *or* quadrumanous.

.5 **fourth, quarter.**

.6 ADVS **fourthly,** in the fourth place; **quarterly,** by quarters.

## 99. FIVE AND OVER

.1 NOUNS **five,** V, cinque, quint, quincunx, **quintet, fivesome, quintuplet;** pentad; five dollars; fiver *or* fin *or* five bucks [all slang]; Phoebe *or* Little Phoebe [both dice slang]; pentagon, pentahedron, pentagram; pentapody, pentameter, pentastich; pentarchy; Pentateuch; pentachord; pentathlon; five-pointed star, pentacle, pentalpha, mullet [her].

.2 **six,** sixer [slang], sise, Captain Hicks [dice slang], **half a dozen, sextet,** sestet, **sextuplet,** hexad; hexagon, hexahedron, hexagram, six-pointed star, estoile [her], Jewish star, star of David, *Magen David* [Heb]; hexameter, hexapody, hexastich;

hexapod; hexarchy; Hexateuch; hexastyle; hexachord.

**.3 seven,** sevener [slang], heptad; heptagon, heptahedron; heptameter, heptastich; heptarchy; Heptateuch; septet, heptachord; septuor, septennate; **week.**

**.4 eight,** eighter [slang]; eighter from Decatur [dice slang]; octagon, octahedron; octave, octavo or 8vo; octad; ogdoad, octonary; octet, octameter, octosyllable; octastyle; utas [archaic], Octateuch.

**.5 nine,** niner [slang], Nina from Carolina [dice slang], ennead; nonage, novena; nonagon, nonuplet; enneastyle.

**.6 ten,** X, tenner [slang], **decade,** Big Dick [dice slang]; decagon, decahedron; decagram, decigram, decaliter, deciliter, decare, decameter, decimeter, decastere; decapod, decastyle, decasyllable; decemvir, decemvirate, decurion; decennium, decennary, Ten Commandments or Decalogue.

**.7** (eleven to ninety) **eleven; twelve, dozen,** boxcar or boxcars [both dice slang], duodecimo or twelvemo or 12mo; **teens; thirteen,** long dozen, baker's dozen; **fourteen,** two weeks, fortnight; **fifteen,** quindecima, quindene, quindecim, quindecennial; **sixteen,** sixteenmo or 16mo; **twenty, score; twenty-four,** four and twenty, two dozen, twenty-fourmo or 24mo; **twenty-five,** five and twenty, quarter of a hundred or century; **thirty-two,** thirty-twomo or 32mo; **forty,** twoscore; **fifty,** L, half a hundred; **sixty,** sexagenary; Sexagesima; sexagenarian; threescore; **sixty-four,** sixty-fourmo or 64mo or sexagesimo-quarto; **seventy,** septuagenarian; threescore and ten; **eighty,** octogenarian, fourscore; **ninety,** nonagenarian, fourscore and ten.

**.8 hundred, century,** C, one C [slang], centred, centrev or centref [both Welsh]; centennium, centennial, centenary; centenarian; cental, centigram, centiliter, centimeter, centare, centistere; hundredweight or cwt; hecatomb; centipede; centumvir, centumvirate, centurion; (120) great or long hundred; (144) gross; (150) sesquicentennial, sesquicentenary; (200) bicentenary, bicentennial; (300) tercentenary, tercentennial, etc.

**.9 five hundred,** D, five centuries; five C's [slang].

**.10 thousand,** M, chiliad; **millennium;** G or grand or thou or yard [all slang]; chiliagon, chiliahedron or chiliaëdron; chiliarchia or chiliarch; millepede; milligram,

milliliter, millimeter, kilogram or kilo, kiloliter, kilometer; kilocycle, kilohertz; **ten thousand,** myriad; **one hundred thousand,** lakh [India].

**.11 million;** ten million, crore [India].

**.12 billion,** thousand million, milliard.

**.13 trillion,** quadrillion, quintillion, sextillion, septillion, octillion, nonillion, decillion, undecillion, duodecillion, tredecillion, quattuordecillion, quindecillion, sexdecillion, septendecillion, octodecillion, novemdecillion, vigintillion; googol, googolplex; zillion or jillion [both informal].

**.14** (division into five or more parts) quinquesection, quinquepartition, sextipartition, etc.; decimation, decimalization; fifth, sixth, etc.; **tenth, tithe,** decima.

**.15** VERBS (divide by five, etc.) quinquesect; decimalize.

**.16** (multiply by five, etc.) fivefold, sixfold, etc.; quintuple, quintuplicate; sextuple, sextuplicate; centuple, centuplicate.

**.17** ADJS **fifth,** quinary; **fivefold, quintuple,** quintuplicate; quinquennial; quinquepartite, pentadic, quinquefid; quincuncial, pentastyle; pentad, pentavalent, quinquevalent; pent(a)– or pen–, quinqu(e)–, quint(i)–.

**.18 sixth,** senary; **sixfold, sextuple;** sexpartite, hexadic, sextipartite, hexapartite; hexagonal, hexahedral, hexangular; hexad, hexavalent; sextuplex, hexastyle; sexennial; hexatomic; hexamerous; hex(a)–, sex(i)–, sexti–.

**.19 seventh,** septimal; **sevenfold, septuple;** septenary; septempartite, heptadic, septemfid; heptagonal, heptahedral, heptangular; heptamerous; hept(a)–, sept(i)–.

**.20 eighth,** octonary; **eightfold, octuple;** octadic; octal, octofid, octaploid; octagonal, octahedral, octan, octangular; octosyllabic; octastyle; oct(a)– or octo–.

**.21 ninth,** novenary, nonary; **ninefold, nonuple,** enneadic; enneahedral, enneastyle; non(a)–, ennea–.

**.22 tenth,** denary, **decimal,** tithe; **tenfold, decuple;** decagonal, decahedral; decasyllabic; deca– or deka–, deci–.

**.23 eleventh,** undecennial; undecennary; undec–, hendec(a)–.

**.24 twelfth,** duodenary, duodenal; duodecimal; dodec(a)–.

**.25 thirteenth,** fourteenth, etc.; eleventeenth, umpteenth [informal]; in one's teens.

**.26 twentieth,** vicenary, vicennial, vigesimal, vicesimal; icos(a)– or icosi–, eicos(a)–.

**.27 sixtieth,** sexagesimal, sexagenary.

.28 **seventieth,** septuagesimal, septuagenary.

.29 **hundredth,** centesimal, **centennial,** centenary, centurial; **hundredfold, centuple,** centuplicate; secular; centigrado; cent(i)–, hect(o)–, hecato(n)–.

.30 **thousandth,** millenary, **millennial; thousandfold;** kilo–, milli–.

.31 millionth, meg(a)–, micro–, billionth, giga–, nano–, trillionth, pico–; quadrillionth, quintillionth, etc.

## 100. PLURALITY

### (more than one)

.1 NOUNS **plurality,** pluralness; a greater number, a certain number; several, a few 102.2, more; plural number, the plural, –s or –es; compositeness, nonsingleness, nonuniqueness; **pluralism** 18.1, variety; numerousness 101.

.2 **majority,** plurality, more than half, the greater number, the greatest number, **most,** preponderance or preponderancy, **bulk, mass;** lion's share.

.3 pluralization, plurification.

.4 **multiplication,** multiplying, proliferation, **increase** 38; multiple, multiplier, multiplicand; tables, multiplication table.

.5 VERBS pluralize, plurify; raise to or make more than one.

.6 **multiply,** proliferate, **increase** 38.4,6.

.7 ADJS **plural,** more than one, more; some, certain; not singular, composite, nonsingle, nonunique; **plurative; pluralistic** 18.3, various; numerous 101.6.

.8 **multiple,** multiplied, multifold, multi–; –fold, **manifold; increased** 38.7; multinomial, polynomial [both math].

.9 majority, **most,** the greatest number.

.10 ADVS in majority, **in the majority;** and others, et al., et cetera 40.14.

## 101. NUMEROUSNESS

.1 NOUNS **numerousness, multiplicity, manyness,** multitudinousness, multifoldness, multifariousness, teemingness, swarmingness, rifeness, profuseness, profusion; **plenty, abundance** 661.2; **countlessness,** innumerability, infinitude.

.2 (indefinite number) **a number,** a certain number, one or two, two or three, **a few, several,** parcel, passel [informal]; eleventeen or umpteen [both informal].

.3 (large number) **multitude, throng** 74.4; plurality, **many; numbers, quantities, lots** 34.4, flocks, **scores;** all kinds or sorts of, quite a few, tidy sum; muchness, **large amount** 34.3,4; **host, army,** legion, rout,

ruck, mob, jam, clutter; **swarm, flock** 74.5, flight, cloud, hail, bevy, covey, shoal, hive, nest, pack, bunch 74.7; a world of, a mass of, worlds of, masses of.

.4 (immense number) **a myriad,** a thousand, **a thousand and one,** a lakh [India], a crore [India], a million, a billion, a quadrillion, a nonillion, etc. 99.10–13; a zillion or jillion [informal].

.5 VERBS **teem with,** overflow with, **abound with,** burst with, bristle with, pullulate with, **swarm with,** throng with, creep with, **crawl with, be alive with;** clutter, crowd, jam, pack; multiply 100.6; outnumber.

.6 ADJS **numerous, many,** not a few, no few; **very many,** full many, **ever so many,** considerable or quite some [both informal]; multi–, myri(o)–, pluri–, poly–, **multitudinous,** multitudinal, multifarious, multifold, multiple, **myriad,** thousand, million, billion; zillion or jillion [both informal]; heaped-up; numerous as the stars, numerous as the sands, numerous as the hairs on the head, "numerous as glittering gems of morning dew" [Edward Young].

.7 **several,** divers, **sundry,** various; fivish, sixish, etc.; some five or six, etc.; upwards of.

.8 **abundant,** copious, ample, plenteous, **plentiful** 661.7.

.9 **teeming, swarming, crowding,** thronging, overflowing, bursting, **crawling, alive with,** populous, prolific, proliferating, crowded, packed, jammed, jam-packed [informal], like sardines in a can [informal], thronged, studded, bristling, rife, lavish, prodigal, superabundant, **profuse,** in profusion, thick, **thick with,** thick-coming, thick as hail or flies; "thick as autumnal leaves that strow the brooks in Vallombrose" [Milton].

.10 **innumerable, numberless,** unnumbered, **countless,** uncounted, untold, incalculable, immeasurable, unmeasured, measureless, inexhaustible, endless, infinite, without end or limit, more than one can tell, more than you can shake a stick at [informal], no end of or to; countless as the stars or sands.

.11 **and many more,** cum multis aliis [L], and what not, and heaven knows what.

.12 ADVS **numerously,** multitudinously, **profusely,** thickly, copiously, **abundantly, prodigally; innumerably, countlessly,** infinitely, incalculably, inexhaustibly, immeasurably; in throngs, in crowds, in swarms, in heaps, *acervatim* [L]; no end [informal].

## 102. FEWNESS

.1 NOUNS **fewness,** infrequency, **sparsity,** sparseness, **scarcity, paucity, scantiness, meagerness,** miserliness, niggardliness, tightness, thinness, stringency, restrictedness; chintziness *or* chinchiness *or* stinginess [all informal], scrimpiness *or* skimpiness [both informal]; **rarity,** exiguity; smallness 35.

.2 **a few,** too few, mere *or* piddling few, only a few, **small number,** limited *or* piddling number, not enough to count *or* matter, **handful, scattering,** sprinkling, trickle.

.3 **minority,** least; the minority, the few; minority group; "we happy few" [Shakespeare].

.4 ADJS **few, not many,** olig(o)–; hardly *or* scarcely any, precious little [informal], of small number, to be counted on one's fingers.

.5 **sparse,** scant, **scanty,** exiguous, **infrequent,** scarce, scarce as hen's teeth [informal], poor, piddling, thin, slim, **meager;** miserly, niggardly, cheeseparing, tight; chintzy *or* chinchy *or* stingy [all informal], scrimpy *or* skimpy [both informal], skimping *or* scrimping [both informal]; **scattered,** sprinkled, spotty, **few and far between; rare,** seldom met with, seldom seen.

.6 **fewer, less,** smaller, not so much *or* many.

.7 **minority,** least.

.8 ADVS **sparsely,** *sparsim* [L], **scantily, meagerly,** exiguously, piddlingly; stingily *or* scrimpily *or* skimpily [all informal], thinly; **scarcely,** rarely, infrequently; **scatteringly,** spottily, in dribs and drabs [informal], **here and there,** in places, in spots.

## 103. REPETITION

.1 NOUNS **repetition, reproduction,** duplication 91, reduplication, doubling, redoubling; **recurrence,** reoccurrence, return, reincarnation, rebirth, reappearance, renewal, resumption, echo, reecho; regurgitation; **quotation;** imitation 22; plagiarism.

.2 **iteration, reiteration, recapitulation,** recap [informal], retelling, recounting, recountal, **recital, rehearsal, restatement,** rehash [informal]; reissue, reprint; review, summary, critique, résumé, summing up; going over *or* through, practicing; reasser-

tion, reaffirmation; elaboration, dwelling upon; **copy** 24.

.3 **redundancy, tautology,** tautologism, pleonasm, macrology, battology; tautophony, stammering, stuttering; padding, filling, expletive.

.4 **repetitiousness,** repetitiveness, stale *or* unnecessary repetition; harping; **monotony,** monotone, drone; **tedium** 884; **humdrum,** dingdong, singsong, chime, jingle, jingle-jangle, trot, pitter-patter; **rhyme, alliteration,** assonance, slant *or* near rhyme; **repeated sounds** 455.

.5 **repeat,** repetend, bis, ditto [informal]; **refrain,** burden, chant, undersong, chorus, bob; bob wheel, bob and wheel; ritornel, *ritornello* [Ital].

.6 **encore,** repeat performance, repeat, reprise; replay, replaying, return match.

.7 VERBS **repeat, redo,** do again, do over, do a repeat, **reproduce, duplicate** 91.3, reduplicate, double, redouble, ditto [informal], **echo,** reecho; regurgitate; renew, reincarnate, revive; come again [slang], say again, repeat oneself, **quote,** repeat word for word *or* verbatim, parrot, repeat like a broken record; **copy, imitate** 22.5; plagiarize.

.8 **iterate, reiterate, rehearse, recapitulate, recount,** rehash [informal], **recite, retell,** retail, **restate,** reword, review, run over, sum up, summarize, resume; reissue, reprint; do *or* say over again, **go over** *or* **through,** practice, say over, go over the same ground, give an encore, quote oneself, go the same round, fight one's battles over again; **tautologize,** battologize, pad, fill; reaffirm, reassert.

.9 **dwell on** *or* **upon,** insist upon, **harp on,** constantly recur *or* revert to, labor, belabor, hammer away at, always trot out, sing the same old song *or* tune, play the same old record, plug the same theme, never hear the last of; **thrash** *or* **thresh over,** go over again and again, go over and over.

.10 **din, ding;** drum 455.4, beat, hammer, pound; **din in the ear,** say over and over.

.11 (be repeated) **repeat, recur,** reoccur, **come again,** come up again, **return, reappear, resume;** resound, reverberate, echo; revert, turn *or* go back; keep coming, come again and again, happen over and over, run through like King Charles's head.

.12 ADJS **repeated,** reproduced, doubled, redoubled; duplicated, reduplicated; regurgitated; **echoed,** reechoed; **quoted,** plagia-

rized; **iterated, reiterated,** reiterate; retold, **twice-told;** warmed up or over, *réchauffé* [Fr].

.13 **recurrent,** recurring, **returning,** reappearing, revenant, ubiquitous, ever-recurring,
cyclical, periodic, thematic, thick-coming,
frequent, incessant, continuous 71.8,
haunting.

.14 **repetitious,** repetitive, repetitional or rep-
etitionary, repeating; **duplicative,** redupli-
cative; **imitative** 22.9, parrotlike; echoing,
reechoing, echoic; **iterative, reiterative,**
reiterant; recapitulative, recapitulatory;
battological, **tautological** or **tautologous,**
**redundant;** tautophon(ic)al.

.15 **monotonous,** monotone; **tedious** 884.8;
harping, labored, belabored, cliché-rid-
den; **humdrum,** singsong, chiming, chanting, dingdong [informal], jog-trot, jingle-
jangle; **rhymed, rhyming, alliterative,** al-
literating, assonant.

.16 ADVS **repeatedly, often, frequently, recurrently, again and again, over and over,**
over and over again, many times over,
time and again, **time after time,** times
without number; year after year, day after day, day by day, "tomorrow and tomorrow and tomorrow" [Shakespeare];
**many times,** several times, a number of
times, many a time, full many a time and
oft; every now and then, every once in a
while; re–; –s or –es.

.17 **again,** over, over again, **once more,** *encore, bis* [both Fr], two times, twice over,
ditto; **anew,** *de novo* [L], afresh; from the
beginning, *da capo* [Ital].

.18 INTERJS **encore!,** bis!, once more!, again!

## 104. INFINITY

.1 NOUNS **infinity,** infiniteness, infinitude;
**boundlessness, limitlessness, endlessness;**
illimitability, interminability, termless-
ness; **immeasurability,** unmeasurability,
immensity, incalculability, innumerability, incomprehensibility; measurelessness,
countlessness, numberlessness; exhaust-
lessness, inexhaustibility; universality,
"world without end" [Bible]; **all-inclu-
siveness,** all-comprehensiveness; **eternity**
112.1,2, **perpetuity** 112, forever; "a dark illimitable ocean, without bound" [Mil-
ton].

.2 VERBS **have no limit** or **bounds,** have or
know no end, be without end, **go on and
on,** go on forever, never cease or end.

.3 ADJS **infinite, boundless, endless, limitless,** termless, shoreless; unbounded, uncircumscribed, **unlimited,** illimited, infi-

nitely continuous or extended, stretching
or extending everywhere, without bound,
without limit or end, no end of or to; illimitable, **interminable,** interminate; **immeasurable,** incalculable, innumerable,
incomprehensible, unfathomable; measureless, countless, sumless; **unmeasured,**
unmeasurable, immense, unplumbed, untold, unnumbered, without measure or
number or term; exhaustless, inexhaustible; **all-inclusive,** all-comprehensive 79.14,
**universal** 79.14; **perpetual, eternal** 112.7;
"as boundless as the sea" [Shakespeare].

.4 ADVS **infinitely, illimitably,** boundlessly,
limitlessly, **interminably; immeasurably,**
measurelessly, immensely, incalculably,
innumerably, incomprehensibly; **endlessly,** without end or limit; *ad infinitum*
[L], to infinity; **forever, eternally** 112.10,
in perpetuity, "to the last syllable of
recorded time" [Shakespeare].

## 105. TIME

.1 NOUNS **time, duration,** *durée* [Fr], lastingness, continuity 71, term, while, tide,
space; tense 586.12; **period** 107; cosmic
time; kairotic time; space-time 179.6;
psychological time; the past 119, the
present 120, the future 121; timebinding;
**chronology** 114.1.

.2 Time, **Father Time,** Cronus, Kronos;
"Old Time, that greatest and longest established spinner of all" [Dickens], "that
old bald cheater, Time" [Ben Jonson];
"Old Time, the clocksetter, that bald
sexton Time", "that old common arbitrator, Time", "the nurse and breeder of all
good" [all Shakespeare], "the soul of the
world" [Pythagoras], "the author of au-
thors", "the greatest innovator" [both
Francis Bacon], "the devourer of things"
[Ovid], "the illimitable, silent, never-rest-
ing thing called Time" [Carlyle], "a short
parenthesis in a long period" [Donne], "a
sandpile we run our fingers in" [Sand-
burg].

.3 tract of time, corridors of time, whirligig
of time, glass or hourglass of time, sands
of time, ravages of time, noiseless foot of
Time, scythe of Time, "the tooth of
time" [Shakespeare].

.4 **passage of time, course of time, lapse of
time,** progress of time, process of time,
succession of time, flow or flux of time,
sweep of time, stream or current or tide
of time, march or step of time, flight of
time, time's caravan, "Time's revolving

wheels" [Petrarch], "Time's wingèd chariot" [Andrew Marvell].

.5 VERBS elapse, lapse, **pass, expire,** run its course, run out, go *or* pass by; flow, run, proceed, advance, roll *or* press on, flit, fly, slip, slide, glide; continue 71.4, last, **endure,** go *or* run *or* flow on.

.6 **spend time, pass time, put in time,** employ *or* use time, fill *or* occupy time, kill time [informal], consume time, take time, take up time, while away the time; find *or* look for time; race with *or* against time, buy time, work against time, run out of time, make time stand still; weekend, winter, summer; keep time, measure time.

.7 ADJS **temporal, chronological,** chron(o)–, –chronous; durational, durative; lasting, continuous 71.8.

.8 ADVS **when, at which time,** at which moment *or* instant, what time, when as [archaic], on which occasion, **upon which, whereupon,** at which, in which time, at what time, in what period, on what occasion, whenever.

.9 **at that time,** on that occasion, at the same time as, at the same time *or* moment that, then, simultaneously, contemporaneously.

.10 in the meantime, meanwhile 109.5; during the time; for the duration; at a stretch.

.11 **then,** thereat, **at that time,** at that moment *or* instant, in that case *or* instance, on that occasion; **again,** at another time, at some other time, anon.

.12 **whenever,** whene'er, whensoever, whensoe'er, **at whatever time,** at any time, anytime, no matter when; if ever, once.

.13 in the year of our Lord, *anno Domini* [L], AD, in the Common *or* Christian Era, CE; *ante Christum* [L], AC, before Christ, BC, before the Common *or* Christian era, BCE; *anno urbis conditae* [L], AUC; *anno regni* [L], AR.

.14 PREPS **during,** pending, durante [law]; **in the course of,** in the process of, in the middle of; **in the time of,** at the time of, in the age *or* era of, intra–; over, through, **throughout,** throughout the course of, **for the period of;** until the conclusion of.

.15 **until, till,** to, unto, **up to,** up to the time of.

.16 CONJS **when, while,** whilst, the while; **during the time that,** at the time that, at the same time that, at *or* during which time; **whereas, as long as,** as far as.

.17 PHRS **time flies,** *tempus fugit* [L], time runs out, time marches on, "Time rolls

his ceaseless course" [Sir Walter Scott], "Time and tide stayeth for no man" [Richard Braithwaite].

## 106. TIMELESSNESS

.1 NOUNS **timelessness,** neverness, datelessness, eternity 112.1,2; no time, no time at all; time out of time, stopping *or* running out of time; everlasting moment.

.2 (a time that will never come) Greek calends, when hell freezes over, the thirtieth of February.

.3 ADJS **timeless, dateless.**

.4 ADVS **never,** ne'er, **not ever,** at no time, on no occasion, not at all; **nevermore;** never in the world, never on earth; not in donkey's years [Brit], never in all one's born days [informal], never in my life, *jamais de la vie* [Fr].

.5 without date, *sine die* [L].

## 107. PERIOD

*(portion or point of time)*

.1 NOUNS **period, point, juncture,** stage; **interval,** space, span, stretch; time lag; **time,** while, **moment,** minute, instant, hour, day, **season;** psychological moment; pregnant *or* fateful moment, kairos, moment of truth; **spell** 108; "this bank and shoal of time" [Shakespeare].

.2 (periods) **moment, second,** millisecond, microsecond; **minute; hour,** man-hour; **day,** sun; weekday; **week;** fortnight; **month,** moon, lunation; calendar month, lunar month; **quarter; semester,** trimester, term, session, academic year; **year,** annum, sun, twelvemonth; common year, regular year, leap year, bissextile year, defective year, perfect *or* abundant year; solar year, lunar year, sidereal year; fiscal year; calendar year; quinquennium, lustrum, luster; **decade,** decennium, decennary; **century; millennium;** –ad.

.3 **term,** time, duration, **tenure;** spell 108.

.4 **age, generation,** time, day, date, cycle; aeon; Platonic year, great year, *annus magnus* [L], indiction, cycle of indiction.

.5 **era, epoch, age;** Golden Age, Silver Age; Ice Age, glacial epoch; Stone Age, Bronze Age, Iron Age, Steel Age; Middle Ages, Dark Ages; Era of Good Feeling; Jacksonian Age; Depression Era; New Deal Era; Prohibition Era.

.6 1870's and 80's, Reconstruction Era, Gilded Age.

.7 1890's, Gay Nineties, Naughty Nineties,

Mauve Decade, Golden Age, Gilded Age.

.8 1920's, Roaring Twenties, Golden Twenties, Mad Decade, Age of the Red-Hot Mamas, Jazz Age.

.9 (modern age) Technological Age, Automobile Age, Air Age, Jet Age, Supersonic Age, Atomic Age, Electronic Age, Computer Age, Space Age, Age of Anxiety.

.10 geological time periods

| | |
|---|---|
| Algonkian | Oligocene |
| Archean | Ordovician |
| Archeozoic | Paleocene |
| Cambrian | Paleozoic |
| Carboniferous | Pennsylvanian |
| Cenozoic | Permian |
| Comanchean | Pleistocene |
| Cretaceous | Pliocene |
| Devonian | Precambrian |
| Eocene | Proterozoic |
| Glacial | Quaternary |
| Holocene | Recent |
| Jurassic | Silurian |
| Lower Cretaceous | Tertiary |
| Lower Tertiary | Triassic |
| Mesozoic | Upper Cretaceous |
| Miocene | Upper Tertiary |
| Mississippian | |

## 108. SPELL

*(period of duty, etc.)*

.1 NOUNS spell, fit, stretch, go [informal].

.2 turn, bout, round, inning, innings [Brit], time, time at bat, place, say, whack [slang], go [informal]; opportunity, chance; relief, spell; one's turn, one's move [informal], one's say.

.3 shift, work shift, tour, tour of duty, stint, bit, watch, trick, time, turn, relay, spell or turn of work; day shift, night shift, swing shift, graveyard shift [informal], dogwatch, anchor watch; lobster trick or tour, sunrise watch; split shift, split schedule; half time, part time, full time; overtime.

.4 term, time; tenure, continuous tenure, tenure in or of office; enlistment, hitch [informal], tour; prison term, stretch [informal].

.5 VERBS take one's turn, have a go; take turns, alternate, turn and turn about; time off, spell or spell off [both informal], relieve, cover, fill in for, take over for; put in one's time, work one's shift; stand one's watch or trick, keep a watch; have one's innings; do a stint; hold office, have tenure or tenure of appointment; enlist, sign up; reenlist, re-up [informal]; do a hitch [informal], do a tour or tour of duty; serve or do time.

## 109. INTERIM

*(intermediate period)*

.1 NOUNS interim, interval, interlude, intermission, intermittence, pause, break, recess, coffee break, half time or half-time intermission, interruption; lull, quiet spell, resting point, point of repose, plateau, letup, relief, vacation, holiday, time off, off-time, downtime, time out; respite 711.2; entr'acte; *intermezzo* [Ital]; interregnum.

.2 meantime, meanwhile, while, the while.

.3 VERBS intervene, interlude, interval, intermit; pause, break, recess, declare a recess; call a break or intermission; call time or time-out; take five or ten, etc., take a break [all informal].

.4 ADJS interim, temporary, tentative, provisional, provisory.

.5 ADVS meanwhile, meantime, in the meanwhile or meantime, in the interim, *ad interim* [L]; between acts or halves or periods, betweenwhiles, betweentimes, between now and then; till or until then; *en attendant* [Fr], in the intervening time, during the interval, at the same time, for the meantime, for the time being, for the nonce, for a time or season; *pendente lite* [L].

## 110. DURABILITY

*(long duration)*

.1 NOUNS durability, endurance, duration, durableness, lastingness, *longueur* [Fr], perennation, abidingness, long-lastingness, perdurability, diuturnity; continuance, maintenance, steadfastness, constancy, stability 142, persistence, permanence 140, standing, long standing; longevity, long-livedness; antiquity, age; survival, survivance, defiance or defeat of time; perpetuity 112.

.2 protraction, prolongation, continuation, extension, lengthening, drawing- or stretching- or dragging- or spinning-out, lingering; procrastination.

.3 length of time, distance of time, vista or stretch or desert of time; corridor or tunnel of time.

.4 long time, long while, long; age or ages [both informal], aeon, century, eternity, years, years on end, coon's age [informal], donkey's years [Brit informal], month of Sundays [informal], right smart spell [dial].

.5 lifetime, life, life's duration, "threescore

years and ten" [Bible], period of existence, all the days of one's life; **generation, age;** all one's born days or natural life [informal].

.6 VERBS **endure, last** or **last out,** bide, **abide,** dwell, perdure, **continue,** run, extend, **go on,** carry on, hold on, keep on, stay on, run on; live, **live on,** continue to be, subsist, exist, tarry, **persist;** maintain, sustain, **remain, stay,** keep, hold, stand, prevail, last long, hold out; **survive,** defy or defeat time; live to fight another day; perennate; live through, tide over; wear, wear well.

.7 **linger on,** linger, tarry, go on, **go on and on, wear on,** crawl, creep, drag, **drag on,** drag along, drag its slow length along, drag a lengthening chain.

.8 **outlast,** outwear, outlive, survive.

.9 protract, **prolong,** continue, **extend, lengthen,** lengthen out, **draw out, spin out,** drag or stretch out; linger on, dwell on; dawdle, procrastinate, temporize, drag one's feet.

.10 ADJS **durable,** perdurable, **lasting, enduring,** perduring, **abiding, continuing,** remaining, staying, **stable** 142.12, persisting, **persistent, perennial,** meno–; inveterate, age-long; **steadfast, constant,** intransient, immutable, unfading, evergreen, sempervirent, **permanent** 140.7, perennial; **long-lasting,** long-standing, of long duration or standing, diuturnal; long-term; **long-lived,** tough, hardy, vital, longevous or longeval; **ancient,** aged, antique; macrobiotic; chronic; **perpetual** 112.7.

.11 **protracted, prolonged,** extended, lengthened; **long,** overlong, interminable, marathon, lasting, **lingering,** languishing; long-continued, long-continuing, long-pending; drawn- or stretched- or dragged- or spun-out, long-drawn, **long-drawn-out;** long-winded.

.12 daylong, nightlong, weeklong, monthlong, yearlong.

.13 lifelong, livelong, lifetime, for life.

.14 ADVS **for a long time, long, for long, interminably,** unendingly, undyingly, persistently, protractedly, enduringly; for ever so long [informal], for many a long day, for life or a lifetime, for an age or ages, for a coon's or dog's age [informal], for a month of Sundays [informal], for donkey's years [Brit informal], **forever and a day, for years on end;** all the year round, all the day long, the livelong day, as the day is long; morning, noon, and night; hour after hour, day after day, month af-

ter month, year after year; day in day out, month in month out, year in year out; till hell freezes over [slang], till you're blue in the face [informal], till the cows come home [informal], till shrimps learn to whistle [informal], till doomsday, from now till doomsday, from here to eternity, till the end of time; since time began, long ago, long since, time out of mind, time immemorial.

## 111. TRANSIENCE

### (short duration)

.1 NOUNS **transience** or transiency, transientness, **impermanence** or impermanency, transitoriness, changeableness 141, **mutability, instability, temporariness,** fleetingness, momentariness; finitude; **ephemerality,** ephemeralness; evanescence, volatility, fugacity, **shortlivedness; mortality,** death, perishability, corruptibility, caducity.

.2 brevity, briefness, shortness; swiftness 269, fleetness.

.3 short time, little while, little, **instant, moment** 113.3, small space, span, spurt, **short spell;** no time, less than no time; bit or **little bit,** a breath, the wink of an eye, pair of winks [informal]; **two shakes** or two shakes of a lamb's tail [both informal].

.4 transient, transient guest or boarder, temporary lodger; sojourner; passer, passerby.

.5 ephemeron, ephemera [pl], ephemeral; ephemerid, ephemeris, ephemerides [pl]; mayfly; bubble, smoke; nine days' wonder, flash in the pan; snows of yesteryear, neiges d'antan [Fr].

.6 VERBS (be transient) flit, **fly,** fleet; pass, **pass away, vanish, evaporate,** evanesce, disappear, fade, melt, sink; fade like a shadow or dream, vanish like a dream, burst like a bubble, go up in smoke, melt like snow.

.7 ADJS **transient, transitory, transitive; temporary, temporal; impermanent,** unenduring, undurable, nondurable, nonpermanent; frail, brittle, fragile, insubstantial; changeable 141.6, **mutable, unstable,** inconstant 141.7; capricious, fickle, impulsive, impetuous; **short-lived, ephemeral,** fly-by-night, evanescent, volatile, **momentary;** deciduous; **passing,** fleeting, flitting, flying, fading, dying; fugitive, fugacious; perishable, mortal, corruptible; "as transient as the clouds" [Robert Green Ingersoll], here today and gone tomorrow.

.8 **brief, short,** quick, brisk, swift 269.19, fleet, speedy, "short and sweet" [Thomas Lodge]; meteoric, cometary, flashing, flickering; short-term, short-termed.

.9 ADVS **temporarily,** for the moment, for the time, *pro tempore* [L], pro tem, for the nonce, **for the time being,** for a time, awhile.

.10 **transiently,** fleetingly, flittingly, flickeringly, **briefly, shortly,** swiftly 269.21, quickly, **for a little while,** for a short time; **momentarily,** for a moment; **in an instant** 113.7.

.11 PHRS "all flesh is grass" [Bible].

## 112. PERPETUITY

*(endless duration)*

.1 NOUNS **perpetuity,** perpetualness; **eternity,** eternalness, sempiternity, infinite duration; everness, foreverness, **everlastingness, permanence** 140, ever-duringness, durability 110, perdurability, indestructibility; **constancy,** stability, immutability, continuance, continualness, perennialness *or* perenniality, **ceaselessness,** unceasingness, incessancy; timelessness 106; **endlessness,** never-endingness, **interminability; infinity** 104; coeternity.

.2 **forever, an eternity,** endless time, **time without end;** "a moment standing still for ever" [James Montgomery], "a short parenthesis in a long period" [Donne], "deserts of vast eternity" [Andrew Marvell].

.3 **immortality,** eternal life, **deathlessness,** imperishability, undyingness, incorruptibility *or* incorruption, athanasy *or* athanasia; eternal youth, fountain of youth.

.4 **perpetuation,** preservation, eternalization, immortalization; eternal re-creation, eternal return *or* recurrence, steady-state universe.

.5 VERBS **perpetuate, preserve,** preserve from oblivion, keep fresh *or* alive, perennialize, **eternalize,** eternize, **immortalize;** monumentalize; freeze, embalm.

.6 last *or* endure forever, **go on forever,** go on and on, live forever, **have no end,** have no limits *or* bounds *or* term, never cease *or* end *or* die *or* pass.

.7 ADJS **perpetual, everlasting,** everliving, ever-being, ever-abiding, ever-during, ever-durable, **permanent** 140.7, perdurable, indestructible; **eternal,** sempiternal, eterne [archaic], **infinite** 104.3, olamic, aeonian; dateless, ageless, timeless, immemorial; **endless,** unending, never-ending,

without end, **interminable,** nonterminous, nonterminating; **continual,** continuous, steady, **constant, ceaseless,** nonstop, unceasing, never-ceasing, **incessant,** unremitting, unintermitting, uninterrupted, "continuous as the stars that shine" [Wordsworth]; coeternal.

.8 **perennial,** indeciduous, **evergreen,** sempervirent, ever-new; ever-blooming, ever-bearing.

.9 **immortal,** everlasting, **deathless,** undying, never-dying, **imperishable,** incorruptible, amaranthine; fadeless, **unfading,** never-fading, ever-fresh; frozen, embalmed.

.10 ADVS **perpetually,** in perpetuity, **everlastingly, eternally, permanently** 140.9, perennially, perdurably, indestructibly, **constantly,** continually, steadily, **ceaselessly,** unceasingly, never-ceasingly, **incessantly,** never-endingly, **endlessly,** unendingly, **interminably,** without end, world without end, time without end, "from everlasting to everlasting" [Bible]; **infinitely,** *ad infinitum* [L] 104.4.

.11 **always, all along, all the time,** all the while, at all times, *semper et ubique* [L, always and everywhere]; ever and always, **invariably,** without exception, never otherwise, *semper eadem* [L, ever the same; Elizabeth I].

.12 **forever, forevermore, for ever and ever,** forever and aye; forever and a day [informal], now and forever, *ora e sempre* [Ital], "yesterday and today and forever" [Bible]; **ever, evermore,** ever and anon, ever and again; aye, for aye; **for good,** for keeps [informal], for good and all, for all time; throughout the ages, from age to age, in all ages, "for ages of ages" [Douay Bible]; **to the end of time,** till time stops *or* runs out, "to the last syllable of recorded time" [Shakespeare], to the crack of doom, to the last trumpet, till doomsday; till you're blue in the face [informal], till hell freezes over [slang], till the cows come home [informal].

.13 **for life,** for all one's natural life, for the term of one's days, while life endures, while one draws breath, in all one's born days [informal]; from the cradle to the grave, from the womb to the tomb; **till death,** till death do us part.

## 113. INSTANTANEOUSNESS

*(imperceptible duration)*

.1 NOUNS **instantaneousness** *or* **instantaneity,** momentariness, **momentaneousness,** immediateness *or* immediacy; simultaneity 118.

.2 **suddenness, abruptness,** precipitateness *or* precipitatousness, precipitance *or* precipitancy; **unexpectedness,** unanticipation, inexpectation 540.

.3 **instant, moment, second,** sec [informal], split second, millisecond, microsecond, half a second, half a mo [Brit informal], minute, trice, twinkle, **twinkling, twinkling** *or* twinkle of an eye, twink, wink, bat of an eye [informal], flash, crack, tick, stroke, coup, breath, twitch; two shakes *or* shake *or* half a shake, **jiffy** *or* jiff *or* half a jiffy [all informal].

.4 ADJS **instantaneous,** instant, momentary, momentaneous, **immediate,** presto, quick as thought *or* lightning; lightning-like.

.5 **sudden, abrupt,** precipitant, **precipitate, precipitous; hasty,** headlong, impulsive, impetuous; speedy, swift, quick; **unexpected** 540.10, unanticipated, unpredicted, unforeseen, unlooked-for; **surprising** 540.11, startling, electrifying, shocking, nerve-shattering.

.6 ADVS **instantly,** instanter, momentaneously, momentarily, momently, **instantaneously, immediately; on the instant,** on the spot, on the dot [informal], on the nail, in half a mo [Brit informal]; just then, just now.

.7 **in an instant, in a trice, in a second,** in a moment, in a bit *or* little bit, in a jiff *or* jiffy *or* half a jiffy [informal], in a flash, in a wink [informal], in a twink, **in a twinkling, in the twinkling of an eye,** in two shakes *or* a shake *or* half a shake [informal], in two shakes of a lamb's tail [informal], before you can say 'Jack Robinson' [informal]; **in no time,** in less than no time, in nothing flat [informal], in short order; at the drop of a hat *or* handkerchief, like a shot, like a shot out of hell [slang]; with the speed of light.

.8 **at once,** at once and on the spot, **then and there, now, right now, right away, right off,** straightway, straightaway, forthwith, this minute, this very minute, **without delay,** without the least delay, in a hurry [informal], *pronto* [Sp], *subito* [Ital]; **simultaneously** 118.6, at the same instant, in the same breath; **all at once,** all together, at one time, at a stroke, at one stroke, at a blow, at one blow, at one swoop, "at one fell swoop" [Shakespeare]; at one jump, *per saltum* [L], *uno saltu* [L].

.9 **suddenly,** sudden, of a sudden, on a sudden, **all of a sudden, all at once: abruptly, sharp; precipitously** *or* precipitately, precipitantly, impulsively, impetuously, hastily; dash; smack, bang, slap, plop, plunk, plump, pop; **unexpectedly** 540.14, on short notice, without notice *or* warning, unawares, **surprisingly** 540.15, startlingly, like a thunderbolt *or* thunderclap, like a flash, like a bolt from the blue.

.10 PHRS no sooner said than done.

## 114. MEASUREMENT OF TIME

.1 NOUNS **chronology,** timekeeping, timing, clocking, horology, **chronometry,** horometry, chronoscopy; watch- *or* clock-making; calendar-making; dating, carbon-14 dating, dendrochronology.

.2 **time of day, time** 105, **the time;** hour, minute; stroke of the hour, time signal, bell.

.3 **standard time,** civil time, zone time, slow time [informal]; mean time, solar time, mean solar time, sidereal time, apparent time, local time; Greenwich time, Greenwich mean time *or* GMT, Eastern time, Central time, Mountain time, Pacific time; Atlantic time; Alaska time, Yukon time; daylight-saving time; fast time [informal], summer time [Brit]; **time zone.**

.4 **date,** point of time, time, day; postdate, antedate; datemark; date line, International Date Line.

.5 **epact,** annual epact, monthly *or* menstrual epact.

.6 **timepiece** 114.17, timekeeper, **timer, chronometer,** ship's watch; horologe, horologium; **clock,** Big Ben, ticker [informal], **watch,** turnip [slang]; watch *or* clock movement, clockworks, watchworks.

.7 **almanac,** The Old Farmer's Almanac, Ephemeris and Nautical Almanac, Information Please Almanac, Nautical Almanac, Poor Richard's Almanac, Reader's Digest Almanac, Whitaker's Almanack, World Almanac.

.8 **calendar,** calends; calendar stone, chronogram; astronomical calendar *or* almanac, ephemeris; perpetual calendar; Chinese calendar, church *or* ecclesiastical calendar, Cotsworth calendar, Gregorian calendar, Hebrew *or* Jewish calendar, Hindu calendar, international fixed calendar, Julian calendar, Muslim calendar, Republican *or* Revolutionary calendar, Roman calendar.

.9 **chronicle, chronology, register,** registry, record; **annals,** journal, diary; time sheet, time book, **log,** daybook; timecard, time ticket, clock card, check sheet; datebook; date slip; timetable; time schedule, time chart; time scale; time study, motion study, time and motion study.

.10 **chronologist,** chronologer, chronographer, horologist, horologer; watchmaker *or* clockmaker; timekeeper, timer; **chronicler,** annalist, diarist; calendar maker, calendarist.

.11 VERBS **time, fix** *or* **set the time,** mark the time; **keep time,** mark time, measure time, beat time; **clock** [informal].

.12 **punch the clock** *or* **punch in** *or* **punch out, time in, time out** [all informal]; ring in, ring out; clock in, clock out; check in, check out; check off.

.13 **date,** be dated, date at *or* from, bear date; fix *or* set the date, make a date; **predate,** backdate, antedate; **postdate; update,** bring up to date; datemark; date-stamp; dateline.

.14 chronologize, chronicle, calendar, intercalate.

.15 ADJS **chronologic(al),** temporal, timekeeping; **chronometric(al),** chronoscopic, chronographic(al), chronogrammatic(al), horologic(al), horometric(al), metronomic(al), calendric(al), intercalary *or* intercalated; dated; annalistic, diaristic; calendarial.

.16 ADVS **o'clock,** of the clock, by the clock; half past, half after [Brit]; a quarter of *or* to, a quarter past *or* after.

.17 **timepieces, clocks, watches**

| | |
|---|---|
| alarm clock | metronome |
| alarm watch | pendule |
| astronomical clock | pendulum clock |
| atomic clock | pneumatic clock |
| box chronometer | pocket chronometer |
| calendar clock | pocket watch |
| calendar watch | program clock |
| chronograph | quartz-crystal clock |
| chronometer | repeater |
| chronopher | Riefler clock |
| chronoscope | sandglass |
| clepsydra | ship's watch |
| cuckoo clock | sidereal clock |
| dial | split-second watch |
| digital clock | stemwinder [informal] |
| digital watch | stop watch |
| egg glass | sundial |
| electric clock | telechron clock |
| electronic clock | telltale |
| gnomon | three-minute glass |
| grandfather clock | time ball |
| half-hour glass | time clock |
| half-minute glass | time lock |
| hourglass | time recorder |
| hunter | time switch |
| independent-seconds watch | traveling clock |
| watch | turret clock |
| isochronon | watchman's clock |
| journeyman | water clock |
| marine chronometer | wristwatch |

## 115. ANACHRONISM

*(false estimation or knowledge of time)*

.1 NOUNS **anachronism,** chronological *or* historical error, **mistiming, misdating,** misdate, postdating, antedating; parachronism, metachronism, prochronism; prolepsis, anticipation; earliness, lateness, tardiness, unpunctuality.

.2 VERBS **mistime, misdate;** antedate, foredate, postdate; lag.

.3 ADJS **anachronous** *or* **anachronistic,** parachronistic, metachronistic, prochronistic; **mistimed, misdated;** antedated, foredated, postdated; ahead of time, **beforehand, early;** behind time, **behindhand, late,** unpunctual, tardy; **overdue,** past due; unseasonable, out of season; out of date, dated.

## 116. PRIORITY

*(previous time)*

.1 NOUNS **priority, previousness, earliness** 131, **antecedence** *or* **antecedency, anteriority, precedence** *or* **precedency** 64, precession; *status quo ante* [L], earlier state; preexistence; **anticipation,** predating, antedating; antedate; **past time** 119.

.2 **antecedent, precedent, premise;** forerunner, precursor 66, ancestor.

.3 VERBS **be prior,** be before *or* early *or* earlier, **precede, antecede,** precurse, **forerun,** come *or* go before; herald, usher in, proclaim, announce, **anticipate,** antedate, predate; preexist.

.4 ADJS **prior, previous, early** 131.7, **earlier,** *ci-devant* [Fr], **former,** fore, prime, first, **preceding** 292.3, precurrent, foregoing, anterior, **anticipatory,** antecedent; preexistent; older, elder, senior; ante– *or* anti–, fore–, pre–, pro–, prot(o)–, proter(o)–, supra–.

.5 **prewar, ante-bellum,** before the war; prerevolutionary; premundane *or* antemundane; prelapsarian, before the Fall; antediluvian, before the Flood; protohistoric, prehistoric 119.10; precultural; pre-Aryan; pre-Christian; premillenarian, premillennial; anteclassical, preclassical, pre-Roman, pre-Renaissance, preromantic, pre-Victorian.

.6 ADVS **previously, priorly, hitherto, heretofore,** theretofore; **before, early** 131.11, **earlier,** ere, erenow, ere then, or ever; already, yet; before all; **formerly** 119.13.

.7 PREPS **prior to, previous to, before,** in advance of, in anticipation of, in preparation for.

## 117. POSTERIORITY

### (later time)

.1 NOUNS **posteriority, subsequence,** sequence, **succession, following** 293, **coming after, lateness** 132; provenience, supervenience, supervention; afterlife, next life; remainder 43, hangover [informal]; postdating; postdate; future time 121.

.2 **sequel** 67, **aftermath,** consequence, effect 154, **conclusion** 494.4; posterity, offspring, descendant, heir, **successor;** line, **lineage,** dynasty.

.3 VERBS **come** or **follow** or **go after, succeed,** replace, displace, overtake, supervene; **ensue,** issue, emanate, attend, **result;** follow up, trail, track, come close on or tread on the heels of, dog the footsteps of; step into the shoes of, take the place of.

.4 ADJS **subsequent, after, later,** posterior, **following, succeeding,** successive, sequent, lineal, consecutive, ensuing, attendant; junior, cadet, puisne, younger.

.5 **posthumous,** afterdeath; **postprandial,** postcibal, postcenal, after-dinner; **postwar,** *postbellum* [L], after the war; **postdiluvian,** postdiluvial, after the flood; postlapsarian, after the Fall; ep(i)– or eph–, infra–, meta–, post–.

.6 ADVS **subsequently, afterwards, after,** after that, after all, **later, next,** since; **thereafter,** thereon, thereupon, therewith, **then;** in the process or course of time, as things worked out, in the sequel; at a subsequent or later time, in the aftermath; *ex post facto* [L].

.7 **after which, on** or **upon which, whereupon,** whereon, whereat, whereto, whereunto, wherewith, wherefore, on, upon; hereinafter.

.8 PREPS **after, subsequent to,** later than, past, beyond, behind.

.9 PHRS *post hoc, ergo propter hoc* [L, after this, therefore on account of this].

## 118. SIMULTANEITY

.1 NOUNS **simultaneity** or **simultaneousness,** coincidence, concurrence, concomitance, coexistence; **contemporaneousness** or contemporaneity, coetaneousness or coetaneity, coevalness or coevalneity; unison; **synchronism,** synchronization; isochronism; accompaniment 73, agreement 26.

.2 **contemporary,** coeval, coexistent, concomitant; dead heat, draw, tie.

.3 VERBS **synchronize,** contemporize; **coincide,** concur, coexist, coextend; **accompany** 73.7, agree 26.6, match, go hand in hand, keep pace with, keep in step; isochronize, put or be in phase, be in time, time.

.4 ADJS **simultaneous, concurrent,** concomitant, collateral; **coexistent, coexisting; contemporaneous,** contemporary, coinstantaneous, coetaneous, coeval; coterminous, conterminous; unison, unisonous; isochronous, isochronal; coeternal; accompanying 73.9, agreeing 26.9.

.5 **synchronous,** synchronized, synchronal or synchronic, in sync [informal]; **in time,** in step, in tempo, in phase, with or on the beat.

.6 ADVS **simultaneously, concurrently,** coinstantaneously; **together,** all together, **at the same time,** at one and the same time, as one, as one man, in concert with, in chorus, with one voice, in unison, in a chorus, in the same breath; at one time, at a clip [informal]; synchronously, isochronously, in phase, in sync [informal], with or on the beat.

## 119. THE PAST

.1 NOUNS **the past,** past, foretime, former times, past times, times past, **days gone by, bygone times** or **days, yesterday, yesteryear,** recent past; history, past history; dead past, dead hand of the past; the years that are past, "the days that are no more" [Tennyson], "the irrevocable Past" [Longfellow], "thou unrelenting past" [William Cullen Bryant], "the eternal landscape of the past" [Tennyson].

.2 **old** or **olden times,** early times, **old days,** the olden time, times of old, **days of old, days** or **times of yore,** yore, yoretime, eld [archaic], good old times or days, lang syne or auld lang syne [both Scot], way back [informal], **long ago,** time out of mind, days beyond recall; old story, same old story.

.3 **antiquity, ancient times,** time immemorial, ancient history, remote age or time, remote or far or dim or **distant past,** distance of time, "the dark backward and abysm of time" [Shakespeare]; ancientness 123; archae(o)– or archeo–.

.4 **memory** 537, **remembrance, recollection, reminiscence, retrospection,** musing on the past, looking back; "the remembrance of things past" [Shakespeare], *"la recherche du temps perdu"* [Proust]; **reliving,** reexperiencing; revival 694.3; youth 124.

.5 [gram terms] past tense, preterit, perfect tense, past perfect tense, pluperfect, historical present tense, past progressive tense; aorist; perfective aspect; preterition.

.6 VERBS **pass**, be past, **be a thing of the past**, elapse, lapse, be gone, be dead and gone, be all over, have run its course, have run out, have had its day; **disappear** 447.2, die.

.7 ADJS **past, gone**, by, **gone-by, bygone**, gone glimmering, bypast, ago, **over**, departed, passed, passed away, elapsed, lapsed, vanished, dead, expired, run out, blown over, finished, forgotten, extinct, dead and buried, defunct, deceased, wound up, passé, obsolete, has-been, dated, antique, antiquated; no more, irrecoverable, never to return; archae(o)– or archeo–, ex–, pale(o)–, praeter– or preter–, retro–; –ed, y– [archaic].

.8 **reminiscent** 537.22, **retrospective, remembered** 537.23, recollected; relived, reexperienced; restored, revived.

.9 [gram terms] past, preterit or preteritive, pluperfect, past perfect; aorist, aoristic; perfective.

.10 **former**, past, fore, **previous**, late, recent, **once, onetime**, sometime, **erstwhile**, then, quondam; **prior** 116.4; **ancient, immemorial**, early, primitive, primeval, prehistoric; **old**, olden.

.11 **foregoing**, aforegoing, **preceding** 64.4; last, latter.

.12 **back**, backward, into the past; early; retrospective, retroactive, ex post facto [L], a priori [L].

.13 ADVS **formerly, previously, priorly** 116.6; **earlier, before**, before now, erenow, erst, whilom, erewhile, **hitherto, heretofore**, aforetime, beforetime, **in the past**, in times past; then; **yesterday**, only yesterday, recently; **historically**, prehistorically, in historic or prehistoric times.

.14 **once**, once upon a time, one day, one fine morning, time was.

.15 **ago, since**, gone by, back, back when; backward, to or into the past; **retrospectively**, reminiscently, retroactively.

.16 **long ago**, long since, **a long while** or **time ago**, some time ago or since, some time back, a way or away back [informal], ages ago, **years ago**, donkey's years ago [Brit informal]; **in times past**, in times gone by, in the old days, in the good old days; **anciently, of old, of yore**, in ancient times, in olden times, in the olden time,

**in days of yore**, early, in the memory of man, time out of mind.

.17 **since**, ever since, until now; **since long ago, long since**, from away back [informal], since days of yore, ages ago, **from time immemorial**, from time out of mind, aeons ago, since the world was made, since the world was young, since time began, since the year one, since Hector was a pup or since God knows when [both slang].

## 120. THE PRESENT

.1 NOUNS **the present**, present, presentness, the present juncture or occasion, the present hour or moment, this instant or second or moment, **the present day** or **time**, the present age, "the living sum-total of the whole Past" [Carlyle]; **today**, this day, **this day and age; this point**, this stage, this hour, **now**, nowadays, the now, the way things are, the nonce, **the time being; the times**, our times, these days; contemporaneousness, contemporaneity, nowness, **newness** 122, modernity; the Now Generation; historical present, present tense [both gram].

.2 ADJS **present, immediate**, instant, immanent, **latest, current**, running, extant, existent, **existing**, actual, being, that is, as is, that be; **present-day**, present-time, present-age, **modern** 122.13; topical; **contemporary**, contemporaneous; up-to-date, up-to-the-minute, fresh, new.

.3 ADVS **now, at present, at this point**, at this juncture, on the present occasion, **at this time**, at this time of day, at this moment or instant, at the present time, "upon this bank and shoal of time" [Shakespeare]; **today**, this day, in these days, **in this day and age**, in our time, **nowadays**; this night, **tonight**; here, hereat, **here and now**, hic et nunc [L], even now, but now, **just now**, as of now, as things are; on the spot; for the nonce, for the time being; for this occasion.

.4 **until now**, till now, **hereunto**, heretofore, until this time, by this time, **up to now**, up to the present, up to this time, to this day, **so far**, thus far, **as yet, to date**, yet, already, still, now or then as previously.

## 121. THE FUTURE

.1 NOUNS **the future**, future, futurity, imminence 152, posteriority 117, eventuality 151.1, **hereafter**, aftertime, afteryears, **time to come**; the morrow, **tomorrow**, mañana [Sp], time just ahead, **immediate** *or* **near future,** immediate prospect, offing; remote *or* deep *or* distant future; **by-and-by,** the sweet by-and-by [informal]; time ahead, course ahead, **prospect,** outlook, expectation, project, probability, prediction, forward look, foresight, prophecy, crystal ball; what is to be *or* come; determinism; future tense; futurism; the womb of time, "the past again, entered through another gate" [Pinero], "the never-ending flight of future days" [Milton].

.2 **destiny** 640.2, **fate;** what bodes *or* looms, what is fated *or* destined *or* doomed, what is in the books; **the hereafter,** the great hereafter, "the good hereafter" [Whittier], a better place, Paradise, Heaven, **afterworld,** otherworld, **next world,** world to come, life *or* world beyond the grave, **the beyond,** the great beyond, the unknown, the great unknown, **the grave,** home, abode *or* world of the dead, eternal home; "They are all gone into the world of light!" [Henry Vaughn], "the great world of light, that lies behind all human destinies" [Longfellow]; **afterlife, postexistence,** future state, **life to come,** life after death.

.3 **doomsday,** doom, day of doom, crack of doom, trumpet *or* trump of doom; **Judgment Day,** Day of Judgment, the Judgment; eschatology, last things, **last days.**

.4 **futurity,** futureness; ultimateness, eventuality, finality.

.5 **advent, coming, approach of time,** time drawing on.

.6 VERBS **come,** come on, **approach,** near, **draw on** *or* **near,** await, stare one in the face; be to be *or* come; be fated *or* destined *or* doomed, be in the books, be in the cards; loom, threaten, be imminent 152.2; lie ahead *or* in one's course; project, plot, plan, predict, expect, foresee, foretell, prophesy; hope, anticipate, look for, look forward to.

.7 **postexist,** live on, survive.

.8 ADJS **future, later,** hereafter; **coming, forthcoming, imminent** 152.3, approaching, nearing, **prospective; eventual** 151.11, ultimate, to-be, **to come; projected,** plotted, planned, looked- *or* hoped-for, desired, emergent, **predicted,** prophesied, probable, extrapolated; determined, fatal, fatidic, fated, destinal, destined; eschatological; futuristic.

.9 ADVS **in the future,** in aftertime, **afterward** *or* afterwards, **later,** at a later time, after a time *or* while, anon; **by and by,** in the sweet by-and-by [informal]; **tomorrow,** *mañana* [Sp], the day after tomorrow; *proximo* [L], prox., **in the near** *or* **immediate future,** just around the corner, **imminently** 152.4, **soon, before long;** probably, predictably, hopefully; fatally, by destiny *or* necessity.

.10 in future, **hereafter,** hereinafter, thereafter, **henceforth, henceforward** *or* henceforwards, thence, **thenceforth,** thenceforward *or* thenceforwards, from this time forward, from this point, from this *or* that time, from then on, **from here** *or* **now on, from now on in** [informal], from here in *or* out [informal], from this moment on.

.11 in time, in due time, in due season *or* course, all in good time, in the fullness of time, in God's good time, in the course *or* process of time, **eventually** 151.12, **ultimately,** in the long run.

.12 **sometime,** somewhen, **someday, some of these days,** one of these days, some fine day *or* morning, one fine day *or* morning, some sweet day, sometime *or* other, **sooner or later,** when all is said and done.

.13 PREPS **about to, at** *or* **on the point of,** on the eve of, on the brink *or* verge of, near to, close upon, in the act of.

## 122. NEWNESS

.1 NOUNS **newness,** freshness, maidenhood, dewiness, pristineness, mint condition, new-mintedness, newbornness, virginity, intactness, greenness, immaturity, rawness, callowness, brand-newness; presentness, nowness; **recentness,** recency, lateness; **novelty,** novelness, gloss of novelty, newfangledness *or* newfangleness; originality; **uncommonness,** unusualness, strangeness, unfamiliarity.

.2 **novelty, innovation,** newfangled device *or* contraption [informal], **new** *or* **latest wrinkle** [informal], **the last word** *or* **the latest thing** [both informal], *dernier cri* [Fr]; what's happening, what's in, the in thing [all informal]; new look, latest fashion *or* fad; advance guard, vanguard, **avant-garde.**

.3 **modernity,** modernness; modernism; modernization, updating, *aggiornamento* [Ital].

.4 **modern,** modern man; modernist; modernizer; neologist, neoterist, neology, neologism, neoterism, neoteric; modern *or* rising *or* new generation; neonate, fledgling, stripling, *novus homo* [L], new man, upstart, arriviste, *nouveau riche* [Fr], parvenu; Young Turk, bright young man, comer [informal].

.5 VERBS **innovate, invent, coin,** new-mint, mint, inaugurate, neologize, neoterize; renew, renovate 694.17.

.6 **modernize, streamline;** update, **bring up to date,** move with the times.

.7 ADJS **new,** young, neoteric, ne(o)–, nov-(o)–; **fresh,** fresh as a daisy, fresh as the morning dew; **unused, firsthand, original;** untried, untouched, unhandled, unhandseled, untrodden, unbeaten; virgin, virginal, intact, maiden, maidenly; green, vernal; dewy, pristine, ever-new, sempervirent, evergreen; immature, undeveloped, raw, callow, fledgling, unfledged, nestling.

.8 **fresh, additional, further,** other, another; renewed.

.9 **new-made,** new-built, new-wrought, new-shaped, new-mown, new-minted, new-coined, uncirculated, in mint condition, mint, new-begotten, new-grown, new-laid; **newborn,** new-fledged; **new-model,** late-model, like new, factory-new.

.10 [informal terms] **brand-new,** fire-new, **brand-spanking new,** spanking, **spanking new; just out,** hot off the fire or griddle or spit, hot off the press; newfangled or newfangle.

.11 **novel, original, unique, different;** strange, unusual, uncommon; unfamiliar, unheard-of.

.12 **recent, late,** newly come, of yesterday; latter, later; cen(o)– or caen(o)–, –cene.

.13 **modern, contemporary, present-day,** present-time, twentieth-century; now [informal], **newfashioned,** fashionable, modish, mod, à la mode [Fr], **up-to-date,** up-to-datish, **up-to-the-minute, in,** abreast of the times; **advanced,** progressive, forward-looking, avant-garde; **ultramodern,** ultra-ultra, ahead of its time, far out, way out, modernistic, modernized, streamlined.

.14 **newest, latest,** last, most recent, newest of the new, farthest out.

•.15 ADVS **newly,** freshly, new, **anew,** once more, from the ground up, from scratch [informal], ab ovo [L], de novo [L], **afresh, again;** as new.

.16 **now, recently, lately,** latterly, **of late,** not long ago, a short time ago, the other day, only yesterday; just now, right now [informal].

## 123. OLDNESS

.1 NOUNS **oldness, age,** eld [archaic], hoary eld; elderliness, seniority, senility, old age 126.5; **ancientness, antiquity,** dust of ages, rust or cobwebs of antiquity; venerableness, eldership, primogeniture, great or hoary age, "the ancient and honourable" [Bible], inveteracy; old order, old style, ancien régime [Fr]; **primitiveness,** primordialism or primordiality, aboriginality; atavism.

.2 **tradition, custom,** common law, **immemorial usage;** Sunna [Muslim]; Talmud, Mishnah [both Jewish]; ancient wisdom, ways of the fathers; traditionalism or traditionality; myth, mythology, legend, lore, folklore, folktale, folk motif; racial memory, archetypal myth or image or pattern, "Spiritus Mundi" [Yeats].

.3 **antiquation, superannuation,** staleness, disuse; **old-fashionedness,** unfashionableness, out-of-dateness; **old-fogyishness,** fogyishness, stuffiness, stodginess, fuddy-duddiness.

.4 **antiquarianism;** classicism, medievalism, Pre-Raphaelitism, longing or yearning or nostalgia for the past; **archaeology** 123.22; archaism.

.5 **antiquarian, antiquary,** laudator temporis acti [L], dryasdust, the Rev. Dr. Dryasdust, Jonathan Oldbuck [both Sir Walter Scott], Herr Teufelsdröckh [Carlyle]; **archaeologist** 123.23; classicist, medievalist, Miniver Cheevy [E. A. Robinson], Pre-Raphaelite; antique dealer, antique collector, antique-car collector; archaist.

.6 **antiquity, antique,** archaism; **relic,** relic of the past, reliquiae [pl]; **remains,** survival, vestige, ruin or ruins; **fossil,** –ite, necr(o)–, oryct(o)–; petrification, petrified wood, petrified forest; **artifact,** eolith, mezzolith, microlith, neolith, paleolith, plateaulith; cave painting, petroglyph; ancient manuscript 602.11.

.7 **ancient,** man of old, **prehistoric man** 123.25; preadamite, antediluvian; anthropoid, humanoid, primate, fossil man, protohuman, prehuman, missing link, apeman, hominid, Hominidae [pl]; **primitive, aboriginal,** aborigine, bushman, autochthon; **caveman,** cave dweller, troglodyte; Stone Age man, Bronze Age man, Iron Age man.

.8 (antiquated person) back number [informal]; pop or pops or dad [all informal], dodo or old dodo [both informal]; fossil or antique or relic [all informal]; mossback [informal], longhair or square [both informal], mid-Victorian, antediluvian; old liner, old believer, conservative, traditionalist, reactionary; has-been; fogy, old fogy, regular old fogy, old poop or crock [informal], fud or fuddy-duddy [both informal]; granny [informal], old woman, matriarch; old man, patriarch, elder, starets [Russ], old-timer [informal], Methuselah.

.9 VERBS age, grow old 126.10; antiquate, fossilize, date, superannuate, outdate; obsolesce, go out of use or style, molder, fust, rust, fade, perish, lose currency or novelty; become obsolete or extinct; belong to the past, be a thing of the past.

.10 ADJS old, age-old, auld [Scot], olden [archaic], old-time; ancient, antique, venerable, hoary; archae(o)– or archeo–, eo–, pale(o)–, proto–; of old, of yore; dateless, timeless, ageless; immemorial, old as Methuselah or Adam, old as history, old as time, old as the hills; elderly 126.16.

.11 primitive, prime, primeval, primogenial, primordial, pristine, atavistic; aboriginal, autochthonous; primoprimitive; ancestral, patriarchal; prehistoric, protohistoric, preglacial, preadamite, antepatriarchal; prehuman, protohuman, humanoid.

.12 traditional; mythological, heroic; legendary, unwritten, oral, handed down; true-blue, tried and true; prescriptive, customary, conventional, understood, admitted, recognized, acknowledged, received; hallowed, time-honored, immemorial; venerable, hoary, worshipful; long-standing, of long standing, long-established, established, fixed, inveterate, rooted; folk, of the folk.

.13 antiquated, grown old, superannuated, antique, archaic, age-encrusted, of other times, old-world; Victorian, mid-Victorian; classical, medieval, Gothic; antediluvian; fossil, fossilized, petrified.

.14 stale, fusty, musty, rusty, dusty, moldy, mildewed; worn, timeworn, time-scarred; moth-eaten, moss-grown, crumbling, moldering, gone to seed, dilapidated, ruined, ruinous.

.15 obsolete, passé, extinct, gone out, dated, out, out of style or use, gone-by, dead, disused, past, run out, outworn.

.16 old-fashioned, oldfangled, old-timey [informal], out-of-date, dated, outdated, outmoded, out of fashion, out of season, unfashionable, styleless, behind the times, of the old school, old hat [infor-

mal], back-number [informal], black-letter, has-been [informal].

.17 old-fogyish, fogyish, old-fogy; fuddy-duddy, stuffy, stodgy; senile, bent or wracked or ravaged with age.

.18 secondhand, used, worn, unnew, not new, pawed-over; hand-me-down or reach-me-down [both informal].

.19 older, senior, Sr., major, elder; oldest, eldest; first-born, firstling, primogenitary; former 119.10.

.20 archaeological, paleological; antiquarian; paleolithic, eolithic, neolithic, mezzolithic.

.21 ADVS anciently 119.16.

.22 archaeology

| | |
|---|---|
| Assyriology | paleohistology |
| Egyptology | paleohydrography |
| epigraphy | paleolatry |
| fossilology | paleolimnology |
| human paleontology | paleolithy |
| micropaleontology | paleology |
| palaeography | paleomammology |
| palaeosophy | paleometeorology |
| palaeotypography | paleontography |
| palaetiology | paleontology |
| paleethnology | paleopathology |
| paleoanthropography | paleophysiography |
| paleoanthropology | paleophysiology |
| paleobiogeography | paleophytology |
| paleobiology | paleopotamology |
| paleobotany | paleopsychology |
| paleochorology | paleornithology |
| paleoclimatology | paleozoology |
| paleocosmology | prehistoric anthropol- |
| paleodendrology | ogy |
| paleoecology | prehistoric archaeol- |
| paleoeremology | ogy |
| paleoethnography | prehistory |
| paleoethnology | protohistory |
| paleogeography | Sumerology |
| paleoglaciology | underwater archaeol- |
| paleography | ogy |
| paleoherpetology | |

.23 archaeologists

| | |
|---|---|
| Assyriologist | paleographer, pale- |
| Egyptologist | ographist |
| epigrapher, epigra- | paleoherpetologist |
| phist | paleolithist |
| fossilologist | paleologist |
| palaeotypographist | paleomammologist |
| palaetiologist | paleometeorologist |
| paleethnographer | paleontologist |
| paleethnologist | paleophysiologist |
| paleoanthropologist | paleophytologist |
| paleobiologist | paleornithologist |
| paleobotanist | paleozoologist |
| paleochorologist | prehistorian |
| paleoclimatologist | protohistorian |
| paleodentrologist | Sumerologist |
| paleoecologist | underwater archaeolo- |
| paleoethnologist | gist |
| paleoglaciologist | |

.24 Stone Age cultures

| | |
|---|---|
| Acheulean | Azilian |
| Aurignacian | Chellean |

Combe-Capelle · Neolithic
Cro-Magnon · Paleolithic
Eolithic · Pre-Chellean
Magdalenian · Solutrean
Mousterian

**.25 prehistoric men and manlike primates**

Aurignacian man · Java man
Australanthropus · Meganthropus
Australopithecus · Neanderthal man
Brünn race · neolithic man
caveman · Oreopithecus
Cro-Magnon man · paleolithic man
Dawn man (the Pilt- · Paranthropus
  down hoax) · Peking man
eolithic man · Piltdown man (hoax)
Florisbad man · Pithecanthropus
Furfooz or Grenelle · Plesianthropus
  man · Rhodesian man
Galley Hill man · Sinanthropus
Gigantopithecus · Stone Age man
Grimaldi man · Swanscombe man
Heidelberg man · Zinjanthropus

**.26 prehistoric animals (including types of dinosaurs)**

allosaur(us) · hesperornis
ammonite · hoplophoneus
anatosaur(us) · hyaenodon
ankylosaur(us) · hyracodont
apatosaur(us) · hyracothere
archaeohippus · ichthyornis
archaeopteryx · ichthyosaur(us)
archaeornis · iguanodon(t)
archaeotherium · imperial mammoth or
archelon ·   elephant
arthrodiran · labyrinthodont
atlantosaur(us) · machairodont
aurochs · mammoth
bothriolepis · mastodon
brachiosaur(us) · megalosaur(us)
brontops · megathere
brontosaur(us) · merodus
brontothere · merychippus
camarasaur(us) · merycoidodon
ceratopsid · merycopotamus
ceratosaur(us) · mesohippus
cetiosaur(us) · miacis
coccostean · mosasaurus
coelodont · nummulite
compsognathus · ornithomimid
coryphodon · ornithopod
cotylosaur · ostracoderm
creodont · palaeodictyopteron
crossopterygian · palaeomastodon
cynodictis · palaeoniscid
diatryma · palaeophis
dimetrodon · palaeosaur
dinichthyid · palaeospondylus
dinothere · pelycosaur
diplodocus · phytosaur
dipnoan · plesiosaur(us)
duck-billed dinosaur · protoceratops
edaphosaurid · protohippus
elasmosaur(us) · protylopus
eohippus · pteranodon
eryopsid · pteraspid
eurypterid · pterichthys
giant sloth · pterodactyl, pterosaur
glyptodont · rhamphorhynchus
gorgosaur(us) · saber-toothed tiger or
hadrosaur(us) ·   cat

sauropod · titanosaur(us)
scelidosaur(us) · titanothere
smilodon · trachodon
stegocephalian · triceratops
stegodon · trilobite
stegosaur(us) · tyrannosaur(us)
struthiomimus · uintathere
teleoceras · urus
therapsid · woolly or northern
theriodont ·   mammoth
theropod

# 124. YOUTH

**.1** NOUNS **youth,** youthhood, youthhead [Scot], **youthfulness,** youthiness [Scot], **juvenility,** juvenescence, **youngness,** tenderness, tender age, early years, school age, *jeunesse* [Fr], prime of life, flower of life, salad days, springtime *or* springtide of life, seedtime of life, flowering time, bloom, florescence, budtime, "the very May-morn of his youth" [Shakespeare], "the summer of your youth" [Edward Moore], "the red sweet wine of youth" [Rupert Brooke], golden season of life, "the glad season of life" [Carlyle], heyday of youth *or* of the blood, young blood, "my burning youth" [Yeats], "my green age" [Dylan Thomas].

**.2 childhood,** "childhood's careless days" [William Cullen Bryant]; **boyhood; girlhood,** maidenhood *or* maidenhead; puppyhood, calfhood; subteens, pre-teens.

**.3 immaturity, undevelopment,** inexperience, **callowness, unripeness,** greenness, rawness, sappiness, freshness, juiciness, dewiness; **minority,** juniority, infancy, nonage.

**.4 childishness,** childlikeness, **puerility; boyishness,** boylikeness; **girlishness,** girllikeness, maidenliness.

**.5 infancy, babyhood,** incunabula, the cradle, the nursery, "my Angel-infancy" [Henry Vaughn].

**.6 adolescence,** maturescence, pubescence, **puberty;** nubility.

**.7 teens,** teen age, **awkward age,** age of growing pains [informal].

**.8** VERBS make young, youthen; **rejuvenate,** reinvigorate.

**.9** ADJS **young,** youngling, **juvenile,** juvenal, juvenescent, **youthful,** youthy [Scot], youthlike, in the flower *or* bloom of youth, florescent, flowering; "towering in confidence of twenty one" [Samuel Johnson].

**.10 immature,** unadult, impubic, inexperienced; **unseasoned, unfledged,** newfledged, **callow, unripe,** ripening, unmellowed, **raw, green,** vernal, primaveral, dewy, juicy, sappy, budding, tender, virginal, intact, innocent, naïve, ingenuous, **undeveloped,** growing, unformed, unlicked, not dry behind the ears; **minor,** underage.

.11 **childish,** childlike, kiddish [informal], **puerile; boyish,** boylike, beardless; **girlish,** girllike, maiden, maidenly; puppyish, puppylike, puplike, calflike, coltish, coltlike.

.12 **infant,** infantine, **infantile; babyish,** babish, baby; dollish, doll-like; kittenish, kittenlike; **newborn,** neonatal; in the cradle *or* crib *or* nursery, in swaddling clothes, in diapers, in nappies [Brit], in arms, at the breast.

.13 **adolescent,** maturescent, pubescent, hebe–; nubile.

.14 **teen-age,** teen-aged, teenish, **in one's teens;** sweet sixteen [slang].

.15 **junior,** Jr.; **younger,** puisne.

.16 PHRS "Young men are fitter to invent than to judge" [Francis Bacon]; "To be young is to be one of the Immortals" [W. C. Hazlitt], "To be young was very Heaven!" [Wordsworth].

## 125. YOUNGSTER

.1 NOUNS **youngster,** young person, **youth, juvenile,** youngling, young'un [dial], juvenal [archaic]; **stripling,** slip, sprig, sapling; fledgling; hopeful, young hopeful; **minor,** infant; **adolescent,** pubescent; **teenager,** teener, teenybopper [informal]; junior, younger, youngest, baby; –ling.

.2 **young people, youth,** young, **younger generation,** rising *or* new generation, young blood, young fry [informal], *ragazze* [Ital]; **children,** tots, childkind; small fry, **kids, little kids,** little guys [all informal]; boyhood, girlhood; babyhood.

.3 **child,** ped(o)– *or* paed(o)–, bairn [Scot]; nipper, kid [informal], **little one,** little fellow *or* guy, little bugger [slang], shaver *or* little shaver [both informal], little squirt [slang], **tot, little tot,** wee tot, peewee, tad *or* little tad, mite, chit [informal]; innocent, little innocent; darling, cherub, lamb, lambkin, kitten, **offspring** 171.3.

.4 **brat,** urchin; **minx, imp,** puck, elf, gamin, little monkey, **whippersnapper,** young whippersnapper, *enfant terrible* [Fr], little terror, holy terror; spoiled brat; snotnose kid [slang]; juvenile delinquent, JD [slang], punk, punk kid [both slang].

.5 **boy, lad,** laddie, **youth,** manchild, young man, *garçon* [Fr], *muchacho* [Sp], fledgling, hobbledehoy; fellow 420.5; pup, puppy, whelp, cub, colt; master; sonny, sonny boy; bud *or* buddy [both informal]; bub *or* bubba [both informal]; buck, young buck; schoolboy.

.6 **girl,** girlie [informal], **maid, maiden, lass,** girlchild, **lassie,** young thing, young creature, **damsel,** damoiselle, demoiselle, *jeune fille* [Fr], *mademoiselle* [Fr], *muchacha* [Sp], miss, missy, little missy, slip, wench [dial *or* slang], colleen; gal, dame, **chick,** tomato, **babe** *or* baby, **broad,** frail, **doll,** skirt, jill, cutie, filly, heifer [all slang]; **schoolgirl,** schoolmaid, schoolmiss, junior miss, subteen, subteener; subdébutante, subdeb [informal]; bobbysoxer [informal], teenybopper [informal], **tomboy,** hoyden, romp; piece [slang], nymphet; virgin.

.7 **infant, baby, babe,** *bambino* [Ital], little darling *or* angel *or* doll *or* cherub, bouncing baby, puling infant, mewling infant, babykins [informal], baby bunting; papoose; **toddler; suckling,** nursling, fosterling, weanling; neonate; yearling, yearold; premature baby, preemie [informal], incubator baby; preschooler.

.8 (animals) **fledgling,** birdling, nestling; **chick,** chicky, chickling; **pullet,** fryer; **duckling;** gosling; **kitten,** kit, catling; **pup,** puppy, whelp; **cub; calf,** dogie, weaner; **colt,** foal; piglet, pigling, shoat; **lamb,** lambkin; **kid,** yeanling; fawn; **tadpole,** polliwog; litter, nest 171.2.

.9 (plants) **sprout, seedling,** set; sucker, shoot, slip; **twig,** sprig, scion, sapling.

.10 (insects) **larva, chrysalis,** aurelia, **cocoon,** pupa; nymph, nympha; wriggler, wiggler; caterpillar, maggot, grub.

## 126. AGE

*(time of life)*

.1 NOUNS **age,** years, "the days of our years", "measure of my days" [both Bible], "slow-consuming age" [Thomas Gray], "a tyrant, which forbids the pleasures of youth on pain of death" [La Rochefoucauld].

.2 **maturity, adulthood, majority,** adultness, grown-upness, fullgrownness, mature age, legal age, voting age, driving age, drinking age, *legalis homo* [L]; age of consent; ripe age, riper years, full age *or* growth *or* bloom, flower of age, prime, prime of life, age of responsibility, age *or* years of discretion, age of matured powers; **manhood,** man's estate, virility, *toga virilis*

[L], manlihood; **womanhood,** womanlihood.

.3 **seniority, eldership,** deanship, primogeniture.

.4 **middle age,** middle life, meridian of life, the middle years, the wrong side of forty, the dangerous age.

.5 **old age, oldness,** eld [archaic], **elderliness,** senectitude, advanced age or years; geront(o)–, presby(o)–; superannuation, pensionable age, age of retirement; **ripe old age,** the golden years, senior citizenship, hoary age, gray or white hairs, vale of years, crabbed age, "an incurable disease" [Seneca]; **decline of life,** declining years, "the downward slope" [Seneca], the shady side [informal]; "the sere, the yellow leaf", "the silver livery of advised age" [both Shakespeare], "a crown of glory" [Bible]; sunset or twilight or evening or autumn or winter of one's days; **decrepitude,** ricketiness, infirm old age, infirmity of age, infirmity, debility, caducity, feebleness; dotage, second childhood; senility 469.10, anility; green or hale old age, longevity.

.6 **maturation,** maturescence, **development,** mellowing, ripening, seasoning, tempering; **aging,** senescence.

.7 **change of life, menopause,** climacteric, grand climacteric.

.8 **geriatrics,** gerontology.

.9 VERBS **mature, grow up,** grow, **develop, ripen,** mellow, season, temper; flower, bloom; fledge, leave the nest, **come of age,** come to maturity, attain majority, **reach one's majority,** reach twenty-one, reach voting age, reach the age of consent, reach manhood or womanhood, write oneself a man, come to or into man's estate, put on long trousers or pants, assume the *toga virilis,* come into years of discretion, be in the prime of life, cut one's wisdom teeth or eyeteeth [informal], have sown one's wild oats, settle down; put up one's hair, not be in pigtails.

.10 **age, grow old,** get on or along, get on or along in years, turn gray or white; **decline,** wane, fade, fail, sink, waste away; **dodder,** totter, shake; wither, wrinkle, shrivel, wizen; **live to a ripe old age,** cheat the undertaker [informal]; be in one's dotage or second childhood.

.11 **have had one's day,** have seen one's day or best days, **have seen better days; show one's age,** show marks of age, have one foot in the grave.

.12 ADJS **adult, mature,** old, **of age,** out of one's teens, big, grown, **grown-up;** old enough to know better; **marriageable,** of marriageable age, marriable, nubile; maturescent.

.13 **mature, ripe,** of full or ripe age, **developed,** fully developed, **full-grown,** full-fledged, full-blown, in full bloom, in one's prime; **mellow** or mellowed, seasoned, tempered, aged.

.14 **middle-aged,** mid-life, *entre deux âges* [Fr], fortyish, matronly.

.15 **past one's prime,** on the shady side [informal], overblown, overripe, of a certain age, over the hill [informal]; "fall'n into the sere, the yellow leaf" [Shakespeare].

.16 **aged, elderly,** old, grown old, in years, **along in years,** years old, advanced, advanced in life or years, **at an advanced age, ancient,** senectuous, **venerable,** old as Methuselah or as the hills; patriarchal; hoary, hoar, **gray,** white, gray- or white-headed, gray- or white-haired, gray- or white-crowned, gray- or white-bearded, gray or white with age; wrinkled; wrinkly, with crow's feet, marked with the crow's foot.

.17 **aging,** growing old, senescent, **getting on** or **along,** getting on or along in years, not as young as one used to be, long in the tooth; **declining,** sinking, waning, fading, wasting, doting.

.18 **stricken in years, decrepit, infirm,** weak, debilitated, feeble, gerontic or gerontal, timeworn, the worse for wear, rusty, moth-eaten or mossbacked [slang], fossilized, wracked or ravaged with age, run to seed; **doddering,** doddery, doddered, tottering, tottery, rickety, shaky, palsied; on one's last legs, with one foot in the grave; **wizened,** crabbed, **withered,** shriveled, like a prune, mummylike, papery-skinned; **senile** 469.23, anile.

## 127. ADULT OR OLD PERSON

.1 NOUNS **adult, grownup,** mature man or woman, grown man or woman, no chicken [informal]; **man, woman;** major, *legalis homo* [L].

.2 **old man, elder,** presbyter [eccl], older, **oldster** [informal]; golden-ager, senior citizen; old chap, old party, **old gentleman,** old gent [informal], old codger [informal], geezer or old geezer [both slang], gramps [slang], gaffer, old duffer [informal], old dog [informal], old-timer [informal], dotard, veteran, pantaloon; **patriarch,** graybeard, reverend or venerable sir;

grandfather 170.11, grandsire; Father Time, Methuselah, Nestor, Old Paar; sexagenarian, septuagenarian, octogenarian, nonagenarian, centenarian; "the quiet-voiced elders" [T. S. Eliot], "a paltry thing, a tattered coat upon a stick" [Yeats].

.3 **old woman, old lady,** dowager, granny, old granny, dame, **grandam,** grammer [Brit dial], trot or old trot [both dial]; old dame or hen or bag or girl [slang]; old battle-ax [slang], war-horse [informal]; **crone,** hag, witch, beldam, frump [informal], old wife; grandmother 170.12.

.4 (elderly couples) Darby and Joan, Baucis and Philemon.

.5 **senior,** Sr., *senex* [L], **elder,** older; dean, *doyen* [Fr], *doyenne* [Fr]; father, sire; firstling, first-born, **eldest,** oldest.

.6 VERBS mature 126.9; grow old 126.10.

.7 ADJS mature 126.12; middle-aged 126.14; aged 126.16, older 123.19.

## 128. SEASON

### (time of year)

.1 NOUNS **season,** time of year, season of the year, "the measure of the year" [Keats], **period,** annual period; dry or rainy or cold season, dead or off season; theatrical or opera or concert season; **social season,** the season; baseball season, football season, basketball season, etc.; seasonality, periodicity 137.2; **seasonableness** 129.1.

.2 **spring,** springtide, **springtime,** seedtime or budtime, Maytime, Eastertide; *primavera* [Ital], prime, prime of the year, "the boyhood of the year" [Tennyson], "Sweet Spring, full of sweet days and roses" [George Herbert], "Daughter of heaven and earth, coy Spring" [Emerson], "the time of the singing of birds" [Bible], "when the hounds of spring are on winter's traces" [Swinburne].

.3 **summer,** summertide, **summertime,** good old summertime; growing season; midsummer; **dog days,** canicular days.

.4 **autumn, fall,** fall of the year, fall of the leaf, harvest, harvest time, harvest home; "Season of mists and mellow fruitfulness!" [Keats].

.5 **Indian summer,** St. Martin's summer, St. Luke's summer, little summer of St. Luke, St. Austin's or St. Augustine's summer, "the dead Summer's soul" [Mary Clemmer].

.6 **winter,** wintertide, **wintertime,** "ruler of th' inverted year" [William Cowper];

midwinter; Christmastime or Christmastide, Yule or Yuletide.

.7 **equinox,** vernal equinox, autumnal equinox; **solstice,** summer solstice, winter solstice.

.8 ADJS **seasonal,** in or out of season, in season and out of season; **spring,** springlike, vernal; **summer,** summery, summerly, summerlike, canicular, aestival; midsummer; **autumn,** autumnal; **winter,** wintry, wintery, hibernal, hiemal, brumal, boreal, arctic 333.14, winterlike; midwinter; equinoctial, solstitial.

## 129. TIMELINESS

.1 NOUNS **timeliness, seasonableness, opportuneness,** convenience; **expedience,** meetness, fittingness, fitness, appropriateness, rightness, propriety, suitability; **favorableness, propitiousness,** auspiciousness, felicitousness; **ripeness,** pregnancy, crucialness, criticality, loadedness, chargedness.

.2 **opportunity, chance, time, occasion;** opening, room, scope, place, liberty; clear stage, fair field, fair game; opportunism; a leg up, stepping-stone, rung of the ladder; time's forelock.

.3 **good opportunity, good chance,** favorable opportunity, golden opportunity, well-timed opportunity; suitable occasion, proper occasion, suitable or proper time, **good time,** high time, due season; well-chosen moment.

.4 **crisis, critical point,** crunch, crucial period, climacteric; **turning point,** hinge, turn, turn of the tide; **emergency, exigency,** juncture or conjuncture or convergence of events, critical juncture, crossroads; **pinch,** clutch [informal], rub, push, pass, strait, extremity.

.5 **crucial moment,** critical moment, loaded or charged moment, decisive moment, kairotic moment, kairos, pregnant moment, moment of truth; **psychological moment;** nick of time, eleventh hour; **zero hour,** H hour, D day, A-day, target date, deadline.

.6 VERBS **be timely,** suit or befit the time or season or occasion.

.7 **take the opportunity,** use the occasion, take the chance; take the bit in the teeth, leap into the breach, take the bull by the horns, **make one's move,** cross the Rubicon, *prendre la balle au bond* [Fr, take the ball on the rebound]; **commit oneself,** make an opening, drive an entering wedge.

.8 **improve the occasion,** "improve each

shining hour" [Isaac Watts], turn to account or good account, avail oneself of, **take advantage of,** put to advantage, profit by, **cash in** or **capitalize on;** take time by the forelock, seize the present hour, seize the day, *carpe diem* [L; Horace], make hay while the sun shines; strike while the iron is hot; not be caught flatfooted, not be behindhand.

.9 ADJS **timely, well-timed, seasonable, opportune,** convenient; **expedient,** meet, fit, fitting, befitting, suitable, sortable, appropriate; **favorable,** propitious, ripe, auspicious, lucky, providential, fortunate, happy, felicitous.

.10 **critical, crucial,** pivotal, climacteric(al), decisive; **pregnant,** kairotic, loaded, charged; exigent, emergent.

.11 **incidental, occasional, casual,** accidental; parenthetical, by-the-way.

.12 ADVS **opportunely, seasonably, propitiously,** auspiciously, in proper time or season, in due time or course or season, in the fullness of time, **in good time,** all in good time; in the nick of time, just in time, at the eleventh hour; now or never.

.13 **incidentally, by the way, by the by; while on the subject,** speaking of, *à propos* [Fr], apropos or apropos of; **in passing,** *en passant* [Fr]; parenthetically, by way of parenthesis, *par parenthèse* [Fr]; for example, *par exemple* [Fr].

## 130. UNTIMELINESS

.1 NOUNS **untimeliness, unseasonableness,** inopportuneness, inopportunity, unripeness, inconvenience, intempestivity; **inexpedience,** inappropriateness, irrelevance, impropriety, unfitness, unfittingness, wrongness, unsuitability; **unfavorableness,** unfortunateness, inauspiciousness, unpropitiousness, infelicity; **intrusion,** interruption; **prematurity** 131.2; **lateness** 132, thinking of it later, *esprit d'escalier* [Fr].

.2 **wrong time, bad time,** unsuitable time, unfortunate time, poor timing; evil hour, unlucky day or hour, off-year, contretemps.

.3 VERBS **not have time,** have other or better things to do, be otherwise occupied, be engaged, be preoccupied, have other fish to fry [informal].

.4 **ill-time,** mistime.

.5 **talk out of turn,** speak inopportunely, interrupt, **put one's foot in one's mouth** [informal], intrude, butt in [informal], **go off half-cocked** [informal], open one's big mouth or big fat mouth [slang], blow it [slang], speak too late or too soon.

.6 **miss an opportunity, miss the chance, miss the boat,** lose the opportunity, ignore opportunity's knock, lose the chance, blow the chance [slang], throw away or waste or neglect the opportunity, allow the occasion to go by, let slip through one's fingers, be left at the starting gate or post, oversleep, lock the barn door after the horse is stolen.

.7 ADJS **untimely, unseasonable, inopportune,** intempestive, **ill-timed,** ill-seasoned, mistimed, unripe, unready, ill-considered, too late or soon, out of phase or time; inconvenient, unhandy; **inappropriate,** irrelevant, improper, unfit, wrong, out of line, off base, unsuitable, **inexpedient,** unfitting, unbefitting, untoward, malapropos, *mal à propos* [Fr], intrusive; **unfavorable,** unfortunate, infelicitous, inauspicious, unpropitious, unhappy, unlucky; **premature** 131.8; **late** 132.16.

.8 ADVS **inopportunely, unseasonably,** inconveniently, inexpediently; **unpropitiously,** inauspiciously, unfortunately, in an evil hour, at just the wrong time.

## 131. EARLINESS

.1 NOUNS **earliness,** early hour, time to spare; head start, running start, ground floor, first crack, beginnings, first or early stage, very beginning; **anticipation, foresight,** prevision, prevenience; a stitch in time, readiness.

.2 **prematurity, prematureness; untimeliness** 130; precocity, **precociousness,** forwardness; precipitation, haste, hastiness, **overhastiness,** rush, impulse, impulsiveness.

.3 **promptness, promptitude, punctuality,** punctualness, readiness; instantaneousness 113, immediateness or immediacy, summariness, decisiveness, **alacrity, quickness** 269.1, speediness, swiftness, rapidity, expeditiousness, expedition, dispatch.

.4 **early bird** [informal], early riser, early comer, first arrival; **precursor** 66.

.5 VERBS **be early,** be ahead of time, take time by the forelock, be up and stirring, be beforehand or betimes, be ready and waiting, be off and running; gain time, draw on futurity or on the future.

.6 **anticipate, foresee,** foreglimpse, foretaste; **forestall,** forerun, go before, **get ahead of,** win the start, get a head start, steal a march on; **jump the gun,** go off half-cocked [informal]; take the words out of one's mouth.

.7 ADJS **early**, bright and early [informal], **beforetime**, in good time *or* season; **forehand**, forehanded; foresighted, **anticipative** *or* **anticipatory**, prevenient; fore–.

.8 **premature, too early, too soon**, oversoon; previous *or* a bit previous [both informal]; **untimely** 130.7; **precipitate**, hasty 113.5, **overhasty**, too soon off the mark, **unprepared**, unripe, impulsive, rushed, unmatured; unpremeditated, unmeditated, ill-considered, **half-cocked** *or* **halfbaked** [both informal], unjelled, uncrystallized, not firm; **precocious, forward, advanced**, far ahead, born before one's time.

.9 **prompt, punctual, immediate, instant**, instantaneous 113.4, **quick** 269.19, speedy, swift, expeditious, summary, decisive, apt, alert, **ready**, Johnny on the spot [informal].

.10 **earlier**, previous 116.4.

.11 ADVS **early, beforehand, beforetime**, betimes, precociously, **ahead of time**, foresightedly, in advance, in anticipation, ahead, before, **with time to spare**.

.12 **in time, in good time, soon enough**, time enough, early enough; just in time, **in the nick of time**, with no time to spare, just under the wire, without a minute to spare.

.13 **prematurely, too soon, oversoon**, untimely, too early, before its *or* one's time; **precipitately**, impulsively, in a rush, hastily, **overhastily**; at half cock [informal].

.14 **punctually, precisely**, exactly, sharp; **on time**, on the minute *or* instant, to the minute *or* second, **on the dot** [informal], at the gun.

.15 **promptly, without delay**, without further delay, directly, **immediately**, immediately if not sooner [informal], **instantly** 113.6, instanter, on the instant, on the spot, **at once**, right off, **right away, straightway**, straightaway, forthwith, *pronto* [Sp], *subito* [Ital], PDQ *or* pretty damned quick [both slang], **quickly** 269.21–23, swiftly, speedily, with all speed, **summarily**, decisively, smartly, expeditiously, apace, in no time, in less than no time; no sooner said than done.

.16 **soon, presently, directly, shortly**, in a short time *or* while, **before long**, ere long, in no long time, in a while, **in a little while, after a while**, by and by, anon, betimes, *bientôt* [Fr], in due time, in due course, at the first opportunity; in a moment *or* minute, *tout à l'heure* [Fr].

## 132. LATENESS

.1 NOUNS **lateness, tardiness, belatedness, unpunctuality**; late hour, small hours; eleventh hour, last minute, high time; unreadiness, unpreparedness; untimeliness 130.

.2 **delay**, delayage, stoppage, jam *or* logjam [both informal], obstruction, tie-up [informal], bind [informal], **block**, blockage, **hang-up** [informal]; delayed reaction, double take, afterthought; **retardation** *or* retardance, slowdown *or* slow-up [both informal], slowness, lag, time lag, lagging, dragging; **detention**, suspension, holdup [informal], hindrance; **wait, halt, stay, stop**, pause, interim 109, respite; reprieve, stay of execution; moratorium; red tape, red-tapery, red-tapeism, bureaucratic delay, *paperasserie* [Fr].

.3 **waiting, tarrying, tarriance, lingering, dawdling**, dalliance, dallying, dillydallying.

.4 **postponement, deferment** *or* **deferral, prorogation**, putting-off, tabling; **prolongation**, protraction, continuation, extension of time; **adjournment** *or* adjournal.

.5 **procrastination**, hesitation 627.3; **temporization, a play for time**, stall [slang], mugwump, hold-off [informal]; Micawberism, Fabian policy; **dilatoriness**, slowness, backwardness, remissness, slackness, laxness.

.6 **latecomer**, late arrival; slow starter; late bloomer *or* developer; retardee; late riser.

.7 VERBS **be late, not be on time**, be overdue, be behindhand, show up late, miss the boat 130.6; keep everyone waiting; **stay late**, stay up late *or* into the small hours, burn the midnight oil, keep late hours; get up late, keep banker's hours; oversleep.

.8 **delay, retard, detain**, make late, slacken, lag, drag, slow down, **hold up** [informal], hold *or* keep back, check, **stay, stop**, arrest, impede, **block**, hinder, obstruct, confine; tie up with red tape.

.9 **postpone, delay, defer, put off**, stave off, shift off, hold off *or* up [informal], reserve, waive, **suspend**, hang up, stay, hang fire; protract, drag *or* stretch out [informal], **prolong, extend**, continue, adjourn, recess, take a recess, prorogue, prorogate; **hold over**, lay over, stand over, let the matter stand, **put aside**, lay *or* set *or* push aside, lay *or* set by, **table**, lay on the table, pigeonhole, **shelve**, put on the shelf put on ice [informal]; consult one's pillow about, sleep on.

.10 **be left behind,** be outrun *or* outdistanced, make a slow start, be slow *or* late *or* last off the mark, be left at the post *or* starting gate; bloom *or* develop late.

.11 **procrastinate,** be dilatory, hesitate, hang, hang back, hang fire; **temporize,** gain *or* make time, **play for time,** drag one's feet [informal], hold off [informal]; **stall,** stall off, **stall for time,** stall *or* stooge around [slang]; talk against time, filibuster.

.12 **wait, delay, stay,** bide, abide, **bide** *or* **abide one's time, take one's time,** take time, mark time; **tarry, linger, loiter,** dawdle, dally, dillydally; hang around *or* about [informal], stick around [slang]; **hold on** [informal], sit tight [informal], hold one's breath; wait a minute *or* second; hold everything *or* hold your horses *or* keep your shirt on [all slang]; wait *or* stay up, sit up; wait and see, bide the issue, see which way the cat jumps, see how the cookie crumbles [informal]; wait for something to turn up; **await** 539.8.

.13 **wait impatiently,** sweat it out [slang], champ *or* chomp at the bit [informal].

.14 **be kept waiting,** be stood up [slang], be left; **kick** *or* **cool one's heels** [informal].

.15 **overstay,** overtarry.

.16 ADJS **late, belated, tardy,** slow, **behindhand,** never on time, backward, back, **overdue; untimely** 130.7; **unpunctual,** unready; latish; **delayed,** detained, **held up** [informal], **retarded, arrested,** blocked, **hung up** *or* in a bind [both informal], obstructed, stopped, jammed [informal]; in abeyance; delayed-action; moratory.

.17 **dilatory, delaying,** Micawberish; slow *or* late *or* last off the mark; **procrastinating,** procrastinative, procrastinatory; **lingering,** loitering, lagging, dallying, dillydallying, slow, sluggish, laggard, foot-dragging, shuffling, backward; easygoing, lazy, **lackadaisical; remiss,** slack, lax.

.18 **later** 117.4; last-minute, **eleventh-hour,** deathbed.

.19 ADVS **late, behind, behindhand,** belatedly, backward, slow, **behind time,** after time; far on, deep into; late in the day, at the last minute, at the eleventh hour, none too soon, in the nick of time.

slow, slowly, deliberately, dilatorishly, lackadaisically, leisurely, leisure, lingeringly.

## 133. MORNING, NOON

.1 NOUNS **morning,** morn, morningtide, morning time, morntime, matins, waking time, **forenoon,** foreday; *ante meridiem* [L], **AM,** Ack Emma [Brit informal]; "dewy morn" [Byron], "incense-breathing morn" [Thomas Gray], "grey-eyed morn", "the morn, in russet mantle clad" [both Shakespeare], "rosy-finger'd morn" [Homer]; this morning, this AM [informal].

.2 **Morning,** Aurora, Eos; "daughter of the dawn" [Homer], "meek-eyed Morn, mother of dews" [James Thomson], "mild blushing goddess" [L. P. Smith].

.3 **dawn,** the dawn of day, dawning, **daybreak,** dayspring, day-peep, **sunrise, sunup** [informal], cockcrow(ing), cocklight [Brit dial], light 335, daylight, aurora; **break of day,** peep of day, **crack of dawn,** prime, prime of the morning, first blush *or* flush of the morning, brightening *or* first brightening; "the opening eyelids of the morn" [Milton], "vestibule of Day" [Bayard Taylor], "golden exhalations of the dawn" [Schiller]; chanticleer.

.4 **foredawn,** twilight, morning twilight, half-light, glow, dawnlight, first light, "the dawn's early light" [Francis Scott Key], crepuscule, aurora; **the small hours;** alpenglow.

.5 **noon, noonday,** noontide, nooning [dial], noontime, high noon, **midday,** meridian, *meridiem* [L], twelve o'clock, 1200 hours, eight bells, noonlight.

.6 ADJS **morning,** matin, matinal, matutinal, **antemeridian;** auroral, dawn, dawning.

.7 **noon, noonday,** noonish, **midday,** meridian, twelve-o'clock; noonlit.

.8 ADVS **in the morning,** before noon, mornings [informal]; at sunrise, at dawn, at dawn of day, at cockcrow, at first light, **at the crack of dawn;** with the sun, with the lark.

.9 at noon, at midday, at twelve-o'clock sharp.

## 134. EVENING, NIGHT

.1 NOUNS **afternoon,** *post meridiem* [L], **PM;** this afternoon, this aft [informal], this PM [informal].

.2 **evening,** eve, even, evensong, **eventide,** vesper; **close of day,** decline *or* fall of day, shut of day, gray of the evening, grayness 366, evening's close, when day is done; **nightfall, sunset, sundown,** setting sun, going down of the sun, cockshut

[dial]; shank of the afternoon or evening [informal], the cool of the evening; "the expiring day" [Dante], "evening's calm and holy hour" [S. G. Bulfinch], "the gray-hooded Ev'n" [Milton], "It is a beauteous evening, calm and free" [Wordsworth], "the pale child, Eve, leading her mother, Night" [Alexander Smith], "the evening is spread out against the sky / Like a patient etherized upon a table" [T. S. Eliot].

.3 **dusk**, duskingtide, dusk-down [dial], **twilight**, crepuscule, crepuscular light, gloam, **gloaming**, glooming; brown of dusk, brownness 367, candlelight, candle-lighting, owllight or owl's light, cocklight [Brit dial], "the pale dusk of the impending night" [Longfellow].

.4 **night, nighttime**, nighttide, **darkness** 337, blackness 365, "sable-vested Night, eldest of things" [Milton], "sable night", "dark-eyed night" [both Shakespeare], "cowlèd night" [Francis Thompson], "empress of silence, and the queen of sleep" [Christopher Marlowe]; dark of night, "the suit of night" [Shakespeare], "the mystic wine of Night" [Louis Untermeyer]; noct(o)– or nocti–, nyct(o)– or nycti–.

.5 eleventh hour, curfew, bedtime.

.6 **midnight, dead of night**, hush of night, witching hour of the night; "the very witching time of night" [Shakespeare], "noonday night", "outpost of advancing day" [both Longfellow].

.7 ADJS **afternoon**, postmeridian.

.8 **evening**, evensong, vesper, vespertine; **twilight**, twilighty, crepuscular; **dusk**, dusky; sunsetty.

.9 **nocturnal**, night, **nightly**, nighttime; nightlong, all-night; night-fallen; midnight.

.10 **benighted**, night-overtaken.

.11 ADVS **nightly**, nights [informal], at or by night; **overnight**, through the night, all through the night, nightlong, the whole night, all night.

## 135. FREQUENCY

.1 NOUNS **frequency**, frequence, **oftenness**; **commonness**, usualness, prevalence, **common occurrence**, routineness, habitualness; incidence, relative incidence.

.2 **constancy, continualness**, steadiness, sustainment, **regularity**, noninterruption or uninterruption, nonintermission or unintermission, incessancy, ceaselessness, constant flow, continuity 71; perpetuity 112; repetition 103; **rapidity** 269.1; rapid recur-

rence or succession, rapid or quick fire, tattoo, **staccato**, chattering, stuttering; pulsation, vibration, **oscillation** 323.

.3 VERBS be frequent, occur often, continue 71.4, recur 137.5, vibrate 323.10.

.4 ADJS **frequent**, oftentime, many, many times, **recurrent, oft-repeated**, thick-coming; **common**, of common occurrence, not rare, **prevalent**, usual, routine, habitual, ordinary, everyday; frequentative.

.5 **constant, continual** 71.8, **perennial**; steady, sustained, **regular; incessant**, ceaseless, unceasing, unintermitting, unintermittent or unintermitted, unremitting, unchanging, unvarying, uninterrupted, unstopped, unbroken; **perpetual** 112.7; repeated 103.12; **rapid** 269.19, **staccato**, stuttering, chattering, machine gun; pulsating, vibrating, **oscillating** 323.15.

.6 ADVS **frequently, commonly**, usually, ordinarily, routinely, habitually; **often**, oft, **oftentimes**, ofttimes; **repeatedly** 103.16, **again and again; most often** or frequently, in many instances, **many times**, many a time, full many a time, many a time and oft, as often as can be, as often as not; **in quick** or **rapid succession**; often enough, not infrequently, not seldom, unseldom; as often as you wish or like, whenever you wish or like.

.7 **constantly, continually** 71.10, **steadily**, sustainedly, **regularly**, right along [informal], unvaryingly, uninterruptedly, unintermittently, **incessantly**, unceasingly, **ceaselessly**, without cease or ceasing, perennially, at all times, ever, ever and anon, on and on, without letup or break or intermission, without stopping; **perpetually, always** 112.10–12; **rapidly** 269.21; every day, every hour, every moment; daily, hourly, daily and hourly; **night and day**, day and night; **morning, noon, and night**; hour after hour, day after day, month after month, year after year; **day in day out**, month in month out, year in year out.

## 136. INFREQUENCY

.1 NOUNS **infrequency**, infrequence, unfrequentness, **seldomness; occasionalness**; rarity, scarcity, **scarceness**, rareness, **uncommonness**, uniqueness, unusualness; sparsity 102.1; **slowness** 270.

.2 ADJS **infrequent**, unfrequent, **rare**, scarce, **uncommon**, unique, unusual, almost unheard-of, seldom met with, seldom seen, few and far between, **sparse** 102.5; **slow** 270.10.

.3 **occasional, casual, incidental; odd**, extra,

side, off, out-of-the-way, spare, spare-time, **part-time.**

**.4** ADVS **infrequently,** unfrequently, **seldom, rarely, uncommonly,** scarcely, hardly, scarcely *or* **hardly ever,** very seldom, not often, only now and then, at infrequent intervals, unoften; **sparsely** 102.8.

**.5 occasionally,** on occasion, **sometimes, at times,** at odd times, every so often [informal], at various times, on divers occasions, **now and then,** every now and then [informal], **once in a while,** every once in a while [informal], once and again, once or twice, betweentimes, betweenwhiles, at intervals, **from time to time;** only occasionally, only when the spirit moves, only when necessary, only now and then, at infrequent intervals, once in a blue moon *or* once in a coon's age [both informal].

**.6 once, one time,** on one occasion, just *or* only once, just this once, once and no more, once for all, once and for all *or* always.

## 137. REGULARITY OF RECURRENCE

**.1** NOUNS **regularity,** clockwork regularity, punctuality, smoothness, **steadiness, evenness, methodicalness,** systematicalness; **repetition** 103; **uniformity** 17; **constancy** 135.2.

**.2 periodicity,** periodicalness, piston motion, pendulum motion, regular wave motion, undulation, **pulsation; rhythm** 463.22, meter, beat; **oscillation** 323; **recurrence,** reoccurrence, reappearance, return, **cyclicalness,** seasonality; **intermittence** *or* intermittency, alternation.

**.3 round, revolution, rotation, cycle,** circle, wheel, **circuit; beat,** upbeat, downbeat, thesis, arsis, **pulse;** systole, diastole; course, series, **bout, turn,** spell 108.

**.4 anniversary, commemoration;** immovable feast, annual holiday; –ennial, biennial, triennial, quadrennial, quinquennial, sextennial, septennial, octennial, decennial, tricennial, jubilee, diamond jubilee; centennial, centenary; quasquicentennial; sesquicentennial; bicentennial, bicentenary; tercentennial, tercentenary; quincentennial, quincentenary; **wedding anniversary,** silver wedding anniversary, golden wedding anniversary; **birthday,** natal day; saint's day, name day; leap year, bissextile day; holy days 1040.15.

**.5** VERBS (occur periodically) **recur, reoccur, return, repeat** 103.7, reappear, **come again,** come up again, be here again,

**come round** *or* **around,** come round again, come in its turn; **rotate, revolve,** turn, circle, wheel, cycle, **roll around,** wheel around; **intermit,** alternate, **come and go;** undulate 323.11; **oscillate** 323.10, **pulse, pulsate** 323.12.

**.6** ADJS **regular, systematic(al), methodical,** ordered, orderly, regular as clockwork; **uniform** 17.5; **constant** 135.5.

**.7 periodic(al), seasonal,** epochal, **cyclic(al),** serial, isochronal, metronomic; measured, steady, even, **rhythmic(al)** 463.28; **recurrent,** recurring, reoccurring; **intermittent,** reciprocal, alternate, every other; circling, wheeling, rotary, wavelike, undulant, undulatory, oscillatory 323.15, pulsing, beating 323.18.

**.8 momentary,** momently, **hourly; daily,** diurnal, quotidian; **weekly,** tertian, hebdomadal, hebdomadary; biweekly, semiweekly; fortnightly; **monthly,** menstrual, catamenial; bimonthly, semimonthly; quarterly; biannual, semiannual, semiyearly, semestral; **yearly, annual;** biennial, triennial, decennial, etc.; centennial, centenary, secular.

**.9** ADVS **regularly, systematically, methodically,** like clockwork, at regular intervals, punctually, steadily; at stated times, at fixed *or* established periods; intermittently, every so often, every now and then; **uniformly** 17.7,8; **constantly** 135.7.

**.10 periodically, recurrently, seasonally,** cyclically, epochally; rhythmically, on the beat, in time, synchronously, **hourly, daily,** etc.; every hour, every day, etc.; hour by hour, day by day, etc.; from hour to hour, from day to day, *de die in diem* [L].

**.11 alternately, by turns, in turns, in rotation,** turn about, **turn and turn about,** reciprocally, every other, one after the other; to and fro, up and down, from side to side; off and on, make and break, round and round.

**.12 anniversaries, holidays**

| | |
|---|---|
| Admission Day [Ariz & Cal] | Day [Vt] |
| Alaska Day | Bill of Rights Day [US] |
| April Fools' *or* All Fools' Day | Bird Day [US] |
| Arbor Day [US] | Boxing Day [England] |
| Armed Forces Day [US] | Bunker Hill Day [Boston] |
| Armistice Day [US] | *Cinco de Mayo* [Mexico Sp, Fifth of May] |
| Army Day [US] | Citizenship Day [US] |
| Bastille Day [France] | Colorado Day |
| Battle of New Orleans Day [La] | Columbus Day [US] |
| Bennington Battle | Confederate Memo- |

rial Day [US]
Constitution Day [US]
Davis' Birthday [US]
Decoration Day [US]
Defenders' Day [Md]
De Hostos' Birthday [Puerto Rico]
Dewali [India]
Discovery Day [Puerto Rico]
Dominion Day [Canada]
Double Ten [China]
Easter Monday [England]
Election Day [US]
Emancipation Day [Puerto Rico]
Empire Day [England]
Evacuation Day [Boston]
Father's Day [US]
Flag Day [US]
Forefathers' Day [New England]
Forrest's Birthday [Tenn]
Foundation Day [Canal Zone]
Fourth of July [US]
Groundhog Day [US]
Halifax Day [NC]
Halloween
Holi [India]
Ides of March
Inauguration Day [US]
Independence Day [US]
Jackson's Birthday [Tenn]
Kamehameha Day [Hawaii]
King's Birthday [England]
Kuhio Day [Hawaii]
Labor Day [US]
Lee-Jackson Day [Va]
Lee's Birthday [US]
Lenin Memorial Day [USSR]
Lincoln's Birthday [US]
Long's Birthday [La]
Loyalty Day [US]
Martin Luther King

Day [US]
Maryland Day
May Day
Mecklenburg Day [NC]
Memorial Day [US]
Midsummer Day
Mother's Day [US]
National Aviation Day [US]
Navy Day [US]
Nevada Day
New Year's Day
New Year's Eve
Orangemen's Day [N Ireland]
Pan American Day [US]
Pascua Florida Day [Fla]
Patriots' Day [Maine & Mass]
Peach Festival [Japan]
Pioneer Day [Utah]
Queen's Birthday [England]
Remembrance Day [Canada]
Rhode Island Independence Day
Roosevelt Day [Ky]
Sadie Hawkins Day [US]
Saint David's Day
Saint Patrick's Day
Saint Swithin's Day
Saint Valentine's Day
San Jacinto Day [Texas]
Seward's Day [Alaska]
Sovereign's Birthday [Canada]
State Day [US]
Tet [Vietnam]
Texas Independence Day
Thanksgiving [US]
United Nations Day
V-E Day
Veterans' Day [US]
Victoria Day [Canada]
Victory Day [RI]
V-J Day
Washington's Birthday [US]
West Virginia Day
Wyoming Day

## 138. IRREGULARITY OF RECURRENCE

.1 NOUNS **irregularity**, unmethodicalness, unsystematicness; **inconstancy**, **unevenness**, **unsteadiness**, uncertainty, desultoriness; **variability**, capriciousness, unpredictability, whimsicality, eccentricity, stagger, wobble, erraticness; roughness; **fitfulness**, **sporadicity** or sporadicness, spasticity, jerkiness, fits and starts, patchi-

ness, spottiness, choppiness, brokenness, disconnectedness, discontinuity 72; **intermittence**, **fluctuation**; nonuniformity 18; arrhythmia, fibrillation [both med].

.2 VERBS **intermit**, **fluctuate**, vary, lack regularity, go by fits and starts.

.3 ADJS **irregular**, unregular, unsystematic, unmethodical or immethodical; **inconstant**, **unsteady**, **uneven**, **unrhythmical**, unmetrical, rough, unequal, uncertain, unsettled; **variable**, deviative, heteroclite; **capricious**, **erratic**, eccentric, wobbly, wobbling, staggering, lurching, careening; **fitful**, **spasmodic**, spastic, spasmatic, spasmic, **jerky**, herky-jerky [slang], halting; **sporadic**, patchy, spotty, scrappy, snatchy, catchy, choppy, **broken**, **disconnected**, **discontinuous** 72.4; **nonuniform** 18.3; **intermittent**, intermitting, **desultory**, **fluctuating**, **wavering**, wandering, rambling, veering; flickering, guttering.

.4 ADVS **irregularly**, unsystematically, unmethodically; **inconstantly**, **unsteadily**, **unevenly**, unrhythmically, roughly, uncertainly; **variably**, capriciously, unpredictably, whimsically, eccentrically, wobblingly, lurchingly, erratically; **intermittently**, **disconnectedly**, **discontinuously** 72.5; **nonuniformly** 18.4; **brokenly**, **desultorily**, patchily, spottily, in spots, in snatches; **by fits and starts**, by fits, by jerks, by snatches, by catches; **fitfully**, **sporadically**, jerkily, spasmodically, haltingly; **off and on**, at irregular intervals, sometimes and sometimes not; when the mood strikes, when the spirit moves, at random.

## 139. CHANGE

.1 NOUNS **change**, **alteration**, **modification**; **variation**, variety, difference, diversity, diversification; **deviation**, diversion, **divergence**; **switch**, **turn**, turnabout, aboutface, **reversal**, flip-flop [informal]; apostasy, defection, change of heart; **shift**, transition, **modulation**, qualification; **conversion**, **renewal**, revival, revivification; remaking, reshaping, re-creation, redesign, restructuring, realignment, **adaptation**, **adjustment**, accommodation, fitting; **reform**, reformation, **improvement**, amelioration, melioration, mitigation, constructive change, **betterment**, change for the better; gradual change, **continuity** 71; **degeneration**, **deterioration**, worsening, degenerative change, change for the worse; sudden change, radical or violent or total change, catastrophic change, upheaval, overthrow, **revolution, break, break with the past, discontinuity** 72; changeableness 141; "the ever whirling wheels of Change" [Spenser], "Nature's mighty law" [Robert Burns], "a sea-change / Into something rich and strange" [Shakespeare], "the changes and chances of this mortal life" [Book of Common Prayer].

.2 **transformation,** transmogrification [informal]; **translation; metamorphosis,** metamorphism; **mutation,** transmutation, permutation, **mutant,** mutated form, sport; **transfiguration** or transfigurement; metastasis, metathesis, transposition, translocation, **displacement,** heterotopia; **transubstantiation,** consubstantiation; transanimation, transmigration, reincarnation, avatar, metempsychosis; metasomatism, metasomatosis; catalysis; metabolism, anabolism, catabolism; metagenesis; transformism; –morphosis, –ody, –tropy.

.3 **innovation, introduction,** discovery, invention; neologism, coinage; **breakthrough,** leap, new phase; **novelty** 122.2.

.4 **transformer,** transmogrifier [informal]; **innovator,** innovationist, introducer; precursor 66; **alterant,** alterer, alterative, **agent,** catalytic agent, catalyst, **leaven,** yeast, ferment; **modifier,** modificator.

.5 VERBS **be changed, change, undergo a change,** go through a change, be converted into, turn into 145.17; **alter,** mutate, modulate; **vary,** checker, diversify; **deviate, diverge,** turn, **shift,** veer, jibe, tack, chop, chop and change, swerve, warp; **revive,** be renewed; **improve,** ameliorate, meliorate, mitigate; **degenerate,** deteriorate, **worsen;** turn aside, take a turn, turn the corner, bottom out [informal]; come about, come round or around, haul around; flop, break.

.6 (make a change) **change, work a change, alter;** mutate; **modify;** adapt; modulate, accommodate, adjust, fit, **qualify; vary, diversify; convert, renew, revamp** [informal], **revive;** remake, reshape, re-create, redesign, **rebuild,** reconstruct, restructure; realign; refit; **reform, improve,** better, ameliorate, meliorate, mitigate; turn upside down, subvert, overthrow, break up, worsen, deform, denature; ring the changes; give a turn to, give a twist to, turn the tide, turn the tables, turn the scale or balance; shift the scene; shuffle the cards; turn over a new leaf; reverse oneself; –en, –ify or –fy, –ize or –ise.

.7 **transform, transfigure, transmute,** trans-

mogrify [informal]; **translate;** transubstantiate, metamorphose; metabolize.

.8 **innovate,** make innovations, invent, discover, **pioneer** 66.3, **revolutionize, introduce,** introduce new blood; neologize, coin.

.9 ADJS **changed, altered, modified,** qualified, **transformed,** transmuted, **metamorphosed;** translated, metastasized; deviant, mutant; divergent; **converted, renewed,** revived, **rebuilt; reformed,** improved, **better; degenerate, worse,** unmitigated; subversive, **revolutionary;** changeable 141.6,7.

.10 innovational, innovative.

.11 **metamorphic, metabolic,** anabolic, catabolic; metastatic, **catalytic;** blast(o)–, meta–, re–, trans–, trop(o)–; –tropic or –trophic.

## 140. PERMANENCE

.1 NOUNS **permanence** or permanency, **immutability, changelessness,** unchangingness, invariableness or invariability; **fixedness, constancy,** steadfastness, firmness, solidity, immovableness or immovability, persistence or persistency, **lastingness, abidingness, endurance,** duration, standing, long standing, inveteracy; **durableness,** durability 110; **perpetualness** 112.1; **stability** 142; **unchangeability** 142.4; **immobility,** stasis, frozenness, hardening, **rigidity; quiescence,** torpor.

.2 **maintenance, preservation** 701, **conservation.**

.3 **conservatism, conservativeness,** opposition or resistance to change, unprogressiveness, fogyism, backwardness, old-fashionedness, standpattism [informal], ultraconservatism; political conservatism, rightism 745.1; laissez-faireism 706.1; old school tie [Brit]; "adherence to the old and tried, against the new and untried" [Lincoln].

.4 **conservative,** conservatist; conservationist 701.4; ultraconservative, **diehard,** standpat or standpatter [both informal], **old fogy,** fogy, stick-in-the-mud [informal], mossback [informal], laudator temporis acti [L], **rightist,** right-winger 745.9, "the leftover progressive of an earlier generation" [Edmund Fuller]; old school.

.5 VERBS **remain, endure** 110.6, last, stay, persist, bide, abide, stand, hold, subsist; be ever the same.

.6 **be conservative,** oppose change, stand on ancient ways; **stand pat** or stand still [both informal]; **let things take their course,** leave things as they are, let be, let or leave alone, let well enough alone, do nothing; stop *or* turn back the clock.

.7 ADJS **permanent, changeless, unchanging, immutable,** unvarying, unshifting; **unchanged,** unvaried, **unaltered,** inviolate, undestroyed, intact; **constant, persistent,** sustained, fixed, firm, solid, steadfast, like the Rock of Gibraltar; unchecked, unfailing, unfading; **lasting, enduring,** abiding, remaining, staying, continuing; **durable** 110.10; **perpetual** 112.7; **stable** 142.12; **unchangeable** 142.17; **immobile, static,** stationary, frozen, rigid; **quiescent,** torpid.

.8 **conservative, preservative,** old-line, **die-hard,** standpat [informal], opposed to change; backward, old-fashioned, **unprogressive,** nonprogressive; ultraconservative, fogyish, **old-fogyish; right-wing** 745.17.

.9 ADVS **permanently,** abidingly, lastingly, steadfastly, unwaveringly, changelessly, unchangingly; enduringly, **perpetually,** invariably, **always** 112.10–12; statically, rigidly, inflexibly.

.10 *in statu quo* [L], as things are, **as is, as usual,** as per usual [informal]; at a stand *or* standstill, without a shadow of turning.

.11 PHRS *plus ça change, plus c'est la même chose* [Fr, the more it changes, the more it's the same thing].

## 141. CHANGEABLENESS

.1 NOUNS **changeableness,** changefulness, **changeability, alterability,** modifiability; **mutability,** permutability, impermanence, **transience,** transitoriness; mobility, movability, plasticity, malleability, rubberiness, fluidity; **resilience, adaptability,** adjustability, **flexibility,** suppleness; **nonuniformity** 18.

.2 **inconstancy, instability,** unstableness, **unsteadiness,** unsteadfastness, unfixedness, unsettledness; **uncertainty,** undependability, inconsistency, shiftiness, unreliability; **variability,** variation, variety, restlessness, deviability; unpredictability, irregularity 138.1; **desultoriness,** waywardness, wantonness; **erraticism, eccentricity;** freakishness, freakery; flightiness, impulsiveness, mercuriality, moodiness, whimsicality, **capriciousness, fickleness** 629.2,3.

.3 **fluctuation,** vicissitude, **variation, alternation,** oscillation, **vacillation,** pendulation; **wavering, shifting,** shuffling, teetering, tottering, seesawing, teeter-tottering.

.4 (comparisons) Proteus, kaleidoscope, chameleon, shifting sands, rolling stone, April showers, cloud shapes; water; wheel of fortune; whirligig; mercury, quicksilver; the weather, weathercock, weather vane; moon, phases of the moon.

.5 VERBS **fluctuate, vary, alternate, vacillate,** oscillate, pendulate; ebb and flow, wax and wane; go through phases, **waver,** shift, shuffle, swing, sway, wobble, flounder, stagger, teeter, totter, **seesaw, teeter-totter;** back and fill, turn, blow hot and cold, ring the changes, have as many phases as the moon.

.6 ADJS **changeable, alterable,** alterative, modifiable; **mutable,** permutable, impermanent, transient, **transitory; variable,** checkered, ever-changing, many-sided, kaleidoscopic; **mobile, movable,** plastic, malleable, rubbery, fluid; **resilient, adaptable,** adjustable, **flexible,** supple, able to adapt, able to roll with the punches *or* bend without breaking; protean, proteiform; metamorphic; **nonuniform** 18.3.

.7 **inconstant, changeable,** changeful, uncertain, inconsistent, shifty, unreliable, undependable, **unstable, unfixed,** infirm, restless, **unsettled,** unstaid, **unsteady,** wishy-washy, spineless, shapeless, amorphous, indecisive, irresolute, unsteadfast, unstable as water; **variable,** deviable; unaccountable, unpredictable; vicissitudinous, vicissitudinary; whimsical, **capricious, fickle** 629.5,6; **erratic, eccentric,** freakish; volatile, giddy, dizzy, scatterbrained, mercurial, moody, flighty, impulsive, impetuous; **fluctuating,** alternating, **vacillating, wavering,** wavery, wavy, mazy, flitting, flickering, fitful, shifting, shuffling; irregular, spasmodic 138.3; **desultory,** rambling, roving, vagrant, wanton, wayward, wandering, afloat, adrift; unrestrained, undisciplined, irresponsible, uncontrolled, fast and loose.

.8 ADVS **changeably, variably, inconstantly,** uncertainly, **unsteadily,** unsteadfastly, capriciously, desultorily, erratically, waveringly; back and forth, to and fro, in and out, off and on, on and off, round and round.

## 142. STABILITY

.1 NOUNS **stability, firmness, soundness, substantiality, solidity;** –stasia *or* –stasis, –pexy; **security,** secureness, rootedness, fastness; reliability 513.4; **steadiness,** steadfastness; constancy, invariability, undeflectability; **imperturbability,** unflappability [informal], nerve, steady *or* unshakable nerves, unshakableness, **cool** [informal], *sang-froid* [Fr]; **equilibrium, balance,** stable state, stable equilibrium, homeostasis; steady state; balanced personality; aplomb; **uniformity** 17.

.2 **fixity,** fixedness, fixture, fixation; infixion, implantation, embedment; **establishment, stabilization,** confirmation, entrenchment; inveteracy, deep-rootedness, **deep-seatedness.**

.3 **immobility,** immovability, unmovability, immovableness, irremovability; inextricability; **firmness,** solidity, unyieldingness, rigidity, **inflexibility** 356.3; inertia, *vis inertiae* [L]; immobilization.

.4 **unchangeableness,** unchangeability, unalterability, unmodifiability, **immutability,** incommutability; lastingness, **permanence** 140; irrevocability, indefeasibility, **irreversibility;** irretrievability, unreturnableness, unrestorableness; intransmutability; inertness.

.5 **indestructibility, imperishability,** incorruptibility, inextinguishability, immortality, **deathlessness;** invulnerability, invincibility, inexpugnability, impregnability; ineradicability, indelibility, ineffaceability, inerasableness.

.6 (comparisons) rock, Rock of Gibraltar, bedrock, pillar, tower, foundation; leopard's spots.

.7 VERBS **stabilize,** stabilitate; firm, firm up [informal]; **steady, balance,** counterbalance, ballast; **immobilize,** freeze, keep, retain; **transfix,** stick, hold, pin *or* nail down [informal].

.8 **secure,** make sure *or* secure, tie, chain, tether, **make fast, fasten,** fasten down; **anchor,** moor; batten, batten down; belay; "build one's house upon a rock" [Bible].

.9 **fix,** define, set, **settle; establish,** found, ground, lodge, seat, **entrench,** confirm, root; infix, ingrain, set in, plant, implant, engraft, bed, embed; **print,** imprint, stamp, inscribe, etch, engrave; impress, impact, pack, jam, **wedge;** deep-dye, **dye in the wool;** stereotype.

.10 (become firmly fixed) root, **take root,** strike root; stick, stick fast, **catch,** jam, lodge.

.11 **stand fast,** stand *or* remain firm, **stand pat** [informal], stay put [informal], hold fast, not budge, not budge an inch, **stand** *or* **hold one's ground,** hold one's own, dig in one's heels, take one's stand, **stick to one's guns,** put one's foot down [informal]; **hold out,** stick it out [informal]; **hold up; weather,** weather the storm, ride it out, get home free [informal]; be im-

perturbable, be unflappable [informal], not bat an eyelash [informal], keep one's cool [informal].

.12 ADJS **stable, substantial, firm, solid, sound;** firm as Gibraltar, solid as a rock; **fast, secure; steady,** unwavering, steadfast; **balanced,** in equilibrium, in a stable state; **well-balanced;** gyr(o)–, stat(o)–; **imperturbable,** unflappable [informal], unshakable, **cool** [informal]; without nerves, without a nerve in one's body, unflinching; **reliable** 513.17, predictable; fiducial.

.13 **established,** stabilized, **entrenched,** vested, firmly established; **well-established,** well-founded, **well-grounded,** on a rock, in *or* on bedrock; old-line, long-established; **confirmed, inveterate; settled,** set; well-settled, well-set; **rooted,** well-rooted; **deep-rooted, deep-seated,** deep-set, deep-settled, deep-fixed, deep-dyed, deep-engraven, deep-grounded, deep-laid; **infixed, ingrained,** implanted, engrafted, embedded, ingrown, inwrought; impressed, indelibly impressed, imprinted; engraved, etched, graven, embossed; **dyed-in-the-wool.**

.14 **fixed,** fastened, anchored, riveted; set, **settled, stated;** staple.

.15 **immovable,** unmovable, **immobile,** immotile, immotive, unmoving, **irremovable, stationary,** frozen, not to be moved, at a standstill; **firm, unyielding,** adamant, adamantine, rigid, **inflexible** 356.12; pat, standpat [informal].

.16 **stuck, fast,** stuck fast, **fixed, transfixed, caught,** fastened, tied, chained, tethered, anchored, moored, held, inextricable; **jammed,** impacted, packed, wedged; aground, grounded, stranded, high and dry.

.17 **unchangeable,** not to be changed, changeless, unchanged, unchanging, unvarying, unvariable, **unalterable,** unaltered, unalterative, **immutable,** incommutable, inconvertible, unmodifiable; unsusceptible, insusceptible of change; **constant, invariable,** undeviating, undeflectable; lasting, unremitting, **permanent** 140.7; irrevocable, indefeasible, **irreversible,** nonreversible, reverseless; irretrievable, unrestorable, unreturnable, nonreturnable; intransmutable, inert, noble [chem].

.18 **indestructible,** undestroyable, **imperishable,** nonperishable, incorruptible; **deathless,** immortal, undying; **invulnerable, invincible,** inexpugnable, impregnable; **ineradicable,** indelible, ineffaceable, inerasable; **inextinguishable,** unquenchable, quenchless, undampable.

.19 PHRS **stet,** let it stand.

.20 **stabilizers**

| | |
|---|---|
| balance | governor |
| balance piston | gyroscope |
| balancer | gyrostabilizer |
| balance rudder | hairspring |
| balance wheel | keel |
| balancing condenser | mordant |
| balancing flap | pendulum |
| ballast | pendulum wheel |
| centerboard damper | shock absorber |
| counterbalance | springs |
| counterweight | stabilizator |
| fin | stiffening |
| fixative | tail plane |
| flywheel | trim tabs |

## 143. CONTINUANCE

*(continuance in action)*

.1 NOUNS **continuance, continuation,** unremittingness, **continualness** 71.1; **prolongation, extension, protraction, perpetuation,** lengthening; **maintenance,** sustenance, sustained action *or* activity; pursuance; run, way, straight *or* uninterrupted course; **progress, progression; persistence, perseverance** 625; **endurance** 110.1; **continuity** 71; **repetition** 103; staying power.

.2 **resumption, recommencement,** rebeginning, **renewal,** reopening, reentrance; **fresh start,** new beginning; another try, another shot *or* crack *or* go [informal].

.3 VERBS **continue** 71.4, **remain,** bide, **abide, stay,** tarry, linger; go on, go along, **keep on,** keep going, carry on, stay on, hold on, hold one's way *or* course *or* path, hold steady, run on, jog on, drag on, slog on, stagger on, put one foot in front of the other; never cease, cease not; **endure** 110.6.

.4 **sustain, protract, prolong, extend,** perpetuate, lengthen; **maintain,** keep, hold, retain, preserve; **keep up,** keep going, keep alive.

.5 **persist, persevere,** keep at it 625.2, stick it out, stick to it, never say die, see it through, hang in *or* hang tough [both informal]; survive, make out, manage, get along, get on, eke out an existence, keep the even tenor of one's way; go on, go on with, go on with the show [informal].

.6 **resume, recommence,** rebegin, **renew,** reenter, reopen, **return to,** go back to, begin again, take up again, make a new beginning, make a fresh start, start all over,

have another try, have another shot *or* crack *or* go [informal].

.7 ADJS **continuing, abiding** 110.10; staying, remaining, sticking; **continuous** 71.8, **unceasing,** unremitting, steady, sustained, undying, indefatigable, **persistent.**

## 144. CESSATION

.1 NOUNS **cessation, discontinuance,** discontinuation, breakoff [informal]; **desistance,** desinence, cease, surcease, **ceasing,** stopping, termination; **close,** closing, shutdown; relinquishment, renunciation, abandonment; –stasia *or* –stasis, stasi–.

.2 **stop, stoppage, halt, stay, arrest,** check, cutoff [informal]; **stand, standstill;** full stop, dead stop, grinding halt; **strike, walkout,** work stoppage, sit-down strike, lockout; **end,** ending, endgame, final whistle, gun, bell, checkmate, stalemate, deadlock, standoff [informal].

.3 **pause, rest, break,** caesura, recess, **intermission,** interim 109, intermittence, interval, interlude, *intermezzo* [Ital], respite, letup [informal], **interruption, suspension;** hesitation, remission, layoff [informal], abeyance, stay, drop, lull, lapse; truce, cease-fire, stand-down; vacation, holiday, day off.

.4 [gram terms] pause, juncture, boundary, caesura; (punctuation) stop *or* point *or* period, comma, colon, semicolon.

.5 (debate) cloture, *clôture* [Fr]; cloture by compartment, kangaroo cloture; guillotine [Brit].

.6 VERBS **cease, discontinue, end, stop, halt,** terminate, abort, cancel, scrub [informal], hold, **quit, stay,** belay [informal]; **desist,** refrain, leave off, lay off [informal], give over, **have done with;** cut it out [slang], drop it [informal], knock it off [informal], relinquish, renounce, abandon; **come to an end** 70.6.

.7 **stop, come to a stop** *or* halt, **halt,** stop in one's tracks, skid to a stop, stop dead; **bring up, pull up,** draw up, **fetch up; stop short,** come up short, bring up short, come to a screaming *or* grinding *or* shuddering halt, stop on a dime [informal], come to a full stop, come to a stand *or* standstill, fetch up all standing; stall, stick, hang fire, cease fire; run into a brick wall.

.8 (stop work) **lay off, knock off** [informal], call it a day [informal], call it quits [informal]; lay down one's tools, **shut up shop,** close shop, shut down, close down, secure [naut informal]; **strike,** walk out, call a strike, go or go out on strike.

.9 **pause, hesitate, rest,** let up [informal]; rest on one's oars; **recess,** take or call a recess.

.10 **interrupt, suspend,** intermit 109.3, **break, break off,** take a break [informal], cut off, break or snap the thread.

.11 **put a stop to, call a halt to,** blow the whistle on [informal], **put an end to** 70.7, put paid to [Brit informal]; **stop, stay, halt, arrest, check,** stall; **block, brake,** dam, stem, stem the tide or current; pull up, draw rein, put on the brakes, hit the brake pedal; **bring to a stand** or **standstill,** freeze, bring to, bring up short, **stop dead** or **dead in one's tracks,** stop cold, stop short, cut short, check in full career; checkmate, stalemate, deadlock.

.12 **turn off, shut off,** shut, shut down, close; kill, cut, switch off.

.13 ADVS de–, un–.

.14 INTERJS **cease!, stop!, halt!,** *halte!* [Fr], hold!, freeze!, stay!, desist!, quit it!; **let up!,** easy!, take it easy!, relax!, **leave off!,** *arrêtez!* [Fr], stop it!, forget it!, no more!, have done!, *tenez!* [Fr], **hold everything!, hold it!,** hold to!, hold on!, whoa!, that's it!, that's enough!, enough!, *basta!* [Ital].

.15 [slang or informal terms] cut it out!, cool it!, can it!, turn it off!, chuck it!, stow it!, drop it!, lay off!, all right already!, come off it!, **knock it off!,** break it off!, break it up!

## 145. CONVERSION

*(change to something different)*

.1 NOUNS **conversion,** reconversion, re-formation, **change-over,** turning into, becoming; **change** 139, **transformation** 139.2; **transition,** transit, switch or switch-over [both informal], passage, **shift;** lapse; **reversal,** about-face or flip-flop [both informal], *volte-face* [Fr]; growth, progress; resolution, reduction, naturalization, assimilation, assumption; alchemy.

.2 **reformation, reform, regeneration, revival, reclamation,** redemption, amendment, improvement 691, renewal, recrudescence, rebirth, renascence, new birth, **change of heart;** change of mind or commitment or allegiance or loyalty or conviction.

.3 apostasy, renunciation, **defection, desertion,** treason, crossing-over; degeneration 692.3.

.4 **rehabilitation,** reconditioning, readjustment, reclamation; **reeducation,** reinstruction; **repatriation.**

.5 **indoctrination,** reindoctrination, counterindoctrination; **brainwashing,** menticide; subversion, alienation, corruption.

.6 **conversion,** proselytization, proselytism, evangelization, persuasion 648.3.

.7 **convert, proselyte,** neophyte, catechumen, disciple.

.8 **apostate, defector,** turncoat, traitor, deserter, **renegade.**

.9 **converter, proselyter,** proselytizer, **missionary, apostle, evangelist** 1038.7.

.10 (instruments) melting pot, crucible, alembic, test tube, caldron, retort, mortar, potter's wheel, anvil, lathe; transformer, transducer, engine, motor, machine 348.4, 21.

.11 VERBS **convert,** reconvert; **change over,** switch or switch over [both informal], shift, make over, do over; **change, transform** 139.6,7; **change into, turn into, become,** resolve into, assimilate to, bring to, reduce to, naturalize; **make,** render; **reverse;** turn back 146.5.

.12 **re-form,** remodel, reshape, refashion; **renew,** new-model; **regenerate, reclaim,** redeem, amend, set straight; **reform,** make a new man of, restore self-respect; mend or change one's ways, **turn over a new leaf,** put on the new man.

.13 **defect, renegade,** renege, turn one's coat, desert, apostatize, change one's colors, turn against, turn traitor; degenerate 692.14.

.14 **rehabilitate,** recondition, reclaim; **reeducate,** reinstruct; **repatriate.**

.15 **indoctrinate, brainwash,** reindoctrinate, counterindoctrinate; subvert, alienate, win away, corrupt 692.14.

.16 **convince, persuade,** wean, bring over, **win over;** proselyte, **proselytize,** evangelize.

.17 be converted into, **turn into** or to, become 1.12, **change into,** alter into, run or fall or pass into, slide or glide into, grow into, ripen into, **develop** or **evolve into,** merge or blend or melt into, shift into, lapse into, open into, resolve itself or settle into, come round to.

.18 ADJS **convertible,** resolvable, transmutable, **transformable, transitional, modifiable.**

.19 **converted, changed, transformed;** naturalized, assimilated; **reformed,** regenerated, renewed, redeemed, reborn.

.20 **apostate, treasonable, traitorous,** degenerate, **renegade.**

## 146. REVERSION

*(change to a former state)*

**.1** NOUNS **reversion,** reverting, retroversion, retrogradation, **retrogression,** retrocession, regress, **regression,** backsliding, slipping back, backing, recidivism, recidivation; reconversion; **reverse, reversal; return,** returning, revulsion; disenchantment, reclamation, return to the fold; reinstatement, rehabilitation, restitution, restoration; turn, turnabout, about-face *or* flip-flop [both informal]; lapse, **relapse** 696.

**.2 throwback,** atavism.

**.3 returnee, repeater;** prodigal son, lost lamb; reversioner, reversionist; recidivist, habitual criminal *or* offender, two-time loser [slang]; backslider.

**.4** VERBS **revert,** retrovert, **regress, retrogress,** retrograde, retrocede, **reverse, return,** return to the fold; backslide, slip back, recidivate, lapse, lapse back, relapse 696.4.

**.5 turn back, change back, go back, hark back,** cry back, break back, **turn,** turn around *or* about; do an about-face *or* flip-flop *or* do a flip-flop [all informal].

**.6 revert to, return to,** recur to, go back to; hark *or* cry back to.

**.7** ADJS **reversionary,** reversional, **regressive,** recessive, **retrogressive, retrograde;** reactionary, revulsionary; recidivist *or* recidivous; retroverse, retrorse; atavistic; revertible, returnable, reversible; re–, retro–.

## 147. REVOLUTION

*(sudden or radical change)*

**.1** NOUNS **revolution, radical** *or* **total change, violent change,** striking alteration, sweeping change, clean sweep, clean slate, tabula rasa; revulsion, transilience; **overthrow,** overturn, upset, *bouleversement* [Fr], convulsion, spasm, subversion, *coup d'état* [Fr]; breakup, breakdown; cataclysm, catastrophe, debacle, *débâcle* [Fr]; revolutionary war, war of national liberation; bloodless revolution, palace revolution; technological revolution, electronic *or* communications *or* computer revolution; counterrevolution; revolt 767.4.

**.2 revolutionism,** anarchism, syndicalism, terrorism; Bolshevism *or* Bolshevikism [both Russia], Carbonarism [Italy], Sinn Feinism [Ireland], Jacobinism [France]; sans-culottism [France], *sans-culotterie* [Fr], Castroism [Cuba], Maoism [China].

**.3 revolutionist,** revolutionary, revolutioner, revolutionizer; **rebel** 767.5; anarchist, anarch, syndicalist, criminal syndicalist, terrorist 162.9; subversive; red; Red Republican [France], *bonnet rouge* [Fr]; Jacobin [France], sans-culotte, sans-culottist; Yankee *or* Yankee Doodle *or* Continental [all US]; Puritan *or* Roundhead [both England]; Bolshevik *or* Bolshevist *or* Bolshie [all Russia], Marxist, Leninist, Communist, Commie [informal], Red, Trotskyite *or* Trotskyist, Castroist *or* Castroite, Guevarist, Maoist; Vietcong, Cong, VC, Charley [all Vietnam]; Mau-Mau [Kenya]; *Carbonaro* [Italy], Carbonarist [Italy]; Sinn Feiner, Fenian [both Ireland]; revolutionary junta.

**.4** VERBS **revolutionize,** revolution, revolute [informal], **make a radical change,** make a clean sweep, break with the past; **overthrow,** overturn, upset; revolt 767.7.

**.5** ADJS **revolutionary,** revolutional; revulsive, revulsionary; transilient; cataclysmic, catastrophic; **radical, sweeping** 56.10; **insurrectionary** 767.11.

**.6 revolutionist,** anarchic(al), syndical(ist), terrorist(ic), agin the government [informal]; Bolshevist(ic), Bolshevik; sans-culottic, sans-culottish; Jacobinic, Carbonarist, Fenian, Marxist, Leninist, Communist, Trotskyist *or* Trotskyite, Guevarist, Castroist *or* Castroite, Maoist, Vietcong, Mau-Mau.

## 148. EVOLUTION

**.1** NOUNS **evolution,** evolving, evolvement; evolutionary change, gradual change, peaceful *or* nonviolent change; **development, growth,** rise; developmental change, natural growth *or* development; flowering, blossoming; ripening, maturation; accomplishment 722; **advance,** advancement, furtherance; **progress,** progression; **elaboration,** enlargement, amplification, **expansion,** explication.

**.2 unfolding,** unfoldment, unrolling, unfurling, unwinding.

**.3** [biol terms] **genesis;** phylogeny, phylogenesis; ontogeny, ontogenesis; physiogeny, physiogenesis; **biological evolution;** natural selection, adaptation; horotely, bradytely, tachytely.

**.4 evolutionism,** theory of evolution; **Darwinism,** Neo-Darwinism, Haeckelism, Lamarckism *or* Lamarckianism, Neo-Lamarckism, Lysenkoism, Weismannism, Spencerianism; social Darwinism, social evolution.

.5 VERBS **evolve**, evolute [informal]; **develop**, **grow**, wax, **progress**, **advance**; ripen, mellow, mature, maturate; **flower**, **bloom**, **blossom**, bear fruit.

.6 **elaborate**, labor, **work out**, enlarge upon, amplify, enlarge, **expand**, detail, go *or* enter into detail, go into, spell out [informal]; complete 722.6.

.7 unfold, unroll, unfurl, unwind, unreel, uncoil.

.8 ADJS **evolutionary**, evolutional, evolutionist *or* evolutionistic; **evolving**, **developing**, **unfolding**; **maturing**, maturational, maturative; **progressing**, **advancing**; genetic, phylogenetic, ontogenetic, physiogenetic; horotelic, bradytelic, tachytelic.

## 149. SUBSTITUTION

*(change of one thing for another)*

.1 NOUNS **substitution**, **exchange**, **change**, switch, commutation, subrogation; vicariousness, **representation**, deputation, **delegation**; deputyship, **agency**, **power of attorney**, **supplanting**, supplantment *or* supplantation; **replacement**, displacement; superseding *or* supersedence *or* supersedure, supersession; tit for tat, *quid pro quo* [L].

.2 **substitute**, sub [informal], **substitution**, **replacement**, second *or* third string [informal], utility player; change, exchange, changeling, secondary, succedaneum; ersatz, phony *or* fake [both informal], counterfeit, imitation 22, copy 24; surrogate; reserves, backup, personnel; spares; **alternate**, alternative, next best thing, supplanter, superseder; **proxy**, dummy; vicar, agent, representative; **deputy** 781; locum tenens, vice-president, vice-regent, etc.; **relief**, fill-in, **stand-in**, **understudy**, **pinch hitter** *or* runner [informal]; double; **equivalent**, equal; ringer [slang]; ghost, ghostwriter; substituent; **analogy**, comparison; **metaphor**, metonymy, synecdoche [all gram]; **symbol**, **sign**, token; makeshift 670.2; allelo–, counter–, pro–, vice–.

.3 **scapegoat**, goat [informal], fall guy *or* patsy [both slang], **whipping boy**.

.4 VERBS **substitute**, **exchange**, **change**, take *or* ask *or* offer in exchange, switch, ring in [informal], **put in the place of**, change for, make way for, give place to; commute, redeem, compound for; rob Peter to pay Paul; dub in; make do with, shift with, put up with.

.5 **substitute for**, sub for [informal], subrogate; **act for**, double for, stand *or* sit in for, understudy for, fill in for, pinch-hit, pinch-run [both informal]; **relieve**, spell *or* **spell off** [both informal]; ghost, ghostwrite; **represent** 781.14; **supplant**, **supersede**, succeed, **replace**, displace, **take the place of**, crowd out, cut out [informal], change places with, swap places with [informal], stand in the stead of, step into the shoes of, fill one's shoes.

.6 [slang *or* informal terms] **cover up for**, **front for**, go to the front for, take the rap for, be the goat *or* patsy.

.7 **delegate**, **deputize**, **commission** 780.9, designate an agent *or* proxy.

.8 ADJS **substitute**, **alternate**, **alternative**, equivalent, token, dummy, pinch, utility, backup, secondary, **vicarious**, ersatz, mock, quasi–, pseudo–, phony *or* fake [both informal], counterfeit, imitation 22.8; **proxy**; makeshift, reserve, **spare**, stopgap, temporary, provisional, tentative.

.9 **substitutional**, substitutionary, substitutive; supersessive.

.10 **replaceable**, substitutable, supersedable, expendable.

.11 ADVS **instead**, **rather**, *faute de mieux* [Fr]; in its stead *or* place; in one's stead, in one's behalf, in one's place, in one's shoes; by proxy; as an alternative; *in loco parentis* [L].

.12 PREPS **instead of**, in the stead of, **in place of**, in the place of, **in** *or* **on behalf of**, **in lieu of**; **for**, as proxy for, as a substitute for, as representing, in preference to, as an alternative to; **replacing**, as a replacement for, *vice* [L].

## 150. INTERCHANGE

*(double or mutual change)*

.1 NOUNS **interchange**, **exchange**, counterchange; **transposition**, transposal; mutual transfer *or* replacement; mutual admiration, mutual support; **cooperation** 786; commutation, permutation, intermutation; alternation; **interplay**, **reciprocation** 13.1, reciprocality, reciprocity, mutuality; **give-and-take**, something for something, *quid pro quo* [L], measure for measure, **tit for tat**, an eye for an eye, "an eye for an eye and a tooth for a tooth" [Bible]; **retaliation**, *lex talionis* [L]; cross fire; battledore and shuttlecock.

.2 **trading**, **swapping** [informal]; trade, swap [informal], even trade, **switch**; barter 827.2; logrolling, back scratching, pork barrel.

**.3 interchangeability,** exchangeability, changeability, standardization; commutability, permutability.

**.4** VERBS **interchange, exchange,** change, counterchange; alternate; **transpose;** commute, permute; **trade, swap** [informal], **switch;** bandy, play at battledore and shuttlecock; **reciprocate,** respond; **give and take,** give a Roland for an Oliver, give as much as one takes, give as good as one gets, return the compliment, pay back, compensate, **requite,** return; **retaliate,** get back at, get even with, be quits with; logroll, scratch each other's back, **cooperate** 786.3.

**.5** ADJS **interchangeable, exchangeable,** changeable, standard; equivalent; **even,** equal; returnable, convertible, **commutable, permutable; commutative;** retaliatory, equalizing; **reciprocative** or **reciprocating, reciprocal; mutual,** give-and-take; **exchanged, transposed,** switched, **swapped** [informal], traded, **interchanged;** allelo-, inter-.

**.6** ADVS **interchangeably, exchangeably; in exchange, in return; even,** au pair [Fr]; **reciprocally** 13.16, mutually; **in turn,** each in its turn, every one in his turn, by turns, turn about, turn and turn about.

## 151. EVENT

**.1** NOUNS **event, eventuality,** eventuation; realization, materialization, coming to be or pass, incidence; contingency, contingent; accident 156.6.

**.2 event, occurrence, incident, episode, experience, adventure,** hap, **happening,** happenstance, **phenomenon,** fact, matter of fact, reality, particular, circumstance, **occasion,** turn of events.

**.3 affair, concern, matter,** thing, concernment, interest, **business,** job [informal], **transaction,** proceeding, doing.

**.4 affairs, concerns, matters,** circumstances, relations, **dealings, proceedings,** doings, goings-on [informal]; course or run of things, the way of things, the way things go, what happens, current of events, march of events; the world, life, the times; order of the day; **conditions, state of affairs,** environing or ambient phenomena, state or condition of things.

**.5** VERBS **occur, happen** 156.11, hap, eventuate, **take place,** come down [slang], **transpire,** be realized, come, **come off, come about,** come true, **come to pass,** pass, pass off, go off, fall, **befall,** betide; **be found,** be met with.

**.6 turn up, show up** [informal], **come along,** come one's way, cross one's path, come into being or existence, chance, **crop up,** spring up, pop up [informal], arise, come forth, come or draw on, appear, approach, materialize, present itself, be destined for one.

**.7 turn out, result** 154.5.

**.8 experience, have, know, feel,** taste; **encounter, meet,** meet with, meet up with [informal], run up against [informal]; **undergo, go through,** pass through, be subjected to, be exposed to, stand under, labor under, **endure, suffer,** sustain, pay, spend.

**.9** ADJS **happening, occurring,** passing, taking place, on, **going on,** ongoing [informal], **current,** prevalent, prevailing, in the wind, afloat, afoot, under way, in hand, **on foot,** ado, doing; incidental, circumstantial, accompanying; accidental; occasional; resultant; eventuating.

**.10 eventful, momentous, stirring,** bustling, full of incident; phenomenal.

**.11 eventual, coming, final,** last, ultimate; **contingent,** collateral, secondary, indirect.

**.12** ADVS **eventually, ultimately, finally,** in the long run; in the course of things, in the natural way of things, as things go, as times go, as the world goes, as the tree falls, the way the cookie crumbles [informal], as things turn out, as it may be or happen or turn out, as luck or fate or destiny wills.

**.13** CONJS **in the event that, if, in case,** just in case, in any case, in either case, in the contingency that, in case that, if it should happen that; **provided** 507.12.

## 152. IMMINENCE

*(future event)*

**.1** NOUNS **imminence, imminency,** impendence, impendency, forthcomingness; **forthcoming,** coming, **approach,** loom; immediate or near future; futurity 121.1.

**.2** VERBS **be imminent, impend, overhang,** hang or lie over, hang over one's head, hover, **threaten, menace,** lower; brew, gather; **come** or **draw on,** draw near or nigh, rush up on one, forthcome, **approach, near,** await, face, **confront,** loom, stare one in the face, be in store, breathe down one's neck, be about to be borning.

**.3** ADJS **imminent, impending,** impendent, **overhanging,** hanging over one's head, waiting, lurking, **threatening,** lowering, menacing, lying in ambush, "in danger imminent" [Spenser]; **brewing,** gathering, preparing; **coming, forthcoming, upcoming, to come,** about to be, about or going to happen, **approaching, nearing,** looming, looming in the distance or future; **near, close,** immediate, instant, **at hand,** near at hand, close at hand; **in the offing,** on the horizon, **in prospect,** already in sight, just around the corner, in view, in one's eye, in store, in reserve, **in the wind,** in the womb of time; on the knees or lap of the gods, in the cards [informal]; that will be, that is to be; future 121.8.

.4 ADVS **imminently,** impendingly; **any time,** any time now, any moment, any minute, any hour, any day; **to be expected,** as may be expected, as may be.

## 153. CAUSE

.1 NOUNS **cause, occasion,** antecedents, call, **grounds,** ground, stimulus, base, **basis,** element, principle, factor; **determinant,** determinative; causation, causality, cause and effect; etiology.

.2 **reason,** reason why, rationale, reason for or behind, underlying reason, rational ground, **explanation, the why,** the wherefore, the whatfor or whyfor [informal], **the why and wherefore,** the idea [informal], the big idea [slang]; stated cause, pretext, pretense, excuse.

.3 **immediate cause,** proximate cause; transient cause, occasional cause; formal cause; efficient cause; ultimate cause, immanent cause, remote cause, causing cause, *causa causans* [L]; first cause; **final cause,** *causa finalis* [L]; provocation, **last straw,** straw that broke the camel's back, match in the powder barrel; causal sequence, chain or nexus of cause and effect.

.4 **author,** agent, originator, generator, begetter, engenderer, producer, maker, beginner, **creator,** mover; **parent, mother, father,** sire; **prime mover,** *primum mobile* [L]; causer, effector; inspirer, instigator, catalyst.

.5 **source, origin,** genesis, original, origination, **derivation, rise, beginning,** conception, inception, commencement, **head;** provenance, provenience; **root,** radix, –rhiza or –rrhiza, radical, taproot, grass roots; stem, stock.

.6 **fountainhead,** headwater, headstream, riverhead, springhead, headspring, **mainspring,** wellspring, wellhead, well, **spring,**

**fountain,** fount, font, *fons et origo* [L]; mine, quarry; cren(o)–.

.7 **egg,** ovum 406.12, **germ,** germen [archaic], spermatozoon 406.11, nucleus 406.7, **seed;** embryo 406.14; bud 411.21; rudiment, *Anlage* [Ger]; loins.

.8 **birthplace, breeding place,** rookery, hatchery; **hotbed,** forcing bed; incubator, brooder; **nest,** nidus; **cradle,** nursery.

.9 **womb,** matrix, uterus, uter(o)–, metr(o)–, –metrium, venter.

.10 (a principle or movement) **cause, principle,** interest, issue, burning issue, commitment, faith, great cause, lifework; reason for being, *raison d'être* [Fr]; **movement,** mass movement, activity; **drive, campaign, crusade.**

.11 VERBS **cause,** be the cause of, lie at the root of; **bring about, bring to pass,** effectuate, **effect,** bring to effect, realize, **occasion, make, create, engender,** generate, **produce,** breed, work, do; –ate, –en, –ise or –ize; **originate,** give origin to, give occasion to, **give rise to,** give birth to, beget, bear, bring forth, labor or travail and bring forth, author, **father,** sire, sow the seeds of; gestate, **conceive;** set up, set afloat, **set on foot;** found, establish, inaugurate, institute.

.12 **induce,** lead, procure, get, obtain, contrive, **effect,** bring, **bring on,** draw on, **call forth, elicit, evoke,** provoke, inspire, instigate, motivate; draw down, open the door to; superinduce.

.13 **contribute to, lead to,** conduce to, redound to; **advance, forward,** influence, subserve; **determine,** decide, turn the scale, have the last word.

.14 ADJS **causal,** causative; occasional; originative, institutive, constitutive; **at the bottom of,** behind the scenes; **formative,** determinative, effectual, decisive, pivotal; etiological; etio– or aetio–, prot(o)–; –facient, –factive, –fic, –ic(al) or –etic.

.15 **original, primary,** primal, primitive, pristine, primordial, primeval, aboriginal, **elementary,** elemental, **basic,** basal, **rudimentary,** crucial, central, radical, **fundamental;** embryonic, in embryo, *in ovo* [L], germinal, seminal, pregnant; **generative,** genetic, protogenic.

## 154. EFFECT

.1 NOUNS **effect, result,** resultant, **consequence,** consequent, sequent, sequence, sequel, sequela; event, eventuality, eventuation, **upshot, outcome,** logical outcome, outgrowth, offshoot, offspring, issue, legacy; **product** 168, precipitate, distillate, **fruit**, harvest; development, corollary; derivative, derivation, by-product.

**.2 conclusion,** end 70, **end** *or* **final result, consummation, culmination,** denouement, catastrophe, termination, completion, finale, last act, climax, bitter end, payoff [slang].

**.3 impact,** force, **repercussion,** reaction; backwash, backlash, reflex, recoil, response; mark, print, imprint, impress, impression; clout [informal].

**.4 aftereffect, aftermath,** aftergrowth, aftercrop, **afterclap,** afterimage, afterglow, aftertaste; wake, trail, track; domino effect.

**.5** VERBS **result, ensue, issue, follow,** attend; **turn out, come out,** fall out, **work out,** pan out [informal], fare; turn out to be, prove, prove to be; **become of,** come of, come about; develop, unfold; **eventuate,** terminate, end.

**.6 result from,** be the effect of, be due to, originate in *or* from, **come from,** come out of, grow from, **grow out of,** follow from *or* on, proceed from, descend from, emerge from, issue from, ensue from, emanate from, flow from, **derive from,** accrue from, rise *or* arise from, take its rise from, **spring from, stem from,** sprout from, bud from, germinate from; **depend on,** hinge *or* pivot *or* turn on, hang on, be contingent on.

**.7** ADJS **resultant, resulting, following, ensuing; consequent,** consequential, sequent, sequential, sequacious; **final** 70.10; derivative, derivational.

**.8 resulting from,** coming from, arising from, deriving *or* derivable from; **owing to, due to;** attributed *or* attributable to, dependent *or* contingent on; **caused by,** occasioned by, **at the bottom of.**

**.9** ADVS **consequently, as a result,** as a consequence, in consequence, naturally, *naturellement* [Fr], necessarily, of necessity, inevitably, of course, as a matter of course, and so, it follows that; **therefore; accordingly** 8.11; **finally** 70.11.

**.10** PHRS one thing leads to another, *post hoc, ergo propter hoc* [L], what goes up must come down.

## 155. ATTRIBUTION

*(assignment of cause)*

**.1** NOUNS **attribution, assignment,** assignation, ascription, imputation, arrogation, placement, application, attachment, saddling, **charge, blame; responsibility,** answerability; **credit,** honor; accounting for, reference to, derivation from, connection with; etiology; palaetiology.

**.2 acknowledgment,** citation, tribute; confession; **reference;** trademark, signature; **by-line,** credit line.

**.3** VERBS **attribute, assign, ascribe, impute,** give, place, put, apply, attach, refer.

**.4 attribute to, ascribe to, impute to,** assign to, **lay to,** put *or* set down to, apply to, refer to, point to; **pin on,** pinpoint [informal], fix on *or* upon, attach to, accrete to, connect with, fasten upon, hang on [slang], **saddle on** *or* **upon,** place upon, **father upon,** settle upon, saddle with; blame, **blame for,** blame on *or* upon [informal], charge on *or* upon, place *or* put the blame on, place the blame *or* responsibility for, **fix the responsibility for,** fix the burden of, **charge to,** lay to one's charge, place to one's account, set to the account of, account for, lay at the door of, bring home to; acknowledge, confess; **credit** *or* **accredit with;** put words in one's mouth.

**.5 trace to,** follow the trail to; **derive from,** trace the origin *or* derivation of; affiliate to, filiate to, father, fix the paternity of.

**.6** ADJS **attributable, assignable, ascribable, imputable,** traceable, referable, accountable, explicable; owing, **due,** assigned *or* referred to, derivable from, derivative, derivational; **charged,** alleged, imputed, putative; **credited, attributed;** ap(o)– *or* aph–, de–, ep(i)–; –genous.

**.7** ADVS **hence, therefore,** therefor, **wherefore,** wherefrom, whence, then, thence, *ergo* [L], for which reason; **consequently** 154.9; **accordingly** 8.11; **because of that,** for that, by reason of that, for that reason, for the reason that, from *or* for that cause, **on that account,** on that ground, thereat; **because of this, on this account,** for this cause, on account of this, *propter hoc* [L], for this reason, hereat; thus, thusly [informal], thuswise.

**.8 why,** whyever, whyfor *or* for why [both dial], how come [informal], how is it that, **wherefore, what for,** for which, **on what account,** on account of what *or* which, for what *or* whatever reason, from what cause, *pourquoi* [Fr].

**.9** PREPS **because of,** by reason of, **as a result of,** by *or* in virtue of, **on account of,** on the score of, for the sake of, **owing to, due to,** thanks to; **considering,** in consideration of, **in view of;** after.

**.10** CONJS **because,** *parce que* [Fr], since, as,

for, **whereas, inasmuch as, forasmuch as,
insofar as, insomuch as,** as things go; in
that, for the cause that, for the reason
that, in view of the fact that, taking into
account that, **seeing that,** seeing as how
[dial], being as how [dial].

## 156. CHANCE

*(absence of assignable cause)*

.1 NOUNS    chance, happenstance, hap,
"heedless hap" [Spenser]; **luck;** good luck
*or* fortune, serendipity, happy chance;
**fortune,** fate, **destiny,** whatever comes,
moira, **lot** 640.2; **fortuity,** fortuitousness,
adventitiousness, indeterminateness *or*
indeterminacy, problematicness, uncertainty 514, flukiness [informal], casualness, flip of a coin, accidentality; break
[informal], the breaks [informal], run of
luck, run *or* turn of the cards, fall *or*
throw of the dice, the way things fall, the
way the cards fall, how they fall, the way
the cookie crumbles *or* the ball bounces
[informal]; uncertainty principle, principle of indeterminacy, Heisenberg's principle; **probability** 511, theory of probability, law of averages, statistical probability,
actuarial calculation; random sample,
**risk, gamble** 515; **opportunity** 129.2.
.2 Chance, Fortune, Lady *or* Dame Fortune, wheel of fortune, Fortuna; Luck,
Lady Luck; "a nickname of Providence"
[de Chamfort], "blind Chance" [Lucan],
"fickle Chance" [Milton], "that Power
which erring men call Chance" [Milton],
"the pseudonym of God when He did
not want to sign" [Anatole France].
.3 **purposelessness, causelessness,** randomness, dysteleology, **unpredictability** 514.1,
designlessness, **aimlessness.**
.4 **haphazard,** chance-medley, **random;** random shot; potluck.
.5 **vicissitudes,** vicissitudes of fortune, ins
and outs, **ups and downs,** ups and downs
of life, chapter of accidents, feast and
famine, "the various turns of chance"
[Dryden], fickle finger of fate; **chain of
circumstances,** concatenation of events,
chain reaction, vicious circle.
.6 (chance event) **happening,** hap, happenstance; **fortuity, accident,** casualty, adventure, hazard; contingent, contingency;
fluke [informal], freak accident; chance
hit, lucky shot, long shot, one in a million, long odds.
.7 **even chance,** even break [informal], fair
shake [informal], even *or* square odds,

touch and go, odds; **half a chance,** fifty-
fifty; toss, **toss-up,** standoff [informal].
.8 **good chance, sporting chance,** good opportunity,    good    possibility,    odds-on,
odds-on chance, **likelihood, possibility**
509, probability 511, favorable prospect,
well-grounded hope; **sure bet,** sure thing
[informal], a lot going for one [informal];
best bet, main chance.
.9 **small chance,** little chance, dark horse,
**poor prospect** *or* prognosis, poor lookout
[informal], little opportunity, poor possibility, **unlikelihood, improbability** 512,
hardly a chance, not half a chance; **off
chance, outside chance** [informal], **remote possibility,** bare possibility, a ghost
of a chance, slim chance, gambling
chance, **fighting chance** [informal]; poor
bet, long odds, long shot [informal], hundred-to-one shot [informal].
.10 **no chance,** not a Chinaman's chance
[slang], not a prayer, not a snowball's
chance in hell [slang]; **impossibility** 510,
hopelessness.
.11 VERBS **chance,** bechance, betide, come *or*
happen by chance, hap, hazard; **happen**
151.5, come, come *or* happen along, **turn
up,** pop up [informal], **befall;** fall to
one's lot, be one's fate.
.12 **risk,** take a chance, **gamble, bet** 515.18–20;
**predict** 543.9, prognosticate, make book
[informal].
.13 have a chance *or* an opportunity, **stand a
chance, run a good chance, bid** *or* **stand
fair to,** admit of; be in it *or* in the running [informal]; have a chance at, have a
fling *or* shot at [informal]; have a small
*or* slight chance, be a dark horse, barely
have a chance.
.14 **not have** *or* **stand a chance,** have no
chance *or* opportunity, not have a prayer,
not have a Chinaman's chance [slang],
not stand a snowball's chance in hell
[slang]; not be in it [informal], be out of
it [informal], **be out of the running.**
.15 ADJS **chance;** chancy [informal], dicey
[Brit informal], **risky** [informal]; **fortuitous, accidental,** aleatory, **casual,** adventitious, incidental, contingent, iffy [infor-
mal]; **causeless,** uncaused; indeterminate,
undetermined; **unexpected** 540.10, **unpredictable** 514.14, unforeseeable, unlooked-
for, **unforeseen;** fluky [informal]; fatal, fatidic, destinal.
.16 **purposeless, causeless,** designless, **aimless,**
driftless, undirected, unmotivated, mind-
less; **haphazard, random,** dysteleological,
stochastic, stray, inexplicable, unaccount-

able, promiscuous, indiscriminate, casual, leaving much to chance.

.17 **unintentional,** unintended, **unmeant, unplanned,** undesigned, unpurposed, unthought-of; **unpremeditated,** unmeditated, unprompted, unguided, unguarded; **unwitting, unthinking,** unconscious, involuntary.

.18 impossible 510.7; **improbable** 512.3; certain 513.13; **probable** 511.6.

.19 ADVS **by chance,** perchance, **by accident, accidentally, casually,** incidentally, **unpredictably, fortuitously;** by a piece of luck, by a fluke [informal], by good fortune; **as it chanced, as luck would have it,** by hazard, as it may happen, as it may be, as the case may be, as it may chance, as it may turn up or out; somehow, in some way, in some way or other, somehow or other, for some reason.

.20 **purposelessly, aimlessly; haphazardly, randomly,** dysteleologically, stochastically, inexplicably, unaccountably, promiscuously, indiscriminately, casually, **at haphazard, at random,** at hazard.

.21 **unintentionally, without design, unwittingly,** unthinkingly, unexpectedly, unconsciously, involuntarily.

## 157. POWER, POTENCY

### (effective force)

.1 NOUNS **power, potency** or potence, prepotency, potentiality, **force, might,** mightiness, **vigor,** vitality, vim, push, drive, charge, puissance [archaic]; dynam(o)-, –dynamia; dint, virtue; moxie or pizzazz or poop or punch or clout or steam [all informal]; powerfulness, forcefulness; virulence, vehemence; **strength** 159; **energy** 161; **virility** 420.2; cogence or cogency, validity, effect, **effectiveness,** effectuality; productivity, productiveness; power structure; **influence** 172, pull; **authority** 739, weight; **superiority** 36; power pack, amperage, wattage; main force, force majeure [Fr], main strength, brute force or strength, compulsion, duress; muscle power, sinew, might and main, beef [informal], strong arm; full force, full blast; superpower; armipotence, power struggle; black power; flower power; mana; charisma.

.2 **ability,** –ability or –ibility, ableness, **capability,** capableness, **capacity,** faculty, facility, fitness, qualification, talent, flair, genius, caliber, **competence,** adequacy, sufficiency, **efficiency,** efficacy; profi-

ciency 733.1; the stuff or the goods or what it takes [all informal]; susceptibility.

.3 **omnipotence, almightiness, all-powerfulness.**

.4 horsepower, manpower; electric power, electropower, hydroelectric power; hydraulic power, water power; steam power, piston power; solar power, atomic power, nuclear power, thermonuclear power; rocket power, jet power; **propulsion, thrust,** impulse.

.5 force of inertia, vis inertiae [L]; dead force, vis mortua [L]; living force, vis viva [L]; force of life, vis vitae [L].

.6 centrifugal force or action, centripetal force or action, force of gravity.

.7 (science of forces) dynamics, statics.

.8 **empowerment, enablement;** investment, endowment.

.9 **work force,** hands, men; **fighting force,** troops, units, the big battalions, firepower; **personnel** 750.11; forces.

.10 VERBS **empower, enable;** invest, clothe, invest or clothe with power, deputize; endue, endow, **authorize** 780.9; arm.

.11 **be able,** be up to [informal], lie in one's **power; can,** may, can do; make it or make the grade [both informal]; hack it or cut it or cut the mustard [all informal]; possess authority 739.13; **take charge** 739.14.

.12 ADJS **powerful, potent,** prepotent, power-packed, **mighty,** irresistible, **forceful,** forcible, dynamic, –dynamous; **vigorous, vital, energetic** 161.12, puissant, ruling, in power; **cogent,** striking, telling, effective, valid, operative, in force; **strong** 159.13; high-powered, high-tension, high-pressure, high-potency; **authoritative** 139.15; armipotent, mighty in battle.

.13 **omnipotent, almighty, all-powerful;** plenipotentiary, absolute, unlimited, **sovereign** 739.17; **supreme** 36.13.

.14 **able,** –able or –ible, –ile, **capable, equal to,** up to, **competent,** adequate, effective, effectual, efficient, efficacious; productive; **proficient** 733.20–22.

.15 ADVS **powerfully, potently, forcefully,** forcibly, mightily, with might and main, **vigorously, energetically** 161.15, dynamically; **cogently,** strikingly, tellingly; **effectively,** effectually; productively; with telling effect, to good account, to good purpose, with a vengeance.

.16 **ably, capably, competently,** adequately, effectively, effectually, **efficiently, well; to the best of one's ability,** as lies in one's power, so far as one can, as best one can; with all one's might, with everything that is in one.

.17 **by force,** by main or brute force, by *force majeure,* with the strong arm, with a high hand, high-handedly; **forcibly,** amain, with might and main; by force of arms, at the point of the sword, by storm.

.18 PREPS by dint of, by virtue of.

## 158. IMPOTENCE

.1 NOUNS **impotence** or impotency, **powerlessness,** impuissance [archaic], forcelessness; feebleness, softness, flabbiness, **weakness** 160; power vacuum.

.2 **inability, incapability, incapacity,** incapacitation, **incompetence** or incompetency, inadequacy, insufficiency, ineptitude, **inferiority** 37, inefficiency, unfitness, imbecility; disability, disablement, disqualification; legal incapacity, wardship, minority, infancy.

.3 **ineffectiveness, ineffectualness,** ineffectuality, inefficaciousness, **inefficacy,** counterproductiveness, counterproductivity, invalidity, **futility, uselessness,** bootlessness, failure 725, fatuity, inanity.

.4 **helplessness, defenselessness,** unprotection; invalidism, debilitation, effeteness.

.5 **emasculation,** demasculinization, effeminization; maiming, castration 42.4.

.6 **impotent,** weakling 160.6, invalid, incompetent; flash in the pan, blank cartridge, dud [informal]; eunuch, *castrato* [Ital], gelding.

.7 VERBS **be impotent,** lack force; be ineffective, avail nothing, not work or do, not take [informal].

.8 **cannot, not be able,** not have it or hack it or cut it or cut the mustard [informal], not make it, not make the grade [both informal].

.9 **disable,** disenable, unfit, **incapacitate,** drain, de-energize; enfeeble, debilitate, **weaken** 160.9,10; cripple, maim, lame, hamstring; wing, clip the wings of; **inactivate,** put out of action, put *hors de combat;* **put out of order,** put out of commission [informal], throw out of gear; bugger [slang], queer or queer the works [both slang], gum up or screw up the works [slang], throw a wrench or monkey wrench in the machinery [informal], sabotage, wreck; kibosh or put the kibosh on [both slang]; spike, spike one's guns, put a spoke in one's wheels.

.10 **disqualify,** invalidate, unfit, knock the bottom out of [informal].

.11 (render powerless) **paralyze,** prostrate, shoot down in flames [informal], knock out [slang], break the neck or back of; hamstring; handcuff, tie the hands of, hobble, enchain, manacle, hog-tie [informal], **tie hand and foot,** truss up; throttle, strangle, get a stranglehold on; muzzle, gag, silence; **disarm,** pull one's teeth, draw the teeth or fangs of; **take the wind out of one's sails,** deflate, knock the props out from under, cut the ground from under, not leave a leg to stand on.

.12 **unman, unnerve, enervate,** exhaust, etiolate, **devitalize; emasculate,** demasculinize, effeminize; desex, desexualize; sterilize; castrate 42.11.

.13 ADJS **impotent, powerless, forceless;** feeble, soft, flabby, **weak** 160.12; –less.

.14 **unable, incapable, incompetent,** inefficient, ineffective; **unqualified,** inept, unendowed, ungifted, untalented, **unfit,** unfitted; **inferior** 37.6; unable to, incapable of.

.15 **ineffective, ineffectual, inefficacious,** counterproductive, feckless, **inadequate** 37.7; **invalid, inoperative,** of no force; nugatory, nugacious; fatuous, fatuitous; **vain, futile, useless,** unavailing, bootless, fruitless; empty, inane, effete, etiolated, barren, sterile.

.16 **disabled, incapacitated; crippled,** hamstrung; disqualified, invalidated; disarmed; paralyzed; hog-tied [informal]; prostrate, **on one's back,** on one's beamends.

.17 **out of action, out of commission** [informal], out of gear; *hors de combat* [Fr], out of the battle, off the field, out of the running; laid on the shelf, obsolete.

.18 **helpless, defenseless, unprotected;** aidless, friendless, unfriended; fatherless, motherless; leaderless, guideless; **untenable,** pregnable, vulnerable.

.19 **unmanned, unnerved, enervated,** debilitated, **devitalized;** nerveless, sinewless, marrowless, pithless, lustless; **castrated,** emasculate, emasculated, gelded, eunuchized, unsexed, deballed [slang], demasculinized, effeminized.

.20 ADVS **beyond one,** beyond one's power or capacity or ability, beyond one's depth, out of one's league [informal], above one's head, too much for.

## 159. STRENGTH

*(inherent power)*

.1 NOUNS **strength, might,** mightiness, powerfulness; **force, potency, power** 157; energy 161; **vigor, vitality,** vigorousness, heartiness, lustiness, lustihood; **stoutness, sturdiness,** stalwartness, robustness, hardiness, ruggedness; **stamina, guts** or gutsiness [both slang], fortitude, intestinal fortitude [informal], **toughness** 359, endurance; strength of will, decisiveness, obstinacy 626; staying or sticking power.

.2 **muscularity,** brawniness; beefiness or huskiness or heftiness [all informal], thewiness, sinewiness; **brawn, beef** [informal]; **muscle,** muscul(o)–, my(o)–, –eus; thew, thews, sinew, sinews; musculature, physique; voluntary muscle 159.22, involuntary muscle; tone, elasticity 358.

.3 **firmness, soundness,** staunchness, **stoutness, sturdiness, stability,** solidity, **hardness** 356, temper.

.4 **impregnability,** impenetrability, **invulnerability,** inexpugnability, inviolability; **unassailability,** unattackableness; resistlessness, **irresistibility; invincibility,** indomitability, insuperability, unconquerableness, unbeatableness.

.5 **strengthening, invigoration,** fortification; hardening, case hardening, tempering; **restrengthening,** reinforcement; **reinvigoration,** refreshment, revivification.

.6 **strong man, stalwart,** tower of strength; powerhouse or muscle man or man mountain or big bruiser [all informal]; strong-arm man, bully, bullyboy, tough, tough guy [informal], gorilla; **giant,** Samson, Goliath; Charles Atlas; Hercules, Atlas, Antaeus, Cyclops, Briareus, colossus, Polyphemus, Titan, Brobdingnagian [Swift], Tarzan [E. R. Burroughs], Superman; the strong, the mighty.

.7 (comparisons) horse, ox, lion; oak, heart of oak; rock, Gibraltar; iron, steel, nails.

.8 VERBS **be strong,** overpower, overwhelm; have what it takes, pack a punch.

.9 **not weaken,** not flag; **bear up, hold up,** keep up, stand up; **hold out,** stay or see it out, stick or sweat it out [informal], stay the distance [informal], not give up, **never say die;** not let it get one down or take it or hang in or hang tough [all informal].

.10 **exert strength,** put beef or one's back into it [informal]; use force, muscle or strong-arm [both informal].

.11 **strengthen, invigorate, fortify,** beef up [informal], brace, buttress, prop, shore up, support, undergird, brace up; gird, gird up one's loins; steel, harden, case harden, stiffen, **toughen,** temper, nerve; confirm, sustain; **restrengthen, reinforce;**

**reinvigorate,** refresh, revive, recruit one's strength.

.12 **proof,** insulate, weatherproof, soundproof, fireproof, waterproof, etc.

.13 ADJS **strong, forceful,** forcible, forcy [Scot], **mighty, powerful,** puissant [dial], **potent** 157.12; **stout, sturdy, stalwart, rugged,** hale; husky or hefty or beefy [all informal], strapping, doughty [dial], **hardy,** hard, hard as nails, iron-hard, steely; **robust,** robustious, gutty or gutsy [both slang]; strong-willed, obstinate 626.8; **vigorous, hearty,** nervy, **lusty,** bouncing, full-or red-blooded; sturdy as an ox, strong as a lion or ox or horse, strong as brandy, strong as strong; full-strength, double-strength.

.14 **able-bodied, well-built,** well-set, well-set-up [informal], well-knit, of good or powerful physique, broad-shouldered, barrel-chested, **athletic; muscular,** thickset, burly, **brawny;** thewy, sinewy, **wiry;** muscle-bound.

.15 **Herculean,** Briarean, Antaean, Cyclopean, Atlantean, gigantic, huge 195.20.

.16 **firm, sound, stout,** sturdy, **staunch, stable,** solid; sound as a dollar, solid as a rock, firm as Gibraltar, made of iron; rigid, unbreakable, infrangible.

.17 **impregnable,** impenetrable, **invulnerable,** inviolable, inexpugnable; **unassailable,** unattackable, insuperable, unsurmountable; resistless, **irresistible; invincible,** indomitable, **unconquerable,** unsubduable, unyielding 626.9, incontestable, unbeatable, more than a match for; overpowering, overwhelming.

.18 **resistant, proof, tight;** proof against, impervious to; foolproof; shatterproof; weatherproof, dampproof, watertight, leakproof; hermetic, airtight; soundproof, noiseproof; punctureproof, holeproof; bulletproof, ballproof, shellproof, bombproof; rustproof, corrosionproof; fireproof, flameproof, fire-resisting; burglarproof.

.19 **unweakened, undiminished,** unallayed, unbated, unabated, unfaded, unwithered, unshaken, unworn, unexhausted; **unweakening, unflagging;** in full force or swing, going strong [informal]; in the plenitude of power.

.20 (of sounds and odors) **intense, penetrating,** piercing; **loud,** deafening, thundering 456.12; **pungent, reeking** 435.10.

.21 ADVS **strongly, stoutly, sturdily,** stalwartly, robustly, ruggedly; **mightily, powerfully, forcefully,** forcibly; **vigorously,** heartily, lustily; soundly, firmly, staunchly; impregnably, invulnerably, invincibly, irresistibly, unyieldingly; resistantly, imperviously; intensely; loudly, deafeningly; pungently.

.22 **voluntary muscles**

| | |
|---|---|
| adductor | plantaris |
| auricularis | platysma |
| biceps | pronator |
| brachialis | psoas |
| brachioradialis | pyriformis |
| buccinator | quadrator |
| coracobrachialis | quadriceps |
| deltoid(eus) | rectus abdominus |
| digastric | rectus femoris |
| extensor | rhomboideus |
| flexor | sacrospinalis |
| frontalis | sartorius |
| gastrocnemius | semimembranosus |
| gemellus | semitendinosus |
| gluteus maximus | serratus |
| gluteus medius | soleus |
| gluteus minimus | sphincter |
| iliacus | spinalis |
| infraspinatus | splenius |
| intercostal | sternocleidomastoid- |
| interosseus | (eus) |
| lacertus fibrosus | sternohyoid |
| latissimus dorsi | subclavius |
| levator | supraspinatus |
| masseter | temporalis |
| mentalis | tensor |
| mylohyoid | teres |
| nasalis | tibialis |
| oblique | trapezius |
| obturator | triangularis |
| occipitalis | triceps |
| omohyoid | vastus intermedius |
| palmaris | vastus lateralis |
| pectineus | vastus medialis |
| pectoralis | zygomaticus |
| peroneus | |

## 160. WEAKNESS

.1 NOUNS **weakness,** weakliness, **feebleness, strengthlessness, flabbiness,** flaccidity, softness, **impotence** 158; gutlessness [slang], cowardice 892; **debility,** debilitation; faintness, gone or blah feeling [informal]; languor, lassitude, languishment, listlessness, weariness, fatigue 717, prostration, dullness, sluggishness; atony, anemia, bloodlessness, etiolation, asthenia, adynamia, cachexia or cachexy.

.2 **frailty,** slightness, **delicacy, daintiness,** lightness; effeminacy, womanishness; **flimsiness, unsubstantiality,** wispiness, sleaziness; **fragility,** frangibility, brittleness, breakability, destructibility, disintegration 53, collapse; human frailty, "amiable weakness" [Henry Fielding]; moral weakness, irresolution, **indecisiveness,** infirmity of will, velleity, changeableness 141; inherent vice.

.3 infirmity, **unsoundness,** incapacity, unfirmness, unsturdiness, **instability, unsubstantiality;** decrepitude; **unsteadiness, shakiness,** ricketiness, wobbliness, caducity, senility, invalidism; wishy-washiness, insipidity, vapidity, wateriness.

.4 **weak point, weak side,** vulnerable point, heel of Achilles; feet of clay.

.5 **weakening, enfeeblement, debilitation,** exhaustion, inanition, attrition, effemination; languishment; **devitalization,** enervation, evisceration; fatigue; attenuation, extenuation; softening, mitigation, damping, abatement, slackening, relaxation, blunting, deadening, dulling; **dilution,** reduction, thinning.

.6 **weakling,** weak or meek soul, weak sister [informal], softy [informal], softling, **jellyfish,** invertebrate, gutless wonder [slang], **baby,** big baby, crybaby, chicken [slang], Milquetoast, sop, **milksop, namby-pamby, mollycoddle,** mama's boy, mother's darling, teacher's pet; sissy or pansy or pantywaist [all slang], pushover [slang], lightweight; poor or weak or dull tool [informal], doormat, nonentity, nebbish or sad sack [both informal].

.7 (comparisons) reed, thread, hair, cobweb, gossamer, matchwood, rope of sand; house of cards, house built on sand, sand castle; water, milk and water, gruel, dishwater, cambric tea.

.8 VERBS (be weak) **shake,** tremble, quiver, cower 892.9, totter, teeter, dodder; halt, limp; be on one's last legs, have one foot in the grave.

.9 (become weak) **weaken,** grow weak or weaker, go soft [informal]; languish, wilt, faint, **droop,** drop, **sink, decline, flag, pine, fade, fail;** crumble, go to pieces, disintegrate 53.3; go downhill, hit the skids [slang], give way, break, collapse, cave in [informal]; give out, conk or peter or poop or peg or fizzle out [informal]; come apart, come apart at the seams, come unstuck; yield; die on the vine [informal]; wear thin or away.

.10 (make weak) **weaken, enfeeble, debilitate,** unstrengthen, unsinew, undermine, soften up [informal], unbrace, unman, unnerve, rattle, shake up [informal], **devitalize, enervate,** eviscerate; **sap,** sap the strength of, exhaust, gruel, take it out of [informal]; shake, unstring; reduce, lay low; attenuate, extenuate, mitigate, abate; blunt, deaden, dull, damp or dampen, take the edge off; cramp, cripple.

.11 **dilute, cut** [informal], **reduce, thin,** attenuate, rarefy; **water,** water down, adulterate, irrigate *or* baptize [both slang].

.12 ADJS **weak,** weakly, **feeble,** asthen(o)–, lept(o)–; **debilitated,** imbecile; **strengthless,** sapless, marrowless, pithless, sinewless, listless, nerveless, lustless; **impotent, powerless** 158.13; spineless, chicken *or* gutless [slang], cowardly 892.10; **unnerved, shook-up** [informal], unstrung, faint, faintish, gone; dull, slack; **soft, flabby,** flaccid, unhardened; **limp,** limber, limp *or* limber as a dishrag, floppy, rubbery; **languorous,** languid, **drooping,** droopy, pooped [informal]; asthenic, anemic, bloodless, effete, etiolated; not what one used to be.

.13 "weak as water" [Bible], weak as milk and water, weak as a drink of water, weak as a child *or* baby, weak as a chicken, weak as a kitten, weak as a mouse, "weak as a rained-on bee" [F. R. Torrence].

.14 **frail, slight, delicate, dainty,** "delicately weak" [Pope]; puny; light, lightweight, womanish, effeminate; namby-pamby, sissified, pansyish; **fragile,** frangible, **breakable,** destructible, shattery, crumbly, brittle; **unsubstantial, flimsy,** sleazy, tacky [informal], wispy, cobwebby, gossamery, papery, pasteboardy; gimcrack *or* gimcracky *or* cheap-jack [all informal]; jerry-built, jerry.

.15 **unsound, infirm,** unfirm, **unstable, unsubstantial,** unsturdy, unsolid, decrepit, crumbling, disintegrating 53.5; poor, poorish; rotten, rotten at *or* rotten to the core.

.16 **unsteady, shaky, rickety,** ricketish, spindly, spidery, teetering, teetery, tottery, tottering, doddering, tumbledown, ramshackle, dilapidated, rocky [informal], groggy, wobbly.

.17 **wishy-washy,** tasteless, bland, **insipid,** vapid, neutral, watery, milky, milk-and-water, mushy; halfhearted, infirm of will *or* purpose, **indecisive,** irresolute, changeable 141.7.

.18 **weakened, enfeebled, disabled,** incapacitated; **devitalized,** drained, exhausted, sapped, burned-out, used up, played out, spent, *ausgespielt* [Ger], effete; **fatigued** 717.6, **enervated,** eviscerated; **wasted, run-down,** worn, worn-out, worn to a frazzle [informal], worn to a shadow, reduced to a skeleton, "weakened and wasted to skin and bone" [Du Bartas].

.19 **diluted, cut** [informal], **reduced, thinned,** rarefied, attenuated; adulterated; watered, watered-down.

.20 **weakening, debilitating, enfeebling;** devitalizing, enervating, sapping, exhausting, fatiguing 717.11, grueling, trying, draining.

.21 **languishing, drooping, sinking, declining, flagging, pining, fading, failing.**

.22 ADVS **weakly, feebly,** strengthlessly, languorously, listlessly; faintly; delicately, effeminately, daintily; infirmly, unsoundly, unstably, unsubstantially, unsturdily, flimsily; shakily, unsteadily, teeteringly, totteringly.

## 161. ENERGY

.1 NOUNS **energy, vigor, force, power, vitality,** strenuousness, **intensity,** dynamism, demonic energy; **potency** 157; **strength** 159; actual *or* kinetic energy; dynamic energy; potential energy, ergal.

.2 **vim, verve,** fire, starch, snap [informal], bang *or* **punch** [both informal], **dash, drive,** push [informal], **aggressiveness, enterprise,** initiative, thrust, spunk, piss and vinegar [slang], get-up-and-go [informal]; pep *or* pepper *or* ginger *or* kick *or* zip *or* zing *or* zizz *or* pizzazz *or* poop [all informal].

.3 **animation, vivacity,** liveliness, **ardor,** glow, warmth, enthusiasm, lustiness, robustness, mettle, **zest,** zestfulness, **gusto,** élan, impetus, impetuosity, *joie de vivre* [Fr], *brio* [Ital], spiritedness, **briskness,** perkiness, pertness, **life, spirit;** activity 707.

.4 **acrimony,** acridity, acerbity, acidity, **bitterness,** tartness, **causticity,** mordancy *or* mordacity, **virulence; harshness,** fierceness, **rigor,** roughness, **severity, vehemence,** violence 162, stringency, astringency, stridency 458.1, **sharpness, keenness, poignancy,** trenchancy; edge, point; bite, teeth, grip, sting.

.5 **energizer, stimulus,** stimulator, arouser, restorative; **stimulant, tonic** 687.8; **activator,** motivating force, motive power; **animator,** spark plug [informal], human dynamo [informal]; life, life of the party.

.6 (units of energy) atomerg, dinamode, dyne, erg, energid, foot-pound, horsepower-hour, horsepower-year, joule, calorie 328.19, kilogram-meter, kilowatt-hour, photon, quantum.

.7 **energizing, invigoration, animation, enlivenment,** quickening, **vitalization,** revival, revitalization; **exhilaration, stimulation.**

.8 **activation,** reactivation; viability.

.9 VERBS **energize,** dynamize; **invigorate, animate, enliven,** liven, vitalize, quicken, exhilarate, stimulate, hearten, galvanize, electrify, fire, inflame, warm, kindle, rouse, arouse, act like a tonic, **pep** *or* snap *or* jazz *or* zip *or* perk up [informal], put pep *or* zip into it [informal].

.10 **have energy**, be energetic, be vigorous, **thrive**, burst *or* overflow with energy, flourish, feel one's oats, be up and doing, be full of beans *or* pep *or* ginger *or* zip [informal], be full of piss and vinegar [slang].

.11 **activate**, reactivate, recharge.

.12 ADJS **energetic, vigorous, strenuous, forceful, forcible, strong, dynamic,** kinetic, intense, acute, keen, incisive, trenchant, vivid, vibrant; **enterprising, aggressive,** take-over *or* take-charge [both informal]; **active, lively,** living, **animated, spirited,** go-go [slang], **vivacious,** brisk, lusty, **robust,** hearty, enthusiastic, mettlesome, zesty, zestful, impetuous, spanking, smacking; snappy *or* zippy *or* peppy *or* full of pep [all informal].

.13 **acrimonious, acrid,** acidulous, acid, **bitter,** tart, **caustic,** escharotic [med], mordant *or* mordacious, **virulent, violent** 162.15, **vehement,** vitriolic; **harsh,** fierce, **rigorous,** severe, rough, stringent, astringent, strident 458.12, **sharp, keen,** incisive, trenchant, **cutting,** biting, stinging, **scathing,** stabbing, **piercing, poignant,** penetrating, edged, double-edged.

.14 **energizing, vitalizing, enlivening,** quickening; tonic, bracing, rousing; **invigorating,** invigorative; **animating,** animative; **exhilarating,** exhilarative; **stimulating,** stimulative; activating; viable.

.15 ADVS **energetically, vigorously, strenuously, forcefully,** forcibly, intensely, zestfully, lustily, heartily, keenly; **actively,** briskly; **animatedly, spiritedly,** vivaciously, with pep [informal], *con brio* [Ital].

## 162. VIOLENCE

### (vehement action)

.1 NOUNS **violence, vehemence, virulence, venom, furiousness, force, rigor,** roughness, harshness, ungentleness, extremity, impetuosity, inclemency, **severity, intensity,** acuteness, **sharpness; fierceness,** ferociousness, viciousness, savagery, destructiveness, vandalism; **terrorism, barbarity, brutality, atrocity,** inhumanity, bloodlust, murderousness, malignity, mercilessness, pitilessness, mindlessness, animality.

.2 **turbulence, turmoil,** chaos, upset, **fury,**

**furor,** *furore* [Ital], **rage, frenzy, passion,** fanaticism, zealousness, zeal, tempestuousness, storminess, wildness, tumultuousness, **tumult, uproar,** racket, cacophony, pandemonium, hubbub, **commotion, disturbance, agitation,** bluster, broil, brawl, embroilment, *brouhaha* [Fr], fuss, flap [Brit informal], row, rumpus, ruckus [informal], foofaraw [informal], ferment, fume, ebullition, fomentation.

.3 **unruliness, disorderliness,** obstreperousness; **riot, rioting;** looting, pillaging, sacking; laying waste, sowing with salt; **attack** 798, **assault,** onslaught, battering; **rape, violation,** forcible seizure; **killing** 409, butchery, massacre, slaughter.

.4 **storm, tempest,** squall, line squall, **tornado, cyclone, hurricane,** typhoon, war of the elements, "Nature's elemental din" [Thomas Campbell], "tempestuous rage", "groans of roaring wind and rain" [both Shakespeare]; stormy weather, rough weather, foul weather, dirty weather; rainstorm 394.2; thunderstorm 394.3; windstorm 403.12–14; **snowstorm** 333.8.

.5 **upheaval, convulsion, cataclysm,** disaster, overthrow, breakup; **fit, spasm, paroxysm,** apoplexy, stroke; climax; **earthquake,** quake, temblor, diastrophism, seismo–, –seism; tidal wave, *tsunami* [Jap].

.6 **outburst, outbreak, eruption,** debouchment, eructation, belch, spew, flare-up; **burst,** dissiliency; **torrent,** rush, gush, spate, cascade, spurt, jet, rapids, **volcano,** volcan, burning mountain.

.7 **explosion, discharge, blowout,** blowup, detonation, fulmination, **blast, burst, report** 456.1–5; flash, flare, fulguration; bang, boom 456.4; backfire.

.8 **concussion, shock, impact,** crunch, smash; percussion, repercussion.

.9 (violent person) **violent,** berserk *or* berserker; **hothead, madcap, hotspur; devil, demon, fiend, brute,** hellhound, hellcat, hellion, hell-raiser; **beast,** wild beast, tiger, dragon, mad dog, wolf, monster, savage; rapist, mugger, killer 409.11; hardnose *or* tough guy *or* tough *or* hoodlum *or* hood [all informal], goon *or* gorilla [both informal], gunsel [slang], Mafioso, terror *or* holy terror [both informal], fire-eater [informal], spitfire, ugly customer [informal]; **fury,** virago, vixen, termagant, beldam, she-wolf, tigress, witch; firebrand, Young Turk; revolutionary 147.3, **terrorist,** incendiary, bomber.

**.10** VERBS **rage, storm, rant, rave,** roar; **rampage,** ramp, **tear,** tear around; go or carry on [informal]; come in like a lion; **destroy, wreck, ruin;** sow chaos or disorder; **terrorize, vandalize, barbarize, brutalize; riot, loot, burn, pillage, sack,** lay waste; **slaughter, butcher** 409.17; **rape,** violate; **attack, assault** 798.15, batter, savage, mug, maul, hammer.

**.11** **seethe, boil, fume,** foam, simmer, stew, ferment, stir, churn.

**.12** **erupt, burst forth** or out, **break out, blow out** or **open,** eruct, belch, **vomit,** spout, spew, disgorge, **discharge,** eject, throw or hurl forth.

**.13** **explode, blow up, go off, blow out,** blast, burst, bust [informal]; **detonate,** fulminate; **touch off,** set off, let off; **discharge,** fire, shoot; backfire.

**.14** **run amok, go berserk,** go on a rampage, cut loose, run riot, run wild.

**.15** ADJS **violent, vehement, virulent, venomous, severe, rigorous, furious, fierce, intense,** sharp, acute, keen, cutting, splitting, piercing; rough, tough [informal]; **drastic, extreme, outrageous, excessive,** exorbitant, unconscionable, intemperate, immoderate, extravagant, great.

**.16** **unmitigated, unsoftened, untempered,** unallayed, unsubdued, unquelled; unquenched, unextinguished, unabated.

**.17** **turbulent, tumultuous, raging, chaotic,** hellish, anarchic, **storming,** stormy, **tempestuous,** troublous, **frenzied, wild, frantic, furious,** infuriate, insensate, mindless, **mad,** angry, ravening, raving; **blustering,** blustery, blusterous; **uproarious,** rip-roaring [informal]; pandemoniac; orgastic, orgasmic.

**.18** **unruly, disorderly,** obstreperous; **unbridled** 762.23; **riotous, wild, rampant;** terrorist(ic), revolutionary 147.5.

**.19** **boisterous, rampageous, rambunctious** [informal], roisterous, wild, rollicking, **rowdy,** rough, harum-scarum [informal]; knockabout, rough-and-tumble, knockdown-and-drag-out [informal].

**.20** **savage, fierce, ferocious, vicious, murderous** 409.24, **atrocious, brutal,** brutish, **bestial,** inhuman, pitiless, ruthless, merciless, bloody, sanguinary, kill-crazy [slang]; malign, malignant; feral, ferine; **wild,** untamed, tameless, ungentle; **barbarous,** barbaric; **uncivilized,** noncivilized.

**.21** **fiery, heated, inflamed,** flaming, scorching, hot, red-hot, white-hot; fanatic, zealous, totally committed, hard-core, ardent, passionate; **hotheaded,** madcap.

**.22** **convulsive,** cataclysmic, disastrous, upheaving; seismic; **spasmodic,** paroxysmal, spastic, jerky, herky-jerky [informal]; orgasmic.

**.23** **explosive,** bursting, detonating, explosible, explodable, fulminating; **volcanic,** eruptive.

**.24** ADVS **violently, vehemently, virulently, venomously, rigorously, severely, fiercely; furiously,** wildly, **madly, like mad,** like fury [informal], like blazes; all to pieces, with a vengeance.

**.25** **turbulently, tumultuously,** riotously, uproariously, stormily, tempestuously, troublously, **frenziedly, frantically, furiously, madly,** insensately, mindlessly, angrily.

**.26** **savagely, fiercely, ferociously, atrociously, viciously, murderously,** brutally or brutishly, bestially, barbarously, inhumanly, ruthlessly, pitilessly, mercilessly; **tooth and nail,** bec et ongles [Fr].

## 163. MODERATION

**.1** NOUNS **moderation,** moderateness; **restraint,** constraint, control; judiciousness, prudence; steadiness, evenness, **stability** 142; **temperateness,** temperance, sobriety; self-abnegation, self-restraint, self-control, self-denial; abstinence, continence, abnegation; **mildness,** lenity, gentleness; calmness, serenity, tranquillity, repose, calm, cool [informal]; unexcessiveness, unextremeness, unextravagance, nothing in excess, meden agan [Gk]; **happy medium, golden mean,** juste-milieu [Fr], middle way or path, via media [L]; moderationism, **conservatism** 140.3; **nonviolence,** pacifism; impartiality, neutrality, dispassion.

**.2** modulation, **abatement,** remission, **mitigation,** diminution, **reduction,** lessening, falling-off; **relaxation,** slackening, **easing,** loosening, letup or letdown [both informal]; **alleviation,** assuagement, allayment, palliation, leniency, lightening, **tempering, softening,** subduement; deadening, dulling, damping, blunting; **pacification, tranquilization,** mollification, demulsion, dulcification, **quieting,** quietening, lulling, **soothing, calming,** hushing.

**.3** **moderator, mitigator,** modulator, stabilizer, temperer, assuager; calming or restraining hand, wiser head; **alleviator,** alleviative, palliative, lenitive; **pacifier, soother,** peacemaker, pacificator, mollifier; anodyne, dolorifuge, soothing syrup, **tranquilizer,** calmative; **sedative** 687.12; **balm, salve;** cushion, shock absorber.

**.4** **moderate,** moderatist, moderationist,

middle-of-the-roader, centrist, neutral, compromiser; **conservative** 140.4.

**.5** VERBS **be moderate, keep within bounds,** keep within compass; practice self-control *or* self-denial, live temperately, do nothing in excess, strike a balance, keep a happy medium *or* the golden mean, steer *or* preserve an even course, keep to the middle path *or* way; keep the peace, not resist, espouse *or* practice nonviolence, be pacifistic; not rock the boat, not make waves *or* static; keep one's cool [informal], keep one's head *or* temper; sober down, settle down; remit, relent; take in sail; go out like a lamb; be conservative 140.6.

**.6 moderate, restrain,** constrain, control, **keep within bounds; modulate, mitigate,** abate, weaken, **diminish, reduce,** slacken, lessen, slow down; **alleviate,** assuage, allay, lay, lighten, palliate, extenuate, **temper,** attemper, lenify; **soften, subdue,** tame, chasten, underplay, play down, downplay, de-emphasize, tone *or* tune down; deaden, dull, blunt, obtund, take the edge off, take the sting *or* bite out; smother, suppress, stifle; damp, dampen, bank the fire, reduce the temperature, throw cold water on, throw a wet blanket on; sober, sober down *or* up.

**.7 calm,** calm down, **stabilize, tranquilize, pacify,** mollify, appease, dulcify; **quiet,** hush, still, rest, compose, **lull, soothe,** gentle, rock, cradle, rock to sleep; cool, **subdue,** quell; ease, steady, smooth, smoothen, smooth over, smooth down, even out; pour oil on troubled waters, pour balm into.

**.8 cushion,** absorb the shock, **soften the blow,** break the fall, deaden, damp *or* dampen, soften, suppress, neutralize, offset; show pity *or* mercy *or* consideration *or* sensitivity, temper the wind to the shorn lamb.

**.9 relax,** unbend; ease, **ease up,** ease off, **let up,** let down; abate, bate, remit, mitigate; **slacken,** slack, slake, slack off, slack up; loose, **loosen;** unbrace, unstrain, unstring.

**.10** ADJS **moderate, temperate,** sober; **mild,** soft, bland, **gentle,** tame; mild as milk *or* mother's milk, mild as milk and water, gentle as a lamb; nonviolent, peaceable, peaceful, pacifistic; judicious, prudent.

**.11 restrained,** constrained, limited, controlled, **stable,** in control, in hand; tempered, **softened,** hushed, **subdued,** quelled, chastened.

**.12 unexcessive,** unextreme, unextravagant, **conservative;** reasonable.

**.13 equable,** even, **cool,** even-tempered, level-headed, dispassionate; tranquil, reposeful, serene, calm 268.12.

**.14 mitigating,** assuaging, abating, **diminishing, reducing,** lessening, allaying, **alleviating, relaxing, easing;** tempering, **softening,** chastening, **subduing;** deadening, dulling, blunting, damping, dampening, cushioning.

**.15 tranquilizing,** pacifying, mollifying, appeasing; **calming,** lulling, gentling, rocking, cradling, hushing, quietening, stilling; **soothing,** soothful, restful; dreamy, drowsy.

**.16 palliative, alleviative,** assuasive, lenitive, **calmative,** calmant, **sedative,** demulcent, anodyne; antiorgastic, anaphrodisiac.

**.17** ADVS **moderately, in moderation,** restrainedly, subduedly, in *or* within reason, within bounds *or* compass, in balance; **temperately,** soberly, prudently, judiciously, dispassionately; composedly, calmly, coolly, evenly, steadily, equably, tranquilly, serenely; soothingly, conservatively.

## 164. OPERATION

**.1** NOUNS **operation,** operance *or* operancy, **functioning, action, performance** *or* **performing,** exercise, practice, work, **working,** workings; agency; management, **conduct, running, carrying-on** *or* -**out,** execution; driving, steering, direction 747; **handling,** manipulation; responsibility 962.1,2; **occupation** 656.

**.2 process, procedure,** proceeding, course; act, motion; step, measure; –age, –al, –ance *or* –ence, –ation, –ing, –ion, –ism, –ization *or* –isation, –ment, –osis, –sis, –th, –ure.

**.3 workability, operability,** performability, negotiability [informal], manageability, compassability, manipulatability, maneuverability; **practicability,** viability.

**.4 operator,** operative, operant; **handler,** manipulator; **driver,** runner, steersman, pilot, engineer; conductor; functionary, agent.

**.5** VERBS **operate, run, work, manage, conduct,** practice, **carry on** *or* **out** *or* **through,** make go; **handle,** manipulate, maneuver; deal with, see to, take care of; **drive,** steer, pilot, direct 147.8; perform on, play; occupy oneself with 656.10; be responsible for 962.6.

**.6 operate on, act on** *or* **upon, work on,** affect, influence; treat, focus or concentrate on; bring to bear upon.

.7 (be operative) **operate, function, work, act, perform, go, run,** be in action or operation or commission; percolate or perk or tick [all informal]; play; be effective, have effect, take effect, militate; have play, have free play.

.8 **function as,** work as, **act as,** act or play the part of, have the function or role or job or mission of.

.9 ADJS **operative, operational,** go [informal], **functional, practical; effective,** effectual, efficient, efficacious.

.10 **workable, operable,** operatable, **performable,** actable, **doable,** manageable, compassable, negotiable [informal], manipulatable, maneuverable; **practicable,** practical, viable.

.11 **operating** or operational, working, **functioning** or functional, acting, active, running, **going,** going on, ongoing; **in operation,** in action, **in practice, in force,** in play, in exercise, at work, on foot; **in process,** in the works, on the fire, in hand.

.12 operational, functional, agential, agentive or agentival; managerial; manipulational.

## 165. PRODUCTIVENESS

.1 NOUNS **productiveness, productivity,** productive capacity, **fruitfulness,** fructiferousness, procreativeness, **fertility,** fecundity, pregnancy; richness, **luxuriance,** lushness, exuberance, prolificacy, generousness, bountifulness, plentifulness, plenteousness, abundance 661.2, superabundance, copiousness, teemingness, swarmingness; teeming womb or loins.

.2 proliferation, prolification, fructification, pullulation, multiplication; **reproduction** 169, **production** 167.

.3 **fertilization, enrichment,** fecundation; insemination, impregnation 169.4.

.4 **fertilizer,** dressing, enrichener; organic fertilizer, manure, muck, night soil, dung, guano, compost, castor-bean meal; commercial fertilizer, inorganic fertilizer, chemical fertilizer, phosphate, superphosphate, ammonia, nitrogen, nitrate.

.5 (goddesses of fertility) Demeter, Ceres, Isis, Astarte or Ashtoreth; (gods) Frey, Priapus, Dionysus, Pan, Baal.

.6 (comparisons) milk cow, rabbit, Hydra, warren, seed plot, hotbed, rich soil, land flowing with milk and honey, mustard.

.7 VERBS **be productive, proliferate,** pullulate, fructify, be fruitful, **multiply,** engender, beget, teem; **reproduce** 169.7,8.

.8 **fertilize, enrich,** fatten; fructify, fecundate, fecundify, prolificate; inseminate, impregnate 169.10; dress, manure.

.9 ADJS **productive, fruitful,** fructiferous, fecund; **fertile,** pregnant, seminal, **rich,** flourishing, thriving, blooming; **prolific,** proliferous, uberous, **teeming,** swarming, bursting, bursting out, plenteous, **plentiful,** copious, generous, bountiful, **abundant** 661.7, superabundant, luxuriant, lush, exuberant; creative 167.19.

.10 **bearing, yielding, producing;** fruitbearing, fructiferous.

.11 **fertilizing, enriching,** richening, fattening, fecundative, fructificative, seminal, germinal.

## 166. UNPRODUCTIVENESS

.1 NOUNS **unproductiveness, unproductivity,** ineffectualness 158.3; **unfruitfulness, barrenness,** dryness, aridity, dearth, famine; sterileness, **sterility,** unfertileness, **infertility,** infecundity; wasted or withered loins, dry womb; **birth control, contraception,** family planning, planned parenthood; impotence 158.

.2 **wasteland, waste,** desolation, barren or **barrens,** barren land, "weary waste" [Southey], "Rock and no water and the sandy road", "An old man in a dry season" [both T. S. Eliot]; heath; **desert,** Sahara, "a barren waste, a wild of sand" [Addison], karroo [Africa], dust bowl, salt flat, Death Valley, Arabia Deserta, lunar waste or landscape; **wilderness,** howling wilderness, wild, wilds; bush, brush, outback [Australia].

.3 VERBS be unproductive, **come to nothing,** come to naught, hang fire, flash in the pan, fizzle or peter out [informal]; **lie fallow.**

.4 ADJS **unproductive,** nonproductive or nonproducing; **infertile,** unfertile or nonfertile; **unfruitful, sterile,** impotent, gelded 158.19, acarpous, infecund, unprolific or nonprolific, ineffectual 158.15; **barren,** desert, arid, gaunt, dry, dried-up, exhausted, drained, leached, sucked dry, wasted, **waste, desolate,** jejune; **childless,** issueless, fruitless, teemless, without issue, sine prole [L]; fallow, unplowed, unsown, untilled, uncultivated; celibate, virgin, menopausal.

.5 **uncreative,** noncreative, nonseminal, nongerminal, unpregnant; uninventive, unoriginal, derivative.

## 167. PRODUCTION, BIRTH

.1 NOUNS production; performance, execution, doing, accomplishment, achievement, realization, bringing to fruition, effectuation, operation 164; overproduction; productiveness 165.

.2 mass production, volume production, assembly-line production; production line, assembly line; modular production or assembly, standardization; division of labor, industrialization.

.3 creation, manufacture or manufacturing, making, producing, devising, fashioning, framing, forming, formation, formulation, casting, shaping, molding, machining, milling, preparation, processing, conversion, assembly, composition, elaboration; construction, building, erection, architecture; fabrication, prefabrication; workmanship, craftsmanship; handiwork, handicraft, crafting; mining, extraction, smelting, refining; growing, cultivation, raising, harvesting; –faction, –fication, –plasia or –plasy, –poiesis.

.4 establishment, foundation, constitution, institution, installation, formation, organization, inauguration, inception, setting-up, realization, materialization, effectuation.

.5 creation, origination, invention, conception, beginning, fabrication, concoction, coinage, mintage, devising, hatching, contriving, contrivance; improvisation, making do; authorship; creative effort, generation 169.6; –genesis, –geny.

.6 bearing, yielding; fruition, fruiting, fructification.

.7 birth, genesis, nativity, nascency, childbirth, childbearing, having a baby, giving birth, birthing [dial], parturition, the stork [informal], delivery, –toky, toco– or toko–; hatching; blessed event [informal]; the Nativity; multiparity; confinement, lying-in, being brought to bed, childbed, accouchement [Fr]; labor, travail, birth throes.

.8 producer, maker, craftsman, wright, smith; manufacturer, industrialist; creator, begetter, engenderer, author, mother, father, sire; ancestors 170.7; precursor 66; generator, mover; originator, initiator, inaugurator, introducer, institutor, beginner, prime mover, instigator; founder, organizer; inventor, discoverer, deviser; builder, constructor, artificer, architect, planner, conceiver, designer, shaper; executor, executrix, engineer;

grower, raiser; effector, realizer; apprentice, journeyman, master, master craftsman, artist, past master; –er or –ier or –yer, –fer, –gen(e), –ist, –ment, –or.

.9 VERBS produce; perform, do, work, act, execute, accomplish, achieve, realize, engineer, effectuate, bring about, bring to fruition or into being, cause 153.11; mass-produce, volume-produce, industrialize; overproduce; be productive 165.7.

.10 create, make, manufacture, produce, form, formulate, evolve, mature, elaborate, fashion, fabricate, prefabricate, cast, shape, mold, extrude, frame; construct, build, erect, put up, set up, run up, raise, rear; make up, get up, prepare, compose, write, indite, devise, concoct, compound; put together, assemble, piece together, patch together, whomp up [slang], fudge together [informal].

.11 process, convert 145.11; mill, machine; carve, chisel; mine, extract, pump, smelt, refine; raise, rear, grow, cultivate, harvest.

.12 establish, found, constitute, institute, install, form, set up, organize, inaugurate, incept, realize, materialize, effect, effectuate.

.13 originate, invent, conceive, discover, make up, devise, contrive, concoct, fabricate, coin, mint, frame, hatch, hatch or cook up, strike out; improvise, make do with; think up, think out, dream up, design, plan, set one's wits to work, strain or crack one's invention; generate, develop, mature, evolve; breed, engender, beget, spawn, hatch; bring forth, give rise to, give being to, bring or call into being; procreate 169.8.

.14 bear, yield, produce, furnish; bring forth, usher into the world; fruit, bear fruit, fructify.

.15 give birth, bear, bear or have young, have; have a baby, bear a child; drop, cast, throw, pup, whelp, kitten, foal, calve, fawn, lamb, yean, farrow, litter; lie in, be confined, labor, travail.

.16 be born, have birth, come forth, issue forth, come into the world; hatch; be illegitimate or born out of wedlock, have the bar sinister; be born on the wrong side of the blanket, come in through a side door [informal].

.17 ADJS productional, creational, formational; executional; manufacturing, manufactural, fabricational, industrial.

.18 constructional, structural, building, housing, edificial; architectural, architectonic.

.19 creative, originative, causative, productive 165.9, **constructive**, formative, fabricative, demiurgic; inventive; generative 169.16; –facient, –factive, –ferous, –fic, –genetic, –genic, –genous, –gerous *or* –igerous, –ic(al) *or* –etic, –ive, –ory, –poietic.

.20 **produced, made, caused, brought about**; effectuated, executed, performed, done; grown, raised; **mass-produced**, volume-produced.

.21 **bearing**, giving birth, –para, –parous, –tokous; **born**, given birth; **hatched**; cast, dropped, whelped, foaled, calved, etc.; "cast naked upon the naked earth" [Pliny the Elder]; née; newborn; stillborn.

.22 **made**, man-made; **manufactured**, created, crafted, formed, shaped, molded, cast, forged, machined, milled, fashioned, **built, constructed**, fabricated; **well-made**, well-built, well-constructed; **homemade**, homespun, **handmade**, handcrafted, self-made; machine-made; **processed; assembled**, put together; **custom-made**, custom-built, custom, made to order; **ready-made**, ready-formed, ready-prepared, ready-to-wear, ready-for-wear; prefabricated, prefab [informal]; **mined**, extracted, smelted, **refined; grown, raised**, harvested, gathered.

.23 **invented**, originated, **conceived**, discovered; fabricated, coined, minted, new-minted; **made-up**, made out of whole cloth.

.24 **manufacturable, producible**, productible, causable.

.25 ADVS **in production**, under construction, in the works, in hand, on foot.

## 168. PRODUCT

.1 NOUNS **product**, end product; **work**, *œuvre* [Fr], **handiwork, artifact**, manufacture, production, **creation**, creature; off-spring, child, fruit; issue, outgrowth, outcome; result, **effect** 154; **invention**, origination, coinage, mintage *or* new mintage, brainchild; concoction, composition; opus, opera [pl], opuscule; **extract, distillation**, essence; apprentice work, journeyman work, **masterwork, masterpiece**, *chef d'œuvre* [Fr], *Meisterstück* [Ger], work of an artist *or* master *or* past master, crowning achievement; –ade, –age, –ate, –gen(e), –ing, –ion, –ite, –ization *or* –isation, –ment, –plast, –state.

.2 **produce**, proceeds, net, **yield, output**, throughput; **crop, harvest**.

.3 **by-product**, outgrowth, offshoot, side issue.

.4 (amount made) make, making; batch, lot, run.

## 169. REPRODUCTION, PROCREATION

.1 NOUNS **reproduction, remaking, re-creation**, refashioning, reshaping, redoing, re-formation, **reconstruction**, rebuilding, redesign, restructuring, **revision**; reedition, reissue, reprinting; reestablishment, **reorganization**, reinstitution, reconstitution; **rebirth**, renascence, resurrection, revival; regeneration, regenesis, palingenesis; **duplication** 91, **imitation** 22, **copy** 24, **repetition** 103; **restoration** 694, renovation; producing *or* making *or* creating over *or* again *or* once more.

.2 **procreation, generation, begetting, breeding**, engenderment; **propagation, multiplication**, –gamy, –gony; proliferation; linebreeding; inbreeding, endogamy; outbreeding, xenogamy; dissogeny; cross-breeding 44.4.

.3 **fertilization**, fecundation; **impregnation**, insemination, getting with child; **pollination**, pollinization; cross-fertilization, cross-pollination; self-fertilization, heterogamy, orthogamy; isogamy, artificial insemination; conjugation, zygosis, zyg(o)–; –spermy, –myxis.

.4 **conception**, conceiving, coming with child; superfetation, superimpregnation.

.5 **pregnancy, gestation, incubation**, parturiency, gravidness *or* gravidity, heaviness, greatness, bigness, the family way [informal]; brooding, sitting, covering.

.6 **birth** 167.7, **generation, genesis; development**; procreation; abiogenesis, archigenesis, biogenesis, blastogenesis, digenesis, dysmerogenesis, epigenesis, eumerogenesis, heterogenesis, histogenesis, homogenesis, isogenesis, merogenesis, metagenesis, monogenesis, oögenesis, orthogenesis, pangenesis, parthenogenesis, phytogenesis, sporogenesis, xenogenesis; spontaneous generation.

.7 VERBS **reproduce, remake**, make *or* do over, **re-create**, regenerate, resurrect, revive, re-form, refashion, **reshape**, redo, **reconstruct**, rebuild, redesign, restructure, **revise**; reprint, reissue; reestablish, reinstitute, reconstitute, refound, **reorganize; duplicate** 91.3, **copy** 22.5, **repeat** 103.7, **restore** 694.11, **renovate**.

.8 **procreate, generate, breed, beget**, get, **engender; propagate, multiply**; proliferate; mother; father, sire; reproduce in kind, reproduce after one's kind, "multiply and replenish the earth" [Bible]; breed true; inbreed, breed in and in; outbreed; crossbreed 44.14; linebreed; copulate 419.23, make love 932.13.

.9 **lay** (eggs), deposit, drop, spawn.

.10 **fertilize,** fructify, fecundate, fecundify; **impregnate, inseminate,** spermatize; **get with child** or **young; pollinate** or pollinize, pollen; cross-fertilize, cross-pollinate or cross-pollinize, cross-pollen.

.11 **conceive, come with child,** (animal) catch, get in the family way [informal]; superfetate.

.12 **be pregnant,** be gravid, be great with child, **be with child** or **young;** be in the family way or have a cake in the oven or be expecting or anticipate a blessed event [all informal], be infanticipating, be knocked up [both slang], be blessedeventing [informal]; gestate, breed, carry, carry young; **incubate, hatch; brood,** sit, set, cover.

.13 **give birth** 167.15.

.14 ADJS **reproductive, re-creative, reconstructive,** re-formative; renascent, regenerative, resurgent, reappearing; reorganizational; revisional; **restorative** 694.22; Hydraheaded, Phoenixlike.

.15 **reproductive, procreative,** procreant, **propagative,** life-giving; spermatic, spermatozoic, seminal, germinal, fertilizing, fecundative; multiparous; gen(o)–, –genic; –spermic.

.16 **genetic, generative,** genial, gametic; genital, genitive; abiogenetic, biogenetic, blastogenetic, digenetic, dysmerogenetic, epigenetic, eumerogenetic, heterogenetic, histogenetic, homogenetic, isogenetic, merogenetic, metagenetic, monogenetic, oögenetic, orthogenetic, pangenetic, parthenogenetic, phytogenetic, sporogenous, xenogenetic.

.17 **bred, impregnated,** inseminated; inbred, endogamic, endogamous; outbred, exogamic, exogamous; crossbred 44.16; linebred.

.18 **pregnant,** enceinte [Fr], **with child** or **young, in the family way** [informal], gestating, breeding, teeming, parturient; heavy with child or young, great or big with child or young, in a delicate condition, gravid, heavy, great, big-laden; carrying, carrying a fetus or embryo; **expecting** [informal], anticipating or anticipating a blessed event [both informal]; preggers [Brit informal]; knocked up [slang]; infanticipating [informal]; superfetate, superimpregnated.

# 170. ANCESTRY

.1 NOUNS **ancestry,** progenitorship; parentage, parenthood; grandparentage, grandfatherhood, grandmotherhood.

.2 **paternity, fatherhood,** fathership; fatherliness, paternalness.

.3 **maternity, motherhood,** mothership; motherliness, maternalness.

.4 **lineage, line, bloodline, descent,** line of descent, succession, **extraction,** derivation, birth, **blood,** breed, **family,** house, **strain,** sept, **stock,** race, stirps, seed; direct line, phylum; **branch,** stem; filiation, affiliation, apparentation; side; male line, spear or sword side; female line, distaff or spindle side; consanguinity, common ancestry 11.1.

.5 **genealogy, pedigree,** stemma, Stammbaum [Ger], genealogical tree, **family tree,** tree.

.6 **heredity, heritage, inheritance, birth;** patrocliny, matrocliny; endowment, inborn capacity or tendency or susceptibility or predisposition; diathesis; inheritability, heritability, hereditability; Mendel's law, Mendelism or Mendelianism; Weismann theory, Weismannism; Altmann theory, De Vries theory, Galtonian theory, Verworn theory, Wiesner theory; **genetics,** pharmacogenetics, genesiology, eugenics; **gene,** factor, inheritance factor, determiner, determinant; **character,** dominant or recessive character, allele or allelomorph; **chromosome,** chromatin, chromatid; genetic code, DNA, RNA, replication.

.7 **ancestors, antecedents, predecessors,** ascendants, **fathers, forefathers, forebears,** progenitors, primogenitors; **grandparents, grandfathers;** patriarchs, elders.

.8 **parent, progenitor, ancestor,** procreator, begetter; grandparent; ancestress, progenitress, progenitrix.

.9 **father, sire,** genitor, paternal ancestor, pater [informal], the old man [slang], governor [informal], abba [Heb]; papa or pa or pap or pappy or pop or pops or dad or daddy or daddums [all informal]; patriarch, paterfamilias; stepfather; foster father.

.10 **mother,** genetrix, dam, maternal ancestor, mater [informal], the old woman [slang]; **mama** or mammy or mam or **ma** or mom or **mommy** or mummy or mumsy or mimsy or motherkin or motherkins [all informal]; matriarch, materfamilias; stepmother; foster mother.

.11 **grandfather; grandpa** or **grampa** or **gramper** or **gramp** or **gramps** or **grandpapa** or **grandpap** or **grandpappy** or **granddad** or **granddaddy** or **granddada** [all informal]; **grandsire** or **gramfer** or **granther** [all dial]; old man 127.2; **great-grandfather.**

.12 **grandmother,** grandam, grannam or gammer [both dial]; **grandma** or granma or grandmamma or grandmammy or **granny** or grammy or gammy [all informal]; old woman 127.3; **great-grandmother.**

.13 ADJS **ancestral,** ancestorial, patriarchal; **parental,** parent; **paternal,** patr(o)– or patri–; fatherly, fatherlike; **maternal,** mother, matr(o)– or matri–; motherly, motherlike; grandparental; grandmotherly, grandmaternal; grandfatherly, grandpaternal.

.14 **lineal,** family, genealogical; direct, in a direct line; phyletic, phylogenetic; diphyletic.

.15 **hereditary,** patrimonial, **inherited,** hered(o)–; **innate** 5.7; genetic, genic; –clinous or –clinic or –clinal, patroclinous, matroclinous.

.16 **inheritable,** heritable, hereditable.

## 171. POSTERITY

.1 NOUNS **posterity, progeny, issue, offspring,** fruit, seed, brood, breed, family, **descent,** succession; lineage 170.4; **descendants,** heirs, inheritors, sons, **children, kids** [informal], little ones, treasures, hostages to fortune, youngsters, younglings; grandchildren, great-grandchildren; new or young or rising generation;

.2 (of animals) **young, brood,** get, nest; (fish) **spawn,** spat, fry; **litter,** drey (of squirrels), farrow (of pigs); (birds) clutch, hatch.

.3 **descendant, offspring, child,** scion; **son,** son and heir, chip of or off the old block, sonny; **daughter,** heiress; grandchild, grandson, granddaughter; stepchild, stepson, stepdaughter; foster child; ped(o)–, proli–, tecno–, toco– or toko–; –id, –ite.

.4 (derived or collateral descendant) **offshoot,** offset, **branch,** sprout, shoot, filiation.

.5 **bastard,** illegitimate, bantling, notho–, illegitimate or bastard child, whore's bird [slang], by-blow, child born out of wedlock, natural or love child, *nullius filius* [L]; illegitimacy, bastardy, bar sinister.

.6 **sonship,** sonhood; **daughtership,** daughterhood.

.7 ADJS **filial,** sonly, sonlike; **daughterly,** daughterlike.

## 172. INFLUENCE

.1 NOUNS **influence,** influentiality; **power** 157, force, clout [informal], potency, pressure, effect, indirect or incidental power, **say,** a lot to do with or to say about [informal], **prestige,** favor, good feeling, credit, esteem, repute, personality, leadership, charisma, magnetism, charm, enchantment; **weight,** moment, consequence, importance, eminence; **authority** 739, control, domination, hold; **sway** 741.1, reign, rule; **mastery,** ascendancy, supremacy, dominance, predominance, preponderance; upper hand, whip hand; leverage, purchase; **persuasion** 648.3, suasion, suggestion, subtle influence, insinuation.

.2 **favor,** special favor, **interest; pull** or drag or suction [all informal]; inside track [informal].

.3 **backstairs influence,** intrigues, deals, schemes, **games,** Machiavellian or Byzantine intrigues, ploys; connections; **wires** or **strings** or ropes [all informal]; **wirepulling** [informal]; **influence peddling;** lobbying, lobbyism.

.4 **sphere of influence,** orbit, ambit; bailiwick, vantage, stamping ground, footing, **territory,** turf, constituency.

.5 **influenceability,** swayableness, movability; **persuadability,** suasibility, openness, open-mindedness, perviousness, accessibility, receptiveness, responsiveness, amenableness; **suggestibility, susceptibility,** impressionability, malleability; weakness 160; putty in one's hands.

.6 (influential person or thing) **influence,** good influence; bad influence, sinister influence; man of influence; heavyweight, big wheel, very important person or VIP [informal]; wheeler-dealer [informal], influencer, **wire-puller** [informal]; **power behind the throne,** gray eminence, *éminence grise* [Fr], hidden hand, manipulator, friend at or in court, kingmaker; **influence peddler,** five-percenter, lobbyist; Svengali, Rasputin; **pressure group,** special-interest group, special interests; lobby; the Establishment, ingroup, court, powers that be 749.15, lords of creation; **key,** key to the city, access, open sesame.

.7 VERBS **influence,** make oneself felt, **affect,** weigh with, **sway,** bias, bend, incline, dispose, predispose, **move,** prompt, lead; color, tinge, tone; **induce, persuade** 648.23; **work,** work or bend to one's will; lead by the nose [informal], wear down, soften up; win friends and influence people, ingratiate oneself.

.8 (exercise influence over) **govern** 741.12, **rule, control** 741.13, order, **regulate**, direct, guide; **determine**, decide, dispose; call the shots *or* be in the driver's seat *or* wear the pants [all informal].

.9 **exercise** *or* **exert influence, use one's influence, bring pressure to bear upon,** act on, **work on,** bear upon, throw one's weight around *or* into the scale, say a few words to the right person *or* in the right quarter; draw, ·draw on, lead on, magnetize; **approach,** go up to with hat in hand, make advances *or* overtures, make up to *or* get cozy with [both informal]; get at *or* get the ear of [informal]; **pull strings** *or* **wires** *or* **ropes,** wire-pull [informal]; lobby, lobby through.

.10 **have influence, be influential, carry weight, weigh, tell, count,** cut ice, throw a lot of weight [informal], have a lot to do with *or* say about [informal]; be the decisive factor *or* the one that counts, have pull *or* suction *or* drag *or* leverage [informal]; have a way with one, have personality *or* magnetism *or* charisma, charm the birds out of the trees, be persuasive; have an in [informal], have the inside track [informal]; have full play.

.11 have influence *or* power *or* a hold over; **lead by the nose, twist** *or* **turn** *or* **wind around one's little finger,** keep under one's thumb, make sit up and beg *or* lie down and turn over; hypnotize, mesmerize, **dominate** 741.15.

.12 gain influence, **get in with** [informal], ingratiate oneself with, get cozy with [informal]; gain a footing, take hold, move in, take root, strike root in; gain a hearing, make one's voice heard, make one sit up and take notice, be listened to, be recognized; get the mastery *or* control of, gain a hold upon; change the preponderance, turn the scale *or* balance, turn the tables.

.13 ADJS **influential, powerful** 157.12, potent, strong; **effective,** effectual, efficacious, telling; **weighty,** momentous, important, consequential, substantial, **prestigious,** estimable, authoritative, reputable; **persuasive,** suasive, personable, **winning,** magnetic, charming, enchanting, charismatic.

.14 (in a position of influence) **dominant** 741.18, **predominant,** preponderant, prepotent, prepollent, regnant, ruling, swaying, prevailing, on the throne, in the driver's seat [informal]; **ascendant,** in the ascendant, in ascendancy.

.15 **influenceable, swayable, movable; persuadable,** persuasible, suasible, open, open-minded, pervious, accessible, receptive, responsive, amenable; **plastic, pliant,** pliable, malleable; **suggestible, susceptible, impressionable,** weak 160.12.

## 173. LACK OF INFLUENCE

.1 NOUNS **lack of influence** *or* **power** *or* **force,** uninfluentiality, **unauthoritativeness,** powerlessness, forcelessness, impotence 158; **ineffectiveness,** inefficaciousness, inefficacy, ineffectuality; **no say,** nothing to do with *or* say about [informal]; unpersuasiveness, lack of personality *or* charm, lack of magnetism *or* charisma; **weakness** 160.

.2 uninfluenceability, unswayableness, unmovability; **unpersuadability,** impersuadability, impersuasibility, unreceptiveness, imperviousness, unresponsiveness; unsuggestibility, **unsusceptibility,** unimpressionability; **obstinacy** 626.

.3 ADJS **uninfluential, powerless,** forceless, impotent 158.13; **weak** 160.12; unauthoritative; **ineffective,** ineffectual, inefficacious; **of no account,** no-account, without any weight, featherweight, lightweight.

.4 **uninfluenceable, unswayable, unmovable; unpliable,** unyielding, inflexible; **unpersuadable** 626.13, impersuadable, impersuasible, unreceptive, unresponsive, unamenable; **impervious,** closed to; **unsuggestible, unsusceptible,** unimpressionable; **obstinate** 626.8.

.5 **uninfluenced, unmoved, unaffected, unswayed.**

## 174. TENDENCY

.1 NOUNS **tendency, inclination, leaning,** penchant, proneness, weakness, susceptibility; liability 175, readiness, willingness, eagerness, aptness, aptitude, **disposition, proclivity, propensity,** predisposition, **predilection,** a thing for [informal], affinity, prejudice, liking, delight, soft spot; conduciveness; instinct *or* feeling for, sensitivity to; diathesis, conatus, tropism; **bent, turn, bias,** cast, warp, twist; probability 511; –ey *or* –y, –itis, –philia, –phoria, –trope; trop(o)–.

.2 **trend, drift, course, current,** stream, mainstream, main current, movement, glacial movement, motion, run, **tenor,** tone, **set,** set of the current, swing, bearing, line, direction, the general tendency or drift, the main course, the course of events, the way the wind blows, **the way things go,** trend of the times, spirit of the age *or* time, time spirit, *Zeitgeist* [Ger]; the way it looks.

.3 VERBS **tend,** have a tendency, **incline,** dispose, **lean, trend,** set, go, head, lead, point, verge, turn, warp, bias, bend to, work *or* gravitate *or* set toward; show a tendency *or* trend *or* set *or* direction, swing toward, point to, look to; **conduce,** contribute, serve, redound to.

.4 ADJS **tending,** tendent, tendentious *or* tendential; **leaning, inclining,** inclinatory, inclinational.

.5 **tending to, conducive to,** leading to, inclined toward, inclining toward, heading *or* moving *or* swinging *or* working toward.

.6 **inclined to, prone to, disposed to,** predisposed to, given to; **apt to, likely to, liable to** 175.5, calculated to, minded to, ready to, in a fair way to; –able *or* –ible, –atory, –ful, –tropic.

## 175. LIABILITY

.1 NOUNS **liability,** liableness, **likelihood** *or* **likeliness,** aptitude, aptness, **possibility** 509, **probability** 511, contingency, chance 156, eventuality 151.1; weakness, **proneness** 174.1; **obligation** 962.1,2.

.2 **susceptibility,** susceptivity, **openness, exposure; vulnerability** 697.4.

.3 VERBS **be liable, be subjected to,** be a pawn *or* plaything of, be the prey of, lie under; **expose oneself to, lay oneself open to,** open the door to; **gamble,** stand to lose *or* gain, stand a chance, **run the chance** *or* **risk, risk,** let down one's guard *or* defenses; **admit of,** open the possibility of, be in the way of, bid *or* stand fair to.

.4 **incur, contract, invite,** welcome, run, **bring on, bring down,** bring upon *or* down upon, bring upon *or* down upon oneself; **be responsible for** 962.6; fall into, fall in with; get, gain, acquire.

.5 ADJS **liable to, subject to,** standing to, in a position to, incident to, dependent on; **susceptible** *or* **prone to,** susceptive to, **open** *or* vulnerable *or* **exposed to,** naked to, in danger of, within range of, at the mercy of; **capable of,** ready for; **likely to, apt to** 174.6; obliged to, responsible *or* answerable for.

.6 CONJS **lest, that, for fear that.**

## 176. INVOLVEMENT

.1 NOUNS **involvement,** involution, **implication, entanglement,** enmeshment, engagement, involuntary presence *or* cooperation, embarrassment; relation 9; **inclusion** 76; **absorption** 530.3.

.2 VERBS **involve, implicate,** tangle, **entangle,** embarrass, enmesh, engage, **draw in,** drag *or* hook *or* suck into, catch up in, **make a party to;** interest, concern; **absorb** 530.13.

.3 ADJS **involved, implicated;** interested, concerned, a party to; **included** 76.5.

.4 **involved in, implicated in,** tangled *or* entangled in, enmeshed in, **caught up in,** tied up in, wrapped up in, all wound up in, dragged *or* hooked *or* sucked into; deeply involved, **up to one's neck** *or* **ears in,** up to one's elbows in, head over heels in, **absorbed in** 530.17, immersed *or* submerged in, far-gone.

## 177. CONCURRENCE

.1 NOUNS **concurrence, collaboration,** coaction, **co-working,** collectivity, combined effort *or* operation, united *or* concerted action, concert, synergy; **cooperation** 786; **agreement** 26; **coincidence,** simultaneity, synchronism; concomitance, accompaniment 73; **union,** junction 47.1,4, **conjunction,** combination 52, association, alliance; conspiracy, collusion, cahoots [informal]; concourse, confluence; **accordance** 794.1, concordance, correspondence, consilience; symbiosis, parasitism; saprophytism.

.2 VERBS **concur, collaborate,** coact, **co-work,** synergize; **cooperate** 786.3; conspire, collude, connive, be in cahoots [informal]; **combine** 52.3, **unite, associate** 52.4, coadunate, join, conjoin; harmonize; **coincide,** synchronize, happen together; **accord** 794.2, correspond, **agree** 26.6.

.3 **go with, go along with, go hand in hand with,** be hand in glove with, team *or* join up with; keep pace with, run parallel to.

.4 ADJS **concurrent,** concurring; **coacting,** coactive, **collaborative,** collective, **co-working,** cooperant, synergetic *or* synergic *or* synergistic; **cooperative** 786.5; conspiratorial, collusive; **united, joint,** conjoint, **combined, concerted,** associated, associate, coadunate; **coincident,** synchronous, coordinate; concomitant, accompanying 73.9; meeting, uniting, combining; **accordant, agreeing** 26.9, concordant, harmonious, consilient, at one with; symbiotic, parasitic, saprophytic.

.5 ADVS concurrently, coactively, jointly, conjointly, concertedly, in harmony or unison with, together; with one accord, with one voice, as one, as one man; hand in hand, hand in glove, shoulder to shoulder, cheek by jowl.

## 178. COUNTERACTION

.1 NOUNS counteraction, counterworking; opposition 790, opposure, counterposition or contraposition, confutation, contradiction; antagonism, repugnance, oppugnance or oppugnancy, antipathy, conflict, friction, interference, clashing, collision; reaction, repercussion, backlash, kick, recoil; resistance, recalcitrance, dissent 522, revolt 767.4, perverseness, nonconformity 83, crankiness, crotchetiness, renitency; going against the current, swimming upstream; contrariety 15.

.2 neutralization, nullification, annulment, cancellation, voiding, invalidation, vitiation, frustration, thwarting, undoing; offsetting, counterbalancing.

.3 counteractant, counteractive, counteragent; counterirritant; antidote, remedy, preventive or preventative, prophylactic; neutralizer, nullifier, offset; antacid, buffer.

.4 counterforce, counterinfluence, counterpressure; counterpoise, counterbalance, counterweight; countercurrent, crosscurrent, undercurrent; counterblast; head wind, foul wind.

.5 countermeasure, counterattack, counterstep; counterblow or counterstroke or countercoup or counterblast, counterfire; counterrevolution, counterinsurgency; backfire; retort, comeback [informal]; defense 799.

.6 VERBS counteract, counter, counterwork, counterattack, countervail; counterpose or contrapose, oppose, antagonize, go in opposition to, go or run counter to, go or work against, go or fly in the face of, run against, beat against, militate against, resist, cross, confute, contradict, contravene, oppugn, conflict, be antipathetic or hostile or inimical, interfere or conflict with, come in conflict with, clash, collide, meet head-on, lock horns; rub or go against the grain; swim upstream or against the current.

.7 neutralize, nullify, annul, cancel, cancel out, negate, negative, negativate, invalidate, vitiate, void, frustrate, stultify,

thwart, come or bring to nothing, undo; offset, counterbalance 33.5; buffer.

.8 ADJS counteractive or counteractant, counteracting, counterworking, countervailing; opposing 790.9, oppositional; contradicting, contradictory; antagonistic, hostile, antipathetic, inimical, oppugnant, repugnant, conflicting, clashing; reactionary; resistant, recalcitrant, dissident, revolutionary, breakaway, nonconformist, perverse, cranky, crotchety, renitent; ant(i)– or anth–, contra–, counter–.

.9 neutralizing, nullifying, stultifying, annulling, canceling, negating, invalidating, vitiating, voiding; offsetting, counterbalancing; antacid, buffering.

.10 ADVS counteractively, antagonistically, opposingly, in opposition to, counter to; de– or des–, dis–, un–.

## 179. SPACE

*(indefinite space)*

.1 NOUNS space, extent, extension, spatial extension; expanse, expansion; spread, breadth; measure, volume; dimension, proportion; area, tract, surface, surface or superficial extension, field, sphere; acreage; empty space, emptiness, void, nothingness, infinite space, outer space, wastes of outer space, interstellar or galactic space; continuum.

.2 range, scope, compass, reach, stretch, radius, sweep, carry; gamut, scale, register, diapason; spectrum.

.3 room, latitude, swing, play, way; spare room, room to spare, room to swing a cat [informal], elbowroom, margin, leeway; sea room; headroom, clearance; air space.

.4 open space, clear space; clearing, clearance, glade; open country, wide-open spaces, terrain, prairie, steppe, plain 387; wilderness, back country, outback [Austral], desert; distant prospect or perspective, empty view, far horizon; territory, living space, *Lebensraum* [Ger], air space.

.5 spaciousness, roominess, commodiousness, capacity, capaciousness, amplitude; extensiveness, expansiveness.

.6 fourth dimension, space-time, time-space, space-time continuum, four-dimensional space; four-dimensional geometry; spaceworld; other continuums; relativity, theory of relativity, Einstein theory, principle of relativity, principle of equivalence, general theory of relativity, special or restricted theory of relativity, continuum theory; cosmic constant.

.7 VERBS **extend, reach, stretch,** sweep, spread, run, **go** or **go out,** cover, carry, **range,** lie; **reach** or stretch or thrust out; span, straddle, take in, hold, encompass, surround, environ.

.8 ADJS **spatial,** space, spatio–, stere(o)–; **dimensional,** proportional; two-dimensional, flat, surface or superficial, three-dimensional, spherical, cubic, volumetric; stereoscopic, 3-D; fourth-dimensional; space-time, spatiotemporal.

.9 **spacious, roomy, commodious, capacious,** ample; **extensive,** expansive, extended; far-reaching, extending, spreading, **vast,** broad, **wide,** deep, amplitudinous, voluminous; widespread 79.13; **infinite** 104.3.

.10 ADVS **extensively, widely,** broadly, vastly, abroad; **far and wide,** far and near; **right and left,** on all sides, on every side; infinitely.

.11 **everywhere,** everywheres [dial], **here, there, and everywhere;** in every place, in every clime or region, in all places, in every quarter, in all quarters; **all over,** all round, all over hell [slang], all over the map [informal], all over the world, the world over, on the face of the earth, under the sun, throughout the world, throughout the length and breadth of the land; from end to end, from pole to pole, from here to the back of beyond [Brit informal], "from Dan to Beersheba" [Bible], from hell to breakfast [slang]; **high and low,** upstairs and downstairs, inside and out, in every nook and cranny or hole and corner; **universally,** in all creation.

.12 **from everywhere,** everywhence, "from the four corners of the earth" [Shakespeare], "at the round earth's imagined corners" [Donne], from all points of the compass, from every quarter or all quarters; everywhere, everywhither, to the four winds, to the uttermost parts of the earth, "unto the ends of the earth" [Bible], to hell and back [slang].

## 180. REGION

.1 NOUNS **region, area, zone,** belt, **territory,** terrain; **place** 184.1; **space** 179; **country** 181, **land** 385, ground, soil; territorial waters, twelve- or three-mile limit, continental shelf, offshore rights; airspace; heartland; hinterland; **district, quarter, section,** department, division; salient, corridor; part, parts; **neighborhood,** vicin-

ity, vicinage, neck of the woods [informal], purlieus; premises, confines, precincts, environs, milieu, –dom, –gaea.

.2 **sphere,** hemisphere, orb, **orbit,** ambit, circle; **circuit,** judicial circuit, **beat, round,** walk; **realm,** demesne, **domain,** dominion, jurisdiction, bailiwick; border, borderland, march; **province,** precinct, department; **field,** pale, arena.

.3 **zone;** climate or clime [both archaic]; **longitude,** longitude in arc, longitude in time; meridian, prime meridian; **latitude,** parallel; equator, the line; tropic, Tropic of Cancer, Tropic of Capricorn; tropics, subtropics, Torrid Zone; Temperate or Variable Zones; Frigid Zones, Arctic Zone or Circle, Antarctic Zone or Circle; horse latitudes, roaring forties.

.4 **plot,** plot of ground or land, parcel of land, plat, **patch, tract, field;** lot; block, square; section (square mile), forty (sixteenth of a section); close, quadrangle, quad, enclave, pale, clos [Fr], croft [Brit], kraal [Africa]; real estate 810.7.

.5 (territorial divisions) **state, territory, province,** region, duchy, electorate, government, principality; **county,** shire, canton, oblast, okrug [both Russ], département [Fr], Kreis [Ger]; **borough, ward,** riding, arrondissement [Fr]; **township,** hundred, commune, wapentake; metropolis, metropolitan area, **city, town** 183; **village,** hamlet; **district,** congressional district, electoral district, precinct; magistracy, soke, bailiwick; shrievalty, sheriffalty, sheriffwick, constablewick [all England]; archdiocese, archbishopric, stake; **diocese,** bishopric, parish.

.6 (regions of the world) continent, landmass; **Old World,** the old country; **New World,** America; **Western Hemisphere, Occident,** West; **Eastern Hemisphere, Orient,** Levant, East, eastland; Far East, Middle East, Near East; Asia, Europe, Eurasia, Asia Major, Asia Minor, Africa; Antipodes, down under, Australasia, Oceania.

.7 (regions of the US) West, westland, wild West, West Coast, the Coast; Northwest, Pacific Northwest, Southwest, Middle West, North Central region; East, eastland, East Coast, Middle Atlantic; Northeast, Southeast; North, northland; South, southland; Dixie, Dixieland; Sunbelt; New England, Down East, Yankeeland [informal].

.8 ADJS **regional, territorial, geographical,** areal, sectional, zonal, topographic or topographical, top(o)–, zon(o)–; locational 184.18.

.9 **local, localized,** of a place, geographically limited, topical, vernacular, parochial, provincial, insular, limited, confined.

## 181. COUNTRY

.1 NOUNS **country,** land; **nation,** nationality, **state,** sovereign nation *or* state, polity, **body politic;** power, superpower; **republic,** people's republic, **commonwealth,** commonweal; **kingdom,** sultanate; **empire,** empery; realm, dominion, domain; **principality,** principate; duchy, dukedom; grand duchy, archduchy, archdukedom, earldom, county, palatinate, seneschalty; chieftaincy, chieftainry; toparchy, *toparchia* [L]; city-state, *polis* [Gk], free city; province, territory, possession; colony, settlement; protectorate, mandate, mandated territory, mandant, mandatee, mandatory; buffer state; ally; satellite, puppet regime *or* government; free nation, captive nation, iron-curtain country; nonaligned *or* unaligned *or* neutralist nation.

.2 **fatherland,** *Vaterland* [Ger], *patria* [L], *la patrie* [Fr], **motherland,** mother country, the old country, **native land,** native soil, one's native heath *or* ground *or* place, **birthplace,** cradle; **home, homeland,** homeground, "home is where one starts" [T. S. Eliot], God's country.

.3 **United States,** United States of America, US, USA, **America,** Columbia, the States, Uncle Sugar [informal], Yankeeland [informal], Land of Liberty, the melting pot; stateside.

.4 **England,** Britain, Great Britain, United Kingdom, Britannia, Albion, Blighty [Brit slang], Limeyland [US slang], Tight Little Island, Land of the Rose, "This royal throne of kings, this scepter'd isle, / This earth of majesty, this seat of Mars, / This other Eden, demi-paradise" [Shakespeare], Sovereign of the Seas; British Empire, Commonwealth of Nations, British Commonwealth of Nations, the Commonwealth.

.5 (national personifications) Uncle Sam *or* Brother Jonathan (US); John Bull (England).

.6 nationhood, peoplehood, **nationality; statehood, sovereignty,** sovereign nationhood *or* statehood, independence, self-government, self-determination; internationality, internationalism; **nationalism.**

.7 [slang or derog terms] dago, Guinea, greaseball, wop (Italian); frog (Frenchman); Kraut, Krauthead, Jerry, Boche (German); Mick, Mickey, Paddy (Irishman); squarehead (Scandanavian); polack (Pole); Hunk, Hunkie, Bohunk (Eastern European); Canuck, Pepsi (French-Canadian); greaser, wetback (Mexican); spic (Latin American); Chink (Chinese); Jap (Japanese); limey (Briton); Aussie (Australian).

## 182. THE COUNTRY

.1 NOUNS **the country,** agricultural region, farm country, farmland, arable land, grazing region *or* country, rural district, rustic region, province *or* **provinces,** countryside, woodland 411.11, grassland 411.8, woods and fields, meadows and pastures, the soil, grass roots; **the sticks** *or* yokeldom *or* hickdom [all slang]; cotton belt, tobacco belt, black belt, farm belt, corn belt, fruit belt, wheat belt, citrus belt; dust bowl; highlands, moors, uplands; lowlands, veld, plains, prairies, steppes, wide-open spaces.

.2 **hinterland, back country,** outback [Austral], up-country, boondock *or* boondocks [both informal]; **the bush,** bush country, bushveld, **woods,** woodlands, **backwoods,** forests, timbers, brush; wilderness, wilds, uninhabited region, virgin land *or* territory; **wasteland** 166.2; **frontier,** borderland, outpost; wild West.

.3 **rusticity, ruralism,** inurbanity, agrarianism, bucolicism, **provincialism,** provinciality, pastorality, simplicity, unspoiledness; yokelism, hickishness, backwoodsiness; **boorishness,** churlishness, unrefinement, uncultivation.

.4 ruralization, countrification, rustication, pastoralization.

.5 VERBS **ruralize, countrify, rusticate,** pastoralize; farm 413.16; return to the soil.

.6 ADJS **rustic, rural, country, provincial, farm, pastoral, bucolic,** Arcadian, **agrarian,** agrestic; **agricultural** 413.20; lowland, upland.

.7 **countrified,** inurbane; country-born, country-bred, up-country, from the sticks [slang]; farmerish, hobnailed, clodhopping; **hick** *or* hicky *or* hickish *or* hickified *or* rube *or* hayseed *or* yokel *or* yokelish [all slang]; **boorish,** clownish, loutish, lumpish, lumpen, cloddish, churlish; **uncouth,** unpolished, uncultivated, uncultured, unrefined; country-style, country-fashion.

.8 **hinterland,** back, **back-country,** up-country, outback [Austral], wild, wilderness, virgin; **waste** 166.4; backwood *or* **backwoods,** back of beyond, backwoodsy; woodland, sylvan.

## 183. TOWN, CITY

.1 NOUNS **town,** township; **city, metropolis,** metropolitan area, greater city, **megalopolis,** conurbation, urban complex, spread city, urban sprawl, **municipality,** *urbs* [L], *polis* [Gk], *ville* [Fr], *Stadt* [Ger], –polis; **borough, burg** [informal], bourg, burgh [Scot]; **suburb,** suburbia, outskirts, *faubourg* [Fr], *banlieue* [Fr]; exurb, exurbia; market town [Brit]; boom town, ghost town.

.2 **village, hamlet;** ham *or* thorp *or* wick [all archaic]; country town, crossroads, wide place in the road; "a little one-eyed, blinking sort o' place" [Thomas Hardy], "a hive of glass, where nothing unobserved can pass" [C. H. Spurgeon].

.3 [slang terms] **one-horse town,** jerkwater town, **tank town** *or* station, **whistle-stop,** jumping-off place; **hick town,** rube town, hoosier town.

.4 **capital,** capital city, **seat,** seat of government; **county seat** *or* county site, county town [Brit], shire town.

.5 **town hall, city hall, municipal building;** courthouse; police headquarters *or* station, precinct house, firehouse, fire station; county building, county courthouse; community center.

.6 (city districts) East Side *or* End, West Side *or* End; downtown, uptown, midtown; city center, central city, core, inner city, suburbs, suburbia, outskirts, greenbelt, residential district, business district *or* section, shopping center; ghetto, Jewtown [derog]; black ghetto, niggertown [derog]; Chinatown, Little Italy, Little Hungary, etc.; barrio; the other side of the tracks, **slum** *or* **slums,** blighted area *or* neighborhood *or* section, urban blight, run-down neighborhood, tenement district, hell's kitchen *or* half-acre; tenderloin, red-light district, Bowery, **skid row** *or* skid road [both slang].

.7 **block,** city block, square.

.8 **square, plaza,** *place* [Fr], *piazza* [Ital], *campo* [Ital], **marketplace,** market, market cross, rialto, mart, forum, agora.

.9 **circle,** circus [Brit]; crescent.

.10 ADJS **urban, metropolitan, municipal,** burghal, **civic,** oppidan; city, town, village; citified; suburban; interurban; downtown, uptown, midtown.

## 184. LOCATION

.1 NOUNS **location, situation, place,** *lieu* [Fr], **placement, emplacement, position,** hole [slang], stead; **whereabouts,** whereabout; **area, district, region** 180; **locality, locale,** *locus* [L]; **abode** 191; **site,** situs; **spot, point,** pinpoint, bench mark; bearings, latitude and longitude; stasi-, top(o)-; –topy; –arium, –ary, –drome, –ery, –ment, –orium, –ory, –ry, –teria, –y.

.2 **station,** status, **stand, standing,** standpoint, viewpoint, angle, perspective, distance, footing, **seat, post,** base, ground, venue.

.3 **position, orientation,** lay, lie, set, **attitude,** aspect, exposure, frontage, **bearing** *or* **bearings,** radio bearing, azimuth; position line *or* line of position; **fix;** celestial navigation, dead reckoning, pilotage.

.4 **place,** stead, lieu.

.5 (act of placing) **placement, positioning, emplacement, situation, location,** localization, **locating, placing,** putting, pinpointing; **allocation,** collocation, **disposition,** assignment, **deployment,** posting, **stationing,** spotting; deposition, reposition, deposit; **stowage,** storage, loading, lading, packing.

.6 **establishment, foundation,** settlement, settling, colonization, population, peopling, plantation; lodgment, fixation, anchorage, mooring; **installation,** installment, inauguration, investiture, initiation.

.7 topography, geography; cartography, chorography; surveying, navigation, geodesy; geodetic satellite, orbiting geophysical observatory, OGO.

.8 VERBS **have place,** be there; have its place *or* slot, **belong, go, fit,** fit in.

.9 **be located** *or* **situated, lie, be found,** stand, rest, repose; lie in, have its seat in.

.10 **locate, situate, place, position;** emplace, spot [informal], **install,** put in place; **allocate,** collocate, **dispose, deploy,** assign; **localize,** narrow *or* pin down; put one's finger on, **fix,** assign *or* consign *or* relegate to a place; **pinpoint,** zero in on, home in on; find *or* fix *or* calculate one's position, triangulate, get a fix *or* navigational fix, navigate.

.11 **place, put, set, lay,** seat, stick [informal], **station, post;** park; pose, posit, submit.

.12 (put violently) **clap,** slap, **thrust, fling, hurl,** throw, cast, chuck, toss; **plump; plunk** *or* **plank** *or* plop [all informal].

.13 **deposit**, repose, reposit, rest, **lay, lodge; put down**, set down, lay down.

.14 **load, lade**, freight, burden; fill 56.7; **stow**, store; **pack**, pack away; ship; pile, heap, heap up, stack, mass; bag, sack, pocket; can, bottle, box, crate, barrel.

.15 **establish, fix, plant**, pitch, seat, **set; found, base**, build, ground, lay the foundation; **install, invest**, vest, put in, put up, set up, build in.

.16 **settle, settle down**, sit down, locate [informal], park [informal], ensconce; take up one's abode or quarters, make one's home, **reside, inhabit** 188.7; **move**, relocate, establish residence, **take up residence**, take residence at, put up or live or stay at, quarter or billet at, hang up one's hat [informal]; take or strike root, place oneself, plant oneself, get a footing, stand, take one's stand or position; anchor, drop anchor, come to anchor, moor; squat, camp, bivouac; perch, roost, nest, hive, burrow; domesticate, **set up housekeeping**, keep house; **colonize**, populate, people; set up in business, go in business for oneself, set up shop, hang up one's shingle [informal].

.17 ADJS **located, placed, situated**, situate, **positioned**, installed, emplaced, spotted [informal], set, seated; stationed, posted, deployed, assigned; **established**, fixed, **settled**, planted, ensconced, embosomed.

.18 **locational**, positional, situational, situal; topographic, geographic, chorographic, cartographic; navigational, geodetic; **regional** 180.8.

.19 ADVS **in place**, in position, −wise; *in situ*, *in loco* [both L].

.20 **where**, whereabouts, in what place, in which place; **whither**, to what or which place.

.21 **wherever**, where'er, **wheresoever**, wheresoe'er, whithersoever, wherever it may be; **anywhere**, anyplace [informal].

.22 **here**, hereat, in this place, just here, on the spot; **hereabouts**, hereabout, in this vicinity; somewhere about or near; aboard, on board, with or among us; **hither**, hitherward, hitherwards, hereto, hereunto, hereinto, to this place.

.23 **there**, thereat, in that place, in those parts; thereabout, **thereabouts**, in that vicinity or neighborhood; **thither**, thitherward, thitherwards, to that place; −ward(s).

.24 **here and there, in places**, in various places, in spots, *passim* [L].

.25 **somewhere, someplace**, in some place, someplace or other.

.26 PREPS **at, in, on, by**, a−; **near, next to; with, among**, in the midst of; **to**, toward 290.28; **from** 301.22.

.27 **over, all over**, here and there on or in, at about, round about; through, **all through, throughout** 56.17.

## 185. DISLOCATION

.1 NOUNS **dislocation, displacement**, −diastasis; disjointing 49.1, disarticulation, unjointing, unhinging, luxation; heterotopia; **shift, removal**, forcible shift or removal; uprooting, ripping out, deracination; **disarrangement** 63; incoherence 51.1; discontinuity 72; Doppler effect, red shift, violet shift [all phys].

.2 **dislodgment**; unplacement, **unseating**, upset, unsaddling, unhorsing; **deposal** 783.

.3 **misplacement, mislaying**, misputting.

.4 displaced person, DP, stateless person, Wandering Jew, man without a country, exile, deportee; displaced or deported population; *déraciné* [Fr].

.5 VERBS **dislocate, displace, disjoint** 49.9, disarticulate, unjoint, luxate, unhinge, put or force or push out of place, **put or throw out of joint**, throw out of gear, **disarrange** 63.2.

.6 **dislodge**, unplace, **uproot**, root up or out, deracinate; depose 783.4, **unseat**, unsaddle; **unhorse**, dismount; throw off, buck off.

.7 **misplace, mislay**, misput.

.8 ADJS dislocatory, dislocating, heterotopic.

.9 **dislocated, displaced; disjointed**, unjointed, unhinged; out, **out of joint**, out of gear; **disarranged** 62.13; ect(o)−.

.10 **unplaced**, unestablished, unsettled; unhoused, unharbored, houseless, homeless, stateless, exiled, outcast.

.11 **misplaced, mislaid**, misput; **out of place**, out of one's element, like a fish out of water, in the wrong place, in the wrong box or pew [informal], in the right church but the wrong pew [informal].

.12 **eccentric, off-center**, off-balance, unbalanced, uncentered.

## 186. PRESENCE

.1 NOUNS **presence**, being here or there, hereness, thereness, physical or actual presence, spiritual presence; **immanence**, indwellingness, **inherence**; whereness, **immediacy**; ubiety; availability, accessibility; **occurrence** 151.2, existence 1.

.2 **omnipresence**, all-presence, **ubiquity**, infinity, everywhereness.

.3 **permeation**, **pervasion**, penetration; **suffusion**, transfusion, diffusion, imbuement; **overrunning**, overspreading, overswarming.

.4 **attendance**, frequenting, frequence; number present; turnout *or* box office *or* draw [all informal].

.5 **attender**, visitor, –goer, **patron**; **fan** *or* buff [both informal], aficionado; **frequenter**, habitué, haunter; spectator 442; theatergoer 611.32; audience 448.6.

.6 VERBS **be present**, be located *or* situated 184.9, be there, be found, be met with; **occur** 151.5, exist 1.8; lie, stand, remain; fall in the way of; dwell in, indwell, inhere.

.7 **pervade**, **permeate**, penetrate; **suffuse**, transfuse, diffuse, leaven, imbue; **fill**, extend throughout, leave no void, occupy; **overrun**, overswarm, overspread, bespread, run through, meet one at every turn; creep with, crawl with, swarm with, teem with; honeycomb.

.8 **attend**, **be at**, be present at, find oneself at, **go** *or* **come to**; **appear**, turn up, show up [informal], show one's face, make *or* put in an appearance, give the pleasure of one's company, make a personal appearance, **visit**, **take in**, do [informal]; catch [informal]; sit in *or* at; be on hand, be on deck [informal]; watch, see; witness, look on, *assister* [Fr].

.9 **revisit**, return to, go back to, come again.

.10 **frequent**, **haunt**, resort to, hang around *or* about at *or* out at [all slang].

.11 **present oneself**, report; report for duty.

.12 ADJS **present**, attendant; **on hand**, on deck [informal], on board; **immediate**, immanent, indwelling, inherent, available, accessible, **at hand**, in view, within reach *or* sight *or* call.

.13 **omnipresent**, all-present, ubiquitous, infinite; everywhere 179.11.

.14 **pervasive**, pervading, suffusive, suffusing.

.15 **permeated**, saturated, shot through, honeycombed; crawling, creeping, swarming, teeming.

.16 ADVS **here, there.**

.17 **in person**, personally, bodily, **in the flesh** [informal], in one's own person, *in propria persona* [L].

.18 PREPS **in the presence of,** in the face of, under the eyes *or* nose of, **before.**

.19 PHRS all present and accounted for; standing room only, SRO.

## 187. ABSENCE

.1 NOUNS **absence**, nonpresence, awayness; nowhereness, **nonexistence** 2; want, lack, blank, deprivation; nonoccurrence, neverness; **subtraction** 42.

.2 **vacancy**, vacuity, voidness, **emptiness**, blankness, hollowness, inanition; **bareness**, barrenness, desolateness, bleakness, desertedness; **nonoccupance** *or* **nonoccupancy**, nonoccupation, noninhabitance, nonresidence; opening, place open, vacant post.

.3 **void**, **vacuum**, blank, empty space, inanity; **nothingness**; *tabula rasa* [L], clean slate; **nothing** 2.2.

.4 **absence**, nonattendance, absenting, leaving, taking leave, **departure** 301; running away, fleeing, abscondence, **disappearance** 447, escape 632; **absentation**, nonappearance, default, unauthorized *or* unexcused absence; **truancy**, **hooky** [informal], French leave, **cut** [informal]; **absence without leave** *or* **AWOL**; **absenteeism**, truantism; **leave**, **leave of absence**, furlough, **vacation**, holiday, day off; authorized *or* excused absence, sick leave; sabbatical leave.

.5 **absentee**, **truant**, no-show.

.6 **nobody**, **no one**, no man, not one, not a single one *or* person, **not a soul** *or* **blessed soul**, never a one, ne'er a one, nary one [dial], nobody on earth *or* under the sun, nobody present.

.7 VERBS **be absent**, **stay away**, keep away, keep out of the way, not come, not show up [informal], turn up missing [informal], stay away in droves [informal], fail to appear, default.

.8 **absent oneself**, take leave *or* a leave of absence, go on leave *or* furlough; slip off *or* away, duck *or* sneak out [informal], slip out, make oneself scarce [informal], leave the scene, bow out, exit, **depart** 301.6, **disappear** 447.2, escape 632.6.

.9 **play truant**, **play hooky** [informal], go **AWOL**, take French leave; jump ship; **cut** *or* **skip** [both informal].

.10 ADJS **absent**, not present, nonattendant, **away**, **gone**, departed, disappeared, vanished, absconded, out of sight; **missing**, wanting, **lacking**, not found, omitted, taken away, subtracted, deleted, nowhere to be found; a– *or* an–, dis–, e–, ectro–, lipo–, lyo–, –less; no longer present *or* with us *or* among us; **nonexistent** 2.7; conspicuous by its absence.

.11 **nonresident**, not in residence, from

home, **away from home,** on leave or vacation or holiday, on sabbatical leave; on tour, on the road; abroad, overseas.

.12 **truant,** absent without leave or **AWOL.**

.13 **vacant, empty,** hollow, inane, **bare, vacuous, void,** without content, with nothing inside, devoid, null, null and void, ken-(o)-, nulli-; **blank,** clear, white, bleached; featureless, unrelieved, characterless, bland, insipid; **barren** 166.4.

.14 **vacant, open, available,** free, **unoccupied,** unfilled, **uninhabited,** unpopulated, unpeopled, untaken, untenanted, tenantless, untended, unmanned, unstaffed; **deserted,** abandoned, forsaken, godforsaken [informal].

.15 ADVS **absently; vacantly, emptily,** hollowly, vacuously, blankly.

.16 **nowhere,** in no place, neither here nor there; nowhither.

.17 **away** 301.21, **elsewhere,** somewhere else, not here; elsewhither.

.18 PREPS void of, empty of, free of, **without** 662.17.

## 188. HABITATION

### (an inhabiting)

.1 NOUNS **habitation,** inhabiting, inhabitation, habitancy, inhabitancy, **tenancy, occupancy,** occupation, **residence** or **residency,** residing, abiding, **living,** nesting, **dwelling,** commorancy, lodging, staying, stopping, sojourning, staying over; squatting; cohabitation; **abode** 191.

.2 **peopling,** peoplement, empeoplement, **population,** inhabiting; **colonization, settlement,** plantation.

.3 **housing,** domiciliation; lodgment, **lodging,** transient lodging, doss [Brit], **quartering,** billeting, hospitality; living quarters 191.3; **housing development,** subdivision, tract; housing problem, housing bill, lower-income housing, slum clearance, urban renewal; assembly-line housing.

.4 **camping,** tenting, **encampment,** bivouacking; camp 191.29.

.5 **sojourn,** sojournment; **stay, stop; stopover,** stop-off, stayover, layover.

.6 **hàbitability,** inhabitability, **livability.**

.7 VERBS **inhabit, occupy,** tenant; **reside, live, dwell, lodge, stay,** remain, **abide,** hang out [slang], domicile, domiciliate; **room,** camp, berth, doss down [Brit]; perch or roost or squat [all informal]; nest, cohabit.

.8 **sojourn,** stop, stay, **stop over,** stay over, lay over.

.9 **people,** empeople, **populate, inhabit,** denizen; colonize, **settle,** settle in, plant.

.10 **house,** domicile, domiciliate; provide with a roof, have as a guest or lodger, shelter, harbor; **lodge, quarter,** put up, billet, room, bed, berth, bunk; stable.

.11 **camp, encamp,** tent; pitch, **pitch camp,** pitch one's tent, drive stakes [informal]; bivouac; go camping, camp out, sleep out, rough it.

.12 ADJS **inhabited, occupied,** tenanted; **peopled,** empeopled, populated, colonized, settled; populous.

.13 **resident,** residentiary, **in residence; residing, living, dwelling,** commorant, lodging, **staying,** remaining, abiding, living in; -cole, -colous, -coline.

.14 **housed,** domiciled, domiciliated, **lodged,** quartered, billeted; stabled.

.15 **habitable,** inhabitable, occupiable, lodgeable, tenantable, **livable, fit to live in;** homelike 191.33.

.16 ADVS **at home,** in the bosom of one's family, *chez soi* [Fr]; in one's element; back home or down home [both informal].

## 189. NATIVENESS

.1 NOUNS **nativeness,** nativity, native-bornness, indigenousness, aboriginality, autochthonousness, **nationality;** nativism.

.2 **citizenship,** native-born citizenship, citizenship by birth, citizenhood, subjecthood; civism.

.3 **naturalization,** naturalized citizenship, citizenship by naturalization or adoption, nationalization, adoption, admission, affiliation, **assimilation;** Americanization, Anglicization, etc.; acculturation, culture shock; papers, citizenship papers.

.4 VERBS **naturalize,** grant or confer citizenship, adopt, admit, affiliate, **assimilate;** Americanize, Anglicize, etc.; acculturate, acculturize; go native [informal].

.5 ADJS **native,** natal, **indigenous,** endemic, autochthonous, vernacular; original, aboriginal, primitive; native-born, homegrown, homebred, native to the soil or place or heath.

.6 **naturalized,** adopted, **assimilated;** indoctrinated, Americanized, Anglicized, etc.; acculturated, acculturized.

## 190. INHABITANT, NATIVE

.1 NOUNS **population, inhabitants,** habitancy, dwellers, **populace, people,** whole people, people at large, citizenry, folk; **public,** general public; community, society, **nation**, commonwealth, constituency; speech *or* linguistic community; ethnic *or* cultural community; socio–.

.2 **inhabitant**, inhabiter, habitant; **occupant**, occupier, **dweller, tenant, denizen**, inmate; **resident**, residencer, residentiary, resider; inpatient; resident physician, intern; house detective; resident *or* live-in maid; writer- *or* poet- *or* artist-in-residence; incumbent, *locum tenens* [L]; sojourner; addressee; –er *or* –ier *or* –yer, –cola, –ese, –ite.

.3 **native**, indigene, autochthon, earliest inhabitant, first comer, primitive settler; primitive; **aborigine**, aboriginal; local *or* local yokel [both informal].

.4 **citizen, national**, subject; **naturalized citizen**, nonnative citizen, citizen by adoption, immigrant, metic; hyphenated American, hyphenate; **cosmopolitan**, cosmopolite, citizen of the world.

.5 **fellow citizen**, fellow countryman, **compatriot**, congener, **countryman**, countrywoman, *landsman* [Yid], *paesano* [Ital], *paisano* [Sp]; fellow townsman, home towner [informal].

.6 **townsman**; townee *or* towner [both informal], **villager**, oppidan, city dweller, city man, big-city man, **city slicker** [informal]; urbanite; suburbanite; exurbanite; burgher, burgess, *bourgeois* [Fr]; townswoman, villageress; townspeople, townfolks, townfolk.

.7 **householder**, freeholder; cottager, cotter, cottier, crofter; head of household.

.8 **lodger, roomer**, paying guest; **boarder**, board-and-roomer, **transient**, transient guest *or* boarder; **renter, tenant**, lessee, underlessee.

.9 **settler**, *habitan(t)* [Can & Louisiana Fr]; **colonist**, colonizer, colonial, immigrant, planter; **homesteader**; **squatter**, nester; **pioneer**; sooner; precursor 66.

.10 **backsettler**, hinterlander, bushman [Austral]; **frontiersman**, mountain man; **backwoodsman**, woodlander, woodsman, woodman, woodhick [informal], forester; **mountaineer**, hillbilly *or* ridge runner [both informal], brush ape *or* briar-hopper [both informal]; cracker *or* redneck [both informal], desert rat [informal], clam digger [informal], piny [informal].

.11 (regional inhabitants) **Easterner**, eastlander; **Westerner**, westlander; **Southerner**, southlander; **Northener**, northlander; Yankee; Northman; New Englander, Down-Easter Yankee.

## 191. ABODE, HABITAT

*(place of habitation or resort)*

.1 NOUNS **abode, habitation, place, dwelling**, dwelling place, abiding place, place to live, where one lives *or* resides, roof over one's head, **residence**, pad *or* crib [both informal]; crash pad; **domicile**, *domus* [L]; **lodging**, lodgment, lodging place; seat, nest; roof, cantonment; address.

.2 **domesticity**, domesticality, homelovingness; housewifery, **housekeeping**, **homemaking**; householding, householdry.

.3 **quarters, living quarters; lodgings**, lodging, lodgment; diggings *or* digs [both Brit informal]; **rooms**, berth, roost, sleeping place, accommodations; **housing** 188.3, shelter, *gîte* [Fr].

.4 **home**, home sweet home, homestead, toft [Brit], home place, home roof, roof, rooftree, place where one hangs his hat; **fireside, hearth**, hearth and home, hearthstone, fireplace, *foyer* [Fr], chimney corner, ingle, ingleside *or* inglenook; **household**, ménage; paternal roof *or* domicile, family homestead, ancestral halls.

.5 **habitat**, home, **range**, locality, native environment; ec(o)– *or* oec(o)– *or* oiko–.

.6 **house**, *casa* [Sp & Ital], dwelling house; **building, structure, edifice**, fabric, erection, skyscraper; roof; lodge; manor house, hall; town house, *rus in urbe* [L]; country house, *dacha* [Russ], country seat; ranch house, farmhouse, farm; prefabricated house, Dymaxion house, living machine; sod house, adobe house; lake dwelling 398.3; houseboat; cave *or* cliff dwelling; penthouse; split-level; parsonage 1042.7, **rectory**, vicarage, deanery, manse; official residence, White House, 10 Downing Street, governor's mansion; presidential palace; embassy, consulate; –age.

.7 **estate**, house and grounds, house and lot, **homestead**, homecroft [Brit], place, home place, messuage [law], farmstead; **ranch**, *rancho, hacienda* [both Sp], toft *or* steading [both Brit], grange.

.8 **mansion**, palatial residence, **villa, château**, *hôtel* [Fr], **castle**, tower; **palace**, *palais* [Fr], *palazzo* [Ital], court.

.9 **cottage**, cot *or* cote, **bungalow**, box; chalet, lodge, snuggery, *pied-à-terre* [Fr]; love nest; **cabin**, cabaña; log cabin, blockhouse.

.10 **hut**, hutch, **shack, shanty**, crib, **shed; lean-to; booth**, bothy *or* boothy [both Scot], stall; tollbooth *or* tollhouse, sentry box, gatehouse, porter's lodge; **outhouse,** outbuilding; **pavilion,** kiosk; Quonset hut *or* Nissen hut.

.11 (Indian houses) wigwam, tepee, hogan, wickiup, jacal, longhouse; tupik, igloo [both Eskimo].

.12 hovel, dump [slang], hole, sty, pigsty, pigpen [both informal], tumbledown shack.

.13 summerhouse, arbor, bower, **gazebo,** pergola, kiosk, alcove, retreat; **conservatory, greenhouse,** glasshouse [Brit], lathhouse.

.14 apartment, flat, tenement, chambers [Brit]; suite, suite *or* set of rooms; walkup, cold-water flat; **penthouse;** garden apartment; duplex apartment; railroad flat.

.15 apartment house, flats, tenement; duplex, duplex house; cooperative apartment house, condominium; high-rise apartment building.

.16 inn, hotel, hostel, hostelry, **tavern,** ordinary [Brit], *posada* [Sp]; **roadhouse,** caravansary, guest house, **hospice; lodging house,** rooming house; **dormitory,** dorm [informal], fraternity *or* sorority house; flophouse *or* fleabag [both slang], doss house [Brit]; **boardinghouse,** *pension* [Fr]; public house, public *or* **pub** [both Brit informal].

.17 motel, motor court, motor inn, motor hotel, auto court; boatel.

.18 trailer, house *or* camp trailer, **mobile home,** camper, caravan [Brit]; trailer court, trailer camp, trailer park.

.19 zoo, menagerie, *Tiergarten* [Ger], zoological garden.

.20 barn, stable, stall; **cowbarn,** cowhouse, cowshed, cowbyre, byre; mews.

.21 kennel, doghouse; pound, dog pound; cattery.

.22 coop, chicken house *or* coop, henhouse, hencote, hennery; brooder.

.23 birdhouse, aviary, bird cage; dovecote, pigeon house *or* loft, columbary; roost, perch, roosting place.

.24 vivarium, terrarium, aquarium; fishpond.

.25 nest, nidus; aerie, eyrie; **beehive, apiary,** hive, bee tree, hornet's nest, wasp's nest, vespiary.

.26 lair, den, cave, **hole,** covert, mew, form; burrow, tunnel, earth, run, couch, lodge.

.27 resort, haunt, purlieu, **hangout** [slang], **stamping ground** [informal]; gathering place, rallying point, meeting place, clubhouse, club; casino, gambling house; health resort 689.29; **spa,** baths, springs, watering place.

.28 (disapproved place) **dive** [slang], **den, lair,** den of thieves; hole *or* dump *or* **joint** [all slang]; gyp *or* clip joint [slang]; **whorehouse,** cathouse [slang], sporting house, brothel, bordello, stews, fleshpots.

.29 camp, encampment, *Lager* [Ger]; bivouac; barrack *or* **barracks,** casern, *caserne* [Fr], cantonment, lines [Brit]; hobo jungle *or* camp; detention camp, concentration camp, *Konzentrationslager* [Ger]; campground *or* campsite.

.30 (deities of the household) lares and penates, Vesta, Hestia.

.31 VERBS **keep house,** housekeep [informal], practice domesticity, maintain a household.

.32 ADJS **residential,** residentiary; domestic, domiciliary, domal; **home, household;** mansional, manorial, palatial.

.33 homelike, homish, **homey** [informal], homely; comfortable, friendly, cheerful, peaceful, cozy, snug, intimate; simple, plain, unpretending.

.34 domesticated, tame, tamed, broken; housebroken.

.35 PHRS "there's no place like home" [J. H. Payne].

## 192. ROOM

*(compartment)*

.1 NOUNS **room, chamber,** *chambre* [Fr], *salle* [Fr]; ballroom, grand ballroom; rotunda.

.2 compartment, chamber, enclosed space; **cavity,** hollow, hole; **cell,** cellule; booth, stall, crib, manger; box, pew; **crypt, vault,** hold.

.3 nook, corner, cranny, niche, recess, cove, bay, oriel, alcove; cubicle, roomlet, carrel, hole in the wall [informal], cubby, **cubbyhole,** snuggery.

.4 hall; assembly hall, exhibition hall, convention hall; gallery; **meetinghouse; auditorium,** opera house, **theater** 611.18, music hall; stadium, **arena** 802, lecture hall, lyceum, amphitheater; concert hall, dance hall; **chapel** 1042.3.

.5 parlor, living room, sitting room, drawing room, front room, best room [informal], foreroom [dial], salon, saloon; sun parlor *or* sunroom, solarium.

.6 library, stacks; **study,** studio, atelier, workroom, office; **loft,** sail loft.

.7 bedroom, boudoir, chamber, bedchamber, sleeping room, cubicle, cubiculum; nursery; dormitory.

.8 (private chamber) **sanctum,** sanctum

sanctorum, holy of holies, adytum; **den,** retreat, closet, cabinet.

.9 (ships) cabin, stateroom; saloon; house, deckhouse, cuddy, shelter cabin.

.10 (trains) drawing room, stateroom, parlor car, saloon [Brit], Pullman car, roomette.

.11 **dining room,** *salle à manger* [Fr], dinette, dining hall, refectory, mess or messroom or mess hall, commons; dining car, dining saloon; **restaurant, cafeteria** 307.15.

.12 **playroom,** recreation room, rec room [informal], family room, game room, **rumpus room** [informal]; **gymnasium** 878.12.

.13 **utility room,** laundry room, sewing room.

.14 **kitchen** 330.3, **storeroom** 660.6, smoking room 434.13.

.15 **closet,** clothes closet, wardrobe, cloakroom; linen closet; dressing room, fitting room.

.16 **attic,** attic room, **garret, loft,** sky parlor; cockloft, hayloft; storeroom, junk room, lumber room [Brit].

.17 **cellar,** cellarage, **basement;** subbasement; wine cellar, potato cellar, storm cellar, cyclone cellar; coal bin or hole, hold, hole, bunker.

.18 **corridor, hall,** hallway; passage, **passageway; gallery,** loggia; arcade, colonnade, pergola, cloister, peristyle; areaway; breezeway.

.19 **vestibule,** portal, **portico,** entry, entryway, entrance, **entrance hall,** entranceway, **threshold; lobby, foyer;** propylaeum, stoa; narthex, galilee.

.20 **anteroom,** antechamber; side room, byroom; **waiting room,** *salle d'attente* [Fr]; **reception room,** presence chamber or room, audience chamber; throne room; lounge, greenroom, wardrobe.

.21 **porch,** stoop, **veranda,** piazza, patio, lanai, gallery; sun porch, solarium, sleeping porch.

.22 **balcony,** gallery, terrace.

.23 **floor, story,** level, flat; first floor or story, ground or street floor, *rez-de-chaussée* [Fr]; mezzanine, mezzanine floor, *entresol* [Fr]; clerestory.

.24 **showroom,** display room, exhibition room, gallery.

.25 **hospital room; ward,** maternity ward, fever ward, charity ward, prison ward, etc.; private room, semi-private room; examining room, consultation room, treatment room; operating room or OR or surgery, labor room, delivery room, recovery room; emergency, intensive care, isolation, X ray, therapy; pharmacy, dispensary; clinic, nursery; laboratory, blood bank; nurses' station.

.26 **bathroom, lavatory, washroom** 681.10, **water closet, WC,** closet, **rest room,** comfort station, **toilet** 311.10.

.27 (for vehicles) **garage,** carport; coach or carriage house; carbarn; roundhouse; hangar; boathouse.

## 193. CONTAINER

.1 NOUNS **container, receptacle** 193.6–19, receiver 819.3, holder, vessel, utensil; –ange, –angium, –coel(e) or –cele, –clinium, –thecium.

.2 **bag** 193.16, **sack,** sac, poke [dial]; **pocket,** fob; **balloon, bladder,** asc(o)– or asci–, cyst(o)– or cysti–, –cyst.

.3 **belly, stomach,** gastr(o)– or gastri– or gaster(o)–, tummy or tum-tum [both informal], **abdomen,** abdomin(o)–, celi(o)–; **crop,** gullet 396.15, **craw,** maw, gizzard; **midriff,** diaphragm, breadbasket [informal]; swollen or distended or protruding or prominent belly, *embonpoint* [Fr], **paunch, gut** [slang], *kishkes* [Yid], spare tire or bay window [both informal]; potbelly or potgut or beerbelly [all slang], pusgut [slang], **pot** [slang], swagbelly [dial]; ventripotence; underbelly; first stomach, rumen, rumeno–; second stomach, reticulum, reticul(o)– or reticuli–, honeycomb stomach; third stomach, psalterium, omasum, manyplies; fourth stomach, abomasum, rennet bag.

.4 ADJS vascular, vesicular; camerated, capsular, cellular, cystic, locular, marsupial, saccular, siliquose; angi(o)–, ascidi(o)–, cotyl(o)– or cotyli–.

.5 **abdominal,** ventral, celiac, –coelous; stomachal or stomachic(al), gastric, ventricular; big-bellied 195.18.

.6 **receptacles**

| | |
|---|---|
| ashcan | crock |
| ashtray | crucible |
| autoclave | dinner pail |
| billy or billycan [both | dinner plate |
| Austral] | dish, dishware |
| bucket | gallipot |
| caddy | garbage can |
| cage | GI can |
| can | hod |
| canister | holdall |
| cannikin | hopper |
| casserole | jerrican |
| catchall | kibble |
| china, chinaware | magazine |
| coal scuttle | messkit |
| coaster | milk pail |
| compote | mortar |
| creamer | mortarboard |
| cream pitcher | oil can |

| | |
|---|---|
| pail | soup bowl *or* plate |
| palette | sugar bowl |
| *patera* [L] | tableware |
| piggin | tin can, tin [Brit] |
| pipkin | trash can |
| pitcher | tray |
| plate | trencher |
| platter | vat |
| powder horn | waiter |
| salver | wastepaper basket |
| saucer | 669.7 |
| scuttle | watering can |
| slop pail | |

## .7 basins

| | |
|---|---|
| barber's basin | punch bowl |
| bathtub | salad bowl |
| bidet | sauce boat |
| bowl | sink 682.12 |
| catch basin *or* drain | sitzbath |
| cereal bowl | terrine |
| cistern | trough |
| finger bowl | tub |
| gravy boat | tureen |
| hip bath | vat |
| porringer | washbasin |
| pottinger | washtub |

## .8 pots

| | |
|---|---|
| biggin | kitchen boiler |
| boiler | *olla* [Sp] |
| bud vase | patella |
| caldron | paten |
| chamber pot | percolator |
| coffeepot | pipkin |
| coffee urn | potty |
| cuspidor | spittoon |
| flower bowl | teakettle |
| flowerpot | teapot |
| honeypot | tea urn |
| jardiniere | urn |
| kettle | vase |

## .9 pans

| | |
|---|---|
| ashpan | pan broiler |
| bakepan | piepan |
| boiler | posnet |
| brazier | roaster |
| bread pan | saucepan |
| broiler | skillet |
| cake pan | spider |
| dishpan | stewpan |
| double boiler | warming pan |
| dustpan | wok |
| frying pan | |

## .10 cups, drinking vessels

| | |
|---|---|
| beaker | jigger |
| beer glass | jorum |
| blackjack | liqueur glass |
| bowl | loving cup |
| brandy snifter | mazer |
| cannikin | mug |
| chalice | noggin |
| coffee cup | pannikin |
| demitasse | pony |
| drinking cup | pottle |
| drinking horn | rummer |
| eggcup | schooner |
| glass | schooper |
| goblet | scyphus |
| highball glass | shell |
| horn | shot glass |

| | |
|---|---|
| stein | Toby-jug *or* Toby |
| tankard | Fillpot jug |
| *tasse* [Fr] | tumbler |
| tassie [Brit] | tyg |
| teacup | wineglass |

## .11 ladles

| | |
|---|---|
| bail | soupspoon |
| calabash | spade |
| cyathus | spatula |
| dessert spoon | spoon |
| dipper | sugar spoon |
| gourd | tablespoon |
| labis [eccl] | teaspoon |
| scoop | trowel |
| shovel | |

## .12 bottles

| | |
|---|---|
| calabash | jar |
| canteen | jeroboam |
| carafe | jug |
| carboy | hipflask |
| caster | hot-water bottle |
| cruet | lota |
| cruse | magnum |
| decanter | mussuk |
| demijohn | *olla* [Sp] |
| ewer | phial |
| fifth | pocket flask |
| flacon | stoup |
| flagon | thermos |
| flask | vacuum bottle |
| flasket | vial |
| gourd | |

## .13 casks

| | |
|---|---|
| barrel | kilderkin |
| breaker | pipe |
| butt | puncheon |
| drum | rundlet |
| firkin | tun |
| harness cask *or* tub | vat |
| hogshead | water butt |
| keg | |

## .14 cases

| | |
|---|---|
| ammunition box | envelope |
| ark | étui |
| attaché case | file |
| bandolier | file folder |
| billfold | filing box *or* case |
| bin | folio |
| boot | glasses *or* spectacle |
| box | case |
| briefcase | holster |
| bunker | hope chest |
| caisson | housewife, hussy |
| canister | hutch |
| capsule, capsula | kit |
| cardcase | letter file |
| carton | matchbox |
| casket | money box |
| cedar chest | monstrance |
| chest | ostensorium |
| cigarette case | packet |
| cist | packing box *or* case |
| coffer | pillbox |
| coffin | pocketcase |
| compact | pod |
| cone | portfolio |
| crate | powder box |
| crib | quiver |
| dispatch box | rack |

reliquary
sarcophagus
scabbard
sheath
skippet
snuffbox
socket

tea chest
till
tinderbox
vanity case
vasculum
wallet

**.15 baskets**

bassinet
breadbasket
buck basket
bushel
clothesbasket
clothes hamper *or* bin
corbeil [archit]
crane
creel
dosser, dorser
flower basket
frail
fruit basket
hamper
pannier, *panier* [Fr]

picnic basket
punnet
reed basket
rush basket
sewing basket
skep
splint basket
stave basket
trug
washbasket
wastebasket
wastepaper basket
wicker basket
wire basket
wooden basket

**.16 bags**

bedroll *or* beddingroll
bindle
budget [dial]
bundle
caddie bag *or* cart
diplomatic pouch
evening bag
game bag
golf bag
gunny, gunny sack
handbag
mail pouch
moneybag
net
nose bag

pack sack
pocketbook
poke
pouch
purse
reticule
sack
saddlebag
schoolbag
scrip [archaic]
sleeping bag
tobacco pouch
vanity bag
wineskin

**.17 luggage, baggage**

attaché case
backpack
bag
bandbox
barracks bag
boodle bag
Boston bag
briefcase
carpetbag
carryall
ditty bag *or* box
duffel bag
flight bag
footlocker
Gladstone, Gladstone
    bag
grip
gripsack
handbag
hatbox
haversack

holdall
kit
kit bag
knapsack
locker box
musette bag
overnight bag
portmanteau
rucksack
*sac de nuit* [Fr]
Saratoga trunk
satchel
sea bag
shoulder bag
suitcase
tote bag *or* sack
traveling bag
trunk
tucker bag [Austral]
valise

**.18 botany, anatomy**

air bladder, phys(o)–
air sac
amnion, amnio–
bladder
bleb
blister
boll

bursa
calyx
cancelli
capsule, capsul(o)– *or*
    capsuli–
cell
cyst, cystis

fistula
follicle
gallbladder
legume
loculus
marsupium
musk bag
pericarp
pocket
pod
sac, sacc(o)– *or* sacci–
saccule
sacculus
saccus

scrotum 419.10
seedcase
silique
sinus
sound
stomach 193.3
theca
udder
utricle
vasculum
ventricle
*vesica* [L]
vesicle

**.19 cupboards**

*armoire* [Fr]
buffet
bunker
bureau
cabinet
Canterbury
cellaret
chest
chest of drawers
chiffonier
chifforobe
closet
clothespress
commode
credenza
davenport
desk
drawer
dresser

*étagère* [Fr]
escritoire
*garderobe* [Fr]
highboy
kitchen cabinet
locker
lowboy
press
*secrétaire* [Fr]
secretary
shelf
shelves
sideboard
tallboy
vargueno
vitrine
wardrobe
whatnot

## 194. CONTENTS

**.1** NOUNS **contents, content,** what is contained *or* included *or* comprised; **insides** 225.4, **innards** [informal], **guts; components, constituents, ingredients,** elements, **items, parts, divisions,** subdivisions; **inventory,** index, census, **list** 88; **part** 55; **whole** 54; **composition** 58.

**.2 load,** lading, **cargo, freight,** charge, **burden; payload;** boatload, busload, carload, cartload, shipload, trailerload, trainload, truckload, vanload, wagonload.

**.3 lining,** liner, –pleura; **interlining,** interlineation; inlayer, **inlay,** inlaying; **filling,** filler; **packing,** padding, wadding, **stuffing;** facing; doubling, doubling; bushing, bush; wainscot; insole.

**.4** (contents of a container) cup, cupful, etc. 28.8.

**.5** (essential content) **substance, stuff, material, matter,** medium, building blocks, fabric; **sum and substance, gist, meat, nub** [informal], core, kernel, marrow, pith, sap, spirit, **essence,** quintessence, elixir, distillate, distillation, distilled essence; irreducible content; heart, soul.

**.6 enclosure,** the enclosed.

**.7** VERBS **fill, pack** 56.7, **load** 184.14; **line,** interline, interlineate; inlay; face; wainscot, ceil; pad, wad, **stuff**; feather, fur.

## 195. SIZE

.1 NOUNS **size, largeness, bigness, greatness** 34, **magnitude**, order of magnitude, amplitude; mass, bulk, **volume**, body; **dimensions, proportions**, dimension, caliber, scantling, proportion; **measure**, measurement, gauge, scale; **extent**, extension, expanse, expansion, scope, reach, range, spread, coverage, area; length, height, depth, breadth, width; girth, diameter, radius; onc(o)– or onch(o)– or onci–.

.2 **capacity, volume, content**, accommodation, room, space, measure, limit, burden; poundage, tonnage, cordage; stowage, tankage; **quantity** 28.

.3 **full size**, full growth; life size.

.4 large size, economy size, family size, **king size**, giant size.

.5 **oversize**, outsize; overlargeness, overbigness; **overgrowth**, wild or uncontrolled growth, overdevelopment; **overweight**, overheaviness; overstoutness, overfatness, overplumpness; gigantism, giantism, titanism; hypertrophy.

.6 **sizableness, largeness, bigness, greatness**, grandness, grandeur, grandiosity; largishness, biggishness; voluminousness, capaciousness, generousness, copiousness, ampleness; tallness, toweringness; broadness, wideness; profundity; extensiveness, expansiveness, comprehensiveness; spaciousness 179.5.

.7 **hugeness, vastness**, enormousness, immenseness, **enormity, immensity**, tremendousness, **prodigiousness**, stupendousness, mountainousness, giantlikeness, giantship, monumentalism; monstrousness, monstrosity.

.8 **corpulence, obesity, stoutness**, *embonpoint* [Fr]; fatness, fattishness, adiposis or adiposity, fleshiness, beefiness, meatiness, heftiness, grossness; **plumpness**, buxomness, rotundity, fubsiness [Brit], tubbiness [informal], roly-poliness; pudginess, podginess; chubbiness, chunkiness [informal], stockiness, squattiness, dumpiness, portliness; paunchiness, bloatedness, puffiness, pursiness, blowziness; hippiness [informal]; steatopygia or steatopygy; bosominess, bustiness [informal].

.9 **bulkiness**, hulkingness or hulkiness, **massiveness**, lumpishness, clumpishness; **ponderousness**, cumbrousness, cumbersomeness; clumsiness, awkwardness, unwieldiness.

.10 **lump**, clump, **hunk** or chunk [both informal]; **mass, bulk, gob** [slang], batch, **wad**, block, loaf; pat (of butter); clod; nugget; **quantity** 28.

.11 (something large) **whopper** or thumper or lunker or whale or jumbo [all informal]; hulk.

.12 (corpulent person) lump [informal], **heavyweight**, heavy [informal], human or man mountain [informal]; **fat man, fatty** or **fatso** [both informal], roly-poly, tub, tub of lard, tun, tun of flesh, blimp [informal], hippo [informal], **potbelly**, gorbelly [archaic or dial], swagbelly.

.13 **giant** 195.26, giantess, **amazon, colossus, titan**, *nephilim* [Heb pl].

.14 **behemoth, leviathan, monster** 85.20; mammoth, mastodon; elephant, jumbo [informal]; whale; hippopotamus, hippo [informal]; **dinosaur** 123.26.

.15 VERBS **size, adjust, grade**, group, range, rank, graduate, sort, match; gauge, **measure** 490.11, proportion; **bulk** 34.5; **enlarge** 197.4–8.

.16 ADJS **large, sizable, big, great** 34.6, **grand, tall** [informal], **considerable, goodly**, healthy, tidy [informal], **substantial**, bumper, **numerous** 101.6; largish, biggish; large-scale; man-sized [informal]; large-size(d), good-size(d); hyper–, macr(o)–, maxi–, meg(a)–, megal(o)–, super–.

.17 **voluminous, capacious, generous, ample**, copious, broad, wide, extensive, expansive, comprehensive; **spacious** 179.9.

.18 **corpulent, stout, fat, overweight**, fattish, **obese**, adipose, gross, fleshy, beefy, meaty, **hefty**; paunchy, paunched, bloated, puffy, blowzy, distended, swollen, pursy; abdominous, big-bellied, full-bellied, potbellied, gorbellied [archaic or dial], swag-bellied, pot-gutted, pussle-gutted [both informal], **plump, buxom**, *zaftig* [Yid], full, rotund, fubsy [Brit], tubby [informal], roly-poly; **pudgy**, podgy; thick-bodied, thick-girthed, **heavyset, thickset, chubby**, chunky [informal], **stocky**, squat, squatty, dumpy, pyknic, endomorphic, square; lusty, strapping [informal], stalwart, brawny, burly; **portly**, imposing; well-fed, corn-fed, grain-fed; chubby-faced, round-faced, moonfaced; hippy [informal], full-buttocked, steatopygic or steatopygous, fat-assed or lard-assed [both slang], broad in the beam [informal]; bosomy, full-bosomed, busty [informal], top-heavy; plump as a dumpling or partridge, fat as a quail, fat as a pig or hog, "fat as a pork hog" [Malory], "fat as a porpoise" [Swift], "fat as a fool" [John Lyly], "fat as butter" [Shakespeare], fat as brawn or bacon.

.19 **bulky, hulky,** hulking, lumpish, lumpy, lumping [informal], clumpish, lumbering, lubberly; **massive,** massy; elephantine, hippopotamic; **ponderous,** cumbrous, cumbersome; **clumsy,** awkward, **unwieldy.**

.20 **huge, immense, vast, enormous,** astronomic(al), tremendous, prodigious, stupendous; great big, larger than life, Homeric, mighty, **titanic, colossal, monumental,** heroic(al), epic(al), towering, mountainous; profound, abysmal, deep as the ocean or as China; monster, monstrous; **mammoth,** mastodonic; **gigantic,** gigantean, gigant(o)–; **giant,** giantlike; Cyclopean, Brobdingnagian, Gargantuan, Herculean, Atlantean; elephantine, jumbo [informal]; dinosaurian, dinotherian; **infinite** 104.3.

.21 [slang terms] **whopping, walloping, whaling, whacking,** spanking, slapping, lolloping, thumping, thundering, bumping, banging.

.22 **full-sized,** full-size, full-scale; **full-grown, full-fledged,** full-blown; full-formed, **life-sized,** large as life.

.23 **oversize,** oversized; **outsize,** outsized, giantsize, **kingsize,** recordsize, **overlarge,** overbig, too big; **overgrown,** overdeveloped; **overweight,** overheavy; overfleshed, overstout, overfat, overplump, overfed.

.24 this big, so big, yay big [informal], this size, about this size.

.25 ADVS largely, on a large scale, in a big way; in the large; as can be.

.26 **giants**

| | |
|---|---|
| Aegaeon | Gargantua |
| Aegir | Geryoneo |
| Alifanfaron | Gog |
| Amarant | Goliath |
| Antaeus | Grantorto |
| Ascapart | Gyes |
| Atlas | Hercules or Heracles |
| Balan | Hlér |
| Bellerus | Hymir |
| Blunderbore | Jötunn |
| Briareüs | Magog |
| Brobdingnagian | Mimir |
| Cormoran | Morgante |
| Cottus | Og |
| Cyclops | Orgoglio |
| Enceladus | Orion |
| Ephialtes | Pantagruel |
| Fafner | Paul Bunyan |
| Fenrir | Polyphemus |
| Ferragus | Titan |
| Fierebras | Tityus |
| Firbauti | Typhon |
| Galapas | Urdar |
| Galligantus | Ymir |

## 196. LITTLENESS

.1 NOUNS **littleness, smallness** 35, smallishness, **diminutiveness,** miniatureness, slightness, exiguity; puniness, pokiness, dinkiness [slang]; tininess, **minuteness;** undersize; petiteness; dwarfishness, stuntedness, runtiness, shrimpiness; **shortness** 203; **scantiness** 102.1.

.2 **infinitesimalness,** microdimensions; inappreciability, evanescence; intangibility, impalpability, tenuousness, imponderability; imperceptibility, invisibility.

.3 (small place) **tight spot** or tight squeeze or **pinch** [all informal]; hole, pigeonhole; hole in the wall; cubby, cubbyhole; cubbyhouse, dollhouse, playhouse, doghouse.

.4 **diminutive, runt, shrimp** [informal], wart [slang], wisp, chit, slip, snip, snippet, minikin [archaic], **peewee** [informal], fingerling, small fry [informal]; lightweight, featherweight; bantam, banty [informal]; pony; minnow, mini, minny [both informal]; mouse, tit, titmouse, tomtit [informal]; nubbin, button.

.5 **miniature, mini,** minny [both informal], subminiature; –cle, –ee, –een, –el, –ella or –illa, –et, –ette, –idium, –idion, –ie or –y or –ey, –ium, –kin, –let, –ling, –ock, –sy, –ula, –ule, –ulum, –ulus; microcosm, microcosmos; baby; doll; puppet; microvolume; Elzevir, Elzevir edition; duodecimo, twelvemo.

.6 **dwarf,** dwarfling, **midget,** midge, **pygmy,** manikin, homunculus, atomy, micromorph, hop-o'-my-thumb; elf, gnome, brownie; dapperling, dandiprat, cocksparrow, pip-squeak; **runt, shrimp** [informal], wart [slang], peewee [informal]; Lilliputian, Pigwiggen, Tom Thumb, Thumbelina, Alberich, Alviss, Andvari, Nibelung, Regin.

.7 (minute thing) minutia, **minutiae** [pl], minim, **drop,** droplet, **mite** [informal], **point,** vanishing point, mathematical point, point of a pin, pinpoint, pinhead, **dot;** mote, fleck, **speck,** flyspeck, jot, tittle, iota; **particle,** crumb, scrap, snip, snippet; grain, grain of sand; barleycorn, millet seed, mustard seed; midge, mite, gnat; microbe, microorganism 196.18.

.8 **atom,** atomy, monad; **molecule,** ion; **electron,** proton, meson, neutrino, quark, parton, subatomic or nuclear particle.

.9 VERBS make small, **contract** 198.7; **shorten** 203.6; **miniaturize,** minify, scale down.

.10 ADJS **little, small** 35.6, smallish, lept(o)–, mei(o)– or mi(o)–, olig(o)–, parvi(o)–,

–cular, –ulous; **slight**, exiguous; **puny**, poky, pindling or piddling [both informal], **dinky** [informal]; cramped, limited; one-horse, two-by-four [informal]; pint-sized [informal], half-pint; knee-high, knee-high to a grasshopper; petite; short 203.8.

.11 **tiny**; teeny or teeny-weeny or eentsy-weentsy [all informal], wee or peewee [informal], bitty or bitsy or little-bitty or little-bitsy or itsy-bitsy or itsy-witsy [all informal]; **minute, fine.**

.12 **miniature, diminutive, minuscule,** mini–, minimal, miniaturized, minikin [archaic], **small-scale,** pony; bantam, banty [informal]; **baby**, baby-sized; pocket, pocket-sized, **vest-pocket; toy;** handy, compact; duodecimo, twelvemo; subminiature.

.13 **dwarf,** dwarfed, dwarfish, nan(o)– or nann(o)–; **pygmy, midget,** nanoid, elfin; Lilliputian, Tom Thumb; **undersized,** undersize, squat, dumpy; **stunted,** runty; shrunk, shrunken, wizened, shriveled; meager, scrubby, scraggy; incipient, rudimentary, rudimental.

.14 **infinitesimal, microscopic,** ultramicroscopic, micr(o)–, ultramicr(o)–; evanescent, thin, tenuous; inappreciable; impalpable, imponderable, intangible; imperceptible, indiscernible, invisible, unseeable; atomic, subatomic; molecular; granular, corpuscular, granul(o)– or granuli–, chondr(o)–; microcosmic(al); embryonic, germinal 406.24.

.15 **microbic,** microbial, **microorganic;** animalcular, bacterial; microzoic; protozoan, microzoan, amoebic or amoeboid.

.16 ADVS smally, **small**, little, **slightly** 35.9; **on a small scale,** in a small compass, in a small way, on a minuscule or infinitesimal scale; **in miniature,** in the small; in a nutshell.

.17 **microscopy**

| | |
|---|---|
| electron microscopy | micromineralogy |
| electrophotomicrography | micropaleontology |
| phy | micropathology |
| microbiology | micropetrography |
| microchemistry | micropetrology |
| microcosmography | microphotography |
| microcosmology | microphysics |
| microcrystallography | microphysiography |
| microgeology | microscopics |
| micrography | microspectroscopy |
| micrology | microtechnic |
| micromechanics | microzoology |
| micrometallography | photomicrography |
| micrometallurgy | photomicroscopy |
| micrometry | |

.18 **microorganisms**

| | |
|---|---|
| amoeba | animalcule |
| arthrospore | nematode, nem(a)– or |
| bacillus, bacill(o)– or | nemo–, nemat(o)– |
| bacilli– | paramecium |
| bacteria, –bacter, bacter(o)– | phage |
| | pneumococcus |
| botulinus | protozoon, protozoa |
| ciliate | [pl] |
| coccus, cocc(o)– or | radiolarian |
| cocci– | rhizopod |
| colon bacillus, col(o)– | rotifer |
| or coli– | salmonella |
| diatom | saprophyte |
| diphtheria bacillus | schizomycete |
| dyad | spirillum |
| entozoon | spirochete |
| euglena | sporozoon |
| filterable virus | staphylococcus, |
| flagellate | staphyl(o)– |
| foraminifer | stentor |
| germ | streptococcus, strep- |
| gonidium | t(o)– |
| gregarine | tetrad |
| infusorian | triad |
| mastigophoran | trypanosome |
| mastigopod | tubercle bacillus, |
| microbe | tubercul(o)– |
| micrococcus | typhoid bacillus |
| microphyte | virus |
| microspore | volvox |
| microzoon, microzoa | vorticellum |
| [pl] | zoogloea |
| microzyme | zoogonidium |
| monad, monas | zoospore |
| moneron | |

## 197. EXPANSION, GROWTH

*(increase in size)*

.1 NOUNS **expansion, extension, enlargement, increase** 38, crescendo, upping, raising, hiking, magnification, aggrandizement, amplification, ampliation [archaic], broadening, widening; **spread,** spreading, fanning out, dispersion, **flare,** splay; deployment; augmentation, **addition** 40; adjunct 41.

.2 **distension,** stretching; **inflation,** sufflation, blowing up; **dilation,** dilatation, diastole; **swelling,** swellage; swell 256.4; puffing, puff, puffiness, **bloating,** bloat, **flatulence** or flatulency, flatus, gassiness, windiness; turgidness or turgidity, turgescence; tumidness or tumidity, tumefaction; tumescence, intumescence; **swollenness,** bloatedness; dropsy, edema; tympanites, tympany, tympanism, meteorism.

.3 **growth, development,** maturation, growing up, upgrowth; vegetation 411.30; reproduction, procreation 169, germination, pullulation; burgeoning, sprouting; budding, gemmation; outgrowth, excrescence; overgrowth 195.5; –auxe, –megaly, –osis, –plasia or –plasy, –trophy; auxo–, plasto–.

.4 VERBS (make larger) **enlarge, expand,** extend, **widen, broaden,** build, build up, aggrandize, **amplify,** crescendo, **magnify, increase** 38.4, augment, add to 40.5, raise, up, hike *or* hike up; develop, bulk *or* bulk out; **stretch, distend, dilate, swell, inflate,** sufflate, **blow up,** puff up, huff, puff, bloat; pump, pump up; rarefy.

.5 (become larger) **enlarge, expand, extend, increase,** greaten, crescendo, **develop, widen, broaden,** bulk; **stretch, distend, dilate, swell, bloat,** tumefy, balloon, puff up, fill out; snowball.

.6 **spread,** spread out, outspread, outstretch; **expand, extend,** widen; open, **open up,** unfold; **flare,** splay; spraddle, sprangle, sprawl; branch, branch out, ramify; fan, fan out, disperse, deploy; spread like wildfire; overrun, overgrow.

.7 **grow, develop,** wax, **increase** 38.4; gather, brew; **grow up,** mature, spring up, **shoot up,** sprout up, upshoot, upspring, upsprout, upspear, overtop, tower; burgeon, **sprout** 411.31, blossom 411.32, reproduce 169.7, procreate 169.8, germinate, pullulate; vegetate 411.31; **flourish, thrive,** grow like a weed; mushroom; outgrow; overgrow, hypertrophy, overdevelop.

.8 **fatten,** fat, plump, pinguefy *or* engross [both archaic]; **gain weight,** gather flesh, take *or* put on weight, become overweight.

.9 ADJS **expansive, extensive;** expansional, extensional; expansile, extensile, elastic; expansible, inflatable; distensive, dilatant; inflationary; –plastic.

.10 **expanded, extended, enlarged, increased** 38.7, upped, raised, hiked, **amplified,** ampliate, crescendoed, widened, broadened, built-up, beefed-up [informal].

.11 **spread, spreading,** patulous; sprawling, sprawly; **outspread, outstretched,** spread-out, stretched-out; open, unfolded; widespread, wide-open; flared, spraddled, sprangled, splayed; flaring, spraddling, sprangling, splaying; splay; fanned, fanning; fanlike, fan-shaped, fan-shape, flabelliform, deltoid.

.12 **grown, full-grown, grown-up,** developed, fully developed, **mature, full-fledged; growing,** sprouting, crescent, budding, flowering 411.35, florescent, **flourishing,** blossoming, blooming, burgeoning, thriving; overgrown, hypertrophied, overdeveloped.

.13 **distended, dilated, inflated,** sufflated, **blown up, puffed up, swollen,** swelled, **bloated,** turgid, tumid, plethoric, incrassate; **puffy,** pursy; flatulent, gassy, windy,

ventose; dropsical, edematous; enchymatous; fat 194.18; phys(o)–.

## 198. CONTRACTION

*(decrease in size)*

.1 NOUNS **contraction,** contracture, systole; **compression,** compressure, compaction, compactedness, coarctation; condensation, concentration, consolidation, solidification; circumscription, narrowing; reduction, diminuendo, decrease 39; abbreviation, curtailment, shortening 203.3; **constriction,** stricture *or* striction, astriction, strangulation, stranglement; bottleneck, hourglass, hourglass figure, nipped *or* wasp waist; neck 47.4, cervix, isthmus, narrow place; astringency, constringency; puckering, pursing; knitting, wrinkling.

.2 **squeezing,** compression, clamping *or* clamping down, tightening; pressure, press, crush; **pinch, squeeze, tweak, nip.**

.3 **shrinking,** shrinkage, atrophy; **shriveling, withering;** searing, parching, drying *or* drying up; attenuation, thinning; wasting, consumption, emaciation, emaceration; preshrinking, preshrinkage, Sanforizing.

.4 **collapse,** prostration, cave-in; implosion; **deflation.**

.5 contractibility, contractility, compactability, **compressibility,** condensability; collapsibility.

.6 contractor, constrictor, clamp, compressor, vise, pincer; **astringent,** styptic; alum, astringent bitters, styptic pencil.

.7 VERBS **contract, compress,** cramp, compact, coarct, condense, concentrate, consolidate, solidify; **reduce, decrease** 39.7; abbreviate, curtail, **shorten** 203.6; **constrict,** constringe, circumscribe, **narrow,** draw, draw in *or* together; strangle, strangulate; **pucker,** pucker up, **purse; knit, wrinkle.**

.8 **squeeze,** compress, clamp, tighten; roll *or* wad up, roll up into a ball, ensphere; **press,** crush; **pinch, tweak, nip.**

.9 **shrink, shrivel, wither,** sear, parch, dry up; **wizen,** weazen; consume, waste, waste away, attenuate, thin, emaciate, macerate, emacerate; preshrink, Sanforize.

.10 **collapse, cave, cave in,** fall in; fold, fold up; implode; **deflate,** let the air out of, take the wind out of; puncture, puncture one's balloon.

.11 ADJS **contractive,** contractional, contractible, contractile, compactable; **astringent,** constringent, styptic; **compressible,** condensable; **collapsible,** foldable; deflationary; consumptive.

.12 **contracted, compressed,** cramped, compact(ed), concentrated, condensed, consolidated, solidified; **constricted,** strangled, strangulated, **squeezed,** clamped, nipped, pinched or pinched-in, waspwaisted; puckered, pursed; knitted, wrinkled.

.13 **shrunk,** shrunken; **shriveled,** shriveled up; **withered,** sear, parched, corky, dried-up; **wasted,** wasted away, consumed, emaciated, emacerated, thin, attenuated; **wizened,** wizen, weazened; wizen-faced; preshrunk, Sanforized.

.14 **deflated, flat.**

## 199. DISTANCE

.1 NOUNS **distance, remoteness,** farness, faroffness; **separation,** divergence, clearance, margin, leeway; **extent, length,** space 179, **reach,** stretch, range, compass, span, stride; way, ways [informal], piece [dial]; perspective, aesthetic distance; astronomical or interstellar or galactic or intergalactic distance, deep space, depths of space, infinity 104; **mileage,** light-years, parsecs.

.2 **long way,** good ways [informal], **great distance,** long chalk [informal], **far cry,** far piece [dial]; long step, tidy step [informal], giant step or stride; long run or haul, long road or trail; long range; apogee, aphelion.

.3 **the distance, remote distance,** offing; **horizon,** where the earth meets the sky, vanishing point, background.

.4 (remote region) jumping-off place, godforsaken place, God knows where, the middle of nowhere [all informal], the back of beyond, the end of the rainbow, Thule or Ultima Thule, Timbuktu, Siberia, Darkest Africa, the South Seas, Pago Pago, the Great Divide, China, Outer Mongolia, pole, antipodes, end of the earth, North Pole, South Pole, Tierra del Fuego, Greenland, Yukon, Pillars of Hercules, remotest corner of the world; outpost, outskirts; the sticks, the boondocks, the tullies [all slang]; nowhere; frontier, outback [Austral]; the moon; outer space.

.5 VERBS **reach out, stretch out,** extend out, go or go out, range out, carry out; outstretch, outlie, outdistance, outrange.

.6 **extend to,** stretch to, stretch away to, **reach to,** lead to, go to, get to, come to, run to, carry to.

.7 **keep one's distance,** remain at a distance,

maintain distance or clearance, keep at a respectful distance, **keep away,** stand off or away; keep away from, keep or stand clear of, **steer clear of** [informal], hold away from, give a wide berth to, keep a good leeway or margin or offing, keep out of the way of, keep at arm's length, keep or stay or stand aloof; maintain one's perspective, keep one's esthetic distance.

.8 ADJS **distant,** distal, **remote, removed, far, far off,** away, **faraway,** at a distance, exotic, separated, apart, asunder; long-distance, long-range; ab-, ap(o)- or aph-, dist(o)- or disti-, over-, tel(e)- or teleo-, trans-, ultra-.

.9 **out-of-the-way,** godforsaken, back of beyond; **out of reach,** inaccessible, ungetatable, unapproachable, untouchable, hyperborean, antipodean.

.10 **thither,** ulterior; **yonder,** yon; **farther, further,** remoter, more distant.

.11 transoceanic, transmarine, ultramarine, oversea, overseas; transatlantic, transpacific; tramontane, transmontane, ultramontane, transalpine; transarctic, transcontinental, transequatorial, transpolar, transpontine, ultramundane.

.12 **farthest, furthest,** farthermost, farthest off, furthermost, ultimate, extreme, remotest, most distant.

.13 ADVS **yonder,** yon; **in the distance,** in the remote distance; **in the offing,** on the horizon, in the background.

.14 **at a distance, away, off,** aloof, at arm's length; distantly, remotely.

.15 **far, far off,** far away, **afar,** afar off, a long way off, a good ways off [informal], a long cry to, "over the hills and far away" [John Gay], as far as the eye can see, out of sight; clear to hell and gone [slang].

.16 **far and wide,** far and near, distantly and broadly, wide, widely, broadly, abroad.

.17 **apart, away, aside,** wide apart, wide away, "as wide asunder as pole and pole" [J. A. Froude], "as far as the east is from the west" [Bible].

.18 **out of reach,** beyond reach, **out of range,** beyond the bounds, out of the way, out of the sphere of; out of sight, à perte de vue [Fr]; out of hearing, out of earshot or earreach.

.19 **wide, clear;** wide of the mark, abroad, all abroad, astray, afield, far afield.

.20 PREPS **as far as, to, all the way to,** the whole way to.

.21 **beyond, past, over, across,** the other or far side of.

## 200. NEARNESS

.1 NOUNS **nearness, closeness,** nighness, **proximity,** propinquity, immediacy; approximation, approach, convergence; **vicinity,** vicinage, **neighborhood,** environs, purlieus, confines, precinct; **foreground,** immediate foreground.

.2 **short distance, short way,** little ways, **step,** short step, brief span, short piece [dial], little; close quarters *or* range *or* grips; **stone's throw,** spitting distance [informal], bowshot, gunshot, pistol shot; earshot, earreach, whoop *or* two whoops and a holler [informal], ace, bit [informal], crack, **hair, hairbreadth** *or* hairsbreadth, hair space, finger's width, inch, span.

.3 **juxtaposition, apposition,** adjacency; **contiguity,** contiguousness, conterminousness *or* coterminousness; abuttal, abutment; adjoiningness, junction 47.1,4, connection, union; **conjunction,** conjugation; appulse, syzygy; perigee, perihelion.

.4 **meeting,** joining, **encounter;** confrontation; rencontre; near-miss, collision course, near thing, narrow squeak *or* brush.

.5 **contact, touch,** touching, *attouchement* [Fr], taction, tangency, contingence; gentle *or* tentative contact, caress, brush, glance, nudge, kiss, rub, graze; impingement, impingence; osculation.

.6 **neighbor,** neighborer, next-door *or* immediate neighbor; borderer; abutter, adjoiner; bystander, onlooker, looker-on; tangent.

.7 VERBS **near, come near,** nigh, draw near *or* nigh, **approach** 296.3; **converge.**

.8 **be near** *or* **around,** be in the vicinity *or* neighborhood of, **approximate, approach,** get warm [informal], come near, begin to.

.9 **adjoin,** join, conjoin, **connect, butt, abut,** abut on *or* upon, be contiguous, be in contact; **neighbor,** border, **border on** *or* **upon,** verge upon; lie by, stand by.

.10 **contact, come in contact, touch, impinge,** hit; osculate; **graze,** caress, kiss, nudge, rub, brush, glance, scrape, sideswipe, skim, skirt, shave; have a near miss, brush *or* graze *or* squeak by.

.11 **meet, encounter; come across, run across,** fall across, cross the path of; **come upon,** run upon, fall upon, light *or* alight upon; come among, fall among; **meet with, meet up with** [informal], come face to face with, **confront,** meet head-on *or* eye-

ball to eyeball; run into, **bump into** [informal], run smack into [informal], come *or* run up against [informal], run *or* fall foul of; burst *or* pitch *or* pop *or* bounce *or* plump upon [all informal]; be on a collision course.

.12 **stay near, keep close to;** stand by, lie by; go with, march with, follow close upon, breathe down one's neck, tread *or* stay on one's heels, stay on one's tail, tailgate [informal]; hang about *or* around, hang upon the skirts of, hover over; **cling to,** clasp, hug, huddle; hug the shore *or* land, keep hold of the land, stay inshore.

.13 **juxtapose** *or* juxtaposit, **appose,** join 47.5, **adjoin, abut,** neighbor; bring near, put with, place *or* set side by side.

.14 ADJS **near, close, nigh,** nearish, nighish, intimate, cheek-by-jowl, side-by-side, hand-in-hand, arm-in-arm, *bras-dessus-bras-dessous* [Fr]; **approaching,** nearing, approximate *or* approximating, proximate, proximal, propinque [archaic]; **in the vicinity** *or* **neighborhood of,** vicinal; near the mark; warm *or* hot *or* burning [all informal]; ad–, circum–, cis–, ep(i) *or* eph–, juxta–, pen(e)–, peri–, plesi(o)–, pros–, proximo–, sub–, vic–.

.15 **nearby, handy, convenient,** convenient to, propinquant *or* propinquous, at hand, ready at hand, easily reached *or* attained.

.16 **adjacent, next,** immediate, contiguous, **adjoining, abutting; neighboring,** neighbor; **juxtaposed,** juxtapositive *or* juxtapositional; **bordering, conterminous** *or* coterminous, connecting; **face to face** 239.6; end to end, endways, endwise; **joined** 47.13.

.17 **in contact,** contacting, **touching, meeting,** contingent; **impinging,** impingent; tangent, tangential; osculatory; grazing, glancing, brushing, rubbing, nudging.

.18 **nearer, nigher, closer.**

.19 **nearest,** nighest, **closest,** nearmost, next, immediate.

.20 ADVS **near, nigh, close;** hard, at close quarters; **nearby, close by,** hard by, fast by, not far *or* far off, at hand, **near** *or* **close at hand; thereabout** *or* thereabouts, hereabout *or* hereabouts; nearabout *or* nearabouts *or* nigh about [all dial]; **about, around** [informal], close about, along toward [informal]; at no great distance, only a step; as near as no matter *or* makes no difference [informal]; **within reach** *or* **range,** within call *or* hearing, within earshot *or* earreach, within a whoop *or* two whoops and a holler [informal], within a stone's throw, in spitting distance [informal], at one's elbow, at one's feet, at one's fingertips, under one's nose, at one's side, within one's grasp; just around the corner, just across the street, just next door.

.21 **in juxtaposition, in conjunction,** in apposition; beside 242.11,12.

.22 **nearly, near,** pretty near [informal], close, closely; almost, all but, not quite, as good as; **well-nigh, just about;** nigh, nighhand.

.23 **approximately,** approximatively, practically [informal], for practical purposes or all practical purposes, at a first approximation, give or take a little, **more or less;** roughly, roundly, in round numbers; **generally,** generally speaking, roughly speaking, say.

.24 PREPS **near, nigh,** near to, **close to,** near upon, close upon, hard on or upon, bordering on or upon, **verging on** or verging upon, on the confines of, at the threshold of, **on the brink** or **verge of,** on the edge of, at next hand, at or on the point of, on the skirts of; **not far from;** next door to, at one's door; nigh about or nearabout or nigh on or nigh onto [all dial].

.25 **against,** up against, on, upon, over against, opposite, nose to nose with, vis-à-vis, in contact with.

.26 **about, around,** just about, *circa* [L], c., somewhere about or near, near or close upon, near enough to, upwards of [informal], –ish; **in the neighborhood** or **vicinity of.**

## 201. INTERVAL

*(space between)*

.1 NOUNS **interval, space** 179, intervening or intermediate space, **interspace,** distance or space between, interstice; **clearance,** margin, leeway, freeboard, **room** 179.3; discontinuity 72, jump, leap, interruption; hiatus, caesura, lacuna; half space, single space, double space, em space, en space, hair space, time interval, interim 109.

.2 **crack, cleft,** cranny, chink, check, chap, **crevice,** fissure, scissure, incision, notch, cut, gash, slit, split, **rift,** rent, rime; **opening,** excavation, cavity, hole; **gap,** gape, **abyss,** abysm, **gulf,** chasm, void 187.3; **breach, break,** fracture, rupture; fault, flaw; slot, groove, furrow, moat, ditch, trench, dike; joint, seam; leak; **ravine, gorge,** dell, flume; kloof, donga; **canyon** or cañon, box canyon, *couloir* [Fr], cou-

lee; **gully, gulch,** arroyo, draw, nullah [India], wadi; clough, cleuch [both Scot]; **crevasse;** chimney, **defile,** pass, passage, col; cwm 257.8, **valley** 257.9.

.3 VERBS **interspace, space,** make a space, interval, set at intervals, **space out, separate,** part, dispart, set or keep apart, remove.

.4 **cleave, crack,** check, incise, **cut, cut apart,** gash, slit, **split,** rive, rent; **open; gap,** breach, break, fracture, rupture; slot, groove, furrow, ditch, trench.

.5 ADJS intervallic, interspatial, interstitial.

.6 **interspaced, spaced,** intervaled, **spaced out,** set at intervals, with intervals or an interval, **separated, parted,** removed.

.7 **cleft, cut,** cloven, **cracked,** sundered, rift, rent, **slit, split;** gaping, gappy, dehiscent; fissured, fissury; rimose, rimulose; chinky.

## 202. LENGTH

.1 NOUNS **length,** longness, lengthiness, longitude, overall length; **extent,** extension, **measure, span, reach, stretch; distance** 199; footage, yardage, mileage; infinity 104; perpetuity 112; long time 110.4; linear measures 490.17.

.2 oblongness, oblongitude.

.3 (a length) **piece, portion,** part; coil, strip, bolt, roll; run.

.4 **line, strip,** bar; stripe 568.6; string 71.2.

.5 **lengthening, prolongation, elongation,** production, protraction, **extension,** stretching, stretching or spinning or stringing out; stretch, tension, strain.

.6 VERBS **be long,** be lengthy, **extend,** be prolonged, **stretch; stretch out,** extend out, reach out; stretch oneself, crane, crane one's neck; stand on tiptoes; outstretch, outreach; sprawl, straggle.

.7 **lengthen, prolong,** prolongate, **elongate, extend,** produce, **protract,** continue; lengthen out, let out, **draw out,** drag out, stretch or string or spin out; **stretch,** draw, pull; tense, tauten, tighten, strain.

.8 ADJS **long, lengthy;** longish, longsome; tall 207.21; **extensive, far-reaching,** fargoing, far-flung; sesquipedalian, sesquipedal; as long as one's arm, a mile long; interminable, without end, no end of or to; dolich(o)–, longi–, macr(o)–, mec(o)–.

.9 **lengthened, prolonged,** prolongated, **elongated, extended, protracted; drawn out,** dragged out, stretched or spun or strung out, straggling; **stretched,** drawn, pulled; tense, taut, taut as a bowstring, tight, strained.

.10 **oblong,** oblongated, oblongitudinal, elongated; rectangular; elliptical.

.11 ADVS lengthily, extensively, at length, *in extenso* [L], *ad infinitum* [L].

.12 **lengthwise** *or* lengthways, longwise *or* longways, longitudinally, along, in length, at length; **endwise** *or* endways, endlong.

## 203. SHORTNESS

.1 NOUNS **shortness, briefness, brevity; succinctness,** curtness, summariness, compendiousness, compactness; **conciseness** 592; littleness 196; lowness 208; transience 111, short time 113.3, instantaneousness 113.

.2 **stubbiness,** stumpiness [informal], **stockiness, fatness** 195.8, chubbiness, chunkiness [informal], blockiness, squatness, squattiness, dumpiness; pudginess, podginess; snubbiness *or* snubbishness.

.3 **shortening, abbreviation; reduction** 39.1; **abridgment, condensation,** compression, conspectus, epitome, epitomization, summary, summation, précis, abstract, recapitulation, recap [informal], synopsis; **curtailment,** truncation, retrenchment; telescoping; elision, ellipsis, syncope, apocope; foreshortening.

.4 **shortener,** cutter, abridger; abstracter, epitomizer *or* epitomist.

.5 **shortcut,** cut, cutoff; shortest way; **beeline,** air line.

.6 VERBS **shorten, abbreviate, cut; reduce** 39.7; **abridge, condense,** compress, contract, **boil down,** abstract, sum up, summarize, recapitulate, recap [informal], synopsize, epitomize, capsulize; **curtail,** truncate, retrench; elide, **cut short,** cut down, cut off short, cut back, take in; **dock,** bob, shear, shave, trim, clip, snub, nip; mow, reap, **crop; prune,** poll, pollard; stunt, check the growth of; telescope; foreshorten.

.7 **take a short cut,** short-cut; **cut across,** cut through; **cut a corner,** cut corners; **make a beeline,** take the air line, go as the crow flies.

.8 ADJS **short,** brachy– *or* brady–; **brief,** abbreviatory, "short and sweet" [Thomas Lodge]; **concise** 592.6; **curt,** curtal, curtate, decurtate; **succinct,** summary, synoptic(al), compendious, compact; **little** 196.10; **low** 208.7; transient 111.7, instantaneous 113.4,5.

.9 **shortened, abbreviated; abridged,** compressed, condensed, epitomized, digested, abstracted, capsule, capsulized; **curtailed,** cut short, short-cut, **docked,** bobbed,

sheared, shaved, trimmed, clipped, snub, snubbed, nipped; mowed, mown, reaped, **cropped; pruned,** polled, pollard; elided, elliptic(al).

.10 **stubby,** stubbed, stumpy [informal], **thickset, stocky,** blocky, **chunky** [informal], **fat** 195.18, **chubby,** tubby [informal], dumpy; **squat,** squatty, squattish; **pudgy,** podgy; pug, **pugged;** snub-nosed; turned-up, *retroussé* [Fr].

.11 **short-legged,** breviped; **short-winged,** brevipennate.

.12 ADVS **shortly, briefly,** summarily, in brief compass, economically, sparely, curtly, succinctly; **concisely** 592.7,8, compendiously, synoptically.

.13 **short, abruptly,** suddenly 113.9, all of a sudden.

## 204. BREADTH, THICKNESS

.1 NOUNS **breadth, width,** broadness, wideness, fullness, amplitude, latitude, distance across *or* crosswise *or* crossways, extent, **span, expanse, spread;** beam.

.2 **thickness,** the third dimension, distance through, depth; **mass, bulk, body;** corpulence, bodily size; **coarseness,** grossness 351.2; fatness 195.8.

.3 **diameter, bore, caliber; radius,** semidiameter.

.4 VERBS **broaden, widen,** deepen; **expand,** extend, extend to the side *or* sides; **spread** 197.6, spread out *or* sidewise *or* sideways, outspread, outstretch.

.5 **thicken,** grow thick, thick; incrassate, inspissate; fatten 197.8.

.6 ADJS **broad, wide,** deep; extensive, spreadout 197.11, **expansive;** spacious, **roomy** 179.9; ample, full; widespread 79.13; "broad as the world" [James Russell Lowell], "wide as a church door" [Shakespeare]; eury–, lati–, plat(y)–.

.7 broad of beam, broad-beamed, broadsterned, beamy; broad-ribbed, wideribbed, laticostate; broad-toothed, widetoothed, latidentate.

.8 **thick,** three-dimensional; **thickset, heavyset,** thick-bodied, broad-bodied, thickgirthed; **massive, bulky** 195.19, corpulent 195.18; coarse, heavy, gross, crass, fat; fullbodied, full, viscous; **dense** 354.12; thicknecked, bullnecked; hadr(o)–, pachy–.

.9 ADVS breadthwise *or* breadthways; widthwise *or* widthways; broadwise *or* broadways; broadside, broad side foremost; sidewise *or* ways; through, depthwise *or* ways.

**.10 broad**

| | |
|---|---|
| broad-backed | wide-armed |
| broad-based | wide-banked |
| broad-billed | wide-bottomed |
| broad-bladed | wide-branched |
| broad-bosomed | wide-breasted |
| broad-bottomed | wide-brimmed |
| broad-breasted | wide-eared |
| broad-brimmed | wide-faced |
| broad-chested | wide-framed |
| broad-eyed | wide-hipped |
| broad-faced | wide-leaved |
| broad-gauge *or* | wide-lipped |
|   -gauged | wide-nosed |
| broad-headed | wide-petaled |
| broad-leaved | wide-rimmed |
| broad-lipped | wide-roving |
| broad-mouthed | wide-set |
| broad-nosed | wide-spaced |
| broad-roomed | wide-spanned |
| broad-shouldered | wide-streeted |
| broad-tailed | wide-tracked |
| broad-winged | wide-wayed |
| wide-angle | wide-winged |
| wide-arched | |

**.11 thick**

| | |
|---|---|
| thick-ankled | thick-leaved |
| thick-barked | thick-legged |
| thick-barred | thick-lipped |
| thick-bottomed | thick-ribbed |
| thick-cheeked | thick-stalked |
| thick-coated | thick-stemmed |
| thick-eared | thick-tailed |
| thick-fingered | thick-toed |
| thick-footed | thick-toothed |
| thick-headed | thick-walled |
| thick-jawed | thick-wristed |
| thick-kneed | |

## 205. NARROWNESS, THINNESS

**.1 NOUNS narrowness, slenderness; closeness,** nearness; **straitness,** restriction, restrictedness, limitation, strictness, confinement; crowdedness, incapaciousness, incommodiousness; **tightness,** tight squeeze; hair, hairbreadth *or* hairsbreadth; finger's breadth; narrow gauge.

**.2 narrowing, tapering,** taper; **contraction** 198; stricture, constriction, coarctation.

**.3 (narrow place) narrow, narrows, strait;** bottleneck; isthmus; channel 396, canal; pass, defile; neck, throat, der(o)–.

**.4 thinness, slenderness, slimness, frailty,** slightness, gracility, lightness, airiness, delicacy, flimsiness, wispiness, laciness, paperiness, gauziness, gossameriness, diaphanousness, insubstantiality, ethereality, mistiness, vagueness; light *or* airy texture; **fineness** 351.3; **tenuity, rarity,** subtility, exility, exiguity; **attenuation;** dilution, dilutedness, wateriness 388.1, weakness.

**.5 leanness, skinniness,** fleshlessness, slightness, frailness, twigginess, spareness, mea-gerness, **scrawniness, gauntness,** lankness, **lankiness,** gawkiness, **boniness,** skin and bones; haggardness, poorness, paperiness, peakedness [informal], puniness, "lean and hungry look" [Shakespeare]; underweight; hatchet face, lantern jaws.

**.6 emaciation,** emaceration, attenuation, atrophy, tabes, marasmus.

**.7 (comparisons)** paper, wafer, lath, slat, **rail,** rake, splinter, slip, shaving, streak, vein; gruel, soup; shadow, mere shadow; **skeleton.**

**.8 (thin person) slim, lanky;** twiggy, **shadow, skeleton,** walking skeleton, corpse, barebones, bag *or* stack of bones; rattlebones *or* **spindleshanks** *or* spindlelegs [all informal], gangleshanks [slang], lathlegs *or* sticklegs [both slang], **bean pole,** beanstalk, broomstick, clothes pole, stilt.

**.9 reducing, slenderizing;** weight-watching, calorie-counting.

**.10 thinner,** solvent 391.4.

**.11 VERBS narrow,** constrict, diminish, draw in, go in; restrict, limit, straiten, confine; **taper,** snape; **contract** 198.7.

**.12 thin,** thin down, thin away *or* off *or* out; **rarefy,** subtilize, attenuate; dilute, water, water down, weaken; **emaciate,** emacerate.

**.13 slenderize, reduce,** reduce *or* lose *or* take off weight, lose flesh, weight-watch, count calories, diet; slim, **slim down,** thin down.

**.14 ADJS narrow, slender;** narrowish, narrowy; **close,** near; **tight, strait,** isthmic, isthmian; close-fitting; **restricted,** limited, circumscribed, **confined,** constricted; **cramped,** cramp; incapacious, incommodious, crowded; **meager,** scant, scanty; narrow-gauge(d); angustifoliate, angustirostrate, angustiseptal, angustisellate; angusti–, dolich(o)–, sten(o)–.

**.15 tapered,** taper, tapering, cone- *or* wedge-shaped.

**.16 thin, slender, slim,** gracile, "imperially slim" [E. A. Robinson]; thin-bodied, thin-set, narrow- *or* wasp-waisted; **svelte,** slinky, sylphlike, willowy; girlish, boyish; thinnish, slenderish, slimmish; **slight,** slight-made; **frail,** delicate, light, airy, wispy, lacy, gauzy, papery, gossamer, diaphanous, insubstantial, ethereal, misty, vague, flimsy, **fine; finespun,** thin-spun, fine-drawn, wiredrawn; threadlike, slender as a thread; **tenuous,** subtle, rare, **rarefied;** attenuated, attenuate, **watery, weak,** diluted, watered *or* watered-down, small; fusi– *or* fuso–, lept(o)–.

.17 **lean,** lean-looking, **skinny** [informal], fleshless, lean-fleshed, thin-fleshed, **spare,** meager, **scrawny,** scraggy, thin-bellied, **gaunt, lank, lanky; gangling** or gangly [both informal], gawky, **spindling,** spindly; flat-chested, flat [informal]; **bony, rawboned,** bare-boned, rattleboned [informal], skeletal, **mere skin and bones;** twiggy; **underweight,** undersized, spidery, thin or skinny as a lath or rail, "lean as a rake" [Chaucer].

.18 lean-limbed, thin-legged, lath- or stick-legged [slang], spindle-legged or -shanked [informal], gangle-shanked [slang], stilt-legged.

.19 lean- or horse- or thin-faced, thin-featured, **hatchet-faced;** wizen- or weazen-faced; lean- or thin-cheeked; lean-jawed or lantern-jawed.

.20 **haggard, poor,** puny, **peaked** or peaky [both informal], **pinched;** shriveled, withered; **wizened,** weazeny; **emaciated,** emaciate, emacerated, **wasted,** attenuated, corpselike, skeletal, hollow-eyed, wraithlike, cadaverous; tabetic, tabid, marantic, marasmic; **starved,** starveling, starved-looking; **undernourished,** underfed, jejune; worn to a shadow, "worn to the bones" [Shakespeare], "weakened and wasted to skin and bone" [Du Bartas].

.21 **slenderizing,** reducing, slimming.

.22 ADVS **narrowly,** closely, nearly, **barely,** hardly, only just, **by the skin of one's teeth.**

.23 thinly, thin; meagerly, sparsely, sparingly, scantily.

## 206. FILAMENT

.1 NOUNS **filament,** fili–; **fiber** 206.8, fibr-(o)–, in(o)–; **thread,** mito–, nem(a)– or nemo– or nemat(o)–, –neme; **strand,** suture; **hair** 230; artificial fiber, natural fiber, animal fiber; threadlet, filamentule; fibril, fibrilla; capillament; cilium, ciliolum, cili(o)–, cilii–; **tendril,** cirrus, cirr(o)– or cirri– or cirrho– or cirrhi–, flagellum, blephar(o)–, mastig(o)–, –kont; gossamer, **web,** cobweb, spider or spider's web; skein, hank; denier.

.2 **cord** 206.9, chord(o)–, line, **string, twine, rope, wire, cable, yarn,** spun yarn; braid, twist, thong, brail; **ligament,** ligature, ligation, syndesm(o)–; **tendon,** teno–.

.3 **cordage,** cording, **ropework,** roping; tackle, tack, gear, rigging; ship's ropes 277.31.

.4 **strip, strap,** strop; shred, slip, list, spill; **band,** bandage, fillet, belt, girdle, fascia, taenia, taen(o)– or taeni–; **ribbon,** ribband; **tape,** tapeline, tape measure, adhesive tape, friction tape, plastic tape, cellophane tape, Scotch tape, masking tape, cloth tape, Mystik tape, ticker tape; slat, lath, batten, spline, strake, plank; ligule, ligula.

.5 **spinner,** spinster; silkworm, spider; spinning wheel, spinning jenny, jenny, mule, mule-jenny; throstle; spinning frame, bobbin and fly frame; spinneret(te).

.6 VERBS (make threads) spin; filament, shred, gin.

.7 ADJS **threadlike,** thready; **stringy,** ropy, wiry; **hairlike** 230.23, hairy 230.24; filamentary, filiform; fibrous, fibered, fibroid, fibrilliform; ligamental; capillary, capilliform; cirrose, cirrous; funicular, funiculate; flagelliform; taeniate, taeniform; ligulate, ligular; gossamery, flossy, silky.

.8 **fibers, threads**

| | |
|---|---|
| acetate rayon | merino |
| Acrilan | mohair |
| alpaca | near-silk |
| angora | nylon |
| Aralac | oakum |
| Avisco | Orlon |
| bast | packthread |
| batting | Polyfibre |
| cashmere | protein fibers |
| Celanese | raffia |
| Chemstrand | raw silk |
| coir | rayon |
| cotton | Rexenite |
| cotton batting | Sarelon |
| Dacron | sericin gum |
| darning cotton | sewing thread |
| Dynel | silk |
| Fiberfrax | sisal, sisal hemp |
| flax | soybean fibers |
| floss, floss silk | spandex |
| Fortisan | spun rayon |
| goat's hair | Terylene |
| harl | tussah |
| hemp | Velon |
| horsehair | Vicara |
| jute | vicuña |
| kapok | Vinyon |
| Lastex | wool |
| linen | worsted |
| llama hair | yarn |
| Manila, Manila hemp | zephyr, zephyr yarn |

.9 **cords**

| | |
|---|---|
| binding twine | lasso |
| braided rope | lead |
| cable | leader |
| catgut | marline |
| clothesline | mason's line |
| fast | monofilament |
| gut | pack twine |
| hamstring | pepper-and-salt rope |
| hawser | rein |
| lace | rope |
| lacing | sail twine |
| lariat | sennit |

ship's ropes 277.31
shoelace
shoestring
sinew
spermatic cord
string

tendon
thew
twine
umbilical cord
whipcord
wire rope

## 207. HEIGHT

.1 NOUNS **height,** heighth [dial], vertical *or* perpendicular distance; **highness, tallness; altitude, elevation,** ceiling; **loftiness,** sublimity, exaltation; hauteur, toploftiness 912.1; eminence, prominence; **stature.**

.2 **height, elevation,** eminence, steep, acr-(o)–, hyps(o)– *or* hypsi–; **rise, raise, uprise,** lift, rising ground, vantage point *or* ground; **heights,** soaring *or* towering *or* Olympian heights, aerial heights, dizzy heights; upmost *or* uppermost *or* utmost *or* extreme height; sky, stratosphere, ether, heaven *or* heavens; zenith, apex, acme.

.3 highland, highlands, upland, uplands, moorland, moors, downs, wold, rolling country.

.4 plateau, tableland, table, mesa, table mountain, bench.

.5 **hill, down,** moor, brae [Scot], barrow, fell [Scot]; **hillock,** monticle, monticule, **knoll, hummock, mound, swell,** knob; anthill, molehill; **dune,** sand dune; butte; drumlin; foothills.

.6 **ridge,** arête [Fr], chine, spine, kame *or* comb [both Scot], esker; saddle, saddleback, col, horseback, hogback, hog's-back.

.7 **mountain, mount, alp,** hump, tor, ore-(o)– *or* oro–; Olympus, Everest; lofty mountains, towering alps; "the wooded mountains" [Vergil], "the hills, rock-ribbed, and ancient as the sun" [William Cullen Bryant].

.8 **peak, pike,** pic [Fr], pico [Sp], **pinnacle,** point, **crest,** spur, tor; **mountaintop; hilltop,** knoll; **summit** 211.2; precipice 213.3; lofty peak, cloud-capped *or* cloud-topped *or* snow-clad peak.

.9 **mountain range,** range, **chain,** cordillera, sierra [both Sp], massif [Fr]; Alps, Rockies, Andes, Himalayas, Caucasus; "alps on alps" [Pope], hill heaped upon hill.

.10 **watershed,** water parting, **divide;** Great Divide, Continental Divide.

.11 **tower; turret,** tour [Fr]; campanile, bell tower, belfry; lighthouse; cupola, lantern; dome; martello, martello tower; barbican; **derrick,** pole; windmill tower, observation tower, fire tower; **mast,** radio *or* television mast, antenna tower; water tower, standpipe; **spire,** pinnacle; **steeple,** flèche [Fr]; minaret; stupa, tope, pagoda; pyramid; pylon; **shaft,** pillar, column; pilaster; obelisk; monument; colossus; skyscraper.

.12 (tall person) **longlegs** *or* longshanks *or* highpockets *or* long drink of water [all informal]; bean pole 205.8; **giant** 195.13; sixfooter, seven-footer, grenadier [Brit].

.13 **high tide,** high water, flood tide, spring tide, flood.

.14 (measurement of height) altimetry, hypsometry, hypsography; altimeter, hypsometer.

.15 VERBS **tower, soar,** spire, "buss the clouds" [Shakespeare]; **rise, uprise, ascend, mount, rear;** stand on tiptoe.

.16 **rise above, tower above** *or* **over,** clear, overtop, o'ertop, outtop, **top, surmount; overlook,** look down upon *or* over; **command,** dominate, overarch, overshadow, command a view of; bestride, bestraddle.

.17 (become higher) **grow,** grow up, upgrow; uprise, **rise** *or* **shoot up,** mount.

.18 **heighten, elevate** 317.5.

.19 ADJS **high,** high-reaching, high-up, **lofty, elevated,** altitudinous, uplifted *or* upreared, **eminent, exalted, prominent, steep, supernal,** superlative, **sublime,** alti–, hyper–, super–; **towering,** towery, **soaring,** spiring, aspiring, mounting, ascending; **topping,** outtopping *or* overtopping; overarching *or* overlooking, dominating; airy, aerial, ethereal; Olympian; monumental, colossal; high as a steeple; topless; high-set, high-pitched; haughty, toplofty.

.20 skyscraping, **sky-high,** heaven-reaching *or* -aspiring, heaven-kissing, "as high as Heaven and as deep as Hell" [Beaumont and Fletcher]; cloud-touching *or* -topped *or* -capped.

.21 **giant** 195.20, gigantic, colossal, statuesque; **tall, lengthy,** long 202.8; **rangy, lanky,** lank, tall as a maypole; **gangling** *or* gangly [both informal]; **long-legged,** long-limbed, leggy.

.22 **highland, upland;** hill-dwelling, mountain-dwelling.

.23 **hilly,** knobby, rolling; **mountainous,** mountained, **alpine,** alpen, alpestrine, alpigene; subalpine, monticuline, monticulous.

.24 **higher,** superior, greater; **over, above,** supra–; **upper,** upmost *or* uppermost; highest 211.10.

.25 altimetric(al), hypsometrical, hypsographic(al).

.26 ADVS **on high,** high up, high; **aloft,** aloof;

up, upward, upwards, straight up, to the zenith; **above, over,** o'er, **overhead;** above one's head, over head and ears; skyward, airward, in the air, in the clouds; on the peak *or* summit *or* crest *or* pinnacle; upstairs, abovestairs; tiptoe, on tiptoe; on stilts; on the shoulders of.

## 208. LOWNESS

.1 NOUNS **lowness, shortness,** squatness, squattiness, stumpiness; **prostration,** supineness, proneness, recumbency, couchancy, lying, lying down, reclining; depression, debasement; subjacency.

.2 **low tide,** low water, dead low water *or* tide, ebb tide, neap tide, neap.

.3 lowland, **lowlands,** bottomland.

.4 **base, bottom** 212, lowest point, nadir; lowest *or* underlying level, lower strata, bedrock.

.5 VERBS **lie low, squat, crouch,** couch; crawl, grovel, lie prone *or* supine *or* prostrate, hug the earth; lie under, underlie.

.6 lower, debase, depress 318.4.

.7 ADJS **low,** unelevated, **short, squat,** squatty, stumpy, runty, chame– *or* chamae–; debased, depressed, prone, supine, prostrate(d), couchant, crouched, stooped, recumbent, laid low, knocked flat; **flat, low-lying,** low-set, low-hung; **low-built,** low-sized, low-statured, lowbodied; low-level, low-leveled; neap; knee-high, knee-high to a grasshopper [informal].

.8 **lower,** hyp(o)–, **infra–, intra–, sub–;** inferior, **under, nether,** subjacent; down; less advanced; earlier; lowest 212.7.

.9 ADVS **low,** near the ground; at a low ebb.

.10 **below,** down below, **under,** *infra* [L]; belowstairs, downstairs, below deck; underfoot; below par, below the mark.

.11 PREPS **below, under, underneath, beneath,** neath, at the foot of, at the base of.

## 209. DEPTH

.1 NOUNS **depth, deepness,** profoundness, profundity; deep-downness, extreme innerness, deep-seatedness, deep-rootedness; bottomlessness, plumblessness, fathomlessness; subterraneity, undergroundness; interiority 225.

.2 **pit, deep, depth,** hole, hollow, **cavity,** shaft, well, **gulf, chasm, abyss,** abysm, yawning abyss; crater; crevasse.

.3 **depths,** deeps, bowels, bowels of the earth; bottomless pit; infernal pit, hell, nether world, underworld; dark *or* unknown *or* yawning *or* gaping depths, unfathomed deeps; outer *or* deep space.

.4 **ocean depths, the deep sea, the deep,** trench, **the deeps, the depths,** bottomless depths, inner space, abyss; bottom waters; abyssal zone, Bassalia, bathyal zone, pelagic zone; **bottom of the sea,** ocean bottom *or* floor *or* bed, ground, benthos, Davy Jones's locker [informal].

.5 **sounding** *or* **soundings,** fathoming, depth sounding; **echo sounding,** echolocation; sonar; oceanography, bathometry, bathymetry; fathomage, water (depth of water).

.6 **draft,** submergence, submersion, sinkage, **displacement.**

.7 **deepening, lowering, depression;** sinking, sinkage; excavation, digging, mining, tunneling; drilling, probing.

.8 VERBS **deepen, lower, depress, sink;** countersink; **dig,** excavate, tunnel, mine, **drill;** pierce to the depths; **dive** 320.6.

.9 **sound, take soundings,** make a sounding, heave *or* cast *or* sling the lead, **fathom, plumb,** plumb-line, plumb the depths.

.10 ADJS **deep, profound,** deep-down, bath(o)– *or* bathy–; deepish, deepsome; **deepgoing,** deep-lying, deep-reaching; **deepset,** deep-laid; deep-sunk, deep-sunken, deep-sinking; **deep-seated, deep-rooted,** deep-fixed, deep-settled; deep-cut, deepengraven; knee-deep, ankle-deep.

.11 **abysmal,** abyssal, yawning, cavernous, gaping, plunging; **bottomless,** without bottom, soundless, unsounded, plumbless, **fathomless,** unfathomed, unfathomable; deep as a well, deep as the sea *or* ocean, deep as hell.

.12 **underground, subterranean,** subterraneous, buried, deep-buried.

.13 **underwater,** subaqueous; **submarine, undersea;** submerged, submersed, immersed, buried, engulfed, inundated, flooded, drowned, sunken.

.14 **deep-sea,** deep-water, blue-water; oceanographic, bathyal, bathysmal, bathybic; benthal, benthonic; abyssal, Bassalian; bathyorographic(al), bathymetric(al); benthopelagic, bathypelagic.

.15 **deepest, deepmost,** bedrock, rock-bottom.

.16 ADVS **deep; beyond one's depth,** out of one's depth; over one's head, over head and ears; at bottom, at the core, at rock bottom.

**.17 depth indicators**

| | |
|---|---|
| bathometer | plumb line |
| bathymeter | plummet |
| bob | probe |
| depth sounder | sonic depth sounder |
| dipsey or deep-sea line | sound |
| or lead | sounding bottle |
| echo sounder | sounding lead |
| fathomer | sounding line |
| Fathometer | sounding machine |
| Kelvin machine | sounding rod |
| lead | sounding tube |
| leadline | space probe |
| plumb | Tanner-Blish machine |
| plumb bob | |

## 210. SHALLOWNESS

.1 NOUNS **shallowness, depthlessness;** shoalness, shoaliness, no water, no depth; **superficiality,** exteriority, triviality, **cursoriness,** slightness; **surface,** superficies, skin 229, rind, epidermis; veneer, gloss; pinprick, scratch, mere scratch.

.2 **shoal, shallow,** shallows, shallow or shoal water, flat, shelf; **bank, bar,** sandbank, sandbar; **reef,** coral reef; ford; wetlands, tidal flats.

.3 VERBS **shallow,** shoal; fill in or up, silt up.

.4 **scratch the surface, touch upon,** hardly touch, skim, skim over, skim or graze the surface, hit the high spots [informal].

.5 ADJS **shallow,** shoal, **depthless,** not deep, unprofound; **surface,** on or near the surface, merely surface; **superficial, cursory,** slight, light, thin, jejune, trivial; **skin-deep,** epidermal; ankle-deep, knee-deep; shallow-rooted, shallow-rooting; shallow-draft or -bottomed or -hulled; shallow-sea.

.6 shoaly, shelfy; reefy; unnavigable.

## 211. TOP

.1 NOUNS **top,** top side, upper side, upside; surface 224.2; topside or topsides; upper story, top floor; clerestory; roof, ridgepole or roofpole; rooftop.

.2 **summit,** top, acr(o)–; **tip-top, peak,** pinnacle; **crest, brow,** loph(o)– or lophi(o)–, –loph; ridge, edge; **crown, cap, tip, point,** spire, pitch; highest pitch, no place higher, **apex,** vertex, **acme,** ne plus ultra [L], **zenith, climax,** apogee, pole; **culmination,** culmen; **extremity, maximum, limit,** upper extremity, highest point, very top, top of the world, extreme limit, utmost or upmost or uppermost, height, "the very acme and pitch" [Pope]; **sky,** heaven or heavens, seventh heaven, cloud nine [informal]; meridian, noon, high noon; mountaintop 207.8.

.3 **topping,** icing, frosting.

.4 (top part) **head,** heading, **headpiece,** cap, *caput* [L], capsheaf, **crown, crest;** topknot; pinhead, nailhead.

.5 **capital,** head, crown, cap; bracket capital; cornice, geisso–.

.6 **head,** headpiece, **pate,** poll [informal], crown, cephal(o)–, corono–; **sconce or noddle or noodle or noggin or bean or dome** [all informal]; brow, ridge; "the dome of Thought, the palace of the Soul" [Byron].

.7 **skull,** cranium, crani(o)–; pericranium, epicranium; brainpan, brain box or case.

.8 **phrenology,** craniology, metoposcopy, physiognomy; phrenologist, craniologist, metoposcopist, physiognomist.

.9 VERBS **top,** top off, **crown, cap,** crest, **head,** tip, peak, surmount; overtop or outtop, have the top place or spot, overarch; **culminate,** consummate, climax; ice, frost (a cake).

.10 ADJS **top,** topmost, **uppermost,** upmost, overmost, **highest;** tip-top, tip-crowning, **maximum,** maximal, ultimate; summital, apical, vertical, zenithal, climactic(al), **consummate;** acmic, acmatic; meridian, meridional; **head,** headmost, capital, chief, paramount, supreme, preeminent.

.11 **topping, crowning, capping,** heading, surmounting, overtopping or outtopping, overarching; culminating, consummating, climaxing.

.12 **topped,** headed, **crowned, capped,** crested, plumed, tipped, peaked.

.13 **topless,** headless, crownless.

.14 cephalic, encephalic, –cephalous.

.15 ADVS **on top,** at or on the top, topside [informal]; at the top of the tree or ladder, on top of the roost or heap; on the crest or crest of the wave; at the head, at the peak or pinnacle or summit.

.16 PREPS atop, on, upon, on top of.

**.17 architectural toppings**

| | |
|---|---|
| abacus | cyma or cima |
| acanthus | cymatium |
| acroterion | dentil |
| annulet | drip |
| antefix | drop |
| architrave | echinus |
| astragal | entablature |
| bell | epistyle |
| campana | fastigium |
| capstone | finial |
| console | frieze |
| coping | frontispiece |
| coping stone | gable end |
| corbel | gorgerin |
| cornice | gutta |
| crown | head |

| | |
|---|---|
| headboard | modillion |
| header | mutule |
| headmold | neck(ing) |
| head molding | neckmold |
| headpiece | neck molding |
| headpost | pediment |
| headsill | sconce |
| hoodmold | taenia |
| hypotrachelium | treenail |
| keystone | triglyph |
| larmier | tympanum |
| lintel | zoophorus |
| metope | |

**.18 capital styles**

| | |
|---|---|
| Byzantine | Ionic |
| Corinthian | Moorish |
| Doric | Roman Corinthian |
| Gothic | Roman Doric |
| Greek | Romanesque |
| Greek Corinthian | Roman Ionic |
| Greek Ionic | Tuscan |

## 212. BOTTOM

.1 NOUNS **bottom,** bottom side, **underside,** nether side, lower side, downside, **underneath,** fundament; belly, underbelly; buttocks 241.4, breech; **rock bottom, bedrock,** bed, hardpan; substratum, underlayer, lowest level *or* layer *or* stratum, nethermost level *or* layer *or* stratum.

.2 **base,** basement, baso– *or* basi–, **foot,** footing, sole, toe; **nadir; foundation** 216.6; baseboard, mopboard, shoemold; wainscot, dado; chassis, frame, keel, keelson.

.3 (ground part) **ground,** earth, *terra firma* [L]; **floor,** flooring; parquet; **deck; pavement,** *pavé* [Fr], paving, surfacing; **cover,** carpet, floor covering.

.4 **bed, bottom, floor,** ground, **basin, channel,** coulee; ocean bottom 209.4.

.5 **foot,** extremity, pes, pedes [pl], *pied* [Fr], ped(o)– *or* pedi–, –pod(e), rhiz(o)–; trotter, pedal extremity, dog, tootsy [informal]; **hoof,** ungula; **paw,** pad, pug, *patte* [Fr]; forefoot, forepaw; harefoot, splayfoot, clubfoot; **toe,** digit, dactyl(o)–; **heel;** sole, pedi(o)–; instep, arch; pastern; fetlock.

.6 VERBS **base on, found on, ground on, build on,** bottom on, bed on, set on; root in; **underlie,** undergird.

.7 ADJS **bottom,** bottommost, **undermost,** nethermost, lowermost, **lowest; rock-bottom,** bedrock; ground.

.8 **basic,** basal, basilar; **underlying, fundamental,** radical, essential, elementary, elemental, primary, primal, primitive, rudimentary, original; nadiral.

.9 **pedal,** plantar; footed, hoofed, ungulate, clawed, taloned, –ped(e), –pelmous, –podous; toed, –dactylous.

## 213. VERTICALNESS

.1 NOUNS **verticalness,** verticality, verticalism; **erectness, uprightness,** straight up-and-downness, up-and-downness, steepness, sheerness, precipitousness, plungingness, **perpendicularity,** plumbness, aplomb; **right-angledness** *or* -angularity, squareness, orthogonality.

.2 **vertical, upright, perpendicular, plumb,** normal; right angle, orthodiagonal; vertical circle, azimuth circle.

.3 **precipice, cliff, steep, bluff,** wall, face, scar; crag, craig [Scot]; scarp, **escarpment; palisade,** palisades.

.4 **erection,** erecting, **elevation; rearing,** raising; **uprearing,** upraising, lofting, uplifting, heaving up *or* aloft; standing on end *or* upright *or* on its feet *or* on its base *or* on its legs.

.5 **rising, uprising;** vertical height, gradient, rise, uprise.

.6 (instruments) **square,** T square, try square, set square, carpenter's square; **plumb,** plumb line, plumb rule, plummet, bob, plumb bob, lead.

.7 VERBS **stand, stand erect, stand up, stand upright, stand up straight,** be erect, be on one's feet; hold oneself straight *or* stiff, have an upright carriage; stand at attention, stand at parade rest, stand at ease [all mil].

.8 **rise, arise,** uprise, **rise up, get up,** get to one's feet; **stand up, stand on end; stick up,** cock up; bristle; **rear, ramp, uprear,** rear up, rise on the hind legs; upheave; sit up, sit bolt upright; jump up, spring to one's feet.

.9 **erect, elevate, rear, raise,** pitch, **set up,** raise *or* lift *or* cast up; raise *or* heave *or* rear aloft; uprear, upraise, uplift, upheave; upright; **upend,** stand upright *or* on end; set on its feet *or* legs *or* base.

.10 **plumb,** plumb-line, set *à plomb;* **square.**

.11 ADJS **vertical, upright,** bolt upright, **erect,** upstanding, standing up, stand-up, orth(o)–, stasi–; rearing, rampant; **upended,** upraised, upreared; downright.

.12 **perpendicular, plumb,** straight-up-and-down, straight-up, **up-and-down;** sheer, steep, precipitous, plunging; **right-angled,** right-angle, right-angular, orthogonal, orthodiagonal.

.13 ADVS **vertically, erectly,** upstandingly, uprightly, **upright,** up, stark *or* bolt upright; **on end,** up on end, right on end, endwise, endways; on one's feet *or* legs, on one's hind legs [informal]; at attention.

.14 perpendicularly, sheer, sheerly; up and down, straight up and down; plumb, *à plomb* [Fr]; at right angles, square.

## 214. HORIZONTALNESS

.1 NOUNS horizontalness, horizontality, horizontalism; levelness, flatness, planeness, evenness, smoothness, flushness.

.2 recumbency, decumbency, accumbency, accubation; prostration, proneness; supineness, reclining, reclination; lying, lounging, repose 711; sprawl, loll.

.3 horizontal, plane, level, flat, homaloid, dead level *or* flat; horizontal plane, level plane; horizontal line, level line; horizontal projection; horizontal parallax; horizontal axis; horizontal fault; water level, sea level, mean sea level; parterre; esplanade, platform, ledge, terrace; ground, earth, floor, steppe, plain, flatland, prairie, sea of grass, bowling green, table, billiard table.

.4 horizon, skyline, rim of the horizon; sea line; apparent *or* local *or* visible horizon, sensible horizon, celestial *or* rational *or* geometrical *or* true horizon, artificial *or* false horizon; azimuth.

.5 VERBS lie, lie down, lay [informal], recline, repose, lounge, sprawl, loll, drape *or* spread oneself, lie limply; lie flat *or* prostrate *or* prone *or* supine, lie on one's face *or* back, lie on a level; grovel, crawl.

.6 level, flatten, even, equalize, align, smooth *or* smoothen, smooth out, flush; grade, roll, roll flat, steamroller *or* steamroll; lay, lay down *or* out; raze, rase, lay level, lay level with the ground; lay low *or* flat; fell 318.5.

.7 ADJS horizontal, level, flat, flattened, plat(y)–; even, smooth, smoothened, smoothed out; tabular, tabloid; flush, homaloidal, homal(o)–; plane, plain, plan-(o)–, plani–; rolled, trodden, squashed, rolled *or* trodden *or* squashed flat; flat as a pancake, "flat as a cake" [Erasmus], flat as a billiard table *or* bowling green *or* tennis court, flat as a board, "flat as a flounder" [John Fletcher], level as a plain.

.8 recumbent, accumbent, procumbent, decumbent; prostrate, prone, flat; supine, resupine; couchant, *couché* [Fr]; lying, reclining, reposing, flat on one's back; sprawling, lolling, lounging; sprawled, spread, draped; groveling, crawling, flat on one's belly *or* nose.

.9 ADVS horizontally, flat, flatly, flatways, flatwise; evenly, flush; level, on a level; lengthwise, lengthways, at full length, on one's back *or* belly *or* nose.

## 215. PENDENCY

.1 NOUNS pendency, pendulousness *or* pendulosity, pensileness *or* pensility; hanging, suspension, dangling *or* danglement, suspense, dependence *or* dependency.

.2 hang, droop, dangle, swing, fall; sag, bag.

.3 overhang, overhanging, impendence *or* impendency, projection, beetling, jutting.

.4 pendant, hanger; hanging, drape; lobe, lobule, lobation, lappet, ear lobe, lob(o)– *or* lobi–; uvula, cion(o)–, staphyl(o)–.

.5 suspender, hanger 215.14, supporter; suspenders, pair of suspenders, braces [Brit], galluses [informal].

.6 VERBS hang, hang down, fall; depend, pend; dangle, swing, flap, flop [informal]; flow, drape, cascade; droop, lop; nod, weep; sag, swag, bag; trail, drag, draggle, drabble, daggle.

.7 overhang, hang over, hang out, impend, impend over, project, project over, beetle, jut, beetle *or* jut *or* thrust over, stick out over.

.8 suspend, hang, hang up, put up, fasten up; sling.

.9 ADJS pendent, pendulous, pendulant, pendular, penduline, pensile; suspended, hung; hanging, pending, depending, dependent; falling; dangling, swinging, falling loosely; weeping; flowing, cascading.

.10 drooping, droopy, limp, loose, nodding, floppy [informal], loppy, lop; sagging, saggy, swag, sagging in folds; bagging, baggy, ballooning; lop-eared.

.11 overhanging, overhung, lowering, impending, impendent, pending; incumbent, superincumbent; projecting, jutting; beetling, beetle; beetle-browed.

.12 lobular, lobar, lobate, lobated.

.13 pendants

| | |
|---|---|
| apronstring | lappet |
| arras | lavaliere |
| bell rope | liripipe |
| bob | pendeloque |
| chandelier | pendicle |
| coattail | pendule |
| curtain | pendulum |
| drape | pigtail |
| drapery | plumb bob |
| drop | queue |
| eardrop | rya |
| earring | skirt |
| flap | stalactite |
| fringe | swing |
| hammock | tail |
| hanging | tailpiece |
| hangnail | tapestry |
| icicle | tassel |

| | |
|---|---|
| tippet | wall-hanging |
| trail | wattle |
| train | |

**.14 suspenders, hangers**

| | |
|---|---|
| bar | horse |
| belt | knob |
| boom | nail |
| button | peg |
| clothes hanger | pendant post |
| clotheshorse | pendant tackle |
| clothesline | pendentive |
| clothespin | picture hook |
| clothes tree | pothanger |
| coat hanger | pothook |
| crane | ring |
| gallows | sock suspenders |
| garter | spar |
| garter belt | stud |
| gibbet | suspensorium |
| hake | suspensory |
| hanger bolt | tenterhook |
| hanging post | yard |
| hat rack | yardarm |
| hook | |

## 216. SUPPORT

**.1 NOUNS support, backing, aid** 785, **upholding, upkeep,** carrying, carriage, maintenance, **sustaining,** sustainment, sustenance, sustentation; subsidy, subvention; **moral support;** emotional or psychological support, security blanket [informal]; supportive relationship, supportive therapy; **reliance** 501.1.

**.2 supporter, support,** 216.26, **upholder,** bearer, carrier, sustainer, maintainer, –fer or –pher, –phor(e); staff 217.2, stave, cane, stick, walking stick, alpenstock, crook, crutch; **advocate** 787.9; **stay, prop,** fulcrum, **bracket** 216.28, **brace,** bracer, guy, guywire or guyline, shroud, rigging, standing rigging; buttress, shoulder, arm; mast, sprit, **mainstay,** backbone, spine, neck, cervix; athletic supporter, jock or jockstrap [both informal], G-string; brassiere, bra [informal], bandeau, corset, girdle, foundation garment; reinforcement, reinforce or reinforcer, strengthener, stiffener; back, backing; rest, resting place.

**.3** (mythology) Atlas, Hercules, Telamon, tortoise that supports the earth.

**.4 buttress,** buttressing; abutment, shoulder; **bulwark,** rampart; **embankment,** bank, retaining wall; **breakwater,** seawall, mole, **jetty,** jutty, groin; **pier,** pier buttress, buttress pier; flying buttress, *arc-boutant* [Fr]; hanging buttress; **beam** 217.7.

**.5 footing, foothold, toehold,** hold, perch, **purchase** 287; **standing,** stand, stance, standing place, *point d'appui* [Fr], *locus standi* [L]; footrest, footplate, footrail.

**.6 foundation,** *fond* [Fr], **base, basis, foot-**ing, basement, pavement, **ground, grounds, groundwork, seat,** sill, floor or flooring, fundament; bed, bedding; **substructure,** substruction, substratum, **understructure,** understruction, underbuilding, undergirding, undercarriage, underpinning, bearing wall; stereobate, stylobate; **fundamental, principle,** radical, rudiment; firm or solid ground, *terra firma* [L]; solid rock or bottom, rock bottom, bedrock; hardpan; riprap.

**.7 foundation stone,** footstone; **cornerstone, keystone,** headstone, first stone, quoin.

**.8 base, pedestal; stand,** standard; **shaft** 217, **upright, column, pillar, post,** jack, pole, staff, stanchion, pier, pile or piling, kingpost, queen-post, pilaster, newel-post, banister, baluster, balustrade, colonnade, caryatid; dado, die; plinth, subbase; surbase; socle; **trunk,** stem, **stalk,** pedicel, peduncle, footstalk.

**.9 sill,** groundsel; mudsill; window sill; doorsill, threshold; doorstone.

**.10 mounting,** mount, **backing, setting;** frame, underframe, infrastructure, chassis, skeleton; bearing, bushing.

**.11 handle** 216.27, **hold,** grip, grasp, haft, helve.

**.12 scaffold,** scaffolding, *échafaudage* [Fr]; stage, staging.

**.13 platform; stage,** estrade, dais, floor; **rostrum, podium, pulpit,** speaker's platform or stand, **soapbox** [informal]; hustings, **stump;** tribune, tribunal; emplacement; catafalque; landing stage, landing; heliport, landing pad; launching pad; **terrace,** step terrace; **balcony, gallery.**

**.14 shelf, ledge,** shoulder, corbel, beam-end; mantel, mantelshelf, mantelpiece; retable, superaltar, gradin, *gradino* [Ital], predella; hob.

**.15 table** 216.29, board, **stand; bench,** workbench; **counter,** bar, buffet; **desk,** writing table, **secretary,** *secrétaire* [Fr], escritoire; **lectern,** ambo, reading desk.

**.16 trestle, horse; sawhorse,** buck or sawbuck; clotheshorse; trestle board or table, trestle and table; trestlework, trestling.

**.17 seat, chair** 216.30; saddle 216.31.

**.18** (saddle parts) **pommel,** horn; jockey; girth, girt, surcingle, bellyband; cinch, stirrup.

**.19 sofa** 216.32, **bed** 216.33, clin(o)–, **couch, bunk;** the sack or the hay or kip or doss [all informal]; bedstead; **litter, stretcher,** gurney [dial].

**.20 bedding,** underbed, underbedding; **mattress,** paillasse, pallet; air mattress, foam-rubber mattress, innerspring mattress; sleeping bag; pad, mat, rug; litter, bedstraw; **pillow**, cushion, bolster; **springs**, bedsprings, box springs.

.21 VERBS **support, bear**, carry, **hold, sustain, maintain, bolster, reinforce, back**, shoulder, give or furnish or afford or supply or lend support; **hold up, bear up**, bolster up, keep up, buoy up, keep afloat, back up; **uphold**, upbear, upkeep; **brace, prop**, crutch, buttress; shore, **shore up**; stay, mainstay; underbrace, undergird, underprop, underpin, underset; **underlie**, be at the bottom of, form the foundation of; craˊdle; cushion, pillow; **subsidize**, subvention or subvenize.

.22 **rest on, stand on, lie on**, recline on, repose on, bear on, **lean on**, abut on; **sit on**, perch, ride; **straddle**, bestraddle, stride, bestride; be based on, rely on.

.23 ADJS **supporting, supportive, bearing**, carrying, burdened, –ferous or –phorous or –iferous; **holding**, upholding, maintaining, sustaining, sustentative, suspensory; bracing, propping, shoring, bolstering, buttressing; stato–.

.24 **supported, borne**, upborne, held, buoyed-up, **upheld, sustained**, maintained; **braced**, guyed, stayed, propped, shored or shored up, bolstered, buttressed; based or founded or grounded on.

.25 ADVS **on, across, astride, astraddle**, straddle, straddle-legged, straddleback, on the back of; horseback, on horseback; pickaback.

.26 **supports**

| | |
|---|---|
| A-frame | raker |
| anvil | ratline |
| back rest | rib |
| bandage | scissors truss |
| block | shoe |
| brace | shore |
| crosstree | shoring |
| cue rest | skid |
| easel | sole |
| guy | splint |
| heel | stand |
| hob | stilts |
| hod | stirrup |
| jack | strut |
| lap | tripod |
| maulstick | trivet |
| music stand | truss |
| prop | umbrella stand |

.27 **handles**

| | |
|---|---|
| bail | handle bar |
| bow | handstaff |
| brace | helm |
| brake | hilt |
| crank | knob |
| crop | knocker |
| doorknob | loom |

| | |
|---|---|
| lug | snatch |
| panhandle | spindle |
| pull | stock |
| rounce | tiller |
| rudder | tote |
| sally | trigger |
| shaft | withe |
| shank | |

.28 **brackets**

| | |
|---|---|
| ancon | corbel |
| angle | cul-de-lampe [Fr] |
| angle bracket | gusset |
| angle iron | modillion |
| brace | shelf bracket |
| cantilever | shelf rest |
| cheek | shoulder |
| consol | strut |

.29 **tables**

| | |
|---|---|
| bar | gate-leg or gate-legged |
| billiard table | table |
| buffet | head table |
| captain's table | high table |
| card table | kitchen table |
| cocktail table | laboratory table |
| coffee table | lampstand |
| conference table | operating table |
| console or console | pool table |
| table | round table |
| counter | sideboard |
| deal table | side table |
| dinette table | taboret |
| dining table | tea table |
| dissecting table | tea wagon |
| dresser | trestle table |
| dressing table | trivet table |
| drop-leaf table | turntable |
| extension table | worktable |
| folding table | |

.30 **seats, chairs**

| | |
|---|---|
| armchair | dentist's chair |
| armless chair | dining chair |
| back seat | draft chair |
| banquette | Eames chair |
| barber chair | easy chair |
| barrel chair | elbowchair |
| bar stool | fan-back chair |
| basket chair | fauteuil [Fr] |
| batwing chair | fender stool |
| bed chair | folding chair |
| bench | foldstool |
| bicycle seat | form |
| Boston rocker | garden chair |
| boudoir chair | hassock |
| bow-back chair | high chair |
| Brewster chair | high seat |
| bucket seat | Hitchcock chair |
| campaign chair | horse |
| camp chair | ladder-back chair |
| campstool | lawn chair |
| captain's chair | long chair |
| channel-back chair | lounge chair |
| club chair | milking stool |
| club lounge chair | Morris chair |
| cocktail chair | occasional chair |
| comb-back chair | ottoman |
| contour chair | overstuffed chair |
| cricket | pew |
| cricket chair | platform rocker |
| deck chair | Priscilla rocker |

pull-up chair
railroad chair
recliner
reclining lounge chair
rocker
rocking chair
rumble seat
saddle seat
sedan chair
settle
shooting stick
snack stool
steamer chair

step stool
stool
straight chair
swing
swing chair
swivel chair
taboret
throne
tub chair
TV chair
Windsor chair
wing chair

**.31 saddles**

aparejo
bicycle saddle
bridal saddle
camel saddle
cavalry saddle
cowboy saddle
English cavalry saddle
English riding saddle
English saddle
howdah
jockey saddle

motorcycle saddle
packsaddle
panel
pillion
racing saddle
riding saddle
sidesaddle
stock saddle
US cavalry saddle
Western saddle

**.32 sofas**

causeuse [Fr]
chaise longue [Fr]
chesterfield
couch
davenport
day bed
divan
lounge

love seat
ottoman
settee
settle
spoonholder
squab
studio couch
tête-à-tête [Fr]

**.33 beds**

bassinet
bed-davenport
berth
bunk
bunk bed
camp bed
Colonial bed
cot
cradle
crib
day bed
door bed
double bed
double bunk
duplex bed
feather bed
fold-away bed
folding bed
four-poster
French bed
hammock

Hollywood bed
hospital bed
king-size bed
lower berth
pallet
panel bed
pipe berth
poster bed
quarter berth
queen-size bed
roll-away bed
single bed
sofa-bed
tester bed
three-quarter bed
trestle bed
truckle bed
trundle bed
twin bed
upper berth
water bed

## 217. SHAFT

**.1 NOUNS shaft, pole, bar, rod, stick,** scape, scapi–; **stalk, stem;** thill; tongue, wagon tongue; pole, flagstaff; totem pole; Maypole; utility or telephone or telegraph pole; tent pole.

**.2 staff,** stave; **cane, stick, walking stick,** handstaff, shillelagh; Malacca cane; baton, marshal's baton, drum-major's baton, conductor's baton; swagger stick, swanking stick; pilgrim's staff, pastoral staff, shepherd's staff, crook; crosier, cross-staff, cross, paterissa; pikestaff, alpenstock; quarterstaff; lituus, thyrsus; **crutch,** crutch-stick.

**.3 beam** 217.7, **timber,** pole, spar.

**.4 post, standard, upright;** king post, queen post, crown post; newel; banister, baluster; balustrade, balustrading; gatepost, swinging or hinging post, shutting post; doorpost, jamb, doorjamb; signpost, milepost; stile, mullion; stanchion; hitching post, snubbing post, Samson post.

**.5 pillar, column,** post, pier, pilaster, cion-(o)–, styl(o)–, –style; colonnette, columella; caryatid; atlas, atlantes [pl]; telamon, telamones [pl]; colonnade, arcade, pilastrade, portico, peristyle.

**.6 leg** 273.16, shank; **stake,** peg; pile, spile; picket, pale, palisade.

**.7 beams**

angle rafter
balk
batten
boom
box girder
breastsummer
corbel
crossbeam
crosstie
footing beam
girder
hammer beam
H beam
hip rafter
I beam
joist
lattice girder
lintel
plate girder
rafter

ridgepole
ridge strut
scantling
sill
sleeper
sprit
stringpiece
strut
stud
studding
summer
summertree
tie
tie beam
transom
transverse
trave
traverse
truss
truss beam

## 218. PARALLELISM

*(physically parallel direction or state)*

**.1 NOUNS parallelism,** coextension, nonconvergence, nondivergence, collaterality, concurrence, equidistance; collineation, collimation; alignment; parallelization; parallelotropism; analogy 491.1.

**.2 parallel,** paralleler; parallel line, parallel dash, parallel bar, parallel file, parallel series, parallel column, parallel trench, parallel vector; parallelogram, parallelepiped or parallelepipedon.

**.3** (instruments) parallel rule or rules or ruler, parallelograph, parallelometer.

**.4 VERBS parallel,** be parallel, coextend; run parallel, go alongside, go beside, run abreast; match, equal.

**.5 parallelize,** place parallel to, equidistance; line up, align, realign; collineate, collimate; match; correspond, follow, equate.

.6 ADJS **parallel**, paralleling, par(a)–; coextending, coextensive, nonconvergent, nondivergent, **equidistant**, equispaced, collateral, concurrent; lined up, aligned; equal, even; parallelogrammic(al), parallelogrammatic(al); parallelepipedal; parallelotropic; parallelodrome, parallelinervate; analogous 491.8.

.7 ADVS **in parallel**, parallelwise, parallelly; side-by-side, alongside, abreast; equidistantly, nonconvergently, nondivergently; collaterally, coextensively.

## 219. OBLIQUITY

.1 NOUNS **obliquity**, obliqueness; **deviation** 291, deviance, divergence, digression, divagation, vagary, excursion, skewness, aberration, squint, declination; deflection, deflexure; nonconformity 83; diagonality, crosswiseness, transverseness; indirection, indirectness, deviousness, circuitousness 321.

.2 **inclination**, **leaning**, lean, angularity; **slant**, slaunch [dial], rake, **slope**, –cline; **tilt**, **tip**, pitch, list, cant, swag, sway; leaning tower, tower of Pisa.

.3 **bias**, **bend**, bent, **crook**, **warp**, **twist**, **turn**, **skew**, slue, **veer**, sheer, **swerve**, lurch.

.4 **incline**, inclination, **slope**, **grade**, gradient, pitch, **ramp**, launching ramp, bank, talus, gentle or easy slope, glacis; rapid or steep slope, stiff climb, scarp, chute; helicline, inclined plane [phys]; **bevel**, bezel, fleam; hillside, side; hanging gardens; shelving beach.

.5 **declivity**, **descent**, dip, drop, fall, falling-off or -away, **decline**; hang, hanging; **downgrade**, downgate [Scot], **downhill**.

.6 **acclivity**, **ascent**, climb, rise, rising, uprise, uprising, rising ground; **upgrade**, **uphill**, upgo, upclimb, uplift, steepness, precipitousness, abruptness, verticalness 213.

.7 **diagonal**, oblique, transverse, bias, bend [her], oblique line, slash, slant, virgule, scratch comma, separatrix, solidus; oblique angle or figure, rhomboid.

.8 **zigzag**, zig, zag; zigzaggery, flexuosity, **crookedness**, crankiness; switchback, hairpin, dogleg; chevron.

.9 VERBS **oblique**, **deviate**, **diverge**, **deflect**, divagate, **bear off**; angle, **angle off**, swerve, shoot off at an angle, **veer**, sheer, sway, slue, **skew**, **twist**, **turn**, bend, bias; crook.

.10 **incline**, **lean**; slope, **slant**, slaunch [dial],

rake, pitch, grade, bank, shelve; **tilt**, **tip**, list, cant, careen, keel, sidle, swag, sway; **ascend**, **rise**, uprise, climb, **go uphill**; descend, decline, dip, drop, fall, fall off or away, go **downhill**; retreat.

.11 cut, cut or slant across, cut crosswise or transversely or diagonally, catercorner, diagonalize, slash, slash across.

.12 **zigzag**, zig, zag, **stagger**, crankle [archaic], wind in and out.

.13 ADJS **oblique**, lox(o)–, plagi(o)–; **devious**, deviant, deviative, divergent, digressive, divagational, deflectional, excursive; **indirect**, side, sidelong; left-handed, sinister, sinistral; backhand, backhanded; circuitous 321.7.

.14 **askew**, **skew**, skewed; skew-jawed, skewgee, askewgee, agee, agee-jawed [all slang]; **awry**, wry; askance, askant, asquint, squinting, **cockeyed** [informal]; **crooked** 249.10; slaunchwise or slaunchways [both informal]; wamper-jawed, catawampous or catawamptious, yaw-ways [all slang], wonky [Brit slang].

.15 **inclining**, **inclined**, inclinatory, inclinational, –clinal, –clinic, clin(o)–; **leaning**, recumbent; **sloping**, sloped, aslope; raking, pitched; **slanting**, slanted, slant, aslant, slantways, slantwise; bias, biased; shelving, shelvy; **tilting**, tilted, atilt, tipped, **tipping**, tipsy, listing, **canting**, careening; sideling, sidelong; out of the perpendicular or square or plumb, bevel, beveled.

.16 (sloping downward) **downhill**, **downgrade**; **descending**, falling, dropping, dipping; **declining**, declined; declivous, declivitous, declivate.

.17 (sloping upward) **uphill**, **upgrade**; **rising**, uprising, **ascending**, climbing; acclivous, acclivitous, acclinate.

.18 **steep**, **precipitous**, **bluff**, plunging, abrupt, bold, **sheer**, sharp, rapid; headlong, breakneck; vertical 213.11.

.19 **transverse**, crosswise or crossways, thwart, athwart, across 221.9; **diagonal**, bendwise; catercorner or **catercornered** or cattycorner or cattycornered or kittycorner or kittycornered; slant, bias, biased, biaswise or biasways.

.20 **crooked**, **zigzag**, zigzagged, zigzaggy, zigzagwise or zigzagways; flexuous, twisty, hairpin, bendy, curvy; staggered, crankled [archaic]; chevrony, chevronwise or chevronways [all archit].

.21 ADVS **obliquely**, **deviously**, deviately, **indirectly**, circuitously 321.9; divergently, digressively, excursively, divagationally;

sideways or sidewise, sidelong, sideling, on or to one side; at an angle.

.22 askew, awry; askance, askant, asquint.

.23 slantingly, slopingly, aslant, aslope, atilt, rakingly, tipsily, slopewise, slopeways, slantwise, slantways, aslantwise, on or at a slant; slaunchwise or slaunchways [both informal]; off plumb or the vertical; downhill, downgrade; uphill, upgrade.

.24 transversely, crosswise or crossways, athwart, across 221.13.

.25 diagonally, diagonalwise; on the bias, bias, biaswise; cornerwise, cornerways; catercornerways or catercorner or cattycorner or kittycorner.

## 220. INVERSION

.1 NOUNS inversion, turning over or around or upside down; eversion, turning inside out, invagination, intussusception, ectropion; introversion, turning inward; reversing, reversal 146.1, turning front to back or side to side; reversion, turning back or backwards, retroversion, retroflexion, revulsion; transposition, transposal; topsy-turvydom or topsy-turviness; pronation, supination, resupination; –trope.

.2 overturn, upset, overset, overthrow, upturn, turnover, spill [informal]; subversion; revolution 147; capsizal, capsize; somersault, somerset, culbute [Fr]; turning head over heels.

.3 [gram terms] metastasis, metathesis; anastrophe, chiasmus, hypallage, hyperbaton, hysteron proteron, palindrome, parenthesis, synchysis, tmesis.

.4 inverse, reverse, converse, opposite 15.2, other side of the cóin or picture.

.5 VERBS invert, inverse, turn over or around or upside down; introvert, turn in or inward; turn down; turn inside out, turn out, evert, invaginate, intussuscept; reverse 146.4, transpose, convert; put the cart before the horse; turn into the opposite, turn about, turn the tables, turn the scale or balance; rotate, revolve, pronate, supinate, resupinate.

.6 overturn, turn over, turn upside down, turn bottom side up, upturn, upset, overset, overthrow, subvert, culbuter [Fr]; go or turn ass over elbows [informal], turn a somersault, go or turn head over heels; turn turtle, turn topsy-turvy, topsy-turvy, topsy-turvify; tip over, keel over, topple over; capsize; careen, set on its beam ends.

.7 ADJS inverted, inversed, back-to-front, backwards, retroverted, reversed, trans-

posed; inside out, outside in, everted, invaginated, wrong side out; upside-down, topsy-turvy, ass over elbows or arsy-varsy [both informal]; capsized, head-over-heels; hyperbatic, chiastic, palindromic; resupinate; introverted.

.8 ADVS inversely, conversely, contrarily, contrariwise, vice versa, the other way around, backwards, turned around; upside down, over, topsy-turvy; bottom up, bottom side up; head over heels, heels over head.

## 221. CROSSING

.1 NOUNS crossing, intercrossing, intersecting, intersection; decussation, chiasma; traversal, transversion; cross section, transection; cruciation.

.2 crossing, crossway, crosswalk, crossroad, crosspoint [Brit], carrefour [Fr], intersection, intercrossing; level crossing, grade crossing; overcrossing, overpass, flyover [Brit], viaduct, undercrossing; traffic circle, rotary; cloverleaf.

.3 network, webwork, weaving 222, meshwork, tissue, crossing over and under, interlacement, intertwinement, intertexture, texture, reticulum, reticulation; crossing-out, cancellation; net, netting; mesh, meshes; web, webbing; weave, weft; lace, lacery, lacing, lacework; screen, screening; sieve, riddle, raddle; wicker, wickerwork; basketwork, basketry; lattice, latticework; hachure, hatching, cross-hatching; trellis, trelliswork; grate, grating, grille, grillwork; grid, gridiron; tracery, fretwork, fret, arabesque, filigree; plexus, plexure; reticle, reticule; wattle; dicty(o)–, reticul(o)– or reticuli–, –spongium.

.4 cross, crux, cruciform, staur(o)–; crucifix, rood; crisscross, christcross; X, ex, exing, chi, St. Andrew's cross, crux decussata [L], saltire [her]; T, tau, crux commisa [L], St. Anthony's cross; Y, thieves' cross, fork cross; ankh, key of the Nile, crux ansata [L]; avellan cross; cross botonée, trefled cross or cross of St. Lazarus; Calvary cross; Celtic or Iona cross; chi-rho, Christogram; crosslet, cross-crosslet; cross fitché; cross fleury, cross of Cleves; cross formée, cross fourchée; Greek cross, St. George's cross; cross grignolée; inverted cross, St. Peter's cross; Jerusalem cross, potent cross; Latin cross, long cross, crux capitata [L], crux immissa [L], crux ordinaria [L], God's mark; cross of Lorraine; Maltese cross; cross moline, cross ancré, cross recercelée; papal cross; patriarchal *or* archiepiscopal cross; cross patée; cross pommée, cross bourdonée; Russian cross; quadrate cross; **swastika,** gammadion, *Hakenkreuz* [Ger], *crux gammata* [L]; voided cross; pectoral cross; crossbones; dagger 586.20.

.5 **crosspiece,** traverse, transverse, transversal, transept, transom, cross bitt; **crossbar,** crossarm; swingletree, singletree, whiffletree, whippletree; doubletree.

.6 VERBS **cross, crisscross,** cruciate; **intersect,** intercross, decussate; **cut across,** crosscut; **traverse,** transverse, lie across; bar, crossbar.

.7 net, web, mesh; lattice, trellis; grate, grid.

.8 ADJS **cross, crossing, crossed; crisscross, crisscrossed; intersecting, intersected,** intersectional; crosscut, cut across; decussate, decussated; chiasmal *or* chiasmic *or* chiastic; secant.

.9 **transverse,** transversal, traverse; **across,** cross, crossway, **crosswise** *or* crossways, thwart, athwart, overthwart; oblique 219.13.

.10 **cruciform, crosslike,** cross-shaped, cruciate, X-shaped, cross, crossed; cruciferous.

.11 **netlike,** retiform, plexiform; **reticulated,** reticular, reticulate, reticulato–; cancellate, cancellated; **netted,** netty; **meshed,** meshy; laced, lacy, lacelike; filigreed; latticed, latticelike; grated, gridded; barred, crossbarred, mullioned; streaked, striped.

.12 **webbed,** webby, weblike, woven, interwoven, interlaced, intertwined; web-footed, palmiped.

.13 ADVS **crosswise** *or* crossways *or* crossway, decussatively; **cross, crisscross, across,** thwart, thwartly, thwartways, **athwart,** athwartwise, overthwart; **traverse,** traversely; **transverse,** transversely, transversally; obliquely 219.21; **sideways** *or* sidewise; contrariwise, contrawise; crossgrained, across the grain; athwartship, athwartships; di(a)–, per–, trans–.

## 222. WEAVING

.1 NOUNS **weaving,** weave, warpage, weftage, warp and woof *or* weft, texture, tissue; **fabric** 378.5, **web; interweaving,** interweavement, intertexture; **interlacing,** interlacement, interlacery; **intertwining,** intertwinement; intertieing, interknitting, interthreading, intertwisting; **lacing,** enlacement; **twining,** entwining, entwinement; wreathing, knitting, twisting; **braiding,** plaiting.

.2 **braid,** plait, **wreath,** wreathwork.

.3 **warp; woof, weft,** filling; shoot, pick.

.4 **weaver,** interlacer, webster [archaic]; weaverbird, weaver finch, whirligig beetle.

.5 **loom,** weaver; hand loom; knitting machine; shuttle.

.6 VERBS **weave,** loom, tissue; **interweave, interlace, intertwine,** interknit, interthread, intertissue, intertie, intertwist; inweave, intort; web, net; **lace,** enlace; **twine,** entwine; **braid,** plait, pleach, **wreathe,** raddle, **knit,** twist, mat, wattle; twill, loop, noose; splice.

.7 ADJS **woven,** loomed, textile; **interwoven, interlaced,** interthreaded, **intertwined,** interknit, intertissued, intertied, intertwisted; handwoven; **laced,** enlaced; **wreathed,** fretted, raddled, knit; **twined,** entwined; **braided,** plaited, platted, pleached.

.8 **weaving, twining,** entwining; **intertwining, interlacing,** interweaving.

## 223. SEWING

.1 NOUNS **sewing, needlework,** stitching, stitchery; suture; **fancywork;** garment making 231.31.

.2 **sewer,** needleworker; **seamstress,** sempstress, needlewoman; seamster, sempster, tailor, needleman [archaic], needler [Brit]; embroiderer, embroideress; knitter; garmentmaker 231.33–35.

.3 **sewing machine,** sewer, Singer.

.4 VERBS **sew, stitch,** needle; sew up; **tailor.**

.5 **sew**

| | |
|---|---|
| appliqué | machine-stitch |
| backstitch | overcast |
| baste | overhand |
| bind | purl |
| buttonhole | quilt |
| chain-stitch | renter |
| crochet | run |
| cross-stitch | saddle-stitch |
| double-stitch | seam |
| embroider | single-stitch |
| fell | tack |
| finedraw | tat |
| gather | whip |
| hemstitch | whipstitch |
| knit | |

.6 **needlework**

| | |
|---|---|
| appliqué | crochet work |
| basting | cross-stitching |
| binding | embroidery |
| binding off | felling |
| buttonholing | finedrawing |
| canvas stitching | gros point |
| casting on | hemming |
| chain-stitching | hemstitching |
| crewelwork | knitting |
| crochet | knitwork |
| crocheting | machine stitching |

macramé
needlepoint
netting
overcasting
petit point
purling

quilting
ribbing
tacking
tatting
whipstitching

**.7 stitches**

backstitch
bargello
buttonhole stitch
cable stitch
carpet stitch
chain stitch
continental stitch
coral stitch
cord(ing) stitch
couching stitch
cross-stitch
damask stitch
double crochet
double stitch
French knot
garter stitch
glover's stitch
half cross stitch
half stitch
hemstitch
lace stitch
lazy daisy stitch
machine stitch
needlepoint

over-and-over stitch
outline stitch
picot
rib stitch
rose stitch
running stitch
saddleback stitch
saddle stitch
saddle wire stitch
satin stitch
shell stitch
side stitch
side thread stitch
side wire stitch
single crochet
single stitch
slip stitch
stockinette
stroke stitch
suture
tent stitch
treble
twist stitch
whipstitch

**.8 needles**

between
blunt
crochet hook
darner
darning needle
embroidery needle
ground-down
knitting needle
knitting pin
knitting wire
long-eyed sharp

sacking needle
sailmaker's needle
sewing-machine nee-
  dle
sewing needle
sharp
straw
tacking needle
three-cornered needle
upholsterer's needle

## 224. EXTERIORITY

**.1** NOUNS **exteriority,** externalness, externality, **outwardness,** outerness; appearance,
outward appearance, seeming, mien,
manner; openness 553.3; extrinsicality 6;
**superficiality, shallowness** 210; extraterri-
toriality, foreignness.

**.2 exterior,** external, **outside; surface,** superficies, covering 228, skin 229, outer skin or
layer, epidermis, integument, envelope,
crust, cortex, rind 229.2, shell 228.16; top,
superstratum; **periphery, fringe,** circumference, outline, lineaments, border; **face,**
outer face or side, façade, front, facet; ex-
trados.

**.3 outdoors,** outside, **the out-of-doors,** the
great out-of-doors, the open, **the open
air;** outland.

**.4 externalization,** exteriorization; objectification, actualization, projection, **extrapolation.**

**.5** VERBS **externalize,** exteriorize; **objectify,**
actualize, project, **extrapolate.**

**.6** ADJS **exterior, external;** extrinsic 6.3;
**outer, outside, out, outward,** outward-fac-
ing, outlying, outstanding; **outermost,**
outmost; surface, superficial 210.5, epidermic, cortical; peripheral, **fringe,** roundabout; apparent, seeming; open 555.10,
public 559.17; exomorphic; e–, ec–, ect-
(o)–, ex– or ef–, ep(i)– or eph–, extra–,
hyper–, peripher(o)–.

**.7 outdoor, out-of-door,** out-of-doors, **outside; open-air,** alfresco.

**.8** extraterritorial, exterritorial; extraterrestrial, exterrestrial, extramundane; extragalactic, extralateral, extraliminal, extramural, extrapolar, extrasolar, extraprovincial,
extratribal; foreign, outlandish, alien.

**.9** ADVS **externally, outwardly,** on the outside, exteriorly; **without, outside, outwards, out;** apparently, to all appearances; openly, publically, to judge by appearances; superficially, on the surface.

**.10** outdoors, out of doors, outside, abroad;
in the open, **in the open air,** alfresco, *en
plein air* [Fr].

## 225. INTERIORITY

**.1** NOUNS interiority, internalness, internality, **inwardness, innerness,** inness; introversion, internalization; **intrinsicality** 5;
depth 209.

**.2 interior, inside,** inner, inward, internal,
intern; inner recess, recesses, **innermost
or deepest recesses,** penetralia, secret
place or places; bosom, heart, heart of
hearts, soul, vitals, vital center; inner self,
inner life, inner landscape, inner or interior man, inner nature; intrados; core,
center 226.2.

**.3 inland,** inlands, **interior,** up-country; **midland,** midlands; **heartland;** hinterland
182.2.

**.4** (inside parts) **insides, innards** [informal],
inwards, internals; inner mechanism,
works [informal]; **guts** [slang], **vitals,** viscera, splanchno–, *kishkes* [Yid], giblets
308.20; **heart,** –cardium, ticker or pump
[both informal], endocardium, end(o)–;
**brain** 466.6,7; **lung** 403.19; **liver,** hepat(o)–,
liver and lights; spleen, splen(o)–; **kidney,**
nephr(o)–, –nephros, reni– or reno–; gizzard, **stomach,** abdomen 193.3; perineum,
perineo–; pylorus, pylor(o)–; **intestine,**
enter(o)–, entrails, bowels, guts; tripes
[dial], stuffings [slang]; large intestine,
small intestine; blind gut, cecum, cec(o)–
or ceci–; foregut, hindgut; midgut, meso-

gaster; colon, col(o)– or coli–; duodenum, duoden(o)–, jejunum, jejun(o)–, ileum, ili(o)– or ile(o)–; **appendix,** vermiform appendix or process, append(o)– or appendic(o)–; rectum, rect(o)–, proct(o)– or procti–; anus 265.6, ano–.

.5 enterology, enterography, splanchnology; internal medicine.

.6 VERBS internalize, put in, keep within; enclose, embed, surround, contain, comprise, include, enfold.

.7 ADJS **interior, internal, inner, inside, inward,** intestine; **innermost,** inmost, **intimate; intrinsic** 5.6; deep 209.10; central 226.11; indoor; en– or em–, end(o)–, ent-(o)–, eso–, infra–, in– or im– or il– or ir–, inter–, intra–, ob–.

.8 **inland, interior,** up-country; hinterland 182.8; **midland,** mediterranean; inshore.

.9 intramarginal, intramural, intramundane, intramontane, intraterritorial, intracoastal, intragroupal.

.10 visceral, splanchnic; abdominal, gastric 193.5; pyloric; **intestinal,** enteric; colonic, colic; cecal, duodenal, ileac, jejunal, mesogastric, appendical, rectal, anal; cardiac, coronary.

.11 ADVS **internally, inwardly,** interiorly, inly, **intimately,** deeply, profoundly, under the surface; **intrinsically** 5.9; centrally 226.16.

.12 **in, inside, within;** herein, therein, wherein.

.13 **inward, inwards, inwardly,** withinward, withinwards; inland, inshore.

.14 **indoors,** indoor, withindoors.

.15 PREPS **in, into; within,** at, inside, **inside of,** in the limits of; to the heart or core of.

## 226. CENTRALITY

.1 NOUNS **centrality,** centralness, middleness, central or middle or mid position; centricity, centricality; concentricity; centripetence, centripetalism.

.2 **center,** centr(o)– or centri–, **middle** 69, **heart, core, nucleus,** nucle(o)–, nuclei–, **kernel; pith,** metr(o)–, **marrow,** myel(o)–, medulla; **nub, hub,** nave, axis, pivot; **navel,** umbilicus, omphalos; bull's-eye; dead center; center of action or area or buoyancy or displacement or curvature or effort or figure or flotation or inversion or origin or oscillation or ossification or percussion or pressure or projection or similitude or suspension or symmetry or volume; metacenter; epicenter, centrum; storm center; center of gravity, center of

mass or inertia, centroid; "the still point of the turning world" [T. S. Eliot].

.3 [biol terms] central body, centriole, centrosome, centrosphere.

.4 **focus,** focal point, prime focus, point of convergence; **center of interest** or attention, focus of attention, center of consciousness; **center of attraction,** cynosure; polestar, lodestar; magnet.

.5 **nerve center,** ganglion, center of activity, vital center.

.6 **headquarters,** HQ, central station, central office, main office, central administration, seat, base, **base of operations,** center of authority; general headquarters, GHQ, command post, CP, company headquarters.

.7 **metropolis, capital;** urban center, art center, medical center, shopping center, shipping center, railroad center, garment center, manufacturing center, tourist center, trade center, etc.

.8 **centralization,** centering; **focalization,** focusing; convergence 298; **concentration,** concentralization, pooling; centralism.

.9 VERBS **centralize, center,** middle; center round, center on or in.

.10 **focus,** focalize, come to a point or focus, bring into focus; **concentrate,** concentralize, concenter; converge 298.2.

.11 ADJS **central,** centric, **middle** 69.4; centermost, middlemost, **midmost;** centralized, concentrated; umbilical, omphalic; axial, **pivotal,** key; centroidal; centrosymmetric; geocentric.

.12 **nuclear,** nucleal, nucleary, nucleate.

.13 **focal,** confocal; converging; centrolineal, centripetal.

.14 **concentric;** homocentric; **coaxial,** coaxal.

.15 ADVS **centrally,** in the center or middle of, at the heart of.

## 227. LAYER

.1 NOUNS **layer,** –cline, thickness; **level, tier,** stage, story, floor, gallery, step, ledge, deck; **stratum,** strati–, seam, couche [Fr], belt, band, **bed, course,** measures; zone; shelf; **overlayer, superstratum,** overstory, topsoil; **underlayer, substratum,** understratum, understory; floor, bedding.

.2 lamina, lamella, lamin(o)– or lamini–, lamell(i)–; **sheet,** leaf, feuille [Fr], foil, pallio–; wafer, disk; **plate,** plating; covering 228, **coat,** coating, veneer, film, patina, scum, membrane, pellicle, peel, skin; **slice,** cut, rasher, collop; **slab,** plank, deal [Brit], slat, tablet, table, plac(o)–, pinac(o)– or pinak–; panel, pane; **fold,** lap, flap, **ply**, plait; laminated glass, safety glass; laminated wood, plywood.

.3 **flake**, flock, floccule, flocculus; lepid(o)–, –lepis, phalid(o)–, squam(o)–; **scale, scurf,** dandruff; chip; shaving, paring.

.4 **stratification, lamination,** lamellation; foliation; delamination, exfoliation; desquamation, furfuration; flakiness, scaliness.

.5 VERBS **layer,** lay down, lay up, **stratify,** arrange in layers or levels or strata or tiers, **laminate;** flake, scale; delaminate, desquamate, exfoliate.

.6 ADJS **layered,** in layers; **laminated,** laminate, laminous; lamellated, lamellate, lamellar, lamelliform; two-ply, three-ply, etc.; **stratified,** stratiform; foliated, foliaceous, leaflike, leafy; spathic, spathose; filmy, scummy; membranous.

.7 **flaky,** flocculent; **scaly,** scurfy, squamous, lentiginous, furfuraceous, lepidote; scabby, scabious, scabrous, asperous.

## 228. COVERING

.1 NOUNS (act of covering) **covering,** coverage, obduction; **coating,** cloaking; **screening,** shielding, hiding, curtaining, **veiling,** clouding, obscuring, masking, mantling, shrouding, blanketing; blocking, blotting out, eclipse, eclipsing, occultation; **wrapping,** enwrapping, enwrapment, sheathing, envelopment; **overlaying,** overspreading, laying on or over, superimposition, superposition; superincumbence; upholstering, upholstery; plasterwork, stuccowork, cementwork, pargeting; incrustation.

.2 **cover** 228.38, **covering,** coverage, covert, coverture, housing, hood, cowl, cowling, **shelter; screen,** shroud, shield, veil, pall, mantle, curtain, hanging, drape, drapery; **coat,** cloak, mask, guise; vestment 231.1; **blanket.**

.3 integument, tegument, tegmen, tegmentum.

.4 **overlayer,** overlay; appliqué; **lap, overlap,** overlapping, imbrication; **flap,** fly, tentfly.

.5 **cover, lid, top, cap;** operculum; stopper 266.4.

.6 **roof** 228.39, roofing, roofage, top, **housetop,** rooftop; roof-deck, roof garden, penthouse; roofpole, ridgepole, rooftree; shingles, slates, tiles; eaves; **ceiling,** plafond [Fr], overhead; skylight, lantern; widow's walk or captain's walk.

.7 **umbrella,** gamp or brolly [both Brit infor-mal], bumbershoot [informal]; **sunshade, parasol,** beach umbrella.

.8 **tent** 228.40, canvas; top, whitetop, round top, big top; tentage.

.9 **rug, carpet** 228.41, floor cover(ing); **mat,** doormat, welcome mat; carpeting, wall-to-wall carpet(ing); drop cloth, ground cloth, ground-sheet; **flooring,** floorboards, duckboards; **tiling; pavement,** pavé.

.10 **blanket, coverlet,** coverlid [dial], cover, **spread,** robe, buffalo robe, **afghan,** rug [Brit]; lap robe; **bedspread; bedcover;** counterpane, counterpin [dial]; **comfort, comforter, quilt,** eiderdown; patchwork quilt; **bedding, bedclothes,** clothes; **linen,** bed linen; **sheet,** sheeting, bedsheet, fitted sheet, contour sheet; **pillowcase,** pillow slip, case, slip.

.11 horsecloth, **horse blanket;** caparison, housing; **saddle blanket,** saddlecloth.

.12 **coating, coat; veneer, facing,** revetment; pellicle, **film, scum,** skin, scale; fur; varnish, enamel, lacquer, paint 362.8.

.13 **plating, plate;** nickel plate, silver plate, gold plate, copperplate, chromium plate, anodized aluminum; electroplating, electrocoating.

.14 **crust, incrustation,** shell; piecrust, pastry shell; stalactite, stalagmite; scale, scab, eschar.

.15 **shell** 228.42, lorication, lorica, –conch; test, testa, episperm, pericarp, elytron, elytr(o)– or elytri–, scute, scutum; **armor,** mail, **shield,** aspid(o)–, scut(i)–; **carapace,** –stegite, –stege, steg(o)–; plate, chitin; **protective covering,** cortex, thick skin.

.16 **hull,** shell, pod, capsule, case, **husk, shuck;** cornhusk, corn shuck; **rind, peel, skin** 229, bark, jacket; chaff, bran, palea.

.17 **case,** casing, encasement; **sheath,** sheathing, cole(o)–, –theca.

.18 **wrapper,** wrapping, gift wrapping, wrap; **binder,** binding; **bandage,** bandaging; **envelope,** envelopment; **jacket,** jacketing; dust jacket.

.19 VERBS **cover,** cover up, obduce; apply to, **put on,** lay on; **superimpose,** superpose; **lay over,** overlay; **spread over,** overspread; **clothe, cloak,** mantle, muffle, blanket, canopy, cope, cowl, hood, **veil,** curtain, **screen, shield,** mask, cloud, obscure, block, eclipse, occult; film, scum.

.20 **wrap,** enwrap, wrap up, wrap about or around; **envelop, sheathe;** surround, lap, smother, enfold, embrace, invest; shroud, enshroud; swathe, swaddle; **box, case,** encase, **crate,** pack, embox, **package,** encapsulate.

.21 **top, cap,** tip, crown; put the lid on, cork, stopper; hood, hat, coif, bonnet; roof, roof in or over; ceil; dome, endome.

.22 **floor; carpet; pave,** causeway, cobblestone, flag, pebble; cement, concrete; blacktop, tar, asphalt, metal [archaic], macadamize.

.23 **face, veneer,** revet; **sheathe;** board, plank, weatherboard, clapboard, lath; shingle, shake; tile, stone, brick, slate; thatch; glass, glaze, fiberglass; paper, wallpaper; wall in or up.

.24 **coat, spread on, spread with;** smear, **smear on,** besmear, slap on, dab, daub, bedaub; lay on, lay it on thick, slather; undercoat, prime; enamel, gild, gloss, lacquer; butter; tar.

.25 **plaster,** parget, stucco, cement, concrete, mastic, grout, mortar; roughcast.

.26 **plate,** chromium-plate, copperplate, goldplate, nickel-plate, silver-plate; **electroplate, galvanize,** anodize.

.27 **crust, incrust,** encrust; loricate; effloresce; scab.

.28 **upholster,** overstuff.

.29 **re-cover,** reupholster, recap.

.30 **overlie,** lie over; **overlap,** lap, **lap over,** override, imbricate, jut, shingle; **extend over,** span, bridge, bestride, bestraddle, arch over, overarch, hang over, overhang.

.31 ADJS **covered,** covert, under cover; **cloaked,** mantled, blanketed, muffled, canopied, coped, cowled, hooded, **shrouded, veiled,** clouded, obscured, eclipsed, occulted, curtained, **screened,** shielded, masked; **housed;** tented, under canvas; roofed, roofed-in or -over; walled, walled-in; **wrapped,** enwrapped, **enveloped,** sheathed, swathed; **boxed, cased,** encased, encapsuled or encapsulated, **packaged; coated,** filmed, scummed; shelled, loricate, loricated; armored, hoplo−; ceiled; paved, floored.

.32 **plated,** chromium-plated, copperplated, gold-plated, nickel-plated, silver-plated; electroplated, galvanized, anodized.

.33 upholstered, overstuffed.

.34 **covering, coating;** cloaking, blanketing, shrouding, **veiling, screening,** shielding; wrapping, **enveloping,** sheathing.

.35 **overlying,** incumbent, superincumbent, superimposed; **overlapping,** lapping, shingled, equitant; imbricate, imbricated; spanning, bridging; overarched, overarching; ep(i)− or eph−.

.36 integumental, integumentary, tegumentary, tegumental, tegmental; vaginal, thecal.

.37 PREPS **on, upon, over,** o'er, **above, on top of.**

.38 **covers**

| | |
|---|---|
| altar cloth or carpet | pall |
| antimacassar | pavilion |
| awning | persienne |
| baldachin | pledget |
| blind | purdah |
| canopy | pyx cloth or veil |
| centerpiece | scarf |
| cerecloth | screen |
| cerement | shade |
| chrismal | shamiana |
| ciborium | sheet |
| cloth | shield |
| cope | shroud |
| corporal | shutter |
| cozy | smoke screen |
| curtain | tablecloth |
| doily | tarpaulin, tarp [informal] |
| dossal | mal] |
| fanon | tester |
| fingerstall | tidy |
| housing | veil |
| jalousie | veiling |
| mantle | venetian blind |
| marquee, marquise | window shade |
| mask | |

.39 **roofs**

| | |
|---|---|
| barrack roof | lean-to roof |
| bulkhead | mansard roof |
| cupola | M roof |
| curb roof | pantile roof |
| dome | penthouse roof |
| flat roof | pitched roof |
| French roof | pyramidal roof |
| gable roof | shed roof |
| gambrel roof | shingle roof |
| geodesic dome | slate roof |
| hip-and-valley roof | thatched roof |
| hip roof | tile roof |
| jerkinhead roof | |

.40 **tents**

| | |
|---|---|
| A-tent | pack tent |
| backpacking tent | pavilion |
| Baker tent | praetorium |
| bell tent | pup tent |
| bungalow tent | pyramidal tent |
| cabin tent | shelter tent |
| canoe tent | Sibley tent |
| circus tent | tepee |
| field tent | tupik |
| fly tent | two-man tent |
| highwall tent | umbrella tent |
| lean-to tent | wall tent |
| marquee, marquise | wigwam |
| mountain tent | |

.41 **rugs, carpets**

| | |
|---|---|
| Axminster | East Indian rug |
| bearskin rug | hooked rug |
| body Brussels | imperial Brussels |
| broadloom | Indian rug |
| Brussels carpet | indoor-outdoor carpeting |
| camel's hair rug | peting |
| Caucasian rug | ingrain |
| chenille carpet or rug | mohair rug |
| Chinese rug | moquette |
| drugget | namda |

nammad, numdah rug
Navaho rug
nylon carpeting
Oriental rug
Persian rug
rag rug
rya
Savonnerie
scatter rug

shag rug
steamer rug
tapestry Brussels
throw rug
Turkish rug
Turkoman rug *or* carpet
Wilton

## .42 shells

abalone shell
armadillo shell
chiton
clam shell
cockleshell
cocoa shell
conch
cowrie
eggshell
limpet
marine shell

nautilus
nutshell
oyster shell
periwinkle
scallop
sea shell
snail shell
tooth shell
turtle shell
whelk
winkle

## .43 covering materials

asbestos tile
asphalt
asphalt tile
blacktop
brick
canvas
carpeting
clapboard
cobblestone
concrete
cork tile
fiber glass, spun glass
flag
flagging
flagstone
flooring
Formica
linoleum
macadam
Masonite
pantile
paper
parquet
pavement
pavestone
paving

plasterboard
plywood
roofing, roofage
roofing paper
roofing tile
shake
sheathing board
sheeting
shingle
shingling
siding
slate
slating
stone
tar paper
thatch
tile
tilestone
tiling
veneer
wainscoting
wallboard
walling
wallpaper
weatherboard
wood

## .44 plaster

adobe
cement
chinking
clay
composition, compo
daubing
grout
mastic
mortar
parget

patching plaster
plaster of Paris
Portland cement
roughcast
scagliola
size, sizing
Spackle
spackling compound
stucco

## 229. SKIN

.1 NOUNS **skin,** dermis, derm(a)– *or* dermo–, scyt(o)–; **cuticle;** rind 228.16; **flesh;** bare skin *or* flesh, the buff; integument, tegument; **pelt, hide** 229.8, **coat, jacket, fell, fleece, fur,** vair [her]; **leather** 229.9, rawhide; imitation leather, leather paper,

Leatheroid, Leatherette; imitation fur; peltry, skins; furring; outer skin *or* layer, sheath, the exterior 224.2.

.2 **peel, peeling, rind** 228.16, **skin,** epicarp; **bark;** cork, phellum, phello–; cortex, cortical tissue, cortic(o)–; periderm, phelloderm; peridium; dermatogen.

.3 **membrane,** membrana, pellicle, chorion, chori(o)–; basement membrane, membrana propria; allantoic membrane, allant(o)–; amnion, amniotic sac, amnio–; arachnoid membrane, arachn(o)–; serous membrane, serosa, membrana serosa; **eardrum,** tympanic membrane, tympanum, membrana tympana, tympan(o)–; **mucous membrane;** velum, vel–; **peritoneum,** periton(o)– *or* peritone(o)–; periosteum, periost(o)– *or* perioste(o)–; pleura, pleur(o)– *or* pleuri–; pericardium, pericardi(o)– *or* pericardo–; meninx [sing], **meninges** [pl], mening(o)– *or* meningi–; perineurium, neurilemma, lemmo–; conjuctiva; **hymen** *or* maidenhead; hymen(o)–.

.4 (skin layers) **epidermis,** epiderm(o)–, scarfskin, ecderon; hypodermis, hypoderma; dermis, derma, corium, cutis, cut(i)–, *cutis vera* [L], true skin; epithelium, pavement epithelium; endothelium, endotheli(o)–; mesoderm, mes(o)–; endoderm, entoderm; blastoderm; ectoderm, epiblast, ectoblast; enderon; connective tissue.

.5 (castoff skin) slough, cast, desquamation, exuviae [pl].

.6 ADJS **cutaneous,** cuticular; skinlike, skinny; skin-deep; **epidermal,** epidermic, ecderonic; hypodermic, hypodermal, subcutaneous; dermal, dermic, –dermatous; ectodermal, ectodermic; endermic, endermatic; cortical; epicarpal; testaceous; furry 230.24.

.7 **leather,** leathern, leathery; buff.

.8 **pelts, furs, hides**

Alaska sable
Australian seal
Baltic leopard
Baltic tiger
bearskin
beaver
beaverette
beaverskin
black fox
black marten
black sable
brook mink
buckskin
calf
calfskin
capeskin

caracul
cat
catskin
chinchilla
chinchillette
coast seal
coney
coney leopard
coney mole
cowhide
deerskin
doeskin
electric beaver
electric mole
electric seal
ermine

erminette
fleece
fox
fox hair
genet
goatskin
golden sable
horsehide
Hudson Bay seal
jaguar
kolinsky
krimmer
lambskin
lapin
leopard
leopardskin
marmink
marmot
marten
merino
miniver
mink
mole
moleskin
monkey
muskrat

New Zealand seal
nutria
otter
Persian lamb
pigskin
polar seal
rabbit
rabbitskin
raccoon
red fox
red sable
Roman seal
sable
seal
sealskin
shagreen
sheepskin
skunk
squirrel
Tartar sable
tiger
water mink
white fox
wool
wool fell, woolskin

**.9 leather**

buff
chamois, chammy
chamois skin
cordovan
cup leather
hat leather
kid
mocha

Morocco
patent leather
sheepskin
shoe leather
suède
tawed leather
whitleather, white
leather

## 230. HAIR, FEATHERS

**.1** NOUNS **hairiness, shagginess,** fuzziness, frizziness, **furriness,** downiness, fluffiness, woolliness, fleeciness, bristliness, stubbliness, burrheadedness, mopheadedness, shockheadedness, hypertrichy, hirsuteness, hirsuties, pilosity, crinosity, hispidity, villosity, pubescence; hirsutism, pilosis, pilosism; –trichia *or* –trichy; –thrix, –coma.

**.2 hair,** chaet(o)–, trich(o)–, pile, pil(o)– *or* pili–, crine, crini–; **fur,** coat; pelt 229.1,8; **fleece,** wool, lan(o)– *or* lani–; camel's hair, horsehair; **mane;** shag, tousled *or* matted hair, **mat of hair;** pubescence, pubes, pubic hair; hairlet, villus, capillament, cilium, ciliolum 206.1; seta, setula; bristle 261.3.

**.3** gray hair, grizzle, silver *or* silvery hair, salt-and-pepper hair *or* beard, graying temples, "hoary hair" [Thomas Gray], "the silver livery of advised age" [Shakespeare], "a crown of glory" [Bible], "silver threads among the gold" [Eben E. Rexford].

**.4 head of hair,** head, crine; **crop,** crop of hair, mat, elflock, **thatch,** mop, **shock,** shag, fleece, **mane;** locks, tresses, helmet

of hair; "her native ornament of hair" [Ovid], "amber-dropping hair" [Milton].

**.5 lock, tress;** flowing locks, flowing tresses; **curl, ringlet,** "wanton ringlets wav'd" [Milton]; earlock, *payess* [Yid]; lovelock; frizz, frizzle; crimp; ponytail.

**.6 tuft, flock,** fleck; forelock, widow's peak, quiff [Brit], fetlock, cowlick; **bang, bangs,** fringe.

**.7 braid,** plait, twist; **pigtail,** rat's-tail *or* rat-tail, tail; **queue,** cue; coil, knot; topknot, scalplock; bun, chignon.

**.8 beard,** pogon(o)–, –pogon, **whiskers;** beaver [informal]; full beard, chin whiskers, side whiskers; **sideburns,** burnsides, **mutton chops; goatee,** tuft; imperial, **Vandyke,** spade beard; adolescent beard, pappus, down, peach fuzz, "the soft down of manhood" [Callimachus], "his phoenix down" [Shakespeare]; **stubble,** bristles.

**.9** (plant beard) awn, brush, arista, pile, pappus.

**.10** (animal and insect whiskers) tactile process, tactile hair, **feeler, antenna,** vibrissa; barb, barbel, barbule; cat whisker.

**.11 mustache,** mustachio, soup-strainer [informal], toothbrush, handle bars *or* handle-bar mustache, tash [informal].

**.12 eyelashes, lashes,** cilia; **eyebrows,** brows.

**.13** false hair, switch, fall, chignon, rat [informal].

**.14 wig,** peruke, **toupee,** hairpiece; **periwig.**

**.15 hairdo, hairstyle, haircut, coiffure,** coif, headdress; wave; marcel, marcel wave; **permanent,** permanent wave; home permanent; cold wave; Afro, natural; process, conk.

**.16 feather, plume,** pinion; **quill;** pinfeather; contour feather, penna, down feather, plume feather, plumule; filoplume; hackle; scapular; **crest,** tuft, topknot, panache; penni– *or* penno–, pinn(i)–, pter(o)–, ptil(o)–, –ptile.

**.17** (parts of feathers) quill, calamus, barrel; barb, shaft, barbule, barbicel, cilium, filament, filamentule.

**.18 plumage, feathers,** feather, feathering; contour feathers, breast feathers, mail (of a hawk); hackle; flight feathers, remiges, primaries, secondaries, tertiaries; covert, tectrices; speculum, wing bay.

**.19 down, fluff,** flue, floss, **fuzz, fur,** pile; eiderdown, eider; swansdown; thistledown; lint.

**.20** VERBS grow hair; whisker, **bewhisker,** beard.

**.21 feather, fledge,** feather out; sprout wings.

**.22** cut *or* dress the hair, trim, **barber,** coiffure, coif, style or shape the hair; pompadour, wave, marcel; process, conk; **bob, shingle.**

.23 ADJS **hairlike,** trichoid, capillary; filamentous, filamentary, filiform; bristlelike 261.10.

.24 **hairy, hirsute,** barbigerous, crinose, crinite, pubigerous, pubescent; pilose, pilous, pileous; **furry,** furred; villous; villose; ciliate, cirrose; hispid, hispidulous; **woolly, fleecy,** lanate, lanated, flocky, flocculent, floccose; woolly-headed, woolly-haired, ulotrichous; bushy, tufty, **shaggy,** shagged; matted, tomentose; mopheaded, burrheaded, shockheaded, unshorn; **bristly** 261.9; fuzzy; dasy–, hebe–; –chaetous, –trichous.

.25 **bearded,** whiskered, **bewhiskered,** barbate, barbigerous; mustached or mustachioed; awned, awny, pappose; goateed; unshaved, **unshaven;** stubbled, stubbly.

.26 **wigged,** periwigged, peruked, toupeed.

.27 **feathery, plumy;** hirsute; featherlike, plumelike, pinnate, pennate, pinnati–; **downy,** fluffy, nappy, velvety, peachy, fuzzy, flossy, furry.

.28 **feathered, plumaged,** flighted, **pinioned, plumed,** pennate, plumate, plumose.

.29 **tufted, crested,** topknotted.

.30 **women's hairdos**

| | |
|---|---|
| Andalusian swirl | personality bob |
| bangs | pigtails |
| bob | pompadour |
| bohemian bob | ponytail |
| boyish bob | Psyche knot |
| chignon bob | roach |
| contour bob | Romanesque bob |
| coquette bob | shag |
| debutante bob | shingle |
| feathercut | short bob |
| Flemish bob | shortcut |
| French knot | straight hair shingle |
| Italian bob | swirl |
| long bob | swirl bob |
| long mane | ultramannish bob |
| mannish bob | updo |
| mannish wavy shingle | upswept hairdo |
| new moon bob | windblown bob |
| page-boy | |

.31 **boys' haircuts**

| | |
|---|---|
| boogie | ducktail |
| brushcut | flattop |
| butch | fuzz cut |
| crewcut | mohawk |
| d.a. | pachuco |

## 231. CLOTHING

.1 NOUNS **clothing, clothes, apparel, wear,** wearing apparel, **dress,** dressing, **raiment,** garmenture, **garb, attire, array,** habit, habiliment, fashion, style 644, guise, costume, gear, fig or full fig [both Brit], toilette, trim, bedizenment; **vestment,** vesture, investment, investiture; **garments, raiments,** robes, robing, rags [slang], drapery, feathers; **toggery** or **togs** or **duds** or threads [all informal], sportswear; work clothes, fatigues; linen; menswear, men's clothing, womenswear, women's clothing; unisex clothing, uniwear.

.2 **wardrobe,** furnishings, things, accouterments, trappings; **outfit,** livery, harness, caparison; turnout or getup or rig [all informal]; wedding clothes, bridal outfit, trousseau.

.3 **garment, raiment,** vestment, vesture, robe, frock, gown, rag [slang], togs or duds [both informal]; –let.

.4 **ready-mades,** ready-to-wear, store or store-bought clothes [dial].

.5 **rags, tatters,** secondhand clothes, old clothes; worn clothes, **hand-me-downs** or reach-me-downs [both informal]; slops.

.6 **suit** 231.48, suit of clothes, **frock,** dress, rig [informal], **costume, habit,** bib and tucker [informal].

.7 **uniform** 231.49, **livery.**

.8 **mufti,** civilian dress or clothes, **civvies** or cits [both informal], plain clothes.

.9 **costume,** character dress; outfit or getup or rig [all informal]; masquerade, disguise; tights, leotards; ballet skirt, tutu; motley, cap and bells; buskin, sock.

.10 **finery, frippery, fancy dress,** fine or full feather [informal], full fig [Brit informal]; **best clothes,** best bib and tucker [informal]; **Sunday best** or Sunday clothes or Sunday-go-to-meeting clothes or Sunday-go-to-meetings [all informal], glad rags [slang], party dress.

.11 **formals,** formal dress, **evening dress, full dress,** white tie and tails, **soup-and-fish** [slang]; dinner clothes; dress suit, full-dress suit, tails [informal]; tuxedo, tux [informal]; **regalia,** court dress; dress uniform, full-dress uniform, special full-dress uniform, social full-dress uniform; evening gown, dinner dress or gown.

.12 **cloak,** overgarment 231.50.

.13 **coat, jacket** 231.51; **overcoat** 231.53, greatcoat, **topcoat,** surcoat.

.14 **waistcoat,** weskit [dial], **vest.**

.15 **waist, shirt** 231.54, **shirtwaist,** linen, sark or shift [both dial]; **blouse,** bodice, corsage; dickey.

.16 **dress** 231.55, **gown, frock; skirt,** jupe [Scot].

.17 **apron,** *tablier* [Fr]; pinafore, bib, tucker; smock.

.18 **pants, trousers** 231.56, pair of trousers, **trews** [Scot], **breeches,** britches [informal], **breeks** [Scot], **pantaloons, jeans, slacks.**

.19 **waistband, belt** 253.3; **loincloth,** breechcloth *or* breechclout, waistcloth, **G-string,** loinguard, dhoti, moocha; **diaper,** dydee [informal], napkins [Brit], nappies [Brit informal].

.20 **dishabille** 231.57, *déshabillé* [Fr], **undress,** something comfortable; **negligee,** *négligé* [Fr]; **wrap,** wrapper; **sport clothes, casual clothes** *or* **dress.**

.21 **nightwear,** night clothes; **nightdress, nightgown, nightie** [informal], **bedgown;** nightshirt; **pajamas,** pyjamas [Brit], PJ's [informal]; **sleepers.**

.22 **underclothes,** underclothing, **undergarments** 231.58, bodywear, **underwear, undies** [informal], Skivvies, body clothes, smallclothes, unmentionables [informal], **lingerie, linen,** underlinen; **flannels, woolens.**

.23 **corset,** stays, foundation garment, corselet; **girdle,** undergirdle, panty girdle; **garter belt.**

.24 **brassiere, bra** [informal], **bandeau,** underbodice, *soutien-gorge* [Fr], **uplift brassiere; falsies** [slang].

.25 **headdress,** headgear, headwear, headclothes, headtire; **millinery;** headpiece, **chapeau, cap, hat** 231.59; **lid** [informal]; headcloth, **kerchief,** coverchief; **handkerchief.**

.26 **veil,** veiling, veiler; *yashmak* [Turk]; **mantilla.**

.27 **footwear,** footgear, *chaussure* [Fr]; **shoes** 231.60, **boots;** clodhoppers *or* gunboats [both slang]; **wooden shoes,** sabots, **pattens.**

.28 **hosiery** 231.61, **hose, stockings; socks.**

.29 **bathing suit,** swim suit, swimming suit, tank suit, *maillot* [Fr]; **trunks; bikini; wet suit.**

.30 **children's wear;** rompers, jumpers; creepers; layette, **baby clothes,** infants' wear, baby linen; **swaddling clothes, swaddle.**

.31 **garment making, tailoring; dressmaking; millinery,** hatmaking, hatting; **shoemaking,** bootmaking, **cobbling;** habilimentation.

.32 **clothier, haberdasher,** draper [Brit], **outfitter;** costumier, costumer; **glover; hosier;** furrier; dry goods dealer, mercer [Brit].

.33 **garmentmaker, garmentworker,** needleworker; cutter, stitcher, finisher.

.34 **tailor,** tailoress, *tailleur* [Fr], **sartor; fitter;** busheler, bushelman; furrier; cloakmaker.

.35 **dressmaker, modiste,** *couturière* [Fr], *couturier* [Fr]; seamstress 223.2.

.36 **hatter,** hatmaker, **milliner.**

.37 **shoemaker,** bootmaker, **booter, cobbler,** souter [Scot].

.38 VERBS **clothe,** enclothe, **dress, garb, attire,** tire, array, **apparel,** raiment, **garment,** habilitate, **tog** [informal], **dud** [slang], robe, enrobe, invest, endue, **deck,** bedeck, **dight,** rag out *or* up [slang]; drape, bedrape; **wrap,** enwrap, lap, envelop, sheathe, shroud, enshroud; wrap *or* bundle *or* muffle up; swathe, swaddle.

.39 **cloak, mantle;** coat, jacket; gown, frock; breech; shirt; coif, bonnet, cap, hat; hood; boot, shoe; stocking, sock.

.40 **outfit,** equip, **accouter,** uniform, caparison, rig, rig out *or* up, fit, **fit out,** turn out, **costume,** habit, suit; disguise, masquerade, cloak oneself.

.41 **dress up, get up, doll** *or* **spruce up** [informal], **primp** *or* prink *or* prank [all informal], gussy up [informal], spiff *or* fancy *or* slick up [slang], pretty up [informal], deck out *or* up, trick out *or* up, tog out *or* up [informal], rag out *or* up [slang], fig out *or* up; titivate, dizen, bedizen; overdress; put on the dog *or* style [slang].

.42 **don, put on,** slip on *or* into, get on *or* into, assume, dress in; change.

.43 **wear, have on,** be dressed in, affect, sport [informal].

.44 ADJS **clothed, clad, dressed, attired, togged** [informal], tired, arrayed, **garbed,** garmented, **habited,** habilimented, decked, bedecked, decked out, tricked out, rigged out, dight [archaic], vested, vestmented, robed, gowned, raimented, **appareled,** invested, endued, liveried, uniformed; **costumed,** in costume, cloaked, mantled, disguised; breeched, trousered, pantalooned; coifed, capped, bonneted, hatted, hooded; **shod,** shoed, booted, *chaussé* [Fr].

.45 **dressed up, dolled** *or* **spruced up** [informal]; spiffed *or* fancied *or* slicked up [slang], gussied up [informal]; **spruce, dressed to advantage,** dressed to the nines, dressed fit to kill [slang]; in Sunday best, *endimanché* [Fr], in one's best bib and tucker [informal], in fine *or* high feather; *en grande tenue* [Fr], *en grande toilette* [Fr], in full dress, in full feather, in white tie and tails, in tails; **well-dressed, chic,** *soigné* [Fr], stylish, modish, well turned-out.

.46 **in dishabille,** *en déshabillé* [Fr], **in negligee; casual,** informal, sporty.

**.47** tailored, custom-made, bespoke [Brit]; ready-made, store-bought [dial], ready-to-wear; vestmental; sartorial.

**.48 suits**

| | |
|---|---|
| business suit | shirtwaist suit |
| casual suit | single-breasted suit |
| combination | ski suit |
| double-breasted suit | sports suit |
| dress suit | summer suit |
| ensemble | sun suit |
| foul-weather suit | sweat suit |
| jump suit | tailored suit |
| mod suit | three-piece suit |
| one-piece suit | town-and-country suit |
| pants suit | track suit |
| rain suit | tropical suit |
| riding habit | two-piece suit |
| sack suit | zoot suit |
| separates | |

**.49 uniforms**

| | |
|---|---|
| blues | olive-drab or OD |
| continentals | regimentals |
| dress blues | sailor suit |
| dress whites | soldier suit |
| fatigues | stripes (prison uniform) |
| full dress | |
| khaki | undress |
| nauticals | whites |

**.50 cloaks, overgarments**

| | |
|---|---|
| academic gown | mantua |
| academic hood | master's gown |
| academic robe | military cloak |
| afghan | monk's robe |
| bachelor's gown | opera cloak or cape |
| blouse | pallium |
| burnoose | pelerine |
| caftan | pelisse |
| cape | peplos |
| capote | peplum |
| cardinal | plaid |
| cashmere, cashmere shawl | poncho |
| | robe |
| cassock | roquelaure |
| chlamys | sagum |
| doctor's gown | serape |
| domino | shawl |
| duster | shoulderette |
| frock | slop |
| gaberdine | smock |
| haik | smock frock |
| houppelande | soutane |
| Inverness cape | stole |
| judge's robe or gown | tabard |
| kimono | talma |
| kirtle | tippet |
| manta | toga |
| manteau | toga virilis |
| mantelet | tunic |
| mantelletta | wrap-around |
| mantellone | wrapper |
| mantilla | wrap-up |
| mantle | |

**.51 coats, jackets**

| | |
|---|---|
| blazer | capuchin |
| blouse | car coat |
| body coat | chaqueta [Sp] |
| bolero | chesterfield |
| bomber jacket | claw-hammer coat, |

| | |
|---|---|
| claw hammer | parka |
| coach coat | peacoat, pea jacket |
| coatee | pilot jacket |
| cutaway coat, cutaway | Prince Albert, Prince Albert coat |
| denim jacket | redingote |
| dinner coat or jacket | reefer |
| dolman | sack |
| double-breasted jacket | sack coat |
| doublet | san benito |
| dress coat | shell jacket |
| dressing jacket | shooting jacket |
| duffel, duffel coat | single-breasted jacket |
| Eisenhower jacket | ski jacket |
| Eton jacket | sleeve waistcoat |
| fingertip coat | smoking jacket |
| fitted coat | spencer |
| frock coat, frock | spiketail coat, spiketail |
| jerkin | |
| jumper | sport coat or jacket |
| jupe [Scot] | swagger coat |
| loden coat | swallow-tailed coat, swallowtail |
| lounging jacket | |
| mackinaw, mackinaw coat | tabard |
| | tail coat, tails |
| Mao jacket | tuxedo coat or jacket |
| maxicoat | watch coat |
| mess jacket | windbreaker |
| midicoat | woolly (woolen jacket) |
| monkey jacket | |
| Nehru jacket | |
| Norfolk jacket | |

**.52 sweaters**

| | |
|---|---|
| bolero | shell |
| bulky | shoulderette |
| cardigan, cardigan jacket | ski sweater |
| | slip-on |
| cashmere sweater | slipover |
| crew-neck sweater | sloppy Joe |
| desk sweater | sweat shirt |
| fisherman's sweater | topper |
| hand-knit | turtleneck sweater |
| jersey | V-neck sweater |
| knittie | windbreaker |
| pull-on sweater | woolly |
| pullover | |

**.53 overcoats**

| | |
|---|---|
| benjamin | paletot |
| Burberry | raglan |
| capote | raincoat |
| chesterfield | slicker |
| cloth coat | slip-on |
| dreadnought | sou'wester |
| duster | surtout |
| fearnought | tarpaulin |
| fur coat | trench coat |
| fur-lined coat | ulster |
| fur-trimmed coat | waterproof |
| Inverness | wet weathers |
| long coat | wrap-around |
| mackintosh, mac | wraprascal |
| oilskins | |

**.54 shirts**

| | |
|---|---|
| basque | dress shirt |
| blouse | evening shirt |
| body shirt | gipon |
| body suit | habit shirt |
| coat shirt | hair shirt |
| dickey | halter |
| doublet | hickory shirt |

jupe [Scot]
middy blouse
olive-drab or OD shirt
overblouse
polo shirt
pourpoint
pullover

sark
shirtwaist
short-sleeved shirt
sport shirt
tank top
top
T-shirt

## .55 dresses, skirts

ballet skirt
cheongsam
chiton
cocktail dress
crinoline
culottes
dinner dress or gown
dirndl
evening gown
farthingale
fillebeg
full skirt
grass skirt
hobble skirt
hoop skirt
jumper
kilt
kirtle
mantua
maxiskirt

microskirt
midiskirt
miniskirt
Mother Hubbard
muu-muu
overdress
overskirt
pannier
peplum
petticoat
pinafore
sack
sari
sarong
sheath
shirtdress
slit skirt
tea gown
tutu

## .56 pants

bags [Brit]
bell-bottoms, bells [in-
    formal]
Bermuda shorts
bloomers
blue jeans
breeks [Scot]
buckskins
Capri pants
chivarras [Sp]
clam diggers
cords
corduroys
culottes
denims
drawers
ducks
dungarees
flannels
gabardines
galligaskins
gym pants
high-water pants
hip-huggers
hot pants
Jamaica shorts
jeans
jodhpurs
kerseys
knee breeches
knee pants
knickerbockers,

knickers
Levi's
long trousers or pants
moleskins
overalls
pajamas
pantalets
pantaloons
pedal-pushers
peg pants
pegtops
plus-fours
riding pants
rompers
sacks
shintiyan
short pants
shorts
short shorts
ski pants
slacks
smallclothes
stretch pants
sweat pants
tights
toreador pants
trews
trouserettes
trunks
tweeds
whites

## .57 dishabille

bathrobe
bed jacket
boudoir dress
brunch coat
dressing gown
dressing sack or jacket

housecoat
kimono
lounging pajamas
lounging robe
morning dress
peignoir [Fr]

robe
robe-de-chambre [Fr]

smoking jacket
wrapper

## .58 undergarments

Balmoral
bloomers
body stocking
brassiere 231.24
briefs
bustle
BVD's
camisole
chemise
combination
corset 231.23
crinoline
drawers
foundation garment
Jockey shorts
long underwear
pannier
panties
pants

petticoat
scanties
shift
shorts
singlet [Brit]
Skivvies
slip
smock
step-ins
tournure [Fr]
T-shirt
underdrawers
underpants
undershirt
underskirt
undervest
union suit
vest [Brit]

## .59 hats, caps

astrakhan
balaclava helmet
Balmoral
baseball cap
beany
bearskin
beaver
beret
billycock hat, billy-
    cock
boater
bonnet
Borsalino
boudoir cap
bowler
brass hat
busby
calash
campaign hat
capote
castor
chapeau bras [Fr]
cloche
cock-and-pinch
cocked hat
coif
coonskin cap
coxcomb
crush hat
derby
dress cap
dunce cap
Dutch cap
fantail
fedora
felt hat
fez
forage cap
fore-and-aft or -after
garrison cap
glengarry
hard hat
helmet
homburg
hood
jockey cap
kaffiyeh
kelly

kepi
leghorn
mobcap
mortarboard
nightcap
opera hat
overseas cap
Panama hat, Panama
peaked cap
picture hat
pillbox
pith hat or helmet
plug hat, plug
poke bonnet, poke
porkpie
puggree
riding hood
rumal
sailor
Salvation Army bon-
    net
scraper
shako
shovel hat
side cap
silk hat
skimmer
skullcap
slouch hat
snood
soft hat
sola topee
sombrero
sou'wester
Stetson
stocking cap
stovepipe hat, stove-
    pipe
straw hat
sunbonnet
sundown
sun hat
sun helmet
tam-o'shanter, tam
tarboosh
ten-gallon hat
three-cornered hat
tin hat

topee
top hat, topper
toque
tricorne
trilby
turban

tyrolean hat
wide-awake hat, wide-
  awake
wimple
wind-cutter
yarmulka

### .60 shoes

arctics
ballet shoes or slippers
Blucher boots or
  shoes, bluchers
bootees
bootikins
boots
brogues, brogans
buskins
button shoes
campus shoes
chopines
chukka boots
clogs
combat boots
cowboy boots
creepers
desert boots
espadrilles
field shoes
flip-flops
gaiters
galoshes
getas
gumshoes, gums
gym shoes
half boots
Hessian boots, hes-
  sians
high-button shoes
high-lows
high-topped shoes
hip boots
hobnailed shoes
horseshoes

jackboots
lace shoes
Loafers
loungers
moccasins
mules
overshoes
Oxford shoes or ties,
  Oxfords
paratrooper boots
pattens
platforms
pumps
riding boots
rope shoes
rubbers
sandals
scuffs
ski boots
slippers
sneakers
snowshoes
socks
stogies
tennis shoes
thigh boots
top boots
veldschoens
Wedgies
Wellington boots,
  Wellingtons
wooden shoes
work shoes
zoris

### .61 hosiery

anklets
argyles
athletic socks
bobbysocks
boothose
boot socks
crew socks
dress sheers
full-fashioned stock-
  ings
garter stockings
half hose
knee socks
lisle hose

nylons
panty-hose
rayon stockings
seamless stockings
sheer stockings, sheers
silk stockings
stocking hose
stretch stockings
sweat socks
tights
trunk hose
varsity socks
work socks

### .62 leggings

antigropelos
chaps, chaparajos [Sp]
gaiters
galligaskins
gamashes
gambados

greaves
leg armor
puttees, putts
spats
spatterdashes

### .63 handwear, gloves

baseball glove or mitt
boxing gloves
brass knuckles
cesta

cestus
gauntlets
hockey gloves
kid gloves, kids

mittens, mitts
mousquetaire gloves,
  mousquetaires

muff
suède gloves, suèdes

### .64 neckwear

ascot, ascot tie
band
bandanna
bertha
boa
bowtie
button-down collar
celluloid collar
chemisette
choke, choker
clerical collar
collar
comforter
cravat
dog collar
fichu
four-in-hand, four-in-
  hand tie
fur
guimpe
high collar

kerchief
muffler
neckband
neckcloth
neckerchief
neckpiece
necktie
plunging neckline
rebato
Roman collar
ruff
scarf
stiff collar
stock
stole
string tie
tallith
tie
tippet
tucker
Windsor tie

### .65 waistbands, belts

baldric
band
bandolier
bellyband
belt
cestus
cincture
cummerbund

fascia
girdle
girt
girth
sash
waist belt
waistcloth

### .66 garment parts

arm
armhole
armlet
bosom
coattail
collar
collarband
cuff
dart
facing
fly
French cuff
gore
gusset
lap
lapel
leg

neck
neckband
pinafore
placket
pocket
pocket flap
seat
shirttail
shoulder pad
shoulder strap
sleeve
stomacher
strap
waist
wristband
yoke
zipper

## 232. DIVESTMENT

.1 NOUNS **divestment**, divestiture, divesture;
   **removal**, de–, dis–, un–; **stripping**, de-
   nudement, denudation; baring, stripping
   or laying bare, uncovering, exposure; indecent exposure, exhibitionism; decorti-
   cation, excoriation; desquamation, exfoliation; exuviation, ecdysis.

.2 **disrobing**, disrobement, **undressing**, un-
   clothing, uncasing; shedding, molting,
   peeling; striptease.

.3 **nudity**, **nakedness**, bareness; **the nude,
   the altogether** or **the buff** [both infor-

mal], **the raw** [slang]; state of nature, **birthday suit** [informal]; not a stitch, not a stitch to one's name or back; décolleté, décolletage, toplessness; nudism, naturism, gymnosophy; nudist, naturist, gymnosophist; stripper, stripteaser, ecdysiast.

.4 **hairlessness, baldness,** acomia, alopecia; beardlessness, bald-headedness or -patedness; baldhead, baldpate, baldy [informal]; shaving, tonsure, depilation; hair remover, depilatory.

.5 VERBS **divest, strip, remove; uncover,** uncloak, unveil, **expose,** lay open, bare, lay or strip bare, **denude,** denudate; fleece, shear; pluck; unsheathe.

.6 **take off, remove, doff,** douse [informal], off with, put off, slip or step out of, cast off, throw off, drop; unwrap, undo.

.7 **undress, unclothe,** undrape, ungarment, unapparel, unarray, disarray; **disrobe,** dismantle, uncase; **strip,** strip to the buff [informal], do a strip-tease.

.8 **peel, pare, skin, strip,** flay, excoriate, decorticate, bark; scalp.

.9 **husk, hull,** pod, **shell,** shuck.

.10 **shed, cast,** throw off, **slough, molt,** exuviate.

.11 **scale, flake,** scale or flake off, desquamate, exfoliate.

.12 ADJS **divested, stripped, bared,** denuded, denudated, exposed, uncovered, stripped or laid bare, unveiled, showing.

.13 **unclad, undressed, unclothed, unattired,** disrobed, ungarmented, undraped, ungarbed, unrobed, unappareled, uncased; **clothesless,** garbless, garmentless, raimentless; half-clothed, underclothed, en déshabillé [Fr], in dishabille, nudish; lownecked, low-cut, décolleté, strapless, topless.

.14 **naked, nude,** gymn(o)–, nudi–; **bare, bald,** peeled, **raw** [slang], **in the raw** [slang], in puris naturalibus [L], in a state of nature, in nature's garb; in one's birthday suit, **in the buff** or in native buff or stripped to the buff, **in the altogether** [all informal], with nothing on, without a stitch, without a stitch to one's name or back; **stark-naked,** bare-ass [slang], bare as the back of one's hand, naked as the day one was born, naked as a jaybird [informal], starkers [Brit informal], "naked as a worm" [Chaucer], "naked as a needle" [William Langland], "naked as my nail" [John Heywood], "in naked beauty more adorned" [Milton]; nudist, naturistic, gymnosophical.

.15 **barefoot,** unshod; discalced, discalceate.

.16 **bare-ankled,** bare-armed, bare-backed, bare-breasted, topless, bare-chested, barefaced, bare-handed, bare-headed, barekneed, bare-legged, bare-necked, barethroated.

.17 **hairless,** depilous; **bald,** acomous; bald as a coot, bald as an egg; **bald-headed,** baldpated, tonsured; **beardless,** whiskerless, shaven, clean-shaven, smooth-shaven, smooth-faced; smooth, glabrous.

.18 **exuvial,** sloughy; desquamative, exfoliatory; denudant or denudatory.

.19 ADVS **nakedly, barely, baldly.**

## 233. ENVIRONMENT

.1 NOUNS **environment, surroundings, environs,** ambience, entourage, circle, circumjacencies, circumambiencies, **circumstances,** environing circumstances, alentours [Fr]; **precincts,** ambit, purlieus, **milieu; neighborhood, vicinity,** vicinage; **suburbs** 183.1; outskirts, outposts, borderlands; periphery, perimeter, compass, circuit; **context, situation;** habitat 191; total environment, gestalt; ec(o)– or oec(o)– or oiko–.

.2 **setting, background, backdrop,** ground, field, scene, arena, theater, locale; back, rear, hinterland, distance; stage, stage setting, stage set, mise-en-scène [Fr].

.3 (surrounding influence or condition) **milieu, atmosphere, climate, air,** aura, spirit, feeling, feel, quality, sense, note, tone, overtone, undertone.

.4 (natural or suitable environment) **element,** medium; ecosystem, ecodeme, ecoclimate; ecology, autecology, synecology, bioecology or bionomics, zoo-ecology.

.5 **surrounding, encompassment,** environment, circumambience or circumambiency, circumjacence or circumjacency; containment, **enclosure** 236; **encirclement,** cincture, encincture, circumcincture, circling, girdling, girding; **envelopment,** enfoldment, embracement; circumposition; circumflexion; inclusion 76, involvement 176.

.6 VERBS **surround, environ,** compass, **encompass,** enclose, close; go round or around, compass about; **envelop,** enfold, lap, wrap, enwrap, embrace, enclasp, embosom, embay, involve, invest.

.7 **encircle, circle,** ensphere, belt, belt in, zone, cincture, encincture; **girdle,** gird, begird, engird; ring, band; loop; wreathe, wreathe or twine around.

.8 ADJS **environing, surrounding,** encompassing, enclosing; **enveloping,** wrapping, enfolding, embracing; **encircling,** circling; circumjacent, circumferential, circumambient, ambient; circumfluent, circumfluous; peripheral; circumflex; **roundabout,** suburban, neighboring.

.9 **environmental,** environal; **ecological.**

.10 **surrounded,** environed, compassed, **encompassed,** enclosed; **enveloped,** wrapped, enfolded, lapped, wreathed.

.11 **encircled, circled,** ringed, cinctured, encinctured, belted, girdled, girt, begirt, zoned.

.12 ADVS **around,** round, **about,** round about, in the neighborhood *or* vicinity, close, close about.

.13 **all round, all about,** on every side, on all sides, on all hands, right and left; amph(i)–, circum–, peri–.

### 234. CIRCUMSCRIPTION

.1 NOUNS **circumscription,** circumscribing, **bounding, demarcation,** delimitation, definition, determination, specification; limit-setting, inclusion-exclusion, circling-in *or* -out, encincture, boundary-marking.

.2 **limitation, restriction,** confinement 236.1, prescription, proscription, restrain, discipline, moderation, continence; qualification; bounds 235, boundary, limit 235.3.

.3 **patent, copyright,** certificate of invention, *brevet d'invention* [Fr]; trademark, registered trademark, trade name, service mark.

.4 VERBS **circumscribe, bound; mark off** *or* **mark out,** stake out, lay off, rope off; **demarcate,** delimit, delimitate, draw *or* mark boundaries, circle in *or* out, set the limit, mark the periphery; **define,** determine, fix, specify; surround 233.6; enclose 236.5.

.5 **limit, restrict, restrain, bound, confine;** straiten, narrow; specialize; stint, scant; **condition,** qualify, hedge about; draw the line, set an end point *or* stopping place; discipline, moderate, contain, **patent, copyright,** register.

.6 ADJS **circumscribed,** circumscript; ringed *or* circled *or* hedged about; **demarcated, delimited, defined,** definite, determined, determinate, specific, stated, set, fixed; surrounded 233.10, encircled 233.11.

.7 **limited, restricted,** bound, **bounded, finite; confined** 236.10, prescribed, proscribed, cramped, strait, straitened, narrow; conditioned, qualified; disciplined, moderated, patented, copyrighted.

.8 **restricted,** out of bounds, off limits.

.9 **limiting, restricting,** defining, confining; limitative, limitary, restrictive, definitive, exclusive.

.10 **terminal,** limital; limitable, terminable.

### 235. BOUNDS

.1 NOUNS **bounds, limits,** boundaries, limitations, **confines, pale,** marches, bourns, verges, edges, outlines, skirts, outskirts, **fringes,** metes, metes and bounds; periphery, **perimeter;** coordinates 490.6, parameters; compass, circumference, circumscription 234.

.2 **outline, contour,** *tournure* [Fr], delineation, lines, lineaments, shapes, figure, figuration, **configuration,** gestalt; features, main features; **profile,** silhouette; relief; skeleton, framework.

.3 **boundary, bound, limit,** limitation, extremity 56.5; delimitation, hedge, break *or* breakoff point, cutoff, cutoff point, terminus, term, deadline, target date, terminal date, time allotment; finish, **end** 70; start, starting line *or* point; **limiting factor,** determinant, limit *or* boundary condition; threshold, limen; upper limit, ceiling, high-water mark; lower limit, floor, low-water mark; **confine,** march, mark, bourn, mete, compass, circumscription; **boundary line, line, border line,** frontier, division line, interface, break boundary, line of demarcation *or* circumvallation.

.4 **border,** bordure, limbus, board, **edge,** limb, **verge, brink,** brow, **brim, rim, margin,** marge, **skirt, fringe,** cross(o)–, thysan(o)–, **hem,** list, selvage, side; sideline; shore, bank, coast; **lip,** labium, labrum, labellum, labio–, chil(o)– *or* cheil(o)–; flange; ledge; frame, enframement; featheredge; ragged edge.

.5 **frontier, border, borderland,** border ground, marchland, march, marches; outskirts, outpost; frontier post; iron curtain, bamboo curtain, Berlin wall; Pillars of Hercules; three-mile *or* twelve-mile limit.

.6 **curb,** kerb [Brit], curbing; border stone, curbstone, kerbstone [Brit], edgestone.

.7 **edging, bordering,** bordure, **trimming,** binding, skirting; fringe, fimbriation, fimbria; hem, selvage, list, welt; frill, frilling; beading, flounce, furbelow, galloon, motif, ruffle, valance.

.8 VERBS **bound,** circumscribe 234.4, surround 233.6, limit 234.5, enclose 236.5, divide, separate.

.9 **outline,** contour; **delineate** 654.12; silhouette, profile, limn.

.10 **border, edge, bound, rim, skirt, hem, fringe,** befringe, lap, list, margin, marge, marginate, march, verge, line, side; **adjoin** 200.9; **frame,** enframe, set off; trim, bind; purl; purfle.

.11 ADJS **bordering, fringing,** rimming, skirting; **bounding, boundary, limiting,** limit, determining or determinant or determinative; threshold, liminal, limbic; extreme, terminal 70.10; **marginal, borderline,** frontier; coastal, littoral.

.12 **bordered,** edged; margined, marged, marginate, marginated; **fringed,** befringed, trimmed, skirted, fimbriate, fimbriated, laciniate, laciniated.

.13 lipped, labial, labiate.

.14 outlinear, delineatory; peripheral, peripher(o)–, perimetric(al), circumferential; outlined, **in outline.**

.15 ADVS **on the verge, on the brink,** on the borderline, on the point, on the edge, on the ragged edge, at the threshold, at the limit or bound; **peripherally,** marginally, at the periphery.

.16 **thus far,** so far, thus far and no farther.

## 236. ENCLOSURE

.1 NOUNS **enclosure; confinement,** circumscription 234, immurement, walling- or hedging- or hemming- or boxing- or fencing-in; imprisonment, incarceration; siege, beleaguerment, blockade, blockading, cordoning, quarantine, besetment; inclusion 76; **envelopment** 233.5.

.2 **packaging, packing,** package; boxing, crating, encasement; canning, tinning [Brit]; bottling.

.3 (enclosed place) **enclosure** 236.12, close, **confine,** enclave, pale, paling, list, cincture; **pen, coop,** fold; **yard,** park, court, courtyard, curtilage, toft; square, quadrangle, quad [informal]; **field,** delimited field, **arena,** theater, ground; **container** 193.

.4 **fence** 236.13, boundary 235.3, **barrier; wall,** stone wall; rail, railing; balustrade, balustrading.

.5 VERBS **enclose,** close in, bound, include, **contain;** compass, encompass; **surround,** encircle 233.7; **shut** or **pen in,** coop in; **fence in,** wall in, rail in; **hem** or **hedge in,** box in, pocket; shut or coop or mew up; pen, coop, corral, cage, impound, mew; **imprison,** incarcerate, jail; **besiege,** beset, beleaguer, leaguer, cordon, cordon off, quarantine, blockade; yard, yard up;

house in; chamber; stable, kennel, shrine, enshrine; **wrap** 228.20.

.6 **confine, immure;** cramp, straiten, encase; cloister, closet, cabin, crib; entomb, coffin, casket; bottle up or in, box up or in.

.7 **fence, wall, pale,** rail, bar; hem, hedge; picket, palisade; bulkhead in.

.8 parenthesize, bracket.

.9 **package, pack, parcel;** box, box up, case, encase, crate, carton; can, tin [Brit]; bottle, jar, pot; barrel, cask, tank; sack, bag; basket, hamper; capsule, encyst.

.10 ADJS **enclosed,** closed-in; **confined,** bound, immured, cloistered, "cabined, cribbed, confined" [Shakespeare]; **imprisoned,** incarcerated, jailed; caged, cramped, restrained, corralled; besieged, beleaguered, leaguered, beset, cordoned, cordoned off, quarantined, blockaded; **shut-in,** pent-up, penned, cooped, mewed, walled- or hedged- or hemmed- or boxed- or fenced-in, fenced, walled, paled, railed, barred; hemmed, hedged.

.11 enclosing, confining, claustral, parietal, parieto–; surrounding 233.8; limiting 234.9.

.12 **enclosures**

| | |
|---|---|
| bailey | henyard |
| barnyard | hutch |
| barton | keddah [India] |
| basecourt | kraal |
| box | manger |
| bullpen | paddock |
| cage | pasture |
| cattlefold | pigpen, pigsty |
| chicken coop | pinfold, penfold |
| chicken yard | polygon |
| close | pound |
| compound | quadrangle, quad |
| corral | rink |
| court | run |
| courtyard | runway |
| crib | sheepcote |
| croft | sheepfold |
| dog pound | shippen |
| dooryard | stall |
| enclave | stockyard |
| farmyard | sty |
| fold | toft |
| hen coop | yard |

.13 **fences, walls**

| | |
|---|---|
| barbed wire | palisade |
| board fence | parapet |
| contravallation, coun- | perpend wall |
| tervallation | picket fence |
| Cyclone fence | quickset hedge |
| dead wall | rail fence |
| dike | railing |
| espalier | rampart |
| garden wall | retaining wall |
| hedge, hedgerow | ring fence |
| hoarding | scarp wall |
| paling | stockade |

stone wall     vallum
trellis     weir
vallation     zigzag fence

## 237. INTERPOSITION

*(a putting or lying between)*

.1 NOUNS interposition, interposure, interlocation, intermediacy, interjacence; **intervention**, intervenience, intercurrence, sandwiching; **intrusion** 238.

.2 interjection, interpolation, introduction, throwing- or tossing-in, **injection**, insinuation, intercalation, interlineation; **insertion** 304; interlocution, remark, parenthetical or side or incidental or casual remark, *obiter dictum* [L], aside, parenthesis; episode; infix, insert.

.3 interspersion, interfusion, interlardment, interpenetration.

.4 **intermediary**, intermedium, mediary, medium; link, **connecting link**, tie, connection, go-between, liaison; middleman, broker, agent, wholesaler, jobber, distributor; **mediator** 805.3.

.5 partition, dividing wall, division, separation, *cloison* [Fr]; septum, interseptum, septulum, dissepiment, sept(o)– or septi–; **wall, barrier**; panel; paries; brattice; bulkhead; diaphragm, midriff, midsection; dividing line, property line, party wall; **buffer, bumper**, fender, cushion, pad, shock pad, collision mat, mat; buffer state.

.6 VERBS interpose, interject, interpolate, intercalate, interjaculate; **intervene**; put between, sandwich; **insert in**, introduce in, insinuate in, inject in, implant in; **foist in**, fudge in, work in, drag in, lug in, drag or lug in by the heels, worm in, squeeze in, smuggle in, throw in, run in, thrust in, edge in, wedge in; **intrude** 238.5.

.7 **intersperse, interfuse**, interlard, interpenetrate; intersow, intersprinkle.

.8 partition, set apart, separate, divide; **wall off**, fence off; panel.

.9 ADJS interjectional, interpolative, intercalary; parenthetical, episodic.

.10 **intervening**, intervenient, **interjacent**, intercurrent; **intermediate**, intermediary, medial, mean, medium, mesne, median, middle, medi(o)–, mes(o)–; inter–, intra–.

.11 partitioned, walled; mural; septal, parietal.

.12 PREPS **between, betwixt**, 'twixt, betwixt and between [informal]; **among, amongst**, 'mongst; **amid, amidst**, mid, 'mid, midst, 'midst; in the midst of, in the thick of.

## 238. INTRUSION

.1 NOUNS intrusion, obtrusion, interloping; interposition 237, interposure, imposition, insinuation, **interference**, intervention, interruption, injection, interjection 237.2; **encroachment**, entrenchment, trespass, trespassing, unlawful entry 824.4; impingement, **infringement**, invasion, incursion, inroad, influx, irruption, infiltration; entrance 302.

.2 meddling, intermeddling; **butting-in** or kibitzing [both informal]; **meddlesomeness, intrusiveness, forwardness**, obtrusiveness; **officiousness**, impertinence, presumption, presumptuousness; inquisitiveness 528.1.

.3 intruder, interloper, trespasser, buttinsky [informal]; crasher or gate-crasher [both informal], unwelcome guest; invader, encroacher, infiltrator.

.4 meddler, intermeddler; busybody, pry, Paul Pry, prier, snoop or snooper, *yenta* [Yid], **kibitzer** [informal]; backseat driver.

.5 VERBS intrude, obtrude, interlope; come between, **interpose** 237.6, intervene, **interfere**, insinuate, impose; **encroach, infringe**, impinge, **trespass**, trench, entrench, invade, infiltrate; **break in upon**, break in, burst in, charge in, crash in, smash in, storm in; **barge in** [informal], irrupt, **cut in**, thrust in 304.7, push in, press in, rush in, throng in, crowd in, squeeze in, elbow in; **butt in** or horn in or chisel in or muscle in [all informal]; appoint oneself; crash or crash the gates [both informal]; creep in, steal in, sneak in, slink in, slip in; foist in, worm or work in, edge in, put in or shove in one's oar; **foist oneself upon**, thrust oneself upon; put on or upon, impose on or upon, put one's two cents in [informal].

.6 interrupt, **put in, cut in, break in**; chime in or chip in [both informal].

.7 meddle, **intermeddle**, busybody, not mind one's business; **meddle with, tamper with**, mix oneself up with, inject oneself into, monkey with, fool with or around with [informal], mess with or around with [informal]; **pry**, Paul-Pry, snoop, nose, **stick** or poke one's nose in, stick one's long nose into; have a finger in, have a finger in the pie; kibitz [informal].

.8 ADJS intrusive, obtrusive, **interfering**, intervenient, invasive, interruptive; xen(o)–.

.9 meddlesome, meddling; officious, overofficious, self-appointed, impertinent, presumptuous; **busybody**, busy; pushing, pushy, forward; **prying**, nosy *or* snoopy [both informal]; inquisitive 528.5.

.10 PHRS **none of your business;** what's it to you?, **mind your own business,** keep your nose out of this, butt out, go soak your head, go sit on a tack, go roll your hoop, go peddle your fish, go fly a kite, go chase yourself, go jump in the lake.

## 239. CONTRAPOSITION

*(a placing over against)*

.1 NOUNS contraposition, anteposition, posing against *or* over against; **opposition,** opposing, opposure; **antithesis,** contrast, ironic *or* contrastive juxtaposition; confrontment, **confrontation;** polarity, polar opposition, **polarization; contrariety** 15; contention 796; hostility 790.2.

.2 **opposites,** antipodes, polar opposites, contraries; **poles,** opposite poles, antipoles, counterpoles, North Pole, South Pole; antipodal points, antipoints; contrapositives, contraposita; night and day, black and white.

.3 opposite side, other side, the other side of the picture *or* coin, other face; **reverse, inverse, obverse, converse;** heads, tails (of a coin).

.4 VERBS contrapose, **oppose,** contrast, match, **set over against,** pose against *or* over against, put in opposition, set *or* pit against one another; **confront,** face, front, stand *or* lie opposite, stand opposed *or* vis-à-vis, be eyeball to eyeball, bump heads, meet head-on; counteract 790.3; contend 796.14; subtend; **polarize;** contraposit.

.5 ADJS contrapositive, **opposite,** opposing, **facing,** confronting, eyeball-to-eyeball, antithetic(al); **reverse, inverse, obverse, converse; antipodal;** polar, polarized, polaric; ant(i)– *or* anth–, cat(a)– *or* cath– *or* kat(a)–, co–, contra–, counter–, enantio–, ob–.

.6 ADVS **opposite, poles apart,** at opposite extremes; contrary, contrariwise, counter; just opposite, **face to face,** vis-à-vis, *front à front* [Fr], nose to nose, eyeball to eyeball [informal], back to back.

.7 PREPS **opposite to,** in opposition to, against, over against; versus, vs.; **facing, across, fronting,** confronting, **in front of;** toward.

## 240. FRONT

.1 NOUNS **front, fore,** forepart, forequarter, foreside, forefront, forehand; priority, anteriority; **frontier;** foreland; foreground, proscenium; frontage; front page; frontispiece; preface, front matter, foreword; prefix; front view, front elevation; **head,** heading; **face,** façade, frontal; false front, window dressing, display; front man; bold *or* brave front, brave face; facet; facia; obverse (of a coin or medal), head (of a coin); lap.

.2 **vanguard,** van, point, **spearhead,** advance guard, **forefront,** avant-garde, outguard; scout, pioneer; precursor 66; front-runner; front, line, front line, battle line, front rank, first line, first line of battle; **outpost,** farthest outpost; **bridgehead,** beachhead, airhead, railhead.

.3 **prow,** prore, **bow, stem,** rostrum, figurehead, nose, beak; bowsprit, jib boom; forecastle, forepeak; foredeck.

.4 **face,** facies, **visage,** prosop(o)–; physiognomy, phiz *or* dial [both informal]; **countenance,** features, lineaments, favor; mug *or* mush *or* pan *or* kisser *or* map *or* puss [all slang].

.5 **forehead, brow.**

.6 **chin,** mentum, mento–, point of the chin, button [slang].

.7 VERBS be *or* stand in front, **lead, head,** head up; come to the front, take the lead, forge ahead; be the front-runner, pioneer.

.8 **confront, front,** affront, **face,** envisage; **meet, encounter,** breast, stem, brave, meet squarely, meet face to face *or* eyeball to eyeball, come face to face with, look in the face; **confront with, face with,** bring face to face with, tell one to one's face, cast *or* throw in one's teeth, present to, **put** *or* **bring before,** set *or* place before, lay before; bring up, bring forward; put it to, put it up to; **challenge,** dare, defy.

.9 **front on, face upon, give upon,** face *or* look toward, look out upon, look over, **overlook.**

.10 ADJS **front, frontal, anterior; fore, forward,** forehand; **foremost, headmost, leading,** first, chief, head, prime, primary; ante–, anti–, ep(i)– *or* eph–, fore–, fronto–, genio–, pre–, pro–, pros–.

.11 **fronting, facing,** opposing, eyeball-to-eyeball.

.12 ADVS **before, ahead,** out *or* up ahead, **in front,** in the front, in the lead, in the van, in advance, **in the forefront,** in the foreground; **to the fore,** to the front; foremost, headmost, first; before one's face *or* eyes, under one's nose.

.13 **frontward,** frontwards, **forward,** forwards, vanward, **headward,** headwards, **onward,** onwards; **facing** 239.7.

### 241. REAR

.1 NOUNS **rear, rear end, hind end,** hind part, hinder part, afterpart, rearward, **posterior, behind,** breech, stern, tail, tail end; **afterpiece,** tailpiece, heelpiece, heel; **back,** back side, reverse (of a coin or medal), tail (of a coin); back door, postern, postern door; back seat, rumble seat; hindhead, occiput, occipit(o)–.

.2 rear guard, rear, rear area.

.3 **back,** dorsum, dors(o)– *or* dorsi–, not(o)–, tergum, ridge; dorsal region, lumbar region; hindquarter; loin, lumb(o)–.

.4 **buttocks, rump,** hips, posterior, derrière, pyg(o)–; croup, crupper; podex; haunches; gluteal region; nates; **butt,** rear, rear end, backside, hind end, behind [all informal].

.5 [slang terms] **ass,** arse, **can,** cheeks, nether cheeks, stern, tail, rusty-dusty, bum, **fanny,** prat, keister, tuchis *or* tushy *or* tush.

.6 **tail,** cauda, caudation, caudal appendage, cerc(o)–, caud(o)– *or* caudi–, ur(o)–, –urus; tailpiece, brush (of a fox), fantail (of fowls); rattail, rat's-tail; dock, stub; **queue,** cue, **pigtail.**

.7 **stern,** heel; poop, counter, fantail, tail end; sternpost, rudderpost.

.8 VERBS (be behind) **bring up the rear,** come last, **follow,** come after; trail, trail behind, lag behind; fall behind, fall back, fall astern; **back up, back,** go back, go backwards, regress 295.5, retrogress; revert 146.4.

.9 ADJS **rear,** rearward, **back,** backward, retrograde, **posterior,** postern, tail; after *or* aft; **hind, hinder; hindmost,** hindermost, hindhand, posteriormost, **aftermost,** aftmost, rearmost; meta–, opisth(o)–, post–, postero–, rere–, retro–, supra–.

.10 (anatomy) posterial, dorsal, retral, tergal, lumbar, gluteal, sciatic, occipital.

.11 **tail,** caudal, caudate, caudated, tailed; taillike, caudiform, –cercal, –urous *or* –ourous.

.12 backswept, swept-back.

.13 ADVS **behind, in the rear, in back of;** in the background; behind the scenes; behind one's back; back to back; tandem.

.14 **after;** aft, abaft, baft, astern.

.15 **rearward,** rearwards, to the rear, **hindward,** hindwards, **backward,** backwards, posteriorly, retrad, tailward, tailwards.

### 242. SIDE

.1 NOUNS **side, flank, hand;** laterality, sidedness, handedness; unilaterality, bilaterality, etc., multilaterality, many-sidedness; border 235.4; bank, shore, coast; siding, planking; beam; broadside; quarter; hip, haunch; **cheek,** mel(o)–, jowl, chop; temple; profile, side-view, half-face view.

.2 **lee side, lee,** leeward; lee shore; lee tide; lee wheel, lee helm, lee anchor, lee sheet, lee tack.

.3 **windward side, windward,** windwards, weather side, weather, weatherboard; weather wheel, weather helm, weather anchor, weather sheet, weather tack, weather rail, weather bow, weather deck; weather roll; windward tide, weather-going tide, windward ebb, windward flood.

.4 VERBS **side, flank;** edge, skirt, border 235.10.

.5 **go sideways, sidle,** lateral, lateralize, **edge, veer, skew,** sidestep; go crabwise; sideslip, skid; make leeway.

.6 ADJS **side,** lateral, later(o)– *or* lateri–, pleur(o)– *or* pleuri–, ali–; flanking, skirting; next-beside; **sidelong,** sideling, **sidewise,** sideway, **sideways,** sideward, **sidewards,** glancing; leeward, lee; windward, par(a)–.

.7 **sided, flanked,** –stichous; handed; lateral, –hedral; **one-sided,** unilateral; **two-sided, bilateral,** dihedral, bifacial; **three-sided, trilateral,** trihedral, triquetrous; **four-sided, quadrilateral,** tetrahedral, etc.; **many-sided, multilateral,** polyhedral.

.8 ADVS **laterally,** laterad; **sideways,** sideway, **sidewise, sidewards,** sideward, sideling, sidling, sidelong, aside, crabwise; **edgeways,** edgeway, **edgewise; askance,** askant, asquint, glancingly; broadside, **broadside on,** on the beam; on its side, on its beamends; on the other hand; right and left.

.9 **leeward,** to leeward, alee, downwind; **windward,** to windward, weatherward, aweather, upwind.

.10 **aside,** on one side, **to one side,** to the side, on the side, sidelong; nearby, in juxtaposition 200.20,21; away.

.11 PREPS **beside, alongside, abreast,** abeam, by, on the flank of, along by, **by the side of,** along the side of.

.12 PHRS **side by side,** cheek to cheek, cheek

by cheek, cheek by jowl, shoulder to shoulder, yardarm to yardarm.

## 243. RIGHT SIDE

.1 NOUNS **right side, right, right hand,** right-hand side, off side (of a horse or vehicle), starboard; Epistle side, decanal side; recto (of a book); right field; starboard tack; right wing; right-winger, conservative, reactionary.

.2 **rightness,** dextrality; dexterity, **right-handedness;** dextroversion, dextrocularity, dextroduction; dextrorotation, dextrogyration.

.3 right-hander; righty [informal].

.4 ADJS **right, right-hand,** dextral, dexter, dextr(o)–; off, **starboard;** dextrorse; dextropedal; dextrocardial; dextrocerebral; dextrocular; **clockwise,** dextrorotary, dextrogyrate, dextrogyratory; right-wing, right-wingish, conservative, reactionary.

.5 **right-handed,** dextromanual, dexterous *or* dextrous.

.6 **ambidextrous,** ambidextral, ambidexter; dextrosinistral, sinistrodextral.

.7 ADVS **rightward,** rightwards, rightwardly, **right, to the right,** dextrally, dextrad; on the right, dexter; starboard, astarboard.

## 244. LEFT SIDE

.1 NOUNS **left side, left, left hand,** left-hand side, wrong side [informal], near *or* nigh side (of a horse or vehicle), portside, port, larboard; Gospel side, cantorial side, verso (of a book); port tack; left wing, left-winger, radical, liberal.

.2 **leftness,** sinistrality, **left-handedness;** sinistration; levoversion, levoduction; levorotation, sinistrogyration.

.3 **left-hander, southpaw** *or* lefty [both informal].

.4 ADJS **left, left-hand,** sinister, sinistral, lev(o)– *or* laev(o)–; near, nigh; **larboard, port;** sinistrorse; sinistrocerebral; sinistrocular; **counterclockwise,** levorotatory, sinistrogyrate; left-wing, left-wingish, radical, liberal.

.5 **left-handed,** sinistromanual, sinistral, southpaw [slang].

.6 ADVS **leftward,** leftwards, leftwardly, **left, to the left,** sinistrally, sinister, sinistrad; on the left; larboard, port, aport.

## 245. STRUCTURE

.1 NOUNS **structure, construction,** architecture, tectonics, architectonics, frame, make, **build,** fabric, tissue, warp and woof *or* weft, web, weave, texture, con-

texture, mold, shape, pattern, plan, fashion, arrangement, **organization,** organism, organic structure, **constitution, composition; makeup, getup** [informal]; setup; **formation,** conformation, format; making, building, creation, production, forging, fashioning, molding, fabrication, manufacture, shaping, structuring, patterning; anatomy, physique; form 246.

.2 **structure, building, edifice, construction,** construct, erection, establishment, architecture, fabric; house 191.6; tower, pile, pyramid, skyscraper; prefabrication, prefab, packaged house; superstructure.

.3 **understructure,** understruction, underbuilding, **substructure,** substruction.

.4 **frame,** framing; **framework, skeleton,** fabric, cadre, chassis, shell; lattice, latticework; sash, casement, case, casing; window case *or* frame, doorframe; picture frame.

.5 **skeleton,** skelet(o)–, anatomy, **carcass,** frame, **bones;** endoskeleton, exoskeleton; axial skeleton, appendicular skeleton.

.6 **bone,** ossicle; osse(o)– *or* ossi– *or* oste(o)–, –ost, –osteon; cartilage, chondr(o)– *or* chondri–; tendon, ligament 206.2.

.7 (science of structure) **anatomy;** morphology, geomorphology, promorphology; tectology; histology; zootomy, anthropotomy; organology, organography; myology, myography; splanchnology, splanchnography; angiology, angiography; osteology, osteography; morphologist, anatomist, histologist.

.8 VERBS **construct** 167.10, structure.

.9 ADJS **structural,** formal, morphological, edificial, tectonic, textural; anatomic(al), organic, organismal; **architectural,** architectonic; constructional; superstructural, substructural.

.10 **skeleton,** skeletal.

.11 **bone,** osteal; **bony,** osseous, ossiferous; ossicular; ossified.

.12 **bones**

| | |
|---|---|
| aitchbone | cranium |
| anklebone | cuboid |
| anvil | edgebone |
| astragalus | ethmoid bone |
| backbone | femur |
| breastbone | fibula |
| calcaneus | floating rib |
| cannon bone | frontal bone |
| carpal, carpus | funny bone |
| cheekbone | hallux |
| chine | hammer |
| clavicle | haunch bone |
| coccyx | heel bone |
| collarbone | hipbone |
| costa | humerus |

| | |
|---|---|
| hyoid bone | radius |
| ilium | rib |
| incus | sacrum |
| inferior maxillary | scaphoid |
| innominate bone | scapula |
| ischium | sesamoid bones |
| jawbone | shinbone |
| kneecap | shoulder blade |
| kneepan | skull |
| malleus | sphenoid |
| mandible | spinal column |
| mastoid | spine |
| maxilla | stapes |
| maxillary | sternum |
| metacarpal, metacarpus | stirrup |
| | talus |
| metatarsal, metatarsus | tarsal, tarsus |
| nasal bone | temporal bone |
| occipital bone | thighbone |
| parietal bone | tibia |
| patella | ulna |
| pelvis | vertebra |
| phalanx, phalanges [pl] | vertebral column |
| | vomer |
| pubis | wishbone |
| rachidial | wristbone |
| rachis | zygomatic bone |

## 246. FORM

.1 NOUNS **form, shape, figure;** figuration, **configuration;** formation, **conformation; structure** 245; **build,** make, frame; makeup, format, layout; cut, set, stamp, type, turn, cast, mold, impression, pattern, matrix, model, mode, modality; archetype, prototype 25.1–6, Platonic form *or* idea; style, fashion; aesthetic form, inner form, significant form; art form, genre; morph(o)–, –morph, –morphism *or* –morphy.

.2 **contour,** *tournure* [Fr], *galbe* [Fr]; broad lines, silhouette, profile, **outline** 235.2.

.3 **appearance** 446, lineaments, features.

.4 (human form) **figure, form,** shape, frame, anatomy, **physique,** build, body-build, person; body 376.3.

.5 **forming, shaping,** molding, modeling, fashioning; **formation,** efformation, formature, conformation, figuration; sculpture; morphogeny, morphogenesis; creation 167.3; –plasis.

.6 [gram terms] form, morph, allomorph, morpheme; morphology, morphemics.

.7 VERBS **form,** formalize, **shape, fashion,** tailor, frame, figure, efform, **lick into shape;** work, knead; set, fix; **forge,** dropforge; **mold,** model, sculpt *or* sculpture; cast, found; thermoform; stamp, mint; carve, cut, chisel, hew; roughhew, roughcast, rough out, block out, lay out, hammer *or* knock out; create 167.10.

.8 (be formed) **form,** shape, **shape up, take shape;** materialize.

.9 ADJS **formative,** formal, formational, plastic, morphotic; morphogen(et)ic; –form *or* –iform, –morphic *or* –morphous.

.10 [biol terms] plasmatic, plasmic, protoplasmic, plastic, metabolic.

.11 [gram terms] morphologic(al), morphemic.

## 247. FORMLESSNESS

.1 NOUNS **formlessness, shapelessness;** amorphousness, amorphism, amorphia; **chaos,** confusion, messiness, orderlessness; **disorder** 62; entropy; anarchy 740.2; **indeterminateness, indefiniteness,** indecisiveness, vagueness, mistiness, haziness, fuzziness, blurriness, unclearness, obscurity.

.2 unlicked cub, diamond in the rough.

.3 VERBS **deform, distort** 249.5; unform, unshape; disorder, jumble, mess up, muddle, confuse; obfuscate, obscure, fog up, blur.

.4 ADJS **formless, shapeless,** featureless, characterless, nondescript, inchoate, lumpen, blobby *or* baggy [both informal], inform; amorphous, amorphic, amorph(o)–; **chaotic, orderless,** disorderly 62.13, unordered, unorganized, confused, anarchic 740.6; kaleidoscopic; **indeterminate, indefinite,** undefined, indecisive, vague, misty, hazy, fuzzy, blurred *or* blurry, unclear, obscure.

.5 **unformed, unshaped,** unshapen, unfashioned, unlicked; uncut, unhewn.

## 248. SYMMETRY

.1 NOUNS **symmetry,** symmetricalness, **proportion,** proportionality, **balance,** equilibrium; **regularity,** uniformity 17, evenness; equality 30; finish; harmony, congruity, consistency, conformity 82, correspondence, keeping; eurythmy, eurythmics; dynamic symmetry; bilateral symmetry, trilateral symmetry, etc., multilateral symmetry; parallelism, polarity; shapeliness.

.2 symmetrization, regularization, balancing, harmonization; evening, equalization; coordination, integration.

.3 VERBS symmetrize, regularize, **balance,** harmonize; **proportion,** proportionate; even, even up, equalize; coordinate, integrate.

.4 ADJS **symmetric(al),** sym–, **balanced,** proportioned, eurythmic, harmonious; **regular,** uniform 17.5, even, equal 30.7; coequal, coordinate, equilateral; **well-balanced,** well-set, well-set-up [informal]; finished.

**.5 shapely, well-shaped, well-proportioned,** well-made, **well-formed,** well-favored; comely 900.17; trim, neat, clean, clean-cut.

## 249. DISTORTION

**.1 NOUNS distortion,** detorsion, torsion, **contortion, crookedness,** tortuosity; **asymmetry,** unsymmetry, disproportion, lopsidedness, imbalance, irregularity, **deviation; twist,** quirk, turn, screw, wring, wrench, wrest; warp, buckle; knot, gnarl; anamorphosis, anamorphism.

**.2 perversion, corruption,** misdirection, misrepresentation, misinterpretation, misconstruction, false coloring; slanting, straining, torturing; misuse 667.

**.3 deformity,** deformation, **malformation,** malconformation, monstrosity, teratology, freakishness, misproportion, misshape; **disfigurement, defacement;** mutilation, truncation; humpback, hunchback, crookback, camelback, kyphosis [med]; swayback, lordosis [med]; wryneck, torticollis [med]; clubfoot, talipes [med], flatfoot, splayfoot; knock-knee; bowlegs; valgus [med]; harelip; cleft palate.

**.4 grimace, wry face,** wry mouth, rictus, snarl; moue, mow, pout.

**.5 VERBS distort, contort,** turn awry; **twist,** turn, screw, wring, wrench, wrest; writhe; warp, buckle, crumple; knot, gnarl; **crook,** bend, spring.

**.6 pervert, garble, put a false construction upon, give a false coloring,** color, varnish, slant, strain, torture; **bias;** misrepresent, misconstrue, misinterpret, misrender, misdirect; misuse 667.4.

**.7 deform,** misshape, disproportion; **disfigure, deface;** mutilate, truncate; blemish, mar.

**.8 grimace, make a face,** make a wry face or wry mouth, pull a face, **screw up one's face,** mug [slang], mouth, make a mouth, mop, mow, mop and mow; pout.

**.9 ADJS distortive,** contortive, contortional, torsional.

**.10 distorted, contorted, warped, twisted, crooked,** plect(o)–, strepsi–, strept(o)–, stroph(o)–; **tortuous,** labyrinthine, buckled, sprung, bent, bowed; cockeyed [informal], crazy; crunched, crumpled; unsymmetric(al), asymmetric(al), as– or asym–, nonsymmetric(al); irregular, deviative, anamorphous; one-sided, lopsided; askew 219.14.

**.11 perverted, twisted, garbled,** slanted, doctored, biased, cooked; strained, tortured; misrepresented, misquoted.

**.12 deformed, malformed, misshapen,** misbegotten, misproportioned, ill-proportioned, ill-made, ill-shaped, **out of shape;** dwarfed, stumpy; bloated; **disfigured,** defaced, blemished, marred; mutilated, truncated; grotesque, monstrous; swaybacked, round-shouldered; bowlegged, bandy-legged, bandy; knock-kneed; rickety, rachitic; club-footed, talipedic; flatfooted, splayfoot(ed), pigeon-toed; pug-nosed, snub-nosed, simous.

**.13 humpbacked, hunchbacked,** bunchbacked, crookbacked, crookedbacked, camelback, humped, gibbous, kyphotic [med].

## 250. STRAIGHTNESS

**.1 NOUNS straightness,** directness, unswervingness, lineality, **linearity,** rectilinearity; verticalness 213; flatness, horizontalness 214.

**.2 straight line,** straight, right line, direct line, –trix; straight course or stretch, straightaway; **beeline;** air line; **shortcut** 203.5; great-circle course; streamline; edge, side, diagonal, secant, transversal, chord, tangent, perpendicular, normal, segment, directrix, diameter, axis, radius, vector, radius vector [all math].

**.3 straightedge, rule,** ruler; square, T square, triangle.

**.4 VERBS be straight,** have no turning; arrow; go straight 289.11.

**.5 straighten, set or put straight,** rectify; **unbend,** unkink, uncurl, unsnarl, disentangle 45.5; straighten up, stand or sit up; straighten out, extend; flatten, smooth 214.6.

**.6 ADJS straight,** orth(o)–, rect(i)–; straightlined, dead straight, straight as an edge or ruler, ruler-straight, even, right, true, straight as an arrow, arrowlike; **rectilinear,** rectilineal; **linear,** lineal, in a line; **direct, undeviating, unswerving,** unbending, undeflected; **unbent, unbowed,** unturned, uncurved, undistorted; **uninterrupted, unbroken;** streamlined; straight-side, straight-front, straight-cut; upright, vertical 213.11; flat, level, smooth, horizontal 214.7.

**.7 ADVS straight,** straightly, on the straight, unswervingly, undeviatingly, **directly** 290.24; straight to the mark; down the alley or down the pipe or in the groove or on the beam [all informal].

## 251. ANGULARITY

.1 NOUNS **angularity,** angularness, crookedness, hookedness; orthogonality, right-angledness, right-angularity, rectangularity; flection, flexure.

.2 **angle,** –gon, goni(o)–, point, bight; vertex, apex 211.2, –ace; **corner,** quoin, coin, nook; **crook, hook,** crotchet; **bend,** swerve, veer, inflection, deflection; ell, L; cant; furcation, bifurcation, fork 299.4; zigzag, zig, zag; chevron; elbow, knee, dogleg [informal]; crank.

.3 (angular measurement) goniometry; trigonometry.

.4 (instruments) goniometer, radiogoniometer; pantometer, clinometer, graphometer, astrolabe; azimuth compass, azimuth circle; theodolite, transit theodolite, transit, transit instrument, transit circle; sextant, quadrant; bevel, bevel square; protractor, bevel protractor.

.5 VERBS **angle, crook, hook, bend,** elbow; crank; angle off or away, swerve, veer, go off on a tangent; furcate, bifurcate, branch, fork 299.7; zigzag, zig, zag.

.6 ADJS **angular,** ang–, anguli– or angulo–; cornered, **crooked, hooked, bent,** akimbo; knee-shaped, geniculate, geniculated; crotched, Y-shaped, V-shaped; furcate, furcal, forked 299.10; sharp-cornered, **sharp, pointed;** zigzag, jagged, serrate, sawtooth or saw-toothed.

.7 **right-angled, rectangular,** right-angular, right-angle; **orthogonal,** orthodiagonal, orthometric; **perpendicular,** normal.

.8 **triangular, trilateral,** trigonal, oxygonal, deltoid, trigon(o)–, hastato–; wedge-shaped, cuneiform, cuneate, cuneated, sphen(o)–.

.9 **quadrangular, quadrilateral,** quadrate, quadriform; **rectangular, square,** quadr(i)– or quadru–; foursquare, orthogonal; tetragonal, tetrahedral; **oblong;** trapezoid(al), rhombic(al), rhomboid(al), rhomb(o)–; **cubic(al),** cubiform, cuboid, cube-shaped, cubed, diced, cub(o)– or cubi–; rhombohedral, trapezohedral.

.10 pentagonal, hexagonal, heptagonal, octagonal, decagonal, dodecagonal, etc.; pentahedral, hexahedral, octahedral, dodecahedral, icosahedral, etc., –hedral.

.11 multilateral, multiangular, polygonal; polyhedral, pyramidal, pyramidic(al), pyramid(o)–; prismatic, prismoid.

.12 **angles**

| | |
|---|---|
| acute angle | obtuse angle |
| oblique angle | reentering angle |
| reflex angle | solid angle |
| right angle | spherical angle |
| salient angle | straight angle |

.13 **angular geometric figures**

| | |
|---|---|
| acute-angled triangle | polygon |
| cube | polyhedron |
| cuboid | prism |
| cusp | prismoid |
| decagon | pyramid |
| dodecagon | quadrangle |
| dodecahedron | quadrant |
| equilateral triangle | quadrature |
| foursquare | quadrilateral |
| frustum of a pyramid | rectangle |
| gnomon | rhombohedron |
| heptagon | rhombus, rhomb, |
| hexagon | rhomboid |
| hexahedron | right-angled triangle, |
| hypercube | right triangle |
| icosahedron | scalene triangle |
| isosceles triangle | square |
| oblong | trapezium, trapeze |
| obtuse-angled triangle | trapezohedron |
| octagon | trapezoid |
| octahedron | tetragon |
| oxygon | tetragram |
| parallelepiped, paral- | tetrahedroid |
| lelepipedon | tetrahedron |
| parallelogram | triangle |
| pentagon | trigon |
| pentahedron | trilateral |
| Platonic body | truncated pyramid |

## 252. CURVATURE

.1 NOUNS **curvature,** curving, curvity, curvation; incurvature, incurvity, incurvation; excurvature, excurvation; decurvature, decurvation; recurvature, recurvity, recurvation; rondure; **arching, vaulting,** arcuation, concameration; aduncity, aquilinity, crookedness, hookedness; sinuosity, sinuousness, tortuosity, tortuousness; circularity 253; convolution 254; rotundity 255; convexity 256; concavity 257.

.2 **curve,** curvi–, sinus; **bow, arc; crook, hook;** parabola, hyperbola; ellipse; caustic, catacaustic, diacaustic; catenary, festoon; conchoid; lituus; tracery; circle 253.2; curl 254.2.

.3 **bend,** bending; **bow,** bowing, oxbow; **turn,** turning, sweep, meander, hairpin turn or bend, S-curve, U-turn; **flexure,** flex, **flection,** conflexure, inflection, deflection; reflection; geanticline, geosyncline; trop(o)–, –tropy, –trope.

.4 **arch, span, vault,** vaulting, concameration, camber; ogive; apse; **dome,** cupola, geodesic dome, igloo, concha; cove; arched roof, ceilinged roof; **arcade, archway,** arcature; voussoir, keystone, skewback.

.5 **crescent, semicircle,** scythe, sickle, meniscus; crescent moon, half-moon; lunula, lunule; horseshoe.

.6 VERBS **curve, turn,** sweep; **crook, hook,** loop; incurve, incurvate; recurve, decurve, bend back, retroflex; sag, swag [dial]; **bend,** flex; deflect, inflect; reflect, reflex; **bow,** embow; **arch,** vault; dome; **hump,** hunch; wind, curl 254.4,5; round 255.6.

.7 ADJS **curved,** curve, curvate, curvated, **curving,** curvy, curvaceous [informal], curvesome, curviform; curvilinear, curvilineal; wavy, undulant, billowy, billowing; sinuous, tortuous, serpentine, mazy, labyrinthine, meandering; **bent;** incurved, incurving, incurvate, incurvated; recurved, recurving, recurvate, recurvated; geosynclinal, geanticlinal; –clastic, –tropic or –trophic; cyrt(o)–, sphing(o)–.

.8 **hooked, crooked, aquiline,** aduncous; **hook-shaped,** hooklike, uncinate, unciform; hamulate, hamate, hamiform; clawlike, unguiform, down-curving; **hooknosed,** beak-nosed, parrot-nosed, aquiline-nosed, Roman-nosed, crooknosed, crookbilled; **beaked,** billed; **beak-shaped,** beak-like; bill-shaped, bill-like; rostrate, rostriform, rhamphoid.

.9 turned-up, upcurving, upsweeping, retroussé.

.10 **bowed,** embowed, bandy; bowlike, bowshaped, oxbow, Cupid's bow; **convex** 256.12, **concave** 257.16, convexoconcave; arcuate, arcuated, arcual, arciform, arclike; **arched,** vaulted; **humped,** hunched, humpy, hunchy; gibbous, gibbose; humpbacked 249.13; tox(o)– or toxi–.

.11 **crescent-shaped,** crescentlike, crescent, crescentic, crescentiform; meniscoid(al), menisciform; S-shaped, sigmoid; **semicircular,** semilunar; horn-shaped, hornlike, horned, corniform; bicorn, two-horned; sickle-shaped, sickle-like, falcate, falciform; moon-shaped, moonlike, lunar, lunate, lunular, luniform; Cynthian; selen(o)– or seleni–.

.12 lens-shaped, lenticular, lentiform.

.13 parabolic(al), saucer-shaped; elliptic(al), ellipsoid; bell-shaped, bell-like, campanular, campanulate, campaniform.

.14 pear-shaped, pearlike, pyriform, obconic(al).

.15 heart-shaped, heartlike; cordate, cardioid, cordiform.

.16 kidney-shaped, kidneylike, reniform.

.17 turnip-shaped, turniplike, napiform.

.18 shell-shaped, shell-like; conchate, conchiform.

.19 shield-shaped, shieldlike, peltate; scutate, scutiform; clypeate, clypeiform.

.20 helmet-shaped, helmetlike, galeiform; cassideous.

.21 **arches**

| | |
|---|---|
| fixed arch | rampant arch |
| flat arch | round arch |
| four-centered or | rowlock arch |
| Tudor arch | segmental arch |
| horseshoe arch | shouldered arch |
| lancet arch | three-centered or bas- |
| ogee arch | ket-handle arch |
| primitive arch | trefoil arch |

## 253. CIRCULARITY

*(simple circularity)*

.1 NOUNS **circularity, roundness,** annularity, annulation.

.2 **circle,** circus, **ring,** annulus, O; **circumference,** radius; **round,** roundel, rondelle; **cycle, circuit;** orbit 375.16; cycl(o)–, gyr(o)–; closed circle or arc; vicious circle, eternal return; magic circle, fairy ring; logical circle; wheel 322.4,18; disk, discus, saucer, disc(o)– or disci–; **loop,** looplet; noose, lasso; crown, diadem, coronet, corona; garland, chaplet, wreath; halo, glory, areola, aureole, stephano–; annular muscle, sphincter.

.3 (thing encircling) **band, belt** 231.65, **cincture,** cingulum, **girdle, girth,** girt, zone, zon(o)–, fascia, fillet; collar, collarband, neckband; necklace, bracelet, armlet; wristlet, wristband, anklet; ring, earring, nose ring, finger ring, dactylio–; hoop, quoit; zodiac, ecliptic, equator, great circle.

.4 **rim,** felly; **tire,** pneumatic tire, balloon tire, tubeless tire, safety tire, nonskid tire, bias tire, belted bias tire, radial tire, belted radial tire, white sidewall tire, winter tire, snow tire, studded tire; retreaded tire, retread.

.5 circlet, **ringlet,** roundlet, annulet, eye, **eyelet,** grommet.

.6 **oval,** ovule, ovoid; ellipse.

.7 cycloid; epicycloid, epicycle; hypocycloid; lemniscate; cardioid; Lissajous figure.

.8 **semicircle,** half circle, hemicycle; crescent 252.5; quadrant, sextant, sector.

.9 **round,** canon; rondo, rondino, rondeau, rondelet.

.10 VERBS **circle, round;** orbit; **encircle** 233.7, surround, encompass, girdle.

.11 ADJS **circular, round,** rounded, circinate, annular, annulate or annulose, ringshaped, ringlike; disklike, discoid; cyclic(al), cycloid(al); coronary, crownlike.

.12 **oval,** ovate, ovoid, oviform, egg-shaped, obovate [bot], ov(o)– *or* ovi–.

## 254. CONVOLUTION

*(complex circularity)*

.1 NOUNS **convolution,** involution, circumvolution, **winding, twisting, turning; meander, meandering;** crinkle, crinkling; circuitousness, circumlocution, circumbendibus, circumambages, ambagiousness, ambages; tortuousness, tortuosity, tortility; torsion, intorsion; sinuousness, **sinuosity,** sinuation, slinkiness; anfractuosity; snakiness; flexuousness, flexuosity; undulation, wave, waving; rivulation.

.2 **coil,** whorl, roll, **curl,** curlicue, ringlet, **spiral,** helix, volute, volution, involute, evolute, gyre, scroll; **kink, twist, twirl;** screw, corkscrew; tendril, cirrus; whirl, swirl, vortex; gyr(o)–, helic(o)–, spir(o)– *or* spiri–, spondyl(o)–, verticill–.

.3 curler, curling iron; curlpaper, papillote.

.4 VERBS convolve, **wind, twine,** twirl, **twist, turn, twist and turn, meander,** crinkle; serpentine, snake, slink, worm; screw, corkscrew; whirl, swirl; whorl; scallop; wring; intort; contort.

.5 **curl, coil;** crisp, kink, crimp.

.6 ADJS **convolutional, winding, twisting,** twisty, **turning; meandering,** meandrous, mazy, labyrinthine; **serpentine,** snaky, anfractuous; roundabout, circuitous, ambagious, circumlocutory; **sinuous,** sinuose, sinuate; **tortuous,** torsional, tortile; flexuous, flexuose; involutional, involute, involuted; rivose, rivulose; sigmoid(al); wreathy, wreathlike; ruffled, whorled.

.7 **snakelike, snaky,** snake-shaped, **serpentine,** serpentile, serpentoid, serpentiform; anguine [archaic], anguiform; eellike, eel-shaped, anguilliform; wormlike, vermiform, lumbriciform.

.8 **spiral,** spiroid, volute, voluted; helical, helicoid(al); anfractuous; screw-shaped, corkscrew, corkscrewy; verticillate, whorled, scrolled; cochlear, cochleate; turbinal, turbinate.

.9 **curly, curled; kinky,** kinked; **frizzly,** frizzy, frizzed; crispy, crisp, crisped.

.10 **wavy, undulatory,** undulative, undulant, undulating, undulate, undulated; **billowy,** billowing, surgy, rolling.

.11 ADVS **windingly, twistingly,** sinuously, tortuously, serpentinely, meanderingly, meandrously; **in and out,** round and round.

## 255. SPHERICITY, ROTUNDITY

.1 NOUNS **sphericity, rotundity, roundness,** rotundness, orbicularity, **sphericalness,** sphericality, globularity, globosity; spheroidity, spheroidicity; belly; cylindricality; convexity 256.

.2 **sphere,** spher(o)– *or* sphaer(o)–, –sphaera; **ball, orb,** orbit, **globe,** rondure; geoid; spheroid, globoid, ellipsoid, oblate spheroid, prolate spheroid; spherule, globule, globelet, orblet; glomerulus, glomerul(o)–; **pellet;** boll; bulb, bulbil, bulblet, bulb(o)–; knob, knot; gob, blob, gobbet, bolus; **balloon,** bladder, bubble.

.3 **drop,** droplet; dewdrop, raindrop, teardrop; bead, pearl.

.4 **cylinder,** cylindroid, cylindr(o)–; pillar, column; barrel, drum, cask; pipe, tube; roll, rouleau, roller, rolling pin; bole, trunk.

.5 **cone,** conoid, conelet, con(o)– *or* coni–; complex cone, cone of a complex; funnel; ice-cream cone, cornet [Brit]; pine cone; cop.

.6 VERBS **round, rotund; round out, fill out;** cone.

.7 **ball, snowball;** sphere, spherify, globe, conglobulate; bead; balloon, mushroom.

.8 ADJS **rotund, round,** rounded, rounded out, round as a ball; bellied, bellylike; convex 256.12, bulging 256.14.

.9 **spheric(al),** spheriform, spherelike, sphere-shaped; **globular, global,** globed, globous, globose, globate, globelike, globe-shaped; orbic(al), orbicular, orbiculate, orbed, orb, orby, orblike; spheroid(al), globoid, ellipsoid(al); hemispheric(al); bulbous, bulblike; ovoid, obovoid [bot].

.10 **beady,** beaded, bead-shaped, bead-like.

.11 **cylindric(al),** cylindroid(al); **columnar,** columnal, columned, columelliform; tubular, tube-shaped; barrel-shaped, drum-shaped.

.12 **conic(al),** coned, cone-shaped, conelike; conoid(al); spheroconic; funnel-shaped, funnellike, funnelled, funnelform, infundibuliform, infundibular; turbinato–.

.13 **balls**

| | |
|---|---|
| ball bearing | eight ball |
| baseball | football |
| basketball | golf ball |
| billiard ball | handball |
| bowling ball, bowl | meatball |
| cannonball | medicine ball |
| clew | mothball |
| cricket ball | pinball |
| croquet ball | Ping-Pong ball |
| cue ball | polo ball |

| | |
|---|---|
| pushball | tea ball |
| rubber ball | tennis ball |
| skittle ball | tetherball |
| snowball | volleyball |
| soccer ball | whiffle ball |
| softball | |

.14 pellets

| | |
|---|---|
| BB | pea |
| bead | pearl |
| buckshot | pebble |
| bullet | pill |
| grapeshot | shot |
| marble 878.16 | |

## 256. CONVEXITY, PROTUBERANCE

.1 NOUNS **convexity,** convexness, convexedness; excurvature, excurvation; camber; gibbousness, gibbosity; tuberousness, tuberosity; bulging, bellying.

.2 **protuberance** or protuberancy, **projection,** protrusion, extrusion; prominence, eminence, salience, boldness, bulging, bellying; gibbousness, gibbosity; excrescence or excrescency; tuberousness, tuberosity; salient; relief, high relief, *altorilievo* [Ital], low relief, bas-relief, *bassorilievo* [Ital], embossment.

.3 **bulge,** bilge, bow, convex; **bump;** thankyou-ma'am, cahot [Can]; hill 207.5, mountain 207.7; **hump,** hunch; **lump,** clump, bunch, blob [informal]; nubbin, nubble, nub; **mole,** nevus [med]; **wart,** papilloma, verruca [med]; **knob,** boss, bulla, button, bulb; stud, jog, joggle, peg, dowel; flange, lip; tab, ear, flap, loop, ring, handle 216.27; **knot,** knur, knurl, gnarl, burl, gall; **ridge,** rib, cost(o)– or costi–, chine, spine, shoulder; welt, wale; blister, bleb, vesicle [anat]; blain; bubble; condyle, condyl(o)–, style, styl(o)– or styli–, tyl(o)–; tubercle or tubercule, tubercul(o)–.

.4 **swelling,** swell, swollenness, edema; **rising, lump, bump,** pimple, papulo–; pock, furuncle, boil, carbuncle; corn; pustule; dilation, dilatation; turgidity, turgescence or turgescency, tumescence, intumescence; tumor, tumidity, tumefaction; wen, cyst, sebaceous cyst; bunion; distension 197.2.

.5 **node,** nodule, nodulus, nodulation, nodosity.

.6 **breast, bosom, bust, chest,** crop, brisket; thorax, thorac(o)– or thoraci–, stern(o)–, steth(o)–; pigeon breast; **breasts;** tits or titties or boobs or boobies or bubbies or jugs or headlights or knockers or knobs [all slang]; *nénés* [Fr slang]; bazoom [slang]; teat, tit or titty or mamma [all slang]; dug; **nipple,** papilla, pap [dial],

mammilla, *mamelon, teton* [both Fr]; mammillation, mamelonation; mammary gland, udder, bag.

.7 **nose,** nas(o)– or nasi–, rhin(o)–, olfactory organ; **snout,** rhynch(o)–, **snoot** [informal], nozzle [slang], **muzzle; proboscis,** antlia, **trunk; beak,** rostrum, rhamph(o)–, rostr(o)– or rostri–; **bill** or pecker [both slang]; nib, neb; smeller or beezer or bugle or schnozzle or schnoz or schnozzola or conk [all slang]; muffle, rhinarium; nostrils, noseholes [Brit dial], nares.

.8 (point of land) **point,** hook, spur, **cape,** tongue, bill; **promontory,** foreland, **headland,** head, mull [Scot]; naze, ness; **peninsula,** chersonese; **delta; spit,** sandspit; **reef,** coral reef; breakwater 216.4.

.9 VERBS **protrude, protuberate, project, extrude;** stick out, jut out, poke out, stand out, shoot out; **stick up,** bristle up, start up, cock up, shoot up.

.10 **bulge,** bilge, bouge [dial], **belly,** bag, balloon, **pouch,** pooch [dial]; pout; **goggle,** bug [dial], pop; **swell, dilate, distend,** billow; swell out, **belly out,** round out.

.11 **emboss, boss,** chase, raise; ridge.

.12 ADJS **convex,** convexed; excurved, excurvate, excurvated; bowed, out-bowed, arched 252.10; gibbous, gibbose; humped 252.10; rotund 255.8.

.13 **protruding, protrusive,** protrudent; **protuberant,** protuberating; **projecting, extruding,** jutting, outstanding; prominent, eminent, salient, bold; prognathous; excrescent, excrescential; protrusile, emissile.

.14 **bulging, swelling,** distended, bloated, potbellied, bellying, pouching; bagging, baggy; rounded, hillocky, hummocky, moutonnée; billowing, billowy, bosomy, ballooning, pneumatic; **bumpy,** bumped; bunchy, bunched; **bulbous,** bulbose; warty, verrucose, verrucated.

.15 **bulged, bulgy;** swollen 197.13, turgid, tumid, turgescent, tumescent, tumorous; bellied, ventricose; pouched, pooched [dial]; goggled, goggle; exophthalmic, bug-eyed [slang], popeyed [informal].

.16 **studded, knobbed, knobby,** knoblike, nubbled, nubby, nubbly, torose; **knotty, knotted; gnarled,** knurled, knurly, burled, gnarly; noded, nodal, nodiform; noduled, nodular; nodulated; tuberculous, tubercular; tuberous, tuberose.

.17 **in relief,** in bold or high relief, bold, raised, *repoussé* [Fr]; chased, bossed, embossed, bossy.

.18 **pectoral,** thoracic; pigeon-breasted; mammary, mammillary, mammiform; mammalian, mammate; papillary, papillose, papulous; breasted, bosomed, chested; teated, titted [slang], nippled.

.19 **peninsular**; deltaic, deltal.

## 257. CONCAVITY

.1 NOUNS **concavity, hollowness;** incurvature, incurvation, incurvity; depression, impression.

.2 **cavity,** concavity, concave; **hollow,** hollow shell, shell; **hole, pit, depression, dip,** sink, fold [Brit]; scoop, pocket; **basin,** trough, **bowl,** punch bowl, cup; **crater;** antrum, antr(o)–; sinus, sinu– or sino–; lacuna; alveola, alveolus, alveolation, alveol(o)–; vug [min]; follicle, crypt; armpit; socket; funnel chest or breast.

.3 **pothole, sinkhole,** pitchhole, chuckhole, **mudhole, rut** 263.1.

.4 **pit, well, shaft,** bothr(o)–; **chasm, gulf, abyss,** abysm; **excavation,** dig, diggings, workings; mine, quarry 383.6.

.5 **cave, cavern,** cove [Scot], **hole, grotto,** grot, antre, subterrane; lair 191.26; **tunnel, burrow,** warren; subway 272.13; bunker, foxhole, dugout, abri [Fr]; sewer.

.6 **indentation,** indent, indention, indenture, **dent,** dint; gouge, **furrow** 263; sunken part or place, **dimple; pit,** pock, pockmark; impression, impress; imprint, print; alveolus, alveolation; honeycomb; **notch** 262.

.7 **recess,** recession, **niche, nook,** inglenook, corner; cove, alcove; bay; pitchhole.

.8 (hollow in the side of a mountain) combe, cwm, cirque, corrie.

.9 **valley, vale, dale, dell,** dingle; **glen,** bottom, bottoms, bottom glade, intervale, strath [Scot], gill [Brit], wadi, grove; trench, trough, lunar rill; gap, pass, ravine 201.2.

.10 **excavator, digger;** sapper; **miner** 383.9; tunneler, sandhog or groundhog [both informal]; driller; steam shovel, navvy [Brit]; dredge, dredger.

.11 **excavation,** digging; mining; indentation, **engraving** 578.2.

.12 VERBS (be concave) **dish,** cup, bowl, hollow; retreat, retire; incurve.

.13 **hollow,** hollow out, concave, **dish,** cup, bowl; cave, cave in.

.14 **indent, dent,** dint, **depress,** press in, stamp, tamp, punch, punch in, impress, imprint; **pit;** pock, pockmark; dimple; **recess,** set back; set in; notch 262.4; engrave 578.10.

.15 **excavate, dig,** dig out, scoop, scoop out, **gouge,** gouge out, grub, shovel, spade,

dike, delve, scrape, scratch, scrabble; dredge; **trench,** trough, furrow, groove; **tunnel, burrow;** drive [min], sink, lower; **mine,** sap; quarry; drill, bore.

.16 ADJS **concave,** concaved, **incurved,** incurving, incurvous, –coelous; **sunk,** sunken; retreating, retiring; **hollow,** hollowed; palm-shaped; dish-shaped, dished, dishing, dishlike, bowl-shaped; bowllike, crater-shaped, craterlike, saucer-shaped; spoonlike; **cupped,** cup-shaped, scyphate, scyph-(o)– or scyphi–; funnel-shaped, infundibular, infundibuliform; funnel-chested, funnel-breasted; boat-shaped, boatlike, navicular, naviform, cymbiform, scaphoid, scaph(o)–; **cavernous,** cavelike.

.17 **indented, dented,** depressed; **dimpled; pitted;** pocked, pockmarked; honeycombed, alveolar, alveolate, faveolate; **notched** 262.5; **engraved** 578.12.

## 258. SHARPNESS

.1 NOUNS **sharpness, keenness, edge;** acuteness, acuity; **pointedness,** acumination; thorniness, prickliness, spinosity, mucronation; acridity 433.1.

.2 (sharp edge) **edge,** cutting edge, knife-edge, razor-edge, featheredge; edge tool 348.2,13; weapon 801.21–25.

.3 **point** 258.18, **tip,** cusp; acumination, mucro; **nib,** neb; needle 223.8, acu–; **drill,** borer, auger, bit; **prick, prickle;** sting, aculeus.

.4 (pointed projection) **projection,** spur, jag, **snag,** snaggle; **tooth,** fang; crag, peak, arête; spire, steeple, flèche; **cog, sprocket,** ratchet; sawtooth; harrow, rake; **comb,** pecten, cten(o)–, pectin(i)–.

.5 **tooth,** dent(o)– or denti–, odont(o)–, **fang, tusk,** tush, scrivello; denticulation, denticle, dentil, dent, dentition; snag, snaggletooth, peg; bucktooth, gagtooth or gang tooth [both dial]; pivot tooth; cuspid, bicuspid; canine tooth, canine, dogtooth, eyetooth; molar, grinder, myl-(o)–; premolar; incisor, cutter, fore tooth; wisdom tooth; milk tooth, baby tooth, deciduous tooth; permanent tooth; gold tooth; crown.

.6 **teeth,** dentition, ivories [informal]; **denture,** false teeth, set of teeth, **plate, bridgework,** dental bridge, uppers and lowers; gums, periodontal tissue, alveolar ridge, gingiv(o)–, ulo–.

.7 **thorn, bramble, brier, nettle,** burr, prickle, sticker [informal]; **spike,** spikelet, spicule, spiculum; **spine;** bristle; quill; **needle,** pine needle; **thistle,** catchweed, cleavers, goose grass, cactus; beggar's-lice, beggar's-ticks; yucca, Adam's-needle; acanth(o)–, echin(o)–.

.8 VERBS come *or* taper to a point, acuminate; prick, sting, stick, bite; be keen, have an edge, cut; bristle with.

.9 sharpen, edge, acuminate, aculeate, spiculate, taper; whet, hone, oilstone, file, grind; strop, strap; set, reset; point, cuspidate; barb, spur.

.10 ADJS sharp, oxy–, keen, edged, acute, acuto– *or* acuti–, fine, cutting, knifelike; sharp-edged, keen-edged, razor-edged, knife-edged, featheredged, sharp as broken glass; acrid 433.6; two-edged, double-edged; sharp as a razor *or* needle *or* tack, "sharp as a two-edged sword" [Bible], "sharper than a serpent's tooth" [Shakespeare]; sharpened, set.

.11 pointed, acuminate, acuate, aculeate, mucronate, acute, unbated; tapered, tapering; cusped, cuspidate; sharp-pointed; needlelike, needle-sharp, needle-pointed, needly, acicular, aculeiform; toothed, –dentate; spiked, spiky, spiculate; barbed, tined, pronged; horned, horny, cornuted, corniculate, cornified; spined, spiny, spinous, hispid, acanthoid, acanthous, "like quills upon the fretful porpentine" [Shakespeare].

.12 prickly, pricky [informal], muricate, echinate, acanaceous, aculeolate; pricking, stinging; thorny, brambly, briery, thistly; bristly.

.13 arrowlike, arrowy, arrowheaded; sagittal, sagittate, sagittiform.

.14 spearlike, hastate; lancelike, lanciform, lanceolate, lanceolar; spindle-shaped, fusiform.

.15 swordlike, gladiate, ensate, ensiform; xiph(o)– *or* xiphi–.

.16 toothlike, dentiform, dentoid, odontoid; dental; molar; bicuspid; toothed, toothy, fanged, tusked; snaggle-toothed, snaggled.

.17 star-shaped, starlike, star-pointed.

.18 points

| | |
|---|---|
| antler | dibble |
| awl | fid |
| barb | fishhook |
| barblet | fork |
| barbule | gaff |
| barbwire, barbed wire | gaffle |
| bodkin | gimlet |
| bradawl | goad |
| caltrop | harpoon |
| carpet tack | hat pin |
| cheval-de-frise, chevaux-de-frise | hook |
| | horn |
| cockspur | icepick |

| | |
|---|---|
| lance | skewer |
| lancet | spearhead |
| marlinespike | spicule |
| nail | spiculum |
| oxgoad | spike |
| pike | spine |
| pin | spit |
| pitchfork | spur |
| prong | staple |
| punch | tack |
| quill | thumbtack |
| rowel | tine, tang [Scot] |

.19 sharpeners

| | |
|---|---|
| Carborundum | oilstone |
| emery | rubstone |
| emery wheel | steel |
| file | strap, strop |
| grindstone | whetrock |
| hone | whetstone |
| novaculite | whittle |

## 259. BLUNTNESS

.1 NOUNS bluntness, dullness, unsharpness, obtuseness, obtundity; bluffness; abruptness; flatness; toothlessness, lack of bite *or* incisiveness.

.2 VERBS blunt, dull, disedge, retund, obtund, take the edge off; turn, turn the edge *or* point of; weaken, repress; draw the teeth *or* fangs; bate.

.3 ADJS blunt, dull, obtuse; bluntish, dullish; unsharp, unsharpened; unedged, edgeless; rounded, faired, smoothed; unpointed, pointless; blunted, dulled; blunt-edged, dull-edged; blunt-pointed, dull-pointed, blunt-ended; bluff, abrupt; ambly(o)–.

.4 toothless, teethless, edentate, edental, biteless.

## 260. SMOOTHNESS

.1 NOUNS smoothness, flatness, levelness, evenness, uniformity, regularity; sleekness, glossiness; slickness, slipperiness, lubricity, oiliness, greasiness, frictionlessness; silkiness, satininess, velvetiness; glabrousness, glabriety; downiness; suavity 936.5.

.2 polish, gloss, glaze, burnish, shine, luster, finish; patina.

.3 (smooth surface) smooth, plane, level, flat; tennis court, bowling alley *or* green, billiard table *or* ball; slide; glass, ice; marble, alabaster, ivory; silk, satin, velvet; mahogany.

.4 smoother, smooth; roller, lawn-roller; sleeker, slicker; polish, burnish; abrasive, abradant.

.5 VERBS smooth, flatten, plane, planish, level, even, equalize; dress, dub, dab; smooth down *or* out, lay; plaster, plaster down; harrow, drag; grade; mow, shave; lubricate, oil, grease.

.6 **press,** hot-press, **iron, mangle,** calender; roll.

.7 **polish, shine, burnish, furbish,** sleek, slick, slick down, gloss, glaze, glance, luster; **rub,** scour, **buff;** wax, varnish; finish.

.8 **grind, file, sand,** sandpaper, emery, pumice; sandblast.

.9 ADJS **smooth,** lio– or leio–, liss(o)–; smooth-textured or -surfaced, **even, level, plane, flat,** regular, uniform, **unbroken;** unrough, unroughened, unruffled, unwrinkled; glabrous, glabrate, glabrescent; downy; smooth as a billiard ball or a baby's ass; leiotrichous, lissotrichous; smooth-shaven 232.17; suave 936.18.

.10 **sleek, slick, glossy,** shiny, gleaming; silky, silken, satiny, velvety; **polished,** burnished, furbished; buffed, rubbed, finished; varnished, lacquered, shellacked, glazed, glacé [Fr]; **glassy,** smooth as glass.

.11 **slippery,** slippy, **slick,** slithery [informal], sliddery [dial], slippery as an eel; lubricious, lubric, oily, greasy, buttery, soaped; lubricated, oiled, greased.

.12 ADVS **smoothly, evenly,** regularly, uniformly; **like clockwork,** on wheels.

.13 **smoothers**

| | |
|---|---|
| buff | mangle |
| buffer | plane 348.17 |
| burnisher | planisher |
| calender | polisher |
| chamois | press |
| drag | presser |
| electric iron | roller |
| flatiron | rolling pin |
| floor polisher | sadiron |
| floor sander | sander |
| glazer | smoothing iron |
| goose | steamroller |
| grader | trouser press |
| harrow | trowel 348.16 |
| hot press | waxer |
| iron | wringer |
| ironing board | |

.14 **polishes, abrasives**

| | |
|---|---|
| aluminum oxide | pumice |
| auto polish | pumice stone |
| colcothar | quartz sand |
| corundum | rasp |
| crocus | rottenstone |
| emery | rouge |
| emery board | sandpaper |
| emery paper | scouring pad |
| ferric oxide | shoe polish |
| file | silicon carbide |
| furniture polish | silver polish |
| garnet | tripoli |
| jeweler's rouge | wax |
| nail file | |

## 261. ROUGHNESS

.1 NOUNS **roughness, unsmoothness, unevenness,** irregularity, ununiformity, nonuniformity 18, inequality, harshness, asperity; **ruggedness,** rugosity; **jaggedness,** raggedness, cragginess, scraggliness; joltiness, bumpiness; rough air, turbulence; choppiness; tooth; granulation; hispidity, bristliness, spininess; nubbiness, nubbliness.

.2 (rough surface) **rough,** broken ground; broken water, chop, lop; **corrugation,** ripple, washboard; washboard or corduroy road, corduroy; gooseflesh, goose bumps, goose pimples, horripilation; sandpaper.

.3 **bristle,** barb, barbel, striga, setule, setula, seta, seti–; **stubble.**

.4 VERBS **roughen,** rough, rough up; coarsen; granulate; gnarl, knob, stud, boss; pimple, horripilate.

.5 **ruffle,** wrinkle, corrugate, crinkle, crumple, **rumple; bristle; rub the wrong way, go against the grain,** set on edge.

.6 ADJS **rough, unsmooth,** trachy–; **uneven,** ununiform, unlevel, inequal, **broken,** irregular, textured; jolty, **bumpy,** rutty, rutted, pitted, pocky, potholed; horripilant, pimply; **corrugated,** ripply, wimpled; **choppy;** ruffled, unkempt; **shaggy,** shagged; **coarse,** rank, unrefined; unpolished; rough-grained, coarse-grained, cross-grained; grainy, granulated; rough-hewn, rough-cast; homespun, linsey-woolsey.

.7 **rugged,** ragged, harsh; rugose, rugous, wrinkled, crinkled, crumpled, corrugated; **jagged,** jaggy; **snaggy,** snagged, snaggled; scraggy, scragged, scraggly; sawtooth, sawtoothed, serrate, serrated; **craggy,** cragged; **rocky,** gravelly, stony; rockbound, ironbound.

.8 **gnarled,** gnarly; **knurled,** knurly; **knotted,** knotty, knobby, knobbly, nodose, nodular, studded, lumpy.

.9 **bristly, bristling,** bristled, hispid, hirsute, barbellate, glochidiate, setaceous, setous, setose; strigal, strigose, strigate, studded; **stubbled,** stubbly; hairy 230.24.

.10 bristlelike, setiform, aristate, setarious.

.11 ADVS **roughly,** rough, in the rough; **unsmoothly,** brokenly, **unevenly,** irregularly, raggedly, choppily, jaggedly.

.12 cross-grained, **against the grain,** the wrong way.

## 262. NOTCH

.1 NOUNS **notch, nick,** nock, **cut,** cleft, **incision, gash,** hack, blaze, scotch, **score,** kerf, crena, depression, jag; jog, joggle; **indentation** 257.6.

.2 **notching, serration,** serrulation; denticulation, dentil, dentil band, dogtooth; crenation, crenelation, crenulation; scallop; rickrack; picot edge, Vandyke edge; deckle edge; cockscomb, crest; saw, saw teeth, pri– or prion(o)–.

.3 battlement, crenel, merlon, embrasure, castellation, machicolation.

.4 VERBS notch, nick, cut, incise, gash, slash, chop, crimp, scotch, score, blaze, jag, scarify; **indent** 257.14; scallop, crenellate, crenulate, machicolate; serrate, pink, mill, knurl, tooth, picot, Vandyke.

.5 ADJS notched, nicked, incised, gashed, scotched, scored, chopped, blazed; **indented** 257.17; serrate, serrated, serrulated, serrato–; crenate, crenated, crenulate, crenellated, battlemented, embrasured; scalloped; dentate, dentated, toothed; **saw-toothed,** sawlike; lacerate, lacerated; **jagged,** jaggy; erose.

## 263. FURROW

.1 NOUNS furrow, groove, scratch, crack, cranny, chase, chink, score, cut, gash, striation, streak, stria, gouge, slit, incision; sulcus, sulcation; rut, ruck [dial], wheeltrack, well-worn groove; wrinkle 264.3; corrugation; flute, fluting, rifling; chamfer, bezel, rabbet, dado; microgroove; engraving 578.2.

.2 trench, trough, channel, ditch, dike, fosse, canal, cut, gutter, kennel [Brit]; moat; sunk fence, ha-ha; aqueduct 396.2; entrenchment 799.5; canalization; pleat, crimp, goffer.

.3 VERBS furrow, groove, score, scratch, incise, cut, carve, chisel, gash, striate, streak, gouge, slit, crack; plow; rifle; channel, trough, flute, chamfer, rabbet, dado; trench, canal, canalize, ditch, dike, gully, rut; corrugate; wrinkle 264.6; pleat, crimp, goffer; engrave 578.10.

.4 ADJS furrowed, grooved, scratched, scored, incised, cut, gashed, gouged, slit, striated; channeled, troughed, fluted, chamfered, rabbeted, dadoed; rifled; sulcate, sulcated; canaliculate, canaliculated; corrugated, corrugate; corduroy, corduroyed, rutted, rutty; wrinkled 264.8, pleated, crimped, goffered; engraved 578.12; ribbed, costate.

## 264. FOLD

.1 NOUNS fold, double, doubling, duplicature; ply; plication, plica, plicature; flec-

tion, flexure; **crease,** creasing; crimp; **tuck, gather;** ruffle, frill, ruche, ruching; flounce; lappet; lapel; dog-ear.

.2 **pleat,** plait, plat [dial]; accordion pleat, box pleat, knife pleat.

.3 **wrinkle, corrugation,** ridge, **furrow, crease,** rivel, crimp, ruck, **pucker,** cockle; **crinkle,** crankle, rimple, ripple, wimple; crumple, rumple; crow's-feet.

.4 **folding, creasing,** infolding, infoldment or enfoldment; plication, plicature; paper-folding, origami [Jap].

.5 VERBS fold, infold or enfold, **double,** ply, plicate; fold over, double over, lap over, turn over or under; **crease, crimp;** crisp; **pleat, plait, plat** [dial]; **tuck, gather;** ruffle, ruff, frill; flounce; twill, quill, flute; dog-ear; interfold.

.6 wrinkle, corrugate, shirr, ridge, furrow, crease, crimp, crimple, cockle, cocker, pucker, purse; knit, knot; ruck, ruckle; crumple, rumple; crinkle, rimple, ripple, wimple.

.7 ADJS folded, doubled; plicate, plicated; pleated, plaited; creased, crimped; tucked, gathered; flounced, ruffled; twilled, quilled, fluted; dog-eared; foldable, folding, flexible, pliable, plicatile.

.8 wrinkled, wrinkly; corrugated, corrugate; creased, rucked, furrowed 263.4, ridged; cockled, cockly; puckered, puckery; pursed, pursy; knitted, knotted; rugged, rugose, rugous; crinkled, crinkly, cranklety [dial], rimpled, rippled; crimped, crimpy; crumpled, rumpled.

## 265. OPENING

.1 NOUNS opening, aperture, hole, hollow, cavity 257.2, orifice, –trema, –pyle, –stome; slot, split, crack, check, leak; opening up, unstopping, uncorking, clearing, throwing open, laying open, broaching; passageway 657.4; inlet 302.5; outlet 303.9; gap, gape, yawn, hiatus, lacuna, gat, space, interval; chasm, gulf; cleft 201.2; fontanel; foramen, fenestra; stoma; pore, poro–; fistula; disclosure 556.

.2 gaping, yawning, oscitation, oscitancy, dehiscence, pandiculation; gape, yawn; the gapes.

.3 perforation, penetration, piercing, empiercement, puncture, goring, boring, puncturing, punching, pricking, lancing, broach, transforation, terebration; acupuncture, acupunctuation; trephining, trepanning; impalement, skewering, fixing, transfixion, transfixation; bore, borehole, drill hole; trypan(o)–, –tresia, –nyxis.

.4 (holes) armhole; bullet-hole, bunghole, keyhole, knothole, loophole, manhole, mousehole, peephole, pigeonhole, pinhole, porthole, punch-hole; placket, placket hole, tap, vent, venthole, air hole, blowhole, spiracle; eye, eyelet, eye of a needle; grommet, cringle, gasket, loop, guide; deadeye.

.5 mouth, oro– or ori–, stomat(o)–, stom(o)–, –stoma, –stomum; maw, oral cavity, gob [dial], gab [Scot]; muzzle, jaw, lips, embouchure; bazoo or kisser or mug or mush or trap or yap [all slang]; jaws, mandibles, chops, chaps, jowls, maxilla, maxill(o)– or maxilli–, geny(o)–, premaxilla.

.6 anus; asshole or bumhole or bunghole [all slang]; bung.

.7 door, doorway 302.6; entrance, entry 302.5.

.8 window, casement; porthole, port, portlight; bull's-eye, œil-de-bœuf [Fr]; casement window; bay window, bow window, bay, window bay, oriel, lancet window, rose window, dormer; picture window; louver window; grille, wicket, lattice; fanlight, fan window; skylight, lantern; transom; windowpane, window glass, pane, light.

.9 porousness, porosity; sievelikeness, cribriformity, cribrosity; screen, sieve, strainer, colander, riddle, cribble, net; honeycomb; sponge.

.10 permeability, perviousness.

.11 opener; can opener, tin opener [Brit]; corkscrew, bottle screw, bottle opener, church key [informal]; latchstring; key, clavis, cleid(o)–; latchkey; passkey, passepartout [Fr], master key, skeleton key; open sesame.

.12 VERBS open, ope, open up; lay open, throw open; fly open, spring open, swing open; tap, broach; cut open, cut, cleave, split, slit, crack, chink, fissure, crevasse, incise; rift, rive; tear open, rent, tear, rip; part, dispart, separate, divide, divaricate; spread, spread out.

.13 unclose, unshut; unfold, unwrap, unroll; unstop, unclog, unblock, clear, unfoul, free, deobstruct; unplug, uncork; unlock, unlatch, undo; unseal, unclench, unclutch; uncover, uncase, unsheathe, unveil, undrape, uncurtain; disclose 556.4, expose, reveal, bare, patefy, manifest.

.14 make an opening, find an opening, make place or space, make way, make room.

.15 breach, rupture; break open, force or pry or prize open, crack or split open, rip or tear open; break into, break through; break in, burst in, bust in [informal], stave or stove in, cave in.

.16 perforate, pierce, empierce, penetrate, puncture, punch, prick, bite, hole; tap, broach; stab, stick, pink, run through; transfix, transpierce, fix, impale, spit, skewer; gore, spear, lance, spike, needle; bore, drill, auger; ream, ream out, countersink, gouge, gouge out; trepan, trephine; punch full of holes, riddle, honeycomb.

.17 gape, gap [dial], yawn, oscitate, dehisce, hang open.

.18 ADJS open, unclosed, uncovered; unobstructed, unstopped, unclogged; clear, cleared, free; wide-open, unrestricted; disclosed 555.10; bare, exposed, unhidden 555.11, naked, bald.

.19 gaping, yawning, oscitant, slack-jawed, openmouthed; dehiscent, ringent; agape, ajar.

.20 apertured, slotted, holey; pierced, perforated, perforate; honeycombed, like Swiss cheese, riddled, criblé [Fr], shot through, peppered; windowed, fenestrated.

.21 porous, porose; sievelike, cribose, cribriform; spongy, spongelike; percolating, leachy.

.22 permeable, pervious, penetrable, openable, accessible.

.23 mouthlike, oral, orificial; mandibular, maxillary.

.24 INTERJS open up!, open sesame!, gangway!, passageway!, make way!

## 266. CLOSURE

.1 NOUNS closure, closing, shutting, shutting up, occlusion, occlus(o)–, –clisis or –cleisis; shutdown; blockade.

.2 imperviousness, impermeability, impenetrability, impassability; imperforation.

.3 obstruction, clog, block, blockade, sealing off, blockage, strangulation, choking, choking off, stoppage, stop, bar, barrier, obstacle, impediment; congestion, jam; gorge; constipation, obstipation, costiveness; infarct, infarction; embolism, embolus; bottleneck; blind alley, blank wall, dead end, cul-de-sac, impasse; cecum, blind gut 225.4.

.4 stopper, stop, stopple, stopgap; plug, cork, bung, spike, spill, spile, tap, faucet, spigot, valve, check valve, cock, sea cock, peg, pin; lid 228.5.

**.5** stopping, **wadding, stuffing,** padding, **packing,** tampon; gland; gasket.

**.6** VERBS **close, shut,** occlude; close up, shut up, contract, constrict, strangle, choke, choke off, squeeze shut, fold, fold up; **fasten,** secure; **lock,** lock up, lock out, key, padlock, latch, bolt, bar, barricade; **seal,** seal up, seal off; plumb; button, button up; snap; zipper, zip up; batten, batten down; put or slap the lid on, **cover;** contain; shut the door, slam, clap, bang.

**.7** stop, stop up; **obstruct, bar,** stay; **block,** block up; **clog,** clog up, foul; **choke,** choke up or off; **fill,** fill up; **stuff,** pack, jam; **congest,** stuff up; **plug,** plug up; stopper, stopple, **cork,** bung, spile; cover; **dam,** dam up; stanch, stench [Scot]; chink; caulk; blockade; constipate, obstipate, bind.

**.8** shut up shop, close shop, **close up** or down, shut up, **shut down,** shutter, put up the shutters; cease 144.6.

**.9** ADJS **closed, shut,** unopen, unopened, cleisto– or clisto–; unvented, unventilated; contracted, constricted, choked, choked off, squeezed shut, strangulated; blank; blind, cecal, dead; dead-end, blind-alley.

**.10** unpierced, pierceless, **unperforated,** imperforate, intact; **untrodden,** pathless, wayless, trackless.

**.11** stopped, stopped up; **obstructed,** infarcted, **blocked; plugged,** plugged up; **clogged,** clogged up; foul, fouled; **choked,** choked up; **full, stuffed,** packed, jammed; **congested,** stuffed up; constipated, obstipated, costive, bound.

**.12** close, tight, compact, fast, shut fast, **snug,** staunch, firm; **sealed;** hermetic(al), hermetically sealed; airtight, dusttight or dustproof, gastight or gasproof, lighttight or lightproof, oiltight or oilproof, raintight or rainproof, smoketight or smokeproof, stormtight or stormproof, watertight or waterproof, windtight or windproof; water-repellant or -resistant.

**.13** impervious, impenetrable, impermeable; **impassable,** unpassable; unpierceable, unperforable; **punctureproof,** nonpuncturable, holeproof.

## 267. MOTION

*(motion in general)*

**.1** NOUNS **motion,** moto–; **movement,** moving, **move,** stir, unrest, restlessness; going, running, stirring; **activity** 707; kinesis, kinetics, kinematics, –kinesia, kin–, kine–

or kino–, kinesi(o)–, kinet(o)–; dynamics; kinesiatrics, kinesipathy, kinesitherapy; **actuation,** motivation; mobilization; **velocity** 269.1,2.

**.2** course, career, set, passage, progress, trend, **advance,** forward motion, traject, trajet, **flow,** flux, flight, **stream, current,** run, rush, onrush, ongoing; drift, driftage; backward motion, **regression,** retrogression, sternway, backing; backflowing, reflowing, refluence, reflux, ebbing, subsiding; downward motion, **descent,** descending, sinking, plunging; upward motion, mounting, climbing, rising, **ascent,** ascending, soaring; oblique motion; sideward motion; radial motion, angular motion, axial motion; random motion, Brownian movement.

**.3** mobility, motivity, motive power, motility, movableness; **locomotion;** motorium.

**.4** rate, gait, pace, tread, step, stride, clip or lick [both informal]; **travel** 273, **progress,** career.

**.5** VERBS move, budge, stir; go, run, flow, stream; **progress,** advance; **back,** back up, regress, retrogress; ebb, subside, wane; **descend,** sink, plunge; **ascend,** mount, rise, climb, soar; go sideways, go round or around, circle, rotate, gyrate, spin, whirl; travel 273.17; move over, get over; shift, change, shift or change place.

**.6** set in motion, move, actuate, motivate, push, shove, nudge, **drive,** impel, propel; mobilize.

**.7** ADJS **moving, stirring, in motion;** transitional; **mobile,** motive, motile, motor; motivational, impelling, propelling, propellant, driving; traveling 273.35; **active** 707.17; moto–, phoro–, plan(o)–, zo(o)–.

**.8** flowing, fluent, passing, streaming, flying, **running, going, progressive,** rushing; drifting; **regressive,** retrogressive, back, **backward;** back-flowing, refluent, reflowing; descending, sinking, plunging, **downward,** down-trending; ascending, mounting, rising, soaring, **upward,** up-trending; sideward; **rotary,** rotatory, rotational; axial, gyrational, gyratory.

**.9** ADVS **under way,** under sail, on one's way, on the go or move or fly or run or march, **in motion, astir;** from pillar to post.

## 268. QUIESCENCE

*(being at rest; absence of motion)*

**.1** NOUNS **quiescence** or quiescency, **stillness,** silence 451, quietness, **quiet,** quietude, "lucid stillness" [T. S. Eliot]; calmness, restfulness, peacefulness, imperturbability, "wise passiveness" [Wordsworth], placidness, placidity, tranquillity, serenity, peace, composure; quietism, contemplation, satori, nirvana, ataraxy or ataraxia; rest, stato–; repose, silken repose, statuelike or marmoreal repose; sleep, slumber.

.2 **motionlessness, immobility; inactivity,** inaction; fixity, fixation 142.2,3.

.3 **standstill, stand,** stillstand; **stop, halt,** cessation 144; dead stop, dead stand, full stop; deadlock, lock, dead set; running or dying down, subsidence, waning, ebbing, wane, ebb.

.4 **inertness, dormancy; inertia,** vis inertiae; passiveness, passivity; suspense, abeyance, latency; torpor, apathy, indifference, indolence, lotus-eating, languor; **stagnation,** stagnancy, **vegetation,** stasis; deathliness, deadliness; catalepsy, catatonia; entropy.

.5 **calm, lull,** lull or calm before the storm; dead calm, flat calm, oily calm, windlessness, deathlike calm; doldrums, horse latitudes; anticyclone.

.6 **airlessness, closeness, oppressiveness,** oppression, **stuffiness.**

.7 VERBS **be still, keep quiet,** lie still; **rest, repose; remain, stay,** tarry; remain motionless, freeze [informal]; **stand, stand still,** be at a standstill; stand or stick fast, stick, stand firm, stay put [informal]; stand like a post; **not stir,** not stir a step; not breathe, hold one's breath; abide, abide one's time, mark time, tread water, coast; rest on one's oars, rest and be thankful.

.8 **quiet,** quieten, **lull, soothe,** quiesce, **calm,** calm down, tranquilize 163.7, pacify; **stop** 144.7, halt, bring to a standstill; **cease** 144.6, wane, subside, ebb, run or die down, dwindle, molder.

.9 **stagnate, vegetate,** fust [archaic]; sleep, slumber; smolder, hang fire; idle.

.10 **sit,** set [dial], **sit down, be seated,** remain seated; perch, roost.

.11 **becalm,** take the wind out of one's sails.

.12 ADJS **quiescent, quiet, still,** stilly [archaic], stillish, hushed; waning, subsiding, ebbing, dwindling, moldering; **at rest,** resting, reposing, restful, reposeful; cloistered, sequestered, sequestrated, isolated, secluded, sheltered; **calm, tranquil, peaceful,** peaceable, pacific, halcyon; **placid, smooth; unruffled, untroubled,** cool, undisturbed, unperturbed, unagitated, unmoved, unstirring; stolid, stoic, impassive;

even-tenored; calm as a mill pond; still as death, "quiet as a street at night" [Rupert Brooke].

.13 **motionless, unmoving,** unmoved, moveless, **immobile,** immotive, aplano–, ankyl(o)–; **still, fixed, stationary,** static, at a standstill; **stock-still,** dead-still; still as a statue, statuelike; still as a mouse; at anchor, riding at anchor; idle, unemployed, out of commission.

.14 **inert, inactive, static, dormant,** passive, sedentary; **latent,** unaroused, suspended, abeyant, in suspense or abeyance; sleeping, slumbering, smoldering; **stagnant,** standing, foul; **torpid, languorous, languid,** apathetic, phlegmatic, **sluggish,** logy, dopey [informal], groggy, heavy, leaden, **dull,** flat, slack, tame, **dead,** lifeless; catatonic, cataleptic.

.15 **untraveled, stay-at-home,** stick-in-the-mud [informal], home-keeping.

.16 **airless,** breathless, breezeless, windless; **close, stuffy, oppressive, stifling, suffocating;** not a breath of air, not a leaf stirring, "not wind enough to twirl the one red leaf" [Coleridge]; ill-ventilated, unventilated, unvented.

.17 **becalmed,** in a dead calm.

.18 ADVS quiescently, **quietly,** stilly, still; **calmly, tranquilly, peacefully; placidly,** smoothly, unperturbedly.

.19 **motionlessly,** movelessly, stationarily, fixedly.

.20 **inertly, inactively,** statically, dormantly, passively, latently; stagnantly; **torpidly, languorously, languidly; sluggishly,** heavily, dully, coldly, lifelessly, apathetically, phlegmatically; stoically, stolidly, impassively.

## 269. SWIFTNESS

.1 NOUNS **velocity, speed,** drom(o)–, tacho–; **rapidity,** celerity, **swiftness,** fastness, **quickness,** snappiness [informal], **speediness;** haste, hurry, flurry, rush, precipitation; dispatch, expedition, promptness, promptitude, instantaneousness; flight, flit; lightning speed; fast or swift rate, smart or rattling or spanking or lively or snappy pace, round pace; air speed, ground speed, speed over the bottom; miles per hour, knots; rpm 322.3.

.2 **speed of sound, sonic speed,** Mach, Mach number, Mach one, Mach two, etc.; subsonic speed; supersonic or ultrasonic or hypersonic or transsonic speed; sound barrier 278.40; escape velocity.

.3 **run, sprint; dash, rush,** plunge, headlong

rush or plunge, race, scurry, scamper, scud, scuttle, **spurt**, burst, **burst of speed**; canter, **gallop**, lope; high lope, hand gallop, full gallop; dead run; **trot**, dogtrot, jog trot; open throttle, flat-out speed [Brit], wide-open speed, heavy right foot, maximum speed; forced draft, flank speed [both naut].

.4 acceleration, **quickening**; pickup, getaway; step-up, speedup; thrust, drive, impetus.

.5 speeder, scorcher or hell-driver [both informal], flier, goer, stepper; hummer or hustler or sizzler [all informal]; **speed demon** or maniac or merchant [informal]; **racer, runner**; horse racer, turfman, jockey; Jehu.

.6 (comparisons) lightning, greased lightning [informal], thunderbolt, flash, streak of lightning, streak, blue streak [informal], bat out of hell [slang], light, electricity, thought, wind, shot, cannonball, rocket, arrow, dart, quicksilver, mercury, express train, jet plane, torrent, eagle, swallow, antelope, courser, gazelle, greyhound, hare, blue darter, striped snake, scared rabbit.

.7 speedometer, accelerometer; cyclometer; tachometer; Mach meter; log, log line, patent log, taffrail log, harpoon log, ground log; wind gauge, anemometer.

.8 VERBS speed, **go fast**, clip [informal], spank or cut along [informal], **tear along, bowl along**, thunder along, storm along, breeze or **breeze along** [both informal], tear up the track or road [informal], eat up the track or road [informal], scorch or sizzle [both informal]; **rip, zip, whiz,** whisk, sweep, brush, nip, **tear**, skim; **fly,** zing [informal], flit, fleet, wing one's way, fly low [informal], outstrip the wind; **highball** [informal], ball the jack [slang], **barrel** [informal], pour it on [informal], boom, **zoom**; make knots, foot; break the sound barrier.

.9 rush, tear, dash, dart, shoot, hurtle, bolt, fling, **scamper, scurry**, skedaddle [informal], **scoot**, scour, scud, scuttle, scramble, **race**, career; **hasten**, haste, make haste, **hurry**, hie, post; **step on it** [informal], step on the gas [informal], hump or hump it [both slang], stir one's stumps [slang]; march in quick or double-quick time.

.10 run, sprint, trip, spring, **bound**, leap; hotfoot or hightail or make tracks [all informal], **step lively** [informal], step or step along [both informal], carry the mail [in-

formal], hop or hop along [both informal], get [slang], git [dial]; gallop, lope, canter; trot, fox-trot.

.11 **go like the wind**, go like a shot or flash, go like lightning or a streak of lightning, go like greased lightning [informal], **go like a bat out of hell** [slang], run like a scared rabbit [informal], run like mad [informal], go hell-bent for election [informal].

.12 **make time**, make good time, **cover ground**, get over the ground, **make strides** or **rapid strides**, make the best of one's way.

.13 go at full blast [informal], go all out [informal], run wide open, go full speed ahead, go at full tilt or steam, go flat out [Brit], let her out [informal], **open her up** [informal].

.14 **accelerate, speed up, step up** [informal], **hurry up, quicken**; step on it [slang]; **hasten** 709.4; get a move on [informal], crack on, put on, put on steam, pour on the coal, put on more speed, open the throttle; quicken one's pace; pick up speed, gain ground; give it the gas or step on its tail or give it the gun [all slang]; race (a motor), rev [informal].

.15 [naut terms] put on sail, crack or pack on sail, crowd sail, press her.

.16 **spurt**, make a spurt or dash, **dash ahead, dart ahead, shoot ahead**, rush ahead, put on or make a burst of speed.

.17 **overtake, outstrip, overhaul**, catch up, **catch up with**, come up with or to, gain on or upon, pass, lap; outpace, outrun, outsail; leave behind, leave standing or looking or flatfooted.

.18 keep up with, keep pace with, run neck and neck.

.19 ADJS fast, swift, speedy, rapid, oxy-, tachy–; **quick**, double-quick, express, **fleet, hasty, expeditious**, hustling, snappy [informal], dashing, flying, galloping, running, –dromous, spanking [informal]; **agile, nimble**, lively, nimble-footed, light-footed, light-legged, light of heel; winged; eagle-winged; mercurial; quick as lightning, quick as thought, swift as an arrow, "swifter than arrow from the Tartar's bow" [Shakespeare]; **breakneck**, reckless, headlong, precipitate; quick as a wink, quick on the trigger [informal], hair-trigger [informal]; **prompt** 131.9.

.20 supersonic, transsonic, ultrasonic, hypersonic, faster than sound; **high-speed**, high-velocity, high-geared.

.21 ADVS swiftly, rapidly, quickly, snappily

[informal], **speedily**, with speed, **fast, quick**, apace, amain, on eagle's wings, *ventre à terre* [Fr]; at a great rate, at a good clip [informal], with rapid strides, with giant strides, *à pas de geant* [Fr], in seven-league boots, **by leaps and bounds**, trippingly; **lickety-split** or lickety-cut [both slang]; hell-bent or hell-bent for election or hell for leather [all slang]; **posthaste, post, hastily**, expeditiously, promptly, with great or all haste, whip and spur, **hand over hand** or fist; double-quick, in double time, in double-quick time, on the double or on the double-quick [both informal]; in high gear, in high; under press of sail, under press of sail and steam, under forced draft, at flank speed [all naut].

.22 **like a shot, like a flash**, like a streak, like a blue streak [informal], like a streak of lightning, like lightning, like greased lightning [informal], **like a bat out of hell** [slang], like a scared rabbit [informal], **like a house afire** [informal]; **like sixty** [informal], **like mad** or crazy or fury [all informal], like sin [informal]; **to beat the band** or the Dutch or the deuce or the devil [all informal].

.23 **in short order, in no time**, instantaneously, immediately if not sooner, in less than no time, in nothing flat [informal]; in a jiff or jiffy [both informal], before you can say 'Jack Robinson', **in a flash**, in a twink, **in a twinkling**, "in the twinkling of an eye" [Bible], *tout de suite* [Fr], pronto [informal].

.24 **at full speed**, with all speed, at full throttle, **at the top of one's bent**, for all one is worth [informal], as fast as one's legs will carry one, as fast as one can lay feet to the ground; **at full blast**, at full drive or pelt; under full steam, in full sail; all out [slang], flat out [Brit], **wide open; full speed ahead**.

## 270. SLOWNESS

.1 NOUNS **slowness, leisureliness**, pokiness, slackness, creeping; **sluggishness, sloth**, laziness, idleness, indolence, sluggardy, languor, inertia, inertness, lentitude or lentor [both archaic]; deliberateness, deliberation, circumspection, tentativeness, cautiousness, reluctance, foot-dragging [informal]; drawl.

.2 **slow motion, leisurely gait**, snail's or tortoise's pace; **creep, crawl; walk**, footpace, dragging or lumbering pace, trudge, waddle, saunter, stroll; slouch, shuffle, plod,

shamble; limp, claudication, hobble; dogtrot, jog trot; jog, rack; mincing steps; slow march, dead or funeral march, andante.

.3 **dawdling, lingering, loitering, tarrying**, dalliance, **dallying**, dillydallying, shilly-shallying, lollygagging, dilatoriness, procrastination 132.5, lag, **lagging**, goofing off [slang].

.4 **slowing, retardation**, retardment, **slackening**, flagging, slowing down; **slowdown**, slowup, **letup, letdown, slack-up**, slack-off, ease-off, ease-up; **deceleration**, negative or minus acceleration; **delay** 132.2, **detention, setback, holdup** [informal], check, arrest, obstruction; lag, drag.

.5 **slowpoke** [informal], plodder, slow goer, **slow-foot**, slowbelly, **lingerer, loiterer, dawdler**, dawdle, **laggard**, procrastinator, foot-dragger, stick-in-the-mud [informal], drone, slug, sluggard, lie-abed, sleepyhead, goof-off [slang], goldbrick [slang]; tortoise, snail.

.6 VERBS **go slow** or slowly, go at a snail's pace, get no place fast [informal]; **drag**, drag out; **creep, crawl**; laze, idle; go dead slow; **inch, inch along**; worm, worm along; **poke, poke along**; shuffle along, stagger along, totter along, toddle along; drag along, drag one's feet, walk, traipse or mosey [both informal]; saunter, stroll, amble, waddle, toddle [informal]; jogtrot, dogtrot; limp, hobble, claudicate.

.7 **plod, plug** [informal], peg, **trudge**, tramp, stump, lumber; **plod along, plug along** [informal], schlep [slang]; rub on, jog on, chug on.

.8 **dawdle, linger, loiter, tarry, delay, dally, dillydally**, shilly-shally, lollygag, waste time, **take one's time**, take one's own sweet time; goof off or around [slang]; lag, drag, trail; flag, falter, halt.

.9 **slow, slow down** or up, **let down** or up, **ease off** or up, **slack off** or up, **slacken**, relax, moderate, lose speed or momentum; **decelerate, retard, delay** 132.8, **detain**, impede, obstruct, arrest, stay, **check**, curb, **hold up, hold back**, keep back, set back, hold in check; draw rein, rein in; throttle down, take one's foot off the gas; brake, **put on the brakes**, put on the drag; reef, take in sail; backwater, backpedal; lose ground; clip the wings.

.10 ADJS **slow**, brady–, **leisurely**, slack, moderate, gentle, **easy**, deliberate, unhurried, relaxed, gradual, circumspect, tentative, cautious, reluctant, foot-dragging [informal]; **creeping, crawling; poking, poky**, slow-poky [informal]; tottering, staggering, toddling, trudging, **lumbering,** ambling, waddling, shuffling, **sauntering,** strolling; **sluggish,** languid, languorous, lazy, slothful, indolent, idle; **slow-going, slow-moving,** slow-creeping, slow-crawling, slow-running, slow-sailing; **slow-footed,** slow-foot, slow-legged, slow-gaited, slow-paced, slow-stepped, easy-paced, slow-winged; snail-paced, snail-like, tortoiselike, turtlelike, "creeping like snail" [Shakespeare]; limping, hobbling, hobbled, halting, claudicant; faltering, flagging; slow as slow, slow as molasses, slow as death, slower than the seven-year itch [informal].

.11 **dawdling, lingering, loitering, tarrying, dallying, dillydallying,** shilly-shallying, lollygagging, procrastinatory or procrastinative, dilatory, delaying 132.17, **lagging,** dragging.

.12 **retarded,** slowed down, **delayed, detained,** checked, **arrested,** impeded, set back, backward, behind; late, **tardy** 132.16.

.13 ADVS **slowly, slow, leisurely,** unhurriedly, relaxedly, easily, moderately, gently; creepingly, crawlingly; pokingly, pokily; **sluggishly,** languidly, languorously, lazily, indolently, idly, deliberately, with deliberation, circumspectly, tentatively, cautiously, reluctantly; **lingeringly,** loiteringly, tarryingly, dilatorily; limpingly, haltingly, falteringly; **in slow motion,** at a funeral pace, with faltering or halting steps; at a snail's or turtle's pace, "in haste like a snail" [John Heywood]; in slow tempo, in march time; with agonizing slowness; in low gear; under easy sail.

.14 **gradually,** little by little 29.6.

## 271. TRANSFERENCE

*(removal from one place to another)*

.1 NOUNS **transference, transfer; transmission,** transmittal, transmittance, –phoresis; transposition, transposal, transplacement, mutual transfer, interchange, metathesis; translocation, **transplantation,** translation; migration, transmigration; import, importation, export, exportation; deportation, extradition, expulsion, **transit,** transition, **passage; communication,** spread, spreading, dissemination, diffusion, contagion; metastasis; transmigration of souls, metempsychosis; passing over; osmosis, diapedesis; transduction, conduction, convection; transfusion, per-

fusion; transfer of property or right 817; delivery 818.1; travel 273.

.2 **removal, movement,** moving, relocation, shift, removement, remotion, amotion; **displacement,** delocalization.

.3 **transportation, conveyance, transport,** carrying, bearing, packing, toting [dial], lugging [informal]; **carriage,** carry, **hauling,** haulage, portage, porterage, waft, waftage; **cartage, truckage,** drayage, wagonage; ferriage, lighterage; telpherage; **freightage,** freight, expressage, railway express; airfreight, air express, airlift; **shipment,** shipping, transshipment; asportation.

.4 transferability, conveyability; transmissibility, transmittability; movability, removability; **portability,** transportability; communicability, impartability.

.5 **carrier, conveyer,** –pher, –phor(e), –phorus, –phorum; transporter, hauler, carter, wagoner, drayman, shipper, trucker, common carrier, truck driver; **bearer, porter,** redcap, skycap; coolie; litter-bearer, stretcher-bearer; caddie; shield-bearer, gun bearer; water carrier or bearer, water boy, bheesty [India]; the Water Bearer, Aquarius; letter carrier 561.5; busboy; cupbearer, Ganymede, Hebe; expressman, express; freighter; stevedore, cargo handler; carrier pigeon, homing pigeon.

.6 **beast of burden; pack** or **draft animal,** pack horse or mule, sumpter, sumpter horse or mule; **horse** 414.10–19, ass 414.20, mule; ox; camel, ship of the desert, dromedary, llama; reindeer; elephant; sledge dog, husky, malamute, Siberian husky.

.7 **freight,** freightage; **shipment, consignment,** goods [Brit]; **cargo,** payload; lading, load, pack; **baggage, luggage,** impedimenta.

.8 [geol terms] **deposit,** sediment; drift, silt, loess, moraine, scree, sinter; alluvium, alluvion, diluvium; detritus, debris.

.9 VERBS **transfer, transmit, transpose,** translocate, transplace, metathesize, switch; **transplant, translate; pass,** pass over, **hand over,** turn over, carry over, make over, consign, assign; **deliver** 818.13; pass on, pass the buck [informal], hand forward, hand on, relay; **import, export;** deport, extradite, expel; communicate, diffuse, disseminate, spread, impart; metastasize; transfuse, perfuse, transfer property or right 817.3.

.10 **remove, move, relocate, shift,** send, shunt; displace, delocalize, dislodge; **take away,** cart away, carry off or away; manhandle; set *or* lay *or* put aside, put *or* set to one side, side.

.11 **transport, convey,** freight, conduct, **take; carry, bear,** pack, tote [dial], lug [informal], manhandle; lift, waft, whisk, wing, fly.

.12 **haul, cart,** dray, truck, bus, van, wagon, coach, wheelbarrow; sled, sledge; ship, boat, barge, lighter, ferry; raft, float.

.13 (convey through a channel) **channel,** put through channels; **pipe,** tube, pipeline, flume, **siphon, funnel,** tap.

.14 **send,** send off *or* away, send forth; **dispatch, transmit,** remit, consign, forward; expedite; **ship,** freight, airfreight, embark, **express,** air-express; **post, mail,** airmail, drop a letter; export.

.15 **fetch, bring,** go get, go and get, go to get, **go after,** go fetch, **go for,** call for, pick up; **get,** obtain, procure, secure; **bring back, retrieve;** chase after, run after, shag, fetch and carry.

.16 **ladle, dip, scoop; bail,** bucket; **dish,** dish out *or* up; cup; **shovel,** spade, fork; spoon; **pour,** decant.

.17 ADJS **transferable, conveyable; transmittable,** transmissible, transmissive, consignable; **movable,** removable; **portable,** portative; **transportable,** transportative, transportive; **conductive,** conductional; **transposable,** interchangeable; **communicable,** contagious, impartable; transfusable; metastatic(al), metathetic(al); mailable, expressable; assignable 817.5.

.18 ADVS by transfer, from hand to hand, from door to door; by freight, by express, by rail, by trolley, by bus, by steamer, by airplane, by mail, by special delivery; trans–.

.19 **on the way,** along the way, on the road *or* high road, **en route, in transit,** *in transitu* [L], on the wing, as one goes; in passing, *en passant* [Fr]; in mid-progress.

## 272. VEHICLE

*(means of conveyance)*

.1 NOUNS **vehicle, conveyance,** carrier, means of carrying *or* transporting, medium of transportation, carriage; watercraft 277.1–9, aircraft 280; –mobile.

.2 **wagon,** waggon [Brit], wain; haywagon, milkwagon; dray, van, caravan; covered wagon, prairie schooner, Conestoga wagon.

.3 **cart,** two-wheeler; oxcart, horsecart, ponycart, dogcart; dumpcart, coup-cart [Scot]; **handcart** 272.28; jinrikisha, ricksha.

.4 **carriage,** four-wheeler, *voiture* [Fr], gharry [India]; **chaise,** shay [dial], "one hoss shay" [O. W. Holmes, Sr.].

.5 **rig, equipage,** turnout [informal], coach-and-four; team, pair, span; tandem, random; spike, spike team, unicorn; three-in-hand, four-in-hand, etc.; three-up, four-up, etc.

.6 **baby carriage,** baby buggy [informal], perambulator, pram [Brit]; gocart; **stroller,** walker.

.7 **wheel chair,** Bath chair.

.8 **cycle** 272.29, wheel [informal]; **bicycle, bike** [informal]; **tricycle, trike** [informal]; **motorcycle,** motocycle, motorbike [informal], iron [slang], road-bike [informal], pig [slang], chopper [informal], trail bike; minibike; pedicab.

.9 **automobile** 272.24, **car, auto,** motorcar, motocar, autocar, **machine,** motor, motor vehicle, motorized vehicle, *voiture* [Fr]; bus *or* buggy *or* wheels *or* heap *or* boat *or* crate *or* tub [all slang]; jalopy [informal], wreck [informal].

.10 **police car, patrol car; prowl car,** squad car, cruiser; **police van,** patrol wagon; wagon *or* paddy wagon *or* Black Maria [all informal]; carryall.

.11 **truck,** lorry [Brit], *camion* [Fr]; **trailer truck,** truck trailer, tractor trailer, semitrailer, semi [informal].

.12 (public vehicles) **bus,** omnibus, chartered bus, autobus, motorbus, motor coach, jitney [informal]; double-decker [informal]; **cab, taxicab, taxi,** hack [informal]; rental car; hired car *or* limousine; stage, **stagecoach,** *diligence* [Fr]; mail *or* post coach.

.13 **train,** railroad train; choo-choo *or* choo-choo train [both informal]; passenger train, Amtrak; local, way train, milk train, accommodation train; shuttle train, shuttle; express train, express; lightning express, flier, cannonball express [informal]; local express; special, limited; parliamentary train *or* parliamentary [Brit]; freight train, goods train [Brit], freight, freighter, rattler [slang]; baggage train, luggage train; electric train, electric [informal]; interurban; cable railroad; funicular; cog railroad *or* railway, rack-and-pinion railroad; subway, *métro* [Fr], tube, underground [Brit]; elevated, el [informal]; monorail; streamliner; rolling stock.

.14 **railway car,** car; passenger car, coach, carriage [Brit]; chair car, day coach; sleeping car, sleeper; Pullman, Pullman car; drawing-room car, palace car, parlor car; drawing room, roomette; dining car *or* compartment, diner; smoking car *or* compartment, smoker; freight car, waggon [Brit], goods waggon [Brit]; boxcar, box waggon [Brit], covered waggon [Brit]; flatcar, flat, truck [Brit]; gondola car, gondola, open waggon [Brit]; baggage car, luggage van [Brit], van [Brit]; mail car, mail van [Brit]; refrigerator car, reefer [slang]; tank car, tank; stockcar; coal car; tender; caboose; dinghy; way car, local.

.15 **streetcar, trolley** *or* trolley car, **tram** *or* tramcar [both Brit]; electric car, electric [informal]; trolley bus, trackless trolley; horsecar, horse box [Brit]; cable car, grip car.

.16 **handcar** [RR], go-devil; push car, trolley, truck car, rubble car.

.17 **tractor** 272.27, traction engine; Caterpillar tractor, Caterpillar, Cat [informal], tracked vehicle; bulldozer, dozer [informal], calfdozer.

.18 **trailer,** trail car; house trailer, mobile home; truck trailer, **semitrailer,** highway trailer; camp(ing) trailer, caravan [Brit]; **camper,** camping bus.

.19 **sled** 272.31, **sleigh,** *traîneau* [Fr]; snowmobile, Sno-Cat, weasel, Skimobile; runner, blade.

.20 **skates,** ice skates, hockey skates, figure skates; roller skates, skateboard, bob skates; **skis, snowshoes.**

.21 **hovercraft,** hovercar, air-cushion vehicle, ACV, cushioncraft, ground-effect machine, GEM, captured-air vehicle, CAV, captured-air bubble, CAB.

.22 ADJS **vehicular,** transportational; automotive, auto–, locomotive.

.23 **carriages**

| | |
|---|---|
| araba | curricle |
| barouche | dearborn |
| berlin | desobligeant |
| break | dogcart |
| britska | *dormeuse* [Fr] |
| brougham | drag |
| buckboard | dray |
| buggy | droshky |
| bullock cart | ekka |
| cabriolet | fiacre |
| calash | fly |
| *calèche* [Fr] | four-in-hand coach |
| Cape cart | gig |
| cariole | glass coach |
| carryall | growler |
| cart | hack |
| charabanc | hackery |
| chariot | hackney, hackney |
| chariotee | coach |
| *charrette* [Fr] | hansom, hansom cab |
| clarence | jaunting *or* jaunty car |
| coach | jigger |
| Concord buggy | jinrikisha |
| coupé | kibitka |
| kittereen | sulky |
| landau | surrey |
| limber | tallyho, tallyho coach |
| mail phaeton | tandem |
| outside jaunting car | tilbury |
| oxcart | tonga |
| phaeton | trap |
| post chaise | troika |
| road cart | trolley |
| rockaway | tumbrel |
| runabout | *vettura* [Ital] |
| shandrydan | victoria |
| sidecar | vis-à-vis |
| sociable, sociable | voiturette |
| coach | wagonette |
| spring wagon | whiskey |
| stanhope | Whitechapel cart |

.24 **automobiles**

| | |
|---|---|
| air cushion car | hot rod |
| ambulance | hovercar |
| armored car | jeep |
| autobolide | landau |
| beach buggy | landaulet |
| beach wagon | land-rover |
| berlin | limousine |
| berlin-landaulet | locomobile |
| blitzbuggy | midget racer |
| brougham | phaeton |
| cabriolet | race car |
| camper | racer |
| carryall | racing car |
| clubmobile | rail |
| coach | roadster |
| combat car | rocket car |
| command car | runabout |
| compact car | saloon [Brit] |
| convertible | scout car |
| convertible coupe | sedan |
| convertible sedan | sedan limousine |
| coupe | shooting brake [Brit] |
| coupelet | sports car |
| crash wagon | staff car |
| double fueler | station wagon |
| dragster | steamer |
| dune buggy | stock car |
| electric brougham | swamp buggy |
| electromobile | torpedo |
| fastback | tourer [Brit] |
| fire engine | touring car |
| fueler | touring coupe |
| funny car | tow car |
| gocart | tractor |
| golf cart | two-seater [Brit] |
| hardtop | wrecker |
| hearse | |

.25 **auto parts**

| | |
|---|---|
| accelerator | choke |
| alternator | clutch |
| ammeter | connecting rod |
| automatic choke | convertible top |
| backup light | cowl |
| bearings | crank |
| bonnet [Brit] | crankcase |
| boot [Brit] | crankshaft |
| brake | cutout |
| bucket seat | cylinder |
| bumper | cylinder head |
| camshaft | dashboard, dash |
| carburetor | differential |
| chassis | directional signal |

disk brakes
distributor
emergency light
exhaust, exhaust pipe
fan
fender
flywheel
gear
gearbox
gearshift
generator
headlight
headrest
hood
horn
ignition
intake, intake mani-
  fold
manifold
muffler
oil gauge
parking light
PCV valve
piston
power brakes
power steering

radiator
radius rod
rear-view mirror
rumble seat
running board
seat belt
seat cover
seat cushion
shock absorber
side mirror
spark plug
speedometer
springs
starter
steering wheel
taillight
tail pipe
top
torsion bar
transmission
universal joint, univer-
  sal
valve
windscreen [Brit]
windshield

**.26 trucks**

auto carrier [Brit]
autotruck
bloodmobile
bookmobile
camper
camping bus
carryall
cart
delivery truck
dolly
dray
duck, DUKW
dump truck
fork *or* forklift truck
freighter
garbage truck

hand truck
motor truck
moving van
panel truck
pickup
railroad truck
refrigerator truck
sedan delivery truck
six-by-six
stake truck
tongue truck
tractor, tractor truck
transfer
van
wagon truck
warehouse truck

**.27 tractors**

amphibian, amphibian
  tractor, amtrac [in-
  formal]
bulldozer
calfdozer
Caterpillar, Caterpil-
  lar tractor
crawler, crawler trac-
  tor
creeper, creeper trac-
  tor
duck, DUKW

farm tractor
go-devil
grader
halftrack
lawn-tractor
LVT (landing vehicle
  tracked)
Rome plow
scraper
tank
tracklayer

**.28 handcarts**

barrow
garden cart
handbarrow
laundry cart
lawn cart
push car

pushcart
serving cart
shopping cart
teacart
wheelbarrow

**.29 cycles**

bicycle
bicycle-built-for-two
folding bicycle
hydrocycle
minibike

monocycle
motorbike
motorcycle
motor scooter
push bicycle

quadricycle
safety bicycle
scooter
sidewalk bike
tandem

tandem bicycle
tricycle
unicycle
velocipede

**.30 litters**

brancard
*cacolet* [Fr]
camel litter
dandy
dolly
doolie
gocart
handbarrow
horse litter

jampan
kajawah [India]
lectica
norimon
palanquin
polki
sedan, sedan chair
stretcher
tonjon

**.31 sleds**

autosled
belly-bumper
bobsled, bobsleigh
cariole
coaster
cutter
dogsled
double-ripper, dou-
  ble-runner
drag

dray
jumper
kick-sled
luge
pung
scoot
skid
sledge
toboggan
troika

## 273. TRAVEL

**.1 NOUNS travel,** traveling, going, journeying, moving, **movement, motion, locomotion, transit, progress, passage,** course, traject, trajet, crossing, commutation; world
travel, globe-trotting [informal]; **tourism,**
touristry.

**.2 travels,** journeys, **journeyings, wanderings,**
voyagings, peregrinations, peripatetics;
odyssey.

**.3 wandering, roving, roaming, rambling,
gadding,** traipsing [dial], wayfaring, flitting, straying, drifting, gallivanting, peregrination, peregrinism, pererration, discursion, errantry, divagation; roam, rove,
ramble; **itinerancy,** itineracy; **nomadism,**
nomadization, gypsydom; vagabonding,
vagabondism, vagabondage, vagabondia;
**vagrancy,** hoboism, waltzing Matilda
[Austral]; bumming [slang]; the open
road; wanderyear, *Wanderjahr* [Ger];
**wanderlust;** "afoot and lighthearted"
[Whitman].

**.4 migration, transmigration,** passage, trek;
run (of fish), flight (of birds and insects);
swarm, swarming (of bees); **immigration,**
in-migration; **emigration,** out-migration,
expatriation; remigration; intermigration.

**.5 journey, trip,** *jornada* [Sp], peregrination,
sally, **trek;** progress, course, run; **tour,**
grand tour; round trip, circuit, turn; **expedition,** campaign; safari, hunting expedition, hunting trip, stalk, shoot; **pilgrimage,** hajj; **excursion, jaunt, junket, outing,**

pleasure trip; sight-seeing trip, rubber-neck tour [slang]; package tour; **voyage** 275.6.

.6 **riding, driving; motoring,** automobiling; busing; motorcycling, bicycling, cycling, pedaling, biking [informal]; **horseback riding,** equitation; horsemanship, ma-nège.

.7 **ride, drive;** spin *or* whirl [both informal]; joyride [informal]; Sunday drive; airing; lift [informal], pickup [slang].

.8 **gliding, sliding,** slipping, slithering, coast-ing, sweeping, flowing, sailing; **skating, skiing, tobogganing, sledding;** glide, slide, slither, sweep, skim, flow.

.9 **creeping, crawling,** going on all fours; sneaking, stealing, slinking, sidling, gum-shoeing *or* pussyfooting [both informal], padding, prowling, nightwalking; worm-ing, snaking; tiptoeing, tiptoe, tippytoe; creep, crawl, scramble, scrabble; all fours; herpet(o)–.

.10 **walking,** ambulation, perambulation, am-bling, pedestrianism, shank's mare, going on foot *or* afoot, footing *or* hoofing, footing it; footwork, legwork [informal]; strolling, sauntering; **tramping, marching, hiking,** backpacking, footslogging, trudg-ing, treading; lumbering, waddling; tod-dling, staggering, tottering; **hitchhiking** *or* hitching [both informal], thumbing *or* thumbing a ride [both informal]; jaywalk-ing.

.11 **nightwalking,** noctambulation, noctam-bulism; night-wandering, noctivagation; **sleepwalking,** somnambulation, somnam-bulism, somnambul–; sleepwalk.

.12 **walk,** ramble, amble, **hike, march, tramp,** trudge, traipse [dial], schlep [slang], mush; **stroll,** saunter; parade; **promenade;** jaunt, airing; **constitutional** [informal], stretch; turn; peripatetic journey *or* exer-cise, peripateticism; walking tour *or* ex-cursion; forced march; –grade.

.13 **step, pace, stride;** footstep, footfall, tread; hoofbeat, clop; hop, jump; skip, hippety-hop [informal].

.14 **gait, pace, walk, step, stride, tread;** saun-ter, stroll, strolling gait; shuffle, shamble, hobble, limp, hitch, waddle; totter, stag-ger, lurch; toddle, paddle; slouch, droop, drag; mince, mincing steps, scuttle, prance, flounce, stalk, strut, swagger; slink, slither, sidle; jog; swing, roll; amble, single-foot, rack, piaffer; trot, gallop 269.3; lock step; velocity 269.1,2; slowness 270.

.15 **march;** quick *or* quickstep march, quick-

step, quick time; double march, double-quick, double time; slow march, slow time; half step; goose step.

.16 **leg, limb, shank,** hind leg, foreleg; podite, pod(e)–; stems *or* trotters *or* hind legs *or* underpinnings [all informal]; pins *or* gams *or* stumps [all slang]; gamb, jamb [her]; bowlegs, baker's legs, scissor-legs; bayonet legs; shin, cnemis; ankle, tarsus, tars(o)–; hock, gambrel; calf; knee; thigh, mer(o)–; popliteal space, ham, drumstick; gigot.

.17 VERBS **travel, go, gang** [Scot], **move, pass,** fare, wayfare, fare forth, fetch, flit, hie, sashay [informal], cover ground; **progress** 294.2; move on *or* along, go along; wend, **wend one's way;** betake oneself, direct one's course, bend one's steps *or* course; course, run, flow, stream; roll, roll on; commute.

.18 (go at a given speed) **go, go at,** reach, **make, do,** hit [informal], clip off [infor-mal].

.19 **traverse, travel over** *or* through, pass through, **go** *or* **pass over, cover,** measure, transit, track, range, range over *or* through, course, do, perambulate, perer-rate, peregrinate, overpass, go over the ground; patrol, reconnoiter, scout; sweep, go *or* make one's rounds, scour, scour the country; ply, voyage 275.13.

.20 **journey,** make *or* take *or* go *or* go on a journey, **take** *or* **make a trip,** fare, **way-fare, trek, jaunt,** peregrinate; **tour;** hit the trail [informal], take the road, go on the road; **cruise, voyage** 275.13; go abroad, go to foreign places *or* shores, range the world, globe-trot [informal]; pilgrimage, pilgrim, go on *or* make a pilgrimage; cam-paign, go overseas, go on an expedition, go on safari; go on a sight-seeing trip, sight-see, rubberneck [informal].

.21 **migrate, transmigrate,** trek; flit, take wing; run (of fish), swarm (of bees); **emi-grate,** out-migrate, expatriate; **immigrate,** in-migrate; remigrate; intermigrate.

.22 **wander, roam, rove, range,** nomadize, **gad,** gad about, wayfare, flit, traipse [dial], gallivant, knock around *or* about [informal], bat around *or* about [slang], mooch [slang], prowl, **drift, stray,** strag-gle, **meander, ramble,** stroll, saunter, jaunt, peregrinate, pererrate, divagate, go *or* run about, go the rounds; **tramp,** hobo, bum *or* go on the bum [both slang], vagabond, vagabondize, take to the road, "travel the open road" [Whit-man], beat one's way; **hit the road** *or* trail [informal], walk the tracks *or* count ties [both informal].

.23 **go for an outing** *or* **airing,** take the air, get some air; go for a walk 273.28; go for a ride 273.32.

.24 **go to, repair to,** resort to, hie to, hie oneself to, arise and go to, direct one's course to, turn one's tracks to, make one's way to, bend one's steps to, betake oneself to, **visit;** make the scene [slang].

.25 **creep, crawl,** scramble, scrabble, grovel, **go on hands and knees,** go on all fours; worm, worm along, worm one's way, snake; inch, inch along; **sneak, steal,** steal along; pussyfoot *or* gumshoe [both informal], slink, sidle, pad, prowl, nightwalk; **tiptoe,** tippytoe, go on tiptoe.

.26 **walk,** ambulate, peripateticate, pedestrianize, traipse [dial]; **step, tread, pace, stride,** pad; foot, foot it; leg, leg it; hoof it, ankle, go on the heel and toe, ride shank's mare *or* pony, ride the shoeleather *or* hobnail express, stump it [slang]; peg *or* jog *or* shuffle on *or* along; perambulate; circumambulate; jaywalk.

.27 (ways of walking) **stroll,** saunter; shuffle, scuff, scuffle, straggle, shamble; stride, straddle; **trudge, plod,** peg, traipse [dial], clump, stump, slog, footslog, drag, **lumber, barge;** stamp, stomp [dial]; swing, roll, lunge; hobble, halt, limp, hitch, lurch; totter, stagger; toddle, paddle; waddle, wobble, wamble, wiggle; slouch; slink, slither, sidle; stalk; **strut, swagger;** mince, sashay [informal], scuttle, prance, tittup, flounce, trip, skip, foot; hop, jump, hippety-hop [informal]; jog, jolt; bundle, bowl along; **amble,** pace; singlefoot, rack; piaffe, piaffer.

.28 **go for a walk, take a walk, take one's constitutional** [informal], take a stretch, stretch the legs; **promenade, parade,** perambulate.

.29 **march,** mush, footslog, **tramp, hike,** backpack; file, defile, file off; **parade,** go on parade; goose-step, do the goose step; do the lock step.

.30 **hitchhike** *or* **hitch** *or* hitch rides [all informal], beat one's way, **thumb** *or* **thumb one's way** [both informal], **catch a ride;** hitch *or* hook *or* bum *or* cadge *or* thumb a ride [informal].

.31 **nightwalk,** noctambulate; **sleepwalk,** somnambulate, walk in one's sleep.

.32 **ride, go for a ride** *or* **drive;** go for a spin [informal], take *or* go for a Sunday drive; **drive, chauffeur; motor,** taxi; bus; bike *or* cycle *or* wheel *or* pedal [all informal];

motorcycle, bicycle; go by rail, entrain; joyride *or* take a joyride [both informal]; catch *or* make a train [informal].

.33 **go on horseback;** ride bareback; mount, take horse; hack; ride hard, clap spurs to one's horse; trot, amble, pace, canter, gallop, tittup, lope; prance, frisk, curvet, piaffe, caracole.

.34 **glide, coast, skim,** sweep, flow; **sail, fly,** flit; **slide,** slip, skid, sideslip, slither, glissade; skate, ice-skate, roller-skate, skateboard; ski; toboggan, sled, sleigh; bellywhop [dial].

.35 ADJS **traveling, going, moving,** trekking, passing; **progressing** 294.5; **itinerant,** itinerary, circuit-riding; **journeying, wayfaring,** strolling; **peripatetic;** ambulant, ambulatory; ambulative; perambulating, perambulatory; peregrine, peregrinative, pilgrimlike; locomotive; **walking, pedestrian, touring,** on tour, globe-trotting [informal], globe-girdling, mundivagant [archaic]; touristic(al), touristy [informal]; expeditionary.

.36 **wandering, roving, roaming,** ranging, **rambling, meandering,** strolling, **straying,** straggling, shifting, flitting, landloping, errant, divagatory, discursive, circumforaneous; **gadding,** traipsing [dial], gallivanting; **nomad,** nomadic, floating, drifting, gypsyish *or* gypsy-like; **transient,** transitory, fugitive; **vagrant,** vagabond; **footloose,** footloose and fancy-free; **migratory,** migrational, transmigratory.

.37 **nightwalking,** noctambulant, noctambulous; night-wandering, noctivagant; **sleepwalking,** somnambulant, somnambular.

.38 **creeping, crawling, on hands and knees, on all fours;** reptant, repent, reptile, reptatorial; **on tiptoe,** on tippytoe, atiptoe, tiptoeing, tiptoe, tippytoe.

.39 **traveled,** well-traveled, cosmopolitan.

.40 **wayworn,** way-weary, road-weary, legweary, **travel-worn,** travel-weary, travel-tired; travel-sated, travel-jaded; travel-soiled, travel-stained, dusty.

.41 ADVS **on the move** *or* **go,** en route, in transit, on the wing *or* fly; on the run, on the jump [informal], on the road, on the tramp *or* march; on the gad [informal], on the bum [informal].

.42 **on foot, afoot,** by foot, footback *or* on footback [both dial]; on the heel and toe, on shank's mare, on shank's pony.

.43 **on horseback,** horseback, by horse, mounted.

## 274. TRAVELER

.1 NOUNS traveler, goer, viator, comers and goers; wayfarer, journeyer, trekker; tourist, tourer, tripper [Brit], visiting fireman; excursionist, sightseer, rubberneck or rubbernecker [both informal]; voyager, *voyageur* [Fr], cruiser, sailor, mariner 276; globe-trotter [informal], globe-girdler, world-traveler, cosmopolite; jet set, jetsetter; pilgrim, palmer, hajji; passenger, fare; commuter, straphanger [informal]; transient; passerby; adventurer, alpinist, climber, mountaineer; explorer, fortyniner, pioneer, pathfinder, voortrekker, trailblazer, trailbreaker; camper; astronaut 282.8.

.2 wanderer, rover, roamer, rambler, stroller, straggler, mover; gad, gadabout [informal], runabout, go-about [dial]; itinerant, peripatetic, rolling stone, peregrine, peregrinator, bird of passage, visitant; drifter or floater [both informal]; Wandering Jew, Ahasuerus, Ancient Mariner [Coleridge], Argonaut, Flying Dutchman, Oisin, Ossian, Gulliver [Swift], Ulysses, Odysseus [Homer]; wandering scholar, Goliard, *vaganti* [L]; strolling player, wandering minstrel, troubadour.

.3 vagabond, vagrant, vag [slang]; bum or bummer [both slang], loafer, wastrel, losel [archaic], *lazzarone* [Ital]; tramp, turnpiker, piker, knight of the road, hobo or bo [both slang], rounder [dial], stiff or bindlestiff [both slang]; landloper, sundowner or swagman or swagsman [all Austral informal]; beggar 774.8; waif, homeless waif, dogie, stray, waifs and strays; ragamuffin, tatterdemalion; gamin, gamine, urchin, street urchin, Arab, street Arab, mudlark, guttersnipe [informal]; beachcomber, loafer, idler; ski bum, beach bum, surf bum, tennis bum; ragman, ragpicker.

.4 nomad, Bedouin, Arab; gypsy, Bohemian, Romany, *zingaro* [Ital], *Zigeuner* [Ger], *tzigane* [Fr].

.5 migrant, migrator, trekker; immigrant, inmigrant; migrant or migratory worker, wetback [informal]; emigrant, out-migrant, *émigré* [Fr]; expatriate; evacuee, *évacué* [Fr]; displaced person, DP, stateless person, exile.

.6 pedestrian, walker, walkist, –bates; foot traveler, foot passenger, hoofer [slang], footbacker [dial], ambulator, peripatetic; hiker, backpacker, trailsman, tramper; marcher, footslogger, foot soldier, infan-tryman, paddlefoot [slang]; hitchhiker [informal]; jaywalker.

.7 nightwalker, noctambulist, noctambule, sleepwalker, somnambulist, somnambulator, somnambule.

.8 rider, equestrian, horseman, horseback rider, horsebacker, caballero, cavalier, knight, chevalier; horse soldier, cavalryman, mounted policeman; horsewoman, equestrienne; cowboy, cowgirl, puncher or cowpuncher [both informal], *vaquero*, *gaucho* [both Sp]; broncobuster [slang], buckaroo; postilion, postboy; roughrider; jockey; steeplechaser; circus rider, trick rider.

.9 driver, reinsman, whip, Jehu, skinner [slang]; coachman, coachy [informal], *cocher* [Fr], *cochero* [Sp], *voiturier* [Fr], *vetturino* [Ital], gharry-wallah [India]; stage coachman; charioteer; harness racer; cabdriver, cabman, cabby [informal], hackman, hack, hacky [both informal], jarvey [Brit slang]; wagoner, wagonman, drayman, truckman; carter, cartman, carman; teamster; muleteer, mule skinner [slang]; bullwhacker; elephant driver, mahout; cameleer.

.10 driver, motorist, automobilist; chauffeur; taxidriver, cabdriver, cabby [informal], hackman, hack [informal], hacky [informal], hackdriver; jitney driver; truck driver, teamster, truckman, trucker; bus driver, busman; speeder 269.5, road hog [informal], Sunday driver, joyrider [informal]; hit-and-run driver; backseat driver.

.11 cyclist, cycler; bicyclist, bicycler; motorcyclist, motorcycler.

.12 engineer, engineman, engine driver [Brit]; hogger or hoghead [both slang]; Casey Jones; motorman; gripman.

.13 trainman, railroad man, railroader; conductor, guard [Brit]; brakeman, brakie [slang]; fireman, footplate man [Brit], stoker; smoke agent or bakehead [both slang]; switchman; yardman; yardmaster; trainmaster, dispatcher; stationmaster; lineman; baggage man, baggagesmasher [slang]; porter, redcap; trainboy; butcher [slang].

## 275. WATER TRAVEL

.1 NOUNS water travel, travel by water, marine or ocean or sea travel, navigation, navigating, seafaring, sailing, steaming, passage-making, voyaging, cruising, coasting, gunkholing [informal]; boating, yachting, motorboating, canoeing, rowing, sculling; circumnavigation, periplus; navigability.

**.2** (methods) celestial navigation, astronavigation; radio navigation, radio beacon; coastal or coastwise navigation; dead reckoning; point-to-point navigation; pilotage; sonar, radar, sofar, loran, consolan, shoran, plane or traverse or spherical or parallel or middle or latitude or Mercator or great-circle or rhumbline or composite sailing; fix, line of position; sextant, chronometer, tables.

**.3 seamanship,** shipmanship; seamanliness, seamanlikeness; weather eye; sea legs.

**.4 pilotship,** pilotry, pilotage, **helmsmanship;** steerage; proper piloting.

**.5** embarkation 301.3; disembarkation 300.2.

**.6 voyage,** ocean or sea trip, **cruise,** sail; course, **run, passage; crossing;** shakedown cruise; leg.

**.7 wake,** track; wash, backwash.

**.8** (submarines) **surfacing,** breaking water; **submergence, dive;** stationary dive, running dive, crash dive.

**.9 way, progress; headway,** steerageway, sternway, leeway, driftway.

**.10 seaway, waterway,** fairway, road, channel, ocean or sea lane, ship route, steamer track or lane; approaches.

**.11** aquatics, **swimming, bathing,** natation, balneation, nect(o)–; **swim, bathe;** crawl, Australian crawl, breaststroke, butterfly, sidestroke, dog paddle, backstroke; treading water; floating; diving 320.3; wading; fin; flipper, flapper; fishtail; waterskiing, aquaplaning, surfboarding; surfing.

**.12 swimmer, bather,** natator, merman; bathing girl, mermaid; bathing beauty; frogman; diver 320.4; –nect.

**.13** VERBS **navigate, sail, cruise,** steam, run, **seafare, voyage,** ply, go on shipboard, go by ship, go on or take a voyage, "go down to the sea in ships" [Bible]; go to sea, sail the sea, sail the ocean blue; **boat, yacht,** motorboat, canoe, row, scull; steamboat; bear or carry sail; cross, traverse, make a passage or run; sail round, circumnavigate; coast.

**.14 pilot,** helm, coxswain, **steer,** guide, be at the helm or tiller, direct, manage, handle, run, operate, **conn** or cond, be at or have the conn; **navigate,** shape or chart a course.

**.15 anchor,** come to anchor, lay anchor, **cast anchor,** let go the anchor, drop the hook; carry out the anchor; kedge, kedge off; **dock, tie up; moor,** pick up the mooring;

run out a warp or rope; lash, lash and tie; foul the anchor; disembark 300.8.

**.16 ride at anchor,** ride, lie, rest; ride easy; ride hawse full; lie athwart; set an anchor watch.

**.17 lay** or **lie to,** lay or lie by; lie near or close to the wind, head to wind or windward, be under the sea; lie ahull; lie off, lie off the land; lay or lie up.

**.18 weigh anchor,** up-anchor, bring the anchor home, break out the anchor, cat the anchor, break ground, loose for sea; **unmoor,** drop the mooring, cast off or loose or away.

**.19 get under way,** put or have way upon, **put** or **push** or **shove off;** hoist the blue Peter; **put to sea,** put out to sea, go to sea, head for blue water, go off soundings; **sail,** sail away; embark 301.16.

**.20 set sail,** hoist sail, unfurl or spread sail, heave out a sail, **make sail,** trim sail; square away, square the yards; **crowd** or **clap** or **crack** or **pack on sail,** put on (more) sail; clap on, crack on, pack on; give her beans [slang].

**.21 make way,** gather way, **make headway,** make sternway; make knots, foot; **go full speed ahead,** go full speed astern; go or run or steam at flank speed.

**.22 run, run** or **sail before the wind,** run or sail with the wind, run or sail down the wind, make a spinnaker run, sail off the wind, sail free, sail with the wind aft, sail with the wind abaft the beam; tack down wind; run or sail with the wind quartering.

**.23 bring off the wind, pay off,** bear off or away, put the helm to leeward, bear or head to leeward, pay off the head.

**.24 sail against the wind,** sail on or by the wind, sail to windward, bear or head to windward; **bring in** or **into the wind,** bring by or on the wind, haul the wind or one's wind; uphelm, put the helm up; haul, haul off, haul up; **haul to, bring to, heave to;** sail in or into the wind's eye or the teeth of the wind; sail to the windward of, weather.

**.25 sail near the wind,** sail close to the wind, lie near or close to the wind, sail full and by, hold a close wind, **sail close-hauled,** close-haul; work or go or beat or eat to windward, **beat, ply;** luff, luff up, sail closer to the wind; sail too close to the wind, sail fine, touch the wind, pinch.

**.26 gain to windward of,** eat or claw to windward of, eat the wind out of, have the wind of, be to windward of.

.27 **chart** or **plot** or **lay out a course;** shape a course, lay or lie a course.

.28 take or follow a course, **keep** or **hold the course** or **a course,** hold on the course or a course, stand on or upon a course, stand on a straight course, maintain or keep the heading, keep her steady, keep pointed.

.29 **drift off course, yaw,** yaw off, pay off, bear off, drift, sag; sag or bear or ride or drive to leeward, make leeway, drive, fetch away; be set by the current, drift with the current, fall down.

.30 **change course,** change the heading, bear off or away, bear to starboard or port; sheer, swerve; **tack,** cast, break, yaw, slew, shift, turn; **cant,** cant round or across; **beat, ply;** veer, wear, **wear ship; jibe** or gybe [both Brit], jibe all standing, make a North River jibe; **put about,** come or go or bring or fetch about, beat about, cast or throw about; bring or swing or heave or haul round; **about ship,** turn or put back, turn on her heel, wind; swing the stern; box off; back and fill; stand off and on; double or round a point; miss stays.

.31 put the rudder hard left or right, put the rudder or helm hard over, put the rudder amidships, ease the rudder or helm, give her more or less rudder; starboard, port, larboard.

.32 **veer** or **wear short,** bring by the lee, **broach to,** lie beam on to the seas.

.33 (come to a stop) **fetch up,** haul up, fetch up all standing.

.34 **backwater,** back, reverse, go astern; **go full speed astern;** make sternway.

.35 **sail for, put away for, make for** or toward, make at, **run for,** stand for, head or steer toward, lay for, **lay a course** or one's **course for,** bear up for; bear up to, **bear down on** or **upon,** run or bear in with, **close with;** make, reach, fetch; heave or go alongside; lay or go aboard; lay or lie in; **put in** or into, put into port, approach anchorage.

.36 **sail away from,** head or steer away from, run from, **stand from,** lay away or off from; **stand off,** bear off, put off, shove off, haul off; stand off and on.

.37 **clear the land,** bear off the land, lay or settle the land, make or get sea room.

.38 **make land,** reach land; close with the land, stand in for the land; sight land; make a landfall.

.39 **coast,** sail coast-wise, stay in soundings, range the coast, skirt the shore, lie along the shore, **hug the shore** or **land** or **coast.**

.40 **weather the storm,** weather, ride, **ride out,** outride, ride or ride out a storm; make heavy or bad weather.

.41 **sail into,** run down, run in or into, **ram; come** or **run foul** or **afoul of, collide,** fall aboard; nose or head into, run prow or end or head on, run head and head; run broadside on.

.42 **shipwreck,** wreck, pile up [informal], cast away; **go** or **run aground,** ground, take the ground, beach, strand, run on the rocks; ground hard and fast.

.43 **careen, list, heel,** tip, cant, heave or lay down, lie along; be on her beam ends.

.44 **capsize, upset,** overset, **overturn,** turn over, turn turtle, upset the boat, keel, keel over or up; pitchpole, somersault; **sink, founder,** be lost, go down, go to the bottom, go to Davy Jones's locker; scuttle.

.45 **go overboard,** go by the board, go over the board or side.

.46 **maneuver,** execute a maneuver; heave in together, keep in formation, maintain position, **keep station,** keep pointed, steam in line, steam in line of bearing; convoy.

.47 (submarines) **surface,** break water; **submerge, dive,** go below; rig for diving; flood the tanks, flood negative.

.48 (activities aboard ship) lay, lay aloft, lay forward, etc.; traverse a yard, brace a yard fore and aft; heave, haul; kedge; warp; boom; heave round, heave short, heave apeak; log, heave or stream the log; haul down, board; spar down; ratline down, clap on ratlines; batten down the hatches; unlash, cut or cast loose; clear hawse.

.49 **trim ship,** trim, trim up; trim by the head or stern, put in proper fore-and-aft trim, give greater draft fore and aft, **put on an even keel; ballast,** shift ballast, wing out ballast; break out ballast, break bulk, shoot ballast; **clear the decks,** clear for action.

.50 **reduce sail,** shorten or take in sail, hand a sail, **reef,** reef one's sails; double-reef; lower sail, dowse sail; run under bare poles; snug down; **furl,** put on a harbor furl.

.51 **take bearings,** cast a traverse; correct distance and maintain the bearings; run down the latitude, **take a sight,** shoot the sun, bring down the sun; **box the compass; take soundings** 209.9.

.52 **signal,** make a signal, speak, hail and

speak; dress ship; unfurl or hoist a banner, unfurl an ensign, break out a flag; hoist the blue Peter; show one's colors, exchange colors; salute, dip the ensign.

.53 row, paddle, ply the oar, pull, scull, punt; give way, row away; catch or cut a crab or lobster [informal]; feather, feather an oar; sky an oar [informal]; row dry [Brit informal]; pace, shoot; ship oars.

.54 float, ride, drift; sail, scud, run, shoot; skim, foot; ghost, glide, slip; ride the sea, plow the deep, walk the waters.

.55 pitch, toss, tumble, toss and tumble, pitch and toss, plunge, hobbyhorse, pound, rear, rock, roll, reel, swing, sway, lurch, yaw, heave, scend, flounder, welter, wallow; make heavy weather.

.56 swim, bathe, go in swimming or bathing; tread water; float, float on one's back, do the deadman's float; wade, go in wading; skinny-dip; dive 320.6.

.57 ADJS nautical, marine, maritime, naval, navigational; seafaring, seagoing, oceangoing, water-borne; seamanly, seamanlike, salty [informal]; pelagic, oceanic 397.8.

.58 aquatic, water-dwelling, water-living, water-growing, water-loving; swimming, balneal, natant, natatory, natatorial; shore, seashore; tidal, estuarine, littoral, grallatorial; deep-sea 209.14.

.59 navigable, boatable.

.60 floating, afloat, awash; water-borne.

.61 adrift, afloat, unmoored, untied, loose, unanchored, aweigh; cast-off, started.

.62 ADVS on board, on shipboard, on board ship, aboard, all aboard, afloat; on deck, topside; aloft; in sail; before the mast; athwart the hawse, athwarthawse.

.63 under way, making way, with steerageway, with way on; at sea, on the high seas, off soundings, in blue water; under sail or canvas, with sails spread; under press of sail or canvas or steam; under steam or power; under bare poles; on or off the heading or course; in soundings, homeward bound.

.64 before the wind, with the wind, down the wind, running free; off the wind, with the wind aft, with the wind abaft the beam, wing and wing, under the wind, under the lee; on a reach, on a beam or broad reach, with wind abeam.

.65 against the wind, on the wind, in or into the wind, up the wind, by the wind, head to wind; in or into the wind's eye, in the teeth of the wind.

.66 near the wind, close to the wind, closehauled, on a beat, full and by.

.67 coastward, landward, to landward; coastwise, coastways.

.68 leeward, to leeward, alee, downwind; windward, to windward, weatherward, aweather, upwind.

.69 aft, abaft, baft, astern; fore and aft.

.70 alongside, board and board, yardarm to yardarm.

.71 at anchor, riding at anchor; lying to, hove to; lying ahull.

.72 afoul, foul, in collision; head and head, head or end or prow on; broadside on.

.73 aground, on the rocks; hard and fast.

.74 overboard, over the board or side, by the board; aft the fantail.

.75 INTERJS (orders, calls) ahoy!, ahoy there!, ship ahoy!; avast!, hold fast!; belay!, belay that or there!; aye, aye!, aye, aye, sir!; heave!, heave ho!, yo-heave-ho!, heave and awash!; lend a hand!; one hand for yourself and one for the ship!; stand by!, stand by to weigh anchor!, stand by the main sheet!, etc.; anchors aweigh!; aloft!, aloft there!; ready about!; turn out!, show a leg!, rise and shine!; man overboard!; aboard!, all aboard!, take ship!, up oars!, give way!, row away!; way enough!, ship oars!

.76 (orders to the helm) up helm!, down helm!, port!, larboard!, starboard!, helm aport!, helm astarboard!, helm alee!, helm aweather!, hard aport!, hard alee!, hard astarboard!, hard aweather!, hard over!, right!, left!, right or left rudder!, right or left standard rudder!, right or left five (ten etc.) degrees rudder!, right or left half rudder!, right or left full rudder!, right or left handsomely!, give her more rudder!, shift the rudder!, meet her!, ease the helm or rudder!, rudder amidships!, nothing to the right or left!, no nearer!, how is your rudder?, how does she head?, keep her so!, steady!, steady so!, steady as you go!, about ship!

.77 (orders to the engine room) starboard or port engine!, all engines!, ahead!, back!, astern!, starboard or port engine ahead!, full speed ahead! or astern!, slow ahead!, slow astern!, all engines ahead!, ahead one-third!, ahead two-thirds!, ahead standard!, ahead full!, back one-third!, back two-thirds!, back full!

.78 (submarine orders) rig for diving!, ventilate inboard!, shift the control!, stations for diving!, secure the engines!, secure the main induction!, close the conning tower hatch!, ahead both motors!, flood the tank!, blow the tank!, flood main bal-

last!, close main vents!, flood 2000
pounds in after trim!

## 276. MARINER

.1 NOUNS **mariner, seaman, sailor,** sailor-
man, **navigator, seafarer,** seafaring man,
**bluejacket,** sea or water dog [informal],
shipman, jack, jacky, jack afloat, jack-tar,
**tar, salt** [informal], hearty, lobscouser
[slang], *matelot* [Fr], windsailor, windjammer; limey or limejuicer [both slang],
lascar [India]; common or ordinary seaman, OD; able or able-bodied seaman,
AB; deep-sea man, saltwater or bluewater
or deepwater sailor; fresh-water sailor;
fair-weather sailor; whaler, fisherman,
lobsterman; viking, sea rover, buccaneer,
privateer, pirate; Jason, Argonaut, Ancient Mariner, Flying Dutchman; Neptune, Poseidon, Varuna, Dylan.

.2 (novice) **lubber, landlubber;** polliwog.

.3 (veteran) **old salt** or old sea dog or shellback or barnacle-back [all informal]; **master mariner.**

.4 **navy man,** man-of-war's man, **bluejacket;**
**gob** or swabbie or swabber [all slang]; **marine, leatherneck** [informal], gyrene, devil
dog [both slang], Royal Marine, jolly
[Brit informal]; horse marine; boot [in-
formal]; **midshipman,** midshipmite,
middy [informal]; cadet, naval cadet;
coastguardsman, Naval Reservist, Seabee,
frogman.

.5 **boatman,** boatsman, boat-handler, **boater,** waterman; **oarsman,** oar, rower,
sculler, punter; galley slave; **yachtsman,**
yachter; **ferryman,** ferrier; **bargeman,**
barger, bargee [Brit], bargemaster;
lighterman, wherryman; **gondolier,** *gon-
doliere* [Ital].

.6 hand, **deckhand,** deckie [Brit], roustabout [informal]; stoker, fireman, bakehead [slang]; black gang; wiper, oiler,
boilerman; cabin boy; yeoman, ship's
writer; purser; ship's carpenter, chips [in-
formal]; ship's cooper, bungs or Jimmy
Bungs [both informal]; ship's tailor, snip
or snips [both informal]; steward, stewardess, commissary steward, mess steward, hospital steward; commissary clerk;
mail orderly; navigator; radio operator,
sparks [informal]; landing signalman;
gunner, gun loader, torpedoman; after-
guard; complement; watch.

.7 (ship's officers) **captain,** shipmaster, **master, skipper** [informal], **commander,** the
Old Man [informal], *patron* [Fr]; navigator, navigating officer, sailing master;

deck officer, officer of the deck, OD;
watch officer, officer of the watch; **mate,**
first or chief mate, second mate, third
mate, boatswain's mate; **boatswain,** bos'n,
pipes [informal]; quartermaster; ser-
geant-at-arms; chief engineer, engine-
room officer; naval officer 749.20.

.8 **steersman, helmsman,** wheelman, wheels-
man, boatsteerer; **coxswain, cox** [infor-
mal]; **pilot,** conner, sailing master; harbor
pilot, docking pilot.

.9 **longshoreman,** wharf hand, dockhand,
docker, dock-walloper [slang]; **stevedore,**
loader; **roustabout** [informal], lumper.

## 277. SHIP, BOAT

.1 NOUNS **ship** 277.22, **boat** 277.21, **vessel,
craft,** bottom, bark, argosy, hull, hulk,
keel, watercraft; tub or bucket or hooker
[all slang], packet; leviathan; "that packet
of assorted miseries which we call a ship"
[Kipling], "the ship, a fragment detached
from the earth" [Joseph Conrad].

.2 **steamer, steamboat, steamship;** motor
ship.

.3 **sailboat, sailing vessel** 277.23, sailing boat,
sailing yacht, sailing cruiser, sailing ship,
tall or taunt ship, sail, sailer, **windjammer**
[informal], windship, windboat; **galley**
277.25.

.4 **motorboat, powerboat,** speedboat;
**launch,** motor launch, steam launch,
naphtha launch; **cruiser,** power cruiser,
**cabin cruiser,** sedan cruiser, outboard
cruiser.

.5 **liner, ocean liner,** ocean greyhound [in-
formal], passenger steamer, floating hotel
or palace, luxury liner.

.6 **warship,** war vessel, naval vessel 277.24,
**man-of-war,** man-o'-war, ship of war, armored vessel; USS, United States Ship;
HMS, His or Her Majesty's Ship; line-of-
battle ship, ship of the line.

.7 **battleship,** battlewagon [informal], capital ship; **destroyer,** can or tin can [both
informal].

.8 **carrier, aircraft carrier,** seaplane carrier,
**flattop** [informal].

.9 **submarine, sub,** submersible, underwater
craft; **U-boat,** *U-boot, Unterseeboot*
[both Ger], pigboat [slang].

.10 **ships, shipping,** merchant or mercantile
marine, merchant navy or fleet, bottoms,
tonnage; **fleet,** flotilla, argosy; line; fishing fleet, whaling fleet, etc.; **navy** 800.26.

.11 **float, raft;** balsa, balsa raft, Kon Tiki; life
raft, Carling float; boom; pontoon; buoy,

life buoy; **life preserver** 701.5; surfboard; cork; bob.

.12 **rigging** 277.31, rig, **tackle**, tackling, **gear**; **ropework**, roping; service, serving, whipping; standing rigging, running rigging; boatswain's stores; ship chandlery.

.13 **spar** 277.29, timber; **mast**, pole, stick *or* tree [both informal]; bare pole.

.14 **sail** 277.30, **canvas**, muslin, cloth, rag [informal]; **full** *or* **plain sail**, press *or* crowd of sail; reduced sail, reefed sail; square sail; fore-and-aft sail; luff, leech, foot, earing, reef point, boltrope, clew, cringle, head.

.15 **oar**, remi–; **paddle**, scull, sweep, pole; steering oar.

.16 **anchor** 277.32, mooring, hook *or* mudhook [both informal]; **anchorage**, moorings; **berth**, slip; mooring buoy.

.17 ADJS **rigged**, decked, trimmed; square-rigged, fore-and-aft rigged, Marconi-rigged, gaff-rigged, lateen-rigged.

.18 **seaworthy**, sea-kindly, fit for sea, **snug**, **bold**; **watertight**, waterproof; A1, A1 at Lloyd's; stiff, tender; weatherly.

.19 **trim**, in trim; apoise, on an even keel.

.20 **shipshape**, Bristol fashion, shipshape and Bristol fashion, trim, trig, neat, tight, taut, ataunt, all ataunto, bungup and bilge-free.

.21 **boats**

| | |
|---|---|
| airboat | dogger |
| almadia | dory |
| ark | double-ender |
| auxiliary, auxiliary boat | drifter |
| | dugout |
| barge | eight-oar |
| bateau | *Faltboat* [Ger] |
| broadhorn | ferry, ferryboat |
| bucentaur | fiber-glass boat |
| bumboat | fireboat |
| bunder boat | fishing boat |
| bungo | fishing dory |
| buss | flatboat |
| caïque | flyboat |
| canalboat | foldboat |
| canoe | four-oar |
| cargo boat | funny |
| catamaran | galley |
| catboat, cat | garvey |
| coble | gig |
| cockboat | glass-bottomed boat |
| cockle | glider |
| cockleboat | gliding boat |
| cockleshell | gondola |
| cog | houseboat |
| coracle | hoy |
| cruiser 277.4 | hydrocycle |
| curragh | hydrofoil |
| cutter | hydroglider |
| cutter-gig | hydroplane |
| dahabeah | jangada |
| dinghy | johnboat |
| dispatch boat | jolly, jolly boat |

| | |
|---|---|
| kayak | rowboat, rowing boat |
| launch 277.4 | runabout |
| lerret | sampan |
| lifeboat | scooter |
| lifesaving boat | scow |
| lighter | scull |
| log canoe | sea sled |
| longboat | shallop |
| mail boat, mailer | shell |
| motorboat | ship's boat |
| nuggar | showboat |
| outboard motorboat, outboard | skiff |
| | small boat |
| outrigger canoe | sneakbox |
| pair-oar | surfboat |
| pilot, pilot boat | towboat |
| pinnace | trawler, trawlboat |
| piragua | trimaran |
| pirogue | trow |
| pontoon | tug, tugboat |
| post boat | tuna clipper |
| pram | umiak |
| punt | wanigan |
| racer | whaleboat |
| racing shell | whale-gig |
| radio-controlled life-boat | wherry |
| | workboat |
| randan | yawl, yawl boat |

.22 **ships**

| | |
|---|---|
| argosy | packet, packet boat *or* ship |
| ark | |
| bathyscaphe | paddle boat *or* steamer |
| buoy-tender | |
| cabin boat | picket ship |
| cable ship | refrigeration ship |
| caravel | revenue cutter |
| cargo ship | rotor, rotor ship |
| coaler, collier | screw steamer |
| coaster | self-propelled barge |
| coast guard cutter | side-wheeler |
| container ship | slaver |
| derelict | spar-decker, spar-deck vessel |
| dredge | |
| excursion steamer | stage boat |
| fishing boat *or* vessel | steamer 277.2 |
| floating drydock | steam schooner |
| freighter | steam yacht |
| hydrofoil | stern-wheeler |
| icebreaker | storeship |
| LASH (lighter aboard ship) | super-tanker |
| | tanker |
| lightship | tender |
| liner 277.5 | tramp steamer |
| mail steamer | transport |
| merchant ship, merchantman | trawler |
| | turbine |
| nuclear-powered ship | turbine steamer |
| ocean-going tug | weather ship |
| oceanographic research ship | whaleback |
| | whaler |
| oiler | |

.23 **sailing vessels**

| | |
|---|---|
| baggala | bugeye |
| bark | bully |
| barkentine | buss |
| bastard schooner | caravel |
| bawley | carrack |
| bilander | cat |
| brig | catamaran |
| brigantine | catboat |

*chasse-marée* [Fr]
Chesapeake canoe
class boat
clipper
corsair
corvette
cutter
dandy
dhow
dogger
dromond
felucca
fishing schooner
fishing smack
flattie
folkboat
fore-and-aft, fore-and-
    after
four-masted bark
four-master
Friendship sloop
frigate
full-rigged ship
gabert
galiot
galleass
galleon
hermaphrodite brig
hooker
hoy
Hudson River sloop
iceboat
ice yacht
junk
keelboat
ketch
knockabout
lateen, lateener
lorcha
lugger
motorsailer
nobby
ocean racer

outrigger
pilot boat
pinnace
piragua
pirogue
polacre, polacca
pram
proa
pungy
racing yacht
rigger
saic
sailing auxiliary
sailing barge
sailing canoe
sailing dinghy
sailing launch
sailing packet
sailing trawler
sampan
sandbagger
schooner
scooter
shallop
sharpie
shipentine
skipjack
sloop
smack
smack boat
snow
square-rigger
tartan
tea-clipper
three-master
topsail schooner
trimaran
well smack
whaler
wool-clipper
xebec
yacht
yawl

ironclad
ironclad ram
ironsides
jeep carrier
landing craft
LC (landing craft)
LCC (landing craft,
    control)
LCI (landing craft, in-
    fantry)
LCM (landing craft,
    mechanized)
LCP (landing craft,
    personnel)
LCT (landing craft,
    tank)
LCV (landing craft,
    vehicle)
LCVP (landing craft,
    vehicle-personnel)
liberty boat
light cruiser
line-of-battle ship
LSD (landing ship,
    dock)
LSM (landing ship,
    medium)
LST (landing ship,
    tank)
mine layer, mine ship
mine sweeper
minisub
monitor
mosquito boat
MTB (motor torpedo
    boat)
naval auxiliary
net-tender
nuclear *or* nuclear-
    powered submarine
patrol boat
patrol torpedo boat
PC (patrol craft)
PCE (patrol craft, es-
    cort)
PCS (patrol craft,
    sweeper)

picketboat
pocket battleship
Polaris submarine
privateer
protected cruiser
PT boat (patrol tor-
    pedo boat)
raider
ram
receiving ship
reconnaissance ship
repair ship
river gunboat
rocket boat
SC (scouting craft)
scout
scout cruiser
seaplane carrier
second-line battleship
second-line destroyer
ship of the line
ship of war
shipplane carrier
sloop of war
spy ship
storeship
storm boat
submarine 277.9
submarine chaser, sub-
    chaser
submarine patrol boat
submarine tender
submersible
superdreadnought
supply ship
sweeper
tanker
target boat
tender
torpedo boat
torpedo-boat de-
    stroyer *or* catcher
transport, transport
    ship *or* vessel
troopship
turret ship
warship

## .24 naval vessels

aircraft carrier 277.8
aircraft tender
AKA boat (auxiliary
    cargo attack)
ammunition ship
APA boat (auxiliary
    personnel attack)
armored *or* protected
    cruiser
assault boat
assault transport
atomic *or* atomic-pow-
    ered submarine
battle cruiser
battleship 277.7
blockship
bomb ketch *or* vessel
capital ship
caravel
carrier 277.8
coast guard cutter
communications ship
convoy
corvette
crash boat
cruiser
cutter

depot ship
destroyer 277.7
destroyer escort
destroyer leader
destroyer tender
dispatch boat
dreadnought
eagle boat
E-boat
escort carrier
escort vessel
fireboat
fire ship
first-rate
flagship
flattop [informal]
fleet submarine
floating battery
frigate
fuel ship
guard ship *or* boat
guided missile cruiser
gunboat
heavy cruiser
hospital ship
hunter-killer subma-
    rine

## .25 galleys

bireme
foist
galiot
galleass
galley foist
half galley
hepteris
hexeris
penteconter

quadrireme
quarter galley
quinquereme
tessaraconter
triaconter
trireme
Venetian galley
war galley

## .26 parts of ships

back
balance rudder
batten
beak, beakhead
beam
beam clamp
bilge keel
bilge keelson
bitt
board
bollard
bollard timber

bow
bracket plate
bridge
bulkhead
bull's-eye
bulwarks
cam cleat
capstan
carling
casemate
cathead
ceiling

centerboard
centerboard trunk
chainplate
cleat
coffee-grinder winch
companion
companion ladder
companionway
conning tower
conning tower hatch
counter
crow's nest
cutwater
daggerboard
davit
deadwood
entrance
false keel
fantail
figurehead
fin keel
forefoot
foresheets
foretop
frame
freeboard
futtock
gangplank
gangway
garboard strake
gudgeon
gunwale, gunnel
hatch
hatchway
hawse, hawsehole
hawsepiece
hawsepipe
hawse timber
head
heel
island
keel
keel and keelson
keelson
kevel
knee
knighthead
larboard
lee, lee side, leeward
leeboard
limber board
limber hole
maintop
mizzentop
monkey rail
nose
paddle wheel

pintle
planking, plank plat-
   ing
Plimsoll marks
poop
port, portside
porthole
post
propeller
prow
pulpit
rail
rib
rubrail
rudder
rudderpost
rudderstock
run
scupper
scuttle
scuttlebutt
shaft tunnel
sheave hole
sheer strake
sheets
shelf, shelfpiece
sister or side keelson
sister rib
skeg
snorkel
spirketing
stanchion
starboard
steering engine
stem
stern
sternpost
stern sheets
strake
stringer
superstructure
tail end
tail shaft
tiller
transom
trimming hatch or
   hole
truck
waterline
waterway
weather, weather side
weatherboard
wheel
winch
windlass
windward, windward
   side

roundhouse
sail loft
sick bay
stateroom

stokehold
topside
wardroom

**.28 decks**

after deck
anchor deck
boat deck
bridge deck
flight deck
forward deck
gun deck
half deck
hurricane deck
landing deck
lower deck
main deck
middle deck
orlop deck

partial hold deck
platform, platform
   deck
poop, poop deck
promenade deck
protective deck
quarterdeck
runway
shelter deck
spar deck
splinter deck
superstructure deck
upper or top deck
weather deck

**.29 spars, masts**

boom
bowsprit
brace bumpkin
bumpkin, boomkin
club
crossjack yard
crosstree
dolphin striker
flying jib boom
fore jack
foremast
foreroyal mast
foreroyal-studding-sail
   boom
foreroyal yard
fore-skysail mast
fore-skysail yard
fore-topgallant mast
fore-topgallant-stud-
   ding-sail boom
fore-topgallant yard
fore-topmast
fore-topmast-stud-
   ding-sail boom
fore-topsail yard
fore-trysail gaff
foreyard
gaff
gooseneck
jack
jack staff
jib boom
jigger mast
king post
lazy jack
lower boom
lower mizzen-topsail
   yard
main-brace bumpkin
mainmast
main-royal mast
main-royal-studding-
   sail boom
main-royal yard

main-skysail mast
main-skysail yard
main-topgallant mast
main-topgallant-stud-
   ding-sail boom
main-topgallant yard
main-topmast
main-topmast-stud-
   ding-sail boom
main-topsail yard
main-trysail gaff
main yard
martingale or dol-
   phin-striker boom
mast
masthead
mizzen, mizzenmast
mizzen-royal mast
mizzen-royal yard
mizzen-skysail mast
mizzen-skysail yard
mizzen-topgallant
   mast
mizzen-topgallant
   yard
mizzen-topmast
mizzen-topsail yard
sheer pole
skysail mast or pole
skysail yard
spanker boom
spanker gaff
spinnaker pole
spreader
sprit
tack bumpkin
topgallant mast
topgallant yard
topmast
trysail gaff
whisker boom
whisker pole
yard
yardarm

**.27 compartments**

below
between-decks,
   'tween-decks
boiler room
brig
bunker
cabin
caboose, camboose
chain locker
chart room, chart
   house
conning tower
engine room, engine

space
forecastle, fo'c'sle
forepeak
galley
head
hold, hole
lazaret
officers' country
paint locker
pilothouse
quarters
radio room, radio
   shack

**.30 sails**

baby jib topsail
balance or French lug
balloon sail or jib, bal-
   looner

batten
batten pocket
club-footed jib
club topsail

crossjack
dipping lug
fly-by-night
flying jib
flying kites
fore gaff-topsail
foreroyal
foreroyal studding sail
foresail
fore-skysail
forestaysail
fore topgallant sail
fore-topgallant stud-
ding sail
fore-topmast staysail
fore-topmast studding
sail
fore-topsail
Genoa, Genoa jib
inner jib
jenny
jib
jigger
jimbo
jolly jumper
kites
lateen sail
leg-of-mutton sail
loose-footed sail
lower studding sail
lug
lugsail
main gaff-topsail
main royal
main-royal staysail
main-royal studding
sail
mainsail
main skysail
main staysail
main-topgallant sail

main-topgallant stud-
ding sail
main-topmast staysail
main-topmast stud-
ding sail
main-topsail
mizzen
mizzen royal
mizzen-royal staysail
mizzen sail
mizzen skysail
mizzen staysail
mizzen-topgallant sail
mizzen-topgallant
staysail
mizzen-topmast stay-
sail
moonraker
moonsail
outer jib
parachute spinnaker
reef
reef point
royal
skysail
skyscraper [informal]
spanker
spinnaker
spitfire
spritsail
square sail
standing lug
staysail
stern staysail
storm trysail
studding sail
topgallant sail
topsail
trysail
working jib

### .31 ropes, rigging

after shroud
anchor chain
anchor rode
backropes
backstay
becket
block
boat line
bobstay
boltrope
boom vang
bow fast
bowline
bowsprit shroud
brace
brail
breast fast
buntline
crossjack brace
crossjack lift
deadeye
downhaul
earing
fast
Flemish horse
flying jib guy
flying jib martingale
flying jib stay
footropes

forebrace
foreganger
fore lift
foreroyal backstay
foreroyal brace
foreroyal lift
foreroyal shroud
foreroyal stay
forerunner
foresheet
fore-skysail backstay
fore-skysail brace
fore-skysail lift
fore-skysail shroud
fore-skysail stay
forestay
foretack
fore-topgallant back-
stay
fore-topgallant brace
fore-topgallant lift
fore-topgallant shroud
fore-topgallant stay
fore-topmast backstay
fore-topmast stay
fore-topmast staysail
stay
fore-topsail lift
fore-trysail peak

halyard
fore-trysail vang
futtock hoop
futtock shroud
gasket
grab rope
guess-rope
guess-warp
guest rope
gunter
guy
halyard
harbor gasket
hawser
head earing
head fast
Jacob's ladder
jib guy
jib martingale
jibstay
lanyard
lee sheet
lee tack
lifeline
lift
lower-boom topping
lift
main brace
main lift
main-royal brace
main-royal lift
main-royal stay
mainsheet
main-skysail brace
main-skysail lift
main-skysail stay
mainstay
main-topgallant brace
main-topgallant lift
main-topgallant stay
main-topmast stay
main-topsail lift
main-trysail peak hal-
yard
main-trysail vang
marline

### .32 anchors

Baldt anchor
bower
center anchor
CQR or CQR plow
anchor
Danforth anchor
dinghy anchor
drag anchor
drogue
Dunn anchor
floating anchor
fluke
grapnel
kedge, kedge anchor
killick
Martin's anchor
mushroom anchor
Navy anchor

### .33 helms

automatic pilot
destroyer wheel
electrohydraulic steer-
ing gear

martingale
messenger
mizzen-royal brace
mizzen-royal lift
mizzen-royal stay
mizzen-skysail brace
mizzen-skysail lift
mizzen-skysail stay
mizzen stay
mizzen-topgallant
brace
mizzen-topgallant lift
mizzen-topgallant stay
mizzen-topmast stay
mizzen-topsail lift
mooring pendant or
pennant
outhaul
painter
pennant hoist
port tack
preventer backstay
quarter fast
ratline
reef earing
roband, ropeband
roller-reefing gear
sea gasket
sheet
shroud
span
spanker peak halyard
spanker sheet
spanker vang
spring, spring line
starboard tack
stay
stern fast
stirrup
swifter
tack
timenoguy
topping lift
vang
weather sheet
whisker jumper

Northill anchor
parachute drogue
plow anchor
port anchor
sacred anchor
sand anchor
screw anchor
sea anchor
shank
sheet anchor
starboard anchor
stern anchor
stock
stockless anchor
stream anchor
Trotman's anchor
yachtman's anchor

gyroscopic pilot
hand gear
lee helm
lever pilot

servo-pilot
steering gear
telemotor

tiller
weather helm
wheel

**.34 equipment**

anemometer
anemoscope
baggywrinkle
barograph
barometer
belaying pin
bilge pump
binnacle
boat hook
caulking cotton
caulking iron
compass
fid
grapnel
grappling iron

hawse bag
hawse hook
holystone
hygrograph
log
marlinespike
mooring swivel or
  shackle
pump
rigger's knife
sounders 209.17
tackle 287.10
thermograph
toggle

## 278. AVIATION

**.1 NOUNS aviation, aeronautics, aer(o)–;** airplaning, skyriding, **flying, flight,** winging, volation, volitation; aeronautism, aerodromics; powered flight, jet flight, subsonic or supersonic flight; cruising, crosscountry flying; bush flying; **gliding,** sailplaning, soaring, sailing; volplaning; ballooning, balloonery, lighter-than-air aviation; barnstorming [informal]; high-altitude flying; blind or instrument flight or flying, instrument flight rules, IFR; contact flying, visual flight or flying, visual flight rules, VFR, pilotage; skywriting; cloud-seeding; in-flight training, ground school; **airline,** air service, feeder airline, scheduled airline, nonscheduled airline or nonsked [informal], short-hop airline; commercial aviation, general aviation, private aviation, private flying; astronautics 282.1; air show, flying circus.

**.2** (allied sciences) aeroballistics, aerocartography, aerodontia, aerodynamics, aerogeography, aerogeology, aerography, aerology, aeromechanics, aerometry, aeronautical engineering, aerophotography, aeronautical meteorology, aerial photography, aerophysics, aeroscopy, aerospace research, aerostatics, aerostation, aerotechnics, aviation technology, aircraft hydraulics, avionics, climatology, acronomy, hydrostatics, jet engineering, kinematics, kinetics, meteorology, micrometry, photometry, pneumatics, rocket engineering, rocketry; supersonics, supersonic aerodynamics; aviation medicine, aeromedicine.

**.3 airmanship,** pilotship; **flight plan;** briefing, brief, rundown [informal], debriefing; flight or pilot training, flying lessons; washout [informal].

**.4** air-mindedness, aerophilia; air legs.

**.5** airsickness; aerophobia, aeropathy.

**.6 navigation,** avigation, aerial or air navigation; celestial navigation, astronavigation; electronic navigation, automatic electronic navigation, radio navigation, navar, radar, consolan, tacan, teleran, loran, shoran; omnidirectional range, omnirange, visual-aural range, VAR.

**.7** (aeronautical organizations) Civil Aeronautics Administration, CAA, Federal Aviation Agency, FAA; Bureau of Aeronautics, BuAer; National Advisory Committee for Aeronautics, NACA; Office of Naval Research, ONR; Civil Air Patrol, CAP; Caterpillar Club; Airline Pilots Association; Aircraft Recognition Society, ARS; Air Force 800.28,29.

**.8 takeoff,** hopoff [informal]; taxiing, takeoff run, takeoff power, rotation; daisy-clipping or grass-cutting [both informal]; ground loop; level-off; jet-assisted takeoff, JATO, booster rocket, takeoff rocket; catapult, electropult.

**.9 flight, trip, run; hop or jump** [both informal]; powered flight; solo flight, solo; inverted flight; supersonic flight; test flight, **test hop** [informal]; **airlift;** airdrop.

**.10 air travel,** air transport, airfreight, air cargo, airline travel; shuttle, air shuttle, shuttle service, shuttle trip, air taxi; weather or meteorological reconnaissance; in-flight refueling; **range,** flying range, radius of action, navigation radius.

**.11** (Air Force) **mission,** flight operation; training mission; gunnery mission; combat rehearsal, **dry run** [informal]; transition mission; reconnaissance mission, reconnaissance, observation flight, search mission; **milk run** [informal]; box-top mission [informal]; combat flight; **sortie,** scramble [informal]; **air raid;** shuttle raid; bombing mission; bombing, strafing 798.7,8; **air support** (for ground troops), **air cover,** cover, umbrella, air umbrella.

**.12** flight formation, formation flying, formation; close formation, loose formation, wing formation; V formation, echelon.

**.13** (maneuvers) acrobatic or tactical evolutions or maneuvers, acrobatics, **aerobatics;** stunting or **stunt flying** [both informal]; rolling, crabbing, banking, porpoising, fishtailing, diving; **dive, nose dive, power dive; zoom,** chandelle; stall, whip stall; **glide,** volplane; spiral, split 'S', lazy eight, sideslip, pushdown, pull-up, pull-out.

.14 **roll, barrel roll,** aileron roll, outside roll, snap roll.

.15 **spin,** autorotation, **tailspin,** flat spin, inverted spin, normal spin, power spin, uncontrolled spin, falling leaf.

.16 **loop,** spiral loop, ground loop, normal loop, outside loop, inverted normal *or* outside loop, dead-stick loop, wingover, looping the loop; Immelmann turn, reverse turn, reversement; flipper turns.

.17 **buzzing,** flathatting *or* **hedgehopping** [both informal].

.18 **landing,** coming in [informal], touching down, touchdown; arrival; landing run, landing pattern; approach, downwind leg, approach leg; holding pattern, stack up [informal]; ballooning in, parachute approach; blind *or* instrument landing, dead-stick landing, glide landing, stall landing, fishtail landing, sideslip landing, level *or* two-point landing, normal *or* three-point landing, Chinese landing [informal], tail-high landing, tail-low landing, thumped-in landing [informal], pancake landing, belly landing, crash landing, noseover, nose-up; practice landing, bounce drill.

.19 (flying and landing guides) marker, pylon; beacon; radio beacon, radio range station, radio marker; fan marker; radar beacon, racon; beam, radio beam; beacon lights 336.10; runway lights, high-intensity runway approach lights, sequence flashers, flare path; wind indicator, wind cone *or* sock, air sleeve; instrument landing system, ILS, touchdown rate of descent indicator, TRODI, ground-controlled approach, GCA; talking-down system, talking down.

.20 **crash, crack-up,** prang [Brit informal]; crash landing; collision, midair collision; near-miss.

.21 **blackout;** grayout; anoxia; useful consciousness; pressure suit, antiblackout suit.

.22 **airport, airfield, airdrome,** aerodrome [Brit], drome, port, air harbor [Can], aviation field, **landing field,** landing, field, airship station; **air base,** air station, naval air station; airpark; **heliport,** helidrome; control tower, island; Air Route Traffic Control Center.

.23 **runway, taxiway,** strip, landing strip, **airstrip, flight strip,** take-off strip; fairway, launching way; stopway; clearway; transition strip; apron; **flight deck,** landing deck.

.24 **hangar,** housing, dock, airdock, shed, airship shed; mooring mast.

.25 aerocurve, aerodynamic *or* air volume, airplane heading, amplitude, aspect ratio, camber, *décalage* [Fr], equivalent monoplane, fineness ratio, flight path, margin of power, positive direction of roll, propulsive efficiency, resultant force, righting *or* restoring moment, skin friction, skin effect, slip, stagger, sweepback, tail force.

.26 (angle) aileron angle, blade angle, coning angle, dihedral angle, drift angle, downwash angle, elevator angle, flapping angle, flight path angle, gliding angle, helix angle, landing angle, rudder angle, trim angle, zero-lift angle, angle of attack, angle of dead rise, angle of heel, angle of incidence *or* wing setting, angle of pitch, angle of roll *or* bank, angle of sideslip, angle of stabilizer setting, angle of yaw.

.27 (center) aerodynamic center, elastic center, center of buoyancy, center of gravity, center of mass, center of pressure, center-of-pressure coefficiency.

.28 (axis) horizontal *or* longitudinal axis, fore-and-aft axis, X axis; lateral axis, Y axis; normal axis, Z axis; elastic axis, wing axis, drag axis, positive lift axis; yawing, yaw, positive direction of yaw.

.29 (stability) automatic stability, directional stability, dynamic stability, inherent stability, lateral stability, longitudinal stability, static stability.

.30 (load) basic load, design load, full load, normal load, ultimate load, useful load; payload, passenger capacity; offensive load; power loading, span loading, unsymmetrical loading, wing loading.

.31 (pressure) altitude *or* height pressure, dynamic pressure, impact pressure, manometer pressure, superpressure; center of pressure; stress, working stress, breathing stress; torsion, torsional stress, torque, propeller torque; structural fatigue.

.32 (thrust) propeller thrust, static propeller thrust, line of thrust *or* flight; jet thrust, pounds of thrust, augmenter *or* thrust augmenter, afterburner, tail-pipe burner, fan-jet; rocket assist.

.33 (propulsion) rocket propulsion, rocket power; **jet propulsion,** jet power; turbojet propulsion, pulse-jet propulsion, ram-jet propulsion, resojet propulsion; constant *or* ram pressure, air ram; reaction propulsion, reaction, action and reaction; aeromotor 280.17, aircraft engine, power plant.

.34 **pitch,** pitch ratio, aerodynamic pitch, effective pitch, geometrical pitch, zero-thrust pitch; angle of pitch, positive direction of pitch.

.35 **lift,** lift ratio, lift force or component, lift direction; aerostatic lift, dynamic lift, gross lift, useful lift, margin of lift.

.36 **drag,** resistance; drag ratio, drag force or component, induced drag, wing drag, parasite or parasitic or structural drag, profile drag, head resistance, drag direction, cross-wind force.

.37 **drift,** drift angle; lateral drift, leeway.

.38 **flow,** air flow, laminar flow; **turbulence,** turbulent flow, burble, burble point, eddies.

.39 **wash,** wake, stream; downwash; backwash, **slipstream,** propeller race, propwash; **exhaust,** jet exhaust, blow wash; **vapor trail,** condensation trail, contrail, vortex.

.40 (speed) **air speed,** true air speed, operating or flying speed, cruising speed, knots, minimum flying speed, hump speed, peripheral speed, pitch speed, terminal speed, sinking speed, get-away or take-off speed, landing speed, ground speed, speed over the ground; **speed of sound** 269.2; zone of no signal, Mach cone; **sound barrier,** sonic barrier or wall; sonic boom, shock wave, Mach wave.

.41 (air, atmosphere) **airspace,** navigable airspace; aerosphere; aeropause; troposphere, tropopause, substratosphere, stratosphere, stratopause, ionosphere; **aerospace;** space, empty space; **ceiling,** ballonet ceiling, service ceiling, static ceiling, absolute ceiling; cloud layer or cover, ceiling zero; visibility, visibility zero; **overcast,** undercast; fog, soup [informal]; high-pressure area, low-pressure area; trough, trough line; front; **air pocket** or air hole, air bump, pocket, hole, bump; **turbulence,** clear-air turbulence, CAT, roughness; head wind, unfavorable wind; tail wind, favorable or favoring wind; crosswind; atmospheric tides; jetstream.

.42 **airway, air lane, air line,** air route, skyway, corridor, lane, path.

.43 **course, heading,** vector; compass heading or course, compass direction, magnetic heading, true heading or course.

.44 (altitude) altitude of flight, absolute altitude, critical altitude, density altitude, pressure altitude, sextant altitude; clearance; ground elevation.

.45 VERBS **fly,** be airborne, flit, wing, take wing, wing one's way, take or make a flight, take to the air, take the air, volitate, be wafted; **jet;** aviate, airplane, aeroplane; travel by air, go or travel by airline, go by plane or by air, take to the airways, ride the skies; hop [informal]; **soar,** drift, hover; **cruise; glide,** sailplane, sail, volplane; hydroplane, seaplane; balloon; ferry; airlift; break the sound barrier; navigate, avigate.

.46 **pilot,** control, be at the controls, fly, manipulate, drive, fly left seat; **copilot,** fly right seat; solo; **barnstorm** [informal]; fly blind, fly by the seat of one's pants [informal]; follow the beam, ride the beam, fly on instruments; fly in formation, take position; peel off.

.47 **take off,** hop or jump off [informal], become airborne, get off or leave the ground, take to the air, go or fly aloft, clear; rotate, power off; **taxi.**

.48 **ascend,** climb, gain altitude, mount; **zoom,** hoick [informal], chandelle.

.49 (maneuver) **stunt** [informal], perform aerobatics; crab, fishtail; **spin,** go into a tail spin; **loop,** loop the loop; **roll,** wingover, spiral, undulate, porpoise, feather, yaw, sideslip, skid, bank, dip, nose down, nose up, pull up, push down, pull out, plow, mush through.

.50 **dive,** nose-dive, power-dive, go for the deck; lose altitude, settle, dump altitude [informal].

.51 **buzz,** flathat or **hedgehop** [both informal].

.52 **land,** set her down [informal], **alight, light,** touch down; **descend,** come down, fly down; come in, come in for a landing; **level off,** flatten out; upwind, downwind; overshoot, undershoot; make a dead-stick landing; pancake, thump in [informal]; bellyland, settle down, balloon in; fishtail down; **crash-land;** ditch [informal]; nose up, nose over; talk down.

.53 **crash, crack up,** prang [Brit informal], spin in, fail to pull out.

.54 **stall,** lose power, conk out [informal]; flame out.

.55 **black out,** gray out.

.56 **parachute, bail out, jump,** make a parachute jump, hit the silk, make a brolly-hop [Brit informal], sky-dive.

.57 **brief,** give a briefing; debrief.

.58 ADJS **aeronautic(al),** aerial; **aviatorial,** aviational; aerodontic, aerospace, aerotechnical, aerostatic(al), aeromechanic(al), aerodynamic(al), avionic, aeronomic, aerophysical; aeromarine; aerobatic; airworthy, air-minded, air-conscious, aeromedical; air-wise; airsick.

.59 **flying,** flitting, winging; volant, volitant, volitational, hovering, fluttering; gliding; **airborne;** jet-propelled, rocket-propelled.

.60 ADVS **in flight, on the wing** or **fly, while airborne.**

.61 **instruments**

| | |
|---|---|
| absolute altimeter | gyrocompass |
| accelerometer | Gyro Flux Gate |
| aerial reconnaissance | gyro horizon |
|   camera | Gyropilot |
| aerograph | gyrosyn |
| aerometer | horn |
| aeroscope | hub dynamometer |
| air log | hygrograph |
| air-speed head | hygrometer |
| air-speed indicator | hypsometer |
| altigraph | inclinometer |
| altimeter | induction compass |
| altitude mixture con- | instrument board or |
|   trol |   panel |
| ammeter | intervalometer |
| anemograph | Joyce stick |
| anemometer | joy stick |
| anemoscope | macaviator |
| aneroid | Mach meter |
| automatic boost con- | magnetic compass |
|   trol | manifold pressure |
| automatic or robot |   gauge |
|   pilot | meteorograph |
| autopilot | micrometer |
| autosyn | nephoscope |
| bank or banking indi- | octant |
|   cator | optical altimeter |
| barometer | ozonometer |
| bearing plate | pelorus |
| bombing locator | photometer |
| bombsight | pitch or pitching indi- |
| Bourdon tube |   cator |
| calorimeter | pitot-static tube |
| carburetor altitude | pluviometer |
|   control | polymeter |
| card compass | position indicator |
| card magnetic com- | potentiometer |
|   pass | pressure altimeter |
| ceiling-height indica- | pyrometer |
|   tor | quadrant |
| chronometer | radar |
| climatometer | radio |
| compass | radio altimeter |
| control rod or column | radio compass |
| control stick | radio direction finder |
| directional gyro | radiogoniometer |
| direction finder | rate-of-climb indicator |
| direction indicator | recording altimeter |
| drift meter | recording anemome- |
| earth inductor or |   ter |
|   induction compass | recording hygrometer |
| electrical capacity | sextant |
|   altimeter | sound-ranging altime- |
| engine gauge |   ter |
| evaporimeter | Sperry antiaircraft |
| flight recorder |   director |
| fuel-flow meter | spirit level |
| fuel quantity indica- | static tube |
|   tor | sting |
| galvanometer | strike radar scanner |
| gosport, gosport tube | sun compass |

| | |
|---|---|
| tachometer | turn-and-bank indica- |
| terrain clearance indi- |   tor |
|   cator | turnmeter |
| thermograph | variometer |
| thermometer | venturi tube |
| thermostat | viscosimeter |
| throttle | yawmeter |
| transit instrument | yoke |

## 279. AVIATOR

.1 NOUNS **aviator,** aeronaut, aeroplaner, airplaner, aeroplanist, airplanist, **airman, flier, pilot,** air pilot; licensed pilot, private pilot, commercial pilot, instructor; wingman; chief pilot, captain; birdman [informal]; copilot; jet pilot, jet jockey [informal]; test pilot; bush pilot; astronaut 282.8; cloud seeder, rainmaker; cropduster; barnstormer [informal]; stunt man, stunt flier.

.2 **aviatrix,** aviatress, **airwoman,** birdwoman [informal].

.3 **military pilot,** naval pilot, combat pilot; fighter pilot; bomber pilot; suicide pilot, kamikaze; observer; **aviation cadet,** air or flying cadet, pilot trainee; flyboy [slang]; ace; air force 800.28,29.

.4 **crew, aircrew,** flight crew; aircrewman; **navigator,** avigator; **bombardier;** gunner, machine gunner, belly gunner, tail gunner; crew chief; aerial photographer; meteorologist; steward, stewardess, hostess, flight attendant.

.5 **ground crew,** landing crew, plane handlers.

.6 **aircraftsman,** aeromechanic, aircraft mechanic, mechanic, grease monkey [slang]; rigger; aeronautical engineer, flight engineer, jet engineer, rocket engineer 281.11; ground tester, flight tester.

.7 **balloonist,** ballooner, aeronaut.

.8 **parachutist,** chutist or chuter [both informal], parachute jumper, sports parachutist; sky diver; smoke jumper; **paratrooper;** paradoctor, paramedic; jumpmaster.

.9 (mythological fliers) Daedalus, Icarus.

## 280. AIRCRAFT

.1 NOUNS **aircraft,** aerocraft, **airplane** 280.15, aeroplane [Brit], **plane, ship,** fixed-wing aircraft, flying machine, *avion* [Fr]; aerodyne, heavier-than-air craft; kite [Brit informal]; lifting body; planform.

.2 **propeller plane,** single-prop, double-prop or twin-prop, multi-prop; tractor, tractor plane; pusher, pusher plane; piston plane; turbo-propeller plane, turbo-prop, propjet.

.3 **jet plane, jet;** turbojet, ramjet, pulse-jet,

blowtorch [informal]; single-jet, twin-jet, multi-jet; Jet Liner, business jet; delta-planform jet, tailless jet, twin-tailboom jet; jumbo jet; subsonic jet; supersonic jet, supersonic transport, SST.

.4 **rocket plane**, repulsor; rocket ship, spaceship 282.2; rocket 281.2.

.5 **rotor plane**, rotary-wing aircraft, rotocraft, rotodyne; gyroplane, gyro, **autogiro**, windmill [informal]; **helicopter**, heli–; copter or whirlybird or chopper or eggbeater [all informal].

.6 **ornithopter**, orthopter, wind flapper, mechanical bird.

.7 **flying platform**, flying ring, Hiller-CNR machine, flying bedstead or bedspring; **hovercraft**, air car, ground-effect machine, air-cushion vehicle, hovercar, cushioncraft; flying crow's nest, flying motorcycle, flying bathtub.

.8 **seaplane**, waterplane, **hydroplane**, aerohydroplane, aeroboat, **floatplane**, float seaplane; **flying boat**, clipper, boat seaplane; **amphibian**, triphibian.

.9 **warplane**, battleplane, combat plane, gun boat, military aircraft; suicide plane, kamikaze; bogey, bandit, enemy aircraft; air fleet, air armada; air force 800.28,29.

.10 **trainer**; Link trainer; **flight simulator**; dual-control trainer; basic or primary trainer, intermediate trainer, advanced trainer; crew trainer, flying classroom; navigator-bombardier trainer, radio-navigational trainer, etc.

.11 **aerostat**, lighter-than-air craft; **airship**, ship, dirigible balloon, **blimp** [informal]; rigid airship, semirigid airship; **dirigible**, zeppelin, Graf Zeppelin; gasbag, ballonet; **balloon** 280.18, ballon [Fr].

.12 **glider**, gliding machine; **sailplane**, soaring plane; rocket glider; student glider; air train, glider train.

.13 **parachute**, para–; **chute** [informal], umbrella [informal], brolly [Brit informal]; pilot chute, drogue chute; rip cord, safety loop, shroud lines, harness, pack, vent; parachute jump, brolly-hop [Brit informal]; sky dive; brake or braking or deceleration parachute.

.14 **kite**, box kite, Eddy kite, Hargrave or cellular kite, tetrahedral kite.

.15 **airplanes**

| | |
|---|---|
| aerobus | airliner |
| aerodone | air scout |
| air ambulance | air-sea rescue amphib- |
| air coach | ian |
| air cruiser | air-sea rescue plane |
| airfreighter | all-weather fighter |
| ambulance | interceptor |
| amphibian transport | intermeshing-rotor he- |
| antique plane | licopter |
| antisubmarine patrol | jet, jet plane 280.3 |
| antisubmarine plane | jet bomber |
| arctic rescue helicop- | jet fighter |
| ter | jet tanker |
| assault transport | jet transport |
| assault-troop plane | killer |
| attack bomber | laminar-flow-control |
| attack plane | plane |
| attack transport | landplane |
| Autogiro | liaison plane |
| avion-canon [Fr] | light bomber |
| biplace [Fr] | light transport |
| biplane | liner |
| bomber | long-range attack air- |
| cabin plane | craft |
| canard | long-range bomber |
| cargo plane | long-range medium or |
| cargo transport | heavy bomber |
| carrier-based plane | long-range patrol |
| carrier fighter | bomber |
| casualty-evacuation | low-wing monoplane |
| plane | mailplane |
| club plane | maritime reconnais- |
| commercial transport | sance plane |
| constant-chord-rotor | medium bomber |
| helicopter | meteorological recon- |
| convertiplane | naissance plane |
| crop-duster | midwing monoplane |
| cruiser | military aircraft |
| Cub | military transport |
| dive bomber | mobile command post |
| drone | monoplace [Fr] |
| escort fighter | monoplane |
| evacuation ambulance | mosquito |
| evacuation plane | multipurpose plane |
| executive plane | naval aircraft |
| fighter | naval bomber |
| fighter-bomber | naval fighter |
| flying banana | naval interceptor |
| flying boxcar | night fighter |
| flying fortress | observation plane |
| flying platform 280.7 | ornithopter 280.6 |
| flying tanker | paraglider |
| flying wing | parasol |
| freighter | passenger plane |
| freight transport | pathfinder |
| general reconnais- | patrol bomber |
| sance | patrol plane |
| glider 280.12 | photo-reconnaissance |
| grasshopper | plane |
| ground-attack fighter | picket patrol plane |
| ground-support air- | pilotless aircraft |
| craft | pou de ciel [Fr] |
| gyrodyne | precision bomber |
| heavy bomber | private plane |
| heavy transport | propeller plane 280.2 |
| helibus | pulse jet helicopter |
| helicopter 280.5 | pursuit plane |
| helicopter gun ship | radar picket plane |
| high-altitude recon- | reconnaissance plane |
| naissance plane | rescue helicopter |
| high-altitude research | rescue plane |
| aircraft | research plane |
| high-wing monoplane | robot plane |
| hovercraft 280.7 | rocket-firing plane |
| hunter | rocket plane 280.4 |
| hurricane hunter | rotor plane 280.5 |
| in-flight refueling | scout, scout plane |
| tanker | seaplane 280.8 |

search plane
service aircraft
sesquiplane
shipboard interceptor
shipboard plane
shipplane
ski-plane
sky truck
sport plane, sports plane
spotter plane
spy plane
STOL (short takeoff and landing)
stratofreighter
stratojet
strike plane
supersonic combat plane
supersonic research plane
tactical support

bomber
tandem plane
tandem-rotor helicopter
target-tug or -tower
taxiplane
torpedo bomber
torpedo strike aircraft
trainer 280.10
trainer-bomber
trainer-fighter
transport
triplane
troop carrier
troop transport
turbojet
utility plane
VTOL (vertical take-off and landing)
warplane 280.9
weather reconnaissance plane

## .16 airplane parts

adjustable propeller
aerothermodynamic duct
afterburner
aileron
air brake
air controls
airfoil
airframe
air intake
air scoop
airscrew
antidrag wire
antilift or landing wire
arresting gear
arrestor hook
astrodome
athodyd
axial-flow unit
balancing flap
ball turret
bay
beaching gear
belly tank
blister
blister canopy
body
bomb bay
bomb rack
bomb release
bonnet
booster rocket unit
bow
brace wire
bubble
bubble canopy
bubble hood
bucket seat
bumper bag
butterfly tail
cabin
canopy
cat strip
channel patch
chassis
chin
coaxial propellers
cockpit

coke-bottle fuselage
contraprops
contra-rotating airscrews
controls
control surface
control wires
cowl
crew compartment
dead stick
deceleron
deck
deicer
delta wing
dihedral
diving rudder
dorsal airdome
dorsal blister
double-bubble
drag strut
drag wire
drift wire
dual controls
ejection seat
ejector
elevating rudder
elevator
elevon
emergency landing gear
empennage
engine controls
fin
finger patch
flame trap
flap
flex wing
float
flotation gear
folding wing
fuel injector
fuselage
gas-shaft hood
gore
gull wing
gun mount
hatch
hood

instruments 278.61
intermeshing rotors
jackstay
jet pipe
jet pod
jury skid
keel
laminar-flow system
landing gear
landing lights
landing skis
launching gear
launching tube
leading edge
lift wire
longeron
monocoque [Fr]
nacelle
navigation lights
navigator's bubble
nose
nose radiator
nose turret
nosewheel
nosewheel undercarriage
oleo gear
oleo leg
pants, wheel parts
parasol wing
Perspex 'chin' housing
pilot plane
pod
pontoon
projector tube
propeller, prop [informal]
propulsive duct
radar nacelle
radar nose
radar scanner
radome
retractable landing gear
rocket launcher
Rogallo wing
rotors
rudder
rudder bar
rudder pedals
ruddervator
runners (for snow or ice)
safety wire

skid fin
skid landing gear
ski landing gear
slitwing
spinner
spoiler
spray strip
stabilizer, stabilizator
stagger or incidence wire
stay
stick, stick control
stressed skin
stringers
strut
stub-wing stabilizer
supersonic wings
tail
tail boom
tail fin
tail pipe
tail plane
tail rotor
tail skid
tail stinger
tail unit
tail wheel
tandem rotors
tandem seat
tractor airscrew
trailing edge
trim controls
trim tab
truss
turbine nozzle
turboprops
turret
turtleback
twin tail wheel
undercarriage
ventral airdome
ventral radome
vertical fin
V tail or vee tail
waist gun blister
walking beam
wheel cowlings
wing
wing radiator
wing rib
wing root air intake
wing roots
wing skid
wing truss

## .17 aircraft engines

aeromotor
arc-jet engine
athodyd
axial-flow turbojet
axial-type engine
cam engine
compound engine
compression-ignition engine
double-row radial engine
fan-jet engine
gas jet
gas turbine jet engine
impulse duct engine
intermittent duct

engine
inverted engine
jet engine
pancake engine
piston engine
propeller-drive gas turbine
propeller-jet engine
propjet
pulse jet
radial engine
ramjet
reaction engine or motor
reciprocating engine
resojet

resonance duct jet
    engine
resonance jet engine
rocket motor
rotary engine
supercharged engine
turbine
turbojet
turboprop

turbo-propeller engine
turboprop-jet
turboram-jet
twin-engines
vertical engine
V-type engine
W-type engine
X-type engine

**.18 balloons**

ballon-sonde [Fr]
barrage balloon
blimp 280.11
captive balloon
ceiling balloon
dirigible balloon, diri-
    gible 280.11
fire balloon
free balloon
gasbag
gas balloon
hot-air balloon
kite balloon or sau-
    sage

montgolfier
observation balloon
pilot balloon
radiosonde balloon
rockoon (rocket-bal-
    loon)
sausage, sausage bal-
    loon
skyhook, skyhook bal-
    loon
sounding balloon
stratosphere balloon
weather balloon

**.19 airship parts**

ballonet
basket
car
catwalk
envelope
gas chamber or
    cell
gondola

landing or mooring
    line
mooring harness
observation car
observation platform
sandbag
side or wing car
subcloud car

## 281. ROCKETRY, MISSILERY

**.1 NOUNS rocketry,** rocket science or engineering or research or technology; **missilery,** missile science or engineering or research or technology; rocket or missile
testing; ground test, firing test, static firing; rocket or missile project or program;
instrumentation; telemetry.

**.2 rocket,** rocket engine or motor, reaction
engine or motor, jet engine; rocket exhaust; plasma jet, plasma engine; ion engine; jetavator.

**.3 rocket,** missile 281.14,15, **ballistic missile,
guided missile;** torpedo 281.16; projectile
rocket, ordnance rocket, combat or military or war rocket; bird [informal]; **payload; warhead,** nuclear or thermonuclear
warhead, atomic warhead; multiple or
multiple-missile warhead.

**.4 rocket bomb,** flying bomb or torpedo,
cruising missile; **robot bomb,** robomb,
Vergeltungswaffe [Ger], V-weapon, P-
plane; **buzzbomb,** bumblebomb, doodlebug.

**.5 multistage rocket, step rocket;** two- or
three-stage rocket, two- or three-step
rocket; single-stage rocket, single step
rocket, one-step rocket; **booster,** booster

unit, booster rocket, takeoff booster or
rocket; piggyback rocket.

**.6 test rocket,** research rocket, high-altitude
research rocket, registering rocket, instrument rocket, instrument carrier, test instrument vehicle, rocket laboratory;
probe.

**.7 proving ground,** testing ground; firing
area; impact area; control center, bunker;
radar tracking station, tracking station,
visual tracking station; meteorological
tower.

**.8 rocket propulsion,** reaction propulsion,
jet propulsion, blast propulsion; **fuel, propellant,** solid fuel, liquid fuel, hydrazine,
liquid oxygen or lox; charge, propelling
or propulsion charge, powder charge or
grain, high-explosive charge; **thrust,** constant thrust; **exhaust,** jet blast, backflash.

**.9 rocket launching** or **firing,** ignition,
launch, shot, shoot; **lift-off,** blast-off;
guided or automatic control, program-
ming; flight, trajectory; **burn; burnout,**
end of burning; velocity peak, Brenn-
schluss [Ger]; altitude peak, ceiling; descent; airburst; impact.

**.10 rocket launcher,** projector; **launching** or
**launch pad,** launching platform or rack,
firing table; **silo;** takeoff ramp; tower projector, launching tower; launching mortar, launching tube, projector tube, firing
tube; rocket gun, bazooka, antitank
rocket, Panzerfaust [Ger]; superbazooka;
multiple projector, calliope, Stalin organ,
Katusha; antisubmarine projector, Mark
10, hedgehog [slang]; Minnie Mouse
launcher, mousetrap [slang]; Meilewagon.

**.11 rocket scientist** or **technician,** rocketeer
or rocketer, rocket or missile man, rocket
or missile engineer.

**.12 VERBS rocket, skyrocket.**

**.13 launch,** project, shoot, fire, blast off.

**.14 rockets, missiles**

AAM (air-to-air mis-
    sile)
AA target rocket
ABM (antiballistic
    missile)
airborne rocket
anchor rocket
antiaircraft rocket
antimine rocket
antimissile
antiradar rocket
antisubmarine or anti-
    sub rocket
antitank rocket
ASM (air-to-surface
    missile)
ATA missile (air-to-
    air)

ATG rocket (air-to-
    ground)
atom-rocket
ATS (air-to-ship)
AUM (air-to-underwa-
    ter missile)
barrage rocket
bat bomb
bazooka rocket
bombardment rocket
chemical rocket
combat high-explosive
    rocket
Congreve rocket
countermissile
demolition rocket
fin-stabilized rocket
fireworks rocket

flare rocket
flying tank
GAPA (ground-to-air pilotless aircraft)
glide bomb
GTA rocket (ground-to-air)
GTG rocket (ground-to-ground)
guided missile
harpoon rocket
high-altitude rocket
homing rocket
HVAR (high velocity aircraft rocket)
ICBM (intercontinental ballistic missile)
incendiary antiaircraft rocket
incendiary rocket
ion rocket
IRBM (intermediate range ballistic missile)
line-throwing rocket
liquid-fuel rocket
long-range rocket
MIRV (multiple independently targetable re-entry vehicle)
MRV (multiple re-entry vehicle)
ram rocket
retro-float light
retro-rocket
rockoon
SAM (surface-to-air missile)
signal rocket

skyrocket
smokeless powder rocket
smoke rocket
snake (antimine)
solid-fuel rocket
space rocket 282.2
spinner
spin-stabilized rocket
SSM (surface-to-surface missile)
STS rocket (ship-to-shore)
submarine killer
supersonic rocket
target missile
torpedo rocket
training rocket *or* missile
trajectory missile
transoceanic rocket
vernier, vernier rocket
window rocket (antiradar)
winged rocket
XAAM (experimental air-to-air missile)
XASM (experimental air-to-surface missile)
XAUM (experimental air-to-underwater missile)
XSAM (experimental surface-to-air missile)
XSSM (experimental surface-to-surface missile)

**.15 rocket and missile names**

Aerobee
Aerojet
Asp
Asroc
Astor
Atlas
Atlas-Agena
Atlas-Centaur
Bomarc
Bullpup
Cajun
Corporal
Corvus
Crossbow
Dart
Davy Crockett
Deacon
Delta
Diamant
Ding-Dong
Dove
Falcon
Firebee
Genie
Hawk
Holy Moses
Honest John
Hound Dog
Jupiter
Lacrosse
Lark

Little John
Lobber
Loki
Loon
Mace
Matador
Mauler
Minnie Mouse
Minuteman
NATIV (North American test instrument vehicle)
Navaho
Nike
Nike Ajax
Nike Hercules
Nike Zeus
Pershing
Petrel
Pofo
Polaris
Poseidon
Private A
Private F
Quail
Ram
Rascal
Redeye
Redstone
Regulus I
Saturn

Scout
Sentinel
Sergeant
Shillelagh
Sidewinder
Skybolt
Snark
Spaerobee
Sparrow
SS-9, SS-10, SS-11
Subroc
Super Talos
Talos

Tartar
Terrier
Thor
Thor Able Star
Thor-Agena
Thor-Delta
Tiny Tim
Titan
V-1, V-2
Viking
WAC-Corporal
Wagtail
Zuni

**.16 torpedoes**

aerial torpedo
bangalore torpedo
homing torpedo
rocket torpedo

spar torpedo
submarine torpedo *or* fish [slang]

## 282. SPACE TRAVEL

**.1 NOUNS** space travel, astronautics, cosmonautics, space flight, navigation of empty space; interplanetary travel, space exploration; space walk; space navigation, astrogation; space science, space technology *or* engineering; aerospace science, aerospace technology *or* engineering; space *or* aerospace research; space *or* aerospace medicine, bioastronautics; astrionics; escape velocity; rocketry 281; multistage flight, step flight, shuttle flights; trip to the moon, trip to Mars, grand tour; space terminal, target planet; science fiction 608.7.

**.2 spacecraft, spaceship, space rocket,** rocket ship, manned rocket, interplanetary rocket; **rocket** 281.2; **capsule, space capsule,** ballistic capsule; module, command module, lunar excursion module, lunar module, LEM, LM; moon ship, Mars ship, etc.; deep-space ship; exploratory ship, reconnaissance rocket; ferry rocket, tender rocket, tanker ship, fuel ship; **multistage rocket** 281.5, shuttle rocket, retro rocket, attitude-control rocket, main rocket; **burn;** space docking, docking, docking maneuver; **orbit,** parking orbit; earth orbit, apogee, perigee; lunar *or* moon orbit, apolune, perilune, apocynthion, pericynthion; soft landing, hard landing; injection, insertion, lunar insertion, Earth insertion; **reentry, splashdown.**

**.3 flying saucer,** unidentified flying object, UFO.

**.4 rocket engine** 281.2; atomic power plant; solar battery.

**.5 space station,** astro station, **space island,** island base, cosmic stepping-stone, halfway station, advance base; manned station; inner station, outer station, transit station; space airport, **spaceport**, space-port station, space dock, launching base; research station, space laboratory, space observatory; tracking station, radar track-ing station; radar station, radio station; radio relay station, radio mirror; space mirror, solar mirror; moon station, moon base, lunar base, lunar city, observatory on the moon.

**.6 artificial satellite, satellite,** space satellite, robot satellite, unmanned satellite, sput-nik; communications satellite, active communications satellite, communica-tions relay satellite, weather satellite, or-biting observatory, geophysical satellite, navigational satellite, geodetic satellite, research satellite, interplanetary monitor-ing satellite, automated satellite; **probe, space probe,** geo probe, interplanetary ex-plorer.

**.7** (satellite telemetered recorders) micro-in-strumentation; aurora particle counter, cosmic ray counter, gamma ray counter, heavy particle counter, impulse recorder, magnetometer, solar ultraviolet detector, solar X-ray detector, telecamera.

**.8 astronaut,** astronavigator, cosmonaut, **spaceman,** space traveler, **rocket man,** rocketeer, rocket pilot; space doctor; space crew; planetary colony, lunar col-ony; extraterrestrial visitor, alien, saucer-man, man from Mars, Martian, little green man.

**.9 rocket society,** American Rocket Society, American Interplanetary Society, British Interplanetary Society, German Society for Space Research.

**.10** (space hazards) cosmic particles, interga-lactic matter, aurora particles, radiation, cosmic ray bombardment; meteors, mete-orites; asteroids; meteor dust impacts, meteoric particles, space bullets; extreme temperatures; the bends, blackout, weightlessness.

**.11 space suit,** pressure suit, G suit, anti-G suit; space helmet.

**.12** VERBS travel in space, go into outer space; orbit the earth, go into orbit, orbit the moon, etc.; navigate in space, astro-gate; escape earth, break free, leave the atmosphere, shoot into space; rocket to the moon, park in space, hang or float in space, space walk.

**.13** ADJS **astronautical,** cosmonautical, space-traveling; astrogational; rocket-borne, spaceborne.

**.14 spacecraft, artificial satellites, space probes**

| | |
|---|---|
| A-1 | Mars probes |
| Alouette | Mercury |
| Anna | Midas |
| Apollo | Molniya |
| Ariel | Nimbus |
| ATDA | OAO (orbiting astro- |
| Atlas-Score | nomical observato- |
| ATS | ry) |
| Aurora 7 (Mercury) | OGO (orbiting geo- |
| Biosatellite | physical observato- |
| Comsat | ry) |
| Cosmos | OSO (orbiting solar |
| Courier | observatory) |
| D1-C | OV1 |
| D2-D | OV3 |
| Diapason | Pageos |
| Discoverer | Pegasus |
| Early Bird | Pioneer |
| Echo | Polyot |
| Elektron | Proton |
| ERS | Ranger |
| ESSA (environmental | Relay |
| survey satellite) | Samos |
| Explorer | San Marco |
| Faith 7 (Mercury) | Secor |
| FR-1 | Sigma 7 (Mercury) |
| Freedom 7 (Mercury) | Skylab |
| Friendship 7 (Mercu- | Soyuz |
| ry) | Sputnik |
| GATV | Surveyor |
| Gemini | Syncom |
| Greb | Telstar |
| Injun | TIROS (television |
| Intelsat | and infrared obser- |
| Lageos (laser geody- | vation satellite) |
| namic satellite) | Transit |
| Lani Bird | Vanguard |
| Liberty Bell 7 (Mercu- | Venus probes |
| ry) | Viking |
| Lofti | Voskhod |
| Luna | Vostok |
| Lunar Orbiter | WRESAT |
| Lunik | Zond |
| Mariner | |

## 283. IMPULSE, IMPACT

*(driving and striking force)*

**.1** NOUNS **impulse,** impulsion, impelling force, impellent; **drive,** driving force or power; **thrust;** motive power, power 157; irresistible force; clout [informal]; **impe-tus; momentum;** moment, moment of force; propulsion 285.1; incitement 648.4, incentive 648.7, compulsion 756.

**.2 thrust, push, shove,** boost [informal]; press, **pressure,** piezo–, tono–; **stress,** bear-ing; **prod, poke, punch, jab,** dig, nudge; **bump,** jog, joggle, jolt; **jostle,** hustle; **butt,** bunt; head (of water, steam, etc.).

**.3 impact, collision, clash,** appulse, encoun-ter, meeting, impingement, **bump, crash,** crump, whomp; **carom,** carambole, can-non; sideswipe [informal]; smash or smashup or crack-up or crunch [all informal]; **shock, brunt;** percussion, concussion; **thrusting, ramming, bulling, bulldozing,** shouldering; hammering, smashing, mauling, sledgehammering; onslaught 798.1.

.4 **hit, blow, stroke, knock, rap, pound,** bat [informal], **slam, bang, crack, whack, smack, thwack,** smash, dash, swipe, **belt** or **clout** [both informal], **swat** [informal], **swing, punch, poke, jab,** dig, drub, thump, pelt, yerk [dial], cut, plunk [informal], chop, **clip** or **lick** [both informal], **sock** [slang], **biff** [informal]; clump or whop or bonk [all informal], dint, slog, **slug** [slang], bash [informal]; **drubbing, drumming,** tattoo, fusillade; **beating** 1010.4.

.5 (boxing blows) backhander, backhand, backstroke; sidewinder; hook; short-arm blow; swing, round-arm blow, roundhouse, Long Melford; uppercut, bolo punch; haymaker; one-two, the old one-two [both slang].

.6 **tap, rap, pat,** dab, chuck, touch, tip; **snap, flick, flip,** fillip, flirt, whisk, brush; **peck, pick.**

.7 **slap, smack,** flap; **box, cuff,** buffet; **spank;** whip, lash, cut, stripe.

.8 **kick, boot;** punt, drop kick, place kick, kicking, calcitration [archaic].

.9 **stamp,** stomp [dial], drub, clump, clop.

.10 VERBS **impel,** give an impetus, **set going** or agoing, put or set in motion, give momentum; **drive, move,** animate, actuate, forward; **thrust,** power; drive or whip on; goad; **propel** 285.10; motivate, incite 648.12–21; compel 756.4.

.11 **thrust, push** 285.10, **shove, boost** [informal]; press, stress, **bear,** bear upon, bring pressure to bear upon; **ram,** ram down, tamp, pile drive, jam, crowd, cram; bull, bulldoze; **drive, force,** run; **prod, goad, poke, punch, jab,** dig, nudge; **bump,** jog, joggle, jolt, shake, rattle; **jostle,** hustle, hurtle; elbow, shoulder; **butt, bunt,** buck [informal], run or bump or butt against, knock or run one's head against; assault 798.15.

.12 **collide,** come into collision, be on a collision course, **clash, meet,** encounter, confront each other, impinge; percuss, concuss; **bump, hit, strike, knock, bang; run into, bump into,** bang into, slam into, smack into, **crash into,** smash into, dash into, carom into; **hit against,** strike against, knock against; foul, fall or run foul or afoul of; hurtle, hurt; **carom,** cannon; **sideswipe** [informal]; **crash,** smash,

crump, whomp; smash up or crack up or crunch [all informal].

.13 **hit, strike, smite, knock,** knock down or out, knock for a loop [informal], knock cold [slang], **deck** [slang], coldcock [slang]; **clobber** or **belt** or **bat** or **clout** [all informal], **bang, slam, dash, bash** [informal], **biff** [informal], **paste** [informal], **poke, punch, jab, thwack, smack,** clap, crack, swipe, **whack;** wham or whop or clump or bonk [all informal], wallop [slang], **clip** [informal], cut, plunk [informal], **swat** [informal], soak or sock [both slang], slog, **slug** [slang], yerk [dial]; **deal,** fetch, deal or fetch a blow, hit a clip [informal], let have it; **thump,** snap; strike at 798.16.

.14 **pound, beat, hammer, maul,** sledgehammer, **knock, rap, bang,** thump, **drub,** buffet, **batter,** pulverize, paste [informal], patter, pommel, **pummel,** pelt, wallop [slang], larrup [informal], baste, lambaste [informal]; thresh, thrash; flail; spank; flap; whip 1010.14.

.15 **tap, rap, pat,** dab, chuck, touch, tip; **snap, flick, flip,** fillip, tickle, flirt, whisk, **graze;** brush; bunt; **peck, pick,** beak.

.16 **slap, smack,** flap; **box, cuff,** buffet; **spank;** whip 1010.14.

.17 **club,** cudgel, blackjack, sandbag, cosh [Brit].

.18 **kick, boot,** calcitrate [archaic]; punt, drop-kick, place-kick; knee.

.19 **stamp,** stomp [dial], trample, tread, drub, clump, clop.

.20 ADJS **impelling, impellent; impulsive,** pulsive, **moving, motive,** animating, actuating, **driving;** thrusting.

.21 concussive, percussive, crashing, smashing.

## 284. REACTION

.1 NOUNS **reaction,** retroaction; **response,** respondence, reply, answer 487.1, **rise** [slang]; **reflex,** reflection, **reflex action;** echo, bounceback, reverberation; return, revulsion; reflux, refluence; sympathetic vibration; action and reaction; predictable response, automatic or autonomic reaction; spontaneous or unthinking response, spur-of-the-moment response; conditioned reflex; –nasty, –taxia or –taxis.

.2 **recoil, rebound,** resilience, repercussion, contrecoup [Fr]; **bounce, bound, spring;** repulse, rebuff; **backlash,** backlashing, kickback, **kick,** recalcitration; **backfire, boomerang;** ricochet, carom.

.3 (a drawing back or aside) **retreat**, recoil, fallback, pullout, pullback; evasion, avoidance, sidestepping; **flinch**, wince, cringe; **side step**, shy; **dodge, duck** [informal].

.4 **reactionary**, reactionist, recalcitrant.

.5 VERBS **react, respond**, reply, answer, riposte, snap back, come back at [informal]; rise to the fly, take the bait.

.6 **recoil, rebound**, resile; **bounce, bound, spring; spring** or **fly back**, bounce or bound back, snap back; repercuss, have repercussions; **kick**, kick back, recalcitrate; **backfire, boomerang**; backlash, lash back; ricochet, carom, cannon, cannon off.

.7 **pull** or **draw back**, retreat, recoil, fade, **fall back**, reel back, hang back, start back, shrink back; **shrink, flinch, wince, cringe**, blink, blench, quail; **shy**, start or turn aside, evade, avoid, sidestep, weasel, weasel out; **dodge, duck** [informal]; jib, swerve, sheer off.

.8 get a reaction, get a response, evoke a response, ring a bell, strike a responsive chord, strike fire, strike or hit home, hit a nerve, get a rise out of [slang].

.9 ADJS **reactive**, reacting; **responsive**, respondent, responding, antiphonal; reactionary; retroactionary, retroactive; revulsive; **reflex**, reflexive; refluent; –tactic, –tropic or –trophic.

.10 recoiling, rebounding, **resilient; bouncing**, bounding, springing; repercussive; recalcitrant.

.11 ADVS **on the rebound**, on the return, on the bounce; on the spur of the moment, off the top of the head.

## 285. PUSHING, THROWING

.1 NOUNS **pushing, propulsion**, pulsion, **propelling**, propelment, **shoving; drive, thrust**, motive power, driving force; push, shove; butt, bunt; shunt, impulsion 283.1.

.2 steam propulsion, gas propulsion, gasoline propulsion, diesel propulsion, diesel-electric propulsion, jet propulsion, turbojet propulsion, pulse-jet propulsion, plasma-jet propulsion, ram-jet propulsion, resojet propulsion, rocket propulsion, reaction propulsion; wind propulsion.

.3 **throwing, projection**, trajection, jaculation, flinging, slinging, **pitching**, casting, hurling, lobbing, chucking, heaving; **shooting**, firing, gunnery, musketry; trapshooting, skeet or skeet shooting; archery.

.4 **throw, fling, sling, cast, hurl**, chuck, chunk, lob, **heave**, shy, **pitch, toss**, peg

[informal]; **flip**; put, shot-put; (football) pass, forward pass, lateral pass, lateral; (tennis) serve, service; bowl; (baseball) fastball, curve, screwball, incurve, outcurve, upcurve, downcurve, sinker, slider, knuckleball, spitball, spitter, change-up, change of pace.

.5 **shot**, discharge; ejection 310; detonation 456.3; gunfire 798.9; **gun, cannon** 801.5,6; bullet 801.13; **salvo, volley**, fusillade, tattoo, spray; bowshot, gunshot, stoneshot, potshot.

.6 **projectile**, trajectile; ejecta, ejectamenta [both pl]; **missile** 801.12; ball 255.13; discus, quoit.

.7 **propeller**, prop [informal], airscrew; propellant, propulsor, driver; **screw**, wheel, screw propeller, twin screws; paddle wheel; turbine, turbo–; fan, impeller, rotor; piston.

.8 **thrower, pitcher**, hurler, chucker, heaver, tosser, flinger, slinger; **bowler**; shotputter; javelin thrower; discus thrower, discobolus.

.9 **shooter**, shot; **gunner, gun, gunman; rifleman**, musketeer, carabineer; cannoneer, artilleryman 800.10; Nimrod, hunter 655.5; trapshooter; archer, bowman, toxophilite; **marksman**, markswoman, targetshooter, **sharpshooter**, sniper; good shot, dead shot, deadeye, **crack shot**.

.10 VERBS **push, propel**, impel, **shove**, thrust 283.11; **drive, move**, forward, advance; sweep, sweep along; butt, bunt; shunt; pole, row; pedal, treadle; **roll**, troll, bowl, trundle.

.11 **throw, fling, sling, pitch, toss, cast, hurl**, hurtle, **heave, chuck**, chunk, lob, peg [informal], shy, fire, launch, dash, let fly; catapult; **flip**, snap, jerk; bowl; pass; serve; put, put the shot; dart, lance, tilt; fork, pitchfork; pelt 798.27,28.

.12 **project**, traject, jaculate.

.13 **shoot, fire**, fire off, let off, let fly, **discharge**, eject 310.13; detonate 456.8; gun [informal], pistol; shoot at 798.22, gun for [informal]; strike, hit, plug [slang]; shoot down, fell, drop, stop in one's tracks; **riddle, pepper**, pelt, pump full of lead [slang]; snipe, pick off; torpedo; pot; potshoot, potshot, take a potshot; load, prime, charge; cock.

.14 **start**, start off, start up, give a start, **put** or **set in motion**, set on foot, set going or agoing, start going; **kick off** or **start the ball rolling** [both informal]; **launch**, float, set afloat; send, send off or forth; bundle, bundle off.

.15 ADJS propulsive, propulsory, pulsive; **propellant,** propelling; motive; **driving, pushing,** shoving.

.16 projectile, trajectile, jaculatory; **ballistic,** missile; ejective 310.28.

.17 jet-propelled, rocket-propelled, steam-propelled, gasoline-propelled, gas-propelled, diesel-propelled, wind-propelled, self-propelled.

## 286. PULLING

.1 NOUNS **pulling, traction, drawing,** draft, heaving, tugging; pulling *or* tractive power, **pull;** tug-of-war; towing, towage; hauling, haulage, drayage; attraction 288; extraction 305.

.2 **pull, draw,** draft, **heave, haul,** lug [informal], **tug,** strain, drag.

.3 **jerk, yerk** [dial], **yank** [informal], quick *or* sudden pull; **twitch, tweak, pluck,** hitch, wrench, snatch, start, bob; **flip, flick, flirt,** flounce; jig, **jiggle;** jog, joggle.

.4 VERBS **pull, draw, heave, haul,** hale, lug, **tug, tow,** take in tow; trail, train; **drag,** draggle, snake [informal]; troll, trawl.

.5 jerk, yerk [dial], **yank** [informal]; **twitch,** tweak, pluck, snatch, hitch, wrench, snake [informal]; **flip, flick, flirt, flounce;** jiggle, jig, jigget, jigger; jog, joggle.

.6 ADJS **pulling, drawing,** tractional, tractive, hauling, tugging, towing; draft.

## 287. LEVERAGE, PURCHASE

*(mechanical advantage applied to
moving or raising)*

.1 NOUNS **leverage,** fulcrumage; **pry,** prize [dial].

.2 **purchase, hold,** advantage; **foothold,** toehold, footing; differential purchase; collier's purchase; traction.

.3 **fulcrum, axis, pivot,** bearing, rest, resting point, *point d'appui* [Fr]; thole, tholepin, rowlock, oarlock.

.4 **lever; pry,** prize [dial]; **bar,** pinch bar, **crowbar,** crow, iron crow, wrecking bar, ripping bar, claw bar; cant hook, peavey; **jimmy;** handspike, marlinespike; boom, spar, beam, outrigger; pedal, treadle, crank; limb.

.5 **arm,** brachi(o)–; forearm; wrist; elbow; upper arm, biceps.

.6 **tackle** 287.10, purchase.

.7 **windlass; capstan; winch,** crab; reel; Chinese windlass, Spanish windlass.

.8 VERBS **get a purchase, get leverage, get a foothold; pry, prize, lever,** wedge; **jimmy,** crowbar.

.9 **reel in,** wind in, draw in, pull in, crank in, trim, tighten, tauten, draw taut; windlass, winch, crank, reel; tackle.

.10 **tackle**

| | |
|---|---|
| Bell's tackle *or* purchase | handy-billy |
| | hatch tackle |
| block | jigger |
| block and fall *or* falls | luff, luff tackle |
| block and tackle | luff upon luff |
| boat falls | pulley |
| boom tackle | pulley tackle |
| burton | runner |
| cat | runner and tackle |
| chain block | runner tackle |
| chain fall | single tackle |
| collier's purchase | single-whip tackle |
| deck tackle | snatch block |
| differential tackle | Spanish burton |
| double *or* twofold tackle | stay tackle |
| | tackle block |
| duplex purchase | threefold, fourfold, |
| fall | etc., tackle |
| fore-and-aft tackle | top burton |
| foretackle | yard tackle |
| gun tackle | |

## 288. ATTRACTION

*(a drawing toward)*

.1 NOUNS **attraction,** traction 286.1, attractiveness, attractivity; attractance *or* attractancy; mutual attraction; pulling power, **pull,** drag, draw, tug; magnetism 342.7; gravity, gravitation, gravit(o)–; centripetal force; capillarity, capillary attraction; adduction; affinity, sympathy; **allurement** 650.

.2 attractor, attractant, attrahent; adductor; cynosure, focus, center, center of attraction *or* attention; **lure** 650.2.

.3 **magnet,** artificial magnet, field magnet, bar magnet, horseshoe magnet, electromagnet, solenoid, paramagnet, electromagnetic lifting magnet, magnetic battery; magnetic needle; lodestone, magnetite; lodestar, polestar.

.4 VERBS **attract, pull, draw,** drag, tug, pull *or* draw towards, have an attraction; **magnetize,** magnet, be magnetic; **lure** 650.4; adduct.

.5 ADJS attracting, drawing, pulling, dragging, tugging; **attractive, magnetic,** magnetized, attrahent; sympathetic; **alluring** 650.7; adductive, adducent.

.6 ADVS attractionally, attractively; magnetically.

## 289. REPULSION

*(a thrusting away)*

.1 NOUNS **repulsion,** repellence *or* repellency, **repelling;** mutual repulsion, polarizization; disaffinity; centrifugal force; magnetic repulsion, diamagnetism; antigravity.

.2 **repulse, rebuff; dismissal,** cold shoulder, snub, spurning, brush-off, cut; refusal.

.3 VERBS **repulse, repel, rebuff, turn back,** put back, beat back, drive or push or thrust back; drive away, chase, chase off or away; send off or away, send about one's business, **send packing,** pack off, dismiss; snub, cut, brush off; spurn, refuse; **ward off,** hold off, keep off, fend off, keep at arm's length.

.4 ADJS **repulsive, repellent, repelling;** diamagnetic, of opposite polarity.

.5 ADVS repulsively, repellently.

## 290. DIRECTION

*(compass direction or course)*

.1 NOUNS **direction,** quarter, line, direction line, line of direction, point, **aim, way,** track, range, **bearing,** azimuth, compass reading, **heading, course;** current, set, tendency, inclination, bent, trend, tenor, run, drift; **orientation,** lay, lie; steering, steerage, helmsmanship, piloting; navigation 275.1,2; line of march.

.2 [naut & aero terms] vector, tack; compass direction, azimuth, compass bearing or heading, magnetic bearing or heading, relative bearing or heading, true bearing or heading or course; lee side, weather side 242.2,3.

.3 **points of the compass,** cardinal points, half points, quarter points, degrees, compass rose; compass card, lubber line; rhumb, loxodrome; **north,** northward, nor', arct(o)–; **south,** southward, austr(o)–, not(o)–; **east,** eastward, orient, sunrise; **west,** westward, occident, sunset; southeast, southwest, northeast, northwest.

.4 easting, westing, northing, southing.

.5 **orientation, bearings;** adaptation, adjustment, accommodation, alignment, collimation; disorientation.

.6 VERBS **direct, point, aim, turn, bend, train,** present, fix, set, determine; point to or at, hold on, fix on, sight on; aim at, level at, turn or train upon; directionize, give a push in the right direction.

.7 **direct to,** give directions to, lead or conduct to, point out to, show, **show** or **point the way,** steer, put on the track, put on the right track, set straight, set or put right.

.8 (have or take a direction) **bear, head,** turn, point, aim, take or hold a heading, lead, go, steer, direct oneself, align oneself; **incline, tend,** trend, set, dispose, verge, tend to go.

.9 wester, west, western; easter, east, eastern; norther, north, northern; souther, south, southern.

.10 **head for, bear for, go for,** make for, hit for [informal], **steer for,** hold for, put for, **set out** or **off for,** strike out for, take off for [informal], bend one's steps for, lay for, bear up for, bear up to, make up to, set in towards; set or direct or shape one's course for, set one's compass for, sail for 275.35; align one's march; **break for,** make a break for [informal], run or dash for, make a run or dash for.

.11 go directly, go straight, follow one's nose, go straight on, **head straight for,** vector for, go straight to the point, steer a straight course, follow a course, keep or hold one's course, hold steady for, arrow for, cleave to the line, keep pointed; **make a beeline,** take the air line, stay on the beam.

.12 **orient,** orientate, orient or orientate oneself, orient the map or chart, **take** or **get one's bearings,** get the lay or lie of the land, see which way the land lies, see which way the wind blows; adapt, adjust, accommodate.

.13 ADJS **direct,** immediate, **straight, straightforward,** straightaway, straightway; **undeviating,** unswerving, unveering; uninterrupted, unbroken; one-way, unidirectional, irreversible.

.14 **directable,** aimable, pointable, trainable; **steerable,** dirigible, guidable, leadable; **directed,** aimed; well-aimed or -directed or -placed; on the mark, on the nose or money [informal]; **directional,** directive.

.15 **northern,** north, northernmost, northerly, northbound, **arctic,** boreal, hyperborean; **southern,** south, southernmost, southerly, southbound, meridional, **antarctic,** austral; **eastern,** east, easternmost or eastermost, easterly, eastbound, **oriental; western,** west, westernmost, westerly, westbound, **occidental; northeastern,** northeast, northeasterly; **southeastern,** southeast, southeasterly; **southwestern,** southwest, southwesterly; **northwestern,** northwest, northwesterly.

.16 ADVS **north, N,** nor', northerly, northward, north'ard, norward, northwards, northwardly; north about.

.17 **south, S,** southerly, southward, south'ard, southwards, southwardly; south about.

.18 **east**, E, easterly, eastward, eastwards, eastwardly, where the sun rises; east-about.

.19 **west**, W, westerly, westernly, westward, westwards, westwardly; westabout.

.20 **northeast**, NE, nor'east, northeasterly, northeastward, northeastwards, northeastwardly; north-northeast, NNE; northeast by east, N by E; northeast by north, NE by N.

.21 **northwest**, NW, nor'west, northwesterly, northwestward, northwestwards, northwestwardly; north-northwest, NNW; northwest by west, NW by W; northwest by north, NW by N.

.22 **southeast**, SE, southeasterly, southeastward, southeastwards, southeastwardly; south-southeast, SSE; southeast by east, SE by E; southeast by south, SE by S.

.23 **southwest**, SW, southwesterly, southwestward, southwestwards, southwestwardly; south-southwest, SSW; southwest by south, SW by S.

.24 **directly**, **direct**, **straight**, straightly, straightforward, straightforwards, **undeviatingly**, unswervingly, unveeringly; **straight ahead**, dead ahead; due, dead, due north, etc.; right, forthright; –way(s), –wise, –ward(s); in a direct or straight line, in line with, in a line for, **in a beeline**, **as the crow flies**, straight across; straight as an arrow.

.25 **squarely**, **square**, **right**, **straight**, flush, full, point-blank; **plump**, plumb, plunk, kerplunk, plop, smack, smack-dab, spang; **exactly**, precisely.

.26 **clockwise**, rightward 243.7; **counterclockwise**, anticlockwise, widdershins, leftward 244.6; **homeward**; landward; seaward; earthward; heavenward; leeward, windward 242.9.

.27 **in every direction**, in all directions, in all manner of ways, every which way [informal], everywhither, **everyway**, **everywhere**, in all directions at once, in every quarter, on every side; around, all round, round about; forty ways or six ways from Sunday [informal]; from every quarter, everywhence; from or to the four corners of the earth, from or to the four winds.

.28 PREPS **toward**, towards, **in the direction of**, **to**, up, on, upon; ad– or ac– or af– or ag– or al– or ap– or as– or at–, pros–; against, over against, versus; headed for, on the way to, on the road or high road to, in transit to, en route to, on route to, in passage to.

.29 **through**, by, passing by or through, **by way of**, by the way of, **via**; over, around, round about, here and there in, all through.

## 291. DEVIATION

*(indirect course)*

.1 NOUNS **deviation**, deviance or deviancy, **deviousness**, **departure**, **digression**, diversion, **divergence**, divarication, branching off, divagation, declination, aberration, aberrancy, **variation**, indirection, exorbitation; detour, excursion, excursus, discursion; obliquity, bias, skew, slant; **circuitousness** 321; **wandering**, rambling, **straying**, errantry, pererration; drift, drifting; turning, shifting, swerving, swinging; **turn**, corner, bend, curve, dogleg, crook, hairpin, zigzag, twist, warp, swerve, **veer**, sheer, sweep; shift, double; tack, yaw; wandering or twisting or zigzag or shifting course or path; –plania.

.2 **deflection**, deflexure, flection, flexure; torsion, distortion; skewness; **refraction**, **diffraction**, **scatter**, diffusion, dispersion.

.3 VERBS **deviate**, **depart from**, **vary**, **diverge**, divaricate, branch off, **digress**, divagate, **turn aside**, go out of the way, detour; **swerve**, **veer**, sheer, curve, **shift**, **turn**, trend, bend, heel, bear off; tack 275.30; alter one's course, change the bearing.

.4 **stray**, go astray, lose one's way, err; take a wrong turn or turning; drift, go adrift; **wander**, ramble, rove, straggle, divagate, excurse, pererrate; meander, wind, twist, snake, twist and turn.

.5 **deflect**, deviate, **divert**, diverge, **turn**, bend, curve, pull, crook, dogleg, hairpin, zigzag; **warp**, bias, twist, distort, skew; refract, diffract, **scatter**, **diffuse**, **disperse**.

.6 **turn aside** or **to the side**, draw aside, side, **turn away**, jib, shy, shy off; avert; gee, haw; **sidetrack**, shove aside, shunt, switch; **head off**, turn back 289.3; **step aside**, sidestep, move aside or to the side, sidle; **steer clear of**, make way for, get out of the way of; go off, bear off, sheer off, veer off, ease off, edge off; fly off, go or fly off at a tangent; glance, glance off.

.7 ADJS **deviative**, deviatory, deviating, **deviant**, departing, aberrant, aberrational, aberrative, shifting, turning, swerving, veering; **digressive**, discursive, excursive, **circuitous**; **devious**, indirect, out-of-the-way; errant, erratic, zigzag, **wandering**, rambling, roving, winding, twisting, meandering, snaky, serpentine, mazy, labyrinthine, vagrant, stray, desultory, planetary, undirected.

.8 **deflective**, inflective, flectional, diffractive, refractive; **refractile**, **refrangible**; deflected, flexed, refracted, diffracted, scattered, diffuse, diffused, dispersed; distorted, skewed, skew.

## 292. LEADING

### (going ahead)

.1 NOUNS **leading**, **heading**, foregoing; anteposition, the lead, le pas [Fr]; **preceding**, precedence 64; priority 116; **front**, van 240; precursor 66.

.2 VERBS **lead**, **head**, spearhead, stand at the head, stand first, head the line; take the lead, go in the lead, **lead the way**, be the bellwether; lead the dance; **light the way**, beacon, guide; get before, get ahead or in front of, come to the front, lap, outstrip, pace, set the pace; get or have the start, get a head start, steal a march upon; **precede** 64.2, **go before** 66.3.

.3 ADJS **leading**, **heading**, precessional, precedent, precursory, foregoing; **first**, **foremost**, headmost; **preceding**, antecedent 64.4; **prior** 116.4; **chief** 36.14.

.4 ADVS **before** 64.6, in front, foremost, headmost, in advance 240.12.

## 293. FOLLOWING

### (going behind)

.1 NOUNS **following**, heeling, **trailing**, tailing [informal], shadowing; **hounding**, dogging, chasing, **pursuit**, pursual, pursuance; sequence 65; sequel 67; series 71.2.

.2 **follower**, successor, tagtail, tail [informal], shadow; **pursuer**, pursuivant; **attendant** 73.4, **satellite**, **hanger-on**, dangler, adherent, appendage, dependent, parasite, stooge [slang], flunky; **henchman**, ward heeler, partisan, supporter, votary, sectary; fan or buff [both informal]; courtier, homme de cour [Fr], cavaliere servente [Ital]; trainbearer; **public**; following 73.6; disciple 566.2.

.3 VERBS **follow**, go after or behind, come after or behind, move behind, **pursue**, **shadow**, tail [informal], **trail**, trail after, follow in the trail of, camp on the trail of, **heel**, follow or tread on the heels of, follow in the steps or footsteps or footprints of, tread close upon, follow in the wake of, hang on the skirts of, stick like the shadow of, sit on the tail of, tailgate [slang], go in the rear of, bring up the

rear, eat the dust of, take or swallow one's dust; tag or **tag after** or tag along [all informal]; string along [informal]; dog, bedog, **hound**, chase, **pursue**.

.4 **lag**, **lag behind**, straggle, drag, trail, **trail behind**, hang back, loiter, linger, **loiter** or **linger behind**, dawdle, get behind, fall behind or behindhand.

.5 ADJS **following**, trailing; succeeding 65.4; consecutive 71.9.

.6 ADVS **behind**, **after**, in the rear, in the train or wake of; in back of 241.13.

## 294 PROGRESSION

### (motion forwards)

.1 NOUNS **progression**, **progress**, progressiveness; **passage**, course, march, career; **advance**, advancing, **advancement**, promotion, **furtherance**, furthering; forward motion, forwarding, forwardal; **ongoing**, ongo, go-ahead [informal], onward course, rolling, rolling on; **headway**, way; travel 273.

.2 VERBS **progress**, **advance**, **proceed**, **go**, go or move forward, step forward, go on, **go ahead**, go along, pass on or along; **move**, travel 273.17; go fast 269.8–18; **make progress**, come on, **get along**, come along [informal], **get ahead**; further oneself; **make headway**, roll, gather head, gather way; make strides or rapid strides, cover ground, get over the ground, make good time, make the best of one's way; make up for lost time, gain ground, make up leeway, make progress against, make head against, stem.

.3 **march on**, run on, rub on, **jog on**, roll on, flow on; drift along, go with the stream.

.4 **make one's way**, **work one's way**, weave or worm or thread one's way, inch forward, feel one's way, muddle through; go slow 270.6–9; carve one's way; push or force one's way, fight one's way; **forge ahead**, drive on or ahead, **push** or **press on** or **onward**, push or press forward, push, crowd.

.5 **advance**, **further**, **promote**, forward, hasten, contribute to, foster.

.6 ADJS **progressive**, progressing, advancing, proceeding, **ongoing**, oncoming, onward, forward, **forward-looking**, go-ahead [informal]; moving 273.35.

.7 ADVS **in progress**, in mid-progress; **going on**.

.8 **forward**, **forwards**, **onward**, **onwards**, **forth**, **on**, along, ahead; on the way to, on the road or high road to, en route to or for.

## 295. REGRESSION

### (motion backwards)

.1 NOUNS **regression**, regress; recession 297; **retrogression**, retrocession, retroflexion, reflux, refluence, retrogradation, retroaction, retrusion, reaction; **return**, reentry; **setback**, backset, throwback, rollback, sternway; **backward motion**, backward step; **backsliding**, lapse, relapse, recidivism, recidivation.

.2 **retreat**, *reculade* [Fr], **withdrawal**, withdrawment, **retirement**, **fallback**, pullout, pullback; advance to the rear; disengagement.

.3 **reverse**, **reversal**, reversing, reversion; **backing**, backing up, backing off, backing out, backup; **about-face**, *volte-face* [Fr], about-turn, right-about, right-about-face, turn to the right-about, U-turn, turnaround, turnabout, swingaround; **back track**, back trail.

.4 **countermotion**, countermovement; countermarching, countermarch.

.5 VERBS **regress**, go backwards, **recede**, return, revert; **retrogress**, retrograde, retroflex, retrocede; pull back, jerk back, cock (the arm, fist, etc.); fall or get or go behind, fall astern, lose ground, slip back; **backslide**, lapse, relapse, recidivate.

.6 **retreat**, sound or beat a retreat, **withdraw**, **retire**, pull out or back, advance to the rear, disengage; **fall back**, move back, go back, stand back; run back; **draw back**, draw off; **back out** or **out of** [informal], back down; give ground, give place.

.7 **reverse**, go into reverse; **back**, **back up**, backpedal, back off or away; **backwater**, make sternway; **backtrack**, backtrail, take the back track; countermarch; reverse one's field; take the reciprocal course.

.8 **turn back**, put back; double, double back, retrace one's steps; turn one's back upon; **return**, go or come back, go or come home.

.9 **turn round** or **around** or **about**, turn, make a U-turn, turn on a dime, turn tail, **come** or **go about**, put about, fetch about; veer, veer around; **swivel**, pivot, pivot about, swing, round, swing round; wheel, wheel about, whirl, spin; heel, turn upon one's heel.

.10 **about-face**, *volte-face* [Fr], right-about-face, **do an about-face** or a right-about-face or an about-turn, perform a *volte-*

*face*, **face about**, turn or face to the right-about, do a turn to the right-about.

.11 ADJS **regressive**, recessive; **retrogressive**, retrocessive, retrograde; retroactive; reactionary.

.12 **reversed**, reflex, **turned around**, back, **backward**; wrong-way, wrong-way around, counter.

.13 ADVS **backwards**, backward, retrad, **hindwards**, hindward, **rearwards**, rearward, arear, astern; **back**, away, fro, *à reculons* [Fr]; **in reverse**, ass-backwards [slang]; against the grain, *à rebours* [Fr]; counterclockwise, anticlockwise, widdershins; an(a)–, re–, retro–.

## 296. APPROACH

### (motion towards)

.1 NOUNS **approach**, approaching, coming toward, coming near, **access**, accession, nearing; approximation, proximation, appropinquation [archaic]; advance, oncoming; **advent**, **coming**, forthcoming; flowing toward, afflux, affluxion; appulse; nearness 200; imminence 152.

.2 **approachability**, **accessibility**, **access**, getatableness or come-at-ableness [both informal], attainability.

.3 VERBS **approach**, **near**, **draw near** or **nigh**, go or come near, come closer or nearer, come to close quarters; **close**, close in, close with; **accost**, encounter, confront; approximate, proximate, appropinquate [archaic]; **advance**, come, **come forward**, come on, come up, bear up, step up; ease or edge or sidle up to; bear down on or upon, be on a collision course with; gain upon, narrow the gap.

.4 ADJS **approaching**, **nearing**, advancing; attracted to, drawn to; **coming**, **oncoming**, **forthcoming**, upcoming, to come; approximate, proximate, approximative; near 200.14; imminent 152.3; –petal, –philic.

.5 **approachable**, **accessible**, getatable or come-at-able [both informal], attainable.

## 297. RECESSION

### (motion from)

.1 NOUNS **recession**, recedence, receding, retrocedence; **retreat**, **retirement**, **withdrawal**; retraction, retractation, retractility.

.2 VERBS **recede**, retrocede; **retreat**, **retire**, **withdraw**; move off or away, stand off or away, stand out from the shore; go, **go away**; **die away**, fade away, drift away; diminish, decline, sink, shrink, dwindle, fade, ebb, wane; go out with the tide, fade into the distance; pull away, widen the distance.

.3 retract, withdraw, draw or pull back, pull out, draw or pull in; draw in one's claws or horns; shrink, wince, cringe, flinch, shy, duck.

.4 ADJS recessive, recessional, recessionary; recedent, retrocedent.

.5 receding, retreating, retiring; diminishing, declining, sinking, shrinking, dwindling, ebbing, waning; fading, dying.

.6 retractile, retractable, retrahent.

## 298. CONVERGENCE

### (coming together)

.1 NOUNS convergence, converging, confluence, concourse, conflux; mutual approach, approach 296; meeting, congress, concurrence; concentration, centralization, focalization 226.8, focus 226.4; collision course, narrowing gap; funnel, bottleneck; hub, spokes; asymptote; radius; tangent; crossing 221.

.2 VERBS converge, come together, approach 296.3, run together, meet, unite; intersect; fall in with; be on a collision course; narrow the gap, close with, close, close up, close in; funnel; taper, pinch, nip; centralize, center, come to a center; concentralize, concenter, concentrate, come or tend to a point; come to a focus 226.10.

.3 ADJS converging, convergent; meeting, uniting; concurrent, confluent, mutually approaching, approaching; connivent; focal, confocal; centrolineal, centripetal; asymptotic(al); radial, radiating; tangent, tangential.

## 299. DIVERGENCE

### (recession from one another)

.1 NOUNS divergence or divergency, divarication; aberration, deviation 291; separation, division, decentralization; centrifugence; spread, spreading, spreading out, splaying, fanning, fanning out, deployment.

.2 radiation, ray, radius, spoke; radiance, diffusion, scattering, dispersion, emanation.

.3 forking, furcation, bifurcation, biforking, trifurcation, divarication; branching, branching off or out, ramification; arborescence, arborization, treelikeness.

.4 fork, prong, trident; Y, V; branch, ramification, stem, offshoot, –dendron; crotch, crutch; fan, delta, Δ; groin, inguen, inguin(o)–; furcula, furculum, wishbone.

.5 VERBS diverge, divaricate; aberrate; separate, divide; spread, spread out, outspread, splay, fan out, deploy; go off or away, fly or go off at a tangent.

.6 radiate, ray, diffuse, emanate, spread, disperse, scatter.

.7 fork, furcate, bifurcate, trifurcate, divaricate; branch, stem, ramify, branch off or out.

.8 ADJS diverging, divergent; divaricate, divaricating; palmate, palmated, palmi–, palmat(i)–; fanlike, fan-shaped; deltoid(al), deltalike, delta-shaped; splayed; centrifugal.

.9 radiating, radial, radiate, radiated, radio–; rayed, spoked; radiative; actin(o)–, actini–, –actinal, –actine.

.10 forked, forking, furcate, biforked, bifurcate, bifurcated, forklike, trifurcate, trifurcated, tridentlike, pronged; crotched, Y-shaped, V-shaped; branched, branching; arborescent, arboreal, arboriform, treelike, tree-shaped, dendriform, dendritic; branchlike, ramous.

## 300. ARRIVAL

.1 NOUNS arrival, coming, advent, approach, appearance, reaching; attainment, accomplishment, achievement.

.2 landing, landfall; docking, mooring, tying up, dropping anchor; disembarkation, disembarkment, debarkation, coming or going ashore.

.3 return, homecoming, recursion; reentrance, reentry; remigration.

.4 welcome, greetings 925.2–4.

.5 destination, goal, bourn [archaic]; port, haven, harbor, anchorage, journey's end; end of the line, terminus, terminal, terminal point; stop, stopping place, last stop.

.6 VERBS arrive, arrive at, arrive in, come, come or get to, approach, reach, hit [informal]; find, gain, attain, attain to, accomplish, achieve, make, make it [informal], fetch, fetch up at, get there, reach one's destination, come to one's journey's end; make or put in an appearance, show up [informal], turn up, pop or bob up [informal]; get in, come in, blow in [slang], pull in, roll in; check in; clock or punch or ring or time in [all informal], sign in; hit town [informal]; come to hand, be received.

.7 **arrive at,** come at, get at, **reach,** arrive upon, **come upon, hit upon,** strike upon, fall upon, light upon, pitch upon, stumble on or upon.

.8 **land,** come to land, make a landfall, set foot on dry land; reach or make land, make port; put in or into, put into port; dock, moor, tie up, drop anchor; go ashore, **disembark,** debark, unboat; **detrain,** debus, deplane, disemplane; alight 316.7, 278.52.

.9 ADJS **arriving,** approaching, entering, **coming,** incoming; inbound, inward-bound; homeward, homeward-bound.

## 301. DEPARTURE

.1 NOUNS **departure, leaving, going,** passing, **parting; exit,** walkout [informal]; exodus, hegira; egress 303; **withdrawal,** removal, retreat 295.2, retirement; evacuation, abandonment; decampment; escape, flight, getaway [informal].

.2 **outset,** outsetting, setout, outstart, **start,** starting, start-off, setoff, takeoff [informal].

.3 **embarkation,** embarkment, boarding; entrainment; enplanement or emplanement, **takeoff,** hopoff [informal].

.4 **leave-taking, leave, parting,** congé; **send-off,** Godspeed; **adieu,** one's adieus, **farewell,** aloha, **good-bye;** valedictory address, valedictory, valediction, parting words; valedictorian; viaticum; stirrup cup, one for the road, *doch-an-dorrach* or *doch-an-dorris* [both Gaelic].

.5 **point of departure, starting place** or **point,** takeoff, **start,** base, basis; line of departure; starting post or gate; stakeboat; port of embarkation.

.6 VERBS **depart,** take one's departure or leave, **leave, go,** up and go [dial], **go away, go off, get off** or **away,** get under way, come away, go one's way, go or get along, be getting along [informal], gang along [Scot], go on, get on; trot or toddle or stagger along [informal]; mosey or sashay [both informal], mosey or sashay off or along [informal]; **buzz off** or along [informal]; take wing or flight, wing it [slang]; move off or away, move out, march off or away; **pull out;** exit 303.11; take or break or tear oneself away, take oneself off.

.7 **set forth,** put forth, go forth, **sally forth,** sally, issue, issue forth, set forward, **set out** or **off,** be off, be on one's way, outset, **start, start out** or **off,** outstart, **strike out,** get off.

.8 **quit, vacate,** evacuate, abandon, turn one's back on; **withdraw,** retreat, **beat a retreat,** retire, remove; abscond, disappear, vanish; **bow out** [informal], make one's exit.

.9 **begone,** get lost or flake off [both slang], get going [informal], shove off or hit the road [both slang], **get out,** be off, take oneself off or away, get or git [both slang]; **clear out** [informal], **get the hell out** [slang], make yourself scarce [informal], vamoose [informal], beat it or scram [both slang].

.10 make off, **take off** [informal], split, dog it [both slang]; skip or skip out [both informal]; lam or take it on the lam [both slang]; powder or take a powder or take a runout powder [all slang]; skedaddle or absquatulate [both slang]; decamp.

.11 **hasten off, hurry away; scamper off, dash off,** whiz off, whip off or away, nip or nip off [both informal], tear off or out, **light out** [slang], dig or skin out [slang].

.12 **fling out** or off, flounce out or off.

.13 **run off** or **away,** run along, flee, take to flight, fly, take to one's heels, cut out or cut and run [both informal], hightail [slang], make tracks [informal]; run for one's life; run away from 631.10.

.14 **check out;** clock or ring or punch out [all informal], sign out.

.15 **decamp, break camp,** strike camp or tent, **pull up stakes.**

.16 **embark, go aboard,** board, go on board; go on shipboard, take ship; hoist the blue Peter; **entrain,** enplane or emplane, embus; weigh anchor, put to sea 275.19,20.

.17 say or bid good-bye or farewell, take leave, make one's adieus; bid Godspeed, give one a send-off, "speed the parting guest" [Pope]; drink a stirrup cup, have one for the road.

.18 **leave home,** go from home; leave the country, emigrate, out-migrate, expatriate.

.19 ADJS **departing, leaving; parting,** last, final, farewell; valedictory; outward-bound.

.20 **departed, left, gone,** gone off or away.

.21 ADVS **hence,** thence, whence; **off, away,** forth, out; therefrom, thereof; ab–, de–.

.22 PREPS **from, away from;** out, out of.

.23 INTERJS **farewell!, good-bye!, adieu!,** so **long!** [informal], cheerio! [Brit], *au revoir!* [Fr], ¡adios! [Sp], ¡hasta la vista! [Sp], ¡hasta luego! [Sp], ¡vaya con Dios! [Sp], *auf Wiedersehen!* [Ger], *addio!* [Ital], *arrivederci!, arrivederla!* [both Ital], *ciao!* [Ital informal], *do svidanye!*

[Russ], *shalom!* [Heb], *sayonara!* [Jap], *vale!, vive valeque!* [both L], aloha!, until we meet again!, until tomorrow!, *à demain!* [Fr], see you later!, see you!, I'll be seeing you!, we'll see you!, *à bientôt!* [Fr], *à toute a l'heure!* [Fr]; be good!, keep in touch!, come again!; *bon voyage!* [Fr], pleasant journey!, have a nice trip!, *tsetchem leshalom!* [Heb], *glückliche Reise!* [Ger], happy landing!; Godspeed!, peace be with you!, *pax vobiscum!* [L]; all good go with you!, God bless you!

.24 good night!, nighty-night! [informal], *bonne nuit!* [Fr], *gute Nacht!* [Ger], *¡buenas noches!* [Sp], *buona notte!* [Ital].

## 302. INGRESS, ENTRANCE

.1 NOUNS ingress, ingression, introgression; entrance, entry, entree, *entrée* [Fr]; access; ingoing, incoming, income; import, importing, importation; input, intake; penetration, interpenetration; infiltration, percolation, seepage, leakage; insinuation; intrusion 238; introduction, insertion 304; admission, reception 306.

.2 influx, influxion, inflow, inflooding, indraft, indrawing, inpour, inrun, inrush; afflux, affluxion, affluence.

.3 immigration, in-migration, incoming population, foreign influx.

.4 incomer, entrant, comer, arrival; visitor, visitant; immigrant, in-migrant; newcomer 78.4; settler 190.9; intruder 238.3.

.5 entrance, entry, entranceway, entryway; inlet, ingress, intake, adit, approach, access, means of access, in [informal], way in; opening 265; passageway, corridor, companionway, hall, passage, way; gangway, gangplank; vestibule 192.19; air lock.

.6 porch, propylaeum; portal, postern, threshold, doorjamb, gatepost, doorpost, lintel; door, doorway, French door; gate, gateway, lych gate, barway, pylon, archway; front door, back door, side door; carriage entrance, porte cochere; cellar door, cellarway; bulkhead; hatch, hatchway, scuttle; storm door; trap door, trap; tollgate; stile, turnstile, turnpike.

.7 VERBS enter, go in *or* into, cross the threshold, come in, find one's way into, put in *or* into; be admitted, gain admittance, have an entree, have an in [informal]; set foot in, step in; get in, jump in, hop in; drop in, look in, visit, pop in [informal]; breeze in, come breezing in; break *or* burst in, bust in *or* come busting in [both slang]; barge in *or* come barging in [both informal]; thrust in, push *or*

press in, crowd in, jam in, wedge in, pack in, squeeze in; slip *or* creep in, wriggle *or* worm oneself into, edge in, work in, insinuate oneself; irrupt, intrude 238.5; take in, admit 306.10; insert 304.3.

.8 penetrate 265.16, interpenetrate, pierce, pass *or* go through, get through, get into, make way into, make an entrance, gain entree.

.9 flow in, inflow, inflood, inpour, inrush, pour in.

.10 filter in, infiltrate, seep in, percolate into, leak in, soak in.

.11 immigrate, in-migrate.

.12 ADJS entering, ingressive, incoming, ingoing; in, inward; inbound, inward-bound; inflowing, inflooding, inpouring, inrushing; invasive, intrusive, irruptive; ingrowing.

.13 ADVS in, inward, inwards, inwardly; en– *or* em–, in– *or* il– *or* im– *or* ir–, ob–.

.14 PREPS into, in, to.

## 303. EGRESS, EMERGENCE

.1 NOUNS egress, egression; exit, exodus; outgoing, outgo, going out; outcoming, outcome, forthcoming; departure 301; extraction 305.

.2 emergence, emersion; surfacing; issue, issuance; extrusion; emission, emanation, vent, discharge.

.3 outburst 162.6, ejection 310.

.4 outflow, outflowing; discharge; outpour, outpouring; effluence, effusion, exhalation; efflux, effluxion, defluxion; exhaust; runoff, flowoff; outfall; drainage, drain; gush 395.4.

.5 leakage, leaking, leak; dripping, drippings, drip, dribble, drop, trickle; distillation.

.6 exudation, transudation; filtration, exfiltration, filtering; straining; percolation, percolating; leaching, lixiviation; effusion, extravasation; seepage, seep; oozing, ooze; weeping, weep; excretion 311.

.7 emigration, out-migration, remigration; exile, expatriation, deportation.

.8 export, exporting, exportation.

.9 outlet, egress, exit, outgo, outcome, out [informal], way out; loophole, escape; opening 265; outfall, estuary; chute, flume, sluice, weir, floodgate; vent, ventage, venthole, port; avenue, channel; spout, tap; debouch; exhaust; door 302.6; outgate, sally port; vomitory; emunctory; pore; blowhole, spiracle.

.10 outgoer, goer, leaver, departer; emigrant, *émigré* [Fr], out-migrant.

.11 VERBS **exit**, make an exit, **make one's exit; egress, go out, get out**, walk out, march out, run out, pass out, bow out [informal]; depart 301.6.

.12 **emerge, come out, issue**, issue forth, extrude, **come forth**, surface, sally, sally forth; emanate, effuse, arise, come; debouch, disembogue; jump out, bail out; burst forth, break forth, erupt, break cover, **come out in the open**; protrude 256.9.

.13 **run out**, empty, find vent; **exhaust** 310.23; **drain**, drain out; **flow out, outflow**, outpour, **pour out**, sluice out, well out, gush *or* spout out, flow, pour, well, surge, gush, jet, spout, spurt, vomit forth, blow out, spew out.

.14 **leak, leak out, drip**, dribble, drop, trickle, trill, weep, distill.

.15 **exude, exudate**, transude, transpire, reek; **emit, discharge**, give off; **filter**, filtrate, exfiltrate; strain; **percolate**; leach, lixiviate; effuse, extravasate; **seep, ooze**; bleed; weep; excrete 311.12.

.16 **emigrate**, out-migrate, remigrate; exile, expatriate, deport.

.17 **export**, send abroad.

.18 ADJS **emerging, emergent; issuing**, arising, surfacing, coming, forthcoming; emanating, emanent, emanative, transeunt, transient.

.19 **outgoing, outbound**, outward-bound; **outflowing**, outpouring, effusive, effluent; effused, extravasated; **extro–**.

.20 **exudative**, transudative; percolative; porous, permeable, pervious, oozy, runny, weepy, leaky; excretory 311.19.

.21 ADVS **forth; out**, outward, outwards, outwardly.

.22 PREPS **out of, ex; from; out.**

## 304. INSERTION

### *(putting in)*

.1 NOUNS **insertion, introduction**, insinuation, injection, infusion, perfusion, inoculation, intromission; entrance 302; penetration 265.3; interjection, interpolation 237.2; graft, grafting, transplant, transplantation; infixion, implantation, embedment, tessellation, impactment, impaction; –phoresis.

.2 **insert**, insertion; **inset, inlay**; tessera.

.3 VERBS **insert, introduce**, insinuate, inject, infuse, perfuse, inoculate, intromit; enter 302.7; penetrate 265.16; **put in, stick in**, set in, throw in, pop in, tuck in, whip in; slip in, ease in; interject 237.7.

.4 **install**, instate, inaugurate, initiate, invest, ordain; enlist, enroll, induct, sign up, sign on.

.5 **inset, inlay; embed** *or* bed, bed in.

.6 **graft**, engraft, **implant**, imp [archaic]; bud; inarch.

.7 **thrust in, drive in, run in, plunge in**, force in, push in, **ram in**, press in, stuff in, crowd in, squeeze in, cram in, jam in, tamp in, pound in, pack in, poke in, knock in, wedge in, impact.

.8 **implant**, infix 142.9, fit in, inlay, tessellate.

## 305. EXTRACTION

### *(taking or drawing out)*

.1 NOUNS **extraction, withdrawal**, removal; **drawing, pulling**, drawing out; ripping *or* tearing *or* wresting out; eradication, **uprooting**, unrooting, deracination; squeezing out, pressing out, expression; avulsion, evulsion, cutting out, exsection, extirpation, excision, enucleation; extrication, evolvement, disentanglement, unravelment; excavation, mining, quarrying, drilling; dredging.

.2 **disinterment, exhumation**, disentombment, **unearthing.**

.3 **drawing**, drafting, sucking, **suction**, aspiration, pipetting; pumping, siphoning, tapping, broaching; milking; drainage, draining, emptying; cupping; bloodletting, bleeding, phlebotomy, venesection.

.4 **evisceration**, gutting, **disembowelment.**

.5 **elicitation**, eduction, drawing out *or* forth, bringing out *or* forth; **evocation**, calling forth; arousal.

.6 **extortion, exaction**, claim, demand; **wresting, wrenching, wringing, rending**, tearing, ripping; wrest, wrench, wring.

.7 (obtaining an extract) **squeezing, pressing**, expression; **distillation**; decoction; **rendering**, rendition; **steeping**, soaking, infusion; concentration.

.8 **extract**, extraction; **essence, quintessence, spirit, elixir**; decoction; **distillate**, distillation; **concentrate**, concentration; infusion; refinement, purification.

.9 **extractor**, separator; siphon; aspirator, pipette; **pump**, vacuum pump; **press**, wringer; corkscrew; forceps, pliers, pincers, tweezers; crowbar.

.10 VERBS **extract, take out, get out, withdraw, remove**; pull, draw; **pull out, draw out**, tear out, rip out, wrest out, pluck out, pick out, weed out, rake out; **pull up**, pluck up; **root up** *or* **out, uproot**, unroot, eradicate, deracinate, pull or pluck up by the roots; cut out, excise, exsect; gouge out, avulse, evulse; extricate, evolve, disentangle, unravel; **dig up or out,** grub up or out, excavate, **unearth,** mine, quarry; dredge, dredge up or out.

.11 **disinter, exhume,** disentomb, unbury, unsepulcher.

.12 **draw off, draft off,** draft, draw, draw from; **suck,** suck out or up, **siphon off;** pipette; pump, pump out; tap, broach; let, let out; bleed; let blood, venesect, phlebotomize; milk; **drain,** decant; exhaust, empty.

.13 **eviscerate, disembowel, gut.**

.14 **elicit,** educe, deduce, induce, derive, obtain, procure, secure; **get from,** get out of; **evoke, call up, summon up,** call or summon forth, call out; rouse, arouse, stimulate; **draw out** or **forth,** bring out or forth, winkle out [Brit], drag out, worm out, bring to light; wangle, wangle out of, worm out of.

.15 **extort, exact,** claim, demand; **wrest, wring from, wrench from, rend from,** wrest or tear from.

.16 (obtain an extract) **squeeze** or **press out,** express, wring, wring out; **distill,** elixirate [archaic]; decoct; **render,** melt down; refine; **steep,** soak, infuse; **concentrate,** essentialize.

.17 ADJS **extractive, eductive; educible; eradicative,** uprooting; elicitory, **evocative,** arousing; **exacting,** exactive; **extortionate,** extortionary, extortive.

.18 **essential,** quintessential, pure 45.6.

## 306. RECEPTION

.1 NOUNS **reception, taking in,** receipt, receiving; welcome, welcoming; refuge 700.

.2 **admission,** admittance, acceptance; immission [archaic], intromission 304.1; **installation,** instatement, inauguration, initiation; baptism, investiture, ordination; enlistment, enrollment, induction.

.3 **entree,** entrée [Fr], in [informal], entry, entrance 302, **access,** opening, **open door,** open arms.

.4 **ingestion,** eating, imbibition, drinking; engorgement, ingurgitation, engulfment; swallowing, gulping; swallow, gulp, slurp.

.5 (drawing in) **suction,** suck, sucking, myzo–; **inhalation,** inhalement, inspiration, aspiration; snuff, snuffle, sniff, sniffle.

.6 sorption, **absorption,** adsorption, chemisorption or chemosorption, engrossment, digestion, **assimilation,** infiltration;

sponging, blotting; seepage, percolation; **osmosis,** osmo–, endosmosis, exosmosis, electroosmosis; absorbency; **absorbent,** adsorbent, **sponge, blotter,** blotting paper.

.7 (bringing in) **introduction; import,** importing, **importation.**

.8 readmission; reabsorption, resorbence.

.9 **receptivity, receptiveness,** invitingness, openness, hospitality, recipience or recipiency; receptibility, admissibility.

.10 VERBS **receive, take in; admit, let in,** immit [archaic], intromit, give entrance or admittance to, give an entree, open the door to, give refuge or shelter or sanctuary to, throw open to.

.11 **ingest,** eat, imbibe, drink; **swallow, devour,** ingurgitate; **engulf,** engorge; **gulp,** gulp down, swill, swill down, wolf down, gobble.

.12 **draw in, suck,** suckle, suck in or up, aspirate; **inhale,** inspire, breathe in; snuff, snuffle, sniff, sniffle, snuff in or up, slurp.

.13 sorb, **absorb,** adsorb, chemisorb or chemosorb, **assimilate,** engross, digest, **drink,** imbibe, take up or in, drink up or in, slurp up, swill up; blot, **blot up, soak up,** sponge; osmose; infiltrate, filter in; **soak in, seep in,** percolate in.

.14 **bring in, introduce, import.**

.15 readmit; reabsorb, resorb.

.16 ADJS **receptive,** recipient; welcoming, open, hospitable, inviting, invitatory; introceptive; **admissive,** admissory; receivable, receptible, admissible; intromissive, intromittent; ingestive, imbibitory; end-(o)–.

.17 sorbent, **absorbent,** adsorbent, chemisorptive or chemosorptive, **assimilative,** digestive; bibulous, imbibitory, thirsty, soaking, blotting; spongy, spongeous; osmotic, endosmotic, exosmotic; resorbent.

.18 **introductory,** introductive; **initiatory,** initiative, baptismal.

## 307. EATING

.1 NOUNS **eating, feeding, dining,** messing; ingestion, consumption, deglutition; **tasting,** relishing, savoring; nibbling, pecking, licking, **munching; devouring,** devourment, gobbling, wolfing; **chewing,** mastication, manducation, rumination; feasting, regalement, epulation; appetite, hunger 634.7; nutrition 309; **dieting** 309.11; gluttony 994; carnivorism, carnivorousness, carnivority; herbivorism, herbivority, herbivorousness, grazing, cropping, pasturing, pasture, vegetarianism, phytophagy; omnivorism, omnivorousness, pantophagy; cannibalism, anthropophagy; omophagia or omophagy; phag(o)–, –phagia or –phagy.

.2 **bite, morsel,** swallow; mouthful, gob [slang]; cud, quid; bolus; **chew,** chaw [dial]; nip, nibble; munch; gnash; champ, chomp [dial]; snap.

.3 **drinking,** imbibing, imbibition, potation; lapping, slipping, tasting, nipping; quaffing, gulping, swigging [informal], swilling or guzzling [both slang], pulling [informal]; compotation, symposium; drunkenness 996.1–4.

.4 **drink,** potation, portion, libation; draft, dram, drench, **swig** [informal], swill or guzzle [both slang], quaff, **sip, sup,** suck, tot, bumper, snort [slang], pull [informal], lap, gulp, slurp [slang]; nip, peg; beverage 308.48,49.

.5 **meal, repast,** feed [informal], mess, spread [informal], table, board, meat, repas [Fr]; **refreshment,** refection, regalement, entertainment, treat.

.6 (meals) **breakfast,** petit déjeuner [Fr]; meat breakfast, déjeuner à la fourchette [Fr]; **brunch** [informal], elevenses [Brit informal]; **lunch, luncheon,** tiffin, hot luncheon; **tea,** teatime, high tea; **dinner,** diner [Fr]; **supper,** souper [Fr]; buffet supper or lunch; TV dinner; **picnic, cookout,** alfresco meal, fête champêtre, **barbecue,** fish fry, clambake, wiener roast or wienie roast; coffee break, tea break, mash [Brit informal].

.7 **light meal,** light repast, light lunch, spot of lunch [informal], collation, **snack** [informal], nosh [informal], **bite** [informal], casse-croûte [Fr], refreshments.

.8 **hearty meal, full meal,** healthy meal, large or substantial meal, heavy meal, **square meal,** man-sized meal, large order.

.9 **feast, banquet,** festal board; lavish or Lucullan feast; bean-feast or beano [both Brit informal], blow or blowout [both informal], groaning board.

.10 **serving,** service; **portion, helping,** help; second helping; **course;** dish, plate; antepast; entree, entrée [Fr], entremets; dessert; cover, place.

.11 (manner of service) service, table service, counter service, self-service; table d'hôte, ordinary; à la carte; cover, couvert [Fr]; cover charge; American plan, European plan.

.12 **menu, bill of fare,** carte.

.13 **gastronomy,** gastronomics, gastrology, **epicurism,** epicureanism.

.14 **eater,** feeder, consumer, devourer; **diner,** luncher; picnicker; mouth, hungry mouth; diner-out, eater-out; boarder, board-and-roomer; **gourmet,** gastronome, epicure, connoisseur of food or wine, bon vivant, high liver, Lucullus, Brillat-Savarin; omnivore, pantophagist; **flesh-eater, meat-eater, carnivore,** omophagist, predacean; **man-eater, cannibal; vegetarian,** lactovegetarian, fruitarian, plant-eater, **herbivore,** phytophagan, phytophage; grass-eater, graminivore; grain-eater, granivore; gourmand, trencherman, **glutton** 994.3; –phage, –vore or –vora.

.15 **restaurant,** eating house, dining room; eatery or beanery or hashery or hash house [all slang]; trattoria [Ital]; **lunchroom,** luncheonette; **café,** caffè [Ital]; tearoom, bistro [Fr]; **coffeehouse,** coffeeroom, **coffee shop,** tavern 191.16; chophouse; **grill,** grillroom; cookshop; buffet, smorgasbord; **lunch counter,** quick-lunch counter; hot-dog stand, hamburger stand, drive-in restaurant, drive-in; fast-food chain; **snack bar,** buvette [Fr], cantina [Sp]; pizzeria; **cafeteria,** automat; mess hall, dining hall; canteen; cookhouse, cookshack, lunch wagon, chuck wagon; diner, dog wagon [slang]; **kitchen** 330.3.

.16 VERBS **feed, dine,** wine and dine, mess; satisfy, gratify; regale; bread, meat; board, sustain; pasture, put out to pasture, graze, grass; forage, fodder; provision 659.9.

.17 **nourish, nurture,** nutrify, aliment, foster; **nurse, suckle,** lactate, breast-feed, wetnurse, dry-nurse; fatten, fatten up, stuff, force-feed.

.18 **eat, feed,** fare, take, partake, partake of, break bread, break one's fast; refresh or entertain the inner man, put on the feed bag [slang], fall to, pitch in [informal]; **taste,** relish, savor; hunger 634.19; **diet,** go on a diet, watch one's weight, count calories.

.19 **dine,** dinner; **sup,** breakfast; lunch; picnic, cook out; **eat out, dine out;** board; mess with, break bread with.

.20 **devour, swallow,** ingest, **consume,** take in, tuck in or away [informal], down, take down, get down, put away [informal]; **eat up;** dispatch or dispose of or get away with [all informal]; surround or put oneself outside of [both slang].

.21 **gobble, gulp, bolt,** wolf, gobble or gulp or bolt or wolf down.

.22 **feast, banquet,** regale; eat heartily, have a good appetite, eat up, lick the platter or

.27 **stuffing, dressing,** forcemeat *or* farce.

.28 **bread,** *pain* [Fr], staff of life; bread stuff; white bread, French bread, Italian bread; garlic bread; dark bread, whole wheat bread, cracked-wheat bread; rye bread, *Bauernbrot* [Ger], pumpernickel, brown bread, black bread; graham bread; salt-rising bread, sourbread, sourdough bread, Irish soda bread; raisin bread, nut bread; unleavened bread, matzo, *matzoth* [Heb pl]; bread stick; **toast;** challah; pita; loaf of bread, tommy [Brit]; crust.

.29 **corn bread;** pone, ash pone, corn pone, corn tash, ash cake, hoecake, johnnycake; dodger, corn dodger, corn dab, hush puppy; cracklin' bread [dial]; *tortilla* [Sp].

.30 **biscuit,** sinker [slang]; hardtack, sea biscuit, ship biscuit, pilot biscuit *or* bread; **cracker,** soda cracker *or* saltine, graham cracker; wafer; rusk, zwieback, Melba toast, Brussels biscuit; pretzel.

.31 **bun, roll, muffin,** English muffin, crumpet, gem; popover, Yorkshire pudding; scone; cross bun, hot cross bun; Danish pastry, Danish; coffee cake; *croissant, brioche* [both Fr]; hard roll, soft roll, crescent roll, kaiser roll, Parker House roll, clover-leaf roll, pinwheel roll, onion roll, bialy *or* bialystoker; bagel.

.32 **sandwich;** double-decker sandwich, club sandwich; open-face sandwich, *canapé* [Fr], *smörgås* [Swed], *smørrebrød* [Dan]; Dagwood sandwich; –burger, **hamburger,** cheeseburger, tunaburger, etc.; **hot dog;** hot roast beef sandwich, Sloppy Joe, barbecued beef; hero sandwich, poor boy, submarine sandwich, grinder, hoagy; toasted *or* grilled cheese sandwich, tuna salad sandwich, egg salad sandwich, bacon-lettuce-tomato sandwich *or* BLT, peanut butter and jelly sandwich, pastrami sandwich, ham sandwich, corned beef sandwich, Swiss cheese sandwich, etc.

.33 **noodles,** *pasta* [Ital], Italian paste, paste; **spaghetti,** spaghettini, ziti, fedellini, fettuccine, vermicelli, **macaroni,** lasagne; ravioli, *kreplach* [Yid pl], won ton; **dumpling;** spaetzle; matzo balls, *knaydlach* [Yid pl].

.34 **cereal,** breakfast food, dry cereal, hot cereal; porridge, gruel, loblolly; **mush,** hasty pudding; oatmeal, rolled oats; farina, millet, hominy grits; grits; kasha; frumenty; cornflakes, wheatflakes, etc.; puffed wheat, puffed rice, etc.

.35 **vegetables** 308.50, produce, *légumes* [Fr];

potherbs; greens; beans, *frijoles* [Sp], *haricots* [Fr]; **potato,** spud [informal], tater [dial], *pomme de terre* [Fr], Irish potato, pratie [dial], white potato; **tomato,** love apple; eggplant, *aubergine* [Fr], mad apple; rhubarb, pieplant; cabbage, *Kraut* [Ger].

.36 **salad,** *salade* [Fr]; **green salad,** combination salad, tossed salad, potato salad, macaroni salad, Waldorf salad, fruit salad, ambrosia, salad niçoise, crab Louis, salmagundi, chef salad, Caesar salad, herring salad, tuna fish salad, chicken salad, etc.; slaw, cole slaw; aspic, molded salad, Jell-O salad.

.37 **fruit** 308.51, fructi–, produce; stone fruit, drupe; citrus fruit, citr(o)– *or* citri–; fruit compote, fruit soup, fruit cocktail.

.38 **nut** 308.52, *noix* [Fr], *noisette* [Fr]; kernel, meat; **Brazil nut** *or* nigger toe [slang]; **peanut;** goober *or* goober pea *or* ground-pea [all dial], groundnut [Brit]; salted peanuts, peanut butter; **almond,** *amande* [Fr]; burnt almond, *amande pralinée* [Fr]; bitter almond, *amande amère* [Fr]; sweet almond, *amande douce* [Fr]; blanched almonds, *amandes mondées* [Fr]; almond paste, *pâté d'amande* [Fr].

.39 **sweets,** sweet stuff, **confectionery; sweet, sweetmeat; confection; candy** 308.54; comfit, confiture; preserve, conserve; jelly, jam; marmalade; gelatin, Jell-O; compote; mousse; blancmange; tutti-frutti; maraschino cherries; honey; icing, frosting, glaze; meringue; whipped cream.

.40 **pastry,** *patisserie* [Fr]; French pastry, Danish pastry; **tart;** turnover; timbale; **pie,** *tarte* [Fr]; pasty, *pâté* [Fr], *pirog* [Russ]; blintz; *quiche* [Fr]; patty, pattycake; patty-shell, *vol-au-vent* [Fr]; rosette; dowdy, pandowdy; trifle, tipsy cake; strudel; baklava; puff, cream puff; éclair, chocolate éclair.

.41 **cake,** *gâteau* [Fr], *Torte* [Ger]; cupcake; *petit four* [Fr]; angel cake, angel food cake; chocolate cake, devil's food cake; white cake, yellow cake; spice cake; gingerbread; fruitcake; pound cake; marble cake; honey cake; sponge cake, génoise; shortcake; coffee cake, tea cake; cheesecake; layer cake, jumble; *baba au rhum* [Fr], savarin; Boston cream pie; upside-down cake; jelly roll, *bûche de Noël* [Fr]; baked Alaska.

.42 **cookie,** biscuit [Brit]; brownie; ginger snap; macaroon; ladyfinger; fruit bar, date bar; shortbread; sugar cookie, oatmeal cookie, chocolate chip *or* Toll House cookie; fortune cookie; gingerbread man; *Pfeffernüsse* [Ger pl].

.43 **doughnut,** friedcake, sinker [slang], cymbal [archaic], olykoek [dial]; French doughnut, raised doughnut; glazed doughnut; fastnacht; **cruller,** twister; jelly doughnut, bismarck; fritter, *beignet* [Fr]; apple fritter, *beignet aux pommes* [Fr].

.44 **pancake,** griddlecake, **hot cake,** battercake, flapcake, **flapjack,** flannel cake; buckwheat cake; chapatty [India]; **waffle;** blintz, cheese blintz, *crêpe, crêpe Suzette* [both Fr], *palacsinta* [Hung], *Pfannkuchen* [Ger].

.45 **pudding;** plum pudding, carrot pudding, steamed pudding, duff; vanilla pudding, chocolate pudding, tapioca pudding, etc.; trifle, Charlotte *or* Charlotte Russe; brown Betty; custard, flan; rennet, junket; syllabub; mousse, chocolate mousse; zabaglione; Bavarian cream.

.46 **ice,** *glace* [Fr], frozen dessert; **ice cream,** ice milk, French ice cream; **sherbet,** water ice [Brit], Italian ice; parfait; sundae, ice-cream sundae, banana split; ice-cream soda; frappé; ice-cream cone; frozen pudding; frozen custard, soft ice cream.

.47 **dairy products,** milk products; **milk,** pasteurized milk, certified milk, raw milk, homogenized milk, half-and-half, powdered milk, nonfat dry milk, evaporated milk, condensed milk, skim milk, buttermilk; **cream,** sour cream, whipping cream, heavy cream, light cream; **butter,** clarified butter, ghee; **margarine,** oleomargarine, oleo; **cheese** 308.53, tyr(o)–; curds, whey, yogurt.

.48 **beverage** 308.49, drink, thirst quencher, potation, potable, drinkable [informal], **liquor,** liquid; **soft drink,** nonalcoholic beverage, –ade; cold drink; carbonated water, soda water, **soda,** pop, soda pop, tonic; milk shake, frosted shake, thick shake, shake *or* frosted [both informal]; malted milk, malt [informal]; hard drink, alcoholic drink 996.38–42.

.49 **beverages, drinks**

| | |
|---|---|
| ade | cider |
| alcoholic beverage 996.38–42 | cocktail |
| | cocoa |
| ambrosia | coffee |
| beef tea | cola |
| birch beer | egg cream |
| bouillon | eggnog |
| buttermilk | *espresso* [Ital] |
| *café au lait* [Fr] | frappé |
| chicory | frosted shake |
| chocolate milk | fruit juice |

| | |
|---|---|
| ginger ale | mocha |
| ginger beer | nectar |
| ginger pop | orangeade |
| ginger punch | orange juice |
| grapefruit juice | phosphate |
| grape juice | pineapple juice |
| hot chocolate | punch |
| hydromel | root beer |
| ice-cream soda | root beer float |
| iced coffee | sarsaparilla |
| iced tea | seltzer |
| ice water | soda |
| juice | spring water |
| koumiss | sweet cider |
| lemonade | tea |
| limeade | tisane |
| malted milk | tomato juice |
| maté | Turkish coffee |
| milk | vichy water |
| milk shake | water |
| mineral water | |

.50 **vegetables**

| | |
|---|---|
| acorn squash | green pepper |
| artichoke | gumbo |
| asparagus | hominy |
| bamboo shoot | horseradish |
| bean | Hubbard squash |
| bean sprout | iceberg lettuce |
| beet, beetroot | kale |
| beet greens | kidney beans |
| bell pepper | kohlrabi |
| Bermuda onion | leaf lettuce |
| Bibb lettuce | leek |
| black-eyed pea | lentil |
| Boston lettuce | lettuce |
| broccoli | lima bean |
| Brussels sprouts | maize |
| butter bean | mushroom |
| butternut squash | mustard greens |
| cabbage | navy bean |
| cardoon | okra |
| carrot | onion |
| cauliflower | oyster plant |
| celery | parsley |
| celery cabbage | parsnip |
| celery root, celeriac | pea |
| celtuce | pea bean |
| chard, Swiss chard | pepper |
| chick-pea | pimento, pimiento |
| chicory | pinto bean |
| chili pepper | popcorn |
| Chinese cabbage | pumpkin |
| chive | radish |
| chive garlic | red cabbage |
| collards, collard greens | red pepper |
| | rhubarb |
| corn | romaine, romaine lettuce |
| cos, cos lettuce | |
| cowpea | rutabaga |
| cress | salsify |
| cucumber | scallion |
| dandelion greens | scarlet runners |
| eggplant | shallot |
| endive, Belgian endive | snap bean |
| escarole | snow pea |
| French bean | sorrel |
| *garbanzos* [Sp] | soy, soya |
| garlic | soybean, soya bean |
| green bean | spinach |
| green onion | squash |
| green pea | string bean |

succory
sugar beet
summer squash
swede, swede turnip
sweet corn
sweet potato
taro
tomato
truffle

turnip
water chestnut
water cress
wax bean
white turnip
winter squash
yam
zucchini

### .51 fruits

akee
alligator pear
ananas
apple
apricot
avocado
banana
barberry
bearberry
berry
bilberry
blackberry
blueberry
boysenberry
breadfruit
cacao
candleberry
canistel
cantaloupe
caprifig
capulin
casaba, casaba melon
Catawba
checkerberry
cherimoya
cherry
citrange
citron
citrus, citrus fruit
civet fruit
crab apple
cranberry
currant
custard apple
damson
date
dewberry
durian
elderberry
feijoa
fig
gooseberry
granadilla
grape
grapefruit
guanabana
guava
hagberry
honeydew, honeydew
  melon
huckleberry
icaco
ilama
imbu
jaboticaba
jackfruit
Jaffa orange
jujube
kumquat
lemon
lime

lingonberry
litchi
loganberry
loquat
mammee apple
mandarin orange
mango
mangosteen
manzanilla
marang
mayapple
medlar
melon
mombin
mulberry
muscadine
muscat, muscatel
muskmelon
navel orange
nectarine
nutmeg melon
olive
orange
papaw
papaya
passion fruit
peach
pear
Persian melon
persimmon
pineapple
pippin
pitanga
plantain, *plátano* [Sp]
plum
plumcot
pomegranate
pond apple
prickly pear
prune
pulasan
quince
raisin
rambutan
raspberry
red currant
rose apple
sapodilla
sapote
Seville orange
soursop
strawberry
sugar apple
sugarplum
sweetsop
tamarind
tangelo
tangerine
ugli fruit
Valencia orange
water lemon

watermelon

### .52 nuts

acorn
almond
beechnut
ben nut
betel nut
black walnut
bonduc nut
Brazil nut
butternut
candlenut
cashew, cashew nut
chestnut
chinquapin
cobnut
coconut
corozo nut
cumara nut
dika nut
English walnut
filbert

whortleberry

groundnut
grugru nut
hazelnut
hickory nut
horse chestnut
kola, kola nut
litchi nut
Macadamia nut
palm nut
peanut
pecan
physic nut
pine nut
piñon
pistachio, pistachio
  nut
sassafras nut
souari nut
walnut

### .53 cheeses

aettekees
Alentejo
Alise Sainte Reine
Allgäuer Bergkäse
Allgäuer Rahmkäse
American cheese
Amou
appetitost
Arrigny
Asco
Asio
Augelot
Aurore
Autun
Azeitão
Backstein
Bagnes
baker's cheese
Banon
Battelmatt
Beaufort
Beaumont
Beaupré de Roybon
Bellelay
Bel Paese
Bitto
bleu, blue cheese
Bleu d'Auvergne
Bleu de Bassilac
Bleu de Salers
Blue Dorset or Blue
  Vinny
Bondes
Bossons Macères
Boule de Lille
Boulette d'Avesnes or
  de Cambrai
Boursin
Bra
brick cheese
Brie
Brie de Coulommiers
Brie de Meaux
Brillat-Savarin
Broccio
Bruxelles
Cacciocavallo

Cachat d'Entrechaux
Caerphilly
Camembert
Canestrato
Cantal
Cardiga
Castelo Branco
Cendré Champenois
  or des Riceys
Cendré d'Aizy
Cendré de La Brie
Chabichou
Chaingy
Champenois
Chaource
Chaumont
Chavignol
Cheddar
Cheshire
Chevret
Chevrotin
Ciclo
Cierp de Luchon
clabber
Cotherstone
cottage cheese
Cottenham
Coulommiers
cream cheese
Crema Danica
Crème des Vosges
Crèmet Nantais
Cremini
croissant demi-sel
Crottin de Chavignol
Danish blue
Dansk Schweizerost
Dauphin
Decize
demi-sel
Domaci Beli Sir
Dorset Vinney
double-crème
Dunlop
Edam
Emmental or Emmen-
  taler

Epoisses
Ercé
Ervy
étuvé
Evarglice
Excelsior
farmer cheese
Feuille de Dreux
Fin de siécle
Fleur de Decauville
Fondue aux raisins
Fontainebleau
Fontina
Fourme d'Ambert
Fourme de Montbri-
son
Fourme de Salers
Friesche Kaas
fromage à la pie or
fromage blanc
Gammelost
Gaperon
Géromé
getmesost
getmjölkost
Gex
gjetost
Gloucester
Glux
goat cheese
Gorgonzola
Gouda
Gournay
Grana
Grana Lombardo
Grana Reggiano
gras
grated cheese
Gruyère
Guéret or Creusois
hand cheese
Harzé
Harzer-Käse
herrgårdsost
Hervé
hushållsost
Ilha
jack cheese
Kackavalj
Kasseri
Kaunas
Kefalotir
kumminost
La Bouillé
Laguiole
Lamothe Bougon or
La Mothe St. Hé-
raye
Lancashire
Langres
Leicester
Les Aydes
Les Laumes
Levroux
Leyden or Leidsche
Kaas or Kummel
Liederkranz
Limburger
Lipski
Liptauer
Livarot
Mainauer

Manicamp
Manuri
Margherita
Maroilles or Marolles
Mascherone
mesost
Metton
Mizitra
Monceau
Montasio
Mont-Cenis
Mont Dore
Morbier
mozzarella
Muenster
Murols
mysost
Nantais
Neufchâtel
New York cheese
Niolo
Nøkkelost
oka cheese
Olivet
Oloron
Óvár
Oxfordshire
Paladru
Pálpuszta
Parmesan
Paski
Pavé de Moyaux
Pecorino
Pélardon de Rioms
Persille de Savoie
Petit Gervais
Petit Gruyère
Petit-Moule
Petit Suisse
Picodon de Dieulefit
Pithiviers au Foin
Pivski
Pommel
Pont l'Évêque
Poona
Port-Salut, Port du
Salut
pot cheese
Pouligny-St. Pierre
primost
process or processed
cheese
Promessi
Provature
Provolone
Puant Macéré
pultost
Pusztadör
Rabaçal
Rahmatour
Ramadoux
Reblochon
Récollet de Gérard-
mer
Reggiano
Remoudou
ricotta
Rigotte de Condrieu
Robbiole
Rocamadur
Rokadur
Rollot

Roma
Romadur
Romano
Roquefort
Rouennais
Saint-Agathon
Saint-Florentin
Saint-Marcellin
Saint-Maure
Saint-Nectaire
Salame
sapsago
Sardo
Sassenage
Sbrinz
Schabzieger
Schmierkäse
Septmoncel
Serra da Estrella
Sjenicki
Slipcote
smaltost
smearcase
Somborski
Sorbais
Soumaintrin
Sposi
Steinbuscher-Käse
Steppe
Stilton

**.54 candies**

bonbon
brittle
bubble gum
butterscotch
candied apple
candy corn
caramel
chewing gum
chocolate
chocolate bar
chocolate drop
cotton candy
cough drop 687.16
cream
divinity
fondant
fudge
glacé
gum
gumdrop
hard candy
honey crisp
horehound
jelly bean, jelly egg
jujube

**.55 condiments, spices**

allspice
amandine
anchovies
angelica
anise
applesauce
basil
bay leaf
bell pepper
black pepper
borage
burnet
caper

store cheese
Stracchino
Suffolk
Sveciaost
Swiss cheese
Székely
Taffel
Tête de Maure
Tête de Moine
Tilsiter
Tomme
Trappe or Trappistes
Travnicki
Triple Aurore
Trôo
Troyes
Truckles
Vacherin
Valençay
Västerbottensost
Västgötaost
Velveeta
Vermont cheese
Vic-en-Bigorre
Vize
Volvet
Weisslacker Käse
Wensleydale
Wilstermarsch Käse
Wisconsin cheese

kiss
licorice
Life Saver
lollipop
lozenge
marshmallow
marzipan, marchpane
mint
nougat
peanut bar
peanut brittle
penuche or panocha
peppermint
popcorn balls
praline
rock candy
saltwater taffy
Scotch kisses
sugar candy
sugarplum
taffy
toffee
torrone [Ital]
tutti-frutti

capsicum
caraway seeds
cardamom
catsup
cayenne, cayenne pep-
per
celery salt
chervil
chili
chili pepper
chili sauce
chili vinegar
chive garlic

chives
chutney
cinnamon
cloves
coriander
cranberry sauce
cubeb
cumin
curry
dahl sauce
dill
dillseed
duck sauce
fagara
fennel, *finnochio*
  [Ital]
filé
five spice powder
garlic
garlic butter
garlic powder
garlic salt
ginger
green pepper
hedge garlic
hoisin sauce
horseradish
hyssop
juniper berries
leek
mace
marinade
marjoram
mayonnaise
mint
monosodium gluta-
  mate, MSG
mustard
nutmeg
onion

onion salt
oregano
paprika
parsley
pepper
peppercorn
peppermint
piccalilli
pickle 432.2
pimento, pimiento
pimpernel
potherb
radish
red pepper
relish
saffron
sage
salad dressing
salt
sauce-alone
savory
seasoned salt
sesame oil
sesame seeds
shallot
soy, soy sauce
spice
star anise
Tabasco, Tabasco
  sauce
tarragon
tartar sauce
thyme
tomato paste
turmeric
vanilla
vinegar
white pepper
Worcestershire sauce

### .56 cold sauces

aïoli sauce
bleu cheese dressing
duck sauce
French dressing
green sauce
Italian dressing
Lorenzo dressing
mayonnaise
Mona Lisa dressing
oil and vinegar
ravigote sauce

rémoulade sauce
Ritz sauce
Russian dressing
salad dressing
sweet-and-sour sauce
tartar sauce
Thousand Island
  dressing
vinaigrette
Vincent sauce

### .57 hot sauces

allemande
barbecue sauce
béarnaise
Bercy
bordelaise
bourguignonne
brown gravy
brown sauce
Colbert
cream sauce
curry sauce
demiglace
egg sauce
espagnole
gravy
hollandaise
marinara

molé
Mornay
mushroom sauce
mustard sauce
Nantua
onion sauce
pan gravy
paprika sauce
pepper sauce
poulette
roux
shallot sauce
Smitane
Soubise
velouté
white sauce

### .58 dishes

arroz con pollo
atole
bacon and eggs
barbecued spareribs
beef Bourguignonne
beef Wellington
boiled dinner
Boston baked beans
bubble and squeak
cannelloni
carbonnade
cheese soufflé
chicken and dump-
  lings
chicken Cacciatore
chicken Marengo
chicken paprikás
chicken Tetrazzini
chili *or* chili con carne
chili and beans
*cholent* [Yid]
chop suey
chow mein
codfish balls, codfish
  cakes
compote
coquilles Saint-
  Jacques
corned beef and cab-
  bage
corned beef hash
Cornish pasty
croquettes
egg foo yong
egg roll
eggs Benedict
enchilada
felafel
fish and chips
fondue
French toast
fried rice
frittata
frog legs
galantine
gefilte fish
goulash
haggis
ham and eggs
hash
jambalaya
kabob
kidney pie
knish
lasagna
liver and onions
lobster Newburg
lobster Thermidor
macaroni and cheese

meatballs
meat loaf
meat pie
mostaccioli
moussaka
osso buco
oysters on *or* in the
  half shell
pasty
pheasant under glass
pigs in blankets
pilaf, pilau
piroshki
pizza, pizza pie
poi
porcupine balls
pork and beans
porkolt
pork pie
potpie
risotto
salmon loaf
sashimi
sauerbraten
sauerkraut
scallopini
scampi
Scotch woodcock
shepherd's pie
shish kebab
souvlaki
spaghetti and meat
  balls
Spanish rice
steak and kidney pie
Stroganoff
stuffed cabbage
stuffed derma
stuffed grape leaves
stuffed peppers
stuffed tomatoes
succotash
sukiyaki
sushi
Swedish meatballs
Swiss steak
taco
tamale
tamale pie
tempura
teriyaki
terrine
tostada
*tsimmes* [Yid]
veal Parmigiana
veal scallopini
Welsh rabbit, Welsh
  rarebit
Wiener schnitzel

## 309. NUTRITION

**.1** NOUNS **nutrition, nourishment,** nutriture, –trophy; alimentation; **food** *or* **nutritive value;** food chain *or* cycle.

**.2 nutritiousness,** nutritiveness, **digestibility,** assimilability.

**.3 nutrient,** nutritive, **nutriment** 308.3; nutrilite, growth factor, growth regulator.

**.4 vitamin,** vitamin complex; provitamin; vitamer; **vitamin A**: vitamin $A_1$ or antiophthalmic factor or axerophthol, vitamin $A_2$, cryptoxanthin, carotene; **vitamin B**, vitamin B complex: vitamin $B_1$ or thiamine or aneurin or antiberi-beri factor, vitamin $B_2$ or vitamin G or riboflavin or lactoflavin or ovoflavin or hepatoflavin, niacin or nicotinic acid, vitamin $B_6$ or pyridoxine or adermin, pantothenic acid or pantothen, inositol, choline, biotin or vitamin H, folic acid or pteroylglutamic acid or vitamin M or vitamin $B_c$, vitamin $B_{12}$ or cobalamin or cyanocobalamin, para-aminobenzoic acid or PABA; **vitamin C** or ascorbic acid; **vitamin D** or calciferol, ergocalciferol, cholecalciferol; **vitamin E** or tocopherol; **vitamin K** or naphthoquinone, menadione; **vitamin P** or bioflavinoid.

.5 **carbohydrate** 309.22, hydroxy aldehyde, hydroxy ketone, saccharide, sacchar(o)– or sacchari–, monosaccharide, disaccharide, trisaccharide, polysaccharide or polysaccharose; **starch**, amyl(o)–; **sugar**, glyc(o)–, sucr(o)–.

.6 **protein**, prote(o)–, proteid or protide, simple protein, conjugated protein, chromoprotein, glycoprotein, lipoprotein, nucleoprotein, phosphoprotein, scleroprotein, albuminoid; protide; **amino acid**, essential amino acid; peptide, dipeptide, polypeptide, etc.

.7 **fat**, glyceride, **lipid**, lipin, lipoid; fatty acid; steroid, sterol; cholesterol; polyunsaturated fat.

.8 **digestion**, ingestion, assimilation, absorption, –pepsia or –pepsy; primary digestion, secondary digestion; predigestion; salivary digestion, gastric or peptic digestion, pancreatic digestion, intestinal digestion; digestive system, alimentary canal, gastrointestinal tract; salivary glands, gastric glands, liver, pancreas; digestive secretions, saliva, gastric juice, pancreatic juice, intestinal juice, bile.

.9 **digestant**, digester, digestive; pepsin, pepsino–; **enzyme** 309.25, proteolytic enzyme; –ase, –in(e), –zyme, zym(o)–.

.10 **metabolism**, basal metabolism, acid-base metabolism, energy metabolism; **anabolism**, assimilation; **catabolism**, disassimilation.

.11 **diet, dieting**, dietary; dietetics; **regimen**, regime; bland diet; soft diet, pap, spoon food or meat, spoon victuals [dial]; balanced diet; diabetic diet, allergy diet, reducing diet, obesity diet; high-calorie diet, low-calorie diet; high-protein diet, low-carbohydrate diet; high-vitamin diet, vitamin-deficiency diet; acid-ash diet, alkaline-ash diet; low-salt diet, low sodium diet, salt-free diet; ulcer diet; vegetarianism, macrobiotic diet; diet book, vitamin chart, calorie chart, calorie counter.

.12 vitaminization, **fortification, enrichment**, restoration.

.13 **nutritionist, dietitian**, vitaminologist, enzymologist.

.14 (science of nutrition) **dietetics**, dietotherapeutics, dietotherapy; vitaminology; enzymology.

.15 VERBS **nourish**, nutrify [archaic]; **sustain**, strengthen.

.16 **digest**, appropriate, **assimilate**, absorb; metabolize; predigest.

.17 **diet**, go on a diet; watch one's weight, count calories.

.18 vitaminize, **fortify, enrich**, restore.

.19 ADJS **nutritious**, nutritive, nutrient, **nourishing**; alimentary, alimental; digestible, assimilable; –trophic, troph(o)–.

.20 **digestive**, assimilative; peptic.

.21 **dietary**, dietetic, dietic [archaic]; regiminal.

.22 **carbohydrates**

| | |
|---|---|
| aldose | levulose |
| altrose | lyxose |
| arbinose | maltose |
| bamboo sugar | malt sugar |
| barley sugar | mannose |
| beet sugar | maple sugar |
| British gum | melibiose |
| cane sugar | milk sugar |
| cellobiose | molasses |
| cellulose | native dextran |
| clinical dextran | nipa sugar |
| corn sugar | palm sugar |
| date sugar | pentosan |
| deoxyribose | pentose sugar |
| dextran | raffinose |
| dextrin | ribose |
| dextro-glucose | saccharose |
| dextrose | sorbose |
| erythrose | starch |
| fructose, fruit sugar | sucrose |
| galactose | tabasheer |
| glucose | tagatose |
| glycogen | talose |
| grape sugar | tree molasses |
| gulose | tree sugar |
| hexose sugar | trehalose |
| idose | wood sugar |
| inulin | xylose |
| lactose | |

.23 **proteins**

| | |
|---|---|
| albumin | chlorophyll |
| albuminoid | chromoprotein |
| amandin | clupeine |
| bynin | coagulated protein |
| casein | collagen |
| caseinogen | cytoglobulin |

edestin
elastin
fibroin
gliadin
globin
globulin
glutelin
glutenin
glycoprotein
helicoprotein
hemoglobin
histone
ichthulin
interferon
keratin
lactalbumin
lecithin
lecithoprotein
lipid
lipoprotein
lysozyme
metaprotein
mucin
nucleohistone

nucleoprotein
oryzenin
osseomucoid
ovalbumin
ovoglobulin
ovovitellin
peptide
peptone
phosphoaminolipide
phospholipide
phosphoprotein
prolamine
protamine
proteolipide
proteose
salmine
serum albumin
serum globulin
sturine
tendomucin
thymus histone
vegetable albumin
vitellin
zein

**24 amino acids**

alanine
arginine
aspartic acid
cystine
glutamic acid
glycine
histidine
isoleucine
leucine
lysine

methionine
phenylalanine
proline
sarcosine
serine
threonine
tryptophan
tyrosine
valine

**.25 enzymes**

alpha-amylase
amidase
aminopeptidase
aminopolypeptidase
amylase
apoenzyme
arginase
beta-amylase
carbohydrase
carboxypeptidase
chymotrypsin
coenzyme
deoxyribonuclease
dextrinogenic enzyme
endopeptidase
esterase
glutaminase
holoenzyme
insulinase

lactase
lecithinase
lipase
lipoxidase
nuclease
nucleotidase
papain
pepsin
peptidase
phosphoglucomutase
phosphorylase
polynucleotidase
protease
proteinase
rennin
ribonuclease
saccharase
saccharifying enzyme
trypsin

**.26 health foods**

acidophilus milk
blackstrap molasses
brewer's yeast
buckwheat flour
caudle
cottonseed flour
fortified flour
fortified milk
fruits
liver
middlings
nonfat milk
nuts

peanut flour
powdered milk
raw vegetables
rice polish
royal jelly
soybeans
soy flour
tiger's milk
unrefined flour
wheat germ
whole wheat
whole wheat flour
yogurt

## 310. EJECTION

.1 NOUNS **ejection**, ejectment, throwing out, **expulsion, discharge**, extrusion, obtrusion, detrusion, ousting, ouster, removal, kicking or booting out [informal]; throwing or kicking downstairs; the bounce, the chuck [Brit slang]; the boot or the bum's rush or the old heave-ho [all slang]; defenestration; rejection; jettison.

.2 **eviction**, ousting, dislodgment, dispossession; ouster.

.3 **depopulation**, dispeoplement, unpeopling; devastation, desolation.

.4 **banishment**, relegation, exclusion 77; **excommunication**, disfellowship; **disbarment**, unfrocking, defrocking; **expatriation, exile**, exilement; outlawing or outlawry, fugitation [Scot law]; **ostracism**, ostracization, blackballing, sending to Coventry; **deportation**, transportation, **extradition**; rustication; degradation, **demotion** 783, stripping, depluming, displuming; deprivation.

.5 **dismissal, discharge**, forced separation, congé [Fr]; **firing** [informal], **cashiering**, drumming out, dishonorable discharge, rogue's march; disemployment, **layoff**, removal, surplusing, displacing, furloughing; suspension; **retirement**; the bounce, the sack [Brit informal], the chuck [Brit slang]; the boot or the gate or the ax [all slang]; walking papers or ticket [both informal], pink slip [informal]; deposal 783.

.6 **evacuation, voidance**, voiding; **elimination**, removal; **clearance, clearing**, clearage; unfouling, scouring or cleaning out; exhaustion, exhausting, venting, emptying, depletion; **unloading**, off-loading, discharging cargo or freight; draining, drainage; egress 303; **excretion**, defecation 311.2,4.

.7 **disgorgement**, disemboguement, **expulsion**, ejaculation, **discharge**, emission; **eruption**, eructation, extravasation, **blowout, outburst**; outpour, jet, spout, squirt, spurt.

.8 **vomiting**, vomition, **disgorgement, regurgitation**, egestion, emesis, pukes or heaves [both slang]; **retching**, heaving, gagging; nausea 686.29; **vomit**, puke or barf [both slang], spew, egesta.

.9 **belch, burp** [informal], **wind, gas**, ructation, eructation; **hiccup**.

.10 **fart** [slang], **flatulence** or flatulency, flatuosity, flatus, gas, wind.

.11 **ejector**, expeller, –fuge; **ouster**, evictor;

**bouncer** or chucker [both informal], chucker-out [Brit informal].

**.12 dischargee,** expellee; ejectee; evictee.

**.13 VERBS eject, expel, discharge,** extrude, obtrude, detrude, exclude, reject, cast, remove; **oust, bounce** [informal], give the hook [informal], **put out, turn out,** thrust out; **throw out,** cast out, chuck out, give the chuck to [Brit slang], toss out, heave out, throw or kick downstairs; kick or boot out [informal]; give the bum's rush or give the old heave-ho or throw out on one's ear [all slang]; defenestrate; jettison, throw overboard, discard, junk, throw away.

**.14 drive out, run out,** chase out, **rout out;** drum out; freeze out [informal], push out, force out; **hunt out,** harry out; **smoke out,** drive into the open; run out of town, ride on a rail.

**.15 evict, oust,** dislodge, dispossess, put out, turn out, **turn out of doors,** turn out of house and home, turn or put out bag and baggage; unhouse, unkennel.

**.16 depopulate,** dispeople, unpeople; devastate, desolate.

**.17 banish, expel, cast out,** thrust out, relegate, **ostracize,** disfellowship, exclude, send down, blackball, spurn, snub, cut, give the cold shoulder, send to Coventry, give the silent treatment; **excommunicate; exile, expatriate, deport,** transport, send away, **extradite; outlaw,** fugitate [Scot law], ban, proscribe; rusticate.

**.18 dismiss, send off** or **away, turn off** or **away,** bundle, bundle off or out, hustle out, pack off, **send packing,** send about one's business, send to the showers [slang]; bow out, **show the door,** show the gate; **give the gate,** give the air [both slang].

**.19 dismiss, discharge, expel, cashier,** drum out, disemploy, separate forcibly or involuntarily, **lay off,** suspend, surplus, furlough, turn off, make redundant, turn out, release, let go, let out, remove, displace, replace, strike off the rolls, give the pink slip; give one his walking papers [informal]; **fire** or **can** [both informal]; **sack** or give the sack to [both Brit informal]; **bump,** bounce, kick, boot, give the ax, give the gate [all slang]; unfrock, defrock; degrade, demote, strip, deplume, displume, deprive; depose, disbar 783.4; break, bust [slang]; **retire,** put on the retired list; pension off, superannuate; read out of; kick upstairs.

**.20 do away with, exterminate,** purge, liqui-

date; **shake off,** shoo, dispel; **throw off,** fling off, cast off; **eliminate,** get rid of 77.5; throw away 668.7.

**.21 evacuate, void; eliminate,** remove; **empty,** empty out, deplete, **exhaust,** vent, drain, clear, purge, clean or scour out, clear of or out or away, unfoul, unclog, blow, blow out, sweep out, make a clean sweep, clear the decks; defecate 311.13.

**.22 unload,** off-load, unlade, unpack, disburden, unburden, **discharge, dump;** unship, break bulk.

**.23 let out, give vent to,** give out or off, throw off, **emit, exhaust,** evacuate; **exhale,** expire, breathe out, let one's breath out, blow, puff; fume, steam, vapor, smoke, reek; open the sluices or floodgates, turn on the tap.

**.24 disgorge,** debouch, disembogue, **discharge, exhaust, expel,** ejaculate, throw out, **cast forth,** send out or forth; **erupt,** eruct, **blow out,** extravasate; **pour out** or **forth,** pour, outpour, decant; **spew,** jet, spout, squirt, **spurt.**

**.25 vomit,** spew, **disgorge, regurgitate,** egest, puke [slang], **throw up,** bring up, barf [slang], be sick, sick up [Brit informal], cast or heave the gorge; upchuck or chuck up or urp [all informal], shoot or toss one's cookies [slang]; **retch, keck, heave, gag;** reject; be seasick, feed the fish.

**.26 belch, burp** [informal], eruct, eructate; **hiccup.**

**.27 fart** [slang], let or lay a fart [slang], let or break wind.

**.28 ADJS ejective, expulsive,** ejaculative, emissive, extrusive, ex(o)–; eliminant; vomitive, vomitory; eructative; flatulent, flatuous.

**.29 INTERJS go away!,** begone!, get you gone!, go along!, get along!, **run along!,** get along with you!, away!, away with you!, off with you!, off you go!, on your way!, go about your business!, be off!, **get out of here!,** get out!, clear out!, leave!, allez! [Fr], allez-vous-en! [Fr], va-t'-en! [Fr], raus mit dir! [Ger], heraus! [Ger], ¡váyase! [Sp], via! or va' via! [Ital], shoo!, scat!, git! [dial], "stand not on the order of your going, but go at once" [Shakespeare], "go and hang yourself" [Plautus].

**.30** [slang terms] **beat it!, scram!,** buzz off!, bug off!, skiddoo!, skedaddle!, vamoose!, cheese it!, make yourself scarce!, **get lost!,** take a walk!, go chase yourself!, get the hell out!, push off!, shove off!, take a powder!, blow!

## 311. EXCRETION

*(bodily discharge)*

.1 NOUNS **excretion**, egestion, extrusion, **elimination, discharge; emission;** eccrisis; exudation, transudation; extravasation, effusion, flux, flow, –rrhea *or* –rrhoea; ejaculation, ejection 310; **secretion** 312.

.2 **defecation,** dejection, **evacuation,** voidance; movement, **bowel movement, BM, stool,** shit *or* crap [both slang]; **diarrhea,** loose bowels, flux; trots *or* runs *or* shits *or* GI's *or* GI shits [all slang]; turistas, Montezuma's revenge [both slang]; lientery; **dysentery,** bloody flux; catharsis, purgation, purge.

.3 **excrement,** dejection, dejecture, discharge, ejection; **waste,** waste matter; **excreta,** excretes, egesta, ejecta, ejectamenta, dejecta; exudation, exudate; transudation, transudate; extravasation, extravasate; **effluent.**

.4 **feces,** feculence, copr(o)–, scat(o)–; defecation, movement, bowel movement *or* BM; **stool,** shit [slang], **ordure,** night soil, jakes [Brit dial], crap [slang], ca-ca [informal]; turd [slang]; dingleberry [slang]; **manure, dung, droppings;** cow pats, cow flops [slang]; cow chips, buffalo chips; guano; coprolite, coprolith; sewage, sewerage.

.5 **urine,** ur(o)–, urin(o)–; water, **piss** [slang], *pish* [Yid], pee, pee-pee *or* wee-wee [both informal], piddle, stale; **urination,** micturition; urea.

.6 **pus,** py(o)–; **matter,** purulence, peccant humor [archaic], ichor, sanies; pussiness; **suppuration, festering,** rankling, mattering, running; gleet, leukorrhea.

.7 **sweat, perspiration,** water, –idrosis; exudation, exudate; diaphoresis, sudor; honest sweat, the sweat of one's brow; beads of sweat, **beaded brow; cold sweat; lather,** swelter, streams of sweat; sudoresis; **body odor, BO,** perspiration odor.

.8 **hemorrhage,** hemorrhea, **bleeding;** nosebleed; ecchymosis, petechia.

.9 **menstruation,** men(o)–, menstrual discharge *or* flow *or* flux, catamenia, catamenial discharge, flowers [archaic], **the curse,** the curse of Eve; **menses, monthlies,** courses, period *or* periods, that time.

.10 **latrine,** convenience, **toilet,** toilet room, water closet, WC [informal]; **john** *or* johnny *or* **can** *or* crapper [all slang]; loo [Brit slang]; **lavatory,** washroom; **bathroom,** basement; **rest room,** comfort station *or* room; ladies' *or* women's *or* girls' *or* little girls' *or* powder room [informal]; men's *or* boys' *or* little boys' room [informal]; head; privy, outhouse, backhouse, shithouse [slang], johnny house [dial], earth closet [Brit], closet *or* necessary [both dial]; urinal.

.11 **toilet, stool, water closet; john** *or* johnny *or* **can** *or* crapper [all slang]; latrine; commode, closestool, potty-chair [informal]; **chamber pot,** chamber, potty [informal], jerry [Brit informal], jordan [Brit dial], thunder mug [slang]; throne [slang]; chemical toilet, chemical closet; urinal; piss pot [slang]; bedpan.

.12 VERBS **excrete,** egest, **eliminate, discharge,** emit, give off, pass; ease *or* relieve oneself, go to the bathroom [informal]; **exude,** exudate, transude; weep; effuse, extravasate; **secrete** 312.5.

.13 **defecate, shit,** crap [both slang], **evacuate,** void, **stool,** dung, have a bowel movement *or* BM, take a shit *or* crap [slang], ca-ca *or* number two [both informal].

.14 **urinate, pass** *or* **make water, wet,** stale, **piss** [slang], piddle, pee; pee-pee *or* wee-wee *or* number one [all informal], spend a penny, pump bilge.

.15 **fester, suppurate, matter, rankle,** run, weep; ripen, come *or* draw to a head.

.16 **sweat, perspire,** exude; break out in a sweat, **get all in a lather** [informal]; sweat like a trooper *or* horse, swelter, wilt.

.17 **bleed, hemorrhage,** lose blood, **shed blood,** spill blood; bloody; ecchymose.

.18 **menstruate,** come sick, come around, have one's period.

.19 ADJS **excretory,** excretive, excretionary; **eliminative,** egestive; **exudative,** transudative; **secretory** 312.7.

.20 **excremental,** excrementary; **fecal,** feculent, shitty *or* crappy [both slang], scatologic *or* scatological, stercoral, stercorous, stercoraceous, dungy; **urinary,** urinative, uric, –uronic.

.21 **festering,** suppurative, rankling, mattering; pussy, purulent.

.22 **sweaty,** perspiry [informal]; sweating, perspiring; wet with sweat, beaded with sweat, **sticky** [informal], **clammy;** bathed in sweat, drenched with sweat, wilted; in a sweat; sudatory, sudoric, sudorific, diaphoretic.

.23 **bleeding, bloody,** hemorrhaging; ecchymosed.

.24 **menstrual,** catamenial.

## 312. SECRETION

.1 NOUNS **secretion,** secreta [pl], secernment, secret(o)–; **excretion** 311; external secretion, internal secretion; lactation; weeping, lacrimation.

.2 digestive secretion *or* juice, salivary secretion, gastric juice, pancreatic juice, intestinal juice; bile, gall, chol(e)– *or* cholo–; endocrine; prostatic fluid, semen, sperm; thyroxin; autacoid, hormone, chalone; mucus; tears; rheum.

.3 **saliva, spittle, sputum, spit, expectoration,** ptyal(o)–, –ptysis; salivation, ptyalism, sialorrhea, sialagogue, **slobber,** slabber, slaver, **drivel,** dribble, **drool;** froth, foam; mouth-watering.

.4 endocrinology, eccrinology, hormonology.

.5 VERBS **secrete,** secern, produce, give out; excrete 311.12; water; lactate; weep, tear.

.6 **salivate,** ptyalize; **slobber,** slabber, slaver, drool, **drivel,** dribble; **expectorate, spit,** spew; hawk, clear the throat.

.7 ADJS **secretory,** secretive, secretional, secretionary; **excretory** 311.19; lymphatic, serous; seminal, spermatic; watery, watering; lactational; lacteal, lacteous; lachrymal, lacrimatory, lachrymose; rheumy; salivary, salivant, salivous, sialoid, sialagogic.

.8 **glandular,** glandulous, aden(o)–; **endocrine,** humoral, exocrine, eccrine, apocrine, holocrine, merocrine; **hormonal** *or* hormonic; adrenal, pancreatic, gonadal; ovarian, ovar(i)– *or* ovaro–; luteal, luteo–; prostatic, prostat(o)–; splenetic, splen(o)–; thymic, thym(o)–; thyroidal, thyro– *or* thyreo–; etc.

.9 **glands**

| | |
|---|---|
| adrenal gland, adrenal | pancreas |
| apocrine gland | parathyroid gland, |
| breast 256.6 | parathyroid |
| corpus luteum | pineal body |
| ductless gland | pituitary gland, pitu- |
| eccrine gland | itary |
| endocrine gland | prostate gland, pros- |
| gonad | tate |
| holocrine gland | salivary gland |
| lacrimal gland | sebaceous gland |
| lacteal gland | spermary |
| liver | suprarenal gland, su- |
| lymph gland | prarenal |
| mamma | sweat gland |
| mammary gland | tear gland |
| merocrine gland | testicle, testis |
| ovary | thymus |
| ovotestis | thyroid gland, thyroid |

.10 **hormones**

| | |
|---|---|
| ACTH (adrenocorti- | adrenosterone |
| cotrophic hormone) | adrenotrophin |
| Allen-Doisy hormone | hydroxydehydrocorti- |
| amniotin | costerone |
| androgen | hydroxydesoxycorti- |
| androsterone | costerone |
| cardiac hormone | insulin |
| cholecystokinin | intermedin |
| chondrotrophic hor- | kinin |
| mone | lactogenic hormone |
| corticosterone | lipocaic |
| cortisone | mammin |
| dehydrocorticosterone | oxytocin |
| desoxycorticosterone | parathyrin |
| dexamethasone | pitocin |
| diiodotyrosine | pitressin |
| enterocrinin | progesterone |
| enterogastrone | progestin |
| epinephrine | prolactin |
| erythropoietin | secretin |
| estradiol | somatrophin |
| estrin | stilbestrol |
| estriol | testosterone |
| estrogen | thyroglobulin |
| estrone | thyrotrophin |
| gonadotrophin | thyroxin |
| growth hormone | vasopressin |
| hydroxycorticosterone | |

## 313. OVERRUNNING

.1 NOUNS **overrunning, overgoing, overpassing;** overrun, overpass; **overspreading,** overgrowth; inundation, overflowing 395.6; exaggeration 617; surplus, excess 663; superiority 36.

.2 **infestation,** infestment; invasion, swarming, swarm, teeming, ravage, plague; **overrunning, overswarming,** overspreading; lousiness, pediculosis.

.3 **overstepping, transgression, trespass,** inroad, usurpation, incursion, intrusion, **encroachment,** infraction, **infringement.**

.4 VERBS **overrun, overgo, overpass,** overreach, go beyond; overstep, overstride; overleap, overjump; **overshoot,** overshoot the mark, overshoot the field; exaggerate 617.3; superabound, exceed, **overdo** 663.8–10.

.5 **overspread,** bespread, spread over; **overgrow,** grow over, run riot, cover, swarm over, teem over.

.6 **infest, beset,** invade, swarm, ravage, plague; **overrun, overswarm,** overspread; **creep with, crawl with,** swarm with.

.7 **run over,** overrun; **ride over,** override, **run down,** ride down; **trample, trample on** *or* **upon,** tread upon, trample underfoot, **ride roughshod over;** hit and run; inundate, overflow 395.17.

.8 **pass, go** *or* **pass by,** get *or* shoot ahead of; bypass; **pass over, cross,** go across, ford; step over, overstride, bestride, straddle.

.9 **overstep, transgress, trespass,** intrude, break bounds, overstep the bounds, go too far, know no bounds, encroach, infringe, invade, irrupt, make an inroad *or* incursion *or* intrusion, advance upon; usurp.

.10 ADJS **overrun, overspread,** overgrown.

.11 **infested,** beset, ravaged, teeming, plagued; lousy, pediculous, pedicular; wormy, grubby; ratty.

## 314. SHORTCOMING

### (motion short of)

.1 NOUNS **shortcoming,** falling short, not measuring up, shortfall, **shortage,** short measure, underage, deficit; **inadequacy** 57.1; insufficiency 662; delinquency; **default,** defalcation; arrear, **arrears,** arrearage; decline, slump; defectiveness, imperfection 678; **inferiority** 37; **failure** 725.

.2 VERBS **fall short, come short, run short,** stop short, not make the course, not reach, not measure up, not hack it [informal], not make it, not make out, not make the grade [informal]; want, lack, **be found wanting,** not answer, not fill the bill, not suffice; not reach to, not stretch; decline, lag, lose ground, slump, collapse, fall away; **fail** 725.8.

.3 **fall through,** fall down, **fall to the ground,** fall flat, **collapse,** break down; get bogged down, get mired, get mired down, get hung up, come to nothing, come to naught, end up *or* go up in smoke; **fizzle out** *or* peter out *or* poop out [all informal]; fall by the wayside, end "not with a bang but a whimper" [T. S. Eliot].

.4 **miss,** miscarry, go amiss, go astray, **miss the mark,** misfire; miss out, miss the boat *or* bus; miss stays, miss one's mooring.

.5 ADJS **short of,** short; **deficient, inadequate** 57.4; **insufficient** 662.9; **inferior** 37.6; lacking, wanting, minus; unreached.

.6 ADVS **behind,** behindhand, **in arrears** *or* arrear.

.7 **amiss, astray, beside the mark,** below the mark, beside the point, far from it, to no purpose, in vain, vainly, fruitlessly, bootlessly.

## 315. ASCENT

### (motion upwards)

.1 NOUNS **ascent,** ascension, levitation, **rise, rising,** uprising, **uprise,** uprisal; **upgoing, upgo,** uphill, upslope, upping, upgang [Scot]; upcoming; **taking off,** leaving the ground, takeoff; **soaring,** zooming, gaining altitude, leaving the earth behind;

spiraling *or* gyring up; shooting *or* rocketing up; jump, vault, spring, saltation, leap 319; mount, **mounting; climb, climbing,** upclimb, anabasis, clamber, escalade; surge, upsurge, upsurgence, upleap, upshoot, uprush; **gush, jet,** spurt, spout, fountain; updraft; upswing, upsweep; upgrowth; upgrade 219.6; **uplift,** elevation 317; increase 38.

.2 **upturn, uptrend,** upcast, upsweep, upbend, upcurve.

.3 **stairs, stairway, staircase,** *escalier* [Fr], **steps,** treads and risers; flight of steps, stepping-stones; spiral staircase, winding staircase; companionway, companion; stile; back stairs; perron; fire escape; landing, landing stage; ramp, incline.

.4 **ladder,** scale; stepladder; folding ladder, extension ladder; Jacob's ladder, companion ladder, accommodation ladder, side ladder, gangway ladder, quarter ladder, stern ladder.

.5 **step, stair, footstep,** rest, footrest, stepping-stone; **rung, round,** rundle, spoke, stave, scale; doorstep; tread; riser; bridgeboard, string; step stool.

.6 **climber,** ascender, upclimber; mountain climber, **mountaineer,** alpinist, rock climber, cragsman.

.7 (comparisons) rocket, skyrocket; lark, skylark, eagle.

.8 VERBS **ascend, rise, mount,** arise, up, uprise, levitate, upgo, **go up,** rise up, come up; go onwards and upwards, go up and up; upsurge, **surge,** upstream, upheave; swarm up, upswarm, sweep up; upwind, upspin, spiral, spire, curl upwards; stand up, **rear,** rear up, **tower,** loom; upgrow, grow up.

.9 **shoot up, spring up,** jump up, **leap up,** vault up, start up, fly up, pop up, bob up; float up, surface, break water; gush, jet, spurt, fountain; upshoot, upstart, upspring, upleap, upspear, rocket, **skyrocket.**

.10 **take off,** leave the ground, leave the earth behind, gain altitude, claw skyward; become airborne; **soar,** zoom, fly, plane, kite, fly aloft; aspire; spire, spiral *or* gyre upward; **hover,** hang, poise, float, float in the air.

.11 **climb,** climb up, upclimb, **mount,** clamber, **clamber up,** scramble *or* scrabble up, claw one's way up, struggle up, shin, shinny *or* shin up [both informal], ramp [dial], work *or* inch one's way up; **scale,** escalade, scale the heights; climb over, surmount.

.12 **mount, get on,** climb on, back; **bestride,**

bestraddle; **board,** go aboard, go on board; **get in,** jump in, hop in, pile in [informal].

.13 **upturn, turn up,** cock up; trend upwards, slope up; upcast, upsweep, upbend, upcurve.

.14 ADJS **ascending,** in the ascendant, **mounting, rising,** uprising, upgoing, upcoming; ascendant, ascensional, ascensive, anabatic; **leaping,** springing, saltatory; spiraling, skyrocketing; **upward,** upwith [Scot]; uphill, uphillward, upgrade, upsloping; uparching, rearing, rampant; climbing, scandent, scansorial.

.15 **upturned, upcast,** uplifted, **turned-up,** retroussé.

.16 ADVS **up, upward, upwards,** upwith [Scot]; skyward, heavenward; uplong, upalong; upstream, upstreamward; uphill; uphillward; upstairs; up attic *or* up steps [both dial]; uptown; up north; an(a)–, ano–, sur–, sursum–.

.17 INTERJS **alley-oop!, upsy-daisy!;** excelsior!, onward and upward!

## 316. DESCENT

### (motion downward)

.1 NOUNS **descent, descending,** descension *or* downcome [both archaic], **comedown, down; dropping, falling,** plummeting, **drop, fall,** *chute* [Fr], **downfall,** debacle, **collapse,** crash; **swoop,** stoop, pounce, downrush, downflow, cascade, waterfall, rapids, cataract; **downpour,** defluxion; downturn, downcurve, downbend, downward trend, downtrend; declension, declination, inclination; gravitation; downgrade 219.5.

.2 **sinkage,** lowering, **decline, slump,** subsidence, submergence, lapse, decurrence; cadence; **droop, sag, swag;** catenary.

.3 **tumble, fall,** *culbute* [Fr], cropper [informal], **flop** [slang], **spill** [informal], forced landing; **header** [informal]; **sprawl;** **pratfall** [informal]; **stumble,** trip; **dive, plunge** 320.

.4 **slide; slip,** slippage; **glide,** coast, glissade; glissando; **slither; skid,** sideslip; **landslide,** landslip, subsidence; **snowslide,** snowslip [Brit]; **avalanche.**

.5 VERBS **descend,** go *or* **come down,** down, dip down, lose altitude; gravitate; **fall, drop,** precipitate, rain, rain *or* pour down, fall *or* drop down; **collapse,** crash; **swoop,** stoop, pounce; **pitch, plunge** 320.6, **plummet;** cascade, cataract; parachute; come down a peg [informal]; **fall**

off, drop off; trend downward, go downhill.

.6 **sink,** go **down,** sink down, submerge; **set, settle,** settle down; **decline,** lower, **subside,** give way, lapse, cave, cave in; **droop,** slouch, **sag,** swag; **slump,** slump down; flump, flump down; flop *or* flop down [both slang]; plump, plop, plump *or* plop down; founder 320.8.

.7 **get down, alight,** touch down, **light; land,** settle, perch; **dismount, get off,** unhorse; climb down.

.8 **tumble, fall, fall down,** come *or* fall *or* get a cropper [informal], take a fall *or* tumble, take a flop [slang], take a spill [informal], precipitate oneself; **sprawl,** take a pratfall [informal], spread-eagle [informal], measure one's length; fall headlong, **take a header** [informal]; fall prostrate, fall flat, fall on one's face; **fall over,** topple down *or* over; capsize, turn turtle; **topple,** lurch, pitch, **stumble,** stagger, totter, careen, list, tilt, trip, flounder.

.9 **slide, slip,** slidder [dial], slip *or* slide down; **glide,** skim, coast, glissade; **slither;** skid, sideslip; avalanche.

.10 **light upon,** alight upon, settle on; **descend upon, come down on, fall on,** drop on, hit *or* strike upon.

.11 ADJS **descending,** descendant, on the descendant; **down,** downward, decurrent, declivitous, deciduous; **downgoing,** downcoming; down-reaching; **dropping, falling, plunging, plummeting,** downfalling; **sinking,** downsinking, foundering, submerging, setting; declining, **subsiding;** collapsing, tumbledown, tottering; drooping, sagging; on the downgrade, downhill 219.16.

.12 **downcast, downturned;** hanging, downhanging.

.13 ADVS **down, downward, downwards,** cat(a)– *or* cath– *or* kat(a)–, cato–; downwith [Scot], adown, below; downright; downhill, downgrade; downstreet; downline; downstream; downstairs; downtown; down south.

## 317. ELEVATION

### (act of raising)

.1 NOUNS **elevation, raising, lifting,** upping, **rearing,** escalation, **erection;** uprearing, uplifting; upbuoying; **uplift,** upheaval, upthrow, upcast, upthrust; **exaltation,** apotheosis, deification, beatification, canonization, enshrinement, assumption; *sursum corda* [L]; height 207; ascent 315.

**.2 lift, boost** [informal], hoist, heave; a leg up.

**.3 lifter, erector;** crane, derrick, gantry crane, crab; **jack,** jackscrew; **hoist, lift,** hydraulic lift; forklift; hydraulic tailgate; lever 287.4; windlass 287.7; tackle 287.10.

**.4 elevator,** *ascenseur* [Fr], **lift** [Brit]; escalator, moving staircase *or* stairway; dumbwaiter.

**.5 VERBS elevate, raise,** rise, **rear,** escalate, up, **erect, heighten, lift,** levitate, boost [informal], **hoist, heist** [dial], heft, heave; raise up, rear up, lift up, hold up, set up, stick up, perk up; buoy up, upbuoy; **upraise, uplift,** uphold, uprear, uphoist; upheave, upthrow, upcast; throw up, cast up; jerk up, hike, hoick; knock up, lob, loft; sky [informal].

**.6 exalt,** apotheosize, deify, beatify, canonize, enshrine; put on a pedestal.

**.7 give a lift,** give a boost, give a leg up [informal], **help up,** put on; mount, horse.

**.8 pick up,** take up, pluck up, **gather up;** draw up, fish up, haul up, drag up; dredge, dredge up.

**.9 ADJS raised, lifted, elevated;** upraised, **uplifted,** upcast; upreared, rampant; upthrown, upflung; **exalted, lofty** 207.19, sublime; stilted, on stilts; **erect, upright** 213.11; **high** 207.19.

**.10 elevating,** elevatory; **lifting, uplifting;** erective, erectile.

### 318. DEPRESSION

*(act of lowering)*

**.1 NOUNS depression, lowering, sinking;** ducking, submergence, pushing *or* thrusting under; detrusion; pushing *or* pulling *or* hauling down; reduction, de-escalation, diminution; demotion, debasement, degradation; concavity, hollowness 257.1; descent 316.

**.2 downthrow,** downcast; **overthrow,** overturn 220.2; **precipitation.**

**.3 crouch, stoop,** bend, squat; **bow,** genuflection, kneeling, kowtow, salaam, reverence, obeisance, **curtsy;** bob, duck, nod; prostration, supination.

**.4 VERBS depress, lower,** let *or* take down, debase, **sink,** bring low, reduce, couch; pull *or* haul down, take down a peg [informal]; bear down, downbear; thrust *or* press *or* push down, detrude; indent 257.14.

**.5 fell, drop, precipitate, bring down,** fetch down, **down** [informal], take down, lay low; **raze,** rase, raze to the ground; **level,** lay level; pull down, pull about one's ears; **cut down,** chop down, hew down, whack down [informal], mow down; **knock down,** dash down, send headlong, floor, deck [slang], ground, **bowl down** *or* **over** [informal], lay out [slang]; trip, topple, tumble; **prostrate,** supinate; **throw,** throw *or* fling *or* cast down; bulldog; spread-eagle [informal]; **blow over** *or* down.

**.6 overthrow,** overturn 220.6.

**.7 drop,** let drop *or* fall.

**.8 crouch,** cringe, **cower; stoop,** bend, squat, get down; hunch, hunch down; scrooch *or* scrouch down [dial]; grovel, wallow, welter.

**.9 bow, bend, kneel,** genuflect, bend the knee, **curtsy,** make a low bow, make a reverence *or* obeisance, salaam, bob, duck; **kowtow,** prostrate oneself.

**.10 sit down,** seat oneself, **be seated** 268.10; squat, get down on one's hunkers [dial].

**.11 lie down,** couch, drape oneself, **recline** 214.5; prostrate, supinate, prone [dial]; flatten oneself, prostrate oneself.

**.12 ADJS depressed, lowered,** debased, reduced, **fallen;** sunk, **sunken,** submerged; downcast, downthrown; prostrate 214.8; low, at a low ebb.

### 319. LEAP

**.1 NOUNS leap, jump, hop, spring, skip, bound,** bounce; **pounce;** upleap, upspring, jump-off; **hurdle; vault,** pole vault; demivolt, curvet, capriole; jeté, grand jeté, tour jeté, saut de basque; jig, galliard, lavolta, Highland fling, morris; standing *or* running *or* flying jump; long jump, broad jump, standing *or* running broad jump; high jump, standing *or* running high jump; leapfrog; jump shot; handspring; buck, buckjump; ski jump, jump turn, geländesprung, gelände jump; steeplechase; hippety-hop [informal]; jump-hop; hop, skip, and jump.

**.2 caper,** dido [informal], **gambol, frisk,** curvet, cavort, capriole; **prance,** caracole; *gambade* [Fr], gambado; falcade.

**.3 leaping, jumping,** bouncing, bounding, hopping, capering, prancing, skipping, **springing,** saltation; **vaulting,** pole vaulting; **hurdling,** the hurdles, hurdle race, timber topping [slang], steeplechase; leapfrogging.

**.4 jumper,** leaper, hopper; broad jumper, high jumper; **vaulter,** pole vaulter; **hurdler,** hurdle racer, timber topper [informal]; jumping jack; bucking bronco, buckjumper, sunfisher [slang]; jumping bean; kangaroo, gazelle, stag, jackrabbit, goat, frog, grasshopper, flea; salmon.

.5 VERBS **leap, jump, vault, spring, skip, hop, bound,** bounce; upleap, upspring, updive; leap over, jump over, etc.; overleap, overjump, overskip, leapfrog; **hurdle,** clear, negotiate; curvet, capriole; buck, buckjump; ski jump; steeplechase; start, start up, start aside; **pounce,** pounce on *or* upon; hippety-hop [informal].

.6 **caper, cut capers,** cut a dido [informal], curvet, cavort, capriole, **gambol,** gambado, **frisk,** flounce, **trip, skip,** bob, bounce, jump about; **romp,** ramp [dial]; **prance;** caracole.

.7 ADJS **leaping, jumping,** springing, hopping, skipping, prancing, bouncing, bounding; saltant, saltatory, saltatorial.

### 320. PLUNGE

.1 NOUNS **plunge, dive, pitch, drop, fall;** header [informal]; swoop, pounce, stoop; swan dive, gainer, jackknife, cannonball; belly flop, belly buster, belly whopper [all informal]; nose dive, power dive; parachute jump, sky dive; crash dive, stationary dive, running dive.

.2 **submergence, submersion, immersion,** immergence, engulfment, inundation, burial; dipping, ducking, dousing, sousing, dunking [informal], sinking; dip, duck, souse; baptism.

.3 diving, plunging; sky diving; fancy diving, high diving, skin diving, pearl diving, deep-sea diving.

.4 diver, plunger; high diver; parachute jumper, jumper, sky diver; skin diver, snorkel diver, scuba diver, free diver, pearl diver, deep-sea diver, frogman; –dytes.

.5 (diving equipment) diving bell, diving chamber, bathysphere, bathyscaphe, benthoscope, aquascope; submarine 277.9; diving boat; scuba, self-contained underwater breathing apparatus, Aqua-Lung; diving goggles, diving mask, swim fins; wet suit; air cylinder; diving suit; diving helmet, diving hood; snorkel, periscope.

.6 VERBS **plunge, dive, pitch, plummet, drop, fall;** plump, plunk, plop; swoop, swoop down, stoop, **pounce,** pounce on *or* upon; nose-dive, make a nose dive; parachute, sky-dive; skin-dive; sound; take a header [informal].

.7 **submerge, submerse, immerse,** immerge, merge, **sink, bury,** engulf, **inundate,** del-

uge, drown, overwhelm, whelm; **dip, duck, dunk** [informal], douse, souse, plunge in water; baptize.

.8 **sink, scuttle,** send to the bottom, send to Davy Jones's locker; **founder, go down,** go to the bottom, sink like lead, go down like a stone; get out of one's depth.

.9 ADJS **submersible,** submergible, immersible, sinkable.

### 321. CIRCUITOUSNESS

.1 NOUNS **circuitousness,** circuitry, circuition [archaic], circulation; **roundaboutness,** indirection, meandering, deviance *or* deviancy, **deviation** 291; deviousness, **digression,** circumlocution 593.5; **excursion,** excursus; **circling, wheeling,** rounding, orbit, **orbiting; spiraling,** spiral, gyring, gyre; circumambulation, circumambience *or* circumambiency, circumflexion, circumnavigation, circummigration; **turning, turn** 291.1; circularity 253.

.2 **circuit, round,** revolution, **circle,** full circle, **cycle,** orbit, ambit; round trip, *aller-retour* [Fr]; **beat,** rounds, **walk,** tour, turn, lap, loop.

.3 **detour, bypass, roundabout way,** roundabout, circuit, circumbendibus [informal], digression, deviation, excursion, ambages.

.4 VERBS **circuit,** make a circuit, **circle,** describe a circle, move in a circle, **circulate; go round** *or* **around,** go about; **wheel,** orbit, round; come full circle, close the circle, make a round trip, return to the starting point; cycle; spiral, gyre; go around in circles, chase one's tail; revolve 322.9; **compass,** encompass, encircle, surround; skirt, flank; go the round, make the round of, make one's rounds, circuiteer [archaic]; lap; circumvent, circumambulate, circummigrate; circumnavigate, girdle, girdle the globe, "put a girdle round about the earth" [Shakespeare].

.5 **turn, go around, round,** turn *or* round a corner, corner, round a bend, double *or* round a point.

.6 detour, make a detour, **go around,** go round about, go the long way around, go out of one's way, **bypass;** deviate 291.3; digress 593.9.

.7 ADJS **circuitous, roundabout, out-of-the-way, devious, oblique, indirect,** meandering, backhanded, ambagious; **deviative** 291.7, **deviating,** digressive, discursive, excursive; **circular** 253.11, **round,** wheelshaped, O-shaped; spiral, helical; orbital; rotary 322.15.

.8 circumambient, circumambulatory, circumforaneous, circumfluent, circumvolant, circumnavigatory, circumnavigable.

.9 ADVS **circuitously, deviously, obliquely, indirectly, round about,** about it and about, in a roundabout way, by a side door, by a side wind; circlewise, wheelwise.

## 322. ROTATION

.1 NOUNS **rotation, revolution,** volution, roll, **gyration, spin,** circulation, turbination; axial motion, rotational motion, angular motion, angular momentum, angular velocity; circumrotation, circumgyration, full circle; **turning, whirling,** swirling, **spinning,** wheeling, reeling, whir; centrifugation; swiveling, pivoting, swinging; **rolling,** volutation, trolling, trundling, bowling.

.2 **whirl, wheel, reel, spin, turn,** round, gyre; pirouette; **swirl,** twirl, **eddy, gurge,** surge; vortex, **whirlpool,** maelstrom, Charybdis; dizzy round, rat race; **whirlwind** 403.14.

.3 revolutions, revs [informal]; revolutions per minute, rpm.

.4 **rotator,** rotor; **roller,** rundle; **whirler,** whirligig, **top,** whirlabout; **merry-go-round,** carousel, roundabout; **wheel,** disk; Ixion's wheel; rolling stone.

.5 **axle, axis,** ax(o)–, axono–; **pivot,** gudgeon, trunnion, **swivel, spindle,** arbor, pole, radiant; fulcrum 216.2; pin, pintle; **hub,** nave; axle shaft, axle spindle, axle bar, axle-tree; distaff; mandrel; gimbal; **hinge,** hingle [dial]; rowlock, oarlock.

.6 **axle box,** journal, journal box; hotbox.

.7 **bearing,** ball bearing, needle bearing, roller bearing, thrust bearing, bevel bearing, bushing; jewel; headstock.

.8 (science of rotation) trochilics, gyrostatics.

.9 VERBS **rotate, revolve, spin, turn,** round, **go round** or **around,** turn round or around; **gyrate,** gyre; circumrotate, circumvolute; circle, circulate; **swivel, pivot, wheel,** swing; pirouette, turn a pirouette; wind, twist, screw, crank; wamble.

.10 **roll, trundle,** troll, **bowl;** roll up, **furl.**

.11 **whirl,** whirligig, twirl, **wheel, reel, spin,** spin like a top or teetotum, whirl like a dervish; centrifuge, centrifugate; **swirl,** gurge, surge, **eddy,** whirlpool.

.12 (move around in confusion) **seethe, mill,** mill around, stir, roil, moil, be turbulent.

.13 (roll about in) **wallow, welter,** grovel, roll, flounder, tumble.

.14 ADJS **rotating, revolving, turning,** gyrat-

ing; **whirling, swirling,** twirling, **spinning,** wheeling, **reeling; rolling,** trolling, bowling; circum–.

.15 **rotary, rotational,** rotatory, rotative, roto–, trocho–; trochilic, vertiginous; circumrotatory, circumvolutory, circumgyratory; gyral, gyratory, gyrational, gyroscopic, gyrostatic, gyr(o)–; whirly, swirly, gulfy; whirlabout, whirligig; vortical, cyclonic, tornadic, whirlwindy, whirlwindish.

.16 ADVS **round, around,** round about, **in a circle; round and round,** in circles, like a horse in a mill; in a whirl, in a spin; head over heels, heels over head; clockwise, counterclockwise, anticlockwise, widdershins.

.17 **rotators**

| | |
|---|---|
| bobbin | rolling pin |
| centrifuge | rotary drill |
| chuck | rotor |
| drill 348.18 | screw |
| extractor | spindle |
| fan | spin-drier |
| governor | spinner |
| gyro | spit |
| gyroplane | spool |
| gyroscope | teetotum |
| gyrostabilizer | top |
| gyrostat | treadmill |
| impeller | turbine |
| jack | turntable |
| propeller | ultracentrifuge |
| reel | whirl drill |
| revolving door | whirling table |
| revolving lever | whorl |
| roller | windmill |

.18 **wheels**

| | |
|---|---|
| balance wheel | paddle wheel |
| bevel gear | pinion |
| buffing wheel | pinwheel |
| cartwheel | potter's wheel |
| caster | prayer wheel |
| Catherine wheel | pulley |
| circular saw | ratchet wheel |
| cog | roulette wheel |
| cogwheel | spinning wheel |
| contrate wheel | sprocket wheel |
| crown wheel | spur gear |
| cycloidal gear | spur pinion |
| drive wheel | spur wheel |
| escape wheel | steering wheel |
| Ferris wheel | truck |
| flywheel | truckle |
| gear | vortex wheel |
| gearwheel | wagon wheel |
| gyrowheel | water wheel |
| idler wheel | wheel of fortune |
| mill wheel | worm wheel or gear |

## 323. OSCILLATION

*(motion to and fro)*

.1 NOUNS **oscillation, vibration,** vibrancy, vibro–, seismo–; harmonic motion, simple harmonic motion; libration, nutation; pendulation; **fluctuation**, vacillation, wavering; libration of the moon, libration in latitude *or* longitude; vibratility; **frequency**, frequency band *or* spectrum; **resonance**, resonant *or* resonance frequency; **periodicity** 137.2.

.2 **waving**, wave motion, **undulation**, undulancy; **brandishing, flourishing**, flaunting, shaking; brandish, flaunt, flourish; wave 395.14.

.3 **pulsation, pulse, beat, throb**; beating, throbbing; rat-a-tat, staccato, rataplan, drumming 455.1; **rhythm, tempo** 463.22–24; **palpitation**, flutter, arrhythmia, pitter-patter, pitapat; **heartbeat, heartthrob**, –crotism.

.4 **wave**, wave motion, **ray**; transverse wave, longitudinal wave; electromagnetic wave, electromagnetic radiation; **light** 335; **radio wave** 344.11; mechanical wave; acoustic wave, **sound wave** 450.1; seismic wave, **shock wave**; de Broglie wave; diffracted wave, guided wave; one- *or* two- *or* three-dimensional wave; periodic wave; standing wave, node, antinode; surface wave, **tidal wave**; amplitude, crest, trough; wavelength; frequency, frequency band *or* spectrum; resonance, resonant *or* resonance frequency; period; wave number; diffraction; reinforcement, interference; in phase, out of phase; wave equation, Schrödinger equation; Huygens' principle.

.5 **alternation, reciprocation**; regular *or* rhythmic play, **coming and going**, to-and-fro, back-and-forth, ebb and flow, *va-et-vien* [Fr], flux and reflux, systole and diastole, ups and downs; sine wave, Lissajous figure *or* curve; **seesawing**, teetering, tottering, **teeter-tottering**; seesaw, teeter, teeter-totter, wigwag.

.6 **swing**, swinging, **sway**, swag; **rock, lurch, roll, reel**, careen; wag, waggle; wave, waver.

.7 **seismicity**, seismism; **seismology, seismography**, seismometry.

.8 (instruments) **oscilloscope, oscillograph**, oscillometer; harmonograph; **vibroscope**, vibrograph; kymograph; **seismoscope, seismograph**, seismometer.

.9 **oscillator, vibrator**; pendulum, pendulum wheel; metronome; **swing; seesaw, teeter**, teeter-totter, teeterboard, teetery-bender; rocker, rocking chair; rocking stone, logan stone, shuttle; shuttlecock.

.10 VERBS **oscillate, vibrate, librate**, nutate; pendulate; **fluctuate**, vacillate, waver,

wave; resonate; **swing, sway**, swag, dangle; **reel, rock, lurch, roll**, careen, toss, pitch; **wag**, waggle; **wobble**, coggle [Brit dial]; bob, bobble; shake, flutter 324.10–12.

.11 **wave, undulate; brandish, flourish**, flaunt, shake, swing, wield; float, fly; **flap, flutter**; wag, wigwag.

.12 **pulsate, pulse, beat, throb**, pant, **palpitate**, go pitapat; tick, ticktock; **drum** 455.4.

.13 **alternate**, reciprocate, swing, **go to and fro**, to-and-fro, **come and go**, pass and repass, ebb and flow, wax and wane, ride and tie, hitch and hike, back and fill; **seesaw**, teeter, **teeter-totter**; shuttle, shuttlecock, battledore and shuttlecock; **wigwag**, wibble-wabble; zigzag.

.14 (move up and down) **pump, shake.**

.15 ADJS **oscillating**, oscillatory; **vibrating**, vibratory, vibratile, harmonic; libratory, nutational; periodic, pendular, pendulous; **fluctuating**, fluctuational, fluctuant; wavering; vacillating, vacillatory; resonant.

.16 **waving, undulating**, undulatory, undulant.

.17 **swinging, swaying**, dangling, **reeling, rocking, lurching**, careening, **rolling**, tossing, pitching.

.18 **pulsative, pulsatory, pulsatile; pulsating, pulsing, beating, throbbing, palpitating**, palpitant, pitapat, staccato; rhythmic 463.28; –crotic.

.19 **alternate, reciprocal**, reciprocative; sinewave; **back-and-forth, to-and-fro**, up-and-down, seesaw.

.20 seismatical, seismological, seismographic, seismometric; succussive, succussatory, sussultatory.

.21 ADVS **to and fro, back and forth**, backward and forward, backwards and forwards, **in and out, up and down**, seesaw, shuttlewise, from side to side, from pillar to post, off and on, ride and tie, hitch and hike, round and round, like buckets in a well.

## 324. AGITATION

*(irregular motion)*

.1 NOUNS **agitation, perturbation**, conturbation [archaic], **trepidation**, trepidity, fidgets *or* jitters [both informal], jumpiness, nervousness, nerviness [Brit], nervosity, twitter, upset, **unrest**, malaise, unease, fever, feverishness, restlessness, **disquiet**, disquietude, inquietude, discomposure; **stir, churn, ferment**, fermentation, foment; seethe, seething, ebullition, boil, boiling; embroilment, roil, turbidity, fume, **disturbance, commotion,** moil, **turmoil, turbulence** 162.2, **swirl, tumult,** tumultuation, hubbub, rout, fuss, row, todo, bluster, fluster, flurry, flutteration, flap, bustle, brouhaha, bobbery, hurlyburly; maelstrom; **excitement** 857; **disorder** 62.

.2 **shaking, quaking, palsy, quivering, quavering, shivering, trembling,** tremulousness, **shuddering, vibration;** succussion; jerkiness, fits and starts, spasms; jactation, jactitation; joltiness, bumpiness, shakes [informal], shivers or cold shivers [both informal], ague, chattering; chorea, St. Vitus's dance.

.3 **shake, quake, quiver, quaver,** falter, tremor, **tremble, shiver, shudder,** twitter, didder, dither; **wobble; bob, bobble; jog,** joggle; **shock, jolt,** jar, jostle; **bounce, bump; jerk, twitch,** tic, grimace, rictus; jig, jiggle, jigget [informal].

.4 **flutter,** flitter, flit, **flicker, waver,** dance; shake, quiver 324.3; **sputter, splutter; flap,** flop [informal]; **beat,** beating; **palpitation,** throb, pitapat, pitter-patter.

.5 **twitching, jerking,** vellication; **fidgets,** fidgetiness; itchiness, formication, pruritus.

.6 **spasm, convulsion,** cramp, **paroxysm,** throes; **orgasm,** sexual climax; epitasis, eclampsia; **seizure,** grip, attack, **fit,** access, ictus; epilepsy, falling sickness; stroke, apoplexy.

.7 **wiggle, wriggle;** wag, waggle; writhe, **squirm.**

.8 **flounder,** flounce, stagger, totter, stumble, falter; wallow, welter, volutation; **roll, rock, reel, lurch,** careen, **swing, sway; toss, tumble,** pitch, plunge.

.9 (instruments) **agitator,** shaker, jiggler, vibrator; beater, paddle, whisk, eggbeater; churn.

10 VERBS **agitate, shake, disturb, perturb,** perturbate, **disquiet, discompose, upset, trouble, stir,** swirl, flurry, fret, roughen, ruffle, rumple, ripple, ferment, convulse; **churn,** whip, whisk, beat, paddle; **stir up,** work up, shake up, churn up, whip up, beat up; roil, rile [dial]; disarrange 63.2; **excite** 857.11.

11 **shake, quake, vibrate,** jactitate; **tremble, quiver, quaver,** falter, **shudder, shiver,** twitter, didder, chatter; shake in one's boots or shoes, quake or shake or tremble like an aspen leaf; have an ague; **wobble; bob,** bobble; **jog, joggle; shock, jolt,** jar, jostle, hustle, jounce, **bounce,** jump, bump.

.12 **flutter,** flitter, flit, flick, **flicker,** gutter, bicker, wave, **waver,** dance; **sputter, splutter; flap,** flop [informal], flip, beat, slat; **palpitate,** pulse, throb, pitter-patter, go pitapat.

.13 **twitch, jerk,** vellicate; itch; **jig, jiggle,** jigger or jigget [both informal]; **fidget,** have the fidgets.

.14 **wiggle, wriggle;** wag, waggle; **writhe, squirm,** twist and turn; have ants in one's pants [informal].

.15 **flounder,** flounce, **stagger,** totter, stumble, falter, blunder, wallop; **struggle,** labor; **wallow, welter;** roll, rock, reel, lurch, careen, career, **swing, sway; toss, tumble,** thrash about, **pitch, plunge,** pitch and plunge, toss and tumble, toss and turn, be the sport of winds and waves; **seethe** 162.11.

.16 ADJS **agitated, disturbed, perturbed, disquieted, discomposed, troubled, upset, ruffled,** flurried, flustered; stirred up, shaken, shaken up; troublous, feverish, fidgety or jittery [both informal], jumpy, nervous, nervy [Brit], restless, **uneasy,** unquiet, unpeaceful; all of a twitter [informal], all of a flutter; **turbulent** 162.17; excited 857.18–25.

.17 **shaking, vibrating,** chattering; **quivering, quavering, quaking, shivering, shuddering, trembling, tremulous,** palsied, aspen; successive, succussatory; **shaky,** quivery, quavery, shivery, trembly; wobbly.

.18 **fluttering, flickering, wavering,** guttering, dancing; sputtering, spluttering, sputtery; fluttery, flickery, flicky, wavery, unsteady, desultory.

.19 **jerky,** twitchy or twitchety, jerking, **twitching, fidgety, jumpy,** jiggety [informal], vellicative; spastic, spasmodic, eclamptic, orgasmic, convulsive; fitful, saltatory.

.20 **jolting,** jolty, **joggling,** joggly, jogglety, **bouncy, bumpy,** choppy, rough; **jarring,** bone-bruising.

.21 **wriggly,** wriggling; **wiggly,** wiggling; squirmy, squirming; writhy, writhing, antsy [slang].

.22 ADVS **agitatedly, troublously, restlessly,** uneasily, unquietly, unpeacefully, nervously, feverishly.

.23 **shakily,** quiveringly, quaveringly, quakingly, **tremblingly,** shudderingly, tremulously; flutteringly, waveringly, unsteadily, desultorily; **jerkily,** spasmodically, fitfully, by jerks, by snatches, saltatorily, by fits and starts, "with many a flirt and flutter" [Pope].

## 325. PHYSICS

.1 NOUNS **physics**; natural *or* physical science; philosophy *or* second philosophy *or* natural philosophy *or* physic [all archaic]; acoustics, applied physics, aerophysics, astrophysics, basic conductor physics, biophysics, classical physics, chemical physics *or* chemicophysics, cryogenics, crystallography, cytophysics, geophysics, macrophysics, mathematical physics, mechanics 347, medicophysics, microphysics, molecular physics, Newtonian physics, nuclear physics 326.1, optics, physicomathematics, psychophysics, radiation physics 327.7, solar physics, solid-state physics, statics, stereophysics, theoretical physics, thermodynamics, zoophysics; physical chemistry, physicochemistry; electron physics, electrophysics, radionics, electronics 343.

.2 **physicist**, aerophysicist, astrophysicist, biophysicist, etc.

.3 ADJS **physical**, physi(o)–, physic(o)–; aerophysical, astrophysical, biophysical, etc.

## 326. ATOMICS

.1 NOUNS **atomics**, atomistics, atomology, atomic science; **nucleonics, nuclear physics**; atomic *or* nuclear chemistry; quantum mechanics, wave mechanics; molecular physics; thermionics; mass spectrometry, mass spectrography; radiology 327.7.

.2 (atomic theory) quantum theory, Bohr theory, Dirac theory, Rutherford theory, Schrödinger theory, Lewis-Langmuir *or* octet theory, Thomson's hypothesis; law of conservation of mass, law of definite proportions, law of multiple proportions, law of Dulong and Petit, law of parity, correspondence principle; atomism.

.3 **atomic scientist, nuclear physicist**; radiologist 327.8.

.4 **atom**; tracer, tracer atom, tagged atom; atomic model, nuclear atom; nuclide; **ion; shell**, subshell, planetary shell, valence shell.

.5 **isotope**; protium, deuterium *or* heavy hydrogen, tritium (isotopes of hydrogen); radioactive isotope, **radioisotope**; carbon 14, strontium 90, uranium 235, etc.; artificial isotope; isotone; isobar, isomer, nuclear isomer.

.6 **elementary particle**, atomic particle, **subatomic particle** 326.24, –on; lepton, meson, baryon, antilepton, antimeson, antibaryon; **atomic nucleus, nucleus**, nucle(o)– *or* nuclei–, *Kern* [Ger]; nuclear particle, nucleon; proton, neutron 326.25;

deuteron (deuterium nucleus), triton (tritium nucleus), alpha particle (helium nucleus); nuclear force, strong interaction; nucleosynthesis; nuclear resonance, Mössbauer effect, nuclear magnetic resonance *or* NMR; strangeness; electron, beta particle, valence electron 343.3; photon, phot(o)–.

.7 atomic cluster, molecule; radical, simple radical, compound radical, chain, straight chain, branched chain, side chain; ring, closed chain, cycle; homocycle, heterocycle; benzene ring *or* nucleus, Kekulé formula; lattice, space-lattice.

.8 **fission, nuclear fission**, fission reaction, fissi–; **atom-smashing**, atom-chipping, **splitting the atom**; atomic reaction; atomic disintegration *or* decay, alpha decay, beta decay, gamma decay; stimulation, dissociation, photodisintegration, ionization, nucleization, cleavage; neutron reaction, proton reaction, etc.; reversible reaction, nonreversible reaction; thermonuclear reaction; **chain reaction**; exchange reaction; breeding; disintegration series; bombardment, atomization; bullet, target; proton gun.

.9 **fusion, nuclear fusion**, fusion reaction, thermonuclear reaction, thermonuclear fusion.

.10 **fissionable material**, nuclear fuel; fertile material; **critical mass**, noncritical mass; parent element, daughter element; end product.

.11 **accelerator** 326.27, **particle accelerator**, atomic accelerator, atom smasher, atomic cannon.

.12 mass spectrometer, mass spectrograph.

.13 **reactor, nuclear reactor, pile**, atomic pile, reactor pile, chain-reacting pile, chain reactor, **furnace**, atomic *or* nuclear furnace, neutron factory; stellarator; power reactor; breeder reactor, power-breeder reactor; homogeneous reactor, heterogeneous reactor; plutonium reactor, uranium reactor, etc.; fast pile, intermediate pile, slow pile; lattice; bricks; rods; radioactive waste.

.14 atomic engine, **atomic** *or* **nuclear power plant**, reactor engine.

.15 **atomic energy, nuclear energy** *or* **power**, thermonuclear power; activation energy, binding energy, mass energy; energy level; atomic research, atomic project; Atomic Energy Commission, AEC.

.16 **atomic explosion, atom blast, A-blast**; **thermonuclear explosion**, hydrogen blast, **H-blast**; ground zero; blast wave, Mach stem; Mach front; mushroom cloud; **fall-out**, airborne radioactivity, fission particles, dust cloud, radioactive dust; flash burn; A-bomb shelter, fallout shelter.

.17 VERBS **atomize**, nucleize; activate, accelerate; bombard, cross-bombard; cleave, fission, **split** or **smash the atom.**

.18 ADJS **atomic**, atomatic, atomistic; atomiferous; monatomic, diatomic, triatomic, tetratomic, pentatomic, hexatomic, heptatomic; heteratomic, heteroatomic; subatomic; dibasic, tribasic; cyclic, isocyclic, homocyclic, heterocyclic; isotopic, isobaric, isoteric.

.19 **nuclear, thermonuclear**, isonuclear, homonuclear, heteronuclear, extranuclear.

.20 **fissionable**, fissile, scissile.

.21 **atoms**

| | |
|---|---|
| acceptor atom | isotopic isobar |
| asymmetric carbon atom | labeled atom |
| | neutral atom |
| discrete atom | normal atom |
| excited atom | nuclear isomer |
| hot atom | radiation atom |
| impurity atom | recoil atom |
| isobar | stripped atom |
| isotere | |

22 **theoretic atoms**

| | |
|---|---|
| Bohr atom | Rutherford atom |
| cubical atom | Schrödinger atom |
| Dirac atom | Thomson atom |
| Lewis-Langmuir atom | |

.23 **valent atoms and radicals**

| | |
|---|---|
| monad | pentad |
| dyad | hexad |
| triad | heptad |
| tetrad | octad |

24 **subatomic particles**

| | |
|---|---|
| antielectron | neutrino |
| antineutrino | neutron |
| antineutron | omega particle |
| antiparticle | phi-meson |
| antiproton | photon |
| beta particle | pion, pi-meson |
| electron | positron, positive electron |
| graviton | |
| hadron | proton |
| hyperon | quark |
| kaon, K-meson or K-particle | rho particle |
| | sigma particle |
| lambda particle | strange particle |
| meson, mesotron | tau-meson |
| muon, mu-meson | xi-particle |

25 **neutrons**

| | |
|---|---|
| fast neutron | resonance neutron |
| monoenergetic neutron | slow neutron |
| | thermal neutron |
| photoneutron | |

26 **atomic units and constants**

| | |
|---|---|
| atom | Avogadro number |
| atomic mass | Boltzmann's constant |
| atomic number | crystal-lattice constant |
| atomic weight | Dulong's constant |

| | |
|---|---|
| elementary quantum of action | Petit's constant |
| | Planck's constant |
| gram atom | quantum |
| gram-atomic weight | quantum number |
| magnetic quantum number | Rydberg number or constant |
| magneton | valence |
| mass number | valence number |

.27 **accelerators**

| | |
|---|---|
| betatron | induction accelerator |
| bevatron | linear accelerator |
| cascade transformer | microwave linear accelerator |
| charge-exchange accelerator | positive-ion accelerator |
| Cockcroft-Walton voltage multiplier | synchrocyclotron |
| cosmotron | synchrotron |
| cyclotron | Van de Graaff generator |
| electron accelerator | |
| electrostatic generator | |

## 327. RADIATION AND RADIOACTIVITY

.1 NOUNS **radiation**, radiant energy; **radioactivity**, activity, radioactive radiation or emanation, atomic or nuclear radiation; natural radioactivity, artificial radioactivity; curiage; specific activity, high specific activity; actinic radiation, actin(o)– or actini–; radiotransparency, radiolucency; radiopacity; radiosensitivity, radiosensibility; half-life; radiocarbon dating; contamination, decontamination; saturation point; radiac or radioactivity detection identification and computation; fallout 326.16.

.2 **radioluminescence**, autoluminescence; cathode luminescence; Cerenkov radiation, synchrotron radiation.

.3 **radiorays**, nuclear rays; alpha ray, beta ray, gamma ray; alpha radiation, beta radiation, gamma radiation; X ray, Roentgen ray, X radiation; Grenz ray, infraroentgen ray; cathode ray, anode ray; Lenard ray; actinic ray; Becquerel ray; positive ray, canal ray; cosmic ray, cosmic radiation; cosmic ray bombardment, electron shower; electron emission 343.5.

.4 **radioactive particle**, radion; alpha particle, beta particle; heavy particle; high-energy particle; meson, mesotron; cosmic particle, solar particle, aurora particle, V-particle.

.5 (radioactive substance) **radiator;** alpha radiator, beta radiator, gamma radiator; fluorescent paint, radium paint; radium dial; fission products; radiocarbon, radiocopper, radioiodine, radiothorium, etc.; mesothorium; **radioelement** 327.12; radioisotope; tracer, tracer element, tracer atom, radioactive waste.

**.6 counter** 327.13, **radioscope**, radiodetector, **atom-tagger**; ionization chamber; ionizing event; X-ray spectrograph, X-ray spectrometer.

**.7 radiation physics**, radiology, radiological physics; radiobiology, radiochemistry, radiometallography, radiography, roentgenography, roentgenology, radiometry, spectroradiometry, radiotechnology, radiopathology; radiotherapy 689.7; radioscopy, curiescopy, roentgenoscopy, radiostereoscopy, fluoroscopy, photofluorography, orthodiagraphy; X-ray photometry, X-ray spectrometry; tracer investigation, atom-tagging.

**.8 radiation physicist**, radiologist, atom-tagger; radiobiologist, radiochemist.

**.9 VERBS radioactivate**, activate, **irradiate**, charge; radiumize; **contaminate**, poison, infect.

**.10 ADJS radioactive**, radio–, activated, radioactivated, irradiated, charged, **hot**; **contaminated**, infected, poisoned; radiferous; radioluminescent, autoluminescent.

**.11 radiable**; radiotransparent, radioparent, radiolucent; radiopaque, radium-proof; radiosensitive.

**.12 radioactive elements**

| | |
|---|---|
| actinium | nobelium |
| americium | plutonium |
| astatine | polonium |
| berkelium | promethium |
| californium | protactinium |
| curium | radium |
| einsteinium | radon, radium emana- |
| fermium | tion |
| francium | technetium |
| hahnium | thorium |
| mendelevium | uranium |
| neptunium | |

**.13 radiation counters and chambers**

| | |
|---|---|
| air-wall ionization chamber | diffusion chamber |
| | electronic counter |
| alpha pulse analyzer | expansion chamber |
| atom counter | externally-quenched |
| atom-tracing spectrometer | counter |
| | extrapolation ioniza- |
| aurora particle counter | tion chamber |
| | free-air ionization |
| beta-ray spectrograph or spectrometer | chamber |
| | gamma ray counter |
| boron counter | gas counter |
| Cerenkov counter | Geiger counter |
| cloud chamber | Geiger-counter tele- |
| coincidence counter | scope |
| compensated ioniza- | Geiger-Klemperer |
| tion chamber | counter |
| cosmic ray counter | Geiger-Müller counter |
| counting tube | heavy particle counter |
| crystal counter | integrating ionization |
| differential ionization | chamber |
| chamber | ion counter |
| ionization chamber | counter |
| kicksorter | scintillation counter |
| minometer | scintillator |
| particle counter | scintillometer |
| proportional counter | screen-wall counter |
| proportional ioniza- | self-quenched counter |
| tion chamber | solar gamma ray |
| pulse analyzer | counter |
| pulse ionization cham- | solar X-ray counter |
| ber | spark chamber |
| radiation pyrometer | spectroradiometer |
| radiometer | spinthariscope |
| radiomicrometer | tube counter |
| Rutherford-Geiger | Wilson chamber |

**.14 radioactive units**

| | |
|---|---|
| curie | millicurie |
| half-life | multicurie |
| megacurie | roentgen |
| microcurie | |

## 328. HEAT

**.1 NOUNS heat, hotness**, heatedness, –thermia or –thermy; superheat, superheatedness; calidity or caloric [both archaic]; **warmth**, warmness; incalescence; radiant heat, thermal radiation, induction heat, convector or convected heat, coal heat, gas heat, oil heat, hot-air heat, steam heat, electric heat, solar heat, dielectric heat, ultraviolet heat, atomic heat, molecular heat; animal heat, body heat, blood heat, hypothermia; fever heat, fever 686.6; heating, burning 329.5.

**.2 (metaphors) ardor**, ardency, **fervor**, fervency, fervidness, fervidity; eagerness 635; excitement 857; **anger** 952.5–10; **sexual desire** 419.5,6; love 931.

**.3 temperature**; boiling point, cocto–; melting point, freezing point; dew point; recalescence point; zero, absolute zero.

**.4 lukewarmness**, tepidness, tepidity; tepidarium.

**.5 torridness**, torridity; extreme heat, intense heat, torrid heat, red heat, white heat, tropical heat, sweltering heat, African heat, Indian heat, Bengal heat, summer heat; "where the sun beats, and the dead tree gives no shelter, the cricket no relief" [T. S. Eliot]; **hot wind** 403.7.

**.6 sultriness, stuffiness, closeness**, oppressiveness; humidity, **humidness, mugginess**, stickiness [informal], swelter, temperature-humidity index, THI.

**.7 hot weather**, sunny or sunshiny weather, sultry weather, stuffy weather, humid weather, muggy weather, sticky weather [informal]; summer, midsummer, high summer; dog days, canicular days, canicule; **heat wave**, hot wave; broiling sun, midday sun; vertical rays; warm weather, fair weather.

.8 **hot day**, summer day; **scorcher** or **roaster**
or broiler or sizzler or swelterer [all infor-
mal].

.9 **hot air**, superheated air; thermal; fire
storm.

.10 **hot water**, boiling water; **steam**, vapor;
volcanic water; hot or warm or thermal
spring, thermae; geyser, Old Faithful.

.11 (hot place) **oven**, **furnace**, fiery furnace,
inferno, hell; steam bath; **tropics**, subtropics, Torrid Zone; equator.

.12 **glow**, incandescence, fieriness; **flush**,
**blush**, **bloom**, redness 368, rubicundity,
rosiness; whiteness 364; thermochromism;
hectic, hectic flush 686.6.

.13 **fire**, igni–, pyr(o)–; **blaze**, **flame**, ingle,
devouring element; **combustion**, **ignition**,
ignition temperature or point, flash or
flashing point; **conflagration**; flicker 335.8,
wavering or flickering flame, "lambent
flame" [Dryden]; smoldering fire, sleeping fire; marshfire, fen fire, ignis fatuus,
will-o'-the-wisp; fox fire; witch fire, St.
Elmo's fire, corposant; **cheerful fire**, cozy
fire, crackling fire, "bright-flaming, heat-
full fire" [Du Bartas]; **roaring fire**,
blazing fire; **raging fire**, sheet of fire, sea
of flames, "whirlwinds of tempestuous
fire" [Milton]; bonfire, balefire; beacon
fire, beacon, signal beacon, watch fire;
alarm fire, two-alarm fire, three-alarm
fire, etc.; wildfire, prairie fire, forest fire;
backfire; open fire; campfire; smudge
fire; death fire, pyre, funeral pyre, crematory; burning ghat.

.14 **flare**, flare-up, **flash**, flash fire, **blaze**,
burst, outburst; deflagration.

.15 **spark**, sparkle; **scintillation**, scintilla;
ignescence.

.16 **coal**, live coal, brand, firebrand, **ember**,
burning ember; **cinder**.

.17 **fireworks** or firework, **pyrotechnics** or pyrotechnic or pyrotechny.

.18 (perviousness to heat) transcalency;
adiathermancy, athermancy.

.19 **thermal unit**; British thermal unit, BTU;
Board of Trade unit, BOT; centigrade
thermal unit; centigrade or Celsius scale,
Fahrenheit scale; **calorie**, mean calorie,
centuple or rational calorie, small calorie,
large or great calorie, kilocalorie, kilo-
gram-calorie; therm.

.20 **thermometer**, mercury, glass; thermostat;
thermal detector.

.21 (science of heat) thermochemistry, ther-
mology, thermotics, thermodynamics;
volcanology; pyrology, pyrognostics; pyro-

technics or pyrotechnic or pyrotechny,
ebulliometry; calorimetry.

.22 VERBS (be hot) **burn**, **scorch**, parch, scald,
**swelter**, **roast**, toast, cook, bake, fry, broil,
boil, seethe, simmer, stew; **be in heat**
419.22; shimmer with heat, give off waves
of heat, radiate heat; **blaze**, combust,
flame, flame up, **flare**, flare up; **flicker**
335.25; **glow**, incandesce, spark, flush,
bloom; smolder; steam; sweat 311.16;
gasp, pant; **suffocate**, **stifle**, smother,
choke.

.23 **smoke**, fume, reek; smudge.

.24 ADJS **warm**, calid [archaic], **thermal**, thermic, therm(o)–, –thermous, mild, genial;
**toasty** [informal], warm as toast; **sunny**,
sunshiny; summery, aestival; **temperate**,
warmish; **tropical**, equatorial, subtropical;
**tepid**, **lukewarm**, luke; room-temperature; blood-warm, blood-hot; unfrozen.

.25 **hot**, **heated**, **torrid**; **sweltering**, sweltry,
canicular; **burning**, parching, scorching,
searing, scalding, blistering, baking, roasting, toasting, broiling, grilling, simmering;
**boiling**, seething, ebullient; **piping hot**,
scalding hot, burning hot, roasting hot,
scorching hot, sizzling hot, smoking hot;
**red-hot**, white-hot; ardent; flushed, sweating, sweaty, sudorific; overwarm, overhot,
overheated; hot as fire, hot as hell or
blazes, hot as the hinges of hell, hot
enough to roast an ox, so hot you can fry
eggs on the sidewalk [informal], like a
furnace or oven; feverish 686.54.

.26 **fiery**, igneous, firelike, pyric; combustive,
conflagrative.

.27 **burning**, **ignited**, kindled, enkindled,
blazing, ablaze, ardent, flaring, flaming,
aflame, inflamed, alight, **afire**, **on fire**, in
flames, in a blaze, flagrant [archaic]; con-
flagrant, comburent; live, living; **glowing**,
aglow, in a glow, incandescent, candescent, candent; sparking, scintillating, scintillant, ignescent; **flickering**, aflicker, guttering; unquenched, unextinguished;
slow-burning; **smoldering**; **smoking**, fuming, reeking.

.28 **sultry**, **stifling**, **suffocating**, **stuffy**, **close**,
oppressive; **humid**, **sticky** [informal],
**muggy**.

.29 **warm-blooded**, hot-blooded.

.30 isothermal, isothermic; centigrade, Fahrenheit.

.31 diathermic, diathermal, transcalent; adi-
athermic, adiathermal, athermanous.

.32 pyrological, pyrognostic, pyrotechnic(al);
pyrogenic or pyrogenous or pyrogenetic;

thermochemical; thermodynamic(al).

**.33 fireworks**

| | |
|---|---|
| bomb | girandole |
| candlebomb | ladyfinger |
| cannon cracker | pinwheel |
| cap | rocket |
| Catherine wheel | Roman candle |
| cherry bomb | serpent |
| cracker | skyrocket |
| cracker bonbon | snake |
| firecracker | sparkler |
| fizgig | squib |
| flare | torpedo |
| flowerpot | whiz-bang |

**.34 thermometers, thermal detectors**

| | |
|---|---|
| barretter | pyrometer |
| black-bulb thermome- | pyrometric cone |
| ter | pyroscope |
| calorimeter | pyrostat |
| candy thermometer | radiation pyrometer |
| centigrade thermome- | radiomicrometer |
| ter | register or self-register- |
| clinical thermometer | ing thermometer |
| cryometer | resistance pyrometer |
| cryoscope | resistance thermome- |
| cryostat | ter |
| dry-bulb thermometer | reversing thermometer |
| electric thermometer | telethermometer |
| Fahrenheit thermom- | thermel |
| eter | thermistor |
| galvanothermometer | thermocouple |
| gas thermometer | thermoelectrometer |
| meat thermometer | thermometrograph |
| metallic thermometer | thermopile |
| optical pyrometer | thermoregulator |
| oven thermometer | thermostat |
| platinum thermome- | wet-bulb thermometer |
| ter | |

## 329. HEATING

**.1 NOUNS heating, warming,** calefaction, torrefaction, increase or raising of temperature; superheating; tepefaction; pyrogenesis; decalescence, recalescence; preheating; stove heating, furnace heating; radiant heating, panel heating; central heating; induction heating, gas heating, steam heating, oil heating, hot-water heating, hot-air heating, electric heating, electronic heating, dielectric heating; solar heating, insolation; heat exchange; cooking 330.

**.2 boiling,** seething, **stewing,** ebullition, ebullience or ebulliency, coction; decoction; **simmering;** boil; simmer; ebullioscope, ebulliometer.

**.3 melting, fusion,** running; **thawing,** thaw; liquation, fusibility; thermoplasticity.

**.4 ignition, lighting,** lighting up or off, **kindling,** firing; flammation, inflammation.

**.5 burning, combustion,** blazing, flaming; **scorching,** parching, singeing; **searing,** branding; **blistering,** vesication; **cauter-**ization, cautery; **incineration,** cineration; **cremation,** concremation; suttee, self-cremation, self-immolation; the stake, burning at the stake, *auto-da-fé* [Pg]; scorification; carbonization; oxidation, oxidization; calcination; cupellation; deflagration; distilling, distillation; refining, smelting; pyrolysis; cracking, thermal cracking, destructive distillation; **spontaneous combustion,** thermogenesis.

**.6 burn,** scald, scorch, singe; sear; brand; sunburn, sunscald; windburn; mat burn; first- or second- or third-degree burn.

**.7 incendiarism, arson,** fire-raising [Brit]; **pyromania;** pyrophilia; pyrolatry, fire worship.

**.8 incendiary, arsonist; pyromaniac, firebug** [infòrmal]; pyrophile, fire buff [informal]; pyrolater, fire worshiper.

**.9 flammability, inflammability,** combustibility.

**.10 heater, warmer; stove, furnace** 329.33; cooker, cookery; firebox; tuyere, tewel [archaic]; burner, jet, gas jet, pilot light or burner, element, heating element; heating pipe, steam pipe, hot-water pipe; heating duct, caliduct.

**.11 fireplace, hearth,** ingle; **fireside,** ingleside, inglenook, ingle cheek [Scot], chimney corner; hearthstone; hob, hub; fireguard, fireboard, fire screen, fender; chimney, flue; smokehole.

**.12 fire iron;** andiron, firedog; tongs, pair of tongs, fire tongs, coal tongs; poker, stove poker, salamander, fire hook; lifter, stove lifter; pothook, crook, crane, chain; trivet, tripod; spit, turnspit; grate, grating; gridiron, grid, griddle, grill, griller; damper.

**.13 incinerator,** cinerator, burner; **crematory,** cremator, crematorium, burning ghat; calcinatory.

**.14 blowtorch,** blast lamp, torch, alcohol torch, butane torch; soldering torch; blowpipe; **burner; welder** 348.24; acetylene torch or welder, cutting torch or blowpipe, oxyacetylene blowpipe or torch, welding blowpipe or torch.

**.15 cauterant,** cauterizer, cauter, cautery; thermocautery, actual cautery; hot iron, **branding iron,** brand iron, brand; moxa; electrocautery; **caustic, corrosive,** mordant, escharotic, potential cautery; acid 379.12; lunar caustic; radium.

**.16** (products of combustion) scoria, sullage, slag, dross; **ashes,** ash; **cinder,** clinker, coal; coke, charcoal, brand, lava, carbon, calx; soot, smut, coom [Brit dial]; smoke, smudge, fume, reek.

.17 VERBS heat, raise or increase the temperature, hot or hot up [both Brit], warm, warm up, fire, fire up, stoke up; chafe; take the chill off; tepefy; gas-heat, oil-heat, hot-air-heat, hot-water-heat, steam-heat, electric-heat; superheat; overheat; preheat; reheat, recook, warm over; mull; steam; foment; cook 330.4.

.18 (metaphors) excite, inflame 857.11; incite, kindle, arouse 648.17–19; anger, enrage 952.21–23.

.19 insolate, sun-dry; sun, bask, bask in the sun, sun oneself, sunbathe.

.20 boil, stew, simmer, seethe; distill.

.21 melt, melt down, run, colliquate, fuse, flux; refine, smelt; render; thaw, thaw out, unfreeze; defrost, deice.

.22 ignite, set fire to, fire, set on fire, build a fire, kindle, enkindle, inflame, light, light up, strike a light, apply the match or torch to, torch, touch off, burn, conflagrate; rekindle, relight, relume; feed, feed the fire, stoke, stoke the fire, add fuel to the flame; bank; poke or stir the fire, blow up the fire, fan the flame; open the draft.

.23 catch on fire, catch fire, catch, take, burn, flame, combust, blaze, blaze up, burst into flame.

.24 burn, torrefy, scorch, parch, sear; singe, swinge; blister, vesicate; cauterize, brand, burn in; char, coal, carbonize; scorify; calcine; pyrolyze, crack; solder, weld; vulcanize; cast, found; oxidize, oxidate; deflagrate; cupel; burn off; blaze, flame 328.22.

.25 burn up, incendiarize, incinerate, cremate, consume, burn or reduce to ashes, burn to a cinder; burn down, burn to the ground, go up in smoke.

.26 ADJS heating, warming, chafing, calorific; calefactory, calefactive, calefacient, calorificient, calorigenic; burning 328.25–27; cauterant, cauterizing; calcinatory.

.27 inflammatory, inflammative, inflaming, kindling, enkindling, lighting; incendiary.

.28 flammable, inflammable, combustible, burnable, accendible, fiery.

.29 heated, het or het up [both dial], hotted up [Brit], warmed, warmed up, centrally heated, gas-heated, oil-heated, hot-water-heated, hot-air-heated, steam-heated, electric-heated; superheated; overheated; reheated, recooked, warmed-over, réchauffé [Fr]; hot 328.25.

.30 burned, burnt, burned to the ground, incendiarized, burned-out or -down, gutted;

scorched, blistered, parched, singed, seared, charred, pyrographic, adust; sunburned; burnt-up, incinerated, cremated, consumed, consumed by fire; ashen, ashy, carbonized, pyrolyzed, pyrolytic.

.31 molten, melted, fused; meltable, fusible; thermoplastic.

.32 heaters

| | |
|---|---|
| Baltimore heater | induction heating machine |
| bedpan | |
| bloom heater | infrared heater |
| brazier | infrared lamp |
| brick oven | ingot heater |
| Bunsen burner | iron heater |
| calefactory | kerosene heater |
| car heater | kiln 576.5 |
| defroster | orchard heater |
| deicer | oven |
| dielectric heater | plate heater |
| dielectric preheater | preheater |
| Dutch oven | radiant heater |
| electric blanket | radiator |
| electric heater | radio-frequency heater |
| electric pad | register |
| electronic heater | rivet heater |
| feed-water heater | sidearm heater |
| fireless heater | solar heater |
| foot warmer | space heater |
| forge | steam heater |
| gas heater | steam radiator |
| gas log | sun lamp |
| geyser [Brit] | superheater |
| heating pad | tire heater |
| heat lamp | warming house |
| high-frequency heater | warming pad |
| hot-water bag, hot-water bottle | warming pan |
| | water heater |
| hot-water heater | water oven |
| induction heater | |

.33 stoves, furnaces

| | |
|---|---|
| arc furnace | gas furnace |
| assay furnace | gas range |
| athanor | gas stove |
| Bessemer furnace | gasoline stove |
| blast furnace | induction furnace |
| boiler | kerosene stove |
| bottle-gas stove | kitchener [Brit] |
| box stove | kitchen range |
| butane stove | Norwegian stove |
| calefactor | oil furnace |
| coal furnace | oil stove |
| coal stove | open-hearth furnace |
| coke oven | potbellied stove |
| cook stove | Primus stove |
| crucible furnace | range |
| cupola furnace | resistance furnace |
| Dutch stove | reverberatory, reverbatory furnace |
| electric-arc furnace | |
| electric furnace | salamander, salamander stove |
| electric range | |
| electric stove | scorifier |
| foot stove | smelter |
| Franklin stove | |

## 330. COOKING

.1 NOUNS cooking, cookery, cuisine, culinary art; home economics, domestic science, culinary science, catering, nutrition 309; baking, toasting, roasting, frying, searing, sautéing, boiling, simmering, stewing, basting, braising, poaching, shirring, barbecuing, steeping, brewing, grilling, broiling, pan-broiling; broil.

.2 **cook**, kitchener, culinarian, culinary artist; **chef**, *chef de cuisine* [Fr], chief cook; fry cook, short-order cook; **baker**, *boulanger* [Fr], pastrycook, pastry chef, *patissier* [Fr].

.3 **kitchen**, cookroom, cookery, **scullery**, cuisine; kitchenette; **galley**, caboose *or* camboose; cookhouse; **bakery**, bakehouse.

.4 VERBS **cook**, prepare food, prepare, do; boil, heat, stew, simmer, parboil, blanch; brew; poach, coddle; bake, fire, ovenbake; scallop; shirr; roast; toast; fry, griddle, pan; sauté, stir-fry; frizz, frizzle; sear, braise, brown; broil, grill, pan-broil; barbecue; fricassee; steam; devil; curry; baste; **do to a turn**, do to perfection.

.5 ADJS **cooking**, culinary, kitchen.

.6 **cooked**, heated, stewed, fried, barbecued, curried, fricasseed, deviled, sautéed, shirred, toasted; roasted, roast; broiled, grilled, pan-broiled; seared, braised, browned; boiled, simmered, parboiled; steamed; poached, coddled; baked, fired, oven-baked; scalloped.

.7 **done**, **well-done**, well-cooked, *bien cuit* [Fr], done to a turn *or* to perfection; overcooked, **overdone**; medium, medium-rare; doneness.

.8 **underdone**, undercooked, not done, **rare**, *saignant* [Fr]; sodden, fallen.

.9 **manners of cooking**

| | |
|---|---|
| à blanc [Fr] | à la macédoine [Fr] |
| à la béarnaise [Fr] | à la Maintenon [Fr] |
| à la bonne femme [Fr] | à la maître d'hôtel [Fr] |
| à la bordelaise [Fr] | à la Marengo |
| à la bourgeoise [Fr] | à la Maryland |
| à la casserole | à la matelote [Fr] |
| à la Chateaubriand [Fr] | à l'américaine [Fr] |
| | à la mode |
| à la cocotte [Fr] | à la mode de Caen [Fr] |
| à la coque [Fr] | |
| à la Crécy [Fr] | à la napolitaine [Fr] |
| à la créole [Fr] | à la Newburg |
| à la Croissy [Fr] | à l'anglaise [Fr] |
| à la dauphine [Fr] | à la normande [Fr] |
| à la dauphinoise [Fr] | à la parisienne [Fr] |
| à la diable [Fr] | à la Périgord [Fr] |
| à la française [Fr] | à la polonaise [Fr] |
| à la godiveau [Fr] | à la printanière [Fr] |
| à la grecque [Fr] | à la ravigote [Fr] |
| à la jardinière [Fr] | à la reine [Fr] |
| à la julienne [Fr] | à la russe [Fr] |
| à la king | à la serviette [Fr] |
| à l'allemande [Fr] | à la Soubise [Fr] |
| à la lyonnaise [Fr] | à la suisse [Fr] |

| | |
|---|---|
| à la tartare [Fr] | au beurre fondu [Fr] |
| à l'aurore [Fr] | au beurre noire [Fr] |
| à la vinaigrette [Fr] | au beurre roux [Fr] |
| al burro [Ital] | au fromage [Fr] |
| al dente [Ital] | au gras [Fr] |
| à l'espagnole [Fr] | au gratin |
| à l'estragon [Fr] | au jus [Fr] |
| à l'etouffée [Fr] | au kirsch [Fr] |
| à l'italienne [Fr] | au maigre [Fr] |
| alla bolognese [Ital] | au naturel [Fr] |
| alla cacciatore [Ital] | au vert pré [Fr] |
| alla diavola [Ital] | au vin blanc [Fr] |
| alla fiorentina [Ital] | aux fines herbes [Fr] |
| alla marinara [Ital] | en casserole |
| alla milanese [Ital] | flambé |
| alla parmigiana [Ital] | fra diavolo [Ital] |
| alla pizzaiola [Ital] | in brodo [Ital] |
| alla romana [Ital] | maître d'hôtel |
| alla siciliana [Ital] | paprikás [Hung] |
| alla veneziana [Ital] | piccante [Ital] |
| al limone [Ital] | piccata [Ital] |
| all'italiana [Ital] | stroganoff |
| al Marsala [Ital] | thermidor |
| a piacere [Ital] | |

.10 **cookers**

| | |
|---|---|
| alcohol stove | fireless cooker |
| baker | fry-cooker |
| barbecue | galley stove |
| boiler | grill |
| broiler | hibachi |
| camp stove | infrared broiler |
| chafer | infrared cooker |
| chafing dish or pan | microwave oven |
| coffee maker | percolator |
| cook stove | pots, pans 193.8,9 |
| corn popper | pressure cooker |
| Dutch oven | roaster |
| electric cooker | samovar |
| electric frying pan | stove 329.33 |
| electric roaster | toaster |
| electric toaster | waffle iron |
| field range | waterless cooker |

## 331. FUEL

.1 NOUNS **fuel**, firing, combustible *or* inflammable *or* flammable material, burnable, combustible, inflammable, flammable; coal 331.10; coke, charcoal, briquette, fireball; peat, turf; carbon, gas carbon; gasoline, kerosene 380.4; paraffin; natural gas; methane, ethane, propane, butane, pentane, hexane, heptane, octane, etc., isooctane; benzine; alcohol, ethanol, methanol; fuel additive, dope, fuel dope; jet fuel, rocket fuel, propellant; oil 380; gas 401.

.2 **slack**, coal dust, coom *or* comb [both Brit dial], culm.

.3 **firewood**, stovewood, wood; **kindling**, kindlings, kindling wood; brush, brushwood; fagot, bavin [Brit]; log, backlog, yule log *or* yule clog [archaic].

.4 **lighter**, light, igniter, sparker; pocket lighter, cigar *or* cigarette lighter, butane lighter; **torch**, flambeau, taper, spill;

brand, firebrand; portfire; **flint,** flint and steel.

.5 **match,** lucifer; friction match, locofoco, safety match, vesuvian, vesta, fusee; Congreve, Congreve match.

.6 **tinder,** touchwood; **punk,** spunk, German tinder, amadou; tinder fungus; pyrotechnic sponge; tinderbox.

.7 **detonator,** exploder; **cap,** blasting cap, percussion cap, mercury fulminate, fulminating mercury; electric detonator or exploder; detonating powder; **primer,** priming; primacord; **fuse,** squib.

.8 VERBS **fuel,** fuel up, fill up, top off; refuel; coal, oil; **stoke, feed,** add fuel to the flame; detonate, explode, fulminate.

.9 ADJS **coaly,** carbonaceous, carboniferous, anthrac(o)–; anthracite, bituminous; lignitic, lign(o)– or ligni–.

.10 **coal**

| | |
|---|---|
| anthracite, hard coal | grate coal |
| bituminous or soft coal | lignite, brown coal |
| | lump coal |
| blind coal | mustard-seed coal |
| broken coal | nut coal |
| buckwheat coal | pea coal |
| cannel, cannel coal | peat |
| chestnut coal | sea coal |
| egg coal | steamboat coal |
| flaxseed coal | stove coal |
| glance coal | |

.11 **fuses**

| | |
|---|---|
| base fuse | friction fuse |
| chemical fuse | point fuse |
| concussion or percussion fuse | proximity fuse |
| | time fuse |
| detonating fuse | variable-time or VT |
| electric fuse | fuse |

## 332. INCOMBUSTIBILITY

.1 NOUNS **incombustibility, uninflammability,** noninflammability, **nonflammability;** unburnableness.

.2 **extinguishing,** extinguishment, extinction, **quenching,** dousing [informal], **snuffing,** putting out; **choking, damping, stifling, smothering,** smotheration; controlling; fire fighting; going out, dying, burning out, flame-out, burnout.

.3 **extinguisher, fire extinguisher;** fire apparatus, fire engine, hook-and-ladder, ladder truck; ladder pipe, snorkel, deluge set, deck gun, water cannon [Brit], pumper, super-pumper; **foam,** carbon-dioxide foam, Foamite, foam extinguisher; dry-powder extinguisher; carbon tetrachloride, carbon tet; water, soda, acid, wet blanket; sprinkler, automatic sprinkler, sprinkler system, sprinkler head; hydrant, fire hydrant, fireplug; fire hose.

.4 **fire fighter, fireman,** fire-eater [informal]; forest fire fighter, fire warden, fire-chaser, smokechaser, smokejumper; volunteer fireman, vamp [informal]; fire department, fire brigade.

.5 **fireproofing,** fire resistance; fireproof or fire-resistant or fire-resisting or fire-resistive or fire-retardant material, fire retardant; asbestos; amianthus, earth flax, mountain flax; asbestos curtain, fire wall; fire break, fire line.

.6 VERBS **fireproof, flameproof.**

.7 **extinguish, put out, quench,** out, douse [informal], **snuff,** snuff out, blow out, stamp out; **choke, damp, smother, stifle,** slack.

.8 **burn out, go out, die,** die out or away; fizzle or fizzle out [both informal]; flame out.

.9 ADJS **incombustible, uninflammable,** noninflammable, **nonflammable,** unburnable; asbestine, asbestic; amianthine.

.10 **fireproof, flameproof,** fireproofed, fire-retarded, fire-resisting or -resistant or -resistive, fire-retardant.

.11 **extinguished,** quenched, snuffed, **out.**

## 333. COLD

.1 NOUNS **cold, coldness; coolness,** coolth, freshness; low temperature, drop or decrease in temperature; **chilliness; chill, nip,** sharp air; **crispness,** briskness, nippiness; **frigidity, iciness,** frostiness, extreme or intense cold, gelidity, algidity; **rawness,** bleakness, keenness, sharpness, bitterness, severity, inclemency, rigor, "a hard, dull bitterness of cold" [Whittier]; cool; freezing point; cryology; cryogenics; absolute zero.

.2 (sensation of cold) **chill,** chilliness, chilling; shivering, **shivers, cold shivers,** didders [Brit dial], dithers, chattering of the teeth; creeps, **cold creeps** [informal]; **gooseflesh, goose pimples,** goose or duck bumps [informal], horripilation; **frostbite, chilblains,** kibe, cryopathy; ache, aching.

.3 **cold weather,** bleak weather, raw weather, bitter weather, wintry weather, **freezing weather,** zero weather, subzero weather; **cold wave,** snap, **cold snap; freeze,** frost; winter, depth of winter, hard winter; "The ways deep and the weather sharp, / The very dead of winter" [T. S. Eliot]; "When icicles hang by the wall" [Shakespeare]; wintry wind 403.8.

.4 (cold place) Siberia, Novaya Zemlya, Alaska, Iceland, the Hebrides, Greenland, "Greenland's icy mountains" [Reginald Heber], the Yukon, Tierra del Fuego, Lower Slobbovia [Al Capp]; North Pole, South Pole; Frigid Zones; the Arctic, Arctic Circle or Zone; Antarctica, the Antarctic; Antarctic Circle or Zone; tundra.

.5 ice, frozen water; ice needle or crystal; icicle, iceshockle [Brit dial]; cryosphere; ice sheet, ice field, ice barrier, ice front; floe, ice floe, ice island, ice raft, ice pack; ice foot, ice belt; shelf ice, pack ice; iceberg, berg, growler; calf; snowberg; icecap, jokul [Iceland]; ice pinnacle, serac, nieve penitente; glacier, glacieret, glaciation, glacio–, ice dike, "motionless torrents, silent cataracts" [Coleridge]; piedmont glacier; icefall; ice banner; ice cave; sleet, glaze, glazed frost; snow ice; névé, granular snow, firn; ground ice, anchor ice, frazil; lolly; sludge, slob; ice cubes; Dry Ice; icequake; ice storm, freezing rain.

.6 hail, hailstone; soft hail, graupel; hailstorm.

.7 frost, Jack Frost; hoarfrost, hoar, rime, rime frost, white frost; black frost; hard frost, sharp frost; killing frost; frost smoke; frost line.

.8 snow, chio– or chion(o)–; granular snow, corn snow, spring corn, spring snow, powder snow, wet snow; "the frolic architecture of the snow" [Emerson]; "a pure and grandfather moss" [Dylan Thomas]; snowfall, "feather'd rain" [William Strode], "the whitening shower" [James Thomson]; snowstorm, snow blast, snow squall, snow flurry, flurry, blizzard; snowflake, snow-crystal, flake, crystal; snow dust; snowdrift, snowbank, snow wreath [Brit dial], snow roller, driven snow; snowcap; snow banner; snow blanket; snow bed, snowfield, mantle of snow; snowscape; snowland; snowshed; snow line; snowball, snowman; snowslide, snowslip, avalanche; snow slush, slush, slosh; snowbridge; snow fence; snowhouse, igloo; mogul.

.9 VERBS be cold, grow cold, lose heat; shiver, quiver, quake, shake, tremble, shudder, didder [Brit dial], dither; chatter; chill, have a chill, have the cold shivers; freeze, freeze to death, freeze one's balls off [informal], perish with cold, horripilate, have goose pimples, have goose or duck bumps [informal]; have chilblains.

.10 (make cold) chill, chill to the bone or marrow, make one shiver, make one's teeth chatter; nip, bite, cut, pierce, penetrate, go through or right through; freeze 334.11; frost, frostbite; numb, benumb; refrigerate 334.10.

.11 hail, sleet, snow; snow in; snow under; frost, ice, ice up, ice over.

.12 ADJS cool, coolish, temperate; chill, chilly, parky [Brit slang]; fresh, bracing, invigorating, stimulating; cool as a cucumber.

.13 unheated, unwarmed; unmelted, unthawed.

.14 cold, cry(o)– or kryo–, frigo–, psychro–; crisp, brisk, nipping, nippy, snappy [informal], raw, bleak, keen, sharp, bitter, biting, pinching, cutting, piercing, penetrating, inclement, severe, rigorous; snowcold; sleety; slushy; icy, icelike, ice-cold, glacial, ice-encrusted; cryospheric; supercooled; frigid, bitter or bitterly cold, gelid, algid; below zero, subzero; freezing, freezing cold, numbing; wintry, wintery, winterlike, winterbound, hiemal, brumal, hibernal; arctic, Siberian, boreal, hyperborean; stone-cold, cold as death, cold as ice, cold as marble, cold as charity, cold as a welldigger's ass, cold as a witch's tit or kiss, cold enough to freeze the tail or balls off a brass monkey, "cold as the north side of a gravestone in winter" [anon], cold as a bastard or bitch, colder than hell or the deuce or the devil.

.15 (feeling cold) cold, cool, chilly; shivering, shivery, shaky, dithery; algid, aguish, aguey; chattering, with chattering teeth; frozen 334.14, half-frozen, frozen to death, chilled to the bone, blue with cold, figé de froid [Fr], so cold one could spit ice cubes.

.16 frosty, frostlike; frosted, frost-beaded, frost-covered, frost-chequered, rimed, hoary, hoar-frosted, rime-frosted; frost-riven, frost-rent; frosty-faced, frosty-whiskered; frostbound, frost-fettered.

.17 snowy, snowlike, niveous, nival; snowblown, snow-drifted, snow-driven; snow-covered, snow-clad, snow-mantled, snow-robed, snow-blanketed, snow-sprinkled, snow-lined, snow-encircled, snow-laden, snow-loaded, snow-hung; snow-capped, snow-crested, snow-crowned, snow-tipped; snow-topped; snow-bearded; snow-feathered; snow-still.

.18 frozen out or in, snowbound, snowed-in, icebound.

.19 cold-blooded, heterothermic, poikilothermic; cryogenic; cryological.

## 334. REFRIGERATION

*(reduction of temperature)*

**.1** NOUNS **refrigeration,** infrigidation, reduction of temperature; **cooling, chilling; freezing,** glacification, glaciation, congelation, congealment; refreezing, regelation; mechanical refrigeration, electric refrigeration, electronic refrigeration, gas refrigeration; food freezing, quick freezing, deep freezing, sharp freezing, blast freezing, dehydrofreezing; adiabatic expansion, adiabatic absorption, adiabatic demagnetization; cryogenics; super-cooling; **air conditioning,** air cooling.

**.2** refrigeration anesthesia, crymoanesthesia, hypothermia *or* hypothermy; crymotherapy, cryo-aerotherapy; cold cautery, cryocautery; cryopathy.

**.3 cooler,** chiller; water cooler, air cooler; ventilator 402.10; fan 403.21; surface cooler; ice cube, ice pail *or* bucket, wine cooler; ice bag, ice pack, cold pack.

**.4 refrigerator,** refrigeratory, **icebox,** ice chest; Frigidaire, fridge [informal], electric refrigerator, electronic refrigerator, gas refrigerator; refrigerator car, refrigerator truck, reefer [informal]; freezer ship.

**.5 freezer, deep freeze,** deep-freezer, quick-freezer, sharp-freezer; ice-cream freezer; ice machine, ice-cube machine, freezing machine, refrigerating machine *or* engine; **ice plant,** icehouse, refrigerating plant.

**.6 cold storage; frozen-food locker,** locker, freezer locker, locker plant; frigidarium; coolhouse; coolerman.

**.7** (cooling agent) **coolant; refrigerant;** cryogen; ice, Dry Ice, ice cubes; freezing mixture, liquid air, ammonia, carbon dioxide, Freon, ether; ethyl chloride; liquid air, liquid oxygen *or* lox, liquid nitrogen, liquid helium, etc.

**.8** antifreeze, alcohol, ethylene glycol.

**.9** refrigerating engineering, refrigerating engineer.

**.10** VERBS **refrigerate,** infrigidate; **cool, chill;** refresh, freshen; ice, ice-cool; water-cool, air-cool; **air-condition;** ventilate 402.11.

**.11 freeze** 333.9,10, ice, glacify, glaciate, congeal; **deep-freeze,** quick-freeze, sharp-freeze, blast-freeze; freeze solid; **nip,** blight, blast; refreeze, regelate.

**.12** ADJS **refrigerative,** refrigeratory, refrigerant, frigorific(al), algific; **cooling, chilling; freezing,** congealing; quick-freezing, deep-freezing, sharp-freezing, blast-freezing; freezable, glaciable.

**.13 cooled, chilled; air-conditioned;** iced, ice-cooled; air-cooled, water-cooled; super-cooled.

**.14 frozen,** frozen solid, glacial, gelid, congealed; **icy,** ice-cold, icy-cold, ice, icelike; deep-frozen, quick-frozen, sharp-frozen, blast-frozen; frostbitten, frostnipped.

**.15** antifreeze, antifreezing.

## 335. LIGHT

**.1** NOUNS **light,** phot(o)–, lumin(o)– *or* lumini–; radiant *or* luminous energy, visible radiation, radiation in the visible spectrum, **illumination, radiation, radiance** *or* radiancy, irradiance *or* irradiancy, irradiation, emanation; "God's first creature" [Francis Bacon], "God's eldest daughter" [Thomas Fuller, D.D.], "offspring of Heav'n firstborn" [Milton], "the first of painters" [Emerson], "the prime work of God" [Milton], "the white radiance of eternity" [Shelley]; highlight; sidelight; photosensitivity; light source 336.

**.2 shine,** shininess, **luster, sheen, gloss,** glint; **glow, gleam,** flush, sunset glow; **incandescence,** candescence; shining light; afterglow; skylight, air glow.

**.3 lightness, luminousness,** luminosity; **lucidity,** lucence *or* lucency, translucence *or* translucency.

**.4 brightness, brilliance** *or* brilliancy, **splendor,** radiant splendor, **glory, radiance** *or* radiancy, resplendence *or* resplendency, **vividness,** flamboyance; effulgence, refulgence *or* refulgency, fulgor; **glare,** blare, blaze; bright light, brilliant light, blazing light, glaring light, dazzling light, blinding light; "the blaze of noon" [Milton]; streaming light, flood of light, burst of light.

**.5 ray, radiation, beam, gleam,** leam [Scot], **stream, streak, pencil, patch,** ray of light, beam of light, etc.; ribbon, ribbon of light, streamer, stream of light; violet ray, ultraviolet ray, infrared ray, X ray, gamma ray, invisible radiation; actinic ray *or* light, actinism; atomic beam, atomic ray; solar rays; radiorays 327.3; photon.

**.6 flash, blaze, flare, flame, gleam, glint, glance;** blaze *or* flash *or* gleam of light; solar flare, solar prominence, facula; Bailey's beads.

**.7 glitter, glimmer, shimmer, twinkle, blink; sparkle,** spark; **scintillation,** scintilla; coruscation; **glisten,** glister, spangle, tinsel, glittering, glimmering, shimmering, twinkling; "shining from shook foil" [G. M. Hopkins]; stroboscopic light, blinking; firefly, glowworm.

.8 **flicker, flutter, dance, quiver;** flickering, fluttering, dancing, quivering, lambency; wavering or flickering light, play, play of light, dancing or glancing light; light show; "the lambent easy light" [Dryden].

.9 **reflection,** reflectance; reflected or incident light, albedo; blink, iceblink, ice sky, snowblink, waterblink, water sky.

.10 **daylight,** dayshine, day glow, light of day; day, daytime, daytide; **sunlight, sunshine,** shine; noonlight, midday sun, noonday or noontide light; broad day or daylight, full sun; dusk, twilight 134.3; dawn 133.3,4; sunburst, sunbreak; **sunbeam,** sun spark, ray of sunshine; green flash.

.11 **moonlight, moonshine, moonglow; moonbeam.**

.12 **starlight,** starshine; earthshine.

.13 **luminescence,** autoluminescence, cathode luminescence, chemiluminescence or chemicoluminescence, crystalloluminescence, electroluminescence, photoluminescence, radioluminescence, thermoluminescence, triboluminescence; bioluminescence, noctiluscence; **fluorescence,** fluor(o)– or fluori–, tribofluorescence; **phosphorescence,** tribophosphorescence; luciferin, luciferase; phosphor, luminophor; ignis fatuus, will-o'-the-wisp, will-with-the-wisp, wisp, jack-o'-lantern, marshfire; friar's lantern; fata morgana; fox fire; St. Elmo's light or fire, witch fire, corposant; double corposant; –escence.

.14 **halo, nimbus,** aura, **aureole,** circle, ring, glory; **rainbow,** irid(o)–; solar halo, lunar halo, ring around the sun or moon; **corona,** solar corona, lunar corona; parhelion, parhelic circle or ring, mock sun, sun dog; anthelion, antisun, countersun; paraselene, mock moon, moon dog.

.15 (nebulous light) nebula 375.7; zodiacal light, Gegenschein, counterglow.

.16 polar lights, **aurora; northern lights, aurora borealis,** merry dancers; southern lights, **aurora australis;** aurora polaris; aurora glory; streamer or curtain or arch aurora; polar ray.

.17 **lightning, flash** or stroke of lightning, fulguration, fulmination, bolt, **bolt of lightning,** bolt from the blue, **thunderbolt,** thunderstroke, thunderball, fireball, firebolt, levin bolt or brand; "flying flame" [Tennyson], "the lightning's gleaming rod" [Joaquin Miller], "oak-cleaving thunderbolts" [Shakespeare]; fork or forked lightning, chain lightning, globular or ball lightning, summer or heat lightning, sheet lightning, dark lightning; Jupiter Fulgur or Fulminator; Thor.

.18 **iridescence,** opalescence, nacreousness, pearliness; **rainbow;** nacre, mother-of-pearl; nacreous or mother-of-pearl cloud.

.19 **lighting, illumination,** enlightenment; radiation, irradiation; tonality; light and shade, black and white, chiaroscuro, clairobscure, contrast, highlights; gaslighting, electric lighting, incandescent lighting, fluorescent lighting, glow lighting; arc lighting; direct lighting, indirect lighting; floodlighting, overhead lighting, stage lighting, decorative lighting, festoon lighting, strip lighting, spot lighting, diffused lighting, cove lighting.

.20 **illuminant,** luminant; electricity; gas, illuminating gas; oil, petroleum, benzine; gasoline, petrol [Brit]; kerosene, paraffin [Brit], coal oil; light source 336.

.21 (measurement of light) **candle power,** luminous intensity, luminous power, luminous flux, flux, intensity, light; quantum, **light quantum, photon;** unit of light, unit of flux; candle, international candle, British candle, Hefner candle; foot-candle, candle-foot; decimal candle, bougie décimale [Fr]; lux, candle-meter, lumen meter, lumeter, lumen, candle lumen; candle-hour, lamp-hour, lumen-hour; **exposure meter,** light meter, ASA scale, Scheiner scale.

.22 (science of light) photics, photology, photometry; **optics,** geometrical optics, physical optics; dioptrics, catoptrics; actinology, actinometry; heliology, heliometry, heliography.

.23 VERBS **shine,** shine forth, **burn, give light,** incandesce; **glow, beam, gleam,** glint, luster, glance; **flash, flare, blaze, flame,** fulgurate; **radiate,** shoot, shoot out rays, send out rays; spread or diffuse light; be bright, shine brightly, beacon; **glare;** daze, blind, dazzle, bedazzle.

.24 **glitter, glimmer, shimmer, twinkle, blink,** spangle, tinsel, coruscate; **sparkle,** spark, **scintillate; glisten,** glister, glisk [Scot].

.25 **flicker,** bicker, **flutter, waver, dance,** play, quiver.

.26 **luminesce,** phosphoresce, fluoresce; iridesce, opalesce.

.27 **grow light,** grow bright, light, **lighten,** brighten; dawn, break.

.28 **illuminate,** illumine, illume, luminate, **light, light up, lighten,** enlighten, brighten, brighten up, irradiate; bathe or flood with light; relumine, relume; **shed light upon,** cast or throw light upon, shed

luster on, shine upon, overshine; spotlight, highlight; floodlight; beacon.

.29 **strike a light,** light, turn or switch on the
**light,** open the light [informal], make a
light, shine a light.

.30 ADJS **luminous,** luminant, luminative, lu-
minificent, luminiferous, luciferous or lu-
cific [both archaic], luciform, illuminant;
**incandescent,** candescent; **lustrous,** orient; **radiant,** irradiative, radio–; **shining,**
shiny, burning, lamping, streaming; **beaming,** beamy; **gleaming,** gleamy, glinting;
**glowing,** aglow, suffused, blushing, flushing; rutilant, rutilous; **sunny, sunshiny,**
bright and sunny, light as day; starry, starlike, starbright.

.31 **light,** lightish, lightsome; **lucid,** lucent, lu-
culent, relucent; **translucent,** translucid,
pellucid, diaphanous, transparent; **clear,**
serene; **cloudless,** unclouded, unobscured.

.32 **bright, brilliant, vivid, splendid,** splendorous, splendent; **resplendent,** bright and
shining; fulgid [archaic], fulgent, efful-
gent, refulgent; **flamboyant,** flaming; **glaring,** glary, garish; **dazzling,** bedazzling,
blinding.

.33 **shiny,** shining, **lustrous, glossy,** glassy,
glacé [Fr], **sheeny, polished,** burnished,
shined.

.34 **flashing,** flashy, **blazing, flaming, flaring,**
**burning,** fulgurant, fulgurating; aflame,
ablaze; meteoric.

.35 **glittering, glimmering, shimmering, twinkling, blinking, glistening,** glistering; glit-
tery, glimmery, glimmerous, shimmery,
twinkly, blinky, spangly, tinselly; **sparkling, scintillating,** scintillant, scintilles-
cent, coruscating, coruscant.

.36 **flickering,** bickering, **fluttering, wavering,**
**dancing,** playing, quivering, lambent;
flickery, flicky [informal], aflicker, fluttery, wavery, quivery; blinking, flashing,
stroboscopic.

.37 **iridescent,** opalescent, nacreous, pearly,
pearl-like; rainbowlike.

.38 **luminescent,** photogenic; electrolumines-
cent, photoluminescent, radioluminescent, thermoluminescent, tribolumines-
cent; chemiluminescent, chemicolumines-
cent; **phosphorescent,** tribophospho-
rescent; **fluorescent,** tribofluorescent;
autoluminescent, self-luminous, self-lumi-
nescent; bioluminescent, noctilucent; luminal; –escent.

.39 **illuminated,** luminous, **lightened,** enlightened, brightened, **lighted, lit, lit up,**
flooded or bathed with light; irradiated,
irradiate; **alight,** aglow, suffused with

light, ablaze, in a blaze; lamplit, lantern-
lit, candlelit, torchlit, gaslit, firelit; sunlit,
moonlit, starlit; spangled, bespangled,
tinseled, studded; star-spangled, star-studded.

.40 **illuminating,** illumining, **lighting, lightening,** enlightening, brightening.

.41 **luminary,** lumi–, photic; photologic(al),
photometric(al); heliological, heliographic; actinic, photoactinic, actin(o)–
or actini–; catoptric(al); luminal.

.42 photosensitive; photophobic; phototrop-
ic.

## 336. LIGHT SOURCE

.1 NOUNS **light source,** source of light, **luminary,** illuminator, luminant, illuminant,
incandescent body or point, **light, glim;**
**lamp,** light bulb, electric light bulb, lantern, candle, taper, torch, flame; match;
phos–; "a lamp unto my feet, and a light
unto my path" [Bible]; fire 328.13; sun,
moon, stars 375.4.

.2 **candle,** taper; dip, farthing dip, tallow
dip; tallow candle; wax candle, bougie;
bayberry candle; rush candle, rushlight;
corpse candle; votary candle.

.3 **torch,** flaming torch, flambeau, cresset,
link [archaic]; **flare,** signal flare, fusee.

.4 **traffic light,** stop-and-go light; stop or red
light, go or green light, caution or amber
light.

.5 **firefly,** lightning bug, lampyrid, **glowworm,** fireworm; fire beetle; lantern fly,
candle fly; luciferin, luciferase; phosphor,
luminophor.

.6 **chandelier,** gasolier, electrolier, hanging
or ceiling fixture, luster; corona, corona
lucis, crown, circlet.

.7 **wick,** taper; candlewick, lampwick.

.8 **lamps, lights**

| | |
|---|---|
| aphlogistic lamp | Coleman lantern |
| arc lamp or light | cresset |
| Argand lamp | dark lantern |
| argon lamp | Davy lamp |
| baby spotlight or spot | daylight lamp |
| barn lantern | desk lamp or light |
| battery lamp | discharge lamp |
| battle lantern | electric-arc lamp |
| bed lamp | electric candle |
| bridge lamp | electric-discharge |
| broadside | lamp or tube |
| bull's-eye, bull's-eye | electric light or lamp |
| lantern | electric torch |
| calcium lamp | filament lamp |
| candle | Finsen light or lamp |
| candlelight | flame lamp |
| carbon light or lamp | flashbulb |
| Carcel lamp | flasher |
| carriage lamp | flashgun |
| Chinese lantern | flash lamp |

flashlight
floodlight, flood lamp
floor lamp
fluorescent light or
    tube
focus lamp
fog light or lamp
footlight
gaslight, gas lamp
gasoline lantern
glow light or lamp
headlight, head lamp
Hefner lamp
high-intensity lamp
hurricane lamp
incandescent electric
    lamp
incandescent light or
    lamp
infrared lamp
instrument lamp or
    light
jack-o'-lantern
Japanese lantern
klieg light
lampion [archaic]
lamplet
lantern
light bulb
limelight
magic lantern
magnetite arc lamp
mercury-arc lamp,
    mercury lamp
mercury-vapor lamp
miner's lamp
moderator lamp
Moore light or lamp
    or tube
navigation light
neon light or lamp or
    tube
Nernst lamp
night light
oil lamp
osmium lamp

photoflash lamp
photoflood lamp
pilot light or lamp
police lantern
projector lamp
quartz lamp
railroad lantern
reading lamp
riding light
running light
rushlight
safety lamp
searchlight, search
    lamp
searchlight lantern
Sheringham daylight
    lamp
shunt lamp
side lamp
side light
sodium-vapor lamp,
    sodium lamp
spotlight, spot
stop light
strobe, strobe light,
    strobotron
stroboscope
student lamp
sun arc, sun spot
sun burner, sunlight
    burner
sun lamp
table lamp
taillight, tail lamp
tantalum lamp
torch, torch light
tornado lantern or
    lamp
tungsten lamp
ultraviolet lamp, uviol
    lamp
vanity lamp
vapor lamp
veilleuse [Fr]
wolfram lamp
zircon light or lamp

**.9 beacons, signal lights**

balefire
beacon fire
flare, flare-up, flare-up
    light
fusee
lighthouse
lightship
magnesium flare
occulting light
pharos

rocket
signal beacon
signal flare
signal lamp
signal lantern
signal rocket
skyrocket
Very flare
watch fire

**.10 aviation beacons**

airport beacon
airway beacon
anchor light
approach light
blinker light
boundary light
ceiling light or projec-
    tor
course light
fixed light
flare path
flashing light

high-intensity runway
    approach light
identification light
landing-direction light
landing light
landmark beacon
Lindbergh light
marker, marker bea-
    con
navigation light
obstruction light
position light

runway light

**.11 light holders**

bracket
candelabrum, candela-
    bra
candlestand
candlestick
chandelier
gas fixture
girandole
lamp holder

sequence flasher

lamp socket
lampstand
light fixture
light socket
sconce
torch holder
torch staff
wall bracket

**.12 burners**

Argand burner
fishtail burner
gas burner
gas jet, jet

gas mantle, incandes-
    cent mantle, mantle
Welsbach mantle

### 337. DARKNESS, DIMNESS

**.1** NOUNS **darkness, dark, lightlessness; obscurity,** obscure, tenebrosity, tenebrousness; **night** 134.4, dead of night, deep night; sunlessness, moonlessness, starlessness; **pitch-darkness,** pitch-blackness, pitchy darkness, utter or thick or total darkness, intense darkness, velvet darkness, Cimmerian or Stygian or Egyptian darkness, Erebus; "obscure darkness" [Bible], "the palpable obscure" [Milton], "darkness visible" [Milton], "a fabulous, formless darkness" [Yeats], "the suit of night" [Shakespeare], "darkness which may be felt" [Bible]; **blackness,** swarthiness 365.2.

**.2 gloom, gloominess, somberness,** sombrousness, somber; lowering, lower.

**.3 shadow, shade, shadiness,** sci(a)- or scio- or skia-; umbra, umbrage, umbrageousness; "shadows numberless" [Keats]; thick or dark shade, gloom; mere shadow, "the shadow of a shade" [Aeschylus]; penumbra; silhouette; skiagram, skiagraph.

**.4 darkishness,** darksomeness, **duskiness,** duskness; **murkiness, murk; dimness,** dim; **semidarkness,** semidark, partial darkness, bad light, dim light, half-light, demi-jour [Fr]; gloaming, **dusk,** twilight 133.4, 134.3.

**.5 dullness, flatness,** lifelessness, **drabness, deadness,** somberness, lackluster, **lusterlessness,** lack of sparkle or sheen; mat, mat finish.

**.6 darkening, dimming; obscuration,** obscurement, obumbration, obfuscation; eclipsing, occulting, blocking the light; **shadowing, shading,** overshadowing, overshading, overshadowment, **clouding,** overclouding, obnubilation, gathering of the clouds, overcast; blackening 365.5; extinguishment 332.2.

**.7 blackout,** dimout, brownout.

**.8 eclipse,** occultation; total eclipse, partial eclipse, central eclipse, annular eclipse; solar eclipse, lunar eclipse.

**.9 VERBS darken,** bedarken; **obscure,** obfuscate, obumbrate; **eclipse,** occult, occultate, block the light; **black out,** brown out; black, brown; blot out; **overcast,** darken over; **shadow, shade,** cast a shadow, spread a shadow *or* shade over, encompass with shadow, overshadow; **cloud,** becloud, encloud, cloud over, .overcloud, obnubilate; gloom, begloom, somber, cast a gloom over, murk; **dim,** bedim, dim out; blacken 365.7.

**.10 dull,** mat, deaden; **tone down.**

**.11 turn** *or* switch off the light, close the light [informal]; extinguish 332.7.

**.12 grow dark, darken,** darkle, lower; gloom [archaic], gloam [Scot]; dusk; **dim, grow dim.**

**.13 ADJS dark, black,** darksome, darkling; **lightless,** beamless, rayless, unlighted, **unilluminated,** unlit; **obscure,** caliginous, obscured, obfuscated, eclipsed, occulted, clothed *or* shrouded *or* veiled *or* cloaked *or* mantled in darkness; tenebrous, tenebrific, tenebrious, tenebrose; **pitch-dark,** pitch-black, pitchy, dark as pitch, "dark as a wolf's mouth" [Sir Walter Scott], dark as the inside of a black cat; ebon, ebony; night-dark, night-black, dark *or* black as night; night-clad, night-cloaked, night-enshrouded, night-mantled, nightveiled, night-hid, night-filled; sunless, moonless, starless; black 365.8.

**.14 gloomy,** gloomful [archaic], glooming, dark and gloomy, Acheronian, Acherontic, **somber,** sombrous; lowering; **funereal;** Cimmerian, Stygian; stormy, cloudy, clouded, overcast; ill-lighted, ill-lit.

**.15 darkish,** darksome, **semidark; dusky,** dusk; subfuscous, subfusc; **murky,** murksome, murk [archaic]; **dim,** dimmish, dimpsy [Brit dial]; dark-colored 365.9.

**.16 shadowy, shady,** shaded, darkling, umbral, umbrageous; overshadowed, overshaded, obumbrate, obumbrated; penumbral.

**.17 lackluster,** lusterless; **dull, dead,** deadened, **lifeless,** somber, **drab,** wan, **flat,** mat.

**.18 obscuring,** obscurant.

**.19 ADVS in the dark,** darkling, in darkness; in the night, in the dark of night, in the dead of night, at *or* by night.

# 338. SHADE

*(a thing that shades)*

**.1 NOUNS shade,** shader, **screen, light shield, curtain,** drape, drapery, blind, veil; **awning,** sunblind [Brit]; **sunshade,** parasol, **umbrella,** beach umbrella; cover 228.2; shadow 337.3.

**.2 eyeshade,** eyeshield, visor; goggles, colored spectacles, smoked glasses, dark glasses, **sunglasses,** shades [slang].

**.3 lamp shade;** moonshade; globe, light globe.

**.4 light filter,** filter, diffusing screen; smoked glass, frosted glass, ground glass; stained glass; butterfly; gelatin filter, Celluloid filter; frosted lens; lens hood; sunscreen.

**.5 VERBS shade, screen,** veil, curtain, shutter, draw the curtains, put up *or* close the shutters; cover 228.19; overshadow 337.9.

**.6 ADJS shading, screening,** veiling, curtaining; covering 228.34.

**.7 shaded, screened,** veiled, curtained; sunproof; shady 337.16.

**.8 shades**

| | |
|---|---|
| awning | roof 228.6,39 |
| baldacchino, baldachin | sash curtain |
| | screen |
| bamboo shade *or* screen | shade tree |
| | shutter |
| belvedere | summerhouse |
| blind | sunbonnet |
| *brise-soleil* [Fr] | sun hat |
| canopy | sun helmet |
| curtain | sunshade |
| gazebo | tent 228.8,40 |
| hat 231.25,59 | topee |
| jalousie | umbrella 228.7 |
| lamp shade | veil |
| occulter, occulting screen | venetian blind |
| | visor |
| parasol | window curtain |
| persienne | window screen |
| pith helmet | window shade |
| portiere | window shutter |
| roller blind *or* shade | |

# 339. TRANSPARENCY

**.1 NOUNS transparency,** transparence, transpicuousness, show-through, transmission *or* admission of light; **lucidity,** pellucidity, **clearness, clarity,** limpidity; nonopacity, uncloudedness; **crystallinity,** crystalclearness; **glassiness,** glasslikeness, vitreousness, vitrescence; vitreosity, hyalescence; **diaphanousness,** diaphaneity, sheerness, thinness, **gossameriness,** filminess, gauziness.

**.2 transparent** substance, diaphane; **glass,** glassware, glasswork; vitrics; stemware;

pane, windowpane, light, windowlight, shopwindow; vitrine; showcase, display case; watch crystal or glass.

.3 VERBS be transparent, show through.

.4 ADJS **transparent,** transpicuous, light-pervious; see-through, peekaboo, revealing; **lucid,** pellucid, **clear,** limpid; nonopaque, unclouded, **crystalline,** crystal, **crystalclear,** clear as crystal; **diaphanous,** diaphane [archaic], sheer, thin; **gossamer,** gossamery, filmy, gauzy.

.5 **glass, glassy,** glasslike, clear as glass, vitric, vitreous, vitriform, hyaline, hyalescent; hyalinocrystalline.

.6 **transparent things, translucent things**

| | |
|---|---|
| aquamarine | gossamer |
| beryl | hyaline |
| carnelian | hyalite |
| cellophane | isinglass |
| Celluloid | Lucite |
| chalcedony | mica |
| chiffon | moonstone |
| chrysolite | morganite |
| chrysoprase | onionskin |
| citrine | Perspex |
| clear plastic | plastic wrap |
| Clearsite | Plexiglas |
| clear varnish or wax or | quartz |
| shellac | Saran wrap |
| crystal | sheers |
| Crystalite | tissue |
| diamond | tissue paper |
| diaphane | veil |
| emerald | voile |
| fixative varnish | water |
| golden beryl | window |

.7 **glass**

| | |
|---|---|
| agate glass | Lalique glass |
| blown glass | laminated glass, laminated safety glass |
| bottle glass | |
| bullet-resisting glass | lead glass |
| camphor glass | milk glass |
| carnival glass | opal glass |
| Cel-o-Glass | opaline |
| CM-glass | optical glass |
| coralene | ornamental glass |
| cranberry glass | Orrefors glass |
| CR-glass | photosensitive glass |
| crown glass | plastic glass |
| cryolite glass | plate glass |
| crystal, crystal glass | porcelain glass |
| custard glass | pressed glass |
| cut glass | prism glass |
| end-of-day glass | Pyrex |
| etched glass | quartz glass |
| fiber glass | rhinestone |
| flashed glass | safety glass |
| flat glass | Sandwich glass |
| flint glass | satin glass |
| float glass | sheet glass |
| Fostoria | stained glass |
| frosted glass | Steuben glass |
| fused quartz | Swedish glass |
| glass bead | tempered glass, tempered safety glass |
| glass brick | |
| ground glass | uranium glass |
| hobnail glass | Venetian glass |

| | |
|---|---|
| Vitaglass | window glass |
| vitreous silica | wire or wired glass |
| Waterford glass | |

## 340. SEMITRANSPARENCY

.1 NOUNS **semitransparency,** semipellucidity, semidiaphaneity; semiopacity.

.2 **translucence, translucency,** lucence, lucency, translucidity, pellucidity, lucidity; transmission or admission of light.

.3 VERBS **frost,** frost over.

.4 ADJS **semitransparent,** semipellucid, semidiaphanous, semiopaque; frosty, frosted.

.5 **translucent,** lucent, translucid, lucid, pellucid; semitranslucent, semipellucid.

## 341. OPAQUENESS

.1 NOUNS **opaqueness,** opacity, intransparency, nontranslucency, imperviousness to light, adiaphanousness; roil, roiledness, turbidity, turbidness; cloudiness; **darkness, obscurity, dimness** 337; opaque.

.2 VERBS opaque, **darken, obscure** 337.9; **cloud,** becloud.

.3 ADJS **opaque,** intransparent, nontranslucent, adiaphanous, impervious to light; **dark, obscure** 337.13, **cloudy,** roiled, roily, grumly [Scot], turbid.

## 342. ELECTRICITY

.1 NOUNS **electricity,** electr(o)–, pyroelectricity, actinoelectricity, photoelectricity, ferroelectricity, piezoelectricity, thermoelectricity, faradic electricity, galvanic electricity, voltaic electricity, animal electricity, bioelectricity, neuroelectricity, organic electricity, atmospheric electricity; static electricity, friction electricity, triboelectricity, dynamic or current electricity; voltaism, galvanism; magnetic electricity, magnetoelectricity; positive electricity, negative electricity.

.2 **electric current,** electric stream or flow, rheo–, juice [informal]; direct current, DC, pulsating direct current; alternating current, AC; free alternating current, single-phase alternating current, three-phase alternating current; delta current; multiphase current, rotary current; high-frequency current, low-frequency current; galvanic current, voltaic current; magnetizing current, exciting current; induced current, induction current; active current, watt current; reactive current, wattless or idle current; absorption current, conduction current, convection current, displacement current, dielectric displacement current, ionization current, oscillating current, thermoelectric current, thermionic current, emission current; stray current, eddy current; cycle.

.3 **electric field,** static field, electrostatic field; tube of electric force, electrostatic tube of force; **magnetic field,** magnetic field of currents; **electromagnetic field;** variable field.

.4 **circuit,** path; galvanic circuit *or* circle, complete circuit, loop, closed circuit, live circuit, hot circuit; open *or* broken circuit, break, dead circuit; branch *or* lateral circuit, leg; multiple circuit *or* connection, multiple series, series multiple *or* parallel; multiplex circuit; magnetic circuit, circuital field, vector field; printed circuit, microcircuit; **short circuit, short.**

.5 **charge,** electric charge, unit quantity; live wire.

.6 **discharge,** electric discharge; aperiodic discharge, arc discharge, brush discharge, disruptive discharge, electrodeless discharge, glow discharge, oscillatory discharge, silent discharge, stratified discharge; **arc,** AC arc, Poulsen arc, arc column; **spark,** electric spark; spark gap; shock, electric shock, galvanic shock.

.7 **magnetism,** magnet(o)–, magnetic attraction; **electromagnetism;** magnetization; diamagnetism, paramagnetism, ferromagnetism; residual magnetism, magnetic remanence; magnetic memory, magnetic retentiveness; magnetic elements; magnetic dip *or* inclination, magnetic variation *or* declination; hysteresis, magnetic hysteresis, hysteresis curve, magnetic friction, magnetic lag *or* retardation, magnetic creeping; permeability, magnetic permeability, magnetic conductivity; magnetic circuit, magnetic curves, magnetic figures; magnetic flux, gilbert, weber, maxwell; magnetic moment; magnetic potential; magnetic viscosity; magnetics.

.8 **polarity,** polarization; **pole, positive pole, negative pole;** magnetic pole, magnetic axis; north pole, N pole; south pole, S pole.

.9 **magnetic force** *or* **intensity,** magnetic flux density, gauss, oersted; magnetomotive force; magnetomotivity; magnetic tube of force; line of force; **magnetic field, electromagnetic field.**

.10 **electroaffinity,** electric attraction; electric repulsion.

.11 **voltage,** volt, **electromotive force** *or* **EMF,** electromotivity, potential difference; **potential, electric potential.**

.12 **resistance,** ohm, ohmage, ohmic resis-

tance, electric resistance; surface resistance, skin effect, volume resistance; insulation resistance; **reluctance,** magnetic reluctance *or* resistance; specific reluctance, reluctivity; **reactance,** inductive reactance, capacitive reactance; **impedance.**

.13 **conduction,** electric conduction; **conductance,** conductivity, mho; superconductivity; gas conduction, ionic conduction, metallic conduction, liquid conduction, photoconduction; **conductor,** semiconductor, superconductor; **nonconductor,** dielectric, insulator.

.14 **induction;** electrostatic induction, magnetic induction, electromagnetic induction, electromagnetic induction of currents; self-induction, mutual induction; **inductance,** inductivity, henry.

.15 **capacitance,** capacity, farad; collector junction capacitance, emitter junction capacitance, resistance capacitance.

.16 **gain,** available gain, current gain, operational gain.

.17 **electric power,** wattage, watts; electric horsepower; hydroelectric power, hydroelectricity; power load.

.18 **powerhouse,** power station, power plant, central station; hydroelectric plant; nuclear *or* atomic power plant.

.19 **electrician, electrotechnician;** radio technician 344.24; **wireman; lineman,** linesman; rigger; groundman.

.20 **electrotechnologist,** electrobiologist, electrochemist, electrometallurgist, electrophysicist, electrophysiologist, **electrical engineer.**

.21 **electrification,** supplying electricity.

.22 **electrolysis;** ionization; galvanization, electrogalvanization; electrocoating, electroplating, electrogilding, electrograving, electroetching; ion, cation, anion; electrolyte, ionogen; nonelectrolyte.

.23 VERBS **electrify, galvanize,** energize, **charge;** shock; **generate,** step up, amplify, stiffen; step down; plug in, loop in; switch on *or* off, turn on *or* off, turn on *or* off the juice [informal]; short-circuit, short.

.24 **magnetize; electromagnetize;** demagnetize, degauss.

.25 **electrolyze;** ionize; galvanize, electrogalvanize; electroplate, electrogild.

.26 **insulate,** isolate; ground.

.27 ADJS **electric(al), electrifying;** galvanic, voltaic; dynamoelectric, hydroelectric, photoelectric, piezoelectric, etc.; electrothermal, electrochemical, electromechanical, electropneumatic, electrodynamic, static, electrostatic, stat–; electromotive; electrokinetic; electroscopic, galvanoscopic; electrometric, galvanometric, voltametric; **electrified,** electric-powered, battery-powered, cordless.

.28 **magnetic, electromagnetic;** diamagnetic, paramagnetic, ferromagnetic; **polar.**

.29 **electrolytic;** hydrolytic; ionic, anionic, cationic; ionogenic.

.30 **electrotechnical;** electroballistic, electrobiological, electrochemical, electrometallurgical, electrophysiological.

.31 **charged, electrified, live, hot;** high-tension, low-tension.

.32 **positive,** plus, electropositive; **negative,** minus, electronegative.

.33 **nonconducting,** nonconductive, insulating, dielectric.

.34 **electrical science**

| | |
|---|---|
| electrical engineering | electrophotomicrogra- |
| electroballistics | phy |
| electrobiology | electrophysics |
| electrochemistry | electrophysiology |
| electrodynamics | electrostatics |
| electrokinematics | electrotechnology, |
| electrokinetics | electrotechnics |
| electromechanics | electrothermics |
| electrometallurgy | galvanism |
| electrometry | magnetics |
| electronics 343 | magnetometry |
| electrooptics | thermionics |

.35 **electric units**

| | |
|---|---|
| abampere | mho |
| abcoulomb | microampere |
| abfarad | microfarad |
| abhenry | microhenry |
| abmho | micromho |
| abohm | micromicrofarad |
| abvolt | microvolt |
| ampere | microwatt |
| ampere-foot | milliampere |
| ampere-hour | millihenry |
| ampere-minute | millivolt |
| ampere-turn | ohm |
| coulomb | ohm-mile |
| farad | picofarad |
| henry | statampere |
| kilovolt | statcoulomb |
| kilovolt-ampere | statfarad |
| kilowatt | statvolt |
| kilowatt-hour | volt |
| megacoulomb | volt-coulomb |
| megampere | volt-second |
| megavolt | watt |
| megawatt | watt-hour |
| megohm | |

.36 **electrical parts and devices**

| | |
|---|---|
| alternator | cap, plug cap |
| anode | capacitor |
| armature | cathode |
| autoconverter | charger |
| autostarter | choking coil |
| autotransformer | circuit breaker |
| battery charger | coil |
| brush | commutator |

| | |
|---|---|
| compensator | oscillator |
| condenser | oscilloscope |
| controller | outlet |
| converter | pile |
| coupling | plug |
| cutout | pocket |
| distributor | points |
| double-pole switch | push button |
| double-throw switch | reactor |
| dynamo | receptacle |
| dynamotor | rectifier |
| electric column | relay |
| electric switch | resistance box |
| electrode | resistor |
| electrolytic inter- | rheostat |
| rupter | rotary gap |
| electrophorus | self-starter |
| electroscope | selsyn |
| electrostatic machine | shunt |
| fuse | socket |
| galvanoscope | spark coil |
| generator | spark plug |
| grid | starter |
| ground | step-down transformer |
| ignition | step-up transformer |
| induction machine | switch |
| inductor | synchronous converter |
| inductoscope | tap |
| insulator | terminal |
| interrupter | thermistor |
| jumper | timer |
| knife switch | time switch |
| lightning rod *or* ar- | toggle switch |
| rester | transformer |
| magnet 288.3 | trickle charger |
| magneto, magneto- | voltage changer |
| electric machine | voltage regulator |
| magnetoscope | voltage transformer |
| mercury switch | voltaic *or* galvanic pile |
| motor-generator | Wimshurst machine |

.37 **batteries**

| | |
|---|---|
| accumulator | Leyden jar |
| alkaline cell | mercury cell |
| atomic battery | nickel-cadmium bat- |
| cell | tery |
| dry battery | primary battery |
| dry cell | secondary battery |
| electronic battery | solar battery |
| fuel cell | storage battery |
| hearing-aid battery | storage cell |
| lead-acid battery | voltaic battery |
| Leyden battery | wet cell |

.38 **electric meters**

| | |
|---|---|
| ammeter, ampereme- | milliammeter |
| ter | millivoltmeter |
| ampere-hour meter | moving-coil meter |
| capillary electrometer | ohm-ammeter |
| coulometer, coulomb | ohmmeter |
| meter | potentiometer |
| dynameter | quadrant electrometer |
| dynamometer, electro- | thermal ammeter |
| dynamometer | thermoammeter |
| electrometer | thermocouple, ther- |
| expansion ammeter | mocouple meter |
| faradmeter | thermoelectrometer |
| galvanometer | thermoelement |
| hysteresis meter | vacuum-tube voltme- |
| magnetometer | ter, VTVM |
| megohmmeter | variometer |
| mhometer | voltameter |

volt-ammeter
volt-ampere-hour
  meter
voltmeter
voltmeter-milliamme-
  ter

volt-ohm meter
volt-ohm-milliamme-
  ter, VOM
watt-hour meter
wattmeter
Wheatstone bridge

**.39 electric wire**

armored cable
battery cable
bell wire
BX cable
coaxial cable
electric cable
electric cord
highline
hookup wire
ignition cable
lead
line

power line
Romex shielded wire
  or cable
telegraph line
telephone line
three-wire cable
transmission line
triaxial cable
underground cable
way wire
wire line

## 343. ELECTRONICS

**.1 NOUNS electronics,** electro–, radionics; electron physics, electrophysics, electron dynamics; electron optics; semiconductor physics, transistor physics; photoelectronics, photoelectricity, phot(o)–; microelectronics; electronic engineering; avionics; electron microscopy; radio 344; television 345; radar 346; automation 349.

**.2** (electron theory) electron theory of atoms, electron theory of electricity, electron theory of solids, free electron theory of metals, band theory of solids.

**.3 electron,** negatron, cathode particle, beta particle; photoelectron; thermion; primary electron, secondary electron; nuclear electron; recoil electron; bound electron, surface-bound electron; bonding electron; free electron, conduction electron, wandering electron; electron capture, electron transfer; spinning electrons, extranuclear electrons, planetary electrons, orbital electron; electron spin; electron state, energy level; ground state, excited state; electron pair, lone pair, shared pair, electron-positron pair, duplet, octet; electron cloud; shells, electron layers, electron shells, valence shell, valence electrons, subvalent electrons; electron affinity, relative electron affinity.

**.4 electronic effect;** Edison effect, photoelectric effect.

**.5 electron emission; thermionic emission;** photoelectric emission, photoemission; collision emission, bombardment emission, secondary emission; field emission; grid emission, thermionic grid emission; electron ray, electron beam, cathode ray, anode ray, positive ray, canal ray; glow discharge, cathode glow, cathodolumines-

cence, cathodofluorescence; electron diffraction.

**.6** electron flow, electron stream; electric current; electron gas, electron cloud, space charge; photoelectric current; thermionic current, ionization current; cathode current, plate current; input current, output current; base current, base signal current; collector current, collector signal current; emitter current, emitter signal current; saturation current.

**.7 electron volt;** ionization potential; input voltage, output voltage; base signal voltage, collector signal voltage, emitter signal voltage; battery supply voltage; screen-grid voltage; inverse peak voltage; voltage saturation.

**.8 electronic circuit;** vacuum-tube circuit, thermionic tube circuit, transistor circuit, semiconductor circuit; equivalent circuit, coupling circuit, flip-flop circuit, trigger circuit, back-to-back switching circuit; rectifier circuit, amplifier circuit, etc.; sinusoidal circuit, nonsinusoidal circuit; astable circuit, monostable circuit, bistable circuit; small signal short circuit, small signal hybrid short circuit; small signal open circuit, small signal hybrid open circuit; printed circuit, microcircuit, wireless circuit; **circuitry.**

**.9 conductance,** input conductance, feedback conductance, transfer conductance, output conductance; grid conductance, electrode conductance, leakage conductance, plate conductance; transconductance, inversion transconductance.

**.10 resistance,** base resistance, collector resistance, emitter resistance, electrode resistance; input resistance, output resistance; image-matched input resistance, image-matched output resistance; reverse transfer resistance, forward transfer resistance; load resistance.

**.11 electron tube,** tube, valve [Brit], thermionic tube; **vacuum tube; radio tube;** discharge tube.

**.12 photoelectric tube** or **cell, phototube,** photocell; electron-ray tube, **electric eye.**

**.13 transistor,** semiconductor or solid-state device; emitter, base, collector; germanium triode, germanium crystal triode, tetrode transistor; conductivity-modulation transistor, filamentary transistor, hook-collector transistor, junction transistor, point-contact transistor, point-junction transistor, unipolar transistor; phototransistor; spacistor.

**.14 electronics engineer,** electronics physicist.

.15 ADJS **electronic;** photoelectronic, photoelectric; autoelectronic; thermionic; an-
odic, cathodic.

.16 **electron tubes**

| | |
|---|---|
| Audion | kenotron |
| beam-power tube | klystron |
| beam tetrode | magnetron |
| Braun tube | mercury-vapor tube |
| cathode-ray tube | monoscope |
| cavity magnetron | multigrid tube |
| cold cathode tube | multiplex tube |
| Crookes tube | oscilloscope tube |
| diode | pentagrid |
| discharge tube | pentode |
| disk-seal tube | permatron |
| duodiode | phanotron |
| duodiode-triode | phasitron |
| duodynatron | pliotron |
| dynatron | reflex klystron |
| electron-beam tube | resnatron |
| electron-ray tube | secondary-emission |
| electron-wave tube | tube |
| excitron | strobotron |
| field-emission X-ray | tetragrid |
| tube | tetrode |
| gas-filled or gas tube | thyratron |
| Geissler tube | trigger tube |
| glow or glow discharge | triode |
| tube | triode-heptode |
| grid-glow tube | twin triode |
| grid-seal tube | vacuum tube |
| heptagrid | vapor tube |
| heptode | variable-mu tube |
| high-mu tube | X-ray diffraction tube |
| hot-cathode tube | X-ray tube |
| ignitron | |

.17 **photoelectric tubes and cells**

| | |
|---|---|
| electron-image tube | plier tube |
| gas phototube | photomultiplier tube |
| high-vacuum photo- | phototube |
| tube | photovoltaic cell |
| multiplier phototube | Photronic cell |
| photoconductor cell | soft phototube |
| photoelectric multi- | vacuum phototube |

.18 **special-purpose tubes**

| | |
|---|---|
| amplifier | mixer tube |
| attenuator | modulator |
| audio-frequency tube | multiplier |
| ballast regulator | multipurpose tube |
| ballast tube | multivibrator |
| beam-switching tube | oscillator |
| convertor | output tube |
| crystal detector | phase inverter |
| current regulator | picture tube 345.18 |
| damper | power tube |
| detector | pulse generator |
| discriminator | radio-frequency tube |
| doubler | receiving tube |
| focus tube | rectifier tube |
| full-wave rectifier tube | regulator |
| generator | repeater |
| iconoscope 345.19 | transducer |
| indicator tube | trigger tube |
| intermediate-fre- | tripler |
| quency tube | TR tube (transmit-re- |
| inverter | ceive) |
| limiter | voltage-reference tube |
| local-oscillator tube | voltage-regulator tube |

.19 **vacuum tube components**

| | |
|---|---|
| anode | loctal base |
| base | octal base |
| bayonet base | photocathode, photo- |
| cathode | electric cathode |
| control grid | plate |
| electrode | screen grid |
| electron gun | shield grid |
| filament | suppressor grid |
| grid | thermionic cathode |
| injection grid | trigatron |

.20 **electronic devices**

| | |
|---|---|
| airborne controls | Flexowriter typewriter |
| amplifier | fluorescent tube or |
| audio amplifier | lamp |
| automatic or robot pi- | germicidal lamp |
| lot | hearing aid |
| battery charger | high-frequency heater |
| calutron | image dissector |
| cathode-ray oscillo- | induction heater |
| graph | infrared cooker |
| cathode-ray oscillo- | isotron |
| scope | laser |
| computer | lie detector |
| cryotron | magnetic drum re- |
| cytoanalyzer | corder |
| depth sounder | magnetic recorder |
| diathermy machine | magnetic tape re- |
| dielectric heater | corder |
| dielectric preheater | magnetic wire re- |
| echo sounder | corder |
| electric eye | maser |
| electrocardiograph | mass spectrograph |
| electroencephalograph | mass spectrometer |
| electrograph | mass spectroscope |
| electron-diffraction | microprocessor |
| camera | microwave diathermy |
| electronic air condi- | machine |
| tioner | microwave oven |
| electronic air filter | neon tube or light |
| electronic altimeter | oscillograph |
| electronic battery | oscilloscope 346.21 |
| electronic clock | pacemaker |
| electronic computer | photoflash bulb |
| 349.16 | polarizing microscope |
| electronic detector | polygraph |
| electronic drum | preamplifier |
| electronic fuel gauge | public-address system |
| electronic heater | radar 346 |
| electronic nutcracker | radio 344 |
| electronic organ | radio direction finder |
| electronic oscillator | radio-frequency heater |
| electronic pilot | radiosonde |
| electronic precipitator | radio telescope |
| electronic recorder | shortwave diathermy |
| electronic refrigerator | machine |
| electronic stenciling | sonar |
| machine | spectroradiometer |
| electronic stethoscope | stereophonic sound |
| electronic switch | system, stereo |
| electronic timer | thermal timing relay |
| electronic typewriter | time-delay relay |
| electronic watch | TR box (transmit-re- |
| electron-image projec- | ceive switch) |
| tor | trickle charger |
| electron lens | ultrasonic electronic |
| electron magnetic | machine tools |
| spectroscope | videotape recorder |
| electron microscope | X-ray microscope |
| Fathometer | |

## .21 electronic meters

count-rate meter
duodial
electronic chronometer
electronic limit gauge
electronic potentiometer
electronic potentiometer pyrometer
electronic voltmeter
events-per-unit-time meter

illuminometer
interferometer
ionization gauge
pH meter
radiomicrometer
sanguinometer
telemeter
tensiometer
thermionic instrument
time-interval meter
vacuum-tube electrometer

## .22 photosensitive devices

electrophotometer
Geiger counter
infrared beam projector
infrared telescope
photoelectric colorimeter
photoelectric counter
photoelectric flame-failure detector
photoelectric image

converter
photoelectric intrusion detector
photoelectric photometer
photoelectric pinhole detector
photoelectric recorder
photoelectric sorter
photoelectric timer
spectrophotometer

## .23 electronic testing equipment

ammeter
audio-frequency oscillator
audio-IF oscillator
electric meter 342.38
field-strength meter
frequency meter
grid-dip meter
grid-dip oscillator
high-voltage probe
Lecher wires
low-capacitance probe
milliammeter
modulation monitor
ohmmeter
oscilloscope
output indicator
pulse generator
RC oscillator

regenerative wavemeter
resonance indicator
signal generator
standing-wave indicator
sweep generator
vacuum-tube voltmeter, VTVM
variable-frequency audio-IF oscillator
vertical amplifier
voltmeter
voltmeter-milliammeter
volt-ohm-milliammeter, VOM
wavemeter

## 344. RADIO

.1 NOUNS **radio, wireless** [Brit]; radiotelephony, radiotelegraphy; communications, telecommunication 560.1–8.

.2 radiotechnology, radio engineering, communication engineering; radio electronics, radioacoustics; radiogoniometry; conelrad (Control of Electromagnetic Radiation for Civil Defense).

.3 **radio, radio receiver;** radio telescope; **radio set, receiver,** receiving set, **wireless** or wireless set [both Brit], set; cabinet, console, housing; chassis.

.4 **radio transmitter, transmitter,** radiator; AM transmitter, FM transmitter, shortwave transmitter; continuous-wave transmitter, CW transmitter; radiotelephone transmitter, RT transmitter; transmitter

receiver, transceiver [informal]; **beacon,** radio beacon, radio range beacon; radio marker, fan marker; radiosonde, radiometeorograph; amateur transmitter, ham transmitter or rig [informal]; radiomicrophone, microphone 450.9.

.5 radiomobile, mobile transmitter, remote-pickup unit.

.6 **radio station,** transmitting station, **studio,** studio plant; AM station, FM station, shortwave station, ultrahigh-frequency station, clear-channel station; direction-finder station, RDF station; relay station, radio relay station, microwave relay station; amateur station, ham station [informal], ham shack [informal].

.7 **control room,** mixing room, monitor room, monitoring booth; **control desk,** console, master control desk, instrument panel, control panel or board, jack field, mixer [informal].

.8 **network,** net, radio links, **hookup,** communications net, circuit, network stations, network affiliations, affiliated stations; coaxial network, circuit network, coast-to-coast hookup.

.9 **radio circuit,** radio-frequency circuit, audio-frequency circuit, superheterodyne circuit, amplifying circuit; electronic circuit 343.8.

.10 **radio signal,** radio-frequency signal, RF signal, direct signal, shortwave signal, AM signal, FM signal; reflected signal, bounce; unidirectional signal, beam; signal-noise ratio; **radio-frequency amplifier,** RF amplifier, radio-frequency stage, RF stage.

.11 **radio wave,** electric wave, electromagnetic wave, hertzian wave; shortwave, long wave, microwave, high-frequency wave, low-frequency wave; ground wave, sky wave; carrier, carrier wave; **wavelength.**

.12 **frequency;** radio frequency, RF, intermediate frequency, IF, audio frequency, AF; high frequency, HF; very high frequency, VHF; ultrahigh frequency, UHF; superhigh frequency, SHF; extremely high frequency, EHF; medium frequency, MF; low frequency, LF; very low frequency, VLF; upper frequencies, lower frequencies; **carrier frequency;** spark frequency; spectrum, frequency spectrum; cycles, CPS, hertz, Hz, **kilocycles,** kilohertz, **megacycles,** megahertz.

.13 **band,** frequency band, standard band, broadcast band, amateur band, citizens band, police band, shortwave band, FM band; **channel**, radio channel, broadcast channel.

.14 **modulation**; amplitude modulation, AM; frequency modulation, FM; phase modulation, PM; sideband, side frequency, single sideband, double sideband.

.15 **amplification**, radio-frequency *or* RF amplification, audio-frequency *or* AF amplification, intermediate-frequency *or* IF amplification, high-frequency amplification.

.16 **radiobroadcasting, broadcasting**, radiocasting, standard broadcasting, AM broadcasting, FM broadcasting, shortwave broadcasting; **transmission, radio transmission;** direction *or* beam transmission, asymmetric *or* vestigial transmission; multipath transmission, multiplex transmission; mixing, volume control, sound *or* tone control, fade-in, fade-out; broadcasting regulation, Federal Communications Commission, FCC.

.17 **pickup**, outside pickup, **remote pickup**, spot pickup.

.18 **radiobroadcast, broadcast**, radiocast, **radio program**; rebroadcast, rerun; newscast, sportscast; radio fare, network show; commercial program, commercial; sustaining program, sustainer; serial, soap opera [informal]; taped program, canned show [informal], electrical transcription; sound effects.

.19 **signature, station identification**, call letters; theme song; **station break,** pause for station identification.

.20 **commercial**, commercial announcement, **spot announcement**, spot *or* plug [both informal].

.21 **reception; fading,** fade-out; **drift,** creeping, crawling; **interference,** noise interference, station interference; **static**, atmospherics; noise; blasting, blaring; blind spot.

.22 **radio listener**, listener-in *or* tuner-inner [both informal]; radio audience, listeners, listenership; hi-fi fan [informal], audiophile.

.23 **broadcaster**, radiobroadcaster, radiocaster; newscaster, sportscaster; commentator, news commentator; anchor man; announcer; disk jockey *or* DJ [both informal]; master of ceremonies, MC *or* emcee [both informal]; program director, programmer; sound-effects man, sound man; American Federation of Radio and Television Artists, AFTRA.

.24 **radioman,** radio technician, radio engineer; radiotrician, radio electrician; **radio**

**operator;** control engineer, volume engineer; mixer; **amateur radio operator, ham** *or* ham operator [both informal], radio amateur; Amateur Radio Relay League, ARRL; monitor; radiotelegrapher 560.16.

.25 VERBS **broadcast,** radiobroadcast, radiocast, **radio, wireless** [Brit], radiate, **transmit,** send; shortwave; beam; newscast, sportscast, put *or* go on the air, sign on; go off the air, sign off.

.26 **monitor,** check.

.27 **listen in, tune in;** tune up, tune down, tune out, tune off.

.28 ADJS **radio, wireless** [Brit]; radiosonic; neutrodyne; heterodyne; superheterodyne; shortwave; radio-frequency, audio-frequency; high-frequency, low-frequency, etc.; radiogenic.

.29 **radios, audio devices**

| | |
|---|---|
| all-wave receiver | radiophone 560.5 |
| AM-FM receiver | radio-phonograph |
| AM receiver | radio-record player |
| AM-FM tuner | railroad radio |
| AM tuner | receiver |
| auto radio | rechargeable-battery |
| aviation radio | radio |
| battery radio | regenerative receiver |
| citizens band *or* CB | relay receiver |
| radio, CB | ship-to-shore radio |
| clock radio | shortwave receiver |
| communications re- | superheterodyne |
| ceiver | table radio |
| crystal set | three-way *or* three- |
| FM receiver | power receiver |
| FM tuner | transceiver |
| mobile radio | transistor radio |
| multiplex receiver | transmit-receiver |
| pocket radio | tuner |
| portable radio | two-way radio |
| radio direction finder, | walkie-talkie |
| RDF | |

.30 **receiver parts**

| | |
|---|---|
| amplifier 450.10 | intermediate-fre- |
| amplitude control | quency amplifier, |
| audio-frequency am- | IF amplifier |
| plifier, audio ampli- | intermediate-fre- |
| fier, AF amplifier | quency oscillator, |
| automatic frequency | IF oscillator |
| control, AFC | intermediate-fre- |
| baffle | quency transformer, |
| beat-frequency oscilla- | IF transformer |
| tor | knob |
| bypass | lead-in wire |
| capacitor | on-off switch |
| chassis | output transformer |
| coil | parasitic suppressor |
| condenser | phase control |
| detector | potentiometer |
| dial | power pack |
| exciter | power plug |
| filter | power supply |
| frequency control | power transformer |
| frequency divider | preamplifier |
| heater | preselector |
| heterodyne | program discriminator |
| inductor | radio-frequency ampli- |

fier, RF amplifier
radio tubes 343.16–18
resistor
rheostat
selector
selsyn
speaker 450.8
tone control
transformer

transistor
trimmer
tuning condenser *or*
  capacitor
variable condenser *or*
  capacitor
vernier dial
volume control
wave trap

**.31 transmitter parts**
amplifier chain
broadcast loop
carrier amplifier
coaxial cable
fader
frequency changer
frequency converter
frequency doubler
frequency meter
litz wire
mixer
modulator
monitor

oscillator
power amplifier
program feed
resonance frequency
  control
signal generator
signal multiplier
transmission line
volume control
volume indicator
wave changer
wave guide

**.32 aerials, antennas**
antenna array
artificial antenna
auto antenna
beam antenna
bowtie antenna
colinear beam an-
  tenna
condenser antenna
dipole
directional antenna
dish
doublet
dummy antenna
eight-ball antenna
flattop antenna
FM antenna
folded dipole
frame aerial
free-space aerial
hank-type antenna
leaky wave-guide an-
  tenna
long-wire antenna
loop antenna
mast
mobile antenna
multiband antenna

nondirectional an-
  tenna
omnidirectional an-
  tenna
open aerial
parabolic antenna
pencil-beam antenna
printed antenna
rabbit ears
radar antenna 346.22
receiving antenna
reflector
resonance wave coil
rhombic antenna
rotary-beam antenna
shortwave antenna
signal squirter
telescope antenna
tower
transmitting antenna
tuned antenna
universal antenna
vertical radiator an-
  tenna
wave antenna
whip antenna
yagi

## 345. TELEVISION

.1 NOUNS **television,** tel(e)–, **TV, video,** telly [Brit informal]; **color television,** dot-sequential *or* field-sequential *or* line-sequential color television; **black-and-white television;** scophony; subscription television, pay TV; cable television; closed-circuit television.

.2 **television broadcast, telecast, TV show;** direct broadcast, live show [informal]; taped show, canned show [informal]; film pickup; colorcast; simulcast; telefilm; videotape.

.3 **televising, telecasting;** facsimile broad-

casting; monitoring, mixing, shading, blanking, switching; scanning, parallel-line scanning, interlaced scanning.

.4 (transmission) photoemission, audioemission; television channel, TV band; video *or* picture channel, audio *or* sound channel; picture carrier, sound carrier; beam, scanning beam, return beam; triggering pulse, voltage pulse, output pulse, timing pulse, equalizing pulse; synchronizing pulse, vertical synchronizing pulse, horizontal synchronizing pulse; video signal, audio signal; IF video signal, IF audio signal; synchronizing signal, blanking signal.

.5 (reception) **picture, image;** definition, blacker than black synchronizing; shading, black spot, hard shadow; test pattern, scanning pattern, grid; vertical interference, rain; granulation, scintillation, snow, snowstorm; flare, bloom, woomp; picture shifts, blooping, rolling; double image, multiple image, ghost; video static, noise, picture noise; signal-to-noise ratio; fringe area.

.6 **television studio, TV station.**

.7 **mobile unit, TVmobile;** video truck, audio truck, transmitter truck.

.8 **transmitter,** televisor; audio transmitter, video transmitter.

.9 **relay links, boosters,** booster amplifiers, relay transmitters, **booster** *or* **relay stations;** microwave link; aeronautical relay, stratovision; communication satellite, satellite relay; Telstar, Intelsat, Syncom; Comsat.

.10 **television camera,** telecamera, pickup camera, pickup; mobile camera.

.11 **television receiver, television** *or* **TV set,** TV, telly [Brit informal], televisor, boob tube *or* idiot box [both informal]; portable television *or* TV set; **screen,** telescreen.

.12 **televiewer,** viewer; television *or* viewing audience.

.13 **television technician,** TV man, television engineer; monitor, sound *or* audio monitor, picture *or* video monitor; pickup unit man, cameraman, sound man.

.14 VERBS **televise, telecast;** colorcast.

.15 **teleview,** watch television.

.16 ADJS **televisional,** televisual, televisionary, video; telegenic, videogenic; in synchronization, in sync [informal], locked in.

.17 **receiver parts**
audio amplifier
audio detector
audio-frequency

detector
blanking amplifier
contrast control

converter
deflection generator
electron tubes 343.16–18
FM detector
horizontal deflector
horizontal synchronizer
limiter
mixer
photocathode
photoelectric cells 343.17

picture control
picture detector
radio units 344.30
screen
shading amplifier
signal separator
sound limiter
synchronizing separator
vertical deflector
vertical synchronizer
video amplifier
video detector

### .18 picture tubes

cathode-ray tube
color kinescope
direct-viewing tube
kinescope
monoscope

Oscilight
projection tube
shadow-mask kinescope

### .19 camera tubes

dissector tube
iconoscope
image dissector
image iconoscope

image orthicon
orthicon
pickup tube
vidicon

### .20 transmitter parts

adder
antenna filter
camera deflection generator
channel filter
encoder
exploring element
monitor screen

reproducing element
signal generator
sound units 344.31
synchronizing generator
Tel-Eye
TV-Eye

## 346. RADAR AND RADIOLOCATORS

.1 NOUNS **radar,** radio detection and ranging, pulse radar, microwave radar, continuous wave or CW radar; radar fence or screen; radar astronomy.

.2 airborne radar, aviation radar; **navar,** navigation and ranging, **teleran,** television radar air navigation; radar bombsight, K-1 bombsight; radar dome, radome.

.3 loran, long range aid to navigation, shoran, short range aid to navigation, GEE navigation, consolan.

.4 direction finder, radio direction finder, RDF, radiogoniometer, high-frequency direction finder, HFDF, huff-duff [informal]; radio compass, wireless compass [Brit].

.5 radar speed meter, electronic cop [informal]; radar highway patrol.

.6 radar station, control station; Combat Information Center, CIC; Air Route Traffic Control Center, ARTCC; beacon station, display station; fixed station, home station; portable field unit, mobile trailer unit; tracking station; direction-finder station, radio compass station; triangulation stations.

.7 **radar beacon, racon;** transponder; radar

beacon buoy, marker buoy, radar marked beacon, ramark.

.8 (radar operations) data transmission, scanning, scan conversion, flector tuning, signal modulation, triggering signals; phase adjustment, locking signals; triangulation, three-pointing; mapping; range finding; tracking, automatic tracking, locking on; precision focusing, pinpointing; radar-telephone relay; radar navigation.

.9 (applications) detection, interception, ranging, ground control of aircraft, air-traffic control, blind flying, blind landing, storm tracking, hurricane tracking.

.10 **pulse,** radio-frequency or RF pulse, high-frequency or HF pulse, intermediate-frequency or IF pulse, trigger pulse, echo pulse.

.11 **signal,** radar signal; transmitter signal; output signal; return signal, echo signal, video signal, reflection, picture, target image, display, signal display, trace, reading, return, **echo, bounces, blips, pips;** spot, CRT spot; three-dimensional or 3-D display, double-dot display; deflection-modulated or DM display, intensity-modulated or IM display; radio-frequency or RF echoes, intermediate-frequency or IF signal; beat signal, Doppler signal, local oscillator signal; beam, beavertail beam.

.12 **radar interference,** deflection, refraction, superrefraction; atmospheric attenuation, signal fades, blind spots, false echoes; clutter, ground clutter, sea clutter.

.13 (radar countermeasure) **jamming;** tinfoil, aluminum foil, chaff, window [Brit].

.14 **radar technician,** radar engineer, radarman; air-traffic controller.

.15 VERBS **transmit, send,** radiate, beam; **jam.**

.16 **reflect,** return, echo, bounce back.

.17 **receive, tune in,** pick up, spot, home on; pinpoint; identify, trigger; lock on; sweep, scan; map.

### .18 radar

AGCA radar (automatic ground control approach)
AI radar (aircraft interception)
airborne intercept radar
airport surveillance radar
antiaircraft or AA radar
antisubmarine radar
ASV radar (air to surface vessel)

CCA radar (close control of aircraft)
DEW Line (distant early warning line)
DME (distance measuring equipment)
Doppler radar
DVOP radar (Doppler velocity and position)
early-warning radar
FC radar (fire control)
GCA radar (ground

control approach)
GCI radar (ground
control of intercep-
tion)
gun-directing radar
H₂S radar (height to
surface, Eng.)
H₂X (height to sur-
face, U.S.)
IFF radar (identifica-
tion, friend or foe)
interception radar
LAW radar (long-
range aircraft warn-
ing)
long-range radar
MAD radar (magnetic
airborne detection)
MADRE radar (mag-
netic drum receiv-
ing equipment)
MEW radar (micro-
wave early warning)
MTI radar (moving
target indication)

Navaglobe
Oboe (beacon bomb-
ing system)
overlap radar
panoramic radar
PAR radar (precision
approach radar)
pulse-modulated radar
radar telescope
RAWIN (radio auto-
matic wind record-
ing)
SARAH (search res-
cue and homing)
SCR (Signal Corps
radar)
search radar
surface or ground
radar
surveillance radar
taxi radar (airport sur-
face detection)
TRW radar (tornado
radar warning)
Volscan

**.22 antennas**
bedspring type
directional antenna
feed-and-reflector unit
mattress type
omnidirectional

antenna
scanner
sontenna
strike radar scanner
(airborne)

**.23 reflectors**
beavertail reflector
corner reflector
dish reflector
horn reflector

orange peel reflector
parabolic reflector
venetian blind reflec-
tor

**.19 radiolocators**
automatic gun direc-
tor, AGD
automatic range
finder, ARF
bombing locator
compensated-loop
direction finder
depth sounder
gun director
height finder

microwave height
finder, MHF
position finder
radio direction finder,
RDF
range finder
spaced-antenna direc-
tion finder
spaced-loop direction
finder

**.20 radar parts**
AFC mixer
altimeter
amplifier
analyzer
ATR box (anti-trans-
mit-receive)
ATR switch
automatic frequency
control, AFC
cascade screen
cathode-ray tube,
CRT
continuous wave or
CW oscillator
demodulator
detector
discriminator
frequency meter
hard-tube pulser
indicator
limiter
local oscillator
magnetron
microwave mixer
mixer
modulator
network pulser
oscillator
plan position indica-

tor, PPI
position data trans-
mitter
position tracker
potentiometer
pulse generator
pulser
pulse transformer
range-marker genera-
tor
range-sweep amplifier
range-sweep generator
receiver
reference-voltage gen-
erator
scan converter
screen
second detector
square-wave generator
synchronizer
timing unit
tracker
transmit-receive or
TR unit
transmitter
TR box (transmit-re-
ceive)
TR switch
trigatron

**.21 oscilloscopes, radarscopes**
A-scope
B-scope
J-scope

PPI-scope
(plan position
indicator scope)

# 347. MECHANICS

**.1** NOUNS **mechanics;** theoretical or analytical mechanics, pure or abstract mechan-
ics, rational mechanics; celestial mechan-
ics; quantum mechanics, matrix mechan-
ics, wave mechanics; animal mechanics,
zoomechanics, biomechanics; microme-
chanics; hydromechanics, fluid mechan-
ics; aeromechanics; electromechanics; telemechanics, servomechanics 349.2; practical mechanics, mechanical arts; applied
mechanics; statistical mechanics; leverage
287.

**.2 statics,** biostatics, electrostatics, geostat-
ics, gyrostatics, rheostatics, stereostatics,
thermostatics, hydrostatics, aerostatics.

**.3 dynamics, kinetics, kinematics,** energet-
ics; astrodynamics, geodynamics, radiodynamics, electrodynamics, photodynamics,
thermodynamics, aerodynamics, pneumo-
dynamics, barodynamics, hydrodynamics,
fluid dynamics, magnetohydrodynamics,
kinesiology, biodynamics, zoodynamics,
myodynamics.

**.4 hydraulics,** hydromechanics, hydrokinet-
ics, fluidics, hydrodynamics, hydrostatics;
hydrology, hydrography, hydrometry, flu-
viology.

**.5 pneumatics,** pneumatostatics; aeromechanics, aerophysics, aerology, aerometry,
aerography, aerotechnics, aerodynamics,
aerostatics.

**.6 engineering,** mechanical engineering, jet
engineering, etc., see engineers 718.9.

**.7** ADJS **mechanical,** mechanistic; locomotive, locomotor; zoomechanical, biome-
chanical, aeromechanical, hydromechanical, etc.

**.8 static;** biostatic, electrostatic, geostatic,
etc.

**.9 dynamic(al), kinetic(al), kinematic(al);**
geodynamic, radiodynamic, electrodynamic, etc.

**.10 pneumatic,** pneumatological; aeromechanical, aerophysical, aerologic(al), aerotechnical, aerodynamic, aerostatic, aero-
graphic(al).

.11 hydrologic, hydrometric(al), hydromechanic(al), hydrodynamic, hydrostatic, hydraulic.

## 348. TOOLS AND MACHINERY

.1 NOUNS tool, instrument, implement, utensil, –labe; apparatus, device, mechanical device, contrivance, contraption [informal], gadget, gizmo, gimcrack, gimmick [informal], means, mechanical means; hand tool; power tool; machine tool; speed tool; precision tool or instrument.

.2 cutlery, edge tools 348.13; knife, ax, dagger, sword, blade, cutter, whittle; steel, cold steel, naked steel; pigsticker or toad stabber or toad sticker [all slang]; perforator, piercer, puncturer, point 258.18; sharpener 258.19.

.3 tableware, dining utensils; silverware, silver, silver plate, stainless-steel ware; flatware, flat silver; hollow ware; cutlery, knives, forks, spoons; tablespoon, teaspoon; chopsticks.

.4 machinery, enginery; machine, mechanism, mechanical device; engine, motor; power plant, power source, drive, motive power; appliance, convenience, facility, utility, home appliance, mechanical aid; fixture; labor-saving device.

.5 mechanism, machinery, movement, movements, action, motion, works, workings, inner workings, innards, what makes it tick; drive train, power train; wheelwork, wheelworks, wheels 322.18, gear, wheels within wheels, epicyclic train; clockworks, watchworks; servomechanism 349.13,30.

.6 gear, gearing, gear train; gearwheel 322.18, cogwheel, rack; gearshift; low, intermediate, high, neutral, reverse; differential, differential gear or gearing; transmission, gearbox; automatic transmission; selective transmission; standard transmission, stick shift; synchromesh; fluid drive, overdrive, freewheel, Hydromatic.

.7 clutch, cone clutch, plate clutch, dog clutch, disk clutch, multiple-disk clutch, rim clutch, friction clutch, cone friction clutch, slip friction clutch, spline clutch, rolling-key clutch.

.8 instrumentation, tooling, tooling up; retooling; industrial instrumentation; servo instrumentation.

.9 mechanic, mechanician; artisan, artificer; machinist, machiner; auto mechanic, aeromechanic, etc.

.10 VERBS tool, instrument; retool; machine, mill; mechanize, motorize; sharpen 258.9.

.11 ADJS mechanical, machinal, machinelike, powered, power-driven, motor-driven; mechanized.

.12 tools

| | |
|---|---|
| awl | nail puller |
| bale breaker | needlenose pliers |
| bar | palette knife |
| battering ram | peavey |
| belt punch | pincers |
| bevel, bevel square | pinch bar |
| bodkin | pitchfork |
| bradawl | planer |
| buffer | pliers |
| calipers | power sander |
| cant hook | puller |
| caulking iron or chisel or tool | punch |
| | puncheon |
| center punch | punch pliers |
| crowbar | putty knife |
| dibble | ram |
| dividers | rammer |
| drum sander | ramrod |
| edger | ripping bar |
| electric riveter | screwdriver |
| electric sander | shaper |
| electric soldering iron | soldering iron, soldering gun |
| emery wheel | |
| file | spatula |
| flail | square |
| forceps | stapler |
| fork | tackle 287.10 |
| grapnel | tamp, tamper |
| grappling iron or hook | tamping bar |
| grease gun | tamping pick |
| grindstone | tamping stick |
| hawk | tap |
| hook | T bevel |
| jack | tire iron |
| jackscrew | tire tool |
| jointer | tongs |
| krenging hook | T square |
| lathe | tweezers |
| level | vise |
| miter box | wrecking bar |
| nail file | |

.13 edge tools

| | |
|---|---|
| adz | knife, drawshave |
| ax 801.25 | electric razor |
| bistoury | gouge |
| bread knife | groover |
| broadax | grub ax |
| bushwhacker | grub hoe |
| butcher knife | hack |
| carving knife | hatchet |
| case knife | hedge trimmer |
| celt | hoe |
| chaser | hunting knife |
| chisel | jackknife |
| chopping knife | knife 801.21 |
| clasp knife | lance |
| cleaver | lancet |
| clipper, clippers | letter-opener |
| cold chisel | linoleum knife |
| colter | machete |
| cutting pliers | mattock |
| dagger 801.22 | nippers |
| drawing knife, draw- | panga |

paper cutter
paper knife
paring knife
penknife
pick
pickax
plowshare
pocketknife
pruning hook
razor
razor blade
rigger's knife
ripping chisel
safety razor
saw knife
sax
scalpel
scissors
scoop

scraper
scuffle hoe
scythe
share
shears
sheath knife
sickle
sidecutters
slotter
snips
spear 801.23
spokeshave
surgical knife
sword 801.24
table knife
tin snips
wedge
wirecutters

core-box plane
dado plane
dovetail plane
edge plane
filletster plane
fore plane
grooving plane
jack plane
jointer, jointer plane
match plane
planer, planing
  machine
rabbet plane

reed plane
routing plane
sash plane
scraper plane
scrub plane
smooth or smoothing
  plane
thumb plane
tonguing plane
toothing plane
trenching plane
trying plane

## .14 saws

backsaw
band saw
belt saw
bow saw
bucksaw
butcher's saw
buzz saw, circular saw
chain saw
compass saw
coping saw
cordwood saw
crosscut saw
diamond saw
double-cut saw
dovetail saw
electric saw
frame saw
fretsaw
hacksaw
handsaw
helicoidal saw
jigsaw
keyhole saw
kitchen saw

lightning or M saw
lumberman's saw
meat saw
mill saw
panel saw
pit saw
plywood saw
portable saw
power saw
pruning saw
ripsaw
rock saw
saw knife
saw machine
scribe saw
scroll saw
splitsaw
surgeon's saw
table saw
two-handed saw
vertical saw
whipsaw
wire saw
wood saw

## .15 shovels

air shovel
air spade
backhoe
bar spade
coal shovel
ditch spade
drain spade
entrenching tool
fire shovel
garden spade
gasoline shovel
gumming spade
irrigating shovel

loy
peat spade
posthole spade
power shovel
salt shovel
scoop, scoop shovel
spade
split shovel
spud
steam shovel
stump spud
trenching spade

## .16 trowels

brick trowel
circle or cove trowel
corner trowel
curbing trowel
garden trowel

guttering trowel
plastering trowel
pointing trowel
radius trowel
slick

## .17 planes

beading plane
bench plane
block plane
bullnose

capping plane
chamfer plane
circular plane
combination plane

## .18 drills

accretion borer
air drill
auger
auger bit
automatic drill
bench drill
bit
bore, borer
bore bit
bow drill
brace and bit
breast auger
breast drill
broach
burr
chamfer bit
compressed-air drill
corkscrew
cross bit
diamond drill
disk drill
drill
drilling bit
drill press
electric drill
expansion bit

extension bit
flat drill
gimlet
gimlet bit
hand drill
keyway drill
portable drill
posthole auger
power drill
pump drill
push drill
ratchet drill
reamer
rotary drill
shell drill
spike bit
star drill
strap drill
tap
taper drill
tapping drill
trepan
trephine
twist bit
twist drill
wimble

## .19 hammers

air hammer
ball peen hammer
beetle
blacksmith's hammer
boilermaker's hammer
brick hammer, brick-
  layer's hammer
chipping hammer
claw hammer
cross peen hammer
die hammer
drop hammer
electric hammer
engineer's hammer
jackhammer

machinist's hammer
mallet
peen hammer
pile hammer
pneumatic hammer
raising hammer
riveting hammer
rubber mallet
sledge, sledgehammer
spalling hammer
steam hammer
stone hammer
tack hammer
tile setter's hammer
triphammer

## .20 wrenches

adjustable wrench
Allen wrench
alligator wrench
box wrench
carriage wrench
chain wrench
end wrench
lug wrench
monkey wrench
open-end wrench
pin wrench

pipe wrench
screw key
socket wrench
spanner
spark-plug wrench
Stillson wrench
S wrench
tappet wrench
tap wrench
tuning wrench
valve wrench

## .21 machinery

adding machine
addressing machine
automatic screw machine
automobile 272.9,24
backhoe
bulldozer
calfdozer
carryall
compressor
crab
crane
crimping machine
cutting machine
cutting press
derrick
dishwasher
dredge, dredger, dredging machine
drop hammer
dryer
dumping machine
edger
elevator dredge
folding machine
gin
grader
hoist, hoisting machine
hydraulic jack
hydraulic press
jackhammer
lawn mower, mower
machine drill
mailing machine
motorcycle 272.8,29
navvy [Brit]

packager
pile driver
planing machine
power mower
power saw
power shovel
press
printing machine
pulp machine
punching machine
pusher
roller
rose engine
ruling machine or engine
sander
saw machine
scraper
screwing machine
screw machine
sewing machine, sewer
snowblower
snowmobile
snowplow
snow-thrower
solar machine
steam hammer
steamroller
steam shovel
tractor 272.17,27
triphammer
typing machine, typewriter
washing machine
water wheel
windlass 287.7

## .22 farm machinery

all-crop harvester
baler
bean harvester
beet harvester
binder
breaker
cast plow
combine
corn picker
cotton picker
cultivator
disk
disk harrow
disk plow
drag
drill
drill plow
four-bottom plow
gang plow
grain harvester
grub hook
harrow
harvester
haymaker
header
hoe drill
lister
lister cultivator
middlebreaker, middlebuster
moldboard plow
mowing machine

peg-tooth harrow
planter
plow
plow drill
prairie breaker
press drill
rake
rotary plow
scooter
seeder
seed plow
shovel plow
snap machine
sprayer
spring-tooth harrow
stag gang
subsoil plow
sulky lister
sulky plow
swather
swivel plow
tedder
three-bottom plow
thresher, thrasher, threshing machine
trench plow
turnplow
two-bottom plow
vineyard plow
walking plow
windrower

## .23 mills

arrastra
ball mill
blooming mill
bone mill
cane mill
cider mill
coffee mill
cotton mill, cotton gin
drag-stone mill
feed mill
flour mill
fulling mill
grinding mill
gristmill
lapidary mill
milling machine
paper mill
pepper mill

planing mill
powder mill
rolling mill
sawmill
sheet mill
silk mill
slab mill
smoothing mill
spice mill
stamp mill
stamps
steel mill
stone mill
sugar mill
treadmill
water mill
windmill
woolen mill

## .24 welders

acetylene welder
AC welder
arc welder
blowtorch 329.14
DC welder
electric welder
gas welder
oxyacetylene welder

pipe welder
spot welder
tack welder
three-phase resistance welder
welding blowpipe or torch
wire welder

## .25 pumps

air lift
air pump
aspirator
beer pump
bicycle pump
bilge pump
booster pump
breast pump
bucket pump
centrifugal pump
cryo-pump
diaphragm pump
displacement pump
donkey pump, donkey
drainage pump
feed pump
float pump
force pump
forcer
hand pump

heat pump
hydraulic ram
jet pump
lift or lifting pump
piston pump
pressure pump
pulsometer
pumping engine
rotary pump
sand pump
shell pump
stirrup pump
stomach pump
suction pump
tire pump
turbine centrifugal pump
vacuum pump
water pump
wobble pump

## .26 engines, motors

aeromotor 280.17
air engine or motor
alternating-current or AC motor
beam engine
blowing engine
caloric engine
cam engine
capacitor motor
commutator motor
compensated motor
compound motor
compression-ignition engine
condensing engine
Corliss engine
diagonal engine
diesel engine

direct-acting engine
direct-current or DC motor
donkey engine
double-acting or double-action engine
double-row radial engine
dynamo
dynamotor
electric motor, electromotor
external-combustion engine
fire engine
four-stroke cycle engine
gas engine

gas turbine engine
generator
heat engine
horizontal engine
hot-air engine
hydraulic engine
hydro-jet
impulse duct engine
inboard-outboard mo-
   tor
inclined engine
induction motor
in-line engine
intermittent duct en-
   gine
internal-combustion
   engine
inverted engine
ion engine, ion rocket
jet, jet engine
locomotive engine
marine engine
mill-type motor
noncondensing engine
oil engine
oscillation-cylinder en-
   gine
oscillation engine
Otto engine
outboard motor
pancake engine
phase-wound rotor
   motor
piston engine
piston-valve engine
plasma engine
polyphase induction
   motor
portable engine
pulse-jet engine
pumping engine
radial engine

ramjet engine, ramjet
reaction motor or en-
   gine
reciprocating engine
refrigerating engine
resojet engine
rocket motor or en-
   gine
rotary engine
rotary-piston engine
rotor motor
series motor
servomotor
shunt motor
single-acting or single-
   action engine
single-phase motor
slide-valve engine
solar engine
split-phase motor
squirrel cage rotor
   motor
stationary engine
steam engine
supercharged engine
synchronous motor
thermal engine
three-phase motor
traction motor
triple-expansion en-
   gine
trunk engine
turbine
turbojet engine, tur-
   bojet
two-stroke cycle en-
   gine
universal motor
variable-speed motor
vernier engine
vertical engine
Wankel engine

.27 **engine parts**

bearings
boiler
cam
camshaft
connecting rod
crankcase
crankshaft
cylinder
cylinder head

differential
electrical parts 342.36
flywheel
gearbox
gears
piston
piston rod
transmission
universal joint

### 349. AUTOMATION

.1 NOUNS **automation,** automatic control; cybernation; **self-action,** self-activity; self-movement, self-motion, **self-propulsion;** self-direction, self-determination, self-government, automatism, self-regulation; automaticity, automatization; servo instrumentation.

.2 autonetics, automatic or automation technology, automatic electronics, automatic engineering, automatic control engineering, servo engineering, **servomechanics,** system engineering, systems analysis, feedback system engineering;

cybernetics; telemechanics; radiodynamics, radio control; systems planning, systems design; circuit analysis; bionics; communication or communications theory, information theory.

.3 **automatic control,** cybernation, servo control, robot control; cybernetic control; electronic control, electronic-mechanical control; feedback control, digital feedback control, analog feedback control; cascade control, piggyback control [informal]; supervisory control; action, control action; derivative or rate action, reset action; control agent; control means.

.4 semiautomatic control; **remote control,** push-button control, remote handling, tele-action; radio control; telemechanics; telemechanism; telemetry, telemeter, telemetering; transponder; bioinstrument, bioinstrumentation.

.5 control system, **automatic control system,** servo system, robot system; closed-loop system; open-sequence system; linear system, nonlinear system; carrier-current system; integrated system, complex control system; data system, data-handling system, data-reduction system, data-input system, data-interpreting system, digital data reducing system; process-control system, annunciator system, flow-control system, motor-speed control system; automanual system; automatic telephone system; electrostatic spraying system; automated factory, automatic or robot factory, push-button plant; servo laboratory, servolab.

.6 **feedback,** closed sequence, feedback loop, closed loop; multiple-feed closed loop; process loop, quality loop; feedback circuit, current-control circuit, direct-current circuit, alternating-current circuit, calibrating circuit, switching circuit, flip-flop circuit, peaking circuit; multiplier channels; open sequence, linear operation; positive feedback, negative feedback; reversed feedback, degeneration.

.7 (functions) accounting, analysis, automatic electronic navigation, automatic guidance, braking, comparison of variables, computation, coordination, corrective action, fact distribution, forecasts, impedance matching, inspection, linear or nonlinear calibrations, manipulation, measurement of variables, missile guidance, output measurement, processing, rate determination, record keeping, statistical communication, steering, system stabilization, ultrasonic *or* supersonic flow detection.

.8 **process control,** bit-weight control, color control, density control, dimension control, diverse control, end-point control, flavor control, flow control, fragrance control, hold control, humidity control, light-intensity control, limit control, liquid-level control, load control, pressure control, precision-production control, proportional control, quality control, quantity control, revolution control, temperature control, time control, weight control.

.9 variable, process variable; simple variable, complex variable; manipulated variable; steady state, transient state.

.10 values, target values; set point; differential gap; proportional band; dead band, dead zone; neutral zone.

.11 time constants; time lead, gain; time delay, dead time; lag, process lag, hysteresis, holdup, output lag; throughput.

.12 automatic device 349.29, automatic; semiautomatic; self-actor, self-mover; **robot, automaton,** mechanical man; cyborg.

.13 **servomechanism,** servo; cybernion, automatic machine; **servomotor;** synchro, selsyn, autosyn; synchronous motor, synchronous machine.

.14 **regulator, control,** controller, **governor;** servo control, servo regulator; control element.

.15 control panel, console; coordinated panel, graphic panel; panelboard, set-up board.

.16 **computer,** electronic computer 349.31, electronic brain; information machine, thinking machine; computer unit, hardware, computer hardware 349.32.

.17 **storage,** storage system *or* unit, **memory,** high-speed memory; random access memory, RAM; memory tubes; tape *or* drum *or* disk memory.

.18 input-output *or* IO device; summing register, relay register; reader, tape reader; magnetic tape, punched tape; punched cards, punch cards; microcards, microfilm, microfiche, recorder, magnetic recorder; alphabetical printer; teletypewriter, Flexowriter typewriter; oscilloscope, oscillograph recorder; digital graph plotter, Teleplotter; **printout,** hard copy, readout.

.19 **data,** information, message, instructions, commands; **computer program,** computer software; computer routine, compiler, assembler; computer *or* machine language,

ALGOL, COBOL, FORTRAN; ruly English; computer code, alphanumeric code; single messages, multiple messages; **input data, output data,** random data, unorganized data; numeric data, alphabetic data; film data, punch-card data, oscillograph data; visible-speech data, ˆsound-level data; angular data, rectangular data, polar data; (quantity to be controlled) input quantity, output quantity, reference quantity, controlled quantity; signals, control signals, block signals, checking signals, error signals, correcting signals, feedback signals; command pulses, feedback pulses; error, bug, play, noise; binary scale *or* system; binary digit, bit; octal system, hexadecimal system; byte.

.20 **data processing,** electronic data processing, EDP, high-speed data handling, data reduction, data retrieval, information retrieval, machine computation, telecomputing; computer typesetting; computing, scanning, analyzing, sorting, collating, integrating, classifying, reporting; computer technology.

.21 process, digital process, analog process; behavior pattern; oscillatory behavior, self-excitation; input oscillation, output oscillation; hunting, feeling; correction of error; overcorrection of error, overshoot; offset (difference between value desired and attained).

.22 **control engineer,** servo engineer, system engineer, systems analyst, automatic control system engineer, feedback system engineer, automatic technician, robot specialist; computer engineer, computer technologist, computer technician, **computer programmer;** cybernetic technologist, cyberneticist.

.23 VERBS **automate,** automatize, robotize; robot-control, servo-control; program.

.24 **self-govern,** self-control, **self-regulate,** self-direct.

.25 ADJS **automated,** cybernated, aut(o)–, automat(o)–, self–; **automatic,** automatous, **spontaneous; self-acting,** self-active; **self-operating,** self-operative, self-working; **self-regulating,** self-regulative, self-governing, self-directing; **self-regulated, self-controlled,** self-governed, self-directed, self-steered; self-adjusting, self-closing, self-cocking, self-cooking, self-dumping, self-emptying, self-lighting, self-loading, self-opening, self-priming, self-rising, self-sealing, self-starting, self-winding, automanual; semiautomatic.

.26 **self-propelled,** self-moved, horseless; **self-**

**propelling,** self-moving, self-propellent; self-driven, self-drive; **automotive,** auto-mobile, automechanical; **locomotive,** locomobile.

**.27 servomechanical,** servo-controlled; **cybernetic; isotronic.**

**.28 remote-control,** remote-controlled, tele-mechanic; telemetered, telemetric; by remote control.

**.29 automatic devices**

airborne controls
antiaircraft gun positioner
artificial feedback kidney
automatic block signal
automatic gun
automatic gun director
automatic heater
automatic iron
automatic piano
automatic pilot
automatic pinspotter
automatic pistol
automatic printer
automatic rifle
automatic sight
automatic sprinkler
automatic stop
automatic telegraph

automatic telephone
automatic telephone exchange
automaton
autopilot
chess-playing machine
guided missile
gyroscopic pilot
lever pilot
mechanical heart
Multiple-Stylus Electronic Printer
radar controls
robot pilot
robot plane
robot submarine
self-starter
speedometer
televox
watcher

**.30 servomechanisms**

alternating-current servo
automatic feed mechanism
direct-current servo
electronic servo
Flettner control
hemostat
hydraulic servo
instrument servo
motor-generator servo
pneumatic servo

power brake
power servo
selsyn
servo brake
servomotor
servotab
sine mechanism
synchro
synchro receiver
synchro transmitter
telemechanism

**.31 electronic computers**

analog computer
Audrey (Automatic Digit Recognizer)
automatic plotter
BINAC (Binary Automatic Computer)
data processor
decimal digital differential analyzer
decoding servomechanism
differential analyzer
digital computer
digital differential analyzer
digital general purpose computer
digital graph plotter
direct-reading computer
ENIAC (Electronic Numerical Integra-

tor and Computer)
ENIAD (Electronic Numerical Integrating and Analyzing Device)
equation solver
ERMA (Electronic Recording Machine—Accounting)
high-speed digit computer
IBM machine
IDA (Integro-Differential Analyzer)
IDP machine (Integrated Data Processing)
Magnetronic Reservisor
OARAC (Office of Air Research Auto-

matic Computer)
printing calculator
Production-Control Quantometer
RAYDAC (Raytheon Data Calculator)
selective calculator
Selective Sequence Electronic Calculator
square root planime-

ter
telecomputer
Teleplotter
Telereader
tristimulus computer
UNIVAC (Universal Automatic Computer)
versatile digit computer

**.32 computer parts**

adder
analytical control unit
analyzer
coder
coefficient component
collator
compiler
decoder
detector
differential
divider
electrostatic storage unit
FOSDIC (Film Optical Sensing Device

for Input to Computers)
integrator
memory tubes
multiplier
phase discriminator
position code converter
position coder
printer
receptor
relay
selector
storage unit
transmitter

**.33 system components**

actuator
amplifier
amplifying generator
calibrating unit
capacitor
clock
control relay
control resistor
converter
discriminating relay
effector
electropneumatic transducer
feedback amplifier
generator
inductor
load-indicating resistor
magnetic amplifier
magnetic relay
meter relay

modulator
oscillator
oscillator relay actuator
phase-discriminating amplifier
pressure transducer
reactor
records-pulse generator
regenerator
relay
reluctance amplifier
resistor
servo amplifier
thermal timing relay
transducer
transmitter
uncommitted amplifier

**.34 control mechanisms**

automatic switch
automatic trip
channel selector
check valve
contour follower
control transformer
control valve
diaphragm motor valve
electrical governor
electromechanical controller
electronic control
electropneumatic valve positioner
emergency control
finder switch
flowmanostat

flow valve
indicating control switch
internal selector
limit switch
line breaker
line switch
manostat
manual control
oscillator relay control
overload breaker
overload circuit
overload switch
phase advancer
positioning mechanism
pressure transmitter
proportioning lever

rectifier
register regulator
safety control
safety fuse
safety stop
safety switch
safety valve
selector switch

sequence switch
servo valve
speed regulator
thermoswitch
timer
voltage regulator
voltage stabilizer

**.35 automatic detectors**

chemical detector
electronic counter
electronic detector
error corrector
error detector
liquid-level sensor
mercury-vapor detec-
    tor
metal detector
photoelectric detector
photoelectric inspec-

tion machine
photoelectric pinhole
    detector
photoelectric sorter
sensor
temperature sensor
ultrasonic detector
ultrasonic flow detec-
    tor
ultrasonic inspector

**.36 automatic analyzers**

analytical spectrome-
    ter
color gauge *or* checker
comparator
$CO_2$ recorder
data analyzer
dew-point hygrometer
direct-reading spec-
    trometer
electronic comparator
gas analyzer
infrared gas and liquid

analyzer
mass spectrograph
mass spectrometer
oxygen recorder
recording analyzer
scanner
stigmatic grating spec-
    trograph
surface analyzer
vibration and stress
    analyzer

**.37 automatic indicators**

control indicator
count-rate meter
current indicator
density indicator
detonation indicator
differential pressure
    gauge
events-per-unit-time
    meter
fault lamp
filled-system ther-
    mometer
flowmeter
galvanometer
humidity indicator
hygrometer
integrating flowmeter
interferometer
ionization gauge
light-intensity indica-
    tor
liquid-level indicator
load indicator

logger
moisture meter
pH meter
potentiometer
pressure indicator
proximity meter
psychometer
pyrometer
radiation pyrometer
resistance thermome-
    ter
square-root flowmeter
strain gauge
tensiometer
thermistor
thermocouple
thermocouple pyrom-
    eter
time-interval meter
turn indicator
vibration meter
voltage indicator

## 350. FRICTION

.1 NOUNS **friction, rubbing,** rub, frottage; frication *or* confrication *or* perfrication [all archaic]; tribo–, –tribe.

.2 **abrasion, attrition, erosion, wearing away, wear,** detrition, ablation; erasure, rubbing away *or* off *or* out; **grinding, filing,** rasping, limation; fretting; galling; chafing, chafe; **scraping,** grazing, scratching, scuff-ing; **scrape,** scratch, **scuff;** scrubbing, scouring; scrub; **polishing,** burnishing, sanding, smoothing, dressing, buffing, shining; sandblasting; abrasive 260.14.

.3 **massage,** massaging, stroking, kneading; **rubdown;** massotherapy; whirlpool bath, vibrator; facial massage, facial.

.4 **massager, masseur, masseuse;** massothera-pist.

.5 (mechanics) force of friction, internal friction, starting friction, static friction, rolling friction, sliding friction, fluid fric-tion, slip friction; force of viscosity; coef-ficient of friction, resistance, frictional re-sistance, drag; skin friction; friction loss, friction head.

.6 VERBS **rub,** frictionize; **massage,** knead, rub down; caress, pet, stroke 425.8.

.7 **abrade,** abrase, gnaw, gnaw away; **erode,** ablate, wear, wear away; erase, rub away *or* off *or* out; grind, **rasp, file, grate; chafe,** fret, gall; **scrape, graze,** raze [archa-ic], **scuff,** bark, skin; **fray,** frazzle; **scrub, scour.**

.8 **buff, burnish, polish,** rub up, sandpaper, **sand,** smooth, dress, shine, furbish, sand-blast.

.9 ADJS **frictional,** friction; fricative; **rub-bing.**

.10 **abrasive,** abradant, attritive, gnawing, erosive, ablative; **grinding, rasping;** chaf-ing, fretting, galling.

## 351. TEXTURE

*(surface quality)*

.1 NOUNS **texture,** surface texture; **surface; finish,** feel; **grain,** granular texture, fine-ness *or* coarseness of grain; **weave,** woof 222.3, wale; **nap,** pile, shag, nub, knub, protuberance 256; **pit,** pock, indentation 257.6; structure 245.

.2 **roughness** 261; **coarseness, grossness, unre-finement,** coarse-grainedness; cross-grainedness; **graininess,** granularity, gran-ulation, grittiness; hardness 356.

.3 **smoothness** 260, **fineness, refinement,** fine-grainedness; **delicacy, daintiness;** filminess, gossameriness 339.1; **down, downiness,** fluff, fluffiness, velvet, velveti-ness, fuzz, fuzziness, peach fuzz, pubes-cence; satin, satininess; silk, silkiness; soft-ness 357.

.4 VERBS **coarsen; grain,** granulate; **tooth, roughen** 261.4; smooth 260.5.

.5 ADJS **textural, textured.**

.6 **rough** 261.6, **coarse, gross, unrefined,**

coarse-grained; cross-grained; grained, grainy, granular, granulated, gritty.

.7 **nappy**, pily, **shaggy**, nubby *or* nubbly, studded, knobbed 256.16; pitted 257.17.

.8 **smooth** 260.9; **fine, refined,** attenuate, attenuated, **fine-grained; delicate, dainty; finespun,** thin-spun, fine-drawn, wiredrawn; gauzy, filmy, gossamer, gossamery 339.4, **downy,** fluffy, velvety, velutinous, fuzzy, pubescent; satin, satiny, silky.

## 352. WEIGHT

.1 NOUNS **weight, heaviness, weightiness, ponderousness,** ponderosity, gravity, heftiness *or* heft [both informal]; body weight, avoirdupois [informal], fatness 195.8, beef *or* beefiness [both informal]; poundage, tonnage; ponderability; deadweight, liveweight; gross weight, gr. wt.; **net weight,** neat weight, nt. wt., net, nett [Brit]; underweight; overweight; overbalance, overweightage.

.2 onerousness, **burdensomeness, oppressiveness, cumbersomeness,** cumbrousness; massiveness, massiness [archaic], bulkiness 195.9, lumpishness, unwieldiness.

.3 (sports) bantamweight, featherweight, flyweight, heavyweight, light heavyweight, lightweight, middleweight, welterweight; catchweight.

.4 **counterbalance** 33.2; makeweight; **ballast,** ballasting.

.5 [phys terms] **gravity, gravitation, G;** specific gravity; gravitational field, gravisphere; graviton; geotropism, positive geotropism, apogeotropism, negative geotropism; G suit, anti-G suit; **mass.**

.6 **weight,** paperweight, letterweight; sinker, lead, plumb, plummet, bob; sandbag.

.7 **burden,** burthen [archaic], pressure, **oppression, deadweight;** burdening, saddling, charging, taxing; overburdening, overtaxing, overweighting, weighing *or* weighting down; charge, load, loading, lading, freight, cargo, bale; cumber, cumbrance, **encumbrance;** incubus; incumbency *or* superincumbency [archaic]; handicap, drag, millstone; surcharge, overload.

.8 (systems of weight) avoirdupois weight, troy weight, apothecaries' weight; atomic weight, molecular weight.

.9 **weighing,** hefting [informal], balancing; weighing-in, weigh-in, weighing-out, weigh-out.

.10 VERBS **weigh,** weight; **heft** [informal], **balance,** weigh in the balance, strike a balance, hold the scales, put on the scales,

lay in the scales; **counterbalance** 33.5; weigh in, weigh out; be heavy, weigh heavy, lie heavy, have weight, carry weight; **tip the scales,** turn *or* depress the scales.

.11 **weigh on** *or* **upon,** rest on *or* upon, bear on *or* upon, lie on, press, press down, press to the ground.

.12 **weight, weigh** *or* **weight down;** hang like a millstone; **ballast;** lead, sandbag.

.13 **burden,** burthen [archaic], **load,** lade, cumber, **encumber, charge, freight,** tax, handicap, hamper, saddle; **oppress, weigh one down, weigh on** *or* **upon, weigh heavy on,** bear *or* rest hard upon, lie hard *or* heavy upon, press hard upon, be an incubus to; **overburden,** overweight, overtax, **overload** 663.15.

.14 **outweigh,** overweigh, overweight, overbalance, **outbalance,** outpoise, overpoise.

.15 **gravitate, descend** 316.5,6, drop, plunge 320.6, precipitate, sink, settle, subside; tend, tend to go, **incline,** point, head, lead, lean.

.16 ADJS **heavy,** bar(o)–, gravi–, hadr(o)–; **ponderous, massive,** massy, weighty, hefty [informal], fat 195.18; **leaden,** heavy as lead; heavyweight; overweight.

.17 **onerous, oppressive, burdensome,** incumbent *or* superincumbent, **cumbersome,** cumbrous; massive; lumpish, **unwieldy.**

.18 **weighted, weighed** *or* **weighted down; burdened, oppressed, laden,** cumbered, **encumbered,** charged, loaded, fraught, freighted, taxed, saddled, hampered; **overburdened,** overloaded, overladen, overcharged, overfreighted, overfraught, overweighted, overtaxed.

.19 **weighable,** ponderable; **appreciable,** palpable, sensible.

.20 **gravitational,** mass.

.21 ADVS **heavily,** heavy, weightily, leadenly; burdensomely, onerously, oppressively; ponderously, cumbersomely, cumbrously.

.22 **weighing instruments**

| | |
|---|---|
| alloy balance | flexure plate scale |
| analytical balance | lever scales |
| assay balance | long-arm balance |
| automatic indicating | Nicholson's hydrome- |
|   scale |   ter |
| balance | pair of scales |
| balance of precision | plate fulcrum scale |
| barrel scale | platform scale *or* bal- |
| beam |   ance |
| bullion balance | precision scale *or* bal- |
| counter scale |   ance |
| cylinder scale | Roman balance |
| Danish balance | scale, scales |
| drum scale | short-arm balance |
| fan scale | spiral balance |

| | |
|---|---|
| spring balance | weighbridge |
| spring scale | weighing machine |
| steelyard | weigh scales |
| torsion scale | Weightometer |
| trone [Scot] | weight voltameter |
| weighbeam | |

**.23 units of weight** *or* **force** *or* **mass**

| | |
|---|---|
| assay ton | microgram, mcg. |
| carat, c. | milligram, mg. |
| carat grain | mole, mol. |
| centigram, cg. | myriagram, myg. |
| decagram, dkg. | net ton |
| decigram, dg. | newton |
| dram, dram avoirdu- | ounce, ounce avoirdu- |
| pois, dr. | pois, oz., oz. av. |
| dram apothecaries', | ounce apothecaries', |
| dr. ap. | oz. ap. |
| dyne | ounce troy, oz. t. |
| grain, gr. | pearl grain |
| gram, g. | pennyweight, dwt. *or* |
| gram equivalent, gram | pwt. |
| equivalent weight | pound, pound avoir- |
| gram molecule, gram- | dupois, lb., lb. av. |
| molecular weight | poundal |
| gross ton | pound apothecaries', |
| hectogram, hg. | lb. ap. |
| hundredweight, cwt. | pound troy, lb. t. |
| international carat | quintal, q. |
| kilogram, kilo, kg. | scruple, s. ap. |
| kiloton | short hundredweight |
| long hundredweight | short ton, s.t. |
| long ton, l. | slug |
| megaton | sthene |
| metric carat | stone, st. |
| metric ton, MT *or* t. | ton, tn. |

## 353. LIGHTNESS

.1 NOUNS **lightness, levity,** unheaviness, lack of weight; **weightlessness; buoyancy,** floatability; levitation, ascent 315; **volatility; airiness,** ethereality; foaminess, frothiness, bubbliness, yeastiness; downiness, fluffiness, gossameriness 339.1; softness, gentleness, delicacy, daintiness, tenderness.

.2 (comparisons) air, ether, feather, down, thistledown, flue, fluff, fuzz, sponge, gossamer, cobweb, fairy, straw, chaff, dust, mote, cork, chip, bubble, froth, foam, spume.

.3 lightening, easing, **easement, alleviation,** relief; disburdening, **disencumberment,** unburdening, **unloading,** unlading, unsaddling, untaxing, unfreighting; unballasting.

.4 leavening, fermentation; leaven, ferment; zym(o)-.

.5 (indeterminacy of weight) **imponderableness** *or* imponderability, unweighableness *or* unweighability; imponderables, imponderabilia.

.6 VERBS **lighten,** make light *or* lighter, reduce weight; unballast; **ease, alleviate,** relieve; **disburden, disencumber,** unburden,

unload, unlade, off-load; **be light, weigh** lightly, have little weight, kick the beam.

.7 **leaven,** raise, **ferment.**

.8 **buoy,** buoy up; float, float high, ride high, waft; **sustain, hold up,** bear up, up hold, upbear, uplift, upraise.

.9 **levitate** (opposed to gravitate), rise, ascend 315.8; hover, **float.**

.10 ADJS **light,** unheavy, **imponderous; weightless; airy, ethereal; volatile;** frothy foamy, bubbly, yeasty; downy, feathery fluffy, gossamery 339.4; *soufflé, moussé, léger* [all Fr]; "lighter than vanity" [Bible], "light as any wind that blows" [Tennyson]; light as air *or* a feather *or* gossamer, etc. 353.2.

.11 **gentle, soft, delicate,** dainty, tender, **easy.**

.12 **lightweight,** bantamweight, feather weight; underweight.

.13 **buoyant,** floaty, floatable; floating, super natant.

.14 levitative, levitational.

.15 **lightening, easing,** alleviating, alleviative relieving, disburdening, unburdening, dis encumbering.

.16 **leavening,** raising, **fermenting,** fermen tative, working; yeasty, barmy; enzymic diastatic.

.17 **imponderable,** unweighable.

.18 **leavens, ferments**

| | |
|---|---|
| bacteria | invertase |
| baking powder | maltase |
| baking soda | mother, mother of |
| barm | vinegar |
| beaten egg | pepsin |
| brewer's yeast | soda |
| buttermilk | sour milk |
| carbon dioxide | vinegar |
| cream of tartar | yeast |
| diastase | zymase |
| enzyme | zyme |
| egg whites | |

## 354. DENSITY

.1 NOUNS **density, denseness, solidity, solid ness,** firmness, **compactness, closeness** dasy–, spissitude [archaic]; crowdedness jammedness, congestedness, congestion impenetrability, impermeability, imporos ity; hardness 356; incompressibility; spe cific gravity, relative density; **consistency** consistence; viscidity, viscosity, viscous ness, **thickness,** gluiness.

.2 **indivisibility, inseparability,** impartibility infrangibility, indiscerptibility; indissolu bility; cohesion, coherence 50.1; unity 89 insolubility, infusibility.

.3 **densification, condensation, compression concentration,** concretion, consolidation hardening, solidification 356.5; agglutination, clumping, clustering.

.4 **thickening,** inspissation; congelation, **congealment, coagulation,** clotting, setting, concretion; gelatinization, gelatination, jellification, jellying, **jelling,** gelling; **curdling,** clabbering.

.5 **precipitation,** deposit, sedimentation; precipitate 43.2.

.6 **solid,** solid body, body, mass; lump, clump, cluster; block, cake; node, knot; concrete, concretion; conglomerate, conglomeration.

.7 **clot,** coagulum, coagulate; blood clot, grume, thrombus, thromb(o)–, embolus, crassamentum; casein, caseinogen, paracasein, legumin; **curd,** clabber, loppered milk or bonnyclabber [both dial], clotted cream, Devonshire cream.

.8 (instruments) densimeter, densitometer; aerometer, hydrometer, lactometer, urinometer, pycnometer.

.9 VERBS **densify,** densen; **condense, compress,** compact, **consolidate, concentrate,** congest, squeeze, **press, crowd,** cram, jam, ram down; **solidify** 356.8.

10 **thicken,** thick [archaic]; inspissate, incrassate; **congeal, coagulate,** clot, set, concrete; gelatinize, gelatinate, jelly, jellify, **jell,** gel; **curdle,** curd, clabber, lopper [dial]; cake, lump, clump, cluster, knot.

11 **precipitate,** deposit, sediment, sedimentate.

12 ADJS **dense, compact, close,** pycn(o)–; close-textured, close-knit, close-woven; serried, **thick, heavy,** thickset, thick-packed, thick-growing, thick-spread, thick-spreading; **condensed, compressed,** compacted, concrete, consolidated, concentrated; **crowded, jammed,** packed, jam-packed, **congested,** crammed, crammed full; **solid, firm,** substantial, massive; impenetrable, impermeable, imporous, nonporous; hard 356.10; incompressible; viscid, viscous or viscose, gluey.

13 **indivisible,** nondivisible, undividable, **inseparable,** impartible, infrangible, indiscerptible, indissoluble; **cohesive, coherent** 50.10; unified 89.10; **insoluble,** indissolvable, infusible.

14 **thickened,** inspissate or inspissated, incrassate; **congealed, coagulated, clotted,** grumous; **curdled,** curded, clabbered; **jellied,** jelled, gelatinized; lumpy, lumpish; caked, cakey.

15 ADVS **densely,** compactly, **close,** closely, **thick,** thickly, heavily; solidly, firmly.

## 355. RARITY

.1 NOUNS **rarity, rareness; thinness, tenuousness,** tenuity; **subtlety,** subtility, subtilty; **fineness,** slightness, flimsiness, **unsubstantiality** or **insubstantiality** 4; **ethereality,** airiness, immateriality, incorporeality, bodilessness, insolidity; "airy nothing", "such stuff as dreams are made on" [both Shakespeare].

.2 **rarefaction,** attenuation, subtilization, etherealization; **thinning,** dilution, adulteration.

.3 VERBS **rarefy, attenuate,** thin, thin out; dilute, adulterate, water, water down, cut; subtilize, **etherealize;** expand 197.4.

.4 ADJS **rare,** rarefied; **subtle,** subtile; **thin,** thinned, dilute, attenuated, attenuate; thinned-out, diluted, adulterated, watered, watered-down, cut; **tenuous, fine,** flimsy, slight, **unsubstantial** or **insubstantial** 4.5; **airy, ethereal,** vaporous, gaseous, windy; uncompact, uncompressed.

.5 rarefactive, rarefactional.

## 356. HARDNESS, RIGIDITY

.1 NOUNS **hardness,** durity [archaic], induration; **callousness,** callosity; stoniness, flintiness, steeliness; **toughness** 359; solidity, impenetrability, density 354; restiveness, resistance 792; obduracy 626.1; hardness of heart 856.3.

.2 **rigidity,** rigidness, rigor [archaic]; **firmness,** renitence, renitency, **stiffness,** starchiness; **tension,** tensity, **tenseness,** tautness, tightness.

.3 **inflexibility,** unpliability, unmalleability, intractability, unbendingness, unlimberness, **stubbornness,** unyieldingness 626.2; **unalterability,** immutability; immovability 142.3; inclasticity, irresilience or irresiliency; inextensibility or unextensibility, unextendibility, inductility.

.4 **temper,** tempering; chisel temper, die temper, razor temper, saw file temper, set temper, spindle temper, tool temper; precipitation hardening, heat treating; hardness scale; indenter.

.5 **hardening, toughening,** induration, firming; **tempering,** case hardening, steeling; **solidification,** setting, concretion; crystallization, granulation; callusing; sclerosis, arteriosclerosis, atherosclerosis; lithification; lapidification [archaic]; **petrification,** petrifaction; fossilization, ossification, –ostosis; cornification, hornification; calcification; vitrification, vitrifaction; **stiffening,** rigidification.

.6 (comparisons) stone, rock 384, adamant, granite, flint, marble, diamond; steel, iron, nails; concrete, cement; brick; oak, heart of oak; bone 245.6,12.

.7 VERBS **harden, indurate,** firm, **toughen; callous; temper,** anneal, **case harden,** steel; **petrify,** lapidify [archaic], **fossilize;** lithify; vitrify; calcify; ossify; cornify, hornify.

.8 **solidify,** concrete, **set,** take a set, cake; condense, thicken 354.10; **crystallize,** granulate, candy.

.9 **stiffen,** rigidify, **strengthen,** back, reinforce, shore up; **tense, tighten,** brace, trice up, screw up.

.10 ADJS **hard, solid,** dure [archaic], **tough** 359.4, scler(a)– or sclero–; resistive, resistant, steely, steellike, iron-hard, ironlike, **stony,** rocky, stonelike, rocklike, lapideous, lithoid or lithoidal, lith(o)–, –lith, –lite or – lyte; diamondlike; flinty, flintlike; marble, marblelike; granitic, granitelike; concrete, cement, cemental; horny, cerat(o)– or kerat(o)–, corneous, –corn; bony, osseous; hard-boiled; hard as nails or a rock, etc. 356.6, "as firm as a stone; yea, as hard as a piece of the nether millstone" [Bible]; dense 354.12; obdurate 626.10; hardhearted 856.12.

.11 **rigid, stiff, firm,** renitent; **tense, taut, tight, unrelaxed;** virgate, rodlike; ramrodstiff, ramrodlike, pokerlike; stiff as a poker, stiff as buckram; starched, starchy.

.12 **inflexible,** unflexible, **unpliable, unpliant, unmalleable, intractable,** untractable, intractile, **unbending,** unlimber, **unyielding** 626.9, ungiving, **stubborn, unalterable,** immutable; **immovable** 142.15; **adamant,** adamantine; **inelastic,** nonelastic, irresilient; inextensile, inextensible, unextensible, inextensional, unextendible, nonstretchable, inductile.

.13 **hardened, toughened,** steeled, indurate, indurated; **case-hardened; callous,** calloused; **solidified,** set; crystallized, granulated; petrified, lapidified [archaic], fossilized; vitrified; sclerotic; ossified; cornified, hornified; calcified; crusted, crusty, incrusted; **stiffened, strengthened,** rigidified, backed, reinforced.

.14 **hardening, toughening,** indurative; petrifying, petrifactive.

.15 **tempered,** heat-treated, **annealed,** oiltempered.

## 357. SOFTNESS, PLIANCY

.1 NOUNS **softness,** nonresistiveness, insolidity, unsolidity, nonrigidity; **gentleness,** easiness, delicacy, morbidezza, tenderness, leniency 759; mellowness; fluffiness, flossiness, downiness, featheriness; velvetiness, plushiness, satininess, silkiness; sponginess, pulpiness.

.2 **pliancy, pliability, plasticity, flexibility,** flexility, flexuousness, ductility, ductibility [archaic], tensileness, tensility, tractility, **tractability,** amenability, adaptability, facility, **elasticity,** give, bendability; **suppleness,** willowiness, springiness, **litheness, limberness; malleability,** moldability, fictility, sequacity [archaic]; **impressionability,** susceptibility, responsiveness, receptiveness, sensibility, sensitiveness; formability, formativeness; extensibility, extendibility; agreeability 622.1; submissiveness 765.3.

.3 **flaccidity,** flaccidness, **flabbiness, limpness,** rubberiness, floppiness; **looseness,** laxness, laxity, laxation.

.4 (comparisons) putty, clay, dough, blubber, rubber, wax, butter, pudding; velvet, plush, satin, silk; wool, fleece; pillow, cushion; kapok; puff; fluff, floss, flue; down, feathers, feather bed, eiderdown, swansdown, thistledown; breeze, zephyr; foam.

.5 **softening,** softening-up; **easing, padding,** cushioning; mollifying, mollification; **relaxation,** laxation; mellowing.

.6 VERBS **soften,** soften up; **ease, cushion;** gentle, mollify, milden; **subdue,** tone or tune down; mellow; tenderize; **relax,** laxate, loosen; **limber,** limber up, supple; massage, knead, plump, fluff, shake up; **mash, smash,** squash, pulp.

.7 **yield, give,** relent, relax, bend, unbend, give way; submit 765.6–11.

.8 ADJS **soft,** malac(o)–; nonresistive, nonrigid; mild, **gentle, easy, delicate, tender;** complaisant 759.8; mellow, mellowy [archaic]; **softened,** mollified; whisper-soft, soft as putty or clay or dough, etc. 357.4, soft as a kiss, soft as a sigh, "soft as sinews of the new-born babe" [Shakespeare].

.9 **pliant, pliable, flexible,** flexile, flexuous, **plastic, elastic, ductile,** sequacious or facile [both archaic], tractile, **tractable, yielding,** giving, bending; adaptable, **malleable,** moldable, shapable, fabricable, fictile; compliant 622.5, submissive 765.12; **impressionable,** impressible, susceptible, responsive, receptive, sensitive; **formable,** formative; **bendable; supple,** willowy, **limber; lithe,** lithesome, lissome, "as lissome as a hazel wand" [Tennyson], springy, whippy; extensile, extensible, extendible; like putty or wax or dough, etc. 357.4.

.10 **flaccid, flabby, limp,** rubbery, flimsy, floppy; **loose,** lax, relaxed.

.11 **spongy,** pulpy, pithy, medullary; edematous.

.12 **pasty, doughy;** loamy, clayey, argillaceous.

.13 **squashy,** squishy, squushy, squelchy.

.14 **fluffy,** flossy, **downy,** pubescent, feathery; fleecy, woolly, lanate; furry.

.15 **velvety,** velvetlike, velutinous; plushy, plush; **satiny,** satinlike; cottony; **silky,** silken, silklike, sericeous, soft as silk.

.16 **softening, easing;** subduing, mollifying, emollient; demulcent; **relaxing,** loosening.

.17 ADVS **softly, gently,** easily, delicately, tenderly; compliantly 622.9, submissively 765.17.

## 358. ELASTICITY

.1 NOUNS **elasticity, resilience** or resiliency, **give; snap, bounce,** bounciness; **stretch,** stretchiness, stretchability; extensibility; tone, tonus, tonicity, –tonia or –tony; **spring, springiness;** rebound 284.2; **flexibility** 357.2; **adaptability,** responsiveness; **buoyancy** or buoyance; **liveliness** 707.2.

.2 **stretching;** extension 202.5; distension 197.2; **stretch, tension, strain.**

.3 **elastic;** elastomer; **rubber, gum** elastic; stretch fabric, Lastex, spandex; gum, chewing gum 389.6; whalebone, baleen; rubber band, rubber ball, handball, tennis ball; spring; springboard; trampoline; racket, battledore; jumping jack.

.4 VERBS **stretch;** extend 202.7; distend 197.4.

.5 **give,** yield 357.7; bounce, spring, spring back 284.6.

.6 **elasticize;** rubberize, rubber; vulcanize.

.7 ADJS **elastic, resilient, springy, bouncy; stretchable, stretchy,** stretch; extensile; **flexible** 357.9; flexile; **adaptable,** adaptive, responsive; buoyant; lively 707.17.

.8 **rubber, rubbery,** rubberlike; rubberized.

.9 **rubber**

| | |
|---|---|
| Buna | elastomer |
| Buna N | foam rubber |
| Buna S | hard rubber |
| Butyl rubber | India rubber |
| caoutchouc | Koroseal |
| caucho | latex |
| Ceará rubber | methyl rubber |
| cis-polyisoprene rubber | natural rubber |
| | neoprene rubber |
| cold rubber | nitrile rubber |
| crepe, crepe rubber | Pará rubber |
| crude rubber | Perbunan |
| ebonite | plantation rubber |

| | |
|---|---|
| polysulfide rubber | sponge rubber |
| polyurethane rubber | synthetic rubber |
| reclaimed rubber | Thiokol |
| rubber tissue | vulcanite |
| silicone rubber | vulcanized rubber |

.10 **springs**

| | |
|---|---|
| balance spring | leaf spring |
| bedspring | mainspring |
| box spring | shock absorber |
| coil spring | spiral spring |
| elliptic spring | volute spring |
| hairspring | |

## 359. TOUGHNESS

.1 NOUNS **toughness, resistance; strength,** hardiness, vitality, stamina 159.1; **stubbornness, stiffness; unbreakableness** or **unbreakability,** infrangibility; cohesiveness, **tenacity,** viscidity 50.3; **durability,** lastingness 110.1; **hardness** 356; **leatheriness,** leatherlikeness; stringiness, ropiness.

.2 (comparisons) leather; gristle, cartilage.

.3 VERBS **toughen,** harden, stiffen, **temper,** strengthen; be tough; endure, hang tough [slang].

.4 ADJS **tough, resistant,** stubborn, stiff; **strong, hardy,** vigorous 159.13; cohesive, **tenacious,** viscid 50.12; **durable,** lasting 110.10; untiring; **hard** 356.10; chewy [informal]; leathery, leatherlike, coriaceous, tough as leather; sinewy, wiry; gristly, cartilaginous; stringy, ropy, fibrous.

.5 **unbreakable,** nonbreakable, infrangible, unshatterable, shatterproof, chip-proof, fractureproof.

.6 **toughened,** hardened, tempered, annealed.

## 360. BRITTLENESS, FRAGILITY

.1 NOUNS **brittleness, crispness,** crispiness; **fragility, frailty,** delicacy 160.2, flimsiness, **breakability,** breakableness, frangibility, fracturableness, crackability, crackableness, crushability, crushableness; laceration; fissility; friability, crumbliness 361; vulnerability 697.4.

.2 (comparisons) eggshell, matchwood, old paper, piecrust, glass, china, parchment, ice, bubble, glass house, house of cards.

.3 VERBS break, shard, shatter 49.12,13; fall to pieces, disintegrate 53.3.

.4 ADJS **brittle, crisp,** crispy; **fragile, frail,** delicate 160.14, flimsy, **breakable,** frangible, crushable, crackable, fracturable; lacerable; **shatterable,** shattery, shivery, splintery; friable, crumbly 361.13; fissile, scissile; brittle as glass; vulnerable 697.16.

## 361. POWDERINESS, CRUMBLINESS

.1 NOUNS powderiness, pulverulence, dustiness; chalkiness; mealiness, flouriness, branniness; efflorescence.

.2 granularity, graininess, granulation; sandiness, grittiness, gravelliness, sabulosity.

.3 friability, pulverableness, crispness, crumbliness; brittleness 360.

.4 pulverization, comminution, trituration, attrition, detrition; levigation; reduction to powder or dust; fragmentation, sharding; brecciation; atomization, micronization; powdering, crumbling; abrasion 350.2; grinding, grating, shredding; granulation, granulization; beating, pounding, mashing, smashing, crushing; disintegration 53.

.5 powder, dust, attritus, coni(o)- or koni-(o)-; dust ball, pussies, kittens, slut's wool, lint; efflorescence; crumb, crumble; meal, bran, flour, farina, aleuro-; grits, groats; filings, raspings, sawdust; soot, smut; airborne particles, air pollution, fallout; cosmic dust.

.6 grain, granule, granulet, granul(o)- or granuli-, chondr(o)-; grit, sand, amm(o)-, psamm(o)-; gravel, shingle; detritus, debris; breccia, collapse breccia.

.7 pulverizer, comminutor, kominuter, triturator, levigator; crusher, rock crusher; mill 348.23; grinder; granulator; grater, nutmeg grater, cheese grater; shredder; pestle, mortar and pestle; masher; millstone, quern, quernstone; roller, steamroller.

.8 koniology; konimeter.

.9 VERBS pulverize, powder, comminute, triturate, contriturate, levigate, bray, pestle, disintegrate, reduce to powder or dust, grind to powder or dust; fragment, shard; brecciate; atomize, micronize; crumble, crumb; granulate, granulize, grain; grind, grate, shred, abrade 350.7; mill, flour; beat, pound, mash, smash, crush, squash, scrunch [informal].

.10 (be reduced to powder) powder, come or fall to dust, crumble, crumble to or into dust, disintegrate 53.3, fall to pieces, break up; effloresce; granulate, grain.

.11 ADJS powdery, dusty, pulverulent, pulverous; pulverized, pulverant, powdered, disintegrated, comminute, gone to dust, reduced to powder; ground, grated, pestled, milled, comminuted, triturated, levigated; sharded, crushed; shredded; fine, impalpable; chalky, chalklike; mealy, floury, farinaceous; branny; furfuraceous, scaly, scurfy; flaky 227.7; detrited, detrital; scobiform, scobicular; efflorescent.

.12 granular, grainy, granulate, granulated; sandy, gritty, sabulous, arenarious, arenaceous; shingly, shingled, pebbled, pebbly; gravelly; breccial, brecciated.

.13 pulverable, pulverizable, pulverulent, triturable; friable, crimp [archaic], crisp, crumbly.

## 362. COLOR

.1 NOUNS color, hue; tint, tinct, tincture, tinge, shade, tone, cast, key; coloring, coloration; color harmony, color balance, color scheme; decorator color; complexion, skin color or coloring or tone; chromatism, chromism; achromatism 363.1; natural color; undercolor; pallor 363.2; -chroia, -chromasia, chrom(o)-, chromat(o)-, -chrome, -chromia, -chromy.

.2 warmth, warmth of color, warm color; blush, flush, glow, healthy glow or hue.

.3 softness, soft color, subtle color, pale color, pastel, pastel color.

.4 colorfulness, color, bright color, pure color, brightness, brilliance, vividness, intensity, saturation; richness, gorgeousness, gaiety; riot of color; Technicolor.

.5 garishness, loudness, luridness, gaudiness 904.3; loud or screaming color [informal]; shocking pink, jaundiced yellow, arsenic green; clashing colors, color clash.

.6 color quality; chroma, Munsell chroma, brightness, purity, saturation; hue, value, lightness; colorimetric quality, chromaticity, chromaticness; tint, tone; chromatic color, achromatic or neutral color; warm color; cool color.

.7 color system, chromaticity diagram, color triangle, Maxwell triangle; hue cycle, color circle, chromatic circle, color cycle or gamut; Munsell scale; color solid; fundamental colors; primary color, primary pigment, primary; secondary color, secondary; tertiary color, tertiary; complementary color; chromaticity coordinate; color mixture curve or function; spectral color, spectrum color, pure or full color; metamer; spectrum, solar spectrum, color spectrum, chromatic spectrum, color index; monochrome; demitint, half tint, halftone.

.8 (coloring matter) color, coloring, colorant, -phyll, tinction, tincture, pigment, pigmento-, stain; chromogen; dye, dyestuff, color filter, color gelatin; paint, distemper, tempera; coat, coating, coat of paint; undercoat, undercoating, primer, priming, prime coat, **ground, flat coat,** dead-color; interior paint, exterior paint, floor enamel; wash, wash coat, flat wash; opaque color, transparent color; medium, vehicle; drier; thinner; turpentine, turps [informal].

**.9** (persons according to hair color) **brunet; blond,** goldilocks; bleached blond, peroxide blond; ash blond, platinum blond, strawberry blond, honey blond; **towhead; redhead,** carrottop.

**.10** (science of colors) chromatology; chromatics, chromatography, chromatoscopy, colorimetry; spectrum analysis, spectroscopy, spectrometry.

**.11** (applying color) **coloring,** coloration; staining, dyeing; **tinting,** tinging, tinction; pigmentation; illumination, emblazonry; color printing; lithography.

**.12** painting, coating, covering; **enameling,** glossing, glazing; **varnishing,** japanning, lacquering, shellacking; staining; **calcimining, whitewashing;** gilding; stippling; frescoing, fresco; undercoating, priming.

**.13** VERBS **color,** hue, lay on color; **tinge, tint,** tinct, **tincture,** tone, complexion; pigment; bedizen; **stain, dye,** dip; imbue; deep-dye, fast-dye, double-dye, dye in the wool; ingrain, grain; shade, shadow; illuminate, emblazon; **paint,** apply paint, **coat,** cover, face; dab, **daub,** bedaub, smear, besmear, brush on paint, slap or slop on paint; **enamel,** gloss, glaze; **varnish,** japan, lacquer, shellac; **calcimine, whitewash,** parget; wash; **gild,** begild, engild; stipple; fresco; distemper; undercoat, prime.

**.14** (be inharmonious) **clash,** conflict, collide, fight.

**.15** ADJS **chromatic,** colorational; **coloring,** colorific, colorative, tinctorial, tingent; pigmentary; –choic, –chroous, monochrome, monochromic, monochromatic; dichromatic; many-colored, parti-colored, medley or motley [both archaic], rainbow, **variegated** 374.9, polychromatic; prismatic, spectral; matching, toning, harmonious; warm, glowing; cool, cold.

**.16 colored,** hued, in color, in Technicolor; **tinged, tinted,** tinctured, tinct, toned; **stained, dyed;** imbued; complexioned, complected [informal]; full-colored, full; deep, deep-colored; wash-colored.

**.17 deep-dyed, fast-dyed,** double-dyed, ·**dyed-in-the-wool;** ingrained, ingrain; colorfast, fast, fadeless, unfading, indelible, constant.

**.18 colorful,** colory; **bright, vivid,** intense, rich, exotic, **brilliant,** burning, **gorgeous, gay,** bright-hued, bright-colored, rich-colored, gay-colored, high-colored, deep-colored.

**.19** garish, lurid, loud, screaming, shrieking, glaring, flaring, flashy, flaunting, crude, blinding, overbright, raw, gaudy 904.20.

**.20 off-color,** off-tone; **inharmonious, discordant,** incongruous, **harsh,** clashing, conflicting, colliding.

**.21** soft-colored, soft-hued, **soft,** softened, **subdued,** light, creamy, pastel, **pale,** subtle, mellow, delicate, quiet, tender, sweet; pearly, nacreous, mother-of-pearl, iridescent, opalescent; patinaed; somber, simple, sober, sad; flat, eggshell, semigloss, gloss.

**.22 dyes**

| | |
|---|---|
| acid color or dye | hydroxyazobenzene |
| acridine dye | lake |
| alizarin, alizarin dye or color | madder |
| | madder bloom |
| amino azobenzene | madder extract |
| aniline, aniline dye | methylene |
| anthracene | mineral pigment |
| artificial or synthetic dye | mordant dye |
| | naphthol |
| azo dye | natural dye or dye-stuff |
| basic dye | |
| biological stain | phthalein |
| chromotrope | phthalocyanine |
| coal-tar dye | pincoffin |
| crocein | rhodamine |
| developing dye | trinitroaniline |
| direct cotton dye | trinitrophenol |
| disazo dye | triphenylmethane dye |
| eosin | vat dye |
| fast dye | vegetable dye |
| food color | woad |
| fuchsine | wool fast dye |
| garancine | xanthene dye |

**.23 paints**

| | |
|---|---|
| acrylic paint | lacquer |
| alkyd paint | latex paint |
| aluminum paint | Lucite paint |
| animé | luminous paint |
| antifouling paint | megilp |
| calcimine | oil-base paint |
| casein paint | oils, oil paints or colors |
| Chinese lacquer | |
| copal | plastic paint |
| copalite, copaline | polyurethane |
| cosmetics 900.11 | poster color |
| deck enamel | radium paint |
| elemi | rubber-base paint |
| emulsion paint | shellac |
| enamel | silicate paint |
| engobe | stain |
| finger paint | synthetic lacquer |
| fluorescent paint | varnish |
| gilt, gilding | washable paint |
| glaze | water-base paint |
| gouache | watercolors |
| greasepaint | water glass |
| japan | whitewash |
| lac | Zanzibar copal |

**.24 color instruments**

| | |
|---|---|
| chromatograph | kaleidoscope |
| chromatometer | monochronometer |
| chromatoscope | prism |
| chromatrope | spectrograph |
| chromometer | spectrohelioscope |
| chromoscope | spectrometer |
| colorimeter | spectroscope 443.15 |

## 363. COLORLESSNESS

.1 NOUNS **colorlessness,** lack *or* absence of color, huelessness, tonelessness, achromatism, achromaticity; dullness, lackluster 337.5.

.2 **paleness, dimness,** weakness, **faintness,** fadedness; lightness, fairness; **pallor,** pallidity, pallidness, pallidi–, prison pallor, **wanness, sallowness,** pastiness, ashiness; muddiness, dullness; **anemia,** hypochromic anemia, hypochromia, chloranemia; bloodlessness, exsanguination; **ghastliness, haggardness,** lividness, sickly hue, sickliness, deadly *or* deathly pallor, deathly hue, cadaverousness.

.3 **decoloration,** decolorizing, decolorization, discoloration, achromatization, lightening; **fading, paling; whitening,** blanching, etiolation; **bleaching,** bleach; market bleach, madder bleach.

.4 **bleach,** bleacher, bleaching agent *or* substance; decolorant, decolorizer.

.5 VERBS decolor, decolorize, discolor, achromatize, etiolate; **fade, wash out; dim, dull, tarnish,** tone down; **pale, whiten,** blanch, drain, drain of color; **bleach,** peroxide, fume.

.6 **lose color, fade,** fade out; **bleach,** bleach out; **pale, turn pale,** grow pale, **change color,** turn white, **whiten, blanch,** wan.

.7 ADJS **colorless, hueless, toneless,** uncolored, achromic, achromatic, achromat(o)–, achro–, achroö–; neutral; dull, flat, mat, dead, dingy, muddy, leaden, lusterless, lackluster 337.17; **faded, washed-out,** dimmed, discolored, etiolated; **pale, dim,** weak, **faint; pallid, wan, sallow,** fallow; **white,** white as a sheet; **pasty,** mealy, waxen; **ashen,** ashy, ashenhued, gray; **anemic,** hypochromic, chloranemic; bloodless, exsanguine, exsanguinated, exsanguineous, bled white; **ghastly,** livid, lurid, **haggard,** cadaverous, sickly, deadly *or* deathly pale; pale as death *or* a ghost *or* a corpse, "pale as a forpined ghost" [Chaucer], "pale as his shirt" [Shakespeare]; pale-faced, tallow-faced, whey-faced.

.8 **bleached,** decolored, decolorized, whit-

ened, blanched, lightened, bleached out, bleached white; drained, drained of color.

.9 **light, fair,** light-colored, light-hued; pastel; whitish 364.8.

.10 **bleaches**

| | |
|---|---|
| benzoyl peroxide | gray sour |
| bleaching clay *or* | hydrochloric acid |
| earth | hydrogen peroxide |
| bleaching powder | Javelle water |
| bleach liquor | lime |
| bluing | lye boil |
| bone charcoal | nitrogen tetroxide |
| calcium hypochlorite | oxalic acid |
| chlorine | peroxide |
| chlorine dioxide | sodium hypochlorite |
| chlorine water | sour |
| Clorox | sulfur dioxide |
| dilute acid | sulfuric acid |
| *eau de Javelle* [Fr] | white sour |

## 364. WHITENESS

.1 NOUNS **whiteness, whitishness;** albescence; **lightness, fairness;** paleness 363.2; silveriness; snowiness, frostiness; chalkiness; pearliness; **creaminess;** blondness; hoariness, grizzliness, canescence; milkiness, lactescence; glaucousness; glaucescence; **white,** silver; albinism, albinoism, achroma, achromasia, achromatosis; albino; leukoderma, vitiligo; white race 418.2,3.

.2 (comparisons) alabaster, chalk, lily, milk, pearl, sheet, swan, fleece, foam, silver, snow, driven snow, paper, flour, ivory, maggot.

.3 **whitening,** albification, blanching; etiolation; **whitewashing; bleaching** 363.3; silvering, frosting, grizzling.

.4 **whiting,** whitening, **whitewash,** calcimine; pipe clay, Blanco [Brit].

.5 VERBS **whiten,** white [archaic], etiolate, **blanch; bleach** 363.5; silver, grizzle, frost, besnow; chalk.

.6 **whitewash,** white [archaic], calcimine; pipe-clay, Blanco [Brit]; chalk.

.7 ADJS **white,** alb(o)–, leuc(o)– *or* leuk(o)–; pure white, **snow-white,** snowy, niveous, white as snow, "whiter than new snow on a raven's back" [Shakespeare], frosty, frosted; **hoary,** hoar, **grizzled,** grizzly, canescent; silver, **silvery,** silvered, argent [her], argentine; platinum; chalky, cretaceous; fleece- *or* fleecy-white; swan-white; foam-white; **milk-white,** milky, lactescent; marble, marmoreal; lily-white, white as a lily, "white as the whitest lily on a stream" [Longfellow]; white as a sheet.

.8 **whitish,** whity, albescent; **light, fair;** pale 363.7; off-white; eggshell; glaucous, glaucescent; pearl, pearly, pearly-white, pearl-white; alabaster, alabastrine; cream, creamy; ivory, ivory-white; gray-white; dun-white; lint-white.

.9 **blond**; flaxen-haired, fair-haired; artificial blond, bleached-blond, peroxide-blond; ash-blond, platinum-blond, strawberry-blond, honey-blond, blond-headed, blond-haired; **towheaded**, tow-haired; golden-haired 370.5.

.10 **albino**, albinic, albinistic, albinal.

.11 **white colors and pigments**

| | |
|---|---|
| alabaster | Kremser white |
| antimony white | lead carbonate |
| bismuth white | off white |
| *blanc d'argent* [Fr] | oyster white |
| *blanc de fard* [Fr] | Paris white |
| *blanc d'Espagne* [Fr] | pearl |
| *blanc fixe* [Fr], bar- | pearl white |
| ium sulfate, baryta | permanent white |
| white | platinum |
| blond | silver |
| bone white | snow white |
| Chinese white | strontium white |
| Dutch white | titanium white |
| eggshell | white lead |
| flake white | zinc oxide, zinc white |
| ivory | zinc sulfide |
| Kremnitz *or* Krems *or* | |

## 365. BLACKNESS

.1 NOUNS **blackness**, nigritude, nigrescence; inkiness; **black, sable, ebony**; melanism; black race 418.2,3; darkness (absence of light) 337; –melane.

.2 **darkness**, **darkishness**, darksomeness, blackishness; **swarthiness**, swartness, swarth; **duskiness**, duskness; soberness, sobriety, **somberness**, graveness, sadness, funereality.

.3 **dinginess**, griminess, smokiness, sootiness, smudginess, smuttiness, blotchiness, dirtiness, **muddiness**, murkiness, fuliginousness, fuliginosity.

.4 (comparisons) ebony *or* ebon [archaic], jet, ink, sloe, pitch, tar, coal, charcoal, smoke, soot, smut, raven, crow, night.

.5 **blackening**, **darkening**, nigrification, melanization, denigration; shading; **smudging**, smutching, **smirching**; smudge, smutch, smirch, smut.

.6 **blacking**, blackening, blackwash; charcoal, burnt cork, black ink; lampblack, carbon black, stove black, gas black, soot.

.7 VERBS **blacken**, black, nigrify, melanize, denigrate; **darken**, bedarken; shade, shadow; blackwash, ink, charcoal, cork; **smudge**, smutch, **smirch**, besmirch, murk; blotch, blot, dinge; smut, soot; smoke, oversmoke; ebonize.

.8 ADJS **black**, atro–, mel(a)– *or* melo–, melan(o)– *or* melam–; **sable** [her], nigrous; **ebony**, "black as ebony" [Shakespeare]; deep black, of the deepest dye; **pitch-black, pitch-dark**, pitchy, black *or* dark as pitch, tar-black, tarry; night-black, night-dark, black *or* dark as night; midnight, black as midnight; **inky**, inky-black, atramentous, ink-black, black as ink; **jet-black**, jetty; **coal-black**, coaly, black as coal; sloe, sloe-black, sloe-colored; raven, **raven-black**, black as a crow, "cyprus black as e'er was crow" [Shakespeare]; **dark** 337.13–16.

.9 **dark**, dark-colored, **darkish**, darksome, blackish; nigrescent; **swarthy**, swart; **dusky**, dusk; **somber**, sombrous, **sober**, **grave**, sad, funereal.

.10 **dark-skinned**, black-skinned, **dark-complexioned**; **black, colored**; melanian, melanic, melanotic, melanistic, melanous, melano.

.11 **dingy**, **grimy**, **smoky**, sooty, **smudgy**, smutty, blotchy, dirty, **muddy**, murky, fuliginous, smirched, besmirched.

.12 **livid, black and blue.**

.13 **black-haired, raven-haired**, raven-tressed, black-locked; brunet.

.14 **black colors and pigments**

| | |
|---|---|
| aniline black | ivory black |
| blue black | japan |
| bone black | lampblack |
| Brunswick black | naphthol blue black |
| carbon black | naphthylamine black |
| chrome black | nigrosine |
| corbeau | raven black |
| direct black | slate black |
| drop black, Frankfort | soot black, sooty |
| black | black |
| ink black | sulfur black |

## 366. GRAYNESS

.1 NOUNS **grayness**, grayishness, canescence; glaucousness, glaucescence; silveriness; smokiness; mousiness; slatiness; leadenness; **gray**, neutral tint; lividness, lividity; dullness, drabness, soberness, somberness.

.2 **gray-haired** *or* **gray-headed person**, grayhair, graybeard, grisard.

.3 VERBS **gray, grizzle**, silver, dapple.

.4 ADJS **gray, grayish**, gray-colored, grayhued, gray-toned, grayed, poli(o)–; canescent; iron-gray, steely, steel-gray; Quaker-gray, Quaker-colored, acier, gray-drab; dove-gray, dove-colored; pearl-gray, pearl, pearly; silver-gray, silver, silvery, silvered; **grizzly**, grizzled, grizzle, griseous; ash-gray, ashen, ashy, cinerous, cinereous, cineritious [archaic], cinereal; dusty, dust-gray; smoky, smoke-gray; charcoal-gray; slaty, slate-colored; stone-colored; leaden, livid, lead-gray; glaucous, glaucescent; mousy, mouse-gray, mouse-colored; taupe; dapple-gray, dappled-gray, dappled, dapple; gray-spotted, gray-speckled, salt-and-pepper; gray-white, gray-black, gray-blue, gray-brown, gray-green, etc.; **dull, dingy,** dismal, **somber, sober, sad, dreary.**

.5 **gray-haired,** gray-headed, silver-headed; hoary, hoary-haired, hoaryheaded; gray-bearded, silver-bearded.

.6 **gray colors and pigments**

| | |
|---|---|
| acier | mouse gray |
| ash | neutral tint |
| ash gray | olive gray |
| bat | opal gray |
| battleship gray | Oxford gray |
| cadet gray | oyster gray |
| charcoal gray | Payne's gray |
| cinder gray | pearl |
| cloud gray | pearl gray |
| crystal gray | pelican |
| dove gray | pepper-and-salt |
| field gray | pigeon's-neck |
| French gray | plumbago gray |
| glaucous gray | powder gray |
| granite gray | Quaker gray |
| grege | salt-and-pepper |
| gun metal | shell gray |
| iron gray | silver gray |
| lead gray | smoke gray |
| light gunmetal | steel gray |
| lilac gray | taupe |
| mole gray | zinc gray |
| moleskin | |

## 367. BROWNNESS

.1 NOUNS **brownness,** brownishness, **brown;** browning, infuscation; brown race 418.2.

.2 VERBS **brown,** embrown, infuscate; rust; **tan, bronze,** suntan; sunburn, burn.

.3 ADJS **brown,** brownish, fusco–, pheo– or phaeo–, pyrr(o)– or pyrrh(o)–, tann(o)–; cinnamon, hazel; fuscous; **brunet,** brune; tawny, fulvous; tan, tan-colored; tan-faced, tan-skinned, tanned, sun-tanned; khaki, khaki-colored; drab, olive-drab; **dun,** dun-brown, dun-drab, dun-olive; beige, grege, ecru; **chocolate,** chocolate-colored, chocolate-brown; cocoa, cocoa-colored, cocoa-brown; coffee, coffee-colored, coffee-brown; toast, toast-brown; nut-brown; walnut, walnut-brown; seal, seal-brown; fawn, fawn-colored; grayish-brown, taupe; snuff-colored, mummy-brown; umber, umber-colored, umber-brown; olive-brown; **sepia;** sorrel; yellowish-brown, brownish-yellow; lurid [archaic]; brown as a berry, berry-brown.

.4 **reddish-brown,** brownish-red; roan; henna; terra-cotta; rufous, foxy; livid-brown; **mahogany,** mahogany-brown; auburn, Titian; **russet,** russety; rust, rust-colored, rusty, ferruginous, rubiginous; liver-colored, liver-brown; **bronze,** bronze-colored, bronzed, brazen; copper, coppery, copperish, cupreous, copper-colored; **chestnut,** chestnut-brown, castaneous; bay, bay-colored; bayard [archaic]; sunburned, adust [archaic].

.5 **brunet;** brown-haired; auburn-haired; xanthous.

.6 **brown colors and pigments**

| | |
|---|---|
| acorn | Italian earth |
| alesan | Italian ocher |
| alizarin brown | ivory brown |
| anthracene brown | leather |
| anthragallol | Manchester brown |
| antique bronze | manganese brown |
| antique brown | maple sugar |
| antique drab | Mars brown |
| antique gold | meadow lark |
| Argos brown | Merida |
| autumn leaf | Mexican red |
| biscuit | mineral brown |
| Bismarck brown | mummy |
| bister | negro |
| bone brown | olive brown |
| Bordeaux | oriole |
| bracken | otter brown |
| brown madder | partridge |
| bunny brown | philamot |
| burnt almond | raw sienna |
| burnt umber | raw umber |
| *cachou de Laval* [Fr] | resorcin dark brown |
| café au lait | Roman umber |
| café noir | Saint Benoit |
| coconut | seal |
| Cologne brown | Sicilian umber |
| Cyprus earth *or* umber | suntan |
| | taupe brown |
| dead leaf | tawny |
| doeskin | tenné |
| drab | terra sienna |
| Dresden brown | terra umbra |
| dun | toast |
| *feuille-morte* [Fr] | topaz |
| foliage brown | Turkey umber |
| fox | umber |
| French nude | Vandyke brown, |
| Havana brown | Verona brown |
| hazel | |

.7 **reddish brown colors and pigments**

| | |
|---|---|
| Arabian red | madder brown |
| beef's blood | Malaga red |
| burgundy | oxblood |
| burnt ocher | oxide brown, oxide |
| burnt sienna | purple |
| Castilian brown | piccolopasso red |
| chestnut | red robin |
| Columbian red | roan |
| coptic | russet |
| cordovan | *sang de bœuf* [Fr] |
| henna | sienna |
| India red | Tanagra |
| Kazak | terra cotta |
| liver brown | Titian |

## 368. REDNESS

**.1** NOUNS **redness, reddishness,** rufosity, rubricity; **red,** *rouge* [Fr], gules; rubicundity, **ruddiness,** color, high color, floridness, floridity; rubor, erythema, erythroderma, "a fire-red cherubim's face" [Chaucer]; erythrism; reddish brown 367.7; red race 418.3; "any color, so long as it's red" [Eugene Field].

**.2 pinkness, pinkishness; rosiness; pink,** rose.

**.3 reddening,** rubefaction, rubification, rubescence, erubescence, rufescence; **coloring,** mantling, crimsoning, **blushing, flushing;** blush, flush, glow, bloom; hectic, hectic flush; rubefacient.

**.4** VERBS (make red) **redden,** rouge, ruddle, rubify, rubric; warm, inflame; crimson, encrimson; vermilion, madder, miniate, henna, rust, carmine; incarnadine, pinkify; red-ink, lipstick.

**.5 redden,** turn *or* grow red, **color,** color up, **mantle, blush, flush, crimson;** flame, glow.

**.6** ADJS **red, reddish,** gules [her], red-colored, red-hued, red-dyed, red-looking; **ruddy,** ruddied, rubicund; rubric(al), rubricate, rubricose; rufescent, rufous, rufulous; warm, hot, glowing; fiery, flaming, flame-colored, flame-red, fire-red, red as fire, lurid, red as a hot *or* live coal; reddened, inflamed; **scarlet, vermilion; crimson;** rubiate; maroon; damask; puce; stammel; cerise; iron-red; cardinal, cardinal-red; cherry, cherry-colored, cherry-red; carmine, incarmined; **ruby,** ruby-colored, ruby-red; wine, port-wine, wine-colored, wine-red, vinaceous; carnation, carnation-red; brick-red, brick-colored, bricky, tile-red, lateritious; rust, rust-red, rusty, ferruginous, rubiginous; lake-colored, laky; beet-red, red as a beet; lobster-red, red as a lobster; red as a turkey-cock; copper-red, carnelian; Titian, Titian-red; infrared; reddish-amber, reddish-gray, etc.; reddish-brown 367.4.

**.7 sanguine,** sanguineous, **blood-red,** blood-colored, bloody-red, bloody, gory, red as blood.

**.8 pink, pinkish,** pinky; **rose, rosy,** rose-colored, rose-hued, rose-red, roseate; primrose; flesh-color, flesh-colored, flesh-pink, incarnadine; coral, coral-colored, coral-red, coralline; salmon, salmon-colored, salmon-pink.

**.9 red-complexioned,** ruddy-complexioned, warm-complexioned, red-fleshed, red-faced, ruddy-faced, **ruddy,** rubicund,

**florid,** sanguine, full-blooded; blowzy, blowzed; rosy, **rosy-cheeked;** glowing, blooming; hectic, flushed, flush; burnt, sunburned; erythematous.

**.10 redheaded,** red-haired, red-polled, red-bearded; erythristic; red-crested, red-crowned, red-tufted; carroty, chestnut, auburn, Titian, xanthous.

**.11** reddening, blushing, flushing, coloring; rubescent, erubescent; rubificative, rubrific; rubefacient.

**.12 red colors and pigments**

| | |
|---|---|
| Adrianople red | light red |
| alizarin | livid brown |
| amidonaphthol red | lobster |
| annatto | madder |
| azogrenadine | madder carmine |
| azolitmin | madder crimson |
| bright rose | madder lake |
| Burgundy | madder pink |
| burnt carmine, burnt | madder purple |
| crimson lake, burnt | madder red |
| lake | madder rose |
| burnt ocher | Majolica earth |
| cardinal | maroon |
| carmine | minium |
| carmine lake | murrey |
| carminette | Naples red |
| carnation | old red |
| carnelian | palladium red |
| casino pink | peach red |
| Chinese red | Persian earth |
| chrome red | Persian red |
| chrome scarlet | phenosafranine |
| cinnabar | Pompeian red |
| claret, claret red, | ponceau |
| claret brown | poppy |
| cochineal | Prussian red |
| Congo rubine | puce |
| copper red | purple lake |
| coquelicot | raisin |
| cordovan | realgar |
| cresol red | red lead |
| cramoisie | red ocher |
| crimson | roccellin |
| crimson madder | royal red |
| damask | rubiate |
| English red | rubine |
| faded rose | ruby |
| fire red | ruddle |
| flame red | scarlet ocher |
| fuchsia red | sienna |
| fuchsine | solferino |
| Goya | stammel |
| gridelin, gris-de-lin | strawberry |
| Harvard crimson | terra rosa |
| hellebore red | tile red |
| Indian red | toluidine red |
| infrared | Turkey red |
| iron red | Vandyke red |
| Japanese red | Venetian red |
| jockey | vermilionette |
| lake | wine |

**.13 pink colors and pigments**

| | |
|---|---|
| amaranth pink | cameo pink |
| annatto | carnation rose |
| begonia | chrome primrose |
| burnt rose | fiesta |

flesh, flesh color
flesh red or pink
incarnadine
India pink
livid pink
madder scarlet
mallow pink
melon
moonlight
opera pink
orchid pink
orchid rose
peach
peachblossom pink

peach red
petal pink
Pompeii
primrose
red pink
rose
rose bengale
rose pink
royal pink
salmon
scarlet madder
shell pink
shocking pink
tea rose

## 369. ORANGENESS

.1 NOUNS orangeness, oranginess; orange.

.2 ADJS orange, orangeish, orangey or orangy, orange-hued, reddish-yellow; ocherous or ochery, ochrous or ochry, ochreous, ochroid, ocherish; old gold; pumpkin, pumpkin-colored; tangerine, tangerine-colored; apricot, peach; carroty, carrot-colored; orange-red, orange-yellow, red-orange, reddish-orange, yellow-orange, yellowish-orange.

.3 orange colors and pigments

apricot
azo-orange
burnt Italian earth
burnt ocher
burnt orange
burnt Roman ocher
burnt sienna
cadmium orange
cadmium yellow
carnelian
carotene
chrome orange
copper
copper red
Dutch orange
Florida gold
helianthin
hyacinth red
madder orange
mandarin
marigold
marigold yellow
Mars orange
methyl orange

ocher brown
ocher orange
ocher red
old gold
orange chrome yellow
orange lead
orange madder
orange mineral
orange ocher
orange vermilion
orpiment
orpiment red
pumpkin
raw sienna
realgar orange
Rubens' madder
Spanish ocher
tangerine
Tangier ocher
terra cotta
Titian
yellow carmine
zinc orange

## 370. YELLOWNESS

.1 NOUNS yellowness, yellowishness; goldenness, aureateness; yellow; gold, or; gildedness; fallowness.

.2 yellow skin, yellow complexion, sallowness; xanthochroism; jaundice, yellow jaundice, icterus, xanthoderma, xanthism; yellow race 418.2,3.

.3 VERBS yellow, turn yellow; gild, begild, engild; aurify; sallow; jaundice.

.4 ADJS yellow, yellowish, chrys(o)–, flav-(o)–, luteo–, xanth(o)–; lutescent, luteous, luteolous; xanthic, xanthous; gold,

golden, or [her], gold-colored, golden-yellow, gilt, gilded, auric, aureate; canary, canary-yellow; citron, citron-yellow, citreous; lemon, lemon-colored, lemon-yellow; sulfur-colored, sulfur-yellow; pale-yellow, sallow, fallow; cream, creamy, cream-colored; straw, straw-colored; flaxen, flaxen-colored, flax-colored; sandy, sand-colored; ocherous or ochery, ochrous or ochry, ochreous, ochroid, ocherish; buff, buff-colored, buff-yellow; beige, ecru; saffron, saffron-colored, saffron-yellow; primrose, primrose-colored, primrose-yellow; topaz-yellow.

.5 yellow-haired, golden-haired, auricomous, xanthous; blond 364.9.

.6 yellow-faced, yellow-complexioned, sallow, yellow-cheeked; jaundiced, xanthodermatous, icterous, icteroid.

.7 yellow colors and pigments

acid yellow
amber
apricot yellow
arsenic yellow
auramine
aureolin
azo flavine
azo yellow
barium chrome or chromate
barium yellow, baryta yellow
brilliant sulpho
buff
butter
cadmium yellow
California green
canarin
canary
Cassel yellow
chamois
champagne
chartreuse yellow
chrome
chrome lemon
chrome yellow
chrysophenin
Claude tint
crash
cream
crocus
curcumin
dandelion
Dutch pink
English pink
euxanthin
flax
gamboge
golden pheasant
goldenrod
golden yellow
grege
honey, honey yellow
Indian yellow
Italian pink
jonquil

king's yellow
lemon chrome
lemon yellow
madder yellow
maize
marigold yellow
massicot
metanil yellow
methyl yellow
middle stone
mikado yellow
milling yellow
naphthol yellow
oil yellow
old gold
old ivory
olivesheen
orpiment
Paris yellow
peach
pebble
permanent yellow
phosphine
primrose
primuline yellow
purree
pyrethrum yellow
quince yellow
quinoline yellow
saffron
sand
snapdragon
stil-de-grain yellow
straw
sulfur
sunflower yellow
tartrazine
yellow madder
yellow ocher
yellowstone
yolk yellow
xanthene
xanthin
xanthophyll
zinc yellow

# 371. GREENNESS

.1 NOUNS **greenness, greenishness; verdant-ness,** verdancy, verdure, virescence, viridescence, viridity; glaucousness, glaucescence; **green;** greensickness, chlorosis, chloremia, chloranemia; chlorophyll.

.2 **verdigris, patina;** patination.

.3 VERBS **green;** verdigris, patinate, patinize.

.4 ADJS **green,** chlor(o)–, verd(o)–; **verdant,** verdurous, vert [her]; grassy, leafy, leaved, foliaged; springlike, summerlike, summery, vernal, vernant, aestival; **greenish,** virescent; **grass-green,** chlorine, green as grass; citrine, citrinous; olive, olive-green, olivaceous; beryl-green, berylline; leek-green, porraceous [archaic]; holly, holly-green; ivy, ivy-green; emerald, emerald-green, smaragdine; chartreuse, yellow-green, yellowish-green, greenish-yellow; glaucous, glaucescent, glaucous-green; blue-green, bluish-green, green-blue, greenish-blue; greensick, chlorotic, chloremic, chloranemic.

.5 verdigrisy, verdigrised; patinous, patinaed, patinated or patinized.

.6 **green colors and pigments**

| | |
|---|---|
| absinthe | jade |
| apple green | Janus green |
| aqua green | Kelly green |
| aquamarine | Kendal green |
| avocado green | Kildare green |
| beryl green | leaf green |
| bice | leek green |
| bottle green | Lincoln green |
| Brunswick green | malachite green |
| celadon | marine green |
| chartreuse | meadow brook |
| chartreuse green | methyl green |
| chartreuse tint | mignonette |
| chrome or chromium green | milori green |
| | Mitis green |
| chrome oxide green | Mittler's green |
| chrysolite green | Montpellier green |
| chrysoprase green | moss green |
| citron green | myrtle |
| civette green | Nile green |
| cobalt green | olive |
| corbeau | Paris green |
| cucumber green | parrot green |
| cypress green | patina green |
| duck green | pea green |
| Egyptian green | pistachio green |
| emerald | Quaker green |
| emeraude | reseda |
| fir, fir green | Rinnemann's green |
| gallein | sap green |
| glauconite | Saxony green |
| glaucous | Schweinfurt green |
| glaucous green | sea or sea-water green |
| grass green | serpentine green |
| green ocher | shamrock |
| Guignet's green | smalt green |
| Guinea green | Spanish green |
| holly green | terre-verte |
| Irish green | turquoise |

| | |
|---|---|
| verdant green | Vienna green |
| verdet | viridian |
| verd gay | viridine green |
| verdigris | Wedgwood green |
| verditer | yew green |
| Veronese green | zinc green |

# 372. BLUENESS

.1 NOUNS **blueness, bluishness;** azureness; **blue, azure;** lividness, lividity; cyanosis, –cyan.

.2 VERBS **blue,** azure.

.3 ADJS **blue, bluish,** cyan(o)–, ind(i)– or indo–, cerulescent; cyanic or cyaneous or cyanean; cerulean or ceruleous; **azure** [her], azurine, azurean or azureous, azured, azure-blue, azure-colored, azure-tinted; sky-blue, sky-colored, sky-dyed; light-blue, lightish-blue, light-bluish, pale-blue; dark-blue, deep-blue; peacock-blue, pavonine, pavonian; beryl-blue, berylline; turquoise, turquoise-blue; sapphire, sapphire-blue, sapphirine; livid; cyanotic.

.4 **blue colors and pigments**

| | |
|---|---|
| Alice blue | indigo white |
| aniline blue | isamine blue |
| aquamarine | Italian blue |
| azo blue | jouvence blue |
| azulene | lacmoid |
| azure | lapis lazuli blue |
| azurite blue | lavender blue |
| baby blue | Leitch's blue |
| benzoazurine | madder blue |
| beryl | marine blue |
| bice | methylene azure |
| *bleu céleste* [Fr] | methylene blue |
| blue turquoise | midnight blue |
| bluing | milori blue |
| Brunswick blue | national blue |
| cadet blue | navy, navy blue |
| calamine blue | new blue |
| Capri blue | old blue |
| cerulean | peacock blue |
| Chinese blue | Persian blue |
| ciba blue | pompadour green |
| cobalt | Pompeian blue |
| Copenhagen blue | powder blue |
| cornflower | Prussian blue |
| cyan | robin's-egg blue |
| cyanine blue | Saxe blue |
| daylight blue | sea blue |
| delft blue | sky blue |
| Dresden blue | smalt |
| electric blue | smoke blue |
| *émail* [Fr] | steel blue |
| Empire blue | trypan blue |
| French blue | Turnbull's blue |
| garter blue | turquoise |
| gentian blue | ultramarine |
| glaucous blue | water blue |
| Gobelin blue | Wedgwood blue |
| hyacinth | wisteria blue |
| indanthrene blue | woad |
| indigo | zaffer |

## 373. PURPLENESS

**.1** NOUNS **purpleness, purplishness,** purpliness; **purple;** lividness, lividity.

**.2** VERBS **purple, empurple, purpurate** [archaic].

**.3** ADJS **purple, purpure** [her], **purpureal** or **purpureous** or **purpurean, purpurate** [archaic], **purpureo–, purpuri–; purplish, purply, purplescent; violet,** violaceous; **plum-colored, plum-purple;** amethystine; **lavender,** lavender-blue; **lilac;** magenta; mauve; mulberry; orchid; pansy-purple, pansy-violet; raisin-colored; livid.

**.4 purple colors and pigments**

| | |
|---|---|
| amethyst | magenta |
| aniline purple | mallow |
| Argyle purple | Mars violet |
| bishop's purple | mauve, mauveine |
| Burgundy violet | methyl violet |
| clematis | monsignor |
| dahlia | mulberry |
| damson | orchid |
| fluorite violet | pansy |
| fuchsia, fuchsia purple | pansy purple |
| fuchsia red | pansy violet |
| grape | Perkin's purple, Perkin's violet |
| grape wine | |
| gridelin | plum |
| heliotrope | pontiff purple |
| Hortense violet | prune purple |
| hyacinth | raisin black |
| hyacinth violet | raisin purple |
| imperial purple | regal purple, royal purple |
| king's purple | |
| lavender | solferino |
| lilac | Tyrian purple |
| livid purple | violet |
| livid violet | wine purple |
| madder violet | |

## 374. VARIEGATION

*(diversity of colors)*

**.1** NOUNS **variegation, multicolor,** particolor; **medley** or **riot of colors;** polychrome, polychromatism; dichromatism, trichromatism, etc.; dichroism, trichroism, etc.

**.2** iridescence, iridization, irisation, **opalescence,** nacreousness, pearliness, **play of colors** or **light;** light show; moiré pattern, burelage.

**.3** spottiness, maculation, freckliness, speckliness, mottledness, dappleness, dappledness, stippledness, spottedness, dottedness; **fleck, speck, speckle;** freckle; **spot,** dot, polka dot, macula, macule, blotch, splotch, patch, splash; **mottle, dapple; stipple,** stippling, pointillism, pointillage.

**.4 check, checker; plaid,** tartan; checkerwork, variegated pattern, harlequin, colors in patches, crazy-work, patchwork;

parquet, parquetry, marquetry, mosaic, tesserae, tessellation; chessboard, checkerboard; crazy-paving [Brit].

**.5 stripe, striping, streak, streaking;** striation, striature, stria; striola, striga; crack, craze; bar, band, belt, list.

**.6** (comparisons) spectrum, rainbow, iris, chameleon, leopard, jaguar, cheetah, ocelot, zebra, barber's pole, candy cane, Dalmatian, firedog, peacock, butterfly, mother-of-pearl, nacre, tortoise shell, opal, serpentine, chrysotile, antigorite, serpentine marble, marble, ophite, mackerel, mackerel sky, confetti, crazy quilt, patchwork quilt, shot silk, moiré, watered silk, marbled paper, Joseph's coat, harlequin.

**.7** VERBS **variegate,** motley; polychrome, polychromize; harlequin; **mottle, dapple,** stipple, **fleck,** flake, **speck, speckle,** bespeckle, freckle, **spot,** bespot, dot, sprinkle, spangle, bespangle, pepper, stud, maculate; blotch, splotch; tattoo, stigmatize [archaic]; **check, checker;** tessellate; **stripe, streak,** striate, band, bar, vein; marble, marbleize; rainbow, iris.

**.8** iridesce, iridize, iris; **opalesce,** opalize; moiré.

**.9** ADJS **variegated, many-colored,** manyhued, divers-colored, **multicolored,** multicolor, multicolorous, **varicolored,** varicolorous, polychrome, polychromic, polychromatic, poecil(o)– or poikil(o)–, parti– or party–; parti-colored, parti-color; of all manner of colors, of all the colors of the rainbow; versicolor, versicolored, versicolorate, versicolorous; motley, medley [archaic], harlequin; colorful, colory; daedal; crazy; thunder and lightning; kaleidoscopic(al); prismatic(al), prismal, spectral; shot, shot through; bicolored, bicolor, dichromic, dichromatic; tricolored, tricolor, trichromic, trichromatic; two-color or -colored, three-color or -colored, two-tone or -toned, etc.

**.10** **iridescent,** iridal, iridial, iridian, irid(o)–; irised, irisated, **rainbowy,** rainbowlike; **opalescent,** opaline, opaloid; nacreous, nacry, *nacré* [Fr], nacred, **pearly,** pearlish, mother-of-pearl; tortoise-shell; peacocklike, pavonine, pavonian; chatoyant; moiré, burelé.

**.11 chameleonlike,** chameleonic.

**.12 mottled, motley; pied, piebald,** skewbald, pinto; **dappled,** dapple; calico; marbled; clouded; pepper-and-salt.

**.13** spotted, **dotted,** polka-dot, sprinkled, peppered, studded, pocked, pockmarked;

spotty, dotty, patchy, pocky; **speckled, specked,** speckledy, speckly, specky; **stippled,** pointillé, pointillistic; **flecked,** fleckered; spangled, bespangled; maculate, maculated, macular, macul(o)– or maculi–; punctate, punctated; freckled, frecked, freckly; blotched, blotchy, splotched, splotchy; flea-bitten.

.14 **checked,** checkered, check; **plaid,** plaided; tessellated, tessellate, mosaic.

.15 **striped,** stripy, **streaked,** streaky; **striated,** striate, striatal, striolate, strigate or strigose; barred, banded, listed; veined; **brindle,** brindled, brinded; tabby; marbled, marbleized; watered.

## 375. UNIVERSE

.1 NOUNS **universe, world, cosmos,** –cosm, cosm(o)–; creation, created universe, created nature, all, **all creation,** all or everything that is, all being, totality, totality of being, sum of things; omneity, allness; nature, system; wide world, whole wide world, "world without end" [Bible]; plenum; macrocosm, macrocosmos, megacosm; metagalaxy; steady-state universe, expanding universe, pulsating universe; Einsteinian universe, Newtonian universe; Ptolemaic universe, Copernican universe; sidereal universe.

.2 **heavens,** heaven, **sky, firmament,** uran(o)–; empyrean, welkin, caelum [L], lift or lifts [both dial]; **the blue,** blue sky, azure, cerulean, the blue serene; **ether, air,** hyaline, "the clear hyaline, the glassy sea" [Milton]; vault, cope, canopy, vault or canopy of heaven, "the arch of heaven" [Vergil], "that inverted bowl they call the sky" [Omar Khayyám], "heaven's ebon vault" [Shelley], starry heaven or heavens, "this majestical roof fretted with golden fire" [Shakespeare]; Caelus [Rom myth].

.3 **space, outer space,** cosmic space, empty space, ether space, pressureless space, celestial spaces, interplanetary or interstellar or intergalactic or intercosmic space, metagalactic space, **the void,** the void above, ocean of emptiness; chaos; outermost reaches of space; astronomical unit, light-year, parsec.

.4 **stars,** fixed stars, starry host, "living sapphires" [Milton], "all the fire-folk sitting in the air" [G. M. Hopkins], "the burning tapers of the sky" [Shakespeare], "the mystical jewels of God" [Robert Buchanan], "golden fruit upon a tree all out of reach" [George Eliot], "bright sentinels

of the sky" [William Habington], "the pale populace of Heaven" [R. Browning]; music or harmony of the spheres; orb, sphere; **heavenly body,** celestial body or sphere; **comet; morning star,** daystar, Lucifer, Phosphor, Phosphorus; **evening star,** Vesper, Hesper, Hesperus, Venus; **North Star,** polestar, polar star, lodestar, Polaris; Dog Star, Sirius, Canicula; Bull's Eye, Aldebaran.

.5 **constellation** 375.28, **configuration,** asterism.

.6 **galaxy, island universe,** galactic nebula, galact(o)–; spiral galaxy or nebula, spiral; barred spiral galaxy or nebula, barred spiral; elliptical or spheroidal galaxy; **Milky Way,** galactic circle, Via Lactea [L]; galactic cluster, supergalaxy; galactic coordinates, galactic pole, galactic latitude, galactic longitude; galactic noise, cosmic noise.

.7 **nebula,** nebulosity; gaseous nebula; dust cloud; planetary nebula; ring nebula; diffuse nebula; bright diffuse nebula; dark nebula, dark cloud, coalsack; Nebula of Lyra or Orion, Crab Nebula, the Coalsack, Black Magellanic Cloud; nebulous stars; nebular hypothesis.

.8 **star,** aster(o)–, astr(o)–, sidero–; fixed star; giant star, red giant star; main sequence star; dwarf star, white dwarf star; binary star, double star; nova, supernova; variable star, Cepheid variable; radio star, quasar, quasi-stellar radio source; pulsar; neutron star; gravity star; black hole; magnitude, stellar magnitude, relative magnitude, absolute magnitude; populations; mass-luminosity law; spectrum-luminosity diagram, Hertzsprung-Russell diagram; star catalog, star chart, sky atlas, Messier catalog, Dreyer's New General Catalog or NGC; star cloud, star cluster, globular cluster, open cluster; Pleiades or Seven Sisters, Hyades, Beehive.

.9 **planet,** wanderer, terrestrial planet, inferior planet, superior planet, secondary planet, major planet; minor planet, planetoid, asteroid; Earth; Jupiter; Mars, areo–; Mercury; Neptune; Pluto; Saturn; Uranus; Venus; solar system.

.10 **Earth, world,** terra [L], tellur(o)– or telluri–; **globe,** terrestrial globe, the blue planet; geosphere, biosphere; vale, vale of tears; "this pendent world", "the little O, the earth", "this goodly frame, the earth", "a stage where every man must play a part" [all Shakespeare], "a seat where gods might dwell" [Milton];

mother earth, Ge or Gaea, Tellus or Terra; whole wide world, four corners of the earth, "the round earth's imagined corners" [Donne], the length and breadth of the land; geography 385.4.

.11 **moon, satellite,** selen(o)- or seleni-; orb of night, queen of heaven, queen of night, "that orbèd maiden" [Shelley], "the wat'ry star" [Shakespeare], "the governess of floods" [Shakespeare], "a ghostly galleon tossed upon cloudy seas" [Alfred Noyes], "Maker of sweet poets" [Keats], "the wandering Moon" [Milton], "bright wanderer, fair coquette of Heaven" [Shelley], "Queen and huntress, chaste and fair" [Ben Jonson], "sovereign mistress of the true melancholy" [Shakespeare], "a ruined world, a globe burnt out, a corpse upon the road of night" [Robert Burton]; silvery moon; **new moon,** wet moon; **crescent moon,** crescent, increscent moon, increscent, waxing moon, waxing crescent moon; decrescent moon, decrescent, waning moon, waning crescent moon; gibbous moon; **half-moon,** demilune; **full moon, harvest moon,** hunter's moon; artificial satellite 282.6,14.

.12 (moon goddess, the moon personified) Diana, Phoebe, Cynthia, Artemis, Hecate or Hekate, Selene, Luna, Astarte, Ashtoreth; man in the moon.

.13 **sun,** heli(o)-; orb of day, daystar; "the glorious lamp of Heav'n, the radiant sun" [Dryden], "that orbed continent, the fire that severs day from night" [Shakespeare], "of this great world both eye and soul" [Milton], "the God of life and poesy and light" [Byron]; photosphere, chromosphere, corona; sunspot; solar flare, solar prominence; solar wind.

.14 (sun god, the sun personified) Sol, Helios, Hyperion, Titan, Phaëthon, Phoebus, Phoebus Apollo, Apollo, Ra or Amen-Ra, Shamash, Surya, Savitar.

.15 **meteor,** meteor(o)-; falling or shooting star, meteoroid, fireball, bolide; **meteorite,** meteorolite; micrometeoroid, micrometeorite; aerolite; chondrite; siderite; siderolite; tektite; meteor dust, cosmic dust; meteor trail, meteor train; meteor swarm; meteor or meteoric shower; radiant, radiant point; meteor crater.

.16 **orbit, circle, trajectory;** circle of the sphere, great circle, small circle; **ecliptic; zodiac;** zone; meridian, celestial meridian; colures, equinoctial colure, solstitial colure; equator, celestial equator, equi-

noctial, equinoctial circle or line; equinox, vernal equinox, autumnal equinox; longitude, celestial longitude, geocentric longitude, heliocentric longitude, galactic longitude, astronomical longitude, geographic or geodetic longitude; apogee, perigee; aphelion, perihelion; period.

.17 **observatory,** astronomical observatory; radio observatory, orbiting astronomical observatory or OAO, orbiting solar observatory or OSO; **planetarium;** orrery; **telescope,** astronomical telescope; reflector, refractor, Newtonian telescope, Cassegrainian telescope; **radio telescope,** radar telescope; **spectroscope,** spectrograph; spectrohelioscope, spectroheliograph; coronagraph or coronograph; heliostat, coelostat.

.18 **cosmology,** cosmography, **cosmogony;** stellar cosmogony, astrogony; cosmism, cosmic philosophy, cosmic evolution; nebular hypothesis; big bang or expanding universe theory, oscillating or pulsating universe theory, steady state or continuous creation theory.

.19 **astronomy, stargazing,** uranology, astrognosy, astrography, uranography, uranometry; astrophotography, stellar photometry; spectrography, spectroscopy, radio astronomy, radar astronomy; **astrophysics,** solar physics; celestial mechanics, gravitational astronomy; astrolithology; meteoritics; astrogeology.

.20 **astrology,** stargazing, astromancy, **horoscopy;** astrodiagnosis; natural astrology; judicial or mundane astrology; genethliacism, genethlialogy, genethliacs, genethliac astrology; **horoscope,** nativity; zodiac, **signs of the zodiac; house,** mansion; house of life, mundane house, planetary house or mansion; aspect.

.21 **cosmologist;** cosmogonist, cosmogoner; cosmographer, cosmographist; cosmic philosopher, cosmist.

.22 **astronomer,** stargazer, uranologist, uranometrist, uranographer, uranographist, astrographer, astrophotographer; radio astronomer, radar astronomer; **astrophysicist,** solar physicist; astrogeologist.

.23 **astrologer,** astrologian, astromancer, stargazer, Chaldean, astroalchemist, horoscoper, horoscopist, genethliac [archaic].

.24 ADJS **cosmic,** cosmical, **universal;** cosmologic(al), cosmogonal, cosmogonic(al); cosmographic(al).

.25 **celestial, heavenly, empyrean,** empyreal; uranic; **astral, starry, stellar,** stellary, sphery; star-spangled, star-studded; sidereal; zodiacal; equinoctial; **astronomic(al)**, **astrophysical**, **astrologic(al)**, astrologistic, astrologous; **planetary**, planetarian, planetal, circumplanetary; planetoidal, planetesimal, asteroidal; **solar**, heliacal; terrestrial 385.6; **lunar**, lunular, lunate, lunulate, lunary, cislunar, translunar, Cynthian; semilunar; meteoric, meteoritic; extragalactic, anagalactic; galactic; nebular, nebulous, nebulose; interstellar, intersidereal; interplanetary; intercosmic.

.26 **extraterrestrial**, exterrestrial, extraterrene, extramundane, alien, space; **transmundane, otherworldly**, transcendental; extrasolar.

.27 ADVS **universally**, everywhere 179.11.

.28 **constellations**

| | |
|---|---|
| Andromeda, the Chained Lady | Corona Australis, the Wreath, the Southern Crown |
| Antlia or Antlia Pneumatica, the Air Pump | Corona Borealis, the Northern Crown |
| Apus, the Bird of Paradise | Corvus, the Crow |
| Aquarius, the Water Bearer | Crater, the Cup Crux, the Cross, |
| Aquila, the Eagle | Cygnus, the Swan |
| Ara, the Altar | Delphinus, the Dolphin |
| Argo or Argo Navis, the Ship Argo | Dorado, the Dorado Fish |
| Aries, the Ram | Draco, the Dragon |
| Auriga, the Charioteer | Equuleus, the Foal |
| Big Dipper, Charles' Wain | Eridanus, the River Po |
| Boötes, the Herdsman | Fornax, the Furnace |
| Caelum or Caela Sculptoris, the Sculptor's Tool | Gemini, the Twins Grus, the Crane Hercules |
| Camelopardalis or Camelopardus, the Giraffe | Horologium, the Clock |
| Cancer, the Crab | Hydra, the Sea Serpent |
| Canes Venatici, the Hunting Dogs | Hydrus, the Water Snake |
| Canis Major, the Larger Dog, Orion's Hound | Indus, the Indian Lacerta, the Lizard Leo, the Lion |
| Canis Minor, the Lesser Dog | Leo Minor, the Lesser Lion |
| Capricorn, the Horned Goat | Lepus, the Hare Libra, the Balance |
| Carina, the Keel | Little Dipper |
| Cassiopeia, the Lady in the Chair | Lupus, the Wolf Lynx, the Lynx |
| Centaurus, the Centaur | Lyra, the Lyre Malus, the Mast |
| Cepheus, the Monarch | Mensa, the Table Microscopium, the |
| Cetus, the Whale | Microscope |
| Chamaeleon, the Chameleon | Monoceros, the Unicorn |
| Circinus, the Compasses | Musca, the Fly Norma, the Rule |
| Columba or Columba Noae, Noah's Dove | Northern Cross Octans, the Octant |
| Coma Berenices, Berenice's Hair | Ophiuchus, the Serpent Bearer |

| | |
|---|---|
| Orion, the Giant Hunter | Sextans, the Sextant Southern Cross |
| Orion's Belt | Taurus, the Bull |
| Orion's Sword | Telescopium, the |
| Pavo, the Peacock | Telescope |
| Pegasus, the Winged Horse | Triangulum, the Triangle |
| Perseus | Triangulum Australe, |
| Phoenix, the Phoenix | the Southern Triangle |
| Pictor, the Painter | gle |
| Pisces, the Fishes | Tucana, the Toucan |
| Piscis Australis, the Southern Fish | Ursa Major, the Great Bear |
| Puppis, the Stern | Ursa Minor, the |
| Reticulum, the Net | Lesser Bear |
| Sagitta, the Arrow | Vela, the Sails |
| Sagittarius, the Archer | Virgo, the Virgin |
| Scorpio or Scorpius, the Scorpion | Volans or Piscis Volans, the Flying Fish |
| Sculptor, the Sculptor | |
| Scutum, the Shield | Vulpecula, the Little |
| Serpens, the Serpent | Fox |

# 376. MATERIALITY

.1 NOUNS **materiality**, materialness; **corporeity**, corporality, corporeality, corporealness, bodiliness, embodiment, –somia; **substantiality**, concreteness 3.1; **physicalness**, physicality, physi(o)–, physic(o)–; flesh, flesh and blood, sarc(o)–, –sarc.

.2 **matter, material**, materiality, **substance** 3.2, **stuff**, hyle, hyl(o)–; brute matter; **element**; chemical element 379.1,10; the four elements; earth, air, fire, water; elementary particle, fundamental particle; elementary unit, building block, unit of being, monad; constituent, component; **atom** 326.4,21; atomic particles 326.6; **molecule**; material world, physical world, nature, natural world; hypostasis, substratum; plenum.

.3 **body**, physical body, material body, corpus [informal], anatomy [informal], person, **figure, form**, frame, **physique**, carcass [informal], bones, flesh, clay, clod, hulk; soma, somat(o)–, –some, –somus; torso, trunk.

.4 **object, article, thing**, material thing, affair, something; what's-its-name 584.2; something or other, etwas [Ger], eppes [Yid], quelque chose [Fr]; artifact; gadget 348.1; thingum, **thingumabob**, thingumadad, thingumadoodle, **thingumajig**, thingumajigger, thingumaree, thingummy, **doodad**, dofunny, **dojigger**, dojiggy, domajig, domajigger, **dohickey**, dowhacky, flumadiddle, gigamaree, **gimmick, gizmo**, dingus, hickey, jigger, hootmalalie, hootenanny, whatchy, widget [all slang or informal].

.5 **materialism**, physicism, epiphenomenalism, identity theory of mind, atomism, mechanism; physicalism, behaviorism, instrumentalism, pragmatism, pragmaticism; historical materialism, dialectical materialism, Marxism; **positivism,** logical positivism, positive philosophy, empiricism, **naturalism;** realism, natural realism, commonsense realism, commonsense philosophy, naïve realism, new realism, critical realism, representative realism, epistemological realism; substantialism; hylomorphism; hylotheism; hylozoism; worldliness, earthliness, animalism, secularism, temporality.

.6 **materialist,** physicist, atomist; historical *or* dialectical materialist, Marxist; **naturalist;** realist, natural realist, commonsense realist, commonsense philosopher, epistemological realist.

.7 **materialization,** corporealization; substantialization, substantiation; **embodiment, incorporation,** personification, **incarnation; reincarnation,** reembodiment, transmigration, metempsychosis.

.8 VERBS **materialize,** corporealize; substantialize, substantify, substantiate; **embody** 3.5, body, **incorporate,** corporify, personify, **incarnate; reincarnate,** reembody, transmigrate.

.9 ADJS **material,** materiate, hylic, **substantial** 3.6; **corporeal,** corporeous, corporal, **bodily; physical,** somatic(al), –somatous; **fleshly;** worldly, earthly, **secular,** temporal, **unspiritual,** nonspiritual.

.10 **embodied,** bodied, **incorporated, incarnate.**

.11 **materialist** *or* **materialistic,** atomistic, mechanist, mechanistic; Marxian, Marxist; **naturalist, naturalistic, positivist,** positivistic; commonsense, **realist,** realistic; hylotheistic; hylomorphous; hylozoic, hylozoistic.

### 377. IMMATERIALITY

.1 NOUNS **immateriality,** immaterialness; incorporeity, incorporeality, incorporealness, **bodilessness; unsubstantiality** 4, unsubstantialness; **intangibility,** impalpability, imponderability; inextension, nonextension; nonexteriority, nonexternality; **unearthliness, unworldliness; supernaturalism** 85.7; **spirituality,** spiritualness, spirituousness [archaic], otherworldliness, ghostliness, shadowiness; occultism 1034, the occult, occult phenomena; psychism, psychics, psychic *or* psychical research, psychicism; spirit world, astral plane.

.2 incorporeal, incorporeity, immateriality, unsubstantiality 4.

.3 **immaterialism, idealism,** philosophical idealism, metaphysical idealism; objective idealism; absolute idealism; epistemological idealism; monistic idealism, pluralistic idealism; critical idealism; transcendental idealism; subjectivism; solipsism; subjective idealism; **spiritualism;** personalism; panpsychism, psychism, animism, hylozoism, animatism; Platonism, Platonic realism, Berkeleianism, Cambridge Platonism, Kantianism, Hegelianism, New England Transcendentalism; Neoplatonism; Platonic idea *or* ideal *or* form, pure form, form, universal; transcendental object; transcendental.

.4 immaterialist, **idealist;** Berkelean, Platonist, Hegelian, Kantian; Neoplatonist; **spiritualist;** psychist, panpsychist, animist.

.5 dematerialization; **disembodiment,** disincarnation; **spiritualization.**

.6 VERBS dematerialize, immaterialize, unsubstantialize, insubstantialize, desubstantialize, **disembody,** disincarnate; **spiritualize,** spiritize.

.7 ADJS **immaterial,** nonmaterial; **unsubstantial** 4.5, insubstantial, **intangible,** impalpable, imponderable; unextended, extensionless; **incorporeal,** incorporate, incorporeous; **bodiless,** unembodied, without body, asomatous; **disembodied,** disbodied, discarnate, decarnate, decarnated; **unphysical,** nonphysical; **unfleshly;** airy, ghostly, phantom, shadowy, ethereal; **spiritual,** astral, psychic(al); **unearthly, unworldly, otherworldly,** extramundane, transmundane; supernatural 85.15; occult 1034.22.

.8 **idealist, idealistic, immaterialist,** immaterialistic; solipsistic; spiritualist, spiritualistic; panpsychist, panpsychistic; animist, animistic; Platonic, Platonistic, Berkeleian, Hegelian, Kantian; Neoplatonic, Neoplatonistic.

### 378. MATERIALS

.1 NOUNS **materials,** substances, stuff; raw **material, staple, stock;** material resources *or* means; store, supply 660; strategic materials; matériel; –ing.

.2 (building materials) sticks and stones, lath and plaster, bricks and mortar; roofing, roofage; walling, siding; flooring, pavement 657.7, paving material, paving; masonry, flag, flagstone, ashlar, stone 384.1,12; covering materials 228.43; mortar, plasters 228.44; cement, concrete, cyclopean concrete, ferroconcrete, prestressed concrete, reinforced concrete; brick, firebrick, clinker, adobe; tile, tiling.

**.3 wood** 378.9, **lumber, timber,** hyl(o)–, lign(o)– *or* ligni–, xyl(o)–; hardwood, softwood; stick, stick of wood, stave; billet; pole, post," beam 217.3, **board,** plank; deal; two-by-four, three-by-four, etc.; slab, puncheon; slat, splat, lath; boarding, timbering, timberwork, planking; lathing, lathwork; sheeting; paneling 378.10, panelboard, panelwork; plywood, plyboard; sheathing,˙ sheathing board; siding, sideboard; weatherboard, clapboard; shingle, shake; log; driftwood; firewood, stovewood; cordwood; cord.

**.4** cane, bamboo, rattan.

**.5 fabric** 378.11, **cloth, rag, textile,** textile fabric, texture, tissue, stuff, weave, weft, woof, web, **material, goods,** drapery, *étoffe, tissu* [both Fr]; napery, table linen, felt, pil(o)– *or* pili–; silk, sereiceo–; wool 230.2; lace 378.12.

**.6 paper** 378.13, papyro–; sheet, leaf, page; quire, ream, stationery 602.29; cardboard.

**.7 synthetic;** synthetic fabric *or* textile *or* cloth; synthetic rubber; **plastic** 378.14, –plast, plasto–; thermoplastic; thermosetting plastic; resin plastic; cellulose plastic; protein plastic; cast plastic, molded plastic, extruded plastic; molding compounds; laminate; adhesive 50.13; plasticizer; polymer.

**.8** VERBS gather *or* procure materials; **store, stock,** stock up 660.10–13; **process,** utilize.

**.9 woods**

| | |
|---|---|
| acacia | hazel, hazelwood |
| alder | hemlock |
| applewood | hickory |
| ash | incense wood |
| balsa | ironwood |
| balsam | juniper |
| banyan | knotty pine |
| bass, basswood | lancewood |
| beech, beechwood | larch |
| birch | lemonwood |
| brierwood, briarwood | lignum vitae |
| burl | linden |
| buttonwood | loblolly pine |
| cedar, cedarwood | locust |
| cherry | logwood |
| chestnut | magnolia |
| cork | mahogany |
| cottonwood | maple |
| cypress | oak |
| dogwood | olive |
| ebony | orangewood |
| elm, elmwood | peachwood |
| eucalyptus | pecan |
| fir | Philippine mahogany |
| fruit wood | pine |
| gum, gumwood | poplar |

| | |
|---|---|
| Port Orford cedar | sycamore |
| redwood | teak, teakwood |
| rosewood | tulipwood |
| sandalwood | tupelo |
| satinwood | walnut |
| spruce | yew |
| sumac | zebrawood |

**.10 panelings**

| | |
|---|---|
| beaver board | Panelyte |
| Celotex | pegboard |
| Coltwood | plasterboard |
| Compoboard | plastic plywood |
| compreg | plyboard |
| fiberboard | plywood |
| firred plywood | Pregwood |
| Formica | pressed hardboard |
| hardboard | Reziwood |
| impreg | Sheetrock |
| Lamicoid | wallboard |
| laminated wood | Weldwood |
| Masonite | |

**.11 fabrics**

| | |
|---|---|
| acetate *or* acetate | chintz |
|   rayon | coating |
| Acrilan | cord |
| alpaca | corduroy |
| Aralac | corseting |
| arras | cotton |
| astrakhan | cotton cambric |
| Avisco | covert cloth |
| awning cloth | crash |
| Axminster | crepe |
| baize | crepe de chine |
| balbriggan | cretonne |
| Banlon | crinoline |
| batik | Dacron |
| batiste | damask |
| blanketing | denim |
| *bouclé* [Fr] | dimity |
| broadcloth | doeskin |
| broadloom | Donegal tweed |
| brocade | double-knit |
| brocatel | *drap d'or* [Fr] |
| buckram | drill |
| bunting | drilling |
| burlap | drugget |
| byssus | duck |
| calico | duffel |
| cambric | dungaree |
| cambric muslin | duvetyn |
| camel's hair | Dynel |
| Canton flannel | faille |
| canvas | felt |
| carpeting | fine linen |
| casheen | flannel |
| cashmere | flannelette |
| cassimere | fleece |
| castor | foulard |
| Celanese | frieze |
| Celanese acetate | fustian |
| challis | gabardine |
| chambray | gauze |
| cheesecloth | Georgette, Georgette |
| chenille |   crepe |
| chenille Axminster | gingham |
| cheviot | gossamer |
| chiffon | grenadine |
| China silk | grogram |
| chinchilla | grosgrain |
| chino | gunny |

haircloth
Harris Tweed
herringbone
hessian
homespun
hop sacking
horsehair
huck
huckaback
Jacquard
jean
jersey
knitwear
lamé
Lastex
lawn
Leatherette
linen
Linene
linenette
linoleum
linsey-woolsey
lisle
list
loden
longcloth
luster
mackinaw
mackintosh
madras
malines, maline
manta
mantua
marquisette
marseilles
mat
matting
melton
messaline
mohair
moiré
moleskin
monk's cloth
mousseline [Fr]
mousseline de soie
  [Fr]
murrey
muslin
nainsook
nankeen
near-silk
net
netting
nylon
oilcloth
oil silk
organdy
organza
Orlon
paisley
panne, panne velvet
pepper-and-salt
percale
permanent-press fab-
  ric
piqué
plaid
plush
polyester
pongee
poplin
print

Qiana
quilting
radium
rayon
rayon casheen
rep
Revolite
rugging
russet
sackcloth
sacking
sailcloth
samite
sarcenet
Sarelon
sateen
satin
say
scrim
seersucker
serge
shalloon
shantung
sharkskin
sheers
sheeting
shirting
shoddy
shot silk
silk
spun rayon
stamin
stammel
stockinette
stuff
suède, suède cloth
swansdown
tabaret
tabby
taffeta, taffety
tapestry
tarpaulin
tartan
terry, terry cloth
Terylene
tick, ticking
toile [Fr]
toweling
tricot
tricotine
tulle
tussah
tussore
tweed
twill
Ultrasuede
veiling
Velon
velours
velure
velvet
velveteen
Vicara
vicuña
Vinyon
voile
wash-and-wear fabric
watered fabric
webbing
wool
worsted

**.12 laces**

Alençon lace
bobbinet
bobbin lace
bobbin net
Brussels point
Carrickmacross lace
Chantilly lace
Dieppe lace
duchesse lace
fillet, filet lace
Greek lace or point
guipure
Mechlin lace

mignonette lace
Milan point
needlepoint
pillow lace
point, point lace
reticella
Roman lace or point
Shetland lace
tambour lace
tatting
Teneriffe lace
Valenciennes
Venetian point

**.13 papers**

art paper
baryta paper
Bible paper
binder's board
blotting paper
blueprint paper
bond paper
butcher paper
carbon, carbon paper
cardboard
cartridge paper
cellophane
cigarette paper
cloth paper
construction paper
copy or copying paper
crepe, crepe paper
crown paper
curlpaper
drawing paper
endpaper
facial tissue
filter paper
flimsy
flypaper
foolscap
gift wrap
graph paper
grass paper
hand paper
hand tissue
ice paper
India paper
kraft paper
lace paper
laid paper
ledger paper
letter paper
litmus paper
manila, Manila paper

matrix paper
millboard
music paper
newspaper
newsprint
note paper
oak tag
onionskin
paperboard
paper toweling
papier-mâché
papyrus
paraffin paper
parchment
pasteboard
plate paper
proof paper
pulpboard
rag paper
rice paper
roofing paper
sepia paper
sheathing paper
shop paper
stipple paper
strawboard
sulfate paper
tar paper
tissue, tissue paper
toilet tissue or paper
tracing paper
transfer paper
typewriter paper
vellum
wallpaper
wastepaper
wax or waxed paper
wrapping paper
writing paper

**.14 plastics**

acetate
acetate nitrate
acrylic
alkyd
aminoplast
Bakelite
Buna
casein plastic
cellophane
Celluloid
cellulose acetate
cellulose ether

cellulose nitrate
cellulosic
coumarone-indene
epoxy
fluorocarbon plastic
Formica
furane
lignin
Lucite
melamine
multiresin
Mylar

neoprene
nitrate
nylon
Perspex
phenolic
phenolic urea
Plexiglas
polyester
polyethylene
polymeric amide
polypropylene
polystyrene
polyurethane
polyvinyl chloride,

PVC
polyvinyl-formalde-
  hyde
resinoid
silicone resin
Styrofoam
Teflon
terpene
tetrafluoroethylene
urea
urea formaldehyde
vinyl
Vinylite

## 379. CHEMICALS

.1 NOUNS **chemical,** chem(o)– *or* chemi–, chemic(o)–; organic chemical, biochemical, inorganic chemical; fine chemicals, heavy chemicals; **element,** chemical element; **radical; ion,** anion, cation; **atom** 326.4,21; **molecule,** macromolecule; **compound;** isomer, pseudoisomer, stereoisomer, diastereoisomer, enantiomer, enantiomorph, alloisomer, chromoisomer, metamer, polymer, copolymer, interpolymer, high polymer, homopolymer, monomer, dimer, trimer, etc., oligomer, –mer(e), –meride; **agent, reagent; acid,** aci–, hydracid, oxyacid, sulfacid; acidity; **base,** basi–, baso–, **alkali,** nonacid; neutralizer, antacid; alkalinity.

.2 **trace element,** microelement, micronutrient, minor element.

.3 **valence,** valency [Brit], positive valence, negative valence; monovalence, univalence, bivalence, trivalence, tervalence, quadrivalence, tetravalence, etc., multivalence, polyvalence; covalence, electrovalence.

.4 **atomic weight,** atomic mass, atomic volume, mass number; **molecular weight,** molecular mass, molecular volume; atomic number, valence number.

.5 **chemicalization;** alkalization, alkalinization; acidification, acidulation, acetification; carbonation, chlorination, hydration, hydrogenation, saturation, hydroxylation, nitration, phosphatization; oxidation, oxidization; reduction; sulfation, sulfatization, sulfonation; isomerization, metamerization, polymerization, copolymerization, homopolymerization; isomerism, geometric isomerism, optical isomerism, position isomerism, tautoisomerism, metamerism, polymerism, copolymerism; fermentation, ferment, working; catalysis 53.2; electrolysis 342.22.

.6 VERBS **chemicalize,** chemical; alkalize, alkalinize, alkalify; acidify, acidulate, ace-

tify; borate, carbonate, chlorinate, hydrate, hydrogenate, hydroxylate, nitrate, oxidize, reduce, pepsinate, peroxidize, phosphatize, sulfate, sulfatize, sulfonate; isomerize, metamerize, polymerize, copolymerize, homopolymerize; ferment, work; catalyze 53.4; electrolyze 342.25.

.7 ADJS **chemical;** biochemical, chemicobiologic; physicochemical, physiochemical, chemicophysical, chemicobiological, chemicophysiologic(al), chemicodynamic, chemicoengineering, chemicomechanical, chemicomineralogical, chemicopharmaceutical, chemurgic, electrochemical, iatrochemical, chemotherapeutic(al), chemophysiologic(al), macrochemical, microchemical, phytochemical, photochemical, radiochemical, thermochemical, zoochemical; elemental, elementary; acid 432.7; alkaline, alkali, nonacid, basic; isomeric, isomerous, metameric, metamerous, heteromerous, polymeric, polymerous, copolymeric, copolymerous, monomeric, monomerous, dimeric, dimerous, etc.

.8 **valent;** univalent, monovalent, monatomic, bivalent, trivalent, tervalent, quadrivalent, tetravalent, etc., multivalent, polyvalent; covalent, electrovalent.

.9 **chemistry**

| | |
|---|---|
| actinochemistry | macrochemistry |
| alchemy | magnetochemistry |
| analytical chemistry | metallurgical chemis- |
| applied chemistry | try |
| astrochemistry | microchemistry |
| atomic chemistry | mineralogical chemis- |
| biochemistry | try |
| biogeochemistry | neurochemistry |
| business chemistry | nuclear chemistry |
| chemiatry | organic chemistry |
| chemical dynamics | pathological chemis- |
| chemical engineering | try, pathochemistry |
| chemicobiology | petrochemistry |
| chemicoengineering | pharmacochemistry |
| chemicophysics | photochemistry |
| chemophysiology | physical chemistry, |
| chemurgy | physicochemistry |
| colloid chemistry | physiological chemis- |
| colorimetry, color- | try, physiochemistry |
|   imetric analysis | phytochemistry |
| crystallochemistry | piezochemistry |
| cytochemistry | polymer chemistry |
| electrochemistry | psychobiochemistry, |
| engineering chemistry |   psychochemistry |
| galactochemistry | pure chemistry |
| geological chemistry, | radiochemistry |
|   geochemistry | soil chemistry |
| hydrochemistry | spectrochemistry |
| iatrochemistry | stereochemistry |
| immunochemistry | structural chemistry |
| industrial chemistry | synthetic chemistry |
| inorganic chemistry | theoretical chemistry |
| lithochemistry | thermochemistry |

topochemistry
ultramicrochemistry
zoochemistry, zoo-

chemy
zymochemistry,
zymurgy

carbide
carbohydrate 309.22
carbonate
carbon dioxide
carbon monoxide
Chile saltpeter
chlorate
chloride
chlorite
chromate
citrate
copperas
cyanide
dehydrated alcohol
dichromate
dioxide
disulfide
ester
ether
ethyl, ethyl alcohol,
ethanol
fluoride
formaldehyde
fulminate
halide
halogen
hydrate
hydride
hydrocarbon
hydroxide
hypochlorite
iodide
isopropyl alcohol, iso-
propanol

ketone
lactate
lye
methane
methyl
methyl alcohol, meth-
anol
monoxide
niter
nitrate
nitride
nitrite
oxalate
oxide
permanganate
peroxide
petrochemical
phosphate
phosphide
potash, potassium hy-
droxide
potassium nitrate
sal ammoniac
salt
saltpeter
silicate
sodium bicarbonate
sodium chloride
sulfate
sulfide
sulfite
tartrate
thiosulfate
trioxide

## .10 chemical elements

actinium, Ac
aluminum, Al
americium, Am
antimony, Sb
argon, Ar or A
arsenic, As
astatine, At
barium, Ba
berkelium, Bk
beryllium, Be
bismuth, Bi
boron, B
bromine, Br
cadmium, Cd
calcium, Ca
californium, Cf
carbon, C
cerium, Ce
cesium, Cs
chlorine, Cl
chromium, Cr
cobalt, Co
columbium, Cb
copper, Cu
curium, Cm
dysprosium, Dy
einsteinium, Es or E
erbium, Er
europium, Eu
fermium, Fm
fluorine, F
francium, Fr
gadolinium, Gd
gallium, Ga
germanium, Ge
gold, Au
hafnium, Hf
hahnium, Ha
helium, He
holmium, Ho
hydrogen, H
indium, In
iodine, I
iridium, Ir
iron, Fe
krypton, Kr
lanthanum, La
lawrencium, Lw
lead, Pb
lithium, Li
lutetium, Lu
magnesium, Mg
manganese, Mn
mendelevium, Md or

Mv
mercury, Hg
molybdenum, Mo
neodymium, Nd
neon, Ne
neptunium, Np
nickel, Ni
niobium, Nb
nitrogen, N
nobelium, No
osmium, Os
oxygen, O
palladium, Pd
phosphorus, P
platinum, Pt
plutonium, Pu
polonium, Po
potassium, K
praseodymium, Pr
promethium, Pm
protactinium, Pa
radium, Ra
radon, Rn
rhenium, Re
rhodium, Rh
rubidium, Rb
ruthenium, Ru
rutherfordium, Rf
samarium, Sm
scandium, Sc
selenium, Se
silicon, Si
silver, Ag
sodium, Na
strontium, Sr
sulfur, S
tantalum, Ta
technetium, Tc
tellurium, Te
terbium, Tb
thallium, Tl
thorium, Th
thulium, Tm
tin, Sn
titanium, Ti
tungsten or wolfram,
W
uranium, U
vanadium, V
xenon, Xe
ytterbium, Yb
yttrium, Y
zinc, Zn
zirconium, Zr

## .11 chemicals

absolute alcohol
acetate
acetone
alcohol
aldehyde
amine
ammonia
amyl alcohol
anhydride
arsenate
arsenite

basic anhydride
benzoate
bicarbonate
bicarbonate of soda
bichloride of mercury
bisulfate
borate
borax
bromide
calcium carbonate
calcium hydroxide

## .12 acids

acetic acid
acetylsalicylic acid, as-
pirin
acrylic acid
amino acid 309.24
ammono acid
aqua fortis
aqua regia
arsenic acid
ascorbic acid
battery acid
benzoic acid
boric acid
butyric acid
carbolic acid
carbonic acid
chloric acid
chlorous acid
chromic acid
citric acid
cyanic acid
fluoric acid
folic acid
formic acid
fumaric acid
gallic acid
hydrobromic acid
hydrochloric acid
hydrocyanic acid
hydrofluoric acid
hydroiodic acid

hypochlorous acid
iodic acid
lactic acid
lauric acid
lignosulphonic acid
linoleic acid
maleic acid
malic acid
muriatic acid
niacin, nicotinic acid
nitric acid
nucleic acid
oil of vitriol
oleic acid
oxalic acid
palmitic acid
pectic acid
perboric acid
perchloric acid
phenol
phosphoric acid
picric acid
prussic acid
salicylic acid
stearic acid
sulfanilic acid
sulfuric acid
tartaric acid
undecylenic acid
uric acid
vitriol

## .13 chemical apparatus

alembic
aspirator
beaker

blowpipe
Büchner funnel
Bunsen burner

| | |
|---|---|
| burette | Kipp's apparatus, |
| capillary tube | Kipp generator |
| centrifuge | matrass |
| condenser | pestle and mortar |
| crucible | pipette |
| deflagrating spoon | precision balance |
| desiccator | reagent bottle |
| distiller | receiver |
| Erlenmeyer flask | reflex condenser |
| etna | retort |
| evaporating dish | separatory funnel |
| funnel | still |
| graduated cylinder, | test tube |
| graduate | volumetric flask |

## 380. OILS, LUBRICANTS

.1 NOUNS oil, ole(o)– or oli–, *oleum* [L]; fat, lipid, lip(o)–, lipar(o)–, grease; ester; cerate; sebum, sebo–, sebi–; tallow, steat(o)–; mineral oil, vegetable oil, animal oil; fixed oil, fatty oil, nonvolatile oil, volatile oil, essential oil; saturated fat, hydrogenated fat, unsaturated fat, polyunsaturated fat; drying oil, semidrying oil, nondrying oil.

.2 lubricant, lubricator, lubricating oil, lubricating agent, antifriction; graphite, plumbago, black lead; silicone; glycerin; wax 380.15, cer(o)–; mucilage, mucus, synovia.

.3 ointment, balm, salve, lotion, cream, unguent, unguentum, inunction, inunctum, unction, chrism; soothing syrup, lenitive, embrocation, demulcent, emollient; spikenard, nard; balsam; pomade, pomatum, brilliantine; cold cream, hand lotion, face cream, lanolin; eye-lotion, eyewash, collyrium.

.4 petroleum, petr(o)– or petri–, rock oil, fossil oil; crude oil, crude; gasoline, gas [informal], petrol [Brit]; aviation gasoline, avgas; ethyl, ethyl gas, premium gas, high-test, high-octane gas; regular, regular gas; low-lead gas, lead-free gas, white gas; kerosene, paraffin 331.1; diesel oil, diesel fuel; motor oil.

.5 oiliness, greasiness, unctuousness, unctiousness, unctuosity; fattiness, fatness, pinguidity; richness; sebaceousness; adiposis, adiposity; soapiness, saponacity or saponaceousness; smoothness, slickness, sleekness, slipperiness, lubricity.

.6 lubrication, lubricating, oiling, greasing, lubrification [archaic]; grease job or lube [both informal]; anointment, unction, inunction; chrismatory, chrismation.

.7 lubritorium, lubritory; grease rack, grease pit.

.8 VERBS oil, grease; lubricate, lubrify [archaic]; anoint, salve, unguent, embrocate, dress, pour oil or balm upon; smear, daub; slick, slick on [informal]; pomade; lard; glycerolate, glycerinate, glycerinize; wax, beeswax; smooth the way, soap the ways, grease the wheels.

.9 ADJS oily, greasy; unctuous, unctional; unguinous; oleaginous, oleic; unguentary, unguent, unguentous; chrismal, chrismatory; fat, fatty, adipose, adip(o)–; pinguid, pinguedinous, pinguescent; rich; sebaceous; blubbery, tallowy, suety; lardy, lardaceous; buttery, butyraceous; soapy, saponaceous; paraffinic; mucoid; smooth, slick, sleek, slippery.

.10 lubricant, lubricating, lubricative, lubricatory, lubricational; lenitive, emollient, soothing.

.11 mineral and fuel oils

| | |
|---|---|
| absorber oil | mineral oil |
| anthracene oil | mineral seal oil |
| asphalt-base oil | mineral sperm oil |
| Barbados tar | mineral spirits |
| benzine | naphtha |
| carbolic oil | naphthalene |
| coal oil | naphthene-base oil |
| creosote | paraffin or paraffine |
| creosote oil | [Brit] |
| derv [Brit] | paraffin-base oil |
| fuel oil | petrolatum |
| furnace oil | petroleum |
| gas oil | petroleum benzine |
| green oil | petroleum jelly |
| hidyne [Brit] | petroleum spirit |
| jet fuel | road oil |
| kerosene | saturating oil |
| lamp oil | shale naphtha or spirit |
| light oil | shale oil |
| liquid petrolatum | signal oil |
| lube oil | stove oil |
| medicinal oil | technical oil |
| middle oil | white oil |

.12 vegetable oils

| | |
|---|---|
| absinthe | flaxseed oil |
| almond oil | fusel oil |
| anise or aniseed oil | grain oil |
| avocado oil | gum spirit |
| bay or bayberry oil | hempseed oil |
| beechnut oil | kekuna oil |
| camphor | kokum butter |
| candlenut oil | laurel butter or oil |
| carapa oil | lemon oil |
| castor or ricinus oil | linseed oil |
| cedarwood oil | Macassar oil |
| China wood oil | mace butter |
| citronella | maize oil |
| clove oil | nut oil |
| cocoa butter | oil of almonds |
| coconut oil or butter | oil or spirits of turpen- |
| colza or rape oil | tine |
| copaiba | oleoresin |
| copra oil | olive oil |
| corn oil | palm-kernel oil, palm |
| cotton or cottonseed | butter |
| oil | palm oil |
| croton oil | peanut oil |
| eucalyptus oil | peppermint oil |

perilla oil
pine-needle oil
pine oil
pine tar
pine-tar oil
poppyseed oil
rapeseed oil
resin oil
rosin grease
rosin oil
safflower oil
sesame oil

soybean oil
spearmint oil
spikenard
sunflower oil
sweet *or* edible oil
tung oil
turpentine
walnut oil
wintergreen oil
wood oil
wood turpentine

**.13 animal oils, fats**

adipose tissue
beef tallow
blubber
bone oil
bottlenose oil
butter
butterfat
cod-liver oil
cod oil
doegling oil
dripping, drippings
fat
fish oil
ghee
goose grease
halibut-liver oil
Haliver Oil
hog lard
lanolin
lard
lard oil
lipid

lipoma
margarine
menhaden oil
mutton tallow
neat's-foot oil
oleo
oleomargarine
oleo oil
porpoise oil
salmon oil
sardine oil
seal oil
shark *or* shark-liver oil
shortening
sperm oil
suet
tallow
tallow oil
tuna oil
whale oil
wool fat *or* grease
wool oil

**.14 glyceryl esters**

glycerin
glycerin jelly
glycerite, glycerole
glycerogel
glycerogelatin
glycerol
margarin

olein
palmitin
stearin
trimargarin
triolein
tripalmitin
tristearin

**.15 waxes**

ader wax
ambergris
beeswax
candelilla wax
carnauba wax
casting wax
cerate
ceresin
fig wax
floor wax
fossil wax
Ghedda wax

gondang wax
lac wax
mineral wax
ozokerite
paraffin scale
paraffin wax
pisang wax
scale wax
sealing wax
ski wax
vegetable wax

## 381. RESINS, GUMS

**.1 NOUNS resin,** resina, resino–, retin(a)– *or* retini–; **gums,** gum resins; oleoresins; hard *or* varnish resins; acaroid resins, gum acaroides, coumarone resins, fossil resins, amber, succin(o)–, lac resins, pine resins, vegetable resins; resinoid, synthetic resin, plastic; resene; resinate, rosin, gum rosin, colophony, colophonium.

**.2 VERBS resin,** resinize, resinate; rosin.

**.3 ADJS resinous,** resinic, resiny; resinoid; rosiny; **gummy,** gummous, gumlike; pitchy.

**.4 resins, gums**

acacia
agar
algin
amber
ambergris
ammoniac
amyrin
animé
asa dulcis
asafetida
balsam
bassorin
Bengal kino
benjamin
benzoin
British Indian gum
butea gum, butea kino
cachibou
camphor
Canada balsam
carob gum
carrageenin
cherry-tree gum
chewing gum
chicle
colophony, colophonium
Congo copal
conima
copaiba
copal
copaline
dammar
dragon's blood
elemi
euphorbium
fossil copal
frankincense
galbanum
garnet lac
ghatti
guacin
guaiac, guaiacum
guar gum
gum ammoniac
gum animé
gum arabic
gum archipin
gum benjamin *or* benzoin
gum butea
gum copal
gum dammar
gum elemi

gum euphorbium
gum galbanum
gum guaiac *or* guaiacum
gum juniper
gum kauri
gum kino
gum labdanum
gum-lac
gum myrrh
gum olibanum
gum opoponax
gum resin
gum rosin
gum sagapenum
gum sandarac
gum shellac
gum storax
gutta-percha
hard resin
herabol myrrh
incense resin
karaya
kauri, kauri resin *or* gum
kino
Kordofan gum
labdanum
lac
lacquer
liquidambar
locust-kernel gum
mastic
megilp
mesquite gum
myrrh
oleoresin
olibanum
opoponax
pitch
quince-seed gum
rosin
sagapenum
sandarac
seed-lac
Senegal gum
shellac
Sonora lac
sterculia gum
stick lac
storax
tragacanth
wood rosin
Zanzibar copal

## 382. INORGANIC MATTER

**.1 NOUNS inorganic matter,** nonorganic matter; inanimate *or* lifeless *or* nonliving matter, inorganized *or* unorganized matter, **brute matter;** mineral kingdom *or* world.

**.2 inanimateness,** inanimation, **lifelessness,** inertness; **insensibility,** insentience, insensateness, senselessness, unconsciousness, unfeelingness.

.3 inorganic chemistry; chemicals 379.

.4 ADJS inorganic, unorganic, nonorganic; mineral, nonbiological; unorganized, inorganized.

.5 inanimate, inanimated, unanimated, exanimate, azoic, abio–, abiotic, nonliving, lifeless, soulless; inert; insentient, unconscious, nonconscious, insensible, insensate, senseless, unfeeling; dumb, mute.

## 383. MINERALS AND METALS

.1 NOUNS mineral; –ine, –ite, –lite or –lyte, –lyth; inorganic substance, lifeless matter found in nature, oryct(o)–; extracted matter or material; mineral world or kingdom; mineral resources; mineraloid, gel mineral, metamict substance; mineralization.

.2 ore, mineral; mineral-bearing material; unrefined or untreated mineral; natural or native mineral.

.3 metal; metallics; native metals, alkali metals, earth metals, alkaline-earth metals, noble metals, precious metals, base metals, rare metals, rare-earth metals or elements; metalloid, semimetal, nonmetal; bullion (gold or silver); gold dust; metal leaf, metal foil; metalwork, metalware; metallicity, metalleity.

.4 alloy, alloyage, fusion, compound; amalgam.

.5 cast, casting; ingot, bullion; pig, sow; sheet metal; button, gate, regulus.

.6 mine, pit; quarry; diggings, workings; open cut, opencast; bank; shaft; coal mine, colliery; strip mine; gold mine, silver mine, etc.

.7 deposit, mineral deposit, pay dirt; vein, lode, dike, ore bed; shoot or chute, ore shoot or ore chute; chimney; stock; placer, placer deposit, placer gravel; country rock; lodestuff, gangue, matrix, veinstone.

.8 mining; coal mining, gold mining, etc.; strip mining; placer mining; hydraulic mining; prospecting; mining claim, lode claim, placer claim; gold fever; gold rush.

.9 miner, mineworker, pitman; coal miner, collier [Brit]; gold miner, gold digger; gold panner; placer miner; quarry .miner; prospector, desert rat, sourdough; fortyniner; hand miner, rockman, powderman, driller, draw man; butty.

.10 mineralogy; mineralogical chemistry; crystallography; petrology, petrography, mi-

cropetrography; geology 385.4; mining geology, mining engineering.

.11 metallurgy; metallography, metallurgical chemistry, metallurgical engineering, physical metallurgy, powder metallurgy, electrometallurgy, hydrometallurgy, pyrometallurgy.

.12 mineralogist; metallurgist, electrometallurgist, metallurgical engineer; petrologist, petrographer; geologist 385.5; mining engineer.

.13 VERBS mineralize; petrify 356.7.

.14 mine; quarry; pan, pan for gold; prospect; hit pay dirt.

.15 ADJS mineral, –litic; inorganic 382.4; mineralized, petrified; asbestine, carbonous, graphitic, micaceous, alabastrine, quartzose, silicic; sulfurous, sulfuric; ore-bearing, ore-forming.

.16 metal, metallic, metallike, metall(o)– or metal(o)–, metalline, metalloid or metalloidal, metalliform; semimetallic; nonmetallic; metallo-organic or metallorganic, organometallic; bimetallic, trimetallic; metalliferous, metalbearing.

.17 brass, brassy, brazen; bronze, bronzy; copper, coppery, cuprous, cupreous; gold, golden, gilt, aureate; nickel, nickelic, nickelous, nickeline; silver, silvery; iron, ironlike, ferric, ferrous, ferruginous; steel, steely; tin, tinny; lead, leaden; pewter, pewtery; mercurial, mercurous, quicksilver; gold-filled, gold-plated, silver-plated, etc.

.18 mineralogical, metallurgical, petrological, crystallographic.

.19 minerals

| | |
|---|---|
| alabaster | clay |
| amphibole | coal 331.10 |
| antimony, stib(o)– or | coke |
|   stibi(o)– | corundum |
| apatite | cryolite |
| aplite | diatomite |
| argillite | elaterite |
| arsenic, ars– | emery |
| asbestos | epidote |
| asphalt | epsomite |
| azurite | feldspar |
| barite | fluorite |
| bauxite | fluorspar |
| bitumen | fool's gold |
| boron, bor(o)– | garnet |
| brimstone | glauconite |
| bromine, brom(o)– | graphite |
| brookite | gypsum |
| brucite | hatchettine |
| calcite | holosiderite |
| carbon, carb(o)– | hornblende |
| celestite | ilmenite |
| chalcedony | iolite |
| chlorite | iron pyrites |
| chromite | jet |

kaolinite
kyanite
lazurite
lignite
lime
magnesite
malachite
maltha
marcasite
marl
meerschaum
mica
mineral charcoal
mineral coal
mineral oil 380.11
mineral salt
mineral tallow
mineral tar
mineral wax
molybdenite
monazite
obsidian
olivine
orthoclase
ozokerite
peat
perlite
phosphate rock
phosphorus, phosph-
  (o)-, phosphor(o)-
pitchblende
pumice

pumicite
pyrite
pyrites
pyroxene
quartz
realgar
red clay
rhodonite
rock crystal
rocks 384
rutile
salt, hal(o)-
selenite
selenium, selen(o)- or
  seleni-
siderite
silica
silicate
silicon, sil-, silic(o)-
spar
spinel
spodumene
sulfur, sulf(o)-
talc, talcum, talc(o)-
tellurium, tellur(o)-,
  telluri-
tourmaline
tripoli
vermiculite
wollastonite
wulfenite
zeolite

## .20 ores

argentite
arsenopyrite
bauxite
cassiterite
chalcocite
chalcopyrite
cinnabar
galena
göthite
hematite
iron ore

ironstone
limonite
lodestone
magnetite
mispickel
pyrite
siderite
stibnite
tinstone
turgite
zincite

## .21 elementary metals

aluminum, aluminium
  [Brit], alumin(o)-
americium
barium
beryllium
bismuth, bismut(o)-
cadmium
calcium, calcio-
cerium
cesium
chromium or chrome,
  chrom(o)-
cobalt, cobalti- or
  cobalto-
copper, cupr(o)- or
  cupri-, chalc(o)- or
  chalk(o)-
dysprosium
erbium
europium
gadolinium
gallium
germanium, germano-
gold, auro-
hafnium

holmium
indium
iridium, irid(o)-
iron, ferro- or ferri-,
  sider(o)-
lanthanum
lead, plumb(o)-,
  molybd(o)-
lithium, lithi(o)-
lutetium
magnesium or magne-
  sia, magnesio-
manganese,
  mangan(o)- or man-
  gani-
mercury, mercur(o)-
molybdenum,
  molybd(o)-
neodymium
nickel
niobium
osmium, osm(o)-
palladium
phosphorus
platinum, platin(o)-

polonium
potassium
praseodymium
promethium
protactinium
radium, radio-
rhenium
rubidium
ruthenium, ruthen(o)-
  or ruthenio-
samarium
scandium
silver, argent(o)- or
  argenti-, argyr(o)-
sodium, natr(o)-
strontium
tantalum, tantal(o)-
  or tantali-

technetium
terbium
thallium
thorium
thulium
tin, stann(o)- or stan-
  ni-
titanium, titan(o)-
tungsten, tungst(o)-,
  wolfram, wol-
  fram(o)-
uranium, uran(o)-
vanadium, vanad(o)-
ytterbium
yttrium
zinc, zinco-
zirconium

## .22 alloys

admiralty metal
air-hardened steel
alloy iron
alloy steel
alnico
aluminum bronze
babbitt or babbitt
  metal
basic iron
bearing steel
bell metal
beryllium bronze
brass, chalc(o)- or
  chalk(o)-
britannia metal
bronze, chalc(o)- or
  chalk(o)-
bush metal
Carboloy
carbon steel
cartridge brass
case-hardened steel
cast iron
cheoplastic metal
chisel steel
chrome or chromium
  steel
chrome-nickel steel
cinder pig
coin nickel
coin silver
constantan
cupronickel
damask or Damascus
  steel
decarbonized iron
dental gold
die steel
drill steel
Duralumin
Duriron
electrum
elinvar
fuse metal
galvanized iron
German silver
gilding metal
graphite steel
green gold
grid metal
gun metal
hard lead

high brass
high-speed steel
hot-work steel
hypernik
inconel
ingot iron
invar
leaded bronze
low brass
manganese bronze
mine pig
misch metal
Monel Metal
Muntz metal
naval brass
nichrome
nickel bronze
nickel silver
ni-hard iron
ni-resist iron
oil-hardened steel
Permalloy
perminvar
pewter
phosphor bronze
pig, pig iron
pig lead
pinchbeck
red brass
rose metal
shot metal
silicon bronze
silicon steel
solder
spiegeleisen
stainless steel
steel
Stellite
sterling silver
structural iron
structural steel
Swedish steel
tin bronze
tombac
tool steel
tula metal
type metal
white gold
white metal
Wood's metal
wrought iron
yellow brass

yellow gold          yellow metal

**.23 leaf metals**

| | |
|---|---|
| aluminum foil | lead foil |
| Dutch foil *or* leaf *or* | silver foil |
|    gold | silver leaf |
| gold foil | tin foil |
| gold leaf | |

## 384. ROCK

**.1** NOUNS **rock, stone,** petr(o)– *or* petri–, saxi–, lith(o)–, –lith; living rock; **igneous rock,** plutonic *or* abyssal rock, hypabyssal rock; volcanic rock, extrusive *or* effusive rock, scoria; magma, intrusive rock; granite, grano–, basalt, porphyry, –phyre; **lava,** aa, pahoehoe, ropy lava, corded pahoehoe, elephant-hide pahoehoe, entrail pahoehoe, festooned pahoehoe, sharkskin pahoehoe, shelly pahoehoe, slab pahoehoe, block lava, pillow lava, ellipsoidal lava *or* basalt; **sedimentary rock;** limestone, sandstone; **metamorphic rock,** blast(o)–, –blast, orth(o)–, par(a)–; schist, gneiss; conglomerate, pudding stone, breccia, –clast; rubble, rubblestone, scree, talus, tuff, tufa, brash; sarsen, sarsen stone, druid stone; monolith; crag, craig [Scot]; bedrock; mantlerock, regolith; saprolite, geest, laterite.

**.2 sand,** amm(o)–, psamm(o)–; grain of sand; sands of the sea; sand pile, sand dune, sand hill; sand reef, sandbar.

**.3 gravel,** shingle, chesil [Brit].

**.4 pebble,** pebblestone, gravelstone, chuckie [Scot]; jackstone *or* checkstone [both dial]; fingerstone; slingstone; drakestone; spall.

**.5 boulder,** river boulder, shore boulder, glacial boulder.

**.6 precious stone, gem,** gem stone, crystal, stone; semiprecious stone; gem of the first water; birthstone.

**.7** petrification, petrifaction, lithification, crystallization.

**.8** geology, petrology, crystallography; petrochemistry.

**.9** VERBS petrify, lithify, crystallize, turn to stone; harden 356.7.

**.10** ADJS **stone, rock;** lithic, –litic; petrified; petrogenic, petrescent; adamant, adamantine; flinty, flintlike; marbly, marblelike; granitic, granitelike; slaty, slatelike.

**.11 stony, rocky,** lapideous; stonelike, rocklike, lithoid *or* lithoidal; sandy, gritty 361.12; gravelly, shingly, shingled; pebbly, pebbled, –clastic; porphyritic, –phyric; trachytic, trachy–; crystal, crystalline, crystall(o)–; bouldery, rock- or boulder-

strewn, rock-studded, rock-ribbed; craggy; monolithic.

**.12 stones**

| | |
|---|---|
| anthraconite | lava |
| aplite | limestone |
| aventurine | lodestone |
| basalt | Lydian stone |
| basanite | marble |
| beetlestone | milkstone |
| brimstone | mudstone |
| brownstone | obsidian |
| buhr, buhrstone | phonolite |
| cairngorm | pitchstone |
| chalk | porphyry |
| clinkstone | pumice |
| corundophilite | quarrystone |
| dendrite | quartz |
| diabase | quartzite |
| diorite | rance |
| dolerite | rottenstone |
| dolomite | sandstone |
| dripstone | serpentine |
| eaglestone | shale |
| emery rock | slabstone |
| fieldstone | slate |
| flag, flagstone | smokestone |
| flint | snakestone |
| floatstone | soapstone |
| freestone | stalactite |
| geode | stalagmite |
| gneiss | starstone |
| goldstone | steatite |
| granite | stinkstone |
| granulite | tinstone |
| greenstone | touchstone |
| grit | trap, traprock |
| gritrock, gritstone | tufa |
| hairstone | wacke |
| ironstone | whitestone |

**.13 gem stones**

| | |
|---|---|
| adamant [archaic] | heliotrope |
| adder stone | hyacinth |
| agate | jacinth |
| alexandrite | jade, jadestone |
| amethyst | jargoon |
| aquamarine | jasper |
| beryl | kunzite |
| black opal | lapis lazuli |
| bloodstone | moonstone |
| brilliant | morganite |
| carbuncle | onyx |
| carnelian | opal |
| cat's-eye | peridot |
| chalcedony | plasma |
| chrysoberyl | rose quartz |
| chrysolite | ruby |
| chrysoprase | sapphire |
| citrine | sard |
| coral | sardonyx |
| demantoid | spinel, spinel ruby |
| diamond | star sapphire |
| emerald | sunstone |
| fire opal | topaz |
| garnet | tourmaline |
| girasol | turquoise |
| harlequin opal | zircon |

**.14 specialized stones**

| | |
|---|---|
| bakestone | capstone |
| bondstone | cobble, cobblestone |

copestone, coping  
stone  
cornerstone  
crowstone  
curbstone  
dogstone  
doorstone  
edgestone  
footstone  
gravestone  
grindstone  
hagstone  
hammerstone  
headstone  
kerbstone [Brit]

keystone  
kneestone  
knockstone  
lapstone  
milestone  
millstone  
oilstone  
pavestone  
rubstone  
stepstone, stepping-  
stone  
tilestone  
tombstone  
topstone  
whetstone

## 385. LAND

.1 NOUNS **land, ground,** earth, ge(o)–, **soil,** agro–, ped(o)–, glebe [archaic], **sod, clod, dirt, dust, clay,** marl, mold [Brit dial]; *terra* [L], **terra firma;** terrain; **dry land;** arable land; marginal land; grassland 411.8, woodland 411.11; crust, earth's crust, lithosphere; regolith; topsoil, subsoil; alluvium, alluvion; eolian *or* subaerial deposit; **real estate,** real property, landholdings, acres, territory, freehold; region 180; the country 182.

.2 **shore, coast,** *côte* [Fr]; **strand,** *playa* [Sp], **beach,** shingle, plage, lido, riviera, sands, berm; waterside, **waterfront;** shoreline, coastline; foreshore; bank, embankment; riverside; **seashore, seacoast, seaside, seaboard,** seabeach, seacliff, seabank, sea margin, tidewater, coastland, littoral; drowned *or* submerged coast; rockbound coast, ironbound coast; loom of the land.

.3 **landsman,** landman, **landlubber.**

.4 (science of land or the earth) **geography,** geographics; physiography, physical geography; geoscopy; geomorphology; geodesy, geodetics 490.9; geophysics; geodynamics; **geology,** geognosy, dynamic geology, hydrogeology, physical geology, physiographic geology, stratigraphic geology, stratigraphy, paleontological geology, cosmical geology, geomorphogeny, historical geology, structural *or* geotectonic geology, mining geology, geological chemistry, geological engineering; mineralogy 383.10; geodesy, geodetics 490.9; soil science, pedology, soil mechanics.

.5 (scientists) **geographer,** physiographer, geodesist 490.10, **geologist,** geognost, geomorphogenist, geophysicist, geological engineer; mineralogist 383.12; soil scientist, pedologist.

.6 ADJS **terrestrial,** terrene [archaic], **earth, earthly,** telluric, tellurian; earthbound; sublunar, subastral; geophilous; terraqueous; fluvioterrestrial.

.7 **earthy,** soily, loamy, marly, gumbo; clayey, clayish; adobe.

.8 **alluvial,** estuarine, fluviomarine.

.9 **coastal, littoral, seaside, shore,** shoreside; shoreward; riparian *or* riparial *or* riparious; riverain, riverine; riverside.

.10 geographic(al), physiographic(al), geodesic, geodetic; geophysical, geologic(al), geognostic(al).

.11 ADVS **on land,** on dry land, on terra firma; onshore, ashore; alongshore; shoreward; by land, overland.

.12 **on earth,** on the face of the earth *or* globe, in the world, in the wide world, in the whole wide world; **under the sun,** under the stars, beneath the sky, under heaven, below, **here below.**

.13 **soils**

| | |
|---|---|
| adobe | latosolic soil |
| alluvial soil | leaf mold |
| argil | lithosol |
| bog soil | loam |
| bole | loess |
| boulder clay | marl |
| chernozemic soil | mold |
| china clay | podsolic soil |
| clay | porcelain clay |
| clunch | potter's clay |
| desertic soil | red clay |
| dust | regosol |
| fuller's earth | regur soil |
| gilgai soil | residual clay |
| gumbo, gumbo soil | sand |
| humus | sedimentary clay |
| indurated clay | silt |
| kaolin | till |
| kaolinite | tundra soil |
| laterite | wiesenboden |

## 386. BODY OF LAND

.1 NOUNS **continent, mainland,** main [archaic], **landmass;** North America, South America, Africa, Europe, Asia, Eurasia, Eurasian landmass, Australia, Antarctica; subcontinent, peninsula 256.8.

.2 **island, isle,** neso–; **islet,** holm, ait [Brit dial]; continental island; oceanic island; **key, cay;** sandbank, sandbar, bar; **reef,** coral reef, coral head; coral island, atoll; archipelago, island group *or* chain; insularity; islandology.

.3 **continental,** mainlander; continentalist.

.4 **islander,** islandman, island-dweller, islesman, insular; islandologist.

.5 VERBS insulate, isolate, island, enisle; island-hop.

.6 ADJS **continental, mainland.**

.7 **insular,** insulated, isolated; island, islandy *or* islandish, islandlike; islanded, isleted, island-dotted; seagirt; archipelagic *or* archipelagian.

## 387. PLAIN

*(open country)*

.1 NOUNS **plain, plains;** peneplain; flat, flat country, flatland, **flats,** level, pedi(o)–; champaign country, champaign, open country, **wide-open spaces; prairie,** grassland 411.8, **steppe, pampas,** *pampa* [Sp], savanna, tundra, vega, campo, llano, sebkha; **veld,** grass veld, bushveld, tree veld; wold, weald; **moor,** moorland, down, **downs,** lande, **heath,** fell [Brit]; lowland, lowlands, bottomland; basin, playa; salt marsh; salt pan; salt flat, alkali flat; **desert** 166.2; **plateau,** upland, tableland, table, **mesa,** mesilla; coastal plain, alluvial plain, delta; mare, lunar mare.

.2 **plainsman,** plainswoman; moorman, moorlander; veldman; plainsfolk, flatlanders, lowlanders.

.3 ADJS champaign, **plain, flat,** open; campestral *or* campestrian.

## 388. LIQUIDITY

.1 NOUNS **liquidity, fluidity,** fluidness, liquidness, liquefaction 391; **fluency, flow,** flux, fluxion, fluxility [archaic]; wateriness; rheuminess; **juiciness,** sappiness, succulence; milkiness, lactescence; lactation; chylifaction, chylification; serosity; suppuration; moisture 392.

.2 **fluid, liquid;** liquor, drink, beverage; liquid extract, fluid extract; **juice, sap,** opo–; blood; latex, milk, whey 308.47; water 392.3; semiliquid 389.5; fluid mechanics, hydraulics, etc. 347.1–4; hydrogeology.

.3 (body fluids) humor, **lymph,** lymph(o)–; chyle, chyl(o)– *or* chyli–, –chylia; rheum; serous fluid, serum, sero–; **pus, matter,** purulence, peccant humor [archaic]; suppuration; ichor, sanies; discharge; gleet, leukorrhea, the whites; **mucus,** mucor, muc(o)– *or* muci–, mucoso–, myx(o)–; **phlegm,** snot [slang]; **saliva** 312.3; **urine** 311.5; **sweat** 311.7; **tear,** teardrop, lachryma; **milk,** lact(o)– *or* lacti–, galact(o)–, mother's milk, colostrum, lactation.

.4 **blood,** hem(o)– *or* hema– *or* hemi–, hemat(o)–, sangui(ni)–, sanguin(o)–; lifeblood, venous blood, arterial blood, **gore,** ichor, humor; grume; **serum,** blood serum; blood substitute; **plasma,** plasm(o)–, plasmato–; synthetic plasma, plasma substitute, dextran, clinical dextran; **blood cell** *or* **corpuscle,** hemocyte; **red corpuscle** *or* **blood cell,** erythrocyte, erythr(o)–; **white corpuscle** *or* **blood cell,** leukocyte, leuk(o)–, leukocyt(o)–, lymphocyte, lym-

ph(o)–, lymphat(o)–, neutrophil, neutro–, phagocyte, phag(o)–; blood platelet; **hemoglobin;** blood pressure; circulation; **blood group** *or* **type,** type O *or* A *or* B *or* AB; Rh-type, Rh-positive, Rh-negative; **Rh factor,** Rhesus factor; antigen, antibody, isoantibody, globulin; opsonin, opson(o)–; blood grouping; blood count, blood picture; hematoscope, hematoscopy, hemometer; bloodstream; hematics, hematology, hematologist; bloodmobile; blood bank, blood donor center; blood donor.

.5 flowmeter, fluidmeter, hydrometer.

.6 ADJS **fluid,** fluidal, fluidic, **fluent, flowing,** fluxible *or* fluxile [both archaic], fluxional, fluxionary [archaic], runny; **liquid,** liquidy; watery 392.16; **juicy,** sappy, succulent.

.7 (physiology) **lymphatic,** rheumy, humoral, phlegmy, ichorous, serous, sanious; chylific, chylifactive, chylifactory; **pussy,** purulent, suppurated *or* suppurating, suppurative; tearlike, **lachrymal,** lacrimatory; bloody 368.7.

.8 **milky,** lacteal, lacteous, **lactic;** lactescent, lactiferous; milk, milch.

## 389. SEMILIQUIDITY

.1 NOUNS semiliquidity, semifluidity; butteriness, creaminess; pulpiness 390.

.2 **viscosity,** viscidity, viscousness, slabbiness, lentor [archaic]; thickness, spissitude, heaviness, stodginess; **stickiness, tackiness,** glutinousness, glutinosity, toughness, tenaciousness, tenacity, adhesiveness, **gumminess,** gauminess [dial], gumlikeness; **ropiness, stringiness;** clamminess, sliminess, mucilaginousness; gooeyness [informal]; **gluiness,** gluelikeness; syrupiness, treacliness [Brit]; gelatinousness, jellylikeness, gelatinity; colloidality; doughiness, pastiness; **thickening,** curdling, clotting, coagulation, incrassation, inspissation, clabbering *or* loppering [dial], jellification.

.3 **mucosity,** mucidness, mucousness, pituitousness [archaic], snottiness [slang].

.4 **muddiness,** muckiness, **slushiness,** sloshiness, sludginess, **sloppiness,** slobbiness, slabbiness [archaic], squashiness, squelchiness, **ooziness,** miriness; **turbidity,** turbidness, dirtiness.

.5 **semiliquid,** semifluid; **goo** *or* **goop** *or* **gook** *or* **gunk** *or* **glop** [all informal], sticky mess, gaum [dial]; **paste,** pap, pudding, putty, **butter,** cream; **pulp** 390.2; **jelly,** gelatin, jell, gel, jam; **glue;** size; **gluten;** mucilage; mucus; **dough,** batter; **syrup,** molasses, treacle [Brit], rob; egg white, albumen, glair; starch, cornstarch; **curd,** clabber, bonnyclabber; gruel, porridge, loblolly [dial]; soup, gumbo, purée.

.6 **gum** 381, chewing gum, bubble gum; chicle, chicle gum.

.7 **emulsion,** emulsoid; emulsification; emulsifier; **colloid,** colloider.

.8 **mud, muck, slush, slosh,** sludge, slob [Ir], squash, **slime,** swill, **slop, ooze, mire;** clay, slip; gumbo; pel(o)–.

.9 **mud puddle, puddle,** loblolly [dial], slop; **mudhole,** slough, muckhole, chuckhole, chughole [dial]; hog wallow.

.10 VERBS **emulsify,** emulsionize; colloid, colloidize; cream; churn, whip, beat up; **thicken,** inspissate, incrassate, curdle, clot, coagulate, clabber or lopper [both dial]; jell, jelly, jellify.

.11 ADJS **semiliquid,** semifluid, semifluidic; buttery; creamy; emulsive, colloidal; **pulpy** 390.6; half-frozen, half-melted.

.12 **viscous, viscid,** viscose, visc(o)–, slabby; **thick,** heavy, stodgy, thickened, inspissated, incrassated; curdled, clotted, grumous, coagulated, clabbered or loppered [both dial]; **sticky, tacky,** tenacious, adhesive, tough; gluey, gluelike, glutinous, glutenous, glutinose, gli(o)–, gloe(o)– or gloio–; gumbo, gumbolike; **gummy,** gaumy [dial], gummous, gumlike, **syrupy;** ropy, stringy; mucilaginous, clammy, slimy, slithery; gooey [informal]; **gelatinous,** jellylike, jellied, jelled, tremelloid or tremellose; glairy; **doughy, pasty;** starchy, amylaceous.

.13 **mucous,** muculent, mucoid, mucinous, pituitous [archaic], snotty [slang]; mucific, muciferous.

.14 **muddy,** mucky, **slushy, sloshy,** sludgy, **sloppy,** slobby, slabby [archaic], splashy, **squashy,** squishy, **squelchy, oozy,** soft, miry, sloughy, plashy, sposhy [dial]; **turbid, dirty.**

### 390. PULPINESS

.1 NOUNS **pulpiness,** pulpousness; **softness** 357; flabbiness; **mushiness,** mashiness, squashiness; **pastiness,** doughiness; **sponginess,** pithiness; fleshiness, succulence.

.2 **pulp, paste, mash, mush,** smash, squash, crush; pudding, porridge, sponge; sauce, butter; poultice, cataplasm, plaster; pith; paper pulp, wood pulp, sulfate pulp, sulfite pulp, rag pulp; pulpwood; pulp lead, white lead; dental pulp.

.3 **pulping,** pulpification, pulpefaction;

blending; digestion; **maceration,** mastication.

.4 **pulper,** pulpifier, macerator, pulp machine or engine, digester; **masher,** smasher, potato masher, beetle.

.5 VERBS **pulp,** pulpify; **macerate,** masticate, chew; **mash,** smash, squash, crush.

.6 ADJS **pulpy,** pulpous, pulpal, pulpar, pulplike, pulped; **pasty,** doughy; pultaceous; **mushy;** macerated, masticated, chewed; **squashy,** squelchy, squishy; soft, flabby; fleshy, succulent; **spongy,** pithy, baccate.

### 391. LIQUEFACTION

.1 NOUNS liquefaction, liquidization, fluidification, fluidization; liquescence or liquescency, deliquescence, deliquium [archaic]; dissolution, solution, dissolving, decoagulation, unclotting, melting, thawing, running, fusing, fusion; solubilization; colliquation; lixiviation, percolation, leaching.

.2 **solubility,** solubleness, dissolvability, dissolvableness, dissolubility, dissolubleness; meltability, fusibility.

.3 **solution,** decoction, infusion, mixture; chemical solution; lixivium, leach, leachate.

.4 **solvent** 391.10, dissolvent, dissolver, dissolving agent, resolvent, resolutive, **thinner,** dilutant or diluent; anticoagulant; liquefier, liquefacient; menstruum; universal solvent, alkahest; flux.

.5 VERBS **liquefy,** liquidize, liquesce, fluidify, fluidize; **melt, run,** thaw, colliquate; melt down; fuse, flux; deliquesce; **dissolve,** solve; thin, cut; solubilize; hold in solution; unclot, decoagulate; leach, lixiviate, percolate; decoct, infuse.

.6 ADJS **liquefied, melted, molten,** thawed, unclotted, decoagulated; in solution, in suspension, liquescent, deliquescent.

.7 **liquefying,** liquefactive; colliquative, **melting,** fusing, thawing; **dissolving,** dissolutive, dissolutional.

.8 **solvent,** dissolvent, resolvent, resolutive; thinning, cutting, diluent; alkahestic.

.9 liquefiable; **meltable,** fusible, thawable; **soluble, dissolvable,** dissoluble.

.10 **solvents**

| | |
|---|---|
| acetone | chloroform |
| alcohol | ether |
| aqua regia | ethyl acetate |
| benzene | furfural |
| benzine, benzol | gasoline |
| carbolic acid | kerosene |
| carbon disulfide | naphtha |
| carbon tetrachloride, | phenol |
| carbon tet | toluene |

turpentine          xylene, xylol
water

## 392. MOISTURE

.1 NOUNS **moisture,** hygr(o)–, **damp, wet;
dampness, moistness,** moistiness, **wetness,**
wettishness, **wateriness,** humor or humectation [both archaic]; soddenness, soppiness, sogginess; swampiness, bogginess,
marshiness; dewiness; mistiness, fogginess
404.3; raininess, pluviosity, showeriness;
rainfall; exudation 303.6.

.2 **humidity,** humidness, **dankness,** dankishness, **mugginess,** stickiness; absolute humidity, relative humidity; dew point; humidification.

.3 **water,** aqua [L], agua [Sp], eau [Fr], hydr-
(o)–, hydrat(o)–, aqui– or aqua–; Adam's
ale or wine, $H_2O$; hydrol; hard water, soft
water; heavy water; drinking water; rain
water, rain 394; ground water, spring water, well water; sea water, salt water; limewater; mineral water or waters; steam,
water vapor; hydrosphere; hydrometeor;
head, hydrostatic head; hydrothermal water; wetting agent, wetting-out agent.

.4 **dew, dewdrops,** dawn dew, night dew,
evening damp; fog drip, false dew.

.5 **sprinkle, spray,** sparge, shower; spindrift,
spume, froth, foam; **splash,** plash, swash,
slosh; **splatter,** spatter.

.6 **wetting, moistening, dampening,** damping; humidification; dewing, bedewing;
**watering, irrigation;** hosing, wetting or
hosing down; **sprinkling, spraying,** sparging, aspersion, aspergation; **splashing,**
swashing, splattering, spattering; affusion,
baptism; bath, bathing, rinsing, laving;
**flooding,** drowning, inundation, deluge;
**immersion, submersion** 320.2.

.7 **soaking,** soakage, soaking through, sopping, **drenching,** imbruement, sousing;
ducking, dunking [informal]; soak,
drench, souse; **saturation,** permeation;
**steeping,** maceration, seething, infusion,
brewing, imbuement; injection, impregnation; infiltration, percolation, leaching,
lixiviation; pulping 390.3.

.8 **sprinkler,** sparger, sparge, sprayer, speed
sprayer, concentrate sprayer, mist concentrate sprayer, spray, spray can, atomizer,
aerosol; nozzle; aspergil, aspergillum;
**shower,** shower bath, shower head, needle
bath; syringe, fountain syringe, douche,
enema, clyster; sprinkling or watering
can, watering pot, watercart; sprinkling
system, sprinkler head.

.9 (science of humidity) hygrology, hygrometry, psychrometry.

.10 (instruments) hygrometer, hair hygrometer, hygrograph, hygrodeik, hygroscope,
hygrothermograph; psychrometer, sling
psychrometer; humidor; hygrostat.

.11 VERBS be damp, not have a dry thread;
**drip,** weep; **seep, ooze,** percolate; exude
303.15; sweat 311.16.

.12 **moisten, dampen,** damp, **wet,** wet down;
humidify, humect or humectate [both archaic]; **water, irrigate;** dew, bedew; **sprinkle,** besprinkle, **spray,** sparge, asperge;
**splash,** dash, **swash, slosh, splatter,** spatter, bespatter; dabble, paddle; slop, slobber; hose, hose down; syringe, douche;
sponge.

.13 **soak, drench,** drouk [Scot], imbrue, **souse,**
sop, sodden; **saturate,** permeate; **bathe,**
lave, wash, rinse, douche, flush; watersoak, waterlog; **steep,** seethe, macerate,
infuse, imbue, brew, impregnate, inject;
infiltrate, percolate, leach, lixiviate.

.14 **flood, float, inundate, deluge,** turn to a
lake or sea, swamp, whelm, drown; duck,
dip, dunk [informal]; **submerge** 320.7;
sluice, pour on, flow on; rain 394.9.

.15 ADJS **moist,** moisty; **damp,** dampish; **wet,**
wettish; undried, tacky; **humid, dank,
muggy, sticky;** dewy, roric; roriferous;
rainy 394.10; marshy, swampy, fenny, boggy.

.16 **watery,** waterish, **aqueous, aquatic;** liquid
388.6; **splashy,** plashy, sloppy, swashy
[Brit]; hydrous, hydrated; hydraulic.

.17 **soaked, drenched,** soused, bathed,
steeped, macerated; **saturated,** permeated; **watersoaked, waterlogged;** soaking,
**sopping; wringing wet,** soaking wet, sopping wet, wet to the skin, like a drowned
rat; **sodden,** soppy, **soggy,** soaky; dripping,
**dripping wet;** dribbling, seeping, weeping, oozing; flooded, overflowed,
whelmed, swamped, engulfed, inundated,
deluged, drowned, submerged, submersed, immersed, dipped, dunked [informal]; awash, weltering.

.18 **wetting,** dampening, moistening, watering, **humectant; drenching, soaking,**
sopping; **irrigational,** irriguous [archaic].

.19 **hygric,** hygrometric, hygroscopic, hygrophilous, hygrothermal.

## 393. DRYNESS

.1 NOUNS **dryness, aridness,** aridity, waterlessness; **drought;** juicelessness, saplessness; **thirst,** thirstiness; corkiness; watertightness, watertight integrity.

.2 (comparisons) dust, bone, parchment, stick, mummy, biscuit, cracker.

.3 **drying, desiccation,** drying up; **dehydration,** anhydration; evaporation; air-drying; insolation; drainage; withering, mummification; dehumidification.

.4 **drier,** desiccator, desiccative, siccative, exsiccative, exsiccator, **dehydrator,** dehydrant; dehumidifier; evaporator; hairdrier, clothes-drier.

.5 VERBS thirst; drink up, soak up, sponge up.

.6 **dry, desiccate,** exsiccate, dry up, **dehydrate,** anhydrate; evaporate; dehumidify; air-dry; insolate, sun, sun-dry; smoke, smoke-dry; cure; torrefy, burn, fire, kiln, **bake, parch,** scorch, sear; **wither, shrivel;** wizen, weazen; mummify; sponge, blot, soak up; **wipe,** rub, swab, brush; towel; drain 305.12.

.7 ADJS **dry, arid,** xer(o)–, scler(a)– or sclero–; **waterless,** unwatered, undamped, anhydrous, anhydr(o)–, dehydr(o)–; **bonedry,** dry as dust, dry as a bone; like parchment; droughty; juiceless, sapless; **thirsty,** thirsting, athirst; high and dry; sandy, dusty; desert, Saharan.

.8 rainless, fine, fair, bright and fair, pleasant.

.9 **dried, dehydrated, desiccated,** dried-up, exsiccated; evaporated; **parched, baked,** sunbaked, burnt, scorched, **seared,** sear or sere, sun-dried, adust; wind-dried, airdried; **withered, shriveled,** wizened, weazened; corky; mummified.

.10 drying, **dehydrating, desiccative,** desiccant, exsiccative, exsiccant, siccative, siccant; evaporative.

.11 **watertight, waterproof,** moistureproof, dampproof, leakproof, seepproof, dripproof, stormproof, stormtight, rainproof, raintight, floodproof.

## 394. RAIN

.1 NOUNS **rain,** ombro–, hyet(o)–; **rainfall,** fall, **precipitation,** moisture, wet; **shower,** sprinkle, flurry, patter, pitter-patter, splatter; streams of rain, sheet of rain, splash or spurt or gout of rain; **drizzle,** mizzle; **mist,** misty rain, Scotch mist; evening mist; rainwater; blood rain; raindrop, unfrozen hydrometeor.

.2 **rainstorm,** brash or scud [both Scot]; **cloudburst,** rainburst, burst of rain, torrent of rain, waterspout, spout, rainspout, **downpour,** downflow, downfall, pour, pouring or pelting or teeming or drowning rain, spate [Scot], plash [dial], **deluge,**

**flood,** heavy rain, driving or gushing rain, drenching or soaking rain, drencher, soaker.

.3 **thunderstorm,** thundersquall, thundergust, thundershower, thunder [dial]; ceraun(o)– or keraun(o)–.

.4 **wet weather, raininess,** rainy weather, stormy or dirty weather, cat-and-dog weather [informal], spell of rain, wet; rainy day; **rains,** rainy or wet season, spring rains, **monsoon;** predominance of Aquarius, reign of St. Swithin.

.5 **rainmaking,** seeding, cloud-seeding, nucleation, artificial nucleation; **rainmaker,** rain doctor, cloud seeder; Dry Ice, silver iodide.

.6 Jupiter Pluvius, Zeus; Thor.

.7 **rain gauge,** pluviometer, pluvioscope, pluviograph; ombrometer, ombrograph, udometer, udomograph; hyetometer, hyetometrograph, hyetograph.

.8 (science of precipitation) hydrometeorology, hyetology, hyetography; pluviography, pluviometry, ombrology.

.9 VERBS **rain, precipitate,** fall; weep, shower, shower down; **sprinkle,** spit [informal], spatter, patter, pitter-patter, **drizzle,** mizzle; **pour,** stream, pour with rain, **pelt,** drum, tattoo, come down in torrents or sheets or buckets, **rain cats and dogs** [informal], "rain dogs and polecats" [Richard Brome], rain tadpoles or bullfrogs or pitchforks [informal], "rain daggers with their points downward" [Robert Burton].

.10 ADJS **rainy, showery;** pluvious or pluviose or pluvial; **drizzly,** drizzling, mizzly, drippy; **misty,** misty-moisty; pouring, streaming, pelting, drumming, driving, blinding, cat-and-doggish [informal].

.11 pluviometric or pluvioscopic or pluviographic, ombrometric or ombrographic, udometric or udographic, hyetometric, hyetographic, hyetometrographic; hydrometeorologic(al), hyetologic(al).

## 395. STREAM

### (running water)

.1 NOUNS **stream, waterway, watercourse** 396.2, channel 396; meandering stream, flowing stream, lazy stream, racing stream, braided stream; spill stream; adolescent stream; **river,** fluvi(o)–; navigable river, underground or subterranean river; "moving road" [Pascal], "a strong brown god" [T. S. Eliot]; wadi, arroyo [Sp]; **brook,** branch; kill, bourn, run [Brit dial]

creek, crick [dial]; **rivulet, rill, streamlet,**
brooklet, runlet, runnel, rundle [dial],
rindle [Brit dial], beck [Brit], gill [Brit],
burn [Scot], sike [Brit dial]; **freshet,** fresh;
millstream, race; midstream, midchannel;
stream action, fluviation.

**.2 headwaters, headstream,** headwater,
head, riverhead; source, fountainhead
153.5,6.

**.3 tributary,** feeder, **branch, fork,** prong
[dial], confluent, confluent stream, affluent; effluent, anabranch; bayou; billa-
bong [Austral]; dendritic drainage pattern.

**.4 flow,** flowing, **flux,** fluency, profluence,
fluid motion or movement, rheo–, –rrhea
or –rrhoea; **stream, current,** set, trend,
tide, water flow; drift, driftage; **course,**
onward course, **surge, gush, rush,** onrush,
spate, run, race; millrace, mill run; undercurrent, undertow; crosscurrent, cross-
flow; affluence, afflux, affluxion, confluence, concourse, conflux; **downflow,**
downpour, defluxion; inflow 302.2; outflow 303.4.

**.5 torrent, river, flood,** waterflood, **deluge;**
spate, **pour,** freshet, fresh; cataract, Niagara.

**.6 overflow,** spillage, spill, spill-over, overflowing, overrunning, alluvion, alluvium,
**inundation, flood, deluge,** whelming, engulfment, submersion 320.2, cataclysm;
the Flood, the Deluge; washout.

**.7 trickle,** tricklet, **dribble, drip,** dripping,
stillicide [archaic], drop, spurtle; percolation, leaching, lixiviation; distillation,
condensation, sweating; seeping, seepage.

**.8 lap, swash, wash, slosh, plash, splash;** lapping, washing, etc.

**.9 jet, spout, spurt,** spurtle, **squirt,** spit,
spew, spray, spritz [dial]; rush, **gush,**
flush; **fountain,** fount, font, jet d'eau
[Fr]; geyser, spouter [informal].

**10 rapids, rapid;** ripple, **riffle,** riff [dial];
chute, shoot, sault.

**11 waterfall, cataract, fall, falls, Niagara,** cascade, force [Brit], linn [Scot], sault;
nappe; watershoot.

**12 eddy,** back stream, gurge, **swirl, twirl,**
whirl; **whirlpool,** vortex, gulf, **maelstrom;**
Maelstrom, Charybdis; countercurrent,
counterflow, counterflux, backflow, reflux, refluence, regurgitation, backwash,
backwater.

**13 tide,** tidal current or stream, tidal flow or
flood, **tide race; tidewater;** tideway, tide
gate; tide rip, **riptide,** rip; direct tide, opposite tide; **spring tide; high tide,** high

water, full tide; **low tide,** low water; **neap
tide,** neap; lunar tide, solar tide; **flood
tide, ebb tide;** rise of the tide, flux, flow,
flood; ebb, reflux, refluence; ebb and
flow, flux and reflux; tidal amplitude,
tidal range; tide chart or table, tidal current chart; tide gauge, thalassometer.

**.14 wave,** cym(o)– or kym(o)–, **billow, surge,
swell,** heave, undulation, lift, rise, send,
scend; trough, peak; **sea,** heavy swell,
ground swell; **roller,** roll; **comber,** comb;
**surf, breakers;** wavelet, **ripple, riffle; tidal
wave,** tsunami; gravity wave, water wave;
tide wave; bore, tidal bore, eagre; **whitecaps,** white horses; rough or heavy sea,
rough water, dirty water or sea, choppy
or chopping sea, popple, lop, chop, choppiness.

**.15 water** gauge, fluviograph, fluviometer;
marigraph; Nilometer.

**.16 VERBS flow, stream, issue, pour, surge,
run, course, rush, gush, flush, flood;** set,
make, trend; flow in 302.9; flow out
303.13; flow back, surge back, ebb, regurgitate.

**.17 overflow,** flow over, **run over, well over,
brim over,** overbrim, overrun, pour out or
over, **spill, slop, slosh,** spill out or over;
**cataract, cascade; inundate,** engulf,
swamp, sweep, whelm, overwhelm, **flood,**
deluge, submerge 320.7.

**.18 trickle, dribble,** dripple, **drip,** drop, spurtle; **filter,** percolate, leach, lixiviate; distill, condense, sweat; seep, weep; **gurgle**
452.11.

**.19 lap, plash, splash, wash, swash, slosh.**

**.20 jet, spout, spurt,** spurtle, **squirt,** spit,
spew, spray, spritz [dial], play, **gush, well,**
surge; vomit, vomit out or forth.

**.21 eddy,** gurge, **swirl,** whirl, purl, reel, spin.

**.22 billow, surge, swell,** heave, lift, rise, send,
scend, toss, popple, **roll,** wave, **undulate;
peak,** draw to a peak, be poised; comb,
**break,** dash, crash, smash; rise and fall,
ebb and flow.

**.23 ADJS streamy,** rivery, brooky, creeky;
streamlike, riverine; fluvial, fluviatile or
fluviatic.

**.24 flowing, streaming, running, pouring,**
fluxive, fluxional, coursing, racing, gushing, rushing, surging, surgy, **fluent,** proflu-
ent, affluent, defluent, decurrent, confluent, diffluent; tidal; gulfy, vortical; meandering, mazy, sluggish, serpentine.

**.25 flooded,** deluged, inundated, engulfed,
swamped, swept, whelmed, drowned,
overwhelmed, afloat, awash; washed, wa-
ter-washed; in flood, at flood, in spate.

## 396. CHANNEL

.1 NOUNS **channel**, conduit, duct, course; way, passage, passageway; trough, troughway, troughing; tunnel; ditch, trench 263.2; adit; ingress, entrance 302; egress, exit 303.1.

.2 **watercourse**, waterway, aqueduct, water channel, water gate, water carrier, culvert; streamway, riverway; **bed**, stream bed, river bed, creek bed, runnel; dry bed; water gap; *arroyo* [Sp], wadi, donga [Africa], nullah [India], gully, gullyhole, gulch; **canal**; swash, swash channel; race, headrace, tailrace; flume; sluice; spillway; spillbox; irrigation ditch, water furrow; waterworks.

.3 **gutter, trough**, eave *or* eaves trough; chute, shoot; pentrough, penstock; guide.

.4 (metal founding) gate, ingate, runner, sprue, tedge.

.5 **drain**, sough [Brit], sluice, scupper; **sink**, sump; piscina; **gutter**, kennel; **sewer**, cloaca, headchute; cloaca maxima.

.6 **tube**, tubi–, solen(o)–; **pipe**, aul(o)–; **tubing**, piping, tubulation; tubulure; nipple, pipette, tubulet, tubule, tubuli–; reed, stem, straw; **hose**, hosepipe, garden hose, fire hose; pipeline; standpipe; water pipe, gas pipe, steam pipe; organ pipe, reed pipe, flue pipe; drainpipe, waste pipe, soil pipe; catheter; **siphon**, siphon(o)– *or* siphoni–; tap; efflux tube, adjutage; funnel; snorkel; siamese, siamese connection *or* joint.

.7 **main**, water main, gas main, fire main.

.8 **spout**, beak, waterspout, downspout; gargoyle.

.9 **nozzle**, bib nozzle, pressure nozzle, spray nozzle, nose, snout; rose, rosehead; shower head, sprinkler head.

.10 **valve**, gate; **faucet, spigot, tap**; cock, petcock, draw cock, stopcock, sea cock, drain cock, ball cock; ball valve; bunghole; needle valve; valvule, valvula.

.11 **floodgate**, flood-hatch, gate, **head gate**, penstock, water gate, **sluice**, sluice gate; tide gate, aboideau [Can]; weir; **lock**, lock gate, dock gate; air lock.

.12 **hydrant**, fire hydrant, **plug**, water plug, fireplug.

.13 (anatomy) **duct, vessel**, canal, angi(o)–, vasi– *or* vaso–; vas, meatus, meat(o)–; thoracic duct, lymphatic, lymphangio–; emunctory [archaic]; pore; intestines 225.4; urethra, ureter, urethr(o)–, uretero–; vagina, vagin(i)–, elytr(o)– *or* elytri–; oviduct, Fallopian tube, fall(o)–; salpinx, salping(o)–; Eustachian tube; ostium; fistula.

.14 **blood vessel; artery**, arteri(o)–, aorta, aort(o)–, pulmonary artery, carotid; **vein**, ven(o)– *or* veni–, phleb(o)–, jugular vein, vena cava, pulmonary vein; portal vein, pyl(o)– *or* pyle–; varicose vein; venation **capillary**, arteriole, veinlet, venule.

.15 **gullet, throat, esophagus**, esophag(o)–, gorge, hals [dial], weasand [archaic] wizen [Brit dial], goozle *or* guzzle [both dial]; fauces, isthmus of the fauces; pharynx, pharyng(o)–.

.16 **windpipe, trachea**, trache(o)–, weasand [archaic], wizen [Brit dial]; bronchus, bronchi [pl], bronchial tube, bronchi(o)–; epiglottis.

.17 **air passage**, air duct, airway, air shaft, shaft, **air hole**, air tube; **blowhole**, breathing hole, spiracle; nostril, naris 256.7; touchhole; spilehole, **vent, venthole**, ventage, ventiduct; **ventilator**, ventilating shaft; transom, louver, louverwork; wind tunnel.

.18 **chimney, flue**, flue pipe, funnel, **stovepipe, stack, smokestack**, smokeshaft, Charley Noble; fumarole.

.19 VERBS **channel**, channelize, canalize, conduct, convey, put through; pipe, funnel, siphon; trench 263.3.

.20 ADJS **tubular**, tubate, tubiform, tubelike tubulo–, pipelike; tubed, piped; cannular, fistular; bronchial, tracheal.

.21 **vascular**, vesicular, vascul(o)–; arterial; venous *or* venose, veinous; capillary.

.22 **throated**, throatlike, jugular.

.23 **valvular**, valval, valvelike.

## 397. OCEAN

.1 NOUNS **ocean, sea**, ocean sea, mari–, thalass(o)–; great *or* main sea, *thalassa* [Gk] main *or* ocean main, the bounding main tide, salt sea, salt water, blue water, **the brine**, the briny [informal], the brine deep, "the vasty deep" [Shakespeare], **the deep**, the deep sea, the deep blue sea drink *or* big drink [both slang], **high sea, high seas**; the seven seas; hydrosphere; ocean depths 209.4.

.2 "great Neptune's ocean", "unpath'd waters", "the always wind-obeying deep" [all Shakespeare], "thou deep and dark blue ocean" [Byron], "Uterine Sea of our dreams and Sea haunted by the true dream", "Sea of a thousand creases, like the infinitely pleated tunic of the god in the hands of women of the sanctuary [both S.-J. Perse], "the great naked se shouldering a load of salt" [Sandburg], "the wine-dark sea" [Homer], "the wavy waste" [Thomas Hood], "old ocean's gray and melancholy waste" [William Cullen Bryant], "the world of waters wild" [James Thomson], "the rising world of waters dark and deep" [Milton], "the glad, indomitable sea" [Bliss Carman], "the clear hyaline, the glassy sea" [Milton].

.3 (oceans) Atlantic, Pacific, Arctic, Antarctic, Indian.

.4 spirit of the sea, "the old man of the sea" [Homer], sea devil, Davy, **Davy Jones;** sea god, **Neptune,** Poseidon, Oceanus, Triton, Nereus, Oceanid, Nereid, Thetis; Varuna, Dylan; **mermaid,** siren; merman, seaman.

.5 (ocean zones) pelagic zone, benthic zone, estuarine area, sublittoral, littoral, intertidal zone, splash zone, supralittoral.

.6 oceanography, thalassography, hydrography, bathymetry; marine biology; aquiculture.

.7 oceanographer, thalassographer, hydrographer.

.8 ADJS oceanic, marine, maritime, pelagic, thalassic, –alian; nautical 275.57; oceanographic(al), hydrographic(al), bathymetric(al), bathyorographical, thalassographic(al); terriginous; deep-sea 209.14.

.9 ADVS **at sea,** on the high seas; afloat 275.62,63; by water, by sea.

10 **oversea, overseas,** beyond seas, over the water, transmarine, across the sea.

11 **oceanward,** oceanwards, **seaward,** seawards, off; offshore, off soundings, out of soundings, in blue water.

### 398. LAKE, POOL

.1 NOUNS **lake,** landlocked water, loch [Scot], lough [Ir], nyanza [Africa], mere, freshwater lake; oxbow lake, bayou lake, glacial lake; volcanic lake; tarn; inland sea; **pool,** lakelet, **pond,** pondlet, limn-(o)– or limni–, –limnion, linn [Scot], dike [Brit dial], *étang* [Fr]; standing water, still water, stagnant water, dead water; **water hole,** water pocket; farm pond; fishpond; millpond, millpool; salt pond, salina, tidal pond or pool; **puddle,** plash, sump [dial]; **lagoon,** *laguna* [Sp]; **reservoir,** artificial lake; dam; **well, cistern,** tank.

.2 **lake dweller,** lacustrian, lacustrine dweller or inhabitant, **pile dweller** or builder; laker.

.3 **lake dwelling,** lacustrine dwelling, **pile house** or **dwelling,** palafitte; crannog.

.4 limnology, limnologist; limnimeter, limnograph.

.5 ADJS **lakish,** laky, lakelike; lacustrine, lacustral, lacustrian; pondy, pondlike, lacuscular; limnologic(al).

### 399. INLET, GULF

.1 NOUNS inlet, **cove,** creek [Brit], arm of the sea, arm, armlet, reach, loch [Scot], **bay, fjord,** bight; **gulf; estuary,** firth or frith, bayou, mouth, *boca* [Sp]; **harbor,** natural harbor; road or roads, roadstead; **strait** or straits, kyle [Scot], **narrow** or narrows, euripus, belt, gut, narrow seas; **sound.**

.2 ADJS gulfy, gulflike; gulfed, bayed, embayed; estuarine, fluviomarine, tidewater.

### 400. MARSH

.1 NOUNS **marsh,** marshland, **swamp,** swampland, fen, fenland, **morass,** mere or marish [both archaic], *marais* [Fr], **bog, mire, quagmire,** sump [dial], wash, baygall; glade, everglade; slough, swale, wallow, hog wallow, buffalo wallow, sough [Brit]; bottom, **bottoms,** bottomland, slob land, holm [Brit], meadow; **moor,** moorland, moss [Scot], peat bog; salt marsh; quicksand; taiga; mud flat, **mud** 389.8,9; helo–, paludi–.

.2 VERBS mire, bemire, sink in, **bog,** mire or bog down, stick in the mud; stodge.

.3 ADJS marshy, swampy, swampish, moory, moorish, fenny, marish [archaic], paludal or paludous; boggy, boggish, miry, mirish, quaggy, quagmiry, spouty, poachy; muddy 389.14; swamp-growing, uliginous.

### 401. VAPOR, GAS

.1 NOUNS vapor, volatile, vapo–, vapori–, atm(o)–; fume, reek, exhalation, breath, effluvium; fluid; miasma, mephitis, malaria [archaic], fetid air; smoke, smudge; wisp or plume or puff of smoke; damp, chokedamp, blackdamp, firedamp, afterdamp; flatus; steam, water vapor; cloud 404.

.2 gas, aer(o)–, mano–, pneum(o)–, pneumat(o)–; rare or noble or inert gas, –on, halogen gas; fluid; atmosphere, air 402; pneumatics, aerodynamics 347.5.

.3 vaporousness, vaporiness; vapor pressure or tension; aeriness; ethereality, etherialism; gaseousness, gaseous state, gassiness, gaseity; flatulence, windiness, flatuosity [archaic]; fluidity.

.4 **volatility,** vaporability, vaporizability, evaporability.

.5 **vaporization, evaporation,** volatilization, gasification; sublimation; distillation, fractionation; etherification; aeration, aerification; fluidization; atomization; exhalation; fumigation; smoking; steaming; etherealization.

.6 **vaporizer, evaporator;** atomizer, aerosol, spray; still, retort.

.7 vaporimeter, manometer, pressure gauge; gas meter, gasometer; pneumatometer, spirometer; aerometer, airometer; eudiometer.

.8 VERBS **vaporize, evaporate,** volatilize, **gasify;** sublimate, sublime; distill, fractionate; etherify; **aerate,** aerify; carbonate, oxygenate, hydrogenate, chlorinate, halogenate, etc.; atomize, spray; fluidize; **reek, fume;** exhale, give off, emit, send out; **smoke; steam;** fumigate, perfume; **etherize.**

.9 ADJS **vaporous,** vaporish, vapory, vaporlike; **airy, aery, aerial, ethereal; gaseous,** in the gaseous state, gasified, gassy, gaslike, gasiform; vaporing; **reeking,** reeky; miasmic or miasmal or miasmatic, mephitic; **fuming,** fumy; smoky, smoking; steamy, steaming; ozonic; oxygenous; oxyacetylene; pneumatic, aerostatic, aerodynamic.

.10 **volatile,** volatilizable; **vaporable,** vaporizable, vaporescent; **evaporative,** evaporable.

.11 **gases**

| | |
|---|---|
| acetylene | marsh gas |
| air gas | methane |
| ammonia | mustard gas |
| argon | natural gas |
| asphyxiating gas | neon |
| butane | nerve gas |
| carbon dioxide | nitrogen, nitr(o)– |
| carbon monoxide | oil gas |
| chlorine, chlor(o)– | oxygen, oxy– |
| coal gas | ozone, ozon(o)– |
| ethane | phosgene |
| ether | poison gas |
| ethylene | propane |
| fluorine, fluor(o)– | radon |
| formaldehyde | sewer gas |
| helium | sneeze gas |
| hydrogen, hydr(o)– | tear gas |
| illuminating gas | vesicatory gas |
| krypton | war gas |
| laughing gas | water gas |
| lewisite | xenon |

## 402. AIR

.1 NOUNS **air,** aero–; ether; ozone [informal]; thin air.

.2 **atmosphere,** atm(o)–; aerosphere, gaseous envelope or environment or medium,

welkin, lift [dial]; biosphere, ecosphere, noosphere.

.3 (atmospheric layers) stratum, layer, belt; lower atmosphere, upper atmosphere, outer atmosphere; troposphere; substratosphere, tropopause; stratosphere, strato–; isothermal region; ionosphere, Heaviside or Heaviside-Kennelly layer or region; Appleton layer, F layer; Van Allen belt or radiation belt; photosphere, chemosphere.

.4 **weather, climate,** clime; **the elements,** forces of nature; microclimate, macroclimate; fair weather, calm weather, halcyon days, good weather; stormy weather 162.4; rainy weather 394.4; windiness 403.15; hot weather 328.7; cold weather 333.3; meteor(o)–.

.5 weather map; isobar, isobaric or isopiestic line; isotherm, isothermal line; isometric, isometric line; high, high-pressure area; low, low-pressure area; front, front(o)–; wind-shift line, squall line; cold front, polar front, cold sector; warm front; occluded front, stationary front; air mass; cyclone, anticyclone.

.6 **meteorology,** weather science, aerology, aerography, weatherology, climatology, climatography, microclimatology, forecasting, long-range forecasting; barometry; pneumatics 347.5; anemology 403.16; nephology 404.4.

.7 **meteorologist,** weather scientist, aerologist, aerographer, weatherologist; climatologist, microclimatologist; **weatherman, weather forecaster,** weather prophet, **weather report,** weather forecast; weather bureau; weather ship; weather station; weather-reporting network.

.8 weather instrument, meteorological or aerological instrument; **barometer,** aneroid barometer, glass, weatherglass; barograph, barometrograph, recording barometer; aneroidograph; vacuometer; hygrometer; weather balloon, radiosonde; weather satellite; hurricane-hunter aircraft; weather vane 403.17.

.9 **ventilation,** cross-ventilation, **airing,** aerage, perflation, refreshment; **aeration; air conditioning,** air cooling; oxygenation, oxygenization.

.10 **ventilator; aerator; air conditioner,** air filter, air cooler, ventilating or cooling system; blower; air passage 396.17; fan 403.21.

.11 VERBS **air,** air out, **ventilate,** cross-ventilate, wind, refresh, freshen; **air-condition,** air-cool; **fan,** winnow; **aerate,** airify; oxygenate, oxygenize.

**.12** ADJS **airy**, aery, **aerial**, aeriform, airlike, **pneumatic**, ethereal; exposed, roomy, light; airish, breezy 403.25; open-air, alfresco; **atmospheric**, tropospheric, stratospheric.

**.13 climatal**, climatic(al), climatographic(al), **elemental**; meteorologic(al), aerologic(al), aerographic(al), climatologic(al); macroclimatic, microclimatic, microclimatologic(al); barometric(al), baric, barographic; isobaric, isopiestic, isometric; high-pressure, low-pressure; cyclonic, anticyclonic.

## 403. WIND

### (air flow)

**.1** NOUNS **wind**, venti– or vento–, current, **air current**, current of air, movement of air, stream, stream of air, flow of air; updraft, downdraft; crosscurrent, undercurrent; monsoon; fall wind, gravity wind, katabatic wind, head wind, tail wind, following wind; jetstream; **draft; inspiration, inhalation, indraft**, inflow, inrush.

**.2** "scolding winds" [Shakespeare], "the felon winds" [Milton], "the wings of the wind" [Bible], "O wild West Wind, thou breath of Autumn's being" [Shelley], "the wind that sang of trees uptorn and vessels tost" [Wordsworth].

**.3** (wind god; the wind personified) Aeolus, Vayu; Boreas (north wind); Eurus (east wind); Zephyr or Zephyrus, Favonius (west wind); Notus (south wind); Caurus (northwest wind); Afer (southwest wind).

**.4 puff**, puff of air or wind, breath, breath of air, flatus, waft, capful of wind, whiff, whiffet, stir of air.

**.5 breeze**, light or gentle wind or breeze, softblowing wind, **zephyr**, gale [archaic], air, light air, moderate breeze; fresh or stiff breeze; cool or cooling breeze; sea breeze, onshore breeze, ocean breeze, cat's-paw.

**.6 gust**, wind gust, **blast**, blow, flaw, **flurry**, scud [Scot].

**.7 hot wind**; snow eater, thawer; chinook, **chinook wind;** simoom, samiel; foehn; khamsin; harmattan; sirocco; solano; Santa Ana; volcanic wind.

**.8 wintry wind**, winter wind, raw wind, chilling or freezing wind, bone-chilling wind, sharp or piercing wind, cold or icy wind, biting wind, the hawk [slang], nipping or nippy wind, "a nipping and an eager air" [Shakespeare], icy blasts; Arctic or boreal or hyperboreal or hyperborean blast.

**.9 north wind, norther**, mistral, bise, tramontane; northeaster, **nor'easter**, Euroclydon, gregale, Tehuantepec wind, Tehuantepecer; northwester, **nor'wester;** southeaster, **sou'easter;** southwester, **sou'wester**, kite-wind; **east wind**, easter, easterly, levanter; **west wind**, wester, westerly; **south wind**, souther, southerly buster [Austral].

**.10** prevailing wind; polar easterlies; prevailing westerlies, antitrades; trade wind, trades; doldrums, wind-equator; horse latitudes; roaring forties.

**.11** [naut terms] **head wind, beam wind, tail wind**, following wind, fair or favorable wind, apparent or relative wind, backing wind, veering wind, slant of wind.

**.12 windstorm**, big or great or fresh or strong or stiff or high or howling or spanking wind, ill or dirty or ugly wind; **storm**, storm wind, stormy winds, **tempest**, tempestuous wind; williwaw; **blow**, violent or heavy blow; **squall**, thick squall, black squall, white squall; squall line, wind-shift line, line squall; line storm; equinoctial; **gale**, half a gale, whole gale; tropical cyclone, **hurricane**, typhoon, tropical storm, **blizzard** 333.8; **thundersquall**, thundergust.

**.13 dust storm, sandstorm**, shaitan, peesash, devil, khamsin, sirocco, simoom, samiel, harmattan.

**.14 whirlwind**, whirlblast, wind eddy; **cyclone, tornado, twister**, rotary storm, typhoon, baguio [Sp]; sandspout, sand column, dust devil; waterspout, rainspout.

**.15 windiness**, gustiness; airiness, **breeziness;** draftiness.

**.16 anemology**, anemometry; **wind direction; wind force, Beaufort scale**, half-Beaufort scale, International scale; wind rose, barometric wind rose, humidity wind rose, hyetal or rain wind rose, temperature wind rose, dynamic wind rose; wind arrow, wind marker.

**.17 weather vane, weathercock**, vane, cock, wind vane, wind indicator, wind cone or sleeve or sock, anemoscope; anemometer, wind-speed indicator, anemograph, anemometrograph.

**.18 breathing, respiration**, aspiration, spiro–, pneumat(o)–, –pnea or –pnoea; **inspiration, inhalation; expiration, exhalation;** insufflation, exsufflation; **breath**, wind, breath of air; pant, puff; wheeze, asthmatic wheeze; broken wind; gasp, gulp; snoring, snore, stertor; sniff, sniffle, snuff, snuffle; sigh, suspiration; sneeze, sternutation; cough, hack; hiccup; **artificial respiration,** mouth-to-mouth resuscitation; inhalator; iron lung; scuba, self-contained underwater breathing apparatus, Aqua-Lung; oxygen mask, oxygen tent.

.19 **lungs,** pneumon(o)–, bellows, lights; **gills,** branchiae, branchi(o)–; ctenidia.

.20 **blower,** bellows; blowpipe, blowtube, blowgun.

.21 **fan,** flabellum, flabelli–, rhipi– or rhipid(o)–; punkah, thermantidote, electric fan, blower, exhaust fan; ventilator 402.10; windsail, windscoop, windcatcher.

.22 VERBS **blow,** waft; **puff,** huff, whiff; **whiffle; breeze;** breeze up, freshen; **gather, brew,** set in, blow up, pipe up, come up, **blow up a storm;** bluster, squall; **storm,** rage, "blow, winds, and crack your cheeks, rage, blow" [Shakespeare], blast, blow great guns, blow a hurricane; blow over.

.23 **sigh,** sough, whisper, mutter, murmur, **sob, moan,** groan, growl, snarl, **wail, howl,** scream, screech, shriek, **roar,** whistle, pipe, sing, sing in the shrouds.

.24 **breathe,** respire; **inhale, inspire,** breathe in; **exhale, expire,** breathe out, exhaust, expel; **puff,** huff, **pant,** suck one's breath or wind, breathe hard or heavily, blow; **gasp,** gulp; snore; wheeze; **sniff,** sniffle, snuff, snuffle, snort; **sigh,** suspire; sneeze; cough, hack; hiccup.

.25 ADJS **windy, blowy; breezy, drafty,** airy, airish; **brisk,** fresh; **gusty,** blasty, puffy, flawy; **squally;** blustery, blustering, blusterous; aeolian, favonian, boreal.

.26 **stormy, tempestuous,** raging, storming, angry; **turbulent** 162.17; dirty, foul; cyclonic, tornadic, typhonic, typhoonish; rainy 394.10; cloudy 404.7.

.27 **windblown,** blown; **windswept,** bleak, raw, exposed.

.28 anemological, anemographic, anemometric(al).

.29 **respiratory,** breathing; inspiratory, expiratory; nasal, rhinal; pulmonary, pulmonic, pneumonic; puffing, huffing, snorting, wheezing, wheezy, asthmatic, stertorous, snoring, panting, heaving; sniffy, sniffly, sniffling, snuffy, snuffly, snuffling; sneezy, sternutative, sternutatory, errhine.

## 404. CLOUD

.1 NOUNS **cloud,** high fog, nepho–, "the clouds—the only birds that never sleep" [Victor Hugo], "the argosies of cloudland" [J. T. Trowbridge], "islands on a

dark-blue sea" [Shelley], "fair, frail, pale aces" [T. B. Aldrich], "the low'ring element" [Milton]; fleecy cloud, cottony cloud, billowy cloud; cloud bank, cloud mass, cloud drift; cloudling, cloudlet nimbus, nimbus cloud, rain cloud, water carrier; storm cloud, squall cloud; thundercloud, thunderhead; **cumulus,** cumulus cloud, woolpack, cloud street, fracto-cumulus; cumulo-nimbus, anvil cloud **stratus,** stratus cloud, strato–, cirro-stratus, cumulo-cirro-stratus, cirro-velum strato-cumulus, cumulo-stratus, snar cloud; mammatocumulus, festoon cloud cloud funnel; alto-cumulus, alto-stratus **cirrus,** cirrus cloud, curl cloud, cirr(o)– o cirri–; cirro-cumulus, cumulo-cirrus, cirro macula; mackerel sky; cirro-nebula, cirru haze; cirro-fillum, cirrus stripe; mare's tail, colt's-tail, cat's-tail, cocktail; goat' hair; banner cloud, cap cloud, cloudcap scud; mushroom cloud, cloudscape, cloud band; cloudland, Cloudcuckooland o Nephelococcygia [Aristophanes].

.2 **fog,** pea soup [informal], peasouper o pea-soup fog [both informal]; London fog, London special [Brit informal]; smog (smoke-fog), smaze (smoke-haze); frost smoke; mist, drizzling mist, drisk [dial] haze, gauze, film; vapor 401.

.3 **cloudiness, haziness, mistiness, fogginess** nebulosity, nubilation, nimbosity, over cast, heavy sky, dirty sky.

.4 nephology, nephelognosy; nephologist.

.5 nephelometer, nepheloscope.

.6 VERBS **cloud,** becloud, encloud, cloud over, overcloud, cloud up, clabber up [dial], **overcast,** overshadow, shadow, shade, **darken** 337.9, darken over, nubilate, obnubilate, obscure; **smoke,** oversmoke; **fog,** befog; smog; **mist,** bemist, enmist; **haze.**

.7 ADJS **cloudy,** nebulous, nubilous, nimbose; **clouded,** overclouded, **overcast;** dirty, heavy; dark 337.13; **gloomy** 337.14; cloud-flecked; cirrous, cirrose; cumulous, cumuliform, stratous, stratiform; lenticularis, mammatus, castellatus; thunderheaded, stormy, squally.

.8 **cloud-covered,** cloud-laden, cloud-curtained, cloud-crammed, cloud-crossed cloud-hidden, cloud-wrapped, cloud-enveloped, cloud-surrounded, cloud-girt, cloud-flecked, cloud-eclipsed, cloud-capped, cloud-topped.

.9 **foggy,** soupy or pea-soupy [both informal]; smoggy; hazy, misty.

.10 nephological.

## 405. BUBBLE

**.1** NOUNS **bubble,** bleb, **globule;** vesicle, bulla, **blister,** blood blister, fever blister; balloon, bladder 193.2; air bubble, soap bubble.

**.2 foam, froth,** aphr(o)–; **spume,** sea foam, scud; **spray, surf,** breakers, white water, spoondrift *or* spindrift, "stinging, ringing spindrift" [Kipling]; **suds, lather,** soapsuds; **scum,** offscum; head, collar; puff, mousse, soufflé, meringue.

**.3 bubbling, bubbliness, effervescence** *or* effervescency, **sparkle,** spumescence, frothiness, frothing, foaming; **fizz,** fizzle, carbonation; ebullience *or* ebulliency; **ebullition,** boiling; **fermentation,** ferment.

**.4** VERBS **bubble,** bubble up, burble; **effervesce, fizz,** fizzle; hiss, **sparkle; ferment,** work; **boil,** seethe, simmer; plop, blubber; guggle, gurgle; bubble over, boil over.

**.5 foam, froth,** spume, cream; **lather,** suds, sud; **scum,** mantle; **aerate,** whip, beat, whisk.

**.6** ADJS **bubbly,** burbly, **bubbling,** burbling; **effervescent,** spumescent, **fizzy, sparkling,** *mousseux* [Fr]; carbonated; ebullient; puffed, soufflé *or* souffléed, beaten, whipped, chiffon; **blistered,** blistery, blebby, vesicated, vesicular; blistering, vesicant, vesicatory.

**.7 foamy,** foam-flecked, **frothy,** spumy, spumous *or* spumose; yeasty, barmy; **sudsy,** suddy, **lathery,** soapy, soapsudsy, soapsuddy; heady, with a head *or* collar on.

## 406. ORGANIC MATTER

**.1** NOUNS **organic matter,** animate *or* living matter, all that lives, living nature, organic nature, organized matter; flesh, tissue, fiber, brawn, plasm, cre(o)– *or* kre(o)–, creat(o)–, hist(o)–, in(o)–, –plasm(a); **flora and fauna,** plant and animal life, animal and vegetable kingdom, biosphere, biota, ecosphere, noosphere.

**.2 organism,** organization, organic being, **living being** *or* **thing,** being, creature, created being, **individual,** genetic individual, physiological individual, morphological individual; zoon, zooid; virus; aerobic organism, anaerobic organism; heterotrophic organism, autotrophic organism; microbe, microorganism 196.18; –ont, –id.

**.3** biological classification *or* taxonomy, kingdom, phylum, etc. 61.5.

**.4 cell,** bioplast, cellule, cellul(o)– *or* cellul(i)–, cyt(o)– *or* cyti–, –cyte, –plast; procaryotic cell, eucaryotic cell; plant cell, animal cell; germ cell, somatic cell; corpuscle; unicellularity, multicellularity; **protoplasm,** energid; trophoplasm; chromatoplasm; cytoplasm, cyt(o)–, plasm-(o)–, plasmato–, plasto–; ectoplasm, endoplasm; cellular tissue, –enchyma; reticulum; plasmodium, coenocyte, syncytium, plasmod(o)– *or* plasmodi(o)–.

**.5** organelle; plastid; chromoplast, plastosome, chloroplast; mitochondrion; Golgi apparatus; ribosome; spherosome, microbody; vacuole; central apparatus, cytocentrum; centroplasm; central body, microcentrum; centrosome; centrosphere; centriole, basal body; pili, cilia, flagella, spindle fibers; aster, astr(o)–; kinoplasm; plasmodesmata; cell membrane.

**.6** metaplasm; cell wall, cell plate; structural polysaccharide; bast, phloem, xylem, xyl-(o)–, cellulose, chitin.

**.7 nucleus,** nucle(o)– *or* nuclei–, kary(o)– *or* cary(o)–; macronucleus, meganucleus; micronucleus; nucleolus, nucleol(o)–, pyren(o)–; plasmosome; karyosome, chromatin strands; nuclear envelope; chromatin, karyotin, chromat(o)–; basichromatin, heterochromatin, oxychromatin.

**.8 chromosome,** –some; allosome; heterochromosome, sex chromosome, idiochromosome; W chromosome; X chromosome, accessory chromosome, monosome; Y chromosome; Z chromosome; euchromosome, autosome; homologous chromosomes; univalent chromosome, chromatid; centromere; gene-string, chromonema; genome; chromosome complement; chromosome number, diploid number, haploid number; polyploidy.

**.9 gene,** gen(o)–; allele; operon; structural gene, regulator gene, operator gene; deoxyribonucleic acid, **DNA;** DNA double helix; nucleotide, codon; ribonucleic acid, **RNA;** messenger RNA, mRNA; transfer RNA, tRNA; ribosomal RNA; anticodon; gene pool, gene complex, gene flow, genetic drift; genotype, biotype; **hereditary character,** heredity 170.6.

**.10 gamete, germ cell,** reproductive cell; macrogamete, megagamete; microgamete; planogamete; genetoid; gamone; gametangium; gametophore; gametophyte; germ plasm, idioplasm.

**.11 sperm, spermatozoa, seed, semen,** scum *or* protein [both slang], sperm(o)– *or* sperm(a)– *or* sperm(i)–, spermat(o)–; seminal *or* spermatic fluid, milt; **sperm cell,** male gamete; spermatozoon, spermatozoid, antherozoid; antheridium; spermatium, spermatiophore or spermatophore, spermagonium; pollen, pollin(i)–; spermatogonium; androcyte, spermatid, spermatocyte.

.12 **ovum, egg, egg cell,** female gamete, oösphere; oöcyte; oögonium; ovicell, ooecium; ovule; stirp.

.13 **spore,** sporule, spor(o)– or spori–, coni(o)–, conidi(o)–; microspore; macrospore, megaspore; swarm spore, zoospore, planospore; spore mother cell, sporocyte; zygospore; sporocarp, cystocarp; basidium, basidi(o)–; sporangium, megasporangium, microsporangium; sporocyst; gonidangium; sporogonium, sporophyte; sporophore; sorus.

.14 **embryo,** embry(o)–, zygote, oösperm, oöspore, blast(o)–, –blast; blastula; *Anlage* [Ger]; **fetus,** fet(o)– or feti– or foet(o)– or foeti–; germ, germen [archaic], rudiment; **larva,** larvi–, nymph.

.15 **egg,** ov(o)– or ovi–, o– or oö–; ovule; bird's egg; **roe,** fish eggs, caviar, spawn; **yolk,** yellow, vitellus, vitell(o)–, lecith(o)–; white, **egg white,** albumen, albumin(o)– or albumini–; glair, eggshell.

.16 **cell division; mitosis,** mit(o)–; amitosis; metamitosis, eumitosis; endomitosis, promitosis; haplomitosis, mesomitosis; karyomitosis; karyokinesis; interphase, prophase, metaphase, anaphase, telophase, diaster, cytokinesis; **meiosis.**

.17 (science of organisms) **biology,** biological science, life science; aerobiology, agrobiology, astrobiology or exobiology or xenobiology, **bacteriology, biochemistry** or biochemy or biochemics, bioecology or ecology or bionomics 233.4, biometry or biometrics, bionics, biophysics, cell physiology, cybernetics, cryobiology, cytology, electrobiology, **embryology,** enzymology, ethnobiology, gnotobiotics, microbiology, molecular biology, paleontology, pharmacology, **physiology,** radiobiology, taxonomy, virology; **anatomy** 245.7; **zoology** 415; **botany** 412; **genetics** 170.6.

.18 **biologist,** bacteriologist, biochemist, biophysicist, biometrist, cytologist, ecologist, embryologist, geneticist, physiologist; naturalist, natural scientist; botanist 412.2; zoologist 415.2; anatomist 245.7.

.19 ADJS **organic,** organ(o)–; organized; **animate, living,** vital, zoetic; **biological,** biotic; physiological, physi(o)–.

.20 **protoplasmic,** plasmic, plasmatic, –plastic; **genetic,** genic, hereditary.

.21 **cellular,** cellulous; unicellular, multicellular; corpuscular.

.22 **gametic,** gamic, sexual; **spermatic,** spermic, **seminal,** spermatozoal, spermatozoan, spermatozoic; sporal, sporous sporoid, –sporic; sporogenous.

.23 **nuclear,** nucleal, nucleary, nucleate; multinucleate; nucleolar, nucleolate, nucleolated; **chromosomal;** chromatinic; –zygous; –ploid, haploid, hapl(o)– or apl(o)–; diploid, dipl(o)–, polyploid; –somic.

.24 **embryonic, germinal,** germinant, germinative, germinational; **larval;** fetal; in the bud; –blastic; germiparous.

.25 **egglike,** ovicular, eggy; ovular; albuminous, albuminoid; yolked, yolky; oviparous.

## 407. LIFE

.1 NOUNS **life, living, vitality,** being alive, having life, animation, animate existence; liveliness, animal spirits, vivacity, spriteliness; long life, longevity; viability; lifetime 110.5; immortality 112.3; birth 167; existence 1; bi(o)–, organ(o)–; –biosis.

.2 "one dem'd horrid grind" [Dickens], "a beauty chased by tragic laughter" [John Masefield], "a little gleam of Time between two eternities" [Carlyle], "a tale told by an idiot, full of sound and fury, signifying nothing" [Shakespeare], "a perpetual instruction in cause and effect" [Emerson], "a flame that is always burning itself out" [G. B. Shaw], "a dome of many-colored glass" [Shelley], "a long lesson in humility" [J. M. Barrie], "a fiction made up of contradiction" [William Blake], "a fatal complaint, and an eminently contagious one" [O. W. Holmes, Sr.], "a play of passion" [Sir W. Raleigh], "a comedy to those who think, a tragedy to those who feel" [H. Walpole].

.3 **life force, soul,** spirit, force of life, living force, *vis vitae, vis vitalis* [both L], **vital force** or vital energy, animating force or power or principle, inspiriting force or power or principle, *élan vital* [Fr], impulse of life, vital principle, **vital spark** or **flame,** spark of life, divine spark, life principle, vital spirit, vital fluid, anima; **breath,** life breath, **breath of life,** breath of one's nostrils, divine breath, life essence, essence of life, pneuma; prana, atman, jivatma, jiva; blood, **lifeblood,** heartblood, heart's blood; **heart,** heartbeat, beating heart; seat of life; growth force, bathmism; **life process;** biorhythm, biological clock, life cycle.

.4 **the living,** the living and breathing, all

animate nature, the quick; the quick and the dead.

.5 vivification, vitalization, animation, quickening.

.6 biosphere, ecosphere, noosphere; biochore, biotope, biocycle.

.7 VERBS **live,** be alive *or* animate *or* vital, have life, exist 1.8, breathe, respire, live and breathe, fetch *or* draw breath, draw the breath of life, walk the earth, subsist.

.8 **come to life,** come into existence *or* being, come into the world, see the light, be incarnated, **be born** *or* begotten *or* conceived; quicken; **revive, come to,** come alive, show signs of life; **awake, awaken;** rise again, live again, rise from the grave, resurge, resuscitate, reanimate, return to life.

.9 vivify, vitalize, **energize, animate, quicken,** inspirit, imbue *or* endow with life, give life to, put life *or* new life into, breathe life into, bring to life, bring *or* call into existence *or* being; conceive 167.13; give birth 167.15.

.10 **keep alive,** keep body and soul together, endure, survive, persist, last, hang on, be spared, have nine lives like a cat; support life; cheat death.

.11 ADJS **living, alive,** having life, live, very much alive, alive and kicking [informal], conscious, breathing, quick [archaic], **animate,** animated, **vital,** zoetic, instinct with life, imbued *or* endowed with life, vivified, enlivened, inspirited; in the flesh, among the living, in the land of the living, on this side of the grave, aboveground; existent 1.13; long-lived, tenacious of life; capable of life *or* survival, viable; –biotic, –coline *or* –colous.

.12 **life-giving,** animating, animative, quickening, vivifying, energizing.

## 408. DEATH

.1 NOUNS **death, dying,** somatic death, clinical death, biological death, **decease, demise,** thanat(o)–, necr(o)–; perishing, release, **passing away,** passing, passing over, "crossing the bar" [Tennyson], leaving life, making an end, departure, parting, going, going off *or* away, exit, ending, end 70, end of life, cessation of life, **loss of life,** ebb of life, expiration, **dissolution, extinction,** bane, annihilation, extinguishment, quietus; doom, summons of death, final summons, sentence of death, death knell, knell; **sleep, rest,** eternal rest *or* sleep, last sleep, last rest; **grave** 410.16; reward, debt of nature, last debt;

last muster, last roundup, curtains [slang]; jaws of death, hand *or* finger of death, shadow *or* shades of death.

.2 "the journey's end", "the undiscovered country from whose bourn no traveler returns", "dusty death" [all Shakespeare], "that dreamless sleep" [Byron], "a debt we all must pay" [Euripides], "the tribute due unto nature" [Laurence Sterne], "the sleeping partner of life" [Horace Smith], "a knell that summons thee to heaven or to hell", "that fell arrest without all bail" [both Shakespeare], "kind Nature's signal of retreat" [Samuel Johnson], "the latter end", "a little sleep, a little slumber, a little folding of the hands to sleep" [both Bible], "the seamouth of mortality" [Robinson Jeffers], "that good night" [Dylan Thomas], "the downward path" [Horace], "the gate of life" [St. Bernard], "the crown of life" [Edward Young], "an awfully big adventure" [J. M. Barrie].

.3 (personifications and symbols) **Death,** "Black Death" [Ovid], "Pale Death" [Horace], "the pale priest of the mute people" [R. Browning], "that grim ferryman", "that fell sergeant" [both Shakespeare], "Hell's grim Tyrant" [Pope], "the king of terrors" [Bible], **Grim Reaper,** Reaper; pale horse; pale horse, pale rider; angel of death, death's bright angel, Azrael; scythe *or* sickle of Death; **skull,** death's-head, grinning skull, crossbones, skull and crossbones; *memento mori* [L]; white cross.

.4 river of death, Styx, Stygian shore, Acheron; Jordan, Jordan's bank; "valley of the shadow of death" [Bible]; Heaven 1018; Hell 1019.

.5 early death, early grave, **untimely end;** sudden death; stroke of death, death stroke; deathblow 409.10.

.6 **violent death;** killing 409; suffocation, smothering, smotheration [informal]; asphyxiation; choking, choke, strangulation, strangling; drowning, watery grave; starvation; liver death, serum death; megadeath.

.7 **natural death;** easy *or* quiet *or* peaceful death *or* end, euthanasia, blessed *or* welcome release.

.8 dying day, deathday, "the supreme day and the inevitable hour" [Vergil]; final *or* fatal hour, dying hour, running-out of the sands, deathtime.

.9 moribundity, extremity, last *or* final extremity; **deathbed;** deathwatch; death struggle, agony, last agony, death agonies, death throes, throes of death; last breath *or* gasp, dying breath; **death rattle,** death groan.

.10 **swan song,** *chant du cygne* [Fr], death song.

.11 **bereavement** 812.1.

.12 **deathliness,** deathlikeness, deadliness; **weirdness, eeriness, uncanniness,** unearthliness; ghostliness, ghostlikeness; **ghastliness, grisliness, gruesomeness,** macabreness; paleness, haggardness, wanness, luridness, pallor; cadaverousness, corpselikeness; *facies Hippocratica* [L], Hippocratic face *or* countenance, mask of death.

.13 **death rate,** death toll; **mortality,** mortalness; transience 111; mutability 141.1.

.14 **obituary,** obit, necrology, necrologue; register of deaths, roll of the dead, death roll, mortuary roll, bill of mortality; casualty list; martyrology; body count.

.15 terminal case; **dying.**

.16 **corpse,** dead body, necr(o)–, dead man *or* woman, dead person, **cadaver, carcass, body;** *corpus delicti* [L]; **stiff** [slang]; **the dead,** the defunct, **the deceased,** the departed, the loved one; **decedent,** late lamented; **remains,** mortal *or* organic remains, bones, skeleton, dry bones, relics, reliquiae; dust, ashes, earth, clay, tenement of clay; **carrion,** crowbait, food for worms; **mummy,** mummification; embalmed corpse.

.17 **dead,** the majority, the great majority; one's fathers, one's ancestors; the choir invisible.

.18 **autopsy, postmortem, inquest,** postmortem examination, ex post facto examination, necropsy, necroscopy, medical examiner, coroner, mortality committee.

.19 VERBS **die, decease, succumb, expire, perish,** be taken by death, up and die [dial], cease to be *or* live, part, depart, quit this world, make one's exit, go, go the way of all flesh, go out, pass, pass on *or* over, **pass away,** meet one's death *or* end *or* **fate,** end one's life *or* days, depart this life, "shuffle off this mortal coil" [Shakespeare], put off mortality, **lose one's life,** fall, be lost, relinquish *or* surrender one's life, resign one's life *or* being, **give up the ghost,** yield the ghost *or* spirit, yield one's breath, take one's last breath, breathe one's last, stop breathing, fall asleep, close one's eyes, take one's last sleep, pay the debt of *or* to nature, go out with the

ebb, "go the way of all earth" [Bible], return to dust *or* the earth.

.20 [slang terms] **croak, go west, kick the bucket,** kick in, **pop off,** drop off, step off, go to the wall, knock off, pipe off, kick off, shove off, pass out, peg out, go for a burton [Brit], take the last count; check out, check in, cash in, hand *or* pass *or* cash in one's checks *or* chips; turn up one's toes, slip one's cable; have one's time *or* have it *or* buy it [all Brit].

.21 **meet one's Maker,** go to glory, go to kingdom come [informal], go to the happy hunting grounds, go to *or* reach a better place *or* land *or* life *or* world, go to one's rest *or* reward, go home, go home feet first [informal], go to one's last home, go to one's long account, go over to *or* join the majority *or* great majority, **be gathered to one's fathers,** join one's ancestors, join the angels, join the choir invisible, die in the Lord, go to Abraham's bosom, pass over Jordan, "walk through the valley of the shadow of death" [Bible], cross the Stygian ferry, give an obolus to Charon; awake to life immortal, "put on immortality" [Bible].

.22 **drop dead, fall dead,** fall down dead, bite the dust [informal]; come to an untimely end.

.23 die in harness, die with one's boots on, make a good end, die fighting, die in the last ditch, die like a man.

.24 die a natural death; die a violent death, be killed 409.21; OD [slang]; **starve, famish; smother, suffocate;** asphyxiate; choke, strangle; **drown,** go to a watery grave, go to Davy Jones's locker [informal]; catch one's death, catch one's death of cold.

.25 lay down *or* give one's life for one's country, **die for one's country,** *"pro patria mori"* [Horace], make the supreme sacrifice, do one's bit.

.26 die out 2.5, become extinct.

.27 be dead, be no more, sleep *or* be asleep with the Lord, sleep with one's fathers *or* ancestors; lie in the grave, lie in Abraham's bosom; push up daisies [informal].

.28 **bereave;** leave, leave behind; orphan, widow.

.29 ADJS **deathly, deathlike, deadly; weird, eerie, uncanny,** unearthly; ghostly, ghostlike; **ghastly, grisly, gruesome, macabre;** pale, deathly pale, wan, lurid, blue, livid, haggard; **cadaverous,** corpselike; mortuary.

.30 **dead, lifeless,** breathless, without life, inanimate 382.5, exanimate, without vital functions, sapro–; **deceased, demised, defunct,** croaked [slang], departed, departed this life, destitute of life, **gone, passed on,** gone the way of all flesh, gone west [informal], dead and gone, done for [informal], dead and done for [informal], no more, finished [informal], taken off or away, released, fallen, bereft of life, gone for a burton [Brit informal]; **at rest,** resting easy [informal], still, out of one's misery; **asleep,** sleeping, reposing; asleep in Jesus, with the Lord, asleep or dead in the Lord; **called home,** out of the world, gone to a better world or place or land, launched into eternity, gone to glory, gone to kingdom come [informal], "gathered to his fathers" [Bible], with the saints, sainted, numbered with the dead; in the grave six feet under, pushing up daisies [both informal]; carrion, food for worms; martyred; death-struck, death-stricken, smitten with death; stillborn; late, late lamented.

.31 **stone-dead;** dead as a doornail, dead as a herring, dead as mutton [all informal]; cold, stone-cold, "as cold as any stone" [Shakespeare], stiff [slang].

.32 **drowned,** in a watery grave or bier, in Davy Jones's locker.

.33 **dying,** expiring, going, slipping, slipping away, sinking, low, despaired of, given up, given up for dead, hopeless, bad, **moribund,** near death, near one's end, at the end of one's rope [informal], done for [informal], at the point of death, **at death's door,** at the portals of death, in articulo mortis [L], in extremis [L], in the jaws of death, facing or in the face of death; **on one's last legs** [informal], with one foot in the grave, tottering on the brink of the grave; on one's deathbed; at the last gasp; terminal; nonviable, incapable of life.

.34 **mortal, perishable,** subject to death, ephemeral, transient 111.7, mutable 141.6.

.35 **bereaved,** bereft, deprived; widowed; orphan, **orphaned,** parentless, fatherless, motherless.

.36 **postmortem,** postmortal, postmortuary, postmundane, post-obit, postobituary, **posthumous.**

.37 ADVS **deathly, deadly;** to the death, à la mort [Fr].

.38 PHRS one's hour is come, one's days are numbered, one's race is run, one's doom is sealed, life hangs by a thread, one's number is up, Death knocks at the door,

Death stares one in the face, the sands of life are running out.

## 409. KILLING

.1 NOUNS **killing, slaying, slaughter, dispatch, extermination, destruction,** destruction of life, taking of life, dealing death, bane; **kill; bloodshed,** bloodletting, blood, gore, flow of blood; mercy killing, euthanasia; ritual murder or killing, immolation, sacrifice; auto-da-fé [Pg], martyrdom, martyrization; lynching; stoning, lapidation; braining; shooting; poisoning; execution 1010.7.

.2 **homicide, manslaughter; murder,** bloody murder [informal]; bumping-off [slang]; foul play; **assassination;** removal, elimination, liquidation, purge, purging; thuggery, thuggism, thuggee.

.3 (killer or killing of) genocide (race), homicide (person), parenticide (parent), patricide (father), matricide (mother), fratricide (brother), sororicide (sister), parricide (kinsman), suicide (self), uxoricide (wife), mariticide (spouse, especially husband), regicide (king), tyrannicide (tyrant), vaticide (prophet), giganticide (giant), infanticide (infant), aborticide or feticide (fetus), pesticide (pest), rodenticide (rodent), vermicide or filaricide (worms), insecticide (insects), microbicide or germicide (germs), fungicide (fungi), herbicide (plants).

.4 **butchery,** butchering, **slaughter,** shambles, occision, slaughtering, hecatomb.

.5 **carnage, massacre, bloodbath, decimation,** saturnalia of blood; **mass murder, mass destruction,** wholesale murder, pogrom, race-murder, genocide, race extermination, **holocaust,** final solution.

.6 **suicide,** self-murder, self-destruction, death by one's own hand, felo-de-se [L], self-immolation, self-sacrifice; **disembowelment,** ritual suicide, hara-kiri, seppuku [both Jap], suttee, sutteeism; car of Jagannath or Juggernaut; mass suicide, race suicide.

.7 **suffocation,** smothering, smotheration, **asphyxiation,** asphyxia; **strangulation,** strangling, burking, throttling, stifling, garrote, garroting; **choking,** choke; **drowning.**

.8 **fatality,** fatal accident, violent death, **casualty,** disaster, calamity.

.9 **deadliness, lethality,** mortality, fatality; **malignance** or malignancy, malignity, **virulence, perniciousness,** banefulness.

.10 **deathblow,** death stroke, final stroke, fatal *or* mortal *or* lethal blow, *coup de grâce* [Fr].

.11 **killer, slayer, slaughterer, butcher,** bloodshedder; massacrer; **manslayer, homicide, murderer,** man-killer, bloodletter, Cain; **assassin,** assassinator; **cutthroat,** thug, desperado, bravo, gorilla [slang], apache, gunman; hit man *or* button man *or* gun *or* trigger man *or* torpedo *or* gunsel [all slang]; **hatchet man;** poisoner; strangler, garroter, burker; cannibal, man-eater, anthropophagus; head-hunter; mercy killer; thrill killer, homicidal maniac; executioner 1010.8; matador; exterminator, eradicator; –cide 409.3, –ctonus; poison, pesticide 676.3.

.12 (place of slaughter) aceldama, field of blood *or* bloodshed; **slaughterhouse,** butchery [Brit], shambles, abattoir; stockyard; gas chamber, concentration camp; Auschwitz, Belsen, etc.

.13 VERBS **kill, slay, put to death,** deprive of life, bereave of life, **take life,** take the life of, take one's life away, **do away with,** make away with, **put out of the way,** put to sleep, end, **put an end to,** end the life of, **dispatch, do to death,** do for, finish, finish off, take off, **dispose of, exterminate, destroy,** annihilate; liquidate, purge; carry off *or* away, remove from life; put down, put away, put one out of one's misery; launch into eternity, send to glory, send to kingdom come [informal], send to one's last account; martyr, martyrize; immolate, sacrifice; lynch; cut off, cut down, nip in the bud; poison; chloroform; starve; execute 1010.19.

.14 [slang terms] **rub out, croak, bump off,** polish off, blot out, erase, **wipe out,** zap, blast, **do in,** off, hit, ice, waste, gun down, lay out, take care of, take for a ride, give the business *or* works, get, fix, settle.

.15 **shed blood,** spill blood, let blood, bloody one's hands with, dye one's hands in blood, pour out blood like water, wade knee-deep in blood.

.16 **murder,** commit murder; **assassinate;** remove, **purge, liquidate,** eliminate, get rid of.

.17 **slaughter, butcher, massacre, decimate,** commit carnage, depopulate, murder *or* kill *or* slay en masse; commit mass murder *or* destruction; murder wholesale, commit genocide.

.18 **strike dead,** fell, bring down, lay low; drop, drop *or* stop in one's tracks; **shoot,** shoot down, pistol, shotgun, machine-gun, gun down, riddle, shoot to death; cut down, cut to pieces *or* ribbons, **put to the sword,** stab to death, jugulate, cut *or* slash the throat; **deal a deathblow,** give the quietus *or* coup de grâce, silence; knock in *or* on the head; **brain,** blow *or* knock *or* dash one's brains out, poleax; **stone,** lapidate, stone to death; blow up, blow to bits *or* pieces *or* kingdom come, frag; disintegrate, vaporize; burn to death, incinerate, burn at the stake.

.19 **strangle, garrote, throttle, choke,** burke; **suffocate, stifle, smother, asphyxiate,** stop the breath; **drown.**

.20 **condemn to death,** sign one's death warrant, strike the death knell of, finger [slang], give the kiss of death to.

.21 **be killed, get killed,** die a violent death, **come to a violent end,** meet with foul play, welter in one's own blood.

.22 **commit suicide, take one's own life, kill oneself,** die by one's own hand, do away with oneself, put an end to oneself; blow one's brains out, take an overdose (of a drug), OD [informal]; commit hara-kiri.

.23 ADJS **deadly, deathly,** deathful, **killing, destructive,** death-dealing, death-bringing, feral [archaic]; savage, brutal; internecine; **fatal, mortal, lethal,** –cidal; **malignant,** malign, **virulent, pernicious,** baneful.

.24 **murderous,** slaughterous; **cutthroat;** redhanded; **homicidal,** man-killing; genocidal; suicidal, self-destructive; cruel 939.24; **bloodthirsty,** bloody-minded; **bloody,** gory, sanguinary.

## 410. INTERMENT

.1 NOUNS **interment, burial,** burying, inhumation, sepulture, **entombment;** encoffinment, inurning, inurnment, urn burial; primary burial; secondary burial, reburial; disposal of the dead; burial *or* funeral *or* funerary customs.

.2 **cremation,** incineration, burning, reduction to ashes; pyre, funeral pile.

.3 **embalmment,** embalming; mummification.

.4 **last offices,** last honors, **last rites,** funeral rites, last duty *or* service, funeral service, burial service, exequies, **obsequies;** Office of the Dead, Memento of the Dead, requiem, requiem mass, dirge [archaic]; **extreme unction;** viaticum; funeral oration *or* sermon, eulogy; **wake,** deathwatch.

.5 **funeral, burial,** burying; funeral procession, cortege; dead march, muffled drum, last post [Brit], taps; dirge 875.5; burial at sea, deep six [slang].

.6 knell, passing bell, death bell, funeral ring, tolling, tolling of the knell.

.7 mourner, griever, lamenter, keener; mute, professional mourner; pallbearer, bearer.

.8 undertaker, mortician, funeral director; embalmer; gravedigger; sexton.

.9 mortuary, morgue, deadhouse [archaic], charnel house, lichhouse [Brit dial] funeral home or parlor, undertaker's establishment; crematorium, crematory, cinerarium, burning ghat.

.10 hearse, funeral car or coach; catafalque.

.11 coffin, casket, burial case, box, kist [Scot]; wooden kimono or overcoat [slang]; sarcophagus; mummy case.

.12 urn, cinerary urn, funerary or funeral urn or vessel, bone pot, ossuary.

.13 bier, litter.

.14 graveclothes, shroud, winding sheet, cerecloth, cerements; pall.

.15 graveyard, cemetery, burial ground or place, burying place or ground, campo santo [Ital], boneyard [slang], burial yard, necropolis, polyandrium, memorial park, city or village of the dead; churchyard, God's acre; potter's field; Golgotha, Calvary; lych-gate.

.16 tomb, sepulcher; grave, burial, pit, deep six [slang]; resting place, "the lone couch of his everlasting sleep" [Shelley]; last home, long home, narrow house, house of death, low house, low green tent; crypt, vault, burial chamber; ossuary, ossuarium; charnel house, bone house; mausoleum; catacombs; mastaba; cist grave, box grave, passage grave, shaft grave, beehive tomb; shrine, reliquary, monstrance, tope, stupa; cenotaph; dokhma, tower of silence; pyramid, mummy chamber; burial mound, tumulus, barrow, cist, cromlech, dolmen.

.17 monument, gravestone 570.12.

.18 epitaph, inscription, hic jacet [L], tombstone marking.

.19 VERBS inter, inhume, bury, sepulture, inearth [archaic], lay to rest, consign to the grave, lay in the grave or earth, lay under the sod, put six feet under [slang]; tomb, entomb, ensepulcher, hearse; enshrine; inurn; encoffin, coffin; hold or conduct a funeral.

.20 cremate, incinerate, burn, reduce to ashes.

.21 lay out; embalm; mummify; lie in state.

.22 ADJS funereal, funeral, funerary, funebrial, funebrous or funebrious, funèbre

[Fr], mortuary, exequial, obsequial, feral; sepulchral, tomblike; cinerary; necrological, obituary, epitaphic; dismal 872.24; mournful 872.26; dirgelike 875.18.

.23 ADVS beneath the sod, underground, six feet under [slang], "in the dark union of insensate dust" [Byron]; at rest, resting in peace.

.24 PHRS RIP, requiescat in pace [L sing], requiescant in pace [L pl], rest in peace; hic jacet [L], ci-gît [Fr], here lies; ashes to ashes and dust to dust [Book of Common Prayer].

## 411. PLANTS

.1 NOUNS plants, vegetation; flora, plant life, vegetable life; vegetable kingdom, plant kingdom; herbage, flowerage, verdure, greenery, greens; botany 412; vegetation spirit 413.4.

.2 growth, stand, crop; plantation, planting; clump, tuft, tussock, hassock.

.3 plant, phyt(o)–, –phyte; vegetable; weed; seedling; cutting; vascular plant; seed plant, spermatophyte; gymnosperm; angiosperm, flowering plant; monocotyledon or monocot or monocotyl; dicotyledon or dicot or dicotyl; polycotyledon or polycot or polycotyl; thallophyte, fungus; gametophyte, sporophyte; exotic, hothouse plant; ephemeral, annual, biennial, triennial, perennial; evergreen, deciduous plant; cosmopolite; aquatic plant, hydrophyte, amphibian.

.4 (varieties) legume, pulse, vetch, bean, pea, lentil, phac(o)– or phak(o)–; herb; succulent; vine, viti–, grapevine, ampel(o)–, creeper, ivy, climber, liana; fern, –pteris, bracken; moss, bry(o)–, musc(o)– or musci–; wort, liverwort; algae, phyc(o)–; brown algae, fucus; green algae, conferva, confervoid; red algae, bluegreen algae; planktonic algae, phytoplankton, diatom; seaweed, kelp, sea moss, rockweed, gulfweed, sargasso or sargassum, sea lentil, wrack, sea wrack; fungus, fungi–, myc(o)–, –mycete, mold, rust, smut, puffball, mushroom, toadstool; lichen; parasitic plant, parasite, saprophyte, perthophyte, heterophyte, autophyte; plant families 412.3–6; fruits and vegetables 308.50,51.

.5 grass, gramin(i)–, gramineous or graminaceous plant, pasture or forage grass, lawn grass, ornamental grass; aftergrass, fog [dial]; cereal, cereal plant, farinaceous plant, grain, grani–, corn [Brit]; sedge, caric(o)–; rush, reed, cane, bamboo.

.6 **turf, sod, sward,** greensward; divot.

.7 **green, lawn;** artificial turf, Astroturf; grassplot, greenyard; grounds; **common, park, village green;** golf course or links, fairway; bowling green, putting green.

.8 **grassland,** grass; **meadow,** meadow land, mead [archaic], swale, lea, haugh or haughland [Scot], vega; **pasture,** pasturage, pasture land, park [Brit dial]; **range,** grazing; **prairie, savanna, steppe,** steppeland, **pampas,** pampa, campo, llano, **veld,** grass veld.

.9 **shrubbery; shrub, bush,** thamn(o)–; scrub, bramble, brier, brier bush.

.10 **tree,** timber, dry(o)–, dendr(o)–, –dendron; shade tree, fruit tree, timber tree; softwood tree, hardwood tree; sapling, seedling; pollard; conifer, evergreen.

.11 **woodland, wood, woods, timberland,** hyl(o)–; **timber,** stand of timber, **forest,** forest land, forest preserve, state or national forest; forestry, dendrology, silviculture; afforestation, reforestation; rain forest, cloud forest; climax forest; sprout forest; selection forest; protection forest; index forest; fringing forest, gallery forest; primeval forest; virgin forest; greenwood; **jungle,** jungles; boondocks [informal]; wildwood, **bush,** scrub; bushveld, tree veld; shrubland, scrubland; pine barrens, palmetto barrens; hanger; **park,** chase [Brit]; park forest; arboretum.

.12 **grove, woodlet;** holt [dial], hurst, spinney [Brit], tope [India], shaw [dial], bosk [archaic]; **orchard;** wood lot; coppice, copse; *bocage* [Fr].

.13 **thicket,** thickset, **copse, coppice,** copsewood, frith [Brit dial]; bosket [archaic], boscage; covert; motte; **brake,** canebrake; chaparral; chamisal; ceja.

.14 **brush, scrub,** bush, **brushwood,** shrubwood, scrubwood.

.15 **undergrowth, underwood, underbrush,** copsewood, undershrubs, boscage, frith [Brit dial].

.16 **foliage, leafage,** leafiness, umbrage, foliation; frondage, frondescence; vernation.

.17 **leaf, frond,** phyll(o)–, –phyllum; leaflet, foliole; ligule, ligul(i)–; lamina, **blade,** spear, spire, pile, flag; **needle,** pine needle; floral leaf, **petal,** sepal; bract, bractlet, bracteole, spathe, involucre, involucrum; glume, lemma; cotyledon, seed leaf, –cotyl; stipule, stipula.

.18 **branch,** fork, **limb, bough;** deadwood; **twig, sprig,** switch; **spray; shoot,** offshoot, spear, frond; scion; **sprout,** sprit, slip, burgeon, thallus, thall(o)– or thalli–, clad-

(o)–; sucker; **runner,** stolon, flagellum, sarmentum, sarment; bine; **tendril;** ramage; branchiness, branchedness, ramification.

.19 **stem, stalk, stock,** axis, *caulis* [L], caul(o)– or cauli–, –dendron; **trunk,** bole, corm(o)–; spear, spire; straw; reed; cane; culm, haulm [Brit]; caudex; footstalk, pedicel, peduncle, pod(o)–; leafstalk, petiole, petiolus, petiolule; seedstalk; caulicle; tigella; funicule, funiculus; stipe, anthrophore, carpophore, gynophore.

.20 **root,** radix, radicle, –rhiza or –rrhiza; rootlet; **taproot,** tap; **rhizome,** rootstock; **tuber,** tubercle; **bulb,** bulbil, bulb(o)–, corm, earthnut.

.21 **bud,** burgeon, gemma; gemmule, gemmula; plumule, acrospire; leaf bud, flower bud.

.22 **flower, posy, blossom, bloom,** flori–, anth(o)–, blow [archaic]; floweret, floret, floscule; **wildflower; gardening,** horticulture, floriculture; hortorium.

.23 **bouquet, nosegay, posy,** boughpot, flower arrangement; **boutonniere,** buttonhole [Brit]; **corsage; spray; wreath;** festoon, **garland,** chaplet, lei.

.24 **flowering,** florescence, efflorescence, flowerage, **blossoming, blooming;** inflorescence; **blossom, bloom,** blowing, blow; unfolding, unfoldment; anthesis, full bloom.

.25 (types of inflorescence) raceme, corymb, umbel, umbell(i)–, panicle, cyme, thyrse, spadix, verticillaster; head, capitulum; spike, spikelet; ament, catkin; strobile, cone, pine cone.

.26 (flower parts) petal, perianth; calyx, calyc(o)–, epicalyx; corolla, corolla tube, corona; androecium, anther, stamen, stamin(i)–, microsporophyll; pistil, pistill–, gynoecium; style, styl(o)– or styli–; stigma, carpel, megasporophyll; receptacle, torus, –clinium.

.27 **ear,** spike; auricle; ear of corn, mealie; cob, corncob.

.28 **seed vessel, seedcase,** seedbox, pericarp, angi(o)–; hull, husk; **capsule, pod,** cod [dial], seed pod; pease cod, legume, legumen, boll, burr, follicle, silique.

.29 **seed,** sperm(o)– or sperma– or spermi–, spermat(o)–; **stone, pit, nut,** pyren(o)–; acorn, balan(o)–; pip; fruit, carp(o)–, –carp, –carpium; **grain, kernel, berry,** cocc(o)– or cocci–; flaxseed, linseed; hayseed; bird seed.

.30 **vegetation, growth;** germination, pullulation; burgeoning, sprouting; budding, lux-uriation.

.31 VERBS **vegetate, grow;** germinate, pullu-late; root, take root, strike root; sprout up, shoot up, upsprout, upspear; **bur-geon,** put forth, burst forth; **sprout,** shoot; **bud,** gemmate, put forth *or* put out buds; **leaf,** leave, leaf out, put out *or* put forth leaves; flourish, luxuriate, riot, grow rank *or* lush; overgrow, overrun.

.32 **flower,** be in flower, **blossom, bloom,** be in bloom, blow, effloresce, floreate, burst into bloom.

.33 ADJS **vegetable,** vegetal, vegetative, vege-tational, vegetarian; **plantlike,** –phytic; **herbaceous,** herbal, herbous, herbose, herby; leguminous, leguminose, legumini-form; cereal, farinaceous; weedy; fruity, fruitlike, –carpic, –carpous; tuberous, bul-bous; rootlike, rhizoid, radicular, radi-cated, radiciform; botanic(al) 412.8.

.34 algal, fucoid, confervoid; phytoplank-tonic, diatomaceous; fungous, fungoid, fungiform.

.35 **floral; flowery, florid** [archaic]; **flowered,** floreate, floriate, floriated, –florate, –flo-rous, –anthous; **flowering, blossoming, blooming,** bloomy, florescent, infiores-cent, efflorescent, in flower, in bloom, in blossom; uniflorous, multiflorous; radici-florous, rhizanthous; **garden,** horticul-tural, hortulan, floricultural.

.36 **arboreal,** arborical, arboresque, arbore-ous, arbory; **treelike,** arboriform, arbo-rescent, dendroid, dendriform, dendritic; deciduous, nondeciduous; evergreen; softwood, hardwood; piny; coniferous; citrous; bushy, shrubby, scrubby, scrub-bly; bushlike, shrublike, scrublike.

.37 **sylvan, woodland, forest,** forestal; dendro-logic(al), silvicultural, afforestational, re-forestational; **wooded,** timbered, for-ested, arboreous; **woody,** woodsy, bushy, shrubby, scrubby; bosky, copsy, braky.

.38 **leafy,** leavy [archaic], bowery; foliated, foliate, foliose, foliaged, leaved, –phyl-lous, –folious; **branched,** branchy, branch-ing, ramified, ramate, ramous *or* ramose; twiggy.

.39 **verdant, verdurous,** verdured; **mossy,** moss-covered, moss-grown; **grassy,** grass-like, gramineous, graminaceous; turfy, swardy, turflike, caespitose, tufted; mead-owy.

.40 **luxuriant,** flourishing, **rank, lush,** riotous, exuberant; dense, impenetrable, thick, heavy, gross; jungly, jungled; overgrown,

overrun; **weedy,** unweeded, weed-choked, weed-ridden; gone to seed.

.41 **perennial,** ephemeral; hardy, half-hardy; **deciduous,** evergreen.

.42 **algae**

| | |
|---|---|
| brown algae | pond scum |
| conferva | red algae |
| dulse | reindeer moss |
| fucoid | rockweed |
| fucus, fuc(o)– *or* fuci– | sargasso, sargassum |
| green algae | scum |
| gulfweed | sea lettuce |
| Iceland moss | sea moss |
| Irish moss | seaweed |
| kelp | sea wrack |
| lichen | stonewort |
| phytoplankton, plank-ton | wrack |

.43 **ferns**

| | |
|---|---|
| adder's fern | lip fern |
| basket fern | maidenhair |
| beech fern | marsh fern |
| bladder fern | moonwort |
| boulder fern | oak fern |
| bracken | osmunda |
| chain fern | ostrich fern |
| cliff brake | rattlesnake fern |
| climbing fern | rock brake |
| curly grass | shield fern |
| grape fern | snuffbox fern |
| hart's tongue | walking fern |
| holly fern | wall fern |
| lady fern | wood fern |

.44 **flowers**

| | |
|---|---|
| acacia | Christmas rose |
| African violet | chrysanthemum |
| amaryllis | cineraria |
| anemone | clematis |
| arbutus | clethra |
| arrowhead | cockscomb |
| asphodel | columbine |
| aster | cornel |
| azalea | cornflower |
| baby-blue-eyes | cosmos |
| baby's breath | cowslip |
| bachelor button | crocus |
| begonia | cyclamen |
| bitterroot | daffodil |
| black-eyed Susan | dahlia |
| bleeding heart | daisy |
| bloodroot | dandelion |
| bluebell | delphinium |
| bluet | dogwood |
| bridal wreath | duckweed |
| broom | Dutchman's-breeches |
| buttercup | edelweiss |
| cactus | eglantine |
| calendula | fireweed |
| camas | flax |
| camellia | *fleur-de-lis* [Fr] |
| camomile | forget-me-not |
| campanula | forsythia |
| candytuft | foxglove |
| carnation | foxtail |
| cat's-paw | fuchsia |
| cattail | gardenia |
| century plant | gentian |
| Chinese lantern | geranium |

gladiolus
goldenrod
groundsel
harebell
hawthorn
heather
hepatica
hibiscus
hollyhock
honeysuckle
horehound
hyacinth
hydrangea
impatience
Indian paintbrush
indigo
iris, irid(o)–
jack-in-the-pulpit
japonica
jasmine
jonquil
knotweed
lady's-slipper
larkspur
lavender
lilac
lily
lily of the valley
lobelia
lotus
love-lies-bleeding
lupine
magnolia
mallow
marguerite
marigold
marshmallow
marsh marigold
mayflower
mignonette
mimosa
moccasin flower
mock orange
monkshood
morning-glory
moss rose
motherwort
myrtle
narcissus
nasturtium
oleander

opium poppy,
  mecon(o)–
orchid
oxalis
pansy, viol–
passion flower
peony
periwinkle
petunia
phlox
pink
poinsettia
poppy
portulaca
primrose
Queen Anne's lace
ranunculus
resurrection plant
rhododendron
rose, rhod(o)–
shooting star
smilax
snapdragon
snowball
snowberry
snowdrop
spiraea
stock
strawflower
sunflower
sweet alyssum
sweet pea
sweet William
trillium
trumpet vine
tulip
umbrella plant
Venus's flytrap
verbena
vetch
viburnum
viola
violet
wallflower
water lily, nymph(o)–
  or nymphi–
wisteria
wolfbane
yarrow
yucca
zinnia

bristly foxtail grass
broomcorn
buckwheat
buffalo grass
bulrush
bunch grass
canary grass
cane
China grass
cocksfoot grass
corn
cotton grass
crab grass
durra
eelgrass
English rye grass
feather grass
finger-comb grass
finger grass
flyaway grass
four-leaved grass
gama or sesame grass
grama or mesquite
  grass
guinea grass
hairgrass
hassock grass
herd's grass
horsetail
Indian corn
Italian rye grass
Japanese lawn grass
Kentucky bluegrass
little quaking grass
lovegrass
lyme grass
maize
meadow fescue
meadow foxtail
meadow grass
millet
myrtle grass

oats
orchard grass
paddy
palm-leaved grass
pampas grass
papyrus
peppergrass
pin grass
plume grass
pony grass
redtop
reed
ribbon grass
rice, oryz(o)– or oryzi–
rush
rye
scutch
sedge
sesame
sheep's fescue
silk grass
sorghum
spear grass
squirrel tail grass
star grass
striped grass
sugar cane
switch grass
sword grass
tear grass
timothy
tufted hair grass
viper's grass
wheat
wild oats
wire grass
wood meadow grass
woolly beard grass
worm grass
yellow-eyed grass
zebra grass
zoysia

## .47 herbs

angelica
anise, anis(o)–
balm
basil
belladonna
boneset
borage
burning bush
calendula
camomile
caraway
cardamom
castor-oil plant
catnip, catmint
chervil
chicory
clover
coriander
Cretan dittany
deadly nightshade
death camas
dill
dittany
fennel
feverroot
figwort
fraxinella, gas plant
ginseng

hemp
henbane
horehound
hyssop
licorice
liverwort
mandrake
marijuana
marjoram
mayapple
mint
monkshood
mullein
mustard
oregano, origanum
parsley
peppermint
rosemary
rue
sage
savory
sorrel
spearmint
sweet cicely
sweet woodruff
tansy
tarragon
thyme

## .45 fungi

blight
blue mold
bread mold
ergot, ergo–
green mold
mildew
mold
mushroom
penicillium
puffball
rot

rust
slime mold
smut
tinea
toadstool
truffle
tuckahoe
verticillium, verticilli–
water mold
yeast

## .46 grasses, grains

alfilaria
bamboo
barley
beach grass
beard grass
Bengal grass

bent, bent grass
Bermuda grass
black bent
bluegrass
bluejoint
bog grass

tobacco
wild marjoram

wintergreen

## .48 mosses

club moss
Florida moss
flowering moss
ground pine
hair cap moss
lycopodium
peat moss

red tipped moss
scale moss
sphagnum moss
staghorn moss
tree moss
white moss

## .49 shrubs

alder
azalea
barberry
bayberry
blackberry
blackthorn
blueberry
box
broom
caper
chokeberry
cinchona, quin(o)–
coca
coffee
cranberry
currant
daphne
elder
forsythia
frangipani
fuchsia
furze
gardenia
genista
gooseberry
gorse
greasewood
guava
guayule
haw
heather
hemp tree
henna
hibiscus
holly
huckleberry
hydrangea
indigo
Juneberry
juniper
jute
kalmia
laurel, laur(o)–

leatherleaf
lilac
magnolia
manzanita
mesquite
milkwort
mock orange
mountain lilac
myrica
myrtle
nandin, nandina
ninebark
oleander
Persian berry
photinia
poison sumac
privet
pussy willow
queen of the meadow
rabbit berry
red brush
rhododendron
rosebay
rosemary
rose of Sharon
sage, sagebrush
sand myrtle
sisal
snowberry
snow wreath
spiraea
sumac
symplocos
syringa
tamarisk
turkey berry
veronica
whin
wintercreeper
witch hazel
yellowroot
zenobia

## .50 trees

acacia
ailanthus
alder
allspice
almond
apple
apricot
ash
aspen
avocado, alligator
   pear
bald cypress
balsa
balsam

banyan
basswood
bay
bayberry
beech
betel palm
birch
boxwood
Brazil-nut
breadfruit
buckeye
butternut
buttonwood
cacao

camphor tree
candleberry
cashew
cassia
catalpa
cedar
cherry
chestnut
chinaberry tree, China
   tree
chinquapin
cinnamon
citron
clove
coconut, coco
cork oak
cottonwood
cypress
date palm
dogwood
ebony
elder
elm
eucalyptus
fig
fir
frankincense
ginkgo
grapefruit
guava
gum
hawthorn
hazel, hazelnut
hemlock
henna
hickory
holly
hop tree
hornbeam
horse chestnut
ironwood
juniper
kumquat
laburnum
lancewood
larch
laurel
lemon
lignum vitae
lime
linden
litchi, litchi nut
locust
logwood

madroña
magnolia
mahogany
mango
mangrove
maple
medlar
mimosa
mountain ash
mulberry
nutmeg
nux vomica
oak
olive
orange
palm, palmi–
papaw
papaya
peach
pear
pecan
persimmon
pine
pistachio
plane
plum
pomegranate
poplar
quince
raffia palm
rain tree
redwood
rosewood
sandalwood
sassafras
satinwood
senna
sequoia
serviceberry
silk oak
spruce
sycamore
tamarack
tamarind
tangerine
teak
thorn tree
tulip oak
tulip tree
upas
walnut
willow
witch hazel
yew

## .51 vines

bittersweet
clematis
dewberry
English ivy
grape
greenbrier
honeysuckle
hop

ivy
jasmine
liana
morning glory
poison ivy
trumpet creeper
Virginia creeper
wisteria

## .52 weeds

beggar's-ticks
bindweed
brake
burdock
burr
Canada thistle

cat's ear
chickweed
chicory
crab grass
crazyweed
creeping buttercup

| | |
|---|---|
| dandelion | prickly lettuce |
| dock | purslane |
| fireweed | quack grass |
| horsetail | ragweed |
| jimsonweed | sandburr |
| knawel | scarlet pimpernel |
| knotweed | sheep's sorrel, sheep |
| lady's thumb | sorrel |
| locoweed | shepherd's purse |
| mallow | skunk cabbage |
| mayweed | smartweed |
| milkweed | speedwell |
| mustard | spotted spurge |
| nettle | spurry |
| pigweed | stinkweed |
| plantain | tarweed |
| poison ivy | thistle |
| poke, pokeweed | tumbleweed |

## 412. BOTANY

.1 NOUNS **botany**, phytology; phytography, phytonomy; algology, phycology, bryology, dendrology, fungology, hydroponics, aquiculture, mycology, paleobotany, physiological botany, phytobiology, phytochemistry, phytoecology, phytogeography, phytomorphology, phytopaleontology, phytopathology, phytotaxonomy, phytoteratology, phytotomy, phytotopography, pomology, structural botany, systematic botany, vegetable or plant anatomy, vegetable or plant pathology, vegetable or plant physiology.

.2 **botanist**, phytologist, herbalist [archaic]; phytographer, phytonomist; algologist, phycologist, bryologist, dendrologist, ecologist, fungologist, herbalist, mycologist, phytobiologist, phytoecologist, phytogeographer, phytopaleontologist, phytopathologist, phytoteratologist, pomologist.

.3 Thallophyta (thallus plants), thallogens, thallophytes: algae; Cyanophyceae (blue-green algae); Chlorophyceae (green algae); Phaeophyceae, Ectocarpales, Fucales (brown algae); Rhodophyceae (red algae); fungi, molds; Schizomycetes (fission fungi, bacteria); Myxomycetes (slime molds); Phycomycetes (algal fungi, water molds); Ascomycetes (sac fungi, lichen, lichen fungi); Penicillium (blue and green molds); Basidiomycetes (basidium fungi, rusts, smuts, puffballs, mushrooms, toadstools).

.4 Bryophyta (moss plants), bryophytes: Hepaticae (liverworts); Musci (mosses).

.5 Pteridophyta (fern plants), pteridophytes: Lycopodiales (ground pines, club mosses, quill worts); Lycopodiaceae (club mosses); Selaginellaceae; Sigillaria, Stigmaria; Equisetaceae, Equisetales (horsetails), equisetum; Calamites, calamite; Filicales, Filices (ferns), filicoids; Cycadofilicales, Cycadofilices (cycad ferns), cycadofilicales; Lepidodendraceae (fossil trees): Lepidodendron, lepidodendroids, lepidodendrids.

.6 Spermatophyta (seed plants), spermatophytes: Gymnospermae (naked-seeded plants), gymnosperms; Cycadales, cycads; Gnetales, gnetums; Ginkgoales, ginkgoes; Pinales or Coniferae (cone-bearing evergreens), conifers; Angiospermae (covered-seeded plants), angiosperms; Monocotyledones, Endogenae (cereals, palms, lilies, orchids, bananas, pineapples, etc.); monocotyledons, endogens; Dicotyledones (oaks, apples, sunflowers, peas, etc.), dicotyledons.

.7 VERBS botanize, herbalize.

.8 ADJS **botanic(al)**, phytologic(al); phytobiological, phytochemical, pomological, etc. 412.1.

## 413. AGRICULTURE

.1 NOUNS **agriculture, farming, husbandry;** cultivation, culture, geoponics, tillage, tilth; agrology, agronomy, agronomics; thremmatology; agrogeology, agricultural geology; dry farming, dryland farming, dirt farming [informal], truck farming, contour farming, mixed farming, intensive farming, subsistence farming, tank farming, hydroponics, grain farming, strip farming, fruit farming, sharecropping; rural economy or economics, farm economy or economics, agrarian economy or economics, agrarianism.

.2 **horticulture, gardening;** landscape gardening, landscape architecture, groundskeeping; truck gardening, market gardening, olericulture; flower gardening, flower-growing, floriculture; viniculture, viticulture; orcharding, fruit-growing, pomiculture, citriculture.

.3 **forestry,** arboriculture, tree farming, silviculture, forest management; Christmas tree farming; forestation, afforestation, reforestation; lumbering, logging; woodcraft.

.4 (agricultural deities) vegetation spirit or daemon, fertility god or spirit, year-daemon, forest god or spirit, corn god, Ceres, Demeter, Gaea or Gaia; Triptolemus or Triptolemos; Dionysus or Dionysos; Persephone, Proserpina or Proserpine or Persephassa, Kore or Cora; Flora; Aristaeus; Pomona; Frey.

.5 **agriculturist,** agriculturalist; agrologist,

agronomist; **farmer,** granger, husbandman, **yeoman,** cultivator, tiller, **tiller of the soil;** peasant, *Bauer* [Ger], rustic 919.8,9; **rancher,** ranchman; **grower,** raiser; **planter,** tea-planter, coffee-planter, etc.; gentleman farmer; dirt farmer [informal]; dry farmer; truck farmer; tree farmer; peasant holder *or* propietor, *kulak, muzhik* [both Russ]; tenant farmer, crofter [Brit]; sharecropper, cropper, collective farm worker, *kolkhoznik* [Russ], *kibbutznik* [Yid]; farmhand, farm laborer, migrant *or* migratory worker *or* laborer, picker; plowman, plowboy; planter, sower; reaper, harvester, harvestman; haymaker.

.6 **horticulturist, nurseryman, gardener;** landscape gardener, landscapist, landscape architect; truck gardener, market gardener, olericulturist; **florist,** floriculturist; vinegrower, viniculturist, viticulturist, vintager, *vigneron* [Fr]; orchardist, orchardman, fruit-grower.

.7 **forester;** arboriculturist, silviculturist, tree farmer; conservationist; **ranger,** forest ranger; woodsman, woodman [Brit], woodcraftsman; **logger, lumberman,** timberman, lumberjack; woodcutter, wood chopper.

.8 **farm,** farmplace, farmstead, farmhold [archaic], farmery [Brit], **grange,** location [Austral], pen [Jamaica]; **plantation,** cotton plantation, etc., *hacienda* [Sp]; **ranch,** rancho, rancheria, station [Austral]; dude ranch; croft, homecroft [Brit]; **homestead,** steading; toft [Brit]; mains [Brit dial]; demesne, homefarm, demesne farm, manor farm; **barnyard,** farmyard, barton [Brit dial]; collective farm, *kolkhoz* [Russ], *kibbutz* [Heb]; dry farm, truck farm, stock farm, grain farm, fur farm, fruit farm, orchard, dairy farm, chicken farm *or* ranch, poultry farm, sheep farm *or* ranch, cattle ranch; factory farm; tree farm; farmland, arable land, plowland, fallow; grassland, pasture 411.8.

.9 **field,** tract, plat, **plot, patch,** piece *or* parcel of land; cultivated land; clearing; hayfield, corn field, wheat field, etc.; paddy, rice paddy.

.10 **garden,** *jardin* [Fr]; paradise; garden spot; kitchen garden, vegetable garden, victory garden, market *or* truck garden, flower garden, rock garden, alpine garden, bog garden, tea garden, roof garden, Japanese garden, ornamental garden, sunken garden; botanical garden, *jardin des plantes* [Fr], arboretum; pinetum; shrubbery;

vineyard, vinery, grapery, grape ranch; bed, **flower bed,** border; **herbarium,** dry garden, hortus siccus; –arium, –etum, –ery.

.11 **nursery; conservatory, greenhouse,** forcing house, summerhouse, glasshouse, lathhouse, **hothouse,** coolhouse; force *or* forcing bed, forcing pit, **hotbed,** cold frame; seedbed; cloche; pinery, orangery.

.12 **growing, raising,** rearing; **green thumb.**

.13 **cultivation,** cultivating, culture, **tilling,** dressing, working; harrowing, plowing, contour plowing, furrowing, listing, fallowing, weeding, hoeing, pruning, thinning.

.14 **planting,** setting; sowing, **seeding,** semination, insemination; **dissemination,** broadcast, broadcasting; transplantation, resetting; retimbering, reforestation.

.15 **harvest,** harvesting, **reaping, gleaning,** gathering, cutting; nutting; crop 811.5.

.16 VERBS **farm, ranch; grow, raise,** rear; crop; dryfarm; sharecrop; **garden.**

.17 **cultivate,** culture, **dress, work, till,** till the soil, dig, delve, spade; mulch; **plow,** list, fallow, backset [W US]; **harrow,** rake; **weed,** weed out, hoe, cut, prune, thin, thin out; force; fertilize 165.8.

.18 **plant,** implant [archaic], **set,** put in; **sow,** seed, seed down, seminate, inseminate; **disseminate,** broadcast, sow broadcast, scatter seed; drill; bed; dibble; **transplant,** reset, pot; forest; **retimber, reforest.**

.19 **harvest, reap,** crop, **glean, gather,** gather in, bring in, get in the harvest, reap and carry; **pick,** pluck; dig, grabble [S US]; mow, cut; hay; nut; crop herbs.

.20 ADJS **agricultural, agrarian,** agro–, geoponic(al), agronomic(al); farm, **farming;** arable; **rural** 182.6.

.21 **horticultural;** olericultural; vinicultural; viticultural; arboricultural, silvicultural.

## 414. ANIMALS, INSECTS

.1 NOUNS **animal life, animal kingdom,** brute creation, **fauna,** Animalia [zool], animality, zo(o)–; birds, beasts, and fish; the beasts of the field, the fowl of the air, and the fish of the sea; domestic animals, livestock, stock [informal], cattle; wild animals *or* beasts, beasts of field, wildlife, denizens of the forest *or* jungle *or* wild, furry creatures; beasts of prey; game, big game, small game.

.2 **animal, creature,** –zoon, critter [dial], living being *or* thing, creeping thing; **brute, beast,** varmint [dial], dumb animal *or* creature, dumb friend.

.3 (varieties) **vertebrate** 415.7–8, **invertebrate** 415.3–6; **biped, quadruped; mammal,** mammalian 414.58; **primate** 414.59, –anthropus; **marsupial,** marsupialian; canine; **feline; rodent,** gnawer; **ungulate; ruminant;** insectivore, herbivore, carnivore, omnivore; cannibal; scavenger; reptile 414.30,31,60,61; amphibian 414.32,62; aquatic; cosmopolite; vermin, varmint [dial].

.4 **pachyderm; elephant,** Jumbo, hathi [India]; **mammoth,** woolly mammoth; **mastodon; rhinoceros,** rhino; **hippopotamus,** hippo, river horse.

.5 (hoofed animals) **deer, buck, doe, fawn;** red deer, **stag, hart, hind;** roe deer, roe, roebuck; musk deer; fallow deer; hogdeer; white-tailed or Virginia deer; mule deer; **elk,** wapiti; **moose; reindeer,** caribou; deerlet; **antelope;** gazelle, kaama, gnu, wildebeest, hartebeest, springbok, dik-dik, eland or Cape elk, koodoo; **camel,** dromedary, ship of the desert; **giraffe,** camelopard, okapi.

.6 **cattle** 414.69, kine [archaic pl], neat; beef cattle, beef, beeves [pl]; dairy cattle or cows; bovine animal, **bovine,** critter [dial]; **cow,** bossy [informal]; milk or milch cow, milker, milcher, dairy cow; **bull,** bullock, tauro– or tauri(o)–, top cow [dial]; **steer,** stot [Brit dial], **ox,** oxen [pl]; **calf, heifer,** yearling, fatling, stirk [Brit]; **dogie,** leppy [both W US]; **maverick** [W US]; hornless cow, butthead, muley head [both dial], muley cow; zebu, Brahman; yak; musk-ox; **buffalo,** water buffalo, Indian buffalo, carabao; bison, aurochs, wisent.

.7 **sheep** 414.70, jumbuck [Austral]; **lamb,** lambkin, yeanling; teg [Brit]; **ewe,** ewe lamb; **ram,** tup [Brit], wether; bellwether; mutton.

.8 **goat;** he-goat, buck, **billy goat** or billy [both informal]; she-goat, doe, **nanny goat** or nanny [both informal]; **kid,** doeling; mountain goat.

.9 **swine** 414.71, **pig, hog,** porker, hyo–, –choerus; **shoat,** piggy, piglet, pigling; sucking or suckling pig; gilt; **boar, sow;** barrow; wild boar, tusker, razorback; babirusa.

.10 **horse** 414.68, hipp(o)–, –hippus; horseflesh, hoss [dial], critter [dial]; **equine, mount, nag** [informal]; **steed,** prancer, dobbin; charger, courser, war-horse, destrier [archaic]; Houyhnhnm [Swift]; **colt, foal, filly; mare,** brood mare; **stallion, studhorse, stud,** top horse [dial], entire

horse, entire; gelding, purebred horse, blood horse; wild horse, Przewalsky's horse, tarpan.

.11 **pony,** Shetland pony, Shetland, shelty, Iceland pony, Galloway.

.12 **bronco,** bronc, range horse, Indian pony, cayuse, mustang; bucking bronco, buckjumper, sunfisher, broomtail; cow-cutting horse, stock horse, roping horse, cow pony.

.13 (colored horses) bay, bayard, chestnut, gray, dapple-gray, grizzle, roan, sorrel, dun, buckskin [W US], pinto, paint, piebald, skewbald, calico pony, painted pony.

.14 (inferior horse) **nag, plug,** hack, jade, crock, garron [Scot & Ir], crowbait [slang], scalawag, rosinante; goat or stiff or dog [all slang]; roarer, whistler; balky horse, balker, jughead; rogue.

.15 (scrawny horse) rackabones, scrag, stack of bones.

.16 **hunter;** stalking-horse; **saddle horse,** saddler, rouncy [archaic], **riding horse,** rider, palfrey, **mount;** remount; polo pony; post-horse; cavalry horse; **driving horse,** road horse, roadster, carriage horse, coach horse, gigster; hack, hackney; **draft horse,** dray horse, cart horse, **workhorse,** plow horse; shaft horse, pole horse, thill horse, thiller, fill horse or filler [both dial]; wheelhorse, wheeler, lead, leader; pack horse, jument [archaic], sumpter, sumpter horse, bidet.

.17 **race horse,** racer, **bangtail,** pony [both slang]; steeplechaser; entry, starter, nomination in the race; stake horse, staker; plate horse, plater; mudder; pole horse; favorite; stable, string.

.18 gaited horse; galloper, trotter, pacer, sidewheeler [slang]; stepper, high-stepper, cob, prancer; ambler, padnag, pad; racker; single-footer.

.19 (famous horses) Al Borak (Mohammed's winged horse of ascension), Baiardo (Rinaldo's bay horse), Black Beauty, Black Bess (Dick Turpin's horse), Black Saladin (Warwick's horse), Bucephalus (Alexander the Great's horse), Buttermilk (Dale Evans' horse), Champion (Gene Autrey's horse), Copenhagen (Wellington's horse at Waterloo), Grani (Sigurd's magic horse), Incitatus (the horse of Caligula, the Roman Emperor), Marengo (Napoleon's white horse), Pegasus (winged horse of the Muses), Roan Barbary (favorite horse of Richard II), Rosinante (Don Quixote's bony horse), Silver (the

Lone Ranger's horse), Sleipnir (Odin's eight-legged horse), Trigger (Roy Rogers' horse), Topper (Hopalong Cassidy's horse), Traveller (Robert E. Lee's horse), Vegliantino or Veillantif (Orlando's horse), White Surrey (favorite horse of Richard III); (race horses) Assault, Citation, Kelso, Man O'War, Nashua, Native Dancer, Seabiscuit, Secretariat, Swaps, Whirlaway.

.20 **ass, donkey, burro,** neddy or cuddy [both Brit dial], moke [Brit slang], Rocky Mountain canary [W US]; **jackass,** jack, dickey [Brit dial]; jenny, jenny ass, jennet.

.21 **mule,** sumpter mule, sumpter; hinny, jennet.

.22 **dog** 414.72, **canine,** cyn(o)-, **pooch** [informal], bowwow [slang]; **pup, puppy,** puppy-dog [informal], **whelp;** bitch, gyp [S US], slut; toy dog, lap dog; working dog; watchdog, bandog; sheep dog, shepherd or shepherd's dog; Seeing Eye dog, guide dog; sled dog; show dog, fancy dog; kennel, pack of dogs.

.23 sporting dog, **hunting dog,** hunter, field dog, bird dog, gun dog, water dog.

.24 **cur, mongrel,** lurcher [Brit], **mutt** [informal]; pariah dog.

.25 **fox,** reynard; **wolf,** lyc(o)-, timber wolf, lobo [W US], **coyote,** brush wolf, prairie wolf, medicine wolf [W US]; dingo, jackal, **hyena;** Cape hunting dog, African hunting dog.

.26 **cat** 414.73, **feline,** ailur(o)- or aelur(o)-; pussy or **puss** or pussycat [all informal], tabby, grimalkin; house cat; **kitten, kitty** or kitty-cat [both informal]; kit, kitling [Brit dial]; **tomcat,** tom; gib or gib-cat [both Brit dial]; mouser; Cheshire cat, Chessycat [informal]; silver cat, Chinchilla cat; blue cat, Maltese cat; tiger cat, tabby cat; tortoise-shell cat, calico cat; alley cat.

.27 (wild cats) **lion,** Leo [informal], simba [Swah]; **tiger,** Siberian tiger; **leopard,** panther, jaguar, cheetah; cougar, painter [S US], puma, mountain lion, catamount or cat-a-mountain; lynx, ocelot; wildcat, bobcat.

.28 (wild animals) **bear,** bar [dial], arct(o)-; guinea pig, cavy; hedgehog, **porcupine,** quill pig [slang]; woodchuck, **groundhog,** whistle-pig [dial]; prairie dog, prairie squirrel; **raccoon,** coon; **opossum,** possum; **weasel,** mousehound [Brit]; **wolverine,** glutton; ferret, monk [informal]; **skunk,** polecat [dial]; zoril, stink cat [S

Africa], Cape polecat; foumart; **ape,** pithec(o)-, -pithecus; **monkey,** monk [informal], chimpanzee, chimp.

.29 **hare,** lag(o)-, leveret, jackrabbit; **rabbit, bunny** [informal], lapin; cottontail; Belgian hare, leporide; buck, doe.

.30 **reptile** 414.60, reptilian; **lizard,** saur(o)-, -saur(us); saurian, dinosaur; crocodile, crocodilian, alligator, gator [informal]; tortoise, turtle, terrapin.

.31 **serpent, snake** 414.61, ophidian, herpet(o)-, ophi(o)-, -ophis; **viper,** pit viper; sea snake.

.32 **amphibian** 414.62, batrachian, croaker, batrach(o)-, -batrachus, paddock [dial]; **frog,** rani-, tree toad or frog, bullfrog; **toad,** hoptoad or hoppytoad; newt, salamander; **tadpole,** polliwog.

.33 **bird** 414.66, **fowl,** -ornis; birdy or birdie [both informal]; fowls of the air, birdlife, avifauna; baby bird, chick, nestling, fledgling; wildfowl, game bird; waterfowl, water bird, wading bird, diving bird; sea bird; shore bird; migratory bird, migrant, bird of passage; **songbird,** oscine bird, warbler, passerine bird, perching bird; cage bird; flightless bird, ratite; seed-eating bird, insect-eating bird, fruit-eating bird, fish-eating bird, bird of prey; **eagle,** aeto-, -aetus, bird of Jove, eaglet; **owl,** bird of Minerva, bird of night; peafowl, peahen, **peacock,** bird of Juno; **swan,** cygnet; **pigeon, dove,** squab; stormy or storm petrel, Mother Carey's chicken; fulmar, Mother Carey's goose.

.34 **poultry, fowl,** domestic fowl, barnyard fowl, barn-door fowl, dunghill fowl; **chicken** 414.67, chick, chicky or chickabiddy [both informal]; **cock, rooster,** chanticleer; **hen,** biddy [informal], partlet; cockerel, pullet; setting hen, brooder, broody hen; capon, poulard; broiler, fryer, spring chicken, roaster, stewing chicken; Bantam, banty [informal]; game fowl; guinea fowl, guinea cock, guinea hen; **goose,** gander, gosling; **duck,** drake, duckling; **turkey,** gobbler, turkey gobbler; turkey-cock, tom, tom turkey; hen turkey; poult.

.35 marine animal 414.63, denizen of the deep; **whale,** cetacean 414.64, cet(o)-; **porpoise, dolphin,** -delphis, sea pig; **sea serpent,** sea snake, Loch Ness monster, sea monster, Leviathan [Bible]; **fish** 414.65, ichthy(o)-, -ichthys, pisci-, game fish, tropical fish, panfish; **shark,** man-eating shark, man-eater; **salmon,** kipper, grilse, smolt, parr, alevin; **minnow** or minny

[dial], fry, fingerling; **sponge**, spongi(o)–
or spong(o)–, –spongia; **plankton**, zoo-
plankton, nekton, benthon, benthos, zoo-
benthos.

.36 **bug; beetle;** arthropod; hexapod, myria-
pod; centipede, chilopod; millipede *or*
millepede, diplopod; **mite,** acar(o)– *or* ac-
ari–; arachnid, **spider,** arachn(o)–; taran-
tula, black widow spider, daddy longlegs
*or* harvestman; **scorpion; tick;** larva, maggot, nymph, **caterpillar,** eruci–, –campa;
**insect** 414.74; **fly,** musci–, myi(o)–, –myia.

.37 **ant,** myrmec(o)–, emmet [dial], pismire,
pissant [dial], antymire [dial]; red ant,
black ant, fire ant, house ant, agricultural
ant, carpenter ant, army ant; slave ant,
slave-making ant; **termite,** termito–,
white ant; queen, worker, soldier.

.38 **bee,** api–; honeybee, bumblebee; queen,
queen bee, worker, drone; **wasp; hornet,**
yellow jacket.

.39 **locust,** acridian; **grasshopper,** hopper,
hoppergrass [dial]; **cricket;** cicada, cicala,
dog-day cicada, seventeen-year locust.

.40 **vermin;** parasite; **louse,** head louse, body
louse, grayback, cootie [slang]; crab, crab
louse; weevil; nit; **flea,** sand flea, dog flea,
cat flea, chigoe, chigger, jigger, red bug,
mite, harvest mite; **roach, cockroach,** *cu-
caracha* [Sp].

.41 **bloodsucker,** parasite; **leech,** bdell(o)–,
–bdella; tick, wood tick; **mosquito,**
skeeter [dial], culex, culic(i)–; bedbug,
housebug [Brit].

.42 **worm** 414.75, vermi–, –scolex; earthworm,
angleworm, fishworm, night crawler,
nightwalker [N US]; measuring worm,
inchworm; tapeworm, helminth, hel-
minth(o)–, ligul(i)–, taen(o)– *or*
taeni(o)–.

.43 ADJS **animal,** animalian, animalic, animalistic, zoic, zooidal; **zoologic**(al); **brutish,
brutal,** brute, brutelike; **bestial, beastly,**
beastlike; subhuman; dumb, "that wants
discourse of reason" [Shakespeare]; instinctual *or* instinctive, mindless, nonrational.

.44 **vertebrate,** chordate, mammalian; marsupial, cetacean.

.45 **canine,** doggish, doggy, doglike; **vulpine,**
foxy, foxlike; **lupine,** wolfish, wolflike.

.46 **feline,** felid, cattish, catty, catlike; kittenish; leonine, lionlike; tigerish, tigerlike.

.47 **ursine,** bearish, bearlike.

.48 **rodent,** rodential; verminous; mousy,
mouselike; ratty, ratlike.

.49 **ungulate,** hoofed, hooved; **equine,** hippic,
horsy, horselike; **equestrian;** asinine, mul-

ish; bovid, ruminant; **bovine,** cowlike,
cowish; bull-like, bullish, taurine; cervine,
deerlike; caprine, caprid, hircine, goatish,
goatlike; ovine, sheepish, sheeplike; porcine, swinish, piggish, hoggish.

.50 elephantlike, elephantine, pachydermous.

.51 **reptile,** reptilian, **reptilelike,** reptiloid,
reptiliform; reptant, repent, creeping,
crawling, slithering; **lizardlike,** saurian;
crocodilian; **serpentine,** serpentile, serpentoid, serpentiform, **serpentlike;** snak-
ish, **snaky, snakelike,** ophidian, anguine
[archaic]; viperish, viperous, vipery, viper-
ine, viperoid, viperiform, viperlike; colu-
brine, colubriform; amphibian, batrachian, froggy, toadish, salamandrian.

.52 **birdlike,** birdy; avian, avicular; gallina-
ceous, rasorial; oscine, passerine, perching; columbine, columbaceous, dovelike;
psittacine; aquiline, hawklike; anserine,
anserous, goosy; nidificant, nesting, nest-
building; nidicolous, altricial; nidifugous,
precocial.

.53 **fishlike,** fishy; piscine, pisciform; piscatorial, piscatory; eellike; selachian, shark-
like, sharkish.

.54 **invertebrate,** invertebral; protozoan, pro-
tozoal, protozoic; crustaceous, crustacean; molluscan, molluscoid.

.55 **insectile, insectlike,** buggy; verminous;
lepidopterous, lepidopteran; weevily.

.56 **wormlike,** vermicular, vermiform; wormy.

.57 planktonic, nektonic, benthonic, zoo-
planktonic, zoobenthoic.

.58 **mammals**

| | |
|---|---|
| aardvark | bassarisk |
| aardwolf | bat, –nycteris |
| addax | bear |
| agouti | beaver |
| alpaca | Belgian hare |
| American lion | bettong |
| Angora goat | bezoar goat |
| anoa | bighorn sheep |
| ant bear | binturong |
| anteater | bison |
| antelope | black bear |
| antelope chipmunk *or* | black buck |
| squirrel | black cat |
| aoudad | black fox |
| apar | black sheep |
| Arctic fox | blue fox |
| Arctic hare | boar |
| argali | bobcat |
| armadillo | brown bear |
| ass | brush deer |
| aurochs | brush wolf |
| babirusa | buffalo |
| Bactrian camel | buffalo wolf |
| badger | burro |
| bandicoot | burro deer |
| banteng | bush baby |
| baronduki | cachalot |

Caffre cat
camel
camelopard
Cape buffalo
capybara, carpincho
carabao
caracal
carcajou
caribou
Cashmere goat
cat
catamount or cat-a-
    mountain
cat squirrel
cattalo
cavy
chamois
cheetah
chevrotain
chickaree
chigetai
chinchilla
chipmunk
cinnamon bear
civet cat
coati
coon
coon cat
cotton mouse
cotton rat
cottontail rabbit
cougar
cow
coyote
coypu
deer
deer mouse
deer tiger
dingo
dog
donkey
dormouse
dromedary
duckbill, duckbill
    platypus
echidna
eland
elephant
elk
ermine
eyra
fallow deer
ferret
field mouse
fisher
fitch
flickertail
flying fox
flying lemur
flying marmot
flying phalanger
flying squirrel
foumart
fox
fox squirrel
gaur
gazelle
gemsbok
genet
gerbil
giant ground sloth
giraffe

glutton
gnu
gnu goat
goat
goat antelope
gopher
grasshopper mouse
gray fox
gray wolf
grison
grizzly bear
groundhog
ground squirrel
guanaco
guib
guinea pig
hackee
hamster
hare
harnessed antelope
hartebeest
harvest mouse
hedgehog
herring hog
hippopotamus
hog
horse
hyena
hyrax
ibex
ice bear
imperial mammoth
Indian buffalo
jabalina
jackal
jackass
jackrabbit
jaguar
jaguarundi
jerboa
jerboa kangaroo
jumping mouse
kaama [Africa]
kangaroo
kangaroo mouse
kangaroo rat
karakul
kiang
kinkajou
kit fox
koala
Kodiak bear
koodoo
lapin
lemming
leopard
leopard cat
lion
llama
loris
lynx
mammoth
manul
mara
Marco Polo's sheep
margay
markhor
marmot
marten
mastodon
mazama
meadow mouse

meerkat
mink
mole, talpi–
mongoose
moose
mouflon
mountain goat
mountain lion
mountain sheep
mouse, my(o)-, –mys
mouse deer
mule
mule deer
muntjac
musk deer
musk hog
musk-ox
muskrat, musquash
nilgai
nutria
ocelot
okapi
onager
oont [India]
opossum
oryx
otter
ounce
ox
pack rat
painter [S US]
Pallas's cat
panda
pangolin
panther
pasang
peba
peccary
peludo
phalanger
pig
pika
pine mouse
platypus
pocket gopher
pocket mouse
pocket rat
polar bear
polar fox
polecat
porcupine
possum
potto
pouched rat
poyou
prairie dog
prairie fox
prairie wolf
pronghorn, pronghorn
    antelope
puma
rabbit
rabbit bandicoot
raccoon
rat
red deer
red fox
red squirrel
reindeer
rhinoceros
ring-tailed cat
rock squirrel

Rocky Mountain goat
roe, roe deer, roebuck
saber-toothed tiger or
    cat
sable
sable antelope
saiga
sambar
sand cat
serval
sheep
shrew
shrew mole
sika
silver fox
skunk
skunk bear
sloth
snowshoe rabbit
springbok
squirrel
steenbok
stoat
suslik
swamp rabbit
swine
Syrian bear
takin
tamandua
tamarin
tapir
tarpan
tatou
tatouay
tatou peba
tayra
Thian Shan sheep
tiger
tiger cat
timber wolf
tree shrew
tree squirrel
tsine
urial
urus
Virginia deer
vole
wallaby
wapiti
warthog
waterbuck
water buffalo or ox
weasel
wharf rat
whistler
white fox
whitetail, whitetailed
    deer
white wolf
wild ass
wild boar
wildcat
wildebeest
wild goat
wild ox
wild pig
wild sheep
wolf
wolverine
wombat
woodchuck
wood mouse

wood rat
woolly mammoth
yak

zebra
zebu
zoril

## .59 primates

angwantibo
anthropoid ape
ape
aye-aye
baboon
Barbary ape
bonnet monkey or
  macaque
capuchin
chacma
chimpanzee
colobus
drill
entellus
gibbon
gorilla
grivet
guenon

guereza
hanuman
langur
lemur
lion-tailed monkey or
  macaque
macaque
man 417
mandrill
marmoset
mountain gorilla
orangutan, orang
proboscis monkey
rhesus
saki
siamang
spider monkey

## .60 reptiles

agama
alligator
alligator lizard
alligator snapper or
  turtle or terrapin
anole
basilisk
beaded lizard
bearded lizard
blindworm
box turtle
butterfly agama
cayman
chameleon
crocodile
diamondback, dia-
  mondback terrapin
dinosaurs 123.26
dragon, flying dragon
false map turtle
gavial
gecko
Gila monster
girdle-tailed lizard
glass snake
green turtle

hawksbill turtle,
  hawksbill
horned toad or lizard,
  horny-toad [dial]
iguana
leatherback
lizard
loggerhead, logger-
  head turtle
matamata
monitor
mugger
sand lizard
sea turtle or tortoise
skink
slow-worm
snapping turtle
soft-shelled turtle
stump-tailed lizard,
  stump tail
teju
terrapin
tortoise
tuatara
turtle

## .61 snakes

adder
anaconda
asp
black snake
blind snake
boa
boa constrictor
bull snake
bushmaster
cobra
cobra de capello
constrictor
copperhead
coral snake
cottonmouth
daboia
diamondback, dia-
  mondback rattle-
  snake

fer-de-lance
garter snake
gopher snake
hamadryad
harlequin snake
hog-nose snake
horned rattlesnake
horned viper
king cobra
king snake
krait
mamba
milk snake
moccasin
pine snake
puff adder
python
racer
rat snake

rattlesnake, rattler
Russell's viper
shovel-nose
sidewinder
spectacled cobra
thunder snake

tic-polonga
urutu
viper
water moccasin
water snake
worm snake

## .62 amphibians

bullfrog
caecilian
congo snake or eel
eft
frog
grass frog
green frog
hellbender
leopard frog
midwife toad
mud puppy

newt
pickerel frog
salamander
siren
spring frog
Surinam toad
toad
tree frog
water dog
wood frog

## .63 marine animals

crustacean 415.5
dugong
elephant seal
fur seal
harbor seal
manatee
mollusk 415.5
octopus, octopod
sea calf

sea cow
sea dog
sea elephant
seal
sea lion
sea urchin, echin(o)–
shellfish 308.25
squid
walrus

## .64 cetaceans

baleen whale
beluga
blackfish
blue whale
cachalot
dolphin
finback
grampus
humpback

killer, killer whale
narwhal
porpoise
right whale
rorqual
sperm whale
sulfur-bottom whale
whalebone whale
zeuglodon

## .65 fish

albacore
alewife
alligator gar
amber jack
anchovy
angel fish
archerfish
argusfish
balloonfish
barbel
barn door skate
barracuda
basking shark
bass
black bass
blackfish
black sea bass
bleak
blind fish
blowfish
blue fish
bluegill
blue shark
bonefish
bonito
bowfin
bream
brook trout
brown trout

buffalo fish
bullhead
burbot
butterfish
candlefish
capelin
carp
catfish
channel bass
char
chimaera
Chinook salmon
chub
cichlid
cisco
cobia
cod, codfish
coelacanth
conger, conger eel
crappie
croaker
cutlass fish
cutthroat trout
dace
darter
devilfish
doctor fish
dogfish
Dolly Varden trout

Holstein, Holstein-
  Friesian
Jersey
Lincoln Red, Lincoln
  Red Shorthorn
Longhorn
Polled Durham *or*
  Shorthorn

Polled Hereford
Red Poll, Red Polled
Santa Gertrudis
Shorthorn
Sussex
Welsh, Welsh Black
West Highland

## 70 breeds of sheep

black face Highland
blackhead Persian
broadtail
Cheviot
Columbia
Corriedale
Cotswold
Dorset Down
Hampshire, Hamp-
  shire Down
Karakul
Kerry Hill
Leicester
Lincoln
Merino
Oxford *or* Oxfordshire

Down
Panama
Rambouillet
Romanov
Romeldale
Romney, Romney
  Marsh
Ryeland
Scottish blackface
Shropshire
Southdown
Suffolk
Targhee
Welsh Mountain
Wensleydale

## .71 breeds of swine

Berkshire
Cheshire
Chester White
Duroc, Duroc-Jersey
Hampshire
Hereford
Landrace
large black

large white
Mangalitza
middle white
Poland China
Spotted Poland China
Tamworth
Wessex saddleback
Yorkshire

## .72 breeds of dogs

affenpinscher
Afghan hound
Airedale, Airedale ter-
  rier
Alaskan malamute
Alsatian
American foxhound
American water span-
  iel
Australian terrier
badger dog
barbet
Basenji
basset, basset hound
beagle
Bedlington terrier
Belgian sheep dog *or*
  shepherd
Bernese mountain dog
Blenheim spaniel
bloodhound, sleuth,
  sleuthhound
boarhound
Border terrier
borzoi
Boston bull *or* terrier
Bouvier des Flandres
boxer
Briard
Brittany spaniel
Brussels griffon
bulldog, bull
bull mastiff
bull terrier

Cairn terrier
Chesapeake Bay
  retriever
Chihuahua
chow, chow chow
clumber spaniel
Clydesdale terrier
cocker spaniel
collie
coonhound
dachshund
Dalmatian, coach dog
Dandie Dinmont ter-
  rier
deerhound
Doberman pinscher
elkhound
English bulldog
English cocker spaniel
English foxhound
English setter
English springer span-
  iel
English toy spaniel
Eskimo dog
field spaniel
flat-coated retriever
foxhound
fox terrier
French bulldog
gazelle hound
German shepherd,
  police dog
German short-haired

pointer
German wire-haired
  pointer
giant schnauzer
golden retriever
Gordon setter
Great Dane
Great Pyrenees
greyhound
griffon
Groenendael
harrier
hound, hound-dog [S
  US]
husky
Irish setter
Irish terrier
Irish water spaniel
Irish wolfhound
Italian greyhound
Japanese spaniel
keeshond
Kerry blue terrier
King Charles spaniel
komondor
kuvasz
Labrador retriever
lakeland terrier
Lhasa apso
malamute
Malinois
Maltese
Manchester terrier
mastiff
Mexican hairless
miniature poodle
miniature pinscher
miniature schnauzer
Newfoundland
Norfolk spaniel
Norwegian elkhound
Norwich terrier
Old English sheep
  dog
otterhound
papillon
Pekingese
pointer
Pomeranian

poodle
pug
puli
rat terrier
retriever
Rhodesian ridgeback
Rottweiler
Russian owtchar
Russian wolfhound
Saluki
St. Bernard
Samoyed
schipperke
schnauzer
Scottish deerhound
Scottish terrier
Sealyham terrier
setter
shepherd dog
Shetland sheep dog
Shih Tzu
Siberian husky
silky terrier
Skye terrier
spaniel
spitz
springer spaniel
staghound
Sussex spaniel
terrier
toy poodle
toy spaniel
toy terrier
turnspit
Vizsla
water spaniel
Weimaraner
Welsh collie
Welsh corgi
Welsh springer span-
  iel
Welsh terrier
West Highland white
  terrier
whippet
wire-haired terrier
wolfhound
Yorkshire terrier

## .73 breeds of cats

Abyssinian cat
Angora cat
Archangel cat
Burmese cat
coon cat [dial]
domestic shorthair cat
Egyptian cat
Havana brown cat

Himalayan cat
Manx cat
Persian cat
Rex cat
Russian blue cat
Siamese cat
Turkish cat

## .74 insects

ant
ant lion
aphid, aphis
assassin bug
bedbug
bee
bee fly
beetle
billbug, billbeetle
blowfly
bluebottle

boll weevil
borer, peachtree
  borer, appletree
  borer, etc.
botfly
bristletail
buffalo bug
buffalo carpet beetle
buprestid beetle
butterfly
caddis fly

Cecropia moth
chafer
chigoe, chigger
chinch, chinch bug
cicada
cicala
cockchafer
cockroach
codling moth
Colorado beetle,
Colorado potato
beetle
cone-nose
crane fly
cricket
Croton bug
cucumber flea beetle
curculio
damselfly
deer fly
dobson fly
dragonfly
drosophila
dung beetle
earwig
elm leaf beetle
ephemerid
firebrat
firefly
flea
flea beetle
flour moth
fly
fruit fly
fruit-tree bark beetle
gadfly
gallfly
glowworm
gnat
grain beetle
grasshopper
greenbottle fly
harlequin cabbage
bug
hawkmoth
hornet
horn fly
horntail
horsefly
housefly
Japanese beetle
jigger, jigger flea
June bug or beetle
katydid
kissing bug

lacewing
ladybug, ladybird,
lady beetle
lantern fly
leafhopper
Lepisma
locust
louse
mantis, praying man-
tis
mayfly
mealworm
mealybug
midge
miller
mole cricket
mosquito
mosquito hawk
moth
pill bug
podura
potato bug or beetle
punkie
roach
robber fly
rose beetle
rove beetle
St. Mark's fly
sawfly
scarab, scarab beetle
scorpion fly
shad fly
silverfish
snout beetle
sow bug
springtail
squash bug
stag beetle
stinkbug
stone fly
syrphus fly
termite
thrips
tiger moth
tsetse fly
tumblebug
walkingstick
wasp
water bug
weevil, grain weevil,
rice weevil, etc.
wood tick
wood wasp
yellow jacket

.75 worms

angleworm
armyworm
bollworm
bookworm
cankerworm
cotton worm
cutworm
earthworm
earworm
fireworm
hellgrammite
inchworm, measuring
worm, looper
leech
nematode

pinworm
planarian
roundworm
shipworm, spileworm
silkworm
tapeworm
teredo
tobacco worm
tomato worm
trematode
tussah
webworm
wireworm
woodworm

## 415. ZOOLOGY

.1 NOUNS zoology, anthropology 417.7, biology 406.17, anatomy 245.7, comparative
anatomy or zootomy, animal physiology
or zoonomy, conchology, ecology, zoo-
ecology, entomology, ethology, helmin-
thology, herpetology, ichthyology, mala-
cology, mammalogy, ophiology, ornithol-
ogy, protozoology, taxonomy or zootaxy,
zoogeography or zoography, zoopathol-
ogy, zoophysics; taxidermy.

.2 zoologist, anthropologist 417.7, biologist
406.18, animal physiologist or zoonomist,
conchologist, ecologist, zoo-ecologist, en-
tomologist or bugologist [informal],
ethologist, helminthologist, herpetologist,
ichthyologist, malacologist, mammalo-
gist, ophiologist, ornithologist, protozool-
ogist, zoographer, zoopathologist, zoo-
physicist, zootaxonomist; taxidermist.

.3 Subkingdom Protozoa (one-celled animals): Protozoa: Mastigophora, Sarco-
dina, Sporozoa, Ciliata, Suctoria.

.4 Subkingdom Parazoa (many-celled animals without a true digestive cavity): Po-
rifera (sponges).

.5 Subkingdom Metazoa (many-celled animals with true digestive cavities): Meso-
zoa; Coelenterata: Scyphozoa (jellyfish-
es), Anthozoa (sea anemones, corals);
Ctenophora (comb jellies); Platyhel-
minthes (flatworms): Turbellaria (free-living flatworms), Trematoda (flukes), Ces-
toda (tapeworms); Nemertinea or Ne-
mertea (ribbon worms); Entoprocta;
Ectoprocta or Bryozoa (moss animals);
Aschelminthes: Rotifera (wheel animal-
cules or wheel worms), Nematoda
(roundworms), Nematomorpha (hair
snakes); Acanthocephala (spiny-headed
worms); Phoronidea; Pogonophora
(beard worms); Brachiopoda (lamp
shells); Echinodermata: Crinoidea (sea
lilies), Asteroidea (starfishes), Ophiuroi-
dea (brittle stars), Echinoidea (sea ur-
chins), Holothurioidea (sea cucumbers);
Chaetognatha (arrowworms); Mollusca:
Gastropoda (univalve mollusks such as
limpets, slugs, snails), Pelecypoda (bi-
valve mollusks such as clams), Cephalo-
poda (octopuses, squids), Scaphopoda
(tooth shells), Amphineura (chitons),
Monoplacophora; Annelida (segmented
worms): Polychaeta (sandworms), Oligo-
chaeta (earthworms), Hirudinea (leech-
es); Sipunculoidea (peanut worms); Pria-

puloidea; Echiuroidea; Arthropoda: Arachnida (spiders), Crustacea (lobsters, shrimp, etc.), Insecta (insects), Chilopoda (centipedes), Diplopoda (millipedes); Chordata.

.6 Phylum Chordata: Hemichordata (tongue worms), Cephalochordata (lancelets), Tunicata (sea squirts), Vertebrata.

.7 Subphylum Vertebrata: Cyclostomata (lampreys, hagfishes), Chondrichtyes (cartilaginous fishes such as sharks, rays, skates), Osteichthyes (bony fishes), Amphibia (amphibians), Reptilia (reptiles), Mammalia (mammals).

.8 Class Mammalia: Monotremata (platypuses, echidnas), Marsupialia (kangaroos, opossums), Insectivora (shrews, moles), Dermoptera (flying lemurs), Chiroptera (bats), Primates (man, apes, monkeys), Edentata (anteaters, armadillos, sloths), Pholidota (pangolin), Lagomorpha (hares, rabbits), Rodentia (rodents), Cetacea (whales, dolphins), Carnivora (carnivores), Tubulidentata (aardvarks), Proboscidea (elephants), Hyracoidea (coneys), Sirenia (manatees or sea cows), Perissodactyla (horses, tapirs, rhinoceroses), Artiodactyla (antelopes, cattle, pigs).

.9 ADJS zoologic(al), entomologic(al); taxidermic, taxidermal.

### 416. ANIMAL HUSBANDRY

.1 NOUNS animal husbandry, animal rearing or raising or culture, stock raising; zooculture, zootechnics, zootechny; thremmatology; gnotobiotics; herding, grazing, keeping flocks and herds, running livestock; breeding, stockbreeding, stirpiculture; horse training, dressage, manège; horsemanship; pisciculture, fish culture; apiculture, bee culture, beekeeping; cattle raising; sheepherding; pig-keeping; dairy-farming, chicken-farming, pig-farming, etc.; cattle-ranching, mink-ranching, etc.

.2 stockman, stock raiser, stockkeeper [Austral]; breeder, stockbreeder; sheepman; cattleman, cow keeper, cowman, grazier [Brit]; rancher, ranchman, ranchero; dairyman, dairy farmer; stableman, stableboy, groom, hostler, equerry; trainer, breaker, tamer; broncobuster or buckaroo [both slang]; horseshoer, farrier.

.3 herder, drover, herdsman, herdboy; shepherd, shepherdess, sheepherder, sheepman; goatherd; swineherd, pigman, pigherd, hogherd; gooseherd, gooseboy, goosegirl; swanherd; cowherd, neatherd

[Brit], cowboy, cowgirl, cowhand, puncher or cowpuncher [both informal], waddy [W US], cowman, cattleman, vaquero [Sp], gaucho; horseherd, wrangler, horse wrangler.

.4 apiarist, apiculturist, beekeeper, beeherd.

.5 animal enclosure 191.19–26, 236.12.

.6 VERBS raise, breed, rear, grow, hatch, feed, nurture, fatten; keep, run; ranch, farm; culture.

.7 tend; groom, rub down, brush, curry, currycomb; water, drench, feed, fodder; bed, bed down, litter; milk; harness, saddle, hitch, bridle, yoke; gentle, handle, manage; tame, train, break.

.8 drive, herd, drove [Brit], punch cattle, shepherd, ride herd on; spur, goad, prick, lash, whip; wrangle, round up; corral, cage.

### 417. MANKIND

.1 NOUNS mankind, humankind, man, human species, human race, race of man, human family, humanity, mortals, mortality, flesh, mortal flesh, clay; generation of man [archaic], le genre humain [Fr], "the plumeless genus of bipeds" [Plato], homo, genus Homo, Homo sapiens, Hominidae, hominid; human nature, frail or fallen humanity, Adam, Adam's seed or offspring.

.2 people 418, persons, folk, folks, gentry, men, people in general; public, populace, population, citizenry, general public; John Q. Public, Everyman, man in the street, common man, you and me, John Doe, everyman, everywoman, everyone, everybody; community, commonwealth, nation, nationality, state; estate [archaic], polity, body politic; society, world, world or community at large.

.3 person, human, human being, man, homo, anthrop(o)–, homin(i)–, prosop(o)–; member of the human race, Adamite; mortal, life, soul, living soul; being, creature, individual, "single, separate person" [Whitman], personage, personality, body; somebody, one, someone; fellow or chap or customer or party or character [all informal]; guy or cat or duck or joker [all slang]; bloke or cove or johnny [all Brit slang]; earthling, groundling, terran, worldling, tellurian; head, hand, nose.

.4 God's image, lord of creation; homo faber, symbol-using animal; "a god in ruins" [Emerson], "the aristocrat amongst the animals" [Heine], "the measure of all things" [Protagoras], "a reasoning animal" [Seneca], "the most intelligent of animals—and the most silly" [Diogenes], "a thinking reed" [Pascal], "a tool-using animal" [Carlyle], "a tool-making animal" [Benjamin Franklin], "the only animal that blushes. Or needs to" [Mark Twain], "an intelligence served by organs" [Emerson], rational animal, animal capable of reason, "an ingenious assembly of portable plumbing" [Christopher Morley], "Nature's sole mistake" [W. S. Gilbert], "that unfeather'd two-legged thing" [Dryden], "but breath and shadow, nothing more" [Sophocles], "this quintessence of dust" [Shakespeare], "political animal" [Aristotle]; "the naked ape" [Desmond Morris].

.5 **humanness, humanity,** mortality; **human nature,** the way you are; **frailty,** human frailty, weakness, **human weakness,** weakness of the flesh, "thy nature's weakness" [Whittier], "one touch of nature" [Shakespeare], the weaknesses human flesh is heir to; human equation.

.6 humanization; **anthropomorphism,** pathetic fallacy, anthropopathism, anthropomorphology.

.7 **anthropology,** science of man; anthropogeny, anthropography, anthropogeography, human geography, demography, human ecology, anthropometry, craniometry, craniology, ethnology, ethnography; behavioral science, sociology, socio–, psychology 690; anatomy 245.7; **anthropologist,** ethnologist, sociologist.

.8 **humanism;** naturalistic humanism, scientific humanism; Religious Humanism; Christian humanism, integral humanism; new humanism; anthroposophy.

.9 VERBS **humanize,** anthropomorphize, make human, civilize.

.10 ADJS **human;** hominal; creaturely, creatural; Adamite or Adamitic; **frail, weak,** fleshly, finite, **mortal; only human;** earthborn, of the earth, earthy, tellurian, unangelic; humanistic; man-centered, homocentric, anthropocentric; anthropological.

.11 **manlike, anthropoid,** humanoid, hominid; anthropomorphic, anthropopathic.

.12 **personal, individual,** private, peculiar, idiosyncratic.

.13 **public, general, common; communal, societal, social;** civic, civil; **national,** state; international, cosmopolitan, supranational, supranational.

.14 ADVS **humanly,** mortally, after the manner of men.

## 418. PEOPLES

.1 NOUNS **people; race,** strain, stock, ethno–, gen(o)–; **culture** 642.3, **society,** speech community, **ethnic group;** community, **nationality, nation.**

.2 (races) **Caucasoid** or **Caucasian** or **white race;** Nordic race, Alpine race, Mediterranean race; xanthochroi, melanochroi; Archaic Caucasoid or archaic white or Australoid race; Polynesian race; **Negroid** or **black race;** Nilotic race, Melanesian race, Papuan race; Pygmoid race; Bushman race; **Mongoloid** or **Mongolian** or **yellow race;** Malayan or Malaysian or brown race; prehistoric races 123.25.

.3 **Caucasian, white man, white;** WASP [informal]; paleface, ofay, the Man, Mister Charley [all slang]; whitey or honky [both derog]; Australian aborigine, blackfellow [Austral]; **Negro, black man, black,** colored person; darky [slang]; spade, nigger, niggra, coon, burrhead, jigaboo, jungle bunny, boy [all derog]; pygmy, Negrito, Negrillo; Bushman; **Indian,** American Indian, Amerind, Red Indian [Brit], red man; injun or redskin [both slang]; Mongolian, yellow man, **Oriental;** gook or slant-eye [both derog]; Malayan, brown man.

.4 **crossbreed, mulatto** 44.9.

## 419. SEX

.1 NOUNS **sex,** gender, gen(o)–; maleness, masculinity 420, femaleness, femininity 421.

.2 **sexuality,** sexualism, gam(o)–; **love** 931, lovemaking 932, marriage 933; **carnality, sensuality** 987; sexiness, voluptuousness, flesh, fleshliness; **libido,** sex drive, sexual instinct or urge; **potency** 420.2; impotence; frigidity, coldness.

.3 **sex appeal,** sexual attraction or attractiveness or magnetism.

.4 **sex object;** piece, meat, piece of meat, ass, piece of ass, hot number [all slang]; sex queen, sex goddess; stud [slang].

.5 **sexual desire,** sensuous or carnal desire, bodily appetite, **biological urge,** venereal appetite or desire, sexual longing, **lust,** desire, lusts or desires of the flesh, itch, **passion,** carnal or sexual passion, fleshly lust, prurience or pruriency, concupiscence, hot blood, aphrodisia, hot pants [slang]; lustfulness, goatishness, horniness, libidinousness; lasciviousness 989.5; **eroticism,** erotism, eroto–; indecency 990; erotomania, eromania, eroticomaniac *hysteria libidinosa* [L]; nymphomania, andromania, *furor uterinus* [L]; satyrism, satyriasis, gynecomania; infantile sexuality, polymorphous perversity.

**.6 heat, rut;** frenzy *or* fury of lust; estrus, estrum, estral cycle, estruation.

**.7 aphrodisiac, love potion,** philter; cantharis, blister beetle, Spanish fly.

**.8 copulation, sex act,** *le sport* [Fr], coupling, mating, coition, **coitus,** pareunia, venery, copula [law], **sex, intercourse, sexual intercourse,** cohabitation, commerce, sexual commerce, congress, sexual congress, sexual union, sexual relations, relations, marital relations, marriage act, act of love, sleeping together *or* sleeping with; screwing, balling, diddling, making it with [all slang]; meat, ass [both slang], intimacy, connection, carnal knowledge, aphrodisia; orgasm, climax, sexual climax; adultery, fornication 989.7; coitus interruptus, onanism; **lovemaking** 932; **procreation** 169; germ cell, sperm, ovum 406.10–12.

**.9 masturbation,** autoeroticism, self-abuse; onanism, manipulation, playing with oneself, hand job [slang]; oral-genital stimulation, fellatio *or* fellation, irrumation, cunnilingus; anal intercourse, buggery, sodomy, pederasty; bestiality.

**.10 genitals,** genitalia, sex organs, reproductive organs, pudenda, private parts, privy parts, privates, ede(o)–, meat [slang]; **male organs; penis, phallus,** phallo–, *lingam* [Skt]; gonads; **testes, testicles,** didym(o)–; balls *or* nuts *or* rocks [all slang], cods [dial], cullions [archaic], ballocks, family jewels [both slang]; spermary; scrotum, bag *or* basket [both slang], cod [archaic], scrot(o)– *or* scroti–; **female organs,** –gyne; **vulva,** vulv(o)–, episio–, *yoni* [Skt]; **vagina;** clitoris; labia, labia majora, labia minora, lips, nymphae, nymph(o)– *or* nymphi–; cervix; ovary, ovar(o)– *or* ovari–; uterus, womb 153.9; secondary sex characteristic, pubic hair, beard 230.8, breasts 256.6.

**.11 sexlessness,** asexuality, neuterness.

**.12 sexual preference;** sexual normality; **heterosexuality; homosexuality,** homosexualism, homoeroticism, sexual inversion; autoeroticism; **bisexuality,** bisexualism, amphierotism, swinging both ways [slang]; **lesbianism,** sapphism, tribadism *or* tribady; paraphilia; zoophilia, zooerastia; pedophilia; algolagnia, algolagny, sadomasochism; active algolagnia, **sadism;** passive algolagnia, **masochism;** fetishism;

narcissism; exhibitionism; necrophilia; coprophilia; scotophilia, voyeurism; transvestitism; **incest,** incestuousness.

**.13 perversion,** sexual deviation, sexual deviance, sexual perversion, sexual abnormality; sexual pathology; psychosexual disorder; sexual psychopathy, *psychopathia sexualis* [L]; **sex crime.**

**.14 intersexuality,** intersexualism, epicenism, epicenity; hermaphroditism, pseudohermaphroditism; androgynism, androgyny, gynandry, gynandrism; transsexuality, transsexualism.

**.15 heterosexual, straight** [slang].

**.16 homosexual,** homosexualist, homophile, invert; homo, queer, faggot, fag, fruit [all derog]; flit, fairy, pansy, nance, auntie [all derog], queen [slang]; catamite, pathic; chicken, punk, gunsel [all derog]; **bisexual,** bi-guy [slang]; **lesbian,** sapphist, tribade, fricatrice [archaic]; dyke *or* bull dyke [both derog], butch, femme [both slang].

**.17 sodomist, sodomite,** bugger; pederast; paraphiliac; zoophiliac; pedophiliac; sadist; masochist; fetishist; transvestite; narcissist; exhibitionist; necrophiliac; coprophiliac; scotophiliac, voyeur; erotomaniac, nymphomaniac, satyr; rapist 989.12.

**.18 pervert, deviant,** deviate, sex *or* sexual pervert, sex *or* sexual deviant, sex *or* sexual deviate; sex fiend, sex criminal, sexual psychopath.

**.19 intersex,** sex-intergrade, epicene; hermaphrodite, pseudohermaphrodite; androgyne, gynandroid; transsexual.

**.20 sexology,** sexologist; sexual customs *or* mores *or* practices; sexual morality; new morality, sexual revolution; sexual freedom, free love; trial marriage.

**.21 VERBS sex,** sexualize.

**.22 lust, lust after,** itch for, have a lech *or* hot pants for [slang], **desire; be in heat** *or* **rut,** rut, come in, estruate.

**.23 copulate, couple, mate,** unite in sexual intercourse, **have sexual relations, have sex,** make out [slang], perform the act of love *or* marriage act, come together, cohabit, be intimate; sleep with, lie with, go to bed with; **screw, lay, ball,** frig, diddle, **make it with** [all slang]; cover, mount, serve *or* service (of animals); commit adultery, fornicate 989.19; **make love** 932.13.

**.24 masturbate,** play with *or* abuse oneself; fellate; sodomize, bugger, ream [slang].

**.25 climax, come,** achieve satisfaction,

achieve or reach orgasm; **ejaculate**, get off [slang].

.26 ADJS **sexual, sex,** sexlike, gamic, libidinal; **erotic,** amorous 931.24; nuptial 933.19; venereal; **carnal, sensual** 987.5,6, voluptuous, fleshly; **sexy; heterosexual, straight** [informal]; erogenous, erogenic, erotogenic; sexed, oversexed, undersexed; procreative 169.15; potent 420.12.

.27 **genital,** genito–; **phallic,** penile, penial; testicular; scrotal; spermatic, seminal, gon-(o)–; vulvar, vulval; vaginal; clitoral; cervical; ovarian; uterine.

.28 **aphrodisiac,** aphroditous, **arousing,** stimulating, eroticizing, venereal.

.29 **lustful, prurient, hot,** steamy, sexy, concupiscent, lickerish, libidinous, **salacious** 990.9, **passionate,** hot-blooded, itching, **horny** [slang], randy, goatish; sex-starved, unsatisfied; lascivious 989.29; **orgasmic,** orgastic, **ejaculatory.**

.30 **in heat, burning, hot; in rut,** rutting, rutty, ruttish; in must, must, musty; estrous, estral, estrual.

.31 **unsexual,** unsexed; **sexless,** asexual, **neuter,** neutral; castrated, emasculated, eunuchized; **cold, frigid; impotent;** frustrated.

.32 **homosexual,** homoerotic, gay [informal], queer [derog]; **bisexual,** bisexed, amphierotic, AC-DC [informal], autoerotic; lesbian, sapphic, tribadistic; mannish 420.13, butch; effeminate 421.14; transvestite; **perverted,** deviant.

.33 **hermaphrodite,** hermaphroditic, pseudohermaphrodite, pseudohermaphroditic, epicene, monoclinous; androgynous, androgynal, gynandrous, gynandrian.

## 420. MASCULINITY

.1 NOUNS **masculinity,** masculineness, maleness; **manliness,** manlihood, **manhood,** manfulness, manlikeness; mannishness; gentlemanliness, gentlemanlikeness.

.2 **virility,** virileness, potence or **potency,** sexual power, manly vigor, *machismo* [Sp]; ultramasculinity.

.3 **mankind, man, men, manhood,** menfolk or menfolks [both dial], sword side; **male sex.**

.4 **male,** male being, masculine; he, him, his; **man,** male person, *homme* [Fr], *hombre* [Sp]; **gentleman;** andr(o)–.

.5 **fellow,** feller, lad, chap, **guy** [all informal]; cat, bird, duck, stud, **joker,** character, jasper, bugger, bastard [all slang]; bloke or cove or johnny [all Brit slang].

.6 **he-man** or two-fisted man [both infor-

mal], jockstrap, jock [both slang], man with hair on his chest; caveman, bucko [both slang].

.7 (forms of address) **Mister, Mr.,** Messrs. [pl], Master; sir; *monsieur, M.* [both Fr], *messieurs, MM.* [both Fr pl]; *signor, signore* [both Ital], *signorino* [Ital], *señor, Sr.* [both Sp], *don* [Sp], *senhor* [Pg]; *Herr* [Ger]; *mein Herr* [Ger]; *mijnheer* [Du], *sahib* [Hind], *bwana* [Swahili].

.8 (male animals) cock, rooster, chanticleer; cockerel; drake; gander; peacock; tom turkey, tom, turkey-cock, bubbly-jock [Scot], gobbler, turkey gobbler; dog; boar; stag, hart, buck; stallion, studhorse, stud, top horse [dial], entire horse, entire; tomcat, tom; he-goat, billy goat, billy; ram, tup [Brit]; wether; bull, bullock, top cow [dial]; steer, stot [Brit dial].

.9 (mannish female) **amazon,** virago, androgyne; lesbian 419.16, butch, dyke [both slang]; **tomboy,** hoyden, romp.

.10 VERBS masculinize, virilize.

.11 ADJS **masculine, male,** bull, he–; **manly, manlike, mannish,** manful, andric; uneffeminate; **gentlemanly,** gentlemanlike.

.12 **virile, potent,** viripotent; ultramasculine; *macho* [Sp], **he-mannish** [informal], two-fisted [informal], broad-shouldered, hairy-chested.

.13 **mannish,** mannified; unwomanly, **unfeminine,** uneffeminate, viraginous; **tomboyish,** hoyden, rompish.

## 421. FEMININITY

.1 NOUNS **femininity,** femineity, feminality, feminacy, feminineness, femaleness; **womanliness,** womanlikeness, womanishness, **womanhood,** womanity, muliebrity; girlishness, little-girlishness; maidenhood, maidenliness; **ladylikeness,** gentlewomanliness; **matronliness,** matronage, matronhood, matronship; the eternal feminine, *"das Ewig-Weibliche"* [Ger; Goethe].

.2 **effeminacy,** unmanliness, effeminateness, epicenity, epicenism, **womanishness,** muliebrity, **sissiness** [informal], prissiness [informal]; androgyny, feminism.

.3 **womankind, woman, women,** femininity, **womanhood,** womenfolk or womenfolks [both dial], distaff side; **female sex;** second sex, **fair sex,** softer sex, **weaker sex,** weaker vessel.

.4 **female,** female being; she, her; –ess, –ette, –ine, –trix; gyne–, gyn(o)–, gyneo–, gyneco–, –gyne.

.5 **woman,** Eve, daughter of Eve, Adam's Rib, *femme* [Fr], distaff [archaic], weaker vessel; frow, *Frau* [Ger], *vrouw* [Du], *donna* [Ital], wahine [Hawaii]; lady, milady, gentlewoman, *domina* [L]; matron, dame, **dowager;** squaw; lass, girl 125.6.

.6 [slang terms] **dame,** hen, biddy, skirt; Jane, **broad, doll, chick,** wench, bird [Brit], tomato, bitch, minx.

.7 "a rag and a bone and a hank of hair" [Kipling], "God's second mistake" [Nietzche], "the last thing civilized by man" [George Meredith], "sphinxes without secrets" [Oscar Wilde], "the female of the human species, and not a different kind of animal" [G. B. Shaw], "O fairest of creation! last and best of all God's works" [Milton], "frailty, thy name is woman!" [Shakespeare], "a necessary evil" [Latin proverb], "a temple sacred by birth, and built by hands divine" [Dryden].

.8 (forms of address) Mistress [archaic], **Mrs.; madam** or ma'am; *madame, Mme* [both Fr]; *mesdames, Mmes* [both Fr pl]; *Frau* [Ger], *vrouw* [Du], *signora* [Ital], *señora* [Sp], *senhora* [Pg], *mem-sahib* [Hind]; dame [archaic], *donna* [Ital], *doña* [Sp], *dona* [Pg], lady; **Ms.; Miss;** *mademoiselle, Mlle* [both Fr]; *Fräulein* [Ger]; *signorina* [Ital], *señorita* [Sp], *senhorita* [Pg].

.9 (female animals) hen, Partlet, biddy; guinea hen; peahen; bitch, slut, gyp; sow; ewe, ewe lamb; she-goat, nanny goat or nanny; doe, hind, roe; jenny; mare, brood mare; filly; cow, bossy; heifer; vixen; tigress; lioness; she-bear, she-lion, etc.

.10 (effeminate male) **mollycoddle,** effeminate; **mother's darling, mama's boy,** Lord Fauntleroy, sissy, Percy, goody-goody; **pantywaist,** nancy or nance, chicken, lily; cream puff, weak sister, milksop; old woman.

.11 feminization, womanization, effemination, effeminization, sissification [informal].

.12 VERBS feminize; womanize, demasculinize, effeminize, effeminatize, effeminate, soften, sissify [informal]; emasculate, castrate, geld.

.13 ADJS feminine, female, she–; gynic, gynecic, gynecoid, –gynous; muliebral, distaff, womanly, womanish, womanlike, petticoat; ladylike, gentlewomanlike, gentlewomanly; matronly, matronal, matronlike; girlish, little-girlish, kittenish; maidenly 124.11.

.14 effeminate, womanish, old-womanish, unmanly, muliebrous, soft, chicken, prissy, sissified, sissy, sissyish.

## 422. SENSATION

### (physical sensibility)

.1 NOUNS sensation, sense, feeling; sense impression, sense-datum or -data, percept, perception, sense perception; experience, sensory experience; **consciousness,** awareness; response, response to stimuli.

.2 sensibility, sensibleness, physical sensibility, sentience or sentiency; openness to sensation, readiness of feeling, receptiveness, receptivity; sensation level, threshold of sensation, limen; impressionability, impressibility, affectibility; **susceptibility,** susceptivity; perceptibility.

.3 sensitivity, sensitiveness; perceptivity, perceptiveness; responsiveness; tact, tactfulness, considerateness, sympathy; empathy, identification; passibility; delicacy, exquisiteness, tenderness, fineness; **oversensitiveness,** oversensibility, hypersensitivity, **thin skin,** hyperesthesia, hyperpathia, supersensitivity, overtenderness; **irritability,** prickliness, soreness, **touchiness,** tetchiness; ticklishness, nervousness 859; allergy, anaphylaxis; sensitization; photophobia.

.4 sore spot, sore point, soft spot, raw, exposed nerve, raw nerve, nerve ending, tender spot, the quick, where the shoe pinches.

.5 senses, **five senses,** sensorium; touch, taste, smell, sight, hearing; sixth sense; sense or sensory organ, sensillum, receptor; synesthesia, chromesthesia, color hearing; phonism, photism.

.6 nerve, nerv(o)– or nervi–, neur(o)–; **neuron;** sensory or afferent neuron, sensory cell; motor or efferent neuron; association or internuncial neuron; axon, dendrite, myelin or medullary sheath; **synapse;** effector organ; nerve trunk; **ganglion,** gangli(o)–; plexus, solar plexus; **spinal cord,** spin(o)– or spini–, myel(o)–; **brain** 466.6,7; cerebral cortex, sensory area, sensorium; gray matter, white matter; **nervous system;** central nervous system, peripheral nervous system; autonomic nervous system; sympathetic or thoracolumbar nervous system, parasympathetic or craniosacral nervous system.

.7 neurology; neurologist, neurosurgeon.

.8 VERBS sense, **feel,** experience, **perceive,** apprehend, be sensible of, be conscious or aware of; taste 427.7, smell 435.8, see 439.12, hear 448.11,12, touch 425.6; respond, respond to stimuli.

.9 sensitize, make sensitive; sensibilize, sensify; sharpen, whet, quicken, stimulate, excite, stir, cultivate, refine.

.10 touch a sore spot, touch a soft spot, touch on the raw, touch to the quick, touch a nerve or nerve ending, touch where it hurts, hit one where he lives [slang].

.11 ADJS **sensory**, sensatory, sensorial, senso-(ri)–; sensitive, receptive; sensuous; sensorimotor, sensimotor.

.12 **neural, nervous,** nerval; neurological.

.13 sensible, sentient, sensile; **susceptible,** susceptive; **receptive,** impressionable, impressive [archaic], impressible; **perceptive;** conscious, cognizant, **aware,** sensitive to, alive to.

.14 sensitive, responsive, sympathetic; empathic, empathetic; passible; delicate, tactful, tender, refined; **oversensitive, thin-skinned;** oversensible, hyperesthetic, hyperpathic, hypersensitive, supersensitive, overtender, overrefined; **irritable, touchy,** tetchy [dial], itchy, ticklish, prickly; goosy, skittish; nervous 859.10; allergic, anaphylactic.

.15 (keenly sensitive) **exquisite,** poignant, **acute,** sharp, **keen,** vivid, intense, extreme, excruciating.

### 423. INSENSIBILITY

*(physical unfeeling)*

.1 NOUNS **insensibility,** insensibleness, **insensitivity,** insensitiveness, insentience, impassibility; **unperceptiveness,** imperceptiveness, imperception, imperceptivity, impercipience, obtuseness; inconsiderateness, **unfeeling,** unfeelingness; thick skin or hide, callousness 856.3; **numbness,** dullness, **deadness,** ambly(o)–, brady–, narc-(o)–; pins and needles; anesthesia, analgesia; narcosis, electronarcosis; narcotization.

.2 **unconsciousness, senselessness;** nothingness, oblivion, obliviousness, nirvana; nirvana principle; **faint, swoon, blackout,** syncope, lipothymy or lipothymia; **coma; stupor;** catalepsy, catatony or catatonia, sleep 712; knockout, KO or kayo [both slang]; semiconsciousness, grayout.

.3 **anesthetic,** analgesic, **pain-killer,** tranquilizer, **sedative,** sleeping pill, knockout drop or Mickey Finn [both slang], dope [slang], drug, narcotic, opiate 687.12.

.4 VERBS (render insensible) **deaden, numb,** benumb, blunt, dull, obtund, **desensitize;** paralyze, palsy; **anesthetize, put to sleep,** slip one a Mickey or Mickey Finn

[slang], chloroform, etherize; narcotize, drug, dope [slang]; freeze, **stupefy, stun,** bedaze, besot; knock unconscious, knock senseless, **knock out,** KO or kayo [both slang], lay out, coldcock [both slang], knock stiff.

.5 **faint, swoon,** drop, succumb, keel over [informal], fall in a faint, fall senseless, **pass out** [informal], **black out,** go out like a light; gray out.

.6 ADJS **insensible, unfeeling, insensitive,** insentient, insensate, impassible; **unperceptive,** imperceptive, impercipient; thickskinned, thick-witted, **dull,** obtuse, obdurate; **numb,** numbed, benumbed, dead, **deadened,** asleep, unfelt; callous 856.12.

.7 **stupefied, stunned,** dazed, bedazed.

.8 **unconscious, senseless, oblivious,** comatose, asleep, dead, **dead to the world,** cold, out, **out cold;** nirvanic; half-conscious, semiconscious; drugged, narcotized; doped, stoned, spaced out, strung out, zonked, zonked out, out of it [all slang]; catatonic, cataleptic.

.9 **deadening,** numbing, dulling; **anesthetic,** analgesic, narcotic; stupefying, stunning.

### 424. PAIN

*(physical suffering)*

.1 NOUNS **pain,** alg(o)–, –algy or –algia, noci–, –odynia, –pathy, –agra; **suffering, hurt, hurting,** misery [dial], **distress,** *Schmerz* [Ger], dolor [archaic]; **discomfort,** malaise; aches and pains.

.2 **pang,** throes; seizure, spasm, paroxysm; **twinge,** twitch, wrench, jumping pain; crick, kink, hitch, cramp or cramps; **nip,** thrill, pinch, tweak, bite, prick, **stab,** stitch, sharp or piercing or stabbing pain, acute pain, **shooting pain,** darting pain, fulgurant pain, lancinating pain, shooting, shoot; gnawing, gnawing or grinding or boring pain; griping, tormen [archaic]; girdle pain; stitch in the side; charley horse [informal].

.3 **smart,** smarting, **sting,** stinging, urtication, **tingle,** tingling; **burn,** burning, burning pain, fire.

.4 **soreness, irritation,** inflammation, tenderness, sensitiveness; algesia; rankling [archaic], festering; sore 686.35; sore spot 422.4.

.5 **ache,** aching, throbbing pain; **headache,** cephalalgia, misery in the head [dial]; splitting headache, **sick headache, migraine,** megrim, hemicrania; **backache; earache,** otalgia; **toothache,** odontalgia;

stomachache, tummyache [informal], bellyache or gut-ache [slang]; colic, collywobbles, gripes, gripe, gnawing, gnawing of the bowels, fret [dial]; heartburn, pyrosis; angina.

.6 agony, anguish, torment, torture, rack, excruciation, crucifixion, martyrdom, martyrization, excruciating or agonizing or atrocious pain.

.7 VERBS pain, give or inflict pain, hurt, wound, afflict, distress, ail; burn; sting; nip, bite, tweak, pinch; pierce, prick, stab, cut, lacerate; irritate, inflame; chafe, gall, fret, rasp, rub, grate; gnaw, grind; gripe; fester, rankle [archaic]; torture, torment, rack, put to torture, put or lay on the rack, agonize, harrow, crucify, martyr, martyrize, excruciate, wring, twist, convulse; prolong the agony, kill by inches.

.8 suffer, feel pain, feel the pangs, anguish 866.19; hurt, ache, have a misery [dial], ail; smart, tingle; throb, pound; shoot; twinge, thrill, twitch; wince, blench or blanch, shrink, make a wry face, grimace; agonize, writhe.

.9 ADJS pained, in pain, hurt, hurting, suffering, afflicted, wounded, distressed, in distress; tortured, tormented, racked, agonized, harrowed, lacerated, crucified, martyred, martyrized, wrung, twisted, convulsed; on the rack, under the harrow.

.10 painful, –pathic; hurtful, hurting, distressing, afflictive; acute, sharp, piercing, stabbing, shooting, stinging, biting, gnawing; poignant, pungent, severe, cruel, harsh, grave, hard; griping, cramping, spasmic, spasmatic, spasmodic, paroxysmal; agonizing, excruciating, atrocious, torturous, tormenting, racking, harrowing.

.11 sore, raw; smarting, tingling, burning; irritated, inflamed, tender, sensitive, fiery, angry, red; algetic; chafed, galled; festering, rankling [archaic].

.12 aching, achy, throbbing; headachy, migrainous, backachy, toothachy, stomachachy, colicky, griping.

.13 irritating, irritative, irritant; chafing, galling, fretting, rasping, grating, grinding, stinging, scratchy.

## 425. TOUCH

.1 NOUNS touch, thigmo–; sense of touch, tactile sense, cutaneous sense; taction, contact 200.5; feel, feeling; hand-mindedness; light touch, lambency, whisper, breath, kiss, caress; lick, lap; brush, graze,

glance; stroke, rub; tap, flick 283.6; fingertip caress, tentative poke.

.2 touching, feeling, fingering, palpation; handling, manipulation; petting, caressing, stroking, rubbing, frottage, friction 350; pressure 283.2.

.3 touchableness, tangibility, palpability, tactility.

.4 feeler, tactile organ, tactor; tactile cell; tactile process, tactile corpuscle, antenna; tactile hair, vibrissa; cat whisker; barbel, barbule; palp, palpus.

.5 finger, digit, digiti–, dactyl(o)–; forefinger, index finger, index; ring finger, annulary; middle finger, medius, dactylion; little finger, pinkie [informal], minimus; thumb, pollex.

.6 VERBS touch, feel, feel of, palpate; finger, pass or run the fingers over, feel with the fingertips, thumb; handle, palm, paw; manipulate, wield, ply; twiddle; poke at, prod 283.11; tap, flick 283.15; come in contact 200.10.

.7 touch lightly, touch upon; kiss, brush, sweep, graze, brush by, glance, scrape, skim.

.8 stroke, pet, caress, fondle; nuzzle, nose, rub noses; feel up [slang]; rub, rub against, massage, knead 350.6.

.9 lick, lap, tongue, mouth.

.10 ADJS tactile, tactual; hand-minded.

.11 touchable, palpable, tangible, tactile.

.12 lightly touching, lambent, playing lightly over, barely touching.

## 426. SENSATIONS OF TOUCH

.1 NOUNS tingle, tingling, thrill, buzz; prickle, prickles, prickling, pins and needles; sting, stinging, urtication; paresthesia.

.2 tickle, tickling, titillation, pleasant stimulation, ticklishness, tickliness.

.3 itch, itching, itchiness, psor(o)–, yeuk [Scot]; pruritus.

.4 creeps or cold creeps or shivers or cold shivers [all informal], creeping of the flesh; gooseflesh, goose bumps, goose pimples; formication.

.5 VERBS tingle, thrill; itch; scratch; prickle, prick, sting.

.6 tickle, titillate.

.7 feel creepy, feel funny, creep, crawl, have the creeps or cold creeps [informal]; have gooseflesh or goose bumps.

.8 ADJS tingly, tingling, atingle; prickly, prickling.

.9 ticklish, tickling, tickly, titillative.

.10 itchy, itching.

.11 creepy, crawly, formicative.

## 427. TASTE

*(sense of taste)*

.1 NOUNS **taste**, gust [archaic], *goût* [Fr]; **flavor**, sapor; **smack, tang; savor, relish,** sapidity; palate, tongue, tooth, stomach; taste in the mouth; sweet, sour, bitter, salt; aftertaste; savoriness 428.

.2 **sip, sup, lick, bite.**

.3 tinge, hint 35.4.

.4 **sample, specimen, taste,** taster, little bite, little smack; example 25.2.

.5 taste bud *or* bulb *or* goblet, taste *or* gustatory cell, taste hair; **tongue,** lingua, lingu(o)– *or* lingui–, gloss(o)–; **palate,** palat(o)–, staphyl(o)–, uran(o)–.

.6 **tasting, savoring,** gustation.

.7 VERBS **taste, sample; savor;** sip, sup [dial], roll on the tongue; **smack, taste of.**

.8 ADJS **gustatory,** gustative; **tastable,** gustable [archaic].

.9 **flavored,** flavorous, flavory, sapid, saporous, saporific; **savory, flavorful** 428.8,9.

.10 **lingual,** glossal; **tonguelike,** linguiform, lingulate.

## 428. SAVORINESS

.1 NOUNS **savoriness, palatableness,** palatability, **tastiness, toothsomeness,** goodness, good taste, right taste, **deliciousness,** gustatory delightfulness, scrumptiousness *or* yumminess [both informal], lusciousness, delectability, **flavorfulness,** flavorsomeness, flavorousness, flavoriness, good flavor, fine flavor, sapidity; full flavor, full-bodied flavor; gourmet quality.

.2 **savor, relish, zest, gusto,** *goût* [Fr].

.3 **flavoring, flavor,** flavorer; **seasoning,** seasoner, **relish, condiment, spice,** condiments 308.55.

.4 VERBS **taste good,** tickle *or* flatter *or* delight the palate, tempt *or* whet the appetite, make the mouth water.

.5 **savor, relish,** like, love, be fond of, be partial to, enjoy, delight in, appreciate; smack the lips; taste 427.7.

.6 **savor of, taste of, smack of,** have a relish of, have the flavor of, taste like.

.7 **flavor, savor; season,** salt, pepper, **spice,** sauce.

.8 ADJS **tasty, good-tasting, savory,** savorous, **palatable, toothsome,** gusty [Scot], gustable [archaic], sapid, **good,** good to eat, nice, agreeable, likable, pleasing, to one's taste, **delicious,** delightful, delectable, exquisite; delicate, dainty, juicy, succulent,

**luscious,** lush; ambrosial, nectarous, nectareous; fit for a king, fit for a gourmet of gourmet quality; scrumptious *or* yummy [both informal].

.9 **flavorful, flavorsome,** flavorous, flavory, well-flavored; full-flavored, full-bodied, nutty, fruity; **rich,** rich-flavored.

.10 **appetizing, mouth-watering, tempting,** tantalizing, provocative, piquant.

## 429. UNSAVORINESS

.1 NOUNS **unsavoriness, unpalatableness,** unpalatability, **distastefulness.**

.2 acridness, acridity, tartness, sharpness, causticity, astringence *or* astringency, acerbity, **sourness** 432; pungency 433; **bitterness,** –picrin; gall, gall and wormwood, wormwood, bitter pill.

.3 **nastiness, foulness, vileness, loathsomeness, repulsiveness, obnoxiousness,** odiousness, offensiveness, disgustingness, nauseousness; **rankness,** rancidity, rancidness, overripeness, rottenness, fetidness; repugnance 867.2; nauseant, emetic, sickener.

.4 VERBS **disgust, repel,** turn one's stomach, nauseate.

.5 ADJS **unsavory, unpalatable, unappetizing,** untasty, ill-flavored, foul-tasting, **distasteful,** dislikable, unlikable, uninviting, unpleasant, unpleasing, displeasing, disagreeable.

.6 **bitter,** picr(o)–, bitter as gall, amaroidal; **acrid,** sharp, caustic, tart, astringent; hard, harsh, rough, coarse; acerb, acerbic, sour 432.6; pungent 433.7.

.7 **nasty, offensive** 864.18, fulsome, noisome, noxious, rebarbative, mawkish, cloying, brackish, **foul, vile,** bad; icky [informal], yucky [slang], **sickening, nauseating,** nauseous, nauseant, vomity *or* barfy [both slang]; poisonous 864.7, rank, rancid, maggoty, weevily, spoiled, overripe, high, rotten, stinking, fetid.

.8 **inedible, uneatable,** not fit to eat *or* drink, undrinkable, impotable; unfit for human consumption.

## 430. INSIPIDNESS

.1 NOUNS **insipidness, insipidity, tastelessness, flavorlessness,** savorlessness, saplessness, unsavoriness; **weakness, thinness,** mildness, **wishy-washiness;** flatness, staleness, lifelessness, deadness; vapidity, inanity, jejunity, jejuneness.

.2 ADJS **insipid, tasteless, flavorless,** spiceless, **savorless,** sapless, unsavory, unflavored; pulpy, pappy, gruelly; **weak, thin, mild,** wishy-washy, washy, watery, watered, watered-down, diluted, dilute, milk-and-water; **flat, stale,** dead, *fade* [Fr]; vapid, inane, jejune; indifferent, neither one thing nor the other.

## 431. SWEETNESS

.1 NOUNS **sweetness,** sweet, sweetishness, saccharinity, dulcitude [archaic]; **sugariness,** syrupiness; oversweetness, mawkishness, cloyingness, sickly-sweetness.

.2 **sweetening,** edulcoration [archaic]; sweetener; sugar 309.5,22; artificial sweetener, saccharin, cyclamates, sodium cyclamate, calcium cyclamate; molasses, blackstrap, treacle [Brit]; syrup, maple syrup, cane syrup, corn syrup, sorghum; **honey,** meli– or melli–, honeycomb, honeypot, comb honey, clover honey; honeydew; **nectar, ambrosia;** sugarcoating; sweets 308.39; sugar-making; sugaring off; saccharification.

.3 VERBS **sweeten,** dulcify, edulcorate *or* dulcorate [both archaic]; **sugar,** honey; sugarcoat, glaze, candy; mull; saccharify; sugar off.

.4 ADJS **sweet,** sweetish, sweetened; sacchar(o)– *or* sacchari–, sacchariferous; **sugary,** sugared, candied, **honeyed,** syrupy; mellifluous, mellifluent [archaic]; melliferous, nectarous, nectareous, ambrosial; sugarsweet, honeysweet, sweet as sugar *or* honey, sweet as a nut; sugarcoated; bittersweet; sour-sweet, sweet-sour, sweet and sour, sweet and pungent.

.5 **oversweet,** saccharine, rich, **cloying,** mawkish, luscious [archaic], sickly-sweet.

## 432. SOURNESS

.1 NOUNS **sourness,** sour, sourishness, **tartness,** tartishness, acerbity, verjuice; acescency; acidity, acidulousness; hyperacidity, subacidity; vinegarishness, vinegariness; unsweetness, **dryness; pungency** 433; greenness, unripeness.

.2 **sour; vinegar,** acidulant; **pickle,** sour pickle, dill pickle, bread-and-butter pickle; verjuice; lemon, lime, crab apple, green apple, chokecherry; sour grapes; sour balls; sourdough; sour cream, yogurt; **acid** 379.1,12.

.3 **souring,** acidification, acidulation, acetification, acescence; fermentation.

.4 VERBS **sour,** turn sour *or* acid, **acidify,** acidulate, acetify; ferment; set the teeth on edge.

.5 ADJS **sour,** soured, sourish; **tart,** tartish; crab, **crabbed;** acerb, acerbic, acerbate;

acescent; **vinegarish,** vinegary, sour as vinegar; pickled; **pungent** 433.6; unsweet, unsweetened, **dry,** sec; green, unripe.

.6 **acid,** acidulous, acidulent, acidulated; acetic, acetous, acetose; hyperacid; subacid, subacidulous.

## 433. PUNGENCY

.1 NOUNS **pungency, piquancy, poignancy; sharpness, keenness,** edge, **causticity,** astringency, mordancy, severity, asperity, trenchancy, cuttingness, bitingness, harshness, roughness, **acridity; bitterness** 429.2; acerbity, acidulousness, acidity, **sourness** 432.

.2 **zest,** zestfulness, zestiness, **briskness,** liveliness, raciness; **nippiness, tanginess,** snappiness; **spiciness,** pepperiness, hotness, fieriness; **tang, spice,** relish; **nip, bite;** punch, snap, zip, ginger; **kick,** guts [slang].

.3 **strength,** strongness; high flavor, highness, rankness, gaminess.

.4 **saltiness, salinity,** brininess; brackishness; **salt,** sali–, salin(o)– *or* salini–; **brine.**

.5 VERBS **bite, nip,** bite the tongue, sting, make the eyes water, go up the nose.

.6 ADJS **pungent, piquant, poignant; sharp, keen,** piercing, penetrating, nose-tickling, stinging, **biting, acrid,** astringent, irritating, harsh, rough, severe, asperous, cutting, trenchant; **caustic,** vitriolic, mordant, escharotic; **bitter** 429.6; acerbic, acid, **sour** 432.6.

.7 **zestful,** zesty, **brisk,** lively, racy, zippy, **nippy,** snappy, **tangy,** with a kick; spiced, seasoned, high-seasoned; **spicy,** curried, **peppery,** hot, burning, hot as pepper.

.8 **strong,** strong-flavored, strong-tasting; **high,** high-flavored, high-tasted; **rank, gamy.**

.9 **salty,** salt, salted, saltish, **saline, briny; brackish;** pickled.

## 434. TOBACCO

.1 NOUNS **tobacco,** *tabac* [Fr], nicotia *or* nicotian [both archaic], nicotin(o)–; **the weed** [informal], fragrant weed, Indian weed *or* drug, filthy weed, sot-weed [archaic], "pernicious weed" [Cowper], "thou weed, who art so lovely fair and smell'st so sweet" [Shakespeare], "sublime tobacco" [Byron], "divine tobacco" [Spenser]; carcinogenic substance.

.2 (tobaccos) flue-cured *or* bright, fire-cured, air-cured; Broadleaf, Burley, Cuban, Havana, Havana seed, Latakia, Turkish, Russian, Maryland, Virginia;

plug tobacco, bird's-eye, canaster, leaf, lugs, seconds, shag.

.3 **smoking tobacco,** smokings [dial], smoke or smokes [both informal].

.4 **cigar,** seegar [dial]; rope or stinker [both slang]; **cheroot, stogie,** corona, belvedere, Havana, colorado, trichinopoly; cigarillo; box of cigars, cigar box, cigar case, humidor; cigar cutter.

.5 **cigarette;** butt or cig or fag or coffin nail or cancer stick [all slang]; cigarette butt, **butt,** stub; snipe [slang]; pack or deck of cigarettes, box or carton of cigarettes, cigarette case.

.6 **pipe,** tobacco pipe; corncob, corncob pipe, Missouri meerschaum; briar pipe, briar; clay pipe, clay, churchwarden [Brit]; meerschaum; water pipe, hookah, nargileh, calean, hubble-bubble; peace pipe, calumet; pipe rack, pipe cleaner, tobacco pouch.

.7 **chewing tobacco,** eating tobacco [dial]; navy or navy plug, cavendish, twist, pigtail, cut plug; **quid,** cud, fid [Brit dial], **chew,** chaw [dial]; tobacco juice.

.8 **snuff,** snoose [slang]; rappee; pinch of snuff; snuff bottle, snuffbox, snuff mill [Scot].

.9 **nicotine,** nicotia [archaic].

.10 **smoking,** smoking habit, habitual smoking; chain-smoke; smoke, puff, drag [slang]; **chewing;** tobacco or nicotine addiction, tobaccoism, tabacosis, tabacism, tabagism, nicotinism.

.11 **tobacco user, smoker,** cigarette or pipe or cigar smoker, chewer, snuffer, snuff dipper.

.12 **tobacconist;** snuffman; tobacco store or shop, cigar store.

.13 **smoking room,** smoking car, **smoker.**

.14 VERBS (use tobacco) **smoke;** inhale, puff, draw, drag [informal], pull; smoke like a furnace or chimney; chain-smoke; **chew,** chaw [dial]; **take snuff,** dip or inhale snuff.

.15 ADJS **tobacco,** tobaccoy, tobaccolike; **nicotinic;** smoking, chewing; snuffy.

## 435. ODOR

.1 NOUNS **odor, smell, scent,** aroma, flavor [archaic], savor, osm(o)–; **essence,** definite odor, redolence, effluvium, emanation, exhalation, fume, breath, subtle odor, whiff, trace, detectable odor; trail, spoor; **fragrance** 436; **stench** 437.

.2 **odorousness, smelliness,** headiness, pungency 433.

.3 smelling, olfaction, nosing, scenting;

sniffing, snuffing, snuffling, whiffing, odorizing, odorization.

.4 **sense of smell,** smell, smelling, scent, olfaction, olfactory sense, –osphresia or –osphrasia.

.5 **olfactory organ;** olfactory pit, olfactory cell, olfactory area, **nose** 256.7; **nostrils,** noseholes [dial], nares; olfactory nerves; **olfactories.**

.6 VERBS (have an odor) **smell,** be aromatic, smell of, be redolent of; emit or emanate or give out a smell, reach one's nostrils, yield an odor or aroma, breathe, exhale; reek, **stink** 437.4.

.7 odorize; scent, perfume 436.8.

.8 **smell, scent, nose; sniff,** snuff, snuffle, inhale, breathe, breathe in; get a noseful of, smell of, catch a smell of, get or take a whiff of, whiff.

.9 ADJS **odorous,** odoriferous, odored, odorant, **smelling,** smellful [Austral], smellsome, **smelly,** redolent, aromatic; effluvious; **fragrant** 436.9; **malodorous** 437.5.

.10 **strong,** strong-smelling, strong-scented; **pungent,** penetrating, nose-piercing, sharp; reeking, suffocating.

.11 **smellable,** sniffable, whiffable.

.12 **olfactory,** olfactive.

.13 **keen-scented,** quick-scented, sharp- or keen-nosed, **with a nose for.**

## 436. FRAGRANCE

.1 NOUNS **fragrance,** fragrancy [archaic], **perfume, aroma, scent,** redolence, balminess, **incense, bouquet,** nosegay [archaic], sweet smell, sweet savor; **odor** 435; spice, spiciness; muskiness; fruitiness.

.2 perfumery, parfumerie [Fr]; **perfume,** parfum [Fr], **scent, essence,** extract; aromatic, ambrosia; attar, essential or volatile oil; aromatic water; balsam, **balm,** aromatic gum; balm of Gilead, balsam of Mecca; myrrh; bay oil, myrcia oil; champaca oil; rose oil, attar of roses, "the perfumed tincture of the roses" [Shakespeare]; lavender oil, heliotrope, jasmine oil, bergamot oil; fixative, musk, civet, ambergris.

.3 **toilet water,** Florida water; rose water, eau de rose [Fr]; lavender water, eau de lavande [Fr]; eau de jasmin [Fr]; cologne, cologne water, eau de Cologne; bay rum; **lotion,** after-shave lotion.

.4 **incense;** joss stick; pastille; frankincense or olibanum; agalloch or aloeswood, calambac, lignaloes or linaloa, sandalwood.

.5 **perfumer,** parfumeur [Fr]; thurifer, censer bearer; **perfuming,** censing, thurification, odorizing.

.6 (articles) perfumer, *parfumoir* [Fr], fumigator, scenter, odorator, odorizer; atomizer, purse atomizer, spray; censer, thurible, incensory, incense burner; vinaigrette, scent bottle, smelling bottle, scent box, scent ball; scent bag, sachet; pomander, pouncet-box [archaic]; potpourri.

.7 VERBS **be fragrant,** smell sweet, **smell good,** please the nostrils.

.8 **perfume, scent,** cense, incense, thurify, aromatize, odorize, fumigate, embalm.

.9 ADJS **fragrant, aromatic,** odoriferous, redolent, perfumy, **perfumed, scented,** odorate *or* essenced [both archaic], **sweet, sweet-smelling,** sweet-scented, savory, balmy, ambrosial, incense-breathing; thuriferous; **odorous** 435.9; sweet as a rose, fragrant as new-mown hay; flowery; fruity; musky; spicy.

### 437. STENCH

.1 NOUNS **stench, stink,** malodor, fetidness, fetidity, fetor, foul odor, offensive odor, offense to the nostrils, bad smell, rotten smell, noxious stench, "the rankest compound of villainous smell that ever offended nostril" [Shakespeare], frowst [Brit], smell *or* stench of decay, **reek,** reeking, nidor; mephitis, miasma, graveolence [archaic]; body odor, BO; halitosis, **bad breath,** foul breath.

.2 **fetidness,** fetidity, malodorousness, **smelliness,** stinkingness, **odorousness,** noisomeness, **rankness, foulness,** putridness, offensiveness; repulsiveness; **mustiness,** funkiness, must, frowst [Brit], moldiness, mildew, fustiness, frowiness [dial], frowziness, frowstiness [Brit], stuffiness; **rancidness,** rancidity, reastiness [Brit dial]; rottenness 692.7.

.3 **stinker,** stinkard; skunk *or* polecat *or* rotten egg; stink ball, stinkpot, stink bomb.

.4 VERBS **stink,** smell, **smell bad,** assail *or* offend the nostrils, stink in the nostrils, smell to heaven *or* high heaven, **reek;** smell up, stink up; stink out.

.5 ADJS **malodorous, fetid,** olid, **odorous, stinking, reeking,** reeky, nidorous, smelling, bad-smelling, ill-smelling, heavy-smelling, **smelly,** smellful [Austral], stenchy; **foul,** vile, putrid, bad, fulsome, noisome, fecal, offensive, repulsive, noxious, sulfurous, graveolent [archaic]; rotten 692.41; **rank,** strong, high, gamy; **rancid,** reasty *or* reasy [both Brit dial], reechy [archaic]; **musty,** funky, fusty,

frowy [dial], frowzy, frowsty [Brit], stuffy, moldy, mildewed, mildewy; mephitic, miasmic, miasmal.

### 438. ODORLESSNESS

.1 NOUNS **odorlessness, inodorousness,** scentlessness, smell-lessness.

.2 **deodorizing,** deodorization, fumigation, ventilation 402.9.

.3 **deodorant,** deodorizer; fumigant, fumigator.

.4 VERBS **deodorize,** fumigate; ventilate 402.11, freshen the air.

.5 ADJS **odorless,** inodorous, nonodorous, smell-less, **scentless,** unscented.

.6 **deodorant,** deodorizing.

### 439. VISION

.1 NOUNS **vision,** seeing, opto–, –opsia *or* –opsy, –opsis; **sight, eyesight,** sightedness, –opy *or* –opia; eye, power of sight, sense of sight, visual sense; **perception,** discernment; perspicacity, perspicuity, sharp *or* acute *or* keen sight, visual acuity, quick sight; farsight, farsightedness; clear sight, unobstructed vision; rod vision, scotopia; cone vision, photopia; color vision, twilight vision, daylight vision, day vision, night vision; eye-mindedness; **field of vision,** visual field, scope, ken, purview, horizon, sweep, range; peripheral vision, peripheral field; field of view 444.3.

.2 **observation,** observance; **looking, watching, viewing,** –scopy; witnessing, espial; **notice,** note, respect, **regard;** watch, lookout; spying, espionage.

.3 **look, sight,** looksee [informal], dekko [Brit informal], eye, view, regard, eyeful [informal]; sidelong look; leer, leering look, lustful leer; sly look; look-in; preview; scene, prospect 446.6.

.4 **glance,** glance of the eye, squiz [Austral], slant [informal], rapid glance, cast, sideglance; **glimpse,** flash, quick sight; **peek, peep;** wink, blink, flicker *or* twinkle of an eye; causal glance, **half an eye;** *coup d'œil* [Fr].

.5 **gaze, stare,** gape, goggle; sharp *or* piercing *or* penetrating look; **ogle,** glad eye, come-hither look [informal], bedroom eyes [slang]; **glare, glower,** glaring *or* glowering look; evil eye, *malocchio* [Ital], whammy [slang].

.6 **scrutiny,** overview, **survey,** contemplation, the eye [slang]; examination, visual examination, vetting [Brit informal], ocular inspection, eyeball inspection [informal], **inspection** 485.3.

.7 **viewpoint, standpoint, point of view,** vantage, vantage point, point or coign of vantage; where one stands; **outlook,** angle, angle of vision; mental outlook 525.2.

.8 observation post or point; **observatory; lookout,** outlook, overlook; **watchtower,** tower; Texas tower; beacon, lighthouse, pharos; gazebo, belvedere; bridge, conning tower, crow's nest; peephole, sighthole, loophole; **ringside,** ringside seat; **grandstand,** bleachers; **gallery,** top gallery; paradise or peanut gallery [informal].

.9 **eye,** visual organ, organ of vision, oculus, optic, **orb,** ocul(o)–, ophthalm(o)–; **peeper** [informal], baby blues [informal]; clear eyes, bright eyes, starry orbs; saucer eyes, banjo eyes [slang], popeyes, goggle eyes; naked eye, unassisted or unaided eye; corner of the eye; eyeball; retina, retin(o)–; lens, phak(o)–; cornea, corne(o)–; sclera, scler(o)–; optic nerve, iris, irid(o)–; pupil; eyelid, lid, blephar(o)–, nictitating membrane.

.10 **sharp eye,** keen eye, piercing or penetrating eye, gimlet eye, X-ray eye; **eagle eye;** peeled eye [informal], watchful eye; **weather eye.**

.11 (comparisons) eagle, hawk, cat, lynx, ferret, weasel; Argus.

.12 VERBS **see, behold, observe, view, witness, perceive, discern, spy,** espy, **sight,** have in sight, make out, pick out, descry, spot [informal], twig [Brit informal], discover, notice, distinguish, recognize, ken [dial], **catch sight of,** get a load of [slang], take in, get an eyeful of [informal], look on or upon, cast the eyes on or upon, **set or lay eyes on, clap eyes on** [informal]; **glimpse,** get or catch a glimpse of; see at a glance, see with half an eye; see with one's own eyes.

.13 **look, peer,** direct the eyes, turn or bend the eyes, cast one's eye, lift up the eyes; **peek, peep,** pry, take a peep or peek; play peekaboo.

.14 **look at,** take a look at, eye, eyeball [informal], have a looksee [informal], look on or upon, gaze at or upon; **watch, observe, view, regard;** keep one's eyes peeled or skinned, be watchful or observant or vigilant, keep one's eyes open; keep in sight or view, hold in view; look after, keep under observation, spy upon, keep an eye on, follow; **reconnoiter,** scout, get the lay of the land.

.15 **scrutinize, survey, eye,** contemplate, look over, give the eye [slang], give the once-over [slang]; **ogle,** ogle at, **leer,** leer at,

give one the glad eye; examine, vet [Brit informal], **inspect** 485.23; **pore,** pore over, peruse; take a close or careful look; take a long, hard look; size up [informal]; take stock of.

.16 **gaze,** gloat [archaic], fix one's gaze, fix or fasten or rivet the eyes upon, keep the eyes upon; **eye, ogle; stare,** stare at, stare hard, look, goggle, gape, **gawk** [informal], gaup [dial], gaze open-mouthed; crane, crane the neck, stand on tiptoe; strain one's eyes; look straight in the eye, look full in the face, hold one's eye or gaze, stare down.

.17 **glare, glower,** look daggers, look black; give one the evil eye, give one a whammy [slang].

.18 **glance, glimpse,** glint, cast a glance, glance at or upon, give a coup d'œil, take a glance at, take a squint at [informal].

.19 **look askance** or askant, give a sidelong look; squint, look asquint; cock the eye; **look down one's nose** [informal].

.20 **look away,** look aside, **avert the eyes,** look another way, break one's eyes away, stop looking, turn away from, turn the back upon; drop one's eyes or gaze, cast one's eyes down; avoid one's gaze.

.21 ADJS **visual, seeing, ocular,** eyeball [informal], **optic(al);** ophthalmic; visible 444.6.

.22 **clear-sighted,** clear-eyed; **farsighted,** farseeing, telescopic; **sharp-sighted,** keensighted, sharp-eyed, **eagle-eyed,** hawkeyed, ferret-eyed, lynx-eyed, cat-eyed, Argus-eyed; eye-minded.

.23 ADVS **at sight,** as seen, visibly, at a glance; by sight, by eyeball [informal], visually; at first sight, **at the first blush,** prima facie [L].

## 440. DEFECTIVE VISION

.1 NOUNS faulty eyesight, bad eyesight, defect of vision or sight, imperfect vision, blurred vision, reduced sight, partial blindness; **astigmatism,** astigmia; nystagmus; albinism; double vision, double sight; tunnel vision; blindness 441.

.2 **dim-sightedness,** dull-sightedness, nearblindness, amblyopia, gravel-blindness, sand-blindness, **purblindness,** dim eyes, ambly(o)–; blurredness, blearedness, bleariness, redness, lippitude [archaic].

.3 **nearsightedness, myopia,** shortsightedness, short sight.

.4 **farsightedness,** hyperopia, longsightedness, long sight; presbyopia.

.5 **strabismus,** heterotropia, –tropia; cast, cast in the eye; **squint,** squinch [dial];

cross-eye, cross-eyedness; convergent strabismus, esotropia; upward strabismus, anoöpsia; walleye, exotropia.

.6 (defective eyes) cross-eyes, cockeyes, squint eyes, swivel eyes [slang], goggle eyes, walleyes, bug-eyes or popeyes [both slang], saucer eyes [slang].

.7 winking, blinking, fluttering the eyelids, nictitation; winker, blinkard [archaic].

.8 VERBS see badly or poorly, barely see, be half-blind; have a mote in the eye; see double.

.9 squint, squinch [dial], squint the eye, look asquint, screw up the eyes, skew, goggle [archaic].

.10 wink, blink, nictitate, bat the eyes [informal].

.11 ADJS poor-sighted; astigmatic(al); nystagmic; nearsighted, shortsighted, myopic, mope-eyed [archaic]; farsighted, longsighted, presbyopic; squinting, squinty, asquint, squint-eyed, squinch-eyed [dial], strabismal, strabismic; winking, blinking, blinky, blink-eyed.

.12 cross-eyed, cockeyed, swivel-eyed [slang], goggle-eyed, bug-eyed or popeyed [both slang], walleyed, saucer-eyed, glare-eyed; one-eyed, monocular; moon-eyed.

.13 dim-sighted, dim, dull-sighted, dim-eyed, weak-eyed, feeble-eyed, mole-eyed; purblind, half-blind, gravel-blind, sand-blind; bleary-eyed, blear-eyed; filmy-eyed, film-eyed.

## 441. BLINDNESS

.1 NOUNS blindness, sightlessness, cecity, ablepsia, unseeingness, sightless eyes, lack of vision, eyelessness; stone-blindness, total blindness; darkness, "ever-during dark", "total eclipse without all hope of day" [both Milton], "the precious treasure of his eyesight lost" [Shakespeare]; economic blindness; partial blindness, reduced sight, blind side; blind spot; dim-sightedness 440.2; snow blindness, niphablepsia; amaurosis, gutta serena [L], drop serene; cataract; glaucoma; trachoma; mental or psychic blindness, mind-blindness, soul-blindness, benightedness, unenlightenment, spiritual blindness; blinding, making blind, depriving of sight, putting out the eyes, excecation [archaic]; blurring the eyes, blindfolding, hoodwinking.

.2 day blindness, hemeralopia; night blindness, nyctalopia; moon blindness, moonblind.

.3 color blindness; dichromatism; monochromatism, achromatopsia; red blind-

ness, protanopia, green blindness, deuteranopia, red-green blindness, Daltonism; yellow blindness, xanthocyanopia; blue-yellow blindness, tritanopia; violet-blindness.

.4 the blind, the sightless, the unseeing; blind man; bat, mole; "blind leaders of the blind" [Bible].

.5 blindfold; eye patch; blinkers, blinds, blinders, rogue's badge.

.6 (aids for the blind) sensory aid, Braille, New York point, Gall's serrated type, Boston type, Howe's American type, Moon or Moon's type, Alston's Glasgow type, Lucas's type, sight-saver type, Frere's type; line letter, string alphabet, writing stamps; noctograph, writing frame, embosser, high-speed embosser; visagraph; talking book; optophone, Visotoner, Optacon; personal sonar, Pathsounder; ultrasonic spectacles; cane; Seeing Eye dog, guide dog.

.7 VERBS blind, blind the eyes, deprive of sight, strike blind, render or make blind, excecate [archaic]; darken, dim, obscure, eclipse; put one's eyes out, gouge; blindfold, hoodwink, bandage; throw dust in one's eyes, benight; dazzle, bedazzle, daze; glare; snow-blind.

.8 be blind, not see, walk in darkness, grope in the dark, feel one's way; go blind, lose one's sight or vision; be blind to, close or shut one's eyes to, wink or blink at, look the other way, blind oneself to, wear blinkers; have a blind spot or side.

.9 ADJS blind, sightless, ableptical, eyeless, visionless, unseeing, undiscerning, unobserving, unperceiving; in darkness, rayless, bereft of light, dark [dial], "dark, dark, dark, amid the blaze of noon" [Milton]; stone-blind, stark blind, blind as a bat, blind as a mole, blind as an owl; amaurotic; dim-sighted 440.13; hemeralopic; nyctalopic; color-blind; mind-blind, soul-blind, mentally or psychically or spiritually blind, benighted, unenlightened.

.10 blinded, excecate [archaic], darkened, obscured; blindfolded, blindfold, hoodwinked; dazzled, bedazzled, dazed; snow-blind, snow-blinded.

.11 blinding, obscuring; dazzling, bedazzling.

## 442. SPECTATOR

.1 NOUNS spectator, observer, −scopus; looker, onlooker, looker-on, watcher, gazer, gazer-on, gaper, goggler, viewer, seer, beholder, perceiver, percipient; spectatress, spectatrix; witness, eyewitness; bystander, passerby; sidewalk superintendent; kibitzer; girl-watcher, ogler, drugstore cowboy [informal]; bird-watcher; television-viewer, televiewer, video-gazer, TV-viewer.

.2 **attender** 186.5; theatergoer 611.32; audience 448.6.

.3 **sightseer**, excursionist, tourist, rubberneck or **rubbernecker** [both slang]; slummer.

.4 **sight-seeing**, rubbernecking [slang], lionism [Brit informal]; excursion, **rubberneck tour** [slang].

.5 VERBS spectate [informal], look on, eye, **ogle, gape** 439.16; take in, **look at, watch** 439.14; attend 186.8.

.6 **sight-see**, see the sights, take in the sights, lionize or see the lions [both Brit informal]; **rubberneck** [slang]; go slumming.

.7 ADJS spectating, spectatorial, –scopic; onlooking; sight-seeing, rubberneck [slang].

### 443. OPTICAL INSTRUMENTS

.1 NOUNS **lens**, glass, phak(o)– or phac(o)–; achromatic lens, astigmatic lens, coated lens; meniscus, concavo-convex lens, concave lens, convex lens, toric lens; telephoto lens; zoom lens, varifocal lens; eyepiece, eyeglass, ocular; objective, object glass; prism, objective prism; hand lens, magnifying glass, magnifier; reading glass, reader; condenser, bull's-eye, burning glass; **camera** 577.11,20.

.2 **spectacles, specs** [informal], **glasses, eyeglasses**, pair of glasses or spectacles, barnacles [Brit slang], cheaters or peepers [both slang]; reading glasses, readers; bifocals, divided spectacles, trifocals, pincenez, nippers [informal]; lorgnette, lorgnon [Fr]; horn-rimmed glasses; harlequin glasses; granny glasses; mini-specs [informal]; colored glasses, sunglasses, sun-specs [informal], dark glasses, Polaroid glasses, shades [slang]; goggles, blinkers; eyeglass, monocle, quizzing glass; contact lens.

.3 **telescope**, scope, **spy glass**, terrestrial telescope, glass, **field glass; binoculars**, zoom binoculars, opera glasses.

.4 **sight**; sighthole; finder, viewfinder; panoramic sight; bombsight; peep sight, open sight, leaf sight.

.5 **mirror**, glass, **looking glass**, seeing glass [Brit dial], reflector, speculum; hand mirror, window mirror, rear-view mirror, cheval glass, pier glass, shaving mirror; steel mirror; convex mirror, concave mirror, distorting mirror.

.6 **optics**, optical physics; **optometry;** microscopy, microscopics, micro–; telescopy; stereoscopy; spectroscopy, spectrometry, spectro–; infrared spectroscopy; spectrophotometry; electron optics; **photography** 577.

.7 **oculist**, ophthalmologist, **optometrist;** microscopist, telescopist; optician.

.8 ADJS **optic(al)**, ophthalmic, ophthalmologic(al), optometrical, optico–, opto–.

.9 –scopic, microscopic, telescopic, etc.; stereoscopic, stereo–, three-dimensional, 3-D.

.10 **spectacled, bespectacled**, four-eyed [informal]; goggled; monocled.

.11 **optical instruments**

| | |
|---|---|
| diffractometer | photometer |
| eriometer | photomultiplier |
| goniometer | prism |
| image orthicon | rangefinder |
| laser | stereopticon |
| microfilm viewer or | thaumatrope |
| reader | viewer |
| optometer | |

.12 **scopes**

| | |
|---|---|
| abdominoscope | pharyngoscope |
| amblyoscope | photoscope |
| bronchoscope | polariscope |
| chromatoscope | polemoscope |
| chromoscope | pseudoscope |
| cystoscope | radarscope |
| diaphanoscope | radioscope |
| epidiascope | retinoscope |
| gastroscope | sniperscope |
| kaleidoscope | snooperscope |
| ophthalmoscope | spectroscope |
| oscilloscope | stereoscope |
| periscope | stroboscope |

.13 **microscopes**

| | |
|---|---|
| binocular microscope | phase contrast micro |
| blink microscope | scope, phase micro |
| compound micro | scope |
| scope | pinion focusing micro |
| dark-field microscope | scope |
| dissecting microscope | polarizing microscope |
| electron microscope | power microscope |
| field ion microscope | projecting microscope |
| fluorescence micro | simple or single micro |
| scope | scope |
| gravure microscope | stereomicroscope, ste |
| laboratory microscope | reoscopic micro |
| metallurgical micro | scope |
| scope | surface microscope |
| optical microscope | ultramicroscope |
| oxyhydrogen micro | ultraviolet microscope |
| scope | X-ray microscope |

.14 **telescopes**

| | |
|---|---|
| astronomical tele | guiding telescope |
| scope | inverting telescope |
| Cassegrainian tele | mercurial telescope |
| scope | Newtonian telescope |
| double-image tele | optical telescope |
| scope | panoramic telescope |
| elbow telescope | prism telescope |
| finder telescope | radio telescope |

reflecting telescope          twin telescope
refracting telescope          vernier telescope
Schmidt telescope             water telescope
spotting scope                zenith telescope,
terrestrial telescope            zenith tube
tower telescope

**.15 spectroscopes, spectrometers**

analytical spectrome-         microspectroscope
ter                           monochromator
diffraction spectro-          ocular spectroscope
scope                         prism spectroscope
direct-reading spec-          reversion spectroscope
trometer                      spectrograph
direct-reading spectro-       spectrophotometer
scope                         spectroradiometer
microspectrophotome-          star spectroscope
ter

## 444. VISIBILITY

**.1** NOUNS **visibility,** visibleness, perceptibility, discernibleness, observability, visual-
ity, seeableness; exposure; manifestation;
outcrop, outcropping; the visible, the
seen, what is revealed, what can be seen;
revelation, epiphany.

**.2 distinctness, plainness,** evidence [archaic],
evidentness, obviousness, patentness,
manifestness; **clearness, clarity,** crystal-
clearness; **definiteness,** definition; percipi;
prominence, conspicuousness, conspicu-
ity; high or low visibility; atmospheric visibility, seeing, ceiling, ceiling unlimited,
visibility unlimited, visibility zero.

**.3 field of view,** field of vision, range or
scope of vision, **sight,** limit of vision,
eyereach, **eyesight,** eyeshot, ken; **vista,**
**view, horizon, prospect, perspective, out-**
**look,** survey, –scape; range, scan, scope;
line of sight, sightliness; naked eye; command, domination, outlook over.

**.4** VERBS **show,** show up, show through,
shine out or through, **appear 446.8, be vis-**
**ible,** be seen, be revealed, be evident, be
noticeable, meet the gaze, impinge on
the eye, present to the eye, meet or catch
or hit or strike the eye; **stand out,** stand
forth, loom large, glare, **stare one in the**
**face,** hit one in the eye, **stick out like a**
**sore thumb.**

**.5 be exposed,** be conspicuous, have high
visibility, stick out, hang out [slang], crop
out; live in a glass house.

**.6** ADJS **visible,** visual, **perceptible,** perceivable, **discernible, seeable,** viewable, wit-
nessable, beholdable, observable, detectable, noticeable, recognizable, to be seen,
phaner(o)–; **in sight,** in view, in plain
sight, in full view, present to the eyes, before one's eyes, under one's eyes, open,
naked, outcropping, hanging out [slang],

exposed, showing, open or exposed to
view; **evident,** in evidence, **manifest, ap-**
**parent;** revealed, disclosed, unhidden, unconcealed, unclouded, undisguised.

**.7 distinct, plain, clear, obvious, evident,**
**patent,** unmistakable, not to be mistaken, plain to be seen, for all to see,
showing for all to see; **definite, defined,**
**well-defined,** well-marked, well-resolved,
in focus; **clear-cut,** clean-cut; crystal-clear,
clear as crystal; as clear as day, as plain as
a pikestaff [informal], as plain as the
nose on one's face, under one's nose, as
plain as plain can be; **conspicuous,** glaring, staring, **prominent,** pronounced,
well-pronounced, in bold or strong or
high relief.

**.8** ADVS **visibly, perceptibly,** perceivably,
discernibly, seeably, recognizably, observably, markedly, noticeably; **manifestly,**
**apparently,** evidently; **distinctly, clearly,**
with clarity or crystal clarity, **plainly,** obviously, patently, definitely, unmistakably; conspicuously, undisguisedly, un-
concealedly, prominently, pronouncedly,
glaringly, starkly, staringly.

## 445. INVISIBILITY

**.1** NOUNS **invisibility,** imperceptibility, un-
perceivability, indiscernibility, unseeable-
ness, viewlessness; nonappearance; disappearance 447; the invisible, the unseen;
unsubstantiality 4, immateriality 377, **se-**
**crecy 614,** concealment 615.

**.2 inconspicuousness,** half-visibility, semivisi-
bility, low profile; **indistinctness, unclear-**
**ness,** unplainness, **faintness,** paleness, feebleness, weakness, **dimness,** bleariness,
darkness, shadowiness, **vagueness,** vague
appearance, indefiniteness, obscurity, uncertainty, indistinguishability; **blurriness,**
blur, soft focus, defocus, **fuzziness, hazi-**
**ness,** mistiness, filminess, fogginess.

**.3** VERBS **be invisible** or **unseen,** escape notice; lie hid 615.8, **blush unseen;** disappear
447.2.

**.4 blur, dim, pale,** soften, film, mist, fog; defocus, lose resolution or sharpness or distinctness, go soft at the edges.

**.5** ADJS **invisible,** aphan(o)–; **imperceptible,**
unperceivable, **indiscernible,** undiscerni-
ble, **unseeable,** viewless, unbeholdable,
unapparent, insensible; **out of sight,** *à*
*perte de vue* [Fr]; **secret 614.11–16; un-**
**seen,** sightless, unbeheld, unviewed, unwitnessed, unobserved, unnoticed, unperceived; behind the curtain or scenes; dis-

guised, camouflaged, hidden, **concealed** 615.11–14; latent, unrealized, submerged.

.6 inconspicuous, half-visible, semivisible, low-profile; **indistinct, unclear,** unplain, **indefinite,** undefined, ill-defined, ill-marked, **faint,** pale, feeble, weak, **dim,** dark, **shadowy, vague, obscure,** indistinguishable, unrecognizable; half-seen, merely glimpsed; uncertain, confused, out of focus, **blurred, blurry,** bleared, bleary, blear, **fuzzy, hazy,** misty, filmy, foggy.

## 446. APPEARANCE

.1 NOUNS **appearance, appearing,** apparition, coming, forthcoming, coming-forth, coming into being, rising, rise, arising, **emergence,** issuance; **materialization** 376.7, materializing, occurrence, **manifestation,** realization, incarnation, revelation, epiphany, theophany, avatar; presentation, disclosure, exposure, opening, unfolding, unfoldment, showing, showing forth, rising of the curtain.

.2 **appearances,** exteriors, externals; **mere externals, façade,** ostent, **show, outward show,** display, front [informal], outward or external appearance, surface appearance, surface show, vain show, apparent character, public image; gaudiness, speciousness, meretriciousness, **superficiality.**

.3 aspect, **look, view;** feature, lineaments; **seeming, semblance, image,** imago, eidolon, likeness, simulacrum; effect, impression, total effect or impression; **form, shape,** figure, configuration, gestalt; **manner,** fashion, wise, guise, style; **respect, regard,** reference, light; **phase,** phasis, phaso–; **facet, side,** angle, viewpoint 439.7, slant [informal], twist [informal].

.4 **looks, features, lineaments,** traits, lines; **countenance, face,** visage, feature, favor, **brow,** physiognomy; cast of countenance, **cut of one's jib** [informal], facial appearance or expression, cast, turn; **air, mien,** demeanor, carriage, bearing, port, posture, stance, presence; guise, garb, complexion, color.

.5 (thing appearing) **apparition, appearance,** phenomenon; **vision, image, shape, form,** figure, presence; false image, mirage, phasm [archaic], **phantom** 1017.1; –phane.

.6 **view, scene, sight;** prospect, outlook, lookout, **vista, perspective;** scenery, scenic view; panorama, sweep; scape, **landscape,** seascape, riverscape, waterscape, airscape, skyscape, cloudscape, cityscape, townscape; bird's-eye view.

.7 **spectacle, sight;** exhibit, **exhibition,** exposition, **show, stage show** 611.4, **display, presentation,** representation; tableau, tableau vivant; panorama, diorama, cosmorama, myriorama, cyclorama, georama; phantasmagoria, shifting scene, light show; psychedelic show; **pageant,** pageantry; parade, pomp.

.8 VERBS **appear,** become visible, **make one's appearance,** make or put in an appearance, appear on the scene, appear to one's eyes, meet or catch or strike the eye, **come in sight** or **view, show,** show oneself, show one's face, **show up** [informal], **turn up,** come, **materialize** 376.8, present oneself, present oneself to view, **manifest oneself,** become manifest, **reveal oneself,** discover oneself, uncover oneself, declare oneself, expose or betray oneself; **come to light,** see the light, see the light of day; **emerge,** issue, issue forth, stream forth, come forth, come out, come forward, come to hand; enter 302.7, come upon the stage; **rise, arise,** rear its head; look forth, peer or peep out; crop out, outcrop; loom, heave in sight, appear on the horizon; fade in.

.9 **burst forth,** break forth, debouch, erupt, irrupt; **pop up, bob up** [informal], start up, spring up, burst upon the view; flare up, flash, gleam.

.10 appear to be, seem to be, **appear, seem, look,** feel, sound, look to be, appear to one's eyes, have or present the appearance of, give the feeling of, strike one as; **appear like, seem like, look like,** have or wear the look of, **sound like; have every appearance of,** have all the earmarks of, have all the features of, have every sign or indication of; assume the guise of, take the shape of, exhibit the form of.

.11 ADJS **apparent,** appearing, **seeming, ostensible;** outward, surface, superficial; **visible** 444.6.

.12 ADVS **apparently, seemingly, ostensibly, to all appearances,** to all seeming, as it seems, to the eye; on the face of it, *prima facie* [L]; on the surface, outwardly, superficially; at first sight or view, at the first blush.

## 447. DISAPPEARANCE

.1 NOUNS **disappearance,** disappearing, **vanishing,** vanishment; going, passing, departure; dissipation, dispersion; dissolution, dissolving, melting, evaporation, evanescence, dematerialization 377.5; fadeout, fading, fadeaway, blackout; wipe, wipe-off, erasure; eclipse, occultation, blocking; vanishing point; elimination 77.2; extinction 693.6.

.2 VERBS **disappear, vanish,** vanish from sight, do a vanishing act [slang], depart, **fly, flee** 631.10, go, be gone, **go away,** pass, pass out *or* away, pass out of sight, exit, leave the scene *or* stage, pass out of the picture, retire from sight, become lost to sight, be seen no more; **perish, die,** die out *or* away, fade, **fade out** *or* **away,** do a fade-out [slang]; sink, sink away, dissolve, melt, melt away, "melt, thaw, and dissolve itself" [Shakespeare], dematerialize 377.6, evaporate, evanesce, **vanish into thin air,** go up in smoke; disperse, dispel, dissipate; cease, cease to exist 2.5, **cease to be;** leave no trace, "leave not a rack behind" [Shakespeare]; waste, waste away, erode, be consumed, wear away, dwindle; undergo *or* suffer an eclipse; hide 615.8.

.3 ADJS **vanishing, disappearing,** passing, fleeting, fugitive, transient, flying, fading, dissolving, melting, evaporating, evanescent.

.4 **gone,** away, gone away, past and gone, extinct, missing, no more, lost, lost to sight *or* view, **out of sight;** nonexistent 2.7.

## 448. HEARING

.1 NOUNS **hearing,** audition, audio–, audit(o)–, –acousia *or* –acusia; sense of hearing, auditory *or* aural sense, ear; listening, heeding, attention, hushed attention, rapt attention, eager attention; auscultation, aural examination, examination by ear; audibility.

.2 **audition,** hearing, tryout [informal], **audience, interview,** conference; attention, favorable attention, ear; **listening,** listening in; **eavesdropping,** wiretapping, electronic surveillance, bugging [informal].

.3 good hearing, refined *or* acute sense of hearing, sensitive ear, nice *or* quick *or* sharp *or* correct ear; **an ear for;** musical ear, ear for music; ear-mindedness; bad ear, no ear, tin ear.

.4 **earshot,** earreach, **hearing,** range, auditory range, reach, carrying distance, **sound.**

.5 **listener,** hearer, auditor, audient, hearkener; **eavesdropper,** overhearer, little pitcher with big ears, snoop, listener-in [informal].

.6 **audience,** auditory [archaic], **house,** congregation; theater, gallery; orchestra, pit; groundling, spectator 442.

.7 **ear,** aur(i)–, oto–, lug [Scot], auditory apparatus; external ear, **outer ear;** auricle, pinna, auriculo–; cauliflower ear; concha, conch, shell; ear lobe, lobe, lobule; auditory canal, acoustic *or* auditory meatus; **middle ear,** tympanic cavity, tympanum; eardrum, drumhead, tympanic membrane; auditory ossicles; malleus, hammer, incus, anvil; stapes, stirrup; mastoid process; Eustachian *or* auditory tube; **inner ear;** round window, secondary eardrum; oval window; bony labyrinth, membraneous labyrinth; perilymph, endolymph; vestibule; semicircular canals; cochlea; basilar membrane, organ of Corti; auditory nerve.

.8 **hearing aid,** hard-of-hearing aid; electronic hearing aid, transistor hearing aid; vacuum-tube hearing aid; ear trumpet; amplifier, speaking trumpet, megaphone; stethoscope.

.9 (science of hearing) otology; otoscopy, auriscopy; otoneurology, otopathy, otography, otoplasty, otolaryngology, otorhinolaryngology; acoustic phonetics, phonetics 594.14; auriscope, otoscope; audiometer.

.10 otologist, ear specialist, otolaryngologist, otorhinolaryngologist, ear, nose, and throat specialist.

.11 VERBS **listen, hark, hearken, heed, hear, attend,** give attention, **give ear,** give *or* lend an ear, bend an ear; **listen to,** listen at [dial], attend to, give a hearing to, give audience to, sit in on; **listen in; eavesdrop,** wiretap, tap, intercept, bug [informal]; **keep one's ears open,** be all ears [informal], listen with both ears, strain one's ears; prick up the ears, cock the ears; hang on the lips of; hear out; auscultate, examine by ear.

.12 **hear,** catch, get [informal], take in; **overhear; hear of,** hear tell of [dial]; get an earful [slang]; have an ear for.

.13 be heard, **fall on the ear,** sound in the ear, catch *or* reach the ear, come to one's ear, register, make an impression, get across [informal]; **have one's ear,** reach, contact, get to; make oneself heard, get through to, gain a hearing, reach the ear of; ring in the ear; caress the ear; assault *or* split *or* assail the ear.

.14 ADJS **auditory,** audio, audile, **hearing, aural,** auricular, otic; audio-visual; audible 449.15; otological, otoscopic, otopathic, etc.; acoustic(al), phonic.

.15 **listening, attentive,** open-eared, **all ears** [informal].

.16 **eared,** auriculate; big-eared, cauliflower-eared, crop-eared, dog-eared, droop-eared, flap-eared, flop-eared, lop-eared, long-eared, mouse-eared, prick-eared; **sharp-eared;** tin-eared; ear-minded.

.17 INTERJS **hark!,** hark ye!, hear ye!, hearken!, hear!, oyez!, hear ye, hear ye!, list!, **listen!, attend!,** attention!, hist!, whisht!, psst!

.18 **phones**

| | |
|---|---|
| autophone | Interphone |
| Dictaphone | kinetophone |
| earphone | magnetophone |
| electrophone | microphone |
| Geophone | optophone |
| headphone | radiophone |
| hydrophone | radiotelephone |
| idiophone | telephone 560.4–6,21 |

## 449. DEAFNESS

.1 NOUNS **deafness, hardness of hearing,** dull hearing, deaf ears, "ears more deaf than adders" [Shakespeare]; **stone-deafness;** nerve-deafness; mind deafness, word deafness; **tone deafness;** impaired hearing, hearing or auditory impairment; loss of hearing, hearing loss; **deaf-muteness,** deaf-mutism, surdimutism [archaic].

.2 **the deaf,** the hard-of-hearing; **deaf-mute,** surdo-mute [archaic], deaf-and-dumb person; lip reader.

.3 deaf-and-dumb alphabet, manual alphabet, finger alphabet; dactylology, sign language; lip reading, oral method.

.4 VERBS **be deaf;** have no ears, be earless; lose one's hearing, suffer hearing loss or impairment, go deaf; shut or stop or close one's ears, **turn a deaf ear;** fall on deaf ears.

.5 **deafen, stun,** split the ears or eardrums.

.6 ADJS **deaf, hard of hearing,** dull or thick of hearing, deaf-eared, dull-eared; surd [archaic]; deafened, stunned; **stone-deaf,** deaf as a stone, deaf as a door or a doorknob or doornail, **deaf as a post,** deaf as an adder, "like the deaf adder that stoppeth her ear" [Bible]; **unhearing;** earless; word-deaf; tone-deaf; half-deaf, quasi-deaf; **deaf and dumb,** deaf-mute.

## 450. SOUND

.1 NOUNS **sound,** sonance, acoustic(al) phenomenon; audio–, audito–, phon(o)–, –phone, –phonia or –phony, son(o)– or soni–; auditory phenomenon or stimulus, auditory effect; noise; ultrasound; sound wave, sound propagation; sound intensity, sound intensity level, amplitude, loudness 453; phone, speech sound 594.13.

.2 **tone, pitch, frequency,** audio frequency, AF; monotone, monotony, tonelessness; overtone, harmonic, partial, partial tone; fundamental tone, fundamental; intonation 594.7; ton(o)–.

.3 **timbre,** tonality, **tone quality,** tone color, color, coloring, clang color or tint, *Klangfarbe* [Ger].

.4 **sounding,** sonation, sonification.

.5 **acoustics,** phonics, radioacoustics; acoustical engineer, acoustician.

.6 **sonics;** subsonics; **supersonics,** ultrasonics; speed of sound 269.2; sound barrier, sonic barrier or wall; sonic boom.

.7 (sound unit) **decibel,** bel, phon.

.8 **loudspeaker, speaker;** dynamic speaker, electrodynamic speaker, excited-field speaker, moving-coil speaker, permanent magnet speaker, coaxial speaker, triaxial speaker, electromagnetic speaker, electrostatic speaker, capacitor speaker; high-fidelity speaker, full-fidelity speaker; **tweeter,** high-frequency speaker; **woofer,** low-frequency speaker; midrange speaker; monorange speaker; speaker unit, speaker system; crossover network; voice coil; cone, diaphragm; acoustical network; horn; **headphone, earphone,** headset.

.9 **microphone, mike** [informal]; radiomicrophone; **bug** [slang].

.10 **audio amplifier, amplifier;** preamplifier, preamp [informal].

.11 sound reproduction system, audio sound system; **high-fidelity** system, **hi-fi** [informal]; **record player, phonograph,** Gramophone, Victrola; **jukebox,** nickelodeon; radio-phonograph combination; monophonic or monaural system, **mono** [informal], stereophonic or binaural system, stereo [informal]; four-channel stereo system, discrete four-channel system, derived four-channel system, quadraphonic sound system; pickup or cartridge, magnetic pickup or cartridge, ceramic pickup or cartridge, crystal pickup, photoelectric pickup; stylus, needle; tone arm; turntable, transcription turntable, record changer, changer; **public-address system,** PA or PA system; sound truck; loudhailer, bullhorn; intercommunication system, **intercom** [informal], squawk box or bitch box [both informal]; **tape recorder,** tape deck; hi-fi fan [informal], audiophile.

.12 **record, phonograph record,** disc, wax; transcription, electrical transcription; recording, wire recording, tape recording; tape, tape cassette, cassette; tape cartridge, cartridge.

.13 **audio distortion, distortion;** scratching, shredding, hum, 60-cycle hum, rumble, hissing, howling, blurping, blooping, woomping, fluttering, flutter, wow, wow-wows, squeals, whistles, birdies, motorboating; feedback; static 344.21.

.14 VERBS **sound,** make a sound *or* noise, give forth *or* emit a sound; noise; speak 594.20; resound.

.15 ADJS **sounding,** sonorous, soniferous; **sounded;** tonal; monotone, monotonic, toneless, droning.

.16 **audible,** hearable; **distinct, clear,** plain, definite, articulate; distinctive, contrastive; high-fidelity, hi-fi [informal].

.17 **acoustic(al),** phonic, **sonic;** subsonic, supersonic, ultrasonic, hypersonic; transonic *or* transsonic, faster than sound.

.18 ADVS **audibly, aloud,** out, **out loud;** distinctly, clearly, plainly.

.19 **microphones**

| | |
|---|---|
| antinoise microphone | phone |
| capacitor microphone | moving-conductor |
| carbon microphone | microphone |
| cardioid microphone | noise-canceling micro- |
| ceramic microphone | phone |
| close-talking micro- | nondirectional micro- |
| phone | phone |
| combination micro- | omnidirectional |
| phone | microphone |
| condenser micro- | parabolic-reflector |
| phone | microphone |
| contact microphone | phase-shift micro- |
| crystal microphone | phone |
| double-button carbon | piezoelectric micro- |
| microphone | phone |
| dynamic microphone | pressure microphone |
| flame microphone | push-pull microphone |
| glow-discharge micro- | ribbon microphone |
| phone | shotgun microphone |
| gradient microphone | single-button carbon |
| hot-wire microphone | microphone |
| lapel microphone | standard microphone |
| lavaliere microphone | stereo microphone |
| line microphone | throat microphone |
| lip microphone | unidirectional micro- |
| magnetostriction | phone |
| microphone | variable-reluctance |
| mask microphone | microphone |
| moving-coil micro- | velocity microphone |

## 451. SILENCE

.1 NOUNS **silence,** silentness, **soundlessness,** noiselessness, **stillness,** "lucid stillness" [T. S. Eliot], **quietness,** quietude, quiescence 268, **quiet, still,** peace, whisht [Scot & Ir], **hush,** mum; lull, rest; golden silence; deathlike silence, tomblike silence, solemn *or* awful silence, silence of the grave *or* tomb; hush *or* dead of night,

dead; tacitness, taciturnity; inaudibility; tranquillity.

.2 **muteness,** mutism, **dumbness,** voicelessness, tonguelessness; speechlessness, wordlessness; inarticulateness; anaudia, aphasia, aphonia; hysterical mutism; deaf-muteness 449.1.

.3 **mute,** dummy; deaf-mute 449.2.

.4 **silencer, muffler,** muffle, **mute,** baffler, quietener, cushion; **damper,** damp; dampener; **soft pedal,** sordine, sourdine, *sordino* [Ital]; hushcloth, silence cloth; **gag, muzzle;** antiknock; **soundproofing,** acoustic tile, sound-absorbing material, soundproofing insulation.

.5 VERBS **be silent,** keep silent *or* silence, **keep still** *or* **quiet; keep one's mouth shut, shut up** [informal], **hold one's tongue,** keep one's tongue between one's teeth, put a bridle on one's tongue, seal one's lips, shut *or* close one's mouth, muzzle oneself, save one's breath [informal], **not breathe a word,** not let out a peep [informal], say nothing, not say 'boo' [informal], forswear speech *or* speaking, **keep mum, hold one's peace,** not let a word escape one, not utter a word; make no sign, keep to oneself, play dumb; not have a word to say, be mute, stand mute.

.6 [slang terms] keep one's trap *or* yap shut, button up, button one's lip, shut one's bazoo, dummy up, clam up, close up like a clam.

.7 **fall silent, hush,** quiet, quieten, quiesce, **quiet down,** pipe down [informal], check one's speech.

.8 **silence, put to silence, hush,** hush-hush, **shush,** quiet, quieten, **still; soft-pedal,** put on the soft pedal; squash, squelch [informal], stifle, choke, choke off, throttle, put the kibosh on [slang], put the lid on *or* shut down on [both informal], put the damper on [informal], **gag, muzzle,** muffle, stop one's mouth, cut one short; strike dumb *or* mute, dumbfound.

.9 **muffle, mute, dull, soften, deaden,** cushion, baffle, damp, **dampen,** deafen; subdue, stop, tone down, **soft-pedal,** put on the soft pedal.

.10 ADJS **silent, still,** stilly, **quiet,** quiescent 268.12, **hushed,** whist [Brit dial], **soundless,** noiseless; echoless; **inaudible,** subaudible, below the limen *or* threshold of hearing, unhearable; quiet as a mouse, mousy; silent as a post *or* stone, "noiseless as fear in a wide wilderness" [Keats], "silent as the shadows" [Coleridge], so quiet that one might hear a feather *or* pin drop; silent as the grave *or* tomb, still as death, "hush as death" [Shakespeare]; **unsounded, unvoiced,** unvocalized, unpronounced, unuttered, unarticulated.

.11 **tacit, wordless, unspoken,** unuttered, unexpressed, unsaid; **implicit** 546.7–9.

.12 **mute, mum, dumb,** voiceless, tongueless, **speechless,** wordless, breathless; inarticulate; **tongue-tied,** stricken dumb, dumbstruck, dumbstricken, dumbfounded; anaudic, aphasic, aphonic.

.13 ADVS **silently,** in silence, **quietly, soundlessly,** noiselessly; inaudibly.

.14 INTERJS **silence!, hush!, shush!, sh!,** sh-sh!, whist! *or* whish! [both Brit dial], whisht! [Scot & Ir], peace!, pax!, *tais toi!* [Fr], **be quiet!, be silent!, be still!, keep still!,** keep quiet!, quiet!, quiet please!, soft!, belay that! *or* there!, stow it!; **hold your tongue!,** hold your jaw! *or* lip!, **shut up!** [informal], **shut your mouth!** [informal], save your breath!, not another word!, not another peep out of you!, mum!, mum's the word!; hush your mouth!, shut your trap!, shut your face!, button your lip!, pipe down!, clam up!, dry up!, can it! [all slang].

## 452. FAINTNESS OF SOUND

.1 NOUNS **faintness, lowness, softness,** gentleness, subduedness, dimness, feebleness, weakness; indistinctness, unclearness, flatness; subaudibility; decrescendo.

.2 muffled tone, veiled voice, *voce velata* [Ital]; **mutedness; dullness, deadness,** flatness.

.3 **thud,** dull thud; **thump,** flump, crump [Brit informal], clop, clump, clunk, plunk, tunk, plump, bump; pad, pat; **patter,** pitter-patter, pitapat; **tap, rap, click,** tick, flick, pop; tinkle, clink, chink.

.4 **murmur,** murmuring, murmuration; **mutter,** muttering; **mumble,** mumbling; soft voice, low voice, small *or* little voice, "still small voice" [Bible]; **undertone,** underbreath, bated breath; susurration, susurrus; **whisper,** whispering, stage whisper, breathy voice; breath, sigh, exhalation, aspiration.

.5 **ripple, splash,** ripple of laughter, ripple of applause.

.6 **rustle,** rustling, froufrou, "a little noiseless noise among the leaves" [Keats].

.7 **hum, humming,** thrumming, low rumbling, booming, bombilation, bombination, **droning, buzzing,** whizzing, whirring, purring.

.8 **sigh, sighing, moaning,** sobbing, whining, soughing.

.9 VERBS **steal** *or* **waft on the ear,** melt in the air, float in the air.

.10 **murmur, mutter, mumble,** mussitate [archaic], maffle [Brit dial]; coo; susurrate; **whisper,** whisper in the ear; breathe, sigh, aspirate.

.11 **ripple, babble, burble, bubble, gurgle, guggle, purl, trill;** lap, plash, splash, swish, swash, slosh, wash.

.12 **rustle,** crinkle; **swish,** whish.

.13 **hum,** thrum, bum [Brit dial], boom, bombilate, bombinate, **drone, buzz,** whiz, whir, burr, birr [Scot], purr.

.14 **sigh, moan, sob, whine,** keen, wail, sough.

.15 **thud, thump, patter,** clop, clump, clunk, plunk; pad, pat; **tap, rap, click,** tick, pop; tinkle, clink, chink.

.16 ADJS **faint, low, soft, gentle, subdued, dim, feeble, weak,** faint-sounding, low-sounding, soft-sounding; soft-voiced, low-voiced, faint-voiced, weak-voiced; murmured, whispered; half-heard, scarcely heard; distant; indistinct, unclear; barely audible, subaudible, near the limit *or* threshold of hearing; piano, pianissimo; decrescendo.

.17 **muffled, muted,** softened, dampened, damped, smothered, stifled, bated, dulled, deadened, subdued; **dull, dead, flat,** *sordo* [Ital].

.18 **murmuring,** murmurous, murmurish, **muttering, mumbling;** susurrous, susurrant; **whispering,** whisper, whispery; **rustling.**

.19 **rippling, babbling, burbling, bubbling, gurgling, guggling, purling, trilling;** lapping, splashing, plashing, sloshing, swishing.

.20 **humming,** thrumming, **droning,** booming, bombinating, **buzzing,** whizzing, whirring, purring, burring, birring [Scot].

.21 ADVS **faintly, softly,** gently, subduedly, hushedly, dimly, feebly, weakly, low; piano, pianissimo; *sordo* [Ital], *sordamente* [Ital], *à la sourdine* [Fr].

.22 **in an undertone,** *sotto voce* [Ital], **under one's breath,** with bated breath, in a whisper, between the teeth; aside, in an aside; out of earshot.

## 453. LOUDNESS

.1 NOUNS **loudness,** loudishness, intensity, volume; fullness, sonorousness, sonority; surge of sound, surge, crescendo, swell, swelling.

.2 **noisiness,** noisefulness, **uproariousness,**

racketiness, tumultuousness, thunderousness, clamorousness, clangorousness, boisterousness, obstreperousness; vociferousness 459.5.

.3 **noise,** loud noise, **blast** 456.3, tintamarre, **racket, din,** chirm [dial], **clamor;** outcry, **uproar,** hue and cry, noise and shouting; howl; clangor, clatter, clap, jangle, rattle; roar, thunder, thunderclap 456.5, brouhaha, **tumult, hubbub,** flap, hullabaloo; row, bobbery [India], fracas, brawl, commotion, drunken brawl, shindy, donnybrook, free-for-all, shemozzle [Brit slang], rumble or rhubarb [both slang], dustup [Brit informal], rumpus [informal], ruckus [informal], ruction [dial], rowdydow [informal]; **pandemonium,** bedlam, hell or bedlam let loose, hell broke loose [slang]; charivari, shivaree [dial]; discord 461.

.4 **blare, blast,** shriek 458.4, peal; **toot,** tootle, **honk,** beep, blat, trumpet; bay, bray; **whistle,** tweedle, squeal; trumpet call, trumpet blast or blare, sound or flourish of trumpets, **fanfare,** tarantara, tantara, tantarara; tattoo; taps.

.5 **noisemaker;** ticktack, bull-roarer, catcall, whizzer, whizgig, snapper, cricket, clapper, clack, clacker, cracker; firecracker, cherry bomb; rattle, rattlebox; horn, Klaxon; whistle, steam whistle, siren; boiler room, boiler factory.

.6 VERBS **din;** boom, thunder 456.9; **resound,** ring, peal, ring or resound in the ears, din in the ear, **blast the ear,** pierce or split or rend the ears, rend or split the eardrums, split one's head; **deafen,** stun; blast 456.8, crash 456.6; **rend the air** or skies or firmament, rock the sky, fill the air, make the welkin ring; shake or rattle the windows; awake or startle the echoes, set the echoes ringing, awake the dead; surge, swell, rise, crescendo.

.7 drown out, outshout, outroar, shout down, overpower, overwhelm; jam.

.8 **be noisy, make a noise** or **racket,** raise a clamor or din or hue and cry, noise, racket, chirm [dial], **clamor,** roar, clangor; brawl, row, rumpus; **make an uproar,** kick up a dust or racket, kick up or raise a hullabaloo, raise the roof, raise Cain or Ned, howl like all the devils of hell, raise the devil, raise hell, whoop it up, maffick [Brit]; not be able to hear oneself think.

.9 **blare, blast;** shriek 458.8; **toot,** tootle, sound, peal, wind, blow, blat; pipe, trumpet, bugle, clarion; bay, bell, bray; **whistle,** tweedle, squeal; **honk,** honk or sound or blow the horn, beep; sound taps, sound a tattoo.

.10 ADJS **loud,** loudish, loud-sounding, stentorian, stentorious, stentoraphonic, forte, fortissimo; **resounding,** ringing, plangent, pealing; full, sonorous; **deafening,** ear-deafening, **ear-splitting,** head-splitting, ear-rending, ear-piercing, piercing; thunderous, tonitruous, tonitruant; booming 456.12; window-rattling, earthshaking, enough to wake the dead or the seven sleepers.

.11 **loud-voiced, loudmouthed,** fullmouthed, full-throated, big-voiced, clarion-voiced, trumpet-voiced, trumpet-tongued, brazen-mouthed, stentorian, boanergean.

.12 **noisy,** noiseful, rackety, clattery, clangorous, clanging, **clamorous,** clamoursome [Brit dial], clamant, blatant, blaring, brassy, brazen, blatting; uproarious, **tumultuous,** turbulent, blustering, brawling, **boisterous,** rip-roaring, rowdy, mafficking [Brit], strepitous, strepitant, obstreperous; vociferous 459.10.

.13 ADVS **loudly, aloud,** loud, lustily; **noisily,** uproariously; ringingly, resoundingly; with a loud voice, at the top of one's voice, at the pitch of one's breath, in full cry, with one wild yell, with a whoop and a hurrah; forte, *fortemente* [Ital], fortissimo.

## 454. RESONANCE

.1 NOUNS **resonance, sonorousness,** sonority, plangency, **vibrancy;** mellowness, richness, fullness; deepness, lowness, bassness; hollowness.

.2 **reverberation, resounding;** rumble, rumbling, thunder, thundering, boom, booming, growl, growling, grumble, grumbling, reboation; rebound, resound, **echo,** re-echo.

.3 **ringing,** tintinnabulation, **pealing, chiming, tinkling,** tingling, **jingling, dinging,** donging; **tolling,** knelling; clangor, clanking, clanging; **ring, peal, chime; toll,** knell; **tinkle,** tingle, **jingle,** dingle, ding, dingdong, ding-a-ling, ting-a-ling; clink, tink, ting, chink; clank, clang; jangle, jingle-jangle; change ringing, peal ringing; tinnitus.

.4 **bell,** tintinnabulum; **gong,** triangle, **chimes;** dinner bell or gong or chimes, doorbell, jingle bell, hand bell, telephone bell, fire bell, sacring bell, passing bell, gong bell, church bell, sleigh bell, cowbell, sheepbell; clapper, tongue.

.5 **resonator,** resounder, reverberator; **sound-**

ing board, sound box; resonant chamber *or* cavity; echo chamber; loud pedal, damper pedal, sustaining pedal.

.6 VERBS **resonate, vibrate,** pulse, throb.

.7 **reverberate, resound,** sound, **rumble,** roll, boom, echo, reecho, rebound, bounce back, be reflected, be sent back, echo back, send back, return.

.8 **ring, tintinnabulate, peal,** sound; **toll, knell,** sound a knell; **chime;** gong; **tinkle, tingle, jingle,** ding, dingdong, dong; clink, tink, ting, chink; clank, clang, clangor; jangle, jinglejangle; ring on the air; ring changes *or* peals; ring in the ear.

.9 ADJS **resonant, vibrant, sonorous,** plangent, rolling; mellow, rich, full; resonating, vibrating, pulsing, throbbing.

.10 **deep, deep-toned,** deep-pitched, deepsounding, deepmouthed, deep-echoing; **hollow, sepulchral; low,** low-pitched, lowtoned, grave, heavy; **bass;** baritone; contralto.

.11 **reverberating, reverberant,** reverberatory, reboant, **resounding,** rebounding, repercussive, sounding; **rumbling, thundering, booming,** growling; echoing, reechoing, echoic; undamped; persistent, lingering.

.12 **ringing, pealing, tolling,** sounding, chiming; **tinkling,** tingling, **jingling,** dinging; tintinnabular *or* tintinnabulary *or* tintinnabulous.

## 455. REPEATED SOUNDS

.1 NOUNS **staccato; drum, thrum, beat, pound, roll;** drumming, tom-tom, beating, pounding, thumping; **throb,** throbbing, pulsation 323.3; **palpitation,** flutter; sputter, spatter, splutter; **patter, pitterpatter,** pitapat; rub-a-dub, rattattoo, rataplan, rat-a-tat, rat-tat, rat-tat-tat, tat-tat, tat-tat-tat; **tattoo,** devil's tattoo, ruff, ruffle, paradiddle; **drumbeat,** drum music; drumfire, barrage.

.2 **clicking, ticking, tick, ticktock,** ticktack, ticktick.

.3 **rattle,** rattling, brattle [Scot], ruckle [Brit dial], rattletybang; **clatter,** clitter, clunter [Brit dial], **clitterclatter, chatter,** clack, clacket [dial]; racket 453.3.

.4 VERBS **drum, thrum, beat, pound, thump, roll;** palpitate, flutter; sputter, splatter, splutter; patter, pitter-patter, go pitapat *or* pitter-patter; **throb,** pulsate 323.12; beat *or* sound a tattoo, beat a devil's tattoo, ruffle, beat a ruffle.

.5 **tick, ticktock,** ticktack.

.6 **rattle,** ruckle [Brit dial], brattle [Scot];

clatter, clitter, **chatter,** clack; rattle around, clatter about.

.7 ADJS **staccato; drumming, thrumming, beating, pounding, thumping; throbbing;** palpitant, fluttering; sputtering, spattering, spluttering; clicking, ticking.

.8 **rattly, rattling,** chattering, **clattery,** clattering.

## 456. EXPLOSIVE NOISE

.1 NOUNS **report, crash, crack, clap, bang, wham,** slam, clash, burst, bust [dial]; **knock, rap, tap,** smack, whack, thwack, whop, whap, swap [dial], whomp, splat, crump [Brit informal], bump, slap, slat [Brit dial], flap, flop.

.2 **snap, crack;** click, clack; **crackle,** snapping, cracking, crackling, crepitation, decrepitation, sizzling, spitting.

.3 **detonation, blast, explosion,** fulmination, **discharge, burst, bang,** pop, crack, bark; **shot,** gunshot; volley, salvo, fusillade.

.4 **boom,** booming, cannonade, **peal, rumble,** grumble, growl, **roll, roar.**

.5 **thunder,** thundering, bront(o)–, ceraun(o)– *or* keraun(o)–; clap *or* crash *or* peal of thunder, **thunderclap,** thunderpeal, thundercrack, thunderstroke; "heaven's artillery", "the thunder, that deep and dreadful organ-pipe", "dread rattling thunder", "deep, dread-bolted thunder" [all Shakespeare], "the crashing of the chariot of God" [William Cullen Bryant], "dry sterile thunder without rain" [T. S. Eliot]; thunderstorm 394.3; Thor *or* Donar, Jupiter Tonans, Indra.

.6 VERBS **crack, clap, crash, wham,** slam, **bang,** clash; **knock, rap, tap,** smack, whack, thwack, whop, whap, swap [dial], whomp, splat, crump [Brit informal], bump, slat [Brit dial], slap, flap.

.7 **snap, crack;** click, clack; **crackle,** crepitate, decrepitate; spit.

.8 **blast, detonate, explode, discharge, burst,** go off, **bang, pop, crack,** bark, fulminate; burst on the ear.

.9 **boom, thunder, peal, rumble,** grumble, growl, **roll, roar.**

.10 ADJS **snapping, cracking, crackling,** crepitant.

.11 **banging,** crashing, bursting, exploding, explosive, blasting, cracking, popping; knocking, rapping, tapping; slapping, flapping, slatting [Brit dial].

.12 **thundering, thunderous,** thundery, fulminating, tonitruous, tonitruant, thunderlike; **booming,** pealing, rumbling, rolling, roaring; cannonading, volleying.

## 457. SIBILATION

*(hissing sounds)*

.1 NOUNS sibilation, sibilance *or* sibilancy; **hiss, hissing**, siss, sissing, white noise; hush, hushing, shush, shushing; sizz, sizzle, sizzling; fizz, fizzle, fizzling, effervescing, effervescence; swish, whish, whoosh; whiz, buzz, zip; siffle; wheeze, *râle* [Fr], rhonchus; whistle, whistling; sneeze, sneezing, sternutation; snort; snore, stertor; sniff, sniffle, snuff, snuffle; spit, sputter, splutter; squash, squish, squelch; sigmatism, lisp; assibilation; frication, frictional rustling.

.2 VERBS sibilate; **hiss**, siss; hush, shush; sizzle, sizz; fizzle, fizz, effervesce; whiz, buzz, zip; swish, whish, whoosh; whistle; wheeze; sneeze; snort; snore; sniff, sniffle, snuff, snuffle; spit, sputter, splutter; squash, squish, squelch; lisp; assibilate.

.3 ADJS **sibilant; hissing**, hushing, sissing; sizzling, fizzling, effervescent; sniffing, sniffling, snuffling; snoring; wheezing, wheezy.

## 458. STRIDOR

*(harsh and shrill sounds)*

.1 NOUNS stridence *or* stridency, **stridor**, stridulousness; **shrillness**, highness, sharpness, acuteness, arguteness; **screechiness, squeakiness**, creakiness, reediness, pipingness.

.2 **raucousness, harshness**, raucity; discord, cacophony 461.1; coarseness, rudeness, ugliness, roughness, gruffness; **raspiness**, scratchiness, scrapiness, **hoarseness**, huskiness, dryness; stertorousness; roupiness [Scot]; gutturalness, gutturalism, gutturality, thickness, throatiness; cracked voice.

.3 **rasp, scratch, scrape**, grind; crunch, craunch, scranch [archaic], scrunch, crump; burr, chirr, buzz; snore; **jangle, clash, jar;** clank, clang, clangor, twang, twanging; blare, blat, bray; croak, caw, cackle; belch; growl, snarl; grumble, groan.

.4 **screech, shriek, scream, squeal**, shrill, keen, squeak, squawk, skirl, screak, skreak [dial], skriech *or* skreigh [both Scot], creak; whistle, pipe; whine, wail, howl, ululation, yammer; caterwaul.

.5 (insect sounds) **stridulation**, cricking, creaking, chirking [Scot]; crick, creak, chirk, chirp, chirrup.

.6 (high voices) soprano, mezzo-soprano, treble; tenor, alto; male alto, counter-

tenor; head register, head voice, head tone, falsetto.

.7 VERBS **stridulate**, crick, creak, chirk, chirp, chirrup.

.8 **screech, shriek**, screak, skreak [dial], skriech *or* skreigh [both Scot], creak, squeak, squawk, **scream, squeal**, shrill, keen; whistle, pipe, skirl; whine, wail, howl, wrawl [Brit dial], yammer, ululate; caterwaul.

.9 (sound harshly) **jangle, clash, jar;** blare, blat, bray; croak, caw, cackle; belch; burr, chirr, buzz; snore; growl, snarl; grumble, groan; clank, clang, clangor; twang.

.10 **grate, rasp, scratch, scrape**, grind; crunch, craunch, scranch [archaic], scrunch, crump.

.11 **grate on,** jar on, grate upon the ear, jar upon the ear, offend the ear, pierce *or* split *or* rend the ears, harrow *or* lacerate the ear, **set the teeth on edge**, get on one's nerves, jangle *or* wrack the nerves, make one's skin crawl.

.12 ADJS **strident**, stridulant, stridulous; strident-voiced.

.13 **high**, high-pitched, high-toned, high-sounding; treble, soprano, mezzo-soprano, tenor, alto, falsetto, countertenor.

.14 **shrill, thin, sharp**, acute, argute, keen, keening, **piercing**, penetrating, ear-piercing; **screechy**, screeching, shrieky, shrieking, **squeaky**, squeaking, screaky, creaky, creaking; whistling, piping, skirling, reedy; whining, wailing, howling, ululating, ululant.

.15 **raucous**, raucid, **harsh**, harsh-sounding; coarse, rude, rough, gruff, ragged; **hoarse, husky**, roupy [Scot], cracked, dry; **guttural**, thick, throaty, croaky, croaking; choked, strangled; squawky, **squawking;** brassy, brazen, tinny, metallic; stertorous.

.16 **grating, jarring**, grinding; **jangling**, jangly; **rasping**, raspy; scratching, scratchy; scraping, scrapy.

## 459. CRY, CALL

.1 NOUNS **cry, call, shout, yell**, hoot; halloo, hollo, yo-ho; **whoop, holler** [informal]; **cheer, hurrah** 867.2; **howl**, yowl, yawl [Brit dial]; bawl, bellow, roar; **scream, shriek**, screech, squeal, squall, caterwaul; yelp, yap, yammer, yawp, bark; war cry, battle cry, war whoop, rallying cry.

.2 **exclamation**, ejaculation, outburst, blurt, ecphonesis; expletive.

.3 hunting cry; tallyho, yoicks [archaic], view halloo.

.4 **outcry, vociferation, clamor,** gaff; hullabaloo, hubbub, **uproar** 453.3; **hue and cry.**

.5 **vociferousness, vociferance, clamorousness, clamoursomeness** [Brit dial], **blatancy; noisiness** 453.2.

.6 VERBS **cry, call, shout, yell, holler** [informal], **hoot; hail, halloo, hollo; whoop; cheer** 876.6; **howl,** yowl, yammer, yawl [Brit dial]; squawk, yawp; **bawl, bellow,** roar, roar or bellow like a bull; **scream, shriek,** screech, squeal, squall, caterwaul; yelp, yap, bark.

.7 **exclaim,** give an exclamation, ejaculate, burst out, blurt, blurt out.

.8 **vociferate,** outcry, **cry out,** call out, bellow out, yell out, holler out [informal], shout out, sing out; pipe up, **clamor** 453.7, make or raise a clamor; make an outcry, **raise a hue and cry,** make an uproar.

.9 cry aloud, raise or lift up the voice, give voice or tongue, shout or cry or thunder at the top of one's voice, split the throat or lungs, strain the voice or throat, rend the air 453.6.

.10 ADJS **vociferous,** vociferant, vociferating; **clamorous,** clamoursome [Brit dial]; **blatant;** obstreperous, brawling; **noisy** 453.12; crying, shouting, **yelling, hollering** [informal], **bawling,** screaming; yelping, yapping, yammering; loudmouthed, openmouthed, boanergean.

.11 **exclamatory,** ejaculatory, blurting.

## 460. ANIMAL SOUNDS

.1 NOUNS animal noise; **call, cry;** mating call or cry; grunt, howl, bark, howling, ululation, barking, etc.; birdcall, note, woodnote, clang; stridulation 458.5.

.2 VERBS cry, call; **howl,** yowl, yawp, yawl [dial], ululate; wail, whine, pule; **squeal,** squall, scream, screech, screak, squeak; troat; **roar; bellow,** blare, **bawl; moo,** low; **bleat,** blate, blat; **bray; whinny, neigh,** whicker, nicker; **bay,** bay at the moon, bell; **bark,** latrate [archaic], give voice or tongue; **yelp, yap,** yip; **mew,** mewl, **meow,** miaow, caterwaul.

.3 **grunt,** gruntle [Brit dial], oink; **snort.**

.4 **growl, snarl,** grumble, gnarl, snap; hiss, spit.

.5 (birds) **warble, sing,** carol, call; pipe, whistle; **trill,** chirr, roll; **twitter,** tweet, twit, chatter, chitter; **chirp,** chirrup, chirk, **cheep,** peep, pip; **quack,** honk, cronk; **croak, caw; squawk,** scold; **crow,** cock-adoodle-doo; **cackle,** gaggle, gabble, guggle, **cluck,** clack, chuck; **gobble; hoot,** hoo; **coo; cuckoo;** drum.

.6 ADJS **howling,** yowling, crying, wailing, whining, puling, bawling, ululant, blatant, etc.; lowing, mugient.

## 461. DISCORD

### (dissonant sounds)

.1 NOUNS **discord,** discordance or discordancy, **dissonance** or dissonancy, diaphony, **cacophony;** stridor 458; **inharmoniousness,** unharmoniousness, disharmony, inharmony; **unmelodiousness,** unmusicalness, unmusicality, untunefulness, tunelessness [archaic]; atonality, atonalism; flatness, sharpness, sourness [informal]; dissonant chord, wolf; sour note or clinker [informal], off note.

.2 **clash, jangle, jar; noise,** mere noise, confusion or conflict or jarring or jostling of sounds; Babel, witches' or devils' chorus; harshness 458.2; clamor 453.3.

.3 VERBS sound or hit a sour note [informal], hit a clinker [informal]; **clash, jar, jangle,** conflict, jostle; grate 458.10,11; untune, unstring.

.4 ADJS **dissonant, discordant, cacophonous,** absonant [archaic], disconsonant, diaphonic; strident, shrill, harsh, raucous, grating 458.12–16; **inharmonious,** unharmonious, disharmonious, disharmonic, inharmonic; **unmelodious,** immelodious, nonmelodious; **unmusical,** musicless, untuneful, tuneless [archaic]; untunable, untuned, atonal; cracked, **out of tune,** out of tone, out of pitch; **off-key, off-tone, off-pitch,** off; flat, sharp, **sour** [informal]; "above the pitch, out of tune, and off the hinges" [Rabelais], "like sweet bells jangled, out of tune and harsh" [Shakespeare].

.5 **clashing, jarring, jangling,** jangly, confused, conflicting, jostling, warring, ajar; **harsh,** grating 458.15,16.

## 462. MUSIC

.1 NOUNS **music,** "the speech of angels" [Carlyle], "the mosaic of the Air" [Andrew Marvell], "the harmonious voice of creation; an echo of the invisible world" [Giuseppe Mazzini], "the only universal tongue" [Samuel Rogers], "the universal language of mankind" [Longfellow], "the poor man's Parnassus" [Emerson], "the brandy of the damned" [G. B. Shaw], "nothing else but wild sounds civilized into time and tune" [Thomas Fuller, D.D.].

.2 **melody,** melodiousness, **tunefulness,** musicalness, musicality; **tune, tone,** musical sound, musical quality, tonality; sweetness, dulcetness, mellifluence, mellifluousness.

**.3 harmony, concord,** concordance, concert, consonance *or* consonancy, consort, accordance, **accord,** monochord, concentus, symphony, diapason; synchronism, synchronization; **attunement,** tune, attune; chime, chiming; unison, unisonance, homophony, monody; **euphony;** light *or* heavy harmony; two-part *or* three-part harmony, etc.; harmony *or* music of the spheres; harmonics 462.

**.4 air,** aria, tune, **melody,** melodia, line, melodic line, refrain, note, **song,** solo, solo part, soprano part, treble, lay, descant, **strain,** measure; canto, cantus; melo–.

**.5 piece,** opus, **composition,** production, work; **score; arrangement,** adaptation, orchestration, harmonization; instrumental music; electronic music; aleatory, aleatory music; **incidental music;** chamber music, string quartet, trio, chamber orchestra, string orchestra; sonata, sonatina; ricercar; absolute music, program music; nocturne, *Nachtmusik* [Ger]; étude, study, exercise; invention; variation, descant, *air varié* [Fr], theme and variations.

**.6 medley,** potpourri; *divertissement* [Fr]; fantasia, *Fantasiestück* [Ger]; caprice, capriccio, humoresque; romance, romanza.

**..7 classical music,** classic; concert music, serious music, longhair music [informal], symphonic music; **symphony,** symphonia, *sinfonietta* [Ital], symphonic ode *or* poem, tone poem *or* poetry; **concerto,** concertino, concertstück, concerto grosso; rhapsody; semiclassic, semiclassical music.

**.8 popular music,** pop music *or* pop, light music, popular song *or* air *or* tune, ballad; hit, song hit, hit tune.

**.9 dance music,** ballroom music, **suite,** musical suite, suite of dances; **dances** 879.7; syncopated music, **syncopation; ragtime** *or* rag; **jazz;** hot jazz, **swing,** jive [slang]; bebop, bop [slang]; mainstream jazz; avant-garde jazz, the new music [informal]; boogie-woogie; rock-and-roll, rock, hard rock, acid rock, folk rock, country rock; rhythm-and-blues.

**.10 folk music,** folk songs, ethnic music, ethnomusicology; folk ballads, balladry; border ballads; country music, hillbilly music; country-and-western music, western swing; old-time country music *or* old-

timey music; bluegrass; field holler; the blues, country blues, city blues.

**.11 march,** martial *or* military music; military march, quick *or* quickstep march; processional march, recessional march; funeral *or* dead march; wedding march.

**.12 vocal music,** song; singing, caroling, warbling, lyricism, vocalism, **vocalization;** operatic singing, bel canto, coloratura, bravura; choral singing; folk singing; croon, crooning; yodel, yodeling; scat, scat singing; intonation; hum, humming; solmization, tonic sol-fa, solfeggio, solfège, sol-fa, sol-fa exercise.

**.13 song,** lay, lied, *chanson* [Fr], carol, **ditty,** canticle, lilt; **ballad,** ballade, *ballata* [Ital]; *canzone* [Ital]; canzonet, *canzonetta* [Ital], cavatina; chant; folk song, *Volkslied* [Ger]; calypso; **art song,** *Kunstlied* [Ger]; drinking song, *brindisi* [Ital]; war song; **love song,** *Liebeslied* [Ger], love-lilt, torch song [informal]; serenade, serenata, *serena* [Provençal]; *matin* [Fr], *aubade* [Fr], *alba* [Provençal], *canso* [Provençal]; blues, blues song; croon, croon song; **carol,** Christmas carol, noël; **anthem,** national anthem; wedding song, bridal hymn, hymeneal, *Brautlied* [Ger], epithalamium, prothalamium; barcarole, boat song, chantey; minstrel song, minstrelsy; theme song; **dirge** 875.5.

**.14 solo; aria;** arietta, arioso; *aria buffa, aria da capo, aria d'agilità, aria da chiesa, aria d'imitazione, aria fugata, aria parlante* [all Ital]; bravura, *aria di bravura* [Ital]; coloratura, *aria di coloratura* [Ital]; cantabile, *aria cantabile* [Ital]; recitative, *recitativo* [Ital].

**.15 lullaby, cradlesong,** *berceuse* [Fr], *Schlummerlied, Wiegenlied* [both Ger].

**.16 sacred music, church music,** liturgical music; **hymn,** hymn-tune, **psalm,** chorale, choral fantasy, anthem; motet; **oratorio;** passion; **mass;** requiem mass, requiem; offertory, offertory sentence *or* hymn; **cantata;** doxology, introit, canticle, paean, prosodion; recessional; **spiritual,** Negro spiritual; white spiritual, gospel music, gospel; psalmody, hymnody, hymnology.

**.17 part music,** polyphonic music, part song, part singing, ensemble music, ensemble singing; **duet,** duo, *duettino* [Ital]; **trio,** terzet, terzetto; **quartet; quintet; sextet,** sestet; **septet,** septuor; **octet.**

**.18 chorus,** choral singing, unison; **glee;** cantata, lyric cantata; madrigal, madrigaletto; oratorio.

**.19 round, rondo,** rondeau, **roundelay,** catch,

troll; rondino, rondoletto; **fugue,** canon, fugato.

.20 **polyphony,** polyphonism; **counterpoint,** contrapunto; Gregorian chant, Ambrosian chant; *faux-bourdon* [Fr]; musica ficta, false music.

.21 monody, monophony, homophony.

.22 **part,** melody *or* voice part, **voice** 463.5, **line;** descant, canto, cantus, cantus planus *or* firmus, plain song, plain chant; prick song, cantus figuratus; soprano, tenor, treble, alto, contralto, baritone, bass, bassus; undersong; **drone; accompaniment;** continuo, basso continuo, figured bass, thorough bass; ground bass, basso ostinato.

.23 **response,** responsory report, answer; echo; antiphon, antiphony, antiphonal chanting *or* singing.

.24 **passage, phrase,** musical phrase, strain, part, **movement;** introductory phrase, anacrusis; statement, exposition, development, variation; division; period, musical sentence; section; **measure;** figure; **verse, stanza;** burden, bourdon; **chorus, refrain,** response; folderol, **ornament** 463.18, cadence 463.23, harmonic close, resolution; **coda,** tailpiece; ritornello; intermezzo, interlude; bass passage; tutti, tutti passage; **bridge,** bridge passage.

.25 (fast, slow, etc. passages) presto, prestissimo; allegro, allegretto; scherzo, scherzando; adagio, adagietto; andante, andantino; largo, larghetto, larghissimo; crescendo; diminuendo, decrescendo; rallentando, ritardando; ritenuto; piano, pianissimo; forte, fortissimo; staccato, marcato, marcando; pizzicato; spiccato; legato; stretto.

.26 **overture, prelude,** *Vorspiel* [Ger], **introduction,** operatic overture, dramatic overture, concert overture, voluntary, descant, vamp; curtain raiser.

.27 **impromptu,** extempore, **improvisation, interpolation;** cadenza, flourish; vamp; lick, hot lick, riff.

.28 **score,** musical score *or* copy, **music,** notation, musical notation, written music, copy, draft, transcript, transcription, version, edition, text, arrangement; part; full *or* orchestral score, compressed *or* short score, piano score, vocal score, instrumental score; tablature, lute tablature; opera score, opera; **libretto;** sheet music; **songbook,** songster; hymnbook, hymnal; music paper; music roll.

.29 **staff,** stave [Brit]; line, ledger line; bar, bar line; space, degree; brace.

.30 **theme,** motive, **motif,** subject, phrase 462.24, figure; leitmotiv.

.31 **execution, performance; rendering,** rendition, music-making, **touch, expression;** fingering; pianism; intonation; repercussion; pizzicato, staccato, spiccato, parlando, legato, cantando, rubato, demilegato, mezzo staccato, slur; glissando.

.32 musicianship; musical talent *or* flair, musicality; virtuosity; musical ear, ear for music; musical sense, sense of rhythm; absolute *or* perfect pitch; relative pitch.

.33 **musicale;** choral service, service of song, sing [informal], singing, community singing *or* sing, singfest, sing-in; folk-sing *or* hootenanny [both informal]; music festival; opera festival; folk-music festival, jazz festival, rock festival; *Sängerfest* [Ger], *eisteddfod* [Welsh]; jam session [informal]; swan song, farewell performance.

.34 **performance,** musical performance, **program,** musical program, program of music; **concert,** symphony concert, chamber concert; Philharmonic concert, philharmonic; popular concert, pops, pop concert [both informal]; promenade concert, prom [informal]; band concert; recital; service of music; concert performance (of an opera); –log(ue).

.35 musical theater, lyric theater, musical stage, lyric stage; **music drama,** lyric drama; song-play, *Singspiel* [Ger]; **opera,** grand opera, light opera, ballad opera; comic opera, *opéra bouffe* [Fr], *opera buffa* [Ital]; **operetta; musical comedy; musical;** Broadway musical; **ballet,** *opéra ballet* [Fr], comedy ballet, *ballet d'action* [Fr], *ballet divertissement* [Fr]; dance drama; chorus show; **song-and-dance act;** minstrel, minstrel show.

.36 VERBS **harmonize,** be harmonious, be in tune *or* concert, chord, **accord,** symphonize, synchronize, **chime, blend,** tune, attune, atone, sound together, sound in tune; assonate; melodize, musicalize.

.37 **tune, tune up,** attune, atone, chord, **put in tune;** voice, string; tone up, tone down.

.38 **strike up,** strike up a tune, **strike up the band,** break into music, pipe up, pipe up a song, yerk out [dial], **burst into song.**

.39 sing, vocalize, carol, descant, lilt; troll; **warble,** trill, tremolo, quaver, shake; **chirp,** chirrup, twit [Brit dial], **twitter;** pipe, whistle, tweedle, tweedledee; **chant; intone,** intonate; **croon; hum;** yodel; roulade; chorus, choir, sing in chorus; **hymn,** anthem, psalm, "make a joyful noise unto the Lord" [Bible]; sing the praises of; minstrel; ballad; **serenade**; sol-fa, do-re-mi, solmizate.

.40 **play, perform, execute, render**, do; interpret; make music; concertize; symphonize; chord; accompany; play by ear.

.41 **strum, thrum, pluck**, plunk, **pick**, twang, sweep the strings.

.42 **fiddle** [informal], play violin or the violin; scrape or saw [both informal], bow.

.43 **blow a horn**, sound or wind the horn, sound, blow, wind, **toot**, tootle, pipe, tweedle; bugle, carillon, clarion, fife, flute, trumpet, whistle; bagpipe, doodle [Brit dial]; lip, tongue, double-tongue, triple-tongue.

.44 **syncopate**, play jazz, swing, jive [slang], rag [informal].

.45 **beat time**, keep time, tap, tap out the rhythm; count, count the beats; beat the drum, **drum** 455.4, play drum or the drums, thrum, beat, thump, pound; tom-tom; ruffle; beat or sound a tattoo.

.46 **conduct, direct**, lead, wield the baton.

.47 **compose, write, arrange, score, set, set to music**, put to music; musicalize, melodize, **harmonize**; orchestrate; instrument, instrumentate; **adapt**, make an adaptation; transcribe, transpose.

.48 ADJS **musical, musically inclined**, musicianly, with an ear for music; virtuoso, virtuose, virtuosic; **music-loving**, music-mad, musicophile, philharmonic.

.49 **melodious**, melodic, **musical**, music-like; **tuneful**, tunable; fine-toned, **pleasant-sounding**, agreeable-sounding, pleasant, appealing, agreeable, catchy, singable; **euphonious** or euphonous or euphonic, **lyric(al)**, melic; songful, songlike; **sweet, dulcet**, sweet-sounding, achingly sweet, sweet-flowing; honeyed, mellifluent, mellifluous, mellisonant, music-flowing; rich, mellow; sonorous, canorous; golden, golden-toned; silvery, silver-toned; sweet-voiced, golden-voiced, silver-voiced, silver-tongued, golden-tongued, music-tongued; ariose, arioso, cantabile.

.50 **harmonious**, harmonic(al), symphonious; harmonizing, **chiming**, blending, well-blended, blended; **concordant**, consonant, accordant, according, **in accord**, in concord, in concert; synchronous, synchronized, in sync [informal], **in tune**, tuned, attuned; in unison, in chorus; unisonous, unisonant; homophonic, monophonic, monodic; assonant, assonantal.

.51 **vocal**, singing; **choral**, choric; operatic; hymnal; psalmic, psalmodic, psalmodial;

sacred, liturgical; treble, soprano, tenor, alto, falsetto; coloratura, lyric, bravura, dramatic, heroic; baritone; bass.

.52 **instrumental**, orchestral, symphonic, concert; dramatico-musical; jazz, syncopated, jazzy, rock, swing.

.53 **polyphonic, contrapuntal**.

.54 ADJS, ADVS (directions, style) legato; staccato; spiccato; pizzicato; forte, fortissimo; piano, pianissimo; sordo; crescendo, accrescendo; decrescendo, diminuendo, morendo; dolce; amabile; affettuoso, con affetto; amoroso, con amore; lamentabile; agitato, con agitazione; leggiero; agilmente, con agilità; capriccioso, a capriccio; scherzando, scherzoso; appassionato, appassionatamente; abbandono; brillante; parlando; a cappella; trillando, tremolando, tremoloso; sotto voce; stretto.

.55 (slowly) largo, larghetto, allargando; adagio, adagietto; andante, andantino, andante moderato; calando; a poco; lento; ritardando, rallentando.

.56 (fast) presto, prestissimo; veloce; accelerando; vivace, vivacissimo; desto, con anima, con brio; allegro, allegretto; affrettando, moderato.

## 463. HARMONICS, MUSICAL ELEMENTS

.1 NOUNS **harmonics**, harmony; melodics; rhythmics; musicality; music, music theory, theory; musicology; musicography.

.2 **harmonization; orchestration, instrumentation**; arrangement, setting, adaptation, transcription; phrasing, modulation, intonation, preparation, suspension, solution, resolution; tone painting.

.3 **tone, tonality** 450.2,3.

.4 **pitch, tune, tone, key, note**, register, tonality; height, depth; classical pitch, high pitch, diapason or normal or French pitch, international or concert or new philharmonic pitch, standard pitch, low pitch, Stuttgart or Scheibler's pitch, philharmonic pitch, philosophical pitch.

.5 **voice**, voce [Ital]; voce di petto [Ital], **chest voice**; voce di testa [Ital], **head voice**; bass, drone, drone bass, bourdon, burden; coloratura, treble, falsetto.

.6 **scale, gamut, register**, compass, range, diapason; tuning, temperament; diatonic scale, chromatic scale, enharmonic scale, major scale, minor scale, natural or harmonic or melodic minor, whole-tone scale; great scale; octave scale, dodecuple scale, pentatonic scale.

.7 **sol-fa**, tonic sol-fa, do-re-mi; Guidonian

syllables, sol-fa syllables, do, re, mi, fa, sol, la, ti, do; fixed-do system, movable-do system; solmization; bobization.

.8 **(diatonic series)** tetrachord, chromatic tetrachord, enharmonic tetrachord, Dorian tetrachord; hexachord, pentachord; –chord.

.9 **octave,** *ottava* [Ital], eighth; *ottava alta* [Ital], *ottava bassa* [Ital]; small octave, great octave; contraoctave, subcontraoctave, double contraoctave; one-line octave, two-line octave, four-line octave, two-foot octave, four-foot octave; twelve-tone row, tone row.

.10 **mode,** octave species; major mode, minor mode; Greek modes, Ionian mode, Dorian mode, Phrygian mode, Lydian mode, mixolydian mode, Aeolian mode, Locrian mode; hypoionian mode, hypodorian mode, hypophrygian mode, hypolydian mode, hypoaeolian mode, hypomixolydian mode, hypolocrian mode; Gregorian *or* ecclesiastical *or* church *or* medieval mode; plagal mode, authentic mode; Indian *or* Hindu mode, raga.

.11 **form,** arrangement, pattern, model, design; song *or* lied form, primary form; sonata form, sonata allegro, symphonic form, canon form, toccata form, fugue form, rondo form.

.12 **notation,** character, mark, symbol, signature, sign, *segno* [Ital]; dot; custos, direct; cancel; bar, measure; measure *or* time signature, key signature; tempo mark, metronome *or* metronomic mark; fermata, hold, pause; *presa* [Ital], lead; slur, tie, ligature, vinculum, enharmonic tie; swell; accent, accent mark, expression mark.

.13 **clef;** C clef, soprano clef, alto clef, tenor clef; F clef *or* **bass clef,** G clef *or* **treble clef.**

.14 **note,** musical note, notes of a scale; **tone** 450.2; **sharp, flat, natural; accidental;** double whole note, breve; whole note, semibreve; half note, minim; quarter note, crotchet; eighth note, quaver; sixteenth note, semiquaver; thirty-second note, demisemiquaver; sixty-fourth note, hemidemisemiquaver; tercet, triplet; sustained note, dominant, dominant note; enharmonic, enharmonic note; staccato, spiccato; responding note, report; shaped note, patent note.

.15 **key,** key signature, tonality; **keynote,** tonic; tonic key; major, minor, major *or* minor key, tonic major *or* minor; supertonic, mediant, submediant, dominant,

subdominant, subtonic; pedal point, organ point.

.16 **harmonic,** harmonic tone, overtone, upper partial tone; flageolet tone.

.17 **chord,** major *or* minor chord, tonic chord, dominant chord; seventh chord, diminished seventh chord, sixth chord; consonant chord, concord; enharmonic chord, enharmonic; broken chord, **arpeggio;** unbroken chord, *concento* [Ital]; key chord, tonic triad, major triad, minor triad, common chord; triad, augmented triad.

.18 **ornament,** grace, arabesque, embellishment, *fioritura* [Ital]; **flourish,** roulade, flight, run; passage, division 462.24; florid phrase *or* passage; coloratura; incidental, incidental note; grace note, appoggiatura; acciaccatura; mordent, single mordent, double *or* long mordent; inverted mordent, pralltriller; turn, back *or* inverted turn; cadence, cadenza.

.19 **trill,** trillo; trillet, *trilleto* [Ital]; **tremolo,** tremolant, tremolando; quaver, quiver, tremble, tremor, flutter, falter, shake; **vibrato,** *Bebung* [Ger].

.20 **interval,** degree, **step,** note, tone; second, third, fourth, fifth, sixth, seventh, octave; prime *or* unison interval, major *or* minor interval, harmonic *or* melodic interval, enharmonic interval, diatonic interval; parallel *or* consecutive intervals, parallel fifths, parallel octaves; whole step, major second; half step, halftone, semitone, minor second; diatonic semitone, chromatic semitone, less semitone, quarter semitone, tempered *or* mean semitone; quarter step, enharmonic diesis; augmented interval; diatessaron, diapason; –chord.

.21 **rest,** pause; whole rest, breve rest, semibreve rest, half rest, minim, quarter rest, eighth rest, sixteenth rest, thirty-second rest, sixty-fourth rest.

.22 **rhythm, beat, meter, measure,** number *or* numbers, movement, **lilt, swing;** prosody, metrics; rhythmic pattern *or* phrase.

.23 **cadence** *or* cadency, authentic cadence, plagal cadence, mixed cadence, perfect *or* imperfect cadence, half cadence, deceptive *or* false cadence, interrupted *or* suspended cadence.

.24 **tempo, time, beat,** time pattern, timing; simple time *or* measure, compound time *or* measure; two-part *or* duple time, three-part *or* triple time, triplet, four-part *or* quadruple time, five-part *or* quintuple time, six-part *or* sextuple time, seven-part *or* septuple time, nine-part *or* nonuple

time; two-four time, six-eight time, etc.;
tempo rubato, rubato; mixed times; **syncopation**, syncope; **ragtime**, rag [informal]; waltz time, three-four or three-quarter time, andante tempo, march tempo,
etc.; largo, etc. 462.55, presto, etc. 462.56.

.25 **accent**, accentuation, rhythmical accent
or accentuation, ictus, emphasis, stress arsis, thesis; grammatical accent, rhetorical
accent; musical or pitch or tone accent,
stress accent; intonation, intonation pattern or contour.

.26 **beat**, throb, pulse, pulsation; downbeat,
upbeat, offbeat; bar beat.

.27 ADJS **tonal**, tonic; chromatic, enharmonic;
semitonic.

.28 **rhythmic(al)**, cadent, cadenced, **measured**, **metric(al)**; in rhythm, in numbers;
beating, throbbing, pulsing, pulsating,
pulsative, pulsatory.

.29 **syncopated**; **ragtime**, ragtimey [informal];
**jazz**; jazzy or jazzed or jazzed up [all informal], hot, swingy [informal].

.30 ADVS **in time**, in tempo 463.24, *a tempo*
[Ital].

## 464. MUSICIAN

.1 NOUNS **musician**, musico, **music maker**,
professional musician, minstrel, minstrelsy, **player**, performer, executant, interpreter, tunester, artiste, artist, concert
artist, **virtuoso**, virtuosa; maestro; recitalist; **soloist**, duettist; –ist.

.2 **syncopator**; ragtimer [informal]; **jazz musician**, **jazzman**; swing musician, swingster
[informal]; Tin Pan Alley.

.3 **instrumentalist**, instrumentist; bandman,
bandsman; orchestral musician; symphonist; concertist; accompanist, accompanyist; ripieno.

.4 **wind musician**, wind-instrumentalist,
horn player, hornist, horner, piper,
tooter; bassoonist, bugler, clarinetist, cornettist, fifer, oboist, piccoloist, saxophonist, trombonist; trumpeter, trumpet major; flutist, flautist.

.5 **string musician**, strummer, picker [informal], thrummer, twanger; banjoist, banjo-picker [informal], citharist, guitarist,
guitar-picker [informal], classical guitarist, folk guitarist, lute player, lutenist, lutanist, lutist, lyrist, mandolinist, theorbist; violinist, fiddler [informal]; bass violinist, bassist, bass player, contrabassist;
violoncellist, cellist or 'cellist, celloist; violist; harpist, harper; zitherist, psalterer.

.6 xylophonist, marimbaist.

.7 **pianist**, pianiste, pianofortist, piano

player, ivory tickler or thumper [slang];
harpsichordist, clavichordist, monochordist; accordionist, concertinist.

.8 **organist**, organ player.

.9 organ-grinder, hurdy-gurdist, hurdy-gurdyist, hurdy-gurdy man.

.10 **drummer**, **percussionist**, timpanist, kettledrummer; taborer.

.11 **cymbalist**, cymbaler; bell-ringer; **carilloneur**, campanologist, campanist.

.12 **orchestra**, **band**, **ensemble**, combo [informal], group; string orchestra, chamber orchestra; **symphony orchestra**, symphony,
Philharmonic; gamelan orchestra; **brass
band**, military band, German band, concert band, ragtime band, string band, dixieland band, steel band or orchestra, **jazz
band**, big band, swing band; street band,
callithumpian band, jug band, skiffle
band; rock-and-roll group; waits; strings,
woodwind or woodwinds, brass or
brasses, string or woodwind or brass section, string or woodwind or brass choir;
desks; trio, **quartet**, quintet, sextet; **string
quartet**, string trio; woodwind quartet,
etc.; brass quintet, etc.

.13 **vocalist**, vocalizer, voice, **singer**, **songster**,
songbird, warbler, canary [slang], lead
singer, caroler, melodist, cantor; songstress, singstress, cantatrice; chanter,
chantress; aria singer, lieder singer, opera
singer, diva, prima donna; improvisator;
blues singer, torch singer [informal];
crooner, rock or rock-and-roll singer; yodeler; psalm singer, hymner; Meistersinger; **bass**, basso, basso profundo, deep
bass, *basso cantante* [Ital], lyric bass;
*basso buffo* [Ital], comic bass; **baritone**,
baritenor; **tenor**, countertenor, lyric
tenor, heroic tenor, *Heldentenor* [Ger];
**soprano**, lyric soprano, coloratura soprano, dramatic soprano, mezzo-soprano;
**alto**, contralto.

.14 **minstrel**, **ballad singer**, balladeer, **bard**,
rhapsode, rhapsodist; wandering or strolling minstrel, **troubadour**, trovatore, trouvère, minnesinger, scop, gleeman, fili,
jongleur; street singer, wait; serenader;
**folk singer**, folk-rock singer; country-and-western singer;

.15 **choral singer**, choir member, chorister,
chorus singer, choralist; choirman, **choirboy**; **chorus girl**, chorine [slang].

.16 **choir**, **chorus**, choral group, choral society, oratorio society, chamber chorus,
*Kammerchor* [Ger], chorale, men's or
women's chorus, mixed chorus, ensemble,
voices; **glee club**, *Liedertafel*, *Lieder-*

*kranz* [both Ger], singing club *or* society; *a cappella* choir; choral symphony.

.17 **conductor,** leader, symphonic conductor, **music director,** director, *Kapellmeister* [Ger]; **orchestra leader, band leader, bandmaster,** band major, drum major.

.18 **choirmaster,** choral director *or* conductor, song leader, *maestro di cappella* [Ital]; choir chaplain, minister of music, precentor, cantor, chorister.

.19 **concertmaster,** concertmeister, *Konzertmeister* [Ger], first violinist.

.20 **composer, scorer, arranger,** musicographer; melodist, melodizer; harmonist, harmonizer; **orchestrator;** symphonist; tone poet; ballad maker *or* writer, balladeer, balladist, balladmonger; madrigalist; lyrist; hymnist, hymnographer, hymnologist; contrapuntist; song writer, songsmith, tunesmith; lyricist, librettist; musicologist, ethnomusicologist.

.21 **music lover,** philharmonic, **music fan,** music buff [both informal], musicophile; musicmonger; concertgoer, operagoer; tonalist.

.22 (patrons) the Muses, the Nine, sacred Nine, tuneful Nine, Pierides; Apollo, Apollo Musagetes; Orpheus; Erato, Euterpe, Polymnia *or* Polyhymnia, Terpsichore.

.23 **songbird,** singing bird, **songster,** feathered songster, warbler; nightingale, Philomel; bulbul, canary, cuckoo, lark, mavis, mockingbird, oriole, ringdove, song sparrow, thrush.

## 465. MUSICAL INSTRUMENTS

.1 **musical instrument,** –ina, –phone, –chord.

.2 **string** *or* **stringed instrument,** chordophone; strings, string choir.

.3 **harp; lyre,** aeolian harp *or* lyre; bell harp; claviharp; Irish harp, clarsach; Autoharp; **cither,** cithara, **zither,** cittern, gittern; psaltery; dulcimer, symphonia; langspiel; polychord, heptachord, hexachord.

.4 **lute,** archlute; theorbo, oud; bandore, *bandurria* [Sp], pandora, pandura; **banjo,** banjer [dial]; banjo-zither; banjorine; **ukulele,** uke [informal]; banjo-ukulele, banjo-uke [informal], banjuke, banjulele; **guitar,** Spanish guitar, Hawaiian guitar, classical guitar, concert guitar, centerhole guitar, F-hole guitar, electric guitar, Dobro guitar, steel guitar, bass guitar; **mandolin,** mandola, mandore, mandolute, mando-bass, mando-cello, balalaika,

tamboura, samisen, troubadour fiddle, vina, sitar.

.5 **viol,** vielle; viol family; violette, viola pomposa; treble viol, descant viol; alto *or* tenor viol, viol *or* viola da braccio; bass viol, viol *or* viola da gamba, viola bastarda, baritone; viol *or* viola d'amore, viol *or* viola da spalla, viol *or* viola di bordone, viol *or* viola di fagotto; rebec; trumpet marine, tromba marina.

.6 **violin, fiddle** [informal], crowd [Brit dial]; violinette, violino piccolo; **kit,** kit violin, pocket *or* kit fiddle; **viola,** tenor violin, violotta; **violoncello, cello** *or* 'cello; violoncello piccolo; **bass viol,** contrabass, **bass, double bass,** violone, **bull fiddle** [informal], *basso da camera* [Ital]; viola alta; Stradivarius, Stradivari, Strad [informal]; Amati, Cremona, Guarnerius; bow, fiddlestick, fiddlebow; bridge, sound hole, soundboard, fingerboard, tuning peg, scroll; string 465.23, G string, D string, A string, E string.

.7 **wind instrument,** wind; aerophone; **horn,** pipe, tooter; mouthpiece, embouchure, lip; valve, bell, reed, double reed, key, slide.

.8 **brass wind,** brass *or* brass-wind instrument; brasses, brass choir; **bugle,** bugle horn; **trumpet,** valve trumpet, key trumpet, pocket trumpet, tromba; **clarion;** post horn; lituus; lur; **cornet,** cornet-à-pistons, cornopean; **trombone;** slide trombone, sliphorn [slang], sackbut, valve trombone; **saxhorn,** saxtuba, saxcornet, flugelhorn; **althorn** *or* alto horn, ballad horn; baritone, tenor tuba, euphonium, double-bell euphonium; **tuba,** helicon, bombardon, bass horn, sousaphone; ophicleide, serpent; **French horn,** horn, orchestral horn, *corno di caccia* [Ital]; hunting horn; mellophone; alphorn, alpenhorn.

.9 **woodwind,** wood *or* woodwind instrument; woods, woodwind choir; **flute;** aul(o)–; recorder, fipple flute *or* pipe, flageolet; **fife;** pipe, tabor pipe; **piccolo;** ocarina, sweet potato [informal]; hornpipe, pibgorn; whistle, tin-whistle, penny-whistle; aulos; reed instrument, **reed;** double-reed instrument, **double reed; oboe,** hautboy, *oboe d'amore* [Ital]; bass *or* basset oboe, heckelphone; tenoroon, *oboe da caccia* [Ital]; musette; shawm, bombard, bombardon, pommer; **bassoon;** double bassoon, contrabassoon, contrafagotto; sonorophone; single-reed instrument, **single reed; clarinet,** licorice stick [slang];

basset horn; **English horn,** *cor anglais* [Fr]; krummhorn, cromorne; **saxophone,** sax [informal]; panpipe, Pandean pipe, oaten reed, syrinx, shepherd's pipe.

.10 **bagpipe** *or* bagpipes, pipes, union pipes, doodlesack, *Dudelsack* [Ger]; cornemuse, musette; sordellina; chanter, drone.

.11 **mouth organ,** mouth harp, harp, French harp [dial], **harmonica,** harmonicon; Jew's harp, mouth bow; kazoo.

.12 **accordion,** piano accordion; **concertina;** squeeze box [informal]; mellophone; bandonion.

.13 **piano,** pianoforte; pianette, pianino; **grand piano,** grand, Steinway; baby grand, parlor grand, concert grand; square piano, upright piano, upright; spinet; cottage piano; clavier, *Klavier* [Ger]; **harpsichord,** clavicymbal, clavicembalo, cembalo, hammer dulcimer, dulcimer harpsichord; **clavichord,** clarichord, monochord, manichord *or* manichordon; clavicittern, clavicytherium; virginal, pair of virginals, couched harp; lyrichord; violin piano, piano-violin, melodion, harmonichord, sostinente pianoforte, melopiano.

.14 **player piano,** mechanical piano, Pianola; street piano; music roll, piano player roll.

.15 **organ,** pipe organ, reed organ, church organ; baroque organ; **electric organ,** Hammond organ, electro-pneumatic organ, tubular-pneumatic organ, tracker-action organ, hydraulic organ; choralcelo, harmonium, melodeon, melodica, organophone, seraphine, symphonion, vocalion; steam organ, calliope, calliophone; orchestrelle.

.16 **hurdy-gurdy,** vielle, **barrel organ,** hand organ, grind organ, street organ.

.17 **music box,** musical box; orchestrion, orchestrina.

.18 **percussion instrument,** percussion, percussive, idiophone; percussions, battery; **cymbals,** potlids [slang], highhat [informal], crash cymbal; sizzler; **triangle; gong,** tam-tam, tonitruone; **bells,** tubular bells, handbells, tintinnabula; chime, **chimes; orchestral bells,** glockenspiel, lyra; **vibraphone,** vibraharp, vibes [informal]; **xylophone, marimba,** metallophone; celesta; gamelan; **clappers,** snappers, **castanets,** finger cymbals, bones, rattle, rattlebones, maraca.

.19 **drum,** membranophone, tympan, tympanum, tympanon, timpani; **kettledrum,** kettle, timbal, naker, nagara [India]; **snare drum,** side drum; tenor drum, bass

drum, tom-tom, tam-tam; **bongo drum; conga; timbrel,** tabor, **tambourine,** tambourin; taboret, tabret; troll-drum; war drum, drumhead, drumskin; snare; drumstick, jazz stick, tymp stick.

.20 **keyboard,** fingerboard; **console, keys,** manual, claviature; piano keys, ivories [slang], eighty-eight [slang], organ manual, great, swell, choir, solo, echo; pedals.

.21 **carillon,** chimes 465.18, chime of bells; electronic carillon.

.22 **stop,** organ stop, rank, register; **foundation stop;** principal, diapason, violin *or* string diapason; **flute stop;** melodia, claribel, octave, piccolo, twelfth; concert flute, harmonic flute, stopped flute, bourdon, gedeckt, stopped diapason, quintaten, rohr flute, koppel flute, block flute; **string stop;** cello, viola, gamba, dulciana, viol d'orchestre; **reed stop,** trumpet, trombone, posaune, cornopean, clarion, cromorna, shawm, bombard, ranket, bassoon, English horn, clarinet, oboe; **mutation stop;** nazard, tierce, quint, larigot, septième; **mixture;** cornet, sesquialtera, fourniture, plein jeu, cymbel; **hybrid stop;** spitz flute, gemshorn; **voix céleste,** vox angelica, unda maris; **tremolo,** vibrato, vox humana.

.23 **string,** chord, steel string, wound string, nylon string; fiddlestring, catgut; horsehair; music wire, piano wire.

.24 **plectrum,** plectron, pick.

.25 (aids) metronome, rhythmometer; tone measurer, monochord, sonometer; tuning fork, tuning bar, diapason; pitch pipe, tuning pipe; mute; music stand, music lyre; baton, conductor's baton, stick [informal].

## 466. INTELLECT

### *(mental faculty)*

.1 NOUNS **intellect, mind,** *mens* [L], menti–, noo–, psych(o)–; mental *or* intellectual faculty, nous, **reason, rationality,** rational *or* reasoning faculty, power of reason, *Vernunft* [Ger], *esprit* [Fr], *raison* [Fr], ratio, discursive reason, "discourse of reason" [Shakespeare], **intelligence,** mentality, mental capacity, **understanding,** reasoning, intellection, conception; **psyche;** brain, **brains,** smarts [slang], gray matter [informal]; head, headpiece.

.2 **wits, senses, faculties,** parts, capacities, intellectual gifts *or* talents; intellectuals [archaic]; consciousness 475.2.

.3 **inmost mind,** inner recesses of the mind,

mind's core, deepest mind, center of the mind; inner man 5.4; subconscious, subconscious mind 690.35; inmost heart 855.2.

.4 **psyche, spirit,** spiritus, **soul,** âme [Fr], **heart, mind,** anima, *anima humana* [L]; shade, shadow, manes; breath, pneuma, breath of life, divine breath; *atman, purusha, buddhi, jiva, jivatma* [all Skt]; ba, khu [both Egypt myth]; *ruach, nephesh* [both Heb]; spiritual being, inner man, "the Divinity that stirs within us" [Addison]; ego, the self, the I.

.5 **life principle,** vital principle, vital spirit *or* soul, **vital force,** prana [Hinduism]; essence *or* substance of life, individual essence, *ousia* [Gk]; divine spark, vital spark *or* flame.

.6 **brain,** cerebr(o)–, encephal(o)–; seat *or* organ of thought, sensory, sensorium; encephalon; gray matter, head, pate *or* sconce *or* noddle [all informal]; noodle *or* noggin *or* bean *or* upper story [all slang]; sensation 422.

.7 (parts of the brain) prosencephalon, forebrain; telencephalon, endbrain; cerebrum; cerebral hemispheres, corpus callosum, cerebral cortex, mantle, pallium, archipallium, neopallium; lobe, frontal lobe, temporal lobe, parietal lobe, occipital lobe, limbic lobe; diencephalon, between brain; hypothalamus, hypothalam(o)–, subthalamus, thalamus, thalam(o)–; midbrain, mesencephalon; pons; optic chiasm; hindbrain, rhombencephalon; metencephalon, myelencephalon; cerebellum, little brain; hippocampus; fornix; corpus striatum, lenticular nucleus, globus pallidus, pallido–; folia, arbor vitae, cerebellar hemispheres, vermis; medulla oblongata; reticular system; brain stem; meninges, dura mater, pia mater, arachnoid; ventricle; convolution, fissure, gyrus; cerebrospinal fluid; pituitary body; pineal body; gray matter, poli(o)–; white matter; glial cells.

.8 ADJS **mental, intellectual, rational, reasoning, thinking,** noetic, conceptive, conceptual, phrenic; intelligent 467.12; noological; endopsychic, psychic(al), psychologic(al), spiritual; cerebral; subjective, internal.

## 467. INTELLIGENCE, WISDOM

*(mental capacity)*

.1 NOUNS **intelligence, understanding,** *Verstand* [Ger], **comprehension,** apprehension, mental *or* intellectual grasp, intellectual power, thinking power, power of mind *or* thought; ideation, conception; integrative power, esemplastic power; rationality, reasoning *or* deductive power; **sense, wit,** mother wit, natural *or* native wit; intellect 466; **intellectuality,** intellectualism; capacity, mental capacity, **mentality,** caliber, reach *or* compass *or* scope of mind; IQ, intelligence quotient, mental ratio, mental age; sanity 472; knowledge 475.

.2 **smartness, braininess,** smarts *or* savvy [both slang], **brightness, brilliance, cleverness,** aptness, aptitude, native cleverness, mental alertness, nous, **sharpness, keenness,** acuity, acuteness, gifts, giftedness, talent, flair, genius; quickness, nimbleness, adroitness, dexterity; sharp-wittedness, keen-wittedness, quick-wittedness, nimble-wittedness; nimble mind, mercurial mind, quick parts, clear *or* quick thinking; ready wit, quick wit, sprightly wit, *esprit* [Fr].

.3 **shrewdness, artfulness, cunning,** cunningness, canniness, **craft, craftiness,** wiliness, guilefulness, slickness, **slyness,** pawkiness [Brit], foxiness [informal], peasant *or* animal cunning, low cunning; subtility, subtilty, **subtlety;** insidiousness, deviousness.

.4 **sagacity,** sagaciousness, **astuteness, acumen,** longheadedness; **foresight,** foresightedness, providence; **farsightedness,** farseeingness, longsightedness; **discernment, insight,** penetration, acuteness, acuity; perspicacity, perspicaciousness, perspicuity, perspicuousness; incisiveness, trenchancy, cogency; **perception,** perceptiveness, percipience, apperception; sensibility 422.2.

.5 **wisdom,** ripe wisdom, seasoned understanding, mellow wisdom, wiseness, sageness, sapience, good *or* sound understanding; Sophia; erudition 475.4,5; **profundity,** profoundness, depth; broadmindedness 526.

.6 **sensibleness, reasonableness,** reason, rationality, sanity, saneness, **soundness; practicality,** practical wisdom, practical mind; **sense,** good *or* common *or* plain sense, **horse sense** [informal]; due sense of; level head, cool head, **levelheadedness,** balance, coolheadedness, coolness; soberness, sobriety, **sober-mindedness.**

.7 **judiciousness, judgment,** good *or* sound judgment, cool judgment, soundness of judgment; **prudence,** prudentialism, providence, policy, polity; weighing, consideration, circumspection, circumspectness, reflection, reflectiveness, **thoughtfulness; discretion**, discreetness; **discrimination**.

.8 **genius**, *Geist* [Ger], spirit, soul; daimonion, demon, daemon; **inspiration**, afflatus, divine afflatus; Muse; fire of genius; **creativity**; talent 733.4; creative thought 535.2.

.9 (intelligent being) **intelligence, intellect**, head, brain, mentality, consciousness; wise man 468.

.10 VERBS **have all one's wits about one**, have all one's marbles [slang], have smarts *or* savvy [slang], have a head on one's shoulders [informal], have one's head screwed on right; use one's head *or* wits; know what's what 733.18, be wise as a serpent *or* owl; be reasonable, listen to reason.

.11 be brilliant, **scintillate**, sparkle, coruscate.

.12 ADJS **intelligent**, intellectual [archaic]; ideational, conceptual, conceptive, discursive; sophic, noetic; **knowing, understanding, reasonable, rational, sensible, bright**; sane 472.4; not so dumb [informal], strong-minded.

.13 **clear-witted**, clearheaded, clear-sighted; awake, **wide-awake**, alive, **alert**, on the ball [slang].

.14 **smart, brainy** [informal], **bright, brilliant**, scintillating; **clever**, apt, **gifted**, talented; **sharp**, keen; **quick**, nimble, adroit, dexterous; **sharp-witted**, keen-witted, needle-witted, **quick-witted**, quick-thinking, steel-trap, nimble-witted, quick on the trigger *or* uptake [informal]; smart as a whip, sharp as a tack [slang]; nobody's fool *or* no dumbbell *or* not born yesterday [all informal].

.15 **shrewd, artful, cunning, knowing, crafty, wily**, guileful, canny, slick, sly, pawky [Brit], foxy [informal], crazy like a fox [slang]; **subtle**, subtile; insidious, devious, Byzantine, calculating.

.16 **sagacious, astute**, longheaded, argute; **understanding, discerning**, penetrating, incisive, acute, trenchant, cogent, piercing; **foresighted**, foreseeing; forethoughted, forethoughtful, provident; **farsighted**, farseeing, longsighted; **perspicacious**, perspicuous; **perceptive** 422.13, percipient, apperceptive, appercipient.

.17 **wise, sage**, sapient, **knowing; learned** 475.21; **profound**, deep; wise as an owl *or* serpent, wise as Solomon; wise beyond one's years, in advance of one's age, wise in one's generation; broad-minded 526.8.

.18 **sensible, reasonable, rational, logical; practical**, pragmatic; philosophical; com-

monsense, commonsensical [informal]; **levelheaded**, balanced, coolheaded, cool, **sound, sane**, sober, **sober-minded**, well-balanced.

.19 **judicious**, judicial, judgmatic(al), **prudent**, prudential, politic, careful, provident, **considerate**, circumspect, **thoughtful**, reflective, reflecting; **discreet**; discriminative, discriminating; **well-advised**, well-judged, enlightened.

.20 ADVS **intelligently, understandingly**, knowingly, discerningly; **reasonably**, rationally, sensibly; **smartly, cleverly; shrewdly**, artfully, cunningly; **wisely**, sagaciously, astutely; **judiciously, prudently**, discreetly, providently, considerately, circumspectly, thoughtfully.

## 468. WISE MAN

.1 NOUNS **wise man, sage**, sapient, man of wisdom; **master**, authority, mastermind, master spirit of the age, oracle; **philosopher**, thinker, lover of wisdom; rabbi; doctor; great soul, mahatma, guru, rishi; *starets* [Russ], elder, wise old man, elder statesman; illuminate; seer; mentor; **intellect**, man of intellect; mandarin, **intellectual** 476; savant, **scholar** 476.3.

.2 Solomon, Socrates, Plato, Mentor, Nestor, Confucius, Buddha, Gandhi.

.3 **the wise**, the intelligent, the sensible, the prudent, the knowing, the understanding.

.4 Seven Wise Men of Greece, Seven Sages, Seven Wise Masters; Solon, Chilon, Pittacus, Bias, Periander, Epimenides, Cleobulus, Thales.

.5 Magi, Three Wise Men, Wise Men of the East, Three Kings; Three Kings of Cologne; Gaspar *or* Caspar, Melchior, Balthasar.

.6 **wiseacre**, wisehead, wiseling, **witling**, wisenheimer [slang], wise guy, smart ass [slang]; wise fool; Gothamite, wise man of Gotham, wise man of Chelm.

## 469. UNINTELLIGENCE

.1 NOUNS **unintelligence**, unintellectuality [archaic], unwisdom, unwiseness, intellectual *or* mental weakness; **senselessness, witlessness, mindlessness**, brainlessness, primal stupidity, *Urdummheit* [Ger], reasonlessness, lackwittedness, lackbrainedness, slackwittedness, slackmindedness; **irrationality; ignorance** 477; **foolishness** 470; incapacity, ineptitude; low IQ.

.2 **unperceptiveness**, imperceptiveness, insensibility, impercipience, undisciningness, unapprehendingness, **incomprehen-**

sion, nonunderstanding; **blindness,** mind-blindness, purblindness; **shortsightedness,** nearsightedness, dim-sightedness.

.3 **stupidity,** stupidness, *bêtise* [Fr], **dumbness** [informal], **doltishness,** boobishness, duncery [archaic], dullardism, blockishness, cloddishness, lumpishness, sottishness, **asininity,** ninnyism, simpletonianism; oafishness, oafdom, yokelism, loutishness; **density,** denseness, opacity; grossness, crassness, crudeness, boorishness; **dullness,** dopiness [slang], **obtuseness,** sluggishness, bovinity, cowishness, slowness, lethargy, stolidity, hebetude; **dim-wittedness,** dimness, **dull-wittedness,** slow-wittedness, beef-wittedness, dull-headedness, **thick-wittedness,** thick-headedness, unteachability, ineducability; wrongheadedness.

.4 [informal terms] **blockheadedness,** woodenheadedness, klutziness, dunderheadedness, jolterheadedness *or* joltheadedness [both Brit], chowderheadedness, chuckleheadedness, beetleheadedness, chumpishness, numskulledness *or* numskullery, cabbageheadedness, sapheadedness, muttonheadedness, fatheadedness, boneheadedness, knuckleheadedness, blunderheadedness.

.5 **muddleheadedness,** addleheadedness, addlepatedness, puzzleheadedness; dizziness [informal].

.6 **empty-headedness,** empty-mindedness, absence of mind; **vacuity,** vacuousness, vacancy, vacuum, emptiness, mental void, blankness, hollowness, inanity, vapidity, jejunity.

.7 **superficiality,** shallowness, **unprofundity,** lack of depth, unprofoundness, thinness; shallow-wittedness, shallow-mindedness; **frivolousness,** flightiness, lightness, fluffiness, frothiness, volatility.

.8 **feeblemindedness,** weak-mindedness; infirmity, weakness, feebleness, softness.

.9 **mental deficiency,** mental retardation, amentia, mental handicap, subnormality, mental defectiveness; **arrested development,** infantilism, retardation, retardment, backwardness; **simplemindedness,** simple-wittedness, simpleness, simplicity; **idiocy,** idiotism [archaic], profound idiocy, **imbecility, half-wittedness,** blithering idiocy; moronity, moronism, **cretinism;** mongolism, mongolianism, mongoloid idiocy, Down's syndrome; insanity 473.

.10 **senility,** senilism, senile weakness, senile debility, caducity, decreptitude, senecti-

tude, decline; **childishness, second childhood,** dotage, dotardism; anility; senile dementia, senile psychosis.

.11 **puerility,** puerilism, immaturity, **childishness; infantilism,** babyishness.

.12 VERBS **be stupid,** etc.; drool, slobber, drivel, dither, blither, blather, maunder, dote, burble; not see an inch beyond one's nose, not have enough sense to come in out of the rain, not find one's way to first base.

.13 ADJS **unintelligent,** unintellectual [archaic], **unthinking, unreasoning, irrational,** unwise, inept, **not bright;** ungifted, untalented; **senseless,** insensate; **mindless, witless, reasonless, brainless,** pin-brained, pea-brained, of little brain, headless; **lackwitted,** lackbrained, slackwitted, slackminded, lean-minded, lean-witted, short-witted; **foolish** 470.8; **ignorant** 477.12.

.14 **undiscerning, unperceptive,** imperceptive, impercipient, insensible, unapprehending, uncomprehending, nonunderstanding; **shortsighted,** myopic, nearsighted, dim-sighted; **blind,** purblind, mind-blind, blind as a bat; blinded, blindfold, blindfolded.

.15 **stupid, dumb,** dullard, **doltish,** blockish, klutzy *or* klutzish [both slang], duncish, duncical, cloddish, clottish [Brit], chumpish [informal], lumpish, **oafish,** boobish, sottish, **asinine,** lamebrained, Boeotian; **dense,** thick [informal], opaque, gross, crass, fat; bovine, cowish, beef-witted, beef-brained, beefheaded; unteachable, ineducable; wrongheaded; dead from the neck up, dead above *or* between the ears, muscle-bound between the ears.

.16 **dull,** dull of mind, **dopey** [slang], **obtuse,** blunt, dim, wooden, heavy, sluggish, slow, **slow-witted,** hebetudinous, **dim-witted, dull-witted,** blunt-witted, dull-brained, dull-headed, dull-pated, **thick witted,** thick-headed, thick-pated, thick skulled, thick-brained, fat-witted, gross witted, gross-headed.

.17 [informal terms] **blockheaded,** wooden headed, stupidheaded, dumbheaded dunderheaded, blunderheaded, jolter headed *or* joltheaded [both Brit], chow derheaded, chuckleheaded, beetleheaded nitwitted, numskulled, cabbageheaded pumpkin-headed, sapheaded, lunkhead ed, muttonheaded, fatheaded, bone headed, knuckleheaded, clodpated, shi headed [slang].

.18 **muddleheaded, fuddlebrained** [informal scramblebrained** [informal], muddled, a

dled, addleheaded, **addlepated,** addlebrained, muddybrained, puzzleheaded,
blear-witted; dizzy [informal], muzzy, foggy.

.19 **empty-headed,** empty-minded, empty-
noddled, empty-pated, empty-skulled;
**vacuous,** vacant, empty, hollow, inane,
vapid, jejune, blank; **rattlebrained,** rattleheaded; scatterbrained 532.16.

.20 **superficial, shallow, unprofound;** shal-
low-witted, shallow-minded, shallow-
brained, shallow-headed, shallow-pated;
**frivolous,** flighty, light, volatile, frothy,
fluffy, **featherbrained, birdwitted, birdbrained.**

.21 **feebleminded, weak-minded,** weak, feeble, infirm, soft, soft in the head, weak in
the upper story [informal].

.22 **mentally deficient,** mentally defective,
mentally handicapped, retarded, **mentally retarded,** backward, arrested, subnormal, not right in the head, **not all
there** [informal]; **simpleminded,** simple-
witted, simple, simpletonian; **half-witted,**
half-baked [informal]; **idiotic, moronic,
imbecile,** imbecilic, cretinous, cretinistic,
mongoloid; crackbrained, cracked, crazy
473.25; babbling, driveling, slobbering,
drooling, blithering, dithering, maundering, burbling.

.23 **senile,** decrepit, doddering, doddery;
**childish,** childlike, in one's second childhood, **doting,** doited [Scot].

.24 **puerile,** immature, **childish;** childlike; **infantile,** infantine; **babyish,** babish.

.25 ADVS **unintelligently, stupidly;** foolishly
470.12.

## 470. FOOLISHNESS

.1 NOUNS **foolishness, folly, foolery, fool-
headedness, stupidity, asininity,** niaiserie
[Fr], bêtise [Fr]; **inanity, fatuity,** fatuous-
ness; ineptitude; **silliness; frivolousness,**
frivolity, giddiness; triviality, triflingness,
nugacity, desipience; **senselessness, witlessness, thoughtlessness,** brainlessness,
mindlessness; **idiocy, imbecility; craziness, madness,** lunacy, **insanity; eccentricity, queerness,** crankiness, crackpot-
tedness; weirdness; screwiness or nuttiness or wackiness or goofiness or
daffiness or battiness or sappiness [all
slang]; zaniness, zanyism, **clownishness,
buffoonery.**

.2 **unwiseness, unwisdom, injudiciousness,
imprudence;** indiscreetness, **indiscretion,**
inconsideration, thoughtlessness, witlessness, inattention, unthoughtfulness; **un-**
reasonableness, unsoundness, unsensible-
ness, senselessness, reasonlessness, **irrationality, unreason,** inadvisability; recklessness; childishness, immaturity, puerility, callowness; inexpedience 671; unintelligence 469; pompousness, stuffiness.

.3 **absurdity,** absurdness, **ridiculousness;** ludicrousness 880.1; **nonsense,** nonsensicality, stuff and nonsense; **preposterousness,**
fantasticalness, monstrousness, wildness,
**outrageousness.**

.4 (foolish act) **folly, stupidity,** act of folly,
absurdity, sottise [Fr], foolish or stupid
thing, dumb thing to do [slang]; fool or
fool's trick, dumb trick [informal]; **imprudence, indiscretion,** imprudent or unwise
step; blunder 518.5.

.5 stultification; infatuation.

.6 VERBS **be foolish;** be stupid 469.12; **act** or
**play the fool;** get funny, do the crazy act
or bit or shtick [slang]; **fool,** tomfool [in-
formal], **trifle,** frivol; **fool around** [infor-
mal], horse around [informal], clown,
clown around; **make a fool of oneself,**
make a monkey of oneself [slang], stultify
oneself, invite ridicule, put oneself out of
court, play the buffoon; **lose one's head,
take leave of one's senses,** go haywire;
pass from the sublime to the ridiculous;
strain at a gnat and swallow a camel.

.7 **stultify, infatuate,** turn one's head, befool; gull, dupe; **make a fool of,** make a
monkey of [slang], play for a sucker
[slang], put on [slang].

.8 ADJS **foolish,** fool [informal], **foolheaded**
[informal], **stupid, dumb** [slang], **asinine,**
wet [Brit]; **buffoonish; silly,** apish, dizzy
[informal]; **fatuous,** fatuitous, **inept,
inane;** futile; **senseless, witless, thoughtless,** brainless; **idiotic,** moronic, imbecile,
**crazy, mad,** daft, **insane;** cockeyed or
screwy or nutty or wacky or goofy or
daffy or loony or batty or sappy or kooky
or flaky [all slang]; infatuated, besotted,
credulous, gulled, befooled, beguiled,
fond, doting, gaga; sentimental, maudlin;
dazed, fuddled.

.9 **unwise, injudicious, imprudent, impolitic; indiscreet;** inconsiderate, thoughtless,
mindless, witless, unthoughtful, unthinking, unreflecting, unreflective; **unreasonable, unsound, unsensible,** senseless, insensate, reasonless, **irrational,** reckless, inadvisable; inexpedient 671.5; **ill-advised,
ill-considered,** ill-gauged, ill-judged, ill-
imagined, ill-contrived, ill-devised, unconsidered; unadvised, misadvised, mis-

guided; undiscerning; unforeseeing, unseeing, shortsighted, myopic.

.10 **absurd, nonsensical,** ridiculous, poppycockish, laughable, ludicrous 880.4; **foolish, crazy;** preposterous, cockamamie [informal], fantastic(al), grotesque, monstrous, wild, weird, **outrageous,** incredible, beyond belief, *outré* [Fr], extravagant, bizarre; high-flown.

.11 foolable, befoolable, gullible; naïve, artless, inexperienced, green.

.12 ADVS **foolishly, stupidly,** sillily, idiotically; **unwisely,** injudiciously, imprudently, indiscreetly, inconsiderately; senselessly, unreasonably, thoughtlessly, witlessly, unthinkingly; absurdly, ridiculously.

## 471. FOOL

.1 NOUNS **fool,** tomfool, perfect fool, born fool; *schmuck* [Yid]; **ass,** jackass, stupid ass, egregious ass; zany, **clown, buffoon,** doodle; sop, milksop; mooncalf, softhead; figure of fun; **lunatic** 473.15; **ignoramus** 477.8.

.2 [slang terms] **chump, booby, boob, sap,** prize sap, klutz, **dingbat,** dingdong, **ding-a-ling,** saphead, **mutt, jerk,** jerk-off, asshole, goof, schlemiel, sawney [Brit], galoot.

.3 **dolt, dunce,** clod, Boeotian, **dullard,** *niais* [Fr], donkey, stupid, **ninny,** ninnyhammer, **nincompoop,** looby, noddy, jobbernowl [Brit informal], thickwit, **dope, nitwit,** dimwit, lackwit, lamebrain, put, lightweight, witling, gaby [Brit dial]; dummy *or* dumb cluck *or* **dumbbell** *or* **dumb bunny** [all slang], block [slang], loon [slang], gowk [Brit dial].

.4 **blockhead,** dolthead, dumbhead, stupidhead, dullhead, bufflehead [dial], bonehead, jughead, thickhead, thickskull, **numskull, lunkhead,** chucklehead, **knucklehead,** chowderhead, jolterhead [Brit informal], muttonhead, beefhead, **meathead,** noodlehead, pinhead, pinbrain, peabrain, cabbagehead, pumpkin head, **fathead,** blubberhead, muddlehead, puzzlehead, addlebrain, addlehead, **addlepate,** tottyhead [archaic], puddinghead, mushhead, blunderhead, dunderhead, dunderpate, clodpate, clodhead, clodpoll.

.5 **oaf, lout,** boor, lubber, **gawk,** gawky, **lummox,** yokel, rube, hick, hayseed, bumpkin, clod, clodhopper.

.6 **silly,** silly Billy, **silly ass, goose.**

.7 **scatterbrain,** scatterbrains, shatterbrain, shatterpate [both archaic], **rattlebrain,** rattlehead, rattlepate, **harebrain,** featherbrain, shallowbrain, shallowpate [archaic], featherhead, giddybrain, giddyhead, giddypate, **flibbertigibbet.**

.8 **simpleton,** simp [slang], juggins *or* jiggins [both slang], clot [Brit], golem, **idiot,** driveling *or* blithering *or* congenital idiot; **imbecile, moron, half-wit,** natural, natural idiot, born fool, natural-born fool, ament, defective; cretin, mongolian *or* mongoloid idiot.

.9 **dotard,** senile; fogy, **old fogy,** fuddy-duddy, old fart *or* fud.

## 472. SANITY

.1 NOUNS **sanity, saneness,** sanemindedness, soundness, **soundness of mind,** soundmindedness, sound mind, healthy mind, right mind [informal], senses, reason, **rationality,** reasonableness, lucidity, balance, wholesomeness; normalness, normality, normalcy; **mental health;** mental hygiene; mental balance *or* poise *or* equilibrium; sobriety, sober senses; a sound mind in a sound body, *"mens sana in corpore sano"* [L; Juvenal]; contact with reality; lucid interval.

.2 VERBS **come to one's senses,** sober down *or* up, recover one's sanity *or* balance *or* equilibrium, get things into proportion; see in perspective; have all one's marbles [slang].

.3 **bring to one's senses,** bring to reason.

.4 ADJS **sane,** sane-minded, **rational,** reasonable, sensible, **lucid,** normal, wholesome, clearheaded, clearminded, balanced, **sound,** mentally sound, of sound mind, *compos mentis* [L], sound-minded, healthy-minded, right, right in the head, **in one's right mind,** in possession of one's faculties *or* senses, together, all there [both slang].

## 473. INSANITY, MANIA

.1 NOUNS **insanity,** insaneness, unsaneness, **lunacy, madness,** *folie* [Fr], **craziness, daftness,** oddness, strangeness, queerness, abnormality; loss of touch *or* contact with reality, loss of mind *or* reason; dementedness, dementia, brainsickness mindsickness, mental sickness, sickness **mental illness, mental disease,** –phrenia brain damage; rabidness, **mania,** furor alienation, aberration, mental disturbance, **derangement,** distraction, disorientation, mental derangement *or* disorder, unbalance, mental instability, unsoundness, **unsoundness of mind** unbalanced mind, diseased *or* unsound mind, **sick mind,** disturbed *or* troubled *or* clouded mind, shattered mind, mind overthrown *or* unhinged, darkened mind, disordered mind *or* reason; senselessness, witlessness, reasonlessness, irrationality; possession, pixilation; mental deficiency 469.1.

.2 [informal terms] **daffiness, nuttiness, battiness,** screwiness, goofiness, kookiness, **wackiness,** dottiness, looniness, **balminess;** bats in the belfry, a screw loose; lame brains.

.3 **psychosis,** psychopathy, psychopathia, psychopathic condition; organic psychosis, metabolic psychosis, toxic psychosis, functional psychosis; reactive *or* situational psychosis; certifiability; **neurosis** 690.19; senile dementia, senile psychosis, senility, Pick's disease; presenile dementia, Alzheimer's disease; syphilitic paresis, dementia paralytica, paralytic dementia, general paresis, general paralysis; arteriosclerotic psychosis; Korsakoff's psychosis *or* syndrome; prison psychosis; psychopathia sexualis, sexual pathology 419.12–14; pathological drunkenness *or* intoxication, dipsomania 993.3; pharmacopsychosis, drug addiction 642.9; moral insanity, psychopathic personality 690.16, *folie du doute* [Fr], abulia 627.4.

.4 **schizophrenia, dementia praecox,** schiz(o)–; mental dissociation, dissociation of personality; **split personality,** alternating personality, dual *or* double personality, multiple personality; catatonic schizophrenia, catatonia, hebephrenia, hebephrenic schizophrenia; schizothymia; schizophasia; **paranoia,** paraphrenia, paranoiac *or* paranoid psychosis; paranoid schizophrenia.

.5 **melancholia,** "moping, melancholy and moonstruck madness" [Milton]; melancholia hypochrondriaca; involutional melancholia *or* involutional psychosis; stuporous melancholia, melancholia attonita; flatuous melancholia; melancholia religiosa; **manic-depressive psychosis;** cyclothymia.

.6 **rabies, hydrophobia,** lyssa, canine madness; dumb *or* sullen rabies, paralytic rabies; furious rabies.

.7 **frenzy, furor,** fury, maniacal excitement, fever, **rage; seizure,** attack, **fit,** paroxysm, spasm, **convulsion;** amok, murderous insanity *or* frenzy; psychokinesia; furor epilepticus.

.8 **delirium,** deliriousness, brainstorm; calenture of the brain, afebrile delirium, lingual delirium, delirium mussitans; incoherence, wandering, raving, ranting.

.9 **delirium tremens,** mania *or* dementia a potu, delirium alcoholicum *or* ebriositatis.

.10 [slang or informal terms] **the DT's,** the horrors, the shakes, **the heebie-jeebies,** the jimjams, the beezie-weezies, the screaming meemies, blue Johnnies, blue devils, pink elephants, pink spiders, snakes, snakes in the boots.

.11 **fanaticism,** fanaticalness, **rabidness, overzealousness,** overenthusiasm, ultrazealousness, zealotry, zealotism, bigotry, perfervidness; extremism, extremeness, extravagance, excessiveness, overreaction; overreligiousness 1028.3.

.12 **mania** 473.36, **craze, infatuation, enthusiasm,** passion, fascination, crazy fancy, **bug** [slang], rage, furore, furor; manic-depressive psychosis.

.13 **obsession,** prepossession, preoccupation, **hang-up** [slang], **fixation,** tic, complex, fascination; hypercathexis; **compulsion,** morbid drive, obsessive compulsion, irresistible impulse; **monomania,** ruling passion, fixed idea, *idée fixe* [Fr], one-track mind; **possession.**

.14 **insane asylum,** asylum, lunatic asylum, **madhouse,** mental institution, mental home, bedlam; **bughouse** *or* nuthouse *or* laughing academy *or* **loonybin** *or* booby hatch [all slang]; mental hospital, psychopathic hospital *or* ward, psychiatric ward; padded cell.

.15 **lunatic, madman,** dement, phrenetic, fanatic [both archaic], *fou, aliéné* [both Fr], noncompos; bedlamite, Tom o' Bedlam; demoniac, energumen; **loon** *or* loony *or* nut *or* **crackpot** *or* **screwball** *or* weirdie *or* weirdo *or* kook *or* flake *or* crackbrain [all slang]; *meshuggenah* [Yid]; **maniac,** raving lunatic; borderline case; idiot 471.8.

.16 **psychotic,** psycho [informal], mental, mental case, certifiable case, **psychopath,** psychopathic case; psychopathic personality; paranoiac, paranoid; schizophrenic, schizophrene, schizoid; schiz *or* schizy *or* schizo [all slang]; catatoniac; hebephreniac; manic-depressive.

.17 **fanatic,** infatuate, **bug** [slang], **nut** [slang], **buff** *or* **fan** [both informal], freak [slang], *fanatico, aficionado* [both Sp], devotee, **zealot, enthusiast,** energumen; **monomaniac,** crank [informal]; lunatic fringe.

.18 psychiatry, alienism; psychiatrist, alienist 690.12.

.19 VERBS **be insane, be out of one's mind,** not be in one's right mind, not be right in the head, **not be all there** [informal], have a demon *or* devil; have bats in the belfry *or* have a screw loose, not have all one's buttons *or* marbles [slang]; **wander, ramble; rave,** rage, **rant;** dote, babble; drivel, drool, slobber, slaver; froth *or* foam at the mouth, run mad, run amok.

.20 **go mad, go crazy, take leave of one's senses,** lose one's senses *or* reason *or* wits, **crack up,** go off one's head [informal].

.21 [slang terms] go off one's nut *or* rocker, go off the track *or* trolley, go out of one's skull, blow one's top *or* stack, flip one's lid *or* wig, go ape, go bananas, go crackers [Brit], blow one's mind, freak out.

.22 addle the wits, **affect one's mind,** go to one's head.

.23 madden, dement, **craze,** mad [archaic], make mad, send mad, **unbalance,** unhinge, undermine one's reason, **derange,** distract, frenzy, shatter, **drive insane** *or* mad *or* crazy, put *or* send out of one's mind, overthrow one's mind *or* reason.

.24 obsess, possess, beset, infatuate, **preoccupy,** be uppermost in one's thoughts, have a thing about [informal]; grip, hold, get a hold on, not let go; **drive, compel, impel.**

.25 ADJS insane, unsane, **mad,** stark-mad, **stark-staring mad,** maddened, **crazy, sick,** crazed, loco [informal], mental, **psycho** [informal], **lunatic,** moon-struck, **daft, non compos mentis,** non compos, **unsound,** of unsound mind, **demented, deranged,** deluded, disoriented, unhinged, **unbalanced,** unsettled, distraught, wandering, mazed, **cracked** [informal], crackbrained, brainsick, sick in the head, not right, not right in the head [informal], not in one's right mind, **touched,** tetched [dial], touched in the head, off one's head [informal], **out of one's mind,** out of one's head [informal], out of one's senses *or* wits, bereft of reason, reasonless, irrational, deprived of reason, senseless, witless, **not all there** [informal], *meshuggah* [Yid]; hallucinated; manic; queer, odd, strange, off, flighty [archaic]; abnormal 85.9, mentally deficient 469.22.

.26 [slang terms] **daffy, dotty,** dippy, **loony, goofy, wacky, balmy** *or* barmy, flaky, **kooky, potty, batty,** bats, **nuts, nutty,** fruity, fruitcakey, **screwy,** screwball, **screwballs,** crackers [Brit], **bananas,** bonk-

ers, loopy, beany, **buggy, bughouse,** bugs, cuckoo, slaphappy, flipped, freaked-out, off the wall, gaga, haywire, out of one's skull, off in the upper story, off one's nut *or* rocker, off the track *or* trolley, off the hinges, round the bend [Brit], minus some buttons, nobody home, with bats in the belfry, just plain nuts.

.27 **psychotic, psychopathic, mentally ill,** mentally sick, certifiable; disturbed, neurotic 690.45; schizophrenic, schizoid, schizy [slang], schizy; manic-depressive; paranoiac, paranoid; catatonic; brain-damaged, brain-injured.

.28 **possessed,** possessed with a demon *or* devil, **pixilated, bedeviled,** demonized, devil-ridden.

.29 **mad as a hatter,** mad as a March hare, crazier than a bedbug *or* coot *or* loon, nutty as a fruitcake [slang].

.30 **rabid, maniac** *or* **maniacal,** raving mad, stark-raving mad, **frenzied, frantic,** frenetic; **mad,** madding, **wild, furious, violent;** desperate; **beside oneself,** like one possessed, uncontrollable; **raving, raging, ranting;** frothing *or* foaming at the mouth; **amok, berserk,** running wild; maenadic, corybantic, bacchic, Dionysiac.

.31 **delirious,** out of one's head [informal], off one's head [informal], off; **giddy,** dizzy, lightheaded; **wandering, rambling, raving, ranting,** babbling, incoherent.

.32 **fanatic(al), rabid;** overzealous, ultrazealous, **overenthusiastic,** zealotic, bigoted, perfervid; **extreme,** extremist, extravagant, inordinate, ultra–, hyper–; **unreasonable, irrational; wild-eyed,** wild-looking, haggard; overreligious 1028.4.

.33 **obsessed, possessed,** prepossessed, infatuated, preoccupied, fixated, **hung-up** [slang], besotted, gripped, held; monomaniac *or* monomaniacal.

.34 **obsessive,** obsessional; obsessing, possessing, **preoccupying,** gripping, holding, driving, impelling, **compulsive,** compelling.

.35 ADVS madly, insanely, crazily; deliriously, fanatically, rabidly, etc.

.36 **manias**

| | |
|---|---|
| abluto– (bathing) | delusions) |
| acro– (incurable insanity) | America– (United States) |
| agora– (open spaces) | andro– (men) |
| agyio– (streets) | Anglo– (England) |
| ailuro– (cats) | antho– (flowers) |
| alcoholo– (alcohol) | aphrodisio– (sexual pleasure) |
| amaxo– (being in vehicles) | api– (bees) |
| ameno– (pleasing | arithmo– (counting) |

auto– (solitude)
autophono– (suicide)
ballisto– (bullets)
biblio– (books)
biblioklepto– (book theft)
bruxo– (gritting one's teeth)
cacodemono– (demonic possession)
chero– (gaiety)
China– (China)
chiono– (snow)
choreo– (dancing)
chremato– (money)
clino– (bed rest)
coprolalo– (foul speech)
cremno– (cliffs)
creso– (great wealth)
cyno– (dogs)
Danto– (Dante)
demo– (crowds)
dipso– (liquor)
dora– (fur)
drapeto– (running away)
dromo– (traveling)
ecdemio– (wandering)
edeo– (genitals)
ego– (one's self)
eleuthro– (freedom)
empleo– (public employment)
eno– (wine)
entheo– (religion)
entomo– (insects)
eremio– (stillness)
ergasio– (activity)
ergo– (work)
erotico– (erotica)
eroto– (sexual desire)
erotographo– (erotic literature)
erythro– (blushing)
ethero– (ether)
flori– (plants)
Franco– (France)
Gallo– (France)
gamo– (marriage)
gephyro– (crossing bridges)
Germano– (Germany)
grapho– (writing)
Greco– (Greece)
gymno– (nakedness)
gyneco– (satyriasis)
hamarto– (sin)
hedono– (pleasure)
helio– (sun)
hiero– (priests)
hippo– (horses)
hodo– (travel)
homicido– (murder)
hydro– (water)
hydrodipso– (drinking water)
hylo– (woods)
hyper– (acute mania)
hypno– (sleep)
hypo– (mild mania)
hystero– (nymphoma-

nia)
ichthyo– (fish)
icono– (icons)
idolo– (idols)
Italo– (Italy)
kaino– (novelty)
kathiso– (sitting)
kineso– (movement)
klepto– (stealing)
lalo– (speech)
letheo– (narcotics)
logo– (talking)
lyco– (lycanthropy)
lype– (deep melancholy)
macro– (becoming larger)
megalo– (own importance)
melo– (music)
mentulo– (the penis)
mesmero– (hypnosis)
metro– (writing verse)
micro– (becoming smaller)
mono– (one subject)
musico– (music)
muso– (mice)
mytho– (lies; exaggerations)
necro– (death; the dead)
nocti– (night)
noso– (imagined disease)
nosto– (return home)
nudo– (nudity)
nympho– (female lust)
ochlo– (crowds)
oestro– (nymphomania)
oiko– (home)
oino– (wine)
oligo– (a few subjects)
onio– (buying)
ophidio– (reptiles)
opio– (opium)
opso– (a special food)
orchido– (testicles)
ornitho– (birds)
para– (joy in complaints)
parousia– (second coming of Christ)
patho– (moral insanity)
phago– (food; eating)
phanero– (picking at growths)
pharmaco– (medicines)
philopatrido– (homesickness)
phono– (noise)
photo– (light)
phronemo– (thinking)
phthisio– (tuberculosis)
pluto– (great wealth)
politico– (politics)
porio– (wanderlust)

pornographo– (pornography)
poto– (drinking; delirium tremens)
pseudo– (falsities)
pyro– (fires)
Russo– (Russia)
satyro– (male lust)
scribble– (writing)
scribo– (writing)
siderodromo– (railroad travel)
sito– (food)
sopho– (one's own wisdom)
squander– (spending)
sub– (mild mania)
symmetro– (symmetry)
Teutono– (Germany)
thalasso– (the sea)
thanato– (death)

theatro– (theater)
theo– (that one is God)
timbro– (postage stamps)
tomo– (surgery)
tricho– (hair)
trichorrhexo– (pinching off one's hair)
trichotillo– (plucking one's hair)
tristi– (melancholia)
tromo– (delirium tremens)
Turko– (Turkey)
typo– (writing for publication)
utero– (nymphomania)
verbo– (words)
xeno– (foreigners)
zoo– (animals)

## 474. ECCENTRICITY

.1 NOUNS eccentricity, **idiosyncrasy**, idiocrasy, **erraticism**, erraticness, **queerness**, oddity, peculiarity, strangeness, singularity, freakishness, freakiness, quirkiness, crotchetiness, dottiness, crankiness, crankism, crackpotism; whimsy, whimsicality; abnormality, anomaly, unnaturalness, irregularity, deviation, deviancy, differentness, divergence, aberration; **nonconformity**, unconventionality 83.2.

.2 **quirk**, **twist**, kink, crank, quip, trick, mannerism, **crotchet**, conceit, whim, maggot, maggot in the brain, bee in one's bonnet or head [informal].

.3 **eccentric**, **erratic**; freak or character or **crank** [all informal]; **crackpot** or **nut** or **screwball** or weirdie or weirdo or kook or queer potato or **oddball** or flake [all slang] 85.4; strange duck [informal]; **nonconformist** 83.3, recluse 924.5.

.4 ADJS **eccentric**, **erratic**, idiocratic(al), idiosyncratic(al), **queer**, queer in the head [informal], **odd**, **peculiar**, strange, fey, singular, anomalous, freakish, funny; unnatural, abnormal, irregular, divergent, deviative, deviant, different, exceptional; unconventional 83.6; **crotchety**, quirky, dotty, maggoty [Brit], cranky, crank, crankish, whimsical, kinky, twisted; screwy or screwball or **nutty** or **wacky** or kooky or flaky or oddball [all slang].

## 475. KNOWLEDGE

.1 NOUNS **knowledge**, knowing, ken, –gnosia or –gnosis or –gnosy, –sophy; **acquaintance**, **familiarity**, intimacy; private knowledge, privity; **information**, data, datum, facts, factual base, corpus; intelligence;

practical knowledge, **experience, know-how**, expertise, technic, technics, technique; self-knowledge; ratio cognoscendi.

.2 **cognizance**; cognition, noesis; **recognition, realization; perception**, insight, apperception; **consciousness, awareness**, mindfulness, note, notice, sensibility; appreciation, appreciativeness.

.3 **understanding, comprehension, apprehension**, intellection, prehension; conception, conceptualization, ideation; savvy [informal]; grasp, mental grasp, grip, command, mastery; precognition, foreknowledge 542.3, clairvoyance 1034.8; intelligence, wisdom 467.

.4 **learning, enlightenment, education, instruction**, edification, illumination; acquirements, acquisitions, attainments, accomplishments; sophistication; store of knowledge; liberal education; acquisition of knowledge 564.

.5 **scholarship, erudition**, eruditeness, **learnedness**, reading, letters; **intellectuality**, intellectualism; **literacy; culture**; book learning, booklore; **bookishness**, bookiness, **pedantry**, pedantism, donnishness [Brit]; bluestockingism; bibliomania, book madness, bibliolatry, bibliophilism; classicism, classical scholarship, humanism, humanistic scholarship.

.6 **profound knowledge**, deep knowledge; specialized or special knowledge; expertise, proficiency 733.1; wide or vast or extensive knowledge, general knowledge, interdisciplinary or cross-disciplinary knowledge, encyclopedic knowledge, polymathy, polyhistory, pansophy; **omniscience**, all-knowingness.

.7 **slight knowledge** 477.6.

.8 **tree of knowledge**, tree of knowledge of good and evil; forbidden fruit.

.9 **lore, body of knowledge**, body of learning, store of knowledge, system of knowledge, treasury of information; literature, literature of the field, publications, materials; bibliography; encyclopedia, cyclopedia.

.10 **science**, ology, **art, study, discipline**, –gnomy, –logy, –nomy, –urgy; **field**, field of inquiry, concern, province, domain, area, arena, sphere, branch or field of study, branch or department of knowledge, specialty, academic specialty, academic discipline; **technology, technics**, technicology, –techny; social science, natural science; applied science, pure science, experimental science.

.11 **scientist**, man of science; **technologist**; practical scientist, experimental scientist, savant, **scholar** 476.3; authority, expert; intellectual 476.

.12 VERBS **know, perceive, apprehend**, prehend, cognize, recognize, discern, see, make out; conceive, conceptualize; realize, appreciate, understand, comprehend, fathom; savvy [informal]; wot or wot of [both Brit dial], ken [Scot]; **have, possess, grasp, seize**; have knowledge of, be informed, be apprised of, have information about, be acquainted with, be conversant with, be cognizant of, be conscious or aware of.

.13 **know well, know full well**, know damn well or darn well [informal], have a good or thorough knowledge of, be well-informed, be learned in, **be up on** [informal], be master of, command, be thoroughly grounded in, **have down pat** or **cold** [both informal], have it taped [Brit informal], have at one's fingers' ends or tips, have in one's head, **know by heart** or rote, **know like a book**, know like the back of one's hand, **know backward**, know backwards and forwards, **know inside out**, know down to the ground [informal], **know one's stuff** or know one's onions [both informal], be expert in, **know the ropes**, know all the ins and outs, know the score [informal], know all the answers [informal]; know what's what 733.18.

.14 **learn** (acquire knowledge) 564.6–15; come to one's knowledge 557.14.

.15 ADJS **knowing**, knowledgeable, –gnostic, **cognizant, conscious, aware, mindful, sensible**; intelligent 467.12; **understanding, comprehending**, apprehensive, apprehending; **perceptive**, insightful, apperceptive, percipient, perspicacious, apperceivient, prehensile; shrewd, sagacious, wise 467.15–17; omniscient, all-knowing.

.16 **cognizant of, aware of, conscious of, mindful of, sensible to** or **of, appreciative of**, no stranger to, seized of [Brit]; privy to, in the secret, let into, in the know [slang], behind the scenes or curtain, alive to, awake to; **wise to** [informal], hep to or on to [both slang]; streetwise; apprised of, informed of; undeceived, undeluded.

.17 [slang or informal terms] **hep, hip**, on the beam, go-go, **with it**, into, really into, groovy.

.18 **informed, enlightened, instructed**, versed, well-versed, educated, schooled, taught; posted, briefed, primed, trained up on, up-to-date, abreast of, *au courant* [Fr].

.19 **versed in**, **informed in**, read *or* well-read in, up on, strong in, at home in, master of, expert *or* authoritative in, proficient in, **familiar with**, at home with, **conversant with**, **acquainted with**, intimate with.

.20 **well-informed**, well-posted, well-educated, **well-grounded**, **well-versed**, **well-read**, widely read.

.21 **learned**, **erudite**, **educated**, **cultured**, cultivated, lettered, literate, civilized, **scholarly**, scholastic, studious; wise 467.17; **profound**, deep, abstruse; **encyclopedic**, pansophic, polymath *or* polymathic, polyhistoric.

.22 **book-learned**, book-read, **literary**, booktaught, book-fed, book-wise, **bookish**, booky, book-minded; book-loving, bibliophilic, bibliophagic; **pedantic**, donnish [Brit], scholastic, inkhorn; **bluestocking**.

.23 **intellectual** 466.8, intellectualistic; **highbrow** *or* highbrowed *or* highbrowish [all informal]; elitist.

.24 **self-educated**, self-taught, autodidactic.

.25 **knowable**, cognizable, recognizable, **understandable**, **comprehensible**, apprehendable, apprehensible, prehensible, graspable, seizable, discernible, conceivable, appreciable, perceptible, distinguishable, ascertainable, discoverable.

.26 **known**, **recognized**, ascertained, conceived, grasped, apprehended, prehended, seized, perceived, discerned, appreciated, **understood**, **comprehended**, realized; pat *or* **down pat** [both informal].

.27 **well-known**, well-kenned [Scot], well-understood, well-recognized, **widely known**, commonly known, universally recognized, generally *or* universally admitted; **familiar**, familiar as household words, household, **common**, **current**; **proverbial**; public, notorious; known by every schoolboy; talked-of, talked-about, in everyone's mouth, **on everyone's tongue**; **commonplace**, trite 883.9, hackneyed, platitudinous, truistic.

.28 **scientific**, scientifico–; **technical**, **technological**, technicological, techno–; **scholarly**; disciplinary.

.29 ADVS **knowingly**, **consciously**, **wittingly**, with forethought, understandingly, intelligently, studiously, learnedly, eruditely, as every schoolboy knows.

.30 **to one's knowledge**, **to the best of one's knowledge**, as far as one can see *or* tell, as far as one knows, as well as can be said.

## 476. INTELLECTUAL

.1 NOUNS **intellectual**, **intellect**, intellectualist, literate, member of the intelligentsia, white-collar intellectual; brainworker, thinker; Brahmin, mandarin, egghead [slang]; **highbrow** [informal]; wise man 468.

.2 **intelligentsia**, literati, illuminati; **intellectual elite**.

.3 **scholar**, scholastic [archaic], clerk *or* learned clerk [both archaic]; a gentleman and a scholar; student 566; **learned man**, man of learning, giant of learning, colossus of knowledge, mastermind, **savant**, pundit; genius 733.12; polymath, polyhistor, mine of information, walking encyclopedia; literary man, *littérateur* [Fr] *or* litterateur, **man of letters**; philologist, philologue; philomath, lover of learning; philosopher, philosophe; bookman; **academician**, schoolman; classicist, classicalist, Latinist, humanist.

.4 **bookworm**, bibliophage; **grind** *or* greasy grind [both slang]; **booklover**, **bibliophile**, bibliophilist, philobiblist, bibliolater, bibliolatrist; bibliomaniac, bibliomane.

.5 **pedant**; **formalist**, **precisionist**, precisian, purist, *précieux* [Fr], **bluestocking**, *bas bleu* [Fr], *précieuse* [Fr fem]; Dr. Pangloss [Voltaire].

.6 **dilettante**, **half scholar**, sciolist, **dabbler**, dabster, amateur, trifler, smatterer; grammaticaster, philologaster, criticaster, philosophaster, Latinitaster.

## 477. IGNORANCE

.1 NOUNS **ignorance**, ignorantness, **unknowingness**, unknowing, nescience; lack of information, knowledge-gap, hiatus of learning; empty-headedness, blankmindedness, vacuousness, vacuity, inanity; tabula rasa; **unintelligence** 469; **unacquaintance**, **unfamiliarity**; **greenness**, greenhornism, rawness, callowness, unripeness, green in the eye, **inexperience** 734.2; innocence, simpleness, simplicity; crass *or* gross *or* primal *or* pristine ignorance; ignorantism, know-nothingism, obscurantism; agnosticism.

.2 "blind and naked Ignorance" [Tennyson], "the mother of devotion" [Robert Burton], "the mother of prejudice" [John Bright], "the dominion of absurdity" [J. A. Froude].

.3 **incognizance, unawareness, unconsciousness, insensibility,** unwittingness, nonrecognition; nonrealization, incomprehension; **unmindfulness;** mindlessness; blindness 441, deafness 449.

.4 **unenlightenment, benightedness,** benightment, dark, darkness; savagery, barbarism, paganism, heathenism, Gothicism; age of ignorance, dark age; rural idiocy.

.5 **unlearnedness, inerudition,** ineducation, unschooledness, unletteredness; **unscholarliness,** unstudiousness; **illiteracy,** illiterateness, functional illiteracy; **unintellectuality,** unintellectualism, Philistinism, bold ignorance.

.6 **slight knowledge,** vague notion, imperfect knowledge, a little learning, glimmering, glimpse [archaic], smattering, **smattering of knowledge,** smattering of ignorance, **half-learning,** semi-learning, semi-ignorance, sciolism; **superficiality,** shallowness, surface-scratching; **dilettantism,** dilettantship, amateurism.

.7 **the unknown,** the unknowable, the strange, the unfamiliar, the incalculable; **matter of ignorance,** sealed book, riddle, enigma, mystery, puzzle 514.3, 549.8,9; *terra incognita* [L], unexplored ground *or* territory; frontier, frontiers of knowledge, **unknown quantity,** x, y, z, n; dark horse.

.8 **ignoramus, know-nothing;** no scholar, puddinghead, dunce, fool 471; **illiterate; lowbrow** [informal]; unintelligentsia, illiterati; **greenhorn,** greeny [informal], tenderfoot; **dilettante,** dabbler 476.6; **middlebrow** [informal].

.9 VERBS **be ignorant,** be green, have everything to learn, **know nothing,** know from nothing [slang], wallow in ignorance; not know any better; **not know what's what,** not know what it is all about, not know the score [informal], not be with it [informal], not know any of the answers; not know the time of day *or* what o'clock it is, not know beans, not know the first thing about, not know one's ass from one's elbow [slang], not know the way home, not know enough to come in out of the rain, not know chalk from cheese, **not know up from down,** not know which way is up.

.10 **be in the dark,** be blind, labor in darkness, walk in darkness, be benighted, grope in the dark, "see through a glass, darkly" [Bible].

.11 **not know,** not rightly know [dial], know not, know not what, know nothing of, wot not of [Brit dial], be innocent of, have no idea *or* notion *or* conception, **not have the first idea, not have the least** *or* **remotest idea,** not have idea one, not have the foggiest [slang], **not pretend to say,** not take upon oneself to say; not know the half of it; not know from Adam, not know from the man in the moon; wonder, wonder whether; half-know, have a little learning, scratch the surface, know a little, smatter, dabble, toy with, coquet with; pass, give up.

.12 ADJS **ignorant, nescient, unknowing,** uncomprehending, **know-nothing;** simple, **dumb** [informal], empty, empty-headed, blankminded, vacuous, inane, **unintelligent** 469.13; **uninformed, unenlightened,** unilluminated, unapprized, unposted [informal]; **unacquainted, unconversant,** unversed, uninitiated, **unfamiliar,** strange to; **inexperienced** 734.17; green, callow, innocent, gauche, awkward, naïve, unripe, raw; groping, tentative, unsure.

.13 **unaware, unconscious, insensible, unknowing, incognizant;** mindless, witless; unprehensive, unrealizing, nonconceiving, **unmindful,** unwitting, unsuspecting; unperceiving, impercipient, unhearing, unseeing, uninsightful; unaware of, in ignorance of, unconscious of, unmindful of, insensible to, out of it [informal], not with it [informal]; **blind to, deaf to,** dead to, a stranger to; asleep, napping, **off one's guard,** caught napping, caught tripping.

.14 **unlearned, inerudite,** unerudite, **uneducated,** unschooled, uninstructed, untutored, unbriefed, untaught, unedified, unguided; ill-educated, misinstructed, misinformed, mistaught, led astray; hoodwinked, deceived; **illiterate,** functionally illiterate, unlettered, grammarless; **unscholarly,** unscholastic, unstudious; **unliterary, unread,** unbookish, unbooklearned, bookless [archaic], unbooked; **uncultured,** uncultivated, unrefined, rude, Philistine; barbarous, pagan, heathen; Gothic; nonintellectual, **unintellectual; lowbrow** *or* lowbrowed *or* lowbrowish [all informal].

.15 **half-learned,** half-baked [informal], halfcocked *or* half-assed [both slang], sciolistic; **shallow, superficial;** immature, sophomoric(al); **dilettante,** dilettantish, smattering, dabbling, amateur, amateurish; **wise in one's own conceit.**

.16 **benighted, dark,** in darkness, in the dark.

.17 **unknown,** unbeknown [informal], unheard [archaic], **unheard-of**, unapprehended, unapparent, unperceived, unsuspected; unexplained, unascertained; uninvestigated, unexplored; unidentified, unclassified, uncharted, unfathomed, unplumbed, virgin, untouched; undisclosed, unrevealed, undivulged, undiscovered, unexposed, sealed; **unfamiliar,** strange; incalculable, **unknowable,** incognizable, undiscoverable; able; enigmatic 549.17, mysterious, puzzling 514.25.

.18 ADVS **ignorantly, unknowingly,** unmindfully, unwittingly, witlessly, unsuspectingly, **unawares;** unconsciously, insensibly; for anything or aught one knows, not that one knows.

.19 INTERJS **God knows!,** God only knows!, Lord knows!, Heaven knows!, nobody knows!, damned if I know!, **it beats me!,** it has me guessing!, it's Greek to me!; **search me!,** you've got me!, I give up!, I pass!, **who knows?,** how should I know?, I don't know what!

## 478. THOUGHT

*(exercise of the intellect)*

.1 NOUNS **thought, thinking, cogitation,** log-(o)–; cerebration, ideation, noesis, mentation, intellection, intellectualization, ratiocination; workings of the mind; **reasoning** 482; **brainwork, headwork,** mental labor or effort, mental act or process, act of thought, mental or intellectual exercise; heavy thinking; straight thinking; conception, conceit [archaic], conceptualization; abstract thought, imageless thought; excogitation, thinking out or through; thinking aloud; **idea** 479; creative thought 535.2.

.2 **consideration, contemplation, reflection, speculation, meditation,** musing, rumination, **deliberation,** lucubration, brooding, study, **pondering,** weighing, revolving, turning over in the mind; advisement, counsel.

.3 **thoughtfulness,** contemplativeness, speculativeness, reflectiveness; **pensiveness,** wistfulness, reverie, musing, melancholy; **preoccupation, absorption, engrossment,** abstraction, brown study, deep or profound thought; **concentration,** study, close study.

.4 **thoughts,** inmost thoughts, secret thoughts, mind's core; **train of thought,** current or flow of thought or ideas, succession or sequence or chain of thought

or ideas; **stream of consciousness; association,** association of ideas.

.5 **mature thought,** developed thought, ripe idea; **afterthought,** *arrière-pensée* [Fr], *esprit d'escalier* [Fr], second thought or thoughts; **reconsideration,** reappraisal, revaluation, rethinking, re-examination, review, thinking over.

.6 **introspection,** self-communion, self-counsel, self-consultation, subjective inspection or speculation.

.7 subject for thought, food for thought, something to chew on, something to get one's teeth into.

.8 VERBS **think, cogitate,** cerebrate, intellectualize, ideate, conceive, conceptualize, form ideas, entertain ideas; **reason** 482.15; **use one's head,** use or exercise the mind, set the brain or wits to work, bethink oneself, put on one's thinking or considering cap [informal].

.9 **think hard,** think one's head off, **rack** or **ransack one's brains,** crack one's brains [informal], **beat** or **cudgel one's brains,** work one's head to the bone, do some heavy thinking, bend or apply the mind; sweat or stew over [informal], hammer or hammer away at; puzzle, **puzzle over.**

.10 **concentrate,** concentrate the mind or thoughts, concentrate on or upon, attend closely to, **focus on** or **upon,** give or devote the mind to, glue the mind to, cleave to the thought of, fix the mind or thoughts upon, bend the mind upon, bring the mind to bear upon; gather or collect one's thoughts, pull one's wits together, focus or fix one's thoughts, marshal or arrange one's thoughts or ideas.

.11 **think about,** cogitate, **give** or **apply the mind to,** put one's mind to, apply oneself to, bend or turn the mind or thoughts to, direct the mind upon, **give thought to, trouble one's head about,** occupy the mind or thoughts with; think through or out, puzzle out, sort out, reason out, excogitate.

.12 **consider, contemplate, speculate, reflect, study, ponder,** perpend, **weigh, deliberate, debate, meditate, muse, brood, ruminate,** chew the cud [informal], digest; introspect, be abstracted; fall into a brown study, retreat into one's mind or thoughts; **toy with, play with,** play around with, flirt or coquet with the idea.

.13 **think over, ponder over, brood over, muse over, mull over, reflect over,** con over, **deliberate over,** run over, **meditate** over, ruminate over, chew over, digest, turn over, **revolve**, revolve in the mind, turn over in the mind, deliberate upon, meditate upon, muse on *or* upon, bestow thought *or* consideration upon.

.14 **take under consideration,** entertain, take under advisement, take under active consideration, inquire into, **think it over,** see about [informal]; **sleep upon,** consult *or* advise with *or* take counsel of one's pillow.

.15 **reconsider, re-examine,** review; revise one's thoughts, reappraise, revaluate, rethink; view in a new light, have second thoughts, think better of.

.16 **think of,** bethink oneself of, **entertain the idea of,** entertain thoughts of; have an idea of, have thoughts about; **have in mind, contemplate, consider;** take it into one's head; **bear in mind, keep in mind,** hold the thought; harbor an idea, keep *or* hold an idea, cherish *or* foster *or* nurse *or* nurture an idea.

.17 (look upon mentally) **contemplate, look upon, view, regard,** see, view with the mind's eye, **envisage,** envision, **visualize** 535.15, imagine, image.

.18 **occur to,** occur to one's mind, occur, **come to mind,** rise to mind, rise in the mind, come into one's head, impinge on one's consciousness, claim one's mind *or* thoughts, pass through one's head *or* mind, dawn upon one, **enter one's mind,** pass in the mind *or* the thoughts, **cross one's mind,** race *or* tumble through the mind, flash on *or* across the mind; **strike,** strike one, strike the mind, grab one [slang], **suggest itself,** present itself, offer itself, present itself to the mind *or* thoughts.

.19 **impress, make an impression, strike,** grab [slang], hit; catch the thoughts, arrest the thoughts, seize one's mind, sink *or* penetrate into the mind, embed itself in the mind, lodge in the mind, **sink in** [informal].

.20 **occupy the mind** *or* **thoughts,** engage the thoughts, monopolize the thoughts, fasten itself on the mind, seize the mind, fill the mind, take up one's thoughts; **preoccupy,** occupy, **absorb, engross,** absorb *or* enwrap *or* engross the thoughts, obsess the mind, run in the head; foster in the mind; come uppermost, be uppermost in the mind; have in *or* on one's mind, **have on the brain** [informal], have constantly in one's thoughts.

.21 ADJS **cognitive,** prehensive, **thought,** conceptive, conceptual, conceptualized, ideative, noetic, mental; **thoughtful,** cogitative, **contemplative, reflective, speculative, deliberative, meditative, ruminative,** ruminant, museful [archaic]; **pensive,** wistful; introspective; thinking, reflecting, contemplating, pondering, deliberating, excogitating, excogitative, meditating, ruminating, musing; sober, serious, deepthinking; concentrating, concentrative.

.22 absorbed *or* engrossed in thought, **absorbed, engrossed,** introspective, rapt, **wrapped in thought, lost in thought,** abstracted, immersed in thought, buried in thought, engaged in thought, occupied, preoccupied.

.23 ADVS **thoughtfully,** contemplatively, reflectively, meditatively, ruminatively, musefully [archaic]; **pensively,** wistfully; on reconsideration, on second thought.

.24 **on one's mind, on the brain** *or* on one's chest [both informal], in the thoughts; in the heart, *in petto* [Ital], in one's inmost thoughts.

## 479. IDEA

.1 NOUNS **idea,** ideo–; **thought,** mental *or* intellectual object, **notion, fancy, concept, conception,** conceit; **perception, impression,** mental impression, image, **mental image,** representation, recept; imago; memory-trace; **sentiment,** apprehension; reflection, observation; **opinion** 501.6; supposition, **theory** 499.

.2 (philosophy) ideatum, ideate; noumenon; universal, universal concept *or* conception; idée-force; Platonic idea *or* form, archetype, prototype, subsistent form, eternal object, transcendent universal, eternal universal, pattern, model, exemplar, ideal, transcendent idea *or* essence, universal essence, innate idea; Aristotelian form, form-giving cause, formal cause; complex idea, simple idea; percept; construct of memory and association; Kantian idea, supreme principle of pure reason, regulative first principle, highest unitary principle of thought, transcendent nonempirical concept; Hegelian idea, highest category, the Absolute, the Absolute Idea, the Self-determined, the realized ideal; noosphere [Teilhard de Chardin]; history of ideas, *Geistesgeschichte* [Ger]; **idealism** 377.3.

.3 **abstract idea, abstraction,** abstract.

.4 **main idea,** leading *or* principal idea, fundamental idea, *idée-maitresse* [Fr], guiding principle, **big idea** [informal].

.5 **novel idea,** new *or* **latest wrinkle** [informal], new slant *or* twist [informal].

.6 **good idea,** not a bad idea; **bright thought,** bright *or* brilliant idea, **brainchild** *or* **brainstorm** [both informal], **inspiration.**

.7 **absurd idea,** crazy idea, fool notion, brainstorm [both informal].

.8 **ideology,** system of ideas, body of ideas, system of theories; world view, *Weltanschauung* [Ger]; philosophy; **ethos.**

.9 ADJS **ideational, ideal, conceptual, notional,** fanciful; **theoretical** 499.13; **ideological.**

.10 **ideaed, notioned,** thoughted.

## 480. ABSENCE OF THOUGHT

.1 NOUNS **thoughtlessness,** thoughtfreeness; **vacuity,** vacancy, **emptiness of mind, empty-headedness,** blankness, mental blankness, blankmindedness; **fatuity,** inanity, foolishness 470; tranquillity, calm of mind; **nirvana;** oblivion; quietism, passivity; blank mind, fallow mind, tabula rasa; unintelligence 469.

.2 VERBS **not think, make the mind a blank,** let the mind lie fallow; **not think of,** not consider, be unmindful of; **not enter one's mind** *or* **head,** be far from one's thoughts.

.3 **get it off one's mind, get it off one's chest** [informal], clear the mind, relieve one's mind; **put it out of one's thoughts,** dismiss from the mind *or* thoughts, push from one's thoughts, put away thought.

.4 ADJS **thoughtless, thoughtfree,** incogitant, **unthinking,** unreasoning; unideaed; **unintellectual; vacuous,** vacant, blank, blankminded, relaxed, empty, **empty-headed,** fatuous, inane 469.19; unoccupied; calm, tranquil; nirvanic; oblivious; quietistic, passive.

.5 **unthought-of, undreamed-of,** unconsidered, unconceived, unconceptualized; unimagined, unimaged; imageless.

## 481. INTUITION

.1 NOUNS **intuition, intuitiveness, sixth sense;** intuitive reason *or* knowledge, direct apprehension, unmediated perception, subconscious perception, unconscious *or* subconscious knowledge, immediate cognition, knowledge without thought *or* reason; **insight,** inspiration, aperçu; anticipation, a priori knowledge; *satori* [Jap], *buddhi* [Skt]; woman's intuition; second sight, second-sightedness,

precognition 542.3, clairvoyance 1034.8; intuitionism, intuitivism.

.2 **instinct,** natural instinct, unlearned capacity, innate *or* inborn proclivity, native *or* natural tendency, **impulse,** blind *or* unreasoning impulse, vital impulse; **libido, id,** primitive self; archetype, archetypal pattern *or* idea; unconscious *or* subconscious urge *or* drive; collective unconscious; "the *not ourselves,* which is in us and all around us" [Matthew Arnold], "an unfathomable Somewhat, which is *Not we*" [Carlyle], "that which is imprinted upon the spirit of man by an inward instinct" [Francis Bacon].

.3 **hunch** [informal], **presentiment, premonition,** preapprehension, intimation, foreboding 544; suspicion, **impression,** intuition, intuitive impression, **feeling,** forefeeling, vague feeling *or* idea, funny feeling [informal], feeling in one's bones.

.4 VERBS **intuit, sense, feel,** feel intuitively, **feel in one's bones** [informal], **have a feeling,** have a funny feeling [informal], **get** *or* **have the impression, have a hunch** [informal], just know, know instinctively.

.5 ADJS **intuitive,** intuitional, sensing, feeling; **second-sighted, precognitive** 542.7, clairvoyant 1034.23.

.6 **instinctive,** natural, **inherent, innate,** unlearned; unconscious, subliminal; **involuntary, automatic,** spontaneous, impulsive; libidinal.

.7 ADVS **intuitively,** by intuition; **instinctively,** automatically, spontaneously, on *or* by instinct.

## 482. REASONING

.1 NOUNS **reasoning, reason,** logical thought, discursive reason, rationalizing, rationalization, ratiocination; **induction,** inductive reasoning, **deduction,** deductive reasoning; rationalism, **rationality,** discourse *or* discourse of reason [both archaic]; sweet reason, reasonableness; demonstration, proof 505; specious reasoning, sophistry 483; philosophy 500.

.2 **logic,** logics, logico–; **dialectics,** dialectic, dialecticism; art of reason, science of discursive thought; formal logic, material logic; doctrine of terms, doctrine of the judgment, doctrine of inference, traditional *or* Aristotelian logic, Ramist *or* Ramistic logic, modern *or* epistemological logic, pragmatic *or* instrumental *or* experimental logic; psychological logic, psychologism; symbolic *or* mathematical logic, logistic; propositional calculus, calculus of individuals, functional calculus, combinatory logic, algebra of relations, algebra of classes, set theory, Boolean algebra.

.3 (methods) a priori reasoning, a fortiori reasoning, a posteriori reasoning; discursive reasoning; **deduction, deductive reasoning,** syllogism, syllogistic reasoning; **induction, inductive reasoning,** epagoge; philosophical induction, inductive *or* Baconian method; **inference; generalization,** particularization; synthesis, analysis; hypothesis and verification.

.4 **argumentation, argument, controversy, dispute, disputation, polemic,** disceptation [archaic], eristic; **contention, wrangling, bickering,** hubbub 453.3, bicker, set-to [informal], rhubarb *or* hassle [both slang], passage of arms; war of words, verbal engagement *or* contest, logomachy, flyting; paper war, *guerre de plume* [Fr]; academic disputation, defense of a thesis; defense, apology, apologia, apologetics; pilpul, casuistry; polemics; litigation.

.5 **argument,** *argumentum* [L]; **case, plea,** pleading, *plaidoyer* [Fr]; special pleading; **reason, consideration; refutation,** elenchus, ignoratio elenchi; pros, cons, **pros and cons;** talking point.

.6 **syllogism;** prosyllogism; mode; figure; mood; pseudosyllogism, paralogism; sorites, progressive *or* Aristotelian sorites, regressive *or* Goclenian sorites; categorical syllogism; enthymeme; dilemma; **rule,** rule of deduction, transformation rule; modus ponens, modus tollens.

.7 **premise, proposition, position,** assumed position, sumption, **assumption,** supposal, presupposition, **hypothesis, thesis, theorem,** lemma, **statement,** affirmation, categorical proposition, assertion, basis, ground, foundation; **postulate, axiom, postulation,** postulatum; data; major premise, minor premise; first principles; a priori principle, apriorism; philosophical proposition, philosopheme; hypothesis ad hoc; sentential *or* propositional function, truth-function, truth table, truth-value.

.8 **conclusion** 494.4.

.9 **reasonableness,** reasonability, **logicalness,** logicality, **rationality, sensibleness, soundness,** justness, justifiability, admissibility; **sense,** common sense, sound sense, sweet reason, **logic, reason;** plausibility 511.3.

.10 **good reasoning, right thinking,** sound reasoning, ironclad reasoning, irrefutable logic; cogent argument, **cogency;** strong argument, knockdown argument; good

case, good reason, sound evidence, strong point.

.11 **reasoner,** ratiocinator, **thinker; rationalist;** rationalizer; **logician,** logistician; logicaster; dialectician; syllogist, syllogizer; sophist 483.6; philosopher 500.6,12,13.

.12 **arguer, controversialist, disputant, debater,** argufier [informal], **wrangler,** mooter, Philadelphia lawyer [informal], guardhouse lawyer [informal], disceptator [archaic], pilpulist, casuist; polemic, polemist, polemicist; logomacher, logomachist; apologist.

.13 **contentiousness,** litigiousness, **quarrelsomeness,** argumentativeness, disputatiousness, combativeness 797.15; ill humor 951.

.14 **side,** interest; **the affirmative,** pro, aye; **the negative,** con, no, nay.

.15 VERBS **reason;** logicalize, logicize; rationalize, provide a rationale; intellectualize; bring reason to bear, apply *or* use reason, put two and two together; **deduce, infer,** generalize; **synthesize, analyze; theorize,** hypothesize; philosophize; syllogize.

.16 **argue,** argufy [informal], **dispute,** discept [archaic], logomachize, polemize, polemicize, moot, **bandy words, chop logic, plead,** pettifog [informal], join issue, give and take, cut and thrust, try conclusions, cross swords, lock horns, **contend, contest,** spar, **bicker, wrangle,** hassle [slang], have it out; thrash out; take one's stand upon, **put up an argument** [informal]; take sides, take up a side; argue to no purpose; **quibble, cavil** 483.9.

.17 **be reasonable, be logical, make sense,** figure [informal], **stand to reason,** be demonstrable, be irrefutable; hold good, hold water [informal]; have a leg to stand on.

.18 ADJS **reasoning, rational,** ratiocinative *or* ratiocinatory; analytic(al).

.19 **argumentative, argumental, dialectic(al), controversial, disputatious, contentious, quarrelsome,** litigious, combative 797.25, ill-humored 951.18–26, eristic(al), polemic(al), logomachic(al), pilpulistic, pro and con.

.20 **logical, reasonable, rational, cogent, sensible, sane, sound,** wholesome, legitimate, just, justifiable, admissible; credible 501.24; plausible 511.7; as it should be, as it ought to be; well-argued, **well-founded, well-grounded.**

.21 **reasoned, advised, considered, calculated,**

meditated, contemplated, deliberated, studied, weighed, thought-out.

.22 dialectic(al), maieutic; syllogistic(al), enthymematic(al), soritical, epagogic, inductive, deductive, inferential, synthetic(al), analytic(al), discursive; a priori, a fortiori, a posteriori; categorical, hypothetical, conditional.

.23 deducible, derivable, infenible; sequential, following.

.24 ADVS reasonably, logically, rationally, by the rules of logic, sensibly, sanely, soundly; syllogistically, analytically; in reason, in all reason, within reason, within the bounds or limits of reason, within reasonable limitations, within bounds, within the bounds of possibility, as far as possible, in all conscience.

## 483. SOPHISTRY

### (specious reasoning)

.1 NOUNS sophistry, sophistication, sophism, philosophism, casuistry, jesuitry, jesuitism, subtlety, oversubtlety; false or specious reasoning, rationalization, evasive reasoning, vicious reasoning, sophistical reasoning, special pleading; fallacy, fallaciousness; speciousness, speciosity, superficial or apparent soundness, plausibleness, plausibility; insincerity, disingenuousness; equivocation, equivocalness; perversion, distortion, misapplication; vicious circle, circularity; mystification, obfuscation, obscurantism.

.2 illogicalness, illogic, illogicality, unreasonableness, irrationality, reasonlessness, senselessness, unsoundness, unscientificness, invalidity, untenableness, inconclusiveness; inconsistency, incongruity, antilogy.

.3 (specious argument) sophism, sophistry, insincere argument, mere rhetoric, philosophism, solecism; paralogism, pseudosyllogism; claptrap, moonshine, empty words, "sound and fury, signifying nothing" [Shakespeare]; bad case, weak point, flaw in an argument, "lame and impotent conclusion" [Shakespeare]; fallacy, logical fallacy, formal fallacy, material fallacy, verbal fallacy; argumentum ad hominem, argumentum ad baculum, argumentum ad captandum, argumentum ad captandum vulgus [all L], crowd-pleasing argument, argument by analogy, tu quoque argument, petitio principii [L], begging the question, circular argument, undis-

tributed middle, non sequitur [L], hysteron proteron [Gk].

.4 quibble, quiddity, quodlibet, quillet [archaic], jesuitism, cavil, quip, quirk, shuffle, dodge.

.5 quibbling, caviling, boggling, captiousness, nit-picking, bickering; logic-chopping, hairsplitting, trichoschistism; subterfuge, chicane, chicanery, pettifoggery; equivocation, tergiversation, prevarication, evasion, hedging, pussyfooting [informal], sidestepping, dodging, shifting, shuffling, fencing, parrying, boggling, paltering.

.6 sophist, sophister, philosophist [archaic], casuist, Jesuit; choplogic [archaic], logic-chopper; paralogist.

.7 quibbler, caviler, pettifogger, hairsplitter, captious or picayune critic, nitpicker; equivocator, mystifier, mystificator, obscurantist, prevaricator, palterer, tergiversator, shuffler, hedger; pussyfoot or pussyfooter [both informal].

.8 VERBS reason speciously, reason ill, paralogize, reason in a circle, argue insincerely, pervert, distort, misapply; rationalize; prove that black is white and white black; not have a leg to stand on.

.9 quibble, cavil, bicker, boggle, chop logic, split hairs, nitpick; equivocate, mystify, obscure, prevaricate, tergiversate, palter, fence, parry, shift, shuffle, dodge, shy, evade, sidestep, hedge, pussyfoot [informal], evade the issue; beat about or around the bush, not come to the point, beg the question; blow hot and cold; strain at a gnat and swallow a camel, pick nits.

.10 ADJS sophistical, sophistic, philosophistic(al) [archaic], casuistic(al), jesuitic(al), fallacious, specious, colorable, plausible, hollow, superficially or apparently sound; deceptive, illusive, empty; overrefined, oversubtle, insincere, disingenuous.

.11 illogical, unreasonable, irrational, reasonless, contrary to reason, senseless, without reason, without rhyme or reason; unscientific, nonscientific, unphilosophical; invalid, inauthentic, unauthentic, faulty, flawed, paralogical, fallacious; inconclusive, inconsequent, inconsequential, not following; inconsistent, incongruous, absonant [archaic], loose, unconnected; contradictory, self-contradictory, self-annulling, self-refuting.

.12 unsound, unsubstantial, insubstantial, weak, feeble, poor, flimsy, unrigorous, inconclusive, unproved, unsustained, poorly argued.

.13 **baseless, groundless,** ungrounded, **unfounded,** ill-founded, unbased, **unsupported,** unsustained, **without foundation,** without basis or sound basis; **untenable, unsupportable,** unsustainable; **unwarranted,** idle, empty, vain.

.14 **quibbling, caviling, equivocatory,** captious, nit-picking [slang], bickering; picayune, petty, trivial, trifling; paltering, shuffling, hedging, pussyfooting [informal], **evasive; hairsplitting,** trichoschistic, logic-chopping, choplogic(al) [archaic].

.15 ADVS **illogically, unreasonably, irrationally, reasonlessly, senselessly;** baselessly, groundlessly; untenably, unsupportably, unsustainably; out of all reason, out of all bounds.

.16 PHRS *post hoc, ergo propter hoc* [L, after this, therefore because of this].

### 484. TOPIC

.1 NOUNS **topic, subject,** subject of thought, **matter, subject matter,** what it is about, **concern,** focus of interest or attention, **theme,** burden, **text,** motif, motive, business at hand, **case,** matter in hand, **question, problem, issue; point,** point at issue, point in question, main point, gist 672.6; item on the agenda; head, heading, chapter, rubric; substance, meat, essence, material part, basis; living issue, topic of the day.

.2 **caption, title, heading, head,** superscription, rubric; **headline;** overline; banner, banner head or line, streamer; **scarehead,** screamer; spread, spreadhead; drop head, dropline, hanger; running head or title, jump head; **subhead, subheading,** subtitle; legend, motto, epigraph; title page.

.3 VERBS **caption, title, head,** head up [informal]; **headline;** subtitle, subhead.

.4 ADJS **topical, thematic.**

### 485. INQUIRY

.1 NOUNS **inquiry,** inquiring, inquirendo, **inquest** 408.18, inquisition; inquiring mind; analysis 48.

.2 **examination,** examen, **exam** [informal], **test, trial, quiz;** oral examination, oral, doctor's oral, master's oral, viva voce examination, viva [informal]; **audition, hearing;** written examination, written [informal], blue book [informal]; midterm, midyear, midsemester; qualifying examination, preliminary examination, prelim [informal]; take-home examination; final

examination, **final** [informal], comprehensive examination, comps [informal], great go [archaic] or greats (Oxford); honors [Brit], tripos (Cambridge).

.3 **examination, inspection, scrutiny,** –opsy; **survey, review, perusal,** perlustration, **study,** look-through, scan, run-through; visitation; overhaul, overhauling; quality control.

.4 **investigation,** indagation [archaic], **research,** legwork [informal], inquiry into; sifting, gathering or amassing evidence; perscrutation, probe, searching investigation, close inquiry, exhaustive study; police inquiry or investigation, criminal investigation, detective work, detection, sleuthing; investigative bureau or agency, bureau or department of investigation; legislative investigation, congressional investigation, hearing; witch-hunt; fishing expedition.

.5 preliminary or tentative examination; quick or cursory inspection, quick look; grope, prod, feel.

.6 **checkup, check;** spot check; physical examination, **physical,** physical checkup, health examination; exploratory examination.

.7 **re-examination,** reinquiry, recheck, **review,** reappraisal, revaluation, rethinking, revision, rebeholding, second or further look.

.8 **reconnaissance;** recce or recco or recon [all slang]; **reconnoitering,** reconnoiter, exploration, **scouting.**

.9 **surveillance,** shadowing, following, trailing, tailing [informal], 24-hour surveillance, observation, stakeout [informal]; **spying, espionage,** espial, **intelligence,** military intelligence, intelligence work, cloak-and-dagger work [informal]; intelligence agency, secret service, secret police; counterespionage, counterintelligence; wiretap, wiretapping, bugging, electronic surveillance.

.10 **question, query, inquiry, demand** [archaic], **interrogation,** interrogatory; interrogative; **problem, issue, topic** 484, case or point in question, bone of contention, controversial point, question before the house, debating point, question or point at issue, **moot point** or case, question mark, *quodlibet* [L]; vexed or knotty question, burning question; leader, leading question; feeler, trial balloon, fishing question; cross-question, rhetorical question; cross-interrogatory; catechism.

.11 **questioning, interrogation, querying,** asking, seeking, pumping, probing, inquiring; **quiz,** quizzing, **examination;** challenge, dispute; interpellation, bringing into question; catechizing, catechization; catechetical method, Socratic method or induction.

.12 **grilling,** the grill [slang], inquisition; police interrogation; **third-degree** [informal]; direct examination, redirect examination, **cross-examination,** cross-interrogation, **cross-questioning.**

.13 **canvass, survey, inquiry, questionnaire,** questionary; poll, **public-opinion poll,** opinion poll or survey, statistical survey, opinion sampling, voter-preference survey, consumer-preference survey; consumer research.

.14 **search,** searching, **quest, hunt,** hunting, stalk, stalking, still hunt, dragnet, frisk [slang]; posse, search party; search warrant; search-and-destroy operation or mission; **rummage,** ransacking, turning over or upside down; **forage;** house-search, perquisition, domiciliary visit; exploration, probe.

.15 **inquirer, asker, prober,** querier, querist, **questioner,** questionist, interrogator; interrogatrix; interpellator; **quizzer,** examiner, catechist; inquisitor, inquisitionist; cross-questioner, cross-interrogator, **cross-examiner;** interlocutor; **pollster,** poller, sampler, opinion-sampler; **interviewer; detective** 781.10; **secret agent** 781.9.

.16 **examiner,** examinant, **tester; inspector,** scrutinizer, scrutator; scrutineer, quality-control inspector, check-out pilot; observer; visitor, visitator; **investigator,** indagator [archaic].

.17 **seeker, hunter, searcher,** perquisitor; rummager, ransacker; digger, delver; zetetic; **researcher,** researchist, research worker.

.18 **examinee,** examinant, examinate, questionee, quizzee; informant, subject, interviewee; witness.

.19 VERBS **inquire, ask, question, query; make inquiry,** take up or institute or pursue or follow up or conduct or carry on an inquiry, ask about, ask questions, put queries; inquire of, require an answer, ask a question, put a question to, pose or set or propose or propound a question; bring into question, interpellate; **demand** [archaic], **want to know.**

.20 **interrogate, question, query, quiz, test, examine;** catechize; **pump,** pump for information, shoot questions at, pick the brains of, worm out of; **interview.**

.21 **grill,** put on the grill [informal], inquisi-

tion, make inquisition; roast [informal], put the pressure on [informal], put the screws to, go over [both slang]; **cross-examine, cross-question,** cross-interrogate; **third-degree** [slang], put through the third degree [informal]; put to the question; extract information, pry or prize out.

.22 **investigate,** indagate [archaic], **sift, explore, look into,** peer into, **search into,** go into, **delve into,** dig into, poke into, pry into; **probe, sound, plumb, fathom.**

.23 **examine, inspect, scrutinize, survey,** canvass, **look at,** peer at, **observe, scan, peruse, study; look over,** run the eye over, cast or pass the eyes over, go over, run over, pass over, pore over; overlook, overhaul; **monitor, review,** pass under review; set an examination, give an examination; **take stock of,** size or size up, take the measure [informal]; **check, check out, check over** or **through; check up on;** autopsy, postmortem 408.18.

.24 **make a close study of, scrutinize,** examine thoroughly, vet [Brit], **go deep into,** look closely at; examine point by point, go over step by step, subject to close scrutiny, view or try in all its phases, get down to nuts and bolts [informal]; perscrutate, perlustrate.

.25 **examine cursorily,** take a cursory view of, give a quick or cursory look, give a dekko [Brit slang], **scan, skim, skim over** or **through,** slur, slur over, slip or skip over or through, **glance at,** give the once-over [slang], pass over lightly, zip through, **dip into, touch upon,** touch upon lightly or in passing, **hit the high spots; thumb through,** flip through the pages, turn over the leaves, leaf or page through.

.26 **re-examine, recheck,** reinquire, **reconsider,** reappraise, revaluate, rethink, **review,** revise, rebehold, take another or a second or a further look; retrace, retrace one's steps, go back over.

.27 **reconnoiter,** make a reconnaissance, case [informal], scout, **scout out,** spy, **spy out,** play the spy, peep; **watch,** put under surveillance, stake out [informal]; bug.

.28 **canvass, survey,** make a survey; **poll,** conduct a poll, sample, **questionnaire** [informal].

.29 **seek, hunt, look** [archaic], **quest, pursue,** go in pursuit of, follow, go in search of, prowl after, see to, try to find; **look up, hunt up; look for,** look around or about for, **search for,** seek for, **hunt for,** cast or beat about for, **fish for, angle for,** bob for, dig for, delve for; **ask for,** inquire for; **gun for,** go gunning for; still-hunt [informal].

.30 **search, hunt, explore;** research; **hunt through, search through, look through, go through;** dig, delve, burrow, root, poke, pry; **look round** or around, poke around, nose around, smell around; beat the bushes; forage; frisk [slang].

.31 **grope,** grope for, **feel for,** fumble, grabble, scrabble, feel around, poke around, pry around, beat about, grope in the dark; **feel** or **pick one's way.**

.32 **ransack, rummage, rake, scour, comb;** rifle; **look everywhere,** look into every hole and corner, **look high and low,** look upstairs and downstairs, **look all over,** look all over hell [slang], search high heaven, turn upside down, turn inside out, **leave no stone unturned;** shake down or shake or toss [all slang].

.33 **search out, hunt out, spy out,** scout out, **ferret out,** fish out, pry out, dig out, root out, grub up.

.34 **trace, stalk, track, trail; follow,** follow up, shadow, tail [informal], dog the footsteps of; nose, nose out, **smell** or **sniff out,** follow the trail or scent or spoor of; follow a clue; **trace down, hunt down, track down, run down,** run to earth.

.35 ADJS **inquiring, questioning, querying,** quizzing; **quizzical, curious; interrogatory,** interrogative, interrogational; **inquisitorial,** inquisitional; catechistic(al), catechetic(al).

.36 **examining,** examinational; examinatorial; **testing,** trying, **tentative;** groping, feeling; **inspectional;** inspectorial; **investigative,** indagative [archaic]; zetetic; heuristic, investigatory, investigational; **exploratory,** explorative, explorational; **fact-finding;** analytic(al).

.37 **searching, probing, prying, nosy** [informal]; poking, digging, fishing, delving; in search or quest of, looking for, **out for,** on the lookout for, **in the market for,** loaded or out for bear [informal]; all-searching.

.38 ADVS **in question, at issue,** in debate or dispute, **under consideration,** under active consideration, **under advisement,** sub judice [L], under examination, under investigation, under surveillance, up or open for discussion; **before the house, on the docket, on the agenda, on the table, on the floor.**

## 486. ANSWER

.1 NOUNS **answer, reply, response,** responsory, responsion, replication; **answering,** respondence; riposte or repost, **retort, rejoinder,** reaction 284, **return, comeback** [slang], back answer, short answer, back talk; **repartee,** backchat, clever or ready or witty reply or retort, snappy comeback [slang]; yes-and-no answer, evasive reply; **acknowledgment,** receipt; rescript, rescription; antiphon; **echo,** reverberation 454.2.

.2 **rebuttal, counterstatement,** counterreply, counterclaim, counterblast, counteraccusation, countercharge, tu quoque [L, you too], contraremonstrance; **rejoinder,** replication, defense, rebutter, surrebutter or surrebuttal, surrejoinder; confutation, refutation.

.3 **answerer, replier, responder, respondent,** responser.

.4 VERBS **answer,** make or give answer, return answer, return for answer, **reply, respond,** say, say in reply; **retort,** riposte, **rejoin,** return, flash back; **come back** or come back at or come right back at [all slang], answer back or talk back [informal], shoot back [informal]; **react; acknowledge,** make or give acknowledgment; echo, reecho, reverberate 454.7.

.5 **rebut,** make a rebuttal; **rejoin,** surrebut, surrejoin; **counterclaim, countercharge;** confute, refute.

.6 ADJS **answering, replying, responsive,** respondent, responding; rejoining, returning; antiphonal; echoing, echoic, reechoing 454.11; confutative, refutative.

.7 ADVS **in answer, in reply, in response, in return,** in rebuttal.

## 487. SOLUTION

*(answer to a problem)*

.1 NOUNS **solution, resolution, answer, reason, explanation** 552.4; **finding,** determination, ascertainment; **outcome, upshot,** denouement, **result,** issue, end 70, end result, accomplishment 722; **solving,** working, **working-out,** finding-out, resolving, **clearing up,** cracking; **unriddling,** riddling, unscrambling, unraveling, sorting out, untwisting, unspinning, unweaving, untangling, disentanglement; **decipherment,** decoding; interpretation 552.

.2 VERBS **solve, resolve,** find the solution or answer, **clear up,** get, get right, do, work, **work out, find out, figure out,** dope or dope out [both slang]; **sort out,** puzzle out; debug; psych *or* psych out [both slang]; **unriddle**, riddle, unscramble, undo, untangle, disentangle, untwist, unspin, unweave, unravel, ravel, ravel out; **decipher, decode, crack; make out,** interpret 552.9; **answer, explain** 552.10; unlock, pick *or* open the lock; find the key of, find a clue to; **get to the bottom of, fathom**, plumb, bottom; have it, hit it, hit upon a solution, hit the nail on the head, hit it on the nose [informal]; guess, divine, guess right.

.3 ADJS **solvable**, soluble, **resolvable**, open to solution, capable of solution, workable, doable, answerable; explainable, explicable, determinable, ascertainable; **decipherable,** decodable.

## 488. DISCOVERY

.1 NOUNS discovery, **finding**, finding out, determining; **detection**, spotting, catching, espial; recognition, determination, distinguishment; **locating, location; disclosure, exposure,** revelation, **uncovering**, unearthing, exhumation, excavation, bringing to light; **find,** trove, treasure trove, *trouvaille* [Fr], strike, lucky strike; accidental *or* chance discovery, casual discovery; serendipity; rediscovery; invention 167.5.

.2 VERBS **discover, find, find out, determine**, get; strike, hit; put *or* lay one's hands on, lay one's fingers on, **locate** 184.10; **hunt down**, trace down, track down, **run down, run to earth**; trace; rediscover; invent 167.13.

.3 **come across, run across, meet with,** meet up with [informal], fall in with, **encounter, run into,** bump into [informal], come *or* run up against [informal], **come on** *or* **upon, hit upon,** light upon, alight upon, tumble on; **chance upon, happen upon, stumble on** *or* **upon,** stub one's toe upon, blunder upon, discover serendipitously.

.4 **uncover, unearth,** disinter, exhume, excavate; **disclose,** expose, reveal, **bring to light; turn up,** dig up, root up, fish up; worm out, ferret out.

.5 **detect, spot** [informal], **spy,** espy, descry, sense, pick up, notice, discern, see, **perceive, make out, recognize,** distinguish, identify.

.6 **scent,** catch the scent of, sniff, smell, **get wind of;** sniff *or* scent *or* smell out, nose out; be on the right scent, be near the truth, be warm [informal], burn [informal].

.7 **catch,** catch out; catch off side, catch off base; catch tripping, **catch napping, catch off-guard** *or* off one's guard, catch asleep at the switch; **catch at,** catch in the act, **catch red-handed,** catch in *flagrante delicto,* **catch with one's pants down** [slang], catch flat-footed, have the goods on [slang].

.8 (detect the hidden nature of) **see through, penetrate,** see as it really is, see in its true colors, see the inside of, see the cloven hoof; open the eyes to, tumble to, catch on to, wise up to [informal]; **be on to, be wise to, be hep to** [slang], have one's measure, **have one's number,** have dead to rights [slang].

.9 **turn up, show up,** be found; discover itself, expose *or* betray itself; hang out [slang]; materialize, **come to light,** come out; come along, come to hand.

.10 ADJS on the right scent, **on the right track,** on the trail of; **hot** *or* **warm** [both informal]; **discoverable,** determinable, findable, **detectable,** spottable, disclosable, exposable, locatable, **discernible.**

.11 INTERJS **eureka!,** I have it!, at last!, at long last!, finally!, *thalassa!, thalatta!* [both Gk].

## 489. EXPERIMENT

.1 NOUNS **experiment, experimentation,** empirio– *or* empirico–; experimental method; testing, trying, **trial;** research and development, R and D; **trial and error,** hit and miss, cut and try [informal]; empiricism, experimentalism, pragmatism, instrumentalism; **rule of thumb;** tentativeness, tentative method; control experiment, controlled experiment, **control;** experimental design; experimental proof *or* verification; noble experiment.

.2 **test, trial, try;** essay; docimasy [archaic], assay; determination, blank determination; **proof,** verification; touchstone, standard, criterion 490.2; crucial test; acid test; ordeal, crucible; probation; **feeling out, sounding out,** kiteflying; test case; first *or* rough draft, *brouillon* [Fr]; rough sketch.

.3 **tryout** *or* **workout** [both informal]; **rehearsal,** practice; pilot plan *or* program; **dry run;** *Gedankenexperiment* [Ger]; road test; **trial run,** practical test; shakedown, shakedown cruise, bench test; flight test, test flight *or* run; audition, hearing.

.4 **feeler, probe,** sound, sounder; **trial balloon,** *ballon d'essai* [Fr], pilot balloon, barometer; weather vane, weathercock;

straw to show the wind, straw vote; sample, random sample, experimental sample.

.5 **laboratory, lab** [informal], research laboratory, research establishment *or* facility, experiment station, field station, research and development *or* R and D establishment; think tank [informal], **proving ground.**

.6 **experimenter,** experimentist, experimentalist, **researcher,** research worker, R and D worker; experimental engineer; **tester,** tryer-out, test driver, test pilot; essayer; assayer; analyst, analyzer.

.7 **experimentee,** testee, patient, **subject,** laboratory animal, experimental *or* test animal, **guinea pig.**

.8 VERBS **experiment,** experimentalize, **research,** make an experiment, **run an experiment,** run a sample *or* specimen; **test, try,** essay, cut and try [informal], **test** *or* **try out,** have a dry run *or* rehearsal *or* test run; put to the test, **put to the proof, prove, verify,** validate, substantiate, confirm, put to trial, bring to test, make a trial of, give a trial to; **give a try,** have a go, give it a go [informal]; sample, taste; assay; play around with [informal], fool around with [slang]; try out under controlled conditions; give a tryout *or* workout [informal], **road-test,** shake down; try one out, put one through his paces; experiment *or* practice upon; try it on; try on, try it for size [informal]; try one's strength, see what one can do.

.9 **sound out, feel out, sound,** get a sounding *or* reading *or* sense, probe, **feel the pulse,** read; **put** *or* **throw out a feeler,** send up a trial balloon, fly a kite; **see which way the wind blows,** see how the land lies; take a straw vote, take a random sample, use an experimental sample.

.10 **stand the test, stand up, hold up, hold up in the wash,** pass, **pass muster,** get by [informal], hack it [slang], meet *or* satisfy requirements.

.11 ADJS **experimental, test, trial;** pilot; testing, proving, trying; probative, probatory; verificatory; probationary; **tentative,** provisional; empirical; trial-and-error, hit-or-miss, cut-and-try; heuristic.

.12 **tried, tested, proved,** verified, confirmed, tried and true.

.13 ADVS **experimentally,** by rule of thumb, by trial and error, by hit and miss, hit or miss, by guess and by God.

.14 **on trial,** under examination, **on** *or* **under probation,** under suspicion, **on approval.**

## 490. MEASUREMENT

.1 NOUNS **measurement, measure,** –metry; mensuration, measuring, gauging; admeasurement; metage; **estimation,** estimate, rough measure, approximation; **quantification,** quantitation, quantization; **appraisal,** appraisement, **assessment,** determination, rating, valuation, evaluation; assizement, assize; **survey,** surveying; triangulation; **instrumentation;** telemetry, telemetering; metric system; English system of measurement; calibration, correction; computation, calculation 87.3.

.2 **measure, gauge,** barometer, **rule, yardstick,** measuring rod *or* stick, **standard,** norm, canon, **criterion,** test, touchstone, check; **pattern,** model, type; **scale,** graduated *or* calibrated scale; meter-reading, reading, readout, value, degree, quantity; parameter.

.3 **extent** (quantity) 28, (degree) 29, (size) 195, (distance) 199, (length) 202, (breadth) 204; **weight** 352.

.4 (measuring device) **measure,** measurer, **gauge,** gauger; **meter;** instrument.

.5 (measures) US liquid measure, British imperial liquid measure, US dry measure, British imperial dry measure, apothecaries' measure, linear measure, square measure, circular measure, cubic measure, volume measure, surface measure, surveyor's measure, land measure, board measure.

.6 **coordinates,** Cartesian coordinates, rectangular coordinates, polar coordinates, cylindrical coordinates, spherical coordinates, equator coordinates; latitude, longitude; altitude, azimuth; declination, right ascension; ordinate, abscissa.

.7 **waterline;** watermark, tidemark, floodmark, **high-water mark;** load waterline, load line mark, Plimsoll mark *or* line.

.8 **measurability,** mensurability, computability, determinability, quantifiability.

.9 (science of measurement) **mensuration;** metrology; **geodesy,** geodetics, geodetic engineering; **surveying;** oceanography, bathymetry; topography, cartography, chorography; cadastration; planimetry; stereometry; goniometry; hypsometry, hypsography, altimetry; craniometry; biometry, biometrics; psychometry; psychometrics.

.10 **measurer,** meter, gauger; **geodesist,** geodetic engineer; **surveyor,** land surveyor, quantity surveyor; topographer, cartographer, oceanographer, chorographer; ap-

**praiser, assessor;** assayer; valuer, valuator, evaluator; estimator.

.11 VERBS **measure, gauge, quantify,** mete [archaic], take the measure of, mensurate, triangulate, apply the yardstick to; quantize; **estimate,** make an approximation; assess, **rate, appraise, valuate, value,** evaluate, appreciate, prize; assay; size *or* size up [both informal], take the dimensions of; **weigh** 352.10; survey; plumb, probe, sound, fathom; span, pace, step; calibrate, graduate; divide; caliper, dial; meter; read the meter, take a reading, check a parameter; compute, calculate 87.11.

.12 **measure off, mark off, lay off,** set off, rule off; **step off,** pace off; **measure out,** mark out, lay out.

.13 ADJS **measuring, metric(al),** mensural, mensurative, mensurational; valuative, valuational; **quantitative,** numerative; approximative, estimative; geodetic(al), geodesic(al), hypsographic(al), hypsometric(al); topographic(al), chorographic(al), cartographic(al), oceanographic(al).

.14 **measured, gauged,** metered, **quantified;** quantized; **appraised, assessed, valuated,** valued; **assayed; surveyed,** plotted, mapped, admeasured, triangulated; known by measurement.

.15 **measurable,** mensurable, **quantifiable,** numerable, meterable, gaugeable, fathomable, **determinable,** computable, calculable; quantizable; estimable; assessable, appraisable; appreciable, perceptible, noticeable.

.16 ADVS **measurably, appreciably, perceptibly, noticeably.**

.17 **linear measures**

| | |
|---|---|
| absolute angstrom | footstep |
| Admiralty mile | furlong, fur. |
| angstrom, angstrom unit, a. *or* å. *or* A. *or* Å. | hand |
| | handbreadth, handsbreadth |
| arpent | hectometer, hm. |
| astronomical unit | inch, in. |
| block | international ang- |
| board foot, bd. ft. | strom |
| cable length | kilometer, km. |
| centimeter, cm. | land mile |
| chain, Gunter's chain, chn. | league |
| | light-year |
| cubit | line |
| decameter, dekameter, dkm. | link, li. |
| | meter, m. |
| decimeter, dm. | micron, $\mu$ |
| ell | mil |
| em | mile, mi. |
| en | millimeter, mm. |
| fathom, fthm. | millimicron, micromil- |
| fingerbreadth, finger | limeter |
| foot, ft. | myriameter, mym. |

| | |
|---|---|
| nail | point, pt. |
| nautical mile, naut. mi. | pole, p. |
| | rod, r. |
| pace | statute mile, stat. mi. |
| palm | step |
| parsec | stride |
| perch | wavelength |
| pica | yard, yd. |

.18 **area measures**

| | |
|---|---|
| acre, a. *or* ac. | rood |
| are, a. | section, sec. |
| arpent | square inch, foot, |
| centare, ca. | mile, etc. |
| hectare, ha. | square meter, kilome- |
| perch | ter, etc. |
| pole, p. | township |

.19 **volume measures**

| | |
|---|---|
| barrel | gill, gi. |
| bushel, bu. | hectoliter, hl. |
| centiliter, cl. | hogshead, hhd. |
| cord, cd. | jeroboam |
| cubic foot, yard, etc. | jigger |
| cubic meter | kiloliter, kl. |
| cup | liquid pint, quart, etc. |
| decaliter, dekaliter, dkl. | liter, l. |
| | magnum |
| decastere, dks. | milliliter, ml. |
| deciliter, dl. | minim, min. |
| drop | peck, pk. |
| dry pint, quart, etc. | pint, pt. |
| fifth | pony |
| finger | quart, qt. |
| fluidounce, fl. oz. | stere, s. |
| fluidram, fl. dr. | tablespoon, tbs. |
| gallon, gal. | teaspoon, ts. |

.20 **gauges**

| | |
|---|---|
| alidade | micrometer caliper |
| calipers | octant |
| chain | plumb 209.17 |
| compass | plumb rule |
| dial | precision block |
| dipstick | protractor |
| dividers | quadrant |
| engineer's chain | rod |
| feeler gauge | rule |
| foot rule | ruler |
| gauge block | scale |
| goniometer | sector |
| gradiometer | set square |
| graduated scale | sextant |
| graduated tape | size stick |
| Gunter's *or* surveyor's chain | spirit level |
| | square |
| Gunter's scale | tape, tapeline, tape |
| Johansson block, Jo block | measure |
| | theodolite |
| level | transit |
| line | transit theodolite |
| log | try square |
| log line | T square |
| measuring machine | vernier |
| meterstick | vernier caliper |
| micrometer | yardstick |

## 491. COMPARISON

.1 NOUNS **comparison, compare,** examining side by side, matching, proportion [archaic], comparative judgment *or* estimate;

likening, comparing, **analogy;** parallelism; comparative relation; weighing, balancing; opposing, opposition, **contrast;** contrastiveness, distinctiveness, distinction 492.3; confrontment, confrontation; **relation** 9; correlation 13; simile, similitude, metaphor, allegory, figure *or* trope of comparison; comparative degree; comparative method; comparative linguistics, comparative grammar, comparative literature, comparative anatomy, etc.

.2 **collation,** comparative scrutiny, point-by-point comparison; **verification, confirmation, checking;** check, cross-check.

.3 **comparability,** comparableness, comparativeness; analogousness, equivalence, commensurability; proportionateness *or* proportionability [both archaic]; ratio, proportion, balance; **similarity** 20.

.4 VERBS **compare, liken,** assimilate, similize, liken to, compare with; **make** *or* **draw a comparison,** run a comparison, do a comparative study, bring into comparison; analogize, bring into analogy; **relate** 9.6; metaphorize; **draw a parallel,** parallel; **match;** examine side by side, view together; weigh *or* measure against; confront, **contrast, oppose,** set in opposition, set off against, set in contrast, **put** *or* **set over against,** place against, counterpose, set over against one another, set against one another; compare and contrast, note similarities and differences; **weigh,** balance.

.5 **collate,** scrutinize comparatively, compare point by point, painstakingly match; **verify, confirm, check, cross-check.**

.6 **compare notes,** exchange views *or* observations, match data *or* findings.

.7 be **comparable, compare, compare to** *or* **with,** not compare with 21.2, admit of comparison, be commensurable, be of the same order, be worthy of comparison, be fit to be compared; **measure up to, come up to,** match up with, stack up with [informal], hold a candle to [informal]; **match, parallel;** vie, vie with, rival; **resemble** 20.7.

.8 ADJS **comparative, relative** 9.7, **comparable,** commensurate, commensurable, parallel, matchable, **analogous;** analogical; collatable; **correlative** 13.10; much at one, much of a muchness [informal]; **similar** 20.10.

.9 **incomparable,** incommensurable, not to be compared, of different orders; **unlike, dissimilar** 21.4.

.10 ADVS **comparatively, relatively; comparably.**

.11 PREPS **compared to, compared with,** as compared with, by comparison with, **in comparison with, beside,** over against, taken with; than.

## 492. DISCRIMINATION

.1 NOUNS **discrimination,** discriminateness, discriminatingness, discriminativeness; seeing *or* making distinctions, appreciation of differences; analytic power *or* faculty; **criticalness; finesse,** refinement, delicacy; niceness of distinction, nicety, subtlety, refined discrimination, critical niceness; **tact, tactfulness,** feel, feeling, sense, **sensitivity** 422.3, **sensibility** 422.2; appreciation, appreciativeness; judiciousness 467.7; taste, discriminating taste, aesthetic *or* artistic judgment; palate, fine *or* refined palate, connoisseurship, selectiveness, fastidiousness 896.

.2 **discernment,** critical discernment, penetration, **perception,** perceptiveness, **insight,** perspicacity; **flair; judgment,** acumen 467.4.

.3 **distinction,** contradistinction, distinctiveness [archaic]; **distinguishment, differentiation** 16.4, separation, division, segregation, demarcation; nice *or* subtle distinction, **nuance,** shade of difference, microscopic distinction; hairsplitting, trichoschistism.

.4 VERBS **be discriminating,** exercise discrimination; **be tactful,** show *or* exercise tact; be tasteful, use one's palate, pick and choose; use advisedly.

.5 **discriminate, distinguish,** contradistinguish, **separate,** divide, analyze, subdivide, **segregate,** sever, severalize, **differentiate,** demark, demarcate, mark the interface, set off, **set apart,** sift, sift out, sieve, sieve out, winnow, screen, screen out, sort, sort out; **pick out, select** 637.14; separate the sheep from the goats, separate the men from the boys, separate the wheat from the tares *or* chaff, winnow the chaff from the wheat; **draw the line,** fix *or* set a limit; **split hairs,** make a fine *or* nice *or* subtle distinction, subtilize.

.6 **make a distinction,** draw distinctions, **distinguish between,** appreciate differences, see nuances *or* shades of difference, see the difference, tell apart, tell one thing from another, know which is which, know what's what [informal], "know a hawk from a handsaw" [Shakespeare], know one's ass from one's elbow [slang].

.7 ADJS **discriminating, discriminate,** discriminative, selective; **tactful, sensitive** 422.14; appreciative; **critical;** distinctive [archaic], **distinguishing;** differential; precise, accurate, exact; nice, fine, delicate, subtle, refined; fastidious 896.9.

.8 **discerning, perceptive** 422.13, perspicacious, insightful; **astute, judicious** 467.16, 19.

.9 ADVS **discriminatingly,** discriminatively, discriminately; with finesse; **tactfully; tastefully.**

## 493. INDISCRIMINATION

.1 NOUNS **indiscrimination,** indiscriminateness, undiscriminatingness, undiscriminativeness, unselectiveness, **uncriticalness, unparticularness;** syncretism; unfastidiousness; lack of refinement, coarseness *or* crudeness *or* crudity of intellect; **casualness,** promiscuousness, **promiscuity; indiscretion,** indiscreetness, **imprudence** 470.2; **untactfulness,** tactlessness, lack of feeling, **insensitivity,** insensibility 423, unmeticulousness, unpreciseness 534.4.

.2 **indistinction,** indistinctness, vagueness 445.2; uniformity 17; **indistinguishableness,** undistinguishableness, indiscernibility; a distinction without a difference.

.3 VERBS **confound, confuse,** mix, muddle, tumble, jumble, jumble together, **blur,** blur distinctions, overlook distinctions.

.4 **use loosely,** use unadvisedly.

.5 ADJS **undiscriminating, indiscriminate,** indiscriminative, undiscriminative, undifferentiating, unselective; wholesale, general, blanket; **uncritical,** uncriticizing, undemanding, nonjudgmental; **unparticular,** unfastidious; unsubtle; **casual, promiscuous;** unexacting, unmeticulous 534.13; **indiscreet,** undiscreet, **imprudent** 470.9; **untactful,** tactless, insensitive.

.6 **indistinguishable,** undistinguishable, undistinguished, indiscernible, **indistinct,** indistinctive, **without distinction,** not to be distinguished, undiscriminated, undifferentiated, **alike,** six of one and half a dozen of the other [informal]; standard, interchangeable, stereotyped, uniform 17.5.

## 494. JUDGMENT

.1 NOUNS **judgment,** judging, adjudgment, adjudication, judicature, deeming [archaic]; arbitrament, arbitration 805.2; good judgment 467.7; **choice** 637; **discrimination** 492.

.2 **criticism, censure** 969.3; **approval** 968; cri-

tique, review, notice, critical notice, report, comment; book review, literary criticism, critical journal, critical bibliography.

.3 **estimate, estimation; view, opinion** 501.6; assessment, assessing, **appraisal,** appraisement, appraising, appreciation, reckoning, valuation, valuing, **evaluation,** evaluating, evaluative criticism, analyzing, weighing, gauging, ranking, **rating;** measurement 490.

.4 **conclusion, deduction, inference,** consequence, consequent, corollary; derivation, illation; induction.

.5 **verdict, decision,** resolution [archaic], **determination, finding;** diagnosis, prognosis; **decree, ruling,** consideration, order, **pronouncement,** deliverance; **award,** action, **sentence; condemnation,** doom; dictum; precedent.

.6 **judge,** judger, adjudicator, justice; arbiter 1002.1; referee, umpire.

.7 **critic,** criticizer; connoisseur, *cognoscente* [Ital]; literary critic, man of letters; textual critic; editor; social critic, muckraker; captious critic, smellfungus, caviler, carper, faultfinder; criticaster, criticule, critickin; **censor,** censurer; **reviewer, commentator,** commenter; scholiast, annotator.

.8 VERBS **judge,** exercise judgment *or* the judgment; adjudge, adjudicate; be judicious *or* judgmental; **consider, regard,** hold, **deem, esteem, count, account,** think of; allow [dial], **suppose, presume** 499.9,10, opine, form an opinion, give *or* pass *or* express an opinion.

.9 **estimate,** form an estimate, make an estimation; **reckon,** call, guess, figure [informal]; **assess, appraise,** give an appreciation, **gauge, rate, rank,** class, mark, **value, evaluate,** valuate, place *or* set a value on, prize, appreciate; size up *or* take one's measure [informal], **measure** 490.11.

.10 **conclude,** draw a conclusion, **come to** *or* **arrive at a conclusion; find; deduce, derive,** take as proved *or* demonstrated, extract, **gather,** collect, glean, fetch; **infer,** draw an inference; induce; **reason,** reason that; put two and two together.

.11 **decide, determine; find,** ascertain; resolve; **settle,** fix; make a decision, come to a decision, **make up one's mind,** settle one's mind.

.12 **sit in judgment,** hold the scales, hold court; **hear,** give a hearing to; **try** 1004.17; referee, umpire, officiate; arbitrate 805.6.

.13 **pass judgment,** utter a judgment, deliver

*or* pronounce judgment; agree on a verdict, return a verdict, **bring in a verdict, find,** find for *or* against; pronounce on, act on, **pronounce,** report, **rule,** decree, order; **sentence,** pass sentence, doom, condemn.

.14 **criticize,** critique; **censure** 969.13,14; **review;** comment upon, annotate; moralize upon.

.15 **rank, rate,** count, be regarded, be thought of, be in one's estimation.

.16 ADJS **judicial, judiciary,** judicative, judgmental; juridic(al), juristic(al); **judicious** 467.19; **critical** 969.24.

.17 ADVS **all things considered, on the whole, taking one thing with another,** on balance, taking everything into consideration *or* account; everything being equal, other things being equal, *ceteris paribus* [L], taking into account, considering, after all, this being so; therefore, wherefore; *sub judice* [L], in court, before the bench *or* bar *or* court.

## 495. PREJUDGMENT

.1 NOUNS **prejudgment,** prejudication, forejudgment; **preconception, presumption, presupposition,** presupposal, presurmise, preapprehension, prenotion, **prepossession; predilection,** predisposition; preconsideration, **predetermination,** predecision, preconclusion, premature judgment; *parti pris* [Fr], **prejudice** 527.3.

.2 VERBS **prejudge,** forejudge; **preconceive, presuppose, presume,** presurmise; **be predisposed;** predecide, predetermine, preconclude, judge beforehand *or* prematurely, judge before the evidence is in, **jump to a conclusion,** go off half-cocked *or* at half cock [informal], jump the gun [slang].

.3 ADJS **prejudged,** forejudged, **preconceived,** preconceptual, **presumed, presupposed,** presurmised; **predetermined,** predecided, preconcluded, judged beforehand *or* prematurely; **predisposed,** predispositional; prejudicial, prejudging, prejudicative.

## 496. MISJUDGMENT

.1 NOUNS **misjudgment,** poor judgment, error in judgment, warped *or* skewed judgment; **miscalculation,** miscomputation, **misreckoning, misestimation,** misappreciation, misevaluation, misvaluation, misconjecture, wrong impression; **misreading,** wrong construction, misconstruction,

misinterpretation 553; error 518; injudiciousness 470.2.

.2 VERBS **misjudge,** judge amiss, **miscalculate, misestimate, misreckon,** misappreciate, misevaluate, misvalue, miscompute, misdeem, misesteem, misthink, misconjecture; misconstrue, **misinterpret** 553.2; err 518.9; fly in the face of facts; put the wrong construction on things, get a wrong impression, misread the situation *or* case.

## 497. OVERESTIMATION

.1 NOUNS **overestimation,** overestimate, **overreckoning,** overcalculation, **overrating,** overassessment, overvaluation, overappraisal; overreaction; **overstatement, exaggeration** 617.

.2 VERBS **overestimate, overreckon,** overcalculate, overcount, overmeasure, **overrate,** overassess, overappraise, overesteem, **overvalue,** overprize, think *or* make too much of, idealize, see only the good points of; overreact to; **overstate, exaggerate** 617.3.

.3 ADJS **overestimated, overrated,** puffed up, overvalued, on the high side; **exaggerated** 617.4.

## 498. UNDERESTIMATION

.1 NOUNS **underestimation,** misestimation, underestimate, **underrating,** underreckoning, undervaluation, misprizing, misprizal, misprision; **belittlement, depreciation,** deprecation, **minimization,** disparagement 971.

.2 VERBS **underestimate,** misestimate, **underrate,** underreckon, **undervalue,** underprize, **misprize; make little of,** attach little importance to, not do justice to, sell short, think little of, make *or* think nothing of, set little by, miss on the low side, set no store by, set at naught, make light of, shrug off; depreciate, minimize, belittle, deprecate, disparage 971.8.

.3 ADJS **underestimated, underrated,** undervalued, on the low side; unvalued, unprized.

## 499. THEORY, SUPPOSITION

.1 NOUNS **theory, theorization,** *theoria* [Gk]; theoretics, theoretic, theoric [archaic]; **speculation,** mere theory; doctrinairism, doctrinality, doctrinarity; analysis, **explanation,** abstraction; theoretical basis *or* justification.

.2 **theory, explanation,** proposed *or* tentative explanation, statement covering the facts or evidence; body of theory, theoretical structure *or* construct; unified theory.

.3 **supposition, supposal,** supposing; **presupposition,** presupposal; **assumption, presumption, conjecture, inference, surmise,** guesswork; **hypothesis,** working hypothesis; **postulate,** postulation, *postulatum* [L], set of postulates; **proposition, thesis,** premise 482.7; **axiom** 517.2.

.4 **guess, conjecture,** unverified supposition, perhaps, **speculation, surmise;** hunch [informal]; shot *or* stab [both informal]; rough guess, wild guess, blind guess, bold conjecture, shot in the dark [informal].

.5 (vague supposition) **suggestion,** bare suggestion, **suspicion, inkling, hint, intimation, impression, notion,** mere notion, sneaking suspicion [informal], trace of an idea, half an idea, vague idea, hazy idea, **idea** 479.

.6 **suppositiousness, presumptiveness,** presumableness, theoreticalness, hypotheticalness, conjecturableness, speculativeness.

.7 **theorist, theorizer,** theoretic, **theoretician,** notionalist [archaic]; **speculator;** hypothesist, hypothesizer; **doctrinaire,** doctrinarian; armchair authority *or* philosopher.

.8 **supposer,** assumer, surmiser, **conjecturer, guesser,** guessworker.

.9 VERBS **theorize, hypothesize, speculate,** have *or* entertain a theory, espouse a theory.

.10 **suppose, assume, presume, surmise,** expect, **suspect, infer, understand, gather, conclude, deduce, consider,** reckon, divine, imagine, **fancy,** dream, conceive, **believe, deem,** repute, feel, **think,** be inclined to think, opine, say, daresay, be afraid [informal]; take, take it, take it into one's head, take for, take to be, take for granted, take as a precondition, **presuppose, presurmise,** prefigure; provisionally accept *or* admit, grant, take it as given, let, let be.

.11 **conjecture, guess,** give a guess, talk off the top of one's head [informal], hazard a conjecture, venture a guess, risk assuming *or* stating, tentatively suggest, go out on a limb [informal].

.12 **postulate, predicate, posit,** set forth, lay down, assert; pose, advance, **propose, propound** 773.5.

.13 ADJS **theoretical,** theoretico–; **hypothetic(al),** postulatory, notional; **speculative,**

**conjectural;** abstract, ideal; academic, moot; impractical, armchair.

.14 **supposed,** suppositive, **assumed,** presumed, **conjectured, inferred,** understood, deemed, **reputed,** putative, alleged, accounted as; suppositional, supposititious; assumptive, **presumptive;** given, granted, taken as *or* for granted; **postulated,** postulational, premised.

.15 **supposable, presumable,** assumable, conjecturable, surmisable, imaginable, premissable.

.16 ADVS **theoretically, hypothetically,** *ex hypothesi* [L], ideally; **in theory,** in idea, in the abstract, on paper.

.17 **supposedly,** supposably, **presumably,** presumedly, assumably, assumedly, presumptively, assumptively, reputedly; suppositionally, supposititiously; **seemingly,** in seeming, quasi; as it were.

.18 conjecturably, **conjecturally;** to guess, to make a guess, **as a guess,** as a rough guess.

.19 CONJS **supposing,** supposing that, **assuming that,** allowing that, on the assumption *or* supposition that, if, as if, as though, by way of hypothesis.

## 500. PHILOSOPHY

.1 NOUNS **philosophy,** "life's guide" [Cicero], "a handmaid to religion" [Francis Bacon]; philosophical inquiry *or* investigation, philosophical speculation; inquiry *or* investigation into first causes; school of philosophy, philosophic system, school of thought; philosophic doctrine, philosophic theory; theory of knowledge, **epistemology,** gnosiology; mental philosophy, moral philosophy; **metaphysics,** ontology, first philosophy, theory *or* science of being, phenomenology, cosmology, casuistry, **ethics** 957; **aesthetics,** theory of beauty; axiology, value theory; **logic;** philosophastry, philosophastering; sophistry 483.

.2 Platonic philosophy, Platonism, philosophy of the Academy; Aristotelian philosophy, Aristotelianism, philosophy of the Lyceum, Peripateticism, Peripatetic school; Stoic philosophy, Stoicism, philosophy of the Porch *or* Stoa; Epicureanism, philosophy of the Garden.

.3 **materialism** 376.5; **idealism** 377.3.

.4 monism, philosophical unitarianism, mind-stuff theory; pantheism, cosmotheism; hylozoism.

.5 pluralism; dualism, mind-matter theory.

.6 **philosopher,** philosophizer, philosophe; philosophaster; **thinker,** speculator; casu-

ist; metaphysician, cosmologist; sophist
483.6.

**.7 VERBS philosophize,** reason 482.15.

**.8 ADJS philosophic(al),** sophistical 483.10;
philosophicohistorical, philosophicolegal,
philosophicojuristic, philosophicopsycho-
logical, philosophicoreligious, philosophi-
cotheological.

**.9** acosmistic, animatistic, animist or animistic, atomistic, cosmotheistic, Cyrenaic,
eclectic(al), Eleatic, empirical, Epicurean, eudaemonistic(al), existential, hedonist or hedonistic, hedonic(al), humanist,
humanistic(al), idealistic(al); materialistic
376.11, mechanistic, Megarian, metaphysical, monistic, naturalistic, nominalist or
nominalistical, panlogical, panlogistical,
pantheistic, positivist, positivistic, pragmatic, pragmatist, instrumentalist, rationalistic, realist or realistic, scholastic,
neo-scholastic, sensationalistic, Stoic, syncretistic, theistic, transcendentalist or
transcendentalistic, utilitarian, vitalistic,
voluntarist or voluntaristic.

**.10** Aristotelian, Peripatetic; Augustinian, Av-
erroist or Averroistic, Bergsonian, Berke-
leian, Cartesian, Comtian or Comptean,
Hegelian, Neo-Hegelian, Heideggerian,
Heraclitean, Humean, Husserlian, Kant-
ian, Leibnizian, Parmenidean, Platonic,
Neoplatonic, pre-Socratic, Pyrrhonic, Pyr-
rhonian, Pythagorean, Neo-Pythagorean,
Sartrian, Schellingian, Schopenhauerian,
Scotist, Socratic, Spencerian, Thomist or
Thomistic, Viconian, Wittgensteinian.

**.11 philosophies**

| | |
|---|---|
| acosmism | dialectical materialism |
| aestheticism | dualism |
| African school | eclecticism |
| agnosticism | egoism |
| Alexandrian school | egoistic hedonism |
| analytic philosophy | Eleaticism, Elean |
| animalism | school |
| animatism | empiricism |
| animism | Epicureanism |
| Aristotelianism | Eretrian school |
| atomism | eristic school |
| Augustinianism | essentialism |
| Averroism | ethicism |
| Bergsonism | ethics 957 |
| Berkeleianism | eudaemonism |
| Bonaventurism | existentialism, existen- |
| Bradleianism | tial philosophy |
| Cartesianism | Fichteanism |
| Comtism | hedonism |
| cosmotheism | Hegelianism |
| criticism, critical phi- | Heideggerianism |
| losophy | Heracliteanism |
| Cynicism | Herbartianism |
| Cyrenaic hedonism, | humanism |
| Cyrenaicism | Humism |
| deism | hylomorphism |

| | |
|---|---|
| hylotheism | nism |
| hylozoism | philosophy of signs |
| idealism | philosophy of the |
| immaterialism | ante-Nicene Fathers |
| individualism | philosophy of the |
| instrumentalism | post-Nicene Fathers |
| intuitionism | physicalism |
| Ionian school | physicism |
| Kantianism | Platonism |
| Leibnizianism | pluralism |
| logical empiricism, | positivism |
| logical positivism | pragmaticism, pragma- |
| Marxism | tism |
| materialism | psychism |
| mechanism | psychological hedo- |
| Megarianism | nism |
| mentalism | Purva Mimamsa |
| Mimamsa | Pyrrhonism |
| monism | Pythagoreanism |
| mysticism | rationalism |
| naturalism | realism |
| neocriticism | Sankhya |
| Neo-Hegelianism | Sartrianism |
| Neoplatonism | Schellingism |
| Neo-Pythagoreanism | Scholasticism |
| neo-scholasticism | Schopenhauerism |
| new ethical move- | Scotism |
| ment | secular humanism |
| nominalism | semiotic, semiotics |
| noumenalism | sensationalism |
| Nyaya | sensism |
| ontologism | skepticism |
| ontology | Socratism |
| optimism | Sophism, Sophistry |
| ordinary language phi- | Spencerianism |
| losophy | Spinozism |
| organicism | Stoicism |
| organic mechanism | substantialism |
| panlogism | syncretism |
| panpneumatism | theism |
| panpsychism | Thomism |
| pantheism | transcendentalism |
| panthelism | universalistic hedo- |
| Parmenidean school | nism |
| patristicism | utilitarianism |
| patristic philosophy | Uttara Mimamsa |
| Peripateticism | vitalism |
| pessimism | voluntarism |
| phenomenalism | zetetic philosophy |
| philosophy of orga- | |

**.12 adherents**

| | |
|---|---|
| acosmist | egoist |
| agnostic | Eleatic |
| analytic philosopher | empiricist |
| animalist | Epicurean |
| animatist | Eretrian |
| animist | eristic |
| Aristotelian | essentialist |
| atomist | eudaemonist |
| Averroist | existentialist, existen- |
| Bergsonian | tial philosopher |
| Berkeleian | Fichtean |
| Cartesian | hedonist |
| Comtist | Hegelian |
| cosmotheist | Heideggerian |
| Cynic | Heraclitean |
| Cyrenaic | Herbartian |
| deist | humanist |
| dialectical materialist | Humist |
| dualist | Husserlian |
| eclectic | hylomorphist |

hylotheist
hylozoist
idealist
immaterialist
individualist
intuitionist
Kantian
Kierkegaardian
Leibnizian
logical empiricist, logi-
  cal positivist
Marxist
materialist 376.6
mechanist
Megarian
mentalist
monist
mystic
naturalist
Neo-Hegelian
Neoplatonist
Neo-Pythagorean
nominalist
ontologist
organicist
organic mechanist
panpsychist
pantheist
Parmenidean
Peripatetic
phenomenalist
physicalist

physicist
Platonist
pluralist
positivist
pragmatist
psychist
Pyrrhonist
Pythagorean
rationalist
realist
Sartrian
Scholastic
Scotist
secular humanist
sensationalist
sensist
skeptic
Socratist
Sophist
Spencerian
Spinozist
Stoic
substantialist
syncretist
theist
Thomist
transcendentalist
utilitarian
vitalist
voluntarist
Wittgensteinian
zetetic

### .13 philosophers

Abelard
Albertus Magnus
Albinus
Alexander, Hartley
  Burr
Alexander, Samuel
Ammonius Saccas
Anaxagoras
Anaximander
Anaximenes
Anselm
Apollonius
Apuleius
Aristippus
Aristotle
Augustine
Averroes
Ayer
Bacon, Francis
Bacon, Roger
Bautain
Bayle
Bentham
Bergson
Berkeley
Boethius
Bonaventure
Boodin
Bosanquet
Bowne
Bradley
Brightman
Broad
Bruno
Cabanis
Caird, Edward
Caird, John
Carnap

Cassirer
Chubb
Cicero
Clifford
Cohen, Hermann
Comte
Condillac
Condorcet
Confucius
Cousin
Croce
Democritus
Descartes
Dewey
d'Holbach
Diderot
Dilthey
Drake
Dreisch
Duns Scotus
Empedocles
Engels
Epictetus
Epicurus
Erigena
Eucken
Euhemerus
Fechner
Feigl
Fichte
Flewelling
Franke
Frege
Fullerton
Gentile
Geulincx
Gilson
Green

Grotius
Haeckel
Hahn
Haldane
Hamann
Harris
Hartmann
Hegel
Heidegger
Heraclitus
Herbart
Herder
Hobbes
Holt
Howison
Hume
Husserl
Hutcheson
Jacobi
James
Jaspers
Kant
Kierkegaard
La Mettrie
Langer
Leibniz
Leucippus
Locke
Lotze
Lovejoy
Lucretius
Mach
Maimonides
Maine de Biran
Malebranche
Marcus Aurelius
Maritain
Marvin
Marx
Maximus
McGilvary
M'Taggart
Mead
Meinong
Mencius
Mendelssohn, Moses
Mill, James
Mill, John Stuart
Moderatus
Montague
Moore
Morgan
Natorp
Neurath
Nietzsche
Numenius
Ockham

Ortega y Gasset
Paley
Parmenides
Pascal
Peirce
Perry
Philo
Plato
Plotinus
Porphyry
Pratt
Pritchard
Protagoras
Pyrrho
Pythagoras
Reid
Reynaud
Rogers
Ross
Rousseau
Royce
Russell
Santayana
Sartre
Scheler
Schelling
Schiller, Ferdinand
Schleiermacher
Schlick
Schopenhauer
Sellars
Seneca
Shaftesbury
Sidgwick
Socrates
Spaulding
Spencer
Spinoza
Stern
Stevenson
Stirling
Strong
Thales
Theophrastus
Thomas Aquinas
Tindal
Toland
Vico
Waismann
Whitehead
Windelband
Wittgenstein
Wolff
Woodbridge
Xenophanes
Zeno of Citium
Zeno of Elea

## 501. BELIEF

.1 NOUNS **belief, credence, credit, faith, trust;** hope; **confidence,** assuredness, **assurance;** sureness, surety, **certainty** 513; reliance, dependence, reliance on or in, dependence on, stock or store [both informal]; acceptation, acception, reception, acquiescence; suspension of disbelief; fideism; **credulity** 502.

.2 a **belief, tenet, dogma,** precept, **principle, principle** or **article** of **faith,** canon, maxim, axiom; **doctrine,** teaching; –ism, –logy or –logia.

.3 **system of belief; religion, faith** 1020.1; **school, cult, ism, ideology,** Weltanschauung [Ger], world view; political faith or belief or philosophy; **creed, credo,** credenda; articles of religion, creedal or doctrinal statement, formulated belief; gospel; catechism;

.4 **statement of belief** or **principles, manifesto,** position paper; solemn declaration; deposition, affidavit.

.5 **conviction, persuasion,** convincement; **firm belief,** implicit or staunch belief, settled judgment, mature judgment or belief, fixed opinion, unshaken confidence, steadfast faith, rooted or deep-rooted belief.

.6 **opinion, sentiment, feeling, impression,** reaction, **notion, idea, thought, mind,** thinking, **way of thinking, attitude,** stance, posture, position, **view,** eye, sight, lights, observation, **conception,** concept, conceit, **estimation,** estimate, consideration, **theory** 499, assumption, presumption, **conclusion, judgment** 494, personal judgment; **point of view** 525.2; public opinion, public belief, general belief, prevailing belief or sentiment, consensus gentium [L], common belief, community sentiment, popular belief, vox populi [L], climate of opinion; ethos; mystique.

.7 **profession, confession, declaration, profession** or **confession** or **declaration of faith.**

.8 **believability,** believableness, **credibility, credit, trustworthiness, plausibility,** tenability, acceptability, conceivability; **reliability** 513.4.

.9 **believer, truster;** religious believer 1028.4; true believer; the assured, the faithful, the believing; fideist.

.10 VERBS **believe, credit, trust, accept,** receive, buy [slang]; give credit or credence to, give faith to, put faith in, take stock in or set store by [informal], attach some weight to; be led to believe; accept implicitly, believe without reservation, take for granted, take or accept for gospel, take as gospel truth [informal], take on faith, take on trust or credit; take at face value; **take one's word for,** trust one's word, take at one's word; swallow 502.6; be certain 513.9.

.11 **think, opine, be of the opinion,** be afraid [informal], **have the idea,** have an idea, **suppose, assume, presume, judge** 494.8, **guess, surmise,** have a hunch [informal], have an inkling, suspect, expect [informal], have an impression, be under the impression, conceive, ween, trow [both archaic], **imagine, fancy, daresay; deem, esteem, hold, regard, consider, maintain,** reckon, estimate; hold as, account as, set down as or for, view as, look upon as, take for, take, take it.

.12 **state, assert,** declare, **affirm,** vow, avow, avouch, warrant, asseverate, confess, swear, profess, express the belief, swear to a belief.

.13 **hold the belief, have the opinion,** entertain a belief or opinion, adopt or embrace a belief; foster or nurture or cherish a belief, be wedded to or espouse a belief; get hold of an idea, get it into one's head, form a conviction.

.14 **be confident,** have confidence, **be satisfied, be convinced, be certain,** be easy in one's mind about, be secure in the belief, **feel sure, rest assured,** rest in confidence; doubt not, **have no doubt,** have no misgivings or diffidence or qualms, have no reservations, have no second thoughts.

.15 **believe in, have faith in,** pin one's faith to, confide in, **have confidence in,** place or repose confidence in, place reliance in, put oneself in the hands of, **trust in,** put trust in, have simple or childlike faith in, rest in, repose in or hope in [both archaic].

.16 **rely on** or **upon, depend on** or **upon,** place reliance on, rest on or upon, repose on, lean on, **count on,** calculate on, reckon on, **bank on** or **upon** [informal]; **trust to** or **unto, swear by,** take one's oath upon; **bet on** or gamble on or lay money on or bet one's bottom dollar on [all informal]; take one's word for.

.17 **trust, confide in, rely on, depend on,** repose, place trust or confidence in, **trust in** 501.15, trust implicitly, deem trustworthy, think reliable or dependable, take one's word.

.18 **convince, convict, convert, win over,** bring over, bring round, talk over, talk one around, bring to reason, bring to one's senses, **persuade, lead to believe;** satisfy, assure; put one's mind at rest on; sell or sell one on [both informal]; carry one's point, bring or drive home to; cram down one's throat; be convincing, carry conviction; inspire belief or confidence.

.19 **convince oneself, persuade oneself,** sell oneself [informal], make oneself easy about, make oneself easy on that score, satisfy oneself on that point, make sure of, make up one's mind.

.20 **find credence, be believed,** be accepted, be received; be swallowed or go down or pass current [all informal]; produce or carry conviction; have the ear of, gain the confidence of.

.21 ADJS **believing, undoubting, undoubtful,** doubtless [archaic]; faithful [archaic], pistic, pious, pietistic, **devout;** under the impression, impressed with; **convinced, confident,** positive, dogmatic, secure, **persuaded,** sold on, **satisfied, assured; sure, certain** 513.13–21; fideistic.

.22 **trusting, trustful,** trusty [archaic], **confiding, unsuspecting, unsuspicious,** without suspicion; childlike, innocent, guileless, naïve 736.5; **credulous** 502.8; relying, depending, reliant, dependent.

.23 **believed, credited, trusted, accepted;** received; **undoubted,** unsuspected, **unquestioned,** undisputed, uncontested.

.24 **believable, credible; tenable,** conceivable, **plausible,** colorable; worthy of faith, trustworthy, trusty; fiduciary; reliable 513.17; unimpeachable, unexceptionable, **unquestionable** 513.15.

.25 fiducial, fiduciary, pistic; convictional.

.26 **convincing,** convictional, **persuasive,** assuring, impressive, satisfying, satisfactory; decisive, absolute, conclusive, determinative; authoritative.

.27 **doctrinal, creedal,** canonical, dogmatic, confessional.

.28 ADVS **believingly, undoubtingly,** undoubtfully, without doubt, unquestioningly; **trustingly,** trustfully, unsuspectingly, unsuspiciously; piously, devoutly; with faith; **with confidence,** on or upon trust, on faith.

.29 **in one's opinion, to one's mind,** in one's thinking, **to one's way of thinking,** the way one thinks, in one's estimation, according to one's lights, as one sees it, to the best of one's belief; in the opinion of, in the eyes of.

## 502. CREDULITY

.1 NOUNS **credulity, credulousness,** inclination or disposition to believe, ease of belief, will or willingness to believe, wishful belief or thinking; **blind faith,** unquestioning belief; uncritical acceptance, premature or unripe acceptation, hasty or rash conviction; **trustfulness, unsuspiciousness,** unsuspectingness; uncriticalness, unskepticalness; overcredulity, overcredulousness, overtrustfulness, overopen-

ness to conviction or persuasion, gross credulity; infatuation, fondness, dotage; one's blind side.

.2 **gullibility, dupability,** cullibility, **deceivability,** seduceability, persuadability, hoaxability; easiness [informal], softness, weakness; **simpleness,** simplicity, **ingenuousness, unsophistication;** greenness, naïveness, **naïveté,** naivety 736.1.

.3 **superstition,** superstitiousness; popular belief, **old wives' tale;** tradition, lore, folklore; charm, spell 1036.

.4 **trusting soul; dupe** 620; sucker or patsy [both slang].

.5 VERBS **be credulous,** accept unquestioningly; not boggle at anything, **believe anything,** be easy of belief or persuasion, be uncritical, believe at the drop of a hat, be a dupe, think the moon is made of green cheese.

.6 [slang or informal terms] kid oneself; **swallow,** swallow anything, swallow whole, not choke or gag on, swallow hook, line, and sinker; **eat up,** lap up, devour, gulp down, gobble up or down; bite, nibble, rise to the fly, take the bait; swing at; go for, **fall for,** tumble for; **be taken in,** be a sucker or patsy or easy mark.

.7 **be superstitious;** knock on wood, keep one's fingers crossed.

.8 ADJS **credulous,** easy of belief, ready or inclined to believe, easily taken in; **undoubting** 501.21; **trustful, trusting; unsuspicious, unsuspecting;** uncritical; unskeptical; **overcredulous, overtrustful, overtrusting, overconfiding; fond, infatuated, doting; superstitious.**

.9 **gullible, dupable,** cullible, **deceivable, foolable, deludable, exploitable,** victimizable, seduceable, **persuadable,** hoaxable, humbugable, hoodwinkable; **soft,** easy [informal], **simple; ingenuous, unsophisticated,** green, naïve 736.5.

## 503. UNBELIEF

.1 NOUNS **unbelief, disbelief,** nonbelief, unbelievingness; refusal or inability to believe; discredit; **incredulity** 504; **denial** 524.2, **rejection** 638; misbelief, heresy 1025.2; infidelity, atheism, **agnosticism** 1031.6; minimifidianism, nullifidianism.

.2 **doubt, doubtfulness, dubiousness,** dubiety; half-belief; **question,** question in one's mind; **skepticism,** skepticalness; total skepticism, Pyrrhonism; suspicion, suspiciousness, wariness, leeriness, **distrust, mistrust, misdoubt,** distrustfulness, mistrustfulness; **misgiving**, self-doubt, diffidence; scruple, scrupulousness [both archaic]; apprehension 891.4; **uncertainty** 514; shadow of doubt.

.3 **unbelievability**, unbelievableness, **incredibility**, **implausibility**, inconceivability, untenableness; **doubtfulness**, **questionableness**; credibility gap; unreliability 514.6.

.4 doubter, doubting Thomas; unbeliever 1031.11,12.

.5 VERBS **disbelieve**, unbelieve, misbelieve, **not believe**, find hard to believe, not admit, refuse to admit, not buy [slang], take no stock in or set no store by [both informal]; **discredit**, refuse to credit, refuse credit or credence to, give no credit or credence to; gag on, **not swallow** 504.3; negate, **deny** 524.3,4; **reject** 638.2.

.6 **doubt**, be doubtful, be dubious, be skeptical, doubt the truth of, beg leave to doubt, **have one's doubts**, have or harbor or entertain doubts or suspicions, half believe, have reservations, **take with a grain of salt**, scruple [archaic], **distrust**, **mistrust**, misgive; **be uncertain** 514.9,10; **suspect**, smell a rat [informal]; **question**, query, **challenge**, **contest**, **dispute**, greet with skepticism, treat with reserve, bring or call in question, raise a question, throw doubt upon, awake a doubt or suspicion; **doubt one's word**, give one the lie; doubt oneself, be diffident.

.7 **be unbelievable**, be incredible, pass belief, be hard to believe, strain one's credulity, **stagger belief**; shake one's faith, undermine one's faith; perplex, stagger, fill with doubt.

.8 ADJS **unbelieving**, **disbelieving**, nonbelieving; faithless, without faith; unconfident, unconvinced, unconverted; nullifidian, minimifidian, creedless; **incredulous** 504.4; repudiative; **heretical** 1025.9; **irreligious** 1031.17.

.9 **doubting**, **doubtful**, in doubt, **dubious**; **questioning**; **skeptical**, Pyrrhonic, from Missouri [informal]; **distrustful**, **mistrustful**, **untrustful**, mistrusting, untrusting; **suspicious**, suspecting, scrupulous [archaic], shy, wary, leery; **agnostic**; **uncertain** 514.14.

.10 **unbelievable**, **incredible**, unthinkable, **implausible**, unimaginable, inconceivable, not to be believed, **hard to believe**, hard of belief, beyond belief, unworthy of belief, not meriting or not deserving belief, tall [informal]; **staggering belief**, passing belief; preposterous, absurd, ridiculous, unearthly, ungodly; **doubtful**, **dubious**, doubtable, dubitable, **questionable**, problematic(al), **unconvincing**, open to doubt or suspicion; **suspicious**, suspect; thin or a bit thin [both informal]; thick or a bit thick or a little too thick [all informal].

.11 unreliable 514.19.

.12 **doubted**, **questioned**, disputed, contested, moot; **distrusted**, mistrusted; **suspect**, suspected, **under suspicion**, under a cloud; **discredited**, exploded, **disbelieved**.

.13 ADVS **unbelievingly**, doubtingly, **doubtfully**, **dubiously**, questioningly, **skeptically**, suspiciously; **with a grain of salt**, with reservations, with some allowance, with caution.

## 504. INCREDULITY

.1 NOUNS **incredulity**, **incredulousness**, uncredulousness, refusal or disinclination to believe, resistance or resistiveness to belief, tough-mindedness, **inconvincibility**, unconvincibility, unpersuadability, unpersuasibility; **suspiciousness**, suspicion, wariness, leeriness, guardedness, cautiousness, caution; **skepticism** 503.2.

.2 **ungullibility**, uncullibility, **undupability**, **undeceivability**, unhoaxability, unseduceability; **sophistication**.

.3 VERBS **refuse to believe**, resist believing, **not allow oneself to believe**, be slow to believe or accept; not kid oneself [slang]; **disbelieve** 503.5; **be skeptical** 503.6; **not swallow**, not be able to swallow or down [informal], not go for or **not fall for** [both slang], not taken in by; **not accept**, **reject** 638.2.

.4 ADJS **incredulous**, uncredulous, **hard of belief**, shy of belief, disposed to doubt, indisposed or disinclined to believe, unwilling to accept; impervious to persuasion, **inconvincible**, unconvincible, unpersuadable, unpersuasible; **suspicious**, **suspecting**, wary, leery, cautious, guarded; **skeptical** 503.9.

.5 **ungullible**, uncullible, **undupable**, **undeceivable**, **unfoolable**, **undeludable**, unhoaxable, unseduceable, hoaxproof; **sophisticated**, **wise**, **hardheaded**, practical, realistic, tough-minded; nobody's fool, not born yesterday, nobody's sucker or patsy [slang].

## 505. EVIDENCE, PROOF

.1 NOUNS **evidence**, **proof**; **reason to believe**, grounds for belief; **grounds**, material grounds, **facts**, **data**, premises, basis for belief; piece or item of evidence, **fact, datum**, relevant fact; **indication, manifestation**, sign, symptom, mark, token, mute witness; **body of evidence**, documentation; **muniments, title deeds and papers; chain of evidence; clue** 568.8; **exhibit.**

**.2 evidence in chief**, primary or secondary evidence, **prima facie evidence**, external or extrinsic evidence, internal or intrinsic evidence, **direct evidence**, indirect evidence, **circumstantial** or **presumptive evidence**, documentary evidence, oral evidence, **word-of-mouth evidence**, ex parte evidence, collateral evidence, **cumulative evidence**, incriminating evidence, **hearsay evidence, hearsay**, state's evidence; *corpus delicti* [L], body of the crime.

**.3 testimony, attestation**, attest [archaic], **witness**; testimonial, testimonium [archaic]; **statement, declaration, assertion**, asseveration, **affirmation** 523, avouchment, avowal, averment, allegation, **admission**, **disclosure** 556, profession, word; **deposition**, legal evidence, sworn evidence or testimony; *procès-verbal* [Fr]; compurgation; affidavit, sworn statement; instrument in proof, *pièce justificative* [Fr].

**.4 proof, demonstration**, ironclad proof; **determination, establishment, settlement; conclusive evidence**, indisputable evidence, incontrovertible evidence, damning evidence, unmistakable sign, **sure sign**, absolute indication; **burden of proof**, onus, *onus probandi* [L]; the proof of the pudding.

**.5 confirmation, substantiation**, proof, proving, **proving out**, bearing out, affirmation, attestation, **authentication, validation, certification, ratification, verification; corroboration, support**, supporting evidence, corroboratory evidence, fortification, **buttressing, bolstering, backing**, backing up, reinforcement, undergirding, strengthening, circumstantiation; **documentation.**

**.6 citation, reference**, quotation; **exemplification**, instance, example, case, case in point, particular, item, illustration, demonstration; cross reference.

**.7 witness, eyewitness**, spectator, **earwitness; bystander**, passerby; **deponent, testifier**, attestant, attester, attestator, voucher, swearer; **informant**, informer; character witness; cojuror, compurgator.

**.8 provability, demonstrability**, determinability; confirmability, supportability, verifiability.

**.9 VERBS evidence, evince**, furnish evidence, show, **go to show**, tend to show; **demonstrate, illustrate**, exhibit, manifest, display, express, **set forth**; approve; **attest**; indicate, **signify**, signalize, symptomatize, mark, **denote, betoken, point to**, give indication of, show signs of; **connote**, imply, **suggest**, involve; argue, breathe, tell, bespeak; **speak for itself**, speak volumes.

**.10 testify, attest, give evidence**, witness, give or **bear witness; disclose** 556.4–7; **vouch**, state one's case, **depose**, depone, **warrant, swear**, take one's oath, acknowledge, avow, **affirm**, avouch, aver, allege, asseverate, **certify, give one's word.**

**.11 prove, demonstrate, show**, afford proof of, prove to be, prove true; **establish, fix**, determine, ascertain, **make out**, remove all doubt; **settle**, settle the matter; **set at rest**; clinch or cinch or **nail down** [all informal]; **prove one's point**, make one's case, **bring home to**, make good, have or make out a case; hold good, hold water; follow, follow from, follow as a matter of course.

**.12 confirm**, affirm, **attest**, warrant, uphold [Brit dial], **substantiate, authenticate, validate, certify**, ratify, **verify**; circumstantiate, **corroborate, bear out**, support, buttress, **sustain**, fortify, bolster, back, **back up**, reinforce, undergird, strengthen; **document**; probate, prove.

**.13 adduce**, produce, **advance, present**, bring to bear, **offer**, allege [archaic], plead, **bring forward**, bring on; rally, marshal, deploy, array.

**.14 cite, name**, call to mind; **instance**, cite a particular or particulars, cite cases or a case in point, itemize, particularize, produce an instance, give a for-instance [informal]; **exemplify**, example [archaic], illustrate, demonstrate; **document; quote**, quote chapter and verse.

**.15 refer to**, direct attention to, **appeal to**, invoke; make reference to; **cross-refer**, make a cross-reference; reference, cross-reference.

**.16 have evidence** or **proof**, have a case, possess incriminating evidence, **have something on** [informal]; **have the goods on** or have dead to rights [both slang].

**.17 ADJS evidential**, evidentiary, **factual**, symptomatic, **significant, indicative**, attestative, attestive, probative; **founded on**, grounded on, based on; implicit, suggestive; **material**, telling, convincing, weighty; overwhelming, damning; **conclusive**, determinative, **decisive**, final, incontrovertible, irresistible, indisputable, irrefutable, sure, certain, absolute; documented, documentary; **valid, admissible;** adducible; firsthand, authentic, reliable 513.17, eye-witness; hearsay, circumstantial, presumptive, nuncupative, cumulative, ex parte.

.18 **demonstrative,** demonstrating, demonstrational; evincive, apodictic.

.19 **confirming,** confirmatory, confirmative; substantiating, **verifying,** verificative; **corroborating,** corroboratory, **corroborative,** supportive, **supporting.**

.20 **provable, demonstrable,** demonstratable, apodictic, evincible, attestable, **confirmable,** checkable, **substantiatable, establishable,** supportable, sustainable, **verifiable,** validatable, authenticatable.

.21 **proved, proven, demonstrated,** shown; **established,** fixed, **settled, determined,** ascertained; **confirmed, substantiated,** attested, **authenticated, certified, validated, verified;** circumstantiated, **corroborated,** borne out.

.22 **unrefuted,** unconfuted, unanswered, uncontroverted, uncontradicted, **undenied; unrefutable** 513.15.

.23 ADVS **evidentially,** according to the evidence, on the evidence, as attested by; **in confirmation, in corroboration of, in support of;** at first hand, at second hand.

.24 **to illustrate, to prove the point,** as an example, as a case in point, to name an instance, by way of example, **for example, for instance,** to cite an instance, as an instance, e.g., *exempli gratia* [L]; as, thus.

.25 **which see,** q.v., *quod vide* [L]; *loco citato* [L], loc. cit.; *opere citato* [L], op. cit.

.26 PHRS **it is proven,** *probatum est* [L], there is nothing more to be said, it must follow; QED, *quod erat demonstrandum* [L].

## 506. DISPROOF

.1 NOUNS **disproof,** disproving, disproval, **invalidation,** disconfirmation, explosion, negation, redargution [archaic]; exposure, exposé; *reductio ad absurdum* [L].

.2 **refutation, confutation,** confounding, refutal, **rebuttal, answer,** complete answer, crushing or effective rejoinder, squelch; discrediting; **overthrow,** overthrowal, upset, upsetting, subversion, undermining, demolition; **contradiction,** controversion, denial 524.2.

.3 **conclusive argument, knockdown argument,** floorer, sockdolager [slang]; **clincher** or crusher or settler or finisher or squelcher [all informal].

.4 VERBS **disprove, invalidate,** disconfirm, discredit, prove the contrary, belie, give the lie to, redargue [archaic]; **negate,** negative; **expose, show up; explode,** blow up, blow sky-high, **puncture,** deflate, shoot or poke full of holes; **knock the bottom out of** [informal], knock the props or chocks out from under, take the ground from under, undercut, cut the ground from under one's feet, not leave a leg to stand on, have the last word, leave nothing to say.

.5 **refute, confute, confound, rebut,** parry, answer, **answer conclusively,** dismiss, dispose of; **overthrow,** overturn, overwhelm, upset, subvert, defeat, demolish, undermine; argue down; floor or finish or settle or squash or squelch [all informal], crush, smash all opposition; silence, put or reduce to silence, shut up, stop the mouth of; nonplus; take the wind out of one's sails; **contradict,** controvert, deny 524.4.

.6 ADJS **refuting, confuting, confounding,** confutative, refutative, refutatory; contradictory, contrary 524.5.

.7 **disproved,** disconfirmed, **invalidated,** negated, negatived, discredited, belied; **exposed,** shown up; **punctured,** deflated, **exploded; refuted,** confuted, confounded; **upset, overthrown,** overturned; **contradicted,** disputed, denied, impugned; dismissed, discarded, rejected 638.3.

.8 **unproved,** not proved, unproven, **undemonstrated,** unshown; **untried,** untested; **unestablished,** unfixed, **unsettled, undetermined,** unascertained; **unconfirmed, unsubstantiated,** unattested, **unauthenticated,** unvalidated, uncertified, **unverified; uncorroborated,** unsustained, **unsupported,** unsupported by evidence, **groundless,** without grounds or basis, **unfounded** 483.13; **inconclusive,** indecisive; not following.

.9 **unprovable,** controvertible, **undemonstrable,** undemonstratable, unattestable, unsubstantiatable, **unsupportable,** unconfirmable, unsustainable, unverifiable.

.10 **refutable,** confutable, **disprovable,** defeasible.

## 507. QUALIFICATION

.1 NOUNS **qualification, limitation, restriction,** circumscription, **modification,** hedge, hedging; specification; **allowance, concession,** cession, grant; grain of salt; **reservation, exception,** waiver, exemption; specialness, special circumstance, special case, special treatment; **mental** reservation, salvo, *arrière-pensée* [Fr]; extenuating circumstances.

.2 **condition, provision, proviso, stipulation,** whereas; **specification,** parameter, given, *donnée* [Fr], limiting condition, boundary condition; **catch** *or* joker *or* kicker [all informal], string, a string to it [informal]; **requisite, prerequisite,** obligation; *sine qua non* [L], *conditio sine qua non* [L]; clause; escape clause, escape hatch, saving clause; escalator clause; **terms,** provisions; grounds; small *or* fine print [informal], fine print at the bottom [informal]; ultimatum.

.3 VERBS **qualify, limit,** condition [archaic], hedge, hedge about, **modify, restrict,** restrain, circumscribe, set limits *or* conditions, box in [informal], narrow; adjust to, regulate by; alter 139.6; **temper, season,** leaven, soften, modulate, moderate, assuage, **mitigate,** palliate, abate, reduce, diminish.

.4 **make conditional,** make contingent, **condition;** make it a condition, attach a condition *or* proviso, **stipulate;** insist upon, make a point of; **have a catch** [informal], have a joker *or* kicker [informal], have a joker in the deck [informal], have a string attached [informal].

.5 **allow for, make allowance for,** provide for, take account of, **take into account** *or* **consideration, consider,** consider the circumstances; allow, **grant, concede,** admit, admit exceptions, see the special circumstances; relax, relax the condition, waive, set aside, lift temporarily; disregard, **discount,** leave out of account; consider the source, **take with a grain of salt.**

.6 **depend,** hang, rest, hinge; **depend on** *or* **upon, hang on** *or* **upon, rest on** *or* **upon,** rest with, repose upon, lie on, lie with, stand on *or* upon, be based on, be bounded *or* limited by, be dependent on, be predicated on, **be contingent** *or* **conditional on; hinge on** *or* **upon, turn on** *or* **upon,** revolve on *or* upon, have as a fulcrum.

.7 ADJS **qualifying,** qualificative, qualificatory, **modifying,** modificatory, altering; **limiting, restricting,** limitative, restrictive, bounding; **extenuating,** extenuatory, **mitigating,** mitigative, mitigatory, modulatory, palliative, assuasive, lenitive, softening.

.8 **conditional, provisional,** provisory, stipulatory; specificative; **specified, stipulated,** fixed, stated, given.

.9 **contingent, dependent, depending;** con-

tingent on, **dependent on, depending on,** predicated on, based on, hanging *or* hinging on, turning on, revolving on; depending on circumstances; circumscribed by, hedged *or* hedged about by; boxed in [informal]; **subject to,** incidental to, incident to.

.10 **qualified, modified, conditioned, limited, restricted,** hedged, hedged about; **tempered, seasoned,** leavened, softened, **mitigated,** modulated.

.11 ADVS **conditionally, provisionally, with qualifications,** with a string *or* catch *or* joker *or* kicker to it [informal]; with a reservation *or* exception, with a grain of salt.

.12 CONJS **provided,** provided that, provided always, **providing,** with this proviso, it being provided; **on condition,** on condition that, **with the stipulation,** with the understanding, according as, subject to.

.13 **granting, admitting, allowing,** admitting that, allowing that; exempting, waiving.

.14 **if,** an *or* an' [both archaic], if and when, only if, if only, if and only if, if it be so, if it be true that, if it so happens *or* turns out.

.15 **so,** just so, so that [archaic], so as, so long as, as long as.

.16 **unless,** unless that, **if not, were it not,** were it not that; **except, excepting,** except that, with the exception that, save, **but.**

## 508. NO QUALIFICATIONS

.1 NOUNS **unqualifiedness,** unlimitedness, **unconditionality,** unrestrictedness, **unreservedness,** uncircumscribedness; categoricalness; **absoluteness,** definiteness, **explicitness;** decisiveness.

.2 ADJS **unqualified, unconditional,** unconditioned, **unrestricted,** unhampered, **unlimited,** uncircumscribed, unmitigated, **categorical,** straight, **unreserved,** without reserve; **implicit,** unquestioning, undoubting, unhesitating; **explicit, express, unequivocal,** clear, unmistakable; **peremptory,** indisputable, inappealable; **without exception,** admitting no exception, unwaivable; **positive, absolute,** definite, definitive, determinate, decided, decisive, fixed, final, conclusive; round, flat, **complete, entire, whole, total,** global, omn(i)–; **utter,** perfect, downright, outright, out-and-out, straight-out [informal], all-out, flat-out [dial].

.3 ADVS [informal terms] **no strings attached,** no holds barred, **no catch** *or* joker *or* kicker, no joker in the deck, no small print *or* fine print, no fine print at the bottom; **no ifs, ands, or buts;** downright.

## 509. POSSIBILITY

**.1** NOUNS **possibility,** possibleness, **the realm of possibility,** the domain of the possible, conceivableness, **conceivability,** thinkability, thinkableness, imaginability; **probability, likelihood** 511; what may be, what might be, what is possible, what one can do, what can be done, the possible, the attainable, the feasible; **potential, potentiality,** virtuality; contingency, eventuality; **chance, prospect; outside chance** [informal], off chance, remote possibility; hope, outside hope, small hope; good possibility, good chance, even chance 156.7,8; bare possibility 156.9.

**.2** practicability, **practicality, feasibility; workability,** operability, actability, performability, realizability, negotiability; **viability,** viableness; **achievability,** doability, compassability, **attainability;** surmountability, superability.

**.3** accessibility, access, **approachability, openness,** reachableness, come-at-ableness, getatableness [both informal]; **penetrability,** perviousness; **obtainability,** obtainableness, **availability, procurability,** procurableness, securableness, gettableness, acquirability.

**.4** VERBS **be possible,** could be, might be, **have** *or* **stand a chance** *or* **good chance, bid fair to.**

**.5** make possible, **enable,** permit, clear the road *or* path for, smooth the way for, open the way for, open up the possibility of.

**.6** ADJS **possible,** within the bounds *or* realm *or* range *or* domain of possibility, in one's power, in one's hands, humanly possible; **probable, likely** 511.6; **conceivable,** conceivably possible, **imaginable, thinkable,** cogitable; plausible 511.7; **potential;** contingent.

**.7** practicable, **practical, feasible; workable,** actable, performable, effectible [archaic], realizable, compassable, operable, negotiable, doable; **viable; achievable, attainable;** surmountable, superable, overcomable.

**.8** accessible, **approachable,** come-at-able *or* getatable [both informal], **reachable,** within reach; **open,** open to; **penetrable,** getinable [informal], pervious; **obtain-**

able, **attainable, available,** procurable, securable, findable, gettable, to be had.

**.9** ADVS **possibly, conceivably,** imaginably, feasibly; **perhaps,** perchance, haply; **maybe,** it may be, for all *or* aught one knows.

**.10** by any possibility, by any chance, by any means, **by any manner of means;** in any way, in any possible way, **at any cost, at all,** if at all, ever; on the bare possibility, on the off chance, by merest chance.

**.11** if possible, if humanly possible, **God willing, wind and weather permitting.**

## 510. IMPOSSIBILITY

**.1** NOUNS **impossibility,** impossibleness, the realm *or* domain of the impossible, **inconceivability,** unthinkability, unimaginability, what cannot be, what can never be, what cannot happen, hopelessness, **no chance** 156.10; **self-contradiction,** absurdity, paradox, oxymoron, logical impossibility; impossible, the impossible, impossibilism.

**.2** impracticability, unpracticability, **impracticality, unfeasibility; unworkability,** inoperability, unperformability; **unachievability, unattainability;** unrealizability, uncompassability; insurmountability, **insuperability.**

**.3** inaccessibility, unaccessibility; **unapproachability,** un-come-at-ableness [informal], unreachableness; **impenetrability,** imperviousness; **unobtainability,** unobtainableness, **unattainability, unavailability,** unprocurableness, unsecurableness, ungettableness [informal], unacquirability; undiscoverability, unascertainableness.

**.4** VERBS **be impossible,** be an impossibility, **not have a chance,** be a waste of time; **contradict itself,** be a logical impossibility, be a paradox; fly in the face of reason.

**.5** attempt the impossible, try for a miracle, look for a needle in a haystack *or* in a bottle of hay, try to be in two places at once, try to fetch water in a sieve *or* catch the wind in a net *or* weave a rope of sand *or* get figs from thistles *or* gather grapes from thorns *or* make bricks from straw *or* make cheese of chalk *or* make a silk purse out of a sow's ear *or* change the leopard's spots *or* get blood from a turnip; ask the impossible, cry for the moon.

**.6** make impossible, rule out, disenable, dis

qualify, close out, **bar,** prohibit, put out of reach, leave no chance.

.7 ADJS **impossible, not possible,** beyond the bounds of possibility *or* reason, contrary to reason, at variance with the facts; **inconceivable, unimaginable, unthinkable, not to be thought of, out of the question;** hopeless; **absurd,** ridiculous, preposterous; **self-contradictory,** paradoxical, oxymoronic, logically impossible; **ruled-out,** excluded, closed-out, **barred,** prohibited.

.8 **impracticable, impractical, unfeasible; unworkable,** unperformable, inoperable, undoable, unnegotiable; **unachievable, unattainable,** uneffectible [archaic]; unrealizable, uncompassable; insurmountable, unsurmountable, **insuperable,** unovercomable; **beyond one,** beyond one's power, beyond one's control, out of one's depth, too much for.

.9 **inaccessible,** unaccessible; **unapproachable,** un-come-at-able [informal]; **unreachable,** beyond reach, out of reach; **impenetrable,** impervious; closed to, denied to, lost to, closed forever to; **unobtainable, unattainable, unavailable,** unprocurable, unsecurable, ungettable [informal], unacquirable; not to be had, **not to be had for love or money;** undiscoverable, unascertainable.

.10 ADVS **impossibly, inconceivably,** unimaginably, unthinkably.

## 511. PROBABILITY

.1 NOUNS **probability, likelihood,** likeliness, liability, aptitude, verisimilitude; **chance, odds; expectation, outlook,** prospect; favorable prospect, well-grounded hope, some *or* reasonable hope, fair expectation; **good chance** 156.8; presumption, presumptive evidence; tendency; probable cause, reasonable ground *or* presumption; probabilism.

.2 **mathematical probability,** statistical probability, statistics, **predictability;** probability theory, game theory, theory of games; operations research; probable error, standard deviation; probability curve, frequency curve, frequency polygon, frequency distribution, probability function, probability density function, probability distribution, cumulative distribution function; **statistical mechanics,** quantum mechanics, uncertainty *or* indeterminacy principle, Maxwell-Boltzmann distribution law, Bose-Einstein statistics, Fermi-Dirac statistics; **mortality table,** actuarial table, life table, com-

bined experience table, Commissioners Standard Ordinary table.

.3 **plausibility; reasonability** 482.9; credibility 501.8.

.4 VERBS **be probable, seem likely,** offer a good prospect, offer the expectation, have *or* run a good chance; **promise,** be promising, make fair promise, **bid fair to,** stand fair to, show a tendency, be in the cards, have the makings of, have favorable odds, lead one to expect; **make probable,** probabilize, make more likely, smooth the way for; increase the chances.

.5 **think likely, daresay,** venture to say; **presume,** suppose 499.10.

.6 ADJS **probable, likely, liable, apt,** verisimilar, in the cards, odds-on; **promising, hopeful,** fair, in a fair way; foreseeable, **predictable; presumable,** presumptive; mathematically *or* statistically probable, predictable within limits.

.7 **plausible,** apparent [archaic]; **reasonable** 482.20; credible 501.24; conceivable 509.6.

.8 ADVS **probably, in all probability** *or* **likelihood,** likely, **most likely, very likely;** very like *or* like enough *or* like as not [all informal]; **doubtlessly,** doubtless, no doubt, indubitably; **presumably,** presumptively; by all odds, ten to one, a hundred to one, dollars to doughnuts.

.9 PHRS **there is reason to believe,** I am led to believe, it can be supposed, it would appear, it stands to reason, it might be thought, one can assume, appearances are in favor of, the chances *or* odds are, you can bank on it, you can make book on it, you can bet on it, you can bet your bottom dollar, you can just bet, you can't go wrong; I daresay, I venture to say.

## 512. IMPROBABILITY

.1 NOUNS **improbability, unlikelihood,** unlikeliness; **doubtfulness,** dubiousness, **questionableness; implausibility,** incredibility 503.3; little expectation, low order of probability, poor possibility, bare possibility, faint likelihood, poor prospect, poor outlook; **small chance** 156.9.

.2 VERBS **be improbable, not be likely,** be a stretch of the imagination, strain one's credulity, go beyond reason, go far afield, go beyond the bounds of reason *or* probability.

.3 ADJS **improbable, unlikely,** unpromising, hardly possible, scarcely to be expected *or* anticipated; **doubtful,** dubious, questionable, doubtable, dubitable, more than doubtful; **implausible**, incredible 503.10.

.4 PHRS **not likely!**, no fear!, never fear!, I ask you!, you should live so long! [slang], don't hold your breath!

## 513. CERTAINTY

.1 NOUNS **certainty, certitude,** certainness, **sureness, surety, assurance, assuredness,** certain knowledge; **positiveness, absoluteness, definiteness,** dead *or* moral *or* absolute certainty; unequivocalness, unmistakableness, **unambiguity,** nonambiguity, univocity, univocality; **infallibility,** infallibilism, inerrability, inerrancy; **necessity,** determinacy, determinateness, noncontingency, Hobson's choice, ineluctability, predetermination, predestination, **inevitability** 639.7; **truth** 516; **proved fact,** probatum.

.2 [slang terms] **sure thing,** dead-sure thing, sure bet, sure card, **cinch,** lead-pipe cinch, **open-and-shut case.**

.3 **unquestionability, undeniability,** indubitability, indubitableness, **indisputability,** incontestability, incontrovertibility, **irrefutability,** unrefutability, unconfutability, irrefragability, unimpeachability; **doubtlessness, questionlessness; demonstrability,** demonstratability, provability, verifiability, confirmability; factuality, **reality,** actuality 1.2.

.4 **reliability, dependability, validity, trustworthiness,** faithworthiness; unerringness; predictability, calculability; stability, substantiality, firmness, **soundness,** solidity, staunchness, steadiness, **steadfastness;** secureness, **security;** invincibility 159.4; **authoritativeness, authenticity.**

.5 **confidence,** confidentness, **conviction,** belief, fixed *or* settled belief, **sureness, assurance, assuredness,** surety, security, certitude; **faith,** subjective certainty; trust 501.1; **positiveness, cocksureness; self-confidence, self-assurance, self-reliance;** poise 858.3; courage 893; **overconfidence, oversureness,** overweening [archaic], overweeningness, hubris; pride 905, arrogance 912, pomposity 904.7, self-importance 909.1.

.6 **dogmatism,** dogmaticalness, **positiveness,** positivism, peremptoriness, **opinionatedness,** self-opinionatedness; bigotry; infallibilism.

.7 **dogmatist,** dogmatizer, opinionist, doctrinaire, bigot; positivist; infallibilist.

.8 **ensuring, assurance;** reassurance, reassurement; **certification;** ascertainment, deter-

mination, establishment; **verification,** substantiation, validation, collation, check, checking; **confirmation** 505.5.

.9 VERBS **be certain, be confident, feel sure, rest assured, have no doubt,** doubt not; **know,** just know, **know for certain; bet on** *or* gamble on *or* bet one's bottom dollar on [all informal]; admit of no doubt; **go without saying,** *aller sans dire* [Fr], be axiomatic *or* apodictic.

.10 **dogmatize,** lay down the law, pontificate, oracle, oraculate, proclaim.

.11 **make sure, make certain,** make sure of, make no doubt, make no mistake; remove *or* dismiss *or* expunge *or* erase all doubt; **assure, ensure,** insure, **certify; ascertain; find out,** get at, see to it, see that; **determine,** decide, **establish,** settle, fix, nail down [informal], clinch *or* cinch [both informal], clear up, sort out, set at rest; assure *or* satisfy oneself, make oneself easy about *or* on that score; **reassure.**

.12 **verify, confirm** 505.12, test, prove, audit, **collate,** validate, **check,** check up *or* on *or* out [informal], check over *or* through, **double-check,** triple-check, cross-check, recheck, check and doublecheck, check up and down, check over and through, check in and out, "make assurance double sure" [Shakespeare].

.13 ADJS **certain, sure,** sure-enough [informal]; **bound; positive, absolute, definite,** perfectly sure, apodictic; **decisive,** conclusive; **clear,** clear as day, clear and distinct, **unequivocal, unmistakable,** unambiguous, nonambiguous, univocal; **necessary,** determinate, ineluctable, predetermined, predestined, **inevitable** 639.15; **true** 516.12.

.14 [informal *or* slang terms] **dead sure,** sure as death, sure as death and taxes, sure as fate, sure as can be, sure as shooting, sure as God made little green apples, sure as hell *or* the devil, as sure as I live and breathe.

.15 **unquestionable, undeniable, indubitable, indisputable, incontestable, irrefutable,** unrefutable, unconfutable, incontrovertible, irrefragable, unanswerable, inappealable, unimpeachable, absolute; admitting no question *or* dispute *or* doubt *or* denial; **demonstrable,** demonstratable, provable, verifiable, testable, confirmable, self-evident, axiomatic; factual, **real,** historical, actual 1.15.

.16 **undoubted,** indubious, **unquestioned,** undisputed, **uncontested,** uncontradicted, unchallenged, uncontroverted, uncontroversial; **doubtless, questionless,** beyond shade or shadow of doubt, past dispute, beyond question.

.17 **reliable, dependable, sure,** surefire [informal], **trustworthy, trusty,** faithworthy, **to be depended** or **relied upon,** to be counted or reckoned on; predictable, calculable; **secure, solid, sound, firm,** fast, **stable, substantial,** staunch, steady, **steadfast, faithful, unfailing;** invincible 159.17; well-founded, well-grounded.

.18 **authoritative, authentic,** magisterial, **official;** cathedral, ex cathedra; standard, approved, accepted, received.

.19 **infallible, inerrable,** inerrant, unerring.

.20 **assured,** made sure; **determined, decided, ascertained; settled, established,** fixed, cinched [informal], set [informal], stated, determinate, secure; **certified,** attested, guaranteed, warranted, tested, tried, proved; **open-and-shut** [informal], nailed down [informal], **in the bag** or on ice [both slang].

.21 **confident, sure,** secure, **assured,** reassured, decided, determined; **convinced,** persuaded, positive, **cocksure; unhesitating,** unfaltering, unwavering; **undoubting** 501.21; **self-confident, self-assured, self-reliant,** sure of oneself; poised 858.13; unafraid 893.19; **overconfident, oversure,** overweening, hubristic; proud 905.8, arrogant 912.9, pompous 904.22, self-important 909.8.

.22 **dogmatic(al),** dogmatizing, pronunciative, **positive,** positivistic, peremptory, pontifical, oracular; **opinionated,** opinioned, opinionative, conceited 909.11; **self-opinionated,** self-opinioned; doctrinarian, doctrinaire; bigoted.

.23 ADVS **certainly, surely, assuredly, positively, absolutely, definitely,** decidedly; decisively, distinctly, clearly, unequivocally, unmistakably; **for certain,** for sure or for a fact [both informal], in truth, certes or forsooth [both archaic], and no mistake [informal]; **for a certainty,** to a certainty, à coup sûr [Fr]; **most certainly,** most assuredly; **indeed,** indeedy [informal]; truly 516.17; **of course,** as a matter of course; **by all means,** by all manner of means; at any rate, at all events; nothing else but [informal], no two ways about it, no buts about it [informal]; no ifs, ands, or buts.

.24 **surely, sure, to be sure,** sure enough; sure thing or surest thing you know [both informal].

.25 **unquestionably, undoubtedly, indubitably, admittedly, undeniably,** indisputa-

bly, **incontestably, incontrovertibly,** irrefutably, irrefragably; **doubtlessly,** doubtless, **no doubt, without doubt,** beyond doubt or question, out of question.

.26 **without fail,** whatever may happen, **come what may,** come hell or high water [slang]; cost what it may, coûte que coûte [Fr]; rain or shine, live or die, sink or swim.

.27 PHRS **it is certain,** there is no question, there is not a shadow of doubt, that's for sure [slang]; that goes without saying, cela va sans dire [Fr]; that is evident, that leaps to the eye, cela saute aux yeux [Fr].

## 514. UNCERTAINTY

.1 NOUNS **uncertainty, incertitude, unsureness,** uncertainness; indemonstrability, unverifiability, unprovability, unconfirmability; **unpredictability,** unforeseeableness, incalculability, unaccountability; **indetermination,** indeterminacy, indeterminism; **randomness, chance,** chanciness, hit-or-missness, **luck; indecision,** indecisiveness, undecidedness, undeterminedness; **hesitation, hesitancy; suspense,** suspensefulness, agony or state of suspense; **fickleness, capriciousness,** whimsicality, **erraticness,** erraticism, **changeableness** 141; **vacillation, irresolution** 627; indeterminacy or uncertainty principle.

.2 **doubtfulness, dubiousness, doubt,** dubiety, dubitancy, dubitation [archaic]; **questionableness, disputability,** contestability, controvertibility, refutability, confutability, deniability; disbelief 503.1.

.3 **bewilderment,** disconcertion, disconcertedness, disconcert, disconcertment, **embarrassment, confoundment,** discomposure, unassuredness, **confusion** 532.3; **perplexity,** puzzlement, baffle, **bafflement,** predicament, plight, **quandary, dilemma,** horns of a dilemma, nonplus; **puzzle, problem,** riddle, mystery, enigma; fix or jam or pickle or scrape or stew [all informal]; perturbation, disturbance, upset, bother, pother.

.4 **vagueness, indefiniteness, indecisiveness, indeterminateness,** indeterminableness, indefinableness, **unclearness, indistinctness,** haziness, fogginess, mistiness, blurriness, fuzziness; **obscurity,** obscuration; **looseness, laxity, inexactness,** inaccuracy, imprecision; **broadness, generality,** sweepingness; ill-definedness, amorphousness, shapelessness, blobbiness; inchoateness, disorder, incoherence.

.5 equivocalness, equivocality, polysemousness, ambiguity 550.

.6 unreliability, undependability, untrustworthiness, unfaithworthiness, treacherousness, treachery; unsureness, insecurity, unsoundness, infirmity, insolidity, unsolidity, instability, insubstantiality, unsubstantiality, unsteadfastness, unsteadiness, desultoriness, shakiness; precariousness, hazard, danger, risk, riskiness, peril, perilousness, ticklishness, slipperiness, shiftiness, shiftingness; speculativeness; unauthoritativeness, unauthenticity.

.7 fallibility, errability, errancy, liability to error.

.8 (an uncertainty) gamble, guess, piece of guesswork, chance, wager, toss-up, touch and go; contingency, double contingency, possibility upon a possibility; question, open question; undecided issue; borderline case; blind bargain, pig in a poke, sight-unseen transaction; leap in the dark.

.9 VERBS be uncertain, feel unsure; doubt, have one's doubts, question, puzzle over, agonize over; wonder, wonder whether; not know what to make of, not be able to make head or tail of; be at sea, float in a sea of doubt; be at one's wit's end, not know which way to turn, be of two minds, not know where one stands, not know whether one stands on one's head or one's heels, be in a dilemma or quandary, flounder, grope, beat about, thrash about, go around in circles; go off in all directions at once.

.10 hang in doubt, stop to consider, think twice; falter, dither, hesitate, vacillate 627.8.

.11 depend, pend [dial], all depend, be contingent or conditional on, hang on or upon; hang, hang in the balance, be touch and go, tremble in the balance, hang in suspense; hang by a thread, hang by the eyelids.

.12 bewilder, disconcert, discompose, upset, perturb, disturb, dismay, abash, embarrass, put out, pother, bother, moider [Brit dial], flummox [informal].

.13 perplex, baffle, confound, boggle [Brit dial], daze, amaze [archaic], maze, addle, fuddle, muddle, buffalo [slang], bamboozle [informal], mystify, puzzle, nonplus, stick [informal], stump [informal], floor [informal], throw [slang], get [informal], beat [informal], lick [slang], put to one's wit's end; keep one guessing, keep in suspense.

.14 make uncertain, obscure, muddle, muddy, fuzz, fog, confuse 532.7.

.15 ADJS uncertain, unsure; doubting, agnostic, skeptical, unconvinced, unpersuaded; chancy, dicey [Brit], touch-and-go; unpredictable, unforeseeable, incalculable, unaccountable, undivinable; indemonstrable, unverifiable, unprovable, unconfirmable; equivocal, polysemous, ambiguous 550.3; fickle, capricious, whimsical, erratic, variable, wavering, changeable 141.6; hesitant, hesitating; indecisive, irresolute 627.9.

.16 doubtful, iffy [informal]; in doubt, in dubio [L]; dubitable, doubtable, dubious, questionable, problematic(al), speculative, conjectural, suppositional; debatable, moot, arguable, disputable, contestable, controvertible, controversial, refutable, confutable, deniable; mistakable; suspicious, suspect; open to question or doubt; in question, in dispute, at issue.

.17 undecided, undetermined, unsettled, unfixed, unestablished; untold, uncounted; pendent, dependent, pending, depending, contingent, conditional, conditioned; open, in question, at issue, in the balance, up in the air, up for grabs [slang], in suspense, in a state of suspense, suspenseful.

.18 vague, indefinite, indecisive, indeterminate, indeterminable, undetermined, unpredetermined, undestined; random, stochastic, chance, chancy [informal], aleatory or aleatoric, hit-or-miss; indefinable, undefined, ill-defined, unclear, unplain, indistinct, fuzzy, obscure, confused, hazy, shadowy, shadowed forth, foggy, blurred, blurry, veiled; loose, lax, inexact, inaccurate, imprecise; nonspecific, unspecified; broad, general, sweeping; amorphous, shapeless, blobby, inchoate, disordered, orderless, chaotic, incoherent.

.19 unreliable, undependable, untrustworthy, unfaithworthy, treacherous, unsure, not to be depended or relied on; insecure, unsound, infirm, unsolid, unstable, unsubstantial, insubstantial, unsteadfast, unsteady, desultory, shaky; precarious, hazardous, dangerous, perilous, risky, ticklish; shifty, shifting, slippery; provisional, tentative, temporary.

.20 unauthoritative, unauthentic, unofficial, nonofficial, apocryphal; uncertified, unverified, unchecked, unconfirmed, uncorroborated, unauthenticated, unva idated, unattested, unwarranted; **undemonstrated, unproved.**

**.21 fallible, errable,** errant, liable or open to error, error-prone.

**.22 unconfident, unsure, unassured, insecure,** unsure of oneself; **unselfconfident, unselfassured,** unselfreliant.

**.23 bewildered, dismayed,** distracted, distraught, abashed, **disconcerted, embarrassed,** discomposed, put-out, **disturbed, upset,** perturbed, **bothered,** all hot and bothered [informal]; **confused** 532.12; clueless, without a clue, guessing, mazed, in a maze; turned around, going around in circles, like a chicken with its head cut off [informal]; in a fix or stew or pickle or jam or scrape [informal]; **lost,** astray, abroad, adrift, **at sea,** off the track, out of one's reckoning, out of one's bearings, disoriented.

**.24 in a dilemma,** on the horns of a dilemma; **perplexed, confounded, mystified, puzzled, nonplussed, baffled,** bamboozled [informal], buffaloed [slang]; **at a loss, at one's wit's end,** fuddled, addled, muddled, dazed, **beat** [informal], licked [slang]; stuck or floored or stumped or thrown [all informal]; **on tenterhooks, in** suspense.

**.25 bewildering, confusing, distracting, disconcerting,** discomposing, **dismaying, embarrassing,** disturbing, **upsetting,** perturbing, bothering; **perplexing, baffling, mystifying, mysterious, puzzling,** confounding; **problematic(al);** intricate 46.4; **enigmatic** 549.17.

**.26 ADVS uncertainly,** in an uncertain state, **unsurely; doubtfully, dubiously;** in suspense, on the horns of a dilemma; perplexedly, disconcertedly, confusedly, dazedly, mazedly, in a daze, in a maze.

**.27 vaguely, indefinitely,** indeterminably, indefinably, **indistinctly,** indecisively, **obscurely; broadly, generally,** in broad or general terms.

## 515. GAMBLE

**.1 NOUNS gamble, chance, risk, hazard; speculation, venture,** play; flier or plunge [both slang]; calculated risk; uncertainty 514; fortune, luck 156.1,2.

**.2 matter of chance,** sporting chance, gambling chance, luck of the draw, chance at odds; hazard of the die, cast or throw of the dice, turn or roll of the wheel, turn of the table, turn of the cards, fall of the cards, flip of the coin; toss-up, toss; heads or tails, touch and go; blind bargain, pig

in a poke; leap in the dark, shot in the dark; potshot, random shot; potluck.

**.3 wager, bet, stake, hazard;** play or chunk or shot [all slang]; **ante;** parlay; book, handbook.

**.4 betting system;** sweepstakes, sweepstake, sweeps; pari-mutuel; daily double, exacta, perfecta; quinella; superfecta; martingale; double-or-nothing.

**.5 pot, jackpot, pool, stakes, kitty; bank,** tiger.

**.6 odds,** price; equivalent odds; **even** or **square odds,** even break; **short odds,** ten-to-one shot; **long odds,** long shot, hundred-to-one shot; even chance, good chance, small chance, no chance 156.10.

**.7 gambling, gaming,** sporting [archaic], **speculation,** play, playing; **betting, wagering,** hazarding, risking, staking; drawing or casting lots, sortition; cardsharping.

**.8 (games of chance)** chuck-a-luck, chuck farthing, crack-loo [slang], **craps,** crap shooting, crap game, fan-tan, hazard, horse racing, keno, lotto, bingo, pinball, policy or the numbers game, the numbers [informal]; pitch and toss or chuck and toss, roulette, *trente-et-quarante, rouge et noir* [both Fr], shell game; sweepstake or sweepstakes; card games 878.35.

**.9 die** [sing]; **dice, bones** [informal]; **ivories** or **cubes** or devil's bones or teeth [all slang]; **craps,** crap shooting, crap game; poker dice; loaded dice, false or crooked dice; bird cage.

**.10 (throw of dice) throw, cast, roll, shot, hazard of the die;** dice throws (snake eyes, etc.) 90.3, 93.1, 96.1, 99.1–7; crap, craps; natural, nick.

**.11 lottery,** drawing, sweepstakes or sweepstake or sweep; draft lottery; **raffle;** lotto, bingo, keno, tombola [Brit], Genoese or number lottery; interest lottery, Dutch or class lottery; numbers pool; tontine; grab bag or barrel or box.

**.12 (gambling device)** gambling wheel, wheel of fortune, Fortune's wheel; roulette wheel; raffle wheel; pinball machine; slot machine, one-armed bandit [informal]; gambling table, crap table.

**.13 pari-mutuel,** pari-mutuel machine; totalizator, totalizer, tote [informal].

**.14 counter, check, chip.**

**.15 gambling house, gaming house,** betting house, betting parlor, gambling hall, sporting house [archaic], **gambling den, gambling hell;** hell or joint or flat or crib [all slang]; casino; poolroom.

.16 bookmaker, bookie [informal]; numbers runner; bagman.

.17 gambler, gamester, player, sportsman or sporting man [both archaic], sport, hazarder [archaic]; venturer, adventurer; bettor, wagerer, punter; speculator, speculatist; plunger [slang]; petty gambler, piker [slang]; tinhorn or tinhorn gambler [both slang]; sharper or sharpie or sharp [all slang]; cardsharp or cardshark, cardsharper; crap shooter [informal], boneshaker [slang]; betting ring; compulsive gambler; tipster, tout [Brit].

.18 VERBS gamble, game, sport [archaic], play, try one's luck or fortune; speculate; draw lots, draw straws, lot, cut lots, cast lots; cut the cards or deck; match coins, toss, flip a coin, call, call heads or tails; shoot craps, play at dice; play the ponies [informal]; raffle off.

.19 chance, risk, hazard, set at hazard, venture, wager, take a flier [informal]; gamble on, take a gamble on; take a chance, take one's chance, take the chances of, try the chance, chance it, "stand the hazard of the die" [Shakespeare]; take or run the risk, run a chance; take chances, tempt fortune; leave or trust to chance or luck, rely on fortune, take a leap in the dark; buy a pig in a poke; take potluck.

.20 bet, wager, gamble, hazard, stake, punt, lay, lay down, make a bet, lay a wager; plunge [slang]; bet on or upon, back; bet or play against; parlay; ante, ante up; meet a bet, see, call, cover, fade; pass; stand pat.

.21 ADJS speculative, uncertain 514.15; hazardous, risky 697.10.

## 516. TRUTH

### (conformity to fact or reality)

.1 NOUNS truth, trueness, verity, very truth, sooth or good sooth [both archaic]; unerroneousness, unfalseness, unfallaciousness; historical truth, objective truth, actuality, historicity, fact, reality 1.2–3; the true, ultimate truth; eternal verities; truthfulness, veracity 974.3.

.2 the truth, the truth of the matter, the case; what's what or how it is or how things are or like it is or where it's at [all informal], the unvarnished truth, the simple truth, the naked truth, the plain truth, the unqualified truth, the honest truth, dinkum oil [Austral slang], the sober truth, the exact truth, the straight truth; the straight of it or the honest-to-

God truth or God's truth [all informal], the absolute truth, the intrinsic truth, the unalloyed truth, the hard truth, the stern truth, gospel, gospel truth, Bible truth, revealed truth; the truth, the whole truth and nothing but the truth.

.3 accuracy, correctness, care for truth, attention to fact, right, rightness, rigor, rigorousness, exactness, exactitude; preciseness, precision; mathematical precision, pinpoint precision, scientific exactness; faultlessness, perfection, absoluteness, flawlessness; faithfulness, fidelity; literalness, literality, literalism, textualism, the letter; strictness, severity, rigidity; niceness, nicety, delicacy, subtlety, fineness, refinement; meticulousness 533.3.

.4 validity, soundness, solidity, substantiality, justness; authority, authoritativeness; cogency, weight, force.

.5 genuineness, authenticity, bona fideness, legitimacy; realness, realism, photographic realism, absolute realism, realistic representation, naturalism, naturalness, truth to nature, lifelikeness, truth to life, true-to-lifeness, verisimilitude, absolute likeness, literalness, literality, literalism, truth to the letter; inartificiality, unsyntheticness; unspuriousness, unspeciousness, unfictitiousness, artlessness, unaffectedness; honesty, sincerity; unadulteration 45.1.

.6 the real thing, the very model, the genuine article, the very thing, it [informal]; the article or the goods or the McCoy or the real McCoy [all slang], the real Simon Pure, not an illusion.

.7 VERBS be true, be the case; conform to fact, square with the facts or evidence; prove true, prove to be, prove out, be so in fact; hold true, hold good, hold water [informal], hold or stick together [informal], hold up, hold up in the wash [slang], wash [informal], stand up, stand the test, be consistent or self-consistent, hold, remain valid; be truthful.

.8 seem true, ring true, sound true, carry conviction, hold the ring of truth.

.9 be right, be correct, be just right; be OK [informal], add up; hit the nail on the head, hit it on the nose [informal], score a bull's eye.

.10 be accurate, dot the i's and cross the t's, draw or cut it fine [informal], be precise, make precise, precise, particularize.

.11 come true, come about, attain fulfillment, turn out, come to pass, happen as expected.

**.12** ADJS **true, truthful, eu−; unerroneous,** not in error, in conformity with the facts *or* evidence; **unfalse, unfallacious, unmistaken; real, veritable, sure-enough** [slang], true to the facts, **factual, actual,** effectual, **historical,** documentary; objectively true; **certain,** undoubted, unquestionable 513.13−16; unrefuted, unconfuted, undenied; **ascertained, proved, verified,** validated, **certified,** demonstrated, confirmed, determined, established, attested, substantiated, **authenticated,** corroborated; true as gospel; substantially true, categorically true; **veracious** 974.16.

**.13** **valid, sound, well-grounded, well-founded,** solid, substantial; consistent, self-consistent, logical; **good, just,** sufficient; **cogent, weighty, authoritative; legal, lawful,** legitimate, binding.

**.14** **genuine, authentic,** veridical, **real, natural,** realistic, naturalistic, true to reality, **true to nature,** lifelike, true to life, verisimilar; **literal,** following the letter, true to the letter; verbatim, verbal, **word-for-word;** true to the spirit; **legitimate,** rightful, lawful; **bona fide,** card-carrying [informal], **good, sure-enough** [slang], **sincere, honest;** candid, honest-to-God [slang], **dinkum** [Austral slang]; **inartificial,** unsynthetic; unspurious, unspecious, unsimulated, unfaked, **unfeigned, undisguised, uncounterfeited, unpretended, unaffected, unassumed; unassuming,** simple, unpretending, unfeigning, undisguising; **unfictitious,** unfanciful, unfabricated, unconcocted, uninvented, unimagined; unromantic; **original,** unimitated, uncopied; unexaggerated, undistorted; unflattering, unvarnished, uncolored, unqualified; **unadulterated** 45.7; **pure,** simon-pure; **sterling,** twenty-four carat, all wool and a yard wide [informal].

**.15** **accurate, correct, right,** proper, just; **all right** *or* **OK** *or* **okay** [all informal], just right, dead right, bang on [Brit informal], straight, straight-up-and-down; **faultless,** flawless, absolute, **perfect;** letter-perfect; **meticulous** 533.12.

**.16** **exact, precise,** express; even, square; absolutely *or* definitely *or* positively right; **faithful;** direct; **unerring, undeviating,** constant; **infallible,** inerrant, inerrable; **strict,** close, severe, **rigorous,** rigid; mathematically exact, mathematical; mechanically *or* micrometrically precise; scientifically exact, scientific; religiously exact, religious; **nice,** delicate, subtle, **fine,** refined; pinpoint, microscopic.

**.17** ADVS **truly, really,** really-truly [informal], **verily,** veritably, forsooth *or* in very sooth [both archaic], **in truth,** in good *or* very truth, **actually,** historically, **in reality, in fact,** factually, in point of fact, as a matter of fact, to tell the truth, to state the fact *or* truth, of a truth, with truth; **indeed,** indeedy [informal]; **certainly,** undoubtedly 513.25; no buts about it [informal], nothing else but.

**.18** **genuinely, authentically, really,** naturally, **legitimately, honestly,** veridically; warts and all; unaffectedly, unassumedly.

**.19** **accurately, correctly,** rightly, properly, straight; **perfectly, faultlessly, flawlessly; just right,** just so; so, sic.

**.20** **exactly, precisely,** expressly; **just, dead,** right, straight, even, square, **plumb,** directly, squarely, point-blank; **unerringly,** undeviatingly; verbatim, **literally,** *literatim* [L], verbally, word for word, word by word, word for word and letter for letter, *verbatim et litteratim* [L], in the same words, *ipsissimis verbis* [L], to the letter, according to the letter, *au pied de la lettre* [Fr]; **faithfully, strictly, rigorously,** rigidly; **definitely, positively, absolutely; in every respect,** in all respects, for all the world, neither more nor less.

**.21** **to be exact, to be precise,** strictly speaking, not to mince the matter, by the book.

**.22** **to a nicety, to a T** *or* **tittle, to a turn,** to a hair, to *or* within an inch.

**.23** PHRS **that's right, that is so,** right on!, amen!, that's it, that's just it, it is that, *c'est ça* [Fr]; **you are right,** right you are, right as rain, you've got it, you better believe it, you've got something there, I'll say, it is for a fact, you speak truly, as you say, right, righto [informal], quite, rather! [informal]; **you said it,** you said a mouthful, now you're talking, you can say that again, you're not kidding, that's for sure, ain't it the truth?, you're darn tootin' [both dial]; don't I know it?, you're telling me?

## 517. MAXIM

**.1** NOUNS **maxim, aphorism, apothegm, epigram, dictum, adage,** axiom, dictate [archaic], **proverb,** gnome, words of wisdom, **saw, saying,** witticism, sentence, expression, phrase, catchword, word, byword, mot, motto, moral; **precept,** prescript, teaching, text, verse, sutra, distich, sloka; golden saying, proverbial saying; common *or* current saying, stock saying, pithy saying, wise saying *or* expression, oracle, sententious expression *or* saying; ana, analects, proverbs, wisdom, wisdom literature, collected sayings.

.2 **axiom, truth,** a priori truth, **postulate, truism,** self-evident truth, general *or* universal truth; **theorem; proposition;** brocard, **principle,** *principium* [L], settled principle; **formula; rule, law,** dictate, **dictum;** golden rule.

.3 **platitude, cliché, commonplace, banality, bromide, chestnut** [informal], **corn** [slang], triticism [archaic], trite saying, hackneyed *or* stereotyped saying, commonplace expression, *lieu commun* [Fr], *locus communis* [L], familiar tune, old song *or* story, old saw; twice-told tale, retold story; reiteration 103.2; prosaicism, prosaism; prose; old joke 881.9.

.4 **motto, slogan,** watchword, catchword, tag line; **device;** epithet; inscription, epigraph.

.5 VERBS aphorize, apothegmatize, epigrammatize, coin a phrase; proverb.

.6 ADJS **aphoristic, proverbial,** epigrammatic(al), **axiomatic(al); sententious, pithy,** gnomic, pungent, succinct, terse, crisp, pointed; formulistic, formulaic; **platitudinous** 883.9.

.7 ADVS **proverbially, as the saying is *or* goes,** as they say, as the fellow says [informal], as it has been said, as it was said of old.

## 518. ERROR

.1 NOUNS **error, erroneousness; untrueness, untruthfulness, untruth; wrongness, wrong; falseness, falsity; fallacy, fallaciousness,** self-contradiction; **fault, faultiness,** defectiveness; sin, sinfulness, peccancy, **flaw, flawedness,** *hamartia* [Gk]; misdoing, misfeasance; errancy, aberrancy, aberration, **deviancy; heresy,** unorthodoxy, heterodoxy; perversion, **distortion;** misconstruction, misapplication; **delusion, illusion** 519; misjudgment 496; **misinterpretation** 553.

.2 **inaccuracy, inaccurateness, incorrectness, uncorrectness, inexactness,** unfactualness, inexactitude, **unpreciseness,** imprecision, looseness, laxity, unrigorousness; tolerance, allowance; negligence; approximation; **deviation,** standard deviation, probable error, predictable error.

.3 **mistake, error,** *erratum* [L], *corrigendum* [L]; **fault,** *faute* [Fr]; human error; **misconception, misapprehension, misunderstanding;** misstatement, misquotation;

misreport; **misprint, typographical error,** typo [informal], printer's error, typist's error; clerical error; misidentification; **misjudgment, miscalculation** 496.1; misplay; misdeal; miscount; misuse; failure, miss, miscarriage.

.4 **slip,** slipup *or* miscue [both informal]; **lapse,** *lapsus* [L], **oversight,** omission, bevue, balk [archaic], inadvertence *or* inadvertency, loose thread; **misstep, trip,** stumble, false *or* wrong step, wrong *or* bad *or* false move; **slip of the tongue,** *lapsus linguae* [L]; **slip of the pen,** *lapsus calami* [L].

.5 **blunder, faux pas,** gaffe, solecism; stupidity, indiscretion 470.4; **botch, bungle** 734.5.

.6 [slang *or* informal terms] goof, boo-boo, foozle, bloomer, **blooper,** boot, **bobble, boner,** bonehead play *or* trick, dumb trick, boob stunt, fool mistake; howler, screamer; **screw-up,** foul-up, muck-up, louse-up; pratfall.

.7 **grammatical error, solecism,** anacoluthon, misusage, missaying, mispronunciation; **bull,** Irish bull, fluff, **malapropism,** malaprop, Mrs. Malaprop [R. B. Sheridan]; Pickwickian sense; spoonerism, marrowsky; hypercorrection, hyperform; folk etymology; catachresis.

.8 VERBS **not hold water** *or* **not hold together** [both informal], **not stand up, not square, not figure** [informal], **not add up, not hold up, not hold up in the wash** *or* **not wash** [both informal].

.9 **err, fall into error, go wrong, go amiss, go astray,** go out of line, go awry, stray, **deviate, wander; lapse, slip, slip up, trip, stumble; miscalculate** 496.2.

.10 **be wrong, be mistaken, be in error, be at fault,** be out of line, be off the track, be in the wrong, miss the truth, miss by a mile [informal], have another think coming [informal]; receive a false impression, take the shadow for the substance, be misled, be misguided; deceive oneself, be deceived, delude oneself; labor under a false impression.

.11 **bark up the wrong tree,** back the wrong horse, count one's chickens before they are hatched.

.12 **misdo, do amiss; misuse, misemploy, misapply; misconduct, mismanage; miscall, miscount, misdeal, misplay, misfield; misprint, miscite, misquote, misread, misreport, misspell.**

.13 **mistake, make a mistake; miscue, make a miscue** [both informal]; **misidentify; mis-**

understand, misapprehend, misconceive, misinterpret 553.2.

.14 blunder, make a blunder, make a faux pas, make a false or wrong step, make a misstep; misspeak, misspeak oneself, trip over one's tongue; blunder into; botch, bungle 734.11.

.15 [slang or informal terms] make or pull a boner or boo-boo or blooper; drop a brick [Brit], goof, fluff, duff [Brit], foozle, boot, bobble, blow; screw up, foul up, muck up, louse up; put one's foot in it or in one's mouth; muff one's cue, fluff one's lines, fall flat on one's face or ass, drop the ball.

.16 ADJS erroneous, untrue, not true, not right; unfactual, wrong, all wrong; peccant, perverse, corrupt; false, fallacious, self-contradictory; illogical 483.11; unproved 506.8; faulty, faultful, flawed, defective, at fault; out, off, all off, off the track or rails; wide [archaic], wide of the mark, beside the mark; amiss, awry, askew, deviant, deviative, deviational; erring, errant, aberrant; straying, astray, adrift; heretical, unorthodox, heterodox; abroad, all abroad; perverted, distorted; delusive, deceptive, illusory 519.9.

.17 inaccurate, incorrect, inexact, unfactual, unprecise, imprecise, loose, lax, unrigorous; negligent; approximate, approximative; out of line, out of plumb, out of true, out of square.

.18 mistaken, in error, erring, under an error, wrong, all wet [slang]; off or out in one's reckoning; in the wrong box, in the right church but the wrong pew.

.19 unauthentic or inauthentic, unauthoritative, unreliable 514.19,20; misstated, misreported, miscited, misquoted, garbled; unfounded 483.13; spurious 616.26.

.20 ADVS erroneously, falsely, fallaciously; faultily, faultfully; untrue [archaic], untruly; wrong, wrongly; mistakenly; amiss, astray.

.21 inaccurately, incorrectly, inexactly, unprecisely.

.22 PHRS you are wrong, you are mistaken, you're all wet [slang], you're way off [informal], you have another guess coming [informal], don't kid yourself [slang].

## 519. ILLUSION

.1 NOUNS illusion, delusion, deluded belief; deception 618, trick; self-deception, self-deceit, self-delusion; dereism, autism; misconception, misbelief, false belief, wrong impression, warped or distorted conception; bubble, chimera, vapor, "airy nothing" [Shakespeare]; ignis fatuus [L], will-o'-the-wisp; dream, dream vision; dreamworld, dreamland; daydream; pipe dream [informal]; trip [informal]; fool's paradise, castle in the air.

.2 illusoriness, illusiveness, delusiveness; falseness, fallaciousness; unreality, unactuality; unsubstantiality, airiness, immateriality; idealization 535.7; seeming, semblance, simulacrum, appearance, false or specious appearance, show, false show, false light; magic, sorcery 1035, illusionism, sleight of hand, prestidigitation, magic show, magic act; magician, sorcerer 1035.5, illusionist, Prospero [Shakespeare].

.3 fancy, imagination 535.

.4 phantom, phantasm, phantasma, wraith, specter; shadow, shade; phantasmagoria; fantasy, wildest dream; figment of the imagination 535.5, phantom of the mind; apparition, appearance; vision, waking dream, image [archaic]; shape, form, figure, presence; eidolon, idolum; "such stuff as dreams are made on" [Shakespeare].

.5 optical illusion, trick of eyesight; afterimage, spectrum, ocular spectrum.

.6 mirage, fata morgana, looming.

.7 hallucination; hallucinosis; tripping [informal], mind-expansion; consciousness-expansion; delirium tremens 473.9,10; dream 535.9.

.8 VERBS go on a trip or blow one's mind [both informal], freak out [slang]; hallucinate; expand one's consciousness.

.9 ADJS illusory, illusive; illusional, illusionary; Barmecide or Barmecidal; delusory, delusive; delusional, delusionary; deluding, pseud(o)-; dereistic, autistic; dreamy, dreamlike; visionary; imaginary 535.19; erroneous 518.16; deceptive 618.19; self-deceptive, self-deluding; chimeric(al), fantastic; unreal, unactual, unsubstantial 4.5,6, airy; unfounded 483.13; false, fallacious, misleading; specious, seeming, apparent, ostensible, supposititious, all in the mind; spectral, apparitional, phantom, phantasmal; phantasmagoric.

.10 hallucinatory, hallucinative, hallucinational; hallucinogenic, psychedelic, consciousness-expanding, mind-expanding, mind-blowing [informal].

## 520. DISILLUSIONMENT

.1 NOUNS disillusionment, disillusion, disenchantment, undeception, unspelling, return to reality, loss of one's illusions, loss of innocence, cold light of reality, enlightenment, bursting of the bubble; awakening, rude awakening, bringing back to earth; disappointment 541; debunking [slang].

.2 VERBS **disillusion,** disillude, disillusionize; **disenchant,** unspell, uncharm, break the spell *or* charm; **disabuse, undeceive;** correct, **set right** *or* **straight,** put straight, tell the truth, enlighten, let in on; clear the mind of; open one's eyes, awaken, wake up, unblindfold; disappoint 541.2; dispel *or* dissipate one's illusions, rob *or* strip one of one's illusions; bring one back to earth, let down easy [informal]; **burst** *or* **prick the bubble,** puncture one's balloon [informal]; let the air out of, take the wind out of; knock the props out from under, take the ground from under; debunk [slang]; expose, show up 556.4.

.3 be disillusioned, be disenchanted, get back to earth, get one's feet on the ground, return to *or* embrace reality; charge to experience.

.4 ADJS **disillusioning,** disillusive, disillusionary, **disenchanting,** disabusing, undeceiving, enlightening.

.5 **disillusioned, disenchanted,** unspelled, uncharmed, **disabused,** undeceived, stripped *or* robbed of illusion, enlightened, set right, put straight; with one's eyes open, sophisticated, **blasé;** disappointed 541.5.

## 521. ASSENT

.1 NOUNS **assent, acquiescence, concurrence, compliance, agreement, acceptance,** accession; eager *or* hearty *or* warm assent, welcome; assentation; agreement in principle, general agreement; support; consent 775.

.2 **affirmative; yes,** yea, aye, amen; nod, nod of assent; thumbs-up; affirmativeness, affirmative attitude, yea-saying.

.3 **acknowledgment, recognition, acceptance;** appreciation; **admission,** confession, concession, allowance; avowal, profession, declaration.

.4 **ratification, endorsement, acceptance, approval,** approbation 968.1, **sanction,** OK *or* okay [both informal], imprimatur, **green light** *or* **go-ahead** [both informal], permission, nod, the nod, **certification, confirmation, validation, authentication,** authorization, warrant; **affirmation,** affirmance; stamp, rubber stamp, **stamp of approval;** seal, signet, sigil; **subscription, signature,** John Hancock [informal];

countersignature; visa, *visé* [Fr]; notarization.

.5 **unanimity,** unanimousness; **like-mindedness, meeting of minds,** one *or* same mind; total agreement; **understanding,** mutual understanding; **concurrence, consent,** general consent, common assent *or* consent, consentaneity, **accord,** accordance, **concord,** concordance, **agreement,** general agreement; **consensus,** consensus of opinion [informal]; *consensus omnium* [L], universal agreement *or* accord, *consensus gentium* [L], agreement of all, sense of the meeting; **acclamation,** general acclamation; unison, harmony, **chorus, concert,** one *or* single voice, one accord; general voice, *vox populi* [L].

.6 **assenter, consenter, accepter,** covenanter, covenantor; assentator, yea-sayer, yes-man.

.7 **endorser, subscriber, ratifier,** approver, upholder, certifier, confirmer; **signer,** signatory; cosigner, cosignatory, party; underwriter, guarantor, insurer; notary, notary public.

.8 VERBS **assent,** give *or* yield assent, **acquiesce, consent** 775.2, **comply, accede, agree,** agree to *or* with; take kindly to *or* hold with [both informal]; **accept,** receive, buy [slang], take one up on [informal]; **subscribe to,** acquiesce in, abide by; yes, **say 'yes' to; nod,** nod assent, give the nod, give a nod of assent; vote for, cast one's vote for, give one's voice for; welcome, hail, cheer, acclaim, applaud, accept *in toto.*

.9 **concur, accord,** coincide, **agree, agree with,** agree in opinion; enter into one's view, enter into the ideas *or* feelings of, **see eye to eye, be at one with,** be of one mind with, go with, **go along with,** fall *or* chime *or* strike in with, close with, meet, conform to, side with, identify oneself with; echo, ditto [informal], say 'ditto' to, say 'amen' to; join in the chorus, go along with the crowd [informal], run with the pack, go *or* float *or* swim with the stream *or* current; get on the bandwagon [informal].

.10 **come to an agreement, agree,** agree with, **agree on** *or* **upon,** arrive at an agreement, **come to an understanding, come to terms,** strike a bargain, covenant, get together [informal]; **shake hands on,** shake on it [informal]; come around to.

.11 **acknowledge, admit, own, confess, allow,** avow, **grant, warrant, concede,** yield [archaic]; **accept, recognize;** agree in principle, express general agreement, go along with, not oppose or deny, agree provisionally or for the sake of argument; assent grudgingly or under protest.

.12 ratify, endorse, second, support, certify, confirm, validate, authenticate, accept, OK [informal], give the green light or go-ahead [informal], give the imprimatur, permit, give permission, approve 968.9; sanction, authorize, warrant, accredit; pass, pass on or upon, give thumbs up [informal]; amen, say amen to; visa, visé [Fr]; underwrite, subscribe to; sign, undersign, sign on the dotted line, put one's John Hancock on [informal], initial, put one's mark or cross on; autograph; cosign, countersign; seal, sign and seal, set one's seal, set one's hand and seal; affirm, swear and affirm, take one's oath, swear to; rubber stamp [informal]; notarize.

.13 ADJS assenting, agreeing, acquiescing, acquiescent, compliant, consenting, submissive, conceding, concessive, assentatious, agreed, content.

.14 accepted, approved, received; acknowledged, admitted, allowed, granted, conceded, recognized, professed, confessed, avowed, warranted; ratified, endorsed, certified, confirmed, validated, authenticated; signed, sealed, signed and sealed, countersigned, underwritten; stamped; sworn to, notarized, affirmed, sworn and affirmed.

.15 unanimous, solid, consentaneous, with one consent or voice; uncontradicted, unchallenged, uncontroverted, uncontested, unopposed; concurrent, concordant, of one accord; agreeing, in agreement, like-minded, of one mind, of the same mind; of a piece, at one, at one with, agreed on all hands, carried by acclamation.

.16 ADVS affirmatively, assentingly, in the affirmative.

.17 unanimously, concurrently, consentaneously, by common or general consent, with one consent, with one accord, with one voice, without contradiction, nemine contradicente [L], nem con, without a dissenting voice, nemine dissentiente [L], in chorus, in unison, to a man, together, all together, all agreeing, as one, as one man, one and all, on all hands; by acclamation.

.18 INTERJS yes, yea, aye, oui [Fr], sí [Sp], da [Russ], ja [Ger]; yeah or yep or uh-huh [all informal]; yes sir, yes ma'am; yes sirree [informal], why yes, mais oui [Fr]; in-

deed, indeedy [informal], yes indeed, yes indeedy [informal]; surely, certainly, assuredly, most assuredly, exactly, precisely, just so, absolutely, positively, really, truly, rather [Brit], quite, to be sure; sure or sure thing or surest thing you know [all slang]; all right, alright [informal], right, righto [informal], alrighty [informal]; OK or okay [both informal], Roger [informal]; fine [informal], good, well and good, good enough, very well, très bien [Fr]; naturally, naturellement [Fr]; of course, as you say, by all means, by all manner of means; amen; hear, hear [Brit].

.19 PHRS so be it, be it so, so mote it be [archaic], so shall it be, amen [Heb]; so it is, so is it; agreed, done; c'est bien [Fr]; that's right 516.23; you bet, you bet your life, you bet your boots [all slang].

## 522. DISSENT

.1 NOUNS dissent, dissidence, dissentience; nonassent, nonconsent, nonconcurrence, nonagreement, agreement to disagree; minority opinion or position; disagreement, difference, variance, diversity, disparity; dissatisfaction, disapproval, disapprobation; repudiation, rejection; opposition 790; dissension, disaccord 795; alienation, withdrawal, dropping out, secession; recusance or recusancy, nonconformity 83; apostasy 628.2; counter-culture, underground.

.2 objection, protest; kick or beef [both informal]; bitch or squawk or howl [all slang], protestation; remonstrance, remonstration, expostulation; challenge; demur, demurrer, scruple, compunction, qualm; complaint, grievance; exception; peaceful or nonviolent protest; demonstration, protest demonstration, rally, march, sit-in, teach-in, boycott, strike, picketing, indignation meeting; grievance committee.

.3 dissenter, dissentient, dissident, recusant; objector, demurrer; minority or opposition voice; protester, protestant; separatist, schismatic; sectary, sectarian, opinionist; nonconformist 83.3; apostate 628.5.

.4 VERBS dissent, dissent from, be in dissent, disagree, discord with, differ, not agree, disagree with, agree to disagree or differ; divide on, be at variance; take exception, withhold assent, take issue, beg to differ, rise to a point of order; be in opposition to, oppose 790.2; with drop out, secede, separate or disjoin one-self.

.5 **object, protest, kick** or **beef** [both informal], put up a struggle or fight; **bitch** or **squawk** or howl or holler or put up a squawk or raise a howl [all slang]; cry out against, yell bloody murder; **remonstrate, expostulate**; raise or press objections, raise one's voice against, enter a protest; complain, state a grievance; **dispute, challenge**, call in question; **demur, scruple, boggle; demonstrate, demonstrate against**, rally, march, sit in, teach in, boycott, strike, picket.

.6 ADJS **dissenting, dissident**, dissentient, recusant; **disagreeing, differing; opposing** 790.8, in opposition; alienated; counterculture, antiestablishment, underground; breakaway [Brit]; at variance with, at odds with; schismatic(al), sectarian, sectary; nonconforming 83.5.

.7 **protesting**, protestant; **objecting**, expostulative, expostulatory, remonstrative, remonstrant; under protest.

## 523. AFFIRMATION

.1 NOUNS **affirmation, affirmance, assertion, asseveration**, averment, **declaration**, vouch [archaic], allegation; **avouchment, avowal; position, stand**, stance; profession, **statement, word**, say, saying, say-so [informal], positive declaration or statement; manifesto, position paper; **creed** 501.3; **pronouncement, proclamation**, announcement, annunciation, enunciation; proposition, conclusion; predication, predicate; protest, protestation; utterance, dictum, *ipse dixit* [L].

.2 **deposition, sworn statement**, statement under oath, notarized statement, sworn testimony, affirmation; **vouching, swearing**; attestation; certification; **testimony** 505.3; **affidavit**.

.3 **oath, vow**, avow [archaic], **word, assurance, guarantee, warrant**, solemn oath or affirmation or word or declaration; pledge 770.1; Bible oath, ironclad oath; judicial oath, extrajudicial oath; oath of office, official oath; oath of allegiance, loyalty oath, test oath.

BS **affirm, assert**, assever [archaic], as-e, aver, protest, lay down, avouch, lare, say, have one's say, speak, out, state, set down, express, lege, profess; stand on or e a manifesto or posi- ifesto; announce, **pro-**ciate, enunciate, **proclaim;**

**maintain**, have, **contend**, argue, **insist, hold**, submit, maintain with one's last breath.

.5 **depose, depone; testify** 505.10; **warrant, attest**, certify, **guarantee, assure; vouch, swear, swear to**, swear the truth, **assert under oath**; make or take one's oath, vow; swear by bell, book, and candle; call heaven to witness, declare or swear to God, swear on the Bible, kiss the book, swear to goodness, hope to die, cross one's heart and hope to die [informal]; swear till one is black or blue in the face [informal].

.6 administer an oath, **place** or **put under oath**, put to one's oath, put upon oath; **swear, swear in**, adjure [archaic].

.7 ADJS **affirmative**, affirming, affirmatory; **assertive**, assertative, assertional; **declarative**, declaratory; predicative, predicational; **positive**, absolute, emphatic, decided.

.8 **affirmed, asserted**, asseverated, avouched, avowed, averred, **declared; alleged**, professed; **stated**, pronounced, announced, enunciated; predicated; manifestoed; **deposed**, warranted, **attested, certified**, vouched, **vouched for**, vowed, pledged, **sworn, sworn to**.

.9 ADVS **affirmatively**, assertively, declaratively, predicatively; **positively**, absolutely, decidedly; emphatically, with emphasis; without fear of contradiction; under oath.

## 524. NEGATION, DENIAL

.1 NOUNS **negation**, abnegation; negativeness, negativity, **negativism**, negative attitude, naysaying; **negative, no**, nay, nix [slang].

.2 **denial, disavowal, disaffirmation, disownment**, disallowance; disclamation, disclaimer; **renunciation, retraction**, retractation, **repudiation**, recantation; revocation, nullification, annulment, abrogation; abjuration, abjurement, forswearing; **contradiction**, flat or absolute contradiction, contravention, contrary assertion, controversion, countering, crossing, gainsaying, impugnment; **refutation, disproof** 506.

.3 VERBS **negate**, abnegate, negative; **say 'no'**; shake the head.

.4 **deny, not admit, not accept**, refuse to admit or accept; **disclaim, disown, disaffirm, disavow, disallow**, abjure, forswear, **renounce, retract**, take back, recant; revoke, nullify, **repudiate; contradict**, cross, assert the contrary, contravene, controvert, impugn, **dispute**, gainsay, **oppose**, **counter**, contest, take issue with, join issue upon; belie, give the lie to, give one the lie direct or in his throat; **refute** 506.5, **disprove** 506.4.

.5 ADJS **negative**, negatory, abnegative; **denying, disclaiming**, disowning, disaffirming, disallowing, disavowing, renunciative, renunciatory, repudiative, recanting, abjuratory, revocative or revocatory; **contradictory**, contradicting, **opposing**, **contrary**, adversative, repugnant; a– or an–, dis–, e– or ef– or ex–, in– or il– or im– or ir–, mis–, non–, nulli–, un–.

.6 ADVS **negatively, in the negative**; in denial, in contradiction.

.7 CONJS **neither**, not either, **nor**, nor yet, or not, and not, also not.

.8 INTERJS **no, nay**, negative, *non* [Fr], *nein* [Ger], *nyet* [Russ]; certainly not, absolutely no; no sir, no ma'am; **not**, not a bit or whit or jot, I think not, not really; to the contrary, *au contraire* [Fr], quite the contrary, far from it; no such thing, nothing of the kind or sort, not so.

.9 **by no means, by no manner of means; on no account**, in no respect, **in no case, under no circumstances, on no condition**, no matter what; **not at all**, not in the least, **never**; in no wise, noways, noway, nohow [dial]; out of the question; **not for the world**, not if one can help it, not if I know it, not at any price, not for love or money, not for the life of me; to the contrary, *au contraire* [Fr], quite the contrary, far from it; God forbid 969.27.

.10 [slang or informal terms] **nope, nix, unhunh**, no sirree; **no way, not on your life**, not by a long chalk, not by a long shot or sight, not by a darn or damn sight, not a bit of it, not much, not a chance, fat chance, **nothing doing, forget it**.

## 525. MENTAL ATTITUDE

.1 NOUNS **attitude**, mental attitude; psychology; **position, posture**, stance; **way of thinking**, way of looking at things; **feeling, sentiment**, the way one feels; feeling tone, affect, affectivity, emotion, emotivity; opinion 501.6.

.2 **outlook**, mental outlook; *Anschauung* [Ger], **point of view, viewpoint, standpoint**; position, stand, place, situation; side; footing, basis; where one is or sits or stands; **view**, sight, light, eye; respect, regard; angle, angle of vision, slant; **frame of reference**, framework, universe of discourse, universe, system, reference system.

.3 **disposition, character, nature, temper, temperament**, mettle, constitution [archaic], makeup, stamp, type, stripe, kidney, make, mold; **turn of mind, inclination**, mind, **tendency**, grain, set, mental set, mind-set, **leaning**, animus, propensity, proclivity, predilection, preference, predisposition; **bent, turn, bias**, slant, cast, warp, twist; idiosyncrasy, eccentricity, individualism; diathesis, aptitude; strain, streak.

.4 **mood, humor, temper, frame of mind, state of mind, morale**, cue or frame [both archaic], tone, note, vein; **mind, heart, spirit** or **spirits**.

.5 (pervading attitudes) **climate**, mental or intellectual climate, spiritual climate, moral climate, mores, norms, climate of opinion, **ethos**, ideology, *Weltanschauung* [Ger], world view.

.6 VERBS **take the attitude**, feel about it, look at it, **view**, look at in the light of; **be disposed to**, tend or incline toward, prefer, lean toward.

.7 ADJS **temperamental, dispositional**, constitutional; emotional, affective; mental, intellectual; spiritual; characteristic 80.13; innate 5.7.

.8 **disposed**, dispositioned, **predisposed, prone, inclined, given**, bent, apt, likely, –tempered, **minded, in the mood** or **humor**.

.9 ADVS **temperamentally, dispositionally**, constitutionally; emotionally; mentally, intellectually; morally, spiritually; **by temperament** or **disposition**, by virtue of mind-set, by the logic of character or temperament; from one's standpoint or viewpoint or angle; within the frame of reference or framework or reference system or universe of discourse.

## 526. BROAD-MINDEDNESS

.1 NOUNS **broad-mindedness**, wide-mindedness, large-mindedness, "the result of flattening high-mindedness out" [George Saintsbury]; **breadth**, broadness, broad gauge, latitude; **unbigotedness**, unhideboundness, unprovincialism, noninsularity, unparochialism, cosmopolitanism; ecumenicity, ecumenicism, ecumenicalism, ecumenism; broad mind, spacious mind.

.2 **liberalness, liberality**, catholicity, **liberalmindedness**; liberalism, libertarianism, latitudinarianism; freethinking, free thought.

.3 open-mindedness, openness, receptiveness, receptivity; persuadableness, persuadability, persuasibility; open mind.

.4 tolerance, toleration; indulgence, lenience or leniency, condonation, lenity; forbearance, patience, long-suffering; easiness, permissiveness; charitableness, charity, generousness, magnanimity 979.2.

.5 unprejudicedness, unbiasedness; impartiality, evenhandedness, equitability, fairness, justness, objectivity, detachment, dispassionateness, disinterestedness; indifference, neutrality; unopinionatedness.

.6 liberal, liberalist; libertarian; freethinker, latitudinarian, ecumenist, ecumenicist; big person, broad-gauge person.

.7 VERBS keep an open mind, be big [informal], judge not, not write off, suspend judgment, listen to reason, open one's mind to, see both sides; live and let live; lean over backwards, tolerate 861.5; accept, be easy with, view with indulgence, condone, brook, abide with, be content with; live with [informal]; shut one's eyes to, look the other way, wink at, blink at, overlook, disregard, ignore; "swear allegiance to the words of no master" [Horace].

.8 ADJS broad-minded, wide-minded, largeminded, broad, wide, broad-gauged, catholic, spacious of mind; unbigoted, unfanatical, unhidebound, unprovincial, cosmopolitan, noninsular, unparochial; ecumenistic, ecumenical.

.9 liberal, liberal-minded, liberalistic; libertarian; freethinking, latitudinarian.

.10 open-minded, open, receptive, admissive; persuadable, persuasible.

.11 tolerant, tolerating; indulgent, lenient, condoning; forbearing, forbearant [archaic], patient, long-suffering; charitable, generous, magnanimous 979.6.

.12 unprejudiced, unbiased, unprepossessed, unjaundiced; impartial, evenhanded, fair, just, equitable, objective, dispassionate, impersonal, detached, disinterested; indifferent, neutral; unswayed, uninfluenced, undazzled.

.13 unopinionated, unopinioned, unwedded to an opinion; unpositive, undogmatic; uninfatuated, unbesotted, unfanatical.

.14 broadening, enlightening.

### 527. NARROW-MINDEDNESS

.1 NOUNS narrow-mindedness, narrowness, illiberality, uncatholicity; little-mindedness, small-mindedness, smallness, littleness, meanness, pettiness; bigotry, bigot-

edness, fanaticism, odium theologicum [L]; insularity, insularism, provincialism, parochialism; hideboundness, straitlacedness, stuffiness [informal]; authoritarianism; shortsightedness, nearsightedness, purblindness; blind side, blind spot, blinders; closed mind, mean mind, petty mind, shut mind; narrow views or sympathies, cramped ideas.

.2 intolerance, intoleration; uncharitableness, ungenerousness; unforbearance.

.3 prejudice, prejudgment, forejudgment, predilection, prepossession, preconception; bias, bent, leaning, inclination, twist; jaundice, jaundiced eye; partiality, partialism, partisanship, favoritism, onesidedness, undispassionateness, undetachment.

.4 discrimination, social discrimination, minority prejudice; xenophobia, know-nothingism; chauvinism, ultranationalism, superpatriotism; fascism; class consciousness, class prejudice, class distinction, class hatred, class war; anti-Semitism; redbaiting [informal]; racism, racialism, race hatred, race prejudice, race snobbery, racial discrimination; white or black supremacy, white or black power; color line, color bar; social barrier, Jim Crow, Jim Crow law; segregation, apartheid, sex discrimination, sexism, male chauvinism.

.5 bigot, intolerant, illiberal, little person; racist; pig [slang]; chauvinist, ultranationalist, jingo, superpatriot; male chauvinist, sexist; dogmatist, doctrinaire 513.7; fanatic 473.17.

.6 VERBS close one's mind, shut the eyes of one's mind, take narrow views, put on blinders, blind oneself, have a blind side or spot, constrict one's views; not see beyond one's nose or an inch beyond one's nose; view with a jaundiced eye, see but one side of the question, look only at one side of the shield.

.7 prejudge, forejudge, judge beforehand, precondemn, prejudicate [archaic], take one's opinions ready-made, accede to prejudice.

.8 discriminate against, draw the line, draw the color line, red-bait.

.9 prejudice, prejudice against, prejudice the issue, prepossess, jaundice, influence, sway, bias, bias one's judgment; warp, twist, bend, distort.

.10 ADJS narrow-minded, narrow, narrowgauged, closed, closed-minded, cramped, constricted, borné [Fr], little-minded, small-minded, mean-minded, petty-minded, narrow-hearted, narrow-souled, narrow-spirited, mean-spirited, small-souled; **small, little, mean, petty;** uncharitable, ungenerous; bigot, **bigoted,** fanatical; **illiberal,** unliberal, uncatholic; provincial, insular, parochial; **hidebound,** creedbound, **straitlaced,** stuffy [informal]; authoritarian; **shortsighted,** nearsighted, purblind; deaf, deaf-minded, deaf to reason.

.11 **intolerant,** untolerating; **unindulgent,** uncondoning, unforbearing.

.12 **prejudiced,** prepossessed, **biased, jaundiced,** colored; **partial,** one-sided, partisan; influenced, swayed, warped, twisted; interested, nonobjective, **undetached,** undispassionate; xenophobic, know-nothing; **chauvinistic,** ultranationalist, superpatriotic; **racist,** anti-Negro, antiblack; anti-Semitic; sexist; dogmatic, doctrinaire, **opinionated** 513.22.

## 528. CURIOSITY

.1 NOUNS **curiosity,** curiousness, **inquisitiveness; interest,** interestedness, lively interest; thirst or desire or lust or itch for knowledge, mental acquisitiveness, inquiring or curious mind; nosiness or snoopiness [both informal], prying; officiousness, meddlesomeness 238.2; morbid curiosity, ghoulishness; voyeurism, scopophilia, prurience, prurient interest.

.2 inquisitive, quidnunc; **inquirer,** questioner, querier, querist, inquisitor, inquisitress; **busybody,** gossip, *yenta* [Yid], **pry,** Paul Pry, **snoop,** snooper, nosy Parker [informal]; sightseer; rubbernecker or rubberneck [slang]; eavesdropper; Peeping Tom, voyeur, scopophiliac; Lot's wife.

.3 VERBS **be curious, want to know, take an interest in,** take a lively interest, burn with curiosity; prick up the ears; interrogate, quiz, question, inquire, query; stare, gape, peer, gawk, rubber or rubberneck [both slang]; seek, dig up, dig around for, nose out, nose around for.

.4 **pry, snoop,** peep, peek, spy, nose, have a long or big nose, poke or stick one's nose in; meddle 238.7.

.5 ADJS **curious, inquisitive,** inquiring, interested, quizzical; burning with curiosity, eaten up or consumed with curiosity, curious as a cat; agape, agog, all agog, openmouthed, open-eyed; gossipy; overcurious, supercurious; morbidly curious, morbid, ghoulish; prurient, itchy, voyeuristic, scopophiliac.

.6 **prying,** snooping, **nosy** or **snoopy** [both informal]; meddlesome 238.9.

## 529. INCURIOSITY

.1 NOUNS **incuriosity,** incuriousness, **uninquisitiveness;** boredom; **uninterestedness,** disinterest, disinterestedness, **unconcern,** uninvolvement, **indifference** 636, indifferentness, indifferentism, **apathy,** impassivity, impassiveness, listlessness, stolidity, **lack of interest;** carelessness, heedlessness, regardlessness, insouciance, unmindfulness; aloofness, detachment, withdrawal; intellectual inertia.

.2 VERBS **take no interest in, not care;** mind one's own business, pursue the even tenor of one's way, glance neither to the right nor to the left.

.3 ADJS **incurious, uninquisitive,** uninquiring; bored; **uninterested,** unconcerned, disinterested, uninvolved, **indifferent, apathetic,** impassive, stolid, phlegmatic, listless; careless, heedless, regardless, insouciant, mindless, unmindful; aloof, detached, distant, withdrawn.

## 530. ATTENTION

.1 NOUNS **attention, attentiveness,** mindfulness, regardfulness, heedfulness; **attention span; heed,** ear; consideration, thought; awareness, consciousness, alertness 533.5; **observation,** observance, advertence, advertency, **note, notice,** remark, **regard,** respect; **intentness,** intentiveness, concentration; diligence, assiduity, assiduousness, earnestness; **care** 533.1.

.2 **interest, concern,** concernment; **curiosity** 528; **enthusiasm,** passion; cathexis; matter of interest, special interest.

.3 **engrossment, absorption, intentness,** single-mindedness, **concentration, application,** study, studiousness, **preoccupation,** engagement, **involvement, immersion,** submersion; obsession, monomania; rapt attention, absorbed attention or interest; deep study, deep or profound thought, contemplation, meditation.

.4 **close attention,** close study, scrutiny, fixed regard, rapt or fascinated attention, whole or total or undivided attention; minute or meticulous attention, attention to detail, finicalness, finickiness; constant or unrelenting attention, harping, strict attention; special consideration.

.5 VERBS **attend to,** look to, **see to,** advert to, be aware of; **pay attention to,** pay regard to, give mind to, pay mind to [informal], not forget, spare a thought for, **give heed to; have a look at; turn to,** give thought to, trouble one's head about; give one's mind to, direct one's attention to, turn or bend or set the mind or attention to; **devote oneself to,** devote the mind or thoughts to, fix or rivet or focus the mind or thoughts on, set one's thoughts on, apply the mind or attention to, apply oneself to, **occupy oneself with, concern oneself with,** give oneself up to, be absorbed or engrossed in, **lose oneself in; hang on one's words,** hang on the lips; **drink in,** drink in with rapt attention.

.6 **heed, attend,** tend, **mind, watch, observe, regard,** look, see, view, mark, remark, animadvert [archaic], **note, notice,** take note or notice.

.7 **hearken to,** hark, **listen, hear,** give ear to, lend an ear to, incline or bend an ear to, prick up the ears, strain one's ears, **keep one's ears open,** unstopper one's ears, have or keep an ear to the ground, listen with both ears, **be all ears.**

.8 **pay attention** or heed, **take heed,** give heed, **look out, watch out** [informal], **take care** 533.7; look lively or alive, **look sharp,** stay or be alert, sit up and take notice; be on the ball or keep one's eye on the ball or not miss a trick or not overlook a bet [all informal]; miss nothing; keep one's eyes open 533.8; attend to business, mind one's business; pay close or strict attention, strain one's attention, not relax one's concern, give one's undivided attention, give special attention to; keep in the center of one's attention, keep uppermost in one's thought; **concentrate on,** focus or fix on; **study,** scrutinize; be obsessed with.

.9 **take cognizance of, take note** or **notice of, take heed of, take account of, take into consideration** or **account, bear in mind,** keep or hold in mind, reckon with, keep in sight or view, not lose sight of, have in one's eye, have an eye to, have regard for.

.10 **call attention to,** direct attention to, **bring under** or **to one's notice,** bring to attention, pick out, focus on, call or bring to notice, direct to the attention; **direct to,** address to; **mention,** specify, mention in passing, touch on, cite, **refer to,** allude to; **point out, point to,** point at, put or lay one's finger on.

.11 **meet with attention,** fall under one's notice; **catch the attention,** draw or hold or focus the attention, catch or meet or strike the eye, attract notice or attention, arrest or engage attention, fix or rivet one's attention, arrest the thoughts, awaken the mind or thoughts, **excite notice,** arouse notice, arrest one's notice, invite or solicit attention, claim or demand attention.

.12 **interest, concern,** involve in or with, affect the interest; **pique, titillate,** tantalize, tickle, **attract,** invite, **fascinate, provoke, stimulate, excite,** pique one's interest, excite interest, excite or whet one's interest, arouse one's passion or enthusiasm, turn one on [slang].

.13 **engross, absorb,** immerse, **occupy, preoccupy, engage,** involve, monopolize, exercise, take up; **obsess; grip, hold, arrest, hold the interest,** fascinate, **enthrall,** spellbind, **hold spellbound,** grab [slang], charm, enchant, mesmerize, hypnotize, catch; absorb the attention, claim one's thoughts, engross the mind or thoughts, engage the attention, involve the interest, occupy the attention, monopolize one's attention, engage the mind or thoughts.

.14 **come to attention,** stand at attention.

.15 ADJS **attentive, heedful, mindful, regardful,** advertent; **intent, intentive,** diligent, assiduous, intense, earnest, concentrated; **careful** 533.10; **observing,** observant; watchful, aware, conscious, alert 533.13,14; agog, openmouthed; open-eared, open-eyed, **all eyes, all ears,** all eyes and ears; on the job [informal], on the ball, Johnny on the spot [both slang]; meticulous, nice, finical, finicky, finicking, niggling.

.16 **interested,** concerned; **curious** 528.5; tantalized, piqued, titillated, tickled, **attracted,** fascinated, excited, turned-on [slang]; keen on or about, enthusiastic, passionate; cathectic.

.17 **engrossed, absorbed,** totally absorbed, single-minded, **occupied, preoccupied, engaged,** devoted, devoted to, intent, intent on, monopolized, obsessed, monomaniacal, swept up, taken up with, **involved, caught up in,** wrapped in, **wrapped up in,** engrossed in, **absorbed in** or with or by, **lost in, immersed in,** submerged in, buried in; over head and ears in, head over heels in [informal], up to one's elbows in, up to one's ears in; contemplating, contemplative, studying, studious, meditative, meditating.

.18 **gripped, held, fascinated, enthralled, rapt, spellbound,** charmed, enchanted, mesmerized, **hypnotized,** fixed, caught, arrested.

.19 **interesting, stimulating, provocative,** provoking, thought-provoking, thought-challenging, thought-inspiring; **titillating,** tickling, **tantalizing, inviting, exciting;** piquant, lively, racy, juicy, succulent, spicy, rich; readable.

.20 **engrossing, absorbing,** consuming, **gripping,** holding, **arresting,** engaging, attractive, **fascinating, enthralling, spellbinding,** enchanting, magnetic, hypnotic, mesmerizing, mesmeric; obsessive, obsessing.

.21 ADVS **attentively,** with attention; **heedfully,** mindfully, regardfully, advertently; observingly, observantly; **interestedly,** with interest; **raptly,** with rapt attention; engrossedly, absorbedly, preoccupiedly; devotedly, **intently,** without distraction, **with undivided attention.**

.22 INTERJS **attention!, look!,** see!, look you!, look here!, looky! [informal], witness!; lo!, behold!, lo and behold!; **hark!, listen!,** hark ye!, hear ye!, oyez!; *nota bene* [L, note well], NB.

.23 **hey!, hail!, ahoy!, hello!, hollo!, hallo!,** halloo!, halloa!, ho!, heigh!, hi!, hist!; hello there!, ahoy there!, etc.

## 531. INATTENTION

.1 NOUNS **inattention,** inattentiveness, **heedlessness, unheedfulness, unmindfulness, thoughtlessness,** inconsideration; **incuriosity** 529, **indifference** 636; inadvertence or inadvertency; unintentness, unintentiveness; disregard, disregardfulness, regardlessness; **flightiness** 532.5, giddiness 532.4, lightmindedness; levity, frivolousness, flippancy; shallowness, superficiality; **inobservance,** unobservance, nonobservance; **unalertness,** unwariness, unwatchfulness; **obliviousness,** unconsciousness, unawareness; **carelessness,** negligence 534.1-4; distraction, **absentmindedness** 532.2.

.2 VERBS **be inattentive, pay no attention,** pay no mind [dial], not attend, not notice, **take no note or notice of,** take no thought or account of, miss, not heed, give no heed, pay no regard to, not listen, hear nothing, not hear a word; **disregard, overlook, ignore,** pass over or by, have no time for, let pass or get by or get past; think little of, **slight,** make light of; **close or shut one's eyes to,** see nothing, be blind to, turn a blind eye, **look the other way, blink at, wink at,** connive at; stick one's head in the sand; **turn a deaf ear to,** stop one's ears, let come in one ear and go out the other; let well enough alone; not trouble oneself with, not trouble one's head with or about; **be unwary,** be off one's guard, be caught out.

.3 **wander, stray,** divagate, wander from the subject; have no attention span, have a short attention span, let one's attention wander, get off the track [informal].

.4 **dismiss,** dismiss or drive from one's thoughts; **put out of mind,** put out of one's head or thoughts, wean one's thoughts from, think nothing of, force one's thoughts from, **think no more of, forget, forget it,** forget about it, **let it go** [informal], let slip, not give it another or a second thought, **drop the subject,** give it no more thought; turn one's back upon, turn away from, turn one's attention from, abandon, leave out in the cold [informal]; put or set or lay aside, push or thrust aside or to one side, put on the back burner [informal]; **turn up one's nose at,** sneeze at; **shrug off, brush off or aside;** laugh off or away, dismiss with a laugh.

.5 **escape notice or attention,** escape one, get by, be missed, pass one by, not enter one's head, fall on deaf ears, not register.

.6 ADJS **inattentive, unmindful,** inadvertent, thoughtless, **incurious** 529.3, **indifferent** 636.6,7; **heedless,** unheeding, unheedful, regardless, *distrait* [Fr], **disregardful,** disregardant; **unobserving,** inobservant, unobservant, unnoticing, unnoting, unremarking, unmarking; **distracted** 532.10; **careless, negligent** 534.10.

.7 **oblivious, unconscious,** insensible, dead to the world; blind, deaf; **preoccupied** 532.11.

.8 **unalert, unwary, unwatchful, unvigilant,** uncautious, incautious; **unprepared,** unready; unguarded, **off one's guard,** offguard; **asleep,** sleeping, nodding, napping, **asleep at the switch** [informal], asleep on the job or **not on the job** [both informal], goofing off or looking out the window [both slang].

## 532. DISTRACTION, CONFUSION

.1 NOUNS **distraction,** distractedness, **diversion,** separation or withdrawal of attention, divided attention; **inattention** 531.

.2 **abstractedness, abstraction,** preoccupation, **absorption,** engrossment, depth of thought, fit of abstraction; **absentmindedness, absence of mind; bemusement,** musing, musefulness [archaic]; woolgathering, mooning [informal], moonraking [archaic], stargazing, **dreaming, daydreaming,** fantasying, pipe-dreaming [informal], castle-building; **brown study,** study, reverie, muse, dreamy abstraction, quiet or muted ecstasy, trance; dream, **daydream,** fantasy, pipe dream [informal]; daydreamer, Walter Mitty.

.3 confusion, fluster, flummox [informal], flutter, flurry, ruffle; disorientation, **muddle, muddlement,** fuddle or fuddlement [both informal], befuddlement, daze, maze [dial]; unsettlement, disorganization, **disorder,** chaos, **mess** [informal], shuffle, jumble, discomfiture, discomposure, disconcertion, discombobulation [informal], **bewilderment, embarrassment, disturbance,** perturbation, **upset,** frenzy, pother, bother, botheration or stew [both informal], pucker [archaic]; tizzy or swivet or sweat [all informal]; haze, fog, mist, cloud; maze; **perplexity** 514.3.

.4 dizziness, vertigo, vertiginousness, spinning head, swimming, swimming of the head, **giddiness,** wooziness [informal], **lightheadedness;** tiddliness [Brit informal], drunkenness 996.1–4.

.5 flightiness, giddiness, volatility, mercuriality; **thoughtlessness,** witlessness, **brainlessness,** empty-headedness, foolishness 470.

.6 VERBS **distract, divert,** detract, distract the attention, divert or detract attention, divert the mind or thoughts, draw off the attention, call away, take the mind off of, relieve the mind of, cause the mind to stray or wander, put off the track, throw off the scent, lead the mind astray, beguile; throw off one's guard.

.7 confuse, throw into confusion, **fluster;** flummox, fuss or fuss up [all informal], **flutter,** put into a flutter, **flurry, rattle, ruffle,** moider [Brit dial], **mix up,** ball up [slang], entangle, **muddle,** fuddle [informal], **befuddle, addle,** addle the wits, **daze, maze, dazzle,** bedazzle; **upset, unsettle,** raise hell, disorganize; throw into a tizzy or swivet, etc.; **disconcert, discomfit, discompose,** discombobulate [informal], disorient, **bewilder, embarrass, put out, disturb, perturb, bother,** pother, bug [slang]; fog, mist, cloud, becloud; **perplex** 514.13.

.8 dizzy, make one's head swim, cause vertigo, send one spinning, whirl the mind, swirl the senses, make one's head reel or whirl or spin or revolve, go to one's head; intoxicate 996.21,22.

.9 muse, moon [informal], dream, daydream, pipe-dream [informal], fantasy; abstract oneself, be lost in thought, let one's attention wander, let one's mind run on other things, dream of or muse on other things; **wander, stray,** divagate, let one's thoughts or mind wander, give oneself up to reverie, **go woolgathering,** let one's wits go bird's nesting, **be in a brown study,** be absent, be somewhere else, stargaze.

.10 ADJS **distracted, distraught,** distrait [Fr]; **wandering, rambling; wild, frantic, beside oneself.**

.11 **abstracted, bemused,** museful [archaic], **musing, preoccupied, absorbed, engrossed,** taken up; **absentminded, absent,** faraway, elsewhere, somewhere else, not there; pensive, meditative; lost, **lost in thought,** wrapped in thought; rapt, transported, ecstatic; dead to the world, **unconscious, oblivious; dreaming, dreamy,** drowsing, nodding, half-awake, betwixt sleep and waking, napping; **daydreaming,** daydreamy, pipe-dreaming [informal]; **woolgathering,** mooning or moony [both informal], moonraking [archaic], castle-building, in the clouds, off in the clouds, stargazing, in a reverie.

.12 confused, **mixed-up,** balled-up [slang]; **flustered,** fluttered, **ruffled, rattled,** fussed [informal]; **upset, unsettled,** disorganized, **disordered,** chaotic, jumbled, in a jumble, shuffled; shaken, shook [slang], **disconcerted, discomposed,** discombobulated [informal], **embarrassed, put-out, disturbed, perturbed,** bothered, all hot and bothered [informal]; in a stew or botheration [informal], in a pucker [archaic]; in a tizzy or swivet or sweat [informal], in a pother; **perplexed** 514.24.

.13 muddled, in a muddle; fuddled [informal], **befuddled;** muddleheaded, fuddlebrained [informal]; puzzleheaded, puzzlepated; **addled,** addleheaded, addlepated, addlebrained; foggy, fogged, in a fog, hazy, muzzy [informal], misted, misty, cloudy, beclouded.

.14 dazed, mazed, **dazzled,** bedazzled, in a daze; **silly,** knocked silly; groggy [informal], **dopey** [slang], woozy [informal]; **punch-drunk** [informal], punchy, **slaphappy** [both slang].

.15 dizzy, giddy, vertiginous, swimming, turned around, going around in circles; lightheaded, tiddly [Brit informal], **drunken** 996.30–33.

.16 scatterbrained, shatterbrained or shatterpated [both archaic], rattlebrained, rattleheaded, rattlepated, scramblebrained, harebrain, harebrained, **giddy, dizzy,** gaga [informal], giddy-brained, giddy-headed, giddy-pated, giddy-witted, giddy as a goose, fluttery, frivolous, featherbrained, featherheaded; **thoughtless, witless, brainless, empty-headed** 469.19.

.17 **flighty,** volatile, mercurial.

## 533. CAREFULNESS

*(close or watchful attention)*

.1 NOUNS **carefulness, care, heed, concern, regard; attention** 530; **heedfulness,** regardfulness, mindfulness, **thoughtfulness;** consideration, solicitude, loving care, tender loving care, TLC [informal]; circumspectness, circumspection; forethought, anticipation, preparedness; **caution** 895.

.2 **painstakingness,** painstaking, **pains; diligence,** assiduousness, assiduity, sedulousness, industriousness, industry; **thoroughness,** thoroughgoingness.

.3 **meticulousness,** exactingness, **scrupulousness,** scrupulosity, **conscientiousness,** punctiliousness, attention to detail, **particularness,** particularity, circumstantiality; **fussiness, criticalness,** criticality; **finicalness,** finickingness, finickiness, finicality; **exactness, exactitude, accuracy, preciseness, precision,** precisionism, precisianism, punctuality, correctness; **strictness,** rigidity, **rigor,** rigorousness; nicety, niceness, delicacy, detail, subtlety, refinement, minuteness, exquisiteness.

.4 **vigilance, wariness,** prudence, **watchfulness,** watching, observance, **surveillance; watch, vigil, lookout;** *qui vive* [Fr]; invigilation, proctoring, monitoring; watch and ward; custody, custodianship, guardianship, stewardship; **guard,** guardedness; watchful eye, weather *or* peeled eye [informal], sharp eye, eagle eye, lidless *or* sleepless *or* unblinking *or* unwinking eye.

.5 **alertness, attentiveness; attention** 530; **wakefulness,** sleeplessness; **readiness,** promptness, promptitude, punctuality; **quickness,** agility, nimbleness; **smartness,** brightness, keenness, sharpness, acuteness, acuity.

.6 VERBS **care, mind, heed,** reck, think, consider, regard, take heed *or* thought of; **take an interest,** be concerned; **pay attention** 530.8.

.7 **be careful, take care** *or* good care, take heed, have a care, exercise care; **be cautious** 895.5; **take pains,** take trouble, be

**painstaking,** go to great pains, go to great lengths, bend over backwards [informal]; mind what one is doing *or* about, mind one's business, **mind one's P's and Q's** [informal]; **watch one's step** [informal], pick one's steps, tread on eggs, place one's feet carefully, feel one's way; treat gently, **handle with gloves** *or* **kid gloves.**

.8 **be vigilant,** be watchful, never nod *or* sleep, **be on the watch** *or* **lookout,** be on the *qui vive*, keep a good *or* sharp lookout, keep in sight *or* view; **keep watch,** keep watch and ward, keep vigil; **watch, look sharp,** look about one, look with one's own eyes, **be on one's guard,** sleep with one eye open, have all one's eyes *or* wits about one, keep one's eyes open, keep a weather eye open [informal], **keep one's eyes peeled** [informal], keep the ears on *or* to the ground, keep a nose to the wind; keep alert, **be on the alert; look out, watch out** [informal]; look lively *or* alive; stop, look, and listen.

.9 **look after, tend, take care of** 699.19.

.10 ADJS **careful, heedful, regardful, mindful, thoughtful, considerate,** solicitous, loving, tender, curious [archaic]; circumspect; **attentive** 530.15; **cautious** 895.8.

.11 **painstaking, diligent, assiduous,** sedulous, **thorough, thoroughgoing,** operose, industrious, elaborate.

.12 **meticulous, exacting, scrupulous, conscientious,** religious, **punctilious, punctual, particular, fussy, critical, attentive,** scrutinizing; **finical,** finicking, finicky; **exact, precise,** precisionistic, precisianistic, **accurate, correct;** close, narrow; **strict,** rigid, **rigorous,** exigent, demanding; nice, delicate, subtle, fine, refined, minute, detailed, exquisite.

.13 **vigilant, wary,** prudent, **watchful,** lidless, sleepless, observant; **on the watch, on the lookout,** *aux aguets* [Fr]; **on guard,** on one's guard, guarded; with open eyes, with one's eyes open, with one's eyes peeled *or* with a weather eye open [both informal]; open-eyed, sharp-eyed, keen-eyed, Argus-eyed, eagle-eyed, hawk-eyed; all eyes, all ears, **all eyes and ears;** custodial.

.14 **alert, on the alert,** on the *qui vive*, on one's toes, **on the job** *or* **on the ball** [both informal], **attentive; awake,** wakeful, **wide-awake,** sleepless, unsleeping, unblinking, unwinking, unnodding, alive, ready, prompt, quick, agile, nimble, quick on the trigger *or* draw [informal]; **smart, bright, keen, sharp.**

.15 ADVS **carefully**, **heedfully**, regardfully, **mindfully**, thoughtfully, **considerately**, solicitously, tenderly, lovingly; circumspectly; **cautiously** 895.12; **with care**, with great care; **painstakingly**, **diligently**, assiduously, industriously, sedulously, thoroughly, thoroughgoingly.

.16 **meticulously**, **exactingly**, **scrupulously**, **conscientiously**, religiously, punctiliously, punctually, fussily; **strictly**, rigorously; exactly, **accurately**, **precisely**, **with exactitude**, **with precision**; nicely, with great nicety, refinedly, minutely, in detail, exquisitely.

.17 **vigilantly**, **warily**, prudently, **watchfully**, observantly; **alertly**, attentively; sleeplessly, unsleepingly, unwinkingly, unblinkingly, lidlessly, unnoddingly.

## 534. NEGLECT

.1 NOUNS **neglect**, neglectfulness, **negligence**, inadvertence or inadvertency, dereliction, *culpa* [L], culpable negligence; **remissness**, laxity, laxness, slackness, looseness, laches; unrigorousness, permissiveness; noninterference, *laissez-faire* [Fr], nonrestriction; **disregard**, slight; **inattention** 531; **oversight**, overlooking; omission, nonfeasance, nonperformance, lapse, failure, default; poor stewardship or guardianship or custody; procrastination 132.5.

.2 **carelessness**, **heedlessness**, **unheedfulness**, disregardfulness, regardlessness; unsolicitude, unsolicitousness, **thoughtlessness**, tactlessness, inconsiderateness, **inconsideration**; unthinkingness, unmindfulness, oblivion, forgetfulness; **unpreparedness**, unreadiness, lack of foresight or forethought; **recklessness** 894.2; **indifference** 636; **laziness** 708.5; perfunctoriness; cursoriness, hastiness, offhandedness, casualness; easiness; nonconcern, insouciance; abandon, careless abandon, *sprezzatura* [Ital].

.3 **slipshodness**, slipshoddiness, **slovenliness**, slovenry, sluttishness, untidiness, **sloppiness** or **messiness** [both informal]; haphazardness; slapdash, slapdashness, a lick and a promise [all informal], loose ends; bad job, sad work, botch, slovenly performance; bungling 734.4.

.4 **unmeticulousness**, unexactingness, **unscrupulousness**, unrigorousness, **unconscientiousness**, unpunctiliousness, unpunctuality, unparticularness, unfussiness, unfinicalness, **uncriticalness**; inexactness,

inexactitude, inaccuracy, imprecision, unpreciseness.

.5 **neglecter**, negligent [archaic], ignorer, disregarder; **procrastinator**, waiter on Providence, Micawber [Dickens]; slacker, shirker, malingerer, dodger, goof-off or goldbrick [both slang], idler; skimper [informal]; trifler 673.9; sloven, slut; bungler 734.8.

.6 VERBS **neglect**, **overlook**, **disregard**, not heed, take for granted, **ignore**; not care for, not take care of; **pass over**, gloss over; **let slip**, **let slide** [informal], **let go**, let ride [slang], let take its course; let the grass grow under one's feet; not think or consider, not give a thought to, take no thought or account of, blind oneself to, turn a blind eye to, leave out of one's calculation; lose sight of, lose track of; **be neglectful** or **negligent**, fail in one's duty, **fail**, lapse, **default**, let go by default; not get involved; nod, sleep [archaic], be caught napping, be asleep at the switch [informal].

.7 **leave undone**, leave, **let go**, leave halfdone, pretermit, **skip**, jump, **miss**, **omit**, cut [informal], let be or alone, pass over, pass up [informal], abandon; leave a loose thread, leave loose ends, let dangle; slack, shirk, malinger, goof off or goldbrick [both slang]; trifle 673.13; **procrastinate** 132.11.

.8 **slight**; turn one's back on, turn a cold shoulder to, cold-shoulder [informal], leave out in the cold; scamp, skimp [informal]; slur, **slur over**, pass over, slubber over, slip or **skip over**, dodge, fudge, blink, carefully ignore; skim, **skim over**, skim the surface, **touch upon**, touch upon lightly or in passing, pass over lightly, go once over lightly, **hit the high spots** or **give a lick and a promise** [both informal]; **cut corners**, cut a corner.

.9 **do carelessly**, do by halves, do in a slipshod fashion, do anyhow, do in any old way [informal]; botch, **bungle** 734.11; **trifle with**, play or play at fast and loose with, mess around or about with [informal]; **do offhand**, dash off, knock off or throw off [both informal], **toss off** or **out** [informal]; **roughhew**, roughcast, rough out; **knock out** [informal], hammer or pound out, bat out [slang]; toss or **throw together**, knock together, patch together, patch, **patch up**, fudge up, fake up, whomp up [informal], lash up [Brit informal], slap up [informal]; jury-rig.

.10 ADJS **negligent**, **neglectful**, neglecting,

derelict, culpably negligent; inadvertent, uncircumspect; **inattentive** 531.6; unwary, unwatchful, off-guard, unguarded; **remiss,** slack, lax, relaxed, loose, unrigorous, permissive, overly permissive; noninterfering, *laissez-faire* [Fr], nonrestrictive; slighting; slurring, scamping, skimping [informal]; procrastinating 132.17.

.11 **careless, heedless, unheeding, unheedful, disregardful,** disregardant, regardless, **unsolicitous,** tactless, respectless, **thoughtless, unthinking, inconsiderate,** untactful, undiplomatic, mindless of, **unmindful,** forgetful, oblivious; **unprepared,** unready; **reckless** 894.8; **indifferent** 636.6,7; lazy 708.18; perfunctory, cursory, casual, offhand; easygoing, *dégagé* [Fr], airy, flippant, insouciant, free and easy.

.12 **slipshod,** slipshoddy, **slovenly,** sloppy *or* messy [both informal], sluttish, untidy; **clumsy, bungling** 734.20; **haphazard, promiscuous, hit-or-miss,** hit-and-miss; deficient, half-assed [slang], botched.

.13 **unmeticulous, unexacting, unpainstaking, unscrupulous,** unrigorous, **unconscientious,** unpunctilious, unpunctual, **unparticular, unfussy, unfinical, uncritical;** inexact, inaccurate, unprecise.

.14 **neglected,** unattended to, untended, unwatched, unchaperoned, uncared-for; **disregarded,** unconsidered, unregarded, **overlooked, missed,** omitted, passed by, passed over, passed up [informal], **ignored, slighted;** unasked, unsolicited; half-done, undone, left undone; deserted, abandoned; in the cold *or* out in the cold [both informal]; shelved, pigeonholed, **put** *or* **laid aside,** sidetracked *or* sidelined [both informal], shunted.

.15 **unheeded, unobserved, unnoticed, unnoted, unperceived, unseen,** undiscerned, undescried, unmarked, unremarked, unregarded, unminded, unconsidered, unthought-of, unmissed.

.16 **unexamined, unstudied,** unconsidered, unsearched, unscanned, unweighed, unsifted, unexplored, unconned.

.17 ADVS **negligently, neglectfully,** inadvertently; **remissly,** laxly, slackly, loosely; **unrigorously,** permissively; nonrestrictively; **slightingly,** lightly, slurringly; scampingly, skimpingly [informal].

.18 **carelessly, heedlessly,** unheedingly, unheedfully, disregardfully, regardlessly, **thoughtlessly, unthinkingly, unsolicitously,** tactlessly, **inconsiderately,** unmindfully, forgetfully; **inattentively, unwarily,** unvigilantly, unguardedly, un-

watchfully; **recklessly** 894.11; perfunctorily; once over lightly, cursorily; casually, offhand, offhandedly, airily; clumsily, bunglingly 734.24; **sloppily** *or* **messily** [both informal]; haphazardly, promiscuously, hit *or* miss, hit and miss, helter-skelter, **slapdash** [both informal], anyhow, any old way, any which way [both informal].

.19 **unmeticulously, unscrupulously, unconscientiously, unfussily, uncritically;** inexactly, inaccurately, unprecisely, imprecisely, unpunctually.

## 535. IMAGINATION

.1 NOUNS **imagination,** imagining, imaginativeness, **fancy, fantasy,** conceit [archaic]; mind's eye, "that inward eye which is the bliss of solitude" [Wordsworth]; flight of fancy, fumes of fancy; fantasticism.

.2 **creative thought,** conception; productive *or* constructive *or* creative imagination, creative power *or* ability, esemplastic imagination *or* power, shaping imagination, poetic imagination, artistic imagination; mythopoeia, *mythopoesis* [Gk]; mythification, mythicization; inspiration, muse; Muses: Calliope (epic poetry), Clio (history), Erato (lyric and love poetry), Euterpe (music), Melpomene (tragedy), Polyhymnia (sacred song), Terpsichore (dancing and choral song), Thalia (comedy), Urania (astronomy); genius 467.8.

.3 **invention, inventiveness, originality, creativity,** creativeness, **ingenuity;** productivity, prolificacy, **fertility,** fecundity; rich *or* teeming imagination, fertile *or* pregnant imagination, seminal *or* germinal imagination, fertile mind.

.4 **lively imagination,** active fancy, **vivid imagination,** colorful *or* highly colored *or* lurid imagination, warm *or* ardent imagination, fiery *or* heated imagination, excited imagination, bold *or* daring *or* wild *or* fervent imagination; verve, vivacity of imagination.

.5 **figment of the imagination,** creature of the imagination, creation *or* coinage of the brain, fiction of the mind, maggot, whim, whimsy, figment, imagination, invention; brainchild; **imagining,** fancy, idle fancy, vapor, fantasque, "thick-coming fancies" [Shakespeare], imagery; **fantasy, make-believe;** phantom, vision, apparition, insubstantial image, eidolon, **phantasm** 519.4; **fiction,** myth, romance; wildest dreams, stretch of the imagination; **chimera, bubble, illusion** 519; hallucination, delirium, sick fancy; trip or drug trip [both slang].

.6 **visualization, envisioning,** envisaging, picturing, objectification, imaging, calling to or before the mind's eye, figuring or portraying or representing in the mind; depicting or delineating in the imagination; conceptualization; **picture, vision, image,** mental image, mental picture, visual image, vivid or lifelike image, eidetic image, concept, **conception,** mental representation or presentation, *Vorstellung* [Ger]; **imagery,** word-painting; poetic image, poetic imagery; imagery study; imagism, imagistic poetry.

.7 **idealism, idealization; ideal,** ideality; visionariness, **utopianism;** flight of fancy, play of fancy, imaginative exercise; **romanticism,** romance; **quixotism,** quixotry; dreamery; **impracticality,** unpracticalness, **unrealism,** unreality; **wishful thinking,** wish fulfillment, wish-fulfillment fantasy, autistic thinking, dereistic thinking, autism, dereism, autistic distortion.

.8 **dreaminess,** dreamfulness, musefulness, pensiveness; dreamlikeness; **dreaming, musing; daydreaming,** pipe-dreaming [informal], dreamery, fantasying, castlebuilding.

.9 **dream,** oneir(o)– or onir(o)–; reverie, **daydream, pipe dream** [informal]; **brown study** 532.2; **vision; nightmare,** incubus, bad dream.

.10 **air castle, castle in the air,** castle in the sky or skies, castle in Spain; Xanadu, pleasure dome of Kubla Khan [both Coleridge].

.11 **utopia** or Utopia [Sir Thomas More], **paradise, heaven** 1018, **heaven on earth;** millennium, kingdom come; dreamland, lotus land, land of dreams, land of enchantment, land of heart's desire, wonderland, cloudland, fairyland, land of faerie, faerie; Eden, Garden of Eden; promised land, land of promise, land of plenty, land of milk and honey, Canaan, Goshen; Shangri-la, New Atlantis [Francis Bacon], Arcadia, Agapemone, Happy Valley [Samuel Johnson], land of Prester John, Eldorado, Seven Cities of Cibola, Quivira; Laputa [Swift]; Cockaigne, Big Rock-Candy Mountain, Fiddler's Green, Never-Never-land [J. M. Barrie], Neverland, Cloudcuckooland or Nephelococcygia [Aristophanes], Erewhon [Samuel Butler], Land of Youth; dystopia or kakotopia; Pandemonium.

.12 **imaginer, fancier,** fantast; fantasist; myth-

maker, mythopoet; mythifier, mythicizer; **inventor; creative artist,** poet.

.13 **visionary, idealist;** prophet, seer; **dreamer, daydreamer,** dreamer of dreams, castlebuilder, lotus-eater, **wishful thinker, romantic,** romanticist, romancer; Quixote, Don Quixote; utopian, utopianist, utopianizer; escapist; enthusiast, rhapsodist.

.14 VERBS **imagine, fancy, conceive,** conceit [archaic], conceptualize, ideate, figure to oneself; **invent, create, originate,** think up, dream up, shape, mold, coin, hatch, concoct, fabricate, produce; **suppose** 499.10; fantasize; fictionalize; give free rein to the imagination, let one's imagination riot or run riot or run wild, allow one's imagination to run away with one; experience imaginatively or vicariously.

.15 **visualize, vision, envision, envisage, picture, image,** objectify; picture in one's mind, picture to oneself, **view with the mind's eye,** contemplate in the imagination, form a mental picture of, represent, **see,** just see, have a picture of; **call up,** summon up, conjure up, **call to mind,** realize.

.16 **idealize,** utopianize, quixotize, rhapsodize; **romanticize,** romance; paint pretty pictures of, paint in bright colors; see through rose-colored glasses; **build castles in the air.**

.17 **dream;** dream of, dream on; **daydream,** pipe-dream [informal], indulge in wishfulfillment; fantasy, conjure up a vision, "see visions and dream dreams" [Bible]; blow one's mind or go on a trip or trip or freak out [all slang].

.18 ADJS **imaginative,** conceptual, conceptive, ideational, ideative, notional; **inventive, original,** originative, esemplastic, shaping, **creative, ingenious; productive, fertile,** fecund, prolific, seminal, germinal, teeming, pregnant; **inspired,** visioned.

.19 **imaginary,** imaginational, notional; **imagined, fancied; unreal,** unactual, nonexistent; fictive, visional, supposititious, **all in the mind;** illusory 519.9.

.20 **fanciful, notional,** notiony [dial], whimsical, maggoty [Brit]; brain-born; **fancybred,** fancy-born, fancy-built, fancyframed, fancy-woven, fancy-wrought; dream-born, dream-built, dream-created; **fantastic(al),** fantasque, extravagant, preposterous, outlandish, wild, baroque, rococo, florid; bizarre, grotesque, Gothic.

.21 **fictitious, make-believe, figmental,** fictional, fictive, pseud(o)–; nonhistorical, nonfactual, nonactual, nonrealistic; **fabu-**

lous, **mythic**(al), mythological, legendary; mythified, mythicized.

.22 **chimeric**(al), **aerial, ethereal,** phantasmal; vaporous, vapory; air-built, cloud-built, cloud-born, cloud-woven.

.23 **ideal, idealized;** utopian, Arcadian, Edenic, paradisal; pie in the sky [informal]; heavenly, celestial; millennial.

.24 **visionary, idealistic,** quixotic(al); **romantic, romanticized,** romancing, romantico–; poetic(al); storybook; **impractical, unpractical, unrealistic;** wish-fulfilling, autistic, dereistic; starry-eyed, dewy-eyed; in the clouds, with one's head in the clouds; airy, **otherworldly,** transmundane, transcendental.

.25 **dreamy, dreamful; dreamy-eyed,** dreamy-minded, dreamy-souled; dreamlike; daydreamy, **dreaming, daydreaming,** pipe-dreaming [informal], castle-building; **entranced,** tranced, in a trance, dream-stricken, enchanted, spellbound, spelled, charmed.

.26 **imaginable, fanciable, conceivable, thinkable,** cogitable; **supposable** 499.15.

## 536. UNIMAGINATIVENESS

.1 NOUNS **unimaginativeness,** unfancifulness; **prosaicness,** prosiness, prosaism, prosaicism, unpoeticalness; **staidness, stuffiness** [informal]; stolidity; **dullness, dryness;** aridness, aridity, barrenness, infertility, infecundity; **unoriginality,** uncreativeness, uninventiveness, dearth of ideas.

.2 (practical attitude) **realism,** realisticness, **practicalness, practicality, practical-mindedness,** sober-mindedness, **hardheadedness, matter-of-factness;** down-to-earthness, earthiness, worldliness, secularism; pragmatism, pragmaticism, positivism, scientism; unidealism, unromanticalness, unsentimentality; sensibleness, saneness, reasonableness, rationality; freedom from illusion, lack of sentimentality; lack of feelings 856.

.3 **realist,** pragmatist, positivist, practical person.

.4 VERBS **keep both feet on the ground,** stick to the facts, call a spade a spade; **come down to earth,** come down out of the clouds.

.5 ADJS **unimaginative, unfanciful;** unideal, unidealized, **unromantic,** unromanticized; **prosaic,** prosy, prosing, unpoetic(al); **literal,** literal-minded; earthbound, mundane; **staid, stuffy** [informal]; stolid;

dull, dry; arid, barren, infertile, infecund; **unoriginal,** uninspired; uninventive 166.5.

.6 **realistic,** realist, **practical;** pragmatic(al), scientific, scientistic, positivistic; **unidealistic,** unideal, **unromantic, unsentimental, practical-minded,** sober-minded, **hardheaded,** straight-thinking, **matter-of-fact, down-to-earth, with both feet on the ground;** worldly, earthy, secular; sensible, sane, reasonable, rational, sound, sound-thinking.

## 537. MEMORY

.1 NOUNS **memory,** –mnesia; **remembrance, recollection,** mind, *souvenir* [Fr]; memory trace, engram; mind's eye, eye of the mind, mirror of the mind, tablets of the memory; corner or recess of the memory, inmost recesses of the memory; Mnemosyne, mother of the Muses; computer memory, information storage, disk memory, tape memory, drum memory, memory bank, memory circuit; collective memory, mneme, race memory; atavism; cover or screen memory, affect memory; anterograde memory; eye or visual memory, kinesthetic memory; skill, verbal response, emotional response.

.2 "that inward eye" [Wordsworth], "the warder of the brain" [Shakespeare], "the treasury and guardian of all things" [Cicero], "storehouse of the mind, garner of facts and fancies" [M. F. Tupper], "the hearing of deaf actions, and the seeing of blind" [Plutarch], "the diary that we all carry around with us" [Oscar Wilde].

.3 **retention, retentiveness,** retentivity, memory span; good memory, retentive memory or mind; total memory, eidetic memory or imagery, photographic memory, total recall; camera-eye.

.4 **remembering, remembrance, recollection,** recollecting, exercise of memory, **recall,** recalling; reflection, reconsideration; **retrospect,** retrospection, hindsight, looking back; flashback, **reminiscence,** review, contemplation of the past, review of things past; **memoir; memorization,** memorizing, **rote,** rote memory, rote learning, study, learning by heart, commitment to memory.

.5 **recognition, identification, reidentification,** distinguishment; realization 475.2.

.6 **reminder, remembrance,** remembrancer; **prompt,** prompter, tickler; prompting, cue, hint; jogger [informal], flapper; *aide-mémoire* [Fr], memorandum 570.4.

.7 **memento, remembrance,** token, trophy,

souvenir, keepsake, relic, remembrancer, favor, token of remembrance; commemoration, memorial 570.12; *memento mori* [L]; **memories, memorabilia,** memorials.

.8 memorability, rememberability.

.9 mnemonics, memory training, mnemotechny, mnemotechnics, mnemonization; mnemonic, mnemonic device, *aide-mémoire* [Fr].

.10 VERBS **remember, recall, recollect, mind** [dial]; reflect; **think of,** bethink oneself [archaic]; **call** *or* **bring to mind,** recall to mind, call up, summon up, conjure up, evoke, reevoke, revive, recapture, call back, bring back, "call back yesterday, bid time return" [Shakespeare]; **think back,** go back, **look back,** cast the eyes back, carry one's thoughts back, look back upon things past, use hindsight, retrospect, **see in retrospect,** go back over, hark back, retrace; review, review in retrospect.

.11 **reminisce,** rake *or* dig up the past.

.12 **recognize, know, tell, distinguish, make out;** identify, place, have; spot *or* nail *or* peg [all informal], **reidentify,** know again, recover *or* recall knowledge of; realize 475.12.

.13 **keep in memory, bear in mind,** keep *or* hold in mind, hold *or* retain the memory of, **keep in view,** have in mind, hold in the thoughts, carry in one's thoughts, retain in the thoughts, store in the mind, **retain, keep;** tax *or* burden the memory, **treasure, cherish,** treasure up in the memory, enshrine *or* embalm in the memory, cherish the memory of; keep up the memory of, keep the memory alive, keep alive in one's thoughts; brood over, dwell on *or* upon, fan the embers.

.14 **be remembered,** sink in the mind, sink in, penetrate, make an impression; live *or* dwell in one's memory, be easy to recall, remain in one's memory, be green *or* fresh in one's memory, remain indelibly impressed on the memory, be stamped on one's memory, **never be forgotten; haunt one's thoughts,** obsess, run in the head, be in one's thoughts, be on one's mind; be burnt into one's memory, plague one; **rankle,** rankle in the breast.

.15 **recur,** recur to the mind, return to mind, come back.

.16 **come to mind,** pop into one's head, come to one, come into one's head, flash on the mind, pass in review.

.17 **memorize, commit to memory,** con; study; **learn by heart,** get by heart, learn *or* get by rote, get letter-perfect, learn word for word, learn verbatim, swot up [Brit informal]; **know by heart, have by heart** *or* **rote, have at one's fingers' ends** *or* **tips;** repeat by heart *or* rote, give word for word, recite, repeat, parrot, repeat like a parrot, say one's lesson.

.18 **fix in the mind** *or* memory, instill, infix, inculcate, impress, imprint, stamp, inscribe, etch, grave, engrave; **impress on the mind, get into one's head,** drive *or* hammer into one's head; **burden the mind with,** task the mind with, load *or* stuff *or* cram the mind with; inscribe *or* stamp *or* rivet in the memory, set in the tablets of memory, etch indelibly in the mind.

.19 **refresh the memory, review,** restudy, **brush up, rub up,** polish up [informal], get up on.

.20 **remind, put in mind, remember,** put in remembrance, bring back to the memory, bring to recollection, refresh the memory of; **remind one of, recall, suggest, put one in mind of; take one back,** carry back, carry back in recollection; **jog the memory,** awaken *or* arouse the memory, flap the memory, give a hint *or* suggestion; **prompt,** prompt the mind, give the cue, hold the promptbook; nudge, pull by the sleeve, nag.

.21 **try to recall,** think hard, rack *or* ransack one's brains, **cudgel one's brains,** crack one's brains [informal]; have on the tip of one's tongue, have on the edge of one's memory *or* consciousness.

.22 ADJS **recollective, memoried;** mnemonic; retentive; **retrospective,** in retrospect; **reminiscent, mindful, remindful, suggestive,** redolent, evocative.

.23 **remembered, recollected, recalled; retained,** pent-up in the memory, kept in remembrance, enduring, lasting, **unforgotten;** present to the mind, lodged in one's mind, stamped on the memory; vivid, eidetic, fresh, green, alive.

.24 **remembering, mindful,** keeping *or* bearing in mind, holding in remembrance; unable to forget, haunted, plagued, obsessed, nagged, rankled.

.25 **memorable, rememberable, recollectable;** notable 672.18.

.26 **unforgettable, never to be forgotten,** never to be erased from the mind, **indelible,** indelibly impressed on the mind, fixed in the mind; haunting, persistent, recurrent, nagging; obsessive.

.27 **memorial, commemorative.**

.28 ADVS **by heart,** *par cœur* [Fr], **by rote, by** *or* **from memory,** without book; **memorably;** rememberingly.

.29 **in memory of,** to the memory of, in remembrance *or* commemoration, *in memoriam* [L]; *memoria in aeterna* [L], in perpetual remembrance.

## 538. FORGETFULNESS

.1 NOUNS **forgetfulness,** unmindfulness, absentmindedness, **memorylessness;** short memory, short memory span, little retentivity *or* recall, mind *or* memory like a sieve; loose memory, vague *or* fuzzy memory, dim *or* hazy recollection; **lapse of memory,** decay of memory; **obliviousness, oblivion,** nirvana; **obliteration;** Lethe, Lethe water, waters of Lethe *or* oblivion, river of oblivion; nepenthe; **forgetting;** heedlessness 534.2; forgiveness 947.

.2 **amnesia,** failure *or* loss of memory, **memory gap,** blackout [informal]; fugue; anterograde amnesia, retrograde amnesia, retroanterograde amnesia; infantile amnesia; lacunar amnesia, partial amnesia; agnosia, unrecognition; paramnesia, false memory, misremembrance; auditory *or* verbal amnesia, word deafness *or* blindness, amnesic *or* amnestic aphasia; tactile amnesia, astereognosis; systematic amnesia; amnesiac.

.3 **block,** blocking, **mental block,** memory obstruction; repression, suppression, defense mechanism, conversion, sublimation, symbolization.

.4 VERBS **be forgetful,** be absentminded, have a short memory, have a mind *or* memory like a sieve, have a short memory span, be unable to retain, have little recall, forget one's own name.

.5 **forget,** clean forget [informal]; **not remember,** disremember *or* disrecollect [both informal], fail to remember, forget to remember, **have no remembrance** *or* **recollection of,** be unable to recollect *or* recall, draw a blank [informal]; lose, lose sight of; have on the tip of the tongue; blow *or* fluff one's lines; misremember, misrecollect.

.6 efface *or* erase from the memory, consign to oblivion, unlearn, obliterate, **dismiss from one's thoughts** 531.4; forgive 947.3–5.

.7 **be forgotten,** escape one, **slip one's mind,** fade *or* die away from the memory, slip *or* escape the memory, drop from one's thoughts; fall *or* sink into oblivion, go in one ear and out the other.

.8 ADJS **forgotten,** clean forgotten [informal], **unremembered,** disremembered *or* disrecollected [both informal], **unrecollected, unretained, unrecalled,** past recollection *or* recall, out of the mind, lost, erased, effaced, obliterated, gone out of one's head *or* recollection, consigned to oblivion, buried *or* sunk in oblivion; out of sight out of mind; misremembered, misrecollected.

.9 **forgetful, forgetting,** inclined to forget, **memoryless, unremembering, unmindful,** absentminded, **oblivious,** insensible to the past, with a mind *or* memory like a sieve; suffering from *or* stricken with amnesia, amnesic, amnestic; blocked, repressed, suppressed, sublimated, converted; heedless 534.11; Lethean.

.10 **forgettable, unrememberable,** unrecollectable.

.11 ADVS **forgetfully, forgettingly,** unmindfully, absentmindedly, **obliviously.**

## 539. EXPECTATION

.1 NOUNS **expectation,** expectance *or* **expectancy,** state of expectancy; **anticipation,** prospect, thought; contemplation; probability 511; confidence, reliance 501.1; certainty 513; imminence 152; unastonishment 921.

.2 **sanguine** *or* **cheerful expectation,** optimism, **hope** 888.

.3 **suspense,** state of suspense, cliff-hanging [informal]; **waiting,** expectant waiting; uncertainty 514; anxiety, dread, pessimism, apprehension 890.1.

.4 **expectations,** prospects, outlook, hopes, apparent destiny *or* fate, future prospects; likelihoods, probabilities.

.5 VERBS **expect,** be expectant, **anticipate, have in prospect,** face, think, **contemplate,** have in contemplation *or* mind, envisage; **hope** 888.7; presume 499.10; dread 891.18; **take for granted;** not be surprised *or* a bit surprised; foresee 542.5.

.6 **look forward to,** reckon *or* calculate *or* count on; look to, **look for, watch for,** look out for, watch out for, be on the watch *or* lookout for, keep a good *or* sharp lookout for; be ready for; forestall.

.7 **be expected,** be one's probable fate *or* destiny, be one's outlook *or* prospect, be in store.

.8 **await,** wait, wait for, wait on *or* upon, stay *or* tarry for; lie in wait for; watch, watch and wait; **bide one's time,** bide, abide, **mark time;** cool one's heels [informal]; be in suspense, hold one's breath, bite one's nails; sweat or sweat out or sweat it or sweat it out [all slang]; **wait up for,** stay up for, sit up for.

.9 **expect to, plan on** 653.4–7.

.10 **be as expected,** be as one thought or looked for, turn out that way, come as no surprise; **be just like one,** be one all over [slang]; **expect it of,** think that way about, **not put it past** [informal]; **impend,** be imminent 152.2; lead one to expect 544.13.

.11 ADJS **expectant,** expecting, in expectation or anticipation; **anticipative,** anticipant, anticipating, anticipatory; **waiting,** awaiting, waiting for; forewarned, forearmed, forestalling, ready, prepared; **looking forward to,** looking for, watching for, on the watch or lookout for; gaping, agape, agog, all agog, eager 635.9; sanguine, optimistic, hopeful 888.11; sure, confident 501.21, 513.21; certain 513.13; unsurprised, not surprised.

.12 **in suspense, on tenterhooks,** on tiptoe, **on edge, with bated breath,** tense, taut, with muscles tense, quivering, keyed-up, biting one's nails; anxious, **apprehensive** 890.6.

.13 **expected, anticipated, awaited, foreseen;** presumed 499.14; probable 511.6; **looked-for,** hoped-for; **due, promised;** long-expected, overdue; **in prospect, prospective; in view,** in one's eye, on the horizon; imminent 152.3.

.14 **to be expected,** as expected, up to or according to expectation, just as one thought, just as predicted, on schedule, **as one may have suspected,** as one might think or suppose; **expected of,** counted on, **taken for granted;** just like one, one all over [slang], in character.

.15 ADVS **expectantly,** expectingly; anticipatively, **anticipatingly,** anticipatorily; hopefully 888.14; **with bated breath,** with breathless expectation; with ears pricked up, with eyes or ears strained.

## 540. INEXPECTATION

.1 NOUNS **inexpectation,** nonexpectation, inexpectance or inexpectancy, no expectation, **unanticipation; unexpectedness;** unforeseeableness, unpredictableness, unpredictability; unreadiness, unpreparedness; the unforeseen, the unlooked-for, the last thing one expects; **improbability** 512.

.2 **surprise,** surprisal; **astonishment** 920.1–2; surpriser, startler, shocker, **blow,** staggerer [informal], **eye-opener,** revelation; **bolt**

out of or **from the blue,** thunderbolt, thunderclap; **bombshell,** bomb; blockbuster, earthshaker; sudden turn or development, *peripeteia* [Gk], switch; surprise ending, kicker or joker or catch [all informal]; surprise package; surprise party.

.3 **start, shock, jar, jolt, turn.**

.4 VERBS **not expect,** hardly expect, **not anticipate, not look for,** not bargain for, **not foresee,** not think of, have no thought of, have no expectation, think unlikely or improbable.

.5 **be startled, be taken by surprise,** be given a start, be given a turn or jar or jolt; **start,** startle, **jump,** jump a mile [informal], jump out of one's skin; **shy,** start aside, flinch.

.6 **be unexpected, come unawares,** come as a surprise or shock, appear unexpectedly, turn up, pop up or bob up [both informal], drop from the clouds, appear like a bolt out of the blue, come or burst like a thunderclap or thunderbolt, burst or flash upon one, come or fall or pounce upon, steal or creep up on.

.7 **surprise, take by surprise,** do the unexpected, spring a surprise [informal], **open one's eyes,** give one a revelation; **catch or take unawares,** catch or take short, pull up short, **catch off-guard** 488.7; come from behind, come from an unexpected quarter, come upon unexpectedly or without warning, spring or pounce upon; spring a mine under, ambush, bushwhack; drop in on [informal]; give a surprise party; **astonish** 920.6,7.

.8 **startle, shock, electrify, jar, jolt, shake,** stun, **stagger, give one a turn** [informal], make one jump out of his skin, take aback, take one's beam ends, bowl down or over [informal], strike all of a heap [informal]; frighten 891.23.

.9 ADJS **inexpectant,** nonexpectant, unexpecting; **unanticipative,** unanticipating; **unsuspecting, unaware,** unguessing; uninformed, unwarned, unforewarned, unadvised, unadmonished; unready, unprepared; off one's guard 531.8.

.10 **unexpected, unanticipated, unlooked for,** unhoped for, unprepared for, undivined, unguessed, unpredicted, **unforeseen;** unforeseeable, unpredictable; **improbable** 512.3; contrary to expectation, beyond or past expectation, out of one's reckoning, more than expected, more than one bargained for; out of the blue, dropped from the clouds, from out in left field [slang]; without warning, unheralded, unannounced; sudden 113.5; out-of-the-way, **extraordinary.**

.11 **surprising, astonishing** 920.12; **startling, shocking,** electrifying, staggering, stunning, jarring, jolting.

.12 **surprised,** struck with surprise; **astonished** 920.9; **taken by surprise,** taken unawares, caught short.

.13 **startled, shocked, electrified,** jarred, jolted, shaken, shook [slang], staggered, **given a turn** or **jar** or **jolt,** taken aback, bowled down or over [informal], struck all of a heap [informal], able to be knocked down with a feather.

.14 ADVS **unexpectedly,** unanticipatedly, improbably, implausibly, unpredictably, **unforeseeably,** *à l'improviste* [Fr], **by surprise,** unawares, against or contrary to all expectation, as no one would have predicted, without notice or warning, in an unguarded moment, like a thief in the night; **out of a clear sky, out of the blue, like a bolt from the blue;** suddenly 113.9.

.15 **surprisingly, startlingly, to one's surprise,** to one's great surprise; shockingly, staggeringly, stunningly, **astonishingly** 920.16.

## 541. DISAPPOINTMENT

.1 NOUNS **disappointment,** sad or sore disappointment, bitter or cruel disappointment, failed or blasted expectation; **dashed hope, blighted hope,** betrayed hope, hope deferred, forlorn hope; **dash** [archaic], dash to one's hopes; blow, buffet; **frustration,** discomfiture, bafflement, defeat, balk, foiling; **comedown, setback, letdown** [informal]; failure, fizzle [informal], fiasco; **disillusionment** 520; tantalization, mirage, tease; dissatisfaction 869.1; fallen countenance.

.2 VERBS **disappoint,** defeat expectation or hope; **dash,** dash or blight or blast or crush one's hope; **balk, bilk, thwart, frustrate, baffle, defeat,** foil, cross; put one's nose out of joint; **let down,** cast down; disillusion 520.2; tantalize, tease; dissatisfy 869.4.

.3 **be disappointing, not come up to expectation,** not live or measure up to expectation, go wrong, turn sour, disappoint one's expectations, come or fall short; peter out or fizzle or fizzle out [all informal], not make it or not hack it [both slang].

.4 **be disappointed,** not realize one's expectations, fail of one's hopes or ambitions, be let down; look blue, laugh on the wrong side of one's mouth [informal]; be crestfallen or chapfallen.

.5 ADJS **disappointed,** bitterly or sorely disappointed; **let down,** betrayed, ill-served, ill done-by; **dashed,** blighted, blasted, crushed; **balked,** bilked, **thwarted, frustrated,** baffled, crossed, dished [Brit], defeated, foiled; hoist by one's own petard, caught in one's own trap; disillusioned 520.5; crestfallen, chapfallen, out of countenance; soured; dissatisfied 869.5; regretful 873.8.

.6 **disappointing,** not up to expectation, falling short, out of the running, not up to one's hopes, second- or third-best; tantalizing, teasing; **unsatisfactory** 869.6.

## 542. FORESIGHT

.1 NOUNS **foresight,** foreseeing, looking ahead, **prevision,** forecast [archaic]; **prediction** 543; **foreglimpse,** foreglance, foregleam; preview, prepublication; **prospect,** prospection; **anticipation,** contemplation, envisionment, envisagement; **foresightedness; farsightedness,** longsightedness, farseeingness; sagacity, providence, discretion, preparation, provision, forehandedness, readiness, prudence 467.4–7.

.2 **forethought, premeditation,** predeliberation, preconsideration 653.3; caution 895.

.3 **foreknowledge,** foreknowing, forewisdom, **precognition,** prescience, presage, presentiment, foreboding 544; clairvoyance 1034.8; foreseeability 543.8.

.4 **foretaste,** antepast [archaic], prelibation.

.5 VERBS **foresee,** see beforehand or ahead, foreglimpse, foretaste, **anticipate,** contemplate, envision, envisage, **look forward to,** look ahead, look beyond, look or pry or peep into the future; **predict** 543.9.

.6 **foreknow,** know beforehand, precognize; smell in the wind, scent from afar; **have a presentiment,** have a premonition 544.11; feel in one's bones [informal], just know, intuit 481.4.

.7 ADJS **foreseeing, foresighted; foreknowing,** precognizant, precognitive, prescient; divinatory 543.11; **forethoughted,** forethoughtful; anticipant, anticipatory; **farseeing, farsighted,** longsighted; sagacious, provident, providential, forehanded, prepared, ready, prudent 467.16–19; intuitive 481.5; clairvoyant 1034.23.

.8 **foreseeable** 543.13; foreseen 543.14.

.9 ADVS **foreseeingly, foreknowingly,** with foresight; against the time when, for a rainy day.

## 543. PREDICTION

.1 NOUNS prediction, foretelling, foreshowing, forecasting, **prognosis**, prognostication, presage [archaic], presaging; **prophecy**, prophesying, vaticination; **soothsaying**, soothsay; prefiguration, prefigurement, prefiguring; preshowing, presignifying, presigning [archaic]; **forecast, promise**; apocalypse; prospectus; foresight 542; presentiment, foreboding 544; omen 544.3,6; **guesswork**, speculation, hariolation; **probability** 511, statistical prediction, actuarial prediction; improbability 512.

.2 **divination**, divining, –mancy; **augury**, haruspication, haruspicy, pythonism, mantic, mantology [archaic]; **fortunetelling**, crystal gazing, palm-reading, palmistry; crystal ball; horoscopy, astrology 375.20; sorcery 1035; clairvoyance 1034.8.

.3 dowsing, witching, water witching; **divining rod** or stick, wand, witch or witching stick, dowsing rod, doodlebug; dowser, water witch or witcher.

.4 predictor, foreteller, prognosticator, seer, foreseer, foreshower, foreknower, presager [archaic], prefigurer; **forecaster**; prophet, prophesier, soothsayer, *vates* [L]; **diviner**, divinator; augur; psychic 1034.13; prophetess, seeress, divineress, pythoness; Druid; **fortuneteller**; crystal gazer; palmist; geomancer; haruspex, astrologer 375.23; weather prophet 402.7; prophet of doom, calamity howler, Cassandra; religious prophets 1022.

.5 [slang terms] **dopester, tipster, tout** or touter.

.6 **sibyl**; Pythia, Pythian, Delphic sibyl; Babylonian or Persian sibyl, Cimmerian sibyl, Cumaean sibyl, Erythraean sibyl, Hellespontine or Trojan sibyl, Libyan sibyl, Phrygian sibyl, Samian sibyl, Tiburtine sibyl.

.7 **oracle**; Delphic or Delphian oracle, Python, Pythian oracle; Delphic tripod, tripod of the Pythia; Dodona, oracle or oak of Dodona.

.8 **predictability**, divinability, foretellableness, **calculability, foreseeability**, foreknowableness.

.9 VERBS **predict**, make a prediction, **foretell**, soothsay, prefigure, **forecast, prophesy, prognosticate**, make a prophecy or prognosis, vaticinate, forebode, presage, see or tell the future, read the future, see in the crystal ball; **foresee** 542.5; **dope** or **dope out** [both slang]; call the turn or call one's shot [both informal]; **divine**; witch or dowse for water; **tell fortunes**, fortune-tell, cast one's fortune; read one's hand, read palms, read tea leaves, cast a horoscope or nativity; **guess**, speculate, hariolate.

.10 **portend**, foretoken 544.10–12.

.11 ADJS **predictive**, predictory, predictional; **foretelling**, forewarning, forecasting; prefiguring, prefigurative, presignifying, presignificative; **prophetic(al)**, fatidic(al), apocalyptic(al); vaticinatory, vaticinal, mantic, sibyllic, sibylline; **divinatory, oracular**, auguring, augural; haruspical; **foreseeing** 542.7; presageful, presaging; **prognostic**, prognosticative, prognosticatory; fortunetelling; weather-wise.

.12 **ominous**, premonitory, foreboding 544.16-17.

.13 **predictable, divinable, foretellable, calculable**, anticipatable; **foreseeable, foreknowable**, precognizable; **probable** 511.6; improbable 512.3.

.14 **predicted**, prophesied, presaged, **foretold, forecast**, foreshown; foreseen, foreglimpsed, **foreknown**.

.15 **forms of divination**

| | |
|---|---|
| aeromancy | halomancy |
| alectryomancy | haruspicy |
| aleuromancy | hieromancy |
| alphitomancy | hieroscopy |
| anthracomancy | hippomancy |
| anthropomancy | horoscopy |
| arithmomancy | hydromancy |
| aspidomancy | I Ching |
| astrodiagnosis | ichthyomancy |
| astrology 375.20 | idolomancy |
| astromancy | lithomancy |
| augury | logomancy |
| austromancy | margaritomancy |
| axinomancy | meteoromancy |
| belomancy | molybdomancy |
| bibliomancy | myomancy |
| botanomancy | necromancy |
| capnomancy | nomancy |
| cephalomancy | numerology |
| ceromancy | oenomancy |
| chalcomancy | omoplatoscopy |
| chirognomy | oneiromancy |
| chiromancy | onomancy |
| chronomancy | onychomancy |
| cleidomancy | ophiomancy |
| cleromancy | ornithomancy |
| coscinomancy | osteomancy |
| crithomancy | palmistry |
| crystallomancy | podomancy |
| cubomancy | psephomancy |
| dactyliomancy | psychomancy |
| extispicy | pyromancy |
| gastromancy | rhabdomancy |
| geloscopy | scapulimancy |
| genethlialogy | scatomancy |
| genethliacs | sciomancy |
| geomancy | scyphomancy |
| gyromancy | sideromancy |

sortes Biblicae [L]
sortes Homericae [L]
sortes Praenestinae
　[L]
sortes Vergilianae [L]
sortilege
spatulamancy

spodomancy
stichomancy
sycomancy
theomancy
xylomancy
zoomancy

## 544. PRESENTIMENT

.1 NOUNS presentiment, premonition, preapprehension, forefeeling, presage, presagement; hunch 481.3; prediction 543.

.2 foreboding, boding; apprehension, misgiving; chill or quiver along the spine, shudder of the flesh.

.3 omen, portent; augury, auspice, soothsay, prognostic, prognostication; premonitory sign or symptom, premonitory shiver or chill, foretoken, foretokening, tokening, betokening, betokenment, foreshowing, prefiguration, presigning [archaic], presignifying, presignification, preindication, indicant, indication, sign, token, type, promise, sign of the times; foreshadow, foreshadowing, shadow, adumbration.

.4 warning, forewarning, "warnings, and portents and evils imminent" [Shakespeare], handwriting on the wall, "mene, mene, tekel, upharsin" [Aramaic; Bible].

.5 harbinger, forerunner, precursor, messenger [archaic], herald, announcer, buccinator novi temporis [L]; presager, premonitor, foreshadower.

.6 (omens) bird of ill omen, owl, raven, stormy petrel, Mother Carey's chicken; gathering clouds, clouds on the horizon, dark or black clouds, angry clouds, storm clouds, thundercloud, thunderhead; black cat; broken mirror; rainbow; ring around the moon; shooting star; halcyon bird.

.7 ominousness, portentousness, portent, bodefulness, presagefulness, suggestiveness, significance, meaning 545; fatefulness, fatality, doomfulness, sinisterness, banefulness, balefulness, direness.

.8 inauspiciousness, unpropitiousness, unfavorableness, unfortunateness, unluckiness, ill-fatedness, ill-omenedness; fatality.

.9 auspiciousness, propitiousness, favorableness; luckiness, fortunateness, prosperousness, beneficence, benignity, benignancy, benevolence; brightness, cheerfulness, cheeriness; good omen, good auspices, auspicium melioris aevi [L].

.10 VERBS foreshow, presage; omen, be the omen of, auspicate [archaic]; foreshadow, shadow, adumbrate, shadow forth, cast

their shadows before; predict 543.9; have an intimation, have a hunch [informal].

.11 forebode, bode, portend, croak; threaten, menace, lower, look black; warn, forewarn; have a premonition or presentiment, apprehend, preapprehend.

.12 augur, hint, divine [archaic]; foretoken, preindicate, presignify, presign, presignal, pretypify, prefigure, betoken, token, typify, signify, mean 545.8, spell, indicate, point to, be a sign of.

.13 promise, suggest, hint, imply, give prospect of, make likely, give ground for expecting, raise expectation, lead one to expect, hold out hope, make fair promise, bid fair, stand fair to.

.14 herald, harbinger, forerun, run before; announce, proclaim, preannounce; give notice, notify.

.15 ADJS augured, foreshadowed, foreshown; indicated, signified; preindicated, prognosticated, foretokened, prefigured, pretypified, presignified, presigned [archaic]; presignaled; presaged; promised, threatened; predicted 543.14.

.16 premonitory, forewarning, augural, monitory, warning, presageful, presaging, foretokening, preindicative, indicative, prognostic, prognosticative, presignificant, prefigurative; significant, meaningful 545.10; foreshowing, foreshadowing; big or pregnant or heavy with meaning; forerunning, precursory, precursive; intuitive 481.5; predictive 543.11.

.17 ominous, portentous, portending; foreboding, boding, bodeful; inauspicious, ill-omened, ill-boding, of ill or fatal omen, of evil portent, loaded or laden or freighted or fraught with doom; fateful, doomful; apocalyptic; unpropitious, unpromising, unfavorable, unfortunate, unlucky; sinister, dark, black, gloomy, somber, dreary; threatening, menacing, lowering; bad, evil, ill, untoward; dire, baleful, baneful, ill-fated, ill-starred, evil-starred.

.18 auspicious, of good omen, of happy portent; propitious, favorable, favoring, fair, good; promising, of promise, full of promise; fortunate, lucky, prosperous; benign, benignant, bright, happy, golden.

.19 ADVS ominously, portentously, bodefully, forebodingly; significantly, sinisterly; threateningly, menacingly, loweringly.

.20 inauspiciously, unpropitiously, unpromisingly, unfavorably, unfortunately, unluckily.

.21 auspiciously, propitiously, promisingly, favorably; fortunately, luckily; brightly.

## 545. MEANING

.1 NOUNS meaning, significance, signification, *significatum* [L], *signifié* [Fr], point,
sense, idea, purport, import; implication,
connotation, reference, referent; inten-
sion, extension; denotation; dictionary
meaning, lexical meaning; emotive *or* affective meaning, undertone, overtone,
coloring; relevance, bearing, relation, pertinence; substance, gist, pith, spirit, essence; drift, tenor; sum, sum and substance; literal meaning, true *or* real
meaning, unadorned meaning; effect,
force, impact, consequence, practical
consequence; totality of associations *or*
references *or* relations, value; syntactic *or*
structural meaning, grammatical meaning; symbolic meaning; metaphorical *or*
transferred meaning; semantic field, semantic cluster; range *or* span of meaning,
scope.

.2 intent, intention, purpose, aim, object,
design, plan.

.3 explanation, definition, construction, interpretation 552.

.4 acceptation, acception, accepted *or* received meaning; usage, acceptance.

.5 meaningfulness, suggestiveness, expressiveness, pregnancy; significance, signifi-
cancy, significantness; intelligibility, interpretability, readability; pithiness,
meatiness, sententiousness.

.6 (units) sign, symbol, signifiant, significant, type, token, icon, lexeme, sememe,
morpheme, glosseme, word, term, phrase,
lexical form *or* item, semantic *or* semiotic
*or* semasiological unit.

.7 semantics, semiotic, semiotics, significs,
semasiology; lexicology.

.8 VERBS mean, signify, denote, connote,
import, spell, have the sense of, be con-
strued as, have the force of; stand for,
symbolize; imply, suggest, argue, breathe,
bespeak, betoken, indicate; refer to.

.9 intend, have in mind 653.7.

.10 ADJS meaningful, meaning, significant,
significative; denotative, connotative, de-
notational, connotational, intensional,
extensional, associational; referential;
symbolic, metaphorical, figurative, alle-
gorical; transferred, extended; intelligible,
interpretable, definable, readable; suggestive, indicative, expressive; pregnant, full
of meaning, loaded *or* laden *or* fraught *or*
freighted *or* heavy with significance;
pithy, meaty, sententious, substantial,
full of substance; pointed, full of point.

.11 meant, implied 546.7, intended 653.9.

.12 semantic, semantological, semiotic, sema
siological; lexologic(al); symbolic, signific
iconic, lexemic, sememic, glossematic
morphemic, verbal, phrasal, lexical.

.13 ADVS meaningfully, meaningly, significantly; suggestively, indicatively; expressively.

## 546. LATENT MEANINGFULNESS

.1 NOUNS latent meaningfulness, latency, la-
tentness, delitescence, latent content; potentiality, virtuality, possibility; dormancy 268.4.

.2 implication, connotation, import, latent
*or* underlying *or* implied meaning, ironic
suggestion *or* implication; meaning 545;
suggestion, allusion; coloration, tinge, undertone, overtone, undercurrent, more
than meets the eye *or* ear, something between the lines, intimation, touch,
nuance, innuendo, hint 557.4; inference,
supposition, presupposition, assumption,
presumption; secondary *or* transferred *or*
metaphorical sense, undermeaning; subsidiary sense, subsense; hidden *or* esoteric
*or* arcane meaning, occult meaning; symbolism, allegory.

.3 VERBS be latent, underlie, lie under the
surface, lurk, lie hid *or* low, lie beneath,
hibernate, lie dormant, smolder; make no
sign, escape notice.

.4 imply, implicate, involve, import, connote, entail 76.4; mean 545.8; suggest,
bring to mind; hint, insinuate, infer, intimate 557.10; allude to, point indirectly to;
write between the lines; allegorize; suppose, presuppose, assume, presume, take
for granted; mean to say *or* imply *or* suggest.

.5 ADJS latent, lurking, lying low, delites-
cent, hidden 615.11, obscured, obfuscated, veiled, muffled, covert, occult,
mystic [archaic], cryptic; esoteric; underlying, under the surface, submerged; between the lines; hibernating, sleeping,
dormant 268.14; potential, unmanifested,
virtual, possible.

.6 suggestive, allusive, allusory, indicative,
inferential; insinuating, insinuative, insin-
uatory; ironic; implicative, implicatory,
implicational; referential.

.7 implied, implicated, involved; meant, indicated; suggested, intimated, insinuated,
hinted; inferred, supposed, assumed, presumed, presupposed.

.8 tacit, implicit, implied, understood,
taken for granted.

.9 **unexpressed,** unpronounced, **unsaid, unspoken, unuttered,** undeclared, unbreathed, unvoiced, wordless, silent; **unmentioned,** untalked-of, **untold,** unsung, unproclaimed, unpublished; unwritten, unrecorded.

.10 **symbolic(al),** allegoric(al), figurative, **metaphoric(al);** anagogic(al).

.11 ADVS **latently,** underlyingly; **potentially,** virtually.

.12 **suggestively, allusively, inferentially,** insinuatingly; impliedly.

.13 **tacitly, implicitly,** unspokenly, wordlessly, silently.

### 547. MEANINGLESSNESS

.1 NOUNS **meaninglessness,** unmeaningness, **senselessness,** nonsensicality; **insignificance,** unsignificancy; **noise,** mere noise, empty sound, talking to hear oneself talk, phatic communion; inanity, emptiness, nullity; "sounding brass and a tinkling cymbal" [Bible], "a tale told by an idiot, full of sound and fury, signifying nothing" [Shakespeare]; purposelessness, aimlessness, futility; dead letter.

.2 **nonsense, stuff and nonsense,** pack of nonsense, **folderol, balderdash,** *niaiserie* [Fr], flummery, trumpery, **rubbish,** trash, *narrishkeit* [Yid], vaporing, fudge; **humbug,** gammon, hocus-pocus; rant, claptrap, fustian, rodomontade, bombast, absurdity 470.3; stultiloquence, **twaddle,** twattle [Brit dial], twiddle-twaddle, fiddle-faddle, fiddledeedee, waffling [Brit], **blather, babble,** babblement, bibble-babble, **gabble,** gibble-gabble, **blabber, gibber, jabber,** prate, **prattle,** palaver, rigmarole *or* rigamarole, galimatias, skimbleskamble, drivel, drool; **gibberish,** jargon, mumbo jumbo, **double-talk,** amphigory, gobbledygook [informal].

.3 [slang terms] **bullshit, shit, crap, bull,** poppycock, bosh, bunkum, **bunk, guff,** gup [Brit], scat, bop, bilge, piffle, moonshine, flapdoodle, tommyrot, **rot, hogwash,** malarkey, hokum, hooey, bushwa, **blah** *or* blah-blah, baloney, tripe, **hot air,** gas, wind.

.4 VERBS **be meaningless, mean nothing,** signify nothing, not mean a thing, not convey anything; not register, not ring any bells.

.5 **talk nonsense, twaddle,** twattle [Brit dial], **piffle,** waffle [Brit], **blather, blabber, babble, gabble,** gibble-gabble, **jabber, gibber,** prate, **prattle,** rattle; talk through one's hat; gas, bull, **bullshit, throw the**

**bull** [all slang]; **drivel,** vapor, drool, run off at the mouth.

.6 ADJS **meaningless,** unmeaning, **senseless,** purportless, importless, nondenotative, nonconnotative; **insignificant,** unsignificant; empty, inane, null; phatic, garbled, scrambled; **purposeless,** aimless, designless, **without rhyme or reason.**

.7 **nonsensical,** silly, poppycockish [informal]; **foolish, absurd** 470.8,10; twaddling, twaddly; rubbishy, trashy; skimble-skamble; Pickwickian.

.8 ADVS **meaninglessly,** unmeaningly, nondenotatively, nonconnotatively, **senselessly, nonsensically;** insignificantly, unsignificantly; **purposelessly,** aimlessly.

### 548. INTELLIGIBILITY

.1 NOUNS **intelligibility, comprehensibility, apprehensibility,** prehensibility, **understandability,** knowability, cognizability, scrutability, penetrability, fathomableness; recognizability, readability; articulateness.

.2 **clearness, clarity; plainness, distinctness,** explicitness, clear-cutness, definition; **lucidity,** limpidity, pellucidity, crystallinity, perspicuity, transpicuity, transparency; **simplicity,** straightforwardness, directness; unmistakableness, unequivocalness, unambiguousness; **coherence,** connectedness, consistency, structure; plain style, plain English, plain speech, unadorned style.

.3 **legibility,** decipherability, **readability.**

.4 VERBS **be understandable, make sense;** be plain *or* clear; **speak for itself,** tell its own tale, speak volumes, have no secrets, put up no barriers; read easily [informal].

.5 (be understood) **get over** *or* **across** [informal], come through, **register** [informal], **penetrate, sink in,** soak in; dawn on, be glimpsed.

.6 **make clear,** make it clear, let it be understood, make oneself understood, get *or* put over *or* across [informal]; **simplify,** put in plain words *or* plain English, put in words of one syllable, spell out [informal]; elucidate, **explain,** explicate, **clarify** 552.10; put one in the picture [Brit]; make available to all, popularize, vulgarize.

.7 **understand, comprehend, apprehend,** have, **know, conceive, realize,** appreciate, ken [Scot], savvy [slang], sense, read, dig [slang], **fathom, follow,** get the idea, b with one *or* with it [informal], get t picture [informal], get into *or* thro one's head or thick head [informal]; **grasp, seize,** get hold of, grasp or seize the meaning, **get** [slang], take, **take in,** catch, **catch on** [informal], get the meaning of, get the hang of, catch or **get the drift** [informal]; **master, learn,** have it taped [Brit informal], assimilate, absorb, **digest.**

.8 **perceive, see, discern, make out,** descry; see the light, see daylight [informal], come alive; **see through,** see to the bottom of, penetrate, see into, pierce, plumb; see at a glance, see with half an eye.

.9 ADJS **intelligible, comprehensible, apprehensible,** prehensible, knowable, cognizable, scrutable, **fathomable, plumbable,** penetrable; **understandable,** easily understood, easy to understand, exoteric; readable; articulate.

.10 **clear, crystal-clear,** clear as crystal, clear as day, clear as the nose on one's face; **plain, distinct; definite,** defined, well-defined, **clear-cut,** clean-cut, crisp; **direct,** simple, **straightforward;** explicit, **express; unmistakable, unequivocal,** univocal, unambiguous, unconfused; **loud and clear; lucid,** pellucid, limpid, crystalline, perspicuous, transpicuous, **transparent,** translucent, luminous; **coherent,** connected, consistent.

.11 **legible, decipherable, readable,** fair; uncoded, unenciphered, in the clear.

.12 ADVS **intelligibly, understandably, comprehensibly,** apprehensibly; articulately; **clearly, lucidly,** limpidly, pellucidly, perspicuously, **simply, plainly, distinctly,** definitely; **coherently;** explicitly, **expressly; unmistakably, unequivocally,** unambiguously; in plain terms or words, in plain English, in no uncertain terms.

.13 **legibly,** decipherably, readably, fairly.

## 549. UNINTELLIGIBILITY

.1 NOUNS **unintelligibility, incomprehensibility,** inapprehensibility, **ununderstandability,** unknowability, incognizability, inscrutability, impenetrability, unfathomableness, unsearchableness, numinousness; **incoherence,** unconnectedness, ramblingness; inarticulateness; ambiguity 550.

abstruseness, reconditeness; crabbedness, ~vedness, knottiness; **complexity,** incomplication 46.1; **hardness,** difficulty, profundity, profoundness, deep~ica.

scuration, obscurantism, ob~ ~mbo jumbo [informal], perplexity; **unclearness,**

unclarity, unplainness, opacity; **vagueness,** indistinctness, indeterminateness, fuzziness, shapelessness, amorphousness; murkiness, murk, mistiness, mist, fogginess, fog, darkness, dark.

.4 **illegibility,** unreadability; undecipherability, indecipherability; scribble, scrawl.

.5 **unexpressiveness,** inexpressiveness, **expressionlessness,** impassivity; straight face, dead pan [slang], poker face [informal].

.6 **inexplicability,** unexplainableness, uninterpretability, indefinability, undefinability, unaccountableness; insolvability, inextricability; **enigmaticalness,** mysteriousness, mystery.

.7 (something unintelligible) Greek, Choctaw, double Dutch; gibberish, babble, jargon, gobbledygook, noise, Babel; scramble, jumble, garble; argot, cant, slang, secret language, Aesopian language, code, cipher, cryptogram; glossolalia, gift of tongues.

.8 **enigma, mystery, puzzle,** puzzlement; Chinese puzzle, crossword puzzle, jigsaw puzzle; **problem,** puzzling or baffling problem, why; question, question mark, vexed or perplexed question, enigmatic question, sixty-four dollar question [informal]; **perplexity;** knot, knotty point, crux, point to be solved; **puzzler,** poser, brain twister or teaser [informal], sticker [slang]; mind-boggler, **floorer** or **stumper** [all informal]; nut to crack, **hard** or **tough nut to crack;** tough proposition [informal], "a perfect nonplus and baffle to all human understanding" [Southey].

.9 **riddle, conundrum,** charade, rebus; logogriph, anagram; riddle of the Sphinx.

.10 VERBS **be incomprehensible, not make sense,** be too deep, go over one's head, be beyond one, beat one [informal], elude or escape one, lose one, need explanation or clarification or translation, be Greek to, pass comprehension or understanding, not penetrate; **baffle, perplex** 514.13, riddle, be sphinxlike, speak in riddles; speak in tongues; talk double Dutch, babble, gibber.

.11 **not understand, be unable to comprehend,** not have the first idea, be unable to get into or through one's head or thick skull; be out of one's depth, be at sea, be lost; **not know what to make of,** make nothing of, not be able to account for, not be able to make head or tail of; be unable to see, not see the wood for the trees; give up, pass [informal].

.12 **make unintelligible, scramble,** jumble

garble; **obscure,** obfuscate, mystify, shadow; **complicate** 46.3.

.13 ADJS **unintelligible, incomprehensible,** inapprehensible, **ununderstandable,** unknowable, incognizable; **unfathomable, inscrutable,** impenetrable, unsearchable, numinous; **ambiguous** 550.3; **incoherent,** unconnected, rambling; **inarticulate; past comprehension,** beyond one's comprehension, beyond understanding; Greek to one.

.14 **hard to understand, difficult, hard,** tough [informal], beyond one, **over one's head,** beyond *or* out of one's depth; knotty, cramp, crabbed; intricate, **complex,** overtechnical, perplexed, **complicated** 46.4; **scrambled,** jumbled, **garbled; obscure,** obscured, obfuscated.

.15 **obscure, vague, indistinct,** indeterminate, fuzzy, shapeless, amorphous; unclear, unplain, opaque, muddy, **clear as mud** *or* clear as ditch water [both informal]; **dark,** dim, blind [archaic], shadowy; **murky,** cloudy, foggy, hazy, misty, nebulous; transcendent.

.16 **recondite, abstruse,** abstract, transcendental; **profound, deep; hidden** 615.11; arcane, **esoteric,** occult; **secret** 614.11.

.17 **enigmatic(al),** cryptic(al); sphinxlike; **perplexing, puzzling** 514.25; riddling, logogriphic.

.18 **inexplicable, unexplainable,** uninterpretable, undefinable, indefinable, **unaccountable; insolvable,** unsolvable, insoluble, inextricable; mysterious, **mystic(al),** shrouded *or* wrapped *or* enwrapped in mystery.

.19 **illegible, unreadable, unclear; undecipherable,** indecipherable.

.20 **inexpressive,** unexpressive, impassive; **expressionless; vacant, empty, blank;** glassy, fishy, wooden; deadpan, poker-faced [informal].

.21 ADVS **unintelligibly, incomprehensibly,** inapprehensibly, ununderstandably.

.22 **obscurely, vaguely, indistinctly,** indeterminately; **unclearly,** unplainly; illegibly.

.23 **reconditely, abstrusely;** esoterically, occultly.

.24 **inexplicably, unexplainably,** undefinably, **unaccountably, enigmatically; mysteriously,** mystically.

.25 **expressionlessly, vacantly, blankly,** emptily, woodenly, glassily, fishily.

.26 PREPS **beyond,** past, above; too deep for.

.27 PHRS **I don't understand, I can't see,** I don't see how *or* why, **it beats me** [informal], you've got me [informal], **it's be-**yond me, it's too deep for me, it has me guessing, I don't have the first idea, it's Greek to me; **I give up,** I pass [informal].

## 550. AMBIGUITY

.1 NOUNS **ambiguity,** ambiguousness; **equivocalness,** equivocacy, equivocality; **double meaning,** amphibology, multivocality, polysemy, polysemousness; punning, paronomasia; double reference, double entendre; uncertainty 514; irony; levels of meaning, richness of meaning, complexity of meaning.

.2 (ambiguous word or expression) **ambiguity,** equivoque, equivocal, equivocality; equivocation, amphibology, double entendre; counterword, portmanteau word; polysemant; weasel word; squinting construction; pun 881.8.

.3 ADJS **ambiguous, equivocal,** equivocatory; multivocal, polysemous, polysemantic, amphibolous, amphibological; uncertain 514.15; ironic; obscure, mysterious, enigmatic 549.14–18.

## 551. FIGURE OF SPEECH

.1 NOUNS **figure of speech, figure, image,** trope, turn of expression, manner *or* way of speaking, ornament, device, flourish, flower; purple passage; imagery, nonliterality, nonliteralness, figurativeness, figurative language; figured *or* florid *or* flowery style, asiaticism, floridity, euphuism.

.2 VERBS metaphorize, figure [archaic]; similize; personify, personalize; symbolize 572.6.

.3 ADJS **figurative,** tropological; **metaphorical,** trolatitious; allusive, referential; **mannered,** figured, ornamented, **flowery** 601.11.

.4 ADVS **figuratively,** tropologically; **metaphorically;** symbolically; **figuratively speaking,** so to say *or* speak, in a manner of speaking, **as it were.**

.5 figures of speech

| | |
|---|---|
| agnomination | catachresis |
| alliteration | chiasmus |
| allusion | circumlocution |
| anacoluthon | climax |
| anadiplosis | conversion |
| analogy | ecphonesis |
| anaphora | emphasis |
| anastrophe | enallage |
| antiphrasis | epanaphora |
| antithesis | epanodos |
| antonomasia | epanorthosis |
| apophasis | epidiplosis |
| aporia | epiphora |
| aposiopesis | eroteme |
| apostrophe | exclamation |

| | |
|---|---|
| gemination | paregmenon |
| hendiadys | parenthesis |
| hypallage | periphrasis |
| hyperbaton | personification |
| hyperbole | pleonasm |
| hypozeugma | ploce |
| hypozeuxis | polyptoton |
| hysteron-proteron | polysyndeton |
| inversion | preterition |
| irony | prolepsis |
| kenning | prosopopoeia |
| litotes | regression |
| malapropism | repetition |
| meiosis | rhetorical question |
| metalepsis | sarcasm |
| metaphor | simile, similitude |
| metonymy | spoonerism |
| onomatopoeia, ono- | syllepsis |
| matopy | symploce |
| oxymoron | synecdoche |
| paradiastole | Wellerism |
| paralepsis | zeugma |

## 552. INTERPRETATION

.1 NOUNS interpretation, construction, reading, way of seeing or understanding or putting; diagnosis; definition, description; meaning 545.

.2 rendering, rendition; text, edited text, diplomatic text, normalized text; version; reading, lection, variant, variant reading; edition, critical or scholarly edition; conflation, composite reading or text.

.3 translation, transcription, transliteration; paraphrase, loose or free translation; decipherment, decoding; amplification, restatement, rewording; metaphrase, literal or verbal or faithful or word-for-word translation; pony or trot or crib [all informal]; interlinear, interlinear translation, bilingual text or edition; gloss, glossary; key, clavis [L].

.4 explanation, explication, elucidation, illumination, enlightenment, light, clarification, éclaircissement [Fr], simplification; exposition, expounding, exegesis; illustration, demonstration, exemplification; reason, rationale; euhemerism, demythologization, allegorization; decipherment, decoding, cracking, unlocking, solution 487; editing, emendation.

.5 (explanatory remark) comment, word of explanation; annotation, notation, note, note of explanation, footnote, gloss, scholium; exegesis; apparatus criticus [L]; commentary, commentation [archaic].

.6 interpretability, construability; definability, describability; translatability; explicability, explainableness, accountableness.

.7 interpreter, exegete, exegetist, exegesist, hermeneut; commentator, annotator, scholiast; critic, textual critic, editor, dia-

skeuast, emender, emendator; cryptographer, cryptologist, decoder, decipherer, cryptanalyst; explainer, lexicographer, definer, explicator, exponent, expositor, expounder, clarifier; demonstrator, euhemerist, demythologizer, allegorist; go-between 781.4; translator, metaphrast, paraphrast; oneirocritic; guide, cicerone [Ital], dragoman.

.8 (science of interpretation) exegetics, hermeneutics; tropology; criticism, literary criticism, textual criticism; paleography, epigraphy; cryptology, cryptography, cryptanalysis; lexicography; diagnostics, symptomatology, semeiology, semeiotics; pathognomy; physiognomics, physiognomy; metoposcopy; oneirology, oneirocriticism.

.9 VERBS interpret, diagnose; construe, put a construction on, take; understand, understand by, take to mean, take it that; read; read into, read between the lines; see in a special light, read in view of, take an approach to, define, describe.

.10 explain, explicate, expound, exposit; give the meaning, tell the meaning of; spell out, unfold; account for, give reason for; clarify, elucidate, clear up, make clear, make plain; simplify, popularize; illuminate, enlighten, shed or throw light upon; rationalize, euhemerize, demythologize, allegorize; tell or show how, show the way; demonstrate, show, illustrate, exemplify; decipher, crack, unlock, find the key to, unravel, solve 487.2; explain oneself; explain away.

.11 comment upon, commentate, remark upon; annotate, gloss; edit, make an edition.

.12 translate, render, transcribe, transliterate put or turn into, transfuse the sense of construe; English.

.13 paraphrase, rephrase, reword, restate, re hash; give a free or loose translation.

.14 ADJS interpretative, interpretive, interpre tational, exegetic(al), hermeneutic(al constructive, constructional; diagnosti symptomatological, semeiological; trope logical; definitional, descriptive.

.15 explanatory, explaining, exegetic(al), e plicative, explicatory; expository, expos tive; clarifying, elucidative; illuminatin illuminative, enlightening; demonstrativ illustrative, exemplificative; glossarial, a notative, critical, editorial, scholiastic; r tionalizing, rationalistic, euhemeristi demythologizing, allegorizing.

.16 translational, translative; paraphrastic, metaphrastic.

.17 interpretable, construable; definable, describable; translatable, renderable; Englishable [archaic]; explainable, explicable, accountable.

.18 ADVS by interpretation, as here interpreted, as here defined, according to this reading; in explanation, to explain; that is, that is to say, id est [L], i.e.; to wit, namely, videlicet [L], viz., scilicet [L], sc.; in other words, in words to that effect.

## 553. MISINTERPRETATION

.1 NOUNS misinterpretation, misunderstanding, malentendu [Fr], misintelligence, misapprehension, misreading, misconstruction, malobservation, misconception; misrendering, mistranslation, eisegesis; misexplanation, misexplication, misexposition; misapplication; gloss; perversion, distortion, wrenching, twisting, contorting, torturing, squeezing, garbling; abuse of terms, misuse of words, catachresis; misquotation, miscitation; "blunders round about a meaning" [Pope]; misjudgment 496; error 518.

.2 VERBS misinterpret, misunderstand, misconceive, mistake, misapprehend; misread, misconstrue, put a false construction on, take wrong, get wrong, get one wrong; misapply; misexplain, misexplicate, misexpound; misrender, mistranslate; quote out of context; misquote, miscite, give a false coloring, give a false impression or idea, gloss; garble, pervert, distort, wrench, contort, torture, squeeze, twist the words or meaning, stretch or strain the sense or meaning, misdeem, misjudge 496.2.

.3 ADJS misinterpreted, misunderstood, mistaken, misapprehended, misread, eisegetical, misconceived, misconstrued; garbled, perverted, distorted, catachrestic(al).

.4 misinterpretable, misunderstandable, mistakable.

## 554. COMMUNICATION

.1 NOUNS communication, communion, congress, commerce, intercourse; speaking, speech, talking, linguistic intercourse, speech situation, speech circuit, converse, conversation 597; contact, touch, connection; intercommunication, intercommunion, interplay, interaction; exchange, interchange; answer, response, reply; one-way communication, two-way communication; dealings, dealing, traffic, truck

[informal]; information 557; message 558.4; ESP, telepathy 1034.8,9; correspondence 604; social intercourse 922.4.

.2 impartation, impartment, imparting, conveyance, telling, transmission, transmittal, transfer, transference, sharing, giving; notification, announcement 559.2, publication 559, disclosure 556.

.3 communicativeness, talkativeness 596, sociability 922; unreserve, unreservedness, unreticence, unrestraint, unconstraint, unrestriction; unrepression, unsuppression; unsecretiveness, untaciturnity; candor, frankness 974.4; openness, plainness, freeness, outspokenness, plainspokenness; accessibility, approachability, conversableness; extroversion, outgoingness.

.4 communicability, impartability, conveyability, transmittability, transmissibility, transferability; contagiousness 686.3.

.5 communications, electronic communications, communications industry, media, communications medium or media, communications network; telecommunication 560.1–3; radiocommunication, wire communication; communication or information theory 557.7.

.6 VERBS communicate, be in touch or contact, be in connection or intercourse, have intercourse, hold communication; intercommunicate, interchange, commune with; commerce with, deal with, traffic with, have dealings with, have truck with [informal]; speak, talk, be in a speech situation, converse 597.9.

.7 communicate, impart, render, convey, transmit, transfer, send, disseminate, broadcast, pass, pass on or along, hand on; report, make known, get across or over; give or send or leave word; signal; share, share with; give 818.12; tell 557.8.

.8 communicate with, get in touch or contact with, contact [informal], make contact with, raise, reach, get to, make or establish connection, get in connection with; make advances, make overtures, approach, make up to [informal]; relate to; keep in touch or contact with, maintain connection; answer, respond or reply to; question, interrogate; correspond 604.11.

.9 ADJS communicational, communicating, communional; transmissional; speech, verbal, linguistic, oral; conversational 597.13; intercommunicational, intercommunicative, intercommunional, interactional, interactive, interacting, interresponsive, responsive, answering; question-

ing, interrogative, interrogatory; telepathic 1034.23.

.10 **communicative, talkative** 596.9, gossipy,
newsy; **sociable** 922.18; **unreserved, unreti-
cent,** unshrinking, **unrestrained, unconstrained,** unhampered, unrestricted; demonstrative, expansive, effusive; **unrepressed, unsuppressed; unsecretive,**
unsilent, untaciturn; candid, **frank** 974.17;
self-revealing, self-revelatory; **open, free,**
outspoken, free-speaking, free-spoken,
free-tongued; **accessible, approachable,**
conversable, easy to speak to; **extroverted,** outgoing.

.11 **communicable, impartable, conveyable,
transmittable,** transmissible, transferable;
contagious 686.58.

## 555. MANIFESTATION

.1 NOUNS    manifestation,    appearance,
–**phany; expression,** evincement; **indication, evidence, proof** 505; **embodiment,**
incarnation, **materialization** 376.7; epiphany, theophany, angelophany, Satanoph-
any, Christophany, pneumatophany, avatar; **revelation, disclosure** 556; dissemination, **publication** 559.

.2 **display, demonstration, show, showing,**
phen(o)– or phaeno–; **presentation,** presentment, ostentation [archaic], **exhibition, exhibit, exposition,** retrospective;
production, performance, representation,
enactment, projection; opening, unfolding, unfoldment; unveiling, exposure, varnishing day, vernissage [Fr].

.3 **manifestness, apparentness, obviousness,
plainness, clearness,** crystal-clearness, perspicuity, distinctness, patentness, palpability, tangibility; evidentness, evidence
[archaic], **self-evidence; openness,** openness to sight, overtness; **visibility** 444; unmistakableness, unquestionability 513.3.

.4 **conspicuousness, prominence, salience** or
saliency, bold or high or strong relief,
boldness, **noticeability,** pronouncedness,
strikingness, outstandingness; obtrusiveness; **flagrance** or flagrancy, arrantness,
blatancy, notoriousness, notoriety; ostentation 904.

.5 VERBS **manifest, show, exhibit, demonstrate, display,** breathe, unfold, develop,
**present,** represent [archaic], **evince, evidence; indicate,** give sign or token, token,
betoken, mean 545.8; **express,** show forth,
set forth; **make plain, make clear;** produce, bring out, roll out, trot out [infor-
mal], bring forth, bring forward or to the
front, bring to notice, expose to view,

bring to or into view; **reveal, divulge, disclose** 556.4; **illuminate,** highlight, spotlight, bring to the fore, place in the foreground, bring out in bold or strong or
high relief; **flaunt,** dangle, wave, **flourish,**
brandish, parade; affect, make a show of;
perform, enact, dramatize; **embody, incarnate, materialize** 376.8.

.6 (manifest oneself) **come out into the
open,** come forth; **show one's colors** or
true colors, wear one's heart upon one's
sleeve; **speak up, speak out,** raise one's
voice, **assert oneself,** let one's voice be
heard, **stand up and be counted,** take a
stand; open up, show one's mind, have
no secrets; **appear, materialize.**

.7 **be manifest,** be there for all to see, be no
secret or revelation, lie on the surface, be
seen with half an eye; need no explanation, **speak for itself,** tell its own story or
tale; go without saying, aller sans dire
[Fr]; **leap to the eye,** sauter aux yeux
[Fr], **stare one in the face,** hit one in the
eye, strike the eye, glare, shout; come
across, project; stand out, stick out, stick
out a mile, stick out like a sore thumb,
hang out [slang].

.8 ADJS **manifest, apparent, evident, self-evident,** axiomatic, indisputable, **obvious,
plain, clear,** perspicuous, distinct, palpable, patent, tangible; **visible, perceptible,
perceivable, discernible,** seeable, observable, **noticeable; to be seen,** easy to be
seen, plain to be seen; plain as day, plain
as the nose on one's face, plain as a pikestaff; **crystal-clear,** clear as crystal; **express,
explicit, unmistakable,** not to be mistaken, open-and-shut [informal]; self-explanatory, self-explaining; **indubitable**
513.15.

.9 **manifesting, manifestative,** showing, dis-
playing, demonstrating, **demonstrative,**
presentational, expository, expositional,
exhibitive, exhibitional, **expressive;** evincive, evidential; **indicative,** indicatory; appearing, incarnating, incarnational, materializing; epiphanic, theophanic, angelo-
phanic, Satanophanic, Christophanic,
pneumatophanic; **revelational,** revelatory,
disclosive 556.10; promulgatory 559.18.

.10 **open, overt,** open to all, open as day; unclassified; **revealed, disclosed, exposed,**
bare, bald, naked.

.11 **unhidden, unconcealed,** unscreened, un-
curtained, unshaded, veilless; **unobscured,**
unobscured, undarkened, unclouded; undisguised, uncamouflaged.

.12 **conspicuous, noticeable, notable,** osten-ble, **prominent, bold, pronounced, salient,** in relief, in bold *or* high *or* strong relief, **striking, outstanding,** in the foreground, sticking *or* hanging out [slang]; obtrusive; **flagrant,** arrant, blatant, notorious; **glaring,** staring, stark-staring.

.13 **manifested,** demonstrated, exhibited, shown, displayed; **manifestable,** demonstrable, exhibitable, displayable.

.14 ADVS **manifestly, apparently, evidently, obviously, patently, plainly, clearly,** distinctly, **unmistakably,** expressly, explicitly, palpably, tangibly; **visibly, perceptibly,** perceivably, discernibly, observably, noticeably.

.15 **openly, overtly,** before one, **before one's eyes** *or* very eyes, under one's nose [informal]; to one's face, face to face; **publicly,** in public; **in the open,** out in the open, in open court, **in plain sight,** in broad daylight, in the face of day *or* heaven, for all to see, in public view, in plain view, in the marketplace; aboveboard, on the table.

.16 **conspicuously, prominently, noticeably,** ostensibly, **notably, markedly, pronouncedly, saliently, strikingly, boldly, outstandingly;** obtrusively; arrantly, flagrantly, blatantly, notoriously; glaringly, staringly.

## 556. DISCLOSURE

.1 NOUNS **disclosure,** disclosing; **revelation,** revealment, revealing, patefaction [archaic]; apocalypse; **discovery,** discovering; manifestation 555; unfolding, unfoldment, **uncovering,** unwrapping, uncloaking, taking the wraps off, taking from under wraps, removing the veil, unveiling, **unmasking; exposure,** exposition, **exposé; baring,** stripping, stripping *or* laying bare; **showing up,** showup.

.2 **divulgence, divulging,** divulgement, divulgation, evulgation, letting out [Brit]; **betrayal,** unwitting disclosure, indiscretion; **leak,** communication leak; **giveaway** *or* dead giveaway [both informal]; **telltale,** telltale sign, obvious clue; **blabbing** *or* blabbering [both informal], babbling; **tattling.**

.3 **confession,** shrift, **acknowledgment, admission,** concession, **avowal, owning,** owning up [informal], unbosoming, unburdening oneself, making a clean breast; rite of confession 1040.4.

.4 VERBS **disclose, reveal, let out, show,** impart, discover, develop [both archaic]; manifest 555.5; **unfold,** unroll; **open, open**

up, lay open, break the seal, bring into the open; **expose, show up; bare,** strip *or* lay bare; take the lid off, **bring to light,** hold up to view; hold up the mirror to; **unmask,** dismask, tear off the mask, **uncover, unveil,** take out from under wraps, take the wraps off, lift *or* draw the veil, raise the curtain, let daylight in, unscreen, uncloak, undrape, unshroud, unfurl, unsheathe, unwrap, unpack, unkennel; show one's hand *or* cards, put *or* lay one's cards on the table.

.5 **divulge,** divulgate, evulgate; **reveal, make known, tell,** breathe, utter, vent, ventilate, air, give vent to, **give out, let out** [Brit], let get around, out with [informal], come out with; break it to, **break the news;** let in on *or* to, **confide,** confide to, let into the secret; **publish** 559.10,11.

.6 **betray,** inform, **inform on** 557.12, talk *or* peach [both informal]; rat *or* stool *or* sing *or* squeal [all slang], turn state's evidence; **leak** [informal], spill [slang], **spill the beans** [informal]; **let the cat out of the bag** [informal], speak before one thinks, be unguarded *or* indiscreet, **give away** *or* give the show away [both informal], betray a confidence, tell secrets, reveal a secret; have a big mouth *or* bazoo [slang], **blab** *or* blabber [both informal]; babble, **tattle,** tell *or* tattle on, tell tales, **tell tales out of school;** talk out of turn, let slip, let fall *or* drop; **blurt, blurt out.**

.7 **confess,** break down and confess, **admit, acknowledge,** allow, avow, concede, grant, **own, own up** [informal], let on, implicate *or* incriminate oneself, come clean [slang]; spill *or* spill it *or* spill one's guts [all slang]; **tell the truth,** tell all, admit everything, let it all hang out [informal], throw off all disguise; **plead guilty,** own oneself in the wrong, cop a plea [slang]; **unbosom oneself, make a clean breast, get it off one's chest** [informal], **get it out of one's system** [informal], disburden *or* unburden one's mind *or* conscience *or* heart, **take the load off one's mind;** out with it *or* spit it out *or* open up [all informal].

.8 **be revealed, become known, come to light,** appear, manifest itself, come to one's ears, transpire, **leak out, get out, come out, out,** break forth, show its face; show its colors, be seen in its true colors, stand revealed, blow one's cover [slang].

.9 ADJS **revealed, disclosed** 555.10.

.10 **disclosive, revealing,** revelatory, revelational, apocalyptic(al); **disclosing,** showing, exposing, betraying; eye-opening; talkative 554.10, 596.9.

.11 confessional, admissive.

## 557. INFORMATION

.1 NOUNS **information**, info [informal], **facts**, datum [sing], **data, knowledge** 475; general information, gen [Brit informal]; factual information, hard information; **evidence, proof** 505; enlightenment, light; incidental information, sidelight; **acquaintance**, familiarization, briefing; **instruction** 562.1; **intelligence**; the know or the dope or the goods or the scoop [all slang]; transmission, **communication** 554; **report, word**, message, presentation, account, **statement**, mention; white paper, white book, blue book, command paper [Brit]; dispatch, bulletin, communiqué, handout [informal], release; publicity, promotional material; **notice**, notification; announcement, publication 559; directory, guidebook 748.10.

.2 **inside information**, private or confidential information; the lowdown or inside dope or inside wire or hot tip [all slang]; insider; pipeline [informal].

.3 **tip** or tip-off or **pointer** [all informal], clue, cue; **steer** or office [both slang]; **advice**; whisper, passing word, **word to the wise**, word in the ear, bug in the ear [informal]; warning, caution, monition, alerting.

.4 **hint**, gentle hint, intimation, indication, suggestion, suspicion, inkling, whisper, glimmer, glimmering; **cue, clue**, index, symptom, sign, spoor, track, scent, telltale; **implication**, insinuation, innuendo; broad hint, gesture, signal, nod, wink, look, nudge, kick, prompt.

.5 **informant, informer, source**, teller, interviewee, enlightener; **adviser**, monitor; **reporter**, notifier, **announcer**, annunciator; spokesman, mouthpiece; communicator, communicant, publisher; **authority**, witness, expert witness; **tipster** [informal], **tout** [slang]; newsmonger, gossipmonger; **information medium** or media, press, radio, television; channel, grapevine; information center; public relations officer.

.6 **informer, betrayer**, delator; **snitch** or snitcher [both slang]; whistle-blower [informal]; **tattler**, tattletale, telltale, talebearer; **blab** or blabber or blabberer or blabbermouth [all informal]; **squealer** or peacher or **stool pigeon** or stoolie or **fink** or narc [all slang]; spy 781.9.

.7 **information** or communication theory; data storage or retrieval, EDP, electronic data processing; signal, noise; encoding, decoding; bit; redundancy, entropy; channel; information or communication explosion.

.8 VERBS **inform, tell, speak**, apprize, **advise, advertise**, advertise of, **give word**, mention to, **acquaint, enlighten**, familiarize, brief, verse, wise up [slang], give the facts, give an account of, give by way of information; **instruct** 562.11; possess or seize one of the facts; **let know, have one to know, give one to understand**; tell once and for all; notify, give notice or notification, serve notice; **communicate** 554.6,7; bring or send or leave word; **report** 558.11; **disclose** 556.4–7; put in a new light, shed new or fresh light upon.

.9 **post** or **keep one posted** [both informal]; fill one in, bring up to date, put one in the picture [Brit].

.10 **hint, intimate, suggest**, insinuate, **imply, indicate**, adumbrate, lead or leave one to gather, justify one in supposing, give or throw out a hint, give an inkling of, **hint at**; **allude to**, make an allusion to, glance at [archaic]; **prompt**, give the cue; put in or into one's head.

.11 **tip** or tip off or **give one a tip** [all informal], alert; **give a pointer to** [informal]; put hep or hip [slang], **let in on**, let in on the know [slang]; let next to or put next to or **put on to** or put on to something hot [all slang]; **confide**, confide to, entrust with information, give confidential information, mention privately or confidentially, whisper, buzz, breathe, whisper in the ear, **put a bug in one's ear** [informal].

.12 **inform on** or **against, tell on** [informal], betray; **tattle, blab** [informal]; **snitch** o squeal or peach or sell out or rat or stoo or fink or narc or put the finger on o snitch on or squeal on [all slang]; turn in former; blow the whistle [informal]; te tify against, **bear witness against**; tur state's evidence, turn king's or queen's e idence [Brit].

.13 **come to know**, have it reported, get th facts, **get wise to** [informal], get hep to next to or on to [all slang]; learn; becom conscious or aware of, become alive awake to, awaken to, open one's eyes to

.14 **be informed** or apprised, have the fac **come to one's knowledge**, come to reach one's ears; be told, **hear**, overhea hear tell of or hear say [both informa get scent *or* wind of; **know** 475.12; **know well** 475.13.

.15 **keep informed,** keep posted [informal], stay briefed, **keep up on,** keep up to date *or* au courant, keep abreast of the times; **keep track of,** keep count *or* account of, keep tab *or* tabs on [informal], keep a check on, keep an eye on.

.16 ADJS informed 475.18–20; informed of, in the know 475.16.

.17 **informative,** informing, informational; **instructive, enlightening;** educative, educational 562.19; advisory, monitory; **communicative** 554.11.

.18 telltale, tattletale.

.19 ADVS from information received, according to reports *or* rumor, from notice given, as a matter of general information, by common report, from what one can gather.

## 558. NEWS

.1 NOUNS news, tidings, intelligence, information, word, advice; newsiness [informal]; newsworthiness; a nose for news; journalism, reportage; the press, the fourth estate, broadcast journalism; news medium *or* media, newspaper, newsletter, newsmagazine, radio, television, press association, news service, news agency, wire service, telegraph agency.

.2 **good news,** good word, **glad tidings;** gospel, evangel; bad news.

.3 **news item,** piece *or* budget of news; **article, story,** piece; copy; scoop *or* beat [both slang], exclusive; spot news.

.4 **message, dispatch, word, communication, communiqué,** advice, release; express [Brit]; embassy, embassage [archaic]; **letter** 604.2; **telegram** 560.14; pneumatogram, *petit bleu* [Fr].

.5 **bulletin,** news report, flash.

.6 **report, rumor,** flying rumor, unverified *or* unconfirmed report, **hearsay,** *on-dit* [Fr], scuttlebutt *or* latrine rumor [both informal]; **talk, whisper, buzz, rumble,** bruit, cry; idea afloat, news stirring; **common talk, town talk, talk of the town,** topic of the day, *cause célèbre* [Fr]; **grapevine;** canard, roorback.

.7 **gossip,** gossiping, gossipry, gossipmongering, back-fence gossip [informal], newsmongering; **talebearing,** taletelling; **tattle,** tittle-tattle, chitchat, **talk,** idle talk; "putting two and two together, and making it five" [Pascal]; piece of gossip, groundless rumor, tale, story.

.8 **scandal, dirt** [informal], **malicious gossip,** "gossip made tedious by morality" [Oscar Wilde]; juicy morsel, tidbit, choice bit of dirt [informal]; **scandalmongering;** gossip column; character assassination, **slander** 971.3; whispering campaign.

.9 **newsmonger, rumormonger, scandalmonger, gossip,** gossipmonger, gossiper, *yenta* [Yid], quidnunc, **busybody,** tabby [informal]; **talebearer,** taleteller, telltale, **tattletale** [informal], tattler, tittle-tattler, "a tale-bearing animal" [J. Harrington]; gossip columnist; reporter, newspaperman 605.22.

.10 (secret news channel) **grapevine, grapevine telegraph,** bush telegraph [Austral]; **pipeline.**

.11 VERBS **report,** give a report, give an account of, tell, relate, rehearse [archaic]; write up, make out *or* write up a report; bring word, tell the news, break the news, give tidings of; bring glad tidings, give the good word; announce 559.12; **rumor** 559.10; **inform** 557.8.

.12 **gossip,** talk over the back fence [informal], **tattle,** tittle-tattle; clatter [Scot], **talk;** retail gossip, **dish the dirt** [informal], tell idle tales.

.13 ADJS **newsworthy,** front-page, with news value, newsy.

.14 **gossipy,** gossiping, newsy; **talebearing,** taletelling.

.15 **reported, rumored,** whispered; rumored about, talked about, whispered about, bruited about, bandied about; **in the news, in circulation, in the air, going around,** going about, **current, rife,** afloat, in every one's mouth, on all tongues, all over the town; made public 559.17.

.16 ADVS as they say, as it is said, **as the story goes** *or* runs, as the fellow says [informal], it is said.

## 559. PUBLICATION

.1 NOUNS **publication, publishing, promulgation,** evulgation, **propagation, dissemination, diffusion, broadcast, broadcasting, spread, spreading,** spreading abroad, **circulation,** ventilation, airing, noising, bandying, bruiting, bruiting about; **display;** issue, issuance; telecasting, videocasting; printing 603; book, periodical 605.

.2 **announcement, annunciation, enunciation; proclamation,** pronouncement, pronunciamento; **report,** communiqué, **declaration, statement;** program, programma, **notice, notification,** public notice; circular, encyclical, encyclical letter; manifesto, position paper; white paper, white book; ukase, edict 752.4; bulletin board.

.3 **press release,** release, handout, bulletin, notice.

.4 **publicity, publicness, notoriety, fame, famousness, celebrity,** *réclame, éclat* [both Fr]; **limelight** *or* **spotlight** [both informal], daylight, bright light, glare, public eye *or* consciousness, **exposure, currency,** common *or* public knowledge, widest *or* maximum dissemination; **ballyhoo** *or* hoopla [both slang]; report, public report; cry, hue and cry; **public relations, PR; publicity story,** press notice; **write-up, puff** [informal], **plug** [slang], **blurb** [informal].

.5 **promotion, buildup** [informal], **flack** [informal], **publicization, publicizing,** promoting, advocating, advocacy, bruiting, drumbeating, tub-thumping, press-agentry; **advertising,** salesmanship 829.2, advertising campaign; advertising agency; advertising medium *or* media.

.6 **advertisement, ad** [informal], notice; **commercial,** message, important message, message from the sponsor; spot commercial *or* spot, network commercial; reader, reading notice; display ad; want ad [informal], classified ad; spread, two-page spread; testimonial.

.7 **poster, bill, placard, sign,** show card, banner, *affiche* [Fr]; **signboard, billboard,** highway sign, hoarding [Brit]; sandwich board; marquee.

.8 **advertising matter,** promotional material, public relations handout *or* release, **literature** [informal]; **leaflet,** leaf, folder, **handbill, bill, flier, throwaway, handout, circular,** broadside, broadsheet.

.9 **publicist,** publicizer, public relations man, public relations officer, PR man, public relations specialist, **publicity man** *or* agent, **press agent,** flack [slang]; **advertiser; adman,** huckster, pitchman [all informal]; ad writer [informal], copywriter; **promoter, booster** [informal], plugger [slang]; **ballyhooer** *or* **ballyhoo man** [both slang]; **barker,** spieler [slang], skywriter; billposter; sandwich boy *or* man.

.10 VERBS **publish, promulgate, propagate, circulate,** circularize, **diffuse, disseminate,** distribute, **broadcast,** televise, telecast, videocast, air, **spread,** spread around *or* about, spread far and wide, publish abroad, **pass the word around,** bruit, **bruit about, advertise,** repeat, retail, put about, **bandy about, noise about,** cry about *or* abroad, noise *or* sound abroad,

set news afloat, **spread a report; rumor,** launch a rumor, voice [archaic], whisper, buzz, **rumor about,** whisper *or* buzz about.

.11 **make public,** bring *or* lay *or* drag before the public, **display,** take one's case to the public, **give** *or* **put out,** give to the world, **make known; divulge** 556.5; **ventilate,** air, give air to, bring into the open, open up, broach.

.12 **announce,** annunciate, enunciate; **declare, state,** declare roundly, affirm, pronounce, give notice; **report,** make an announcement *or* report, make *or* issue a statement, publish *or* issue a manifesto, present a position paper, issue a white paper, hold a press conference.

.13 **proclaim,** cry, cry out, **promulgate,** celebrate, **herald,** herald abroad; **blazon,** blaze, blaze *or* blazon about *or* abroad, blare, blare forth *or* abroad, thunder, declaim, shout, trumpet, trumpet *or* thunder forth, announce with flourish of trumpets *or* beat of drum; shout from the housetops, proclaim at the crossroads *or* market cross, proclaim at Charing Cross [Brit].

.14 **issue, bring out, put out, get out,** get off, emit, put *or* give *or* send forth, offer to the public.

.15 **publicize,** give publicity; bring *or* drag into the limelight, throw the spotlight on [informal]; **advertise, promote,** build up, cry up, sell, puff [informal], **boost** [informal], **plug** [slang], **ballyhoo** [slang]; put on the map, make a household word of, establish; bark, spiel [both slang]; make a pitch for *or* beat the drum for *or* thump the tub for [all informal]; **write up,** give a write-up, press-agent [informal]; circularize; bulletin; bill; **post bills,** post, post up, placard; skywrite.

.16 (be published) **come out,** break, **issue,** go *or* come forth, find vent, **see the light,** become public; **circulate, spread,** spread about, have currency, **get around** *or* about, get abroad, get afloat, get exposure, go *or* fly *or* buzz *or* blow about, **go the rounds,** pass from mouth to mouth, be on everyone's lips, go through the length and breadth of the land; spread like wildfire.

.17 ADJS **published, public,** made public, **circulated,** in circulation, promulgated, propagated, **disseminated,** spread, diffused, distributed; in print; **broadcast,** telecast, televised; **announced,** proclaimed, declared, **stated,** affirmed; reported, brought to notice; common knowledge, common property, current; **open,** accessible, open to the public.

.18 publicational, promulgatory, propagatory; proclamatory, annunciatory, enunciative; declarative, declaratory; heraldic.

.19 ADVS **publicly, in public; openly** 555.15; in the public eye, in the glare of publicity, in the limelight *or* spotlight [informal].

## 560. COMMUNICATIONS

.1 NOUNS **communications,** signaling, telecommunication, tel(e)– *or* telo–; electronic communication, electrical communication; wire communication, wireless communication; communication engineering, communication technology; communications engineer; media, communications medium *or* media; communication *or* information theory 557.7; communication *or* information explosion.

.2 **telegraphy,** telegraphics; railroad telegraphy, submarine telegraphy; simplex telegraphy, multiplex telegraphy, duplex telegraphy, quadruplex telegraphy; single-current telegraphy, closed-circuit telegraphy; teleprinter, teletypewriter, Teletype, typotelegraph, teleprinter exchange *or* telex; TelAutograph, facsimile telegraph; wire service, Teletype network, Teletyping, teletypewriting, typotelegraphy, TelAutography; **ticker,** stock ticker, news ticker; code 614.6; electricity 342; **key,** interrupter, transmitter, sender; receiver, **sounder.**

.3 **radio** 344, **radiotelephony, radiotelegraphy,** wireless [Brit], wireless telephony, wireless telegraphy; line radio, wire *or* wired radio, wired wireless [Brit], wire wave communication; radiophotography; **television** 345; electronics 343.

.4 **telephone, phone** [informal], telephone set; telephony, telephonics, telephone mechanics, telephone engineering; high-frequency telephony; receiver, telephone receiver; mouthpiece, transmitter; telephone extension, extension; wall telephone, desk telephone; dial telephone, push-button telephone; telephone booth, call box [Brit], public telephone, coin telephone, pay station.

.5 **radiophone, radiotelephone,** wireless telephone, wireless; headset, headphone 450.8.

.6 **intercom** [informal], Interphone, intercommunication system.

.7 **telephone exchange,** telephone office, central office, **central;** automatic exchange, machine-switching office; step-by-step switching, panel switching, crossbar switching, electronic switching.

.8 **switchboard; PBX,** private branch *or* business exchange; in *or* A board, out *or* B board.

.9 **telephone operator, operator,** switchboard operator, telephonist, **central;** long distance; PBX operator.

.10 **telephone man;** telephone mechanic; telephonic engineer; lineman 342.19.

.11 **telephoner,** phoner [informal], caller, **party,** calling party.

.12 telephone number, **phone number** [informal]; telephone directory, phone book [informal]; telephone exchange, exchange; telephone area, area code.

.13 telephone call, **phone call** [informal], **call, ring** *or* buzz [both informal]; local call, toll call, long-distance call; long distance, direct distance dialing, DDD; station-to-station call, person-to-person call; collect call; mobile call; dial tone, busy signal.

.14 **telegram, telegraph, wire** [informal], telex; **cablegram, cable; radiogram,** radiotelegram; **day letter, night letter;** fast telegram.

.15 **Telephoto,** Wirephoto, facsimile, telephotograph, radiophotograph, Photoradiogram.

.16 **telegrapher,** telegraphist, telegraph operator; **sparks** *or* brass pounder *or* dit-da artist [all informal]; radiotelegrapher; wireman, wire chief.

.17 **line,** wire line, telegraph line, telephone line; private line, party line; trunk, trunk line; WATS *or* wide area telecommunications service, WATS line; cable, telegraph cable; concentric cable, coaxial cable, co-ax [informal].

.18 VERBS **telephone, phone** [informal], **call,** call on the phone [informal], put in *or* make a call, **call up, ring,** ring up, give a ring *or* buzz [informal], buzz [informal]; dial; listen in; hold the phone *or* wire; hang up, ring off [Brit].

.19 **telegraph,** telegram, flash, **wire** *or* send a wire [both informal], telex; **cable;** Teletype; radio; sign on, sign off.

.20 ADJS **communicational,** telecommunicational, **communications,** communication, signal; **telephonic,** magnetotelephonic, microtelephonic, monotelephonic, thermotelephonic; **telegraphic; Teletype;** Wirephoto, facsimile; phototelegraphic, telephotographic; **radio,** wireless [Brit]; radiotelegraphic.

**.21 telephones**

| | |
|---|---|
| carbon telephone | Picturephone |
| dial telephone | push-button tele- |
| extension phone | phone |
| field telephone | radiotelephone |
| French telephone, | sound-powered tele- |
|   hand set | phone |
| light-beam telephone | string telephone |
| magnetotelephone | thermophone, ther- |
| mechanical telephone | motelephone |
| microtelephone | wall telephone |
| monotelephone | wireless telephone |
| pantelephone | |

**.22 telegraphs**

| | |
|---|---|
| autotelegraph | multiplex |
| dial telegraph | needle telegraph |
| disk telegraph | pantelegraph |
| electric telegraph | phototelegraph |
| engine-room telegraph | quadruplex |
| facsimile telegraph | radiotelegraph |
| field telegraph | semaphore telegraph |
| heliograph | solar telegraph |
| indicator telegraph | TelAutograph |
| magnetotelegraph | telectrograph |
| marconigraph | telegraphoscope |
| Morse telegraph | typewriting telegraph |
| multiple telegraph | writing telegraph |

**.23 teleprinters**

| | |
|---|---|
| news ticker | Teletypesetter |
| printer | teletypewriter |
| printing telegraph | TFX |
| stock ticker | ticker |
| telecon | typewriting telegraph |
| teleprinter | typotelegraph |
| Teletype | |

**.24 telegraph recorders**

| | |
|---|---|
| phototransceiver | telegraphonograph |
| siphon recorder | telegraphophone |
| telegraphone | |

## 561. MESSENGER

**.1** NOUNS **messenger,** message-bearer, **dispatch-bearer,** commissionaire [Brit], nuncio [archaic], **courier,** diplomatic courier, carrier, **runner,** express [Brit], dispatchrider, post [archaic], postboy, postrider, *estafette* [Fr]; **go-between** 781.4; **emissary** 781.6; Mercury, Hermes, Iris, Pheidippides, Paul Revere.

**.2 herald, harbinger,** forerunner; **evangel,** evangelist, bearer of glad tidings; herald angel, Gabriel.

**.3 announcer,** annunciator, enunciator; nunciate [archaic]; **proclaimer; crier, town crier,** bellman.

**.4 errand boy,** office boy, copyboy; bellhop [slang], bellboy, bellman, callboy, caller.

**.5 postman, mailman,** mail carrier, letter carrier; **postmaster,** postmistress; postal clerk.

**.6** (mail carriers) carrier pigeon, carrier,

homing pigeon, homer [informal]; pigeon post; post-horse, poster; post coach, mail coach; post boat, packet boat *or* ship; mail boat, mail packet, mailer [archaic]; mail train, mail car, post car, post-office car, railway mail car; mail truck; mailplane.

## 562. TEACHING

**.1** NOUNS **teaching, instruction, education, schooling, tuition; edification, enlightenment,** illumination; tutelage, tutorage, tutorship; tutoring, coaching, private teaching; spoon-feeding; direction, guidance; **pedagogy,** pedagogics, didactics; catechization; programmed instruction; self-teaching, self-instruction; information 557; reeducation 145.4.

**.2 inculcation, indoctrination,** catechization, inoculation, **implantation,** infixation, infixion, **impression, instillment,** instillation, impregnation, **infusion,** imbuement; **absorption** and **regurgitation;** dictation; conditioning, brainwashing; reindoctrination 145.5.

**.3 training, preparation,** readying [informal], **conditioning, grooming,** cultivation, development, improvement; **discipline;** breaking, housebreaking; **upbringing, bringing-up,** fetching-up [dial], **rearing, raising, breeding, nurture,** nurturing, fostering; **practice,** rehearsal, **exercise, drill,** drilling; **apprenticeship,** in-service training, on-the-job training; military training, basic training; manual training, sloyd; vocational training *or* education.

**.4 preinstruction,** pre-education; **priming,** cramming [informal].

**.5 elementary education; initiation, introduction,** propaedeutic; **rudiments,** first steps, elements, **ABC's;** reading, writing, and arithmetic, **three R's;** primer, hornbook, abecedarium, abecedary.

**.6 instructions, directions, orders; briefing,** final instructions.

**.7 lesson, teaching, instruction, lecture,** lecture-demonstration, harangue, **discourse,** disquisition, exposition, **talk;** homily, **sermon,** preachment; chalk talk [informal]; skull session [informal]; **recitation,** recital; **assignment, exercise,** task, set task; homework; **moral,** morality, moralization, moral lesson; object lesson.

**.8 study,** branch of learning; **discipline,** subdiscipline; **field, specialty,** academic specialty, area; **course,** course of study, **curriculum; subject; major, minor;** elective; refresher course; **seminar,** proseminar;

classical education; scientific education, technical education; religious education; liberal arts, humanities, trivium, quadrivium; general education, general studies, core curriculum.

.9 physical education, physical culture, gymnastics, calisthenics, eurythmics.

.10 primary education, elementary education; secondary education, higher education; vocational education; liberal education; graduate education, professional education, graduate-professional education; postgraduate education; continuing education, adult education.

.11 VERBS teach, instruct, give instruction, give lessons in, educate, school; edify, enlighten, civilize, illumine; direct, guide; inform 557.8; show, show how, demonstrate; give an idea of; put in the right, set right; improve one's mind, enlarge or broaden the mind; sharpen the wits, open the eyes or mind; teach a lesson, give a lesson to; ground, teach the rudiments or elements; catechize; teach an old dog new tricks; reeducate 145.14.

.12 tutor, coach; prime, cram [informal], cram with facts, stuff with knowledge.

.13 inculcate, indoctrinate, catechize, inoculate, instill, infuse, imbue, impregnate, implant, infix, impress; impress upon the mind or memory, urge on the mind, beat into, beat or knock into one's head; condition, brainwash, program.

.14 train; drill, exercise; practice, rehearse; keep in practice, keep one's hand in; prepare, ready, condition, groom, fit, put in tune, form, lick into shape [informal]; rear, raise, bring up, fetch up [dial], bring up by hand; breed; cultivate, develop, improve; nurture, foster, nurse; discipline, take in hand; put through the mill or grind [informal]; break, break in, housebreak, house-train [Brit]; put to school, send to school, apprentice.

.15 preinstruct, pre-educate; initiate, introduce.

.16 give instructions, give directions; brief, give a briefing.

.17 expound, exposit; explain 552.10; lecture, discourse, harangue, hold forth, give or read a lesson; preach, sermonize; moralize, point a moral.

.18 assign, give or make an assignment, give homework, set a task, set hurdles; lay out a course, make a syllabus.

.19 ADJS educational, educative, educating, teaching, instructive, instructional, tuitional, tuitionary; cultural, edifying, en-

lightening, illuminating; informative 557.17; didactic, preceptive; self-instructional, self-teaching, autodidactic; lecturing, preaching, hortatory, exhortatory, homiletic(al); initiatory, introductory, propaedeutic; disciplinary; coeducational.

.20 scholastic, academic, schoolish; scholarly; pedagogical 565.12; graduate, professional, graduate-professional, postgraduate; interdisciplinary, cross-disciplinary; curricular.

.21 extracurricular, extraclassroom; nonscholastic, noncollegiate.

## 563. MISTEACHING

.1 NOUNS misteaching, misinstruction; misguidance, misdirection, misleading; sophistry 483; perversion, corruption; mystification, obscuration, obfuscation, obscurantism; misinformation, misknowledge; the blind leading the blind; college of Laputa.

.2 propaganda; propagandism, indoctrination; propagandist, agitprop.

.3 VERBS misteach, misinstruct, miseducate; misinform; misadvise, misguide, misdirect, mislead; pervert, corrupt; mystify, obscure, obfuscate.

.4 propagandize, carry on a propaganda; indoctrinate.

.5 ADJS mistaught, misinstructed; misinformed; misadvised, misguided, misdirected, misled.

.6 misteaching, misinstructive, miseducative, misinforming; misleading, misguiding, misdirecting.

## 564. LEARNING

.1 NOUNS learning, intellectual acquirement or acquisition or attainment, stocking or storing the mind, mental cultivation, mental culture, improving or broadening the mind; mastery of skills; self-education, self-instruction; knowledge, erudition 475.5,6; education 562.1; memorization 537.4.

.2 absorption, ingestion, imbibing, assimilation, taking-in, soaking-up, digestion.

.3 study, studying, application, conning; reading, perusal, –lexia; restudy, restudying, review; contemplation 478.2; inspection 485.3; engrossment 330.3; brainwork, headwork, lucubration, mental labor; exercise, practice, drill; grind or grinding or boning [all informal], cramming or cram [both informal], swotting [Brit informal]; extensive study, wide reading; subject 562.8.

.4 **studiousness, scholarliness,** scholarship; bookishness 475.4, diligence 707.6.

.5 **teachableness, teachability, educability,** trainableness; aptness, aptitude, quickness, **readiness; receptivity,** mind like a blotter; **willingness, motivation;** docility, **malleability,** moldability, pliability, facility, plasticity, **impressionability,** susceptibility, formability; brightness, cleverness, **intelligence** 467.

.6 VERBS **learn,** get, get hold of [informal], get into one's head; **gain knowledge,** pick up information, gather *or* collect *or* glean knowledge *or* learning; stock *or* store the mind, improve *or* broaden the mind; stuff *or* cram the mind; burden *or* load the mind; **find out, ascertain, discover,** find, determine; **become informed,** gain knowledge *or* understanding of, acquire information *or* intelligence about, **learn about, find out about;** acquaint oneself with, make oneself acquainted with, become acquainted with; be informed 557.14.

.7 **absorb, get by osmosis, take in,** ingest, imbibe, **assimilate, digest, soak up,** drink in; **soak in, seep in,** percolate in.

.8 **memorize** 537.17; fix in the mind 537.18.

.9 **master,** attain mastery of, make oneself master of, **gain command of, become adept in,** become familiar *or* conversant with, become versed *or* well-versed in, **get up in** *or* **on,** gain a good *or* thorough knowledge of, **learn all about, get down pat** [informal], get down cold [slang], get taped [Brit informal]; **get the hang** *or* **knack of; learn the ropes,** learn the ins and outs; know well 475.13.

.10 **learn by experience,** learn by doing, **live and learn,** go through the school of hard knocks; **learn a lesson,** be taught a lesson.

.11 **receive instruction, undergo schooling,** pursue one's education, attend classes, go to *or* attend school, take lessons; **train,** prepare oneself, ready oneself, go into training; serve an apprenticeship; apprentice oneself to; **study with,** read with, sit at the feet of, learn from, have as one's master.

.12 **study,** regard studiously, apply oneself to, con; **read, peruse,** go over; restudy, **review; contemplate** 478.12; **examine** 485.23; give the mind to 530.5; **pore over,** vet [Brit informal]; bury oneself in, wade through, plunge into; **dig** *or* **grind** *or* **bone** [all informal], swot [Brit informal]; lucubrate, elucubrate, **burn the midnight oil;** make a study of; **practice, drill.**

.13 **browse, scan, skim, dip into,** thumb over *or* through, run over *or* through, glance *or* run the eye over *or* through, turn over the leaves, have a look at, hit the high spots.

.14 **study up, brush up,** polish up [informal], rub up, get up; **study up on, read up on, get up on; cram** *or* cram up [both informal], **bone up** [slang].

.15 **study to be, study for, read for,** read law, etc.; **specialize in, go in for,** make one's field; major in, minor in.

.16 ADJS educated, **learned** 475.18–23; self-taught, self-instructed, autodidactic.

.17 **studious,** devoted to studies, **scholarly,** scholastic, academic, professorial, donnish; owlish; rabbinic, mandarin; pedantic, dryasdust; bookish 475.22; diligent 707.22.

.18 **teachable, instructable, educable,** schoolable, trainable; **apt,** quick, **ready,** ripe for instruction; **receptive, willing,** motivated; thirsty for knowledge; docile, **malleable, moldable,** pliable, facile, plastic, **impressionable,** susceptible, formable; bright, clever, **intelligent** 467.12.

## 565. TEACHER

.1 NOUNS **teacher, instructor, educator,** educationist, preceptor, **mentor;** rabbi, *melamed* [Heb], pandit, pundit, guru, *mullah* [Per], *starets* [Russ]; **master,** maestro; **pedagogue,** pedagogist; **schoolteacher, schoolmaster,** schoolkeeper; dominie [Scot], abecedarian [archaic], certified teacher; professor, docent, don [Brit], doctor, fellow; guide 748.7.

.2 **instructress,** educatress, preceptress, **mistress; schoolmistress; schoolma'am** *or* **schoolmarm,** dame, schooldame; tutoress; **governess,** duenna.

.3 **schoolman, academician.**

.4 (academic ranks) professor, associate professor, assistant professor, instructor, tutor, associate, assistant, lecturer, reader [Brit]; visiting professor; emeritus, professor emeritus, retired professor.

.5 **teaching fellow, teaching assistant;** teaching intern, intern; **practice teacher,** apprentice teacher, **student** *or* **pupil teacher; teacher's aide,** paraprofessional; monitor, proctor, prefect, praepostor [Brit]; **student assistant,** graduate assistant.

.6 **tutor,** tutorer; **coach,** coacher; **private instructor,** *Privatdocent, Privatdozen* [both Ger]; crammer [Brit informal].

**.7 trainer, handler, groomer;** driller, drillmaster; **coach,** athletic coach.

**.8 lecturer,** lector, **reader** [Brit], praelector, **preacher,** homilist.

**.9 principal, headmaster,** headmistress; president, chancellor, vice-chancellor, rector, provost, master; **dean,** academic dean, dean of the faculty, dean of women, dean of men; administrator, educational administrator; administration.

**.10 faculty,** faculty members, professorate, professoriate, professors, professordom, teaching staff.

**.11 instructorship, teachership,** preceptorship, schoolmastery; **tutorship,** tutorhood, tutorage, tutelage; **professorship,** professorhood, professorate, professoriate; **chair,** chair of English, etc.; lectureship, readership [Brit]; fellowship.

**.12** ADJS **pedagogic(al),** preceptorial, tutorial; **teacherish,** teachery, teacherlike, teachy, **schoolteacherish,** schoolteachery, **schoolmasterish,** schoolmasterly, schoolmastering, schoolmasterlike; schoolmistressy, schoolmarmish [dial]; **professorial,** professorlike, academic, donnish; pedantic 475.22.

## 566. STUDENT

**.1** NOUNS **student, pupil, scholar,** learner, studier, educatee, **trainee,** élève [Fr]; inquirer; self-taught person, autodidact; auditor; monitor, prefect, praepostor [Brit]; –log or –logue.

**.2 disciple, follower,** apostle; convert, proselyte 145.7.

**.3** self-taught man, autodidact.

**.4 school child,** school kid [informal]; **schoolboy,** school lad; **schoolgirl;** preschool child, preschooler, nursery school child, infant [Brit]; kindergartner, grade schooler, primary schooler, intermediate schooler; secondary schooler, prep schooler, preppie [informal], high schooler; schoolmate, schoolfellow, fellow student, classmate.

**.5 college student, collegian,** collegiate, **varsity student** [Brit informal], college boy or girl; co-ed [informal]; seminarian, seminarist; bahur [Heb], yeshiva bocher [Yid].

**.6 undergraduate,** undergrad [informal], cadet, midshipman; underclassman, **freshman,** freshie [informal], plebe, **sophomore,** soph [informal]; **upperclassman, junior, senior.**

**.7** [Brit terms] commoner, pensioner, sizar, servitor [archaic], exhibitioner, fellow commoner; sophister, questionist [both archaic]; wrangler, optime; passman.

**.8 graduate,** grad [informal]; **alumnus,** alumni [pl], alumna [fem], alumnae [fem pl]; **graduate student,** master's degree candidate, doctoral candidate; **postgraduate,** postgrad [informal]; degrees 917.6,9; college graduate, college man, educated man, educated class; meritocracy.

**.9 novice,** novitiate, **tyro,** abecedarian, alphabetarian, **beginner** 68.2, entrant, **neophyte, tenderfoot** or **greenhorn** [both informal], freshman, **fledgling;** catechumen, initiate, debutant; new boy, newcomer 78.4; ignoramus 477.8; **recruit, raw recruit,** inductee, **rookie** [informal], boot; **probationer,** probationist, postulant; **apprentice,** articled clerk.

**.10 grind** or greasy grind [both informal], swotter or mugger [both Brit informal]; bookworm 476.4; overachiever; failing student, flunkee [informal], underachiever.

**.11 class, form** [Brit], **grade;** track.

**.12** ADJS **studentlike,** schoolboyish, schoolgirlish; undergraduate, graduate, postgraduate; **collegiate,** college-bred; sophomoric(al); autodidactic; **studious** 564.17; **learned, bookish** 475.21,22.

**.13 probationary,** probational, on probation.

## 567. SCHOOL

**.1** NOUNS **school, educational institution,** teaching institution, academic or scholastic institution, teaching and research institution, **institute, academy,** seminary, Schule [Ger], école [Fr], escuela [Sp].

**.2 public school,** common school, district school; union school, regional school, **central school, consolidated school; private school;** day school, country day school; **boarding school,** pensionat [Fr]; **finishing school;** dame school, blab school; **special school,** school for the handicapped; **night school,** evening school; **summer school,** vacation school; correspondence school, extension, university extension; school of continuing education, continuation school; platoon school; progressive school; free school, nongraded school, informal school, open classroom school; alternate or alternative school, street academy, storefront school, school without walls.

**.3** [Brit terms] provided school, council school, board school; voluntary school, nonprovided school, national school, charity school.

**.4 preschool,** infant school [Brit], nursery,

nursery school; day nursery, **day-care center**, crèche; **kindergarten.**

.5 **elementary school, grade school** or graded school, the grades; **primary school;** junior school [Brit]; **grammar school;** folk school, *Volksschule* [Ger].

.6 **secondary school,** middle school, **academy,** *Gymnasium* [Ger]; *lycée* [Fr], lyceum; **high school,** high [informal]; **junior high school,** junior high [informal], intermediate school; **senior high school,** senior high [informal]; **preparatory school,** prep school [informal], public school [Brit], seminary; **grammar school** [Brit], Latin school, *Progymnasium* [Ger]; *Realschule* [Ger]; *Realgymnasium* [Ger].

.7 **college,** four-year college, degree-granting institution, institution of higher learning; alma mater; college of general studies, university college, college of liberal arts, liberal-arts college; **university,** varsity [Brit informal], *université* [Fr]; multiversity; **junior college,** two-year college; **community college; graduate school,** postgraduate school; teachers' college, college or school of education; normal school, normal; law school, medical school, library school, journalism school, school of communications, school or college of business administration; engineering school, college of engineering, institute of technology; coeducational school; academe, academia, the groves of Academe, **the campus,** the halls of learning, ivied halls.

.8 **vocational school, trade school,** occupational school; business college or school, commercial school, secretarial school; industrial school; technical school, technical training institute, technological school or institute; polytechnic school, polytechnic; manual arts school; school of arts and crafts.

.9 **conservatory,** *conservatoire* [Fr]; school of fine arts; **art school,** school of art, school of graphic arts, school of design; school or college of architecture; school of the performing arts; **music school,** college or academy of music; singing school, choir school, schola cantorum; **dancing school,** *salle de danse* [Fr]; acting school, school or college of dramatic arts, school of drama.

.10 **religious school,** denominational school, **church school, parochial school,** parish school; convent school; Hebrew school, *heder* [Yid], Talmud Torah; yeshiva, mesivta; **seminary,** divinity school, theological seminary, theological school; **Bible school,** Bible institute; **Sunday school,** Sabbath school; vacation church school.

.11 **gymnasium,** palaestra; wrestling school; fencing school, *salle d'armes* [Fr].

.12 **riding school** or academy, manège.

.13 **military school** or academy; US Military Academy, West Point; Royal Military Academy (at Woolwich); Royal Military College, Sandhurst; *Ecole Speciale Militaire Interarmes*, St. Cyr; naval school or academy; US Naval Academy, Annapolis; US Coast Guard Academy (at New London); US Merchant Marine Academy, Kings Point; Royal Naval College, Dartmouth; *École Navale* (at Brest); US Air Force Academy (at Colorado Springs); Royal Air Force College, Cranwell; *École de l'Air* (at Salon-de-Provence); war college, naval college, staff college, command and general staff school, air university.

.14 **reform school, reformatory,** industrial school, training school; borstal or borstal school or remand school [all Brit].

.15 **schoolhouse,** school building; little red schoolhouse; classroom building; hall; campus.

.16 **schoolroom, classroom;** recitation room; lecture room or hall; auditorium; theater, amphitheater.

.17 **governing board, board;** board of education, school board; college board, board of regents, board of trustees, board of visitors.

.18 ADJS **scholastic, academic,** institutional, **school,** classroom; **collegiate; university;** preschool; interscholastic, intercollegiate, extramural; intramural.

## 568. INDICATION

.1 NOUNS **indication,** signification, identification, differentiation, denotation, **designation,** denomination; characterization, highlighting; specification, naming, pointing, pointing out or to, fingering [informal], picking out, selection; symptomaticness, indicativeness; **meaning** 545; hint, suggestion 557.4; **expression, manifestation** 555; show, showing, disclosure 556.

.2 **sign,** telltale sign, sure sign, **index,** indicant, **indicator,** signal [archaic], measure; **symptom;** note, keynote, **mark, earmark,** hallmark, **badge,** device, banner, stamp, signature, sigil, seal, trait, **characteristic,** character, peculiarity, idiosyncrasy, **property,** differentia; image, picture, **representation,** representative; **insignia** 569.

.3 **symbol, emblem, token,** cipher [archaic], type; **allegory; symbolism, symbology,** iconology, charactery; conventional symbol; symbolic system; **symbolization; ideogram,** logogram, pictogram; logotype; **totem,** totem pole; love knot.

.4 **pointer,** index, lead; **direction, guide;** fist, index finger *or* mark; **arrow;** hand, hour hand, minute hand, **needle,** compass needle, lubber 'line; **signpost,** guidepost, finger post, direction post; milepost; blaze; guideboard, signboard 559.7.

.5 **mark, marking;** watermark; **scratch,** scratching, engraving, graving, **score,** scotch, cut, hack, gash, blaze; nick, notch 262; **scar,** cicatrix, scarification, cicatrization; **brand, earmark; stigma; stain,** discoloration 679.2,3; blemish, macula, **spot,** blotch, splotch, flick, patch, splash; mottle, dapple; **dot,** point; polka dot; tittle, jot; **speck, speckle,** fleck; tick, **freckle,** lentigo, mole; birthmark, strawberry mark, nevus; caste mark; **check,** checkmark; prick, puncture; tattoo, tattoo mark.

.6 **line,** score, **stroke,** slash, virgule, diagonal, **dash, stripe, strip, streak, striation,** striping, streaking, bar, band; hairline; dotted line; lineation, delineation; sublineation, **underline,** underlining, underscore, underscoring; hatching, cross-hatching, hachure.

.7 **print, imprint, impress, impression;** dint, dent, indent, indentation, indention, concavity; sitzmark; **stamp,** seal, sigil, signet; colophon; **fingerprint,** thumbprint, thumbmark, dactylogram, dactylograph; **footprint,** footmark, footstep, step, vestige; pad, paw print, pawmark, pug, pugmark; fossil print *or* footprint, ichnite, ichnolite; **bump,** boss, stud, pimple, lump, excrescence, convexity, embossment.

.8 **track, trail, path, course,** *piste* [Fr], **line, wake;** vapor trail, contrail, condensation trail; **spoor,** signs, traces, **scent.**

.9 **clue, cue, key,** tip-off [informal], telltale, straw in the wind; **trace, vestige, spoor,** scent, whiff; **lead** [informal], hot lead [informal]; catchword, cue word, key word; **evidence** 505; **hint, intimation, suggestion** 557.4.

.10 **marker, mark;** bookmark; **landmark,** seamark; bench mark; **milestone,** milepost; cairn, menhir, catstone; lighthouse, lightship, tower, platform, watchtower, pharos; monument 570.12.

.11 **identification,** identification mark;

badge, identification badge, identification tag, dog tag [mil], **ID card,** tessera, **card,** calling card, visiting card, *carte de visite* [Fr], press card; letter of introduction; signature, initials, monogram, calligram; credentials; serial number; countersign, countermark.

.12 **password, watchword, countersign,** tessera; token; open sesame; secret grip; shibboleth.

.13 **label, tag;** ticket, docket [Brit], tally; **stamp, sticker; seal,** sigil, signet; cachet; stub, counterfoil; **token,** check; **brand, trade name,** trademark name; **trademark,** registered trademark; government mark, government stamp, broad arrow [Brit]; **hallmark,** countermark; price tag; plate, bookplate, book stamp, colophon, *ex libris* [L], logotype *or* logo; masthead, imprint, title page; letterhead, billhead; running head *or* title.

.14 **gesture, gesticulation; motion,** movement; carriage, bearing, posture, poise, pose, stance, way of holding oneself; body language, kinesics; beck, beckon; shrug; charade, dumb show, **pantomime;** sign language, gesture language; dactylology, deaf-and-dumb alphabet; hand signal; chironomy.

.15 **signal, sign; high sign** *or* the wink *or* the nod [all informal]; wink, flick of the eyelash, glance, leer; look in one's eyes, tone of one's voice; nod; nudge, elbow in the ribs, poke, kick, touch; **alarm** 704; **beacon,** signal beacon, marker beacon, radio beacon; signal light, signal lamp *or* lantern; blinker; signal fire, beacon fire, watch fire, balefire; **flare,** parachute flare; rocket, signal rocket, Roman candle; signal gun, signal shot; signal siren *or* whistle, signal bell, bell, signal gong, **police whistle,** watchman's rattle; aid to navigation, sailing aid; fog signal *or* alarm, fog bell, **foghorn,** fog whistle; **buoy,** spar buoy, bell buoy, gong buoy; **traffic signal,** traffic light, red *or* stop light, amber *or* caution light, green *or* go light; heliograph; signal flag; **semaphore,** semaphore telegraph, semaphore flag; **wigwag,** wigwag flag; international alphabet flag, international numeral pennant; red flag; white flag; yellow flag, quarantine flag; blue peter; pilot flag *or* jack; signal post, signal mast, signal tower; telecommunications 560.1–3.

.16 **call, summons;** whistle; moose call, birdcall, duck call, hog call, goose call, crow call, hawk call, dog whistle; **bugle call,** trumpet call; **reveille, taps,** last post [Brit]; alarm, alarum; **battle cry,** war cry, rebel yell, rallying cry; Angelus, Angelus bell.

.17 VERBS **indicate,** be indicative of, be an indication of, be significant of, connote, denominate, argue, bespeak, be symptomatic *or* diagnostic of, symptomize, symptomatize, **characterize, mark,** highlight, be the mark *or* sign of, give token, **betoken, signify,** stand for, identify, differentiate, note [archaic], **denote, mean** 545.8; testify, give evidence 505.10; **show, express, display, manifest** 555.5, **hint,** suggest 557.10, reveal, **disclose** 556.4; entail, involve 76.4.

.18 **designate, specify;** denominate, name, denote; stigmatize; **symbolize, stand for,** typify, be taken as, symbol, emblematize, figure [archaic]; **point to,** refer to, advert to, allude to, make an allusion to; pick out, select; **point out,** point at, put *or* lay one's finger on, finger [slang].

.19 **mark,** make a mark, put a mark on; pencil, chalk; mark out, demarcate, delimit, define; **mark off, check, check off,** tick, tick off, chalk up; punctuate, point; **dot, spot,** blotch, splotch, dash, **speck, speckle,** fleck, freckle; mottle, dapple; blemish; **brand,** stigmatize; **stain, discolor** 679.6; stamp, seal, punch, impress, imprint, **print, engrave** 578.12; **score, scratch,** gash, scotch, scar, scarify, cicatrize; nick, notch 262.4; **blaze,** blaze a trail; **line, seam,** trace, **stripe, streak, striate;** hatch; **underline, underscore;** prick, puncture, tattoo, riddle, pepper.

.20 **label, tag,** tab, ticket; stamp, seal; **brand, earmark;** hallmark.

.21 **gesture, gesticulate; motion,** motion to; beckon, wiggle the finger at; wave the arms, saw the air; shrug, shrug the shoulders; pantomime, mime.

.22 **signal,** signalize, sign, give a signal, make a sign; speak; flash; **give the high sign** *or* **the nod** [informal]; nod; nudge, poke, kick, dig one in the ribs, touch; wink, glance, raise one's eyebrows, leer; hold up the hand; **wave,** wave the hand, wave a flag, **flag,** flag down; **unfurl a flag,** hoist a banner, break out a flag; **show one's colors,** exchange colors; **salute,** dip; dip a flag, hail, hail and speak; half-mast; give *or* sound an alarm, raise a cry; beat the drum, sound the trumpet.

.23 ADJS **indicative,** indicatory; connotative, indicating, signifying, signalizing; **significant,** significative, meaningful; symptom-

atic, symptomatologic(al), diagnostic, pathognomonic(al); evidential, **designative,** denotative, denominative, naming; **suggestive,** implicative; **expressive,** demonstrative, exhibitive; representative 572.10, 11; identifying, identificational; individual, peculiar, idiosyncratic; **emblematic(al); symbolic(al),** symbolistic, symbological, typical; figurative, figural, metaphorical; ideographic; semiotic, semantic.

.24 **gestural,** gesticulative, gesticulatory; kinesic; pantomimic, **in pantomime,** in dumb show.

## 569. INSIGNIA

.1 NOUNS **insignia, regalia,** ensigns, **emblems, badges, symbols,** markings; badge, badge of office, mark of office, chain, chain of office, collar; wand, verge, *fasces* [L], mace, staff, baton; livery, uniform, mantle, dress; tartan, tie, old school tie, regimental tie; ring, school ring, class ring; pin, button, lapel pin *or* button; cap and gown, mortarboard; cockade; brassard; figurehead, eagle; cross 221.4, skull and crossbones, swastika, hammer and sickle, rose, thistle, shamrock, fleur-de-lis; medal, **decoration** 916.5,6; **heraldry,** armory, blazonry, sigillography, sphragistics.

.2 [her terms] heraldic device, achievement, bearings, coat of arms, arms, armorial bearings, armory, blazonry, blazon; hatchment; shield, escutcheon, scutcheon, lozenge; charge, field; crest, torse, wreath, garland, bandeau, chaplet, mantling, helmet; crown, coronet; device, motto; pheon, broad arrow; animal charge, lion, unicorn, griffin, yale, cockatrice, falcon, alerion, eagle, spread eagle; marshaling, quartering, impaling, impalement, dimidiating, differencing, difference; ordinary, bar, bend, bar sinister, bend sinister, baton, chevron, chief, cross, fess, pale, paly, saltire; subordinary, billet, bordure, canton, flanch, fret, fusil, gyron, inescutcheon, mascle, orle, quarter, rustre, tressure; fess point, nombril point, honor point; cadency mark, file, label, crescent, mullet, martlet, annulet, fleur-de-lis, rose, cross moline, octofoil; tincture, gules, azure, vert, sable, purpure, tenne; metal, or, argent; fur, ermine, ermines, erminites, erminois, pean, vair; heraldic officials 749.21.

.3 (royal insignia) regalia; scepter, rod, rod of empire; orb; armilla; purple, ermine, robe of state *or* royalty; purple pall crown, royal crown, coronet, tiara, diadem; cap of maintenance *or* dignity *or* estate, triple plume, Prince of Wales's feathers; uraeus; seal, signet, great seal, privy seal.

**.4** (ecclesiastical insignia) tiara, triple crown; ring, keys; miter, crosier, crook, pastoral staff; pallium; cardinal's hat, red hat.

**.5** (military insignia) insignia of rank, grade insignia, chevron, stripe; star, bar, eagle, spread eagle, chicken [slang], pip [Brit], oak leaf; branch of service insignia, insignia of branch *or* arm; unit insignia, organization insignia, shoulder patch, patch; shoulder sleeve insignia, badge, aviation badge *or* wings; parachute badge, submarine badge; service stripe, hash mark [informal], overseas bar, Hershey bar [slang]; epaulet.

**.6** flag, **banner**, oriflamme, **standard**, gonfalon *or* gonfanon, guidon, *vexillum* [L], *labarum* [L]; **pennant**, pennon, pennoncel, banneret, banderole, swallowtail, burgee, **streamer**; **bunting**; coachwhip, long pennant; **national flag, colors**; royal standard; **ensign**, merchant flag, jack, Jolly Roger, black flag; house flag; (US) Old Glory, Stars and Stripes, Star-Spangled Banner, red, white, and blue; (Confederacy) Stars and Bars; (France) tricolor, *le drapeau tricolore* [Fr]; (Britain) Union Jack, Union Flag, white *or* red *or* blue ensign; (Denmark) Dannebrog; signal flag 568.15.

## 570. RECORD

**.1** NOUNS **record, recording**, documentation, –gram; **chronicle, annals**, history; roll, **rolls**, pipe roll [Brit]; **account; register, registry**, rota, roster, scroll, catalog, inventory, table, list 88; letters, correspondence; **vestige, trace**, memorial, token, relic, remains.

**.2** archives, public records, government archives, government papers, presidential papers, historical documents, historical records, memorabilia; cartulary; biographical records, life records, biographical material, papers, ana; parish rolls *or* register *or* records.

**.3** registry, register office; archives, files; chancery.

**.4** memorandum, memo [informal], memoir, *aide-mémoire* [Fr], memorial; reminder 537.6; **note, notation**, annotation, jotting, docket, marginal note, marginalia, scholium, scholia, adversaria, foot-

note; **entry**, register, **registry**, item; **minutes**.

**.5** document, official document, legal document, legal paper, legal instrument, instrument, writ, **paper, parchment**, scroll, roll, **writing**, script, scrip; holograph, chirograph; **papers**, ship's papers; docket, file, personal file, **dossier**; blank, form.

**.6** certificate, certification, **ticket; authority**, authorization; **credential, voucher, warrant**, warranty, testimonial; note; **affidavit**, sworn statement, notarized statement, deposition, witness, attestation, *procès-verbal* [Fr]; **visa**, *visé* [Fr]; **bill of health**, clean bill of health; navicert [Brit]; **diploma**, sheepskin [informal]; certificate of proficiency, testamur [Brit].

**.7** report, bulletin, brief, statement, account, accounting; account rendered, *compte rendu* [Fr]; **minutes**, the record, proceedings, transactions, acta; **yearbook**, annual; **returns**, census report *or* returns, election returns, tally.

**.8** (official documents) state paper, white paper; blue book, green book, Red Book [Brit], white book, yellow book, *livre jaune* [Fr]; gazette, official journal, Congressional Record, Hansard.

**.9** (registers) genealogy, pedigree, studbook; Social Register, blue book; directory; Who's Who; Almanach de Gotha, Burke's Peerage; Red Book, Royal Kalendar; Lloyd's Register.

**.10** (recording media) bulletin board; scoresheet, scorecard, scoreboard; tape, magnetic tape, videotape, ticker tape; phonograph record, disc, platter [informal]; film, motion-picture film; slip, card, index card, filing card; library catalog, catalog card; microcard, microfiche, microdot, microfilm; file 88.3.

**.11** (record books) notebook, pocketbook, pocket notebook, blankbook; loose-leaf notebook, spiral notebook; **memorandum book**, memo book [informal], commonplace book, adversaria; address book; workbook; **blotter**, police blotter; docket, court calendar; **calendar**, desk calendar, appointment calendar, appointment schedule, engagement book; **tablet**, table [archaic], writing tablet; diptych, triptych; pad, **scratch pad; scrapbook**, memory book, **album; diary, journal; log**, ship's log, **logbook; account book, ledger**, daybook; **cashbook**, petty cashbook; Domesday Book; catalog, classified catalog; yearbook, annual.

**.12** monument, monumental *or* memorial

record, **memorial**; necrology, obituary, **memento**, remembrance, testimonial; cup, trophy, prize, ribbon, plaque; **marker**; inscription; **tablet**, stone, hoarstone [Brit], boundary stone, memorial stone; **pillar**, stela, shaft, column, memorial column, rostral column; cross; arch, memorial arch; memorial statue, bust; monolith, obelisk, **pyramid**; **tomb**, grave 410.16; **gravestone, tombstone**; memorial tablet, brass; headstone, footstone; mausoleum; cenotaph; cairn, mound, barrow, cromlech, dolmen, megalith, menhir, cyclolith; **shrine**, reliquary, tope, stupa.

.13 recorder, registrar 571.1.

.14 register, recording instruments 571.3.

.15 **registration, register, registry; recording,** record keeping, recordation; minuting, **enrollment**, matriculation, enlistment; impanelment; **listing, tabulation, cataloging,** inventorying, indexing; chronicling; **entry**, insertion, entering, posting; docketing, inscribing, **inscription**; **booking, logging.**

.16 VERBS record, put or place upon record; **inscribe**, enscroll; **register, enroll**, matriculate, check in; impanel; poll; **file**, index, catalog, calendar, **tabulate, list,** docket; **chronicle**; minute, put in the minutes or on the record, spread on the record; **write**, commit or reduce to writing, put in writing, put in black and white, put on paper; **write out; make out**, fill out; **write up**, chalk, chalk up; **write down, mark down, jot down, put down, set down, take down**; note, note down, make a note, make a memorandum; **post**, post up; **enter**, make an entry, insert, write in; **book**, log; cut, carve, grave, engrave, incise; put on tape, tape, tape-record; record, cut; videotape.

.17 ADJS recording, recordative [archaic], registrational; self-recording.

.18 recorded, registered; inscribed, written down, down; **filed**, indexed, enrolled, **entered**, logged, booked, posted; documented; minuted; **on record**, on file, on the books; official, legal, of record.

.19 documentary, documentational, documental, archival; epigraphic, inscriptional; necrological, obituary; testimonial.

### 571. RECORDER

.1 NOUNS **recorder**, recordist; **registrar**, register, prothonotary; archivist, documentalist; master of the rolls [Brit], *custos rotulorum* [L]; librarian; **clerk**, record clerk,

filing clerk; bookkeeper, accountant; **scribe**, scrivener; **secretary**, amanuensis; **stenographer** 602.17; notary, notary public; marker; scorekeeper, scorer, official scorer, timekeeper; engraver, stonecutter.

.2 annalist, genealogist, chronicler, historian 608.11.

.3 **recording instruments**

| | |
|---|---|
| anemograph | recording meter |
| autograph, auto- | register |
| graphic recorder | seismochronograph |
| barograph camera | seismograph |
| cash register | seismoscope |
| chronograph | self-registering barom- |
| Dictaphone | eter, thermometer, |
| differential recorder | etc. |
| dynagraph | siphon recorder |
| electrograph | sound recorder |
| facsimile telegraph | spectrograph |
| frequency recorder | sphygmograph |
| Gramophone | stethograph |
| Graphophone | tape recorder |
| hydrograph | TelAutograph |
| hygrograph | telegraphone |
| kymograph | Teletype, teletype- |
| odometer | writer |
| oscillograph | telltale |
| pari-mutuel, pari-mu- | thermograph, ther- |
| tuel machine | mometrograph |
| pedometer, passome- | ticker |
| ter | time clock |
| pluviograph | totalizator |
| pneumatograph, pneu- | turnstile |
| mograph | videotape recorder |
| recording barometer, | voting machine |
| potentiometer, | votograph |
| pyrometer, etc. | wire recorder |

### 572. REPRESENTATION

.1 NOUNS **representation, delineation,** presentment, drawing, **portrayal, portraiture, depiction,** depictment, rendering, rendition, characterization, charactering [archaic], picturization, figuration, limning, imaging; prefigurement; **illustration,** exemplification, demonstration; projection, **realization**; imagery, iconography; **art** 574; **drama** 611.1,4–6; conventional representation, plan, diagram, schema, blueprint, chart, map; **notation**, mathematical notation, musical notation, score, tablature, dance notation, choreography; writing, script, alphabet, syllabary; letter, ideogram, pictogram, logogram, logograph, hieroglyphic; printing 603; **symbol** 568.3.

.2 **impersonation,** personation; mimicry, mimicking, miming, pantomime, pantomiming, aping, dumb show; mimesis, **imitation** 22; personification, embodiment, incarnation; **characterization**, portrayal; **acting**, playing, enacting, enactment, performing, performance; **posing**, masquerade.

.3 image, likeness, eid(o)–; **resemblance,** semblance, similitude, simulacrum; **effigy, icon, idol; copy 24; picture 574.12;** portrait 574.16; photograph 577.3–7; perfect *or* exact likeness, duplicate, double; match, fellow, mate, companion, twin; living image, very image, very picture, living picture, dead ringer [informal], spitting image *or* spit and image [both slang]; miniature, model; **reflection,** shadow, mirroring; trace, tracing; rubbing.

.4 figure, figurine; **doll,** dolly [informal]; **puppet, marionette,** fantoccini [pl]; **mannequin** *or* manikin, model, dummy, lay figure; wax figure, waxwork; scarecrow, man of straw, snowman, gingerbread man; **sculpture, bust, statue, statuette,** statuary, monument [archaic]; portrait bust *or* statue; carving, wood carving; figurehead.

.5 representative, representation, **type, specimen,** typification, embodiment; **cross section;** exponent; **example 25.2.**

.6 VERBS **represent, delineate, depict,** render, characterize, hit off, character [archaic], **portray, picture,** picturize, limn, draw, paint 574.20; register, convey an impression of; take *or* catch a likeness; notate, write, print, map, chart, diagram, schematize; trace, trace out, trace over; rub, take a rubbing; **symbolize 568.18.**

.7 **go for, pass for,** count for, answer for, stand in the place of, be taken as, be regarded as, be the equivalent of; **pass as, serve as,** go as, be accepted for.

.8 **image, mirror,** hold the mirror up to nature, reflect, figure; **embody,** body forth, incarnate, **personify,** personate, impersonate; **illustrate,** demonstrate, exemplify; project, realize; shadow, shadow forth; **prefigure, pretypify,** foreshadow, adumbrate.

.9 **impersonate,** personate; **mimic,** mime, pantomime, take off, do *or* give an impression of; ape, copy; **pose as, masquerade as,** affect the manner *or* guise of, pass for, pretend to be, represent oneself to be; **act,** enact, perform, do; **play, act as,** act *or* play a part, act the part of, act out.

.10 ADJS representational, **representative, depictive, delineatory; illustrative,** illustrational; pictorial, graphic, vivid; ideographic, pictographic, figurative; **representing, portraying,** limning, illustrating; **typifying, symbolizing,** personifying, incarnating, embodying; imitative, mimetic, simulative, apish, mimish; echoic, onomatopoeic.

.11 **typical,** typic, typal; exemplary, sample; **characteristic,** distinctive, distinguishing, quintessential; **realistic, naturalistic;** natural, normal, usual, regular; **true to type, true to form,** the nature of the beast [informal].

## 573. MISREPRESENTATION

.1 NOUNS misrepresentation, **perversion, distortion,** deformation, garbling, twisting, slanting; inaccuracy; **coloring,** miscoloring, **false coloring; falsification 616.9;** misteaching 563; injustice, unjust representation; misdrawing, mispainting; misstatement, misreport, misquotation; nonrepresentationalism, nonrealism, abstractionism, expressionism, calculated distortion; overstatement, exaggeration, hyperbole, overdrawing; understatement, litotes.

.2 bad likeness, **daub,** botch; scribble, scratch; distortion, distorted image, anamorphosis; travesty, parody, caricature, burlesque.

.3 VERBS **misrepresent, belie,** give a wrong idea; put in a false light, **pervert, distort, garble, twist,** warp, wrench, slant, twist the meaning of; **color, miscolor, give a false coloring,** put a false construction *or* appearance upon, falsify 616.16–23; misteach 563.3; **disguise,** camouflage; misstate, misreport, misquote; overstate, exaggerate, overdraw; understate; travesty, parody, caricature, burlesque.

.4 **misdraw, mispaint;** daub, botch, scribble, scratch.

## 574. ART

.1 NOUNS **art,** the arts; **fine arts,** *beaux arts* [Fr]; arts of design, **design,** designing; art form; abstract art, representative art; **graphic arts;** plastic art; **arts and crafts;** primitive art, cave art; folk art; calligraphy; sculpture 575; ceramics 576; photography 577; etching, engraving 578.2; decoration 901.1; artist 579.

.2 "a treating of the commonplace with the feeling of the sublime" [J. F. Millet], "the conveyance of spirit by means of matter" [Salvador de Madariaga], "the expression of one soul talking to another" [Ruskin], "an instant arrested in eternity" [James Huneker], "a handicraft in flower" [George Iles], "science in the flesh" [Jean Cocteau], "life upon the larger scale" [E. B. Browning], "the perfection of nature" [Sir Thomas Browne], "the conscious utterance of thought, by speech or action, to any end" [Emerson], "the wine of life" [Jean Paul Richter], "a shadow of the divine perfection" [Michelangelo], "life seen through a temperament" [Zola], "a form of catharsis" [Dorothy Parker].

.3 **craft, manual art,** industrial art, **handicraft,** artisan work, craftwork, artisanship; industrial design; woodcraft, metalcraft, stonecraft; techno–.

.4 **architecture,** "frozen music", "music in space" [both Schelling], "the art of significant forms in space" [Claude Bragdon], "the printing press of all ages" [Lady Morgan]; landscape architecture, landscape gardening; civil architecture; functionalism.

.5 (act or art of painting) **painting,** coloring, –chromy, "a noble and expressive language" [Ruskin]; the brush; **portraiture** 572.1; **illustration,** picturization; watercoloring, *gouache* [Fr], oil painting, acrylic painting, tempera painting, encaustic painting, encaustic cerography, wash, wash drawing; grisaille, impasto; finger painting; monochrome; portrait painting, historical painting, still-life painting, nude painting, landscape painting, marine painting, genre painting; mural painting, fresco painting, poster painting, decorative painting, flower painting, miniature painting; illumination; sand painting.

.6 (art of drawing) **drawing, sketching, delineation; black and white,** charcoal; mechanical drawing, drafting; freehand drawing.

.7 scenography, ichnography, orthographic *or* orthogonal projection.

.8 **artistry, art, talent,** artistic skill, flair, artistic flair, artistic invention; artiness *or* arty-craftiness *or* artsy-craftiness [all informal]; artistic temperament; virtu, artistic quality.

.9 **style,** pencil; lines; genre; **school,** movement; the grand style.

.10 **treatment; technique,** draftsmanship, brushwork, painterliness; **composition, design,** arrangement; grouping; balance; **color,** values; atmosphere, tone; shadow, shading; **line;** perspective.

.11 **work of art, object of art,** *objet d'art* [Fr], art object, art work, artistic production, piece, **work, study, design,** composition; creation, brainchild; virtu, article *or* piece of virtu; **masterpiece,** *chef d'œuvre*

[Fr], masterwork, master [archaic], old master, classic; museum piece; grotesque; statue 572.4; mobile, stabile; nude, still life; pastiche, *pasticcio* [Ital]; artware, artwork; bric-a-brac; kitsch.

.12 **picture,** picto–; **image, likeness, representation,** tableau; "a poem without words" [Horace]; photograph 577.3; **illustration,** illumination; miniature; copy, reproduction; print, color print; engraving 578.2, stencil 578.5, block print; daub; abstraction, abstract; mural, fresco, wall painting; cyclorama, panorama, montage, collage; still life, study in still life; tapestry, mosaic, stained glass window, **icon,** altarpiece, diptych, triptych.

.13 **scene, view, scape; landscape;** waterscape, riverscape, seascape, seapiece; airscape, skyscape, cloudscape; snowscape; cityscape, townscape; farmscape; pastoral; treescape; diorama; exterior, interior.

.14 **drawing,** –gram; **delineation;** line drawing; **sketch, draft; black and white,** chiaroscuro; **charcoal, crayon, pen-and-ink,** pencil drawing, charcoal drawing, pastel, pastel painting; silhouette; vignette; doodle; rough draft *or* copy, rough outline, cartoon, sinopia, **study,** design; *brouillon, ébauche, esquisse* [all Fr]; diagram, graph; silver-print drawing, tracing.

.15 **painting, canvas,** easel-picture, "a pretty mocking of the life" [Shakespeare], "silent poetry" [Simonides], "the intermediate somewhat between a thought and a thing" [Coleridge]; **oil painting,** oil; **watercolor,** water, aquarelle, wash, wash drawing; finger painting; tempera, egg tempera; *gouache* [Fr].

.16 **portrait, portraiture, portrayal;** head; profile; silhouette, shadow figure; miniature.

.17 **cartoon, caricature; comic strip;** comic section, comics [both informal], funny paper *or* funnies [both slang]; comic book; animated cartoon.

.18 **studio,** *atelier* [Fr]; **gallery** 660.9.

.19 (art equipment) palette; easel; paintbox; art paper, drawing paper; sketchbook, sketchpad; canvas, artists' canvas; canvas board; scratchboard; lay figure; camera obscura, camera lucida; maulstick; palette knife, spatula; brush, paintbrush; air brush, spray gun; pencil, drawing pencil; crayon, charcoal, chalk, pastel; stump; painter's cream; ground; pigments, medium; siccative, drier; fixative, varnish; **paint** 362.8,23.

.20 VERBS **portray, picture,** picturize, **depict, limn,** draw *or* paint a picture; **paint**

362.13; color, tint; spread *or* lay on a color; **daub** [informal]; scumble; **draw, sketch, delineate; draft;** pencil, chalk, crayon, charcoal; dash off, scratch [informal]; doodle; design; diagram; cartoon; copy, trace; stencil; hatch, crosshatch, shade.

.21 ADJS **artistic,** painterly; **arty** *or* arty-crafty *or* artsy-craftsy [all informal]; **art-minded,** art-conscious; **aesthetic; tasteful; beautiful** 900.16; **ornamental** 901.10; **well-composed,** well-grouped, well-arranged, well-varied; of consummate art; in the grand style.

.22 **pictorial,** pictural, graphic, **picturesque;** picturable; photographic 577.17; scenographic; painty, pastose; scumbled; monochrome, polychrome; freehand.

.23 **art schools, groups, movements**

| | |
|---|---|
| American | Mannerist |
| Art Nouveau | Milanese |
| Ashcan school, the | Modenese |
| Eight | Momentum |
| Barbizon | 'N' |
| Bauhaus | Neapolitan |
| Bolognese | New Objectivity |
| British | New York |
| classical abstraction | Origine |
| Cobra | Paduan |
| Der Blaue Reiter | Parisian |
| De Stijl | Phases |
| Die Brücke | plein-air |
| Dutch | Pre-Raphaelite |
| eclectic | Raphaelite |
| Flemish | Reflex |
| Florentine | Restany |
| Fontainebleau | Roman |
| French | Scottish |
| Honfleur | Sienese |
| Hudson River | Spur |
| Italian | Suprematism |
| L'Age d'or | The Ten |
| letrist | Tuscan |
| Lombard | Umbrian |
| Madinensor | Venetian |
| Madrid | Washington |

.24 **art styles**

| | |
|---|---|
| abstract classicism | cubism |
| abstract expressionism | Dadaism |
| abstractionism | display art |
| action painting | divisionism |
| activist art | earth art |
| analytical cubism | elementarism |
| *art autre* [Fr] | existentialism |
| *art brut* [Fr] | expressionism |
| art deco | expressionistic abstraction |
| art nouveau | |
| attitude art | Fauvism |
| baroque | free abstraction |
| baroque formalism | free expressionism |
| classicism, classicalism | futurism |
| cloisonnism | geometricism |
| conceptual art | gesture calligraphy |
| concrete art | gesture painting |
| constructivism | Gothicism |
| conventionalism | hallucinatory painting |

| | |
|---|---|
| idealism | photomontage |
| impressionism | poetic kinetics |
| informalism | poetic realism |
| intimism | poetic tachism |
| intuitionism | pointillism |
| invisible painting | pop art |
| kinetic art | poptical art |
| linear chromatism | postconcretism |
| luminodynamism | postexpressionism |
| lyrical abstraction | postimpressionism |
| magic realism | postpainterly abstraction |
| matter informalism | |
| matter painting | pre-Columbian art |
| minimal art | preimpressionism |
| modernism | primitivism |
| mysticism | purism |
| naturalism | quietistic painting |
| neoclassicism | realism |
| neoconcrete art | representationism, representationalism |
| neoconstructivism | |
| neocubism | romanticism |
| neodadaism | social realism |
| neoexpressionism | spatialism |
| neofigural postsurrealism | suprarational automatism |
| neoimpressionism | suprematism |
| neoplasticism | surrealism |
| neotraditionalism | surrealist tachism |
| nonaction calligraphy | symbolism |
| nonobjectivism | synchromism |
| nonrepresentationalism | synthesism |
| | tachism |
| nuagism | traditionalism |
| objectivism | unism |
| op art | vorticism |
| ornamentalism | |

.25 **architecture styles**

| | |
|---|---|
| academic | high Renaissance |
| baroque | international |
| Bauhaus | Italian |
| Beaux Arts | medieval |
| Byzantine | Mesopotamian |
| early Renaissance | modern |
| Egyptian | Neo-Gothic |
| English | new brutalism |
| French | Persian |
| German | Renaissance |
| Gothic | Roman |
| Greco-Roman | Romanesque |
| Greek | Spanish |
| Greek Revival | |

## 575. SCULPTURE

.1 NOUNS **sculpture, sculpturing;** plastic art, **modeling; statuary;** monumental sculpture, architectural sculpture, decorative sculpture, garden sculpture, portrait sculpture; stone sculpture, clay sculpture, glass sculpture, metal sculpture, wire sculpture, paper sculpture, CYSP sculpture, earth art; **stonecutting;** gem-cutting; **wood carving,** xyloglyphy; whittling; bone-carving, shell-carving, ivory-carving, scrimshaw; wax modeling, ceroplastics; relief-carving, relief, relievo, glyptic, anaglyphy, anaglyptics, anaglyptography; embossing, **engraving** 578.2, **chasing,** toreutics, founding, casting, molding, plaster casting, lost-wax process, *cire perdue* [Fr]; sculptor 579.6,14.

.2 (sculptured piece) **sculpture; statue** 572.4; marble, bronze, terra cotta; mobile, stabile; cast 24.6.

.3 **relief,** relievo; **embossment, boss;** half relief, *mezzo-rilievo* [Ital]; high relief, *alto-rilievo* [Ital]; low relief, bas-relief, *basso-rilievo* [Ital], *rilievo stiacciato* [Ital]; sunk relief, *cavo-rilievo* [Ital], coelanaglyphic sculpture, **intaglio,** *intaglio rilievo, intaglio rilevato* [both Ital]; *repoussé* [Fr]; glyph, anaglyph; glyptograph; **mask;** plaquette; **medallion; medal; cameo,** cameo glass, sculptured glass; cut glass.

.4 (tools, materials) chisel, point, mallet, modeling tool, spatula; cutting torch, welding torch, soldering iron; solder; modeling clay, Plasticine, sculptor's wax.

.5 VERBS **sculpture,** sculp *or* sculpt [both informal], insculpture [archaic]; **carve,** chisel, cut, grave, engrave, chase; weld, solder; assemble; **model, mold;** cast, found.

.6 ADJS **sculptural,** sculpturesque, sculptitory; statuary; **statuesque,** statuelike; **monumental,** marmoreal.

.7 **sculptured,** sculpted; sculptile; **molded, modeled,** ceroplastic; **carved,** chisled; **graven,** engraven; in relief, in high *or* low relief; glyphic, glyptic, anaglyphic, anaglyptic; anastatic; embossed, chased, hammered, toreutic; *repoussé* [Fr].

## 576. CERAMICS

.1 NOUNS **ceramics, pottery.**

.2 **ceramic ware,** ceramics; **pottery, crockery; china, porcelain;** enamelware; refractory; cement; bisque, biscuit; pot, crock, vase, urn, jug, bowl; tile, tiling; brick, firebrick, refractory brick, adobe; glass 339.2.

.3 (materials) clay, argill(o)– *or* argilli–; potter's clay *or* earth, fireclay, refractory clay; porcelain clay, kaolin, china clay; china stone, petuntse; flux; slip; glaze.

.4 **potter's wheel,** wheel; kick wheel, pedal wheel, power wheel.

.5 **kiln, oven, stove, furnace;** acid kiln, brick-kiln, cement kiln, enamel kiln, muffle kiln, limekiln, reverberatory, reverberatory kiln; pyrometer, pyrometric cone, Seger cone.

.6 VERBS pot, shape, **throw,** throw *or* turn a pot; mold; **fire,** bake; glaze.

.7 ADJS **ceramic,** clay, enamel, china, porcelain; refractory.

.8 **ceramics**

| | |
|---|---|
| Albion ware | jasper, jasper ware |
| Allervale pottery | Kinkozan ware |
| basalt, basaltes | Leeds pottery |
| Belleek ware | Limoges, Limoges |
| Berlin ware | ware |
| biscuit ware | Lowestoft ware |
| blackware | lusterware, luster pottery |
| bone china | |
| Castleford ware | majolica |
| Castor ware | Meissen ware |
| champlevé, champlevé enamel | Nabeshima ware |
| | Old Worcester ware |
| china, chinaware | Palissy ware |
| clayware | Parian ware |
| cloisonné, cloisonné enamel | porcelain |
| | queensware |
| cottage china | refractory ware |
| crackle, crackleware | Rockingham ware |
| crouch ware | salt-glazed ware |
| Crown Derby ware | Satsuma ware |
| delft, delftware | Seto ware |
| Dresden china | Sèvres, Sèvres ware |
| earthenware | soft-paste porcelain |
| eggshell porcelain | Spode |
| enamel, enamelware | spongeware |
| faience | Staffordshire ware |
| glassware 339.2,7 | stoneware |
| glazed ware | terra cotta |
| gombroon | ting ware |
| hard-paste porcelain | Toft ware |
| Hirado ware | Wedgwood ware |
| Hizen porcelain | whiteware, white pottery |
| Imari ware | tery |
| ironstone, ironstone china | Worcester ware |
| Jackfield ware | yi tsing ware |

## 577. PHOTOGRAPHY

.1 NOUNS **photography,** picture-taking; **cinematography,** motion-picture photography; color photography; photochromy, heliochromy; **3-D,** three-dimensional photography; photofinishing; photogravure; radiography, X-ray photography; photogrammetry, phototopography.

.2 photographer 579.5.

.3 **photograph, photo** [informal], heliograph, **picture,** shot [informal]; **snapshot,** snap [informal]; black-and-white photograph; color photograph, color print, heliochrome; slide, diapositive, transparency; candid photograph; still, still photograph; photomural; montage, photomontage; aerial photograph, photomap; telephotograph, Telephoto, Wirephoto; photomicrograph, microphotograph; metallograph; microradiograph; electron micrograph; photochronograph, chronophotograph; **portrait;** pinup [informal], cheesecake *or* beefcake [both slang]; **mug** *or* mug shot [both slang]; rogues' gallery; photobiography.

.4 **tintype** *or* ferrotype, ambrotype, daguerreotype, calotype or talbotype, collotype, photocollotype, autotype, vitrotype.

**.5 print,** photoprint, positive; glossy, matte, semi-matte; **enlargement, blowup;** photocopy, Photostat, photostatic copy, Xerox, Xerox copy; microprint, microcopy; blueprint, cyanotype; **slide,** transparency, lantern slide; contact printing, projection printing; photogravure; hologram.

**.6** shadowgraph, shadowgram, skiagraph, skiagram; radiograph, radiogram, scotograph; **X ray,** X-ray photograph, roentgenograph, roentgenogram; photofluorogram; photogram.

**.7** spectrograph, spectrogram; spectroheliogram.

**.8** (motion pictures) **shot; take, retake;** close-up, long shot, medium shot, full shot, group shot, deuce shot, matte shot, process shot, boom shot, travel shot, trucking shot, follow-focus shot, pan shot or panoramic shot, rap shot, reverse or reverse-angle shot, wild shot, zoom shot; motion picture 611.16; kinescope.

**.9 exposure,** time exposure; shutter speed; f-stop, lens opening; film rating, **film speed,** film gauge, ASA exposure index, DIN number; exposure meter, light meter.

**.10 film; negative;** printing paper, photographic paper; **plate;** dry plate; vehicle; motion-picture film, panchromatic film, monochromatic film, orthochromatic film, black-and-white film, color film, color negative film, color reversal film; microfilm, bibliofilm; sound-on-film, sound film; sound track, soundstripe; roll, cartridge; pack, bipack, tripack; frame; emulsion, dope, backing.

**.11 camera,** Kodak; motion-picture camera, cinematograph or kinematograph [both Brit].

**.12 projector;** motion-picture projector, cinematograph or kinematograph [both Brit], vitascope; **slide projector,** magic lantern, stereopticon; slide viewer.

**.13 processing solution;** developer, soup [informal]; fixer, fixing bath, sodium thiosulfate or sodium hyposulfite or hypo; stop bath, short-stop, short-stop bath.

**.14** VERBS **photograph, shoot** [informal], take a photograph, **take a picture,** take one's picture; **snap,** snapshot, snapshoot; **film,** get or capture on film; **mug** [slang]; daguerreotype, talbotype, calotype; Photostat; Xerox; microfilm; photomap; pan; **X-ray,** radiograph, roentgenograph.

**.15 process; develop; print;** blueprint; **blow up, enlarge.**

**.16 project, show, screen.**

**.17** ADJS **photographic,** photo; **photogenic;** photosensitive, photoactive; panchromatic; telephotographic, telephoto; tintype; three-dimensional, 3-D.

**.18 types of photography**

| | |
|---|---|
| aerophotography, aerial photography, air photography | miniature photography |
| animation photography | phonophotography |
| | photoheliography |
| | photomacrography |
| astrophotography | photomicrography |
| candid photography | pyrophotography |
| chronophotography | radiography |
| cinematography | schlieren photography |
| cinephotomicrography | skiagraphy |
| color photography | spectroheliography |
| electrophotography | spectrophotography |
| heliophotography | stereophotography |
| holography | stroboscopic photography |
| infrared photography | |
| integral photography | telephotography |
| laser photography | uranophotography |
| macrophotography | xerography |
| microphotography | X-ray photography |

**.19 photographic equipment**

| | |
|---|---|
| burning-in tool | lens hood |
| changing bag | light meter |
| closeup lens | periscopic lens |
| darkroom | photoelectric cell |
| darkroom timer | meter |
| developing tank | photoflash, photoflash |
| diaphragm | lamp |
| dodging tool | photoflood, photo- |
| dryer | flood lamp |
| drying blotter | photographometer |
| easel | photometer |
| electronic-flash unit | polarizing filter |
| enlarger | portrait lens |
| exposure meter | range finder |
| filter | reflected light meter |
| finder | reflector |
| fisheye lens | safelight |
| flashbulb | self-timer |
| flashcube | shutter |
| flashgun | stroboscopic or strobe |
| flashlight | light |
| flash powder | telephoto lens |
| flash synchronizer | timer |
| flash tube | tripod |
| gadget bag | varifocal lens |
| incident light meter | viewfinder |
| iris diaphragm | wide-angle lens |
| lens | zoom lens |
| lens cover | |

**.20 cameras**

| | |
|---|---|
| aerial reconnaissance camera | flash camera |
| | folding camera |
| astrograph | hand camera |
| box camera | Iconoscope |
| camera obscura | image orthicon |
| candid camera | laboratory camera |
| cinematograph [Brit] | magazine camera |
| color camera | microcamera |
| electron-diffraction camera | miniature camera, minicam |

motion-picture camera, movie camera
photochronograph
photocopier
photographic telescope
photomicrographic camera
photomicroscope
photopitometer
photospectroscope
Photostat
pinhole camera
Polaroid Land camera
portrait camera
precision camera

press camera
reflex camera
single-lens reflex, SLR
spectroscopic camera
stereo camera
still camera
telescopic camera
television camera
tripod camera
twin-lens reflex
vest-pocket camera
Xerox machine
X-ray diffraction camera
X-ray machine

## 578. GRAPHIC ARTS

.1 NOUNS **graphic arts, graphics; printmaking; painting** 574.5; **drawing** 574.6; **relief-carving** 575.1; **photography** 577; **printing** 603; graphic artist 579.8.

.2 **engraving,** engravement, graving, enchasing, **tooling,** chiseling, incising, incision, lining, scratching, slashing, scoring; **inscription,** inscript; gem-engraving, glyptic, glyptography; glass-cutting; type-cutting; **marking,** line, scratch, slash, score; hatching, cross-hatching; etch, etching; stipple, stippling; tint, demitint, half tint; burr.

.3 (engraving processes) steel engraving, zincography, plate engraving, copperplate engraving, chalcography; relief method; woodcut, wood engraving, xylography; linocut; metal cut, *manière criblée* [Fr], cribbling; relief etching, zinc etching; intaglio; drypoint, etching, soft-ground etching, aquatint, mezzotint, stipple engraving, crayon engraving; cerography; pyrography, pyrogravure, woodburning, xylopyrography; photoengraving 603.1.

.4 **lithography,** planography, autolithography, artist lithography; chromolithography; photolithography, offset lithography 603.1.

.5 stencil printing, stencil; silk-screen printing, serigraphy; monotype; glass printing, decal, decalcomania; cameography.

.6 **print,** imprint, impression, impress; negative; color print; engraving, engravement; **etching;** aquatint, mezzotint; **lithograph;** autolithograph; chromolithograph; lithotype; copperplate, copperplate print *or* engraving; crayon engraving, graphotype; **block, block print,** linoleum-block print, rubber-block print, wood engraving, **woodprint,** xylograph, **cut, woodcut,** woodblock; vignette.

.7 **plate,** steel plate, copperplate, chalcograph; zincograph; stone, lithographic stone; printing plate 603.8.

.8 **proof,** artist's proof, proof before letter, open-letter proof, remarque proof.

.9 **engraving tool, graver,** burin, style, point, etching point, needle, etching needle; etching ball; etching ground *or* varnish; scorper; rocker; **die,** punch, stamp, intaglio, seal.

.10 VERBS **engrave, grave, tool, enchase, incise, sculpture, inscribe,** character, **mark,** line, crease, score, scratch, scrape, cut, carve, chisel; groove, furrow 263.3; stipple, cribble; hatch, crosshatch; lithograph, autolithograph; **be a printmaker** *or* graphic artist; **make prints** *or* graphics; print 603.14.

.11 **etch,** eat, eat out, corrode, bite, bite in.

.12 ADJS **engraved, graven,** graved, glypt(o)–; tooled, enchased, inscribed, incised, marked, lined, creased, cut, carved, glyphic, **sculptured,** insculptured, "insculp'd upon" [Shakespeare]; grooved, furrowed 263.4; **printed, imprinted, impressed,** stamped.

.13 glyptic(al), glyptographic, lapidary, lapidarian; xylographic, wood-block; lithographic, autolithographic, chromolithographic; aquatint, aquatinta, mezzotint.

## 579. ARTIST

.1 NOUNS **artist,** *artiste* [Fr], "a dreamer consenting to dream of the actual world" [Santayana], creator, maker; master, **old master;** dauber, daubster; copyist; **craftsman, artisan** 718.6.

.2 limner, delineator, depicter, picturer, portrayer, imager; **illustrator;** illuminator; calligrapher; commercial artist.

.3 **drawer,** sketcher, delineator; **draftsman,** architectural draftsman; crayonist, charcoalist, pastelist; **cartoonist, caricaturist.**

.4 **painter,** *artiste-peintre* [Fr]; **colorist;** luminist, luminarist; **oil painter,** oil-colorist; **watercolorist;** aquarellist; finger painter; monochromist, polychromist; genre painter, historical painter, landscapist, miniaturist, portrait painter, portraitist, marine painter, still-life painter; pavement artist; scene painter, scenewright, scenographer.

.5 **photographer,** photographist, **cameraman; cinematographer;** snapshotter, snap shooter, shutterbug [informal]; daguerreotypist, calotypist, talbotypist; skiagrapher, shadowgraphist, radiographer, X-ray photographer.

.6 **sculptor,** sculptress, sculpturer; earth artist; statuary; figurer, *figuriste* [Fr], **modeler,** molder, wax modeler, clay modeler;

graver, chaser, carver; stonecutter, mason, monumental mason, wood carver, xyloglyphic artist, whittler; ivory carver, bone carver, shell carver; gem carver, glyptic *or* glyptographic artist.

.7 **ceramist, ceramicist, potter;** china decorator *or* painter, tile painter, majolica painter; glassblower, glazer, glass decorator, pyroglazer, glass cutter; enamelist, enameler.

.8 **printmaker,** graphic artist; **engraver,** graver, burinist; inscriber, carver; **etcher;** line engraver, **lithographer,** autolithographer, chromolithographer; serigrapher, silk-screen artist; cerographer, cerographist; chalcographer; gem engraver, glyptographer, lapidary; wood engraver, xylographer; pyrographer, xylopyrographer; zincographer.

.9 **designer, stylist,** styler; costume designer, dress designer, *couturier* [Fr], *couturière* [Fr fem]; furniture designer, rug designer, textile designer.

.10 **architect,** civil architect; landscape architect, landscape gardener; city *or* urban planner, urbanist; functionalist.

.11 **decorator,** expert in decor, ornamentist, ornamentalist; **interior decorator,** house decorator, room decorator, floral decorator, table decorator; window decorator *or* dresser; confectionery decorator.

.12 **stylists**

| | |
|---|---|
| abstract classicist | idealist |
| abstract expressionist | impressionist |
| abstractionist | informalist |
| actionist | intimist |
| action painter | kineticist |
| activist | linear chromatist |
| analytical cubist | luminist |
| attitudist | luminodynamist |
| baroque formalist | lyrical abstractionist |
| classicist | magic realist |
| conceptual artist | mannerist |
| concretist | matter informalist |
| constructivist | modernist |
| conventionalist | mystic |
| cubist | naturalist |
| Dadaist | neoclassicist |
| divisionist | neoconcretist |
| earth artist | neoconstructivist |
| eclectic | neocubist |
| elementarist | neodadaist |
| existentialist | neoexpressionist |
| expressionist | neofigural postsurrealist |
| expressionistic abstractionist | |
| Fauvist | neoimpressionist |
| free abstractionist | neoplasticist |
| free expressionist | neotraditionalist |
| futurist | nonaction calligraphist |
| geometricist | nonobjectivist |
| gesture calligraphist | nonrepresentationist |
| gesturist | nuagist |

| | |
|---|---|
| objectivist | representationist, representationalist |
| op artist | romanticist |
| plein-airist | social realist |
| poetic kineticist | spatialist |
| poetic realist | suprarational automatist |
| poetic tachist | |
| pointillist | suprematist |
| pop artist | surrealist |
| poptical artist | surrealist tachist |
| postconcretist | symbolist |
| postexpressionist | synchromist |
| postimpressionist | synthesist |
| postpainterly abstractionist | tachist |
| preimpressionist | traditionalist |
| primitive, primitivist | unist |
| purist | vorticist |
| realist | |

.13 **painters**

| | |
|---|---|
| Albright | Grosz |
| Bacon | Guardi |
| Baziotes | Hals |
| Bellini | Hobbema |
| Bellows | Hodler |
| Benton | Hogarth |
| Blake | Hokusai |
| Boccioni | Holbein |
| Bonnard | Homer |
| Botticelli | Hopper |
| Boucher | Ingres |
| Braque | Jongkind |
| Brueghel | Kandinsky |
| Buffet | Kent |
| Carrà | Kirchner |
| Cassatt | Klee |
| Cézanne | Kline |
| Chagall | Kokoschka |
| Chardin | Kollwitz |
| Chirico | LeBrun |
| Constable | Léger |
| Copley | Leonardo |
| Corot | Limburg |
| Correggio | Lippi |
| Courbet | Lorenzetti |
| Dali | Manet |
| Daumier | Mantegna |
| David | Marc |
| da Vinci | Marin |
| Degas | Marquet |
| de Kooning | Masaccio |
| Delacroix | Masolino |
| Dubuffet | Masson |
| Duchamp | Matisse |
| Dufy | Michelangelo |
| Dürer | Millet |
| Eakins | Miró |
| El Greco | Modigliani |
| Ensor | Mondrian |
| Ernst | Monet |
| Feininger | Moses |
| Fra Angelico | Motherwell |
| Fragonard | Munch |
| Friesz | Murillo |
| Gainsborough | Nolde |
| Gauguin | Orozco |
| Giotto | Ozenfant |
| Gleizes | Picabia |
| Goya | Picasso |
| Graves | Pissarro |
| Greuze | Pollock |
| Gris | Poussin |

Raphael
Redon
Rembrandt
Remington
Renoir
Reynolds
Riley
Rivera
Rockwell
Romney
Rosa
Rossetti
Rothko
Rouault
Rousseau
Rubens
Ryder
Sargent
Schmidt-Rottluff
Seurat
Severini
Signac
Siqueiros
Sisley
Soutine

Stella
Stuart
Tintoretto
Titian
Tobey
Toulouse-Lautrec
Turner
Utrillo
van der Weyden
Vandyke
van Eyck
van Gogh
van Ruisdael
Velázquez
Vermeer
Veronese
Vlaminck
Vuillard
Warhol
Watteau
Whistler
Wood
Wyeth
Zadkine

**.14 sculptors**

Arp
Borglum
Brancusi
Calder
Cellini
della Robbia
Donatello
Epstein
French
Ghiberti
Giacometti
Lipchitz

Maillol
Michelangelo
Milles
Moore
Oldenburg
Phidias
Picasso
Pisano
Praxiteles
Rodin
Saint-Gaudens

## 580. LANGUAGE

.1 NOUNS language, speech, tongue, *lingua* [L], lingu(o)– or lingui–, gloss(o)–, glott-(o)–; talk, parlance, locution, phraseology, idiom, lingo [informal]; dialect; idiolect, personal usage, individual speech habits or performance, parole; code or system of oral communication, individual speech competence, langue; usage.

.2 dead language, ancient language, lost language; parent language; classical language; living language, vernacular.

.3 mother tongue, native language or tongue, native speech, vernacular.

.4 standard language, standard or prestige dialect; national language, official language; educated speech or language; literary language, written language, formal written language; classical language; correct or good English, Standard English, the King's or Queen's English, Received Standard, Received Pronunciation.

.5 informal language or speech, informal standard speech, spoken language, colloquial language or speech, vernacular language or speech, vernacular; colloquialism, colloquial usage, conversationalism, vernacularism; informal English, conversational English, colloquial English, English as it is spoken.

.6 substandard language or speech, nonstandard language or speech; vernacular language or speech, vernacular, vulgate, vulgar tongue, common speech, uneducated speech, illiterate speech; substandard usage; slang.

.7 dialect, idiom; class dialect; regional or local dialect; subdialect; folk speech or dialect, patois; provincialism, localism, regionalism, regional accent 594.9; Canadian French, French Canadian; Pennsylvania Dutch, Pennsylvania German; Yankee, New England dialect; Brooklynese; Cockney; Yorkshire; Midland, Midland dialect; Anglo-Indian; Australian English; Gullah; Acadian, Cajun; dialect atlas, linguistic atlas; isogloss, bundle of isoglosses; speech community; linguistic community, linguistic ambience; speech or linguistic island, relic area; dialect dictionary, Dictionary of American Regional English.

.8 (idioms) Anglicism, Briticism, Englishism; Americanism, Yankeeism; Gallicism, Frenchism; Irishism, Hibernicism; Canadianism, Scotticism, Germanism, Russianism, Latinism, etc.

.9 jargon, lingo [informal], cant, argot, patois, patter, vernacular; vocabulary, phraseology; gobbledygook, mumbo jumbo, gibberish; slang; taboo language, vulgar language; obscene language, scatology.

.10 (jargons) Academese, cinemese, collegese, economese, sociologese, legalese, pedagese, societyese, stagese, telegraphese, Varietyese, Wall Streetese, journalese, newspaperese, officialese, federalese, Pentagonese, Washingtonese, medical Greek, medicalese, businessese, computerese, commercialism, business English; shoptalk.

.11 lingua franca, jargon, pidgin, trade language; auxiliary language, interlanguage; creolized language, creole language, creole; koine; pidgin English, talkeetalkee, Bêche-de-Mer, Beach-la-mar; Kitchen Kaffir; Chinook or Oregon Jargon; Sabir; artificial international languages 580.24.

.12 linguistics, linguistic science, science of language; glottology, glossology [archaic]; linguistic analysis; historical linguistics, comparative linguistics, general linguistics, descriptive linguistics, structural linguistics, structuralism, theoretical linguistics, areal linguistics, dialectology, geolinguistics, dialect or linguistic geography, glottochronology or lexicostatistics, computational or mathematical linguistics, psycholinguistics, sociolinguistics, metalinguistics; transformational linguistics, glossematics; etymology, derivation; **philology**; bowwow theory, dingdong theory, pooh-pooh theory; lexicology 582.15; semantics 545.7; syntactics, linguistic structure; **grammar** 586; phonology, phonemics, phonetics 594.14; morphophonemics, morphology 582.3; graphemics, paleography; language study, foreign-language study.

.13 **linguist,** linguistic scientist, linguistician, linguistic scholar; philologist, philologer, philologian; philologaster; **grammarian,** grammatist; grammaticaster; **etymologist,** etymologer; **lexicologist; lexicographer,** glossographer, glossarist; phoneticist, phonetician, phonemicist, phonologist, orthoepist; dialectician, dialectologist; semanticist, semasiologist; paleographer.

.14 **polyglot,** linguist, **bilingual** or diglot, trilingual, multilingual, –glot.

.15 **colloquializer;** jargonist, jargoneer, jargonizer; slangster.

.16 VERBS **speak, talk,** use language, communicate orally or verbally; use informal speech or style, colloquialize, vernacularize; jargon, jargonize, cant; patter.

.17 ADJS **linguistic,** lingual, glottological; descriptive, structural, glottochronological, lexicostatistical, psycholinguistic, sociolinguistic, metalinguistic; **philological;** lexicological, lexicographic(al); syntactic(al), **grammatic(al);** semantic 545.12; phonetic 594.31, phonemic, phonological; morphological 582.22; morphophonemic, graphemic, paleographic(al).

.18 **vernacular, colloquial, conversational, unliterary, informal,** spoken; unstudied, familiar, common, everyday; **substandard,** nonstandard, uneducated.

.19 **jargonish,** jargonal; **slang,** slangy; taboo; scatological.

.20 **idiomatic; dialect,** dialectal, dialectological; provincial, regional, local.

.21 **types of languages**

| | |
|---|---|
| affixing | inflectional |
| agglutinative | isolating |
| analytic | monosyllabic |
| fusional | polysyllabic |
| incorporative | polysynthetic |

polytonic
symbolic

.22 **groups of languages**

| | |
|---|---|
| Adamawa-Eastern | Latinian |
| Afro-Asiatic | Luorawetlan |
| Algonquian | Malayo-Polynesian, |
| Anatolic, Anatolian | Malayo-Indonesian |
| Annam-Muong | Manchu |
| Araucanian | Mande |
| Arawakan | Mayan |
| Aryan | Melanesian |
| Athapaskan | Micronesian |
| Austric | Mongolic |
| Austroasiatic | Mon-Khmer |
| Austronesian | Munda |
| Aymara | Muran |
| Baltic | Muskogean |
| Balto-Slavic | Na-dene |
| Bantu | Nahuatlan |
| Berber | Niger-Congo |
| Brythonic | Nilotic |
| Bushman | Osco-Umbrian |
| Caddoan | Otomanguean |
| Cariban | Paleo-Asiatic, Paleo- |
| Caspian | Siberian |
| Caucasian | Papuan |
| Celtic | Penutian |
| Chad | Permian |
| Chari-Nile | Piman |
| Chibchan | Polynesian |
| Chinookan | Quechuan |
| Cushitic | Ritwan |
| Dard | Romance, Romanic |
| Dravidian | Sabellian |
| Eskimo-Aleut | Salish |
| Finnic | Samoyed, Samoyedic |
| Finno-Ugric, Finno- | Sanskritic |
| Ugrian | Scandinavian |
| Germanic | Semitic |
| Goidelic | Shahaptian |
| Gur | Shoshonean |
| Haida | Sino-Tibetan |
| Hamitic | Siouan |
| Hamito-Semitic | Skittagetan |
| Hellenic | Slavic, Slavonic |
| Hokan | Sudanic |
| Hokan-Coahuiltecan, | Tagala |
| Hokaltecan | Takilman |
| Hokan-Siouan | Tanoan |
| Indic, Indo-Aryan | Taracahitian |
| Indo-Chinese | Tarascan |
| Indo-European, Indo- | Teutonic |
| Germanic | Thraco-Illyrian |
| Indo-Hittite | Thraco-Phrygian |
| Indo-Iranian | Tibeto-Burman, |
| Indonesian | Tibeto-Burmese |
| Iranian | Tsimshian |
| Iroquoian | Tungusic |
| Italic | Tupi-Guaranian |
| Jicaquean | Turanian |
| Karankawa | Turkic, Turko-Tartar |
| Kartvelian | Ugric |
| Kechumaran | Ural-Altaic |
| Keresan | Uralian |
| Khoin | Uto-Aztecan |
| Khoisan | Xincan |
| Kitunahan | Yeniseian |
| Koluschan | Yukaghir |
| Kuki-Chin | Yukian |
| Kunama | Zuñian |
| Kwa | |

synthetic

## .23 languages

| | | | |
|---|---|---|---|
| Abnaki | Dalmatian | Kabyle | Makassar |
| Afghan, Afghani | Danish | Kachin | Malagasy |
| Afrikaans | Dinka | Kafiri | Malay |
| Ainu | Dutch | Kalmuck | Malayalam |
| Akan | Dyak | Kamasin | Maltese |
| Akkadian | Edo | Kamchadal, Kamchat- | Malto |
| Albanian | Efatese | kan | Manchu |
| Aleut | Egyptian | Kanarese | Mandarin |
| Algonquin | Elamitic | Kara-Kalpak | Mandingo |
| Amharic | English | Karamojong | Mangarevan |
| Andaman | Eskimo | Karankawa | Manobo |
| Anglo-French, Anglo- | Estonian | Karelian | Manx |
| Norman | Ethiopic | Karen | Maori |
| Anglo-Saxon | Euskarian | Kashmiri | Marathi |
| Annamese | Ewe | Kashubian | Marquesan |
| Anzanite | Faeroese | Kazan Tatar | Marshall, Marshallese |
| Apache | Faliscan | Keres | Maya |
| Arabic | Fijian | Ket | Meithei |
| Aramaic | Finnish | Khamti | Mende |
| Araucanian | Flemish | Kharia | Messapian |
| Arawak | Fox | Khasi | Middle English |
| Armenian | French | Khmer | Middle Greek |
| Assamese | Frisian | Khondi | Middle High German |
| Austral | Fulani, Fula | Khosa | Middle Persian |
| Avestan | Gadaba | Khotanese | Mishmi |
| Aymara | Gaelic | Khowar | Mishongnovi |
| Aztec | Galcha | Kickapoo | Misima |
| Balinese | Galla | Kiowa | Miskito |
| Baluchi | Garo | Kiowa Apache | Mon |
| Bashkir | Gaulish | Kiranti | Mongolian |
| Basque | Geez | Kirghiz | Mordvin, Mordvinian |
| Batak | Georgian | Kiriwina | Moro |
| Bellacoola | German | Kodagu | Mru |
| Bengali | Gilbertese | Kohistani | Mundari |
| Berber | Gold, Goldi | Koiari | Muong |
| Bhili | Gondi | Kolami | Mura |
| Bihari | Gothic | Komi | Murmi |
| Bikol | Greek | Kongo | Muskogee |
| Bini | Guanche | Konkani | Naga |
| Blackfoot | Guarani | Korean | Nepali |
| Brahui | Gujarati | Korwa | Newari |
| Breton | Gypsy | Koryak | Ngala |
| Buginese | Haida | Kui | Ngbaka |
| Bulgarian | Haitian Créole | Kuki | Niasese |
| Burmese | Hausa | Kumyk | Nicobarese |
| Burushaski | Hawaiian | Kunama | Niuean |
| Buryat | Hebrew | Kurdish | Nogai |
| Byelorussian | High German | Kurukh | Nootka |
| Cantonese | Hindustani | Kutchin | Norwegian |
| Carib | Hittite | Kutenai | Old English |
| Carolinian | Ho | Ladino | Oraon |
| Castilian | Hopi | Lahnda | Oriya |
| Catalan | Hottentot | Lampong | Oscan |
| Cham | Iban | Lamut | Osmanli |
| Chamorro | Ibanag | Lao | Ossetic |
| Cheremis | Ibo | Lapp | Ostyak |
| Cherokee | Icelandic | Latin | Pahari |
| Chibcha | Igorot | Latvian, Lettish | Pahlavi |
| Chin | Illyrian | Libyan | Palaic |
| Chinese | Ilocano | Ligurian | Palau |
| Choctaw | Irish, Irish Gaelic | Limbu | Palaung |
| Chukchi | Italian | Lithuanian | Pali |
| Chuvash | Ivatan | Livonian | Pampango |
| Coptic | Jagatai | Loucheux | Pangasinan |
| Cornish | Jakun | Low German | Panjabi, Punjabi |
| Cuman | Japanese | Lusatian | Pashto |
| Czech | Javanese | Luwian | Paya |
| Dafla | Juang | Lycian | Persian |
| Dagomba | Judeo-German | Lydian | Phrygian |
| Dakota | Judeo-Spanish | Macedonian | Plattdeutsch |
| | | Madurese | Polabian |
| | | Magyar | Polish |

445

Portuguese
Prakrit
Provençal, *langue d'oc* [Fr]
Punic
Punjabi
Puyi
Quechua
Quiché
Rajasthani
Riffian
Romaic
Romansh, Rhaeto-Romanic, Rhaetian
Romany
Ronga
Ruanda
Rumanian
Rundi
Russian
Ruthenian
Sabellian
Saharan
Saho
Sakai
Salar
Samoan
Sanskrit
Santali
Sardinian
Sasak
Savara
Scottish Gaelic
Selung
Semang
Serbo-Croatian
Shan
Shina
Shluh, Shilha
Siamese
Sindhi
Sinhalese
Slovak
Slovene, Slovenian
Sogdian
Somali
Sorbian
Soyot
Spanish
Sumerian
Susian
Swahili
Swedish
Syriac
Syryenian
Taal
Tagalog

Tagula
Tahitian
Tajiki
Takelma
Talamanca
Talishi
Tamashek
Tamaulipec
Tamil
Tatar
Tavgi
Taw-Sug
Teleut
Telugu
Thracian
Tibetan
Tigre
Tigrinya
Tino
Tipura
Tocharian
Toda
Tonga
Tuamotu
Tuareg
Tulu
Tungus
Tupi
Turkish
Turkoman
Ugaritic
Uighur
Ukrainian
Umbrian
Urdu
Uzbek
Venetic
Veps
Vietnamese
Visayan
Vogul
Vote
Votyak
Wa
Welsh
Wendish
White Russian
Xhosa
Yakut
Yenisei
Yiddish
Yoruba
Yurak
Zenaga
Zulu
Zuñi

**.24 artificial languages**

Antido
Arulo
Blaia Zimondal
Esperantido
Esperanto
Europan
Idiom Neutral
Ido
Interlingua
Latinesce
Latino, Latino sine flexione
Lingualumina

Lingvo Kosmopolita
Monario
Nov-Esperanto
Novial
Nov-Latin
Occidental
Optez
Pasigraphy
Ro
Romanal
Solresol
Volapük

**581. LETTER**

**.1** NOUNS letter, written character, character, sign, symbol, graph, grapheme, allograph, alphabetic character or symbol, phonetic character or symbol; logographic or lexigraphic character or symbol; ideographic or ideogrammic or ideogrammatic character or symbol; syllabic character or symbol, syllabic, syllabogram; pictographic character or symbol; cipher, device; monogram; graphy, *mater lectionis* [L]; writing 602.

**.2** (phonetic and ideographic symbols) phonogram; phonetic symbol; logogram, logograph, grammalogue; word letter; ideogram, ideograph, phonetic, radical, determinative; pictograph, pictogram; hieroglyphic, hieroglyph, hieratic symbol, demotic character; rune, runic character or symbol; cuneiform, character; wedge, arrowhead, ogham; kana, hiragana, katakana; shorthand 602.8; hieroglyphics.

**.3** writing system, script, letters; alphabet, letters of the alphabet, ABC's; christcross-row; phonetic alphabet, International Phonetic Alphabet, IPA; Initial Teaching Alphabet, ITA; phonemic alphabet; runic alphabet, futhark; alphabetism; syllabary; alphabetics, alphabetology, graphemics; paleography; speech sound 594.13.

**.4** spelling, orthography; phonetic spelling, phonetics, phonography; spelling reform; spelling match or bee, spelldown; bad spelling, cacography; spelling pronunciation.

**.5** lettering, initialing; inscription, epigraph, graffito; alphabetization; transliteration, transcription.

**.6** VERBS letter, initial, inscribe, character, sign, mark; capitalize; alphabetize, alphabet; transliterate, transcribe.

**.7** spell, orthographize; spell out, write out, trace out; spell backward; outspell, spell down; syllabify, syllabize, syllable, syllabicate.

**.8** ADJS literal, lettered; alphabetic(al); abecedarian; graphemic, allographic; large-lettered, majuscule, majuscular, uncial; capital, capitalized, upper-case; small-lettered, minuscule, minuscular, lower-case; logographic, logogrammatic, lexigraphic, ideographic, ideogrammic, ideogrammatic, pictographic; transliterated, transcribed.

## .9 writing systems

| | |
|---|---|
| Arabic | kanji |
| Armenian | katakana |
| Assyrian | Kharoshthi |
| Avestan | Korean |
| Babylonian | Latin |
| Berber | Lemnian |
| Brahmi | Libyan |
| Chalcidian | Linear A |
| Cherokee | Linear B |
| Coptic | Lycian |
| Cretan | Lydian |
| Cypriot | Manchu |
| Cypro-Minoan | Mayan |
| Cyrillic | Minoan |
| Devanagari | Mitannic |
| Egyptian demotic | Mongolian |
| Egyptian hieratic | Nagari |
| Egyptian hieroglyphic | Nubian |
| Elamitic | ogham |
| Ethiopian | Oscan |
| Etruscan | Pahlavi |
| Georgian | Permian |
| Glagolitic | Persian |
| Gothic | Phoenician |
| Grantha | Phrygian |
| Greek | runic |
| Hebrew | Sanskrit |
| hiragana | Scandinavian |
| Hittite hieroglyphic | Semitic |
| Iberian | Sinaitic |
| Indus Valley | Sogdian |
| Initial Teaching | Sumerian |
| Alphabet | Szeklian |
| International Pho- | Tuareg |
| netic Alphabet | Turkish runic |
| Ionian | Uighur |
| Irish | Umbrian |
| Kalmuck | Vietnamese |
| kana | |

## 582. WORD

.1 NOUNS **word**, log(o)–, onomato–, –onym, –onymy; **term**, expression, locution, linguistic form, lexeme, free form, minimum free form, *logos* [Gk], *verbum* [L]; verbalism, vocable, utterance, articulation; **usage**; syllable, polysyllable; homonym, homophone, homograph; monosyllable; synonym; metonym; antonym.

.2 **root**, etymon, primitive; eponym; derivative, derivation; cognate; doublet.

.3 **morphology**, morphemics; morphophonemics; **morpheme**; morph, allomorph; bound morpheme *or* form, free morpheme *or* form; difference of form, formal contrast; accidence; **inflection**, conjugation, declension; paradigm; derivation, word-formation; formative; root, radical; theme, stem; **affix, suffix, prefix,** infix; proclitic, enclitic; affixation, infixation, suffixation, prefixation; morphemic analysis, immediate constituent *or* IC analysis, cutting; morphophonemic analysis.

.4 **word form,** formation, construction; back formation; clipped word; spoonerism; **compound;** *tatpurusha, dvandva, karmadharaya, dvigu, avyayibhava, bahuvrihi* [all Skt]; endocentric compound, exocentric compound; acronym, acrostic; paronym, conjugate.

.5 **technical term,** technicality; jargon word.

.6 **barbarism,** corruption, vulgarism, impropriety, taboo word; **colloquialism, slang,** localism 582.6.

.7 **loan word,** borrowing, borrowed word, paronym; loan translation, calque; foreignism.

.8 **neologism,** neology, neoterism, new word *or* term, newfangled expression; **coinage;** new sense *or* meaning; nonce word; ghost word *or* name.

.9 **catchword,** catch phrase, shibboleth, slogan, cry; **pet expression,** byword; vogue word, fad word, cliché.

.10 long word, hard word, jawbreaker [informal], polysyllable; sesquipedalian, sesquipedalia [pl]; lexiphanicism, grandiloquence 601.

.11 hybrid word, **hybrid;** macaronicism, macaronic; hybridism, contamination; blend-word, blend, portmanteau word, portmanteau, portmantologism, telescope word.

.12 **portmanteau word,** portmanteau, **counterword.**

.13 **archaism,** archaicism, antiquated word *or* expression; obsoletism, obsolete.

.14 **vocabulary, lexis, words, wordage, verbiage,** wordhoard, stock of words; phraseology; thesaurus; lexicon 605.7.

.15 **lexicology; lexicography,** lexigraphy, glossography; onomastics, onomatology; onomasiology; semantics, semasiology.

.16 **etymology, derivation, origin,** word history, semantic history; historical linguistics, comparative linguistics; eponymy, folk etymology.

.17 echoic word, onomatopoeic word, onomatope; onomatopoeia; bowwow theory.

.18 **neologist, word-coiner,** neoterist; phraser, phrasemaker, phrasemonger.

.19 ADJS **verbal,** vocabular, vocabulary.

.20 lexical, lexicologic(al); lexigraphic(al), **lexicographic(al),** glossographic(al); etymologic(al), derivative; onomastic, onomatologic; onomasiologic(al); echoic, onomatopoeic; conjugate, paronymous, paronymic.

.21 neological, neoteric(al).

.22 **morphological,** morphemic; morphophonemic; inflective, inflectional, paradigmatic, derivational; affixal, prefixal, infixal, suffixal.

## 583. NOMENCLATURE

.1 NOUNS **nomenclature, terminology,** orismology, glossology [archaic]; onomatology, onomastics; toponymy, place-names, place-naming; antonomasia; polyonymy; **taxonomy,** classification, systematics, biosystematy, biosystematics, cytotaxonomy, binomial nomenclature, binomialism, Linnaean method, trinomialism; kingdom, phylum, class, order, family, genus, species.

.2 **naming, calling, denomination,** appellation, designation, styling, terming, definition, identification; **christening,** baptism; dubbing; nicknaming.

.3 **name,** onomato-, –onym, –onymy; **appellation,** appellative, **denomination, designation, style,** *nomen* [L], **cognomen,** cognomination; proper name *or* noun; moniker *or* handle [both slang]; **title,** honorific; empty title *or* name; **label, tag; epithet,** byword; **scientific name,** trinomen, trinomial name, binomen, binomial name; nomen nudum, hyponym; tautonym; typonym; middle name; eponym; namesake; secret name, cryptonym, euonym.

.4 **first name,** forename, **Christian name,** given name, baptismal name.

.5 **surname,** last name, **family name, cognomen,** byname; **maiden name;** married name; patronymic, matronymic.

.6 (Latin terms) *praenomen, nomen, agnomen, cognomen.*

.7 **nickname,** sobriquet, byname, cognomen; **pet name,** diminutive, hypocoristic, affectionate name.

.8 **alias,** pseudonym, anonym, **assumed name,** false *or* fictitious name, *nom de guerre* [Fr]; **pen name,** nom de plume; stage name, *nom de theatre* [Fr], professional name; John Doe, Jane Doe, Richard Roe.

.9 **misnomer,** wrong name.

.10 **signature,** sign manual, **autograph, hand, John Hancock** [informal]; mark, mark of signature, cross, christcross, X; initials; subscription; countersignature, countersign, countermark, counterstamp; endorsement; visa, *visé* [Fr]; monogram, cipher, device; seal, sigil, signet.

.11 VERBS **name, denominate, nominate, designate, call, term, style, dub;** specify; define, identify; **title, entitle; label, tag; nickname; christen,** baptize.

.12 **misname,** misnomer, **miscall,** misterm, misdesignate.

.13 **be called, be known by** *or* as, go by, go as, **go by the name of,** go *or* pass under the name of, bear the name of, rejoice in the name of; go under an assumed *or* false name, have an alias.

.14 ADJS **named, called,** yclept [archaic], **styled, titled,** denominated, denominate [archaic], **known as,** known by the name of, designated, termed, dubbed, identified as; christened, baptized; what one may well *or* fairly *or* properly *or* fitly call.

.15 **nominal,** cognominal; **titular, in name only,** nominative, formal; **so-called,** quasi; would-be, *soi-disant* [Fr]; **self-called, self-styled,** self-christened; honorific; epithetic(al); hypocoristic, diminutive; by name, by whatever name, under any other name.

.16 **denominative,** nominative, appellative; eponymous, eponymic.

.17 **terminological,** nomenclatural, orismological; onomastic; toponymic, toponymous; taxonomic, classificatory, binomial, Linnaean, trinomial.

## 584. ANONYMITY

.1 NOUNS **anonymity, anonymousness, namelessness; incognito;** anonym.

.2 **what's-its-name** *or* **what's-his-name** *or* what's-his-face *or* what's-her-name *or* **what-you-may-call-it** *or* what-you-may-call-'em *or* what-d'ye-call-'em *or* what-d'ye-call-it *or* whatzit [all informal]; *je ne sais quoi* [Fr], I don't know what; such-and-such; **so-and-so,** certain person, Mr. X; you-know-who.

.3 ADJS **anonymous, anon.; nameless, unnamed,** unidentified, undesignated, unspecified, innominate, without a name, **unknown;** undefined; unacknowledged; **incognito;** cryptonymous, cryptonymic.

## 585. PHRASE

.1 NOUNS **phrase, expression, locution, utterance,** usage, term, verbalism, –logy *or* –logia; **word-group,** construction, endocentric construction, headed group, syntagm; syntactic structure; noun phrase, verb phrase, verb complex, adverbial phrase, adjectival phrase, prepositional phrase; **clause; sentence,** period, periodic sentence; **paragraph; idiom,** idiotism, phrasal idiom; turn of phrase *or* expression, peculiar expression, manner *or* way of speaking; set phrase *or* term; conventional *or* common *or* standard phrase; phraseogram, phraseograph.

.2 **diction, phrasing** 588.1.

.3 **phraser, phrasemaker, phrasemonger,** phraseman.

.4 ADJS **phrasal, phrase;** phrasey.

.5 ADVS in set phrases *or* terms, in good set terms, in round terms.

## 586. GRAMMAR

.1 NOUNS **grammar,** rules of language; "the rule and pattern of speech" [Horace]; grammaticalness, grammaticality, grammatical theory; traditional grammar, school grammar; descriptive grammar, structural grammar, phrase-structure grammar; generative grammar, transformational grammar, transformational generative grammar; tagmemic analysis; glossematics; stratificational grammar; **parsing,** grammatical analysis; **morphology** 582.3; **phonology** 594.14.

.2 **syntax, structure, syntactic structure,** word order, word arrangement; syntactics, syntactic analysis; immediate constituent analysis, IC analysis, cutting; phrase structure; surface structure, shallow structure, deep structure, underlying structure; levels, ranks, strata; tagmeme, form-function unit, slot, filler, slot and filler; **function, subject, predicate, complement, object,** direct object, indirect object, **modifier,** qualifier, sentence *or* construction modifier, appositive, attribute, attributive.

.3 **part of speech,** form class, major form class, function class; function *or* empty *or* form word; **adjective,** adjectival, attributive; **adverb,** adverbial; **preposition;** verbal adjective, gerundive; **participle,** present participle, past participle, perfect participle; **conjunction,** subordinating conjunction, coordinating conjunction, conjunctive adverb, adversative conjunction, copulative, copulative conjunction, correlative conjunction, disjunctive, disjunctive conjunction; **interjection,** exclamatory noun *or* adjective; **particle.**

.4 **verb,** transitive, transitive verb, intransitive, intransitive verb, impersonal verb, neuter verb, deponent verb, defective verb, finite verb, linking verb, copula; verbal; **infinitive; auxiliary verb,** auxiliary, modal auxiliary; verb phrase.

.5 **noun, pronoun,** substantive, common noun, proper noun, abstract noun, collective noun, quotation noun, hypostasis,

adherent noun, adverbial noun; verbal noun, gerund; nominal; noun phrase.

.6 **article,** definite article, indefinite article; determiner, noun determiner, determinative.

.7 **person;** first person; second person, proximate; third person; fourth person, obviative.

.8 number; singular, dual, trial, plural.

.9 **case;** common case, subject case, nominative; object *or* objective case, accusative, dative, possessive case, genitive; local case, locative, essive, superessive, inessive, adessive, abessive, lative, allative, illative, sublative, elative, ablative, delative, terminative, approximative, prolative, perlative, translative; comitative, instrumental, prepositional, vocative; oblique case.

.10 **gender,** masculine, feminine, neuter, common gender; grammatical gender, natural gender; animate, inanimate.

.11 **mood,** mode; indicative, subjunctive, imperative, conditional, potential, obligative, permissive, optative, jussive.

.12 **tense; present;** historical present; **past,** preterit; aorist; imperfect; future; **perfect,** present perfect, future perfect; past perfect, **pluperfect;** progressive tense, durative; point tense.

.13 **aspect;** perfective, imperfective, inchoative, iterative, frequentative, desiderative.

.14 **voice;** active voice, active, passive voice, passive; middle voice, middle; medio-passive; reflexive.

.15 **punctuation,** punctuation marks; diacritical mark *or* sign; reference mark, reference; point, tittle; stop, end stop.

.16 VERBS grammaticize; **parse,** analyze; inflect, **conjugate, decline; punctuate,** mark, point; parenthesize, hyphenate, bracket.

.17 ADJS **grammatic(al), correct, syntactic(al),** formal, structural; tagmemic, glossematic; **functional;** substantive, nominal, pronominal; verbal, transitive, intransitive; linking, copulative; attributive, adjectival, adverbial, participial; prepositional, postpositional; conjunctive.

.18 **punctuation marks**

| | |
|---|---|
| ampersand (&) | periods (. . . *or* |
| angle brackets (⟨ ⟩) | * * *) |
| apostrophe (') | exclamation mark *or* |
| braces ({ }) | point (!) |
| brackets ([ ]) | hyphen (-) |
| colon (:) | parentheses, parens |
| comma (,) | [informal] ( ) |
| dash (—, -) | period, full stop |
| ellipsis, suspension | [Brit], point, deci- |

mal point, dot (.)
question mark, inter-
  rogation mark or
  point (?)
quotation marks,
  quotes (" ")

semicolon (;)
single quotation
  marks, single quotes
  (' ')
virgule, diagonal, soli-
  dus, slash mark (/)

## .19 diacritical marks

acute accent (´)
breve (˘)
cedilla (̦)
circumflex accent (^ ,
  ˆ , or ˜)

diaeresis, umlaut (¨)
grave accent (`)
haček [Cz], wedge (ˇ)
macron (¯)
tilde (˜)

## .20 reference marks

asterisk, star (*)
asterism (*̣*)
bullet, centered dot
  (●)
caret (∧)
dagger, obelisk (†)
ditto mark (")
double dagger,

diesis (‡)
double prime (″)
index, fist (☛)
leaders (. . . .)
paragraph (¶)
parallels (‖)
prime (′)
section (§)

## 587. UNGRAMMATICALNESS

.1 NOUNS **ungrammaticalness,** bad or faulty grammar, faulty syntax; lack of concord or agreement, faulty reference, misplaced or dangling modifier, shift of tense, shift of structure, anacoluthon, faulty subordination, faulty comparison, faulty coordination, faulty punctuation, lack of parallelism, sentence fragment, comma fault, comma splice; abuse of terms, corruption of speech, broken speech, talkee-talkee.

.2 **solecism,** ungrammaticism, **misusage, missaying, misconstruction,** barbarism, infelicity; corruption; antiphrasis, malapropism 518.7.

.3 VERBS solecize, commit a solecism, use faulty or inadmissible or inappropriate grammar, ignore or disdain or violate grammar, murder the King's or Queen's English, break Priscian's head [archaic].

.4 ADJS **ungrammatic(al),** solecistic(al), **incorrect,** barbarous; faulty, erroneous 518.16; infelicitous, improper 27.7; careless, slovenly, slipshod 62.15; loose, imprecise 518.17.

## 588. DICTION

.1 NOUNS **diction,** use or choice of words, **phraseology,** phrase, **phrasing, wording, wordage, verbiage,** rhetoric, speech, talk [informal], **language,** dialect, parlance, locution, expression, formulation; **grammar;** usage, usus loquendi [L]; **idiom;** composition.

.2 **style; mode, manner,** strain, vein; fashion, way 657; **rhetoric; manner of speaking,** mode of expression, literary style, style of writing, command of language or idiom,

form of speech, expression of ideas; feeling for words or language, sense of language, Sprachgefühl [Ger]; power or grace of expression; linguistic tact or finesse; personal style; mannerism, trick, peculiarity; affectation; "the dress of thoughts" [Dickens], "a certain absolute and unique manner of expressing a thing, in all its intensity and color" [Walter Pater]; inflation, exaggeration, grandiloquence 601; the grand style, the sublime style, the sublime; the plain style; **stylistics,** stylistic analysis.

.3 **stylist,** master of style; rhetorician, rhetor, rhetorizer [archaic]; mannerist.

.4 VERBS **phrase, express,** find a phrase for, give expression or words to, **word,** state, **frame,** conceive, style, couch, **put in words,** clothe or embody in words, couch in terms, express by or in words, find words to express; put, present, set out; **formulate,** formularize; paragraph; rhetorize [archaic].

.5 ADJS **phrased,** expressed, worded, formulated, styled, put, presented, couched.

## 589. ELEGANCE

*(of language)*

.1 NOUNS **elegance,** elegancy; **grace,** gracefulness, gracility; **taste,** tastefulness, good taste; **correctness,** seemliness, comeliness, **propriety; refinement,** discrimination, restraint; **polish, finish,** terseness, neatness; smoothness, flow, **fluency; felicity,** felicitousness, **ease;** clarity, clearness, lucidity, limpidity, pellucidity, perspicuity; distinction, dignity; **purity,** chastity, chasteness; **plainness,** straightforwardness, directness, **simplicity,** naturalness, unaffectedness, Atticism, Attic quality; classicism, classicalism; well-rounded or well-turned periods, flowing periods; the right word in the right place, fittingness, appropriateness.

.2 **harmony, proportion,** symmetry, **balance,** equilibrium, order, orderedness, measure, measuredness, concinnity; rhythm; **euphony,** sweetness, beauty.

.3 (affected elegance) **affectation,** affectedness, studiedness, **pretentiousness, mannerism,** manneredness, artifice, artfulness, **artificiality,** unnaturalness; **euphuism,** Gongorism, Marinism; **preciousness,** preciosity; euphemism; purism; overelegance, overelaboration, overniceness, overrefinement, hyperelegance, etc.

.4 **purist,** classicist, Atticist, plain stylist.

.5 euphuist, Gongorist, Marinist, *précieux* [Fr], *précieuse* [Fr fem]; phrasemaker, phrasemonger.

.6 ADJS **elegant, tasteful, graceful,** gracile, **polished,** finished, **round,** terse; **neat,** trim, **refined, restrained; clear,** lucid, limpid, pellucid, perspicuous; **simple, unaffected, natural,** unlabored, **easy; pure,** chaste; **plain,** straightforward, direct; classic(al); Attic, Ciceronian.

.7 **appropriate, fit, fitting,** just [archaic], **proper, correct, seemly,** comely; **felicitous,** happy, **apt,** well-chosen, **well-put,** well-expressed, inspired.

.8 **harmonious, balanced,** symmetrical, orderly, ordered, measured, concinnate, concinnous; **euphonious,** euphonic, euphonical [archaic], sweet; **smooth,** tripping, smooth-sounding, fluent, flowing.

.9 (affectedly elegant) **affected,** euphuistic(al); **elaborate,** elaborated; **pretentious, mannered, artificial, unnatural,** studied; precious, *précieux, précieuse* [both Fr], overnice, overrefined, overelegant, overelaborate, hyperelegant, etc.; Gongoristic, Gongoresque, Marinistic.

## 590. INELEGANCE

*(of language)*

.1 NOUNS **inelegance,** inelegancy; inconcinnity, infelicity; **clumsiness,** cumbrousness, leadenness, heaviness, stiltedness, **ponderousness,** unwieldiness; sesquipedalianism, sesquipedality; turgidity, bombasticness, pompousness 601.1; **gracelessness,** ungracefulness; **tastelessness,** bad taste, **impropriety,** indecorousness, unseemliness; incorrectness, impurity; **vulgarity,** vulgarism, Gothicism [archaic], barbarism, barbarousness, **coarseness, unrefinement,** roughness, grossness, rudeness, crudeness, uncouthness; dysphemism; cacology, poor diction; cacophony, uneuphoniousness, harshness; loose *or* slipshod construction, ill-balanced sentences; lack of finish *or* polish.

.2 ADJS **inelegant, clumsy, graceless,** ungraceful, inconcinnate, inconcinnous, infelicitous, unfelicitous; **tasteless,** in bad taste, offensive to ears polite; **incorrect, improper; indecorous, unseemly,** uncourtly, undignified; **unpolished, unrefined;** impure, unclassical; **vulgar,** barbarous, barbaric, rude, **crude, uncouth,** Doric, outlandish; low, gross, **coarse,** dysphemistic, doggerel; cacologic(al), ca-

cophonous, uneuphonious, harsh, ill-sounding.

.3 **stiff, stilted, formal,** Latinate, *guinde* [Fr], **labored,** ponderous, elephantine, lumbering, cumbrous, leaden, heavy, unwieldy, sesquipedalian, inkhorn, turgid, bombastic, pompous 601.8; **forced,** awkward, cramped, halting.

## 591. PLAIN SPEECH

.1 NOUNS **plain speech,** plain speaking, plain style, unadorned style, **plain English,** plain words, common speech, vernacular, household words; **plainness,** simpleness, simplicity; soberness, restrainedness; severity, austerity; spareness, leanness, baldness, bareness, starkness, unadornedness; naturalness, unaffectedness; directness, straightforwardness, calling a spade a spade, making no bones about it [informal]; unimaginativeness, prosaicness, matter-of-factness, prosiness, unpoeticalness; homespun, rustic style; candor, frankness, openness.

.2 VERBS **speak plainly,** waste no words, **call a spade a spade,** come to the point, not beat about the bush, make no bones about it *or* talk turkey [both informal].

.3 ADJS **plain-speaking,** simple-speaking; **plain,** common; **simple,** unadorned, unvarnished, pure, neat; sober, severe, austere, ascetic, spare, lean, bald, bare, stark, Spartan; **natural, unaffected;** direct, straightforward; commonplace, homely, homespun, rustic; candid, plain-spoken, frank, open; **prosaic,** prosing, prosy; unpoetical, unimaginative, dull, dry, **matter-of-fact.**

.4 ADVS **plainly, simply,** naturally, unaffectedly, matter-of-factly; in plain words, **in plain English,** in words of one syllable; point-blank, to the point.

## 592. CONCISENESS

.1 NOUNS **conciseness,** concision, briefness brachylogy, **brevity,** "the soul of wit" [Shakespeare]; shortness, compactness **curtness,** brusqueness, **crispness, terseness** summariness; taciturnity 613.2, reserve 613.3; **pithiness,** succinctness, pointedness sententiousness; compendiousness.

.2 laconicness, laconism, laconicism, economy of language; laconics.

.3 aphorism, epigram 517.1; abridgment 607.

.4 **abbreviation,** shortening, clipping, cutting, pruning, truncation; ellipsis, aposiopesis, contraction, syncope, apocope, elision, crasis, syneresis [all gram].

.5 VERBS **be brief, come to the point, make a long story short,** cut the matter short, be telegraphic, waste no words, put it in few words, give more matter and less art; shorten, condense, **abbreviate** 203.6.

.6 ADJS **concise, brief, short,** "short and sweet" [Thomas Lodge]; **condensed, compressed,** tight, close, compact; compendious 203.8; **curt,** brusque, **crisp, terse,** summary; taciturn 613.9; reserved 613.10; **pithy, succinct; laconic,** Spartan; **abridged, abbreviated,** synopsized, shortened, clipped, cut, pruned, contracted, truncated, docked; elliptic, aposiopestic; sententious, epigrammatic(al), gnomic, aphoristic(al) 517.6, **pointed,** to the point.

.7 ADVS **concisely, briefly, shortly;** laconically; **curtly,** brusquely, **crisply, tersely,** summarily; **pithily, succinctly,** pointedly; sententiously, aphoristically, epigrammatically.

.8 **in brief, in short,** in substance, in epitome, in outline, **in a nutshell,** in a capsule; **in a word,** in two words, in a few words, without wasting words; **to be brief,** to come to the point, to cut the matter short, **to make a long story short.**

## 593. DIFFUSENESS

.1 NOUNS **diffuseness, diffusiveness, diffusion; formlessness** 247; **profuseness,** profusiveness, profusion; **effusiveness, effusion,** gush, gushing; outpour, tirade; logorrhea, talkativeness 596, cloud of words; **copiousness, exuberance,** rampancy, amplitude, extravagance, prodigality, fertility, fecundity, rankness, teemingness, prolificity, prolificacy, productivity, abundance, overflow, fluency [archaic]; superfluity, superflux, superabundance; redundancy, pleonasm, repetitiveness, reiterativeness, reiteration, tautology, macrology; repetition for effect or emphasis, palilogy.

.2 **wordiness, verbosity,** verbiage, verbalism, verbality; **prolixity, long-windedness,** longiloquence; flow or flux of words, cloud of words; logorrhea, talkativeness 596.

.3 discursiveness, desultoriness, digressiveness, aimlessness; rambling, maundering, meandering, wandering, roving.

.4 **digression, departure,** deviation, **discursion,** excursion, excursus, sidetrack, side path, side road, byway, bypath; episode.

.5 **circumlocution, roundaboutness,** circuitousness, ambages [archaic]; deviousness, obliqueness, **indirection;** periphrase, periphrasis.

.6 **expatiation, amplification, enlargement,** expansion, dilation; elaboration; development, explication, unfolding, working-out.

.7 VERBS **expatiate, amplify, dilate, expand,** enlarge, **enlarge upon,** elaborate; relate or rehearse in extenso; detail, particularize; **develop,** evolve, unfold; work out, explicate; descant, relate at large.

.8 **protract, extend, spin out,** string out, draw out, stretch out, **drag out,** run out; pad, fill out; perorate, **speak at length,** spin a long yarn, never finish; chatter, talk one to death 596.5,6.

.9 **digress,** wander, **get off the subject, wander from the subject,** get sidetracked, excurse, ramble, maunder, stray, go astray; depart, deviate, turn aside; **go off on a tangent,** go up blind alleys.

.10 circumlocute [informal], **go round about,** go around and around, **beat around or about the bush,** go round Robin Hood's barn; periphrase.

.11 ADJS **diffuse,** diffusive; **formless** 247.4; **profuse,** profusive; **effusive,** gushing, gushy; copious, exuberant, extravagant, prodigal, fecund, teeming, prolific, productive, abundant, superabundant, overflowing; redundant, pleonastic, repetitive, reiterative, tautologous.

.12 **wordy, verbose; talkative** 596.9; prolix, windy [informal], **long-winded,** longiloquent; **protracted,** extended, de longue haleine [Fr], lengthy, long, **long-drawn-out,** long-spun, spun-out, endless, unrelenting; padded, filled out.

.13 **discursive, aimless,** loose; **rambling, maundering, wandering,** roving; excursive, **digressive,** deviative, **desultory,** episodic; by the way.

.14 **circumlocutory,** circumlocutional, **roundabout, circuitous,** ambagious [archaic], oblique, indirect; periphrastic.

.15 **expatiating,** dilative, dilatative, enlarging, amplifying, expanding; **developmental.**

.16 ADVS **at length,** at large, in full, in extenso [L], in detail.

## 594. SPEECH

### (utterance)

.1 NOUNS **speech,** log(o)–, lalo–, phon(o)–; **language** 580, **talk,** talking, speaking, **discourse,** oral communication, comment, parole, **palaver, prattle, gab** [informal]; rapping or yakking or yakkety-yak [all slang]; **words, accents;** chatter 596.3; conversation 597; elocution 599.1.

.2 "the mirror of the soul" [Publilius Syrus],

"the image of life" [Democritus], "a faculty given to man to conceal his thoughts" [Talleyrand], "but broken light upon the depth of the unspoken" [George Eliot].

.3 **utterance, speaking,** locution [archaic], phonation; **parole,** speech act, linguistic act or behavior; **string,** utterance string, sequence of phonemes; **voice, tongue;** word of mouth, parol, the spoken word; vocable, **word** 582.

.4 **remark, statement, comment, crack** [slang], one's two cents' worth [informal], **word,** say, **saying, utterance, observation, reflection, expression; note,** thought, **mention; assertion,** averment, allegation, affirmation, pronouncement, position, dictum; **declaration;** interjection, exclamation; question 485.10; answer 486; address, greeting, apostrophe; **sentence, phrase;** subjoinder, Parthian shot.

.5 **articulateness,** articulacy, readiness or facility of speech; eloquence 600.

.6 **articulation, phonation, voicing, vocalization; pronunciation, enunciation,** utterance; **delivery, attack.**

.7 **intonation, inflection, modulation;** intonation pattern or contour, intonation or inflection of voice, speech tune or melody; **suprasegmental,** suprasegmental phoneme; **tone, pitch;** pitch accent.

.8 **manner of speaking,** way of saying, mode of expression; **tone of voice, voice,** voce [Ital], **tone;** voice quality, **timbre;** voice qualifier; paralinguistic communication.

.9 **regional accent,** foreign accent, **accent;** brogue, twang, burr, drawl, broad accent.

.10 **juncture,** open juncture, close juncture; **terminal,** clause terminal, rising terminal, falling terminal; **sandhi;** word boundary, clause boundary; pause.

.11 **accent, accentuation,** stress accent; **emphasis, stress;** ictus, beat, rhythmical stress; **rhythm,** rhythmic pattern, **cadence;** prosody, prosodics, metrics 609.8; stress pattern; level of stress; primary stress, secondary stress, tertiary stress, weak stress.

.12 **vowel quantity, quantity,** mora; long vowel, short vowel, full vowel, reduced vowel.

.13 **speech sound,** phone, vocable; articulation, manner of articulation; **stop,** plosive, explosive, mute, check, occlusive, **affricate,** continuant, **liquid,** lateral, **nasal;** point or place of articulation; labial, bilabial, labiodental, labiovelar, dental, apico-dental, alveolar, apico-alveolar, pala-

tal, cerebral, cacuminal, retroflex, velar, guttural, pharyngeal, glottal, laryngeal; lingual; voice, voicing, sonority; aspiration, palatalization, labialization, pharyngealization, glottalization; surd, voiceless sound; sonant, voiced sound; **consonant; semivowel,** glide, transition sound; vocalic, syllabic nucleus, syllabic peak, peak; vocoid; **vowel;** monophthong, **diphthong,** triphthong; **phoneme,** segmental phoneme, morphophoneme; modification, assimilation, dissimilation; **allophone;** parasitic vowel, epenthetic vowel, svarabhakti vowel, prothetic vowel; **syllable.**

.14 **phonetics,** articulatory phonetics, acoustic phonetics; phonology; morphophonemics; orthoepy; sound or phonetic law; sound shift, Lautverschiebung [Ger]; umlaut, mutation, ablaut, gradation; rhotacism, betacism; Grimm's law, Verner's law, Grassmann's law.

.15 **phonetician,** phonetist, phoneticist; orthoepist.

.16 **ventriloquism,** ventriloquy; **ventriloquist.**

.17 **talking machine,** sonovox, voder, vocoder.

.18 **talker, speaker,** sayer, utterer, patterer; chatterbox 596.4; conversationalist 597.8.

.19 **vocal** or **speech organ,** articulator; tongue, apex, tip, blade, dorsum, back; vocal cords or bands, vocal processes, vocal folds; voice box, larynx, Adam's apple, laryng(o)–; syrinx; arytenoid cartilages; glottis, vocal chink; lips, teeth, palate, hard palate, soft palate, velum, alveolus, teeth ridge, alveolar ridge; nasal cavity, oral cavity; pharynx, throat or pharyngeal cavity.

.20 VERBS **speak, talk; patter** or **gab** or wag the tongue [all informal]; mouth; chatter 596.5; converse 597.9; declaim 599.10.

.21 [slang terms] yap, yak, yakkety-yak, spiel, chin, jaw, shoot off one's face, shoot off the bat the breeze, beat the gums.

.22 **speak up, speak out, pipe up, open one's mouth,** open one's lips, say out, lift or raise one's voice, break silence; take the floor; put in a word, get in a word edgewise.

.23 **say, utter, breathe,** sound, voice, vocalize, phonate, **articulate, enunciate, pronounce,** lip, give voice, give tongue, give utterance; whisper; **express,** give expression, verbalize, put in words, find words to express; **word,** formulate, phrase 588; **present,** deliver; **emit,** give, raise, **let out** with, come or give out with, put forth, set forth, pour forth; throw off, fling off chorus, chime; **tell, communicate** 554.6,7; **convey, impart, disclose** 556.4,5; have *or* say one's say, speak one's mind.

.24 **state, declare, assert,** aver, affirm, asseverate, allege; **relate, recite;** quote; proclaim, nuncupate.

.25 **remark, comment, observe, note; mention,** speak [archaic], let drop *or* fall, say by the way, make mention of; refer to, allude to, make reference to, call attention to; muse, reflect; opine [dial]; interject; blurt, blurt out, exclaim.

.26 (utter in a certain way) murmur, mutter, mumble, whisper, breathe, buzz, sigh; gasp, pant; exclaim, yell 459.6–9; sing, lilt, warble, chant, coo, chirp; pipe, flute; cackle, crow; bark, yelp, yap; growl, snap, snarl; hiss, sibilate; grunt, snort; roar, bellow, blare, trumpet, bray, blat, bawl, thunder, rumble, boom; scream, shriek, screech, squeal, squawk, yawp, squall; whine, wail, keen, blubber, sob; drawl, twang.

.27 **address, speak to, talk to,** bespeak, beg the ear of; **appeal to,** invoke; apostrophize; **approach; buttonhole,** take by the button *or* lapel; take aside, talk to in private, closet oneself with; **accost, call to, hail,** halloo, greet, salute, speak, speak fair.

.28 **pass one's lips,** escape one's lips, fall from the lips *or* mouth.

.29 inflect, modulate, intonate.

.30 ADJS **speech,** linguistic, lingual; **spoken, uttered, said,** vocalized, **voiced,** pronounced, sounded, articulated, enunciated; vocal, voiceful; **oral, verbal, unwritten,** *viva voce* [L], nuncupative, parol; acroamatic(al).

.31 **phonetic,** phonic; intonated; pitched, pitch, **tonal,** tonic, oxytone, oxytonic, paroxytonic, barytone; **accented, stressed,** strong, heavy; unaccented, unstressed, weak, light, pretonic, atonic, posttonic; articulated; stopped, muted, checked, occlusive, nasal, nasalized, twangy, continuant, liquid, lateral, affricated; labial, bilabial, labiodental, labiovelar, dental, apico-dental, alveolar, apico-alveolar, palatal, cerebral, cacuminal, retroflex, velar, guttural, throaty, thick, pharyngeal, glottal; lingual, glossal; apical, laminal, dorsal; low, high, mid, open, broad, close; front, back, central; wide, lax, tense, narrow; voiced, sonant, voiceless, surd; rounded, unrounded, flat; aspirated; labialized; palatalized, soft, *mouillé* [Fr]; unpalatalized, hard; pharyngealized, glottal-

ized; **consonant,** consonantal, semivowel, glide, **vowel;** vowellike, vocoid, vocalic, syllabic; monophthongal, diphthongal, triphthongal; **phonemic;** assimilated, dissimilated.

.32 **speaking, talking;** articulate, talkative 596.9; eloquent 600.8, well-spoken; true-speaking, clean-speaking, plain-speaking, plain-spoken, **outspoken,** free-speaking, free-spoken, loud-speaking, loud-spoken, soft-speaking, soft-spoken; English-speaking, etc.

.33 ventriloquial, ventriloquistic.

.34 ADVS **orally, vocally, verbally, by word of mouth,** *viva voce* [L]; from the lips of, from his own mouth.

## 595. IMPERFECT SPEECH

.1 NOUNS **speech defect,** speech impediment, impairment of speech, –lalia *or* –laly, –phasia *or* –phasy, –phemia, –phonia, –phrasia; dysarthria, dysphasia, dysphrasia; dyslalia, dyslogia; idioglossia, idiolalia; **broken speech,** cracked *or* broken voice, broken tones *or* accents; indistinct *or* blurred *or* muzzy speech; loss of voice, aphonia; **nasalization,** nasal tone *or* accent, **twang,** nasal twang, talking through one's nose; **falsetto,** childish treble, artificial voice; **shake, quaver,** tremor; **lisp,** lisping; hiss, sibilation; **croak,** choked voice, hawking voice; crow; harshness, dysphonia, hoarseness 458.2.

.2 **inarticulateness,** inarticulacy; thickness of speech.

.3 **stammering, stuttering,** hesitation, faltering, traulism, dysphemia, *balbuties* [L]; palilalia; stammer, stutter.

.4 **mumbling, muttering,** maundering; droning, drone; mumble, mutter; jabber, jibber, gibber, gibbering, gabble; whispering, whisper, susurration; mouthing; murmuring.

.5 **mispronunciation,** misspeaking, cacology, cacoepy; lallation, lambdacism, paralambdacism; rhotacism, pararhotacism; gammacism; mytacism; **corruption.**

.6 **aphasia,** motor aphasia, paraphasia, jargon aphasia, paranomia; aphrasia; loss of speech, mutism, muteness 451.2.

.7 VERBS **speak poorly,** talk incoherently, be unable to put two words together; have an impediment in one's speech, have a bone in one's neck *or* throat; speak thickly; **croak; lisp; shake, quaver; drawl;** mince, clip one's words.

.8 **stammer, stutter,** hesitate, falter, halt,

mammer [Brit dial], stumble; hem, haw, hum, **hum and haw**, hem and haw.

.9 **mumble, mutter,** maunder; drone; swallow one's words, speak drunkenly or incoherently; jabber, gibber, gabble; splutter, sputter; blubber, sob; whisper, susurrate; murmur; mouth.

.10 **nasalize, speak through one's nose,** twang, snuffle.

.11 **mispronounce,** misspeak, missay, **murder the King's** or **Queen's English.**

.12 ADJS (imperfectly spoken) inarticulate, indistinct, blurred, muzzy; **mispronounced; shaky,** shaking, **quavering,** tremulous, titubant; **drawling,** drawly; **lisping; throaty, guttural,** thick, velar; stifled, choked, choking, strangled; **nasal, twangy,** breathy, adenoidal, snuffling; croaking, hawking; harsh, dysphonic, hoarse 458.12–16.

.13 **stammering, stuttering,** halting, hesitating, faltering, stumbling, balbutient.

## 596. TALKATIVENESS

.1 NOUNS **talkativeness, loquacity,** loquaciousness; overtalkativeness, loose tongue, big mouth [informal]; gabbiness or windiness or gassiness [all informal]; **garrulousness,** garrulity; **long-windedness,** prolixity, verbosity 593.2; multiloquence, multiloquy; **volubility, fluency, glibness;** fluent tongue, flowing tongue, gift of gab [informal]; openness, candor, frankness 974.4; effusion, gush, slush; gushiness, **effusiveness** 593.1; flow or flux or spate of words; *flux de bouche, flux de mots, flux de paroles* [all Fr]; **communicativeness** 554.3; gregariousness, sociability, conversableness 922.

.2 logomania, logorrhea, diarrhea of the mouth, verbal diarrhea, *cacoëthes loquendi, furor loquendi* [both L].

.3 **chatter, jabber,** gibber, **babble,** babblement, prate, **prating, prattle, palaver,** chat, natter [Brit], **gabble, gab** [informal], blab, **blabber, blather,** blether, blethers [Scot], clatter, clack, cackle, talkee-talkee; *caquet, caqueterie, bavardage* [all Fr], twaddle, twattle, **gibble-gabble, bibble-babble, chitter-chatter, prittle-prattle, tittle-tattle,** mere talk, idle talk or chatter, "the hare-brained chatter of irresponsible frivolity" [Disraeli]; **guff** or **gas** or **hot air** or blah-blah or **yak** or **yakkety-yak** [all slang]; gossip; nonsense talk 547.2.

.4 **chatterer, chatterbox, babbler, jabberer,** prater, **prattler, gabbler,** gibble-gabbler, gabber [informal], **blabberer,** blatherer,

patterer, word-slinger, *moulin à paroles* [Fr], blab, rattle, "agreeable rattle" [Goldsmith]; magpie, jay; **windbag** or gasbag or windjammer or hot-air artist [all slang]; idle chatterer, talkative person, **big** or **great talker** [informal], spendthrift of one's tongue.

.5 VERBS **chatter, chat, prate, prattle, patter, palaver, babble, gab** [informal], natter [Brit], **gabble, gibble-gabble,** tittle-tattle, **jabber,** gibber, **blab, blabber, blather,** blether, clatter, twaddle, twattle, rattle, clack, waffle [Brit], haver [Brit], dither, **spout** or **spout off** [both informal], pour forth, gush, talk to hear one's head rattle [informal]; **jaw** or **gas** or **yak** or **yakketyyak** or run off at the mouth or beat one's gums [all slang], **shoot off one's mouth** or **face** [slang]; reel off; **talk on,** talk away, **go on** [informal], run on, rattle on, run on like a mill race; ramble on; talk oneself hoarse, talk till one is blue in the face, talk oneself out of breath; "varnish nonsense with the charms of sound" [Charles Churchill]; **talk too much;** gossip; talk nonsense 549.5.

.6 **talk one to death, talk one's head** or **ear off,** talk one deaf and dumb, talk one into a fever, talk the hind leg off a mule.

.7 **outtalk,** outspeak, **talk down,** outlast; filibuster.

.8 be loquacious or garrulous, be a windbag or gasbag [slang]; have a big mouth or bazoo [slang].

.9 ADJS **talkative, loquacious, talky, bigmouthed** [informal], overtalkative, garrulous, chatty; gossipy, newsy; gabby or windy or gassy [all slang], all jaw [slang], multiloquent, multiloquious, **long winded, prolix, verbose** 593.12; **voluble, fluent; glib,** flip [informal], smooth; candid, frank 974.17; **effusive,** gushy; expansive, **communicative** 554.11; conversational; gregarious, sociable 922.18.

.10 **chattering, prattling, prating,** gabbling, jabbering, gibbering, blabbing, blabbering, blathering.

.11 ADVS **talkatively, loquaciously,** garrulously; **volubly, fluently,** glibly; effusively, gushingly.

## 597. CONVERSATION

.1 NOUNS **conversation, converse,** conversing, rapping [slang]; interlocution, colloquy; **exchange;** verbal intercourse, interchange of speech, give-and-take; discourse, colloquial discourse; **communion, intercourse, communication** 554.

.2 **the art of conversation,** "a game of circles", "our account of ourselves" [both Emerson]; "the sweeter banquet of the mind", "the feast of reason and the flow of soul" [both Pope].

.3 **talk, palaver, speech, words;** confabulation, **confab** [informal]; **chinfest** or **talkfest** or **bull session** [all informal]; **dialogue,** duologue, trialogue; question-and-answer session.

.4 **chat,** cozy chat, friendly chat or talk, **little talk,** coze, causerie, **visit** [informal], gam, *tête-à-tête* [Fr], **heart-to-heart talk.**

.5 **chitchat,** chitter-chatter, tittle-tattle, **small talk,** cocktail-party chitchat, beauty-parlor chitchat, tea-table talk, table talk, idle chat or gossip, backchat.

.6 **conference, congress, convention, parley,** palaver, **confab** [informal], confabulation, **conclave, powwow, huddle** [informal], **consultation,** *pourparler* [Fr], **meeting;** session, sitting, séance; exchange or interchange of views; **council,** council of war; **discussion; interview, audience; news conference,** press conference; high-level talk, conference at the summit, summit, summit conference; summitry; negotiations, bargaining, bargaining session; confrontation, eyeball-to-eyeball encounter [informal]; council fire.

.7 **discussion, debate,** debating, **deliberation, dialogue,** exchange of views, canvassing, ventilation, airing, review, **treatment, consideration,** investigation, **examination, study, analysis,** logical analysis; logical discussion, dialectic; buzz session [informal], rap or rap session [both slang]; panel discussion, open discussion, joint discussion, symposium, colloquium, conference, seminar; forum, open forum, town meeting.

.8 **conversationalist,** converser, conversationist; talker, discourser, confabulator; colloquist, colloquialist, collocutor; conversational partner; interlocutor, interlocutress or interlocutrice or interlocutrix; parleyer, palaverer; dialogist; Dr. Johnson.

.9 VERBS **converse, talk together, talk** or **speak with,** converse with, visit with [informal], discourse with, **commune with,** communicate with, take counsel with, commerce with, **have a talk with,** have a word with, **chin** [slang], **chew the rag** or **fat** [slang], **shoot the breeze** [slang], hold or carry on or join in or engage in a conversation; confabulate, confab [informal]; colloque, colloquize; "inject a few raisins of conversation into the tasteless dough

of existence" [O. Henry]; **bandy words; communicate** 554.6,7.

.10 **chat, visit** [informal], gam, coze, have a friendly or cozy chat; **have a little talk,** have a heart-to-heart talk, let one's hair down; talk with one in private, talk with one *tête-à-tête,* be closeted with, make conversation or talk; **prattle,** prittle-prattle, tittle-tattle; **gossip.**

.11 **confer,** hold conference, parley, palaver, powwow, sit down together, meet around the conference table, **go into a huddle** [informal], deliberate, take counsel, counsel, lay or put heads together; collogue; **confer with,** sit down with, **consult with, advise with, discuss with, take up with,** reason with; **discuss,** talk over; **consult,** refer to, call in; **compare notes,** exchange observations or views; have conversations; negotiate, bargain.

.12 **discuss, debate, reason, deliberate,** deliberate upon, exchange views or opinions, talk, **talk over,** talk of or about, rap [slang], comment upon, reason about, discourse about, **consider, treat,** handle, deal with, take up, go into, examine, investigate, **analyze,** sift, **study,** canvass, review, pass under review, controvert, ventilate, air, thresh out, reason the point, consider pro and con; **kick** or **knock around** [slang].

.13 ADJS **conversational, colloquial,** confabulatory, interlocutory; **communicative** 554.11; chatty, chitchatty, cozy.

.14 ADVS **conversationally, colloquially;** *tête-à-tête* [Fr].

## 598. SOLILOQUY

.1 NOUNS **soliloquy,** monology; **monologue;** aside; solo; monodrama.

.2 **soliloquist,** soliloquizer, Hamlet; **monologist.**

.3 VERBS **soliloquize,** monologize; **talk to oneself,** say to oneself, tell oneself, think out loud or aloud; address the four walls; say aside; do all the talking, monopolize the conversation, hold forth without interruption.

.4 ADJS **soliloquizing,** monologic(al), apostrophic; soloistic; monodramatic.

## 599. PUBLIC SPEAKING

.1 NOUNS **public speaking, declamation, speechmaking, speaking,** speechification [informal], lecturing, speeching; **oratory,** platform oratory or speaking; campaign oratory, stump speaking; **elocution; rhet-**

oric, art of public speaking; eloquence 600; forensics, **debating**; speechcraft, wordcraft; homiletics; demagogism, demagoguery, rabble-rousing; **pyrotechnics**.

.2 **speech**, speeching, speechification [informal], **talk, oration, address,** declamation, harangue; public speech *or* address, formal speech, set speech, prepared speech *or* text; say; **tirade**, screed, **diatribe,** jeremiad, philippic, invective; after-dinner speech; funeral oration, eulogy; allocution, exhortation, hortatory address, forensic, forensic address; **recitation,** recital, reading; salutatory, salutatory address; valediction, valedictory, valedictory address; inaugural address, inaugural; chalk talk [informal]; pep talk [informal]; pitch, sales talk 829.5; talkathon, filibuster; peroration; debate.

.3 **lecture,** prelection, **discourse,** log(o)–, –log(ue), –logia, –logy; **sermon,** sermonette, homily, religious discourse; preachment, preaching, preachification [informal]; travelogue.

.4 **speaker, talker, public speaker, speechmaker,** speecher, speechifier [informal], spieler *or* jawsmith [both slang]; after-dinner speaker; **spokesman,** spokeswoman; **demagogue,** rabble-rouser; declaimer, ranter, tub-thumper [informal], haranguer, spouter [informal]; panelist, debater.

.5 **lecturer,** praelector, discourser, reader; **preacher;** sermonizer, sermonist, sermoner, homilist [archaic], pulpitarian, pulpiteer, Boanerges; **expositor,** expounder; chalk talker [informal].

.6 **orator, public speaker,** platform orator *or* speaker; rhetorician, rhetor; silver-tongued orator, **spellbinder;** Demosthenes, Cicero, Franklin D. Roosevelt, Winston Churchill, William Jennings Bryan; soapbox orator, soapboxer, stump orator.

.7 **elocutionist,** elocutioner; **recitationist,** reciter, diseur, diseuse; reader; improvisator, *improvvisatore* [Ital].

.8 **rhetorician,** teacher of rhetoric, rhetor, elocutionist.

.9 VERBS **make a speech, give a talk, deliver an address,** speechify [informal], **speak, talk, discourse; address;** stump [informal], go on *or* take the stump; platform, soapbox; take the floor.

.10 **declaim,** hold forth, **orate,** elocute [informal], spout [informal], spiel [informal], mouth; **harangue, rant,** "out-herod Herod" [Shakespeare], tub-thump, perorate,

rodomontade; **recite,** read; debate; demagogue, rabble-rouse.

.11 **lecture,** prelect, read *or* deliver a lecture; **preach,** preachify [informal], **sermonize,** read a sermon.

.12 ADJS **declamatory, elocutionary, oratorical, rhetorical,** forensic; eloquent 600.8; demagogic(al).

## 600. ELOQUENCE

.1 NOUNS **eloquence, rhetoric, silver tongue,** eloquent tongue, facundity; **articulateness;** gift of gab [informal], **glibness,** smoothness, slickness; **felicitousness,** felicity; **oratory** 599.1; expression, **expressiveness,** command of words *or* language, gift of expression, vividness, graphicness; pleasing *or* effective style; **meaningfulness** 545.5.

.2 **fluency, flow;** smoothness, **facility, ease; grace,** gracefulness, poetry; **elegance** 589.

.3 **vigor, force,** power, strength, vitality, drive, sinew, sinewiness, nervousness, nervosity, vigorousness, forcefulness, effectiveness, impressiveness, punch *or* guts [both informal]; incisiveness, trenchancy, cuttingness, poignancy, bitingness, bite, mordancy; strong language, "thoughts that breathe and words that burn" [Thomas Gray].

.4 **spirit,** pep [informal], liveliness, raciness, sparkle, vivacity, dash, verve, vividness; piquancy, poignancy, pungency.

.5 **vehemence, passion,** impassionedness, enthusiasm, **ardor,** ardency, **fervor,** fervency, fire, fieriness, glow, warmth.

.6 **loftiness,** elevation, sublimity; grandeur, **nobility,** stateliness, majesty, gravity, solemnity, dignity.

.7 VERBS **have the gift of gab** [informal], have a tongue in one's head; spellbind; shine, "pour the full tide of eloquence along" [Pope].

.8 ADJS **eloquent, silver-tongued,** silver; well-speaking, well-spoken, **articulate,** facund; **glib, smooth,** smooth-spoken, smooth-tongued, **slick; felicitous;** spellbinding; Demosthenic, Demosthenian; Ciceronian, Tullian.

.9 **fluent, flowing,** tripping; **smooth,** pleasing, facile, **easy, graceful, elegant** 589.6.

.10 **expressive, graphic, vivid,** suggestive, imaginative; **meaningful** 545.10.

.11 **vigorous,** strong, **powerful,** imperative, **forceful,** forcible, vital, driving, sinewy, sinewed, nervous, punchy *or* gutsy [both informal], **striking, telling, effective,** impressive; incisive, trenchant, cutting, biting, piercing, poignant, penetrating, slashing, mordant, acid, corrosive; sensational.

.12 **spirited, lively,** peppy [informal], racy, sparkling, vivacious; piquant, poignant, pungent.

.13 **vehement,** emphatic, **passionate, impassioned,** enthusiastic, **ardent,** fiery, **fervent,** burning, glowing, warm; urgent, stirring, exciting, stimulating, provoking.

.14 **lofty, elevated, sublime, grand, majestic,** noble, stately, grave, solemn, dignified; serious, weighty; moving, inspiring.

.15 ADVS **eloquently; fluently,** smoothly, glibly, trippingly on the tongue; **expressively,** vividly, graphically; **meaningfully** 545.13; **vigorously,** powerfully, forcefully, spiritedly; tellingly, strikingly, effectively, impressively; **vehemently, passionately,** ardently, fervently, warmly, glowingly, in glowing terms.

## 601. GRANDILOQUENCE

.1 NOUNS **grandiloquence,** magniloquence, lexiphanicism, **pompousness,** pomposity, orotundity; **rhetoric,** mere rhetoric, rhetoricalness; high-flown diction, big or tall talk [informal]; grandioseness, grandiosity; loftiness, stiltedness; fulsomeness; **pretentiousness,** pretension, **affectation** 589.3; ostentation; showiness, flashiness, gaudiness, meretriciousness, bedizenment, garishness; sensationalism, luridness, Barnumism; **inflation, inflatedness,** swollenness, turgidity, turgescence, flatulence or flatulency, tumidness, tumidity; sententiousness, pontification; swollen phrase or diction, swelling utterance; platitudinous ponderosity, polysyllabic profundity, pompous prolixity; Johnsonese; prose run mad; convolution, tortuosity, tortuousness, ostentatious complexity or profundity.

.2 **bombast,** bombastry, **fustian,** highfalutin [informal], **rant,** rodomontade; **hot air** [slang]; balderdash, gobbledygook [slang].

.3 high-sounding words, lexiphanicism, hard words; **sesquipedalian word,** big or long word, two-dollar word [slang], **jawbreaker,** jawtwister, mouthful; antidisestablishmentarianism, honorificabilitudinitatibus [Shakespeare], pneumonoultramicroscopicsilicovolcanoconiosis; polysyllabism, sesquipedalianism, sesquipedality; Latinate diction; academic choctaw, technical jargon.

.4 **ornateness, floweriness,** floridness, floridity, lushness, luxuriance; flourish, flourish of rhetoric, flowers of speech or rhetoric,

purple patches or passages, beauties, fine writing; **ornament,** ornamentation, **adornment, embellishment,** elegant variation, embroidery, **frill,** colors or colors of rhetoric [both archaic], **figure, figure of speech** 551.

.5 **phrasemonger,** rhetorician; phraseman, phrasemaker, fine writer, wordspinner; euphuist, Gongorist, Marinist; pedant.

.6 VERBS **talk big** [informal], talk highfalutin [informal], **pontificate, blow** [slang], **vapor,** Barnumize; inflate, bombast, lay or pile it on [informal], lay it on thick or lay it on with a trowel [both informal]; smell of the lamp.

.7 **ornament, decorate, adorn, embellish, embroider,** enrich; overcharge, overlay, overload, load with ornament, festoon, weight down with ornament, flourish [archaic]; **gild,** trick out, varnish; paint in glowing colors, tell in glowing terms; "to gild refined gold, to paint the lily, to throw a perfume on the violet" [Shakespeare]; elaborate, convolute, involve.

.8 ADJS      **grandiloquent,** magniloquent, **pompous, orotund; grandiose;** fulsome; lofty, elevated, tall [informal], **stilted; pretentious, affected** 589.9; overdone, overwrought; **showy, flashy, ostentatious,** gaudy, meretricious, flamboyant, flaming, bedizened, flaunting, garish; lurid, sensational, sensationalistic; **high-flown, highfalutin** [informal], high-flying; high-flowing, **high-sounding, big-sounding,** greatsounding, grandisonant [archaic], sonorous; **rhetorical,** declamatory; **pedantic,** inkhorn, lexiphanic [archaic]; sententious, Johnsonian; convoluted, tortuous, labyrinthine, overelaborate, overinvolved; euphuistic, Gongoresque.

.9 **bombastic,** fustian, mouthy, **inflated, swollen,** swelling, turgid, turgescent, tumid, tumescent, flatulent, windy or gassy [both informal].

.10 **sesquipedalian,** sesquipedal, polysyllabic, jawbreaking [informal].

.11 **ornate, purple** [informal], colored, **fancy;** adorned, **embellished, embroidered,** decorated, festooned, overcharged, overloaded, befrilled; **flowery, florid,** lush, luxuriant; figured, **figurative** 551.3.

.12 ADVS **grandiloquently,** magniloquently, **pompously,** grandiosely, loftily, stiltedly, pretentiously; **ostentatiously,** showily; **bombastically,** turgidly, tumidly, flatulently, windily [informal].

.13 **ornately,** fancily; **flowerily,** floridly.

## 602. WRITING

.1 NOUNS **writing,** scrivening *or* scrivenery [both archaic], inscription, lettering, grapho–, –graphy, –graphia; engrossment; pen, **pen-and-ink;** inkslinging *or* ink spilling [both slang], pen *or* pencil driving *or* pushing [slang]; **typing, typewriting;** macrography, micrography; stroke *or* dash of the pen, *coup de plume* [Fr]; secret writing, cryptography 614.6.

.2 **authorship, writing,** authorcraft, pencraft, **composition,** inditement; pen; **creative writing,** literary composition, literary production, verse-writing, short-story writing, novel-writing, playwriting, drama-writing; essay-writing; **expository writing;** technical writing; journalism, editorial-writing, feature-writing, rewriting; songwriting, lyric-writing, libretto-writing; artistry, literary power, literary artistry, literary talent *or* flair, skill with words *or* language, facility in writing, ready pen; **writer's itch,** graphomania, scribblemania, graphorrhea, *cacoethes scribendi* [L]; automatic writing; writer's cramp, graphospasm.

.3 **handwriting, hand, script,** scription, fist [informal], chirography, **calligraphy,** autography; **manuscript,** scrive [Scot]; **penmanship,** penscript, pencraft; stylography; graphology, graphanalysis, graphometry; paleography.

.4 (style of handwriting) **longhand,** cursive; bold hand, round hand, slanting hand, perpendicular hand, letter hand, book hand, Spencerian writing, Italian hand, law hand, court hand, charter hand, chancery hand, text hand, copperplate hand; cursive hand, minuscule script; uncial, majuscule script; **printing,** handprinting, block letter, **lettering.**

.5 (good writing) **calligraphy,** fine writing, elegant penmanship, **good hand,** fine hand, good fist [informal], fair hand, copybook hand.

.6 (bad writing) **cacography, bad hand,** poor fist [informal], cramped *or* crabbed hand, botched writing, childish scrawl, illegible handwriting, *griffonage* [Fr].

.7 **scribbling,** scribblement; **scribble,** scrabble, **scrawl, scratch,** *barbouillage* [Fr]; *pattes de mouche* [Fr], hen tracks, hen scratches, pothookery, pothooks, pothooks and hangers.

.8 **stenography, shorthand,** brachygraphy, tachygraphy; Speedwriting; phonography, stenotypy; contraction.

.9 **letter, written character** 581.1; **alphabet, writing system** 581.3,9; punctuation 586.15, 18–20.

.10 (written matter) **writing, piece,** –graph, –gram; piece of writing, screed; **copy, matter;** printed matter, literature, reading matter; the written word, *literae scriptae* [L]; nonfiction; fiction 608.7,8; **composition, work,** opus, production, literary production, literary artefact *or* artifact, lucubration, brainchild; essay, article 606.1; poem 609.6; play 611.4–6; letter 604.2; **document** 570.5-8; **paper,** parchment, scroll; **script,** scrip, scrive [Scot]; **penscript, typescript; manuscript, MS., Ms., ms.,** holograph, autograph; **draft,** first draft, second draft, etc., recension, **version;** edited version, finished version, final draft; transcription, transcript, fair copy, engrossment; flimsy; original, author's copy; printout, computer printout.

.11 (ancient manuscript) **codex;** scroll; palimpsest, *codex rescriptus* [L]; papyrus, parchment.

.12 **literature, letters, belles lettres,** polite literature, humane letters, *litterae humaniores* [L], republic of letters; serious literature; **classics,** ancient literature; medieval literature, Renaissance literature, etc.; national literature, English literature, French literature, etc.; contemporary literature; underground literature; pseudonymous literature; folk literature; travel literature; wisdom literature; erotic literature, erotica, pornographic literature, pornography, porn [slang], obscene literature, scatological literature; popular literature, pop literature [slang]; kitsch.

.13 **writer, scribbler** [slang], **penman,** pen, penner, –grapher; pen *or* pencil driver *or* pusher [slang], word-slinger, **inkslinger** *or* ink spiller [both slang], knight of the plume *or* pen *or* quill [informal]; **scribe, scrivener, amanuensis, secretary,** recording secretary, **clerk;** letterer; **copyist,** copier, transcriber; chirographer, calligrapher.

.14 **writing expert,** graphologist, handwriting expert, graphometrist; paleographer.

.15 **author, writer,** scribe [informal], composer, inditer; authoress, penwoman; **creative writer,** *littérateur* [Fr], literary artist, literary craftsman *or* artisan *or* journeyman, belletrist, man of letters, literary man; wordsmith, word painter; freelance, free-lance writer; ghostwriter, ghost [informal]; collaborator, coauthor; prose writer, logographer; story writer, **short**

story writer; storyteller 608.10; **novelist,** novelettist; diarist; **newspaperman** 605.22; **annalist** 608.11; **poet** 609.13; **dramatist** 611.27, humorist 881.12; scriptwriter, scenario writer, scenarist; nonfiction writer; article writer, magazine writer; **essayist;** monographer; reviewer, critic, literary critic, music critic, art critic, drama critic, dance critic; columnist; pamphleteer; technical writer; copywriter, advertising writer; compiler, encyclopedist, bibliographer.

.16 **hack writer,** hack, literary hack, Grub Street writer [Brit], **penny-a-liner,** scribbler [slang], **potboiler** [informal].

.17 **stenographer,** brachygrapher, tachygrapher; phonographer, stenotypist.

.18 **typist;** printer.

.19 VERBS **write, pen, pencil,** drive or push the pen or pencil [slang]; stain or spoil paper [informal], shed or spill ink [informal], **scribe,** scrive [Scot]; inscribe, scroll; superscribe; enface; take pen in hand; **put in writing,** put in black and white; **draw up, draft, write out,** make out; **write down,** record 570.16; take down in shorthand; **type; transcribe,** copy out, engross, make a fair copy, copy; trace; **rewrite, revise, edit,** recense, make a recension, make a critical revision.

.20 **scribble, scrabble, scratch, scrawl;** doodle.

.21 **write, author, compose, indite,** formulate, produce, prepare; dash off, knock off or out [informal], throw on paper; free-lance; collaborate, coauthor; ghostwrite, ghost [informal]; novelize; scenarize; pamphleteer; editorialize.

.22 ADJS **written,** penned, penciled; **inscribed;** engrossed; **in writing, in black and white,** on paper; scriptural, scriptorial, **graphic;** calligraphic, chirographic(al); stylographic(al); manuscript, autograph, autographic(al), holograph, holographic(al), in one's own hand, under one's hand; **longhand, in longhand; shorthand,** in shorthand; italic, italicized; cursive, running, flowing; graphologic(al), graphometric(al); graphoanalytic(al); typewritten; printed.

.23 **scribbled, scrabbled, scratched, scrawled; scribbly, scratchy, scrawly.**

.24 **literary,** belletristic; classical.

.25 auctorial, authorial; polygraphic; graphomaniac(al), scribblemaniac(al), scripturient [archaic].

.26 **alphabetic,** ideographic, etc. 581.8.

.27 stenographic(al), tachygraphic(al), **shorthand,** in shorthand; phonographic(al).

.28 **clerical, secretarial.**

.29 **stationery**

| | |
|---|---|
| biblus | paper |
| bond paper | papyrus |
| carbon paper | parchment |
| copy or copying paper | rice paper |
| demy | scratch pad |
| flimsy | scroll |
| foolscap | stencil |
| lambskin (parchment) | tracing paper |
| legal-size paper | typing paper |
| letter paper | vellum |
| note paper | writing paper |
| pad | |

.30 **writing materials**

| | |
|---|---|
| ballpoint pen | lettering pen |
| blackboard | nib |
| cartridge pen | pen |
| chalk | penpoint |
| China or Chinese ink | plume |
| copying ink | printer's ink |
| crayon | quill |
| drawing ink | reed |
| eraser | secret or invisible or |
| felt-tip pen |   sympathetic ink |
| fountain pen | slate |
| India or Indian ink | snorkel pen |
| ink | stencil |
| ink cartridge | style |
| ink eradicator | stylograph, stylograph |
| ink eraser |   pen |
| inkhorn | stylus |
| inkpot | table |
| inkstand | tablet |
| inkwell | typewriter ribbon |
| lead pencil | writing brush |

.31 **writing machines**

| | |
|---|---|
| addressing machine | stenotype |
| Addressograph | teleprinter |
| Composaline | Teletype, teletype- |
| electric typewriter |   writer |
| Flexowriter | ticker, stock ticker |
| Selectric | typewriter |
| stenograph | VariTyper |

### 603. PRINTING

.1 NOUNS **printing,** publishing, publication, –typy; photographic reproduction, photochemical process, phototypography, phototypy; **photoengraving; letterpress,** relief printing, **typography,** letterpress photoengraving; zincography, photozincography; line engraving, halftone engraving; stereotypy; wood-block printing, xylotypography, chromoxylography; intaglio printing, **gravure;** rotogravure, rotary photogravure; planographic printing, planography, **lithography,** typolithography, photolithography, lithogravure, lithophotogravure; offset lithography, offset, dry offset, photo-offset; photogelatin process, albertype, collotype; electronography, electrostatic printing, onset, xerography, xeroprinting; stencil, mimeograph, silk-screen

printing; color printing, chromotypography, chromotypy, two-color printing, three-color printing; book printing, job printing, sheetwork; history of printing, palaeotypography; photography 577; **graphic arts, printmaking** 578.1.

.2 composing, composition, typesetting, setting; hand composition, machine composition; hot-metal typesetting, cold-type typesetting, photosetting, photocomposition; imposition; justification; composing stick, galley chase, furniture, quoin; typesetting machine, Linotype, Intertype, Monotype, phototypesetter, phototypesetting machine; computerized typesetting; line of type, slug; layout, dummy.

.3 **print, imprint, stamp, impression, impress,** letterpress; reprint, reissue; offprint; offcut; offset, setoff, mackle.

.4 copy, printer's copy, manuscript, typescript; **matter;** composed matter, live matter, dead matter, standing matter.

.5 **proof,** proof sheet, pull [Brit], trial impression; galley, **galley proof,** slip; page proof, foundry proof, plate proof, stone proof, press proof, cold-type proof, color proof, computer proof, engraver's proof, reproduction or repro proof, blueprint, blue [informal], vandyke, progressive proof; author's proof; revise.

.6 **type, print, stamp, letter;** type body or shank or stem, body, shank, stem, shoulder, belly, back, bevel, beard, feet, groove, nick, face, counter; ascender, descender, serif; lower case, minuscule; upper case, majuscule; capital, cap [informal], small capital, small cap [informal]; ligature, logotype; bastard type, bottle-assed type, fat-faced type; **pi;** type lice; **font; face,** typeface; type class, roman, sans serif, script, italic, black letter; case, typecase; point, pica; en, em; typefounders, typefoundry.

.7 **space,** patent space, justifying space, justification space; spaceband, slug; quadrat, quad; em quad, en quad; em, en; three-em space, thick space; four-em space, five-em space, thin space; hair space.

.8 **printing surface, plate,** printing plate; typeform, locked-up page; duplicate plate, electrotype, stereotype, plastic plate, rubber plate; zincograph, zincotype; stone.

.9 **presswork,** makeready; **press, printing press,** printing machine [Brit]; platen press, flatbed cylinder press, cylinder press, rotary press, web press, rotogravure press; bed, platen, web.

.10 **printed matter; reading matter, text,** letterpress [Brit]; advertising matter; advance sheets.

.11 **press,** printing office, printshop, printery, printers; publishers, **publishing house; pressroom,** composing room, proofroom.

.12 **printer,** pressman; **compositor, typesetter,** typographer, Linotyper; keyboarder; stoneman, makeup man; proofer; stereotyper, stereotypist, electrotyper; apprentice printer, devil, **printer's devil.**

.13 **proofreader,** reader, printer's reader [Brit]; **copyreader,** copy editor, copyholder.

.14 VERBS **print; imprint, impress, stamp,** enstamp [archaic]; engrave 578.10; run, run off, strike; **publish, issue, bring out, put out, get out;** put to press, put to bed, see through the press; prove, proof, prove up, make or pull a proof, pull; overprint; reprint, reissue; mimeograph, hectograph; multigraph.

.15 autotype, electrotype, linotype, monotype, palaeotype, stereotype; keyboard.

.16 **compose,** set, set in print; **make up,** impose; justify, overrun; pi, pi a form.

.17 **copy-edit; proofread,** read, read or correct copy.

.18 (be printed) go to press, come out, appear in print.

.19 ADJS **printed, in print;** typeset.

.20 **typographic(al);** phototypic, phototypographic; chromotypic, chromotypographic; stereotypic, palaeotypographic(al); **boldface,** bold-faced, blackface, black-faced, full-faced; **lightface,** lightfaced; **upper-case, lower-case.**

.21 **typesetting machines**

| | |
|---|---|
| Alphatype | Ludlow |
| Composaline | Monophoto |
| Diatype | Monotype |
| Elrod | Monotype caster |
| Fotomatic | Monotype keyboard |
| Fotosetter | Photon |
| Fototronic | phototypesetter |
| Intertype | Tapetron |
| Linasec | VideoComp |
| Linofilm | V-I-P |
| Linotron | Zip |
| Linotype | |

.22 **type sizes**

| | |
|---|---|
| 3-point, excelsior | 10-point, elite or long |
| 3½-point, brilliant | primer |
| 4-point, gem | 11-point, small pica |
| 4½-point, diamond | 12-point, pica |
| 5-point, pearl | 14-point, English |
| 5½-point, agate, ruby | 16-point, Columbian |
| 6-point, nonpareil | 18-point, great primer |
| 7-point, minion | 20-point, paragon |
| 8-point, brevier | 48-point, canon |
| 9-point, bourgeois | |

**.23 type styles, typefaces**

| | |
|---|---|
| antique | bold |
| Baskerville | extracondensed |
| blackface | Futura |
| black letter | Garamond |
| block-serifed | German text |
| Bodoni | Gothic |
| boldface, bold | Goudy |
| Bulmer | Granjon |
| Caledonia | grotesque |
| Caslon | Ionic |
| Caslon Old Style | italic |
| Century | Janson |
| Clarendon | lightface |
| condensed | modern |
| cursive | Old English |
| display | old style |
| Doric | roman |
| Egyptian | sans serif |
| Electra | script |
| Elzevir | Times Roman |
| expanded | Transitional |
| extended | Typewriter |
| extraboldface, extra- | |

**.24 presses**

| | |
|---|---|
| copying press | Multigraph |
| cylinder press | offset lithography |
| electrotype press | press |
| flatbed press, flat | perfecting press |
| press | platen press |
| foundry press | proof press |
| four-color press | rotary press |
| galley press | sheet-fed press |
| gravure press | two-color press |
| hand press | web press, web-fed |
| letterpress | press |

**.25 copying machines**

| | |
|---|---|
| Ditto | Multigraph |
| duplicator | pantograph |
| hectograph | spirit duplicator |
| mimeograph | Xerox machine |

**.26 printing equipment**

| | |
|---|---|
| bearer | galley |
| bed | gripper |
| bevel | guide |
| blanket | gutter, gutter stick |
| boss | ink bell, inking bell |
| box | inking roller |
| brayer | line gauge |
| burr | matrix |
| case | overlay |
| chase | page gauge |
| composing frame | platen |
| composing rule | quoin |
| composing stick | ratchet |
| drawsheet | reglet |
| footstick | rounce |
| form | turtle |
| frame | tympan, tympan sheet |
| frisket | type mold |
| furniture | underlay |

### 604. CORRESPONDENCE

**.1** NOUNS **correspondence, letter writing,** written communication, epistolary inter-course *or* communication; personal corre-spondence, business correspondence.

**.2 letter, epistle, message, communication, dispatch, missive,** favor [archaic]; per-sonal letter, business letter; **note, line,** chit, billet [archaic]; **reply, answer, ac-knowledgment,** rescript.

**.3** air letter, aerogram; airgraph [Brit], V-mail; drop letter; fan letter; love letter, *billet-doux* [Fr]; poison-pen letter; open letter; chain letter; form letter; circular letter, newsletter, encyclical, encyclical letter; round robin; bull, apostolic *or* pa-pal brief; monitory, monitory letter; pas-toral letter, Pastoral Epistle; paschal let-ter; dimissory letter, dimissorial; letter of credence, letters credential, letters overt, letters patent, letters rogatory, letters tes-tamentary; letters of marque; letter of delegation, letters of request, letter of credit; letter of introduction; dead letter, nixie; letter book.

**.4 card, postcard, postal card,** lettercard; picture postcard.

**.5 mail, post** [Brit], **letters, correspondence;** airmail, surface mail, seapost, sea mail; **parcel post, PP;** letter post, printed pa-per, halfpenny post, newspaper post, book post [all Brit]; first-class *or* second-class *or* third-class *or* fourth-class mail; junk mail [informal]; rural free delivery, RFD, rural delivery, RD; **special delivery,** special handling, express *or* express deliv-ery [both Brit]; registered mail, certified mail; frank; letter bag; post day [Brit]; mailing list; direct mail, direct-mail ad-vertising *or* selling, mail-order selling; fan mail.

**.6 postage;** stamp, postage stamp; frank; postmark, cancellation.

**.7 mailbox,** postbox, letter box, pillar box [Brit]; drop, letter drop; mailing ma-chine; mailbag, postbag [Brit].

**.8 postal service, postal system; post office,** PO, general post office, GPO, sub post office, sea post office.

**.9 correspondent, letter writer,** writer, com-municator; pen pal [informal]; addressee.

**.10 address,** name and address, direction [ar-chaic], **destination,** superscription; zone, postal zone, zip code; letterhead, bill-head.

**.11** VERBS **correspond,** correspond with, **com-municate with, write, write to,** write a letter, send a letter to, send a note, **drop a line** [informal]; use the mails; keep up a correspondence, exchange letters.

**.12 reply, answer, acknowledge;** reply by re-turn mail.

**.13 mail, post,** dispatch, send; airmail.

.14 address, direct, superscribe.

.15 ADJS epistolary, epistolatory; **postal**, post.

.16 PHRS please reply, RSVP, *répondez s'il vous plaît* [Fr].

## 605. BOOK, PERIODICAL

.1 NOUNS book, volume, tome, biblio–; **publication, writing, work, opus, production; title;** opusculum, opuscule; magnum opus, great work, classic; standard work, definitive work; nonbook; folio; serial; paperback, pocket book, soft-cover, soft-bound book, limp-cover book; cloth-bound book, hardback, hard-cover book, hard book, bound book, cased book; playbook 611.26; songbook 462.28; note-book 570.11; storybook, **novel** 608.8; best seller; trade book; children's book, juvenile book, juvenile; picture book; coloring book, sketchbook; prayer book, psalter, psalmbook.

.2 edition, issue; volume, **number;** printing, impression; copy; series, set, collection, library; library edition; back number; **trade edition, trade book;** subscription edition, subscription book; school edition, text edition.

.3 **rare book,** early edition; first edition; Elzevir, Elzevir book *or* edition; Aldine, Aldine book *or* edition; manuscript, scroll, codex; incunabulum, cradle book.

.4 **compilation, omnibus; symposium;** collection, collectanea, miscellany; collected works, selected works, complete works, *œuvres* [Fr], canon; **miscellanea,** analects; ana; chrestomathy, delectus; **anthology,** garland, florilegium; flowers, beauties; garden; *Festschrift* [Ger]; quotation book; album, photograph album; scrapbook.

.5 **handbook, manual,** enchiridion, vade mecum, gradus, how-to book [informal]; cookbook, cookery book [Brit]; nature book, field guide; travel book, **guidebook** 748.10.

.6 **reference book,** work of reference; **encyclopedia,** cyclopedia; **concordance; catalog;** calendar; index; classified catalog, *catalogue raisonné* [Fr], dictionary catalog; **directory,** city directory; telephone directory, telephone book, phone book [informal]; **atlas, gazetteer;** studbook; polyglot, diatesseron, harmony; source book, casebook; record book 570.11.

.7 **dictionary, lexicon, wordbook, Webster's; glossary,** gloss, **vocabulary,** onomasticon, nomenclator; **thesaurus, Roget's,** storehouse *or* treasury of words, thesaurus dic-

tionary, synonym dictionary, synonymy; phrase book; gradus; general dictionary, unabridged dictionary, semi-unabridged dictionary, desk dictionary, college dictionary; specialized dictionary; bilingual dictionary, foreign-language dictionary, polyglot dictionary; dialect dictionary; idiom dictionary, slang dictionary; rhyming dictionary; etymological dictionary; etymologicon; children's dictionary, juvenile dictionary, school dictionary, elementary dictionary; biographical dictionary; geographical dictionary, gazetteer; dictionary of quotations; science dictionary, electronics dictionary, geological dictionary, chemical dictionary, psychological dictionary, etc.

.8 **textbook, text, schoolbook, manual,** manual of instruction; **primer,** alphabet book, abecedary, abecedarium; hornbook, battledore; gradus, exercise book, workbook; **grammar, reader;** spelling book, speller, casebook.

.9 **booklet, pamphlet, brochure, chapbook, leaflet, folder, tract;** circular 559.8; comic book.

.10 **periodical, serial, journal,** gazette; ephemeris; **magazine,** pulp magazine, slick magazine, newsmagazine, women's magazine, men's magazine, children's magazine, trade magazine; pictorial; review; organ, **house organ;** daily, weekly, biweekly, bimonthly, fortnightly, monthly, quarterly; annual, yearbook; daybook, diary 570.11.

.11 **newspaper,** news, **paper,** sheet *or* rag [both slang], **gazette,** daily newspaper, daily, weekly newspaper, weekly, neighborhood newspaper, national newspaper; newspaper of record; **tabloid,** extra, special, extra edition, special edition.

.12 **makeup;** front matter, preliminaries, text, back matter; head, fore edge, back, tail; page, leaf, folio; type page; trim size; flyleaf, endpaper, endleaf, endsheet, signature; recto, verso *or* reverso; title page, half-title page; title, bastard title, binder's title, subtitle, running title; copyright page, imprint, printer's imprint, colophon; catchword, catch line; dedication, inscription; acknowledgments, preface, foreword, introduction; contents, contents page, table of contents; errata; bibliography; index.

.13 **part, section,** book, volume; article; serial, installment, *livraison* [Fr]; fascicle; **passage,** phrase, clause, verse, paragraph, chapter, column.

.14 (sizes) –mo; folio; quarto, 4to; octavo,

8vo; duodecimo, twelvemo, 12mo; sexto-decimo, sixteenmo, 16mo; octodecimo, eighteenmo, 18mo; imperial, super, royal, medium, crown.

.15 **bookbinding**, bibliopegy; **binding, cover, book cover,** case, bookcase, hard binding, soft binding, mechanical binding, spiral binding, plastic binding; library binding; headband, footband, tailband; jacket, book jacket, dust jacket, dust cover, wrapper; slipcase, slipcover; book cloth, binder's cloth, binder's board, binder board; folding, tipping, gathering, collating, sewing; **signature;** collating mark, niggerhead; Smyth sewing, side sewing, saddle stitching, wire stitching, stapling, perfect binding; smashing, gluing-off, trimming, rounding, backing, lining, lining-up; casemaking, stamping, casing-in.

.16 (bookbinding styles) Aldine, Arabesque, Byzantine, Canevari, cottage, dentelle, Etruscan, fanfare, Grolier, Harleian, Jansenist, Maioli, pointillé, Roxburgh.

.17 **library,** bookroom, bookery [archaic], *bibliothèque* [Fr], *bibliotheca* [L], athenaeum; **public library, circulating library, lending library** [Brit]; **rental library; book wagon, bookmobile;** Bibliothèque Nationale, Bodleian Library, British Museum, Deutsche Bücherei, Library of Congress, Vatican Library; American Library Association, ALA.

.18 **bookstore, bookshop,** *librairie* [Fr], bookseller's; **bookstall,** bookstand; **book club.**

.19 **bibliography,** bibliography of bibliographies, annual bibliography, annotated bibliography, critical bibliography; index, Art Index, Education Index, etc.; periodical index, Reader's Guide to Periodical Literature; Bibliography Index; Books in Print, Paperbound Books in Print; Cumulative Book Index; National Union Catalog, Library of Congress Catalog, General Catalogue of Printed Books [Brit], Union List of Serials; **publisher's catalog,** publisher's list, backlist.

.20 **bookholder, bookrest,** book support, **book end; bookcase,** revolving bookcase *or* bookstand, bookrack, bookstand, **bookshelf;** stack, bookstack; book table, book tray, book truck; folder, folio; **portfolio.**

.21 **bookman,** bibliographer, bibliognost; **bookmaker; publisher,** book publisher; **editor,** trade editor, reference editor, juvenile editor, textbook editor, dictionary editor, college editor, acquisitions editor, executive editor, managing editor,

editor-in-chief, copy editor, production editor, permissions editor; **printer,** book printer; **bookbinder,** bibliopegist; **bookdealer, bookseller,** book agent, book salesman; bibliopole, bibliopolist; **librarian,** bibliothec, bibliothecary, *bibliothécaire* [Fr], reference librarian, cataloger, children's librarian; chief librarian, library director, curator; **booklover,** philobiblist, bibliophile, bibliolater, book collector, bibliomane, bibliomaniac, bibliotaph; **bookworm,** bibliophage; book-stealer, biblioklept.

.22 **journalist, newspaperman, newsman,** pressman [Brit], newswriter, gazetteer [archaic], gentleman *or* representative of the press; **reporter, leg man** [informal], interviewer; **cub reporter;** newspaperwoman, sob sister [slang]; **correspondent, foreign correspondent,** war correspondent, special correspondent, own correspondent; publicist; rewriter, **rewrite man;** reviser, diaskeuast; **editor,** subeditor, managing editor, city editor, news editor, sports editor, woman's editor, feature editor, **copy editor,** copyman, copy chief, slotman; reader, **copyreader;** editorial writer, leader writer [Brit]; **columnist,** paragrapher, paragraphist.

.23 **the press,** public press, **fourth estate;** print medium *or* media, public print; Fleet Street; **journalism;** Associated Press, AP; United Press International, UPI; Reuters; **publishing,** book publishing, magazine publishing; publishing industry, communications, communications industry.

.24 **bibliology,** bibliography; **bookcraft, bookmaking,** book production, book manufacturing, bibliogenesis, bibliogony; **bookselling,** bibliopolism.

.25 ADJS **bibliological,** bibliographic(al); bibliothecal, bibliothecary; bibliopolic; bibliopegic.

.26 **journalistic,** journalese [informal]; **periodical,** serial; magazinish, magaziny; newspaperish, newspapery; **editorial; reportorial.**

## 606. TREATISE

.1 NOUNS **treatise,** piece, treatment, tractate, tract, –logy *or* –logia; examination, survey, **discourse, discussion,** disquisition, descant, exposition, screed; homily; memoir; dissertation, **thesis; essay,** theme; pandect; excursus; **study,** lucubration, étude; **paper,** research paper, term paper; **sketch,** outline, aperçu; causerie; **monograph,** research monograph; *morceau* [Fr], paragraph, **note**; preliminary study, introductory study, first approach, prolegomenon; **article**, feature, special article.

.2 **commentary**, commentation [archaic]; **comment**, remark; **criticism**, critique, *compte-rendu critique* [Fr], analysis; **review**, critical review, **report**, notice, **write-up** [informal]; **editorial**, leading article *or* leader [both Brit]; gloss, running commentary.

.3 **discourser**, disquisitor, expositor; descanter; **essayist**; monographer, monographist; tractation, tractator [archaic]; **writer, author** 602.15.

.4 **commentator**, commenter; expositor, expounder; annotator, scholiast; glossarist, glossographer; **critic**; **reviewer**, book reviewer; **editor**; editorial writer, editorialist, leader writer [Brit]; news analyst; publicist.

.5 VERBS **write upon**, touch upon, **discuss, treat, treat of, deal with**, take up, handle, go into, inquire into, survey; discourse, dissert, dissertate, descant; **comment upon**, remark upon; **criticize, review**, write up.

.6 ADJS dissertational, disquisitional, discoursive; expository, expositorial, expositive; essayistic; monographic(al); commentative, commentatorial; critical.

## 607. ABRIDGMENT

.1 NOUNS **abridgment**, compendium, compend, *abrégé* [Fr], **condensation**, short *or* shortened version, condensed version, abbreviation, abbreviature, brief, digest, **abstract**, epitome, **précis, capsule**, sketch, thumbnail sketch, **synopsis**, conspectus, syllabus, apercu, **survey, review**, overview, pandect, bird's-eye view; **outline**, skeleton, draft; topical outline; head, rubric.

.2 **summary**, résumé, recapitulation, **recap** [informal], rundown, run-through; **summation**; sum, substance, sum and substance; pith, meat, gist, core, essence, main point 672.6.

.3 **excerpt**, extract, selection, extraction, excerption; passage, selected passage.

.4 **excerpts**, *excerpta* [L], **extracts, gleanings**, cuttings, clippings, flowers, florilegium, **anthology** 605.4; fragments; analects; **miscellany**, miscellanea; **collection**, collectanea; ana.

.5 VERBS **abridge, condense; summarize**, brief, **outline, sketch**, sketch out, hit the high spots; capsule, capsulize; nutshell,

**put in a nutshell**; synopsize; shorten 203.6.

.6 ADJS **abridged**, condensed; compendious, **brief** 203.8.

.7 ADVS in brief, in summary, in sum, in a nutshell 592.8.

## 608. DESCRIPTION

.1 NOUNS **description, portrayal**, portraiture, **depiction**, rendering, rendition, **delineation**, limning, **representation** 572; imagery; **word painting** *or* **picture, picture, portrait, image**, photograph; evocation, impression; **sketch**, vignette, cameo; **characterization**, character, character sketch, profile; vivid description, exact description, realistic *or* naturalistic description, slice of life, *tranche de vie* [Fr], graphic account; specification, particularization, details, itemization, catalog, cataloging.

.2 **narration, narrative, relation, recital**, rehearsal, telling, retelling, recounting, recountal, review; **storytelling**, tale-telling, yarn spinning *or* yarning [both informal].

.3 **account, statement, report, word**.

.4 **chronicle, record** 570; **history, annals**, chronicles, memorabilia, chronology; **biography, memoir**, memorial, **life**, story, **life story**, adventures, fortunes, experiences; life and letters; legend, saint's legend, hagiology, hagiography; **autobiography, memoirs**, memorials; **journal, diary**, confessions; **profile, biographical sketch**, résumé, curriculum vitae; obituary, necrology, martyrology; photobiography; case history; historiography, theory of history; Clio, Muse of history.

.5 (history) "a set of lies agreed upon" [Napoleon], "the unrolled scroll of prophecy" [Garfield], "the chart and compass for national endeavor" [Sir Arthur Helps], "a voice forever sounding across the centuries the laws of right and wrong" [J. A. Froude], "a cyclic poem written by Time upon the memories of man" [Shelley], "the crystallisation of popular belief" [Donn Piatt], "philosophy learned from examples" [Dionysius of Halicarnassus], "history is bunk" [Henry Ford], "history is merely gossip" [Oscar Wilde].

.6 **story, tale, yarn, account, narrative**, narration, chronicle; **anecdote**, anecdotage; **epic**, epos, saga.

.7 **fiction**, work of fiction; **fairy tale**, *Märchen* [Ger]; **legend, myth**, mythos, mythology, folktale, folk story, **fable**, *fabliau* [Fr], **parable, allegory**, apologue; **fantasy**;

**romance,** gest; love story; bedtime story; nursery tale; adventure story; suspense story, thriller *or* shocker [both informal]; detective story *or* yarn, whodunit [informal]; mystery story, mystery; ghost story; Western story, Western, Westerner, horse opera [informal]; **science fiction,** sci-fi; space fiction, space opera [informal], scientifiction [archaic].

.8 (fictional forms) **short story,** storiette; short-short; vignette; **novel,** *roman* [Fr]; novelette; novella, *nouvelle* [Fr]; **dime novel,** dreadful, penny dreadful, shilling shocker [Brit informal]; epistolary novel, historical novel, psychological novel, novel of ideas, comic novel, picaresque novel, *roman à clef* [Fr], *roman-fleuve* [Fr], river novel, thesis novel, novel of manners, detective novel, sociological novel, sentimental novel, propaganda novel, proletarian novel, novel of character, novel of incident, novel of the soil, regional novel, Gothic novel, problem novel, satirical novel, novel of sensibility, science-fiction novel, *Bildungsroman* [Ger], stream-of-consciousness novel; erotic novel, pornographic novel.

.9 (story elements) **plot,** fable, argument, story, line, subplot, secondary plot, mythos; plan, **structure,** architecture, architectonics, scheme, design; subject, topic, theme, motif; thematic development, development, continuity; **action,** movement; incident, episode; **complication;** rising action, falling action, *peripeteia* [Gk], switch [informal]; *anagnorisis* [Gk], recognition; denouement, catastrophe; *deus ex machina* [L]; device, contrivance, **gimmick** [informal]; angle *or* slant *or* twist [all informal]; **characterization; tone, atmosphere,** mood; background, color, **local color.**

10 **narrator,** relator, reciter, recounter, *raconteur* [Fr]; anecdotist; **storyteller,** storier, taleteller, teller of tales, spinner of yarns *or* yarn spinner [both informal]; word painter; short-story writer; **novelist,** novelettist, fictionist; fabulist, fableist, fabler, mythmaker, mythopoet; romancer, romancist; sagaman.

11 **chronicler,** annalist; **historian,** historiographer; **biographer,** memorialist, Boswell; autobiographer, autobiographist; diarist.

12 VERBS **describe, portray, picture,** render, **depict, represent, delineate,** limn, **paint,** draw; evoke, bring to life, make one see; outline, sketch; **characterize,** character;

**express,** set forth, give words to; **write** 602.21.

.13 **narrate, tell, relate, recount,** report, recite, rehearse, give an account of; tell a story, unfold a tale, fable, fabulize; storify, fictionalize; romance; novelize; mythicize, mythify, mythologize, allegorize; retell.

.14 **chronicle,** historify; biograph, **biography,** biographize; **record** 570.16.

.15 ADJS **descriptive, depictive,** expositive, **representative, delineative; expressive, vivid, graphic,** well-drawn; realistic, naturalistic, true to life, lifelike, faithful.

.16 **narrative, narrational;** storied, storified; **anecdotal,** anecdotic; epic(al).

.17 **fictional;** fictionalized; mythic(al), mythological, **legendary, fabulous;** mythopoeic, mythopoetic(al); parabolic(al), allegoric(al); **romantic,** romanticized.

.18 historic(al), historiographic(al), historied, historico–; chronologic(al); **traditional, legendary;** biographical, autobiographical; hagiographic(al), martyrologic(al); necrologic(al).

.19 ADVS **descriptively,** representatively; **expressively, vividly, graphically;** faithfully, realistically, naturalistically.

## 609. POETRY

.1 NOUNS **poetry, poesy, verse, song, rhyme;** "musical thought", "the harmonious unison of man with nature" [both Carlyle], "the supreme fiction" [Wallace Stevens], "the spontaneous overflow of powerful feelings recollected in tranquility" [Wordsworth], "the rhythmical creation of beauty" [Poe], "painting with the gift of speech" [Simonides], "the poet's innermost feeling issuing in rhythmic language" [John Keble], "the record of the best and happiest moments of the happiest and best minds" [Shelley], "the journal of a sea animal living on land, wanting to fly in the air", "the achievement of the synthesis of hyacinths and biscuits" [both Sandburg], "the best words in the best order" [Coleridge], "the rhythmic, inevitably narrative, movement from an overclothed blindness to a naked vision" [Dylan Thomas], "not the thing said but a way of saying it" [A. E. Housman], "the art of uniting pleasure with truth, by calling imagination to the help of reason" [Samuel Johnson], "the emotion of life rhythmically remembering beauty" [Fiona MacLeod], "the music of the soul, and above all of great and of feeling souls" [Voltaire].

.2 **poetics,** poetcraft, versecraft, versification, versemaking, *ars poetica* [L]; "my craft and sullen art" [Dylan Thomas]; **poetic language,** poeticism; **poetic license, poetic justice.**

.3 **bad poetry,** versemongering, poetastering, poetastery; poesy.

.4 **lyric poetry,** melic poetry, elegiac poetry *or* verse; **narrative poetry,** epic poetry *or* verse, epos, *épopée* [Fr], runic verse, heroic poetry, –ad; mock-heroic poetry, Hudibrastic verse; dramatic poetry, amoebean verse, stichomythia; pastoral poetry, didactic poetry, metaphysical poetry, erotic poetry, satirical poetry, satire, Goliardic verse, light verse, society verse, *vers de société* [Fr], occasional verse; modernist verse, imagist verse, symbolist verse, cubist poetry, concrete poetry; oral poetry; polyphonic prose, prose poetry.

.5 **doggerel,** crambo, crambo clink *or* jingle [Scot], Hudibrastic verse; nonsense verse, amphigory; macaronics, macaronic verse; lame verses, limping meters, halting meters.

.6 **poem, verse, rhyme,** "imaginary gardens with real toads in them" [Marianne Moore]; verselet, versicle; **jingle;** anacreontic, ballad, ballade, cento, clerihew, dithyramb, epode, elegy, epigram, ghazel, limerick, lyric, madrigal, nursery rhyme, ode, Pindaric ode, Sapphic ode, Horatian ode, narrative poem, palinode, satire, sestina, sonnet, English sonnet, Shakespearean sonnet, Italian sonnet, Petrarchan sonnet, sonnet sequence, sloka, song, villanelle; troubadour poem, Provençal poem, canso, chanson, balada, tenso, tenzone, pastourelle, pastorela, alba; epic, epos, *épopée* [Fr], epopoeia; pastoral, eclogue, idyll, pastoral elegy, bucolic, georgic; rondeau, rondel, roundel, roundelay, triolet, virelay; haiku, tanka; epithalamium, prothalamium; dirge, threnody, monody.

.7 **book of verse,** garland, anthology 605.4; poetic works, poesy.

.8 **metrics,** prosody, versification; **scansion,** scanning; metrical pattern *or* form, prosodic pattern *or* form, meter, numbers, measure; quantitative meter, syllabic meter, accentual meter; free verse, *vers libre* [Fr]; alliterative meter, *Stabreim* [Ger].

.9 **meter,** measure, numbers; **rhythm,** cadence, movement, lilt, jingle, swing;

sprung rhythm; **accent,** accentuation, metrical accent, stress, emphasis, ictus, **beat;** arsis, thesis; quantity, mora; metrical unit; foot, metrical foot; triseme, tetraseme; metrical group, metron, colon; period; dipody, syzygy, tripody, tetrapody, pentapody, hexapody, heptapody, iamb *or* iambus *or* iambic, anapest, trochee, dactyl, spondee, pyrrhic; amphibrach, antispast, bacchius, chloriambus *o* chloriamb, cretic *or* amphimacer, dochmiac, epitrite, ionic, molossus, paeon, proceleusmatic, tribrach; dimeter, trimeter, tetrameter, pentameter, hexameter, heptameter; **iambic pentameter, dactylic hexameter;** Alexandrine; Saturnian meter; elegiac, elegiac couplet *or* distich, elegiac pentameter; heroic couplet; counterpoint; caesura, diaeresis, masculine caesura, feminine caesura; catalexis; anacrusis; –stich.

.10 **rhyme;** clink, crambo; **consonance, assonance; alliteration;** eye rhyme; male *o* masculine *or* single rhyme, female *o* feminine *or* double rhyme; initial rhyme, end rhyme; tail rhyme, rhyme royal; near rhyme, slant rhyme; rhyme scheme; rhyming dictionary; unrhymed poetry, blank verse.

.11 (poetic divisions) **measure, strain; syllable; line; verse; stanza,** stave; strophe, antistrophe, epode; **canto,** book; **refrain, chorus,** burden; envoi; monostich, distich, tristich, tetrastich, pentastich, hexastich, heptastich, octastich; **couplet;** triplet, tercet, *terza rima* [Ital]; **quatrain;** sextet, sestet; septet; octave, octet, *ottava rima* [Ital]; rhyme royal; Spenserian stanza.

.12 **Muse;** the Muses, Pierides, *Camenae* [L], Apollo, Apollo Musagetes; Calliope, Polyhymnia, Erato, Euterpe; Helicon, Parnassus; Castilian Spring, Pierian Spring, Hippocrene; Bragi; **poetic genius,** poesy, afflatus, fire of genius, **creative imagination** 535.2, inspiration 467.8.

.13 **poet,** poetess, poetress [archaic], maker [archaic]; "the painter of the soul" [Disraeli], "a nightingale who sits in darkness and sings to cheer its own solitude with sweet sounds", "the unacknowledged legislators of the world" [both Shelley], "all who love, who feel great truths, and tell them" [Philip James Bailey], "literalists of the imagination" [Marianne Moore]; ballad maker, balladmonger; **bard, minstrel,** scop, fili, skald, jongleur, troubadour, *trovatore* [Ital], trouveur, *trouvère* [Fr], *Meistersinger* [Ger], minnesinger minor poet, major poet, arch-poet; laureate, **poet laureate;** occasional poet; **lyric poet;** epic poet; pastoral poet, pastoralist, idyllist, bucoliast [archaic]; rhapsodist, rhapsode; vers-librist, *vers libriste* [Fr]; elegist, librettist; lyricist, lyrist; odist; satirist; sonneteer; modernist, imagist, symbolist; Parnassian; beat poet.

14 **bad poet;** rhymester, rhymer; metrist; versemaker, versesmith, versifier, verseman, versemonger; poetling, **poetaster,** poeticule; balladmonger.

15 VERBS **poetize, versify,** verse, write *or* compose poetry, build the stately rime, sing deathless songs, make immortal verse; tune one's lyre, climb Parnassus, mount Pegasus; sing, "lisp in numbers" [Pope]; elegize; poeticize.

16 **rhyme,** assonate, alliterate; **scan;** jingle; cap verses *or* rhymes.

17 ADJS **poetic(al),** poetlike; **lyric(al), narrative,** dramatic, lyrico-dramatic; bardic; runic, skaldic; epic, heroic; mock-heroic, Hudibrastic; pastoral, bucolic, eclogic, idyllic, Theocritean; didactic; elegiac(al); dithyrambic, rhapsodic(al), Alcaic, Anacreontic, Homeric, Pindaric, sapphic; Castalian, Pierian; poetico-mythological; poetico-mystical, poetico-philosophic.

18 **metric(al),** prosodic(al); **rhythmic(al), measured,** cadenced, –semic; scanning; iambic, dactylic, spondaic, pyrrhic, trochaic, anapestic, antispastic; –stichous.

19 **rhyming; assonant,** assonantal; **alliterative;** jingling.

20 ADVS **poetically, lyrically; metrically, rhythmically,** in measure.

### 610. PROSE

.1 NOUNS **prose,** "words in their best order" [Coleridge]; prose fiction, nonfiction prose, expository prose; prose rhythm; prose style; poetic prose, polyphonic prose, prose poetry.

.2 **prosaism, prosaicism, prosaicness,** prosiness, **unpoeticalness; matter-of-factness,** unromanticism, unidealism; **unimaginativeness** 536; **plainness,** commonness, commonplaceness, unembellishedness; insipidness, flatness, vapidity; **dullness** 883.

.3 VERBS **prose,** write prose *or* in prose.

.4 ADJS **prose,** in prose; unversified, nonpoetic, nonmetrical.

.5 **prosaic, prosy,** prosing; unpoetic(al), poetryless; **plain, common, commonplace, ordinary,** unembellished, mundane; **matter-of-fact, unromantic, unidealistic,** unimpassioned; pedestrian, **unimaginative**

536.5; insipid, vapid, flat; humdrum, tiresome, **dull** 883.6.

### 611. SHOW BUSINESS

.1 NOUNS **show business,** show biz [informal], entertainment industry; **the theater, the footlights, the stage, the boards,** the scenes [archaic], traffic of the stage; stagedom, theater world, stage world, stageland, playland; **drama,** legitimate stage *or* theater, legit [slang], Broadway, off Broadway, off-off-Broadway; repertory drama *or* theater, stock; summer stock, strawhat *or* strawhat circuit [both informal]; **vaudeville,** variety; **burlesque; circus,** carnival; theatromania, theatrophobia.

.2 **dramatics;** dramaticism, dramatism; **theatrics,** theatricism, **theatricalism,** theatricality, staginess; theatricals, amateur theatricals; **histrionics,** histrionism; dramatic *or* histrionic *or* Thespian art; dramatic stroke, *coup de théâtre* [Fr]; **melodramatics,** sensationalism; **dramaturgy,** dramatic structure, play construction, dramatic form; dramatic irony.

.3 **theatercraft, stagecraft,** stagery, scenecraft; **showmanship.**

.4 **stage show, show; play,** stage play, piece, vehicle, work; **drama,** dramatic play; comedy drama; playlet, skit, sketch; well-made play, *pièce bien faite* [Fr]; closet drama; straight drama, legitimate drama; **melodrama,** sensational play; Grand Guignol; suspense drama, cliff hanger [slang]; Tom show; sociodrama, psychodrama; problem play; **pageant,** spectacle, extravaganza; mystery play, mystery, miracle play, miracle, morality play, morality; Passion play; pastoral, pastoral drama; masque, antimasque; charade; pantomime 568.14; improvisational drama, a happening; experimental theater, total theater; epic theater; documentary drama; theater of the absurd; theater of cruelty; tableau, *tableau vivant* [Fr]; dramalogue; monologue, monodrama; duologue, duodrama; dialogue; **vaudeville show,** vaudeville; **variety show; revue** *or* review, musical revue; minstrel show; burlesque show; music drama, opera, ballet 462.35; television drama *or* play *or* show, teleplay; radio drama *or* play *or* show; broadcast drama; dramatic series, serial, daytime serial, soap opera *or* soap [both informal]; quiz show, giveaway, giveaway show, panel show, talk show [informal]; situation comedy, sitcom [informal]; telethon; **hit** or hit show [both informal], gasser [slang], success, critical success, audience success, word-of-mouth success; failure, **flop** or bomb [both slang].

.5 **tragedy,** tragic drama; classical tragedy, Greek tragedy, Aeschylean tragedy, Sophoclean tragedy, Euripidean tragedy, Senecan tragedy; Renaissance tragedy; revenge tragedy, romantic tragedy, domestic tragedy; tragic flaw; buskin, cothurnus; tragic muse, Melpomene.

.6 **comedy;** tragicomedy; sentimental comedy, *comédie larmoyante* [Fr]; light comedy, comedietta; comedy of ideas, comedy of manners, realistic comedy, romantic comedy, comedy of humors, comedy of intrigue, domestic comedy, comedy of situation, **situation comedy,** black comedy, dark comedy, high comedy; comedy of character; genteel comedy; low comedy, broad or raw comedy, *comédie rosse* [Fr]; **burlesque;** mime, satyr play; **slapstick,** slapstick comedy; **farce,** farce comedy, exode; camp, high camp, low camp [all slang]; commedia dell'arte; harlequinade, *arlequinade* [Fr]; musical comedy, **musical** [informal]; comedy ballet; comic opera, burletta, *opera buffa* [Ital], *comédie bouffe* [Fr]; comic relief, comedy relief; comic muse, Thalia.

.7 (comedy symbols) sock, coxcomb, cap and bells, motley, bladder, slapstick.

.8 **act, scene, number, turn,** bit or shtick [both slang], routine [informal]; curtain raiser or lifter; introduction; expository scene; **prologue,** epilogue; **entr'acte,** intermezzo, intermission, interlude, *divertissement* [Fr], *divertimento* [Ital]; **finale,** afterpiece; exodus, exode; chaser [slang]; curtain call, curtain; hokum or hoke act [slang]; song and dance; burlesque act, striptease; stand-up comedy act; sketch, skit.

.9 **acting, playing,** playacting, performing, **performance,** taking a role or part; representation, portrayal, characterization, projection; impersonation, personation, miming, mimicking, mimicry, mimesis; pantomiming, mummery; ham or hammy acting or hamming or hamming up [all slang], overacting; stage presence; stage directions, **business,** stage business, *jeu de théâtre* [Fr], acting device; stunt or gag [both informal]; hokum or hoke [both slang]; buffoonery, slapstick; patter; stand-up comedy [informal].

.10 **repertoire, repertory;** stock.

.11 **role, part,** piece [slang]; cue, lines, side;

cast; **character,** person, personage; lead starring or lead role, fat part, leading man, leading woman or lady, hero, heroine; antihero; title role, protagonist, principal character; supporting role, supporting character; ingenue, *jeune première* [Fr]; soubrette; villain, heavy [informal] antagonist; bit, bit part, minor role feeder, straight part; walking part, walking on; actor 612.2.

.12 **engagement,** playing engagement, booking; **run; stand,** one-night stand; **circuit** vaudeville circuit, borscht circuit; tour date.

.13 **theatrical performance, performance show, presentation,** presentment, **production,** entertainment, stage presentation or performance; bill; **exhibit, exhibition** benefit performance, benefit; personal appearance, flesh show [slang]; tryout premiere, premier performance, debut farewell performance, swan song [slang].

.14 **production,** mounting, staging, putting on; stage management; **direction,** *mise-en-scène* [Fr]; **rehearsal,** dress rehearsal, walk-through, run-through.

.15 (shows) repertory show, rep show [slang]; **floor show;** variety show, vaudeville show; leg or girl or girly show [slang], burlesque show, hootchy-kootchy show, cooch or coochie show [slang]; magic show; **rodeo; circus,** the big top, **carnival, sideshow; puppet show,** fantoccini [pl], Punch-and-Judy show; peep show, raree-show; galanty show, shadow show, *ombres chinoises* [Fr]; light show.

.16 **motion picture, moving picture, movie** [informal], **picture,** picture show, motion-picture show, moving-picture show, **film,** flicker or flick [both informal], cinema [Brit], photoplay, photodrama, cine–; silent film, silent; talkie [informal], talking picture; **feature;** preview, sneak preview, trailer; selected short subject, **short;** documentary film, **documentary;** educational film; newsreel; Grade B movie; Western, horse opera or shoot-'em-up [both slang], spaghetti Western [informal]; horror picture; thriller or chiller or creepie [all slang]; pornographic film, nudie [informal], porno or skin flick [both slang]; animated cartoon, cartoon; 3-D; Cinemascope, Cinerama; black-and-white film, color film; Technicolor, underground film or movie; experimental film.

.17 **the cinema, the movies** or the pictures [both informal], the screen, the silver screen; art film, *cinéma vérité, nouvelle vague* [both Fr].

.18 **theater,** theatr(o)–; **playhouse, house,** theatron, odeum; **auditorium; opera house,** opera; **hall,** music hall, concert hall; **amphitheater;** circle theater, arena theater, theater-in-the-round; vaudeville theater; burlesque theater; **little theater,** community theater; open-air theater, outdoor theater; Greek theater; Elizabethan theater, Globe Theatre; showboat; cabaret, nightclub, club, night spot, *boîte de nuit* [Fr].

.19 **motion-picture theater,** moving-picture theater, movie theater [informal], movie house, picture palace *or* picture house [both Brit], cinema *or* cinema theater [both Brit], cinematograph *or* kinematograph [both Brit]; drive-in, drive-in theater; nickelodeon.

.20 **auditorium;** parquet, orchestra, **pit** [Brit]; **orchestra circle,** parquet circle, parterre; **dress circle;** fauteuil *or* theatre stall *or* **stall** [all Brit]; **box,** box seat, **loge,** *baignoire* [Fr]; **stage box;** proscenium boxes, parterre boxes; **balcony,** gallery; **peanut gallery** *or* paradise *or* nigger heaven [all slang]; standing room.

.21 **stage,** the boards; acting area, playing *or* performing area; apron, apron stage, forestage; proscenium stage, proscenium arch, proscenium; bridge; revolving stage; orchestra, pit, orchestra pit; **bandstand,** shell, band shell; stage right, R; stage left, L; backstage; **wings,** coulisse; dressing room, greenroom; flies, fly gallery, fly floor; gridiron, grid [informal]; board, lightboard, switchboard; dock; prompter's box.

.22 (stage requisites) **property, prop;** practical piece *or* prop [informal]; costume 231.9; theatrical makeup, makeup, greasepaint, blackface, clown white; spirit gum.

.23 **lights; footlights,** foots [informal], floats; floodlight, flood; bunch light; **limelight, spotlight,** spot [informal], arc light, arc, klieg light; color filter, medium, gelatin; dimmer; marquee; light plot.

.24 **setting, stage setting,** stage set, set, *mise-en-scène* [Fr].

.25 **scenery,** decor; **scene;** screen, **flat;** cyclorama; stage screw; side scene, **wing,** coulisse; border; tormentor, **teaser;** wingcut, woodcut; transformation, transformation scene; flipper; batten; counterweight; **curtain,** rag [slang], hanging; **drop,** drop scene, drop curtain, scrim, cloth; **backdrop,** back cloth [Brit]; act drop *or* cur-

tain; tab, tableau; fire curtain, curtain board, asbestos, asbestos board.

.26 **playbook, script,** text, libretto; promptbook; book; **score; scenario,** continuity, shooting script; scene plot; lines, actor's lines, cue, side.

.27 **dramatist; playwright,** playwriter, dramaturge; play doctor *or* play fixer [both informal]; dramatizer; **scriptwriter, scenario writer,** scenarist, scenarioist, **screenwriter; gagman,** joke writer, jokesmith; **librettist;** tragedian, comedian; farcist, *farceur, farceuse* [both Fr], farcer; melodramatist; monodramatist; mimographer; **choreographer.**

.28 **theater man,** theatrician; **showman,** exhibitor, **producer, impresario; director,** auteur; stage director, **stage manager;** set designer, scenewright; costume designer, costumer, *costumier, costumière* [both Fr]; wigmaker; makeup man *or* artist; prompter; callboy; playreader; master of ceremonies, MC *or* emcee [both informal]; ticket collector; usher, usherer, usherette; ringmaster, equestrian director; barker, ballyhoo man *or* spieler [both informal].

.29 **stage technician, stagehand,** machinist [archaic], sceneman, **sceneshifter;** flyman; carpenter; **electrician;** scene painter, scenic artist, scenewright.

.30 **agent, actor's agent,** playbroker, ten-percenter [slang]; **booking agent;** advance agent, advance man; publicity man *or* agent.

.31 **patron,** patroness; **backer, angel** [informal]; Dionysus.

.32 **playgoer, theatergoer;** attender 186.5, spectator 442, audience 448.6; moviegoer [informal], **motion-picture fan** [informal]; first-nighter; standee, groundling [archaic]; *claqueur* [Fr], hired applauder; pass holder, deadhead [informal].

.33 VERBS **dramatize,** theatricalize; melodramatize; scenarize; **present, stage, produce,** mount, **put on,** put on the stage; **put on a show;** try out, preview; give a performance; premiere; **open,** open a show, open a show cold [informal]; set the stage; ring up the curtain, ring down the curtain; **star, feature** [informal], bill, **headline,** give top billing to; succeed, make *or* be a hit [informal], be a gas *or* gasser [slang]; fail, flop *or* bomb [both slang].

.34 **act, perform, play,** playact, tread the boards, strut one's stuff [slang]; appear, **appear on the stage;** act like a trouper;

register; emotionalize, emote [informal]; pantomime, mime; patter; sketch; troupe, barnstorm [informal]; steal the show, upstage; make one's debut or bow, come out; act as foil or feeder, stooge [slang], be straight man for; star, play the lead, get top billing, have one's name in lights.

.35 enact, act out; represent, depict, portray; act or play or perform a part or role, take a part, sustain a part, act or play the part of; create a role or character; impersonate, personate; play opposite, support.

.36 overact, overdramatize, chew up the scenery [informal], act all over the stage; ham or ham it up [both informal]; mug [slang], grimace; spout, rant, roar, declaim, "out-herod Herod" [Shakespeare]; milk a scene; underact, throw away [informal].

.37 rehearse, practice, go through, run through, go over; go through one's part, read one's lines; con or study one's part; be a fast or slow study.

.38 ADJS dramatic, dramatical [archaic], dramaturgic(al); theatrical, histrionic, thespian; scenic; stagy; theaterlike, stagelike, spectacular; melodramatic; ham or hammy [both slang]; overacted, overplayed, milked [informal]; underacted, underplayed, thrown away; film, filmic, movie [informal], cinematic, cinematographic; monodramatic; vaudevillian; operatic; ballet, balletic; legitimate; stellar, all-star; stagestruck, starstruck; stageworthy, actor-proof.

.39 tragic, heavy; buskined, cothurned.

.40 comic, light; tragicomic(al), farcical, slapstick; camp or campy [both slang].

.41 ADVS on the stage or boards, before an audience, before the footlights; in the limelight or spotlight; onstage; downstage, upstage; backstage, off stage, behind the scenes; down left, DL; down right, DR; up left, UL; up right, UR.

## 612. ENTERTAINER

.1 NOUNS entertainer, public entertainer, performer; artist, artiste; impersonator, female impersonator; vaudevillian, vaudevillist; dancer 879.3, hoofer [slang]; song and dance man; chorus girl, show girl, chorine [informal]; coryphée; chorus boy or man; burlesque queen [informal], stripteaser, exotic dancer, ecdysiast; stripper or peeler or stripteuse [all slang]; dancing girl, nautch girl, belly dancer; go-go dancer; geisha, geisha girl; mountebank; magician, conjurer, prestidigitator,

sleight-of-hand artist; mummer, guiser or guisard [both Scot]; singer, musician 464.

.2 actor, player, stage player or performer, playactor, histrion, histrio, thespian, Roscius, theatrical [informal], trouper; actress; child actor; mummer, pantomime, pantomimist; monologist, diseur, diseuse, reciter; dramatizer; mime, mimer, mimic; strolling player, stroller; barnstormer [informal]; character actor, character man or woman, character; villain, antagonist; bad guy or heavy [both informal]; juvenile, ingenue; soubrette; foil, feeder or stooge [both slang], straight man; utility man; protean actor; matinee idol [informal].

.3 circus artist or performer; trapeze artist, aerialist, flier [informal]; high-wire artist, tightrope walker, slack-rope artist, equilibrist; acrobat, tumbler; bareback rider; juggler; lion tamer, sword swallower; snake charmer; clown; ringmaster, equestrian director.

.4 motion-picture actor, movie actor [informal]; movie star [informal], film star; starlet.

.5 ham or ham actor [both informal]; grimacer.

.6 lead, leading man or lady, principal, star, superstar, headliner, headline or feature attraction; hero, heroine, protagonist; juvenile lead, jeune premier, jeune première [both Fr]; first tragedian, heavy lead [informal]; prima donna, diva, singer 464.13; première danseuse, prima ballerina, danseur noble [Fr].

.7 supporting actor; support, supporting cast; supernumerary, super or supe [both informal], spear-carrier [informal], extra; bit player; walking gentleman or lady [slang], walk-on, mute; figurant, figurante; understudy, stand-in, standby, substitute.

.8 tragedian, tragedienne.

.9 comedian, comedienne, comic, funnyman; farcist, farcer, farceur, farceuse [both Fr]; stand-up comic or comedian [informal], light comedian, genteel comedian, low comedian, slapstick comedian, hokum or hoke comic [slang].

.10 buffoon, buffo [Ital], clown, fool, jester, zany, merry-andrew, jack-pudding, pickle-herring, motley fool, motley, wearer of the cap and bells; harlequin; Pantaloon, Pantalone; Punch, Punchinello, Pulcinella, Polichinelle; Punch and Judy; Hanswurst; Columbine; Harlequin; Scaramouch.

**.11 cast,** cast of characters, characters, persons of the drama, *dramatis personae* [L]; supporting cast; **company,** acting company, **troupe;** repertory company, stock company; ensemble, chorus, *corps de ballet* [Fr]; circus troupe.

### 613. UNCOMMUNICATIVENESS

**.1** NOUNS **uncommunicativeness,** closeness, indisposition to speak, disinclination to communicate; unconversableness, **unsociability** 923; **secretiveness** 614.1; lack of message *or* meaning, meaninglessness 547.

**.2 taciturnity, untalkativeness,** unloquaciousness; **silence** 451; **speechlessness,** wordlessness, dumbness, **muteness** 451.2; obmutescence; quietness, quietude; laconicalness, laconism, curtness, shortness, terseness; brusqueness, briefness, brevity, conciseness, economy *or* sparingness of words, pauciloquy [archaic].

**.3 reticence** *or* reticency; **reserve,** reservedness, restraint, **constraint;** guardedness, discreetness, discretion; suppression, repression; subduedness; backwardness, retirement; **aloofness, standoffishness,** distance, remoteness, **detachment,** withdrawal, withdrawnness; impersonality; **coolness,** coldness, frigidity, iciness, frostiness, chilliness; **inaccessibility, unapproachability; undemonstrativeness,** unexpansiveness, unaffability, uncongeniality; **introversion;** modesty, bashfulness 908.1–4; expressionlessness, blankness, impassiveness, impassivity.

**.4 prevarication, equivocation,** tergiversation, evasion, shuffle, fencing, dodging, parrying; *suppressio veri* [L]; weasel words.

**.5 man of few words,** clam [informal], laconic [archaic]; Spartan, Laconian.

**.6** VERBS **keep to oneself,** keep one's own counsel; not open one's mouth, not say a word, stand mute, **hold one's tongue** 451.5; have little to say, refuse comment, say neither yes nor no, waste no words, save one's breath; retire; **keep one's distance,** keep at a distance, keep oneself to oneself, **stand aloof,** hold oneself aloof; keep secret 614.7.

**.7 prevaricate, equivocate,** waffle [informal], tergiversate, evade, dodge, sidestep, parry, duck, weasel [informal], palter; hum and haw, **hem and haw,** back and fill; **mince words,** mince the truth, euphemize.

**.8** ADJS **uncommunicative,** indisposed *or* disinclined to communicate; unconversa-

tional, unconversable [archaic]; **unsociable** 923.5; **secretive** 614.15; meaningless 547.6.

**.9 taciturn, untalkative,** unloquacious, indisposed to talk; **silent, speechless,** wordless, mum; **mute** 451.12, dumb, quiet; close, closemouthed, close-tongued, snug [dial], tight-lipped; tongue-tied, word-bound; **laconic,** curt, brief, terse, brusque, short, concise, **sparing of words,** economical of words.

**.10 reticent, reserved,** restrained, constrained; **suppressed,** repressed; subdued; guarded, discreet; backward, **retiring,** shrinking; **aloof, standoffish,** offish [informal], standoff, **distant,** remote, removed, **detached,** Olympian, withdrawn; impersonal; **cool,** cold, frigid, icy, frosty, chilled, chilly; **inaccessible, unapproachable,** forbidding; **undemonstrative,** unexpansive, unaffable, uncongenial, ungenial; **introverted;** modest, bashful 908.9–12; expressionless, blank, impassive.

**.11 prevaricating, equivocal,** tergiversating, tergiversant, **evasive,** weasel-worded.

### 614. SECRECY

**.1** NOUNS **secrecy,** secretness, airtight secrecy, close secrecy; crypticness; the dark; hiddenness, **concealment** 615; **secretiveness,** closeness; discreetness, discretion, **uncommunicativeness** 613; **evasiveness,** evasion, subterfuge; hugger-mugger, hugger-muggery.

**.2 privacy,** retirement, isolation, sequestration, seclusion; incognito, anonymity; **confidentialness,** confidentiality; closed meeting, executive session, private conference.

**.3 veil of secrecy, veil,** curtain, pall, wraps; iron curtain, "curtains of fog and iron" [Churchill], bamboo curtain; wall *or* barrier of secrecy; **suppression,** repression, stifling, smothering; **censorship,** blackout [informal], **hush-up; seal of secrecy,** official secrecy; security, ironbound security; pledge *or* oath of secrecy.

**.4 stealth,** stealthiness, **furtiveness, clandestineness,** clandestinity, clandestine behavior, **surreptitiousness, covertness,** slyness, shiftiness, sneakiness, slinkiness, underhand dealing, undercover *or* underground activity; prowl, prowling; stalking.

**.5 secret, confidence;** private *or* personal matter, privity [archaic]; confidential *or* **privileged communication;** deep, dark secret; solemn secret; guarded secret, classified information, restricted information;

mystery, enigma, arcanum; esoterica, cabala, the occult, hermetism, hermeticism, hermetics; deep *or* profound secret, sealed book, mystery of mysteries; skeleton in the closet *or* cupboard.

.6 **cryptography,** cryptanalysis, cryptoanalytics; **code, cipher;** secret language; **secret writing,** coded message, cryptogram, cryptograph; secret *or* invisible *or* sympathetic ink; cryptographer.

.7 VERBS **keep secret, keep mum, veil,** keep dark; keep it a deep, dark secret; secrete, conceal 615.7; keep to oneself 613.6, keep *in petto,* bosom, keep close, keep snug [dial], keep back, keep from, **withhold,** hold out on [slang]; not let it go further, keep within these walls, keep within the bosom of the lodge, keep between us; **not tell,** hold one's tongue 451.5, never let on [informal], make no sign, not breathe a word, be the soul of discretion; **not give away** [informal], "tell it not in Gath" [Bible], **keep it under one's hat** [informal], keep under wraps [informal], keep buttoned up [informal], keep one's own counsel; play dumb; not let the right hand know what the left is doing; keep in ignorance, keep *or* leave in the dark; classify; file and forget.

.8 **hush up, hush,** hush-hush, shush, huggermugger; **suppress,** repress, **stifle,** muffle, **smother,** squash, quash, squelch, kill, sit on *or* upon, put the lid on [slang]; **censor,** black out [informal].

.9 **tell confidentially,** tell for one's ears only, mention privately, **whisper, breathe, whisper in the ear;** tell one a secret; take aside, see one alone, talk to in private, speak in privacy.

.10 **code, encode, encipher, cipher.**

.11 ADJS **secret,** close, closed, cryptic, dark; unuttered, unrevealed, undivulged, undisclosed, unspoken, untold; **hush-hush** [informal], **top secret,** classified, restricted, under wraps [informal], under security *or* security restrictions; **censored,** suppressed, stifled, smothered, hushed-up, under the seal *or* ban of secrecy; **unrevealable, undivulgable, undisclosable, untellable,** unwhisperable, unbreatheable, unutterable; latent, ulterior, concealed, hidden 615.11; arcane, esoteric, occult, cabalistic, hermetic; enigmatic, mysterious 549.18.

.12 **covert, clandestine,** quiet, unobtrusive, hugger-mugger, hidlings [Scot], **surreptitious, undercover,** underground, under-the-counter, under-the-table, back-door,

hole-and-corner [informal], underhand, **underhanded; furtive, stealthy,** privy, backstairs, **sly, shifty, sneaky,** sneaking, skulking, slinking, slinky, feline.

.13 **private, privy; intimate, inmost,** innermost, interior, inward, **personal;** closet; **secluded, sequestered,** isolated, withdrawn, retired; incognito, anonymous.

.14 **confidential,** auricular, inside [slang], esoteric; *in petto* [Ital], close to one's chest [informal], under one's hat [informal]; **off the record,** not for the record, not to be minuted, within these four walls, in the bosom of the lodge, for no other ears, eyes-only, between us; not to be quoted, not for publication *or* release; not for attribution; unquotable, unpublishable, sealed; sensitive, privileged, under privilege.

.15 **secretive,** secret, close, dark; discreet; evasive, shifty; **uncommunicative, closemouthed** 613.8,9.

.16 coded, encoded; ciphered, enciphered; cryptographic(al).

.17 ADVS **secretly, in secret,** in *or* up one's sleeve; nobody the wiser; **covertly,** in hidlings [Scot], **undercover,** *à couvert* [Fr], under the cloak of; **behind the scenes,** in the background, in a corner, in the dark, in darkness, behind the veil *or* curtain, behind the veil of secrecy; *sub rosa* [L], under the rose; underground; *sotto voce* [Ital], under the breath, with bated breath, in a whisper.

.18 **surreptitiously, clandestinely, secretively,** furtively, stealthily, slyly, shiftily, sneakily, sneakingly, skulkingly, slinkingly, slinkily; by stealth, **on the sly, on the quiet,** on the q.t. [both slang], *à la dérobée* [Fr], *en tapinois* [Fr], behind one's back, by a side door, **like a thief in the night,** underhand, underhandedly, under the table, in holes and corners *or* in a hole-and-corner way [both informal].

.19 **privately,** privily, **in private,** in privacy, in privy; apart, aside; **behind closed doors,** *januis clausis* [L], *à huis clos* [Fr], *in camera* [L], in chambers, in secret *or* closed meeting, in executive session, in private conference.

.20 **confidentially, in confidence,** in strict confidence, under the seal of secrecy, **off the record; between ourselves,** strictly between us, *entre nous* [Fr], *inter nos* [L], for your ears only, between you and me, from me to you, between you and me and the bedpost *or* lamppost [informal].

## 615. CONCEALMENT

.1 NOUNS concealment, hiding, secretion; burial, burying, interment, putting away; covering, covering up, masking, screening 228.1; mystification, obscuration; darkening, obscurement, clouding 337.6; hiddenness, concealedness, covertness, occultation; secrecy 614; uncommunicativeness 613; invisibility 445; subterfuge, deception 618.

.2 veil, curtain, cover, screen 228.2; wraps; disguise 618.10.

.3 ambush, ambushment, ambuscade, guetapens [Fr]; surveillance, shadowing 485.9; lurking hole or place; blind, stalkinghorse; booby trap, trap 618.11.

.4 hiding place, hideaway, hideout, hidey hole [slang], hiding, concealment, cover, secret place; recess, corner, dark corner, nook, cranny, niche; hole, bolt-hole, foxhole, funk hole, dugout, lair, den; asylum, sanctuary, retreat, refuge 700; covert, coverture, undercovert; cache, stash [informal]; cubbyhole, cubby.

.5 secret passage, covert way, secret exit; back way, back door, side door; bolt-hole, escape route, escape hatch; secret staircase, escalier dérobé [Fr], back stairs; underground, underground route, underground railroad.

.6 VERBS conceal, hide, ensconce; cover, cover up, blind, screen, cloak, veil, curtain, blanket, shroud, enshroud, envelop; disguise, camouflage, mask, dissemble; whitewash [informal]; gloss over, varnish, slur over; distract attention from; obscure, obfuscate, cloud, becloud, befog, throw out a smoke screen, shade, throw into the shade; eclipse, occult; put out of sight, sweep under the rug, keep under cover; cover up one's tracks, lay a false scent, hide one's trail; hide one's light under a bushel.

.7 secrete, hide away, keep hidden, put away, store away, stow away, file and forget, bottle up, lock up, seal up, put out of sight; keep secret 614.7; cache, stash [informal], deposit, plant [slang]; bury; bosom, embosom [archaic].

.8 (hide oneself) hide, conceal oneself, take cover, hide out [informal], hide away, go into hiding, go to ground; stay in hiding, lie hid or hidden, lie low [informal], lie perdue, lie snug or close [dial], lie doggo or sit tight [both slang], burrow [archaic], hole up [slang], go underground; play peekaboo or bopeep or hide and seek;

keep out of sight, retire from sight, drop from sight, disappear 447.2, crawl or retreat into one's shell, keep in the background, stay in the shade; disguise oneself, masquerade, take an assumed name, change one's identity, go under an alias, remain anonymous, be incognito, go under false colors, wear a mask.

.9 lurk, couch; lie in wait, lay wait; sneak, skulk, slink, prowl, nightwalk, steal, creep, pussyfoot [slang], gumshoe [slang], tiptoe; stalk, shadow 485.34.

.10 ambush, ambuscade, waylay; lie in ambush, lay wait for, lie in wait for, lay for [informal]; set a trap for 618.18.

.11 ADJS concealed, hidden, hid, occult, recondite [archaic], blind, adel(o)–, crypt-(o)– or krypt(o)–; covered 228.31; covert, under cover, under wraps [informal]; obscured, obfuscated, clouded, clouded over, wrapped in clouds, in a cloud or fog or mist or haze, beclouded, befogged; eclipsed, in eclipse, under an eclipse; in the wings; buried; underground; close, secluded, secluse, sequestered; in purdah, under house arrest, incommunicado; obscure, abstruse, mysterious 549.15–18; secret 614.11,12; unknown 477.17, latent 546.5.

.12 unrevealed, undisclosed, undivulged, unexposed; unapparent, invisible, unseen, unperceived, unspied, undetected; undiscovered, unexplored, untraced, untracked; unexplained, unsolved.

.13 disguised, camouflaged, in disguise; masked, masquerading; incognito, incog [informal].

.14 in hiding, hidden out, under cover, in a dark corner, lying hid, doggo [slang]; in ambush or ambuscade; waiting concealed, lying in wait; in the wings; lurking, skulking, prowling, sneaking, stealing; pussyfooted, pussyfoot, on tiptoe; stealthy, furtive, surreptitious 614.12.

.15 concealing, hiding, obscuring; covering 228.34; unrevealing, nonrevealing, undisclosing.

## 616. FALSENESS

.1 NOUNS falseness, falsehood, falsity, inveracity, untruth, truthlessness, untrueness; fallaciousness, fallacy, erroneousness 518.1.

.2 spuriousness, phoniness [slang], bogusness [informal], ungenuineness, unauthenticity, unrealness, artificiality, factitiousness, syntheticness.

.3 sham, fakery, faking, falsity, feigning, pretending; feint, pretext, **pretense**, hollow pretense, **pretension, false pretense** *or* **pretension;** humbug, humbuggery; **bluff,** bluffing, four-flushing [informal]; speciousness, meretriciousness; cheating, fraud; imposture 618.6; deception, delusion 618.1; acting, playacting; representation, **simulation,** simulacrum; dissembling, **dissemblance, dissimulation;** seeming, semblance, appearance, face, ostentation, **show, false show,** outward show, false air; window dressing, front, **false front, façade,** gloss, varnish; gilt; color, coloring, false color; masquerade, disguise 618.10; posture, pose, posing, attitudinizing; affectation 903.

.4 **falseheartedness, falseness,** doubleheartedness, doubleness of heart, doubleness, **duplicity, two-facedness,** double-facedness, **double-dealing,** ambidexterity; **dishonesty,** improbity, lack of integrity, Machiavellianism, bad faith; low cunning, **cunning,** artifice, wile 735.1–3; **deceitfulness** 618.3; faithlessness, treachery 975.5,6.

.5 **insincerity, uncandidness,** uncandor, **unfrankness,** disingenuousness; emptiness, hollowness; mockery, hollow mockery; crossed fingers, tongue in cheek, unseriousness; sophistry, jesuitry, casuistry 483.1.

.6 **hypocrisy,** hypocriticalness; Tartuffery, Tartuffism, Pecksniffery, pharisaism, **sanctimony** 1029, sanctimoniousness, religiosity, false piety, ostentatious devotion; **mealymouthedness, unctuousness,** oiliness; **cant,** mummery, snuffling [archaic], **mouthing; lip service;** tokenism; token gesture, empty gesture; sweet talk *or* soft soap [both informal]; crocodile tears.

.7 **quackery,** quackishness, quackism, **mountebankery, charlatanry,** charlatanism; **imposture; humbug,** humbuggery.

.8 **untruthfulness, dishonesty,** falsehood, **unveracity,** unveraciousness, truthlessness, mendaciousness, **mendacity;** credibility gap; **lying, fibbing,** fibbery, pseudology; pathological lying, mythomania, *pseudologia phantastica* [L].

.9 **falsification,** falsifying; confabulation; **perversion, distortion,** straining; **misrepresentation,** misconstruction, misstatement, coloring, false coloring, miscoloring; **exaggeration** 617; **prevarication,** equivocation 613.4; **perjury,** false swearing, oath breaking.

.10 **fabrication, invention, concoction;** canard; **forgery; fiction,** figment, **myth,** fable, romance, extravaganza.

.11 **lie, falsehood,** falsity, **untruth,** untruism, mendacity, **prevarication, fib,** taraddidle [informal], flimflam *or* flam, *blague* [Fr]; **fiction,** pious fiction, legal fiction; **story** [informal], **trumped-up story,** farrago; **yarn** [informal], **tale,** fairy tale [informal], ghost story; farfetched story, tall tale *or* **tall story** [both informal], **cock-and-bull story,** fish story [informal]; exaggeration 617; half-truth, stretching of the truth, slight stretching, white lie, little white lie; *suggestio falsi* [L]; a pack of lies.

.12 monstrous lie, consummate lie, deep-dyed falsehood, out-and-out lie, **whopper** [informal], gross *or* flagrant *or* shameless falsehood, **barefaced lie, dirty lie** [slang]; **slander, libel** 971.3; the big lie.

.13 **fake, fakement** [informal], **phony** [slang], **rip-off** [slang], **sham, mock, imitation,** simulacrum, dummy; paste, tinsel, *clinquant* [Fr], pinchbeck, shoddy, junk; **counterfeit, forgery;** put-up job *or* frame-up [both informal], put-on [informal]; **hoax, cheat, fraud, swindle** 618.7–9; whited sepulcher, whitewash job [informal]; impostor 619.6.

.14 **humbug,** humbuggery; **bunk** [slang], **bunkum;** hooey *or* hoke *or* hokum [all slang], **bosh** [informal], bull *or* **bullshit** *or* balls *or* crap [all slang], baloney [slang], flimflam, flam, claptrap, moonshine, eyewash, hogwash, gammon [informal], *blague* [Fr], jiggery-pokery [Brit].

.15 VERBS ring false, **not ring true.**

.16 **falsify, belie, misrepresent,** miscolor; misstate, misquote, misreport, miscite; overstate, understate; **pervert, distort,** strain, warp, **slant, twist;** garble; put a false appearance upon, give a false coloring, give a color to, **color, gild, gloss, gloss over,** whitewash, varnish; fudge [informal], dress up, titivate, embellish, embroider, trick *or* prink out; deodorize, make smell like roses; **disguise, camouflage, mask.**

.17 **tamper with, manipulate, fake, juggle,** sophisticate, **doctor** *or* **cook** [both informal], rig; pack, stack; **adulterate** 44.13; retouch; **load; salt,** plant [slang], salt a mine.

.18 **fabricate, invent, manufacture, trump up, make up, hatch, concoct, cook up** [informal], fudge [informal], fake, hoke up [slang]; **counterfeit, forge;** fantasize, fantasize about.

.19 **lie, tell a lie,** falsify, speak falsely, speak with forked tongue [informal], be untruthful, trifle with the truth, deviate from the truth, **fib, story** [informal]; **stretch the truth,** strain *or* bend the truth; draw the longbow; **exaggerate** 617.3; lie flatly, lie in one's throat, lie through one's teeth, lie like a trooper, **prevaricate**, equivocate 613.7; deceive, mislead 618.13,15.

.20 swear falsely, forswear oneself [archaic], perjure oneself, bear false witness.

.21 **sham, fake** [informal], **feign, counterfeit, simulate,** gammon [informal]; **pretend,** make a pretense, **make believe, make a show of,** make like [informal], make as if *or* as though; go through the motions [informal]; let on, let on like [informal]; **affect,** profess, **assume, put on; dissimulate, dissemble,** cover up; **act, play, playact, put on an act** [informal], act *or* play a part; **put up a front** [informal], put on a front *or* false front [informal]; four-flush [slang], **bluff,** pull *or* put up a bluff [informal]; **play possum** [informal], roll over and play dead.

.22 **pose as, masquerade as,** impersonate, pass for, assume the guise *or* identity of, set up for, act the part of, represent oneself to be, claim *or* pretend to be, **make false pretenses,** go under false pretenses, **sail under false colors.**

.23 **be hypocritical, act** *or* **play the hypocrite;** cant, be holier than the Pope, reek of piety; snuffle [archaic], snivel, mouth; give mouth honor, render *or* give lip service; sweet-talk, soft-soap, blandish 970.5.

.24 **play a double game** *or* **role, play both ends against the middle,** work both sides of the street, have it both ways at once, have one's cake and eat it too, run with the hare and hunt with the hounds [Brit]; two-time [informal].

.25 ADJS **false, untrue, truthless, not true,** void *or* devoid of truth, contrary to fact, in error, **fallacious, erroneous** 518.16; unfounded 483.13.

.26 **spurious, ungenuine, unauthentic,** suppositious, bastard, **pseudo, quasi,** apocryphal, **fake** [informal], **phony** [slang], **sham, mock, counterfeit,** colorable, **bogus, queer** [slang], **dummy, make-believe,** so-called, **imitation** 22.8, noth(o)–; not what it is cracked up to be [slang]; **falsified;** dressed up, titivated, embellished, embroidered; garbled; twisted, distorted, warped, perverted; **simulated, faked, feigned,** colored, fictitious, fictive, **counterfeited, pretended, affected, assumed, put-on; artificial, synthetic,** ersatz; unreal; factitious, unnatural, man-made; illegitimate; *soi-disant* [Fr], self-styled;

pinchbeck, brummagem [Brit], tinsel, shoddy, tin, junky.

.27 **specious, meretricious,** gilded, tinsel, **seeming,** apparent, colored, colorable, plausible, **ostensible.**

.28 **quack, quackish; charlatan, charlatanish,** charlatanic.

.29 **fabricated,** invented, manufactured, **concocted, hatched, trumped-up, made-up,** put-up, cooked-up [informal]; **forged;** fictitious, fictional, **figmental, mythical,** fabulous, legendary; fantastic, fantasied, fancied.

.30 **tampered** with, **manipulated,** cooked *or* doctored [both informal], juggled, **rigged,** engineered; packed.

.31 **falsehearted, false,** false-principled, false-dealing; **double,** duplicitous, ambidextrous, **double-dealing,** doublehearted, double-minded, double-tongued, double-faced, **two-faced,** Janus-faced; Machiavellian, dishonest; **crooked, deceitful** 618.20; artful, cunning, crafty 735.12; faithless, perfidious, treacherous 975.20,21.

.32 **insincere, uncandid, unfrank, mealy-mouthed,** disingenuous; dishonest; **empty, hollow;** tongue in cheek, unserious; sophistic(al), jesuitic(al), casuistic 483.10.

.33 **hypocritic(al),** canting, Pecksniffian, pharisaic(al), pharisean, **sanctimonious, goody-goody** [informal], holier than the Pope, holier-than-thou, simon-pure; **mealymouthed, unctuous, oily.**

.34 **untruthful, dishonest, unveracious,** unveridical, truthless, **lying, mendacious;** perjured, forsworn; prevaricating, equivocal 613.11.

.35 ADVS **falsely, untruly,** truthlessly; **erroneously** 518.20; **untruthfully,** unveraciously; **spuriously,** ungenuinely; artificially, synthetically; unnaturally, factitiously; speciously, seemingly, apparently, plausibly, ostensibly; nominally, in name only.

.36 **insincerely,** uncandidly; emptily, hollowly; unseriously; **hypocritically,** mealymouthedly, unctuously.

## 617. EXAGGERATION

.1 NOUNS **exaggeration, exaggerating; overstatement,** big *or* tall talk [informal], **hyperbole,** hyperbolism; **superlative; extravagance,** profuseness, **prodigality** 854; **magnification, enlargement,** amplification [archaic], dilation, dilatation, **inflation,** expansion, blowing up, puffing up, aggrandizement; **heightening,** enhancement; **stretching,** overemphasis; overestimation 497; **exaggerated lengths, extreme,** overkill, exorbitance, inordinacy, **excess** 663; burlesque, travesty, caricature; sensationalism, puffery *or* ballyhoo [both informal], touting, huckstering; grandiloquence 601.

.2 **overreaction, much ado about nothing,** storm *or* tempest in a teapot, making a mountain out of a molehill.

.3 VERBS **exaggerate,** hyperbolize; **overstate,** overspeak [archaic], overreach, **overdraw,** overcharge; overstress; **overdo, carry too far, go to extremes;** overestimate 497.2; overpraise, oversell, tout, puff *or* ballyhoo [both informal]; **stretch,** stretch the truth, draw the longbow; **magnify,** amplify [archaic]; aggrandize, build up; pile *or* lay it on [informal], **lay it on thick** [informal], lay it on with a trowel [slang]; pile Pelion on Ossa; talk big [informal], talk in superlatives, deal in the marvelous, make much of; **overreact,** make a mountain out of a molehill; caricature, travesty, burlesque.

.4 ADJS **exaggerated,** hyperbolic(al), **magnified,** amplified [archaic], **inflated,** aggrandized; **stretched,** disproportionate, **blown up out of all proportion;** overpraised, oversold, touted, puffed *or* ballyhooed [both informal]; overemphasized, overemphatic, overstressed; **overstated, overdrawn; overdone,** overwrought; overestimated 497.3; overlarge, overgreat; **extreme,** exorbitant, inordinate, **excessive** 663.16; **superlative, extravagant,** profuse, **prodigal** 854.8; high-flown, grandiloquent 601.8.

.5 **exaggerating, exaggerative,** hyperbolic(al).

## 618. DECEPTION

.1 NOUNS **deception, calculated deception, deceptiveness, subterfuge,** snow job [slang], song and dance [informal], **trickiness; falseness** 616; fallaciousness, fallacy; self-deception, fond illusion, wishful thinking, willful misconception; vision, hallucination, phantasm, mirage, will-o'-the-wisp, **delusion,** delusiveness, illusion 519; deceiving, **victimization, dupery;** bamboozlement [informal], hoodwinking; swindling, defrauding, conning, flimflam *or* flimflammery [both informal]; fooling, befooling, tricking, **kidding** *or* putting on [both informal]; spoofing *or* spoofery [both informal]; bluffing; circumvention, overreaching, outwitting; ensnarement, entrapment, enmeshment, entanglement.

.2 **misleading, misguidance, misdirection;** bum steer [slang]; misinformation 563.1.

.3 **deceit, deceitfulness, guile, falseness,** insidiousness, **underhandedness; shiftiness, furtiveness,** surreptitiousness, indirection; hypocrisy 616.6; **falseheartedness, duplicity** 616.4; **treacherousness** 975.6; **artfulness, craft, cunning** 735; sneakiness 614.4; sneak attack.

.4 **chicanery,** chicane, **skulduggery** [informal], **trickery,** dodgery, pettifogging, pettifoggery, *supercherie* [Fr], **artifice,** sleight, machination; **sharp practice, underhand dealing, foul play;** connivery, connivance, collusion, conspiracy, covin.

.5 **juggling,** jugglery, **trickery,** *escamotage* [Fr], prestidigitation, conjuration, **legerdemain, sleight of hand;** mumbo jumbo, **hocus-pocus,** hanky-panky [informal], monkey business, hokey-pokey [informal], jiggery-pokery [Brit].

.6 **trick, artifice, device,** ploy, gambit, stratagem, **scheme,** design, *ficelle* [Fr], **subterfuge,** blind, **ruse, wile,** chouse [informal], shift, **dodge,** artful dodge, sleight, pass, feint, fetch, chicanery; **bluff;** gimmick, joker, catch; curve, curve-ball; googly *or* bosey *or* wrong'un [all Brit informal]; **dirty trick,** dirty deal, fast deal, scurvy trick; sleight of hand, sleight-of-hand trick, hocus-pocus [archaic]; juggle, juggler's trick; **bag of tricks,** tricks of the trade.

.7 **hoax, deception,** spoof [informal], **humbug, flam, fake** *or* fakement [both informal], **rip-off** [slang], sham; mare's nest.

.8 **fraud, fraudulence** *or* fraudulency, **dishonesty;** imposture; imposition, cheat, **cheating,** cozenage, diddle *or* diddling [both slang], **swindle,** scam [slang], flimflam *or* flam, dodge [slang], **gyp** [slang], ramp [Brit slang], fishy transaction, piece of sharp practice; **gyp joint** [slang]; racket [informal], illicit business 826; **graft** [informal], grift [slang]; bunco; cardsharping; ballot-box stuffing, gerrymandering.

.9 **confidence game, con game** [slang], **skin game** [slang], **bunco game; shell game,** thimblerig, thimblerigging; bucket shop, boiler room [slang]; goldbrick.

.10 **disguise, camouflage,** protective coloration; **false colors, false front** 616.3; **incognito;** smoke screen; **masquerade,** masque, mummery; **mask,** visor, vizard, vizard mask [archaic], false face, domino, domino mask.

.11 **trap, gin; pitfall,** trapfall, deadfall; flytrap, mousetrap, mole trap, rattrap, bear trap; deathtrap, firetrap; Venus's flytrap, Dionaea; spring gun, set gun; baited trap; **booby trap, mine; decoy** 619.5, 650.2.

.12 **snare**, springe; noose, lasso, lariat; bola; **net**, trawl, dragnet, seine, purse seine, pound net, gill net; cobweb; **meshes, toils; fishhook, hook, sniggle; bait**, ground bait; **lure**, fly, jig, squid, plug, wobbler, spinner; lime, birdlime.

.13 VERBS **deceive, beguile, trick, hoax, dupe, gammon, gull**, pigeon, **bamboozle** [informal], snow [slang], **hornswaggle** [slang], diddle [slang], **humbug, take in,** hocuspocus [informal], string along, **put something over or across,** slip one over on [informal], pull a fast one on; **delude,** mock; **betray,** let down, leave in the lurch, leave holding the bag, play one false, **doublecross** [informal], cheat on; two-time [informal]; juggle, conjure; **bluff;** cajole, **circumvent,** get around, forestall; **overreach,** outreach, outwit, outmaneuver, outsmart.

.14 **fool,** befool, make a fool of, practice on one's credulity, **pull one's leg,** make an ass of; **trick; spoof or kid** [both informal], put one on [informal]; **play a trick on,** play a practical joke upon, send on a fool's errand; fake out [slang].

.15 **mislead, misguide, misdirect,** lead astray, lead up the garden path, **give a bum steer** [slang]; throw off the scent, put on a false scent, drag or draw a red herring across the trail; throw a curve or curve ball, bowl a googly or bosey or wrong 'un [Brit informal]; misinform 563.3.

.16 **hoodwink,** blindfold, blind, blind one's eyes, blear the eyes of [archaic], throw dust in one's eyes, **pull the wool over one's eyes.**

.17 **cheat, victimize, gull,** pigeon, fudge, **swindle, defraud,** practice fraud upon, scam [slang], euchre, **con,** finagle, **fleece,** shave [dial], mulct, beat [informal], rook [informal], **gyp,** fob [archaic], **bilk, flam** or flimflam [both informal], **diddle** [slang], **screw, have** [informal], ramp [Brit slang], **stick** [informal], **sting** [slang], burn [informal], **gouge** [informal], **chisel** [slang], cozen, cog [archaic]; chouse or hocus or hocus-pocus [all informal]; **do out of,** chouse out of [informal], beguile of or out of; **play or take for a sucker** [slang], make a patsy of [slang], **sell one a bill of goods** [informal], do in [slang], obtain under false pretenses; live by one's wits; bunco, play a bunco game; sell gold bricks [informal]; shortchange, shortweight; stack the cards or deck, pack the

deal [slang], deal off the bottom of the deck, play with marked cards; cog the dice, load the dice; thimblerig; crib [slang]; throw a fight or game [informal], take a dive [slang].

.18 **trap,** entrap, gin, catch, catch out, catch in a trap; **ensnare, snare, hook, hook in,** sniggle, noose; inveigle 650.4; net, mesh, **enmesh,** snarl [archaic], ensnarl, wind, tangle, entangle, entoil, enweb; trip, trip up; **set or lay a trap for,** bait the hook, spread the toils; lime, birdlime; **lure,** allure, **decoy** 650.4.

.19 ADJS **deceptive, deceiving, misleading,** beguiling, **false, fallacious,** delusive, delusory; hallucinatory, illusive, **illusory** 519.9; tricky, trickish, tricksy [archaic], catchy; fishy [informal], questionable, dubious.

.20 **deceitful, false;** fraudulent, sharp, **guileful, insidious,** slippery, **shifty, tricky,** trickish, finagling, chiseling [slang]; underhand, **underhanded, furtive, surreptitious,** indirect; collusive, covinous; **falsehearted, two-faced** 616.31; **treacherous** 975.21; sneaky 614.12; **cunning,** artful, **wily, crafty** 735.12; calculating, scheming 654.14.

.21 ADVS **deceptively,** beguilingly, **falsely,** fallaciously, delusively, **trickily, misleadingly,** with intent to deceive; under false colors, under cover of, under the garb of, in disguise.

.22 **deceitfully, fraudulently, guilefully,** insidiously, **shiftily, trickily; underhandedly,** furtively, surreptitiously, indirectly, like a thief in the night; **treacherously** 975.25.

## 619. DECEIVER

.1 NOUNS **deceiver, deluder, duper,** misleader, **beguiler, bamboozler** [informal]; actor, playactor [informal], role-player; **dissembler,** dissimulator; **double-dealer,** Machiavelli, Machiavel, Machiavellian; dodger, Artful Dodger [Dickens], **counterfeiter, forger, faker;** plagiarizer, plagiarist; entrancer, **enchanter,** charmer, befuddler, hypnotizer, mesmerizer; **seducer,** Don Juan, Casanova; tease, teaser; jilt, jilter; gay deceiver; **fooler, joker,** jokester, **hoaxer,** practical joker; spoofer, **kidder,** ragger, leg-puller [all informal].

.2 **trickster,** tricker; **juggler,** sleight-of-hand performer, magician, illusionist, conjurer, **prestidigitator,** escamoteur [Fr].

.3 **cheat, cheater; swindler, defrauder,** cozener, **gypper or gyp artist** [both slang], flimflammer or flimflam man [both informal], **blackleg** [informal], magsman

[Brit slang], **chiseler** [slang], bilker [informal], diddler [informal], **crook** [slang], juggler; two-timer [informal].

.4 **sharper, sharp,** sharpie [informal], **shark,** jackleg [informal], slicker [informal]; spieler, pitchman; **confidence man, con man** or **con artist** [both informal], **bunco artist, bunco steerer** [slang], carpetbagger; **horse trader,** horse coper [Brit]; **cardsharp,** cardsharper; thimblerigger; shortchanger; **shyster** or pettifogger [both informal]; land shark, land pirate, landgrabber, mortgage shark; crimp.

.5 **shill,** decoy, **come-on man** [slang], plant, capper, stool pigeon, stoolie [informal]; *agent provocateur* [Fr].

.6 **impostor, ringer; impersonator; pretender;** sham, shammer, **humbug,** *blagueur* [Fr], **fraud** [informal], **fake** or **faker** [both informal], **phony** [slang], **fourflusher** [slang], bluff, bluffer; **charlatan, quack,** quacksalver, quackster, **mountebank,** saltimbanco; **wolf in sheep's clothing,** ass in lion's skin, jackdaw in peacock's feathers; poser, poseur; malingerer.

.7 **masquerader,** masker; **impersonator,** personator; mummer, guiser or guisard [both Scot]; incognito, incognita.

.8 **hypocrite, phony** [slang], sanctimonious fraud, pharisee, whited sepulcher, **canter,** snuffler, mealymouth, "a saint abroad and a devil at home" [Bunyan]; Tartuffe, Pecksniff, Uriah Heep, Joseph Surface; false friend, fair-weather friend; summer soldier.

.9 **liar, fibber,** fibster, fabricator, fabulist, pseudologist; falsifier; **prevaricator,** equivocator, palterer; **storyteller;** yarner, yarn spinner, spinner of yarns [all informal]; Ananias; Satan, Father of Lies; Baron Munchausen; Sir John Mandeville; consummate liar, "liar of the first magnitude" [Congreve], *menteur à triple étage* [Fr], dirty liar; pathological liar, mythomaniac, pseudologue, confirmed or habitual liar; **perjurer,** false witness.

.10 **traitor, treasonist, betrayer, quisling, rat** [slang], serpent, snake, cockatrice, **snake in the grass, double-crosser** [slang], double-dealer; double agent; trimmer, timeserver 628.4; turncoat 628.5; informer 557.6; archtraitor; Judas, Judas Iscariot, Benedict Arnold, Quisling, Brutus; **schemer, plotter,** intriguer, *intrigant* [Fr], conspirer, **conspirator,** conniver, machinator.

.11 **subversive; saboteur, fifth columnist; fellow traveler,** crypto; security risk; **collaborationist,** collaborator, fraternizer; fifth column, underground; Trojan horse.

## 620. DUPE

.1 NOUNS **dupe, gull,** cull [Brit dial]; pigeon, patsy, fall guy [all slang]; mug [Brit slang], **sucker** or **fish** [both informal], gudgeon, *gobe-mouches* [Fr]; **victim; gullible** or **dupable** or **credulous person, easy mark** [informal], **sitting duck,** trusting soul, innocent, *naïf* [Fr], babe, babe in the woods; pushover or cinch or leadpipe cinch [all informal], easy pickings, greenhorn, greeny or greener [both informal]; **toy, plaything;** monkey, chump [informal], boob [slang], schlemiel [slang], sap or saphead or prize sap [all slang], fool 471; stooge, **cat's-paw** 658.3.

## 621. WILL

.1 NOUNS **will, volition,** –boulia or –bulia; **choice,** determination, **decision** 637.1; **wish,** velleity, **mind, fancy, discretion, pleasure, inclination, disposition,** liking, appetence, appetency, desire 634; appetite, passion, lust, sexual desire 419.5; animus, **objective, intention** 653; **command** 752; free choice, one's own will or choice or discretion or initiative, free will 762.6; conation, conatus; will power, **resolution** 624.

.2 VERBS **will,** see or think fit, think good, think proper, **choose to, have a mind to; choose,** determine, decide 637.13–16; **resolve** 624.7; command, decree 752.9; wish, desire 634.14–20.

.3 have one's will, **have one's way, write one's own ticket,** have it all one's way, do or go as one pleases, please oneself; take the bit in one's teeth, take charge of one's destiny; stand on one's rights; take the law into one's own hands; have the last word, impose one's will.

.4 ADJS **volitional; willing, voluntary;** conative; –willed, –boulic or –bulic.

.5 ADVS **at will,** at choice, at pleasure, *al piacere* [Ital], **at one's pleasure,** *a beneplacito* [Ital], at one's will and pleasure, at one's own sweet will, **at one's discretion,** *à discrétion* [Fr], **ad arbitrium** [L], *ad libitum* [L], ad lib; as one wishes, as it pleases or suits oneself, **in one's own way,** in one's own sweet way [informal], **as one thinks best,** as it seems good or best, as far as one desires; of one's own free will, of one's own accord, on one's own; without coercion, unforced.

## 622. WILLINGNESS

**.1** NOUNS **willingness, gameness** [informal], readiness; **unreluctance,** unloathness, ungrudgingness; agreeableness, **agreeability,** favorableness; **acquiescence, consent** 775; **compliance,** cooperativeness; receptivity, receptiveness, responsiveness; amenability, tractableness, tractability, docility, pliancy, pliability; **eagerness,** promptness, forwardness, alacrity, zeal, zealousness, ardor, enthusiasm; goodwill, cheerful consent; **willing heart** or **mind** or **humor, favorable disposition,** right or receptive mood, willing ear.

**.2 voluntariness,** volunteering; **gratuitousness; spontaneity,** spontaneousness, unforcedness; **self-determination,** self-activity, self-action, autonomy, autonomousness, independence, free will 762.5–7; voluntaryism, voluntarism; volunteer.

**.3** VERBS **be willing, be game** [informal], be ready; be of favorable disposition, find one's heart [archaic], have a willing heart; **incline, lean** 173.3; look kindly upon; be open to, **agree,** be agreeable to; **acquiesce, consent** 775.2,3; not hesitate to, would as lief, would as leave [dial], would as lief as not, not care or mind if one does [informal]; **go along with** [informal]; be eager, be dying to, be spoiling for, be champing at the bit; **enter with a will,** go into heart and soul, plunge into; **cooperate,** collaborate 786.3; lend or give or turn a willing ear.

**.4 volunteer,** do voluntarily, **do of one's own accord,** do of one's own volition, **do of one's own free will** or **choice;** do independently.

**.5** ADJS **willing, willinghearted, ready, game** [informal]; **disposed, inclined, minded, willed,** fain, prone [archaic]; **well-disposed,** well-inclined, favorably inclined or disposed; predisposed; **favorable, agreeable, cooperative; compliant,** content [archaic], **acquiescent,** consenting 775.4; **eager;** prompt, quick, alacritous, forward, ready and willing, zealous, ardent, enthusiastic; in the mood or vein or humor or mind, in a good mood; receptive, responsive; amenable, tractable, docile, pliant.

**6 ungrudging,** ungrumbling, **unreluctant,** unloath, **nothing loath,** unaverse, unshrinking.

**7 voluntary, volunteer; gratuitous; spontaneous, free, freewill,** willful [archaic]; offered, proffered; **discretionary,** discretional, nonmandatory, **optional,** elective;

arbitrary; **self-determined,** self-determining, autonomous, independent, self-active, self-acting; **unsought,** unbesought, **unasked,** unrequested, **unsolicited,** uninvited, unbidden, uncalled-for; **unforced,** uncoerced, unpressured, unrequired, uncompelled; unprompted, uninfluenced.

**.8** ADVS **willingly, with a will,** with good will, with right good will, de bonne volonté [Fr]; **eagerly,** with zest, with relish, with open arms, zealously, ardently, enthusiastically; **readily,** promptly, at the drop of a hat [informal].

**.9 agreeably, favorably, compliantly;** lief, lieve [dial], fain, as lief, as lief as not; **ungrudgingly,** ungrumblingly, **unreluctantly, nothing loath,** without reluctance or demur or hesitation.

**.10 voluntarily, freely, gratuitously, spontaneously,** willfully [archaic]; optionally, electively, by choice; **of one's own accord,** of one's own free will, of one's own volition, of one's own choice, at one's own discretion; without coercion or pressure or compulsion or intimidation; independently 762.32.

## 623. UNWILLINGNESS

**.1** NOUNS **unwillingness, disinclination,** nolition, **indisposition,** indisposedness, **reluctance,** renitency, renitence, grudgingness, grudging consent; unenthusiasm, lack of enthusiasm or zeal or eagerness, slowness, backwardness, dragging of the feet or foot-dragging [both informal]; sullenness, sulk, sulks, sulkiness; cursoriness, perfunctoriness; recalcitrance or recalcitrancy, disobedience, refractoriness, fractiousness, intractableness, indocility, mutinousness; averseness, aversion, repugnance, antipathy, distaste, disrelish; **obstinacy, stubbornness** 626.1; **refusal** 776; opposition 790; **resistance** 792; **disagreement,** dissent 795.2,3.

**.2 demur,** demurral, **scruple, qualm,** qualm of conscience, compunction; **hesitation,** hesitancy or hesitance, pause, boggle, **falter;** qualmishness, scrupulousness, scrupulosity; **stickling,** boggling; **faltering;** shrinking; shyness, **diffidence,** modesty, bashfulness; recoil; **protest, objection** 522.2.

**.3** VERBS be unwilling, **would rather not, not care to,** not feel like [informal], not find it in one's heart to, not have the heart or stomach to; **mind,** object to, draw the line at, **balk at;** grudge, begrudge.

.4 **demur, scruple,** have qualms *or* scruples; **stickle, stick at,** boggle, strain; falter, waver; **hesitate,** pause, haīng back, hang off, hold off; **fight shy of,** shy at, shy, shrink, recoil, blench, flinch, wince, quail, pull back; make bones about *or* of.

.5 ADJS **unwilling, disinclined, indisposed,** not in the mood, averse; **unconsenting** 776.6; opposed 790.8; **resistant** 792.5; **disagreeing,** differing, at odds 795.15,16; disobedient, recalcitrant, refractory, fractious, sullen, sulky, indocile, mutinous; cursory, perfunctory; **involuntary, forced.**

.6 **reluctant,** renitent, **grudging, loath;** backward, laggard, dilatory, slow, slow to; unenthusiastic, unzealous, indifferent, apathetic, perfunctory; balky, balking, restive.

.7 **demurring, qualmish,** boggling, stickling, squeamish, **scrupulous; diffident,** shy, modest, bashful; **hesitant,** hesitating, faltering; shrinking.

.8 ADVS **unwillingly, involuntarily, against one's will,** *à contre cœur* [Fr]; under compulsion *or* coercion *or* pressure; in spite of oneself, *malgré soi* [Fr].

.9 **reluctantly, grudgingly,** sullenly, sulkily; unenthusiastically, perfunctorily; with dragging feet, with a bad *or* an ill grace, **under protest;** with a heavy heart, with no heart *or* stomach.

## 624. RESOLUTION

.1 NOUNS **resolution,** resolvedness, **determination, decision, resolve,** fixed *or* firm resolve, **will, purpose; resoluteness, determinedness,** determinateness, decisiveness, decidedness, **purposefulness;** definiteness; **earnestness, seriousness,** sincerity, devotion, dedication, commitment, total commitment; "the dauntless spirit of resolution", "the native hue of resolution" [both Shakespeare]; single-mindedness, relentlessness, persistence, tenacity, perseverance 625; self-will, obstinacy 626.

.2 **firmness,** firmness of mind *or* spirit, **staunchness,** settledness, steadiness, constancy, steadfastness, fixedness; concentration; flintiness, steeliness; inflexibility, rigidity, unyieldingness 626.2; trueness, loyalty 974.7.

.3 **pluck, spunk** [informal], **mettle, backbone** [informal], **grit,** true grit, spirit, stamina, **guts** *or* moxie [both slang], pith [archaic], bottom, **toughness** [informal]; pluckiness, spunkiness [informal], **gameness,** mettlesomeness; courage 893.

.4 **will power, will,** power, **strong-minded-**

**ness,** strength of mind, strength *or* fixity of purpose, strength, fortitude, **moral fiber; iron will,** will of iron; a will *or* mind of one's own; the courage of one's convictions, moral courage.

.5 **self-control, self-command, self-possession,** self-mastery, self-government, self-domination, **self-restraint,** self-conquest, self-discipline, **self-denial;** control, restraint, constraint, discipline; composure, possession, aplomb; **independence** 762.5.

.6 **self-assertion,** self-assertiveness, forwardness, **nerve** *or* pushiness [both informal], importunateness, importunacy; self-expression, self-expressiveness.

.7 VERBS **resolve, determine, decide, will, purpose, make up one's mind,** make *or* take a resolution, make a point of; **settle,** fix, seal; conclude, come to a determination *or* conclusion, determine once for all.

.8 **be determined,** be resolved; **have a mind** *or* **will of one's own,** know one's own mind; **be in earnest, mean business** [informal], mean what one says; have blood in one's eyes *or* be out for blood [both informal], **set one's mind** *or* **heart upon;** put one's heart into, devote *or* commit *or* dedicate oneself to, give oneself up to; buckle oneself, buckle down, buckle to; steel oneself, brace oneself, grit one's teeth, set one's teeth *or* jaw; put *or* lay *or* set one's shoulder to the wheel; take the bull by the horns, take the plunge, cross the Rubicon; nail one's colors to the mast, burn one's bridges *or* boats, go for broke [slang], kick down the ladder, throw away the scabbard; never say die, die hard, die fighting, die with one's boots on.

.9 **remain firm, stand fast** *or* **firm, hold out,** hold fast, **take one's stand,** set one's back against the wall, **stand** *or* **hold one's ground,** keep one's footing, hold one's own, hang in *or* hang in there *or* hang tough [all slang], dig in, dig one's heel in; **stick to one's guns,** stick, stick fast, stick to one's colors, adhere to one's principles; not listen to the voice of the siren, take what comes, stand the gaff; **put one's foot down** [informal], stand no nonsense.

.10 **not hesitate,** think nothing of, think little of, **make no bones about** [informal], have *or* make no scruple of [archaic], **stick at nothing,** stop at nothing; not look back, go the whole hog [informal], carry through, face out.

**.11** ADJS **resolute, resolved, determined,** bound or bound and determined [both informal], **decided,** decisive, **purposeful;** definite; **earnest, serious,** sincere; devoted, dedicated, committed, wholehearted; single-minded, relentless, persistent, tenacious, persevering 625.7; **obstinate** 626.8.

**.12** **firm, staunch,** fixed, settled, steady, steadfast, constant, set or sot [both dial], flinty, steely; unshaken, not to be shaken, unflappable [informal]; undeflectable, **unswerving,** not to be deflected; immovable, unbending, inflexible, **unyielding** 626.9; true, loyal 974.20.

**.13** **unhesitating,** unhesitant, **unfaltering,** unflinching, unshrinking; stick-at-nothing [informal].

**.14** **plucky, spunky** [informal], gritty [informal], gutty or gutsy [both slang], **mettlesome,** dauntless, **game,** game to the backbone, game to the last or end; **courageous** 893.17–21.

**.15** **strong-willed, strong-minded,** firm-minded; **self-controlled,** controlled, self-disciplined, self-restrained; **self-possessed; self-assertive,** self-asserting, forward, pushy [informal], importunate; self-expressive; **independent** 762.21.

**.16** **determined upon,** resolved upon, decided upon, intent upon, fixed upon, settled upon, **set on,** dead set on [informal], sot on [dial], **bent on,** hell-bent on [slang].

**.17** ADVS **resolutely, determinedly, decidedly,** decisively, resolvedly, **purposefully, with a will;** firmly, steadfastly, steadily, fixedly, with constancy, staunchly; **seriously,** in all seriousness, **earnestly,** in earnest, in good earnest, sincerely; devotedly, with total dedication, committedly; hammer and tongs, tooth and nail, bec et ongles [Fr]; heart and soul, with all one's heart, wholeheartedly; **unswervingly;** single-mindedly, relentlessly, persistently, tenaciously, like a bulldog, like a leech, perseveringly 625.8; obstinately, unyieldingly, inflexibly 626.14,15.

**18** **pluckily, spunkily** [informal], mettlesomely, **gamely,** dauntlessly, manfully, like a man; on one's mettle; **courageously, heroically** 893.22.

**19** **unhesitatingly,** unhesitant, **unfalteringly,** unflinchingly, unshrinkingly.

**20** **come what may,** venga lo que venga [Sp], vogue la galère [Fr], **cost what it may,** coûte que coûte [Fr], whatever the cost, at any price or cost or sacrifice, at all risks or hazards, **whatever may happen,** ruat caelum [L], though the heavens may fall, at all events, live or die, survive or perish, sink or swim, rain or shine, come hell or high water; in some way or other.

## 625. PERSEVERANCE

**.1** NOUNS **perseverance, persistence** or persistency, insistence or insistency, singleness of purpose; resolution 624; **steadfastness, steadiness,** stability 142; **constancy, permanence** 140.1; loyalty, fidelity 974.7; single-mindedness, concentration, unswerving attention, engrossment, preoccupation 530.3; **endurance, stick-to-itiveness** [informal], staying power, **pertinacity,** pertinaciousness, **tenacity,** tenaciousness, **doggedness,** unremittingness, relentlessness, dogged perseverance, bulldog tenacity; plodding, plugging, slogging; **obstinacy, stubbornness** 626.1; **diligence,** application, sedulousness, sedulity, industry, industriousness, assiduousness, assiduity; **tirelessness, indefatigability, stamina; patience,** patience of Job 861.1.

**.2** VERBS **persevere, persist, carry on,** go on, **keep on,** keep up, keep at, **keep at it,** keep going, keep driving, keep trying, try and try again, **keep the ball rolling,** keep the pot boiling, keep up the good work; not take 'no' for an answer; not accept compromise or defeat; **endure, last, continue** 110.6.

**.3** keep doggedly at, **plod,** drudge, slog or slog away, put one foot in front of the other, peg away or at or on; **plug,** plug at, plug away or along; pound or hammer away; **keep one's nose to the grindstone.**

**.4** **stay with it, hold on,** hold fast, **hang on,** hang on for dear life [informal], hang on like a bulldog or leech, hang in or hang in there or hang tough [all slang]; **stick to it** or **stick with it** [both informal], stick [slang], **stick to one's guns;** not give up, **never say die,** not give up the ship [informal], not strike one's colors; come up fighting, come up for more; **stay it out, stick it** or **stick it out** [both informal], tough it out [slang], stick out, hold out; hold up, **bear up,** stand up; **live with it,** live through it; stay the distance [informal]; "wear this world out to the ending doom", "bears it out even to the edge of doom" [both Shakespeare]; brazen it out.

**.5** prosecute to a conclusion, **go through with it, carry through,** follow through, **see it through** [informal], see out, follow out or up; go to the bitter end, go all the

way, go to any length, go the whole
length; go the limit, go the whole hog, go
all out, go for broke [all slang]; leave no
stone unturned, leave no avenue unexplored, overlook nothing, exhaust every
move; move heaven and earth, go
through fire and water, go through hell
and high water [informal].

.6 die trying, die in the last ditch, die in
harness, die with one's boots on or die in
one's boots, die at one's post, die in the
attempt, die game, die hard, go down
with flying colors.

.7 ADJS persevering, perseverant, persistent,
persisting, insistent; enduring, permanent, constant, lasting; continuing 140.7;
stable, steady, steadfast 142.12; immutable, inalterable 142.17; resolute 624.11; diligent, assiduous, sedulous, industrious;
dogged, plodding, slogging, plugging; pertinacious, tenacious, stick-to-itive [infor-
mal]; loyal, faithful 974.20; unswerving,
unremitting, unabating, unintermitting,
uninterrupted; single-minded, utterly attentive; rapt, preoccupied 530.17,18; unfaltering, unwavering, unflinching; relentless, unrelenting; obstinate, stubborn
626.8; unrelaxing, unfailing, untiring, un-
wearying, unflagging, never-tiring, tireless,
weariless, indefatigable, unwearied, unsleeping, undrooping, unnodding, unwinking, sleepless; undiscouraged, undaunted, indomitable, unconquerable, invincible, game to the end; patient,
patient as Job 861.9.

.8 ADVS perseveringly, persistently, persist-
ingly, insistently; resolutely 624.17; loyally,
faithfully, devotedly 974.25; diligently, industriously, assiduously, sedulously; doggedly, sloggingly, ploddingly; pertinaciously, tenaciously; unremittingly, un-
abatingly, unintermittingly, uninterruptedly; unswervingly, unwaveringly, unfalteringly, unflinchingly; relentlessly,
unrelentingly; indefatigably, tirelessly,
wearilessly, untiringly, unwearyingly,
unflaggingly, unrestingly, unsleepingly;
patiently 861.12.

.9 through thick and thin, through fire and
water, come hell or high water, through
evil report and good report, rain or shine,
fair or foul, in sickness and in health;
come what may 624.20.

## 626. OBSTINACY

.1 NOUNS obstinacy, obstinateness, pertinacity, restiveness, stubbornness, willfulness,
self-will, hardheadedness, headstrongness,

strongheadedness; mind or will of one's
own, set or fixed mind, inflexible will;
doggedness, determination, tenaciousness, tenacity, "tough tenacity of purpose" [J. A. Symonds], perseverance 625;
bullheadedness, pigheadedness, mulish-
ness; obduracy, unregenerateness; stiff
neck, stiff-neckedness; sullenness, sulkiness; balkiness; uncooperativeness; bitter-
endism [informal]; dogmatism, opinionatedness 513.6; overzealousness, fanaticism 473.11; intolerance, bigotry 527.1,2.

.2 unyieldingness, unbendingness, stiff temper, inflexibility, inelasticity, impliability,
ungivingness, obduracy, toughness, firmness, stiffness, adamantness, rigorism, rigidity; hard-bittenness, hard-nosedness
[informal]; unalterability, unchangeability, immutability, immovability; irreconcilability, uncompromisingness, intransigence or intransigency, intransigeance
[Fr], intransigentism; implacability, inexorability, relentlessness, unrelentingness;
sternness, grimness, dourness, flintiness,
steeliness.

.3 perversity, perversité [Fr], perverseness,
contrariness, wrongheadedness, waywardness, frowardness, difficultness, cross-
grainedness, cantankerousness, orneriness
[informal], cussedness or pure cussedness
[both informal]; sullenness, sulkiness,
dourness, stuffiness [informal]; irascibility
951.2.

.4 ungovernability, unmanageability, uncontrollability; indomitability, untam-
ableness, intractability, refractoriness,
shrewishness; incorrigibility; unsubmissiveness, unbiddability [Brit], indocility;
irrepressibility, insuppressibility; unmalleability, unmoldableness; recalcitrance or
recalcitrancy, contumacy, contumaciousness; unruliness, obstreperousness, restiveness, fractiousness, wildness, breachiness
[dial]; defiance 793; resistance 792.

.5 unpersuadableness, deafness, blindness;
positiveness, dogmatism 513.6.

.6 (obstinate person) mule, donkey, ass, perverse fool; bullethead or pighead [both
slang]; hardnose [informal]; standpat or
standpatter [both informal], stickler; intransigent, intransigeant [Fr], maverick,
dogmatist, positivist, bigot, fanatic, purist; diehard, bitter-ender [informal], last
ditcher.

.7 VERBS balk, stickle; hold one's ground,
not budge, stand pat [informal], no
yield an inch, stick to one's guns; hol
out, stand out; take no denial, not tak

'no' for an answer; take the bit in one's teeth; die hard; persevere 625.2.

.8 ADJS **obstinate, stubborn, pertinacious, restive; willful, self-willed,** strong-willed, hardheaded, **headstrong,** strongheaded, *entêté* [Fr]; **dogged,** bulldogged, **tenacious,** persevering 625.7; **bullheaded,** bulletheaded [informal], **pigheaded, mulish,** stubborn as a mule; set, set in one's ways, case-hardened, stiff-necked; sullen, sulky; balky, balking; unregenerate, uncooperative; bigoted, intolerant 527.11, overzealous, fanatic(al) 473.32; dogmatic, opinionated 513.22.

.9 **unyielding, unbending, inflexible, hard,** inelastic, impliable, ungiving, **firm, stiff, rigid,** rigorous; rock-ribbed; **adamant,** adamantine; unmoved, unaffected; **immovable,** not to be moved; **unalterable,** unchangeable, immutable; **uncompromising,** intransigent, irreconcilable, hardshell, hard-core [both informal]; implacable, inexorable, **relentless,** unrelenting; stern, grim, dour; iron, cast-iron, flinty, steely.

.10 **obdurate,** tough, **hard,** hard-set, hardmouthed, hard-bitten, hard-nosed [informal].

.11 **perverse, contrary, wrongheaded, wayward, froward, difficult,** cross-grained, cantankerous, ornery [informal]; sullen, sulky, stuffy [informal]; irascible 951.19.

.12 **ungovernable, unmanageable, uncontrollable, indomitable, untamable, intractable, refractory;** shrewish; **incorrigible; unsubmissive,** unbiddable [Brit], **indocile;** irrepressible, insuppressible; unmalleable, unmoldable; **recalcitrant,** contumacious; obstreperous, **unruly, restive,** wild, fractious, breachy [dial]; beyond control, out of hand; resistant, resisting 792.5; defiant 793.7.

.13 **unpersuadable,** deaf, blind; positive; dogmatic 513.22.

.14 ADVS **obstinately, stubbornly,** pertinaciously; willfully, headstrongly; **doggedly,** tenaciously; **bullheadedly,** pigheadedly, mulishly; unregenerately; uncooperatively; with set jaw, with sullen mouth, with a stiff neck.

.15 **unyieldingly, unbendingly, inflexibly, adamantly,** obdurately, **firmly,** stiffly, rigidly, rigorously; unalterably, unchangeably, immutably, immovably, unregenerately; uncompromisingly, intransigently, irreconcilably; implacably, inexorably, relentlessly, unrelentingly; sternly, grimly, dourly.

.16 **perversely, contrarily,** contrariwise, waywardly, wrongheadedly, frowardly, crossgrainedly, cantankerously, sullenly, sulkily.

.17 **ungovernably, unmanageably, uncontrollably,** indomitably, untamably, intractably; shrewishly; incorrigibly; unsubmissively; irrepressibly, insuppressibly; contumaciously; unrulily, obstreperously, restively, fractiously.

## 627. IRRESOLUTION

.1 NOUNS **irresolution, indecision,** unsettlement, unsettledness, irresoluteness, undeterminedness, **indecisiveness,** undecidedness, infirmity of purpose; mugwumpery, mugwumpism, fence-sitting, fence-straddling; double-mindedness, **ambivalence,** ambitendency; dubiety, dubiousness, **uncertainty** 514; **instability, inconstancy,** changeableness 141; capriciousness, mercuriality, fickleness 629.2,3; change of mind, second thoughts, tergiversation 628.1.

.2 **vacillation, fluctuation,** oscillation, pendulation, **wavering,** wobbling, shillyshally, **shilly-shallying,** blowing hot and cold; equivocation 613.4.

.3 **hesitation, hesitance, hesitancy,** hesitating; falter, faltering, shilly-shally, shillyshallying; diffidence, tentativeness, caution, cautiousness.

.4 **weak will, weak-mindedness;** feeblemindedness [archaic], **weakness,** feebleness, faintness, faintheartedness, **frailty, infirmity; spinelessness,** invertebracy; abulia; fear 891; cowardice 892; **pliability** 357.2.

.5 **vacillator, shillyshallyer,** shilly-shally, **waverer,** wobbler; mugwump, fence-sitter, fence-straddler; ass between two bundles of hay; weakling, jellyfish, Milquetoast.

.6 VERBS **not know one's own mind,** not know where one stands, **be of two minds;** have two minds; stagger, stumble, boggle.

.7 **hesitate, pause, falter, hang back,** hover; shilly-shally, hum and haw, **hem and haw;** wait to see how the cat jumps *or* the wind blows, scruple, jib, demur [archaic], stick at, stickle, strain at; think twice about, stop to consider, ponder, debate, deliberate, see both sides of the question, balance, weigh one thing against another, consider both sides of the question; come down squarely in the middle, sit on *or* straddle the fence, fall between two stools; yield, back down 765.7; retreat, withdraw 295.6; pull back, shy 284.7; fear

891.9; not face up to, hide one's head in the sand 633.13.

.8 **vacillate, waver, fluctuate,** pendulate, oscillate, wobble, teeter, totter [archaic], dither, swing from one thing to another, **shilly-shally,** back and fill, keep off and on, will and will not; blow hot and cold 629.4; **equivocate** 613.7; change one's mind, tergiversate 628.6; vary, **alternate** 141.5; shift, **change** 139.5.

.9 ADJS **irresolute,** irresolved, **unresolved; undecided, indecisive, undetermined,** unsettled, infirm of purpose; dubious, **uncertain** 514.15; at loose ends, at a loose end; **of two minds,** double-minded, ambivalent, ambitendent; changeable, mutable 141.6; capricious, mercurial, fickle 629.5,6; mugwumpian, mugwumpish, fence-sitting, fence-straddling.

.10 **vacillating,** vacillatory, oscillatory, wobbly, **wavering, fluctuating,** pendulating, oscillating, **shilly-shallying,** shilly-shally, "at war 'twixt will and will not" [Shakespeare].

.11 **hesitant,** hesitating; faltering; shilly-shallying; diffident, tentative, timid, cautious; scrupling, jibbing, demurring [archaic], sticking, straining, stickling.

.12 **weak-willed, weak-minded,** feebleminded [archaic], weak-kneed, **weak,** feeble, faint, fainthearted, **frail, infirm; spineless,** invertebrate; without a will of one's own, unable to say 'no'; abulic; afraid 891.30–34, cowardly 892.10–13; **pliable** 357.9.

.13 ADVS **irresolutely,** irresolvedly, **undecidedly, indecisively, undeterminedly; uncertainly** 514.26; hesitantly, hesitatingly, falteringly; waveringly, vacillatingly, shilly-shally, shilly-shallyingly.

### 628. CHANGE OF ALLEGIANCE

.1 NOUNS **tergiversation,** tergiversating; **reverse, reversal,** flip or flip-flop [both slang], turnabout, turnaround, **about-face,** volte-face [Fr], right-about-face, right-about, a turn to the right-about; **change of mind;** second thoughts, better thoughts, afterthoughts, mature judgment.

.2 **apostasy,** recreancy; treason, misprision of treason, betrayal, turning traitor, ratting [slang], going over, **defection;** bolt, secession, breakaway; **desertion** 633.2; recidivism, recidivation, backsliding 696.2; faithlessness, disloyalty 975.5.

.3 **recantation, withdrawal, disavowal, denial,** reneging, **unsaying, repudiation,** palinode, palinody, **retraction,** retractation;

**disclaimer,** disclamation, **disownment,** disowning, abjurement, abjuration, revokement or revocation [both archaic]; **renunciation,** renouncement, forswearing; expatriation.

.4 **timeserver,** timepleaser [archaic], temporizer, formalist, trimmer, weathercock; chameleon, Vicar of Bray.

.5 **apostate, turncoat,** turnabout, **recreant, renegade,** renegado, renegate [archaic], runagate, **defector,** tergiversator, tergiversant; **deserter, turntail,** quisling, fifth columnist, collaborationist, collaborator, traitor 619.10; strikebreaker 789.6; **bolter,** mugwump, **seceder,** secessionist, **separatist,** schismatic; **backslider,** recidivist; reversionist; convert, proselyte.

.6 VERBS **change one's mind, tergiversate, change one's song** or **tune** or **note,** sing a different tune; come round, wheel, do an about-face, reverse oneself, do a flip-flop [slang]; swing from one thing to another; think better of it, have second thoughts, be of another mind.

.7 **be a timeserver,** trim, temporize, change with the times.

.8 **apostatize** or apostacize, go over, change sides, switch, switch over, change one's allegiance, **defect; turn one's coat,** turn cloak; secede, break away, bolt, fall off or away; desert 633.6.

.9 **recant, retract, repudiate, withdraw, take back,** renege, **abjure, disavow, disown, deny, disclaim, unsay,** revoke [archaic]; **renounce, forswear,** eat one's words, swallow, eat crow, eat humble pie; **back down** or **out,** climb down, crawfish out [informal], backwater.

.10 ADJS **timeserving, trimming, temporizing;** supple, neither fish nor fowl.

.11 **apostate, recreant,** renegade, tergiversating, tergiversant; treasonous, treasonable, traitorous, collaborative; faithless, disloyal 975.20.

.12 **repudiative,** repudiatory; abjuratory, revocatory [archaic]; renunciative, renunciatory; schismatic; **separatist,** secessionist, breakaway [informal], mugwumpian, mugwumpish.

### 629. CAPRICE

.1 NOUNS **caprice, whim,** capriccio [Ital] boutade [Fr], humor, **whimsy,** freak, whim-wham; **fancy,** fantasy, **conceit,** notion, flimflam, toy, freakish inspiration, crazy idea, fantastic notion, fool notion [informal], harebrained idea, brainstorm, vagary, megrim; **fad, craze, passing fancy**

**quirk, crotchet,** crank, kink; maggot, maggot in the brain, bee in one's bonnet [informal], flea in one's nose [informal].

.2 **capriciousness,** caprice, **whimsicalness,** whimsy, whimsicality; humorsomeness, **fancifulness,** fantasticality, **freakishness;** crankiness, crotchetiness, quirkiness; **moodiness,** temperamentalness; petulance 951.5; **arbitrariness,** motivelessness.

.3 **fickleness, flightiness,** skittishness, inconstancy, **lightness, levity,** *légèreté* [Fr]; volatility, mercurialness, mercuriality; faddishness, faddism; **changeableness** 141; unpredictability 514.1; unreliability, undependability 975.4; coquettishness 932.8; frivolousness 469.7.

.4 VERBS **blow hot and cold,** keep off and on, have as many phases as the moon, chop and change, **fluctuate** 141.5, vacillate 627.8.

.5 ADJS **capricious, whimsical,** freakish, humorsome, vagarious; **fanciful, notional,** fantasied [archaic], fantastic(al), maggoty, **crotchety,** kinky, harebrained, cranky, flaky [slang], quirky; wanton, wayward, vagrant; **arbitrary, unreasonable,** motiveless; **moody, temperamental;** petulant 951.21; unrestrained 762.23.

.6 **fickle, flighty,** skittish, **light;** coquettish, flirtatious, toying; versatile, **inconstant, changeable** 141.7; **vacillating** 627.10; volatile, mercurial, quicksilver; faddish; unpredictable 514.15; unreliable, undependable 975.19.

.7 ADVS **capriciously, whimsically,** fancifully, at one's own sweet will [informal]; **flightily, lightly;** arbitrarily, unreasonably, without rhyme or reason.

## 630. IMPULSE

.1 NOUNS **impulse;** natural impulse, blind impulse, **instinct,** urge, drive; vagrant *or* fleeting impulse; involuntary impulse, reflex, automatic response; gut response [slang]; **notion, fancy; sudden thought,** flash, inspiration, brainstorm, brain wave, quick hunch.

.2 **impulsiveness, impetuousness,** impetuosity; **hastiness,** overhastiness, haste, quickness, suddenness; **precipitateness,** precipitance, precipitancy, precipitation; **recklessness, rashness** 894; impatience 862.

.3 **thoughtlessness,** unthoughtfulness, **heedlessness, carelessness,** inconsideration, inconsiderateness; caprice 629.

.4 **unpremeditation,** indeliberation, **undeliberateness,** uncalculatedness, undesignedness, **spontaneity, spontaneousness,**

unstudiedness; involuntariness 639.5; snap judgment *or* decision; snap shot, offhand shot.

.5 **improvisation, extemporization,** improvision, extempore [archaic], **impromptu, ad lib,** ad-libbing *or* playing by ear [both informal]; extemporaneousness, extemporariness; temporary measure *or* arrangement, *pro tempore* measure *or* arrangement, **stopgap, makeshift,** jury-rig [naut].

.6 **improviser,** improvisator, *improvvisatore, improvvisatrice* [both Ital], **extemporizer,** ad-libber [informal].

.7 VERBS **act on the spur of the moment,** obey one's impulse, let oneself go; **blurt out,** come out with, say what comes uppermost, say the first thing that comes into one's head.

.8 **improvise, extemporize,** improvisate, talk off the top of one's head [informal], throw away *or* depart from the prepared text, throw away the speech, scrap the plan, **ad-lib** [informal], **do offhand,** wing it [slang], vamp, fake [informal], play by ear [informal]; **dash off, strike off,** knock off, throw off, toss off *or* out; make up, whip up, **cook up,** whomp up [informal], lash up [Brit], throw together; jury-rig.

.9 ADJS **impulsive, impetuous, hasty,** overhasty, quick, sudden, **precipitate,** headlong; **reckless, rash** 894.7–9; impatient 862.6.

.10 **unthinking, unreasoning, unreflecting,** uncalculating, unthoughtful, **thoughtless, inadvertent,** reasonless, **heedless, careless,** inconsiderate; unguarded; arbitrary, capricious 629.5.

.11 **unpremeditated,** unmeditated, **uncalculated,** undeliberated, **spontaneous, undesigned, unstudied;** unintentional, unintended, inadvertent, unwilled, **indeliberate,** undeliberate; **involuntary,** reflex, reflexive, automatic, gut [slang], unconscious; **unconsidered,** unadvised, snap, casual; **ill-considered,** ill-advised, ill-devised.

.12 **extemporaneous, extemporary,** extempore, **impromptu,** unrehearsed, **improvised,** improvisatory, improvisatorial, improviso, *improvisé* [Fr]; **ad-lib,** *ad libitum* [L]; stopgap, makeshift, jury-rigged; **offhand,** off-the-cuff [informal].

.13 ADVS **impulsively, impetuously, hastily,** suddenly, quickly, **precipitately,** headlong; **recklessly, rashly** 894.10,11.

.14 **on impulse,** on a sudden impulse, **on the spur of the moment; without premeditation,** unpremeditatedly, uncalculatedly, undesignedly; unthinkingly, unreflectingly, unreasoningly, unthoughtfully, thoughtlessly, heedlessly, carelessly, inconsiderately, unadvisedly; unintentionally, inadvertently, without willing, indeliberately, involuntarily.

.15 extemporaneously, extemporarily, extempore, *à l'improviste* [Fr], impromptu, ad lib, offhand, out of hand; at *or* on sight; by ear, off the hip [slang], off the cuff [informal]; at short notice.

## 631. AVOIDANCE

.1 NOUNS avoidance, shunning; forbearance, refraining; hands-off policy, nonintervention, noninvolvement, neutrality; evasion, elusion; getting around [informal], circumvention; prevention, forestalling, forestallment 730.2; escape 632; evasive action, the runaround [slang]; zigzag, jink, slip, dodge, duck, side step, shy; shunting off, sidetracking; evasiveness, elusiveness; equivocation 613.4; avoiding reaction, defense mechanism *or* reaction.

.2 shirking, slacking, goldbricking [informal], soldiering, goofing *or* goofing off [both slang]; clock-watching; malingering, skulking [Brit]; dodging, ducking; welshing [slang]; truancy; tax evasion, tax dodging.

.3 shirker, shirk, slacker, eye-servant *or* eye-server [both archaic], soldier *or* old soldier, goldbricker, goldbrick [informal]; clock watcher; welsher [slang]; malingerer, skulker *or* skulk [both Brit]; truant; tax dodger.

.4 flight, fugitation, exit, quick exit, making oneself scarce *or* getting the hell out [both informal], bolt, disappearing act [slang], hasty retreat; running away, decampment; skedaddle, skedaddling, scramming, absquatulation [all slang]; elopement; disappearance 447; French leave, absence without leave, AWOL; desertion 633.2; hegira.

.5 fugitive, fleer, runaway, runagate, bolter, skedaddler [informal]; absconder, eloper; refugee, evacuee, *émigré* [Fr]; displaced person, DP, stateless person; escapee 632.5.

.6 VERBS avoid, shun, fight shy of, keep from, keep away from, keep clear of, steer clear of [informal], give a miss to [informal], keep *or* get out of the way of, give a wide berth, keep remote from, stay detached from; make way for, give place to; keep one's distance, keep at a respectful distance, keep *or* stand *or* hold aloof; give the cold shoulder to [informal], have

nothing to do with, have no association with, have no truck with [informal]; not meddle with, let alone, let well enough alone, keep hands off, not touch, not touch with a ten-foot pole; turn away from, turn one's back upon, slam the door in one's face.

.7 evade, elude, beg, get out of, shuffle out of, circumvent, skirt, double, get around [informal]; give one the run-around; ditch *or* shake *or* shake off [all slang], get away from; throw off the scent; play at hide and seek; lead one a chase *or* merry chase, lead one a dance *or* pretty dance; escape 632.6–9.

.8 dodge, duck; shy, shy off *or* away; swerve, sheer off; pull away *or* clear; pull back, shrink, recoil 284.6,7; sidestep, step aside; parry, fence, ward off; shift, shift *or* put off; hedge, pussyfoot [informal], be *or* sit on the fence, beat around *or* about the bush, hem and haw, beg the question, equivocate 613.7.

.9 shirk, slack, lie *or* rest upon one's oars, not pull fair; lie down on the job [informal]; soldier, duck duty, goof off *or* dog it [both slang], goldbrick [informal]; malinger, skulk [Brit]; get out of, sneak *or* slip out of, slide out of, dodge, duck; welsh [slang].

.10 flee, fly, take flight, take to flight, take wing, fugitate, run, cut and run [informal], make a precipitate departure, run off *or* away, run away from, decamp, absquatulate *or* skedaddle [both informal], take to one's heels, make off, clear out [informal], depart 301.6, do the disappearing act, make a quick exit, make oneself scarce [informal], get the hell out [informal], beat a retreat, turn tail, show the heels, show a clean *or* light pair of heels, run for it, "show it a fair pair of heels and run for it" [Shakespeare], bolt, make a break for it [informal], run for one's life; advance to the rear, make a strategic withdrawal; take French leave, go AWOL, slip the cable; desert 633.6; ski *or* skip out [both informal], jump [informal]; abscond, levant [Brit], elope, run away with; skip *or* jump bail.

.11 [slang terms] beat it, blow, scram, lam, take it on the lam, take a powder *or* run out powder, split, skin out, duck out, duck and run, dog it; vamoose.

.12 slip away, steal away, sneak off, slink off, slide off, slither off, skulk away, mooch off [slang], duck out [slang], slip out of.

.13 not face up to, hide one's head in the

sand, not come to grips with, put off, procrastinate, temporize.

.14 ADJS **avoidable, escapable,** eludible; evadable; preventable.

.15 **evasive, elusive,** elusory; **shifty, slippery,** cagey [slang]; shirking, malingering.

.16 **fugitive, runaway,** in flight, on the lam [slang], hot [slang]; disappearing 447.3; –fugal.

## 632. ESCAPE

.1 NOUNS **escape; getaway** or **break** or **breakout** [all informal]; **deliverance; delivery,** riddance, **release,** setting-free, freeing, **liberation, extrication, rescue;** emergence, issuance, issue, outlet, vent; **leakage,** leak; jailbreak, prisonbreak; evasion 631.1; flight 631.4; escapism.

.2 **narrow escape,** hairbreadth escape, **close call** [informal], **close shave** [informal], **near miss,** near go or near thing [both Brit informal], near or narrow squeak [Brit informal], close squeak or tight squeeze [both informal].

.3 (means of escape) bolt-hole, escape hatch, fire escape, life net, lifeboat, life raft, life buoy, lifeline, sally port, slide, inflatable slide, ejection seat, emergency exit.

.4 **loophole, way out,** way of escape, hole to creep out of, escape hatch, escape clause, saving clause; pretext 649; **alternative,** choice 637.

.5 **escapee,** escaper; escape artist; escapist; **fugitive** 631.5.

.6 VERBS **escape,** make or effect one's escape, make good one's escape; **get away, make a getaway** [informal]; **free oneself,** deliver oneself, gain one's liberty, **get free, get clear of,** bail out, **get out, get out of,** get well out of; **break loose,** cut loose, break away, break one's bonds or chains, slip the collar, shake off the yoke; **jump** or **skip** [both informal]; **break jail** or **prison,** escape prison, fly the coop [slang]; leap over the wall; evade 631.7; flee 631.10.

.7 **get off, go free,** win freedom, go at liberty, **go scot free,** escape with a whole skin, escape without penalty; **get away with** [slang], get by, get away with murder, **get off cheap;** cop a plea or cop out [both slang].

.8 scrape or squeak through, escape with or by the skin of one's teeth.

.9 **slip away, give one the slip,** slip through one's hands or fingers; **slip** or **sneak** through; **slip out of,** slide out of, crawl or

creep out of, sneak out of, wiggle or wriggle or squirm or shuffle or worm out of, find a loophole.

.10 **find vent,** issue forth, come forth, exit, **emerge, issue,** debouch, erupt, break out, break through, come out, run out, **leak out,** ooze out.

.11 ADJS **escaped, loose,** on the loose, disengaged, out of, well out of; **fled, flown;** fugitive, runaway; scot-free; at large, **free** 762.19.

## 633. ABANDONMENT

.1 NOUNS **abandonment, forsaking, leaving,** lipo–; jettison, jettisoning, throwing overboard or away, casting away; **withdrawal,** evacuation, pulling out, absentation; cessation 144; disuse, desuetude.

.2 **desertion, defection,** ratting [slang]; dereliction; **secession,** bolt, breakaway, walkout; betrayal 975.8; schism, apostasy 628.2; deserter 628.5.

.3 (giving up) **relinquishment, surrender, resignation, renouncement,** renunciation, abdication, waiver, abjurement, abjuration, cession, handing over, **yielding, forswearing; withdrawing, dropping out** [informal].

.4 **derelict,** castoff; jetsam, flotsam, lagan, **flotsam and jetsam;** waifs and strays; rubbish, junk, trash, refuse; waif, orphan, dogie [dial]; **castaway;** foundling; wastrel, reject, discard 668.3.

.5 VERBS **abandon, forsake; quit, leave,** leave behind, take leave of, depart from, absent oneself from, turn one's back upon, turn one's tail upon, say goodbye to, bid a long farewell to; **withdraw, back out, drop out** [informal], pull out, stand down [informal]; **go back on, go back on one's word;** cry off [Brit], beg off, renege; **vacate,** evacuate; quit cold or leave flat [both informal]; jilt, throw over [informal]; maroon; **jettison,** discard 668.7; let fall into disuse or desuetude.

.6 **desert, leave in the lurch,** rat [slang], let down, **walk** or **run out on** [informal], turn one's back upon; apostatize 628.8; **defect, secede, bolt,** break away, pull out [informal], withdraw one's support; sell out [slang], betray 975.14.

.7 **give up, relinquish, surrender, yield,** waive, **forgo, resign, renounce,** throw up, abdicate, **abjure, forswear, have done with,** cede, hand over, lay down, wash one's hands of, drop, drop all idea of, drop like a hot potato; **cease** 144.6, **desist from,** leave off, give over; hold or stay one's hand, cry quits, acknowledge defeat, throw up the cards, throw in the sponge, throw in the towel 765.8.

.8 ADJS **abandoned, forsaken, deserted,** left; disused; **derelict,** castaway, jettisoned; marooned; discarded 668.11.

## 634. DESIRE

.1 NOUNS **desire, wish,** wanting, **want, need,** desideration; **hope; fancy; will, mind, pleasure,** will and pleasure; heart's desire; **urge,** drive, libido, pleasure principle; concupiscence; horme; wish fulfillment, fantasy; passion, ardor, sexual desire 419.5; **curiosity,** intellectual curiosity, thirst for knowledge, lust for learning; **eagerness** 635; –philia, –orexia.

.2 **liking, likes** [pl], **love, fondness;** infatuation, crush; **affection;** relish, taste, gusto, gust [Scot]; **passion, weakness** [informal].

.3 **inclination,** penchant, partiality, fancy, favor, predilection, **preference,** propensity, proclivity, leaning, bent, turn, bias, **affinity;** mutual affinity or attraction; **sympathy,** fascination.

.4 **wistfulness,** wishfulness, yearnfulness, **nostalgia;** wishful thinking; sheep's eyes, longing or wistful eye; daydream, daydreaming.

.5 **yearning, yen** [informal]; **longing,** desiderium, **hankering** [informal], **pining,** honing [dial], aching; languishment, languishing; **nostalgia, homesickness,** *Heimweh* [Ger], *mal du pays, maladie du pays* [both Fr]; nostomania.

.6 **craving,** coveting; **hunger, thirst, appetite,** "an universal wolf" [Shakespeare], appetition, appetency or appetence; aching void; **itch, itching,** prurience or pruriency; **sexual desire** 419.5; cacoëthes, mania 473.12.

.7 **appetite,** stomach, relish, taste; **hunger,** hungriness, –phagia; tapeworm [slang], eyes bigger than the stomach, wolf in the stomach, canine appetite; empty stomach, emptiness [informal], hollow hunger; **thirst,** thirstiness, drought [dial], dryness; polydipsia; torment of Tantalus; sweet tooth [informal].

.8 **greed,** greediness, graspingness, **avarice, cupidity, avidity, voracity, rapacity, lust,** avariciousness, –lagnia or –lagny; avidness, esurience, wolfishness; voraciousness, ravenousness, rapaciousness, sordidness, **covetousness,** acquisitiveness; itching palm; grasping; **piggishness, hoggishness,** swinishness; **gluttony** 994; inordinate

desire, fury or frenzy of desire, overgreediness; insatiable desire, insatiability; incontinence, intemperateness 993.1.

.9 **aspiration,** hitching one's wagon to a star, reaching high, upward looking; "the desire of the moth for the star" [Shelley]; high goal or aim or purpose, dream, ideals; **idealism** 535.7.

.10 **ambition,** ambitiousness, vaulting ambition; climbing, status-seeking, social climbing, careerism; power-hunger; "the mind's immodesty" [D'Avenant], "the way in which a vulgar man aspires" [Henry Ward Beecher], "the evil shadow of aspiration" [George Macdonald], "the avarice of power" [G. G. Coulton], "avarice on stilts and masked" [W. S. Landor]; noble or lofty ambition, magnanimity [archaic]; "the spur that makes man struggle with destiny" [Donald G. Mitchell].

.11 (object of desire) **desire,** heart's desire, desideration, *desideratum* [L]; wish; **hope;** catch, plum, prize, trophy; forbidden fruit, temptation; lodestone, magnet; golden vision, glimmering goal; land of heart's desire 535.11; something to be desired, "a consummation devoutly to be wish'd" [Shakespeare]; dearest wish, ambition, the height of one's ambition.

.12 **desirer,** wisher, wanter, hankerer [informal], yearner, coveter; fancier, collector; addict, freak [slang], devotee, votary 635.6; **aspirant,** aspirer, solicitant, hopeful [informal], candidate; **lover,** suitor 931.11.

.13 **desirability; agreeability,** acceptability, unobjectionableness; **attractiveness,** attraction, magnetism, **appeal,** seductiveness, provocativeness; likability, lovability 931.7.

.14 VERBS **desire,** desiderate, be desirous of, **wish,** lust after, **want,** have a mind to, choose [dial]; would fain do or have, would be glad of; **like,** fancy, take to, **take a fancy to,** have a fancy for; have an eye to, have one's eye on, aim at; set one's cap for, have designs on; wish very much, wish to goodness; **love** 931.18; lust 419.22; prefer, favor 637.17.

.15 **want to, wish to, like to,** love to, dearly love to, choose to; **itch to,** burn to; ache to [informal], long to, **be dying to.**

.16 **wish for, hope for, yearn for,** yen for or have a yen for [both informal], **itch for,** lust for, pant for, **long for, pine for,** hone for [dial], ache for, be hurting for [dial], weary for, languish for, **be dying for,** thirst for, sigh for, gape for [archaic]; cry for, clamor for; spoil for [informal].

.17 want with all one's heart, want in the worst way; set one's heart on, have one's heart set on, give one's kingdom in hell for or one's eyeteeth for [slang].

.18 crave, covet, hunger after, thirst after, crave after, lust after, pant after, run mad after, hanker after [informal]; crawl after; aspire after, be consumed with desire.

.19 hunger, hunger for, feel hungry, starve [informal]; be ravenous, raven; have a good appetite, be a good trencherman, have a tapeworm [slang], have a wolf in one's stomach; eye hungrily, lick one's chops [informal]; thirst, thirst for.

.20 aspire, be ambitious; aspire to, try to reach; aim high, keep one's eyes on the stars, "hitch one's wagon to a star" [Emerson].

.21 ADJS desirous, desiring, desireful [archaic], lickerish, wanting, wishing, needing, hoping; tempted; appetitive, desiderative, optative, libidinous, libidinal; hormic; eager 635.9; lascivious, lustful 419.29.

.22 desirous of or to, keen on, set on [dial], bent on; fond of, with a liking for, partial to [informal]; fain of or to; inclined toward, leaning toward; itching for or to, aching for or to, dying for or to; spoiling for [informal]; mad on or for, wild to or for [informal], crazy to or for [informal].

.23 wistful, wishful; longing, yearning, yearnful, hankering [informal], languishing, pining, honing [dial]; nostalgic, homesick.

.24 craving, coveting; hungering, hungry, thirsting, thirsty, athirst; itching, prurient; fervid; devoured by desire, in a frenzy or fury of desire, mad with lust, consumed with desire.

.25 hungry, hungering, peckish [dial]; empty [informal], unfilled; ravening, ravenous, voracious, sharp-set, wolfish, dog-hungry [slang], hungry as a bear; starved, famished, starving, famishing, perishing or pinched with hunger; fasting; half-starved, half-famished.

.26 thirsty, thirsting, athirst; dry, parched, droughty [dial].

.27 greedy, avaricious, avid, voracious, rapacious, esurient, ravening, grasping, grabby [slang], acquisitive, mercenary, sordid, overgreedy; ravenous, gobbling, devouring; miserly, money-hungry, money-mad, venal; covetous, coveting; piggish, hoggish, swinish, a hog for, greedy as a hog; gluttonous 994.6; omnivorous, all-devour-

ing; insatiable, insatiate, unsatisfied, unsated, unappeased, unappeasable, limitless, bottomless, unquenchable, quenchless, unslaked, unslakeable, slakeless.

.28 aspiring, ambitious, sky-aspiring, upward-looking, high-reaching; high-flying, social-climbing, careerist, careeristic, on the make [informal]; power-hungry.

.29 desired, wanted, coveted; wished-for, hoped-for, longed-for; in demand, popular.

.30 desirable, to be desired, much to be desired; enviable, worth having; likable, pleasing, after one's own heart; agreeable, acceptable, unobjectionable; attractive, taking, winning, seductive, provocative, tantalizing, exciting 650.7; appetizing, tempting, toothsome, mouth-watering; lovable, adorable 931.23.

.31 ADVS desirously, wistfully, wishfully, longingly, yearningly, piningly, languishingly; cravingly, itchingly; hungrily, thirstily; aspiringly, ambitiously.

.32 greedily, avariciously, avidly, ravenously, raveningly, voraciously, rapaciously, covetously, graspingly, devouringly; wolfishly, piggishly, hoggishly, swinishly.

## 635. EAGERNESS

.1 NOUNS eagerness, anxiousness, anxiety; avidity, avidness, keenness, forwardness, readiness, promptness, quickness, alacrity, cheerful readiness, empressement [Fr]; keen desire, appetite 634.7; zest, zestfulness, gusto, gust [Scot], verve, liveliness, life, vitality, vivacity, élan, spirit, animation; impatience, breathless impatience 862.1.

.2 zeal, ardor, ardency, fervor, fervency, fervidness, spirit, warmth, fire, heat, heatedness, passion, passionateness, impassionedness, heartiness, intensity, abandon, vehemence; intentness, resolution 624; devotion, devoutness, devotedness, dedication, commitment, committedness; earnestness, seriousness, sincerity; loyalty, faithfulness, faith, fidelity 974.7.

.3 enthusiasm, enthusiasticalness; keen interest, fascination; craze 473.12.

.4 overzealousness, overeagerness, overanxiousness, overanxiety; overenthusiasm, infatuation; overambitiousness; frenzy, fury; zealotry, zealotism; mania, fanaticism 473.11.

.5 enthusiast, zealot, infatuate, energumen, eager beaver [informal], rhapsodist, great one for [informal]; addict; hound, fiend, demon, freak, nut, bug [all slang]; faddist; pursuer; sucker for [slang]; hobbyist, collector; **fanatic** 473.17; visionary 535.13.

.6 devotee, votary, **fan** or **buff** [both informal], **fancier,** admirer, **follower; groupie;** worshiper, idolizer, idolater; amateur, dilettante; collector; rooter or booster [both informal].

.7 VERBS **jump at,** catch, grab, grab at, snatch, snatch at, fall all over oneself, get excited about; desire 634.14–20.

.8 be enthusiastic, **rave, enthuse** [informal]; **rhapsodize, carry on over** [informal], make much of, **make a fuss over,** make an ado or much ado about, make a to-do over [informal], take on over [informal], go on over or about [informal], rave about [informal], whoop it up about [slang]; gush, gush over; effervesce, bubble over.

.9 ADJS **eager, anxious,** agog, all agog; **avid, keen,** forward, prompt, quick, ready, ready and willing, alacritous, bursting to, raring to; **zestful, lively,** full of life, vital, vivacious, vivid, spirited, **animated; impatient** 862.6; breathless, panting, champing at the bit; **desirous** 634.21.

.10 **zealous, ardent, fervent, fervid,** perfervid, **spirited, intense,** hearty, vehement, abandoned, **passionate,** impassioned, **warm,** heated, hot, hot-blooded, red-hot, fiery, white-hot, flaming, burning, afire, on fire; **devout, devoted;** dedicated, committed; **earnest, sincere, serious,** in earnest; loyal, faithful 974.20; intent, intent on, resolute 624.11.

.11 **enthusiastic, enthused** [informal], glowing, full of enthusiasm, gung-ho [slang]; enthusiastic about, infatuated with, **keen on** or **about.**

.12 [slang terms] **wild about, crazy about, mad about,** ape about or over, gone on, all in a dither over, gaga over, starry-eyed over, all hopped up about, hepped up over, hot about or for or on, steamed up about, **turned-on;** hipped on, **cracked on,** bugs on, freaked-out, **nuts on** or **over** or **about.**

.13 **overzealous,** ultrazealous, **overeager,** overanxious; **overambitious;** overdesirous; **overenthusiastic, infatuated;** feverish, perfervid, febrile, at fever pitch; hectic, frenetic, furious, **frenzied,** frantic, **wild,** hysteric(al), delirious; **insane** 473.25–34; **fanatical** 473.32.

.14 ADVS **eagerly, anxiously; impatiently,** breathlessly; **avidly,** promptly, quickly, keenly, readily; zestfully, vivaciously, animatedly; **enthusiastically,** with enthusi-

asm; **with alacrity,** with zest, with gusto, with relish, with open arms.

.15 zealously, **ardently, fervently, fervidly,** perfervidly, heatedly, heartily, vehemently, **passionately,** impassionedly; intently, intensely; **devoutly, devotedly;** earnestly, sincerely, seriously.

## 636. INDIFFERENCE

.1 NOUNS **indifference,** indifferentness; indifferentism; halfheartedness, zeallessness, perfunctoriness, fervorlessness; **coolness,** coldness, chilliness, chill, iciness, frostiness; tepidness, **lukewarmness,** Laodiceanism; **neutrality,** neutralness, neuterness; insipidity, vapidity.

.2 **unconcern, disinterest, detachment; disregard, dispassion,** insouciance, **carelessness,** regardlessness; easygoingness; **heedlessness,** mindlessness, inattention 531; **unmindfulness, incuriosity** 529; disregardfulness, recklessness, negligence 534.1,2; unsolicitousness, unanxiousness; pococurantism; **nonchalance,** inexcitability 858; ataraxy or ataraxia; indiscrimination, casualness 493.1; **listlessness,** lackadaisicalness, lack of feeling or affect, sloth, accidia, acedia, **apathy** 856.4.

.3 **undesirousness,** desirelessness; nirvana; lovelessness, passionlessness; uneagerness, **unambitiousness;** lack of appetite, inappetence, anorexia, anorexia nervosa.

.4 VERBS **not care, not mind, not give** or **care a damn,** not give a hoot or shit [slang], care nothing for or about, not care a straw about; shrug off; **take no interest in,** have no desire for, have no taste or relish for; hold no brief for.

.5 **not matter to,** be all one to, take it or leave it.

.6 ADJS **indifferent, halfhearted,** zealless, perfunctory, fervorless; **cool, cold** 929.9; tepid, **lukewarm,** Laodicean; neither hot nor cold, neither one thing nor the other, "neither fish, nor flesh, nor good red herring" [John Heywood]; **neuter, neutral.**

.7 **unconcerned, uninterested, disinterested,** turned-off, **dispassionate,** insouciant, **careless,** regardless; easygoing; incurious 529.3; mindless, **unmindful, heedless,** inattentive 531.6, perfunctory, disregardful; **devil-may-care,** reckless, negligent 534.10, 11; unsolicitous, unanxious; pococurante, **nonchalant,** inexcitable 858.10; ataractic; **blasé;** undiscriminating, casual 493.5; **listless,** lackadaisical; **apathetic** 856.13.

.8 **undesirous,** unattracted, desireless; loveless, passionless; inappetent; nirvanic; **un-**

enthusiastic, uneager; **unambitious,** unaspiring.

.9 ADVS **indifferently, with indifference,** with utter indifference; coolly, coldly; lukewarmly, halfheartedly; perfunctorily; for aught one cares.

.10 **unconcernedly, uninterestedly, disinterestedly,** dispassionately, insouciantly, **carelessly,** regardlessly; mindlessly; **unmindfully, heedlessly,** recklessly, negligently 534.17,18; nonchalantly; listlessly, lackadaisically; **apathetically** 856.14,15.

.11 PHRS **who cares?,** I don't care, I couldn't care less; it's a matter of sublime indifference; never mind!, **what does it matter?,** what's the difference?, what's the diff? [slang], what are the odds?, what of it?, what boots it?, **so what?,** what the hell [slang], it's all one to me, it's all the same to me [slang].

.12 **I should worry?,** I should fret?, that's your lookout, I feel for you but I can't reach you; that's your pigeon [slang], that's your tough luck, tough titty *or* tough shit [both slang].

## 637. CHOICE

.1 NOUNS **choice, selection, election,** preference, decision, **pick, choosing,** free choice; alternativity; co-option, co-optation; **will,** volition, free will 762.6,7; preoption, first choice; the pick 674.8.

.2 **option, discretion, pleasure,** will and pleasure; optionality; possible choice, alternative, alternate choice.

.3 **dilemma,** Scylla and Charybdis, the devil and the deep blue sea; *embarras de choix* [Fr]; choice of Hercules; Hobson's choice, no choice, only choice.

.4 **adoption, embracement,** acceptance, espousal; affiliation.

.5 **preference, predilection,** proclivity, bent, affinity, prepossession, predisposition, partiality, inclination, leaning, bias, tendency, taste; favor, fancy; prejudice; personal choice, particular choice [archaic], chosen kind *or* sort, style, cup of tea [informal], type, bag *or* thing [both slang]; druthers [dial].

.6 **vote,** voting, **suffrage,** franchise, enfranchisement, voting right, right to vote; **voice, say;** representation; **poll,** polling, canvass, canvassing, division, counting heads *or* noses; **ballot,** secret ballot, Australian ballot; **plebiscite,** plebiscitum, **referendum;** yeas and nays, yea, aye, yes, nay, no; voice vote, *viva voce* vote; rising vote; hand vote, show of hands; absentee

vote, proxy; casting vote, deciding vote; write-in vote, write-in; fagot vote [Brit]; graveyard vote; single vote, plural vote; transferable vote, nontransferable vote; Hare system, list system, cumulative voting, preferential voting, proportional representation; straw vote, record vote, snap vote, plumper [Brit].

.7 **selector,** chooser, optant, elector, **voter; electorate.**

.8 **nomination, designation,** naming, proposal.

.9 **election, appointment;** political election 744.15.

.10 **selectivity,** selectiveness, picking and choosing; **choosiness** 896.1; eclecticism; **discrimination** 492.

.11 **eligibility, qualification, fitness,** fittedness, **suitability,** acceptability, worthiness, desirability; eligible.

.12 **elect,** elite, chosen; chosen people.

.13 VERBS **choose, elect,** opt, opt for, co-opt, make *or* take one's choice, make choice of, use *or* take up *or* exercise one's option; pick and choose.

.14 **select,** make a selection; **pick, handpick, pick out, single out,** choose out; extract, excerpt; **decide between;** cull, glean, winnow, sift; separate the wheat from the chaff *or* tares, separate the sheep from the goats.

.15 **adopt;** approve, ratify, pass, carry; **take up, go in for** [informal]; accept, **embrace,** espouse; affiliate.

.16 **decide upon, determine upon,** settle upon, fix upon; make *or* take a decision, **make up one's mind.**

.17 **prefer,** have preference, **favor, like better** *or* **best,** prefer to, set before *or* above, regard *or* honor before; rather [dial], **had** *or* **have rather,** choose rather; think proper, see *or* think fit, think best, please; incline *or* lean *or* tend toward, have a bias *or* partiality.

.18 **vote,** cast one's vote, ballot, cast a ballot; hold up one's hand, stand up and be counted; plump [Brit]; divide; poll, canvass.

.19 **nominate, name, designate;** put up, propose, submit, name for office; run, run for office.

.20 **elect, vote in,** place in office; **appoint.**

.21 **put to choice,** offer, present, set before; put to vote, have a show of hands.

.22 ADJS **elective;** volitional, voluntary; **optional,** discretional; **alternative,** disjunctive.

.23 **selective,** selecting, choosing; eclectic(al);

elective, electoral; appointing, appointive, constituent; adoptive; discriminating 492.7; **choosy** [informal], particular 896.9.

.24 **eligible, qualified, fit,** fitted, **suitable,** acceptable, admissible, worthy, desirable; with voice, with vote, with voice and vote, enfranchised.

.25 **preferable,** of choice or preference, **better,** preferred, **to be preferred,** more desirable, favored; preferential, preferring, favoring.

.26 **chosen, selected, picked;** select, elect; handpicked; **adopted,** accepted, embraced, espoused, approved, ratified, passed, carried; **elected,** unanimously elected, elected by acclamation; appointed; **nominated,** designated, named.

.27 ADVS **at choice, at one's will,** at one's will and pleasure, at one's pleasure, electively, at one's discretion, at the option of, if one wishes; on approval; **optionally;** alternatively.

.28 **preferably, by choice** or **preference,** in preference; by vote, by election or suffrage; **rather than,** sooner than, first, sooner, rather, before.

.29 CONJS or, either . . . or; and/or.

## 638. REJECTION

.1 NOUNS **rejection, repudiation;** abjurement, abjuration, renouncement 633.3; disownment, disclamation, recantation 628.3; **exclusion,** exception 77.1; **disapproval, nonacceptance,** nonapproval, declining, declination, refusal 776; contradiction, denial 524.2; passing by or up [informal], ignoring, nonconsideration, discounting, dismissal, disregard 531.1; throwing out or away, putting out or away, chucking or chucking out [both informal]; discard 668.3; turning out or away, repulse, rebuff 289.2; **spurning,** scouting, despising, despisal, contempt 966.

.2 VERBS **reject, repudiate,** abjure, forswear, **renounce** 633.7, **disown, disclaim, recant** 628.9, except, **exclude** 77.4; **disapprove, decline, refuse** 776.3; contradict, **deny** 524.4; pass by or up [informal], waive, ignore, refuse to consider, discount, **dismiss; disregard** 531.2; throw out or away, chuck or chuck out [both informal], **discard** 668.7; turn out or away, shove away, brush aside, push aside, repulse, repel, rebuff 289.2; **spurn,** scout, **disdain,** contemn, **despise** 966.3.

.3 ADJS **rejected, repudiated; renounced,** forsworn, **disowned; denied,** refused; excluded, excepted; **disapproved, declined;** ignored, discounted, not considered, **dismissed,** dismissed out of hand; **discarded;** repulsed, rebuffed; **spurned,** scouted, **disdained, scorned,** contemned, **despised;** out of the question, not to be thought of, declined with thanks.

.4 rejective; renunciative, abjuratory; declinatory; dismissive; contemptuous, despising, **scornful,** disdainful.

## 639. NECESSITY

.1 NOUNS **necessity,** necessariness, necessitude [archaic], necessitation; mandatoriness, mandatedness, obligatoriness, **obligation,** obligement; compulsoriness, **compulsion, duress** 756.3.

.2 **requirement, requisite,** requisition; **necessity, need, want,** occasion; need for, **call for, demand,** demand for; desideratum, desideration; **prerequisite,** prerequirement; **must,** must item; **essential,** indispensable; the necessary, the needful; necessities, necessaries, essentials, bare necessities.

.3 **needfulness,** requisiteness; **essentiality,** essentialness, vitalness; **indispensability,** indispensableness; irreplaceability; irreducibleness, irreducibility.

.4 **urgent need, dire necessity;** exigency or exigence, **urgency,** imperative, imperativeness, immediacy, pressingness, pressure; "necessity's sharp pinch" [Shakespeare]; matter of necessity, case of need, **matter of life and death; predicament** 731.4.

.5 **involuntariness,** unwilledness, **instinctiveness;** compulsiveness; reflex action, conditioning, automatism; echolalia, echopraxia; automatic writing; **instinct,** impulse 630; blind impulse or instinct, sheer chemistry.

.6 **choicelessness,** no choice, no alternative, **Hobson's choice,** only choice; that or nothing; not a pin to choose, six of one and half a dozen of the other, distinction without a difference; indiscrimination 493.

.7 **inevitability,** inevitableness, **unavoidableness,** necessity, inescapableness, inevasibleness, unpreventability, undeflectability, ineluctability; irrevocability, indefeasibility; uncontrollability; relentlessness, inexorability, unyieldingness, inflexibility; fatefulness, **certainty,** sureness; force majeure, vis major, act of God, inevitable accident, unavoidable casualty; **predetermination, fate** 640.2,3.

.8 VERBS **necessitate, oblige,** dictate, **constrain;** insist upon, **compel** 756.4.

.9 **require, need, want,** feel the want of, have occasion for, be in need of, be hurting for [dial], stand in need of, not be able to dispense with, not be able to do without; **call for,** cry for, cry out for, clamor for; **demand,** ask, claim, exact; prerequire [archaic]; need or want doing, take doing [informal], be indicated.

.10 be **necessary,** lie under a necessity, be one's fate; can't be avoided, can't be helped; be under the necessity of, be in for; be obliged, **must,** need or needs must [archaic], **have to,** have got to [informal], should, need, **need to,** have need to; can't keep from, can't help, **cannot help but,** cannot do otherwise; be forced or driven.

.11 **have no choice** or **alternative,** have one's options reduced or eliminated, have no option but, cannot choose but, be robbed or relieved of choice; be pushed to the wall, be driven into a corner; take it or leave it [informal], have that or nothing.

.12 ADJS **necessary, obligatory, compulsory,** mandatory; **exigent, urgent,** necessitous, importunate, **imperative;** choiceless, without choice, out of one's hands or control.

.13 **requisite, needful, required,** needed, necessary, **wanted, called for,** indicated; **essential, vital, indispensable,** unforgoable, irreplaceable; **irreducible,** irreductible; prerequisite.

.14 **involuntary, instinctive, automatic, mechanical,** reflex, reflexive, conditioned; **unconscious,** unthinking, blind; **unwitting,** unintentional, independent of one's will, unwilling, unwilled, against one's will; **compulsive;** forced; **impulsive** 630.9–12.

.15 **inevitable, unavoidable,** necessary, **inescapable,** inevasible, unpreventable, undeflectable, ineluctable, irrevocable, indefeasible; uncontrollable, unstoppable; relentless, inexorable, unyielding, inflexible; irresistible, resistless; **certain,** fateful, **sure,** sure as fate, sure as death, sure as death and taxes; **fated** 640.9.

.16 ADVS **necessarily,** needfully, requisitely; **of necessity,** from necessity, need or needs [both archaic], perforce; without choice; **willy-nilly,** nolens volens [L], willing or unwilling, bon gré mal gré [Fr], whether one will or not; come what may; compulsorily 756.12.

.17 **if necessary, if need be,** if worst comes to

worst; for lack of something better, faute de mieux [Fr].

.18 **involuntarily, instinctively, automatically, mechanically,** by reflex, reflexively; blindly, **unconsciously,** unthinkingly; **unwittingly,** unintentionally; **compulsively; unwillingly** 623.8.

.19 **inevitably, unavoidably,** necessarily, **inescapably,** inevasibly, unpreventably, ineluctably; irrevocably, indefeasibly; uncontrollably; relentlessly, inexorably, unyieldingly, inflexibly; fatefully, **certainly, surely.**

.20 PHRS **it is necessary, it must be,** it needs must be or it must needs be [both archaic], it will be, there's no two ways about it, it must have its way; it cannot be helped, there is no helping it or help for it, that's the way the cookie crumbles or the ball bounces [informal], what will be will be, it's God's will; the die is cast; it is fated 640.11.

## 640. PREDETERMINATION

.1 NOUNS **predetermination, predestination,** foredestiny, **preordination,** foreordination, foreordainment; decree; foregone conclusion; **necessity** 639; foreknowledge, prescience 542.3.

.2 **fate, fatality, fortune, lot,** cup, **portion,** appointed lot, kismet, weird, moira [Gk], future 121; **destiny,** destination, **end,** final lot; **doom,** foredoom [archaic], God's will, will of Heaven; **inevitability** 639.7; handwriting on the wall; book of fate; Fortune's wheel, wheel of fortune or chance; astral influences, stars, planets, constellation, astrology 375.20; unlucky day, ides of March, Friday, Friday the thirteenth, dies funestis [L].

.3 **Fates,** Fata [L], Parcae, Moirai [Gk], Clotho, Lachesis, Atropos; Nona, Decuma, Morta; Weird Sisters, Weirds; Norns; Urdur, Verthandi, Skuld; Fortuna, Lady or Dame Fortune, Tyche [Gk]; Providence, Heaven, "a divinity that shapes our ends, rough-hew them how we will" [Shakespeare].

.4 **determinism, fatalism,** necessitarianism, necessarianism, predeterminism; predestinarianism, Calvinism, election.

.5 **determinist, fatalist,** necessitarian, necessarian; predestinationist, predestinarian, Calvinist.

.6 VERBS **predetermine, predecide,** preestablish; **predestine,** predestinate, **preordain,** foreordain.

.7 **destine,** destinate [archaic], **ordain, fate,**

mark, appoint [archaic]; have in store for; **doom**, foredoom, devote.

.8 ADJS **predetermined, predecided,** preestablished, **predestined,** predestinate, **preordained,** foreordained; forgone.

.9 **destined, fated,** fateful, fatal [archaic], ordained, written, in the cards, marked, appointed [archaic], in store; **doomed,** foredoomed, devoted; inevitable 639.15.

.10 **deterministic, fatalistic,** necessitarian, necessarian.

.11 PHRS it is fated, it is written, it's in the cards; what will be will be, *che sarà sarà* [Ital], *que será será* [Sp].

### 641. PREARRANGEMENT

.1 NOUNS **prearrangement,** preordering, preconcertedness; **premeditation, plotting, planning, scheming; put-up job** [informal], **frame-up** [slang], packed *or* rigged jury [slang], setup [slang], packed deal *or* stacked deck [both slang]; directed verdict.

.2 **schedule, program,** programma, **bill,** card, **calendar,** docket, slate; playbill; batting order, **lineup** [informal], **roster;** blueprint, budget; **prospectus;** schedule *or* program of operation, **order of the day,** things to be done, **agenda,** list of agenda; protocol; **bill of fare, menu,** *carte du jour* [Fr].

.3 VERBS **prearrange,** precontrive, predesign [archaic], preorder, preconcert; premeditate, plot, plan, scheme; **fix** *or* **rig** [both informal]; pack [slang], set up *or* cook up [both slang]; **stack the cards** *or* pack the deal [both slang]; put in the bag *or* sew up [both slang]; frame *or* frame up [both slang].

.4 **schedule, line up** [informal], **slate, book,** bill, program, calendar, docket, budget, put on the agenda.

.5 ADJS **prearranged,** precontrived, predesigned [archaic], preordered, preconcerted, cut out; premeditated, plotted, planned, schemed; **fixed** *or* rigged [both informal], packed *or* stacked [both slang], **put-up** [informal], set-up *or* cooked-up [both slang]; **in the bag** *or* on ice *or* cinched *or* sewed up [all slang]; cut-and-dried, cut-and-dry.

.6 **scheduled, slated,** booked, billed, to come.

### 642. CUSTOM, HABIT

.1 NOUNS **custom, convention,** use, **usage,** standard usage, standard behavior, **wont,** wonting, **way,** established way, time-honored practice, **tradition,** standing custom, **folkway,** manner, **practice,** praxis, prescription, **observance,** ritual, consuetude, **mores** [pl]; proper thing, what is done, social **convention** 645; *bon ton* [Fr], **fashion** 644; manners, etiquette 646.3; conformity 82.

.2 "a sort of second nature" [Cicero], "the universal sovereign" [Pindar], "that unwritten law, by which the people keep even kings in awe" [D'Avenant], "often only the antiquity of error" [Cyprian].

.3 **culture, society, civilization;** trait, culture trait; key trait; complex, culture complex, trait-complex; culture area; culture center; **folkways, mores,** system of values, **ethos, culture pattern;** cultural change; cultural lag; culture conflict; acculturation, culture contact [Brit], cultural drift.

.4 **habit,** habitude, **custom, second nature;** use, **usage,** trick, wont, **way,** practice, praxis; bad habit; stereotype; "the petrifaction of feelings" [L. E. Landon]; pattern, **habit pattern;** stereotyped behavior; force of habit; creature of habit; automatism 639.5; peculiarity, characteristic 80.4.

.5 **rule,** procedure, **common practice,** form, prescribed *or* set form; common *or* ordinary run of things, matter of course; standard operating procedure, SOP, drill [Brit]; standing orders [pl].

.6 **routine,** run, **round,** beat, track, beaten path; jog trot, **rut, groove,** well-worn groove; **treadmill,** squirrel cage; grind *or* daily grind [both informal]; **red tape,** redtapeism, **bureaucracy,** bureaucratism, *chinoiserie* [Fr].

.7 **customariness,** accustomedness, wontedness, **habitualness; inveteracy,** inveterateness, confirmedness, settledness, fixedness; commonness, prevalence 79.2.

.8 **habituation, accustoming; conditioning,** seasoning, training; **familiarization,** naturalization [archaic], breaking-in [informal], orientation; **domestication, taming,** breaking, housebreaking; acclimation, acclimatization; **inurement,** hardening, case hardening; adaption, adjustment, accommodation 82.1.

.9 **addiction,** addictedness; dependence, psychological dependence, drug dependence; craving 634.6; habituation; cocainism; physical dependence; **drug addiction,** a habit [informal]; tolerance, acquired tolerance; withdrawal sickness, withdrawal symptoms; amphetamine withdrawal symptoms, crash [slang]; opiate addiction, morphinism; barbiturism, barbiturate addiction; **alcoholism** 996.3, chronic alcoholism, acute alcoholism, dipsomania; nicotine addiction 434.10, chain smoking; drug culture.

.10 **addict,** fiend [informal], habitual; **drug user,** user [informal], tripper [slang], drug abuser; doper or freak or **head** [all slang]; marijuana smoker, **pothead** [slang]; cocaine sniffer, cokie or snowbird [both slang]; pillhead [slang]; methhead or **speed freak** [both slang]; LSD user; **acid freak** or acidhead or cubehead [all slang]; **drug addict;** narcotics addict; opium eater; **dope fiend** [informal]; **junkie** or hype or hophead [all slang]; **alcoholic,** dipsomaniac, **drunkard** 996.10,11; heavy smoker, **chain smoker,** nicotine addict [informal]; glue sniffer.

.11 VERBS accustom, habituate, wont; **condition,** season, train; familiarize, naturalize [archaic], break in [informal], orient, orientate; **domesticate,** domesticize, **tame,** break, gentle, housebreak; acclimatize, acclimate, inure, harden, case harden; adapt, adjust, accommodate 26.7; confirm, fix, establish 142.9.

.12 **become a habit,** take root, grow on one, take hold of one, take one over.

.13 **be used to, be wont,** wont, **make a practice of;** get used to, get into the way of, **take to,** accustom oneself to; contract or fall into a habit, addict oneself to.

.14 **get in a rut, be in a rut,** move or travel in a groove or rut, run on in a groove, follow the beaten path, go round like a horse in a mill, go on in the old jog-trot way.

.15 ADJS **customary, wonted,** consuetudinary; traditional, time-honored; familiar, everyday, ordinary, **usual** 84.8; **established,** received, accepted; set, prescribed, prescriptive; **normal** 84.7; **standard,** regular, stock, regulation; prevalent, widespread, obtaining, generally accepted, popular, **current** 79.12; **conventional** 645.5; conformable 82.5.

.16 **habitual, regular,** frequent, constant, persistent; repetitive, recurring, recurrent; stereotyped; automatic 639.14; **routine,** well-trodden, well-worn, beaten; trite, hackneyed 883.9.

.17 **accustomed, wont,** wonted, used to; **conditioned,** trained, seasoned; experienced; **familiarized,** naturalized [archaic], broken-in, run-in [informal], oriented, orientated; acclimated, acclimatized; inured,

hardened, case-hardened; adapted, adjusted, accommodated.

.18 **used to, familiar with,** conversant with, **at home in** or **with,** no stranger to, an old hand at.

.19 **habituated,** *habitué* [Fr]; **in the habit of,** used to; **addicted to, hooked on** [slang], dependent on; never free from; **in a rut; addicted, hooked** or strung out or spaced out or hyped [all slang], dependent.

.20 **addictive, habit-forming,** habituating, conditioning; hard [informal], physiologically addictive, psychologically addictive.

.21 **confirmed, inveterate, chronic, established,** long-established, **fixed, settled,** rooted, thorough; incorrigible, irreversible; **deep-rooted,** deep-set, deep-settled, **deep-seated,** deep-fixed, deep-dyed; **infixed, ingrained,** fast, dyed-in-the-wool; implanted, inculcated, instilled; set, **set in one's ways,** settled in habit.

.22 ADVS **customarily,** conventionally, accustomedly, wontedly; normally, **usually** 84.9; **as is the custom;** as is usual, *comme d'habitude* [Fr]; as things go, as the world goes.

.23 **habitually, regularly,** routinely, frequently, persistently, repetitively, recurringly; **inveterately, chronically; from habit, by** or **from force of habit,** as is one's wont.

# 643. UNACCUSTOMEDNESS

.1 NOUNS **unaccustomedness,** unwontedness, disaccustomedness, unusedness, unhabituatedness; **unfamiliarity,** unacquaintance, unconversance, unpracticedness, newness to; inexperience 734.2; ignorance 477.

.2 VERBS **disaccustom, cure, break of,** stop, **wean.**

.3 **break the habit, cure oneself of,** disaccustom oneself, wean oneself from, break the pattern, break one's chains or fetters; **give up,** leave off, **abandon,** drop, stop, discontinue, kick or shake [both slang], throw off, rid oneself of; get on the wagon, swear off 992.8.

.4 ADJS **unaccustomed,** disaccustomed, **unused, unwonted;** uninured, unseasoned, untrained, unhardened; **unhabituated, not in the habit of;** out of the habit of, rusty; weaned; **unused to, unfamiliar with,** unacquainted with, unconversant with, unpracticed, new to, a stranger to; inexperienced 734.17; ignorant 477.12.

## 644. FASHION

.1 NOUNS **fashion, style, mode, vogue,** trend, prevailing taste; proper thing, *bon ton* [Fr], custom 642; convention 645.1,2; swim [informal], current *or* stream of fashion; height of fashion; the new look, the season's look; high fashion, *haute couture* [Fr].

.2 **fashionableness,** *bon ton* [Fr], fashionability, **stylishness, modishness,** voguishness; **popularity,** prevalence, currency 79.2.

.3 **smartness, chic,** elegance; style-consciousness, clothes-consciousness; **spruceness, nattiness,** neatness, trimness, sleekness, **dapperness,** jauntiness; sharpness *or* spiffiness *or* classiness *or* niftiness [all slang]; swankness *or* **swankiness** [both informal]; foppery, foppishness, coxcombry, dandyism.

.4 **the rage,** the thing, **the last word** [informal], *le dernier cri* [Fr], **the latest thing,** the latest wrinkle [informal].

.5 **fad, craze, rage;** wrinkle [informal]; novelty 122.2; faddishness, faddiness [informal], faddism; **faddist.**

.6 **society,** *société* [Fr], fashionable society, **polite society, high society,** high life, *beau monde, haut monde* [both Fr], good society; best people, people of fashion, right people; *monde* [Fr], world of fashion, Vanity Fair; **smart set** [informal]; the Four Hundred, **upper crust** *or* upper cut [both informal]; **cream of society,** elite, carriage trade; café society, jet set; beautiful people, in-crowd; *jeunesse dorée* [Fr]; drawing room, salon; social register.

.7 person of fashion, fashionable, man-about-town, man *or* woman of the world, *mondain, mondaine* [both Fr], leader *or* arbiter of fashion, taste-maker, trend-setter, tone-setter, *arbiter elegantiae* [L]; ten best-dressed, fashion plate, clothes-horse, "the glass of fashion and the mold of form" [Shakespeare], Beau Brummel; fop, dandy 903.9; **socialite** [informal]; **clubwoman,** clubman; jet setter; swinger [informal]; **debutante,** subdebutante, deb *or* subdeb [both informal].

.8 VERBS **catch on,** become popular, **become the rage.**

.9 **be fashionable,** be the style, be the rage, be the thing; have a run; cut a figure in society [informal], give a tone to society, set the fashion *or* style *or* tone; dress to kill.

.10 **follow the fashion, get in the swim** [informal], get *or* jump on the bandwagon [slang], join the parade, follow the crowd, go with the stream *or* tide *or* current; keep in step, do as others do; keep up, **keep up appearances,** keep up with the Joneses.

.11 ADJS **fashionable, in fashion, smart, in style, in vogue; all the rage,** all the thing; **popular,** prevalent, current 79.12; **up-to-date,** up-to-datish, up-to-the-minute, hip *or* mod [both slang], trendy [informal], newfashioned, modern, new 122.9–14; **in the swim.**

.12 **stylish, modish,** voguish, vogue; *soigné or soignée* [both Fr]; *à la mode* [Fr], in the mode.

.13 **chic, smart,** elegant; style-conscious, clothes-conscious; **well-dressed,** well-groomed, *soigné or soignée* [both Fr], dressed to advantage, dressed to kill, dressed to the teeth, dressed to the nines, well-turned-out; **spruce, natty,** neat, trim, sleek, smug, trig, tricksy [archaic]; **dapper,** dashing, jaunty, braw [Scot]; sharp *or* spiffy *or* classy *or* nifty *or* snazzy [all slang]; **swank** *or* **swanky** [both informal], posh [informal], ritzy [informal], swell *or* nobby [both slang]; genteel; exquisite, *recherché* [Fr]; cosmopolitan, sophisticated 733.26.

.14 **ultrafashionable,** ultrastylish, ultrasmart; chichi; foppish, dandified, dandyish, dandiacal.

.15 **faddish,** faddy [informal].

.16 socially prominent, in society, high-society, elite; café-society, jet-set; lace-curtain, silk-stocking.

.17 ADVS **fashionably, stylishly, modishly,** *à la mode* [Fr], in the latest style *or* mode.

.18 smartly, chicly, elegantly, exquisitely; **sprucely, nattily,** neatly, trimly, sleekly; **dapperly,** jauntily, dashingly, swankly *or* swankily [both informal]; foppishly, dandyishly.

## 645. SOCIAL CONVENTION

.1 NOUNS **social convention, convention,** conventional usage, **social usage, form, formality;** custom 642; conformity 82; **propriety, decorum,** decorousness, correctness, *convenance, bienséance* [both Fr], decency, seemliness, civility [archaic], good form, etiquette 646.3; **conventionalism, conventionality,** Grundyism; **Mrs. Grundy.**

.2 **the conventions,** the proprieties, the mores, the right things, accepted *or* sanctioned conduct, what is done, civilized behavior; **dictates of society,** dictates of Mrs. Grundy.

.3 conventionalist, Grundy, Mrs. Grundy; conformist 82.2.

.4 VERBS **conform,** observe the proprieties, play the game, follow the rules 82.3,4.

.5 ADJS **conventional, decorous,** orthodox, **correct,** right, **proper,** decent, seemly, meet; **accepted, recognized,** acknowledged, received, admitted, approved, being done; *comme il faut, de rigueur* [both Fr]; **traditional, customary** 642.15; formal 646.7; conformable 82.5.

.6 ADVS **conventionally,** decorously, orthodoxly; **customarily, traditionally;** correctly, properly, as is proper, as it should be, *comme il faut* [Fr]; according to use *or* custom, according to the dictates of society *or* Mrs. Grundy.

### 646. FORMALITY

.1 NOUNS **formality, form, formalness; ceremony,** ceremonial, **ceremoniousness; ritual,** rituality; extrinsicality, impersonality 6.1; formalization, stylization, conventionalization; **stiffness, stiltedness,** primness, rigidness, starchiness, buckram [archaic], **dignity,** gravity, weight, solemnity 871; **pomp** 904.6; pomposity 904.7.

.2 **formalism, ceremonialism, ritualism;** legalism; pedantry, pedantism, pedanticism; precisianism, preciseness, preciousness, preciosity, purism; punctiliousness, punctilio, scrupulousness.

.3 **etiquette,** social code, rules of conduct; **formalities,** social procedures, social conduct; **manners,** good manners, exquisite manners, quiet good manners, **politeness,** *politesse* [Fr], natural politeness, comity, civility 936.1; **amenities,** decencies, civilities, elegancies, **social graces, mores, proprieties;** decorum, good form; **courtliness,** elegance 589; **protocol,** diplomatic code; punctilio, point of etiquette; convention, social usage.

.4 (ceremonial function) **ceremony,** ceremonial; **rite, ritual, formality; solemnity, service, function,** office, **observance,** performance; **exercise,** exercises; **celebration,** solemnization; **liturgy,** religious ceremony 1040.3; **rite of passage,** *rite de passage* [Fr]; convocation; commencement, commencement exercises; graduation, graduation exercises; baccalaureate service; inaugural, inauguration; initiation; formal; empty formality *or* ceremony, mummery.

.5 VERBS **formalize,** ritualize, solemnize, cel-

ebrate, dignify; **observe;** conventionalize, stylize.

.6 **stand on ceremony,** observe the formalities, follow protocol.

.7 ADJS **formal,** formulary; **formalist, formalistic;** legalistic; pedantic(al); stylized, conventionalized; extrinsic, outward, impersonal 6.3; surface, **superficial** 224.6, nominal 583.15.

.8 **ceremonious, ceremonial; ritualistic, ritual;** hieratic(al), sacerdotal, liturgic 1040.22; **solemn** 871.3; **pompous** 904.22; **stately** 904.21; well-mannered 936.16; **conventional,** decorous 645.5.

.9 **stiff, stilted,** prim, rigid, starch, starched, buckram, in buckram.

.10 **punctilious, scrupulous, precise,** precisian, precisionist, precious, puristic; exact, meticulous 533.12; **orderly, methodical** 59.6.

.11 ADVS **formally,** in due form, in set form; **ceremoniously, ritually,** ritualistically; solemnly 871.4; for form's sake, *pro forma* [L], **as a matter of form.**

.12 **stiffly, stiltedly,** starchly, primly, rigidly.

### 647. INFORMALITY

.1 NOUNS **informality, informalness, unceremoniousness; casualness,** offhandedness, **ease, easiness,** easygoingness; **relaxedness;** affability, graciousness, cordiality, sociability 922; Bohemianism, unconventionality 83.2; **familiarity; naturalness,** simplicity, plainness, homeliness, homeyness, folksiness [informal], common touch, **unaffectedness,** unpretentiousness 902.2; unconstraint, unconstrainedness, looseness; irregularity.

.2 VERBS **not stand on ceremony,** let one's hair down [slang], be oneself, come as you are.

.3 ADJS **informal, unceremonious; casual, offhand,** offhanded, unstudied, easy, easygoing, free and easy; *dégagé* [Fr]; **relaxed;** affable, gracious, cordial, sociable 922.18; Bohemian, unconventional 83.6; **familiar; natural,** simple, plain, homely, homey, folksy [informal], *haymish* [Yid]; **unaffected, unassuming** 902.7; unconstrained, loose; irregular; unofficial.

.4 ADVS **informally, unceremoniously,** without ceremony, *sans cérémonie, sans façon* [both Fr]; **casually,** offhand, offhandedly; relaxedly; familiarly; **naturally,** simply, plainly; **unaffectedly, unassumingly** 902.11; unconstrainedly, unofficially; *en famille* [Fr].

## 648. MOTIVATION, INDUCEMENT

.1 NOUNS motive, reason, **cause**, source, spring, mainspring; matter, score, consideration; **ground, basis** 153.1; sake; **goal** 653.2; **ideal**, principle, **ambition**, aspiration, inspiration, guiding light or star, lodestar; calling, vocation; intention 653; ulterior motive.

.2 motivation, moving, actuation, **prompting**, stimulation, animation; direction, inner-direction, other-direction; influence 172.

.3 inducement, enlistment, engagement, solicitation, **persuasion**, suasion; exhortation, hortation, preaching, preachment; selling, sales talk, salesmanship; jawboning [informal]; lobbying; coaxing, wheedling, working on [informal], cajolery, cajolement, conning, snow job [slang], blandishment, sweet talk or soft soap [both informal]; **allurement** 650.

.4 incitement, incitation, instigation, stimulation, arousal, excitement, excitation, fomentation, agitation, inflammation, firing, stirring, stirring-up, impassioning, whipping-up, rabble-rousing; **provocation,** irritation, exasperation; pep talk, pep rally.

.5 urging, pressure, pressing; **encouragement**, abetment; **insistence,** instance; goading, prodding, spurring, pricking, needling.

.6 urge, urgency; impulse, impulsion, compulsion; press, **pressure,** drive, push; sudden or rash impulse; constraint, exigency, stress, pinch.

.7 incentive, inducement, encouragement, persuasive, invitation, provocation, incitement; stimulus, stimulation, stimulative, fillip, whet; carrot; reward, payment 841; **profit** 811.3; bait, **lure** 650.2; bribe 651.2; sweetening or sweetener [both informal], interest, percentage, what's in it for one [informal].

.8 goad, spur, prod, prick [archaic], sting, gadfly; oxgoad; rowel; whip, lash, whiplash, gad [dial].

.9 inspiration, infusion, infection; fire, firing; **animation, exhilaration,** enlivenment; afflatus, divine afflatus; genius, animus, moving or animating spirit.

.10 prompter, mover, prime mover, impeller, energizer, galvanizer, inducer, **actuator, animator,** moving spirit; **encourager,** abettor, **inspirer,** firer, spark, sparker, spark plug [informal]; persuader; **stimula-**tor, gadfly; **tempter** 650.3; coaxer, coax [informal], wheedler, cajoler, pleader.

.11 instigator, inciter, exciter, urger; provoker, *provocateur* [Fr], *agent provocateur* [Fr], catalyst; **agitator, fomenter,** inflamer; agitprop; **rabble-rouser,** rouser, **demagogue; firebrand, incendiary;** seditionist, seditionary; **troublemaker,** mischief-maker, ringleader.

.12 VERBS motivate, move, set in motion, actuate, move to action, impel, propel; egoinvolve; stimulate, energize, galvanize, animate, spark; promote, foster; force, compel 756.4.

.13 prompt, provoke, evoke, elicit, call up, summon up, muster up, call forth, inspire; bring about, cause 153.11.

.14 urge, press, push, work on [informal], twist one's arm [slang]; importune, nag, pressure, high-pressure, bring pressure to bear upon, throw one's weight around, throw one's weight into the scale, jawbone [informal]; lobby; coax, wheedle, cajole, blandish, plead with, sweet-talk or soft-soap [both informal], exhort, call on or upon, advocate, recommend; insist, insist upon 753.7.

.15 goad, prod, poke [archaic], nudge, spur, prick, sting, needle; whip, lash, flog [Brit].

.16 urge on or along, egg on [informal], hound on, hie on, hasten on, hurry on, speed on; goad on, spur on, drive on, whip on; cheer on, root on [informal].

.17 incite, instigate, put up to [slang]; set on, sic on; foment, ferment, agitate, arouse, excite, stir up, work up, whip up; rally; inflame, incense [archaic], fire, heat, heat up, impassion; provoke, pique, whet; tickle; nettle; lash into a fury or frenzy; pour oil on the fire, feed the fire, add fuel to the flame, fan, fan the flame, blow the coals, stir the embers.

.18 kindle, enkindle, fire, spark, trigger, touch off, set off, light the fuse.

.19 rouse, arouse, raise, raise up, waken, awaken, wake up, turn on [slang], stir, stir up, set astir, pique.

.20 inspire, inspirit, spirit, spirit up; fire, fire one's imagination; animate, exhilarate, enliven; infuse, infect, inject, inoculate, imbue or embue, inform.

.21 encourage, give encouragement, pat or clap on the back; invite, ask for; abet, aid and abet, countenance, keep in countenance; foster, nurture, nourish, feed.

.22 induce, prompt, move one to, influence, sway, incline, dispose, carry, bring, lead,

lead one to; lure 650.4; tempt 650.5; determine, decide; enlist; procure, engage [archaic], interest in, get to do.

.23 persuade, prevail on or upon, prevail with, sway, convince, bring round, bring to reason, bring to one's senses; win, win over, bring over, draw over, gain, gain over; talk over, talk into, argue into, outtalk [informal]; wangle, wangle into; hook or hook in [both slang], con, sell or sell one on [both informal], charm, captivate 650.6; wear down, overcome one's resistance, twist one's arm [slang].

.24 persuade oneself, make oneself easy about, make sure of, make up one's mind; be persuaded, rest easy.

.25 ADJS motivating, motivational, motive, moving, animating, actuating, impelling, impulsive, inducive [archaic], directive; urgent, pressing, driving; compelling 756.9; causal, causative 153.14.

.26 inspiring, inspirational, inspiriting; infusive; animating, exhilarating, enlivening.

.27 provocative, provoking, piquant, exciting, challenging, prompting, rousing, stirring, stimulating, stimulant, stimulative, energizing, galvanizing, galvanic; encouraging, inviting, alluring 650.7; auxo–.

.28 incitive, inciting, incentive; instigative, instigating; agitative, agitational; inflammatory, incendiary, fomenting, rabble-rousing.

.29 persuasive, suasive, persuading; wheedling, cajoling; hortative, hortatory; exhortative, exhortatory.

.30 moved, motivated, prompted, impelled, actuated; stimulated, animated; minded, inclined, of a mind to, with half a mind to; inner-directed, other-directed.

.31 inspired, fired, afire, on fire.

### 649. PRETEXT

.1 NOUNS pretext, pretense, pretension, lying pretension, show, ostensible or announced or public motive; front, façade, sham 616.3; excuse, apology, protestation, poor excuse, lame excuse; put-off; handle, peg to hang on, leg to stand on, locus standi [L]; subterfuge, refuge, device, stratagem, feint, trick 618.6; dust thrown in the eye, smoke screen, screen, cover, stalking-horse, blind; guise, semblance; mask, cloak, veil; gloss, varnish, color; cover-up, cover story, alibi.

.2 claim, profession, allegation.

.3 VERBS pretext, make a pretext of, take as an excuse or reason or occasion, urge as a motive, pretend, make a pretense of; put

up a front or false front; allege, claim, profess, purport, avow; protest too much.

.4 hide under, cover oneself with, shelter under, take cover under, wrap oneself in, cloak or mantle oneself with, take refuge in; conceal one's motive with.

.5 ADJS pretexted, pretended, alleged, claimed, professed, purported, avowed; ostensible, hypocritical, specious; so-called, in name only.

.6 ADVS ostensibly, allegedly, purportedly, professedly, avowedly; for the record, for public consumption; under the pretext of, as a pretext, as an excuse, as a cover or cover-up or alibi.

### 650. ALLUREMENT

.1 NOUNS allurement, allure, enticement, inveiglement, invitation, agacerie [Fr], blandishment, cajolery; inducement 648.7; temptation, tantalization; seduction, seducement; beguilement, beguiling, come-hither [dial]; fascination, captivation, enthrallment, entrapment, snaring; enchantment, witchery, bewitchery, bewitchment; attraction, interest, charm, glamour, appeal, magnetism; charisma; sex appeal, SA [slang]; attractiveness, charmingness, seductiveness, winsomeness, winning ways; song of the Sirens, voice of the tempter; forbidden fruit; wooing 932.6; flirtation 932.8.

.2 lure, charm, come-on [slang], drawing card, drawcard; decoy, decoy duck; bait, ground bait, baited trap; snare, trap, hook; endearment 932.

.3 tempter, seducer, enticer, inveigler, charmer, enchanter, fascinator, tantalizer, teaser; coquette, flirt; Don Juan; Pied Piper of Hamelin; temptress, enchantress, seductress, siren; Siren, Circe, Lorelei, Parthenope; vampire, vamp [slang], femme fatale [Fr].

.4 VERBS lure, allure, entice, seduce, inveigle, decoy, draw, draw on, lead on; give the come-on or bat the eyes at [both slang], flirt with, flirt 932.18; woo 932.19; coax, cajole, blandish; ensnare 618.18; draw in, suck in or rope in [both slang]; bait, offer bait to, bait the hook, angle with a silver hook.

.5 attract, interest, appeal, engage, fetch [informal], attract one's interest, be attractive, take or tickle one's fancy; invite, summon, beckon; tempt, tantalize, titillate, tickle, tease, whet the appetite, make one's mouth water, dangle before one.

**.6 fascinate, captivate, charm,** becharm, spell, spellbind, cast a spell, put under a spell, **beguile, intrigue, enthrall,** infatuate, **enrapture, transport, enravish, entrance, enchant,** witch, **bewitch,** vamp [slang], carry away, turn one's head; hypnotize, mesmerize.

**.7** ADJS **alluring, fascinating, captivating, charming, glamorous,** exotic, **enchanting,** spellful, **spellbinding, entrancing,** ravishing, **enravishing, intriguing, enthralling,** witching; **bewitching; attractive, interesting, appealing,** engaging, taking, fetching [informal], catching, winning, winsome, prepossessing; exciting; charismatic; **seductive,** seducing, **beguiling, enticing, inviting,** come-hither [informal]; flirtatious, coquettish; coaxing, cajoling, blandishing; **tempting, tantalizing,** teasing, **titillating,** titillative, tickling; **provocative,** *provoquant* [Fr]; appetizing, mouth-watering, piquant; **irresistible;** siren, sirenic; hypnotic, mesmeric.

**.8** ADVS **alluringly, fascinatingly,** captivatingly, charmingly, enchantingly, entrancingly, enravishingly, intriguingly, beguilingly, glamorously, bewitchingly; attractively, appealingly, engagingly, winsomely; **enticingly, seductively,** with bedroom eyes [slang]; **temptingly,** provocatively; **tantalizingly,** teasingly; piquantly, appetizingly; irresistibly; hypnotically, mesmerically.

## 651. BRIBERY

**.1** NOUNS **bribery,** bribing, subornation, **corruption, graft,** bribery and corruption.

**.2 bribe,** bribe money, sop, sop to Cerberus, gratuity, gratification [archaic], payoff [informal], boodle [slang]; hush money [slang]; payola [slang]; protection.

**.3** VERBS **bribe,** throw a sop to; grease [informal], **grease the palm** or **hand,** tickle the palm or tickle in the palm; **purchase;** buy or **buy off** or pay off [all informal]; suborn, **corrupt,** tamper with; reach or get at or get to [all informal]; approach, try to bribe; **fix, take care of.**

**.4** ADJS **bribable,** corruptible, purchasable, buyable; approachable; fixable; on the take [slang], on the pad [slang]; **venal, corrupt.**

## 652. DISSUASION

**.1** NOUNS **dissuasion,** talking out of [informal], remonstrance, expostulation, admonition, monition, **warning,** caveat, **caution,** cautioning; intimidation, deter-

ment, deterrence, scaring or frightening off.

**.2 deterrent,** determent; **discouragement,** disincentive; damp, damper, **wet blanket,** cold water, chill.

**.3** VERBS **dissuade,** convince to the contrary, **talk out of** [informal], kid out of [slang]; unconvince, unpersuade; remonstrate, expostulate, admonish, cry out against; **warn, caution;** intimidate, scare or frighten off, daunt 891.26.

**.4 disincline, indispose,** disaffect, disinterest; **deter,** repel, turn from, turn away or aside; divert, deflect; distract, put off or turn off [both slang]; wean from; **discourage; throw cold water on,** throw or lay a wet blanket on, damp, dampen, cool, chill, quench, blunt.

**.5** ADJS **dissuasive, dissuading, disinclining, discouraging; deterrent;** expostulatory, admonitory, monitory, cautionary; intimidating.

## 653. INTENTION

**.1** NOUNS **intention, intent,** intendment, **aim,** effect, counsel [archaic], meaning, view, study, animus, **point, purpose,** function, set or settled or fixed purpose; sake; **design, plan,** project, idea; **proposal,** prospectus; **resolve,** resolution, mind, will; **motive** 648.1; determination 624.1; desideratum, desideration, **ambition,** aspiration, **desire** 634; striving, nisus.

**.2 objective, object, aim, end, goal,** destination, mark, pursuit, object in mind, **end in view; target,** butt, bull's-eye, quintain; quarry, prey, game; reason for being, *raison d'être* [Fr]; by-purpose, by-end; final cause, ultimate aim, "the be-all and the end-all" [Shakespeare], teleology.

**.3 intentionality, deliberation, deliberateness,** express intention, expressness, premeditation, predeliberation, preconsideration, **calculation, calculatedness, predetermination,** preresolution, forethought, aforethought.

**.4** VERBS **intend, purpose, plan,** purport, **mean,** have every intention, think, **propose; resolve,** determine 624.7; project, **design,** destine; **aim,** aim at, drive at, aspire to or after, set one's sights on, go for, be after, set before oneself, purpose to oneself; harbor a design; **desire** 634.14–20.

**.5 intend to, mean to, aim to,** propose to, resolve to.

**.6 plan on, figure on,** count on, calculate

on, reckon on, bank on *or* upon; bargain for.

.7 **contemplate, meditate; envisage,** envision, **have in mind, have in view;** have an eye to, **have a mind to,** have half a mind to, have a good *or* great mind to.

.8 **premeditate, calculate, preresolve, predetermine,** predeliberate, preconsider, forethink, **work out beforehand;** plan 654.9; plot, scheme 654.10.

.9 ADJS **intentional, intended,** proposed, purposed, **projected, designed,** of design, aimed, aimed at, **meant, purposeful,** purposive, **willful, voluntary, deliberate;** deliberated; considered, studied, advised, **calculated, contemplated, envisaged,** envisioned, meditated, **conscious,** knowing, witting; planned 654.13; teleological.

.10 **premeditated, predeliberated,** preconsidered, **predetermined, preresolved, prepense, aforethought.**

.11 ADVS **intentionally, purposely,** purposefully, purposively, **on purpose,** with purpose, **deliberately, designedly, willfully, voluntarily;** pointedly; **wittingly, consciously, knowingly;** advisedly, **calculatedly,** contemplatedly, meditatedly, premeditatedly, **with premeditation, with intent,** with full intent, **by design,** with one's eyes open; with malice aforethought, in cold blood.

.12 PREPS, CONJS for, to; **in order to** *or* **that,** so, **so that, so as to;** for the purpose of, to the end that, with the intent that, with the view of, **with a view to,** with an eye to; in contemplation of, in consideration of; **for the sake of.**

## 654. PLAN

.1 NOUNS **plan, scheme, design, method, program,** device, contrivance, game, envisagement, conception, enterprise, **idea;** organization, rationalization, systematization, schematization; charting, mapping, graphing, blueprinting; **planning,** calculation, figuring; planning function; longrange planning, long-range plan; master plan, the picture *or* the big picture [both informal]; approach, attack; way, procedure 657.1; **arrangement,** prearrangement, system, disposition, layout, setup, lineup; schedule; schema, schematism, scheme of arrangement; blueprint, **guidelines,** program of action; methodology; working plan, ground plan, tactical plan, strategic plan; tactics, **strategy;** operations research; **intention** 653; forethought, foresight 542.

.2 **project, projection; proposal,** prospectus, proposition; scenario, game plan [informal].

.3 **diagram, plot, chart, blueprint,** graph, table; **design, pattern,** copy [archaic], cartoon; **sketch, draft, drawing,** working drawing, rough; *brouillon, ébauche, esquisse* [all Fr]; **outline, delineation,** skeleton, figure, profile; house plan, ground plan, ichnography; elevation, projection.

.4 **map, chart;** general reference map, special map, thematic map; political map; road map, transportation map; physical map, terrain map, relief map, contour map, topographic chart; photomap; **globe,** terrestrial globe, celestial globe; **atlas;** mariner's chart, hydrographic chart; aeronautical chart; weather map, weather chart, climatic chart; celestial chart, astronomical chart, heliographic chart; hachure, contour line, isoline, layer tint; **scale,** graphic scale, representative fraction; **legend;** grid line, meridian, parallel, latitude, longitude; index; **projection,** map projection; azimuthal projection, azimuthal equidistant projection, gnomonic projection; cylindrical projection, Mercator projection, Miller projection; conic projection, Lambert conformal conic projection *or* Lambert conformal projection, polyconic projection; sinusoidal projection; **cartography,** chorography, topography, photogrammetry, phototopography; **cartographer, map maker, mapper,** chorographer, topographer, photogrammetrist.

.5 **policy, polity, principles,** guiding principles; **procedure,** course, line, plan of action; creed 501.3; **platform;** position paper.

.6 **intrigue,** web of intrigue, **plot, scheme,** deep-laid plot *or* scheme, underplot, game *or* little game [both informal], trick, stratagem, finesse; counterplot; **conspiracy,** confederacy, covin, complot [archaic], cabal; **complicity, collusion, connivance;** artifice 735.3; **contrivance,** contriving; **scheming,** schemery, plotting; finagling [informal], **machination,** manipulation, **maneuvering,** engineering, rigging; frame-up [informal]; wire-pulling [informal].

.7 **planner, designer,** deviser, contriver, framer, projector; enterpriser, entrepreneur; organizer, promoter, developer; **architect, tactician, strategist, strategian.**

.8 **schemer, plotter,** counterplotter, finagler [informal], Machiavellian; **intriguer,** *intri-*

gant, *intrigante* [both Fr]; **conspirer, conspirator,** coconspirator, **conniver;** maneuverer, machinator, operator [informal], opportunist, exploiter; wire-puller [informal].

.9 VERBS **plan, devise, contrive, design,** frame, shape, cast, concert, lay plans; organize, rationalize, systematize, schematize, methodize; **arrange,** prearrange, make arrangements, set up, work up, work out; **schedule;** lay down a plan, shape *or* mark out a course; program; **calculate,** figure; **project,** cut out, make a projection, forecast [archaic], plan ahead; intend 653.4.

.10 **plot, scheme, intrigue,** be up to something; **conspire, connive,** collude, complot [archaic], cabal; **hatch, hatch up,** cook up [informal], brew, concoct, hatch *or* lay a plot; **maneuver,** machinate, finesse, operate [informal], engineer, rig, wangle [informal], angle, finagle [informal]; frame *or* frame up [both informal]; counterplot, countermine.

.11 **plot, map, chart, blueprint; diagram,** graph; **sketch;** draw up a plan; map out, plot out, **lay out,** sketch out, set out, mark out; lay off, mark off.

.12 **outline,** line, **delineate,** chalk out, brief; **sketch, draft,** trace; block in *or* out; rough in, rough out.

.13 ADJS **planned, devised, designed,** shaped, set, **blueprinted,** charted, **contrived; plotted;** arranged; organized, rationalized, systematized, schematized, methodized; worked out, calculated, figured; **projected; scheduled,** on the agenda, in the works, on the calendar, on the docket, on the anvil, on the carpet, on the tapis [archaic], *sur le tapis* [Fr]; tactical, **strategic,** strategetic.

.14 **scheming, calculating, designing, contriving, plotting, intriguing;** Machiavellian, Byzantine; **conniving,** connivent [archaic], conspiring, collusive; stratagemical; up to.

.15 schematic, diagrammatic.

## 655. PURSUIT

.1 NOUNS **pursuit,** pursuing, pursuance, prosecution [archaic]; **quest,** seeking, hunting, searching 485.14; **following,** follow, follow-up; tracking, trailing, tracking down, dogging, shadowing, stalking; **chase,** hot pursuit; hue and cry.

.2 **hunting,** gunning, shooting, venery, cynegetics, sport, sporting; **hunt, chase, chevy** *or* **chivy** [both Brit], shikar [India], coursing; fox hunting; hawking, falconry; stalking, still hunt.

.3 **fishing,** fishery, **angling,** piscation, halieutics; rod and reel; harpooning; whaling; casting, fly fishing; still-fishing; trolling; trawling; jigging; guddling.

.4 **pursuer,** pursuant, **chaser,** follower; hunter, quester, **seeker.**

.5 **hunter, huntsman,** sportsman, **Nimrod;** huntress, sportswoman; stalker; courser; trapper; big game hunter, shikari [India], white hunter; jacklighter, jacker, beater.

.6 **fisher, fisherman, angler,** *piscator* [L], piscatorian, piscatorialist; Waltonian, "the compleat angler" [Izaak Walton]; dibber, dibbler, troller, trawler, jacker, jigger, guddler, drifter, drift netter, whaler.

.7 **quarry, game, prey,** venery, beasts of venery, victim, the hunted; kill; big game.

.8 VERBS **pursue,** prosecute [archaic], **follow,** follow up, **go after,** take out after [informal], run after, run in pursuit of, make after, go in pursuit of; raise the hunt, raise the hue and cry, hollo after; **chase, give chase,** chivy; hound, dog; **quest,** quest after, **seek,** seek out, hunt, search 485.29,30.

.9 **hunt,** go hunting, hunt down, chase, run, shikar [India], sport; shoot, gun; course; ride to hounds, follow the hounds; **track,** trail; **stalk,** prowl after, still-hunt; hound, dog; hawk, falcon; fowl; flush, start; drive, beat; jack, jacklight.

.10 **fish,** go fishing, **angle;** cast one's hook *or* net; bait the hook; shrimp, whale, clam, grig; still-fish, fly-fish, troll, bob, dap, dib *or* dibble, gig, jig, spin; torch, jack, jacklight; guddle; net, trawl, seine; drive.

.11 ADJS **pursuing,** pursuant, following; **questing, seeking, searching** 485.37; **in pursuit,** in hot pursuit, in full cry; hunting, cynegetic, fishing, piscatory, piscatorial, halieutic(al).

.12 PREPS **after, in pursuit** *or* **pursuance of,** in search of, on the lookout for, in the market for, out for; on the track *or* trail of, on the scent of.

.13 INTERJS (hunting cries) view halloo!, yoicks! [archaic]; so-ho!, tallyho!, tallyho over!, tallyho back!

## 656. BUSINESS, OCCUPATION

.1 NOUNS **business, occupation, employment, service,** employ, **activities,** activity, function, enterprise, undertaking, **work, affairs,** labor; thing *or* bag [both slang]; **affair, matter, concern,** concernment, interest, lookout [informal]; what one is doing or about; commerce 827.

.2 **task, work, stint, job,** labor, job of work, piece of work, **chore,** chare, odd job; **assignment, charge,** project, errand, **mission,** commission, **duty,** service, exercise; things to do, matters in hand, irons in the fire, fish to fry; homework; busywork, make-work.

.3 **function, office,** duty, job, province, place, **role,** *rôle* [Fr], part; **capacity,** character, **position.**

.4 (sphere of work or activity) **field, sphere,** province, department, area, discipline, subdiscipline, orb, orbit, realm, domain, demesne, walk; beat, round.

.5 **position, situation, job,** employment, service, **office, post,** –ate, –cy, –dom, –ship, –ure, –y; **place,** station, berth, billet, **appointment,** engagement, gig [slang]; incumbency, tenure; opening, vacancy; second job, moonlighting [informal].

.6 **vocation, occupation, business, work, line, line of work,** line of business or endeavor, number [informal], walk, **walk of life, calling,** mission, **profession, practice,** pursuit, specialty, specialization, *métier* [Fr], mystery [archaic], **trade,** racket or game [both slang]; **career,** lifework, life's work; **craft,** art, handicraft; careerism, career building.

.7 **avocation, hobby,** hobbyhorse [archaic], sideline, by-line, side interest, pastime, spare-time activity.

.8 **professionalism,** professional standing or status.

.9 **nonprofessionalism, amateurism,** amateur standing or status.

.10 VERBS **occupy, engage, busy,** devote, spend, **employ,** occupy oneself, busy oneself, go about one's business, devote oneself; pass or employ or spend the time; occupy one's time, take up one's time; attend to business, attend to one's work; mind one's business, mind the store [informal], stick to one's last or knitting.

.11 **busy oneself with, do,** occupy or engage oneself with, employ oneself in or upon, pass or employ or spend one's time in; **engage in, take up,** devote oneself to, apply oneself to, address oneself to, have one's hands in, turn one's hand to; concern oneself with, make it one's business; **be about, be doing,** be occupied with, be engaged or employed in, be at work on; practice, follow as an occupation 705.7.

.12 **work,** work at, work for, have a job, be employed, **ply one's trade,** labor in one's

vocation, do one's number [informal], follow a trade, practice a profession, carry on a business or trade, keep up; **do** or **transact business,** carry on business 827.14; set up shop, set up in business, hang out one's shingle [informal]; stay employed, hold down a job [informal]; moonlight [informal]; labor, toil 716.13, 14.

.13 **officiate, function, serve; perform as, act as,** act or play one's part, **do duty,** discharge or perform or exercise the office or duties or functions of, serve in the office or capacity of.

.14 **hold office,** fill an office, occupy a post.

.15 ADJS **businesslike, working;** practical, realistic 536.6; banausic, moneymaking, breadwinning, utilitarian 665.18; materialistic 1031.16; workaday, workday, prosaic 883.8; **commercial** 827.21.

.16 **occupational, vocational,** functional; **professional,** pro [informal]; official; technical, industrial; all in the day's work.

.17 **avocational,** amateur, nonprofessional.

.18 ADVS **professionally, vocationally;** as a profession or vocation; in the course of business.

## 657. WAY

.1 NOUNS **way, wise, manner, means, mode,** form [archaic], **fashion, style,** tone, guise [archaic]; **method,** methodology, **system;** algorithm [math]; **approach,** attack, tack; **technique, procedure, process,** proceeding, course, practice; order; lines, line, line of action; *modus operandi* [L], mode of operation, MO, manner of working, mode of procedure; **routine;** the way of, the how, the drill [Brit].

.2 **route, itinerary, course,** path, track, run, line, road; trajectory, traject, *trajet* [Fr]; circuit, tour, orbit; walk, beat, round; trade route, **sea lane, air lane,** flight path; path of least resistance, primrose path; shortcut 202.5.

.3 **path, track, trail,** –ode; **pathway,** footpath, footway; walkway, catwalk; **sidewalk, walk,** fastwalk, *trottoir* [Fr], foot pavement [Brit]; boardwalk; hiking trail; public walk, promenade, esplanade, alameda, parade, *prado* [Sp], mall; towpath or towing path; bridle path or road or trail or way; bicycle path; berm; run, runway; beaten track or path, rut, groove; garden path.

.4 **passageway, pass, passage,** defile; avenue, artery; corridor, aisle, alley, lane; channel, conduit 396.1; ford, ferry, traject, *trajet*

[Fr]; opening, aperture; access, inlet 302.5; exit, outlet 303.9; connection, communication; covered way, gallery, arcade, portico, colonnade, cloister, ambulatory; underpass, overpass; tunnel, railroad tunnel, vehicular tunnel; junction, interchange, **intersection** 221.2.

.5 **byway, bypath,** byroad, by-lane, bystreet, side road, side street; **bypass, detour,** roundabout way; bypaths and crooked ways; back way, back stairs, back door, side door; back road, back street.

.6 **road, roadway,** carriageway [Brit], right-of-way; **main road,** main drag [slang], **thoroughfare, arterial,** artery; **highway,** highroad [Brit], arterial highway, primary highway, **freeway, superhighway, expressway, turnpike,** pike, **thruway,** speedway, **parkway,** motorway [Brit], *Autobahn* [Ger], *autostrada* [Ital], *autoroute* [Fr]; state highway, US highway, interstate highway, *route nationale* [Fr], King's or Queen's highway, royal road, *camino real* [Sp]; secondary road, local road, county road, township road; private road, byway, driveway; highways and byways; dirt road, gravel road, paved road, *pavé* [Fr], plank road, corduroy road; **street,** through street, arterial street, **avenue, boulevard, drive;** place, row, court, lane, terrace, crescent, vennel [Scot]; **alley,** alleyway, mews, wynd [Scot], close [Brit], dead-end street, blind alley, cul-de-sac; toll road or highway; controlled access highway; post road; bypass, circumferential, belt highway, ring road; causeway, causey, *chaussée* [Fr], dike; roadbed.

.7 **pavement,** paving; macadam, blacktop, bitumen, asphalt, tarmacadam, Tarmac, Tarvia, bituminous macadam; cement, concrete; tile, brick, paving brick; stone, paving stone, pavestone, flag, flagstone, flagging; cobblestone, cobble; road metal; gravel; washboard; curbstone, kerbstone [Brit], edgestone; curb, kerb [Brit], curbing.

.8 **railway, railroad,** rail, line, track, railway or railroad or rail line; tram or tramline or tramway or tramroad [all Brit], trolley line, streetcar line, street railway; elevated railway; elevated or el or L [all informal]; subway, underground [Brit], *métro* [Fr], tube [Brit informal]; electric railway, cable railway, horse railway; cog railway, rack railway, rack-and-pinion railway; gravity-operated railway; monorail; light railroad; main line, trunk, trunk line; branch, feeder, feeder line; siding,

sidetrack, turnout; switchback; junction; terminus, terminal, the end of the line; roadway, roadbed, embankment, trestle.

.9 **cableway,** ropeway, wireway, wire ropeway, cable or rope railway, funicular or funicular railway; telpher, telpherway, telpher ropeway, telpher line or railway; ski lift.

.10 **bridge, span, viaduct;** overpass, overcrossing, overbridge or flyover [both Brit]; drawbridge, bascule bridge, lift bridge, swing bridge; floating bridge, bateau bridge, pontoon bridge; **suspension bridge;** cantilever bridge; arch bridge; footbridge; gangplank, gangboard, gangway, catwalk; rope bridge; toll bridge; stepping-stone, stepstone; Bifrost.

.11 ADVS **how, in what way** or **manner,** by what mode or means; to what extent; in what condition; by what name; at what price; after this fashion, in this way, in such wise, along these lines; **thus, so,** thus and so; as, like, on the lines of; a–, –ally, –ling, –ly, –wise, –way or –ways.

.12 **anyhow, anyway,** anywise, in any way, by any means, by any manner of means; in any event, at any rate, in any case; **nevertheless, nonetheless, however, regardless,** irregardless [informal]; at all, nohow [dial].

.13 **somehow, in some way,** in some way or other, someway [informal], by some means, **somehow or other,** somehow or another, in one way or another, in some such way, after a fashion; no matter how, **by hook or by crook,** by fair means or foul.

## 658. MEANS

.1 NOUNS **means, ways, ways and means,** means to an end; **wherewithal,** wherewith; funds 835.14; **resources,** disposable resources, capital 835.15; stock, supply 660; power, capacity, ability 157.1,2; recourses, resorts, devices; method 657.1, –ment.

.2 **instrumentality, agency;** machinery, **mechanism;** mediation, going between, intermediation, service; **expedient,** recourse, resort, device 670.2.

.3 **instrument, tool, implement, appliance,** device; contrivance, lever, mechanism; **vehicle, organ; agent** 781; medium, mediator, intermedium, intermediary, intermediate, interagent, go-between 781.4; midwife, servant, slave, handmaid, handmaiden, *ancilla* [L]; **cat's-paw, puppet, dummy, pawn,** creature, minion, stooge [slang], Charlie McCarthy [informal]; toy, plaything; dupe 620.

.4 VERBS **find means, find a way,** provide the wherewithal; get by hook or by crook, obtain by fair means or foul; beg, borrow, or steal.

.5 be instrumental, serve, subserve, minister to, act for, act in the interests of, promote, advance, forward, assist, facilitate; mediate, go between.

.6 ADJS instrumental, implemental; agential, agentive, agentival; **useful,** handy, employable, **serviceable; helpful,** conducive, forwarding, favoring, promoting, assisting, facilitating; subservient, ministering, ministerial; mediating, mediatorial, intermediary.

.7 ADVS, PREPS **by means of, by** or **through the agency of,** by or through the good offices of, through the instrumentality of, by the aid of, thanks to, by use of, **by way of,** by dint of, by the act of, through the medium of, by or in virtue of, at the hand of, at the hands of; **with;** herewith, therewith, wherewith, wherewithal; whereby, thereby, hereby; **through, by,** per; on, upon [archaic].

## 659. PROVISION, EQUIPMENT

.1 NOUNS **provision,** providing; **equipment, accouterment,** fitting out, outfitting; **supply,** supplying, finding; **furnishing,** furnishment; chandlery, **retailing, selling** 829.2; logistics; procurement 811.1; investment, endowment, subvention, subsidy, subsidization; provisioning, victualing, purveyance, catering; armament; resupply, replenishment, reinforcement; **preparation** 720.

.2 provisions, supplies 660.1; provender 308.5; **merchandise** 831.

.3 **accommodations,** accommodation, facilities; **lodgings** 188.3; bed, board; **board and room,** bed and board; **subsistence,** keep.

.4 **equipment,** matériel, equipage, munitions; **furniture, furnishings, furnishments** [archaic]; **fixtures, fittings, appointments, accouterments, appurtenances,** installations, plumbing; **appliances, utensils, conveniences; outfit, apparatus, rig,** machinery; stock-in-trade; **plant, facility, facilities;** paraphernalia, things, **gear,** impedimenta [pl], **tackle;** rigging; armament, munition; **kit,** duffel.

.5 **harness,** caparison, trappings, tack, tackle; headgear, bridle, halter, headstall, cavesson, hackamore, jaquima; bit, snaffle,

curb, noseband, chinband, cheekpiece, blinds, blinders, winker braces, browband, crownband, gag swivel, side check, breeching, britchen [dial], bellyband, girth, cinch, surcingle; collar; reins, lines, ribbons; yoke, tug, hames, hametugs, shaft tug; jerk line, checkrein, bearing rein, martingale or pole strap; saddle or back band; backstrap, crupper, hip straps.

.6 **provider, supplier, furnisher;** donor 818.11; patron; **purveyor,** provisioner, caterer, victualer, sutler; *vivandier, vivandière* [both Fr]; chandler, retailer, merchant 830.2,3; commissary, commissariat, quartermaster, storekeeper, stock clerk, steward, manciple.

.7 VERBS **provide, supply,** find, **furnish;** accommodate; invest, clothe, endow, fund, subsidize; donate, give, afford, contribute, yield, present 818.12,14; make available; stock, store; provide for, make provision or due provision for; prepare 720.6; support, maintain, keep; fill, fill up; replenish, recruit.

.8 **equip, furnish, outfit,** gear, prepare, fit, fit up or out, **rig,** rig up or out, **turn out,** appoint, accouter, dress; arm, heel [slang], munition; man, staff; –ate, –ize.

.9 provision, provender, cater, victual; feed; forage; fuel, gas, gas up, fill up, top off, coal, oil, bunker; **purvey,** sell 829.8,9.

.10 accommodate, furnish accommodations; lodge 188.10; **put up,** board.

.11 **make a living,** earn a living or livelihood, **make** or **earn one's keep.**

.12 **support oneself,** make one's way; **make ends meet, keep body and soul together, keep the wolf from the door,** keep or hold one's head above water, keep afloat; **survive, subsist, cope, eke out,** make out, scrape along, manage, get by.

.13 ADJS **provided, supplied, furnished,** provisioned, purveyed, catered; invested, endowed; **equipped, fitted,** fitted out, outfitted, rigged, accoutered; armed, heeled [slang]; **prepared** 720.16.

.14 **well-provided, well-supplied, well-furnished,** well-stocked, well-found; **well-equipped, well-fitted,** well-appointed; well-armed.

## 660. STORE, SUPPLY

.1 NOUNS **store, hoard, treasure,** treasury; **plenty, plenitude, abundance,** cornucopia; heap, mass, stack, pile, dump, rick; **collection, accumulation,** cumulation, **amassment,** budget, **stockpile; backlog;** repertory, repertoire; stock-in-trade; in-

ventory, stock, supply on hand; **stores,
supplies, provisions,** provisionment, rations; larder, commissariat, commissary;
munitions; matériel; material, materials
378.

.2 **supply, fund, resource, resources; means,
assets,** liquid assets, balance, **capital,** capital goods, capitalization, available means
*or* resources; grist, grist to the mill; holdings, property 810.

.3 **reserve, reserves,** reservoir, resource,
stockpile, **cache,** reserve supply, something in reserve *or* in hand, something to
fall back on, reserve fund, **nest egg, savings,** sinking fund; backlog, unexpended
balance, ace in the hole [slang], a card up
one's sleeve.

.4 **source of supply,** source, staple, resource;
well, fountain, fount, font [archaic],
spring, wellspring; mine, **gold mine, bonanza;** quarry, lode, vein; cornucopia.

.5 **storage, stowage;** preservation, conservation, safekeeping, warehousing; cold storage, dry storage, dead storage; storage
space, shelf-room; custody, guardianship
699.2.

.6 **storehouse, storeroom,** stock room, lumber room, store, storage, **depository, repository,** conservatory [archaic], reservoir,
repertory, depot, supply depot, supply
base, magazine, *magasin* [Fr], warehouse,
godown; bonded warehouse, *entrepôt*
[Fr]; dock; hold, cargo dock; attic, cellar,
basement; closet, cupboard; wine cellar,
buttery; **treasury,** treasure house, treasure
room, exchequer; bank, vault 836.12,13;
archives, library, stack room; armory, arsenal, dump; lumberyard; drawer, shelf;
bin, bunker, bay, crib; rack, rick; vat,
tank; crate, box; chest, locker, hutch;
bookcase, stack, glory hole.

.7 **garner, granary,** grain bin, elevator, grain
elevator, **silo;** mow, haymow, hayloft,
hayrick; crib, corncrib.

.8 **larder, pantry,** buttery [dial]; spence [Brit
dial], stillroom [Brit]; root cellar; dairy,
dairy house *or* room.

.9 **museum; gallery,** art gallery, picture gallery, pinacotheca; salon; Metropolitan
Museum, National Gallery, Museum of
Modern Art, Guggenheim Museum,
Tate Gallery, British Museum, Louvre,
Hermitage, Prado, Uffizi, Rijksmuseum;
museology, curatorship.

.10 VERBS **store, stow,** lay in store; **lay in,** lay
in a supply *or* stock *or* store, store away,
stow away, **put away, lay away,** pack
away, bundle away, lay down, stow down,

salt down *or* away [informal]; **deposit,** reposit, lodge; **cache,** stash [slang]; **bank,**
coffer, hutch [archaic]; warehouse, reservoir; file, file away.

.11 **store up, stock up, lay up,** put up, **save
up,** hoard up, treasure up, garner up,
**heap up,** pile up, build up a stock *or* inventory; **accumulate,** cumulate, **collect,
amass, stockpile;** backlog; garner, gather
into barns; **hoard,** treasure, save, keep,
hold, squirrel, squirrel away; hide, secrete
615.7.

.12 **reserve, save, conserve, keep,** retain, husband, husband one's resources, keep *or*
hold back, withhold; **keep in reserve,**
keep in store, keep on hand, keep by
one; **preserve** 701.7; **set** *or* **put aside,** set *or*
put apart, put *or* lay *or* set by; save up,
save to fall back upon, keep as a nest egg,
**save for a rainy day,** provide for *or*
against a rainy day.

.13 **have in store** *or* **reserve,** have to fall back
upon, have something to draw on, have
something laid by, have something laid
by for a rainy day.

.14 ADJS **stored, accumulated,** amassed, laid
up; gathered, garnered, collected; **stockpiled;** backlogged; **hoarded,** treasured.

.15 **reserved, preserved, saved,** conserved, put
by, kept, retained, held, withheld, held
back, kept *or* held in reserve; spare.

.16 ADVS **in store,** in stock, in supply, **on
hand.**

.17 **in reserve,** back, aside, by.

## 661. SUFFICIENCY

.1 NOUNS **sufficiency,** sufficientness, **adequacy,** adequateness, **enough,** competence *or* competency, satisfactoriness, satisfaction, satisfactory amount; good *or*
adequate supply; exact measure, right
amount, no more and no less; bare sufficiency, minimum, bare minimum, just
enough, enough to get by on.

.2 **plenty, plenitude, plentifulness,** plenteousness; myriad, myriads, numerousness
101; **amplitude,** ampleness; substantiality,
substantialness; **abundance, copiousness;**
exuberance, riotousness; **bountifulness,**
bountiousness, liberalness, **liberality,** generousness, **generosity; lavishness, extravagance,** prodigality; luxuriance, fertility,
teemingness, productiveness 165; **wealth,
opulence** *or* opulency, richness, affluence,
more than enough; maximum; **fullness,**
full measure, repletion, repleteness; overflow, outpouring, flood, flow, shower,
spate, stream, gush, avalanche; landslide

prevalence, profuseness, **profusion**, riot; **superabundance** 663.2; great abundance, great plenty, "God's plenty" [Dryden], quantities, much, lots, scads 34.4; bumper crop, rich harvest, foison [archaic]; rich vein, bonanza; ample sufficiency, enough and to spare, enough and then some; fat of the land.

.3 cornucopia, horn of plenty, horn of Amalthea, endless supply.

.4 VERBS **suffice, do,** just do, serve, **answer;** work, be equal to, **avail;** answer or serve the purpose; qualify, meet, fulfill, **satisfy,** meet requirements; **pass muster,** make the grade [informal], hack it [slang], **fill the bill** [informal]; get by [slang], do it, do'er [dial], do in a pinch, **pass,** pass in the dark [informal]; hold, stand, stand up, take it, bear; stretch [informal], reach, go around.

.5 **abound,** exuberate [archaic], teem, **teem with,** creep with, crawl with, swarm with, bristle with; proliferate 165.7; **overflow,** run over; flow, stream, rain, pour, shower, gush.

.6 ADJS **sufficient,** sufficing; **enough, ample,** substantial, **plenty, satisfactory, adequate,** decent, due; competent, up to the mark; commensurate, proportionate, corresponding 26.9; suitable, fit 26.10; good, **good enough,** plenty good enough [informal]; sufficient for or to or unto, up to, equal to; barely sufficient, minimal, minimum.

.7 **plentiful,** plenty, **plenteous,** plenitudinous, "plenty as blackberries" [Shakespeare]; **galore** [informal], in plenty, in quantity or quantities, aplenty [informal]; numerous 101.6; much, many 34.8; **ample,** all-sufficing; wholesale; wellstocked, well-provided, well-furnished, well-found; abundant, abounding, **copious,** exuberant, riotous; flush; **bountiful,** bounteous, **lavish, generous, liberal,** extravagant, prodigal; **luxuriant,** fertile, productive 165.9, **rich,** fat, **wealthy, opulent, affluent;** maximal; **full,** replete, wellfilled, running over, overflowing; inexhaustible, exhaustless, bottomless; **profuse,** profusive, effuse, diffuse; **prevalent,** prevailing, rife, rampant, epidemic; teeming 101.9; **superabundant** 663.19; a dime a dozen.

.8 ADVS **sufficiently, amply,** substantially, **satisfactorily, enough;** competently, **adequately;** minimally.

.9 **plentifully,** plenteously, **aplenty** [informal], **in plenty,** in quantity or quantities, in good supply; **abundantly,** in abundance, copiously, no end [informal]; **superabundantly** 663.24; **bountifully,** bounteously, **lavishly, generously, liberally,** extravagantly, prodigally; maximally; **fully,** in full measure, to the full, overflowingly; inexhaustibly, exhaustlessly, bottomlessly; exuberantly, luxuriantly, riotously; richly, opulently, affluently; **profusely,** diffusely, effusely.

## 662. INSUFFICIENCY

.1 NOUNS **insufficiency, inadequacy,** insufficientness, inadequateness, –penia; short supply, seller's market, none to spare; nonsatisfaction, nonfulfillment, coming or falling short or shy; too little, too late; incompetence, unqualification, unsuitability 27.3.

.2 **meagerness,** exiguousness, exiguity, scrimpiness, skimpiness, scantiness, scantness, spareness; meanness, miserliness, niggardliness, narrowness [dial], stinginess, parsimony; smallness, slightness, puniness, paltriness; thinness, leanness, slimness, slim pickings [informal], slenderness, scrawniness; jejuneness, jejunity; austerity; Lenten fare.

.3 **scarcity,** scarceness; **sparsity,** sparseness; **scantiness,** scant sufficiency; **dearth, paucity,** poverty, **rarity,** rareness, uncommonness.

.4 **want, lack, need, deficiency, deficit, shortage,** shortfall, wantage, **incompleteness,** defectiveness, shortcoming 314, imperfection; **absence,** omission; **destitution,** impoverishment, beggary, deprivation; starvation, famine, drought.

.5 **pittance,** dole, scrimption [dial]; drop in the bucket; **mite,** bit 35.2; short allowance, short commons, half rations, cheeseparings and candle ends; mere subsistence, starvation wages.

.6 **dietary deficiency,** vitamin deficiency, **malnutrition** 686.10.

.7 VERBS **want, lack, need, require;** miss, feel the want of; run short of.

.8 **be insufficient,** not qualify, be found wanting, not make it [informal], kick the beam, not hack it [slang], **fall short,** fall shy, come short, not come up to; run short; want, lack, fail, fail of or in.

.9 ADJS **insufficient,** unsufficing, **inadequate,** hyp(o)–, mal–, olig(o)–, sub–, –privic; found wanting, defective, incomplete, imperfect, deficient, lacking, failing, wanting; too little, not enough; unsatisfactory, unsatisfying; unequal to, incompetent, unqualified, not up to snuff.

.10 **meager, slight,** scrimpy, scrimp, skimp, skimpy, exiguous; scant, **scanty,** spare; miserly, niggardly, stingy, narrow [dial], parsimonious, mean; austere, Lenten, Spartan, abstemious, ascetic; stinted, frugal, sparing; poor, impoverished; small, puny, paltry; thin, lean, slim, slender, scrawny; dwarfish, dwarfed, stunted; straitened, limited; jejune, watered, watery, unnourishing, unnutritious; subsistence, starvation.

.11 scarce, sparse, scanty; in short supply, at a premium; **rare,** uncommon; scarcer than hen's teeth [informal]; not to be had, not to be had for love or money, not to be had at any price; out of print, out of stock *or* season.

.12 **ill-provided,** ill-furnished, ill-equipped, ill-found, ill off; **unprovided,** unsupplied, unreplenished; bare-handed; unfed, underfed, undernourished; shorthanded, undermanned; **empty-handed, poor,** pauperized, impoverished, beggarly; starved, half-starved, on short commons, starving, starveling, famished.

.13 **wanting, lacking, needing, missing, in want of;** for want of, in default of, in the absence of; short, **short of,** scant of; shy, **shy of** *or* **on;** out of, destitute of, bare of, void of, empty of, devoid of, forlorn of, bereft of, deprived of, denuded of, unpossessed of, unblessed with; bankrupt in; out of pocket; at the end of one's rope *or* tether.

.14 ADVS **insufficiently; inadequately,** unsubstantially, incompletely.

.15 **meagerly, slightly,** sparely, punily, scantily, poorly, frugally, sparingly.

.16 **scarcely, sparsely, scantily,** skimpily, scrimpily; **rarely,** uncommonly.

.17 PREPS **without,** minus, less, sans.

## 663. EXCESS

.1 NOUNS **excess, excessiveness, inordinance,** inordinacy [archaic], inordinateness, nimiety, **immoderateness,** immoderacy, immoderation, **extravagance** *or* extravagancy, intemperateness, incontinence, overindulgence, **intemperance** 993; unrestrainedness, abandon; gluttony 994; **extreme,** extremity, **extremes; boundlessness** 104.1; overlargeness, overgreatness, monstrousness, enormousness 34.1; overgrowth, overdevelopment, hypertrophy, gigantism, giantism; **overmuch,** overmuchness, too much, too-muchness; **exor-**

bitance *or* exorbitancy, undueness, **outrageousness,** unconscionableness, **unreasonableness;** radicalism, extremism 745.4; egregiousness; fabulousness, hyperbole, **exaggeration** 617.

.2 **superabundance,** overabundance, superflux, **plethora,** redundancy, overprofusion, **overplentifulness,** overplenteousness, overplenty, **oversupply,** overaccumulation, **oversufficiency,** overmuchness, overcopiousness, overlavishness, overluxuriance, overbounteousness, overnumerousness; lavishness, **extravagance** *or* extravagancy, **prodigality; plenty** 661.2; **more than enough, enough and to spare,** enough in all conscience; **overdose,** overmeasure, "enough, with over-measure" [Shakespeare]; too much of a good thing, egg in one's beer [slang]; drug on the market; spate, avalanche, landslide, deluge, flood, inundation; *embarras de richesses* [Fr], money to burn [informal]; overpopulation.

.3 **overfullness,** plethora, **surfeit, glut;** satiety 664; engorgement, repletion, congestion; hyperemia; **saturation,** supersaturation; **overload,** overburden, overcharge, surcharge, overfreight, overweight; **overflow,** overbrimming, overspill.

.4 **superfluity,** superfluousness, fat; **redundancy,** redundance; unnecessariness, needlessness; featherbedding, payroll padding; duplication, duplication of effort, overlap; **luxury,** extravagance, frill *or* **frills** [both informal]; frippery, overadornment, bedizenment, gingerbread; **ornamentation, embellishment** 901.1; expletive, padding, filling; pleonasm, tautology; verbosity, prolixity 593.2; more than one really wants to know.

.5 **surplus,** surplusage, plus, **overplus,** overstock, **overage,** overset, overrun, **overmeasure, oversupply;** margin; remainder, **balance, leftover, extra, spare,** something extra *or* to spare; bonus, dividend, lagniappe [dial], gratuity, tip, *pourboire* [Fr].

.6 **overdoing,** overcarrying, **overreaching,** supererogation; overimportance, overemphasis; overuse; overreaction; **overwork, overexertion,** overexercise, overexpenditure, overtaxing, overstrain, tax, strain; too many irons in the fire, too much at once.

.7 **overextension, overdrawing,** drawing *or* spreading too thin, **overstretching,** overstrain, overstraining, stretching, straining stretch, strain, tension, extreme tension snapping *or* breaking point; **overexpansion;** inflation, distension, overdistension, ˙swelling, bloat, bloating 197.2.

.8 VERBS **superabound,** overabound, **know no bounds, swarm,** pullulate, run riot, luxuriate, **teem;** overflow, flood, overbrim, overspill, spill over, overrun, overspread, overswarm, overgrow, fill; meet one at every turn; hang heavy on one's hands, remain on one's hands.

.9 **exceed, surpass, pass, transcend, go beyond;** overpass, overstep, overrun, **overreach,** overshoot, overshoot the mark.

.10 overdo, go too far, pass all bounds, know no bounds, overact, **carry too far,** overcarry, go to an extreme, **go to extremes, go overboard; run into the ground;** overemphasize, overstress; overplay, overplay one's hand [informal]; overreact, protest too much; overreach oneself; **overtax, overtask, overexert, overexercise, overstrain,** overdrive, overspend, exhaust, overexpend, overuse; overtrain; **overwork,** overlabor; overelaborate, overdevelop, tell more than one wants to know; overstudy; burn the candle at both ends; have too many irons in the fire, do too many things at once; **exaggerate** 617.3; **overindulge** 993.5.

.11 **pile it on,** lay it on, **lay it on thick,** lay it on with a trowel [slang].

.12 **carry coals to Newcastle,** teach fishes to swim, teach one's grandmother to suck eggs, kill the slain, beat *or* flog a dead horse, labor the obvious, butter one's bread on both sides, paint *or* gild the lily, "to gild refined gold, to paint the lily, to throw a perfume on the violet" [Shakespeare].

.13 **overextend, overdraw, overstretch, overstrain,** stretch, strain; reach the breaking *or* snapping point; **overexpand,** overdistend, overdevelop, inflate, swell 197.4.

.14 **oversupply, overprovide,** overlavish, overfurnish, overequip; **overstock;** overprovision, overprovender; overdose; flood the market, oversell; **flood, deluge,** inundate, engulf, swamp, whelm, overwhelm; lavish with, be prodigal with.

.15 **overload,** overlade, **overburden,** overweight, **overcharge,** surcharge; **overfill,** stuff, crowd, cram, jam, pack, jam-pack, **congest,** choke; **overstuff,** overfeed; gluttonize 994.4; **surfeit, glut, gorge,** satiate 664.4; **saturate,** soak, drench, supersaturate, supercharge.

.16 ADJS **excessive, inordinate,** arch–, hyper–, super–, sur–, ultra–; **immoderate,** over-

weening, **intemperate, extravagant,** incontinent; **unrestrained, unbridled,** abandoned; gluttonous 994.6; **extreme; overlarge, overgreat,** overbig, **monstrous, enormous,** gigantic 34.7; overgrown, overdeveloped, hypertrophied; **overmuch,** too much, a bit much; **exorbitant, undue, outrageous,** unconscionable, **unreasonable;** fancy *or* high *or* stiff *or* steep [all informal]; **out of bounds** *or* **all bounds,** out of sight *or* out of this world [both informal], **boundless** 104.3; **egregious;** fabulous, hyperbolic, **exaggerated** 617.4.

.17 **superfluous, redundant; excess,** in excess; unnecessary, unessential, nonessential, expendable, dispensable, **needless,** unneeded, gratuitous, uncalled-for; expletive; pleonastic, tautologous, tautologic(al); verbose, prolix 593.12; *de trop* [Fr], supererogatory, supererogative; spare, to spare; on one's hands.

.18 **surplus,** overplus; **remaining,** unused, **leftover;** over, over and above; **extra, spare,** supernumerary, for lagniappe [dial], as a bonus.

.19 **superabundant,** overabundant, plethoric, **overplentiful,** overplenteous, overplenty, **oversufficient, overmuch; lavish, prodigal,** overlavish, overbounteous, overgenerous, overliberal; overcopious, overluxuriant, riotous, overexuberant; overprolific, overnumerous; **swarming,** pullulating, **teeming,** overpopulated, overpopulous; plentiful 661.7.

.20 **overfull, overloaded, overladen, overburdened,** overfreighted, overfraught, overweighted, **overcharged,** surcharged, **saturated,** drenched, soaked, supersaturated, supercharged; **surfeited, glutted,** gorged, overfed, satiated 664.6, **stuffed,** overstuffed, **crowded, crammed,** jammed, packed, jam-packed; choked, **congested,** stuffed up; **overstocked, oversupplied; overflowing,** in spate, running over, filled to overflowing; plethoric, hyperemic; **bursting,** ready to burst, bursting at the seams, at the bursting point, overblown, distended, **swollen, bloated** 197.13.

.21 **overdone,** overwrought; **overdrawn,** overstretched, overstrained.

.22 ADVS **excessively, inordinately, immoderately, intemperately,** overweeningly, **overly,** over, **overmuch,** too much; **too,** too-too [informal]; **exorbitantly, unduly, unreasonably,** unconscionably, **outrageously.**

.23 **in** *or* **to excess, to extremes,** to the extreme, all out [informal], flat out [Brit informal], to a fault, too far, out of all proportion.

.24 **superabundantly**, overabundantly, **lavishly**, **prodigally**, **extravagantly**; more than enough, plentifully 661.9; without measure, out of measure, beyond measure.

.25 **superfluously**, **redundantly**, supererogatorily; tautologously; unnecessarily, needlessly, beyond need, beyond reason, overplus [archaic].

.26 PREPS **in excess of**, over, beyond, past, above, **over and above**, above and beyond.

## 664. SATIETY

.1 NOUNS **satiety**, **satiation**, **satisfaction**, **fullness**, **surfeit**, **glut**, repletion, engorgement; **fill**, **bellyful** or skinful [both informal], snootful [slang]; **saturation**, saturatedness, supersaturation; saturation point; more than enough, enough in all conscience, all one can stand or take; too much of a good thing, much of a muchness [informal].

.2 **satedness**, surfeitedness, cloyedness, jadedness; overfullness, fed-upness [informal].

.3 **cloyer**, surfeiter, sickener; **overdose**; a diet of cake; warmed-over cabbage, "cabbage repeatedly" [Juvenal].

.4 VERBS **satiate**, **sate**, **satisfy**, slake, allay; **surfeit**, **glut**, **gorge**, engorge; **cloy**, **jade**, pall; **fill**, fill up; saturate, oversaturate, supersaturate; **stuff**, overstuff, cram; **overfill**, overgorge, overdose, overfeed.

.5 **have enough**, have about enough of, have quite enough, **have one's fill**; have too much, have too much of a good thing, **have a bellyful** or skinful [informal], have a snootful [slang], have an overdose of, **be fed up** [informal], have all one can take or stand, have it up to here [informal], have had it.

.6 ADJS **satiated**, **sated**, **satisfied**, slaked, allayed; **surfeited**, **gorged**, replete, engorged, **glutted**; **cloyed**, jaded; **full**, full of, with one's fill of, **overfull**, saturated, oversaturated, supersaturated; **stuffed**, overstuffed, crammed, overgorged, overfed; **fed-up** or fed to the gills or fed to the teeth [all informal], stuffed to the gills [informal]; **with a bellyful** or skinful [informal], with a snootful [slang], with enough of; disgusted, **sick of**, tired of, sick and tired of.

.7 **satiating**, sating, satisfying, filling; surfeiting, overfilling; jading, **cloying**, cloysome.

## 665. USE

.1 NOUNS **use**, **employment**, employ [archaic], **usage**; **exercise**, **exertion**, active use; good use; ill use, wrong use, misuse 667; hard use, hard or rough usage; **application**, appliance; using up, **consumption** 666.

.2 **usage**, **treatment**, **handling**, management; way or means of dealing; stewardship, custodianship, guardianship, care.

.3 **utility**, **usefulness**, **usability**, **use**, utilizability, **serviceability**, helpfulness, functionality, profitability, applicability, availability, **practicability**, practicality, practical utility, operability, **effectiveness**, efficacy, efficiency.

.4 **benefit**, use, service, avail, profit, **advantage**, point, percentage [informal], what's in it for one [slang], convenience; interest, behalf, behoof; **value**, **worth**.

.5 **function**, use, purpose, role, end use, immediate purpose, ultimate purpose, operational purpose, operation; work, duty, office.

.6 **functionalism**, **utilitarianism**; pragmatism, pragmaticism; functional design, functional furniture or housing, etc.

.7 [law terms] usufruct, imperfect usufruct, perfect usufruct, right of use, user, enjoyment of property; jus primae noctis [L], droit du seigneur [Fr].

.8 **utilization**, using; **employment**, management, manipulation, handling, working, operation, **exploitation**.

.9 **user**, employer; **consumer**, enjoyer.

.10 VERBS **use**, **utilize**, **make use of**, do with; **employ**, practice, ply, work, manage, handle, manipulate, operate, **wield**, play; **have** or **enjoy the use of**; exercise, exert.

.11 **apply**, **put to use**, carry out, put into execution, **put in practice** or operation, put in force, enforce; bring to bear upon.

.12 **treat**, **handle**, manage, use, **deal with**, cope with, contend with, do with; steward, care for.

.13 **spend**, consume, expend, **pass**, employ, **put in**; devote, bestow, give to or give over to, devote or consecrate or dedicate to; while, while away, wile; use up 666.2.

.14 **avail oneself of**, **resort to**, have recourse to, **turn to**, look to, recur to, refer to, take to [informal], betake oneself to; revert to, fall back upon; convert or turn to use, put in or into requisition, press or enlist into service, impress, call or bring into play.

.15 **take advantage of**, make the most of, use

to the full, make good use of, improve, turn to use or profit or account or good account, turn to one's advantage, use to advantage, put to advantage, find one's account or advantage in; improve the occasion 129.8; profit by, benefit from, reap the benefit of; exploit, capitalize on, make capital of, make a good thing of [informal], make hay [informal], trade on, cash in on [informal]; make the best of, make a virtue of necessity.

.16 (take unfair advantage of) exploit, take advantage of, use, make use of, use for one's own ends; make a pawn or cat's-paw of, play for a sucker [slang]; manipulate, work on, work upon, stroke, play on or upon; impose upon, presume upon; use ill, ill-use, abuse, misuse 667.4,5; milk, bleed, bleed white [informal]; drain, suck the blood of or from, suck dry; exploit one's position, feather one's nest [informal].

.17 avail, be of use, serve, suffice, do, answer, answer or serve the purpose, serve one's need, fill the bill or do the trick [both informal]; bestead [archaic], stand one in stead or good stead, be handy, stand one in hand [dial]; advantage, be of advantage or service to; profit, benefit, pay or pay off [both informal], give good returns, yield a profit.

.18 ADJS useful, employable, of use, of service, serviceable, commodious [archaic]; good for; helpful, of help 785.21; advantageous, beneficial 674.12; practical, banausic, pragmatic, functional, utilitarian, of general utility or application; fitting, proper, appropriate, expedient 670.5.

19 handy, convenient; available, accessible, ready, at hand, to hand, on hand, on tap, on deck [informal], on call, at one's call or beck and call, at one's elbow, at one's fingertips, just around the corner, at one's disposal; versatile, adaptable, all-around [informal], of all work.

20 effectual, effective, active, efficient, efficacious, operative.

21 valuable, of value, profitable, yielding a return, well-spent, worthwhile, rewarding; gainful, remunerative 811.15.

22 usable, utilizable; applicable, appliable; practical, operable; reusable; exploitable; manipulable, pliable, compliant 765.12–14.

23 used, employed, exercised, exerted, applied, techno–; secondhand 123.18.

24 in use, in practice, in force, in effect, in service, in operation, in commission.

.25 ADVS usefully, to good use; profitably, advantageously, to advantage, to profit, to good effect; effectually, effectively, efficiently; serviceably, functionally, practically; handily, conveniently.

## 666. CONSUMPTION

.1 NOUNS consumption, using or eating up; burning up; absorption, assimilation, digestion, ingestion, expenditure, expending, spending; squandering, wastefulness 854.1; finishing; depletion, drain, exhaustion, impoverishment, waste, wastage, wasting away, erosion, ablation, wearing down, wearing away, attrition.

.2 VERBS consume, spend, expend, use up; absorb, assimilate, digest, ingest, eat, eat up, swallow, swallow up, gobble, gobble up; burn up; finish, finish off; exhaust, deplete, impoverish, drain, drain of resources; suck dry, bleed white [informal], suck one's blood; wear away, erode, ablate; waste away; squander 854.3,4.

.3 be consumed, be used up, waste; run out, give out, peter out [informal]; run dry, dry up.

.4 ADJS used up, consumed, eaten up, burnt up; finished, gone; spent, exhausted, effete, dissipated, depleted, impoverished, drained, worn-out; worn away, eroded, ablated; wasted 854.9.

.5 consumable, expendable, spendable; replaceable; disposable, throwaway, no-deposit, no-deposit-no-return.

## 667. MISUSE

.1 NOUNS misuse, misusage, abuse; misemployment, misapplication; mishandling, mismanagement, poor stewardship; corrupt administration, malversation, breach of public trust, maladministration; diversion, defalcation, misappropriation, conversion, embezzlement, peculation, pilfering; perversion, prostitution; profanation, violation, pollution, fouling, befoulment, desecration, defilement, debasement; malpractice, abuse of office, misconduct, malfeasance, misfeasance.

.2 mistreatment, ill-treatment, maltreatment, ill-use, ill-usage, abuse; molestation, violation, outrage, violence, injury, atrocity; cruel and unusual punishment.

.3 persecution, oppression, harrying, hounding, tormenting, harassment, victimization; witch-hunting, witch-hunt, red-baiting [informal], McCarthyism.

.4 VERBS misuse, misemploy, abuse, misapply; mishandle, mismanage, maladminis-

ter; divert, misappropriate, convert, defal-
cate [archaic], embezzle, pilfer, peculate,
feather one's nest [informal]; pervert,
prostitute; profane, violate, pollute, foul,
foul one's own nest, befoul, desecrate,
defile, debase.

.5 **mistreat, maltreat, ill-treat, ill-use, abuse,**
injure, molest; do wrong to, do wrong by;
outrage, do violence to, do one's worst
to; mishandle, manhandle; buffet, batter,
bruise, savage, maul, knock about, rough,
rough up.

.6 **persecute,** oppress, **torment,** victimize,
**harass,** molest, harry, hound, beset; pursue, hunt 654.8,9.

## 668. DISUSE

.1 NOUNS **disuse, disusage, desuetude; nonuse,** nonemployment, abstinence, abstention; nonprevalence, unprevalence; **obsolescence,** obsoleteness, obsoletism, obso-
letion; superannuation, retirement, pensioning off.

.2 **discontinuance,** cessation, desistance; relinquishment, forbearance, resignation,
renunciation, renouncement, abjurement,
abjuration; waiver, nonexercise; abeyance, suspension, cold storage [informal];
**abandonment** 633.

.3 **discard, discarding,** jettison, deep six
[slang], disposal, dumping; **scrapping,
junking** [informal]; removal, elimination
77.2; **rejection** 638; **reject,** throwaway,
castaway, castoff, rejectamenta [pl];
**refuse** 669.4,5.

.4 VERBS **cease to use,** relinquish, **discontinue, disuse,** quit, stop, drop [informal],
give up, give over, put behind one, let go,
leave off, come off [slang], cut out, desist, have done with; waive [archaic], resign, renounce, abjure; nol-pros, not pursue with or proceed with.

.5 **not use, do without,** dispense with, **let
alone,** not touch, hold off; **abstain, refrain,** forgo, forbear, spare, waive; keep or
hold back, reserve, save, keep in hand,
have up one's sleeve.

.6 **put away,** lay away, **put aside,** lay or set
or push aside, sideline [informal], lay or
set by; stow, store 660.10; **pigeonhole,
shelve,** put on the shelf, put in mothballs; **table,** lay on the table; table the
motion, pass to the order of the day;
postpone, delay 132.8.

.7 **discard, reject, throw away, throw out,**
chuck [informal], eighty-six [slang], cast,
cast off or away or aside; **get rid of,** get
quit of, get shut or shet of [dial], rid one-

self of, **dispose of,** slough, **dump, ditch**
[informal], **jettison, throw** or **heave** or
**toss overboard,** deep-six [slang], throw
out the window, throw or cast to the
dogs, cast to the winds; throw over, jilt;
part with, give away; **abandon** 633.5; remove, eliminate 77.5.

.8 **scrap, junk** [informal], consign to the
scrap heap, throw on the junk heap [in-
formal]; superannuate, retire, pension
off, put out to pasture or grass.

.9 **obsolesce,** fall into disuse, go out, pass
away; be superseded; superannuate.

.10 ADJS **disused, abandoned,** deserted, **discontinued,** done with; out, **out of use;**
old; relinquished, resigned, renounced,
abjured; **outworn,** worn-out, past use, not
worth saving; **obsolete,** obsolescent, superannuated, superannuate; superseded,
outdated, out-of-date, outmoded; retired,
pensioned off; on the shelf; antique, antiquated, old-fashioned, archaic.

.11 **discarded,** rejected, **cast-off,** castaway.

.12 **unused,** unutilized, **unemployed,** unap-
plied, unexercised; in abeyance, suspended; waived; **unspent,** unexpended,
unconsumed; held back, held out, put by,
put aside, saved, held in reserve, in hand,
spare, to spare, extra, reserve; stored
660.14; untouched, unhandled; untapped;
untrodden, unbeaten; **new,** original, pristine, fresh, mint.

## 669. USELESSNESS

.1 NOUNS **uselessness,** inutility; **needlessness**
unnecessity; unserviceability, **unusability**
unemployability, inoperativeness, inoper
ability, disrepair; unhelpfulness; inappli
cability, unsuitability, unfitness; function
lessness; otiosity; **superfluousness** 663.4.

.2 **futility,** vanity, emptiness, hollowness
**fruitlessness,** bootlessness, unprofitable
ness, profitlessness, unprofitability, otios
ity, worthlessness, valuelessness; triviality
nugacity; unproductiveness 166; **ineffectu
ality,** ineffectiveness, inefficacy 158.3; im
potence 158.1; **pointlessness,** meaningles
ness, purposelessness, aimlessness, fee
lessness; the absurd, absurdity; inanit
fatuity; vicious circle; **rat race** [informal]

.3 **labor in vain,** labor lost, labor of Sis
phus; work of Penelope, Penelope's we
**wild-goose chase,** snipe hunt, bootless e
rand; waste of labor, waste of breat
waste of time.

.4 **refuse, waste,** wastage, waste matter, 
fal; **leavings,** sweepings, dust [Bri
**scraps,** orts; **garbage,** gash [slang], sw

slop, slops, hogwash [informal]; draff, lees, **dregs** 43.2; **offscourings, scourings,** rinsings, dishwater; parings, raspings, filings, shavings; **scum;** chaff, stubble, husks; weeds, tares; deadwood; rags, bones, wastepaper, shards, potsherds; scrap iron; slag, culm, slack.

.5 **rubbish, rubble, trash, junk** [informal], shoddy, riffraff, raff [Brit dial], **scrap,** dust [Brit], **debris, litter,** lumber, clam-jamfry [Scot], truck [informal].

.6 **trash pile,** rubbish heap, dustheap, midden, kitchen midden; wasteyard, **junkyard** [informal], **dump.**

.7 wastepaper basket, wastebasket; wastebin, garbage can, dustbin [Brit], trash can.

.8 VERBS **labor in vain, go on a wild-goose chase,** beat the air, lash the waves, tilt at windmills, sow the sand, bay at the moon, waste one's breath, preach *or* speak to the winds, beat *or* flog a dead horse, roll the stone of Sisyphus, milk the ram, milk a he-goat into a sieve, pour water into a sieve, hold a farthing candle to the sun, look for a needle in a haystack, lock the barn door after the horse is stolen.

.9 ADJS **useless,** of no use, no go [informal]; **aimless,** meaningless, **purposeless,** of no purpose, **pointless, feckless; unavailing,** of no avail; ineffective, **ineffectual** 158.15; impotent 158.13–19; **superfluous** 663.17.

.10 **needless, unnecessary, unessential,** nonessential, **unneeded, uncalled-for,** unrequired.

.11 **worthless, valueless, good-for-nothing,** good-for-naught, no-good *or* NG [both informal], no-account [dial], dear at any price, worthless as tits on a boar [dial], not worthwhile, not worth having, not worth mentioning *or* speaking of, not worth a thought, not worth a rap *or* a continental *or* a damn, not worth the powder to blow it to hell, not worth the powder and shot, not worth the pains, of no earthly use, fit for the junk yard [informal]; trivial, nugatory, nugacious; **junk** *or* **junky** [both informal]; **cheap,** shoddy, trashy, **shabby** 673.18.

.12 **fruitless,** gainless, profitless, bootless, otiose, **unprofitable,** unremunerative, nonremunerative, **unrewarding,** rewardless; abortive; barren, sterile, unproductive 166.4.

.13 **vain, futile,** hollow, empty, "weary, stale, flat, and unprofitable" [Shakespeare], idle; absurd; inane, fatuous, fatuitous.

.14 **unserviceable, unusable,** unemployable, inoperative, inoperable, unworkable; out of order, out of whack [informal], in disrepair; **unhelpful,** unconducive; inapplicable; unsuitable, unfit; functionless, nonfunctional, otiose, nonutilitarian.

.15 ADVS **uselessly; needlessly,** unnecessarily; bootlessly, fruitlessly; **futilely, vainly;** purposelessly, to little purpose, to no purpose, **aimlessly, pointlessly,** fecklessly.

## 670. EXPEDIENCE

.1 NOUNS **expedience** *or* **expediency, advisability,** politicness, **desirability,** recommendability; **fitness, fittingness, appropriateness,** propriety, decency [archaic], seemliness, **suitability,** rightness, feasibility, **convenience;** seasonableness, timeliness, **opportuneness; usefulness** 665.3; **advantage, advantageousness,** beneficialness, **profit,** profitability, percentage [informal], worthwhileness, fruitfulness; wisdom, prudence 467.5–7.

.2 **expedient, means,** means to an end, **measure, step, action,** effort, **stroke,** stroke of policy, coup, **move,** countermove, **maneuver,** demarche, course of action; tactic, **device,** contrivance, artifice, stratagem, **shift; gimmick** *or* dodge *or* trick [all informal]; **resort,** resource; answer, solution; working proposition, working hypothesis; **temporary expedient, improvisation,** ad hoc measure, jury-rigged expedient, **makeshift,** stopgap, shake-up, jury-rig; last expedient, **last resort** *or* resource, *pis aller* [Fr], last shift, trump.

.3 VERBS **expedite one's affair,** work to one's advantage, not come amiss, be just the thing, be just what the doctor ordered [informal]; forward, advance, promote, profit, advantage, benefit; **work, serve,** answer, fill the bill *or* do the trick [both informal]; suit the occasion, **be fitting, fit,** befit, be right.

.4 **make shift, make do,** make out [dial], cope, manage, manage with, get along on, get by on, do with; do as well as one can.

.5 ADJS **expedient, desirable,** to be desired, much to be desired, **advisable, politic,** recommendable; **appropriate, meet, fit,** fitten [dial], **fitting,** befitting, **right, proper,** good, decent [archaic], **becoming,** seemly, likely, congruous, **suitable,** sortable, **feasible, convenient,** happy, felicitous; timely, seasonable, opportune, well-timed; **useful** 665.18; **advantageous,** favorable; **profitable,** fructuous, worthwhile, worth one's while; **wise** 467.17–19.

**.6 practical,** practicable, pragmatic(al), banausic; feasible, workable, operable, realizable; **efficient,** effective, **effectual** 665.20.

**.7 makeshift,** makeshifty, **stopgap,** band-aid [informal], improvised, improvisational, **jury-rigged; ad hoc;** temporary, provisional, tentative.

**.8** ADVS **expediently, fittingly,** fitly, **appropriately, suitably,** sortably, congruously, rightly, properly, decently [archaic], feasibly, conveniently; practically; seasonably, opportunely; desirably, advisably; advantageously, to advantage, all to the good.

## 671. INEXPEDIENCE

**.1** NOUNS **inexpedience** or inexpediency, **undesirability, inadvisability,** impoliticness or impoliticalness; unwiseness 470.2; **unfitness, unfittingness, inappropriateness, unsuitability,** incongruity, **unmeetness,** wrongness, unseemliness, inconvenience or inconveniency [both archaic], ineptitude, inaptitude; unseasonableness, untimeliness, inopportuneness; unfortunateness, infelicity; disadvantageousness, unprofitableness, unprofitability, worthlessness, futility, uselessness 669.

**.2 disadvantage, drawback, liability; detriment,** impairment, prejudice, loss, damage, hurt, harm, mischief, injury; step backward, loss of ground; **handicap** 730.6.

**.3 inconvenience,** discommodity, incommodity, disaccommodation [archaic], **trouble, bother;** inconvenientness, inconveniency, **unhandiness,** awkwardness, clumsiness, unwieldiness, troublesomeness.

**.4** VERBS **inconvenience,** put to inconvenience, **put out, discommode,** incommode, disaccommodate [archaic], disoblige, **trouble, bother,** put to trouble, **impose upon;** harm, disadvantage 675.6.

**.5** ADJS **inexpedient, undesirable, inadvisable,** impolitic(al), not to be recommended; **ill-advised, ill-considered, unwise** 470.9; **unfit, unfitting,** unbefitting, **inappropriate, unsuitable,** unmeet, inapt, inept, unseemly, improper, wrong, bad, out of place, incongruous, ill-suited; malapropos, *mal à propos* [Fr], inopportune, untimely, ill-timed, unseasonable; infelicitous, unfortunate, unhappy; unprofitable 669.12; futile 669.13.

**.6 disadvantageous,** unadvantageous, **unfavorable;** unprofitable, unrewarding, worthless, useless 669.9–11; **detrimental,** deleterious, injurious, harmful, prejudicial, disserviceable.

**.7 inconvenient, incommodious,** discommodious; **unhandy, awkward,** clumsy, unwieldy, troublesome.

**.8** ADVS **inexpediently, inadvisably,** impoliticly or impolitically, **undesirably; unfittingly, inappropriately, unsuitably,** ineptly, inaptly, incongruously; inopportunely, unseasonably; infelicitously, unfortunately, unhappily.

**.9 disadvantageously,** unadvantageously, unprofitably, unrewardingly; uselessly 669.15; **inconveniently,** unhandily, with difficulty, ill.

## 672. IMPORTANCE

**.1** NOUNS **importance, significance, consequence,** consideration, **import,** note, mark, **moment, weight;** materiality; concern, concernment, interest; **first order,** high order, high rank; **priority,** primacy, precedence, preeminence, paramountcy, superiority, **supremacy;** value, worth, merit, excellence 674.1; emphasis, stress, accent; consequentiality, self-importance 909.1.

**.2 notability, noteworthiness,** remarkableness, salience, memorability; **prominence, eminence, greatness,** distinction; prestige, esteem, repute, reputation, honor, glory, renown, dignity, fame 914.1.

**.3 gravity, seriousness,** solemnity, weightiness; no joke, no laughing matter.

**.4 urgency,** imperativeness, exigency; **press,** pressure, high pressure, **stress,** tension, **pinch;** clutch or crunch [both informal]; **crisis, emergency.**

**.5 matter of importance,** thing of interest, point of interest, matter of concern, object of note, one for the book or something to write home about [both informal], something special; vital concern or interest, matter of life or death; notabilia, memorabilia, great doings.

**.6 salient point,** cardinal point, high point, great point; important thing, chief thing, **the point, main point,** main thing, essential matter, **essence,** the bottom line [informal], substance, gravamen, *sine qua non* [L], issue, real issue, prime issue, name of the game [informal]; **essential,** fundamental, substantive point, material point; **gist, nub** [informal], **heart,** mean, pith, kernel, **core; crux,** crucial or pivotal or critical point, pivot; turning point, climax, crisis; keystone, cornerstone; landmark, milestone, bench mark.

.7 **feature, highlight,** high spot, outstanding feature.

.8 **personage, important person,** person of importance *or* consequence, **great man,** big man [informal], man of mark *or* note, **somebody,** something [informal], **notable,** notability, figure; **celebrity,** famous person, person of renown, lion [informal], personality; name, big name, big gun [informal]; nabob, **mogul,** panjandrum, person to be reckoned with, very important person, **VIP** [informal], **bigwig** [informal]; sachem; brass hat [informal]; **worthy,** pillar of society, elder, father; **dignitary,** dignity; **magnate;** tycoon [informal], baron; power; power elite, Establishment; interests; brass, top brass; top people, the great; ruling circle, lords of creation, "the choice and master spirits of the age" [Shakespeare]; the top, the summit.

.9 [slang terms] **big shot,** wheel, **big wheel,** big cheese, big noise, big-timer, big-time operator, **high-muck-a-muck** *or* high-muckety-muck, his nibs; big man on campus, BMOC.

.10 **chief, principal,** paramount, biggest frog in the pond [slang]; honcho [slang], top dog *or* Mr. Big [both slang]; **king,** electronics king, etc.; leading light, luminary, master spirit, **star,** superstar, prima donna, lead 612.6.

.11 VERBS **matter,** import [archaic], signify, **count, tell, weigh,** carry weight, cut ice *or* cut some ice [both informal], be prominent, stand out, mean much; be something, be somebody, amount to something; have a key to the executive washroom; be featured, star, get top billing.

.12 **value, esteem, treasure, prize,** appreciate, **rate highly,** think highly of, think well of, **think much of,** set store by; give *or* attach *or* ascribe importance to; make much of, make a fuss *or* stir about, make an ado *or* much ado about.

.13 **emphasize, stress,** lay emphasis *or* stress upon, place emphasis on, give emphasis to, **accent, accentuate, punctuate, point up,** bring to the fore, put in the foreground; **highlight,** spotlight; **star, underline, underscore,** italicize; overemphasize, overstress, overaccentuate, rub in; harp on; dwell on, belabor; attach too much importance to, make a federal case of, make a mountain out of a molehill.

.14 **feature,** headline [informal]; **star,** give top billing to.

.15 **dramatize, play up** [informal], splash, make a production of.

.16 ADJS **important, major, consequential, momentous, significant, considerable, substantial, material, great,** grand, big; superior, world-shaking, earthshaking; bigtime *or* big-league *or* major-league *or* heavyweight [all informal]; high-powered [informal], double-barreled [slang]; bigwig *or* bigwigged [both informal]; name *or* big-name [both informal], self-important 909.8.

.17 **of importance, of significance, of consequence,** of note, of moment, of weight; of concern, of concernment, of interest, not to be overlooked *or* despised, not to be sneezed at [informal]; viable.

.18 **notable, noteworthy, celebrated, remarkable, marked,** of mark, signal; **memorable,** rememberable, unforgettable, never to be forgotten; **striking, telling,** salient; **eminent, prominent,** conspicuous, noble, **outstanding, distinguished;** prestigious, esteemed, estimable, reputable 914.15–19; **extraordinary,** out of the ordinary, exceptional, **special,** rare.

.19 **weighty, heavy, grave,** sober, solemn, serious, earnest; portentous, fateful, fatal; formidable, awe-inspiring, imposing.

.20 **emphatic, decided, positive, forceful,** forcible; **emphasized, stressed,** accented, accentuated, punctuated, pointed; underlined, underscored, starred, italicized; in red letters, in letters of fire.

.21 **urgent, imperative,** imperious, **compelling, pressing,** high-priority, high-pressure, crying, clamorous, insistent, instant, exigent; crucial, critical, pivotal, acute.

.22 **vital,** of vital importance, life-and-death *or* life-or-death; **essential,** fundamental, indispensable, basic, substantive, bedrock, material; **central,** focal.

.23 **paramount, principal, leading, foremost, main, chief,** premier, **prime, primary,** preeminent, **supreme,** capital [archaic], cardinal; highest, uppermost, topmost, toprank, ranking, of the first rank, **dominant,** predominant, master, controlling, **overruling,** overriding, all-absorbing.

.24 ADVS **importantly, significantly,** consequentially, **materially,** momentously, greatly, grandly; eminently, prominently, conspicuously, outstandingly, saliently, signally, notably, markedly, remarkably.

## 673. UNIMPORTANCE

.1 NOUNS **unimportance, insignificance,** inconsequence, inconsequentiality, indifference, **immateriality**; inessentiality; ineffectuality; unnoteworthiness, unimpressiveness; inferiority, secondariness, low order of importance, low priority; marginality; **smallness**, littleness, slightness, inconsiderableness, negligibility; **pettiness**, puniness, pokiness, picayune, picayunishness; irrelevance 10.1.

.2 **paltriness**, poorness, **meanness**, sorriness, sadness, pitifulness, contemptibleness, pitiableness, despicableness, miserableness, wretchedness, vileness, crumminess [slang], shabbiness, shoddiness, cheapness, beggarliness, worthlessness, unworthiness, meritlessness; meretriciousness, gaudiness 904.3.

.3 **triviality**, trivialness, triflingness, nugacity; **superficiality**, shallowness; slightness, slenderness, flimsiness, **frivolity**, frivolousness, lightness, levity; **foolishness**, silliness; inanity, emptiness, vacuity; triteness, vapidity; vanity, idleness, futility; **much ado about nothing**, tempest or storm in a teacup or teapot, much cry and little wool, big deal [slang].

.4 **trivia**, **trifles**; **trumpery**, gimcrackery, knickknackery, bric-a-brac; **rubbish**, trash, chaff; peanuts, chicken feed or chickenshit [both slang], small change; small beer; froth, "trifles light as air" [Shakespeare]; minutiae, details, minor details.

.5 **trifle**, triviality, bagatelle, fribble, **gimcrack**, gewgaw, frippery, **trinket**, bibelot, curio, **bauble**, gaud, toy, **knickknack**, knickknackery, kickshaw, minikin [archaic], whim-wham, folderol; pin, button, hair, straw, rush, feather, fig, bean, hill of beans [informal], molehill, row of pins or buttons [informal], sneeshing [Brit dial], pinch of snuff; bit, snap; a curse, a continental, a hoot [informal], a damn, a darn, shit [slang], a tinker's damn; picayune, rap, sou, halfpenny, farthing, brass farthing, cent, red cent, two cents, twopence or tuppence [both Brit]; peppercorn; drop in the ocean, drop in the bucket; fleabite, pinprick; joke, jest, farce, mockery, child's play.

.6 **insignificancy**, inessential, marginal matter or affair, trivial or paltry affair, small or trifling or minor matter, **no great matter**; a little thing, peu de chose [Fr], hardly or scarcely anything, matter of no importance or consequence, matter of indifference; **nothing**, naught, mere nothing, nothing in particular, nothing to signify, nothing to speak or worth speaking of, nothing to think twice about, nothing

to boast of, nothing to write home about, thing of naught, rien du tout [Fr], nullity, nihility; **technicality**.

.7 **a nobody**, **insignificancy**, jackstraw [archaic], **little fellow**, little guy [informal], **man in the street**; common man 79.3; **nonentity**, nebbish [informal], obscurity, a nothing, cipher, "an O without a figure" [Shakespeare], nobody one knows; lightweight, mediocrity; whippersnapper, whiffet, pip-squeak, squirt, shrimp, scrub, runt [all informal]; squit [Brit informal], punk [slang]; small potato, small potatoes; man of straw, dummy, figurehead 749.4; **small fry**, Mr. and Mrs. Nobody, John Doe and Richard Roe or Mary Roe; Tom, Dick, and Harry; Brown, Jones, and Robinson.

.8 **trifling**, dallying, **dalliance**, flirtation, coquetry; toying, fiddling, playing, fooling, monkeying or monkeying around [both informal], horsing or fooling or kidding or messing or playing or screwing or mucking or farting around [informal]; jerking off [slang]; **puttering**, tinkering, pottering, piddling; dabbling, smattering; loitering, idling 708.4.

.9 **trifler**, dallier, fribble; **putterer**, potterer, piddler, smatterer, dabbler; amateur, dilettante, Sunday painter; **flirt**, coquet.

.10 VERBS **be unimportant**, be of no importance, not signify, **not matter**, not count, cut no ice [informal], signify nothing, matter little, **not make any difference**, **not amount to anything**, not amount to a hill of beans [informal], not amount to a damn [slang].

.11 **attach little importance to**, give little weight to; make little of, underplay, deemphasize, downplay, play down, minimize, **make light of**, think little of, **make or think nothing of**, take no account of, set little by, set no store by, set at naught; snap one's fingers at; not care straw about; not give a shit or a hoot or two hoots for [slang], not give a damn about, not give a dime a dozen for; depreciate, depreciate 971.8.

.12 **make much ado about nothing**, make mountains out of molehills, have a storm or tempest in a teacup or teapot.

.13 **trifle**, dally; **flirt**, coquet; toy, fiddle, fiddle-faddle [informal], fribble, frivol [informal], **play**, fool, monkey or monkey around [both informal], horse or fool or play or mess or kid or screw or muck or fart around [informal]; jerk off [slang]; putter, potter, tinker, piddle; dabble smatter; toy with, fiddle with, fool with, play with, finger with, fidget with, twiddle; idle, loiter 708.11–13.

.14 ADJS **unimportant,** of no importance, of little or small importance, of no great importance, **of no account,** of no significance, of no concern, of no matter, of little or no consequence, no great shakes [informal]; no skin off one's nose or elbow [informal]; inferior, secondary, of a low order of importance, low-priority; marginal.

.15 **insignificant, inconsequential, immaterial;** nonessential, unessential, inessential, **not vital,** back-burner [informal], dispensable; unnoteworthy, unimpressive; **inconsiderable,** inappreciable, negligible; **small, little,** minute, dinky [slang], petit [archaic], minor, inferior; technical; irrelevant 10.6.

.16 **trivial, trifling;** fribble, fribbling, nugacious, nugatory; catchpenny; **slight,** slender, flimsy; **superficial, shallow; frivolous, light,** windy, airy, frothy; idle, futile, vain, otiose; **foolish,** fatuous, asinine, **silly; inane,** empty, vacuous; trite, vapid; unworthy of serious consideration.

.17 **petty, puny,** measly [slang], **poky, piddling,** piffling, niggling, pettifogging, picayune, picayunish; **small-time** or two-bit or tinhorn or punk [all slang]; **one-horse** or **two-by-four** or jerkwater [all informal]; small-beer.

18 **paltry, poor,** common, **mean, sorry, sad, pitiful,** pitiable, pathetic, **despicable, contemptible,** beneath contempt, **miserable, wretched,** beggarly, vile, **shabby,** scrubby, scruffy, shoddy, scurvy, scuzzy [slang], scummy, **crummy** or cheesy [both slang], **trashy,** rubbishy, garbagey [informal], trumpery, gimcracky [informal]; tinpot [slang]; **cheap,** worthless, valueless, twopenny or twopenny-halfpenny [both Brit], two-for-a-cent or -penny, dime-adozen; meretricious, gaudy 904.20.

9 **unworthy, worthless,** meritless, unworthy of regard or consideration, beneath notice.

0 ADVS **unimportantly, insignificantly, inconsequentially,** immaterially, unessentially; **pettily,** paltrily; **trivially,** triflingly; superficially, shallowly; frivolously, lightly, idly.

PHRS **it does not matter,** it matters not, it does not signify, **it is of no consequence** or **importance, it makes no difference,** it cannot be helped, it is all the same; *n'importe, de rien, ça ne fait rien* [all Fr]; it will all come out in the wash [informal], it will be all the same a hundred years from now.

.22 **no matter, never mind,** think no more of it, do not give it another or a second thought, don't lose any sleep over it, let it pass, let it go [informal], ignore it, forget it [informal], skip it or drop it [both slang].

.23 **what does it matter?, what matter?, what's the difference?,** what's the diff? [slang], what do I care?, what of it?, what boots it?, what's the odds?, so what?, what else is new?; for aught one cares, big deal [informal].

## 674. GOODNESS

### *(good quality or effect)*

.1 NOUNS **goodness, excellence, quality, class** [informal]; **virtue,** grace; **merit,** desert; **value, worth; fineness,** goodliness, fairness, niceness; **superiority,** first-rateness, **skillfulness** 733.1; wholeness, **soundness,** healthiness 683.1; **virtuousness** 980.1; **kindness, benevolence,** benignity 938.1; beneficialness, helpfulness 785.10; favorableness, auspiciousness 544.9; expedience, advantageousness 670.1; **usefulness** 665.3; pleasantness, agreeableness 863.1; cogency, validity 516.4; profitableness, rewardingness 811.4.

.2 **superexcellence,** supereminence, preeminence, supremacy, primacy, paramountcy, peerlessness, unsurpassedness, matchlessness, superfineness; **superbness,** exquisiteness, **magnificence,** splendidness, splendiferousness, marvelousness.

.3 **tolerableness,** tolerability, goodishness, passableness, fairishness, **adequateness, satisfactoriness,** acceptability, admissibility; sufficiency 661.

.4 **good, welfare,** well-being, **benefit; interest, advantage; behalf,** behoof; blessing, benison, boon; **profit,** avail [archaic], gain; world of good.

.5 **good thing,** a thing to be desired, "a consummation devoutly to be wish'd" [Shakespeare]; **treasure,** gem, jewel, diamond, pearl; boast, pride, **pride and joy;** prize, trophy, plum; winner [informal]; catch, find [informal], *trouvaille* [Fr]; godsend, windfall.

.6 **first-rater** or topnotcher [both informal]; wonder, prodigy, genius, virtuoso, star, superstar; luminary, leading light, one in a thousand.

.7 [slang or informal terms] **dandy, jim-**

dandy, dilly, **humdinger**, **pip**, pippin, **peach**, ace, beaut, **lulu**, **daisy**, darb, honey, sweetheart, dream, lollapaloosa, corker, whiz, **crackerjack**, knockout, killer-diller, the nuts, the cat's pajamas *or* meow.

.8 **the best**, the very best, the best ever, the tops [informal]; **quintessence**, prime, optimum, superlative; **choice**, **pick**, **select**, **elect**, **elite**, *corps d'élite* [Fr], chosen; **cream**, **flower**, fat; cream of the crop, *crème de la crème* [Fr], salt of the earth; *pièce de résistance* [Fr]; prize, champion, queen; nonesuch, paragon, nonpareil; gem of the first water.

.9 **harmlessness**, hurtlessness, uninjuriousness, **innocuousness**, benignity, benignancy; unobnoxiousness, inoffensiveness; innocence.

.10 VERBS **do good**, **profit**, avail; do a world of good; **benefit**, **help**, **serve**, advance, advantage, favor 785.11–19; be the making of, make a man of; do no harm, break no bones.

.11 **be as good as**, equal, emulate, rival, vie, vie with, challenge comparison.

.12 ADJS **good**, **excellent**, eu–, *bueno* [Sp], *bon* [Fr], bonny [Brit], **fine**, **nice**, goodly, fair; **splendid**, **capital**, **grand**, elegant [informal], braw [Scot], famous [informal], noble; royal, regal, fit for a king; very good, *très bon* [Fr]; commendable, laudable, **estimable** 968.20; skillful 733.20–26; **sound**, healthy 683.5; virtuous 980.7; **kind**, benevolent 938.13–17; beneficial, helpful 785.21; profitable 811.15; favorable, auspicious 544.18; expedient, advantageous 670.5; useful 665.18; pleasant 863.6; cogent, valid 516.13.

.13 [slang terms] **great**, **swell**, **dandy**, jimdandy, neat, cool, bully, tough, mean, heavy, bad, groovy, out of sight, fab, marvy, gear, something else, ducky, keen, hot, nifty, spiffy, spiffing, ripping, nobby, peachy, peachy-keen, delicious, scrumptious, out of this world, hunky-dory, crackerjack, boss, stunning, corking, smashing, solid, all wool and a yard wide; rum *or* wizard [both Brit], bonzer [Austral]; bang-up, jam-up, slap-up, ace-high, fine and dandy, just dandy, but good, OK, okay, A-OK.

.14 **superior**, above par, crack [informal]; **high-grade**, **high-class**, **high-quality**, high-caliber, high-test.

.15 **first-rate**, **first-class**, in a class by itself, first-chop [informal]; tip-top, top-notch, topflight, top-drawer, tops [all informal];

topping *or* top-hole [both Brit informal]; A1 *or* A number 1 [both informal].

.16 **up to par**, up to standard, **up to snuff** [informal]; **up to the mark**, up to the notch *or* up to scratch [both informal].

.17 **superb**, super [slang], **superexcellent**, supereminent, superfine, **exquisite**; **magnificent**, splendid, splendiferous, tremendous, immense, **marvelous**, **wonderful**, glorious, divine, heavenly, terrific, sensational; sterling, golden; gilt-edged *or* giltedge [both informal]; of the highest type, of the best sort, of the first water, as good as good can be, as good as they come, as good as they make 'em [informal], out of this world [slang].

.18 **best**, very best, greatest [informal], **prime**, optimum, optimal, aristo–; **choice**, **select**, **elect**, elite, **picked**, handpicked; **prize**, **champion**; **supreme**, paramount, **unsurpassed**, surpassing, unparalleled, unmatched, unmatchable, matchless, **peerless**; quintessential; for the best, all for the best.

.19 **tolerable**, **goodish**, **fair**, **fairish**, moderate, tidy [informal], **decent**, respectable, presentable, good enough, **pretty good**, **not bad**, not amiss, not half bad, not so bad, **adequate**, **satisfactory**, **all right**, OK *or* okay [both slang]; better than nothing **acceptable**, admissible, **passable**, unobjectionable, unexceptionable; workmanlike sufficient 661.6.

.20 **harmless**, hurtless, unhurtful, **uninjurious** undamaging, **innocuous**, innoxious, innocent; unobnoxious, inoffensive; nonmalignant, **benign**; nonpoisonous, nontoxic nonvirulent, nonvenomous.

.21 ADVS **excellently**, **nicely**, finely, **capitally splendidly**, **famously**, royally; **well**, very well, **fine** [informal], right, aright.

.22 **superbly**, exquisitely, **magnificently**, tremendously, immensely, terrifically, **marvelously**, **wonderfully**, gloriously, divinely out–.

.23 **tolerably**, **fairly**, fairishly, moderately, respectably, **adequately**, **satisfactorily**, passably, **acceptably**, unexceptionably, presentably, decently; fairly well, well enough, pretty well; **rather**, **pretty**.

## 675. BADNESS

*(bad quality or effect)*

.1 NOUNS **badness**, **evilness**, viciousness damnability, reprehensibility; moral badness, peccancy, wickedness 981.4; unhealthiness 684.1; inferiority 680.3; unsk fulness 734.1; unkindness, malevolence 939; inauspiciousness, unfavorableness 544.8; inexpedience 671; unpleasantness 864; invalidity 158.3; inaccuracy 518.2; improperness 959.1.

.2 **terribleness, dreadfulness,** direness, **awfulness** [informal], horribleness; **atrociousness, outrageousness,** heinousness, nefariousness; **notoriousness, egregiousness,** scandalousness, shamefulness, **infamousness; abominableness,** odiousness, **loathsomeness, detestableness,** despicableness, contemptibleness, hatefulness; **offensiveness,** grossness, obnoxiousness; squalor, squalidness, sordidness, **wretchedness,** filth, **vileness,** fulsomeness, **nastiness,** rankness, **foulness,** noisomeness; disgustingness, repulsiveness; uncleanness 682; beastliness, bestiality, brutality; **rottenness** or lousiness [both informal], the pits [slang]; shoddiness, shabbiness; scurviness, **baseness** 915.3; **worthlessness** 673.2.

.3 **evil, bad, wrong, ill; harm, hurt, injury, damage, detriment; destruction** 693; despoliation 824.5; mischief, havoc; outrage, atrocity; abomination, grievance, vexation, woe, crying evil; poison 676.3; blight, venom, toxin, **bane** 676; **corruption,** pollution, infection, befoulment, defilement; fly in the ointment, worm in the apple or rose; skeleton in the closet; snake in the grass; "something rotten in the state of Denmark" [Shakespeare]; ills the flesh is heir to, "all ills that men endure" [Abraham Cowley]; the worst.

.4 **bad influence,** malevolent influence, evil star, **ill wind;** evil genius, **hoodoo** or **jinx** [both informal], **Jonah;** curse, enchantment, whammy [slang], spell, hex, voodoo; evil eye, *malocchio* [Ital].

.5 **harmfulness, hurtfulness,** injuriousness, banefulness, balefulness, detrimentalness, deleteriousness, perniciousness, mischievousness, noxiousness, venomousness, poisonousness, toxicity, virulence, noisomeness, **malignance** or **malignancy,** malignity, viciousness; unhealthiness 684.1; deadliness, lethality 409.8; ominousness 544.7.

.6 VERBS **work evil, do ill; harm, hurt; injure,** scathe, wound, **damage; destroy** 693.10–21; despoil 824.16, prejudice, disadvantage, impair, disserve, distress; **wrong,** do wrong, do wrong by, aggrieve, do evil, do a mischief, do an ill office to; **molest,** afflict; lay a hand on; get into trouble; abuse, outrage, violate, maltreat, mistreat 667.5; torment, harass, persecute, savage,

crucify, torture 866.18; play mischief or havoc with, wreak havoc on, play hob with [informal]; **corrupt,** deprave, taint, pollute, infect, befoul, defile 682.19; poison, envenom, blight; curse, hex, jinx, bewitch; threaten, menace 973.2; doom; condemn 1008.3.

.7 ADJS **bad, evil, ill,** untoward, cac(o)– or kako–, dis– or dys–, mal–; black, sinister; **wicked, wrong,** peccant, **vicious, sinful** 981.16; criminal 982.6; unhealthy 684.5; **inferior** 680.9,10; unskillful 734.15–20; unkind, malevolent 939.14–24; inauspicious, unfavorable 544.17; inexpedient 671.5; unpleasant 864.17; invalid 158.15; inaccurate 518.17; improper 959.3.

.8 [slang terms] **dirty,** punk, bum, shitty, crappy, cheesy, **crummy,** grim, putrid, icky, yecchy, vomity, barfy, stinking, stinky, creepy, hairy, godawful, goshawful.

.9 **terrible, dreadful, awful** [informal], dire, horrible, horrid; **atrocious, outrageous,** heinous, villainous, nefarious; enormous, monstrous; **deplorable,** lamentable, regrettable, pitiful, pitiable, woeful, grievous, sad 864.20; flagrant, **scandalous,** shameful, **shocking,** infamous, **notorious,** arrant, **egregious;** unclean 682.20–25; shoddy, schlock [slang], shabby, scurvy, **base** 915.12; **odious, obnoxious,** offensive, gross, **disgusting,** repulsive, loathsome, **abominable, detestable, despicable, contemptible,** beneath contempt, hateful; blameworthy, **reprehensible** 969.26; rank, fetid, foul, filthy, vile, **rotten** or **lousy** [both informal], fulsome, noisome, **nasty,** squalid, sordid, **wretched;** beastly, brutal; as bad as they come, as bad as they make 'em [informal], as bad as bad can be; worst; too bad; worthless 673.19

.10 **execrable, damnable;** cursed 972.9,10; infernal, hellish, devilish, fiendish, satanic, ghoulish, demoniac, demonic(al), diabolic(al), ungodly.

.11 evil-fashioned, ill-fashioned, evil-shaped, ill-shaped, evil-qualitied, evil-looking, ill-looking, evil-favored, ill-favored, evil-hued, evil-faced, evil-minded, evil-eyed, ill-affected [archaic], evil-gotten, ill-gotten, ill-conceived.

.12 **harmful, hurtful,** scatheful, **baneful,** baleful, distressing, **injurious, damaging, detrimental,** deleterious, counterproductive, **pernicious,** mischievous; noxious, venomous, venenate, poisonous, venenous, veneniferous, toxic, virulent, noisome; **malignant,** malign, malevolent, malefic, vicious; prejudicial, disadvantageous, disserviceable; corruptive, corrupting, corrosive, corroding 692.45; deadly, lethal 409.23; ominous 544.17.

.13 ADVS **badly**, bad [informal], **ill**, evil, evilly, wrong, wrongly, amiss; to one's cost.

.14 **terribly, dreadfully**, dreadful [dial], **horribly**, horridly, **awfully** [informal], **atrociously, outrageously**; flagrantly, scandalously, shamefully, shockingly, infamously, notoriously, egregiously, grossly, offensively, nauseatingly, fulsomely, odiously, **vilely**, obnoxiously, **disgustingly**, loathsomely; wretchedly, sordidly, shabbily, basely, abominably, detestably, despicably, contemptibly, foully, nastily; brutally, bestially, savagely, viciously; something fierce or terrible [informal].

.15 **harmfully, hurtfully, banefully**, balefully, **injuriously, damagingly, detrimentally**, deleteriously, counterproductively, **perniciously**, mischievously; noxiously, venomously, poisonously, toxically, virulently, noisomely; **malignantly**, malignly, malevolently, malefically, **viciously**; prejudicially, disadvantageously, disserviceably; corrosively, corrodingly.

## 676. BANE

.1 NOUNS **bane, curse, affliction**, infliction, visitation, **plague, pestilence**, pest, calamity, scourge, **torment**, open wound, running sore, grievance, woe, burden, crushing burden; disease 686; death 408; evil, harm 675.3; destruction 693; vexation 866.2; thorn, thorn in the flesh or side, pea in the shoe; bugbear, *bête noire* [Fr], nemesis.

.2 **blight**, blast; canker, cancer; mold, fungus, mildew, smut, must, rust; rot, dry rot; **pest**; worm, worm in the apple or rose; moth [archaic], "moth and rust" [Bible].

.3 **poison, venom**, venin, virus [archaic], toxic, toxin, toxicant, tox(o)– or toxi–; eradicant, **pesticide; insecticide**, insect powder, **bug bomb** [informal]; roach powder, roach paste; stomach poison, contact poison, systemic insecticide or systemic, fumigant, chemosterilant; chlorinated hydrocarbon insecticide, organic chlorine; organic phosphate insecticide; carbamate insecticide; miticide, acaricide, vermicide, anthelmintic; rodenticide, rat poison; **herbicide**, defoliant, **weed killer**; fungicide; microbicide, germicide, antiseptic, disinfectant, antibiotic; **toxicology**.

.4 **miasma, mephitis**, malaria [archaic]; effluvium, exhaust, exhaust gas; coal gas, chokedamp, blackdamp, firedamp.

.5 sting, stinger, dart; **fang, tang** [dial]; beesting, snakebite.

.6 **poisons**

| | |
|---|---|
| aconite | hydrocyanide |
| aldrin | hydrogen cyanide |
| alkaloid | hyoscyamine |
| antimony | lead |
| arsenic | lead arsenate |
| arsenic trioxide, arse- | lindane |
| nious oxide | Malathion |
| arsenious acid | mercuric chloride |
| beryllium | mercury |
| bichloride of mercury | methoxychlor, |
| cadmium | methoxy DDT |
| calcium arsenate | mustard gas |
| carbolic acid | nerve gas |
| carbon monoxide | nicotine |
| carbon tetrachloride | parathion |
| chlordane | Paris green |
| chlorine | phenol |
| corrosive sublimate | poison gas |
| curare | potassium cyanide |
| cyanide | prussic acid |
| cyanide gas | pyrethrum |
| DDD | red squill |
| (dichlorodiphenyl- | rotenone |
| dichloroethane) | selenium |
| DDT | strychnine |
| (dichlorodiphenyl- | tartar emetic |
| trichloroethane) | 2,4-D |
| dieldrin | 2,4,5-T |
| endrin | warfarin |
| hydrocyanic acid | white arsenic |

.7 **poisonous plants**

| | |
|---|---|
| aconite | locoweed |
| amanita | mayapple |
| banewort | mescal bean |
| bearded darnel | monkshood |
| belladonna | nightshade |
| black henbane | nux vomica |
| black nightshade | ordeal tree |
| castor-oil plant | poison bean |
| corn cackle | poisonberry |
| datura | poison bush |
| deadly nightshade | poison hemlock, poi- |
| death camas | son parsley |
| death cup, death | poison ivy |
| angel | poison oak |
| ergot | poison rye grass |
| foxglove | poison sumac |
| Gastrolobium | poison tobacco |
| hellebore | poisonweed |
| hemlock | pokeweed |
| henbane | sheep laurel |
| horsetail | upas |
| jequirity, jequirity | water hemlock |
| bean | white snakeroot |
| jimsonweed | wolfsbane |
| larkspur | |

## 677. PERFECTION

.1 NOUNS **perfection**, finish; **faultlessness flawlessness**, defectlessness, indefectibil ity, impeccability, absoluteness; infallibility; spotlessness, stainlessness, taintlessness, purity, immaculateness; sinlessness 980.4; chastity 988.

.2 soundness, integrity, intactness, wholeness, entireness, completeness; fullness, plenitude.

.3 acme of perfection, pink, pink of perfection, culmination, perfection, height, top, acme, ultimate, summit, pinnacle, peak, highest pitch, climax, consummation, *ne plus ultra* [L], last word.

.4 pattern *or* standard *or* mold *or* norm of perfection, very model, quintessence; archetype, prototype, exemplar, mirror; classic, masterwork, masterpiece, *chef d'œuvre* [Fr]; ideal 25.4; paragon 985.4.

.5 VERBS perfect, develop, ripen, mature; improve 691.7; crown, culminate, complete 722.6; do to perfection 722.7.

.6 ADJS perfect, ideal, faultless, flawless, unflawed, defectless, not to be improved, impeccable, absolute; just right; spotless, stainless, taintless, unblemished, untainted, unspotted, immaculate, pure, uncontaminated, unadulterated, unmixed; sinless 980.9; chaste 988.4; indefective [archaic], indefectible; infallible; beyond all praise, irreproachable, unfaultable, *sans peur et sans reproche* [Fr], peerless 36.15.

.7 sound, intact, whole, entire, complete, integral; full; total, utter, unqualified 508.2.

.8 undamaged, unharmed, unhurt, uninjured, unscathed, unspoiled, virgin, inviolate, unimpaired; harmless, scatheless; unmarred, unmarked, unscarred, unscratched, undefaced, unbruised; unbroken, unshattered, untorn; undemolished, undestroyed; undeformed, unmutilated, unmangled, unmaimed; unfaded, unworn, unwithered, bright, fresh, untouched, pristine, mint.

.9 perfected, finished, polished, refined; classic(al), masterly, masterful, expert, proficient; ripened, ripe, matured, mature, developed, fully developed; consummate, quintessential, archetypical, exemplary, model.

.10 ADVS perfectly, ideally; faultlessly, flawlessly, impeccably; just right; spotlessly; immaculately, purely; infallibly; wholly, entirely, completely, fully, thoroughly, totally, absolutely 56.14,15.

.11 to perfection, to a turn, to a T [informal], to a finish, to a nicety; to a fare-thee-well *or* fare-you-well *or* fare-ye-well [informal].

## 678. IMPERFECTION

.1 NOUNS imperfection, imperfectness; unperfectedness; faultiness, defectiveness, defectibility; shortcoming, deficiency, lack, want, shortage, inadequacy, inadequateness; erroneousness, fallibility; inaccuracy, inexactness, inexactitude 518.2; unsoundness, incompleteness, patchiness, sketchiness, unevenness; impairment 692; mediocrity 680; immaturity, undevelopment 721.4; impurity, adulteration 44.3.

.2 fault, *faute* [Fr], defect, deficiency, inadequacy, imperfection, kink, defection [archaic]; flaw, hole, bug [slang]; something missing; catch [informal], fly in the ointment, problem, little problem, snag, drawback; crack, rift; weakness, frailty, infirmity, failure, failing, foible, shortcoming; weak point, Achilles' heel, vulnerable place, chink in one's armor, weak link; blemish, taint 679.

.3 VERBS fall short, come short, miss, miss out, not qualify, fall down [slang], not measure up, not come up to par, not come up to the mark, not come up to scratch [informal], not pass muster, not bear inspection, miss the mark, not hack it [slang], not make it [informal], not make the grade.

.4 ADJS imperfect, not perfect, atel(o)–; unperfected; defective, faulty, inadequate, deficient, short, lacking, wanting, found wanting, "weighed in the balance and found wanting" [Bible]; off; erroneous, fallible; inaccurate, inexact, imprecise 518.17; unsound, incomplete, unfinished, partial, patchy, sketchy, uneven, unthorough; makeshift 670.7; damaged, impaired 692.29–44; mediocre 680.7,8; blemished 679.8; immature, undeveloped 721.11,12; impure, adulterated, mixed 44.15.

.5 ADVS imperfectly, inadequately, deficiently; incompletely, partially; faultily, defectively.

## 679. BLEMISH

.1 NOUNS blemish, disfigurement, disfiguration, defacement; scar, keloid, cicatrix; needle scar, track *or* crater [both slang]; scratch; scab; blister, vesicle, bulla, bleb; weal, wale, welt, wen, sebaceous cyst; port-wine stain *or* port-wine mark, hemangioma, strawberry mark; pock, pustule; pockmark, pit; nevus, birthmark, mole; freckle, lentigo; milium, whitehead, blackhead, comedo, pimple, hickey, sty; wart, verruca; crack, craze, check, rift, split; **deformity,** deformation, warp, twist, kink, **distortion; flaw, defect, fault** 678.2.

.2 **discoloration,** discolorment, discolor [archaic]; bruise 692.9.

.3 **stain, taint, tarnish;** mark, brand, **stigma;** maculation, macule, macula; **spot, blot, blur, blotch,** patch, speck, speckle, fleck, flick, flyspeck; daub, dab; **smirch, smudge,** smutch *or* smouch, smut, **smear;** splotch, splash, splatter, spatter; bloodstain; eyesore; macul(o)– *or* maculi–.

.4 VERBS **blemish, disfigure,** deface, **flaw, mar;** scab; scar, cicatrize, scarify; **crack,** craze, check, split; **deform,** warp, twist, kink, **distort.**

.5 **spot,** bespot, **blot, blotch, speck, speckle,** bespeckle, maculate [archaic]; freckle; flyspeck; **spatter, splatter,** splash, splotch.

.6 **stain,** bestain, **discolor,** smirch, besmirch, **taint,** attaint, **tarnish; mark, stigmatize,** brand; smear, besmear, daub, bedaub, slubber [Brit dial]; blur, slur [dial]; **darken, blacken;** smoke, besmoke; scorch, singe, sear; dirty, **soil** 682.16.

.7 **bloodstain, bloody,** ensanguine.

.8 ADJS **blemished, disfigured,** defaced, **marred,** scarred, keloidal, cicatrized, scarified, scabbed, scabby; pimpled, pimply; cracked, crazed, checked, split; deformed, warped, twisted, kinked, distorted; faulty, flawed, defective 678.4.

.9 **spotted, spotty,** maculate, maculated, macular, blotched, **blotchy,** splotched, splotchy; **speckled,** speckly, bespeckled; freckled, freckly, freckle-faced; spattered, splattered, splashed.

.10 **stained, discolored,** foxed, foxy, **tainted, tarnished,** smirched, besmirched; stigmatized, stigmatic, stigmatiferous; darkened, blackened, murky, smoky, inky; **soiled** 682.21.

.11 **bloodstained,** blood-spattered, **bloody,** sanguinary, **gory,** ensanguined.

## 680. MEDIOCRITY

.1 NOUNS **mediocrity,** mediocreness, fairishness, modestness, modesty, moderateness, middlingness, **indifference;** respectability, passableness, **tolerableness** 674.3; **dullness,** lackluster, tediousness 883.1.

.2 **ordinariness,** averageness, normality, **commonness, commonplaceness;** common *or* garden variety [informal]; unexceptionality, unremarkableness, unnoteworthiness; conventionality.

.3 **inferiority,** inferiorness, poorness, lowliness, humbleness, baseness, meanness,

**commonness,** coarseness; **second-rateness,** third-rateness, fourth-rateness.

.4 **low grade,** low class, low quality; second best.

.5 **mediocrity, second-rater,** third-rater, fourth-rater, nothing *or* nobody special, no prize, not much of a bargain, small potatoes *or* small beer [both slang]; tinhorn [slang]; nonentity 673.7; middle class, middle order *or* orders, bourgeoisie, burgherdom; suburbia; Middle America, silent majority.

.6 **irregular,** second, third; *schlock, schmatte* [both Yid].

.7 ADJS **mediocre, middling, indifferent, fair, fairish, fair to middling** [informal], moderate, modest, medium, betwixt and between; respectable, passable, **tolerable** 674.19; **so-so,** *comme ci comme ça* [Fr]; of a kind, of a sort, of sorts [informal]; nothing to brag about, not much to boast of, nothing to write home about; "not below mediocrity nor above it" [Johnson]; dull, lackluster, tedious 883.6; insipid, vapid, wishy-washy, namby-pamby.

.8 **ordinary, average,** normal, **common, commonplace,** garden *or* garden-variety [both informal], run-of-mine *or* -mill, run-of-the-mine *or* -mill; **unexceptional, unremarkable, unnoteworthy,** unspectacular, no great shakes [informal]; conventional; middle-class, bourgeois, plastic [slang]; suburban; usual, regular 84.8.

.9 **inferior, poor,** punk [slang], **base, mean, common,** coarse, cheesy *or* tacky [both informal], tinny; shabby, seedy 692.34; cheap, Mickey Mouse [informal], paltry 673.18; irregular; second-best; **second-rate,** third-rate, fourth-rate; **second-class,** third-class, fourth-class; **low-grade, low-class,** low-quality, low-test.

.10 **below par,** below standard, **below the mark** [informal], substandard, **not up to scratch** [informal], not up to snuff [informal], not up to sample *or* standard *or* specification, off.

.11 ADVS **mediocrely, middlingly,** fairly, fairishly, middling well, fair to middling [informal], moderately, modestly, **indifferently, so-so;** passably, **tolerably** 674.23.

.12 **inferiorly, poorly,** basely, meanly, commonly.

## 681. CLEANNESS

.1 NOUNS **cleanness, cleanliness; purity,** pureness; **immaculateness,** immaculacy; **spotlessness,** unspottedness, stainlessness, whiteness; freshness; fastidiousness, daintiness, cleanly habits; asepsis, sterility, hospital cleanliness; tidiness 59.3.

.2 **cleansing, cleaning, detersion; purge,** purging, purgation, abstersion [archaic]; **purification,** lustration, catharsis; expurgation, bowdlerization; dry cleaning, steam cleaning.

.3 **sanitation, hygiene,** hygenics; **disinfection, decontamination, sterilization,** antisepsis; pasteurization, flash pasteurization; fumigation, disinfestation, delousing.

.4 **refinement, clarification, purification,** depuration; **straining,** colature; elution, elutriation; extraction 305.8; **filtering,** filtration; **percolation,** leaching, edulcoration [archaic], lixiviation; **sifting,** separation, **screening,** sieving, bolting, riddling, winnowing; essentialization; sublimation; **distillation,** destructive distillation, spiritualization [archaic].

.5 **washing, ablution;** lavation, laving, lavage; lavabo; **wash,** washup; soaping, lathering; rinse, rinsing; sponge, sponging; shampoo; washout, elution, elutriation; irrigation, flush, flushing, flushing out; douche, douching; enema; **scrub,** scrubbing, swabbing, mopping, scouring; **cleaning up** or **out,** washing up, scrubbing up or out, mopping up, wiping up.

.6 **laundering, laundry,** tubbing; **wash, washing;** washday.

.7 **bathing, balneation,** balne(o)–.

.8 **bath,** bathe [Brit], tub [informal]; **shower,** shower bath, needle bath, hot or cold shower; douche; sponge bath, sponge; hip bath, sitz bath; sweat bath, Turkish bath, hummum, Russian bath, Swedish bath, Finnish bath, sauna or sauna bath, Japanese bath, whirlpool bath, plunge bath.

.9 **dip, bath;** acid bath, mercury bath, fixing bath; sheep dip.

.10 **bathing place, bath,** baths, public baths, **bathhouse,** bagnio [archaic], sauna; *balneum, balneae, thermae* [all L]; mikvah; watering place, spa; lavatory, washroom, bathroom; steam room, sweat room, sudatorium, sudarium, caldarium, tepidarium; rest room.

.11 **washery, laundry;** washhouse, washshed; **Laundromat, launderette,** coin laundry, coin-operated laundry; automatic laundry; hand laundry; car wash.

12 **washbasin, washbowl,** washdish, basin; lavatory, washstand; **bathtub,** tub, bath; bidet; **shower,** showers, shower room,

shower bath, shower stall, shower head, shower curtain; **sink,** kitchen sink; dishwasher, automatic dishwasher; washing machine; washer; piscina, lavabo, ewer, aquamanile; washtub, washpot, washing pot, wash boiler, dishpan; finger bowl; wash barrel.

.13 **refinery; refiner,** purifier, clarifier; **filter; strainer,** colander; **percolator,** lixiviator; **sifter, sieve, screen,** riddle, cribble; winnow, winnower, winnowing machine, winnowing basket or winnowing fan; cradle, rocker.

.14 **cleaner,** cleaner-up, cleaner-off, cleaner-out; **janitor,** janitress, custodian; cleaning woman or lady or man, charwoman or char [both Brit].

.15 **washer,** launderer; **laundress,** laundrywoman, **washerwoman,** washwoman, washerwife [Scot]; **laundryman,** washerman, washman; dry cleaner; **dishwasher,** pot-walloper [slang], scullion, scullery maid; dishwiper.

.16 **sweeper; street sweeper,** crossing sweeper, whitewing, cleanser or scavenger [both Brit]; **chimney sweep** or **sweeper,** sweep, flue cleaner.

.17 **cleanser, cleaner;** cleaning agent; lotion, cream; cold cream, cleansing cream, **soap, detergent,** synthetic detergent, abstergent; shampoo; rinse; **solvent** 391.10, cleaning solvent; purifier, depurant; mouthwash, wash; dentifrice, **toothpaste, tooth powder;** pumice stone, holystone; purge, purgative, cathartic, enema, diuretic, emetic, nauseant.

.18 VERBS **clean, cleanse, purge,** deterge, depurate; **purify,** lustrate; sweeten, **freshen;** whiten, bleach; clean up or out, clear out, sweep out; reform, clean house, delouse; spruce, **tidy** 60.12; scavenge; **wipe,** wipe up or out, wipe off; dust, dust off; steam-clean, **dry-clean;** expurgate, bowdlerize.

.19 **wash, bathe, bath** [Brit], shower, lave; **launder,** tub; wash up or out; **rinse,** rinse out, flush, flush out, irrigate, sluice, sluice out; ritually immerse, baptize, *toivel* [Yid]; sponge; **scrub,** scrub up or out, **swab, mop,** mop up; **scour,** holystone; soap, lather; shampoo; syringe; douche; gargle.

.20 **groom,** dress, fettle [Brit dial], **brush up; preen,** plume; manicure.

.21 **comb,** curry, card, hackle or hatchel, heckle [dial], rake.

.22 **refine, clarify,** clear, purify, rectify, depurate, decrassify; try; **strain;** elute, elutriate; **extract** 305.10; **filter,** filtrate; **percolate,** leach, lixiviate, edulcorate [archaic]; **sift,** separate, sieve, **screen,** bolt, winnow; sublimate, sublime; **distill,** spiritualize [archaic], essentialize.

.23 **sweep,** sweep up or out, **brush,** brush off, whisk, **broom; vacuum** [informal], vacuum-clean.

.24 **sanitize,** sanitate, hygienize; **disinfect, decontaminate, sterilize,** antisepticize; autoclave, boil; pasteurize, flash-pasteurize; disinfest, fumigate, delouse; chlorinate.

.25 ADJS **clean, pure; immaculate, spotless,** stainless, white, fair, dirt-free, soil-free; **unsoiled, unsullied,** unmuddied, unsmirched, unbesmirched, unblotted, unsmudged, unstained, untarnished, **unspotted,** unblemished; smutless, smut-free; bleached, whitened; bright, shiny 335.32, 33; **unpolluted,** nonpolluted, untainted, unadulterated, **undefiled;** kosher, *tahar* [Heb], ritually pure or clean; clean as a whistle or a new penny or a hound's tooth; sweet, **fresh; cleanly,** fastidious, dainty, of cleanly habits; well-washed, well-scrubbed, tubbed [informal].

.26 **cleaned, cleansed,** cleaned up; purged, purified; expurgated, bowdlerized; reformed; refined; spruce, spick and span, **tidy** 59.8.

.27 **sanitary, hygienic, prophylactic; sterile,** aseptic, antiseptic, **uninfected;** disinfected, decontaminated, sterilized; autoclaved, boiled; pasteurized.

.28 **cleansing, cleaning;** detergent, abstergent, depurative; **purifying,** purificatory, lustral; expurgatory; purgative, purging, cathartic, diuretic, emetic.

.29 ADVS **cleanly,** clean; **purely, immaculately, spotlessly.**

.30 **cleansers**

| | |
|---|---|
| anion detergent | cation detergent |
| benzine, benzol | cleaning fluid |
| bleach 363.10 | detergent |
| borax | lye |
| Carbona | sodium carbonate, sal |
| carbon tetrachloride, | soda, soda |
| carbon tet [informal] | washing powder |
| mal] | washing soda |

.31 **soaps**

| | |
|---|---|
| amole | kosher soap |
| bar soap | laundry soap |
| bath soap | lead soap |
| brown soap | lime soap |
| castile soap, castile | liquid soap |
| deodorant soap | marine soap |
| floating soap | metallic soap |
| glycerin soap | milled soap |
| granulated soap | neat soap |
| green soap | olive-oil castile soap |

| | |
|---|---|
| powdered soap, soap | soda soap |
| powder | soft soap |
| pumice soap | tar soap |
| saddle soap | toilet soap |
| shaving soap | wash ball |
| soap flakes | |

.32 **cleaning devices**

| | |
|---|---|
| autoclave | nail brush |
| automatic washer | napkin |
| automatic washer- | paper towel |
| dryer | pumice stone |
| bath brush | purificator |
| bath towel | push broom |
| broom, besom | rag mop |
| brush | rake |
| carpet cleaner or | scouring pad |
| sweeper | scraper |
| chamois cloth | scrubber |
| cleansing tissue | scrub or scrubbing |
| comb | brush |
| currycomb | serviette [Brit] |
| dishcloth | soap pad |
| dishmop | sponge |
| dishrag | sponge mop |
| dish towel | steam cleaner |
| dishwasher | sterilizer |
| doormat | sudarium, sudary [ar- |
| dustcloth | chaic] |
| duster | swab |
| dust mop, dry mop | toilet paper |
| dustpan | toothbrush |
| eyeglass cloth | toothpick |
| facecloth | towel |
| face towel | Turkish towel |
| feather duster | vacuum cleaner |
| hackle | washboard |
| hairbrush | washcloth |
| hand brush | washer |
| handkerchief | washing engine |
| hand towel | washing machine |
| holystone | washrag |
| hose | whisk broom, whisk |
| mop | wisp [Brit] |
| mop bucket or pail | wringer |
| mundatory | wringer washer |

## 682. UNCLEANNESS

.1 NOUNS **uncleanness,** immundity; **impurity,** unpureness; **dirtiness,** grubbiness, dinginess, griminess, messiness [informal], scruffiness, slovenliness, untidiness 62.6; miriness, muddiness 389.4; uncleanliness.

.2 **filthiness, foulness,** vileness, scumminess [informal], feculence, shittiness [slang], muckiness, ordurousness, nastiness, ickiness [informal]; scurfiness, scabbiness; rottenness, putridness 692.7; rankness, fetidness 437.2; odiousness, repulsiveness 864.2; nauseousness, disgustingness 429.3; hoggishness, piggishness, swinishness beastliness.

.3 **squalor,** squalidness, squalidity, **sordidness;** slumminess [informal].

.4 **defilement, befoulment,** dirtying, soiling besmirchment; **pollution, contamination** infection; abomination; ritual uncleanness or impurity or contamination.

.5 **soil,** soilure, soilage, smut; **smirch, smudge,** smutch, smear, **spot,** blot, blotch, **stain** 679.3.

.6 **dirt, grime;** dust; soot, smut; **mud** 389.8.

.7 **filth, muck,** slime, mess, sordes, foul matter; ordure, **excrement** 311.3,4; mucus, snot [slang]; scurf, furfur, dandruff; scuz [slang]; putrid matter, pus, corruption [dial], gangrene, decay, carrion, **rot** 692.7; obscenity, smut [informal] 990.4.

.8 **slime, slop,** scum, sludge, slush, splosh [dial], slosh, slab [dial], slob [dial], glop or gunk [both informal], **muck, mire,** ooze.

.9 **offal,** slough, **offscourings,** scurf, scum, riffraff, scum of the earth; **carrion; garbage, swill,** slop, slops; dishwater, ditchwater, bilgewater, bilge; **sewage,** sewerage; **refuse** 669.4.

.10 **dunghill, manure pile,** midden, mixen [Brit dial], colluvies; compost heap; dump, garbage dump, kitchen midden, refuse heap.

.11 **sty, pigsty,** pigpen; **stable,** Augean stables; dump or hole [both slang], tenement; warren, **slum,** rookery; the slums; plague spot, pesthole; hovel 191.12.

.12 (receptacle of filth) **sink;** sump, cesspool, septic tank; **sewer,** drain, *cloaca, cloaca maxima* [both L]; **dump,** garbage dump; swamp, bog, mire, quagmire, marsh.

.13 **pig, swine, hog,** slut, sloven, slattern 62.7; Struwwelpeter.

.14 VERBS wallow in the mire, live like a pig.

.15 **dirty,** dirty up, dirt [archaic], grime, **begrime;** muck, muck up [informal]; **muddy,** bemud [archaic]; mire, bemire; slime; dust; soot, smoke, besmoke.

.16 **soil,** besoil; black, **blacken; smirch,** besmirch, sully, slubber [Brit dial], smutch or smouch, besmutch, smut, **smudge, smear,** besmear, daub, bedaub; spot, stain 679.5,6.

.17 **defile, foul, befoul; sully;** nasty or benasty [both dial], mess or mess up [both informal]; **pollute, corrupt, contaminate, infect; taint,** tarnish.

.18 spatter, splatter, splash, **bespatter,** dabble, bedabble, spot, splotch.

.19 draggle, bedraggle, **drabble,** bedrabble, daggle [archaic], drabble in the mud.

.20 ADJS **unclean,** unwashed, unbathed, unscrubbed, unscoured, unswept, unwiped; **impure,** unpure; **polluted, contaminated, infected, corrupted;** ritually unclean or impure or contaminated, *tref* [Yid], *terefah* [Heb], nonkosher; not to be handled without gloves; **uncleanly.**

.21 **soiled, sullied, dirtied, smirched,** besmirched, smudged, spotted, **tarnished,** tainted, **stained; defiled,** fouled, **befouled;** draggled, drabbled, bedraggled.

.22 **dirty, grimy, grubby,** grungy [slang], smirchy, dingy, messy [informal]; scruffy, slovenly, untidy 62.15; miry, **muddy** 389.14; **dusty;** smutty, smutchy, smudgy; sooty, smoky; snuffy.

.23 **filthy, foul, vile,** mucky, **nasty,** icky or yecchy [both informal]; malodorous, mephitic, rank, **fetid** 437.5; **putrid, rotten** 692.41; nauseating, disgusting; **odious, repulsive** 864.18; **slimy,** scummy [informal]; barfy or vomity or puky [all slang]; sloppy, sludgy, slushy, sloshy, sposhy [dial], slabby [archaic], gloppy or gunky [both informal], scurfy, scabby; wormy, maggoty, flyblown; feculent, ordurous, crappy or shitty [both slang], fecal 311.20.

.24 **hoggish, piggish, swinish,** beastly.

.25 **squalid, sordid,** wretched, shabby; slumlike, slummy.

.26 ADVS **uncleanly, impurely,** unpurely; **dirtily,** grimily; **filthily, foully,** nastily, vilely.

## 683. HEALTHFULNESS

.1 NOUNS **healthfulness, healthiness, salubrity,** salubriousness, salutariness, **wholesomeness,** beneficialness, goodness.

.2 **hygiene,** hygienics; sanitation 681.3; public health, epidemiology; health physics; preventive medicine, prophylaxis, preventive dentistry, prophylactodontia; prophylactic psychology, mental hygiene.

.3 **hygienist,** hygeist, sanitarian; public health doctor or physician, epidemiologist; health physicist; preventive dentist, prophylactodontist; dental hygienist.

.4 VERBS **make for health,** conduce to health, **be good for,** agree with.

.5 ADJS **healthful, healthy, salubrious, salutary,** wholesome, health-preserving, health-enhancing, **beneficial,** benign, good, **good for; hygienic(al),** hygeian, sanitary; constitutional, for one's health; bracing, refreshing, invigorating, tonic.

## 684. UNHEALTHFULNESS

.1 NOUNS **unhealthfulness, unhealthiness, insalubrity,** insalubriousness, unsalutariness, **unwholesomeness,** badness; noxiousness, noisomeness, injuriousness, harmfulness 675.5; pathenogenicity; health hazard, threat or danger or menace to health; contamination, pollution, environmental pollution, air *or* water *or* noise pollution.

.2 **innutritiousness, indigestibility.**

.3 **poisonousness, toxicity, venomousness; virulence** *or* virulency, **malignancy,** noxiousness, destructiveness, deadliness; **infectiousness,** infectivity, contagiousness, communicability; poison, venom 676.3.

.4 VERBS **disagree with,** not be good for.

.5 ADJS **unhealthful, unhealthy, insalubrious, unsalutary, unwholesome,** peccant, bad, **bad for;** noxious, noisome, injurious, harmful 675.12; **polluted,** contaminated, tainted, foul, septic; unhygienic, unsanitary, insanitary; morbific, pathogenic, pestiferous.

.6 **innutritious, indigestible,** unassimilable.

.7 **poisonous, toxic(al),** toxicant; **venomous,** envenomed, venenate, venenous; veneniferous, toxiferous; **virulent, noxious, malignant,** malign, destructive, deadly; pestiferous, pestilential; mephitic, miasmal, miasmic, miasmatic; **infectious,** infective, contagious, communicable, catching.

## 685. HEALTH

.1 NOUNS **health, well-being; fitness,** physical fitness; bloom, flush, glow, rosiness; mental health, emotional health; physical condition; Hygeia.

.2 **healthiness,** healthfulness, **soundness,** wholesomeness; healthy body, good *or* healthy constitution; **good health,** good state of health, "good estate of body" [Bible], *"mens sana in corpore sano"* [L; Juvenal], a sound mind in a sound body; **robust health,** rugged health, rude health, glowing health, picture of health, "health that snuffs the morning air" [Grainger]; **fine fettle,** fine whack [informal], fine *or* high feather [informal], **good shape,** good trim, fine shape, top shape [informal], good condition, mint condition; eupepsia, good digestion; clean bill of health.

.3 **haleness, heartiness, robustness,** vigorousness, ruggedness, **vitality,** lustiness, hardiness, strength, vigor; longevity.

.4 **immunity, resistance,** nonproneness *or* nonsusceptibility to disease; acquired immunity, artificial immunity, congenital immunity, familial immunity, inherent immunity, inherited immunity, innate *or* racial immunity, natural immunity, nonspecific immunity, specific immunity, opsonic immunity, phagocytic immunity, toxin-antitoxin immunity, active immunity, passive immunity; **immunization** 689.17; antibody, antigen 687.27.

.5 VERBS **enjoy good health,** have a clean bill of health, be in the pink; be in the best of health; **feel good,** feel fine, feel like a million [informal], never feel better; feel one's oats, be full of pep; burst with health, bloom, glow, flourish; keep fit, stay in shape; wear well, stay young.

.6 **get well,** mend, recuperate 694.19; recover 694.20.

.7 ADJS **healthy, healthful,** enjoying health, **fine,** in health, in shape, in condition, **fit, fit and fine; in good health, in the pink** [informal], in the pink of condition, in mint condition, in good case, **in good** *or* **fine shape, in fine fettle,** in fine whack [informal], in fine *or* high feather [informal], chipper [informal], fit as a fiddle [informal]; alive and kicking [informal], bursting with health, full of life and vigor, bright-eyed and bushy-tailed; full of beans *or* of piss and vinegar [slang], feeling one's oats; eupeptic.

.8 **well, unailing, unsick, unsickly,** unfrail; all right, doing nicely, up and about, sitting up and taking nourishment.

.9 **sound,** whole, wholesome; unimpaired 677.8; sound of mind and body, sound in wind and limb, sound as a dollar [informal].

.10 **hale, hearty,** hale and hearty, **robust,** robustious, robustuous, vital, **vigorous, strong,** strong as a horse, stalwart, stout, sturdy, **rugged,** rude, hardy, lusty, bouncing, flush [archaic].

.11 **fresh,** green, youthful, **blooming;** flush, flushed, **rosy,** rosy-cheeked, ruddy, pink, pink-cheeked; fresh as a daisy *or* rose, fresh as April.

.12 **immune, resistant,** nonprone *or* nonsusceptible to disease.

## 686. DISEASE

.1 NOUNS **disease, illness, sickness, malady, ailment, indisposition, disorder, complaint,** morbidity, *morbus* [L], **affliction** affection, distemper [archaic], **infirmity** –ia, –iasis, –pathy, –sis, nos(o)–; **disability,** defect, handicap; deformity 249.3 birth defect, congenital defect; abnormality, condition, pathological condition **signs, symptoms, pathology,** symptomatology, symptomology, syndrome; **sickishness,** malaise, seediness *or* rockiness [both informal], the pip [informal]; complication, secondary disease *or* condition contageous *or* infectious disease; bacterial disease, protozoan disease; worm disease; fungus disease, –osis *or* –ose; viru disease; allergy, allergic disease; nutritional disease, deficiency disease; geriatric disease; congenital disease, genetic disease, hereditary disease; iatrogenic disease; occupational disease; degenerative disease, wasting disease, atrophy, necr-(o)–; organic disease, functional disease; psychogenic *or* psychosomatic disease; circulatory disease, cardiovascular disease, respiratory disease, endocrine disease, gastrointestinal disease, urinogenital *or* urogenital disease, muscular disease, neurological disease; epidemic disease, pandemic disease, endemic disease, endemic; acute disease *or* condition, chronic disease *or* condition; plant disease, blight 676.2.

**.2 unhealthiness,** healthlessness; **ill health,** poor health, delicate *or* shaky *or* frail *or* fragile health; **sickliness,** peakedness [informal], **feebleness,** delicacy, weakliness, fragility, **frailty** 160.2; **infirmity, unsoundness,** debility, debilitation, enervation, exhaustion, decrepitude; wasting, languishing, languishment [archaic], cachexia *or* cachexy; chronic ill health, invalidity, invalidism; unwholesomeness, morbidity, morbidness; hypochondria, hypochondriasis, valetudinarianism.

**.3 infection, contagion,** contamination, taint, virus; aerial infection, airborne infection, contact infection, direct infection, cryptogenic infection, droplet infection, dust infection, hand infection, indirect infection, phytogenic infection, primary infection, pyogenic infection, secondary infection, subclinical infection, waterborne infection, zoogenic infection; **contagiousness, infectiousness, communicability;** epidemicity, inoculability; carrier, vector; epidemiology.

**.4 epidemic, plague, pestilence,** pest, pandemic, pandemia, scourge; epizootic, epiphytotic, murrain; bubonic plague, black plague, hemorrhagic plague, ambulatory plague, larval plague, glandular plague, cellulocutaneous plague, defervescing plague, pneumonic plague, premonitory plague, septicemic plague, siderating plague, black death; white plague, tuberculosis 686.15; pesthole, plague spot.

**.5 seizure, attack,** access, visitation; arrest; blockage, stoppage, occlusion, thrombosis, thromboembolism; **stroke,** ictus, apoplexy; **spasm, throes, fit, paroxysm, convulsion,** eclampsia, frenzy; **epilepsy,** epilept(o)– *or* epilepti–, falling sickness; grand mal, haute mal, epilepsia major,

epilepsia gravior; petit mal, epilepsia minor, epilepsia mitior; abdominal epilepsy, acquired epilepsy, activated epilepsy, affect epilepsy, akinetic epilepsy, autonomic epilepsy, cardiac epilepsy, cortical epilepsy, cursive epilepsy, diurnal epilepsy, focal epilepsy, hysterical epilepsy, Jacksonian epilepsy *or* Rolandic epilepsy, larval epilepsy *or* latent epilepsy, laryngeal epilepsy, matutinal epilepsy, menstrual epilepsy, musicogenic epilepsy, myoclonus epilepsy *or* Unterricht's disease, nocturnal epilepsy, epilepsia nutans, physiologic epilepsy, psychic epilepsy, psychomotor epilepsy, reflex epilepsy, epilepsia, rotatoria *or* torsion spasm, sensory epilepsy, serial epilepsy, epilepsia tarda *or* tardy epilepsy, tonic epilepsy, traumatic epilepsy, ucinate epilepsy; cryptogenic *or* essential *or* idiopathic epilepsy; tonic spasm, tetany, lockjaw, trismus, tetanus; laryngospasm, laryngismus; clonic spasm, clonus; cramp.

**.6 fever, feverishness,** febrility, febricity, pyrexia, febri–, pyr(o)–, pyret(o)–; hyperpyrexia, hyperthermia; **heat, fire, fever heat;** flush, hectic flush; calenture; hectic fever *or* hectic; intermittent fever, remittent fever *or* remittent, continued fever, eruptive fever, recurrent *or* relapsing fever; irritation fever, water fever, protein fever, vaccinal fever, urethral fever, urinal fever; traumatic fever, wound fever; childbed fever, puerperal fever; delirium 473.8.

**.7 collapse, breakdown, crackup** [informal], **prostration,** exhaustion; nervous prostration *or* breakdown *or* exhaustion, neurasthenia; circulatory collapse.

**.8 (disease symptoms)** anemia; ankylosis; asphyxiation, anoxia, cyanosis; ataxia; bleeding, hemorrhage; colic; dizziness, vertigo; ague, chill, chills; dropsy, hydrops, edema; fainting; fatigue 717; fever 686.6; constipation; diarrhea, flux, dysentery; indigestion, upset stomach, dyspepsia 686.28; inflammation 686.9; necrosis 686.37; insomnia; itching, pruritus; jaundice 686.21, icterus, ictero–; backache, lumbago; vomiting, nausea 686.29; paralysis 686.25; skin eruption, rash 686.33,34; sore, abscess 686.35; hypertension, high blood pressure; hypotension, low blood pressure; tumor, growth 686.36; shock 686.24; convulsion, seizure, spasm 686.5; pain 424; fibrillation, tachycardia; labored breathing, apnea, dyspnea, asthma; blennorhea; nasal discharge, rheum, coughing, sneezing; wasting, cachexia or cachexy, tabes, tabo–, marasmus, emaciation, atrophy, necr(o)–; sclerosis.

.9 **inflammation,** –itis; acute inflammation, adhesive inflammation, chronic inflammation, catarrhal inflammation, diffuse inflammation, exudative inflammation, focal inflammation, hyperplastic inflammation, hypertrophic inflammation, metastatic inflammation, necrotic inflammation, obliterative inflammation, reactive inflammation, seroplastic inflammation, serous inflammation, simple inflammation, specific inflammation, suppurative inflammation, toxic inflammation, traumatic inflammation; atrophic inflammation, cirrhotic inflammation, fibroid inflammation, sclerosing inflammation; **appendicitis; arthritis;** rheumatoid arthritis, atrophic arthritis, arthritis deformans, chronic infectious arthritis, proliferative arthritis, arthritis pauperum, poor man's gout, osseous rheumatism; **gout,** podagra, gouty arthritis, uratic arthritis; gonococcal arthritis, gonorrheal arthritis, blennorrhagic arthritis, urethral arthritis, syphilitic arthritis; tuberculous arthritis, arthritis fungosa; menopausal arthritis, climactic arthritis; hypertrophic arthritis, degenerative arthritis; acute arthritis, dysenteric arthritis, hemophilic arthritis, infectional arthritis, suppurative arthritis, vertebral arthritis; osteoarthritis; **rheumatism,** rheumatiz or rheumatics [both dial]; gonorrheal rheumatism, rheumatism of the heart, Heberden's rheumatism, subacute rheumatism, tuberculous rheumatism or Poncet's rheumatism, visceral rheumatism; **bursitis,** bunion, housemaid's knee, tennis elbow; **colitis,** ulcerative colitis, mucous colitis, irritable bowel syndrome, spastic colon; nephritis, pyonephritis; **hepatitis,** infectious hepatitis, serum hepatitis; gastritis, enteritis; catarrh; bronchitis; **laryngitis;** pharyngitis; carditis, pericarditis, endocarditis; arteritis; phlebitis, thrombophlebitis, milk leg; capillaritis; mastoiditis; meningitis, cerebral meningitis, cerebrospinal meningitis, spinal meningitis, alcoholic meningitis, mumps meningitis, brain fever, cerebritis, cerebellitis, encephalitis, equine encephalomyelitis, myelitis; neuritis; osteitis, osteomyelitis; peritonitis; adrenitis; penitis or priapitis, orchitis or testitis, prostatitis; vaginitis, vulvitis, clitoritis, metritis or uteritis, ovaritis; ureteritis, cystitis, urethritis; lymphangitis; otitis; glossitis; tonsilitis, adenoiditis; ophthalmia, ophthalitis, conjunctivitis; rhinitis; sinusitis; pyorrhea, pyorrhea alveolaris, paradental pyorrhea, gingivitis, periodontitis, Rigg's disease; wryneck or torticollis, lumbago or lumbar rheumatism, collagen disease.

.10 (deficiency diseases) anemia, deficiency anemia, pernicious anemia, chlorosis, greensickness; goiter, struma; protein deficiency, kwashiorkor; malnutrition, cachexia; vitamin deficiency; night blindness, keratomalacia, xerophthalmia; pellagra, Italian or Lombardy leprosy, maidism; ariboflavinosis, beriberi; scurvy; rickets or rachitis, osteomalacia, osteoporosis; dermatitis.

.11 (genetic diseases) sickle-cell anemia or disease, thalassemia; hemophilia; dichromatic vision, achromatic vision, color blindness; mongolism or mongolianism, Down's syndrome; Turner's syndrome; Christmas disease; Hartnup disease; maple syrup urine disease; Milroy's disease; Niemann-Pick disease, lipid histiocytosis; Tay-Sachs disease; Werdnig-Hoffmann disease; cystic fibrosis, pancreatic fibrosis, mucoviscidosis; albinism; Huntington's chorea; muscular dystrophy; ichthyosis; dysautonomia.

.12 (infectious diseases) **dysentery,** amebic dysentery, amebiasis, bacillary dysentery, viral dysentery; anthrax, splenic fever, woolsorter's disease, ragsorter's disease, milzbrand, anthrac(o)–; bubonic plague, black death 686.4; **cholera,** Asiatic cholera; **chicken pox,** varicella; cowpox, vaccinia; **smallpox,** variola; diphtheria; elephantiasis; erysipelas, St. Anthony's fire; dengue or dengue fever, dandy fever, breakbone fever; histoplasmosis; leprosy, lepra, hansenosis, Hansen's disease; influenza, **flu** [informal], grippe 686.14; herpes, herpes simplex, herpet(o)–; herpes zoster, zoster, zona, shingles; jungle rot; kala azar, black fever, dumdum fever, cachectic fever, ponos; **hepatitis** 686.21; loaiasis, loa loa; hookworm; **malaria,** malarial fever, malari(o)–, ague, blackwater fever Chagres fever, marsh fever; yellow fever yellow jack; meningitis 686.9; **mononucleosis,** infectious mononucleosis, glandular fever, kissing disease [slang]; **measles,** rubeola; **German measles,** bastard measles, rubella; mumps, parotitis; leptospirosis, swamp fever; osteomyelitis; paratyphoid fever; pneumonia 686.14; infantile paralysis, poliomyelitis, polio [informal]; strep throat, septic sore throat, streptococcu tonsilitis; scarlet fever, scarlatina; rheumatic fever, acute articular rheumatism, inflammatory rheumatism, cerebral rheumatism, polyarthritis rheumatism; ringworm, tinea; rabies, hydrophobia, lyssa, madness; rat-bite fever, Haverhill fever; Rocky Mountain spotted fever; rickettsialpox, Kew Gardens spotted fever; schistosomiasis, snail fever; sleeping sickness, sleepy sickness [Brit], African lethargy, encephalitis lethargica; **tetanus, lockjaw,** tetan(o)–; trench fever, five-day fever; trench mouth, Vincent's infection; tularemia, deer fly fever, rabbit fever, alkali disease; psittacosis, parrot fever, ornithosis; tuberculosis 686.15; typhoid fever *or* typhoid, enteric fever, typh(o)–; typhus *or* typhus fever, jail fever, spotted fever; famine fever, relapsing fever; brucellosis, undulant fever; whooping cough, pertussis; thrush; yaws, frambesia; venereal disease 686.16.

.13 (eye diseases) **conjunctivitis,** pink eye; trachoma, blepharitis, iritis, sty, keratitis, choroiditis, uveitis, optic neuritis; detached retina; glaucoma; cataract; esotropia, cross-eye, walleye; retinoblastoma; amaurosis, gutta serena; eye defect, defective vision 440.

.14 (respiratory diseases) **bronchitis,** acute bronchitis, chronic bronchitis; catarrh, rheum, **cold,** common cold, coryza, the sniffles, the snuffles; influenza, flu [informal], grippe, *la grippe* [Fr]; Asian *or* Asiatic flu, Hong Kong flu; swine flu; bronchiectasis; pleurisy, pleuritis, dry pleurisy, wet pleurisy; **pneumonia,** pneum(o)–; lobar pneumonia, pneumococcal pneumonia, croupous pneumonia, fibrinous pneumonia, lung fever, pneumonic fever; atypical pneumonia, virus pneumonia; bronchopneumonia, bronchial pneumonia, bronchiolitis; double pneumonia; empyema; **emphysema;** epidemic pleurodynia, devil's grip; pneumothorax, collapsed lung; pneumoconiosis, coniosis, silicosis, silic(o)–, aluminosis, asbestosis, berylliosis, byssinosis, chalicosis, siderosis, siderosilicosis, mason's lung, farmer's lung; bituminosis, anthracosis, anthracosilicosis, coal-miner's lung, miner's lung, miner's asthma, miner's consumption, miner's phthisis, black lung [informal]; lipoid pneumonia; lung cancer; whooping cough; hay fever, asthma 686.32; tonsilitis, amygdalitis, quinsy, adenoiditis; croup; pharyngitis, sore throat; laryngitis.

.15 **tuberculosis, TB,** tubercul(o)–, white plague, phthisis, **consumption;** pulmonary tuberculosis *or* phthisis; inhalation *or* aerogenic tuberculosis; scrofula, tuberculosis of the lymphatic glands; scrofuloderma, colliquation, tuberculosis cutis, lupus vulgaris, tuberculosis luposa; cerebral tuberculosis, tuberculous meningitis; tuberculosis of the bones and joints, tuberculosis of the intestines, tuberculosis of the kidney and bladder, tuberculosis of the larynx, tuberculosis of the serous membranes; miliary *or* disseminated tuberculosis.

.16 **venereal disease, VD,** social disease, Cupid's itch *or* Venus's curse, dose [slang]; **syphilis,** syph [informal], syphil(o)–, pox, great pox, French disease *or* pox *or* plague [archaic], Italian *or* Spanish pox [archaic], *morbus Gallicus* [L]; acquired syphilis, congenital syphilis; primary *or* secondary *or* tertiary syphilis, latent syphilis, constitutional syphilis; paresis, general paresis, paralytic dementia, cerebral tabes, syphilitic meningoencephalitis; tabes, tabes dorsales, syphilitic posterior spinal sclerosis, locomotor ataxia; **gonorrhea,** clap *or* claps [both slang], dose of clap *or* claps [slang]; chancre, hard chancre, chancroid, simple chancre, soft chancre; granuloma inguinale, granuloma venereum, pudendal ulcer; lymphogranuloma venereum, Frei's disease, Nicolas-Favre disease, fifth venereal disease, climatic bubo, tropical bubo; balanitis gangrenosa.

.17 (cardiovascular diseases) heart disease, heart condition; angina, angina pectoris; congenital heart disease, rheumatic heart disease, coronary *or* ischemic heart disease, hypertensive heart disease; carditis, endocarditis, myocarditis, pericarditis, pyopericarditis; palpitation of the heart, palpitation, tachycardia, arrhythmia, extrasystole, premature beat, paroxysmal tachycardia, atrial fibrillation, auricular fibrillation, ventricular fibrillation; cardiac insufficiency, coronary insufficiency, myocardial insufficiency, myovascular insufficiency, pseudoaortic insufficiency; insufficiency of the valves, aortic insufficiency, mitral insufficiency, pulmonary insufficiency, tricuspid insufficiency; cardiac stenosis, aortic stenosis, mitral stenosis, pulmonary stenosis, tricuspid stenosis; **heart attack, heart failure,** heart *or* cardiac shock, cardiac arrest; cardiac *or* myocardial infarction, heart block; thrombosis, cardiac thrombosis, coronary thrombosis, coronary; sclerosis, atherosclerosis, arteriosclerosis, hardening of the arteries; armored heart, beriberi heart, chaotic heart, encased heart, fat *or* fatty heart, cor adiposum, hairy heart *or* cor villosum, fibroid heart, flask-shaped heart, frosted heart, round heart, stony heart, tabby-cat *or* thrush-breast *or* tiger *or* tiger-lily heart, turtle heart, ox heart *or* cor bovinum, cor juvenum; cor biloculare, cor pseudotriloculare biatriatum, cor triloculare biatriatum, cor triloculare biventriculare, cor triatriatum; hypertension, high blood pressure, systolic hypertension, diastolic hypertension; apoplexy, stroke, apoplectic stroke, paralytic stroke; arterial aneurism; varicose veins, varix, hemorrhoid, pile, lingual hemorrhoid.

.18 (blood diseases) **anemia;** hypochromic anemia, iron deficiency anemia, pernicious anemia, macrocytic anemia, microcytic anemia, aplastic anemia, hypoplastic anemia, Fanconi's syndrome, hemolytic anemia, primary anemia; hemoglobinopathy, sickle-cell anemia *or* disease, thalassemia *or* Mediterranean anemia; polycythemia *or* erythrocytosis; purpura, idiopathic thrombocytopenic purpura, purpura hemorrhagica; hemophilia, bleeder's disease, hemophilia A; Christmas disease, hemophilia B; hemophilia C; angiohemophilia, pseudohemophilia, vascular hemophilia; afibrinogenemia; neutropenia, cyclic neutropenia, Banti's syndrome, Felty's syndrome; panhematopenia; leukemia, acute leukemia, chronic leukemia, lymphoid *or* lymphogenous *or* lymphatic leukemia, myeloid *or* myelogenous leukemia, monocytic leukemia, lymphosarcoma; lymphoma; Hodgkin's disease, infectious granuloma, malignant granuloma, malignant lymphoma, anemia lymphatica, pseudoleukemia; reticulum cell sarcoma, lymphoblastoma, leukemic reticuloendotheliosis, Gaucher's disease, Letterer-Siwe syndrome, xanthomatosis, Hand-Schuller-Christian disease; multiple myeloma, plasma cell leukemia, plasmacytoma.

.19 (gland diseases) acromegaly, giantism, dwarfism, sexual precocity, sexual infantilism, panhypopituitarism, persistent lactation, diabetes insipidus; hyperthyroidism, thyrotoxicosis, toxic goiter, Graves' disease, hypothyroidism, cretinism, myxedema; hyperparathyroidism, hypoparathyroidism; Addison's disease, hypercorticoidism, Cushing's disease, androgenital syndrome, pheochromocytoma; eunuchoidism, choriocarcinoma, Kleinfelter's syndrome; hypo-ovarianism, hyperovarianism; diabetes, diabetes mellitus, hypoglycemia; hyperglycemia.

.20 (metabolic diseases) acidosis, alkalosis, ketosis; gout, podagra; galactosemia, lactose intolerance, fructose intolerance; phenylketonuria *or* PKU, maple syrup urine disease, congenital hypophosphatasia.

.21 (liver diseases) **jaundice** *or* icterus, **cirrhosis, hepatitis,** infectious hepatitis, serum hepatitis, hepatoma; cholecystitis, gallstone *or* biliary calculus, cholangitis.

.22 (kidney diseases) nephritis, Bright's disease, glomerulonephritis; nephrosis, nephrosclerosis, nephrolithosis, uremia, hematuria, renal hematuria; kidney stone, nephrolith, renal calculus.

.23 nervous disorder, neuropathy, brain disease; neuritis, shingles *or* herpes zoster, sciatica *or* sciatic neuritis, writer's cramp, polyneuritis, pressure neuropathy, Bell's palsy, radiculitis; neuralgia, ischialgia, glossopharyngeal neuralgia, trigeminal neuralgia, *tic douloureux* [Fr]; **headache,** cephalalgia, **migraine; epilepsy,** falling sickness 686.5; palsy, shaking palsy, paralysis agitans, Parkinson's disease, Parkinsonism; cerebral palsy, spastic paralysis; chorea, the jerks [informal], St. Vitus's dance, Huntington's chorea; multiple sclerosis *or* MS, amyotrophic lateral sclerosis *or* Lou Gehrig's disease; brain tumor; priapism; organic psychosis, toxic psychosis 473.3; emotional disorder 690.17.

.24 **shock,** traumatism; secondary shock; allergic shock, anaphylactic shock, histamine shock, serum shock, cardiogenic shock, cerebral shock, hematogenic shock, neurogenic shock; protein shock; insulin shock, hypoglycemic shock; postoperative shock, surgical shock, traumatic shock, wound shock; mental shock, **trauma;** thanatosis; shell shock, combat *or* battle fatigue 690.19.

.25 paralysis, paralyzation, palsy, impairment of motor function, –plegia *or* –plegy, –lysis; stroke, apoplexy; paresis; motor paralysis, sensory paralysis; hemiplegia, paraplegia, diplegia; cataplexy, catalepsy; infantile paralysis, poliomyelitis, polio [informal].

.26 **heatstroke;** heat prostration *or* exhaustion; sunstroke, *coup de soleil* [Fr], siriasis, insolation; calenture, thermic fever.

.27 (diseases of the digestive tract) stomach

condition; gastritis; **ulcer,** peptic ulcer, stomach ulcer, duodenal ulcer, esophagal ulcer; esophagitis, duodenitis; hiatal hernia, abdominal hernia, diverticulosis; diverticulitis, peritonitis; megacolon; polyp; colitis 686.9.

**.28 indigestion,** dyspepsia; heartburn, cardialgia, pyrosis; colic, gripe, gripes; cholera morbus; **constipation, irregularity,** obstipation, costiveness; **diarrhea,** dysentery, flux, trots [slang], lientery, looseness of the bowels.

**.29 nausea,** nauseation, queasiness, squeamishness, qualmishness; qualm, pukes [slang]; motion sickness, seasickness, *mal de mer* [Fr], airsickness, car sickness; vomiting 310.8.

**.30 poisoning,** intoxication, venenation; septic poisoning, blood poisoning, sepsis, septicemia, toxemia, pyemia, septicopyemia; autointoxication; food poisoning, ptomaine poisoning, milk sickness, ergotism, St. Anthony's fire.

**.31** (environmental and occupational diseases) motion sickness 686.29; jet lag; altitude sickness, anoxia, anoxemia, anoxic anoxia; frostbite, chilblain, immersion foot, trench foot; radiation sickness, radionecrosis; lead poisoning; Minamata disease, mercury poisoning; *itai* [Jap], cadmium poisoning; sunstroke 686.26; aeroembolism, caisson disease, decompression sickness, diver's palsy, the bends [informal]; red-out; pneumoconiosis, black lung [informal] 686.14; writer's cramp *or* palsy *or* spasm; housemaid's knee; anthrax, woolsorter's disease.

**.32 allergy,** allergic disorder; allergic rhinitis, **hay fever,** rose cold, pollinosis; **asthma,** bronchial asthma; **hives,** urticaria; eczema; conjunctivitis; cold sores; allergic gastritis; cosmetic dermatitis; allergen.

**.33** (skin diseases) dermatosis, dermatitis, –derma; **eczema,** tetter; **acne,** acne vulgaris; dermamycosis, **athlete's foot,** jungle rot; itch, scabies, pruigo, pruritus; psora, psoriasis; erysipelas, St. Anthony's fire; erythema; elephantiasis; herpes, herpes simplex; herpes zoster, shingles; ringworm; hives; impetigo; lichen, lichen primus; miliaria, prickly heat, heat rash; pemphigus; lupus, lupus vulgaris; leprosy; skin cancer, epithelioma; exanthem.

**.34 skin eruption,** eruption, **rash,** efflorescence, breaking out, –anthema, –id(e); diaper rash; drug rash, vaccine rash; prickly heat, heat rash; hives, urticaria, nettle rash; papular rash; rupia.

**.35 sore, lesion;** pustule, papule, papula, papulo–, fester, pimple; pock; ulcer, ulceration; bed sore; tubercle; blister, bleb, bulla, blain; whelk, wheal, welt, wale; boil, furuncle, furunculus; carbuncle; canker; canker sore; cold sore, fever blister; sty; abscess, gathering, aposteme [archaic]; gumboil, parulis; whitlow, felon, paronychia; bubo; chancre; soft chancre, chancroid; hemorrhoids, piles; bunion; chilblain, kibe; polyp; stigma, petechia; scab, eschar; fistula; suppuration, festering; wound 692.8; swelling, rising 256.4.

**.36 growth,** neoplasm, –phyte; **tumor,** intumescence, –cele, –oma, onch(o)– *or* onchi– *or* onci–; benign tumor, nonmalignant tumor, innocent tumor; malignant tumor, malignant growth, metastatic tumor, **cancer,** carcin(o)–, sarcoma, carcinoma; morbid growth; excrescence, outgrowth; proud flesh; exostosis; cyst, wen; fungus, fungosity; callus, callosity, **corn,** clavus; **wart,** verruca; **mole,** nevus.

**.37 gangrene,** mortification, necrosis, sphacelus, sphacelation; noma; moist gangrene, dry gangrene, gas gangrene; caries, cariosity; slough; necrotic tissue.

**.38** (animal diseases) anthrax, splenic fever, charbon, milzbrand, malignant pustule; malignant catarrh *or* malignant catarrhal fever; bighead; blackleg, black quarter, quarter evil *or* ill; cattle plague, rinderpest; glanders; foot-and-mouth disease, hoof-and-mouth disease, aphthous fever; distemper; gapes; heaves, broken wind; hog cholera; loco, loco disease, locoism; mange, scabies; pip; rot, liver rot, sheep rot; staggers, megrims, blind staggers, mad staggers; swine dysentery, bloody flux; stringhalt; Texas fever, blackwater; John's disease, paratuberculosis, pseudotuberculosis; rabies, hydrophobia.

**.39 germ,** pathogen, bug [informal], disease-causing agent, disease-producing microorganism; **microbe,** microorganism; **virus,** filterable virus, nonfilterable virus, adenovirus, echovirus, reovirus, rhinovirus, enterovirus, picornavirus; rickettsia; **bacterium, bacteria** [pl], coccus, streptococcus, staphylococcus, bacillus, spirillum, vibrio, spirochete, gram-positive bacteria, gram-negative bacteria, aerobe, aerobic bacteria, anaerobe, anaerobic bacteria; protozoon, protozoa [pl], amoeba, trypanosome; fungus, mold, spore.

**.40 sick person,** sufferer, –path; valetudinarian, **invalid, shut-in;** incurable, terminal case; **patient, case;** inpatient, outpatient;

apoplectic, consumptive, dyspeptic, epileptic, rheumatic, arthritic, spastic; **the sick, the infirm.**

.41 **carrier,** vector, biological vector, mechanical vector; Typhoid Mary.

.42 **cripple,** defective, **handicapped person,** incapable; amputee; paraplegic, quadriplegic, paralytic; deformity 249.3; the crippled, the handicapped, "the halt, the lame, and the blind" [Bible]; idiot, imbecile 471.8.

.43 VERBS **ail, suffer,** labor under, be affected with, complain of; **feel ill,** feel under the weather, feel awful [informal], feel something terrible, not feel like anything [informal], feel like the walking dead; look green about the gills [informal].

.44 **take sick** or **ill, sicken; catch, contract, get,** take, sicken for [Brit], **come down with** [informal], be stricken or seized by, fall a victim to; catch cold; take one's death [dial]; **break out,** break out with, break out in a rash, erupt; run a temperature, fever; be laid by the heels, be struck down, be brought down, be felled; drop in one's tracks, **collapse;** overdose, OD [slang]; go into shock, be traumatized.

.45 **fail, weaken, sink, decline,** run down, lose strength, lose one's grip, dwindle, droop, flag, wilt, wither, wither away, fade, **languish,** waste, waste away, pine, peak, "dwindle, peak, and pine" [Shakespeare].

.46 **go lame,** founder.

.47 **afflict, disorder, derange; sicken, indispose; weaken, enfeeble,** enervate, reduce, debilitate, devitalize; **invalid,** incapacitate, **disable;** lay up, hospitalize.

.48 **infect, disease, contaminate,** taint.

.49 **poison,** empoison [archaic], envenom.

.50 ADJS **unhealthy, healthless,** in poor health; **infirm, unsound,** invalid, valetudinary, valetudinarian, debilitated, cachectic, enervated, exhausted, drained; **sickly,** peaky or peaked [both informal]; **weakly, feeble, frail** 160.12–18,21; weakened, with low resistance, **run-down,** reduced, reduced in health; moribund, languishing, failing 160.21; pale 363.7.

.51 **unwholesome, unhealthy,** unsound, morbid, diseased, pathological, path(o)–.

.52 **ill, ailing, sick, unwell, indisposed,** taken ill, down, bad, on the sick list; **sickish, seedy** or **rocky** [both informal], **under the weather, out of sorts** [informal], below par [informal], off-color, off one's feed [informal]; not quite right, not oneself; faint, faintish, feeling faint; feeling awful,

feeling something terrible [both informal]; sick as a dog, laid low; in a bad way, critically ill, in danger, on the critical list; mortally ill, sick unto death.

.53 **nauseated,** nauseous, **queasy, squeamish, qualmish,** qualmy; **sick to one's stomach,** sick to or sick at the stomach; pukish or puky or barfy [all slang]; seasick, carsick, airsick.

.54 **feverish,** fevered, feverous, in a fever, febrile, pyretic; **flushed,** inflamed, **hot, burning,** fiery, hectic; hyperpyretic, hyperthermic; delirious 473.31.

.55 **laid up, invalided,** hospitalized, in hospital [Brit]; **bedridden, bedfast, sick abed; down,** prostrate, flat on one's back; in childbed, confined.

.56 **diseased, morbid, pathological,** bad, **infected, contaminated,** tainted, peccant, –pathic, kako– or caco–; **poisoned,** septic; cankerous, cankered, ulcerous, ulcerated, gangrenous, gangrened, mortified, sphacelated.

.57 anemic, chlorotic; bilious; dyspeptic, colicky; dropsical, edematous, hydropic; gouty, podagric; neuritic, neuralgic; palsied, paralytic; pneumonic, pleuritic, tubercular, tuberculous, phthisic, consumptive; rheumatic, arthritic, rickety, rachitic; syphilitic, pocky, luetic; tabetic, tabid [archaic]; allergic; apoplectic; hypertensive; diabetic; encephalitic; epileptic; laryngitic; leprous; malarial; measly; nephritic; scabietic, scorbutic, scrofulous; variolous, variolar; tumorous; cancerous, malignant; carcinogenic, tumorigenic.

.58 **contagious, infectious,** infective, **catching,** taking, spreading, **communicable,** zymotic, inoculable; pestiferous, pestilential, **epidemic,** epidemial, pandemic; epizootic, epiphytotic; endemic; sporadic.

## 687. REMEDY

.1 NOUNS **remedy, cure, corrective,** alterative, remedial measure, sovereign remedy; **relief, help, aid, assistance,** succor; balm, balsam; healing agent; restorative, analeptic; healing quality or virtue; specific, specific remedy; **prescription,** recipe, receipt.

.2 **nostrum,** patent medicine, quack remedy; snake oil.

.3 **panacea, cure-all,** universal remedy, theriac, catholicon; polychrest, broad-spectrum drug or antibiotic; elixir, elixir of life,'elixir vitae [L].

.4 **medicine, medicament, medication,** medicinal, theraputant, **drug, physic,** preparation, mixture, pharmacon, phar-mac(o)–; herbs, medicinal herbs, simples, vegetable remedies, "the physic of the field" [Pope]; balsam, balm; tisane, pti-san; drops; powder; inhalant; electuary, elixir, syrup, lincture, linctus; officinal; prescription drug, ethical drug; over-the-counter drug, nonprescription drug, pro-prietary medicine or drug, proprietary, patent medicine; proprietary name, ge-neric name; materia medica.

.5 **dangerous drug, drug;** dope, junk, candy, stuff [all informal]; hard drug, hard stuff [informal]; addictive drug.

.6 **dose, draft, potion,** portion, **shot,** injec-tion; broken dose; booster, booster dose, recall dose, booster shot; narcotic shot; overdose; **fix** or **hit** or **bang** [all slang], mainlining [slang]; popping or skin-pop-ping [both slang]; dropping; drug packet, bag or deck [both slang].

.7 **pill,** bolus, **tablet, capsule,** lozenge, troche.

.8 **tonic, bracer,** cordial, restorative, analep-tic, roborant, **pick-me-up** [informal]; **shot in the arm** [slang]; vitamin shot.

.9 **stimulant** 687.52, upper [slang]; cocaine, coke or snow [both slang], C [slang]; am-phetamine, pep pill [informal], jolly bean [slang]; amphetamine sulfate, Benze-drine, Benzedrine pill, bennie or benzie [both slang]; dextroamphetamine sulfate, Dexedrine, Dexedrine pill; dexie or heart or football [all slang]; Dexamyl, Dexamyl pill, purple heart [slang]; methampheta-mine hydrochloride, Methedrine, Meth-edrine pill; meth or speed or crystal or businessman's trip [all slang].

.10 **palliative, alleviative, lenitive, assuasive,** assuager.

.11 **balm** 687.51, **lotion, salve, ointment, un-guent,** unguentum [L], cerate, unction, balsam, oil, emollient, demulcent; **lini-ment,** embrocation; vulnerary; collyrium, eyesalve, eyewater [archaic], eyewash.

.12 **sedative, depressant** 687.54, depressor, downer [slang]; **calmative, tranquilizer** 687.55, soother, soothing syrup, quietener, pacifier; **analgesic** 687.56, **anodyne,** pare-goric [archaic], **pain killer** or pain pill [both informal]; hypnotic, soporific, som-nifacient, sleep-inducer, sleeping draught, **sleeping pill,** goofball or sleeper [both slang]; barbiturate, barbiturate pill, barb [slang]; phenobarbital sodium, Nembu-tal, Nembutal pill; yellow jacket or yel-low or nemmie [all slang]; secobarbital sodium, Seconal, Seconal pill, red or red

devil [both slang]; amobarbital sodium, Amytal, Amytal pill; blue, blue angel, blue heaven, blue bird, blue devil [all slang]; Tuinal, Tuinal pill, rainbow or tooie [both slang]; sodium thiopental, phenobarbital, Luminal, Luminal pill, purple heart [slang]; chloral hydrate, knockout drops or Mickey Finn [both slang]; **narcotic,** narc(o)–; **opiate; opium,** mecon(o)–; pen yan, hop, tar, black stuff [all slang]; codeine, codeine cough syrup, turps [slang]; tincture of opium, lauda-num; paregoric, blue velvet [slang]; mor-phine, morphia, M or Miss Emma [both slang]; diacetyl morphine, heroin; **H,** hard stuff, **horse, junk, scag, shit, smack,** white stuff [all slang]; meperidine, Dem-erol; methadone, Dolophine, dolly [slang]; lotus; alcohol, liquor 996.12–14.

.13 **psychoactive drug,** psychochemical, mind-altering drug; **tranquilizer** 687.55, at-aractic; psychic energizer, antidepressant; **hallucinogen, psychedelic,** psychedelic drug, mind-expanding drug, mind-blow-ing drug, psychotomimetic; lysergic acid diethylamide, LSD-25, **LSD, acid** or 25 [both slang]; STP; dimethyltryptamine, DMT; diethyltryptamine, DET; psilocy-bin, psilocin; mescal, mescal button, pey-ote, mescaline, mesc [slang]; mescal bean; morning glory seeds; kava; **marijuana;** gage, **grass,** hay, **pot,** tea, hemp, weed, Mary Jane [all slang]; marijuana ciga-rette; **joint** or **stick** or reefer [all slang], roach [slang]; hashish, hash [slang]; ganja [India]; tetrahydrol cannabinol, THC.

.14 **antipyretic** 687.64, febrifuge, fever-re-ducer, fever pill [informal].

.15 **anesthetic** 687.57; local or topical or gen-eral anesthetic; differential anesthetic.

.16 **cough medicine,** cough syrup, cough drops; horehound.

.17 **laxative** 687.62, **cathartic, physic, purge, purgative,** aperient, carminative, diuretic, –agogue.

.18 **emetic,** vomitive or vomit [both archaic], nauseant.

.19 **enema,** clyster, clysma, lavage, lavement [archaic].

.20 **prophylactic, preventive,** preventative, protective.

.21 **antiseptic** 687.58, **disinfectant** 687.59, fu-migant, fumigator, **germicide,** bacteri-cide, microbicide.

.22 **dentifrice, toothpaste,** tooth powder; mouthwash, gargle.

.23 **contraceptive,** birth control device, pro-phylactic; condom; **rubber** or skin or bag [all slang]; oral contraceptive, **birth control pill, the pill** [informal]; diaphragm, pessary; spermicide, spermicidal jelly, contraceptive foam; intrauterine device, IUD.

.24 **vermifuge,** vermicide, worm medicine, anthelmintic.

.25 **antacid** 687.63, gastric antacid, alkalizer.

.26 **antidote,** counterpoison, alexipharmic, theriaca *or* theriac.

.27 **antitoxin,** antitoxic serum; **antivenin; serum,** antiserum; interferon; **antibody,** antigen-antibody product, anaphylactic antibody, incomplete antibody, inhibiting antibody, sensitizing antibody; gamma globulin, serum gamma globulin, immune globulin, antitoxic globulin; lysin, precipitin, agglutinin, anaphylactin, bactericidin; antiantibody; antigen, Rh antigen, Rh factor; allergen; **immunosuppressive drug.**

.28 **vaccine,** stock vaccine, bovine vaccine, humanized vaccine; univalent vaccine, homologous *or* autogenous vaccine, heterogenous vaccine, multivalent *or* polyvalent vaccine; live-virus vaccine, killed-virus vaccine; T.A.B. vaccine, typhoid-paratyphoid A and B vaccine, triple vaccine; measles vaccine; rubella vaccine; BCG vaccine (bacillus Calmette-Guérin), Calmette's vaccine; polio vaccine, Salk vaccine, Sabin vaccine; toxoid, tetanus toxoid, diphtheria toxoid.

.29 **miracle drugs, wonder drugs,** magic bullets; **antibiotic** 687.60; bacteriostat; **sulfa drug** 687.61, sulfa, sulfanilamide, sulfonamide.

.30 **diaphoretic,** sudorific.

.31 **vesicant,** vesicatory, epispastic.

.32 (other drugs) antihistamine; antiperiodic; antiphlogistic; antispasmodic; counterirritant; decongestant; carminative; adjuvant; expectorant; emmenagogue; maturative; vasodilator, vasoconstrictor; **hormone** 312.10; **vitamin** 309.4.

.33 **dressing, application,** epithem [archaic]; plaster, court plaster, mustard plaster, sinapism; **poultice,** cataplasm; formentation; **compress,** pledget; stupe; tent; tampon; **bandage, bandaging,** band [archaic], binder, cravat, triangular bandage, roller *or* roller bandage, four-tailed bandage; bandage compress, adhesive compress, Band-Aid; elastic bandage, Ace elastic bandage, Ace bandage; rubber bandage; plastic bandage; **tourniquet;** sling; splint, brace; cast, plaster cast; tape, **adhesive tape;** lint, cotton, gauze, sponge.

.34 **pharmacology, pharmacy, pharmaceutics;** posology; materia medica.

.35 **pharmacist,** pharmaceutist, pharmacopolist, **druggist, chemist** [Brit], **apothecary,** dispenser, gallipot; pharmacologist, pharmaceutical chemist, posologist.

.36 **drugstore, pharmacy,** chemist *or* chemist's shop [both Brit], apothecary's shop, dispensary, dispensatory.

.37 **pharmacopoeia,** pharmacopedia, dispensatory.

.38 VERBS remedy, cure 694.13–15; prescribe; treat 689.30.

.39 ADJS **remedial, curative, therapeutic, healing, corrective,** alterative, restorative, analeptic, sanative, sanatory; adjuvant; **medicinal,** medicative, theriac(al), iatric.

.40 **palliative, lenitive, alleviative, assuasive,** soothing, balmy, balsamic, demulcent, emollient.

.41 **antidotal,** alexipharmic; **antitoxic; antibiotic,** bacteriostatic, antimicrobial; antiluetic, antisyphilitic; antiscorbutic; antiperiodic; antipyretic, febrifugal; vermifugal, anthelmintic; **antacid.**

.42 **prophylactic, preventive,** protective.

.43 **antiseptic, disinfectant, germicidal,** bactericidal.

.44 **tonic, stimulating, bracing, invigorating,** reviving, refreshing, restorative, analeptic, strengthening, roborant, corroborant.

.45 **sedative, calmative,** calmant, depressant, **soothing, tranquilizing, quietening; narcotic,** opiatic; **analgesic,** anodyne, paregoric [archaic]; **hypnotic,** soporific, somniferous, somnifacient, sleep-inducing.

.46 **psychochemical,** psychoactive; ataractic; antidepressant; hallucinogenic, **psychedelic,** mind-expanding, psychotomimetic.

.47 **anesthetic,** deadening, numbing.

.48 **cathartic,** laxative, purgative, aperient; carminative; diuretic.

.49 **emetic,** vomitive, vomitory [archaic].

.50 **pharmaceutic(al),** pharmacological.

.51 **balms**

| | |
|---|---|
| arnica | menthol |
| balm of Gilead | Mentholatum |
| balsam | mercurial ointment |
| blue ointment | olive oil |
| glycerin | petrolatum, petroleum jelly |
| glycerite, glycerole | |
| glycerogel, glycerogelatin | Vaseline |
| glycerol | Vicks Vaporub |
| lanolin | witch hazel |
| melissa | zinc ointment |

.52 **stimulants**

| | |
|---|---|
| Adrenalin, adrenaline | ammonium carbonate |
| aloes | amphetamine |

amphetamine sul-
phate
arnica
aromatic spirits of
ammonia
Benzedrine
benzoin
caffeine
chocolate
cocaine
cocoa
coffee
colocynth
desoxyephedrine
Dexamyl
Dexedrine, dex-
troamphetamine

sulfate
digitalin, digitalis
epinephrine
kola nut, kola
Methedrine, meth-
amphetamine
hydrochloride
nikethamide
nux vomica
picrotoxin
quassia
quinine
smelling salts, salts
sodium phosphate
strychnine
tea

### .53 hallucinogens, psychoactive drugs

belladonna
cannabis, bhang
DET, diethyltrypt-
amine
DMT, dimethyl-
tryptamine
hashish
hemp, ganja
hyoscyamus, henbane
Indian hemp
jimsonweed
LSD, lysergic acid

diethylamide
marijuana
mescal
mescaline
morning glory seeds
peyote
psilocin
psilocybin
stramonium
THC, tetrahydrol can-
nabinol

### .54 depressants

aconite
alcohol
Amytal, amobarbital
sodium
atropine
barbital, barbitone
[Brit]
barbituric acid
belladonna
bromide
chloral hydrate, chlo-
ral
codeine
Demerol
Dial, diallylbarbituric
acid
heroin
hyoscyamine
laudanum
Luminal

meperidine
methadone
morphine
Nembutal
opium
paraldehyde
pentobarbital
phenobarbital
Quaalude
reserpine
scopolamine
Seconal, secobarbital
sodium
sodium bromide
Sulfonal, sulfonmeth-
ane
thalidomide
Trional, sulfonethyl-
methane
Tuinal

### .55 tranquilizers

chlorpromazine
Equanil
Librium
meprobamate
Miltown
phenoglycodol
phenothiazine
rauwolfia

reserpine
Serpasil
thalidomide
thioridazine
Thorazine
Triavil
Valium

### .56 analgesics

acetanilide
acetophenetidin
aminopyrine
Anacin
aspirin, acetylsalicylic
acid
Bufferin, buffered
aspirin

Darvon
Empirin
Excedrin
headache powder
phenacetin
Pyramidon
sodium salicylate

### .57 anesthetics

A.C.E. mixture (alco-
hol, chloroform and
ether)
anesthyl
Avertin
benzocaine
butacaine sulfate,
butacaine
C.E. mixture (chloro-
form and ether)
chloroform
cocaine
cyclopropane
dibucaine
ether
ethyl chloride
ethylene
gas

halocaine
laughing gas
menthol
Metycaine
nitrous oxide
novocaine, Novocain
Nupercaine
Pantocain
piperocaine
procaine
protoxide of nitrogen
tetracaine
thiopental sodium,
Pentothal, truth
serum
tribromoethanol
trichloromethane
urethane

### .58 antiseptics

A.B.C. powder (boric
acid, bismuth subni-
trate and calomel)
alcohol
Argyrol
boric acid
calomel
camphor
carbolic acid
chloramine, chlora-
mine-T
cresol
gentian violet
gramicidin
hexachloraphene
hydrogen peroxide

iodine
iodoform
Mercurochrome, mer-
bromin
mercurous chloride
Merthiolate
peroxide
phenol
phenyl salicylate
resorcinol
Salol
silver vitellin
spirits of camphor
thimerosal
thymol
tincture of iodine

### .59 disinfectants

bichloride of mercury
bleaching powder
carbolic acid
chlorine
chloride of lime
cresol
formaldehyde
hypochlorous acid
lye

Lysol
mercuric chloride,
mercury chloride
phenol
potassium permanga-
nate
sodium hydroxide
sodium hypochlorite

### .60 antibiotics

actinomycin
amphotericin
ampicillin
antimycin A
Aureomycin
azaserine
bacitracin
carbomycin
cephaloridine
Chloromycetin, chlor-
amphenicol
chlortetracycline
cloxacillin
cycloserine
dihydrostreptomycin
erythromycin
fradicin
gramicidin
griseofulvin
kanamycin
methicillin
mitomycin

mycomycin
neomycin
novobiocin
nystatin
oxacillin
oxytetracycline
penicillin
phenethicillin
polymyxin
pyocyanase
pyocyanin
spectinomycin
Staphcillin
streptomycin
streptothricin
subtilin
Terramycin
tetracycline
tylocin
tyrothricin
vancomycin
viomycin

## .61 sulfa drugs

| | |
|---|---|
| Gantrisin | sulfamethazine |
| Neoprontosil | sulfanilamide |
| phthalylsulfathiazole | sulfapyrazine |
| Prontosil | sulfapyridine |
| succinylsulfathiazole | Sulfasuxidine |
| sulfadiazine | Sulfathalidine |
| sulfadimethoxine | sulfathiazole |
| sulfaguanidine | sulfisoxazole |
| sulfamerazine | |

## .62 laxatives

| | |
|---|---|
| agar | magnesia, magnesium |
| aloes | oxide |
| bran | mercurous chloride |
| calomel | milk of magnesia, |
| cascara, cascara | magnesium hydrox- |
| sagrada | ide |
| castor oil | mineral oil |
| citrate of magnesia, | mineral water |
| magnesium citrate | phenolphthalein |
| colocynth | podophyllin |
| Culver's root | prunes |
| epsom salts, epsom | psyllium seed |
| salt | Rochelle powders |
| figs | salts |
| Glauber's salt | Seidlitz powders |
| jalop | senna |
| leptandra | sodium phosphate |

## .63 antacids

| | |
|---|---|
| Alka-Seltzer | magnesium hydrox- |
| bicarbonate of soda | ide |
| Brioschi | Pepto-Bismol |
| Bromo Seltzer | Rolaids |
| calcium carbonate | seltzer, seltzer water |
| Maalox | sodium bicarbonate |
| magnesia, magnesium | sodium phosphate |
| oxide | Tums |
| milk of magnesia, | |

## .64 antipyretics

| | |
|---|---|
| acetanilide | phenazone |
| antipyrine | quinacrine |
| aspirin, acetylsalicylic | quinidine |
| acid | quinine |
| Atabrine | sodium salicylate |
| mepacrine [Brit] | |

## .65 miscellaneous drugs

| | |
|---|---|
| ammonium chloride | ergot |
| Antabus | ipecac, ipecacuanha |
| atropine, belladonna | milk of bismuth |
| bismuth | podophyllin |
| curare | quassia |
| Dilantin, diphenylhy- | sal ammoniac |
| dantoin | sassafras |
| ephedrine | syrup of ipecac |

## 688. HEALING ARTS

**.1** NOUNS **medicine,** leechcraft, physic or leechdom [both archaic]; therapy 689; anatomic medicine, biomedicine, comparative medicine, clinical medicine, constitutional medicine, dosimetric medicine, experimental medicine, folk medicine, general medicine, group medicine, holistic medicine, industrial medicine, internal medicine, materia medica, neo-Hippocratic medicine, physical medicine, preclinical medicine, preventive medicine, public health medicine, tropical medicine, veterinary medicine; psychosomatic medicine 690.4; socialized medicine, state medicine, federal medicine; Medicare, Medicaid; forensic or legal medicine, medical jurisprudence; military medicine, naval medicine, air medicine, aviation medicine, aerospace medicine, space medicine.

**.2** (systems) osteopathy; chiropractic, chiropraxis; Galenic medicine; naturopathy; eclectic medicine, eclecticism; allopathy; homeopathy; ayurveda, ayurvedic medicine.

**.3 surgery,** −chirurgia; operative surgery, clinical surgery, general surgery; major surgery, minor surgery; veterinary surgery; aseptic surgery, antiseptic surgery; dental surgery or oral surgery, neurosurgery; brain surgery, urological surgery, orthopedic surgery, thoracic surgery, heart surgery, open-heart surgery, plastic surgery or reconstructive surgery, chiroplasty, reparative surgery, prosthetics, cryosurgery; microsurgery; electrosurgery; radiosurgery; operation 689.21−25; organ transplantation.

**.4 dentistry,** general dentistry; operative dentistry, oral surgery, surgical dentistry; prosthetic dentistry, prosthodontics, prosthodontia; orthodontics, orthodontia; periodontics, periodontia; exodontics, exodontia; endodontics, endodontia; radiodontics, radiodontia.

**.5 healer, therapist,** therapeutist, **medic,** −path, −iatrist, iatro−; bonesetter; oculist; **optometrist; midwife;** homeopath, homeopathist; **osteopath; chiropractor.**

**.6 doctor,** doc [informal], **physician,** Doctor of Medicine, MD, **medical practitioner, medical man, medico** [informal], leech [archaic], croaker or sawbones [both slang]; allopath, allopathist; general practitioner, GP; family doctor; country doctor; **intern; resident,** house physician, resident physician; physician in ordinary; medical attendant, attending physician; **medical examiner,** coroner.

**.7 quack,** quacksalver, **charlatan, medicaster,** medicine man, medicine monger, horse doctor.

**.8 specialist; orthopedist; pediatrician,** pediatrist; **chiropodist, podiatrist,** foot doctor; **dermatologist,** skin man [slang]; **internist; cardiologist; neurologist; psychia-**

trist 690.12,13; gynecologist; obstetrician; gerontologist, geriatrician; otolaryngologist, eye-ear-nose-throat specialist; **oculist,** ophthalmologist, eye doctor; otologist; **pathologist;** immunologist, serologist; anesthesiologist; radiologist.

.9 **surgeon,** sawbones [slang]; operator, operative surgeon.

.10 **dentist,** tooth doctor, toothdrawer; **dental surgeon,** operative dentist; DDS, Doctor of Dental Surgery; DDSc, Doctor of Dental Science; DMD, Doctor of Dental Medicine; **orthodontist,** periodontist, prosthodontist, exodontist, endodontist; radiodontist.

.11 **veterinary, veterinarian, vet** [informal], veterinary surgeon [Brit]; horse doctor.

.12 **nonmedical therapist;** theotherapist; Christian *or* spiritual *or* divine healer; **Christian Science practitioner,** healer; **faith healer.**

.13 **nurse,** sister *or* nursing sister [both Brit]; trained nurse, graduate nurse; registered nurse, RN; practical nurse, licensed practical nurse, LPN; charge nurse, general-duty nurse, private-duty nurse, surgical nurse, scrub nurse; community nurse, district nurse, visiting nurse, public health nurse, school nurse; student nurse; probe [informal], **probationer,** probationist.

.14 (hospital staff) paramedic; orderly, attendant, nurse's aide; dresser; anesthetist; radiographer, X-ray technician; laboratory technician; radiotherapist; physical therapist, physiotherapist; dietitian; hospital administrator.

.15 **Hippocrates,** Galen; Aesculapius, Asclepius.

.16 **practice of medicine,** medical practice; general practice, restricted practice; internship; residency; Hippocratic oath.

.17 VERBS **practice medicine,** doctor [informal]; treat 689.30; intern.

.18 ADJS **medical,** medico–, iatric, surgical; chiropodic, pediatric, orthopedic, obstetric(al), neurological; dental, dent(o)– *or* denti–; orthodontic, periodontic, prosthodontic, exodontic; osteopathic, chiropractic, naturopathic, hydropathic, allopathic, homeopathic; clinical, clinico–.

.19 **branches of medicine**

| | |
|---|---|
| anatomy | dentistry |
| anesthesiology | dermatology |
| audiology | diagnostics |
| bacteriology | embryology |
| cardiography | endocrinology |
| cardiology | epidemiology |
| chiropody | etiology |
| dental surgery | exodontics |

| | |
|---|---|
| fluoroscopy | otolaryngology |
| general medicine | otology |
| geriatrics, gerontology | parasitology |
| gynecology | pathology |
| hematology | pediatrics |
| hygiene | periodontics |
| immunochemistry | physical medicine |
| immunology | physiopathology |
| internal medicine | podiatry |
| materia medica | psychiatry |
| mental hygiene | psychoanalysis |
| midwifery | psychology 690 |
| mycology | radiology |
| neurology | serology |
| neurosurgery | surgery |
| nosology | surgical anatomy |
| nutrition | symptomatology, |
| obstetrics | semeiology |
| ophthalmology | teratology |
| optometry | therapeutics 689.1 |
| orthodontics | tocology |
| orthopedics | toxicology |

## 689. THERAPY

.1 NOUNS **therapy, therapeutics,** therapeusis, **treatment, medical care** *or* **treatment,** medication, –iatric(s) *or* –iatry, –pathic(s) *or* –pathy, –praxis; healing arts 688; psychotherapy 690; medicines 687.

.2 actinotherapy, aerosol therapy, aerotherapy *or* aerotherapeutics, arsenotherapy, autoserum therapy, bacterial therapy, bacteriotherapy, bibliotherapy, biotherapy, buffer therapy, cardiotherapy, chemotherapy, chrysotherapy, climatotherapy, cold therapy, collapse therapy, constitutional therapy, contact therapy, crymotherapy, dermatotherapy, dietotherapy 309.14, dye therapy, endocrinotherapy, fever therapy, frigotherapy, galactotherapy, glandular therapy, gold therapy, hemotherapy, heterovaccine therapy, hyperbaric therapy, immunization therapy, infrared therapy, intravenous therapy, iodotherapy, maggot therapy, malariotherapy, mechanotherapy, Metrazol therapy, nonspecific therapy, occupational therapy, opsonic therapy, organotherapy, oxygen therapy, pharmacotherapy, physical therapy *or* physiotherapy, phototherapy, protein therapy, pyretotherapy, radium therapy, ray therapy, replacement therapy, serotherapy, shock therapy 690.7, specific therapy, substitution therapy, suggestion therapy 690.6, surgicotherapy, ultrasonic therapy, ultraviolet therapy, vaccine therapy, X-ray therapy.

.3 **nonmedical therapy;** theotherapy; **healing;** Christian *or* spiritual *or* divine healing; **faith healing.**

.4 **hydrotherapy,** hydrotherapeutics; hydropathy, water cure; cold-water cure; contrast bath, whirlpool bath.

.5 **heat therapy,** thermotherapy; heliotherapy, solar therapy; fangotherapy; hot bath, sweat bath, sunbath.

.6 **diathermy,** medical diathermy; electrotherapy, electrotherapeutics; **radiothermy,** high-frequency treatment; shortwave diathermy, ultrashortwave diathermy, microwave diathermy; ultrasonic diathermy; surgical diathermy, radiosurgery, electrosurgery, electroresection, electrocautery, electrocoagulation.

.7 **radiotherapy,** radiotherapeutics, radio–; curietherapy, ray therapy, radiation therapy, irradiation therapy, irradiation; interstitial irradiation therapy, intercavitary irradiation therapy; X-ray therapy, roentgenotherapy or roentgentherapy, roentgen ray therapy, roentgenization; X-ray dosimetry, roentgenometry; isotope therapy; radium therapy, radiumization; cobalt therapy.

.8 **radiology,** radiography, radioscopy, fluoroscopy, etc. 327.7.

.9 (radiotherapeutic substances) radium; cobalt; radioisotope, tracer, labeled or tagged element, radioelement; radiocarbon, carbon 14, radiocalcium, radiopotassium, radiosodium, radioiodine; atomic cocktail.

.10 (diagnostic pictures and graphs) **X ray,** radiograph, radiogram, roentgenogram or roentgenograph; photofluorograph; X-ray movie; chest X-ray; pyelogram; orthodiagram; encephalograph, encephalogram; electroencephalograph, electroencephalogram, EEG; electrocorticogram; electrocardiogram, ECG, EKG; electromyogram.

.11 case history, medical history, anamnesis; associative anamnesis; catamnesis, follow-up.

.12 **diagnostics,** prognostics; symptomatology, semeiology, semeiotics.

.13 **diagnosis,** differential diagnosis, postmortem diagnosis; biological diagnosis, clinical diagnosis, laboratory diagnosis; cytodiagnosis, serum diagnosis or serodiagnosis; physical diagnosis, anatomic diagnosis; examination, physical examination, digital examination, oral examination, etc.; study, test, work-up [informal]; urinalysis, uroscopy; biopsy; Pap test or smear; electrocardiography, electroencephalography, electromyography; mammography.

.14 **prognosis,** prognostication; prognostic, **symptom,** sign.

.15 **treatment,** medical treatment or attention; **cure,** curative measures; **medication,** medicamentation; regimen, regime; first aid; hospitalization.

.16 (methods) prophylaxis or prophylaxy, preventive treatment; active treatment, adjuvant treatment, causal treatment, conservative treatment, empiric treatment, expectant treatment, palliative treatment, perennial treatment, preseasonal treatment, rational treatment, specific treatment, supporting treatment, symptomatic treatment; antigen treatment, crossfire treatment, cross-firing, diathermic treatment, dietetic treatment, drip treatment, drug treatment, electrotherapeutic treatment, fever treatment, heat treatment, hot-air treatment, light treatment, radiotherapeutic treatment, shock treatment, starvation treatment, surgical treatment, tonic treatment, vibration treatment.

.17 **immunization;** immunization therapy, immunotherapy; vaccine therapy, vaccinotherapy; toxin-antitoxin immunization; serum therapy, serotherapy, serotherapeutics; tuberculin test, scratch test, patch test; **immunology,** immunochemistry; immunity theory, side-chain theory; immunity.

.18 **inoculation, vaccination; injection,** hypodermic, hypodermic injection, shot [informal], hypospray or jet injection; booster, booster shot [informal]; antitoxin, vaccine 687.27,28; narcotic injection; bang or fix or hit [all slang]; mainlining or shooting up or skin-popping [all slang].

.19 (methods of injection) cutaneous, percutaneous, subcutaneous, intradermal, intramuscular, intravenous, intramedullary, intracardiac, intrathecal, intraspinal.

.20 **transfusion,** blood transfusion; arterial transfusion, direct transfusion, drip transfusion, exchange transfusion, exsanguination transfusion, exsanguino transfusion, plasma transfusion, reciprocal transfusion, replacement transfusion, serum transfusion, venous transfusion; serum 388.4; blood bank, blood donor center, bloodmobile; blood donor; perfusion.

.21 **surgery,** surgical treatment; cautery, cauterization; bloodless surgery; electrolysis, electrolyzation; electrocautery, electrosurgery, surgical diathermy, electroresection; laser surgery; radiosurgery.

.22 **operation,** surgical operation, surgical intervention, surgical technique *or* measure, the knife [informal]; major operation, minor operation; capital operation, serious operation; ablative operation, anastomotic operation, bloodless operation, compensating operation, crescent operation, elective operation, emergency operation, exploratory operation, fenestration operation, interval operation, palliative operation, radical operation; **section, resection; excision,** removal; **amputation; transplant,** organ transplant *or* transplantation, heart transplant, kidney transplant, corneal transplant.

.23 (surgical removal) –ectomy, adenoidectomy, appendectomy, arteriectomy, cervicectomy, cholecystectomy, craniectomy, cricoidectomy, cystectomy, enterectomy, gastrectomy, hemorrhoidectomy, hysterectomy, mammectomy *or* mastectomy, mastoidectomy, nephrectomy, omphalectomy, oophorectomy *or* ovariectomy, oophorocystectomy, orchidectomy, pancreatectomy, penectomy, pericardiectomy, phrenicectomy, pneumonectomy, prostatectomy, salpingectomy, stapedectomy, tonsillectomy, ureterectomy, urethrectomy, vasectomy, venectomy; castration.

.24 (surgical incision) –tomy, amygdalotomy, ankylotomy, arteriotomy, blepharotomy, cardiotomy, cecotomy, celiotomy, cholecystotomy, cirsotomy, coccygotomy, colpotomy, craniotomy, cystotomy, duodenotomy, elytrotomy, embryotomy, enterotomy, gastroenterotomy, gastrotomy, glossotomy, hebotomy, herniotomy, hysterotomy, laparotomy, lithotomy, lobotomy, mastotomy, nephrotomy, neurotomy, ovariotomy, pancreatotomy, phrenicotomy, pneumonotomy, prostatotomy, salpingotomy, sclerotomy, thoracotomy, thyrotomy, tonsillotomy, ureterotomy, urethrotomy; prefrontal lobotomy, psychosurgery; caesarean, caesarean section *or* operation.

.25 **plastic surgery,** –plastic *or* –plasty; reparative surgery, plastic operation, reconstructive operation, cosmetic operation; **facelifting;** balanoplasty, blepharoplasty, batrachoplasty, bronchoplasty, canthoplasty, colpoplasty, cystoplasty, dermoplasty, genyoplasty, heteroplasty, labioplasty, mammilloplasty, otoplasty, rhinoplasty.

.26 bloodletting, bleeding, venesection, phlebotomy; leeching; cupping.

.27 **hospital,** *hôpital* [Fr], **infirmary;** sick bay *or* berth; **clinic,** polyclinic, inpatient clinic, outpatient clinic, policlinic, well-baby clinic; general hospital, teaching hospital, special hospital; community hospital, government hospital, public hospital, voluntary hospital, private hospital, proprietary hospital; veterans hospital, VA hospital; surgical hospital, osteopathic hospital, convalescent hospital, children's hospital, maternity *or* lying-in hospital, mental hospital 473.14; base hospital, field hospital, station hospital, evacuation hospital; **sanatorium;** asylum, home; **nursing home,** convalescent home, *maison de santé* [Fr]; rest home, ward, sickroom; sickbed.

.28 **pesthouse,** lazar house, lazaretto *or* lazaret, lock hospital [Brit]; isolation ward.

.29 **health resort, spa, watering place,** baths; mineral spring, warm *or* hot spring; pump room, pump house.

.30 VERBS **treat, doctor,** minister to, care for, give care to; **diagnose;** nurse; **cure, remedy, heal;** dress the wounds, bandage, poultice, plaster, strap, splint; lick one's wounds; bathe; massage, rub; operate on; physic, purge, flux [archaic].

.31 **medicate,** medicine, drug, dope [slang], dose; salve, oil, anoint, embrocate.

.32 **irradiate,** radiumize, **X-ray,** roentgenize.

.33 bleed, let blood, leech, phlebotomize; cup; **transfuse,** give a transfusion; perfuse.

.34 **immunize, inoculate, vaccinate,** shoot [informal].

.35 **undergo treatment,** take the cure, doctor [dial], take medicine; go under the knife [informal].

.36 **medical and surgical instruments**

| | |
|---|---|
| artificial heart | heat lamp |
| artificial kidney | hemostat |
| aspirator | hypodermic, hypo |
| bedpan | [slang], hypodermic |
| bistoury | needle, hypodermic |
| bronchoscope | syringe |
| cardiograph | kidney basin |
| cardioscope | lancet, lance |
| catheter | laparotomy pack, lap |
| clinical thermometer | pack [informal] |
| cystoscope | manometer |
| dialysis machine | mechanical heart |
| diaphanoscope | microscope |
| diathermy machine | microwave diathermy |
| drain | machine |
| drain tube | nebulizer |
| electrocardiograph | needle |
| electroencephalograph | ophthalmoscope |
| electromyograph | orthodiagraph |
| fluoroscope | orthoscope |
| forceps | otoscope |
| gastroscope | percussion hammer |
| germicidal lamp | pneumatometer |
| heart-lung machine | pneumograph, |

pneumatograph
probe
pus basin
radio knife
resectoscope
respirometer
roentgenoscope
rubber gloves
scalpel
shortwave diathermy
   machine
sound
specimen bottle
speculum
sphygmograph
sphygmomanometer
sphygmometer
spirograph
spirometer

splint
stethograph
stethometer
stethoscope
stomach pump
stomach tube
stylet
surgical or suture nee-
   dle
suture
swab
syringe
tongue depressor or
   blade
trephine, trepan
trocar
urinalysis kit
X-ray machine

**.37 respirators**

heart-lung machine
inhalator
inspirator
iron lung
oxygen mask

oxygen tank
oxygen tent
Pulmotor
resuscitator

## 690. PSYCHOLOGY AND PSYCHOTHERAPY

**.1** NOUNS **psychology,** psych(o)–; science of the mind, science of human behavior; mental philosophy; psychonomics, psychonomy; reactology, reflexology; abnormal psychology, academic psychology, analytical psychology, applied psychology, animal psychology, association psychology, child psychology, clinical psychology, cognitive psychology, comparative psychology, constitutional psychology, criminal psychology, depth psychology, developmental psychology, differential psychology, dynamic psychology, ecological psychology, educational psychology, experimental psychology, existential psychology, faculty psychology, folk psychology, functional psychology, genetic psychology, group psychology, hormic psychology, individual psychology, industrial psychology, morbid psychology, neuropsychology, phenomenological psychology, popular psychology, physiological psychology, race psychology, rational psychology, self psychology, social psychology, structural psychology; parapsychology 1034.4; psychobiochemistry, psychobiology, psychodiagnostics, psychodynamics, psychogenetics, psychogeriatrics, psycholinguistics, psychometrics, psychopathology, psychopharmacology, psychophysics, psychophysiology, psychosociology; psychosomatics, psychotechnics, psychotechnology, psychothera-peutics; psychological medicine, psychological warfare.

**.2** (systems) Freudian psychology, Freudianism, psychoanalysis, psychoanalytic theory, metapsychology; Jungian psychology, analytical psychology, Adlerian psychology; Reichian psychology, orgone theory; Horneyan psychology; Gestalt psychology, configurationism; behavior or behavioristic psychology, **behaviorism,** stimulus-response psychology, Watsonian psychology, Skinnerian psychology, Pavlovian psychology; structuralism; association psychology, associationism, mental chemistry; apperceptionism; dianetics.

**.3 psychiatry,** psychological medicine; neuropsychiatry; social psychiatry; prophylactic psychiatry.

**.4 psychosomatic medicine,** psychological medicine, medicopsychology; psychosocial medicine.

**.5 psychotherapy,** psychotherapeutics, mind cure; group therapy, group psychotherapy, conjoint therapy; humanistic therapy; gestalt therapy, psychodrama, bioenergetics, encounter therapy, rational-emotive therapy, marriage encounter, confrontation therapy; training group or T-group, sensitivity training, sensory awareness training or SAT, consciousness raising, group sensitivity training, group relations training; marathon, est or Erhard Seminars Training; New Consciousness, behavior modification, behavior therapy; biofeedback; transpersonal therapy, Arica movement, psychosynthesis, transcendental meditation or TM; transactional analysis or TA, assertiveness training; regression therapy, primal therapy, scream therapy; family training, radical therapy, feminist therapy; occupational therapy, vocational therapy; recreational therapy, play therapy; reality therapy; release therapy; supportive therapy; directive therapy, nondirective therapy; narcotherapy, narcoanalysis, narcosynthesis, Pentothal interview; sleep treatment, prolonged narcosis; hypnotherapy, hypnoanalysis; hypnotism, hypnosis, narcohypnosis; psychosurgery; **counseling,** psychological counseling; pastoral counseling.

**.6 suggestion therapy,** suggestionism; hypnotherapy, hypnotism, hypnosis, hypnotic suggestion, posthypnotic suggestion; **autosuggestion,** self-suggestion, self-hypnosis; suggestibility, power of suggestion.

**.7 shock therapy,** shock treatment; convulsive therapy; electroshock therapy, electroshock, electronarcosis, Metrazol shock therapy; hypoglycemic shock therapy, insulin shock therapy.

.8 **psychoanalysis, analysis,** psychanalysis, the couch [informal]; psychoanalytic therapy, psychoanalytic method; **depth psychology,** psychology of depths; group analysis; psychognosis, psychognosy; dream analysis, interpretation of dreams, dream symbolism; depth interview.

.9 **psychodiagnostics,** psychodiagnosis, psychological or psychiatric evaluation; Rorschach method.

.10 **psychometrics,** psychometry; **intelligence testing;** psychological screening; psychography; psychogram, psychograph, psychological profile; psychometer, IQ meter [informal]; lie detector, polygraph, psychogalvanometer.

.11 **psychological test,** mental test; standardized test; achievement test; **aptitude test,** Oseretsky test, Stanford scientific aptitude test; **personality test,** Bernreuter personality inventory, Brown personality inventory, Minnesota multiphasic personality inventory; interest inventory; **association test,** word association test, controlled association test, free association test; **apperception test,** thematic apperception test, TAT; **Rorschach test,** inkblot test; Szondi test; **intelligence test,** IQ test; alpha test, beta test, Babcock-Levy test, Binet or Binet-Simon test, Stanford-Binet test, Stanford revision, Goldstein-Sheerer test, Kent mental test; Wechsler-Bellevue intelligence scale, Gesell's development schedule, Minnesota preschool scale, Cattell's infant intelligence scale; intelligence quotient, IQ.

.12 **psychologist,** psychologue; clinical psychologist; **psychiatrist,** alienist; neuropsychiatrist; psychopathist, psychopathologist; psychotechnologist, industrial psychologist; psychobiologist, psychochemist, psychophysiologist, psychophysicist; psychographer; somatist; Freud, Adler, Jung, Reich, Horney, Watson, Skinner, Pavlov.

.13 **psychotherapist,** psychotherapeutist; **clinical psychologist; psychiatrist;** narcotherapist; hypnotherapist; behavior therapist; **psychoanalyst,** psychoanalyzer, **analyst;** headshrinker or shrinker or shrink [all slang].

.14 **personality tendency,** complexion [archaic], humor; somatotype; **introversion,** introvertedness, ingoingness; inner-directedness; **extroversion,** extrovertedness, outgoingness; other-directedness; syntony, ambiversion; schizothymia, schizothymic or schizoid personality; cyclothymia, cyclothymic or cycloid personality; mesomorphism, mesomorphy; endomorphism, endomorphy; ectomorphism, ectomorphy.

.15 (personality type) **introvert, extrovert,** syntone, ambivert; schizothyme, schizoid; cyclothymic, cyclothyme, cycloid; choleric, melancholic, sanguine, phlegmatic; endomorph, mesomorph, ectomorph.

.16 (pathological personality types) neurotic personality, **neurotic, psychoneurotic,** neuropath; weak personality, maladjusted personality, inadequate personality, inferior personality, immature personality, disordered personality, disturbed personality, emotionally unstable personality, perverse personality, hostile personality; paranoid personality; schizoid personality, schizoid; dual personality, double personality, multiple personality, split personality, alternating personality; seclusive personality, shut-in personality; escapist; antisocial personality, sociopath, psychopathic personality, moral insanity, **psychopath;** psychotic personality, **psychotic** 473.16; mentally defective personality, idiot 471.8; hypochondriac, hypochondriast, valetudinarian, valetudinary, imaginary invalid, *malade imaginaire* [Fr]; alcoholic 996.10,11; drug user 642.10; sexual psychopath 419.16–19.

.17 **mental disorder, emotional disorder,** functional nervous disorder; reaction; emotional instability; **maladjustment,** social maladjustment; nervous breakdown, crack-up [slang]; problems in living; **insanity, mental illness** 473.1; psychosis 473.3; **schizophrenia,** schiz(o)–; **paranoia** 473.4; **manic-depressive psychosis,** melancholia 473.5; **neurosis;** personality disorder; brain disease, nervous disorder 686.23.

.18 **personality disorder, character disorder,** moral insanity, sociopathy, **psychopathy; psychopathic personality;** sexual pathology, sexual psychopathy 419.12–14.

.19 **neurosis, psychoneurosis,** neuroticism, neurotic or psychoneurotic disorder; psychasthenia; accident neurosis, anxiety neurosis, association neurosis, blast neurosis, compensation neurosis, conversion neurosis, expectation neurosis, fixation neurosis, fright neurosis, homosexual neurosis, hypochondria or hypochondriasis, occupational neurosis, pathoneurosis, regression neurosis, traumatic neurosis, transference neurosis, compulsion neurosis, obsessional neurosis, obsessive-compulsive neurosis; hysteria; anxiety hysteria, conversion hysteria; phobia 891.1; reactive neurosis, situational neurosis; combat or war neurosis, combat or battle fatigue, shell shock, psychopathia martialis.

.20 (neurotic reactions) anxiety reaction, avoidance reaction, compensatory reaction, conversion reaction, depressive reaction, dissociation reaction, emotional instability reaction, flight reaction, immaturity reaction, neurotic-depressive reaction, obsessive-compulsive reaction, passive-aggressive reaction, passive-dependence reaction, phobic reaction, psychasthenic reaction, somatization reaction, shock reaction, stress reaction.

.21 **psychological stress, stress; frustration,** external frustration, internal frustration; conflict, ambivalence, ambivalence of impulse; trauma, traumatism, mental or emotional shock, decompensation.

.22 (psychosomatic symptoms) analgesia, anesthesia, bulimia, depraved appetite, neurasthenia, paresthesia, parorexia, pica; anxiety equivalent; speech abnormality.

.23 (symptoms of emotional disorder) mental distress, psychalgia; emotionalism; anxiety, anxiety state, anxiety equivalent, free-floating anxiety; hysteria, hysterics, hyster(o)–; melancholia, hypochondria, psycholepsy, **depression,** dejection; detachment, alienation, withdrawal, abstraction, preoccupation; **apathy,** lethargy, indifference, unresponsiveness, insensibility; stupor, catatonic stupor; psychomotor disturbance, tic, twitching; amimia, paramimia; euphoria, elation; folie du doute [Fr], pathological indecisiveness, abulia; mania 473.12,36; obsession, compulsion 473.13.

.24 (thought disturbances) blocking, **block,** psychological block, mental block; paralogia; mental confusion, disorientation; agnosia; flight of ideas; **delusion,** delusion of persecution, delusion of grandeur, paranoid delusion, delusion of reference; nihilism, nihilistic delusion; hallucination, hallucinosis 519.7; delirium 473.8.

.25 (speech abnormalities) dysarthria, dysphasia; aphonia, hysterical aphonia, psychophonasthenia; incoherence; echolalia, verbigeration; schizophasia; mutism; imper-

fect speech, speech defect 595.1; aphasia 595.6.

.26 (trance states) **trance,** daze, stupor; catatonic stupor, catalepsy; cataplexy; dream state, reverie, daydreaming 532.2; somnambulism, sleepwalking; hypnotic trance; fugue, fugue state; **amnesia** 538.2.

.27 **dissociation,** mental or emotional dissociation, disconnection; dissociation of personality, personality disorganization or disintegration; **schizoid personality;** double or dual personality; multiple personality, split personality, alternating personality; schizoidism, schizothymia, **schizophrenia** 473.4; depersonalization; **paranoid personality; paranoia** 473.4.

.28 **fixation,** libido fixation or arrest, **arrested development;** infantile fixation, pregenital fixation, father fixation, Freudian fixation, mother fixation, parent fixation; **regression,** retreat to immaturity.

.29 **complex,** inferiority complex, superiority complex, parent complex, Oedipus complex, mother complex, Electra complex, father complex, Diana complex, persecution complex; castration complex.

.30 **defense mechanism,** defense reaction; ego defense, psychotaxis; biological or psychological or sociological adjustive reactions; resistance; dissociation 690.27; **negativism, alienation; escapism,** escape mechanism, avoidance mechanism; escape, flight, **withdrawal; isolation,** emotional insulation; **fantasy,** fantasizing, escape into fantasy, dreamlike thinking, autistic or dereistic thinking, wishful thinking, autism, dereism; wish-fulfillment, wish-fulfillment fantasy; **compensation,** overcompensation, decompensation; substitution; **sublimation; projection,** blame-shifting; displacement; **rationalization.**

.31 **suppression, repression, inhibition,** resistance, restraint, censorship; block, psychological block, blockage, blocking; reaction formation; rigid control; **suppressed desire.**

.32 **catharsis,** purgation, abreaction, motor abreaction, psychocatharsis, **emotional release,** outlet; release therapy, acting-out, psychodrama.

.33 **conditioning,** classical or Pavlovian conditioning; instrumental conditioning, operant conditioning; psychagogy, reeducation, reorientation; conditioned reflex, conditioned stimulus, conditioned response; reinforcement, positive reinforcement, negative reinforcement; simple reflex, unconditioned reflex, **reflex** 284.1; **behavior** 737.

.34 **adjustment**, adjustive reaction; **readjustment**, **rehabilitation**; psychosynthesis, integration of personality; fulfillment, self-fulfillment; integrated personality, syntonic personality.

.35 **psyche**, psychic apparatus, **personality**, **self; mind** 466.1–5; preconscious, foreconscious, coconscious; **subconscious, unconscious**, subconscious *or* unconscious mind, submerged mind, subliminal, subliminal self; **libido**, psychic *or* libidinal energy, motive force, vital impulse, ego-libido, object libido; **id**, primitive self, pleasure principle, life instinct, death instinct; **ego**, conscious self; **superego**, ethical self, conscience; ego ideal; ego-id conflict; anima, persona; collective unconscious, racial unconscious.

.36 **engram**, memory trace, traumatic trace *or* memory; unconscious memory; archetype, archetypal pattern *or* image *or* symbol; imago, image, father image, etc.; **memory** 537.

.37 **symbol**, universal symbol, father symbol, mother symbol, phallic symbol, fertility symbol, etc.; symbolism, symbolization.

.38 **surrogate**, substitute; father surrogate, father figure, father image; mother surrogate, mother figure.

.39 **gestalt**, pattern, figure, configuration, sensory pattern; figure-ground.

.40 **association, association of ideas**, mental linking; controlled association, free association, association by contiguity, association by similarity; association by sound, clang association; stream of consciousness; transference, identification, positive transference, negative transference; **synesthesia** 422.5.

.41 **cathexis**, desire concentration; charge, energy charge, cathectic energy; anticathexis, countercathexis, counterinvestment; hypercathexis, overcharge.

.42 VERBS **psychologize, psychoanalyze.**

.43 ADJS **psychological; psychiatric**, neuropsychiatric; psychometric; **psychopathic**, psychopathological; **psychosomatic**, psychophysical, psychophysiological, psychobiological; psychogenic, psychogenetic, functional; psychodynamic, psychoneurological, psychosexual, psychosocial, psychotechnical; **psychotic** 473.27.

.44 **psychotherapeutic**; psychiatric, psychoanalytic(al).

.45 **neurotic, psychoneurotic**, disturbed, dis- ordered; neurasthenic, psychasthenic; hysteric(al), hypochondriac, phobic.

.46 **introverted**, introvert, introversive, **subjective, ingoing**, inner-directed.

.47 **extroverted**, extrovert, extroversive, **outgoing**, extrospective; other-directed.

.48 **subconscious, unconscious**; subliminal, extramarginal; preconscious, foreconscious, coconscious.

## 691. IMPROVEMENT

.1 NOUNS **improvement, betterment**, bettering, change for the better; melioration, **amelioration; mend**, mending, **amendment; progress**, progression, headway; **advance**, advancement; upward mobility; **promotion, furtherance**, preferment; **rise**, ascent, **lift, uplift**, upswing, uptrend, upbeat; upping *or* boost *or* pickup [all informal]; Great Leap Forward; **enhancement, enrichment**; euthenics, eugenics; **restoration**, revival, recovery 692.2,8.

.2 **development, refinement**, elaboration, **perfection;** beautification, embellishment; maturation, ripening, evolution, seasoning.

.3 **cultivation, culture, refinement, polish**, civility; cultivation of the mind; **civilization;** acculturation; enculturation, socialization; enlightenment, education 475.4, 562.1–3.

.4 **revision**, revise, revisal; revised edition; **emendation, amendment, correction, rectification;** editing, redaction, recension; revampment; **rewrite**, rewriting, rescript, rescription [archaic].

.5 **reform, reformation;** regeneration 145.2; **transformation** 139.2; **conversion** 145; reformism, meliorism; gradualism, Fabianism, revisionism; utopianism; progressivism, progressism; radical reform, extremism, radicalism 745.4; revolution 147.

.6 **reformer**, reformist, meliorist; gradualist, Fabian, revisionist; utopian, utopist; progressive, progressivist, progressionist, progressist; radical, extremist 745.12; revolutionary 147.3.

.7 VERBS (get better) **improve, grow better**, show improvement, **mend**, amend [archaic], meliorate, ameliorate; **look up** *or* **pick up** *or* **perk up** [all informal]; **develop**, shape up; **advance, progress, make progress, make headway, gain**, gain ground, go forward, get *or* go ahead, come on, come along [informal], get along; make strides *or* rapid strides, take off *or* skyrocket [both informal], make up for lost time; graduate.

**.8 rally,** come about or round, **take a favorable turn,** take a turn for the better, gain strength; **recuperate, recover** 694.19,20.

**.9** (make better) **improve, better,** change for the better, make an improvement; transform, transfigure 139.7; improve upon, refine upon, **mend, amend,** emend [archaic]; meliorate, **ameliorate; advance, promote,** foster, favor, nurture, forward, bring forward; **lift,** elevate, **uplift,** raise, boost [informal]; upgrade; **enhance, enrich,** fatten, lard [archaic]; make one's way, better oneself; be the making of; **reform;** reform oneself, turn over a new leaf, mend one's ways, straighten out, straighten oneself out, go straight [informal]; **civilize,** acculturate, socialize; enlighten, edify; **educate** 562.11.

**.10 develop,** elaborate; beautify, embellish; **cultivate, refine,** polish, finish, **perfect;** mature, ripen, evolve, season.

**.11 touch up,** tone up, **brush up, furbish,** furbish up, spruce, **spruce up,** freshen, vamp, vamp up, rub up, brighten up, polish, polish up, shine [informal]; retouch; **revive, renovate** 694.16,17; **repair, fix** 694.14.

**.12 revise,** redact, recense, **revamp, rewrite,** redraft, **rework,** work over; **emend, amend,** emendate, **rectify,** correct; **edit,** blue-pencil.

**.13** ADJS **improved, bettered,** eu–; changed for the better, advanced, ameliorated, enhanced, enriched; developed, perfected; beautified, embellished; **reformed; transformed,** transfigured, converted; **cultivated,** cultured, **refined,** polished, civilized; **educated** 475.18.

**.14 better,** better off, better for, all the better for.

**.15 improving, bettering;** meliorative, ameliorative; progressive, progressing, advancing, ongoing; mending, **on the mend;** on the lift or rise or upswing or upbeat or upgrade [informal], looking up [informal].

**.16 emendatory, corrective;** revisory, revisional; reformatory, reformative, reformational; **reformist,** reformistic, melioristic; gradualistic, Fabian, revisionist; utopian; radical 745.20; revolutionary 147.5.

**.17 improvable,** ameliorable, corrigible, perfectible; **emendable** 694.25.

## 692. IMPAIRMENT

**.1** NOUNS **impairment, damage, injury, harm,** mischief, scathe, **hurt, detriment,** loss, weakening, sickening; disablement, incapacitation; encroachment, inroad, infringement 238.1; **disrepair, dilapidation,** ruinousness; breakage; **breakdown, collapse,** crack-up [informal]; bankruptcy; hurting, spoiling, ruination; sabotage; mayhem, mutilation, crippling, hobbling, laming, maiming; destruction 693.

**.2 corruption, pollution, contamination,** vitiation, **defilement,** fouling, befouling; **poisoning,** envenoming; infection, festering, suppuration; **perversion,** prostitution, misuse 667; denaturing, adulteration.

**.3 deterioration, decadence** or decadency, **degradation, debasement,** derogation, deformation; **degeneration,** degeneracy, degenerateness, effeteness; loss of tone, failure of nerve; depravation, depravedness; **retrogression,** retrogradation, retrocession, **regression;** devolution, involution; demotion 783; downward mobility; **decline,** declination, declension, comedown, **descent,** downtrend, downward trend, downturn, depreciation, **drop, fall,** falling-off, slippage, slump, lapse, fading, dying, failing, failure, wane, ebb.

**.4 waste,** wastage, **consumption;** withering, atrophy, wilting, marcescence; emaciation 205.6.

**.5 wear,** use; **wear and tear; erosion, weathering,** ablation, ravages of time.

**.6 decay, decomposition, disintegration, dissolution,** resolution, degradation, biodegradation, breakup, disorganization, **corruption,** spoilage, **dilapidation;** corrosion, oxidation, oxidization, rust; mildew, mold 676.2; degradability, biodegradability.

**.7 rot, rottenness, foulness, putridness,** putridity, rancidness, rancidity, rankness, **putrefaction,** putrescence, spoilage, decay, decomposition; **mortification,** necrosis, gangrene, sphacelation, sphacelus, slough; caries, tooth decay, carrion; dry rot.

**.8** (an impairment) **injury, hurt, lesion; wound, trauma; sore** 686.35; cut, incision, scratch, gash; puncture, stab, stab wound; laceration, mutilation; abrasion, scuff, scrape, chafe, gall; frazzle, fray; run, **rip, rent,** slash, **tear;** burn, scald, scorch, first- or second- or third-degree burn; flash burn; break, fracture, rupture; crack, chip, craze, check, crackle; wrench; concussion; mortal wound, "wounds immedicable" [Milton]; **blemish** 679.

**.9 bruise, contusion,** ecchymosis, **black-and blue mark; black eye,** shiner or mouse [both slang].

**.10 wreck, ruins, ruin,** hulk, carcass, skeleton

mere wreck, wreck of one's former self; nervous wreck; rattletrap.

.11 VERBS **impair, damage,** endamage, **injure, harm, hurt,** irritate; **worsen, make worse,** deteriorate, put back, aggravate, exacerbate, embitter; **weaken; dilapidate;** add insult to injury, rub salt in the wound.

.12 **spoil, mar,** botch, **ruin, wreck, blight, play havoc with; destroy** 693.10–21.

.13 [slang or informal terms] **queer, screw up, foul up,** louse up, snafu, snarl up, bugger, bugger up, gum up, ball up, bollix, bollix up, **mess up,** hash up, muck up; play hob with, play hell with, play merry hell with, play the devil with; cook, sink, shoot down in flames.

.14 **corrupt, debase, degrade, degenerate, deprave, debauch, defile,** violate, desecrate, deflower, ravish, ravage, despoil; **contaminate,** confound, **pollute, vitiate, poison, infect, taint;** canker, ulcerate; **pervert,** warp, twist, distort; prostitute, misuse 667.4; denature; **cheapen,** devalue; coarsen, vulgarize, drag in the mud; adulterate, alloy.

.15 (inflict an injury) **injure, hurt;** wound, scotch [archaic]; **traumatize;** stab, stick, pierce, puncture; cut, incise, slit, slash, gash, scratch; abrade, scuff, scrape, chafe, fret, gall, bark, skin; break, fracture, rupture; crack, chip, craze, check; lacerate, claw, tear, rip, rend; run; frazzle, fray; burn, scorch, scald; mutilate, maim, make mincemeat of, maul, savage; sprain, strain, wrench; bloody; **blemish** 679.4–7.

.16 **bruise, contuse,** bung or bung up [both slang]; **buffet,** batter, bash [informal], maul, pound, beat, beat black and blue; give a black eye.

.17 **cripple, lame,** maim; hamstring, hobble; wing; emasculate, castrate; incapacitate, disable 158.9.

.18 **undermine,** sap, mine, sap the foundations of, honeycomb; sabotage.

19 **deteriorate, sicken, worsen, get or grow worse,** get no better fast [informal], disimprove, **degenerate;** slip back, **retrogress,** retrograde, regress, relapse, fall back; go to the bad 693.24; let oneself go, let down, slacken; be the worse for, be the worse for wear, have seen better days.

.20 **decline, sink, fail, fall,** slip, fade, die, wane, ebb, subside, lapse, **run down,** go down, **go downhill, fall away, fall off,** go off [informal], slide, slump, hit a slump; hit the skids [slang]; reach the depths, hit or touch bottom, hit rock bottom, have no lower to go.

.21 **languish, pine, droop, flag, wilt;** fade, fade away; **wither, shrivel,** shrink, diminish, **dry up,** desiccate, wizen, sear; "fall'n into the sere, the yellow leaf" [Shakespeare].

.22 **waste, waste away, wither away,** atrophy, consume, consume away, emaciate, pine away; trickle or dribble away; run to waste, run to seed.

.23 **wear, wear away, wear down, wear off;** abrade, fret, rub off; fray, frazzle, tatter, wear ragged; **wear out;** weather, erode, ablate.

.24 **corrode, erode,** eat, gnaw, eat into, eat away, nibble away, gnaw at the root of; canker; **oxidize, rust.**

.25 **decay, decompose, disintegrate;** go or fall into decay, go or fall to pieces, break up, crumble, crumble into dust; **spoil,** corrupt, canker, **go bad; rot, putrefy,** putresce; fester, suppurate, rankle [informal]; **mortify,** necrose, gangrene, sphacelate; mold, molder, mildew.

.26 **break, break up,** fracture, **come apart,** come unstuck, **come** or **fall to pieces, disintegrate;** burst, rupture; crack, split, fissure; snap; break open, give way or away, start, spring a leak, come apart at the seams.

.27 **break down, founder, collapse;** cave or fall in, come crashing or tumbling down, topple, topple down or over, tremble or nod or totter to one's fall; totter, sway.

.28 **get out of order, get out of whack** [informal], **get out of kilter** [informal], get out of commission [informal], get out of gear; get out of joint; go wrong, go kaput [slang], **go on the blink** or **fritz** [slang], go haywire [slang], give out, **break down,** pack up [Brit informal], conk out [slang].

.29 ADJS **impaired, damaged, hurt, injured, harmed; deteriorated, worsened,** aggravated, exacerbated, irritated, embittered; **weakened; worse,** worse off, the worse for, all the worse for; imperfect 676.4; lacerated, mangled, cut, split, rent, torn, slit, slashed, mutilated; **broken** 49.24, **shattered, smashed,** in bits, in pieces, in shards, burst, busted [dial], ruptured, sprung; cracked, chipped, crazed, checked; burned, scorched, scalded.

.30 **spoiled** or spoilt, **marred,** botched, blighted, **ruined,** wrecked; **destroyed** 693.28.

.31 [slang or informal terms] queered, **screwed up, fouled up,** loused up, snafued, buggered, buggered up, gummed up, snarled up, balled up, bollixed up, messed up, hashed up, mucked up; cooked, sunk, shot.

.32 crippled, game [informal], bad, handicapped, maimed; lame, halt, halting, hobbling, limping; hamstrung; spavined; disabled, incapacitated; emasculated, castrated.

.33 worn, well-worn, deep-worn, worn-down, the worse for wear, dog-eared; timeworn; shopworn, shelfworn; worn to the stump, worn to the bone; worn ragged, worn to rags, worn to threads; threadbare, bare, sere [archaic].

.34 shabby, shoddy, seedy, scruffy, tacky [informal], dowdy, tatty, ratty; holey, full of holes; raggedy, ragged, tattered, torn; patchy; frayed, frazzled; in rags, in tatters, in shreds; out at the elbows, out at the heels, down-at-heel or -heels, down-at-the-heel or -heels.

.35 dilapidated, ramshackle, decrepit, tottery, slummy [informal], tumbledown, broken-down, run-down, in ruins, ruinous, ruined, derelict, gone to wrack and ruin, the worse for wear; battered, beaten up, beat-up [informal].

.36 weatherworn, weather-beaten, weathered, weather-battered, weather-wasted, weather-eaten, weather-bitten, weather-scarred; eroded; faded, washed-out, bleached, blanched.

.37 wasted, atrophied, shrunken; withered, sere, shriveled, wilted, wizened, dried-up, desiccated; wrinkled, wrinkled like a prune; brittle, papery, parchmenty; emaciated 205.20; worn to a shadow, reduced to a skeleton, "worn to the bones" [Shakespeare].

.38 worn-out, used up [informal], worn to a frazzle, frazzled, fit for the dust hole or wastepaper basket; exhausted, tired, fatigued, pooped [slang], spent, effete, played out, ausgespielt [Ger], shotten [dial], jaded, emptied, done or done up [both informal]; run-down, laid low, at a low ebb, in a bad way, far-gone, on one's last legs.

.39 in disrepair, out of order, out of working order, out of condition, out of repair, inoperative, out of whack or kilter or kelter [informal], out of commission [informal], out of tune, out of gear; out of joint; on the fritz or on the blink [both slang], haywire [slang], packed-up [Brit informal]; broken 49.24.

.40 putrefactive, putrefacient, rotting, septic; saprogenic, saprogenous; saprophilous, saprophytic, saprobic, sapro–.

.41 decayed, decomposed; spoiled, corrupt, peccant, bad, gone bad; rotten, rotting, putrid, putrefied, foul; putrescent, mortified, necrosed, necrotic, sphacelated, gangrened, gangrenous; carious; cankered, ulcerated, festering, suppurating, suppurative; rotten at or to the core.

.42 tainted, off, blown, frowy [dial]; stale; sour, soured, turned; rank, reechy [archaic], rancid, strong [informal], high, gamy.

.43 blighted, blasted, ravaged, despoiled; blown, flyblown, wormy, weevily, maggoty; moth-eaten, worm-eaten; moldy, moldering, mildewed, smutty, smutted; musty, fusty, frowzy or frowsy, frowsty [Brit].

.44 corroded, eroded, eaten; rusty, rust-eaten, rust-worn, rust-cankered.

.45 corrupting, corruptive; corrosive, corroding; erosive, eroding, damaging, injurious 675.12.

.46 deteriorating, worsening, disintegrating, coming apart or unstuck, crumbling, cracking, fragmenting, going to pieces; decadent, degenerate, effete; retrogressive, retrograde, regressive, from better to worse; declining, sinking, failing, falling, waning, subsiding, slipping, sliding, slumping; languishing, pining, drooping, flagging, wilting; ebbing, draining, dwindling; wasting, fading, withering, shriveling; tabetic, marcescent.

.47 on the wane, on the decline, on the downgrade, on the downward track, on the skids [slang]; tottering, nodding to its fall.

.48 degradable, biodegradable, decomposable, putrefiable, putrescible.

## 693. DESTRUCTION

.1 NOUNS destruction, ruin, ruination, blue ruin [slang]; perdition, damnation, eternal damnation; universal ruin; wreck wrack [dial]; wrack and ruin; devastation ravage, havoc, holocaust, hecatomb, carnage, shambles, slaughter, bloodbath desolation; waste, consumption; decimation; dissolution, disintegration, breakup disruption, disorganization, undoing, lysis; vandalism, depredation, spoliation despoliation, despoilment; the road to ruin.

.2 end, fate, doom, death, death knell bane, deathblow, coup de grâce [Fr], quietus.

.3 fall, downfall, prostration; overthrow overturn, upset, upheaval, boulevers *ment* [Fr]; convulsion, **subversion,** sabotage.

.4 **debacle, disaster, cataclysm, catastrophe; breakup,** breaking up; **breakdown, collapse; crash,** smash, **smashup,** crack-up [informal]; **wreck,** wrack, shipwreck; cave-in, cave; washout; total loss.

.5 **demolition,** demolishment; **wrecking,** wreckage, leveling, razing, flattening, smashing, tearing down, bringing to the ground; **dismantlement,** disassembly, unmaking.

.6 **extinction, extermination, elimination, eradication,.** extirpation; rooting out, deracination, uprooting, tearing up root and branch; **annihilation,** extinguishment, **snuffing out; abolition,** abolishment; annulment, **nullification,** voiding, **negation; liquidation, purge; suppression;** choking, choking off, suffocation, stifling, strangulation; silencing.

.7 **obliteration, erasure, effacement,** expunction, blot [archaic], blotting, **blotting out, wiping out;** washing out, scrubbing [informal], cancellation, cancel; deletion.

.8 **destroyer, wrecker,** demolisher, –clast; **vandal,** hun; exterminator, annihilator; **iconoclast,** idoloclast, idol breaker; biblioclast; nihilist; terrorist, syndicalist; **bomber,** dynamiter, dynamitard; burner, arsonist.

.9 **eradicator,** expunger; **eraser,** rubber, India rubber, sponge.

.10 VERBS **destroy,** deal *or* unleash destruction, unleash the hurricane; **ruin,** ruinate [dial], bring to ruin, lay in ruins; throw into disorder, upheave; **wreck,** wrack, shipwreck; damn, seal the doom of, **condemn,** confound; **devastate, desolate,** waste, **lay waste, ravage,** havoc, wreak havoc, despoil, depredate; vandalize; **decimate;** devour, consume, engorge, gobble, gobble up, swallow up; gut, gut with fire, incinerate, vaporize, ravage with fire and sword; dissolve, lyse.

.11 **do for, fix** [informal], settle, sink, cook [informal], cook one's goose, dish, scuttle, put the kibosh on [slang], do in, **undo,** knock in *or* on the head, torpedo, knock out, KO [slang], deal a knockout blow to, shoot down *or* shoot down in flames [both informal]; break the back of; make short work of; **defeat** 727.6.

.12 **put an end to,** make an end of, **end, finish,** finish off [informal], put paid to [Brit], give the *coup de grâce* to, give the quietus to, deal a deathblow to, dispose of, get rid of, do away with; cut off, take off, be the death of, sound the death knell of; put out of the way, put out of existence, **slaughter,** make away with, kill 409.13; nip, nip in the bud *or* head; cut short.

.13 **abolish, nullify,** void, abrogate, annihilate, annul, repeal, revoke, negate, negative, invalidate, **undo, cancel,** bring to naught.

.14 **exterminate, eliminate, eradicate,** deracinate, **extirpate, annihilate; wipe out** [informal]; cut out, root up *or* out, uproot, pull *or* pluck up by the roots, cut up root and branch, strike at the root of, lay the ax to the root of; **liquidate, purge;** remove, sweep away.

.15 **extinguish, quench, snuff out,** put out, stamp *or* trample out, trample underfoot; **smother,** choke, stifle, strangle, suffocate; silence; **suppress, quash,** squash *or* squelch [both informal], **quell,** put down.

.16 **obliterate, expunge, efface, erase,** raze [archaic], blot, sponge, **wipe out,** wipe off the map, rub out, **blot out,** sponge out; cancel, strike out, cross out, scratch, scratch out, rule out; delete, dele.

.17 **demolish, wreck,** total *or* wrack up [both slang], undo, unbuild, unmake, **dismantle, disassemble; take apart, tear apart, rend, take** *or* **pull** *or* **pick** *or* **tear to pieces,** pull in pieces, tear to shreds *or* rags *or* tatters; sunder, cleave, **split; disintegrate, fragment,** break to pieces, make mincemeat of, reduce to rubble, atomize, pulverize, **smash,** shatter 49.13.

.18 **blow up,** blast, spring, blow to pieces *or* bits, bomb, bombard, blitz; mine.

.19 **raze,** rase, **fell, level,** flatten, smash, prostrate, raze to the ground *or* dust; steamroller, bulldoze; **pull down, tear down, take down,** bring down, bring down about one's ears, bring tumbling *or* crashing down, break down, throw down, cast down, beat down, knock down *or* over; cut down, chop down, mow down; blow down; burn down.

.20 **overthrow, overturn; upset,** overset, upend, **subvert,** throw down *or* over; undermine, honeycomb, sap, sap the foundations, **weaken.**

.21 **overwhelm,** whelm, swamp, engulf; inundate.

.22 (be destroyed) **fall,** fall to the ground, tumble, come tumbling *or* crashing down, topple, tremble *or* nod to its fall, bite the dust [informal]; **break up,** crumble, crumble to dust, disintegrate, go *or* fall to pieces; go by the board, go out the window, go up the spout [informal].

.23 perish, expire, succumb, die, cease, end, come to an end, go, pass, pass away, vanish, disappear, fade away, run out, peg or conk out [slang], come to nothing or naught, be no more, be done for; be all over with, be all up with [informal].

.24 go to ruin, go to wrack and ruin, go to rack and manger [archaic], go to the bad, go wrong, go to the dogs or go to pot [both informal], go to the deuce or devil [informal], go to hell [slang], go to the wall, go to perdition or glory [informal]; go up [informal], go under; go to smash, go to shivers, go to smithereens [informal].

.25 drive to ruin, drive to the bad, force to the wall, drive to the dogs [informal], hound or harry to destruction.

.26 ADJS destructive, destroying, –clastic, ant(i)– or anth–; ruinous, ruining; demolishing, demolitionary; disastrous, calamitous, cataclysmic, cataclysmal, catastrophic; fatal, fateful, doomful, baneful; deadly 409.23; consumptive, consuming, withering; devastating, desolating, ravaging, wasting, wasteful, spoliative, depredatory; vandalic, vandalish, vandalistic; subversive, subversionary; nihilist, nihilistic; suicidal, self-destructive; fratricidal, internecine, internecive.

.27 exterminative, exterminatory, annihilative, eradicative, extirpative, extirpatory; all-destroying, all-devouring, all-consuming.

.28 ruined, destroyed, wrecked, blasted, undone, done for [informal], done in [informal], finished, ausgespielt [Ger], kaput [slang]; down-and-out, broken, bankrupt; spoiled 692.30; irremediable 889.15; fallen, overthrown; devastated, desolated, ravaged, blighted, wasted; ruinous, in ruins; gone to wrack and ruin, gone to pot or gone to the dogs [both informal].

## 694. RESTORATION

.1 NOUNS restoration, restitution, reestablishment, reinstatement, reinstation, reformation [archaic], reinvestment, reinvestiture, instauration, reversion, reinstitution, reconstitution, replacement, rehabilitation, redintegration [archaic], reconversion, reactivation, reenactment; improvement 691.

.2 reclamation, recovery, retrieval, redemption, salvation, salvage.

.3 revival, revivification, revivescence or re-

vivescency, renewal, resurrection, resuscitation, reanimation, resurgence, recrudescence; refreshment 695; second wind; renaissance [Fr], renascence, rebirth, new birth; rejuvenation, rejuvenescence, second youth, new lease on life; regeneration, regeneracy, regenerateness; regenesis, palingenesis, palingenesy.

.4 renovation, renewal; refreshment, reconditioning, furbishment, refurbishment; retread or retreading [both informal]; face-lifting or face-lift; slum clearance, urban renewal.

.5 reconstruction, re-creation, remaking, remodeling, rebuilding, refabrication, refashioning; reassembling, reassembly; reformation.

.6 reparation, repair, repairing, fixing, mending; overhaul, overhauling; troubleshooting [informal]; rectification, correction, remedy; redress, making right, amends, satisfaction, compensation, recompense.

.7 cure, curing, healing, remedy 687; therapy 689.

.8 recovery, rally, comeback [informal], return; recuperation, convalescence.

.9 restorability, reparability, curability, recoverability, reversibility, remediability, retrievability, redeemability, corrigibility.

.10 mender, fixer, doctor [informal], restorer, renovator, repairer, repairman, maintenance man, serviceman; trouble man or troubleshooter [both informal]; Mr. Fixit or little Miss Fixit [both informal]; mechanic or mechanician; tinker; cobbler.

.11 VERBS restore, put back, replace, return, place in statu quo ante; reestablish, reform [archaic], reinstate, reenact, reinstall, reinvest, revest, reinstitute, reconstitute, recruit, rehabilitate, reintegrate, reconvert, reactivate; refill, replenish; give back 823.4.

.12 redeem, reclaim, recover, retrieve; ransom; rescue; salvage, recycle; win back, recoup.

.13 remedy, rectify, correct, right, emend, amend, redress, make good or right, put right, set right, put or set to rights, put straight, set straight, set up, make all square; pay reparations, give satisfaction, requite, recompense, compensate, remunerate.

.14 repair, mend, fix, fix up [informal], do up, doctor [informal], put in repair, put in shape, set to rights, put in order or condition; condition, recondition, commission, put in commission, ready; service, overhaul; patch, patch up; tinker

tinker up; cobble; sew up, darn; recap, re-tread.

.15 **cure**, work a cure, recure [archaic], **remedy, heal, restore to health,** bring round *or* around, pull round *or* around, give a new *or* fresh lease on life, make better, make well, fix up, pull through, set on one's feet *or* legs; snatch from the jaws of death.

.16 **revive**, revivify, **renew, recruit; reanimate,** reinspire, **regenerate, rejuvenate, revitalize,** put *or* breathe new life into; **refresh** 695.2; **resuscitate,** bring to; recharge; **resurrect,** bring back, call back, recall to life, raise from the dead; rewarm, warm up *or* over; **rekindle,** relight, reheat the ashes, stir the embers.

.17 **renovate, renew; recondition,** refit, revamp, furbish, refurbish; refresh, face-lift.

.18 **remake,** reconstruct, remodel, re-create, **rebuild,** refabricate, re-form, refashion, reassemble.

.19 **recuperate,** recruit, **gain strength,** recruit *or* renew one's strength, **get better; improve** 691.7; **rally, pick up,** perk up *or* brace up [both informal], take a new *or* fresh lease on life; **take a favorable turn,** turn the corner, be out of the woods, take a turn for the better; **convalesce;** sleep it off.

.20 **recover, rally, revive, get well, get over, pull through,** pull round *or* around, come round *or* around [informal], come back [informal], make a comeback [informal]; get about, get back in shape [informal], be oneself again; **survive,** weather the storm; **come to,** come to oneself, show signs of life; come up smiling, bounce back [both informal]; come *or* pull *or* snap out of it [informal].

.21 **heal,** heal over, close up, scab over, cicatrize, granulate; heal *or* right itself; **knit, set.**

.22 ADJS **restorative, restitutive,** restitutory, analeptic; **reparative,** reparatory; **remedial, curative** 687.39.

.23 **recuperative,** recuperatory; **reviviscent; convalescent;** buoyant, resilient, elastic.

.24 **renascent,** *redivivus* [L], resurrected, renewed, revived, reborn, resurgent, recrudescent, reappearing.

.25 **remediable, curable,** medicable; **emendable,** amendable, **correctable,** rectifiable, corrigible; **improvable,** ameliorable; **reparable,** repairable, **mendable, fixable;** restorable, recoverable, retrievable, reversible, reclaimable, recyclable, redeemable.

## 695. REFRESHMENT

.1 NOUNS **refreshment,** refection, refreshing, **bracing, exhilaration, stimulation,** enlivenment, vivification, **invigoration,** reinvigoration, reanimation, revival, revivification, revivescence *or* revivescency, renewal, recreation; regalement, regale; tonic, bracer, pick-me-up [informal], cordial.

.2 VERBS **refresh, freshen,** refreshen, freshen up, fresh up [informal]; **revive,** revivify, **reinvigorate,** reanimate; **exhilarate, stimulate, invigorate,** fortify, enliven, animate, vivify, quicken, brisk, brisken; brace, **brace up,** buck up *or* pick up [both informal], perk up *or* chirk up [both informal], set up, set on one's legs *or* feet [informal]; renew one's strength, put *or* breathe new life into; renew, recreate; **regale, cheer,** refresh the inner man.

.3 ADJS **refreshing,** refreshful, **fresh,** brisk, crisp, crispy, zesty, zestful, **bracing, tonic,** cordial, **exhilarating, stimulating, invigorating,** rousing, energizing; regaling, cheering.

.4 **refreshed, invigorated, exhilarated,** stimulated, energized, recharged, animated, reanimated, **revived,** renewed, recreated.

.5 **unwearied, untired, unfatigued, unexhausted.**

## 696. RELAPSE

.1 NOUNS **relapse, lapse,** falling back; **reversion, regression** 146.1; **reverse, reversal,** backward deviation, **setback,** backset; **return,** recurrence, renewal, recrudescence; throwback, atavism.

.2 **backsliding,** backslide; **fall, fall from grace;** recidivism, recidivation; apostasy 628.2.

.3 **backslider,** recidivist, reversionist; apostate 628.5.

.4 VERBS **relapse, lapse, backslide,** slide back, lapse back, **slip back,** sink back, **fall back,** have a relapse, **return to, revert to,** recur to, yield again to, fall again into, recidivate; revert, **regress** 146.4; **fall, fall from grace.**

.5 ADJS **relapsing, lapsing, backsliding,** recidivous; recrudescent; **regressive** 146.7; apostate 628.11.

## 697. DANGER

.1 NOUNS **danger, peril, jeopardy, hazard, risk; endangerment, imperilment;** cause for alarm, **menace, threat** 973; **crisis, emergency,** pass, pinch, strait, plight, predicament 731.4; rocks or breakers ahead, gathering clouds, storm clouds; dangerous ground, yawning or gaping chasm, quicksand, thin ice; house of cards, cardhouse.

.2 **dangerousness, hazardousness, riskiness,** chanciness [informal], diceyness [Brit informal], **perilousness; unsafeness,** unhealthiness [informal]; criticalness; **precariousness, ticklishness,** slipperiness, touchiness, delicacy, ticklish business [informal]; **insecurity,** unsoundness, instability, unsteadiness, shakiness, totteriness; sword of Damocles; **unreliability,** undependability, untrustworthiness 514.6; **unsureness,** unpredictability, **uncertainty,** doubtfulness, dubiousness 514.1,2.

.3 **exposure, openness,** liability, nonimmunity, susceptibility; **unprotectedness, defenselessness,** nakedness, helplessness.

.4 **vulnerability, pregnability,** penetrability, assailability, vincibility; weakness 160; vulnerable point, **weak link, weak point, soft spot,** heel of Achilles, chink, chink in one's armor, "the soft underbelly of Europe" [Sir Winston Churchill].

.5 (hidden danger) snags, rocks, reefs, ledges; coral heads; shallows, shoals; sandbank, sandbar, sands; quicksands; rockbound or ironbound coast, lee shore; undertow, undercurrent; **pitfall** 618.11; snake in the grass.

.6 VERBS **endanger, imperil,** peril, periclitate; **risk, hazard, gamble, gamble with; jeopardize,** jeopard, jeopardy, compromise, put in danger, **put in jeopardy,** put on the spot or lay on the line [both slang]; **expose,** lay open; incur danger, run into or encounter danger.

.7 **take chances, take a chance, chance, risk, gamble,** hazard, **run the chance or risk or hazard;** go out on a limb [informal], expose oneself, lower one's guard, **lay oneself open to,** open the door to; **tempt Providence,** forget the odds, **defy danger,** skate on thin ice, court destruction, dance on the razor's edge, go in harm's way, stand or sleep on a volcano, sit on a barrel of gunpowder, build a house of cards, put one's head in the lion's mouth, "beard the lion in his den" [Sir Walter Scott], march up to the cannon's mouth, play with fire, go through fire and water, go out of one's depth, go to sea in a sieve, carry too much sail, sail too near the wind; risk one's life, **take one's life in one's hand, dare, face up to, brave** 893.10, 11.

.8 **be in danger,** be in peril, be in extremis, be in desperate case, have one's name on the danger list, have the chances or odds against one; be despaired of; hang by a thread; tremble on the verge, totter on the brink; feel the ground sliding from under one; have to run for it; be threatened, be on the spot [informal].

.9 ADJS **dangerous,** dangersome [dial], **perilous,** periculous, parlous, jeopardous, bad, ugly, serious, critical, explosive, attended or beset or fraught with danger; alarming, **menacing, threatening** 973.3.

.10 **hazardous, risky, chancy** [informal], dicey [Brit informal], aleatory, riskful, full of risk; **adventurous,** venturous, venturesome; **speculative,** wildcat.

.11 **unsafe,** unhealthy [informal]; **unreliable, undependable, untrustworthy,** treacherous, **insecure, unsound,** unstable, unsteady, shaky, tottery, rocky; **unsure, uncertain,** unpredictable, doubtful, dubious 514.15,16.

.12 **precarious, ticklish, touchy,** touch-and-go, **critical, delicate;** slippery, slippy; on thin ice, on slippery ground; hanging by a thread, trembling in the balance.

.13 **in danger, in jeopardy, in peril,** in a bad way; **endangered, imperiled, jeopardized;** at the last extremity, in extremis [L], in desperate case; threatened, on the spot [informal]; between the hammer and the anvil, between Scylla and Charybdis, between two fires, between the devil and the deep blue sea; in a predicament 731.20; cornered 731.23.

.14 **unprotected, unshielded, unsheltered,** uncovered, unscreened, **unguarded,** unde fended, unattended, unwatched, unforti fied; unarmored, **unarmed,** bare-handed, weaponless, anopl(o)–; guardless, ungarri soned, **defenseless, helpless;** unwarned, unsuspecting.

.15 **exposed, open,** out in the open, nake out on a limb [informal]; liable, suscept ble, nonimmune.

.16 **vulnerable, pregnable,** penetrable, e pugnable; assailable, attackable, su mountable; conquerable, beatable [info mal], vincible; weak 160.12–17.

.17 ADVS **dangerously, perilously,** hazar ously, **riskily,** critically, unsafely; preca ously, ticklishly.

## 698. SAFETY

.1 NOUNS **safety, safeness, security,** sure [archaic], assurance; risklessness, imm nity, clear sailing; **protection,** safegua

699.3; harmlessness 674.9; invulnerability 159.4.

.2 VERBS **be safe, be on the safe side; keep safe, come through;** weather, ride out, weather the storm; keep one's head above water, tide over; land on one's feet; save one's bacon [informal], save one's neck; lead a charmed life, possess nine lives.

.3 **play safe** [informal], **keep on the safe side,** give danger a wide berth, take precautions 895.6; assure oneself, make sure, look before one leaps; **save** 701.7, **protect** 699.18.

.4 ADJS **safe, secure, safe and sound;** immune, immunized; insured; **protected** 699.21; on the safe side; unthreatened, unmolested; unhurt, unharmed, unscathed, intact, untouched, with a whole skin, undamaged.

.5 **unhazardous, undangerous, unperilous, unrisky,** riskless, **unprecarious;** fail-safe; guaranteed, warranteed; dependable, reliable, trustworthy, sound, stable, steady, firm 513.17; "founded upon a rock" [Bible]; as safe as houses; harmless 674.20; invulnerable 159.17.

.6 **in safety, out of danger,** past danger, out of the meshes *or* toils, home free [informal], **in the clear, out of harm's reach** *or* **way;** under cover, under lock and key; in shelter, in harbor *or* port, at anchor *or* haven, in the shadow of a rock; on sure *or* solid ground, on *terra firma,* high and dry, above water.

.7 snug, cozy; airworthy, seaworthy, seakindly.

.8 ADVS **safely, securely,** reliably, dependably; with safety, **with impunity.**

.9 INTERJS **all's well!,** all clear!, all serene!; ally-ally out'n free!

.10 PHRS the danger is past, the storm has blown over, the coast is clear.

## 699. PROTECTION

.1 NOUNS **protection, guard, safekeeping; eye,** watchful eye; protective custody; safety 698; **shelter, cover,** shade, shadow [archaic], lee; **refuge** 700; preservation 701; **defense** 799.

.2 **protectorship, guardianship,** stewardship, custodianship; **care, charge, keeping, custody; hands,** safe hands, wing; **auspices, patronage, tutelage, guidance; ward,** wardship, wardenship, watch and ward; cure, pastorship, pastorage, pastorate; **oversight,** jurisdiction, management, min-

istry, administration, government, governance.

.3 **safeguard,** palladium, **guard; shield,** scut(i)–, aspid(o)–, –aspis; **screen,** aegis; umbrella, protective umbrella; patent, copyright; **bulwark** 799.4; backstop; **fender,** mudguard, **bumper, buffer, cushion,** pad, padding; seat belt; protective clothing; shin guard, knuckle guard, knee guard, nose guard, hand guard, arm guard, ear guard, finger guard, foot guard; goggles, mask, face mask, welder's mask, fencer's mask; safety shoes; helmet, hard hat [informal], crash helmet, sun helmet; cowcatcher, pilot; dashboard; windshield, windscreen [Brit], dodger; life preserver 701.5; lifeline, safety rail, guardrail, handrail; governor; safety, safety switch, interlock; safety valve, safety plug; fuse, circuit breaker; insulation; safety glass, laminated glass; lightning rod, lightning conductor; prophylactic, preventive 687.20; contraceptive 687.23.

.4 **insurance,** assurance [Brit]; group insurance, fraternal insurance; reciprocal insurance, interinsurance; term insurance; reinsurance; straight *or* ordinary life insurance, limited payment insurance, endowment insurance, family income policy, family maintenance policy, retirement income insurance, joint life insurance, industrial life insurance, group life insurance, business life insurance, savings bank life insurance, credit life insurance; **casualty insurance; health insurance,** hospitalization insurance, hospital service contract, major medical insurance, disability insurance, accident insurance, workmen's compensation insurance; **automobile insurance,** collision insurance; nofault insurance; aviation insurance; fire insurance, flood insurance; burglary insurance, theft insurance, robbery insurance, fidelity insurance, fidelity bond, forgery bond; credit insurance; bond, surety bond, license bond, permit bond, customs bond, bail bond, court bond; business interruption insurance; title insurance; liability insurance, public liability insurance, automobile liability insurance, malpractice insurance; marine insurance, ocean marine insurance, inland marine insurance; **annuity,** variable annuity; government insurance, **social security** 745.7; **insurance company,** stock company, mutual company; **insurance policy, policy, certificate of insurance; deductible; insurance man, underwriter, insurance broker, insurance agent, insurance adjuster, actuary.

.5 **protector**, protectress, safekeeper; **patron**, patroness; tower, pillar, tower of strength, rock; champion, **defender** 799.7.

.6 **guardian, warden**, governor; **custodian**, steward, **keeper, caretaker**, warder [Brit], attendant; next friend, prochein ami, guardian *ad litem*; **curator**, conservator; janitor; castellan; **shepherd**; game warden, gamekeeper; ranger, forest ranger; lifeguard, lifesaver [Brit]; air warden; guardian angel 1014.22.

.7 **chaperon**, duenna; **governess**.

.8 **nurse**, nursemaid, nurserymaid, nanny [informal], amah, ayah [India], mammy [dial]; dry nurse, wet nurse; **baby-sitter**, sitter [informal].

.9 **guard**, guarder, guardsman [archaic], warder; **outguard, outpost; picket**, outlying picket, inlying picket; advance guard, **vanguard**, van; **rear guard**; coast guard; armed guard, security guard; jailer 761.10; bank guard; railway *or* train guard; goalkeeper, goaltender, goalie [informal]; **garrison**; cordon, *cordon sanitaire* [Fr].

.10 **watchman, watch**, watcher, watchkeeper; **lookout**, lookout man; **sentinel**, picket, **sentry; scout**, vedette; forward observer, spotter; **patrol, patrolman**, patroller, roundsman; night watchman, Charley [slang]; fireguard, fire patrolman, fire warden; airplane spotter; Argus.

.11 **watchdog**, bandog, guard dog; Cerberus.

.12 **doorkeeper, doorman, gatekeeper**, cerberus, warden, **porter, janitor**, *concierge* [Fr], ostiary, usher; receptionist.

.13 **picket**, picketer, demonstrator; picket line.

.14 **bodyguard**, safeguard; **convoy, escort**; guards, praetorian guard; guardsman; yeoman *or* yeoman of the guard *or* beefeater, gentleman-at-arms, Life Guardsman [all England].

.15 **policeman, constable**, officer, **police officer**, *flic* [Fr slang], *gendarme* [Fr], *carabiniere* [Ital]; peace officer, law enforcement agent, arm of the law; military policeman, MP; detective 781.10; policewoman, police matron; patrolman, police constable [England]; trooper, mounted policeman; reeve, portreeve; **sheriff, marshal**; deputy sheriff, deputy, bound bailiff, catchpole, beagle [slang], bombailiff [Brit slang]; sergeant, police sergeant; roundsman; lieutenant, police lieutenant; captain, police captain; inspector, police inspector; superintendent,

chief of police; commissioner, police commissioner; government man, federal, fed *or* G-man [both informal]; narc [slang]; **bailiff**, tipstaff, tipstaves [pl]; mace-bearer, lictor, sergeant at arms; beadle.

.16 [slang *or* informal terms] cop, copper, John Law, bluecoat, bull, flatfoot, gumshoe, gendarme, shamus, dick, flattie, bobby *or* peeler [both Brit], pig, Dogberry; the cops, the law, the fuzz; New York's finest.

.17 **police, police force**, law enforcement agency; **constabulary**; state police, troopers, highway patrol, county police, provincial police; security force; special police; tactical police, riot police; **posse**, *posse comitatus* [L]; **vigilantes**, vigilance committee; secret police, political police; FBI, Federal Bureau of Investigation; military police, MP; shore patrol, SP; Scotland Yard [England]; Sûreté [France]; Cheka, NKVD, MVD, OGPU [all USSR]; Gestapo [Germany]; Royal Canadian Mounted Police, RCMP, Mounties [all Canada]; Interpol, International Criminal Police Commission.

.18 VERBS **protect, guard, safeguard, secure, keep**, bless, make safe, police; keep from harm; **insure**, underwrite; ensure, guarantee 772.9; patent, copyright, register; **cushion**; champion, go to bat for [slang], ride shotgun for [informal], fend, defend 799.8; **shelter, shield, screen, cover**, cloak, shroud [archaic]; **harbor, haven**; nestle; compass about, fence; arm, armor.

.19 **care for, take care of**; preserve, conserve; provide for, support; take charge of, **take under one's wing**, make one a *protégé*; **look after**, see after, **attend to, minister to**, look *or* see to, look *or* watch out for [informal], keep an eye on *or* upon, keep a sharp eye on *or* upon, **watch over**, keep watch over, **watch, mind, tend**; keep tab *or* tabs on [informal]; **shepherd**, ride herd on [slang]; **chaperon**, matronize; baby-sit [informal]; **foster, nurture, cherish, nurse**; **mother**, be a mother *or* father to.

.20 **watch, keep watch, keep guard, keep vigil**, keep watch and ward; stand guard, stand sentinel; be on the lookout 533.8; mount guard; **police, patrol**, go on one's beat.

.21 ADJS **protected, guarded**, safeguarded, defended; safe 698.4–7; patented, copyrighted; **sheltered, shielded**, screened, covered, cloaked; policed; armed 799.14; invulnerable 159.17,18.

.22 **under the protection of,** under the shield of, under the aegis of, **under one's wing,** under the wing of, under the shadow of one's wing.

.23 **protective, custodial,** guardian, tutelary; vigilant, watchful; prophylactic, preventive; immunizing; protecting, guarding, safeguarding, sheltering, **shielding,** screening, covering; fostering, parental; defensive 799.11.

## 700. REFUGE

.1 NOUNS **refuge, sanctuary,** safehold, **asylum, haven, port,** harborage, **harbor;** harbor of refuge, port in a storm, snug harbor, safe haven; game sanctuary, bird sanctuary, preserve, forest preserve, game preserve; stronghold 799.6.

.2 **recourse, resource, resort;** last resort or resource, *dernier ressort, pis aller* [both Fr]; **hope; expedient** 670.2.

.3 **shelter, cover, covert,** coverture; concealment 615; *abri* [Fr], dugout, cave, earth, funk hole [informal], foxhole; bunker; trench; storm cellar, storm cave, cyclone cellar; air-raid shelter, bomb shelter, bombproof, fallout shelter, safety zone or isle or island.

.4 **asylum, home,** retreat; **poorhouse,** almshouse, workhouse [Brit], poor farm; **orphanage; hospice,** hospitium; old folks' home, rest home, nursing home, old soldiers' home, sailors' snug harbor; foster home; halfway house.

.5 **retreat,** recess, hiding place, **hideaway,** hideout; **sanctum, sanctum sanctorum,** holy of holies, adytum; privacy [archaic], secret place; **den,** lair, mew; **cloister,** hermitage, ashram, cell; **ivory tower.**

.6 **harbor, haven, port, seaport;** harborage, **anchorage,** anchorage ground, protected anchorage, moorings; **roadstead,** road, roads; berth, slip; **dock,** dockage, marina, basin; dry dock; shipyard, dockyard; **wharf, pier,** quay; landing, landing place or stage, jetty, jutty [archaic]; breakwater, mole, groin; seawall, embankment, bulkhead.

.7 VERBS **take refuge, take shelter,** seek refuge, **claim sanctuary,** run into port; fly to, throw oneself into the arms of; bar the gate, lock or bolt the door, raise the drawbridge, let the portcullis down; take cover 615.8.

.8 **find refuge** or sanctuary, make port, reach safety.

## 701. PRESERVATION

.1 NOUNS **preservation,** preserval, **conservation,** conservancy, **saving, salvation,** salvage, **keeping, safekeeping,** maintenance, upkeep, support; protection 699; conservationism, environmental conservation; soil conservation, forest conservation, forest management, wildlife conservation, stream conservation, water conservation, wetlands conservation.

.2 (means of preservation) **curing,** seasoning, salting, brining, pickling, marination, corning; **drying,** dry-curing, jerking; dehydration, anhydration, evaporation, desiccation; **smoking,** fuming, smoke-curing, kippering; **refrigeration,** freezing, quick-freezing, blast-freezing; freeze-drying, lyophilization; irradiation; **embalming,** mummification; taxidermy, stuffing; **canning,** tinning [Brit]; bottling, potting.

.3 **preservative,** preservative medium; salt, brine, vinegar, formaldehyde, Formalin, embalming fluid.

.4 **preserver,** saver, conservator, keeper, safekeeper; taxidermist; lifesaver, rescuer, deliverer, savior; **conservationist,** preservationist; National Wildlife Service, Audubon Society, Sierra Club; ranger, forest ranger, game warden.

.5 **life preserver,** life jacket, life vest, life belt, cork jacket, Mae West [informal]; life buoy, life ring, buoy; water wings; breeches buoy; lifeboat, life raft, rubber dinghy [Brit]; life net; lifeline; safety belt; **parachute,** ejection seat or ejector seat, ejection capsule.

.6 (place set apart for conservation) **preserve, reserve, reservation; park,** paradise; national park; forest preserve or reserve; national or state forest; wilderness preserve; Indian reservation; game reserve, bird sanctuary, wildlife preserve, **sanctuary** 700.1; museum, library, archives, bank, store 660.

.7 VERBS **preserve, conserve, save,** spare; **keep,** keep safe, keep inviolate or intact; patent, copyright, register; not endanger, not destroy; not use up, not waste, not expend; **guard, protect** 699.18; **maintain, sustain,** uphold, support, **keep up,** keep alive.

.8 (preserve from decay) preservatize; **cure,** season, salt, brine, marinate or marinade, pickle, corn, **dry, dry-cure,** jerk, dry-salt; dehydrate, anhydrate, evaporate, desiccate; **smoke,** fume, **smoke-cure,** smoke-dry, kipper; **refrigerate,** freeze, quick-freeze, blast-freeze; freeze-dry, lyophilize; irradiate; **embalm,** mummify; stuff.

.9 **put up,** do up; **can,** tin [Brit]; bottle, jar, pot.

.10 ADJS **preservative,** preservatory, conservative, conservatory; **conservational,** conservationist; preserving, conserving, saving, keeping; **protective** 699.23.

.11 **preserved,** conserved, **kept,** saved, spared; protected 699.21; **untainted, unspoiled;** intact, undamaged 677.7,8; **well-preserved,** well-conserved, **well-kept,** in a good state of preservation.

## 702. RESCUE

.1 NOUNS **rescue, deliverance,** delivery, **saving;** lifesaving; **extrication, release, freeing, liberation** 763; **salvation,** salvage, redemption, ransom; **recovery, retrieval.**

.2 **rescuer,** lifesaver, lifeguard; coast guard, lifesaving service, air-sea rescue; savior 942.2; lifeboat.

.3 VERBS **rescue,** come to the rescue, **deliver, save,** be the saving of, **redeem,** ransom, **salvage; recover,** retrieve 823.6; **free,** set free, **release, extricate,** extract, **liberate** 763.4–6; snatch from the jaws of death; save one's bacon *or* save one's neck *or* bail one out [all informal].

.4 ADJS **rescuable, savable;** redeemable; deliverable, extricable.

## 703. WARNING

.1 NOUNS **warning, caution, caveat, admonition,** monition, admonishment; **notice,** notification; **word to the wise,** *verbum sapienti* [L], verb. sap.; flea in one's ear [informal]; hint, tip-off [informal]; **lesson,** object lesson, **example,** deterrent example, warning piece; moral, moral of the story; **alarm** 704; final warning *or* notice, ultimatum; **threat** 973.

.2 **forewarning, prewarning, premonition,** precautioning; advance notice, plenty of notice, prenotification, prenotice; presentiment, **foreboding** 544; portent, "warnings, and portents and evils imminent" [Shakespeare].

.3 **warning sign, premonitory sign, danger sign;** preliminary sign *or* signal; **symptom,** early symptom, premonitory symptom, prodrome, prodroma, prodromata [pl]; **precursor** 66; omen 544.3,6; **handwriting on the wall,** *"mene, mene, tekel, upharsin"* [Aramaic; Bible]; straw in the wind; gathering clouds, clouds on the horizon; thundercloud, thunderhead; falling barometer *or* glass; storm *or* stormy petrel,

Mother Carey's chicken; **red light,** red flag; quarantine flag, yellow flag, yellow jack; death's-head, skull and crossbones; **high sign** [slang], **warning signal.**

.4 **warner,** cautioner, admonisher, monitor; prophet of doom, Cassandra, Jeremiah; **lookout, lookout man; sentinel, sentry; signalman,** signaler, flagman; lighthouse keeper.

.5 VERBS **warn, caution, advise, admonish; give warning,** give fair warning, utter a caveat, address a warning to, put a flea in one's ear [informal], say a word to the wise; tip *or* tip off [both informal]; notify, give notice, tell once and for all; issue an ultimatum; **threaten** 973.2; **alert,** warn against, put on one's guard; **give the high sign** [slang]; cry havoc, sound the alarm 704.3.

.6 **forewarn,** prewarn, precaution, premonish; prenotify, tell in advance, give advance notice; **portend, forebode** 544.10.

.7 ADJS **warning,** cautioning, **cautionary; monitory,** monitorial, admonitory, admonishing; notifying, notificational; exemplary, deterrent.

.8 **forewarning, premonitory; portentous,** foreboding 544.17; **precautionary,** precautional; precursive, precursory, forerunning, prodromal, prodromic.

## 704. ALARM

.1 NOUNS **alarm,** alarum, alarm signal, **alert;** hue and cry; note of alarm; air-raid alarm; all clear; tocsin, alarm bell; signal of distress, SOS, Mayday, upside-down flag; fiery cross, crostarie; storm warning, storm flag *or* pennant *or* cone, hurricane warning, gale warning, small-craft warning; fog signal *or* alarm, foghorn, fog bell; burglar alarm; fire alarm, fire bell, fire flag, still alarm; siren, whistle, horn, Klaxon; hooter [Brit], buzzer; police whistle, watchman's rattle; alarm clock; five-minute gun, two-minute gun; lighthouse, beacon; blinking light, flashing light, occulting light.

.2 **false alarm,** cry of wolf; bugbear, bugaboo; bogy; flash in the pan, dud [informal].

.3 VERBS **alarm, alert, arouse,** put on the alert; **warn** 703.5; fly storm warnings; **sound the alarm,** give *or* raise *or* beat o[...] turn in an alarm, ring *or* sound the toc[...] sin, cry havoc, raise a hue and cry; give [...] false alarm, **cry wolf; frighten** 891.23, star[...] tle 540.8.

.4 ADJS alarmed, aroused; alerted; frightened 891.33; startled 540.13.

## 705. ACTION

*(voluntary action)*

.1 NOUNS action, act, acting, doing, –ade, –esis, –ice, –y; not words but action; practice, praxis, –praxia; exercise; operation, working, function, functioning; operations; workings, movements; employment, work, occupation; swing, play; activism; activity 707; behavior 737.

.2 performance, execution, enactment; transaction; discharge, dispatch; conduct, handling, management, administration [archaic]; achievement, accomplishment, effectuation, implementation; commission, perpetration; completion 722.2.

.3 act, action, deed, doing, thing, thing done; turn; feat, stunt [informal], *tour de force* [Fr], exploit, adventure, gest, enterprise, achievement, accomplishment, performance, production; effort, endeavor, job, undertaking; transaction, passage; operation, proceeding, step, measure, maneuver, move; coup, stroke; blow, go [informal]; accomplished fact, *fait accompli* [Fr]; overt act [law]; *acta, res gestae* [both L], doings, dealings; works; work, handiwork, hand.

.4 VERBS act, serve, function; operate, work, practice, do one's stuff [slang]; do one's thing [slang]; move, proceed; make, play, behave 737.4.

.5 take action, take steps *or* measures; proceed, proceed with; do something, do something about, act on *or* upon, get with it [slang]; go; lift a finger, take *or* bear a hand; play a role *or* part in; stretch forth one's hand, strike a blow; maneuver.

.6 do, effect, effectuate, make; bring about, bring to pass, bring off, produce, achieve, accomplish, realize 722.4,5; render, pay; inflict, wreak, do to; commit, perpetrate; pull off [informal]; go and do, up and do *or* take and do [both dial].

.7 practice, exercise, employ, use; carry on, conduct, prosecute, wage; follow, pursue; engage in, work at, devote oneself to, do, apply oneself to, employ oneself in; take up, take to, undertake, tackle, take on, address oneself to, have a go at, turn one's hand to, go in *or* out for [informal], make it one's business, follow as an occupation; specialize in 81.4.

.8 perform, execute, enact; transact; discharge, dispatch; conduct, manage, handle; dispose of, take care of, deal with, cope with; make, accomplish, complete 722.4–6.

.9 carry out, carry through, go through, fulfill, work out; bring off, carry off; put through, get through; implement; put into effect, put in *or* into practice, carry into effect, carry into execution, translate into action; suit the action to the word; rise to the occasion, come through [informal].

.10 ADJS acting, performing, practicing, serving, functioning, functional, operating, operational, working; in action 164.11; behavioral 737.7.

## 706. INACTION

*(voluntary inaction)*

.1 NOUNS inaction, passiveness, "a wise passiveness" [Wordsworth], passivity, passivism; passive resistance, nonviolent resistance; nonresistance, nonviolence; pacifism; neutrality, neutralness, neutralism, nonparticipation, noninvolvement; standpattism [informal]; do-nothingism, do-nothingness, do-nothing policy, *laissez-faire* policy, laissez-faireism; *laissez-faire, laissez-aller* [both Fr]; watching and waiting, watchful waiting, waiting game; inertia, inertness, immobility, dormancy, stagnation, stagnancy, vegetation, stasis, paralysis; procrastination; idleness, indolence, inactivity 708; quiescence 268; quietism, contemplation, meditation, passive self-annihilation; contemplative life, *vita contemplativa* [L].

.2 VERBS do nothing, not stir, not budge, not lift a finger *or* hand, not move a foot, sit back, sit on one's hands [informal], sit on one's ass *or* butt *or* duff [slang], sit on the sidelines, be a sideliner, sit it out, fold one's arms, twiddle one's thumbs; cool one's heels [informal]; bide one's time, delay, watch and wait, wait and see, play a waiting game, hang fire; lie *or* rest upon one's oars, rest, be still 268.7; repose on one's laurels; drift, coast; stagnate, vegetate, lie dormant, hibernate; idle 708.11.

.3 refrain, abstain, hold, spare, forbear, forgo, keep from; hold *or* stay one's hand.

.4 let alone, leave alone, leave *or* let well enough alone; not make waves, not rock the boat; let be, leave be [slang], let things take their course, let it have its way; leave things as they are, let sleeping dogs lie; *laisser faire, laisser passer, laisser aller* [all Fr], live and let live; **take no part in,** not get involved in, **have nothing to do with,** have no hand in, stand *or* hold aloof.

.5 **let go, let pass, let slip, let slide** *or* let ride [both informal]; procrastinate.

.6 ADJS **passive;** neutral, neuter; standpat [informal], **do-nothing;** *laissez-faire, laissez-aller* [both Fr]; **inert,** immobile, dormant, **stagnant,** stagnating, vegetative, vegetable, **static,** stationary, motionless, paralyzed, paralytic; procrastinating; **inactive, idle** 708.16,17; quiescent 268.12; quietist, quietistic, contemplative, meditative.

.7 ADVS **at a stand** *or* **standstill,** at a halt.

## 707. ACTIVITY

.1 NOUNS **activity, action,** activeness; **movement,** motion, stir; **proceedings, doings, goings-on,** –fest, –ics; **activism,** political activism, **militancy;** business 656.

.2 **liveliness, animation, vivacity,** vivaciousness, sprightliness, spiritedness, bubbliness, ebullience, effervescence, **briskness,** breeziness, peppiness [informal]; **life, spirit, verve,** energy; moxie *or* pizzazz *or* piss and vinegar [all slang], pep [informal], vim 161.2.

.3 **quickness, swiftness,** speediness, alacrity, **readiness,** smartness, sharpness, briskness; **promptness,** promptitude; dispatch, expeditiousness, expedition; **agility, nimbleness,** spryness.

.4 **bustle, fuss,** flurry, flutter, fluster, scramble, ferment, stew, sweat, whirl, swirl, vortex, maelstrom, **stir,** hubbub, hullabaloo, flap [informal], feery-fary [Scot], ado, to-do, bother, botheration, pother; fussiness, flutteriness; tumult, commotion, **agitation** 857.3; **restlessness,** unquiet, fidgetiness 857.4; **spurt, burst,** fit, spasm.

.5 **busyness, press of business;** plenty to do, many irons in the fire; the battle of life, the rat race [informal].

.6 **industry,** industriousness, assiduousness, **assiduity,** diligence, application, concentration, laboriousness, sedulity, **sedulousness,** unsparingness, relentlessness, zealousness, ardor, fervor, vehemence; **energy,** energeticalness, strenuousness, tirelessness, indefatigability.

.7 **enterprise,** enterprisingness, dynamism, **initiative,** aggression, **aggressiveness,** force, forcefulness, pushfulness, pushingness, **pushiness, push, drive, hustle, go,** getup, get-up-and-get *or* **get-up-and-go,**

**go-ahead, go-getting, go-to-itiveness** [informal], **up-and-comingness;** adventurousness, venturousness, venturesomeness, adventuresomeness; **spirit,** gumption *or* spunk [both informal]; **ambitiousness** 634.10.

.8 **man of action, doer,** man of deeds; **hustler** [informal], bustler; go-getter *or* ball of fire *or* live wire *or* powerhouse *or* human dynamo [all informal]; beaver, busy bee, **eager beaver** [informal]; operator *or* big-time operator *or* wheeler-dealer [all slang]; winner [informal]; **activist,** political activist, **militant;** enthusiast 635.5; new broom, take-charge guy [slang].

.9 **overactivity,** hyperactivity; hyperkinesia *or* hyperkinesis; franticness, frenziedness; overexertion, overextension; officiousness 238.2.

.10 VERBS **be busy, have one's hands full,** have many irons in the fire; not have a moment to spare, not have a moment that one can call one's own; have other things to do, have other fish to fry; **work, labor, drudge** 716.12–14; **busy oneself** 656.10,11.

.11 **stir,** stir about, **bestir oneself,** stir one's stumps [informal], be up and doing.

.12 **bustle, fuss,** make a fuss, **flutter,** rush around *or* about, tear around, hurry about, buzz *or* whiz about, dart to and fro, go around like a chicken with its head cut off.

.13 **hustle** [informal], **drive,** drive oneself, **push, scramble,** go all out [informal], **make things hum,** step lively [informal], make the sparks *or* chips fly; make up for lost time; press on, drive on; go ahead, forge ahead, shoot ahead, go full steam ahead.

.14 [slang terms] **hump,** get cutting, break one's neck, bear down on it, **hit the ball,** pour it on, lean on it, shake a leg, go to town on.

.15 **keep going, keep on,** keep on the go, **carry on,** peg *or* plug away [informal], **keep at it,** keep moving, keep driving, **keep the pot boiling,** keep the ball rolling; keep busy, **keep one's nose to the grindstone,** stay on the treadmill.

.16 **make the most of one's time,** improve the shining hour, make hay while the sun shines, not let the grass grow under one's feet; get up early.

.17 ADJS **active, lively, animated, spirited,** bubbly, ebullient, effervescent, **vivacious,** sprightly, chipper *or* perky [both informal], **pert; spry, breezy, brisk, energetic** smacking, spanking; alive, live, full of life, full of pep or full of go [both informal]; **peppy** or snappy or zingy [all informal]; frisky, bouncing, bouncy; mercurial, quicksilver; **activist**, activistic, **militant.**

.18 **quick, swift, speedy, expeditious,** alacritous, dispatchful [archaic], **prompt,** ready, smart, sharp, quick on the trigger [informal]; **agile, nimble, spry.**

.19 **astir, stirring,** afoot, **on foot;** in full swing.

.20 **bustling,** fussing, fluttering, **fluttery,** fussy; **fidgety,** restless, fretful, jumpy, unquiet, unsettled 857.25; **agitated, turbulent** 857.21,22.

.21 **busy,** full of business; occupied, engaged, **employed, working;** at it; **at work,** on duty, on the job, in harness; hard at work, **hard at it; on the move, on the go,** on the run, **on the hop** or **jump** [informal]; busy as a bee or beaver, busier than a one-armed paper hanger [informal]; up to one's ears or elbows in; tied up.

.22 **industrious, assiduous, diligent, sedulous,** laborious, **hardworking;** hard, unremitting, unsparing, relentless, zealous, ardent, fervent, vehement; **energetic,** strenuous; never idle; sleepless, unsleeping; tireless, unwearied, unflagging, indefatigable 625.7.

.23 **enterprising, aggressive, dynamic,** driving, forceful, **pushing,** pushful, **pushy, up-and-coming, go-ahead** or **hustling** [both informal]; adventurous, venturous, venturesome, adventuresome; **ambitious** 634.28.

.24 **overactive, hyperactive;** hectic, frenzied, frantic, frenetic; **hyperkinetic;** intrusive, officious 238.8,9.

.25 ADVS **actively, busily;** lively, sprightly, **briskly, breezily, energetically, animatedly, vivaciously, spiritedly,** with life and spirit; allegro, allegretto; **full tilt, in full swing,** all out [informal].

.26 **quickly, swiftly, expeditiously,** with dispatch, readily, **promptly; agilely, nimbly, spryly.**

.27 **industriously, assiduously, diligently, sedulously,** laboriously; unsparingly, relentlessly, zealously, ardently, fervently, vehemently; **energetically,** strenuously, tirelessly, indefatigably.

## 708. INACTIVITY

.1 NOUNS **inactivity, inaction, inactiveness;** lull, suspension; suspended animation; dormancy, hibernation; immobility, motionlessness, quiescence 268; **inertia** 706.1; underactivity.

.2 **idleness,** unemployment, otiosity, inoccupation; idle hands, idle hours, time hanging on one's hands; "a life of dignified otiosity" [Thackeray].

.3 **unemployment,** inoccupation; layoff, furlough; normal unemployment, seasonal unemployment, technological unemployment, cyclical unemployment; unemployment insurance.

.4 **idling, loafing,** lazing, flânerie [Fr], goofing off [slang], goldbricking [informal]; dolce far niente [Ital]; trifling, dallying, dillydallying, mopery, dawdling; loitering, tarrying, lingering; lounging, lolling.

.5 **indolence, laziness, sloth,** slothfulness, lotus-eating; laggardness, slowness, dilatoriness, remissness, do-nothingness, faineancy, fainéantise [Fr]; inexertion, inertia; **shiftlessness,** dolessness [dial], hoboism, vagrancy; spring fever; ergophobia.

.6 **languor,** languidness, languorousness, languishment [archaic], lackadaisicalness, **listlessness,** lifelessness, inanimation, enervation, slowness, lenitude or lentor [both archaic], **dullness, sluggishness,** heaviness, dopiness [informal], hebetude, supineness, **lassitude, lethargy,** oscitancy, kef; phlegm, apathy, indifference, passivity; torpidness, **torpor,** torpitude, torpidity; stupor, stupefaction; **sloth,** slothfulness, acedia; **sleepiness, somnolence, drowsiness** 712.1; **weariness, fatigue** 717; jadedness, satedness 664.2; world-weariness, ennui, boredom 884.3.

.7 **lazybones,** lazyboots, lazylegs, indolent, lie-abed, slugabed.

.8 **idler, loafer, lounger,** loller, lotus-eater, flâneur, flâneuse [both Fr], **do-nothing,** dolittle, fainéant [Fr], goof-off [slang], goldbrick or goldbricker [both informal]; **sluggard,** slug, slouch, sloucher, lubber, stick-in-the-mud [informal], gentleman of leisure; **time waster,** time killer; **dallier, dillydallier,** mope, moper, doodler, diddler [informal], **dawdler,** dawdle, laggard, **loiterer,** lingerer; waiter on Providence; trifler, **putterer,** potterer; clock watcher.

.9 **bum,** stiff [slang], derelict, skid-row bum, Bowery bum, lazzarone [Ital]; beachcomber; **good-for-nothing,** good-for-naught, **ne'er-do-well,** wastrel; vagrant, hobo, tramp 274.3; beggar 774.8.

.10 **nonworker, drone;** cadger, bummer or moocher [both slang], **sponger,** freeloader, lounge lizard [informal], social parasite, parasite, spiv [Brit]; beggar, mendicant, panhandler [slang]; **the unemployed;** the unemployable; lumpen proletariat; leisure class, rentiers, coupon clippers, idle rich.

.11 VERBS idle, do nothing, laze, lazy [informal], take one's ease, take one's time, loaf, lounge; lie around, lounge around, loll around, lollop around [Brit informal], moon, moon around, sit around, sit on one's ass or butt or duff [slang], stand around, hang around, loiter about or around, slouch, slouch around, bum around or mooch around [both slang]; goof off or lie down on the job [both slang]; sleep at one's post; let the grass grow under one's feet; twiddle one's thumbs, fold one's arms.

.12 waste time, consume time, kill time, idle or trifle or fritter or fool away time, loiter away or loiter out the time, beguile the time, while away the time, pass the time, lose time, waste the precious hours, burn daylight [archaic]; trifle, dabble, fribble, footle, putter, potter, piddle, diddle, doodle.

.13 dally, dillydally, piddle, diddle, diddle-daddle, doodle, dawdle, loiter, lollygag [dial], linger, lag, poke, take one's time.

.14 take it easy, take things as they come, drift, drift with the current, swim with the stream, coast, lead an easy life, live a life of ease, eat the bread of idleness, lie or rest upon one's oars; rest or repose on one's laurels, lie back on one's record.

.15 lie idle, lie fallow; aestivate, hibernate, lie dormant; lie or lay off, recharge one's batteries [informal]; lie up, lie on the shelf; ride at anchor, lay or lie by, lay or lie to; have nothing to do, have nothing on [slang].

.16 ADJS inactive, unactive; stationary, static, at a standstill; sedentary; quiescent, motionless 268.12–14.

.17 idle, fallow, otiose; unemployed, unoccupied, disengaged, désœuvré [Fr], jobless, out of work, out of employ, out of a job, out of harness; free, available, at liberty, at leisure; at loose ends; unemployable, lumpen; leisure, leisured; off duty, off work, off.

.18 indolent, lazy, bone-lazy, slothful, work-shy, ergophobic; do-nothing, fainéant [Fr], laggard, slow, dilatory, procrastinative, remiss, slack, lax; easy; shiftless, do-less [dial]; unenterprising, nonaggressive; good-for-nothing, ne'er-do-well; drony, dronish, spivvish [Brit], parasitic, cadging, sponging, scrounging.

.19 languid, languorous, listless, lifeless, inanimate, enervated, debilitated, pepless [in-

formal], lackadaisical, slow, wan, lethargic, hebetudinous, supine, lymphatic, apathetic, sluggish, dopey [slang], drugged, droopy, dull, heavy, leaden, lumpish, torpid, stultified, inert, stagnant, stagnating, vegetative, vegetable, dormant; phlegmatic, numb, benumbed; moribund, dead, exanimate; sleepy, somnolent 712.21; pooped [slang], weary 717.6; jaded, sated 664.6; blasé, world-weary, bored 884.10,11.

## 709. HASTE

.1 NOUNS haste, hurry, scurry, rush, race, dash, drive, scuttle, scamper, scramble, hustle [informal], bustle, flutter, flurry, hurry-scurry, helter-skelter; no time to be lost.

.2 hastiness, hurriedness, quickness, swiftness, expeditiousness, alacrity, promptness 707.3; speed 269.1,2; furiousness, feverishness; precipitousness, precipitance or precipitancy, precipitation; suddenness, abruptness; impetuousness, impetuosity, impulsiveness, rashness.

.3 hastening, hurrying, festination, speeding, forwarding, quickening, acceleration; forced march, double time, double-quick time, double-quick.

.4 VERBS hasten, haste, hurry, accelerate, speed, speed up, hurry up, hustle up [informal], rush, quicken, hustle [informal], bustle, bundle, precipitate, forward; dispatch, expedite; whip, whip along, spur, urge 648.14–16; push, press; crowd, stampede; hurry on, hasten on, drive on, hie on, push on; hurry along, rush along, speed along, speed on its way; push through, railroad through [informal].

.5 make haste, hasten, festinate, hurry, get moving or going [informal], get a move on [informal], hurry up, race, run, post, rush, chase, tear, dash, spurt, leap, plunge, scurry, hurry-scurry, scamper, scramble, scuttle, hustle [informal], bundle, bustle; bestir oneself, move quickly 269.8–13; hurry on, dash on, press or push on, crowd; double-time, go at the double; break one's neck or fall all over oneself [both informal]; lose no time, not lose a moment; rush through, hurry through; dash off; make short work of, make the best of one's time or way, make up for lost time.

.6 [slang terms] step on it, snap to it, hop to it, hotfoot, bear down on it, shake it up, get cracking, get the lead out, get the lead out of one's ass, get one's ass in gear, hump, hump it, hump oneself, shag ass, tear ass, **get a hustle** or **move** or **wiggle on,** stir one's stumps, not spare the horses.

.7 **rush into, plunge into,** dive into, plunge, plunge headlong; **not stop to think,** go off half-cocked or at half cock [informal], leap before one looks.

.8 **be in a hurry,** have no time to lose or spare, not have a moment to spare, work against time, work under pressure.

.9 ADJS **hasty, hurried,** festinate, **quick,** flying, **expeditious,** prompt 707.18; **immediate,** instant, on the spot; **swift, speedy** 269.19; **urgent** 672.21; furious, feverish; slap-bang, slapdash, **cursory,** passing, snap [informal]; superficial; last-minute.

10 **precipitate,** precipitant, precipitous; **sudden,** abrupt; **impetuous, impulsive, rash;** headlong, breakneck; breathless, panting.

11 **hurried, rushed,** pushed, **pressed,** crowded, **pressed for time,** hard-pushed or -pressed, hard-run; double-time, double-quick, on or at the double.

12 ADVS **hastily, hurriedly, quickly; expeditiously,** promptly, with dispatch; apace, amain, hand over fist, **immediately,** instantly, at once; **swiftly, speedily** 269.21; with haste, with great or all haste, with a rush; furiously, feverishly, in a sweat or lather of haste, hotfoot; by forced marches; **helter-skelter, hurry-scurry,** pellmell; slapdash, cursorily, superficially, on the run or fly, in passing.

13 **posthaste,** in posthaste; post, express; by express, by airmail, by return mail; by cable, by telegraph.

14 **in a hurry, in haste,** in hot haste, in all haste; in short order 269.23; against time, against the clock.

15 **precipitately,** precipitantly, precipitously, slap-bang; **suddenly,** abruptly; **impetuously, impulsively, rashly;** headlong, headfirst, headforemost, head over heels, heels over head [archaic], à corps perdu [Fr].

16 INTERJS **make haste!,** make it quick!, **hurry up!; now!; at once!,** rush!, immediate!, **urgent!,** instanter!; **step lively!,** look alive!, on the double!

17 [slang terms] **step on it!,** snap to it!, **make it snappy!, get a move on!,** get a wiggle on!, **chop-chop!, shake a leg!,** stir your stumps!, get the lead out!, **get moving!, get going!,** get cracking!, get with it!, hop to it!, move your tail!, move your fanny!, **get on the ball!,** don't spare the horses!

.1 NOUNS **leisure, ease, convenience,** freedom; retirement, semiretirement; **rest,** repose 711; **free time, spare time,** goof-off time [slang], odd moments, idle hours; time to spare or burn or kill, time on one's hands, time at one's disposal or command; time, one's own sweet time [informal].

.2 **leisureliness, unhurriedness,** unhastiness, hastelessness, relaxedness; dolce far niente [Ital]; inactivity 708; **slowness** 270; deliberateness, deliberation.

.3 VERBS **have time,** have time enough, have time to spare, have plenty of time, have nothing but time, be in no hurry.

.4 **take one's leisure,** take one's ease, **take one's time, take one's own sweet time** [informal], do at one's leisure or convenience or pleasure; go slow 270.6–9.

.5 ADJS **leisure, leisured;** idle, unoccupied, free, open, spare; retired, semiretired.

.6 **leisurely, unhurried,** unhasty, hasteless, easy, relaxed; deliberate; inactive 708.16, 17; **slow** 270.10.

.7 ADVS **at leisure,** at one's leisure, at one's **convenience,** at one's own sweet time [informal], when one gets around to it, when it is handy, when one has the time, when one has a minute to spare, when one has a moment to call one's own.

.1 NOUNS **rest, repose, ease, relaxation;** slippered or unbuttoned ease; **comfort** 887; restfulness, quiet, tranquillity 268.1; inactivity 708; sleep 712.

.2 **respite, recess, rest, pause,** halt, stay, lull, **break,** surcease, suspension, interlude, **intermission,** spell [Austral], letup [informal], **time out** [informal], time to catch one's breath; **breathing spell,** breathing time, breathing place, breathing space, breath, **breather;** coffee break, tea break, cigarette break; cocktail hour, happy hour [informal]; enforced respite, downtime.

.3 **vacation,** holiday [Brit]; **time off;** paid vacation, paid holiday [Brit]; **leave, leave of absence, furlough;** liberty, shore leave; **sabbatical,** sabbatical leave or year; **weekend;** busman's holiday.

.4 **holiday** 137.12, **day off;** red-letter day, gala day, fete day, festival day, day of festivities; legal holiday, bank holiday [Brit]; High Holiday, High Holy Day; holy day 1040.14,15; feast, feast day, high day, church feast, fixed feast, movable feast; half-holiday.

.5 **day of rest,** *dies non* [L]; **Sabbath,** Sunday, Lord's day, First day.

.6 VERBS **rest, repose,** take rest, take one's ease, **take it easy** [informal], rest from one's labors, take life easy; go to rest, settle to rest; lie down, go to bed, snug down, curl up, bed, bed down, couch, recline, lounge, drape oneself, sprawl, loll; take off one's shoes, unbuckle one's belt.

.7 **relax,** unlax [slang], unbend, unwind, slack, slacken, **ease; ease up, let up,** slack up, slack off, **ease off,** let down, **slow down,** let up on.

.8 **take a rest, take a break, break, take time out** [informal], pause, lay off, **knock off** [informal], recess, **take a recess,** take ten *or* take five [both slang]; stop for breath, catch one's breath, breathe; stop work, suspend operations, call it a day.

.9 **vacation,** holiday, take a holiday, make holiday; **take a leave of absence,** take leave, go on leave, go on furlough, take one's sabbatical; weekend; Sunday, Christmas, etc.

.10 ADJS **vacational, holiday,** ferial [archaic], festal; sabbatical; **comfortable** 887.11,12; **restful,** quiet 268.12.

.11 ADVS **at rest, at ease,** at one's ease; abed, in bed.

.12 **on vacation,** on leave, on furlough; off duty, on one's own time.

## 712. SLEEP

.1 NOUNS **sleepiness, drowsiness,** doziness, heaviness, lethargy, oscitation, somnolence *or* somnolency, yawning, stretching, oscitancy, pandiculation; **languor** 708.6; sand in the eyes, heavy eyelids; REM sleep.

.2 **sleep, slumber,** narc(o)–, somni–; **repose,** silken repose, *somnus* [L], the arms of Morpheus; bye-bye *or* beddy-bye [both informal]; doss [Brit slang], blanket drill *or* shut-eye [both slang]; light sleep, fitful sleep, **doze, drowse,** snoozle [dial]; beauty sleep [informal]; sleepwalking, somnambulism; somniloquy; **land of Nod,** slumberland, sleepland, dreamland; hibernation, winter sleep, aestivation; bedtime, sack time [slang]; **unconsciousness** 423.2.

.3 **nap, snooze** [informal], **cat nap, wink, forty winks** [informal], wink of sleep, spot of sleep; **siesta,** blanket drill [slang].

.4 **sweet sleep, balmy sleep, downy sleep,** soft sleep, gentle sleep, smiling sleep, golden slumbers; "folded sleep" [Tenny-

son], "dewy-feathered sleep" [Milton], "care-charmer Sleep, son of the sable night" [Samuel Daniel], "the honey-heavy dew of slumber" [Shakespeare]; peaceful sleep, sleep of the just; restful sleep, good night's sleep, "sleep that knits up the ravell'd sleave of care" [Shakespeare], "Brother of Death" [Sir Thomas Browne].

.5 **deep sleep,** profound sleep, heavy sleep, **sound sleep,** unbroken sleep, wakeless sleep, drugged sleep, dreamless sleep, the sleep of the dead, "sleep such as makes the darkness brief" [Martial].

.6 **stupor,** sopor, **coma, swoon,** lethargy [archaic]; **trance;** narcosis, narcohypnosis, narcoma, narcotization, narcotic stupor *or* trance; sedation; high [slang]; nod [informal]; narcolepsy; catalepsy; thanatosis, **shock** 686.24; sleeping sickness, encephalitis lethargica.

.7 **hypnosis,** mesmeric *or* **hypnotic sleep** *or* **trance,** somnipathy, hypnotic somnolence; lethargic hypnosis, somnambulistic hypnosis, cataleptic hypnosis, animal hypnosis; narcohypnosis; autohypnosis, self-hypnosis; **hypnotherapy** 690.5.

.8 **hypnotism, mesmerism;** hypnology; hypnotization, mesmerization; **animal magnetism,** od, odyl, odylic force; hypnotic suggestion, posthypnotic suggestion, autosuggestion.

.9 **hypnotist, mesmerist,** hypnotizer, mesmerizer; Svengali, Mesmer.

.10 **sleep-inducer,** sleep-producer, sleep-provoker, sleep-bringer, hypnotic, soporific, somnifacient; poppy, mandrake, mandragora, opium, opiate, morphine, morphia; nightcap; **sedative** 687.12; anesthetic 687.57; **lullaby** 462.15.

.11 **Morpheus,** Somnus, Hypnos; "sweet father of soft rest" [Wm. Drummond]; sandman, dustman [Brit].

.12 **sleeper, slumberer;** sleeping beauty, **sleepyhead,** lie-abed, slugabed, sleepwalker, somnambulist; somniloquist.

.13 VERBS **sleep, slumber,** rest in the arms of Morpheus; **doze, drowse; nap,** take a nap, catch a wink; sleep soundly, **sleep like a top** *or* **log,** sleep like the dead; snore, saw wood *or* saw logs [both slang]; oversleep.

.14 [slang *or* informal terms] **snooze, get some shut-eye,** get some sack time, take forty winks; pound the ear, kip *or* doss [both Brit].

.15 **hibernate,** aestivate, lie dormant.

.16 **go to sleep,** settle to sleep, go off to sleep, **fall asleep, drop asleep, drop off** "drift gently down the tides of sleep" [Longfellow]; **doze off, drowse off,** nod off, dope off [slang]; close one's eyes, "let fall the shadow of mine eyes" [Shakespeare].

.17 **go to bed, retire;** lay me down to sleep; bed, bed down; go night-night *or* go bye-bye *or* go beddy-bye [all informal].

.18 [slang *or* informal terms] **hit the hay, hit the sack,** crash, turn in, crawl in, flop, sack out, sack up, kip down *or* doss down [both Brit].

.19 **put to bed,** bed; nestle, cradle; **tuck in.**

.20 **put to sleep; lull to sleep,** rock to sleep; **hypnotize, mesmerize,** magnetize; **entrance,** trance, put in a trance; narcotize, drug, dope [slang]; anesthetize, put under; sedate.

.21 ADJS **sleepy, drowsy,** dozy, snoozy [informal], **slumberous,** slumbery, dreamy; **half asleep,** asleep on one's feet; sleepful, sleep-filled; yawny, stretchy [informal], oscitant, yawning, napping, **nodding,** ready for bed; heavy, **heavy-eyed, heavy with sleep,** sleep-swollen, sleep-drowned, sleep-drunk, drugged with sleep; **somnolent,** soporific; **lethargic,** comatose, narcose *or* narcous, stuporose *or* **stuporous, in a stupor,** out of it [informal]; narcoleptic; cataleptic; narcotized, drugged, doped [slang]; sedated; anesthetized; **languid** 708.19.

.22 **asleep, sleeping, slumbering,** in the arms *or* lap of Morpheus, in the land of Nod; **sound asleep, fast asleep,** dead asleep, deep asleep, in a sound sleep, flaked-out [slang]; **unconscious, oblivious, out;** comatose; dormant; dead, **dead to the world;** unwakened, unawakened.

.23 **sleep-inducing,** sleep-producing, sleep-bringing, sleep-causing, sleep-compelling, sleep-inviting, sleep-provoking, sleep-tempting; **narcotic, hypnotic, soporific, somniferous,** somnifacient; sedative 687.45.

.24 **hypnotic,** hypnoid(al), **mesmeric;** odylic; narcohypnotic.

### 713. WAKEFULNESS

.1 NOUNS **wakefulness,** wake; **sleeplessness,** restlessness, tossing and turning; **insomnia,** insomnolence *or* insomnolency, "the wakey nights" [Sir Thomas Wyatt]; vigil, all-night vigil, lidless vigil, *pervigilium* [L]; insomniac; consciousness, sentience; alertness 533.5.

.2 **awakening, wakening,** rousing, **arousal;** rude awakening; reveille [mil].

.3 VERBS **keep awake,** keep one's eyes open; keep alert, be vigilant 533.8; **stay awake, toss and turn,** not sleep a wink, not shut one's eyes, count sheep.

.4 **awake, awaken, wake, wake up, get up,** rouse, come alive [informal]; open one's eyes, stir [informal].

.5 (wake someone up) **awaken, waken, rouse, arouse,** awake, wake, **wake up,** shake up, knock up [Brit].

.6 **get up, get out of bed, arise, rise, rise and shine** [informal], greet the day, **turn out** [informal]; roll out *or* pile out *or* show a leg *or* hit the deck [all slang].

.7 ADJS **wakeful, sleepless,** slumberless, unsleeping, insomniac, insomnious; restless.

.8 **awake, conscious, up; wide-awake,** broad awake; alert 533.14.

.9 ADVS **sleeplessly,** unsleepingly; **wakefully,** with one's eyes open; alertly 533.17.

### 714. ENDEAVOR

.1 NOUNS **endeavor,** effort, striving, struggle, strain; **exertion** 716; determination, resolution 624.

.2 **attempt, trial, effort, essay,** assay [archaic], **endeavor, undertaking;** approach, move; stroke, step; **try** *or* go *or* fling *or* shot [all informal]; **crack** *or* whack *or* stab *or* lick [all slang]; gambit, offer, **bid, strong bid;** experiment, tentative; tentation, trial and error.

.3 **one's best, one's level best** [informal], **one's utmost,** one's damndest *or* darndest [slang], one's best effort *or* endeavor, the best one can, the best one knows how, all one can do, all one's got *or* one's all [both informal], the top of one's bent, as much as in one lies.

.4 VERBS **endeavor, strive, struggle,** strain, sweat, sweat blood, labor, **exert oneself,** apply oneself; spend oneself; seek, study, aim; resolve, be determined 624.7–9.

.5 **attempt, try, essay,** assay, offer; **undertake** 715.3, **approach,** come to grips with, engage, take the bull by the horns; venture, venture on *or* upon, chance; **make an attempt** *or* effort, lift a finger *or* hand.

.6 [slang *or* informal terms] **tackle, take on, make a try, give a try,** try on for size, **have a fling at,** give a fling, take a fling at, have a go at, give a go, give a whirl, **take a crack** *or* whack at, make a stab at, have a shot at.

.7 **try to,** try and [informal], **attempt to, endeavor to,** strive to, seek to, study to, aim to, venture to, dare to, pretend to.

.8 **try for, strive for,** strain for, struggle for,

contend for, pull for [informal], bid for, make a bid *or* strong bid for, make a play for [informal].

.9 **see what one can do,** see what can be done, see if one can do, do what one can, use one's endeavor; try anything once; **try one's hand,** try one's luck; make a cautious *or* tentative move, experiment, feel one's way.

.10 **make a special effort, go out of the way,** go out of one's way, **put oneself out,** put oneself out of the way, lay oneself out *or* bend over backwards [both informal], trouble oneself, **go to the trouble,** take trouble, **take pains,** redouble one's efforts.

.11 **try hard, push** [informal], make a bold push, **put one's back to *or* into,** put one's heart into, try until one is blue in the face, knock oneself out [slang], break one's neck [informal], bust one's ass [slang], rupture oneself, do it or break a leg, do it or bust a gut [slang]; die trying, **try and try;** try, try again; exert oneself 716.9.

.12 **do one's best,** do one's level best [informal], **do one's utmost,** try one's best *or* utmost, do *or* try one's damndest *or* darndest [slang], **do all *or* everything one can,** do the best one can, **do the best one knows how,** do all in one's power, do as much as in one lies, do what lies in one's power; put all one's strength into, put one's whole soul in, **strain every nerve; go all out *or* go the limit** [both informal], go for broke *or* shoot the works [both slang], give it one's all *or* give it all one's got [both informal]; be on one's mettle.

.13 **make every effort, spare no effort *or* pains, go all lengths, go to great lengths,** go the whole length, go through fire and water, not rest, not relax, not slacken, move heaven and earth, leave no stone unturned, leave no avenue unexplored.

.14 ADJS trial, tentative, experimental; venturesome, willing; determined, resolute 624.11,12.

.15 ADVS **out for,** out to, trying for, **on the make** [informal].

.16 **at the top of one's bent,** to one's utmost, as far as possible.

## 715. UNDERTAKING

.1 NOUNS **undertaking, enterprise, operation,** work, venture, project, proposition *or* deal [both informal]; **program, plan** 654; **affair, business, task** 656.2; effort, attempt 714.2; engagement, contract, obligation, commitment 770.2.

.2 **adventure,** emprise, **mission;** quest, pilgrimage; expedition, exploration.

.3 VERBS **undertake, assume,** accept, **take on, take upon oneself,** take upon one's shoulders, **tackle,** attack; engage *or* contract *or* obligate *or* commit oneself; **put *or* set *or* turn one's hand to,** engage in, **devote oneself to,** apply oneself to, betake oneself to [archaic], address oneself to, give oneself up to; busy oneself with 656.11; **take up,** move into, go into, go in *or* out for [informal], **enter on *or* upon,** proceed to, embark in *or* upon, **venture upon,** go upon, launch forth, set forward, set going, get under way; set about, go about, lay about, go to do; **set to, turn to, buckle to, fall to;** pitch into [informal], plunge into, fall into, **launch into** *or* upon; go at, set at, have at [informal], knuckle *or* buckle down to; put one's hand to the plow, put *or* lay one's shoulder to the wheel; take the bull by the horns; **endeavor, attempt** 714.4,5.

.4 **have in hand, have one's hands in,** have on one's hands *or* shoulders.

.5 **be in progress *or* process,** be on the anvil, be in the fire, be in the works *or* hopper *or* pipeline [informal], **be under way.**

.6 **bite off more than one can chew** [informal], overextend *or* overreach oneself, have too many irons in the fire.

.7 ADJS **undertaken, assumed,** accepted, **taken on** [informal]; **ventured,** attempted, chanced; **in hand,** on the anvil, in the fire, **in progress *or* process,** in the works *or* hopper *or* pipeline [informal], **under way.**

.8 **enterprising,** venturesome, adventurous.

## 716. EXERTION

.1 NOUNS **exertion, effort, energy,** elbow grease; **endeavor** 714; **trouble, pains;** great *or* mighty effort, might and main, muscle, nerve and sinew, hard *or* strong *or* long pull, "a long pull, a strong pull, and a pull all together" [Dickens].

.2 **strain, straining, stress, stressfulness, stress and strain,** taxing, **tension,** stretch, rack; tug, pull, haul, heave; overexertion, overstrain, overtaxing, overextension, overstress.

.3 **struggle, fight, battle, tussle, scuffle, wrestle,** hassle [informal].

.4 **work,** erg(o)–; **labor, employment, industry, toil,** moil, travail, toil and trouble, sweat of one's brow; **drudgery, sweat,** slavery, spadework, donkeywork; rat race [informal]; treadmill; unskilled labor, hewing of wood and drawing of water; dirty work, scut work; tedious or stupid or idiot or tiresome work, grind [informal], fag; manual labor, handwork, handiwork; hand's turn, stroke of work, stroke; lick or lick of work or stitch of work [all informal]; task 656.2; fatigue 717.

.5 hard work or labor, backbreaking work, warm work, uphill work, hard or tough grind [informal]; hard job 731.2; laboriousness, toilsomeness, effortfulness, strenuousness, arduousness, operosity, operoseness; onerousness, oppressiveness, burdensomeness; troublesomeness.

.6 exercise, exercising; practice, drill, workout; athletics, gymnastics, calisthenics, gymnastic exercises, physical jerks [Brit], setting-up exercises, daily dozen, isometric exercises, isometrics; yoga; constitutional [informal], stretch; violent exercise, breather [informal]; physical education.

.7 exerciser; horizontal bar, parallel bars, horse, side horse, long horse, rings; trapeze; trampoline; Indian club; medicine ball; punching bag; rowing machine; weight, dumbbell, barbell.

.8 VERBS exert, exercise, ply, employ, use, put forth, put out [informal].

.9 exert oneself, put forth one's strength, bend one's effort, bend might and main, spare no effort, tax one's energies; put oneself out or lay oneself out or go all out [all informal]; endeavor 714.4; do one's best 714.12; apply oneself; hump or hump it or hump oneself [all slang], buckle down or knuckle down [both informal], bear down on it [slang], lay to; lay to the oars, ply the oar.

.10 strain, tense, stress, stretch, tax, press, rack; pull, tug, haul, heave; strain the muscles, strain every nerve or every nerve and sinew; put one's back into it [informal]; sweat blood; overexert, overstrain, overtax, overextend; drive or whip or flog oneself.

.11 struggle, strive, contend, fight, battle, buffet, scuffle, tussle, wrestle, hassle [informal], work or fight one's way, agonize, huff and puff, grunt and sweat, sweat it [slang], make heavy weather of it.

.12 work, labor; busy oneself 656.10,11; turn a hand, do a hand's turn, do a lick of work; chore, do the chores, char or do chars, chare [Brit].

.13 work hard; scratch or hustle or sweat [all

informal], slave, sweat and slave [informal]; hit the ball or bear down on it or pour it on [all slang]; work one's head off [informal], work one's fingers to the bone; work like a horse or cart horse or dog, work like a slave or galley slave, work like a coal heaver, work like a Trojan; work overtime, do double duty, work double hours or tides, work day and night, work late, burn the midnight oil; lucubrate, elucubrate; overwork 663.10.

.14 drudge, grind or dig [both informal], fag, grub, toil, moil, toil and moil, travail, plod, slog, peg, plug [informal], hammer, peg away or along, plug away or along [informal], hammer away, pound away, work away; keep one's nose to the grindstone; wade through.

.15 set to work, get busy, roll up one's sleeves, spit on one's hands; fall to work, fall to, buckle or knuckle down to [informal], turn to, set to or about, put or set one's hand to, start in, enter on or upon, launch into or upon; get on the job or get going [both informal]; go to it or get with it or get cracking or have at it [all slang]; hop or jump to it [slang]; attack, set at, tackle [informal]; plunge into, dive into; pitch in or into [informal]; light into or wade into or tear into or sail into [all informal], put or lay one's shoulder to the wheel, put one's hand to the plow; take on, undertake 715.3.

.16 task, work, busy, keep busy, fag, sweat [informal], drive, tax; overtask, overtax, overwork, overdrive; burden, oppress 352.13.

.17 ADJS laboring, working; struggling, striving, straining; drudging, toiling, slaving, sweating or grinding [both informal], grubbing, plodding, slogging, pegging, plugging [informal]; hardworking 707.21.

.18 laborious, toilsome, arduous, strenuous, painful, effortful, operose, troublesome, onerous, oppressive, burdensome; wearisome 717.11; heavy, hefty [informal], tough [informal], uphill, backbreaking, grueling, punishing, crushing, killing, Herculean; labored, forced, strained; hard-fought, hard-earned.

.19 ADVS laboriously, arduously, toilsomely, strenuously, operosely; effortfully, with effort, hard, by the sweat of one's brow; the hard way; with all one's might, for all one is worth, with a will, with might and main, with a strong hand, manfully; hammer and tongs, tooth and nail, bec et *ongles* [Fr], heart and soul; **industriously** 707.27.

## 717. FATIGUE

.1 NOUNS **fatigue, tiredness, weariness, wearifulness**; overtiredness, overstrain; faintness, goneness, weakness, enfeeblement, enervation, debility, debilitation 160.1; jadedness; lassitude, languor 707.6; tension fatigue, stance fatigue; mental fatigue, brain fag [informal]; strain, mental strain, heart strain, eyestrain; sleepiness 712.1.

.2 **exhaustion,** exhaustedness, draining; **collapse,** prostration, breakdown, crack-up [informal], nervous exhaustion or prostration.

.3 **breathlessness, shortness of breath,** windedness, short-windedness; panting, gasping; dyspnea, labored breathing.

.4 VERBS **fatigue, tire, weary, exhaust, fag** or **tucker** [both informal], wilt, flag, jade, harass, frazzle, beat, **poop** [slang]; **wear, wear on** or **upon, wear down; tire out, wear out, fag out** or **tucker out** [both informal], knock out or poop out [both slang], burn out; **use up,** do up or knock up [both informal]; take the tuck out of, **do in;** wind, put out of breath; overtire, overweary, overfatigue, overstrain; weaken, enervate, debilitate 160.10; weary or tire to death; prostrate.

.5 **get tired, grow weary, tire, weary, fatigue,** jade; flag, droop, faint, sink, wilt; **play out, poop out** [slang], peter out [informal], run out, run down, burn out; gasp, wheeze, pant, puff, blow, puff and blow, puff like a grampus; collapse, break down, crack up [informal], give out, drop, drop in one's tracks, succumb.

.6 ADJS **fatigued, fagged** [informal], **tired, weary,** wearied, weariful, jaded, **frazzled,** run ragged, run-down, good and tired; unrefreshed, unrestored, in need of rest, ready to drop; **faint,** fainting, feeling faint, **weak,** enfeebled, enervated, debilitated, seedy [informal], weakened 160.12, 13,18; drooping, droopy, wilting, flagging, sagging; languid 708.19; worn, worn-down, **worn to a frazzle** or shadow, toilworn, weary-worn; wayworn, way-weary; footweary, weary-footed, footsore; tired-armed; tired-winged, weary-winged; weary-laden, "tired and weary-laden" [Bible].

.7 **tired-looking,** weary-looking, tired-eyed, tired-faced, haggard, hollow-eyed, ravaged, drawn, worn, wan.

.8 **exhausted,** drained, **spent,** gone; **tired out, worn-out, fagged out** [informal], **tuckered out** [informal], **played out; pooped out** or knocked out or wiped out [all slang]; used up or done up or beat up [all informal], washed-up [informal]; **all in** or bushed or pooped or beat [all slang], whacked [Brit informal], beaten; done or done in [both informal]; bonetired, bone-weary; **dog-tired,** dog-weary; dead [informal], **dead-tired,** dead beat, **tired to death,** weary unto death, dead-alive or dead-and-alive, more dead than alive, dead on one's feet, ready to drop, on one's last legs; prostrate.

.9 **overtired, overweary,** overwearied, overstrained, overdriven, overfatigued, overspent.

.10 **breathless, winded;** wheezing, puffing, panting, **out of breath,** short of breath or wind; short-winded, short-breathed, broken-winded, touched in the wind, dyspneic.

.11 **fatiguing, wearying,** wearing, **tiring,** straining, stressful, trying, **exhausting,** draining, **grueling,** punishing, killing; **tiresome,** fatiguesome, **wearisome,** weariful; toilsome 716.18.

.12 ADVS **out,** to the point of exhaustion.

## 718. WORKER, DOER

.1 NOUNS **doer, actor, performer, worker, practitioner,** perpetrator; **producer, maker,** creator, fabricator, **author,** mover, prime mover; **architect; agent,** medium; **executor,** executant, executrix; **operator,** operative, operant; subject; –ant or –ent, –arian, –ator, –ee, –eer, –er or –ier or –yer, –ist, –ster.

.2 (working person) **worker, laborer, toiler,** moiler; proletarian, blue-collar worker, laboring man, stiff or working stiff [both slang]; **workman, workingman; workwoman, workingwoman,** working girl, workgirl; industrial worker, factory worker; white-collar worker, office worker; **jobholder,** wageworker, **wage earner,** salaried worker; **breadwinner;** wage slave; employee, servant 750; **hand, workhand;** common laborer, unskilled laborer, navvy [Brit], day laborer, roustabout; casual, casual laborer; migrant worker, migrant; menial, flunky; pieceworker, jobber; full-time worker, part-time worker; temporary employee, temporary, office temporary; free-lance worker, free lance, free-lancer; self-employed person.

**.3 drudge, grub, hack, fag, plodder, slave,** galley slave, **workhorse**, beast of burden, slogger; "hewers of wood and drawers of water" [Bible]; grind or greasy grind [both slang], swot [Brit informal].

**.4 professional,** professionist, pro or old pro [both informal], seasoned professional; gownsman; the profession.

**.5 amateur, nonprofessional;** layman.

**.6 craftsman, handicraftsman;** craftswoman; **artisan,** artificer, artist [archaic], mechanic; wright; **technician;** apprentice, prentice [informal]; **journeyman,** skilled laborer; **master,** master craftsman, master workman, master carpenter, etc.

**.7 smith,** farrier [Brit], forger, forgeman, metalworker; Vulcan, Hephaestus, Wayland or Völund.

**.8 craftsmen, workers**

| | |
|---|---|
| architect | manicurist |
| armorer | mason |
| barber | mechanic |
| beautician | miller |
| brazier | paperhanger |
| bricklayer | plumber |
| builder | potter |
| cabinetmaker | puddler |
| carpenter | puttier |
| carver | rigger |
| chandler | roofer |
| contractor | saddler |
| cooper | spinner |
| electrician | steam fitter |
| farmhand | steeplejack |
| fitter | stonecutter |
| forger | stonemason |
| founder | tanner |
| fuller | tinker |
| gas fitter | tinner |
| glassblower | turner |
| glazer | upholsterer |
| glazier | weaver |
| hairdresser | welder |
| lather | woodcutter |
| machinist | wrecker |

**.9 engineers**

| | |
|---|---|
| aeronautical engineer | hydraulic engineer |
| aerospace engineer | illuminating engineer |
| agricultural engineer | industrial engineer |
| architectural engineer | irrigation engineer |
| army engineer | marine engineer |
| automotive engineer | mechanical engineer |
| ceramic engineer | metallurgical engineer, metallurgist |
| chemical engineer | |
| civil engineer | military engineer |
| communications engineer | mining engineer |
| | municipal engineer |
| construction engineer | naval engineer |
| electrical engineer | nuclear engineer |
| electronics engineer | ordnance engineer |
| fire-protection engineer | petroleum engineer |
| | power engineer |
| fuel engineer | power-supply engineer |
| furnace engineer | product engineer |
| geological engineer | radar engineer |
| highway engineer | radio engineer |
| railroad engineer | textile engineer |
| refrigerating engineer | tool engineer |
| research engineer | transportation engineer |
| rocket engineer | |
| sanitary engineer | ventilation engineer |
| steam engineer | water-supply engineer |
| structural engineer | welding engineer |
| telephone engineer | |

**.10 smiths**

| | |
|---|---|
| anglesmith | keysmith |
| arrowsmith | knifesmith |
| blacksmith | locksmith |
| bladesmith | runesmith |
| brightsmith | shoeingsmith |
| bronzesmith | silversmith |
| chainsmith | stonesmith |
| clocksmith | tinsmith |
| coppersmith | toolsmith |
| goldsmith | versesmith 609.14 |
| gunsmith | wagonsmith |
| hammersmith | weaponsmith |
| housesmith | whitesmith |
| ironsmith | wiresmith |
| jawsmith 599.4 | wordsmith 602.15 |
| jokesmith 881.12 | |

**.11 wrights**

| | |
|---|---|
| cartwright | scenewright |
| housewright | shipwright |
| millwright | wagonwright, wainwright |
| pitwright | |
| playwright 611.27 | wheelwright |
| plowwright | woodwright |

**.12 makers**

| | |
|---|---|
| anvil maker | cake maker |
| arrow maker | candlemaker |
| ax maker | candymaker |
| bag maker | canvas maker |
| balance maker | cap maker |
| barrel maker | carpet maker |
| basket maker | cart maker |
| bed maker | casemaker |
| beer maker | cement maker |
| bell maker | chain maker |
| bellows maker | chairmaker |
| belt maker | cheese maker |
| blanket maker | chest maker |
| block maker | chisel maker |
| board maker | cider maker |
| bobbin maker | cigarette maker |
| bodice maker | cigar maker |
| body maker | cloak maker |
| boilermaker | clockmaker |
| bolt maker | clog maker |
| bookmaker | cloth maker |
| boot maker | coach maker |
| bottle maker | coffin maker |
| bow maker | collar maker |
| box maker | combmaker |
| brake maker | cord maker |
| bread maker | coremaker |
| brickmaker | couch maker |
| bridge maker | cradle maker |
| broom maker | crate maker |
| brush maker | cup maker |
| bucket maker | diemaker |
| bullet maker | dish maker |
| butter maker | doll maker |
| button maker | door maker |
| cabinetmaker | dressmaker |

dye maker
fan maker
felt maker
fiddle maker
file maker
garment maker
glassmaker
glove maker
glue maker
gunmaker
harness maker
hat maker
hook maker
hub maker
ice maker
ink maker
iron maker
kettle maker
lace maker
lamp maker
leather maker
lens maker
lockmaker
lute maker
map maker
matchmaker 933.13
model maker
nail maker
needle maker
netmaker
papermaker
patternmaker
pen maker
pie maker
pinmaker
plate maker
porcelain maker

pot maker
powder maker
ribbon maker
road maker
rope maker
rug maker
sack maker
saddle maker
safe maker
sailmaker
salt maker
sausage maker
saw maker
scale maker
scarf maker
screw maker
scythe maker
shirtmaker
shoemaker
soapmaker
steelmaker
sugar maker
sword maker
tentmaker
thread maker
tile maker
tool-and-die maker
toolmaker
tubemaker
tub maker
wagonmaker
watchmaker
web maker
wheel maker
whip maker
wigmaker
wine maker

**.13 workers**

brainworker
brassworker
clothworker
fieldworker
flintworker
garmentworker
glassworker
goldworker
ironworker
laceworker
leatherworker
metalworker
millworker
mineworker

needleworker
plateworker
saltworker
sawworker
shellworker
silverworker
steelworker
stoneworker
tinworker
waxworker
wireworker
woodworker
woolworker

## 719. WORKPLACE

.1 NOUNS **workplace,** work site, **workshop, shop,** –ery, –y; work space, working space, loft; **bench,** workbench, worktable; **desk;** establishment, facility, installation; **company,** institution, house, firm, concern, agency, organization, **corporation;** workhouse; sweatshop; workroom; studio, atelier; parlor, beauty parlor, funeral parlor, etc.; barbershop, beauty shop, butcher shop, etc.

.2 hive, hive of industry, beehive; factory or mill or manufacturing town; hub of industry, center of manufacture.

.3 **plant; factory,** manufactory, manufacturing plant, *usine* [Fr]; main plant, assembly plant, subassembly plant, feeder plant; push-button plant, automated or cybernated or automatic or robot factory; assembly or production line; defense plant, munitions plant, armory, arsenal; **power plant** 342.18; atomic energy plant; **machine shop; mill,** sawmill, flour mill, etc. 348.23; **yard,** yards, brickyard, shipyard, dockyard, boatyard; mint; refinery, oil refinery, sugar refinery, etc.; distillery, brewery, winery; boilery; bindery, bookbindery; packing house; cannery; dairy, creamery; pottery; tannery; **factory district,** industrial zone, industrial park, factory belt, manufacturing quarter.

.4 **works,** bleachworks, bottling works, brassworks, copperworks, dye works, gasworks, glassworks, ironworks, metalworks, paper works, printworks, saltworks, scrapworks, soapworks, starchworks, steelworks, tileworks, tubeworks, tryworks, waterworks, wireworks.

.5 **foundry,** metalworks; steelworks, steel mill; forge, furnace, bloomery; smelter; smithy, smithery, stithy, blacksmith shop or blacksmith's shop.

.6 **repair shop,** fix-it shop [informal]; **garage;** roundhouse; hangar.

.7 **laboratory, lab** [informal]; research laboratory, research installation or facility or center.

.8 **office,** shop [informal]; home or head or main office, headquarters, executive office, corporate headquarters; chambers; closet, cabinet [archaic], **study,** den; embassy, consulate, legation, chancery, chancellery; box office, booking office, ticket office; branch, branch office, local office.

## 720. PREPARATION

.1 NOUNS **preparation,** preparing, prep or prepping [both informal], fixing [informal], **readying,** making ready, makeready; warm-up; mobilization; **prearrangement** 641; **planning** 654.1; trial, **tryout** 489.2,3; **provision, arrangement;** preparatory or preliminary act or measure or step; **preliminary, preliminaries,** clearing the decks [informal]; propaedeutic, preparatory study or instruction; basic training, familiarization, briefing; prerequisite; processing, treatment, pretreatment; equipment 659; training 562.3; manufacture 167.3; **spadework,** groundwork, foundation 216.6.

**.2 fitting, fit** [informal]; **conditioning; adaptation, adjustment,** tuning; **qualification,** capacitation, enablement; **equipment, furnishing** 659.1.

**.3** (a preparation) **concoction,** decoction, *decoctum* [L], **brew, confection; composition, mixture** 44.5, **combination** 52.

**.4 preparedness, readiness; fitness, fittedness,** suitedness, suitableness, **suitability;** condition, trim; **qualification,** qualifiedness, **competence** or competency, **ability, capability, proficiency,** mastery; ripeness, maturity, seasoning, tempering.

**.5 preparer,** preparator, preparationist; trainer, coach, instructor, mentor, teacher; **trailblazer, pathfinder; forerunner** 66.1; **paver of the way.**

**.6** VERBS **prepare, make** or **get ready, prep** [informal], trim [archaic], **ready, fix** [informal]; provide [archaic], **arrange; make preparations** or **arrangements,** sound the note of preparation, clear the decks [informal], clear for action, settle preliminaries; **mobilize, marshal, deploy; prearrange** 641.3; **plan** 654.9; **try out** 489.8; fix up or ready up [both informal], put in or into shape; dress; treat, pretreat, process; cure, tan.

**.7 make up, get up, fix up** [informal]; **concoct,** decoct, brew; **compound, compose, put together, mix** 44.11; **make** 167.10.

**.8 fit, condition, adapt, adjust,** suit, tune, attune, put in tune or trim or working order; **qualify,** enable, capacitate; **equip, furnish** 659.7–9.

**.9 prime, load,** charge, cock, set; wind, wind up; steam up, get up steam, warm up.

**.10 prepare to, get ready to,** get set for [informal], fix to [dial]; be about to, be on the point of; ready oneself to, hold oneself in readiness.

**.11 prepare for, provide for, arrange for,** make arrangements or dispositions for, look out for, **make provision** or **due provision for;** provide against, make sure against, forearm, **provide for** or **against a rainy day,** prepare for the evil day; lay in provisions, lay up a store, keep as a nest egg, save to fall back upon, lay by, husband one's resources, salt or squirrel something away; set one's house in order.

**.12 prepare the way, pave the way,** smooth the path or road, **clear the way,** open the way, open the door to; **break the ice;** go in advance; **blaze the trail; prepare the ground,** cultivate the soil, sow the seed; do the spadework, lay the groundwork or

foundation, lay the first stone; lead up to.

**.13 prepare oneself, brace oneself, get ready, get set** [informal], strip for action, roll up one's sleeves, spit on one's hands, limber up, warm up, flex one's muscles, gird up one's loins, buckle on one's armor, get into harness, shoulder arms; sharpen one's tools, whet the knife or sword.

**.14 be prepared, be ready,** stand by, stand ready, hold oneself in readiness, keep one's powder dry, "put your trust in God, my boys, and keep your powder dry" [Cromwell].

**.15** (be fitted) **qualify, measure up,** check out [informal], have the qualifications or prerequisites.

**.16** ADJS **prepared, ready,** prepped [informal], in readiness or ready state, all ready, good and ready, prepared and ready, psyched up [informal]; **vigilant** 533.13; **ripe, mature; set** or **all set,** on the mark [informal]; **prearranged** 641.5; **planned** 654.13; **primed,** loaded, cocked, **loaded for bear** [slang]; familiarized, briefed, informed, put into the picture [Brit informal]; groomed, coached; ready for anything, "prepared for either course" [Vergil]; in the saddle, booted and spurred; armed and ready, in arms, up in arms, **armed** 799.14; in battle array, mobilized; **provided, equipped** 659.13; **well-prepared.**

**.17 fitted, adapted, adjusted, suited; qualified, fit, competent, able, capable,** proficient; checked out [informal]; **well-qualified, well-fitted, well-suited.**

**.18 prepared for, ready for,** alert for, set or all set for [informal]; loaded for, primed for; up for [slang]; equal to, up to.

**.19 ready-made, ready-formed, ready-mixed, ready-furnished, ready-dressed, ready-cooked; ready-built, prefabricated, prefab** [informal]; **ready-to-wear, ready-for-wear; ready-cut, cut-and-dried** or **cut-and-dry.**

**.20 preparatory, preparative; propaedeutic; prerequisite; provident, provisional.**

**.21** ADJS, ADVS **in readiness, in store, in reserve; in anticipation.**

**.22 in preparation,** in course of preparation, **in progress** or **process, under way, going on,** in embryo, **in production,** on stream, under construction, **in the works** or hopper or pipeline [informal], on the way, **in the making, in hand,** on the anvil, on the fire, in the oven; under revision; brewing, forthcoming.

**.23 afoot, on foot, afloat, astir.**

.24 PREPS in preparation for, against, for; in order to.

## 721. UNPREPAREDNESS

.1 NOUNS **unpreparedness, unreadiness,** unprovidedness, nonpreparedness, nonpreparation, lack of preparation; vulnerability 697.4; extemporaneousness, improvisation, ad lib [informal], planlessness; **unfitness,** unfittedness, unsuitedness, unsuitableness, **unsuitability, unqualifiedness,** unqualification, **disqualification,** incompetence, incapability.

.2 **improvidence, thriftlessness, unthriftiness,** poor husbandry, lax stewardship; **shiftlessness,** fecklessness, thoughtlessness, heedlessness; happy-go-luckiness; hastiness 709.2; negligence 534.1.

.3 (raw or original condition) **naturalness,** inartificiality; **natural state,** nature, **state of nature,** nature in the raw; pristineness, intactness, virginity; natural man, "unaccommodated man" [Shakespeare]; artlessness 736.

.4 **undevelopment,** nondevelopment; **immaturity,** immatureness, callowness, unfledgedness, **rawness, unripeness, greenness; unfinish,** unfinishedness, unpolishedness, **unrefinement, uncultivation; crudity,** crudeness, **rudeness, coarseness,** roughness, the rough; **oversimplification,** oversimplicity, simplism, reductionism.

.5 **raw material;** crude, crude stuff [informal]; ore, rich ore, rich vein; unsorted or unanalyzed mass; rough diamond, **diamond in the rough;** unlicked cub; **virgin soil.**

.6 VERBS **be unprepared** or **unready,** not be ready; go off half-cocked or at half cock [informal]; be taken unawares or aback, be caught napping, be caught with one's pants down [slang], be surprised; **extemporize,** improvise, ad-lib or play by ear [both informal]; have no plan, be innocent of forethought.

.7 **make no provision,** take no thought of tomorrow or the morrow, seize the day, *carpe diem* [L; Horace], let tomorrow take care of itself, live for the day, live like the grasshopper, live from hand to mouth; eat, drink, and be merry.

.8 ADJS **unprepared, unready,** unprimed; surprised, caught short, caught napping, caught with one's pants down [slang], taken by surprise, taken aback, taken unawares, caught off balance, caught off base [informal], tripped up; **unarranged,** unorganized, haphazard; makeshift,

rough-and-ready, **extemporaneous,** extemporized, improvised, ad-lib or off the top of one's head [both informal]; impromptu, snap [informal]; **unmade,** unmanufactured, unconcocted, unhatched, uncontrived, undevised, unplanned, unpremeditated, undeliberated, unstudied; hasty, precipitate 709.9–11; unbegun.

.9 **unfitted, unfit,** ill-fitted, **unsuited, unadapted, unqualified,** disqualified, incompetent, incapable; **unequipped, unfurnished,** unarmed, ill-equipped, ill-furnished, **unprovided,** ill-provided 662.12.

.10 **raw, crude;** uncooked, unbaked, unboiled; underdone, undercooked, rare, red.

.11 **immature, unripe,** underripe, unripened, impubic, **raw, green,** callow, unfledged, fledgling, unseasoned, unmellowed; ungrown, half-grown, adolescent, juvenile; undigested, ill-digested; half-baked [informal]; half-cocked or at half cock [both informal].

.12 **undeveloped, unfinished,** unlicked, unformed; unfashioned, unwrought, unlabored, unworked, unprocessed, untreated; unblown; uncut, unhewn; **underdeveloped;** backward, arrested, stunted; **crude, rude, coarse, unpolished, unrefined; uncultivated, uncultured; rough,** roughcast, roughhewn, **in the rough; rudimentary,** rudimental, lyo–, pro–; embryonic, in embryo, *in ovo* [L]; **oversimple,** simplistic, reductive, reductionistic.

.13 (in the raw or original state) **natural, native, in a state of nature,** in the raw; inartificial, artless 736.5; virgin, virginal, pristine, untouched, unsullied.

.14 **fallow, untilled, uncultivated, unsown.**

.15 **improvident,** unproviding; **thriftless, unthrifty,** uneconomical; grasshopper; hand-to-mouth; **shiftless, feckless, thoughtless, heedless;** happy-go-lucky; negligent 534.10, 11.

## 722. ACCOMPLISHMENT

*(act of accomplishing; entire performance)*

.1 NOUNS **accomplishment, achievement, fulfillment, performance, execution, effectuation,** implementation, carrying out or through, **discharge, dispatch, consummation, realization, attainment,** production, fruition; success 724; *fait accompli* [Fr], accomplished fact; mission accomplished.

.2 **completion,** completing, **finish, finishing,**

conclusion, end, ending, **termination, terminus, close, windup** [informal], rounding off or out, topping off; **perfection,** culmination 677.1,3; ripeness, maturity, maturation, full development.

.3 **finishing touch,** final touch, last touch, last stroke, final or finishing stroke, **finisher** [informal], copestone, capstone, crown, crowning of the edifice; climax 211.2.

.4 VERBS **accomplish, achieve, effect, effectuate, compass, consummate, do, execute, produce, make,** enact, **perform, discharge, fulfill, realize, attain,** fetch [dial]; **work,** work out; **dispatch, dispose of,** knock off [informal], polish off [slang], take care of [informal], **deal with,** put away, make short work of; succeed, manage 724.6–12; do the job [informal], **do** or turn the trick [slang].

.5 **bring about, bring to pass,** bring to effect, bring to a happy issue; **implement, carry out, carry through,** carry into execution; **bring off, carry off, pull off** [informal]; **put through, get through, put over** or **across** [informal]; come through with [informal].

.6 **complete, perfect, finish, finish off, conclude, terminate, end,** carry to completion, prosecute to a conclusion; **get through, get done;** get through with, get it over, get it over with, **finish up;** clean up or wind up or button up or wrap up or mop up [all informal], close up or out; put the lid on it [slang], call it a day [informal]; **round off** or **out, top off;** top out, crown, cap 211.9; climax, culminate; **give the finishing touches** or **strokes,** put the finishing touches or strokes on, finalize.

.7 **do to perfection,** do up brown [slang], **do to a turn,** do to a T [informal], do to a frazzle [slang], do down to the ground [informal], not do by halves, do oneself proud [informal], leave no loose ends, leave nothing hanging; go all lengths, go to all lengths, go the whole length or way; go the limit or go whole hog or go all out or shoot the works or go for broke [all slang].

.8 **ripen,** ripe [dial], **mature, maturate;** bloom, blow, blossom, flourish; come to fruition, bear fruit; **mellow;** grow up, reach maturity, reach its season; come or draw to a head; bring to maturity, bring to a head.

.9 ADJS **completing, completive, completory, finishing,** consummative, culminat-

ing, terminative, conclusive, **concluding,** fulfilling, finalizing, crowning; ultimate, **last, final,** terminal.

.10 **accomplished, achieved, effected,** effectuated, implemented, **consummated, executed, discharged, fulfilled, realized,** compassed, **attained; dispatched, disposed of,** set at rest; wrought, wrought out.

.11 **completed, done, finished, concluded, terminated, ended,** finished up; cleaned up or wound up or wrapped up or mopped up [all informal]; washed up [informal], **through,** done with; all said and done, all over but the shouting; perfective.

.12 **complete, perfect, consummate,** polished; exhaustive, thorough 56.10; fully realized.

.13 **ripe, mature,** matured, maturated, seasoned, **mellow,** full-grown, fully developed; tel(o)– or tele–.

.14 ADVS **to completion,** to the end, to the full, to the limit; to a turn, to a T [informal], to a finish, to a frazzle [slang].

## 723. NONACCOMPLISHMENT

.1 NOUNS **nonaccomplishment, nonachievement, nonperformance,** inexecution, nonexecution, nondischarging, **noncompletion,** nonconsummation, nonfulfillment, unfulfillment; nonfeasance, omission; neglect 534; loose ends, rough edges; endless task, work of Penelope, Sisyphean labor or toil or task; failure 725.

.2 VERBS neglect, leave undone 534.7, fail 725.8–16.

.3 ADJS **unaccomplished, unachieved, unperformed,** unexecuted, undischarged, unfulfilled, unconsummated, unrealized, unattained; **unfinished, uncompleted, undone;** neglected 534.14.

## 724. SUCCESS

.1 NOUNS **success, successfulness;** go [informal]; fortunate outcome, prosperous issue; **prosperity** 728; accomplishment 722; victory 726.

.2 sure success, **winner** or **natural** [both informal]; shoo-in or **sure thing** or sure bet or **cinch** or lead-pipe cinch [all slang].

.3 **great success,** howling or roaring success [informal], **triumph,** resounding triumph, brilliant success, striking success, meteoric success; **killing** [informal]; **hit** or big hit [both informal]; **smash** or smash hit or gas or gasser or riot or wow or sensation or overnight sensation [all slang]; brief or momentary success, nine days' wonder, flash in the pan, fad; best seller.

.4 score, hit, bull's-eye; goal, touchdown; slam, grand slam; strike; hole, hole in one; home run, homer [informal].

.5 (successful person) winner, star, star in the firmament, success; comer [slang]; victor 726.2.

.6 VERBS succeed, prevail, be successful, be crowned with success, meet with success; go, come off, go off; prosper 728.7; fare well, work well, do or work wonders, go to town or go great guns [both informal]; make a hit [informal], click or connect [both slang], catch on or take [both informal]; go over [informal], go over big [slang]; pass, graduate, qualify, win one's spurs, get one's credentials, be blooded; come through or pass with flying colors.

.7 achieve one's purpose, gain one's end or ends, secure one's object, attain one's objective, do what one set out to do, reach one's goal; make one's point; play it or handle it just right [informal], not put a foot wrong, play it like a master.

.8 score a success, score, hit it, hit the mark, ring the bell [informal], turn up trumps, break the bank or make a killing [both informal], hit the jackpot [slang].

.9 make good, come through, achieve success, make a success, make it [informal], make one's mark, give a good account of oneself, bear oneself with credit, do all right by oneself or do oneself proud [both informal]; advance, progress, make one's way, make headway, get on, come on [informal], get ahead [informal]; go places, go far; rise, rise in the world, work one's way up, claw or scrabble one's way up, mount the ladder of success; arrive, get there [slang], make the scene [informal]; come out on top, come out on top of the heap [slang]; be a success, have it made [informal], have the world at one's feet; make a noise in the world [informal], cut a swath, set the world or river or Thames on fire; break through, score or make a breakthrough.

.10 succeed with, crown with success; make a go of it; accomplish, compass, achieve 722.4; bring off, carry off, pull off [informal], turn or do the trick [informal], put through, bring through; put over or across [informal]; get away with it or get by [both slang].

.11 manage, contrive, succeed in; make out, get on or along [informal], come on or along [informal], go on; scrape along,

worry along, muddle through [Brit], get by, manage somehow; make it [informal], make the grade, cut the mustard or hack it [both slang]; clear, clear the hurdle; negotiate [informal], engineer; swing [informal], put over [slang], put through, swing the deal.

.12 win through, win out [informal], come through [slang], rise to the occasion, beat the game or beat the system [both informal]; triumph 726.3; weather out, weather the storm, live through, keep one's head above water; come up fighting or smiling, not know when one is beaten, persevere 625.2–6.

.13 ADJS successful, succeeding, crowned with success; prosperous, fortunate 728.12–14; triumphant 726.8; ahead of the game, out in front, on top, on top of the heap [slang]; assured of success, surefire, made; coming or on the up-and-up [both informal].

.14 ADVS successfully, swimmingly [informal], well, to some purpose, to good purpose; beyond all expectation, beyond one's fondest dreams.

## 725. FAILURE

.1 NOUNS failure, unsuccessfulness, unsuccess, successlessness, nonsuccess; no go [informal]; ill success; futility, uselessness 669; defeat 727; losing game; "lame and impotent conclusion" [Shakespeare]; nonaccomplishment 723; bankruptcy 842.3.

.2 [slang or informal terms] flop, floperoo, bust, frost, fizzle, lemon, washout, turkey, bomb, flat failure, dull thud, total loss.

.3 collapse, crash, smash, comedown, breakdown, fall, pratfall [slang], stumble, tumble, downfall, cropper [informal]; nose dive or tailspin [both slang]; deflation, bursting of the bubble.

.4 miss, near-miss; slip, slipup [informal], slip 'twixt cup and lip; error, mistake 518.3.

.5 abortion, miscarriage, miscarrying, abortive attempt, vain attempt; wild-goose chase, merry chase; misfire, flash in the pan, wet squib, dud [slang].

.6 fiasco, botch, bungle, hash, mess, muddle, foozle or bollix [both informal], flunk [informal], washout [slang].

.7 (unsuccessful person) failure, loser [informal]; flop or washout or false alarm [all slang], flash in the pan, dud [slang], also-ran; bankrupt 842.4.

**.8** VERBS **fail,** be unsuccessful, fail of success, not work or not come off [both informal], come to grief, **lose;** not make the grade, be found wanting, not come up to the mark; not pass, **flunk** or **flunk out** [both informal]; go to the wall, **go on the rocks;** labor in vain 669.8; go bankrupt 842.7.

**.9** [slang or informal terms] **lose out,** get left, **not make it,** not hack it, not get to first base, drop the ball, **flop,** flummox, lay an egg, go over like a lead balloon, draw a blank, bomb, drop a bomb; **fold,** fold up; take it on the chin, take the count; crap out; strike out, fan, whiff.

**.10** sink, founder, go down, go under [informal]; **slip,** go downhill, be on the skids [slang].

**.11** fall, **fall down** [slang], fall down on the job [informal]; **fall short, fall through,** fall to the ground; **fall between two stools; fall dead,** fall stillborn; **fall flat,** fall on one's face or fall flat on one's face [both informal], fall on one's ass [slang]; **collapse,** fall in; **crash,** go to smash [informal].

**.12** come to nothing, hang up or get nowhere [both informal]; **poop out** or go phut [both slang]; be all over or up with; fail miserably or ignominiously; fizz out or **fizzle** or fizzle out [all informal]; **misfire,** flash in the pan; **blow up, explode, end** or **go up in smoke,** go up like a rocket and come down like a stick.

**.13** miss, **miss the mark,** miss one's aim; **slip,** slip up [informal], goof [slang], bungle, blunder, foozle [informal]; err 518.9.

**.14** miscarry, abort; **go amiss,** go astray, **go wrong,** go on a wrong tack, take a wrong turn.

**.15** stall, stick, die, go dead, conk out [slang], sputter and stop, run out of steam, come to a shuddering halt, come to a dead stop.

**.16** flunk or flunk out [both informal]; **fail,** pluck or plough [both Brit slang], bust or wash out [both slang].

**.17** ADJS unsuccessful, successless, failing; failed, manqué [Fr], stickit [Scot]; **unfortunate** 729.14; abortive, par(a)–; miscarrying, miscarried, stillborn; fruitless, bootless, futile, useless 669.9–14; lame, **ineffectual,** ineffective, inefficacious, of no effect.

**.18** ADVS unsuccessfully, successlessly, **without success;** fruitlessly, bootlessly, ineffectually, ineffectively, inefficaciously; to little or no purpose, **in vain.**

## 726. VICTORY

**.1** NOUNS victory, triumph, conquest, subduing, subdual; a feather in one's cap [informal]; total victory, grand slam; championship; **winning,** win [informal]; knockout, KO [slang]; easy victory, walkover or walkaway [both informal], pushover or picnic [both slang]; runaway victory, landslide victory, landslide; Pyrrhic victory, Cadmean victory; moral victory; winning streak [informal]; **success** 724; ascendancy 739.6,7; mastery 741.2.

**.2** victor, winner, triumpher; **conqueror,** defeater, **vanquisher,** subduer, subjugator, conquistador [Sp]; top dog [informal]; master, master of the situation; hero, conquering hero; champion, champ [slang]; easy winner, sure winner, shoo-in [slang]; pancratiast; runner-up.

**.3** VERBS triumph, prevail, be victorious, come out on top [informal], chain victory to one's car; **succeed** 724.6; break the record, set a new mark [informal].

**.4** win, gain, capture, carry; win out [informal], win through, carry it, carry off or away; **win** or **carry** or **gain the day,** win the battle, come out first, finish in front, make a killing [informal], remain in possession of the field; **win the prize,** win the palm or bays or laurels, bear the palm, **bring home the bacon** [informal], take the cake [slang], win one's spurs; fluke or win by a fluke [both slang].

**.5** win hands down or win going away [both informal], win in a canter or walk or waltz [all informal], romp home or breeze [both informal], **walk off** or **away with,** waltz off with [informal], walk off with the game, **walk over** [informal]; have the game in one's own hands, have it all one's way; **take** or **carry by storm,** sweep aside all obstacles, carry all before one, make short work of.

**.6** triumph over, prevail over, best, beat [informal], **get the better** or **best of; surmount, overcome,** rise above, **defeat** 727.6.

**.7** gain the ascendancy, get on top [slang], **get the advantage, gain the upper** or **whip hand,** dominate the field, get the edge on or jump on or drop on [slang], get a leg up on [slang], get a stranglehold on.

**.8** ADJS victorious, triumphant, triumphal, **winning, prevailing;** conquering, vanquishing, defeating, overcoming; ascendant, in the ascendant, in ascendancy, dominant 741.18; successful 724.13; flushed with success or victory.

.9 undefeated, unbeaten, unvanquished, unconquered, unsubdued, unquelled, unbowed.

.10 ADVS triumphantly, victoriously, in triumph.

## 727. DEFEAT

.1 NOUNS defeat; beating, drubbing, thrashing, hiding, lathering, whipping, lambasting, trimming, licking [all informal], trouncing; vanquishment, conquest, conquering, mastery, subjugation, subduing, subdual; overthrow, overturn, overcoming; fall, downfall, collapse, smash, crash, undoing, ruin, debacle, destruction 693; deathblow, quietus; Waterloo; failure 725.

.2 discomfiture, rout, repulse, rebuff; frustration, bafflement, confusion; checkmate, check, balk, foil [archaic]; reverse, reversal, setback.

.3 utter defeat, total defeat, overwhelming defeat, crushing defeat, smashing defeat, decisive defeat; no contest; smearing or pasting or creaming or clobbering or shellacking or whopping or whomping [all slang]; whitewash or whitewashing [both informal], shutout.

.4 ignominious defeat, abject defeat, inglorious defeat, disastrous defeat, utter rout, bitter defeat, stinging defeat.

.5 loser, defeatee [informal]; the vanquished; good loser, game loser, sport or good sport [both informal]; underdog, also-ran; booby or duck [both slang]; stooge or fall guy [both slang]; victim 866.11.

.6 VERBS defeat, worst, best, get the better or best of, be too good for, be too much for, be more than a match for; outdo, outgeneral, outmaneuver, outclass, outshine, outpoint, outsail, outrun, outfight, etc.; triumph over 726.6; beat, drub, lick, whip, thrash, trim, hide, lather, trounce, lambaste [all informal]; skin or skin alive [both slang]; fix or settle or settle one's hash or make one say 'uncle' or put one's nose out of joint [all informal]; do in [slang], knock on the head, deal a deathblow to, put hors de combat; undo, ruin, destroy 693.10–21; lick to a frazzle [informal], beat hollow or all hollow [informal]; beat by a nose [informal].

.7 overcome, surmount; overpower, overmaster, overmatch; overthrow, overturn, overset; put the skids to [informal]; up-

set, trip, trip up, lay by the heels, send flying or sprawling; silence, floor, deck, make bite the dust; overcome oneself, master oneself; kick one's habit [slang].

.8 overwhelm, whelm, snow under [informal], overbear, defeat utterly, deal a crushing or smashing defeat; bulldoze or steamroller [both informal]; smear or paste or cream or clobber or shellac or whop or skunk or whomp [all slang]; schmear [Yid], blank or whitewash [both informal], shut out.

.9 discomfit, rout, put to rout, put to flight, scatter, stampede, panic; confound; put out of court.

.10 conquer, vanquish, quell, suppress, put down, subdue, subjugate, put under the yoke, master; reduce, prostrate, fell, flatten, break, smash, crush, humble, bend, bring one to his knees; roll or trample in the dust, tread or trample underfoot, trample down, ride down, ride or run roughshod over, override.

.11 thwart, frustrate, dash, check, deal a check to, checkmate 730.15,16.

.12 lose, lose out [informal], lose the day, come off second best, get or have the worst of it, meet one's Waterloo; fall, succumb, tumble, bow, go down, go under, bite or lick the dust, take the count [slang]; snatch defeat from the jaws of victory; throw in the towel, say uncle; have enough.

.13 ADJS lost, unwon.

.14 defeated, worsted, bested, outdone; beaten, beat, licked, whipped, trimmed, lathered, trounced, lambasted, settled, fixed [all informal]; skinned or skinned alive [both slang], thrown for a loss [slang]; discomfited, put to rout, routed, scattered, stampeded, panicked; confounded; overcome, overthrown, upset, overturned, overmatched, overpowered, overwhelmed, whelmed, overmastered, overborne, overridden; fallen, down; floored, silenced; done in [slang], undone, done for [informal], ruined, on the skids [informal], hors de combat [Fr]; all up with [informal].

.15 shut out, blanked or whitewashed [both informal], unscoring.

.16 conquered, vanquished, quelled, suppressed, put down, subdued, subjugated, mastered; reduced, prostrate(d), felled, flattened, smashed, crushed, broken, humbled, brought to one's knees.

.17 overpowering, overcoming, overwhelming, overmastering, overmatching.

## 728. PROSPERITY

.1 NOUNS **prosperity**, prosperousness, thriving or flourishing condition; **success** 724; **welfare, well-being,** weal, happiness, felicity; comfortable or easy circumstances, **comfort, ease,** security; **life of ease,** the life of Riley [informal], **the good life; clover** or **velvet** [both informal], **bed of roses, luxury,** lap of luxury, Easy Street [informal]; **the affluent life, gracious life,** gracious living; fat of the land; fleshpots, fleshpots of Egypt; milk and honey, loaves and fishes; a chicken in every pot, a car in every garage; purple and fine linen; high standard of living; upward mobility; **affluence, wealth** 837.

.2 **good fortune** or **luck,** happy fortune, **fortune, luck,** the breaks [slang]; **fortunateness, luckiness,** felicity [archaic]; blessing, smiles of fortune, fortune's favor.

.3 **stroke of luck,** piece of good luck; blessing; **fluke** or **lucky strike** or **scratch hit** or **break** [all slang], **good** or **lucky break** [slang]; **run** or **streak of luck** [informal].

.4 **good times,** piping times, bright or palmy or halcyon days, rosy era; heyday; prosperity, era of prosperity; fair weather, sunshine; golden era, **golden age,** golden time, Saturnian age, reign of Saturn, *Saturnia regna* [L]; age of Aquarius, millennium; utopia 535.11; heaven 1018.

.5 **roaring trade, land-office business** [informal], bull market, seller's market; booming economy, **boom** [informal], expanding economy.

.6 **fortunate, lucky dog** [informal], fortune's favorite, favorite of the gods, fortune's child, destiny's darling; man of substance 837.6.

.7 VERBS **prosper,** enjoy prosperity, **fare well,** get on well, do well, have everything going one's way, get on swimmingly; **turn out well, go well,** take a favorable turn; **succeed** 724.6; come on or along [informal], get on [informal]; **advance,** progress, make progress, make headway, get ahead [informal].

.8 **thrive, flourish,** boom; blossom, bloom, flower; batten, fatten, grow fat; be fat, dumb, and happy [informal].

.9 **be prosperous, make good, make one's mark,** rise or get on in the world, make a noise in the world [informal], do all right by oneself [informal], **make one's fortune;** grow rich 837.9; drive a roaring trade, do a land-office business [informal], rejoice in a seller's market.

.10 **live well, live in clover** or on velvet [informal], **live a life of ease,** live the life of Riley, **live high, live high on the hog** [informal], live on or off the fat of the land, roll in the lap of luxury; bask in the sunshine, have one's place in the sun; have a good or fine time of it.

.11 **be fortunate, be lucky,** be in luck, have all the luck, have one's moments [informal], **lead** or **have a charmed life;** fall into the shithouse and come up with a five-dollar gold piece [slang]; **get a break** or get the breaks [both slang]; hold aces or turn up trumps [both informal]; have a run of luck or hit a streak of luck [both informal]; have it break good for one [slang], have a stroke of luck; strike it lucky or make a lucky strike or strike oil [all slang], **strike it rich** [informal], hit big [slang], strike a rich vein, come into money, drop into a good thing.

.12 ADJS **prosperous,** in good case; **successful** 724.13; **affluent, wealthy** 837.13; **comfortable,** comfortably situated, **easy;** on Easy Street [informal], **in clover** or on velvet [both informal], on a bed of roses, in luxury, high on the hog [informal]; up in the world, on top of the heap [slang].

.13 **thriving, flourishing, prospering, booming** [informal]; vigorous, exuberant; in full swing, going strong [informal]; halcyon, palmy, balmy, rosy, piping, clear, fair; blooming, blossoming, flowering, fruiting; fat, sleek, in good case; fat, dumb, and happy [informal].

.14 **fortunate, lucky, providential; in luck; blessed,** blessed with luck, favored; born under a lucky star, born with a silver spoon in one's mouth, born on the sunny side of the hedge; **auspicious** 544.16.

.15 ADVS **prosperously, thrivingly, flourishingly,** boomingly, swimmingly [informal].

.16 **fortunately, luckily, providentially.**

## 729. ADVERSITY

.1 NOUNS **adversity,** adverse circumstances, difficulties, hard knocks [informal], **hardship, trouble,** troubles, "sea of troubles" [Shakespeare]; rigor, vicissitude, care, stress, pressure, stress of life; hardcase, **hard life,** a dog's life, vale of tears; wretched or miserable or hard or unhappy lot, hard row to hoe [informal], ups and downs of life, things going against one; **bummer** or **downer** [both slang]; annoyance, irritation, aggravation; **difficulty** 731; **trial,** tribulation, cross, curse, blight, **affliction** 866.8; plight, predicament 731.4.

.2 **misfortune, mishap,** ill hap, **misadventure, mischance,** *contretemps* [Fr], grief; **disaster, calamity, catastrophe, cataclysm, tragedy; shock, blow,** hard *or* nasty *or* staggering blow; **accident,** casualty; collision, crash; **wreck,** shipwreck; smash *or* smashup *or* crack-up *or* pileup [all informal], "the slings and arrows of outrageous fortune" [Shakespeare].

.3 **reverse, reversal,** reverse of fortune, **setback,** check, severe check, backset, throwback [informal]; **comedown,** descent, down.

.4 **unfortunateness, unluckiness,** lucklessness, ill success; unprosperousness; starcrossed *or* ill-fated life; inauspiciousness 544.8.

.5 **bad luck,** ill luck, **hard luck,** hard lines [Brit], **tough** *or* **rotten luck** [informal], raw deal [slang], bad *or* tough *or* rotten break [informal], devil's own luck; **ill fortune,** bad fortune, evil fortune, evil star, ill wind, evil dispensation; frowns of fortune.

.6 **hard times,** bad times, sad times; evil day, rainy day; hard *or* stormy *or* heavy weather; **depression,** recession, **slump,** economic stagnation, **bust** [informal].

.7 **unfortunate,** poor unfortunate, the plaything *or* toy *or* sport of fortune, fortune's fool; **loser** *or* sure loser [both informal]; hardcase *or* sad sack *or* hard-luck guy [all slang]; *schlemiel, schlimazel* [both Yid]; the wretched of the earth; victim 866.11.

.8 VERBS **go hard with,** go ill with; run one hard; **oppress, weigh on** *or* **upon,** weigh heavy on, weigh down, **burden,** overburden, load, overload, bear hard upon, lie on, lie hard *or* heavy upon; try one, put one out.

.9 **have trouble;** be born to trouble, be born under an evil star, be "born unto trouble, as the sparks fly upward" [Bible]; **have a hard time of it,** be up against it [informal], make heavy weather of it, meet adversity, have a bad time; bear the brunt, bear more than one's share; be put to one's wit's end, not know which way to turn.

.10 **come to grief,** have a mishap, suffer a misfortune, be stricken *or* staggered, be poleaxed, be felled, be clobbered [slang]; run aground, go on the rocks *or* shoals, split upon a rock; sink, drown, founder.

.11 **fall on evil days, go down in the world,** go downhill, slip, be on the skids [slang], come down, have a comedown, fall from one's high estate; **deteriorate,** degenerate, sink, decline; **go to pot** [informal], go to the dogs; reach the depths, touch bottom, hit rock bottom; have seen better days.

.12 **bring bad luck; hoodoo** *or* **hex** *or* **jinx** *or* Jonah *or* put the jinx on [all informal]; put the evil eye on, whammy [slang].

.13 ADJS **adverse, untoward, detrimental, unfavorable,** mis–; **sinister;** hostile, antagonistic, inimical; contrary, counter, counteractive, conflicting, opposing, opposed, opposite, in opposition; **difficult, troublesome, troublous, hard,** trying, rigorous, stressful; wretched, miserable 866.26; **not easy** 731.16; harmful 675.12.

.14 **unfortunate, unlucky, unprovidential,** unblessed, **unprosperous,** sad, unhappy, hapless, fortuneless, luckless, donsie [Brit dial]; **out of luck,** short of luck; **down on one's luck** [informal], badly *or* ill off, down in the world, in adverse circumstances; underprivileged, depressed; ill-starred, evil-starred, born under a bad sign, born under an evil star, planet-stricken, planet-struck, star-crossed; fatal, dire, doomful, funest, **ominous, inauspicious** 544.17.

.15 **disastrous, calamitous, catastrophic, cataclysmic,** cataclysmal, **tragic,** ruinous, wreckful [archaic], fatal, dire, black, grievous; destructive 693.26.

.16 ADVS **adversely, untowardly,** detrimentally, **unfavorably;** contrarily, conflictingly, opposingly, oppositely.

.17 **unfortunately, unluckily,** unprovidentially, sadly, unhappily, **as ill luck would have it;** by ill luck, by ill hap; in adverse circumstances, if worst comes to worst.

.18 **disastrously,** calamitously, catastrophically, cataclysmically, grievously, tragically, crushingly, shatteringly.

## 730. HINDRANCE

.1 NOUNS **hindrance,** hindering, **hampering,** let, let or hindrance; **check, arrest,** arrestment, arrestation; fixation; **impediment,** holdback; **resistance, opposition** 790; suppression, **repression, restriction, restraint** 760; **obstruction,** blocking, blockage, clogging, occlusion; **interruption,** interference; **retardation,** retardment, **detention,** detainment, **delay,** holdup, setback; **inhibition;** constriction, squeeze, stricture, cramp, stranglehold; **closure,** closing up *or* off; obstructionism, negativism, foot dragging [informal]; nuisance value.

.2 **prevention, stop, stoppage, stopping,** arrestation, estoppel; **stay, halt; prohibition,** forbiddance; debarment; **determent,** deterrence, **discouragement; forestalling,** preclusion, obviation, foreclosure.

.3 **frustration, thwarting, balking, foiling;** discomfiture, disconcertion, **bafflement,** confounding; **defeat,** upset; check, checkmate, balk, foil [archaic].

.4 **obstacle, obstruction, obstructive; hangup** [informal]; **block,** blockade, cordon, curtain; **difficulty,** hurdle, hazard; **deterrent,** determent; **drawback,** objection; **stumbling block,** stumbling stone, stone in one's path; fly in the ointment, one small difficulty [informal], **hitch, catch,** joker [informal], **rub, snag; bottleneck.**

.5 **barrier, bar;** gate, portcullis; **fence; wall,** stone wall, brick wall; seawall, jetty, groin, mole, breakwater; **bulwark, rampart,** defense, buffer, bulkhead, parapet, breastwork, work, earthwork, mound; bank, embankment, levee, dike; ditch, moat; dam, weir, leaping weir, barrage, milldam, beaver dam, cofferdam, wicket dam, shutter dam, bear-trap dam, hydraulic-fill dam, rock-fill dam, arch dam, archgravity dam, gravity dam; boom, jam, logjam; roadblock; backstop; iron curtain, bamboo curtain.

.6 **impediment,** embarrassment, hamper; encumbrance, cumbrance; **trouble,** difficulty 731; **handicap,** disadvantage, inconvenience, penalty; white elephant; **burden** or burthen [archaic], imposition, onus, cross, weight, deadweight, millstone around one's neck; **load,** pack, cargo, freight, charge; impedimenta, lumber.

.7 **curb, check,** countercheck, arrest, **stay, stop,** damper, holdback; **brake,** clog, drag, drogue, remora; chock, scotch, spoke, spoke in one's wheel; doorstop; checkrein, bearing rein, martingale; bit, snaffle, pelham, curb bit; shackle, chain, fetter, trammel 760.4; sea anchor, drift anchor, drift sail, drag sail or sheet.

.8 **hinderer,** impeder, **marplot,** obstructer; frustrater, thwarter; obstructionist, negativist; filibuster, filibusterer.

.9 **spoilsport,** wet blanket, **killjoy,** grouch, sourpuss [informal], malcontent, **dog in the manger** [informal].

0 VERBS **hinder, impede, inhibit, arrest, check,** countercheck, scotch, **curb, snub; resist, oppose** 790.3; **suppress, repress** 760.8; **interrupt,** intercept [archaic]; **intervene, interfere,** intermeddle, meddle

238.7; **damp, dampen,** throw cold water on; **retard,** slacken, **delay, detain, hold back, keep back,** set back, hold up [informal]; **restrain** 760.7; keep or hold in check, bottle up, dam up.

.11 **hamper, impede, cramp,** embarrass; trammel, entrammel, **enmesh, entangle,** ensnarl, **entrap, entwine, involve,** entoil, toil, net, lime, tangle, snarl; **fetter, shackle;** tie one's hands; **encumber,** cumber, **burden,** lumber, saddle with; weigh down, press down; hang like a millstone round one's neck; **handicap,** put at a disadvantage; **lame, cripple,** hobble, hamstring.

.12 **obstruct, stand in the way; dog, block,** blockade, block up, occlude; **jam,** crowd, pack; **bar,** barricade, bolt, lock; **debar,** shut out; shut off, **close,** close off or up, close tight, shut tight; constrict, squeeze, squeeze shut, strangle, strangulate, stifle, suffocate, **choke,** choke off, chock; stop up 266.7.

.13 **stop, stay, halt,** bring to a stop, put a stop or end to; **brake,** slow down, put on the brakes; **block, stall, stymie,** deadlock; nip in the bud.

.14 **prevent, prohibit, forbid; bar,** estop; **save, help, keep from; deter, discourage,** dishearten; **avert, keep off, ward off, stave off, fend off,** fend, repel, deflect, turn aside; **forestall, foreclose, preclude,** exclude, debar, **obviate,** anticipate; rule out.

.15 **thwart, frustrate, foil, cross, balk,** stonewall [slang]; spike, scotch, checkmate; **counter,** contravene, counteract, countermand, counterwork; stand in the way of, confront, brave, defy, challenge; **defeat** 727.6–11; **discomfit,** upset, **disrupt, confound,** flummox [slang], discountenance, put out of countenance, **disconcert, baffle,** nonplus, perplex, stump [informal], throw on one's beam ends; **circumvent,** elude; sabotage, **spoil, ruin,** dish [informal], dash, blast; **destroy** 693.10; throw a wrench in the machinery, **throw a monkey wrench into the works** [informal]; put a spoke in one's wheel, scotch one's wheel, spike one's guns, put one's nose out of joint [informal], upset one's applecart; take the wind out of one's sails, steal one's thunder, cut the ground from under one, knock the chocks or props from under one, knock the bottom out of [informal]; tie one's hands, clip the wings of.

.16 [slang terms] **queer, crab, foul up, louse**

up, snafu, bollix, gum, **gum up**, gum up the works; crimp, cramp, **put a crimp in,** cramp one's style.

.17 ADJS **hindering**, hindersome [dial], troublesome; **inhibitive**, inhibiting, suppressive, repressive; constrictive, strangling, stifling, choking; restrictive 760.12; **obstructive**, obstructing, occlusive, obstruent [archaic]; contrary, crosswise; counterproductive; interruptive, interrupting; in the way.

.18 hampering, impeding, impedimental, impeditive; onerous, oppressive, burdensome, cumbersome, cumbrous, encumbering.

.19 preventive, preventative, prophylactic, ant(i)– or anth–; prohibitive, forbidding; deterrent, deterring, discouraging; preclusive, forestalling.

.20 frustrating, confounding, disconcerting, baffling, defeating.

.21 ADVS under handicap, at a disadvantage, on the hip [archaic], with everything against one.

## 731. DIFFICULTY

.1 NOUNS **difficulty**, difficultness; **hardness, toughness,** rigor, rigorousness, ruggedness; **arduousness**, laboriousness, strenuousness, toilsomeness; **troublesomeness**, bothersomeness; onerousness, oppressiveness, burdensomeness; formidability, hairiness [slang]; complication, intricacy, complexity 46; abstruseness 549.2.

.2 **tough proposition** [informal], large or tall order [informal]; **hard job, tough job** [informal], backbreaker, ballbuster [slang], **chore,** man-sized job; brutal task, Herculean task, Augean task; **uphill work or going,** rough go [informal], **heavy sledding,** hard pull [informal], dead lift [archaic]; tough lineup to buck [slang], hard road to travel; tough nut to crack or hard row to hoe or hard row of stumps [all informal]; bitch [slang]; **handful** [informal], all one can manage.

.3 **trouble, matter;** headache [slang], problem, besetment, **inconvenience, disadvantage; ado,** great ado; peck of troubles, "sea of troubles" [Shakespeare]; hornet's nest, Pandora's box, can of worms [informal]; **evil** 675.3; **bother,** annoyance 864.7; **anxiety, worry** 890.1,2.

.4 predicament, plight, pickle or hobble [both informal], strait, straits, parlous straits, pinch, bind, pass, clutch, crunch [informal]; pretty pass, pretty pickle [informal], nice or pretty predicament, sorry

plight, fine kettle of fish [informal], how-do-you-do or fine how-do-you-do [both informal]; spot or tight spot or squeeze or tight squeeze [all informal], tightrope, ticklish or tricky spot [informal], sticky wicket [Brit informal]; scrape or jam or hot water [all informal]; tail in a gate or tit in the wringer [both slang]; slough, quagmire, morass, swamp, quicksand; embarrassment, embarrassing position or situation; complication, imbroglio, mess, holy or unholy mess [informal], mix or stew [both informal]; the devil to pay, hell to pay [slang].

.5 impasse, corner or box or hole [all informal]; cul-de-sac, blind alley, dead end, dead-end street; extremity, end of one's rope or tether, wit's end, nowhere to turn; stalemate, deadlock; stand, standstill, halt, stop.

.6 dilemma, horns of a dilemma, quandary, nonplus; vexed question, thorny problem, knotty point, knot, crux, node, nodus, Gordian knot, poser, teaser, perplexity, puzzle, enigma 549.8; paradox, oxymoron; asses' bridge, pons asinorum [L].

.7 crux, hitch, pinch, rub, snag, catch, joker [informal], where the shoe pinches.

.8 unwieldiness, unmanageability; unhandiness, inconvenience, impracticality; awkwardness, clumsiness; cumbersomeness, ponderousness, bulkiness, hulkiness.

.9 VERBS be difficult, present difficulties, take some doing [informal].

.10 have difficulty, have trouble, have a hard time of it, have one's hands full, be hard put, have much ado with; labor under difficulties, labor under a disadvantage, struggle, flounder, beat about, make heavy weather of it; swim against the current; walk on eggshells or hot coals, dance on a hot griddle.

.11 get into trouble, plunge into difficulties, let oneself in for, put one's foot in it [informal]; get in a jam or hot water or the soup [informal], get into a scrape [informal], get in a mess or hole or box or bind [informal]; paint oneself into a corner [informal], get one's ass in a bind or put oneself in a spot [both slang], put one foot in one's mouth; have a tiger by the tail; burn one's fingers; get all tangled or snarled or wound up, get all balled up or bollixed up [slang].

.12 trouble, beset; bother, pother, disturb, perturb, irk, plague, torment, harass, vex, distress 866.13–16; inconvenience, put out, put out of the way, discommode 671 concern, **worry** 890.3,4; **puzzle, perplex** 514.13; put to it, give one trouble, complicate matters; give one a hard time *or* give one a bad time *or* make it tough for [all informal]; be too much for; ail, be the matter.

.13 **cause trouble,** bring trouble, "sow the wind and reap the whirlwind" [Bible]; bring down upon one, bring down upon one's head, bring down around one's ears; **stir up a hornet's nest,** bring a hornet's nest about one's ears, open Pandora's box, open a can of worms [informal]; **raise hob** *or* **hell** [informal]; raise merry hell *or* play hob *or* play hell [all informal], play the deuce *or* devil [informal].

.14 **put in a hole** [informal], put in a spot [slang]; **embarrass; involve,** enmesh, entangle.

.15 **corner,** run *or* drive into a corner [both informal], **tree** [informal], chase up a tree *or* stump [informal], drive *or* force to the wall, put one's back to the wall, have one on the ropes [informal].

.16 ADJS **difficult,** difficile, dys– *or* dis–; **not easy,** no picnic; **hard, tough, rough, rugged,** rigorous, brutal, severe; wicked *or* mean *or* hairy [all slang], **formidable; arduous, strenuous, toilsome, laborious,** operose, Herculean; steep, uphill; hard-fought; hard-earned; jawbreaking; knotty, knotted; thorny, spiny, set with thorns; delicate, ticklish, tricky, critical, easier said than done; exacting, demanding; intricate, complex 46.4; abstruse 549.16.

.17 **troublesome,** besetting; **bothersome,** irksome, vexatious, painful, plaguey [informal], annoying 864.22; **burdensome,** oppressive, onerous, heavy *or* hefty [both informal], crushing, backbreaking; **trying,** grueling.

.18 **unwieldy, unmanageable, unhandy;** inconvenient, impractical; **awkward, clumsy, cumbersome,** unmaneuverable; contrary, perverse, crosswise; ponderous, bulky, hulky, hulking.

.19 **troubled,** beset, sore beset; **bothered, vexed,** irked, annoyed 866.21; **plagued, harassed** 866.24; distressed, perturbed 866.22; inconvenienced, embarrassed; put to it *or* hard put to it [both informal]; **worried, anxious** 890.6,7; puzzled 514.24.

.20 **in a predicament,** in a sorry plight, in a pretty pass; **in a mess** *or* **in a scrape** *or* **in a jam** *or* **in hot water** *or* **in the soup** [all informal]; **in a spot** *or* **in a fix** *or* **in a tight spot** *or* **in a hole** *or* in a bind *or* in a box [all informal], **in a pickle** [informal],

in a nice *or* pretty pickle [informal]; **in trouble,** in Dutch [slang], **on the spot** *or* **behind the eight ball** [both informal]; on Queer Street [informal]; out on a limb [informal]; in deep water, out of one's depth.

.21 **in a dilemma,** on the horns of a dilemma, **in a quandary;** between two stools; between Scylla and Charybdis, between the devil and the deep blue sea.

.22 **at an impasse,** at one's wit's end, at a loss, at a stand *or* standstill; **nonplussed,** at a nonplus; **baffled, perplexed, bewildered,** mystified, stuck *or* stumped [both informal].

.23 **cornered,** in a corner, with one's back to the wall; **treed** *or* **up a tree** *or* up a stump [all informal]; at bay, *aux abois* [Fr].

.24 **straitened,** reduced to dire straits, in desperate straits, **pinched,** sore *or* sorely pressed, **hard pressed, hard up** [slang], **up against it** [slang]; driven from pillar to post; **desperate, in extremities,** *in extremis* [L], **at the end of one's rope** *or* tether.

.25 **stranded, grounded,** aground, **on the rocks,** high and dry; **stuck,** stuck *or* set fast; foundered, swamped; castaway, marooned, wrecked, shipwrecked.

.26 ADVS **with difficulty,** difficultly, with much ado, mogi–; hardly, painfully; **the hard way, arduously, strenuously, laboriously,** toilsomely.

.27 **unwieldily, unmanageably, unhandily,** inconveniently; **awkwardly, clumsily, cumbersomely;** ponderously.

## 732. FACILITY

.1 NOUNS **facility, ease, easiness,** facileness, **effortlessness;** lack of hindrance, **smoothness,** freedom; clear coast, clear road *or* course; smooth road, royal road, highroad; easy going, plain sailing, smooth *or* straight sailing; clarity, intelligibility 548; uncomplexity, uncomplicatedness, simplicity 45.

.2 **wieldiness,** wieldableness, **manageability,** manageableness, maneuverability, handiness; **convenience,** practicality, untroublesomeness; **flexibility,** pliancy, pliability, ductility, malleability; adaptability, feasibility.

.3 **easy thing,** mere child's play, simple twist of the wrist; **cinch** *or* **snap** *or* **pushover** *or* setup *or* breeze *or* duck soup *or* velvet *or* picnic *or* pie [all slang], piece of cake [Brit slang]; easy target, sitting duck [informal]; sinecure.

.4 **facilitation, easing,** smoothing; **speeding,** expediting, expedition, quickening, hastening; streamlining; simplifying, **simplification, clarification.**

.5 **disembarrassment, disentanglement, disencumbrance,** disinvolvement, uncluttering, unscrambling, unsnarling, disburdening, unhampering; **extrication,** disengagement, **freeing,** clearing.

.6 VERBS **facilitate, ease; grease the wheels** [informal]; **smooth, smooth** or **pave the way,** grease the ways, soap the ways [both informal], prepare the way, **clear the way,** make all clear for, make way for; run interference for [informal], open the way, open the door to; **open up, unclog,** unblock, unjam, unbar, loose 763.6; **lubricate,** remove friction, grease, oil; **speed, expedite,** quicken, hasten; **help along,** help on its way; **aid** 785.11; **explain** 552.11, make clear 548.6; **simplify** 45.4,5.

.7 **do easily,** make short work of, do with one's hands tied behind one's back, do with both eyes shut.

.8 **disembarrass, disencumber,** disburden, unhamper; **disentangle,** disembroil, disinvolve, unclutter, unscramble, unsnarl; **extricate,** disengage, **free,** free up, clear; **liberate** 763.4.

.9 **go easily, run smoothly,** work well, work like a machine, go like clockwork; present no difficulties, give no trouble, be painless, be effortless; flow, roll, glide, slide, coast, sweep, sail.

.10 **have it easy, have it soft** [informal], have it all one's own way, have the game in one's hands; win easily; breeze in or walk over the course or win in a walk or win in a canter or win hands down [all informal].

.11 **take it easy** or **go easy** [both informal], swim with the stream, drift with the current, go with the tide; cool it or not sweat it [both slang]; take it in one's stride, make little or light of, think nothing of.

.12 ADJS **easy, facile, effortless,** smooth, casual, painless; soft [informal], cushy [slang]; plain, uncomplicated, straightforward, **simple** 45.6–9, Mickey Mouse [informal], simple as ABC [informal], easy as pie or easy as falling off a log [both informal], like shooting fish in a barrel, like taking candy from a baby; **clear** 548.10; glib; **light,** unburdensome; nothing to it.

.13 **smooth-running,** frictionless, easy-running, easy-flowing; well-oiled, well-greased.

.14 **wieldy,** wieldable; tractable; flexible, pliant, yielding, malleable, ductile, pliable, **manageable,** maneuverable; handy, **convenient,** foolproof, practical, untroublesome; adaptable, feasible.

.15 ADVS **easily,** facilely, **effortlessly, readily, simply,** lightly, swimmingly [informal], without difficulty; no sweat or like nothing or slick as a whistle [all slang]; hands down [informal], with one hand tied behind one's back, with both eyes closed; **smoothly,** like clockwork; on easy terms.

## 733. SKILL

.1 NOUNS **skill,** skillfulness, **expertness, proficiency,** craft, expertise, **cleverness; dexterity,** dexterousness or dextrousness; **adroitness,** address, **adeptness, deftness,** handiness, practical ability; coordination, timing; quickness, readiness; **competence,** capability, capacity, ability; efficiency; **facility, prowess;** grace, style, finesse; **tact, tactfulness, diplomacy;** savoir-faire [Fr]; **artistry;** artfulness; **craftsmanship,** workmanship, artisanship; **know-how** [informal], savvy [slang]; technical skill, **technique;** technical brilliance, technical mastery, **virtuosity,** bravura, wizardry; brilliance 467.2; **cunning** 735; **ingenuity,** ingeniousness, resource, resourcefulness, wit; **mastery,** mastership, **command,** control, grip; marksmanship, seamanship, airmanship, horsemanship, etc.; –ery or –ry, –ics, –ship, –manship, –urgy.

.2 **agility, nimbleness,** spryness, lightness, featliness.

.3 **versatility, ambidexterity,** many-sidedness, all-roundedness [informal], Renaissance versatility; **adaptability,** adjustability, flexibility; Renaissance man.

.4 **talent,** flair, strong flair, **gift, endowment,** dowry, dower, natural gift or endowment, **genius,** instinct, **faculty,** bump [informal], **power,** ability, **capability, capacity,** potential; caliber; **forte,** speciality, métier, long suit, strong point; **equipment, qualification;** talents, powers, naturals [archaic], parts; the goods or the stuff or what it takes [all slang], makings.

.5 **aptitude,** inborn or innate aptitude, aptness, felicity, flair; **bent, turn,** propensity, leaning, inclination, tendency; turn for, capacity for, gift for, genius for; an eye for, an ear for, a hand for.

.6 **knack, art, hang, trick,** way; **touch,** feel.

.7 **art, science, craft;** skill; **technique,** technic, **technics,** technology, technical knowledge or skill, technical know-how [informal]; **mechanics**, mechanism; method 657.1.

.8 **accomplishment**, acquirement, attainment; finish.

.9 **experience**, **practice**, practical knowledge or skill; background, past experience, seasoning, tempering; **worldly wisdom**, knowledge of the world, blaséness, sophistication; sagacity 467.4.

.10 **masterpiece**, masterwork, *chef d'œuvre* [Fr]; **master stroke**, *coup de maître* [Fr]; **feat**, *tour de force* [Fr].

.11 **expert**, **adept**, proficient, –an or –ean or –ian, –ician, –ist; **artist**, craftsman, artisan, skilled workman, journeyman; technician; seasoned or experienced hand; shark or sharp [both informal], no slouch [slang]; graduate; **professional**, **pro** [informal]; **jack-of-all-trades**, handy man, Admirable Crichton [J. M. Barrie]; **authority**, professor, **consultant**, expert consultant, attaché, technical adviser, savant 476.3; diplomatist, diplomat; politician, statesman, elder statesman; connoisseur, *connaisseur* [Fr]; *cordon bleu* [Fr]; marksman, crack shot, dead shot.

.12 **talented person**, **talent**, man of parts, gifted person, prodigy, **genius**; mental genius, intellectual genius, intellectual prodigy, mental giant; gifted child, **child prodigy**, boy wonder [informal]; natural [informal].

.13 **master**, past master; master hand, **good hand**, skilled or practiced hand; ace or star or superstar or crackerjack or great or all-time great or topnotcher or first-rater [all informal]; **prodigy**, **wizard** or whiz [both informal], magician; **virtuoso**; **genius**, man of genius; mastermind; mahatma, sage 468.1.

.14 **champion**, champ [slang], world champion; **record holder**, world-record holder; laureate; medal winner, Olympic medal winner, medalist, award winner, prizeman, prizetaker, **prizewinner**; hall-of-famer.

.15 **veteran**, vet [informal], seasoned veteran, **old pro** [informal]; old hand, old-timer [informal]; old campaigner, war-horse [informal]; salt or old salt or old sea dog [all informal], shellback [slang].

.16 **sophisticate**, man of experience, **man of the world**; slicker or city slicker [both informal]; man-about-town; **cosmopolitan**, cosmopolite, citizen of the world.

.17 VERBS **excel in** or **at**, shine in or at [informal], be master of; be at home in; **have a gift** or **flair** or **talent** or **bent** or **faculty** or

**turn for**, have a bump for [informal], **have a good head for**, have an ear for, have an eye for, be born for, show aptitude or talent for; have the knack or touch, have the hang of it; have something on the ball or plenty on the ball [slang].

.18 **know backwards and forwards**, **know one's stuff** or **know one's onions** [both slang], **know the ropes** or **know all the ins and outs** [both informal], know from A to Z or from alpha to omega, know from the ground up, know all the tricks, know all the tricks of the trade, know all the moves of the game; **know what's what**, **know a thing or two**, **know what it's all about**, **know the score** or know all the answers [both slang], "know a hawk from a handsaw" [Shakespeare]; have savvy [slang]; **know one's way about**, know the ways of the world, have been around [slang], have been through the mill [informal], have cut one's wisdom teeth or eyeteeth [informal], be long in the tooth, **not be born yesterday**; get around [informal].

.19 **exercise skill**, handle oneself well, demonstrate one's ability, **strut one's stuff** [slang], show expertise; cut one's coat according to one's cloth, play one's cards well.

.20 ADJS **skillful**, **good**, goodish, excellent, **expert**, **proficient**; **dexterous** or dextrous, **adroit**, **deft**, **adept**, **coordinated**, well-coordinated, **apt**, no mean, **handy**; quick, ready; **clever**, cute or slick [both informal], neat, clean; fancy, graceful, stylish; some or quite some or quite a or every bit a [all informal]; **masterly**, **masterful**; magisterial; authoritative, professional; the compleat or the complete; crack or crackerjack [both informal]; virtuoso, bravura, technically superb; **brilliant** 467.14; cunning 735.12; tactful, diplomatic, politic, statesmanlike; **ingenious**, resourceful, daedal, Daedalian; **artistic**; workmanlike, **well-done**.

.21 **agile**, **nimble**, **spry**, sprightly, fleet, featly, peart [dial], light, graceful, nimble-footed, light-footed, sure-footed; nimble-fingered, neat-fingered, neat-handed.

.22 **competent**, **capable**, **able**, efficient, qualified, **fit**, **fitted**, suited, worthy; journeyman; fit or fitted for; **equal to**, up to; up to snuff [slang], up to the mark [informal], *au fait* [Fr]; well-qualified, well-fitted, well-suited.

.23 **versatile**, **ambidextrous**, two-handed, all-around [informal], **many-sided,** generally capable; **adaptable,** adjustable, flexible, resourceful, supple; amphibious.

.24 **skilled, accomplished; practiced; professional,** career; trained, coached, prepared, primed, finished; at one's best, at concert pitch; initiated, initiate; technical; conversant 475.20.

.25 **skilled in,** proficient in, adept in, versed in, **good at,** expert at, **handy at, a hand** or **good hand at,** master of, strong in, at home in; **up on,** well up on, well-versed 475.19,20.

.26 **experienced, practiced,** mature, matured, ripe, ripened, **seasoned,** tried, tried and true, **veteran,** old, an old dog at [informal]; sagacious 467.16–19; **worldly, worldly-wise,** world-wise, wise in the ways of the world, knowing, **sophisticated,** cosmopolitan, cosmopolite, blasé, dry behind the ears, not born yesterday, long in the tooth.

.27 **talented, gifted, endowed,** with a flair; born for, made for, cut out for [informal], with an eye for, with an ear for, with a bump for [informal].

.28 **well-laid, well-devised,** well-contrived, well-designed, well-planned, well-worked-out; well-invented, *ben trovato* [Ital]; **well-weighed, well-reasoned,** well-considered, well-thought-out; **cunning, clever.**

.29 ADVS **skillfully, expertly, proficiently,** excellently, well; **cleverly,** neatly, ingeniously, resourcefully; cunningly 735.13; **dexterously** or dextrously, **adroitly, deftly, adeptly,** aptly, handily; agilely, nimbly, featly, spryly; **competently, capably, ably,** efficiently; **masterfully;** brilliantly, superbly, with genius, with a touch of genius; **artistically,** artfully; with skill, with consummate skill, with finesse.

## 734. UNSKILLFULNESS

.1 NOUNS **unskillfulness,** skill-lessness, **inexpertness, unproficiency, uncleverness;** unintelligence 469; inadeptness, **undexterousness** or undextrousness, indexterity, **undeftness;** inefficiency; **incompetence** or incompetency, **inability, incapability, incapacity,** inadequacy; **ineffectiveness, ineffectuality; mediocrity,** pedestrianism; **inaptitude,** inaptness, unaptness, **ineptness,** maladroitness; unfitness, unfittedness; untrainedness, unschooledness; thoughtlessness, inattentiveness; maladjustment; rustiness [informal].

.2 **inexperience,** unexperience, unexperiencedness, unpracticedness; **rawness, greenness,** unripeness, callowness, unfledgedness, immaturity; ignorance 477; **unfamiliarity,** unacquaintance, unacquaintedness, unaccustomedness; **amateurishness,** amateurism, unprofessionalness, unprofessionalism.

.3 **clumsiness, awkwardness,** bumblingness, **maladroitness, unhandiness,** left-handedness, heavy-handedness, ham-handedness [informal]; handful of thumbs; **ungainliness,** uncouthness, **ungracefulness,** gracelessness, inelegance; **gawkiness,** gawkishness; **lubberliness, oafishness,** loutishness, boorishness, clownishness, lumpishness; **cumbersomeness,** hulkiness, **ponderousness; unwieldiness, unmanageability** 731.8.

.4 **bungling, blundering,** boggling, **fumbling,** muffing, **botching,** botchery, blunderheadedness; **sloppiness, carelessness** 534.2; too many cooks.

.5 **bungle, blunder, botch,** flub, boner or bonehead play [both slang], boggle, bobble or boo-boo [both slang], foozle [informal], bevue; **fumble, muff, fluff,** miscue [slang]; **slip, trip, stumble;** *gaucherie, étourderie, balourdise* [all Fr]; **hash** or **mess** [both informal]; bad job, sad work, clumsy performance; off day; **error, mistake** 518.3.

.6 **mismanagement, mishandling,** misdirection, misguidance, misconduct, **misgovernment,** misrule; misadministration, maladministration; malfeasance, malpractice, misfeasance, wrongdoing 982; nonfeasance, omission, **negligence,** neglect 534.6; bad policy, impolicy, inexpedience or inexpediency 671.

.7 **incompetent,** incapable; dull tool, mediocrity, **no conjuror;** one who will not set the Thames on fire [Brit]; greenhorn 477.8.

.8 **bungler, blunderer,** blunderhead, boggler, slubberer, bumbler, **fumbler, botcher;** bull in a china shop, ox; lubber, looby, lout, oaf, gawk, gowk [Brit dial], *klutz* [Yid], boor, **clown,** slouch; clodhopper, clodknocker, yokel; **clod,** clot [Brit], **dolt,** blockhead 471.3,4; awkward squad.

.9 [slang or informal terms] goof, goofer, goofball, foul-up, foozler, clumsy, fumble-fist, **butterfingers,** muff, muffer, stumblebum, stumblebunny, duffer, lummox, **slob,** lump, dub; rube, hick.

.10 VERBS not know how, not have the knack, not have it in one [informal]; not be up to [informal]; not be versed.

.11 **bungle, blunder,** bumble, boggle, muff, muff one's cue, **fumble,** be all thumbs, have a handful of thumbs; **flounder, muddle, lumber;** stumble, **slip, trip,** trip over one's own feet, miss one's footing, miscue; commit a *faux pas*, commit a gaffe; blunder on *or* upon *or* into; blunder away, be not one's day; **botch,** mar, **spoil, butcher, murder,** make sad work of; play havoc with, play the mischief with.

.12 [slang *or* informal terms] bobble, **goof,** put one's foot in it, stub one's toe, drop a brick, bonehead into it; bitch, bitch up, hash up, **mess up,** flub, **make a mess** *or* **hash of,** foul up, goof up, **screw up,** louse **up, gum up,** gum up the works, bugger, bugger up, play the deuce *or* devil *or* hell *or* merry hell with; go at it ass-backwards.

.13 **mismanage, mishandle, misconduct,** misdirect, **misguide, misgovern, misrule;** misadminister, maladminister; be negligent 534.6.

.14 not know what one is about, not know one's interest, make an ass of oneself, make a fool of oneself, stultify oneself, put oneself out of court, stand in one's own light, not know on which side one's bread is buttered, kill the goose that lays the golden egg, cut one's own throat, dig one's own grave, behave self-destructively, play with fire, burn one's fingers, jump out of the frying pan into the fire, "sow the wind and reap the whirlwind" [Bible], lock the barn door after the horse is stolen, count one's chickens before they are hatched, buy a pig in a poke, aim at a pigeon and kill a crow, put the cart before the horse, put a square peg into a round hole, run before one can walk.

.15 ADJS **unskillful,** skill-less, artless, **inexpert, unproficient, unclever;** inefficient; **undexterous** *or* undextrous, **undeft, inadept, unfacile; unapt, inapt, inept,** half-assed [slang], **poor;** mediocre, pedestrian; thoughtless, inattentive; unintelligent 469.13.

16 **unskilled, unaccomplished, untrained,** untaught, **unschooled, untutored,** uncoached, **uninitiated, unprepared,** unprimed, **unfinished, unpolished; untalented, ungifted, unendowed; amateurish,** unprofessional, unbusinesslike, semiskilled.

7 **inexperienced,** unexperienced, unversed, unconversant, **unpracticed;** undeveloped, unseasoned; **raw, green,** green as grass, unripe, callow, unfledged, immature, unmatured, fresh, not dry behind the ears,

**untried;** unskilled in, unpracticed in, unversed in, unconversant with, unaccustomed to, unused to, unfamiliar *or* unacquainted with, new to, uninitiated in, a stranger to, a novice *or* tyro at; ignorant 477.12.

.18 **out of practice,** out of training *or* form, soft [informal], out of shape *or* condition, stiff, **rusty;** gone *or* run to seed [informal], not what one used to be [informal], losing one's touch, slipping, on the downgrade.

.19 **incompetent, incapable, unable,** inadequate, **unequipped, unqualified,** ill-qualified, **unfit, unfitted,** unadapted, not equal *or* up to, not cut out for [informal]; **ineffective, ineffectual;** unadjusted, maladjusted.

.20 **clumsy, awkward, bungling, blundering,** blunderheaded, bumbling, fumbling; **maladroit, unhandy,** left-hand, left-handed, heavy-handed, ham-handed *or* ham-fisted [both informal], clumsy-fisted, butterfingered [informal], **all thumbs,** fingers all thumbs, with a handful of thumbs; stiff; **ungainly, uncouth, ungraceful,** inelegant, *gauche* [Fr]; **gawky,** gawkish; **lubberly, loutish, oafish,** boorish, clownish, lumpish, slobbish [slang]; **sloppy, careless** 534.11; **ponderous, cumbersome,** lumbering, hulking, hulky; **unwieldy** 731.18.

.21 **botched, bungled,** fumbled, muffed, spoiled, **butchered,** murdered; **ill-managed,** ill-done, ill-conducted, ill-devised, ill-contrived, ill-executed; mismanaged, misconducted, **misdirected, misguided;** impolitic, ill-considered, ill-advised 470.9; negligent 534.10–13.

.22 [slang *or* informal terms] bobbled, bitched, bitched up, hashed up, **messed up,** fouled up, **screwed up, loused up,** gummed up, buggered, buggered up; assbackwards.

.23 ADVS **unskillfully, inexpertly, unproficiently, uncleverly;** inefficiently; **incompetently, incapably,** inadequately, unfitly; **undexterously, undeftly, inadeptly,** unfacilely; **unaptly, inaptly, ineptly,** poorly.

.24 **clumsily, awkwardly; bunglingly, blunderingly; maladroitly,** unhandily; **ungracefully,** gracelessly, inelegantly, uncouthly; **ponderously, cumbersomely,** lumberingly, hulkingly, hulkily; ass-backwards [slang].

## 735. CUNNING

.1 NOUNS **cunning,** cunningness, **craft, craftiness,** callidity, **artfulness, art, artifice,** wiliness, wiles, guile, **slyness,** insidiousness, suppleness [Scot], **foxiness,** slipperiness, shiftiness, trickiness; gamesmanship *or* one-upmanship [both informal]; **canniness, shrewdness,** sharpness, acuteness, astuteness, **cleverness** 733.1; resourcefulness, ingeniousness, wit, inventiveness, readiness; subtlety, subtilty, subtleness, Italian hand, fine Italian hand, finesse; sophistry 483; "the dark sanctuary of incapacity" [Chesterfield], "the ape of wisdom" [Locke]; satanic cunning, the cunning of the serpent; sneakiness, **stealthiness,** stealth 614.4; cageyness [informal], wariness 895.2.

.2 **Machiavellianism,** Machiavellism; **politics, diplomacy,** diplomatics; jobbery, jobbing.

.3 **stratagem, artifice,** art [archaic], **craft, wile,** strategy, **device,** wily device, **contrivance, expedient, design, scheme, trick,** cute trick, fetch, fakement [informal], gimmick [slang], **ruse, red herring, shift,** tactic, **maneuver,** move, coup, gambit, **ploy, dodge,** artful dodge; **game,** little game, racket *or* grift [both slang]; **plot,** conspiracy, **intrigue** 654.6; sleight, feint, jugglery; **subterfuge,** blind, dust in the eyes; chicanery, knavery, deceit, trickery 618.3,4.

.4 **machination, manipulation, wire-pulling** [informal]; influence, political influence, behind-the-scenes influence *or* pressure; **maneuvering,** maneuvers, tactical maneuvers; **tactics,** devices, expedients.

.5 **circumvention,** getting round *or* around; **evasion,** elusion, the slip [informal]; the runaround *or* buck-passing *or* passing the buck [all informal]; **frustration, foiling, thwarting** 730.3; **outwitting,** outsmarting, outguessing, **outmaneuvering.**

.6 **slyboots,** sly dog [informal], **fox,** reynard, dodger, Artful Dodger [Dickens], crafty rascal, smooth *or* slick citizen [informal], glib tongue, smooth *or* sweet talker, charmer; **trickster,** shyster [slang], Philadelphia lawyer [informal]; horse trader, Yankee horse trader; **swindler** 619.3.

.7 **strategist, tactician;** maneuverer, **machinator, manipulator, wire-puller** [informal]; calculator, schemer, **intriguer** 654.8.

.8 **Machiavellian,** Machiavel, Machiavellianist; **diplomat,** diplomatist, **politician** 746; political realist; influence peddler *or* power broker [both informal].

.9 VERBS **live by one's wits,** play a deep game; use one's fine Italian hand, finesse; shift, dodge, twist and turn, zig and zag;

hide one's hand, cover one's path; **trick, deceive** 618.13–18.

.10 **maneuver, manipulate,** pull strings *or* wires; **machinate, contrive,** angle [informal], **jockey, engineer;** play games [informal]; **plot, scheme, intrigue** 654.10; **finagle, wangle;** gerrymander.

.11 **outwit, outsmart,** outguess, outfigure, **outmaneuver,** outgeneral, outflank, outplay; get the better *or* best of, go one better, know a trick worth two of that; **overreach,** outreach; **circumvent,** get round *or* around, **evade,** stonewall [slang], **elude, frustrate, foil,** give the slip *or* runaround [informal]; pass the buck [informal]; pull a fast one [slang], steal a march on; make a fool of, make a sucker *or* patsy of [slang]; be too much for, be too deep for; **deceive, victimize** 618.13–18.

.12 ADJS **cunning, crafty, artful, wily,** guileful, **sly,** insidious, supple [Scot], **shifty,** pawky [Brit], arch, **smooth, slick** [informal], **slippery,** snaky, serpentine, **foxy,** vulpine, feline; **canny, shrewd,** knowing, sharp, cute, acute, astute, **clever** 733.20; resourceful, ingenious, inventive, ready; subtle, subtile; sophistical 483.10; **tricky,** trickish, tricksy [archaic]; **Machiavellian,** Machiavellic, politic, diplomatic; strategic, tactical; deep, deep-laid; cunning as a fox *or* serpent, crazy like a fox [slang], slippery as an eel, too clever by half; sneaky, **stealthy** 614.12; cagey [informal], wary 895.9; **scheming, designing** 654.14; **deceitful** 618.20.

.13 ADVS **cunningly, craftily, artfully,** wilily, guilefully, insidiously, shiftily, foxily, trickily, smoothly, slick [slang]; **slyly,** on the sly; **cannily, shrewdly,** knowingly, astutely, **cleverly** 733.29; subtlely, subtilely, cagily [informal], warily 895.13.

## 736. ARTLESSNESS

.1 NOUNS **artlessness, ingenuousness, guilelessness; simplicity,** simpleness, plainness; simpleheartedness, simplemindedness; **unsophistication,** unsophisticatedness; **naïveté** [Fr], naïvety, naïveness, childlikeness; **innocence;** trustfulness, trustingness, unguardedness, unwariness, unsuspiciousness; **openness,** openheartedness, sincerity, candor 974.4; single-heartedness, single-mindedness, singleness *of* heart; directness, bluffness, bluntness, 'outspokenness.

.2 **naturalness,** naturalism, nature; state *of* nature; unspoiledness; **unaffectedness,** unaffectation, **unassumingness,** unpr tendingness, unpretentiousness, undisguise; **inartificiality,** unartificialness, genuineness.

**.3 unsophisticate,** simple soul, naïf, **ingenue, innocent, child,** mere child, infant, **babe,** babe in the woods, lamb, dove; child of nature, noble savage; yokel, rube *or* hick [both slang]; oaf, lout 471.5; dupe 620.

**.4** VERBS wear one's heart on one's sleeve, look one in the face.

**.5** ADJS **artless, simple,** plain, **guileless;** simplehearted, simpleminded; **ingenuous, ingénu** [Fr]; **unsophisticated, naïve;** childlike, born yesterday; **innocent;** trustful, trusting, unguarded, unwary, unreserved, confiding, unsuspicious; **open,** openhearted, sincere, candid, **frank** 974.17; single-hearted, single-minded; direct, bluff, blunt, outspoken.

**.6 natural,** naturelike, native; in the state of nature; unspoiled; **unaffected, unassuming, unpretending,** unpretentious, unfeigning, undisguising, undissimulating, undissembling, undesigning; **genuine, inartificial,** unartificial, unadorned, unvarnished, unembellished; homespun; pastoral, rural, arcadian, bucolic.

**.7** ADVS **artlessly, ingenuously, guilelessly;** simply, plainly; naturally, genuinely; naïvely; openly, openheartedly.

### 737. BEHAVIOR

**.1** NOUNS **behavior, conduct, deportment, comportment, manner, manners, demeanor, mien,** *maintien* [Fr], **carriage, bearing,** port, poise, posture, guise, **air,** address, presence; –phoria; tone, style, lifestyle; way of life, modus vivendi; way, ways; methods, method, methodology; practice, praxis; procedure, proceeding; **actions,** acts, goings-on, doings, movements, moves, tactics; action, doing 705.1; activity 707; objective *or* observable behavior; motions, gestures; pose, affectation 903; pattern, behavior pattern; culture pattern, behavioral norm, folkway, **custom** 642; behavioral science, social science.

**.2 good behavior,** sanctioned behavior; good citizenship; good manners, correct deportment, etiquette 646.3; courtesy 936; sociability 922; bad *or* poor behavior, misbehavior 738; discourtesy 937.

**.3 behaviorism,** behavior *or* behavioristic psychology; behavior therapy.

**.4** VERBS **behave, act, do,** go on; **behave oneself, conduct oneself,** manage oneself, **handle oneself,** guide oneself, **comport**

oneself, **deport oneself,** demean oneself, **bear oneself, carry oneself;** acquit oneself, quit oneself [archaic]; proceed, move; misbehave 738.4.

**.5 behave oneself, behave,** act well, **be good,** be nice, **do right,** do what is right, do the right *or* proper thing, keep out of mischief, play the game *or* mind one's P's and Q's [both informal], be on one's good *or* best behavior.

**.6 treat, use, do by,** deal by, **act** *or* **behave toward,** conduct oneself toward, act with regard to, conduct oneself vis-à-vis *or* in the face of; **deal with,** cope with, **handle;** respond to.

**.7** ADJS **behavioral;** behaviorist, behavioristic; **behaved,** behaviored, **mannered,** demeanored, –phoric.

### 738. MISBEHAVIOR

**.1** NOUNS **misbehavior, misconduct,** misdemeanor [archaic]; unsanctioned *or* nonsanctioned behavior; frowned-upon behavior; **naughtiness,** badness; impropriety; venial sin; **disorderly conduct,** disorder, disorderliness, disruptiveness, disruption, **rowdiness,** rowdyism, ruffianism, hooliganism; vandalism; roughhouse, horseplay; discourtesy 937; vice 981; misdoing, wrongdoing 982.

**.2 mischief, mischievousness;** devilment, deviltry, devilry; **roguishness,** roguery, scampishness; **waggery,** waggishness; **impishness,** devilishness, puckishness, elfishness; **prankishness,** pranksomeness; sportiveness, playfulness, *espièglerie* [Fr]; high spirits, youthful spirits; foolishness 470.

**.3 mischief-maker,** mischief, **rogue, devil,** knave, **rascal,** rapscallion, scapegrace, **scamp; wag** 881.12; buffoon 612.10; funmaker, joker, jokester, practical joker, prankster, life of the party, **cutup** [slang]; **rowdy,** ruffian, hoodlum, hood [informal], hooligan; **imp, elf, puck,** pixie, **minx,** bad boy, bugger *or* booger [both informal], little devil, little rascal, little monkey, *enfant terrible* [Fr].

**.4** VERBS **misbehave,** misdemean [archaic], **misbehave oneself, misconduct oneself,** misdemean oneself [archaic], behave ill; get into mischief; **act up** *or* **carry on** *or* carry on something scandalous [all informal], sow one's wild oats; **cut up** [slang], horse around [informal], roughhouse *or* cut up rough [both slang]; play the fool 470.6.

**.5** ADJS **misbehaving,** unbehaving; **naughty, bad;** improper, not respectable; out-of-order *or* off-base *or* out-of-line [all informal]; **disorderly,** disruptive, **rowdy,** rowdyish, **ruffianly.**

.6 **mischievous,** mischief-loving, full of mischief; **roguish,** scampish, scapegrace, arch, knavish; **devilish; impish, puckish, elfish,** elvish; **waggish, prankish,** pranky, **pranksome,** trickish, tricksy; **playful,** sportive, high-spirited, *espiègle* [Fr]; foolish 470.8–10.

.7 ADVS **mischievously, roguishly,** knavishly, scampishly, devilishly; impishly, puckishly, elfishly; waggishly; prankishly, playfully, sportively, in fun.

## 739. AUTHORITY

.1 NOUNS **authority, prerogative, right, power,** faculty, competence *or* competency; regality, royal prerogative; constituted authority, vested authority; inherent authority; legal *or* lawful *or* rightful authority, legitimacy; derived *or* delegated authority, vicarious authority, indirect authority; **the say** *or* **the say-so** [both informal]; divine right, *jus divinum* [L]; absolute power, absolutism 741.9,10.

.2 **authoritativeness, authority, power,** powerfulness, magisterialness, **potency** *or* potence, puissance, **strength,** might, mightiness, clout [slang].

.3 **authoritativeness, masterfulness, lordliness,** magistrality, magisterialness; **arbitrariness,** peremptoriness, imperativeness, **imperiousness,** autocraticalness, highhandedness, dictatorialness, overbearingness, overbearance, overbearing, domineering, domineeringness, tyrannicalness, authoritarianism, bossism [informal].

.4 **prestige, authority, influence,** influentialness; pressure, **weight,** weightiness, moment, **consequence;** eminence, **stature,** rank, seniority, priority, precedence; **greatness** 34; **importance, prominence** 672.1,2.

.5 **governance, authority, jurisdiction, control, command, power, rule, reign,** regnancy, **dominion,** sovereignty, empire, empery, raj [India], **sway; government** 741; administration, disposition 747.3; **grip,** claws, **clutches,** hand, hands, iron hand, talons.

.6 **dominance** *or* dominancy, **dominion, domination;** preeminence, **supremacy, superiority** 36; **sovereignty,** suzerainty, suzerainship, **overlordship;** primacy, principality, **predominance** *or* predominancy, predomination, prepotence *or* prepotency; preponderance, **ascendance** *or* ascendancy; **upper** *or* **whip hand,** balance of power; eminent domain.

.7 **mastership,** masterhood, masterdom, **mastery; leadership, headship, lordship;** hegemony; supervisorship, directorship 747.4; hierarchy, nobility, aristocracy, **ruling class** 749.15; chairmanship; chieftainship, chieftaincy, chieftainry, chiefery *or* chiefry; presidentship, presidency; premiership, prime-ministership, prime-ministry; governorship; princeship, princedom, principality; rectorship, rectorate; suzerainty, suzerainship; regency, regentship; prefectship, prefecture; proconsulship, proconsulate; provostship, provostry; protectorship, protectorate; seneschalship, seneschalsy; pashadom, pashalic; sheikhdom; emirate, viziership, vizierate; magistrateship, magistrature, magistracy; mayorship, mayoralty; sheriffdom, sheriffcy, sheriffalty, shrievalty; consulship, consulate; chancellorship, chancellery, chancellorate; seigniory; tribunate, aedileship; deanery; patriarchate, patriarchy [archaic]; bishopric, episcopacy; archbishopric, archiepiscopacy, archiepiscopate; metropolitanship, metropolitanate; popedom, popeship, popehood, papacy, pontificate, pontificality; dictatorship, dictature.

.8 **sovereignty, royalty,** regnancy, **majesty,** empire, empery, imperialism, **emperorship; kingship,** kinghood; queenship, queenhood; kaisership, kaiserdom; czardom; rajaship; sultanship, sultanate; caliphate; **the throne, the crown, the purple;** royal insignia 569.3.

.9 **scepter, rod, staff,** staff *or* rod of office, wand, wand of office, baton, mace, truncheon, fasces; crosier, crook, cross-staff, caduceus; gavel; mantle; chain of office, portfolio.

.10 (seat of authority) **saddle** [informal] **helm, driver's seat** [informal]; seat, chair, bench; woolsack [England]; seat of state, seat of power; curule chair; dais.

.11 **throne, royal seat;** musnud *or* gaddi [both India]; Peacock throne.

.12 (acquisition of authority) **accession; su**ccession, rightful *or* legitimate succession; **usurpation,** arrogation, assumption, ta**k**ing over, seizure; anointment, anointing, consecration, coronation; **delegation,** deputation, assignment, **appointmen**t, election; **authorization,** empowerment.

.13 VERBS **possess** *or* **wield authority, ha**ve **power,** have the power, have the righ**t,** have the say *or* say-so· [informal], ho**l** the prerogative; carry authority, have clout [slang], have what one says go, have one's own way; show one's authority, crack the whip, throw one's weight around [informal]; rule 741.14, dominate 741.15, govern 741.12, control 741.13; supervise 747.10.

.14 take command, take charge, take over, take the helm, take the reins of government, take the reins into one's hand, get the power into one's hands, gain *or* get the upper hand, take the lead; ascend *or* mount *or* succeed to *or* accede to the throne; assume command, assume, usurp, arrogate, seize; usurp *or* seize the throne *or* crown *or* mantle, usurp the prerogatives of the crown; seize power, execute a *coup d'état*.

.15 ADJS authoritative, clothed with authority, commanding, imperative; governing, controlling, ruling 741.18; preeminent, supreme, leading, superior 36.12–14; powerful, potent, puissant, mighty; dominant, ascendant, hegemonic, hegemonistic; influential, prestigious, weighty, momentous, consequential, eminent, substantial, considerable; great 34.6; important, prominent 672.18; ranking, senior; authorized, empowered, duly constituted, competent; official, *ex officio* [L]; authoritarian; absolute, autocratic, monocratic; totalitarian.

.16 imperious, imperial, masterful, authoritative, feudal, aristocratic, lordly, magistral, magisterial; arrogant 912.9; arbitrary, peremptory, imperative; absolute, absolutist, absolutistic; dictatorial, authoritarian; bossy [informal], domineering, high-handed, overbearing, overruling; autocratic, monocratic, despotic, tyrannical; tyrannous, grinding, oppressive 864.24; repressive, suppressive 760.11; strict, severe 757.6.

.17 sovereign; regal, royal, majestic, purple; kinglike, kingly, "every inch a king" [Shakespeare]; imperial, imperious *or* imperatorious [both archaic]; imperatorial; monarchic(al), monarchal, monarchial; tetrarchic; princely, princelike; queenly, queenlike; dynastic.

.18 ADVS authoritatively, with authority; commandingly, imperatively; powerfully, potently, puissantly, mightily; influentially, weightily, momentously, consequentially; officially, *ex cathedra* [L].

.19 imperiously, masterfully, magisterially; arbitrarily, peremptorily; autocratically, dictatorially, high-handedly, domineer-

ingly, overbearingly, despotically, tyrannically.

.20 by authority of, in the name of, in *or* by virtue of.

.21 in authority, in power, in charge, in control, in command, at the reins, at the head, at the helm, at the wheel, in the saddle *or* driver's seat [informal], on the throne; "drest in a little brief authority" [Shakespeare].

## 740. LAWLESSNESS

*(absence of authority)*

.1 NOUNS lawlessness; licentiousness, license, uncontrol, unrestraint 762.3; indiscipline, insubordination, mutiny, disobedience 767; irresponsibility, unaccountability; willfulness, unchecked *or* rampant will; interregnum, power vacuum.

.2 anarchy, anarchism; disorderliness, unruliness, misrule, disorder, disruption, disorganization, confusion, turmoil, chaos, primal chaos, tohubohu; antinomianism; nihilism; syndicalism, anarcho-syndicalism, criminal syndicalism, lynch law, mob rule *or* law, mobocracy, ochlocracy; law of the jungle; revolution 147; rebellion 767.4.

.3 anarchist, anarch; antinomian; nihilist, syndicalist, anarcho-syndicalist; revolutionist 147.3; mutineer, rebel 767.5.

.4 VERBS reject *or* defy authority, enthrone one's own will; take the law in one's own hands, act on one's own responsibility; do *or* go as one pleases, indulge oneself; be a law unto oneself, answer to no man, "swear allegiance to the words of no master" [Horace].

.5 ADJS lawless; licentious, ungoverned, undisciplined, unrestrained 762.33; insubordinate, mutinous, disobedient 767.8–11; uncontrolled, uncurbed, unbridled, unchecked, rampant, unreined, reinless; irresponsible, wildcat, unaccountable; self-willed, willful, headstrong, heady.

.6 anarchic(al), anarchial, anarchistic; unruly, disorderly, disorganized, chaotic; antinomian; nihilistic, syndicalistic.

.7 ADVS lawlessly, licentiously; anarchically, chaotically.

## 741. GOVERNMENT

.1 NOUNS government, governance, discipline, regulation; direction, management, administration, dispensation, disposition, oversight, supervision 747.2; regime, regimen; rule, sway, sovereignty, reign, regnancy; empire, empery; civil government, political government; form or system of government, political organization, polity; –archy, –cracy or –ocracy.

.2 **control, mastery, mastership, command, power, jurisdiction, dominion, domination;** hold, grasp, grip, gripe; hand, hands, iron hand, clutches; talons, claws; helm, reins of government.

.3 **the government, the authorities; the powers that be,** the Establishment; Uncle Sam, Washington; John Bull, the Crown, His or Her Majesty's Government, Whitehall.

.4 (governments) federal government, federation; unitary government; republic, commonwealth, democracy, representative government, representative democracy, direct or pure democracy; constitutional or parliamentary government; "government of the people, by the people, for the people" [Lincoln]; social democracy, welfare state; mob rule, tyranny of the majority, mobocracy [informal], ochlocracy; pantisocracy; aristocracy, hierarchy, oligarchy; feudal system; monarchy, absolute monarchy, constitutional monarchy, limited monarchy; dictatorship, tyranny, autocracy, autarchy; dyarchy, duarchy, duumvirate; triarchy, triumvirate; totalitarian government or regime, police state; stratocracy, military government, militarism, garrison state; martial law, rule of the sword; regency; hierocracy, theocracy, thearchy; patriarchy, patriarchate; gerontocracy; technocracy, meritocracy; autonomy, self-government, home rule, self-determination; heteronomy, dominion rule, colonial government, colonialism, neocolonialism; provisional government; coalition government.

.5 matriarchy, matriarchate, gynarchy, gynocracy, gynecocracy; petticoat government.

.6 [slang or informal terms] foolocracy, gunocracy, mediocracy, moneyocracy, landocracy, cottonocracy, beerocracy, oiligarchy, parsonarchy, pedantocracy, pornocracy, snobocracy, squirearchy.

.7 **supranational government,** supergovernment, **world government,** World Federalism; League of Nations, United Nations 743.

.8 (principles of government) democratism, republicanism; constitutionalism, parliamentarism, parliamentarianism; monarchism, royalism; feudalism, feudality; imperialism; fascism, neofascism, Nazism, national socialism; statism, governmental-

ism; collectivism, communism 745.5, socialism 745.6; federalism; centralism; pluralism; political principles 745.

.9 **absolutism, dictatorship, despotism,** tyranny, autocracy, autarchy, monarchy, absolute monarchy; **authoritarianism;** totalitarianism; one-man rule, one-party rule; Caesarism, Stalinism, kaiserism, czarism; benevolent despotism, paternalism.

.10 **despotism, tyranny, fascism,** domineering, domination, oppression; heavy hand, high hand, iron hand, iron heel or boot; big stick, *argumentum baculinum* [L]; **terrorism,** reign of terror; thought control.

.11 **officialism, bureaucracy;** beadledom, bumbledom; **red-tapeism,** red-tapery, **red tape** [all informal]; official jargon 744.37.

.12 VERBS **govern, regulate; wield authority** 739.13; **command,** officer, captain, **head, lead,** be master, be at the head of, **preside over,** chair; **direct, manage, supervise, administer,** administrate 747.8–11; discipline; stand over.

.13 **control, hold in hand,** have in one's power, gain a hold upon; hold the reins, hold the helm, be in the driver's seat or the saddle [informal]; have control of, **have under control, have in hand** or **well in hand;** be master of the situation, have it all one's own way, have the game in one's own hands; pull the strings or wires.

.14 **rule, sway, reign,** bear reign, have the sway, wield the scepter, wear the crown, sit on the throne; rule over, overrule.

.15 **dominate, predominate,** preponderate, prevail; **have the ascendancy, have the upper** or **whip hand,** have at a disadvantage, have on the hip [archaic]; **master** have the mastery of; bestride; dictate, lay down the law; **rule the roost** or wear the pants [both informal]; take the lead, play first fiddle; **lead by the nose, twist** o **turn around one's little finger; kee under one's thumb,** bend to one's will.

.16 **domineer,** domineer over, **lord it ove** browbeat, henpeck [informal], intimidate, bully, cow, bulldoze [informal walk over, walk all over; castrate, unmardaunt, terrorize 891.26–28; **tyrannize,** tyrannize over, despotize; **grind, grin** down, break, **oppress,** suppress, repres weigh or press heavy on; keep unde keep down, beat down, clamp down c [informal]; overbear, overmaster, ove awe; override, ride over, trample stamp or tread upon, trample or tre down, **trample** or **tread underfoot,** cru under an iron heel, **ride roughshod over;** hold *or* keep a tight hand upon, rule with a rod of iron, rule with an iron hand *or* fist; enslave, subjugate 764.8; compel, coerce 756.4–7.

.17 ADJS **governmental, gubernatorial; political, civil,** civic; **official,** bureaucratic; democratic, republican, fascist, fascistic, oligarchal, oligarchic(al), aristocratic(al), theocratic, **federal,** federalist, federalistic, **constitutional,** parliamentary, parliamentarian; monarchic(al), monarchial, monarchal [archaic]; autocratic, monocratic, absolute, **authoritarian;** despotic, **dictatorial; totalitarian;** pluralistic; patriarchal, patriarchic(al); matriarchal, matriarchic(al); heteronomous; autonomous, self-governing.

.18 **governing, controlling, regulating,** regulative, regulatory, **commanding; ruling, reigning, sovereign,** regnant; **master, chief,** general, **boss** [informal]; **head; dominant, predominant,** predominate, preponderant, preponderate, prepotent, prepollent, prevalent, **leading, paramount, supreme,** hegemonic, hegemonistic; ascendant, in the ascendant, in ascendancy; at the head, in chief; in charge 739.21.

.19 **executive, administrative,** ministerial; official, bureaucratic; **supervisory, directing, managing** 747.12–14.

.20 ADVS **under control, in hand,** well in hand; **in one's power,** under one's control.

## 742. LEGISLATURE, GOVERNMENT ORGANIZATION

.1 NOUNS **legislature,** legislative body; **parliament, congress, assembly,** general assembly, house of assembly, legislative assembly, **national assembly, chamber of deputies,** federal assembly, diet, soviet, court; unicameral legislature, bicameral legislature; legislative chamber, upper chamber *or* house, lower chamber *or* house; state legislature, state assembly; provincial legislature, provincial parliament; city council, city board, board of aldermen, common council, commission; representative town meeting, town meeting.

.2 **Parliament** (Afghanistan, Austria, Barbados, Belgium, Canada, Ethiopia, Fiji, France, West Germany, India, Iran, Italy, Jamaica, Laos, Liechtenstein, Malagasy Republic, Malaysia, Rhodesia, Singapore, South Africa, Swaziland, Trinidad and Tobago, United Kingdom), Federal Parliament (Australia), National Assembly (Bhutan, Botswana, Bulgaria, Republic of China, El Salvador, Gabon, Guinea, Equatorial Guinea, Guyana, Hungary, Ivory Coast, Jordan, Kenya, South Korea, Kuwait, Malawi, Mauritania, Pakistan, Rwanda, Senegal, Tanzania, Thailand, Tunisia, Uganda, Upper Volta, North Vietnam, Zaïre, Zambia), Legislative Assembly (Costa Rica, Mauritius, Nauru, Western Samoa, Tonga), Federal Assembly (Czechoslovakia, Switzerland, Yugoslavia), Federal National Assembly (Cameroon), Grand National Assembly (Rumania, Turkey), People's Assembly (Albania, Egypt), Supreme People's Assembly (North Korea), **Congress** (Chile, Colombia, Honduras, Liberia, Mexico, US, Venezuela), National Congress (Brazil, Dominican Republic, Ecuador, Guatemala), National People's Congress (People's Republic of China), People's Consultative Congress (Indonesia), House of Representatives (Cyprus, Gambia, Malta, New Zealand, Sierra Leone), People's Council (Maldive Islands, Syria), Great and General Council (San Marino), Council of the Valleys (Andorra), National Council (Monaco), Chamber of Deputies (Lebanon, Luxembourg), Legislative Chamber (Haiti), Chamber of Representatives (Morocco), Diet (Japan), Cortes (Spain), Eduskunta (Finland), Folketing (Denmark), Riksdag (Sweden), Althing (Iceland), Great People's Khural (Mongolia), Storting (Norway), States General (Netherlands), Supreme Soviet (USSR), Knesset (Israel), Volkskammer (East Germany), Oireachtas (Ireland), Sejm (Poland).

.3 **upper house, upper chamber; Senate** (Australia, Barbados, Belgium, Brazil, Canada, Chile, Colombia, Dominican Republic, Ecuador, Ethiopia, Fiji, France, Iran, Ireland, Italy, Jamaica, Liberia, Malagasy Republic, Malaysia, Mexico, Nicaragua, Paraguay, Philippines, Rhodesia, South Africa, Swaziland, Trinidad and Tobago, US, Venezuela), House of Elders (Afghanistan), Chamber of Nations (Czechoslovakia), Bundesrat (Austria, West Germany), Rajya Sabha (India), House of Councillors (Japan), Chamber of Notables (Jordan), King's Council (Laos), First Chamber (Netherlands), Lagting (Norway), Corporative Chamber (Portugal), Council of Nationalities (USSR), Council of States (Switzerland), Republican Senate (Turkey), **House of Lords** (United Kingdom).

.4 **lower house,** lower chamber; **House of Representatives,** House [informal] (Australia, Fiji, Jamaica, Japan, Liberia, Malaysia, Philippines, US), House of the People (Afghanistan), House of Assembly (Barbados, Rhodesia, South Africa, Swaziland), Chamber of Representatives (Belgium, Colombia), **Chamber of Deputies** (Brazil, Chile, Dominican Republic, Ecuador, Ethiopia, Italy, Jordan, Mexico, Nicaragua, Paraguay, Venezuela), National Assembly (France, Laos, Malagasy Republic, Portugal, Turkey), **House of Commons** (Canada, United Kingdom), Chamber of the People (Czechoslovakia), Bundestag (West Germany), Lok Sabha (India), Majlis (Iran), Dáil (Ireland), Second Chamber (Netherlands), Odelsting (Norway), Council of the Union (USSR), National Council (Switzerland).

.5 (US Senate committees) Aeronautical and Space Sciences; Agriculture and Forestry; Appropriations; Armed Services; Banking, Housing and Urban Affairs; Budget; Commerce; District of Columbia; Finance; Foreign Relations; Government Operations; Interior and Insular Affairs; Judiciary; Labor and Public Welfare; Post Office and Civil Service; Public Works; Rules and Administration; Veterans' Affairs.

.6 (US House of Representatives committees) Agriculture; Appropriations; Armed Services; Banking, Currency and Housing; Budget; District of Columbia; Education and Labor; Government Operations; House Administration; Interior and Insular Affairs; Internal Security; International Relations; Interstate and Foreign Commerce; Judiciary; Merchant Marine and Fisheries; Post Office and Civil Service; Public Works and Transportation; Rules; Science and Technology; Small Business; Standards of Official Conduct; Veterans' Affairs; Ways and Means.

.7 (US executive departments) Department of State; Department of the Treasury; Department of Justice; Department of Defense; Department of the Interior; Department of Agriculture; Department of Commerce; Department of Labor; Department of Health, Education, and Welfare; Department of Housing and Urban Development; Department of Transportation.

.8 **cabinet,** ministry, **council,** advisory council, council of state, privy council, divan; shadow cabinet; kitchen cabinet, camarilla.

.9 (US Cabinet) Secretary of State; Secretary of the Treasury; Secretary of Defense; Secretary of the Interior; Secretary of Agriculture; Secretary of Commerce; Secretary of Labor; Secretary of Health, Education, and Welfare; Attorney General; Secretary of Housing and Urban Development; Secretary of Transportation.

.10 (British Cabinet) Prime Minister; First Lord of the Treasury; Chief Secretary, Treasury; Lord Chancellor; Lord President of the Council; Lord Privy Seal; Chancellor of the Exchequer; First Secretary of State; Secretary of State for Foreign and Commonwealth Affairs; Secretary of State for the Home Department; Secretary of State for Employment and Productivity; Secretary of State for Defence; Secretary of State for Economic Affairs; Secretary of State for Scotland; Secretary of State for Education and Science; Secretary of State for Wales; First Lord of the Admiralty; President of the Board of Trade; Paymaster-General; Minister of Housing and Local Government; Minister of Technology; Minister of Transport; Minister of Power; President of the Board of Education; Minister of Agriculture, Fisheries and Food.

.11 (US Agencies) ACTION; Administrative Conference of the United States; Agency for International Development; American Battle Monuments Commission; American National Red Cross; Appalachian Regional Commission; Architect of the Capitol; Atomic Energy Commission, AEC; Central Intelligence Agency, CIA; Civil Aeronautics Board, CAB; Commission of Fine Arts; Commission on Civil Rights; Council of Economic Advisors; Council on Environmental Quality; Council on International Economic Policy; District of Columbia; Domestic Council; Economic Development Administration, EDA; Energy Research Development Administration; Environmental Protection Agency, EPA; Equal Employment Opportunity Commission, EEOC; Export-Import Bank of the United States, EIB; Farm Credit Administration, FCA; Federal Aviation Agency,

FAA; Federal Bureau of Investigation, FBI; Federal Communications Commission, FCC; Federal Deposit Insurance Corporation, FDIC; Federal Energy Administration; Federal Home Loan Bank Board; Federal Maritime Commission; Federal Mediation and Conciliation Service; Federal Power Commission, FPC; Federal Reserve System; Federal Trade Commission, FTC; Food and Drug Administration, FDA; Foreign Claims Settlement Commission of the United States; General Accounting Office, GAO; General Services Administration, GSA; Government Printing Office; Indian Claims Commission; Interstate Commerce Commission, ICC; Library of Congress; National Academy of Sciences; National Academy of Engineering; National Aeronautics and Space Administration, NASA; National Aeronautics and Space Council; National Credit Union Administration; National Foundation on the Arts and the Humanities; National Labor Relations Board, NLRB; National Mediation Board; National Science Foundation, NSF; National Security Council; Occupational Safety and Health Review Commission; Office of Consumer Affairs; Office of Economic Opportunity, OEO; Office of Intergovernmental Relations; Office of Management and Budget; Office of Science and Technology; Office of the Special Representative for Trade Negotiations; Panama Canal Company; Railroad Retirement Board; Renegotiation Board; St. Lawrence Seaway Development Corporation; Securities and Exchange Commission, SEC; Selective Service System; Small Business Administration; Smithsonian Institution; Tennessee Valley Authority, TVA; United States Arms Control and Disarmament Agency; United States Civil Service Commission; United States Information Agency, USIA; United States Postal Service; United States Tariff Commission; United States Tax Court; Veterans Administration, VA.

.12 **capitol, statehouse; courthouse;** city hall.

.13 **legislation, lawmaking,** legislature [archaic]; **enactment,** enaction, constitution, passage, passing; **resolution,** concurrent resolution, joint resolution; act 998.3.

.14 (legislative procedure) introduction, first reading, committee consideration, tabling, filing, second reading, deliberation, **debate,** third reading, **vote,** division, roll

call; **filibustering,** filibuster, talkathon [slang]; cloture 144.5; **logrolling;** steamroller methods.

.15 **veto,** executive veto, absolute veto, qualified or limited veto, suspensive or suspensory veto, item veto, pocket veto; veto power; veto message; senatorial courtesy.

.16 **referendum,** constitutional referendum, statutory referendum, optional or facultative referendum, compulsory or mandatory referendum; **mandate; plebiscite,** plebiscitum; initiative, direct initiative, indirect initiative; recall.

.17 **bill,** omnibus bill, hold-up bill, companion bills amendment; **clause, proviso;** enacting clause, dragnet clause, escalator clause, saving clause; **rider;** joker [informal]; **calendar, motion;** question, previous question, privileged question.

.18 VERBS **legislate,** make or enact laws, **enact, pass,** constitute, ordain, put in force; **put through, jam** or **steamroller** or **railroad through** [informal], lobby through; table, pigeonhole; take the floor, get the floor, have the floor; yield the floor; **filibuster; logroll,** roll logs; **veto, pocket, kill; decree** 752.9.

.19 ADJS **legislative,** legislatorial, lawmaking; deliberative; **parliamentary, congressional;** senatorial; bicameral, unicameral.

## 743. UNITED NATIONS, INTERNATIONAL ORGANIZATIONS

.1 NOUNS **United Nations, UN;** League of Nations.

.2 (organs) Secretariat; General Assembly; Security Council; Trusteeship Council; International Court of Justice; Economic and Social Council, ECOSOC.

.3 (agencies) Food and Agricultural Organization, FAO; General Agreement on Tariffs and Trade, GATT; Intergovernmental Maritime Consultative Organization, IMCO; International Atomic Energy Agency, IAEA; International Bank for Reconstruction and Development, World Bank; International Civil Aviation Organization, ICAO; International Development Association, IDA; International Finance Corporation, IFO; International Labor Organization, ILO; International Monetary Fund, the Fund; International Telecommunication Union, ITU; United Nations Children's Fund, UNICEF; United Nations Educational, Scientific, and Cultural Organization, UNESCO; Universal Postal Union, UPU; World Health Organization,

WHO; World Meteorological Organization, WMO.

.4 (ECOSOC commissions) Statistical Commission; Commission on Human Rights, Subcommission on Prevention of Discrimination and the Protection of Minorities; Social Development Commission; Commission on the Status of Women; Commission on Narcotic Drugs; Population Commission; Economic Commission for Europe, ECE; Economic Commission for Asia and the Far East, ECAFE; Economic Commission for Latin America, ECLA; Economic Commission for Africa.

.5 (non-UN international organizations) World Council of Churches, WCC; Organization for Economic Cooperation and Development, OECD; North Atlantic Treaty Organization, NATO; Council of Europe; European Economic Community, Common Market, EEC; European Coal and Steel Community, ECSC; European Atomic Energy Community, Euratom; European Free Trade Association, EFTA; Colombo Plan for Cooperative Development in South and Southeast Asia, Colombo Plan; Central Treaty Organization, CENTO; Organization of American States, OAS; Latin American Free Trade Association, LAFTA; Central American Common Market, CACM; Arab League, AL; Organization of Petroleum Exporting Countries, OPEC; Organization of African Unity, OAU; Southeast Asia Treaty Organization, SEATO; ANZUS Council; African-Malagasy-Mauritius Common Organization, OCAM; Asian and Pacific Council, ASPAC; Bank for International Settlements, BIS; Council for Mutual Economic Assistance, COMECON; Eastern European Mutual Assistance Treaty, Warsaw Pact; French Community; International Bureau of Weights and Measures; International Committee of the Red Cross, ICRC; International Criminal Police Organization, Interpol; Nordic Council; Commonwealth of Nations, British Commonwealth [informal].

## 744. POLITICS

.1 NOUNS politics, polity, the art of the possible, "economics in action" [Robert La Follette]; practical politics, Realpolitik [Ger]; empirical politics; party or partisan politics, partisanism, –partism; reform politics; power politics, Machtpolitik [Ger]; machine politics, bossism [informal], Tammany Hall, Tammanism [informal]; pressure-group politics; confrontation politics; consensus politics; career politics; petty politics, peanut politics [slang]; pork-barrel politics; kid-glove politics [slang]; silk-stocking politics [slang]; ward politics.

.2 political science, poli-sci [slang], politics, government, civics; political philosophy, political theory; political behavior; political economy, comparative government, international relations, public administration; political geography, geopolitics, Geopolitik [Ger].

.3 statesmanship, statecraft, political or governmental leadership, national leadership; transpartisan or suprapartisan leadership; "the wise employment of individual meanness for the public good" [Lincoln]; kingcraft, queencraft; senatorship.

.4 policy, polity, public policy; line, party line, party principle or doctrine or philosophy, position, bipartisan policy; noninterference, nonintervention, laissez-faire [Fr], laissez-faireism; free enterprise; go-slow policy; government control, governmentalism; planned economy, managed currency; price supports, pump-priming [informal]; autarky, economic self-sufficiency; free trade; protection, protectionism; bimetallism; strict constructionism; localism, sectionalism, states' rights, nullification.

.5 foreign policy, foreign affairs; world politics; diplomacy, diplomatic or diplomatics [both archaic]; shirt-sleeve diplomacy; shuttle diplomacy; dollar diplomacy, dollar imperialism; brinkmanship; nationalism, internationalism; expansionism, imperialism, manifest destiny, colonialism, neocolonialism; spheres of influence; balance of power; containment; deterrence; militarism, preparedness; tough policy, the big stick [informal], twisting the lion's tail; nonresistance, isolationism neutralism, coexistence, peaceful coexistence; détente; compromise, appeasement; peace offensive; good-neighbor policy; open-door policy, open door Monroe Doctrine; Truman Doctrine; Eisenhower Doctrine; Nixon Doctrine.

.6 program; Square Deal [Theodore Roosevelt], New Deal [F. D. Roosevelt], Fair Deal [Truman], New Frontier [J. F. Kennedy], Great Society [L. B. Johnson]; austerity program; Beveridge Plan [Brit five-year plan; Cultural Revolution [China]; Point Four; Marshall Plan.

.7 **platform**, party platform, **program**, declaration of policy; **plank; issue;** keynote address, keynote speech.

.8 **political convention, convention;** conclave, powwow [informal]; national convention, quadrennial circus [informal]; state convention, county convention, preliminary convention, nominating convention; constitutional convention.

.9 **caucus,** legislative or congressional caucus, packed caucus; secret caucus.

.10 **candidacy,** candidature [Brit], **running, running for office,** throwing one's hat in the ring [informal], standing or standing for office [both Brit].

.11 **nomination,** caucus nomination, direct nomination, petition nomination; acceptance speech.

.12 **electioneering,** campaigning, politicking [informal], **stumping** or **whistle-stopping** [both informal]; **rally,** clambake [informal]; campaign dinner, $100-a-plate dinner, fund-raising dinner.

.13 **campaign,** all-out campaign, hard-hitting campaign, hoopla or hurrah campaign [informal]; **canvass, solicitation;** front-porch campaign; grass-roots campaign; stump excursion or stumping tour or **whistle-stop campaign** [all informal]; TV or media campaign; campaign commitments or promises; campaign fund, campaign contribution; campaign button.

.14 **smear campaign,** mudslinging campaign; **whispering campaign;** muckraking, **mudslinging** or **dirty politics** [both informal], character assassination; political canard, roorback; last-minute lie.

.15 **election,** general election, by-election; congressional election, presidential election; partisan election, nonpartisan election; **primary,** primary election; direct primary, open primary, closed primary, nonpartisan primary, mandatory primary, optional primary, preference primary, presidential primary, presidential preference primary, runoff primary; caucus 744.9; runoff, runoff election; disputed or contested election; referendum.

.16 **election district, precinct, ward, borough;** congressional district; safe district; swing district [informal]; close borough, pocket borough, rotten borough [all Brit]; gerrymander, gerrymandered district, shoestring district; silk-stocking district or ward; single-member district or constituency.

.17 **suffrage, franchise, the vote,** right to vote; universal suffrage, manhood suffrage, woman or female suffrage; suffragism, suffragettism; suffragist, woman-suffragist, suffragette; household franchise; one man, one vote.

.18 **voting,** going to the polls, casting one's ballot; preferential voting, preferential system, alternative vote; proportional representation, PR, cumulative system or voting, Hare system, list system; single system or voting, single transferrable vote; plural system or voting; single-member district 744.16; absentee voting; proxy voting, card voting; voting machine; election fraud, colonization, floating, repeating, ballot-box stuffing; vote 637.6.

.19 **ballot, slate, ticket,** proxy [dial]; straight ticket, split ticket; Australian ballot; Massachusetts ballot, office-block ballot; Indiana ballot, party-column ballot; absentee ballot; long ballot, blanket ballot, jungle ballot [informal]; short ballot; nonpartisan ballot; sample ballot; party emblem.

.20 **polls,** poll, polling place, polling station [Brit], balloting place; voting booth, polling booth; ballot box; voting machine; pollbook.

.21 **returns,** election returns, **poll,** count, official count; **recount;** landslide, tidal wave.

.22 **electorate,** electors; **constituency,** constituents; electoral college.

.23 **voter, elector, balloter;** registered voter; fraudulent voter, floater, repeater, ballot-box stuffer; proxy.

.24 **political party, party,** major party; minor party, third party, splinter party; "the madness of many for the gain of a few" [Pope]; Republican Party, GOP (Grand Old Party); Democratic Party; Conservative Party, Liberal Party, Socialist Party, Socialist Labor Party, Socialist Workers Party, Communist Party, Prohibition Party; Anti-Masonic Party, Anti-Monopoly Party, Constitutional Union Party, Democratic-Republican Party, States' Rights Democratic Party or Dixiecrats [informal], Farmer-Labor Party, Federalist Party, Free Soil Party, Greenback Party, American Party or Know-Nothing Party, Liberal Republican Party, Liberty Party, National Republican Party, People's Party or Populist Party, Progressive Party, Bull Moose Party, Whig Party; Conservative Party or Tory Party, Liberal Party, Labour Party [all England]; party in power, opposition party, loyal opposition; **faction, camp; machine,** political *or* party machine, Tammany Hall; city hall; one-party system, two-party system, multiple party system.

.25 **partisanism,** partisanship, partisanry; Republicanism; Conservatism, Toryism; Liberalism; Whiggism, Whiggery.

.26 **nonpartisanism, independence,** neutralism; mugwumpery, mugwumpism.

.27 **partisan, party member,** party man; regular, stalwart, loyalist; wheelhorse, party wheelhorse; heeler, ward heeler, **party hack;** party faithful; Republican, Democrat, etc.; registered Republican, registered Democrat; Labourite, Conservative, Tory, Liberal, Whig [all England].

.28 **nonpartisan, independent, neutral, mugwump,** undecided *or* uncommitted voter; swing vote.

.29 **political influence, wire-pulling** [informal]; **social pressure, public opinion, special-interest pressure,** group pressure; **influence peddling; lobbying,** lobbyism; **logrolling,** back scratching.

.30 **wire-puller** [informal]; **influence peddler,** four-percenter, power broker, fixer [informal], five-percenter [slang]; logroller.

.31 **pressure group,** interest group, special-interest group, **special interests;** vested interests; financial interests, farm interests, labor interests, etc.; minority interests, ethnic vote, black vote, Jewish vote, Italian vote, etc.; **Black Power, White Power,** Polish Power, etc.

.32 **lobby,** legislative lobby, special-interest lobby; **lobbyist,** registered lobbyist, lobbyer, parliamentary agent [England].

.33 **front, movement,** coalition, political front; popular front, people's front, communist front, etc.; grass-roots movement, ground swell.

.34 (political corruption) **graft,** boodling [slang], jobbery; pork-barrel legislation *or* pork-barreling; political intrigue.

.35 **spoils of office; graft,** boodle [slang]; slush fund [slang]; campaign fund, campaign contribution; public tit *or* public trough [both slang]; spoils system; cronyism, nepotism.

.36 **political patronage, patronage, favors of office,** pork *or* pork barrel [both informal], plum, melon [informal].

.37 **political** *or* **official jargon;** officialese, federalese, Washingtonese, gobbledygook [all informal]; bafflegab [slang]; political doubletalk, bunkum [informal]; pussyfooting; pointing with pride and viewing with alarm.

.38 VERBS **politick** [informal], **politicize;** look after one's fences *or* mend one's fences [both informal]; caucus; gerrymander.

.39 **run for office,** run; **throw** *or* **toss one's hat in the ring** [informal], enter the lists *or* arena, stand *or* stand for office [both Brit]; contest a seat [Brit].

.40 **electioneer, campaign; stump,** take the stump, take to the stump, stump the country, take to the hustings, hit the campaign trail, whistle-stop [all informal]; **canvass,** go to the voters *or* electorate, solicit votes, ring doorbells; shake hands and kiss babies.

.41 **support, back** *or* **back up** [both informal], **endorse;** go with the party, follow the party line; **get on the bandwagon** [informal]; **nominate, elect, vote** 637.18–20.

.42 **hold office,** hold *or* occupy a post, fill an office, be the incumbent, be in office.

.43 ADJS **political, politic, politico–;** governmental, civic; geopolitical; statesmanlike; diplomatic; suffragist; politico-commercial, politico-diplomatic, politico-ecclesiastical, politico-economic(al), politico-ethical, politico-geographical, politico-judicial, politico-military, politico-moral, politico-religious, politico-scientific, politico-social, politico-theological.

.44 **partisan, party;** bipartisan, biparty, two-party.

.45 **nonpartisan, independent, neutral,** mugwumpian *or* mugwumpish [both informal], **on the fence.**

### 745. POLITICO-ECONOMIC PRINCIPLES

.1 NOUNS **conservatism, conservativeness, rightism;** "an unhappy crossbreed, the mule of politics that engenders nothing" [Disraeli]; old school tie [Brit]; standpattism, unprogressiveness, backwardness; **ultraconservatism, reaction,** reactionism, reactionarism, reactionaryism, reactionariness, die-hardism [informal], Toryism, Bourbonism; extreme rightism, radical rightism, know-nothingism; extreme right, extreme right wing; social Darwinism; laissez-faireism 706.1; **royalism, monarchism.**

.2 **moderatism, moderateness,** moderantism; middle of the road, moderate position, fence [informal], **center,** third force.

.3 **liberalism, progressivism, leftism; left, left wing.**

.4 **radicalism, extremism,** ultraism; radicalization; revolutionism; ultraconservatism 745.1; extreme left, extreme left wing, left-wing extremism; New Left, Old Left; Jacobinism, sans-culottism, *sans-culotterie* [Fr]; anarchism, nihilism, syndicalism, anarcho-syndicalism, criminal syndicalism.

.5 **communism, Bolshevism, Marxism,** Marxism-Leninism, Leninism, Trotskyism, Stalinism, Maoism, Titoism, Castroism, revisionism; Marxian socialism; dialectical materialism; democratic centralism; dictatorship of the proletariat; **Communist Party;** Communist International, Comintern; Communist Information Bureau, Cominform; iron curtain 730.5.

.6 **socialism,** collective ownership, public ownership; **collectivism;** creeping socialism; state socialism, *Staatsozialismus* [Ger]; guild socialism; Fabian socialism, Fabianism; utopian socialism; Marxian socialism, Marxism 745.5; phalansterism; Owenism; Saint-Simonianism, Saint-Simonism; **nationalization.**

.7 **welfarism,** welfare statism; womb-to-tomb security, cradle-to-grave security; social welfare; social security, social insurance; old-age and survivors insurance; unemployment compensation, unemployment insurance; workmen's compensation, workmen's compensation insurance; health insurance, Medicare, Medicaid, state medicine, **socialized medicine;** sickness insurance; public assistance, **welfare, relief,** welfare payments, aid to dependent children, ADC, old-age assistance, aid to the blind, aid to the permanently and totally disabled; guaranteed income, guaranteed annual income; welfare state; welfare capitalism.

.8 **capitalism,** capitalistic system, **free enterprise,** private enterprise, free-enterprise economy, free-enterprise system, free economy; finance capitalism; *laissez-faire* [Fr], laissez-faireism; private sector; private ownership; state capitalism; **individualism,** rugged individualism.

.9 **conservative,** conservatist, **rightist, right-winger;** Bircher; "a person who has something to conserve" [Edward Young], "the leftover progressive of an earlier generation" [Edmund Fuller]; standpat *or* standpatter [both informal]; hard hat; social Darwinist; ultraconservative, extreme right-winger, **reactionary,** reactionarist, reactionist, diehard, Bourbon, Tory; **royalist, monarchist,** imperialist; **right, right wing; radical right.**

.10 **moderate,** moderatist, moderationist,

moderantist, centrist, middle-of-the-roader [informal]; center.

.11 **liberal,** liberalist, **progressive,** progressivist, **leftist, left-winger;** welfare stater; Lib-Lab [Brit informal]; **left.**

.12 **radical, extremist,** ultra, ultraist; **revolutionary,** revolutionist; subversive; extreme left-winger, left-wing extremist, red [informal], Bolshevik; yippie; Jacobin, sansculotte; **anarchist,** nihilist, syndicalist, anarcho-syndicalist; Wobbly [slang]; mild radical, parlor Bolshevik [informal], pink *or* parlor pink [both slang], pinko [derog]; lunatic fringe.

.13 **Communist,** Bolshevist; **Bolshevik, Red** [informal], bolshie [slang], commie [derog]; Marxist, Leninist, Marxist-Leninist, Trotskyite *or* Trotskyist, Stalinist, Maoist, Titoist, Castroite, revisionist; card-carrying Communist, avowed Communist; fellow traveler, Communist sympathizer, comsymp [slang].

.14 **socialist,** collectivist; state socialist; Fabian, Fabian socialist; Marxist 745.13; utopian socialist; Fourierist, phalansterian; Saint-Simonian; Owenite.

.15 **capitalist,** individualist, rugged individualist; rich man 837.6,7.

.16 VERBS **politicize;** democratize, republicanize, socialize, communize; nationalize 815.7.

.17 ADJS **conservative, right-wing,** right of center; old-line, die-hard, standpat [informal], unprogressive, nonprogressive; ultraconservative, **reactionary,** reactionist.

.18 **moderate,** centrist, middle-of-the-road [informal].

.19 **liberal,** liberalistic, liberalist, **progressive,** progressivistic; **leftist, left-wing,** on the left, left of center.

.20 **radical, extreme, extremist,** extremistic, ultraist, ultraistic; revolutionary, revolutionist; subversive; ultraconservative 745.17; extreme left-wing, red [informal]; anarchistic, nihilistic, syndicalist, anarcho-syndicalist; mildly radical, pink [slang].

.21 **Communist, communistic,** Bolshevik, Bolshevist, bolshie [slang], Red [informal], commie [derog]; **Marxist,** Leninist, Marxist-Leninist, Trotskyite *or* Trotskyist, Stalinist, Maoist, Titoist, Castroite, revisionist.

.22 **socialist, socialistic,** collectivistic; Fabian; Fourieristic, phalansterian; Saint-Simonian.

.23 **capitalist, capitalistic,** bourgeois, individualistic, nonsocialistic, free-enterprise, private-enterprise.

## 746. POLITICIAN

.1 NOUNS **politician,** politico, political leader, professional politician, –crat *or* –ocrat; party leader, party boss *or* party chieftain [both informal]; machine politician, political hack, Tammany man; pol [informal]; old campaigner, war-horse; wheelhorse; reform politician, reformer.

.2 **statesman,** stateswoman, solon, public man, national leader; "a politician who is held upright by equal pressure from all directions" [Eric Johnston], "a successful politician who is dead" [Thomas B. Reed]; elder statesman.

.3 **legislator,** lawmaker, solon, lawgiver; **congressman,** congresswoman, Member of Congress; **senator; representative;** Speaker of the House; majority leader, minority leader; floor leader; whip, party whip; Member of Parliament, MP; state senator, assemblyman, chosen freeholder, councilman, alderman, city father.

.4 (petty politician) **two-bit** *or* **peanut politician** [slang], politicaster, statemonger [archaic], political dabbler; hack, party hack.

.5 (corrupt politician) **dirty** *or* **crooked politician** [informal], jackleg politician [slang]; **grafter,** boodler [informal]; spoilsman, spoilsmonger; influence peddler 744.30.

.6 (political intriguer) strategist, machinator, gamesman, wheeler-dealer [slang]; operator *or* finagler *or* **wire-puller** [all informal]; **logroller,** pork-barrel politician; Machiavellian 654.8; behind-the-scenes operator, gray eminence, *éminence grise* [Fr], power behind the throne, kingmaker [informal].

.7 (political leader) **boss** [slang], cacique, sachem, man higher up [informal]; keynoter [informal], policy maker; standardbearer; ringleader 648.11.

.8 **henchman,** hanger-on; heeler *or* **ward heeler** [both informal]; hatchet man.

.9 **candidate, aspirant,** hopeful *or* political hopeful [both informal], office seeker *or* hunter, baby kisser [slang]; running mate; **dark horse;** stalking-horse; favorite son; presidential timber; defeated candidate, also-ran *or* dud [both slang]; lame duck.

.10 **campaigner,** electioneer, **stumper** [informal], whistle-stopper [slang], stump speaker *or* orator [informal].

.11 **officeholder,** office-bearer [Brit], jack-in-office, public servant, public official, incumbent, holdover, lame duck; new broom [slang]; president-elect; ins, the powers that be.

.12 **political worker, committeeman,** committeewoman, precinct captain, precinct leader, district leader; party chairman, state chairman, national chairman, chairman of the national committee.

.13 ADJS **statesmanlike,** statesmanly.

## 747. DIRECTION, MANAGEMENT

.1 NOUNS **direction, management, managing,** managery [archaic], **handling, running** [informal], **conduct;** governance, **command, control, government** 741; **authority** 739; **regulation,** ordering, husbandry; **manipulation; guidance, lead, leading; steering,** steerage, pilotage, the conn, the helm, the wheel.

.2 **supervision, superintendence,** intendance, **bossing** [informal]; **surveillance, oversight, eye; charge, care, auspices, jurisdiction; responsibility,** accountability 962.2.

.3 **administration,** executive function *or* role, command function; **decision-making; disposition,** disposal, **dispensation;** officiation.

.4 **directorship, directorate, managership, leadership,** headship, governorship, chairmanship, convenership [Brit], presidency, generalship, captainship; mastership 739.7; dictatorship, sovereignty 739.8; superintendence *or* **superintendency,** intendancy, foremanship, overseership, supervisorship; stewardship, custody, guardianship, proctorship.

.5 **helm,** rudder, tiller, wheel, **reins,** reins of government.

.6 **domestic management, housekeeping,** homemaking, housewifery, ménage, husbandry [archaic]; domestic economy, home economics.

.7 **efficiency engineering,** scientific management, industrial engineering, management engineering, management consulting; management theory; efficiency expert, management consultant; time and motion study, time-motion study, time study.

.8 VERBS **direct, manage, regulate, conduct, carry on, handle, run** [informal]; **control, command, govern** 741.12; pull the strings *or* **mastermind** [both informal]; quarterback, call the signals; **order, prescribe;** lay down the law, make the rules; **head, head up, officer, captain, skipper** [informal];

**lead,** take the lead, lead on; manipulate, maneuver, engineer; take command 739.14; be responsible for.

.9 **guide, steer, drive, run** [informal]; herd, shepherd; **pilot, take the helm,** be at the helm *or* wheel *or* tiller *or* rudder, hold the reins, **be in the driver's seat.**

.10 **supervise, superintend, boss** [informal], oversee, overlook, ride herd on [informal], stand over, keep an eye on *or* upon, keep in order; cut work out for; strawboss [informal]; take care of 699.19.

.11 **administer,** administrate; **officiate; preside,** preside over, preside at the board; chair, chairman, occupy the chair.

.12 ADJS **directing, directive, directory, directorial; managing, managerial; commanding, controlling, governing** 741.18; **regulating, regulative, regulatory; head, chief; leading, guiding.**

.13 **supervising, supervisory,** overseeing, **superintendent, boss** [informal]; **in charge** 739.21.

.14 **administrative, administrating;** ministerial, **executive; officiating, presiding.**

.15 ADVS in the charge of, in the hands of, in the care of; **under the auspices of,** under the aegis of; in one's charge, on one's hands, under one's care, under one's jurisdiction.

## 748. DIRECTOR

.1 NOUNS **director,** *directeur* [Fr], **governor,** rector, **manager, administrator,** intendant, **conductor;** person in charge, responsible person; ship's husband, supercargo; impresario, producer; deputy, agent 781.

.2 **superintendent, super** [informal]; **supervisor, foreman, monitor, head,** headman, overman, Big Brother [Orwell], **boss** [informal], chief, gaffer, ganger [both Brit], taskmaster; sirdar [India], **overseer,** overlooker; inspector, surveyor, visitor; proctor; subforeman, **straw boss** [informal]; slave driver; boatswain; floorman, floorwalker, floor manager; noncommissioned officer 749.19; controller, comptroller, auditor.

.3 **executive,** executive officer, executive director, executive secretary; officer, official; **president,** prexy [slang], chief executive officer, chief executive, managing director, provost, prefect, warden, archon; magistrate; **chairman of the board; chancellor,** vice-chancellor; vice-president, VP, veep [informal]; secretary; treasurer;

dean; **management,** the administration 748.11.

.4 **steward,** bailiff [Brit], factor [Scot], seneschal; majordomo, butler, housekeeper, *maître d'hôtel* [Fr]; master of ceremonies, MC *or* emcee [both informal], master of the revels; proctor, procurator, attorney; guardian, custodian 699.6–12; curator, librarian; landreeve; croupier.

.5 **chairman,** chairwoman, **chair,** convener [Brit], speaker, presiding officer.

.6 **leader,** conductor [archaic]; file leader, fugleman; pacemaker, pacesetter; bellwether, bell mare, bell cow, Judas goat; standard-bearer, torchbearer; **leader of men,** born leader, charismatic leader *or* figure, inspired leader; messiah, Mahdi; führer, duce; forerunner 66.1; ringleader 648.11; precentor, coryphaeus, choragus, symphonic conductor, choirmaster 464.17, 18.

.7 **guide,** guider; **shepherd,** herd, herdsman, drover, cowherd, goatherd, etc.; tour guide, tour director *or* conductor, cicerone, mercury [archaic], courier, dragoman; **pilot,** river pilot, navigator, **helmsman,** timoneer, steersman, steerer, coxswain, boatsteerer, boatheader; automatic pilot, Gyropilot; pointer, guidepost 568.4.

.8 **guiding star,** cynosure [archaic], **polestar,** polar star, lodestar, Polaris, **North Star.**

.9 **compass,** magnetic compass, gyrocompass, gyroscopic compass, gyrostatic compass, Gyrosin compass, surveyor's compass, mariner's compass; needle, magnetic needle; direction finder, radio compass, radio direction finder, RDF; inertial guidance *or* inertial navigation system; loran, shoran.

.10 **directory, guidebook,** handbook, Baedeker; city directory, business directory; telephone directory, telephone book, phone book [informal], classified directory, Yellow Pages; **bibliography;** catalog, index, handlist, checklist, finding list; itinerary, road map, roadbook; reference book 605.6.

.11 **directorate,** directory, **management, the administration,** the brass *or* top brass [both informal], the people upstairs *or* the people in the front office [both informal], executive hierarchy; the executive, executive arm *or* branch; **cabinet; board,** governing board *or* body, board of directors, board of trustees, board of regents; steering committee, executive committee, interlocking directorate; cadre, executive council; infrastructure; council 755.

## 749. MASTER

.1 NOUNS **master, lord, lord and master,**
overlord, **seigneur** or **seignior, paramount,**
lord paramount, **liege,** liege lord, *padrone* [Ital], *patron, chef* [both Fr], patroon; **chief** or **boss** [both informal], sahib [India], *bwana* [Swahili]; employer;
husband, man of the house, master of
the house, goodman [archaic or dial], paterfamilias; patriarch, elder; teacher,
rabbi, guru, starets; church dignitary, ecclesiarch 1038.9.

.2 **mistress,** governess, dame, madam; **matron, housewife,** homemaker, goodwife
[Scot], lady of the house, chatelaine;
housemistress, housemother; rectoress,
abbess, mother superior; great lady, first
lady; matriarch, dowager.

.3 **chief,** principal; top dog or kingpin or
kingfish [all informal]; master, dean,
doyen, doyenne [fem], high priest [infor-
mal]; superior, senior; **leader** 748.6; important person, personage 672.8–10.

.4 **figurehead,** nominal head, dummy, lay
figure, front man or front [both infor-
mal], stooge or Charlie McCarthy [both
slang], puppet, creature.

.5 **governor, ruler,** –arch, –crat or –ocrat;
**captain,** master, **commander,** commandant, intendant, castellan, chatelain,
chatelaine; **director, manager, executive**
748.3.

.6 **head of state, chief of state; premier,**
**prime minister, chancellor,** grand vizier,
dewan [India]; doge; **president,** chief executive, the man in the White House.

.7 **potentate, sovereign, monarch, ruler,**
**prince,** dynast, **crowned head, emperor,**
*imperator* [L], king-emperor, **king,**
anointed king, majesty, royalty, royal,
royal personage; petty king, tetrarch,
kinglet; grand duke; paramount, lord paramount, suzerain, overlord, overking,
high king; **chief, chieftain,** high chief;
prince consort 918.7.

.8 (rulers) **caesar,** *Kaiser* [Ger], **czar;** Holy
Roman Emperor; Dalai Lama; **pharaoh;**
pendragon, rig, ardri; **mikado,** tenno; shogun, tycoon; khan or cham; shah, padi-
shah; negus; bey; **sheikh;** sachem, saga-
more; Inca; cacique; kaid.

.9 (princes of India) **raja, maharaja,** rana, nizam, jam; Great Mogul, Mogul.

.10 (Muslim rulers) **sultan,** Grand Turk,
grand seignior; caliph, imam; hakim;
khan or cham; nizam, nawab, emir; Great
Mogul, Mogul.

.11 **sovereign queen, sovereign princess, princess, queen,** queen regent, queen regnant,
**empress, czarina,** *Kaiserin* [Ger]; rani,
maharani [both India]; grand duchess;
queen consort.

.12 **regent,** protector, prince regent, queen
regent.

.13 (regional governors) **governor,** governor-
general, **lieutenant governor; viceroy,**
vice-king, exarch, proconsul, khedive,
stadtholder; nabob, nawab, subahdar [all
India]; gauleiter; eparch; palatine; tetrarch; burgrave; collector; hospodar,
vaivode; dey, bey or beg, beglerbeg, wali
or vali, satrap; provincial.

.14 **tyrant, despot,** warlord; **autocrat,** autarch;
oligarch; absolute ruler or master or monarch, omnipotent or all-powerful ruler;
**dictator,** duce, führer, commissar, pharaoh, caesar, czar; usurper, arrogator; **op-
pressor, hard master,** driver, **slave driver,**
Simon Legree [Harriet B. Stowe]; **martinet, disciplinarian,** stickler.

.15 **the authorities, the powers that be,** ruling
class or classes, **the Establishment,** the interests, the power elite, the power structure; **they, them;** the inner circle; the ins
or the ingroup [both informal]; **management, the administration;** higher eche-
lons, **top brass** [informal]; higher-ups, the
people upstairs or the people in the front
office [all informal]; **the top** [informal],
the corridors of power; prelacy, hierarchy;
ministry; **bureaucracy, officialdom;** directorate 748.11.

.16 **official, officer,** officiary, functionary or
functionnaire, *fonctionnaire* [Fr]; **public
official,** public servant; officeholder, office-bearer or placeman [both Brit]; civil
servant; bureaucrat, mandarin, red-tapist;
petty tyrant, jack-in-office.

.17 (public officials) **minister,** secretary, secretary of state [Brit], undersecretary, cabinet minister, cabinet member, minister
of state [Brit]; chancellor; warden; archon; magistrate; syndic; commissioner;
commissar; county commissioner; city
manager, mayor, *maire* [Fr], lord mayor,
burgomaster or burghermaster; headman,
induna [Africa]; **councilman,** council-
woman, councillor, city councilman, elder, city father, alderman, bailie [Scot];
selectman; supervisor, county supervisor;
reeve, portreeve; legislator 746.3.

.18 **commissioned officer, officer; top brass,**
the brass [both informal]; **commander in
chief,** generalissimo, captain general; het-
man, sirdar; general of the army, genera

of the air force, five-star general [informal], **marshal**, *maréchal* [Fr], field marshal; general officer, **general**, four-star general [informal]; lieutenant general, three-star general [informal]; major general, two-star general [informal], brigadier general, one-star general [informal], brigadier [Brit]; field officer; **colonel**, chicken colonel [slang]; lieutenant colonel; **major;** company officer; **captain,** subahdar, risaldar [both India]; subaltern [Brit], **lieutenant,** jemadar [India]; first lieutenant; second lieutenant, shavetail [slang], sublieutenant [Brit]; **commander,** commandant, the Old Man [slang]; **commanding officer,** CO, executive officer, exec [slang]; chief of staff; aide, aide-de-camp, ADC; officer of the day, OD, orderly officer [Brit]; staff officer; senior officer, junior officer.

.19 **noncommissioned officer,** noncom [informal], NCO; warrant officer, chief warrant officer; centurion; sergeant, sarge [slang], havildar [India]; first sergeant, top sergeant [informal], topkick [slang]; sergeant major, master sergeant, sergeant first class, technical sergeant, platoon sergeant, staff sergeant, mess sergeant, color sergeant, acting sergeant, lance sergeant [Brit]; **corporal,** naik [India]; acting corporal, lance corporal [Brit], lance-jack [Brit slang].

.20 **naval officer; fleet admiral,** navarch, **admiral,** vice admiral, rear admiral, **commodore, captain, commander,** lieutenant commander, **lieutenant,** lieutenant junior grade, ensign; warrant officer; petty officer, master chief petty officer, senior chief petty officer, chief petty officer, petty officer first class, petty officer second class, petty officer third class; skipper.

.21 (heraldic officials) herald, king of arms, king at arms, earl marshal; Garter, Garter King of Arms, Clarenceux, Clarenceux King of Arms, Norroy and Ulster, Norroy and Ulster King of Arms, Norroy, Norroy King of Arms, Lyon, Lyon King of Arms; College of Arms.

## 750. SERVANT, EMPLOYEE

.1 NOUNS **retainer,** dependent, follower; myrmidon, yeoman; vassal, liege, liege man, feudatory, homager; inferior, **underling, subordinate,** understrapper; **minion,** creature, hanger-on, lackey, flunky, stooge [informal]; peon, serf, slave 764.7.

.2 **servant,** servitor, help; domestic, domes-

tic servant, house servant; **menial,** drudge, slavey [informal]; scullion, turnspit.

.3 **employee;** pensioner, **hireling, mercenary,** myrmidon; hired man, hired hand, man *or* girl Friday, right-hand man, assistant 787.6; worker 718.

.4 **man,** manservant, serving man, gillie [Scot], **boy,** *garçon* [Fr], houseboy, houseman; butler; valet, *valet de chambre* [Fr], gentleman, gentleman's gentleman; driver, chauffeur, coachman; gardener; lord-in-waiting, lord of the bedchamber, equerry.

.5 **attendant,** tender, usher, squire, yeoman; errand boy, errand girl, gofer [slang], office boy, office girl, copyboy; page, footboy; bellboy, bellman, bellhop; cabin boy; printer's devil; chore boy; caddie; bootblack, boots [Brit]; trainbearer; cupbearer, Ganymede, Hebe; orderly, batman [Brit]; steward, **stewardess, hostess,** airline stewardess, airline hostess.

.6 **lackey, flunky,** livery *or* liveried servant; **footman,** *valet de pied* [Fr].

.7 **waiter, waitress;** carhop; counterman, soda jerk [informal]; busboy; headwaiter, *maître d'hôtel* [Fr], maitre d' [informal]; hostess; wine steward, sommelier; bartender, barkeeper *or* barkeep, barman, barmaid [Brit].

.8 **maid, maidservant,** servitress, **girl,** servant girl, *bonne* [Fr], serving girl, wench, biddy [informal], hired girl; lady-help [Brit], au pair girl, ayah [India], amah [China]; live-in maid, live-out maid; **handmaid,** handmaiden; **lady's maid,** waiting maid *or* woman, gentlewoman, abigail, soubrette; lady-in-waiting, maid-in-waiting, lady of the bedchamber; companion; chaperon; betweenmaid, tweeny [both Brit]; duenna; parlormaid; kitchenmaid, scullery maid; cook; housemaid, chambermaid, *femme de chambre*, *fille de chambre* [both Fr], upstairs maid; nursemaid 699.8.

.9 **factotum, do-all** [archaic], general servant [Brit], man of all work; maid of all work, domestic drudge, slavey [informal].

.10 **majordomo, steward,** house steward, butler, chamberlain, *maître d'hôtel* [Fr], seneschal; **housekeeper.**

.11 **staff, personnel, employees,** help, hired help, the help, **crew, gang,** men, force, servantry, retinue 73.6.

.12 **service,** servitude [archaic], servitorship, *servitium* [L]; **employment, employ; min-**

istry, ministration, attendance, tendance; serfdom, peonage, slavery 764.1.

.13 VERBS serve, work for, be in service with; minister *or* administer to, pander to, do service to; help 785.11; care for, do for [informal], look after, take care of; wait, wait on *or* upon, attend, tend, attend on *or* upon, dance attendance upon, wait on hand and foot; lackey, valet, maid, chore; drudge 716.14.

.14 ADJS serving, servitorial, servitial, ministering, waiting, attending, attendant; in the train of, in one's pay *or* employ; helping 785.20; menial, servile 907.12.

## 751. PRECEPT

.1 NOUNS precept, prescript, prescription, teaching; instruction, direction, charge, commission, injunction, dictate; order, command 752.

.2 rule, law, canon, rubric, maxim, dictum, moral; norm, convention; formula, form; rule of action *or* conduct, moral precept; commandment, *mitzvah* [Heb]; ordinance, imperative, regulation, *règlement* [Fr]; principle, principium, settled principle, general principle *or* truth, tenet; standard; guideline, working rule, working principle; guiding principle, golden rule; code.

.3 formula, form [archaic], recipe, receipt; prescription; formulary.

.4 ADJS preceptive, didactic, instructive, prescriptive; prescript, prescribed, mandatory, hard and fast, binding, dictated; formulary, standard, regulation, official, authoritative, canonical, statutory, rubric(al).

## 752. COMMAND

.1 NOUNS command, commandment, order, direct order, bidding, behest, hest [archaic], imperative, dictate, dictation, will, pleasure, say-so [informal], word, word of command, *mot d'ordre* [Fr]; special order.

.2 injunction, charge, commission, mandate.

.3 direction, directive, instruction, rule, regulation; prescript, prescription, precept 751; general orders.

.4 decree, decreement [archaic], decretum, decretal, rescript, fiat, edict, *edictum* [L]; law 998.3; rule, ruling, dictum, ipse dixit; ordinance, *ordonnance* [Fr], appointment [archaic]; proclamation, pronouncement, pronunciamento, declaration, ukase; bull, brevet [archaic]; decree-law,

*décret loi* [Fr]; *senatus consultum* [L], senatus consult; diktat.

.5 summons, bidding, beck, call, calling, nod, beck and call, preconization; convocation, evocation, calling forth, invocation; requisition, indent [Brit].

.6 (legal order) injunction, interdict, mandatory injunction, prohibitory injunction; mandate; writ, process, precept; notice, notification; warrant, bench warrant, justice's warrant, search warrant, death warrant, warrant of arrest, warrant of attorney; mittimus, mandamus, caveat, capias, nisi prius [Brit], fieri facias, levari facias, elegit, habere facias possessionem, habere facias seisinam.

.7 summons, writ of summons, subpoena, citation, monition; certiorari; venire *or* venire facias, venire facias de novo *or* venire de novo; habeas corpus, writ of habeas corpus, habeas corpus ad faciendum et recipiendum *or* habeas corpus cum causa, habeas corpus ad prosequendum, habeas corpus ad subjiciendum, habeas corpus ad testificandum; garnishment.

.8 process server, summoner.

.9 VERBS command, order, dictate, direct, instruct, mandate, bid, enjoin, charge, commission, call on *or* upon; issue a writ *or* injunction; decree, rule, ordain, promulgate; give an order *or* direct order, issue a command, say the word, give the word *or* word of command; call the tune [informal], call the signals *or* play [slang]; order about *or* around; proclaim, declare, pronounce 559.12,13.

.10 prescribe, require, demand, dictate, impose, lay down, set, appoint, make obligatory *or* mandatory; authorize 777.11.

.11 lay down the law, put one's foot down [informal], read the riot act.

.12 summon, call, demand, preconize; call for, send for *or* after, bid come; cite, summons [informal], subpoena, serve; page; convoke, convene, call together; call away; muster, invoke, conjure; order up, summon up, muster up, call up, conjure up; evoke, call forth, summon forth, call out; recall, call back, call in; requisition, indent [Brit].

.13 ADJS mandatory, mandated, imperative, compulsory, prescript, prescriptive, obligatory, must [informal]; dictated, imposed, required, entailed, decretory; decisive, final, peremptory, absolute, hard-and-fast, ultimate, conclusive, binding, irrevocable, without appeal.

.14 commanding, imperative, jussive, peremptory; **directive, instructive; mandating,** dictating, compelling, obligating, **prescriptive, preceptive;** decretory, decretive, decretal.

.15 ADVS **commandingly, imperatively,** peremptorily.

.16 **by order** or **command,** at the word of command, as ordered or required, to order; mandatorily, compulsorily, obligatorily.

## 753. DEMAND

.1 NOUNS **demand, claim, call; requisition,** requirement, order, rush order, indent [Brit]; **call for, demand for;** heavy demand, draft, drain, levy, tax, taxing; imposition, impost, tribute, duty, contribution; **insistent demand,** rush; **exorbitant** or **extortionate demand,** exaction, extortion, blackmail; **ultimatum,** nonnegotiable demand; notice, warning 703.

.2 **stipulation, provision,** proviso, condition, term, string [informal], exception, reservation; **qualification** 507.

.3 **insistence, importunity,** importunateness, importunacy, **demandingness,** pertinaciousness, pertinacity; pressure, pressingness, urgency, exigency 672.4; persistence 625.1.

.4 VERBS **demand, ask, ask for,** make a demand; **call for,** call on or upon one for; appeal to one for; cry for, clamor for; **claim,** challenge, **require;** levy, **impose,** impose on one for; **exact, extort,** screw; blackmail; **requisition,** make or put in requisition, indent [Brit]; **order,** put in or place an order, order up; deliver or issue an ultimatum; warn 703.5.

.5 **claim, pretend to, lay claim to, challenge;** assert or vindicate a claim or right or title to.

.6 **stipulate,** stipulate for, specifically provide, set conditions or terms, make reservations; **qualify** 507.3,4.

.7 **insist, insist on** or **upon,** stick to [slang], set one's heart or mind upon; **take one's stand upon,** stand on or upon; stand upon one's rights, **put one's foot down** [informal]; brook or take no denial, not take 'no' for an answer; **maintain, contend,** assert 523.4; urge, press 648.14; **persist** 625.2–6.

.8 ADJS **demanding, exacting,** exigent; draining, taxing, exorbitant, extortionate, grasping; **insistent,** instant, **importunate,** urgent, pertinacious, pressing, loud, clamant, crying, clamorous; persistent 625.7.

.9 requisitorial, requisitory.

.10 ADVS **demandingly, exactingly,** exigently; exorbitantly, extortionately; **insistently, importunately, urgently,** pressingly, clamorously, loudly, clamantly.

.11 **on demand,** at demand, **on call,** upon presentation.

## 754. ADVICE

.1 NOUNS **advice, counsel, recommendation, suggestion;** proposal; **advising, advocacy; direction, instruction, guidance, briefing; exhortation,** hortation, expostulation, remonstrance; **admonition,** monition, caution, caveat, **warning** 703; **idea, thought,** opinion 501.6; **consultation,** parley 597.6; council 755.

.2 piece of advice, **word of advice, word to the wise,** verbum sapienti [L], verb. sap. or verbum sap., word in the ear, **flea in the ear** [informal], **tip** [informal], a few words of wisdom, one's two cents' worth [informal].

.3 **adviser, counsel, counselor, consultant,** professional consultant, expert; instructor, guide, **mentor,** nestor, orienter; confidant, personal adviser; admonisher, monitor, Dutch uncle; Polonius [Shakespeare], preceptist; **teacher** 565; meddler, buttinsky [slang], kibitzer or backseat driver [both informal].

.4 advisee, counselee.

.5 VERBS **advise, counsel, recommend, suggest, advocate,** propose, submit; **instruct,** coach, guide, direct, brief; prescribe; give a piece of advice, put a flea in one's ear [informal], speak words of wisdom; meddle, kibitz [informal]; confer, consult with 597.11.

.6 **admonish, exhort,** expostulate, remonstrate, preach; **enjoin, charge,** call upon one to; caution, issue a caveat; warn 703.5,6; move, prompt, **urge, incite, encourage, induce, persuade** 648.12–23.

.7 take or accept advice, **follow advice,** follow, follow implicitly; solicit advice, desire guidance, implore counsel; **be advised by;** have at one's elbow, take one's cue from.

.8 ADJS **advisory,** recommendatory; consultative, consultatory; directive, instructive; **admonitory,** monitory, monitorial, cautionary, **warning** 703.7; **expostulative,** expostulatory, **remonstrative,** remonstratory, remonstrant; **exhortative,** exhortatory, hortative, hortatory, preachy [informal], **didactic,** moralistic, sententious.

## 755. COUNCIL

.1 NOUNS **council,** *concilium* [L], deliberative *or* advisory body, deliberative assembly, consultative assembly; chamber,
**board,** court, bench; **congress,** diet,
synod, soviet; legislature 742; **cabinet,** divan, council of ministers, council of state,
US Cabinet 742.9, British Cabinet 742.10;
kitchen cabinet, camarilla; staff; junta, directory; Sanhedrin; privy council, common council, county council, parish
council, borough council, city council;
brain trust [informal], group *or* corps *or*
body of advisers; council of war; council
fire; syndicate, **association** 788; **conference** 597.6; **assembly** 74.2; tribunal 1001.

.2 **committee,** subcommittee, standing committee, special committee, ad hoc committee; committee of one.

.3 **forum,** discussion group, **round table,
panel;** open forum.

.4 **ecclesiastical council,** chapter, classis,
conclave, conference, congregation, con-
sistory, convention, convocation, presbytery, session, synod, vestry; parochial
council, parochial church council; diocesan conference, diocesan court; provincial
court, plenary council; ecumenical council; Council of Nicaea, Council of Trent,
Lateran Council, Vatican Council; con-
ciliarism.

.5 ADJS **conciliar,** council; consultative, deliberative, advisory; synodal, synodic(al).

.6 ADVS **in council, in conference, in consultation, in a huddle** [slang], in conclave; **in session,** sitting.

## 756. COMPULSION

.1 NOUNS **compulsion, obligation,** obligement; **necessity** 639; **inevitability** 639.7; **irresistibility, compulsiveness; forcing,** enforcement; **constraint,** coaction; **restraint**
760.

.2 **force,** *ultima ratio* [L]; **brute force,** naked force, rule of might, big battalions,
**main force,** physical force; the right of
the strong, the law of the jungle; **tyranny**
741.10; steamroller [informal].

.3 **coercion,** intimidation, **duress; the strong
arm** *or* **strong-arm tactics** [both informal],
the sword, the mailed fist, the bludgeon,
the boot in the face, the jackboot, the
big stick, the club, *argumentum baculinum* [L]; **pressure, high pressure,** high-
pressure methods; **violence** 162.

.4 VERBS **compel, force, make;** have, cause,
cause to; **constrain, bind,** tie, tie one's

hands; **restrain** 760.7; enforce, **drive,** impel; use force upon, force one's hand.

.5 **oblige, necessitate, require,** exact, demand, **dictate,** impose, call for; take *or*
brook no denial; leave no option *or* escape, admit of no option.

.6 **press; pressure** *or* **high-pressure** *or* lean on
*or* squeeze [all informal], twist one's arm
[slang]; ram *or* cram down one's throat;
**bring pressure to bear upon, put pressure
on,** bear down on, bear down upon, bear
against, bear hard upon; put the screw *or*
screws on [informal], put the screw *or*
screws to [informal].

.7 **coerce,** use violence, intimidate, **strong-
arm** [slang], bully, steamroller *or* bulldoze [both informal], bludgeon, blackjack; hijack, shanghai, dragoon.

.8 **be compelled, be coerced,** have to 639.10.

.9 ADJS **compulsory, compulsive,** compulsa-
tory, **compelling; pressing, driving,** imperative, imperious; constraining, coactive;
**restraining** 760.11; irresistible.

.10 **obligatory, compulsory,** imperative, mandatory, required, dictated, **binding;** involuntary; **necessary** 639.12; **inevitable** 639.15.

.11 **coercive, forcible;** steamroller *or* bulldozer *or* sledgehammer *or* strong-arm [all
informal]; **violent** 162.15.

.12 ADVS **compulsively,** compulsorily, **com-
pellingly,** imperatively, imperiously.

.13 **forcibly, by force,** by main force, by *force
majeure,* by a strong arm; by force of
arms, *vi et armis* [L].

.14 **obligatorily,** compulsorily, mandatorily,
by stress of, under press of; at the point
of a gun, at the point of the sword *or*
bayonet, at bayonet point; under the
lash; of necessity.

## 757. STRICTNESS

.1 NOUNS **strictness, severity, harshness,
stringency,** astringency; **discipline,** strict
*or* tight *or* rigid discipline, regimentation;
**austerity, sternness,** grimness, ruggedness,
**toughness** [informal]; Spartanism; authoritarianism; demandingness, exactingness;
**meticulousness** 533.3.

.2 **firmness, rigor, rigorousness,** rigidness, rigidity, stiffness, **hardness,** obduracy, obdurateness, **inflexibility,** inexorability, unyieldingness, unbendingness, impliability,
unrelentingness, **relentlessness; uncompromisingness;** stubbornness, obstinacy
626; purism; precisianism, puritanism,
fundamentalism, orthodoxy.

.3 **firm hand, iron hand,** heavy hand, strong
hand, tight hand, tight rein; tight ship.

.4 VERBS **hold** or **keep a tight hand upon,** keep a firm hand on, keep a tight rein on, rule with an iron hand, rule with a rod of iron; regiment, discipline; run a tight ship, keep in line; maintain the highest standards, not spare oneself nor anyone else.

.5 **deal hardly** or **harshly with,** deal hard measure to, lay a heavy hand on, bear hard upon, not pull one's punches [slang]; throw one's back at [informal].

.6 ADJS **strict, exacting,** exigent, demanding, not to be trifled with, **stringent,** astringent; **severe, harsh,** dour, unsparing; **stern, grim, austere,** rugged, **tough** [informal]; Spartan, Spartanic; authoritarian; **meticulous** 533.12.

.7 **firm, rigid, rigorous,** rigorist, rigoristic, stiff, **hard,** iron, obdurate, **inflexible,** ironhanded, inexorable, dour, **unyielding,** unbending, impliable, **relentless,** unrelenting, procrustean, muscle-bound; **uncompromising;** stubborn, obstinate 626.8; purist, puristic; puritan, puritanic(al), fundamentalist, orthodox; ironbound, rockbound, ironclad [informal]; straitlaced or straightlaced, hidebound.

.8 ADVS **strictly, severely, stringently, harshly;** sternly, grimly, **austerely,** ruggedly, toughly [informal].

.9 **firmly, rigidly, rigorously,** stiffly, hardly, obdurately, **inflexibly,** impliably, inexorably, unyieldingly, unbendingly; **uncompromisingly, relentlessly,** unrelentingly; ironhandedly, with a firm or strong or heavy or tight or iron hand.

## 758. LAXNESS

.1 NOUNS **laxness, laxity, slackness, looseness,** relaxedness; loosening, relaxation; imprecision, sloppiness [informal], carelessness, remissness, negligence 534.1–4; indifference 636; leniency 759; permissiveness; overpermissiveness, overindulgence, softness; easygoingness, easiness; weakness 160; impotence 158; unrestraint 762.3.

.2 **unstrictness,** nonstrictness, undemandingness, unsevereness, unharshness; unsternness, unaustereness; flexibility, pliancy.

.3 VERBS **hold a loose rein, give free rein to,** give the reins to, **give one his head,** give a free course to, give rope enough to; permit all or anything.

.4 ADJS **lax, slack, loose,** relaxed; imprecise, sloppy [informal], careless, slipshod; remiss, negligent 534.10–13; indifferent 636.6–8; lenient 759.7; permissive; overpermissive, overindulgent, soft; easy, easygo-

ing; weak 160.12; impotent 158.13–15; unrestrained 762.23.

.5 **unstrict,** undemanding, **unexacting;** unsevere, **unharsh; unstern,** unaustere; **flexible, pliant,** yielding.

## 759. LENIENCY

.1 NOUNS **leniency** or **lenience,** lenientness, lenity; **clemency,** clementness, **mercifulness, mercy, humaneness,** humanity, pity, **compassion** 944.1; **mildness, gentleness,** tenderness, softness, moderateness; **easiness,** easygoingness; laxness 758; **forbearance,** forbearing, patience 861; **acceptance, tolerance** 526.4.

.2 **compliance, complaisance,** obligingness, accommodatingness, **agreeableness;** affability, graciosity, graciousness, generousness, decency, amiability; kindness, kindliness, benignity, **benevolence** 938.

.3 **indulgence, humoring,** obliging; favoring, gratification, pleasing; **pampering,** cosseting, **coddling,** mollycoddling, spoiling; **permissiveness,** overpermissiveness, overindulgence.

.4 **spoiled child,** *enfant gâté* [Fr], pampered darling, mama's boy, mollycoddle; *enfant terrible* [Fr], naughty child.

.5 VERBS **be easy on,** handle with kid gloves or velvet gloves, use a light hand or light rein, spare the rod; **tolerate,** bear with 861.5.

.6 **indulge, humor, oblige;** favor, please, gratify, satisfy, **cater to; give way to,** yield to, let one have his own way; **pamper,** cosset, **coddle,** mollycoddle, spoil; spare the rod and spoil the child.

.7 ADJS **lenient, mild, gentle,** tender, humane, compassionate, **clement,** merciful 944.7; soft, moderate, **easy,** easygoing; lax 758.4,5; forgiving 947.6; **forbearing,** forbearant, patient 861.9; accepting, tolerant 526.11.

.8 **indulgent, compliant,** complaisant, **obliging, accommodating, agreeable,** amiable, gracious, generous, benignant, affable, decent, kind, kindly, benign, benevolent 938.13–15; permissive, overpermissive, overindulgent.

.9 **indulged, pampered, coddled, spoiled,** spoiled rotten [informal].

## 760. RESTRAINT

.1 NOUNS **restraint, constraint;** inhibition; legal restraint, injunction, interdict; **control, curb, check,** rein, arrest, arrestation; **retardation,** deceleration, slowing down; cooling or cooling off or cooling down [all informal]; retrenchment, curtailment; self-control 624.5; **hindrance** 730; rationing; thought control; restraint of trade, monopoly, protection, protectionism, protective tariff, tariff wall; **prohibition** 778.

.2 **suppression, repression; subdual,** quelling, putting down, smashing, crushing; quashing, squashing or squelching [both informal]; smothering, stifling, suffocating, strangling, throttling; extinguishment, quenching; crackdown [informal]; censorship.

.3 **restriction, limitation, confinement;** circumscription 234; stint, cramping, cramp; qualification 507.

.4 **shackle,** restraint, **restraints, fetter, hamper,** trammel, trammels, **manacle,** gyves, bond, **bonds,** irons, chains, Oregon boat; stranglehold; **handcuffs,** cuffs; stocks, bilbo, pillory; hobbles, hopples; straitjacket or straightjacket, strait-waistcoat [Brit], camisole; yoke, collar; bridle, halter; **muzzle, gag;** tether; leash, leading strings; reins.

.5 **lock,** bolt, bar, padlock; barrier 730.5.

.6 **restrictionist, protectionist, monopolist;** censor.

.7 VERBS **restrain, constrain, control, govern,** guard, contain, keep under control, put or lay under restraint; **inhibit,** straiten [archaic]; enjoin, prohibit 778.3; **curb, check, arrest, bridle,** rein, snub; **retard,** slow down, decelerate; **cool** or **cool off** or **cool down** [all informal]; retrench, curtail; hold, keep, withhold, hold up [informal], **keep from;** hinder 730.10; **hold back, keep back,** pull, set back; **hold in, keep in,** pull in, rein in; **hold** or **keep in check, hold at bay,** dompt, hold in leash; hold fast, keep a tight hand on; restrain oneself, not go too far, not go off the deep end [informal].

.8 **suppress, repress,** stultify; **keep down,** hold down, keep under; **subdue, quell, put down,** smash, **crush; quash, squash** or **squelch** [both informal]; **extinguish,** quench, stanch, damp down, pour water on, drown, kill; **smother, stifle,** suffocate, asphyxiate, strangle, throttle, choke off, **muzzle, gag;** censor, silence; sit on or sit down on [both slang]; jump on or crack down on or clamp down on or shut down on [all informal], put or keep the lid on [slang]; bottle up, cork, cork up.

.9 **restrict, limit, narrow, confine,** tighten; circumscribe 234.4; keep in or within bounds, keep from spreading, localize,

hem, hem in, box, box in or up; **cramp,** stint; qualify 507.3.

.10 **bind, restrain, tie,** tie up, **strap,** lash, leash, pinion, fasten, secure, make fast; **hamper, trammel,** entrammel; rope; **chain,** enchain; **shackle, fetter, manacle,** gyve, **put in irons; handcuff, tie one's hands; tie hand and foot,** hog-tie [informal]; straitjacket; hobble, hopple; tether, picket, moor, anchor; tie down, pin down, peg down; get a stranglehold on, put a half nelson on [informal]; **bridle.**

.11 ADJS **restraining, constraining; inhibiting,** inhibitive; **suppressive, repressive,** stultifying.

.12 **restrictive,** limitative, restricting, **narrowing, limiting, confining,** cramping.

.13 **restrained, constrained, inhibited,** pent-up; guarded; controlled, curbed, bridled; **under restraint,** under control, in check, under discipline; slowed down, retarded, arrested, in remission; in or on leash, in leading strings.

.14 **suppressed, repressed; subdued,** quelled, put down, smashed, crushed; quashed, squashed or squelched [both informal]; smothered, stifled, suffocated.

.15 **restricted, limited, confined;** circumscribed 234.6, hemmed in, hedged in or about, boxed in; landlocked; weatherbound, windbound, icebound, snowbound; cramped, stinted; qualified 507.10.

.16 **bound, tied,** tied up, tied down, strapped, hampered, trammeled, shackled, handcuffed, fettered, manacled, tethered; **in bonds,** in irons or chains, ironbound.

## 761. CONFINEMENT

.1 NOUNS **confinement,** locking up, lockup, caging, penning, impoundment, **restraint,** restriction; check, constraint 760.1.

.2 **quarantine, isolation,** cordoning off, segregation, separation, seclusion; sanitary cordon, cordon sanitaire [Fr], cordon; quarantine flag, yellow flag, yellow jack.

.3 **imprisonment, jailing, incarceration, internment,** immurement, immuration; **detention, captivity,** duress, durance, durance vile; close arrest, house arrest; term of imprisonment.

.4 **commitment,** committal, consignment; recommitment, remand; mittimus [law].

.5 **custody,** custodianship, keep [archaic], **keeping, care, charge, ward,** guarding, hold, protective or preventive custody; protection, safekeeping 699.1.

.6 **arrest,** arrestment, arrestation, pinch or

bust [both slang]; **capture, apprehension, seizure,** netting [informal].

**.7 place of confinement;** limbo, hell, purgatory; pound, pinfold *or* penfold; **cage; enclosure,** pen, coop 236.3.

**.8 prison, prisonhouse, penitentiary,** pen [slang], keep, penal institution, bastille, state prison, federal prison; house of detention, detention home; **jail, gaol** [Brit], jailhouse, lockup, tollbooth [Scot], bridewell [Brit]; maximum-security prison, minimum-security prison; **guardhouse, stockade; brig; dungeon,** oubliette, black hole; **reformatory,** house of correction, reform school, training school, industrial school, borstal *or* borstal institution [both Brit]; debtor's prison, sponging house; **prison camp,** internment camp, detention camp, labor camp, forced-labor camp, **concentration camp;** prisoner-of-war camp *or* stockade, POW camp; **cell;** bullpen; solitary confinement, the hole [slang]; condemned cell, death cell, death house *or* death row; penal settlement *or* colony, Devil's Island.

**.9** [slang *or* informal terms] **jug, can, coop, cooler,** hoosegow, slammer, stir, clink, pokey, quod *or* chokey [both Brit].

**.10 jailer, gaoler** [Brit], **keeper, warder,** prison guard, **turnkey,** bull *or* screw [both slang]; **warden,** governor [Brit], commandant, principal keeper; custodian, guardian 699.6; **guard** 699.9.

**.11 prisoner, captive,** *détenu* [Fr], cageling; **convict,** con [slang]; **jailbird** [informal], gaolbird [Brit informal], stir bird [slang]; **internee; prisoner of war, POW;** political prisoner; lifer [informal]; trusty; parolee; ticket-of-leave man *or* ticket-of-leaver [both Brit]; ex-convict; chain gang.

**.12 VERBS confine, shut in,** coop in, hem in, fence in, wall in, rail in; **shut up, coop up, pen up,** box up, mew up, bottle up, cork up, seal up, **impound;** pen, coop, pound [archaic], crib, mew, cloister, immure, cage, encage; **enclose** 236.5; **hold, keep in,** hold *or* keep in custody, **detain,** keep in detention, constrain, **restrain,** hold in restraint; check, inhibit 760.7; restrict 760.9; shackle 760.10.

**.13 quarantine, isolate, segregate, separate,** seclude; **cordon, cordon off,** seal off, rope off.

**.14 imprison, incarcerate, intern, immure; jail, gaol** [Brit], **jug** [slang], throw into jail, throw under the jailhouse [dial]; throw *or* cast in prison, clap up, clap in jail *or* prison; **lock up,** lock in, bolt in,

put *or* keep under lock and key; hold captive, hold prisoner, hold in captivity; hold under close *or* house arrest.

**.15 arrest,** make an arrest, put under arrest, pick up, **take captive, take prisoner, apprehend, capture,** seize, net [informal], lay by the heels, **take into custody.**

**.16** [slang *or* informal terms] **bust, pinch,** make a pinch, nab, pull in, **run in,** collar.

**.17 commit,** consign, commit to prison, send to jail, send up *or* send up the river [both slang]; **commit to an institution,** institutionalize; recommit, remit, remand.

**.18 be imprisoned, do** *or* **serve time** [informal].

**.19 ADJS confined,** in confinement, **shut-in,** pent, **pent-up,** kept in, under restraint; "cabined, cribbed, confined" [Shakespeare]; impounded; **detained;** restricted 760.15; cloistered, enclosed 236.10.

**.20 quarantined,** isolated, segregated, separated; cordoned, cordoned *or* sealed *or* roped off.

**.21 jailed,** jugged [slang], **imprisoned, incarcerated, interned,** immured; **in prison,** in stir [slang], in captivity, **behind bars,** locked up, under lock and key, in durance vile.

**.22 under arrest, in custody,** in hold, in charge [Brit], under *or* in detention; under close arrest, under house arrest.

## 762. FREEDOM

**.1 NOUNS freedom, liberty;** license, loose [archaic]; run *or* the run of [both informal], "the right to live as we wish" [Epictetus], "the will to be responsible to ourselves" [Nietzsche], "political power divided into small fragments" [Thomas Hobbes], "the choice of working or starving" [Samuel Johnson]; the Four Freedoms [F. D. Roosevelt], freedom of speech and expression, freedom of worship, freedom from want, freedom from fear; constitutional freedom; academic freedom, *Lehrfreiheit, Lernfreiheit* [both Ger].

**.2 right, rights, civil rights,** civil liberties, constitutional rights, legal rights; Bill of Rights, Petition of Right, Declaration of Right, Declaration of the Rights of Man, Magna Charta *or* Magna Carta; **unalienable rights, human rights,** natural rights, "life, liberty, and the pursuit of happiness" [Thomas Jefferson].

**.3 unrestraint, unconstraint,** noncoercion, nonintimidation; **unreserve,** irrepressibility, uninhibitedness; immoderacy, intem-

perance, incontinence, uncontrol, unruliness, indiscipline; **abandon,** abandonment, **licentiousness,** wantonness, riotousness, wildness; permissiveness, unstrictness, laxness 758.

.4 **latitude, scope, room,** range, way, field,
maneuvering space *or* room; **margin,**
clearance, **space,** open space, elbowroom,
**leeway** [informal], sea room, wide berth;
**tolerance; free scope,** full *or* ample scope,
**free hand,** free play, free course; **carte
blanche,** blank check; no holds barred;
swing, play, full swing; rope, long rope *or*
tether, rope enough to hang oneself.

.5 **independence, self-determination, self-
government,** self-direction, **autonomy,**
home rule; autarky, autarchy, self-containment, self-sufficiency; **individualism,**
rugged individualism, **self-reliance,** self-
dependence; inner-direction; Declaration
of Independence.

.6 **free will,** free choice, **discretion,** option,
choice, say, say-so [informal], free decision; **full consent;** absolute *or* unconditioned *or* noncontingent free will.

.7 **own free will, own account, own accord,
own hook** *or* own say-so [both informal],
own discretion, own choice, **own initiative,** personal initiative, own responsibility, personal *or* individual responsibility,
own volition, own authority, own power;
own way, own sweet way [informal].

.8 **exemption,** exception, **immunity; release,**
discharge; **franchise, license,** charter,
patent, liberty; diplomatic immunity,
congressional *or* legislative immunity;
privilege 958.4; permission 777.

.9 **noninterference, nonintervention;** isolationism; laissez-faireism, let-alone principle *or* doctrine *or* policy; *laissez-faire,
laissez-aller* [both Fr]; liberalism, free enterprise, free competition, self-regulating
market; capitalism 745.8; free trade.

.10 **liberalism,** libertarianism, latitudinarianism; broad-mindedness, open-minded-
ness, toleration, tolerance; unbigotedness
526.1; libertinism, **freethinking,** free
thought; **liberation** 763.

.11 **freeman,** freewoman; citizen, free citizen,
burgess; franklin; freedman, freedwoman,
deditician.

.12 **independent, free lance; individualist,**
rugged individualist; free spirit; **liberal,**
libertarian, latitudinarian; libertine, freethinker; free trader; **nonpartisan,** neutral,
mugwump; isolationist; nonaligned nation; third world, third force.

.13 VERBS **liberalize,** ease; **free, liberate** 763.4.

.14 **exempt, free, release,** discharge, **let go** *or*
**let off** [both informal], **excuse,** spare, except, grant immunity, dispense from; give
dispensation from; dispense with, save
the necessity; remit, remise; absolve
1007.4.

.15 **give a free hand,** let one have his head,
**give one his head; give the run of** [infor-
mal], give the freedom of; give one leeway [informal], give full play; give one
scope *or* space *or* room; **give rein** *or* **free
rein to,** give the reins to, give bridle to,
give one line, give one rope; **give one
carte blanche, give one a blank check;** let
go one's own way, let one go at will.

.16 **not interfere, leave** *or* **let alone, let be,**
leave be [informal], leave *or* let well
enough alone, let sleeping dogs lie; **keep
hands off,** not tamper, not meddle, not
involve oneself, not get involved, butt
out *or* not butt in [both slang], let it take
its course, live and let live, leave to oneself; mind one's own business.

.17 **be free,** feel free, feel at liberty; **go at
large,** breathe the air of freedom; **have
free scope,** have a free hand, have the run
of [informal]; be at home, feel at home.

.18 **let oneself go,** let go, let loose *or* cut
loose [both informal], **give way to,** open
up, let it all hang out [informal]; go all
out, go flat out [Brit], pull out all the
stops; go unrestrained, run wild, have
one's fling, sow one's wild oats.

.19 (be independent *or* self-sufficient) **shift
for oneself, fend for oneself,** strike out
for oneself, look out for number one
[slang]; **go it alone, be one's own man,**
pull a lone oar, play a lone hand [infor-
mal], **paddle one's own canoe** [informal];
stand on one's own legs *or* own two feet,
stand on one's own [informal], suffice to
oneself, do for oneself, make one's own
way; ask no favors, ask no quarter; **be
one's own boss** [informal], ask leave of no
man; **go one's own way,** take one's own
course; do on one's own, do on one's
own initiative, do on one's own hook *or*
say-so [informal], do in one's own sweet
way [informal]; **have a will of one's own,**
have one's own way, do what one likes *or*
wishes *or* chooses, **do as one pleases,** go
as one pleases, please oneself [informal],
**suit oneself;** have a free mind, free-lance.

.20 ADJS **free,** eleuther(o)–; **at liberty, a**
**large,** on the loose, **loose,** unengaged, disengaged, detached, unattached, uncommitted, uninvolved, clear, in the clear,
go-as-you-please, easygoing, footloose

footloose and fancy-free, "afoot and lighthearted" [Whitman], free and easy; free as air, free as a bird, free as the wind; scot-free; **freeborn; freed, liberated, emancipated,** released.

**.21 independent,** self-dependent, self–; freespirited, freewheeling, **self-determined,** self-directing, one's own man; inner-directed, **individualistic;** self-governed, **self-governing, autonomous,** sovereign; self-reliant, self-sufficient, self-subsistent, selfsupporting, self-contained, autarkic, autarchic; nonpartisan, neutral, **nonaligned;** third-world, third-force.

**.22 free-acting,** free-going, free-moving, freeworking; freehand, freehanded; **free-spoken,** outspoken, **plain-spoken, open,** direct, candid, blunt 974.17.

**.23 unrestrained, unconstrained, unforced,** uncompelled, uncoerced; unmeasured, **uninhibited, unsuppressed, unrepressed, unreserved,** go-go; **uncurbed, unchecked, unbridled,** unmuzzled; **unreined,** reinless; **uncontrolled,** unmastered, unsubdued, ungoverned, **unruly;** out of control, out of hand, out of one's power; **abandoned,** intemperate, immoderate, **incontinent, licentious,** loose, wanton, rampant, riotous, wild; irrepressible; lax 758.4,5.

**.24 nonrestrictive,** unrestrictive; **permissive;** indulgent 759.8; lax 758.4,5; **liberal,** libertarian, latitudinarian; broad-minded, open-minded, tolerant; unbigoted 526.8; libertine; freethinking.

**.25 unhampered, untrammeled, unhandicapped, unimpeded,** unhindered, unprevented, unclogged, unobstructed; **clear,** unencumbered, unburdened, unladen, unembarrassed, disembarrassed.

**.26 unrestricted, unconfined, uncircumscribed,** unbound [archaic], unbounded, unmeasured; **unlimited,** limitless, illimitable; unqualified, unconditioned, **unconditional,** without strings, no strings; **absolute,** perfect, unequivocal, full, plenary, open, **wide-open** [informal].

**.27 unbound,** untied, **unfettered,** unshackled, unchained; **unmuzzled, ungagged;** uncensored.

**.28 unsubject,** ungoverned, unenslaved, **unenthralled;** unvanquished, unconquered, unsubdued, unquelled, untamed, unbroken.

**.29 exempt, immune;** exempted, **released, excused,** excepted, let off [informal], spared; **privileged, licensed,** favored, chartered; permitted; **unliable,** unsubject, ir-

responsible, unaccountable, unanswerable.

**.30 quit, clear, free, rid;** free of, clear of, quit of, rid of, **shut of** [informal], shed of [dial].

**.31 ADVS freely, free; without restraint,** without stint, **unreservedly,** with abandon; outright.

**.32 independently, alone, by oneself,** all by one's lonesome [informal], under one's own power, **on one's own** *or* **on one's own hook** [both informal], on one's own initiative; **on one's own account** *or* **responsibility,** on one's own say-so [informal]; **of one's own free will, of one's own accord,** of one's own volition, at one's own discretion.

## 763. LIBERATION

**.1 NOUNS liberation, freeing,** setting free, setting at liberty; **deliverance, delivery;** rescue 702; **emancipation,** disenthrallment, manumission; enfranchisement, affranchisement; Emancipation Proclamation; women's liberation 958.6; gay liberation.

**.2 release,** unhanding, **loosing, unloosing;** unbinding, untying, unbuckling, unshackling, unfettering, unlashing, unstrapping, untrussing *or* unpinioning [both archaic], unmanacling, unleashing, unchaining, untethering, unhobbling, unharnessing, unyoking, unbridling; unmuzzling, ungagging; unlocking, unlatching, unbolting, unbarring; unpenning, uncaging; **discharge, dismissal;** parole; demobilization, separation from the service.

**.3 extrication,** freeing, releasing, clearing; **disengagement,** disentanglement, untangling, unsnarling, unraveling, disentwining, disinvolvement, unknotting, disembarrassment, disembroilment; dislodgment, breaking out *or* loose.

**.4 VERBS liberate, free, deliver, set free,** set at liberty, set at large; **emancipate,** manumit, disenthrall; enfranchise, affranchise; rescue 702.3.

**.5 release, unhand,** let go, let loose, **turn loose,** cast loose, let out, let off, let go free; **discharge, dismiss;** let out on bail, grant bail to, go bail for [informal]; parole, put on parole; demobilize, separate from the service.

**.6 loose, loosen, unloose, unloosen; unbind, untie,** unstrap, unbuckle, unlash, untruss *or* unpinion [both archaic]; **unfetter, unshackle,** unmanacle, unchain, unhandcuff, untie one's hands; **unleash,** untether, unhobble; unharness, unyoke, unbridle; unmuzzle, ungag; unlock, unlatch, unbolt, unbar; unpen, uncage.

.7 extricate, free, release, clear, get out; disengage, disentangle, untangle, unsnarl, unravel, disentwine, disinvolve, unknot, disembarrass, disembroil; dislodge, break out or loose, cut loose, tear loose.

.8 free oneself from, deliver oneself from, get free of, get quit of, get rid of, get clear of, get out of, get well out of; throw off, shake off; escape 632.6.

.9 go free, go scot free, go at liberty, get off, get off scot-free, get out of.

.10 ADJS liberated, freed, emancipated, released; delivered, rescued, ransomed, redeemed; extricated, unbound, untied, unshackled, etc.; free 762.20; on parole.

## 764. SUBJECTION

.1 NOUNS subjection, subjugation; domination 741.2; restraint, control 760.1; bondage, captivity; thrall, thralldom, enthrallment; slavery, enslavement; servitude, compulsory or involuntary servitude, servility, bond service, indentureship; serfdom, serfhood, villenage, vassalage; helotry, helotism; debt slavery, peonage; feudalism, feudality; absolutism, tyranny 741.9,10; deprivation of freedom, disenfranchisement, disfranchisement.

.2 subservience or subserviency, subjecthood, subordinacy, subordination, juniority, inferiority; lower status, subordinate role, satellite status; service, servitorship 750.12.

.3 dependence or dependency, tutelage, chargeship, wardship; clientship, clientage.

.4 subdual, quelling, crushing, trampling or treading down, reduction, humbling, humiliation; breaking, taming, domestication, gentling; conquering 727.1; suppression 760.2.

.5 subordinate, junior, secondary, inferior; underling, understrapper, low man on the totem pole [informal]; assistant, helper 787.6; right-hand man 787.7; servant, employee 750.

.6 dependent, charge, ward, client, protégé, encumbrance; pensioner, pensionary; public charge, ward of the state.

.7 subject, vassal, liege, liege man, liege subject, homager; captive; slave, servant, chattel, chattel slave, bondsman, bondman, bondslave, theow, thrall; indentured servant; bondwoman, bondswoman, bondmaid; odalisque, concubine; galley slave; serf, helot, villein; churl; debt slave, peon.

.8 VERBS subjugate, subject, subordinate; dominate 741.15; disfranchise, disenfranchise, divest or deprive of freedom; enslave, enthrall, make a chattel of; take captive, lead captive or into captivity; hold in subjection, hold in bondage, hold captive, hold in captivity; hold down, keep down, keep under; keep under one's thumb, have tied to one's apron strings, hold in leash, hold in leading strings, hold in swaddling clothes, hold or keep at one's beck and call; vassalize, make dependent or tributary; peonize.

.9 subdue, master, overmaster, quell, crush, reduce, beat down, break, break down, overwhelm; tread underfoot, trample underfoot, roll in the dust, trample in the dust, drag at one's chariot wheel; suppress 760.8; conquer 727.10; tyrannize 741.16; unman 158.12; bring low, bring to terms, humble, humiliate, bend, bring one to his knees, bend to one's will.

.10 have subject, twist or turn or wind around one's little finger, make lie down and roll over, have eating out of one's hand, lead by the nose, make a puppet of, make putty of, make a sport or plaything of; use as a doormat, treat like dirt under one's feet.

.11 domesticate, tame, break, bust [slang]; gentle [informal], break in, break to harness; housebreak.

.12 depend on, be at the mercy of, be the sport or plaything or puppet of, be putty in the hands of; not dare to say one's soul is one's own.

.13 ADJS subject, dependent, tributary, client; subservient, subordinate, inferior; servile; liege, vassal, feudal, feudatory.

.14 subjugated, subjected, enslaved, enthralled, captive, bond, unfree; disenfranchised, disfranchised, oppressed, suppressed 760.14; in subjection, in bondage, in captivity, in slavery, in bonds, in chains; under the lash, under the heel; in one's power, in one's control, in one's hands or clutches, in one's pocket, under one's thumb, at one's mercy, under one's command or orders, at one's beck and call, at one's feet.

.15 subdued, quelled, crushed, broken, reduced, humbled, humiliated, brought to one's knees, brought low, made to grovel; tamed, domesticated, broken to harness, housebroken or housebroke.

.16 downtrodden, downtrod [archaic], kept

down or under, ground down, overborne, trampled, **oppressed; abused,** misused; **henpecked, browbeaten,** led by the nose, in leading strings, tied to one's apron strings, ordered around [informal], regimented, tyrannized; slavish, servile, submissive 765.12–16; unmanned 158.19; treated like dirt under one's feet.

.17 PREPS **under, below, beneath,** underneath, subordinate to; at the feet of; under the heel of; at the beck and call of.

## .765. SUBMISSION

.1 NOUNS **submission,** submittal, **yielding; compliance,** complaisance, **acquiescence, acceptance;** going along with [informal], assent 521; consent 775; **obedience** 766; subjection 764; **resignation,** resignedness; **deference,** homage, kneeling, obeisance; **passivity,** passiveness, supineness, nonresistance, nonopposition, nonopposal, nondissent.

.2 **surrender, capitulation;** renunciation, giving over, abandonment, relinquishment, **cession;** giving up or in, backdown [informal]; retreat, recession, recedence.

.3 **submissiveness,** docility, tractability, biddability, yieldingness, compliableness [archaic], pliancy, pliability, flexibility, malleability, moldability, ductility, plasticity, facility; agreeableness, agreeability; subservience, **servility** 907.

.4 **manageability, governability, controllability,** manipulability, manipulatability, corrigibility, untroublesomeness; **tameness,** housebrokenness; tamableness, domesticability.

.5 **meekness, gentleness, tameness, mildness,** peaceableness, quietness, lamblikeness, dovelikeness; humility 906.

.6 VERBS **submit, comply, take, accept,** go along with [informal], **acquiesce,** be agreeable, accede, **assent** 521.8; **consent** 775.2; **relent, succumb,** resign, resign oneself, not resist; take one's medicine, swallow the pill, face the music; **knuckle down or under,** knock under [archaic], take it, swallow it; take it lying down; put up with it, grin and bear it, make the best of it, **live with it;** obey 766.2.

.7 **yield, give way, give ground, back down, give up, give in,** cave in [informal], withdraw from or quit the field, break off combat, cease resistance, have no fight left.

.8 **surrender, capitulate,** acknowledge defeat, **cry quits,** cry pax [Brit], **say uncle** [informal], beg a truce, pray for quarter,

implore mercy, **throw in the towel, throw in the sponge** [both informal], show or wave the white flag, lower or haul down or strike one's flag or colors, throw down or lay down or deliver up one's arms, hand over one's sword, yield the palm, pull in one's horns [informal], come to terms; renounce, abandon, relinquish, **cede,** give over.

.9 **submit to, yield to, defer to,** bow to, give way to, knuckle under to, succumb to.

.10 **bow down,** bow, bend, stoop, crouch, **bow one's head,** bend the neck, bow submission; genuflect, curtsy; **bow to,** bend to, knuckle to [informal], bend or bow to one's will, bend to one's yoke; kneel to, **bend the knee to, fall on one's knees before,** crouch before, **fall at one's feet,** throw oneself at the feet of, prostrate oneself before, **truckle to,** cringe to; kowtow, bow and scrape, grovel, do obeisance or homage.

.11 **eat dirt, eat crow, eat humble pie,** lick the dust, kiss the rod.

.12 ADJS **submissive, compliant,** compliable [archaic], complaisant, complying, **acquiescent,** consenting 775.4; **assenting,** accepting, agreeable; subservient, abject, **obedient** 766.3; servile; **resigned,** uncomplaining; unassertive; **passive,** supine, **unresisting,** nonresisting, unresistant, nonresistant, nonresistive, nonopposing, nondissenting.

.13 **docile, tractable,** biddable, **yielding,** pliant, pliable, flexible, malleable, moldable, ductile, plastic, facile [archaic], like putty in one's hands.

.14 **manageable, governable, controllable,** manipulable, manipulatable, handleable, corrigible, restrainable, untroublesome; domitable, tamable, domesticable.

.15 **meek, gentle, mild,** peaceable, pacific, quiet; **subdued, chastened, tame,** tamed, broken, housebroken, domesticated; lamblike, gentle as a lamb, dovelike; humble 906.9.

.16 **deferential, obeisant; subservient, obsequious,** servile 907.12,13; crouching, prostrate, prone, on one's belly, on one's knees, on one's marrowbones [informal], on bended knee.

.17 ADVS **submissively, compliantly,** complaisantly, acquiescently, agreeably; **obediently** 766.6; **resignedly,** uncomplainingly, with resignation; **passively,** supinely, unresistingly, unresistantly, nonresistively.

.18 **docilely, tractably,** biddably, **yieldingly,**

pliantly, pliably, malleably, flexibly, plastically, facilely [archaic].

.19 meekly, gently, tamely, mildly, peaceably, pacifically, quietly, like a lamb.

## 766. OBEDIENCE

.1 NOUNS obedience *or* obediency, compliance; acquiescence, submission, submissiveness 765.1–5; servility 907; willingness, dutifulness, duteousness; **service**, servitium, homage, fealty, **allegiance**, loyalty, faith, suit and service *or* suit service, observance [archaic]; conformity 82; lawabidingness.

.2 VERBS **obey, mind, heed, keep, observe,** listen *or* hearken to; **comply, conform** 82.3; stay in line *or* not get out of line *or* not get off base [all informal], toe the line *or* mark, obey the rules, follow the book, **do what one is told;** do as one says, do the will of, defer to, do one's bidding, come at one's call, lie down and roll over for [slang]; take orders, attend to orders, do suit and service, follow the lead of; submit 765.6–11.

.3 ADJS **obedient, compliant,** complying; **acquiescent, submissive** 765.12–15; willing, dutiful, duteous; loyal, faithful, devoted; conforming; law-abiding.

.4 at one's command, at one's pleasure, at one's disposal, at one's nod, at one's call, **at one's beck and call.**

.5 henpecked, **tied to one's apron strings,** on a string, on a leash, in leading strings.

.6 ADVS **obediently, compliantly; acquiescently, submissively** 765.17; willingly, **dutifully,** duteously; loyally, faithfully, devotedly; in obedience to, in compliance *or* conformity with.

.7 at your service *or* command *or* orders, as you please, as you will, as thou wilt [archaic].

## 767. DISOBEDIENCE

.1 NOUNS disobedience, nonobedience, **noncompliance; undutifulness,** unduteousness; willful disobedience; **insubordination,** indiscipline; **unsubmissiveness, intractability,** indocility 626.4, recusancy; nonconformity 83; lawlessness, waywardness, frowardness, naughtiness; violation, transgression, infraction, infringement, lawbreaking; civil disobedience, passive resistance; uncooperativeness, noncooperation.

.2 refractoriness, recalcitrance *or* recalcitrancy, recalcitration, contumacy, **contumaciousness,** obstreperousness, defiance,

defiance of authority, **unruliness,** restiveness, fractiousness, orneriness [informal]; wildness, breachiness [dial]; **obstinacy, stubbornness** 626.1.

.3 rebelliousness, mutinousness; riotousness; insurrectionism, insurgentism; factiousness, **sedition,** seditiousness; treasonableness, traitorousness, subversiveness; extremism 745.4.

.4 revolt, rebellion, revolution, mutiny, insurrection, insurgence *or* insurgency, *émeute* [Fr], **uprising,** rising, outbreak, general uprising, *levée en masse* [Fr], riot, civil disorder; peasant revolt, *jacquerie* [Fr]; putsch, *coup d'état* [Fr].

.5 rebel, revolter; **insurgent,** insurrectionary, insurrecto, **insurrectionist;** malcontent, *frondeur* [Fr]; **mutineer,** rioter, brawler; maverick [informal], insubordinate, nonconformist 83.3; agitator 648.11; extremist 745.12; revolutionary, revolutionist 147.3; traitor, subversive 619.10,11.

.6 VERBS **disobey,** not mind, not heed, not keep *or* observe, not listen *or* hearken, pay no attention to, **ignore, disregard, defy,** set at defiance, fly in the face of, snap one's fingers at, scoff at, flout, go counter to, set at naught, set naught by, care naught for; be a law unto oneself, refuse to cooperate; not conform 83.4; **violate,** transgress 769.4; break the law 999.5.

.7 revolt, rebel, kick over the traces, reluct, reluctate; **rise up,** rise, arise, rise up in arms, mount the barricades; **mutiny,** mutineer [archaic]; insurge, insurrect, **riot,** run riot; revolutionize, revolution, revolute, subvert, overthrow 147.4; strike 789.8.

.8 ADJS **disobedient, transgressive,** uncom plying, violative, lawless, wayward, fro ward, naughty; recusant, nonconforming 83.5; **undutiful,** unduteous; **self-willed** willful, obstinate 626.8; **undisciplined, il** disciplined, indisciplined.

.9 insubordinate, unsubmissive, indocile **uncompliant, uncooperative,** noncoope ative, noncooperating, **intractable** 626.12.

.10 refractory, recalcitrant, contumaciou obstreperous, defiant, unruly, restive, in patient of control *or* discipline, fractiou ornery [informal]; wild, breachy [dial].

.11 rebellious, rebel, breakaway; **mutinou** mutineering; **insurgent, insurrectiona** riotous, turbulent; factious, **seditious, s** ditionary; revolutionary, revolution: traitorous, treasonable, subversive; e treme, extremistic 745.20.

.12 ADVS **disobediently,** uncompliant against *or* contrary to order and dis pline; **insubordinately, unsubmissively,** indocilely, **uncooperatively;** unresignedly; disregardfully, floutingly, **defiantly;** intractably 626.17; obstreperously, contumaciously, restively, fractiously; **rebelliously,** mutinously; riotously.

## 768. OBSERVANCE

.1 NOUNS **observance,** observation; **keeping,** adherence, heeding; compliance, conformance, conformity, accordance; **performance, practice,** execution, discharge, carrying out *or* through; acquittal, acquittance [both archaic], fulfillment, satisfaction; respect, heed, care 533.1.
.2 VERBS **observe, keep, heed, follow;** regard, **respect,** attend to, **comply with,** conform to; hold by, **abide by,** adhere to; **live up to,** act up to, **be faithful to,** keep faith with, do justice to, do the right thing by; **fulfill, fill, meet, satisfy; make good,** keep *or* make good one's word *or* promise, be as good as one's word, redeem one's pledge, stand to one's engagement.
.3 **perform, practice,** do, execute, discharge, carry out *or* through, carry into execution, do one's office, fulfill one's role, discharge one's function.
.4 ADJS **observant,** regardful, mindful; **faithful,** devout, devoted, true, loyal, constant; dutiful, duteous; as good as one's word; practicing, active; compliant, conforming; punctual, punctilious, scrupulous, meticulous, conscientious 533.12.

## 769. NONOBSERVANCE

.1 NOUNS **nonobservance,** inobservance, unobservance, nonadherence; nonconformity, disconformity, **nonconformance, noncompliance;** inattention, **disregard** 531.1; laxity 758.1; **nonfulfillment, nonperformance,** nonfeasance, failure, dereliction, delinquency, omission, default, slight, oversight; **negligence; neglect** 534.
.2 **violation, infraction, breach,** breaking; **infringement, transgression, trespass,** contravention; offense 999.4; breach of promise, breach of contract, breach of trust *or* faith, bad faith, breach of privilege; breach of the peace.
.3 VERBS **disregard,** pay no regard to 531.3; **neglect** 534.6.
.4 **violate, break; infringe, transgress, trespass,** contravene, trample on *or* upon, trample underfoot, do violence to, make a mockery of; **defy,** set at defiance, flout, set at naught, set naught by; take the law

into one's own hands; break one's promise, break one's word, etc.
.5 ADJS **nonobservant,** inobservant, unobservant, nonadherent; **nonconforming,** unconforming, noncompliant, uncompliant; inattentive, **disregardful** 531.6; **negligent** 534.10; unfaithful, untrue, unloyal, inconstant.

## 770. PROMISE

.1 NOUNS **promise, pledge,** troth, plight, faith, parole, **word, word of honor,** solemn declaration *or* word; **oath, vow** 523.3; avouch, avouchment; **assurance, guarantee,** warranty.
.2 **engagement, undertaking, commitment, agreement,** obligation, recognizance; **understanding,** gentlemen's agreement; verbal agreement, informal agreement, pactum [law]; contract 771.1,3; preengagement.
.3 **betrothal,** betrothment, espousal, **engagement,** handfasting *or* affiance [both archaic]; troth, marriage contract *or* vow, plighted troth *or* faith *or* love; banns, banns of matrimony.
.4 VERBS **promise,** give *or* make a promise, hold out an expectation; **pledge,** plight, troth, vow; **give one's word,** pledge *or* pass one's word, give one's parole, **give one's word of honor,** plight one's troth *or* faith, pledge *or* plight one's honor; **swear** 523.5; vouch, avouch, **warrant, guarantee, assure;** underwrite, countersign.
.5 **engage, undertake, commit,** obligate, bind, **agree to,** answer for, be answerable for, take on oneself, be responsible for, be security for, go bail for, accept obligation *or* responsibility, bind oneself to; have an understanding; enter into a gentlemen's agreement; take the vows *or* marriage vows; shake hands on; contract 771.6.
.6 **affiance, betroth,** troth, **plight, engage,** contract, contract an engagement, pledge *or* promise in marriage; **plight one's troth, become engaged;** publish the banns.
.7 ADJS **promissory,** votive; under *or* upon oath, on one's word, on one's word of honor, on the Book, under hand and seal.
.8 **promised, pledged, bound, committed,** compromised, **obligated; sworn,** warranted, **guaranteed,** assured, underwritten; contracted 771.12; **engaged, plighted, affianced, betrothed,** intended.

## 771. COMPACT

.1 NOUNS **compact, pact, contract,** legal contract, valid contract, **covenant,** convention, transaction, paction [Scot], accord, **agreement,** mutual agreement, formal agreement, legal agreement, stipulation, **understanding,** arrangement, **bargain,** dicker *or* **deal** [both informal]; union contract, wage contract, employment contract, collective agreement; cartel, consortium; protocol; bond, binding agreement, ironclad agreement, covenant of salt; gentleman's agreement *or* gentlemen's agreement; promise 770.

.2 **treaty,** international agreement, *entente, entente cordiale* [both Fr], concord, concordat, cartel, convention, paction, capitulation; **alliance, league;** nonaggression pact, mutual-defense treaty; NATO, North Atlantic Treaty Organization; SEATO, Southeast Asia Treaty Organization.

.3 (contracts) indenture, indent; **deed,** deed poll, title deed, contract by deed; deed of arrangement, arrangement; specialty contract, specialty, formal contract, special contract; parol contract, simple contract; quasi contract, contract quasi, implied contract; deed *or* covenant of indemnity, recognizance; contract of record; insurance policy, policy, group policy; bond, promissory note, debenture, debenture bond; mortgage deed, deed of trust.

.4 arrangement, settlement; signing, signature, sealing, closing, conclusion; adjustment, accommodation; solemnization.

.5 execution, completion; transaction; **carrying out, discharge, fulfillment,** prosecution, effectuation; enforcement; observance 768.

.6 VERBS **contract, compact, covenant, bargain, agree, engage,** undertake, make a deal [informal], do a deal [Brit informal], stipulate, agree to, bargain for; **promise** 770.4.

.7 **treat with, negotiate, bargain,** make terms, sit down with, sit down at the bargaining table.

.8 **sign, shake hands,** seal, formalize, make legal and binding; agree on terms, come to an agreement 521.10; strike a bargain 827.18.

.9 **arrange, settle; adjust,** accommodate, **compose,** fix, make up, straighten out, work out; **conclude, close, close with,** settle with.

.10 **execute, complete, transact,** promulgate, **make;** make out, fill out; **discharge, fulfill,** render, administer; **carry out,** carry through, put through, prosecute; effect, effectuate, implement; enforce, put in force; **abide by, honor,** adhere to, observe 768.2.

.11 ADJS contractual, covenantal, conventional.

.12 **contracted,** compacted, **covenanted, agreed, bargained for,** stipulated; engaged, undertaken; **promised** 770.8; arranged, settled; under hand and seal, **signed,** sealed; signed, sealed, and delivered.

.13 ADVS **as agreed upon, as promised,** as contracted for, according to the contract *or* bargain *or* agreement.

## 772. SECURITY

*(thing given as a pledge)*

.1 NOUNS **security, surety,** indemnity, **guaranty, guarantee, warranty, warrant,** insurance, **assurance; bond,** tie; stocks and bonds 834.1–4.

.2 **pledge, gage,** *pignus, vadium* [both L]; undertaking; **earnest,** earnest money, god's penny, handsel; escrow; token payment; pawn, hock [slang]; **bail,** bond, vadimonium, replevin, replevy, recognizance; mainprise; **hostage, surety.**

.3 **deposit, stake,** forfeit; caution money, caution; **collateral,** collateral security *o* warranty; margin.

.4 **mortgage,** mortgage deed, deed of trus' lien, security agreement; vadium mortu um *or* mortuum vadium; dead pledge vadium vivum, living pledge, antichresi hypothec, hypothecation, bottomry, bo tomry bond; adjustment mortgage, bla ket mortgage, chattel mortgage, close mortgage, participating mortgage, insta' ment mortgage, leasehold mortgage, tru mortgage; first mortgage, second mo' gage, third mortgage.

.5 **lien,** general lien, particular lien; pign legale, common-law lien, statutory lie judgment lien, pignus judiciale, tax lie mechanic's lien; mortgage bond.

.6 **guarantor, warrantor,** guaranty, guar tee; **mortgagor; insurer,** underwrit sponsor, surety; godparent, godfath godmother; bondsman, bailsman, ma pernor.

.7 **warrantee,** mortgagee; insuree, poli holder; godchild, godson, goddaughter

.8 guarantorship, **sponsorship,** sponsion.

.9 VERBS secure, guarantee, guaranty, warrant, assure, insure, ensure, bond, certify; countersecure; sponsor, be sponsor for, sign for, sign one's note, back, stand behind, stand up for; endorse; sign, underwrite, undersign, subscribe to; confirm, attest 505.12.

.10 pledge, impignorate, handsel [Brit], deposit, stake, post, put up, put up as collateral; pawn, put in pawn, spout or put up the spout [both archaic], hock or put in hock [both informal]; mortgage, hypothecate, bottomry, bond; go bail.

.11 ADJS secured, covered, guaranteed, warranted, certified, insured, ensured, assured; certain, sure 513.13.

.12 pledged, staked, posted, deposited, put up, put up as collateral; on deposit, at stake; as earnest; pawned, in pawn, in hock [informal], up the spout [archaic].

.13 in trust, held in trust, held in pledge, fiduciary; in escrow.

### 773. OFFER

.1 NOUNS offer, offering, proffer, presentation, bid, submission; advance, overture, approach, invitation; hesitant or tentative or preliminary approach, feeler [informal]; asking price.

.2 proposal, proposition, suggestion, instance; motion, resolution; sexual advance or approach or invitation or overture, indecent proposal, pass [slang], improper suggestion; request 774.

.3 ultimatum, last word, final offer, firm price.

.4 VERBS offer, proffer, present, tender, put up, submit, extend, prefer [archaic], hold out, hold forth, place in one's way, lay at one's feet, put or place at one's disposal.

.5 propose, submit, prefer; suggest, recommend, advance, proposition [informal], commend to attention, propound, pose, put forward, bring forward, put or set forth, put it to, put or set or lay or bring before; bring up, broach, moot, introduce, open up, launch, start; move, make a motion, offer a resolution; postulate 499.12.

.6 bid, bid for, make a bid.

.7 make advances, approach, overture, make an overture; make a pass or throw a pass [both slang], proposition [informal], solicit, importune.

.8 urge upon, press upon, ply upon, push upon, force upon, thrust upon; press, ply; insist 753.7.

.9 volunteer, come or step forward, offer or proffer or present oneself, be at one's service, not wait to be asked, not wait for an invitation, need no prodding.

### 774. REQUEST

.1 NOUNS request, asking; the touch [slang]; desire, wish, expressed desire; petition, petitioning, impetration, address; application; requisition, indent [Brit]; demand 753.

.2 entreaty, appeal, plea, bid, suit, call, cry, clamor, cri du cœur [Fr]; supplication, prayer, rogation, beseechment, imploring, imploration, obsecration, obtestation, adjuration, imprecation; invocation, invocatory plea or prayer.

.3 importunity, importunateness, urgency, pressure, urging, pressing, plying; buttonholing; dunning; teasing, pestering, plaguing, nagging; coaxing, wheedling, cajolery, cajolement, blandishment.

.4 invitation, invite or bid [both informal], engraved invitation, bidding, biddance, call, calling, summons.

.5 solicitation, canvass; suit, addresses; courting, wooing.

.6 beggary, mendicancy, mendicity; begging, cadging, scrounging; mooching or bumming or panhandling [all slang].

.7 petitioner, supplicant, suppliant, suitor; solicitor 830.7; applicant, solicitant, claimant; aspirant, seeker; candidate, postulant; bidder.

.8 beggar, mendicant, scrounger, cadger; bum or bummer or moocher or panhandler [all informal]; schnorrer [Yid]; hobo, tramp 274.3; loafer 708.8; mendicant friar; mendicant order.

.9 VERBS request, ask, make a request, beg leave, make bold to ask; desire, wish, express a wish for, crave; ask for, order, put in an order for, bespeak, call for, trouble one for; whistle for [informal]; requisition, make a requisition, indent [Brit]; make application, apply for, file for, put in for; demand 753.4.

.10 petition, present or prefer a petition, sign a petition, circulate a petition; pray, sue; apply to, call on or upon; memorialize.

.11 entreat, implore, beseech, beg, crave, plead, appeal, pray, supplicate, impetrate, obtest; adjure, conjure; invoke, imprecate [archaic], call on or upon, cry on or upon, appeal to, cry to, run to; go cap in hand to; kneel to, go down on one's knees to, fall on one's knees to, go on bended knee to, throw oneself at the feet of, get or come down on one's marrowbones [informal]; plead for, clamor for, cry for; call for help.

.12 importune, urge, press, pressure [informal], apply or exert pressure, push, ply; dun; beset, buttonhole, besiege; work on [informal], tease, pester, plague, nag, nag at, bug [slang]; coax, wheedle, cajole, blandish.

.13 invite, ask, call, summon, call in, bid come, extend or issue an invitation, request the presence of, request the pleasure of one's company.

.14 solicit, canvass; court, woo, address, sue, sue for, pop the question [informal]; seek, bid for, look for; fish for, angle for.

.15 beg, scrounge, cadge; mooch or bum or panhandle [all informal]; hit or hit up or touch or put the touch on or make a touch [all slang]; pass the hat [informal].

.16 ADJS supplicatory, suppliant, supplicant, supplicating, prayerful, precative; petitionary; begging, mendicant, cadging, scrounging, mooching [slang]; on one's knees or bended knees, on one's marrowbones [informal]; with joined or folded hands.

.17 imploring, entreating, beseeching, begging, pleading, appealing, precatory, precative, adjuratory.

.18 importunate; teasing, pestering, plaguing, nagging, dunning; coaxing, wheedling, cajoling; insistent, demanding, urgent 753.8.

.19 invitational, inviting, invitatory.

.20 INTERJS please, prithee [archaic], pray, do, pray do; be so good as to, be good enough, have the goodness; will you, may it please you; if you please, s'il vous plaît [Fr]; I beg you, je vous en prie [Fr]; for God's or goodness or heaven's or mercy's sake.

## 775. CONSENT

.1 NOUNS consent, assent, agreement, accord [archaic], acceptance, approval, blessing, approbation, sanction, endorsement, ratification; affirmation, affirmative, affirmative voice or vote, aye, okay or OK [both informal]; permission 777; willingness, readiness, promptness, promptitude, eagerness, unreluctance, unloathness, ungrudgingness, tacit or unspoken or silent or implicit consent, connivance; acquiescence, compliance; submission 765.

.2 VERBS consent, assent, give consent, yield assent, accede to, accord to or grant [both archaic], say yes, say aye, vote affirmatively, vote aye, nod, nod assent; ac-

cept, agree to, go along with [informal]; be in accord with, be in favor of, take kindly to, approve of, hold with; approve, give one's blessing to, okay or OK [both informal]; sanction, endorse, ratify; consent to silently or by implication, wink at, connive at; be willing, turn a willing ear; deign, condescend 906.7; have no objection, not refuse; permit 777.9.

.3 acquiesce, comply, comply with, fall in with, be persuaded, come round or around, come over, come to [dial]; submit 765.6–11.

.4 ADJS consenting, assenting, affirmative, approving, agreeing, favorable, accordant, consentient; sanctioning, endorsing, ratifying; acquiescent, compliant, compliable [archaic]; submissive 765.12–16; willing, agreeable, content; ready, prompt, eager, unreluctant, unloath, nothing loath, ungrudging, unrefusing; permissive 777.14.

.5 ADVS consentingly, assentingly, affirmatively, approvingly, favorably, agreeably, accordantly; acquiescently, compliantly; willingly 622.8; yes 521.18.

## 776. REFUSAL

.1 NOUNS refusal, rejection, turndown or turning down [both informal]; thumbsdown [informal]; nonconsent, nonacceptance; declining, declination, declension, declinature; denial, disclamation, disclaimer, disallowance; repudiation 638.1; disagreement, dissent 522; recantation 628.3; contradiction 524.2; negation, abnegation, negative, negative answer, nay, no, nix [slang]; unwillingness 623; disobedience 767; noncompliance, nonobservance 769; withholding, holding back, retention, deprivation.

.2 repulse, rebuff, peremptory or flat or point-blank refusal, summary negative; slap in the face [informal], kick in the teeth [slang]; short shrift.

.3 VERBS refuse, decline, not consent, refuse consent, reject, turn down [informal], decline to accept, not buy [slang]; not think of, not hear of [both informal]; say no, say nay, vote nay, vote in the negative, disagree, dissent 522.4; vote negatively, shake one's head, negative, negate; turn thumbs down on [informal]; be unwilling 623.3; turn one's back upon, turn a deaf ear to, set oneself against, set one's face against, be unmoved, harden one's heart, resist entreaty or persuasion; stand aloof, have nothing to do with, wash one's hands of; hold out against; put or se one's foot down [informal], refuse point-blank or summarily; decline politely or with thanks, beg off; **repudiate**, disallow, disclaim 638.2.

.4 **deny, withhold**, hold back; grudge, be-grudge; close the hand or purse; deprive one of.

.5 **repulse, rebuff, repel**, slap one in the face [informal], kick one in the teeth [slang], give one short shrift, shut or slam the door in one's face, turn one away, send to the right-about [informal]; deny one-self to, refuse to receive, not be at home to, cut, **snub** 966.5–7.

.6 ADJS **unconsenting**, nonconsenting, **negative; unwilling** 623.5; **uncompliant**, un-complying, uncomplaisant, inacquiescent, uncooperative; disobedient 769.8–11; re-jective, declinatory; deaf to, not willing to hear of.

.7 PHRS I refuse, I won't, I will not, I will no such thing; over my dead body, far be it from me, not if I can help it, not likely, not on your life, count me out, in-clude me out, I'm not taking any, I won't buy it, it's no go, like hell I will, I'll be hanged if I will, try and make me, you have another guess coming, you should live so long, I'll see you in hell first, noth-ing doing [all informal]; out of the ques-tion, not to be thought of, impossible; **no**, by no means.

## 777. PERMISSION

.1 NOUNS **permission, leave, allowance**, vouchsafement; **consent** 775; permission to enter, admission, ticket, ticket of ad-mission; **license**, liberty 762.1; **okay or OK or the go-ahead or the green light** [all in-formal]; special permission, charter, patent, dispensation, release, waiver.

.2 **sufferance, tolerance**, toleration, **indul-gence**; winking, overlooking, connivance; permissiveness.

.3 **authorization, authority, sanction**, coun-tenance, **warrant**, warranty, fiat; em-powerment, enabling, entitlement, en-franchisement, certification; clearance, security clearance; ratification 521.4.

.4 **carte blanche**, blank check [informal], **full authority**, full power, free hand, open mandate.

.5 **grant, concession**; charter, franchise, lib-erty, diploma, patent, letters patent, bre-vet; royal grant.

.6 **permit, license, warrant**; building permit, learner's permit; driver's license, marriage license, hunting license, fishing license, etc.; nihil obstat, imprimatur.

.7 **pass, passport, safe-conduct**, safeguard, protection; visa; clearance, clearance pa-pers; bill of health, clean bill of health, pratique, full pratique.

.8 **permissibility**, permissibleness, **allowable-ness; admissibility**, admissibleness; justifi-ableness, warrantableness, sanctionable-ness; **validity**, legitimacy, lawfulness, licit-ness, legality.

.9 VERBS **permit, allow, admit, let**, leave [dial], give permission, give leave, make possible; consent 775.2; **grant**, accord, vouchsafe; **okay or OK or give the go-ahead or give the green light** [all infor-mal], say the word or give the word [both informal]; dispense, release.

.10 **suffer, countenance**, have, **tolerate**, brook, condone, endure, stomach, bear, bear with, put up with, stand for, hear of [informal]; indulge 759.6; shut one's eyes to, wink at, blink at, overlook, connive at; leave the door or way open.

.11 **authorize, sanction, warrant**; give official sanction or warrant, legitimize, validate, legalize; empower, give power, enable, entitle; **license, privilege**; charter, patent, enfranchise, franchise; certificate, certify; ratify 521.12.

.12 **give carte blanche**, issue or accord or give a blank check [informal], give full power or authority, give an open mandate, give a free hand, leave alone, leave it to one; permit all or anything, open the flood-gates, remove all restrictions.

.13 **may**, can, have permission, **be permitted or allowed**.

.14 ADJS **permissive**, admissive, permitting, al-lowing; consenting 775.4; **unprohibitive**, nonprohibitive; tolerating, **suffering, tol-erant; indulgent**, lenient 759.7; lax 758.4,5.

.15 **permissible, allowable, admissible**; justifi-able, warrantable, sanctionable; licit, law-ful, legitimate, legal, legitimized, legal-ized.

.16 **permitted, allowed**, admitted; tolerated, on sufferance; unprohibited, unforbid-den.

.17 **authorized**, empowered, entitled; **war-ranted, sanctioned; licensed, privileged**; chartered, patented; franchised, enfran-chised.

.18 ADVS **permissively**, admissively; **toler-antly, indulgently**.

.19 **permissibly, allowably**, admissibly; with permission, by one's leave; licitly, law-fully, legitimately, legally.

.20 PHRS **by your leave,** with your permission, if you please, may I?

## 778. PROHIBITION

.1 NOUNS **prohibition, forbidding,** forbiddance; **ruling out, disallowance,** denial, rejection 633; refusal 776; **repression, suppression** 760.2; **ban, embargo, injunction,** prohibitory injunction, **proscription,** inhibition, **interdict,** *interdictum* [L], interdiction; index, index expurgatorius, index librorum prohibitorum; **taboo;** thou-shalt-not *or* don't *or* no-no [all informal]; law, statute 998.3; preclusion, exclusion, **prevention** 730.2; forbidden fruit, contraband; Eighteenth Amendment, Volstead Act, Prohibition Party; sumptuary laws *or* ordinances; zoning, zoning laws, restrictive covenants.

.2 **veto,** negative [archaic]; absolute veto, qualified *or* limited negative *or* veto, suspensive *or* suspensory veto, item veto, pocket veto.

.3 VERBS **prohibit, forbid; disallow, rule out;** deny, reject 638.2; say no to, **refuse** 776.3; **bar, debar, preclude, exclude,** exclude from, shut out, shut the door to, **prevent** 730.14; **ban, put under the ban, outlaw; repress, suppress** 760.8; **enjoin, put under an injunction,** issue an injunction against, issue a prohibitory injunction; **proscribe,** inhibit, **interdict, put** *or* **lay under an interdict** *or* **interdiction; put on the Index;** embargo, lay *or* **put an embargo on; taboo.**

.4 **not permit** *or* **allow, not have, not suffer** *or* **tolerate,** not endure, not stomach, not bear, not bear with, not countenance, not brook, brook no, not condone, not accept, not put up with, not go along with [informal]; not stand for *or* not hear of [both informal], put *or* set one's foot down on [informal].

.5 **veto, put one's veto upon,** decide *or* rule against, **negative,** kill.

.6 ADJS **prohibitive, prohibitory, prohibiting, forbidding;** inhibitive, inhibitory, **repressive, suppressive** 760.11,12; proscriptive, interdictive, interdictory; **preclusive, exclusive, preventive** 730.19.

.7 **prohibited, forbidden,** forbade, forbid, *verboten* [Ger], **barred; vetoed; unpermissible,** nonpermissible, not permitted *or* allowed, **unallowed;** disallowed, ruled out; off limits, out of bounds; unauthorized, **unsanctioned,** unlicensed; banned, under the ban, **outlawed,** contraband; taboo, tabooed, untouchable; **illegal,** unlawful, illicit.

## 779. REPEAL

.1 NOUNS **repeal, revocation,** revoke, revokement, renege, **rescinding,** rescindment, rescission, **abrogation,** cassation, reversal; suspension; waiving, **waiver, setting aside; countermand,** counterorder; **annulment,** nullification, withdrawal, **invalidation,** voiding, voidance, vacation, vacatur, defeasance; **cancellation,** canceling, cancel, write-off; **abolition,** abolishment; **recall,** retraction, recantation 628.3.

.2 VERBS **repeal, revoke, rescind,** reverse, **abrogate,** renege, renig [informal]; suspend; **waive, set aside; countermand,** counterorder; **abolish,** do away with; **cancel,** write off; **annul,** nullify, disannul, withdraw, **invalidate,** void, vacate, make void, declare null and void; **overrule,** override; **recall,** retract, recant 628.9.

.3 ADJS **repealed, revoked, rescinded,** etc.; **invalid,** void, **null and void.**

## 780. COMMISSION

.1 NOUNS **commission,** commissioning, **delegation,** devolution, devolvement, **deputation;** commitment, entrusting, entrustment, **assignment,** consignment; **errand, task, office; care,** cure, **responsibility,** purview, jurisdiction; **mission,** legation, embassy; **authority,** authorization, power to act, **full power,** plenipotentiary power, empowerment, vicarious *or* delegated authority; **warrant,** license, **mandate, charge, trust,** brevet, exequatur; **agency,** agentship, factorship; regency, regentship; lieutenancy; trusteeship, executorship; **proxy,** procuration, power of attorney.

.2 **appointment, assignment,** designation, **nomination,** naming, selection, tabbing [informal]; **ordainment,** ordination; posting, transferral.

.3 **installation,** installment, **instatement,** induction, placement, **inauguration,** investiture, taking office; **accession,** accedence, coronation, enthronement.

.4 **engagement, employment, hiring, appointment,** taking on [informal]; retainment, briefing [Brit]; preengagement, bespeaking; reservation, booking.

.5 **rental,** rent; **lease,** let [Brit]; hire, hiring, sublease, subrent; **charter,** bareboat charter; lend-lease.

.6 **enlistment, enrollment;** conscription, **draft, drafting, induction,** impressment, press; call, draft call, call-up, summons call to the colors, letter from Uncle Sam [informal]; **recruitment,** recruiting; **muster,** levy; mobilization; selective service, compulsory military service.

.7 indenture, binding over; **apprenticeship.**

.8 **assignee, appointee,** selectee, nominee, candidate; licensee, licentiate; deputy, agent 781.

.9 VERBS **commission, authorize,** empower, accredit; **delegate,** devolute, devolve, devolve upon, depute, **deputize; assign,** consign, **commit, charge, entrust,** give in charge; license, charter, warrant; detail, detach, post, transfer, send out, mission, send on a mission.

.10 **appoint, assign,** designate, **nominate,** name, select, tab [informal]; **ordain,** ordinate [archaic].

.11 **install,** instate, induct, **inaugurate,** invest, put in, place, **place in office;** chair; crown, throne, enthrone, anoint.

.12 **be instated, take office,** accede; take or mount the throne; attain to.

.13 **employ, hire,** give a job to, take into employment, take into one's service, take on [informal], recruit, **engage,** sign up or on [informal]; retain, brief [Brit]; bespeak, preengage; sign up for [informal], **reserve,** book.

.14 **rent, lease,** let [Brit], hire, job, **charter; sublease, sublet,** underlet.

.15 **rent out, rent; lease,** lease out; let or let off or let out [all Brit]; **hire out,** hire; charter; **sublease, sublet,** underlet; lend-lease, lease-lend; lease-back; farm, farm out; job.

.16 **enlist,** list [archaic], **enroll, sign up** or on [informal]; **conscript, draft, induct,** press, impress, commandeer; detach, detach for service; summon, call up, call to the colors; **mobilize,** call to active duty; **recruit, muster,** levy, raise, muster in; join 788.14.

.17 indenture, article, bind, bind over; **apprentice.**

.18 ADJS **commissioned, authorized, accredited;** delegated, deputized, appointed.

19 **employed, hired, hireling, paid,** mercenary; rented, leased, let [Brit]; sublet, subleased; chartered.

20 **indentured,** articled, bound over; **apprenticed, apprentice,** prentice or 'prentice.

21 ADVS **for hire, for rent,** to let, to lease.

## 781. DEPUTY, AGENT

.1 NOUNS **deputy, proxy, representative, substitute, vice,** vicegerent, **alternate,** backup or backup man [both informal], alter ego, **surrogate,** procurator, secondary, stand-in, understudy, pinch hitter [informal], utility man; second in command, executive officer; exponent, advocate, pleader, paranymph, attorney, champion; lieutenant, vicar, vicar general; locum tenens, locum [informal]; amicus curiae; co–; dummy, figurehead 749.4.

.2 **delegate,** legate; **commissioner,** commissary, *commissionaire* [Fr], commissar; **messenger,** herald, **emissary, envoy; minister,** secretary.

.3 **agent, instrument,** implement, **tool; steward** 748.4; **functionary; official** 749.16; clerk, **secretary;** amanuensis; factor, consignee; general agent, special agent; actor's agent, baggage agent, business agent or walking delegate, claim agent, commercial agent, commission agent, customer agent, federal agent, Federal [informal], fed [slang], freight agent, insurance agent, land agent, law agent, literary agent, loan agent, news agent, passenger agent, press agent, parliamentary agent, purchasing agent, real estate agent, sales agent, station agent, theatrical agent, ticket agent, travel agent; puppet, cat's-paw 658.3; dupe 620.

.4 **go-between, middleman, intermediary, medium,** intermedium, intermediate, interagent, **internuncio,** broker; connection [slang], **contact; negotiator,** negotiant; interpleader; arbitrator, mediator 805.3.

.5 **spokesman,** spokeswoman, official spokesman, speaker, **voice,** mouthpiece [informal]; herald; prolocutor, prolocutress or prolocutrix; reporter, rapporteur.

.6 **diplomat,** diplomatist, diplomatic agent, diplomatic [archaic]; **emissary, envoy, legate, minister,** foreign service officer; **ambassador,** ambassadress, ambassador-at-large; envoy extraordinary, plenipotentiary, **minister plenipotentiary;** nuncio, internuncio, apostolic delegate; vice-legate; resident, minister resident; *chargé d'affaires* [Fr], chargé; secretary of legation, chancellor [Brit]; **attaché,** commercial attaché, military attaché; **consul,** consul general, vice-consul, consular agent; career diplomat.

.7 **foreign office, foreign service,** diplomatic service; diplomatic mission, diplomatic staff or corps, *corps diplomatique* [Fr]; **embassy, legation;** consular service.

.8 vice-president, vice-chairman, vice-governor, vice-director, vice-master, vice-chancellor, vice-premier, vice-warden, vice-consul, vice-legate; vice-regent, viceroy, vicegerent, vice-king, vice-queen, vice-reine.

.9 **secret agent**, operative, cloak-and-dagger operative, **undercover man**, inside man [slang]; **spy**, espionage agent; counterspy, double agent; spotter; scout, reconnoiterer; **intelligence agent** or **officer**; CIA man, military-intelligence man, naval-intelligence man; spy-catcher [informal], counterintelligence agent.

.10 **detective**, operative, investigator, sleuth, Sherlock Holmes [A. Conan Doyle]; police detective, Bow Street runner or officer [England], **plainclothesman**; private detective, private investigator, inquiry agent [Brit]; hotel detective, house detective, house dick [slang], store detective; arson investigator; narcotics agent, narc [slang]; FBI agent, G-man [informal], treasury agent, T-man [informal], revenuer [slang], Federal [informal], fed [slang]; Federal Bureau of Investigation, FBI; Secret Service.

.11 [slang or informal terms] **dick**, gumshoe, gumshoe man, hawkshaw, sleuthhound, beagle, flatfoot, tec; eye, private eye; skip tracer, spotter.

.12 **secret service**, intelligence service, intelligence bureau or department; intelligence, military intelligence, naval intelligence; **counterintelligence**.

.13 (group of delegates) delegation, deputation, commission, mission; committee, subcommittee.

.14 VERBS **represent**, **act for**, act on behalf of, substitute for, appear for, answer for, speak for, hold the proxy of, hold a brief for, act in the place of, stand in for, stand in the stead of, serve in one's stead, pinch-hit for [informal]; understudy, back up [informal]; front for [slang]; deputize, commission 780.9.

.15 ADJS **deputy**, deputative; **acting**, representative; vice–.

.16 **diplomatic**, ambassadorial, consular, ministerial, plenipotentiary.

.17 ADVS by proxy, indirectly; in behalf of 149.12.

## 782. PROMOTION

.1 NOUNS **promotion**, preferment, **advancement**, **advance**, upping [informal], rise, elevation, upgrading, step up, step up the ladder; **raise**, pay raise, **boost** [informal]; exaltation, aggrandizement; **ennoblement**, knighting; graduation, passing.

.2 VERBS **promote**, **advance**, prefer [archaic], up [informal], elevate, upgrade; kick upstairs [informal]; **raise**, raise one's pay, up one's pay or boost one's pay [both informal]; exalt, aggrandize; **ennoble**, knight; pass, graduate.

## 783. DEMOTION, DEPOSAL

.1 NOUNS **demotion**, **degrading**, degradation, disgrading, downgrading, **debasement**, abasement, humbling, casting down, **reduction**, bump or bust [both slang]; stripping of rank, depluming, displuming.

.2 **deposal**, **deposition**, **removal**, displacement, deprivation, **ousting**, unseating; **cashiering**, **firing** [informal], **dismissal** 310.5; forced resignation; kicking upstairs [informal]; **superannuation**, pensioning off, **retirement**; **suspension**; impeachment; purge, **liquidation**; **overthrow**, overthrowal; **dethronement**, disenthronement, discrownment; **disbarment**, disbarring; unfrocking, defrocking, unchurching; deconsecration, expulsion, excommunication 310.1,4.

.3 VERBS **demote**, **degrade**, disgrade, downgrade, debase, abase, humble, **lower**, **reduce**, bump or bust [both slang]; strip of rank, cut off one's spurs, deplume, displume.

.4 **depose**, **remove from office**, give the gate [slang], divest or deprive or strip of office, **remove**, displace, **oust**; **suspend**; **cashier**, drum out, strip of rank, **break**, bust [slang]; **dismiss** 310.19; **purge**, **liquidate**; **overthrow**; **retire**, superannuate, pension, pension off, put out to pasture [informal]; kick upstairs [informal]; **unseat**, unsaddle; **dethrone**, disenthrone, unthrone, uncrown, discrown; **disbar**; **unfrock**, defrock, unchurch; strike off the roll, read out of; **expel**, excommunicate 310.13,17; deconsecrate.

## 784. RESIGNATION

*(retirement from office)*

.1 NOUNS **resignation**, demission, **withdrawal**, **retirement**, retiral [Brit], superannuation, emeritus status; **abdication**; voluntary resignation; forced resignation, deposal 783; relinquishment 633.3.

.2 VERBS **resign**, demit, **quit**, leave, **vacate**, withdraw from; **retire**, superannuate, be superannuated, be pensioned or pensioned off, be put out to pasture [informal]; relinquish, give up 633.7; retire from office, stand down, stand or step aside, give up one's post, hang up one's spurs

[informal]; **tender** *or* **hand in one's resignation,** send in one's papers, turn in
one's badge *or* uniform; **abdicate,** renounce the throne, give up the crown;
pension off 783.4.

.3 ADJS **retired,** in retirement, superannuated, on pension, pensioned, pensioned
off, emeritus, emerita [fem].

## 785. AID

.1 NOUNS **aid, help, assistance, support,** succor, relief, comfort, ease, remedy; **service,
benefit** 665.4; ministry, ministration, office, offices, good offices; yeoman's service; therapy 689; protection 699; rescue
702.

.2 **assist, helping hand, hand, lift; boost** *or*
**leg** *or* **leg up** [all informal]; help in time
of need.

.3 **support, maintenance, sustainment,** sustentation, **sustenance, subsistence,** provision; **keep, upkeep; livelihood, living,**
meat, bread, daily bread; **nurture, nourishment;** mothering, care, tender loving
care, TLC [informal]; manna, manna in
the wilderness; economic support, price
support, subsidy, subsidization, subvention, endowment.

.4 **patronage, fosterage, tutelage, sponsorship, auspices,** aegis, care, guidance,
**championship;** seconding; interest, advocacy, encouragement, **backing, abetment;**
countenance, **favor, goodwill,** charity,
**sympathy.**

.5 **furtherance, helping along, advancement,**
advance, **promotion, forwarding,** facilitation, speeding, easing *or* smoothing of
the way, clearing of the track, greasing of
the wheels, expedition, expediting, rushing; special *or* preferential treatment.

.6 **self-help,** self-helpfulness, **self-support,**
self-sustainment, self-improvement; independence 762.5.

.7 helper, assistant 787.6; benefactor 942.

.8 **reinforcements, support, relief,** auxiliaries, reserves, reserve forces.

.9 **facility, accommodation, appliance, convenience,** amenity, appurtenance; advantage.

10 **helpfulness,** aidfulness [archaic]; serviceability, utility, **usefulness** 665.3; **advantageousness,** profitability, favorableness,
beneficialness 674.1.

11 VERBS **aid, help, assist,** comfort, abet [ar-
chaic], **succor, relieve, ease,** doctor, remedy; be of some help; do good, do a
world of good, **benefit, avail** 674.10; **favor,
befriend; give help,** render assistance,

proffer aid, come to the aid of, rush *or*
fly to the assistance of, lend one aid, **give**
*or* **lend** *or* **bear a hand** *or* **helping hand,**
stretch forth *or* hold out a helping hand;
take by the hand, take in tow; **give an assist, give a leg up** [informal], give a lift *or*
give a boost [both informal], help a lame
dog over a stile; **save,** redeem, bail out
[informal], **rescue** 702.3; protect 699.18–20;
set up, put on one's feet; give new life to,
resuscitate, rally, reclaim, revive, **restore**
694.11–21; be the making of; see one
through.

.12 **support, lend support,** give *or* furnish *or*
afford support; **maintain, sustain, keep,**
upkeep [Brit]; **uphold,** hold up, bear, upbear, **bear up,** bear out; reinforce, undergird, bolster, **bolster up,** buttress, shore,
shore up, prop, prop up, crutch; **finance,**
fund, subsidize, subvention, subvention-
ize; pick up the tab *or* check [informal].

.13 **back, back up, stand behind, stand back
of,** get behind, get in behind, get in back
of; **stand by,** stick by *or* **stick up for**
[both informal], **champion; second, take
the part of,** take up *or* adopt *or* espouse
the cause of, **go to bat for** [informal],
take up the cudgels for, run interference
for [informal]; **side with,** take sides with,
associate oneself with, join oneself to,
align oneself with, come down *or* range
oneself on the side of.

.14 **abet, aid and abet, encourage,** hearten,
embolden, comfort [archaic]; **advocate,**
hold a brief for [informal], countenance,
keep in countenance, **endorse, lend oneself to,** lend one's countenance to, lend
one's favor *or* support to, lend one's offices, put one's weight in the scale,
plump for *or* thump the tub for [both in-
formal], lend one's name to, give one's
support *or* countenance to, give moral
support to, hold one's hand, make one's
cause one's own; subscribe [Brit], **favor,
go for** [informal], smile upon, shine
upon.

.15 **patronize, sponsor, take up.**

.16 **foster, nurture, nourish,** mother, care for,
lavish care on, feed, sustain, cultivate,
**cherish;** pamper, coddle, cosset, fondle
[archaic]; **nurse,** suckle, cradle; dry-nurse,
wet-nurse; spoon-feed.

.17 **further, forward, advance, promote,** encourage, **boost** [informal], favor, advantage, **facilitate,** set *or* put *or* push forward, give an impulse to; speed, expedite,
quicken, hasten, lend wings to; conduce
to, make for, contribute to.

.18 **serve,** render service to, do service for, **work for, labor in behalf of; minister to,** pander to, cater to; attend 750.13.

.19 **oblige, accommodate, favor,** do a favor, do a service.

.20 ADJS **helping,** assisting, serving; **assistant, auxiliary,** adjuvant, subservient, subsidiary, ancillary, accessory; ministerial, ministering, ministrant; fostering, nurtural, nutricial; instrumental 658.6.

.21 **helpful,** aidful [archaic]; **profitable, salutary,** good for, **beneficial** 674.12; remedial, therapeutic; **serviceable, useful** 665.18–22; contributory, conducive, constructive, positive, furthersome [archaic]; at one's service, at one's command, at one's beck and call.

.22 **favorable, propitious;** kind, kindly, kindly-disposed, **well-disposed,** well-affected, well-intentioned, well-meant, **well-meaning;** benevolent, beneficent, benign, benignant; friendly, amicable, neighborly; cooperative.

.23 self-helpful, self-helping, self-improving; **self-supporting, self-sustaining;** self-supported, self-sustained; independent 762.21.

.24 ADVS **helpfully,** helpingly; **beneficially,** favorably, profitably, advantageously, to advantage, to the good; serviceably, **usefully** 665.25.

.25 PREPS helped by, with the help or assistance of, by the aid of; **by means of** 658.7.

.26 **for, on** or **in behalf of,** in aid of, in the name of, on account of, **for the sake of,** in the service of, in furtherance of, in favor of; remedial of.

.27 **behind, back of** [informal], supporting, **in support of.**

# 786. COOPERATION

.1 NOUNS **cooperation, collaboration, coaction,** concurrence, synergy, synergism; community, harmony, concordance, concord, fellowship, fellow feeling, solidarity, concert, **teamwork;** pulling together, joining of forces, pooling, pooling of resources; bipartisanship, mutualism, mutuality, mutual assistance, coadjuvancy; reciprocity; joint effort, common effort, combined or joint operation, common enterprise or endeavor, collective or united action, mass action; coagency; coadministration, cochairmanship, codirectorship, duet, duumvirate; trio, triumvirate, troika; quartet, quintet, sextet, septet, octet; symbiosis, commensalism; **cooperativeness, collaborativeness, team**

spirit, morale, esprit, *esprit de corps* [Fr]; communism, communalism, communitarianism, collectivism; ecumenism, ecumenicism, ecumenicalism; **collusion,** complicity 654.6.

.2 **affiliation, alliance, alignment, association,** combination, **union, unification, coalition,** fusion, merger, coalescence, coadunation, amalgamation, **league, federation, confederation,** confederacy, consolidation, incorporation, inclusion, integration; hookup or tie-up or tie-in [all informal]; **partnership,** copartnership, copartnery, cahoots [slang]; colleagueship, collegialism, collegiality; **fraternity,** confraternity, fraternization, fraternalism; sorority; **fellowship,** sodality, comradeship, freemasonry.

.3 VERBS **cooperate, collaborate,** do business with or **play ball** [both slang], coact, concur; concert, harmonize, concord; **join, band, league, associate, affiliate,** ally, **combine, unite,** fuse, merge, coalesce, amalgamate, federate, confederate, consolidate; hook up or tie up or tie in [all informal]; partner, be in league, go **into partnership with,** go partners [informal], go or be in cahoots with; **join together,** club together, league together, band together, etc.; **work together,** get together or team up [both informal], work as a team, act together, act in concert, **pull together; hold together, hang together,** keep together, **stand together,** stand shoulder to shoulder; lay or put or get heads together; make common cause, throw in together [slang], unite efforts, join in; reciprocate; **conspire, collude** 654.10.

.4 **side with,** take sides with, **unite with; join, join with;** join up with or get together with or team up with [all informal], strike in with [archaic]; **throw in with** or string along with or swing in with [all informal], **go along with; line up with** [informal], align with, align oneself with, range with, range oneself with, stand in with [slang]; **join hands with,** be hand in glove with, go hand in hand with; act with, take part with, **go in with;** cast in one's lot with, join one's fortunes with, stand shoulder to shoulder with, be cheek by jowl with, sink or swim with, stand or fall with; make common cause with, pool one's interests with; enlist under the banner of, rally round, flock to.

.5 ADJS **cooperative, cooperating, cooperan-**

collaborative, coactive, coacting, coefficient, synergetic, synergic(al), synergistic(al); **fellow, co–;** concurrent, concurring, concerted; harmonious, harmonized, concordant, **common, communal,** collective; **mutual,** reciprocal; **joint, combined** 52.5; coadjuvant, coadjutant; symbiotic, commensal; uncompetitive, noncompetitive, communalist, communalistic, communist, communistic, communitarian, collectivist, collectivistic, ecumenic(al); **conniving, collusive** 654.14.

.6 ADVS cooperatively, cooperatingly, coactively, coefficiently, concurrently, **jointly,** combinedly, **conjointly,** concertedly, in concert with; harmoniously, concordantly; communally, collectively, **together;** as one, with one voice, unanimously, in chorus, in unison, as one man; **side by side, hand in hand, hand in glove, shoulder to shoulder, back to back,** "all for one, one for all" [Dumas père].

.7 in cooperation, in collaboration, in partnership, in cahoots [slang], in collusion, in league.

.8 PREPS with, in cooperation with, etc.

### 787. ASSOCIATE

.1 NOUNS associate, confederate, consociate, colleague, fellow member, companion, fellow, bedfellow, crony, consort, cohort, compeer, compatriot, confrere, brother, brother-in-arms, ally, adjunct, coadjutor; comrade 928.3; –ster; co–.

.2 partner, pardner or pard [both dial], mate, teammate, comate, copemate or copesmate [both archaic], copartner, side partner, buddy [informal], sidekick or sidekicker [both slang]; playmate, messmate, tentmate, roommate, classmate, pewmate, waymate, cupmate, shopmate, shipmate, jailmate, schoolmate, tablemate, cradlemate, bedmate, housemate, lovemate, shelfmate, couchmate, birthmate, watchmate, clubmate; nominal or holding-out or ostensible or quasi partner, general partner, special partner, silent partner, secret partner, dormant or sleeping partner.

.3 accomplice, cohort, confederate, fellow conspirator, coconspirator, partner or accomplice in crime; particeps criminis, socius criminis [both L]; accessory, accessory before the fact, accessory after the fact; abettor.

.4 collaborator, cooperator; coauthor; collaborationist.

.5 co-worker, workfellow, fellow worker,

buddy [informal], butty [Brit informal]; **teammate, yokefellow,** yokemate; benchfellow, shopmate.

.6 assistant, helper, auxiliary, aider, aid, aide, paraprofessional; help, helpmate, helpmeet; deputy, agent 781; attendant, second, acolyte, acolythist [archaic]; best man, paranymph; servant 750; adjutant, aide-de-camp; lieutenant, executive officer; coadjutant, coadjutor; coadjutress, coadjutrix; supporting actor or player, supporting instrumentalist, sideman.

.7 right-hand man, right hand, strong right hand, man Friday, fidus Achates, second self, alter ego, confidant.

.8 man, henchman, gillie; hanger-on, satellite, follower, disciple, adherent, votary; creature, lackey, flunky, stooge [slang], jackal, minion, myrmidon; sycophant 907.3; goon [slang], thug 943.3–4; puppet, cat's-paw 658.3; dummy, figurehead 749.4.

.9 supporter, upholder, maintainer, sustainer; support, mainstay, standby [informal], stalwart, reliance, dependence; abettor, seconder, second; endorser, sponsor; backer, promoter, angel [slang], patron, Maecenas; friend at or in court; champion, defender, apologist, advocate, –arian, –ist, –ite, paranymph, exponent, protagonist; well-wisher, favorer, encourager, sympathizer; partisan, sider [archaic], sectary, votary; fan or buff [both informal], aficionado, admirer, lover.

### 788. ASSOCIATION

.1 NOUNS association, society, body; alliance, coalition, league, union; council; bloc, axis; partnership; federation, confederation, confederacy; grouping, assemblage 74; combination, combine; Bund, Verein [both Ger]; gang or ring or mob [all informal]; machine, political machine; economic community, common market, free trade area, customs union; credit union; cooperative, cooperative society, consumer cooperative, Rochdale cooperative; college, group, corps, band 74.3.

.2 community, society, commonwealth; body; kinship group, clan, moiety, totem, phyle, phratry or phratria, gens, caste, subcaste, endogamous group; family, extended family, nuclear family; order, class, social class, economic class; colony, settlement; commune, ashram; socio–.

.3 fellowship, sodality; society, guild, order; brotherhood, fraternity, confraternity, confrerie, fraternal order; **sisterhood, sorority; club,** country club; secret society.

**.4 party, interest, camp, side;** interest group, pressure group, ethnic group; minority group, vocal minority; silent majority; **faction,** division, **sect, wing, caucus,** splinter, splinter group, breakaway group, offshoot; **political party** 744.24.

**.5 school, sect,** class, order; **denomination, communion,** confession, faith, church; **persuasion, ism; disciples, followers,** adherents.

**.6 clique, coterie, set, circle, ring, junto,** junta, cabal, camarilla, **clan, group; crew** or mob or **crowd** or **bunch** or outfit [all informal]; cell; cadre, inner circle; closed or charmed circle; ingroup, we-group; elite, elite group.

**.7 team, squad, string;** eleven, nine, eight, five; **crew,** rowing crew; varsity, first team, first string; reserves, second team, second string, third string; platoon; complement; **cast,** company.

**.8 organization, establishment, foundation, institution, institute.**

**.9 company, firm, concern, house,** *compagnie* [Fr], *compañía* [Sp]; **business,** industry, **enterprise,** business establishment, commercial enterprise; **partnership,** copartnership; joint-stock association, joint-stock company, *Aktiengesellschaft* [Ger], *aktiebolag* [Swed]; **corporation,** corporate body, body corporate, conglomerate corporation, conglomerate, diversified corporation; holding company, consolidating company; **trust, syndicate, cartel,** combine, pool, consortium, plunderbund [slang]; combination in restraint of trade; stock company 833.15; operating company; utility, public utility; chamber of commerce, junior chamber of commerce; trade association.

**.10 branch, organ, division,** wing, arm, offshoot, **affiliate; chapter,** lodge, post; **local;** branch office.

**.11 member, affiliate,** belonger, insider, initiate, one of us, cardholder, card-carrier, card-carrying member; **enrollee,** enlistee; **associate,** socius, **fellow; brother, sister;** comrade; honorary member; life member; member in good standing, dues-paying member; charter member; clubman, clubwoman, clubber [informal]; fraternity man, Greek [slang], sorority woman, sorority girl; guildsman; committeeman; conventionist, conventioner, conventioneer; joiner [informal]; pledge.

**.12 membership,** members, associates, affiliates, body of affiliates, constituency.

**.13 partisanism,** partisanship, **partiality; factionalism, sectionalism,** faction; sectarianism, denominationalism; **cliquism,** cliquishness, cliqueyness; **clannishness,** clanship; exclusiveness; ethnocentricity; party spirit, *esprit de corps* [Fr]; the old college spirit.

**.14** VERBS **join,** join up [informal], **enter, go into,** come into, get into, make oneself part of, swell the ranks of; **enlist, enroll, affiliate, sign up** or on [informal], take up membership, take out membership; inscribe oneself, put oneself down; associate oneself with, affiliate with, league with, team or team up with; sneak in, creep in, insinuate oneself into; **combine, associate** 52.3,4.

**.15 belong,** hold membership, be a member, be on the rolls, be inscribed, subscribe, hold or carry a card.

**.16** ADJS **associated, corporate,** incorporated; **combined** 52.5.

**.17 associational, social, society, communal;** organizational; coalitional; sociable 922.18.

**.18 cliquish, cliquey, clannish;** ethnocentric.

**.19 partisan, party; partial,** interested; **factional, sectional,** sectarian, sectary, denominational.

**.20** ADVS **in association, conjointly** 786.6,7.

## 789. LABOR UNION

**.1** NOUNS **labor union,** trade union, trade guild [Brit]; organized labor; collective bargaining; craft union, horizontal union; industrial union, vertical union; **local,** union local, local union; company union.

**.2 union shop,** preferential shop, **closed shop;** open shop; nonunion shop; **labor contract, union contract;** maintenance of membership.

**.3 labor unionist, trade unionist, union member,** unionist, cardholder; shop steward, bargainer, negotiator; business agent; union officer; union or labor organizer, organizer.

**.4 striker;** sitdown striker; holdout [informal].

**.5** (strike enforcer) **picket; goon** [slang], strong-arm man; flying squadron or squad, goon squad [slang].

**.6 strikebreaker, scab** or **rat** or **fink** or scis sorbill [all slang], **blackleg** [Brit].

**.7 strike, walkout** or tie-up [both informal] turnout [Brit informal], job action; slow down, rulebook slowdown, sick-in or sick out [both informal]; work stoppage, sit-down strike, sit-down, wildcat strike, outlaw strike; sympathy strike; **boycott**, boycottage; buyer's or consumer's strike; **lockout**; revolt 767.4.

**.8** VERBS **organize, unionize.**

**.9 strike, go on strike, go out, walk out;** shut it down; slow down; sit down; **boycott**; picket; hold out [informal]; **lock out**; revolt 767.7.

**.10 break a strike; scab** or **rat** or **fink** [all slang], **blackleg** [Brit].

## 790. OPPOSITION

**.1** NOUNS **opposition**, opposing, opposure, crossing, traversal, oppugnation, bucking [informal], standing against; contraposition 15.1; **resistance** 792; **contention** 796; negation 524; **rejection** 638; **counteraction**, counterworking 178.1; refusal 776; **contradiction**, challenge, contravention, contraversion, rebutment, rebuttal, denial, impugnation, impugnment; crosscurrent, undercurrent, head wind.

**.2 hostility, antagonism, repugnance,** oppugnancy, **antipathy,** enmity, bad blood, inimicalness; contrariness, contrariety, perverseness, **obstinacy** 626; fractiousness, refractoriness, recalcitrance 767.2; uncooperativeness, noncooperation, negativeness; **friction, conflict,** clashing, **collision,** cross-purposes, dissension, disaccord 795; rivalry, vying, competition 796.2.

**.3** VERBS **oppose, counter, cross, traverse, go** or **act in opposition to, go against,** run against, **run counter to,** fly in the face of, fly in the teeth of; **protest** 522.5; set oneself against, set one's face against, be or play at cross-purposes; **take issue with, take one's stand against,** declare oneself against, stand and be counted against, vote against; make a stand against, make a dead set against; join the opposition; not put up with, not abide, not be content with; counteract, counterwork, countervail 178.6; **resist,** withstand 792.3.

**.4 contend against,** militate against, **contest, combat, battle,** reluct, reluctate, **fight against, strive against,** struggle against, labor against, **take on** [informal], grapple with, join battle with, close with, antagonize [archaic], **fight, buck** [informal], buffet, beat against, beat up against, breast, stem, breast or stem the tide or current or flood, breast the wave, buffet the waves; rival, compete with or against, vie with or against; offer resistance 792.3.

**.5 confront, affront, front, meet, face;** en-counter 796.16.

**.6 contradict,** cross, traverse, contravene, controvert, rebut, deny, **gainsay;** challenge, contest; oppugn, call into question; **belie,** be contrary to, come in conflict with, negate 524.3,4; **reject** 638.2.

**.7 be against,** be agin [dial]; discountenance 969.10,11; not hold with, not have anything to do with; have a crow to pluck or pick, have a bone to pick.

**.8** ADJS **oppositional, opponent, opposing, opposed; anti** [informal], enantio–; **adverse, adversary,** adversative, oppugnant, antithetic(al), repugnant, con [informal], **contrary, counter; negative; opposite,** oppositive; overthwart [archaic], cross; **contradictory;** unfavorable, unpropitious 544.17; **hostile, antagonistic,** unfriendly, enemy, inimical, alien, antipathetic(al); fractious, refractory, recalcitrant 767.10; uncooperative, noncooperative; perverse, obstinate 626.8–11; **conflicting, clashing,** dissentient, disaccordant 795.15; rival, competitive 796.26.

**.9** ADVS **in opposition, in confrontation,** eyeball-to-eyeball [slang], **at variance, at cross-purposes, at odds,** at issue, at war with, up in arms, with crossed bayonets, at daggers drawn, at daggers, in hostile array, poised against one another; contra, contrariwise, counter, cross, athwart; against the tide or wind or grain.

**.10** PREPS **opposed to, adverse to,** counter to, **in opposition to,** in conflict with, at cross-purposes with; **against,** agin [dial], dead against, athwart; **versus, vs.; con,** contra, face to face with, *vis-à-vis* [Fr].

## 791. OPPONENT

**.1** NOUNS **opponent, adversary, antagonist, assailant, foe,** foeman, **enemy;** adverse or opposing party, opposite camp, **the opposition,** the loyal opposition; **combatant** 800.

**.2 competitor, contestant,** contender, vier, player, entrant; **rival,** corrival, emulator; the field.

**.3 oppositionist,** opposer; obstructionist, obstructive, negativist, naysayer; **objector, protester,** dissident, dissentient; **resister;** noncooperator; **disputant,** litigant, plaintiff, defendant; quarreler, irritable man, scrapper [slang], wrangler, brawler; die-hard, bitter-ender, last-ditcher, intransigent, irreconcilable.

## 792. RESISTANCE

.1 NOUNS **resistance**, withstanding, renitence or renitency, repellence or repellency; **defiance** 793; **opposition** 790; **stand**; **repulsion**, repulse, rebuff; **objection**, protest, remonstrance, **dispute**, challenge, demur, **complaint**; dissentience, **dissent** 522; reaction, hostile or combative reaction, counteraction 178; revolt 767.4; recalcitrance or recalcitrancy, recalcitration, fractiousness, refractoriness 767.2; **reluctance** 623.1; **obstinacy** 626; passive resistance, noncooperation; uncooperativeness, negativism.

.2 VERBS **resist**, withstand; **stand**; endure 861.5; **stand up, bear up, hold up, hold out**; **defy** 793.3–6; be proof against, bear up against; **repel, repulse**, rebuff.

.3 **offer resistance**, not turn the other cheek, show fight, **withstand**, stand, **take one's stand**, make a stand, make a stand against, take one's stand against, **stand up to**, stand up against, stand at bay; front, **confront**, meet head-on, **face up to**, face down, face out; **object, protest**, remonstrate, **dispute**, challenge, **complain**, complain loudly, **dissent** 522.4,5; reluct, make a determined resistance; kick against, recalcitrate, "kick against the pricks" [Bible]; put up a fight or struggle [informal], not take lying down; **revolt** 767.7; **oppose** 790.3; **contend with** 796.18; **strive against** 790.4.

.4 **stand fast, stand** or **hold one's ground**, make a resolute stand, **hold one's own**, remain firm, stick or stick fast [both informal], **stick to one's guns, stay it out, stick it out** [informal], **hold out**, not back down, not give up, not submit, **never say die; fight to the last ditch**, die hard, sell one's life dearly, go down with flying colors.

.5 ADJS **resistant, resistive**, resisting, renitent, **withstanding**, repellent; obstructive, retardant, retardative; **unyielding**, unsubmissive 626.9–12; rebellious 767.11; **proof against** 159.18; **objecting, protesting**, disputing, disputatious, complaining, dissentient, dissenting 522.6,7; recalcitrant, fractious, refractory 767.10; **reluctant** 623.5–7; noncooperative, uncooperative; up in arms, on the barricades, not lying down.

## 793. DEFIANCE

.1 NOUNS **defiance**, defying, defial [archaic]; **daring**, daringness, **audacity**, boldness, bold front, brash bearing, brashness,

brassiness [informal], brazenness, bravado, insolence; arrogance 912; sauciness, cheekiness [informal], pertness, impudence, impertinence; bumptiousness, cockiness; **contempt**, contemptuousness, derision, **disdain**, disregard, despite.

.2 **challenge, dare**, double dare; **defy** or defi; gage, gage of battle, gauntlet, glove, chip on the shoulder, slap of the glove, invitation or bid to combat; war cry, war whoop, battle cry, rebel yell.

.3 VERBS **defy**, bid defiance, hurl defiance, snarl or shout or scream defiance; **dare**, double-dare, outdare; **challenge**, call out, throw or fling down the gauntlet or glove or gage, knock the chip off one's shoulder; beard, face, face out, stare down, **confront, affront**, front; pluck by the beard, slap one's face, double or shake one's fist at; show fight, show one's teeth, bare one's fangs; dance the war dance; **brave** 893.11.

.4 **flout**, disregard, **slight**, slight over, treat with contempt, set at defiance, fly in the teeth or face of, **snap one's fingers at; thumb one's nose at**, cock a snook at, bite the thumb at; **disdain, despise, scorn** 966.3; laugh at, laugh to scorn, laugh out of court, laugh in one's face; hold in derision, scout, scoff at, **deride** 967.8,9.

.5 **show** or **put up a bold front**, bluster, throw out one's chest, crow, look big, stand with arms akimbo.

.6 **take a dare**, accept a challenge, **take one up on** or **call one's bluff** [both informal]; take up the gauntlet.

.7 ADJS **defiant**, defying, challenging; **daring, bold**, brash, brassy [informal], brazen, **audacious**, insolent; arrogant 912.9–14; saucy, cheeky [informal], pert, impudent, impertinent; bumptious, cocky; **contemptuous**, disdainful, derisive, disregardful, greatly daring, regardless of consequences.

.8 ADVS **in defiance of**, in the teeth of, in the face of, under one's very nose.

## 794. ACCORD

### (harmonious relationship)

.1 NOUNS **accord**, accordance, **concord**, concordance, **harmony**, symphony; **rapport**, good vibrations [informal], good vibe [slang]; amity 927.1; frictionlessness; rapprochement [Fr]; **sympathy**, empathy, identity, feeling of identity, fellow feeling, **fellowship**, kinship, **affinity; agreement, understanding**, like-mindedness congeniality, **compatibility; oneness,** unity, unison, union; **community,** communion, community of interests; solidarity, team spirit, esprit, *esprit de corps* [Fr]; mutuality, sharing, reciprocity, mutual supportiveness; bonds of harmony, ties of affection, cement of friendship; happy family; peace 803; **love,** *agape* [Gk], charity, *caritas* [L], brotherly love; correspondence 26.1.

.2 VERBS **get along,** harmonize, **agree with, agree, get along with,** get on with, cotton to or hit it off with [both informal], harmonize with, **be in harmony with,** be in tune with, fall or chime in with, blend in with, go hand in hand with, **be at one with;** sing in chorus, be on the same wavelength [informal]; **sympathize,** empathize, identify with, respond to, understand one another, enter into one's views, enter into the ideas or feelings of; **accord,** correspond 26.6; reciprocate, interchange 150.4.

.3 ADJS **in accord,** accordant [archaic], **harmonious, in harmony,** in tune, attuned, agreeing, in concert, **in rapport,** *en rapport* [Fr], amicable 927.14–20; frictionless; **sympathetic,** empathic, empathetic, **understanding,** sympathetico– or sympatho–; **like-minded,** akin, of the same mind, of one mind, at one, united, together; concordant, corresponding 26.9; agreeable, congenial, **compatible; peaceful** 803.9,10.

## 795. DISACCORD

### (unharmonious relationship)

.1 NOUNS **disaccord, discord,** discordance or discordancy, **unharmoniousness,** inharmoniousness, disharmony, inharmony, disaffinity, incompatibility, incompatibleness; noncooperation; **conflict,** open conflict, friction, rub; jar, jangle, clash, clashing; strained relations, **tension; unpleasantness;** mischief; **contention** 796; **enmity** 929; Eris, Discordia.

.2 **disagreement, difficulty, misunderstanding, difference,** difference of opinion, agreement to disagree, **variance,** division, dividedness; **odds,** cross-purposes; polarity of opinion, polarization; disparity 27.1.

.3 **dissension, dissent,** dissidence, flak [informal]; bickering, infighting, faction, factiousness, partisanship, partisan spirit; **divisiveness; quarrelsomeness;** litigiousness; pugnacity, bellicosity, combativeness, **aggressiveness,** contentiousness, belligerence

797.15; irritability, shrewishness, irascibility 951.2.

.4 **falling-out, breach of friendship,** parting of the ways; **alienation, estrangement, disaffection,** disfavor; **breach, break, rupture, schism, split, rift,** cleft, **disunity, disunion, disruption,** separation, cleavage, divergence, division, dividedness; division in the camp, house divided against itself; open rupture, breaking off of negotiations, recall of ambassadors.

.5 **quarrel,** open quarrel, **dispute, argument,** polemic, slanging match [Brit], fliting [archaic or dial], **controversy,** altercation, **fight, squabble, contention,** strife, **tussle,** bicker, wrangle, snarl, **tiff, spat,** fuss; **fracas,** donnybrook or donnybrook fair; broil, embroilment, imbroglio; words, sharp words, logomachy; **feud,** blood feud, vendetta; brawl 796.5.

.6 [slang or informal terms] **row, rumpus,** ruckus, ruction, shindy, barney [Brit], set-to, run-in, **scrap, hassle,** rhubarb, dustup; knock-down-and-drag-out, knock-down-and-drag-out quarrel or fight.

.7 **bone of contention,** apple of discord, sore point, tender spot, delicate or ticklish issue, rub; **bone to pick,** crow to pluck or pick or pull; *casus belli* [L], grounds for war.

.8 VERBS **disaccord, disagree, differ,** differ in opinion, hold opposite views, **be at variance,** not get along, pull different ways, be at cross-purposes, have no measures with, misunderstand one another; **conflict, clash,** collide, jostle, jangle, jar; live like cat and dog, live a cat-and-dog life.

.9 **have a bone to pick with,** have a crow to pluck with or pick with or pull with.

.10 **fall out,** have a falling-out, **break with, split,** separate, **diverge,** divide, agree to disagree, **part company,** come to or reach a parting of the ways.

.11 **quarrel, dispute,** differ [archaic], flite [archaic or dial], altercate, **fight, squabble,** tiff, spat, **bicker, wrangle,** spar, broil, have words, set to, join issue, make the fur fly; **feud; brawl** 796.14.

.12 [slang or informal terms] **row, scrap, hassle,** make or kick up a row; lock horns, bump heads.

.13 **pick a quarrel,** fasten a quarrel on, look for trouble, pick a bone with, pluck a crow with; have a chip on one's shoulder.

.14 **sow dissension,** stir up trouble, make trouble; **alienate, estrange,** separate, **divide, disunite,** disaffect, **come between;**

irritate, provoke, aggravate; **set at odds,** set at variance; **set against,** pit against, **sic on** *or* **at, set on,** set by the ears, set at one's throat; fan the flame, pour oil on the blaze, light the fuse.

.15 ADJS **disaccordant, unharmonious,** inharmonious, disharmonious, **discordant,** out of accord, dissident, dissentient, **disagreeing, differing; conflicting,** clashing, colliding; like cats and dogs.

.16 **at odds, at variance, at loggerheads,** at square [archaic], at cross-purposes; at war, at strife, at feud, at daggers *or* at daggers drawn, up in arms.

.17 **partisan,** polarizing, **divisive,** factional, factious; **quarrelsome,** bickering, disputatious, wrangling, eristic(al), polemic(al); litigious, pugnacious, combative, **aggressive,** bellicose, belligerent 797.25; irritable, shrewish, irascible 951.19.

## 796. CONTENTION

.1 NOUNS **contention, contest,** contestation, **combat, conflict, strife, war, struggle,** cut and thrust; **warfare** 797; **hostility,** enmity 929; **quarrel, altercation, controversy,** polemic, debate, argument, dispute, **disputation,** litigation; words, war of words, paper war, logomachy; **fighting,** scrapping [slang]; **quarreling, bickering, wrangling, squabbling;** contentiousness, **quarrelsomeness** 795.3; cat-and-dog life; Kilkenny cats.

.2 **competition, rivalry,** vying, emulation, jockeying [informal]; cutthroat competition; run for one's money; gamesmanship, lifemanship, one-upmanship.

.3 **contest, engagement, encounter, match,** matching, meet, meeting, derby, **trial, test,** *concours, rencontre* [both Fr]; fight, bout, go [informal]; joust, tilt; **tournament,** tourney; rally; **game** 878.9,34,35; **games,** Olympic games, Olympics, gymkhana.

.4 **fight, battle, fray,** affray, combat, action, conflict, embroilment, **clash; brush, skirmish,** scrimmage; tussle, **scuffle, struggle,** scramble, shoving match; exchange of blows, *passage d'arms* [Fr], passage at *or* of arms, clash of arms; **quarrel** 795.5; pitched battle, battle royal, hand-to-hand fight, stand-up fight [informal], running fight *or* engagement; tug-of-war; bullfight, tauromachy; dogfight, cockfight; street fight, rumble [informal]; air *or* aerial combat, sea *or* naval combat, ground combat, armored combat, infantry combat, fire fight, hand-to-hand combat, house-to-house combat.

.5 **free-for-all,** knock-down-and-drag-out [informal], **brawl,** broil, melee, scrimmage, **fracas,** donnybrook *or* donnybrook fair; riot; rumpus, ruckus, ruction, row [all informal].

.6 **death struggle, life-and-death** *or* **life-or-death struggle, fight to the death,** *guerre à mort, guerre à outrance* [both Fr], all-out war, total war, last-ditch fight, fight to the last ditch.

.7 **duel,** single combat, monomachy, satisfaction, **affair of honor.**

.8 **fencing, swordplay.**

.9 **boxing, fighting,** noble *or* manly art of self-defense, **fisticuffs, pugilism, prizefighting,** the fights [informal], the ring; **boxing match, prizefight,** spar, bout; shadowboxing; close fighting, infighting, the clinches [informal]; Chinese boxing; savate.

.10 **wrestling,** rassling [dial], grappling, *sumo* [Jap]; **martial arts;** jujitsu, judo, karate, *aikido* [all Jap], *t'ai chi chu'an, kung-fu, wu-su* [all Chin], *tae-kwan-do* [Korean]; catch-as-catch-can; wrestling match, wrestling meet; Greco-Roman wrestling, Cornish wrestling, Westmorland wrestling, Cumberland wrestling.

.11 **racing, track,** track sports; **horse racing,** the turf, the sport of kings; dog racing, automobile racing.

.12 **race,** contest of speed *or* fleetness; derby; **heat, lap;** footrace, **run,** dash, hundred-yard dash, etc.; sprint, sprint race; marathon, marathon race; relay, relay race; torch race, match race, obstacle race, hurdle race, cross-country race, point-to-point race, three-legged race, sack race, potato race; walk; automobile race, road race, endurance race, track race *or* speedway race, stock-car race, drag race; Grand Prix, Le Mans, Indianapolis 500; motorcycle race, bicycle race; boat race, yacht race, regatta; air race; dog race.

.13 **horse race,** flat race, harness race, trotting race, quarter-horse race, steeplechase *or* chase, hurdle race; invitational race, claiming race, plate race [informal], purse race, stake race *or* stake, sweepstakes *or* sweepstake, sweep [informal], handicap race *or* handicap; Kentucky Derby, Preakness Stakes, Belmont Stakes; Grand National, Derby.

.14 VERBS **contend, contest,** jostle; **fight, battle, combat, war,** put up a fight [informal]; wage war 797.18; **strive, struggle,** scramble, **tussle, scuffle; quarrel** 795.11,12; clash, collide; **wrestle,** rassle [dial], grapple, grapple with, go to the mat with; **come to blows,** close, **mix it up** [slang], exchange blows or fisticuffs, box, spar, give and take; cut and thrust, **fence,** thrust and parry; **joust, tilt, tourney,** run a tilt or a tilt at, break a lance with; **duel,** fight a duel, give satisfaction; **feud;** skirmish; fight one's way; fight the good fight; **brawl, broil; riot.**

.15 **lift** or **raise one's hand against;** make war on 797.19; draw the sword against, take up the cudgels, couch one's lance; square up or off [informal], come to the scratch; have at, jump; lay on, lay about one; **pitch into** or **sail into** [both informal], light into or lay into [both slang], strike the first blow, draw first blood; **attack** 798.15.

.16 **encounter, come up against,** fall or run foul or afoul of; close with, come to close quarters, bring to bay, meet or fight hand-to-hand.

.17 **engage, take on** [informal], enter the ring or arena with, put on the gloves with, match oneself against; **join issue,** try conclusions, **join battle, do** or **give battle,** engage in battle.

.18 **contend with, engage with,** cope with, **fight with, strive` with, struggle with,** wrestle with, grapple with, bandy with [archaic], try conclusions with, measure swords with, tilt with, **cross swords with;** exchange shots, shoot it out with [informal]; **lock horns** or **bump heads** [both informal], fall or go to loggerheads [archaic]; **tangle with** or **mix it up with** [both slang], have a brush with; have it out, fight or battle it out, settle it; fight tooth and nail, fight like devils, ask and give no quarter, make blood flow freely, battle *à outrance,* fight to the death.

.19 **compete, compete with, challenge,** jockey [informal], **vie, vie with,** cope [archaic], enter into competition with, **meet;** try or test one another; **rival,** emulate, outvie.

.20 **race,** race with, run a race; horse-race, boat-race.

.21 **contend for, strive for, struggle for, fight for,** vie for; stickle for, stipulate for, make a point of.

.22 **dispute, contest,** take issue with; **fight over,** quarrel over, wrangle over, squabble over, bicker over, strive or contend about.

.23 ADJS **contending,** contesting; **contestant,**

disputant; **striving, struggling; fighting, battling, warring; warlike** 797.25; **quarrelsome** 795.17.

.24 **competitive, competing, vying, rivaling, rival,** emulous, in competition, in rivalry; **cutthroat.**

## 797. WARFARE

.1 NOUNS **warfare, war,** warring, warmaking, **combat, fighting,** *la guerre* [Fr], –machy; armed conflict, armed combat, military operations, the sword, arbitrament of the sword, appeal to arms or the sword, resort to arms, force or might of arms, bloodshed; **state of war, hostilities,** belligerence or belligerency, open war or warfare or hostilities; **hot war, shooting war;** total war, all-out war; **wartime; battle** 796.4; **attack** 798.

.2 "an epidemic insanity" [Emerson], "a brain-spattering, windpipe-slitting art", "the feast of vultures, and the waste of life" [both Byron], "the business of barbarians" [Napoleon], "the trade of kings" [Dryden], "a by-product of the arts of peace" [Ambrose Bierce], "a conflict which does not determine who is right— but who is left" [anon], "the continuation of politics by other means" [von Clausewitz], "an emblem, a hieroglyphic, of all misery" [Donne], "politics with bloodshed" [Mao Tse-tung].

.3 civil war, revolutionary war, religious war or holy war or jihad, war of independence, people's war, war of national liberation; limited war, brushfire war, police action; undeclared war; preventive war, war to end war; world war, general war, global war; Armageddon.

.4 air or aerial warfare, sea or naval warfare, amphibious warfare, land warfare, three-dimensional war; submarine warfare; trench warfare, siege warfare, underground warfare; offensive warfare, defensive warfare; war of movement, mobile warfare; motorized warfare, mechanized warfare; position warfare, war of position; irregular warfare, guerrilla warfare, bushfighting; jungle warfare; chemical warfare, gas warfare; biological warfare, bacteriological warfare, virus warfare, germ warfare; psychological warfare; conventional war or warfare; atomic war or warfare, atom war, A-war, H-war; push-button warfare, technological warfare, slide-rule warfare, missile warfare; war of attrition.

.5 **cold war,** inactive war, phony war, twilight war, armed neutrality; **psychological warfare, war of nerves;** economic warfare.

.6 **battle array,** order of battle, **disposition, deployment;** open order; close formation; echelon.

.7 **campaign,** war, **drive, expedition,** hostile expedition; **crusade,** holy war, jihad.

.8 **operation,** action; **movement; mission; operations,** military operations, naval operations; combined operations, joint operations, coordinated operations; active operations, amphibious operations, airborne operations, fluid operations, major operations, minor operations, night operations, overseas operations; war plans, staff work; logistics; war game, dry run, kriegspiel, maneuver, maneuvers.

.9 **strategy, tactics;** applied tactics; offensive strategy, defensive strategy; aerial tactics, infantry tactics, airborne tactics, paratroop tactics, cavalry tactics, guerrilla tactics, mobile tactics, armored tactics, columnar tactics, mob tactics, fire tactics, barrier tactics, shock tactics, blitzkrieg tactics, scorched-earth tactics, linear tactics, grand tactics, maneuver tactics; diversion, feint, diversionary movement; encirclement, investment, encircling movement, pincers movement; infiltration.

.10 **warcraft,** war, arms, **military science,** art or rules or science of war; siegecraft; **generalship,** soldiership; chivalry, knighthood, knightly skill.

.11 **declaration of war,** challenge; defiance 793.

.12 **call to arms, call-up,** call to the colors, **rally; mobilization; muster,** levy; conscription, recruitment 780.6; **rallying cry,** slogan, watchword, catchword, exhortation; **battle cry,** war cry, war whoop, rebel yell; banzai, gung ho, St. George, Montjoie, Geronimo, go for broke; **bugle call,** trumpet call, clarion, clarion call.

.13 **service,** duty; active service or duty; military obligation; selective service, national service [Brit].

.14 **militarization,** activation, **mobilization;** war or wartime footing, national emergency; martial law, suspension of civil rights; garrison state, military dictatorship; remilitarization, reactivation; arms race; war clouds, war scare.

.15 **warlikeness,** unpeacefulness, war or warlike spirit, ferocity, fierceness; **combativeness, contentiousness;** hostility, antagonism; unfriendliness 929.1; aggression, **aggressiveness; belligerence** or belligerency,

**pugnacity,** pugnaciousness, bellicosity, **truculence,** fight [informal]; chip on one's shoulder [informal]; militancy, **militarism,** martialism, militaryism; saber rattling; **chauvinism, jingoism,** hawkishness [informal], bellicism, **warmongering,** waving of the bloody shirt; warpath; quarrelsomeness 795.3.

.16 (rallying devices and themes) battle flag, banner, colors, gonfalon, bloody shirt, fiery cross or crostarie, atrocity story, enemy atrocities; martial music, war song, battle hymn, national anthem; national honor, face; foreign threat, totalitarian threat, Communist threat, colonialist or neocolonialist or imperialist threat, Western imperialism, yellow peril; expansionism, manifest destiny; independence, self-determination.

.17 war-god, Mars, Ares, Odin or Woden or Wotan, Tyr or Tiu or Tiw; war-goddess, Athena, Minerva, Bellona, Enyo, Valkyrie.

.18 VERBS **war, wage war, make war, carry on war** or **hostilities,** engage in hostilities, wield the sword; battle, **fight** 796.14; spill or shed blood.

.19 **make war on,** levy war on, "let slip the dogs of war" [Shakespeare]; **attack** 798.15–28; **declare war, challenge,** throw or fling down the gauntlet; defy 793.3–6; open hostilities, plunge the world into war; launch a holy war on, go on a crusade against.

.20 **go to war,** break the peace, take up the gauntlet, **go on the warpath, rise up in arms, take** or **resort to arms,** take arms, take up arms, take up the cudgels or sword, fly or appeal to the sword, unsheathe one's weapon, come to cold steel; take the field.

.21 **campaign,** undertake operations, pursue a strategy, make an expedition, go on a crusade.

.22 **serve,** do duty; fulfill one's military obligation, wear the uniform; **soldier,** see or do active duty; **bear arms,** carry arms, shoulder arms, shoulder a gun; see action or combat, hear shots fired in anger.

.23 **call to arms, call up,** call to the colors, **rally; mobilize; muster,** levy; conscript, recruit 780.16; give the battle cry, wave the bloody shirt, beat the drums, blow the bugle or clarion.

.24 **militarize, activate, mobilize,** go on a wartime footing, gird or gird up one's loins, muster one's resources; reactivate, remilitarize, take out of mothballs [informal].

.25 ADJS **warlike, militant,** fighting, warring, battling; **martial, military,** soldierly, soldierlike; **combative, contentious,** gladiatorial; trigger-happy [informal]; **belligerent, pugnacious, truculent, bellicose,** scrappy [slang], full of fight; **aggressive,** offensive; fierce, ferocious, savage, bloody, bloody-minded, bloodthirsty, sanguinary, sanguineous; **unpeaceful,** unpeaceable, unpacific; **hostile, antagonistic, enemy,** inimical; unfriendly 929.9; quarrelsome 795.17.

.26 militaristic, warmongering, saber-rattling; **chauvinistic,** chauvinist, **jingoistic,** jingoist, jingoish, jingo; hawkish [informal], of the war party.

.27 embattled, battled, engaged, at grips, in combat; arrayed, deployed, ranged, in battle array, in the field; armed 799.14.

.28 ADVS at war, up in arms; in the midst of battle, in the thick of the fray or combat; in the cannon's mouth, at the point of the gun; at swords' points, at the point of the bayonet or sword.

.29 **wars**

| | |
|---|---|
| Algerian War | Peloponnesian Wars |
| American Revolution | Persian Wars |
| Arab-Israeli War | Punic Wars |
| Balkan Wars | Russian Revolution |
| Boer War | Russo-Japanese War |
| Civil War (American) | Samnite Wars |
| Civil War (English) | Seven Weeks' War |
| Civil War (Spanish) | Seven Years' War |
| Civil Wars (Chinese) | Sino-Japanese War |
| Civil Wars (Roman) | Six Day War |
| Crimean War | Southeast Asian War |
| Crusades | Spanish-American |
| Franco-Prussian War | War |
| French and Indian | Thirty Years' War |
| War | Vietnam War |
| French Revolution | War Between the |
| Gallic Wars | States |
| Greco-Persian Wars | War of 1812 |
| Hundred Years' War | War of the Austrian |
| Indian Wars | Succession |
| Indochina War | War of the Polish |
| Italian Wars of Inde- | Succession |
| pendence | War of the Spanish |
| Korean War | Succession |
| Macedonian-Persian | Wars of the French |
| War | Revolution |
| Manchurian War | Wars of the Roses |
| Mexican War | World War I |
| Napoleonic Wars | World War II |

.30 **battles**

| | | |
|---|---|---|
| Actium | Arbela-Gaugamela | Battle of Britain | Marne River |
| Adrianople | Ardennes | Battle of the Bulge | Marston Moor |
| Aegates Isles | Austerlitz | Belleau Wood | Metaurus River |
| Aegospotami | Ayacucho | Bennington | Meuse River-Argonne |
| Agincourt | Balaclava | Bismarck Sea | Forest |
| Antietam | Bannockburn | Blenheim | Midway |
| Anzio | Bataan-Corregidor | Borodino | Minden |
|  |  | Bosworth Field | Monmouth |
|  |  | Bouvines | Mukden |
|  |  | Boyne | Naseby |
|  |  | Brunanburh | Nashville |
|  |  | Buena Vista | Navarino |
|  |  | Bull Run | New Orleans |
|  |  | Bunker Hill | Nile River |
|  |  | Cannae | Normandy |
|  |  | Caporetto | Novgorod |
|  |  | Caudine Forks | Okinawa |
|  |  | Chaeronea | Omdurman |
|  |  | Châlons-sur-Marne | Orleans |
|  |  | Chancellorsville | Panipat |
|  |  | Château-Thierry | Passero Cape |
|  |  | Chattanooga | Pearl Harbor |
|  |  | Chickamauga | Petersburg |
|  |  | Constantinople | Pharsalus |
|  |  | Coral Sea | Philippi |
|  |  | Crécy | Philippine Sea |
|  |  | Cunaxa | Plassey |
|  |  | Cynoscephalae | Plataea |
|  |  | Dardanelles | Plevna |
|  |  | Dienbienphu | Poitiers |
|  |  | Drogheda | Port Arthur |
|  |  | Dunkirk | Pydna |
|  |  | El Alamein | Quebec |
|  |  | Flodden | Ravenna |
|  |  | Fontenoy | Rocroi |
|  |  | Fredericksburg | Rossbach |
|  |  | Gaza | Saint-Mihiel |
|  |  | Gettysburg | Saipan |
|  |  | Granicus River | Salamis |
|  |  | Guadalcanal | Salerno |
|  |  | Hampton Roads | Santiago de Cuba |
|  |  | Hastings | Saratoga |
|  |  | Hohenlinden | Sedan |
|  |  | Inchon | Sempach |
|  |  | Ipsus | Sevastopol |
|  |  | Issus | Shiloh |
|  |  | Ivry-la-Bataille | Singapore |
|  |  | Iwo Jima | Soissons |
|  |  | Jena-Auerstedt | Solferino |
|  |  | Jutland | Somme River |
|  |  | Khartoum | Spanish Armada |
|  |  | Kwajalein-Eniwetok | Spotsylvania |
|  |  | Lake Erie | Stalingrad |
|  |  | Lake Trasimenus | Syracuse |
|  |  | Langside | Tannenberg |
|  |  | Leipzig | Tarawa-Makin |
|  |  | Leningrad | Tertry |
|  |  | Lepanto | Teutoburger Wald |
|  |  | Leuctra | Thermopylae |
|  |  | Lexington and Con- | Tours |
|  |  | cord | Trafalgar |
|  |  | Leyte | Valmy |
|  |  | Long Island | Verdun |
|  |  | Lucknow | Vicksburg |
|  |  | Lüleburgaz | Vienna |
|  |  | Lützen | Wagram |
|  |  | Maldon | Wake Island |
|  |  | Manila Bay | Waterloo |
|  |  | Mantinea | Yalu River |
|  |  | Marathon | Yorktown |
|  |  | Marengo | Ypres |
|  |  | Mariana Islands | Zama |

## 798. ATTACK

.1 NOUNS **attack, assault,** assailing, assailment; **offense, offensive; aggression; onset, onslaught; strike;** descent on or upon; **charge,** rush, dead set at, run at or against; **drive, push** [informal]; **sally, sortie;** infiltration; *coup de main* [Fr]; frontal attack or assault, head-on attack, flank attack; mass attack; banzai attack or charge; hit-and-run attack; breakthrough; **counterattack, counteroffensive;** amphibious attack; gas attack; diversionary attack, diversion; assault and battery, simple assault, mugging [informal], aggravated assault, armed assault, unprovoked assault; **blitzkrieg, blitz,** lightning attack, lightning war, panzer warfare, sudden or devastating or crippling attack, shock tactics; atomic or thermonuclear attack, first-strike capacity, megadeath, overkill.

.2 **surprise attack,** surprise, surprisal, unforeseen attack, **sneak attack** [informal]; Pearl Harbor.

.3 **thrust,** pass, lunge, swing, cut, stab, jab; feint; home thrust.

.4 **raid, foray,** razzia; invasion, incursion, inroad, irruption; **air raid, air strike,** air attack, shuttle raid, fire raid, saturation raid; escalade, scaling, boarding.

.5 **siege, besiegement, beleaguerment;** encompassment, investment, encirclement, envelopment; blockading, blockade; cutting of supply lines; vertical envelopment; pincer movement.

.6 **storm,** storming, taking by storm.

.7 **bombardment, cannonade;** strafe, strafing; air raid, blitzkrieg, blitz, lightning attack, lightning war.

.8 **bombing, blitz,** dive-bombing, glide-bombing, skip-bombing, shuttle bombing, area bombing, interdiction bombing, pattern bombing, carpet bombing, precision bombing, pinpoint bombing, saturation bombing, tactical bombing, strategic bombing, high-altitude bombing, low-altitude bombing.

.9 **gunfire, fire, firing,** musketry, **shooting,** fireworks or gunplay [both informal]; gunfight, shoot-out; shellfire; rocket fire; antiaircraft fire, flak or flack; automatic-weapons fire, cross fire, curtain fire, direct fire, dry fire, file fire, ground fire, horizontal fire, interdiction fire, machine-gun fire, mortar fire, vertical fire, percussion fire, pistol fire, platoon fire, plunging fire, high-angle fire, raking fire, rapid fire, ricochet fire, rifle fire, rolling fire, time fire, zone fire, fire of demolition; firepower.

.10 **volley, salvo, burst, spray, fusillade,** drumfire, **cannonade,** cannonry, **broadside,** enfilade; **barrage,** antiaircraft barrage, box barrage, emergency barrage, mortar barrage, normal barrage, standing barrage, rolling or creeping barrage.

.11 **stabbing,** piercing; **knifing,** bayonetting; the sword; **impalement, transfixion.**

.12 **stoning,** lapidation.

.13 **assailant,** assailer, **attacker;** assaulter, mugger [informal]; **aggressor;** invader, raider.

.14 **zero hour,** H hour; D day, target day.

.15 VERBS **attack, assault, assail,** harry, assume or take the offensive; commit an assault upon, mug [informal]; **strike, hit, pound** 283.13,14; **go at, come at,** have at, lay at [dial], go for [informal], **launch out against,** make a set or dead set at; **pitch into** or **light into** or **sail into** or wade into or lay into [all informal]; **fall on** or **upon, set on** or **upon, descend on** or upon, come down on, swoop down on; pounce upon, land on, land on like a ton of bricks, crack down on [informal]; **lift** or **raise a hand against,** draw the sword against, take up the cudgels against; **lay hands on,** lay a hand on, bloody one's hands with; gang up on, attack in force; jump or bushwhack [both informal], surprise, **ambush;** blitz, attack or hit like lightning.

.16 **lash out at,** let drive at, let fly at, strike out at; **strike at,** hit at, poke at, thrust at, **swing at;** swing on, **take a swing** or **crack** or **swipe** or **poke** or **shot at** [informal], make a thrust or pass at, lunge at, aim or deal a blow at, flail at, flail away at, take a fling or shy at; cut and thrust; feint.

.17 **launch an attack,** kick off an attack, mount an attack, **push, thrust,** mount or open an offensive; **drive; advance against** or **upon, march upon** or **against,** bear down upon; **infiltrate; strike;** flank; press the attack, follow up the attack; **counterattack; gas.**

.18 **charge,** rush, **rush at, fly at,** run at, dash at, make a dash or rush at; tilt at, go full tilt at, make or run a tilt at, ride full tilt against; **jump off,** go over the top [informal].

.19 **besiege, lay siege to,** encompass, surround, **encircle,** envelop, invest, set upon on all sides, get in a pincers, close the jaws of the pincers or trap; **blockade;** beset, beleaguer, harry, harass, drive or press one hard; soften up.

.20 raid, foray, make a raid; invade, inroad, make an inroad, make an irruption into; escalade, scale, scale the walls, board; storm, take by storm, overwhelm, inundate.

.21 pull a gun on, draw a gun on; get the drop on or beat to the draw [both slang].

.22 fire upon, fire at, shoot at, pop at or take a pop at [both slang], take or fire or let off a shot at; open fire, commence firing, open up on [slang]; aim at, take aim at, zero in on, take dead aim at, draw a bead on; snipe, snipe at; bombard, blast, strafe, shell, cannonade, mortar, barrage, blitz; pepper, fusillade, fire a volley; rake, enfilade; pour a broadside into; cannon; torpedo; shoot 285.13.

.23 bomb, drop a bomb, lay an egg [slang]; dive-bomb, glide-bomb, skip-bomb, pattern-bomb, etc.; atom-bomb, hydrogen-bomb.

.24 mine, plant a mine, trigger a mine.

.25 stab, stick [informal], pierce, plunge in; run through, impale, spit, transfix, transpierce; spear, lance, poniard, bayonet, saber, sword, put to the sword; knife, dirk, dagger, stiletto; spike.

.26 gore, horn, tusk.

.27 pelt, stone, lapidate [archaic], pellet; brickbat or egg [both informal].

.28 hurl at, throw at, cast at, heave at, chuck at [informal], fling at, sling at, toss at, shy at, fire at, let fly at; hurl against, hurl at the head of.

.29 ADJS attacking, assailing, assaulting, charging, driving, thrusting, advancing; invading, invasive, invasionary, incursive, incursionary, irruptive.

.30 offensive, combative, on the offensive or attack; aggressive 797.25.

.31 ADVS under attack, under fire; under siege.

.32 INTERJS attack!, advance!, charge!, over the top!, up and at 'em!, give 'em hell!, let 'em have it!, fire!, open fire!; banzai!

## 799. DEFENSE

.1 NOUNS defense, defence [Brit], guard, ward; protection 699; resistance 792; self-defense, self-protection, self-preservation; deterrent capacity; defense in depth; the defensive; defenses, psychological defenses, ego defenses, defense mechanism, escape mechanism, avoidance reaction, negative taxis or tropism.

.2 civil defense; Office of Emergency Planning, OEP, Office of Civil Defense, OCD, Air Defense Command; conelrad (control of electromagnetic radiation for civil defense), Emergency Broadcast System, EBS, Civil Defense Warning System; radar defenses, distant early warning or DEW Line; antimissile missile, anti-ballistic-missile system, ABM.

.3 armor, armature; armor plate; body armor, suit of armor, plate armor; panoply, harness; mail, chain mail, chain armor, coat of mail, hauberk, habergeon; bullet-proof vest; shield, buckler; protective covering, cortex, thick skin, shell 228.15; spines, needles.

.4 fortification; bulwark, rampart, parapet, battlement, merlon; vallation [archaic], vallum, contravallation, circumvallation; earthwork, work, bank [archaic], dike, mound, parados; stockade, palisade; barricade; abatis; entanglement, barbed-wire entanglement; fieldwork; casemate; breastwork; mantelet; ravelin; redan; lunette; bastion, demibastion, banquette, curtain, tenaille; advanced work, outwork, barbican, redoubt, sconce, fortalice [archaic]; glacis; scarp, escarp, escarpment, counterscarp; machicolation, loophole, balistraria; bartizan; drawbridge, portcullis, cheval-de-frise or chevaux-de-frise; postern gate, sally port; fence, barrier 730.5; enclosure 236.3.

.5 entrenchment, trench, ditch, fosse; moat; dugout, abri; bunker; foxhole, slit trench; approach trench, communication trench, fire trench, gallery, parallel, coupure; tunnel, fortified tunnel; sap, single or double sap, flying sap; mine, countermine.

.6 stronghold, hold, safehold, fasthold, fastness, keep, ward, bastion, donjon, citadel, castle, tower, tower of strength, strong point; mote or motte; fort, fortress, post; bunker, pillbox, blockhouse, garrison, garrison house; acropolis; peel, peel tower; rath; martello tower, martello; bridgehead, beachhead.

.7 defender, champion, advocate; upholder; supporter 787.9; vindicator, apologist; protector 699.5; guard 699.9; paladin.

.8 VERBS defend, guard, shield, screen, secure, guard against; defend tooth and nail; safeguard, protect 699.18–20; stand by the side of, flank; advocate, champion 1006.10.

.9 fortify, embattle, battle [archaic]; arm; armor, armor-plate; man; garrison, man the garrison; barricade, blockade; bulwark, wall, palisade, fence; castellate, crenellate; bank; entrench, **dig in**; mine.

.10 **fend off, ward off, stave off, hold off,** keep off, beat off, parry, fend, counter, turn aside; **hold** or **keep at bay,** keep at arm's length; stop, check, block, hinder, obstruct; **repel, repulse, rebuff, drive back,** put back, push back; go on the defensive, fight a holding or delaying action, fall back to prepared positions.

.11 ADJS **defensive,** defending, **guarding,** shielding, screening; **protective** 699.23; self-defensive, self-protective, self-preservative.

.12 **fortified,** battlemented, embattled, battled [archaic]; castellated, crenellated, casemated, machicolated.

.13 **armored,** armor-plated; in armor, panoplied, armed cap-a-pie, armed at all points, in harness, "in complete steel" [Shakespeare]; mailed, mailclad, ironclad; loricate, loricated.

.14 **armed,** hoplo–; heeled or carrying [both slang]; accoutered, **in arms,** bearing or wearing or carrying arms, under arms, sword in hand; **well-armed,** heavy-armed, full-armed, bristling with arms, **armed to the teeth;** light-armed.

.15 **defensible, defendable,** tenable.

.16 ADVS **defensively, in defense,** in self-defense; **on the defensive,** on guard; **at bay,** *aux abois* [Fr], with one's back to the wall.

.17 **armor**

| | |
|---|---|
| aegis | habergeon |
| armet | hauberk |
| backplate | headpiece |
| bard | heaume |
| basinet | helm |
| beaver | helmet |
| brassard | jamb |
| breastplate | jambeau |
| brigandine | knee plate |
| buckler | lorica |
| bulletproof vest | mail |
| burganet | morion |
| byrnie | nasal |
| cabasset | nosepiece |
| camail | pallette |
| casque | pavise |
| casquetel | *Pickelhaube* [Ger] |
| chamfron | plate |
| coif | rerebrace |
| corselet | rondel |
| cubitiere | sallet |
| cuirass | shield |
| cuisse | skirt of tasses |
| épaulière | solleret |
| face guard | tasse |
| gas mask | tuille |
| gauntlet | vambrace |
| gorget | visor |
| greaves | |

## 800. COMBATANT

.1 NOUNS **combatant, fighter, battler,** scrapper [slang]; **contestant, contender, competitor, rival;** disputant, wrangler, squabbler, bickerer, quarreler; struggler, tussler, scuffler; brawler, rioter; feuder; **belligerent,** militant; gladiator; jouster, tilter; **knight,** belted knight; swordsman, blade, sword, *sabreur, beau sabreur* [both Fr]; fencer, foilsman, swordplayer [archaic]; duelist; gamecock, fighting cock; **tough,** rough, rowdy, **ruffian,** thug, **hoodlum, hood** [informal], hooligan, streetfighter, bully, bullyboy, bravo; gorilla or goon or plug-ugly [all slang], hatchet man or enforcer [both informal], strong-arm man, strong arm, strong-armer; swashbuckler.

.2 **pugilist,** pug or palooka [both slang], **boxer, fighter, prizefighter,** fisticuffer, bruiser, sparrer; flyweight, bantamweight, featherweight, lightweight, welterweight, middleweight, light heavyweight, heavyweight; judo or jujitsu or karate expert, brown belt, black belt; Chinese boxer; savate expert.

.3 **wrestler,** rassler [dial], grappler, scuffler, matman.

.4 **bullfighter,** toreador, *torero* [Sp]; banderillero, picador, matador.

.5 **militarist, warmonger,** war dog or hound, war hawk, **hawk** [informal]; **chauvinist, jingo,** jingoist.

.6 **serviceman,** military man; navy man 276.4; air serviceman 279.3,4; **soldier, warrior,** brave, fighting man, legionary, hoplite, **man-at-arms,** rifleman, rifle; **cannon fodder,** food for powder; warrioress, Amazon; spearman, pikeman, halberdier.

.7 (common soldiers) GI, GI Joe, **doughboy, Yank;** Tommy Atkins or **Tommy** or Johnny or swaddy [all Brit]; redcoat; *poilu* [Fr]; Aussie, Anzac, digger [all Austral]; jock [Scot]; Fritz, Jerry, Heinie, Hun [derog], Boche [derog], Kraut [derog] (German soldier); Janissary (Turkish soldier); sepoy [India]; askari [Africa].

.8 **enlisted man,** noncommissioned officer 749.19; **common soldier, private,** buck private [slang]; private first class, pfc.

.9 **infantryman, foot soldier;** footslogger or paddlefoot or doughfoot or dogface or grunt [all slang]; light infantryman, chasseur, *Jäger* [Ger], Zouave; **rifleman,** rifle, musketeer; fusileer, carabineer; **sharpshooter,** marksman, expert rifleman, *bersagliere* [Ital]; **sniper;** grenadier.

.10 **artilleryman,** artillerist, **gunner,** guns

[slang], cannoneer, machine gunner; bomber, bomb thrower, bombardier.

.11 **cavalryman,** mounted infantryman, **trooper;** dragoon, light *or* heavy dragoon; lancer, lance, uhlan, hussar; cuirassier; spahi; cossack.

.12 **tank corpsman, tanker,** tank crewman.

.13 **engineer,** combat engineer, pioneer, Seabee; sapper, sapper and miner.

.14 **elite troops,** special troops, **shock troops,** storm troops, elite corps; commandos, rangers, Special Forces, Green Berets, marines, paratroops, guardsmen, Schutzstaffel, SS, Waffen-SS, Gurkhas.

.15 **irregular,** casual; **guerrilla,** partisan, franctireur; **bushfighter,** bushwhacker [slang]; underground, resistance, maquis; Vietcong, VC, Charley [slang]; *maquisard* [Fr], underground *or* resistance fighter.

.16 **mercenary, hireling,** *condottiere* [Ital], free lance, free companion, **soldier of fortune,** adventurer; gunman, gun, hired gun, hired killer, professional killer.

.17 **recruit,** rookie [slang], **conscript,** drafted man, **draftee, inductee, selectee, enlistee,** enrollee, trainee, boot [slang]; **raw recruit,** tenderfoot; awkward squad [slang]; draft, levy.

.18 **veteran,** vet [informal], campaigner, old campaigner, old soldier, war-horse [informal].

.19 (military units) **unit, organization,** tactical unit, **outfit** [informal]; **army,** field army, army group, corps, **division,** wing, regiment, battle group, battalion, garrison, **company,** troop, brigade, legion, phalanx, cohort, **platoon,** section, **battery,** maniple, combat team, combat command; task force; **squad,** squadron, detachment, detail, posse; kitchen police, KP; column, flying column; rank, file; train, field train; cadre.

.20 **corps;** army corps, *corps d'armée* [Fr]; corps troops; air corps, armored corps, tank corps, engineer corps, corps of engineers, army service corps, drum corps, bugle corps, quartermaster corps, signal corps, corps of signals, medical corps, rifle corps, marine corps, staff corps, motor corps, adjutant general corps, judge advocate general corps, ordnance corps, chemical corps, transportation corps, dental corps, veterinary corps, army nurse corps, military police corps; corps of cadets.

.21 **arm, branch, service,** arm *or* branch of the service.

.22 **army,** this man's army [slang], **armed force, armed service,** fighting machine;

the **military,** military establishment; **soldiery, forces, troops, host,** array, legions; ranks, rank and file; **standing army, regular army,** regulars, professional *or* career soldiers; the line, troops of the line; line of defense, first *or* second line of defense; ground forces, ground troops; storm troops; paratroops, ski troops; occupation force.

.23 **militia,** organized militia, national militia, mobile militia, territorial militia, reserve militia; home reserve; **National Guard,** Air National Guard, state guard; home guard; minutemen, trainband, yeomanry.

.24 **reserves,** auxiliaries, **second line of defense,** landwehr, army reserves, home reserves, territorial reserves, territorial *or* home defense army, supplementary reserves, organized reserves; US Army Reserve, US Naval Reserve, US Marine Corps Reserve, US Air Force Reserve, US Coast Guard Reserve.

.25 **volunteers,** volunteer army, volunteer militia, volunteer navy.

.26 **navy,** naval forces, **first line of defense;** fleet, flotilla, argosy, armada, squadron, escadrille, division, task force, task group; mosquito fleet; United States Navy, USN; Royal Navy, RN; marine, mercantile *or* merchant marine, merchant navy, merchant fleet; naval militia; naval reserve; coast guard; Seabees, Naval Construction Battalion.

.27 **marines,** sea soldiers, Marine Corps, Royal Marines; **leathernecks** *or* devil dogs *or* gyrenes [all slang], jollies [Brit informal].

.28 **air force,** air corps, air service, air arm; strategic air force, tactical air force; squadron, escadrille, flight, wing.

.29 **air force;** US Air Force, USAF; US Army Air Force, USAAF; Royal Air Force, RAF; Royal Canadian Air Force, RCAF; Royal Australian Air Force, RAAF; US National Air Service, USNAS; Naval Air Division, NAD, Navy Air, Fleet Air Arm; Army-Navy Air Corps, ANAC; Far East Air Force, FEAF; Air Command, Bomber Command, Coastal Command; Strategic Air Command, SAC, Air Transport Command, ATC; Air Transport Service, ATS; Military Air Transport Service, MATS; Naval Air Transport Service, NATS; Carrier Aircraft Service Unit, CASU; Airborne Reconnaissance Force, ARF.

.30 (women's services) Women Accepted for

Volunteer Emergency Service, WAVE, Waves; Women's Army Corps, WAC, Wacs; Women's Royal Army Corps, WRAC, Wracs; Women's Army Auxiliary Corps, WAAC, Waacs; Women's Royal Naval Corps, WREN, Wrens; Women's Air Force, WAF, Wafs; Women's Royal Air Force, WRAF, Wrafs; Women's Auxiliary Air Force, WAAF, Waafs; Women's Air Force Service Pilots, WASP, Wasps; Women's Reserve of the Marine Corps, WAM, Wams; Women's Auxiliary of the US Coast Guard, Spars; Army Nurse Corps, Navy Nurse Corps.

.31 guards, household troops; yeomen of the guard, beefeaters, Life Guards, Horse Guards, Foot Guards, Grenadier Guards, Coldstream Guards, Scots Guards, Irish Guards; Swiss Guards.

.32 war-horse, charger, courser, trooper.

## 801. ARMS

.1 NOUNS arms, weapons, deadly weapons, instruments of destruction; weaponry, armament, munitions, ordnance, munitions of war, apparatus belli [L]; musketry; missilery; small arms; side arms; stand of arms; conventional weapons, nonnuclear weapons; nuclear weapons, atomic weapons, thermonuclear weapons, A-weapons; biological weapons; weapons of mass destruction.

.2 armory, arsenal, magazine, dump; ammunition depot, ammo dump [informal]; park, gun park, artillery park, park of artillery; atomic arsenal, thermonuclear arsenal.

.3 ballistics, gunnery, musketry, artillery; rocketry, missilery; archery.

.4 sword, blade, good or trusty sword; steel, cold steel; Excalibur.

.5 gun, firearm; shooting iron or gat or rod or heater or piece [all slang]; shoulder weapon or gun or arm; rifle, musket, recoilless rifle; shotgun, smoothbore gun or weapon, sawed-off shotgun; pistol, handgun, automatic, repeater, revolver, six-shooter or six-gun [both informal], Saturday night special [informal]; flame-thrower, flame projector; blowgun, blowpipe, sumpit or sumpitan; peashooter.

.6 artillery, cannon, cannonry, ordnance, engines of war; field artillery; heavy artillery, heavy field artillery; siege artillery, bombardment weapons, breakthrough weapons; siege engine; mountain artil-

lery, coast artillery, trench artillery, antiaircraft artillery, flak [slang]; battery.

.7 antiaircraft gun, AA gun, ack-ack [slang], pom-pom [informal], Fliegerabwehrkanone [Ger], skysweeper, Bofors, Oerlikon.

.8 ammunition, ammo [informal], powder and shot, iron rations [informal].

.9 explosive, high explosive; powder, nitro powder, smokeless powder; gunpowder, "villanous saltpetre" [Shakespeare]; guncotton, nitrocotton; cellulose nitrate, pyroxylin, nitroglycerin, melinite, cordite, gelignite, lyddite, Ballistite; TNT, trinitrotoluene, trinitrotoluol; dynamite, giant powder; plastic explosive.

.10 charge, load; blast; warhead, payload.

.11 cartridge, cartouche, shell; ball cartridge; blank cartridge, dry ammunition.

.12 missile, projectile, bolt; brickbat, stone, rock, Irish confetti [slang]; boomerang; bola; throwing-stick, throw stick, waddy [Austral]; countermissile; rocket 281.2–6, 14,15; torpedo 281.16.

.13 shot, bar shot, bird shot, buckshot, canister shot, cannon shot, case shot, chain shot, crossbar shot, duck shot, langrage or langrel shot, round shot, split shot, swan shot; grapeshot, grape; ball, cannonball, rifle ball, minié ball; bullet, slug, pellet; dumdum bullet, expanding bullet, explosive bullet, manstopping bullet, manstopper; tracer bullet, tracer; shell, high-explosive shell, shrapnel.

.14 bomb, bombshell; time bomb, infernal machine; grenade, hand grenade, rifle grenade, concussion grenade, smoke grenade, incendiary grenade, wall grenade, gas grenade, tear-gas grenade; petard, carcass; depth charge, depth bomb, ash can [slang]; aerial bomb, fire bomb, incendiary bomb, antipersonnel bomb.

.15 atomic bomb, atom bomb, A-bomb, fission bomb, nuclear explosive, atomic warhead, nuclear warhead, thermonuclear warhead; hydrogen bomb, H-bomb, fusion bomb, thermonuclear bomb, superbomb, hell bomb; cobalt bomb; plutonium bomb; clean bomb, dirty bomb; nuclear artillery, tactical nuclear weapons, low-yield or limited nuclear weapons, nukes [slang].

.16 arrow, shaft, dart, reed, bolt, tox(o)– or toxi–; quarrel; chested arrow, footed arrow, bobtailed arrow, cloth yard shaft; arrowhead, barb; flight, volley.

.17 bow, crossbow, longbow, carriage bow; bow and arrow.

**.18 sling, slingshot;** throwing-stick, throw stick, spear-thrower, atlatl, wommera; **catapult,** arbalest, ballista, trebuchet.

**.19 launcher,** projector, bazooka; rocket launcher 281.10.

**.20 brass knuckles; knucks** or **brass knucks** [both informal], knuckles, knuckle-dusters.

**.21 knives**

| | |
|---|---|
| barong | shiv [slang] |
| bolo | switchblade knife, |
| bowie knife, bowie | switchblade |
| edge tool 348.2,13 | throwing knife or iron |
| gravity knife | trench knife |
| machete | yataghan |
| parang | |

**.22 daggers**

| | |
|---|---|
| bayonet | misericord |
| dirk | poniard, poignard |
| dudgeon [archaic] | skean, skean dhu |
| kris | stiletto |
| kuttar | |

**.23 spears**

| | |
|---|---|
| assegai | lance |
| bill | partisan |
| gisarme | pike |
| halberd | spontoon |
| javelin | |

**.24 swords**

| | |
|---|---|
| backsword | glaive [archaic] |
| bilbo | rapier |
| broadsword | saber |
| claymore | scimitar |
| cutlass | smallsword |
| épée | Toledo |
| falchion | tuck [archaic] |
| foil | |

**.25 axes**

| | |
|---|---|
| battle-ax | Lochaber ax |
| broadax | poleax |
| halberd | tomahawk |
| hatchet | |

**.26 clubs**

| | |
|---|---|
| bastinado | mace |
| bat | morning star |
| billy, billy club | nightstick |
| blackjack | paddle |
| bludgeon | quarterstaff |
| cane | ram, battering ram |
| clavi– | sandbag |
| cosh [Brit slang] | shillelagh |
| cudgel | spontoon |
| ferule | staff |
| knobkerrie | stave |
| knobstick | stick |
| life preserver | truncheon |
| loaded cane | war club |

**.27 guns and launchers**

| | |
|---|---|
| air gun | antitank gun |
| air pistol | antitank rifle |
| air rifle | arquebus |
| antiaircraft gun, AA | atomic cannon |
| gun | atomic gun, atom gun |
| antisubmarine mortar | automatic |

| | |
|---|---|
| automatic pistol | M-14 |
| automatic rifle, auto- | mine thrower, Minen- |
| rifle | werfer [Ger] |
| ball-turret gun | mitrailleuse [Fr] |
| bazooka | M-1 |
| BB gun | mortar |
| belly-gun | mountain gun |
| Big Bertha | M-16 |
| blunderbuss | musket |
| bolt-action rifle | musketoon |
| bombard | muzzle-loader |
| breechloader | needle gun |
| Bren gun, Bren | pedrero |
| brown Bess | petronel |
| Browning automatic | pistol |
| rifle, BAR | pom-pom |
| bulldog | popgun |
| burp gun [informal] | pump gun |
| caliver | recoilless rifle |
| cane gun | repeater |
| cannon | revolver |
| carbine | rifle |
| carronade | riot gun |
| chassepot | rocket launcher |
| culverin | semiautomatic rifle, |
| dart gun | semiautomatic |
| derringer | shotgun |
| escopeta | shoulder arm or gun |
| falconet | or weapon |
| field gun, fieldpiece | siege gun |
| firelock | six-gun, six-shooter |
| flintlock | [informal] |
| forty-five, .45 | skysweeper |
| forty-four, .44 | smoothbore |
| fowling piece | Sten gun, Sten |
| fusil | submachine gun |
| Garand rifle, Garand | swivel, swivel gun |
| Gatling gun | tear-gas gun |
| hackbut | thirty-eight, .38 |
| handgun | thirty-thirty, .30-30 |
| harpoon gun | thirty-two, .32 |
| harquebus | Thompson subma- |
| hedgehog | chine gun, tommy |
| horse pistol | gun [informal] |
| howitzer | trench mortar |
| lever-action rifle | turret gun |
| Lewis gun | twenty-two, .22 |
| Long Tom | wind-gun [archaic] |
| machine gun | Y-gun |
| machine pistol | zip gun |
| matchlock | |

**.28 gun makes**

| | |
|---|---|
| Armstrong | Marlin |
| Benet-Mercie | Martini-Henry |
| Beretta | Mauser |
| Bofors | Maxim |
| Browning | Minié |
| Colt | Mossberg |
| Enfield | Oerlikon |
| Flobert | Paixhans |
| Garand | Parrott |
| Garling | Remington |
| Gatling | Savage |
| Hotchkiss | Smith and Wesson |
| Krupp | Snider |
| Lancaster | Spandau |
| Lee-Enfield | Springfield |
| Lee-Metford | Stevens |
| Lewis | Vickers |
| Luger | Vickers-Maxim |
| Mannlicher | Webley-Scott |

Westley Richards     Winchester
Whitworth

**.29 gun parts**

| | |
|---|---|
| barrel | hair trigger |
| bolt | hammer |
| breech | lock |
| butt | magazine |
| chamber | muzzle |
| cock | receiver |
| cylinder | sear |
| flintlock | sear pin |
| gun carriage | sight |
| gunflint | stock |
| gunlock | trigger |
| gunstock | |

**.30 bombs**

| | |
|---|---|
| aerial bomb | hydrobomb |
| antipersonnel bomb | hydrogen bomb, |
| antisubmarine bomb |   H-bomb |
| atomic bomb, | incendiary, incendiary |
|   A-bomb |   bomb |
| azon bomb, azon | petard |
| blockbuster | pipe bomb |
| citybuster | plutonium bomb |
| concussion bomb | razon bomb |
| delayed-action bomb | robot bomb |
| demolition bomb | roc |
| depth bomb, depth | rocket bomb 281.4 |
|   charge | satchel charge |
| dynamite bomb | smoke bomb |
| fireball | stench bomb, stink |
| fire bomb |   bomb |
| fission bomb | tear-gas bomb |
| fragmentation bomb | thermonuclear bomb |
| fusion bomb | time bomb |
| gas bomb | |

**.31 mines**

| | |
|---|---|
| aerial mine | land mine |
| antenna mine | Leon mine |
| antipersonnel mine | limpet mine |
| antitank mine | magnetic mine |
| booby trap | oyster mine |
| buoyant mine | pressure mine |
| castrator mine | set gun |
| Claymore mine | sonic mine, acoustic |
| floating mine |   mine |
| fougasse | spring gun |
| ground mine | submarine mine |

## 802. ARENA

.1 NOUNS **arena,** scene of action, site, scene, setting, background, **field, ground,** terrain, sphere, place, locale, milieu, precinct, purlieu; course, range, walk [archaic]; campus; **theater,** stage, stage set or setting, scenery; **platform; forum,** agora, marketplace, open forum, public square; **amphitheater,** circus, **hippodrome,** coliseum, colosseum, **stadium, bowl; hall, auditorium;** gymnasium, gym [informal], palaestra; **lists,** tiltyard, tilting ground; floor, **pit,** cockpit; bear garden; **ring,** prize ring, boxing ring, canvas, squared circle [informal], wrestling ring, mat, bull ring; parade ground; athletic field 878.12.

.2 **battlefield, battleground,** battle site, **field,** combat area, **field of battle;** field of slaughter, field of blood or bloodshed, aceldama, killing ground, shambles; **the front,** front line, **line,** enemy line or lines, firing line, battle line, line of battle; combat zone; **theater, theater of operations,** theater or seat of war; communications zone, zone of communications; no-man's-land; demilitarized zone, DMZ; jump area, landing beach.

.3 campground, camp, encampment, bivouac, tented field.

## 803. PEACE

.1 NOUNS **peace,** *pax* [L]; **peacetime,** piping time of peace, the storm blown over; freedom from war, cessation of combat, exemption from hostilities, public tranquillity, "liberty in tranquillity" [Cicero]; **harmony,** accord 794.

.2 **peacefulness, tranquillity, serenity, calmness, quiet,** peace and quiet, quietude, quietness, quiet life, restfulness; order, orderliness, law and order.

.3 **peace of mind,** peace of heart, peace of soul or spirit, peace of God, "peace which passeth all understanding" [Bible].

.4 **peaceableness, unpugnaciousness,** uncontentiousness, nonaggression; irenicism, dovishness [informal], **pacifism,** pacificism; peaceful coexistence; **nonviolence.**

.5 **noncombatant,** nonbelligerent, nonresistant, nonresister; **civilian,** citizen.

.6 **pacifist,** pacificist, peacenik [informal], **peace lover, dove,** dove of peace [both informal]; pacificator, peacemaker, peacemonger; **conscientious objector,** conchie [slang].

.7 VERBS **keep the peace,** remain at peace, wage peace; refuse to shed blood, keep one's sword in its sheath; forswear violence, beat one's swords into plowshares; pursue the arts of peace.

.8 [Bible] "be at peace among yourselves", "follow after the things which make for peace", "follow peace with all men", "as much as lieth in you, live peaceably with all men", "seek peace, and pursue it", "have peace one with another", "be of one mind, live in peace".

.9 ADJS **pacific, peaceful, peaceable; tranquil, serene;** idyllic, pastoral; halcyon, soft, piping, **calm, quiet,** restful, **untroubled,** orderly, **at peace;** concordant 794.3; bloodless; peacetime.

.10 **unbelligerent, unhostile,** unbellicose, **unpugnacious, uncontentious,** unmilitant unmilitary, **nonaggressive**, noncombative, nonmilitant; noncombatant, civilian; **pacific, peaceable**, peace-loving, dovish [informal]; **pacifistic**, pacifist, irenic; **nonviolent**; conciliatory 804.12.

.11 INTERJS **peace!, peace be with you!,** peace be to you!, *pax vobiscum!, pax tecum!* [both L]; *shalom!, shalom aleichem!* [both Heb], *salaam aleikum!* [Arab]; "peace be to this house!", "peace be within thy walls, and prosperity within thy palaces", "let the peace of God rule in your hearts" [all Bible]; go in peace!, *vade in pace!* [L].

## 804. PACIFICATION

.1 NOUNS **pacification, peacemaking,** peacemongering, **conciliation, propitiation, placation, appeasement, mollification,** dulcification; **calming, soothing,** tranquilization 162.2; **détente,** relaxation of tension, easing of relations; mediation 805; placability; peace-keeping force, United Nations troops.

.2 **peace offer,** offer of parley, parley; **peace feelers; peace offering,** propitiatory gift; **olive branch; white flag,** truce flag, flag of truce; calumet, peace pipe, **pipe of peace;** downing of arms, hand of friendship, empty hands, outstretched hand.

.3 **reconciliation,** reconcilement, *rapprochement* [Fr], **reunion,** shaking of hands, making up *or* kissing and making up [both informal].

.4 **adjustment, accommodation, resolution,** composition of differences, compromise, arrangement, settlement, terms.

.5 **truce, armistice, peace;** pacification, treaty of peace, suspension of hostilities, **cease-fire,** stand-down, breathing spell, cooling-off period; Truce *or* Peace of God, Pax Dei, Pax Romana; temporary arrangement, *modus vivendi* [L]; hollow truce, *pax in bello* [L]; demilitarized zone, buffer zone, neutral territory.

.6 **disarmament,** reduction of armaments; **demilitarization, deactivation,** disbanding, disbandment, **demobilization,** mustering out, reconversion, decommissioning.

.7 VERBS **pacify, conciliate, placate, propitiate, appease, mollify,** dulcify; **calm, soothe,** tranquilize 163.7; **smooth,** smooth over, smooth down, smooth one's feathers; allay, lay, lay the dust; pour oil on troubled waters, pour balm on, take the edge off of, take the sting out of; cool [slang], defuse.

.8 **reconcile, bring to terms, bring together,** reunite, heal the breach; bring about a détente; **harmonize,** restore harmony, put in tune; adjust, settle, compose, accommodate, arrange matters, settle differences, resolve, compromise; **patch things up,** fix up [informal], patch up a friendship *or* quarrel, weave peace between, smooth it over; mediate 805.6.

.9 **make peace,** cease hostilities, raise a siege; **bury the hatchet, smoke the pipe of peace;** negotiate a peace, dictate peace; make a peace offering, hold out the olive branch, hoist *or* show *or* wave the white flag.

.10 **make up** *or* **kiss and make up** *or* make it up *or* make matters up [all informal], **shake hands,** come round, come together, come to an understanding, **come to terms,** let the wound heal, let bygones be bygones, forgive and forget, put it all behind one, settle *or* compose one's differences.

.11 **disarm, lay down one's arms,** down *or* ground one's arms, sheathe the sword, turn swords into plowshares; **demilitarize, deactivate, demobilize, disband,** reconvert, decommission.

.12 ADJS **pacificatory, pacific,** irenic, **conciliatory, reconciliatory, propitiatory,** propitiative, **placative,** placatory, **mollifying,** appeasing; **pacifying, soothing** 163.15.

.13 **pacifiable, placable, appeasable.**

## 805. MEDIATION

.1 NOUNS **mediation,** intermediation, **intercession; intervention,** interposition, putting oneself between, stepping in, declaring oneself in, involvement, interagency.

.2 **arbitration,** arbitrament, compulsory arbitration, binding arbitration; umpirage, refereeship, mediatorship.

.3 **mediator,** intermediator, **intermediate agent,** intermediate, intermedium, **intermediary,** interagent, internuncio; **medium; intercessor,** interceder; ombudsman; **intervener,** interventor, interventionist; **go-between, middleman** 781.4; connection [slang]; front *or* front man [both slang]; deputy, agent 781; **spokesman,** spokeswoman, **mouthpiece; negotiator,** negotiant, negotiatress *or* negotiatrix.

.4 **arbitrator, arbiter, impartial arbitrator,** third party, unbiased observer; **moderator; umpire, referee, judge;** magistrate 1002.1.

.5 **peacemaker,** make-peace, reconciler,

smoother-over; **pacifier,** pacificator; **conciliator,** propitiator, **appeaser;** marriage counselor, family counselor.

.6 VERBS **mediate,** intermediate, **intercede,** go between; **intervene,** interpose, step in, declare oneself a party, involve oneself, put oneself between disputants, use one's good offices, act between; represent 781.14; **negotiate,** bargain, **treat with,** make terms, meet halfway; **arbitrate,** moderate; **umpire, referee,** judge.

.7 **settle, arrange,** adjust, straighten out, bring to terms *or* an understanding; make peace 804.9.

.8 ADJS **mediatory,** mediatorial, mediative, mediating, going *or* coming between; intermediatory, intermediary, intermedial, intermediate, **middle,** intervening, mesne, interlocutory; interventional, arbitrational, arbitrative; **intercessory,** intercessional; pacificatory 804.12.

### 806. NEUTRALITY

.1 NOUNS **neutrality, neutralism,** strict neutrality; **noncommitment, noninvolvement; independence, nonpartisanism, nonalignment;** anythingarianism *or* nothingarianism [both informal]; mugwumpery, mugwumpism, fence-sitting; **evasion, cop-out** [slang], abstention; **impartiality** 976.4.

.2 **indifference,** indifferentness, Laodiceanism; passiveness 706.1; apathy 856.4.

.3 **middle course** *or* **way,** *via media* [L]; **middle ground,** neutral ground, center, **middle of the road,** fence [informal]; medium, **happy medium;** mean, **golden mean;** moderation, moderateness 163.1; compromise 807; halfway measures, half measures, half-and-half measures.

.4 **neutral,** neuter; **independent, nonpartisan;** mugwump, fence-sitter; anythingarian *or* nothingarian [both informal]; third force, third world.

.5 VERBS **remain neutral,** stand neuter, sit it out [informal], **keep in the middle of the road,** sit on the fence *or* straddle [both informal], trim; **evade,** evade the issue, duck the issue [informal], **cop out** [slang], abstain.

.6 **steer a middle course,** hold *or* keep *or* preserve a middle course, walk a middle path, follow the *via media,* strike *or* preserve a balance, **keep a happy medium,** keep the golden mean, avoid both Scylla and Charybdis; be moderate 163.5.

.7 ADJS **neutral,** neuter; **noncommitted, uncommitted,** noninvolved, uninvolved; **in-**different, Laodicean; passive 706.6; apathetic 856.13; neither one thing nor the other, neither hot nor cold; even, half-and-half, fifty-fifty [informal]; **on the fence** [informal], **in the middle of the road,** centrist, moderate, midway; **independent, nonpartisan; nonaligned,** third-force, third-world; **impartial** 976.10.

### 807. COMPROMISE

*(mutual concession)*

.1 NOUNS **compromise,** composition, adjustment, accommodation, settlement, mutual concession, give-and-take; abatement of differences; bargain, deal [informal], arrangement, understanding; **concession,** giving way, yielding; surrender, desertion of principle, evasion of responsibility, cop-out [slang].

.2 VERBS **compromise,** make *or* reach a compromise, compound, compose, accommodate, adjust, settle, make an adjustment *or* arrangement, **make a deal** [informal], come to an understanding, strike a bargain; strike a balance, take the mean, **meet halfway,** split the difference, go fifty-fifty [informal], give and take; play politics; steer a middle course 806.6; **make concessions,** give way, yield; surrender, desert one's principles, evade responsibility, duck responsibility [informal], cop out [slang].

### 808. POSSESSION

.1 NOUNS **possession,** possessing, **owning,** having title to; seisin, nine points of the law, *de facto* possession, *de jure* possession, lawful *or* legal possession; property rights, proprietary rights; **title,** derivative title, original title; adverse possession, squatting, squatterism, squatter's right; claim, legal claim; usucapion, prescription; **occupancy,** occupation; **hold, holding, tenure;** tenancy, tenantry, **lease,** leasehold, sublease, underlease, undertenancy; gavelkind; villenage, villein socage, villeinhold; socage, free socage; burgage; frankalmoign, lay fee; tenure in chivalry, knight service; fee fief, fiefdom, feud, feodum; freehold, alodium; fee simple, fee tail, fee simple absolute, fee simple conditional, fee simple defeasible *or* fee simple determinable; fee position; dependency, colony, mandate; prepossession [archaic], preoccupation, preoccupancy, chose in possession, bird in hand; property 810.

**.2 ownership,** possessorship, *dominium* [L], **proprietorship,** proprietary; lordship, overlordship, seigniory; dominion, sovereignty 739.5; landownership, landowning, landholding, land tenure.

**.3 monopoly,** monopolization; **corner,** cornering, a corner on [all informal]; exclusive possession; engrossment, forestallment.

**.4 VERBS possess, have, hold,** have and hold, **occupy, fill, enjoy,** boast; be possessed of, have tenure of, have in hand, be seized of, have in one's grip *or* grasp, have in one's possession, be enfeoffed of; **command,** have at one's command *or* pleasure *or* disposition *or* disposal; claim, usucapt; squat, squat on, claim squatter's right.

**.5 own,** have for one's own *or* very own, have to one's name, call one's own, have title to, have the deed for, hold in fee simple.

**.6 monopolize,** hog [slang], take it all, have all to oneself, have exclusive possession of *or* exclusive rights to; engross, forestall, tie up; **corner** *or* get a corner on *or* corner the market [all informal].

**.7 belong to,** pertain to, appertain to; vest in.

**.8 ADJS possessed, owned,** held; –an *or* –ean *or* –ian; in seisin, in fee, in fee simple, free and clear; **own,** of one's own; **in one's possession, in hand,** in one's grip *or* grasp, at one's command *or* disposal; on hand, by one, in stock, in store.

**.9 possessing, having, holding,** having and holding, **occupying, owning; in possession of, possessed of,** seized of, master of; tenured; enfeoffed; endowed with, blessed with; worth; propertied, property-owning, landed, landowning, landholding; –ed *or* –'d.

**.10 possessive,** possessory, **proprietary.**

**.11 monopolistic,** monopoloid, monopolizing, hogging *or* hoggish [both slang].

### 809. POSSESSOR

**.1 NOUNS possessor, holder, keeper,** haver, enjoyer, –er; have [informal].

**.2 proprietor,** proprietary, **owner;** *rentier* [Fr]; titleholder, deedholder; proprietress, proprietrix; **master, mistress, lord,** laird [Scot]; **landlord, landlady;** lord of the manor, mesne lord, mesne, feudatory, feoffee; squire, country gentleman; householder; beneficiary, cestui, cestui que trust, cestui que use.

**.3 landowner,** landholder, property owner,

propertied *or* landed person, man of property, freeholder; landed interests, landed gentry, slumlord, rent gouger; absentee landlord.

**.4 tenant, occupant,** occupier, incumbent, **resident; lodger,** roomer, paying guest; **renter,** hirer [Brit], **lessee,** leaseholder; subtenant, sublessee, underlessee, undertenant; tenant at sufferance, tenant at will; tenant from year to year, tenant for years, tenant for life; squatter; homesteader.

**.5 trustee,** fiduciary, holder of the legal estate; depository, depositary.

### 810. PROPERTY

**.1 NOUNS property, properties, possessions, holdings,** havings, goods, chattels, goods and chattels, **effects,** estate and effects, what one can call one's own, what one has to one's name; hereditament, corporeal hereditament, incorporeal hereditament; acquest.

**.2 belongings, appurtenances,** trappings, paraphernalia, appointments, accessories, perquisites, appendages, appanages, choses local; **things,** material things, mere things; choses, choses in possession, choses in action; personal effects, chattels personal, movables, choses transitory; one's all.

**.3 impedimenta,** luggage, dunnage, baggage, bag and baggage, traps, tackle, apparatus, gear, outfit, duffel.

**.4 estate, interest, equity, stake,** part, percentage; **right, title, claim,** holding; use, trust, benefit; absolute interest, vested interest, contingent interest, beneficial interest, equitable interest; easement, right of common, common, right of entry; limitation; settlement, strict settlement.

**.5 (estates)** particular estate, legal estate, equitable estate, paramount estate, vested estate, estate at sufferance, estate at will, estate in possession, estate for years, estate for life, estate pour autre vie; feudal estate, fee, feud, feod [archaic], feodum, fief, estate in fee; fee simple; fee tail, estate tail *or* in tail; copyhold; lease, leasehold; remainder; reversion; estate in expectancy.

**.6 freehold,** estate of freehold; alodium, alod; frankalmoign, lay fee, tenure in *or* by free alms; mortmain, dead hand.

**.7 real estate, realty,** real property, chattels real, tenements; *praedium* [L], landed property *or* estate, **land, lands,** property, grounds, acres; lot, lots, parcel, plot, plat, quadrat; demesne, domain [archaic]; messuage, manor, honor, toft [Brit].

.8 **assets, means, resources;** stock, stock-in-trade; one's worth, what one is worth; circumstances, funds 835.14; wealth 837; **material assets,** tangible assets, tangibles; intangible assets, intangibles; current assets, deferred assets, fixed assets, frozen assets, liquid assets, quick assets, assets and liabilities, net assets, net worth; assessed valuation.

.9 ADJS **propertied,** proprietary; **landed.**

.10 real, praedial; manorial, seignioral, seigneurial; feudal, feudatory, feodal.

.11 freehold, leasehold, copyhold; alodial.

## 811. ACQUISITION

.1 NOUNS **acquisition,** gaining, getting, getting hold of [informal], coming by, **acquirement, obtainment,** obtention, **attainment,** securement, winning; trover; accession; addition 40; **procurement,** procural, procurance, procuration; **earnings,** making, pulling or dragging down [slang], moneymaking, moneygetting, moneygrubbing.

.2 **collection, gathering,** gleaning, bringing together, assembling, **accumulation,** cumulation, **amassment.**

.3 **gain, profit,** percentage [informal], get [Brit dial], **take,** take-in [informal], rake-off [slang]; **gains, profits, earnings, winnings, return, returns, proceeds,** gettings, makings; **income** 841.4; **receipts** 844; pickings, gleanings; pelf, lucre, filthy lucre; perquisite, perk or perks [both Brit]; cleanup or killing [both slang]; net or neat profit, clean or clear profit, net; gross profit, gross; paper profits; capital gains; interest, dividends; hoard, store 660; wealth 837.

.4 **profitableness, profitability,** gainfulness, remunerativeness, rewardingness.

.5 **yield, output, make,** production; **proceeds,** produce, product; **crop, harvest,** fruit, vintage, bearing; second crop, aftermath; bumper crop.

.6 **find,** finding, **discovery;** trove, trouvaille [Fr]; treasure trove, buried treasure; foundling; waifs, waifs and strays; **windfall,** windfall money, windfall profit, **bonus, gravy** [slang], bunce [Brit slang].

.7 **godsend, boon, blessing;** manna, manna from heaven, loaves and fishes.

.8 VERBS **acquire, get, gain, obtain, secure, procure; win,** score; **earn, make,** pull down or drag down [both slang]; **reap, harvest;** contract; take, catch, capture,

corral [informal]; **net,** bag, sack; come or enter into possession, **come into, come by,** come in for, be seized of; draw, derive.

.9 **take possession, take up,** take over, get hold of [informal], get at, **lay hands on,** get one's fingers or hands on, make one's own; grab, glom on to [both slang], annex.

.10 **collect, gather, glean, pick, pluck,** cull, **take up,** pick up, get or gather in, gather to oneself, bring or get together, scrape together; amass, assemble, accumulate 660.11; **scrape up,** rake up, **dig up,** grub, grub up, round up, scare up [informal].

.11 **profit, make** or **draw** or **realize** or **reap profit, make money;** coin money, make a killing, clean up; gain by, **capitalize on,** commercialize, make capital out of, **cash in on** or make a good thing of [both informal], turn to profit or account, **realize on,** make money by, obtain a return, turn a penny or an honest penny; **gross, net; realize, clear.**

.12 **be profitable, pay,** repay, pay off [informal], yield a profit, be gainful, be worthwhile or worth one's while, be a good investment.

.13 ADJS **obtainable, attainable, available,** accessible, to be had.

.14 **acquisitive,** acquiring; **grasping, grabby** [slang]; **greedy** 634.27.

.15 **gainful,** productive, **profitable, remunerative, lucrative,** fat, **paying,** well-paying; advantageous, worthwhile; banausic, moneymaking, breadwinning.

.16 ADVS **profitably, gainfully,** remuneratively, lucratively, **at a profit,** in the black; for money; advantageously, to advantage, to profit, to the good.

## 812. LOSS

.1 NOUNS **loss, losing,** privation, **deprivation, bereavement,** taking away; stripping, dispossession, despoilment, spoliation, robbery; divestment, denudation; **sacrifice, forfeit, forfeiture,** denial, nonrestoration; expense, cost, debit; detriment, injury, damage; destruction, ruin, perdition, total loss, dead loss; losing streak [informal]; **loser** 727.5.

.2 **waste,** wastage, **exhaustion, depletion,** depreciation, dissipation, wearing, wearing away, erosion, ablation, using, using up consumption, expenditure, impoverishment, drain, shrinkage, leakage, evaporation; decrement, decrease 39.

.3 **losses, losings.**

**.4** VERBS **lose,** incur loss, **suffer loss,** undergo privation *or* deprivation, be bereaved of *or* bereft of, have no more, meet with a loss; drop, kiss good-bye [both slang]; let slip, let slip through one's fingers; **forfeit,** default; **sacrifice; miss,** wander from, go astray from; **mislay,** misplace; lose out.

**.5** waste, **deplete, depreciate,** dissipate, wear, wear away, erode, ablate, consume, drain, **shrink,** dribble away; decrease 39.6; squander 854.3,4.

**.6** go to waste, come to nothing, come to naught, go up in smoke *or* go down the drain [both informal]; run to waste, go to pot [informal], run *or* go to seed; dissipate, leak, leak away, scatter to the winds, "waste its sweetness on the desert air" [Thomas Gray].

**.7** ADJS **lost, gone; forfeited,** forfeit; by the board, out the window; long-lost; lost to; wasted, consumed, depleted, dissipated, expended, worn away, eroded, ablated, used, used up, shrunken; squandered 854.9; irretrievable 889.15.

**.8** bereft, bereaved, divested, denuded, **deprived of,** shorn of, parted from, bereaved of, stripped of, dispossessed of, despoiled of, robbed of; **out of,** minus [informal], wanting, lacking; cut off, cut off without a cent.

**.9** ADVS **at a loss, unprofitably,** to the bad [informal]; in the red [slang]; out, out of pocket.

## 813. RETENTION

**.1** NOUNS **retention,** retainment, **keeping, holding, maintenance, preservation;** prehension; keeping *or* holding in, **bottling up** *or* corking up [both informal], locking in, suppression, repression, inhibition, retentiveness, retentivity; **tenacity** 50.3.

**.2** hold, purchase, grasp, **grip,** gripe, **clutch, clamp, clinch, clench;** seizure 822.2; bite, nip; **cling,** clinging; toehold, foothold, footing; **clasp, hug, embrace,** bear hug; grapple; firm hold, tight grip, iron grip, grip of steel, death grip.

**.3** (wrestling holds) half nelson, full nelson, quarter nelson, three-quarter nelson, stranglehold, toehold, lock, hammerlock, headlock, scissors, bear hug.

**.4** (prehensile organs) **clutches, claws, talons,** pounces, unguals, *ungues, ungulae* [both L], chel(i)–, onych(o)–, ungui–; **nails,** fingernails; **pincers,** nippers, chelae; **tentacles; fingers,** digits, hooks [slang]; **hands,** paws, meathooks, mitts [both

slang]; palm, palmi–; prehensile tail; jaws, mandibles, maxillae; **teeth,** fangs.

**.5** VERBS **retain, keep, save,** save up, **maintain, preserve;** keep *or* hold in, **bottle up** *or* cork up [both informal], lock in, suppress, repress, inhibit, keep to oneself; persist in; hold one's own, hold one's ground.

**.6** hold, grip, gripe, **grasp, clutch, clip, clinch, clench;** bite, nip; grapple; **clasp, hug, embrace; cling, cling to,** cleave to, stick to, adhere to, freeze to; **hold on to,** hold fast *or* tight, hang on to, keep a firm hold upon; **hold on, hang on** [informal], hold on like a bulldog, stick like a leech, cling like a winkle, hang on for dear life; keep hold of, never let go.

**.7** hold, keep, harbor, bear, have, have and hold, hold on to; **cherish,** fondle, entertain, treasure, treasure up; **foster, nurture, nurse;** embrace, hug, clip [Brit dial], cling to; bosom *or* embosom [both archaic], take to the bosom.

**.8** ADJS **retentive,** keeping, holding, gripping, grasping; **tenacious,** clinging; viselike.

**.9** prehensile, raptorial; fingered, digitate *or* digitated, digital; clawed, taloned, jawed, toothed, dentate, fanged.

**.10** incommunicable, noncommunicable, **unimpartable;** inalienable, indefeasible; noninfectious, noncontagious, not catching.

**.11** ADVS **for keeps** [informal], to keep, for **good,** for good and all, for always; forever 112.12.

**.12** gripping instruments

| | |
|---|---|
| chuck | grip |
| clamp | holdfast |
| clasp | jaws |
| clinch | nippers |
| clip | paper clip |
| cramp | pincers |
| dog | pincette |
| forceps | pliers |
| grab | tie clip |
| grabhook | tongs |
| grapnel, grapple, grappler | tweezers |
| | vise |
| grappling iron *or* hook | wrench 348.20 |

## 814. RELINQUISHMENT

**.1** NOUNS **relinquishment, release,** giving up, letting go, dispensation; **disposal,** disposition, riddance, getting rid of, dumping 668.3; **renunciation,** forgoing, forswearing, swearing off, resignation, abjuration, **abandonment** 633; recantation, retraction 628.3; **surrender,** cession, **yielding;** sacrifice.

.2 waiver, quitclaim, deed of release.

.3 VERBS relinquish, give up, render up, surrender, yield, cede; spare; resign, vacate; drop, waive, dispense with; forgo, do without, get along without, forswear, abjure, renounce, swear off, abandon 633.5–7; recant, retract 628.9; disgorge, throw up; have done with, wash one's hands of; part with, give away, dispose of, rid oneself of, get rid of, dump 668.7; kiss goodbye [slang]; sacrifice, make a sacrifice; quitclaim.

.4 release, let go, leave go [dial], let loose of, unhand, unclutch, unclasp, relax one's grip or hold.

.5 ADJS relinquished, released, disposed of; waived, dispensed with; forgone, forsworn, renounced, abjured, abandoned 633.8; recanted, retracted; surrendered, ceded, yielded; sacrificed.

## 815. PARTICIPATION

.1 NOUNS participation, partaking, sharing, having a part or share or voice, contribution, association; involvement, engagement; complicity; voting 744.18, suffrage 744.17; partnership, copartnership, copartnery, joint control, cochairmanship, joint chairmanship; joint tenancy, cotenancy; joint ownership, condominium.

.2 communion, community, communal effort or enterprise, cooperation, cooperative society; collectivity, collectivism, collective enterprise, collective farm, kibbutz, kolkhoz; democracy, participatory democracy, town meeting; collegiality; common ownership, public ownership, state ownership, communism, socialism 745.5,6; profit sharing; sharecropping.

.3 communization, communalization, socialization, nationalization, collectivization.

.4 participator, participant, partaker, sharer; party, a party to, accomplice, accessory; partner, copartner; cotenant; shareholder.

.5 VERBS participate, partake, contribute, chip in, involve or engage oneself; have a hand in, have a finger in, have a finger in the pie, have to do with, have a part in, be an accessory to, be implicated in, be a party to; participate in, partake of or in, take part in, take an active part in, join, join in, make oneself part of, join oneself to, associate oneself with, play or perform a part in, get in the act [slang]; have a voice in, help decide, be in on the decisions, vote, have suffrage, be enfranchised; enter into, go into; make the

scene [slang]; sit in, sit in on; bear a hand, pull an oar.

.6 share, share in, come in for a share, go shares, be partners in, have a stake in, have a percentage or piece of [informal], divide with, divvy up with [slang], halve, go halves; go halvers or go fifty-fifty or go even stephen [all informal], split the difference, share and share alike; do one's share or part, pull one's weight; cooperate 786.3; apportion 816.6.

.7 communize, communalize, socialize, collectivize, nationalize.

.8 ADJS participating, participative, participant, participatory; involved, engaged; implicated, accessory; partaking, sharing.

.9 communal, common, general, public, collective, popular, social, societal; mutual, commutual [archaic], reciprocal, associated, joint, conjoint, in common, share and share alike; cooperative 786.5; profit-sharing; collectivistic, communistic, socialistic 745.21,22.

## 816. APPORTIONMENT

.1 NOUNS apportionment, portioning, division, divvy [slang], partition, repartition, partitionment, partitioning, parceling, budgeting, rationing, dividing, sharing, sharing out, splitting, cutting, slicing, cutting the pie [informal], divvying up [slang].

.2 distribution, dispersion, disposal, disposition; dole, doling, doling out, giving out, passing around; dispensation, administration, issuance; disbursal, disbursement, paying out.

.3 allotment, assignment, appointment, setting aside, earmarking, tagging; appropriation; allocation.

.4 dedication, commitment, devotion, consecration, hallowing, ordainment, ordination.

.5 portion, share, interest, part, stake, stock piece, bit, segment, –ile; bite or cut o slice or chunk [all informal], a piece o the action [informal], lot, allotment, en[informal], proportion, percentage, mea sure, quantum, quota, deal or dole [bot: archaic], meed, moiety, mess, helping contingent; dividend; commission, rake off [slang]; equal share, half, halver [in formal]; lion's share, bigger half, big en [slang]; small share, modicum; allowanc ration, budget; fate, destiny 640.2.

.6 VERBS apportion, portion, parcel, part tion, part, divide, share; share with, sha and share alike, divide with, go halvers fifty-fifty *or* even stephen with [informal]; divide into shares, **share out** *or* **around,** divide up, divvy up [slang], **split,** split up, carve, cut, slice, carve up, slice up, cut up, cut *or* slice the pie *or* melon [informal].

.7 **proportion,** proportionate, prorate, divide *pro rata.*

.8 **parcel out, portion out, measure out,** spoon out, **deal out, dole out, mete out,** ration out, give out, pass around; mete, dole, deal; **distribute, disperse; dispense,** dispose [archaic], issue, administer; disburse, pay out.

.9 **allot,** lot, **assign, appoint,** set, detail; **allocate,** make assignments *or* allocations, schedule; **set apart** *or* **aside, earmark,** tag, mark out for; set off, mark off, portion off; assign to, appropriate to *or* for; reserve, restrict to, restrict 234.5; **ordain, destine, fate.**

.10 **budget, ration;** allowance, put on an allowance.

.11 **dedicate, commit, devote, consecrate,** set apart.

.12 ADJS **apportioned,** portioned out, parceled, allocated, etc.; **apportionable,** divisible, distributable, dispensable, severable.

.13 **proportionate,** proportional; prorated, *pro rata* [L]; half; halvers *or* fifty-fifty *or* even stephen [all informal], half-and-half, equal; **distributive,** distributional; **respective,** particular, per head, per capita, several.

.14 ADVS **proportionately, in proportion,** *pro rata* [L]; **distributively; respectively,** severally, each to each; share and share alike, in equal shares, half-and-half; fifty-fifty *or* even stephen [both informal].

## 817. TRANSFER OF PROPERTY OR RIGHT

.1 NOUNS **transfer,** transference; **conveyance,** conveyancing; **giving** 818; **delivery,** deliverance; **assignment,** assignation; **consignment,** consignation; conferment, conferral, settling, settlement; vesting; bequeathal 818.10; **sale** 829; surrender, cession; transmission, transmittal; disposal, disposition; demise; alienation, abalienation; amortization, amortizement; enfeoffment; deeding; bargain and sale; lease and release; **exchange,** barter, trading.

.2 devolution, succession, reversion; shifting use, shifting trust.

.3 VERBS **transfer, convey, deliver,** hand,

pass, negotiate; **give** 818.12–21; **hand over, turn over, pass over; assign, consign,** confer, settle, settle on; cede, surrender; bequeath 818.18; **sell** 829.8–12; **make over, sign over,** sign away; transmit, **hand down, hand on, pass on,** devolve upon; demise; alienate, alien, abalienate, amortize; enfeoff; **deed,** deed over, give title to; **exchange,** barter, trade.

.4 **change hands,** change ownership; devolve, pass on, descend, succeed [archaic].

.5 ADJS **transferable, conveyable,** negotiable, alienable; **assignable,** consignable; devisable, bequeathable; heritable, inheritable.

## 818. GIVING

.1 NOUNS **giving, donation, bestowal,** bestowment; **endowment,** gifting [informal], **presentation,** presentment; **award,** awarding; **grant, granting; accordance,** vouchsafement [archaic]; **conferment,** conferral; investiture; **delivery,** deliverance, surrender; **concession,** communication, impartation, impartment; **contribution,** subscription; accommodation, supplying, furnishment, provision 659; **offer** 773; **liberality** 853.

.2 **commitment, consignment, assignment,** delegation, relegation, commendation, remanding, **entrustment;** enfeoffment, infeudation *or* infeodation.

.3 **charity,** almsgiving; **philanthropy** 938.4.

.4 **gift, present,** presentation, *cadeau* [Fr], **offering,** fairing [Brit]; tribute, **award;** oblation 1032.7; handsel; box [Brit]; Christmas present *or* gift, birthday present *or* gift; peace offering; white elephant [informal].

.5 **gratuity, largess, bounty,** liberality, donative, sportula; perquisite, perks [Brit informal]; consideration, fee [archaic], **tip,** *pourboire* [Fr], *Trinkgeld* [Ger], sweetener, inducement; grease *or* salve *or* palm oil [all slang]; **premium, bonus,** something extra, **gravy** [slang], bunce [Brit slang], lagniappe; honorarium; incentive pay, time and a half, double time; bribe 651.2.

.6 **donation,** donative; **contribution, subscription; alms,** pittance, **charity, dole, handout** [slang], alms fee, widow's mite; Peter's pence; **offering,** offertory, votive offering, collection; tithe.

.7 **benefit,** benefaction, benevolence, **blessing, favor, boon,** grace; manna.

.8 **subsidy,** subvention, subsidization, support, price support, depletion allowance, tax benefit or write-off; **grant, grant-in-aid,** bounty; **allowance, stipend, allot-ment;** **aid,** assistance, financial assistance; **help,** pecuniary aid; scholarship, fellowship; **welfare,** public welfare, public assistance, relief, relief or welfare payments, welfare aid, dole, aid to dependent children; guaranteed annual income; alimony; annuity; pension, old-age insurance, retirement benefits.

.9 **endowment,** investment, **settlement,** foundation; **dowry,** dot [Fr], portion, marriage portion; **dower,** widow's dower; jointure, legal jointure, thirds; appanage.

.10 **bequest,** bequeathal, **legacy,** devise; inheritance 819.2; **will, testament,** last will and testament; probate, attested copy; codicil.

.11 **giver, donor,** donator, gifter [informal], presenter, bestower, conferrer, grantor, awarder, imparter, vouchsafer; fairy godmother, lady bountiful, Santa Claus, sugar daddy [informal]; cheerful giver; **contributor, subscriber,** supporter, backer, financer, funder, angel [informal]; patron, patroness, Maecenas; almsgiver, almoner; **philanthropist** 938.8; assignor, consignor; settler; testate, testator, testatrix; feoffor.

.12 VERBS **give, present, donate,** slip [slang], let have; **bestow, confer, award, allot, render,** bestow on; impart, communicate; **grant,** accord, **allow,** vouchsafe, yield, afford; **tender,** proffer, offer, extend, issue, dispense, administer; serve, help to; deal, dole, mete; **give out, deal out, dole out, mete out, hand out** or dish out [both informal], fork out or shell out [both slang]; make a present of, gift or gift with [both informal], give as a gift; be generous or liberal with, give freely; pour, shower, rain, snow, heap, lavish 854.3.

.13 **deliver, hand, pass,** reach, forward, render, put into the hands of; transfer 271.9; **hand over,** give over, deliver over, fork over [slang], **pass over, turn over,** come across with [informal]; hand out, give out, pass out, distribute, circulate; hand in, give in; **surrender,** resign.

.14 **contribute, subscribe, chip in** [informal], kick in [slang], give one's share or fair share; put oneself down for, pledge; contribute to, give to, **donate to, gift** or gift with [both informal]; put something in the pot, sweeten the kitty.

.15 **furnish, supply, provide, afford,** provide for; **accommodate with,** favor with, in-

dulge with; **heap upon,** pour on, shower down upon, **lavish upon.**

.16 **commit, consign, assign, delegate,** relegate, confide, commend, remit, remand, give in charge; **entrust,** trust, give in trust; enfeoff, infeudate.

.17 **endow,** invest, vest; endow with, favor with, bless with, grace with, vest with; **settle on** or **upon; dower.**

.18 **bequeath, will,** will and bequeath, **leave, devise, will to,** hand down, hand on, pass on, transmit; **make a will,** draw up a will, execute a will, make a bequest, write one's last will and testament, write into one's will; add a codicil; entail.

.19 **subsidize, finance,** fund; **aid, assist, support, help,** pay the bills, pick up the check or tab [informal]; pension, pension off.

.20 **thrust upon, force upon, press upon,** push upon, obtrude on, ram or cram down one's throat.

.21 **give away,** dispose of, part with, sacrifice, spare.

.22 ADJS philanthropic, eleemosynary, **charitable** 938.15; **generous** 853.4.

.23 **giveable, presentable, bestowable;** impartable, communicable; bequeathable, devisable; allowable.

.24 **given,** allowed, accorded, granted, vouchsafed, bestowed, etc.; gratuitous 850.5; God-given, providential.

.25 **donative,** contributory; concessive; testate, testamentary; intestate.

.26 **endowed,** dowered, invested; dower, dowry, dotal; subsidiary, stipendiary, pensionary.

.27 ADVS as a gift, gratis, on one, on the house, free; to his heirs, to the heirs of his body, to his heirs and assigns, to hi executors or administrators and assigns.

## 819. RECEIVING

.1 NOUNS **receiving,** receival, **receipt, ge ting, taking; acquisition** 811; derivation assumption, **acceptance;** admission, a mittance; **reception** 306.

.2 **inheritance,** heritance [archaic], **heritag** patrimony, **birthright, legacy, beques** bequeathal; reversion; entail; heirshi **succession,** line of succession, mode succession, law of succession; primoger ture, ultimogeniture, postremogenitu borough-English, coheirship, coparcenar gavelkind; hereditament, corporeal or corporeal hereditament; **heritable; he** loom.

.3 **recipient, receiver,** accepter, getter, tak

acquirer, obtainer, procurer; payee, endorsee; addressee, consignee; holder, trustee; **hearer,** viewer, beholder, audience, auditor, listener, looker, spectator; –ee.

.4 **beneficiary,** allottee, **donee, grantee, patentee; assignee, assign; devisee, legatee,** legatary [archaic]; feoffee; almsman, almswoman; stipendiary; pensioner, pensionary; annuitant; –ee.

.5 **heir,** heritor, inheritor, *heres* [L]; **heiress,** inheritress, inheritrix; coheir, joint heir, fellow heir, coparcener; heir portioner [Scot]; heir expectant; **heir apparent,** apparent heir; **heir presumptive,** presumptive heir; statutory next of kin; legal heir, heir at law, heir general, heir of line *or* heir whatsoever [both Scot]; heir of inventory *or* beneficiary heir [both Scot]; heir of provision [Scot], heir by destination; heir of the body; heir in tail, heir of entail; fideicommissary heir, fiduciary heir; reversioner; remainderman; **successor,** next in line.

.6 VERBS **receive, get, gain, secure,** have, come by, be in receipt of; **obtain, acquire** 811.8–10; **admit, accept, take,** take off one's hands, **take in** 306.10; **assume, take on,** take over; **derive, draw,** draw *or* derive from; have an income of, drag down *or* pull down [both slang]; have coming in, have in prospect, come in for.

.7 **inherit,** heir [dial], **come into,** come in for, come by, step into a fortune; step into the shoes of, succeed to.

.8 **be received, come in,** come to hand, pass *or* fall into one's hands, go into one's pocket, come *or* fall to one, fall to one's share *or* lot; **accrue,** accrue to.

.9 ADJS **receiving,** on the receiving end; **receptive, recipient** 306.16.

10 **received, accepted, admitted, recognized, approved.**

## 820. LENDING

.1 NOUNS **lending, loaning;** moneylending, lending at interest; **advance, advancing, advancement; usury,** loan-sharking *or* shylocking [both slang]; lend-lease.

.2 **loan, lend** [dial], **advance, accommodation;** secured loan, collateral loan; unsecured loan; call loan, call money, demand loan; time loan, time money; term loan, long-term loan, short-term loan; installment loan; clearance loan, day loan, morning loan; selfliquidating loan; bank loan, Wall Street loan; policy loan; foreign loan, external loan.

.3 **lender, loaner;** loan officer; **moneylender,** moneymonger; money broker; banker 836.10; **usurer,** Shylock, loan shark [informal]; **pawnbroker;** mortgagee, mortgage holder.

.4 **lending institution,** savings and loan association, finance company *or* corporation, loan office, mortgage company; **bank** 836.13; **credit union; pawnshop, pawnbroker,** pawnbrokery, **hock shop** [informal], *mont-de-piété* [Fr], sign of the three balls.

.5 VERBS **lend, loan, advance,** accommodate with; loan-shark [slang]; float *or* negotiate a loan; lend-lease, lease-lend.

.6 ADJS **loaned, lent.**

.7 ADVS **on loan,** on security; in advance.

## 821. BORROWING

.1 NOUNS **borrowing,** money-raising; touching *or* hitting *or* hitting-up [all slang]; **pawning, pledging,** hocking [slang]; financing, mortgaging; installment buying, installment plan, hire purchase [Brit]; debt, debtor 840.4.

.2 **adoption, appropriation, taking,** deriving, derivation, assumption; **imitation,** simulation, copying, mocking; borrowed plumes; **plagiarism,** plagiary, pastiche, pasticcio; infringement, pirating.

.3 VERBS **borrow,** borrow the loan of, get on credit *or* trust, get on tick *or* get on the cuff [both informal]; get a loan, float *or* negotiate a loan, go into the money market, **raise money; touch** *or* **hit up** *or* hit one for [all slang]; run into debt 840.6; pawn 772.10.

.4 **adopt, appropriate, take, take on,** take over, assume, make use of, derive from; **imitate, simulate, copy, mock,** steal one's stuff [slang]; **plagiarize,** steal; **pirate,** infringe.

## 822. TAKING

.1 NOUNS **taking, possession,** taking possession, taking away; **claiming,** staking one's claim; **acquisition** 811; **reception** 819.1; theft 824.

.2 **seizure, grab,** grabbing, snatching, snatch, –lepsy; **kidnapping, abduction,** forcible seizure; power grab, coup, *coup d'état* [Fr], seizure of power; hold 813.2; **catch,** catching; **capture,** collaring [informal], nabbing [slang]; **apprehension,** prehension; **arrest,** arrestation, taking into custody; picking up *or* taking in *or* running in [all informal]; dragnet.

.3 **sexual possession,** taking; sexual assault,

ravishment, rape, violation; defloration, deflowerment, devirgination.

.4 **appropriation, taking over, takeover** [informal], **adoption, assumption, usurpation,** arrogation; requisition, indent [Brit]; preoccupation, prepossession, preemption; **conquest,** occupation, subjugation, enslavement, colonization.

.5 (seizure and appropriation) **attachment, annexation,** annexure [Brit]; **confiscation,** sequestration; impoundment; **commandeering, impressment;** expropriation, nationalization, socialization, communalization, communization, collectivization; levy; distraint, distress; garnishment; execution; eminent domain, angary, right of eminent domain, right of angary.

.6 **deprivation,** deprivement, **privation, divestment, bereavement;** relieving, disburdening, disburdenment; curtailment, abridgment [archaic]; disentitlement.

.7 **dispossession,** disseisin, expropriation; reclaiming, repossessing, **repossession,** foreclosure; **eviction** 310.2; disendowment; **disinheritance,** disherison, disownment.

.8 **extortion, shakedown** [informal], **blackmail,** bloodsucking, vampirism; protection racket; badger game.

.9 **rapacity,** rapaciousness, ravenousness, sharkishness, wolfishness, **predaciousness,** predacity; pillaging, looting 824.5.

.10 **take, catch, bag,** capture, seizure, **haul;** booty 824.11.

.11 **taker;** partaker; **catcher, captor,** capturer.

.12 **extortionist,** extortioner, **blackmailer,** racketeer, shakedown artist [informal], **bloodsucker,** leech, **vampire;** raptor, predator, harpy, **vulture,** shark; profiteer; rackrenter.

.13 VERBS **take,** possess, take possession; **get,** get into one's hold or possession; pocket, palm; draw off, drain off; **claim,** stake one's claim, enforce one's claim; partake; **acquire** 811.8–11; **receive** 819.6; **steal** 824.13–19.

.14 **seize,** take or get hold of, **lay hold of,** catch or grab hold of, glom on to [slang], **lay hands on,** lay one's hands on, clap hands on [informal], get into one's grasp or clutches; get one's fingers or hands on, get between one's finger and thumb; **grab, grasp, grip,** gripe [archaic], **grapple,** snatch, nip, nail [slang], **clutch,** claw, clinch, clench; **clasp, hug, embrace;** snap up, nip up, whip up, catch up; pillage, loot 824.16; take by assault or storm; **kidnap, abduct,** carry off; shanghai; take by the throat, throttle.

.15 **possess sexually,** take; **rape, ravish,** violate, assault sexually, lay violent hands on; deflower, deflorate, devirginate.

.16 **seize on** or **upon,** fasten upon; spring or pounce upon, jump [informal], swoop down upon; **catch at, snatch at,** snap at, jump at, make a grab for, scramble for.

.17 **catch, take,** land or nail [both informal], hook, **snag, snare,** sniggle, spear, harpoon; ensnare, enmesh, entangle, tangle, foul, tangle up with; **net,** mesh; **bag,** sack; **trap,** entrap; lasso, rope, noose.

.18 **capture, apprehend, collar** [informal], **nab** [slang], grab [informal], lay by the heels, take prisoner; **arrest,** place or put under arrest, take into custody; pick up or take in or run in [all informal].

.19 **appropriate, adopt, assume, usurp,** arrogate, accroach; requisition, indent [Brit]; **take possession of,** possess oneself of, take for oneself, arrogate to oneself, take up, **take over, help oneself to,** make use of, make one's own, make free with, dip one's hands into; take it all, take all of, hog, monopolize, sit on; preoccupy, prepossess, preempt; jump a claim; **conquer,** overrun, occupy, subjugate, enslave, colonize; squat on.

.20 (seize and appropriate) **attach, annex; confiscate,** sequester, sequestrate, impound; **commandeer,** press, **impress;** expropriate, nationalize, socialize, communalize, communize, collectivize; exercise the right of eminent domain, exercise the right of angary; levy, distrain, replevy, replevin; garnishee, garnish.

.21 **take from,** take away from, **deprive of,** relieve one of, disburden one of, lighten one of, ease one of; **deprive, bereave, divest;** tap, milk, mine, drain, bleed, curtail, abridge [archaic]; cut off; disentitle.

.22 **wrest,** wring, wrench, **rend,** rip; **extort,** exact, squeeze, screw, **shake down** [informal], **blackmail,** levy blackmail, badger or play the badger game [both slang]; **force from, wrest from, wrench from, wring from, tear from, rip from, rend from,** snatch from, pry loose from.

.23 **dispossess,** disseise, expropriate, foreclose; **evict** 310.15; disendow; **disinherit,** disherison, **disown,** cut out of one's will, **cut off,** cut off with a shilling, cut off without a cent.

.24 **strip,** strip bare or clean, **fleece** [informal], **shear,** denude, skin or pluck [both slang], flay, **despoil, divest,** pick clean, pick the bones of; deplume, displume, **milk; bleed, bleed white;** exhaust, drain dry, suck dry; **impoverish**, eat out of house and home.

.25 ADJS **taking, catching**; privative, deprivative; confiscatory, annexational, expropriatory; **thievish** 824.20,21.

.26 **rapacious, ravenous**, ravening, vulturous, vulturine, sharkish, **wolfish**, lupine, predacious, **predatory**, raptorial; vampirish, **bloodsucking**, parasitic; **extortionate; grasping**, grabby [slang]; all-devouring, all-engulfing.

## 823. RESTITUTION

.1 NOUNS **restitution, restoration**, restoring, giving back, sending back, **return**; reddition [archaic]; extradition, rendition; repatriation; recommitment, remandment, remand; remitter.

.2 **reparation, recompense**, paying back, squaring [informal], repayment, reimbursement, refund, **compensation, indemnification**, retribution, **atonement**, redress, satisfaction, **amends**, making good, **requital.**

.3 **recovery**, regainment; **retrieval**, retrieve; **recuperation**, recoup, recoupment; **retake**, retaking, recapture; **repossession**, resumption, reoccupation; **reclamation**, reclaiming, revindication; **redemption**, ransom, salvage, trover; replevin, replevy; revival, restoration 694.

.4 VERBS **restore, return, give back, take back**, bring back, put back; remit, send back; repatriate; extradite; recommit, remand.

.5 **make restitution**, make reparation, **make amends**, make good, make up for, atone, give satisfaction, redress, **recompense**, pay back, square [informal], repay, reimburse, refund, **compensate, requite**, indemnify, make it up to; pay damages, pay reparations; pay conscience money.

.6 **recover, regain**, retrieve, recuperate, **recoup, get back**, come by one's own; **redeem**, ransom; **reclaim**, revindicate; **repossess**, resume, reoccupy; **retake**, recapture, take back; replevin, replevy; revive, renovate, restore 694.11–18.

.7 ADJS **restitutive**, restitutory, **restorative**; compensatory, indemnificatory, retributive, reparative; reversionary, reversional, revertible; redeeming, redemptive, redemptional.

8 ADVS **in restitution**, in reparation, in recompense, in compensation, in retribution, in requital, in amends, in atonement, to atone for.

## 824. THEFT

.1 NOUNS **theft, thievery**, stealage, **stealing**, thieving, **purloining**, klept(o)–; swiping or lifting or snatching or snitching or pinching [all slang]; conveyance [archaic], **appropriation**, conversion, liberation [slang], annexation [informal]; **pilfering**, pilferage, **filching**, scrounging [informal], moonlight requisition [informal]; abstraction; sneak thievery; shoplifting, boosting [slang]; poaching; **graft; embezzlement** 667.1; **fraud, swindle** 618.8.

.2 **larceny**, petit or petty larceny, petty theft, grand larceny, grand theft, simple larceny, mixed or aggravated larceny.

.3 **robbery**, robbing; bank robbery; banditry, **highway robbery**; armed robbery, **holdup**, heist or stickup [both slang], holdup or stickup job [slang]; assault and robbery, **mugging** [slang]; purse snatching; **pocket picking; hijacking** [informal]; asportation; cattle stealing, **cattle rustling** or cattle lifting [both informal]; **extortion** 822.8.

.4 **burglary**, burglarizing, housebreaking, **breaking and entering**, break and entry, break-in, unlawful entry; second-story work [slang]; safebreaking, **safecracking** or safeblowing [both informal].

.5 **plundering, pillaging, looting, sacking**, freebooting, ransacking, rifling, spoiling, **despoliation**, despoilment, despoiling; rapine, spoliation, depredation, direption [archaic], **raiding**, reiving [Scot], ravage, ravaging, ravagement, rape, ravishment; **pillage, plunder**, sack; brigandage, brigandism, banditry; **marauding**, foraging; raid, foray, razzia.

.6 **piracy, buccaneering, privateering, freebooting**; letters of marque, letters of marque and reprisal; air piracy, airplane hijacking, skyjacking.

.7 **plagiarism**, plagiarizing, plagiary, **piracy**, literary piracy, appropriation, borrowing, cribbing; infringement of copyright; autoplagiarism.

.8 **abduction, kidnapping; shanghaiing**, impressment, crimping.

.9 **grave-robbing**, body-snatching [informal], resurrectionism.

.10 **theft, steal**, grab, filch, pinch or lift [both slang]; rip-off [slang]; **heist** or **job** or caper [all slang]; robbery, burglary, etc.

.11 **booty**, spoil, **spoils, loot, swag** [slang], illgotten gains, **plunder**, prize, haul, take, pickings, stealings, stolen goods, hot goods or items [slang]; **boodle** or squeeze or **graft** [all informal]; perquisite, perks

[Brit informal], pork barrel, spoils of office, public trough; till, public till; blackmail.

.12 **thievishness,** larcenousness, taking ways [slang], light fingers, sticky fingers; kleptomania, bibliokleptomania.

.13 VERBS **steal, thieve, purloin, appropriate,** annex or borrow [both informal], **take,** snatch, palm, bag [informal], **make off with,** walk off with, run off or away with, abstract, disregard the distinction between *meum* and *tuum;* **lift** or hook or crib or **cop** or **pinch** or nip or snitch or snare [all slang], have one's hand in the till; **pilfer, swipe** [slang], **filch,** scrounge [informal]; shoplift, boost [slang]; poach; rustle; embezzle 667.4; defraud, swindle 618.17; extort 822.22.

.14 **rob,** commit robbery; pick one's pockets; hold up, stick up [informal]; mug [slang]; hijack [informal]; heist or knock over [both slang], rip off [slang].

.15 **burglarize,** burgle [informal], commit burglary, crack a crib [slang]; crack or blow a safe [informal].

.16 **plunder, pillage, loot, sack,** ransack, rifle, freeboot, spoil, spoliate, despoil, depredate, prey on or upon, **raid,** reive [Scot], ravage, ravish, raven, sweep, gut; **fleece** 822.24; maraud, foray, forage.

.17 **pirate,** buccaneer, privateer, freeboot.

.18 **plagiarize, pirate,** borrow or crib [both informal], appropriate; **pick one's brains;** infringe a copyright.

.19 **abduct,** abduce, spirit away, **carry off** or **away,** run off or away with; **kidnap,** snatch [slang], hold for ransom; skyjack; **shanghai,** impress.

.20 ADJS **thievish, thieving, larcenous, lightfingered, sticky-fingered;** kleptomaniac(al), burglarious; brigandish, piratic(al), piratelike; fraudulent 618.20.

.21 **plunderous, plundering, looting,** pillaging, ravaging, marauding, spoliatory; predatory, predacious.

.22 **stolen,** pilfered, purloined; pirated, plagiarized; hot [informal].

## 825. THIEF

.1 NOUNS **thief, robber,** stealer, purloiner, lifter [slang], *ganef* [Yid], **crook** [informal]; larcenist, larcener; **pilferer, filcher,** petty thief, chicken thief, scrounger [slang]; sneak thief, prowler; shoplifter, booster [slang]; poacher; **grafter,** petty grafter; jewel thief; **swindler,** con man 619.3,4; land pirate, land shark, land-grabber; grave robber, body snatcher, resur-

rectionist, ghoul; embezzler, peculator, white-collar thief; den of thieves.

.2 **pickpocket,** cutpurse, fingersmith or dip [both slang]; mobsman or swell-mobsman [both Brit]; **purse snatcher;** light-fingered gentry.

.3 **burglar,** yegg or cracksman [both slang]; housebreaker, cat burglar, cat man, second-story thief or worker; **safecracker,** safebreaker, safeblower; pete blower or pete man or peterman [all slang].

.4 **bandit, brigand,** dacoit; **gangster** [informal], mobsman, mobster, racketeer; **thug, hoodlum** 943.4.

.5 **robber, holdup man** or stickup man [both informal]; highwayman, highway robber, footpad, road agent, bushranger [Austral]; mugger [slang], sandbagger; train robber; bank robber, **hijacker** [informal].

.6 **plunderer, pillager, looter, marauder,** rifler, sacker, spoiler, despoiler, spoliator, depredator, **raider,** moss-trooper, freebooter, rapparee, reiver [Scot], forayer, forager, ravisher, ravager; wrecker.

.7 **pirate, corsair, buccaneer, privateer,** sea rover, rover, picaroon; viking, sea king; Blackbeard (Edward Teach), Captain Kidd, Jean Lafitte, Henry Morgan; Captain Hook [J. M. Barrie], Long John Silver [Stevenson]; air pirate, airplane hijacker, skyjacker.

.8 cattle thief, abactor, rustler or **cattle rustler** [both informal].

.9 **plagiarist,** plagiarizer, cribber [informal], **pirate,** literary pirate, copyright infringer.

.10 **abductor, kidnapper; shanghaier,** crimp, crimper.

.11 (famous thieves) Barabbas, Robin Hood, Jesse James, Clyde Barrow, John Dillinger, Claude Duval, Jack Sheppard Willie Sutton, Dick Turpin, Jonathan Wild; Autolycus, Macheath [John Gay] Thief of Baghdad, Jean Valjean [Hugo] Jimmy Valentine [O. Henry], Raffles [E W. Hornung], Bill Sikes [Dickens].

## 826. ILLICIT BUSINESS

.1 NOUNS illicit business, illegitimate business, illegal operations, illegal commerce or traffic, shady dealings, **racket** [informal]; **the rackets** [informal], the syndicate, **organized crime, Mafia, Cosa Nostra; black market,** gray market; narcotics traffic; prostitution, traffic in women, white slavery; usury, loan-sharking [slang] protection racket; bootlegging, moonshining [informal]; gambling 515.7.

.2 **smuggling,** contrabandage, contraband; narcotics smuggling, dope smuggling [slang], jewel smuggling, cigarette smuggling; gunrunning, rumrunning.

.3 **contraband,** smuggled goods; narcotics, drugs, dope [slang], jewels, cigarettes; bootleg liquor 996.17; stolen goods *or* property, hot goods *or* items [slang].

.4 **racketeer;** Mafioso; **black marketeer,** gray marketeer; **bootlegger,** moonshiner [informal]; **pusher** *or* **dealer** [both informal], narcotics *or* dope *or* drug pusher [informal].

.5 **smuggler,** contrabandist, runner; gunrunner, rumrunner.

.6 **fence,** receiver, **receiver of stolen goods,** swagman *or* swagsman [both slang].

.7 VERBS (deal in illicit goods) push *or* shove [both slang]; **sell under the counter; black-market,** black-marketeer; bootleg, moonshine [informal]; fence [informal].

.8 **smuggle,** run, sneak.

## 827. COMMERCE, ECONOMICS

.1 NOUNS **commerce, trade, traffic,** truck, intercourse, **dealing, dealings; business,** business dealings *or* affairs *or* relations, commercial affairs *or* relations; the business world, the world of trade *or* commerce, the marketplace; merchantry, mercantile business; **market,** marketing, state of the market, buyers' market, sellers' market; **industry** 716.4; big business, small business; fair trade, free trade, reciprocal trade, unilateral trade, multilateral trade; balance of trade; restraint of trade.

.2 **trade, trading, doing business, trafficking;** barter, bartering, **exchange,** interchange, swapping [informal]; give-and-take, horse trading [informal], **dealing,** wheeling and dealing [informal]; **buying and selling; wholesaling,** jobbing; brokerage, agency; **retailing,** merchandising 829.2.

.3 **negotiation, bargaining, haggling,** higgling, **dickering, chaffering,** chaffer, haggle; hacking out *or* working out *or* hammering out a deal, coming to terms; collective bargaining, package bargaining, pattern bargaining.

.4 **transaction,** business *or* commercial transaction, **deal,** business deal, negotiation [archaic], operation, turn; package deal.

.5 **bargain, deal** [informal], dicker; **trade, swap** [informal]; horse trade [informal]; trade-in; blind bargain, pig in a poke; hard bargain.

.6 **custom,** patronage, trade; **goodwill,** repute, good name.

.7 **economy, economic system,** national economy, world economy, local economy, town economy, urban economy, village economy, farm economy, rural economy, handicraft economy, industrial economy, mercantile economy, barter economy, diversified economy, consumer economy, war economy, planned economy, collectivized economy, capitalist *or* capitalistic economy, free-enterprise *or* private-enterprise economy, *laissez-faire* economy, socialist *or* socialistic economy; hot *or* overheated economy; healthy *or* sound economy; **gross national product, GNP.**

.8 **standard of living,** standard of life, standard of comfort; real wages, take-home pay *or* take-home; **cost of living;** cost-of-living index, consumer price index.

.9 **business cycle, economic cycle,** business fluctuations; peak, peaking; low, bottoming out [informal]; prosperity, boom [informal]; crisis, recession, **depression,** slowdown, cooling off, slump *or* bust [both informal], downturn; upturn, expanding economy, recovery; **growth,** economic growth, high growth rate, expansion, market expansion, economic expansion.

.10 **economics,** eco *or* econ [both informal], economic science, the dismal science; political economy; dynamic economics; theoretical economics, plutology; classical economics; Keynesian economics, Keynesianism; econometrics; economism, economic determinism; economic man.

.11 **economist,** economic expert *or* authority; political economist.

.12 **commercialism,** mercantilism; industrialism; Mercury, Hermes.

.13 **commercialization;** industrialization.

.14 VERBS **trade, deal, traffic, truck, buy and sell, do business; barter; exchange,** change, interchange, give in exchange, take in exchange, **swap** [informal], switch; swap horses *or* horse-trade [both informal]; trade off; trade in; trade sight unseen, make a blind bargain, sell a pig in a poke; **ply one's trade** 656.12.

.15 **deal in, trade in, traffic in, handle,** carry, be in; market, merchandise, **sell,** retail, wholesale, job.

.16 **trade with, deal with, traffic with, do business with,** have dealings with, have truck with, transact business with; frequent as a customer, shop at, trade at, **patronize,** take one's business *or* trade to;

open an account with, have an account with.

.17 **bargain, drive a bargain, negotiate, haggle,** higgle, chaffer, huckster, **dicker,** hack out *or* work out *or* hammer out a deal; **bid,** bid for, cheapen, beat down, jew down [derog]; underbid, outbid; drive a hard bargain.

.18 **strike a bargain,** make a bargain, make a dicker, **make a deal,** get oneself a deal, put through a deal, shake hands, shake on it [informal]; bargain for, agree to; **come to terms** 521.10; be a bargain, be a go *or* be a deal [both informal], be on [slang].

.19 put on a business basis *or* footing, make businesslike; commercialize; industrialize.

.20 (adjust the economy) cool *or* cool off the economy; heat *or* heat up the economy.

.21 ADJS **commercial, business, trade,** trading, **mercantile,** merchant; commercialistic, mercantilistic; industrial; wholesale, retail.

.22 **economic;** socio-economic, politico-economic(al); ec(o)– *or* oec(o)– *or* oik(o)–.

## 828. PURCHASE

.1 NOUNS **purchase, buy,** emption; **buying, purchasing; shopping, marketing;** window-shopping; impulse buying; shopping spree; repurchase, rebuying; mail-order buying, catalog buying; installment buying, hire purchase [Brit]; buying up, cornering, coemption [archaic]; buying power, purchasing power; consumer sovereignty, consumer power, consumerism; money illusion.

.2 emption, right of emption, right of sole emption; **option,** first option, **first refusal,** refusal, preemption, right of preemption, prior right of purchase.

.3 **clientele,** clientage, **patronage, custom,** trade, carriage trade; **market,** public, purchasing public; urban market, rural market, youth market, suburban market, etc.

.4 **customer, client; patron,** patronizer [informal], regular customer *or* buyer, regular; **prospect;** mark *or* sucker [both slang].

.5 **buyer,** purchaser, emptor, **consumer,** vendee; **shopper,** marketer; window-shopper, browser; purchasing agent, customer agent.

.6 **by-bidder,** decoy, come-on man *or* shill [both slang].

.7 VERBS **purchase, buy,** procure, make *or* complete a purchase, make a buy, make a deal for, blow oneself to [slang]; **buy up,** regrate, **corner,** monopolize, engross; buy

out; buy off; buy in, buy into, buy a piece of; repurchase, rebuy, buy back; buy on credit, buy on the installment plan.

.8 **shop, market, go shopping,** go marketing; window-shop, browse.

.9 **bid,** make a bid, offer, offer to buy, make an offer; give the asking price; by-bid, shill [slang]; bid up; bid in.

.10 ADJS **purchasing, buying,** in the market; cliental.

.11 **bought,** store-bought, boughten *or* store-boughten [both dial], purchased.

## 829. SALE

.1 NOUNS **sale; wholesale, retail; market, demand,** outlet; buyers' market, sellers' market; mass market; conditional sale; tie-in sale, tie-in; turnover; bill of sale.

.2 **selling, merchandising, marketing;** wholesaling, jobbing; **retailing;** mail-order selling, direct-mail selling, catalog selling; **vending, peddling, hawking, huckstering;** market *or* marketing research, consumer research, consumer preference study, consumer survey; sales campaign, promotion, sales promotion; **salesmanship,** high-pressure salesmanship, hard sell [informal], low-pressure salesmanship, soft sell [informal]; sellout.

.3 **sale,** closing-out sale, going-out-of-business sale, inventory-clearance sale, distress sale, fire sale; bazaar; rummage sale, white elephant sale, garage sale, flea market; tax sale.

.4 **auction,** auction sale, vendue, outcry, sale at *or* by auction, sale to the highest bidder; Dutch auction; **auction block, block.**

.5 **sales talk, sales pitch,** patter; **pitch** *or* spiel *or* ballyhoo [all slang].

.6 **sales resistance,** consumer *or* buyer resistance.

.7 **salability,** salableness, merchandisability, **marketability,** vendibility.

.8 VERBS **sell, merchandise, market,** move, turn over, sell off, make *or* effect a sale; convert into cash, turn into money; **sell out,** close out; sell up [Brit]; **retail,** sell retail, sell over the counter; **wholesale,** sell wholesale, job, be jobber *or* wholesaler for; dump, unload, flood the market with; sacrifice, sell at a sacrifice *or* loss; resell, sell over; undersell, undercut, cut under; sell short; sell on consignment.

.9 **vend,** dispense, **peddle, hawk, huckster.**

.10 **put up for sale,** put up, ask bids *or* offers for, offer for sale, offer at a bargain.

.11 **auction, auction off, auctioneer,** sell a

auction, sell by auction, put up for auction, **put on the block**, bring under the hammer; knock down, sell to the highest bidder.

.12 **be sold, sell,** bring, realize, sell for.

.13 ADJS **sales,** selling, market, **marketing, merchandising, retail,** retailing, wholesale, wholesaling.

.14 **salable, marketable,** retailable, merchandisable, merchantable, vendible; in demand.

.15 **unsalable,** nonsalable, **unmarketable;** on one's hands, on the shelves, not moving, not turning over, unbought, unsold.

.16 ADVS **for sale,** to sell, up for sale, in or on the market, in the marts of trade; at a bargain, marked down.

.17 **at auction,** at outcry, at public auction or outcry, by auction, **on the block,** under the hammer.

## 830. BUSINESSMAN, MERCHANT

.1 NOUNS **businessman,** businesswoman; enterpriser, entrepreneur, man of commerce; small or little businessman; big businessman, magnate, tycoon [informal], baron, king, top executive, business leader; director, manager 748.1; big boss; **industrialist,** captain of industry; banker, financier 836.9,10.

.2 **merchant,** merchandiser, marketer, **trader,** trafficker, **dealer,** monger, chandler; **tradesman,** tradeswoman; **storekeeper, shopkeeper;** regrater; **wholesaler,** jobber, middleman; importer, exporter; **distributor; retailer,** retail merchant, retail dealer or seller.

.3 (merchants) grocer, groceryman; greengrocer; fruiterer; butcher; baker; poulterer; fishmonger, fishwife; ironmonger [Brit], hardwareman; drysalter [Brit]; perfumer; haberdasher, furnisher, clothing merchant; draper; shoe or footwear merchant; bookseller, bookdealer; chandler; confectioner; florist; furrier; jeweler; newsdealer; saddler; stationer; tobacconist; wine merchant, vintner, liquor merchant.

.4 **salesman,** seller, salesperson, salesclerk; **saleswoman,** saleslady, salesgirl; **clerk,** shop clerk, store clerk, shop assistant; floorwalker; **agent, sales agent,** selling agent; scalper or ticket scalper [both informal]; sales engineer; sales manager; salespeople, sales force, sales personnel.

.5 **traveling salesman, traveler, commercial traveler,** traveling agent, traveling man or woman, knight of the road, bagman [Brit], drummer; detail man; door-to-door salesman, canvasser.

.6 **vendor, peddler, huckster, hawker,** higgler, cadger [Scot], colporteur, chapman [Brit]; cheap-jack or cheap-john [both informal]; coster or costermonger [both Brit]; sidewalk salesman.

.7 **solicitor,** canvasser; tout, touter, **pitchman, barker, spieler,** ballyhooer, **ballyhoo man** [all informal].

.8 **auctioneer,** auction agent.

.9 **broker,** note broker, bill broker [Brit], discount broker, cotton broker, hotel broker, insurance broker, mortgage broker, diamond broker, furniture broker, ship broker, grain broker; stockbroker 833.10; pawnbroker 820.3; money broker, money changer, cambist; land broker, real estate broker, Realtor, real estate agent, estate agent [Brit].

.10 **ragman,** old-clothesman, rag-and-bone man [Brit]; **junkman,** junk dealer.

.11 **tradesmen, tradespeople,** tradesfolk, **merchantry.**

## 831. MERCHANDISE

.1 NOUNS **merchandise, commodities, wares, goods,** effects, vendibles, **consumer goods,** consumer items, goods for sale; stock, staples, stock-in-trade; inventory; line, line of goods; sideline; job lot; mail-order goods, catalog goods.

.2 **commodity, ware,** vendible, **product, article, item,** article of commerce or merchandise; staple, staple item, standard article; special, feature, leader, lead item, loss leader; seconds; drug, drug on the market.

.3 **dry goods, soft goods;** textiles 378.5,11; yard goods, white goods, linens, napery; men's wear, ladies' wear, children's wear, infants' wear; sportswear, sporting goods; leatherware, leather goods.

.4 **hard goods, durables,** durable goods; fixtures, white goods, appliances 659.4; tools and machinery 348; **hardware,** ironmongery [Brit]; sporting goods, **housewares,** housefurnishings, kitchenware; tableware, dinnerware; flatware, hollow ware; metalware, brassware, copperware, silverware, ironware, tinware; woodenware; glassware; chinaware, earthenware, clayware, stoneware, graniteware; enamelware; ovenware.

.5 **furniture,** furnishings, home furnishings.

.6 **notions, sundries,** novelties, knickknacks, odds and ends; toilet goods, toiletries; cosmetics; giftware.

.7 **groceries**, grocery [Brit], food items, baked goods, packaged goods, canned goods, tinned goods [Brit]; green goods, **produce**, truck.

## 832. MARKET

*(place of trade)*

.1 NOUNS **market, mart, store, shop**, salon, boutique, wareroom, emporium, house, establishment, *magasin* [Fr]; **retail store; wholesale house, discount store, discount house**, warehouse, mail-order house; **general store**, country store; **department store; co-op** [informal], cooperative; **variety store**, variety shop, **dime store; ten-cent store** *or* five-and-ten *or* five-and-dime [all informal]; chain store; concession; **trading post**, post; **supermarket**; countinghouse.

.2 **marketplace, mart, market, open market,** market overt; **shopping center**, shopping plaza, plaza, shopping mall, shopping *or* shop *or* commercial complex; emporium, rialto; staple; **bazaar, fair,** trade fair, show, auto show, boat show, etc., exposition; flea market, flea fair, street market, *marché aux puces* [Fr].

.3 **booth, stall, stand**; newsstand, kiosk, news kiosk.

.4 (stores) hardware store, ironmongery [Brit]; stationery store, stationers; toy shop; hobby shop; novelty shop; confectionery, candy store, sweet shop; drugstore, pharmacy, apothecary, chemist *or* chemist's shop [both Brit]; tobacco store, cigar store, tobacconists, smoke shop; secondhand store, secondhand shop, thrift shop; antique store; gift shop; bookstore 605.18; trimming store, dry goods store; clothing store, clothiers, sweater shop, dress shop, specialty shop, haberdashery, men's-wear shop, ladies'-wear shop, children's shop; florists; fur salon; furniture store; jewelry store, jewelers; leather goods store, luggage shop; saddlery; shoe store, bootery; hat shop, milliners; sporting goods store; liquor store, package store; automobile showroom, used-car lot; schlock shop *or* schlock house [both slang].

.5 **grocery**, grocery store, food store, food shop; **supermarket**; *bodega* [Sp], superette, groceteria; delicatessen, deli [informal], appetizing store; health food store; vegetable store *or* market, greengrocery, fruit stand; butcher shop, meat market,

pork store, *charcuterie* [Fr]; bakery, bakeshop; dairy, creamery.

.6 **commissary, canteen, post exchange, PX.**

.7 **gas station, filling station, service station.**

.8 **vending machine**, vendor, coin machine, coin-operated machine, slot machine, **automat.**

.9 **salesroom**, wareroom; showroom; auction room.

.10 **counter**, shopboard [archaic]; notions counter; showcase; peddler's cart, pushcart.

## 833. STOCK MARKET

.1 NOUNS **stock market, the market, Wall Street**; ticker market; open market, competitive market; steady market, strong market, hard *or* stiff market; unsteady market, spotty market; weak market; long market; top-heavy market; market index, stock price index, Dow-Jones Industrial Average.

.2 **active market**, brisk market, lively market.

.3 **inactive market**, slow market, stagnant market, flat market, tired market, sick market; investors on the sidelines.

.4 **rising market**, booming market, buoyant market; **bull market**, bullish market.

.5 **declining market**, sagging market, retreating market, off market, soft market; **bear market**, bearish market; **slump**, sag; break, break in the market; **crash**, smash.

.6 **rigged market**, manipulated market, pegged market, put-up market.

.7 **stock exchange, exchange**, Wall Street, 'change [Brit], **stock market**, bourse, **board;** the Exchange, New York Stock Exchange, the Big Board; American Stock Exchange, Amex, curb, curb market, curb exchange; over-the-counter market, telephone market, outside market; third market; exchange floor; commodity exchange, pit, corn pit, wheat pit, etc.; quotation board; **ticker**, stock ticker; ticker tape.

.8 **financial district**, Wall Street, the Street; Lombard Street.

.9 **stockbrokerage**, brokerage, brokerage house, brokerage office; wire house; bucket shop, boiler room [both slang].

.10 **stockbroker**, sharebroker [Brit], **broker** jobber, stockjobber, dealer, stock dealer Wall Streeter; stock-exchange broker *agent de bourse* [Fr]; floor broker, floor trader, floorman, specialist; pit man; curb broker; odd-lot dealer; two-dollar broker broker's agent, customer's broker *or* cus tomer's man, registered representative; bond crowd.

.11 **speculator,** adventurer, operator; big operator, smart operator; **plunger,** gunslinger; scalper; stag [Brit]; lame duck; margin purchaser.

.12 **bear,** short, short seller; shorts, short interest, short side; short account, bear account.

.13 **bull,** long, longs, long interest, long side; long account, bull account.

.14 **stockholder,** stockowner, **shareholder;** bondholder, coupon clipper [slang]; stockholder of record.

.15 **stock company,** joint-stock company; issuing company; stock insurance company.

.16 **trust,** investment company; investment trust, holding company; closed-end investment company, closed-end fund; open-end fund, mutual fund; load fund, no-load fund; growth fund, income fund, dual purpose fund.

.17 **pool,** bear pool, bull pool, blind pool.

.18 **stockbroking,** brokerage, stockbrokerage, jobbing, stockjobbing, stockjobbery, stock dealing; bucketing, legal bucketing.

.19 **speculation,** agiotage; stockjobbing, stockjobbery; **venture,** flutter; flier, plunge; scalping; liquidation, profit taking; arbitrage; buying in, covering shorts; short sale; spot sale; round trade or transaction, turn; risk or venture capital, equity capital.

.20 **manipulation, rigging; raid,** bear raid, bull raid; **corner,** corner in, corner on the market, monopoly; washing, washed or wash sale.

.21 **option,** stock option, right, **put, call,** put and call, right of put and call; straddle, spread; strip; strap.

.22 **panic,** bear panic, rich man's panic.

.23 VERBS **speculate,** venture, operate, **play the market,** buy or sell or deal in futures; **plunge,** take a flier; scalp; bucket, bucketshop; stag or stag the market [both Brit]; trade on margin; pyramid; be long, go long, be long of the market, be on the long side of the market; be short, be short of the market, be on the short side of the market; margin up, apply or deposit margin; wait out the market, hold on; be caught short, miss the market, overstay the market; scoop the market, make a scoop or killing.

.24 **sell,** convert, liquidate; throw on the market, dump, unload; **sell short,** go short, make a short sale; cover one's short, fulfill a short sale; make delivery, clear the trade; close out, sell out, terminate the account.

.25 **manipulate the market, rig the market;** bear, **bear the market;** bull, **bull the market;** raid the market; hold or peg the market; whipsaw; wash sales.

.26 **corner,** get a corner on, **corner the market;** monopolize, engross; buy up, absorb.

## 834. SECURITIES

.1 NOUNS **securities, stocks and bonds,** investment securities; active securities, marketable securities; obsolete securities; digested securities, undigested securities; gilt-edged securities; speculative securities, cats and dogs [slang]; international securities, foreign securities, American Depository Receipts; government securities, governments, treasury bill, treasury note, treasury certificate, treasury bond, short-term note; municipal securities; corporation securities; outstanding securities; registered securities, unregistered securities; senior securities, junior securities; listed securities; unlisted securities, outside securities, over-the-counter securities; negotiable securities, negotiables; callable securities, subject to call; noncallable securities, not subject to call; convertible securities, convertibles; stamped securities; margined securities; legal securities; certificate of deposit; banker's acceptance; note; warrant; futures contract; portfolio.

.2 **stock, stocks,** shares [Brit], equity, equities, equity security, corporate stock, capital stock; authorized capital stock, issued capital stock, unissued capital stock; floating stock; treasury stock; active stock, inactive stock; **preferred stock,** preference stock [Brit], cumulative preferred stock, convertible preferred stock, cumulative convertible preferred stock, participating preferred stock; **common stock,** ordinary shares [Brit]; voting stock; nonvoting stock, voting-right certificate; assessable stock; nonassessable stock; no-par stock; letter stock; guaranteed stock; deferred stock; ten-share unit stock; quarter stock, eighth stock; high-grade stock, quality stock, seasoned stock, standard stock, blue chip stock, blue chip, pale blue chip; fancies [slang]; penny stock; speculative stock; growth stock; income stock; cyclical stock; defensive stock, protective stock; specialty stock; hot issue, glamour issue, high-flier [informal]; new issue; special situation stock; long stock, short stock; borrowed stock, loaned stock; hypothecated stock; watered stock; industrials, rails, utilities, steels, coppers, etc.; stock split, split; reverse split; stock list; stock ledger, share ledger [Brit].

.3 **share, lot;** preference share; dummy share; holding, holdings, stockholding, stockholdings; block; round lot, full lot, even lot, board lot; odd lot, fractional lot.

.4 **bond, debenture;** negotiable bond, nonnegotiable bond; long-term bond, short-term bond; government bond; savings bond, Series E bond, appreciation bond, Series H bond, current income bond; war bond, defense bond, Liberty bond; treasury bond; Federal Agency bond, Fannie Mae, Ginnie Mae; municipal bond, tax-exempt bond, corporation stock [Brit], state bond, revenue bond, general obligation bond, turnpike bond, bond anticipation note, tax anticipation note; corporate bond; bearer bond, bearer certificate, coupon bond; registered bond, registered certificate; interchangeable bond; callable bond, redeemable bond; noncallable bond; optional bond; convertible bond, convertible debenture; participating bond; installment bond; serial bond; perpetual bond, annuity bond; consolidated annuities, consolidated stock, consols; tax-free bond; definitive bond; guaranteed bond; interim bond; deferred bond, extended bond; refunding bond; assented bond; assumed bond; adjustment bond; joint bond; voting bond; income bond; small bond, baby bond; secured bond, unsecured bond; sinking-fund bond; mortgage bond, general mortgage bond, trustee mortgage bond, purchase money bond, first mortgage bond, firsts [pl], second mortgage bond, seconds [pl]; collateral trust bond; equipment bond, equipment note, equipment trust bond, equipment trust certificate, equipment trust; high-grade bond; premium bond; par bond; discount bond, deep-discount bond; indenture, trust indenture; nominal rate, coupon rate, current yield, yield to maturity.

.5 **stock certificate,** certificate of stock; street certificate; interim certificate; **coupon.**

.6 **issue,** issuance; **flotation;** stock issue, secondary issue; bond issue.

.7 **dividend;** regular dividend; extra dividend, special dividend, plum or melon

[both slang]; cumulative dividend, accumulated dividends, accrued dividends; interim dividend; cash dividend; stock dividend; optional dividend; scrip dividend; liquidating dividend; phony dividend; **interest** 840.3.

.8 **assessment,** Irish dividend.

.9 **price, quotation;** bid-and-asked prices, bid price, asked or asking or offering price; actual or delivery or settling price, put price, call price; opening price, closing price; high, low; market price, quoted price, flash price; issue price; fixed price; parity; **par,** issue par; par value, nominal value, face value; stated value; book value; market value; bearish prices, bullish prices; swings, fluctuations; flurry, flutter; rally, decline.

.10 **margin;** thin margin, shoestring margin; exhaust price.

.11 (commodities) spots, spot grain, etc.; futures, future grain, etc.

.12 VERBS **issue, float,** put on the market; issue stock, go public [informal]; float a bond issue.

.13 **declare a dividend,** cut a melon [slang].

.14 ADVS dividend off, ex dividend; dividend on, cum dividend; coupon off, ex coupon; coupon on, cum coupon; warrants off, ex warrants; warrants on, cum warrants; when issued.

## 835. MONEY

.1 NOUNS **money, currency, legal tender, medium of exchange,** circulating medium, sterling [Brit], **cash,** hard cash, cold cash; specie, coinage, mintage, coin of the realm, gold; **silver;** dollars; pounds, shillings, and pence; **the wherewithal,** the wherewith; lucre, **filthy lucre** [informal], the almighty dollar, pelf, root of all evil, mammon; "the sinews of war" [Libanius], "the sinews of affairs" [Laertius], "the ruling spirit of all things" [Publilius Syrus], "coined liberty" [Dostoyevsky]; **hard currency,** soft currency; fractional currency, postage currency, postal currency; managed currency; necessity money, scrip, emergency money.

.2 [slang or informal terms] **dough, bread, jack, kale,** mazuma, mopus, gelt, gilt, rhino, spondulics, oof, ooftish, wampum, possibles, moolah, boodle, blunt, dinero, **sugar,** brass, tin, rocks, simoleons, shekels, berries, chips, **bucks,** green, green stuff, the needful, grease, ointment, oil of palms, cabbage.

.3 **wampum,** wampumpeag, peag, sewan, roanoke; cowrie.

.4 **specie,** hard money; coin, piece, piece of money, piece of silver or gold; roll of coins, rouleau; **gold piece;** ten-dollar gold piece, eagle; five-dollar gold piece, half eagle; twenty-dollar gold piece, double eagle; guinea, sovereign, pound sovereign, crown, half crown; doubloon; ducat; napoleon, louis d'or; moidore.

.5 **paper money; bill,** dollar bill, etc.; note, negotiable note, legal-tender note; **bank note,** Federal Reserve note; national bank note; government note, treasury note; silver certificate; gold certificate; scrip; fractional note, shinplaster [slang]; fiat money, assignat.

.6 [slang or informal terms] **folding money,** the long green, mint leaves, lettuce, greenbacks, frogskins, skins.

.7 (US denominations) mill; cent, penny, copper, red cent [informal]; five cents, nickel; ten cents, dime; twenty-five cents, quarter, two bits [informal]; fifty cents, half dollar, four bits [informal]; dollar, dollar bill; buck or smacker or frogskin or fish or skin [all slang]; silver dollar, cartwheel or iron man [both slang]; two-dollar bill, two-spot [slang]; five-dollar bill; fiver or five-spot or fin [all slang]; ten-dollar bill; tenner or ten-spot or sawbuck [all slang]; twenty-dollar bill, double sawbuck [slang]; fifty-dollar bill, half a C [slang]; hundred-dollar bill; C or C-note or century [all slang]; five hundred dollars, half grand [slang], five-hundred-dollar bill, half G [slang]; thousand dollars, G or grand [both slang], thousand-dollar bill, G-note or yard [both slang].

.8 (British denominations) mite; farthing; halfpenny or ha'penny, bawbee [Brit informal], mag or meg [both Brit dial]; penny; pence, p; new pence, np; twopence or tuppence; threepence or thrippence, threepenny bit or piece; fourpence, fourpenny, groat; sixpence, tanner [Brit slang], teston; shilling, bob [Brit slang]; florin; half crown, half dollar [Brit informal]; crown, dollar [Brit informal]; pound, quid [slang]; guinea; fiver (£5), tenner (£10), pony (£25), monkey (£500), plum (£100,000), marigold (£1,000,000) [all Brit slang].

.9 (foreign denominations) afghani (Afghanistan), anna, pie or pai (India), azteca (Mexico), baht or tical (Thailand), balboa (Panama), bolivar (Venezuela), cent (Australia, Netherlands, etc.), centavo (Portugal, Argentina, Mexico, etc.), centesimo (Italy, Uruguay); centime (Belgium, France, Switzerland), centimo (Spain, Venezuela, etc.), colón (Costa Rica, El Salvador), conto, cruzeiro (Brazil), cordoba (Nicaragua), dinar (Algeria, Kuwait, Iraq, Iran, Yugoslavia); dirham (Morocco); dollar (Australia, Liberia, Malaysia, etc.), dong (North Vietnam), drachma (Greece); ekpwele (Equatorial Guinea), escudo (Chile, Portugal), florin, guilder, gulden, stiver (Netherlands), forint (Hungary), franc (France, Belgium, Switzerland, Burundi, Cameroon, Central African Republic, Chad, Congo, Dahomey, Gabon, Guinea, Ivory Coast, Luxembourg, Malagasy Republic, Mali, Niger, Rwanda, Senegal, Togo, Upper Volta), gourde (Haiti), groschen (Austria), guaraní (Paraguay), kip (Laos), kopeck, ruble (Russia), koruna (Czechoslovakia), krona (Sweden); krone (Denmark, Norway, Austria), kwacha (Malawi, Zambia), kyat (Burma), lek (Albania), lempira (Honduras), leone (Sierra Leone), leu (Romania), lev (Bulgaria), lilangeni (Swaziland), lira (Italy, Turkey); Mark, Deutschmark, Reichsmark, Pfennig (Germany), markka (Finland), piaster (South Vietnam), milreis, reis (Brazil), ouguiya (Mauritania), peseta (Spain), peso (Argentina, Mexico, etc.), pistareen, piece of eight (Spain), pound (United Kingdom, Cyprus, United Arab Republic, Gambia, Ghana, Ireland, Israel, Lebanon, Malta, New Zealand, Nigeria, Sudan, Syria, Turkey), quetzal (Guatemala), rand (South Africa), rial (Iran), riel (Cambodia), riyal (Saudi Arabia), rupee (India, Pakistan, etc.), rupiah (Indonesia), schilling (Austria), shekel (ancient Near East), shilling (Kenya, Tanzania, Uganda), sol (Peru), sucre (Ecuador), soldo (Italy), sou (France), taka (Bangladesh), tugrik (Mongolia), won (South Korea), yen (Japan), yuan (China), zaïre (Zaïre), zloty (Poland).

.10 **counterfeit,** counterfeit money, phony or bogus money [informal], false or bad money, queer [slang], base coin, green goods [slang]; **forgery,** bad check, rubber check or kite [both slang].

.11 **negotiable instrument** or **paper,** commercial paper, paper, bill; **bill of exchange,** bill of draft; certificate, certificate of deposit, CD; **check,** cheque [Brit]; blank check; bank check, teller's check; treasury check; cashier's check, certified check;

traveler's check or banker's check; letter of credit, commercial letter of credit; **money order, MO**; postal order or post-office order [both Brit]; draft, warrant, voucher, debenture; **promissory note, note, IOU**; note of hand; acceptance, acceptance bill, bank acceptance, trade acceptance; due bill; demand bill, sight bill, demand draft, sight draft; time bill, time draft; exchequer bill or treasury bill [both Brit]; checkbook.

.12 **token, counter, slug; scrip, coupon; check, ticket,** tag; hat check, baggage check.

.13 **sum,** amount of money; round sum, lump sum.

.14 **funds, finances, moneys,** exchequer, purse, budget, pocket; treasure, substance, **assets,** resources, **pecuniary resources, means,** wherewithal, command of money; balance; pool, **fund, kitty** [informal]; checking account, bank account; Swiss bank account, unnumbered or unregistered bank account; reserves, cash reserves; savings, savings account, nest egg [informal]; life savings; bottom dollar [informal].

.15 **capital, fund;** moneyed capital; principal, corpus; circulating capital, floating capital; fixed capital, working capital, equity capital, risk or venture capital; capital structure; capital gains distribution; capitalization.

.16 **money market,** supply of short-term funds; tight money, cheap money; **borrowing** 821; **lending** 820; discounting, note discounting, note shaving, dealing in commercial paper.

.17 **bankroll;** roll or wad [both slang]; shoestring [informal].

.18 **ready money,** the ready [informal], available funds, **cash, money in hand, cash in hand,** balance in hand, immediate resources, liquid assets, cash supply; treasury.

.19 **petty cash, pocket money, pin money,** spending money, **change,** small change.

.20 precious metals; **gold,** yellow stuff [slang]; nugget, gold nugget; **silver, copper, nickel,** coin gold or silver; bullion, ingot, bar.

.21 standard of value, gold standard, silver standard; monometallism, bimetallism; money of account.

.22 (science of coins) **numismatics,** numismatology; numismatist, numismatologist.

.23 monetization; issuance, circulation; re-

monetization; demonetization; revaluation, devaluation.

.24 **coining,** coinage, mintage, striking, stamping; **counterfeiting, forgery;** coinclipping.

.25 **coiner,** minter, mintmaster, moneyer; **counterfeiter, forger;** coin-clipper.

.26 VERBS monetize; **issue, utter, circulate;** remonetize, reissue; demonetize; revalue, devalue, devaluate.

.27 discount, discount notes, deal in commercial paper, shave; borrow 820.3, lend 820.5.

.28 **coin, mint; counterfeit, forge;** utter, pass or shove the queer [slang].

.29 **cash,** cash in [informal], liquidate, convert into cash.

.30 ADJS **monetary, pecuniary,** nummary, **financial;** capital; fiscal; sumptuary; numismatic; sterling.

.31 convertible, liquid, negotiable.

## 836. FINANCE, INVESTMENT

.1 NOUNS **finance, finances, money matters;** world of finance, **high finance,** investment banking, international banking, Wall Street banking, Lombard Street; economics 851.

.2 **financing, funding, backing,** financial backing, **sponsorship, patronization,** support, financial support; **stake or grubstake** [both informal]; subsidy 818.8; provision of capital, capitalization; deficit financing.

.3 **investment, venture, risk,** plunge [informal], speculation; prime investment.

.4 **banking,** money dealing, money changing; investment banking.

.5 **financial condition,** state of the exchequer; **credit rating,** Dun and Bradstreet rating.

.6 **solvency,** soundness, solidity; credit standing; unindebtedness.

.7 **crisis,** financial crisis; dollar crisis, dollar gap.

.8 **financier,** moneyman, **capitalist,** finance capitalist; Wall Streeter; investor; financial expert, economist, authority on money and banking.

.9 **financer, backer,** funder, **sponsor, patron supporter,** angel [slang]; staker or grubstaker [both informal], meal ticket [slang].

.10 **banker, money dealer,** moneymonger, money broker; discounter, note broker, bill broker [Brit]; moneylender 820.3, money changer, cambist; investment banker; bank president, bank manager, bank officer, loan officer, trust officer, banking executive; bank clerk, cashier, teller.

.11 **treasurer**, financial officer, bursar, purser, purse bearer, **cashier**, cashkeeper; accountant, auditor, controller *or* comptroller, bookkeeper; chamberlain, curator, steward, trustee; depositary, depository; receiver, liquidator; **paymaster**; Secretary of the Treasury, Chancellor of the Exchequer.

.12 **treasury**, treasure-house; subtreasury; **depository**, repository; storehouse 660.6; gold depository, Fort Knox; **strongbox, safe**, money chest, **coffer, locker, chest**; piggy bank, penny bank, bank; **vault**, strong room; safe-deposit *or* safety-deposit box *or* vault; cashbox, coin box, cash register, **till**; bursary; exchequer, fisc; public treasury, pork barrel, public crib *or* trough *or* till [informal].

.13 **bank**; **commercial bank, trust company**; national bank, state bank; **savings bank**, mutual savings bank; savings and loan association; central bank, branch bank; Federal Reserve bank, reserve bank, member bank, nonmember bank; land bank, federal land bank, federal intermediate credit bank, federal home loan bank, farm loan bank *or* association; moneyed corporation; investment banking house, investment bank, Wall Street bank, Lombard Street bank; international bank; Bank of England, Old Lady of Threadneedle Street; Bank of France; Swiss bank; World Bank, International Monetary Fund; clearing house.

.14 **purse, wallet, pocketbook, bag, handbag**, porte-monnaie, **billfold**, money belt, money clip, poke [slang], pocket; moneybag; purse strings.

.15 VERBS **finance, back, fund, sponsor, patronize, support**, provide for, capitalize, provide capital *or* money for, pay for, bankroll [informal], angel [slang], put up the money; **stake** *or* **grubstake** [both informal]; subsidize 818.19; set up, set up in business; refinance.

.16 **invest**, place, put, sink; **risk, venture**; make an investment, lay out money, place out *or* put out at interest; reinvest, plow back into [informal]; **invest in, put money in**, sink money in, pour money into, tie up one's money in; buy in *or* into, buy a piece *or* share of; financier; plunge [informal], speculate 833.23.

.17 ADJS **solvent, sound**, substantial, solid,

good, sound as a dollar; **able to pay**, good for, unindebted 841.23.

.18 **insolvent**, unsound, indebted 840.8.

## 837. WEALTH

.1 NOUNS **wealth, riches, opulence** *or* **opulency** 661.2, **luxuriousness** 904.5; richness, wealthiness; **prosperity**, prosperousness, **affluence**, comfortable *or* easy circumstances, independence; **money**, lucre, pelf, gold, mammon; **substance, property, possessions**, material wealth; **assets** 835.14; **fortune, treasure**, handsome fortune; full *or* heavy *or* well-lined *or* bottomless *or* fat *or* bulging purse, moneybags [informal]; *embarras de richesses* [Fr], money to burn [informal]; high income, six-figure income; high tax bracket, upper bracket.

.2 **large sum**, good sum, tidy sum *or* **pretty penny** [both informal], king's ransom, mint, pot *or* potful [both informal]; power *or* mint *or* barrel *or* raft *or* load of money [informal]; heaps of gold, pile *or* wad [both slang]; thousands, millions, cool million.

.3 (rich source) **mine**, mine of wealth, **gold mine**, bonanza, lode, rich lode, mother lode, Eldorado, Golconda, Seven Cities of Cibola; gravy train [informal]; rich uncle.

.4 **the golden touch**, Midas touch; philosophers' stone; Pactolus.

.5 **the rich, the wealthy**, the well to do, the haves [informal]; **plutocracy, timocracy**.

.6 **rich man**, wealthy man, warm man [Brit informal], **moneyed man**, man of wealth, **man of means** *or* **substance**, fat cat [slang], richling, moneybags [informal], Daddy Warbucks [Harold Gray], **nabob**; **capitalist, plutocrat**, bloated plutocrat; **millionaire**, multimillionaire, billionaire; parvenu 919.10.

.7 **Croesus, Midas, Plutus, Dives**, Timon of Athens, Danaë; Rockefeller, Vanderbilt, Whitney, DuPont, Ford, Getty, Rothschild, Onassis, Hughes, Hunt.

.8 VERBS **enrich, richen**.

.9 **grow rich, get rich**, fill *or* line one's pockets, feather one's nest, **make** *or* **coin money**, have a gold mine, have the golden touch, **make a fortune**, make one's pile [slang]; **strike it rich**; come into money; make good, get on in the world, do all right by oneself [informal].

.10 **have money**, command money, **be loaded** [informal], have the wherewithal, have means, have independent means; **afford,** well afford.

.11 **live well,** live high, live high on the hog [informal], **live in clover,** roll *or* wallow in wealth, roll in the lap of luxury; have all the money in the world, have a mint, have money to burn [informal].

.12 worship mammon, worship the golden calf.

.13 ADJS **wealthy, rich, loaded** [informal], warm [Brit informal], **affluent, moneyed,** in the money [informal], in funds *or* cash, **well-to-do,** well-to-do in the world, **well-off, well-situated, well-fixed** [informal], **prosperous,** comfortable, provided for, well provided for, fat, **flush,** flush with *or* of money, abounding in riches, made of money, **rolling in money,** rolling *or* wallowing in wealth, worth a great deal, frightfully rich, disgustingly rich, big-rich [dial], rich as Croesus; **well-heeled** *or* oofy *or* lousy rich *or* filthy rich [all slang]; independent, independently rich, independently wealthy; **luxurious** 904.21; **opulent** 661.7.

## 838. POVERTY

.1 NOUNS **poverty, poorness,** impecuniousness, impecuniosity; **straits,** difficulties, **hardship** 729.1; distress, embarrassment, **embarrassed** *or* **reduced** *or* **straitened circumstances,** tight squeeze, hard pinch, slender *or* narrow means, insolvency, light purse; unprosperousness; broken fortune; genteel poverty; vows of poverty, voluntary poverty.

.2 **indigence, penury, pennilessness,** moneylessness; **pauperism,** pauperization, **impoverishment,** grinding poverty, chronic pauperism; **beggary,** beggarliness, mendicancy; homelessness; **destitution, privation, deprivation; neediness, want,** need, lack, pinch, gripe, necessity, disadvantagedness, necessitousness; **hand-to-mouth existence,** bare subsistence, wolf at the door, bare cupboard, empty purse *or* pocket.

.3 **the poor, the needy, the have-nots** [informal], **the down-and-out,** the disadvantaged, the underprivileged, the distressed; the urban poor, ghetto-dwellers, barrio-dwellers; welfare rolls, welfare clients, welfare families; "wretched of the earth" [E. Pottier]; the other America; the forgotten man, "the forgotten man at the bottom of the economic pyramid" [F. D. Roosevelt]; depressed population, de-

pressed area, chronic poverty area; underdeveloped nation.

.4 **poor man,** poorling, poor devil, down-and-out, **down-and-outer, pauper,** indigent, penniless man, hardcase, starveling; **beggar** 774.8; welfare client; almsman, almswoman, charity case, casual; bankrupt 842.4.

.5 VERBS **be poor,** be hard up [informal], find it hard going, have seen better days, be on one's uppers, be pinched *or* strapped, **be in want,** want, need, lack; **starve,** not know where one's next meal is coming from, **live from hand to mouth,** eke out *or* squeeze out a living; **not have a penny** *or* **sou,** not have a penny to bless oneself with, not have one dollar to rub against another; go on welfare.

.6 **impoverish,** reduce, **pauperize, beggar;** eat out of house and home; **bankrupt** 842.8.

.7 ADJS **poor, ill off,** badly *or* poorly off, **hard up** [informal], **impecunious, unmoneyed; unprosperous;** reduced, in reduced circumstances; **straitened, in straitened circumstances,** narrow, in narrow circumstances, feeling the pinch, strapped, **embarrassed,** distressed, **pinched,** squeezed, put to one's shifts *or* last shifts, at the end of one's rope, on the edge *or* ragged edge [informal], down to bedrock, in Queer Street; short, **short of money** *or* **funds** *or* **cash,** out of pocket; unable to make ends meet, unable to keep the wolf from the door; poor as a church mouse, "poor as Job" [John Gower]; land-poor.

.8 **indigent, poverty-stricken; needy,** necessitous, **in need, in want,** disadvantaged, deprived, underprivileged; **beggared,** beggarly, mendicant; **impoverished, pauperized,** starveling; ghettoized; bereft, bereaved; stripped, fleeced; **down at heels,** down at the heel, on *or* down on one's uppers, out at the heels, out at elbows, in rags; on welfare, on relief, on the dole [Brit].

.9 **destitute, down-and-out,** in the gutter; **penniless,** moneyless, fortuneless, out of funds, **without a sou,** without a penny to bless oneself with, without one dollar to rub against another; insolvent, in the red, **bankrupt** 842.11; homeless; propertyless, landless.

.10 [slang terms] **broke,** busted, **flat, flat broke, stone-broke,** stony, **strapped,** skint [Brit], beat, oofless; down to one's last penny *or* cent.

## 839. FINANCIAL CREDIT

.1 NOUNS **credit, trust,** tick [informal]; borrowing power *or* capacity; commercial credit, cash credit, bank credit, book credit, tax credit, investment credit; line of credit; installment plan, installment credit, consumer credit, hire purchase plan *or* never-never [both Brit]; rating, credit rating, Dun and Bradstreet rating; credit insurance; credit union.

.2 **account,** credit account, charge account; bank account, savings account, checking account; bank balance; expense account.

.3 **credit instrument;** paper credit; **letter of credit,** *lettre de créance* [Fr], circular note; credit slip, deposit slip, certificate of deposit; negotiable instruments 835.11; **credit card,** charge card, charge plate.

.4 **creditor,** creditress; debtee; mortgagee, mortgage-holder; note-holder; credit man; bill collector, collection agent; dunner, dun.

.5 VERBS **credit,** accredit; **credit to one's account,** place to one's credit *or* account.

.6 **give** *or* **extend credit,** sell on credit, trust, entrust; give tick [informal]; carry, carry on one's books.

.7 **receive credit,** take credit, **charge,** charge to one's account, keep an account with, go on tick [informal], buy on credit, buy on the cuff [informal], buy on the installment plan; go in hock for [slang]; have one's credit good for.

.8 ADJS **accredited,** credited, of good credit, **well-rated.**

.9 ADVS **to one's credit** *or* **account,** to the credit *or* account of, to the good.

.10 **on credit, on account, on trust,** on tick *or* **on the cuff** [both informal]; on terms, on good terms, on easy terms, on budget terms, in installments.

## 840. DEBT

.1 NOUNS **debt, indebtedness,** indebtment, **obligation, liability,** financial commitment, **due, dues,** score, pledge, unfulfilled pledge, amount due, outstanding debt; **bill, bills,** chits, **charges;** floating debt; funded debt; accounts receivable; accounts payable; borrowing 821; maturity; bad debts, uncollectibles; national debt, public debt.

.2 **arrears,** arrear, arrearage, back debts, back payments; **deficit,** default, deferred payments; overdraft, bounced *or* bouncing check; dollar gap, unfavorable balance of payments; deficit financing.

.3 **interest, premium, price, rate;** interest rate, rate of interest, prime interest rate, bank rate, price of money; discount rate; **usury,** excessive *or* exorbitant interest; mortgage points; simple interest, compound interest; net interest, gross interest; compensatory interest; lucrative interest; penal interest.

.4 **debtor,** borrower; mortgagor.

.5 VERBS **owe, be indebted,** be obliged *or* obligated for, be financially committed, lie under an obligation, be bound to pay.

.6 **go in debt,** get into debt, run into debt, plunge into debt, incur *or* contract a debt, go in hock [slang], **run up a bill** *or* a score *or* an account; run *or* show a deficit, operate at a loss; borrow 820.3.

.7 **mature, accrue, fall due.**

.8 ADJS **indebted, in debt,** plunged in debt, in difficulties, embarrassed, in embarrassed circumstances, in the hole [informal], in the red, in hock [slang], encumbered, mortgaged, mortgaged to the hilt, tied up, involved; deep in debt, involved *or* deeply involved in debt, burdened with debt, head over heels in debt, up to one's ears in debt.

.9 **chargeable, obligated, liable,** pledged, responsible, answerable for.

.10 **due, owed, owing, payable,** receivable, redeemable, mature, **outstanding, unpaid,** in arrear *or* arrears, back.

## 841. PAYMENT

.1 NOUNS **payment, paying,** paying off, paying up [informal], payoff; **defrayment,** defrayal; paying out, doling out, **disbursal** 843.1; **discharge, settlement, clearance, liquidation, amortization,** amortizement, retirement, satisfaction; quittance; acquittance *or* acquitment *or* acquittal [all archaic]; debt service, interest payment, sinking-fund payment; remittance; installment, installment plan; hire purchase *or* hire purchase plan *or* never-never [all Brit]; regular payments, monthly payments, weekly payments, quarterly payments, etc.; down payment, deposit, earnest, earnest money, binder; god's penny; cash, spot cash, cash payment, cash on the nail *or* cash on the barrelhead [both informal]; prepayment; payment in kind.

.2 **reimbursement,** recoupment, return, restitution; **refund,** refundment, kickback [informal]; **repayment** 823.2.

.3 **recompense, remuneration, compensation;** requital, requitement, quittance, **retribution, reparation, redress,** satisfaction, atonement, amends, return, restitution 823; blood money, wergild; **indemnity,** in**demnification;** price, consideration; re**ward,** meed, guerdon; honorarium; workmen's compensation, solatium, damages, smart money; salvage.

**.4** **pay, payment, remuneration, compensation,** total compensation, wages plus fringe benefits, pay and allowances, financial remuneration; **salary, wage, wages, income, earnings,** hire; real wages, purchasing power; take-home pay, takehome [informal], pay or income or wages after taxes, pay or income or wages after deductions, net income or wages or pay or earnings, taxable income; gross income; living wage; minimum wage, base pay; portal-to-portal pay; severance pay, discontinuance or dismissal wage; wage scale; escalator plan, escalator clause, sliding scale; payroll; wage freeze, wage rollback, wage reduction, wage control; guaranteed annual wage, guaranteed income plan.

**.5** **fee, stipend, allowance,** emolument, tribute; **reckoning,** account, bill; assessment, scot; initiation fee, footing [archaic]; retainer, retaining fee; hush money, blackmail; blood money; mileage.

**.6** (extra pay or allowance) **bonus, premium, fringe benefit** or **benefits,** bounty, perquisite, perquisites, perks [Brit informal], gravy [slang], lagniappe, solatium; **tip** 818.5; overtime pay; bonus system.

**.7** **dividend; royalty; commission,** rake-off or cut [both slang].

**.8** (the bearing of another's expense) **treat,** standing treat, picking up the check or tab [informal]; paying the bills, maintenance, support 785.3; subsidy 818.8.

**.9** **payer,** remunerator, compensator, recompenser; paymaster, purser, bursar, cashier, treasurer 836.11; defrayer; liquidator; taxpayer, ratepayer [Brit].

**.10** VERBS **pay,** render, tender; **recompense, remunerate, compensate, reward,** guerdon, indemnify, satisfy; salary, fee; remit; prepay; pay by installments, pay on, pay in.

**.11** **repay,** pay back, **reimburse,** recoup; re**quite,** quit, atone, redress [archaic], **make amends,** make good, make up for, make up to, make restitution, make reparation 823.4,5; pay in kind, pay one in his own coin, give tit for tat; **refund,** kick back [informal].

**.12** **settle with,** reckon with, account with [archaic], pay out, **settle** or **square** ac-

counts **with,** square oneself with, get square with, **get even** or quits with; even the score [slang], wipe or clear off old scores, pay old debts, clear the board.

**.13** **pay in full, pay off, pay up** [informal], **discharge, settle, square, clear, liquidate, amortize,** retire, take up, lift, take up and pay off, honor, acquit oneself of [archaic]; satisfy; meet one's obligations or commitments, redeem, redeem one's pledge or pledges, tear up or burn one's mortgage, have a mortgage-burning party, settle or square accounts, make accounts square, strike a balance; pay the bill, pay the shot.

**.14** **pay out, fork out** or **shell out** [both slang]; **expend** 843.5.

**.15** **pay over,** hand over; **ante, ante up,** put up; put down, lay down, lay one's money down.

**.16** [slang or informal terms] **kick in, fork over,** pony up, cough up, stump up [Brit], come across, come through with, come across with, come down with, come down with the needful, plank down, plunk down, post, tickle or grease the palm, cross one's palm with, lay on one; pay to the tune of.

**.17** **pay cash,** make a cash payment, cash, **pay spot cash, pay cash down,** pay cash on the barrelhead [informal], plunk down the money or put one's money on the line [both slang], pay at sight; pay in advance; pay as you go; pay cash on delivery, pay COD.

**.18** **pay for,** pay or stand the costs, **bear the expense** or **cost,** pay the piper [informal]; **finance, fund** 836.15; **defray,** defray expenses; pay the bill, **foot the bill** [informal], pick up the check or tab [informal]; honor a bill, acknowledge, redeem; pay one's way; pay one's share, chip in [informal], go Dutch [informal].

**.19** **treat, treat to, stand treat,** go treat, stand to [informal], pick up the check or tab [informal], pay the bill, set up, blow to [slang]; stand drinks; maintain, support 785.12; subsidize 818.19.

**.20** **be paid, draw wages,** be salaried, work for wages, be remunerated, collect for one's services, **earn,** get an income, pull down or drag down [both slang].

**.21** ADJS **paying, remunerative; compensating,** compensative, compensatory; retributive, retributory; **rewarding,** rewardful; lucrative, moneymaking, profitable 811.15; repaying, satisfying, reparative.

**.22** **paid,** discharged, settled, liquidated, acquitted [archaic], paid in full, receipted, remitted; **spent, expended;** salaried, waged, hired; prepaid, postpaid.

.23 **unindebted,** unowing, **out of debt,** above water, **clear,** all clear, free and clear, all straight; solvent 836.17.

.24 ADVS **in compensation,** as compensation, in recompense, for services rendered, for professional services, **in reward,** in requital, in reparation, in retribution, in restitution, **in amends,** in atonement, to atone for.

.25 **cash,** cash on the barrelhead [informal], strictly cash; **cash down, money down,** down; cash on delivery, **COD;** on demand, on call; pay-as-you-go.

## 842. NONPAYMENT

.1 NOUNS **nonpayment, default, delinquency,** delinquence [archaic], nondischarge of debts, nonremittal, failure to pay; defection; protest, repudiation; dishonor, dishonoring; bad debt, uncollectible, dishonored or protested bill.

.2 **moratorium,** grace period; **write-off,** cancellation, obliteration 693.7.

.3 **insolvency, bankruptcy,** receivership, **failure; crash,** collapse, bust [slang]; run upon a bank; insufficient funds, overdraft, overdrawn account, bounced or bouncing check, kited check.

.4 **insolvent,** insolvent debtor, lame duck [informal]; **bankrupt,** failure.

.5 **defaulter,** delinquent, nonpayer; **welsher** [slang], levanter; tax evader, tax dodger [informal].

.6 VERBS **not pay;** dishonor, repudiate, disallow, protest, stop payment, refuse to pay; **default, welsh** [slang], levant; button up one's pockets, draw the purse strings.

.7 **go bankrupt, go broke** [informal], go into receivership, become insolvent or bankrupt, **fail,** break, bust [slang], crash, collapse, **fold, fold up,** go up or **go under** [both informal], shut down, shut one's doors, go out of business, **be ruined,** go to ruin, go on the rocks, go to the wall, go to pot [informal], go to the dogs.

.8 **bankrupt, ruin, break,** bust [slang]; put out of business, drive to the wall, scuttle, sink; impoverish 838.6.

.9 **declare a moratorium; write off,** absolve, cancel, nullify, wipe the slate clean; wipe out, obliterate 693.16.

.10 ADJS **defaulting,** nonpaying, **delinquent;** behindhand, in arrear or arrears.

.11 **insolvent, bankrupt,** in receivership, broken, **broke** [informal], busted [slang],

**ruined,** failed, unable to pay one's creditors, unable to meet one's obligations, on the rocks; destitute 838.9.

.12 **unpaid, unremunerated,** uncompensated, unrecompensed, **unrewarded,** unrequited.

.13 **unpayable,** irredeemable, inconvertible.

## 843. EXPENDITURE

.1 NOUNS **expenditure, spending,** disbursal, **disbursement;** debit, debiting; budgeting, scheduling; costing, costing-out; **payment** 841; deficit spending.

.2 **spendings,** outgoings, outgo, outflow, **outlay,** money going out.

.3 **expenses, costs,** charges, budget, budget items, disbursals, liabilities; **expense, cost,** burden of expenditure; **overhead,** operating expense or expenses or costs or budget, general expenses; expense account, swindle sheet [slang]; direct costs, indirect costs; distributed costs, undistributed costs; material costs; labor costs; carrying charge; unit cost; replacement cost; prime cost; cost of living, cost-of-living index, cost-of-living allowance.

.4 **spender,** expender, expenditor, disburser.

.5 VERBS **spend, expend, disburse, pay out,** fork or shell out [slang], **lay out,** outlay; **pay** 841.10; put one's hands in one's pockets, open the purse, loosen or untie the purse strings; throw money around [informal], go on a spending spree, splurge, spend money as if it were going out of style, go or run through, **squander** 854.3; **invest,** sink money in [informal], put out; **incur costs** or **expenses;** budget, schedule, cost, cost out.

.6 **be spent,** burn in one's pocket, burn a hole in one's pocket.

.7 **afford,** well afford, spare, **spare the price,** bear, stand, support, endure, undergo, meet the expense of.

## 844. RECEIPTS

.1 NOUNS **receipts,** receipt, **income, revenue, profits, earnings, returns, proceeds,** avails [archaic], **take,** takings, intake, take-in [informal], get [Brit dial]; credit, credits; gains 811.3; gate receipts, gate, box office; net receipts, net; gross receipts, gross; net income, gross income; earned income, unearned income; dividend, dividends; royalties, commissions; receivables; disposable income; make, produce, **yield, output** 168.2.

.2 (written acknowledgment) **receipt, acknowledgment, voucher,** warrant [Brit]; canceled check; **receipt in full,** receipt in full of all demands, release, acquittance, quittance, discharge.

.3 VERBS receive 819.6; acquire 811.8–12; acknowledge receipt of, receipt, mark paid.

.4 yield, bring in, afford, pay, pay off [informal], return; gross, net.

## 845. ACCOUNTS

.1 NOUNS accounts; outstanding accounts, uncollected or unpaid accounts; accounts receivable, receipts, assets; accounts payable, expenditures, liabilities; budget, budgeting, costing-out.

.2 account, reckoning, tally, score; profit and loss account, debtor and creditor account, open or running account, cash account, suspense account, income account, revenue account, selling account, stock account, control account, provision account, valuation account, sales account; account current; account rendered, *compte rendu* [Fr], account stated; balance.

.3 statement, bill, itemized bill, bill of account, account, reckoning, check, *l'addition* [Fr], score or tab [both slang]; dun; invoice, manifest, bill of lading.

.4 account book, ledger, journal, daybook; register, registry, record book, books; log, logbook; cashbook; purchase ledger, accounts payable ledger, sales ledger, sales journal, accounts receivable ledger, card ledger, suspense ledger, stock ledger, bank ledger, stores ledger, inventory, cost ledger, factory ledger; bankbook, passbook; balance sheet; cost sheet, cost card.

.5 entry, item, minute, note, notation; single entry, double entry; credit, debit.

.6 accounting, accountancy, bookkeeping, double-entry bookkeeping or accounting, single-entry bookkeeping or accounting; business or commercial or monetary arithmetic; cost accounting, cost system, cost-accounting system; audit, auditing.

.7 accountant, bookkeeper; clerk, actuary [archaic], registrar, recorder, journalizer; calculator, reckoner; cost accountant, cost keeper; certified public accountant, CPA; chartered accountant or CA [both Brit]; auditor, bank examiner; bank accountant; accountant general; comptroller or controller.

.8 VERBS keep accounts, keep books, make up or cast up accounts; make an entry, enter, post, post up, journalize, book, docket, log, note, minute; credit, debit; charge off; capitalize; carry, carry on one's books; carry over; balance, balance

accounts, balance the books, strike a balance; close the books, close out.

.9 take account of, take stock, overhaul; inventory; audit, examine or inspect the books.

.10 falsify accounts, garble accounts, cook or doctor accounts [informal], salt; surcharge.

.11 bill, send a statement; invoice; call, call in, demand payment, dun.

.12 ADJS accounting, bookkeeping.

## 846. PRICE, FEE

.1 NOUNS price, cost, expense, expenditure, charge, –age; rate, figure, amount, price tag [informal]; damage or score or tab [all slang].

.2 quotation, quoted price; cash price; bargain price, cut price; asking price, offered price, bid, bid price; selling price; current price, going price, market price, price current, current quotation; wholesale price, trade price; list price, recommended price; net or neat price, net; fixed price; controlled price, managed price, fair-trade price; flat rate; *prix fixe* [Fr]; package price; unit price; piece price; price list, prices current; stock market quotations 834.9.

.3 worth, value, account, rate; face value, face; par value; market value; net worth; conversion factor or value; money's worth, pennyworth, value received.

.4 valuation, evaluation, pricing, price determination, assessment, appraisal, appraisement, apprizal, estimation, rating; unit pricing, dual pricing.

.5 price index, business index; consumer price index; cost-of-living index; price level; price ceiling, ceiling price, ceiling, top price; floor price, floor, bottom price; demand curve; rising prices, inflation, inflationary spiral.

.6 price controls, price-fixing, valorization; managed prices, fair-trading, fair trade, fair-trade agreement; price supports, rigid supports, flexible supports; price freeze; rent control.

.7 fee, dues, toll, charge, charges, demand, exaction, exactment, scot, shot, scot and lot; hire; fare, carfare; license fee; entrance or admission fee, admission; cover charge; portage, towage; wharfage, anchorage, dockage; pilotage; storage, cellarage; brokerage; salvage.

.8 freightage, freight, haulage, carriage, cartage, drayage, expressage, lighterage; poundage, tonnage.

**.9 rent, rental;** rent-roll; rent charge; rack rent, quitrent.

**.10 tax, taxation, duty, tribute,** contribution, **assessment,** cess [Brit], **levy, toll, impost,** imposition; **tithe;** surtax, supertax; direct tax, indirect tax; progressive tax or taxation, graduated taxation; proportional tax, ad valorem tax; regressive tax or taxation; single tax; withholding tax, tax withholding; tax return, separate returns, joint return; tax dodging, tax evasion; conscience money; tax exemption, tax-exempt status; tax structure, tax base; taxable income or goods or land or property, ratables [Brit].

**.11** (kinds of tax) excise, excise tax, internal revenue tax; **duty,** customs, customs duty, **tariff,** tariff duty, specific duty, ad valorem duty, revenue tariff, protective tariff; import tax, export tax; poll tax, poll, head tax, capitation tax, capitation; salt tax, gabelle; federal tax, state tax, provincial tax, local tax, rates [Brit]; property tax, land tax, property-increment tax, personal property tax; school tax; death tax, estate tax, death duty or estate duty [both Brit], inheritance tax; liquor tax, alcohol tax; capital gains tax, corporation tax, excess profits tax, value added tax, VAT; gift tax; income tax; license tax, franchise tax; automobile registration tax, gasoline tax; telephone tax, luxury tax, window tax, nuisance tax; amusement tax; doomage, assessment on default; sales tax, use tax; severance tax.

**.12 taxer, taxman; tax collector,** publican, collector of internal revenue, internal revenue agent; tax farmer, farmer; assessor, **tax assessor;** exciseman [Brit], revenuer; Internal Revenue Service, IRS; customs, US Customs Service, Bureau of Customs and Excise [Eng]; customhouse.

**.13 VERBS price,** set a price on, fix the price of; place a value on, **value, evaluate,** valuate, **appraise, assess, rate,** prize; quote a price; set an arbitrary price on, control or manage the price of, valorize; fair-trade.

**.14 charge, demand, ask,** require; **exact, assess, levy, impose; tax,** assess a tax upon, slap a tax on [slang], lay or put a duty on, make dutiable, subject to a tax or fee or duty, collect a tax or duty on; tithe; prorate, assess pro rata; charge for, stick for [informal].

**.15 cost, sell for, fetch, bring,** bring in, afford [archaic], set one back [slang]; **come to,** run to or into, **amount to,** mount up to, come up to, total up to.

**.16 ADJS priced, valued,** evaluated, assessed, appraised, rated, prized; **worth,** valued at; good for; ad valorem, pro rata.

**.17 chargeable, taxable,** ratable [Brit], assessable, dutiable, leviable; tithable.

**.18 tax-free, nontaxable, nondutiable,** tax-exempt; deductible, tax-deductible.

**.19 ADVS at a price,** for a consideration; to the amount of, to the tune of [informal].

## 847. DISCOUNT

**.1 NOUNS discount, cut, deduction,** abatement, reduction, price reduction, price-cutting, price-cut, rollback [informal]; underselling; rebate, rebatement; bank discount, cash discount, chain discount, time discount, trade discount; write-off, charge-off; **depreciation; allowance,** concession; setoff; drawback, **refund,** kickback [slang]; **premium,** percentage, agio, contango, backwardation [both Brit]; breakage, salvage; tare, tret; penalty, penalty clause.

**.2 VERBS discount, cut, deduct,** bate, abate; **take off,** write off, charge off; **depreciate,** reduce; **allow,** make allowance; rebate, **refund,** kick back [slang]; take a premium or percentage.

**.3 ADVS at a discount,** at a reduction, below par.

## 848. EXPENSIVENESS

**.1 NOUNS expensiveness, dearness,** high or great cost, **costliness,** highness, stiffness or steepness [both informal], priceyness [Austral]; richness, sumptuousness, luxuriousness.

**.2 preciousness, dearness, value,** high or great value, **worth,** extraordinary worth, price or great price [both archaic], **valuableness; pricelessness, invaluableness.**

**.3 high price,** high or big price tag [informal], **fancy price,** good price, steep or stiff price [informal], luxury price, pretty penny or an arm and a leg [both informal], exorbitant or unconscionable or extortionate price; famine price, scarcity price; rack rent; inflationary prices, rising or soaring or spiraling prices, soaring costs; sellers' market; **inflation,** inflationary trend or pressure, hot economy, inflationary spiral, inflationary gap.

**.4 exorbitance,** exorbitancy [archaic], **extravagance,** excess, **excessiveness,** inordinateness, immoderateness, immoderation, undueness, unreasonableness, outrageousness, preposterousness; unconscionableness, extortionateness.

.5 **overcharge,** surcharge, overassessment;
usury, shylocking *or* loan-sharking [both
slang]; **extortion,** exploitation, **holdup** *or*
highway robbery [both slang]; profiteering.

.6 VERBS **cost much,** cost money *or* cost you
[both informal], cost a pretty penny *or*
an arm and a leg [informal], cost a
packet, **run into money;** be overpriced,
price out of the market.

.7 **overprice,** set the price tag too high;
**overcharge,** surcharge, overtax; **hold up** *or*
soak *or* stick *or* sting *or* clip [all slang],
**make pay through the nose, gouge;** victimize, swindle 618.13–18; exploit, skin
[slang], fleece, screw, bleed, bleed white;
profiteer; rack *or* rack up the rents, rack-
rent.

.8 **overpay,** overspend, pay too much, pay
more than it's worth, **pay dearly,** pay exorbitantly, pay, **pay through the nose,** be
had [informal].

.9 **inflate,** heat *or* heat up the economy.

.10 ADJS **precious, dear, valuable,** worthy,
rich, golden, of great price [archaic],
worth a pretty penny [informal], worth a
king's ransom, worth its weight in gold,
good as gold, precious as the apple of
one's eye; **priceless, invaluable,** inestima-
ble, **beyond price,** not to be had for love
or money, too precious for words.

.11 **expensive, dear, costly,** of great cost,
dear-bought, **high, high-priced,** premium,
top; **fancy** *or* stiff *or* steep [all informal],
pricey [Austral]; beyond one's means, not
affordable, more than one can afford; unpayable; rich, sumptuous, **luxurious**
904.21.

.12 **overpriced,** grossly overpriced, **exorbitant,
excessive, extravagant, inordinate, immoderate,** undue, unwarranted, unreasonable, fancy, unconscionable, outrageous,
preposterous, out of bounds, out of sight
[informal], **prohibitive; extortionate,** cutthroat, **gouging, usurious,** exacting; **inflationary,** spiraling, skyrocketing.

.13 ADVS **dear, dearly;** at a high price, at
great cost, at a premium, at a great rate,
at heavy cost, at great expense.

.14 **preciously, valuably,** worthily; pricelessly,
invaluably, inestimably.

.15 **expensively,** richly, sumptuously, luxuriously.

.16 **exorbitantly, excessively,** grossly, **extravagantly, inordinately,** immoderately, unduly, unreasonably, unconscionably, outrageously, preposterously; **extortionately,**
usuriously, gougingly.

## 849. CHEAPNESS

.1 NOUNS **cheapness, inexpensiveness,** reasonableness, modesty, moderateness,
nominalness; **drug** *or* glut on the market;
shabbiness, shoddiness 673.2.

.2 **low price, nominal price,** reasonable
price, modest *or* manageable price, sensible price, moderate price; low *or* nominal
*or* reasonable charge; **bargain prices,** budget prices, economy prices, easy prices,
popular prices, rock-bottom prices; buyers' market; low *or* small price tag [infor-
mal], low tariff [informal]; **reduced price,**
cut price, sale price; cheap *or* reduced
rates.

.3 **bargain,** advantageous purchase, **buy** [in-
formal], **good buy, steal** [slang]; money's
worth, pennyworth, good pennyworth.

.4 **cheapening, depreciation, devaluation,**
reduction, lowering; deflation, cooling *or*
cooling off of the economy; decline,
plummet, plummeting, plunge, dive, nose
dive *or* slump *or* sag; price fall, break;
**price cut** *or* **reduction,** cut, slash, **markdown.**

.5 VERBS **be cheap,** cost little, not cost anything *or* cost nothing [both informal],
cost next to nothing; **buy dirt cheap,** buy
for a song, buy for nickels and dimes, buy
at a bargain, buy for a mere nothing; get
one's money's worth, get a good pennyworth; buy at wholesale prices *or* at cost.

.6 **cheapen, depreciate, devaluate,** lower, reduce, **mark down, cut prices, cut,** slash,
shave, trim, pare, knock the bottom out
of [informal]; deflate, cool *or* cool off
the economy; beat down, jew down [de-
rog]; come down *or* fall in price; **fall,** decline, plummet, dive, nose-dive [infor-
mal], head for the bottom, plunge, sag,
slump; break, give way; reach a new low.

.7 ADJS **cheap, inexpensive,** unexpensive,
low, **low-priced,** frugal, reasonable, sensible, manageable, modest, moderate, to
fit the pocketbook, budget, easy, economy, economic(al); within means; nominal, token; worth the money, well worth
the money; cheap *or* good at the price,
cheap at half the price; shabby, shoddy
673.18.

.8 **dirt cheap,** cheap as dirt, dog-cheap [in-
formal], **a dime a dozen,** two-for-a-penny,
twopenny-halfpenny, sixpenny, bargain-
basement, five-and-ten, dime-store.

.9 **reduced,** cut, slashed, **marked down;** cut-
rate; half-price; giveaway [informal], sacri-
ficial; **lowest,** rock-bottom, bottom, best.

.10 ADVS **cheaply, cheap,** on the cheap [Brit informal]; **inexpensively,** reasonably, moderately, nominally; **at a bargain,** *à bon marché* [Fr], for a song *or* mere song, for pennies, for nickels and dimes, at small cost, at a low price, at budget prices, at piggy-bank prices, at a sacrifice; at cost *or* cost price, at prime cost, wholesale, at wholesale; at reduced rates.

## 850. COSTLESSNESS

### *(absence of charge)*

.1 NOUNS **costlessness,** gratuitousness, gratuity, **freeness,** expenselessness, complimentariness, no charge; free ride [informal]; freebie [slang]; labor of love; gift 818.4–6.

.2 **complimentary ticket, pass,** free pass *or* ticket, paper [slang], free admission, guest pass *or* ticket, Annie Oakley [slang]; discount ticket, twofer [informal].

.3 **freeloader,** free rider, pass holder, deadhead [informal], paper [slang]; paper house [informal].

.4 VERBS **give, present** 818.12; freeload, sponge 907.11.

.5 ADJS **gratuitous, gratis, free, free of charge,** for free, **for nothing,** free for nothing, free for the asking, free gratis *or* free gratis for nothing [both informal], for love, free as air; freebie *or* freebee *or* freeby [all slang]; costless, expenseless, untaxed, without charge, free of cost *or* expense; unbought, unpaid-for; **complimentary, on the house;** given 818.24; giftlike; eleemosynary, charitable 938.15.

.6 ADVS **gratuitously, gratis, free, free of charge,** for nothing, for the asking, without charge, with the compliments of the management, as our guest.

## 851. ECONOMY

.1 NOUNS **economy, thrift, thriftiness,** economicalness, savingness, sparingness, unwastefulness, **frugality,** frugalness; tight purse strings; parsimony, parsimoniousness 852.1; false economy; carefulness, care, chariness, canniness; **prudence,** providence, forehandedness; **husbandry,** management, good management *or* stewardship, prudent *or* prudential administration; austerity, austerity program; economic planning; economy of means 852.1.

.2 **economizing,** economization, reduction of spending *or* government spending; **saving,** scrimping, skimping [informal], scraping, sparing, cheeseparing; retrench-ment, curtailment, reduction of expenses, cutback, slowdown, cooling, cooling off *or* down, low growth rate.

.3 **economizer,** economist, **saver.**

.4 VERBS **economize, save,** make *or* enforce economies; **scrimp, skimp** [informal], **scrape,** scrape and save; **manage, husband,** husband one's resources; keep within compass [archaic], keep within one's means *or* budget, balance income with outgo, live within one's income, make ends meet, cut one's coat according to one's cloth; put something aside, save for a rainy day, have a nest egg.

.5 **retrench, cut down,** cut *or* pare down expenses, **curtail expenses;** cut corners, tighten one's belt, cut back, roll back [informal], take a reef, slow down.

.6 ADJS **economic(al), thrifty, frugal,** unwasteful, conserving, **saving,** economizing, spare, **sparing;** Scotch; **prudent,** prudential, provident, forehanded; careful, chary, canny; scrimping, skimping [informal], cheeseparing; penny-wise; parsimonious 852.7; labor-saving, time-saving, money-saving.

.7 ADVS **economically, thriftily, frugally,** husbandly [archaic]; prudently, providently; carefully, charily, cannily; sparingly, with a sparing hand.

## 852. PARSIMONY

.1 NOUNS **parsimony,** parsimoniousness; frugality 851.1; **stinting, pinching, scrimping,** skimping, cheeseparing; economy, economy of means, economy of assumption, law of parsimony, Ockham's razor, elegance.

.2 **niggardliness,** penuriousness, **meanness,** minginess, shabbiness, sordidness.

.3 **stinginess, ungenerosity, illiberality, cheapness** *or* tightness [both informal], tight purse strings, nearness, closeness, closefistedness, closehandedness [archaic], tightfistedness, hardfistedness, **miserliness,** penny-pinching, hoarding; **avarice** 634.8.

.4 **niggard, tightwad** [slang], **miser,** hard man with a buck [slang], **skinflint,** scrooge, penny pincher, pinchfist, pinchgut [archaic], churl, curmudgeon [archaic], muckworm, save-all [dial], Harpagon [Molière], Silas Marner [George Eliot].

.5 VERBS **stint, scrimp, skimp, scamp,** scant, screw, **pinch,** starve, famish; **pinch pennies,** rub the print off a dollar bill, rub the picture off a nickel; live upon nothing; grudge, begrudge.

.6 **withhold, hold back,** hold out on [slang].

.7 ADJS **parsimonious, sparing,** cheeseparing, **stinting, scamping, scrimping, skimping; frugal** 851.6; too frugal, overfrugal, frugal to excess; **penny-wise,** penny-wise and pound-foolish.

.8 **niggardly, niggard, pinchpenny, penurious, grudging, mean,** mingy, shabby, sordid.

.9 **stingy, illiberal, ungenerous, miserly,** saveall, **cheap** or **tight** [both informal], **near, close, closefisted,** closehanded [archaic], **tightfisted,** pinchfisted, **hardfisted;** near as the bark on a tree, "as close as a vise" [Hawthorne]; **pinching, penny-pinching; avaricious** 634.27.

.10 ADVS **parsimoniously,** stintingly, scrimpingly, skimpingly.

.11 **niggardly, stingily,** illiberally, ungenerously, closefistedly, tightfistedly; **meanly,** shabbily, sordidly.

## 853. LIBERALITY

.1 NOUNS **liberality,** liberalness, freeness, freedom; **generosity,** generousness, largeness, **unselfishness, munificence,** largess; **bountifulness,** bounteousness, **bounty;** hospitality, welcome, graciousness; **openhandedness,** freehandedness, open or free hand, easy purse strings; **givingness;** openheartedness, bigheartedness, largeheartedness, greatheartedness, freeheartedness; open heart, big or large or great heart; **magnanimity** 979.2.

.2 **cheerful giver,** free giver.

.3 VERBS **give freely, give cheerfully,** give with an open hand, give with both hands, put one's hands in one's pockets, open the purse, loosen or untie the purse strings; **spare no expense,** spare nothing, not count the cost, let money be no object; **heap upon,** lavish upon, shower down upon; give the coat or shirt off one's back, give more than one's share, **give until it hurts;** give of oneself, give of one's substance, not hold back, offer oneself; keep the change!

.4 ADJS **liberal, free,** free with one's money, free-spending; **generous, munificent,** large, princely, handsome; **unselfish, ungrudging; unsparing, unstinting,** stintless, unstinted; **bountiful,** bounteous, **lavish,** profuse; hospitable, gracious; **openhanded,** freehanded, open; **giving;** openhearted, **bighearted,** largehearted, greathearted, freehearted; **magnanimous** 979.6.

.5 ADVS **liberally, freely; generously, munificently,** handsomely; **unselfishly,** ungrudgingly; **unsparingly, unstintingly; bountifully,** bounteously, **lavishly,** profusely; hospitably, graciously; **openhandedly,** freehandedly; **openheartedly, bigheartedly,** largeheartedly, greatheartedly, freeheartedly; with open hands, with both hands, with an unsparing hand, without stint.

## 854. PRODIGALITY

.1 NOUNS **prodigality, overliberality,** overgenerousness, overgenerosity; **profligacy, extravagance,** pound-foolishness, reckless spending or expenditure; **incontinence, intemperance** 993; lavishness, profuseness, profusion; **wastefulness, waste; dissipation, squandering,** squandermania; carpe diem; slack or loose purse strings, leaking purse; conspicuous consumption or waste.

.2 **prodigal, wastrel,** waster, **squanderer; spendthrift,** wastethrift, spender, spendall, big-time spender [informal]; Diamond Jim Brady; prodigal son.

.3 VERBS **squander, lavish,** slather, blow [slang], play ducks and drakes with; **dissipate,** scatter [archaic], sow broadcast, scatter to the winds; **run through,** go through; **throw away,** throw one's money away, **spend money like water,** hang the expense, let slip or flow through one's fingers, spend as if money grew on trees, spend money as if it were going out of style, throw money around, spend like a drunken sailor; gamble away; burn the candle at both ends; seize the day, live for the day, let tomorrow take care of itself.

.4 **waste, consume, spend, expend, use up, exhaust;** lose; spill, pour down the drain or rathole; pour water into a sieve, cast pearls before swine, kill the goose that lays the golden egg, manger son blé en herbe [Fr], throw out the baby with the bath water.

.5 **fritter away,** fool away, fribble away, dribble away, drivel away, **trifle away,** dally away, potter away, piss away [slang], muddle away, diddle away [informal], squander in dribs and drabs; idle away, while away.

.6 **misspend, throw good money after bad,** throw the helve after the hatchet.

.7 **overspend,** spend more than one has, spend what one hasn't got; **overdraw,** overdraw one's account, live beyond one's means, have champagne tastes on a beer budget.

.8 ADJS **prodigal, extravagant, lavish,** profuse, **overliberal,** overgenerous, overlavish, **spendthrift, wasteful,** profligate, dissipative; incontinent, intemperate 993.7; pound-foolish, penny-wise and pound-foolish; easy come, easy go.

.9 **wasted, squandered, dissipated,** consumed, spent, used, lost; **gone to waste,** run to seed; down the drain or spout or rathole [informal]; misspent.

## 855. FEELINGS

.1 NOUNS feelings, emotions, affections, sentiments, passions, sensibilities, susceptibilities, **sympathies,** tender susceptibilities, finer feelings; the logic of the heart; emotional life; affectivity, affective faculty; feeling tone.

.2 (seat of affections; hence, affections, deepest feelings) **heart, soul, spirit,** *esprit* [Fr], **breast, bosom,** inmost heart or soul, heart of hearts, secret or inner recesses of the heart, secret places, heart's core, heartstrings, cockles of the heart, bottom of the heart, being, innermost being, core of one's being; viscera, pit of one's stomach, guts [slang]; bones.

.3 **feeling, emotion, affection,** emotional charge, path(o)–, thym(o)–; **sentiment, passion,** heartthrob; sense, deep or profound sense, **sensation** 422; impression, undercurrent; presentiment 481.3; foreboding 544; experience; affect; reaction, response, gut reaction [informal]; feeling tone, emotional shade or nuance.

.4 (capacity of emotion) **sensibility, sensitivity, sensitiveness,** delicacy, affectivity, susceptibility, impressionability 422.2.

.5 **sympathetic response, sympathy, fellow feeling,** responsiveness, relating, caring, concern; response, echo, chord, sympathetic chord, vibrations, vibes [slang]; **empathy,** identification; involvement, sharing; pathos.

.6 **tender feeling, tenderness,** softness, gentleness, delicacy; **tenderheartedness,** softheartedness, warmheartedness, tender or sensitive or warm heart, soft place or spot in one's heart; fondness, weakness 634.2.

.7 **bad feeling, hard feelings;** immediate dislike, disaffinity, personality conflict, **hostility,** animosity 929.3,4; **hardheartedness** 856.3.

.8 **sentimentality, sentiment, sentimentalism,** oversentimentality, oversentimentalism, bathos; nostalgia, nostomania; romanticism; sweetness and light, hearts-and-flowers; bleeding heart; mawkish-

ness, cloyingness, maudlinness, namby-pamby, namby-pambyness, namby-pambyism; mushiness or sloppiness [both informal]; **mush** or slush or slop or goo or schmaltz [all slang]; sob story or tearjerker [both slang], soap opera.

.9 **emotionalism,** emotionality, emotionalizing, emotionalization; emotiveness, emotivity, visceralness; nonrationalness, unreasoningness; demonstrativeness; theatricality, theatrics, histrionics, making scenes; **sensationalism, melodrama,** melodramatics, blood and thunder, yellow journalism; emotional appeal, human interest, love interest.

.10 **fervor, fervency,** fervidness, **passion,** passionateness, impassionedness, **ardor, ardency,** *empressement* [Fr], warmth of feeling, **warmth, heat, fire,** verve, furor, fury, vehemence; heartiness, gusto, relish, savor; spirit, heart, soul; **liveliness** 707.2; **zeal** 635.2; **excitement** 857; ecstasy 857.7.

.11 VERBS **feel,** entertain or harbor or cherish or nurture a feeling; **feel deeply,** feel in one's viscera or bones, feel in one's guts [slang]; experience 151.8; have a sensation, get or receive an impression, **sense, perceive** 422.8.

.12 **respond, react,** be moved, be affected or touched, be inspired, echo, catch the flame or infection, be in tune, be turned on to [slang], enter into the spirit of, be imbued with the spirit of; care about, sympathize with, empathize with, identify with, relate to emotionally, dig [slang], be turned on by [slang], be involved, share; color with emotion, change color.

.13 **take to heart,** lay to heart, nourish in one's bosom, feel in one's breast, cherish at the heart's core, treasure up in the heart; lie at the heart.

.14 **have deep feelings, be all heart, have a tender heart,** be a man of heart or sentiment; have a soft place or spot in one's heart; be a prey to one's feelings; **love** 931.18–20; **hate** 930.5.

.15 **emotionalize, emote** [informal], give free play to the emotions, make a scene; be theatrical, theatricalize, ham it up [informal]; **sentimentalize,** gush [informal], slobber over [slang], slop over [informal].

.16 **affect, touch, move, stir; melt, soften,** melt the heart; **penetrate,** pierce, go through one, go deep; touch a chord, **touch a sympathetic chord, touch one's heart,** tug at the heart or heartstrings, go to one's heart; come home to; **touch to** the quick, touch on the raw, flick one on the raw, smart, sting.

.17 impress, affect, strike, hit, smite, rock; make an impression, make a dent in, make an impact upon, sink in [informal], strike home, come home to, hit the mark [informal]; tell, have a strong effect, traumatize, strike hard, impress forcibly.

.18 impress upon, bring home to, make it felt; stamp, stamp on, etch, engrave, engrave on.

.19 ADJS emotional, emotive, affectional, affective, feeling; soulful, of soul, of heart, of feeling, of sentiment; visceral, gut [slang]; glandular; emotiometabolic, emotiomotor, emotiomuscular, emotiovascular; demonstrative, overdemonstrative.

.20 emotionalistic, emotive, overemotional, hysteric(al), sensational, sensationalistic, melodramatic, theatrical, histrionic, hammy [informal], nonrational, unreasoning.

.21 sensitive, sensible, emotionable, passible, delicate; responsive, sympathetic, receptive; susceptible, impressionable 422.13; tender, soft, tenderhearted, softhearted, warmhearted.

.22 sentimental, sentimentalized, soft, mawkish, maudlin, cloying; sticky or gooey or schmaltzy or sappy [all slang], oversentimental, oversentimentalized, bathetic; mushy or sloppy or gushing or teary or beery [all informal]; tear-jerking [slang]; namby-pamby, romantic; nostalgic, nostomanic.

.23 fervent, fervid, passionate, impassioned, intense, ardent; hearty, cordial, enthusiastic, exuberant, unrestrained, vigorous; keen, breathless, excited 857.18–25; lively 707.17; zealous 635.10; warm, burning, heated, hot, red-hot, fiery, flaming, glowing, ablaze, afire, on fire, boiling over, steaming, steamy; delirious, fevered, feverish, febrile, flushed; intoxicated, drunk.

.24 affecting, touching, moving, emotive, pathetic.

.25 affected, moved, touched, impressed; impressed with or by, penetrated with, seized with, imbued with, devoured by, obsessed, obsessed by; wrought up by; stricken, wracked, racked, torn, agonized, tortured.

.26 deep-felt, deepgoing, heartfelt, homefelt [archaic]; deep, profound, indelible; pervading, absorbing; penetrating, piercing; poignant, keen, sharp, acute.

.27 ADVS feelingly, emotionally, affectingly, touchingly, movingly, with feeling, poignantly.

.28 fervently, fervidly, passionately, impassionedly, intensely, ardently, zealously; keenly, breathlessly, excitedly; warmly, heatedly, glowingly; heartily, cordially; enthusiastically, exuberantly, vigorously; kindly, heart and soul, with all one's heart, from the bottom of one's heart.

.29 sentimentally, mawkishly, maudlinly, cloyingly; mushily or sloppily or gushingly [all informal].

## 856. LACK OF FEELINGS

.1 NOUNS unfeeling, unfeelingness, lack of affect, lack of feeling or feeling tone, emotional deadness or numbness or paralysis, anesthesia, emotionlessness, unemotionalism, unexcitability; dispassion, dispassionateness, unpassionateness, objectivity; passionlessness, spiritlessness, heartlessness, soullessness; coldness, coolness, frigidity, chill, chilliness, frostiness, iciness; coldheartedness, cold-bloodedness; cold heart, cold blood; unresponsiveness, unsympatheticness; lack of touch or contact, autism, self-absorption, withdrawal, catatonia; unimpressionableness, unimpressibility; insusceptibility, unsusceptibility; impassiveness, impassibility, impassivity; straight face or poker face [both informal], dead pan [slang]; immovability, untouchability; dullness, obtuseness; inexcitability 858.

.2 insensibility, insensibleness, unconsciousness, unawareness, obliviousness, oblivion.

.3 callousness, callosity, callus; insensitivity, insensitiveness, Philistinism; hardness, hardenedness, hardheartedness, hardness of heart, hard heart, heart of stone, stoniness, flintiness; obduracy, obdurateness, induration, inuredness; imperviousness, thick skin, rhinoceros hide, thick or hard shell, armor, formidable defenses.

.4 apathy, indifference, unconcern, disinterest; withdrawnness, aloofness, detachment, ataraxy or ataraxia, dispassion; passiveness, passivity, supineness, insouciance, nonchalance; inappetence, lack of appetite; listlessness, spiritlessness, blah or blahs [both slang], heartlessness, plucklessness, spunklessness; lethargy, phlegm, lethargicalness, phlegmaticalness, phlegmaticness, hebetude, dullness, sluggishness, languidness; soporifousness, sopor, comatoseness, torpidness, torpor, torpidity, stupor, stupefaction; acedia, sloth;

resignation, resignedness; **numbness,** benumbedness; hopelessness 889.

.5 VERBS not be affected by, remain unmoved, not turn a hair; have a thick skin, have a heart of stone; be cold as ice, be a cold fish, be an icicle.

.6 **callous, harden,** case harden, **harden one's heart,** ossify, steel, indurate, inure; brutalize.

.7 **dull, blunt,** desensitize, obtund, hebetate.

.8 **numb, benumb,** paralyze, **deaden,** anesthetize, freeze, **stun, stupefy,** drug.

.9 ADJS **unfeeling, unemotional,** nonemotional, emotionless, affectless, emotionally dead or numb or paralyzed, anesthetized, drugged; **unpassionate, dispassionate,** unimpassioned, **objective;** passionless, **spiritless, heartless,** soulless; **cold, cool, frigid,** frozen, chill, chilly, arctic, frosty, frosted, icy, **coldhearted, coldblooded,** cold as charity; **unaffectionate,** unloving; **unresponsive,** unresponding, **unsympathetic;** out of touch or contact; in one's shell or armor, behind one's defenses; autistic, self-absorbed, catatonic; unimpressionable, unimpressible, insusceptible, unsusceptible; **impassive,** impassible; immovable, untouchable; dull, obtuse, blunt; **inexcitable** 858.10.

.10 **insensible, unconscious,** unaware, **oblivious,** blind to, deaf to, dead to, lost to.

.11 **unaffected, unmoved, untouched,** unimpressed, unstruck, **unstirred,** unruffled, unanimated, uninspired.

.12 **callous, calloused,** insensitive, Philistine; **thick-skinned,** pachydermatous; **hard, hardhearted, hardened,** case-hardened, indurated, stony, flinty, steely, impervious, inured, steeled against, proof against, as hard as nails.

.13 **apathetic, indifferent, unconcerned,** uncaring, Laodicean, **disinterested, uninterested; withdrawn, aloof, detached,** Olympian; **passive,** supine; stoic; insouciant, nonchalant, blasé; **listless, spiritless,** blah [slang], heartless, pluckless, spunkless; **lethargic, phlegmatic,** hebetudinous, **dull,** desensitized, sluggish, torpid, languid, slack, soporific, comatose, **stupefied,** in a stupor, **numb,** numbed, benumbed; resigned; hopeless 889.12.

.14 ADVS **unfeelingly, unemotionally,** emotionlessly; with a straight or poker face [informal], deadpan [slang]; **dispassionately,** unpassionately; **spiritlessly, heartlessly,** coldly, coldheartedly, cold-bloodedly, **in cold blood;** with dry eyes.

.15 **apathetically, indifferently, unconcernedly,** disinterestedly, uninterestedly, impassively; **listlessly, spiritlessly,** heartlessly, plucklessly, spunklessly; **lethargically, phlegmatically,** dully, numbly.

## 857. EXCITEMENT

.1 NOUNS **excitement,** emotion, excitedness, **arousal, stimulation, exhilaration;** a high [slang], manic state or condition.

.2 **thrill, sensation,** titillation; **tingle,** tingling; **quiver,** shiver, shudder, tremor, **tremor of excitement,** rush [slang]; flush, rush of emotion, surge of emotion; **kick** or charge or boot or bang or lift [all slang], jollies [slang].

.3 **agitation, perturbation,** ferment, **turbulence, turmoil,** tumult, embroilment, uproar, **commotion,** disturbance, ado, brouhaha [Fr], feery-fary [Scot], to-do [informal]; pell-mell, **flurry,** ruffle, bustle, stir, swirl, swirling, whirl, vortex, eddy, hurry, hurry-scurry, hurly-burly; fermentation, yeastiness, effervescence, ebullience, ebullition; fume.

.4 **trepidation,** trepidity; **disquiet,** disquietude, inquietude, **unrest, restlessness,** fidgetiness; **fidgets** or **shakes** or shivers or dithers [all informal]; **quivering, quavering, quaking, shaking,** trembling; **quiver,** quaver, shiver, shudder, didder [Brit dial], twitter, **tremor,** tremble, flutter; palpitation, pitapatation [informal], pitapat, pitter-patter; **throb,** throbbing; panting, heaving.

.5 **dither, tizzy** [informal], swivet, foofaraw, **pucker** [informal], **twitter,** twitteration [informal], **flutter, fluster,** flusteration or flustration [both informal], **fret, fuss,** pother, bother, lather or stew [both informal], flap.

.6 **fever of excitement,** fever, heat, fever heat, fire; sexual excitement, rut 419.6.

.7 **fury, furor,** furore [Brit], fire and fury; **ecstasy,** transport, **rapture,** ravishment; intoxication, abandon; **passion, rage,** raging or tearing passion, towering rage or passion; **frenzy,** orgy, orgasm; madness, craze, **delirium,** hysteria.

.8 **outburst,** outbreak, **burst, flare-up,** blaze, **explosion,** eruption, irruption, upheaval, convulsion, spasm, seizure, fit, paroxysm; storm, tornado, whirlwind, cyclone, hurricane, gale, tempest, gust.

.9 **excitability,** excitableness, perturbability, agitability; emotional instability, explosiveness, eruptiveness, inflammability, combustibility, tempestuousness, violence, latent violence; **irascibility** 951.2; irritability, edginess, touchiness, prickliness, **sensitivity** 422.3; skittishness, startlishness, **nervousness** 859; emotionalism 855.9.

.10 **excitation, excitement, arousal,** arousing, **stirring,** stirring up, working up, working into a lather [informal], lathering up, whipping up, steaming up, **agitation, perturbation; stimulation, stimulus, exhilaration,** animation; electrification, galvanization; **provocation, irritation,** aggravation, exasperation, exacerbation, fomentation, inflammation, infuriation, **incitement** 648.4.

.11 VERBS **excite, impassion, arouse, rouse,** blow up [archaic], **stir, stir up,** set astir, stir the feelings, stir the blood, play on the feelings; **work up,** work into, work up into a lather [informal], lather up, whip up, **key up,** steam up; **move** 648.12; **foment, incite** 648.17; turn on [slang]; **awaken,** awake, wake, waken, wake up; call up, summon up, call forth; **kindle,** enkindle, light up, light the fuse, **fire, inflame,** heat, warm, set fire to, set on fire, fire or warm the blood; fan, fan the fire or flame, blow the coals, stir the embers, feed the fire, add fuel to the fire or flame, pour oil on the fire; raise to a fever heat or pitch, bring to the boiling point; overexcite; **annoy, incense** 952.22; **enrage, infuriate** 952.23; frenzy, madden 473.23.

.12 **stimulate, whet, sharpen,** pique, provoke, quicken, enliven, pick up, jazz up [slang], animate, **exhilarate,** invigorate, galvanize, fillip, give a fillip to; infuse life into, give new life to, revive, renew, resuscitate.

.13 **agitate, perturb, disturb, trouble, disquiet, discompose,** discombobulate [informal], unsettle, stir, **ruffle, shake, shake up, shock, upset,** jolt, jar, rock, stagger, electrify, bring or pull one up short, give one a turn [informal]; fuss [slang], flutter, flurry, rattle, disconcert, **fluster.**

.14 **thrill, tickle,** titillate, flush, give a thrill, **give one a kick** or boot or charge or bang or lift [informal]; intoxicate, fascinate, take one's breath away.

.15 **be excitable,** have a short fuse [informal], excite easily; **get excited,** get into a dither or tizzy or swivet or pucker, get into a stew [informal]; catch the infection, **work oneself up,** work oneself into a sweat or lather [informal], get hot under the collar [informal], run a temperature or race one's motor [both slang]; turn a hair; ex-

plode, **blow up** [informal], blow one's top or stack [informal], blow one's cool [slang], flip or flip one's lid [both slang], blow a gasket [slang]; **flare up,** flash up, flame up, fire up, catch fire, take fire; **fly into a passion, fly off the handle** or **hit the ceiling** [both informal]; go into hysterics, have a tantrum or temper tantrum, come apart; **rage, rave, rant,** rant and rave, bellow, **storm,** ramp; be angry, smolder, **seethe** 952.15.

.16 (be excited) **thrill,** tingle, **tingle with excitement,** glow; swell, swell with emotion, be full of emotion; thrill to; flip out [slang]; turn on to or get high on or freak out on [all slang]; heave, pant; **throb,** palpitate, go pitapat; **tremble, shiver, quiver, quaver, quake,** flutter, twitter, **shake,** shake like an aspen leaf, have the shakes [informal]; shit in one's pants [slang]; **fidget,** have the fidgets [informal]; toss and turn, toss, tumble, twist and turn, wriggle, wiggle, writhe, squirm; twitch, jerk.

.17 **change color,** turn color, go all colors; **pale,** whiten, blanch, turn pale; darken, look black; turn blue in the face; **flush, blush,** crimson, glow, mantle, color, redden, turn red.

.18 ADJS **excited,** impassioned; **thrilled,** agog, tingling, tingly, atingle, aquiver, atwitter; **stimulated, exhilarated, high** [slang]; manic; **moved, stirred,** stirred up, **aroused, roused,** on one's mettle, fired, inflamed, **wrought up, worked up,** worked up into a lather [informal], lathered up, whipped up, steamed up, keyed up, hopped up [slang]; turned-on [slang]; carried away; bursting, ready to burst; effervescent, yeasty, ebullient.

.19 **in a dither, in a tizzy** [informal], in a swivet, in a foofaraw, **in a pucker** [informal], in a quiver, **in a twitter,** in a flutter, all of a twitter or flutter, in a fluster, in a flurry, in a pother, in a bother, in a ferment, in a turmoil, in an uproar, in a stew or in a sweat [both informal], in a lather [slang].

.20 **heated, passionate, warm, hot,** red-hot, flaming, **burning, fiery, glowing, fervent, fervid; feverish,** febrile, hectic, flushed; sexually excited, in rut 419.30; burning with excitement, het up [dial], hot under the collar [informal]; seething, boiling, boiling over, steamy, steaming.

.21 **agitated, perturbed, disturbed, troubled, disquieted, upset,** unsettled, **discomposed, flustered,** ruffled, **shaken.**

.22 **turbulent**, tumultuous, tempestuous, boisterous, clamorous, uproarious.

.23 **frenzied**, **frantic**; **ecstatic**, transported, enraptured, ravished, in a transport or ecstasy; intoxicated, abandoned; orgiastic, orgasmic; raging, raving, roaring, bellowing, ramping, storming, howling, ranting, fulminating, frothing or foaming at the mouth; **wild**, hog-wild [slang]; **violent**, fierce, ferocious, feral, **furious**; **mad**, madding, **rabid**, maniac(al), demoniac(al), possessed; carried away, **distracted, delirious, beside oneself**, out of one's wits; uncontrollable, running mad, amok, berserk; **hysterical**, in hysterics; wild-eyed, wild-looking, haggard; blue in the face.

.24 **overwrought**, overexcited; **overcome**, overwhelmed, overpowered, overmastered; **upset**, *bouleversé* [Fr].

.25 **restless**, restive, **uneasy**, unquiet, unsettled, unrestful, tense; **fidgety**, fussy, fluttery.

.26 **excitable**, **emotional**, highly emotional, perturbable, agitable; emotionally unstable; explosive, volcanic, eruptive, inflammable; irascible 951.19; irritable, edgy, touchy, prickly, **sensitive** 422.13; **skittish**, startlish; **high-strung**, high-spirited, mettlesome, high-mettled; **nervous** 859.10.

.27 **passionate**, **fiery**, vehement, hotheaded, **impetuous**, violent, furious, fierce, **wild**; tempestuous, stormy, tornadic; simmering, volcanic, ready to burst forth.

.28 **exciting**, **thrilling**, thrilly [informal], **stirring, moving, breathtaking**, excito–; agitating, perturbing, disturbing, upsetting, troubling, disquieting, unsettling, distracting, jolting, jarring; heart-stirring, heart-thrilling, heart-swelling, heart-expanding, soul-stirring, spirit-stirring, deepthrilling, mind-blowing [slang]; impressive, striking, telling; **provocative** 648.27, provoking, piquant, tantalizing 650.7; **inflammatory** 648.28; **stimulating**, stimulative; exhilarating, heady, intoxicating, maddening, ravishing; **electric**, galvanic, charged; **overwhelming**, overpowering, overcoming, overmastering, more than flesh and blood can bear; suspensive, **suspenseful**, cliff-hanging [informal].

.29 **penetrating**, **piercing**, stabbing, cutting, stinging, biting, keen, brisk, sharp, caustic, astringent.

.30 **sensational**, **lurid**, yellow, **melodramatic**, Barnumesque; spine-chilling; blood-and-thunder, cloak-and-dagger.

.31 ADVS **excitedly**, **agitatedly**, perturbedly; with beating or leaping heart, with heart beating high, with heart going pitapat or pitter-patter, thrilling all over, with heart in mouth; with glistening eyes, all agog, all aquiver or atwitter or atingle; in a sweat or stew or dither or tizzy.

.32 **heatedly**, **passionately**, warmly, hotly, glowingly, fervently, fervidly, **feverishly**.

.33 **frenziedly**, **frantically**, wildly, furiously, violently, fiercely, madly, rabidly, distractedly, deliriously, till one is blue in the face.

.34 **excitingly**, **thrillingly**, stirringly, movingly; **provocatively**, provokingly; stimulatingly, exhilaratingly.

## 858. INEXCITABILITY

.1 NOUNS **inexcitability**, inexcitableness, unexcitableness, **imperturbability**, imperturbableness, unflappability [informal]; inirritability, unirritableness; **dispassion**, dispassionateness, unpassionateness, ataraxy or ataraxia; steadiness; stoicism; **even temper**, steady or smooth temper, good or easy temper; unnervousness 860; **patience** 861; **impassiveness**, impassivity, stolidity; bovinity, dullness.

.2 **composure**, countenance; **calmness**, calm disposition, **placidity**, **serenity**, tranquillity, soothingness, peacefulness; mental composure, peace or calm of mind; calm or quiet mind, easy mind; philosophicalness, philosophy, philosophic composure; quiet, quietude; imperturbation, indisturbance, unruffledness; **coolness**, coolheadedness, cool [slang], sangfroid; icy calm; Oriental calm, Buddha-like composure.

.3 **equanimity**, equilibrium, equability, balance; **levelheadedness**, level head, well-balanced or well-regulated mind; poise, aplomb, **self-possession**, self-control, self-command, self-restraint, restraint, possession, **presence of mind**; confidence, assurance, **self-confidence, self-assurance**.

.4 **sedateness**, **staidness**, soberness, sobriety, sober-mindedness, seriousness, gravity, solemnity, sobersidedness; temperance, moderation; sobersides.

.5 **nonchalance**, casualness, offhandedness; easygoingness, lackadaisicalness; **indifference**, unconcern 636.2.

.6 VERBS **compose, calm** 163.7; **set one's mind at ease** or **rest**, make one easy.

.7 **compose oneself, control oneself**, restrain oneself, collect oneself, **get hold of oneself**, get organized [informal], master one's feelings; **calm down, cool off**, sober down, simmer down [informal], cool it [slang]; **relax, unwind, take it easy** [informal].

.8 (control one's feelings) **suppress, repress,** keep under, smother, stifle, inhibit; sublimate.

.9 **keep cool,** keep one's cool [slang], **keep calm,** keep one's head, keep one's shirt on [slang], not turn a hair; take things as they come, roll with the punches [informal]; keep a stiff upper lip.

.10 ADJS **inexcitable, imperturbable,** undisturbable, **unflappable** [informal]; **unirritable,** inirritable; **dispassionate,** unpassionate; **steady;** stoic(al); **even-tempered; impassive,** stolid; bovine, dull; unnervous 860.2; **patient** 861.10.

.11 **unexcited, unperturbed,** undisturbed, untroubled, unagitated, **unruffled,** unflustered, unstirred, unimpassioned.

.12 **calm, placid,** quiet, **tranquil, serene,** peaceful; **cool, coolheaded,** cool as a cucumber [informal]; philosophical.

.13 **composed, collected,** recollected, **level-headed; poised,** together [slang], in equipoise, equanimous, equilibrious, **balanced,** well-balanced; **self-possessed,** self-controlled, self-restrained; confident, assured, **self-confident, self-assured.**

.14 **sedate, staid,** sober, sober-minded, serious, grave, solemn, sobersided; temperate, moderate.

.15 **nonchalant, blasé; indifferent,** unconcerned 636.6,7; **casual, offhand; easygoing,** easy, free and easy, devil-may-care, lackadaisical, *dégagé* [Fr].

.16 ADVS inexcitably, **imperturbably,** inirritably, **dispassionately;** steadily; stoically; **calmly, placidly,** quietly, **tranquilly, serenely; coolly, composedly,** levelheadedly; impassively, stolidly, stodgily, stuffily.

.17 sedately, staidly, soberly, sobersidedly.

.18 nonchalantly, casually, offhandedly, easygoingly, lackadaisically.

## 859. NERVOUSNESS

.1 NOUNS **nervousness, nerves,** nervosity, uneasiness, apprehensiveness; undue *or* morbid excitability, excessive irritability, state of nerves, case of nerves, spell of nerves, attack of nerves; **agitation, trepidation** 857.3,4; **fear** 891; panic, panickiness; **fidgets,** fidgetiness; twitching, tic, vellication; stage fright, buck fever [informal]; nervous stomach.

.2 [slang or informal terms] **jitters, willies, heebie-jeebies,** jimjams, **jumps, shakes,** quivers, trembles, dithers, all-overs, butterflies, shivers, cold shivers, sweat, cold sweat.

.3 **tension,** tenseness, tautness, **strain, stress,** stress and strain, mental strain, nervous tension *or* strain, pressure.

.4 frayed nerves, frazzled nerves, jangled nerves, shattered nerves, raw nerves, twanging nerves; neurosis 690.19; neurasthenia, nervous prostration, nervous breakdown 686.7.

.5 **nervous wreck,** wreck, a bundle of nerves.

.6 VERBS **fidget,** have the fidgets; jitter, have the jitters, etc.; **tremble** 857.16.

.7 lose self-control, go into hysterics; lose courage 892.8; **crack** *or* **crack up** [informal], go haywire [slang]; **flip** *or* flip one's lid *or* wig [slang], **go to pieces,** have a nervous breakdown, come unstuck *or* come apart [both informal], go up the wall [informal].

.8 **get on one's nerves,** jangle the nerves, **grate on, jar on,** put on edge, **set the teeth on edge,** go against the grain; **irritate** 866.14.

.9 **unnerve, unman, undo, unstring,** unbrace, **demoralize, shake, upset,** psych out [informal], dash, knock down, **crush,** overcome, prostrate.

.10 ADJS **nervous,** nervy [Brit informal]; **high-strung,** overstrung, all nerves; **uneasy, apprehensive;** nervous as a cat; **excitable** 857.26; **irritable,** edgy, on edge, nerves on edge, on the ragged edge [informal], panicky, fearful, frightened 891.31–33.

.11 **jittery** [informal], **jumpy,** skittery [dial], twittery, all-overish [informal]; **shaky,** shivery, quivery, in a quiver; tremulous, tremulant, trembly; jumpy as a cat on a hot tin roof; **fidgety,** fidgeting; fluttery, all of a flutter *or* twitter; twitchy; **agitated** 857.21; shaking, trembling, quivering, shivering; shook up *or* all shook up [both slang].

.12 **tense,** uptight [informal], **strained,** stretched tight, taut, unrelaxed, **under a strain.**

.13 **unnerved, unmanned, unstrung,** undone, reduced to jelly, unglued [informal], **demoralized, shaken, upset,** dashed, stricken, **crushed; shot,** shot to pieces; neurasthenic, prostrate, prostrated, overcome.

.14 **nerve-racking,** nerve-rending, nerve-shaking, nerve-jangling, nerve-trying, nerve-stretching; jarring, grating.

.15 ADVS **nervously, shakily,** shakingly, tremulously, tremblingly, quiveringly.

## 860. UNNERVOUSNESS

.1 NOUNS unnervousness, nervelessness; **calmness, inexcitability** 858; unshakiness, untremulousness; **steadiness,** steady-handedness, steady nerves; no nerves, strong nerves, iron nerves, nerves of steel, icy nerves; cool head.

.2 ADJS **unnervous, nerveless,** without a nerve in one's body; strong-nerved, iron-nerved, steel-nerved; coolheaded, **calm, inexcitable** 858.10−12; cool, calm, and collected; **steady,** rock-steady, steady-nerved, steady-handed; unshaky, unshaken, unquivering, untremulous, without a tremor; unflinching, unfaltering, unwavering, unshrinking, unblenching, unblinking; **relaxed,** unstrained.

## 861. PATIENCE

.1 NOUNS **patience,** patientness; **tolerance,** toleration, **acceptance; indulgence,** lenience, leniency 759; sweet reasonableness; **forbearance,** forbearing, forbearingness; **sufferance, endurance; long-suffering,** long-sufferance, longanimity; **stoicism,** fortitude, self-control; patience of Job; "the art of hoping" [Vauvenargues], "a minor form of despair, disguised as a virtue" [Ambrose Bierce]; waiting game, waiting it out; **perseverance** 625.

.2 **resignation, meekness,** humility, humbleness; obedience; amenability; submission, **submissiveness** 765.3; acquiescence, compliance, uncomplainingness; nonresistance, quietism, passivity, **passiveness** 706.1; passive resistance, nonviolent resistance; Quakerism.

.3 **stoic,** Spartan, man of iron.

.4 VERBS **be patient,** forbear, bear with composure, **wait,** wait it out, play a waiting game, watch for one's moment, keep one's shirt on [slang], not hold one's breath [informal]; contain oneself, possess oneself, possess one's soul in patience; carry on, carry through; "have patience and endure" [Ovid].

.5 **endure, bear, stand,** support, sustain, **suffer, tolerate, abide,** bide; persevere, **stick** [informal]; hang in or hang in there or hang tough [all slang]; **bear with, put up with,** take up with, abide with, stand for [informal], brook, brave; lump or lump it [both informal].

.6 **accept, condone, countenance;** overlook, not make an issue of, let go by, let pass; **reconcile oneself to,** resign oneself to,

yield or submit to, obey; accustom oneself to, accommodate oneself to, adjust oneself to; accept one's fate, lay in the lap of the gods, take things as they come, roll with the punches [informal]; **make the best of it,** make the most of it, make the best of a bad bargain, make a virtue of necessity; submit with a good grace, **grin and bear it,** grin and abide, shrug, shrug it off; take in good part, take in one's stride; rise above.

.7 **take, pocket, swallow,** down, stomach, eat, digest, disregard, turn a blind eye, ignore; swallow an insult, pocket the affront, turn the other cheek, take it lying down, turn aside provocation.

.8 **bear up under, bear the brunt,** stand the gaff [slang], **take it** [informal], take it on the chin [slang], take it like a man, not let it get one down [informal].

.9 ADJS **patient,** armed with patience, with a soul possessed in patience, patient as Job; **tolerant,** tolerative, tolerating, accepting; understanding, **indulgent,** lenient 759.8; **forbearing;** philosophical; **long-suffering,** longanimous; **enduring,** endurant; stoic(al), Spartan; disciplined, self-controlled; **persevering** 625.7.

.10 **resigned,** reconciled; **meek,** humble; obedient, amenable, **submissive** 765.12; acquiescent, compliant; accommodating, adjusting, adapting, adaptive; unresisting, **passive** 706.6; **uncomplaining.**

.11 ADVS **patiently,** enduringly, stoically; **tolerantly, indulgently,** leniently, forbearantly, forbearingly, philosophically, more in sorrow than in anger; "like patience on a monument smiling at grief" [Shakespeare]; perseveringly 625.8.

.12 **resignedly, meekly, submissively,** passively, acquiescently, compliantly, uncomplainingly.

## 862. IMPATIENCE

.1 NOUNS **impatience,** impatientness, unpatientness, breathless impatience; **anxiety, eagerness** 635; tense readiness, **restlessness,** restiveness, ants in one's pants [slang]; disquietude, unquietness, uneasiness; sweat or lather or stew [all informal], **fretfulness,** fretting, chafing; **impetuousness** 630.2; **haste** 709; **excitement** 857.

.2 **intolerance,** intoleration, unforbearance, nonendurance.

.3 **the last straw,** the straw that breaks the camel's back, the limit, the limit of one's patience, all one can bear or stand.

.4 VERBS **be impatient,** hardly wait; hasten

709.4–8; itch to, burn to; **champ at the bit, pull at the leash,** not be able to sit down *or* stand still; **chafe, fret, fuss,** squirm; **stew,** sweat, sweat and stew, get into a dither, get into a stew [informal], work oneself into a lather *or* sweat [informal], get excited 857.15; wait impatiently, sweat it out [slang]; jump the gun [informal].

.5 **have no patience with,** be out of all patience; **lose patience,** run out of patience, call a halt, have had it [informal], blow the whistle [slang].

.6 ADJS **impatient,** unpatient; breathless; champing at the bit, rarin' to go [slang]; **anxious, eager** 635.9; hopped-up [slang], in a lather [informal], in a sweat *or* stew [informal], excited 857.18,19; edgy, **on edge; restless,** restive, unquiet, uneasy; **fretful,** fretting, chafing, antsy-pantsy *or* antsy [both slang], squirming, squirmy, about to piss one's pants [slang]; **impetuous** 630.9; **hasty** 709.9–11.

.7 **intolerant, unforbearing, unindulgent.**

.8 ADVS **impatiently,** breathlessly; **anxiously** 635.14; fretfully; restlessly, restively, uneasily; intolerantly.

### 863. PLEASANTNESS

.1 NOUNS **pleasantness,** pleasingness, pleasance, pleasure, pleasurefulness, **pleasurableness,** pleasurability, pleasantry [archaic], felicitousness, **enjoyableness; bliss, blissfulness;** sweetness, mellifluousness, *douceur* [Fr]; mellowness; **agreeableness,** agreeability, complaisance, rapport, harmoniousness; compatibility; welcomeness; geniality, congeniality, cordiality, affability, amicability, amiability; amenity, graciousness; goodness, goodliness, niceness.

.2 **delightfulness,** exquisiteness, loveliness; **charm,** winsomeness, grace, **attractiveness, appeal,** appealingness, winningness; **glamour;** captivation, enchantment, entrancement, bewitchment, witchery, enravishment, **fascination** 650.1; invitingness, temptingness, tantalizingness; voluptuousness, sensuousness; luxury.

.3 **delectability,** delectableness, deliciousness, lusciousness; tastiness, flavorsomeness, savoriness; juiciness, succulence.

.4 **cheerfulness;** brightness, sunniness; sunny side, bright side; fair weather.

.5 VERBS make pleasant, brighten, sweeten, gild, gild the lily *or* pill.

.6 ADJS **pleasant, pleasing, pleasureful, pleasurable,** hedy–; fair, fair and pleasant, **en**joyable, pleasure-giving; felicitous, felicific; **likable, desirable,** to one's liking, to one's taste, to *or* after one's fancy, after one's own heart; **agreeable,** complaisant, harmonious, *en rapport* [Fr], compatible; **blissful;** sweet, mellifluous, honeyed, dulcet; mellow; **gratifying,** satisfying, rewarding, heart-warming, grateful; **welcome,** welcome as the roses in May; genial, congenial, cordial, affable, amiable, amicable, gracious; good, goodly, nice, fine; cheerful 870.11.

.7 **delightful, exquisite, lovely; thrilling,** titillative; **charming, attractive, engaging, appealing,** prepossessing, **enchanting,** bewitching, witching, entrancing, enthralling, intriguing, fascinating 650.7; captivating, irresistible, ravishing, enravishing; **winning,** winsome, taking, fetching, heart-robbing; inviting, tempting, tantalizing; voluptuous, sensuous; luxurious.

.8 **blissful,** beatific, saintly, divine; sublime; **heavenly,** paradisiac(al), paradisial, paradisian, paradisic(al), empyreal *or* empyrean, Elysian; out of this world [slang].

.9 **delectable, delicious,** luscious; tasty, flavorsome, savory; juicy, succulent.

.10 **bright, sunny,** fair, mild, balmy; halcyon, Saturnian.

.11 ADVS **pleasantly, pleasingly, pleasurably,** fair, **enjoyably; blissfully; gratifyingly,** satisfyingly; agreeably, genially, affably, cordially, amiably, amicably, graciously, kindly; cheerfully 870.17.

.12 **delightfully, exquisitely; charmingly, engagingly, appealingly, enchantingly,** bewitchingly, entrancingly, intriguingly, fascinatingly 650.8; ravishingly, enravishingly **winningly,** winsomely; invitingly, temptingly, tantalizingly, voluptuously, sensuously; luxuriously.

.13 **delectably,** deliciously, lusciously, tastily succulently.

### 864. UNPLEASANTNESS

.1 NOUNS **unpleasantness,** unpleasingnes displeasingness, displeasure; **disagreeabl ness,** disagreeability, *désagrément* [Fr **undesirability,** unappealingness, unattra tiveness, unengagingness, uninvitingnes **distastefulness,** unsavoriness, unpalatab ity, **undelectability; ugliness** 899.

.2 **offensiveness,** objectionability, objectio ableness; repugnance, contrariety, **odio ness, repulsiveness,** repellence *or* rep lency, rebarbativeness, disgustingne nauseousness; **loathsomeness,** hatefulne beastliness [informal]; **vileness, foulne** putridness, putridity, rottenness, noxiousness; nastiness, fulsomeness, noisomeness, **obnoxiousness**, abominability, heinousness; contemptibility, despicability, despicableness, baseness, ignobility; harshness; unspeakableness; grossness, crudeness, obscenity.

.3 **dreadfulness, horribleness,** horridness, atrociousness, atrocity, hideousness, terribleness, awfulness [informal]; grimness, direness, banefulness.

.4 **agony,** agonizingness, excruciation, excruciatingness, **torture,** torturesomeness, torturousness, **torment,** tormentingness; desolation, desolateness, heartbreak, heartsickness.

.5 **distressfulness, distress, grievousness, grief; painfulness,** pain 424; bitterness, sharpness; lamentability, lamentableness, deplorability, deplorableness, pitiableness, pitifulness, pitiability, regrettableness; **sadness, sorrowfulness, mournfulness,** lamentation, woefulness, woebegoneness, pathos, poignancy; comfortlessness, discomfort; dreariness, cheerlessness, joylessness, dismalness, **depression,** bleakness.

.6 **mortification,** humiliation, embarrassment; disconcertedness, awkwardness.

.7 **vexatiousness, irksomeness, annoyance,** annoyingness, aggravation, exasperation, provocation, provokingness, tiresomeness, wearisomeness; **troublesomeness, bothersomeness,** harassment; worrisomeness, plaguesomeness, peskiness or pestiferousness [both informal].

.8 **oppressiveness, burdensomeness,** onerousness, weightiness, heaviness.

.9 **intolerability,** intolerableness, unbearableness, insupportableness, insufferableness, **unendurability.**

10 VERBS **be unpleasant; displease;** be disagreeable or undesirable or distasteful, etc.

11 **offend,** give offense, **repel,** put off, re**volt, disgust,** nauseate, sicken, make one sick, make one sick to or in the stomach, make one vomit or puke or retch, turn the stomach, gross out [slang]; stink in the nostrils; stick in one's throat, stick in one's crop or craw or gizzard [informal]; **horrify, appall,** shock; make the flesh creep or crawl, make one shudder.

2 **agonize,** excruciate, **torture, torment,** desolate.

3 **mortify,** humiliate, embarrass, disconcert, disturb.

.14 **distress, dismay,** grieve, mourn, lament, sorrow; pain, discomfort.

.15 **vex, irk, annoy, aggravate,** exasperate, provoke; **trouble, worry,** plague, harass, bother.

.16 **oppress, burden,** weigh upon, weight down, wear one down, be heavy on one, crush one; **tire, exhaust,** weary, wear out, wear upon one; prey on the mind, prey on or upon; **haunt,** haunt the memory, obsess.

.17 ADJS **unpleasant, unpleasing, unenjoyable; displeasing, disagreeable; unlikable,** dislikable; **undesirable,** unattractive, unappealing, unengaging, uninviting, unalluring; unwelcome, thankless; **distasteful,** untasteful, **unpalatable,** unsavory, unappetizing, undelicious, **undelectable;** ugly 899.6–11; sour, **bitter.**

.18 **offensive, objectionable, odious, repulsive,** repellent, rebarbative, **repugnant, revolting,** forbidding; **disgusting, sickening, loathsome,** beastly [informal], **vile, foul, nasty, nauseating** 429.7; fulsome, mephitic, miasmal, miasmic, malodorous, stinking, fetid, noisome, noxious; gross, crude, obscene; **obnoxious, abhorrent, hateful, abominable,** heinous, **contemptible, despicable,** detestable, execrable, beneath or below contempt, **base,** ignoble.

.19 **horrid, horrible,** horrific, **horrifying,** horrendous, unspeakable; **dreadful, atrocious, terrible, rotten,** awful or beastly [both informal], hideous; **tragic;** dire, grim, baneful; appalling, shocking.

.20 **distressing,** distressful, dismaying; afflicting, afflictive; **painful,** sore, **bitter,** sharp; **grievous,** dolorous, dolorific, dolorogenic; **lamentable, deplorable,** regrettable, pitiable, piteous, rueful, woeful, woebegone, **sad,** sorrowful, wretched, mournful, **depressing,** depressive; **pathetic,** affecting, touching, moving, saddening, poignant; comfortless, discomforting, uncomfortable; dreary, cheerless, joyless, dismal, bleak.

.21 **mortifying,** humiliating, **embarrassing,** crushing, disconcerting, awkward, disturbing.

.22 **annoying, irritating,** galling, provoking, **aggravating** [informal], **exasperating; vexatious,** vexing, irking, **irksome,** tiresome, wearisome; **troublesome, bothersome, worrisome,** bothering, troubling, disturbing, plaguing, plaguesome, plaguey [informal], pestilent, pestilential, **pesky** or pestiferous [both informal]; tormenting, ha rassing, worrying; pestering, teasing; importunate, importune.

.23 agonizing, excruciating, harrowing, racking, rending, desolating, consuming; tormenting, torturous; heartbreaking, heartrending, heartsickening, heartwounding.

.24 oppressive, burdensome, onerous, heavy, weighty; harsh, wearing, wearying, exhausting; overburdensome, tyrannous, grinding.

.25 insufferable, intolerable, insupportable, unendurable, unbearable, past bearing, not to be borne or endured, too much or a bit much [informal], more than flesh and blood can bear, enough to drive one mad, enough to provoke a saint, enough to make a preacher swear [informal], enough to try the patience of Job.

.26 ADVS unpleasantly, unpleasingly; displeasingly, offensively, objectionably, odiously, repulsively, repellently, rebarbatively, repugnantly, revoltingly, disgustingly, sickeningly, loathsomely, vilely, foully, nastily, fulsomely, mephitically, malodorously, fetidly, noisomely, noxiously, obnoxiously, abhorrently, hatefully, abominably, contemptibly, despicably, detestably, execrably, nauseatingly.

.27 horridly, horribly, dreadfully, terribly, hideously; tragically; grimly, direly, banefully; appallingly, shockingly.

.28 distressingly, distressfully; painfully, sorely, grievously, lamentably, deplorably, pitiably, ruefully, woefully, sadly, pathetically; agonizingly, excruciatingly, harrowingly, heartbreakingly.

.29 annoyingly, irritatingly, aggravatingly [informal], provokingly, exasperatingly; vexatiously, irksomely, tiresomely, wearisomely; troublesomely, bothersomely, worrisomely.

.30 insufferably, intolerably, unbearably, unendurably, insupportably.

.31 INTERJS eeyuck! or yeeuck! or yeeuch!, phew! or pugh!, ugh!; feh! [Yid].

## 865. PLEASURE

.1 NOUNS pleasure, enjoyment; quiet pleasure, euphoria, well-being, contentment, content, ease, comfort 887; coziness; gratification, satisfaction, great satisfaction, hearty enjoyment, keen pleasure or satisfaction; self-gratification, self-indulgence; luxury; relish, zest, gusto, joie de vivre [Fr]; sweetness of life, douceur de vivre [Fr]; kicks [informal], fun, entertainment, amusement 878; intellectual pleasure, pleasures of the mind; physical pleasure, creature comforts, bodily pleasure, sense or sensuous pleasure; sexual pleasure, voluptuousness, sensual pleasure, volupté [Fr], animal pleasure, animal comfort, bodily comfort, fleshly or carnal delight; forepleasure, titillation, endpleasure, fruition.

.2 happiness, gladness, delight, delectation; joy, joyfulness, joyance; cheer, cheerfulness, exhilaration, exuberance, high spirits, glee, sunshine; gaiety 870.4, overjoyfulness, overhappiness; intoxication; rapture, ravishment, bewitchment, enchantment, unalloyed happiness; elation, exaltation; ecstasy, ecstatics, transport; bliss, blissfulness; beatitude, beatification, blessedness, felicity; paradise, heaven, seventh heaven, cloud nine.

.3 treat, regalement, regale, revelment, feast, round of pleasures, mad round, banquet, feast or banquet of the soul; festivity, celebration, merrymaking, revel, revelry, jubilation, joyance.

.4 pleasure-loving, pleasure principle, hedonism, hedonics; epicureanism, Cyrenaicism, eudaemonism.

.5 VERBS please, give pleasure, afford one pleasure, be to one's liking, sit well with one, meet one's wishes, take or strike one's fancy, strike one right, hit the spot [slang], be just the ticket or be just what the doctor ordered [both informal], make a hit [informal], go over big [slang].

.6 gratify, satisfy, sate, satiate; slake, appease, allay, assuage, quench; regale, feed, feast; do one's heart good, warm the cockles of the heart.

.7 gladden, make happy, happify; bless, beatify; cheer 870.7.

.8 delight, delectate, tickle, titillate, thrill, tickle to death or tickle pink [both informal]; wow or slay or knock out or knock dead [all slang]; enrapture, enthrall, enchant, entrance, fascinate, captivate, bewitch, charm, becharm; enravish, ravish, imparadise; transport, carry away, send or freak out [both slang].

.9 be pleased, feel happy, sing, purr, smile, laugh, be wreathed in smiles, beam; delight, joy, take great satisfaction; like the cat that swallowed the canary, walk or tread on air, be in heaven or seventh heaven or paradise, be on cloud nine; fall or go into raptures; die with delight or pleasure.

.10 enjoy, be pleased with, receive or derive pleasure from, take delight or pleasure in, get a kick or boot or bang or charge lift out of [slang]; like, love, adore [informal]; **delight in, rejoice in,** indulge in, luxuriate in, revel in, riot in, bask in, wallow in, swim in; groove on or get high on or freak out on [all slang]; feast on, gloat over or on; **relish, appreciate,** roll under the tongue, savor, smack the lips; devour, eat up.

.11 **enjoy oneself,** have a good time.

.12 ADJS **pleased, delighted; glad,** gladsome; **charmed,** intrigued [informal]; **thrilled; tickled,** tickled to death or tickled pink [both informal], exhilarated; **gratified, satisfied;** pleased with, taken with, favorably impressed with, sold on [slang]; pleased as Punch, pleased as a child with a new toy; euphoric, eupeptic; **content, contented,** easy, **comfortable** 887.11,12, cozy, in clover.

.13 **happy, glad, joyful, joyous,** flushed with joy, radiant, beaming, glowing, starry-eyed, sparkling, laughing, smiling, smirking, chirping, purring, singing, dancing, leaping, capering, **cheerful, gay** 870.11–16; **blissful,** "throned on highest bliss" [Milton]; blessed; beatified, beatific; thrice happy, "thrice and four times blessed" [Vergil]; happy as a lark, happy as a king, happy as the day is long, happy as a baby boy, happy as a clam at high water.

.14 **overjoyed,** overjoyful, overhappy, bursting with happiness; **rapturous,** raptured, **enraptured, enchanted,** entranced, enravished, ravished, rapt, possessed; sent or high or freaked out [all slang], **in raptures,** transported, in a transport of delight, **carried away,** rapt or ravished away, beside oneself, beside oneself with joy, all over oneself [slang]; **ecstatic,** in ecstasies, rhapsodic(al); imparadised, **in paradise,** in heaven, in seventh heaven, on cloud nine; **elated,** elate, exalted, jubilant, exultant, flushed.

.15 **pleasure-loving,** pleasure-seeking, fun-loving, hedonic, hedonistic; epicurean, Cyrenaic, eudaemonic.

.16 ADVS **happily, gladly, joyfully, joyously, delightedly,** with pleasure, to one's delight; blissfully, blessedly; **ecstatically,** rhapsodically, **rapturously; elatedly,** jubilantly, exultantly.

.17 INTERJS **goody!,** goody, goody!, goody gumdrops!, good-o!; whee!, **wow!,** u-mm!, mmmm!, oooo!, oo-la-la!; oh boy!, boy oh boy!, boy!, man!, hot dog!, hot ziggety!, hot diggety!, wowie zowie!, out of sight! or outa sight!, groovy!, keen-o!, keen-o-peachy!

### 866. UNPLEASURE

.1 NOUNS unpleasure, **lack of pleasure,** joylessness, cheerlessness; unsatisfaction, nonsatisfaction, ungratification, nongratification; grimness; discontent 869; **displeasure, dissatisfaction, discomfort,** uncomfortableness, malaise, **painfulness; disquiet,** inquietude, **uneasiness,** unease, discomposure, vexation of spirit, **anxiety;** angst, anguish, dread, nausea, existential woe, existential vacuum; the blahs [slang]; **dullness,** flatness, staleness, tastelessness, savorlessness; ashes in the mouth; **boredom,** ennui, tedium, tediousness, spleen; emptiness, spiritual void, death of the heart or soul; unhappiness 872.2; dislike 867.

.2 annoyance, **vexation,** bothersomeness, exasperation, **aggravation** [informal]; **nuisance, pest, bother,** botheration [informal], **trouble, problem,** difficulty, trial; **bore,** crashing bore [informal]; **drag,** downer [both slang]; **worry,** worriment [informal]; bad news [informal]; headache [informal], **pain in the neck** or pain in the ass [both slang]; **harassment,** molestation, persecution, dogging, hounding, harrying; devilment, bedevilment; vexatiousness 864.7.

.3 **irritation,** exacerbation, salt in the wound, embitterment, **provocation;** fret, gall, chafe; irritant; pea in the shoe.

.4 **mortification, chagrin, distress;** embarrassment, abashment, **discomfiture,** disconcertion, disconcertment, discountenance, discomposure, disturbance, confusion; skeleton in the closet.

.5 **pain, distress, grief,** stress, stress of life, suffering, passion, dolor; ache, aching; pang, wrench, throes, cramp, spasm; wound, injury, hurt; **sore,** sore spot, tender spot, lesion; cut, stroke; shock, blow, hard or nasty blow.

.6 **wretchedness, despair,** bitterness, infelicity, **misery, anguish, agony, woe,** bale; **melancholy,** melancholia, **depression, sadness, grief** 872.10; **heartache,** aching heart, heavy heart, bleeding heart, broken heart, agony of mind or spirit; suicidal despair; **desolation,** prostration, crushing; extremity, depth of misery.

.7 **torment, torture,** cruciation, crucifixion, passion, rack, laceration, clawing, lancination; persecution; martyrdom; purgatory, "frigid purgatorial fires" [T. S. Eliot], hell, hell upon earth; holocaust; nightmare, horror.

.8 affliction, infliction; **curse, woe,** distress, grievance, **sorrow,** *tsures* [Yid]; **trouble,** peck *or* pack of troubles, "sea of troubles" [Shakespeare]; **care,** burden of care, cankerworm of care; **burden, oppression, cross, load,** encumbrance, weight, albatross around one's neck, millstone around one's neck; **thorn,** thorn in the side, crown of thorns; bitter pill, bitter draft, bitter cup, cup *or* waters of bitterness; gall, gall and wormwood; "the thousand natural shocks that flesh is heir to" [Shakespeare], "all the ills that men endure" [Abraham Cowley].

.9 **trial, tribulation,** trials and tribulations; **ordeal,** fiery ordeal, the iron entering the soul.

.10 **tormentor, torment; pest,** pesterer, nag, nudzh [slang], *nudnik* [Yid]; **tease,** teaser; annoyer, harasser, harrier, badgerer, **heckler,** plaguer, persecutor; sadist; **bully.**

.11 **sufferer,** victim, prey; **wretch,** poor devil, object of compassion; martyr.

.12 VERBS **give no pleasure** *or* joy *or* cheer *or* comfort, **disquiet,** discompose, leave unsatisfied; discontent 869.4; taste like ashes in the mouth; **bore,** be tedious.

.13 **annoy, irk, vex, nettle, provoke, pique,** miff *or* peeve [both informal], distemper, **ruffle, disturb,** discompose, roil, rile [informal], **aggravate** [informal], **exasperate,** exercise, try the patience; **put one's back up,** bristle; **gripe;** give one a pain [informal]; **get, get one's goat;** get under one's skin, get in one's hair; burn up *or* brown off [both slang]; **torment, molest, bother,** pother; **harass,** harry, drive up the wall [informal], **hound,** dog, nag, nudzh [slang], **persecute; heckle,** badger, hector, bait, bullyrag, worry, nip at the heels of, chivy, fash [Scot]; **bug** [slang], be on the back of *or* be at *or* ride [all slang], **pester, tease, needle,** devil, **bedevil, pick on** [informal], tweak the nose, pluck the beard, give a bad time to [slang]; **plague, beset.**

.14 **irritate,** exacerbate, rub salt in the wound, provoke, **gall, chafe, fret, grate,** grit *or* gravel [both informal], rasp; **get on one's nerves, grate on,** set on edge, **set the teeth on edge,** go against the grain; **rub the wrong way.**

.15 **chagrin, embarrass, abash, discomfit, disconcert,** discompose, confuse, throw into confusion, **upset,** confound, cast down, mortify, put out, put out of face *or* countenance, put to the blush.

.16 **distress, afflict, trouble,** burden, load with care, **bother, disturb, perturb,** disquiet, discomfort, agitate, upset, put to it.

.17 **pain, grieve, aggrieve, anguish; hurt, wound,** bruise, **hurt the feelings;** pierce, prick, stab, cut, sting; **cut up** [informal], **cut to the heart,** wound *or* sting *or* cut to the quick; touch a soft spot *or* tender spot, touch a raw nerve, touch where it hurts, hit one where he lives [slang]; step on one's corns; barb the dart, twist the knife.

.18 **torture, torment, agonize, harrow,** savage, **rack,** scarify, crucify, impale, excruciate, lacerate, claw, rip, bloody, lancinate, macerate, convulse, wring; prolong the agony, kill by inches; martyr, martyrize; punish 1010.10.

.19 **suffer, hurt, ache, bleed;** anguish, **suffer anguish; agonize,** writhe; go hard with, have a bad time of it; quaff the bitter cup, drain the cup of misery to the dregs, be nailed to the cross.

.20 ADJS **pleasureless,** joyless, cheerless, depressed 872.22, grim; **sad, unhappy** 872.20–28; unsatisfied, unfulfilled, ungratified; **bored;** anguished, anxious, suffering angst *or* dread *or* nausea, uneasy, unquiet, prey to malaise; **repelled,** revolted, **disgusted,** sickened, nauseated, nauseous.

.21 **annoyed, irritated,** bugged [slang]; galled, chafed; **bothered, troubled, disturbed, ruffled, roiled,** riled [informal]; **irked, vexed, piqued, nettled, provoked, peeved** *or* miffed [both informal], griped, **aggravated** [informal], **exasperated;** burnt-up *or* browned-off [both slang], resentful, angry 952.24–29.

.22 **distressed, afflicted, put-upon,** beset, **troubled, bothered, disturbed, perturbed, disquieted,** discomforted, discomposed, agitated; hung up [informal]; **uncomfortable,** uneasy, ill at ease; **chagrined, embarrassed,** abashed, discomfited, disconcerted, **upset, confused,** mortified, put out, out of countenance, cast down, chapfallen.

.23 **pained, grieved, aggrieved; wounded, hurt,** injured, **bruised,** mauled; **cut, cut to the quick; stung;** anguished, aching, bleeding.

.24 **tormented, plagued, harassed, harried,** dogged, **hounded, persecuted,** beset, nipped at, worried, chivied, **heckled,** badgered, hectored, baited, bullyragged, ragged, **pestered, teased, needled,** deviled, **bedeviled, picked on** [informal], **bugged** [slang].

.25 **tortured, harrowed,** savagèd, **agonize**

convulsed, wrung, racked, crucified, impaled, lacerated, clawed, ripped, bloodied, lancinated; on the rack, under the harrow.

26 wretched, miserable; woeful, woebegone; crushed, stricken, cut up [informal], heartsick, heart-stricken, heart-struck; deep-troubled; desolate, disconsolate, suicidal.

27 ADVS to one's displeasure, to one's disgust.

## 867. DISLIKE

.1 NOUNS dislike, distaste, disrelish; disaffection, disfavor, disinclination; disaffinity; displeasure, disapproval, disapprobation.

.2 hostility, antagonism, enmity 929; hatred, hate 930; aversion, repugnance, repulsion, antipathy, allergy [informal], abomination, abhorrence, horror, mortal horror; disgust, loathing; nausea; shuddering, cold sweat, creeping flesh.

.3 VERBS dislike, mislike, disfavor, not like, have no liking for, have no use for [informal], not care for, have a disaffinity for, entertain or conceive or take a dislike to, not be able to bear or endure or abide, disapprove of; disrelish, have no taste for, not have the stomach for; be hostile to; hate, abhor, loathe 930.5.

.4 feel disgust, be nauseated, sicken at, choke on, have a bellyful of [slang]; gag, retch, keck, heave, vomit, puke, upchuck or barf [both slang].

.5 shudder at, have one's flesh creep or crawl at the thought of; shrink from, recoil, revolt at; grimace, make a wry face or wry mouth; turn up one's nose at, look down one's nose at, look askance at, take a dim view of, show distaste for, disapprove of.

.6 repel, disgust 864.11.

.7 ADJS unlikable, distasteful, mislikable, dislikable, uncongenial, displeasing, unpleasant 864.17; not to one's taste, not one's sort, not one's cup of tea, against one's grain, counter to one's preferences, offering no delight, uninviting; unlovable; abhorrent, odious 864.18; intolerable 864.25.

8 averse, allergic [informal], undelighted, out of sympathy, disaffected, disenchanted, disinclined, displeased, put off [informal], not charmed; unfriendly, hostile 929.9–13; –phobic.

9 disliked, uncared-for, unvalued, unprized; despised, lowly; unpopular, out of favor,

gone begging; unappreciated, misunderstood, misprized; unsung, thankless; unwept, unlamented, unmourned, undeplored, unmissed, unregretted.

.10 unloved, unbeloved, uncherished, loveless; lovelorn, forsaken, rejected, jilted, thrown over [informal], spurned, crossed in love.

.11 unwanted, unwished, undesired; unwelcome, unasked, unbidden, uninvited, uncalled-for, unasked-for.

## 868. CONTENTMENT

.1 NOUNS contentment, content, contentedness, satisfiedness; satisfaction, entire satisfaction, fulfillment; ease, peace of mind, composure 858.2; comfort 887; well-being, euphoria; happiness 865.2; acceptance, resignation, reconcilement, reconciliation.

.2 complacence or complacency, bovinity; smugness, self-complacence or self-complacency, self-satisfaction, self-content, self-contentedness.

.3 satisfactoriness, adequacy, sufficiency 661; acceptability, admissibility, tolerability, agreeability, unobjectionability, unexceptionability, tenability, viability.

.4 VERBS content, satisfy; gratify 865.6; put or set at ease, set one's mind at ease or rest, achieve inner harmony.

.5 be content, rest satisfied, rest easy, rest and be thankful, be reconciled to, take the good the gods provide, accept one's lot, let well enough alone; come to terms with oneself, learn to live in one's own skin; have no kick coming [slang], can't complain; content oneself with, settle for; be pleased 865.9.

.6 be satisfactory, suffice 661.4.

.7 ADJS content, contented, satisfied; pleased 865.12; happy 865.13; easy, at ease, at one's ease, easygoing; composed 858.13; comfortable 887.11,12, of good comfort; euphoric, eupeptic; without care, sans souci [Fr]; accepting, resigned, reconciled; uncomplaining, unrepining.

.8 untroubled, unbothered, undisturbed, unperturbed 858.11, unworried, unvexed, unplagued, untormented.

.9 well-content, well-pleased, well-contented, well-satisfied, highly satisfied.

.10 complacent, bovine; smug, self-complacent, self-satisfied, self-content, self-contented.

.11 satisfactory, satisfying; sufficient 661.6, sufficing, adequate, commensurate, proportionate, proportionable, ample, equal to.

.12 acceptable, admissible, agreeable, unobjectionable, unexceptionable, tenable, viable; OK or okay or all right or alright [all informal]; passable, good enough.

.13 tolerable, bearable, endurable, supportable, sufferable.

.14 ADVS contentedly, to one's heart's content; satisfiedly, with satisfaction; complacently, smugly, self-complacently, self-satisfiedly, self-contentedly.

.15 satisfactorily, satisfyingly; acceptably, agreeably, admissibly; sufficiently, adequately, commensurately, amply, enough; tolerably, passably.

.16 to one's satisfaction, to one's delight, to one's great glee; to one's taste, to the king's or queen's taste.

## 869. DISCONTENT

.1 NOUNS discontent, discontentment, discontentedness; dissatisfaction, unsatisfaction, dissatisfiedness, unfulfillment; resentment, envy 954; restlessness, restiveness, uneasiness; rebelliousness 767.3; disappointment 541; unpleasure 866; unhappiness 872.2; ill humor 951; disgruntlement, sulkiness, sourness, petulance, peevishness, querulousness; vexation of spirit; cold comfort; divine discontent; Faustianism.

.2 unsatisfactoriness, dissatisfactoriness; inadequacy, insufficiency 662; unacceptability, inadmissibility, unsuitability, undesirability, objectionability, untenability, indefensibility; intolerability 864.9.

.3 malcontent, frondeur [Fr]; complainer, complainant, faultfinder, grumbler, growler, murmurer, mutterer, griper, croaker, peevish or petulant or querulous person, whiner, kvetch [Yid]; kicker or grouch or crank or crab or grouser or beefer [all informal]; bellyacher or bitcher or sorehead [all slang]; reactionary, reactionist; rebel 767.5.

.4 VERBS dissatisfy, discontent, disgruntle, displease, disappoint, dishearten, put out [informal].

.5 ADJS discontented, dissatisfied, disgruntled, unaccepting, unaccommodating, displeased, disappointed; unsatisfied, ungratified, unfulfilled; resentful, dog-in-the-manger; envious 954.4; restless, restive, uneasy; rebellious 767.11; malcontent, malcontented, complaining, complaintful, faultfinding, grumbling, growling, murmuring, muttering, griping, croaking,

peevish, petulant, sulky, querulous, querulant, whiny; grouchy or cranky or beefing or crabby or crabbing or grousing [all informal]; bellyaching or bitching [both slang]; unhappy 872.21; out of humor 951.17.

.6 unsatisfactory, dissatisfactory; unsatisfying, ungratifying, unfulfilling; displeasing 864.17, disappointing, disheartening, not up to expectation, not good enough; inadequate, incommensurate, insufficient 662.9.

.7 unacceptable, inadmissible, unsuitable, undesirable, objectionable, exceptionable, impossible, untenable, indefensible, intolerable 864.25.

.8 ADVS discontentedly, dissatisfiedly.

.9 unsatisfactorily, dissatisfactorily; unsatisfyingly, ungratifyingly; inadequately, insufficiently; unacceptably, inadmissibly, unsuitably, undesirably, objectionably; intolerably 864.30.

## 870. CHEERFULNESS

.1 NOUNS cheerfulness, cheeriness, good cheer, cheer, cheery vein or mood; blitheness, blithesomeness; gladness, gladsomeness; happiness 865.2; pleasantness, winsomeness, geniality, brightness, radiance, sunniness; sanguineness, sanguinity, sanguine humor, euphoric or eupeptic mien, optimism, rosy expectation, hopefulness.

.2 good humor, good spirits; high spirits, exhilaration, rare good humor.

.3 lightheartedness, lightsomeness, lightness, levity; buoyancy, resilience, bounce [informal]; jauntiness, perkiness, debonairness, carefreeness; breeziness, airiness, pertness, chirpiness, light heart.

.4 gaiety, gayness, allégresse [Fr]; liveliness, vivacity, vitality, life, animation, spiritedness, spirit, esprit, élan, sprightliness, zestfulness, zest, vim, zip [informal], vigor, verve, gusto, exuberance, heartiness; spirits, animal spirits; piss and vinegar [slang]; friskiness, skittishness, coltishness, rompishness, rollicksomeness, capersomeness; sportiveness, playfulness, frolicsomeness, gamesomeness.

.5 merriment, merriness; hilarity, hilariousness; joy, joyfulness, joyousness; glee, gleefulness, high glee; jollity, jolliness, joviality, jocularity, jocundity; frivolity, levity; mirth, mirthfulness, amusement 87; fun; laughter 876.4.

.6 VERBS exude cheerfulness, radiate cheer, beam, glow, sparkle, sing, lilt, whistle, chirp, chirrup, chirp like a cricket, dan-

skip, caper, frolic, gambol, romp, caracole; **smile, laugh** 876.7,8.

.7 **cheer, gladden, brighten,** put in good humor; **encourage, hearten,** pick up [informal]; **inspire,** inspirit, warm the spirits, **raise the spirits,** elevate one's mood, buoy up, boost, give a lift [slang], put one on top of the world *or* on cloud nine [both informal]; **exhilarate,** animate, invigorate, liven, enliven, vitalize; **rejoice,** rejoice the heart, do the heart good.

.8 **elate, exalt,** elevate, lift, uplift, flush.

.9 **cheer up, take heart,** drive dull care away; **brighten up,** light up, **perk up; buck up** *or* brace up *or* chirk up [all informal]; come out of it, snap out of it [slang], revive.

.10 **be of good cheer,** bear up, **keep one's spirits up,** keep one's chin up [informal], keep one's pecker up [Brit informal], keep a stiff upper lip [slang], grin and bear it.

.11 ADJS **cheerful, cheery,** of good cheer, in good spirits; in high spirits, exalted, elated, exhilarated, high [slang]; irrepressible; **blithe,** blithesome; **glad, gladsome; happy** 865.13; **pleasant, genial,** winsome; **bright, sunny,** bright and sunny, **radiant,** riant, sparkling, beaming, glowing, flushed, rosy, smiling, laughing; sanguine, sanguineous, euphoric, eupeptic; optimistic, hopeful.

.12 **lighthearted,** light, lightsome; **buoyant,** corky [informal], resilient; **jaunty, perky, debonair, carefree,** free and easy; **breezy,** airy.

.13 **pert,** peart [dial], chirk [dial], chirrupy, **chirpy, chipper** [informal].

.14 **gay,** gay as a lark; **spirited,** sprightly, **lively, animated, vivacious,** vital, zestful, zippy [informal], **exuberant, hearty; frisky,** antic, skittish, coltish, rompish, capersome; **full of beans** *or* feeling one's oats [both informal], full of piss and vinegar [slang]; **sportive, playful,** playful as a kitten, **frolicsome,** gamesome; rollicking, rollicky, rollicksome.

.15 **merry, mirthful, hilarious; joyful, joyous,** rejoicing 876.9; **gleeful,** gleesome; **jolly,** buxom; **jovial,** jocund, jocular; **frivolous;** laughter-loving, mirth-loving, risible; merry as a cricket *or* grig, "as merry as the day is long" [Shakespeare].

.16 **cheering, gladdening; encouraging, heartening,** heart-warming; **inspiring,** inspiriting; **exhilarating,** animating, enlivening, invigorating; **cheerful, cheery, glad,** joyful.

.17 ADVS **cheerfully,** cheerily, with good cheer, with a cheerful heart; irrepressibly; **lightheartedly,** lightly; jauntily, perkily, airily; **pleasantly,** genially, blithely; **gladly, happily, joyfully,** smilingly; optimistically, hopefully.

.18 **gaily, exuberantly, heartily, spiritedly, animatedly, vivaciously,** zestfully, with zest, with vim, with élan, with zip [informal], with verve, with gusto.

.19 **merrily, gleefully, hilariously;** jovially, jocundly, jocularly; frivolously; **mirthfully,** laughingly.

## 871. SOLEMNITY

.1 NOUNS **solemnity, solemnness, soberness, sobriety, gravity,** weightiness, **somberness, grimness;** sedateness, staidness; demureness, decorousness; **seriousness, earnestness, thoughtfulness, sober-mindedness,** sobersidedness; **sobersides;** long face, straight face; **formality** 646.

.2 VERBS **keep a straight face,** look serious, compose one's features, wear an earnest frown, repress a smile, not crack a smile [slang], wipe the smile off one's face, keep from laughing.

.3 ADJS **solemn, sober, grave,** unsmiling, weighty, **somber,** frowning, **grim; sedate, staid;** demure, decorous; **serious, earnest, thoughtful,** serio–; **sober-minded,** sobersided; straight-faced, long-faced, grim-faced, grim-visaged, stone-faced; sober as a judge, grave as an undertaker; **formal** 646.7–10.

.4 ADVS **solemnly, soberly,** gravely, somberly, grimly; sedately, staidly, demurely, decorously; **seriously, earnestly,** thoughtfully, sober-mindedly, sobersidedly; with a straight face; **formally** 646.11,12.

## 872. SADNESS

.1 NOUNS **sadness, sadheartedness; heaviness, heavyheartedness,** heavy heart, **heaviness of heart;** pathos, bathos.

.2 **unhappiness,** infelicity; **displeasure** 866.1; **discontent** 869; **uncheerfulness,** cheerlessness; **joylessness,** unjoyfulness; **mirthlessness,** unmirthfulness, humorlessness, infestivity; **grimness; wretchedness, misery.**

.3 **dejection, depression, oppression,** dejectedness, **downheartedness,** downcastness; **discouragement, disheartenment,** dispiritedness; *Schmerz, Weltschmerz* [both Ger]; malaise 866.1; lowness, lowness *or* depression *or* oppression of spirit, downer, down trip [both slang]; **low spirits,** drooping spirits, sinking heart; despondence or **despondency,** despondentness, spiritlessness, heartlessness; black or blank despondency, Slough of Despond; hopelessness 889, **despair** 889.2, pessimism 889.6, suicidal despair, death wish, self-destructive urge, weariness of life, *taedium vitae* [L].

.4 **hypochondria,** hypochondriasis, morbid anxiety.

.5 **melancholy, melancholia,** melancholiness; gentle melancholy, romantic melancholy; **pensiveness, wistfulness,** tristfulness.

.6 **blues** or blue devils [both informal], mulligrubs [slang], mumps, **dumps** [informal], **doldrums,** dismals, dolefuls [informal], blahs [informal], mopes, megrims, sulks.

.7 **gloom, gloominess,** darkness, **dismalness, bleakness,** grimness, **somberness,** gravity, **solemnity; dreariness,** drearisomeness; wearifulness, wearisomeness.

.8 **glumness,** grumness, **moroseness, sullenness,** sulkiness, **moodiness,** mumpishness, dumpishness; mopishness, mopiness [informal].

.9 **heartache,** aching heart, bleeding heart; heartsickness, heartsoreness; **heartbreak, broken heart,** brokenheartedness, heartbrokenness.

.10 **sorrow,** sorrowing, **grief, care,** carking care, **woe;** heartgrief, heartfelt grief; languishment, pining; **anguish, misery, agony;** prostration; lamentation 875.

.11 **sorrowfulness, mournfulness,** ruefulness, **woefulness, dolefulness,** dolorousness, **plaintiveness,** plangency, grievousness, aggrievedness, lugubriousness, funerealness; tearfulness 875.2.

.12 **disconsolateness,** disconsolation, **inconsolability,** comfortlessness; **desolation,** desolateness; forlornness.

.13 **sourpuss** or gloomy Gus [both slang]; mope, brooder; melancholic, melancholiac; depressive.

.14 **killjoy, spoilsport,** crepehanger [informal]; damp, damper, **wet blanket;** skeleton at the feast; pessimist 889.7.

.15 VERBS hang one's head, pull or make a long face, look blue, sing the blues [informal]; hang crepe [informal].

.16 **despond,** lose heart, give way, give oneself up or over to; despair 889.10, be or become suicidal, lose the will to live; **droop,** sink, languish; reach or plumb the depths, touch bottom, hit rock bottom.

.17 **grieve, sorrow;** mourn 875.8–14; be dumb with grief; **pine,** pine away; **brood over,** mope, fret, take on [informal]; **eat one's heart out,** break one's heart over; **agonize,** ache, bleed.

.18 **sadden,** darken, cast a pall or gloom upon, weigh or weigh heavy upon; **deject, depress, oppress,** press down, **cast down,** lower, lower the spirits, get one down [informal], **discourage, dishearten,** take the heart out of, **dispirit;** damp, dampen, damp or dampen the spirits; dash, knock down, beat down; sink, sink one's soul, plunge one into despair.

.19 **aggrieve,** oppress, **grieve, sorrow,** plunge one into sorrow, embitter; draw tears, bring to tears; **anguish, cut up** [informal], wring or pierce or lacerate or rend the heart, pull at the heartstrings; afflict 866.16, torment 866.18; **break one's heart, make one's heart bleed;** desolate, leave an aching void; prostrate, break down, crush, inundate, overwhelm.

.20 ADJS **sad,** saddened; sadhearted, **sad of heart; heavyhearted,** heavy; oppressed, weighed upon, weighed or weighted down, burdened or laden with sorrow; sad-faced, long-faced; sad-eyed; sad-voiced.

.21 **unhappy, uncheerful,** uncheery, **cheerless, joyless, unjoyful,** unsmiling; mirthless, unmirthful, humorless, infestive; **grim; out of humor,** out of sorts, in bad humor or spirits; **sorry,** sorryish; discontented 869.5; **wretched, miserable;** pleasureless 866.20–26.

.22 **dejected, depressed, downhearted, down, downcast, cast down,** bowed-down, subdued; **discouraged, disheartened, dispirited,** dashed; **low,** feeling low, low-spirited, **in low spirits; down in the mouth** [informal], **in the doldrums, in the dumps** or in the doleful dumps [both informal], **in the depths; despondent,** desponding; **despairing** 889.12, weary of life, suicidal, world-weary; pessimistic 889.16, spiritless, heartless, **woebegone; drooping,** droopy, languishing, pining; hypochondriac or hypochondriacal.

.23 **melancholy,** melancholic, **blue** [informal], funky; atrabilious, atrabiliar; pensive, **wistful,** tristful.

.24 **gloomy, dismal, bleak, grim, somber,** sombrous, **solemn, grave,** *triste* [Fr], **funereal,** funebrial, crepehanging [informal], saturnine; **dark,** black, gray; **dreary,** drear, drearisome; weary, weariful, wearisome.

.25 **glum, grum, morose, sullen,** sulky, mumpish, dumpish, long-faced, crestfallen, chapfallen; **moody,** moodish, **brooding,** broody; mopish, mopey [informal], moping.

.26 **sorrowful, sorrowing, sorrowed, mournful, rueful, woeful, doleful, plaintive,** plangent; anguished; dolorous, **grievous, lamentable,** lugubrious; **tearful** 875.17; **careworn;** grieved, **grief-stricken, griefful,** aggrieved, in grief, plunged in grief, dumb with grief.

.27 **sorrow-stricken, sorrow-wounded,** sorrow-struck, sorrow-torn, sorrow-worn, sorrow-wasted, sorrow-beaten, sorrow-blinded, sorrow-clouded, sorrow-shot, sorrow-burdened, sorrow-laden, sorrow-sighing, sorrow-sobbing, sorrow-sick.

.28 **disconsolate, inconsolable,** unconsolable, comfortless, forlorn; desolate, *désolé* [Fr]; sick, **sick at heart, heartsick,** soul-sick, heartsore.

.29 **overcome,** crushed, overwhelmed, inundated, **stricken, cut up** [informal], desolated, prostrate(d), broken-down, undone; **heart-stricken,** heart-struck; **heartbroken,** brokenhearted.

.30 **depressing,** down [slang], depressive, depressant, **oppressive; discouraging, disheartening, dispiriting.**

.31 ADVS **sadly, gloomily, dismally, drearily,** heavily, bleakly, grimly, somberly, sombrously, solemnly, funereally, gravely, with a long face.

.32 **unhappily, uncheerfully,** cheerlessly, joylessly, unjoyfully.

.33 **dejectedly, downheartedly; discouragedly, disheartenedly, dispiritedly; despondently,** despairingly, spiritlessly, heartlessly; **disconsolately,** inconsolably, unconsolably, forlornly.

.34 **melancholily, pensively,** wistfully, tristfully.

.35 **glumly, grumly, morosely, sullenly; moodily,** moodishly, broodingly, broodily; mopishly, mopily [informal], mopingly.

.36 **sorrowfully, mournfully, ruefully, woefully, dolefully,** dolorously, **plaintively, grievously,** grieffully, lugubriously; **heartbrokenly,** brokenheartedly; **tearfully,** with tears in eyes.

## 873. REGRET

.1 NOUNS **regret,** regretting, regretfulness; **remorse,** remorsefulness, remorse of conscience, ayenbite of inwit [archaic]; **shame,** shamefulness, shamefacedness, shamefastness; **sorrow, grief, sorriness,** repining; **contrition,** contriteness, attrition; bitterness; regrets, apologies; wistfulness 634.4.

.2 **compunction, qualms,** scruples, pangs, **pangs of conscience,** throes, sting *or* pricking *or* twinge *or* twitch of conscience, touch of conscience, **voice of conscience,** pricking of heart, **better self.**

.3 **self-reproach,** self-reproachfulness, **self-accusation, self-condemnation,** self-conviction, self-punishment, self-humiliation, self-debasement, self-hatred, self-flagellation; self-analysis, soul-searching, examination of conscience.

.4 **penitence, repentance, change of heart; apology,** humble *or* heartfelt apology, abject apology; reformation 145.2; deathbed repentance; *mea culpa* [L]; *saeta* [Sp]; **penance** 1012.3; wearing a hairshirt *or* sackcloth *or* sackcloth and ashes, mortification of the flesh.

.5 **penitent,** confessor, "a sadder and a wiser man" [Coleridge]; **prodigal son,** prodigal returned; Magdalen.

.6 VERBS **regret, deplore, repine, be sorry for; rue,** rue the day; **bemoan, bewail;** curse one's folly, **reproach oneself,** kick oneself [slang], bite one's tongue, accuse *or* condemn *or* blame *or* convict *or* punish oneself, flagellate oneself, humiliate *or* debase oneself, hate oneself for one's actions; examine one's conscience, search one's soul, analyze *or* search one's motives; cry over spilled milk, waste time in regret.

.7 **repent, think better of,** change one's mind; plead guilty, own oneself in the wrong, humble oneself, **apologize** 1012.5, beg pardon *or* forgiveness, throw oneself on the mercy of the court; **do penance** 1012.6; reform.

.8 ADJS **regretful, remorseful,** full of remorse, **ashamed,** shameful, shamefaced, shamefast, **sorry, rueful, repining,** unhappy about; **conscience-stricken,** conscience-smitten; **self-reproachful,** self-reproaching, self-accusing, self-condemning, self-convicting, self-punishing, self-flagellating, self-humiliating, self-debasing, self-hating; wistful 634.23.

.9 **penitent, repentant;** penitential, penitentiary; **contrite,** abject, humble, humbled, sheepish, apologetic, touched, softened, melted.

.10 **regrettable,** much to be regretted; **deplorable** 675.9.

.11 ADVS **regretfully, remorsefully,** sorrily, ruefully, unhappily.

.12 **penitently,** repentantly, penitentially; **contritely,** abjectly, **humbly** 906.15, sheepishly, apologetically.

## 874. UNREGRETFULNESS

.1 NOUNS unregretfulness, **unremorseful-ness, unsorriness,** unruefulness; **remorse-lessness,** regretlessness, sorrowlessness; **shamelessness,** unashamedness.

.2 **impenitence,** impenitentness; nonrepentance, irrepentance; **uncontriteness,** unabjectness; seared conscience, **heart of stone,** callousness 856.3; **hardness of heart,** hardness, induration, obduracy; insolence 913.

.3 VERBS **harden one's heart,** steel oneself; **have no regrets,** not look backward, not cry over spilled milk; **have no shame.**

.4 ADJS **unregretful,** unregretting, **unre-morseful, unsorry, unsorrowful,** unrueful; **remorseless,** regretless, sorrowless, grief-less; unsorrowing, ungrieving, unrepining; **shameless,** unashamed.

.5 **impenitent, unrepentant, unrepenting; uncontrite,** unabject; untouched, unsoftened, unmelted, callous 856.12; **hard,** hardened, obdurate; insolent 913.8–10.

.6 **unregretted, unrepented.**

.7 ADVS **unregretfully, unremorsefully,** un-ruefully; **remorselessly,** sorrowlessly, impenitently, shamelessly, unashamedly; **without regret,** without looking back, **without remorse,** without compunction, without any qualms or scruples.

## 875. LAMENTATION

.1 NOUNS **lamentation,** lamenting, **mourn-ing, moaning, grieving, sorrowing, wail-ing, bewailing, bemoaning,** keening, howling, ululation, "weeping and gnashing of teeth" [Bible]; **sorrow** 872.10.

.2 **weeping, sobbing, crying, bawling, greet** [Scot]; blubbering, whimpering, sniveling; **tears,** flood of tears, fit of crying; cry or good cry [both informal]; **tearfulness,** weepiness [informal], lachrymosity, melting mood; **tearful eyes,** swimming or brimming or overflowing eyes; **tear, tear-drop,** lachryma, dacry(o)–; lacrimatory, tear bottle.

.3 **lament, plaint,** planctus [L]; **murmur,** mutter; **moan, groan; whine, whimper; wail,** wail of woe; **sob,** cri du cœur [Fr], **cry, outcry, scream, howl, yowl, bawl,** yawp, keen, ululation; jeremiad, tirade, dolorous tirade.

.4 **complaint, grievance, peeve,** pet peeve, **groan;** dissent, protest 522; **beef** or **kick** or **gripe** or **grouse** [all informal]; **bellyache** or **howl** or **holler** or **squawk** or **bitch** [all slang]; **complaining,** scolding, groaning,

faultfinding 969.4, sniping, destructive criticism, **grumbling, murmuring;** beefing or grousing or kicking or griping [all informal]; **bellyaching** or **squawking** or **bitching** or **yapping** [all slang]; whining, petulance, peevishness, querulousness.

.5 **dirge, funeral** or **death song,** coronach, keen, **elegy,** epicedium, **requiem,** monody, threnody, threnode, **knell, death knell,** passing bell, funeral or dead march, muffled drums; eulogy, funeral or graveside oration.

.6 (mourning garments) **mourning, weeds, widow's weeds, crape,** black; deep mourning; sackcloth, sackcloth and ashes; cypress, cypress lawn, yew; mourning band; mourning ring.

.7 **lamenter, griever, mourner** 410.7; **com-plainer,** malcontent 869.3.

.8 VERBS **lament, mourn, moan, grieve, sor-row, keen,** weep over, **bewail, bemoan, deplore, repine, sigh,** give sorrow words; sing the blues [informal], elegize, **dirge, knell.**

.9 **wring one's hands,** tear one's hair, gnash one's teeth, beat one's breast, roll on the ground.

.10 **weep, sob, cry, greet** [Scot], **bawl, boo-hoo; blubber, whimper, snivel; shed tears,** drop a tear; **burst into tears,** give way to tears, melt or dissolve in tears, break down, break down and cry; cry one's eyes out, cry oneself blind.

.11 **wail, ululate; moan, groan; howl,** yowl, yawl [Brit dial]; **cry, squall, bawl,** yawp, **yell, scream,** shriek; cry out, make an outcry; bay at the moon; tirade.

.12 **whine, whimper,** yammer [dial], pule.

.13 **complain, groan;** kick or gripe or beef [all informal], **grumble, murmur, mutter, grouch** [informal], growl, clamor, croak, grunt, yelp, howl or raise a howl [both informal], put up a squawk or howl [slang] **squawk** or holler or **crab** or **grouse** [all informal]; **bitch** or **bellyache** or yap [all slang]; **take on** [informal], **fret, fuss,** make a fuss about, fret and fume; air a grievance, lodge or register a complaint.

.14 **go into mourning;** put on mourning, wear mourning.

.15 ADJS **lamenting, grieving, mourning, moaning, sorrowing; wailing, bewailing, bemoaning; in mourning,** in sackcloth and ashes.

.16 **plaintive, plangent, mournful,** moanful, wailful, lamentive, ululant; **sorrow-ful** 872.26,27; **complaining, faultfinding** 969.24, **querulous, fretful,** petulant, pevish; **howling**, Jeremianic; whining, whiny, whimpering, puling.

.17 **tearful**, teary, **weepy** [informal]; lachrymal, lachrymose, lacrimatory; in the melting mood, on the edge of tears, ready to cry; **weeping**, **sobbing**, **crying**; blubbering, whimpering, sniveling; **in tears**, with tears in one's eyes, with tearful or watery eyes, with swimming or brimming or overflowing eyes, with eyes suffused, bathed or dissolved in tears, "like Niobe, all tears" [Shakespeare].

.18 **dirgelike**, knell-like, elegiac(al), epicedial, threnodic.

.19 ADVS **lamentingly**, plaintively, **mournfully**, moanfully, wailfully; **sorrowfully** 872.36; complainingly, groaningly, querulously, fretfully, petulantly, peevishly.

## 876. REJOICING

.1 NOUNS **rejoicing**, jubilation, jubilance, jubilant display, jubilee, show of joy, raucous happiness; **exultation**, elation, triumph; whoopee or hoopla [both informal], festivity 878.3,4, merriment 870.5; celebration 877.

.2 **cheer**, hurrah, huzzah, hurray, hooray, yippee, rah; **cry, shout, yell**; hosanna, hallelujah, alleluia, paean, paean or chorus of cheers; **applause** 968.2.

.3 **smile**, smiling; bright smile, gleaming or glowing smile, beam; silly smile or grin; **grin**, grinning; broad grin, ear-to-ear grin, toothful grin; stupid grin, idiotic grin; sardonic grin, **smirk, simper**.

.4 **laughter**, laughing, hilarity 870.5, risibility; **laugh**; boff or boffola or yuck [all slang]; **titter**; **giggle**; **chuckle, chortle**; cackle, crow; **snicker**, snigger, snort; ha-ha, hee-haw, hee-hee, ho-ho, tee-hee, yuk-yuk; guffaw, horselaugh; **hearty laugh**, **belly laugh** [slang], Homeric laughter, cachinnation; **shout, shriek**, shout of laughter, burst or outburst of laughter, peal or roar of laughter, gales of laughter; fit of laughter, convulsion, "laughter holding both his sides" [Milton].

.5 VERBS **rejoice**, jubilate, **exult**, glory, joy, **delight**, bless or thank one's stars, congratulate oneself, hug oneself, rub one's hands, clap hands; dance or skip for joy, dance, skip, frisk, rollick, revel, frolic, caper, gambol, caracole, romp; sing, carol, chirp, chirrup, chirp like a cricket, whistle, lilt.

.6 **cheer**, give a cheer, **cry, shout, yell**, cry for joy, yell oneself hoarse; huzzah, hurrah, hurray, hooray; shout hosanna or hal-

lelujah, "make a joyful noise unto the Lord" [Bible]; **applaud** 968.10.

.7 **smile**, crack a smile [slang], break into a smile; **beam**, smile brightly; **grin**, grin like a Cheshire cat or chessy-cat [informal]; **smirk, simper**.

.8 **laugh**, burst out laughing, burst into laughter, burst out, laugh outright; laugh it up [slang]; **titter**; **giggle**; **chuckle, chortle**; cackle, crow; **snicker**, snigger, snort; ha-ha, hee-haw, hee-hee, ho-ho, tee-hee, yuk-yuk; **guffaw**, horselaugh; **shout**, **shriek**, give a shout or shriek of laughter; **roar**, cachinnate, roar with laughter; shake with laughter, shake like jelly; be convulsed with laughter, go into convulsions; burst or split with laughter, break up [slang], split [informal], **split one's sides**, laugh fit to burst or bust [slang], bust a gut or pee one's pants laughing [both slang], **be in stitches** [informal], hold one's sides; laugh oneself sick or silly or limp, die or nearly die laughing; laugh in one's sleeve, laugh up one's sleeve, laugh in one's beard.

.9 ADJS **rejoicing**, delighting, exulting; **jubilant, exultant, elated**, elate, flushed.

.10 ADVS **rejoicingly**, delightingly, exultingly; **jubilantly, exultantly, elatedly**.

## 877. CELEBRATION

.1 NOUNS **celebration**, celebrating; **observance**, formal or solemn or ritual observance, **solemnization**; marking the occasion; **commemoration**, memorialization, remembrance, memory; jubilee; holiday 711.4; anniversaries 137.12; **festivity** 878.3,4; **revel** 878.6; rejoicing 876; **ceremony**, rite 646.4; religious rites 1040; ovation, triumph; **tribute**; testimonial, testimonial banquet or dinner; toast; **salute**; salvo; flourish of trumpets, fanfare, fanfaronade; dressing ship.

.2 VERBS **celebrate, observe, keep, mark**, solemnly mark, honor; **commemorate**, memorialize; **solemnize**, signalize, hallow, mark with a red letter; hold jubilee, jubilize, jubilate, maffick [Brit informal]; **make merry** 878.26; kill the fatted calf; sound a fanfare, blow the trumpet, beat the drum, fire a salute; dress ship.

.3 ADJS **celebrative**, celebrating; **commemorative**, commemorating; memorial; solemn.

.4 ADVS **in honor of, in commemoration of**, in memory or remembrance of, to the memory of.

## 878. AMUSEMENT

**.1** NOUNS amusement, entertainment, diversion, solace, divertisement, *divertissement* [Fr], recreation, relaxation, regalement; pastime, *passe-temps* [Fr]; **mirth** 870.5; pleasure, enjoyment 865.

**.2** fun, action [informal]; funmaking, fun and games, play, sport, game; good time, lovely time, pleasant time; big time or high time or high old time [all informal], picnic or laughs or lots of laughs or ball [all slang], great fun, time of one's life; a short life and a merry one.

**.3** festivity, merrymaking, merriment, gaiety, jollity, jollification [informal], joviality, conviviality, whoopee or hoopla [both informal]; larking [informal], skylarking, racketing, mafficking [Brit informal], holiday-making; revelry, revelment, reveling, revels.

**.4** festival, festivity, festive occasion, *fiesta* [Sp], fete, –fest, gala, gala affair, blowout [slang], jamboree [slang]; high jinks, do, great doings [all informal]; *fête champêtre* [Fr]; feast, banquet 307.9; picnic 307.6; party 922.11; waygoose [Brit dial], wayzgoose; fair, carnival; kermis; *Oktoberfest* [Ger]; Mardi Gras; Saturnalia; field day, gala day, feria.

**.5** frolic, play, romp, rollick, frisk, gambol, caper, dido [informal].

**.6** revel, lark, escapade, ploy; **celebration** 877; spree, bout, fling, wingding, randy [Scot], randan [dial]; bust or tear or bender or binge or toot or bat [all slang]; carouse, carousal; orgy, debauch; drinking bout 996.5.

**.7** round of pleasure, mad round, whirl, merry-go-round, the rounds, the dizzy rounds.

**.8** sports; athletics, agonistics; gymnastics, palaestra; acrobatics, tumbling; track, track and field; soccer, association football; Rugby, rugger [informal]; swimming, bathing, natation.

**.9** game, sport 878.34; play; contest 796.3; race 796.12; event, meet; bout, match, go [informal]; singles, doubles; twosome, threesome, foursome; double-header; pentathlon, decathlon; play-off, runoff; games of chance 515.8.

**.10** tournament, tourney, gymkhana, field day; rally; regatta; carousel; meet, track meet; games, Olympic games, the Olympics; Olympiad, Highland games.

**.11** entertainment industry; show business, show biz [informal]; theater 611.18–20;

cabaret, tavern, roadhouse; café dansant, café chantant; nightclub, night spot or nitery [both informal], *boîte, boîte de nuit* [both Fr]; juke joint [slang], discothèque; dance hall, dancing pavilion, ballroom, dance floor; casino; amusement park, fun-fair [Brit]; resort 191.27.

**.12** playground; field, athletic field, playing field; football field, gridiron; baseball field, diamond; infield, outfield; soccer field; archery ground, cricket ground, polo ground, croquet ground or lawn, bowling green; bowling alley; links, golf links, golf course; fairway, putting green; gymnasium, gym [informal]; court, badminton court, basketball court, tennis court, racket court, squash court; billiard parlor, poolroom, pool hall; racecourse, track, course, turf, oval; stretch; rink, glaciarium, ice rink, skating rink; playroom 192.12.

**.13** swimming pool, pool, swimming bath [Brit], plunge, plunge bath, natatorium; swimming hole; wading pool.

**.14** park, public park, pleasure garden or ground, pleasance, paradise, common, commons.

**.15** merry-go-round, carousel, roundabout, whirligig, whip, flying horses; Ferris wheel; seesaw, teeter-totter; swing; roller coaster; chutes, chute-the-chutes; –drome.

**.16** toy, plaything, sport; bauble, knickknack, gimcrack, gewgaw, kickshaw, whim-wham, trinket; doll, paper doll, rag doll, puppet, marionette, toy soldier; dollhouse, doll carriage; hobbyhorse, cockhorse, rocking horse; top, teetotum; pinwheel; jack-in-the-box; jacks, jackstones; jackstraws, pick-up sticks; blocks; checkerboard, chessboard; marble, mig, agate, steelie, taw; athletic equipment; ball 255.13; racket, battledore; bat, baseball bat, cricket bat; cue; club, golf club.

**.17** playing cards, cards; picture cards, face cards, court cards: king, queen, jack or knave; bower, right or left bower, best bower; spot cards: ace, deuce, trey; joker; diamonds, hearts, clubs, spades; hand; dummy; royal flush, flush, full house, straight, three of a kind, pair; singleton; trump, ruff; trick; rubber, round; pack, deck.

**.18** chessman, man, piece; bishop, knight, king, queen, pawn, rook or castle.

**.19** player, frolicker, frisker, funmaker, gamboler; pleasure-seeker, pleasurer, pleasurist, playboy [slang]; reveler, merrymaker rollicker, skylarker, **carouser**, cutup [slang]; contestant 791.2.

**.20 athlete**, jock [slang], **player**, amateur athlete, professional athlete, competitor, sportsman, sport, gamester, games-player; ballplayer, baseballer, cricketer; batter, catcher, baseman, infielder, outfielder, shortstop, outfield, battery; footballer, lineman, offensive lineman, defensive lineman, halfback, blocking back, wingback, tailback, quarterback, fullback, end, tackle; center; guard, linebacker; golfer; poloist; pugilist; wrestler 800.2,3; racer 269.5; jumper 319.4; skater; archer, bowman, toxophilite; coach, games master or mistress [Brit].

**.21 gymnast**, palaestrian; pancratiast; acrobat, tumbler, contortionist; funambulist, high wire artist, ropewalker, tightrope walker, ropedancer; aerialist, man on the flying trapeze; weightlifter.

**.22 master of ceremonies**, MC or emcee [both informal], marshal; **toastmaster**; master of the revels, revel master; Lord of Misrule, Abbot of Unreason [Scot]; social director.

**.23 VERBS amuse, entertain, divert**, regale, beguile, solace, recreate, refresh, enliven, exhilarate, put in good humor; **relax**, loosen up; **delight, tickle, titillate**, tickle the fancy; raise a smile or laugh, convulse, set the table on a roar, be the death of one; wow or slay or knock dead or kill or break one up or fracture one [all slang].

**.24 amuse oneself**, take one's pleasure, give oneself over to pleasure, be on pleasure bent; **relax**, let oneself go, loosen up; **have fun, have a good time**, have a ball or have lots of laughs [both slang], live it up or laugh it up [both slang]; drown care, drive dull care away; beguile the time, kill time, while away the time.

**.25 play, sport, disport; frolic, rollick, gambol, frisk, romp, caper**, cut capers [informal], antic, curvet, cavort, caracole, flounce, trip, skip, dance; **cut up** [slang], cut a dido [informal], horse around [slang], fool around, carry on [informal].

**.26 make merry, revel, roister**, jolly, lark [informal], skylark, **make whoopee** [slang], let oneself go, **blow or let off steam**; cut loose, let loose, let go, whoop it up, **kick up one's heels**; hell around or raise hell or blow off the lid [all slang]; step out [informal], go places and do things, go on the town, see life, **paint the town red** [slang]; go the dizzy rounds, go on the

merry-go-round [slang]; **celebrate** 877.2; spree, **go on a spree**, go on a bust or toot or bender or binge or rip or tear [all slang]; **carouse**, jollify [informal], wanton, debauch, **sow one's wild oats, have one's fling**.

**.27** "eat, drink, and be merry" [Bible], feast, banquet.

**.28 ADJS amused, entertained; diverted, delighted, tickled, titillated;** "pleased with a rattle, tickled with a straw" [Pope].

**.29 amusing, entertaining, diverting**, beguiling; **fun** [informal], more fun than a barrel of monkeys [informal]; recreative, recreational; **delightful**, titillative, titillating; humorous 880.4.

**.30 festive, festal; merry, gay, jolly, jovial, joyous, joyful**, gladsome, convivial, gala, hilarious; merrymaking, on the loose [informal].

**.31 playful, sportive**, sportful; **frolicsome**, gamesome, rompish, larkish, capersome; waggish 738.6.

**.32 sporting, sports; athletic**, agonistic; **gymnastic**, palaestral; **acrobatic**.

**.33 ADVS in fun**, for amusement, **for fun**, for the fun of it; for kicks or for laughs [both slang], for the heck or hell of it [slang], for the devil of it [slang]; just to be doing.

**.34 sports, games**

| | |
|---|---|
| acey-deucy | cricket |
| acrostics | croquet |
| anagrams | curling |
| archery | deck tennis |
| association football | discus |
| backgammon | dominoes |
| badminton | draughts |
| bagatelle | fencing |
| ball | fishing |
| balloon ball | fives |
| bandy | football |
| baseball | fox and geese |
| basketball | French and English |
| battledore and shut- | Frisbee |
|    tlecock | ghost |
| billiards | gliding |
| bingo, beano | go |
| blindman's buff | gobang |
| bobsledding | golf |
| boccie | go maku |
| boloball | Halma |
| bowling, bowls | hammer throwing |
| boxing 796.9 | handball |
| captain ball | hide-and-seek |
| cat | hiking |
| catch | hockey |
| charades | hopscotch |
| checkers | horseshoes |
| chess | hunting |
| Chinese checkers | hurdling |
| climbing | ice hockey |
| court tennis | ice skating |
| crambo | jacks, jackstones |

| | |
|---|---|
| jackstraws | shinny |
| jai alai | shogi |
| keno | shooting |
| lacrosse | shot-put |
| lawn tennis | shuffleboard, shovel- |
| leapfrog | board |
| lotto | skating |
| luging | skeet, skeet shooting |
| Mah-Jongg | skiing |
| marbles | ski-jumping |
| merels | skin-diving |
| Monopoly | skittles |
| motorcycling | sky-diving |
| mountaineering | sledding |
| mumble-the-peg, | snowmobiling |
| mumblety-peg | snooker |
| ninepins | snorkel diving |
| paddle tennis | soccer |
| pall-mall | softball |
| pallone | squash, squash rac- |
| parachuting | quets |
| Parcheesi | stickball |
| pelota | surfing |
| Ping-Pong | table tennis |
| polo | tennis |
| pool | tenpins |
| post office | tent pegging |
| pushball | tetherball |
| pyramids | three-dimensional |
| quintain | chess |
| quoits | ticktacktoe |
| racquets | tiddlywinks |
| riding | tilting |
| roller skating | tipcat |
| rounders | tivoli |
| rowing | tobogganing |
| Rugby | trap bat and ball |
| sailing | trapshooting |
| sailplaning | tug of war |
| Scrabble | volleyball |
| scuba diving | water polo |
| sculling | waterskiing |
| sharpshooting | wrestling 796.10 |

**.35 card games**

| | |
|---|---|
| all fours | flinch |
| auction bridge | fright |
| authors | frog |
| baccarat | gin |
| banker | gin rummy |
| beggar-my-neighbor | goat |
| bezique | go fish |
| blackjack | hearts |
| blind poker | keno |
| bluff | lansquenet |
| Boston | loo |
| brag | lottery |
| bridge | lotto |
| canasta | matrimony |
| casino | Milles Bornes |
| commerce | monte |
| commit | napoleon |
| connections | old maid |
| contract bridge, con- | ombre |
| tract | pairs |
| cribbage | patience |
| draw poker | penny ante |
| Earl of Coventry | picquet |
| écarté | pinochle |
| euchre | Pit |
| faro | poker |
| five hundred | Polish bank |

| | |
|---|---|
| put-and-take | snipsnapsnorum |
| quadrille | solitaire |
| quinze | speculation |
| reverse | squeezers |
| rouge et noir | straight poker |
| rum | stud poker |
| rummy | thirty-one |
| Russian bank | twenty-one |
| seven-up | vingt-et-un |
| skat | whist |

## 879. DANCING

.1 NOUNS **dancing,** terpsichore, dance, chore(o)–, chorio–; the light fantastic; **choreography; ballet,** classical ballet, modern ballet, comedy ballet; **modern dance;** dance drama, choreodrama; **hoofing** [slang]; tap dancing, soft-shoe dancing, clog dancing; solo dancing, choral dancing, ballroom dancing, social dancing, folk dancing, country dancing, square dancing, round dancing, couple dancing.

.2 **dance, hop** [informal], **shindig** or shindy [both slang]; **ball, bal** [Fr]; masked ball, masque, mask, masquerade ball, masquerade, *bal masqué* [Fr], *bal costumé* [Fr], fancy-dress ball; promenade, **prom** [informal]; country dance, square dance, barn dance; mixer, stag dance; record hop; tea dance, *thé dansant* [Fr]; gay dance [informal].

.3 **dancer,** *danseur* [Fr], terpsichorean, **hoofer** [slang], step dancer, tap dancer, clog dancer, heel-and-toe dancer; solo dancer, choral dancer, ballroom dancer, social dancer, folk-dancer, country dancer, square-dancer, round-dancer; figure dancer, figurant, figurante; skirt dancer; ballet dancer, ballet girl, **ballerina,** danseuse, coryphée; *première danseuse* [Fr], *danseur noble* [Fr]; **modern dancer;** chorus girl, chorus boy or man; geisha or geisha girl; nautch girl, bayadere; hula girl; taxi dancer.

.4 **ballroom, dance hall,** dancery; dance palace; casino.

.5 VERBS **dance, trip the light fantastic,** trip, skip, hop, foot, prance [informal], **hoof** [slang], clog, tap-dance; shake, shimmy, shuffle; waltz, one-step, two-step, foxtrot, etc.

.6 ADJS **dancing, dance,** terpsichorean; balletic; choreographic.

.7 **dances**

| | |
|---|---|
| allemande | *ventre* [Fr] |
| apache dance | bolero |
| barn dance | boogaloo |
| beguine | bourrée |
| belly dance, *danse du* | boutade |

branle
breakdown
bubble dance
bunny hop
cakewalk
can-can
cantico
Castle walk
cha-cha
Charleston
chonchina
clog
conga
cotillion
country dance
courante
eagle rock
fan dance
fandango
flamenco
fling
folk dance
fox trot
frug
funky chicken
furlana
galliard
gallopade
galop
gavotte
german, german cotillion
habañera
Highland fling
hokey-pokey
hootchy-kootchy
hopak
hora
hornpipe
hula, hula-hula
hustle
interpretative dance
jig
jota
juba
kola
Lambeth Walk
lancers
limbo
lindy, lindy hop
longways dance
malagueña

mambo
mazurka
merengue
Mexican hat dance
minuet
monkey
morris dance
one-step
ox dance
pachanga
pas de deux
paso doble
passamezzo
pas seul
peabody
polka
polonaise
Portland fancy
quadrille
rain dance
reel
rigadoon
Road to the Isles
round dance
rumba
salsa
saltarello
samba
saraband
schottische
Scotch reel
shimmy
Sir Roger de Coverley
skirt dance
snake dance
square dance
strathspey
swim
sword dance
tango
tap dance
tarantella
trepak
turkey trot
twist
two-step
Virginia reel
waltz, valse
war dance
Watusi
ziganka

**.8 dance steps**

arabesque
buck-and-wing
chassé
coupé
double shuffle
gambado, gambade

grapevine
heel-and-toe
pas
pigeonwing
quickstep
shuffle

## 880. HUMOROUSNESS

.1 NOUNS **humorousness, funniness,** amusingness, laughableness, laughability, hilarity; **wittiness** 881.2; **drollness,** drollery; **whimsicalness,** quizzicalness; **ludicrousness, ridiculousness, absurdity,** absurdness, quaintness, eccentricity, incongruity, bizarreness, bizarrerie; richness, pricelessness [informal]; the funny side.

.2 **comicalness,** comicality; farcicalness, **farcicality,** slapstick quality, broadness.

.3 bathos; anticlimax, comedown.

.4 ADJS **humorous, funny, amusing; witty** 881.15; **droll, whimsical,** quizzical; **laughable,** risible, good for a laugh; **ludicrous, ridiculous, hilarious, absurd,** quaint, eccentric, incongruous, bizarre; rich, priceless [informal], screaming, too funny *or* too killing for words [informal].

.5 **comic** *or* **comical; farcical,** slapstick, broad; **burlesque** 967.14; tragicomic, seriocomic, mock-heroic.

.6 ADVS **humorously, amusingly,** funnily, **laughably;** wittily 881.18; drolly, whimsically, quizzically; **comically,** farcically, broadly; **ludicrously, ridiculously, absurdly,** quaintly, eccentrically, incongruously, bizarrely.

## 881. WIT, HUMOR

.1 NOUNS **wit, humor,** pleasantry, *esprit* [Fr], salt, spice *or* savor of wit; Attic wit *or* salt, Atticism; ready wit, quick wit, nimble wit, agile wit, pretty wit; dry wit, subtle wit; **comedy** 611.6; black humor, sick humor, gallows humor; satire, sarcasm, irony; parody, lampoon, travesty, caricature, burlesque, squib; farce, mere farce; slapstick, slapstick humor, broad humor; visual humor.

.2 **wittiness, humorousness, funniness; facetiousness,** pleasantry, **jocularity,** jocoseness, jocosity; **joking,** joshing [informal]; smartness, cleverness, brilliance; pungency, saltiness; keenness, sharpness; keen-wittedness, quick-wittedness, nimble-wittedness.

.3 **drollery,** drollness; **whimsicality,** whimsicalness, humorsomeness, antic wit.

.4 **waggishness, waggery;** roguishness 738.2; **playfulness,** sportiveness, **levity,** frivolity, flippancy, merriment 870.5; **prankishness,** pranksomeness; trickery, trickiness, trickiness, trickishness.

.5 **buffoonery,** buffoonism, clownery, harlequinade; **clownishness,** buffoonishness; **foolery,** fooling, **tomfoolery;** horseplay; shenanigans *or* monkeyshines [both informal]; **banter** 882.

.6 **joke, jest, gag** [informal], **wheeze,** jape; **fun, sport, play;** story, yarn, **funny story,** good story; dirty story *or* joke, blue story *or* joke, *double entendre* [Fr]; shaggy-dog story; sick joke [informal]; ethnic joke; capital joke, good one, laugh, belly laugh, rib tickler, sidesplitter, howler, wow, scream, riot, panic; visual joke, sight gag [informal]; **point, cream of the jest; jest-book.**

.7 **witticism, pleasantry,** *plaisanterie,* **bou-tade** [both Fr]; **play of wit,** *jeu d'esprit* [Fr]; **crack** *or* **smart crack** *or* **wisecrack** [all informal]; **quip,** conceit, bright *or* happy thought, bright *or* brilliant idea; **mot, bon mot,** smart saying, stroke of wit; epigram, turn of thought, aphorism, apothegm; flash of wit, scintillation; **sally,** flight of wit; **repartee,** retort, riposte, snappy comeback [slang]; facetiae [pl], quips and cranks; **gibe, dirty** *or* **nasty** crack [informal]; persiflage 882.1.

.8 **wordplay, play on words,** *jeu de mots* [Fr], missaying, corruption, paronomasia, *calembour* [Fr], abuse of terms; **pun,** punning; equivoque, equivocality; anagram, logogram, logogriph, metagram; acrostic, double acrostic; amphiboly, amphibologism; palindrome; spoonerism; malapropism.

.9 **old joke,** old wheeze, old turkey, **trite joke,** hoary-headed joke, joke with whisk-ers; **chestnut** *or* **corn** *or* **corny joke** *or* **old-ie** [all slang]; Joe Miller, Joe Millerism; twice-told tale, retold story, warmed-over cabbage [informal].

.10 **prank, trick, practical joke,** waggish trick, *espièglerie* [Fr], antic, caper, frolic; **mon-keyshines** *or* **shenanigans** [both slang].

.11 **sense of humor, risibility,** funny bone.

.12 **humorist, wit, funnyman, comic,** *bel-es-prit* [Fr], life of the party; **joker,** jokester, gagman [informal], **jester, quipster, wise-cracker** *or* gagster [both informal]; **wag,** wagwit; zany, madcap, cutup [slang]; **prankster; comedian,** banana [slang]; **clown** 612.10; punster, punner; epigram-matist; satirist, ironist; burlesquer, carica-turist, parodist, lampooner; reparteeist; witling; gag writer [slang], jokesmith.

.13 VERBS **joke, jest, wisecrack** *or* **crack wise** [both informal], utter a mot, **quip,** jape, josh [informal], fun [informal], make fun, **kid** *or* **kid around** [both informal]; **make a funny** [informal]; **crack a joke,** get off a joke, tell a good story; pun, play on words; scintillate, sparkle; **make fun of,** gibe at, fleer at, mock, scoff at, poke fun at, make the butt of one's humor, be merry with; ridicule 967.8–11.

.14 **trick, play a practical joke,** play tricks *or* pranks, **play a joke** *or* **trick on,** make merry with; pull one's leg, put one on [slang].

.15 ADJS **witty,** *spirituel* [Fr]; **humorous, funny; jocular,** joky [informal], **joking,**

jesting, jocose; **facetious,** joshing [infor-mal], **whimsical, droll,** humorsome; smart, clever, brilliant, scintillating, spar-kling, sprightly; keen, sharp, rapier-like, pungent, pointed, biting, mordant; salty, salt, Attic; **keen-witted, quick-witted,** nimble-witted.

.16 **clownish, buffoonish.**

.17 **waggish;** roguish 738.6; **playful, sportive; prankish,** pranky, pranksome; tricky, trickish, tricksy.

.18 ADVS **wittily, humorously; jocularly,** jo-cosely; **facetiously; whimsically, drolly.**

.19 **in fun, in sport, in play, in jest,** in joke, as a joke, jokingly, jestingly, with tongue in cheek; **for fun,** for sport.

## 882. BANTER

.1 NOUNS **banter, badinage, persiflage, pleasantry, fooling, fooling around, kid-ding** *or* **kidding around** [both informal], **raillery,** rallying, **sport,** good-natured ban-ter, harmless teasing; ridicule 967; **chaff, twit,** jest, joke, jape, josh [informal]; jive [slang]; **exchange,** give-and-take.

.2 **bantering, twitting, chaffing, joking, jest-ing,** japing, **fooling, teasing,** hazing, josh-ing [informal]; **jollying** *or* **kidding** [both informal]; **ribbing** *or* **ragging** *or* **razzing** *or* roasting [all slang].

.3 **banterer,** *persifleur* [Fr], **chaffer, twitter; jollyer** *or* **kidder** *or* josher [all informal]; **ribber** *or* roaster *or* razzer *or* ragger [all slang].

.4 VERBS **banter, twit, chaff, rally, joke, jest,** jape, **tease,** haze; **jolly** *or* **kid** *or* josh *or* put on [all informal], ride *or* needle [both informal]; rib *or* rag *or* razz *or* roast *or* jive [all slang].

.5 ADJS **bantering, chaffing, twitting; jolly-ing** *or* **kidding** *or* joshing [all informal], **fooling, teasing,** quizzical.

## 883. DULLNESS

*(being uninteresting)*

.1 NOUNS **dullness, dryness,** dustiness, unin-terestingness; **stuffiness, stodginess,** wood-enness, stiffness; barrenness, sterility, aridity, jejunity; **insipidness,** insipidity, vapidness, vapidity, inanity, hollowness, emptiness, superficiality, **flatness,** taste-lessness; characterlessness, colorlessness, pointlessness; **deadness,** lifelessness, spirit-lessness, bloodlessness, paleness, pallor, etiolation, effeteness; **slowness,** pokiness, dragginess [informal], unliveliness; **te-diousness** 884.2; **dreariness,** drearisomeness, dismalness; **heaviness,** leadenness, ponderousness; inexcitability 858; solemnity 871; lowness of spirit 872.3.

.2 **prosaicness,** prosiness; prosaism, prosaicism, prose, plainness; **matter-of-factness,** unimaginativeness; matter of fact.

.3 **triteness,** corniness *or* squareness [both slang], **banality,** banalness, unoriginality, **hackneyedness, commonplaceness,** commonness, familiarness, platitudinousness; **staleness,** mustiness, fustiness; cliché 517.3.

.4 VERBS **fall flat,** fall flat as a pancake; leave one cold, go over like a lead balloon [slang], lay an egg, bomb [slang]; **wear thin.**

.5 prose, platitudinize, sing a familiar tune.

.6 ADJS **dull, dry,** dusty, dryasdust; **stuffy, stodgy,** wooden, stiff; arid, barren, blank, sterile, jejune; **insipid,** vapid, inane, hollow, empty, superficial; fade, blah [informal], **flat,** tasteless; characterless, colorless, pointless; **dead,** lifeless, spiritless, bloodless, pale, pallid, etiolated, effete; cold; **slow,** poky, draggy [informal], pedestrian, plodding, unlively; **tedious** 884.8; **dreary,** drearisome, dismal; **heavy,** leaden, ponderous, elephantine; ho-hum [informal]; dull as dish water, "weary, stale, flat and unprofitable" [Shakespeare]; inexcitable 858.10; solemn 871.3; low-spirited 872.22.

.7 **uninteresting,** uneventful, **unexciting; unentertaining,** unenjoyable, **unamusing,** unfunny, unwitty.

.8 **prosaic,** prose, prosy, prosing, plain; **matter-of-fact,** unimaginative, unimpassioned.

.9 **trite;** corny *or* square *or* square-John *or* Clyde [all slang], fade, **banal,** unoriginal, platitudinous, **stereotyped,** stock, set, **commonplace, common,** truistic, **familiar,** bromidic [slang], old hat [informal], back-number, bewhiskered, warmed-over, **cut-and-dried; hackneyed,** hackney; well-known 475.27; **stale,** musty, fusty; **worn,** timeworn, well-worn, moth-eaten, threadbare, **worn thin.**

.10 ADVS **dully, dryly,** dustily, **uninterestingly;** stuffily, stodgily; aridly, barrenly, jejunely, **insipidly, vapidly,** inanely, hollowly, emptily, superficially, tastelessly, **colorlessly,** pointlessly; lifelessly, spiritlessly, bloodlessly, pallidly, effetely; slowly, draggily [informal], ploddingly; **tediously** 884.12; drearily, drearisomely, dismally; heavily, ponderously.

.11 **tritely,** cornily [slang], banally, commonplacely, commonly, familiarly, hackneyedly, unoriginally, truistically, stalely.

## 884. TEDIUM

.1 NOUNS **tedium, monotony, humdrum,** irksomeness, irk; **sameness,** sameliness, samesomeness [dial], wearisome sameness, the same old thing, the same damn thing [slang]; broken record; undeviation, unvariation, invariability; the round, the daily round, the weary round, the treadmill, the squirrel cage, the beaten track *or* path; time on one's hands, time hanging heavily on one's hands.

.2 **tediousness, monotonousness; humdrumness,** humdrumminess; **dullness** 883; **wearisomeness,** wearifulness; **tiresomeness, irksomeness,** drearisomeness; **boresomeness,** boringness; prolixity, long-windedness.

.3 **weariness, tiredness,** wearifulness; jadedness, fed-upness, satiation, satiety; **boredom,** boredness; **ennui,** spleen, melancholy, life-weariness, *taedium vitae* [L], world-weariness, dispiritedness 872.3.

.4 **bore,** crashing bore [informal], frightful bore; **pest, nuisance; headache** *or* **pain in the neck** *or* pain in the ass [all slang]; dryasdust, dusty, humdrum; drag [slang], proser, twaddler; **drip** *or* **pill** *or* **flat tire** [all slang]; **wet blanket;** buttonholer.

.5 VERBS **be tedious, drag on,** go on forever; have a certain sameness, be infinitely repetitive; **weary, tire, irk,** wear, wear on *or* upon, **make one tired,** fatigue, weary *or* tire to death, jade; give one a swift pain in the ass *or* give one a bellyful *or* make one fed-up [all slang], pall, satiate, glut.

.6 **bore,** leave one cold, set *or* send to sleep; **bore stiff** [informal], bore to tears, bore to death *or* extinction, bore to distraction, bore out of one's life, bore out of all patience; buttonhole.

.7 **harp on** *or* **upon, dwell on** *or* **upon,** harp upon one *or* the same string, play *or* sing the same old song *or* tune, play the same broken record.

.8 ADJS **tedious, monotonous, humdrum,** singsong, jog-trot, treadmill, unvarying, invariable, uneventful, broken-record, harping, everlasting, too much with us [informal]; blah [informal], **dreary,** drearisome, dry, dryasdust, dusty, **dull** 883.6; prolix, long-winded.

.9 **wearying,** wearing, **tiring; wearisome,** weariful, fatiguing, **tiresome,** irksome; **boring, boresome,** stupefyingly boring, stuporific, yawny [informal].

**.10 weary,** weariful; **tired,** wearied, irked; good and tired, tired to death, weary unto death; sick, **sick of, tired of, sick and tired of;** jaded, satiated, fed-up [slang]; **blasé;** splenetic, melancholy, melancholic, life-weary, world-weary, tired of living, dispirited 872.22.

**.11 bored, uninterested;** bored stiff [slang], bored to death *or* extinction, bored to tears, stupefied *or* stuporous with boredom.

**.12 ADVS tediously, monotonously,** harpingly, everlastingly, unvaryingly, endlessly; longwindedly; **boringly,** boresomely; **wearisomely,** fatiguingly, wearyingly, **tiresomely, irksomely,** drearisomely; dully 883.10.

**.13** on a treadmill, in a squirrel cage, on the beaten track, on the same old round; without a change of menu *or* scenery *or* pace.

**.14 PHRS** ho, hum!, heigh ho!, what a life!; *plus ça change, plus c'est la même chose* [Fr, the more it changes, the more it's the same thing]; so what else is new?

## 885. AGGRAVATION

**.1 NOUNS aggravation, worsening; exacerbation,** embittering, embitterment, souring; deterioration; **intensification, heightening,** sharpening, deepening, increase, enhancement, amplification, enlargement, magnification, augmentation; **exasperation, annoyance, irritation** 866.2,3; deliberate aggravation, provocation; contentiousness 797.15.

**.2 VERBS aggravate, worsen,** make worse; **exacerbate,** embitter, sour; deteriorate; **intensify, heighten,** sharpen, make acute *or* more acute, bring to a head, deepen, increase, enhance, amplify, enlarge, magnify, build up; augment; rub salt in the wound, add insult to injury, pour oil on the fire, heat up [informal], hot up [slang]; **exasperate, annoy, irritate** 866.13, 14; provoke, be an *agent provocateur.*

**.3 worsen,** get *or* grow worse, go from push to shove; **go from bad to worse, jump out of the frying pan into the fire,** avoid Scylla and fall into Charybdis, "sow the wind and reap the whirlwind" [Bible].

**.4 ADJS aggravated, worsened, worse,** exacerbated, embittered, soured; **intensified, heightened,** increased, enhanced, amplified, magnified, enlarged, augmented, heated up [informal], hotted up [slang]; **exasperated, irritated, annoyed** 866.21; provoked, deliberately provoked.

**.5 aggravating,** aggravative; **exasperating,** exasperative; **annoying, irritating** 864.22; provocative; contentious.

**.6 ADVS aggravatingly, exasperatingly; annoyingly** 864.29.

**.7 from bad to worse,** worse and worse, out of the frying pan into the fire.

## 886. RELIEF

**.1 NOUNS relief, easement, easing, ease; reduction,** diminishment, diminution, lessening, abatement; **remedy** 687; **alleviation, mitigation, palliation,** softening, assuagement, allayment, appeasement, mollification, subduement; soothing, salving; lulling; dulling, deadening, numbing, anesthesia, anesthetizing, analgesia.

**.2 release, deliverance, freeing,** removal; suspension, intermission, respite, surcease, reprieve; discharge; catharsis, purging, purgation, purge, cleansing, cleansing away, emotional release.

**.3 lightening, disburdening,** unburdening, unweighting, unloading, disencumbrance, disembarrassment, easing of the load, a load off one's mind, something out of one's system.

**.4 sense** *or* **feeling of relief,** sigh of relief.

**.5 VERBS relieve,** give relief; **ease,** ease matters; **reduce,** diminish, lessen, abate; **alleviate, mitigate, palliate,** soften, pad, cushion, assuage, allay, lay, appease, mollify, subdue, soothe; salve, pour balm into, pour oil on; poultice, foment, stupe; slake, slacken; lull; **dull, deaden,** dull *or* deaden the pain, numb, benumb, anesthetize; temper the wind to the shorn lamb, lay the flattering unction to one's soul.

**.6 release, free, deliver,** reprieve, remove, free from; suspend, intermit, give respite *or* surcease; discharge; act as a cathartic, purge, purge away, cleanse, cleanse away; give release.

**.7 lighten, disburden,** unburden, unweight, unload, unfreight, disencumber, disembarrass, ease one's load; **set one's mind at ease** *or* **rest,** set at ease, **take the load off one's mind,** smooth the ruffled brow of care.

**.8 be relieved, feel relief,** feel better about it, get something out of one's system, feel *or* be oneself again; **breathe easy** *or* **easier,** breathe more freely, breathe again; **heave a sigh of relief,** draw a long *or* deep breath.

**.9 ADJS relieving, easing, alleviative,** alleviating, **mitigative,** mitigating, **palliative,** lenitive, assuasive, softening, subduing, soothing, demulcent, emollient, balmy, balsamic; **remedial** 687.39; dulling, deadening, numbing, benumbing, anesthetic, analgesic, anodyne, pain-killing; cathartic, purgative, cleansing.

## 887. COMFORT

.1 NOUNS **comfort, ease, well-being;** contentment 868; clover, velvet [slang], bed of roses; life of ease 728.1; solid comfort.

.2 **comfortableness, easiness; restfulness,** reposefulness, peace, peacefulness; softness, cushiness [informal], cushioniness; **coziness, snugness;** friendliness, warmness; **homelikeness,** homeyness [informal], homeliness; **commodiousness,** roominess, convenience; luxuriousness 904.5; hospitality 925.

.3 **creature comforts, comforts, conveniences,** excellent accommodations, amenities, good things of life, cakes and ale, egg in one's beer [slang], all the comforts of home, all the heart can desire.

.4 **consolation, solace,** solacement, easement, heart's-ease, **encouragement,** aid and comfort, **assurance, reassurance,** support, **comfort,** crumb or shred of comfort, "kind words and comfortable" [William Cowper]; condolence 946, sympathy; **relief** 886.

.5 **comforter,** consoler, solacer, encourager, paraclete.

.6 VERBS **comfort, console, solace,** give comfort, bear up; condole with, sympathize with; ease, **put** or **set at ease;** relieve 886.5; **assure, reassure; encourage, hearten,** pat on the back; **cheer** 870.7; wipe away the tears, "rejoice with them that do rejoice, and weep with them that weep" [Bible].

.7 **be comforted, take comfort, take heart,** pull oneself together, pluck up one's spirits.

.8 **be at ease,** be or feel easy, stand easy [Brit]; **make oneself comfortable,** make oneself at home, feel at home; **relax,** be relaxed; live a life of ease 728.10.

.9 **snug,** snug down or up; tuck in.

.10 **snuggle, nestle, cuddle,** croodle [Brit dial], cuddle up, curl up; bundle; snuggle up to, snug up or together [archaic].

.11 ADJS **comfortable,** comfy [informal]; contented 868.7–10; **easy,** easeful; **restful,** reposeful, peaceful, **relaxing;** soft, cushioned, cushy [informal], cushiony; **cozy, snug,** snug as a bug in a rug; friendly, warm; **homelike,** homey [informal],

homely, lived-in; **commodious,** roomy, convenient; luxurious 904.21.

.12 **at ease, at one's ease,** easy, relaxed, at rest; **at home,** in one's element.

.13 **comforting, consoling,** consolatory, of good comfort; condoling, condolent, condolatory, sympathetic; **assuring, reassuring,** supportive; **encouraging, heartening; cheering** 870.16; relieving 886.9; hospitable 925.11.

.14 ADVS **comfortably, easily,** with ease; **restfully,** reposefully, peacefully; **cozily, snugly; commodiously,** roomily, conveniently; luxuriously, voluptuously.

.15 **in comfort,** in ease, **in clover,** on or in velvet [slang], on a bed of roses.

.16 **comfortingly, consolingly,** assuringly, reassuringly, supportively, encouragingly, hearteningly; hospitably.

## 888. HOPE

.1 NOUNS **hope, hopefulness,** hoping, **hopes,** fond or fervent hope, good hope, good cheer; aspiration, **desire** 634; **expectation** 539; sanguine expectation, happy or cheerful expectation; **trust, confidence, faith,** assured faith, **reliance,** dependence; conviction, assurance, security, well-grounded hope; assumption, presumption; **promise,** prospect, prospects, good or bright or fair prospect, good or hopeful prognosis; great expectations, high hopes; hoping against hope, prayerful hope; doomed hope or hopes.

.2 "the second soul of the unhappy" [Goethe], "the dream of those that wake" [Matthew Prior], "the thing with feathers that perches in the soul" [Emily Dickinson], "the worst of all evils, because it prolongs the torments of man" [Nietzsche].

.3 **optimism,** optimisticalness, Pollyannaism, cheerful or bright or rosy outlook; **cheerfulness** 870; bright side, silver lining; "the noble temptation to see too much in everything" [Chesterton], "the mania of maintaining that everything is well when we are wretched" [Voltaire]; philosophical optimism, Leibnizian optimism, utopianism, perfectionism, perfectibilism; millenarianism, chiliasm, millennialism.

.4 **ray of hope,** gleam or glimmer of hope; faint hope.

.5 **airy hope,** unreal hope, dream, golden dream, pipe dream [informal], bubble, chimera, fool's paradise, quixotic ideal, utopia 535.11.

.6 **optimist,** hoper, Pollyanna [Eleanor Porter], ray of sunshine [slang], irrepressible optimist; "a proponent of the doctrine that black is white" [Ambrose Bierce], "one who makes the best of it when he gets the worst of it" [anon], "one who makes the most of all that comes and the least of all that goes" [Sara Teasdale], Leibnizian optimist, philosophical optimist, utopian, perfectionist, perfectibilist, perfectibilitarian; millenarian, chiliast, millennialist, millennian; aspirer, aspirant, hopeful [informal].

.7 VERBS **hope,** be or live in hopes, entertain or harbor the hope, cling to the hope, cherish or foster or nurture the hope; **expect** 539.5; trust, confide, presume, feel confident, rest assured; pin one's hope upon, put one's trust in, hope in, rely on, count on, lean upon, bank on; hope for, **aspire to,** desire 634.14–16; **hope against hope,** hope and pray, hope to God [informal].

.8 **be hopeful,** get one's hopes up, keep one's spirits up, never say die, take heart, be of good hope, be of good cheer, keep hoping, keep hope alive; **hope for the best,** knock on wood, keep one's fingers crossed, allow oneself to hope; catch at straws.

.9 **be optimistic, look on the bright side, look through rose-colored glasses,** voir en couleur de rose [Fr], think positively or affirmatively, be upbeat [informal], think the best of, **make the best of it,** say that all is for the best, put a good or bold face upon, put the best face upon; count one's chickens before they are hatched, count one's bridges before they are crossed.

.10 **give hope, raise hope,** yield or afford hope, hold out hope, justify hope, inspire hope, **raise one's hopes,** raise expectations, **lead one to expect; cheer** 870.7; inspire, inspirit; **assure, reassure, support; promise,** hold out promise, augur well, bid fair or well, make fair promise, have good prospects.

.11 ADJS **hopeful, hoping, in hopes,** full of hope, in good heart, of good hope, of good cheer; **aspiring** 634.28; **expectant** 539.11; **sanguine,** fond; **confident,** assured; undespairing.

.12 **optimistic,** upbeat [informal], **bright, sunny; cheerful** 870.11–15; **rosy,** roseate, rose-colored, couleur de rose [Fr]; Leibnizian, utopian 535.23, perfectionist, perfectibilitarian, millenarian, chiliastic, millennialistic.

.13 **promising,** of promise, full of promise, bright with promise, pregnant of good, **favorable,** looking up; **auspicious,** propitious 544.18; **inspiring,** inspiriting, **encouraging,** cheering, reassuring, supportive.

.14 ADVS **hopefully,** hopingly; **expectantly** 539.15; **optimistically; cheerfully** 870.17; sanguinely, fondly; confidently.

## 889. HOPELESSNESS

.1 NOUNS **hopelessness,** unhopefulness, no hope, not a prayer [informal], small hope, bleak outlook or prospect or prognosis, blank future; inexpectation 540; futility 669.2; impossibility 510.

.2 **despair, desperation,** desperateness; no way [informal], no way out, no exit, despondency 872.3; disconsolateness 872.12; forlornness; cave of despair, cave of Trophonius; acedia, sloth; apathy 856.4.

.3 **irreclaimability, irretrievability,** irredeemability, irrecoverableness, unsalvageability, unsalvability; incorrigibility, irreformability; irrevocability, **irreversibility; irreparability, incurability,** irremediableness, curelessness, remedilessness, immedicableness; unrelievability, unmitigability.

.4 **forlorn hope,** vain expectation, doomed or foredoomed hope, counsel of perfection.

.5 **dashed hopes,** blighted hope, hope deferred; disappointment 541.

.6 **pessimism, cynicism,** malism, nihilism; uncheerfulness 872.2; **gloominess,** dismalness, gloomy outlook; negativism; defeatism; retreatism; "the name that men of weak nerve give to wisdom" [Bernard De Voto].

.7 **pessimist, cynic,** malist, nihilist; killjoy 872.14, calamity howler [informal], worrywart [slang], seek-sorrow, Job's comforter, prophet of doom, Cassandra, Eeyore; negativist; defeatist; retreatist; "one who is not happy except when he is miserable" [anon], "a man who feels bad when he feels good for fear he'll feel worse when he feels better" [George Burns], "one who is always building dungeons in the air" [John Galsworthy], "a man who thinks everybody as nasty as himself, and hates them for it" [G. B. Shaw].

.8 **hopeless case; goner** or gone goose or gosling or dead duck [all slang]; terminal case.

.9 VERBS **be hopeless,** have not a hope or prayer, look bleak or dark; **be pessimistic, look on the dark side,** be or think downbeat [informal], think negatively, think o make the worst of, put the worst face upon; "fancy clouds where no clouds be" [Thomas Hood].

.10 **despair, despair of, despond** 872.16, falter, lose hope, **lose heart, abandon hope,** give up hope, **give up,** give up all hope *or* expectation, give way, fall *or* sink into despair, give oneself up *or* yield to despair, turn one's face to the wall.

.11 **shatter one's hopes,** dash *or* crush *or* blight one's hope, dash the cup from one's lips, disappoint 541.2, drive to despair *or* desperation.

.12 ADJS **hopeless,** unhopeful, without hope, affording no hope, bleak, grim, dismal, cheerless, comfortless; **desperate, despairing, in despair;** despondent 872.22; disconsolate 872.28; forlorn; apathetic 856.13.

.13 futile, vain 669.13; doomed, foredoomed.

.14 **impossible,** out of the question, not to be thought of, no go [informal].

.15 **past hope, beyond recall,** past praying for; **irretrievable, irrecoverable, irreclaimable,** irredeemable, unsalvageable, unsalvable; incorrigible, irreformable; irrevocable, **irreversible; irremediable, irreparable,** inoperable, **incurable,** cureless, remediless, immedicable, beyond remedy, terminal; unrelievable, unmitigable; **ruined,** undone; lost, gone.

.16 **pessimistic,** pessimist, downbeat [informal], **cynical,** nihilistic; uncheerful 872.21; **gloomy,** dismal; negative, negativistic; defeatist; Cassandran *or* Cassandrian, Cassandra-like.

.17 ADVS **hopelessly, desperately,** forlornly; impossibly.

.18 **irreclaimably, irretrievably, irrecoverably,** irredeemably, unsalvageably, unsalvably; irrevocably, **irreversibly; irremediably,** incurably, irreparably.

## 890. ANXIETY

### (troubled thought)

.1 NOUNS **anxiety, anxiousness; apprehension, apprehensiveness,** misgiving, foreboding, forebodingness, suspense, strain, tension, nervous strain *or* tension; **dread, fear** 891; **concern,** concernment, anxious concern, **solicitude,** zeal 635.2; **care,** cankerworm of care; **distress,** trouble, vexation; **uneasiness, perturbation, disturbance,** upset, **agitation, disquiet,** disquietude, inquietude, unquietness; **nervousness** 859; malaise, angst 866.1; pucker *or* stew *or* all-overs [all informal], pins and needles; overanxiety; anxious seat *or*

bench; anxiety neurosis 690.19, anxiety hysteria 690.19.

.2 **worry, worriment** [informal], **worriedness; worries,** worries and cares; worrying, fretting; harassment, torment.

.3 VERBS **concern,** give concern, **trouble, bother, distress, disturb, upset,** frazzle, **disquiet, agitate;** rob one of ease *or* sleep *or* rest, keep one on edge *or* on tenterhooks *or* on pins and needles.

.4 (make anxious) **worry, vex, fret, harass,** harry, **torment,** dog, hound, plague, persecute, haunt, beset.

.5 (feel anxious) **worry,** worry oneself, worry one's head about, worry oneself sick, be a prey to anxiety; **fret, fuss, chafe,** stew *or* take on [both informal], fret and fume; bite one's nails.

.6 ADJS **anxious, concerned, apprehensive,** foreboding, misgiving, suspenseful, strained, tense; **fearful** 891.31,32; **solicitous,** zealous 635.9,10; **troubled, bothered; uneasy, perturbed, disturbed, disquieted, agitated; nervous** 859.10–12; **on pins and needles,** on tenterhooks, on the anxious seat *or* bench; anxioused up [dial], all hot and bothered [slang]; all-overish *or* in a pucker *or* in a stew [all informal]; overanxious, overapprehensive.

.7 **worried, vexed,** fretted; **harassed,** harried, tormented, dogged, hounded, persecuted, haunted, beset, plagued; worried sick, worried to a frazzle, worried stiff [slang].

.8 **careworn,** heavy-laden.

.9 **troublesome,** bothersome, **distressing,** distressful, **disturbing, upsetting, disquieting; worrisome,** worrying; fretting, chafing; **harassing,** tormenting, plaguing; **annoying** 864.22.

.10 ADVS **anxiously, concernedly, apprehensively,** misgivingly, **uneasily;** worriedly; solicitously, zealously 635.14,15.

## 891. FEAR, FRIGHTENINGNESS

.1 NOUNS **fear, fright,** affright, phob(o)–; **scare, alarm, consternation, dismay; dread,** unholy dread, awe; **terror, horror,** horrification, mortal *or* abject fear; **phobia;** funk *or* blue funk [both informal]; **panic,** panic fear *or* terror; stampede; **cowardice** 892.

.2 **frighteningness, frightfulness, awfulness, scariness,** fearfulness, fearsomeness, alarmingness, dismayingness, disquietingness, startlingness, disconcertingness, terribleness, **dreadfulness,** horribleness, **hideousness,** appallingness, direness, **ghastliness,** grimness, grisliness, **gruesomeness,** ghoulishness; **creepiness, spookiness,** eeriness, weirdness, uncanniness.

.3 **fearfulness,** afraidness; **timidity, timorousness, shyness;** shrinkingness, bashfulness, diffidence, stage fright, mike fright [informal]; skittishness, startlishness, jumpiness.

.4 **apprehension,** apprehensiveness, **misgiving,** qualm, qualmishness, all-overs [informal]; **anxiety** 890; doubt 503.2; foreboding 544.

.5 **trepidation,** trepidity, perturbation, **fear and trembling; quaking, agitation** 857.3,4; **uneasiness, disquiet,** disquietude, inquietude; nervousness 859; palpitation, heartquake; shivers or cold shivers [both informal], creeps or cold creeps [both informal], chills of fear or terror, icy fingers or icy clutch of dread, jimjams [slang]; horripilation, gooseflesh, goose bumps [informal]; sweat, cold sweat; thrill of fear, spasm or quiver of terror; sinking stomach.

.6 **frightening, intimidation,** bullying, browbeating, cowing, bulldozing [informal], hectoring; **demoralization,** psychological warfare, war of nerves.

.7 **terrorization,** horrification, scaremongering; **terrorism,** terror or terroristic tactics, *Schrecklichkeit* [Ger], rule by terror, reign of terror.

.8 **alarmist,** scaremonger; **terrorist,** bomber, assassin.

.9 **frightener, scarer;** scarebabe, **bogey,** bogey man, **bugaboo,** bugbear; hobgoblin; **scarecrow; horror, terror,** holy terror; **ogre,** ogress, **monster,** vampire, werewolf, ghoul, bête noire, fee-faw-fum; incubus, succubus, nightmare; **ghost,** specter, phantom, revenant; Frankenstein, Dracula, Wolf-man; mythical monsters 85.20.

.10 (fear of people, etc.) androphobia (men), gynephobia (women), parthenophobia (young girls), pedophobia (children); tyrannophobia (tyrants), hagiophobia (saints), hierophobia (priests), papaphobia (the Pope), anthropophobia (people), agoraphobia or demophobia (crowds), ochlophobia (mobs), harpaxophobia (robbers); xenophobia (foreigners), Anglophobia (English), Francophobia or Gallophobia (French), Germanophobia or Teutonophobia (Germans), gringophobia (gringos), Japanophobia (Japanese), Judeophobia (Jews), Negrophobia (Negroes), Russophobia (Russians), Sinophobia (Chinese); theophobia (God), Satanophobia (Satan), demonophobia (demons), phasmophobia (ghosts), pneumatophobia (spirits).

.11 (fear of animals) ailurophobia (cats), cynophobia (dogs), hippophobia (horses), musophobia (mice), taurophobia (bulls), zoophobia (animals); batrachophobia or herpetophobia (reptiles), ophiciophobia or ophiophobia or snakephobia (snakes); ornithophobia (birds); ichthyophobia (fish); vermiphobia or helminthophobia (worms); acarophobia (mites), apiphobia (bees), arachnephobia (spiders), entomophobia (insects), pediculophobia (lice); bacillophobia or microbiophobia (microbes), bacteriophobia (bacteria), spermophobia or spermatophobia (germs); teratophobia (monsters).

.12 (fear of things) anthophobia (flowers), aulophobia (flutes), ballistophobia (bullets), belonephobia (needles), crystallophobia (crystals), eisoptrophobia (mirrors), enetophobia (pins); koniophobia or amathophobia (dust), linonophobia (string), mysophobia (dirt), necrophobia (corpses); hydrophobia (water); metallophobia (metal), aurophobia (gold), chrometophobia (money); mechanophobia (machinery), ochophobia (vehicles), telephonophobia (telephone); chaetophobia or trichophobia (hair), dermatosiophobia (skin), doraphobia (fur), odontophobia (teeth), ommetaphobia (eyes), pogonophobia (beards), pteronophobia (feathers), rectophobia (rectum); blennophobia or myxophobia (slime), coprophobia (feces), hemaphobia or hematophobia or hemophobia (blood), proteinphobia (protein), urophobia (urine); cibophobia or sitophobia or sitiophobia (food), potophobia (drink), pharmacophobia (drugs), toxiphobia or toxophobia or toxicophobia (poison); microphobia (small things), neophobia (new things), monophobia (one thing), panphobia or pantophobia (everything).

.13 (fear of natural phenomena) cometophobia (comets), heliophobia (sun), siderophobia (stars); barophobia (gravity); astraphobia or astrapophobia (lightning), brontophobia or tonitrophobia or keraunophobia (thunder), ancraophobia (wind), aerophobia (draft), homichlophobia (fog); nephophobia (clouds); chionophobia (snow); antlophobia (floods), cymophobia (waves); cheimaphobia or cheimatophobia (cold), thermophobia (heat), pyrophobia (fire); photophobia (light), selaphobia (light flashes), electrophobia (electricity); eosophobia (dawn), achluophobia *or* scotophobia (darkness), sciophobia (shadows), nyctophobia (night); acousticophobia (sound); bromidrosiphobia (body odor); cryophobia (ice, frost).

.14 (fear of diseases) acarophobia (the itch), albuminurophobia (albumin in the urine), anemophobia (anemia), cancerphobia *or* cancerophobia *or* carcinophobia (cancer), cardiophobia (heart disease), cholerophobia (cholera), cnidophobia (insect stings), coprostasophobia (constipation), dermatopathophobia (skin disease), diabetophobia (diabetes), diplopiaphobia (double vision), emetophobia (vomiting), febriphobia (fever), helminthophobia (worms), hormephobia (shock), hydrophobophobia (rabies), lyssophobia *or* maniaphobia (insanity), meningitophobia (meningitis), nephophobia *or* pathophobia (disease), parasitophobia (parasites), pellagraphobia (pellagra), scabiophobia (scabies), syphilophobia (syphilis), traumatophobia (wound, injury), trichinophobia (trichinosis), trichopathophobia (hair disease), tuberculophobia *or* phthisiophobia (tuberculosis), venereophobia (venereal disease).

.15 (fear of situations) acerophobia *or* acerbophobia (sourness), acrophobia (sharpness), anginophobia (narrowness), asthenophobia (weakness), bathophobia (depth), hygrophobia (dampness); algophobia (pain), dikephobia (justice), eleutherophobia (freedom), hedonophobia (pleasure), kopophobia (fatigue), peniaphobia (poverty), phobophobia (fear), poinephobia (punishment), zelophobia (jealousy); chromophobia (color), chronophobia (duration), dromophobia *or* kinetophobia (motion), symmetrophobia (symmetry), tachophobia (speed), tredecaphobia *or* triskaidekaphobia (13); autophobia *or* monophobia *or* ermitophobia (being alone), atephobia (ruin), atelophobia (imperfection), hypegiaphobia (responsibility), kakorraphiaphobia (failure); erotophobia *or* genophobia (sex), gametophobia (marriage), patroiophobia (heredity), gymnophobia *or* nudophobia (nudity); ideophobia (ideas), logophobia (words), onomatophobia (names), philosophobia (philosophy), politicophobia (politics), rhabdophobia (magic); apeirophobia (infinity), kenophobia (void).

.16 (fear of places) agoraphobia (open places), claustrophobia (enclosed places), ac-

rophobia *or* altophobia *or* batophobia *or* hypsophobia (high places); cremnophobia (precipices), limnophobia (lakes), potamophobia (rivers), thalassophobia (sea); ecclesiophobia (church), ecophobia *or* oecophobia *or* oikophobia (home); uranophobia *or* ouranophobia (heaven), hadephobia *or* stygiophobia (hell); topophobia (certain places).

.17 (fear of activities) agyrophobia (crossing a street), gephyrophobia (crossing a bridge), batophobia (passing high buildings), hodophobia (travel); clinophobia (going to bed), coitophobia (coitus), ergophobia (work), graphophobia (writing), hypnophobia (sleep), kleptophobia (stealing), lalophobia *or* laliophobia *or* glossophobia *or* phonophobia (speech), phagophobia (swallowing), rypophobia (soiling), stasophobia (standing), thaasophobia (being idle); erythrophobia (blushing), geumatophobia (taste), haptophobia *or* haphophobia *or* thixophobia (touch), olfactophobia *or* osmophobia *or* ophresiophobia (smell), phronemophobia (thinking), tremophobia (trembling); katagelophobia (ridicule), mastigophobia (beating), pnigophobia *or* pnigerophobia (smothering), trypanophobia *or* vaccinophobia (inocculation); tocophobia (childbirth), thanatophobia (death); musicophobia (music); hamartophobia *or* peccatiphobia (sin).

.18 VERBS **fear, be afraid; apprehend,** have qualms, misgive, eye askance; **dread,** stand in dread *or* awe of, be in mortal dread of, stand aghast; be on pins and needles, sit upon thorns; have one's heart in one's mouth.

.19 **take fright,** take alarm, push the panic button [informal]; funk *or* go into a funk [both informal], get wind up [Brit slang]; lose courage 892.8; pale, grow *or* turn pale, change *or* turn color; look as if one had seen a ghost; freeze, be paralyzed with fear; shit in one's pants [slang].

.20 **start,** startle, **jump,** jump out of one's skin, jump a mile, leap like a startled gazelle; **shy,** fight shy, start aside, boggle, jib; **panic,** stampede, skedaddle [informal].

.21 **flinch, shrink,** draw back, recoil, funk [informal], **quail, cringe, wince, blench,** blink.

.22 **tremble, shake, quake, shiver, quiver, quaver; tremble** *or* **quake in one's boots** *or* **shoes,** tremble like an aspen leaf, quiver like a rabbit, shake all over.

.23 **frighten,** fright, affright, funk [informal]; **scare,** spook [slang]; give one a fright *or* scare *or* turn; **alarm,** disquiet, raise apprehensions; shake, stagger; **startle** 540.8; **unnerve, unman,** unstring; give one gooseflesh, horripilate, make one's flesh creep, chill one's spine, make one's nerves tingle, make one's hair stand on end, make one's blood run cold, freeze *or* curdle the blood, make one's teeth chatter, make one tremble, take one's breath away, make one shit one's pants [slang].

.24 **put in fear,** put the fear of God into, **throw a scare into** [slang], scare the life out of, scare the pants off of, scare hell out of *or* scare the shit out of [both slang]; **panic,** stampede, send scuttling, throw blind fear into.

.25 **terrify, awe,** strike terror into; **horrify, appall, shock,** make one's flesh creep; **frighten out of one's wits** *or* **senses,** frighten from one's propriety, **scare stiff** *or* **shitless** [slang], scare to death; strike dumb, **stun, stupefy, paralyze, petrify,** freeze.

.26 **daunt, deter,** shake, stop; **discourage, dishearten;** faze [informal]; **awe, overawe.**

.27 **dismay, disconcert, appall, astound, confound, abash, discomfit, put out, take aback** [informal].

.28 **intimidate, cow, browbeat, bulldoze** [informal], bludgeon, dragoon; **bully, hector, harass,** huff; bluster, bluster out of *or* into; **terrorize,** put in bodily fear, use terror *or* terroristic tactics, pursue a policy of *Schrecklichkeit,* systematically terrorize; threaten 973.2; **demoralize.**

.29 **frighten off, scare away,** bluff off, put to flight.

.30 ADJS **afraid, scared,** spooked [slang]; feared *or* afeared [both dial]; **fearstricken, fear-struck;** haunted with fear; –**phobic.**

.31 **fearful,** fearing, fearsome, **in fear;** cowardly 892.10; **timorous,** timid, shy, rabbity *or* mousy [both informal]; **shrinking,** bashful, diffident; scary; **skittish,** skittery [dial], startlish, jumpy, goosy [slang], trigger-happy [informal]; **tremulous,** trembling, trepidant, shaky, shivery; **nervous** 859.10.

.32 **apprehensive, misgiving,** all-overish [informal], qualmish, qualmy; anxious 890.6.

.33 **frightened,** affrighted, in a fright, in a funk *or* blue funk [informal]; **alarmed,** disquieted; consternated, **dismayed,**
daunted; **startled** 540.13; more frightened than hurt.

.34 **terrified,** terror-stricken, terror-struck, terror-smitten, terror-shaken, terror-troubled, terror-riven, terror-ridden, terror-driven, terror-crazed, terror-haunted; awestricken, awestruck; **horrified,** horrorstricken, horror-struck; **appalled, astounded, aghast;** frightened out of one's wits, **scared to death, scared stiff** *or* **shitless** [slang]; unnerved, unstrung, unmanned, undone, **cowed,** awed, **intimidated; stunned, petrified, stupefied,** paralyzed, frozen; white as a sheet, pale as death *or* a ghost, deadly pale, ashen, blanched, pallid, gray with fear.

.35 **panicky,** panic-prone, panicked, in a panic, panic-stricken, panic-struck, out of one's mind with fear, prey to blind fear.

.36 **frightening, frightful; fearful,** fearsome, fear-inspiring; **scary** [informal], scaring, chilling; **alarming, startling,** disquieting, dismaying, disconcerting; **daunting,** deterring, **deterrent,** discouraging, disheartening, fazing, awing, overawing.

.37 **terrifying,** terrorful, terror-striking, terror-inspiring, terror-bringing, terror-giving, terror-breeding, terror-breathing, terror-bearing, terror-fraught; **bloodcurdling, hair-raising** [informal]; petrifying, paralyzing, stunning, stupefying; **terror, terroristic.**

.38 **terrible,** terrific, tremendous, din(o)– *or* dein(o)–; **horrid, horrible, horrifying,** horrific, horrendous, *schrecklich* [Ger]; **dreadful, dread,** dreaded; **awful;** awesome, awe-inspiring; **shocking, appalling,** astounding; **dire,** direful, fell; formidable, redoubtable; **hideous, ghastly,** morbid, grim, grisly, gruesome, ghoulish, macabre.

.39 **creepy, spooky, eerie, weird, uncanny,** unco *or* uncolike [both Scot].

.40 ADVS **fearfully, apprehensively, diffidently,** for fear of; **timorously, timidly, shyly,** mousily [informal], bashfully, shrinkingly; tremulously, tremblingly, quakingly, **with** *or* **in fear and trembling;** with heart in mouth, with bated breath.

.41 **in fear, in terror,** in awe, in alarm, in consternation; in mortal fear, in fear of one's life.

.42 **frightfully, fearfully; alarmingly, startlingly,** disquietingly, dismayingly, disconcertingly; **shockingly, appallingly,** astoundingly; **terribly,** terrifically, tremendously; **dreadfully, awfully; horridly, horribly,** horrifyingly, horrifically, horrendously.

## 892. COWARDICE

**.1** NOUNS **cowardice**, **cowardliness**; **fear** 891; **faintheartedness**, **faintheart**, **weakheartedness**, **chickenheartedness**, **henheartedness**, **pigeonheartedness**; **yellowness**, **white-liveredness** or **lily-liveredness** or **chicken-liveredness** [all informal], **weakkneedness**; **weakness**, **softness**; **unmanliness**, **unmanfulness**; **timidness**, **timidity**, **timorousness**, **milksoppiness**, **milksoppishness**, **milksopism**.

**.2** **uncourageousness**, **unvaliantness**, **unvalorousness**, **unheroicness**, **ungallantness**, **unintrepidness**; **plucklessness**, **spunklessness** or **gritlessness** [both informal], **gutlessness** [slang], **spiritlessness**, **heartlessness**.

**.3** **dastardliness**, **pusillanimousness**, **pusillanimity**, **poltroonery**, **poltroonishness**, **poltroonism**, **baseness**, **cravenness**; **desertion under fire**, **skedaddling** [informal].

**.4** **cold feet** [slang], **weak knees**, **faint heart**, **chicken heart**, **yellow streak** [slang], **white feather**.

**.5** **coward**, **jellyfish**, **invertebrate**, **weakling**, **weak sister** [informal], **milksop**, **Milquetoast**, **mouse**, **sissy**, **baby**, **big baby**, **chicken** [slang]; **white liver** or **lily liver** or **chicken liver** [all informal], **white feather**; **fraid-cat** or **fraidy-cat** or **scaredy-cat** [all slang]; **funk** or **funker** [both informal]; "one who in a perilous emergency thinks with his legs" [Ambrose Bierce]; –**phobe**.

**.6** **dastard**, **craven**, **poltroon**, **recreant**, **caitiff**, **arrant coward**; **sneak**.

**.7** VERBS **dare not**; **have a yellow streak** [slang], **have cold feet** [slang], **be unable to say 'boo' to a goose**.

**.8** **lose one's nerve**, **lose courage**, **get cold feet** [slang], **show the white feather**; **falter**, **boggle**, **funk** [informal], **chicken** [slang]; **back out**, **funk out** [informal], **chicken out** [slang]; **desert under fire**, **skedaddle** [informal], **run scared** [slang], **scuttle**.

**.9** **cower**, **quail**, **cringe**, **crouch**, **skulk**, **sneak**, **slink**.

**.10** ADJS **cowardly**, **coward**; **afraid**, **fearful** 891.30–35; **timid**, **timorous**, **overtimorous**, **overtimid**, **rabbity** or **mousy** [both informal]; **fainthearted**, **weakhearted**, **chickenhearted**, **henhearted**, **pigeonhearted**; **white-livered** or **lily-livered** or **chicken-livered** or **milk-livered** [all informal]; **yellow** or **with a yellow streak** [both informal]; **weak-kneed**, **chicken** [slang], **afraid of one's shadow**; **weak**, **soft**; **unmanly**, **un-**

manful, **sissy**, **sissified**; **milksoppy**, **milksoppish**; **panicky**, **panic-prone**, **funking** or **funky** [both informal]; **daunted**, **dismayed**, **unmanned**, **cowed**, **intimidated**.

**.11** **uncourageous**, **unvaliant**, **unvalorous**, **unheroic**, **ungallant**, **unintrepid**, **undaring**, **unable to say 'boo' to a goose**; **unsoldierlike**, **unsoldierly**; **pluckless**, **spunkless** or **gritless** [both informal], **gutless** [slang], **spiritless**, **heartless**.

**.12** **dastardly**, **dastard**; **poltroonish**, **poltroon**; **pusillanimous**, **base**, **craven**, **recreant**, **caitiff**; **dunghill**, **dunghilly**.

**.13** **cowering**, **quailing**, **cringing**; **skulking**, **sneaking**, **slinking**, **sneaky**, **slinky**.

**.14** ADVS **cravenly**, **poltroonishly**, **like a coward**, **uncourageously**, **unvaliantly**, **unvalorously**, **unheroically**, **ungallantly**, **unintrepidly**, **undaringly**; **plucklessly**, **spunklessly** or **gritlessly** [both informal], **spiritlessly**, **heartlessly**; **faintheartedly**, **weakheartedly**, **chickenheartedly**.

## 893. COURAGE

**.1** NOUNS **courage**, **courageousness**; **bravery**, **braveness**, **boldness**, **valor**, **valorousness**, **valiance**, **valiancy**, **gallantry**, **conspicuous gallantry**, **gallantry under fire**, **gallantness**, **intrepidity**, **intrepidness**, **prowess**, **virtue**; **doughtiness**, **stalwartness**, **stoutness**, **stoutheartedness**, **lionheartedness**, **greatheartedness**; **heroism**, **heroicalness**; **chivalry**, **chivalrousness**, **knightliness**; **military** or **martial spirit**, **soldierly quality** or **virtues**; **manliness**, **manfulness**, **manhood**; **Dutch courage** [informal], **pot-valor**.

**.2** "fear that has said its prayers" [Dorothy Bernard], "fear holding on a minute longer" [George Patton], "taking hard knocks like a man when occasion calls" [Plautus], "doing without witnesses that which we would be capable of doing before everyone" [La Rochefoucauld].

**.3** **fearlessness**, **dauntlessness**, **undauntedness**, **unfearfulness**, **unfearingness**, **unafraidness**, **unapprehensiveness**; **confidence** 513.5; **untimidness**, **untimorousness**, **unshrinkingness**, **unshyness**, **unbashfulness**.

**.4** **fortitude**, **hardihood**, **hardiness**; **pluckiness**; **spunkiness** or **grittiness** or **nerviness** [all informal], **mettlesomeness**; **gameness**, **gaminess**; **resolution** 624, **resoluteness**, **tenaciousness**, **tenacity**, **pertinaciousness**, **pertinacity**, **bulldog courage**.

**.5** **nerve**, *chutzpah* [Yid], **spunk** [informal], **pluck**, **grit**, **stamina**, **toughness**, **backbone** [informal], **pith**, **mettle**, **bottom**; **guts** or gutsiness or guttiness [all slang], **intestinal fortitude** [informal]; **heart, spirit; stout heart, heart of oak.**

.6 **daring,** derring-do; **bravado,** bravura; **audacity,** audaciousness, overboldness, balls [slang]; **adventurousness,** venturousness, venturesomeness, adventuresomeness, enterprise; foolhardiness 894.3.

.7 **exploit, feat, deed, enterprise, achievement, adventure,** gest, **bold stroke,** heroic act or deed; aristeia.

.8 (brave person) **hero, heroine;** brave, stalwart, gallant, valiant, **man of courage** or mettle, a man, valiant knight, good soldier; demigod, paladin; demigoddess; the brave; decorated hero; Hector, Achilles, Roland, David, Samson; lion, tiger, bulldog, fighting cock, gamecock; chutzpanik [Yid].

.9 **encouragement, heartening, inspiration,** inspiriting, inspiritment, emboldening, assurance, reassurance, pat or clap on the back.

.10 VERBS **dare, venture, make bold to,** make so bold as to, **have the nerve, have the guts** [slang], have the courage of one's convictions, be a man, "dare do all that may become a man" [Shakespeare], "be strong, and quit yourselves like men" [Bible]; defy 793.3.

.11 **brave, face, confront,** affront. front, look straight in the eyes, meet eyeball to eyeball [informal], meet, **meet boldly; set at defiance** 793.4; speak up, speak out, stand up and be counted; **face up to, stand up to,** not flinch or shrink from, bite the bullet [informal], look full in the face, put a bold face upon, show or present a bold front, **meet head-on,** face up, face the music [informal]; **brazen,** brazen out or through; beard, "beard the lion in his den" [Sir Walter Scott]; put one's head in the lion's mouth, fly into the face of danger, take the bull by the horns, march up to the cannon's mouth, bell the cat, go through fire and water, go in harm's way, run the gauntlet, take one's life in one's hands, put one's life on the line [informal].

.12 **outbrave, outdare; outface,** face down, face out; **outbrazen,** brazen out; **outlook,** outstare, stare down, stare out of countenance.

.13 **steel oneself,** get up nerve, nerve oneself, muster or summon up or gather courage, pluck up heart, screw up one's nerve or courage, "screw your courage to the sticking place" [Shakespeare], stiffen one's backbone [informal].

.14 **take courage, take heart,** take heart of grace; **brace up** or buck up [informal].

.15 keep up one's courage, bear up, **keep one's chin up** [informal], **keep a stiff upper lip** [informal], hold up one's head, take what comes; hang in or hang in there or hang tough or stick it out [all slang], stick to one's guns.

.16 **encourage, hearten, embolden, nerve,** pat or clap on the back, **assure, reassure,** bolster, support; **inspire,** inspirit; buck up or brace up [both informal]; put upon one's mettle, make a man of; cheer 870.7.

.17 ADJS **courageous, brave, bold, valiant, valorous, gallant, intrepid,** doughty, **hardy,** stalwart, stout, stouthearted, ironhearted, lionhearted, greathearted, bold-spirited, bold as a lion; **heroic,** herolike; **chivalrous,** chivalric, knightly, knightlike, soldierly, soldierlike; **manly,** manful.

.18 **plucky; spunky** or gritty or nervy [all informal], **gutsy** or gutty [both slang], tough, **resolute, game,** gamy; **spirited,** spiritful, red-blooded, **mettlesome;** bulldoggish, tenacious, pertinacious.

.19 **unafraid, unfearing, unfearful; unapprehensive,** undiffident; **confident** 513.21; **fearless, dauntless,** aweless, dreadless; **unfrightened,** unscared, unalarmed, unterrified; **untimid,** untimorous, unshy, unbashful.

.20 **undaunted, undismayed, uncowed, unintimidated,** unappalled, unabashed, unawed; **unflinching, unshrinking, unquailing,** uncringing, unwincing, unblenching, unblinking.

.21 **daring, audacious, overbold; adventurous, venturous, venturesome,** adventuresome, enterprising; foolhardy 894.9.

.22 ADVS **courageously, bravely, boldly, heroically, valiantly,** valorously, **gallantly, intrepidly,** doughtily, stoutly, hardily, stalwartly; **pluckily, spunkily** [informal], gutsily [slang], **resolutely, gamely,** tenaciously, pertinaciously, bulldoggishly, **fearlessly,** unfearingly, unfearfully; **daringly,** audaciously; chivalrously, knightly, yeomanly; **like a man,** like a soldier.

## 894. RASHNESS

.1 NOUNS **rashness, brashness,** brazen boldness, **incautiousness, overboldness, imprudence, indiscretion,** injudiciousness, improvidence; **unwariness,** unchariness; overcarelessness; **overconfidence,** oversureness, overweeningness; **impudence,** insolence 913; gall or brass or cheek [all informal], *chutzpah* [Yid]; hubris; temerity, temerariousness; heroics.

.2 **recklessness**, devil-may-careness; **heedlessness**, **carelessness** 534.2; **impetuousness** 630.2, impetuosity, hotheadedness; **haste** 709, **hastiness**, hurriedness, overeagerness; overzealousness, overenthusiasm; **furiousness**, desperateness, wantonness, wildness; **precipitateness**, precipitousness, precipitance, precipitancy, precipitation.

.3 **foolhardiness**, harebrainedness; **audacity**, audaciousness; *courage fou* [Fr]; forwardness, boldness, **presumption**, presumptuousness; **daring**, daredeviltry, daredevilry, fire-eating; playing with fire, flirting with death, courting disaster, stretching one's luck, going for broke [slang], brinkmanship; adventurousness 893.6.

.4 **daredevil**, devil, **madcap**, madbrain, wild man, hotspur, hellcat, rantipole, harum-scarum or fire-eater [both informal]; **adventurer**, adventuress; brazenface.

.5 VERBS **be rash**, be reckless, carry too much sail, sail too near the wind, go out of one's depth, go too far, go to sea in a sieve, take a leap in the dark, buy a pig in a poke, count one's chickens before they are hatched, catch at straws, lean on a broken reed, put all one's eggs in one basket, live in a glass house; go out on a limb [informal], leave oneself wide open [slang], drop one's guard, stick one's neck out or ask for it [both slang].

.6 **court danger**, mock or defy danger, thumb one's nose at the consequences, **tempt Providence**, tweak the devil's nose, bell the cat, play a desperate game, ride for a fall; play with fire, flirt with death, stretch one's luck, go for broke [slang], march up to the cannon's mouth, put one's head in a lion's mouth, beard the lion in his den, sit on a barrel of gunpowder, sleep on a volcano, play Russian roulette.

.7 ADJS **rash**, **brash**, **incautious**, overbold, **imprudent**, **indiscreet**, injudicious, **improvident**; **unwary**, **unchary**; overcareless; overconfident, oversure, overweening, **impudent**, insolent, brazenfaced, brazen 913.8–10; hubristic; temerarious.

.8 **reckless**, devil-may-care; careless 534.11; **impetuous**, hotheaded; **hasty** 709.9–11, hurried, overeager, overzealous, overenthusiastic; **furious**, desperate, mad, wild, wanton, harum-scarum [informal]; precipitate, **precipitous**, **precipitant**;

headlong, breakneck; slapdash, slap-bang; accident-prone.

.9 **foolhardy**, **harebrained**, madcap, **wild**, wild-ass [slang], madbrain, madbrained; **audacious**; forward, bold, **presumptuous**; **daring**, daredevil, fire-eating, death-defying; adventurous 893.21.

.10 ADVS **rashly**, **brashly**, **incautiously**, **imprudently**, **indiscreetly**, injudiciously, improvidently; **unwarily**, uncharily; overconfidently, overweeningly, **impudently**, insolently, **brazenly**, hubristically, temerariously.

.11 **recklessly**, happen what may; heedlessly, **carelessly** 534.18; **impetuously**, hotheadedly; **hastily**, hurriedly, overeagerly, overzealously, overenthusiastically; **furiously**, desperately, wildly, wantonly, **madly**, like mad [informal], like crazy [slang]; **precipitately**, precipitously, precipitantly; **headlong**, headfirst, headforemost, **head over heels**, heels over head, *à corps perdu* [Fr]; slapdash, slap-bang or slam-bang [both informal]; helter-skelter, ramble-scramble [informal], hurry-scurry, holus-bolus.

.12 **foolhardily**, **daringly**, **audaciously**, presumptuously, harebrainedly.

## 895. CAUTION

### *(provident care)*

.1 NOUNS **caution**, **cautiousness**; slowness to act or commit oneself or make one's move; **care**, **heed**, **solicitude**; **carefulness**, **heedfulness**, mindfulness, regardfulness, thoroughness; **gingerliness**, guardedness; uncommunicativeness 613; **tentativeness**, hesitation, unprecipitateness, slow and careful steps, deliberate stages, wait and see policy; **prudence**, prudentialness, **circumspection**, **discretion**, canniness [Scot], pawkiness [Brit], judiciousness; calculation, **deliberateness**, deliberation, careful consideration, prior consultation; **safeness**, safety first, no room for error; **hedge**, **hedging**, hedging one's bets, cutting one's losses.

.2 **wariness**, **chariness**, **cageyness** or **leeriness** [both slang]; **suspicion**, suspiciousness; **distrust**, distrustfulness, mistrust, mistrustfulness.

.3 **precaution**, precautiousness; **forethought**, **foresight**, foresightedness, forehandedness, forethoughtfulness; **providence**, provision, forearming; precautions, steps, measures, steps and measures; **safeguard**, protection 699, preventive measure; insurance.

.4 overcaution, overcautiousness, overcarefulness, overwariness.

.5 VERBS be cautious, be careful; think twice, give it a second thought; make haste slowly, take it easy [informal]; put the right foot forward, take one step at a time, pick one's steps, go step by step, feel one's ground or way; pussyfoot, tiptoe, go on tiptoe, walk on eggshells; draw in one's horns.

.6 take precautions, take steps or measures, take steps and measures; prepare or provide for or against, forearm; guard against, make sure against, make sure, "make assurance double sure" [Shakespeare]; play safe [informal], keep on the safe side; leave no stone unturned, forget or leave out nothing, overlook no possibility, leave no room for error, leave nothing to chance, consider every angle; look before one leaps; see how the land lies or the wind blows, see how the cat jumps [informal]; clear the decks, batten down the hatches, shorten sail, reef down, tie in or tuck in or take in a reef, get out a sheet-anchor, have an anchor to windward; hedge, provide a hedge, hedge one's bets, cut one's losses; take out insurance; keep something for a rainy day.

.7 beware, take care, have a care, take heed, take heed at one's peril; keep at a respectful distance, keep out of harm's way; mind, mind one's business; be on one's guard, be on the watch or lookout, be on the qui vive; look out, watch out [informal]; look sharp, keep one's eyes open, keep a weather eye open [informal], keep one's eye peeled [slang], watch one's step [slang], look about one; stop, look, and listen; not stick one's neck out [slang], not go out on a limb [informal], not expose oneself, not be too visible, lie low, stay in the background; hold one's tongue 451.5–7.

.8 ADJS cautious, careful, heedful, mindful, regardful, thorough; prudent, circumspect, slow to act or commit oneself or make one's move, canny [Scot], pawky [Brit], discreet, politic, judicious, noncommittal; unadventurous, unenterprising, undaring; gingerly; guarded, on guard, on one's guard; uncommunicative 613.8–10; tentative, hesitant, unprecipitate; deliberate; safe, on the safe side, leaving no stone unturned, forgetting or leaving out nothing, overlooking no possibility, leaving no room for error.

.9 wary, chary, cagey [slang], leery [slang], suspicious, suspecting, distrustful, mistrustful, shy.

.10 precautious, precautionary, precautional; forethoughtful, forethoughted, foresighted, foreseeing, forehanded; provident, provisional.

.11 overcautious, overcareful, overwary.

.12 ADVS cautiously, carefully, heedfully, mindfully, regardfully; prudently, circumspectly, cannily [Scot], pawkily [Brit], discreetly, judiciously; gingerly, guardedly, easy [informal], with caution, with care.

.13 warily, charily, cagily [slang]; askance, askant, suspiciously, leerily [slang], distrustfully.

.14 INTERJS careful!, be careful!, take care!, have a care!, look out!, watch out!, watch your step!, watch it!, steady!, look sharp!, easy!, take it easy!, easy does it!, go easy!

## 896. FASTIDIOUSNESS

.1 NOUNS fastidiousness, particularity, particularness; scrupulousness, scrupulosity; punctiliousness, punctilio; preciseness, precision; meticulousness, conscientiousness, criticalness; taste 897; sensitivity, discrimination 492, discriminatingness, discriminativeness; selectiveness, selectivity, pickiness [slang], choosiness; strictness 533.3, perfectionism, precisianism, purism; puritanism, priggishness, prudishness, censoriousness.

.2 finicalness, finickiness, finickingness, finicality; fussiness, pernicketiness or persnicketiness [both informal]; squeamishness, queasiness, pawkiness [Brit].

.3 nicety, niceness, delicacy, delicateness, daintiness, exquisiteness, fineness, refinement.

.4 overfastidiousness, overscrupulousness, overparticularity, overconscientiousness, overmeticulousness, overniceness, overnicety; overcriticalness, hypercriticism, hairsplitting; overrefinement; oversqueamishness, oversensitivity, hypersensitivity, morbid sensibility.

.5 exclusiveness, selectness, selectiveness, selectivity; cliquishness, clannishness; snobbishness, snobbery, snobbism.

.6 perfectionist, precisian, precisianist, stickler, nitpicker [slang], captious critic 494.7.

.7 fuss-budget or fusspot [both informal], fuss, fusser, fuddy-duddy [slang], granny, old woman, old maid.

.8 VERBS be hard to please, fuss, pick and choose; turn up one's nose at, look down one's nose at, disdain, scorn, spurn.

.9 ADJS fastidious, particular, scrupulous

meticulous, conscientious, exacting, precise, punctilious; **sensitive, discriminating** 492.7, discriminative; **selective,** picky [slang], choosy, choicy [slang]; critical 969.24, "nothing if not critical" [Shakespeare]; **strict** 533.12, perfectionistic, precisianistic, puristic; puritanic(al), priggish, prudish, censorious.

.10 **finical, finicky,** finicking, finikin; **fussy,** fuss-budgety [informal]; **squeamish,** queasy, pawky [Brit], pernickety or persnickety [both informal], difficult, hard to please.

.11 **nice, dainty, delicate,** délicat [Fr], **fine,** refined, exquisite.

.12 overfastidious, overparticular, overscrupulous, overconscientious, overmeticulous, overnice, overprecise; overcritical, hypercritical, ultracritical, hairsplitting; overrefined; oversqueamish, oversensitive, hypersensitive, morbidly sensitive.

.13 **exclusive,** selective, **select,** elect; cliquish, clannish; **snobbish,** snobby.

.14 ADVS **fastidiously, particularly,** scrupulously, meticulously, conscientiously, critically, punctiliously; discriminatingly, discriminatively, selectively; **finically,** finickily, finickingly; **fussily; squeamishly,** queasily.

## 897. TASTE, TASTEFULNESS

.1 NOUNS **taste, good taste,** sound critical judgment, discernment or appreciation of excellence, preference for the best, goût raffiné [Fr]; **tastefulness,** quality, excellence, choiceness, **elegance,** grace, gracefulness, gracility, graciousness, graciosity; **refinement,** finesse, **polish, culture, cultivation,** civilizedness, refined or cultivated or civilized taste; niceness, nicety, delicacy, daintiness, subtlety, sophistication, discrimination 492, fastidiousness 896; acquired taste, "caviare to the general" [Shakespeare].

.2 "good sense delicately put in force" [Chévier], "the microscope of the judgment" [Rousseau], "a fine judgment in discerning art" [Horace], "the literary conscience of the soul" [Joseph Joubert], "the enemy of creativeness" [Picasso].

.3 **decorousness, decorum,** decency, properness, propriety, rightness, **seemliness,** becomingness, fittingness, fitness, appropriateness, suitability, meetness, happiness, felicity; gentility, genteelness; civility, urbanity 936.1.

.4 **restraint,** restrainedness, understatement,

unobtrusiveness, quietness, subduedness, quiet taste; simplicity 902.1.

.5 **aesthetic** or **artistic taste,** virtuosity, virtu, **expertise,** expertism, connoisseurship; dilettantism; fine art of living; epicurism, epicureanism; gastronomy, friandise [Fr]; aesthetics.

.6 **aesthete,** man of taste, lover of beauty.

.7 **connoisseur,** connaisseur [Fr], cognoscente [Ital]; **judge, good judge, critic, expert,** authority, maven [slang], **arbiter,** arbiter of taste, arbiter elegantiarum [L]; **epicure,** epicurean; **gourmet, gourmand,** bon vivant [Fr], good or refined palate; **virtuoso; dilettante,** amateur; collector.

.8 ADJS **tasteful, in good taste,** in the best taste; **excellent,** of quality, of the best; **aesthetic, artistic,** pleasing, well-chosen, **choice,** of choice; **pure, chaste;** classic(al), Attic, **restrained, understated,** unobtrusive, quiet, subdued, simple, unaffected 902.6,7.

.9 **elegant,** graceful, gracile, gracious; **refined, polished, cultivated,** civilized, **cultured; nice, fine, delicate, dainty,** subtle, sophisticated, **discriminating** 492.7,8, fastidious 896.9.

.10 **decorous,** decent, **proper,** right, **seemly, becoming,** fitting, **appropriate,** suitable, meet, happy, felicitous; genteel; civil, urbane 936.14.

.11 ADVS **tastefully, with taste,** in good taste, in the best taste; aesthetically, artistically; elegantly, gracefully; decorously, genteelly, decently, properly, seemly, becomingly; quietly, unobtrusively; simply 902.10.

## 898. VULGARITY

.1 NOUNS **vulgarity,** vulgarness, vulgarism; **inelegance** or inelegancy, **indelicacy, impropriety,** indecency, **indecorum,** indecorousness, unseemliness, unbecomingness, unfittingness, inappropriateness, unsuitableness, unsuitability; ungentility; **untastefulness,** tastelessness, unaestheticness, unaestheticism; low or bad or poor taste, mauvais goût [Fr]; vulgar taste, bourgeois taste, Babbittry, philistinism; popular taste, pop culture or pop [both slang]; campiness, camp, high or low camp; kitsch.

.2 **coarseness, grossness,** grossièreté [Fr], **rudeness, crudeness,** crudity, **crassness,** rawness, roughness, **earthiness;** ribaldness, ribaldry; **obscenity** 990.4; meretriciousness, **loudness** [informal], gaudiness 904.3.

.3 **unrefinement, uncouthness,** uncultivation, uncultivatedness, unculturedness; uncivilizedness, wildness; impoliteness, incivility, ill breeding 937.1; **barbarism,** barbarousness, barbarity, philistinism, Gothicism; **savagery,** savagism; **brutality,** brutishness, bestiality, animality; Neanderthalism, troglodytism.

.4 **boorishness, churlishness,** carlishness, **loutishness, lubberliness, lumpishness,** cloddishness, clownishness, yokelism; ruffianism, rowdyism, hooliganism; parvenuism, arrivism, upstartness.

.5 **commonness, commonplaceness,** ordinariness, homeliness; **lowness, baseness, meanness;** ignobility, plebeianism.

.6 **vulgarian,** low or vulgar or ill-bred fellow, mucker [slang], guttersnipe [informal], épicier [Fr]; Babbitt, Philistine, bourgeois; parvenu, arriviste, nouveau riche [all Fr], upstart; bounder [informal], cad, **boor,** churl, clown, **lout,** looby, peasant, groundling, yokel; rough, **ruffian,** roughneck [slang], **rowdy,** hooligan; vulgarist, ribald.

.7 **barbarian, savage,** Goth, animal, brute; Neanderthal, troglodyte.

.8 vulgarization, coarsening; popularization; haute vulgarisation [Fr].

.9 VERBS vulgarize, coarsen; popularize.

.10 ADJS **vulgar, inelegant, indelicate, indecorous, indecent, improper, unseemly,** unbeseeming, unbecoming, unfitting, inappropriate, unsuitable, **ungenteel,** undignified; **untasteful,** tasteless, in bad or poor taste, chintzy; **offensive,** offensive to gentle ears.

.11 **coarse, gross, rude, crude, crass,** raw, rough, **earthy;** ribald; obscene 990.5–9; meretricious, **loud** [informal], **gaudy** 904.20.

.12 **unrefined, unpolished, uncouth,** unkempt, uncombed, unlicked; **uncultivated, uncultured; uncivilized,** noncivilized, impolite, uncivil, ill-bred 937.4–6; **wild,** untamed, agrio–; **barbarous,** barbaric, barbarian; outlandish, Gothic; primitive; **savage, brutal,** brutish, bestial, animal; Neanderthal, troglodytic; wild-and-woolly, rough-and-ready.

.13 **boorish, churlish,** carlish, **loutish,** lubberly, lumpish, cloddish, clownish, loobyish, yokelish 182.7; rowdy, **rowdyish, ruffianly,** roughneck [slang], hooliganish, raffish, raised in a barn.

.14 **common, commonplace, ordinary;** plebeian 919.11; homely, homespun; **general, public, popular,** pop [slang]; vernacular;

Babbittish, Philistine, bourgeois; campy, high-camp, low-camp, kitschy.

.15 **low, base, mean, ignoble,** vile, scurvy, sorry, scrubby, beggarly; low-minded, base-minded.

.16 ADVS **vulgarly, uncouthly, inelegantly,** indelicately, indecorously, indecently, improperly, unseemly, untastefully, offensively; **coarsely, grossly, rudely, crudely,** crassly, roughly; ribaldly.

## 899. UGLINESS

.1 NOUNS **ugliness, unsightliness, unattractiveness,** uncomeliness, unhandsomeness, unbeautifulness, unprettiness, unloveliness, unaestheticness, unpleasingness 864.1; unprepossessingness, ill-favoredness, inelegance; **homeliness,** plainness; unshapeliness, shapelessness; ungracefulness, gracelessness, clumsiness, ungainliness 734.3; **uglification, uglifying, disfigurement,** defacement; dysphemism; cacophony.

.2 **hideousness,** horridness, horribleness, frightfulness, dreadfulness, terribleness, awfulness [informal]; **repulsiveness** 864.2, repugnantness, offensiveness, forbiddingness, loathsomeness; ghastliness, gruesomeness, grisliness; **deformity,** misshapenness.

.3 forbidding countenance, vinegar aspect, wry face, face that would stop a clock.

.4 **eyesore,** blot, blemish, **sight** [informal], **fright,** mess, no beauty, ugly duckling; baboon; scarecrow, gargoyle, monster, **monstrosity,** teratism; witch, bag or dog [both slang], hag, harridan.

.5 VERBS **offend** 864.9, offend the eye, offend one's aesthetic sensibilities, **look bad;** look something terrible or look like hell or look like the devil or look a sight or look a fright or look a mess or look like something the cat dragged in [all informal]; **uglify, disfigure,** deface, blot, blemish, mar, spoil; dysphemize.

.6 ADJS **ugly, unsightly, unattractive, unhandsome, unpretty, unlovely,** uncomely, **inelegant; unbeautiful,** unbeauteous, beautiless, unaesthetic, unpleasing 864.17; **homely, plain;** not much to look at, no much for looks, short on looks [informal], hard on the eyes [slang]; ugly as sin, ugly as the wrath of God, ugly as hell, homely as a mud fence, homely enough to sour milk, homely enough to stop a clock, not fit to be seen; **uglified, disfigured,** defaced, blotted, blemished, marred, spoiled; dysphemized, dysphemistic; cacophonous, cacophonic.

.7 **unprepossessing, ill-favored,** hard-favored, evil-favored, ill-featured; **ill-looking,** evil-looking; hard-featured, hard-visaged; grim, grim-faced, grim-visaged.

.8 **unshapely,** shapeless, **ill-shaped,** ill-made, ill-proportioned; **deformed,** misshapen, misproportioned, malformed, misbegotten; grotesque, scarecrowish, gargoylish; monstrous, teratic, cacogenic.

.9 **ungraceful,** ungraced, graceless; clumsy, ungainly 734.20.

.10 **inartistic,** unartistic, **unaesthetic;** unornamental, undecorative.

.11 **hideous, horrid, horrible, frightful, dreadful, terrible, awful** [informal]; **repulsive** 864.18, repelling, **repugnant,** offensive, foul, forbidding, loathsome, revolting; **ghastly,** gruesome, grisly.

.12 ADVS **uglily,** homelily, uncomelily, **unattractively,** unhandsomely, unbeautifully, unprettily.

.13 **hideously, horridly, horribly, frightfully, dreadfully, terribly, awfully** [informal]; **repulsively, repugnantly,** offensively, forbiddingly, loathsomely, revoltingly; gruesomely, ghastly.

## 900. BEAUTY

.1 NOUNS **beauty, beautifulness,** beauteousness, **prettiness, handsomeness, attractiveness** 863.2, **loveliness, pulchritude, charm, grace, elegance, exquisiteness;** bloom, glow; the beautiful; source of aesthetic pleasure or delight; beauty unadorned.

.2 "truth's smile when she beholds her own face in a perfect mirror" [Tagore], "the sensible image of the Infinite" [Bancroft], "God's handwriting" [Emerson], "a form of genius" [Oscar Wilde], "the power by which a woman charms a lover and terrifies a husband" [Ambrose Bierce].

.3 **comeliness, fairness,** sightliness, personableness, becomingness, pleasingness 863.1, goodliness, bonniness, agreeability, agreeableness.

.4 **good looks,** good appearance, good effect; good proportions, aesthetic proportions; **shapeliness,** good figure, good shape, belle tournure [Fr], nice body, lovely build, physical or bodily charm, curvaceousness, curves [informal], pneumaticness, sexy body; bodily grace, **gracefulness,** gracility; good points, **beauties, charms, delights,** perfections, good features.

.5 **daintiness, delicacy,** delicateness; **cuteness** or cunningness [both informal].

.6 **gorgeousness,** ravishingness; **gloriousness,** heavenliness, sublimity; **splendor,** splendidness, splendorousness, splendrousness, resplendence; **brilliance,** brightness, radiance, luster; **glamour** 650.1.

.7 **thing of beauty, vision, picture** [informal], **poem, eyeful** [informal], **sight** or **treat for sore eyes** [slang].

.8 **beauty, charmer,** charmeuse [Fr]; **beaut** or **dream** or **looker** or **good looker** or **stunner** or **dazzler** or **fetcher** or **peach** or **knockout** or **raving beauty** [all slang]; **beauty queen,** beauty contest winner, Miss America, bathing beauty, cover girl, model, pinup girl, pinup, bunny, **cute** or **slick chick** [slang], **pussycat** or **sex kitten** [both slang]; **belle,** reigning beauty, great beauty, lady fair; beau ideal, paragon; enchantress 650.3; "the face that launch'd a thousand ships" [Marlowe].

.9 (famous beauties) Venus, Venus de Milo; Aphrodite, Hebe; Adonis, Apollo, Apollo Belvedere, Hyperion, Antinoüs; Narcissus; Astarte; Balder, Freya; Helen of Troy, Cleopatra; the Graces, houri, peri.

.10 **beautification,** prettification, **adornment;** decoration 901.1; beauty treatment; **facial** [informal]; manicure; hairdressing.

.11 **makeup, cosmetics; war paint** or drugstore complexion [both informal]; powder, talcum, talcum powder; rouge, paint, lip rouge; nail polish; greasepaint, clown white; mascara, eye shadow; cold cream, hand cream or lotion, vanishing cream, foundation cream; foundation, base; mudpack; lipstick; eyebrow pencil; puff, powder puff; compact, vanity case.

.12 **beautician,** beautifier; hairdresser, coiffeur, coiffeuse [both Fr]; barber; manicurist.

.13 **beauty parlor** or salon or shop, salon de beauté [Fr]; barbershop.

.14 VERBS **beautify, prettify; pretty up** or **gussy up** or **doll up** [all informal], **grace, adorn; decorate** 901.8; set off, set off to advantage or good advantage, become one; glamorize.

.15 **look good; look like a million** or **look fit to kill** or **knock dead** or **knock one's eyes out** [all slang]; take the breath away, beggar description; **shine, beam, bloom, glow.**

.16 ADJS **beautiful, beauteous,** endowed with beauty, cal(o)- or call(o)- or cali- or calli-; **heavy** [slang]; **pretty, handsome, at-**

tractive 863.7, pulchritudinous, **lovely, graceful, gracile, habro–**; elegant, fine, exquisite, flowerlike; aesthetic, aesthetically appealing; eye-filling or easy on the eyes or not hard to look at or long on looks or looking fit to kill [all slang]; pretty as a picture, "lovely as the day" [Longfellow], "fair as is the rose in May" [Chaucer]; tall, dark, and handsome.

.17 **comely, fair, good-looking,** well-favored, **personable,** presentable, agreeable, becoming, pleasing 863.6, goodly, bonny, likely [dial], **sightly, braw** [Scot]; pleasing to the eye, lovely to behold; **shapely,** well-built, built, well-shaped, well-proportioned, well-made, well-formed, stacked, well-stacked, curvaceous, curvy [slang], pneumatic, amply endowed, built for comfort or built like a brick shithouse [both slang], buxom, callipygian, callipygous; Junoesque, statuesque, goddess-like; slender 205.16.

.18 **dainty, delicate;** *mignon* [Fr], **cute,** cunning [informal], cute as a bug's ear.

.19 **gorgeous, ravishing;** raving or **devastating** or **stunning** or killing [all slang]; **glorious,** heavenly, divine, sublime; **resplendent,** splendorous, splendrous, splendid, resplendently beautiful; **brilliant,** bright, radiant, shining, beaming, glowing, blooming, sparkling, **dazzling; glamorous** 650.7.

.20 **beautifying,** cosmetic; decorative 901.10.

.21 ADVS **beautifully,** beauteously, **prettily, handsomely, attractively, becomingly,** comelily; elegantly, exquisitely.

.22 **daintily, delicately; cutely,** cunningly [informal].

.23 **gorgeously, ravishingly;** ravingly or devastatingly or stunningly [all slang]; **gloriously,** divinely, sublimely; **resplendently,** splendidly, splendorously, splendrously; **brilliantly,** brightly, radiantly, glowingly, dazzlingly.

## 901. ORNAMENTATION

.1 NOUNS ornamentation, **ornament; decoration,** decor; **adornment, embellishment,** embroidery, elaboration; nonfunctional addition or adjunct; garnish, garnishment, garniture; trimming, trim; flourish; emblazonment, emblazonry; illumination; **color,** color patterns, color compatibility, color design, color arrangement; **arrangement,** flower arrangement, floral decoration, furniture arrangement; table setting or decoration; window dressing; **interior decoration** or decorating, room decoration.

.2 **ornateness, elegance, fanciness,** fineness, **elaborateness; ostentation** 904; richness, luxuriousness, luxuriance; **floweriness,** floridness, floridity; flamboyance; **overelegance,** overelaborateness, overornamentation; baroqueness, baroque, rococo, arabesque, moresque, chinoiserie.

.3 **finery, frippery, gaudery,** gaiety, bravery, trumpery, flashery [slang], folderol, trickery, chiffon, trappings, festoons, superfluity; **frills,** frills and furbelows, **frillery,** frilling, frilliness; foofaraw [dial], fuss [informal], froufrou; gingerbread; **tinsel,** clinquant, pinchbeck, paste; gilt, gilding.

.4 **trinket,** gewgaw, **knickknack,** knack, **gimcrack,** kickshaw, whim-wham, **bauble,** fribble, bibelot, toy, gaud; bric-a-brac.

.5 **jewelry,** bijouterie, ice [slang]; costume jewelry, glass, paste, junk jewelry [informal], scatter pins.

.6 **jewel,** bijou, **gem,** stone, precious stone, dactylio–; rhinestone; pin, brooch, stickpin, breastpin, chatelaine; ring, circle, earring, nose ring; bracelet, wristlet, wristband, armlet, anklet; chain, necklace, torque; locket; beads, chaplet, wampum; bangle; charm; fob; crown, coronet, diadem, tiara.

.7 **motif,** ornamental motif, **figure, detail,** form, touch, repeated figure; **pattern, theme,** design, ornamental theme, ornamental or decorative composition; foreground detail, background detail; **background,** setting, foil, **style,** ornamental or decorative style, national style, period style.

.8 VERBS **ornament, decorate, adorn, dress, trim, garnish,** array, **deck,** bedeck, dizen, bedizen; prettify, **beautify** 900.14; **redecorate,** refurbish, redo 694.17; **embellish, furbish,** embroider, enrich, grace, set off or out, paint, color, blazon, emblazon, paint in glowing colors; **dress up; spruce up** or gussy up or doll up or fix up [all informal], **primp up,** prink up, prank up, trick up or out, deck out, fig out; primp, prink, prank, preen; smarten, smarten up, dandify, titivate.

.9 **figure, filigree; spangle, bespangle;** bead, tinsel; **jewel, bejewel, gem,** diamond; ribbon, beribbon; flounce; flower, garland, wreathe; feather, plume; flag; illuminate, paint 362.13; engrave 578.10.

.10 ADJS **ornamental, decorative,** adorning, embellishing.

.11 **ornamented, adorned, decorated, embellished, bedecked,** decked out, tricked out, garnished, trimmed, bedizened; f ured; flowered; festooned, befrilled, wreathed; spangled, bespangled, spangly; jeweled, bejeweled; beaded; studded; plumed, feathered; beribboned.

.12 ornate, elegant, fancy, fine, chichi, pretty-pretty; picturesque; elaborate, labored, high-wrought; ostentatious 904.18–22; rich, luxurious, luxuriant; flowery, florid; flamboyant; fussy, frilly; overelegant, overelaborate, overlabored, overworked, overwrought, busy; baroque, rococo, arabesque, moresque.

.13 ornamentations

| | |
|---|---|
| aglet | frostwork |
| aigrette | garland |
| appliqué | graffito |
| arabesque | guilloche |
| arras | hanging |
| batik | helix |
| beading | imbrication |
| beaten work | inlay |
| bouquet | lacework |
| boutonniere | metalwork |
| bow | motif |
| bugle | niello |
| chaplet | nosegay |
| coronal | openwork |
| corsage | panache |
| crown | panelwork |
| cul-de-lampe [Fr] | parquetry |
| cuspidation | passementerie |
| cutwork | plume |
| damascene, damask | pom-pom |
| decoupage | posy |
| diaper, diapering | quilting |
| drapery | reeding |
| drawnwork | rosette |
| egret | ruffle |
| embroidery | scroll |
| epaulet | sequin |
| fancywork | snood |
| feather | spangle |
| festoon | spiral |
| figure work | stenciling |
| filigree | strapwork |
| fillet | striping |
| finial | tapestry |
| fleuron [Fr] | tassel |
| foliage | tooling |
| foliation | tracery |
| fretwork | vermiculation |
| fringe | vignette |
| frog | wreath |

4 architectural ornamentations

| | |
|---|---|
| acanthus | cyma |
| apophyge | fascia |
| astragal | fillet |
| beading | finial |
| beak | foil |
| billet | fret |
| boss | frieze |
| cartouche | listel |
| cavetto | molding |
| cinquefoil | ogee |
| congé [Fr] | ovolo |
| cornice | patera |
| cusp | pendant |

| | |
|---|---|
| quatrefoil | terminal |
| reed | torus |
| scotia | trefoil |
| scrollhead | volute |
| splay | |

## 902. PLAINNESS

### (unaffectedness)

.1 NOUNS plainness, simplicity, simpleness, ordinariness, commonness, commonplaceness, homeliness, prosaicness, prosiness, matter-of-factness; purity, chasteness, classic or classical purity, Attic simplicity.

.2 naturalness, inartificiality; unaffectedness, unassumingness, unpretentiousness; directness, straightforwardness.

.3 unadornment, unembellishment, unornamentation; uncomplexity, uncomplication, uncomplicatedness, unsophistication, unadulteration; bareness, baldness, nakedness, nudity, undress, beauty unadorned.

.4 inornateness, unelaborateness, unfanciness, unfussiness; austerity, severity, starkness, Spartan simplicity.

.5 VERBS simplify, chasten, restrain, purify.

.6 ADJS simple, plain, ordinary, nondescript, common, commonplace, prosaic, prosy, matter-of-fact, homely, homespun, everyday, workday, workaday, household, garden, common- or garden-variety; pure, pure and simple, chaste, classic or classical, Attic.

.7 natural, native; inartificial, unartificial; unaffected, unpretentious, unpretending, unassuming, unfeigning, direct, straightforward, honest, candid.

.8 unadorned, undecorated, unornamented, unembellished, ungarnished, unfurbished, unvarnished, untrimmed; uncomplex, uncomplicated, unsophisticated, unadulterated; undressed, undecked, unarrayed; bare, bald, blank, naked, nude.

.9 inornate, unornate, unelaborate, unfancy, unfussy; austere, severe, stark, Spartan.

.10 ADVS plainly, simply, ordinarily, commonly, commonplacely, prosaically, matter-of-factly.

.11 unaffectedly, naturally, unpretentiously, unassumingly, directly, straightforwardly.

### 903. AFFECTATION

.1 NOUNS affectation, affectedness; pretension, pretense, airs, putting on airs, put-on [informal]; show, false show, mere show; front, false front [informal], façade, mere façade, image, public image; feigned belief, hypocrisy 616.6; sham

616.3; artificiality, unnaturalness, insincerity; prunes and prisms, airs and graces; stylishness, mannerism.

.2 **mannerism**, *minauderie* [Fr], **trick of behavior**, trick, **quirk**, habit, peculiarity, peculiar trait, idiosyncrasy, trademark; –ism.

.3 **posing, pose, posturing**, attitudinizing, attitudinarianism; peacockery, peacockishness.

.4 **foppery, foppishness, dandyism**, coxcombry, puppyism, conceit.

.5 **overniceness**, overpreciseness, **overrefinement, elegance**, exquisiteness, preciousness, preciosity; goody-goodyism *or* goody-goodness [both informal]; purism, formalism, formality, pedantry, precisionism, precisianism; euphuism; euphemism.

.6 **prudery, prudishness, priggishness, primness, smugness, stuffiness** [informal], old-maidishness, **straitlacedness**, stiff-neckedness, hideboundness, narrowness, censoriousness, sanctimony, sanctimoniousness, **puritanicalness**, Quakerishness; **false modesty**, overmodesty, demureness, demurity, *mauvaise honte* [Fr].

.7 **affecter**; mannerist; **phony** [slang], **fake** *or* **fraud** [informal], **pretender**, actor, playactor [informal], performer; paper tiger, hollow man, straw man, man of straw; deceiver 619.

.8 **poser**, poseur, striker of poses, **posturer**, posturist, posture maker, attitudinarian, attitudinizer.

.9 **dandy, fop**, coxcomb, macaroni, gallant, dude *or* swell [both informal], sport [slang], exquisite, blood, fine gentleman, puppy, jackanapes, jack-a-dandy, fribble, clotheshorse, fashion plate; beau, Beau Brummel, spark, blade, ladies' man, lady-killer [slang], masher; man-about-town, boulevardier.

.10 **fine lady**, *grande dame*, *précieuse* [both Fr]; belle, toast.

.11 **prude**, prig, puritan, bluenose, goody-goody [informal], old maid; Victorian, mid-Victorian.

.12 VERBS **affect, assume, put on**, assume *or* put on airs, wear, **pretend, simulate, counterfeit, sham, fake** [informal], **feign**, make out like [informal], make a show of, play, playact [informal], act *or* play a part, play a scene, do a bit [informal], put up a front [slang], dramatize, histrionize, lay it on thick [informal], overact, tug the heartstrings.

.13 **pose, posture, attitudinize**, peacock, strike a pose, strike an attitude, pose for effect.

.14 **mince**, mince it, prink [Brit dial]; **simper**, smirk, bridle.

.15 ADJS **affected, pretentious**, la-di-da; **mannered**, *maniéré* [Fr]; **artificial, unnatural**, insincere; theatrical, stagy, histrionic; overdone, overacted.

.16 **assumed, put-on, pretended**, simulated, **phony** [slang], **fake** *or* **faked** [informal], feigned, counterfeited; spurious, sham 616.26; hypocritical 616.33.

.17 **foppish, dandified**, dandy, coxcombical, conceited.

.18 (affectedly nice) **overnice**, overprecise, precious, *précieuse* [Fr], exquisite, **overrefined, elegant**, mincing, simpering, namby-pamby; **goody-goody** *or* goody good-good [both informal]; puristic, formalistic, pedantic, precisionistic, precisian, precisianistic, euphuistic, euphemistic.

.19 **prudish, priggish, prim, smug, stuffy** [informal], old-maidish, **overmodest**, demure, **straitlaced**, stiff-necked, hidebound, narrow, censorious, sanctimonious, **puritanical**, Quakerish, Victorian, mid-Victorian.

.20 ADVS **affectedly, pretentiously**; elegantly, mincingly; for effect, for show.

.21 **prudishly, priggishly**, primly, smugly, stuffily [informal], straitlacedly, stiff-neckedly, puritanically.

## 904. OSTENTATION

.1 NOUNS **ostentation**, ostentatiousness, os tent; **pretentiousness, pretension, pre tense**; loftiness, lofty affectations.

.2 **pretensions**, vain pretensions; **airs**, loft airs, vaporing, highfalutin *or* highfalutin ways [informal], side, swank [informal].

.3 **showiness, flashiness**, flamboyance, pa nache, dash, jazziness [slang], jauntines sportiness [informal], gaiety, glitter, glar dazzle, dazzlingness; extravaganza; **gaud ness**, gaudery, **tawdriness**, meretriciou ness; gorgeousness, colorfulness; **garisl ness**, loudness [informal], **blatancy**, fl grancy, shamelessness, brazenness, l ridness, extravagance, sensationalisr obtrusiveness, vulgarness, crudeness, e travagation.

.4 **display, show, demonstration**, manifes tion, **exhibition, parade**, *étalage* [F **pageantry**, pageant, **spectacle**; vaunt, fa faronade, blazon, flourish, flaunt, flau ing; daring, brilliancy, éclat, bravu flair; dash *or* splash *or* splurge [all inf mal]; figure; **exhibitionism**, showing-c

theatrics, histrionics, dramatics, staginess; false front, sham 616.3.

.5 **grandeur,** grandness, grandiosity, **magnificence,** gorgeousness, **splendor,** splendidness, splendiferousness, resplendence, brilliance, glory; nobility, proudness, **state, stateliness, majesty;** impressiveness, imposingness; **sumptuousness, elegance, elaborateness, lavishness, luxuriousness;** ritziness or poshness or plushness or swankness or swankiness [all informal]; **luxury,** barbaric or Babylonian splendor.

.6 **pomp,** circumstance, pride, **state,** solemnity 871, formality 646; **pomp and circumstance,** "pride, pomp, and circumstance" [Shakespeare]; heraldry, "trump and solemn heraldry" [Coleridge].

.7 **pompousness, pomposity,** pontification, pontificality, **stuffiness** [informal], **self-importance,** inflation; grandiloquence 601, turgidity, orotundity.

.8 **swagger, strut,** swank [informal], bounce, brave show; swaggering, strutting; swash, **swashbucklery,** swashbuckling, swashbuckling; peacockishness, peacockery.

.9 **stuffed shirt** [slang], blimp [slang], Colonel Blimp; bloated aristocrat.

.10 **strutter, swaggerer,** swanker [Brit], swash, swasher, swashbuckler, peacock, miles gloriosus.

.11 **show-off** [informal], **exhibitionist,** flaunter; **grandstander** or grandstand player or hot dog or hotshot or showboat [all slang].

.12 VERBS **put** or **thrust oneself forward,** come forward, step to the front or fore, step into the limelight, take center stage, attract attention, make oneself conspicuous.

.13 **cut a dash,** make a show, put on a show, make one's mark, cut a swath, **cut** or **make a figure;** make a splash or a splurge [informal]; splurge or splash [both informal]; shine, glitter, glare, dazzle.

.14 **give oneself airs, put on airs,** put on, put on side, put on the dog [informal], put up a front [slang], ritz it [slang], look big, swank [slang], swell, swell it, act the grand seigneur; pontificate, play the pontiff.

.15 **strut, swagger,** swank [Brit], prance, stalk, peacock, swash, swashbuckle.

.16 **show off** [informal], **grandstand** or hot dog [both slang], play to the gallery or galleries [informal], please the crowd; exhibit or parade one's wares [informal], strut one's stuff [slang], go through one's paces, show what one has.

.17 **flaunt,** vaunt, **parade, display,** demonstrate, manifest, **exhibit,** air, put forward, put forth, hold up, flash or sport [both informal]; advertise; **flourish,** brandish, wave; dangle, dangle before the eyes; emblazon, blazon forth; trumpet, trumpet forth.

.18 ADJS **ostentatious, pretentious,** ambitious, vaunting, **lofty, highfalutin** or highfaluting [both informal], **high-flown,** high-flying; **high-toned,** tony [both informal], **fancy,** classy [slang], flossy [informal].

.19 **showy, flaunting, flashy,** snazzy, flashing, glittering, **jazzy** [slang], splashy or splurgy [both informal]; exhibitionistic, showoffy [informal], bravura; **gay,** jaunty, rakish, **dashing;** gallant, brave, braw [Scot], daring; **sporty** or dressy [both informal]; frilly [informal], frothy, chichi.

.20 **gaudy, tawdry;** gorgeous, colorful; garish, loud [informal], **blatant, flagrant,** shameless, **brazen,** brazenfaced, lurid, extravagant, sensational, **spectacular,** glaring, flaring, flaunting, screaming [informal], obtrusive, vulgar, crude; meretricious.

.21 **grandiose, grand, magnificent, splendid,** splendiferous [informal], splendacious [slang], **glorious,** superb, fine, superfine, fancy, superfancy, swell [slang]; **imposing, impressive,** awful, awe-inspiring; **noble, proud, stately, majestic,** princely; **sumptuous, elegant, elaborate, luxurious,** extravagant, deluxe; plush or posh or ritzy or swank or swanky [all informal], Corinthian; palatial, Babylonian; barbaric.

.22 **pompous, stuffy** [informal], **self-important,** impressed with oneself, pontifical; **inflated, swollen,** bloated, tumid, turgid, flatulent, gassy [informal], stilted; grandiloquent, **bombastic** 601.8,9; solemn 871.3, formal 646.7–10.

.23 **strutting, swaggering;** swashing, **swashbuckling,** swashbuckling; peacockish, peacocky.

.24 **theatrical, stagy, dramatic,** histrionic; spectacular.

.25 ADVS **ostentatiously, pretentiously,** loftily; with flourish of trumpet, with beat of drum, with flying colors.

.26 **showily, flauntingly,** flashily, with a flair, glitteringly; gaily, jauntily, **dashingly;** gallantly, bravely, daringly.

.27 **gaudily, tawdrily;** gorgeously, colorfully; garishly, **blatantly, flagrantly,** shamelessly, **brazenly,** brazenfacedly, luridly, sensationally, **spectacularly,** glaringly, flaringly, obtrusively.

.28 **grandiosely, grandly, magnificently,**

splendidly, splendiferously, splenda-
ciously, gloriously, superbly; nobly,
proudly, majestically; imposingly, impressively; **sumptuously, elegantly,** elabo-
rately, luxuriously, **extravagantly;** palatial-
ly.

.29 pompously, stuffily [informal], **self-importantly;** stiltedly; **bombastically** 601.12.

## 905. PRIDE

.1 NOUNS **pride,** proudness, pridefulness;
**self-esteem, self-respect,** self-confidence,
self-reliance, self-consequence, face, independence, self-sufficiency; pardonable
pride; obstinate or stiff-necked pride,
stiff-neckedness; **vanity, conceit** 909.4;
haughtiness, **arrogance** 912; boastfulness
910.1; purse-pride.

.2 **proud bearing,** pride of bearing, **dignity,**
dignifiedness, **stateliness,** courtliness,
grandeur, **loftiness;** pride of place; **nobility,** lordliness, princeliness; **majesty,** regality, kingliness, queenliness; worthiness,
augustness, venerability; **sedateness, solemnity** 871, gravity, sobriety.

.3 proudling, highflier; stiff neck; egoist
909.5; boaster 910.5; the proud.

.4 VERBS **be proud,** hold up one's head,
hold one's head high, stand up straight,
hold oneself erect, never stoop; look one
in the face or eye.

.5 **pride oneself, preen oneself,** plume oneself on, pique oneself, **congratulate oneself,** hug oneself; **be proud of, take pride
in,** glory in, exult in.

.6 **make proud,** do proud [informal], **gratify,
elate,** flush, turn one's head.

.7 save face, save one's face, preserve one's
dignity, guard or preserve one's honor, be
jealous of one's repute or good name.

.8 ADJS **proud, prideful,** proudful [dial]; **self-
esteeming, self-respecting;** self-confident,
self-reliant, independent, self-sufficient;
proudhearted, proud-minded, proud-spir-
ited, proud-blooded; proud-looking; as
proud as Punch, proud as Lucifer, proud
as a peacock; erect, stiff-backed, stiff-
necked; purse-proud, house-proud.

.9 **vain, conceited** 909.8–12; haughty, **arrogant** 912.9; boastful 910.10.

.10 **puffed up,** swollen, bloated, swollen or
bloated with pride; elated, flushed,
flushed with pride.

.11 **lofty, elevated,** high, high-flown, highfalutin or highfaluting [both informal], high-
toned [informal]; high-minded, lofty-
minded; high-headed, high-nosed [infor-
mal].

.12 **dignified, stately, imposing, grand,
courtly,** magisterial, aristocratic; **noble,**
lordly, princely; **majestic,** regal, royal,
kingly, queenly; worthy, august, **venerable;** statuesque; **sedate, solemn** 871.3, sober, grave.

.13 ADVS **proudly,** pridefully, **with pride;** self-
esteemingly, self-respectingly, self-confi-
dently, self-reliantly, independently, self-
sufficiently; erectly, with head erect, with
head held high, with nose in air; stiff-
neckedly; like a lord, *en grand seigneur*
[Fr].

.14 **dignifiedly, with dignity;** nobly, stately,
imposingly, loftily, grandly, magisterially;
majestically, regally, royally; worthily, au-
gustly, venerably; sedately, solemnly, soberly, gravely.

## 906. HUMILITY

.1 NOUNS **humility, humbleness, meekness;
lowliness,** lowlihood, poorness, meanness, smallness, ingloriousness, undistin-
guishedness; unimportance 673; innocuousness 674.9; teachableness 564.5; submissiveness 765.3; **modesty,** unpretentiousness
908.1; plainness, simpleness, homeliness.

.2 **humiliation, mortification;** embarrassment 866.4; **abasement,** debasement, **letdown,** setdown, put-down, dump [infor-
mal], **comedown,** descent, deflation,
wounded or humbled pride; self-dimin-
ishment, **self-abasement, self-abnegation**
979.1; **shame, disgrace;** shamefacedness,
shamefastness, hangdog look.

.3 **condescension,** condescendence, deign-
ing, lowering oneself, stooping from one's
high place.

.4 VERBS **humiliate, humble;** mortify, **embarrass** 866.15; put out, put out of face or
countenance; **shame, disgrace,** put to
shame, put to the blush; **deflate,** prick
one's balloon, let down; take it out of
take the shine out of [informal], take the
wind out of one's sails, take the starch
out of [slang]; put one's nose out of join
[informal], put a tuck in one's tail o
make one sing small [both informal].

.5 **abase, debase, crush,** abash, **degrade,** re
duce, diminish, **demean,** lower, **brin
low,** bring down, trip up, take down, se
down, put down, dump or dump o
[both informal], knock one off his perc
take down a peg or a peg or two [info
mal].

.6 **humble oneself, demean oneself,** aba
oneself, climb down [informal], get dov
from one's high horse [informal]; p

one's pride in one's pocket; **eat humble pie**, eat crow, eat dirt, swallow one's pride, lick the dust; come on bended knee, come hat in hand; go down on one's knees; draw in one's horns *or* sing small [both informal], lower one's note *or* tone, tuck one's tail; come down a peg *or* a peg or two; **deprecate** *or* **depreciate oneself**, diminish oneself, discount oneself, belittle oneself.

.7 **condescend, deign, vouchsafe; stoop, descend**, lower oneself, set one's dignity aside *or* to one side; be so good as to, so forget oneself.

.8 **be humiliated**, be put out of countenance; **be crushed, feel small, feel cheap**, look foolish *or* silly, could sink through the floor; **take shame, be ashamed, feel ashamed of oneself**, be put to the blush, have a very red face; hang one's head, hide one's face, not dare to show one's face, not have a word to say for oneself; drink the cup of humiliation to the dregs.

.9 ADJS **humble, lowly, low, poor, mean**, small, inglorious, undistinguished; unimportant 673.14–19; innocuous 674.20; teachable 564.18; **modest, unpretentious** 908.9; **plain, simple**, homely; humble-looking, humble-visaged; humblest, lowliest, lowest, least.

.10 humblehearted, humble-minded, humble-spirited, poor in spirit; **meek, meekhearted, meek-minded, meek-spirited; abject**, submissive 765.12–16.

.11 **self-abasing, self-abnegating, self-deprecating,** self-depreciating, self-doubting.

.12 **humbled**, reduced, diminished, lowered, brought down, brought low, set down, bowed down, in the dust; on one's knees, on one's marrowbones [informal].

.13 **humiliated,** humbled, mortified, **embarrassed, chagrined, abashed, crushed,** out of countenance; blushing, red-faced, **ashamed,** shamed, ashamed of oneself, shamefaced, shamefast; crestfallen, chapfallen, hangdog.

.14 **humiliating,** humiliative, humbling, chastening, mortifying, **embarrassing,** crushing.

.15 ADVS **humbly, meekly;** modestly 908.14; with due deference, with bated breath, "with bated breath and whispering humbleness" [Shakespeare]; submissively 765.17–19; **abjectly,** on bended knee, **on one's knees,** on one's marrowbones [informal], on all fours, with one's tail between one's legs, hat in hand.

## 907. SERVILITY

.1 NOUNS **servility, slavishness,** subservience *or* subserviency, menialness, abjectness, **baseness,** meanness; **submissiveness** 765.3; slavery, helotry, helotism, serfdom, peonage.

.2 **obsequiousness, sycophancy,** fawnery, **toadyism,** flunkyism, parasitism, sponging; ingratiation, insinuation; **truckling, fawning, toadying,** toadeating, groveling, cringing, footlicking, **bootlicking** [slang], backscratching, tufthunting; **apple-polishing** *or* **handshaking** [both informal]; asslicking *or* ass-kissing *or* brown-nosing [all slang]; timeserving; obeisance, prostration; mealymouthedness.

.3 **sycophant, flatterer, toady,** toad, toadeater, footlicker, bootlick *or* **bootlicker** [both slang], lickspit, lickspittle, **truckler, fawner,** courtier, led captain, tufthunter, kowtower, groveler, cringer, spaniel; **backslapper,** backscratcher, clawback [dial]; **handshaker** *or* **apple-polisher** *or* **yes-man** [all informal]; suck *or* ass-licker *or* asskisser *or* brown-nose *or* brown-noser *or* brownie [all slang]; flunky, lackey, stooge [slang], jackal; timeserver; creature, **puppet,** minion, **tool,** cat's-paw, dupe, instrument, faithful servant, slave, helot, serf, peon; mealymouth.

.4 **parasite,** barnacle, leech, parasit(o)– *or* parasiti–; **sponger,** sponge [informal], freeloader [slang], smell-feast; beat *or* deadbeat [both slang].

.5 **hanger-on,** adherent, dangler, appendage, **dependent, satellite, follower,** retainer, servant, man, shadow, tagtail, **henchman,** heeler *or* ward heeler [both informal].

.6 VERBS **fawn, truckle; flatter; toady,** toadeat; **bootlick** [slang], lickspittle, lick one's shoes, lick the feet of; **grovel,** crawl, creep, cower, cringe, crouch, stoop, kneel, bend the knee, fall on one's knees, prostrate oneself, throw oneself at the feet of, fall at one's feet, kiss one's feet, kiss the hem of one's garment, lick the dust, make a doormat of oneself; **kowtow, bow, bow and scrape.**

.7 **toady to, truckle to, pander to, cater to; wait on** *or* **upon,** wait on hand and foot, do service, fetch and carry, do the dirty work of, do *or* jump at the bidding of.

.8 **curry favor, court, pay court to,** make court to, run after [informal], dance attendance on; **shine up to,** make up to [informal]; **suck up to** *or* **play up to** *or* act up to [all slang]; be a yes man [informal], agree to anything; fawn upon, fall over or all over [slang]; **handshake** or **polish the apple** [both informal]; lick one's ass or kiss one's ass or brown-nose [all slang].

.9 **ingratiate oneself, insinuate oneself,** worm oneself in, creep into the good graces of, get next to [informal], **get on the good** or **right side of,** rub the right way [informal].

.10 **attach oneself to,** pin or fasten oneself upon, hang about or around, dangle, hang on the skirts of, hang on the sleeve of, become an appendage of, **follow,** follow at heel; follow the crowd, get on the bandwagon, go with the stream, hold with the hare and run with the hounds.

.11 **sponge** or **sponge on** [both informal]; feed on, fatten on, batten on, live off of, use as a meal ticket.

.12 ADJS **servile, slavish,** subservient, **menial, base, mean; submissive** 765.12.

.13 **obsequious, flattering, sycophantic**(al), **toadyish, fawning, truckling, ingratiating, toadying,** toadeating, **bootlicking** [slang], footlicking, backscratching; **groveling,** sniveling, cringing, cowering, crouching, crawling; **parasitic,** leechlike, sponging [informal], par(a)–; timeserving; **abject,** beggarly, hangdog; obeisant, prostrate, on one's knees, on one's marrowbones [slang], on bended knee; mealymouthed.

.14 ADVS **servilely, slavishly,** subserviently, menially, "in a bondman's key" [Shakespeare]; **submissively** 765.17.

.15 **obsequiously, sycophantically, ingratiatingly, fawningly, trucklingly;** hat-in-hand, cap-in-hand; **abjectly,** obeisantly, grovelingly, on one's knees; parasitically.

## 908. MODESTY

.1 NOUNS **modesty, meekness; humility** 906; **unpretentiousness,** unassumingness, unpresumptuousness, **unostentatiousness,** unambitiousness, unobtrusiveness, unboastfulness.

.2 **self-effacement, self-depreciation,** self-deprecation, self-detraction, undervaluing of self, self-doubt, **diffidence;** weak ego, lack of self-confidence or self-reliance, self-distrust.

.3 **reserve, restraint, constraint,** backwardness, retiring disposition.

.4 **shyness, timidity,** timidness, timorousness, **bashfulness,** shamefacedness, shamefastness, **coyness, demureness,** demurity, skittishness, mousiness; self-consciousness, embarrassment; stammering, confusion; stagefright, mikefright [informal].

.5 **blushing, flushing,** coloring, mantling, reddening, crimsoning; **blush, flush,** suffusion; pudicity, pudency.

.6 shrinking violet, modest violet, mouse.

.7 VERBS **efface oneself,** depreciate or deprecate or doubt or distrust oneself; reserve oneself, retire, shrink, **retire into one's shell, keep in the background,** keep oneself to oneself, keep one's distance, remain in the shade, take a back seat [informal], hide one's face, hide one's light under a bushel, avoid the limelight; pursue the noiseless tenor of one's way, blush unseen, "do good by stealth and blush to find it fame" [Pope].

.8 **blush, flush,** mantle, **color,** change color, color up, redden, crimson, turn red, get red in the face, blush up to the eyes; stammer; squirm with self-consciousness or embarrassment.

.9 ADJS **modest, meek; humble** 906.9; **unpretentious,** unpretending, **unassuming,** unpresuming, unpresumptuous, **unostentatious,** unobtrusive, unimposing, unboastful; unambitious, unaspiring.

.10 **self-effacing, self-depreciative, self-depreciating, self-deprecating; diffident,** deprecatory, deprecative, self-doubting, unselfconfident, unselfreliant, self-distrustful.

.11 **reserved, restrained, constrained;** quiet; **backward, retiring, shrinking.**

.12 **shy, timid,** timorous, **bashful,** shamefaced, shamefast, **coy, demure,** skittish, mousy; self-conscious, conscious, confused; stammering, inarticulate.

.13 **blushing,** blushful; **flushed,** red, ruddy red in the face; **sheepish; embarrassed.**

.14 ADVS **modestly, meekly;** humbly 906.15 **unpretentiously,** unpretendingly, **unas**sumingly, unpresumptuously, **unostenta**tiously, unobtrusively; quietly, withou ceremony, *sans façon* [Fr].

.15 **shyly, timidly,** timorously, **bashfully** coyly, **demurely,** diffidently; **shame**facedly, shamefastly, **sheepishly,** blush ingly, with downcast eyes.

## 909. VANITY

.1 NOUNS **vanity, vainness;** overproudnes overweening pride; **self-importance,** co sequentiality, **self-esteem,** self-respec self-assumption; **self-admiration,** self-d light, self-worship, self-endearment, se love, *amour-propre* [Fr], self-infatuatio narcissism, narcism; autoeroticism, aut erotism; **self-satisfaction, self-content,** e trip [informal], self-approbation, self-cc gratulation, self-gratulation, self-comp

cency, **smugness**, complacency, self-sufficiency; vainglory, vaingloriousness; "an
itch for the praise of fools" [R. Brow-
ning].

.2 **pride** 905; arrogance 912; **boastfulness**
910.1.

.3 **egotism, egoism,** egoisticalness, egotisti-
calness, **ego** [informal], self-interest, individualism, "the tongue of vanity" [Cham-
fort]; **egocentricity,** egocentrism, self-centeredness, self-centerment; selfishness 978.

.4 **conceit,** conceitedness, **self-conceit, self-**
**conceitedness, immodesty,** side, self-
assertiveness; **stuck-upness** [informal],
chestiness [slang], swelled-headedness,
swelled head; **cockiness** [informal], pertness, perkiness; aggressive self-confidence,
obtrusiveness, bumptiousness.

.5 **egotist, egoist, egocentric,** individualist;
**swellhead** [slang], narcissist, narcist, Narcissus; **braggart** 910.5, know-it-all, smart aleck 913.5, no modest violet, "a person of
low taste, more interested in himself than
in me" [Ambrose Bierce].

.6 VERBS **be stuck on oneself** [slang], be impressed or overly impressed with oneself;
ego-trip, be or go on an ego trip [all in-
formal]; think well of oneself, think one
is it or one's shit doesn't stink [slang], get
too big for one's breeches, have a swelled
head, know it all, have no false modesty,
have no self-doubt, love the sound of
one's own voice, be blinded by one's own
glory, lay the flattering unction to one's
soul; fish for compliments; toot one's
own horn, **boast** 910.6–8; be vain as a peacock, give oneself airs 904.14.

.7 **puff up, inflate,** swell; go to one's head,
turn one's head.

.8 ADJS **vain, vainglorious,** overproud, overweening; **self-important, self-esteeming,**
self-respecting, self-assuming, consequential; **self-admiring,** self-delighting, self-
worshiping, self-loving, self-endeared, self-
infatuated, narcissistic, narcistic, narcissan, narcissine; **self-satisfied, self-content,**
self-contented, self-approving, self-gratu-
lating, self-gratulatory, self-congratulat-
ing, self-congratulatory, self-complacent,
**smug,** complacent, self-sufficient.

.9 **proud** 905.8; arrogant 912.9; **boastful**
910.10.

.10 **egotistic(al),** egoistic(al), self-interested;
**egocentric,** egocentristic, self-centered,
narcissistic, narcistic, narcissan, narcissine;
selfish 978.5.

11 **conceited, self-conceited, immodest,** self-
opinionated; **stuck-up** [informal], **puffed**

up, chesty [slang], **swelled-headed,** too
big for one's shoes or britches; biggety
[dial]; **cocky** [informal], pert, perk, perky;
peacockish, peacocky; know-it-all, smart-
alecky 913.9, overwise, wise in one's own
conceit; aggressively self-confident, obtrusive, bumptious.

.12 **stuck on oneself** [informal], impressed
with oneself, pleased with oneself, full of
oneself, all wrapped up in oneself.

.13 ADVS **vainly,** self-importantly; **egotisti-**
**cally,** egoistically; **conceitedly,** self-con-
ceitedly, immodestly; cockily [informal],
pertly, perkily.

## 910. BOASTING

.1 NOUNS **boasting, bragging,** vaunting;
**boastfulness, braggadocio, braggartism;**
**boast, brag,** vaunt; side, bombast, bravado, vauntery, fanfaronade, gasconade,
gasconism, rodomontade; bluster, swagger 911.1; vanity, conceit 909.4; jactation,
jactitation; heroics.

.2 [slang or informal terms] **big talk,** fine
talk, fancy talk, tall talk, highfalutin or
highfaluting, **hot air,** gas, bunk, bunkum,
**bullshit;** tall story, fish story.

.3 **self-approbation,** self-praise, self-lauda-
tion, self-gratulation, self-applause, self-
puffery, self-vaunting, self-advertising,
self-advertisement, self-glorification; vainglory, vaingloriousness.

.4 **crowing,** exultation, elation, triumph, jubilation; **gloating.**

.5 **braggart, boaster,** brag, braggadocio, hector, fanfaron, Gascon, gasconader, miles
gloriosus; **blowhard** or blower or big
mouth or bullshit artist or hot-air artist
or gasbag or windbag or big bag of wind
or windjammer or windy [all slang]; blusterer 911.2; Texan, Fourth-of-July orator;
Braggadocchio [Spenser], Captain Boba-
dil [Ben Jonson], Thraso [Terence], Pa-
rolles [Shakespeare].

.6 VERBS **boast, brag,** make a boast of,
vaunt, flourish, gasconade, vapor, puff,
draw the longbow, advertise oneself,
**blow one's own trumpet, toot one's own**
**horn,** sing one's own praises, exaggerate
one's own merits; bluster, swagger 911.3;
speak for Buncombe.

.7 [slang or informal terms] **blow,** blow off,
**blow hard, talk big,** shoot the shit, spread
oneself, lay it on thick, brag oneself up.

.8 **flatter oneself,** conceit oneself, **congratu-**
**late oneself,** hug oneself, shake hands
with oneself, **pat oneself on the back,**
take merit to oneself.

.9 **exult,** triumph, glory, delight, joy, jubilate; **crow** or crow over, crow like a rooster or cock; **gloat,** gloat over.

.10 ADJS **boastful, boasting, braggart, bragging,** thrasonical, thrasonic, big-mouthed [slang], vaunting, vaporing, gasconading, Gascon, fanfaronading, fanfaron; vain, conceited 909.8–12; **vainglorious,** self-glorious, self-lauding, self-applauding, self-praising, self-flattering, self-vaunting, self-advertising.

.11 **inflated, swollen, windy** or gassy [both informal], **bombastic,** high-swelling, **highflown, highfalutin** or highfaluting [both informal], **pretentious,** extravagant, big, tall [informal].

.12 **crowing,** exultant, exulting, elated, elate, jubilant, **triumphant, flushed,** cock-a-hoop, in high feather; **gloating.**

.13 ADVS **boastfully,** boastingly, braggingly, vauntingly, vaingloriously.

.14 **exultantly,** exultingly, elatedly, jubilantly, triumphantly, in triumph; **gloatingly.**

## 911. BLUSTER

.1 NOUNS **bluster,** blustering, hectoring, bullying, **swagger,** swashbucklery, side; **bravado,** rant, rodomontade, fanfaronade; sputter, splutter; fuss, bustle, fluster, flurry; bluff, bluster and bluff; intimidation 891.6; **boastfulness** 910.1.

.2 **blusterer, swaggerer,** swasher, swashbuckler, fanfaron, bravo, **bully,** bullyboy, bucko, roisterer, cock of the walk, vaporer, blatherskite [informal]; ranter, raver, hectorer, hector, Herod; slanger [Brit]; bluff, bluffer; **braggart** 910.5.

.3 VERBS **bluster,** hector; **swagger,** swashbuckle; **bully;** bounce, vapor, roister, rollick, gasconade, kick up a dust [informal]; sputter, splutter; rant, rage, rave, storm, "out-herod Herod" [Shakespeare]; slang [Brit]; bluff, bluster and bluff, put up a bluff [informal]; intimidate 891.28; **brag** 910.6.

.4 ADJS **blustering,** blustery, blusterous, hectoring, **bullying, swaggering,** swashing, swashbuckling, boisterous, roisterous, roistering, rollicking; ranting, raging, raving, storming; tumultuous 162.17; noisy, "full of sound and fury" [Shakespeare].

## 912. ARROGANCE

.1 NOUNS **arrogance,** arrogantness; overbearingness, overbearing pride, overweening pride, stiff-necked pride, assumption of superiority, domineering, domineeringness; **pride,** proudness; superbia, sin of pride, chief of the deadly sins; **haughtiness, hauteur; loftiness,** Olympian loftiness or detachment; **toploftiness** or stuckupness or uppishness or uppityness [all informal], side, hoity-toitiness, hoity-toity; haughty airs, airs of de haut en bas, cornstarchy airs [informal]; high horse [informal]; **condescension,** condescendence, patronizing, patronization, patronizing attitude; purse-pride.

.2 **presumptuousness,** presumption, overweening, overweeningness, assumption, total self-assurance; hubris; **insolence** 913.

.3 **lordliness, imperiousness,** masterfulness, magisterialness, **high-and-mightiness,** aristocratic presumption; elitism.

.4 **aloofness, standoffishness,** offishness [informal], chilliness, coolness, distantness, remoteness.

.5 **disdainfulness, disdain,** aristocratic disdain, **contemptuousness, superciliousness,** contumeliousness, cavalierness, you-be-damnedness [slang].

.6 **snobbery, snobbishness,** snobbiness, snobbism; **priggishness, priggery,** priggism; snootiness or snottiness or sniffiness or high-hattedness or high-hattiness [all slang]; tufthunting.

.7 **snob, prig;** elitist; **highbrow** or egghead [both slang], Brahmin, mandarin; namedropper, tufthunter; "he who meanly admires a mean thing" [Thackeray].

.8 VERBS **give oneself airs** 904.14; **hold one's nose in the air, look down one's nose,** toss the head, bridle; mount or get on one's high horse or ride the high horse [informal]; **condescend, patronize,** deal with or treat de haut en bas.

.9 ADJS **arrogant, overbearing, superior,** domineering, **proud, haughty; lofty, toplofty** [informal] 207.19; high-flown, highfalutin or high-faluting [both informal]; high-headed; high-nosed or **stuck-up** or uppish or uppity or **upstage** [all informal]; **hoity-toity,** big, big as you please, six feet above contradiction; on one's high horse; **condescending, patronizing,** de haut en bas [Fr]; purse-proud.

.10 **presumptuous,** presuming, assuming, overweening, would-be, self-elect, self-elected, self-appointed; **insolent** 913.8.

.11 **lordly, imperious,** aristocratic, totally self-assured; hubristic; masterful, magisterial, **high and mighty;** elitist; U [Brit informal]; dictatorial 739.16.

.12 **aloof, standoffish,** standoff, offish [informal], chilly, cool, distant, remote, above all that; Olympian.

.13 **disdainful,** dismissive, **contemptuous, supercilious,** contumelious, cavalier, you-be-damned [slang].

.14 **snobbish,** snobby, **priggish,** snippy [informal]; **snooty** or **snotty** or sniffy [all slang]; **high-hat** or high-hatted or high-hatty [all slang]; patronizing, condescending.

.15 ADVS **arrogantly, haughtily, proudly,** aloofly; **condescendingly, patronizingly,** de haut en bas [Fr]; loftily, toploftily [informal]; imperiously, magisterially; Olympianly; **disdainfully, contemptuously,** superciliously, contumeliously; with nose in air, with nose turned up, with head held high, with arms akimbo.

.16 **presumptuously,** overweeningly, aristocratically; hubristically; **insolently** 913.11.

.17 **snobbishly,** snobbily, **priggishly;** snootily or snottily [both slang].

### 913. INSOLENCE

.1 NOUNS **insolence,** procacity, bumptiousness, contumely; **audacity, effrontery,** boldness, assurance, hardihood; hubris; **presumption,** presumptuousness, overweening, overweeningness; **arrogance** 912, uppishness or uppityness [both informal], obtrusiveness, pushiness [informal].

.2 **impudence, impertinence,** flippancy, **cockiness** or cheekiness [both informal], freshness [slang], **brazenness,** brazenfacedness, brassiness [informal], face of brass, **rudeness** 937.1, brashness, disrespectfulness, contempt 966, derision, ridicule 967.

.3 **cheek** or face or brass [all informal]; **nerve** or gall or crust [all slang]; chutzpah [Yid].

.4 **sauciness,** sassiness [informal], **sauce** [informal], sass [dial], lip [slang], **back talk** or backchat [both informal].

.5 (impudent person) malapert, saucebox [informal]; minx, hussy; whippersnapper, puppy, pup, upstart; smarty or smart-ass or wise-ass [all slang], **smart aleck** or smarty-pants [both informal], wise guy [slang]; boldface, brazenface; chutzpanik [Yid]; swaggerer 911.2.

.6 VERBS **have the audacity, have the cheek; have the gall** or have a nerve or have one's nerve [all informal]; **get fresh** [slang], get smart [informal], forget one's place, **dare, presume,** take liberties, make bold; hold in contempt 966.3–6, ridicule, taunt, deride 967.8–10.

.7 **sauce** [informal], sass [dial], **talk back,** answer back [informal], lip or give one the lip [both slang], provoke.

.8 ADJS **insolent,** insulting, **audacious,** procacious, bumptious, contumelious; **arrogant** 912.9, uppish or uppity [both informal]; hubristic; **presumptuous,** presuming, over-presumptuous, overweening; forward, pushy [informal], obtrusive, familiar; cool, cold, **disdainful** 912.13.

.9 **impudent, impertinent, pert,** malapert, flip [informal], flippant, **cocky** or cheeky [both informal], **fresh** [slang], facy [dial]; crusty or gally or nervy [all slang], chutzpadik [Yid]; uncalled-for, gratuitous, biggety [dial]; **rude** 937.4–7, **disrespectful,** contemptuous 966.8, derisive 967.12, brash, bluff; **saucy,** sassy [dial]; **smart** or smart-alecky [both informal], smart-ass or wise-ass [both slang].

.10 **brazen,** brazenfaced, boldfaced, barefaced, brassy [informal], **bold,** bold as brass [informal], unblushing, unabashed, aweless, **shameless,** dead or lost to shame; swaggering 911.4.

.11 ADVS **insolently, audaciously,** procaciously, bumptiously, contumeliously; **arrogantly** 912.15; **presumptuously,** obtrusively, pushily [informal].

.12 **impudently, impertinently,** pertly, flippantly, **cockily** or cheekily [both informal], saucily; **rudely** 937.8, brashly, disrespectfully, contemptuously 966.9, derisively 967.15, in a smart-alecky way [informal], in a smart-ass fashion [slang].

.13 **brazenly,** brazenfacedly, **boldly,** boldfacedly, **shamelessly,** unblushingly.

### 914. REPUTE

.1 NOUNS **repute, reputation,** "the bubble reputation" [Shakespeare]; **name,** character, figure; **fame, famousness, renown,** "that last infirmity of noble mind" [Milton], **kudos,** report, **glory;** éclat, **celebrity, popularity,** recognition, a place in the sun; **acclaim, public acclaim,** réclame, publicity, vogue, **notoriety,** notoriousness, talk of the town.

.2 **reputability,** reputableness; good reputation, good name, **good** or **high repute,** good report, good odor, fair name, name to conjure with; jealousy of one's repute, maintenance of one's good name; face-saving.

.3 **esteem,** estimation, **honor, regard, respect,** approval, approbation, account, favor, consideration, credit, worth.

.4 **prestige,** kudos, **dignity; face; rank, standing,** stature, high place, position, station, **status.**

.5 **distinction, mark, note; importance,** consequence, significance; **notability, prominence, eminence, greatness**, conspicuousness, outstandingness; elevation, exaltation, loftiness, high mightiness; nobility, grandeur, sublimity; excellence 674.1, supereminence 674.2.

.6 **illustriousness,** luster, brilliance *or* brilliancy, radiance, splendor, resplendence *or* resplendency, glory, blaze of glory, nimbus, halo, aura, envelope; charisma, mystique, glamour, numinousness, magic.

.7 (posthumous fame) **memory, remembrance,** legend, heroic legend *or* myth; **immortality,** lasting *or* undying fame, niche in the hall of fame, secure place in history; immortal name, "ghost of a great name" [Lucan].

.8 **glorification, ennoblement,** dignification, exaltation, elevation, magnification, aggrandizement; enthronement; immortalization, enshrinement; beatification, canonization, sainting, sanctification; deification, apotheosis; lionization.

.9 **celebrity,** man of mark *or* note, person of note *or* consequence, **notable, notability, luminary, great man,** master spirit, worthy, name, **big name,** figure, public figure, **somebody; important person, personage** 672.8; cynosure, "the observed of all observers" [Shakespeare], idol, popular idol, lion, social lion; hero, heroine, popular hero, pop hero [slang], folk hero; star, superstar; immortal; luminaries, galaxy, pleiad, constellation.

.10 VERBS **be somebody,** be something; figure, make *or* cut a figure, cut a dash *or* make a splash [both informal], **make a noise in the world,** make *or* leave one's mark; live, flourish; shine, glitter, gleam, glow.

.11 **gain recognition,** be recognized, come into one's own, come to the front *or* fore, come into vogue.

.12 **honor,** confer *or* bestow honor upon; **dignify,** adorn, grace; **distinguish,** signalize, confer distinction on.

.13 **glorify,** glamorize; **exalt,** elevate, raise, uplift, set up, **ennoble,** aggrandize, magnify, exalt to the skies; crown; throne, enthrone; immortalize, enshrine, hand one's name down to posterity, make legendary; beatify, canonize, saint, sanctify; deify, apotheosize, apotheose; **lionize.**

.14 **reflect honor on,** shed a luster on, redound to one's honor.

.15 ADJS **reputable,** highly reputed, **estimable, esteemed,** much *or* highly esteemed, **honorable,** honored; meritorious, noble,

worthy, creditable; respected, respectable, highly respectable; revered, reverend, venerable, venerated, worshipful; **well-thought-of,** highly regarded, held in esteem, in good odor, in favor, in high favor; in one's good books; prestigious.

.16 **distinguished,** distingué; **noted, notable,** marked, of note, of mark; **famous, famed,** honored, **renowned, celebrated, popular,** acclaimed, much acclaimed, **notorious, well-known,** in everyone's mouth, on everyone's tongue *or* lips, talked-of, talked-about; far-famed, far-heard; fabled, legendary, mythical.

.17 **prominent, conspicuous, outstanding, to the front,** in the limelight [informal]; **important,** consequential, significant.

.18 **eminent, high, exalted,** elevated, lofty, sublime, held in awe, awesome; immortal; **great,** big [informal], **grand;** excellent 674.12–15, supereminent 674.17,18, mighty, high and mighty; glorified, ennobled, magnified, aggrandized; enthroned, throned; immortalized, shrined, enshrined; beatified, canonized, sainted, sanctified; deified, apotheosized.

.19 **illustrious,** lustrous, glorious, brilliant, radiant, splendid, splendorous, splendrous, splendent, resplendent, bright, shining; charismatic, glamorous, numinous, magic(al).

.20 ADVS **reputably, estimably, honorably,** nobly, respectably, worthily, creditably.

.21 **famously, notably, notedly, notoriously,** popularly, celebratedly; **prominently, eminently,** conspicuously, outstandingly; illustriously, gloriously.

## 915. DISREPUTE

.1 NOUNS **disrepute, ill repute, bad repute,** bad *or* poor reputation, evil repute *or* reputation, ill fame, shady *or* unsavory reputation, **bad name,** bad odor, bad report, bad character; **disesteem, dishonor,** public dishonor, **discredit; disfavor,** ill-favor; disapprobation 969.1.

.2 **disreputability,** disreputableness, **notoriety;** discreditableness, dishonorableness, unsavoriness, **unrespectability;** disgracefulness, **shamefulness.**

.3 **baseness, lowness, meanness, crumminess** [slang], poorness, pettiness, paltriness, smallness, littleness, pokiness, beggarliness, shabbiness, shoddiness, squalor, scrubbiness, scumminess, scabbiness, scurviness, scruffiness, abjectness, wretchedness, miserableness, despicableness, contemptibleness, contemptibility, abominbleness, execrableness, obnoxiousness, **odiousness, vileness** 864.2, foulness, rankness, fulsomeness, grossness, nefariousness, heinousness, **atrociousness,** monstrousness, enormity; degradation, debasement, depravity.

.4 **infamy,** infamousness; **ignominy,** ignominiousness; ingloriousness, **ignobility,** odium, obloquy, opprobrium, "a long farewell to all my greatness" [Shakespeare]; depluming, displuming, loss of honor *or* name *or* repute, degradation, demotion 783.

.5 **disgrace, scandal, humiliation; shame,** dirty shame *or* low-down dirty shame [both slang], crying *or* burning shame; **reproach,** byword, byword of reproach, a disgrace to one's name.

.6 **stigma,** stigmatism, onus; **brand,** badge of infamy; **slur,** reproach, censure, reprimand, imputation, aspersion, reflection, stigmatization; pillorying; **black eye** [informal], black mark; **disparagement** 971; **stain, taint,** attaint, **tarnish,** blur, **smirch,** smutch, smudge, smear, spot, blot, blot on *or* in one's escutcheon *or* scutcheon; bend *or* bar sinister [her]; baton, champain, point champain [all her]; mark of Cain; broad arrow [Brit].

.7 VERBS **incur disgrace,** incur disesteem *or* dishonor *or* discredit, be shamed, earn a bad name, forfeit one's good opinion, fall into disrepute, seal one's infamy; lose one's good name, **lose face,** lose countenance, lose credit, **lose caste; disgrace oneself,** lower oneself, demean oneself, degrade *or* debase oneself, act beneath oneself, derogate, stoop, descend, ride to a fall, fall from one's high estate, foul one's own nest; put one's good name in jeopardy; compromise oneself.

.8 **disgrace, dishonor, discredit,** reflect discredit upon, bring into discredit, reproach, cast reproach upon, be a reproach to; **shame, put to shame,** impute shame to, hold up to shame; hold up to public shame *or* public scorn *or* public ridicule, pillory, bring shame upon; **humiliate** 906.4; **degrade, debase** 783.3, deplume, displume, defrock, unfrock, bring low.

.9 **stigmatize, brand; stain,** tarnish, taint, attaint, blot, **blacken, smear,** bespatter, sully, soil, defile, vilify, **slur,** cast a slur upon, blow upon; disapprove 969.10–15; **disparage, defame** 971.8,9; censure, reprimand, **give a black eye** [informal], give a black mark, put in one's bad *or* black

books; give a bad name, give a dog a bad name; expose, expose to infamy; pillory, gibbet; burn *or* hang in effigy.

.10 ADJS **disreputable, discreditable, dishonorable,** unsavory, shady, seamy, sordid, **unrespectable, ignoble, ignominious, infamous,** inglorious; notorious; unpraiseworthy 969.25,26; derogatory 971.13.

.11 **disgraceful, shameful,** pitiful, deplorable, opprobrious, sad, sorry, too bad; degrading, debasing, demeaning, beneath one, beneath one's dignity, *infra indignitatem* [L], infra dig [informal], unbecoming, unworthy of one; cheap, gutter; **humiliating,** humiliative; **scandalous,** shocking, outrageous.

.12 **base, low,** low-down [informal], **mean,** crummy [slang], poor, petty, paltry, small, little, **shabby, shoddy,** squalid, lumpen, scrubby, scummy, scabby, **scurvy,** scruffy, mangy [informal], measly *or* cheesy [both slang], poky, beggarly, **wretched, miserable,** abject, **despicable, contemptible,** abominable, execrable, obnoxious, **disgusting, odious** 864.18, vile, foul, dirty, rank, fulsome, gross, flagrant, grave, arrant, nefarious, heinous, reptilian, **atrocious,** monstrous, unmentionable; degraded, debased, depraved.

.13 **in disrepute,** in bad repute, in bad odor; **in disfavor,** in discredit, **in bad** [informal], in one's bad *or* black books, out of favor, out of countenance, at a discount; **in disgrace,** in Dutch [informal], **in the doghouse** [slang], under a cloud; stripped of reputation, disgraced, discredited, dishonored, shamed, loaded with shame, unable to show one's face.

.14 **unrenowned,** renownless, nameless, inglorious, **unnotable, unnoted,** unnoticed, unremarked, **undistinguished, unfamed,** uncelebrated, unsung, unhonored, unglorified, unpopular; no credit to; **unknown,** little known, obscure, unheard-of, *ignotus* [L].

.15 ADVS **disreputably, discreditably, dishonorably, unrespectably, ignobly, ignominiously, infamously,** ingloriously.

.16 **disgracefully, scandalously,** shockingly, deplorably, outrageously; **shamefully,** to one's shame, to one's shame be it spoken.

.17 **basely, meanly,** poorly, pettily, **shabbily, shoddily,** scurvily, **wretchedly, miserably,** abjectly, **despicably, contemptibly,** abominably, execrably, obnoxiously, **odiously** 864.26, **vilely,** foully, grossly, flagrantly, arrantly, nefariously, heinously, **atrociously,** monstrously.

## 916. HONOR

### (token of esteem)

.1 NOUNS **honor,** great honor, distinction, glory, credit, ornament; "blushing honors" [Shakespeare].

.2 **award, reward, prize;** first prize, second prize; consolation prize; booby prize; Nobel Prize, Pulitzer Prize; sweepstakes; jackpot; Oscar, Academy Award.

.3 **trophy,** laurel, **laurels,** bays, palm, palms, crown, chaplet, wreath, garland, **feather in one's cap** [informal]; civic crown or garland or wreath; **cup,** loving cup, pot [slang]; America's Cup, Old Mug.

.4 **citation,** eulogy, mention, honorable mention, kudos, **accolade, tribute, praise** 970.1.

.5 **decoration,** decoration of honor, order, ornament; ribbon, riband; blue ribbon, *cordon bleu* [Fr]; red ribbon, red ribbon of the Legion of Honor; cordon, grand cordon; garter; star, gold star.

.6 **medal,** order, medallion; military medal, service medal, war medal, soldier's medal; Congressional Medal of Honor, Medal of Honor, Distinguished Service Medal, Distinguished Service Cross, Navy Cross, Distinguished Flying Cross, Air Medal, Silver Star Medal, Bronze Star Medal, Order of the Purple Heart, Unit Citation, Distinguished Unit Citation; Distinguished Conduct Medal, Military Cross, Victoria Cross, Distinguished Service Order; Croix de Guerre, Médaille Militaire; Carnegie hero's medal.

.7 scholarship, fellowship.

.8 VERBS **honor, do honor,** pay regard to, give or pay or render honor to; **cite; decorate,** pin a medal on; crown, crown with laurel; pay tribute, praise 970.5.

.9 ADJS **honored, distinguished;** laureate, crowned with laurel.

.10 **honorary, honorific, honorable.**

.11 ADVS **with honor,** with distinction; *cum laude, magna cum laude, summa cum laude, insigne cum laude, honoris causa* [all L].

## 917. TITLE

### (appellation of dignity or distinction)

.1 NOUNS **title, honorific, honor,** title of honor; **handle** or handle to one's name [both slang].

.2 (honorifics) Excellency, Eminence, Reverence, Grace, Honor, Worship, Your or His or Her Excellency; Lord, My Lord, milord, Lordship, Your or His Lordship; Lady, My Lady, milady, Ladyship, Your or Her Ladyship; Highness, Royal Highness, Imperial Highness, Serene Highness, Your or His or Her Highness; Majesty, Royal Majesty, Imperial Majesty, Serene Majesty, Your or His or Her Majesty.

.3 Sir, sire, sirrah; Esquire; Master, Mister 420.7; mirza, effendi, sirdar, emir, khan, sahib.

.4 Mistress, madame 421.8.

.5 (ecclesiastical titles) Reverend, His Reverence, His Grace; Monsignor; Holiness, His Holiness; Dom, Brother, Sister, Father, Mother; Rabbi.

.6 **degree,** academic degree; **bachelor,** baccalaureate, *baccalaureus* [L], bachelor's degree; **master,** master's degree; **doctor,** doctorate, doctor's degree.

.7 ADJS **titular,** titulary; honorific.

.8 the Noble, the Most Noble, the Most Excellent, the Most Worthy, the Most Worshipful; the Honorable, the Most Honorable, the Right Honorable; the Reverend, the Very Reverend, the Right Reverend, the Most Reverend.

.9 **academic degrees**

| | |
|---|---|
| AA, Associate of Arts | MBA, Master in Business Administration |
| AB, Bachelor of Arts (Artium Baccalaureus) | MD, Doctor of Medicine |
| AdjA, Adjunct in Arts | MDiv, Master of Divinity |
| AM, Master of Arts (Artium Magister) | MFA, Master of Fine Arts |
| BA, Bachelor of Arts | MLS, Master of Library Science |
| BD, Bachelor of Divinity | MRE, Master of Religious Education |
| BS, Bachelor of Science | MS, Master of Science |
| DD, Doctor of Divinity | MusD, Doctor of Music |
| DDS, Doctor of Dental Surgery | PhD, Doctor of Philosophy |
| DEd, Doctor of Education | SB, Bachelor of Science |
| DPhil, Doctor of Philosophy | ScD, Doctor of Science |
| EdD, Doctor of Education | SM, Master of Science |
| JD, Doctor of Jurisprudence | STD, Doctor of Sacred Theology |
| LittD, Doctor of Letters | ThD, Doctor of Theology |
| LLD, Doctor of Laws | |
| MA, Master of Arts | |

## 918. NOBILITY

### (noble rank or birth)

.1 NOUNS **nobility,** nobleness; **aristocracy,** aristocraticalness; **gentility,** genteelness, quality, rank, distinction; birth, high b noble birth, ancestry, high *or* honorable descent; blood, **blue blood;** royalty 739.8.

.2 **nobility,** noblesse, **aristocracy,** aristo–; **elite,** elect, the classes, **upper classes** *or* circles, upper cut *or* **upper crust** [both informal], upper ten [Brit informal], **upper ten thousand,** the Four Hundred, high society, high life, *haut monde* [Fr]; old nobility, *ancienne noblesse* [Fr], *noblesse de robe, noblesse d'épée* [both Fr]; First Families of Virginia, FFVs; **peerage,** baronage, lords temporal and spiritual; baronetage; knightage, chivalry; royalty.

.3 **gentry,** gentlefolk, gentlefolks, gentlepeople, better sort; lesser nobility, *petite noblesse* [Fr]; *samurai* [Jap]; landed gentry, squirearchy.

.4 **nobleman, noble, gentleman;** peer; **aristocrat, patrician,** Brahman, **blue blood,** thoroughbred, silk-stocking, lace-curtain, swell *or* upper-cruster [both slang]; **grandee,** magnifico, magnate, optimate; **lord,** laird [Scot], lordling; seignior, seigneur, *hidalgo* [Sp]; **duke,** grand duke, archduke, marquis, **earl, count,** viscount, **baron,** daimio, **baronet;** squire; esquire, armiger; palsgrave, waldgrave, margrave, landgrave.

.5 **knight,** cavalier, chevalier, *caballero* [Sp], *Ritter* [Ger], "a verray parfit gentil knight" [Chaucer]; **knight-errant,** knight-adventurer; companion; bachelor, knight bachelor; baronet, knight baronet; banneret, knight banneret; Bayard, Gawain, Lancelot, Sidney, Sir Galahad, Don Quixote.

.6 **noblewoman, peeress, gentlewoman; lady,** dame, *doña* [Sp], khanum; **duchess,** grand duchess, archduchess, marchioness, viscountess, **countess, baroness,** margravine.

.7 **prince,** *Prinz, Fürst* [both Ger], knez, atheling, sheikh, sherif, mirza, khan, emir, shahzada [India]; princeling, princelet; crown prince, heir apparent; heir presumptive; prince consort; prince regent; **king** 749.7; princes of India 749.9; Muslim rulers 749.10.

.8 **princess,** *princesse* [Fr], *infanta* [Sp], rani, maharani, begum, shahzadi, kumari *or* kunwari, raj-kumari, malikzadi; crown princess; **queen** 749.11.

.9 (rank or office) lordship, ladyship; dukedom, marquisate, earldom, barony, baronetcy; viscountship, viscountcy, viscounty; knighthood, knight-errantship; seigniory, seigneury, seignioralty; pasha-

ship, pashadom; princeship, princedom; kingship, queenship 739.8.

.10 ADJS **noble,** of rank, high, exalted; **aristocratic, patrician; gentle,** genteel, of gentle blood; gentlemanly, gentlemanlike; ladylike, quite the lady; knightly, chivalrous; ducal, archducal; princely, princelike; kingly, kinglike, "every inch a king" [Shakespeare]; queenly, queenlike; titled.

.11 **wellborn, well-bred, blue-blooded,** of good breed; **thoroughbred,** purebred, pure-blooded, *pur sang* [Fr], full-blooded; **highborn,** highbred; born to the purple.

## 919. COMMONALTY

.1 NOUNS **commonalty,** commonality, commonage, commoners, commons; **common people,** *vulgus* [L], ordinary people, common sort, plain people, plain folks, common run [informal], rank and file, neither nobility nor clergy, the third estate, the salt of the earth; **proletariat,** working class, working people, toiling class, toilers, laborers, lumpen proletariat; **bourgeoisie,** middle class, middle orders, upper middle class, lower middle class, linendrapers, shopkeepers, small tradesmen; **lower classes,** lower orders, the lower cut [informal], the other half; peasantry.

.2 **the people, the populace,** *hoi polloi* [Gk], the population, the citizenry, **the public,** the general public, John Q. Public; *demos* [Gk]; Tom, Dick, and Harry; Brown, Jones, and Robinson.

.3 **the masses, the hoi polloi,** the many, **the multitude,** the crowd, **the mob,** the horde, the million, **the majority,** the mass of the people, the herd, the great unnumbered, the great unwashed, **the vulgar** *or* **common herd;** *profanum vulgus, ignobile vulgus, mobile vulgus* [all L]; "the multitude of the gross people" [Erasmus], "many-headed multitude" [Sir Philip Sidney], "the beast with many heads" [Shakespeare], "the blunt monster with uncounted heads, the still-discordant wavering multitude" [Shakespeare].

.4 **rabble,** rabblement, rout, ruck, common ruck, canaille, ragtag [informal], "the tagrag people" [Shakespeare], **ragtag and bobtail;** rag, tag, and bobtail.

.5 **riffraff,** raff, chaff, trash, **rubbish,** dregs, sordes, offscourings, offscum, **scum, scum of the earth, dregs** *or* **scum** *or* **offscum** *or* **offscourings of society,** swinish multitude, vermin, cattle.

.6 **the underprivileged,** the disadvantaged, the poor, ghetto-dwellers, slum-dwellers, welfare cases, chronic poor, depressed class, poverty subculture, the wretched of the earth, outcasts, the dispossessed, the powerless.

.7 **common man, commoner,** little man, **little fellow, average man,** ordinary man, typical man, **man in the street,** one of the people, man of the people, Everyman; **plebeian,** pleb [slang]; **proletarian,** bourgeois, *roturier* [Fr]; Cockney; Joe Doakes, John Smith, Mr. *or* Mrs. Brown *or* Smith.

.8 **peasant, countryman,** countrywoman, **provincial,** son of the soil, tiller of the soil; peon, hind, fellah, muzhik; sons of Martha, "hewers of wood and drawers of water" [Bible].

.9 **rustic,** bucolic [informal]; **yokel, hick, rube, hayseed** [all slang], **bumpkin,** country bumpkin, clod, **clodhopper** [informal], hillbilly *or* woodhick [both slang], **boor,** clown, lout, looby, **farmer** 413.5.

.10 **upstart, parvenu,** adventurer, sprout [slang], "an upstart crow beautified in our feathers" [Robert Greene]; *bourgeois gentilhomme* [Fr], would-be gentleman; *nouveau riche, nouveau roturier* [both Fr], **newly-rich,** pig in clover [slang]; social climber, name-dropper, tufthunter; status seeker.

.11 ADJS **common,** commonplace, **plain, ordinary, lowly,** low, mean, **humble,** homely; **lowborn, lowbred,** baseborn, earthborn, plebeian; non-noble, nonclerical; third-estate; ungenteel, shabby-genteel; vulgar, rude 898.10–15; below the salt; cockney, born within sound of Bow bells.

.12 **middle-class, bourgeois; proletarian,** working-class.

.13 **parvenu, upstart,** mushroom, risen from the ranks; **newly-rich,** *nouveau-riche* [Fr].

## 920. WONDER

.1 NOUNS **wonder, wonderment,** sense of wonder, marveling, marvel, **astonishment, amazement,** amaze, **astoundment;** dumbfoundment, stupefaction; **surprise, awe,** breathless wonder *or* awe, sense of mystery, admiration; beguilement, fascination 650.1; bewilderment, puzzlement 514.3.

.2 **marvel, wonder, prodigy, miracle, phenomenon,** astonishment, amazement, marvelment, wonderment, wonderful thing, nine days' wonder, amazing *or* astonishing thing, quite a thing, really

something, **sensation,** stunner [slang]; one for the book *or* something to brag about *or* something to shout about *or* something to write home about *or* something else [all informal]; **rarity,** nonesuch, exception, one in a thousand, one in a way; **curiosity,** gazingstock, sight, spectacle; wonders of the world.

.3 **wonderfulness,** wondrousness, **marvelousness,** miraculousness, phenomenalness, prodigiousness, stupendousness, remarkableness, extraordinariness; beguilingness, fascination, enchantingness, enticingness, seductiveness, glamorousness; awesomeness, mysteriousness, mystery, numinousness.

.4 **inexpressibility, ineffability,** inenarrability, noncommunicability, noncommunicableness, incommunicability, incommunicableness, indescribability, indefinableness, **unutterability, unspeakability,** unnameableness, innominability, unmentionability.

.5 VERBS **wonder, marvel,** be astonished *or* amazed *or* astounded, be seized with wonder; **gaze, gape,** look *or* stand aghast *or* agog, gawk, **stare,** stare openmouthed, open one's eyes, rub one's eyes, hold one's breath; not be able to account for, not know what to make of, not believe one's eyes *or* ears *or* senses.

.6 **astonish, amaze, astound, surprise,** startle, stagger, bewilder, perplex 514.12,13, flabbergast [informal], confound, overwhelm, boggle; **awe, awestrike,** strike with wonder *or* awe; **dumbfound,** dumbfounder, strike dumb, strike dead; strike all of a heap *or* throw on one's beam ends [both informal], bowl down *or* over [informal], dazzle, bedazzle, daze, bedaze; stun, stupefy, petrify, paralyze.

.7 take one's breath away, turn one's head, make one's head swim, make one's hair stand on end, make one's tongue cleave to the roof of one's mouth, make one stare, make one sit up and take notice, carry one off his feet.

.8 beggar *or* baffle description, stagger belief.

.9 ADJS **wondering,** wrapped *or* rapt in wonder, marveling, **astonished, amazed,** surprised, **astounded,** flabbergasted [informal], **bewildered,** puzzled 514.23,24, confounded, **dumbfounded,** dumbstruck, staggered, overwhelmed, unable to believe one's senses *or* eyes; **aghast,** agape, agog, all agog, gazing, gaping, at gaze, staring, gauping, wide-eyed, popeyed open-eyed, openmouthed, **breathless; thunderstruck,** wonder-struck, wonder-stricken, awestruck, struck all of a heap [informal]; awed, in awe, in awe of; spellbound, fascinated, captivated, under a charm, beguiled, enthralled, enraptured, enravished, enchanted, entranced, bewitched, hypnotized, mesmerized, stupefied, lost in wonder or amazement.

.10 **wonderful, wondrous, marvelous, miraculous,** fantastic, fabulous, phenomenal, prodigious, stupendous, unheard-of, unprecedented, extraordinary, exceptional, rare, unique, **remarkable,** striking, **sensational; strange,** passing strange, "wondrous strange" [Shakespeare]; **beguiling, fascinating** 650.7; incredible, inconceivable, outlandish, unimaginable, incomprehensible; **bewildering, puzzling** 514.25, enigmatic.

.11 **awesome,** awful, awing, awe-inspiring; **mysterious,** numinous; weird, eerie, uncanny, bizarre.

.12 **astonishing, amazing, surprising,** startling, **astounding,** confounding, staggering, stunning [slang], eye-opening, breathtaking, overwhelming, mind-boggling; **spectacular.**

.13 **indescribable, ineffable,** inenarrable, inexpressible, unutterable, unspeakable, noncommunicable, incommunicable, indefinable, undefinable, unnameable, innominable, unwhisperable, unmentionable.

.14 ADVS **wonderfully,** wondrously, **marvelously, miraculously,** fantastically, fabulously, phenomenally, prodigiously, stupendously, extraordinarily, exceptionally, remarkably, strikingly, **sensationally;** strangely, outlandishly, incredibly, inconceivably, unimaginably, incomprehensibly, **bewilderingly, puzzlingly,** enigmatically; **beguilingly, fascinatingly** 650.8.

.15 **awesomely,** awfully, awingly, awe-inspiringly; **mysteriously,** numinously, weirdly, eerily, uncannily, bizarrely.

.16 **astonishingly, amazingly, astoundingly,** staggeringly, confoundingly; **surprisingly,** startlingly, to one's surprise or great surprise, to one's astonishment or amazement; for a wonder, strange to say.

.17 **indescribably, ineffably,** inexpressibly, unutterably, unspeakably, inenarrably, indefinably, unnameably, unmentionably.

.18 in wonder, in astonishment, in amazement, in bewilderment, in awe, in admiration, with gaping mouth.

.19 INTERJS (astonishment or surprise) my word!, I declare!, well I never!, of all things!, as I live and breathe!, what!, indeed!, really!, surely!, how now!, what on earth!, what in the world!, I'll be jiggered!, holy Christ!, holy Christmas!, holy cow!, holy mackerel!, holy Moses!, holy smoke!, holy shit! [slang], hush or shut my mouth!, blow me down!, strike me dead!, shiver my timbers!

.20 oh!, O!, ah!, la!, lo!, lo and behold!, hello!, halloo!, hey!, whew!, phew!, wow!, yipes!, yike!

.21 my!, oh, my!, dear!, dear me!, goodness!, gracious!, goodness gracious!, gee!, my goodness!, my stars!, good gracious!, good heavens!, good lack!, lackadaisy!, welladay!, hoity-toity!, zounds!, 'sdeath!, gadzooks!, gad so!, bless my heart!, God bless me!, heavens and earth!, for crying out loud! [slang].

.22 imagine!, fancy!, fancy that!, just imagine!, only think!, well!, I never!, can you feature that!, can you beat that!, it beats the Dutch!, do tell!, you don't say!, the devil or deuce you say!, I'll be!, what do you know!, what do you know about that!, how about that!, who would have thought it!, did you ever!, can it be!, can such things be?, will wonders never cease!

## 921. UNASTONISHMENT

.1 NOUNS **unastonishment, unamazement,** unamazedness, nonastonishment, nonamazement, nonamazedness, nonwonder, nonwondering, nonmarveling, unsurprise, unsurprisedness, awelessness, wonderlessness, calmness, coolness, **cool** [slang], cool or calm or nodding acceptance, composure, inexcitability 858, expectation 539, unimpressibleness, refusal to be impressed or awed or amazed.

.2 VERBS **accept, take for granted,** take as a matter of course, treat as routine, show no amazement, refuse to be impressed, not blink an eye, not turn a hair, keep one's cool [slang].

.3 ADJS **unastonished, unsurprised, unamazed,** unmarveling, unwondering, unastounded, undumbfounded, unbewildered; undazzled, undazed; unawed, aweless, wonderless; **unimpressed,** unmoved; calm, **cool,** composed, inexcitable 858.10–15; expecting, expected 539.11–14.

## 922. SOCIABILITY

.1 NOUNS **sociability,** sociality, sociableness, fitness or fondness for society, social-mindedness, **gregariousness, affability,** companionability, compatibility, geniality, **congeniality**; hospitality 925; **clubbability** [informal], clubbishness, clubbism; intimacy, familiarity; amiability, **friendliness** 927.1; **communicativeness** 554.3; social grace, civility, urbanity, courtesy 936.

.2 **camaraderie**, comradery, comradeship, **fellowship**, **good-fellowship**; consorting, hobnobbing.

.3 **conviviality**, joviality, jollity, gaiety, heartiness, cheer, good cheer, festivity, merrymaking, merriment, revelry.

.4 **social intercourse**, social activity, **intercourse**, communication, **communion**, intercommunion, **fellowship**, intercommunication, **community**, collegiality, commerce, congress, converse, conversation, social relations.

.5 (social grouping) **social circle** or **set**, social class, one's crowd or set; **association** 788.

.6 **association**, consociation, affiliation, **fellowship**, companionship, company, society; fraternity, **fraternization**; membership, participation, partaking, sharing, cooperation 786.

.7 **visit**, **social call**, call; formal visit, duty visit, required visit; visiting, visitation; round of visits; social round, social whirl, mad round.

.8 **appointment**, **engagement**, **date** [informal], double date, blind date [both informal]; arrangement, interview; engagement book.

.9 **rendezvous**, **tryst**, **assignation**, **meeting**; trysting place, meeting place, place of assignation; assignation house; love nest [informal].

.10 **social gathering**, **social**, sociable, social affair, affair, gathering, get-together [informal]; **reception**, at home, salon, levee; soiree; matinee; reunion, family reunion; wake.

.11 **party**, **entertainment**, blowout [slang]; **festivity** 878.3,4; shindig or shindy; **ball** 879.2; stag or stag party [both informal]; hen party [slang]; house party; housewarming, house-raising; shower, donation party; surprise party; garden party, lawn party, *fête champêtre* [Fr]; costume party, masquerade party, masquerade, masque, mask; coffee party, coffee klatch, *Kaffeeklatsch* [Ger]; cocktail party; dinner party, dinner; smoker [informal].

.12 **tea**, afternoon tea, five-o'clock tea, high tea; **tea party**.

.13 **bee**, quilting bee, raising bee, husking bee, cornhusking, corn shucking, husking.

.14 **debut**, **coming out** [informal], presentation, coming-out party [informal].

.15 (sociable person) joiner, mixer or **good mixer** [both informal], good or pleasant company, excellent companion, life of the party, bon vivant; man-about-town, playboy, social lion, nightclub habitué; clubman, clubwoman.

.16 VERBS **associate with**, assort with, sort with, consort with, hobnob with, **mingle with**, **mix with**, **touch elbows** or **shoulders with**, eat off the same trencher; **fraternize**, fellowship, join in fellowship; **keep company with**, bear one company, walk hand in hand with; join, take up with [informal], tie up with [slang]; **flock together**, herd together, club together, clique or clique with [both informal], gang up with [slang], hang around with [informal], hunt or run in couples; chum, **chum with** or chum together [both informal]; pal or pal with [both informal], pal up with or around with [slang], run around with, run with, hang out with.

.17 **visit**, make or pay a visit, **call on** or **upon**, **drop in**, run in, look in, look one up, see, stop off or over [informal], drop or run or stop by; leave one's card.

.18 ADJS **sociable**, **social**, social-minded, fit for society, fond of society, **gregarious**, **affable**; **companionable**, companionate, compatible, genial, **congenial**; hospitable 925.11; clubby, clubbable [both informal], clubbish; **communicative** 554.10; amiable, **friendly** 927.14; civil, urbane, courteous 936.14–17.

.19 **convivial**, boon, free and easy, hail-fellow-well-met; **jovial**, **jolly**, hearty, festive, gay.

.20 **intimate**, **familiar**, cozy, chatty, tête-à-tête.

.21 ADVS **sociably**, socially, gregariously, affably; companionably, arm in arm, hand in hand.

## 923. UNSOCIABILITY

.1 NOUNS **unsociability**, insociability, unsociableness, dissociability; **ungregariousness**, uncompanionability; unclubbableness or unclubbability [both informal]; ungeniality, **uncongeniality**; incompatibility, social incompatibility; **unfriendliness** 929.1; **uncommunicativeness** 613; sullenness, mopishness, moroseness; self-sufficiency, self-containment; autism; bashfulness 908.4.

.2 **aloofness**, **standoffishness**, offishness

withdrawnness, **remoteness,** distance, detachment; **coolness,** coldness, frigidity, chill, chilliness, iciness, frostiness; inaccessibility, unapproachability.

.3 seclusiveness, exclusiveness; **seclusion** 924.

.4 VERBS **keep to oneself,** keep oneself to oneself, enjoy or prefer one's own company, stay at home, shun companionship, **stand aloof,** hold oneself aloof or apart, keep one's distance, keep at a distance, keep in the background, retire, retire into the shade, creep into a corner.

.5 ADJS **unsociable,** insociable, dissociable, unsocial; **ungregarious,** nongregarious; **uncompanionable,** ungenial, uncongenial; incompatible, socially incompatible; unclubbable [informal]; **unfriendly** 929.9; **uncommunicative** 613.8; sullen, mopish, mopey, morose; close, snug; self-sufficient, self-contained; autistic; bashful 908.12.

.6 aloof, standoffish, offish, standoff, **distant, remote,** withdrawn, removed, detached, Olympian; **cool,** cold, frigid, chilly, icy, frosty; seclusive, exclusive; inaccessible, unapproachable.

## 924. SECLUSION

.1 NOUNS **seclusion,** reclusion, **retirement, withdrawal, retreat,** recess; renunciation or forsaking of the world; **sequestration,** quarantine, separation, detachment, apartness; segregation, apartheid, Jim Crow; **isolation,** "splendid isolation" [Sir William Goschen]; **privacy,** privatism, secrecy; rustication; privatization; isolationism.

.2 **hermitism,** hermitry, eremitism, anchoritism, cloistered monasticism.

.3 **solitude,** solitariness, **aloneness,** loneness, singleness; **loneliness, lonesomeness.**

.4 **forlornness,** desolation; friendlessness, kithlessness, fatherlessness, motherlessness, homelessness; helplessness, defenselessness; abandonment, desertion.

.5 **recluse, loner,** solitaire, solitary, solitudinarian; **shut-in,** invalid, bedridden invalid; cloistered monk or nun; **hermit,** eremite, anchorite; marabout; hermitess, anchoress; **ascetic;** closet cynic; stylite, pillarist, pillar saint; Hieronymite, Hieronymian; Diogenes, Timon of Athens, St. Simeon Stylites, St. Anthony, desert saints; desert fathers; outcast, pariah 926.4; **stay-at-home,** homebody; isolationist, seclusionist.

.6 VERBS **seclude oneself,** go into seclusion, **retire,** go into retirement, retire from the world, abandon or forsake the world, live in retirement, lead a retired life, lead a cloistered life, be or remain incommunicado, shut oneself up, live alone, live apart; stay at home; rusticate; take the veil; cop out [slang], opt out or drop out of society.

.7 ADJS **secluded, retired, withdrawn;** isolated, shut off, insular, **separate,** separated, **apart,** detached, removed; segregated, quarantined; **remote, out-of-the-way,** in a backwater, out-of-the-world; **unfrequented,** unvisited.

.8 **private,** privy, **secret, hidden.**

.9 **recluse,** sequestered, cloistered, shut up or in; **hermitic(al),** eremitic(al), hermitish; anchoritic(al); stay-at-home, domestic.

.10 **solitary,** alone; in solitude, by oneself, all alone; **lonely, lonesome, lone.**

.11 **forlorn,** lorn; **abandoned, forsaken,** deserted, desolate, godforsaken [informal], friendless, unfriended, kithless, fatherless, motherless, homeless; helpless, defenseless; outcast 926.10.

.12 ADVS **in seclusion, in retirement,** in retreat, in solitude; in privacy, in secrecy; "far from the madding crowd's ignoble strife" [Thomas Gray], "the world forgetting by the world forgot" [Pope].

## 925. HOSPITALITY, WELCOME

.1 NOUNS **hospitality,** hospitableness, receptiveness; **cordiality,** amiability, graciousness, **friendliness,** neighborliness, geniality, heartiness, bonhomie, **generosity,** liberality, openheartedness, warmth, warmness, warmheartedness; open door.

.2 **welcome,** welcoming, **reception,** accueil [Fr]; cordial or warm or hearty welcome, pleasant or smiling reception, the glad hand [slang], open arms; embrace, hug; welcome mat.

.3 **greetings, salutations,** salaams; **regards,** best wishes 936.8.

.4 **greeting, salutation,** salute; **hail, hello,** how-do-you-do; accost, address; nod, bow, bob; curtsy 964.2; wave; handshake, hand-clasp; embrace, hug, kiss; smile, smile of recognition.

.5 **host,** mine host; hostess, receptionist; landlord 809.2.

.6 **guest, visitor,** visitant, xen(o)–; **caller,** company; frequenter, habitué; uninvited guest, gate-crasher [informal]; moocher or freeloader [both slang].

.7 VERBS **receive, admit,** accept, take in, let in, open the door to; **be at home to,** have the latchstring out, keep a light in the window, put out the welcome mat, keep the door open, keep an open house.

.8 entertain, entertain guests, guest; host, preside, do the honors [informal]; give a party, throw a party [slang]; spread oneself [informal].

.9 welcome, make welcome, bid one welcome, make one feel welcome or at home, hold out the hand, extend the right hand of friendship; glad hand, give the glad hand or glad eye [all informal]; embrace, hug, receive with open arms; give a warm reception to, "kill the fatted calf" [Bible].

.10 greet, hail, accost, address; salute, make one's salutations; bid or say hello, bid good day or good morning, etc.; exchange greetings, pass the time of day; give one's regards 936.13; shake hands, shake [slang], press or squeeze one's hand; nod to, bow to; curtsy 964.6; tip the hat to, lift the hat, touch the hat or cap; take one's hat off to, uncover; pull the forelock; kiss, greet with a kiss, kiss hands or cheeks.

.11 ADJS hospitable, receptive, welcoming; cordial, amiable, gracious, friendly, neighborly, genial, hearty, open, openhearted, warm, warmhearted; generous, liberal; –xenous.

.12 welcome, welcome as the roses in May; agreeable, desirable, acceptable; grateful, gratifying, pleasing.

.13 ADVS hospitably, with open arms.

.14 INTERJS welcome!, soyez le bienvenu! [Fr], ¡bien venido! [Sp], benvenuto! [Ital], Willkommen! [Ger]; glad to see you!

.15 greetings!, salutations!, hello!, hullo!, hail!, hey! or heigh!, hi!, aloha!, ¡hola! [Sp]; how do you do?, how are you?, comment allez-vous?, comment ça va? [both Fr], ¿cómo está Usted? [Sp], come sta? [Ital], wie geht's? [Ger]; good morning!, guten Morgen! [Ger]; good day!, bon jour! [Fr], ¡buenos días! [Sp], buon giorno! [Ital], guten Tag! [Ger]; good afternoon!, ¡buenas tardes! [Sp]; good evening!, bon soir! [Fr], buona sera! [Ital], guten Abend! [Ger].

.16 [informal terms] howdy!, howdy-do!, how-de-do!, how-do-ye-do!, how-d'ye-do!, how you doin'?, hi ya!; how's things?, how's tricks?, how goes it?, how's every little thing?, how's the world treating you?

## 926. INHOSPITALITY

.1 NOUNS inhospitality, inhospitableness, unhospitableness, unreceptiveness; uncordialness, ungraciousness, unfriendliness, unneighborliness; nonwelcome, nonwelcoming.

.2 unhabitability, uninhabitability, unlivability.

.3 ostracism, ostracization; banishment 310.4; proscription, ban; boycott, boycottage; blackball, blacklist.

.4 outcast, social outcast, outcast of society, castaway, derelict, Ishmael; pariah, untouchable, leper; outcaste; déclassé [Fr]; outlaw; expellee, evictee; displaced person, DP; exile, expatriate, man without a country; undesirable; persona non grata [L], unacceptable person.

.5 VERBS have nothing to do with, have no truck with [informal], refuse to associate with, steer clear of [informal], spurn, turn one's back upon; deny oneself to, refuse to receive, not be at home to; shut the door upon.

.6 ostracize, disfellowship; banish 310.17; proscribe, ban, outlaw, put under the ban; boycott, blackball, blacklist.

.7 ADJS inhospitable, unhospitable; unreceptive, closed; uncordial, ungracious, unfriendly, unneighborly.

.8 unhabitable, uninhabitable, nonhabitable, unoccupiable, untenantable, unlivable, unfit to live in, not fit for man or beast.

.9 unwelcome, unwanted; unagreeable, undesirable, unacceptable; uninvited, unasked, unbidden.

.10 outcast, cast-off, castaway, derelict; outside the pale, outside the gates; rejected, disowned; abandoned, forsaken 924.11.

## 927. FRIENDSHIP

.1 NOUNS friendship, friendliness; amicability, amicableness, amity, peaceableness, unhostility; amiability, amiableness, congeniality, well-affectedness; neighborliness, neighborlikeness; sociability 922; love 931; kindness 938.

.2 fellowship, companionship, comradeship, colleagueship, chumship [informal], palship [slang], freemasonry, consortship, boon companionship; brotherhood, fraternity, fraternalism, sodality, confraternity; sisterhood, sorority; brotherliness, sisterliness; community of interest, esprit de corps [Fr].

.3 good terms, good understanding, good

footing, friendly relations; **harmony,** sympathy, fellow feeling, **rapport** 794.1; **favor, goodwill, good graces, regard,** respect, mutual regard, favorable regard, the good or right side of [informal]; an in [informal].

.4 **acquaintance,** acquaintedness, close acquaintance; **introduction,** presentation, knockdown [slang].

.5 **familiarity, intimacy,** intimate acquaintance, closeness, nearness, inseparableness; affinity, special affinity; chumminess [informal], palliness [slang], mateyness [Brit informal].

.6 **cordiality, geniality,** heartiness, bonhomie, ardency, warmth, warmness, warmheartedness; hospitality 925.

.7 **devotion, devotedness;** dedication, commitment; fastness, steadfastness, firmness, constancy, staunchness; triedness, trueness, tried-and-trueness.

.8 cordial friendship, warm or ardent friendship, devoted friendship, bosom friendship, intimate or familiar friendship, sincere friendship, beautiful friendship, fast or firm friendship, staunch friendship, loyal friendship, lasting friendship, undying friendship.

.9 VERBS **be friends,** have the friendship of, have the ear of; **know, be acquainted with;** associate with 922.16; cotton to or hit it off [both informal], get on well with, hobnob with, fraternize with; be close friends with, be inseparable; **be on good terms,** enjoy good or friendly relations with; keep on good terms, have an in with [informal].

.10 **befriend, make friends with,** gain the friendship of, **strike up a friendship,** get to know one another, take up with [informal], shake hands with, **get acquainted,** make or scrape acquaintance with, pick up an acquaintance with; get chummy with [informal], buddy up [slang]; play footsie with [slang]; win friends, win friends and influence people.

.11 **cultivate,** cultivate the friendship of, **court,** pay court to, pay addresses to, seek the company of, **run after** [informal], **shine up to,** make up to [informal], play up to or suck up to [both slang], hold out or extend the right of friendship or fellowship; **make advances,** approach, break the ice.

.12 **get on good terms with, get into favor,** win the regard of, **get in the good graces of, get in good with,** get in with [informal], get on the in with or get next to

[both informal], **get on the good** or **right side of** [informal].

.13 **introduce, present, acquaint,** make acquainted, give an introduction, give a knockdown [slang], do the honors [informal].

.14 ADJS **friendly, friendlike; amicable, peaceable,** unhostile; **harmonious** 794.3; **amiable, congenial,** simpático [Sp], simpatico [Ital], sympathique [Fr], pleasant, agreeable, favorable, well-affected, well-disposed, well-intentioned, well-meaning, well-meant; brotherly, fraternal; sisterly; neighborly, neighborlike; sociable 922.18; kind 938.13–17.

.15 **cordial, genial,** hearty, ardent, warm, warmhearted; hospitable 925.11.

.16 **friends with,** friendly with, at home with; **acquainted.**

.17 **on good terms,** on a good footing, on friendly or amicable terms, **on speaking terms,** on a first-name basis, on visiting terms; **in good with,** in with [informal], on the in with, in [both slang], **in favor, in one's good graces,** in one's good books, on the good or right side of [informal].

.18 **familiar, intimate, close,** near, inseparable, on familiar or intimate terms; handin-hand, hand and glove; **thick, thick as thieves** [informal].

.19 **chummy** [informal], matey [Brit informal]; pally or palsy or palsy-walsy or buddy-buddy [all slang].

.20 **devoted,** dedicated, committed, **fast,** steadfast, constant, faithful, staunch; tried, true, **tried and true,** tested.

.21 ADVS **amicably,** friendly, friendliwise; **amiably, congenially,** pleasantly, agreeably, favorably; **cordially, genially,** heartily, ardently, warmly, with open arms; familiarly, intimately; arm in arm, hand in hand.

## 928. FRIEND

.1 NOUNS **friend, acquaintance,** close acquaintance; **confidant,** confidante, repository; **intimate,** familiar, **close friend,** intimate or familiar friend; **bosom friend,** friend of one's bosom, inseparable friend, **best friend;** alter ego, other self; brother, fellow, fellowman, fellow creature, neighbor; **sympathizer,** well-wisher, partisan, advocate, favorer, backer, **supporter** 787.9; casual acquaintance; pickup [informal]; lover 931.11,12.

.2 **good friend,** great friend, devoted friend, warm or ardent friend, **faithful friend,** trusted or trusty friend, fidus Achates

[L], constant friend, staunch friend, fast friend, "a friend that sticketh closer than a brother" [Bible]; **friend in need,** friend indeed.

.3 **companion, fellow,** fellow companion, **comrade,** *camarade* [Fr], amigo [informal], mate [Brit], comate, company, **associate** 787, consociate, compeer, confrere, consort, **colleague, partner,** pardner or pard [both slang], copartner, side partner, **sidekick** [slang], **crony,** old crony, gossip; **chum** or **buddy** or buddy-boy or bosom buddy [all informal], **pal** [informal], ace [slang], butty [Brit informal]; girl friend [informal]; **roommate,** chamberfellow; bunkmate, bunkie [informal]; bedfellow, bedmate; **schoolmate,** schoolfellow, classmate, classfellow, school companion, school chum, fellow student or pupil; **playmate,** playfellow; **teammate,** yokefellow, yokemate; workfellow 787.5; shipmate; messmate.

.4 **boon companion,** boonfellow; **good fellow,** jolly fellow, hearty, *bon vivant* [Fr]; pot companion.

.5 (famous friendships) Achilles and Patroclus, Castor and Pollux, Damon and Pythias, David and Jonathan, Diomedes and Sthenelus, Epaminondas and Pelopidas, Hercules and Iolaus, Nisus and Euryalus, Pylades and Orestes, Theseus and Pirithoüs, Christ and the beloved disciple; The Three Musketeers.

## 929. ENMITY

.1 NOUNS **enmity, unfriendliness,** inimicality; **uncordiality,** unamiability, ungeniality, disaffinity, incompatibility, incompatibleness; personal conflict, strain, **tension;** coolness, coldness, chilliness, chill, frost, iciness; inhospitality 926, unsociability 923.

.2 **disaccord** 795; ruffled feelings, strained relations, alienation, estrangement 795.4.

.3 **hostility, antagonism, repugnance, antipathy,** spitefulness, spite, despitefulness, malice, malevolence, malignity, **hatred, hate** 930; **conflict, contention** 796, collision, clash, clashing, **friction;** quarrelsomeness 795.3; belligerence 797.15.

.4 **animosity,** animus; **ill will,** ill feeling, bitter feeling, **hard feelings,** no love lost; **bad blood,** ill blood, feud, vendetta; **bitterness,** sourness, soreness, **rancor,** acrimony, virulence, venom, vitriol.

.5 **grudge,** spite, crow to pick or pluck or pull, bone to pick; peeve or pet peeve [both informal].

.6 **enemy, foe, foeman, adversary, antagonist;** bitter enemy; sworn enemy; open enemy; public enemy; archenemy, devil; "my nearest and dearest enemy" [Thomas Middleton].

.7 VERBS **antagonize,** set against, set at odds, set at each other's throat, sick on each other [informal]; aggravate, exacerbate, heat up, **provoke,** envenom, **embitter,** infuriate, madden; **alienate,** estrange 795.14.

.8 **bear ill will,** bear malice, have it in for [informal], hold it against, be down on [informal]; **bear a grudge,** owe a grudge, have a bone to pick with; have a crow to pick or pluck or pull with; hate 930.5.

.9 ADJS **unfriendly, inimical, unamicable; uncordial,** unamiable, ungenial, incompatible; strained, tense; disaccordant, unharmonious 795.16; cool, cold, chill, chilly, frosty, icy; inhospitable 926.7; unsociable 923.5.

.10 **hostile, antagonistic,** repugnant, antipathetic, set against, spiteful, despiteful, malicious, malevolent, malignant, hateful, full of hate or hatred; virulent, **bitter,** sore, rancorous, acrid, caustic, venomous, vitriolic; conflicting, clashing, colliding; quarrelsome 795.17; belligerent 797.25.

.11 **alienated, estranged,** disaffected, separated, divided, disunited, torn; irreconcilable.

.12 **at outs, on the outs** [informal], at enmity, at variance, **at odds,** at loggerheads, at cross-purposes, at sixes and sevens, at each other's throat, at daggers drawn.

.13 **on bad terms,** not on speaking terms; in bad with [informal], in bad odor with, in one's bad or black books, on one's shitlist [slang].

.14 ADVS **unamicably,** inimically; **uncordially,** unamiably, ungenially; coolly, coldly, chillily, frostily; **hostilely, antagonistically.**

## 930. HATE

.1 NOUNS **hate, hatred,** mis(o)–; dislike 867; **detestation, abhorrence, aversion, antipathy,** repugnance, **loathing,** execration, **abomination,** odium; **spite,** spitefulness, despitefulness, **malice, malevolence,** malignity; vials of hate or wrath; misanthropy, misandry, misogyny; anti-Semitism; race hatred, racism; bigotry; Anglophobia, Russophobia, xenophobia, etc. 891.10–17.

.2 **enmity** 929; bitterness, **animosity** 929.4.

.3 (hated thing) **anathema, abomination**

detestation, aversion, abhorrence, antipathy, execration, hate; peeve, pet peeve; phobia.

.4 **hater**, man-hater, woman-hater, misanthropist, misanthrope, misogynist, anti-Semite, racist, bigot; Anglophobe, Russophobe, xenophobe, etc.

.5 VERBS **hate, detest, loathe, abhor**, execrate, **abominate**, hold in abomination, take an aversion to, shudder at, utterly detest.

.6 **dislike**, disrelish 867.3.

.7 ADJS **hating, abhorrent**, loathing; averse to 867.8; disgusted 866.20.

.8 **hateful**, detestable 864.18; despiteful; unlikable 867.7.

## 931. LOVE

.1 NOUNS **love, affection, attachment, devotion**, phil(o)–, –phily; **fondness**, sentiment, weakness [informal], like, **liking**, fancy, shine [slang]; **passion**, tender feeling or passion, **ardor**, ardency, fervor, heart, flame; physical love, Amor, Eros, bodily love, libido, sexual love, sex 419; desire, yearning 634.1–5; lasciviousness 989.5; charity, *caritas* [L], brotherly love, Christian love, *agape* [Gk]; spiritual love, Platonic love; **adoration**, worship, hero worship; **regard**, admiration; idolization, idolism, idolatry; popular regard, popularity; faithful love, truelove; married love, conjugal love, uxoriousness; free love, free-lovism; **lovemaking** 932.

.2 "an insatiate thirst of enjoying a greedily desired object" [Montaigne], "the heart's immortal thirst to be completely known and all forgiven" [Henry Van Dyke], "Nature's second sun" [George Chapman], "tyrant sparing none" [Corneille], "the blood of life, the power of reunion of the separated" [Tillich], "the reflection of a man's own worthiness from other men" [Emerson], "a spiritual coupling of two souls" [Ben Jonson].

.3 **amorousness**, amativeness, lovingness, meltingness, **affection, affectionateness**, demonstrativeness; sexiness; goatishness, horniness [slang]; romanticism, **sentimentality**, susceptibility; lovesickness, lovelornness; ecstasy, rapture 857.7; enchantment 865.2.

.4 **infatuation**, infatuatedness, passing fancy; **crush** or mash or pash or case [all slang]; **puppy love** or calf love [both informal].

.5 **parental love**, natural affection, mother or maternal love, father or paternal love; filial love.

.6 **love affair, affair**, affair of the heart, **amour, romance**, romantic tie or bond, something between, liaison, entanglement, intrigue; flirtation, hanky-panky; triangle, eternal triangle; illicit love, forbidden love, adulterous affair, adultery, unfaithfulness, infidelity, cuckoldry.

.7 **lovability, likability, adorability**, sweetness, loveliness, lovesomeness, amiability, attractiveness 863.2, desirability, agreeability; **charm, appeal**, allurement 650; winsomeness, winning ways.

.8 (gods) Love, Cupid, Amor, Eros, Kama; (goddesses) Venus, Aphrodite, Astarte, Freya.

.9 (symbols) **cupid**, cupidon, amor, amourette, amoretto, *amorino* [Ital].

.10 **sweetheart**, sweetie [informal], sweet patootie [slang]; honey 932.5; date [informal]; steady [slang]; flirt, coquette; vampire, vamp; conquest, catch, captive.

.11 **lover, admirer**, adorer, amorist, –phile; infatuate, paramour, **suitor, wooer**, pursuer, follower.

.12 **beau, inamorato, swain**, man, gallant, cavalier, squire, esquire, *caballero* [Sp]; *amoroso, cavaliere servente* [both Ital]; sugar daddy [slang]; gigolo; **boyfriend** or **fellow** or young man or flame [all informal]; old man [informal]; love-maker; petter or necker [both slang]; seducer, lady-killer, ladies' man, sheik, philanderer; Lothario, Casanova, Romeo, Don Juan.

.13 **loved one, love, beloved, darling, dear, dear one**, dearly beloved, well-beloved, truelove, beloved object, **object of one's affections**, light of one's eye or life, light of love; crush.

.14 **lady love, inamorata**, *amorosa* [Ital], lady, mistress; old lady [informal]; **girl** or girl friend or best girl or dream girl [all informal], lass, lassie, jo [Scot], gill, jill, Dulcinea.

.15 **favorite**, preference; **darling**, idol, jewel, apple of one's eye, man after one's own heart; **pet**, fondling, cosset, minion; spoiled child or darling, *enfant gâté* [Fr]; teacher's pet; matinee idol.

.16 **fiancé, fiancée**, bride-to-be, affianced, betrothed, future, intended [informal].

.17 **loving couple**, soul mates, lovebirds, turtledoves, bill-and-cooers; Romeo and Juliet, Antony and Cleopatra, Tristan and Isolde, Pelléas and Mélisande, Abélard and Héloïse, Daphnis and Chloë, Aucassin and Nicolette.

.18 VERBS **love, be fond of,** be in love with, **care for, like, fancy,** have a fancy for, have eyes for [informal], go for [slang], take an interest in, **dote on** or **upon,** be sweet on [informal]; have a crush or mash or case on [slang]; be desperately in love, have it bad [slang], burn with love; be partial to, have a soft spot in one's heart for, have a weakness or fondness for.

.19 **cherish, hold dear,** prize, treasure; **admire, regard,** esteem, revere; **adore, idolize,** worship, dearly love, think worlds or the world of, love to distraction.

.20 **fall in love, lose one's heart, become enamored,** be smitten [informal]; take to, **take a liking** or **fancy to,** take a shine to or fall for [both slang], cotton to [informal], become attached to, bestow one's affections on; fall head and ears or head over heels in love, be swept off one's feet.

.21 **enamor, endear;** win one's heart, win the love or affections of, take the fancy of, make a hit with [slang]; **charm, becharm, infatuate,** hold in thrall, **fascinate,** attract, allure, **captivate,** bewitch, enrapture, carry away, sweep off one's feet, turn one's head, inflame with love; **seduce,** vamp [slang], draw on, tempt, tantalize.

.22 ADJS **beloved, loved, dear, darling, precious;** pet, favorite; **adored, admired,** esteemed, revered; **cherished,** prized, treasured, held dear; **well-liked,** popular; **well-beloved,** dearly beloved, dear to one's heart, after one's heart or own heart, dear as the apple of one's eye.

.23 **lovable, likable, adorable,** admirable, lovely, lovesome, sweet, winning, winsome; **charming** 650.7; angelic, seraphic; caressable, kissable; cuddlesome, cuddly.

.24 **amorous,** amatory, amative, erotic; **sexual** 419.26–30; loverly, loverlike; **passionate, ardent,** impassioned; desirous 634.21–28; lascivious 989.29.

.25 **loving,** lovesome, **fond, adoring, devoted, affectionate,** –philic, –philous; demonstrative, **romantic, sentimental, tender,** soft [informal], melting; lovelorn, lovesick, languishing; wifely, husbandly, conjugal, uxorious, faithful; parental, paternal, maternal, filial.

.26 **enamored, charmed,** becharmed, **fascinated, captivated,** bewitched, enraptured 857.23, enchanted 865.14; **infatuated,** infatuate; **smitten** [informal], heartsmitten.

.27 **in love,** head over heels in love, over head and ears in love.

.28 **fond of, enamored of,** partial to, **sweet on** or **upon** [informal], **stuck on** [slang], **in love with,** attached to, wedded to, devoted to, wrapped up in; **taken with,** smitten with [informal], struck with; gone on or far gone on or hipped on or keen about or **wild about** or **mad about** or crazy about [all informal]; nuts about [slang], have a thing about [informal].

.29 ADVS **lovingly, fondly, affectionately, tenderly,** dearly, **adoringly,** devotedly; amorously, ardently, passionately; with love, with affection, with all one's love.

## 932. LOVEMAKING, ENDEARMENT

.1 NOUNS **lovemaking,** dalliance, amorous dalliance, billing and cooing; **petting** or **necking** or spooning [all informal], smooching [slang], lollygagging [dial]; **fondling, caressing,** hugging, kissing; cuddling, snuggling, nestling, nuzzling; bundling; sexual intercourse 419.8.

.2 **embrace, hug,** squeeze, clasp, enfoldment, bear hug [informal].

.3 **kiss,** buss, smack, smooch [slang], **osculation.**

.4 **endearment;** caress, pat; sweet talk, soft words, honeyed words, sweet nothings; blandishments, artful endearments.

.5 **darling, dear,** deary, **sweetheart, sweetie, sweet,** sweets, sweetkins, **honey,** hon, **honey bunch,** honey child, sugar, love, lover, precious, precious heart, pet, petkins, babe, **baby, doll,** baby-doll, cherub, angel, chick, chickabiddy, buttercup, duck, duckling, lamb, lambkin, snookums.

.6 **courtship, courting, wooing;** court, suit, suing, amorous pursuit, addresses; gallantry; serenade.

.7 **proposal,** marriage proposal, offer of marriage; engagement 770.3.

.8 **flirtation, coquetry,** dalliance; flirtatiousness, coquettishness, coyness; sheep's eyes, goo-goo eyes [slang], amorous looks, coquettish glances, come-hither look; ogle, side-glance.

.9 **philandering,** philander, lady-killing [slang]; lechery, licentiousness, unchastity 989.

.10 **flirt, coquette,** gold digger or vamp [both slang]; strumpet, whore 989.14–16.

.11 **philanderer,** philander, woman chaser, **ladies' man,** heartbreaker, masher, ladykiller, wolf, skirt chaser, man on the make *or* make-out artist [both slang]; libertine, lecher, seducer 989.10–12.

.12 **love letter,** billet-doux, mash note [slang]; valentine.

.13 VERBS **make love,** bill and coo; **pet** *or* **neck** *or* spoon [all informal], make out [slang], smooch [slang], lollygag [dial]; dally, toy, trifle, wanton; sweet-talk [dial], whisper sweet nothings; copulate 419.23.

.14 **caress, pet, pat; fondle,** dandle, coddle, cocker, cosset; pat on the head *or* cheek, chuck under the chin.

.15 **cuddle, snuggle, nestle,** nuzzle; lap; bundle.

.16 **embrace, hug, clasp, press, squeeze** [informal], fold, **enfold,** bosom, embosom, put *or* throw one's arms around, take to one's arms, fold to the heart, press to the bosom.

.17 **kiss, osculate,** buss, smack, smooch [slang]; blow a kiss.

.18 **flirt, coquet;** gold-dig; **philander,** gallivant, run around, play around; **make eyes at, ogle,** eye, cast coquettish glances, cast sheep's eyes at, make goo-goo eyes at [slang], *faire les yeux doux* [Fr], look sweet upon [informal].

.19 **court, woo,** sue, press one's suit, **pay court** *or* **suit to,** make suit to, pay one's court to, address, pay one's addresses to, pay attention to, lay siege to, throw oneself at the head of; **pursue,** follow; chase [slang]; set one's cap at *or* for [informal]; serenade; spark [informal], squire, esquire, beau, sweetheart [informal], swain.

.20 **propose, pop the question** [informal], ask for one's hand; become engaged 770.6.

.21 ADJS amatory, amative 931.24; sexual 419.26–30; caressive; **flirtatious, flirty; coquettish,** coy.

## 933. MARRIAGE

.1 NOUNS **marriage, matrimony, wedlock,** –gamy; holy matrimony, holy wedlock, match, union, matrimonial union, alliance, "a world-without-end bargain" [Shakespeare], "a dignified and commodious sacrament" [T. S. Eliot], marriage sacrament, sacrament of matrimony, bond of matrimony, wedding knot, conjugal bond *or* tie *or* knot, nuptial bond *or* tie *or* knot; married state *or* status, wedded state *or* status, wedded bliss, weddedness, wifehood, husbandhood, spousehood; coverture, cohabitation; bed, marriage bed, bridebed; intermarriage, mixed marriage, interfaith mar-

riage, interracial marriage; miscegenation; misalliance, *mésalliance* [Fr], ill-assorted marriage.

.2 (kinds of marriage) **monogamy,** monogyny, monandry; serial polygamy; digamy, deuterogamy; **bigamy;** trigamy, **polygamy,** polygyny, polyandry; morganatic marriage, left-handed marriage; marriage of convenience, *mariage de convenance* [Fr]; love match; levirate, leviration; beena marriage; companionate marriage, trial marriage; common-law marriage; picture marriage; concubinage; homosexual marriage.

.3 **marriageability,** nubility, ripeness.

.4 **wedding, marriage,** marriage ceremony, nuptial mass; church wedding, civil wedding, civil ceremony; espousement, bridal; banns; **nuptials,** spousals, espousals, hymeneal rites; *chuppah* [Heb], wedding canopy; wedding song, marriage song, nuptial song, prothalamium, epithalamium, epithalamy, hymen, hymeneal; wedding veil, saffron veil *or* robe; bridechamber, bridal suite, nuptial apartment; **honeymoon;** forced marriage, shotgun wedding; Gretna Green wedding, elopement.

.5 **wedding party;** wedding attendant, usher; **best man,** bridesman, groomsman; paranymph; **bridesmaid,** bridemaiden, maid *or* matron of honor.

.6 **newlywed; bridegroom, groom; bride,** plighted bride, blushing bride; war bride, GI bride [slang]; honeymooner.

.7 **spouse, mate,** yokemate, partner, consort, **better half** [informal], "bone of my bones, and flesh of my flesh" [Bible].

.8 **husband, married man,** man, benedict, goodman [archaic], old man [slang].

.9 **wife, married woman,** wedded wife, goodwife *or* goody [both archaic], squaw, woman, lady, matron, old lady *or* old woman [both slang], feme, feme covert, **better half** [informal], **helpmate,** helpmeet, rib, wife of one's bosom; wife in name only; wife in all but name, concubine, common-law wife.

.10 **married couple,** wedded pair, **man and wife,** husband and wife, man and woman, *vir et uxor* [L], one flesh; newlyweds, **bride and groom.**

.11 **harem, seraglio,** serai, gynaeceum; zenana, purdah.

.12 **monogamist,** monogynist; **bigamist;** digamist, deuterogamist; trigamist; **polygamist,** polygynist, polyandrist; Mormon; Bluebeard.

.13 **matchmaker, marriage broker,** matrimonial agent, *shadchen* [Yid]; matrimonial agency *or* bureau.

.14 (god) Hymen; (goddesses) Hera, Teleia; Juno, Pronuba; Frigg.

.15 VERBS (join in marriage) **marry,** wed, nuptial, **join, unite, hitch** [slang], **splice** [informal], couple, match, make *or* arrange a match, join together, **unite in marriage,** join *or* unite in holy wedlock, tie the nuptial *or* wedding knot, make one; give away, give in marriage; marry off, find a mate for, find a husband *or* wife for.

.16 (get married) **marry, wed,** contract matrimony, mate, couple, espouse, wive, **take to wife,** take to oneself a wife, **get hitched** [slang], be spliced [informal], become one, be made one, pair off, give one's hand to, bestow one's hand upon, lead to the altar, take for better or for worse; remarry, rewed; intermarry, interwed, miscegenate.

.17 **honeymoon,** go on a honeymoon.

.18 **cohabit,** live together, live as man and wife, share one's bed and board.

.19 ADJS **matrimonial, marital, conjugal, connubial, nuptial,** wedded, married, hymeneal; epithalamic; spousal, husbandly, wifely; bridal; –gamous.

.20 **monogamous,** monogynous, monandrous; **bigamous,** digamous; **polygamous,** polygynous, polyandrous; morganatic; miscegenetic.

.21 **marriageable,** nubile, ripe, of age, of marriageable age.

.22 **married, wedded,** one, one bone and one flesh, mated, matched, coupled, partnered, paired.

## 934. CELIBACY

.1 NOUNS **celibacy, singleness,** single blessedness, single state *or* condition; unwed state *or* condition; **bachelorhood,** bachelordom, bachelorism, bachelorship; **spinsterhood,** maidenhood, maidenhead, **virginity,** maiden *or* virgin state; **monasticism,** monachism; misogamy, misogyny; continence 988.3.

.2 **celibate,** *célibataire* [Fr]; monk, monastic, priest, nun; misogamist, misogynist; unmarried, single [informal].

.3 **bachelor,** bach *or* old bach [both slang], confirmed bachelor, **single man.**

.4 **spinster,** spinstress, **old maid,** maid, maiden, bachelor girl, single girl, single woman, lone woman, maiden lady, feme sole; **virgin,** vestal, vestal virgin; parthen(o)–.

.5 VERBS **be unmarried, be single, live alone,** enjoy single blessedness, **bach** *or* **bach it** [both slang], keep bachelor quarters, keep one's freedom.

.6 ADJS **celibate; monastic,** monachal, **monkish;** misogamic, misogynous.

.7 **unmarried, unwedded, unwed, single,** sole, spouseless, wifeless, husbandless; **bachelorly,** bachelorlike; **spinsterly,** spinsterish, spinsterlike; **old-maidish,** old-maidenish; maiden, maidenly; virgin, virginal.

## 935. DIVORCE, WIDOWHOOD

.1 NOUNS **divorce,** divorcement, grasswidowhood, **separation,** legal *or* judicial separation, separate maintenance; interlocutory decree; dissolution of marriage; annulment, decree of nullity; broken marriage, broken home.

.2 **divorcée,** divorced person, divorced man, *divorcé* [Fr], divorced woman, *divorcée* [Fr]; divorcer; grass widow, grass widower.

.3 **widowhood,** viduity [archaic]; **widowerhood,** widowership; weeds, widow's weeds.

.4 **widow,** widow woman [dial], relict; dowager, queen dowager, etc.; **widower,** widowman [dial].

.5 VERBS **divorce, separate,** part, split up [informal], unmarry, put away, obtain a divorce, come to a parting of the ways, untie the knot, sue for divorce, file suit for divorce; grant a divorce, grant a final decree; grant an annulment, grant a decree of nullity, annul a marriage, put asunder.

.6 **widow,** bereave.

.7 ADJS widowly, widowish, widowlike; **widowed,** widowered; **divorced;** separated, legally separated.

## 936. COURTESY

.1 NOUNS **courtesy,** courteousness, **politeness, civility,** amenity, agreeableness, urbanity, comity, affability; **graciousness,** gracefulness; complaisance; **thoughtfulness, considerateness,** tactfulness, tact, solicitousness, solicitude; **respect,** respectfulness, deference.

.2 **gallantry,** gallantness, **chivalry,** chivalrousness, knightliness; courtliness, courtly politeness, *noblesse oblige* [Fr].

.3 **mannerliness, manners, good manners,** excellent *or* exquisite manners, good *or* po lite deportment, good *or* polite behavior, *bienséance* [Fr]; *savoir-faire, savoir-vivre* [both Fr]; correctness, correctitude.

.4 **good breeding, breeding; refinement, polish, culture, cultivation; gentility,** gentleness, genteelness, elegance; **gentlemanliness,** gentlemanlikeness, ladylikeness.

.5 **suavity, suaveness, smoothness, smugness,** blandness, **unctuousness,** oiliness, **glibness,** fulsomeness; sweet talk, fair words, soft words *or* tongue, sweet *or* honeyed words *or* tongue, incense; soft soap *or* butter [both informal].

.6 **courtesy, civility,** amenity, urbanity, attention, polite act, act of courtesy *or* politeness, graceful gesture; favor 938.7.

.7 **amenities, civilities,** gentilities, graces, elegancies; dignities; **formalities,** ceremonies, rites, rituals.

.8 **regards, compliments, respects,** *égards, devoirs* [both Fr]; **best wishes,** one's best, good wishes, best regards, kind *or* kindest regards, love, best love; greetings 925.3; remembrances, kind remembrances; compliments of the season.

.9 **gallant, cavalier,** chevalier, **knight,** "a verray parfit gentil knight" [Chaucer].

.10 "the very pink of courtesy" [Shakespeare], "the very pineapple of politeness" [R. B. Sheridan], "the mirror of all courtesy" [Shakespeare].

.11 VERBS **mind one's manners,** mind one's P's and Q's [informal]; keep a civil tongue in one's head; mend one's manners; observe etiquette, observe *or* follow protocol.

.12 **pay one's respects to, make one's compliments to,** present oneself, pay attentions to, do service, wait on *or* upon.

.13 **give one's regards, give one's compliments,** give one's love, give one's best regards, give one's best, send one's regards *or* compliments, etc.; wish one joy, wish one luck, bid Godspeed.

.14 ADJS **courteous, polite, civil, urbane, gracious,** graceful, agreeable, affable, fair; complaisant; obliging, accommodating; **thoughtful, considerate,** tactful, solicitous; respectful, deferential, attentive.

.15 **gallant, chivalrous,** chivalric, **knightly; courtly; formal,** ceremonious; old-fashioned, old-world.

.16 **mannerly, well-mannered,** good-mannered, **well-behaved,** well-spoken; **correct,** correct in one's manners *or* behavior.

.17 **well-bred,** highbred, **well-brought-up;** cultivated, cultured, polished, refined, gen-

teel, **gentle; gentlemanly,** gentlemanlike, ladylike.

.18 **suave, smooth, smug,** bland, **glib,** unctuous, oily, soapy *or* buttery [both informal], fulsome, ingratiating, disarming; suave-spoken, fine-spoken, fair-spoken, soft-spoken, smooth-spoken, smooth-tongued, oily-tongued, honey-tongued, honey-mouthed.

.19 ADVS **courteously, politely, civilly,** urbanely, mannerly; **gallantly, chivalrously,** courtly, knightly; **graciously,** gracefully, with a good grace; complaisantly, complacently; obligingly, accommodatingly; respectfully, attentively, deferentially.

## 937. DISCOURTESY

.1 NOUNS **discourtesy,** discourteousness; **impoliteness,** unpoliteness; **rudeness, incivility,** inurbanity, **ungraciousness, ungallantness,** uncourtliness, ungentlemanliness, **unmannerliness,** mannerlessness, bad *or* ill manners, **ill breeding,** conduct unbecoming a gentleman, caddishness; inconsiderateness, unsolicitousness, tactlessness, insensitivity; grossness, gross behavior, vulgarity, offensiveness, coarseness, crudeness, loutishness.

.2 disrespectfulness 965.1; **insolence** 913.

.3 **gruffness, brusqueness,** *brusquerie* [Fr], **curtness,** shortness, sharpness, abruptness, bluntness, brashness; **harshness,** roughness, severity; truculence, aggressiveness 797.15; **surliness,** crustiness, bearishness, beastliness, churlishness, **boorishness,** nastiness.

.4 ADJS **discourteous,** uncourteous; **impolite,** unpolite; **rude, uncivil, ungracious, ungallant,** uncourtly, inaffable, uncomplaisant, unaccommodating; disrespectful 965.5; **insolent** 913.8.

.5 **unmannerly,** unmannered, mannerless, **ill-mannered, ill-behaved,** ill-conditioned.

.6 **ill-bred, ungenteel,** ungentle, caddish; inconsiderate, unsolicitous, tactless, insensitive; **ungentlemanly,** ungentlemanlike; **unladylike,** unfeminine; **vulgar, boorish, unrefined** 898.10–13, offensive, coarse, crude, loutish, louty, nasty.

.7 **gruff, brusque, curt,** short, sharp, snippy [informal], abrupt, **blunt,** bluff, brash, cavalier; **harsh,** rough, severe; truculent, aggressive 797.25; **surly,** crusty, bearish, beastly, churlish.

.8 ADVS **discourteously, impolitely, rudely,** uncivilly, ungraciously, ungallantly, ungenteelly, caddishly; inconsiderately, unsolicitously, tactlessly, insensitively.

.9 gruffly, brusquely, curtly, shortly, sharply, snippily [informal], abruptly, bluntly, bluffly, brashly, cavalierly; harshly, crustily, bearishly, churlishly, boorishly, nastily.

## 938. KINDNESS, BENEVOLENCE

.1 NOUNS kindness, kindliness, kindly disposition; benignity, benignancy; goodness, niceness; graciousness; kindheartedness, warmheartedness, softheartedness, tenderheartedness, affectionateness, warmth, goodness or warmth of heart, loving kindness, "milk of human kindness" [Shakespeare]; soul of kindness, heart of gold; brotherhood, fellow feeling, sympathy, compassion, fraternal feeling, feeling of kinship; humaneness, humanity.

.2 good nature, good humor, good disposition, good temper, sweetness, sweet temper or nature, goodnaturedness, goodhumoredness, goodtemperedness, bonhomie; amiability, affability, geniality, cordiality; gentleness, mildness, lenity.

.3 considerateness, consideration, thoughtfulness, mindfulness, heedfulness, regardfulness, attentiveness, solicitousness, solicitude, thought, regard, concern, delicacy, tact, tactfulness; indulgence, toleration, leniency 759; complaisance, accommodatingness, helpfulness, obligingness, agreeableness.

.4 benevolence, benevolentness, benevolent disposition, well-disposedness, beneficence, charity, charitableness, philanthropy; altruism, philanthropism, humanitarianism, welfarism, do-goodism; utilitarianism, Benthamism, greatest good of the greatest number; goodwill, grace, brotherly love, Christian charity or love, caritas [L], love of mankind, good will to or toward man, love, agape [Gk], flower power; BOMFOG (brotherhood of man and fatherhood of God); bigheartedness, largeheartedness, greatheartedness; generosity 853; giving 818.

.5 welfare; welfare work, social service, social welfare, social work; child welfare, etc.; commonweal, public welfare; welfare state, welfare statism, welfarism.

.6 benevolences, philanthropies, charities; works, good works.

.7 kindness, favor, mercy, benefit, benefaction, benevolence, benignity, blessing, service, turn, good turn, good or kind deed, mitzvah [Heb], office, good or kind offices, obligation, grace, act of grace, courtesy, act of kindness, kindly act, labor of love.

.8 philanthropist, altruist, benevolist, humanitarian, man of good will, do-gooder, well-doer, power for good; welfare worker, social worker; welfare statist; almsgiver, almoner; Robin Hood.

.9 VERBS be kind, be good or nice to, show kindness to; treat well, do right by; favor, oblige, accommodate.

.10 be considerate, consider, respect, regard, think of, be thoughtful of, have consideration or regard for.

.11 be benevolent, bear good will, wish well, have one's heart in the right place; practice the golden rule, do as you would be done by, do unto others as you would have others do unto you; make love, not war.

.12 do a favor, do good, do a kindness, do a good turn, do a good or kind deed, use one's good offices, render a service, confer a benefit; benefit, help 785.11.

.13 ADJS kind, kindly, kindly-disposed; benign, benignant; good, nice, decent; gracious; kindhearted, warm, warmhearted, softhearted, tenderhearted, tender, loving, affectionate; sympathetic, sympathizing, compassionate; brotherly, fraternal; humane, human; Christian, Christly, Christlike.

.14 good-natured, well-natured, good-humored, good-tempered, bonhomous, sweet, sweet-tempered; amiable, affable, genial, cordial; gentle, mild; easy, easy-natured, easy to get along with, agreeable.

.15 benevolent, charitable, beneficent, philanthropic, altruistic, humanitarian; bighearted, largehearted, greathearted, freehearted; generous 853.4; almsgiving, eleemosynary; welfare, welfarist(ic), welfare statist.

.16 considerate, thoughtful, mindful, heedful, regardful, solicitous, attentive, delicate, tactful, mindful of others; complaisant, accommodating, accommodative, helpful, agreeable, obliging, indulgent, tolerant, lenient 759.7,8.

.17 well-meaning, well-meant, well-affected, well-disposed, well-intentioned.

.18 ADVS kindly, benignly, benignantly; good, nicely, well, favorably; kindheartedly, warmly, warmheartedly, softheartedly, tenderheartedly; humanely, humanly.

.19 good-naturedly, good-humoredly, bonhomously; sweetly; amiably, affably, genially, cordially; graciously, in good part.

.20 benevolently, beneficently, charitably

philanthropically, altruistically, bigheartedly, with good will.

.21 **considerately, thoughtfully,** mindfully, heedfully, regardfully, tactfully, solicitously, attentively; well-meaningly, well-disposedly.

## 939. UNKINDNESS, MALEVOLENCE

.1 NOUNS **unkindness, unkindliness;** unbenignity, unbenignness; **unamiability,** uncordiality, ungraciousness, inhospitality, inhospitableness, ungeniality, unaffectionateness; unsympatheticness, uncompassionateness; disagreeableness.

.2 **unbenevolentness, uncharitableness,** ungenerousness.

.3 **inconsiderateness, inconsideration, unthoughtfulness,** unmindfulness, unheedfulness, **thoughtlessness, heedlessness,** respectlessness, disregardfulness, forgetfulness; **unhelpfulness,** unobligingness, unaccommodatingness.

.4 **malevolence, ill will,** bad will, bad blood, bad temper, ill nature, ill-disposedness, ill *or* evil disposition; evil eye, *malocchio* [Ital], whammy [slang], blighting glance.

.5 **malice, maliciousness,** maleficence; **malignance** *or* **malignancy, malignity; meanness** *or* orneriness *or* cussedness *or* bitchiness [all informal], hatefulness, nastiness, invidiousness; **wickedness,** iniquitousness 981.4; deviltry, devilry, devilment; malice prepense *or* aforethought, evil intent; **harmfulness, noxiousness** 675.5.

.6 **spite,** despite; **spitefulness,** cattiness; gloating pleasure, unwholesome *or* unholy joy, *Schadenfreude* [Ger].

.7 **rancor, virulence,** venomousness, **venom,** vitriol, gall.

.8 **causticity,** causticness, corrosiveness, mordancy, mordacity, bitingness; **acrimony,** asperity, acidity, acidness, acidulousness, acridity, acerbity, **bitterness,** tartness; sharpness, keenness, incisiveness, piercingness, stabbingness, trenchancy; "sharp-toothed unkindness" [Shakespeare].

.9 **harshness, roughness,** ungentleness; **severity,** austerity, hardness, sternness, grimness, inclemency; stringency, astringency.

.10 **heartlessness, unfeeling,** unnaturalness, unresponsiveness, insensitivity, coldness, **coldheartedness,** coldbloodedness; **hardheartedness,** hardness, hardness of heart, heart of stone; **callousness,** callosity; obduracy; **pitilessness, unmercifulness** 945.1.

.11 **cruelty,** cruelness, sadistic cruelty, sadism, wanton cruelty; **ruthlessness** 945.1; inhumaneness, **inhumanity,** atrociousness;

brutality, brutalness, brutishness, bestiality, beastliness, animality; **barbarity,** barbarousness, vandalism; **savagery, viciousness,** violence, fiendishness, truculence; fierceness, ferociousness, ferocity; bloodthirst, bloodthirstiness, bloodlust, bloodiness, bloody-mindedness, sanguineousness; cannibalism.

.12 (brutal act) **atrocity,** cruelty, brutality, barbarity, inhumanity.

.13 **bad deed, disservice,** ill service, **ill turn,** bad turn.

.14 ADJS **unkind, unkindly,** ill; **unbenign,** unbenignant; **unamiable,** disagreeable, **uncordial, ungracious,** inhospitable, ungenial, unaffectionate, unloving; **unsympathetic,** unsympathizing, **uncompassionate,** uncompassioned.

.15 **unbenevolent,** unbeneficent, **uncharitable,** unphilanthropic, unaltruistic, ungenerous.

.16 **inconsiderate, unthoughtful,** unmindful, unheedful, disregardful, **thoughtless,** heedless, respectless, mindless, unthinking, forgetful; uncomplaisant; **unhelpful, unaccommodating, unobliging,** disobliging, uncooperative.

.17 **malevolent, ill-disposed,** evil-disposed, ill-natured, ill-affected, ill-conditioned, ill-intentioned.

.18 **malicious,** maleficent, malefic; **malignant,** malign; **mean** *or* **ornery** *or* cussed *or* bitchy [all informal], hateful, nasty, baleful, invidious; **wicked,** iniquitous 981.16; **harmful, noxious** 675.5.

.19 **spiteful,** despiteful; **catty,** cattish.

.20 **rancorous, virulent,** vitriolic; **venomous,** venenate, envenomed.

.21 **caustic,** mordant, mordacious, corrosive, corroding; **acrimonious,** acrid, acid, acidic, acidulous, acidulent, acerb, acerbate, acerbic, **bitter,** tart; **sharp,** keen, incisive, trenchant, **cutting,** penetrating, piercing, biting, **stinging,** stabbing, **scathing, scorching,** withering.

.22 **harsh, rough,** rugged, ungentle; **severe,** austere, **stringent,** astringent, hard, stern, dour, grim, inclement, unsparing.

.23 **heartless, unfeeling,** unnatural, unresponsive, insensitive, **cold,** cold of heart, **coldhearted, coldblooded; hard, hardened,** hard of heart, **hardhearted,** stonyhearted, marblehearted, flinthearted; **callous,** calloused; obdurate; **unmerciful** 945.3.

.24 **cruel,** cruel-hearted, sadistic; **ruthless** 945.3; **brutal,** brutish, brute, bestial, beastly, animal; subhuman, dehumanized, brutalized; sharkish, wolfish, slavering; **barbarous**, barbaric, uncivilized, unchristian; **savage, ferocious**, feral, **vicious, fierce, atrocious**, truculent, fell; **inhumane**, inhuman, unhuman; fiendish, fiendlike; demoniac *or* demoniacal, diabolic(al), devilish, satanic, hellish, infernal; **bloodthirsty**, bloody-minded, bloody, sanguineous, sanguinary; cannibalistic, anthropophagous; murderous 409.24; Draconian, Tartarean.

.25 ADVS unkindly, ill; **unbenignly**, unbenignantly; **unamiably**, disagreeably, uncordially, ungraciously, inhospitably, ungenially, unaffectionately, unlovingly; unsympathetically, uncompassionately.

.26 **unbenevolently**, unbeneficently, **uncharitably**, unphilanthropically, unaltruistically, ungenerously.

.27 **inconsiderately**, unthoughtfully, thoughtlessly, heedlessly, unthinkingly; unhelpfully, uncooperatively.

.28 **malevolently, maliciously**, maleficently, **malignantly; meanly** *or* ornerily *or* cussedly *or* bitchily [all informal], hatefully, nastily, invidiously, balefully; **wickedly**, iniquitously 981.19; **harmfully, noxiously** 675.15, **spitefully**, in spite; with bad intent, with malice prepense *or* aforethought.

.29 **rancorously, virulently**, vitriolically; venomously, venenately.

.30 **caustically**, mordantly, mordaciously, corrosively, corrodingly; **acrimoniously**, acridly, acidly, acerbly, acerbically, **bitterly**, tartly; **sharply**, keenly, incisively, trenchantly, **cuttingly**, penetratingly, piercingly, bitingly, **stingingly**, stabbingly, **scathingly**, scorchingly, witheringly.

.31 **harshly**, roughly; **severely**, austerely, stringently, sternly, grimly, inclemently, unsparingly.

.32 **heartlessly, unfeelingly, callously**, cold-heartedly; cold-bloodedly, **in cold blood**.

.33 **cruelly, brutally**, brutishly, bestially, subhumanly, sharkishly, wolfishly, slaveringly; **barbarously, savagely, ferociously**, ferally, **viciously**, fiercely, **atrociously**, truculently; **ruthlessly** 945.4; **inhumanely**, inhumanly, unhumanly; fiendishly, diabolically, devilishly.

### 940. MISANTHROPY

.1 NOUNS **misanthropy**, misanthropism, Timonism, cynicism, antisociality, antisocial sentiments *or* attitudes; unsociability 923.

.2 **misanthrope**, misanthropist; man-hater,

cynic; misogynist, woman-hater; sexist; Alceste, Timon.

.3 ADJS **misanthropic**, Timonistic, **antisocial**; unsociable 923.5,6; man-hating, cynical; misogynous, woman-hating; sexist.

### 941. PUBLIC SPIRIT

.1 NOUNS **public spirit**, social consciousness; **civism**, citizenship, citizenism.

.2 **patriotism**, love of country; "the last refuge of a scoundrel" [Samuel Johnson]; **nationalism**, nationality, ultranationalism; Americanism, Anglicism, Briticism, etc.; **chauvinism, jingoism**, overpatriotism; patriotics, flag waving.

.3 **patriot;** nationalist; ultranationalist; **chauvinist**, chauvin, **jingo**, jingoist; patrioteer [informal], flag waver, superpatriot, hard hat [informal], hundred-percenter, hundred-percent American.

.4 ADJS **public-spirited, civic; patriotic; nationalistic;** ultranationalist, ultranationalistic; overpatriotic, superpatriotic, flag-waving, **chauvinist(ic)**, jingoist(ic).

### 942. BENEFACTOR

.1 NOUNS **benefactor**, benefactress, **benefiter**, succorer, befriender; ministrant, ministering angel; Samaritan, **good Samaritan; helper**, aider, assister, help, aid, helping hand, "a very present help in time of trouble" [Bible]; jack-at-a-pinch; **patron, backer** 787.9; **good person** 985.

.2 **savior, redeemer**, deliverer, **liberator**, rescuer, freer, **emancipator**, manumitter.

### 943. EVILDOER

.1 NOUNS **evildoer, wrongdoer**, worker of ill *or* evil, **malefactor**, malfeasant, malfeasor, misfeasor, malevolent, public enemy, **sinner, villain**, transgressor, delinquent; **criminal**, outlaw, felon, **crook** [informal], lawbreaker, gangster *or* mobster [both informal], racketeer, thief; **bad person** 986; deceiver 619.

.2 **troublemaker, mischief-maker;** agitator 648.11.

.3 **ruffian**, rough, bravo, **rowdy, thug**, desperado, cutthroat, kill-crazy animal, mad dog; gunman; **bully, bullyboy, bucko** devil, hellcat, hell-raiser; killer 409.11.

.4 [slang *or* informal terms] **roughneck, tough**, bruiser, mug, mugger, ugly customer, **hoodlum, hood, hooligan**, gorilla, plug-ugly, strong-arm man, muscle man, **goon;** gun, gunsel, trigger man, rodman, torpedo, hatchet man; hellion, terror, holy terror.

.5 savage, barbarian, brute, beast, animal, tiger, shark, hyena; wild man; cannibal, man-eater, anthropophagite; **wrecker, vandal,** nihilist, destroyer.

.6 **monster, fiend,** fiend from hell, **demon, devil,** devil incarnate, hellhound, hellkite; **vampire,** lamia, **harpy, ghoul;** werewolf, ape-man; ogre, ogress; Frankenstein's monster.

.7 **witch, hag, vixen,** hellhag, hellcat, she-devil, virago, termagant, grimalkin, Jezebel, beldam, she-wolf, tigress, wildcat, bitch-kitty [slang], siren, fury.

## 944. PITY

.1 NOUNS **pity, sympathy,** feeling, fellow feeling in suffering, commiseration, condolence; **compassion, mercy,** ruth, humanity; **clemency,** quarter, reprieve, mitigation, relief 886, favor, grace; **leniency,** forbearance 759.1; **kindness, benevolence** 938; pardon, **forgiveness** 1007.1; self-pity; **pathos.**

.2 **compassionateness, mercifulness,** ruthfulness, softheartedness, tenderness, lenity, gentleness; bowels of compassion *or* mercy; bleeding heart.

.3 VERBS **pity, be** *or* **feel sorry for,** feel sorrow for; **commiserate,** compassionate; sympathize, **sympathize with,** feel for, weep for, lament for, bleed, bleed for, have one's heart bleed for, condole with 946.2.

.4 **have pity, have mercy upon, take pity on** *or* **upon;** melt, thaw; relent, forbear, relax, give quarter, spare, temper the wind to the shorn lamb, go easy on *or* let up on [both informal], reprieve, pardon, forgive 1007.4; put out of one's misery; be cruel to be kind.

.5 (excite pity) **move, touch,** affect, reach, **soften,** melt, melt the heart, appeal to one's better feelings; sadden, grieve 872.17,18.

.6 **beg for mercy,** ask for pity, cry for quarter, beg for one's life; fall on one's knees, throw oneself at the feet of.

.7 ADJS **pitying, sympathetic,** sympathizing, commiserative, condolent, understanding; **compassionate, merciful,** ruthful, **clement,** gentle, soft, melting, bleeding, tender, **tenderhearted,** softhearted, warmhearted; **humane, human;** lenient, forbearant 759.7,8; charitable 938.15.

.8 **pitiful, pitiable, pathetic, piteous,** touching, moving, affecting, heartrending, grievous, doleful 872.26.

.9 self-pitying, self-pitiful, sorry for oneself.

.10 ADVS **pitifully,** sympathetically; **compassionately, mercifully,** ruthfully, clemently, humanely.

## 945. PITILESSNESS

.1 NOUNS **pitilessness, unmercifulness, uncompassionateness,** unsympatheticness, mercilessness, **ruthlessness,** unfeelingness, inclemency, relentlessness, inexorableness, unyieldingness 626.2, unforgivingness; **heartlessness,** hardness, flintiness, harshness, **cruelty** 939.10,11; remorselessness, unremorsefulness; short shrift, tender mercies.

.2 VERBS **show no mercy,** give no quarter, turn a deaf ear to, claim one's pound of flesh, harden one's heart.

.3 ADJS **pitiless, unpitying, unpitiful; unsympathetic,** unsympathizing; **uncompassionate,** uncompassioned; **merciless, unmerciful,** without mercy, **ruthless,** dog-eat-dog; unfeeling, bowelless, inclement, relentless, inexorable, unyielding 626.9, unforgiving; **heartless,** hard, flinty, harsh, **cruel** 939.23,24; remorseless, unremorseful.

.4 ADVS **pitilessly,** unsympathetically; mercilessly, **unmercifully, ruthlessly,** uncompassionately, inclemently, relentlessly, inexorably, unyieldingly, unforgivingly; **heartlessly,** harshly, cruelly 939.33; remorselessly, unremorsefully.

## 946. CONDOLENCE

.1 NOUNS **condolence, condolement, consolation,** comfort, balm, soothing words, **commiseration, sympathy,** sharing of grief *or* sorrow.

.2 VERBS **condole with, commiserate, sympathize with,** feel with, express sympathy for, send one's condolences; **console,** wipe away one's tears, comfort, speak soothing words, bring balm to one's sorrow; sorrow with, share *or* help bear one's grief, grieve *or* weep with, grieve *or* weep for, share one's sorrow, "weep with them that weep" [Bible].

.3 ADJS condolent, consolatory, comforting, commiserative, **sympathetic.**

## 947. FORGIVENESS

.1 NOUNS **forgiveness, forgivingness;** unresentfulness, unrevengefulness; **condonation,** overlooking, disregard; patience 861; **indulgence, forbearance,** longanimity, long-suffering; **kindness, benevolence** 938; **magnanimity** 979.2; **tolerance** 526.4.

.2 **pardon,** excuse, sparing, **amnesty,** indemnity, exemption, immunity, reprieve, grace; **absolution**, shrift, remission, remission of sin; redemption; **exoneration, exculpation** 1007.1.

.3 VERBS **forgive, pardon, excuse,** give *or* grant forgiveness, spare; amnesty, grant amnesty to, grant immunity *or* exemption; **absolve,** remit, give absolution, shrive, grant remission; **exonerate, exculpate** 1007.4; blot out one's sins, wipe the slate clean.

.4 **condone, overlook, disregard, ignore,** take [informal], pass over, let it go [informal], give one another chance, let one off this time *or* let one off easy [both informal], close *or* shut one's eyes to, **blink** *or* **wink at,** connive at; allow for, make allowances for; bear with, endure, regard with indulgence; pocket the affront, leave unavenged, turn the other cheek.

.5 **forget, forgive and forget,** dismiss from one's thoughts, think no more of, not give it another *or* a second thought, let it go [informal], let it pass, **let bygones be bygones;** write off, charge off, charge to experience; bury the hatchet.

.6 ADJS **forgiving,** sparing, placable, conciliatory; **kind, benevolent** 938.13–17; **magnanimous, generous** 979.6; **patient** 861.9,10; **forbearing,** longanimous, long-suffering; unresentful, unrevengeful; **tolerant** 526.11, more in sorrow than in anger.

.7 **forgiven, pardoned, excused,** spared, amnestied, reprieved, remitted; overlooked, disregarded, forgotten, not held against one, wiped away, removed from the record, blotted, canceled, **condoned,** indulged; absolved, shriven; redeemed; exonerated, exculpated, acquitted; unresented; unavenged, unrevenged; uncondemned.

## 948. CONGRATULATION

.1 NOUNS **congratulation,** gratulation, **felicitation,** blessing, **compliment,** pat on the back; good wishes, best wishes.

.2 VERBS **congratulate,** gratulate, **felicitate,** bless, **compliment,** tender *or* offer one's congratulations *or* felicitations *or* compliments; shake one's hand, pat on the back; **rejoice with,** wish one joy.

.3 ADJS **congratulatory,** congratulant, congratulational; gratulatory, gratulant; **complimentary.**

.4 INTERJS **congratulations!,** take a bow!; nice going!, bravo!, well done!, right on! [slang], good show! [Brit].

## 949. GRATITUDE

.1 NOUNS **gratitude, gratefulness, thankfulness, appreciation, appreciativeness;** obligation, sense of obligation *or* indebtedness.

.2 **thanks, thanksgiving,** praise, hymn, paean, benediction; grace, prayer of thanks; **thank-you; acknowledgment,** cognizance, **credit,** crediting, recognition; thank offering.

.3 VERBS **be grateful, be obliged,** feel *or* be *or* lie under an obligation, be obligated *or* indebted, be in the debt of; **be thankful,** thank God, thank *or* bless one's stars; **appreciate,** be appreciative of; never forget; overflow with gratitude.

.4 **thank,** bless; give one's thanks, **express one's appreciation; offer thanks, give thanks,** tender *or* render thanks, return thanks; acknowledge, make acknowledgments of, credit, recognize, give *or* render credit *or* recognition; fall on one's knees.

.5 ADJS **grateful, thankful; appreciative,** sensible; **obliged, much obliged,** beholden, indebted to, crediting, under obligation, acknowledging, cognizant of.

.6 INTERJS **thanks!, thank you!,** I thank you!, *merci!* [Fr], *¡gracias!* [Sp], *grazie!* [Ital], *danke!, danke schön!* [both Ger], gramercy!, **much obliged!,** many thanks!, thank you kindly!; I thank you very much!, *merci beaucoup!, je vous remercie beaucoup!* [both Fr].

## 950. INGRATITUDE

.1 NOUNS **ingratitude, ungratefulness, unthankfulness,** thanklessness, unappreciation, **unappreciativeness;** nonacknowledgment, nonrecognition, denial of due *or* proper credit; "benefits forgot" [Shakespeare]; grudging *or* halfhearted thanks.

.2 **ingrate,** ungrateful wretch.

.3 VERBS **be ungrateful,** feel no obligation, **not appreciate,** owe one no thanks; look a gift horse in the mouth; bite the hand that feeds one.

.4 ADJS **ungrateful, unthankful,** thankless, unappreciative, unmindful.

.5 unthanked, unacknowledged, unrecognized, uncredited, denied due *or* proper credit, unrequited, unrewarded, forgotten, neglected, unduly *or* unfairly neglected, ignored; ill-requited, ill-rewarded.

## 951. ILL HUMOR

.1 NOUNS **ill humor,** bad humor, **bad temper,** ill temper, ill nature, filthy *or* rotten *or* evil humor; sourness, biliousness; choler, bile, gall, spleen; causticity, corrosiveness, asperity 939.8; **anger** 952.5; discontent 869.

.2 **irascibility, irritability,** excitability, **crossness,** crabbedness, **crankiness, testiness,** crustiness, huffiness, huffishness, **cantankerousness** [informal], churlishness, bearishness, snappishness, waspishness; **meanness** *or* **orneriness** *or* **bitchiness** *or* cussedness [all informal], disagreeability, ugliness [informal]; **perversity,** crossgrainedness, fractiousness.

.3 **hot temper, temper,** quick *or* short temper, irritable temper, warm temper, fiery temper, fierce temper, short fuse [slang], pepperiness, spunkiness [informal], **hotheadedness,** hot blood.

.4 **touchiness, tetchiness,** ticklishness, prickliness, quickness to take offense, **sensitiveness,** oversensitiveness, hypersensitiveness, sensitivity, oversensitivity, hypersensitivity, thin skin; temperamentalness.

.5 **petulance** *or* **petulancy, peevishness,** pettishness, **querulousness, fretfulness,** resentfulness; shrewishness, vixenishness.

.6 **grouchiness, crabbiness, grumpiness,** grumpishness, gruffness.

.7 **contentiousness, quarrelsomeness** 795.3; **disputatiousness, argumentativeness,** litigiousness; **belligerence** 797.15.

.8 **sullenness, sulkiness, surliness, moroseness, glumness,** grumness, grimness, mumpishness. dumpishness, *bouderie* [Fr]; **moodiness,** moodishness; mopishness, mopiness [informal]; dejection, melancholy 872.3–5.

.9 **scowl, frown,** lower, **glower, pout,** moue, mow, grimace, wry face; sullen looks, black looks, **long face.**

.10 **sulks,** sullens, **mopes,** mumps, dumps, grumps [informal], frumps [Brit dial], **blues,** blue devils, mulligrubs, dorts *or* dods [both Scot], **pouts.**

.11 (ill-humored person) **sorehead, grouch, crank, crosspatch,** feist [dial], **bear,** grizzly bear; fury, Tartar, dragon, ugly customer [slang]; **hothead,** hotspur; fire-eater.

.12 **bitch** [slang], **shrew, vixen,** virago, termagant, fury, witch, beldam, cat, tigress, she-wolf, she-devil, spitfire; fishwife; **scold,** common scold; battle-ax [slang].

13 VERBS **have a temper,** have a short fuse [slang], **have a devil in one,** be possessed of the devil.

14 **sulk, mope;** grump *or* grouch *or* bitch [all informal], **fret;** get oneself in a sulk.

15 **look sullen,** look black, look black as

thunder, gloom, pull *or* make a long face; **frown, scowl,** knit the brow, lower, **glower, pout,** make a moue *or* mow, grimace, make a wry face, make a lip, hang one's lip.

.16 **sour,** acerbate, exacerbate; **embitter,** bitter, envenom.

.17 ADJS **out of humor,** out of temper, out of sorts, **in a bad humor,** in a shocking humor, feeling evil [slang]; caustic, corrosive, acid 939.21; **angry** 952.26; discontented 869.5.

.18 **ill-humored, bad-tempered,** ill-tempered, evil-humored, evil-tempered, **ill-natured,** ill-affected, ill-disposed.

.19 **irascible, irritable,** excitable, **cross, cranky, testy,** feisty, crusty, huffy, huffish, shirty [Brit slang], **cantankerous** [informal], cankered, crabbed, spiteful, spleeny, splenetic, churlish, bearish, snappish, waspish; **mean** *or* **ornery** *or* cussed *or* **bitchy** [all informal], disagreeable, ugly [informal]; **perverse,** fractious, crossgrained.

.20 **touchy, tetchy,** miffy, ticklish, prickly, quick to take offense, **thin-skinned, sensitive,** oversensitive, hypersensitive, highstrung, temperamental.

.21 **peevish, petulant,** pettish, **querulous, fretful,** resentful; catty; shrewish, vixenish, vixenly; nagging, naggy.

.22 **grouchy, crabby, grumpy,** grumpish, gruff, grumbly, grumbling, growling.

.23 **sour,** soured, **sour-tempered,** vinegarish; **choleric, dyspeptic, bilious,** jaundiced; **bitter,** embittered.

.24 **sullen, sulky, surly, morose,** dour, mumpish, dumpish, **glum,** grum, grim; **moody,** moodish; **mopish,** mopey [informal], moping; **glowering,** lowering, **scowling, frowning;** dark, black; black-browed, beetle-browed; dejected, melancholy 872.22, 23.

.25 **hot-tempered, hotheaded,** passionate, hot, fiery, peppery, spunky [informal], **quick-tempered, short-tempered;** hasty, quick, "sudden and quick in quarrel" [Shakespeare], explosive, volcanic, combustible.

.26 **contentious, quarrelsome** 795.17; **disputatious,** controversial, litigious, polemic(al); **argumentative,** argumental; scrappy [slang], fighty [dial]; cat-and-doggish, cat-and-dog; **belligerent** 797.25.

.27 ADVS **ill-humoredly, ill-naturedly; irascibly, irritably,** crossly, crankily, testily, huffily, cantankerously [informal], crabbedly, sourly, churlishly, crustily, bearishly, snappily; perversely, fractiously, cross-grainedly.

.28 peevishly, petulantly, pettishly, **querulously, fretfully.**

.29 grouchily [informal], **crabbily, grumpily, grumblingly.**

.30 sullenly, sulkily, surlily, morosely, mumpishly, glumly, grumly, grimly; moodily, mopingly; gloweringly, loweringly, scowlingly, frowningly.

## 952. RESENTMENT, ANGER

.1 NOUNS resentment, resentfulness; **displeasure,** disapproval, disapprobation, dissatisfaction, **discontent; vexation,** irritation, **annoyance,** aggravation [informal], exasperation.

.2 **offense, umbrage, pique;** glower, scowl, angry look, dirty look [slang], glare, frown.

.3 **bitterness, bitter resentment,** bitterness of spirit, heartburning; **rancor,** virulence, **acrimony,** acerbity, asperity; causticity 939.8; **choler,** gall, bile, spleen, acid, acidity, acidulousness; hard feelings, **animosity** 929.4; soreness, rankling, slow burn [informal]; gnashing of teeth.

.4 **indignation,** indignant displeasure, righteous indignation.

.5 **anger, wrath, ire,** *saeva indignatio* [L], mad [informal]; angriness, irateness, wrathfulness, soreness [informal], "a transient madness" [Horace]; infuriation, enragement; vials of wrath, grapes of wrath; **heat,** more heat than light [informal].

.6 **temper,** dander *or* Irish [both informal], monkey [Brit slang]; bad temper 951.1.

.7 **dudgeon,** high dudgeon; **huff, pique, pet,** tiff, miff *or* stew [both informal], fret, fume, ferment.

.8 **fit,** fit of anger, fit of temper, rage, wax [Brit slang], **tantrum,** temper tantrum; duck fit *or* cat fit *or* **conniption** *or* conniption fit [all informal], paroxysm, convulsion.

.9 **outburst,** outburst of anger, burst, **explosion,** eruption, blowup *or* **flare-up** [both informal], access, blaze of temper; **storm, scene,** high words.

.10 **rage, passion; fury,** furor; towering rage *or* passion, blind *or* burning rage, raging *or* tearing passion, furious rage; vehemence, violence; the Furies, the Eumenides, the Erinyes; Nemesis; Alecto, Tisiphone, Megaera.

.11 **provocation, affront, offense,** "head and front of one's offending" [Shakespeare]; *casus belli* [L], red rag, red rag to a bull,

sore point, sore spot, tender spot, raw nerve, slap in the face.

.12 VERBS **resent,** be resentful, feel *or* harbor *or* nurse resentment, feel hurt, smart, feel sore *or* have one's nose out of joint [both informal].

.13 **take amiss,** take ill, **take in bad part,** take to heart, not take it as a joke, **mind; take offense, take umbrage,** get miffed *or* huffy [informal].

.14 (show resentment) redden, color, flush, mantle; **growl, snarl,** gnarl, **snap,** show one's teeth, spit; gnash *or* grind one's teeth; **glower, lower, scowl, glare, frown,** give a dirty look [slang], look daggers.

.15 (be angry) **burn, seethe, simmer,** sizzle, smoke, smolder; be pissed *or* pissed off *or* browned off [all slang], be livid, be beside oneself, **fume,** stew [informal], boil, fret, chafe; foam at the mouth; breathe fire and fury; **rage, storm, rave,** rant, bluster; take on *or* go on *or* carry on [all informal], rant and rave, kick up a row *or* dust *or* shindy [slang]; raise Cain *or* raise hell *or* raise the devil *or* raise the roof [all slang], tear up the earth; throw a fit, have a conniption *or* conniption fit *or* duck fit *or* cat fit [informal], go into a tantrum; stamp one's foot.

.16 vent one's anger, vent one's rancor *or* choler *or* spleen, pour out the vials of one's wrath; **snap at, bite** *or* **snap one's nose off, bite** *or* **take one's head off, jump down one's throat;** expend one's anger on, take it out on [informal].

.17 (become angry) **anger, lose one's temper,** forget oneself, let one's angry passions rise; **get mad** *or* **get sore** [both informal]; **get one's gorge up,** get one's blood up, **get one's dander** *or* **Irish up** [informal], get one's monkey up [Brit slang]; **bridle,** bridle up, **bristle,** bristle up, raise one's hackles, get one's back up; **see red** [informal]; **get hot under the collar** [slang], flip out [slang], work oneself into a lather *or* sweat *or* stew [informal], do a slow burn [informal], reach boiling point, boil over.

.18 **flare up, blaze up,** fire up, flame up, spunk up, ignite, kindle, take fire.

.19 **fly into a rage** *or* **passion** *or* **temper,** fly out, fly off at a tangent; **fly off the handle** *or* **hit the ceiling** *or* go into a tailspin *or* have a hemorrhage [all slang]; **explode, blow up** [informal]; blow one's top *or* stack [slang], blow a fuse *or* gasket [slang], flip one's lid *or* wig [slang].

.20 **offend, give offense, give umbrage,** affront, outrage; grieve, aggrieve; wound hurt, **sting**, hurt the feelings; step *or* tread on one's toes.

.21 **anger, make angry, make mad** *or* **sore** [informal], tick off [slang], raise one's gorge *or* choler, raise one's dander [informal], **put** *or* **get one's dander** *or* **Irish up** [informal], put *or* get one's monkey up [Brit slang], get one's mad up [informal]; make hot under the collar *or* burn one up [both slang]; piss one off [slang].

.22 **provoke, incense,** arouse, inflame, embitter; **vex, irritate, annoy, aggravate** [informal], **exasperate, nettle,** fret, chafe; **pique, peeve** *or* miff [both informal], **huff; ruffle, roil, rile** [informal], ruffle one's feathers, **rankle;** bristle, put *or* get one's back up, set up, put one's hair *or* fur *or* bristles up; stick in one's craw [informal]; **stir up, work up,** stir one's bile, stir the blood.

.23 **enrage, infuriate, madden,** drive one mad, frenzy, lash into fury, work up into a passion, **make one's blood boil.**

.24 ADJS **resentful,** resenting; **bitter,** embittered, rancorous, virulent, **acrimonious,** acerb, acerbic, acerbate; caustic 939.21; **choleric,** splenetic, acid, acidic, acidulous, acidulent; **sore** [informal], rankled, burning *or* stewing [both informal].

.25 **provoked, vexed, piqued; peeved** *or* miffed *or* huffy [all informal], **nettled, irritated, annoyed,** aggravated [informal], exasperated, put-out.

.26 **angry,** angered, **incensed, indignant, irate,** ireful; pissed *or* pissed-off *or* PO'd *or* teed off *or* TO'd *or* ticked off *or* browned-off [all slang], livid, livid with rage, beside oneself, **wroth, wrathful,** wrathy, **mad** *or* **sore** [both informal], **cross,** waxy [Brit slang]; wrought-up, worked up, riled up [informal].

.27 **hot** [slang], het up [dial], **hot under the collar** [slang]; **burning, seething,** simmering, smoldering, sizzling, boiling; flushed with anger.

.28 **in a temper, in a huff, in a pet,** in a stew [informal], in a wax [Brit slang], **in high dudgeon.**

.29 **infuriated,** infuriate, in a rage *or* passion *or* fury; **furious,** fierce, wild, savage; raving mad [informal], **rabid,** foaming *or* frothing at the mouth; **fuming,** in a fume; **enraged, raging, raving, ranting, storming;** mad as a hornet, mad as a wet hen; fighting mad *or* roaring mad *or* good and mad *or* hopping mad [all informal], fit to be tied [slang].

.30 ADVS **angrily, indignantly, irately,** wrathfully, infuriatedly, infuriately, furiously, heatedly; **in anger,** in hot blood, in the heat of passion.

## 953. JEALOUSY

.1 NOUNS **jealousy,** *jalousie* [Fr], **jealousness, heartburning, heartburn, jaundice,** jaundiced eye, green in the eye [informal], "the jaundice of the soul" [Dryden]; "green-eyed jealousy", "green-eyed monster", "a monster begot upon itself, born on itself" [all Shakespeare], Othello's flaw, horn-madness; envy 954.

.2 **suspiciousness,** suspicion, doubt, misdoubt, mistrust, distrust, distrustfulness.

.3 VERBS suffer pangs of jealousy, have green in the eye [informal], be possessive *or* overpossessive, view with a jaundiced eye; **suspect,** distrust, mistrust, doubt, misdoubt.

.4 ADJS **jealous, jaundiced,** jaundice-eyed, yellow-eyed, green-eyed, yellow, green, green with jealousy; horn-mad; invidious, **envious** 954.4; **suspicious,** distrustful.

## 954. ENVY

.1 NOUNS **envy, enviousness, covetousness;** invidia, deadly sin of envy, invidiousness; grudging, grudgingness; **jealousy** 953; rivalry.

.2 "the tax which all distinction must pay" [Emerson], "emulation adapted to the meanest capacity" [Ambrose Bierce], "a kind of praise" [John Gay].

.3 VERBS **envy,** be envious *or* covetous of, **covet,** cast envious eyes, desire for oneself; **grudge, begrudge.**

.4 ADJS **envious,** envying, invidious, green with envy; **jealous** 953.4; **covetous,** desirous of; **grudging, begrudging.**

## 955. RETALIATION

.1 NOUNS **retaliation, reciprocation,** exchange, interchange, give-and-take; **retort, reply,** return, comeback [informal]; **counter, counterblow, counterstroke,** counterblast, recoil, boomerang.

.2 **reprisal, requital, retribution;** recompense, compensation 33, reward, comeuppance [informal], desert, deserts, just deserts, what is merited, what is due *or* condign, what one has coming [informal]; quittance, return of evil for evil; revenge 956; **punishment** 1010.

.3 **tit for tat, measure for measure,** like for like, quid pro quo, something in return, blow for blow, a Roland for an Oliver, a game two can play, **an eye for an eye,** a tooth for a tooth, "eye for eye, tooth for tooth, hand for hand, foot for foot" [Bible], law of retaliation *or* equivalent retaliation, *lex talionis* [L], talion.

.4 VERBS **retaliate, retort,** counter, **strike back,** hit back at [informal], give in return; **reciprocate,** give in exchange, give and take; **get back at** [slang], come back at [informal], turn the tables upon.

.5 **requite,** quit, make requital *or* reprisal *or* retribution, get satisfaction, recompense, compensate, make restitution, indemnify, reward, redress, make amends, **repay, pay, pay back,** pay off; **give one his comeuppance** [informal], give one his deserts, serve one right, give one what is coming to him [informal].

.6 **give in kind,** cap, match, give as good as was sent; repay in kind, **pay one in his own coin** *or* **currency, give one a dose of his own medicine** [informal]; return the like, return the compliment; return like for like, **return evil for evil;** return blow for blow, **give one tit for tat,** give a quid pro quo, give as good as one gets, give measure for measure, give *or* get an eye for an eye and a tooth for a tooth, follow *or* observe the *lex talionis*.

.7 **get even with** [informal], even the score, **settle with, settle** *or* **square accounts** [informal], settle the score [informal], fix [informal], pay off old scores, pay back in full measure, be *or* make quits; **take revenge** 956.4; **punish** 1010.10–12.

.8 ADJS **retaliatory,** retaliative; **retributive,** retributory; reparative, compensatory, restitutive, recompensing, recompensive, reciprocal; punitive 1010.25.

.9 ADVS **in retaliation, in exchange,** in reciprocation; **in return,** in reply; **in requital, in reprisal,** in retribution, in reparation, in amends; **in revenge,** *en revanche* [Fr].

## 956. REVENGE

.1 NOUNS **revenge, vengeance, avengement,** sweet revenge, getting even, evening of the score; revanche, revanchism; **retaliation, reprisal** 955.2; vendetta, feud, blood feud.

.2 **revengefulness, vengefulness, vindictiveness,** rancor, grudgefulness, irreconcilableness, unappeasableness, implacableness, implacability.

.3 **avenger, vindicator;** revanchist; Nemesis, the Furies, the Erinyes, the Eumenides.

.4 VERBS **revenge, avenge, take revenge,** have one's revenge, wreak one's ven-

geance; **retaliate, even the score, get even with** 955.4–7; launch a vendetta.

.5 **harbor revenge,** breathe vengeance; have accounts to settle, have a crow to pick *or* pluck *or* pull with; nurse one's revenge, brood over, dwell on *or* upon, keep the wound open.

.6 ADJS **revengeful, vengeful,** avenging; **vindictive,** vindicatory; revanchist; **punitive,** punitory; rancorous, grudgeful, irreconcilable, unappeasable, implacable, unwilling to forgive and forget, unwilling to let bygones be bygones; **retaliatory** 955.8.

## 957. ETHICS

.1 NOUNS **ethics, principles,** standards, **morals,** moral principles; code, ethical *or* moral code, **ethic,** code of morals *or* ethics, ethical system, value system, axiology; **norm,** behavioral norm, normative system; moral climate, ethos, *Zeitgeist* [Ger]; Ten Commandments, decalogue; new morality; social ethics, professional ethics, medical ethics, legal ethics, business ethics, etc.

.2 ethical *or* moral philosophy, ethology, ethonomics, aretaics, eudaemonics, casuistry, deontology, empiricism, evolutionism, hedonism, ethical formalism, intuitionism, perfectionism, Stoicism, utilitarianism, categorical imperative, golden rule; egoistic ethics, altruistic ethics, Christian ethics, situation ethics; comparative ethics.

.3 **morality, morals,** morale; virtue 980; ethicality, ethicalness.

.4 **amorality,** unmorality; amoralism.

.5 **conscience,** grace, **sense of right and wrong;** inward monitor, inner arbiter, moral censor, censor, ethical self, superego; **voice of conscience,** still small voice within; tender conscience; social conscience; conscientiousness 974.2; twinge of conscience 873.2.

.6 ADJS **ethical, moral,** moralistic; ethological; axiological.

.7 **amoral,** unmoral, nonmoral.

## 958. RIGHT

.1 NOUNS **right,** rightfulness, rightness; what is right *or* proper, what should be, what ought to be, the seemly, the thing, the proper thing, the right *or* proper thing to do, what is done.

.2 **propriety, decorum, decency;** correctness, correctitude, rightness, properness, decorousness, goodness, niceness, seemliness, fitness, fittingness, appropriateness, suability 670.1; normativeness, normality; proprieties, decencies; righteousness 980.1.

.3 (a right or privilege) **right, due,** droit; **prerogative,** power, authority; faculty, appurtenance; **claim,** proper claim, demand, **interest, title,** pretension, pretense, prescription; birthright; natural right, presumptive right, inalienable right; divine right; vested right or interest; property right; conjugal right.

.4 **privilege, license, liberty, freedom, immunity;** franchise, patent, copyright, grant, warrant, blank check, carte blanche; favor, indulgence, **special favor,** dispensation.

.5 **human rights,** rights of man; constitutional rights, **civil rights** 762.2.

.6 **women's rights,** rights of women; **feminism, women's liberation,** women's lib [informal], women's liberation movement, sisterhood.

.7 **women's rightist, feminist, women's liberationist,** women's liberation advocate or adherent or activist, women's libber, libber [both informal]; **suffragette,** suffragist.

.8 ADJS **right,** rightful; **fit, suitable** 670.5; **proper, correct, decorous,** good, nice, decent, seemly, **due, appropriate,** fitting, condign, **right and proper,** as it should be, as it ought to be; kosher, according to Hoyle [both informal]; in the right; normative, normal; righteous 980.7–9; orth(o)–.

.9 ADVS **rightly, rightfully,** right; **by rights, by right,** with good right, **as is right** or **only right; properly,** correctly, as is proper or fitting, **duly, appropriately,** fittingly, condignly, **in justice,** in equity; in reason, in all conscience.

## 959. WRONG

.1 NOUNS **wrong, wrongfulness, wrongness; impropriety, indecorum;** incorrectness, improperness, indecorousness, unseemliness; unfitness, unfittingness, inappropriateness, unsuitability 671.1; infraction, violation, delinquency, criminality, illegality, unlawfulness; abnormality, deviance or deviancy, aberrance or aberrancy; sinfulness, wickedness, unrighteousness 981.3–5.

.2 **abomination,** terrible thing; **scandal, disgrace, shame, pity,** atrocity, profanation, desecration, violation, sacrilege, infamy, ignominy.

.3 ADJS **wrong, wrongful; improper, incorrect, indecorous,** undue, unseemly; unfit,

unfitting, inappropriate, unsuitable 671.5; **delinquent, criminal, illegal, unlawful;** abnormal, deviant, aberrant; **evil, sinful, wicked, unrighteous** 981.16; not the thing, hardly the thing, not done; **off-base** or **out-of-line** or **off-color** [all informal]; abominable, terrible, scandalous, disgraceful, shameful, shameless, atrocious, sacrilegious, infamous, ignominious; mis–.

.4 ADVS **wrongly, wrongfully,** wrong; **improperly,** incorrectly, indecorously.

## 960. DUENESS

.1 NOUNS **dueness, entitlement,** entitledness, deservingness, deservedness, meritedness, expectation, just or justifiable expectation; **justice** 976.

.2 **due,** one's due, what one merits, what one has earned, what is owing, what one has coming, what is coming to one, acknowledgment, cognizance, credit, crediting, recognition; **right** 958.3.

.3 **deserts,** just deserts, deservings, merits, dues, due reward or punishment, **comeuppance** [informal], all that is coming to one.

.4 VERBS **be due,** be one's due, **be entitled to,** have a right or title to, have a rightful claim to or upon, claim as one's right, **have coming.**

.5 **deserve, merit, earn,** rate or be in line for [both informal], **be worthy of,** be deserving, richly deserve.

.6 **get one's deserts,** get one's dues, **get one's comeuppance** [informal], get his or get hers [both slang], get what is coming to one; get justice; serve one right, be rightly served; get for one's pains, reap the fruits or benefit of, reap where one has sown.

.7 ADJS **due, owed, owing,** payable, redeemable, coming, **coming to.**

.8 **rightful,** condign, appropriate, proper 958.8; fit, becoming 670.5; **fair, just** 976.8–10.

.9 **warranted, justified, entitled,** qualified, worthy; **deserved, merited,** richly deserved, earned, well-earned.

.10 **due, entitled to,** with a right to; **deserving, meriting, meritorious, worthy of;** attributable, ascribable.

.11 ADVS **duly, rightfully,** condignly, as is one's due or right.

## 961. UNDUENESS

.1 NOUNS **undueness, undeservedness,** undeservingness, unentitledness, unentitlement, unmeritedness; disentitlement; lack of claim *or* title, false claim *or* title, invalid claim *or* title, no claim *or* title, empty claim *or* title; **inappropriateness** 671.1; **impropriety** 959.1; **excess** 663.

.2 **presumption, assumption, imposition; license,** licentiousness, **undue liberty,** liberties, familiarity, **presumptuousness,** freedom *or* liberty abused, hubris; lawlessness 740.

.3 (taking to oneself unduly) **usurpation, arrogation,** seizure, **appropriation,** assumption, adoption, infringement, encroachment, invasion, trespass, trespassing; playing God.

.4 **usurper,** arrogator, pretender.

.5 VERBS **not be entitled to,** have no right *or* title to, have no claim upon, not have a leg to stand on.

.6 **presume, assume, venture, hazard, dare,** pretend, attempt, **make bold,** make free, **take the liberty,** take upon oneself.

.7 **presume on** *or* **upon, impose on** *or* **upon,** encroach upon, obtrude upon; **take liberties,** take a liberty, overstep, overstep one's rights *or* bounds *or* prerogatives, make free with *or* of, abuse one's rights, abuse a privilege, give an inch and take an ell; **inconvenience,** bother, trouble, cause to go out of one's way.

.8 (take to oneself unduly) **usurp, arrogate,** seize, **appropriate,** assume, adopt, take over, arrogate *or* accroach to oneself, pretend to, infringe, encroach, invade, trespass; play God.

.9 ADJS **undue, unowed, unowing,** not coming, not outstanding; **undeserved, unmerited,** unearned; **unwarranted, unjustified;** unentitled, undeserving, unmeriting, nonmeritorious, unworthy; preposterous, outrageous.

.10 **inappropriate** 671.5; **improper** 959.3; **excessive** 663.16–21.

.11 **presumptuous, presuming, licentious;** hubristic.

## 962. DUTY

### (moral obligation)

.1 NOUNS **duty, obligation,** charge, onus, burden, mission, devoir, must, ought, imperative, **bounden duty,** proper *or* assigned task, what ought to be done, what one is responsible for, "stern daughter of the voice of God" [Wordsworth], deference, respect 964, fealty, allegiance, loyalty, homage, devotion, dedication, commitment, self-imposed duty; **business,**

place 656.3; ethics 957; line of duty; call of duty; duties and responsibilities.

.2 **responsibility,** incumbency; **liability,** accountability, accountableness, answerability, answerableness, amenability; **responsibleness, dutifulness,** duteousness, devotion *or* dedication to duty, sense of duty *or* obligation.

.3 VERBS **should, ought to,** had best, had better, be expedient.

.4 **behoove, become,** befit, beseem, be bound, be obliged *or* obligated, be under an obligation; **owe it to,** owe it to oneself.

.5 **be the duty of, be incumbent on** *or* **upon,** stand on *or* upon, be a must *or* an imperative for, duty calls one to.

.6 **be responsible for,** stand responsible for, **be liable for,** be answerable *or* accountable for, have to answer for.

.7 **be one's responsibility,** be one's office, be one's charge *or* mission, **rest with,** lie upon, devolve on, rest on the shoulders of, lie on one's head, lie at one's door, fall to one, fall to one's lot.

.8 **incur a responsibility,** become bound to, become sponsor for.

.9 **take** *or* **accept the responsibility, take upon oneself,** take upon one's shoulders, commit oneself, **answer for,** respect *or* defer to one's duty; sponsor, be *or* stand sponsor for; do at one's own risk *or* peril; **take the blame,** take the rap for [slang].

.10 **do one's duty,** perform *or* fulfill *or* discharge one's duty, do what one has to do, pay one's dues [informal], **do what is expected,** do the needful, do justice to, do *or* act one's part, play one's proper role; answer the call of duty, do one's bit

.11 **meet an obligation,** satisfy one's obligations, stand to one's engagement, stand up to, **acquit oneself, make good,** redeem one's pledge.

.12 **obligate, oblige, require,** make incumbent *or* imperative, tie, **bind,** pledge, commit, saddle with, put under an obligation.

.13 ADJS **dutiful, duteous;** moral, ethical, conscientious, scrupulous, observant; obedient 766.3; deferential, respectful 964.8.

.14 **incumbent on** *or* **upon,** chargeable to, behooving.

.15 **obligatory, binding, imperative,** imperious, peremptory, mandatory, must, *de rigueur* [Fr]; **necessary,** required 639.12,13

.16 **obliged, obligated,** obligate, **under obligation; bound, duty-bound,** in duty bound, tied, pledged, committed, saddled, holden, bounden; **obliged to,** beholden to, bound *or* bounden to, **indebted to.**

.17 **responsible, answerable; liable, accountable,** amenable, unexempt from, chargeable; **responsible for,** at the bottom of; **to blame.**

.18 ADVS **dutifully, duteously, in the line of duty,** as in duty bound; **beyond the call of duty.**

### 963. IMPOSITION

*(a putting or inflicting upon)*

.1 NOUNS **imposition, infliction,** laying on, charging, taxing, tasking; burdening, weighting, freighting, loading, loading down, imposing an onus; **exaction, demand** 753; unwarranted demand, obtrusiveness, presumptuousness 913.1; inconvenience, trouble, bother; inconsiderateness 939.3.

.2 administration, giving, bestowal; applying, application, dosing, dosage, meting out, prescribing; forcing, forcing on, enforcing.

.3 **charge, duty, tax,** task; **burden,** weight, freight, cargo, load, onus.

.4 VERBS **impose, impose on** *or* **upon, inflict on** *or* **upon, put on** *or* **upon, lay on** *or* **upon,** enjoin; **put, place, set, lay, put down; levy, exact, demand** 753.4; **tax, task, charge,** burden with, weight *or* freight with, weight down with, yoke with, **fasten upon,** saddle with; subject to.

.5 **inflict, wreak, do to,** bring, bring upon, bring down upon, visit upon.

.6 administer, give, bestow; **apply, put on** *or* **upon,** lay on *or* upon, dose, dose with, mete out to, prescribe for; **force, force upon,** enforce upon.

.7 impose on *or* upon, **take advantage of** 665.16; **presume upon** 961.7; **deceive** 618.13, play *or* work on, put on *or* upon, put over *or* across [slang]; palm *or* pass off on, fob *or* foist on; shift the blame *or* responsibility, **pass the buck** [informal].

### 964. RESPECT

NOUNS **respect, regard,** consideration, appreciation, favor, approbation, approval; **esteem, estimation,** prestige; **reverence, veneration,** awe; **deference,** deferential *or* reverential regard; **honor, homage,** duty; great respect, high regard, admiration, adoration, breathless adoration, exaggerated respect, worship, hero worship, idol-

ization 1033.8; idolatry, deification, apotheosis; courtesy 936.

.2 **obeisance,** reverence, homage; **bow, nod, bob,** bend, inclination, inclination of the head, **curtsy, salaam, kowtow,** scrape, bowing and scraping, making a leg; **genuflection,** kneeling, bending the knee; prostration; salute, salutation, presenting arms, dipping the colors *or* ensign, standing at attention; **submissiveness, submission** 765; **obsequiousness, servility** 907.

.3 **respects, regards,** *égards* [Fr], duties, *devoirs* [Fr], attentions.

.4 VERBS **respect,** entertain respect for, accord respect to, **regard, esteem,** hold in esteem *or* consideration, favor, **admire,** think much of, think well of, think highly of, have *or* hold a high opinion of; **appreciate, value,** prize; **revere, reverence,** hold in reverence, **venerate, honor,** look up to, **defer to,** exalt, put on a pedestal, **worship,** hero-worship, **deify, apotheosize, idolize, adore,** worship the ground one walks on, stand in awe of.

.5 **do** *or* **pay homage to,** show *or* demonstrate respect for, pay respect to, pay tribute to, **do** *or* **render honor to; doff one's cap to, take off one's hat to;** salute, present arms, dip the colors *or* ensign, stand at *or* to attention.

.6 **bow, make obeisance, salaam, kowtow,** make one's bow, bow down, **nod,** incline *or* bend *or* bow the head, bend the neck, **bob,** bob down, **curtsy,** bob a curtsy, bend, make a leg, scrape, **bow and scrape; genuflect, kneel,** bend the knee, get down on one's knees, throw oneself on one's knees, fall on one's knees, fall down before, fall at the feet of, prostrate oneself, kiss the hem of one's garment.

.7 **command respect,** inspire respect, stand high, have prestige, rank high, be widely reputed; **awe** 920.6.

.8 ADJS **respectful, regardful,** attentive; **deferential,** conscious of one's place, dutiful, honorific, ceremonious, cap in hand; **courteous** 936.14.

.9 **reverent, reverential;** admiring, **adoring, worshiping,** worshipful, hero-worshiping, **idolizing,** idolatrous, deifying, apotheosizing; **venerative,** venerational; **awestruck,** awestricken, awed, in awe; solemn 871.3.

.10 **obeisant,** prostrate, on one's knees, on bended knee; **submissive** 765.12–16; **obsequious** 907.13.

.11 **respected, esteemed, revered,** reverenced, adored, worshiped, **venerated, honored,** well-thought-of, admired, much-admired, appreciated, valued, prized, in high esteem or estimation, highly considered, well-considered, held in respect or regard or favor or consideration, prestigious.

.12 **venerable, reverend, estimable, honorable,** worshipful, august, awe-inspiring, awesome, awful, dreadful; time-honored.

.13 ADVS, PREPS **in deference to,** with due respect, with all respect, **with all due respect to** or for, saving, excusing the liberty, saving your reverence, sir-reverence.

## 965. DISRESPECT

.1 NOUNS **disrespect, disrespectfulness,** lack of respect, **disesteem,** dishonor, **irreverence;** ridicule 967; disparagement 971; **discourtesy** 937; **impudence,** insolence 913.

.2 **indignity, affront, offense, injury,** humiliation; scurrility, contempt 966, contumely, despite, flout, flouting, mockery, jeering, jeer, mock, scoff, gibe, taunt, brickbat [informal]; **insult, aspersion,** uncomplimentary remark, left-handed or backhanded compliment, slap in the face, damning with faint praise; cut, "most unkindest cut of all" [Shakespeare]; dump or **put-down** [both slang]; **outrage, atrocity,** enormity.

.3 VERBS **disrespect,** not respect, **disesteem,** hold a low opinion of, rate or rank low, hold in low esteem, not care much for; **show disrespect for,** show a lack of respect for, **be disrespectful,** treat with disrespect, be overfamiliar with; trifle with, make bold or free with, take a liberty, take liberties with, play fast and loose with; **ridicule** 967.8–11; **disparage** 971.8–12.

.4 **offend, affront,** give offense to, disoblige, outrage; dishonor, humiliate, treat with indignity; flout, mock, jeer at, scoff at, fleer at, gibe at, taunt; insult, call names, hurl a brickbat [informal], slap in the face, damn with faint praise, take or pluck by the beard; dump on or put down [both slang]; **add insult to injury.**

.5 ADJS **disrespectful, irreverent,** aweless; **discourteous** 937.4; **insolent, impudent** 913.8,9; ridiculing, **derisive** 967.12–14; **disparaging** 971.13.

.6 **insulting, insolent, abusive,** offensive, humiliating, degrading, contumelious, calumnious; scurrilous, scurrile; backhand, backhanded, left-handed; **outrageous,** atrocious, unspeakable.

.7 **unrespected, unregarded, unrevered,** unvenerated, unhonored, unenvied.

## 966. CONTEMPT

.1 NOUNS **contempt, disdain, scorn,** contemptuousness, disdainfulness, superciliousness, snootiness, snottiness, sniffiness, toploftiness, scornfulness, despite, contumely, sovereign contempt; snobbishness; clannishness, cliquishness, exclusiveness; hauteur, airs, arrogance 912; **ridicule** 967; **insult** 965.2; **disparagement** 971.

.2 **snub, rebuff,** repulse; **slight,** humiliation, spurning, spurn, disregard, the go-by [slang]; cut, cut direct, **the cold shoulder** [informal]; sneer, snort, sniff.

.3 VERBS **disdain, scorn, despise,** contemn, disprize, misprize, rate or rank low, be contemptuous of, feel contempt for, **hold in contempt,** hold cheap, look down upon, feel superior to, be above, hold beneath one or beneath contempt, look with scorn upon, view with a scornful eye; **put down** or dump on [both slang]; deride, **ridicule** 967.8–11; **insult** 965.4; **disparage** 971.8–12; thumb one's nose at, sniff at, sneeze at, snap one's fingers at, sneer at, snort at, curl one's lip at, shrug one's shoulders at; care nothing for, couldn't care less about, think nothing of, set at naught.

.4 **spurn, scout, turn up one's nose at,** scorn to receive or accept, not want any part of; spit upon.

.5 **snub, rebuff,** repulse; **high-hat** or upstage [both slang]; **look down one's nose at,** look cool or coldly upon; cold-shoulder or turn a cold shoulder upon or give the cold shoulder or give or turn the shoulder [informal]; turn one's back upon, turn away from, turn on one's heel, set one's face against, slam the door in one's face, show one his place, put one in his place, not be at home to, not receive.

.6 **slight, ignore,** pooh-pooh [informal], make little of, dismiss, pretend not to see, disregard, overlook, neglect, pass by, pass up or give the go-by [both slang], leave out in the cold [informal], take no note or notice of, look right through [informal], pay no attention or regard to, refuse to acknowledge or recognize; cut or cut dead [both informal].

.7 **avoid** 631.6, shun, dodge, steer clear of, have no truck with [both informal]; **keep one's distance,** keep at a respectful distance, **keep** or **stand** or **hold aloof;** keep at a distance, keep at arm's length; **stuck-up** [informal], act holier than thou, give oneself airs.

**.8** ADJS **contemptuous, disdainful,** supercilious, **snooty, snotty,** sniffy, toplofty, toploftical, **scornful,** sneering, withering, contumelious; snobbish, snobby; clannish, cliquish, exclusive; haughty, arrogant 912.9.

**.9** ADVS **contemptuously, scornfully, disdainfully;** in or with contempt, in disdain, in scorn; sneeringly, with a sneer, with curling lip.

**.10** INTERJS **bah!, pah!, phooey!, boo!, phoo!,** pish!, ecch!, yeech!, eeyuck! or eeyuch!, yeeuck!, *feh!* [Yid].

## 967. RIDICULE

**.1** NOUNS **ridicule, derision, mockery, raillery,** rallying, chaffing; panning or razzing or roasting or ragging [all slang], **scoffing, jeering, sneering,** snickering, sniggering, smirking, grinning, leering, fleering, snorting, levity, flippancy, smartness, smart-aleckiness or joshing [both informal], fooling, twitting, taunting, booing, hooting, catcalling, hissing; **banter** 882.

**.2** gibe, scoff, jeer, fleer, flout, mock, barracking [Brit], **taunt, twit,** quip, jest, jape, put-on or leg-pull [both informal], foolery; scurrility, caustic remark; **cut,** cutting remark, verbal thrust; dump or put-down or rank-out or dirty dig [all slang], crack [slang], **slap, slam** or **swipe** [both informal], jab [slang], dig [informal], gibing retort, rude reproach, short answer, back answer, comeback [slang], parting shot, Parthian shot.

**.3** boo, booing, **hoot, catcall; Bronx cheer** or **raspberry** or razz [all slang]; **hiss, hissing,** the bird [slang].

**.4** scornful laugh or smile, snicker, snigger, **smirk,** sardonic grin, leer, fleer, **sneer,** snort.

**.5** sarcasm, irony, cynicism, satire, satiric wit or humor, invective, innuendo; causticity 939.8.

**.6** burlesque, lampoon, squib, **parody, satire,** farce, mockery, imitation, wicked imitation or pastiche, takeoff [informal], **travesty, caricature.**

**.7** laughingstock, jestingstock, gazingstock, derision, mockery, **figure of fun,** byword, byword of reproach, jest, joke, **butt,** target, stock, goat [informal], toy, game, **fair game,** victim, dupe, fool, everybody's fool, monkey, mug [Brit slang].

**.8** VERBS **ridicule, deride,** ride [informal], make a laughingstock or mockery of; **pan** or razz or roast or rag [all slang]; **make fun** or **game of, poke fun at,** make merry

with, put one on or pull one's leg [both informal]; **laugh at,** laugh in one's face, grin at, smile at, snicker or snigger at; **laugh to scorn,** hold in derision, laugh out of court; point at, point the finger of scorn; pillory.

**.9** scoff, jeer, gibe, barrack [Brit], **mock, revile, rail at, rally,** chaff, **twit, taunt,** jape, flout, scout, have a fling at, cast in one's teeth; cut at; dump on or put down or rank out [all slang], slap at, slam or swipe [both informal], jab, jab at, dig at; pooh, **pooh-pooh;** sneer, **sneer at,** fleer, curl one's lip.

**.10** boo, hiss, hoot, catcall, give the raspberry or Bronx cheer [slang], give the bird [slang], whistle at.

**.11** burlesque, lampoon, satirize, parody, caricature, travesty, hit or take off on.

**.12** ADJS **ridiculing, derisive,** derisory; **mocking,** railing, rallying, chaffing; panning or razzing or roasting or ragging [all slang], **scoffing,** jeering, sneering, snickering, sniggering, smirking, grinning, leering, fleering, snorting, flippant, smart, smart-alecky [informal], smart-ass [slang], joshing [informal], fooling, twitting, taunting, booing, hooting, catcalling, hissing, bantering, kidding, teasing, quizzical.

**.13** sarcastic, ironic(al), sardonic, cynical, satiric(al), Rabelaisian, dry; caustic 939.21.

**.14** burlesque, satiric(al), farcical, parodic, caricatural, macaronic, doggerel.

**.15** ADVS **derisively, mockingly, scoffingly,** jeeringly, sneeringly, "with scoffs and scorns and contumelious taunts" [Shakespeare].

## 968. APPROVAL

**.1** NOUNS **approval, approbation;** sanction, acceptance, countenance, **favor;** admiration, esteem, respect 964; endorsement, vote, favorable vote, yea vote, yea, voice, adherence, blessing, seal of approval, nod, stamp of approval, OK 521.4.

**.2** applause, plaudit, éclat, **acclaim, acclamation; popularity;** clap, handclap, **clapping,** handclapping, clapping of hands; **cheer** 876.2; burst of applause, peal or thunder of applause; round of applause, hand, big hand; ovation, standing ovation; encore.

**.3** commendation, good word, acknowledgment, recognition, appreciation; boost or buildup [both slang]; **puff,** promotion; **blurb** or **plug** or promo or hype [all slang]; honorable mention.

**.4** recommendation, recommend [Brit informal]; **advocacy,** advocating, advocation, patronage; **reference, credential,** voucher, **testimonial;** character reference, character, certificate of character; letter of introduction.

.5 **praise,** bepraisement; **laudation, laud; glorification,** glory, exaltation, magnification, **honor;** eulogy, *eloge,* *hommage* [both Fr], eulogium; **encomium,** accolade, kudos, panegyric; paean; **tribute,** homage, meed of praise; congratulation 948.1; flattery 970; overpraise, excessive praise, idolizing, idolatry, deification, apotheosis, adulation, lionizing, hero worship.

.6 **compliment,** polite commendation, complimentary *or* flattering remark; **bouquet** *or* **posy** [both informal], trade-last *or* TL [both informal].

.7 **praiseworthiness, laudability,** laudableness, commendableness, estimableness, meritoriousness, exemplariness, admirability.

.8 **commender,** eulogist, eulogizer; **praiser,** lauder, extoller, encomiast, panegyrist, **booster** [informal], puffer, promoter; plugger *or* tout *or* touter [all slang]; **applauder,** claqueur; claque; rooter *or* fan *or* buff [all informal], adherent; appreciator.

.9 VERBS **approve, approve of,** think well of; **sanction, accept; admire, esteem, respect** 964.4; endorse, bless, OK 521.12; **countenance,** keep in countenance; hold with, uphold; **favor,** be in favor of, view with favor, take kindly to.

.10 **applaud, acclaim, hail; clap,** clap the hands, give a hand *or* big hand, hear it for [slang]; **cheer** 876.6; root for [informal], cheer on; encore; cheer *or* applaud to the very echo.

.11 **commend, speak well** *or* **highly of,** speak in high terms of, speak warmly of, have *or* say a good word for; boost *or* give a boost to [both informal], puff, promote, cry up; plug *or* tout *or* hype [all slang]; **recommend, advocate,** put in a word *or* good word for, support, back, lend one's name *or* support *or* backing to.

.12 **praise,** bepraise; **laud,** belaud; **eulogize,** panegyrize, pay tribute, salute; **extol, glorify,** magnify, exalt, bless; cry up, blow up, puff, puff up; boast of, brag about [informal], make much of; celebrate, emblazon, sound *or* resound the praises of, ring one's praises, sing the praise of, trumpet; praise to the skies, *porter aux nues* [Fr]; flatter 970.5; overpraise, praise

to excess, idolize, deify, apotheosize, adulate, lionize, hero-worship.

.13 **espouse,** take up, take for one's own; **campaign for, crusade for,** put on a drive for; carry the banner of, march under the banner of; beat the drum for, thump the tub for; lavish oneself on, fight the good fight for; devote *or* dedicate oneself to, spend *or* give *or* sacrifice oneself for.

.14 **compliment, pay a compliment,** make one a compliment, give a bouquet *or* posy [informal], say something nice about; hand it to *or* have to hand it to [both slang], pat on the back, take off one's hat to, doff one's cap to, congratulate 948.2.

.15 **meet with approval,** find favor with, pass muster, recommend itself, do credit to; redound to the honor of; ring with the praises of.

.16 ADJS **approbatory, commendatory, complimentary, laudatory,** acclamatory, eulogistic, panegyric, encomiastic, **appreciative; admiring, regardful, respectful** 964.8; flattering 970.8.

.17 **approving, favorable,** favoring, in favor of, **pro,** well-disposed, well-inclined, supporting, backing, **advocating.**

.18 **uncritical,** uncriticizing, **uncensorious,** unreproachful; overpraising, overappreciative, unmeasured *or* excessive in one's praise, idolatrous, adulatory, lionizing, hero-worshiping, fulsome.

.19 **approved,** favored, backed, advocated, supported; favorite; **accepted,** received, admitted; recommended, highly touted [informal], **admired** 964.11, **applauded,** well-thought-of, in good odor, **acclaimed,** cried up; **popular.**

.20 **praiseworthy,** worthy, **commendable,** estimable, **laudable,** admirable, meritorious, creditable; exemplary, model, unexceptionable; deserving, well-deserving; beyond all praise, *sans peur et sans reproche* [Fr].

.21 PREPS **in favor of, for, pro,** all for.

.22 INTERJS bravo!, bravissimo!, **well done!,** ¡ole! [Sp], *bene!* [Ital], hear, hear!, aha! hurrah!; **good!, fine!,** excellent!, great! beautiful!, swell!, good for you!, good enough!, not bad!, now you're talking! attaboy!, attababy!, attagirl!, attagal! good boy!, good girl!; that's the idea! that's the ticket!; encore!, *bis!* [Fr], take a bow!, one cheer more!

.23 hail!, all hail!, *ave!* [L], *vive!* [Fr], *viva! evviva!* [both Ital], long life to!, glory b to!, honor be to!

## 969. DISAPPROVAL

.1 NOUNS disapproval, disapprobation, disfavor, disesteem, disrespect 965; dim view, poor or low opinion, low estimation; displeasure, distaste, dissatisfaction, discontent, discontentment, discontentedness, disgruntlement, indignation, unhappiness; disillusion, disillusionment, disenchantment, disappointment; disagreement, opposition 790, opposure; rejection, thumbs-down, exclusion, ostracism, blackballing, blackball, ban; complaint, protest, objection, dissent 522.

.2 deprecation, discommendation, dispraise, denigration, disvaluation; ridicule 967; depreciation, disparagement 971; contempt 966.

.3 censure, reprehension, stricture, reprobation, blame, denunciation, denouncement, decrial, impeachment, arraignment, indictment, condemnation, damnation, fulmination, anathema; castigation, flaying, skinning alive [informal], fustigation, excoriation; pillorying.

.4 criticism, adverse criticism, hostile criticism, flak [informal], bad notices, bad press, animadversion, imputation, reflection, aspersion, stricture, obloquy; knock or swipe or slam or rap or hit [all informal], home thrust; minor or petty criticism, niggle, cavil, quibble, exception, nit [informal]; censoriousness, reproachfulness, priggishness; faultfinding, taking exception, carping, caviling, pettifogging, quibbling, captiousness, niggling, nit-picking, pestering, nagging; hypercriticism, hypercriticalness, overcriticalness, hairsplitting, trichoschistism.

.5 reproof, reproval, reprobation; rebuke, reprimand, reproach, reprehension, scolding, chiding, rating, upbraiding, objurgation; admonishment, admonition; correction, castigation, chastisement, spanking, rap on the knuckles; lecture, lesson, sermon.

.6 [slang or informal terms] piece or bit of one's mind, talking-to, speaking-to, roasting, raking-down, raking-over, raking over the coals, dressing, dressing-down, setdown; bawling-out, cussing-out, callingdown, jacking-up, going-over, chewingout, chewing, reaming-out, reaming, asschewing, ass-reaming, what-for.

7 berating, rating, jawing [slang], tonguelashing; revilement, vilification, blackening, execration, abuse, vituperation, invective, contumely, hard or cutting or

bitter words; tirade, diatribe, jeremiad, screed, philippic; attack, assault, onslaught, assailing.

.8 reproving look, dirty or nasty look [slang], black look, frown, scowl.

.9 faultfinder, frondeur [Fr], momus; critic 494.7, captious critic, criticizer, nitpicker [informal], smellfungus, belittler, censor, censurer, carper, caviler, quibbler, pettifogger; scold, common scold.

.10 VERBS disapprove, disapprove of, not approve; disfavor, view with disfavor, frown at or upon, look black upon, look askance at, make a wry face at, grimace at, turn up one's nose at, shrug one's shoulders at; take a dim view of [informal], not think much of, think ill of, think little of, not take kindly to, not hold with, hold no brief for [informal]; not go for or not get all choked up over or be turned off by [all slang]; not want or have any part of, wash one's hands of, dissociate oneself from; object to, take exception to; oppose 790.3-7, set oneself against, set one's face against; reject, categorically reject, disallow, not hear of; turn thumbs down on or thumb down [both informal], frown down, exclude, ostracize, blackball, ban; say no to, shake one's head at; dissent from, protest, object 522.4,5.

.11 discountenance, not countenance, not tolerate, not brook, not condone, not suffer, not abide, not endure, not bear with, not put up with, not stand for [informal].

.12 deprecate, discommend, dispraise, disvalue, not be able to say much for, denigrate, put down [slang]; ridicule 967.8-11; depreciate, disparage 971.8; hold in contempt, disdain, despise 966.3.

.13 censure, reprehend; blame, lay or cast blame upon; reproach, impugn; condemn, damn, damn with faint praise; fulminate against, anathematize, anathemize, put on the Index; denounce, denunciate, accuse 1005.7-11, decry, cry down, impeach, arraign, indict, call to account, exclaim or declaim or inveigh against, cry out against, cry out on or upon, cry shame upon, raise one's voice against, raise a hue and cry against, shake up [archaic]; reprobate, hold up to reprobation; animadvert on or upon, reflect upon, cast reflection upon, cast a reproach or slur upon, complain against; throw a stone at, cast or throw the first stone.

**.14 criticize;** pan or knock or slam or hit or rap or take a rap or swipe at [all informal], snipe at.

**.15 find fault,** take exception, fault-find, pick holes, cut up, pick or pull or tear apart, **pick** or **pull** or **tear to pieces; carp, cavil,** quibble, **nitpick,** pettifog, catch at straws.

**.16 nag,** niggle, **carp at, fuss at, fret at,** yap at or **pick at** [both informal], peck at, nibble at, **pester, henpeck, pick on** [informal], bug or hassle [both slang].

**.17 reprove, rebuke, reprimand,** reprehend, **scold, chide, rate, admonish, upbraid,** objurgate, have words with; **lecture,** read a lesson or lecture to; **correct,** rap on the knuckles, **chastise,** spank, turn over one's knees; **take to task,** call to account, bring to book, call on the carpet, read the riot act; take down, set down, set straight, straighten out.

**.18** [informal terms] **call down, dress down, speak** or **talk to, tell off,** tell a thing or two, **give a piece** or **bit of one's mind, rake** or **haul over the coals,** rake up one side and down the other, give it to, trim, come down on or upon, jump on, jump all over, jump down one's throat.

**.19** [slang terms] **bawl out,** give a bawling out, chew, **chew out,** chew ass, ream, ream out, ream ass, cuss out, jack up, sit on or upon, lambaste, give a going-over, tell where to get off; **give what-for,** give the deuce or devil, give hell, give hail Columbia.

**.20 berate,** rate, betongue, jaw [slang], clapper-claw [dial], **tongue-lash, rail at,** rag, thunder or fulminate against, rave against, yell at, bark or yelp at; **revile, vilify,** blacken, **execrate, abuse,** vituperate, load with reproaches.

**.21** (criticize or reprove severely) **attack, assail** 798.15; **castigate, flay,** skin alive [informal], lash, slash, **excoriate,** fustigate, scarify, scathe, **roast** [informal], scorch, blister, trounce.

**.22** ADJS **disapproving, disapprobatory,** unapproving, turned-off, **displeased, dissatisfied,** discontented, disgruntled, indignant, **unhappy;** disillusioned, disenchanted, disappointed; **unfavorable,** low, poor, **opposed** 790.8, opposing, **con,** against, agin [informal], **dissenting** 522.6, 7; **uncomplimentary;** unappreciative.

**.23 condemnatory, censorious,** damnatory, **denunciatory, reproachful,** blameful, reprobative, objurgatory, priggish, judgmental; deprecative, deprecatory; **derisive, ridiculing, scoffing** 967.12–14; deprecia-

tive, disparaging 971.13; contemptuous 966.8; invective, inveighing; reviling, vilifying, blackening, execrating, execrative, execratory, abusive, vituperative.

**.24 critical, faultfinding,** carping, caviling, quibbling, pettifogging, captious, cynical; nagging, niggling; hypercritical, ultracritical, overcritical, hairsplitting, trichoschistic.

**.25 unpraiseworthy, illaudable;** uncommendable, discommendable; **objectionable,** exceptionable, unacceptable, not to be thought of.

**.26 blameworthy,** blamable, to blame; **reprehensible,** censurable, reproachable, reprovable, open to criticism or reproach; **culpable,** chargeable, impeachable, accusable, indictable, arraignable, imputable.

**.27** ADVS **disapprovingly, askance,** askant, **unfavorably;** censoriously, critically, reproachfully; captiously.

**.28** INTERJS **God forbid!,** Heaven forbid!, Heaven forfend!, forbid it Heaven!; by no means!, not for the world!, not on your life!, over my dead body!, not if I know it!, nothing doing!, no way!, perish the thought!, I'll be hanged or damned if . . . !

## 970. FLATTERY

**.1** NOUNS **flattery, adulation; praise** 968.5; **blandishment,** palaver, **cajolery,** cajolement, wheedling; **blarney** or bunkum or **soft soap** or soap or butter salve [all informal], oil, grease, eyewash [slang]; sweet talk, fair or sweet or honeyed words, soft or honeyed phrases, incense, pretty lies, sweet nothings; **compliment** 968.6; **fawning, sycophancy** 907.2.

**.2 unction,** "that flattering unction" [Shakespeare]; **unctuousness,** oiliness; slobber gush, smarm; flattering tongue; insincerity 616.5.

**.3 overpraise,** overprizing, excessive praise overcommendation, overlaudation, over estimation; idolatry 968.5.

**.4 flatterer,** *flatteur* [Fr], adulator, courtier cajoler, **wheedler; backslapper,** back scratcher; blarneyer or soft-soaper [bot informal]; **sycophant** 907.3.

**.5** VERBS **flatter,** adulate, conceit; **cajol wheedle, blandish,** palaver; slaver or slob ber over, beslobber, beslubber; oil th tongue, lay the flattering unction t one's soul, make fair weather; **prais compliment** 968.12,14; fawn upon 907.6–9

**.6** [slang or informal terms] **soft-soap,** bu ter, honey, **butter up,** soften up; strok blarney, jolly, pull one's leg; lay it on, lay it on thick, overdo it, soap, oil; string along, kid along; play up to, get around; lay it on with a trowel.

.7 **overpraise,** overprize, overcommend, overlaud; overesteem, overestimate; idolize 968.12.

.8 ADJS **flattering, adulatory; complimentary** 968.16; **blandishing, cajoling, wheedling,** blarneying *or* soft-soaping [both informal]; fair-spoken, fine-spoken, smoothspoken, smooth-tongued, **mealymouthed,** honey-mouthed, honey-tongued, honeyed, oily-tongued; fulsome, slimy, slobbery, gushing, smarmy, insinuating, oily, buttery [informal], soapy [slang], **unctuous,** smooth, bland; insincere 616.32; courtly, courtierly; **fawning, sycophantic, obsequious** 907.13.

## 971. DISPARAGEMENT

.1 NOUNS **disparagement, depreciation, detraction,** derogation, running down *or* knocking [both informal], putting down [slang], **belittling;** sour grapes; slighting, minimizing, faint praise, lukewarm support, discrediting, decrial; disapproval 969; contempt 966; indignity, disgrace, comedown [informal].

.2 **defamation,** malicious defamation, defamation of character, injury of *or* to one's reputation; **vilification,** revilement, defilement, blackening, denigration; **smear,** character assassination, *ad hominem* attack, name-calling, smear word, smear campaign; **muckraking, mudslinging.**

.3 **slander, scandal, libel,** traducement; calumny, calumniation; backbiting, cattiness *or* bitchiness [both informal].

.4 **aspersion,** slur, **reflection,** imputation, insinuation, suggestion, sly suggestion, innuendo, whispering campaign; disparaging *or* uncomplimentary remark; personality, personal remark.

.5 **lampoon,** pasquinade, pasquin, pasquil, squib, **satire,** malicious parody, **burlesque** 967.6; poison pen, hatchet job.

.6 **disparager, depreciator,** decrier, detractor, belittler, debunker, deflater, slighter, derogator, **knocker** [informal], caustic critic, hatchet man; **slanderer, libeler,** defamer, backbiter; calumniator, traducer; **muckraker, mudslinger,** social critic; cynic, railer, Thersites.

.7 **lampooner,** lampoonist, **satirist,** pasquinader; poison-pen writer.

.8 VERBS **disparage, depreciate, belittle,** slight, minimize, make little of, degrade,

debase, **run down** *or* **knock** [informal], **put down** [slang]; **discredit,** bring into discredit, reflect discredit upon, disgrace; detract from, derogate from, cut down to size [slang]; **decry,** cry down; speak ill of, speak slightingly of, not speak well of; disapprove of 969.10; hold in contempt 966.3; submit to indignity *or* disgrace, bring down, bring low.

.9 **defame, malign, bad-mouth** [informal]; **asperse, cast aspersions on,** cast reflections on, injure one's reputation, damage one's good name; **slur,** cast a slur on, do a number on [informal]; give a bad name, give a dog a bad name.

.10 **vilify, revile, defile, sully, soil, smear,** smirch, besmirch, bespatter, tarnish, **blacken,** denigrate, blacken one's good name, give a black eye [informal]; stigmatize 915.9; **muckrake, throw mud at,** heap dirt upon, drag through the mud; call names, engage in personalities.

.11 **slander, libel;** calumniate, traduce; stab in the back, backbite, speak ill of behind one's back.

.12 **lampoon, satirize,** pasquinade, dip the pen in gall, **burlesque** 967.11.

.13 ADJS **disparaging, derogatory,** derogative, **depreciatory,** depreciative, deprecatory, slighting, belittling, minimizing, detractory, pejorative, back-biting, catty *or* bitchy [both informal], contumelious, contemptuous, derisive, derisory, ridiculing 967.12; censorious 969.23; **defamatory,** vilifying, **slanderous, scandalous, libelous;** calumnious, calumniatory; **abusive,** scurrilous, scurrile.

## 972. CURSE

.1 NOUNS **curse, malediction,** malison, damnation, denunciation, commination, imprecation, execration; **blasphemy;** anathema, fulmination, thundering, excommunication; ban, proscription; hex, evil eye, *malocchio* [Ital], whammy [slang].

.2 **vilification, abuse,** revilement, **vituperation, invective,** opprobrium, obloquy, contumely, calumny, scurrility, blackguardism.

.3 **cursing,** cussing [informal], **swearing, profanity,** profane swearing, foul *or* profane *or* obscene *or* blue *or* bad *or* strong *or* unparliamentary *or* indelicate language, vulgar language, vile language, colorful language, unrepeatable expressions, dysphemism, billingsgate, ribaldry, evil speaking, **dirty language** *or* **talk** [informal], obscenity, scatology, **filthy language, filth.**

.4 **oath,** profane oath, curse; **cuss** or cuss word or dirty word or four-letter word or **swearword** [all informal], naughty word, no-no [informal], foul invective, **expletive, epithet,** dirty name [slang], dysphemism, obscenity.

.5 VERBS **curse,** accurse, **damn,** darn, **confound,** blast, anathematize, fulminate or thunder against, execrate, imprecate; excommunicate; call down evil upon, call down curses on the head of; put a curse on; curse up hill and down dale; curse with bell, book, and candle; blaspheme; hex, give the evil eye, throw a whammy [slang].

.6 **curse, swear, cuss** [informal], curse and swear, execrate, rap out or rip out an oath, take the Lord's name in vain; swear like a trooper, cuss like a sailor, make the air blue, swear till one is blue in the face; **talk dirty** [informal], scatologize, dysphemize.

.7 **vilify, abuse, revile,** vituperate, blackguard, call names, epithet, epithetize; **swear at,** damn, cuss out [informal].

.8 ADJS **cursing, maledictory,** imprecatory, **damnatory,** denunciatory, epithetic(al); **abusive,** vituperative, contumelious; calumnious, calumniatory; execratory, comminatory, fulminatory, excommunicative, excommunicatory; scurrilous, scurrile; blasphemous, profane, foul, vile, **dirty** [informal], **obscene,** dysphemistic, scatologic(al); ribald, Rabelaisian, raw, risqué.

.9 **cursed,** accursed, bloody [Brit slang], **damned, damn, damnable,** goddamned, goddamn, **execrable.**

.10 (euphemisms) **darned,** danged, **confounded,** deuced, **blessed, blasted,** dashed, blamed, goshdarn, doggone or doggoned, goldarned, goldanged, dadburned; blankety-blank; ruddy [Brit].

.11 INTERJS damn!, damn it!, God damn it! or goddam it!, confound it!, hang it!, devil take!, a plague upon!, a pox upon!, *parbleu!* [Fr].

.12 (euphemistic oaths) darn!, dern!, dang!, dash!, drat!, blast!, doggone!, goldarn!, goldang!, golding!, gosh-darn!

## 973. THREAT

.1 NOUNS **threat, menace,** threateningness, threatfulness, promise of harm, knife poised at one's throat, arrow aimed at one's heart, sword of Damocles; denunciation, commination; imminence 152;

foreboding 544; **warning** 703; saber rattling, bulldozing, **intimidation** 891.6; veiled or implied threat, idle or hollow or empty threat.

.2 VERBS **threaten, menace,** bludgeon, bulldoze, **intimidate** 891.28; utter threats against, shake or double or clench one's fist at; hold over one's head; denounce, comminate; **lower,** look threatening; **be imminent** 152.2; **forebode** 544.11; **warn** 703.5.

.3 ADJS **threatening, menacing,** threatful, minatory, minacious; **lowering; imminent** 152.3; **ominous,** foreboding 544.17; denunciatory, comminatory, abusive; fear-inspiring, **intimidating,** bludgeoning, bulldozing, browbeating, bullying, hectoring, blustering, terrorizing, terroristic.

## 974. PROBITY

.1 NOUNS **probity,** assured probity, **honesty, integrity, rectitude, uprightness,** upstandingness, erectness, **virtue,** virtuousness, **righteousness, goodness;** cleanness, **decency; honor,** honorableness, worthiness, estimableness, reputability, nobility; unimpeachableness, unimpeachability, irreproachableness, irreproachability, blamelessness; immaculacy, unspottedness, stainlessness, pureness, purity; respectability; **principles,** high principles, high ideals, high-mindedness; **character,** good character, moral strength, moral excellence; **fairness,** justness, justice 976.

.2 **conscientiousness, scrupulousness,** scrupulosity, **scruples,** punctiliousness, meticulousness; scruple, point of honor, punctilio; qualm 623.2; twinge of conscience 873.2; overconscientiousness, overscrupulousness; fastidiousness 896.

.3 **veracity,** veraciousness, verity, **truthfulness,** truth, veridicality, truth-telling, truth-speaking; truth-loving; credibility, absolute credibility.

.4 **candor, candidness, frankness,** sincerity, genuineness, plain dealing; ingenuousness; artlessness 736; **openness,** openheartedness; freedom, freeness; **unreserve,** unrestraint, unconstraint; **forthrightness, directness, straightforwardness; outspokenness,** plainness, plainspokenness, plainspeaking, roundness, broadness; **bluntness,** bluffness, brusqueness.

.5 **undeceptiveness, undeceitfulness, guilelessness.**

.6 **trustworthiness,** faithworthiness, **trustiness,** trustability, **reliability, dependability,** responsibility, sureness; unfalseness unperfidiousness, untreacherousness; incorruptibility, inviolability.

.7 **fidelity, faithfulness, loyalty, faith; constancy, steadfastness,** staunchness, firmness; trueness, troth, true blue; good faith, *bona fides* [L], *bonne foi* [Fr]; **allegiance, fealty, homage;** bond, tie; attachment, adherence, adhesion; devotion, devotedness.

.8 **man of honor,** man of his word, gentleman, *gentilhomme* [Fr], *galantuomo* [Ital]; **honest man,** good man; woman of honor, woman of her word, lady, real lady; honest woman, good woman; salt of the earth; square *or* straight shooter [informal]; true blue, truepenny; trusty, faithful.

.9 VERBS **keep faith,** not fail, **keep one's word** *or* **promise,** keep troth, be as good as one's word, redeem one's pledge, play by the rules, acquit oneself, make good.

.10 shoot straight [informal], draw a straight furrow, **put one's cards on the table,** level with [slang].

.11 **speak** *or* **tell the truth,** speak *or* tell true, paint in its true colors, tell the truth and shame the devil; tell the truth, the whole truth, and nothing but the truth.

.12 **be frank, speak plainly,** speak out, speak one's mind, say what one thinks, **call a spade a spade,** tell it like it is.

.13 ADJS **honest, upright,** uprighteous, **upstanding,** erect, right, **righteous, virtuous, good,** clean, **decent; honorable,** full of integrity, **reputable,** estimable, creditable, worthy, noble, sterling, manly, yeomanly, Christian [informal]; unimpeachable, irreproachable, blameless, immaculate, spotless, stainless, unstained, unspotted, unblemished, untarnished, unsullied, undefiled, pure; **respectable,** highly respectable; **ethical, moral; principled, high-principled,** high-minded, rightminded; uncorrupt, uncorrupted, inviolate; truehearted, true-souled, true-spirited; true-dealing, true-disposing, true-devoted; **law-abiding,** law-loving, law-revering; fair, just 976.8–10.

14 **straight, square,** foursquare, **fair and square; square-dealing,** square-shooting, straight-shooting, up-and-up, **on the up-and-up, on the level,** on the square; open, **aboveboard, open and aboveboard;** bona fide, good-faith; authentic, veritable, genuine 516.14; single-hearted; honest as the day is long.

15 **conscientious,** tender-conscienced; **scrupulous,** careful 533.10–14; punctilious,

punctual, meticulous, religious, strict, nice; fastidious 896.9; overconscientious, overscrupulous.

.16 **veracious, truthful,** true, veridical; truth-telling, truth-speaking, truth-declaring, truth-passing, truth-bearing, truth-loving, truth-seeking, truth-desiring, truth-guarding, truth-filled; true-speaking, true-meaning, true-tongued.

.17 **candid, frank, sincere,** genuine, ingenuous, frankhearted; **open,** openhearted, transparent; artless 736.5; **straightforward, direct,** straight [informal], **forthright,** downright, straight-out [informal]; plain, broad, round; **unreserved,** unrestrained, unconstrained, unchecked; unguarded; free; **outspoken, plain-spoken,** free-spoken, free-speaking, free-tongued; explicit, unequivocal; **blunt,** bluff, brusque; heart-to-heart.

.18 **undeceptive, undeceitful, undissembling,** undissimulating, undeceiving, undesigning, uncalculating; **guileless,** unbeguiling, unbeguileful; unassuming, unpretending, unfeigning, undisguising, unflattering; undissimulated, undissembled; unassumed, unaffected, unpretended, unfeigned, undisguised, unvarnished, untrimmed.

.19 **trustworthy, trusty,** trustable, faithworthy, **reliable, dependable, responsible,** straight [slang], sure, to be trusted, **to be depended** *or* **relied upon,** to be counted *or* reckoned on, as good as one's word; tried, true, **tried and true,** tested, proven; unfalse, unperfidious, untreacherous; incorruptible, inviolable.

.20 **faithful, loyal,** devoted; **true, true-blue,** true to one's colors; **constant, steadfast,** steady, consistent, stable, unfailing, staunch, firm, "marble-constant" [Shakespeare].

.21 ADVS **honestly, uprightly, honorably,** upstandingly, erectly, **virtuously, righteously, decently,** worthily, reputably, nobly; unimpeachably, irreproachably, blamelessly, immaculately, unspottedly, stainlessly, purely; high-mindedly, morally; **conscientiously, scrupulously,** punctiliously, meticulously, fastidiously 896.14.

.22 **truthfully, truly,** veraciously; to tell the truth, to speak truthfully; in truth, in sooth [archaic], of a truth, with truth, in good *or* very truth.

.23 **candidly, frankly, sincerely,** genuinely, in all seriousness *or* soberness, in all conscience; in plain words *or* English, straight from the shoulder, not to mince the matter, not to mince words, without equivocation, with no nonsense, all joking aside or apart; **openly,** openheartedly, **unreservedly,** unrestrainedly, unconstrainedly, **forthrightly, directly, straightforwardly,** outspokenly, **plainly,** plain-spokenly, broadly, roundly, **bluntly,** bluffly, brusquely.

.24 **trustworthily,** trustily, **reliably, dependably, responsibly;** undeceptively, undeceitfully, guilelessly; incorruptibly, inviolably.

.25 **faithfully, loyally,** devotedly; **constantly, steadfastly,** steadily, responsibly, consistently, staunchly, firmly; in or with good faith, *bona fide* [L].

## 975. IMPROBITY

.1 NOUNS **improbity, dishonesty,** dishonor; **unscrupulousness, unconscientiousness; corruption,** corruptness, corruptedness; **crookedness, criminality,** feloniousness, **fraudulence** or fraudulency, underhandedness, unsavoriness, fishiness or shadiness [both informal], indirection, shiftiness, slipperiness, deviousness, evasiveness, unstraightforwardness, trickiness.

.2 **knavery, roguery, rascality,** rascalry, **villainy,** reprobacy, scoundrelism; chicanery 618.4; knavishness, roguishness, scampishness, villainousness; **baseness, vileness,** degradation, turpitude, moral turpitude.

.3 **deceitfulness** 618.4; falseheartedness 616.4; perjury, forswearing, untruthfulness 616.8, credibility gap; **insincerity,** unsincereness, uncandidness, uncandor, unfrankness, disingenuousness; sharp practice 618.4; fraud 618.8; artfulness, craftiness 735.1; intrigue 654.6.

.4 **untrustworthiness,** unfaithworthiness, untrustiness, **unreliability, undependability,** irresponsibility.

.5 **infidelity, unfaithfulness,** unfaith, faithlessness, trothlessness; **inconstancy, unsteadfastness,** fickleness; **disloyalty,** unloyalty; **falsity,** falseness, untrueness; disaffection, recreancy, dereliction; bad faith, *mala fides* [L], Punic faith; breach of promise, breach of trust or faith, barratry.

.6 **treachery,** treacherousness; **perfidy,** perfidiousness, falseheartedness; **duplicity, double-dealing, foul play;** dirty work or dirty pool or dirty trick [all slang].

.7 **treason,** petty treason, misprision of treason, high treason; lese majesty, sedition; quislingism, fifth-column activity; collaboration, fraternization.

.8 **betrayal,** betrayment, letting down [informal], **double cross** [slang], sellout [slang], Judas kiss, stab in the back.

.9 **corruptibility, venality,** bribability, purchasability.

.10 criminal 986.10, scoundrel 986.3, traitor 619.10, deceiver 619.

.11 VERBS (be dishonest) live by one's wits; shift, shift about, evade; deceive 618.13; cheat 618.17; falsify 616.16; lie 616.19.

.12 **be unfaithful,** not keep faith with, **go back on** [informal], **fail,** break one's word or promise, go back on one's word [informal], break faith, perjure or forswear oneself; forsake, desert 633.5,6; pass the buck [informal]; shift the responsibility or blame.

.13 **play one false,** prove false; **stab in the back,** knife [slang]; bite the hand that feeds one; play dirty pool [slang].

.14 **betray, double-cross** or two-time [both slang], sell out or sell down the river [both slang], turn in; let down or let down one's side [both informal]; inform on 557.12.

.15 **act the traitor,** quisle, turn against, go over to the enemy, turn one's coat, sell oneself; collaborate, fraternize.

.16 ADJS **dishonest, dishonorable; unconscientious,** unconscienced, conscienceless, unconscionable, shameless, without shame or remorse, **unscrupulous, unprincipled,** unethical, immoral, amoral; **corrupt,** corrupted, rotten; **crooked, criminal,** felonious, **fraudulent;** underhand, underhanded; shady [informal], not kosher, unsavory, dark, sinister, insidious, indirect, slippery, devious, tricky, shifty, evasive, unstraightforward; fishy [informal], questionable, suspicious, doubtful, dubious; ill-gotten, ill-got.

.17 **knavish, roguish, scampish, rascally, scoundrelly,** blackguardly, villainous, reprobate, recreant, **base, vile,** degraded; **infamous, notorious.**

.18 **deceitful** 618.20; falsehearted 616.31; perjured, forsworn, untruthful 616.34; **insincere,** unsincere, uncandid, unfrank, disingenuous; artful, crafty 735.12; calculating scheming 654.14.

.19 **untrustworthy,** unfaithworthy, untrusty, trustless, **unreliable, undependable,** fly-by-night, irresponsible, unsure, not to be trusted, not to be depended or relied upon.

.20 **unfaithful,** faithless, of bad faith, trothless; **inconstant, unsteadfast,** fickle; **disloyal,** unloyal; false, **untrue,** not true to disaffected, recreant, derelict, barratrous

.21 **treacherous, perfidious,** falsehearted; **shifty,** slippery, tricky; **double-dealing,** double, ambidextrous; **two-faced** 616.31.

.22 **traitorous,** turncoat, double-crossing *or* two-timing [both slang], betraying; Judas-like, Iscariotic; **treasonable,** treasonous; quisling, quislingistic, fifth-column, Trojan-horse.

.23 **corruptible, venal,** bribable, purchasable, mercenary, hireling.

.24 ADVS **dishonestly, dishonorably; unscrupulously,** unconscientiously; **crookedly,** criminally, feloniously, **fraudulently,** underhandedly, like a thief in the night, insidiously, deviously, shiftily, evasively, fishily [informal], suspiciously, dubiously, by fair means or foul; **deceitfully** 618.22; knavishly, roguishly, villainously; basely, vilely; infamously, notoriously.

.25 **perfidiously,** falseheartedly; **unfaithfully,** faithlessly; **treacherously;** traitorously, treasonably.

## 976. JUSTICE

.1 NOUNS **justice, justness; equity,** equitableness, evenhandedness, measure for measure, give-and-take; **right, rightness,** rightfulness, meetness, properness, propriety, what is right; dueness 960; **justification, justifiableness,** justifiability, warrantedness, warrantability, defensibility; poetic justice; retributive justice, nemesis; summary justice, drumhead justice, rude justice; scales of justice; lawfulness, legality 998.

.2 "truth in action" [Disraeli], "right reason applied to command and prohibition" [Cicero], "the firm and continuous desire to render to everyone that which is his due" [Justinian].

.3 **fairness,** fair-mindedness, candor; the fair thing, the right *or* proper thing, the handsome thing [informal]; **square deal** [informal], **fair shake** [slang]; **fair play,** cricket [informal]; sportsmanship, good sportsmanship, sportsmanliness, sportsmanlikeness.

.4 **impartiality,** detachment, **dispassion,** loftiness, Olympian detachment, **dispassionateness, disinterestedness,** disinterest, unbias, unbiasedness, a fair field and no favor; **neutrality** 806; selflessness, unselfishness 979.

.5 (personifications) Justice, Justitia, blind *or* blindfolded Justice; Rhadamanthus, Minos; (deities) Jupiter Fidius, Deus Fidius; Fides, Fides publica Romani, Fides populi Romani; Nemesis, Dike, Themis; Astraea.

.6 VERBS **be just, be fair,** do the fair thing, do the handsome thing [informal], do the right thing by; **do justice to,** see justice done, see one righted *or* redressed, redress a wrong *or* injustice, remedy an injustice, serve one right, shoot straight with *or* **give a square deal** [both informal], give a fair shake [slang]; give the Devil his due; give and take; bend over backwards, lean over backwards.

.7 **play fair, play the game** [informal], be a good sport, show a proper spirit.

.8 ADJS **just, fair,** square, **fair and square; equitable,** balanced, level [informal], **even,** evenhanded; **right, rightful;** justifiable, justified, warranted, warrantable, defensible; **due** 960.7–10, deserved, merited; meet, meet and right, right and proper, fit, **proper, good,** as it should *or* ought to be; lawful, legal 998.10.

.9 **fair-minded; sporting, sportsmanly,** sportsmanlike; square-dealing *or* square-shooting [both informal].

.10 **impartial, impersonal,** candid, **dispassionate, disinterested,** detached, lofty, Olympian; **unbiased,** uninfluenced, unswayed; **neutral** 806.7; selfless, unselfish 979.5,6.

.11 ADVS **justly, fairly,** fair, in a fair manner; rightfully, rightly, duly, deservedly, meetly, properly; **equitably, equally, evenly,** upon even terms; justifiedly, justifiably, warrantably, warrantedly; **impartially, impersonally,** dispassionately, disinterestedly, without distinction, without regard *or* respect to persons, without fear or favor.

.12 **in justice,** in equity, in reason, in all conscience, in all fairness, **to be fair,** as is only fair *or* right, as is right *or* just *or* fitting *or* proper.

## 977. INJUSTICE

.1 NOUNS **injustice, unjustness; inequity,** iniquity, inequitableness, iniquitousness; **wrong, wrongness,** wrongfulness, unmeetness, improperness, **impropriety;** undueness; what should not be, what ought not *or* must not be; unlawfulness, illegality 999.

.2 **unfairness;** unsportsmanliness, **unsportsmanlikeness;** foul play, foul, a hit below the belt.

.3 **partiality, one-sidedness; bias,** leaning, inclination; undispassionateness, undetachment, interest, involvement, **partisanism,** partisanship, parti pris; unneutrality; **fa-**

voritism, preference, nepotism; unequal *or* preferential treatment, discrimination, unjust legal disability, inequality.

.4 injustice, wrong, injury, grievance, disservice, raw deal [slang]; imposition; mockery *or* miscarriage of justice; great wrong, grave *or* gross injustice; atrocity, outrage.

.5 unjustifiability, unwarrantability, indefensibility; inexcusability, unconscionableness, unpardonability, unforgivableness, inexpiableness, irremissibility.

.6 VERBS not play fair, hit below the belt, give a raw deal [slang].

.7 do one an injustice, wrong, do wrong, do wrong by, do one a wrong, do a disservice; do a great wrong, do a grave *or* gross injustice, commit an atrocity *or* outrage.

.8 favor, prefer, show preference, play favorites, treat unequally, discriminate.

.9 ADJS unjust, inequitable, unequitable, iniquitous, unbalanced, uneven, unequal; wrong, wrongful, unrightful; undue, unmeet, undeserved, unmerited; unlawful, illegal 999.6,7.

.10 unfair, not fair; unsporting, unsportsmanly, unsportsmanlike, not cricket [informal]; foul, below the belt.

.11 partial, interested, involved, partisan, unneutral, one-sided, all on one side, undetached, undispassionate, biased, warped, influenced, swayed.

.12 unjustifiable, unwarrantable, unallowable, unreasonable, indefensible; inexcusable, unconscionable, unpardonable, unforgivable, inexpiable, irremissible.

.13 ADVS unjustly, unfairly; wrongfully, wrongly, undeservedly; inequitably, iniquitously, unequally, unevenly; partially, interestedly, one-sidedly, undispassionately; unjustifiably, unwarrantably, unallowably, unreasonably, indefensibly; inexcusably, unconscionably, unpardonably, unforgivably, inexpiably, irremissibly.

## 978. SELFISHNESS

.1 NOUNS selfishness, selfism, self-seeking, self-serving, self-pleasing, self-indulgence, self-advancement, careerism, personal ambition, self-devotion, self-jealousy, self-sufficiency, self-consideration, self-solicitude, self-absorption, ego trip, self-occupation; self-containment, autism, remoteness 923.1,2; self-interest, self-interestedness, interest; self-esteem, self-admiration 909.1; self-centeredness, narcissism, egotism 909.3; possessiveness, greed, graspingness, acquisitiveness; individualism 762.5,

personalism, privatism, private *or* personal desires, private *or* personal aims.

.2 ungenerousness, unmagnanimousness, illiberality, meanness, smallness, littleness, paltriness, minginess, pettiness; niggardliness, stinginess 852.2,3.

.3 self-seeker, self-pleaser, self-advancer; narcissist, egotist 909.5; timepleaser, timeserver, temporizer; fortune hunter, tufthunter; self-server, careerist; monopolist, hog, road hog; dog in the manger; individualist, loner *or* lone wolf [both informal].

.4 VERBS please oneself, gratify oneself; egotrip, be *or* go on an ego trip [all informal]; indulge *or* pamper *or* coddle oneself, consult one's own wishes, look after one's own interests, take care of *or* look out for number one [both informal].

.5 ADJS selfish, self-seeking, self-serving, self-pleasing, self-advancing, careerist, ambitious for self, self-indulgent, self-jealous, self-sufficient, self-interested, self-considerative, self-besot, self-devoted, self-occupied, self-absorbed, wrapped up in oneself, self-contained, autistic, remote 923.5, 6; self-esteeming, self-admiring 909.8; self-centered, narcissistic, egotistical 909.10; possessive, greedy, grasping, acquisitive; individualistic 762.21, personalistic, privatistic.

.6 ungenerous, illiberal, unchivalrous, mean, small, little, paltry, mingy, petty; niggardly, stingy 852.8,9.

.7 ADVS selfishly, for oneself, in one's own interest, from selfish *or* interested motives, to gain some private ends.

## 979. UNSELFISHNESS

.1 NOUNS unselfishness, selflessness; altruism; self-subjection, self-subordination, self-abasement, self-effacement; humility 906; modesty 908; self-neglect, self-neglectfulness, self-forgetfulness; self-renunciation, self-renouncement; self-denial, self-abnegation; self-sacrifice, sacrifice, self-immolation, self-devotion, devotion, dedication, commitment, consecration; disinterest, disinterestedness; unpossessiveness, unacquisitiveness.

.2 magnanimity, magnanimousness, generosity, generousness, openhandedness, liberality, liberalness; bigness, bigheartedness, greatheartedness, largeheartedness, big *or* large *or* great heart, greatness of heart *or* soul; noble-mindedness, high-mindedness, idealism; nobleness, nobility, princeliness, greatness, loftiness, elevation, exaltation sublimity; chivalry, chivalrousness, knightliness, errantry, knight-errantry; heroism.

.3 VERBS not have a selfish bone in one's body, think only of others; put oneself out, go out of the way, lean over backwards; sacrifice, make a sacrifice; subject oneself, subordinate oneself, abase oneself.

.4 observe the golden rule, do as one would be done by, do unto others as you would have others do unto you.

.5 ADJS **unselfish, selfless**; altruistic; self-unconscious, self-forgetful, self-abasing, self-effacing; **humble** 906.9; **unpretentious, modest** 908.9–13; self-neglectful, self-neglecting; **self-denying**, self-renouncing, self-abnegating, self-abnegatory; **self-sacrificing**, self-immolating, sacrificing, self-devotional, self-devoted, devoted, dedicated, committed, consecrated, unsparing of self, disinterested; unpossessive, unacquisitive.

.6 **magnanimous, generous**, openhanded, liberal; **big, bighearted**, greathearted, largehearted, great of heart or soul; noble-minded, high-minded, idealistic; **noble**, princely, handsome, great, high, elevated, **lofty**, exalted, sublime; chivalrous, knightly; heroic.

.7 ADVS **unselfishly, altruistically**, forgetful of self; for others.

.8 **magnanimously, generously**, openhandedly, **liberally**; **bigheartedly**, greatheartedly, largeheartedly; **nobly**, handsomely; chivalrously, knightly.

## 980. VIRTUE

### (moral goodness)

.1 NOUNS **virtue, virtuousness, goodness, righteousness**, rectitude, right conduct, the straight and narrow; probity 974; **morality**, moral rectitude or virtue, morale; **saintliness**, saintlikeness, angelicalness; godliness 1028.2.

.2 "the health of the soul" [Joseph Joubert], "the fount whence honour springs" [Marlowe], "the adherence in action to the nature of things" [Emerson], "victorious resistance to one's vital desire to do this, that or the other" [James Branch Cabell], "to do unwitnessed what we should be capable of doing before all the world" [La Rochefoucauld].

.3 **purity**, immaculacy, **chastity** 988; guiltlessness, innocence 984.

.4 **uncorruptness**, uncorruptedness, incorruptness; **unsinfulness**, sinlessness; un-

wickedness, uniniquitousness; undegenerateness, undepravedness, undissoluteness, undebauchedness.

.5 **cardinal virtues**, natural virtues; prudence, justice, temperance, fortitude; theological virtues or supernatural virtues; faith, hope, charity or love.

.6 VERBS **be good**, do no evil; keep in the right path, walk the straight path, follow the straight and narrow, keep on the straight and narrow way or path; fight the good fight.

.7 ADJS **virtuous, good, moral**; **upright, honest** 974.13–20; **righteous, just, straight**, right-minded; **angelic**, seraphic; **saintly**, saintlike; **godly** 1028.9.

.8 **chaste, immaculate, pure** 988.4; guiltless, innocent 984.6.

.9 **uncorrupt**, uncorrupted, incorrupt, incorrupted; **unsinful**, sinless; **unwicked**, uniniquitous, unerring, unfallen; undegenerate, undepraved, undemoralized, undissolute, undebauched.

## 981. VICE

### (moral badness)

.1 NOUNS **vice**, viciousness; criminality, **wrongdoing** 982; **immorality**, unmorality, **evil**; **amorality** 957.4; **unvirtuousness**, ungoodness; **unrighteousness**, ungodliness, unsaintliness, unangelicalness; **uncleanness**, impurity, **unchastity** 989; waywardness, wantonness, prodigality; delinquency, moral delinquency; peccability; backsliding, recidivism; **evil nature, carnality** 987.2.

.2 **vice, weakness**, weakness of the flesh, **flaw**, moral flaw, frailty, infirmity; failing, failure; weak point, weak side, foible; bad habit, besetting sin; **fault, imperfection** 678.

.3 **iniquity, evil**, bad, wrong, error, obliquity, villainy, knavery, reprobacy, peccancy, **abomination, atrocity**, shame, disgrace, scandal, **infamy**; sin 982.2.

.4 **wickedness, badness**, naughtiness, evilness, **viciousness, sinfulness, iniquitousness; baseness**, rankness, vileness, foulness, arrantness, nefariousness, heinousness, villainousness, flagitiousness; fiendishness, hellishness; devilishness, devilry, deviltry.

.5 **turpitude, moral turpitude**; corruption, corruptedness, corruptness, rottenness, moral pollution or pollutedness; **decadence** or decadency, debasement, degradation, demoralization, abjection; degeneracy, degenerateness, degeneration, reprobacy, **depravity**, depravedness, depravation; **dissoluteness, profligacy**; abandonment, abandon.

.6 **obduracy, hardheartedness, hardness, callousness**, heartlessness, hardness of heart, heart of stone.

.7 sink, **sink of corruption; den of iniquity**, den, **fleshpots, hellhole**; hole or joint [both slang]; Sodom, Gomorrah, Babylon; brothel 989.9.

.8 VERBS do wrong, sin 982.5.

.9 **go wrong**, go astray, **err**, deviate from the path of virtue, leave the straight and narrow; **fall, lapse, slip, trip; degenerate** 692.19; go to the bad 693.24; backslide 696.4.

.10 **demoralize**, vitiate, drive to the dogs; **corrupt** 692.14; **sully, soil, defile**.

.11 ADJS **vice-laden, vice-prone, vicious**, steeped in vice; **immoral, unmoral; amoral**, nonmoral.

.12 **unvirtuous**, virtueless, ungood; **unrighteous, ungodly, unsaintly**, unangelic; **unclean**, impure, **unchaste** 989.23; fleshly, carnal 987.6, wayward, wanton, prodigal; **erring, fallen, lapsed**, postlapsarian; frail, weak, infirm; Adamic; peccable; backsliding, recidivist, recidivistic; of easy virtue 989.26.

.13 **diabolic(al), devilish**, demoniac or demoniacal, satanic, Mephistophelian; **fiendish**, fiendlike; **hellish, hellborn, infernal**.

.14 **corrupt**, corrupted, vice-corrupted, polluted, morally polluted, rotten, tainted, contaminated, vitiated; **warped, perverted; decadent**, debased, degraded, reprobate, **depraved, debauched, dissolute, degenerate**, profligate, abandoned, gone to the bad or dogs, sunk or steeped in iniquity, rotten at or to the core.

.15 **evil-minded, evilhearted, blackhearted; base-minded**, low-minded; low-thoughted, dirty or dirty-minded [all slang].

.16 **wicked, evil, vicious, bad, naughty, wrong, sinful, iniquitous, peccant**, reprobate; dark, black; **base, low, vile, foul**, rank, flagrant, **arrant**, nefarious, heinous, villainous, criminal, knavish, flagitious; abominable, atrocious, monstrous, unspeakable, execrable, damnable; **shameful**, disgraceful, scandalous, **infamous, unpardonable**, unforgivable; **improper**, reprehensible, blamable, blameworthy, unworthy.

.17 **hardened, hard, case-hardened, obdurate**, inured, indurated; **callous, calloused**,

seared; **hardhearted**, heartless; **shameless**, lost to shame, lost to all sense of honor, conscienceless, unblushing, **brazen**.

.18 **irreclaimable**, irredeemable, unredeemable, unregenerate, **irreformable**, incorrigible, past praying for; shriftless, graceless; **lost**.

.19 ADVS **wickedly, evilly, sinfully, iniquitously**, peccantly, **viciously**; basely, vilely, foully, rankly, arrantly, flagrantly, flagitiously.

## 982. WRONGDOING, SIN

.1 NOUNS **wrongdoing, evildoing**, misdoing, wrong conduct, **misconduct, misdemeanor**, misfeasance, malfeasance, malversation, **malpractice**, evil courses, machinations of the devil; **sin**, "thou scarlet sin" [Shakespeare], "the transgression of the law" [Bible]; **crime, criminality**, lawbreaking, feloniousness, criminal tendency, criminosis; viciousness, **vice** 981; misprision, negative or positive misprision, misprision of treason or felony.

.2 **misdeed, misdemeanor**, misfeasance, malfeasance, malefaction, criminal or guilty or sinful act, **offense**, injustice, injury, **wrong, iniquity, evil**, peccancy, *malum* [L]; **tort; error, fault**, breach; **impropriety**, slight or minor wrong, venial sin, **indiscretion**, peccadillo, trip, slip, lapse; **transgression**, trespass; **sin**, "deed without a name" [Shakespeare]; deadly or mortal sin, grave or heavy sin, unutterable sin, unpardonable or unforgivable or inexpiable sin; sin against the Holy Ghost; sin of commission; sin of omission, nonfeasance, omission, failure, dereliction, delinquency; **crime, felony**; capital crime; war crime, crime against humanity, genocide; **outrage, atrocity**, enormity.

.3 **deadly sin, seven deadly sins: pride**, superbia; **envy**, invidia; **avarice**, greed, avaritia; **sloth**, acedia; **wrath**, anger, ira; **gluttony**, gula; **lust**, luxuria.

.4 **original sin, fall from grace, fall, fall of man**, fall of Adam or Adam's fall, sin of Adam.

.5 VERBS **do wrong**, do amiss, misdemean oneself, **err, offend; sin**, commit sin; **transgress**, trespass.

.6 ADJS **wrongdoing, evildoing**, malefactory, malfeasant; **wrong**, iniquitous, **sinful**, **wicked** 981.16; **criminal**, felonious.

## 983. GUILT

.1 NOUNS **guilt**, guiltiness; **criminality**, peccancy; **culpability**, reprehensibility, blam ability, blameworthiness; chargeability, censurability, censurableness, reproachability, reproachableness, reprovability, reprovableness, inculpation, implication, involvement, complicity, impeachability, impeachableness, indictability, indictableness, arraignability, arraignableness; red-handedness, dirty hands, red or bloody hands, "hangman's hands" [Shakespeare]; guilty conscience, guilt-feelings; onus, burden.

.2 VERBS be guilty, look guilty, look like the cat that swallowed the canary, blush, stammer.

.3 ADJS guilty, peccant, criminal, to blame, at fault, faulty, on one's head; culpable, reprehensible, censurable, reproachable, reprovable, inculpated, implicated, involved, impeachable, indictable, arraignable.

.4 ADVS red-handed, red-hand, in the act, in the very act, in flagrante delicto [L].

.5 guiltily, shamefacedly, sheepishly, with a guilty conscience.

## 984. INNOCENCE

.1 NOUNS innocence, innocency, innocentness; unfallen or unlapsed or prelapsarian state; unguiltiness, guiltlessness, faultlessness, blamelessness, reproachlessness, sinlessness, offenselessness; spotlessness, stainlessness, taintlessness, unblemishedness; purity, cleanness, cleanliness, whiteness, immaculacy, impeccability; clean hands, clean slate, clear conscience, nothing to hide.

.2 childlikeness 736.1; lamblikeness, dovelikeness, angelicness; unacquaintance with evil, uncorruptedness, incorruptness, pristineness, undefiledness.

.3 inculpability, unblamability, unblamableness, unblameworthiness, irreproachability, irreproachableness, impeccability, impeccableness, unexceptionability, unexceptionableness, irreprehensibility, irreprehensibleness, uncensurability, uncensurableness, unimpeachability, unimpeachableness, unindictableness, unarraignableness.

.4 innocent, babe, newborn babe, infant, babe in the woods, child, mere child, lamb, dove, angel.

.5 VERBS know no wrong, have clean hands, have a clear conscience, look as if butter would not melt in one's mouth.

.6 ADJS innocent; unfallen, unlapsed, prelapsarian; unguilty, not guilty, guiltless, faultless, blameless, reproachless, sinless,

offenseless, with clean hands, "blameless in life and pure of crime" [Horace]; clear, in the clear; without reproach, sans reproche [Fr]; innocent as a lamb, lamblike, dovelike, angelic, childlike 736.5; unacquainted with or untouched by evil, uncorrupted, incorrupt, pristine, undefiled.

.7 spotless, stainless, taintless, unblemished, unspotted, untainted, unsoiled, unsullied, undefiled; pure, clean, immaculate, impeccable, white, "without unspotted, innocent within" [Dryden].

.8 inculpable, unblamable, unblameworthy, irreproachable, irreprovable, irreprehensible, uncensurable, unimpeachable, unindictable, unarraignable, unobjectionable, unexceptionable, above suspicion.

.9 ADVS innocently, guiltlessly, unguiltily, with a clear conscience; unknowingly, unconsciously, unawares.

## 985. GOOD PERSON

.1 NOUNS good person, good man or woman or child, worthy, prince, nature's nobleman, man after one's own heart; persona grata [L], acceptable person; good fellow, capital fellow, good sort, right sort, a decent sort of fellow, good lot [Brit informal], no end of a fellow; real man or woman, mensch [Yid]; gentleman, perfect gentleman, a gentleman and a scholar; lady, perfect lady; gem, jewel, pearl, diamond; rough diamond, diamond in the rough; honest man 974.8.

.2 [slang or informal terms] good guy, crackerjack, brick, trump, good egg, stout fellow, nice guy, good Joe, likely lad, no slouch, doll, pussycat.

.3 good or respectable citizen, excellent or exemplary citizen, good neighbor, burgher, pillar of society, pillar of the church, salt of the earth; Christian or true Christian [both informal].

.4 paragon, ideal, beau ideal, nonpareil, chevalier sans peur et sans reproche [Fr], good example, shining example; exemplar, model, pattern, standard, mirror, "the observed of all observers" [Shakespeare]; Übermensch [Ger; Nietzsche]; one in a thousand or ten thousand, man of men, a man among men.

.5 hero, god, demigod, phoenix; heroine, goddess, demigoddess; idol.

.6 holy man; great soul, mahatma; guru, rishi [Skt]; starets [Russ]; saint, angel 1017.

## 986. BAD PERSON

.1 NOUNS **bad person, bad man** or **woman** or **child,** unworthy or disreputable person, unworthy, disreputable, **undesirable,** *persona non grata* [L], unacceptable or unwanted or objectionable person, bad news [informal]; bad example; –eer.

.2 **wretch,** mean wretch, **beggarly fellow, beggar, blighter** [Brit slang]; **bum** or **bummer** or **lowlifer** or **lowlife** or **mucker** [all slang], caitiff, budmash [India], pilgarlic; devil, **poor devil,** *pauvre diable* [Fr], poor creature, *mauvais sujet* [Fr]; **sad case,** sad sack or sad sack of shit [both slang]; **good-for-nothing, good-for-naught, nogood** [informal], **ne'er-do-well,** wastrel, *vaurien* [Fr], worthless fellow; **derelict,** skid-row bum, Bowery bum, tramp, hobo, beachcomber, **drifter,** drunkard, vagrant, vag [informal], vagabond, truant, stiff or bindlestiff [both slang], swagman or sundowner [both Austral]; human wreck.

.3 **rascal,** precious rascal, rogue, knave, **scoundrel,** villain, blackguard, **scamp, scalawag** [informal], spalpeen [Ir], rapscallion, **devil;** shyster; sneak.

.4 "a rascally yeaforsooth knave", "a foulmouthed and calumnious knave", "poor cuckoldy knave", "a poor, decayed, ingenious, foolish, rascally knave", "an arrant, rascally, beggarly, lousy knave", "a slipper and subtle knave, a finder of occasions", "a whoreson, beetle-headed, flap-ear'd knave", "filthy, worsted-stocking knave; a lily-livered, action-taking knave", "a knave; a rascal; an eater of broken meats; a base, proud, shallow, beggarly, threesuited, hundred-pound, filthy, worstedstocking knave" [all Shakespeare].

.5 **reprobate,** recreant, **miscreant,** bad or sorry lot [both Brit informal], bad egg [informal], bad'un or wrong'un [both slang]; scapegrace, black sheep; lost soul, lost sheep, *âme damnée* [Fr], backslider, recidivist, fallen angel; degenerate, pervert; profligate, **lecher** 989.10,11; trollop, **whore** 989.14–16; **pimp** 989.18.

.6 [slang or informal terms] **bastard, son of a bitch, SOB, jerk, creep,** mother, **shit,** turd, shithead, fart, **louse, meanie, heel, shitheel, rat, stinker,** stinkard, pill, bugger; **hood, hooligan** 943.3,4.

.7 **beast, animal; cur,** dog, hound, whelp, mongrel; **reptile,** viper, serpent, snake; vermin, varmint [dial], hyena; **swine,** pig; **skunk,** polecat; insect, worm.

.8 **cad, bounder** or **rotter** [both informal].

.9 **wrongdoer, malefactor, sinner,** transgressor, delinquent; **malfeasor,** misfeasor, nonfeasor; misdemeanant, misdemeanist; **culprit, offender; evil person, evil man** or **woman** or **child, evildoer** 943.

.10 **criminal, felon, crook** [informal], public enemy, **lawbreaker,** scofflaw; **gangster** or mobster [both informal], **racketeer;** swindler 619.3,4; thief 825; thug 943.3,4; **desperado,** desperate criminal; **outlaw,** fugitive, **convict,** jailbird, gaolbird [Brit]; gallows bird [informal]; **traitor,** betrayer, quisling, Judas, double-dealer, two-timer [slang], **deceiver** 619.

.11 **the underworld,** gangland, gangdom, **organized crime,** the rackets, the mob, the syndicate, the Mafia, Cosa Nostra, Black Hand.

.12 **the wicked,** the bad, the evil, the unrighteous, the reprobate; sons of men, sons of Belial, sons or children of the devil, limbs of Satan, children of darkness; **scum of the earth,** dregs of society.

## 987. SENSUALITY

.1 NOUNS **sensuality,** sensualness, sensualism; appetitiveness, appetite; **voluptuousness,** luxuriousness, luxury; **unchastity** 989; **pleasure-seeking;** sybaritism; **hedonism,** Cyrenaic hedonism, Cyrenaicism, ethical hedonism, psychological hedonism, hedonics, hedonic calculus; epicurism, epicureanism; pleasure principle, *Lustprinzip* [Ger].

.2 **carnality,** carnal-mindedness; **fleshliness,** flesh; animal or carnal nature, the flesh, the beast, Adam, the Old Adam, the offending Adam, fallen state or nature, lapsed state or nature, postlapsarian state or nature; **animality, animalism, bestiality,** beastliness, brutishness, **brutality;** coarseness, grossness; swinishness; **earthiness,** unspirituality, nonspirituality, materialism.

.3 **sensualist,** sensuist; **voluptuary, pleasure-seeker,** sybarite, Cyrenaic, Sardanapalus, Heliogabalus, **hedonist,** *bon vivant* [Fr] carpet knight; epicure, epicurean; gourmet, gourmand; swine.

.4 VERBS **sensualize, carnalize,** coarsen, brutify.

.5 ADJS **sensual;** appetitive; **voluptuous,** luxurious; **unchaste** 989.23, **hedonistic,** pleasure-seeking, pleasure-bent, bent on pleasure, luxury-loving, epicurean, sybaritic, Cyrenaic.

.6 **carnal,** carnal-minded, **fleshly, bodily,** physical; Adamic, fallen, lapsed, postlapsarian; animal, animalistic; **brutish, brutal,** brute; **bestial,** beastly, beastlike; Circean; coarse, gross; swinish; orgiastic; **earthy,** unspiritual, nonspiritual, material, materialistic.

## 988. CHASTITY

.1 NOUNS **chastity, virtue,** virtuousness, honor; **purity,** cleanness, cleanliness; whiteness, snowiness; **immaculacy,** immaculateness, spotlessness, stainlessness, taintlessness, blotlessness, unspottedness, unstainedness, unblottedness, untaintedness, unblemishedness, unsoiledness, unsulliedness, undefiledness, untarnishedness; uncorruptness 980.4; sexual innocence, innocence 984.

.2 **decency,** seemliness, propriety, **decorum,** decorousness, elegance, delicacy; **modesty,** shame, pudicity, pudency.

.3 **continence** or **continency;** abstinence 992.2; celibacy; **virginity,** intactness, maidenhood, maidenhead; Platonic love; marital fidelity or faithfulness.

.4 ADJS **chaste, virtuous; pure,** purehearted, pure in heart; **clean,** cleanly; **immaculate, spotless,** blotless, stainless, taintless, white, snowy; **unsoiled, unsullied, undefiled,** untarnished, unstained, unspotted, untainted, unblemished, unblotted, uncorrupt 980.9; "as chaste as Diana", "as chaste as unsunn'd snow" [both Shakespeare], "chaste as morning dew" [Edward Young]; sexually innocent, innocent 984.6–8.

.5 **decent, modest, decorous,** delicate, elegant, proper, becoming, seemly.

.6 **continent;** abstinent 992.10; celibate; virginal, **virgin,** maidenly, vestal, intact; Platonic.

.7 **undebauched, undissipated, undissolute,** unwanton, unlicentious.

## 989. UNCHASTITY

.1 NOUNS **unchastity,** unchasteness; unvirtuousness; **impurity,** uncleanness, uncleanliness, taintedness, soiledness, sulliedness, maculacy; **indecency** 990.

.2 **incontinence,** uncontinence; intemperance 993; unrestraint 762.3.

.3 **profligacy, dissoluteness, licentiousness,** license, unbridledness, wildness, fastness, rakishness, gallantry, **libertinism,** libertinage; **dissipation, debauchery,** debauchment; venery, wenching, whoring, womanizing.

.4 **wantonness, waywardness; looseness,** laxity, lightness, loose morals, easy virtue, whorishness, chambering, **promiscuity,** sleeping around [informal]; swinging [informal].

.5 **lasciviousness, lechery, lecherousness, lewdness,** bawdiness, **dirtiness,** salacity, salaciousness, **carnality,** animality, fleshliness, **sexuality, sexiness, lust, lustfulness,** prurience or pruriency; **obscenity** 990.4; concupiscence, lickerishness, libidinousness, randiness, horniness [slang], lubricity, lubriciousness, **sensuality,** eroticism, goatishness; satyrism, satyriasis, gynecomania; nymphomania, furor uterinus, hysteromania, uteromania, clitoromania; erotomania, eroticomania, aphrodisiomania.

.6 **seduction,** seducement, **betrayal; violation,** abuse; **debauchment, defilement,** ravishment, ravage, despoilment, fate worse than death; priapism; defloration, deflowering; **rape,** sexual or criminal assault.

.7 (illicit sexual intercourse) **adultery,** criminal conversation or congress or cohabitation, extramarital or premarital sex, extramarital or premarital relations, extracurricular sex or relations [informal], **fornication;** free love, free-lovism; **incest;** concubinage; cuckoldry.

.8 **prostitution, harlotry,** whoredom, **streetwalking;** soliciting, solicitation; Mrs. Warren's profession; whoremonging, whoremastery, pimping, pandering.

.9 **brothel, house of prostitution,** house of assignation, house of joy or ill repute or ill fame, **whorehouse,** bawdyhouse, sporting house, disorderly house, **cathouse, bordello,** bagnio, stew, dive, den of vice, den or sink of iniquity, crib, joint; panel house or panel den; red-light district, tenderloin, stews, street of fallen women.

.10 **libertine, swinger** [informal], **profligate, rake,** rakehell, rip [informal], **roué,** wanton, womanizer, walking phallus, debauchee, rounder [archaic], **wolf** [slang], woman chaser, skirt chaser [slang], gay dog, gay deceiver, gallant, philanderer, lover-boy [informal], lady-killer, Lothario, Don Juan, Casanova.

.11 **lecher, satyr, goat, old goat, dirty old man;** whorer or whoremonger [both archaic], whoremaster, whorehound [slang]; Priapus; gynecomaniac; erotomaniac, eroticomaniac, aphrodisiomaniac.

.12 **seducer, betrayer,** deceiver; **debaucher, ravisher,** ravager, violator, despoiler, defiler; raper, **rapist.**

.13 adulterer, fornicator; adulteress, fornicatress, fornicatrix.

.14 strumpet, trollop, wench, hussy, slut, jade, baggage, *cocotte* [Fr], grisette; tart *or* chippy *or* floozy *or* broad [all slang], bitch, drab, trull, quean, harridan, Jezebel, wanton, whore [informal], bad woman, loose woman, easy woman [informal], easy lay [slang], woman of easy virtue, frail sister; pickup; nymphomaniac, nympho [slang], hysteromaniac, uteromaniac, clitoromaniac; nymphet.

.15 demimonde, demimondaine, demirep; courtesan, adventuress, seductress, femme fatale, vampire, vamp, temptress; hetaera, houri, harem girl, odalisque; Jezebel, Messalina, Delilah, Thais, Phryne, Aspasia, Lais.

.16 prostitute, harlot, whore, *fille de joie* [Fr], daughter of joy, call girl *or* B-girl [both informal], scarlet woman, unfortunate woman, painted woman, fallen woman, erring sister, streetwalker, hustler *or* hooker [both slang], woman of the town, *poule* [Fr], stew, meretrix, Cyprian, Paphian; white slave.

.17 mistress, woman, kept woman, kept mistress, paramour, concubine, doxy, playmate, spiritual *or* unofficial wife.

.18 procurer, pimp, pander *or* panderer, *maquereau* [Fr], bawd; gigolo, fancy man; procuress, madam [informal]; white slaver.

.19 VERBS be promiscuous, sleep around, swing [informal]; debauch, wanton, rake, chase women, womanize, whore, sow one's wild oats; philander 932.18; dissipate 993.6; fornicate, commit adultery; grovel, wallow, wallow in the mire.

.20 seduce, betray, deceive, mislead, lead astray; debauch, ravish, ravage, despoil, ruin; deflower, pop one's cherry [slang]; defile, soil, sully; violate, abuse; rape, force.

.21 prostitute; pimp, procure, pander.

.22 cuckold, father upon; wear horns, wear the horn.

.23 ADJS unchaste, unvirtuous, unvirginal; impure, unclean; indecent 990.5; soiled, sullied, smirched, besmirched, defiled, tainted, maculate.

.24 incontinent, uncontinent; orgiastic; intemperate 993.7; unrestrained 762.23.

.25 profligate, licentious, unbridled, free; dissolute, dissipated, debauched, abandoned; wild, fast, gallant, gay, rakish; rakehell, rakehellish, rakehelly.

.26 wanton, wayward, Paphian; loose, lax, slack, loose-moraled, of loose morals, of easy virtue, easy [informal], light, no better than she should be, whorish, chambering, promiscuous.

.27 freeloving; adulterous, illicit, extramarital, premarital; incestuous.

.28 prostitute, prostituted, whorish, harlot, scarlet, fallen, meretricious, streetwalking, hustling [slang], on the town *or* streets, on the *pavé*.

.29 lascivious, lecherous, sexy, salacious, carnal, animal, sexual, lustful, ithyphallic, hot, prurient, concupiscent, lickerish, libidinous, randy, horny [slang], lubricious; lewd, bawdy, dirty, obscene 990.9; erotic, sensual, fleshly; goatish, satyric, priapic, gynecomaniacal; nymphomaniacal, hysteromaniacal, uteromaniacal, clitoromaniacal; erotomaniacal, eroticomaniacal, aphrodisiomaniacal.

## 990. INDECENCY

.1 NOUNS indecency, indelicacy, inelegance *or* inelegancy, indecorousness, indecorum, impropriety, inappropriateness, unseemliness, indiscretion, indiscreetness; unchastity 989.

.2 immodesty, unmodestness, impudicity; exhibitionism; shamelessness, unembarrassedness; brazenness, forwardness, boldness, flagrancy, notoriousness.

.3 vulgarity, uncouthness, coarseness, grossness, rankness, rawness; earthiness, frankness; raciness, saltiness, spiciness.

.4 obscenity, dirtiness, bawdry, ribaldry, pornography, porno *or* porn [both informal], hard-core *or* soft-core pornography, salacity, smut, dirt, filth; lewdness, bawdiness, salaciousness, smuttiness, foulness, filthiness, nastiness, vileness, offensiveness; scurrility, fescenninity; Rabelaisianism; erotic art *or* literature, pornographic art *or* literature; sexploitation; blue movie *or* dirty movie *or* porno film *or* skin flick [all slang], stag film [informal], X-rated movie; pornographomania, erotographomania, iconolagny.

.5 ADJS indecent, indelicate, inelegant, indecorous, improper, inappropriate, unseemly, unbecoming, indiscreet.

.6 immodest, unmodest; exhibitionistic; shameless, unashamed, unembarrassed, unabashed, unblushing, brazen, brazenfaced; forward, bold, flagrant, notorious.

.7 risqué, risky, racy, salty, spicy, off-color, suggestive, scabrous.

.8 **vulgar, uncouth, coarse, gross,** rank, raw, broad, low; gutter; **earthy,** frank.

.9 **obscene, lewd, bawdy,** ithyphallic, **ribald, pornographic, salacious,** sultry [informal], lurid, **dirty, smutty,** raunchy [slang], blue, smoking-room, impure, unchaste, unclean, **foul, filthy, nasty,** vile, fulsome, offensive, unprintable, unrepeatable, not fit for mixed company; scurrilous, scurrile, Fescennine; foul-mouthed, foul-tongued, foul-spoken; Rabelaisian.

## 991. ASCETICISM

.1 NOUNS **asceticism, austerity, self-denial,** rigor; **puritanism,** eremitism, anchoritism, anchorite or anchoritic monasticism, monasticism, monachism; Sabbatarianism; Albigensianism, Waldensianism, Catharism; Yoga; mortification, self-mortification, maceration, flagellation; **abstinence** 992.2; fasting 995; voluntary poverty, mendicantism, Franciscanism; Trappism.

.2 **ascetic, puritan,** Sabbatarian; Albigensian, Waldensian, Catharist; **abstainer** 992.4; anchorite, **hermit** 924.5; yogi, yogin; sannyasi, bhikshu, dervish, fakir, flagellant; mendicant, Franciscan; Trappist.

.3 ADJS **ascetic, austere,** self-denying, rigoristic, **puritanical,** eremitic, anchoritic 924.9, Sabbatarian; Albigensian, Waldensian, Catharist; **abstinent** 992.10; mendicant, wedded to poverty, Franciscan; Trappist; flagellant.

## 992. TEMPERANCE

.1 NOUNS **temperance,** temperateness, **moderation,** moderateness, sophrosyne; golden mean; nothing in excess, sobriety, soberness, frugality, forbearance, abnegation; renunciation, renouncement; denial, **self-denial;** restraint, constraint, **self-restraint; self-control,** self-mastery, self-discipline.

.2 **abstinence,** abstention, abstainment, **abstemiousness,** refraining, refrainment, avoidance, eschewal, passing up [informal]; **total abstinence, teetotalism,** nephalism, Rechabitism; the pledge; Encratism, Shakerism; Pythagorism, Pythagoreanism; sexual abstinence, celibacy 934; chastity 988; gymnosophy; Stoicism; vegetarianism, fruitarianism; plain living, spare diet, simple diet; Spartan fare, Lenten fare; fish day, Friday, banyan day; fast 995.2,3; **continence** 988.3; asceticism 991.

.3 **prohibition,** prohibitionism; Eighteenth Amendment, Volstead Act.

.4 **abstainer,** abstinent; **teetotaler,** teetotalist; nephalist, Rechabite, hydropot, water-drinker; vegetarian, fruitarian; banian, banya; gymnosophist; Pythagorean, Pythagorist; Encratite, Apostolici, Shaker; ascetic 991.2.

.5 **prohibitionist, dry** [slang]; Anti-Saloon League; Women's Christian Temperance Union, WCTU.

.6 VERBS **restrain oneself,** constrain oneself, curb oneself, hold back, **avoid excess; limit oneself, restrict oneself; control oneself,** control one's appetites, repress or inhibit one's desires, contain oneself, discipline oneself, master oneself, exercise self-control or self-restraint, keep oneself under control, keep in or within bounds, keep within compass or limits, know when one has had enough; live plainly or simply or frugally; mortify oneself, mortify the flesh, control the fleshly lusts, control the carnal man or the old Adam, "let the passions be amenable to reason" [Cicero]; eat to live, not live to eat; eat sparingly.

.7 **abstain,** abstain from, refrain, **refrain from, forbear, forgo,** spare, withhold, hold back, **avoid, shun,** eschew, **pass up** [informal], **keep from,** keep or stand or hold aloof from, have nothing to do with, take no part in, have no hand in, **let alone,** let well enough alone, let go by, **deny oneself,** do without, not or never touch.

.8 **swear off, renounce,** forswear, **give up,** abandon, stop, discontinue; take the pledge, get on the wagon or water wagon [slang].

.9 ADJS **temperate, moderate,** sober, frugal, restrained, **sparing,** stinting, measured.

.10 **abstinent,** abstentious, **abstemious;** teetotal, sworn off, on the wagon or water wagon [slang]; nephalistic, Rechabite; Encratic, Apostolic, Shaker; Pythagorean; sexually abstinent, celibate, chaste; Stoic; vegetarian, fruitarian; Spartan, Lenten; **continent** 988.6; ascetic 991.3.

.11 prohibitionist, antisaloon, **dry** [informal].

.12 ADVS **temperately, moderately, sparingly,** stintingly, frugally, in moderation, within compass or bounds.

## 993. INTEMPERANCE

.1 NOUNS **intemperance,** intemperateness, **indulgence, self-indulgence; overindulgence,** overdoing; **unrestraint,** unconstraint, indiscipline, uncontrol; **immoderation,** immoderacy, immoderateness; inordinacy, inordinateness; excess, excessiveness, too much, too-muchness [informal]; prodigality, extravagance; crapulence or crapulency, crapulousness; incontinence 989.2; swinishness, gluttony 994; drunkenness 996.1.

.2 dissipation, licentiousness; riotous living, free living, high living [informal], fast or killing pace; debauchery, debauchment; carousal, carouse; debauch, orgy, saturnalia.

.3 dissipater, rounder [archaic], free liver, high liver [informal]; nighthawk or night owl [both informal].

.4 VERBS indulge, indulge oneself, indulge one's appetites, "indulge in easy vices" [Samuel Johnson], deny oneself nothing or not at all; give oneself up to, give free course to, give free rein to; live well or high, live high on the hog [slang], live off the fat of the land; indulge in, luxuriate in, wallow in; roll in.

.5 overindulge, overdo, carry to excess, carry too far, go the limit, go whole hog [slang], not know when to stop; dine not wisely but too well.

.6 dissipate, plunge into dissipation, debauch, wanton, carouse, run riot, live hard or fast, squander one's money in riotous living, burn the candle at both ends, keep up a fast or killing pace, sow one's wild oats, have one's fling, "eat, drink, and be merry" [Bible].

.7 ADJS intemperate, indulgent, self-indulgent; overindulgent, overindulging, unthrifty, unfrugal, immoderate, inordinate, excessive, too much, prodigal, extravagant, extreme, unmeasured, unlimited; crapulous, crapulent; undisciplined, uncontrolled, unbridled, unconstrained, unrestrained 762.23; incontinent 989.24; swinish, gluttonous 994.6; bibulous 996.34.

.8 licentious, dissipated, riotous, dissolute, debauched; free-living, high-living [informal].

.9 orgiastic, saturnalian, corybantic.

.10 ADVS intemperately, prodigally, immoderately, inordinately, excessively, in or to excess, to extremes, beyond all bounds or limits, without restraint; high, high on the hog [slang].

## 994. GLUTTONY

.1 NOUNS gluttony, gluttonousness, greed, greediness, voraciousness, voracity, ravenousness, edacity, crapulence or crapulency, gulosity, rapacity, insatiability; omnivorousness; piggishness, hoggishness,

swinishness, "swinish gluttony" [Milton]; overindulgence, overeating, polyphagia, hyperphagia; intemperance 993.

.2 epicurism, epicureanism, gourmandise, gastronomy.

.3 glutton, greedy eater, hefty or husky eater [informal], trencherman, trencherwoman, belly-god, greedygut or greedyguts [both slang], gorger, gourmand, gourmandizer, gormand, gormandizer, guttler, cormorant; hog or pig [both informal].

.4 VERBS gluttonize, gormandize, indulge one's appetite, live to eat; gorge, engorge, glut, cram, stuff, batten, guttle, guzzle, devour, raven, bolt, gobble, gulp, wolf, gobble or gulp or bolt or wolf down, eat like a horse, eat one's head off [informal], eat out of house and home.

.5 overeat, overgorge, overindulge, make a pig or hog of oneself.

.6 ADJS gluttonous, greedy, voracious, ravenous, edacious, rapacious, insatiable, polyphagic, hyperphagic, Apician; piggish, hoggish, swinish; crapulous, crapulent; intemperate 993.7; omnivorous, all-devouring; gorging, cramming, glutting, guttling, stuffing, guzzling, wolfing, bolting, gobbling, gulping, gluttonizing.

.7 overfed, overgorged, overindulged.

.8 ADVS gluttonously, greedily, voraciously, ravenously, edaciously; piggishly, hoggishly, swinishly.

## 995. FASTING

.1 NOUNS fasting, abstinence from food; starvation; restriction of intake; punishment of Tantalus.

.2 fast, lack of food; spare or meager diet, Lenten diet, Lenten fare, "Lenten entertainment" [Shakespeare]; short commons or rations, starvation diet, bread and water, bare subsistence; xerophagy, xerophagia; Barmecide or Barmecidal feast.

.3 fast day, jour maigre [Fr]; Lent, Quadragesima; Yom Kippur, Tishah B'Av or Ninth of Av; Ramadan.

.4 VERBS fast, not eat, go hungry, dine with Duke Humphrey; eat sparingly.

.5 ADJS fasting, uneating, unfed; Lenten, quadragesimal.

## 996. INTOXICATION

.1 NOUNS intoxication, inebriation, inebriety, insobriety, besottedness, sottedness, drunkenness, tipsiness, befuddlement, fuddle, fuddlement, fuddledness, tipsification or tiddliness [both informal]; a high; Dutch courage, pot-valiance *or* pot-valiancy, pot-valor; hangover, katzenjammer, morning after [informal].

.2 **bibulousness,** bibacity, bibaciousness, bibulosity, sottishness; serious drinking; crapulence, crapulousness; **intemperance** 993; bacchanalianism; Bacchus, Dionysus.

.3 **alcoholism, dipsomania,** oenomania *or* oinomania, alcoholic psychosis *or* addiction, pathological drunkenness, problem drinking, heavy drinking, habitual drunkenness, ebriosity; delirium tremens 473.9, 10; grog blossom *or* bottle nose [both informal]; gin drinker's liver, cirrhosis of the liver.

.4 **drinking,** imbibing; social drinking; tippling, guzzling, gargling, bibbing; winebibbing, winebibbery; toping, **boozing** *or* swilling [both informal], **hitting the booze** *or* bottle *or* sauce [slang].

.5 **spree,** drinking bout, bout, **celebration,** potation, compotation, symposium, wassail, guzzle, **carouse, carousal,** drunken carousal *or* revelry; **binge, drunk,** bust, tear; **bender** *or* **toot** *or* **bat** *or* **jag** [all slang], pub-crawl [Brit informal]; bacchanal, bacchanalia, bacchanalian; **debauch, orgy.**

.6 **drink,** dram, potation, potion, libation, **nip,** draft, drop, spot, finger *or* two, sip, sup, suck, drench, guzzle, gargle, jigger; peg, swig, swill, pull; **snort, jolt, shot,** snifter, wet; round; round of drinks.

.7 **bracer,** refresher, reviver, pickup *or* **pick-me-up** [both informal], hair of the dog *or* hair of the dog that bit one [both informal].

.8 **drink, cocktail, highball,** mixed drink 996.42; **punch; eye-opener** [informal], **nightcap** [informal], sundowner [Brit informal]; **chaser** [informal], *pousse-café* [Fr], *apéritif* [Fr]; parting cup, stirrup cup, doch-an-dorrach *or* wee doch-an-dorrach [both Scot]; Mickey Finn *or* Mickey *or* knockout drops [all slang].

.9 **toast, pledge.**

.10 **drinker,** imbiber, **social drinker,** tippler, bibber; winebibber, oenophilist; **drunkard, drunk, inebriate,** *shikker* [Yid], sot, toper, guzzler, swiller, soaker, lovepot, tosspot, barfly, thirsty soul, **serious drinker,** devotee of Bacchus; **boozer** [informal], swigger; hard drinker, heavy drinker, big drunk [slang]; **alcoholic, dipsomaniac, problem drinker,** chronic alcoholic, chronic drunk, pathological drinker, alcoholic addict; carouser, reveler, wassailer; bacchanal, bacchanalian; pot companion.

.11 [slang terms] **lush,** lusher, **soak,** sponge, hooch hound, **boozehound,** ginhound, elbow bender *or* crooker, bottle sucker, swillbelly, swillpot, swillbowl; **souse, stew,** bum, rummy, rum hound; wino.

.12 **liquor,** intoxicating liquor, "the luscious liquor" [Milton], **hard liquor,** schnapps, **spirits, ardent spirits,** strong waters, **intoxicant,** toxicant, inebriant, **potable,** potation, **beverage, drink, strong drink,** alcoholic drink *or* beverage, **alcohol,** aqua vitae, water of life, brew, **grog,** social lubricant, nectar of the gods; **booze** [informal]; **rum,** the Demon Rum, John Barleycorn; the bottle, the cup, the cup that cheers, "the ruddy cup" [Sir Walter Scott], little brown jug; punch bowl, the flowing bowl.

.13 [slang terms] **likker, hooch, sauce,** firewater, tiger milk; **medicine,** snake medicine, corpse reviver.

.14 (bad liquor) **rotgut, poison,** rat poison, formaldehyde, embalming fluid, shellac, panther piss [all slang].

.15 **beer** 996.38, "barmy beer" [Dryden]; swipes [Brit informal], suds [informal]; small beer.

.16 **wine** 996.39, *vin* [Fr], *vino* [Sp & Ital], oen(o)- *or* en(o)-; vintage wine, nonvintage wine; red wine, white wine, rosé wine, pink wine; dry *or* sweet wine, heavy *or* light wine, full *or* thin wine, rough *or* smooth wine, still wine, sparkling wine; extra sec *or* demi-sec *or* sec *or* brut champagne; new wine, must; imported wine, domestic wine.

.17 **bootleg liquor, moonshine** [informal]; hooch *or* shine *or* mountain dew [all slang], white lightning *or* white mule [both slang]; bathtub gin; home brew.

.18 **liquor dealer,** liquor store owner; **vintner,** wine merchant; **bartender,** mixologist, barkeeper, barkeep, barman [Brit]; tapster, publican [Brit]; barmaid, tapstress; **brewer,** brewmaster; **distiller; bootlegger, moonshiner** [informal].

.19 **bar,** barroom, bistro, cocktail lounge; taproom; **tavern, pub,** pothouse, alehouse, rumshop, grogshop, dramshop, groggery, gin mill [slang], **saloon,** drinking saloon, saloon bar [Brit]; public house [Brit]; public *or* local [both Brit informal]; beer parlor, beer garden, rathskeller; **nightclub, cabaret;** café, wine shop; barrel house *or* honky-tonk *or* dive [all slang]; **speakeasy** *or* blind tiger *or* blind pig *or* after-hours joint [all slang].

.20 distillery, still, distiller; **brewery, brewhouse; winery,** wine press; bottling works.

.21 VERBS **intoxicate, inebriate, addle, befuddle,** bemuse, besot, go to one's head, make one see double, make one tiddly.

.22 [slang or informal terms] **plaster,** pickle, swack, crock, stew, souse, stone, pollute, tipsify, booze up, boozify, fuddle, overtake.

.23 **tipple, drink,** dram [Brit], nip; grog, **guzzle, gargle; imbibe,** have a drink *or* nip *or* dram *or* guzzle *or* gargle, soak, bib, quaff, sip, sup, lap, lap up, take a drop, slake one's thirst, cheer *or* refresh the inner man, drown one's sorrows, commune with the spirits; toss off *or* down, toss one's drink, knock back, drink off *or* up, drain the cup, drink bottoms-up, drink deep; **drink hard,** drink like a fish, drink seriously, **tope;** take to drink *or* drinking, "follow strong drink" [Bible].

.24 [slang or informal terms] **booze,** swig, swill, moisten *or* wet one's whistle; **liquor, liquor up,** lush, souse, tank up, **hit the booze** *or* **bottle** *or* **sauce,** exercise *or* bend *or* crook *or* raise the elbow, dip the beak, splice the main brace; chug-a-lug, chug.

.25 **get drunk,** be stricken drunk, get high, put on a high, take a drop too much; **get plastered** *or* **pickled,** etc. [slang], tie one on *or* get a bun on [both slang].

.26 **be drunk,** be intoxicated, have a drop too much, have more than one can hold, have a jag on [slang], see double, be feeling no pain; **stagger, reel; pass out** [slang].

.27 **go on a spree;** go on a binge *or* drunk *or* toot *or* bat *or* bender [slang], **carouse, spree,** revel, wassail, debauch, "eat, drink, and be merry" [Bible], paint the town red [slang], pub-crawl [Brit informal].

.28 **drink to, toast, pledge,** drink a toast to, drink *or* pledge the health of, give you.

.29 **distill; brew;** bootleg, moonshine [informal], moonlight [slang].

.30 ADJS **intoxicated, inebriated,** inebriate, inebrious, **drunk, drunken,** *shikker* [Yid], **tipsy,** in liquor, **in one's cups, under the influence,** the worse for liquor; nappy, beery; **tiddly, giddy, dizzy,** muddled, addled, flustered, bemused, reeling, seeing double; **mellow, merry,** jolly, happy, gay, glorious; **full,** fou [Scot]; **besotted,** sotted, sodden, drenched, far-gone; drunk as a lord, drunk as a fiddler *or* piper, drunk as an owl; **staggering drunk, blind drunk;** crapulent, crapulous; **maudlin.**

.31 [slang or informal terms] **fuddled,** muzzy, boozy, overtaken; **swacked, plastered,** stewed, **pickled,** pissed, **soused,** soaked, boiled, fried, canned, tanked, potted, corned, bombed, smashed; bent, **crocked,** crocko, shellacked, tight, lushy, squiffy, afflicted, jug-bitten, oiled, lubricated, polluted, raddled, organized, **high,** elevated, high as a kite, lit, **lit up,** lit to the gills, illuminated, **loaded, stinko,** stinking drunk, pie-eyed, pissy-eyed, cockeyed, cockeyed drunk, roaring *or* rip-roaring drunk, skunk-drunk; half-seas over, three sheets to the wind.

.32 **full of Dutch courage, pot-valiant,** potvalorous.

.33 **dead-drunk,** blind drunk, blind [informal], overcome, out [informal], **out cold** *or* passed out [both slang], blotto *or* stiff [both slang], helpless, under the table; paralyzed [informal], **stoned** [slang].

.34 **bibulous,** bibacious, drunken, sottish, liquorish, given *or* addicted to drink, **liquor-loving,** liquor-drinking, drinking, swilling [informal], toping, tippling, winebibbing.

.35 **intoxicating,** intoxicative, **inebriating,** inebriative, inebriant, heady.

.36 **alcoholic, spirituous, ardent, strong, hard,** with a kick [slang]; winy, vinous.

.37 INTERJS (toasts) skoal!, *skôl!* [Norw], prosit! *or* prost!, *à votre santé!* [Fr], ¡salud! [Sp], *l'chaim!* [Heb], *sláinte!* [Ir], *salute!* [Ital], *na zdorov'e!* [Russ], *nazdrowie!* [Pol], to your health!, cheerio!, cheers!, down the hatch!, bottoms up!, here's how!, here's to you!, here's looking at you!, here's mud in your eye!, here's good luck!, here's to absent friends!

.38 **brews**

| | |
|---|---|
| ale | metheglin |
| beer | Munich beer |
| bitters [Brit] | near beer |
| bock beer | Pilsner |
| dark beer | porter |
| half-and-half | pulque |
| kvass | sake |
| lager beer | schenk beer |
| light beer | stout |
| malt liquor | weiss beer |
| mead | |

.39 **wines**

| | |
|---|---|
| abboccato | amontillado |
| Aglianico del Vulture | amoroso |
| Alba Flora | Anjou |
| Alban(a) | apple wine |
| Algarve | apricot wine |
| Algerian wine | Argentine wine |
| Alicante | Assmannshausen |
| Aloxe-Corton | Asti Spumante |
| Alsace | Aszú |
| altar wine | Bad Kreuznach |

Badacsonyi
Banyuls
Barbaresco
Barbera
Bardolino
Barolo
Barsac
Beaujolais
Beaune
Bernkasteler
blackberry wine
blanc de blancs
blanc de noirs
Blanquette de
   Limoux
Bockstein
Bordeaux
bual
Bucelas
Burgundy
Byrrh
Cabernet
Cabernet Sauvignon
Cahors
California wine
Canary
Carignan
Castelli Romani
Catawba
Chablis
Chalonnais
Chambertin
Champagne
champagne cider
Chardonnay
Châteauneuf-du-Pape
Chenin blanc
cherry wine
Chian
Chianti
Chianti classico
Chiaretto
Chilean wine
Clairette de Die
claret
Colares
cold duck
Concord wine
Constantia
consumo
Cortaillod
Cortese
Corton
Corvo
Côte de Nuits
Côte d'Or
Côte Rotie
Côtes de Provence
Côtes du Rhone
cowslip wine
cream sherry
crémant
currant wine
damson wine
dandelion wine
Dão
Deidesheimer
Delaware
dessert wine
Dôle
Dubonnet
Échézeaux

Egri Bikavér
Eiswein
elderberry wine
Eszencia
Etna
Falerno
Fendant de Sion
Fixin
fortified wine
Frascati
Frecciarossa
frizzante
Gamay
Geisenheimer
Gewürztraminer
ginger wine
gooseberry wine
Gragano
Grands Échézeaux
Graves
Grenache
Grignolino
Grinzig
Grumello
Gumpoldskirchner
hard cider
Hattenheimer
Haut Sauternes
hawthorn wine
Hermitage
Hochheimer
hock
Hospices de Beaune
Inferno
Johannisberger
jug wine
Jura
Jurançon
Kaffia
kosher wine
Kremser
Lacrima Christi
Lambrusco
Liebfraumilch
Livermore Valley
Ljutomer
loganberry wine
Lugana
Mâcon(nais)
Madeira
Málaga
malmsey
Malvasia
Mamertino
Manzanilla
Marsala
Mavrodaphne
May wine
Médoc
Meursault
milk sherry
Monbazillac
Monchhof
Montefiascone
Montepulciano
Montmélian
Montrachet
Moroccan wine
Moselblümchen
Moselle
mulberry wine
Muscadet

Muscat
muscatel
Musigny
Nackenheimer
Napa Valley
Neckar
Neuchâtel
New York State wine
Nuits-St.-Georges
Oeil de Perdrix
oloroso
Orvieto
Pallini
Palomino
parsnip wine
Passover wine
peach wine
Peruvian wine
pink or rosé cham-
   pagne
Pinot
Pinot blanc
Pinot Chardonnay
Pinot noir
plum wine
pomace
Pomerol
Pommard
pop wine
port
Pouilly-Fuissé
Pouilly-Fumé
Priorato
Prošek
quince wine
raisin wine
raspberry wine
red wine
retsina
Reuilly
Rhenish wine
Rhine
Rhône
rhubarb wine
Ribero
Riesling
Rioja
Riquewihr
riserva
Romanée Conti
rosé
Roussillon
ruby port
Rüdesheimer
Ruppertsberger
sack
sacramental wine

**.40 spirits, liquor**

absinthe
alcool blanc [Fr]
Amer Picon
Angostura bitters
aquavit or akvavit
arak
Armagnac
bitters
blended whiskey
bourbon
brandy
Campari
Canadian whiskey,

sage wine
St.-Denis
St.-Émilion
St. Raphael
Sancerre
Sangiovese
Santa Clara Valley
Sassella
Saumur
sauterne
Sauternes
Sauvignon blanc
Sekt
Sémillon
sercial
Seyssel
sherry
soave
solera sherry
Somlo
Sonoma Valley
sparkling Burgundy
sparkling wine
Steinwein
stone wine
straw wine
Sylvaner
Szekszárd
Szomorodni
table wine
Tarragona
Tavel
tawny port
Tokay
Touraine
Traminer
Tulare County
Valdepeñas
Valpolicella
Valtellina
verbesserte
verdelho
Verdicchio
vermouth
Vernaccia
Vesuvio
vinho verde
vin-jaune
vin mousseux
vin ordinaire
vin rosé
Volnay
Vougeot
Vouvray
white wine
Zinfandel
zucco

   Canadian
clean rum
Cognac
corn whiskey
eau de vie [Fr]
Fernet Branca
geneva
gin
Grand Champagne
Grand Fine Cham-
   pagne
grappa
grog

Holland gin, Hollands
Irish whiskey, Irish
Jamaica gin
Jamaica rum
Kirsch
light whiskey
malt whiskey
marc
marc de Burgogne
mescal
moonshine
ouzo
*pastis* [Fr]
Pernod

Petite Champagne
plum brandy
Punt e Mes
raki
rum
rye whiskey, rye
schnapps
Scotch whiskey,
    Scotch
slivovitz
tequila
vodka
whiskey

sidecar
silver fizz
sling
smash
sour
swizzle
toddy

Tom and Jerry
Tom Collins
vermouth cassis
vodka martini
wassail
whiskey smash
whiskey sour

## 997. SOBRIETY

### (unintoxicated state)

**.1** NOUNS **sobriety, soberness;** unintoxicatedness, uninebriatedness, undrunkenness;
temperance 992.

**.2** VERBS **sober up,** sober off; sleep it off;
bring one down, take off a high [slang].

**.3** ADJS **sober,** in one's sober senses, in one's
right mind, in possession of one's faculties; **unintoxicated, uninebriated,** unine-
briate, uninebrious, undrunk, undrunken,
untipsy; cold sober [informal], **sober as a
judge;** able to walk the chalk, able to
walk the chalk mark *or* line [informal];
temperate 992.9.

**.4** **unintoxicating,** nonintoxicating, unine-
briating; **nonalcoholic, soft.**

## 998. LEGALITY

**.1** NOUNS **legality, legitimacy, lawfulness, le-
gitimateness, licitness,** rightfulness, validity, scope, applicability; **jurisdiction** 1000;
actionability, justiciability, **constitution-
ality,** constitutional validity; legal process, legal form, **due process;** legalism,
constitutionalism; **justice** 976.

**.2** **legalization, legitimatization,** validation,
authorization, sanction; legislation, enactment 742.13.

**.3** **law,** *lex, jus* [both L], **statute,** rubric,
**canon,** institution; **ordinance,** ordonnance; **act, enactment, measure,** legislation 742.13; **rule, ruling; prescript,** prescription; **regulation, *règlement*** [Fr]; **dictate,** dictation; form, formula, formulary,
formality; standing order; bylaw; **edict,
decree** 752.4; **bill** 742.17.

### .41 liqueurs, cordials.

anisette
apple brandy
applejack
apricot brandy
Benedictine
Calvados
Chartreuse
Cointreau
Cordial Médoc
Crema de Lima
crème d'amande
crème de cacao
crème de cassis
crème de menthe
crème de moka
crème de noyau
crème Yvette
Curaçao
Danzig brandy

Danziger Goldwasser
Drambuie
framboise
Galliano
goldwater
Grand Marnier
green Chartreuse
Irish Mist
Kümmel
maraschino
parfait amour
pear brandy
poire
pousse-café
rainbow cordial
sloe gin
Strega
Triple Sec
yellow Chartreuse

### .42 mixed drinks

Americano
apricot sour
Bacardi
bishop
Black Russian
Bloody Mary
bourbon and branch
    water
bowle
brandy Alexander
brandy and soda, BS
brandy smash
Bronx cocktail
Bull Shot
buttered rum
champagne cocktail
church parade
cobbler
cocktail
coffee royale
collins
cooler
Cuba Libre
Daiquiri
dry martini
Dubonnet cocktail
eggnog
fizz
flip
gimlet
gin and tonic
gin fizz
gin rickey
gin sling
Glühwein

grasshopper
Green Dragon
Guggenheim
Harvey Wallbanger
highball
hot buttered rum
hot toddy
Irish coffee
Jersey Lily
julep
lamb's wool
Mai-Tai
Manhattan
Margarita
martini
mint julep
Moscow mule
Negroni
negus
old-fashioned
orange blossom
pink lady
pink squirrel
planter's punch
posset
purl
rickey
rince pichon
Rob Roy
rum punch
sangria
Sazerac
Scotch and soda
Scotch and water
screwdriver

**.4** (laws) common law, *jus commune* [Fr];
chancery law, equity; substantive law; unwritten law, *lex non scripta* [L]; written
*or* statute law, *lex scripta* [L], *jus scrip-
tum* [L], positive law; constitutional law;
civil law, *jus civile* [L]; criminal law;
crown law [Brit]; penal law; public law,
*jus publicum* [L]; decree law; martial law;
case law; international law, law of nations, *jus inter gentes* [L], *droit des gen.*
[Fr]; local law, law of the place, *lex loci*
*lex situs* [both L]; law of the land, *lex ter-
rae* [L]; law of the domicile, *lex domicili*

[L]; law of general application, *lex generalis* [L]; law of the forum, *lex fori* [L]; mercantile law, *lex mercatorum, lex mercatoria* [both L]; commercial law, business law, corporation law, law merchant; maritime law, sea law, admiralty law; canon *or* ecclesiastical law, *jus ecclesiasticum* [L], Corpus Juris Canonici; Roman law, Corpus Juris Civilis; blue law; dry law; gag law.

.5 **code, digest,** pandect, capitulary, **body of law,** corpus juris, code of laws, digest of law; equity; codification; civil code, penal code; Napoleonic code, *Code Napoléon* [Fr].

.6 **constitution,** written constitution, unwritten constitution; constitutional amendment; Bill of Rights, constitutional guarantees.

.7 **jurisprudence, law,** legal science; nomology, nomography; forensic *or* legal medicine, medical jurisprudence, medico-legal medicine; forensic psychiatry; forensic *or* legal chemistry; criminology.

.8 VERBS **legalize, legitimize,** legitimatize, legitimate, make legal, declare lawful, validate; **authorize, sanction;** constitute, ordain, establish, put in force; prescribe, formulate; regulate, make a regulation; **decree** 752.9; **legislate, enact** 742.18.

.9 **codify,** digest.

.10 ADJS **legal, legitimate,** legit [slang], kosher [informal], competent, licit, **lawful,** rightful, according to law, within the law; actionable, justiciable, within the scope of the law; **judicial,** juridical; **authorized,** sanctioned, valid, applicable; **constitutional;** statutory, statutable; **legislative, lawmaking** 742.19; lawlike; **just** 976.8–10.

.11 jurisprudent, jurisprudential; **legalistic; forensic;** nomistic, nomothetic; criminological.

.12 ADVS **legally, legitimately,** licitly, **lawfully,** by law, *de jure* [L], in the eyes of the law.

## 999. ILLEGALITY

.1 NOUNS **illegality, unlawfulness, illicitness, lawlessness,** wrongfulness; unauthorization, impermissibility, **unconstitutionality;** legal *or* technical flaw, legal irregularity; **criminality,** criminalism; **outlawry; anarchy,** collapse *or* breakdown *or* paralysis of authority, anomie; illicit business 826.

.2 **illegitimacy, illegitimateness,** illegitimation; **bastardy,** bastardism, noth(o)–; bend *or* bar sinister, baton.

.3 **lawbreaking, violation of law,** breach of law, infringement, contravention, infraction, **transgression,** trespass, trespassing.

.4 **offense, wrong,** illegality; **violation** 769.2; **wrongdoing** 982; **crime, felony;** misdemeanor; tort; delict, delictum.

.5 VERBS **break the law, violate the law,** breach the law, infringe, contravene, infract, violate 769.4, **transgress, trespass,** disobey the law, offend against the law, fly in the face of the law, set the law at defiance, set the law at naught, circumvent the law, disregard the law, **take the law into one's own hands,** twist *or* torture the law to one's own ends *or* purposes; commit a crime; live outside the law.

.6 ADJS **illegal, unlawful, illegitimate, illicit,** nonlicit, nonlegal, lawless, wrongful, **against the law; unauthorized,** unallowed, impermissible, unwarranted, unwarrantable, unofficial; unstatutory; **unconstitutional,** nonconstitutional; flawed, irregular, contrary to law; actionable, chargeable, justiciable; triable, punishable; **criminal, felonious; outlaw, outlawed; contraband,** bootleg, black-market; under-the-table, under-the-counter; anarchic, anarchistic, anomic.

.7 **illegitimate, spurious,** false; **bastard,** misbegot, **misbegotten,** miscreated, baseborn, born out of wedlock, without benefit of clergy.

.8 ADVS **illegally, unlawfully, illegitimately, illicitly;** impermissibly; **criminally,** feloniously; contrary to law, in violation of law.

## 1000. JURISDICTION

### (administration of justice)

.1 NOUNS **jurisdiction,** legal authority *or* power *or* right; original *or* appellate jurisdiction, exclusive *or* concurrent jurisdiction, civil *or* criminal jurisdiction, common-law *or* equitable jurisdiction, *in rem* jurisdiction, *in personam* jurisdiction; voluntary jurisdiction.

.2 **judiciary,** judicature, judicatory, legal system, the courts; **justice,** the wheels of justice, judicial process; **judgment** 494.

.3 **magistracy,** magistrature, magistrateship; **judgeship,** justiceship; mayoralty, mayorship.

.4 **bureau, office, department;** secretariat, ministry, commissariat; municipality, bailiwick; **constabulary,** constablery, sheriffry, sheriffalty, shrievalty; constablewick, sheriffwick.

.5 VERBS **administer justice,** administer, administrate; preside, preside at the board; sit in judgment 1004.17; judge 494.8.

.6 ADJS **jurisdictional**, jurisdictive; **judicatory**, judicatorial, judicative, **juridic(al)**; **judicial, judiciary**; magisterial.

## 1001. TRIBUNAL

.1 NOUNS **tribunal, forum, board**, curia, Areopagus; judicature, judicatory, judiciary; council 755; inquisition, the Inquisition.

.2 **court, law court, court of law** *or* **justice**, court of arbitration, legal tribunal, judicature.

.3 (courts) circuit court, civil court, common-law court, county court, criminal court, district court, divorce court, juvenile court, police court, prize court, superior court, court of claims, court of domestic relations, family court, court of errors, court of first instance, court of record, court of requests, court of wards; appellate court, court of review, court of appeals, court of last resort; court of common pleas; assizes, court of assize; chancery, chancery court, court of chancery; conciliation court; court of inquiry, court of honor; court of conscience, equity court, court of equity; small-claims court; small-debts court; hustings, hustings court; probate court, court of probate; sessions, court of sessions, petty *or* quarter *or* special *or* general sessions; night court; traffic court; kangaroo court [informal], mock court, moot court.

.4 (US courts) Supreme Court, United States Supreme Court; United States District Court, United States Circuit Court of Appeals, Federal Court of Claims, Court of Private Land Claims.

.5 (British courts) court of admiralty, Court of Appeal, Court of Criminal Appeal, Court of Common Pleas, Court of Common Bank, Court of Common Council, Court of Divorce and Matrimonial Causes, Court of Exchequer, Court of Exchequer Chamber, Court of Queen's *or* King's Bench, Court of the Duchy of Lancaster, High Court, High Court of Appeal, High Court of Justice, High *or* Supreme Court of Judicature, Judicial Committee of the Privy Council, Lords Justices' Court, Palatine Court, Rolls Court, Stannary Court, superior courts of Westminster, Vice Chancellor's Court; court of attachments, woodmote; ward-mote, wardmote court; Green Cloth, Board of Green Cloth; Court of Session

[Scot], Teind Court [Scot]; court of piepoudre *or* dustyfoot.

.6 (ecclesiastical courts) Papal Court, Curia, Rota, Sacra Romana Rota, Court of Arches [Brit], Court of Peculiars [Brit].

.7 **military court, court-martial**, general *or* special *or* summary court-martial, drumhead court-martial.

.8 **seat of justice, judgment seat**, mercy seat, **bench**; woolsack [Brit].

.9 **courthouse, court**; town hall, town house; **courtroom**; jury box; witness stand *or* box, dock.

.10 ADJS **tribunal, judicial**, judiciary, curial; appellate.

## 1002. JUDGE, JURY

.1 NOUNS **judge, magistrate, justice**, indicator, bencher, beak [Brit slang]; **justice of the peace, JP; arbiter, arbitrator, moderator; umpire, referee**; his honor, his worship, his lordship; Mr. Justice; critic 494.6, 7.

.2 (historical) tribune, praetor, ephor, archon, syndic, podesta; Areopagite; justiciar, justiciary; dempster, deemster, doomster, doomsman.

.3 [Muhammadan] mullah, ulema, hakim, mufti, cadi.

.4 (special judges) judge advocate, JA, presiding judge, probate judge, police judge *or* justice *or* magistrate, PJ; circuit judge; justice in eyre; ordinary, judge ordinary; judge *or* justice of assize; puisne judge *or* justice; military judge; lay judge; assessor, legal assessor; barmaster [Brit], chancellor, vice-chancellor, jurat, recorder, master, amicus curiae; ombudsman.

.5 Chief Justice, Associate Justice, Justice of the Supreme Court; Lord Chief Justice, Lord Justice, Lord Chancellor, Master of the Rolls, Baron of the Exchequer; Judge Advocate General.

.6 Pontius Pilate, Solomon, Minos, Rhadamanthus, Aeacus.

.7 **jury, panel**, jury of one's peers, sessions [Scot], country, twelve men in a box; inquest, jury of inquest; grand jury, petit jury, coroner's jury, special jury, trial jury, jury of the vicinage, jury of matrons *or* women, blue-ribbon jury *or* panel; police jury; jury panel, jury list, venire; hung jury.

.8 **juror, juryman**, veniremen, jurywoman; talesman; foreman of the jury, foreman, jury chancellor [Scot]; grand-juror, grand-juryman; petit-juror, petit-juryman; recognitor.

## 1003. LAWYER

.1 NOUNS **lawyer, attorney, attorney-at-law,** barrister, barrister-at-law, **counselor,** counselor-at-law, **counsel,** legal counselor, legal adviser, legal expert, **solicitor, advocate, pleader, mouthpiece** [slang]; member of the bar, legal practitioner, officer of the court; proctor, procurator; friend at or in court, amicus curiae; deputy, agent 781; intercessor 805.3; sea lawyer, latrine lawyer, self-styled lawyer, legalist.

.2 legist, jurist, jurisprudent, jurisconsult; law member of a court-martial.

.3 [derog terms] **shyster, ambulance chaser,** pettifogger, Philadelphia lawyer.

.4 (special lawyers) **district attorney, DA; prosecuting attorney, prosecutor;** trial judge advocate; public prosecutor; United States or US attorney; special pleader; private attorney, attorney in fact; court-appointed lawyer, public defender; **defense counsel;** criminal lawyer, mouthpiece [slang]; constitutional lawyer; corporation lawyer; law agent or writer to the signet [both Scot]; sergeant-at-law [Brit]; civilian; publicist; conveyancer; leader [Brit]; **attorney general, AG; solicitor general, SG;** Solicitor Supreme Court, SSC; King's or Queen's Counsel, KC, QC, silk, silk gown, silk-gownsman [Brit]; junior barrister or counsel, stuff gown, stuff-gownsman.

.5 bar, legal profession, members of the bar; representation, counsel, pleading, attorneyship.

.6 VERBS **practice law,** practice at the bar; take silk, be admitted to the bar.

.7 ADJS **lawyerly,** lawyerlike, barristerial; representing, of counsel.

## 1004. LEGAL ACTION

.1 NOUNS **lawsuit, suit,** suit in or at law; **litigation, prosecution, action, legal action,** proceedings, legal proceedings, legal process; legal remedy; **case,** cause, cause in court, legal case; judicial process.

.2 summons, subpoena 752.7; writ, warrant 752.6.

.3 arraignment, indictment, impeachment; charge 1005.1; presentment; information; bill of indictment, true bill; **bail** 772.2.

.4 jury selection, impanelment, venire, venire facias, venire facias de novo.

.5 trial, jury trial, trial by jury, trial at the bar, **hearing, inquiry,** inquisition, inquest, assize; court-martial; **examination,** cross-

examination 485.11,12; mistrial; change of venue.

.6 **pleadings,** arguments at the bar; **plea,** pleading, argument; **defense,** statement of defense; demurrer, general or special demurrer; refutation 506.2; rebuttal 486.2.

.7 **declaration, statement,** allegation, allegation or statement of facts, procès-verbal; **deposition,** affidavit; claim; complaint; bill, bill of complaint; libel, narratio; nolle prosequi, nol. pros.; nonsuit.

.8 **testimony** 505.3; **evidence** 505; **argument,** presentation of the case; resting of the case; **summing up,** summation, charge to the jury, charging of the jury.

.9 **judgment, decision,** landmark decision; **verdict, sentence** 494.5; acquittal 1007; condemnation 1008, penalty 1009.

.10 **appeal,** appeal motion, application for retrial, appeal to a higher court; writ of error; certiorari, writ of certiorari.

.11 **litigant, litigator,** litigationist; suitor, **party,** party to a suit; **plaintiff** 1005.5; **defendant** 1005.6; **witness** 505.7; accessory, accessory before or after the fact; panel, parties litigant.

.12 VERBS **sue, litigate, prosecute,** go into litigation, **bring suit,** put in suit, sue or prosecute at law, **go to law,** seek in law, appeal to the law, seek justice or legal redress, implead, **bring action against,** prosecute a suit against, take or institute legal proceedings against, **take** or **have the law of** or **on** [informal], law [informal], take to court, bring into court, hale or haul or drag into court, bring a case before the court or bar, bring to justice, bring to trial, **put on trial,** bring to the bar, take before the judge; set down for hearing.

.13 **summons,** subpoena 752.12.

.14 **arraign, indict, impeach,** find an indictment against, present a true bill, prefer or file a claim, have or pull up [informal], bring up for investigation; **prefer charges** 1005.7.

.15 **impanel a jury,** impanel, panel.

.16 **call to witness,** bring forward, put on the stand; swear in 523.6; take oath 523.5; testify 505.10.

.17 **try,** try a case, conduct a trial, **hear,** give a hearing to; charge the jury, deliver one's charge to the jury; **judge, sit in judgment.**

.18 **plead,** implead, conduct pleadings, argue at the bar; **plead** or **argue one's case,** present one's case, make a plea, tell it to the judge [informal]; hang the jury [informal]; rest, rest one's case; sum up one's case.

.19 **bring in a verdict, pass sentence** 494.13; acquit 1007.4; convict 1008.3; penalize 1009.4.

.20 ADJS litigious, litigant, litigatory; causidical; litigable, actionable.

.21 PHRS **in litigation,** in court, in chancery, in jeopardy, **at law,** at bar, at the bar, **on trial,** up for investigation or hearing, before the court or bar or judge, *sub judice* [L].

## 1005. ACCUSATION

.1 NOUNS **accusation,** accusal, **charge, complaint,** plaint, count, **blame, imputation,** delation, reproach, taxing; **accusing, bringing of charges,** laying of charges, bringing to book; **denunciation,** denouncement; **impeachment, arraignment, indictment,** true bill; **allegation,** allegement; insinuation, implication, innuendo, veiled accusation, unspoken accusation; information, information against, bill of particulars; gravamen of a charge; prosecution, suit, lawsuit 1004.1.

.2 **incrimination,** crimination, **inculpation,** implication, **citation,** involvement, impugnment; attack, assault; **censure** 969.3.

.3 **recrimination,** retort, countercharge.

.4 **trumped-up charge,** false witness; **put-up job** or **frame-up** or **frame** [all slang].

.5 **accuser,** accusant, accusatrix; incriminator, delator, allegator, impugner; informer 557.6; impeacher, indictor; **plaintiff, complainant,** claimant, appellant, petitioner, libelant, suitor, **party,** party to a suit; **prosecutor,** the prosecution.

.6 **accused, defendant,** respondent, correspondent, libelee, suspect, prisoner.

.7 VERBS **accuse,** bring accusation; **charge, press charges, prefer** or **bring charges,** lay charges; complain, **lodge a complaint,** lodge a plaint; **impeach, arraign, indict,** bring in or hand up an indictment, return a true bill, article, **cite,** cite on several counts; book; **denounce,** denunciate; **finger** or point the finger at or put the finger on [all slang], inform on or against; allege, insinuate, imply; impute, fasten on or upon, pin on [informal], hang something on [slang], bring to book; tax, task, take to task or account; **reproach,** twit, taunt with; report, put on report.

.8 **blame,** blame on or upon [informal], hold against, **lay the blame on,** lay or cast blame upon, place or fix the blame or responsibility for.

.9 **accuse of, charge with,** tax or task with, saddle with, lay to one's charge, place to one's account, lay to one's door, bring home to, cast or throw in one's teeth, throw or thrust in the face of.

.10 **incriminate,** criminate, **inculpate,** implicate, involve; cry out against, cry out on or upon, cry shame upon, raise one's voice against; attack, assail, impugn; **censure** 969.13; throw a stone at, cast or throw the first stone.

.11 **recriminate,** countercharge, retort an accusation.

.12 **trump up a charge, bear false witness; frame,** frame up, put up a job [all slang].

.13 ADJS **accusing, accusatory,** accusative; imputative, denunciatory; recriminatory; **condemnatory** 969.23.

.14 **incriminating,** incriminatory, criminatory; delatorian; inculpative, inculpatory.

.15 **accused, charged, blamed,** tasked, taxed, reproached, **denounced, impeached, indicted, arraigned; incriminated,** inculpated, implicated, involved, in complicity; **cited,** impugned; under attack, under fire.

## 1006. JUSTIFICATION

.1 NOUNS **justification, vindication; clearing,** clearing of one's name, clearance, purging, purgation, destigmatizing, destigmatization, **exculpation** 1007.1; explanation, rationalization; reinstatement, restoration, rehabilitation.

.2 **defense, plea,** pleading; argument, statement of defense; answer, reply, counterstatement, response, riposte; **refutation** 506.2, **rebuttal** 486.2; demurrer, general or special demurrer; denial, objection, exception; **special pleading.**

.3 **apology,** apologia, apologetic.

.4 **excuse, cop-out** [slang], **alibi** or **out** [both informal]; lame excuse, poor excuse, likely story.

.5 **extenuation, mitigation, palliation,** softening; extenuative, palliative; **whitewash, whitewashing,** decontamination; gilding, gloss, varnish, color, putting the best color on; qualification, allowance; extenuating circumstances.

.6 **warrant, reason,** good reason, **cause,** call, **right, basis,** substantive or material basis, **ground, grounds,** foundation, substance.

.7 **justifiability,** vindicability, defensibility, explainability, explicability; excusability, pardonableness, forgivableness, remissibility, veniality; warrantableness, allowabl ness, admissibility, reasonableness, reasonability, legitimacy.

**.8 justifier, vindicator; defender,** pleader; **advocate,** successful advocate *or* defender, proponent, **champion; apologist,** apologizer, apologete; whitewasher.

**.9** VERBS **justify, vindicate,** do justice to, make justice *or* right prevail; **warrant,** account for, show sufficient grounds for, give good reasons for; **rationalize,** explain; cry sour grapes, "make a virtue of necessity" [Shakespeare]; **exculpate** 1007.4; **clear,** clear one's name, purge, destigmatize, reinstate, restore, rehabilitate.

**.10 defend,** offer *or* say in defense, allege in support *or* vindication, **support, uphold, sustain, maintain,** assert; **answer,** reply, respond, riposte, counter; refute 506.5, **rebut** 486.5; **plead for,** make a plea, offer as a plea, plead one's case *or* cause; **advocate,** champion, espouse, join *or* associate oneself with, stand *or* stick up for, speak up for, contend for, speak for, argue for, urge reasons for, put in a good word for.

**.11 excuse,** alibi [informal], offer excuse for, give as an excuse, cover with excuses; plead ignorance; **apologize for,** make apology for; alibi out of [informal], crawl *or* worm *or* squirm out of, lie out of.

**.12 extenuate, mitigate, palliate,** soften, lessen, diminish, **ease,** mince; **soft-pedal;** slur over, ignore, pass by in silence, give the benefit of the doubt, not hold it against one, **gloss over,** put a gloss upon, put a good face upon, varnish, **whitewash,** color, lend a color to, put the best color on, show in the best colors; **allow for,** make allowance for; give the Devil his due.

**13** ADJS **justifying,** justificatory; **vindicative,** vindicatory, rehabilitative; refuting 506.6; **excusing,** excusatory; **apologetic(al); extenuating,** extenuative, **palliative.**

**14 justifiable, vindicable, defensible; excusable, pardonable, forgivable,** expiable, remissible, exemptible, venial; **condonable,** dispensable; **warrantable,** allowable, admissible, reasonable, legitimate; unobjectionable, inoffensive.

## 1007. ACQUITTAL

**1** NOUNS **acquittal, acquittance,** quittance; **exculpation,** disculpation, verdict of acquittal *or* of not guilty; **exoneration, absolution, vindication, remission,** compurgation, purgation, purging, clearing, clearance, destigmatizing, destigmatization, quietus; **pardon, excuse, forgiveness; dis-**charge, release, dismissal;** quashing of the charge *or* indictment.

**.2 exemption, immunity,** impunity; **amnesty,** indemnity, nonprosecution, non prosequitur, nolle prosequi; stay.

**.3 reprieve,** respite, grace.

**.4** VERBS **acquit, exculpate, exonerate, absolve,** give absolution, bring in *or* return a verdict of not guilty; **vindicate,** justify; **pardon, excuse, forgive;** remit, grant remission, remit the penalty of; amnesty, grant amnesty to; **discharge, release, dismiss, free, set free,** let off [informal], let go; quash the charge *or* indictment, withdraw the charge; **exempt,** grant immunity, exempt from, dispense from; clear, clear the skirts of, shrive, purge; blot out one's sins, wipe the slate clean; **whitewash,** decontaminate; destigmatize; nonpros.

**.5 reprieve,** respite, give *or* grant a reprieve.

## 1008. CONDEMNATION

**.1** NOUNS **condemnation, damnation, doom,** guilty verdict, verdict of guilty; proscription, excommunication, anathematizing; **denunciation,** denouncement; **censure** 969.3; **conviction; sentence, judgment,** rap [slang]; death sentence, death warrant.

**.2** attainder, attainture, attaintment; bill of attainder.

**.3** VERBS **condemn, damn, doom; denounce,** denunciate; **censure** 969.13; **convict,** find guilty, bring home to; proscribe, excommunicate, anathematize; blacklist, put on the Index; pronounce judgment 494.13; **sentence,** pronounce sentence, pass sentence on; penalize 1009.4; attaint; sign one's death warrant.

**.4 stand condemned,** be convicted, be found guilty.

**.5** ADJS **condemnatory, damnatory,** denunciatory, proscriptive; **censorious** 969.23.

## 1009. PENALTY

**.1** NOUNS **penalty,** penalization, penance, penal retribution; **punishment** 1010; compensation, price; the devil to pay.

**.2 handicap,** disability, **disadvantage** 730.6.

**.3 fine,** mulct, amercement, sconce, damages; distress, distraint; forfeit, forfeiture; escheat, escheatment.

**.4** VERBS **penalize,** put *or* impose *or* inflict a penalty on; **punish** 1010.10; **handicap,** put at a disadvantage.

**.5 fine,** mulct, amerce, sconce, estreat; distrain, levy a distress.

.6 ADVS on pain of, under *or* upon pain of, on *or* under penalty of.

## 1010. PUNISHMENT

.1 NOUNS punishment, punition, chastisement, chastening, correction, discipline, disciplinary measures *or* action, castigation, infliction, scourge, ferule, what-for [slang]; pains, pains and punishments; pay, payment; retribution, retributive justice, nemesis; judicial punishment; punishment that fits the crime, condign punishment, well-deserved punishment; penalty, penal retribution; penology; cruel and unusual punishment; judgment; deserts 960.3.

.2 (forms of punishment) penal servitude, jailing, imprisonment, incarceration, confinement; hard labor, rock pile; galleys; torture, torment, martyrdom; the gantlet, keelhauling, tar-and-feathering, railriding, picketing, the rack, impalement, dismemberment; strappado, estrapade.

.3 slap, smack, whack, whomp, cuff, box, buffet; blow 283.4; rap on the knuckles, box on the ear, slap in the face; slap on the wrist, token punishment.

.4 corporal punishment, whipping, beating, thrashing, spanking, flogging, flagellation, scourging, flailing, swingeing [dial], trouncing, basting, drubbing, buffeting, belaboring; lashing, lacing, stripes; horsewhipping; strapping, belting, rawhiding, cowhiding; switching; clubbing, cudgeling, caning, truncheoning, fustigation, bastinado; pistol-whipping; battery.

.5 [informal terms] licking, larruping, walloping, whaling, lathering, leathering, hiding, tanning, dressing-down; paddling.

.6 [slang terms] strap oil, hazel oil, hickory oil, birch oil; dose of strap oil, etc.

.7 capital punishment, execution; legal *or* judicial murder; hanging, the gallows, the rope *or* noose; lynching, necktie party *or* sociable [slang]; crucifixion; electrocution, the chair [informal], the hot seat [slang]; gassing, the gas chamber; decapitation, decollation, beheading, the guillotine, the ax, the block; strangling, strangulation, garrote; shooting, fusillade; burning, burning at the stake; poisoning, hemlock; stoning, lapidation; defenestration.

.8 punisher, discipliner, chastizer; executioner, executionist, deathsman [archaic], Jack Ketch [Brit]; hangman; lyncher; electrocutioner; headsman, beheader, de-

capitator; strangler, garroter; sadist torturer.

.9 penologist; jailer 761.10.

.10 VERBS punish, chastise, chasten, discipline, correct, castigate, penalize; take to task, bring to book, bring *or* call to account; deal with, settle with, settle *or* square accounts, give one his deserts, serve one right; inflict upon, visit upon; give a lesson to, make an example of; pillory; masthead.

.11 [informal terms] attend to, do for, take care of, serve one out, give it to, take *or* have it out of; pay, pay out, fix, settle, settle one's hash, settle the score, give one his gruel, give one his comeuppance; come down on *or* upon.

.12 [slang terms] give what-for, give a going-over, climb one's frame, let have it, light into, land on, mop *or* wipe up the floor with.

.13 slap, smack, whack, whomp, cuff, box, buffet; strike 283.13; slap the face, box the ears, give a rap on the knuckles.

.14 whip, give a whipping *or* beating *or* thrashing, beat, thrash, spank, flog, scourge, flagellate, flail, whale; whop *or* wallop *or* swinge [all dial], smite, thump, trounce, baste, pummel, drub, buffet, belabor, lay on; lash, lace, cut, stripe; horsewhip; knout; strap, belt, rawhide, cowhide; switch, birch, give the stick; club, cudgel, cane, truncheon, fustigate, bastinado; pistol-whip.

.15 [informal terms] lick, larrup, wallop, whale, welt, trim, flax, lather, leather, hide, tan, tan one's hide, dress down, give a dressing-down; paddle.

.16 [slang terms] lambaste, clobber, dus[t] one's jacket, give a dose of birch oil o[r] strap oil *or* hickory oil *or* hazel oil, tak[e] it out of one's hide *or* skin.

.17 thrash soundly, batter, beat up [slang] beat to a jelly, bruise, beat black an[d] blue, beat the shit *or* tar out of [slang].

.18 torture, put to the question; rack, put o[n] *or* to the rack; dismember, tear lim[b] from limb; draw and quarter, break o[n] the wheel, tar and feather, ride on a ra[il]; picket, keelhaul, impale, grill.

.19 execute, put to death, inflict capital pu[n]ishment; electrocute, burn [slang]; se[nd] to the gas chamber; behead, decapita[te] decollate, guillotine, bring to the blo[ck] crucify; shoot, execute by firing squa[d] burn, burn at the stake; strangle, garro[te] bowstring; stone, lapidate; defenestrate

.20 hang, hang by the neck; string up, sc[r]

or stretch [all informal]; gibbet, noose, neck, bring to the gallows; **lynch**; hang, draw, and quarter.

.21 **be hanged,** suffer hanging, **swing,** dance upon nothing, kick the air or wind or clouds.

.22 **be punished, suffer,** suffer for, **suffer the consequences** or **penalty,** get it, **catch it** [both informal], get or catch it in the neck [slang]; get one's deserts 960.6; be doubly punished, get it coming and going [slang], sow the wind and reap the whirlwind.

.23 **take one's punishment, take the consequences, take** one's **medicine,** swallow the bitter pill, pay the piper, face the music [informal], make one's bed and lie on it; take the rap [slang].

.24 **deserve punishment,** have it coming, be for it or in for it, be heading for a fall.

.25 ADJS **punishing, chastising,** chastening, **corrective,** disciplinary; **retributive; grueling** [informal]; **penal, punitive,** punitory, inflictive; castigatory; penological.

## 1011. INSTRUMENTS OF PUNISHMENT

.1 NOUNS **whip, lash, scourge,** flagellum, mastig(o)–; strap, thong, **rawhide,** cowhide, blacksnake, kurbash, sjambok, belt, razor strap; knout; **bullwhip, bullwhack; horsewhip;** crop; quirt; rope's end; **cat,** cat-o'-nine-tails; whiplash.

.2 **rod, stick, switch; paddle,** ruler, ferule, pandybat; birch, rattan; cane; club 801.26.

.3 (devices) **pillory, stocks,** finger pillory; cucking stool, ducking stool, trebuchet; whipping post, branks, triangle or triangles, wooden horse, treadmill, crank.

.4 (instruments of torture) **rack,** wheel, Iron Maiden of Nuremberg; screw, **thumbscrew; boot,** iron heel, scarpines; Procrustean bed, bed of Procrustes.

.5 (instruments of execution) **scaffold; block, guillotine,** ax, maiden; **stake; cross; gallows,** gallows-tree, **gibbet,** tree, drop; **hangman's rope, noose,** rope, halter, hemp, hempen collar or necktie or bridle [slang]; **electric chair,** death chair, the **chair** [informal], hot seat [slang]; **gas chamber,** lethal chamber, death chamber.

## 1012. ATONEMENT

.1 NOUNS **atonement, reparation, amends,** making amends, **restitution, propitiation, expiation, redress, recompense,** compensation, making right or good, making up, squaring, **redemption,** reclamation, satis-

faction, quittance; **indemnity,** indemnification; **compromise,** composition; expiatory offering or sacrifice, piaculum, peace offering.

.2 **apology, excuse, regrets;** acknowledgment, **penitence, contrition,** breast-beating, mea culpa, confession 556.3; abject apology.

.3 **penance, penitence, repentance;** penitential act or exercise, **mortification,** maceration, **flagellation,** lustration; **asceticism** 991, **fasting** 995; **purgation,** purgatory, "cold purgatorial fires" [T. S. Eliot]; **sackcloth and ashes;** hair shirt; Day of Atonement, Yom Kippur.

.4 VERBS **atone, atone for, propitiate, expiate,** compensate, **recompense, redress, redeem, repair, satisfy, give satisfaction, make amends, make reparation** or **compensation** or **expiation, make good,** make right, **make up for,** make matters up, square it, square things, pay the forfeit or penalty, pay one's dues [informal], wipe off old scores, set one's house in order; live down.

.5 **apologize, beg pardon, ask forgiveness,** beg indulgence, express regret; take back 628.9; get or fall down on one's knees, get down on one's marrowbones [slang].

.6 **do penance,** flagellate oneself, mortify oneself, mortify one's flesh, shrive oneself, purge oneself, cleanse oneself of guilt, stand in a white sheet, repent in sackcloth and ashes, wear a hairshirt, wear sackcloth or sackcloth and ashes; receive absolution.

.7 ADJS **atoning, propitiatory, expiatory,** piacular, **reparative, reparatory, restitutive,** restitutory, restitutional, **redressing,** recompensing, **compensatory,** compensational, **righting, squaring; redemptive, redeeming,** reclamatory, satisfactional; **apologetic(al);** repentant, repenting; **penitential,** purgative, purgatorial; lustral, lustrative, lustrational, **cleansing, purifying; ascetic** 991.3.

## 1013. DEITY

.1 NOUNS **deity, divinity,** divineness; **godliness,** godlikeness; **godhood,** godhead, godship, Fatherhood.

.2 **God,** the(o)–; **Lord, Jehovah, Providence, Heaven, the Deity, the Divinity, the Supreme Being, God Almighty, the Almighty, Almighty God,** the All-powerful, the Omnipotent, Omnipotence, **the Infinite,** the Infinite Being, the Everlasting, the Eternal, the Eternal Being, Alpha and Omega, the Absolute, the Absolute Being, the Omniscient, Omniscience, the All-wise, the All-knowing, the All-merciful, the All-holy, the Infinite Spirit, the Supreme Soul, **King of Kings,** Lord of Lords, Lord of hosts, Demiurge, Demiourgos, I Am, the Preserver, **the Maker, the Creator,** the First Cause, Author *or* Creator of all things; the Unmoved Mover; the ground of being; ultimate concern.

.3 *Deus* [L], *Theos* [Gk], *Dieu* [Fr], *Gott* [Ger]; *Yahweh, Adonai, Elohim* [all Heb]; **Allah;** the Great Spirit, Manitou.

.4 (Hinduism) **Brahma,** the Supreme Soul, the Essence of the Universe; **Atman,** the Universal Ego *or* Self; **Vishnu,** the Preserver; **Shiva** *or* Siva, the Destroyer, the Regenerator.

.5 (Buddhism) **Buddha,** the Blessed One, the Teacher, **the Lord Buddha,** bodhisattva.

.6 (Zoroastrianism) **Ahura Mazda,** Ormazd, Mazda, the Lord of Wisdom, the Wise Lord, the Wise One, the King of Light, the Guardian of Mankind.

.7 (Christian Science) **Mind, Divine Mind,** Spirit, Soul Principle, Life, Truth, Love.

.8 **world spirit** *or* **soul,** *anima mundi* [L], universal life force, world principle, **world-self,** universal ego *or* self, infinite spirit, supreme soul *or* principle, **oversoul, nous,** archeus, **Logos,** World Reason.

.9 **Nature, Mother Nature,** Dame Nature, "Beldame Nature" [Milton].

.10 **Godhead, Trinity,** Holy Trinity, Triune, Triunity, Triune God, Trinity in Unity, Threefold Unity, Three in One and One in Three; **Father, Son, and Holy Ghost;** Trimurti, Hindu trinity *or* triad.

.11 **God the Father, the Father,** the All-father, the Everlasting Father, the Holy Father, Our Father, Our Father which art in Heaven, the Creator.

.12 **God the Son, Christ,** the Christ, **Jesus,** Jesu, **Jesus Christ,** Christ Jesus, Jesus of Nazareth, the Nazarene, the Galilean, the Man of Sorrows, **Messiah,** the Anointed, God-man, **Savior, Redeemer,** the Mediator, the Intercessor, the Advocate, the Judge, **Son of God, Son of Man,** Son of David, the son of Mary, the only son of Mary, the Only-Begotten, Only-Begotten Son, **Our Lord,** Lord Jesus, the Lamb, **Lamb of God, Immanuel,** Emmanuel, **the Master, King of Kings,** Lord of Lords, King of Kings and Lord of Lords, King of Heaven, King of Glory,

King of the Jews, Lord our Righteousness, the Sun of Righteousness, **Prince of Peace, the Good Shepherd,** the Risen, the Door, the Way, the Truth, the Life, the Bread of Life, the Light of the World, the Vine, the True Vine; the Christ Child, the Infant Jesus; Christo–.

.13 **the Word, Logos,** the Word Made Flesh, **the Incarnation,** the Hypostatic Union.

.14 God the Holy Ghost, **the Holy Ghost, the Holy Spirit,** the Spirit of God, the Spirit of Truth, Paraclete, the Comforter, the Consoler, the Intercessor, the Dove.

.15 (divine attributes) infinity, eternity; infinite goodness, infinite justice, infinite truth, infinite love, infinite mercy; omniscience *or* omnisciency, infinite wisdom; omnipotence *or* omnipotency, infinite power; omnipresence, ubiquity; unity, immutability; holiness, glory, light; majesty, sovereignty.

.16 (divine functions) creation, preservation, dispensation; providence, dealings *or* dispensations *or* visitations of providence.

.17 (functions of Christ) salvation, redemption; atonement, propitiation; mediation, intercession; judgment.

.18 (functions of the Holy Ghost) inspiration, unction, regeneration, sanctification, comfort, consolation, grace, witness.

.19 ADJS **divine,** heavenly, celestial, empyrean; **godly, godlike** 1028.9; **transcendent,** superhuman, supernatural; self-existent; Christly, Christlike, redemptive, salvational, propitiative, propitiatory, mediative, mediatory, intercessive, intercessional; incarnate, incarnated, made flesh.

.20 **almighty, omnipotent,** all-powerful; creating, creative, making, shaping; **omniscient,** all-wise, all-knowing, all-seeing; **infinite,** boundless, limitless, unbounded, unlimited, undefined, omnipresent, ubiquitous; eternal, everlasting, timeless, perpetual, immortal, permanent; one; immutable, unchanging, changeless, eternally the same; supreme, sovereign, highest; holy, hallowed, sacred, numinous; glorious, radiant, luminous; majestic; good; just, loving, merciful.

## 1014. MYTHICAL AND POLYTHEISTIC GODS AND SPIRITS

.1 NOUNS **the gods,** the immortals; the major deities, the greater gods, *di majores* [L]; the minor deities, the lesser gods, *di minores* [L]; pantheon; theogony.

.2 **god,** *deus* [L]; **deity, divinity,** immortal

heathen god, pagan deity or divinity; **goddess,** *dea* [L]; deva, devi, the shining ones; **idol,** false god, devil-god.

**.3** godling, godlet, godkin; **demigod,** half-god, hero; demigoddess, heroine.

**.4** (gods and goddesses) deities of fertility 165.5; deities of the household 191.30; earth goddesses 375.10; moon goddesses 375.12; sun gods 375.14; sea gods 397.4; rain gods 394.6; wind gods 403.3; thunder gods 456.5; gods of lightning 335.17; agricultural deities 413.4; gods of commerce 827.12; war gods 797.17; love deities 931.8; gods of marriage 933.14; Muses 535.2, poetry Muses 609.12; music Muses 464.22; Fates 640.3; water gods 1014.20; forest gods 1014.21; goddesses of discord 795.1; gods of evil 1016.6; deities of the nether world 1019.5, deities of justice 976.5.

**.5** (Greek and Roman deities) Olympic gods, Olympians; Zeus, Jupiter, Jove; Jupiter Fulgur or Fulminator, Jupiter Tonans, Jupiter Pluvius, Jupiter Optimus Maximus, Jupiter Fidius; Helios, Hyperion, Phaëthon; Apollo, Apollon, Phoebus, Phoebus Apollo; Mars, Ares; Mercury, Hermes; Neptune, Poseidon; Vulcan, Hephaestus; Bacchus, Dionysus; Pluto, Hades, Dis, Orcus; Saturn, Kronos or Cronus; Cupid, Amor, Eros; Hymen; Momus; Juno, Hera or Here; Demeter, Ceres; Persephone, Proserpina, Proserpine, Persephassa, Kore or Cora, Despoina; Diana, Artemis; Athena, Minerva; Nike; Venus, Aphrodite; Hestia, Vesta; Ge or Gaea or Gaia, Tellus; Ate; Mithras; Cybele, Agdistis, Great Mother, Magna Mater, Rhea, Ops.

**.6** (Norse and Germanic deities) Aesir, Vanir; Balder, Bor, Bori, Bragi, Forseti, Frey or Freyr, Heimdall, Höder or Hödr, Hoenir, Loki, Nerthus or Hertha, Njorth or Njord, Odin or Woden or Wotan, Reimthursen, Thor or Donar, Tyr or Tiu, Ull or Ullr, Vali, Vitharr or Vidar, Ymir; Völund, Weland, Wayland; Wyrd; Ing; Freya or Freyja, Frigg or Frigga, Hel, Nanna, Ithunn or Idun, Sif, Sigyn.

**7** (Celtic deities) Aine, Amaethon, Angus Og, Arawn, Arianrhod, Blodenwedd, Bóann, Bodb, Brigit, Dagda, Danu, Dôn, Dylan, Epona, Goibniu, Lir, Llew Llaw Gyffes, Lug, Macha, Manannán, Morrigan, Neman.

(Hindu deities) Aditi, Agni, Aryaman, Asapurna, Avalokita or Avalokitesvara, Bhaga, Bhairava, Brahma, Brihaspati, Chitragupta, Daksha, Devaki, Dharma,

Dyaus, Ganesa or Ganesha or Ganapati, Garuda, Himavat, Hanuman, Indra, Ka, Kala, Kama, Kamsa, Karttikeya, Marut, Mitra, Parjanya, Pushan, Rahu, Rhibhus, Rudra, Savitar, Shiva, Sita, Soma, Surya, Vaja, Varuna, Varuni, Vayu, Vibhu, Vishnu, Yama, Dharti Mai, Bhudevi; Devi, Bhairavi, Chandi, Durga, Gauri, Jaganmati, Kali, Parvati, Uma; Lakshmi, Sarasvati, Ushas; Asvins.

**.9** (avatars of Vishnu) Buddha, Kalki, Krishna, Kurma, Matsya, Narsinh, Parshuram, Rama, Vaman, Varah; Juggernaut, Jagannath.

**.10** (Egyptian deities) Anubis, Bast, Horus, Isis, Khem, Min, Neph, Nephthys, Nut, Osiris, Ptah, Ra or Amen-Ra, Set, Thoth.

**.11** (Semitic deities) Adad, Adapa, Anshar, Antu, Anu, Anunaki, Ashur, Baal, Baba, Bau, Beltu, Dagon, Damkina, Dumuzi, Ea, Enki, Enkimdu, Enlil, Ereshkigal, Gibil, Girru, Gish Bar, Gishzida, Gula, Igigi, Inanna, Ishtar, Isimud, Ki, Kishar, Lahamu, Lahmu, Mama, Marduk or Bel-Merodach or Merodach, Moloch, Mylitta, Nabu or Nebo, Nammu, Namtar, Nanna, Nergal, Neti, Nina, Ningal, Ninhursag or Ninmah or Nintoo, Ninib, Ninkur, Ninlil, Ninsar, Ninshubur, Ninurta or Ningirsu, Nusku, Papsukai, Ramman, Shala, Shamash, Sin, Tammuz, Tashmit, Utnapishtim, Uttu, Utu, Zarpanit, Zubird.

**.12** (animistic spirits and powers) manitou, huaca, nagual, mana, pokunt, tamanoas, wakan, zemi.

**.13** (Chinese deities) Chang Fei, Chang Hsien, Chang Kuo, Ch'eng Huang, Cheng Wu, Han Chung-li, Heu Chi, Hou T'u, Hsi Wang Mu, Kuan Ti, Kuan Yin, Kuei Hsing, Lei Kung, Lung Wang, Lü Tung Pin, Ma Wang, Niu Wang, Tsai Shen, Tsao Chün, Ts'ao Kuo-ch'iu, Tung Wang Kung, T'u Ti, Wen Ch'ang, Yang Chin, Yen Lo.

**.14** (Japanese deities) Amaterasu Omikami, Amatsumara, Hachiman, Hiruko, Hotei, Inari, Izanagi, Izanami, Kwannon, Ninigino-Mikoto, Susanoo.

**.15 spirit,** intelligence, supernatural being; **genius,** daemon, demon; atua; **specter** 1017; **evil spirits** 1016.

**.16 elemental,** elemental spirit; sylph, gnome, salamander, undine.

**.17 fairyfolk,** elfenfolk, shee or sidhe, **the little people** or **men,** the good folk or people, denizens of the air; **fairyland,** faerie.

**.18 fairy, sprite, fay,** fairy man or woman; **elf,**

brownie, pixie, **gremlin**, ouphe, hob, clu-
ricaune, puca *or* pooka *or* pwca, kobold,
nisse, peri; **imp, goblin** 1016.8,9; **gnome,
dwarf; sylph,** sylphid; **banshee;** leprechaun; fairy queen; Ariel, Mab, Oberon,
Titania, Béfind, Corrigan, Finnbeara.

.19 **nymph;** nymphet, nymphlin, nymph(o)–
*or* nymphi–; **dryad,** hamadryad, wood
nymph; vila *or* willi; tree nymph; oread,
mountain nymph; limoniad, meadow *or*
flower nymph; Napaea, glen nymph;
Hyades; Pleiades, Atlantides.

.20 **water god, water spirit** *or* **sprite** *or*
**nymph;** undine, nix, nixie, kelpie; naiad,
limniad, fresh-water nymph; Oceanid,
Nereid, sea nymph, ocean nymph, **mermaid,** sea-maid, sea-maiden, siren; Thetis;
**merman,** man fish; **Neptune,** "the old
man of the sea" [Homer]; Oceanus, Poseidon, Triton; Davy Jones, Davy.

.21 **forest god, sylvan deity,** vegetation spirit
*or* daemon, field spirit, fertility god, corn
spirit, **faun, satyr,** silenus, panisc, panis-
cus, panisca; **Pan,** Faunus; Cailleac; Priapus; Vitharr *or* Vidar, the goat god.

.22 **familiar spirit,** familiar; **genius, good genius,** daemon, demon, *numen* [L], totem;
**guardian, guardian spirit, guardian angel,**
angel, good angel, ministering angel, **fairy
godmother, guide, control,** attendant
godling *or* spirit, invisible helper, special
providence; **tutelary** *or* **tutelar god** *or* **genius** *or* **spirit,** tutelary; *genius tutelae, genius loci, genius domus, genius familiae*
[all L]; **household gods;** *lares familiaris,
lares praestites, lares compitales, lares
viales, lares permarini* [all L]; penates,
lares and penates; ancestral spirits;
manes, pitris.

.23 **Santa Claus,** Santa, Saint Nicholas, Saint
Nick, Kriss Kringle, Father Christmas.

.24 **mythology,** mythicism; **legend, lore, folklore,** mythical lore; fairy lore, fairyism.

.25 ADJS **mythic(al), mythological,** myth-
ic(o)–; **fabulous, legendary.**

.26 **divine, godlike** 1013.19,20.

.27 **fairy,** faery, **fairylike,** fairyish, fay; sylph-
ine, sylphish, sylphy, sylphidine, sylphlike;
**elfin,** elfish, elflike; gnomish, gnomelike;
pixieish.

.28 nymphic, nymphal, nymphean, nymph-
like.

### 1015. ANGEL, SAINT

.1 NOUNS **angel,** celestial, celestial *or* heavenly being; messenger of God; **seraph,**
seraphim [pl], angel of love; **cherub, cherubim** [pl], angel of light; **principality,**
archangel; recording angel; **saint,** hagi-
(o)–; beatified soul, canonized mortal;
patron saint; martyr; redeemed *or* saved
soul, soul in glory.

.2 **heavenly host,** host of heaven, choir invis-
ible, angelic host, heavenly hierarchy,
Sons of God, ministering spirits; Amesha
Spentas.

.3 (celestial hierarchy of Pseudo-Dionysius)
seraphim, cherubim, thrones; domina-
tions *or* dominions, virtues, powers; prin-
cipalities, archangels, angels; angelology.

.4 Azrael, angel of death, death's bright angel; Abdiel, Chamuel, Gabriel, Jophiel,
Michael, Raphael, Uriel, Zadkiel.

.5 **Madonna, Holy Mary; Our Lady,** *Notre
Dame* [Fr]; **Mother of God,** *Dei Mater*
[L], Deipara, Theotokos; *mater dolorosa*
[L], the Sorrowful Mother; Queen of
Heaven, *Regina Coeli* [L]; Queen of An-
gels, *Regina Angelorum* [L]; Star of the
Sea, *Stella Maris* [L]; **the Virgin,** the
Blessed Virgin, **the Virgin Mary,** the Vir-
gin Mother; *Sancta Virgo Virginum* [L],
Holy Virgin of Virgins; *Virgo Sponsa
Dei* [L], Virgin Bride of the Lord; *Virgo
Clemens* [L], Virgin Most Merciful;
*Virgo Gloriosa* [L], Virgin Most Glori-
ous; *Virgo Potens* [L], Virgin Most Pow-
erful; *Virgo Praedicanda* [L], Virgin
Most Renowned; *Virgo Sapientissima*
[L], Virgin Most Wise; *Virgo Veneranda*
[L], Virgin Most Venerable; *hortus clu-
sus* [L]; Immaculate Conception; Mariol-
ogy; Mariolatry.

.6 ADJS **angelic, seraphic, cherubic; heavenly, celestial;** archangelic; **saintly,
sainted,** beatified, canonized; martyred,
saved, redeemed, glorified, in glory.

### 1016. EVIL SPIRITS

.1 NOUNS **evil spirits, demons, demonkind,**
powers of darkness, spirits of the air, host
of hell, hellish host, denizens of hell, inhabitants of Pandemonium, souls in hell,
damned spirits, lost souls, the lost, the
damned.

.2 **devil,** *diable* [Fr], *diablo* [Sp], *diabolus*
[L], deil [Scot], *Teufel* [Ger], diabol(o)–.

.3 **Satan,** Satanas, **the Devil, Lucifer,** the
Demon, the Fiend, the Foul Fiend, the
Arch-fiend, the Wicked One, **the Evil
One,** the Evil Spirit, **the Tempter,** the
Adversary, the archenemy, the Common
Enemy, the Old Enemy, the Devil Incar-
nate, the Author *or* Father of Evil, the
Father of Lies, the serpent, the Old Ser-
pent, the Prince of the Devils, the Prince

of Darkness, the Prince of this world, the Prince of the power of the air, His Satanic Majesty, the angel of the bottomless pit.

.4 [slang terms] the Deuce, the Dickens, **Old Harry**, Old Nick, Old Ned, Old Horny, Old Scratch, Old Gooseberry, Old Bendy, Old *or* Auld Clootie, Old Poker, the Old Gentleman.

.5 Beelzebub, Belial, Eblis, Azazel, Ahriman *or* Angra Mainyu; Mephistopheles, Mephisto; Shaitan, Sammael, Asmodeus; Abaddon, Apollyon; Lilith; Aeshma, Pisacha, Putana, Ravana.

.6 (gods of evil) Set, Typhon, Loki; Nemesis; gods of the nether world 1019.5.

.7 **demon, fiend**, fiend from hell, **devil**, satan, daeva, rakshasa, dybbuk, shedu, gyre [Scot], bad *or* evil spirit, unclean spirit; **hellion** [informal]; cacodemon, incubus, succubus; **jinni**, genie, genius, jinniyeh, afreet; evil genius; barghest; **ghoul**, lamia, Lilith, yogini, Baba Yaga, **vampire**, the undead.

.8 **imp, pixie, sprite, elf, puck**, kobold, *diablotin* [Fr], tokoloshe, poltergeist, **gremlin**, Dingbelle, Fifinella, **bad fairy**, bad peri; little *or* young devil, devilkin, deviling; erlking; Puck, Robin Goodfellow, Hob, Hobgoblin.

.9 goblin, hobgoblin, hob, ouphe.

.10 bugbear, bugaboo, bogey, bogle, boggart; **booger, bugger**, bug [archaic], **boogerman**, bogeyman, boogeyman; bête noire, fee-faw-fum, Mumbo Jumbo.

.11 Fury, avenging spirit; the Furies, the Erinyes, the Eumenides, the Dirae; Alecto, Megaera, Tisiphone.

.12 changeling, elf child.

.13 werefolk, were-animals; werewolf, lycanthrope, *loup-garou* [Fr]; werejaguar, jaguar-man, uturuncu; wereass, werebear, werecalf, werefox, werehyena, wereleopard, weretiger, werelion, wereboar, werecrocodile, werecat, werehare.

.14 devilishness, demonishness, fiendishness; devilship, devildom; horns, the cloven hoof, the Devil's pitchfork.

.15 Satanism, diabolism, demonism, devilry, diablerie, demonry; demonomy, demonianism; black magic; Black Mass; sorcery 1035; demonolatry, demon *or* devil *or* chthonian worship; demonomancy; demonology, diabolology *or* diabology, demonography, devil lore.

.16 Satanist, diabolist, demonist; demonomist, demoniast; demonologist, demonologer; demonolater, chthonian, devil

worshiper, demon worshiper, Satan worshiper; sorcerer 1035.5.

.17 VERBS demonize, devilize, diabolize; possess, **obsess; bewitch**, bedevil 1036.10.

.18 ADJS demoniac *or* demoniacal, demonic(al), demonish, demonlike; **devilish**, devil-like; **satanic, diabolic(al); hellish** 1019.8; **fiendish**, fiendlike; ghoulish, ogreish; inhuman.

.19 impish, puckish, elfish, elvish; mischievous 738.6.

## 1017. SPECTER

.1 NOUNS **specter, ghost**, spectral ghost, **spook** [informal], **phantom**, phantasm, phantasma, **wraith, shade**, shadow, **apparition**, appearance, presence, shape, form, eidolon, idolum, revenant, larva; **spirit**, pneumat(o)-, psych(o)-, thymo-; sprite, shrouded spirit, disembodied spirit, departed spirit, wandering soul, soul of the dead, dybbuk; oni; Masan; astral spirit, astral; unsubstantiality, immateriality, incorporeal, incorporeity, incorporeal being *or* entity; walking dead man, zombie; duppy; vision, theophany; materialization; haunt *or* hant [both dial]; banshee; poltergeist; control, guide; manes, lemures; grateful dead.

.2 White Lady, White Lady of Avenel [Scot], White Ladies of Normandy; Brocken specter; Wild Hunt; Flying Dutchman.

.3 **double**, etheric double *or* self, co-walker, *Doppelgänger* [Ger], doubleganger, fetch, wraith.

.4 eeriness, ghostliness, weirdness, uncanniness, spookiness [informal].

.5 possession, obsession, spirit control.

.6 VERBS haunt, hant [dial], spook [informal]; **possess, obsess.**

.7 ADJS spectral, specterlike; **ghostly**, ghostish, ghosty, ghostlike; **spiritual**, psychic(al); **phantomlike**, phantom, phantomic(al), phantasmal, phantasmic, **wraithlike**, wraithy, shadowy; etheric, ectoplasmic, astral, ethereal 4.6; incorporeal 377.7; **supernatural** 85.15.

.8 disembodied, discarnate, decarnate, decarnated.

.9 weird, eerie, eldritch, uncanny, unearthly, macabre; **spooky** *or* spookish [both informal].

.10 haunted, hanted [dial], spooked *or* spooky [both informal], spirit-haunted, ghost-haunted, specter-haunted; **possessed, obsessed**, ghost-ridden.

## 1018. HEAVEN

*(abode of the deity and blessed dead)*

.1 NOUNS Heaven, Paradise, glory, eternity, **kingdom come** [informal], a better place, happy hunting ground, Land of the Leal [Scot], the happy land, the Promised Land, the world above, otherworld, better world, heaven above, high heaven, eternal home, abode of the blessed, inheritance of the saints in light, realm of light; Beulah, Beulah Land, Land of Beulah; **kingdom of heaven,** God's kingdom, heavenly kingdom, kingdom of God, kingdom of glory; God's presence, presence of God; Abraham's bosom.

.2 "my Father's house" [Bible], "God's residence" [Emily Dickinson], "mansions in the sky" [Isaac Watts], "the bosom of our rest" [Cardinal Newman], "the treasury of everlasting joy" [Shakespeare], "the great world of light, that lies behind all human destinies" [Longfellow].

.3 **the hereafter,** afterworld, afterlife 121.2.

.4 Holy City, **Zion,** New Jerusalem, Heavenly *or* Celestial City, City Celestial, Heavenly City of God, City of God, *Civitas Dei* [L], "heaven's high city" [Francis Quarles].

.5 **heaven of heavens, seventh heaven,** the empyrean, throne of God, God's throne, celestial throne, the great white throne.

.6 (Christian Science) bliss, harmony, spirituality, the reign of Spirit, the atmosphere of Soul.

.7 (Mormon) celestial kingdom, terrestrial kingdom, telestial kingdom.

.8 (Mohammedan) Alfardaws, Assama; Falak al aflak.

.9 (Hindu, Buddhist, and Theosophical) nirvana; Buddha-field; devaloka, land of the gods; kamavachara, kamaloka; devachan.

.10 (mythological) Olympus, Mount Olympus; Elysium, Elysian fields; fields of Aalu; Islands *or* Isles of the Blessed, Happy Isles, Fortunate Isles *or* Islands; Avalon; garden of the Gods, garden of the Hesperides, Bower of Bliss; Tir-na-n'Og, Annwfn.

.11 (Norse) Valhalla, Asgard, Fensalir, Glathsheim, Vingolf, Valaskjalf, Hlithskjalf, Thruthvang *or* Thruthheim, Bilskirnir, Ydalir, Sökkvabekk, Breithablik, Folkvang, Sessrymnir, Noatun, Thrymheim, Glitnir, Himinbjorg, Vithi.

.12 (removal to heaven) apotheosis, resurrection, translation, gathering, ascension, the Ascension; **assumption,** the Assumption; removal to Abraham's bosom.

.13 ADJS **heavenly,** heavenish; **paradisal, paradisaic(al),** paradisiac(al), paradisic(al); **celestial,** supernal, ethereal; **unearthly,** unworldly; **otherworldly,** extraterrestrial, extramundane, transmundane, transcendental; Elysian, Olympian; blessed, beatified, beatific(al), glorified, in glory; from on high.

.14 ADVS **celestially,** paradisally, supernally, ethereally; in heaven, in Abraham's bosom, *in sinu Abraham* [L], on high, among the blest, in glory.

## 1019. HELL

.1 NOUNS **hell, Hades,** Sheol, Gehenna, Tophet, Abaddon, Naraka, jahannan, avichi, **perdition,** Pandemonium, **inferno,** the pit, **the bottomless pit,** the abyss, "a vast, unbottom'd, boundless pit" [Robert Burns], **nether world,** lower world, underworld, infernal regions, abode *or* world of the dead, abode of the damned, place of torment, the grave, shades below; **purgatory; limbo.**

.2 **hellfire,** fire and brimstone, lake of fire and brimstone, everlasting fire *or* torment, "the fire that never shall be quenched" [Bible].

.3 (mythological) **Hades,** Orcus, Tartarus, Avernus, Acheron, pit of Acheron; Amenti, Aralu; Hel, Niflhel, Niflheim, Naströnd.

.4 (rivers of Hades) Styx, Stygian creek; Acheron, River of Woe; Cocytus, River of Wailing; Phlegethon, Pyriphlegethon, River of Fire; Lethe, River of Forgetfulness.

.5 (deities of the nether world) Pluto, Orcus, Hades *or* Aides *or* Aidoneus, Dis *or* Dis pater, Rhadamanthus, Erebus, Charon, Cerberus, Minos; Osiris; Persephone, Proserpine, Proserpina, Persephassa, Despoina, Kore *or* Cora; Hel, Loki; Satan 1016.3.

.6 VERBS **damn,** doom, send *or* consign to hell, cast into hell, doom to perdition, condemn to hell *or* eternal punishment.

.7 go to hell, be damned, go the other way [informal].

.8 ADJS **hellish, infernal,** sulfurous, chthonic, chthonian; pandemonic, pandemoniac; devilish 1016.18; Plutonic, Plutonian; Tartarean; Stygian; Lethean; Acherontic; purgatorial, hellborn.

.9 ADVS **hellishly, infernally,** in hell, in hell fire, below, in torment.

## 1020. RELIGIONS, CULTS, SECTS

.1 NOUNS **religion**, religio–; religious belief or faith, **belief, faith**, teaching, doctrine, creed, credo, theology 1023, orthodoxy 1024; system of beliefs; tradition.

.2 **cult, ism;** cultism; **mystique.**

.3 **sect** 1020.32, sectarism, religious order, **denomination, persuasion,** faction, **church,** communion, community, group, fellowship, affiliation, order, school, party, society, body, organization; branch, variety, version, segment; offshoot; **schism,** division.

.4 **sectarianism,** sectarism, **denominationalism,** partisanism, the clash of creeds; schismatism; syncretism, eclecticism.

.5 **theism; monotheism; polytheism,** multitheism, myriotheism; **ditheism,** dyotheism, dualism; **tritheism;** tetratheism; **pantheism,** cosmotheism, theopantism, acosmism; physitheism, psychotheism, animotheism; physicomorphism; hylotheism; anthropotheism, anthropomorphism; anthropolatry; allotheism; monolatry, henotheism; autotheism; zootheism, theriotheism; **deism.**

.6 **Christianity,** Christianism, Christendom; Latin or Roman or Western Christianity; Eastern or Orthodox Christianity; Protestant Christianity; Judeo-Christian religion or tradition or belief.

.7 **Catholicism,** Catholicity; **Roman Catholicism,** Romanism, Rome; papalism; popery, popeism, papism, papistry [all derog]; ultramontanism; Catholic Church, **Roman Catholic Church,** Church of Rome; Eastern Rites, Uniate Rites, Uniatism, Alexandrian or Antiochian or Byzantine Rite.

.8 Orthodoxy; **Eastern Orthodox Church, Holy Orthodox Catholic Apostolic Church,** Greek Orthodox Church, Russian Orthodox Church; patriarchate of Constantinople, patriarchate of Antioch, patriarchate of Alexandria, patriarchate of Jerusalem.

.9 **Protestantism,** Reform, Reformationism; Evangelicalism; Zwinglianism; dissent 522; apostasy 628.2; new theology.

.10 **Anglicanism;** High-Churchism, Low-Churchism; Anglo-Catholicism; Church of England, Established Church; High Church, Low Church, Broad Church, Free Church.

.11 **Judaism;** Hebraism, Hebrewism; Israelitism; Orthodox Judaism, Conservative Judaism, Reform Judaism, Reconstruction-ism; Hasidism; rabbinism, Talmudism; Pharisaism; Sadduceeism; Karaism or Karaitism.

.12 **Islam, Muhammadanism, Mohammedanism, Muslimism, Moslemism,** Islamism; Sufism, Wahabiism, Sunnism, Shiism; Black Muslimism.

.13 **Christian Science;** New Thought, Higher Thought, Practical Christianity, Mental Science, Divine Science Church.

.14 **religionist,** religioner; **believer** 1028.4; cultist, ist.

.15 **theist; monotheist; polytheist,** multitheist, myriotheist; ditheist, dualist; tritheist; tetratheist; **pantheist,** cosmotheist; psychotheist; physitheist; hylotheist; anthropotheist; anthropolater; allotheist; henotheist; autotheist; zootheist, theriotheist; **deist.**

.16 **Christian,** Nazarene, Nazarite.

.17 **sectarian,** sectary, **denominationalist,** factionist, schismatic.

.18 **Catholic,** Roman Catholic, RC [informal], Romanist, papist [derog]; ultramontane; Eastern-Rite Christian, Uniate.

.19 **Protestant,** non-Catholic, Reformed believer, Reformationist; Evangelical; Zwinglian; dissenter 522.3; apostate 628.5.

.20 **Jew, Hebrew,** Judaist, Israelite; Orthodox or Conservative or Reform Jew, Reconstructionist; Hasid; Rabbinist, Talmudist; Pharisee; Sadducee; Karaite.

.21 **Mormon,** Latter-day Saint, Josephite [informal].

.22 **Muslim, Muhammadan** or **Mohammedan** [both derog], Mussulman, Moslem, Islamite; Shiite, Shia, Sectary; Motazilite, Sunnite, Wahabi, Sufi; dervish; abdal; Black Muslim.

.23 **Christian Scientist,** Christian Science Practitioner.

.24 ADJS **religious, theistic; monotheistic; polytheistic,** ditheistic, tritheistic; **pantheistic,** cosmotheistic; physicomorphic; anthropomorphic, anthropotheistic; **deistic.**

.25 **sectarian,** sectary, **denominational,** schismatic(al).

.26 **nonsectarian, undenominational, nondenominational;** interdenominational.

.27 **Protestant,** non-Catholic, Reformed, Reformationist, Evangelical; Lutheran, Calvinist, Calvinistic, Zwinglian; dissentient 522.6; apostate 628.11.

.28 **Catholic; Roman Catholic,** RC [informal], Roman; Romish, popish, papish, papist, papistic(al) [all derog]; ultramontane.

.29 **Jewish, Hebrew,** Judaical, Israelite, Israelitic, Israelitish; Orthodox, Conservative, Reform, Reconstructionist; Hasidic.

.30 **Muslim, Islamic,** Muhammadan, Mohammedan, Moslem, Islamitic, Islamistic.

.31 (Oriental) Buddhist, Buddhistic; Brahmanic, Brahmanistic; Vedic, Vedantic; Confucian, Confucianist; Taoist, Taoistic, Shintoist, Shintoistic; Zoroastrian, Zarathustrian, Parsee.

### .32 religions and sects

| | |
|---|---|
| anthroposophy | Parsiism, Parsism |
| Babism, Babi | Reconstructionism |
| Bahaism | Reform Judaism |
| Brahmanism | reincarnationism |
| Brahmoism | Sabaeanism |
| Buddhism | Saivism |
| Ch'an Buddhism | Shaivite Hinduism |
| Chen Yen Buddhism | Shiite Muslimism |
| Ching-t'u Buddhism | Shin Buddhism |
| Christianity 1020.6,33 | Shingon Buddhism |
| Confucianism | Shinto, Shintoism |
| Conservative Judaism | Sikhism |
| Dakshincharin Hinduism | Soka Gakkai Buddhism |
| Eleusinianism | Sufism |
| Ethical Culture | Taoism |
| Gnosticism | Tendai Buddhism |
| gymnosophy | Theosophy |
| Hinduism | Theravada or Hinayana Buddhism |
| Jainism | |
| Jodo Buddhism | T'ien-t'ai Buddhism |
| Judaism 1020.11 | Unitarianism |
| Lamaism | Vaishnavite Hinduism |
| Lingayat Hinduism | Vajrayana Buddhism |
| Magianism | Vamacharin Hinduism |
| Mahayana Buddhism | |
| Mandaeism | Vedanta, Vedantism |
| Mithraism | Wahabiism |
| Muhammadanism 1020.12 | Yoga, Yogism |
| | Zen, Zen Buddhism |
| Nichiren Buddhism | Zoroastrianism, Zoroastrism |
| Orphism | |
| Orthodox Judaism | |

### .33 Christian denominations

| | |
|---|---|
| Adventism, Second Adventism | Laudism, Laudianism |
| | Liberal Catholicism |
| Amish | Lutheranism |
| Anabaptism | Mennonitism |
| Anglicanism 1020.10 | Methodism |
| Anglo-Catholicism | Moral Rearmament |
| antinomianism | Mormonism |
| Arianism | New Thought |
| Athanasianism | Origenism |
| Boehmenism | Orthodox Christianity |
| Calvinism | Oxford Movement |
| Catholicism 1020.7 | Practical Christianity |
| Christian Science 1020.13 | Presbyterianism |
| | Puritanism |
| Congregationalism | Puseyism |
| Eastern Orthodox Christianity | Quakerism |
| | quietism |
| Episcopalianism | Roman Catholicism |
| Erastianism | Rosicrucianism |
| homoiousianism | Sabellianism |
| homoousianism | Salvation Army |
| Jansenism | Socinianism |
| latitudinarianism | Stundism |

| | |
|---|---|
| Swedenborgianism | Unitarianism |
| Tractarianism | Universalism |
| Trinitarianism | Wesleyanism, Wesleyism |
| Ubiquitarianism | |
| Uniatism | |

### .34 religionists

| | |
|---|---|
| anthroposophist | Magian, Magus |
| Babist | Mandaean |
| Brahman, Brahmanist | Muhammadan |
| Buddhist | 1020.22 |
| Christian 1020.16,35 | Parsee |
| Confucianist | reincarnationist |
| Gentoo | Sabaean |
| Gheber | Shintoist |
| Gnostic | Sikh |
| gymnosophist | Taoist |
| Hindu | Theosophist |
| Jain, Jaina | Vedantist |
| Jew 1020.20 | Yogi, Yogin, Yogist |
| Lamaist, Lamaite | Zoroastrian |

### .35 Christian sectarians

| | |
|---|---|
| Adventist, Second Adventist | Huguenot |
| | Independent |
| Amish, Amish Mennonite | Irvingite |
| | Jacobite |
| Anabaptist | Jansenist |
| Anglican | Jehovah's Witness |
| Anglo-Catholic | Jovinianist |
| antinomian | Latitudinarian |
| Arian | Latter-day Saint |
| Athanasian | Laudist, Laudian |
| Baptist | Liberal Catholic |
| Bible Christian | Low-Churchman |
| Boehmenist | Lutheran |
| Bryanite | Mennonite |
| Calvinist | Methodist |
| Campbellite | Mormon |
| Catholic | Nestorian |
| Christadelphian | Presbyterian |
| Christian Scientist 1020.23 | Protestant 1020.19 |
| | Protestant Episcopal |
| Churchman | Puritan |
| Congregationalist | Puseyite |
| Coptic Christian | Quaker |
| Davidist | quietist |
| Disciple of Christ | Restitutionist |
| Doukhobor | Roman Catholic |
| Dunker | Rosicrucian |
| Ebionite | Russian Orthodox |
| Episcopalian | Sandemanian |
| Erastian | Seventh-Day Adventist |
| Eusebian | |
| Evangelical Congregationalist | Shaker |
| | Stundist |
| Familist | Swedenborgian |
| Friend | Tractarian |
| German Baptist | Trinitarian |
| Gideon | Ubiquitarian |
| Glassite | Uniate |
| Greek Orthodox | Unitarian |
| High-Churchman | Universalist |
| Homoiousian | Wesleyan |
| Homoousian | |

## 1021. SCRIPTURE

.1 NOUNS **scripture, scriptures, sacred writings, Bible;** canonical writings or books, sacred canon.

.2 **Bible, Holy Bible,** biblic(o)–; **Scriptur**

the Scriptures, Holy Scripture, Holy Writ, the Book, the Good Book, the Book of Books, the Word, the Word of God; Vulgate, Septuagint, Douay Bible, Authorized *or* King James Version, Revised Version, American Revised Version; Revised Standard Version; Jerusalem Bible; Testament; canon.

.3 **Old Testament,** Tenach; Hexateuch, Octateuch; Pentateuch, Chumash, Five Books of Moses, **Torah,** the Law, the Jewish *or* Mosaic Law, Law of Moses; the Prophets, Nebiim, Major *or* Minor Prophets; the Writings, Hagiographa, Ketubim; Apocrypha, noncanonical writings.

.4 New Testament; **Gospels,** Evangels, the Gospel, Good News, Good *or* Glad Tidings; Synoptic Gospels, Epistles, Pauline Epistles, Catholic Epistles, Johannine Epistles; Acts, Acts of the Apostles; Apocalypse, Revelation.

.5 **Talmud,** Mishnah, Gemara; Masorah.

.6 **Koran;** Avesta, **Zend-Avesta;** Granth, Adigranth; Tripitaka, agama; Tao Tê Ching; Analects of Confucius; the Eddas; Arcana Caelestia; **Book of Mormon;** Science and Health with Key to the Scriptures.

.7 (Hindu) **the Vedas, Veda,** Rig-Veda, Yajur-Veda, Sama-Veda, Atharva-Veda; Brahmana, Upanishad, Aranyaka; Samhita; shastra, sruti, smriti, purana, tantra; Bhagavad-Gita.

.8 (Buddhist) Vinaya Pitaka, Sutta Pitaka, Abhidamma Pitaka; Dhammapada, Jataka; The Diamond-Cutter, The Lotus of the True Law, Prajna-Paramita Sutra, Pure Land Sutras.

.9 **revelation, divine revelation; inspiration,** afflatus, divine inspiration; theopneusty, theopneustia; theophany, theophania, epiphany; direct *or* immediate communication, mystical experience, mysticism, direct intuition, mystical intuition; **prophecy,** prophetic revelation, apocalypse.

10 ADJS **scriptural, Biblical,** Old-Testament, New-Testament, Gospel, Mosaic, Yahwist, Yahwistic, Elohist, revealed, revelational, prophetic, apocalyptic(al); inspired, theopneustic; evangelic(al), evangelistic, gospel; apostolic(al); textual, textuary; canonical.

11 Talmudic, Mishnaic, Gemaric, Masoretic; rabbinic.

12 epiphanic, mystic(al).

.3 Koranic; Avestan; Eddic; Mormon.

.14 Vedic; tantrist.

## 1022. PROPHETS, RELIGIOUS FOUNDERS

.1 NOUNS **prophet** 543.4, *vates sacer* [L]; Abraham, Amos, Daniel, Ezekiel, Habakkuk, Haggai, Hosea, Isaac, Isaiah, Jacob, Jeremiah, Joel, Jonah, Joseph, Joshua, Malachi, Micah, Moses, Nahum, Obadiah, Samuel, Zechariah, Zephaniah.

.2 (Christian founders) **evangelist, apostle, disciple,** saint; Matthew, Mark, Luke, John; Paul; Peter; **the Fathers,** Apostolic Fathers, ante-Nicene Fathers, Primitive Fathers; Barnabas, Clement of Rome, Hermas, Ignatius, Papias, Polycarp; Apologetic Fathers, Justin Martyr, Theophilus, Irenaeus, Clement of Alexandria, Tertullian, Origen, Cyprian of Carthage, Dionysius of Alexandria, Gregory Thaumaturgus; post-Nicene Fathers, Eusebius of Caesarea, Athanasius, Basil, Ephrem Syrus, Cyril of Jerusalem, Gregory of Nazianzus, Gregory of Nyssa, Epiphanius of Salamis, John Chrysostom, Cyril of Alexandria, Lactantius Firmianus, Hilary of Poitiers, Ambrose of Milan, Jerome, Augustine of Hippo.

.3 Martin Luther, John Calvin, John Wycliffe, Jan Hus, John Wesley, John Knox, George Fox (Protestant reformers); Swedenborg (Church of the New Jerusalem); Mary Baker Eddy (Christian Science); Joseph Smith (Church of Jesus Christ of Latter-day Saints).

.4 Buddha, Gautama Buddha (Buddhism); Mahavira *or* Vardhamana *or* Jina (Jainism); Mirza Ali Muhammad of Shiraz *or* the Bab (Babism); Muhammad *or* Mohammed (Islam); Confucius (Confucianism); Lao-tzu (Taoism); Zoroaster *or* Zarathustra (Zoroastrianism); Nanak (Sikhism); Ram Mohan Roy (Brahmo-Samaj).

## 1023. THEOLOGY

.1 NOUNS **theology, religion, divinity;** theologism; doctrinism, doctrinalism, doctrinal theology; canonics; dogmatics, dogmatic theology; systematic theology, systematics; philosophical theology; dialogical theology; patristic theology, patristics; physicotheology; natural *or* rational theology; hierology, hagiology; hierography, hagiography; soteriology, Christology, logos theology, logos Christology; apologetics; eschatology; theological hermeneutics; secularism; rationalism; school theology, scholastic theology; Mercersburg theology; crisis theology, neoorthodox theology, neoorthodoxy; existential theology; phenomenological theology; Buddhology; Mariology, Mariolatry.

.2 **doctrine, dogma** 501.2; **creed,** credo; credenda, articles of religion *or* faith; Apostles' Creed, Nicene Creed, Athanasian Creed; Catechism.

.3 **theologian,** theologist, theologizer, theologer, theologician; **divine;** scholastic, schoolman; theological *or* divinity student, theological, theologue; canonist.

.4 ADJS **theological,** the(o)–, **religious,** religio–, **divine;** doctrinal, doctrinary; canonic(al); physicotheological; Buddhological; Mariological.

## 1024. ORTHODOXY

.1 NOUNS **orthodoxy,** orthodoxism; orthodoxness, orthodoxicalness; **soundness,** soundness of doctrine, rightness, right belief *or* doctrine; **authoritativeness,** authenticity, canonicalness, canonicity; traditionalism; **the truth,** religious truth, gospel truth.

.2 **the faith, true faith,** apostolic faith, primitive faith, "the faith once delivered unto the saints" [Bible]; old-time religion, faith of our fathers.

.3 **the Church, the true church,** Holy Church, Church of Christ, the Bride of the Lamb, body of Christ, temple of the Holy Ghost, body of Christians, members in Christ, disciples *or* followers of Christ; apostolic church; universal church, the church universal; church visible, church invisible; church militant, church triumphant.

.4 **true believer,** orthodox Christian; Sunni Muslim; Orthodox Jew; orthodox, orthodoxist; textualist, textuary; canonist; fundamentalist; the orthodox.

.5 **strictness,** strict interpretation, scripturalism, evangelicalism; hyperorthodoxy, puritanism, puritanicalness, purism; staunchness; straitlacedness, stiff-neckedness, hideboundness; **bigotry** 527.1; **dogmatism** 513.6; **fundamentalism,** literalism, precisianism; bibliolatry; Sabbatarianism; sabbatism.

.6 **bigot** 527.5; **dogmatist** 513.7.

.7 ADJS **orthodox,** orthodoxical; of the faith, of the true faith; **sound,** firm, faithful, true, true-blue; **Christian; evangelical; scriptural,** canonical; traditional, traditionalistic; literal, textual; standard, customary, conventional; **authoritative,** au-

thentic, accepted, received, approved; correct, right, proper.

.8 **strict,** scripturalistic, evangelical; hyperorthodox, puritanical, purist *or* puristic, straitlaced; staunch; hidebound, creedbound; **bigoted** 527.10; **dogmatic** 513.22; **fundamentalist,** precisianist *or* precisianistic, literalist *or* literalistic; Sabbatarian.

## 1025. UNORTHODOXY

.1 NOUNS **unorthodoxy,** heterodoxy; unorthodoxness, **unsoundness,** un-Scripturality; **unauthoritativeness,** unauthenticity, uncanonicalness, uncanonicity; **nonconformity** 83.

.2 **heresy,** false doctrine, **misbelief; fallacy, error** 518; antinomianism, Arianism, Donatism, Ebionitism, emanatism, Erastianism, Gnosticism, hylotheism, Jansenism, Jovinianism, Manichaeism *or* Manichaeanism, pantheism, Sabellianism, Montanism, Monophysitism *or* Monophysism, Pelagianism; Albigensianism, Waldensianism, Catharism; Wyclifism, Lollardy.

.3 **infidelity,** infidelism; unchristianity; gentilism; **atheism, unbelief** 1031.5.

.4 **paganism, heathenism;** paganry, heathenry; pagandom, heathendom; pagano-Christianism; allotheism; animism, animatism; idolatry 1033.

.5 **heretic, misbeliever;** heresiarch; **nonconformist** 83.3; antinomian, Arian, Donatist, Ebionite, emanationist, Erastian, Gnostic, hylotheist, Jansenist, Jovinian, Manichaean, pantheist, Sabellian, Montanist, Monophysite, Pelagian; Albigensian, Waldensian, Cathar; Wyclifite, Lollard.

.6 **gentile;** non-Christian; **non-Jew,** goy, goyim [pl], *shegets* [Yid masc], *shiksa* [Yid fem]; non-Muslim, non-Moslem, non-Muhammadan, non-Mohammedan; *giaour* [Turk], kaffir; zendik, zendician, zendikite; non-Mormon; infidel; unbeliever 1031.11.

.7 **pagan, heathen;** allotheist; animist; idolater 1033.4.

.8 VERBS **misbelieve, err,** stray, deviate, wander, go astray, go wrong, fall into error; be wrong, be mistaken, be in error; serve Mammon.

.9 ADJS **unorthodox,** nonorthodox, **heterodox, heretical; unsound; unscriptural,** uncanonical, apocryphal; **unauthoritative,** unauthentic, unaccepted, unreceived, unapproved; **fallacious,** erroneous 518.1; antinomian, Arian, Donatist, Ebionitic, emanationist, Erastian, Gnostic, hylotheist *or* hylotheistic, Jansenist *or* Jansenistic, Jovinianist *or* Jovinianistic, Manichaean, pantheist *or* pantheistic, Sabellian, Montanist *or* Montanistic, Monophysite *or* Monophysitic, Pelagian; Albigensian, Waldensian, Catharist; Wyclifite, Lollard.

.10 **infidel,** infidelic, misbelieving; **atheistic,** unbelieving 1031.19; **unchristian,** non-Christian; gentile, non-Jewish, goyish, uncircumcised; non-Muslim, non-Muhammadan, non-Mohammedan, non-Moslem, non-Islamic; non-Mormon.

.11 **pagan, paganish,** paganistic; **heathen, heathenish;** pagano-Christian; allotheistic; animist, animistic; idolatrous 1033.7.

## 1026. SANCTITY

*(sacred quality)*

.1 NOUNS **sanctity,** sanctitude; **sacredness, holiness,** hallowedness, numinousness; sacrosanctness, sacrosanctity; heavenliness, divineness; venerableness, **venerability, blessedness;** awesomeness, awfulness; inviolableness, **inviolability;** ineffability, unutterability, unspeakability, inexpressibility, inenarrability; godliness 1028.2; odor of sanctity.

.2 **the sacred,** the holy, the holy of holies, the numinous, the ineffable, the unutterable, the unspeakable, the inexpressible, the inenarrable.

.3 **sanctification, hallowing; purification;** beatification, beatitude, blessing; **glorification,** exaltation; **consecration,** dedication, devotion, setting apart; sainting, canonization, enshrinement; **sainthood, blessedness; grace,** state of grace; justification, justification by faith, justification by works.

.4 **redemption,** redeemedness, **salvation,** conversion, regeneration, new life, reformation, adoption; rebirth, new birth, second birth; circumcision, spiritual purification *or* cleansing.

.5 VERBS **sanctify, hallow; purify,** cleanse, wash one's sins away; **bless,** beatify; **glorify,** exalt; **consecrate,** dedicate, devote, set apart; saint, canonize, enshrine.

.6 **redeem,** regenerate, reform, convert, save, give salvation.

.7 ADJS **sacred,** sacr(o)–, **holy,** hier(o)–, hagi(o)–, numinous, **sacrosanct, religious, spiritual,** heavenly, divine; **venerable,** awesome, awful; inviolable, **inviolate,** untouchable; **ineffable,** unutterable, unspeakable, inexpressible, inenarrable.

.8 **sanctified, hallowed; blessed,** beatified; consecrated, devoted, dedicated, set apart; **saintly,** sainted, canonized.

.9 **redeemed, saved,** converted, regenerated, regenerate, justified, reborn, born again, renewed; circumcised, spiritually purified *or* cleansed.

## 1027. UNSANCTITY

.1 NOUNS **unsanctity,** unsanctitude; **unsacredness, unholiness,** unhallowedness, unblessedness; **profanity,** profaneness; unregenerateness, reprobation.

.2 **the profane,** the unholy; the temporal, the secular, the worldly, the fleshly, the mundane.

.3 ADJS **unsacred,** nonsacred, **unholy,** unhallowed, unsanctified, unblessed; **profane,** secular, temporal, worldly, fleshly, mundane; unregenerate, reprobate.

## 1028. PIETY

.1 NOUNS **piety, piousness,** pietism; **religion, faith; religiousness,** religionism, religious-mindedness; theism; **devoutness,** devotion, devotedness, worship, worshipfulness, prayerfulness, cultism; faithfulness, dutifulness, observance, churchgoing, conformity 82; **reverence,** veneration; love of God, adoration.

.2 **godliness,** godlikeness; fear of God; **sanctity,** sanctitude; odor of sanctity, beauty of holiness; **righteousness, holiness,** goodness; **spirituality,** spiritual-mindedness, holy-mindedness, heavenly-mindedness, godly-mindedness; **purity,** pureness, pureheartedness, pureness of heart; **saintliness,** saintlikeness; saintship, sainthood; **Christianity, Christliness,** Christlikeness; angelicalness, seraphicalness; heavenliness; **unworldliness,** unearthliness, otherworldliness.

.3 **zeal,** zealousness, zealotry, zealotism; **revival,** revivalism; pentecostalism, charismatic movement, charismatic renewal, baptism in the spirit; charismatic gift, gift of tongues, glossolalia; **overreligiousness,** overpiousness, overrighteousness, **overzealousness,** overdevoutness; bibliolatry; **fanaticism** 473.11; sanctimony 1029.

.4 **believer,** truster, accepter, receiver, –arian; God-fearing man, pietist, religionist, saint, theist; **devotee,** devotionalist, votary, **zealot; Christian,** good Christian; **churchgoer,** churchman, churchite; pillar of the church; communicant, daily communicant; **convert,** proselyte, neophyte, catechumen; disciple, follower; **fanatic** 473.17.

.5 **the believing, the faithful, the righteous, the good;** the elect, the chosen, the saved; the children of God, the children of light; Christendom.

.6 VERBS **be pious, be religious; have faith,** trust in God, love God, fear God, **believe** 501.10; keep the faith, fight the good fight, let one's light shine, praise and glorify God, walk humbly with one's God.

.7 **be converted, get religion** [informal], receive or accept Christ, stand up for Jesus, be washed in the blood of the Lamb.

.8 ADJS **pious,** pietistic; **religious,** religious-minded; theistic; **devout,** devoted, worshipful, prayerful, cultish, cultist, cultistic; **reverent,** reverential, venerative, venerational, adoring, solemn; faithful, dutiful; believing 501.21; Christian, Christianly, Christianlike.

.9 **godly,** godlike; God-fearing; **righteous, holy,** good; **spiritual,** spiritual-minded, holy-minded, godly-minded, heavenly-minded; **pure,** purehearted, pure in heart; **saintly,** saintlike; Christly, **Christlike; angelic(al),** seraphic(al); heavenly; **unworldly,** unearthly, otherworldly, not of the earth, not of this world.

.10 **regenerate,** regenerated, **converted, redeemed, saved,** reborn; sanctified 1026.8.

.11 **zealous,** zealotic; **overreligious,** ultrareligious, overpious, overrighteous, **overzealous,** overdevout; **fanatical** 473.32; sanctimonious 1029.5.

## 1029. SANCTIMONY

.1 NOUNS **sanctimony, sanctimoniousness; pietism,** piety, piousness, pietisticalness, false piety; religionism, religiosity; **self-righteousness;** goodness or goody-goodiness [both informal]; pharisaism, pharisaicalness; Tartuffery, Tartuffism; **falseness, insincerity, hypocrisy** 616.6; affectation 903; **cant,** mummery, snivel, snuffle; unction, unctuousness, oiliness, mealymouthedness.

.2 **lip service, mouth honor,** lip homage, lip worship, lip devotion, lip praise, lip reverence; formalism, solemn mockery; BOMFOG, brotherhood of man and fatherhood of God.

.3 **pietist,** religionist, **hypocrite,** religious hypocrite, canting hypocrite, pious fraud, religious or spiritual humbug, whited sepulcher, **pharisee,** Holy Willie [Robert Burns], "a saint abroad and a devil at home" [Bunyan]; **canter,** ranter, snuffler,

sniveler; dissembler, dissimulator; affecter, poser 903.7,8; **lip server,** lip worshiper, formalist; Pharisee, scribes and Pharisees; Tartuffe, Pecksniff, Mawworm, Joseph Surface.

.4 VERBS be sanctimonious, be hypocritical 616.23; cant, snuffle, snivel; give mouth honor, render lip service.

.5 ADJS **sanctimonious,** sanctified, **pious, pietistic(al),** self-righteous, pharisaic(al), holier-than-thou; goody or goody-goody [both informal]; **false, insincere, hypocritical** 616.25–34; affected 903.15; Tartuffish, Tartuffian; canting, sniveling, unctuous, mealymouthed.

## 1030. IMPIETY

.1 NOUNS **impiety, impiousness; irreverence,** undutifulness; desertion, renegadism, apostasy, recreancy; backsliding, recidivism, lapse, fall or lapse from grace; **atheism, irreligion** 1031.1.

.2 **sacrilege, blasphemy,** impiety; **profanity,** profaneness; sacrilegiousness, blasphemousness; **desecration, profanation.**

.3 sacrilegist, **blasphemer,** Sabbath-breaker; deserter, renegade, apostate, recreant; backslider, recidivist; **atheist,** unbeliever 1031.11.

.4 VERBS **desecrate, profane,** dishonor, unhallow, commit sacrilege.

.5 **blaspheme;** vilify, abuse 972.7; curse, swear 972.6; take in vain.

.6 ADJS **impious, irreverent,** undutiful; **profane,** profanatory; **sacrilegious, blasphemous;** renegade, apostate, recreant, backsliding, recidivist or recidivistic, lapsed, fallen, lapsed or fallen from grace; atheistic, **irreligious** 1031.17.

## 1031. NONRELIGIOUSNESS

.1 NOUNS **nonreligiousness, unreligiousness, undevoutness;** indevoutness, indevotion undutifulness, nonobservance; adiapho rism, indifferentism, Laodiceanism, luke warm piety; indifference 636.

.2 **worldliness,** earthliness, earthiness, mun daneness; **unspirituality,** carnality, worldly-mindedness, earthly-mindedness carnal-mindedness; materialism, Philistir ism.

.3 **ungodliness,** godlessness, **unrighteousnes** irreligion, unholiness, unsaintliness, unar gelicalness; unchristianliness, un-Christ ness; impiety 1030; **wickedness, sinfulne** 981.4.

.4 **unregeneracy,** unredeemedness, **repr bacy,** gracelessness, shriftlessness.

.5 **unbelief, disbelief** 503.1; infidelity, infidelism, faithlessness; **atheism;** nullifidianism, minimifidianism; secularism.

.6 **agnosticism; skepticism, doubt, incredulity,** Pyrrhonism, Humism; scoffing 967.1.

.7 **freethinking,** free thought, **latitudinarianism; humanism,** secular humanism.

.8 **antireligion;** antichristianism, antichristianity; antiscripturism.

.9 **iconoclasm,** iconoclasticism, image breaking.

.10 **irreligionist; worldling,** earthling; **materialist** 376.6; iconoclast, idoloclast; antichristian, antichrist.

.11 **unbeliever, disbeliever, nonbeliever; atheist, infidel, pagan, heathen;** nullifidian, minimifidian; secularist; **gentile** 1025.6.

.12 **agnostic; skeptic, doubter,** dubitante, **doubting Thomas,** scoffer, Pyrrhonist, Humist.

.13 **freethinker, latitudinarian,** *esprit fort* [Fr]; humanist, secular humanist.

.14 VERBS **disbelieve, doubt** 503.5,6; **scoff** 967.9.

.15 ADJS **nonreligious, unreligious; undevout,** indevout, indevotional, undutiful, nonobservant; adiamorphic, indifferentist or indifferentistic, Laodicean, lukewarm, indifferent 636.6.

.16 **worldly, earthly,** earthy, terrestrial, **mundane,** temporal; **unspiritual, profane,** carnal, secular; worldly minded, earthly minded, carnal-minded; **materialistic,** material, Philistine.

.17 **ungodly, godless, irreligious, unrighteous, unholy,** unsaintly, unangelic(al); **unchristian,** un-Christly; impious 1030.6; **wicked, sinful** 981.16.

.18 **unregenerate,** unredeemed, **unconverted,** godless, reprobate, graceless, shriftless, **lost, damned.**

.19 **unbelieving, disbelieving, faithless; infidel,** infidelic; **pagan, heathen; atheistic,** atheist; nullifidian, minimifidian; unchristian.

.20 **agnostic; skeptic(al), doubtful, dubious, incredulous,** Humean, Pyrrhonic.

.21 **freethinking, latitudinarian.**

.22 **antireligious;** antichristian; antiscriptural; iconoclastic.

## 1032. WORSHIP

.1 NOUNS **worship, worshiping, adoration, devotion, homage, veneration, reverence,** "transcendent wonder" [Carlyle]; **cult,** cultus, cultism; latria, dulia, hyperdulia; falling down and worshiping, prostration; co-worship; idolatry 1033.

.2 **glorification,** glory, **praise,** laudation, laud, exaltation, magnification.

.3 **paean,** laud; hosanna, hallelujah, alleluia; **hymn,** hymn of praise, doxology, psalm, **anthem,** motet, canticle, chorale; **chant,** versicle; mantra, Vedic hymn or chant; Introit, Miserere; Gloria, Gloria in Excelsis, Gloria Patri; Te Deum, Agnus Dei, Benedicite, Magnificat, Nunc Dimittis; response, responsory, report, answer; Trisagion; antiphon, antiphony; offertory, offertory sentence or hymn; hymnody, hymnology, hymnography, psalmody.

.4 **prayer, supplication, invocation,** imploration, impetration, entreaty, beseechment, appeal, petition, suit, aid prayer, bid or bidding prayer, orison, obsecration, obtestation, rogation, **devotions;** silent prayer, meditation, contemplation, communion; intercession; **grace, thanks, thanksgiving;** litany; breviary, canonical prayers; collect, collect of the Mass, collect of the Communion; Angelus; Paternoster, the Lord's Prayer; Hail Mary, Ave, Ave Maria; Kyrie Eleison; chaplet; rosary, beads, beadroll; prayer wheel or machine.

.5 **benediction, blessing,** benison, invocation, benedicite; sign of the cross; laying on of hands.

.6 **propitiation,** appeasement 804.1; atonement 1012.

.7 **oblation, offering, sacrifice, immolation,** incense; libation, drink offering; burnt offering, holocaust; thank offering, votive or ex voto offering; heave offering, peace offering, sacramental offering, sin or piacular offering, whole offering; human sacrifice, mactation, infanticide, hecatomb; self-sacrifice, self-immolation; sutteeism; scapegoat, suttee; offertory, collection.

.8 **divine service, service,** public worship, liturgy 1040.3, office, duty, exercises, **devotions;** meeting; church service, church; **revival,** revival meeting, camp meeting, tent meeting, praise meeting; watch meeting, watch-night service, watch night; **prayer meeting,** prayers, prayer; morning devotions or services or prayers, matins, lauds; prime, prime song; tierce, undersong; sext; none, nones; novena; evening devotions or services or prayers, vesper, vespers, vigils, evensong; compline, night song or prayer; bedtime prayer; Mass 1040.9.

.9 **worshiper,** adorer, venerator, votary, communicant, daily communicant, celebrant, churchgoer, chapelgoer; prayer, suppliant, supplicant, supplicator, petitioner; beadsman; revivalist, evangelist; congregation; **idolater** 1033.4.

**.10** VERBS **worship, adore, reverence, venerate, revere, honor,** do or pay homage to, pay divine honors to, do service, lift up the heart, bow down and worship, humble oneself before; **idolize** 1033.5,6.

**.11 glorify, praise, laud, exalt, extol,** magnify, bless, celebrate; praise God, praise or glorify the Lord, bless the Lord, praise God from whom all blessings flow; praise Father, Son, and Holy Ghost; sing praises, sing the praises of, sound or resound the praises of; doxologize, hymn.

**.12 pray, supplicate,** invoke, petition, make supplication; **implore, beseech** 774.11; offer a prayer, send up a prayer, commune with God; **say one's prayers;** tell one's beads, recite the rosary; **say grace, give** or **return thanks;** pray over.

**.13 bless, give one's blessing,** give benediction, confer a blessing upon, invoke benefits upon; cross, make the sign of the cross over or upon; lay hands on.

**.14 propitiate,** make propitiation; appease 804.7; **offer sacrifice,** sacrifice, make sacrifice to, immolate before, offer up an oblation.

**.15** ADJS **worshipful,** worshiping; **adoring,** adorant; **devout,** devotional; **reverent,** reverential; **venerative,** venerational; solemn; at the feet of; **prayerful, supplicatory,** supplicant, suppliant, precatory, precative, imploring, on one's knees, on bended knee; prone or prostrate before, in the dust.

**.16** INTERJS **hallelujah!,** alleluia!, **hosanna!, praise God!,** praise the Lord!, praise ye the Lord!, "praise ye Him . . . all His hosts!" [Bible], Heaven be praised!, glory to God!, glory be to God!, glory be to God in the highest!, bless the Lord!, "bless the Lord, O my soul: and all that is within me, bless His holy name!", "hallowed be Thy Name!" [both Bible]; thanks be to God!, Deo gratias! [L]; (Hinduism) om!, om mani padme hum!

**.17** O Lord!, our Father which art in heaven!; God grant!, pray God that!; God bless!, God save!, God forbid!

## 1033. IDOLATRY

**.1** NOUNS **idolatry, idolatrousness, idolism, idolodulia, idol worship;** heathenism, paganism; image worship, iconolatry, iconoduly; **fetishism; demonism, demonolatry,** demon or devil worship; animal worship, snake worship, fire worship, pyrolatry, Parsiism, Zoroastrianism; sun worship, star worship, Sabaism; tree worship, plant worship, Druidism, nature worship; phallic worship, phallicism; hero worship; idolomancy; –latry.

**.2 idolization** 1033.8, fetishization; **deification,** apotheosis.

**.3 idol,** idolo– or eidolo–; **fetish,** joss; **graven image, golden calf;** devil-god, "the god of my idolatry" [Shakespeare]; Baal, Juggernaut.

**.4 idolater,** idolatress, idolizer, idolatrizer, idolist, idol worshiper; fetishist; demon or devil worshiper, demonolater, chthonian; animal worshiper, zoolater, theriolater, therolater, snake worshiper, ophiolater; fire worshiper, pyrolater, Parsi, Zoroastrian; sun worshiper, heliolater; star worshiper, Sabaist; tree worshiper, arborolater, dendrolater, plant worshiper, Druid, nature worshiper; phallic worshiper; anthropolater, archaeolater, etc.; –later.

**.5** VERBS **idolatrize,** idolize, idolify, idol; fetishize, fetish; **make an idol of, deify,** apotheosize.

**.6 worship idols,** worship the golden calf, adorer le veau d'or [Fr].

**.7** ADJS **idolatrous,** idolatric or idolatrical, **idol worshiping;** idolistic, fetishistic; heathen, pagan; demonolatrous, chthonian; heliolatrous; bibliolatrous; zoolatrous.

**.8 idolatries, idolization**

| | |
|---|---|
| anthropolatry | logolatry |
| arborolatry | lordolatry |
| archaeolatry | mammonolatry |
| astrolatry | martyrolatry |
| autolatry | mobolatry |
| Bardolatry | monolatry |
| bibliolatry | neolatry |
| classicolatry | onolatry |
| cosmolatry | ophiolatry |
| curatolatry | Oxonolatry |
| demonolatry | palaeolatry |
| dendrolatry | papolatry |
| diabolatry | parsonolatry |
| ecclesiolatry | parthenolatry |
| episcopolatry | patriolatry |
| geniolatry | physiolatry |
| grammatolatry | phytolatry |
| gyneolatry | plutolatry |
| hagiolatry | pseudolatry |
| heliolatry | pulpitolatry |
| hierolatry | pyrolatry |
| hydrolatry | Russolatry |
| hygeiolatry | selenolatry |
| ichthyolatry | sermonolatry |
| iconolatry | Shakespearolatry |
| idiolatry | sociolatry |
| idolatry | statolatry |
| Japanolatry | staurolatry |
| juvenolatry | symbolatry |
| litholatry | taurolatry |

Teutolatry                  topolatry
thaumatolatry               uranolatry
theriolatry                 urbanolatry
therolatry                  verbolatry
titanolatry                 zoolatry

## 1034. OCCULTISM

.1 NOUNS occultism, mysticism; esoterics, esotericism, esoterism, esotery; cabalism, cabala; yoga, yogism, yogeeism; theosophy, anthroposophy; symbolics, symbolism; anagogics; anagoge; mystery; mystification, hocus-pocus, mumbo jumbo.

.2 supernaturalism, supranaturalism, preternaturalism, transcendentalism; the supernatural, the supersensible.

.3 metaphysics, hyperphysics, transphysical science, the first philosophy or theology.

.4 psychics, psychism, psychicism; parapsychology, psychical research; metapsychics, metapsychism; psychosophy; panpsychism; psychic monism.

.5 spiritualism, spiritism; mediumism; necromancy; séance, sitting; spirit 1017.1.

.6 psychic(al) phenomena, spirit manifestation; materialization; spirit rapping, table tipping or turning; poltergeistism, poltergeist; telekinesis, psychokinesis, power of mind over matter, telesthesia, teleportation; levitation; trance speaking; psychorrhagy; automatism, psychography, automatic or trance or spirit writing; Ouija board, Ouija; planchette.

.7 ectoplasm, exteriorized protoplasm; aura, emanation, effluvium; ectoplasy.

.8 extrasensory perception, ESP; clairvoyance, lucidity, second sight, insight, sixth sense; intuition 481; foresight 542; premonition 544.1; clairsentience, clairaudience, crystal vision, psychometry, metapsychosis.

.9 telepathy, mental telepathy, mind reading, thought transference, telepathic transmission; telepathic dream, telepathic hallucination.

.10 divination 543.2,15; sorcery 1035.

.11 occultist, esoteric, mystic, mystagogue, cabalist, supernaturalist, transcendentalist; adept, mahatma; yogi, yogin, yogist; theosophist, anthroposophist.

.12 psychist, psychicist; parapsychologist; metapsychist; panpsychist; metaphysician, metaphysicist.

.13 psychic; spiritualist, spiritist, medium, ecstatic, spirit rapper, automatist, psychographist; necromancer.

.14 clairvoyant; clairaudient; psychometer, psychometrist.

.15 telepathist, mental telepathist, mind reader, thought reader.

.16 diviner 543.4; sorcerer 1035.5–9.

.17 astral body, astral, linga sharira, design body, subtle body, vital body, etheric body, bliss body, Buddhic body, spiritual body, soul body; kamarupa, desire or kamic body; causal body; mental or mind body.

.18 (seven principles of man, theosophy) spirit, atman; mind, manas; soul, buddhi; life principle, vital force, prana; astral body, linga sharira; physical or dense or gross body, sthula sharira; principle of desire, kama.

.19 spiritualization, etherealization, idealization; dematerialization, immaterialization, unsubstantialization; disembodiment, disincarnation.

.20 VERBS spiritualize, spiritize; etherealize; idealize; dematerialize, immaterialize, unsubstantialize; disembody, disincarnate.

.21 practice spiritualism, hold a séance or sitting; call up spirits 1035.11.

.22 ADJS occult, esoteric(al), mystic(al), mysterious, mystico–; anagogic(al); metaphysic(al); cabalic, cabalistic; supernatural 85.15; theosophical, theosophist.

.23 psychic(al), spiritual; spiritualistic, spiritistic; mediumistic; clairvoyant, secondsighted, clairaudient, clairsentient, telepathic; extrasensory, psychosensory; supersensible, supersensual, pretersensual; telekinetic, psychokinetic; automatist.

## 1035. SORCERY

.1 NOUNS sorcery, necromancy, magic, sortilege, wizardry, theurgy, gramarye [archaic], rune, glamour; witchcraft, spellcraft, spellbinding, spellcasting; witchery, witchwork, bewitchery, enchantment; voodooism, voodoo, hoodoo, wanga, juju, jujuism, obeah, obeahism; shamanism; magism, magianism; fetishism; vampirism; thaumaturgy, thaumaturgia, thaumaturgics, thaumaturgism; alchemy; white or natural magic; sympathetic magic; divination 543.2,15; spell, charm 1036.

.2 black magic, the black art; diabolism, demonism, Satanism 1016.15.

.3 (practices) magic circle; ghost dance; Sabbat, witches' meeting or Sabbath; ordeal, ordeal by battle or fire or water or lots.

.4 conjuration, conjurement, evocation, invocation; exorcism, exorcisation; exsufflation; incantation 1036.4.

.5 sorcerer, necromancer, wizard, wonderworker, warlock, theurgist; thaumaturge, thaumaturgist, miracle-worker; **conjurer; diviner** 543.4; dowser, water witch; diabolist 1016.16; Faust, Comus.

.6 **magician**, mage, magus, magian; Merlin; illusionist 619.2.

.7 **witchman**, witch master; **shaman**, shamanist; **voodoo**, voodooist, wangateur, **witch doctor**, obeah doctor, **medicine man**, mundunugu, isangoma; witchhunter, witch-finder; **exorcist**, exorciser; unspeller.

.8 **sorceress**, shamaness; **witch**, witchwoman [dial], witchwife [Scot], **hex, hag,** lamia; witch of Endor; coven, witches' coven, Weird Sisters [Shakespeare].

.9 **bewitcher, enchanter, charmer, spellbinder; enchantress, siren,** vampire; Circe; Medusa, Medea, Gorgon, Stheno, Euryale.

.10 VERBS sorcerize, shamanize; wave a wand, rub the ring or lamp; ride a broomstick.

.11 **conjure, conjure up,** evoke, invoke, raise, summon, call up; **call up spirits,** conjure or conjure up spirits, summon spirits, raise ghosts, evoke from the dead, "call spirits from the vasty deep" [Shakespeare].

.12 **exorcise,** lay; lay ghosts, **cast out devils;** unspell.

.13 cast a spell, bewitch 1036.7–10.

.14 ADJS sorcerous, necromantic, **magic(al),** magian, numinous, thaumaturgic(al), cantrip or weird [both Scot], wizardlike, wizardly; shaman, shamanic, shamanist or shamanistic; witchlike, witchy, witch; voodoo, hoodoo [informal], voodooistic; incantatory, incantational; talismanic.

## 1036. SPELL, CHARM

.1 NOUNS **spell,** magic spell, **charm,** glamour, weird or cantrip [both Scot], wanga; hand of glory; evil eye, *malocchio* [Ital], whammy [slang]; **hex, jinx, curse;** exorcism.

.2 **bewitchment, witchery, bewitchery; enchantment, entrancement,** fascination, captivation; illusion, maya; bedevilment; possession, obsession.

.3 **trance,** ecstasy, ecstasis, **rapture;** yoga trance, dharana, dhyana, samadhi; hypnosis 712.7.

.4 **incantation, conjuration,** magic words or formula; hocus-pocus, abracadabra, mumbo jumbo; open sesame.

.5 **charm, amulet, talisman, fetish,** periapt, phylactery; voodoo, hoodoo, juju, obeah, mumbo jumbo; **good-luck charm,** goodluck piece, **lucky piece,** rabbit's-foot,

lucky bean, whammy [slang]; mascot; madstone; love charm, philter; scarab, scarabaeus, scarabee; veronica, sudarium; swastika, fylfot, gammadion.

.6 **wish-bringer,** wish-giver; **wand, magic wand,** Aaron's rod; Aladdin's lamp, magic ring, magic belt, magic spectacles, magic carpet, seven-league boots; wishing well, wishing stone; wishing cap, Fortunatus's cap; cap of darkness, Tarnkappe, Tarnhelm; fern seed; wishbone, wishing bone, merrythought [Brit].

.7 VERBS **cast a spell,** spell, **spellbind; entrance,** trance, put in a trance; **hypnotize, mesmerize.**

.8 **charm,** becharm, enchant, fascinate, captivate, glamour.

.9 **bewitch,** witch, hex, jinx; voodoo, hoodoo; **possess, obsess;** bedevil, diabolize, demonize; hagride; overlook, look on with the evil eye, cast the evil eye.

.10 **put a curse on,** put a hex on, put a juju on, put obeah on, give the evil eye, give the *malocchio,* give a whammy [slang].

.11 ADJS **bewitching, witching;** illusory, illusive, illusionary; **charming, enchanting, entrancing, spellbinding, fascinating,** glamorous, Circean.

.12 **enchanted, charmed,** becharmed, charmstruck, charm-bound; **spellbound,** spellstruck, spell-caught; **fascinated,** captivated; **hypnotized, mesmerized;** under a spell, in a trance.

.13 **bewitched,** witched, witch-charmed, witch-held, witch-struck; hag-ridden; **possessed, obsessed.**

## 1037. THE MINISTRY

.1 NOUNS **the ministry,** pastorate, pastorage, pastoral care, cure or care of souls, **the church,** the cloth, the pulpit, the desk; **priesthood,** priestship; apostleship; call, vocation, sacred calling; holy orders; rabbinate.

.2 ecclesiasticalism, ecclesiology, priestcraft.

.3 **clericalism,** sacerdotalism; priesthood priestism; episcopalianism; ultramontanism.

.4 **monasticism,** monachism, monkery, **monkhood,** friarhood; celibacy 934.

.5 (ecclesiastical offices and dignities) cardinalate, cardinalship; primacy, primateship; prelacy, prelature, prelateship, prelatehood; archbishopric, archiepiscopate archiepiscopacy; bishopric, bishopdom episcopate, episcopacy; deanery, deanship; prebend, prebendaryship, prebend stall; canonry, canonicate; curacy; recto ate, rectorship; vicariate, vicarship; pastorate, pastorship; deaconry, deaconship; archdeaconry; chaplaincy, chaplainship; abbacy; presbytery, presbyterate.

.6 **papacy**, papality, **pontificate**, popedom, the Vatican, Apostolic See, See of Rome.

.7 hierarchy, hierocracy; theocracy.

.8 **diocese, see,** archdiocese, bishopric, archbishopric; province; synod, conference; **parish.**

.9 **benefice,** living, **incumbency,** glebe, advowson; curacy, cure, charge, cure or care of souls; prelacy, rectory, vicarage.

.10 **holy orders, orders** 1038.4, major orders, apostolic orders, minor orders; calling, election, nomination, appointment, preferment, induction, institution, installation, investiture; conferment, presentation; **ordination,** ordainment, consecration, canonization, reading in [Brit].

.11 VERBS **be ordained, take holy orders,** take orders, take vows, read oneself in [Brit]; **take the veil,** wear the cloth.

.12 **ordain,** frock, **canonize, consecrate;** saint.

.13 ADJS **ecclesiastic(al), churchly; ministerial, clerical,** sacerdotal, **pastoral; priestly,** priestish; prelatic(al), prelatial; episcopal, episcopalian; archiepiscopal; canonical; capitular, capitulary; abbatical, abbatial; ultramontane; **evangelistic;** rabbinic(al); priest-ridden.

.14 **monastic,** monachal, **monasterial, monkish;** conventual.

.15 **papal, pontifical,** apostolic(al); **popish** or papist or papistic(al) [all derog], papish [dial].

.16 **hierarchic(al),** hierarchal; theocratic, theocratist.

.17 **ordained;** in orders, in holy orders, of the cloth.

## 1038. CLERGY

.1 NOUNS **clergy,** clerico–, **ministry,** the cloth; clerical order, clericals; **priesthood;** priestery; presbytery; prelacy; Sacred College; rabbinate.

.2 **clergyman,** man of the cloth, **divine, ecclesiastic, churchman, cleric,** clerical; clerk, clerk in holy orders, tonsured cleric; **minister, minister of the Gospel, parson, pastor,** abbé, curé [both Fr], **rector,** curate, man of God, servant of God, shepherd, sky pilot or Holy Joe [both slang], reverend [informal]; supply minister or preacher, supply clergy; **chaplain;** military chaplain, padre [informal]; the Reverend, the Very or Right Reverend; Doctor of Divinity, DD.

.3 **preacher,** sermoner, sermonizer, sermonist; pulpiter, pulpiteer; predicant, predikant; preaching friar; circuit rider.

.4 holy orders, major orders, priest or presbyter, deacon or diaconus, subdeacon or subdiaconus; minor orders, acolyte or acolytus, exorcist or exorcista, reader or lector, doorkeeper or ostiarius.

.5 **priest,** gallach [Heb], **father,** father in Christ, **padre,** cassock, presbyter; curé, parish priest; confessor, father confessor, spiritual father or director or leader; penitentiary.

.6 **clergywoman,** priestess, ministress, pastoress, parsoness, preacheress.

.7 **evangelist,** revivalist; **missionary,** missioner; missionary apostolic, missionary rector, colporteur.

.8 benefice-holder, beneficiary, **incumbent;** resident, residentiary.

.9 (church dignitaries) ecclesiarch, hierarch, **patriarch, high priest; pope,** pontiff, papa, Holy Father, servant of the servants of God; antipope; **cardinal,** cardinal bishop, cardinal priest, cardinal deacon, primate, exarch, metropolitan, abuna, archpriest, **archbishop, bishop,** prelate, diocesan, suffragan, coadjutor, bishop coadjutor, dean, subdean, archdeacon, prebendary, canon, rural dean, **rector, vicar, chaplain,** curate; penitentiary, Grand Penitentiary; devil's advocate, promoter of the faith.

.10 (minor and lay officers) clerk, parish clerk, Bible clerk; reader, Bible reader, lay reader, lecturer, lector, anagnost; capitular, capitulary; elder, elderman, teaching elder, lay elder, ruling elder; deacon, deaconess; churchwarden; sidesman; almoner; verger, vergeress; beadle, bedral [Scot], suisse [Fr], shames [Yid]; sacristan, sacrist; acolyte, thurifer, choir chaplain, precentor, succentor.

.11 (Mormon) deacon, teacher, priest, elder, Seventy, high priest, bishop, patriarch, apostle; Aaronic priesthood, Melchizedek priesthood.

.12 (Jewish) **rabbi,** rabbin; chief rabbi; baal kore [Yid]; cantor; priest, kohen [Heb], high priest; Levite; scribe.

.13 (Muslim) imam, qadi, sheikh, mullah, murshid, mufti, hajji, muezzin, dervish, abdal, fakir, santon.

.14 (Hindu) Brahman, pujari, purohit, pundit, guru, bashara, vairagi or bairagi, Ramwat, Ramanandi; sannyasi; yogi, yogin; bhikshu, bhikhari.

.15 (Buddhist) bonze, bhikku, poonghie, talapoin; lama; Grand Lama, Dalai Lama, Panchen Lama.

.16 (pagan) Druid, Druidess; flamen; hierophant, hierodule, hieros, daduchus, mystes, epopt.

.17 religious, *religieux* [Fr]; **monk,** monastic; brother, lay brother; cenobite, conventual; caloyer, hieromonach; **mendicant, friar;** pilgrim, palmer; stylite, pillarist, pillar saint; beadsman; prior, claustral *or* conventual prior, grand prior, general prior; abbot; lay abbot, abbacomes; hermit 924.5; ascetic 991.2; celibate 934.2.

.18 (religious orders) Franciscan, Gray Friar, Friar Minor, Minorite, Observant, Recollect *or* Recollet, Conventual, Capuchin; Dominican, Black Friar, Friar Preacher, preaching friar *or* brother; Carmelite, White Friar; Augustinian, Augustinian Hermit, Austin Friar, begging hermit; Benedictine, Black Monk; Jesuit, Loyolite; Crutched Friar, Crossed Friar; Templar, Hospitaler; Bernardine, Bonhomme, Carthusian, Cistercian, Cluniac, Gilbertine, Lorettine, Maturine, Premonstratensian, Trappist; Brigittine; Marist; Maryknoll; Oratorian; Redemptorist.

.19 nun, sister, *religieuse* [Fr], clergywoman, conventual; abbess, prioress; **mother superior,** lady superior, superioress, the reverend mother; canoness, regular *or* secular canoness; novice, postulant.

## 1039. LAITY

.1 NOUNS laity, laymen, nonclerics, nonordained persons, seculars; brethren, people; flock, fold, sheep; **congregation,** parishioners, churchgoers, assembly; *minyan* [Heb]; **parish,** society; class.

.2 layman, laic, secular, churchman, **parishioner,** church member; brother, sister, lay brother, lay sister; laywoman, churchwoman; catechumen; communicant.

.3 ADJS lay, laic *or* laical; **nonecclesiastical,** nonclerical, nonministerial, nonpastoral, nonordained; nonreligious; **secular,** secularist, secularistic; temporal, popular, civil; congregational.

## 1040. RELIGIOUS RITES

.1 NOUNS **ritualism,** rituality, **ceremonialism, formalism,** liturgism; symbolism, symbolics; **cult,** cultus, cultism; sacramentalism, sacramentarianism; sabbatism, Sabbatarianism; ritualization, **solemnization,** solemn observance; **celebration;** liturgics, liturgiology.

.2 ritualist, ceremonialist, liturgist, formal-

ist, formulist, formularist; sacramentalist, sacramentarian; sabbatist, Sabbatarian; High-Churchman, High-Churchist.

.3 **rite, ritual,** rituality, **liturgy,** holy rite; order of worship; **ceremony, ceremonial; observance,** ritual observance; **formality,** solemnity; **form,** formula, formulary, form of worship *or* service, mode of worship; prescribed form; service, function, duty, office, practice; **sacrament,** sacramental, mystery; ordinance; institution.

.4 (rites) celebration, high celebration; processional; litany, greater *or* lesser litany; invocation, invocation of saints; confirmation, imposition *or* laying on of hands; confession, auricular confession, the confessional, the confessionary; sign of the cross; pax, kiss of peace; love feast, agape; reciting the rosary, telling of beads; thurification, incense; aspersion, asperges; lustration; circumcision; bar mitzvah, bas mitzvah.

.5 **seven sacraments,** mysteries: baptism, confirmation, the Eucharist, penance, extreme unction, holy orders, matrimony.

.6 **unction,** sacred unction, sacramental anointment, chrism *or* chrisom, chrismation, chrismatory; **extreme unction, last rites,** viaticum; ointment; chrismal.

.7 **baptism,** baptizement; **christening; immersion,** total immersion; **sprinkling,** aspersion, aspergation; affusion, infusion; baptism for the dead; baptismal regeneration; baptismal gown *or* dress *or* robe, chrismal; baptistery, **font.**

.8 **Eucharist, Lord's Supper, Last Supper, Communion,** Holy Communion, **the Sacrament,** the Holy Sacrament; intinction; consubstantiation, impanation, subpanation, transubstantiation; real presence; elements, consecrated elements, bread and wine, body and blood of Christ; Host, wafer, loaf, bread, altar bread, consecrated bread; Sacrament Sunday.

.9 **Mass,** *Missa* [L], Eucharistic rites; **the Liturgy,** the Divine Liturgy; High Mass, *Missa solemnis* [L]; Low Mass, *Missa bassa* [L]; Rosary Mass, Rosary, Rosary of the Seven Dolors of Mary; Lady Mass, Dry Mass, *Missa sicca* [L]; Liturgy of the Presanctified, *Missa praesanctificatorum* [L]; *Missa publica, Missa privata, Missa cantata, Missa media, Missa adventitia, Missa manualis, Missa capitularis, Missa legata* [all L]; requiem, Requiem Mass, dirge, Memento of the Dead.

.10 (parts of the Mass) Prayers at Foot of the Altar, Introit, Kyrie, Kyrie Eleison, Gloria, Collect, Epistle, Gradual, Alleluia, Tract, Gospel, Credo, Offertory, Lavabo, Secreta, Preface, Sanctus, Tersanctus; Canon, Memento of the Living, Consecration, Elevation of the Host, Anamnesis, Memento of the Dead; Paternoster, Fraction, Agnus Dei, Pax, Communion, Post-Communion, Dismissal, Blessing, Last Gospel.

.11 (sacred and ritualistic articles) relics, sacred relics; monstrance, ostensorium; Host; eucharistial, pyx, ciborium; tabernacle; ark; crucifix, cross, rood, holy cross or rood; osculatory, pax; Agnus Dei; icon, icon(o)– or ikon(o)– or eikon(o)–; bambino [Ital], veronica, Pietà [Ital]; sacramental; holy water; holy-water sprinkler, aspergillum, asperges, asperger; thurible, censer, incensory; cruet, urceole; rosary, beads, beadroll; chaplet; prayer wheel or machine; candle, votive candle, vigil light, paschal candle; Sanctus bell, sacring bell; Sangraal, Holy Grail; menorah, shofar, sukkah, matzo [all Heb]; tallith [Heb], prayer shawl; tefillin [Heb], phylacteries; mezuzah [Heb]; mikvah [Heb].

.12 (ritualistic manual) missal, Mass book; ritual, rituale [L], manual, formulary, church book, service book; rubric, canon, ordinal, breviary; farse; lectionary; pontifical; Virginal; prayer book; siddur, machzor, haggadah [all Heb]; Book of Common Prayer, euchologion or euchology, litany; Torah, Torah scroll, Sefer Torah [Heb].

.13 psalter, psalmbook; Psalm Book, Book of Common Order; the Psalms, Book of Psalms, the Psalter, the Psaltery.

.14 holy day, hallowday [dial], holytide; feast, fast; Sabbath; Sunday, Lord's day; saint's day; church calendar, ecclesiastical calendar.

.15 (Christian holy days) Advent; Christmas; Candlemas, Candlemas Day; Epiphany, Three Kings' Day, Twelfth-tide, Twelfthnight, Twelfth-day; Septuagesima; Shrove Tuesday, Mardi Gras, Carnival, Pancake Day; Ash Wednesday; Lent, Lententide; Quadragesima, Quadragesima Sunday; Holy Week, Passion Week; Palm Sunday, Holy Thursday or Maundy Thursday, Good Friday; Easter, Eastertide, Easter Saturday, Easter Sunday, Easter Monday; Annunciation, Annunciation Day, Lady Day; Ascension Day or Holy Thursday; Pentecost, Whitsuntide, Whitsun, Whitweek; Whitsunday, Whitmonday, Whit-Tuesday, White Sunday,

etc.; Trinity Sunday, Corpus Christi; Lammas, Lammas Day, Lammastide; Michaelmas, Michaelmas Day, Michaelmastide; Hallowmas, Allhallowmas, Allhallowtide, Halloween; Allhallows, All Saints' Day; All Souls' Day; Martinmas; Ember days.

.16 (Jewish holy days) Passover, Pesach; Pentecost, Shabuoth, Feast of Weeks; Rosh Hashanah, New Year; High Holy Days; Yom Kippur, Day of Atonement; Sukkoth, Feast of Tabernacles; Simhath Torah, Rejoicing over the Law; Hanukkah, Feast of the Dedication; Purim; Fast of Av, Ninth of Av, Tishah b'Av.

.17 (Muslim holy days) Ramadan (month), Bairam, Muharram.

.18 VERBS celebrate, observe, keep, solemnize; celebrate Mass; communicate, administer Communion; attend Communion, receive the Sacrament, partake of the Lord's Supper; attend Mass.

.19 minister, officiate, do duty, perform a rite, perform service or divine service; administer a sacrament, administer the Eucharist, etc.; anoint, chrism; confirm, impose, lay hands on; make the sign of the cross.

.20 baptize, christen; dip, immerse; sprinkle, asperge.

.21 confess, make confession, receive absolution; shrive, hear confession; absolve, administer absolution; administer extreme unction.

.22 ADJS ritualistic, ritual; ceremonial, ceremonious; formal, formular, formulary; liturgic(al), liturgistic(al); High-Church; sacramental, sacramentarian; eucharistic(al), baptismal; paschal.

## 1041. ECCLESIASTICAL ATTIRE

.1 NOUNS canonicals, clericals [informal], robes, cloth; vestments, vesture; liturgical garments, ceremonial attire; pontificals, pontificalia, episcopal vestments.

.2 robe, frock, mantle, gown, cloak.

.3 staff, pastoral staff, crosier, cross, crossstaff, crook, paterissa.

.4 ADJS vestmental, vestmentary.

.5 clerical garments

| | |
|---|---|
| alb | calotte |
| almuce | cap |
| amice | capuche, capuchin |
| apron | cardinal's hat |
| bands | cassock |
| biretta | chasuble |
| bishop's ring | chimere |
| black gown | cincture |
| buskins | cingulum |

| | |
|---|---|
| clerical collar | rochet |
| cope | Roman collar |
| cotta | rosary |
| cowl | Salvation Army bon- |
| crucifix | net |
| cuculla | sandals |
| dalmatic | scapular |
| dog collar [slang] | scarf |
| episcopal ring | shovel hat |
| fanon | simar |
| Geneva bands | skullcap |
| Geneva cloak or gown | soutane |
| habit | stole |
| hood | subcingulum |
| lawn sleeves | succinctorium |
| maniple | surplice |
| mantelletta | tiara |
| mantellone | tippet |
| miter | triple crown |
| mozzetta | tunic |
| pallium | tunicle |
| pectoral cross | vakass, vagas |
| rabat, rabbi | zucchetto |
| reversed collar | |

## 1042. RELIGIOUS BUILDINGS

.1 NOUNS **church**, kirk [Scot], bethel, **meetinghouse**, church house, **house of God**, place of worship, house of worship or prayer; **mission**; basilica, major or patriarchal basilica, minor basilica; **cathedral**, cathedral church, *duomo* [Ital].

.2 **temple**, fane; **tabernacle**; **synagogue**, *shul* [Yid]; **mosque**, masjid; dewal, girja; pagoda; kiack; pantheon.

.3 **chapel**, chapel of ease, chapel royal, side chapel, school chapel, sacrament chapel, Lady chapel, oratory, oratorium; chantry; sacellum, sacrarium.

.4 **shrine**, holy place, dagoba, naos; sacrarium, delubrum; tope, stupa; reliquary, *reliquaire* [Fr].

.5 **sanctuary**, holy of holies, sanctum, sanctum sanctorum, adytum, sacrarium.

.6 **cloister**, monastery, house, abbey, friary; priory, priorate; lamasery; **convent, nunnery.**

.7 **parsonage**, pastorage, pastorate, manse, church house, clergy house; presbytery, **rectory**, vicarage, deanery; glebe.

.8 bishop's palace; **Vatican**; Lambeth, Lambeth Palace.

.9 (church interior) vestry, sacristy, sacrarium, diaconicon or diaconicum; baptistery; ambry, apse, blindstory, chancel, choir, cloisters, confessional, confessionary [archaic], crypt, Easter sepulcher, nave, porch, presbytery, rood loft, rood stair, rood tower or spire or steeple, transept, triforium.

.10 (church furnishings) piscina; stoup, holy-water stoup or basin; baptismal font; paten; reredos; jube, rood screen, chancel screen; altar cloth, cerecloth, chrismal; communion or sacrament cloth, corporal, fanon, oblation cloth; rood cloth; baldachin, *baldacchino* [Ital]; kneeling stool, *prie-dieu* [Fr]; prayer rug or carpet or mat.

.11 (vessels) cruet; chalice; ciborium, pyx; chrismal, chrismatory; monstrance, ostensorium; reliquary; font, holy-water font.

.12 **altar**, scrobis; bomos, eschara, hestia; **Lord's table**, holy table, **Communion table**, chancel table, table of the Lord, God's board; rood altar; altar desk, missal stand; credence, prothesis, table or altar of prothesis; predella; superaltar, retable, retablo, ancona, gradin; altarpiece, altar side, altar rail, altar carpet, altar stair; altar facing or front, frontal; altar slab, altar stone, mensal.

.13 **pulpit**, **rostrum**, ambo; **lectern**, desk, reading desk.

.14 (seats) **pew**; **stall**; mourners' bench, anxious bench or seat, penitent form; amen corner; sedilia.

.15 ADJS **churchly**, churchish, **ecclesiastical**; churchlike, templelike; cathedral-like, cathedralesque; tabernacular; synagogical, synagogal; pantheonic.

.16 **claustral**, **cloistered**; **monastic**, monachal, **monasterial**; **conventual**, conventical.

# INDEX

# HOW TO USE THIS INDEX

Numbers after index entries refer to categories and paragraphs in the front section of this book, not to page numbers. The part of the number before the decimal point refers to the category in which synonyms and related words to the word you are looking up are found. The part of the number after the decimal point refers to the paragraph or paragraphs within the category. Look at the first index entry on the next page:

**aardvark** 415.8, 58

This entry listing tells you that you can find words related to **aardvark** both in paragraph 8 and paragraph 58 of category 415.

Words, of course, frequently have more than one meaning. Each of those meanings may have synonyms or associated related words. Look at the entry for **abhor**:

**abhor** dislike 867.3

hate 930.5

This tells you that you will find synonyms for **abhor** in the sense meaning "dislike" in category 867, paragraph 3. It also tells you that you will find synonyms for **abhor**, meaning "hate," in category 930, paragraph 5.

In many cases, words are spelled the same as nouns, verbs, adjectives, etc. Look at the entry for **abandon** and notice that here you are directed to **abandon** when it is used as a noun and when it is used as a verb in a variety of meanings. Here, as in the examples above, you are referred to the category and paragraph number.

Not all words in the main part of the book are included in the index. In order to save space, many adverbs ending with **-ly** have been left out of the index; but you will find the common adverbs ending in **-ly** here, such as lightly or easily. If you can't find the adverb ending in **-ly** that you are looking for, look up the word in its adjective form and go to that category. Frequently, you can use the words in the adjective paragraphs you find and convert them into the adverb you are looking for by simply adding **-ly** to the adjective.

To make it easier to find phrases, we have indexed them according to their first word. You do not have to guess what the main word of the phrase is to find it in the index. Simply look up the first word in the phrase. For example, **hot air** will be found in the Hs, **fat cat** in the Fs, and **let go** in the Ls.

# INDEX

wrong 959.3
**abominate** 930.5
**abomination**
  defilement 682.4
  dislike 867.2
  evil 675.3
  hate 930.1
  hated thing 930.3
  iniquity 981.3
  wrong 959.2
**aboriginal**
  beginning 68.15
  causal 153.15
  native 189.5
  primitive 123.11
**aborigine** native 190.3
  prehistoric man 123.7
**abort** cease 144.6
  end 70.5
  fail 725.14
**abortion** failure 725.5
  monstrosity 85.6
**abortive**
  fruitless 669.12
  unsuccessful 725.17
**aboulia** see **abulia**
**abound**
  be numerous 101.5
  exuberate 661.5
**about**
  *adv.* in the vicinity
    233.12
  near 200.20
  some 28.6
  *prep.* in relation to
    9.13
  near 200.26
**about-face**
  *n.* change 139.1
  conversion 145.1
  regression 295.3
  reversion 146.1
  turnabout 628.1
  *v.* turn around 295.10
**about ship**
  change course 275.30
  sailing 275.76
**about to** 121.13
**above**
  *adj.* high 207.24
  superior 36.12
  *adv.* additionally
    40.11
  over 207.26
  preceding 64.6
  *prep.* in excess of
    663.26
  on 228.37
  unintelligible 549.26
**above all** 36.17
**above all that** 912.12
**above and beyond**
  663.26
**aboveboard**
  *adj.* honest 974.14
  *adv.* overtly 555.15
**above suspicion** 984.8
**above water**
  in safety 698.6
  unindebted 841.23
**ab ovo** anew 122.15
  essential 5.8

from the beginning
  68.18
**abracadabra** 1036.4
**abrade** injure 692.15
  pulverize 361.9
  rub 350.7
  subtract 42.9
  wear 692.23
**abrasion** friction 350.2
  impairment 692.8
  pulverization 361.4
  subtraction 42.1
**abrasive**
  *n.* abrasion 350.2
  smoother 260.4
  types of 260.14
  *adj.* rubbing 350.10
**abreast**
  *adv.* in parallel 218.7
  *prep.* beside 242.11
**abreast of** 475.18
**abridge** condense 607.5
  delete 42.12
  reduce 39.7
  shorten 203.6
  take from 822.21
**abridged** concise 592.6
  condensed 607.6
  shortened 203.9
**abridgment**
  compendium 607
  conciseness 592.3
  decrease 39.1
  deletion 42.5
  deprivation 822.6
  shortening 203.3
**abroad**
  *adj.* absent 187.11
  bewildered 514.23
  erroneous 518.16
  *adv.* astray 199.19
  extensively 179.10
  far and wide 199.16
  outdoors 224.10
  overseas 78.6
**abrogate** abolish 693.13
  repeal 779.2
**abrogation** denial 524.2
  repeal 779.1
**abrupt** blunt 259.3
  gruff 937.7
  precipitate 709.10
  steep 219.18
  sudden 113.5
**abruptly** gruffly 937.9
  precipitously 709.15
  short 203.13
  suddenly 113.9
**abscess**
  disease symptom
    686.8
  sore 686.35
**abscissa** 490.6
**abscond** flee 631.10
  leave 301.8
**absconded** 187.10
**absconder** 631.5
**absence**
  non-attendance 187.4
  nonexistence 2.1
  nonpresence 187
  want 662.4

**absent**
  abstracted 532.11
  not present 187.10
**absentee** 187.5
**absentminded**
  abstracted 532.11
  forgetful 538.9
**absentmindedness**
  abstractedness 532.2
  forgetfulness 538.1
  inattention 531.1
**absolute**
  accurate 516.15
  asserting 523.7
  authoritative 739.15
  certain 513.15
  convincing 501.26
  evidential 505.17
  governmental 741.17
  imperious 739.16
  mandatory 752.13
  omnipotent 157.13
  outright 34.12
  particular 80.12
  perfect 677.6
  positive 513.13
  real 1.15
  simple 45.7
  sole 89.9
  thorough 56.10
  unqualified 508.2
  unrestricted 762.26
**absolutely**
  *adv.* assertingly 523.9
  certainly 513.23
  exactly 516.20
  extremely 34.22
  perfectly 677.10
  really 1.16
  totally 56.15
  *interj.* yes 521.18
**absolute zero**
  cold 333.1
  temperature 328.3
**absolution**
  acquittal 1007.1
  pardon 947.2
**absolutism**
  authority 739.1
  dictatorship 741.9
  subjection 764.1
**absolve** acquit 1007.4
  administer rites
    1040.21
  debts 842.9
  exempt 762.14
  forgive 947.3
**absorb** consume 666.2
  digest 309.16
  engross 530.13
  involve 176.2
  learn 564.7
  occupy the mind
    478.20
  sorb 306.13
  stock market 833.26
  understand 548.7
**absorbed**
  absorbed in thought
    478.22
  abstracted 532.11
  engrossed 530.17

  involved in 176.4
**absorbent** 306.6
**absorbing**
  deep-felt 855.26
  engrossing 530.20
**absorption**
  abstractedness 532.2
  consumption 666.1
  digestion 309.8
  engrossment 530.3
  involvement 176.1
  learning 564.2
  sorption 306.6
  thoughtfulness 478.3
**absquatulate**
  flee 631.10
  leave 301.10
**abstain** not do 706.3
  not use 668.5
  refrain from 992.7
  remain neutral 806.5
**abstainer** ascetic 991.2
  teetotaler 992.4
**abstemious**
  abstinent 992.10
  meager 662.10
**abstention**
  abstinence 992.2
  disuse 668.1
  neutrality 806.1
**abstinence**
  abstemiousness 992.2
  asceticism 991.1
  chastity 988.3
  disuse 668.1
  fasting 995.1
  moderation 163.1
**abstract**
  *n.* abridgment 203.3
  abstract idea 479.3
  picture 574.12
  summary 607.1
  *v.* eliminate 77.5
  shorten 203.6
  steal 824.13
  subtract 42.9
  *adj.* general 79.11
  recondite 549.16
  theoretical 499.13
**abstracted**
  absorbed in thought
    478.22
  bemused 532.11
  shortened 203.9
**abstraction**
  abstractedness 532.2
  abstract idea 479.3
  emotional symptom
    690.23
  generalization 79.8
  picture 574.12
  separation 49.1
  subtraction 42.1
  theft 824.1
  theorization 499.1
  thoughtfulness 478.3
**abstruse**
  concealed 615.11
  difficult 731.16
  profound 475.21
  recondite 549.16
**absurd** foolish 470.10

confess 556.7
correspond 604.12
pay 841.18
recognize 521.11
testify 505.10
thank 949.4
**acknowledged**
conventional 645.5
recognized 521.14
traditional 123.12
**acknowledgment**
answer 486.1
apology 1012.2
attribution 155.2
book 605.12
commendation 968.3
confession 556.3
due 960.2
letter 604.2
receipt 844.2
recognition 521.3
thanks 949.2
**acme** completion 56.5
culmination 677.3
height 207.2
ideal 25.4
summit 211.2
supremacy 36.3
**acne** 686.33
**acolyte** assistant 787.6
churchman 1038.10
holy orders 1038.4
**acoustic**(al)
auditory 448.14
phonic 450.17
**acoustics** phonics 450.5
physics 325.1
**acquaint** inform 557.8
introduce 927.13
**acquaintance**
friend 928.1
friendship 927.4
information 557.1
knowledge 475.1
**acquiesce** assent 521.8
be willing 622.3
consent 775.3
submit to 765.6
**acquiescence**
assent 521.1
belief 501.1
conformity 82.1
consent 775.1
obedience 766.1
resignation 861.2
submission 765.1
willingness 622.1
**acquiescent**
agreeing 521.13
conformable 82.5
consenting 775.4
obedient 766.3
resigned 861.10
submissive 765.12
willing 622.5
**acquire** get 811.8
incur 175.4
receive 819.6
take 822.13
**acquisition** gaining 811
learning 475.4
receiving 819.1

taking 822.1
**acquisitive**
acquiring 811.14
greedy 634.27
selfish 978.5
**acquit**
bring in a verdict
1004.19
exculpate 1007.4
**acquittal**
exculpation 1007
legal decision 1004.9
observance 768.1
payment 841.1
**acquitted**
forgiven 947.7
paid 841.22
**acreage** 179.1
**acres** land 385.1
much 34.3
real estate 810.7
**acrid**
acrimonious 161.13
bitter 429.6
caustic 939.21
hostile 929.10
pungent 433.6
sharp 258.10
**acridity**
acrimony 161.4
causticity 939.8
pungency 433.1
sharpness 258.1
unpleasant taste
429.2
**acrimonious**
acrid 161.13
caustic 939.21
resentful 952.24
**acrimony** acridity 161.4
animosity 929.4
bitterness 952.3
causticity 939.8
**acrobat**
circus artist 612.3
gymnast 878.21
**acrobatics**
air maneuver 278.13
sports 878.8
**acronym** 582.4
**acropolis** 799.6
**across**
*adj.* crosswise 221.9
transverse 219.19
*adv.* crosswise 221.13
on 216.25
transversely 219.24
*prep.* beyond 199.21
opposite 239.7
**across the board**
comprehensive 76.7
wholly 54.13
**acrostic** word 582.4
wordplay 881.8
**acrylic** 378.14
**act**
*n.* behavior 737.1
deed 705.3
doing 705.1
law 998.3
legislation 742.13
process 164.2

stage show 611.8
*v.* behave 737.4
do 705.4
fake 616.21
operate 164.7
perform 611.34
produce 167.9
represent 572.9
**acta** acts 705.3
reports 570.7
**act as** do duty 656.13
function as 164.8
represent 572.9
**act for**
be instrumental
658.5
represent 781.14
substitute for 149.5
**acting**
*n.* doing 705.1
fakery 616.3
impersonation 572.2
playing 611.9
*adj.* deputy 781.15
operating 164.11
performing 705.10
**acting-out** 690.32
**actini–**
actinic radiation
327.1
luminary 335.41
radiating 299.9
**action** activeness 707.1
automation 349.3
behavior 737.1
deed 705.3
doing 705
expedient 670.2
fight 796.4
fun 878.2
judgment 494.5
lawsuit 1004.1
mechanism 348.5
military operation
797.8
operation 164.1
story element 608.9
**actionable** illegal 999.6
legal 998.10
litigable 1004.20
**activate** atomics 326.17
energize 161.11
militarize 797.24
radioactivate 327.9
**activator** 161.5
**active**
*n.* voice 586.14
*adj.* effectual 665.20
energetic 161.12
lively 707.17
moving 267.7
observant 768.4
operating 164.11
**active duty** 797.13
**activism** action 705.1
activity 707.1
**activist** 707.8
**activity** action 705.1
activeness 707
animation 161.3
behavior 737.1
business 656.1

cause 153.10
motion 267.1
radiation 327.1
**act like** 22.5
**act of God** 639.7
**act on** influence 172.9
operate on 164.6
pass judgment 494.13
take action 705.5
**actor** affecter 903.7
deceiver 619.1
doer 718.1
player 612.2
role 611.11
**act out** act 611.35
represent 572.9
**actress** 612.2
**actual** certain 513.15
present 120.2
real 1.15
true 516.12
**actuality**
certainty 513.3
reality 1.2
truth 516.1
**actually**
positively 34.19
really 1.16
truly 516.17
**actuarial table** 511.2
**actuary**
accountant 845.7
calculator 87.8
insurance man 699.4
**actuate** impel 283.10
motivate 648.12
set in motion 267.6
**actuation** motion 267.1
motivation 648.2
**act up** 738.4
**acuity** alertness 533.5
intelligence 467.2
sagacity 467.4
sharpness 258.1
**acumen**
discrimination 492.2
sagacity 467.4
**acute** cunning 735.12
deep-felt 855.26
energetic 161.12
painful 424.10
pointed 258.11
sagacious 467.16
sensitive 422.15
sharp 258.10
shrill 458.14
urgent 672.21
violent 162.15
**acutely** 34.20
**ad** 559.6
**AD** 105.13
**adage** 517.1
**adagio**
*n.* music 462.25
*adv.* music 462.55
**adamant**
immovable 142.15
rigid 356.12
stone 384.10
unyielding 626.9
**Adam's apple** 594.19
**adapt** accustom 642.11

change 139.6
conform 82.3
make agree 26.7
music 462.47
orient 290.12
prepare 720.8
**adaptable**
changeable 141.6
conformable 82.5
handy 665.19
pliant 357.9
resilient 358.7
versatile 733.23
wieldy 732.14
**adaptation**
adjustment 26.4
change 139.1
conformity 82.1
development 148.3
fitting 720.2
harmonization 463.2
music 462.5
orientation 290.5
**adapted**
accustomed 642.17
apt 26.10
fitted 720.17
in conformity with
82.9
**add** adjoin 40.4
calculate 87.11
combine 52.3
**addendum**
adjunct 41.1
nonessential 6.2
sequel 67.1
**add fuel to the flame**
excite 857.11
fuel 331.8
incite 648.17
increase 38.5
stoke 329.22
**addict** desirer 634.12
drug user 642.10
enthusiast 635.5
**addicted** 642.19
**addiction** 642.9
**addictive** 642.20
**adding** addition 40.3
calculation 87.3
**adding machine**
addition 40.3
calculator 87.19
**add insult to injury**
aggravate 885.2
impair 692.11
offend 965.4
**addition**
acquisition 811.1
adjunct 41.1
affiliation 9.1
annex 41.3
augmentation 40
combination 52.1
expansion 197.1
increase 38.1
mathematics 87.4
nonessential 6.2
**additional**
additive 40.8
renewed 122.8
supplementary 40.10

unessential 6.4
**additive**
*n.* adjunct 41.1
*adj.* additional 40.8
**addle** confuse 532.7
make drunk 996.21
perplex 514.13
**addled**
intoxicated 996.30
muddled 532.13
perplexed 514.24
stupid 469.18
**addlepate** 471.4
**addlepated**
muddled 532.13
stupid 469.18
**address**
*n.* abode 191.1
behavior 737.1
greeting 925.4
mail 604.10
remark 594.4
request 774.1
skill 733.1
speech 599.2
*v.* court 932.19
greet 925.10
make a speech 599.9
solicit 774.14
speak to 594.27
write destination
604.14
**address book** 570.11
**addressee**
correspondent 604.9
recipient 819.3
resident 190.2
**address oneself to**
busy oneself with
656.11
practice 705.7
undertake 715.3
**add to** augment 40.5
increase 38.4
make larger 197.4
**adduction** 288.1
**add up** add 40.6
be OK 516.9
calculate 87.12
total 54.8
**adenoidal** 595.12
**adept**
*n.* expert 733.11
occultist 1034.11
*adj.* skilled in 733.25
skillful 733.20
**adequate** able 157.14
satisfactory 868.11
sufficient 661.6
tolerable 674.19
**adhere** be joined 47.11
cohere 50.6
**adherence**
approval 968.1
cohesion 50.1
fidelity 974.7
observance 768.1
**adherent** adherer 50.4
commender 968.8
follower 293.2
hanger-on 907.5
man 787.8

philosophy 500.12
**adhere to** fulfill 771.10
hold 813.6
observe 768.2
**adhesive**
*n.* adherent 50.4
connection 47.3
types of 50.13
*adj.* adherent 50.12
sticky 389.12
**adhesive tape**
medical dressing
687.33
tape 206.4
**ad hoc** 670.7
**ad hominem attack**
971.2
**adieu**
*n.* departure 301.4
*interj.* farewell! 301.23
**ad infinitum**
continuously 71.10
infinitely 104.4
lengthily 202.11
perpetually 112.10
throughout 56.17
¡adios! 301.23
**adipose**
corpulent 195.18
oily 380.9
**adit** channel 396.1
entrance 302.5
**adjacent** 200.16
**adjective** 586.3
**adjoin** add 40.4
be near 200.9
border 235.10
juxtapose 200.13
**adjoining** 200.16
**adjourn** 132.9
**adjournment** 132.4
**adjudicate** 494.8
**adjunct** addition 40.1
associate 787.1
attendant 73.3
component 58.2
expansion 197.1
nonessential 6.2
ornamentation 901.1
part 55.1
relationship 9.1
thing added 41
**adjure** entreat 774.11
place under oath
523.6
**adjust** accept 861.6
accustom 642.11
arrange 771.9
change 139.6
compromise 807.2
conform 82.3
equalize 30.6
make agree 26.7
mediate 805.7
organize 60.10
orient 290.12
prepare 720.8
qualify 507.3
reconcile 804.8
size 195.15
**adjustable**
changeable 141.6

conformable 82.5
versatile 733.23
**adjusted**
accustomed 642.17
fitted 720.17
**adjustment**
adaptation 26.4
adjustive reaction
690.34
change 139.1
compacting 771.4
compromise 807.1
condition 7.3
conformity 82.1
equalization 30.2
fitting 720.2
habituation 642.8
organization 60.2
orientation 290.5
reconciliation 804.4
**adjutant** 787.6
**adjuvant**
*n.* adjunct 41.1
drug 687.32
*adj.* helping 785.20
remedial 687.39
**ad lib**
*n.* improvisation 630.5
unpreparedness 721.1
*adv.* at will 621.5
extemporaneously
630.15
**ad-lib**
*v.* be unprepared
721.6
improvise 630.8
*adj.* extemporaneous
630.12
unprepared 721.8
**adman** 559.9
**administer**
administer justice
1000.5
apportion 816.8
execute 771.10
give 818.12
govern 741.12
impose 963.6
manage 747.11
**administer to** 750.13
**administration**
apportionment 816.2
educators 565.9
governance 739.5
government 741.1
imposition 963.2
management 747.3
performance 705.2
protectorship 699.2
**administration, the**
directorate 748.11
executives 748.3
the rulers 749.15
**administrative**
directing 747.14
governing 741.19
**administrator**
director 748.1
educator 565.9
**admirable**
lovable 931.23
praiseworthy 968.20

admiral 749.20
admiration
approval 968.1
love 931.1
respect 964.1
wonder 920.1
admire approve 968.9
cherish 931.19
respect 964.4
admired
approved 968.19
beloved 931.22
respected 964.11
admirer devotee 635.6
lover 931.11
supporter 787.9
admissibility
fitness 26.5
inclusion 76.1
justifiability 1006.7
permissibility 777.8
reasonableness 482.9
receptivity 306.9
satisfactoriness 868.3
tolerableness 674.3
admissible
acceptable 868.12
eligible 637.24
evidential 505.17
justifiable 1006.14
logical 482.20
permissible 777.15
receptive 306.16
relevant 9.11
tolerable 674.19
admission
acknowledgment
521.3
admittance 306.2
confession 556.3
entrance 302.1
fee 846.7
inclusion 76.1
naturalization 189.3
permission 777.1
receiving 819.1
testimony 505.3
admissive
disclosive 556.11
open-minded 526.10
permitting 777.14
receptive 306.16
admit
acknowledge 521.11
allow 507.5
confess 556.7
enter 302.7
include 76.3
naturalize 189.4
permit 777.9
receive 819.6
take in 306.10
welcome 925.7
admit of
be liable 175.3
have a chance 156.13
admitted
acknowledged 521.14
approved 968.19
conventional 645.5
permitted 777.16
received 819.10

traditional 123.12
admitting 507.13
admixture
compound 44.5
mixture 44.1
admonish advise 754.6
dissuade 652.3
reprove 969.17
warn 703.5
admonition
advice 754.1
dissuasion 652.1
reproof 969.5
warning 703.1
ado bustle 707.4
disturbance 62.4
excitement 857.3
trouble 731.3
adobe
n. building material
378.2
ceramic ware 576.2
adj. earthy 385.7,13
adolescence 124.6
adolescent
n. youngster 125.1
adj. undeveloped
721.11
young 124.13
Adonis 900.9
adopt
appropriate 822.19
borrow 821.4
choose 637.15
naturalize 189.4
usurp 961.8
adopted chosen 637.26
naturalized 189.6
adoption
appropriation 822.4
borrowing 821.2
embracement 637.4
naturalization 189.3
redemption 1026.4
usurpation 961.3
adorable
desirable 634.30
lovable 931.23
adoration love 931.1
piety 1028.1
respect 964.1
worship 1032.1
adore cherish 931.19
enjoy 865.10
respect 964.4
worship 1032.10
adored beloved 931.22
respected 964.11
adoring loving 931.25
pious 1028.8
reverent 964.9
worshipful 1032.15
adorn beautify 900.14
dignify 914.12
make grandiloquent
601.7
ornament 901.8
adorned
high-flown 601.11
ornamented 901.11
adornment
beautification 900.10

flowery language
601.4
ornamentation 901.1
adrift afloat 275.61
astray 518.16
bewildered 514.23
inconstant 141.7
irrelevant 10.6
unfastened 49.22
adroit
intelligent 467.14
skillful 733.20
adsorb 306.13
adsorbent
n. sorption 306.6
adj. sorbent 306.17
adsorption 306.6
adulation flattery 970.1
praise 968.5
adult
n. grownup 127
adj. mature 126.12
adulterate
corrupt 692.14
dilute 355.3
mix with 44.13
tamper with 616.17
weaken 160.11
adulterated
imperfect 678.4
thinned 355.4
weakened 160.19
adulterer 989.13
adulteress 989.13
adulterous 989.27
adultery
copulation 419.8
love affair 931.6
unchastity 989.7
adulthood 126.2
adumbrate hint 557.10
portend 544.10
represent 572.8
advance
n. approach 296.1
course 267.2
development 148.1
help along 785.5
improvement 691.1
increase 38.1
lending 820.1
loan 820.2
offer 773.1
progression 294.1
promotion 782.1
v. adduce evidence
505.13
approach 296.3
attack 798.17
be expedient 670.3
be instrumental
658.5
cause 153.13
do good 674.10
elapse 105.5
encourage 785.17
encroach 313.9
evolve 148.5
further 294.5
get better 691.7
increase 38.6
lend 820.5

make better 691.9
make good 724.9
move 267.5
postulate 499.12
progress 294.2
promote 782.2
propose 773.5
prosper 728.7
push 285.10
interj. attack! 798.32
advanced aged 126.16
improved 691.13
modern 122.13
preceding 66.4
premature 131.8
advance guard
guard 699.9
the latest thing 122.2
vanguard 240.2
advance man 611.30
advancement
development 148.1
furtherance 785.5
improvement 691.1
lending 820.1
progression 294.1
promotion 782.1
advance notice 703.2
advantage
n. benefit 665.4
expedience 670.1
facility 785.9
good 674.4
leverage 287.2
superiority 36.2
v. be expedient 670.3
be of use 665.17
do good 674.10
further 785.17
advantageous
expedient 670.5
gainful 811.15
good 674.12
useful 665.18
advantageously
expediently 670.8
favorably 36.19
gainfully 811.16
helpfully 785.24
usefully 665.25
advent approach 296.1
arrival 300.1
coming 121.5
Advent 1040.15
adventitious
chance 156.15
circumstantial 8.7
unessential 6.4
adventure act 705.3
biography 608.4
chance event 156.6
courageous act 893.7
event 151.2
undertaking 715.2
adventurer
gambler 515.17
mercenary 800.16
reckless person 894.4
stock speculator
833.11
traveler 274.1
upstart 919.10

**adventuresome**
daring 893.21
enterprising 707.23
**adventuress**
reckless person 894.4
unchaste woman
989.15
**adventurous**
daring 893.21
dynamic 707.23
enterprising 715.8
foolhardy 894.9
hazardous 697.10
**adverb** 586.3
**adversary**
*n.* enemy 929.6
opponent 791.1
*adj.* opposing 790.8
**adverse** contrary 15.6
opposing 790.8
untoward 729.13
**adversity** 729
**advertent** 530.15
**advertise** flaunt 904.17
inform 557.8
publicize 559.15
publish 559.10
**advertisement** 559.6
**advertising** 559.5
**advice** counsel 754
message 558.4
news 558.1
tip 557.3
**advisable** 670.5
**advise** counsel 754.5
inform 557.8
warn 703.5
**advised**
considered 482.21
intentional 653.9
**advisement** 478.2
**adviser** counselor 754.3
informant 557.5
**advisory**
admonitory 754.8
conciliar 755.5
informative 557.17
**advocacy** advice 754.1
patronage 785.4
promotion 559.5
recommendation
968.4
**advocate**
*n.* associate 787.9
defender 799.7
deputy 781.1
friend 928.1
justifier 1006.8
lawyer 1003.1
supporter 216.2
*v.* abet 785.14
advise 754.5
commend 968.11
defend 1006.10
urge 648.14
**aegis** armor 799.17
patronage 785.4
safeguard 699.3
**aeon** age 107.4
long time 110.4
**aeonian** 112.7
**aer(o)–** air 402.1

aviation 278.1
gas 401.2
**aerate** add gas 401.8
air 402.11
foam 405.5
**aerial**
*n.* radio 344.32
*adj.* aeronautic(al)
278.58
airy 402.12
high 207.19
imaginary 535.22
vaporous 401.9
**aerialist**
circus artist 612.3
gymnast 878.21
**aerie** 191.25
**aeriness** 401.3
**aerobatics** 278.13
**aerodynamic(al)**
aeronautic 278.58
gas 401.9
pneumatic 347.10
**aerodynamics**
aeronautics 278.2
dynamics 347.3
gas 401.2
pneumatics 347.5
**aerography**
aeronautics 278.2
meteorology 402.6
pneumatics 347.5
**aerology**
aeronautics 278.2
meteorology 402.6
pneumatics 347.5
**aeromechanics**
aeronautics 278.2
mechanics 347.1
pneumatics 347.5
**aeromedicine** 278.2
**aeronaut** aviator 279.1
balloonist 279.7
**aeronautic(al)** 278.58
**aeronautics** 278.1
**aeroplane** see **airplane**
**aerosol**
moisturizer 392.8
vaporizer 401.6
**aerospace**
*n.* aviation 278.41
*adj.* aeronautic 278.58
**aerospace science** 282.1
**aerosphere**
atmosphere 402.2
aviation 278.41
**aerostatics**
aeronautics 278.2
pneumatics 347.5
statics 347.2
**aerotechnics**
aeronautics 278.2
pneumatics 347.5
**aery** airy 402.12
ethereal 401.9
**aesthete** 897.6
**aesthetic** artistic 574.21
beautiful 900.16
tasteful 897.8
**aesthetics**
aesthetic taste 897.5
philosophy 500.1

**aestival** green 371.4
summer 128.8
warm 328.24
**afar** 199.15
**affable** agreeable 759.8
courteous 936.14
good-natured 938.14
informal 647.3
pleasant 863.6
sociable 922.18
**affair** business 656.1
concern 151.3
object 376.4
romance 931.6
social gathering
922.10
undertaking 715.1
**affair of honor** 796.7
**affairs** business 656.1
concerns 151.4
dealings 9.1
**affect**
*n.* emotion 855.3
mental attitude 525.1
*v.* affect emotionally
855.17
entail 76.4
excite pity 944.5
fake 616.21
imitate 22.5
influence 172.7
operate on 164.6
put on airs 903.12
relate to 9.5
show 555.5
stir feelings 855.16
wear 231.43
**affectation**
affectedness 903
behavior 737.1
fakery 616.3
grandiloquence 601.1
preciosity 589.3
style 588.2
**affected** elegant 589.9
falsified 616.26
grandiloquent 601.8
moved 855.25
pretentious 903.15
sanctimonious 1029.5
**affecting**
sympathetic 944.8
touching 855.24
unpleasant 864.20
**affection**
amorousness 931.3
disease 686.1
emotion 855.3
feelings 855.1
liking 634.2
love 931.1
**affectionate**
kind 938.13
loving 931.25
**affianced**
*n.* fiancée 931.16
*adj.* promised 770.8
**affidavit**
certificate 570.6
deposition 523.2
legal statement
1004.7

statement of belief
501.4
testimony 505.3
**affiliate**
*n.* branch 788.10
member 788.11
*v.* accept 637.15
ally 52.4
cooperate 786.3
join 788.14
naturalize 189.4
trace to 155.5
*adj.* joined 52.6
related 9.9
**affiliated**
associated 9.9
joined 52.6
related 11.6
**affiliation**
adoption 637.4
ancestry 170.4
blood relationship
11.1
combination 52.1
cooperation 786.2
naturalization 189.3
relationship 9.1
religion 1020.3
sociability 922.6
**affinity** accord 794.1
agreement 26.1
attraction 288.1
friendship 927.5
inclination 634.3
marriage relationship
12.1
preference 637.5
relationship 9.1
similarity 20.2
tendency 174.1
**affirm**
announce 559.12
assert 523.4
confirm 505.12
express belief 501.12
ratify 521.12
speak 594.24
testify 505.10
**affirmation**
assertion 523
confirmation 505.5
consent 775.1
deposition 523.2
premise 482.7
ratification 521.4
remark 594.4
testimony 505.3
**affirmative**
*n.* affirmative expres-
sion 521.2
consent 775.1
side of controversy
482.14
*adj.* agreeing 26.9
asserting 523.7
consenting 775.4
**affirmed** asserted 523.8
made public 559.17
ratified 521.14
**affix**
*n.* addition 41.2
morphology 582.3

breeze 403.5
element 376.2
gas 401.2
heavens 375.2
lightness 353.2
looks 446.4
melody 462.4
milieu 233.3
spirit 4.3
*v.* broadcast 559.10
discuss 597.12
divulge 556.5
flaunt 904.17
make public 559.11
ventilate 402.11
**airborne** 278.59
**air-built**
imaginary 535.22
tenuous 4.6
**airburst** 281.9
**air-condition** air 402.11
refrigerate 334.10
**air-conditioned** 334.13
**air conditioner** 402.10
**air conditioning**
refrigeration 334.1
ventilation 402.9
**air corps**
air force 800.28
corps 800.20
**air cover** 278.11
**aircraft**
airplane 280.1,15
vehicle 272.1
**aircraft carrier** 277.8,24
**aircraft engine**
aviation 278.33
types of 280.17
**aircrew** 279.4
**air current** 403.1
**air-cushion vehicle**
aircraft 280.7
hovercraft 272.21
**air express** 271.3
**airfield** 278.22
**air force**
air corps 800.28
aircraft 280.9
air service 800.29
aviator 279.3
**Air Force** 278.7
**airfreight**
*n.* air travel 278.10
transportation 271.3
*v.* send 271.14
**air hole**
air passage 396.17
aviation 278.41
hole 265.4
**airiness** frailness 205.4
illusoriness 519.2
lightheartedness
870.3
lightness 353.1
rarity 355.1
unsubstantiality 4.1
windiness 403.15
**airing** discussion 597.7
publication 559.1
ride 273.7
ventilation 402.9
walk 273.12

**air lane** aviation 278.42
route 657.2
**airless** 268.16
**airlift**
*n.* flight 278.9
transportation 271.3
*v.* fly 278.45
**airline** 278.1
**air line** aviation 278.42
shortcut 203.5
straight line 250.2
**air lock** entrance 302.5
lock 396.11
**airmail**
*n.* mail 604.5
*v.* mail 604.13
send 271.14
**airman** 279.1
**airmanship**
pilotship 278.3
skill 733.1
**air mass** 402.5
**airplane**
*n.* aircraft 280.1,15
parts 280.16
*v.* fly 278.45
**air pocket** 278.41
**air pollution**
powder 361.5
unhealthfulness 684.1
**airport** 278.22
**air raid**
bombardment 798.7
flight 278.11
raid 798.4
**air route** 278.42
**airs** affectation 903.1
contempt 966.1
ostentation 904.2
**air shaft** 396.17
**airship** aircraft 280.11
parts 280.19
**air show** 278.1
**air shuttle** 278.10
**airsick**
aeronautic 278.58
nauseated 686.53
**airspace**
aviation 278.41
region 180.1
**air space**
headroom 179.3
space 179.4
**air speed**
aviation 278.40
speed 269.1
**air strike** 798.4
**airstrip** 278.23
**air support** 278.11
**airtight**
impenetrable 266.12
resistant 159.18
**air-traffic controller**
346.14
**air travel** 278.10
**airway**
air passage 396.17
aviation 278.42
**airworthy**
aeronautic 278.58
safe 698.7
**airy** aery 402.12

careless 534.11
high 207.19
illusory 519.9
immaterial 377.7
light 353.10
lighthearted 870.12
rare 355.4
tenuous 4.6
thin 205.16
trivial 673.16
vaporous 401.9
visionary 535.24
windy 403.25
**aisle** 657.4
**ajar** clashing 461.5
gaping 265.19
**akimbo** 251.6
**akin** in accord 794.3
related 9.10
related by blood 11.6
similar 20.13
**à la** 22.12
**alabaster**
mineral 383.19
smooth surface 260.3
white comparisons
364.2
**à la carte** 307.11
**alacrity** eagerness 635.1
hastiness 709.2
promptness 131.3
quickness 707.3
willingness 622.1
**Aladdin's lamp** 1036.6
**à la mode**
fashionably 644.17
modern 122.13
stylish 644.12
**alarm**
*n.* alarm signal 704
fear 891.1
signal 568.15
summons 568.16
warning 703.1
*v.* alert 704.3
frighten 891.23
**alarmed** aroused 704.4
frightened 891.33
**alarming**
dangerous 697.9
frightening 891.36
**alarmist** 891.8
**albeit** 33.8
**albinism**
faulty eyesight 440.1
genetic disease
686.11
whiteness 364.1
**albino**
*n.* whiteness 364.1
*adj.* white 364.10
**album**
compilation 605.4
record book 570.11
**albumen**
egg white 406.15
semiliquid 389.5
**alchemy**
conversion 145.1
sorcery 1035.1
**alcohol**
antifreeze 334.8

antiseptic 687.58
chemical 379.11
depressant 687.54
fuel 331.1
liquor 996.12
sedative 687.12
solvent 391.10
**alcoholic**
*n.* addict 642.10
drunkard 996.10
pathological type
690.16
*adj.* spirituous 996.36
**alcoholism**
addiction 642.9
intoxication 996.3
**alcove** nook 192.3
recess 257.7
summerhouse 191.13
**alderman**
legislator 746.3
public official 749.17
**aleatory**
*n.* music 462.5
*adj.* chance 156.15
circumstantial 8.7
hazardous 697.10
uncertain 514.18
**Alecto** Fury 1016.11
rage 952.10
**alee** downwind 275.68
leeward 242.9
**alehouse** 996.19
**alert**
*n.* alarm 704.1
*v.* alarm 704.3
inform 557.11
warn 703.5
*adj.* attentive 530.15
awake 713.8
clear-witted 467.13
prepared for 720.18
prompt 131.9
vigilant 533.14
**alfresco**
*adj.* airy 402.12
outdoor 224.7
*adv.* outdoors 224.10
**algae** plant 411.4; 412.3
types of 411.42
**algebraic(al)** 87.17
**algesia** 424.4
**algid** cold 333.14
feeling cold 333.15
**algorithm**
mathematics 87.2
number system 86.2
way 657.1
**alias**
*n.* pseudonym 583.8
*adv.* otherwise 16.11
**alibi**
*n.* excuse 1006.4
pretext 649.1
*v.* excuse 1006.11
**alien**
*n.* odd person 85.4
outsider 77.3
spaceman 282.8
stranger 78.3
*adj.* external 224.8
extraterrestrial 375.26

**allowance**
  acknowledgment
    521.3
  discount 847.1
  extenuation 1006.5
  fee 841.5
  inaccuracy 518.2
  permission 777.1
  portion 816.5
  qualification 507.1
  rations 308.6
  subsidy 818.8
**allowed**
  acknowledged 521.14
  given 818.24
  permitted 777.16
**allow for**
  condone 947.4
  extenuate 1006.12
  take into account
    507.5
**alloy**
  *n.* compound 44.5
  metal 383.4,22
  *v.* corrupt 692.14
  mix 44.11
**all-pervading**
  thorough 56.10
  universal 79.14
**all-powerful**
  godlike 1013.20
  omnipotent 157.13
**all-present** 186.13
**all right**
  acceptable 868.12
  accurate 516.15
  tolerable 674.19
  well 685.8
  yes! 521.18
**all round**
  all around 233.13
  everywhere 179.11
  in every direction
    290.27
**All Saints' Day** 1040.15
**all-seeing** 1013.20
**all set** 720.16
**All Souls' Day** 1040.15
**all the time** 112.11
**all the way**
  as far as 199.20
  to the end 70.12
  utterly 56.16
**all things considered**
  generally 79.17
  judgment 494.17
  on the average 32.5
**all thumbs** 734.20
**all together**
  at once 113.8
  jointly 47.18
  simultaneously 118.6
  unanimously 521.17
**allude to**
  call attention to
    530.10
  designate 568.18
  hint 557.10
  imply 546.4
  remark 594.25
**allurement**
  attraction 288.1

enticement 650
  inducement 648.3
  lovability 931.7
**alluring**
  attracting 288.5
  fascinating 650.7
  provocative 648.27
**allusion** 546.2
**allusive** figurative 551.3
  suggestive 546.6
**alluvial** 385.8
**alluvium** deposit 271.8
  land 385.1
  overflow 395.6
  sediment 43.2
**ally**
  *n.* associate 787.1
  country 181.1
  likeness 20.3
  *v.* cooperate 786.3
  join 52.4
  relate 9.6
**alma mater** 567.7
**almanac** 114.7
**almighty**
  *adj.* godlike 1013.20
  omnipotent 157.13
  *adv.* very 34.18
**almond** 308.38,52
**almost** 200.22
**alms** 818.6
**almsgiver** giver 818.11
  philanthropist 938.8
**almshouse** 700.4
**almsman**
  beneficiary 819.4
  poor person 838.4
**aloft**
  *adv.* on board 275.62
  up 207.26
  *interj.* sailing 275.75
**aloha**
  *n.* departure 301.4
  *interj.* farewell! 301.23
  greetings! 925.15
**alone**
  *adj.* secluded 924.10
  sole 89.9
  solitary 89.8
  *adv.* independently
    762.32
  simply 45.11
  singly 89.13
**along** beside 242.11
  forward 294.8
  lengthwise 202.12
**alongside**
  *adv.* beside 275.70
  in parallel 218.7
  *prep.* beside 242.11
**along with**
  in addition 40.12
  together with 73.12
**aloof**
  *adj.* alone 89.8
  apathetic 856.13
  disconnected 51.4
  incurious 529.3
  reticent 613.10
  standoffish 912.12
  unsociable 923.6

*adv.* at a distance
  199.14
  up 207.26
**aloud** audibly 450.18
  loudly 453.13
**alp** 207.7
**alpen** 207.23
**alpha** beginning 68.1
  first 68.3
**alphabet** basics 68.6
  representation 572.1
  writing system 581.3
**alphabetarian** 566.9
**alphabetic(al)**
  literal 581.8
  written 602.26
**alphabetize**
  classify 61.6
  letter 581.6
**alpha particle**
  atomics 326.6
  radiation 327.4
**alpine** 207.23
**Alps** 207.9
**already**
  previously 116.6
  until now 120.4
**alright** see all right
**also**
  *adv.* additionally
    40.11
  *conj.* and 40.13
**also-ran**
  defeated candidate
    746.9
  loser 727.5
  unsuccessful person
    725.7
**altar** 1042.12
**altarpiece**
  church part 1042.12
  picture 574.12
**alter** be changed 139.5
  become 145.17
  castrate 42.11
  change 139.6
  qualify 507.3
**alteration** change 139.1
  differentiation 16.4
**altercation**
  contention 796.1
  quarrel 795.5
**alter ego** deputy 781.1
  friend 928.1
  likeness 20.3
  right-hand man 787.7
  self 80.5
**alternate**
  *n.* deputy 781.1
  substitute 149.2
  *v.* fluctuate 141.5
  interchange 150.4
  oscillate 323.13
  recur 137.5
  take turns 108.5
  vacillate 627.8
  *adj.* periodic 137.7
  reciprocal 323.19
  substitute 149.8
**alternate school** 567.2
**alternating current**
  342.2

**alternation**
  fluctuation 141.3
  interaction 13.3
  interchange 150.1
  oscillation 323.5
  periodicity 137.2
**alternative**
  *n.* loophole 632.4
  option 637.2
  substitute 149.2
  *adj.* elective 637.22
  substitute 149.8
**althorn** 465.8
**although** 33.8
**altimeter** 207.14
**altimetry**
  height measurement
    207.14
  mensuration 490.9
**altitude**
  aviation 278.44
  coordinates 490.6
  height 207.1
**alto** high voice 458.6
  music 462.22
  vocalist 464.13
**altogether**
  additionally 40.11
  completely 56.14
  generally 79.17
  wholly 54.13
**altogether, the** 232.3
**alto-rilievo** relief 256.2
  sculpture 575.3
**altruism**
  benevolence 938.4
  unselfishness 979.1
**altruist** 938.8
**altruistic**
  benevolent 938.15
  unselfish 979.5
**alum** 198.6
**alumnus** 566.8
**alveolar**
  indented 257.17
  phonetic 594.31
**alveolus** cavity 257.2
  indentation 257.6
  vocal organ 594.19
**always** constantly 135.7
  permanently 140.9
  perpetually 112.11
  regularly 17.8
  universally 79.18
**AM** modulation 344.14
  morning 133.1
**amah** maid 750.8
  nurse 699.8
**amalgam** alloy 383.4
  compound 44.5
**amalgamate**
  combine 52.3
  cooperate 786.3
  mix 44.11
**amalgamation**
  affiliation 786.2
  combination 52.1
  mixture 44.1
**amanuensis** agent 781.3
  recorder 571.1
  writer 602.13
**amaranthine** 112.9

*adj.* froglike 414.51
**amphibious**
  mixed 44.15
  versatile 733.23
**amphitheater**
  arena 802.1
  hall 192.4
  schoolroom 567.16
  theater 611.18
**ample** abundant 101.8
  broad 204.6
  much 34.8
  plentiful 661.7
  satisfactory 868.11
  spacious 179.9
  sufficient 661.6
  voluminous 195.17
**amplification**
  aggravation 885.1
  development 148.1
  exaggeration 617.1
  expansion 197.1
  expatiation 593.6
  increase 38.1
  interpretation 552.3
  radio 344.15
**amplified**
  aggravated 885.4
  exaggerated 617.4
  expanded 197.10
  increased 38.7
**amplifier**
  audio amplifier 450.10
  electronic 343.18,20
  hearing aid 448.8
**amplify**
  aggravate 885.2
  develop 148.6
  electricity 342.23
  exaggerate 617.3
  expatiate 593.7
  increase 38.4
  make larger 197.4
**amplitude**
  aviation 278.25
  breadth 204.1
  diffuseness 593.1
  fullness 56.2
  greatness 34.1
  plenty 661.2
  quantity 28.1
  size 195.1
  sound 450.1
  spaciousness 179.5
  wave 323.4
**amply**
  abundantly 34.20
  satisfactorily 868.15
  sufficiently 661.8
**amputate** excise 42.10
  sever 49.11
**amputation**
  excision 42.3
  separation 49.2
  surgical operation 689.22
**amputee** 686.42
**amuck** see amok
**amulet** 1036.5
**amuse** 878.23
**amused** 878.28

**amusement**
  entertainment 878
  merriment 870.5
  pleasure 865.1
**amusing**
  entertaining 878.29
  humorous 880.4
**ana** archives 570.2
  collection 74.11
  compilation 605.4
  maxim 517.1
  selections 607.4
**anabolism**
  metabolism 309.10
  transformation 139.2
**anachronism** 115
**anachronistic** 115.3
**anaerobe** 686.39
**anagram** riddle 549.9
  wordplay 881.8
**anal** conformist 82.6
  intestinal 225.10
  tidy 59.8
**analects**
  compilation 605.4
  maxim 517.1
  selections 607.4
**analeptic**
  remedial 687.39
  restorative 694.22
  tonic 687.44
**analgesia**
  insensibility 423.1
  psychosomatic symptom 690.22
  relief 886.1
**analgesic**
  *n.* depressant 423.3
  sedative 687.12
  types of 687.56
  *adj.* deadening 423.9
  relieving 886.9
  sedative 687.45
**analogous**
  comparable 491.8
  parallel 218.6
  reciprocal 13.13
  similar 20.11
**analogue** correlate 13.4
  likeness 20.3
**analogy**
  comparison 491.1
  parallelism 218.1
  similarity 20.1
  substitute 149.2
**analysis**
  automation 349.7
  breakdown 48
  classification 61.1
  commentary 606.2
  differentiation 16.4
  discussion 597.7
  inquiry 485.1
  logic 482.3
  mathematics 87.18
  particularization 8.5
  psychoanalysis 690.8
  separation 49.5
  theorization 499.1
**analyst** analyzer 48.5
  psychotherapist 690.13

  tester 489.6
**analytic(al)**
  classificatory 48.9
  dialectic(al) 482.22
  examining 485.36
  mathematical 87.17
  reasoning 482.18
**analyze**
  break down 48.6
  classify 61.6
  differentiate 16.6
  discriminate 492.5
  discuss 597.12
  dissect 49.17
  grammaticize 586.16
  reason 482.15
**analyzer** analyst 48.5
  automatic 349.36
  separator 49.7
  tester 489.6
**analyzing**
  data processing 349.20
  judgment 494.3
**anapest** 609.9
**anaphylactic** 422.14
**anaphylaxis** 422.3
**anarchic(al)**
  confused 62.16
  formless 247.4
  illegal 999.6
  lawless 740.6
  revolutionary 147.6
  violent 162.17
**anarchism**
  lawlessness 740.2
  radicalism 745.4
  revolutionism 147.2
**anarchist** anarch 740.3
  radical 745.12
  revolutionist 147.3
**anarchistic** illegal 999.6
  lawless 740.6
  radical 745.20
**anarchy** confusion 62.2
  disorder 51.1
  formlessness 247.1
  illegality 999.1
  lawlessness 740.2
**anathema** curse 972.1
  disapproval 969.3
  hated thing 930.3
**anatomic(al)** 245.9
**anatomize** analyze 48.6
  differentiate 16.6
  dissect 49.17
  particularize 8.6
**anatomy** analysis 48.1
  biology 406.17
  body 376.3
  dissection 49.5
  human form 246.4
  science 245.7
  science of man 417.7
  skeleton 245.5
  structure 245.1
  zoology 415.1
**ancestor**
  antecedent 116.2
  parent 170.8
  precursor 66.1

**ancestors**
  antecedents 170.7
  producer 167.8
**ancestral**
  parental 170.13
  primitive 123.11
**ancestry**
  blood relationship 11.1
  kinsmen 11.2
  nobility 918.1
  progenitorship 170
**anchor**
  *n.* mooring 277.16
  types of 277.32
  *v.* fasten 47.7
  moor 275.15
  restrain 760.10
  settle 184.16
  stabilize 142.8
**anchorage**
  anchor 277.16
  destination 300.5
  fee 846.7
  harbor 700.6
  settlement 184.6
**anchored** fixed 142.14
  held 142.16
**anchorite** ascetic 991.2
  recluse 924.5
**anchor man** 344.23
**anchors aweigh!** 275.75
**ancient**
  *n.* man of old 123.7
  *adj.* aged 126.16
  enduring 110.10
  former 119.10
  old 123.10
**ancient times** 119.3
**ancillary**
  additional 40.10
  helping 785.20
**and** 40.13
**andante**
  *n.* music 462.25
  slowness 270.2
  tempo 463.24
  *adv.* music 462.55
**andiron** 329.12
**andr(o)–** 420.4
**androgynous** 419.33
**androgyny**
  effeminacy 421.2
  intersexuality 419.14
**anecdotal** 608.16
**anecdote** 608.6
**anemia**
  blood disease 686.18
  colorlessness 363.2
  deficiency disease 686.10
  disease symptom 686.8
  weakness 160.1
**anemic** colorless 363.7
  diseased 686.57
  weak 160.12
**anemology**
  meteorology 402.6
  wind 403.16
**anemometer**
  speed meter 269.7

wind instrument 403.17

**anesthesia**
insensibility 423.1
psychosomatic symptom 690.22
relief 886.1
unfeeling 856.1

**anesthetic**
*n.* depressant 423.3
medicine 687.15,57
sleep-inducer 712.10
*adj.* deadening 423.9
numbing 687.47
relieving 886.9

**anesthetist** 688.14

**anesthetize**
make unfeeling 856.8
put to sleep 712.20
relieve 886.5
render insensible 423.4

**anesthetized**
sleepy 712.21
unfeeling 856.9

**anew** again 91.7
newly 122.15
repeatedly 103.17

**anfractuous**
spiral 254.8
winding 254.6

**angel**
celestial being 1015
celestial hierarchy 1015.3
endearment 932.5
financer 836.9
giver 818.11
good person 985.6
guardian angel 1014.22
innocent person 984.4
play backer 611.31
supporter 787.9

**angelic** innocent 984.6
lovable 931.23
pious 1028.9
seraphic 1015.6
virtuous 980.7

**Angelus** prayer 1032.4
signal 568.16

**anger**
*n.* heat 328.2
ill humor 951.1
sin 982.3
wrath 952.5
*v.* become angry 952.17
make angry 952.21
make hot 329.18

**angina** ache 424.5
cardiovascular disease 686.17

**angle**
*n.* aspect 446.3
aviation 278.26
corner 251.2
mental outlook 525.2
standpoint 184.2
story element 608.9
types of 251.12

viewpoint 439.7
*v.* bend 251.5
fish 655.10
maneuver 735.10
oblique 219.9
plot 654.10

**angle for** seek 485.29
solicit 774.14

**angler** 655.6

**Anglicanism** 1020.10

**Anglicism** idiom 580.8
patriotism 941.2

**Anglicize** 189.4

**angling** 655.3

**angry** annoyed 866.21
ill-humored 951.17
sore 424.11
stormy 403.26
violent 162.17
wrathful 952.26

**angst** anxiety 890.1
unpleasure 866.1

**anguish**
*n.* despair 866.6
pain 424.6
sorrow 872.10
unpleasure 866.1
*v.* make grieve 872.19
pain 866.17
suffer 866.19
suffer pain 424.8

**anguished**
pained 866.23
pleasureless 866.20
sorrowful 872.26

**angular** 251.6

**angularity**
angularness 251
inclination 219.2

**anhydrous** 393.7

**anility** old age 126.5
senility 469.10

**anima** life force 407.3
mind 466.4
psyche 690.35

**animadversion** 969.4

**animal**
*n.* bad person 986.7
barbarian 898.7
creature 414.2,58
prehistoric 123.26
savage 943.5
*adj.* animalian 414.43
carnal 987.6
cruel 939.24
lascivious 989.29
uncouth 898.12

**animal diseases** 686.38

**animal husbandry** 416

**animalism**
carnality 987.2
materialism 376.5

**animalistic**
animal 414.43
carnal 987.6

**animality**
animal life 414.1
carnality 987.2
cruelty 939.11
lasciviousness 989.5
uncouthness 898.3
violence 162.1

**animal kingdom**
animal life 414.1
class 61.4
stock 11.4

**animal life** 414

**animal magnetism** 712.8

**animal noise** 460

**animal spirits**
gaiety 870.4
life 407.1

**animal worship** 1033.1

**animate**
*v.* cheer 870.7
energize 161.9
impel 283.10
inspire 648.20
motivate 648.12
refresh 695.2
stimulate 857.12
vivify 407.9
*adj.* gender 586.10
living 407.11
organic 406.19

**animated** eager 635.9
energetic 161.12
gay 870.14
lively 707.17
living 407.11
motivated 648.30
refreshed 695.4

**animated cartoon**
cartoon 574.17
motion picture 611.16

**animation**
eagerness 635.1
energizing 161.7
excitation 857.10
gaiety 870.4
infusion 648.9
life 407.1
liveliness 707.2
stimulation 648.2
vivacity 161.3
vivification 407.5

**animism** idealism 377.3
paganism 1025.4

**animist** idealist 377.4
pagan 1025.7

**animosity**
bad feeling 855.7
bitterness 952.3
enmity 929.4
hate 930.2

**animus** animosity 929.4
inspiration 648.9
intention 653.1
trait of character 525.3
will 621.1

**anion** chemical 379.1
electrolysis 342.22

**ankh** 221.4

**ankle** joint 47.4
leg 273.16

**ankle-deep** deep 209.10
shallow 210.5

**annalist** author 602.15
chronicler 608.11
chronologist 114.10
recorder 571.2

**annals** chronicle 114.9
history 608.4
record 570.1

**annealed**
hardened 356.15
toughened 359.6

**annex**
*n.* addition 41.3
adjunct 41.1
*v.* acquire 811.9
add 40.4
appropriate 822.20
fasten 47.7
steal 824.13

**annexation**
addition 40.1
adjunct 41.1
appropriation 822.5
connection 47.3
theft 824.1

**annihilate**
abolish 693.13
destroy 693.14
eradicate 42.10
exterminate 2.6
kill 409.13

**annihilation**
death 408.1
destruction 693.6
excision 42.3

**anniversary**
celebration 877.1
commemoration 137.4,12

**annotate**
comment upon 552.11
judge 494.14

**annotation**
comment 552.5
record 570.4

**announce** affirm 523.4
forerun 116.3
presage 544.14
proclaim 559.12
report 558.11

**announcement**
affirmation 523.1
impartation 554.2
information 557.1
proclamation 559.2

**announcer**
broadcaster 344.23
harbinger 544.5
informant 557.5
precursor 66.1
proclaimer 561.3

**annoy** aggravate 885.2
excite 857.11
irk 866.13
provoke 952.22
vex 864.15

**annoyance**
adversity 729.1
aggravation 885.1
resentment 952.1
trouble 731.3
unpleasantness 864.7
vexation 866.2

**annoyed**
aggravated 885.4
irritated 866.21

**antidote**
counteractant 178.3
counterpoison 687.26
**antiestablishment** 522.6
**antifreeze** 334.8
**antigen**
antibody 687.27
blood 388.4
immunity 685.4
**antigravity** 289.1
**antihero** 611.11
**antihistamine** 687.32
**antinomian**
anarchistic 740.6
unorthodox 1025.9
**antinomy**
contrariety 15.3
inconsistency 27.2
**antipasto** 308.9
**antipathetic(al)**
contrary 15.6
counteractive 178.8
disagreeing 27.6
hostile 929.10
opposing 790.8
**antipathy**
contrariety 15.1
counteraction 178.1
dislike 867.2
hate 930.1
hated thing 930.3
hostility 929.3
opposition 790.2
unwillingness 623.1
**antiphon** answer 486.1
hymn 1032.3
music 462.23
**antipodal**
diametric 15.7
polarized 239.5
**antipodes**
opposite 15.2
poles 239.2
remote region 199.4
**Antipodes** 180.6
**antipole**
contraposition 239.2
opposite 15.2
**antipyretic**
*n.* fever reducer
687.14,64
*adj.* curative 687.41
**antiquarian**
*n.* archaist 123.5
*adj.* archaeological
123.20
**antiquate** 123.9
**antiquated**
archaic 123.13
disused 668.10
past 119.7
**antique**
*n.* antiquated person
123.8
relic 123.6
*adj.* antiquated
123.13
disused 668.10
enduring 110.10
old 123.10
past 119.7

**antiquity**
ancient times 119.3
durability 110.1
oldness 123.1
relic 123.6
**antireligion** 1031.8
**antireligious** 1031.22
**anti-Semitism**
hate 930.1
prejudice 527.4
**antiseptic**
*n.* disinfectant
687.21,58
poison 676.3
*adj.* disinfectant
687.43
sanitary 681.27
**antisocial** 940.3
**antithesis**
contraposition 239.1
contrariety 15.1
opposite 15.2
**antithetic(al)**
contrary 15.6
facing 239.5
opposing 790.8
**antitoxic** 687.41
**antitoxin**
antitoxic serum
687.27
injection 689.18
**antitype** 25.1
**antonym** opposite 15.2
word 582.1
**anus** opening 265.6
rectum 225.4
**anvil**
auditory organ 448.7
converter 145.10
**anxiety**
apprehension 891.4
eagerness 635.1
emotional symptom
690.23
expectancy 539.3
impatience 862.1
tension 890
trouble 731.3
unpleasure 866.1
**anxious**
concerned 890.6
eager 635.9
fearful 891.32
impatient 862.6
in suspense 539.12
pleasureless 866.20
troubled 731.19
**anxiously**
concernedly 890.10
eagerly 635.14
impatiently 862.8
**any**
*n.* anything 79.5
some 28.3
*adj.* every 79.15
one 89.7
quantifier 28.5
**anybody** 79.5
**anyhow** anyway 657.12
carelessly 534.18
**any old way** 534.18
**anyone** any 79.5

whoever 79.7
**anything** any 79.5
some 28.3
**anytime**
whenever 105.12
imminently 152.4
**anyway** 657.12
**anywhere** 184.21
**A1**
*n.* superior 36.4
*adj.* best 36.13
first-rate 674.15
seaworthy 277.18
**aorta** 396.14
**apace** fast 269.21
hastily 709.12
promptly 131.15
**apart**
*adj.* alone 89.8
distant 199.8
secluded 924.7
separate 49.20
unrelated 10.5
*adv.* away 199.17
in half 92.8
privately 614.19
separately 49.28
singly 89.13
**apartheid**
exclusiveness 77.3
prejudice 527.4
seclusion 924.1
**apartment** 191.14
**apathetic** aloof 856.13
hopeless 889.12
incurious 529.3
inert 268.14
languid 708.19
neutral 806.7
reluctant 623.6
unconcerned 636.7
**apathy** despair 889.2
emotional symptom
690.23
incurious 529.1
inertia 268.4
languor 708.6
neutrality 806.2
unconcern 636.2
unfeeling 856.4
**ape**
*n.* imitator 22.4
mammals 415.8
primate 414.59
wild animal 414.28
*v.* imitate 22.6
impersonate 572.9
resemble 20.7
*adj.* enthusiastic
635.12
**aperçu**
abridgment 607.1
insight 481.1
treatise 606.1
**apéritif**
alcoholic drink 996.8
appetizer 308.9
**aperture** opening 265.1
passageway 657.4
**apex** height 207.2
summit 211.2
vertex 251.2

vocal organ 594.19
**aphasia**
imperfect speech
595.6
mental symptom
690.25
muteness 451.2
**aphorism**
conciseness 592.3
maxim 517.1
witticism 881.7
**aphoristic(al)**
concise 592.6
proverbial 517.6
**aphrodisiac** 419.7
**Aphrodite**
beautiful woman
900.9
goddess 1014.5
love goddess 931.8
**apiary** 191.25
**apiece** 80.19
**apish** foolish 470.8
imitative 22.9
representational
572.10
**aplenty**
*adj.* plentiful 661.7
*adv.* plentifully 661.9
**aplomb**
equanimity 858.3
self-control 624.5
stability 142.1
verticalness 213.1
**apocalypse**
disclosure 556.1
prediction 543.1
revelation 1021.9
**Apocalypse** 1021.4
**apocalyptic(al)**
disclosive 556.10
ominous 544.17
predictive 543.11
scriptural 1021.10
**apocryphal**
spurious 616.26
unauthoritative
514.20
unorthodox 1025.9
**apogee**
astronomy 375.16
climax 56.5
distance 199.2
spacecraft 282.2
summit 211.2
**Apollo**
beautiful man 900.9
god 1014.5
Muse 609.12
music patron 464.22
spacecraft 282.14
sun god 375.14
**apologetic(al)**
atoning 1012.7
justifying 1006.13
penitent 873.9
**apologetics**
argumentation 482.4
theology 1023.1
**apologia**
argumentation 482.4
justification 1006.3

**apologist**
advocate 1006.8
arguer 482.12
defender 799.7
supporter 787.9
**apologize**
beg pardon 1012.5
excuse 1006.11
repent 873.7
**apology**
argumentation 482.4
excuse 1012.2
justification 1006.3
penitence 873.4
pretext 649.1
regret 873.1
**apoplexy**
cardiovascular disease
686.17
paralysis 686.25
paroxysm 162.5
seizure 686.5
stroke 324.6
**apostasy** change 139.1
conversion 145.3
defection 628.2
desertion 633.2
dissent 522.1
impiety 1030.1
religion 1020.9
**apostate**
*n.* defector 145.8
dissenter 522.3
impious person
1030.3
turncoat 628.5
*adj.* impious 1030.6
recreant 628.11
treasonable 145.20
**apostatize**
convert 145.13
defect 628.8
desert 633.6
**apostle** converter 145.9
disciple 566.2
Mormon priest
1038.11
religious founder
1022.2
**apostolic(al)**
papal 1037.15
scriptural 1021.10
**apostrophize** 594.27
**apothecary**
pharmacist 687.35
store 832.4
**apothegm** maxim 517.1
witticism 881.7
**apotheosis**
exaltation 317.1
glorification 914.8
ideal 25.4
idolization 1033.2
praise 968.5
removal to heaven
1018.12
respect 964.1
**appall** dismay 891.27
offend 864.11
terrify 891.25
**appalling**
disagreeable 864.19

remarkable 34.10
terrifying 891.38
**appanage** adjunct 41.1
endowment 818.9
property 810.2
**apparatus**
belongings 810.3
chemical 379.13
equipment 659.4
tool 348.1
**apparel** 231.1
**apparent**
appearing 446.11
false 616.27
illusory 519.9
manifest 555.8
probable 511.7
superficial 224.6
visible 444.6
**apparently**
externally 224.9
falsely 616.35
manifestly 555.14
seemingly 446.12
visibly 444.8
**apparition**
appearance 446.5
emergence 446.1
phantom 519.4
specter 1017.1
thing imagined 535.5
**appeal**
*n.* allurement 650.1
desirability 634.13
entreaty 774.2
legal action 1004.10
lovability 931.7
pleasantness 863.2
prayer 1032.4
*v.* attract 650.5
entreat 774.11
**appealing**
alluring 650.7
imploring 774.17
melodious 462.49
pleasant 863.7
**appeal to**
address 594.27
cite 505.15
demand 753.4
entreat 774.11
**appear** act 611.34
appear to be 446.10
attend 186.8
become visible 446.8
be revealed 556.8
be visible 444.4
manifest oneself
555.6
occur 151.6
**appearance**
apparition 446.5
appearing 446
arrival 300.1
exteriority 224.1
façade 446.2
fakery 616.3
form 246.3
illusoriness 519.2
manifestation 555.1
phantom 519.4
specter 1017.1

**appear for** 781.14
**appease** calm 163.7
gratify 865.6
pacify 804.7
relieve 886.5
worship 1032.14
**appeasement**
foreign policy 744.5
pacification 804.1
relief 886.1
worship 1032.6
**appellation** name 583.3
naming 583.2
**append** add 40.4
place after 65.3
**appendage**
adjunct 41.1
attendant 73.3
belongings 810.2
follower 293.2
hanger-on 907.5
nonessential 6.2
part 55.4
**appendectomy** 689.23
**appendicitis** 686.9
**appendix** addition 41.2
intestine 225.4
sequel 67.1
**appertaining**
relative 9.7
relevant 9.11
**appertain to**
belong to 808.7
relate to 9.5
**appetite** craving 634.6
eagerness 635.1
eating 307.1
sensuality 987.1
stomach 634.7
will 621.1
**appetizer** 308.9
**appetizing**
alluring 650.7
desirable 634.30
mouth-watering
428.10
**applaud** acclaim 968.10
assent 521.8
cheer 876.6
**applause** acclaim 968.2
cheer 876.2
**apple of one's eye**
931.15
**apple-polisher** 907.3
**apple-polishing** 907.2
**appliance**
equipment 659.4
facility 785.9
hard goods 831.4
instrument 658.3
machinery 348.4
use 665.1
**applicable** apt 26.10
legal 998.10
relevant 9.11
usable 665.22
**applicant** 774.7
**application**
attribution 155.1
engrossment 530.3
giving 963.2
industry 707.6

medical dressing
687.33
perseverance 625.1
relevance 9.4
request 774.1
study 564.3
use 665.1
**appliqué**
*n.* cover 228.4
*v.* sew 223.5
**apply** administer 963.6
attribute 155.3
cover 228.19
petition 774.10
put to use 665.11
relate 9.6
request 774.9
**apply oneself**
endeavor 714.4
exert oneself 716.9
**apply oneself to**
attend to 530.5
busy oneself with
656.11
practice 705.7
study 564.12
think about 478.11
undertake 715.3
**appoint** allot 816.9
assign 780.10
choose 637.20
destine 640.7
equip 659.8
prescribe 752.10
**appointee** 780.8
**appointment**
accession to power
739.12
allotment 816.3
assignment 780.2
consecration 1037.10
decree 752.4
engagement 922.8
hiring 780.4
position 656.5
selection 637.9
**appointments**
belongings 810.2
equipment 659.4
**apportion** allot 816.6
distribute 60.9
portion 49.18
quantify 28.4
share 815.6
**apposite** apt 26.10
relevant 9.11
**apposition** 200.3
**appraisal** analysis 48.3
judgment 494.3
measurement 490.1
valuation 846.4
**appraise** analyze 48.8
judge 494.9
measure 490.11
price 846.13
**appraiser** 490.10
**appreciable**
knowable 475.25
measurable 490.15
substantial 3.6
weighable 352.19

**appreciably**
measurably 490.16
to a degree 35.10
**appreciate**
be grateful 949.3
enjoy 865.10
increase 38.6
judge 494.9
know 475.12
measure 490.11
rate highly 672.12
respect 964.4
savor 428.5
understand 548.7
**appreciation**
acknowledgment 521.3
cognizance 475.2
commendation 968.3
discrimination 492.1
gratitude 949.1
increase 38.1
judgment 494.3
respect 964.1
**appreciative**
approbatory 968.16
cognizant of 475.16
discriminating 492.7
grateful 949.5
**apprehend**
arrest 761.15
capture 822.18
fear 891.18
have foreboding 544.11
know 475.12
sense 422.8
understand 548.7
**apprehension**
anxiety 890.1
arrest 761.6
doubt 503.2
expectancy 539.3
fearfulness 891.4
foreboding 544.2
idea 479.1
intelligence 467.1
seizure 822.2
understanding 475.3
**apprehensive**
anxious 890.6
fearful 891.32
in suspense 539.12
knowing 475.15
nervous 859.10
**apprentice**
*n.* artisan 718.6
novice 566.9
producer 167.8
trainee 68.2
*v.* indenture 780.17
train 562.14
*adj.* indentured 780.20
**apprenticed** 780.20
**apprenticeship**
indenture 780.7
training 562.3
**apprise** 557.8
**apprised of** 475.16
**approach**
*n.* arrival 300.1

attempt 714.2
coming 296
convergence 298.1
entrance 302.5
imminence 152.1
landing 278.18
nearness 200.1
offer 773.1
plan 654.1
similarity 20.1
way 657.1
*v.* accost 296.3
address 594.27
appear 151.6
arrive 300.6
attempt 714.5
befriend 927.11
be imminent 152.2
be in the future 121.6
be near 200.8
bribe 651.3
communicate with 554.8
converge 298.2
influence 172.9
make advances 773.7
near 200.7
resemble 20.7
**approachable**
accessible 296.5
bribable 651.4
communicative 554.10
possible 509.8
**approaching**
arriving 300.9
converging 298.3
future 121.8
imminent 152.3
near 200.14
nearing 296.4
**approbation**
approval 968.1
consent 775.1
esteem 914.3
ratification 521.4
respect 964.1
**appropriate** allot 816.9
borrow 821.4
digest 309.16
plagiarize 824.18
steal 824.13
take 822.19
usurp 961.8
**appropriate** apt 26.10
characteristic 80.13
decorous 897.10
due 960.8
expedient 670.5
relevant 9.11
right 958.8
timely 129.9
useful 665.18
well-chosen 589.7
**appropriation**
allotment 816.3
borrowing 821.2
plagiarism 824.7
taking over 822.4
theft 824.1
usurpation 961.3

**approval**
approbation 968
consent 775.1
esteem 914.3
ratification 521.4
respect 964.1
**approve** accept 968.9
adopt 637.15
consent 775.2
evidence 505.9
ratify 521.12
**approved**
accepted 968.19
acknowledged 521.14
authoritative 513.18
chosen 637.26
conventional 645.5
orthodox 1024.7
received 819.10
**approximate**
*v.* approach 296.3
be near 200.8
resemble 20.7
similarize 20.8
*adj.* approaching 296.4
inaccurate 518.17
near 200.14
relative 9.8
similar 20.14
**approximately**
nearly 200.23
some 28.6
virtually 54.14
**approximation**
approach 296.1
inaccuracy 518.2
mathematics 87.4
measurement 490.1
nearness 200.1
relationship 9.1
similarity 20.1
**appurtenance**
adjunct 41.1
component 58.2
facility 785.9
nonessential 6.2
privilege 958.3
**appurtenances**
belongings 810.2
equipment 659.4
**a priori** back 119.12
dialectic(al) 482.22
**apron** runway 278.23
stage 611.21
clothing 231.17
**apropos**
*adj.* apt 26.10
relevant 9.11
*adv.* incidentally 129.13
**apse** arch 252.4
church part 1042.9
**apt** apposite 26.10
inclined 525.8
intelligent 467.14
probable 511.6
prompt 131.9
skillful 733.20
teachable 564.18
well-chosen 589.7
**aptitude** fitness 26.5

intelligence 467.2
likelihood 175.1
probability 511.1
talent 733.5
teachability 564.5
tendency 174.1
trait of character 525.3
**aptitude test** 690.11
**apt to**
inclined to 174.6
liable to 175.5
**Aqua-Lung**
breathing 403.18
diving equipment 320.5
**aquarium** abode 191.24
collection 74.11
**aquatic**
water-dwelling 275.58
watery 392.16
**aquatint**
engraving process 578.3
print 578.6
**aqueduct** trench 263.2
watercourse 396.2
**aqueous** 392.16
**aquiculture**
botany 412.1
oceanography 397.6
**aquiline** avian 414.52
curved 252.8
**Arab** nomad 274.4
waif 274.3
**arabesque** music 463.18
network 221.3
ornateness 901.2,13
**Arabic numerals** 86.2
**arable** 413.20
**arbiter** arbitrator 805.4
connoisseur 897.7
judge 1002.1
**arbitrarily**
capriciously 629.7
imperiously 739.19
**arbitrary**
capricious 629.5
discretionary 622.7
imperious 739.16
impulsive 630.10
**arbitrate** judge 494.12
mediate 805.6
**arbitration**
judgment 494.1
mediation 805.2
**arbitrator**
go-between 781.4
judge 1002.1
mediator 805.4
**arbor** axis 322.5
summerhouse 191.13
**arboreal**
branched 299.10
treelike 411.36
**arboretum**
garden 413.10
woodland 411.11
**arc** curve 252.2
electric discharge 342.6

theater lighting
611.23
**arcade** arch 252.4
colonnade 217.5
corridor 192.18
passageway 657.4
**Arcadian**
idealized 535.23
natural 736.6
rustic 182.6
**arcane**
recondite 549.16
secret 614.11
supernatural 85.15
**arch**
*n.* curve 252.4
foot 212.5
memorial 570.12
types of 252.21
*v.* cover 228.30
curve 252.6
*adj.* chief 36.14
cunning 735.12
mischievous 738.6
**archae(o)–**
antiquity 119.3
old 123.10
past 119.7
**archaeological** 123.20
**archaeologist** 123.5,23
**archaeology** 123.4,22
**archaic**
antiquated 123.13
disused 668.10
**archaism**
antiquarianism 123.4
antique 123.6
word 582.13
**archangel** angel 1015.1
celestial being 1015.3
**archbishop** 1038.9
**archbishopric**
church office 1037.5
diocese 1037.8
district 180.5
mastership 739.7
**arched** bowed 252.10
convex 256.12
**archer** athlete 878.20
shooter 285.9
**archery** ballistics 801.3
throwing 285.3
**archetype**
engram 690.36
form 246.1
idea 479.2
instinct 481.2
original 23.2
pattern of perfection
677.4
type 25.1
**archetypic(al)**
model 25.9
perfect 677.9
**archipelago** 386.2
**architect** artist 579.10
doer 718.1
planner 654.7
producer 167.8
**architectural**
constructional 167.18
structural 245.9

**architectural
ornamentation**
901.14
**architectural topping**
211.17
**architecture** art 574.4
building 245.2
manufacture 167.3
story element 608.9
structure 245.1
styles of 574.25
**archives** preserve 701.6
public records 570.2
registry 570.3
storage place 660.6
**archivist** 571.1
**archway** arch 252.4
entrance 302.6
**arctic** cold 333.14
northern 290.15
unfeeling 856.9
winter 128.8
**ardent** alcoholic 996.36
amorous 931.24
burning 328.27
cordial 927.15
fanatic 162.21
fervent 855.23
hot 328.25
industrious 707.22
vehement 600.13
willing 622.5
zealous 635.10
**ardor** animation 161.3
desire 634.1
fervor 855.10
heat 328.2
industry 707.6
love 931.1
vehemence 600.5
willingness 622.1
zeal 635.2
**arduous**
difficult 731.16
laborious 716.18
**area** location 184.1
region 180.1
science 475.10
size 195.1
space 179.1
specialty 81.1
sphere of work 656.4
study 562.8
**area measure** 490.18
**areaway** 192.18
**arena** enclosure 236.3
hall 192.4
region 180.2
scene of action 802
science 475.10
setting 233.2
**areola** 253.2
**Ares** god 1014.5
war god 797.17
**argosy** fleet 277.10
navy 800.26
ship 277.1,22
**argot** jargon 580.9
unintelligibility 549.7
**arguable** 514.16
**argue** contend 523.4
dispute 482.16

evidence 505.9
indicate 568.17
mean 545.8
**argument**
argumentation 482.4
case 482.5
contention 796.1
justification 1006.2
legal argument
1004.8
legal plea 1004.6
mathematics 86.9
quarrel 795.5
story element 608.9
**argumentative**
contentious 951.26
controversial 482.19
**aria** melody 462.4
solo 462.14
**arid** barren 166.4
dry 393.7
unimaginative 536.5
uninteresting 883.6
**Ariel** 1014.18
**arise** appear 446.8
ascend 315.8
begin 68.13
emerge 303.12
occur 151.6
result from 154.6
revolt 767.7
stand 213.8
wake up 713.6
**aristocracy**
gentility 918.1
government 741.4
mastership 739.7
peerage 918.2
superiors 36.5
**aristocrat** 918.4
**aristocratic(al)**
arrogant 912.11
dignified 905.12
governmental 741.17
imperious 739.16
noble 918.10
**arithmetic** 87.18
**arithmetic(al)**
mathematical 87.17
numerical 86.8
**ark** 1040.11
**arm**
*n.* affiliate 788.10
bay 399.1
limb 287.5
military unit 800.21
part 55.4
supporter 216.2
*v.* empower 157.10
equip 659.8
fortify 799.9
protect 699.18
**armada** 800.26
**armadillo** 414.58; 415.8
**Armageddon** 797.3
**armament** arms 801.1
equipment 659.4
provision 659.1
**armchair** 499.13
**armed**
embattled 797.27
in arms 799.14

prepared 720.16
protected 699.21
provided 659.13
**armed force** 800.22
**arm in arm**
amicably 927.21
near 200.14
sociably 922.21
together 73.10
**armistice** 804.5
**armor** callousness 856.3
defense 799.3,17
shell 228.15
**armored**
covered 228.31
defended 799.13
**armory** arsenal 801.2
heraldic insignia
569.2
insignia 569.1
plant 719.3
storage place 660.6
**arms**
heraldic insignia
569.2
warcraft 797.10
weapons 801
**arms race** 797.14
**army**
armed force 800.22
flock 74.5
large number 101.3
military unit 800.19
throng 74.4
**aroma**
characteristic 80.4
fragrance 436.1
odor 435.1
**aromatic** fragrant 436.9
odorous 435.9
**around**
*adv.* in every direction
290.27
in the vicinity 233.12
near 200.20
round 322.16
*prep.* near 200.26
through 290.29
**arousal**
awakening 713.2
elicitation 305.5
excitement 857.1
incitement 648.4
stimulation 857.10
**arouse** alarm 704.3
awaken 713.5
elicit 305.14
energize 161.9
excite 857.11
incite 648.17
induce 648.19
make hot 329.18
provoke 952.22
**aroused** alarmed 704.4
excited 857.18
**arousing**
*n.* excitation 857.10
*adj.* aphrodisiac
419.28
elicitory 305.17
**arpeggio** 463.17
**arraign** accuse 1005.7

censure 969.13
indict 1004.14
**arraignment**
accusation 1005.1
disapproval 969.3
indictment 1004.3
**arrange** classify 61.6
contract 771.9
mediate 805.7
music 462.47
order 60.8
organize 59.4
plan 654.9
prepare 720.6
**arranged**
contracted 771.12
orderly 59.6
placed 60.14
planned 654.13
**arrangement**
appointment 922.8
artistry 574.10
classification 61.1
compact 771.1
composition 462.5
compromise 807.1
conclusion 771.4
deed 771.3
harmonization 463.2
music form 463.11
ordering 60
organization 59.1
ornamentation 901.1
plan 654.1
preparation 720.1
reconciliation 804.4
score 462.28
structure 245.1
**arrant** bad 675.9
conspicuous 555.12
evil 981.16
outright 34.12
paltry 915.12
**array**
*n.* army 800.22
arrangement 60.1
clothing 231.1
order 59.1
row 71.2
*v.* align 71.5
arrange evidence 505.13
clothe 231.38
distribute 60.9
order 59.4
ornament 901.8
**arrayed** arranged 60.14
clothed 231.44
embattled 797.27
**arrearage** debt 840.2
deficiency 57.2
shortcoming 314.1
**arrears** debt 840.2
shortcoming 314.1
**arrest**
*n.* confinement 761.6
curb 730.7
disease 686.5
hindrance 730.1
restraint 760.1
seizure 822.2
slowing 270.4

stop 144.2
*v.* capture 822.18
delay 132.8
engross 530.13
hinder 730.10
restrain 760.7
slow 270.9
stop 144.11
take prisoner 761.15
**arrested**
engrossed 530.18
incomplete 57.4
late 132.16
mentally deficient 469.22
restrained 760.13
retarded 270.12
undeveloped 721.12
**arrested development**
mental deficiency 469.9
psychological fixation 690.28
**arrival** coming 300
incomer 302.4
landing 278.18
**arrive** make good 724.9
reach 300.6
**arrive at**
hit upon 300.7
reach 300.6
**arrivederci!** 301.23
**arriviste** modern 122.4
newcomer 78.4
vulgar person 898.6
**arrogance**
contempt 966.1
defiance 793.1
haughtiness 912
insolence 913.1
pride 905.1
sureness 513.5
vanity 909.2
**arrogant**
contemptuous 966.8
defiant 793.7
haughty 912.9
imperious 739.16
insolent 913.8
proud 905.9
sure 513.21
vain 909.9
**arrogate**
appropriate 822.19
take command 739.14
usurp 961.8
**arrogation**
accession to power 739.12
appropriation 822.4
attribution 155.1
usurpation 961.3
**arrow** missile 801.16
pointer 568.4
speed 269.6
**arsenal** armory 801.2
plant 719.3
storage place 660.6
**arsenic** 676.6
**arson** 329.7
**arsonist** destroyer 693.8

incendiary 329.8
**arsy-varsy**
*adj.* confused 62.16
reversed 220.7
*adv.* contrarily 15.9
**art** cunning 735.1
fine arts 574
knack 733.6
representation 572.1
schools and movements 574.23
science 475.10
skill 733.7
stratagem 735.3
styles of 574.24
talent 574.8
vocation 656.6
**arterial**
*n.* road 657.6
*adj.* vascular 396.21
**arteriosclerosis**
cardiovascular disease 686.17
hardening 356.5
**artery**
blood vessel 396.14
passageway 657.4
road 657.6
**artful** cunning 735.12
deceitful 618.20
falsehearted 616.31
insincere 975.18
shrewd 467.15
**Artful Dodger**
cunning person 735.6
deceiver 619.1
**artfulness**
cunning 735.1
deceit 618.3
insincerity 975.3
preciosity 589.3
shrewdness 467.3
skill 733.1
**arthritic**
*n.* sick person 686.40
*adj.* diseased 686.57
**arthritis** 686.9
**article**
*n.* book part 605.13
commodity 831.2
individual 89.4
news 558.3
particular 8.3
part of speech 586.6
part of writing 55.2
thing 376.4
treatise 606.1
written matter 602.10
*v.* accuse 1005.7
indenture 780.17
**articulate**
*v.* fasten 47.8
join 47.5
say 594.23
*adj.* audible 450.16
eloquent 600.8
intelligible 548.9
jointed 47.17
speaking 594.32
**articulation**
continuity 71.2
joining 47.1

joint 47.4
phonation 594.6
speech sound 594.13
word 582.1
**artifact** antiquity 123.6
object 376.4
product 168.1
**artifice** chicanery 618.4
cunning 735.1
expedient 670.2
falseheartedness 616.4
intrigue 654.6
preciosity 589.3
stratagem 735.3
trick 618.6
**artificial**
affected 903.15
elegant 589.9
ungenuine 616.26
**artillery** ballistics 801.3
cannon 801.6
**artilleryman**
shooter 285.9
soldier 800.10
**artisan** artist 579.1
craftsman 718.6
expert 733.11
mechanic 348.9
**artist** artisan 718.6
creator 579.1,12
entertainer 612.1
expert 733.11
musician 464.1
producer 167.8
**artistic**
painterly 574.21
skillful 733.20
tasteful 897.8
**artistry** skill 733.1
talent 574.8
writing 602.2
**artless** candid 974.17
foolable 470.11
ingenuous 736.5
undeveloped 721.13
unskillful 734.15
**artlessness**
authenticity 516.5
candor 974.4
ingenuousness 736
original condition 721.3
**art song** 462.13
**artsy-craftsy** 574.21
**art work** 574.11
**arty** 574.21
**as**
*adv.* equally 30.11
for instance 505.24
in the same way as 657.11
*conj.* because 155.10
**as a rule**
generally 79.17
normally 84.9
**asbestos**
fireproofing 332.5
scenery 611.25
**ascend** be high 207.15
fly 278.48
incline 219.10

levitate 353.9
move 267.5
rise 315.8
**ascendancy**
dominance 739.6
influence 172.1
superiority 36.1
victory 726.1
**ascendant**
ascending 315.14
authoritative 739.15
dominant 741.18
influential 172.14
superior 36.12
victorious 726.8
**ascending**
flowing 267.8
high 207.19
rising 315.14
sloping upward
219.17
**ascension** ascent 315.1
removal to heaven
1018.12
**ascent** acclivity 219.6
course 267.2
exaltation 317.1
improvement 691.1
increase 38.1
lightness 353.1
rise 315
**ascertain** decide 494.11
learn 564.6
make sure 513.11
prove 505.11
**ascertained**
known 475.26
made sure 513.20
proved 505.21
true 516.12
**ascetic**
*n.* abstainer 992.4
puritan 991.2
recluse 924.5
religious 1038.17
*adj.* abstinent 992.10
atoning 1012.7
austere 991.3
in plain style 591.3
meager 662.10
**asceticism**
abstinence 992.2
austerity 991
penance 1012.3
**ascorbic acid** 309.4
**ascribable**
attributable 155.6
due 960.10
**ascribe** 155.3
**aseptic** 681.27
**asexual** 419.31
**as far as** to 199.20
when 105.16
**ash** cinders 329.16
residue 43.2
**ashamed**
humiliated 906.13
regretful 873.8
**ashen** burned 329.30
colorless 363.7
gray 366.4
terrified 891.34

**ashes** cinders 329.16
corpse 408.16
**ashore** 385.11
**ashram**
commune 788.2
retreat 700.5
**Ash Wednesday**
1040.15
**aside**
*n.* interjection 237.2
soliloquy 598.1
*adv.* apart 199.17
in an undertone
452.22
in reserve 660.17
on one side 242.10
privately 614.19
sideways 242.8
**aside from**
excluding 77.9
separately 49.28
**as if** 499.19
**asinine** foolish 470.8
stupid 469.15
trivial 673.16
ungulate 414.49
**as is** as usual 140.10
identically 14.9
present 120.2
**as it were**
figuratively 551.4
so to speak 20.19
supposedly 499.17
**ask** charge 846.14
demand 753.4
inquire 485.19
invite 774.13
request 774.9
require 639.9
**askance** askew 219.22
disapprovingly 969.27
sideways 242.8
**askew**
*adj.* asymmetric
249.10
disorderly 62.13
erroneous 518.16
oblique 219.14
*adv.* awry 219.22
**ask for** demand 753.4
encourage 648.21
request 774.9
seek 485.29
**ask for it** 894.5
**asking price** offer 773.1
price 846.2
stock price 834.9
**asleep** dead 408.30
inattentive 531.8
insensible 423.6
sleeping 712.22
unaware 477.13
unconscious 423.8
**as long as**
provided 507.15
when 105.16
**as one** coactively 177.5
cooperatively 786.6
jointly 47.18
simultaneously 118.6
unanimously 521.17
**aspect** astrology 375.20

**component** 58.2
grammatical form
586.13
look 446.3
particular 8.3
position 184.3
**aspen** 324.17
**asperity**
bitterness 952.3
causticity 939.8
ill humor 951.1
pungency 433.1
roughness 261.1
**aspersion**
baptism 1040.7
disapproval 969.4
indignity 965.2
rite 1040.4
slur 971.4
**asphalt**
covering material
228.43
mineral 383.19
pavement 657.7
**asphyxiate** die 408.24
strangle 409.19
suppress 760.8
**asphyxiation**
disease symptom
686.8
suffocation 409.7
violent death 408.6
**aspic** meat 308.12
salad 308.36
**aspirant** desirer 634.12
optimist 888.6
petitioner 774.7
political candidate
746.9
**aspirate** suck 306.12
whisper 452.10
**aspiration**
ambition 634.9
breathing 403.18
extraction 305.3
hope 888.1
inhalation 306.5
intention 653.1
motive 648.1
murmur 452.4
speech sound 594.13
**aspire** aim at 653.4
be ambitious 634.20
be hopeful 888.7
crave 634.18
soar 315.10
**aspirin** analgesic 687.56
antipyretic 687.64
**aspiring**
ambitious 634.28
high 207.19
hopeful 888.11
**ass**
beast of burden
271.6
buttocks 241.5
copulation 419.8
donkey 414.20
fool 471.1
obstinate person
626.6
sex object 419.4

**assail** attack 798.15
criticize severely
969.21
incriminate 1005.10
**assailant**
attacker 798.13
opponent 791.1
**assassin**
frightener 891.8
killer 409.11
**assassinate** 409.16
**assassination** 409.2
**assault**
*n.* accusation 1005.2
attack 798.1
berating 969.7
violence 162.3
*v.* attack 798.15
terrorize 162.10
thrust 283.11
**assay**
*n.* analysis 48.1
attempt 714.2
test 489.2
*v.* analyze 48.6
attempt 714.5
measure 490.11
try out 489.8
**ass-backwards**
*adj.* bungled 734.22
confused 62.16
*adv.* backwards 295.13
clumsily 734.24
**assemblage** all 54.3
assembling 74.14
association 788.1
collection 74
composition 58.1
hodgepodge 44.6
**assemble** collect 811.10
come together 74.16
compose 58.3
create 167.10
gather 74.18
join 47.5
sculpture 575.5
**assembled**
collected 74.21
joined 47.13
made 167.22
**assembly** bunch 74.14
collection 74.1
composition 58.1
council 755.1
laity 1039.1
legislature 742.1
manufacture 167.3
meeting 74.2
**assembly line**
assembling 74.14
plant 719.3
production 167.2
**assemblyman** 746.3
**assent**
*n.* acquiescence 521
agreement 26.1
consent 775.1
submission 765.1
*v.* acquiesce 521.8
agree 26.6
consent 775.2
submit to 765.6

**assenting**
acquiescing 521.13
consenting 775.4
submissive 765.12
**assert** affirm 523.4
defend 1006.10
express belief 501.12
insist 753.7
postulate 499.12
state 594.24
**assertion**
affirmation 523.1
premise 482.7
remark 594.4
testimony 505.3
**assertive** 523.7
**assert oneself** 555.6
**assess** analyze 48.8
charge 846.14
judge 494.9
measure 490.11
price 846.13
**assessed**
measured 490.14
priced 846.16
**assessment**
analysis 48.3
fee 841.5
judgment 494.3
measurement 490.1
stock assessment
834.8
tax 846.10
valuation 846.4
**assessor** judge 1002.4
measurer 490.10
taxer 846.12
**assets** accounts 845.1
funds 835.14
property 810.8
resources 660.2
wealth 837.1
**asseverate** affirm 523.4
express belief 501.12
state 594.24
testify 505.10
**asshole** anus 265.6
fool 471.2
**assiduity**
attention 530.1
industry 707.6
painstakingness 533.2
perseverance 625.1
**assiduous**
attentive 530.15
industrious 707.22
painstaking 533.11
persevering 625.7
**assign** allot 816.9
appoint 780.10
assign lessons 562.18
attribute 155.3
commission 780.9
commit 818.16
locate 184.10
specify 80.11
transfer 271.9
transfer property
817.3
**assignation**
attribution 155.1
meeting 74.2

property transfer
817.1
rendezvous 922.9
**assignee**
appointee 780.8
beneficiary 819.4
**assignment**
accession to power
739.12
allotment 816.3
appointment 780.2
attribution 155.1
commission 780.1
commitment 818.2
lesson 562.7
placement 184.5
property transfer
817.1
specification 80.6
task 656.2
**assimilate**
combine 52.3
compare 491.4
conform 82.3
consume 666.2
convert 145.11
digest 309.16
include 76.3
learn 564.7
make agree 26.7
make uniform 17.4
naturalize 189.4
similarize 20.8
sorb 306.13
understand 548.7
**assimilated**
combined 52.5
converted 145.19
naturalized 189.6
phonetic 594.31
**assimilation**
adjustment 26.4
combination 52.1
consumption 666.1
conversion 145.1
digestion 309.8
inclusion 76.1
learning 564.2
metabolism 309.10
naturalization 189.3
similarity 20.1
sorption 306.6
speech sound 594.13
**assist**
*n.* helping hand 785.2
*v.* aid 785.11
be instrumental
658.5
subsidize 818.19
**assistance** aid 785.1
remedy 687.1
subsidy 818.8
**assistant**
academic rank 565.4
helper 785.7
partner 787.6
retainer 750.3
subordinate 764.5
**assizes** 1001.3
**ass-kisser** 907.3

**associate**
*n.* academic rank
565.4
companion 928.3
confederate 787
likeness 20.3
member 788.11
*v.* accompany 73.7
affiliate 788.14
be friends 927.9
be sociable 922.16
concur 177.2
cooperate 786.3
join 47.5
league 52.4
relate 9.6
**associated**
accompanying 73.9
communal 815.9
concurrent 177.4
corporate 788.16
joined 47.13
leagued 52.6
related 9.9
**association**
affiliation 786.2
combination 52.1
company 73.2
concurrence 177.1
council 755.1
participation 815.1
psychology 690.40
relationship 9.1
sociability 922.6
social grouping 922.5
society 788
thoughts 478.4
**assonance**
repetitiousness 103.4
rhyme 609.10
similar sound 20.6
**assonant**
harmonious 462.50
repetitious 103.15
rhyming 609.19
similar sounding
20.17
**assort** arrange 60.11
classify 61.6
**assorted** arranged 60.14
classified 61.8
different 16.7
diversified 19.4
**assortment**
grouping 60.3
hodgepodge 44.6
miscellany 74.13
**assuage** gratify 865.6
moderate 163.6
qualify 507.3
relieve 886.5
**assuasive**
palliative 163.16
qualifying 507.7
relieving 886.9
remedial 687.40
**assume**
appropriate 822.19
believe 501.11
borrow 821.4
don 231.42
entail 76.4

fake 616.21
imitate 22.5
imply 546.4
put on airs 903.12
receive 819.6
suppose 499.10
take command
739.14
take the liberty 961.6
undertake 715.3
usurp 961.8
**assumed**
falsified 616.26
implied 546.7
put-on 903.16
supposed 499.14
undertaken 715.7
**assumed name** 583.8
**assuming that** 499.19
**assumption**
accession to power
739.12
appropriation 822.4
belief 501.6
borrowing 821.2
conversion 145.1
entailment 76.2
exaltation 317.1
hope 888.1
implication 546.2
premise 482.7
presumption 961.2
presumptuousness
912.2
receiving 819.1
removal to heaven
1018.12
supposition 499.3
usurpation 961.3
**assurance** belief 501.1
certainty 513.1
comfort 887.4
confidence 513.5
encouragement 893.9
equanimity 858.3
hope 888.1
insolence 913.1
insurance 699.4
making certain 513.8
oath 523.3
promise 770.1
safety 698.1
security 772.1
**assure** affirm 523.5
comfort 887.6
convince 501.18
encourage 893.16
give hope 888.10
guarantee 772.9
make sure 513.11
promise 770.4
**assured**
believing 501.21
composed 858.13
guaranteed 772.11
hopeful 888.11
made sure 513.20
promised 770.8
sure 513.21
**assuredly**
*adv.* certainly 513.23
positively 34.19

*interj.* yes 521.18
**Astarte**
　beautiful woman
　　900.9
　fertility goddess
　　165.5
　love goddess 931.8
　moon goddess 375.12
**astern** aft 275.69
　behind 241.14
　in reverse 295.13
**asteroid** planet 375.9
　space hazard 282.10
**as the crow flies** 290.24
**asthma**
　allergic disorder
　　686.32
　disease symptom
　　686.8
　respiratory disease
　　686.14
**asthmatic** 403.29
**as though** 499.19
**astigmatism** 440.1
**astir**
　*adj.* stirring 707.19
　*adv.* in motion 267.9
　preparation 720.23
**astonish** amaze 920.6
　surprise 540.7
**astonishing**
　amazing 920.12
　remarkable 34.10
　startling 540.11
**astound** astonish 920.6
　dismay 891.27
**astounded**
　astonished 920.9
　terrified 891.34
**astounding**
　astonishing 920.12
　terrible 891.38
**astral**
　*n.* astral body 1034.17
　specter 1017.1
　*adj.* celestial 375.25
　ghostly 1017.7
　immaterial 377.7
**astray**
　*adj.* bewildered
　　514.23
　erroneous 518.16
　*adv.* afield 199.19
　amiss 314.7
　erroneously 518.20
**astride** 216.25
**astringency**
　acrimony 161.4
　constriction 198.1
　pungency 433.1
　strictness 757.1
　unkindness 939.9
　unpleasant taste
　　429.2
**stringent**
　*n.* contractor 198.6
　*adj.* acrimonious
　　161.13
　bitter 429.6
　contractive 198.11
　penetrating 857.29
　pungent 433.6

strict 757.6
　unkind 939.22
**astro–** aster 406.5
　star 375.8
**astrogate** 282.12
**astrologer**
　astrology 375.23
　predictor 543.4
**astrology**
　divining 543.2,15
　fate 640.2
　horoscopy 375.20
**astronaut** aviator 279.1
　spaceman 282.8
　traveler 274.1
**astronautics**
　aviation 278.1
　space travel 282.1
**astronomic(al)**
　celestial 375.25
　huge 195.20
　immeasurable 34.7
**astronomy** 375.19
**astrophysical**
　celestial 375.25
　physical 325.3
**astrophysics**
　astronomy 375.19
　physics 325.1
**astute** cunning 735.12
　discriminating 492.8
　sagacious 467.16
**asunder**
　*adj.* distant 199.8
　separate 49.20
　*adv.* in half 92.8
　separately 49.28
**as usual** as is 140.10
　normally 84.9
**as well**
　additionally 40.11
　equally 30.11
**asylum**
　hiding place 615.4
　home 700.4
　infirmary 689.27
　insane asylum 473.14
　refuge 700.1
**asymmetric(al)**
　distorted 249.10
　unequal 31.4
**asymmetry**
　distortion 249.1
　inconsistency 27.2
　inequality 31.1
**asymptote** 298.1
**at** by 184.26
　in 225.15
**at all** anyhow 657.12
　by any possibility
　　509.10
　of any kind 61.9
**at a loss**
　at an impasse 731.22
　perplexed 514.24
　unprofitably 812.9
**at any cost**
　by any possibility
　　509.10
　come what may
　　624.20
　in spite of 33.9

**at any rate**
　anyhow 657.12
　at least 35.10
　certainly 513.23
　notwithstanding 33.8
**atar** see **attar**
**ataraxy**
　detachment 856.4
　inexcitability 858.1
　quiescence 268.1
　unconcern 636.2
**at a standstill**
　as is 140.10
　at an impasse 731.22
　at a stand 706.7
　immovable 142.15
　inactive 708.16
　motionless 268.13
**atavism** memory 537.1
　oldness 123.1
　relapse 696.1
　reversion 146.2
**atavistic** innate 5.7
　primitive 123.11
　reversionary 146.7
**at bay** cornered 731.23
　defensively 799.16
**at cross-purposes**
　alienated 929.12
　at odds 795.16
　contrary 15.6
　disagreeing 27.6
　in opposition 790.9
　opposed to 790.10
**at ease**
　at one's ease 887.12
　at rest 711.11
　contented 868.7
**atelier** art 574.18
　studio 192.6
　workplace 719.1
**at fault**
　erroneous 518.16
　guilty 983.3
**at hand**
　convenient 200.15
　handy 665.19
　imminent 152.3
　near 200.20
　present 186.12
**atheism** impiety 1030.1
　nonreligiousness
　　1031.5
　unbelief 503.1
　unorthodoxy 1025.3
**atheist**
　impious person
　　1030.3
　unbeliever 1031.11
**atheistic**
　impious 1030.6
　unbelieving 1031.19
　unorthodox 1025.10
**Athena** goddess 1014.5
　war goddess 797.17
**atherosclerosis**
　cardiovascular disease
　　686.17
　hardening 356.5
**athlete** 878.20
**athlete's foot** 686.33

**athletic**
　sporting 878.32
　strong 159.14
**athletics** exercise 716.6
　sports 878.8
**at home**
　*n.* meeting 74.2
　social gathering
　　922.10
　*adj.* at ease 887.12
　*adv.* with one's family
　　188.16
**at home with**
　acquainted 927.16
　used to 642.18
　versed in 475.19
**athwart**
　*adj.* oblique 219.19
　transverse 221.9
　*adv.* crosswise 221.13
　in opposition 790.9
　obliquely 219.24
　*prep.* opposed to
　　790.10
**at issue**
　in opposition 790.9
　in question 485.38
　moot 514.16
　uncertain 514.17
**at large**
　at length 593.16
　escaped 632.11
　free 762.20
　generally 79.17
　scatteringly 75.12
　wholly 54.13
**atlas** map 654.4
　pillar 217.5
　reference book 605.6
**Atlas** giant 195.26
　rocket 281.15
　strong man 159.6
　supporter 216.3
**at last** discovery 488.11
　finally 70.11
**at length**
　at large 593.16
　finally 70.11
　fully 8.13
　lengthily 202.11
　lengthwise 202.12
**at liberty** free 762.20
　idle 708.17
**atman** life force 407.3
　psyche 466.4
　theosophy 1034.18
**atmosphere**
　aerosphere 402.2
　art 574.10
　gas 401.2
　milieu 233.3
　story element 608.9
**atmospheric** 402.12
**at most** 35.10
**at odds**
　alienated 929.12
　at variance 795.16
　different 16.7
　disagreeing 27.6
　dissenting 522.6
　in opposition 790.9
　unwilling 623.5

atoll 386.2
atom atomics 326.4
 chemical 379.1
 matter 376.2
 one 89.3
 particle 196.8
 small amount 35.2
 substance 3.2
 theoretic 326.22
 types of 326.21
 valent 326.23
atom bomb 801.15,30
atomic
 infinitesimal 196.14
 nuclear 326.18
 one 89.7
Atomic Age 107.9
atomic constants
 326.26
atomic energy 326.15
atomics 326
atomic scientist 326.3
atomic units 326.26
atomic weight
 chemistry 379.4
 system of weight
 352.8
atomism
 atomic theory 326.2
 materialism 376.5
 philosophy 500.11
atomization
 bombardment 326.8
 differentiation 16.4
 disintegration 53.1
 particularization 8.5
 pulverization 361.4
 vaporization 401.5
atomize atomics 326.17
 demolish 693.17
 differentiate 16.6
 disintegrate 53.3
 particularize 8.6
 pulverize 361.9
 shatter 49.13
 vaporize 401.8
atomizer
 scent article 436.6
 sprinkler 392.8
 vaporizer 401.6
atom-smashing 326.8
atonal 461.4
at once
 concurrently 47.18
 hastily 709.12
 instantly 113.8
 make haste! 709.16
 promptly 131.15
atone compensate 33.4
 harmonize 462.36
 make amends 1012.4
 make restitution
 823.5
 put in tune 462.37
 repay 841.11
at one agreeing 26.9
 in accord 794.3
 unanimous 521.15
atonement
 compensation 33.1
 recompense 841.3
 reparation 1012

restitution 823.2
 worship 1032.6
at one's disposal
 at one's command
 766.4
 handy 665.19
 owned 808.8
at one's fingertips
 handy 665.19
 near 200.20
at one's wit's end
 at an impasse 731.22
 perplexed 514.24
atony 160.1
at random
 haphazardly 62.18
 irregularly 138.4
 purposelessly 156.20
at rest at ease 711.11
 dead 408.30
 in the grave 410.23
 quiescent 268.12
 relaxed 887.12
atrocious bad 675.9
 base 915.12
 cruel 939.24
 disagreeable 864.19
 evil 981.16
 insulting 965.6
 painful 424.10
 savage 162.20
 wrong 959.3
atrociously
 badly 675.14
 basely 915.17
 cruelly 939.33
 savagely 162.26
atrocity
 brutal act 939.12
 crime 982.2
 evil 675.3
 indignity 965.2
 iniquity 981.3
 injustice 977.4
 mistreatment 667.2
 scandal 959.2
 unpleasantness 864.3
 violence 162.1
atrophy
 n. deterioration 692.4
 disease 686.1
 disease symptom
 686.8
 emaciation 205.6
 shrinking 198.3
 v. deteriorate 692.22
at sea
 bewildered 514.23
 on the high seas
 397.9
 under sail 275.63
attach add 40.4
 appropriate 822.20
 attribute 155.3
 fasten 47.7
attaché diplomat 781.6
 expert 733.11
attached to 931.28
attachment
 addition 40.1
 adjunct 41.1
 appropriation 822.5

attribution 155.1
 connection 47.3
 fidelity 974.7
 love 931.1
attack
 n. accusation 1005.2
 articulation 594.6
 assault 798
 berating 969.7
 disorderliness 162.3
 frenzy 473.7
 plan 654.1
 seizure 686.5
 spasm 324.6
 warfare 797.1
 way 657.1
 v. assault 798.15
 contend 796.15
 criticize severely
 969.21
 incriminate 1005.10
 make war on 797.19
 set to work 716.15
 terrorize 162.10
 undertake 715.3
 interj. advance!
 798.32
attacker 798.13
attain
 accomplish 722.4
 arrive 300.6
 be instated 780.12
attainable
 accessible 509.8
 approachable 296.5
 obtainable 811.13
 possible 509.7
attainment
 accomplishment
 722.1
 acquisition 811.1
 arrival 300.1
 learning 475.4
 skill 733.8
attar 436.2
attempt
 n. trial 714.2
 undertaking 715.1
 v. endeavor 714.5
 presume 961.6
 try to 714.7
 undertake 715.3
attend accompany 73.7
 be a spectator 442.5
 be at 186.8
 ensue 117.3
 escort 73.8
 heed 530.6
 help 785.18
 listen 448.11
 result 154.5
 serve 750.13
attendance
 following 73.6
 presence 186.4
 service 750.12
attendant
 n. accompanier 73.4
 assistant 787.6
 concomitant 73.3
 entourage 73.6
 follower 293.2

guardian 699.6
 hospital staff 688.14
 servant 750.5
 adj. accompanying
 73.9
 present 186.12
 serving 750.14
 subsequent 117.4
attending
 accompanying 73.9
 serving 750.14
attend to
 care for 699.19
 listen 448.11
 observe 768.2
 pay attention to
 530.5
 punish 1010.11
attention
 n. alertness 533.5
 audience 448.2
 carefulness 533.1
 courtesy 936.6
 hearing 448.1
 heed 530
 respects 964.3
 interj. hark! 448.17
 look! 530.22
attentive alert 533.14
 careful 533.10
 considerate 938.16
 courteous 936.14
 heedful 530.15
 listening 448.15
 meticulous 533.12
 respectful 964.8
attenuate dilute 160.11
 dissipate 75.5
 etherialize 4.4
 rarefy 355.3
 reduce 39.8
 shrink 198.9
 thin 205.12
 weaken 160.10
attenuated
 diluted 160.19
 reduced 39.10
 shrunk 198.13
 smooth 351.8
 thin 205.16
 thinned 355.4
 wasted 205.20
attest affirm 523.5
 confirm 505.12
 evidence 505.9
 guarantee 772.9
 testify 505.10
attestation
 certificate 570.6
 confirmation 505.5
 deposition 523.2
 statement 505.3
attested affirmed 523.8
 decided 513.20
 proved 505.21
 true 516.12
at the end of one's rope
 dying 408.33
 in trouble 731.24
 poor 838.7
 wanting 662.13

at the same time
  additionally 40.11
  at that time 105.9
  notwithstanding 33.8
  simultaneously 118.6
  till then 109.5
  when 105.16
attic garret 192.16
  storage place 660.6
Attic polished 589.6
  simple 902.6
  tasteful 897.8
  witty 881.15
attire
  n. clothing 231.1
  v. clothe 231.38
attitude belief 501.6
  mental attitude 525
  position 184.3
attitudinize 903.13
attorney deputy 781.1
  lawyer 1003.1
  manager 748.4
attract enamor 931.21
  interest 530.12
  lure 650.5
  pull 288.4
attracted
  approaching 296.4
  interested 530.16
attraction
  allurement 650.1
  desirability 634.13
  pull 288
  pulling 286.1
attractive
  alluring 650.7
  attracting 288.5
  beautiful 900.16
  desirable 634.30
  engrossing 530.20
  pleasant 863.7
attributable
  assignable 155.6
  due 960.10
  resulting from 154.8
attribute
  n. characteristic 80.4
  syntax 586.2
  v. ascribe to 155.4
  assign 155.3
attribution
  designation 80.6
  imputation 155
attrition abrasion 350.2
  consumption 666.1
  pulverization 361.4
  reduction 42.2
  regret 873.1
  waste 39.3
  weakening 160.5
attune
  harmonize 462.36
  make agree 26.7
  prepare 720.8
  put in tune 462.37
attuned
  in accord 794.3
  music 462.50
at variance
  alienated 929.12
  at odds 795.16

different 16.7
  disagreeing 27.6
  dissenting 522.6
  in opposition 790.9
at war at odds 795.16
  disagreeing 27.6
  in opposition 790.9
  up in arms 797.28
auburn
  reddish-brown 367.4
  redheaded 368.10
au courant 475.18
auction
  n. sale 829.4
  v. sell 829.11
auctioneer 830.8
audacious
  daring 893.21
  defiant 793.7
  foolhardy 894.9
  insolent 913.8
audacity courage 893.6
  defiance 793.1
  insolence 913.1
  recklessness 894.3
audible
  auditory 448.14
  hearable 450.16
audience
  attender 186.5
  audition 448.2
  conference 597.6
  listeners 448.6
  playgoer 611.32
  recipient 819.3
  spectator 442.2
audio 448.14
audio– hearing 448.1
  sound 450.1
audio devices 344.29
audio frequency
  radio frequency
    344.12
  tone 450.2
audio-visual 448.14
audit
  n. accounting 845.6
  v. check 87.14
  make certain 513.12
  take account of 845.9
audition
  examination 485.2
  hearing 448.2
  sense of hearing
    448.1
  tryout 489.3
auditor
  accountant 845.7
  financial officer
    836.11
  listener 448.5
  recipient 819.3
  student 566.1
  supervisor 748.2
auditorium arena 802.1
  hall 192.4
  schoolroom 567.16
  seating 611.20
  theater 611.18
auditory 448.14
auger drill 348.18
  sharpness 258.3

aught any 79.5
  nothing 2.2
  some 28.3
augment add to 40.5
  aggravate 885.2
  increase 38.4
  make larger 197.4
augur
  n. predictor 543.4
  v. hint 544.12
augur well 888.10
augury
  divining 543.2,15
  omen 544.3
august dignified 905.12
  eminent 34.9
  venerable 964.12
aunt 11.3
au pair girl 750.8
aura
  illustriousness 914.6
  light 335.14
  milieu 233.3
  occultism 1034.7
aural 448.14
aureole halo 253.2
  light 335.14
auricular
  auditory 448.14
  confidential 614.14
aurora dawn 133.3
  foredawn 133.4
  light 335.16
Aurora 133.2
ausgespielt
  ruined 693.28
  weakened 160.18
  worn-out 692.38
auspices
  patronage 785.4
  protectorship 699.2
  supervision 747.2
auspicious
  fortunate 728.14
  good 674.12
  of good omen 544.18
  promising 888.13
  timely 129.9
austere ascetic 991.3
  meager 662.10
  plain 902.9
  plainspoken 591.3
  simple 45.6
  strict 757.6
  unkind 939.22
austerity
  asceticism 991.1
  economy 851.1
  meagerness 662.2
  plainness 902.4
  plain speech 591.1
  strictness 757.1
  unkindness 939.9
autarchy
  absolutism 741.9
  government 741.4
  independence 762.5
auteur 611.28
authentic
  authoritative 513.18
  evidential 505.17
  honest 974.14

natural 516.14
  original 23.5
  orthodox 1024.7
  real 1.15
authenticate
  confirm 505.12
  ratify 521.12
authenticated
  proved 505.21
  ratified 521.14
  true 516.12
authenticity
  genuineness 516.5
  originality 23.1
  orthodoxy 1024.1
  reality 1.2
  reliability 513.4
author
  n. creator 153.4
  discourser 606.3
  doer 718.1
  producer 167.8
  writer 602.15
  v. originate 153.11
  write 602.21
authoritarian
  governmental 741.17
  imperious 739.16
  narrow-minded
    527.10
  powerful 739.15
  strict 757.6
authoritative
  authentic 513.18
  commanding 739.15
  convincing 501.26
  imperious 739.16
  influential 172.13
  orthodox 1024.7
  powerful 157.12
  prescriptive 751.4
  skillful 733.20
  specialized 81.5
  valid 516.13
  versed in 475.19
authorities, the
  the government
    741.3
  the rulers 749.15
authority
  authoritativeness
    739.2
  certificate 570.6
  commission 780.1
  connoisseur 897.7
  direction 747.1
  expert 733.11
  governance 739.5
  influence 172.1
  informant 557.5
  power 157.1
  prerogative 739
  prestige 739.4
  privilege 958.3
  sanction 777.3
  scientist 475.11
  specialist 81.3
  supremacy 36.3
  validity 516.4
  wise man 468.1

**authorization**
accession to power
739.12
certificate 570.6
commission 780.1
legalization 998.2
ratification 521.4
sanction 777.3
supremacy 36.3
**authorize**
commission 780.9
empower 157.10
legalize 998.8
prescribe 752.10
ratify 521.12
sanction 777.11
**authorized**
authoritative 739.15
commissioned 780.18
empowered 777.17
legal 998.10
**authorship**
creation 167.5
writing 602.2
**autism**
defense mechanism
690.30
fantasy 535.7
illusion 519.1
selfishness 978.1
unfeeling 856.1
unsociability 923.1
**autistic**
daydreaming 535.24
illusory 519.9
selfish 978.5
unfeeling 856.9
unsociable 923.5
**auto**
automobile 272.9,24
parts 272.25
**auto–**
automatic 349.25
automotive 272.22
identical 14.7
individual 80.12
**autobiography** 608.4
**autochthonous**
beginning 68.15
native 189.5
primitive 123.11
**autocrat** 749.14
**autocratic**
governmental 741.17
imperious 739.16
powerful 739.15
**auto-da-fé**
burning 329.5
killing 409.1
**autodidactic**
educational 562.19
learned 475.24
studentlike 566.12
taught 564.16
**autoeroticism**
masturbation 419.9
sexual preference
419.12
vanity 909.1
**autograph** original 23.3
signature 583.10
written matter 602.10

**automat**
restaurant 307.15
vending machine
832.8
**automate** 349.23
**automated** 349.25
**automatic**
n. gun 801.5,27
robot 349.12
adj. automated
349.25
habitual 642.16
instinctive 481.6
involuntary 639.14
methodical 17.5
unpremeditated
630.11
**automatically**
instinctively 481.7
involuntarily 639.18
**automatic analyzer**
349.36
**automatic detector**
349.35
**automatic indicator**
349.37
**automatic writing**
automatism 639.5
occultism 1034.6
writing 602.2
**automation**
electronics 343.1
self-action 349
**automatism**
automation 349.1
habit 642.4
involuntariness 639.5
occultism 1034.6
**automaton** 349.12,29
**automobile**
car 272.9,24
parts 272.25
**automotive**
self-propelled 349.26
vehicular 272.22
**autonomous**
governmental 741.17
independent 762.21
voluntary 622.7
**autonomy**
government 741.4
independence 762.5
voluntariness 622.2
**autopsy**
n. post-mortem
408.18
v. examine 485.23
**autosuggestion**
hypnotism 712.8
suggestion therapy
690.6
**autumn**
n. fall 128.4
adj. autumnal 128.8
**auxiliaries**
military reserves
800.24
reinforcements 785.8
**auxiliary**
n. aide 787.6
nonessential 6.2
verb 586.4

adj. additional 40.10
helping 785.20
unessential 6.4
**avail**
n. benefit 665.4
good 674.4
v. aid 785.11
be of use 665.17
do good 674.10
suffice 661.4
**availability**
accessibility 509.3
presence 186.1
utility 665.3
**available**
accessible 509.8
handy 665.19
idle 708.17
obtainable 811.13
present 186.12
vacant 187.14
**avalanche**
overabundance 663.2
plenty 661.2
slide 316.4
snow 333.8
**avant-garde**
n. precursor 66.1
the latest thing 122.2
vanguard 240.2
adj. advanced 66.4
modern 122.13
original 23.5
**avarice** greed 634.8
sin 982.3
stinginess 852.3
**avaricious**
greedy 634.27
stingy 852.9
**avatar**
appearance 446.1
manifestation 555.1
transformation 139.2
Vishnu 1014.9
**Ave Maria** 1032.4
**avenge** 956.4
**avenger** 956.3
**avenue** outlet 303.9
passageway 657.4
road 657.6
**aver** affirm 523.4
state 594.24
testify 505.10
**average**
n. generality 79.3
mean 32.1
v. middle 69.3
strike a balance 32.2
adj. mediocre 680.8
medium 32.3
middle 69.4
ordinary 79.12
usual 84.8
**average man**
common man 919.7
generality 79.3
**averse** displeased 867.8
hating 930.7
unwilling 623.5
**aversion** dislike 867.2
hate 930.1
hated thing 930.3

unwillingness 623.1
**avert** prevent 730.14
turn aside 291.6
**avian** 414.52
**aviary** 191.23
**aviate** 278.45
**aviation** 278
**aviation beacon** 336.10
**aviation instrument**
278.61
**aviator** 279
**avid** eager 635.9
greedy 634.27
**avidity** eagerness 635.1
greed 634.8
**avidly** eagerly 635.14
greedily 634.32
**avocation** 656.7
**avocational** 656.17
**avoid** abstain 992.7
pull back 284.7
shun 631.6
snub 966.7
**avoidable** 631.14
**avoidance**
abstinence 992.2
evasion 631
retreat 284.3
**avoirdupois** 352.1
**avoirdupois weight**
352.8
**avouch** affirm 523.4
express belief 501.12
promise 770.4
testify 505.10
**avow**
acknowledge 521.11
affirm 523.4
confess 556.7
express belief 501.12
purport 649.3
testify 505.10
**avowal**
acknowledgment
521.3
affirmation 523.1
confession 556.3
testimony 505.3
**avowed**
acknowledged 521.14
affirmed 523.8
professed 649.5
**await**
be imminent 152.2
be in the future
121.6
loiter 132.12
wait for 539.8
**awake**
v. awaken 713.5
excite 857.11
revive 407.8
wake up 713.4
adj. alert 533.14
clear-witted 467.13
unsleeping 713.8
**awaken** arise 713.4
become informed
557.13
disillusion 520.2
excite 857.11
revive 407.8

**back down**
be irresolute 627.7
recant 628.9
retreat 295.6
yield 765.7
**backdrop**
scenery 611.25
setting 233.2
**backed**
approved 968.19
hardened 356.13
**backer**
benefactor 942.1
financer 836.9
friend 928.1
giver 818.11
play backer 611.31
supporter 787.9
**backfire**
*n.* countermeasure
178.5
explosion 162.7
fire 328.13
recoil 284.2
*v.* explode 162.13
recoil 284.6
**backflow** 395.12
**background**
arena 802.1
experience 733.9
horizon 199.3
motif 901.7
setting 233.2
story element 608.9
**backhanded**
circuitous 321.7
insulting 965.6
oblique 219.13
**backing**
*n.* bookbinding
605.15
confirmation 505.5
course 267.2
film 577.10
financing 836.2
mounting 216.10
patronage 785.4
regression 295.3
reversion 146.1
support 216.1
supporter 216.2
*adj.* favoring 968.17
**backlash** effect 154.3
reaction 178.1
recoil 284.2
**backlist** 605.19
**backlog** firewood 331.3
reserve 660.3
store 660.1
**back matter**
book 605.12
part of writing 55.2
sequel 67.1
**back number**
antiquated person
123.8
edition 605.2
**back-number**
old-fashioned 123.16
trite 883.9
**back of beyond**
backwoods 182.8

out-of-the-way 199.9
remote region 199.4
**back off** 295.7
**back out**
abandon 633.5
be a coward 892.8
recant 628.9
retreat 295.6
**backpack** 273.29
**backpedal** retreat 295.7
slow 270.9
**back scratching**
exchange 150.2
obsequiousness 907.2
political influence
744.29
**back-scratching** 907.13
**back seat** back 241.1
inferiority 37.1
**backseat driver**
advisor 754.3
driver 274.10
meddler 238.4
**backsettler** 190.10
**backside** 241.4
**backslapper**
flatterer 970.4
sycophant 907.3
**backslide**
go wrong 981.9
regress 295.5
relapse 696.4
revert 146.4
**backsliding**
*n.* apostasy 628.2
immorality 981.1
impiety 1030.1
regression 295.1
relapse 696.2
reversion 146.1
*adj.* impious 1030.6
relapsing 696.5
unrighteous 981.12
**backstage**
*n.* stage 611.21
*adv.* theater 611.41
**backstairs** 614.12
**back stairs** byway 657.5
secret passage 615.5
stairs 315.3
**backstop** barrier 730.5
safety equipment
699.3
**backstroke**
boxing 283.5
swimming 275.11
**back talk** answer 486.1
insolence 913.4
**back to back**
behind 241.13
cooperatively 786.6
opposite 239.6
**backtrack** 295.7
**backup**
*n.* deputy 781.1
regression 295.3
substitute 149.2
*adj.* substitute 149.8
**back up**
confirm 505.12
go back 241.8
move 267.5

represent 781.14
retreat 295.7
second 785.13
support 216.21
support politically
744.41
**backward**
*adj.* back 119.12
conservative 140.8
dilatory 132.17
flowing 267.8
inside out 220.7
late 132.16
mentally deficient
469.22
modest 908.11
rear 241.9
reluctant 623.6
retarded 270.12
reticent 613.10
reversed 295.12
undeveloped 721.12
*adv.* ago 119.15
in reverse 295.13
inversely 220.8
late 132.19
rearward 241.15
**backwash**
aviation 278.39
eddy 395.12
effect 154.3
water travel 275.7
**backwater**
*n.* eddy 395.12
*v.* recant 628.9
retreat 295.7
sail 275.34
slow 270.9
**back way** byway 657.5
secret passage 615.5
**back when** 119.15
**backwoods**
*n.* hinterland 182.2
*adj.* country 182.8
**backwoodsman** 190.10
**bacon** 308.16
**bacteria** germ 686.39
microorganism
196.18
**bacterial** 196.15
**bactericide** 687.21
**bacteriology** 406.17
**bad**
*n.* evil 675.3
iniquity 981.3
*adj.* crippled 692.32
dangerous 697.9
decayed 692.41
diseased 686.56
dying 408.33
evil 675.7
excellent 674.13
inexpedient 671.5
malodorous 437.5
misbehaving 738.5
ominous 544.17
sick 686.52
unhealthful 684.5
unsavory 429.7
wicked 981.16
*adv.* badly 675.13

**bad blood**
animosity 929.4
malevolence 939.4
opposition 790.2
**bad boy** 738.3
**bad breath** 437.1
**bad character** 915.1
**bad check** 835.10
**bad debt** debt 840.1
nonpayment 842.1
**bad deed** 939.13
**bad faith**
falseheartedness
616.4
infidelity 975.5
violation 769.2
**badge**
characteristic 80.4
identification 568.11
insignia 569.1
military insignia
569.5
sign 568.2
**badger** annoy 866.13
wrest from 822.22
**badgered** 866.24
**bad guy** 612.2
**bad habit** habit 642.4
vice 981.2
**bad hand** 602.6
**badinage** 882.1
**bad influence**
influential person
172.6
malevolent influence
675.4
**bad job** bungle 734.5
slipshodness 534.3
**bad language** 972.3
**bad lot** 986.5
**bad luck** 729.5
**badly off** poor 838.7
unfortunate 729.14
**bad-mouth** 971.9
**bad move** 518.4
**bad name** 915.1
**bad news** news 558.2
trouble 866.2
undesirable person
986.1
**bad notices** 969.4
**bad person**
evildoer 943.1
undesirable 986
**bad press** 969.4
**bad taste**
literary inelegance
590.1
vulgarity 898.1
**bad temper**
anger 952.6
ill humor 951.1
malevolence 939.4
**bad-tempered** 951.18
**bad time** 130.2
**bad turn** 939.13
**bad will** 939.4
**baffle**
*n.* perplexity 514.3
*v.* be incomprehensi-
ble 549.10
disappoint 541.2

perplex 514.13
silence 451.9
thwart 730.15
**baffled**
at an impasse 731.22
disappointed 541.5
perplexed 514.24
**bafflement**
defeat 727.2
disappointment
541.1
frustration 730.3
perplexity 514.3
**baffling**
bewildering 514.25
frustrating 730.20
**bag**
*n.* business 656.1
container 193.2
contraceptive 687.23
drug dose 687.6
preference 637.5
purse 836.14
sag 215.2
scrotum 419.10
specialty 81.1
take 822.10
types of 193.16
udder 256.6
ugly thing 899.4
*v.* acquire 811.8
bulge 256.10
catch 822.17
hang 215.6
package 236.9
put in 184.14
steal 824.13
**bagatelle**
small amount 35.5
trifle 673.5
**bagel** 308.31
**baggage**
belongings 810.3
freight 271.7
types of 193.17
unchaste woman
989.14
**baggy** bulging 256.14
drooping 215.10
formless 247.4
loose 51.5
**bagman**
gambling 515.16
traveling salesman
830.5
**bagpipe** 465.10
**bah!** 966.10
**bail**
*n.* arraignment 1004.3
pledge 772.2
*v.* scoop out 271.16
**bail bond** 699.4
**bailiff** manager 748.4
peace officer 699.15
**bailiwick** district 180.5
jurisdiction 1000.4
region 180.2
sphere of influence
172.4
**bail out** aid 785.11
emerge 303.12
escape 632.6

parachute 278.56
rescue 702.3
**bairn** 125.3
**bait**
*n.* incentive 648.7
lure 650.2
snare 618.12
*v.* annoy 866.13
lure 650.4
**baited** 866.24
**bake** be hot 328.22
cook 330.4
dry 393.6
make ceramics 576.6
**baked** cooked 330.6
dried 393.9
**baker** cook 330.2,3
merchant 830.3
**baker's dozen** 99.7
**bakery** kitchen 330.3
store 832.5
**baking**
*n.* cooking 330.1
*adj.* hot 328.25
**balance**
*n.* account 845.2
artistry 574.10
average 32.1
comparability 491.3
correlation 13.1
difference 42.8
equality 30.1
equanimity 858.3
funds 835.14
literary elegance
589.2
offset 33.2
reasonableness 467.6
remainder 43.1
resources 660.2
sanity 472.1
stability 142.1
surplus 663.5
symmetry 248.1
*v.* be irresolute 627.7
check 87.14
compare 491.4
equal 30.5
equalize 30.6
keep accounts 845.8
make uniform 17.4
offset 33.5
stabilize 142.7
symmetrize 248.3
weigh 352.10
**balanced**
composed 858.13
harmonious 589.8
just 976.8
poised 30.9
sane 472.4
sensible 467.18
stable 142.12
symmetric 248.4
uniform 17.5
**balance of power**
ascendancy 739.6
foreign policy 744.5
**balance of trade** 827.1
**balance sheet** 845.4
**balancing**
*n.* comparison 491.1

compensation 33.1
symmetrization 248.2
weighing 352.9
*adj.* compensating
33.6
contrary 15.6
**balcony** gallery 192.22
platform 216.13
theater part 611.20
**bald** hairless 232.17
in plain style 591.3
manifest 555.10
naked 232.14
open 265.18
unadorned 902.8
**Balder**
beautiful man 900.9
Norse deity 1014.6
**balderdash**
bombast 601.2
nonsense 547.2
**bale**
*n.* bundle 74.8
burden 352.7
despair 866.6
*v.* bundle 74.20
**balefire** fire 328.13
signal 568.15
**baleful** harmful 675.12
malicious 939.18
ominous 544.17
**balk**
*n.* an error 518.4
defeat 727.2
disappointment
541.1
frustration 730.3
*v.* be obstinate 626.7
be unwilling 623.3
disappoint 541.2
thwart 730.15
**balked** 541.5
**ball**
*n.* dance 879.2
fun 878.2
meeting 74.2
party 922.11
plaything 878.16
projectile 285.6
shot 801.13
sphere 255.2
types of 255.13
*v.* copulate 419.23
round 255.7
**ballad** poem 609.6
popular music 462.8
song 462.13
**balladeer**
composer 464.20
singer 464.14
**balladmonger**
composer 464.20
poet 609.13,14
**balladry** 462.10
**ballast**
*n.* offset 33.2
weight 352.4
*v.* sail 275.49
stabilize 142.7
weigh down 352.12
**ballbuster** 731.2

**balled-up**
confused 532.12
disordered 62.16
mixed up 46.4
spoiled 692.31
**ballerina** 879.3·
**ballet** dancing 879.1
music drama 462.35
stage show 611.4
**balletic** dancing 879.6
theatrical 611.38
**ballistic** 285.16
**ballistics** 801.3
**ball of fire** 707.8
**balloon**
*n.* aircraft 280.11
ball 255.2
bubble 405.1
container 193.2
types of 280.18
*v.* ball 255.7
become larger 197.5
bulge 256.10
fly 278.45,52
increase 38.6
**ballooning**
*n.* aviation 278.1
increase 38.1
*adj.* bulging 256.14
drooping 215.10
**ballot**
political ballot
744.19
vote 637.6
**ballplayer** 878.20
**ballroom**
amusement 878.11
dance hall 879.4
room 192.1
**balls** audacity 893.6
humbug 616.14
testes 419.10
**ball the jack** 269.8
**ball up** complicate 46.3
confuse 532.7
disarrange 63.3
spoil 692.13
**ballyhoo**
*n.* exaggeration 617.1
publicity 559.4
sales talk 829.5
*v.* exaggerate 617.3
publicize 559.15
**ballyhoo man**
publicist 559.9
showman 611.28
solicitor 830.7
**balm** alleviative 163.3
condolence 946.1
healing ointment
687.11
medicine 687.4,51
ointment 380.3
perfume 436.2
remedy 687.1
**balmy** fragrant 436.9
insane 473.26
pleasant 863.10
prosperous 728.13
relieving 886.9
remedial 687.40

causal 153.15
essential 5.8
basalt 384.1
base
  n. bottom 212.2
  cause 153.1
  chemical 379.1
  foundation 216.6
  headquarters 226.6
  lowness 208.4
  make-up 900.11
  pedestal 216.8
  point of departure
    301.5
  station 184.2
  transistor 343.13
  v. establish 184.15
  found on 212.6
  adj. bad 675.9
  dastardly 892.12
  dishonest 975.17
  disreputable 915.12
  evil 981.16
  inferior 37.7
  mediocre 680.9
  offensive 864.18
  servile 907.12
  vulgar 898.15
baseboard 212.2
baseborn bastard 999.7
  common 919.11
based on
  contingent 507.9
  evidential 505.17
  supported 216.24
baseless groundless 4.8
  unfounded 483.13
basement
  bottom 212.2
  cellar 192.17
  foundation 216.6
  rest room 311.10
  storage place 660.6
baseness badness 675.2
  dastardliness 892.3
  dishonesty 975.2
  disrepute 915.3
  inferiority 37.3
  mediocrity 680.3
  offensiveness 864.2
  servility 907.1
  vulgarity 898.5
  wickedness 981.4
base pay 841.4
bash
  n. hit 283.4
  v. bruise 692.16
  hit 283.13
bashful
  demurring 623.7
  fearful 891.31
  reticent 613.10
  shy 908.12
  unsociable 923.5
basic causal 153.15
  chemical 379.7
  essential 5.8
  simple 45.6
  underlying 212.8
  vital 672.22
basics 68.6

basic training
  preparation 720.1
  training 562.3
basilar 212.8
basilica 1042.1
basin bed 212.4
  harbor 700.6
  pit 257.2
  plain 387.1
  types of 193.7
  washing equipment
    681.12
basis cause 153.1
  foundation 216.6
  justification 1006.6
  mental outlook 525.2
  motive 648.1
  point of departure
    301.5
  premise 482.7
  topic 484.1
bask enjoy 865.10
  sun 329.19
basket
  n. scrotum 419.10
  types of 193.15
  v. package 236.9
basketwork 221.3
bas-relief relief 256.2
  sculpture 575.3
bass
  n. music 462.22
  viol 465.6
  vocalist 464.13
  voice 463.5
  adj. deep 454.10
  vocal 462.51
basso 464.13
bassoon
  organ stop 465.22
  wood wind 465.9
basso-rilievo
  relief 256.2
  sculpture 575.3
bastard
  n. bad person 986.6
  illegitimate 171.5
  man 420.5
  adj. illegitimate 999.7
  spurious 616.26
bastardize 44.13
bastardy
  illegitimacy 999.2
  posterity 171.5
baste cook 330.4
  pound 283.14
  punish 1010.14
bastille 761.8
bastion
  fortification 799.4
  stronghold 799.6
bat
  n. blind 441.4
  hit 283.4
  mammal 414.58;
    415.8
  plaything 878.16
  revel 878.6
  spree 996.5
  v. hit 283.13
batch amount 28.2
  bunch 74.7

lump 195.10
  much 34.4
  product 168.4
bate blunt 259.2
  decrease 39.6
  discount 847.2
  reduce 39.8
  relax 163.9
  subtract 42.9
bated muffled 452.17
  reduced 39.10
bated breath 452.4
bath bathe 681.8
  bathing place 681.10
  dip 681.9
  washing equipment
    681.12
  wetting 392.6
bathe
  n. bath 681.8
  swimming 275.11
  v. soak 392.13
  swim 275.56
  treat 689.30
  wash 681.19
bather 275.12
bathhouse 681.10
bathing
  balneation 681.7
  sports 878.8
  swimming 275.11
  wetting 392.6
bathing beauty
  beautiful person
    900.8
  swimmer 275.12
bathing suit 231.29
bathos
  ludicrousness 880.3
  sadness 872.1
  sentimentality 855.8
bathroom
  bathing place 681.10
  rest room 311.10
  room 192.26
baths
  bathing place 681.10
  health resort 689.29
  resort 191.27
bathtub 681.12
bathtub gin 996.17
bathymetry
  depth measurement
    209.5
  mensuration 490.9
  oceanography 397.6
bathysmal 209.14
bathysphere 320.5
batman 750.5
baton bastardy 999.2
  emblem of authority
    739.9
  heraldic insignia
    569.2
  insignia 569.1
  music 465.25
  staff 217.2
  stigma 915.6
bat out 534.9
batrachian
  n. amphibian 414.32
  adj. amphibian 414.51

bats 473.26
battalion group 74.3
  military unit 800.19
batten
  n. scenery 611.25
  strip 206.4
  v. close 266.6
  fasten 47.8
  gluttonize 994.4
  stabilize 142.8
  thrive 728.8
batter
  n. athlete 878.20
  semiliquid 389.5
  v. bruise 692.16
  mistreat 667.5
  pound 283.14
  punish 1010.17
  terrorize 162.10
battered 692.35
battering 162.3
battery artillery 801.6
  athlete 878.20
  military unit 800.19
  percussion section
    465.18
  punishment 1010.4
  set 74.12
  types of 342.37
battery-powered 342.27
bat the breeze 594.21
bat the eyes lure 650.4
  wink 440.10
battle
  n. fight 796.4
  struggle 716.3
  warfare 797.1,30
  v. contend 796.14
  fortify 799.9
  oppose 790.4
  struggle 716.11
  war 797.18
battle array 797.6
battle-ax 951.12
battle cry
  call to arms 797.12
  challenge 793.2
  cry 459.1
  signal 568.16
battled
  embattled 797.27
  fortified 799.12
battledore
  elastic object 358.3
  plaything 878.16
  textbook 605.8
battle fatigue
  combat neurosis
    690.19
  shock 686.24
battlefield 802.2
battlement
  fortification 799.4
  notching 262.3
battle royal 796.4
battleship 277.7
batty foolish 470.8
  insane 473.26
bauble ornament 901.4
  toy 878.16
  trifle 673.5
bawd 989.18

**bawdy**
  lascivious 989.29
  obscene 990.9
**bawdyhouse** 989.9
**bawl**
  *n.* cry 459.1
  lament 875.3
  *v.* animal sound 460.2
  cry 459.6
  utter 594.26
  wail 875.11
  weep 875.10
**bawling-out** 969.6
**bawl out** 969.19
**bay**
  *n.* arm of the sea
    399.1
  compartment 192.3
  horse 414.13
  loud sound 453.4
  recess 257.7
  storage place 660.6
  trophy 916.3
  window 265.8
  *v.* animal sound 460.2
  blare 453.9
  *adj.* reddish-brown
    367.4
**bayard**
  *n.* horse 414.13
  *adj.* reddish-brown
    367.4
**bayonet**
  *n.* dagger 801.22
  *v.* stab 798.25
**bayou**
  arm of the sea 399.1
  tributary 395.3
**bay window**
  abdomen 193.3
  window 265.8
**bazaar**
  marketplace 832.2
  sale 829.3
**bazoo** 265.5
**bazooka**
  rocketry 281.10
  weapon 801.19,27
**BC** 105.13
**be** 1.8
**be above** 966.3
**beach**
  *n.* shore 385.2
  *v.* shipwreck 275.42
**beachcomber**
  bad person 986.2
  bum 708.9
  vagrant 274.3
**beachhead**
  outpost 240.2
  stronghold 799.6
**beacon** alarm 704.1
  aviation 278.19
  fire 328.13
  luminary 336.10
  observation post
    439.8
  radio transmitter
    344.4
  signal 568.15
  types of 336.9

**bead**
  *n.* drop 255.3
  jewel 901.6
  *v.* ball 255.7
  ornament 901.9
**beaded** beady 255.10
  ornamented 901.11
**beading** 235.7
**beadle**
  churchman 1038.10
  peace officer 699.15
**beads** prayer 1032.4
  sacred article 1040.11
**beady** 255.10
**beagle** detective 781.11
  peace officer 699.15
**beak** conduit 396.8
  front 240.3
  judge 1002.1
  nose 256.7
**beaked** 252.8
**be-all and end-all**
  all 54.3
  supremacy 36.3
**beam**
  *n.* aviation 278.19
  breadth 204.1
  buttress 216.4
  lever 287.4
  radar signal 346.11
  radio signal 344.10
  ray 335.5
  side 242.1
  smile 876.3
  television transmis-
    sion 345.4
  timber 217.3
  types of 217.7
  wood 378.3
  *v.* be cheerful 870.6
  broadcast 344.25
  feel happy 865.9
  give light 335.23
  look beautiful 900.15
  smile 876.7
  use radar 346.15
**beaming**
  cheerful 870.11
  gorgeous 900.19
  happy 865.13
  luminous 335.30
**bean** brain 466.6
  food 308.35,50
  head 211.6
  legume 411.4
  trifle 673.5
**beanery** 307.15
**bean pole**
  tall person 207.12
  thin person 205.8
**bear**
  *n.* animal 414.28,58
  ill-humored person
    951.11
  speculator 833.12
  *v.* afford to pay 843.7
  aid 785.12
  be patient 861.5
  engender 68.14
  give birth 167.15
  harbor 813.7
  head 290.8

  manipulate the mar-
    ket 833.25
  originate 153.11
  permit 777.10
  stand up 661.4
  support 216.21
  thrust 283.11
  transport 271.11
  yield 167.14
**bearable** 868.13
**bear a grudge** 929.8
**bear arms** 797.22
**beard**
  *n.* printing 603.6
  sex characteristic
    419.10
  whiskers 230.8
  *v.* defy 793.3
  face up to 893.11
  grow hair 230.20
**bearded** 230.25
**beardless**
  childish 124.11
  hairless 232.17
**bear down**
  depress 318.4
  exert oneself 716.9
  hurry 709.6
  hustle 707.14
  work hard 716.13
**bear down on**
  approach 296.3
  attack 798.17
  compel 756.6
  sail for 275.35
**beard the lion in his**
  **den**
  be reckless 894.6
  defy danger 697.7
  face up to 893.11
**bearer** carrier 271.5
  mourner 410.7
  supporter 216.2
**bear false witness**
  accuse 1005.12
  swear falsely 616.20
**bear fruit** bear 167.14
  evolve 148.5
  reach perfection
    722.8
**bear hug**
  embrace 932.2
  hold 813.2,3
**bearing**
  *n.* ball bearing 322.7
  behavior 737.1
  direction 290.1
  fulcrum 287.3
  gesture 568.14
  looks 446.4
  meaning 545.1
  mounting 216.10
  position 184.3
  pressure 283.2
  production 167.6
  relevance 9.4
  transportation 271.3
  trend 174.2
  yield 811.5
  *adj.* giving birth
    167.21
  supporting 216.23

  yielding 165.10
**bearings**
  heraldic insignia
    569.2
  location 184.1
  orientation 290.5
  position 184.3
  state 7.1
**bear in mind**
  remember 537.13
  take cognizance of
    530.9
  think of 478.16
**bearish** gruff 937.7
  irascible 951.19
  ursine 414.47
**bear market** 833.5
**bear off**
  change course 275.30
  deviate 291.3
  drift off course
    275.29
  oblique 219.9
  sail 275.23
  sail away from 275.36
  turn aside 291.6
**bear out**
  confirm 505.12
  support 785.12
**bear the brunt**
  endure 861.8
  have trouble 729.9
**bear up** aid 785.12
  approach 296.3
  be cheerful 870.10
  buoy up 353.8
  comfort 887.6
  endure 861.8
  have courage 893.15
  not weaken 159.9
  persevere 625.4
  resist 792.2
  support 216.21
**bear upon**
  be heavy upon
    352.11
  influence 172.9
  relate to 9.5
  rest on 216.22
  thrust 283.11
**bear with**
  be lenient 759.5
  be patient 861.5
  condone 947.4
  permit 777.10
**bear witness** 505.10
**bear witness against**
  557.12
**beast animal** 414.2
  bad person 986.7
  savage 943.5
  violent person 162.9
**beastly animal** 414.43
  bad 675.9
  carnal 987.6
  cruel 939.24
  filthy 682.24
  gruff 937.7
  horrid 864.19
  offensive 864.18
**beast of burden**
  drudge 718.3

pack animal 271.6
**beat**
*n.* circuit 321.2
flutter 324.4
meter 609.9
music 463.26
news 558.3
parasite 907.4
periodicity 137.2
pulsation 323.3
region 180.2
rhythm 463.22
round 137.3
route 657.2
routine 642.6
speech accent 594.11
sphere of work 656.4
staccato sound 455.1
tempo 463.24
*v.* agitate 324.10
best 36.7
bruise 692.16
change course 275.30
cheat 618.17
defeat 727.6
fatigue 717.4
flutter 324.12
foam 405.5
hunt 655.9
make staccato sounds
455.4
music 462.45
perplex 514.13
pound 283.14
pulsate 323.12
pulverize 361.9
punish 1010.14
repeat 103.10
sail 275.25
triumph over 726.6
*adj.* defeated 727.14
exhausted 717.8
nonconformist 83.6
perplexed 514.24
poor 838.10
**beatable** 697.16
**beat about**
be uncertain 514.9
change course 275.30
grope 485.31
have difficulty 731.10
seek 485.29
**beat around the bush**
circumlocute 593.10
dodge 631.8
equivocate 483.9
**beat back** 289.3
**beat down**
bargain 827.17
cheapen 849.6
domineer 741.16
make sad 872.18
raze 693.19
subdue 764.9
**beaten** bubbly 405.6
defeated 727.14
exhausted 717.8
habitual 642.16
**beaten path** path 657.3
routine 642.6
tedium 884.1
**beater** agitator 324.9

hunter 655.5
mixer 44.10
**beatification**
exaltation 317.1
glorification 914.8
happiness 865.2
sanctification 1026.3
**beatified**
eminent 914.18
happy 865.13
heavenly 1018.13
saintly 1015.6
sanctified 1026.8
**beatify** exalt 317.6
gladden 865.7
glorify 914.13
sanctify 1026.5
**beating**
*n.* defeat 727.1
flutter 324.4
hit 283.4
pulsation 323.3
pulverization 361.4
punishment 1010.4
staccato sound 455.1
*adj.* music 463.28
periodic 137.7
pulsating 323.18
staccato 455.7
**beat into** 562.13
**beat it** depart 301.9
flee 631.11
go away! 310.30
**beatitude**
happiness 865.2
sanctification 1026.3
**beatnik** 83.3
**beat off** 799.10
**beat one's breast** 875.9
**beat the drum**
call to arms 797.23
celebrate 877.2
espouse 968.13
music 462.45
publicize 559.15
signal 568.22
**beat the system** 724.12
**beat up** agitate 324.10
make viscid 389.10
punish 1010.17
**beat-up**
dilapidated 692.35
exhausted 717.8
slovenly 62.15
**beau** dandy 903.9
inamorato 931.12
**Beau Brummel**
dandy 903.9
fashionable 644.7
**beaucoup** 34.15
**Beaufort scale** 403.16
**beaut**
beautiful person
900.8
good thing 674.7
**beauteous** 900.16
**beautician** 900.12
**beautification**
improvement 691.2
prettification 900.10
**beautified** 691.13

**beautiful**
*adj.* artistic 574.21
beauteous 900.16
*interj.* approval
968.22
**beautiful people** 644.6
**beautify**
improve 691.10
ornament 901.8
prettify 900.14
**beauty**
beautifulness 900
beautiful person
900.8
literary elegance
589.2
**beauty parlor**
beauty salon 900.13
workplace 719.1
**beauty queen** 900.8
**beaux arts** 574.1
**beaver** beard 230.8
man of action 707.8
**bebop** 462.9
**be born** begin 68.13
come forth 167.16
come to life 407.8
**becalm** 268.11
**becalmed** 268.17
**be careful**
*v.* be cautious 895.5
take care 533.7
*interj.* caution 895.14
**because** 155.10
**because of** 155.9
**bechance** 156.11
**becharm** delight 865.8
enamor 931.21
enchant 1036.8
fascinate 650.6
**becharmed**
enamored 931.26
enchanted 1036.12
**beck** gesture 568.14
running water 395.1
summons 752.5
**beck and call** 752.5
**beckon** attract 650.5
gesture 568.21
**becloud** cloud 404.6
conceal 615.6
confuse 532.7
darken 337.9
opaque 341.2
**beclouded**
concealed 615.11
muddled 532.13
**become**
be converted into
145.17
begin 68.13
behoove 962.4
come to be 1.12
convert 145.11
**become of** 154.5
**becoming** apt 26.10
beautiful 900.17
decent 988.5
decorous 897.10
due 960.8
expedient 670.5

**bed**
*n.* accommodations
659.3
bottom 212.1
couch 216.19
floor 212.4
foundation 216.6
garden 413.10
layer 227.1
marriage 933.1
printing press
603.9,26
types of 216.33
watercourse 396.2
*v.* base 212.6
embed 304.5
go to bed 712.17
house 188.10
implant 142.9
plant 413.18
put to bed 712.19
rest 711.6
tend animals 416.7
**bed and board** 659.3
**bedaub** blemish 679.6
coat 228.24
color 362.13
soil 682.16
**bedazzle** astonish 920.6
blind 441.7
confuse 532.7
give light 335.23
**bedazzled**
blinded 441.10
dazed 532.14
**bedbug** 414.41,74
**bedchamber** 192.7
**bedclothes** 228.10
**bedding**
bedclothes 228.10
foundation 216.6
underbedding 216.20
underlayer 227.1
**bedeck** clothe 231.38
ornament 901.8
**bedecked**
clothed 231.44
ornamented 901.11
**bedevil** annoy 866.13
bewitch 1036.9
demonize 1016.17
**bedeviled**
insane 473.28
tormented 866.24
**bedfast** 686.55
**bedfellow**
associate 787.1
companion 928.3
**bedizen** color 362.13
dress up 231.41
ornament 901.8
**bedizened**
grandiloquent 601.8
ornamented 901.11
**bedlam**
insane asylum 473.14
noise 453.3
pandemonium 62.5
**bedmate**
companion 928.3
partner 787.2

**bed of roses**
  comfort 887.1
  prosperity 728.1
**Bedouin** 274.4
**bedpan** 311.11
**bedraggle** 682.19
**bedraggled**
  slovenly 62.15
  soiled 682.21
**bedrape** 231.38
**bedridden** 686.55
**bedrock**
  *n.* bottom 212.1
  foundation 216.6
  lowest level 208.4
  stability 142.6
  stone 384.1
  *adj.* bottom 212.7
  deepest 209.15
  vital 672.22
**bedroom** 192.7
**bedroom eyes** 439.5
**bedspread** 228.10
**bedspring** 216.20
**bedstead** 216.19
**bedtime**
  eleventh hour 134.5
  sleep 712.2
**bedwarf** 39.9
**bee** insect 414.38,74
  party 922.13
**beef**
  *n.* cattle 414.6
  complaint 875.4
  meat 308.13
  objection 522.2
  power 157.1
  strength 159.2
  weight 352.1
  *v.* complain 875.13
  object 522.5
**beefcake** 577.3
**beefeater**
  bodyguard 699.14
  household troop
  800.31
**beefed-up**
  expanded 197.10
  increased 38.7
**beefhead** 471.4
**beefheaded** 469.15
**beefing**
  *n.* complaint 875.4
  *adj.* discontented
  869.5
**beefsteak** 308.18
**beef up** increase 38.5
  strengthen 159.11
**beefy** corpulent 195.18
  strong 159.13
**beehive** apiary 191.25
  workplace 719.2
**bee in one's bonnet**
  caprice 629.1
  eccentricity 474.2
**beekeeper** 416.4
**beeline** shortcut 203.5
  straight line 250.2
**Beelzebub** 1016.5
**beep**
  *n.* noise 453.4
  *v.* honk 453.9

**beer** 996.15,38
**beerbelly** 193.3
**beer garden** 996.19
**beery**
  intoxicated 996.30
  sentimental 855.22
**beetle**
  *n.* bug 414.36,74
  pulper 390.4
  *v.* overhang 215.7
  *adj.* overhanging
  215.11
**beetle-browed**
  overhanging 215.11
  sullen 951.24
**befall** happen 156.11
  occur 151.5
**befit**
  be expedient 670.3
  behoove 962.4
**befitting** apt 26.10
  expedient 670.5
  timely 129.9
**befog** cloud 404.6
  conceal 615.6
**before**
  *adv.* ahead 240.12
  early 131.11
  formerly 119.13
  in front 292.4
  preceding 64.6
  preferably 637.28
  previously 116.6
  *prep.* in the presence
  of 186.18
  prior to 116.7
**beforehand**
  *adj.* ahead of time
  115.3
  *adv.* early 131.11
**before long**
  in the future 121.9
  soon 131.16
**before one's eyes**
  in front 240.12
  overtly 555.15
  visible 444.6
**before the house** 485.38
**beforetime**
  *adj.* early 131.7
  *adv.* early 131.11
  formerly 119.13
**befoul** defile 682.17
  misuse 667.4
  work evil 675.6
**befouled** 682.21
**befriend** aid 785.11
  make friends with
  927.10
**befrilled**
  high-flown 601.11
  ornamented 901.11
**befuddle** confuse 532.7
  make drunk 996.21
**befuddled** 532.13
**beg** entreat 774.11
  evade 631.7
  scrounge 774.15
**beg, borrow, or steal**
  658.4
**beget**
  be productive 165.7

**engender** 68.14
  invent 167.13
  originate 153.11
  procreate 169.8
**beggar**
  *n.* bad person 986.2
  bum 708.9
  mendicant 774.8
  nonworker 708.10
  poor person 838.4
  vagabond 274.3
  *v.* impoverish 838.6
**beggar description**
  baffle description
  920.8
  look beautiful 900.15
**beggared** 838.8
**beggarly** base 915.12
  ill-provided 662.12
  indigent 838.8
  paltry 673.18
  servile 907.13
  vulgar 898.15
**beggary**
  indigence 838.2
  mendicancy 774.6
  want 662.4
**begging**
  *n.* beggary 774.6
  *adj.* imploring 774.17
  petitionary 774.16
**begild** color 362.13
  yellow 370.3
**begin** 68.7
**begin again** 143.6
**beginner** creator 153.4
  neophyte 68.2
  novice 566.9
  producer 167.8
**beginning**
  *n.* commencement 68
  creation 167.5
  earliness 131.1
  origin 68.4
  source 153.5
  *adj.* initial 68.15
**beg leave** 774.9
**beg off** abandon 633.5
  refuse 776.3
**be gone**
  disappear 447.2
  pass 119.6
**be good**
  behave oneself 737.5
  be virtuous 980.6
**beg pardon**
  apologize 1012.5
  repent 873.7
**begrime** 682.15
**begrudge**
  be parsimonious
  852.5
  be unwilling 623.3
  envy 954.3
  refuse 776.4
**beg the question**
  dodge 631.8
  equivocate 483.9
**beg to differ** 522.4
**beguile** amuse 878.23
  cheat 618.17
  deceive 618.13

**distract** 532.6
  fascinate 650.6
**beguiled**
  astonished 920.9
  foolish 470.8
**beguiling** alluring 650.7
  amusing 878.29
  deceptive 618.19
  wonderful 920.10
**begum** 918.8
**behalf** benefit 665.4
  good 674.4
**behave** act 705.4
  act toward 737.6
  behave oneself 737.5
  conduct oneself
  737.4
**behaved** 737.7
**behavior** action 705.1
  conditioning 690.33
  conduct 737
**behavioral**
  acting 705.10
  of behavior 737.7
**behaviorism**
  behavior 737.3
  materialism 376.5
  psychology 690.2
**behaviorist(ic)** 737.7
**behead** 1010.19
**behemoth** 195.14
**behest** 752.1
**behind**
  *n.* buttocks 241.4
  rear 241.1
  *adj.* retarded 270.12
  *adv.* after 293.6
  in arrears 314.6
  in the rear 241.13
  late 132.19
  *prep.* after 117.8
  supporting 785.27
**behindhand**
  *adj.* anachronous
  115.3
  defaulting 842.10
  late 132.16
  *adv.* in arrears 314.6
  late 132.19
**behind one's back**
  behind 241.13
  furtively 614.18
**behind the eight ball**
  731.20
**behind the scenes**
  *adj.* causal 153.14
  cognizant of 475.16
  unseen 445.5
  *adv.* behind 241.13
  secretly 614.17
  theater 611.41
**behind the times**
  123.16
**behind time**
  anachronous 115.3
  late 132.19
**behold**
  *v.* see 439.12
  *interj.* attention!
  530.22
**beholden**
  grateful 949.5

thanks 949.2
**benefaction** gift 818.7
good deed 938.7
**benefactor**
helper 785.7
patron 942
**benefice** 1037.9
**beneficence**
auspiciousness 544.9
benevolence 938.4
**beneficent**
benevolent 938.15
helpful 785.22
**beneficial** good 674.12
healthful 683.5
helpful 785.21
useful 665.18
**beneficiary**
clergyman 1038.8
donee 819.4
proprietor 809.2
**benefit**
*n.* aid 785.1
estate 810.4
gift 818.7
good 674.4
good deed 938.7
theatrical perfor-
mance 611.13
use 665.4
*v.* aid 785.11
be expedient 670.3
be of use 665.17
do a favor 938.12
do good 674.10
**benefit from** 665.15
**benevolence**
auspiciousness 544.9
charity 938.4
forgiveness 947.1
gift 818.7
good deed 938.7
goodness 674.1
indulgence 759.2
pity 944.1
**benevolent**
charitable 938.15
forgiving 947.6
good 674.12
helpful 785.22
indulgent 759.8
**benighted** blind 441.9
ignorant 477.16
night 134.10
**benign**
auspicious 544.18
harmless 674.20
healthful 683.5
helpful 785.22
indulgent 759.8
kind 938.13
**benignity**
auspiciousness 544.9
good deed 938.7
goodness 674.1
harmlessness 674.9
indulgence 759.2
kindness 938.1
**bennie** 687.9
**bent**
*.* aptitude 733.5
bias 219.3

direction 290.1
inclination 634.3
preference 637.5
prejudice 527.3
tendency 174.1
trait of character
525.3
*adj.* angular 251.6
curved 252.7
distorted 249.10
drunk 996.31
minded 525.8
**benthonic**
deep-sea 209.14
life 414.57
**benthos**
ocean depths 209.4
plankton 414.35
**bent on**
desirous of 634.22
determined upon
624.16
**benumb** chill 333.10
make unfeeling 856.8
relieve 886.5
render insensible
423.4
**benumbed**
apathetic 856.13
insensible 423.6
languid 708.19
**Benzedrine** 687.9,52
**benzine** fuel 331.1
illuminant 335.20
**be off** depart 301.9
go away! 310.29
start out 301.7
**be on to** 488.8
**bequeath**
transfer property
817.3
will 818.18
**bequeathal**
inheritance 819.2
legacy 818.10
property transfer
817.1
**bequest**
inheritance 819.2
legacy 818.10
**be quiet!** 451.14
**berate** 969.20
**berating** 969.7
**bereave** die 408.28
take from 822.21
widow 935.6
**bereaved** bereft 408.35
deprived of 812.8
indigent 838.8
**bereavement**
deprivation 822.6
loss 812.1
**bereft** bereaved 408.35
deprived of 812.8
indigent 838.8
wanting 662.13
**berg** 333.5
**beribbon** 901.9
**beribboned** 901.11
**beriberi** 686.10
**berm** path 657.3
shore 385.2

**berry** fruit 308.51
seed 411.29
**berserk** excited 857.23
mad 473.30
**berth**
*n.* anchorage 277.16
harbor 700.6
lodgings 191.3
position 656.5
*v.* house 188.10
inhabit 188.7
**beseech** entreat 774.11
pray 1032.12
**beseechment**
entreaty 774.2
prayer 1032.4
**beset**
*v.* annoy 866.13
besiege 798.19
enclose 236.5
importune 774.12
make anxious 890.4
obsess 473.24
overrun 313.6
persecute 667.6
trouble 731.12
*adj.* distressed 866.22
enclosed 236.10
in difficulty 731.19
infested 313.11
tormented 866.24
worried 890.7
**besetting**
prevalent 79.12
troublesome 731.17
**beside**
*adv.* additionally
40.11
near 200.21
*prep.* alongside 242.11
compared to 491.11
excluding 77.9
**beside oneself**
angry 952.26
distracted 532.10
excited 857.23
mad 473.30
overjoyed 865.14
**beside the point**
amiss 314.7
irrelevant 10.6
**besiege** attack 798.19
enclose 236.5
importune 774.12
**besiegement** 798.5
**besmear** blemish 679.6
coat 228.24
color 362.13
soil 682.16
**besmirch** blacken 365.7
blemish 679.6
soil 682.16
vilify 971.10
**besmirched**
blemished 679.10
dingy 365.11
soiled 682.21
unchaste 989.23
**besmoke** blemish 679.6
dirty 682.15
**besot**
make drunk 996.21

render insensible
423.4
**besotted** fooled 470.8
intoxicated 996.30
obsessed 473.33
**bespangle**
ornament 901.9
variegate 374.7
**bespangled**
illuminated 335.39
ornamented 901.11
spotted 374.13
**bespatter**
moisten 392.12
spatter 682.18
stigmatize 915.9
vilify 971.10
**bespeak** address 594.27
engage 780.13
evidence 505.9
indicate 568.17
mean 545.8
request 774.9
**bespeckle**
blemish 679.5
variegate 374.7
**bespeckled** 679.9
**bespoke** 231.47
**best**
*v.* defeat 727.6
excel 36.6
outdo 36.7
triumph over 726.6
*adj.* cheap 849.9
prime 674.18
superlative 36.13
**best, the**
good thing 674.8
superiors 36.5
**best bet** 156.8
**bested** 727.14
**bestial** animal 414.43
carnal 987.6
cruel 939.24
savage 162.20
uncouth 898.12
**bestiality**
badness 675.2
carnality 987.2
cruelty 939.11
sex act 419.9
uncouthness 898.3
**be still**
*v.* do nothing 706.2
keep quiet 268.7
*interj.* silence! 451.14
**bestir oneself**
be active 707.11
make haste 709.5
**best man**
assistant 787.6
wedding attendant
933.5
**bestow** give 818.12
impose 963.6
use 665.13
**bestowal** giving 818.1
imposition 963.2
**bestowed** 818.24
**best part** 54.6
**bestraddle**
be high 207.16

price 846.2
*v.* bargain 827.17
bid at auction 828.9
command 752.9
offer 773.6
**bid come** invite 774.13
summon 752.12
**bidder** 774.7
**bidding**
command 752.1
invitation 774.4
summons 752.5
**biddy**
female animal 421.9
maid 750.8
poultry 414.34
woman 421.6
**bide** await 539.8
be patient 861.5
continue 143.3
endure 110.6
remain 140.5
wait 132.12
**bide one's time**
do nothing 706.2
expect 539.8
wait 132.12
**bidet** horse 414.16
washing equipment
681.12
**bid price** price 846.2
stock price 834.9
**biennial**
*n.* anniversary 137.4
plant 411.3
*adj.* recurring 137.8
**bier** 410.13
**biff**
*n.* hit 283.4
*v.* hit 283.13
**bifocals** 443.2
**bifurcation** angle 251.2
bisection 92.1
duality 90.1
forking 299.3
▶**big** adult 126.12
arrogant 912.9
boastful 910.11
eminent 914.18
important 672.16
large 195.16
magnanimous 979.6
▶**igamist** 933.12
▶**igamy** 933.2
▶**ig bang theory** 375.18
▶**ig Board, the** 833.7
▶**ig Brother** 748.2
▶**ig business** 827.1
▶**ig deal** triviality 673.3
what does it matter?
673.23
▶**ig Dipper** 375.28
▶**ig game**
animal life 414.1
quarry 655.7
▶**ggety**
conceited 909.11
impudent 913.9
▶**g gun** 672.8
▶**g hand** 968.2
▶**ghearted**
benevolent 938.15

liberal 853.4
magnanimous 979.6
**bight** angle 251.2
arm of the sea 399.1
**big-league** 672.16
**big mouth**
braggart 910.5
talkativeness 596.1
**big name**
famous person 914.9
personage 672.8
**big-name** 672.16
**bigot** dogmatist 513.7
hater 930.4
intolerant person
527.5
obstinate person
626.6
orthodox 1024.6
**bigoted**
dogmatic 513.22
fanatical 473.32
narrow-minded
527.10
obstinate 626.8
orthodox 1024.8
**bigotry**
dogmatism 513.6
fanaticism 473.11
hate 930.1
narrow-mindedness
527.1
obstinacy 626.1
orthodoxy 1024.5
**big shot** 672.9
**big talk** boasting 910.2
exaggeration 617.1
grandiloquence 601.1
**big talker** 596.4
**big time** 878.2
**big-time** 672.16
**big-time operator**
important person
672.9
man of action 707.8
**big-time spender** 854.2
**big top, the** 611.15
**big wheel**
important person
672.9
influential person
172.6
**bigwig** personage 672.8
superior 36.5
**bijou** 901.6
**bike**
*n.* bicycle 272.8
*v.* ride 273.32
**bikini** 231.29
**bilabial**
*n.* speech sound
594.13
*adj.* phonetic 594.31
**bilateral** bipartite 90.6
double 91.4
sided 242.7
**bile** bitterness 952.3
digestion 309.8
ill humor 951.1
secretion 312.2
**bilge** bulge 256.3
nonsense 547.3

offal 682.9
**bilingual** 580.14
**bilious** diseased 686.57
ill-humored 951.23
**bilk** cheat 618.17
disappoint 541.2
**bilker** 619.3
**bill**
*n.* advertising 559.8
beak 256.7
debt 840.1
fee 841.5
law 998.3
legal statement
1004.7
legislative bill 742.17
list 88.5
negotiable instru-
ment 835.11
paper money 835.5
point of land 256.8
poster 559.7
schedule 641.2
statement 845.3
theatrical perfor-
mance 611.13
*v.* give a show 611.33
publicize 559.15
schedule 641.4
send a statement
845.11
**bill and coo** 932.13
**billboard** 559.7
**bill collector**
collector 74.15
creditor 839.4
**billed** curved 252.8
scheduled 641.6
**billet**
*n.* heraldic insignia
569.2
letter 604.2
position 656.5
wood 378.3
*v.* house 188.10
settle 184.16
**billet-doux** letter 604.3
love letter 932.12
**billfold** 836.14
**billion**
immense number
101.4
large number 86.4
number 99.12
**billionaire** 837.6
**bill of fare** list 88.5
menu 307.12
schedule 641.2
**bill of health**
certificate 570.6
pass 777.7
**bill of lading**
account 845.3
list 88.5
**bill of particulars**
1005.1
**Bill of Rights**
constitution 998.6
liberties 762.2
**bill of sale** 829.1
**billow**
*n.* wave 395.14

*v.* bulge 256.10
surge 395.22
**billowy** bulging 256.14
curved 252.7
wavy 254.10
**billy goat** goat 414.8
male animal 420.8
**bin** 660.6
**binary** 91.4
**bind**
*n.* delay 132.2
predicament 731.4
*v.* border 235.10
compel 756.4
indenture 780.17
obligate 962.12
promise 770.5
relate 9.6
restrain 760.10
stick together 50.9
stop 266.7
tie 47.9
**binder**
medical dressing
687.33
payment 841.1
wrapper 228.18
**binding**
*n.* bookbinding
605.15
connection 47.3
edging 235.7
wrapper 228.18
*adj.* compulsory
756.10
joining 47.16
mandatory 752.13
obligatory 962.15
prescriptive 751.4
valid 516.13
**bind up** bundle 74.20
tie 47.9
**binge** revel 878.6
spree 996.5
**bingo** game 878.34
game of chance 515.8
lottery 515.11
**binoculars** 443.3
**binomial** bipartite 92.7
terminological 583.17
**bio–** 407.1
**biochemical**
*n.* chemical 379.1
*adj.* chemical 379.7
**biochemist** 406.18
**biochemistry** 406.17
**biodegradable**
decomposable 692.48
disintegrable 53.5
**biofeedback** 690.5
**biographer** 608.11
**biographical** 608.18
**biography** 608.4
**biological** 406.19
**biological classification**
406.3
**biological clock** 407.3
**biological urge** 419.5
**biologist**
biology 406.18
zoologist 415.2

biology
  biological science
    406.17
  zoology 415.1
bionics
  automation 349.2
  biology 406.17
bionomics
  biology 406.17
  ecology 233.4
biophysicist
  biologist 406.18
  physicist 325.2
biophysics
  biology 406.17
  physics 325.1
biopsy 689.13
biorhythm 407.3
biosphere
  atmosphere 402.2
  Earth 375.10
  ecosphere 407.6
  organic matter 406.1
biotic 406.19
bipartisan
  bipartite 90.6
  partisan 744.44
bipartisanship 786.1
bipartite bifid 92.7
  separate 49.20
  two 90.6
biped
  *n.* animal 414.3
  *adj.* bipartite 92.7
Bircher 745.9
bird fowl 414.33,66
  man 420.5
  missile 281.3
  woman 421.6
birdbrained 469.20
bird cage
  birdhouse 191.23
  dice 515.9
birdcall
  animal sound 460.1
  signal 568.16
birdhouse 191.23
bird in hand 808.1
bird sanctuary
  preserve 701.6
  refuge 700.1
bird's-eye 76.7
bird's-eye view
  abridgment 607.1
  view 446.6
birds of a feather 20.5
birth
  *n.* ancestry 170.4
  childbirth 167.7
  generation 169.6
  heredity 170.6
  life 407.1
  nobility 918.1
  origin 68.4
  *v.* engender 68.14
birth control 166.1
birth control device
  687.23
birthday 137.4
birthday suit 232.3
birth defect 686.1

birthmark
  blemish 679.1
  mark 568.5
birthplace
  breeding place 153.8
  native land 181.2
birthright
  inheritance 819.2
  privilege 958.3
birthstone 384.6
biscuit
  ceramic ware 576.2,8
  cookie 308.42
  dryness 393.2
  food 308.30
bisect halve 92.4
  middle 69.3
  sever 49.11
bisexual
  *n.* homosexual 419.16
  *adj.* bipartite 92.7
  sexual 419.32
bishop
  chessman 878.18
  clergyman 1038.9
  Mormon priest
    1038.11
bishopric
  church office 1037.5
  diocese 1037.8
  district 180.5
  mastership 739.7
bishop's palace 1042.8
bison 414.6
bisque
  ceramic ware 576.2
  soup 308.10
bistro
  restaurant 307.15
  saloon 996.19
bit act 611.8
  computer 349.19
  curb 730.7
  drill 258.3
  harness 659.5
  information theory
    557.7
  number 86.1
  piece 55.3
  pittance 662.5
  portion 816.5
  role 611.11
  shift 108.3
  short distance 200.2
  short time 111.3
  small amount 35.2
  trifle 673.5
bit, a scarcely 35.9
  to a degree 29.7
bit by bit
  gradually 29.6
  piece by piece 55.9
bitch
  *n.* complaint 875.4
  difficult thing 731.2
  dog 414.22
  female animal 421.9
  ill-humored woman
    951.12
  objection 522.2
  unchaste woman
    989.14

woman 421.6
  *v.* be ill-humored
    951.14
  bungle 734.12
  complain 875.13
  object 522.5
bitch box 450.11
bitchy
  disparaging 971.13
  irascible 951.19
  malicious 939.18
bite
  *n.* acrimony 161.4
  eloquence 600.3
  hold 813.2
  light meal 307.7
  morsel 307.2
  pain 424.2
  portion 816.5
  pungency 433.2
  taste 427.2
  *v.* be credulous 502.6
  be pungent 433.5
  be sharp 258.8
  chew 307.25
  chill 333.10
  etch 578.11
  hold 813.6
  hurt 424.7
  puncture 265.16
bite off more than one
  can chew 715.6
bite one's nails
  await 539.8
  feel anxious 890.5
bite the bullet 893.11
bite the dust
  be defeated 727.12
  be destroyed 693.22
  die 408.22
bite the hand that feeds
  one
  be dishonest 975.13
  be ungrateful 950.3
biting
  acrimonious 161.13
  caustic 939.21
  cold 333.14
  eloquent 600.11
  exciting 857.29
  painful 424.10
  pungent 433.6
  witty 881.15
bit much, a
  excessive 663.16
  insufferable 864.25
bitter
  *n.* taste 427.1
  *adj.* acrimonious
    161.13
  caustic 939.21
  cold 333.14
  distressing 864.20
  hostile 929.10
  ill-humored 951.23
  pungent 433.6
  resentful 952.24
  unpleasant 864.17
  unsavory 429.6
bitter end
  extremity 70.2
  result 154.2

bitterly
  caustically 939.30
  distressingly 34.21
bitterness
  acrimony 161.4
  animosity 929.4
  bitter resentment
    952.3
  causticity 939.8
  cold 333.1
  despair 866.6
  distressfulness 864.5
  hate 930.2
  pungency 433.1
  regret 873.1
  unpleasant taste
    429.2
bitter pill
  affliction 866.8
  bitterness 429.2
bituminous 331.9,10
bivouac
  *n.* camp 191.29
  military camp 802.3
  *v.* camp 188.11
  settle 184.16
biweekly
  *n.* periodical 605.10
  *adj.* periodically 137.8
bizarre abnormal 85.13
  awesome 920.11
  fanciful 535.20
  foolish 470.10
  humorous 880.4
blab
  *n.* chatter 596.3
  chatterer 596.4
  informer 557.6
  *v.* chatter 596.5
  divulge 556.6
  inform on 557.12
blabber
  *n.* chatter 596.3
  informer 557.6
  nonsense 547.2
  *v.* chatter 596.5
  divulge 556.6
  talk nonsense 547.5
blabbermouth 557.6
black
  *n.* blackness 365.1
  colors 365.14
  mourning garment
    875.6
  race 418.3
  *adj.* bad 675.7
  color 365.8
  comparisons 365.4
  dark 337.13
  dark-skinned 365.10
  disastrous 729.15
  evil 981.16
  gloomy 872.24
  lightless 337.13
  ominous 544.17
  sullen 951.24
black-and-blue 365.12
black-and-blue mark
  692.9
black and white
  drawing 574.6
  lighting 335.19

opposites 239.2
picture 574.14
**black art, the** 1035.2
**blackball**
  *n.* disapproval 969.1
  ostracism 926.3
  *v.* disapprove 969.10
  eject 310.17
  ostracize 926.6
**black belt** fighter 800.2
  the country 182.1
**black cat** 544.6
**blackdamp**
  miasma 676.4
  vapor 401.1
**black death**
  infectious disease
    686.12
  plague 686.4
**blacken** berate 969.20
  blemish 679.6
  darken 337.9
  make black 365.7
  soil 682.16
  stigmatize 915.9
  vilify 971.10
**black eye** bruise 692.9
  stigma 915.6
**blackface** 611.22
**blackguard** 986.3
**Black Hand** 986.11
**blackhead** 679.1
**blackhearted** 981.15
**black hole** prison 761.8
  star 375.8
**black humor** 881.1
**blackjack**
  *n.* card game 878.35
  club 801.26
  *v.* coerce 756.7
  hit 283.17
**blackleg**
  *n.* animal disease
    686.38
  cheat 619.3
  strikebreaker 789.6
  *v.* break a strike
    789.10
**blacklist**
  *n.* ostracism 926.3
  *v.* condemn 1008.3
  ostracize 926.6
**black look**
  disapproval 969.8
  scowl 951.9
**black lung**
  occupational disease
    686.31
  respiratory disease
    686.14
**black magic**
  Satanism 1016.15
  sorcery 1035.2
**blackmail**
  *n.* booty 824.11
  demand 753.1
  extortion 822.8
  fee 841.5
  *v.* demand 753.4
  wrest from 822.22
**black man** 418.3
**Black Maria** 272.10

**black mark** 915.6
**black market** 826.1
**black-market**
  *v.* deal illicitly 826.7
  *adj.* illegal 999.6
**Black Mass** 1016.15
**blackout** amnesia 538.2
  aviation 278.21
  darkening 337.7
  disappearance 447.1
  keeping secret 614.3
  space hazard 282.10
  unconsciousness
    423.2
**black out**
  aviation 278.55
  darken 337.9
  faint 423.5
  hush up 614.8
**black power**
  power 157.1
  prejudice 527.4
  pressure group 744.31
**black sheep**
  bad person 986.5
  intruder 78.2
**blacktop**
  *n.* pavement 657.7
  *v.* cover 228.22
**bladder** ball 255.2
  bubble 405.1
  comedy 611.7
  container 193.2,18
**blade** combatant 800.1
  cutlery 348.2
  dandy 903.9
  leaf 411.17
  sled part 272.19
  sword 801.4
  vocal organ 594.19
**blah**
  *n.* apathy 856.4
  nonsense 547.3
  *adj.* apathetic 856.13
  tedious 884.8
  uninteresting 883.6
**blah feeling** 160.1
**blahs** apathy 856.4
  sadness 872.6
  unpleasure 866.1
**blame**
  *n.* accusation 1005.1
  attribution 155.1
  disapproval 969.3
  *v.* accuse 1005.8
  attribute to 155.4
  censure 969.13
**blamed**
  accused 1005.15
  damned 972.10
**blameless**
  honest 974.13
  innocent 984.6
**blameworthy** bad 675.9
  culpable 969.26
  evil 981.16
**blanch**
  become excited
    857.17
  cook 330.4
  decolor 363.5
  lose color 363.6

  suffer pain 424.8
  whiten 364.5
**blanched**
  bleached 363.8
  terrified 891.34
  weatherworn 692.36
**bland** flattering 970.8
  general 79.11
  moderate 163.10
  suave 936.18
  vacant 187.13
  weak 160.17
**blandish**
  be hypocritical
    616.23
  flatter 970.5
  importune 774.12
  lure 650.4
  urge 648.14
**blandishment**
  allurement 650.1
  endearment 932.4
  flattery 970.1
  importuning 774.3
  inducement 648.3
**blank**
  *n.* absence 187.1
  document 570.5
  void 187.3
  *adj.* closed 266.9
  inexpressive 549.20
  reticent 613.10
  stupid 469.19
  thoughtless 480.4
  unadorned 902.8
  uninteresting 883.6
  vacant 187.13
**blank check**
  full permission 777.4
  latitude 762.4
  negotiable instru-
    ment 835.11
  right 958.4
**blanket**
  *n.* cover 228.2
  coverlet 228.10
  *v.* conceal 615.6
  cover 228.19
  *adj.* comprehensive
    76.7
  undiscriminating
    493.5
**blankety-blank** 972.10
**blankminded**
  ignorant 477.12
  thoughtless 480.4
**blank verse** 609.10
**blank wall** 266.3
**blare**
  *n.* glare 335.4
  harsh sound 458.3
  loud sound 453.4
  *v.* animal sound 460.2
  blast 453.9
  proclaim 559.13
  sound harshly 458.9
  utter 594.26
**blaring**
  *n.* radio reception
    344.21
  *adj.* noisy 453.12
**blarney** 970.1

**blasé** apathetic 856.13
  bored 884.10
  disillusioned 520.5
  languid 708.19
  nonchalant 858.15
  unconcerned 636.7
  worldly-wise 733.26
**blaspheme** curse 972.5
  profane 1030.5
**blasphemous**
  cursing 972.8
  impious 1030.6
**blasphemy** curse 972.1
  sacrilege 1030.2
**blast**
  *n.* blight 676.2
  detonation 456.3
  explosion 162.7
  explosive charge
    801.10
  gust 403.6
  loud sound 453.4
  noise 453.3
  *v.* blare 453.9
  blow 403.22
  curse 972.5
  destroy 693.18
  detonate 456.8
  din 453.6
  explode 162.13
  fire upon 798.22
  freeze 334.11
  kill 409.14
  thwart 730.15
  *interj.* curse 972.12
**blasted** damned 972.10
  disappointed 541.5
  ruined 693.28
  spoiled 692.43
**blasting**
  *n.* radio reception
    344.21
  *adj.* banging 456.11
**blasting cap** 331.7
**blast off** begin 68.7
  rocket 281.13
**blast-off** beginning 68.1
  rocketry 281.9
**blasty** 403.25
**blat**
  *n.* harsh sound 458.3
  loud sound 453.4
  *v.* animal sound 460.2
  blare 453.9
  sound harshly 458.9
  utter 594.26
**blatancy**
  conspicuousness
    555.4
  showiness 904.3
  vociferousness 459.5
**blatant**
  animal sound 460.6
  conspicuous 555.12
  gaudy 904.20
  noisy 453.12
  vociferous 459.10
**blatantly**
  conspicuously 555.16
  flagrantly 34.21
  gaudily 904.27

**blather**
*n.* chatter 596.3
nonsense 547.2
*v.* be unintelligent
469.12
chatter 596.5
talk nonsense 547.5
**blaze**
*n.* emotional outburst
857.8
fire 328.13
flash 328.14
glare 335.4
light 335.6
mark 568.5
notch 262.1
pointer 568.4
*v.* become angry
952.18
be hot 328.22
burn 329.23
give light 335.23
heat 329.24
mark 568.19
notch 262.4
proclaim 559.13
**blazer** 231.51
**blazing**
*n.* burning 329.5
*adj.* burning 328.27
flashing 335.34
**blazon**
*n.* display 904.4
heraldic insignia
569.2
*v.* flaunt 904.17
ornament 901.8
proclaim 559.13
**bleach**
*n.* decolorant 363.4
decoloration 363.3
types of 363.10
*v.* clean 681.18
decolor 363.5
lose color 363.6
whiten 364.5
**bleached** clean 681.25
decolored 363.8
vacant 187.13
weatherworn 692.36
**bleachers** 439.8
**bleaching**
decoloration 363.3
whitening 364.3
**bleak** cold 333.14
gloomy 872.24
hopeless 889.12
unpleasant 864.20
wind-blown 403.27
**bleary** 445.6
**bleary-eyed** 440.13
**bleat** 460.2
**bleb** blemish 679.1
blister 256.3
bubble 405.1
sore 686.35
**blebby** 405.6
**bleed** despoil 822.24
exploit 665.16
extract 305.12
exude 303.15
grieve 872.17

hemorrhage 311.17
let blood 689.33
overcharge 848.7
pity 944.3
suffer 866.19
take from 822.21
**bleeding heart**
compassionateness
944.2
despair 866.6
heartache 872.9
sentimentality 855.8
**bleed white**
consume 666.2
despoil 822.24
exploit 665.16
overcharge 848.7
**blemish**
*n.* disfigurement 679
fault 678.2
impairment 692.8
impurity 78.2
mark 568.5
ugly thing 899.4
*v.* be ugly 899.5
deform 249.7
disfigure 679.4
injure 692.15
mark 568.19
**blemished**
deformed 249.12
disfigured 679.8
imperfect 678.4
ugly 899.6
**blench** demur 623.4
flinch 891.21
pull back 284.7
suffer pain 424.8
**blend**
*n.* combination 52.1
compound 44.5
hybrid word 582.11
*v.* combine 52.3
harmonize 462.36
mix 44.11
**blended**
combined 52.5
harmonious 462.50
mixed 44.15
**blend into** 145.17
**bless** approve 968.9
congratulate 948.2
endow 818.17
give one's blessing
1032.13
gladden 865.7
praise 968.12
protect 699.18
sanctify 1026.5
thank 949.4
worship 1032.11
**blessed** damned 972.10
fortunate 728.14
happy 865.13
heavenly 1018.13
sanctified 1026.8
**blessed event** 167.7
**blessed with** 808.9
**blessing** approval 968.1
benediction 1032.5
boon 674.4
congratulation 948.1

consent 775.1
gift 818.7
godsend 811.7
good deed 938.7
prosperity 728.2
sanctification 1026.3
stroke of luck 728.3
**blight**
*n.* adversity 729.1
blast 676.2
disease 686.1
evil 675.3
*v.* freeze 334.11
impair 692.12
work evil 675.6
**blighted**
damaged 692.30
disappointed 541.5
ruined 693.28
spoiled 692.43
**blighter** 986.2
**blimp** aircraft 280.11
balloon 280.18
corpulent person
195.12
pompous person
904.9
**blind**
*n.* blinder 441.5
bridle part 659.5
concealment 615.3
pretext 649.1
shade 338.1,8
stratagem 735.3
trick 618.6
*v.* blind the eyes 441.7
conceal 615.6
dazzle 335.23
hoodwink 618.16
*adj.* closed 266.9
concealed 615.11
drunk 996.33
inattentive 531.7
involuntary 639.14
obscure 549.15
sightless 441.9
undiscerning 469.14
unpersuadable 626.13
**blind, the** 441.4
**blind alley**
impasse 731.5
obstruction 266.3
road 657.6
**blinded** blind 441.10
undiscerning 469.14
**blinders**
blindfold 441.5
bridle part 659.5
narrow-mindedness
527.1
**blind faith** 502.1
**blindfold**
*n.* blinder 441.5
*v.* blind 441.7
hoodwink 618.16
**blindfolded**
blinded 441.10
undiscerning 469.14
**blind impulse**
impulse 630.1
instinct 481.2
involuntariness 639.5

**blinding**
*n.* blindness 441.1
*adj.* bright 335.32
garish 362.19
obscuring 441.11
rainy 394.10
**blindness**
faulty eyesight 440.1
incognizance 477.3
sightlessness 441
unperceptiveness
469.2
unpersuadableness
626.5
**blind spot**
blindness 441.1
narrow-mindedness
527.1
radar interference
346.12
radio reception
344.21
**blind to**
insensible 856.10
unaware 477.13
**blink**
*n.* glance 439.4
light 335.7
reflection 335.9
*v.* flinch 891.21
glitter 335.24
neglect 534.8
pull back 284.7
wink 440.10
**blink at** be blind 441.8
be broad-minded
526.7
condone 947.4
disregard 531.2
permit 777.10
**blinker** 568.15
**blinking**
*n.* light 335.7
winking 440.7
*adj.* flickering 335.36
glittering 335.35
poor-sighted 440.11
**blintz** pancake 308.44
pastry 308.40
**blips** 346.11
**bliss** happiness 865.2
heaven 1018.6
pleasantness 863.1
**blissful** happy 865.13
pleasant 863.6
sublime 863.8
**blister**
*n.* blemish 679.1
bubble 405.1
ridge 256.3
sore 686.35
*v.* burn 329.24
criticize severely
969.21
**blistered** blistery 405.
burned 329.30
**blistering**
*n.* burning 329.5
*adj.* bubbly 405.6
hot 328.25
**blistery** 405.6
**blithe** 870.11

**blither** 469.12
**blithering** 469.22
**blithering idiot** 471.8
**blithesome** 870.11
**blitz**
  *n.* attack 798.1
  bombardment 798.7
  bombing 798.8
  *v.* attack 798.15
  blow up 693.18
  fire upon 798.22
**blitzkrieg** attack 798.1
  bombardment 798.7
**blizzard** snow 333.8
  windstorm 403.12
**bloat**
  *n.* distension 197.2
  overextension 663.7
  *v.* become larger
    197.5
  increase 38.6
  make larger 197.4
**bloated** bulging 256.14
  corpulent 195.18
  deformed 249.12
  distended 197.13
  increased 38.7
  overfull 663.20
  pompous 904.22
  proud 905.10
**blob** ball 255.2
  bulge 256.3
**blobby** formless 247.4
  vague 514.18
**bloc** 788.1
**block**
  *n.* auction 829.4
  city block 183.7
  clog 266.3
  defense mechanism
    690.31
  delay 132.2
  dolt 471.3
  instrument of execu-
    tion 1011.5
  lump 195.10
  mental block 538.3
  obstacle 730.4
  plaything 878.16
  print 578.6
  set 74.12
  shares 834.3
  solid 354.6
  thought disturbance
    690.24
  tract 180.4
  *v.* cover 228.19
  delay 132.8
  end 144.11
  fend off 799.10
  obstruct 730.12
  prevent 730.13
  stop up 266.7
**ockade**
  . closure 266.1
  enclosure 236.1
  exclusion 77.1
  hindrance 730.4
  obstruction 266.3
  siege 798.5
  . besiege 798.19
  enclose 236.5

exclude 77.4
  fortify 799.9
  obstruct 730.12
  stop 266.7
**blockage**
  defense mechanism
    690.31
  delay 132.2
  hindrance 730.1
  obstruction 266.3
  seizure 686.5
**blockbuster** 540.2
**blocked** clogged 266.11
  forgetful 538.9
  late 132.2
**blockhead**
  bungler 734.8
  dolt 471.4
**blockheaded** 469.17
**blockhouse**
  cottage 191.9
  stronghold 799.6
**blockish** 469.15
**block letter** 602.4
**block out** analyze 48.7
  form 246.7
  outline 654.12
**blocky** 203.10
**bloke** man 420.5
  person 417.3
**blond**
  *n.* hair color 362.9
  *adj.* fair-haired 364.9
  yellow-haired 370.5
**blood** ancestry 170.4
  blood relationship
    11.1
  body fluid 388.4
  class 61.2
  dandy 903.9
  diseases 686.18
  fluid 388.2
  killing 409.1
  kind 61.3
  kinsmen 11.2
  nobility 918.1
  race 11.4
  seat of life 407.3
**blood and thunder**
    855.9
**blood-and-thunder**
    857.30
**blood bank**
  blood 388.4
  hospital room 192.25
  transfusion 689.20
**bloodbath**
  carnage 409.5
  destruction 693.1
**blood brother** 11.3
**blood clot** 354.7
**bloodcurdling** 891.37
**bloodied** 866.25
**bloodless**
  colorless 363.7
  pacific 803.9
  uninteresting 883.6
  weak 160.12
**bloodletting**
  bleeding 689.26
  extraction 305.3
  killing 409.1

**bloodline** 170.4
**bloodlust**
  cruelty 939.11
  violence 162.1
**bloodmobile**
  blood 388.4
  transfusion 689.20
**blood money** fee 841.5
  recompense 841.3
**blood-red** 368.7
**blood relationship**
  consanguinity 11
  relationship 9.3
**blood relative** 11.2
**bloodshed** killing 409.1
  warfare 797.1
**bloodstain**
  *n.* blemish 679.3
  *v.* bloody 679.7
**bloodstained** 679.11
**bloodstream** 388.4
**bloodsucker**
  extortionist 822.12
  parasite 414.41
**bloodthirsty**
  cruel 939.24
  murderous 409.24
  warlike 797.25
**blood type** 388.4
**blood vessel** 396.14
**bloody**
  *v.* bleed 311.17
  bloodstain 679.7
  injure 692.15
  torture 866.18
  *adj.* bleeding 311.23
  blood red 368.7
  bloodstained 679.11
  cruel 939.24
  damned 972.9
  fluid 388.7
  murderous 409.24
  savage 162.20
  warlike 797.25
**bloody-minded**
  cruel 939.24
  murderous 409.24
  warlike 797.25
**bloom**
  *n.* beauty 900.1
  blossom 411.22
  flowering 411.24
  health 685.1
  heat 328.12
  reddening 368.3
  television reception
    345.5
  youth 124.1
  *v.* be healthy 685.5
  be hot 328.22
  evolve 148.5
  flower 411.32
  look beautiful 900.15
  mature 126.9
  reach perfection
    722.8
  thrive 728.8
**blooper** 518.6
**blooping**
  audio distortion
    450.13

television reception
    345.5
**blossom**
  *n.* bloom 411.22
  flowering 411.24
  *v.* evolve 148.5
  flower 411.32
  grow 197.7
  reach perfection
    722.8
  thrive 728.8
**blot**
  *n.* blemish 679.3
  obliteration 693.7
  soil 682.5
  stigma 915.6
  ugly thing 899.4
  *v.* be ugly 899.5
  blacken 365.7
  blemish 679.5
  dry 393.6
  obliterate 693.16
  sorb 306.13
  stigmatize 915.9
**blotch**
  *n.* blemish 679.3
  mark 568.5
  soil 682.5
  spottiness 374.3
  *v.* blacken 365.7
  blemish 679.5
  mark 568.19
  variegate 374.7
**blotchy**
  blemished 679.9
  dingy 365.11
  spotted 374.13
**blot out** darken 337.9
  delete 42.12
  kill 409.14
  obliterate 693.16
**blotter** absorbent 306.6
  record book 570.11
**blotto** 996.33
**blouse** 231.15,54
**blow**
  *n.* act 705.3
  blossom 411.22
  disappointment
    541.1
  distress 866.5
  feast 307.9
  flowering 411.24
  gust 403.6
  hit 283.4
  misfortune 729.2
  punishment 1010.3
  surprise 540.2
  windstorm 403.12
  *v.* be bombastic 601.6
  become exhausted
    717.5
  blare 453.9
  blunder 518.15
  boast 910.7
  breathe 403.24
  eject 310.21
  flee 631.11
  flower 411.32
  play music 462.43
  puff 310.23

reach perfection
722.8
squander 854.3
wind 403.22
**blow about** 559.16
**blow down**
knock down 318.5
raze 693.19
**blower** bellows 403.20
braggart 910.5
fan 403.21
ventilator 402.10
**blow for blow** 955.3
**blowgun** blower 403.20
weapon 801.5
**blowhard** 910.5
**blow hard** 910.7
**blowhole**
air passage 396.17
opening 265.4
outlet 303.9
**blow hot and cold**
be capricious 629.4
equivocate 483.9
fluctuate 141.5
vacillate 627.8
**blow in** 300.6
**blown** spoiled 692.43
tainted 692.42
wind-blown 403.27
**blown up out of all
proportion** 617.4
**blow off** boast 910.7
dissipate 75.5
**blow off steam** 878.26
**blow one's mind**
fantasy 535.17
go crazy 473.21
have hallucinations
519.8
**blow one's top**
become angry 952.19
get excited 857.15
go crazy 473.21
**blowout** banquet 307.9
ejection 310.7
explosion 162.7
festival 878.4
party 922.11
**blow out** eject 310.24
erupt 162.12
explode 162.13
extinguish 332.7
flow out 303.13
unclog 310.21
**blow over** end 70.6
knock down 318.5
stop blowing 403.22
**blowpipe**
blower 403.20
blowtorch 329.14
weapon 801.5
**blow the whistle**
be impatient 862.5
inform 557.12
put a stop to 144.11
**blow to** 841.19
**blowtorch**
aircraft 280.3
burner 329.14
**blowup**
explosion 162.7

increase 38.2
outburst 952.9
photoprint 577.5
**blow up**
become angry 952.19
come to nothing
725.12
demolish 693.18
disprove 506.4
excite 857.11
explode 162.13
get excited 857.15
increase 38.5
make larger 197.4
praise 968.12
process photos
577.15
set in 403.22
strike dead 409.18
**blowy** 403.25
**blowzy**
corpulent 195.18
red-complexioned
368.9
slovenly 62.15
**blubber**
n. softness 357.4
v. bubble 405.4
speak poorly 595.9
utter 594.26
weep 875.10
**blubbery** 380.9
**bludgeon** coerce 756.7
intimidate 891.28
threaten 973.2
**blue**
n. barbiturate 687.12
blueness 372.1
colors 372.4
trial print 603.5
v. make blue 372.2
adj. bluish 372.3
deathly 408.29
melancholy 872.23
obscene 990.9
**blue, the** 375.2
**Bluebeard** 933.12
**blue blood**
nobility 918.1
nobleman 918.4
**blue-blooded** 918.11
**blue book**
examination 485.2
information 557.1
official document
570.8
register 570.9
**blue chip** 834.2
**blue-collar worker** 718.2
**blue devil** 687.12
**blue devils**
delirium tremens
473.10
ill humor 951.10
sadness 872.6
**bluegrass** 462.10
**blue in the face** 857.23
**bluejacket**
navy man 276.4
sailor 276.1
**blue language** 972.3
**blue movie** 990.4

**bluenose** 903.11
**blue-pencil**
delete 42.12
revise 691.12
**blueprint**
n. diagram 654.3
outline 48.4
photograph 577.5
plan 654.1
representation 572.1
schedule 641.2
trial print 603.5
v. plot 654.11
process photos
577.15
**blue ribbon**
award 916.5
supremacy 36.3
**blues** folk music 462.10
ill humor 951.10
sadness 872.6
song 462.13
**bluestocking**
n. pedant 476.5
adj. book-learned
475.22
**blue streak** 269.6
**blue velvet** 687.12
**bluff**
n. bluster 911.1
blusterer 911.2
fakery 616.3
impostor 619.6
precipice 213.3
trick 618.6
v. bluster 911.3
deceive 618.13
fake 616.21
frighten off 891.29
adj. artless 736.5
blunt 259.3
candid 974.17
gruff 937.7
impudent 913.9
steep 219.18
**blunder**
n. an error 518.5
bungle 734.5
foolish act 470.4
v. bungle 734.11
err 518.14
fail 725.13
flounder 324.15
**blunderhead**
bungler 734.8
dolt 471.4
**blunderheaded**
clumsy 734.20
stupid 469.17
**blunder upon**
bungle 734.11
find 488.3
**blunt**
v. desensitize 856.7
disincline 652.4
dull 259.2
moderate 163.6
numb 423.4
weaken 160.10
adj. artless 736.5
candid 974.17
dull 259.3

free-spoken 762.22
gruff 937.7
stupid 469.16
unfeeling 856.9
**blunted** 259.3
**blur**
n. blemish 679.3
indistinctness 445.2
stigma 915.6
v. be undiscriminating
493.3
blemish 679.6
deform 247.3
lose distinctness
445.4
**blurb**
commendation 968.3
publicity 559.4
**blurred** formless 247.4
imperfectly spoken
595.12
indistinct 445.6
uncertain 514.18
**blurt** divulge 556.6
exclaim 459.7
remark 594.25
**blurt out** 630.7
**blush**
n. blushing 908.5
heat 328.12
reddening 368.3
warmth 362.2
v. become excited
857.17
become red 368.5
flush 908.8
look guilty 983.2
**bluster**
n. agitation 324.1
boasting 910.1
swagger 911
violence 162.2
v. be angry 952.15
blow 403.22
boast 910.6
intimidate 891.28
show a bold front
793.5
swagger 911.3
**blustering** noisy 453.12
swaggering 911.4
threatening 973.3
violent 162.17
windy 403.25
**BM** defecation 311.2
feces 311.4
**BMOC** 672.9
**BO** stench 437.1
sweat 311.7
**boar** male animal 420.8
swine 414.9
**board**
n. accommodations
659.3
council 755.1
directorate 748.11
edge 235.4
food 308.1
meal 307.5
rations 308.6
school board 567.17
stage 611.21

stock exchange 833.7
table 216.15
tribunal 1001.1
wood 378.3
*v.* accommodate
659.10
cover 228.23
eat 307.19
embark 301.16
feed 307.16
mount 315.12
raid 798.20
sail 275.48
**boarder** eater 307.14
lodger 190.8
**boardinghouse** 191.16
**boards, the**
stage 611.21
theater 611.1
**boardwalk** 657.3
**boast**
*n.* boasting 910.1
good thing 674.5
*v.* be vain 909.6
brag 910.6
possess 808.4
**boastful**
boasting 910.10
proud 905.9
vain 909.9
**boast of** 968.12
**boat**
*n.* automobile 272.9
ship 277.1,21
*v.* haul 271.12
sail 275.13
**boathouse** 192.27
**boating** 275.1
**boatman** 276.5
**boatswain**
ship's officer 276.7
supervisor 748.2
**boatyard** 719.3
**bob**
*n.* British money
835.8
crouch 318.3
float 277.11
greeting 925.4
jerk 286.3
obeisance 964.2
plumb 213.6
repeat 103.5
shake 324.3
weight 352.6
*v.* bow 318.9
cut off 42.10
fish 655.10
jump 319.6
make obeisance
964.6
oscillate 323.10
shake 324.11
shorten 203.6
style the hair 230.22
**bobble**
. an error 518.6
bungle 734.5
shake 324.3
blunder 518.15
bungle 734.12
oscillate 323.10

shake 324.11
**bobby** 699.16
**bob up** appear 446.9
arrive 300.6
ascend 315.9
be unexpected 540.6
**bode** 544.11
**bodega** 832.5
**bodice** 231.15
**bodiless**
immaterial 377.7
unsubstantial 4.5
**bodily**
*adj.* innate 5.7
material 376.9
sensual 987.6
*adv.* in person 186.17
wholly 54.13
**body**
*n.* association 788.1
collection 74.11
community 788.2
corpse 408.16
entity 3.3
group 74.3
major part 54.6
person 417.3
physical body 376.3
physique 246.4
printing 603.6
religion 1020.3
size 195.1
solid 354.6
substantiality 3.1
thickness 204.2
*v.* embody 376.8
**body-build** nature 5.3
physique 246.4
**body count**
death list 408.14
numeration 87.5
**bodyguard** escort 73.5
guard 699.14
**body language** 568.14
**body odor** stench 437.1
sweat 311.7
**body of knowledge**
475.9
**body politic**
country 181.1
people 417.2
**body-snatching** 824.9
**bog**
*n.* filthy place 682.12
marsh 400.1
*v.* bog down 400.2
**bogey** aircraft 280.9
evil spirit 1016.10
frightener 891.9
**bogeyman**
evil spirit 1016.10
frightener 891.9
**boggle**
*n.* bungle 734.5
demur 623.2
*v.* be a coward 892.8
be frightened 891.20
be irresolute 627.6
bungle 734.11
demur 623.4
object 522.5
overwhelm 920.6

perplex 514.13
quibble 483.9
**boggy** marshy 400.3
moist 392.15
**bogus** 616.26
**Bohemian**
*n.* nomad 274.4
nonconformist 83.3
*adj.* informal 647.3
nonconformist 83.6
**boil**
*n.* agitation 324.1
dish 308.7
heating 329.2
sore 686.35
swelling 256.4
*v.* be angry 952.15
be hot 328.22
bubble 405.4
cook 330.4
sanitize 681.24
seethe 162.11
stew 329.20
**boil down** 203.6
**boiler room**
fraud 618.9
noisemaker 453.5
stockbrokerage 833.9
**boiling**
*n.* agitation 324.1
bubbling 405.3
cooking 330.1
heating 329.2
*adj.* angry 952.27
excited 857.20
hot 328.22
**boiling over**
excited 857.20
fervent 855.23
**boisterous**
blustering 911.4
excited 857.22
noisy 453.12
rampageous 162.19
**bold** brazen 913.10
conspicuous 555.12
courageous 893.17
defiant 793.7
foolhardy 894.9
immodest 990.6
in relief 256.17
protruding 256.13
seaworthy 277.18
steep 219.18
**bold-faced**
brazen 913.10
typographical 603.20
**boldly** brazenly 913.13
conspicuously 555.16
courageously 893.22
**bole** cylinder 255.4
plant stem 411.19
**boll** ball 255.2
seed vessel 411.28
**bollixed up**
confused 62.16
spoiled 692.31
**bollix up** confuse 63.3
spoil 692.13
**bologna** 308.21
**Bolshevik**
Communist 745.13

radical 745.12
revolutionist 147.3
**bolster**
*n.* bedding 216.20
*v.* confirm 505.12
encourage 893.16
support 216.21
sustain 785.12
**bolt**
*n.* apostasy 628.2
arrow 801.16
bundle 74.8
desertion 633.2
flight 631.4
length 202.3
lightning 335.17
restraint 760.5
weapon 801.12
*v.* apostatize 628.8
arrange 60.11
close 266.6
desert 633.6
eat 307.21
fasten 47.8
flee 631.10
gluttonize 994.4
obstruct 730.12
refine 681.22
rush 269.9
separate 77.6
**bolt-hole** escape 632.3
hiding place 615.4
secret passage 615.5
**bolt out of the blue**
540.2
**bolt upright** 213.11,13
**bolus** ball 255.2
bite 307.2
pill 687.7
**bomb**
*n.* bombshell
801.14,30
failure 725.2
stage show 611.4
surprise 540.2
*v.* attack 798.23
be a flop 611.33
be uninteresting
883.4
blow up 693.18
fail 725.9
**bombard**
atomize 326.17
blow up 693.18
fire upon 798.22
**bombardier**
artilleryman 800.10
aviation 279.4
**bombardment**
attack 798.7
fission 326.8
**bombast**
boasting 910.1
grandiloquence 601.2
nonsense 547.2
**bombastic**
boastful 910.11
fustian 601.9
literary inelegance
590.3
pompous 904.22

bomber
 artilleryman 800.10
 destroyer 693.8
 frightener 891.8
 violent person 162.9
bombinate 452.13
bombing attack 798.8
 flight 278.11
bombshell
 bomb 801.14
 surprise 540.2
bona fide
 authentic 516.14
 faithfully 974.25
 honest 974.14
bonanza plenty 661.2
 rich source 837.3
 source of supply
  660.4
bond
 n. compact 771.1
 connection 47.3
 contract 771.3
 debenture 834.4
 fidelity 974.7
 insurance 699.4
 joining 47.1
 pledge 772.2
 relationship 9.1
 restraint 760.4
 security 772.1
 v. join 47.5
 pledge 772.10
 secure 772.9
bondage 764.1
bondholder 833.14
bondsman
 guarantor 772.6
 slave 764.7
bone
 n. dryness 393.2
 hardness 356.6
 structure 245.6,12
 v. study 564.12
 adj. osteal 245.11
bonehead 471.4
bone of contention
 discord 795.7
 question 485.10
boner an error 518.6
 bungle 734.5
bones body 376.3
 corpse 408.16
 dice 515.9
 percussion instrument
  465.18
 refuse 669.4
 seat of affections
  855.2
 skeleton 245.5
bone to pick
 bone of contention
  795.7
 grudge 929.5
bonhomie
 cordiality 927.6
 good nature 938.2
 hospitality 925.1
bonkers 473.26
bon mot 881.7
bonny beautiful 900.17
 good 674.12

bon ton custom 642.1
 fashion 644.1
 fashionableness 644.2
bonus extra 41.4
 extra pay 841.6
 gratuity 818.5
 surplus 663.5
 windfall 811.6
bon vivant
 companion 928.4
 connoisseur 897.7
 gourmet 307.14
 sensualist 987.3
 sociable person
  922.15
bon voyage! 301.23
bony bone 245.11
 hard 356.10
 lean 205.17
boo
 n. hoot 967.3
 v. hiss 967.10
 interj. contempt
  966.10
boob dupe 620.1
 fool 471.2
 teat 256.6
boo-boo an error 518.6
 bungle 734.5
boob tube 345.11
booby fool 471.2
 loser 727.5
 teat 256.6
booby hatch 473.14
booby prize 916.2
booby trap
 concealment 615.3
 trap 618.11
boodle booty 824.11
 bribe 651.2
 money 835.2
 spoils of office
  744.35
boogie-woogie 462.9
boohoo 875.10
book
 n. book part 605.13
 part of writing 55.2
 playbook 611.26
 poetic division
  609.11
 publication 559.1
 volume 605
 wager 515.3
 v. accuse 1005.7
 engage 780.13
 keep accounts 845.8
 list 88.8
 record 570.16
 schedule 641.4
bookbinding 605.15
bookcase
 bookbinding 605.15
 bookholder 605.20
 storage place 660.6
book collector 605.21
bookdealer
 bookman 605.21
 merchant 830.3
booked
 recorded 570.18
 scheduled 641.6

book end 605.20
bookie 515.16
booking
 engagement 780.4
 playing engagement
  611.12
 recording 570.15
booking agent 611.30
bookish
 book-learned 475.22
 studentlike 566.12
 studious 564.17
bookkeeper
 accountant 845.7
 calculator 87.8
 financial officer
  836.11
 recorder 571.1
bookkeeping
 n. accounting 845.6
 adj. accounting
  845.12
book-learned 475.22
booklet 605.9
booklover
 bookman 605.21
 bookworm 476.4
bookmaker
 bookman 605.21
 gambling 515.16
bookmobile 605.17
bookrest 605.20
book review 494.2
book reviewer 606.4
books
 account book 845.4
 list 88.5
bookseller
 bookman 605.21
 merchant 830.3
bookstore
 bookshop 605.18
 store 832.4
book value 834.9
bookworm
 bibliophage 476.4
 bookman 605.21
 student 566.10
boom
 n. barrier 730.5
 business cycle 827.9
 explosion 162.7
 float 277.11
 increase 38.1
 lever 287.4
 loud noise 456.4
 prosperity 728.5
 reverberation 454.2
 v. din 453.6
 hum 452.13
 increase 38.6
 reverberate 454.7
 sail 275.48
 speed 269.8
 thrive 728.8
 thunder 456.9
 utter 594.26
boomerang
 n. recoil 284.2
 retaliation 955.1
 weapon 801.12
 v. recoil 284.6

booming
 n. boom 456.4
 hum 452.7
 reverberation 454.2
 adj. humming 452.20
 loud 453.10
 reverberating 454.11
 thriving 728.13
 thundering 456.12
boon
 n. gift 818.7
 godsend 811.7
 good 674.4
 adj. convivial 922.19
boondocks
 hinterland 182.2
 remote region 199.4
 woodland 411.11
boor
 awkward person
  734.8
 oaf 471.5
 rustic 919.9
 vulgar person 898.6
boorish churlish 898.13
 clumsy 734.20
 countrified 182.7
 discourteous 937.6
boost
 n. assist 785.2
 commendation 968.3
 improvement 691.1
 increase 38.1
 promotion 782.1
 raise 317.2
 thrust 283.2
 v. cheer 870.7
 commend 968.11
 elevate 317.5
 further 785.17
 increase 38.4
 make better 691.9
 publicize 559.15
 steal 824.13
 thrust 283.11
booster
 commender 968.8
 devotee 635.6
 dose 687.6
 injection 689.18
 publicist 559.9
 rocket 281.5
 television relay 345.9
 thief 825.1
boot
 n. an error 518.6
 footwear 231.27,60
 instrument of torture
  1011.4
 kick 283.8
 novice 566.9
 recruit 800.17
 sailor 276.4
 thrill 857.2
 v. blunder 518.15
 clothe 231.39
 dismiss 310.19
 kick 283.18
boot, the
 dismissal 310.5
 ejection 310.1
bootblack 750.5

**booth**
  compartment 192.2
  hut 191.10
  store 832.3
**bootleg**
  v. deal illicitly 826.7
  make liquor 996.29
  adj. illegal 999.6
**bootlegger**
  liquor maker 996.18
  racketeer 826.4
**bootless**
  fruitless 669.12
  ineffective 158.15
  unsuccessful 725.17
**bootlicker** 907.3
**booty** loot 824.11
  take 822.10
**booze**
  n. liquor 996.12
  v. drink 307.27
  liquor 996.24
**bop** music 462.9
  nonsense 547.3
**bordello** brothel 989.9
  disapproved place
    191.28
**border**
  n. edge 235.4
  exterior 224.2
  frontier 235.5
  garden 413.10
  region 180.2
  scenery 611.25
  side 242.1
  v. adjoin 200.9
  edge 235.10
  side 242.4
**bordering**
  n. edging 235.7
  adj. adjacent 200.16
  fringing 235.11
**bordering on** 200.24
**borderland**
  environment 233.1
  frontier 235.5
  hinterland 182.2
  region 180.2
**borderline** 235.11
**borderline case**
  an uncertainty 514.8
  lunatic 473.15
**bore**
  n. annoyance 866.2
  boring person 884.4
  puncture 265.3
  thickness 204.3
  wave 395.14
  v. excavate 257.15
  give no pleasure
    866.12
  leave one cold 884.6
  puncture 265.16
**boreal** cold 333.14
  northern 290.15
  windy 403.25
  winter 128.8
**boreas** 403.3
**bored** incurious 529.3
  languid 708.19
  pleasureless 866.20
  uninterested 884.11

**boredom**
  incurious 529.1
  languor 708.6
  tedium 884.3
  unpleasure 866.1
**boring**
  n. puncture 265.3
  adj. monotonous 17.6
  wearying 884.9
**born** given birth 167.21
  innate 5.7
  thorough 56.10
**borne** 216.24
**borne out** 505.21
**born for** 733.27
**born out of wedlock**
    999.7
**born yesterday** 736.5
**borough** city 183.1
  district 180.5
  election district
    744.16
**borrow**
  deal in money 835.27
  go in debt 840.6
  imitate 22.5
  plagiarize 824.18
  raise money 821.3
  steal 824.13
**borrower** 840.4
**borrowing** debt 840.1
  loan word 582.7
  money market 835.16
  money-raising 821
  plagiarism 824.7
**borrowing power** 839.1
**borscht circuit** 611.12
**borstal** prison 761.8
  reform school 567.14
**boscage** thicket 411.13
  undergrowth 411.15
**bosh** humbug 616.14
  nonsense 547.3
**bos'n** 276.7
**bosom**
  n. breast 256.6
  inner nature 5.4
  interior 225.2
  seat of affections
    855.2
  v. embrace 932.16
  harbor 813.7
  keep secret 614.7
  secrete 615.7
**bosomy** bulging 256.14
  corpulent 195.18
**boss**
  n. knob 256.3
  mark 568.7
  master 749.1
  political leader 746.7
  relief 575.3
  superior 36.4
  supervisor 748.2
  v. emboss 256.11
  roughen 261.4
  supervise 747.10
  adj. excellent 674.13
  governing 741.18
  supervising 747.13

**bossism**
  authoritativeness
    739.3
  politics 744.1
**bossy**
  n. cow 414.6
  female animal 421.9
  adj. imperious 739.16
  in relief 256.17
**botanic(al)**
  herbaceous 411.33
  phytological 412.8
**botanist**
  biologist 406.18
  phytologist 412.2
**botany** biology 406.17
  phytology 412
  plants 411.1
**botch**
  n. an error 518.5
  bungle 734.5
  fiasco 725.6
  misrepresentation
    573.2
  slipshodness 534.3
  v. bungle 734.11
  do carelessly 534.9
  err 518.14
  impair 692.12
  misrepresent 573.4
**botched**
  bungled 734.21
  damaged 692.30
  slipshod 534.12
**both**
  n. two 90.2
  adj. two 90.7
**bother**
  n. annoyance 866.2
  bustle 707.4
  commotion 62.4
  confusion 532.3
  dither 857.5
  imposition 963.1
  inconvenience 671.3
  perplexity 514.3
  trouble 731.3
  v. annoy 866.13
  be unpleasant 864.15
  bewilder 514.12
  confuse 532.7
  disquiet 890.3
  distress 866.16
  inconvenience 671.4
  take liberties 961.7
  vex 731.12
**bothered**
  annoyed 866.21
  anxious 890.6
  bewildered 514.23
  confused 532.12
  distressed 866.22
  troubled 731.19
**bothersome**
  annoying 864.22
  troublesome 731.17
  worrisome 890.9
**bottle**
  n. types of 193.12
  v. enclose 236.6
  package 236.9
  preserve 701.9

  put in 184.14
**bottleneck**
  constriction 198.1
  convergence 298.1
  narrow place 205.3
  obstacle 730.4
  obstruction 266.3
**bottle up**
  confine 761.12
  enclose 236.6
  hinder 730.10
  retain 813.5
  secrete 615.7
  suppress 760.8
**bottom**
  n. base 208.4
  bed 212.4
  bottom side 212
  courage 893.5
  marsh 400.1
  pluck 624.3
  ship 277.1
  valley 257.9
  adj. bottommost
    212.7
  cheap 849.9
**bottom dollar** end 70.2
  funds 835.14
**bottomland**
  lowland 208.3
  marsh 400.1
  plain 387.1
**bottomless** deep 209.11
  greedy 634.27
  plentiful 661.7
**bottomless pit**
  depths 209.3
  hell 1019.1
**bottom line, the**
  crucial point 672.6
  the whole story 86.5
**bottom out** 139.5
**boudoir** 192.7
**bough** branch 411.18
  offshoot 55.4
**bought** 828.11
**bouillabaisse**
  soup 308.10
  stew 308.11
**bouillon** beef 308.13
  soup 308.10
**boulder** 384.5
**boulevard** 657.6
**bounce**
  n. elasticity 358.1
  leap 319.1
  lightheartedness
    870.3
  ostentation 904.8
  radar signal 346.11
  radio signal 344.10
  recoil 284.2
  shake 324.3
  v. be elastic 358.5
  bluster 911.3
  dismiss 310.19
  eject 310.13
  jump 319.6
  leap 319.5
  recoil 284.6
  shake 324.11

**bounce back**
radar 346.16
recoil 284.6
recover 694.20
reverberate 454.7
**bouncing** leaping 319.7
lively 707.17
recoiling 284.10
robust 685.10
strong 159.13
**bound**
*n.* leap 319.1
limit 235.3
recoil 284.2
*v.* border 235.10
circumscribe 234.4
enclose 236.5
leap 319.5
limit 234.5
recoil 284.6
run 269.10
separate 235.8
*adj.* blocked 266.11
certain 513.13
enclosed 236.10
joined 47.13
limited 234.7
obliged 962.16
promised 770.8
related 9.9
resolute 624.11
restrained 760.16
**boundary**
*n.* divider 92.3
end 70.2
fence 236.4
joint 47.4
limit 235.3
limitation 234.2
pause 144.4
*adj.* bordering 235.11
final 70.10
**bounder**
bad person 986.8
vulgar person 898.6
**boundless**
excessive 663.16
godlike 1013.20
infinite 104.3
large 34.7
**bound over** 780.20
**bountiful** liberal 853.4
plentiful 661.7
productive 165.9
**bounty** extra pay 841.6
gratuity 818.5
liberality 853.1
subsidy 818.8
**bouquet** bundle 74.8
compliment 968.6
flowers 411.23
fragrance 436.1
**bourgeois**
*n.* common man
919.7
conformist 82.2
townsman 190.6
vulgar person 898.6
*adj.* capitalist 745.23
conformist 82.6
mediocre 680.8
middle-class 919.12

vulgar 898.14
**bourn** boundary 235.3
destination 300.5
running water 395.1
**bourse** 833.7
**bout** boxing 796.9
contest 796.3
game 878.9
revel 878.6
spell 108.2
spree 996.5
turn 137.3
**boutique** 832.1
**boutonniere** 411.23
**bovine**
*n.* cattle 414.6
*adj.* complacent
868.10
inexcitable 858.10
stupid 469.15
ungulate 414.49
**bow**
*n.* bend 252.3
bulge 256.3
curve 252.2
viol 465.6
weapon 801.17
*v.* curve 252.6
fiddle 462.42
**bow**
*n.* crouch 318.3
front 240.3
greeting 925.4
obeisance 964.2
*v.* be defeated 727.12
bend 318.9
be servile 907.6
bow down 765.10
make obeisance
964.6
**bowdlerize**
clean 681.18
delete 42.12
**bowel movement**
defecation 311.2
feces 311.4
**bowels** depths 209.3
intestine 225.4
**bower**
playing card 878.17
summerhouse 191.13
**bowery** 411.38
**bowl**
*n.* arena 802.1
ceramic ware 576.2
pit 257.2
throw 285.4
*v.* be concave 257.12
make concave 257.13
push 285.10
roll 322.10
throw 285.11
**bowlegged** 249.12
**bowl over**
astonish 920.6
knock down 318.5
startle 540.8
**bow out**
absent oneself 187.8
dismiss 310.18
exit 303.11
leave 301.8

**box**
*n.* coffin 410.11
compartment 192.2
cottage 191.9
gift 818.4
impasse 731.5
punishment 1010.3
slap 283.7
storage place 660.6
theater part 611.20
*v.* contend 796.14
package 236.9
punish 1010.13
put in 184.14
restrain 760.9
slap 283.16
wrap 228.20
**boxcar** 272.14
**boxcars** 99.7
**boxer** 800.2
**box in** confine 236.6
enclose 236.5
qualify 507.3
restrain 760.9
**boxing** packaging 236.2
pugilism 796.9
**box office**
attendance 186.4
office 719.8
receipts 844.1
**box springs** 216.20
**boy**
*n.* child 125.5
male servant 750.4
race 418.3
*interj.* pleasure 865.17
**boycott**
*n.* exclusion 77.1
ostracism 926.3
protest 522.2
strike 789.7
*v.* object 522.5
ostracize 926.6
strike 789.9
**boyfriend** 931.12
**boyhood**
childhood 124.2
young people 125.2
**boyish** childish 124.11
thin 205.16
**boy wonder** 733.12
**bra** brassiere 231.24
supporter 216.2
**brace**
*n.* medical dressing
687.33
music 462.29
support 216.2,26
two 90.2
*v.* bind 47.9
refresh 695.2
stiffen 356.9
strengthen 159.11
support 216.21
**bracelet** circle 253.3
jewel 901.6
**brace oneself**
be determined 624.8
prepare oneself
720.13
**bracer** drink 996.7
refresher 695.1

supporter 216.2
tonic 687.8
**braces** 215.5
**brace up**
cheer up 870.9
encourage 893.16
recuperate 694.19
refresh 695.2
strengthen 159.11
take courage 893.14
**bracing** cool 333.12
energizing 161.14
healthful 683.5
refreshing 695.3
supporting 216.23
tonic 687.44
**bracken** 411.4,43
**bracket**
*n.* class 61.2
supporter 216.2,28
*v.* join 47.5
pair 90.5
parenthesize 236.8
punctuate 586.16
relate 9.6
**brackish** salty 433.9
unsavory 429.7
**bract** 411.17
**brag**
*n.* boasting 910.1
braggart 910.5
*v.* bluster 911.3
boast 910.6
**brag about** 968.12
**braggart**
*n.* blusterer 911.2
boaster 910.5
egotist 909.5
*adj.* boastful 910.10
**bragging**
*n.* boasting 910.1
*adj.* boastful 910.10
**Bragi**
Norse deity 1014.6
poetic inspiration
609.12
**Brahma** God 1013.4
Hindu deity 1014.8
**Brahman**
Hindu priest 1038.14
nobleman 918.4
religionist 1020.34
**Brahmin**
intellectual 476.1
snob 912.7
**braid**
*n.* cord 206.2
hair 230.7
weaving 222.2
*v.* weave 222.6
**Braille** 441.6
**brain**
*n.* intellect 466.1
intelligent being
467.9
seat of thought 466.₁
sensory area 422.6
vitals 225.4
*v.* strike dead 409.18
**brainchild**
good idea 479.6
product 168.1

thing imagined 535.5
work of art 574.11
written matter 602.10
**brain damage** 473.1
**brainless** foolish 470.8
  scatterbrained 532.16
  unintelligent 469.13
**brainstorm**
  absurd idea 479.7
  caprice 629.1
  delirium 473.8
  good idea 479.6
  impulse 630.1
**brain trust** 755.1
**brainwash**
  alienate 145.15
  indoctrinate 562.13
**brain wave** 630.1
**brainwork** study 564.3
  thought 478.1
**brainy** 467.14
**braise** 330.4
**brake**
  *n.* curb 730.7
  thicket 411.13
  *v.* prevent 730.13
  slow 270.9
  stop 144.11
**bramble** adherent 50.4
  shrubbery 411.9
  thorn 258.7
**bran** grain 308.4
  hull 228.16
  powder 361.5
**branch**
  *n.* affiliate 788.10
  ancestry 170.4
  biology 61.5
  bough 411.18
  class 61.2
  collateral descendant
    171.4
  fork 299.4
  limb 55.4
  military unit 800.21
  office 719.8
  railway 657.8
  religion 1020.3
  running water 395.1
  tributary 395.3
  *v.* angle 251.5
  bisect 92.4
  deviate 291.3
  fork 299.7
  spread 197.6
**branching**
  *n.* bisection 92.1
  forking 299.3
  *adj.* branched 411.38
  forked 299.10
  halved 92.6
**branch out**
  disperse 75.4
  fork 299.7
  spread 197.6
**brand**
  *n.* ashes 329.16
  blemish 679.3
  burn 329.6
  burner 329.15
  characteristic 80.4
  coal 328.16

kind 61.3
label 568.13
lighter 331.4
mark 568.5
nature 5.3
stigma 915.6
*v.* blemish 679.6
  burn 329.24
  label 568.20
  mark 568.19
  stigmatize 915.9
**brandish** flaunt 904.17
  indicate 555.5
  wave 323.11
**brand-new** 122.10
**brash** defiant 793.7
  gruff 937.7
  impudent 913.9
  rash 894.7
**brass**
  *n.* brass wind 465.8
  insolence 913.3
  memorial 570.12
  money 835.2
  orchestra 464.12
  rashness 894.1
  *adj.* metal 383.17
**brass, the**
  directorate 748.11
  important persons
    672.8
  officer 749.18
  superiors 36.5
**brassiere**
  supporter 216.2
  undergarment
    231.24,58
**brass knuckles** 801.20
**brass tacks** 1.4
**brassy** see **brazen**
**brat** 125.4
**bravado** bluster 911.1
  boasting 910.1
  courage 893.6
  defiance 793.1
**brave**
  *n.* brave person 893.8
  soldier 800.6
  *v.* confront 240.8
  defy 793.3
  defy danger 697.7
  endure 861.5
  stand up to 893.11
  thwart 730.15
  *adj.* courageous
    893.17
  showy 904.19
**bravery** courage 893.1
  ornamentation 901.3
**bravo!** approval 968.22
  congratulations 948.4
**bravura**
  *n.* aria 462.14
  courage 893.6
  display 904.4
  skill 733.1
  vocal music 462.12
  *adj.* showy 904.19
  skillful 733.20
  vocal 462.51
**braw** beautiful 900.17
  chic 644.13

excellent 674.12
showy 904.19
**brawl**
  *n.* commotion 62.4
  free-for-all 796.5
  meeting 74.2
  noise 453.3
  quarrel 795.5
  violence 162.2
  *v.* be noisy 453.8
  contend 796.14
  quarrel 795.11
**brawler**
  combatant 800.1
  oppositionist 791.3
  rebel 767.5
**brawling** noisy 453.12
  vociferous 459.10
**brawn** flesh 406.1
  strength 159.2
**brawny**
  corpulent 195.18
  strong 159.14
**bray**
  *n.* harsh sound 458.3
  loud sound 453.4
  *v.* animal sound 460.2
  blare 453.9
  pulverize 361.9
  sound harshly 458.9
  utter 594.26
**brazen**
  *v.* face up to 893.11
  *adj.* defiant 793.7
  gaudy 904.20
  immodest 990.6
  metal 383.17
  noisy 453.12
  rash 894.7
  raucous 458.15
  reddish-brown 367.4
  shameless 913.10
  wicked 981.17
**brazen out**
  face up to 893.11
  outbrave 893.12
  persevere 625.4
**breach**
  *n.* break 49.4
  crack 201.2
  discontinuity 72.2
  falling-out 795.4
  misdeed 982.2
  violation 769.2
  *v.* begin 68.12
  break 49.12
  cleave 201.4
  open 265.15
**breach of promise**
  infidelity 975.5
  violation 769.2
**bread** Eucharist 1040.8
  food 308.1
  money 835.2
  support 785.3
  types of 308.28
**breadth**
  broad-mindedness
    526.1
  size 195.1
  space 179.1
  width 204

**breadwinner** 718.2
**breadwinning**
  businesslike 656.15
  gainful 811.15
**break**
  *n.* chance 156.1
  change 139.1
  cheapening 849.4
  crack 201.2
  discontinuity 72.2
  electric circuit 342.4
  escape 632.1
  falling-out 795.4
  gap 57.2
  impairment 692.8
  interim 109.1
  pause 144.3
  respite 711.2
  separation 49.4
  stock market 833.5
  stroke of luck 728.3
  *v.* accustom 642.11
  bankrupt 842.8
  be changed 139.5
  be damaged 692.26
  be made public
    559.16
  billow 395.22
  change course 275.30
  cheapen 849.6
  cleave 201.4
  conquer 727.10
  depose 783.4
  disaccustom 643.2
  disagree 27.5
  discontinue 72.3
  dismiss 310.19
  domesticate 764.11
  domineer 741.16
  drive animals 416.7
  fracture 49.12
  go bankrupt 842.7
  grow bright 335.27
  injure 692.15
  interrupt 144.10
  not observe 769.4
  recess 109.3
  show fragility 360.3
  subdue 764.9
  take a rest 711.8
  train 562.14
  weaken 160.9
**breakable** brittle 360.4
  frail 160.14
**breakage**
  discount 847.1
  impairment 692.8
  separation 49.4
**breakaway**
  *n.* apostasy 628.2
  desertion 633.2
  *adj.* counteractive
    178.8
  dissenting 522.6
  nonconformist 83.6
  rebellious 767.11
  reputative 628.12
  unusual 85.10
**break away**
  apostatize 628.8
  desert 633.6
  escape 632.6

**brickbat**
indignity 965.2
weapon 801.12
**bridal** 933.19
**bride** 933.6
**bride and groom** 933.10
**bridegroom** 933.6
**bridesmaid** 933.5
**bridge**
n. card game 878.35
dental 258.6
music division 462.24
observation post
439.8
span 657.10
stage 611.21
viol 465.6
v. cover 228.30
join 47.5
**bridgehead**
outpost 240.2
stronghold 799.6
**bridle**
n. harness 659.5
restraint 760.4
v. affect 903.14
be arrogant 912.8
become angry 952.17
bind 47.10
drive animals 416.7
restrain 760.7
shackle 760.10
**brief**
n. abridgment 607.1
airmanship 278.3
record 570.7
v. abridge 607.5
advise 754.5
aviation 278.57
engage 780.13
give instructions
562.16
inform 557.8
outline 654.12
adj. abridged 607.6
concise 592.6
short 203.8
taciturn 613.9
transient 111.8
**briefed**
informed 475.18
prepared 720.16
**briefing** advice 754.1
airmanship 278.3
engagement 780.4
information 557.1
instructions 562.6
preparation 720.1
**briefly** concisely 592.7
shortly 203.12
transiently 111.10
**rier** adherent 50.4
shrubbery 411.9
thorn 258.7
**rig** 761.8
**rigade** group 74.3
military unit 800.19
**rigadier** 749.18
**rigand** 825.4
**right** alert 533.14
auspicious 544.18
brilliant 335.32

cheerful 870.11
clean 681.25
colorful 362.18
gorgeous 900.19
illustrious 914.19
intelligent 467.12
optimistic 888.12
pleasant 863.10
sharp-witted 467.14
teachable 564.18
undamaged 677.8
**brighten** cheer 870.7
grow bright 335.27
illuminate 335.28
make pleasant 863.5
**brightness**
alertness 533.5
auspiciousness 544.9
beauty 900.6
brilliance 335.4
cheerfulness 870.1
colorfulness 362.4
color quality 362.6
intelligence 467.2
pleasantness 863.4
teachability 564.5
**bright side**
optimism 888.3
pleasantness 863.4
**Brigit** 1014.7
**brilliance** beauty 900.6
brightness 335.4
colorfulness 362.4
grandeur 904.5
illustriousness 914.6
intelligence 467.2
skill 733.1
wittiness 881.2
**brilliant** bright 335.32
colorful 362.18
gorgeous 900.19
illustrious 914.19
intelligent 467.14
skillful 733.20
witty 881.15
**brim** 235.4
**brimming** 56.11
**brim over** 395.17
**brindle** 374.15
**brine**
preservative 701.3
salt 433.4
**bring** be sold 829.12
bring on 153.12
cost 846.15
entail 76.4
fetch 271.15
induce 648.22
inflict 963.5
**bring about**
accomplish 722.5
cause 153.11
change course 275.30
do 705.6
produce 167.9
prompt 648.13
**bring back** fetch 271.15
remember 537.10
restore 823.4
revive 694.16
**bring before**
confront 240.8

propose 773.5
**bring charges** 1005.7
**bring down**
disparage 971.8
fell 318.5
humiliate 906.5
incur 175.4
raze 693.19
strike dead 409.18
**bring down upon**
cause trouble 731.13
incur 175.4
inflict 963.5
**bring forth** bear 167.14
create 167.13
elicit 305.14
indicate 555.5
originate 153.11
**bring forward**
adduce evidence
505.13
call to witness
1004.16
confront 240.8
indicate 555.5
make better 691.9
propose 773.5
**bring home to**
accuse of 1005.9
attribute to 155.4
condemn 1008.3
convince 501.18
impress upon 855.18
prove 505.11
**bring in** cost 846.15
harvest 413.19
introduce 306.14
yield 844.4
**bring off**
bring about 722.5
carry out 705.9
do 705.6
succeed with 724.10
**bring on**
adduce evidence
505.13
incur 175.4
induce 153.12
**bring out** elicit 305.14
indicate 555.5
issue 559.14
print 603.14
**bring round**
change course 275.30
convince 501.18
persuade 648.23
restore to health
694.15
**bring to** convert 145.11
revive 694.16
sail 275.24
stop 144.11
**bring to light**
disclose 556.4
elicit 305.14
uncover 488.4
**bring to mind**
imply 546.4
remember 537.10
resemble 20.7
**bring to pass**
bring about 722.5

cause 153.11
do 705.6
**bring up** begin 68.11
confront 240.8
propose 773.5
stop 144.7
train 562.14
vomit 310.25
**brink** 235.4
**brinkmanship**
foreign policy 744.5
recklessness 894.3
**brio** 161.3
**brisk** brief 111.8
cold 333.14
energetic 161.12
exciting 857.29
lively 707.17
pungent 433.7
refreshing 695.3
windy 403.25
**bristle**
n. barb 261.3
beard 230.8
hair 230.2
thorn 258.7
v. annoy 866.13
become angry 952.17
be sharp 258.8
provoke 952.22
rise 213.8
roughen 261.5
**bristle with**
be numerous 101.5
teem with 661.5
**bristling** crowded 74.22
rough 261.9
teeming 101.9
**bristly** hairy 230.24
prickly 258.12
rough 261.9
**Britain** 181.4
**britches** 231.18
**brittle** crisp 360.4
deteriorated 692.37
frail 160.14
transient 111.7
**broach** begin 68.11
extract 305.12
make public 559.11
open 265.12
propose 773.5
puncture 265.16
**broad**
n. girl 125.6
unchaste woman
989.14
woman 421.6
adj. broad-minded
526.8
candid 974.17
comic 880.5
compounds 204.10
extensive 79.13
general 79.11
phonetic 594.31
spacious 179.9
vague 514.18
voluminous 195.17
vulgar 990.8
wide 204.6

**broadcast**
 *n.* dispersion 75.1
  planting 413.14
  publication 559.1
  radio broadcast
   344.18
 *v.* communicate 554.7
  disperse 75.4
  plant 413.18
  publish 559.10
  radiobroadcast
   344.25
 *adj.* dispersed 75.9
  made public 559.17
**broadcaster** 344.23
**broadcasting**
  dispersion 75.1
  planting 413.14
  publication 559.1
  radio broadcasting
   344.16
**broaden** augment 38.4
  become larger 197.5
  generalize 79.9
  make larger 197.4
  spread 38.6
  widen 204.4
**broadening** 526.14
**broadly**
  candidly 974.23
  extensively 179.10
  far and wide 199.16
  generally 79.17
  humorously 880.6
  vaguely 514.27
**broad-minded**
  liberal 762.24
  tolerant 526.8
  wise 467.17
**broad-shouldered**
  strong 159.14
  virile 420.12
**broadside**
 *n.* advertising 559.8
  gunfire 798.10
  side 242.1
 *adv.* breadthwise
   204.9
  sideways 242.8
**Broadway** 611.1
**brochure** 605.9
**brogue** 594.9
**broil**
 *n.* commotion 62.4
  cooking 330.1
  dish 308.7
  free-for-all 796.5
  quarrel 795.5
  violence 162.2
 *v.* be hot 328.22
  contend 796.14
  cook 330.4
  quarrel 795.11
**broiler** cooker 330.10
  food 308.22
  hot day 328.8
  poultry 414.34
**broke** insolvent 842.11
  poor 838.10
**broken**
  conquered 727.16
  damaged 692.29

  disconnected 51.4
  discont.nuous 72.4
  domesticated 191.34
  in disrepair 692.39
  insolvent 842.11
  irregular 138.3
  rough 261.6
  ruined 693.28
  ruptured 49.24
  subdued 764.15
  weak 765.15
**broken-down**
  dilapidated 692.35
  heartbroken 872.29
**broken heart**
  despair 866.6
  heartache 872.9
**broken-in** 642.17
**broken off** 72.4
**broker** dealer 830.9
  intermediary 237.4
  middleman 781.4
  stockbroker 833.10
**brokerage** fee 846.7
  stockbrokerage 833.9
  stockbroking 833.18
  trade 827.2
**brolly** parachute 280.13
  umbrella 228.7
**bromide** cliché 79.8
  platitude 517.3
**bronchial tube** 396.16
**bronchitis**
  inflammation 686.9
  respiratory disease
   686.14
**bronco** 414.12
**broncobuster**
  animal handler 416.2
  rider 274.8
**Bronx cheer** 967.3
**bronze**
 *n.* sculpture 575.2
 *v.* brown 367.2
 *adj.* metal 383.17
  reddish-brown 367.4
**brooch** 901.6
**brood**
 *n.* animal young 171.2
  family 11.5
  posterity 171.1
  race 11.4
 *v.* be pregnant 169.12
  consider 478.12
**brooder**
  birthplace 153.8
  coop 191.22
  poultry 414.34
  sad person 872.13
**brood mare**
  female animal 421.9
  horse 414.10
**brood over**
  grieve 872.17
  harbor revenge 956.5
  remember 537.13
  think over 478.13
**brook**
 *n.* running water
   395.1
 *v.* be broad-minded
   526.7

  be patient 861.5
  permit 777.10
**broom** 681.32
**broth** 308.10
**brothel**
  disapproved place
   191.28
  house of prostitution
   989.9
  place of vice 981.7
**brother** associate 787.1
  friend 928.1
  layman 1039.2
  likeness 20.3
  member 788.11
  religious 1038.17
  sibling 11.3
**brotherhood**
  blood relationship
   11.1
  friendship 927.2
  guild 788.3
  kindness 938.1
**brotherly**
  friendly 927.14
  kind 938.13
**brotherly love**
  accord 794.1
  benevolence 938.4
  love 931.1
**brought about** 167.20
**brouhaha**
  agitation 324.1
  commotion 62.4
  excitement 857.3
  noise 453.3
  violence 162.2
**brow** border 235.4
  front 240.5
  hair 230.12
  head 211.6
  looks 446.4
  summit 211.2
**browbeat**
  domineer 741.16
  intimidate 891.28
**browbeaten** 764.16
**brown**
 *n.* brownness 367.1
  colors 367.6
 *v.* cook 330.4
  darken 337.9
  embrown 367.2
 *adj.* brownish 367.3
**browned-off**
  angry 952.26
  annoyed 866.21
**brownie** cookie 308.42
  dwarf 196.6
  fairy 1014.18
  sycophant 907.3
**brown-nose** 907.3
**brownout** 337.7
**brown study**
  abstractedness 532.2
  dream 535.9
  thoughtfulness 478.3
**browse** eat 307.26
  scan 564.13
  shop 828.8
**bruise**
 *n.* contusion 692.9

  discoloration 679.2
 *v.* mistreat 667.5
  pain 866.17
  punish 1010.17
  wound 692.16
**bruiser** pugilist 800.2
  roughneck 943.4
**bruit about** 559.10
**brumal** cold 333.14
  winter 128.8
**brunch** 307.6
**brunet**
 *n.* hair color 362.9
 *adj.* black-haired
   365.13
  brown 367.3
  brown-haired 367.5
**brunt** 283.3
**brush**
 *n.* art equipment
   574.19
  brushwood 411.14
  contact 200.5
  fight 796.4
  firewood 331.3
  hinterland 182.2
  plant beard 230.9
  tail 241.6
  tap 283.6
  touch 425.1
  wilderness 166.2
 *v.* dry 393.6
  graze 200.10
  speed 269.8
  sweep 681.23
  tap 283.15
  tend animals 416.7
  touch lightly 425.7
**brush aside**
  disregard 531.4
  reject 638.2
**brush off**
  disregard 531.4
  send away 289.3
  sweep 681.23
**brush-off** 289.2
**brush up**
  furbish 691.11
  groom 681.20
  refresh the memory
   537.19
  study up 564.14
**brusque** candid 974.17
  concise 592.6
  gruff 937.7
  taciturn 613.9
**brutal** animal 414.43
  bad 675.9
  carnal 987.6
  cruel 939.24
  difficult 731.16
  fatal 409.23
  savage 162.20
  uncouth 898.12
**brutality** badness 675.2
  barbarity 939.12
  carnality 987.2
  cruelty 939.11
  uncouthness 898.3
  violence 162.1
**brutalize**
  make unfeeling 856.

wreck 162.10
**brute**
  *n.* animal 414.2
  barbarian 898.7
  savage 943.5
  violent person 162.9
  *adj.* animal 414.43
  carnal 987.6
  cruel 939.24
**brute force** force 756.2
  power 157.1
**BTU** 328.19
**bub** boy 125.5
  brother 11.3
**bubble**
  *n.* air 405
  ball 255.2
  blister 256.3
  fragility 360.2
  hope 888.5
  illusion 519.1
  lightness 353.2
  spirit 4.3
  thing imagined 535.5
  transient 111.5
  *v.* be enthusiastic
    635.8
  bubble up 405.4
  make a liquid sound
    452.11
**bubbly** bubbling 405.6
  light 353.10
  lively 707.17
**buccaneer** pirate 825.7
  sailor 276.1
**buck**
  *n.* boy 125.5
  goat 414.8
  hoofed animal 414.5
  jump 319.1
  male animal 420.8
  rabbit 414.29
  trestle 216.16
  US money 835.2,7
  *v.* contend against
    790.4
  jump 319.5
  thrust 283.11
  unseat 185.6
**buckaroo**
  animal handler 416.2
  rider 274.8
**bucket**
  *n.* ship 277.1
  *v.* ladle 271.16
  speculate in stocks
    833.23
**bucket shop**
  fraud 618.9
  stockbrokerage 833.9
**buck fever** 859.1
**buckle**
  *n.* distortion 249.1
  *v.* distort 249.5
  fasten 47.8
**buckle down**
  be determined 624.8
  exert oneself 716.9
**buck-passing** 735.5
**buckshot** 801.13
**buckskin** hide 229.8
  horse 414.13

**buck up** cheer up 870.9
  encourage 893.16
  refresh 695.2
  take courage 893.14
**bucolic**
  *n.* poem 609.6
  rustic 919.9
  *adj.* natural 736.6
  poetic 609.17
  rustic 182.6
**bud**
  *n.* boy 125.5
  brother 11.3
  burgeon 411.21
  source 153.7
  *v.* graft 304.6
  sprout 411.31
**Buddha** God 1013.5
  religious founder
    1022.4
  Vishnu 1014.9
  wise man 468.2
**budding**
  beginning 68.15
  growing 197.12
  immature 124.10
**buddy** boy 125.5
  brother 11.3
  co-worker 787.5
  friend 928.3
  partner 787.2
**buddy-buddy** 927.19
**budge** 267.5
**budget**
  *n.* accounts 845.1
  accumulation 660.1
  amount 28.2
  bundle 74.8
  expenses 843.3
  funds 835.14
  portion 816.5
  schedule 641.2
  *v.* plan expenditures
    843.5
  ration 816.10
  schedule 641.4
  *adj.* cheap 849.7
**buff**
  *n.* attender 186.5
  commender 968.8
  devotee 635.6
  fanatic 473.17
  follower 293.2
  specialist 81.3
  supporter 787.9
  *v.* polish 260.7
  rub 350.8
  *adj.* leather 229.7
  yellow 370.4,7
**buff, the** nudity 232.3
  skin 229.1
**buffalo**
  *n.* cattle 414.6
  *v.* perplex 514.13
**buffer**
  *n.* barrier 730.5
  neutralizer 178.3
  partition 237.5
  safety equipment
    699.3
  smoother 260.13
  tool 348.12

*v.* neutralize 178.7
**buffer state**
  country 181.1
  partition 237.5
**buffet**
  counter 216.15,29
  restaurant 307.15
**buffet**
  *n.* disappointment
    541.1
  lash 283.7
  punishment 1010.3
  *v.* bruise 692.16
  contend against
    790.4
  mistreat 667.5
  pound 283.14
  punish 1010.13
  slap 283.16
  struggle 716.11
  whip 1010.14
**buffoon** comic 612.10
  fool 471.1
  mischief-maker 738.3
**buffoonery**
  acting 611.9
  clownishness 881.5
  foolishness 470.1
**bug**
  *n.* beetle 414.36
  computer 349.19
  enthusiast 635.5
  evil spirit 1016.10
  fanatic 473.17
  fault 678.2
  germ 686.39
  mania 473.12
  microphone 450.9
  *v.* annoy 866.13
  bulge 256.10
  confuse 532.7
  discompose 63.4
  importune 774.12
  listen 448.11
  nag 969.16
  spy on 485.27
**bugbear** bane 676.1
  evil spirit 1016.10
  false alarm 704.2
  frightener 891.9
**bug-eyed**
  bulging 256.15
  defective eyes 440.12
**bugger**
  *n.* bad person 986.6
  evil spirit 1016.10
  man 420.5
  mischief-maker 738.3
  sex deviant 419.17
  *v.* anal sex 419.24
  bungle 734.12
  disable 158.9
  spoil 692.13
**buggy**
  *n.* automobile 272.9
  *adj.* insane 473.26
  insectile 414.55
**bughouse** 473.14
**bugle**
  *n.* brass wind 465.8
  nose 256.7
  *v.* blare 453.9

play music 462.43
**bugle call**
  call to arms 797.12
  signal 568.16
**bugs**
  enthusiastic 635.12
  insane 473.26
**build**
  *n.* form 246.1
  physique 246.4
  structure 245.1
  *v.* compose 58.3
  create 167.10
  establish 184.15
  increase 38.4
  make larger 197.4
**builder**
  craftsman 718.8
  producer 167.8
**building**
  composition 58.1
  edifice 245.2
  house 191.6
  manufacture 167.3
  structure 245.1
**building block**
  content 194.5
  element 376.2
  substance 3.2
**build on** 212.6
**buildup**
  commendation 968.3
  composition 58.1
  increase 38.1
  promotion 559.5
**build up**
  aggravate 885.2
  compose 58.3
  exaggerate 617.3
  increase 38.4
  make larger 197.4
  publicize 559.15
**built** beautiful 900.17
  made 167.22
**bulb** ball 255.2
  knob 256.3
  plant root 411.20
**bulbous** bulging 256.14
  globular 255.9
  herbaceous 411.33
**bulge**
  *n.* advantage 36.2
  protuberance 256.3
  *v.* protrude 256.10
**bulging** full 56.11
  rotund 255.8
  swelling 256.14
**bulk**
  *n.* greatness 34.1
  lump 195.10
  majority 100.2
  major part 54.6
  quantity 28.1
  size 195.1
  thickness 204.2
  *v.* assemble 74.18
  become larger 197.5
  loom 34.5
  make larger 197.4
**bulkhead** barrier 730.5
  entrance 302.6
  harbor 700.6

partition 237.5
**bulky** large 34.7
  massive 195.19
  substantial 3.7
  thick 204.8
  unwieldy 731.18
**bull**
  *n.* animal 414.6
  decree 752.4
  error in speech 518.7
  humbug 616.14
  jailer 761.10
  letter 604.3
  male animal 420.8
  nonsense 547.3
  policeman 699.16
  speculator 833.13
  *v.* manipulate the market 833.25
  talk nonsense 547.5
  thrust 283.11
  *adj.* masculine 420.11
**bulldog** adherent 50.4
  brave person 893.8
**bulldogged**
  obstinate 626.8
  persistent 50.12
**bulldoze** coerce 756.7
  domineer 741.16
  intimidate 891.28
  overwhelm 727.8
  raze 693.19
  threaten 973.2
  thrust 283.11
**bulldozer** 272.17,27
**bullet** discharge 285.5
  fission 326.8
  shot 801.13
**bulletin**
  information 557.1
  news report 558.5
  press release 559.3
  record 570.7
**bullfight** 796.4
**bullfighter** 800.4
**bullheaded**
  obstinate 626.8
  persistent 50.12
**bullion**
  currency metals 835.20
  metal 383.3
  metal casting 383.5
**bull market**
  prosperity 728.5
  stock market 833.4
**bull session** 597.3
**bull's-eye** center 226.2
  lens 443.1
  objective 653.2
  score 724.4
  window 265.8
**bullshit**
  *n.* boasting 910.2
  humbug 616.14
  nonsense 547.3
  *v.* talk nonsense 547.5
**bullwhack** 1011.1
**bullwhacker** 274.9
**bully**
  *n.* beef 308.13
  blusterer 911.2

combatant 800.1
  evildoer 943.3
  strong man 159.6
  tormentor 866.10
  *v.* bluster 911.3
  coerce 756.7
  domineer 741.16
  intimidate 891.28
  *adj.* excellent 674.13
**bulwark** barrier 730.5
  buttress 216.4
  fortification 799.4
  safeguard 699.3
**bum**
  *n.* bad person 986.2
  beggar 774.8
  buttocks 241.5
  derelict 708.9
  drunkard 996.11
  vagabond 274.3
  *v.* beg 774.15
  hum 452.13
  wander 273.22
  *adj.* bad 675.8
**bum around** 708.11
**bumble** 734.11
**bumbledom** 741.11
**bumbling** 734.20
**bummer**
  adversity 729.1
  bad person 986.2
  beggar 774.8
  nonworker 708.10
  vagabond 274.3
**bump**
  *n.* aviation 278.41
  bulge 256.3
  demotion 783.1
  explosive noise 456.1
  faint sound 452.3
  impact 283.3
  mark 568.7
  push 283.2
  shake 324.3
  swelling 256.4
  talent 733.4
  *v.* collide 283.12
  demote 783.3
  dismiss 310.19
  make explosive noise 456.6
  shake 324.11
  thrust 283.11
**bumper**
  *n.* drink 307.4
  full measure 56.3
  partition 237.5
  safety equipment 699.3
  *adj.* large 195.16
**bump into**
  collide 283.12
  find 488.3
  meet 200.11
**bumpkin** oaf 471.5
  rustic 919.9
**bump off** 409.14
**bumptious**
  conceited 909.11
  defiant 793.7
  insolent 913.8
**bumpy** bulging 256.14

jolting 324.20
  rough 261.6
**bum's rush, the** 310.1
**bum steer** 618.2
**bun** hair 230.7
  roll 308.31
**bunch**
  *n.* amount 28.2
  bulge 256.3
  clique 788.6
  cluster 74.7
  conglomeration 50.5
  flock 74.5
  group 74.3
  large number 101.3
  *v.* assemble 74.18
  cohere 50.6
  come together 74.16
  join 52.4
**bunco** 618.8
**bunco artist** 619.4
**buncombe see bunkum**
**bundle**
  *n.* package 74.8
  *v.* bind 47.9
  cuddle 932.15
  dismiss 310.18
  make haste 709.5
  package 74.20
  push 709.4
  snuggle 887.10
  start 285.14
  walk 273.27
**bundle off**
  dismiss 310.18
  start 285.14
**bundle up**
  clothe 231.38
  package 74.20
**bungalow** 191.9
**bungle**
  *n.* an error 518.5
  blunder 734.5
  fiasco 725.6
  *v.* blunder 734.11
  do carelessly 534.9
  err 518.14
  fail 725.13
**bungler**
  blunderer 734.8
  neglecter 534.5
**bungling**
  *n.* blundering 734.4
  slipshodness 534.3
  *adj.* clumsy 734.20
  slipshod 534.12
**bunion**
  inflammation 686.9
  sore 686.35
  swelling 256.4
**bunk**
  *n.* bed 216.19,33
  boasting 910.2
  humbug 616.14
  nonsense 547.3
  *v.* house 188.10
  inhabit 188.7
**bunker** cellar 192.17
  entrenchment 799.5
  rocketry 281.7
  shelter 700.3
  storage place 660.6

stronghold 799.6
  tunnel 257.5
**bunkum** boasting 910.2
  flattery 970.1
  humbug 616.14
  nonsense 547.3
  political doubletalk 744.37
**bunny**
  beautiful person 900.8
  rabbit 414.29
**bunt**
  *n.* push 283.2
  pushing 285.1
  *v.* push 285.10
  tap 283.15
  thrust 283.11
**bunting** 569.6
**buoy**
  *n.* float 277.11
  life preserver 701.5
  signal 568.15
  *v.* float 353.8
**buoyancy**
  lightheartedness 870.3
  lightness 353.1
  resilience 358.1
**buoyant** light 353.13
  lighthearted 870.12
  recuperative 694.23
  resilient 358.7
**buoy up** cheer 870.7
  elevate 317.5
  float 353.8
  support 216.21
**burble**
  be unintelligent 469.12
  bubble 405.4
  make a liquid sound 452.11
**burden**
  *n.* affliction 866.8
  bane 676.1
  capacity 195.2
  charge 963.3
  duty 962.1
  guilt 983.1
  impediment 730.6
  load 194.2
  music division 462.24
  poetic division 609.11
  repeat 103.5
  topic 484.1
  voice 463.5
  weight 352.7
  *v.* add 40.4
  distress 866.16
  exhaust 864.16
  freight 184.14
  hamper 730.11
  impose 963.4
  load 352.13
  oppress 729.8
  task 716.16
**burdened** fraught 56.1
  supporting 216.23
  weighted 352.18

busty 195.18
busy
  *v.* occupy 656.10
    task 716.16
  *adj.* active 707.21
    meddlesome 238.9
    ornate 901.12
busybody
  curious person 528.2
  meddler 238.4
  newsmonger 558.9
busywork 656.2
but
  *adv.* notwithstanding
    33.8
  *conj.* unless 507.16
butch
  *n.* homosexual 419.16
    mannish female
    420.9
  *adj.* bisexual 419.32
butcher
  *n.* killer 409.11
    merchant 830.3
    trainman 274.13
  *v.* bungle 734.11
    destroy 162.10
    murder 409.17
    sever 49.11
butchered
  botched 734.21
  mutilated 57.5
butler
  majordomo 750.10
  male servant 750.4
  manager 748.4
butt
  *n.* buttocks 241.4
    cigarette 434.5
    end 70.2
    ham 308.16
    joint 47.4
    laughingstock 967.7
    objective 653.2
    piece 55.3
    push 283.2
    pushing 285.1
    remainder 43.1
    stub 434.5
  *v.* adjoin 200.9
    fasten 47.8
    push 285.10
    thrust 283.11
butte 207.5
butter
  *n.* food 308.47
    pulp 390.2
    semiliquid 389.5
    softness 357.4
    suavity 936.5
  *v.* coat 228.24
    flatter 970.6
butterfingers 734.9
butterflies 859.2
butt in intrude 238.5
  talk out of turn 130.5
buttinsky advisor 754.3
  intruder 238.3
buttocks 241.4
button
  *n.* chin 240.6
    fastener 47.20

insignia 569.1
  knob 256.3
  little thing 196.4
  metal casting 383.5
  trifle 673.5
  *v.* close 266.6
    fasten 47.8
buttonhole
  address 594.27
  bore 884.6
  importune 774.12
button up
  be silent 451.6
  close 266.6
  complete 722.6
butt out
  none of your business
    238.10
  not interfere 762.16
buttress
  *n.* bulwark 216.4
    supporter 216.2
  *v.* aid 785.12
    confirm 505.12
    strengthen 159.11
    support 216.21
buxom
  beautiful 900.17
  corpulent 195.18
  merry 870.15
buy
  *n.* bargain 849.3
    purchase 828.1
  *v.* assent 521.8
    believe 501.10
    bribe 651.3
    purchase 828.7
buyer 828.5
buyers' market
  commerce 827.1
  low prices 849.2
  sale 829.1
buy in buy 828.7
  invest 836.16
buy off bribe 651.3
  buy 828.7
buy up purchase 828.7
  stock market 833.26
buzz
  *n.* harsh sound 458.3
    monotone 71.2
    rumor 558.6
    sensation 426.1
    sibilation 457.1
    telephone call 560.13
  *v.* bustle 707.12
    fly 278.51
    hum 452.13
    inform 557.11
    publish 559.10
    sibilate 457.2
    sound harshly 458.9
    telephone 560.18
    utter 594.26
buzzer 704.1
buzzing
  *n.* air maneuver
    278.17
    hum 452.7
  *adj.* humming 452.20
buzz off depart 301.6
  go away! 310.30

by
  *adv.* in reserve 660.17
  *prep.* at 184.26
    beside 242.11
    by means of 658.7
    in conformity with
    82.9
    through 290.29
by all means
  certainly 513.23
  yes 521.18
by and by
  in the future 121.9
  soon 131.16
by and large
  generally 79.17
  on the whole 54.14
by chance
  haphazardly 62.18
  unpredictably 156.19
by choice
  preferably 637.28
  voluntarily 622.10
by degrees
  gradually 29.6
  piece by piece 55.9
by design 653.11
by ear 630.15
by far 34.17
bygone 119.7
by heart 537.28
bylaw 998.3
by-line
  attribution 155.2
  avocation 656.7
by means of
  by the agency of
    658.7
  helped by 785.25
by no means
  disapproval 969.28
  negation 524.9
  noway 35.11
  refusal 776.7
by oneself
  independently 762.32
  singly 89.13
  solitary 924.10
bypass
  *n.* byway 657.5
    detour 321.3
    road 657.6
  *v.* detour 321.6
    pass 313.8
by-product
  aftermath 67.3
  outgrowth 168.3
  result 154.1
byre 191.20
bystander
  neighbor 200.6
  spectator 442.1
  witness 505.7
by the book
  according to rule
    82.8
  exactly 516.21
by the way
  discursive 593.13
  incidentally 129.13
  occasional 129.11

by virtue of
  because of 155.9
by authority of
  739.20
by dint of 157.18
  by means of 658.7
byway bypath 657.5
  digression 593.4
  road 657.6
by way of
  by means of 658.7
  through 290.29
byword disgrace 915.5
  laughingstock 967.7
  maxim 517.1
  name 583.3
  phrase 582.9
Byzantine devious 46.4
  scheming 654.14
  shrewd 467.15

## C

cab 272.12
cabal clique 788.6
  combination 52.1
  group 74.3
  intrigue 654.6
cabala
  occultism 1034.1
  secrets 614.5
caballero beau 931.12
  knight 918.5
  rider 274.8
cabaña 191.9
cabaret
  amusement 878.11
  saloon 996.19
  theater 611.18
cabbage food 308.35,50
  money 835.2
cabdriver
  coachman 274.9
  driver 274.10
cabin cottage 191.9
  ship room 192.9
cabin boy
  attendant 750.5
  sailor 276.6
cabin cruiser 277.4
cabinet council 755.1
  cupboard 193.19
  directorate 748.11
  ministry 742.8
  office 719.8
  radio receiver 344.3
  sanctum 192.8
cable
  *n.* communications
    560.17
    cord 206.2;9
    electric 342.39
    telegram 560.14
  *v.* communicate
    560.19
caboose kitchen 330.3
  railway car 272.14
cache
  *n.* hiding place 615.4
    reserve 660.3
  *v.* secrete 615.7
    store 660.10

**cachet**
  characteristic 80.4
  label 568.13
**cackle**
  *n.* chatter 596.3
  harsh sound 458.3
  laughter 876.4
  *v.* bird sound 460.5
  laugh 876.8
  sound harshly 458.9
  utter 594.26
**cacography**
  bad handwriting
    602.6
  spelling 581.4
**cacophony**
  dissonance 461.1
  literary inelegance
    590.1
  pandemonium 62.5
  raucousness 458.2
  ugliness 899.1
  uproar 162.2
**cactus** 258.7
**cad** bad person 986.8
  vulgar person 898.6
**cadaver** 408.16
**cadaverous**
  colorless 363.7
  deathly 408.29
  wasted 205.20
**caddie** attendant 750.5
  carrier 271.5
**cadence** fall 316.2
  meter 609.9
  music 463.18
  music division 462.24
  speech accent 594.11
  types of 463.23
**cadenza**
  improvisation 462.27
  music 463.18
**cadet** sailor 276.4
  student 566.6
**cadge** 774.15
**cadger** beggar 774.8
  nonworker 708.10
  vendor 830.6
**cadre** clique 788.6
  directorate 748.11
  frame 245.4
  military unit 800.19
**caduceus** 739.9
**caducity** old age 126.5
  senility 469.10
  transience 111.1
  weakness 160.3
**caesar** autocrat 749.14
  ruler 749.8
**caesura**
  discontinuity 72.2
  interval 201.1
  meter 609.9
  pause 144.3
  punctuation 144.4
**café** restaurant 307.15
  saloon 996.19
**cafeteria**
  dining room 192.11
  restaurant 307.15

**cage**
  *n.* place of confine-
    ment 761.7
  *v.* confine 761.12
  drive animals 416.8
  enclose 236.5
**cagey** cautious 895.9
  cunning 735.12
  evasive 631.15
**cahoots**
  affiliation 786.2
  concurrence 177.1
**cairn** mark 568.10
  memorial 570.12
**cajole** deceive 618.13
  flatter 970.5
  importune 774.12
  lure 650.4
  urge 648.14
**cake**
  *n.* pastry 308.41
  solid 354.6
  *v.* solidify 356.8
  thicken 354.10
**calamitous**
  destructive 693.26
  disastrous 729.15
**calamity** bane 676.1
  fatality 409.8
  misfortune 729.2
**calcify** 356.7
**calcimine** color 362.13
  whitewash 364.6
**calcination** 329.5
**calculable**
  computable 87.16
  measurable 490.15
  predictable 543.13
  reliable 513.17
**calculate**
  compute 87.11
  measure 490.11
  plan 654.9
  premeditate 653.8
**calculated**
  intentional 653.9
  logical 482.21
  planned 654.13
**calculate on**
  believe in 501.16
  expect 539.6
  plan on 653.6
**calculating**
  deceitful 618.20
  insincere 975.18
  numerative 87.15
  scheming 654.14
  shrewd 467.15
**calculation**
  caution 895.1
  computation 87.3
  intentionality 653.3
  measurement 490.1
  plan 654.1
**calculator**
  accountant 845.7
  addition 40.3
  cunning person 735.7
  mathematician 87.8
  types of 87.19
**calculus** 87.3,18
**caldron** 145.10

**calefaction** 329.1
**calendar**
  *n.* calendar of bills
    742.17
  chronology 114.8
  list 88.6
  record book 570.11
  reference book 605.6
  schedule 641.2
  *v.* chronologize 114.14
  list 88.8
  record 570.16
  schedule 641.4
**calf** animal 414.6
  ice 333.5
  leg 273.16
  young cow 125.8
**caliber** ability 157.2
  degree 29.1
  intelligence 467.1
  size 195.1
  talent 733.4
  thickness 204.3
**calibrate** grade 29.4
  measure 490.11
**caliper** 490.11,20
**caliph** 749.10
**calisthenics**
  exercise 716.6
  physical education
    562.9
**calk** see **caulk**
**call**
  *n.* animal sound 460.1
  cause 153.1
  cry 459.1
  demand 753.1
  enlistment 780.6
  entreaty 774.2
  invitation 774.4
  justification 1006.6
  signal 568.16
  stock option 833.21
  summons 752.5
  telephone call 560.13
  the ministry 1037.1
  visit 922.7
  *v.* animal sound 460.2
  bet 515.20
  bill 845.11
  bird sound 460.5
  cry 459.6
  gamble 515.18
  invite 774.13
  judge 494.9
  name 583.11
  summon 752.12
  telephone 560.18
**call a spade a spade**
  be honest 974.12
  be practical 536.4
  speak plainly 591.2
**call attention to**
  direct attention to
    530.10
  remark 594.25
**call down** 969.18
**caller** errand boy 561.4
  guest 925.6
  telephoner 560.11
**call for**
  *n.* demand 753.1

  requirement 639.2
  *v.* demand 753.4
  entail 76.4
  fetch 271.15
  oblige 756.5
  request 774.9
  require 639.9
  summon 752.12
**call forth** elicit 305.14
  evoke 153.12
  excite 857.11
  prompt 648.13
  summon 752.12
**call girl** 989.16
**calligraphy** arts 574.1
  fine writing 602.5
  handwriting 602.3
**call in** bill 845.11
  confer with 597.11
  invite 774.13
  summon 752.12
**calling**
  consecration 1037.10
  invitation 774.4
  motive 648.1
  naming 583.2
  summons 752.5
  vocation 656.6
**calling card** 568.11
**calliope** organ 465.15
  rocketry 281.10
**call it a day**
  complete 722.6
  stop work 144.8
  take a rest 711.8
**call off** end 70.7
  number 87.10
**call on** command 752.9
  entreat 774.11
  petition 774.10
  urge 648.14
  visit 922.17
**call one's bluff** 793.6
**callous**
  *v.* harden 356.7
  make unfeeling 856.6
  *adj.* hardened 356.13
  heartless 939.23
  impenitent 874.5
  insensible 423.6
  unfeeling 856.12
  wicked 981.17
**callousness**
  hardness 356.1
  heartlessness 939.10
  impenitence 874.2
  insensibility 423.1
  insensitivity 856.3
  obduracy 981.6
**call out** defy 793.3
  elicit 305.14
  summon 752.12
  vociferate 459.8
**callow** ignorant 477.12
  immature 124.10
  incomplete 57.4
  inexperienced 734.17
  new 122.7
  undeveloped 721.11
**call time** 109.3
**call up**
  call to arms 797.23

support 216.1
transportation 271.3
vehicle 272.1
**carriage trade**
clientele 828.3
society 644.6
**carried away**
excited 857.18
frenzied 857.23
overjoyed 865.14
**carrier** carter 271.5
infection 686.3
mail carrier 561.6
messenger 561.1
radio wave 344.11
supporter 216.2
vector 686.41
vehicle 272.1
warship 277.8,24
**carrier pigeon**
carrier 271.5
message carrier 561.6
**carrion** corpse 408.16
filth 682.7
offal 682.9
rotting 692.7
**carrottop** 362.9
**carry**
*n.* range 179.2
transportation 271.3
*v.* adopt 637.15
be pregnant 169.12
deal in 827.15
extend 179.7
give credit 839.6
induce 648.22
keep accounts 845.8
support 216.21
transport 271.11
win 726.4
**carry away**
abduct 824.19
come apart 49.8
delight 865.8
enamor 931.21
fascinate 650.6
kill 409.13
remove 271.10
win 726.4
**carrying**
*n.* support 216.1
transportation 271.3
*adj.* armed 799.14
pregnant 169.18
supporting 216.23
**carry off** abduct 824.19
bring about 722.5
carry out 705.9
kill 409.13
remove 271.10
seize 822.14
succeed with 724.10
win 726.4
**carry on**
be angry 952.15
be disorderly 62.11
be enthusiastic 635.8
be industrious 707.15
be patient 861.4
continue 143.3
direct 747.8
endure 110.6

misbehave 738.4
operate 164.5
persevere 625.2
play 878.25
practice 705.7
rage 162.10
**carry out** apply 665.11
be distant 199.5
bring about 722.5
do 705.9
execute 771.10
observe 768.3
operate 164.5
**carry over**
keep accounts 845.8
transfer 271.9
**carry through**
be patient 861.4
bring about 722.5
carry out 705.9
execute 771.10
not hesitate 624.10
observe 768.3
operate 164.5
persevere 625.5
**carry weight**
be important 672.11
have influence 172.10
weigh 352.10
**carsick** 686.53
**cart**
*n.* vehicle 272.3,28
*v.* haul 271.12
**cart away** 271.10
**carte blanche**
full permission 777.4
latitude 762.4
right 958.4
**cartel** association 788.9
combination 52.1
compact 771.1
treaty 771.2
**carter** carrier 271.5
coachman 274.9
**cartilage**
structure 245.6
toughness 359.2
**cartography**
location 184.7
map 654.4
mensuration 490.9
**carton**
*n.* container 193.14
*v.* package 236.9
**cartoon**
caricature 574.17
diagram 654.3
motion picture
611.16
picture 574.14
**cartoonist** 579.3
**cartridge** film 577.10
shell 801.11
sound recording
450.12
sound reproduction
system 450.11
**carve** apportion 816.6
engrave 578.10
form 246.7
groove 263.3
produce 167.11

record 570.16
sculpture 575.5
slice 49.11
**carver**
printmaker 579.8
sculptor 579.6
**carving** 572.4
**Casanova** beau 931.12
deceiver 619.1
unchaste person
989.10
**cascade**
*n.* descent 316.1
eruption 162.6
waterfall 395.11
*v.* descend 316.5
hang 215.6
overflow 395.17
**case**
*n.* argument 482.5
bookbinding 605.15
citation 505.6
example 25.2
frame 245.4
grammatical form
586.9
hull 228.16
lawsuit 1004.1
love 931.4
odd person 85.4
particular 8.3
pillowcase 228.10
printing 603.6
sheath 228.17
sick person 686.40
state 7.1
topic 484.1
types of 193.14
*v.* package 236.9
reconnoiter 485.27
wrap 228.20
**case, the** fact 1.3
the truth 516.2
**casebook**
reference book 605.6
textbook 605.8
**case-hardened**
accustomed 642.17
callous 856.12
hardened 356.13
obstinate 626.8
wicked 981.17
**case history**
biography 608.4
medical history
689.11
**casein** 354.7
**case in point**
citation 505.6
example 25.2
**casement** frame 245.4
window 265.8
**Casey Jones** 274.12
**cash**
*n.* money 835.1
payment 841.1
ready money 835.18
*v.* cash in 835.29
pay 841.17
*adv.* in cash 841.25
**cashbook**
account book 845.4

record book 570.11
**cashbox** 836.12
**cashier**
*n.* banker 836.10
financial officer
836.11
payer 841.9
*v.* depose 783.4
dismiss 310.19
**cash in on**
improve the occasion
129.8
profit by 811.11
take advantage of
665.15
**casino**
amusement 878.11
ballroom 879.4
gambling house
515.15
resort 191.27
**cask**
*n.* cylinder 255.4
types of 193.13
*v.* package 236.9
**casket**
*n.* coffin 410.11
*v.* enclose 236.6
**Cassandra**
pessimist 889.7
predictor 543.4
warner 703.4
**casserole** 308.7
**cassette** 450.12
**cassock** 1038.5
**cast**
*n.* actors 612.11
castoff skin 229.5
characteristic 80.4
color 362.1
copy 24.6
defective vision 440.5
disposition 525.3
form 246.1
glance 439.4
group 74.3
kind 61.3
looks 446.4
medical dressing
687.33
metal casting 383.5
model 25.6
nature 5.3
role 611.11
sculpture 575.2
small amount 35.4
sum 86.5
team 788.7
tendency 174.1
throw 285.4
throw of dice 515.10
*v.* attack 798.28
calculate 87.11
change course 275.30
create 167.10
discard 668.7
eject 310.13
form 246.7
give birth 167.15
heat 329.24
hurl 184.12
plan 654.9

cervix
  constriction 198.1
  joint 47.4
  sex organ 419.10
  supporter 216.2
cesarean 689.24
cessation
  abandonment 633.1
  closing 70.3
  discontinuance 668.2
  discontinuity 72.2
  end 70.1
  standstill 268.3
  stopping 144
cession
  abandonment 633.3
  property transfer
    817.1
  qualification 507.1
  relinquishment 814.1
  surrender 765.2
cesspool 682.12
cetacean 414.35,64
chafe
  n. abrasion 350.2
  impairment 692.8
  irritation 866.3
  v. abrade 350.7
  be angry 952.15
  be impatient 862.4
  feel anxious 890.5
  heat 329.17
  hurt 424.7
  injure 692.15
  irritate 866.14
  provoke 952.22
chaff
  n. banter 882.1
  hull 228.16
  lightness 353.2
  rabble 919.5
  radar countermeasure
    346.13
  refuse 669.4
  residue 43.1
  trifles 673.4
  v. banter 882.4
  ridicule 967.9
chagrin
  n. mortification 866.4
  v. embarrass 866.15
chagrined
  distressed 866.22
  humiliated 906.13
chain
  n. atomics 326.7
  continuity 71.2
  curb 730.7
  fireplace 329.12
  insignia 569.1
  jewel 901.6
  mountains 207.9
  restraint 760.4
  v. bind 47.9
  connect 71.4
  join 47.5
  restrain 760.10
  stabilize 142.8
chain gang 761.11
chain of circumstances
  156.5

chain reaction
  continuity 71.2
  fission 326.8
  vicissitudes 156.5
chair
  n. instructorship
    565.11
  manager 748.5
  seat 216.17,30
  seat of authority
    739.10
  v. administer 747.11
  govern 741.12
  install 780.11
chair, the
  capital punishment
    1010.7
  electric chair 1011.5
chairman 748.5
chaise 272.4
chalet 191.9
chalice 1042.11
chalk
  n. art equipment
    574.19
  white 364.2
  writing material
    602.30
  v. mark 568.19
  picture 574.20
  record 570.16
  whiten 364.5
  whitewash 364.6
chalk talk lesson 562.7
  speech 599.2
chalk up mark 568.19
  record 570.16
chalky powdery 361.11
  white 364.7
challenge
  n. dare 793.2
  declaration of war
    797.11
  objection 522.2
  opposition 790.1
  questioning 485.11
  resistance 792.1
  v. be doubtful 503.6
  claim 753.5
  compete 796.19
  confront 240.8
  contradict 790.6
  defy 793.3
  demand 753.4
  make war on 797.19
  object 522.5
  offer resistance 792.3
  thwart 730.15
challenging
  defiant 793.7
  exciting 648.27
chamber
  bedroom 192.7
  compartment 192.2
  council 755.1
  radiation 327.13
  room 192.1
  toilet 311.11
chamberlain
  financial officer
    836.11
  majordomo 750.10

chambermaid 750.8
chamber music 462.5
chamber of commerce
  788.9
chamber pot 311.11
chambers
  apartment 191.14
  office 719.8
chameleon
  changeableness 141.4
  mind-changer 628.4
  reptile 414.60
  variegation 374.6
champ
  n. bite 307.2
  expert 733.14
  victor 726.2
  v. chew 307.25
champaign 387.1
champ at the bit
  be impatient 862.4
  wait 132.13
champion
  n. advocate 1006.8
  defender 799.7
  deputy 781.1
  expert 733.14
  protector 699.5
  superior 36.4
  supporter 787.9
  the best 674.8
  victor 726.2
  v. back 785.13
  defend 799.8
  protect 699.18
  uphold 1006.10
  adj. best 674.18
  chief 36.14
championship
  patronage 785.4
  supremacy 36.3
  victory 726.1
chance
  n. an uncertainty
    514.8
  gamble 515.1
  happenstance 156
  liability 175.1
  opportunity 129.2
  possibility 509.1
  probability 511.1
  turn 108.2
  uncertainty 514.1
  v. attempt 714.5
  gamble 515.19
  happen 156.11
  occur 151.6
  risk 697.7
  adj. uncertain 514.18
  unpredictable 156.15
Chance 156.2
chancel 1042.9
chancellery
  mastership 739.7
  office 719.8
chancellor
  diplomat 781.6
  educator 565.9
  executive 748.3
  judge 1002.4
  premier 749.6
  public official 749.17

chancery court 1001.3
  office 719.8
  registry 570.3
chance upon 488.3
chancre sore 686.35
  venereal disease
    686.16
chancy chance 156.15
  hazardous 697.10
  uncertain 514.15
  vague 514.18
chandelier 336.6,11
chandler
  merchant 830.3
  provider 659.6
  tradesman 830.2
change
  n. alteration 139
  alternate 149.2
  conversion 145.1
  differentiation 16.4
  petty cash 835.19
  substitution 149.1
  v. alter 139.6
  be changed 139.5
  convert 145.11
  differentiate 16.6
  don 231.42
  interchange 150.4
  move 267.5
  substitute 149.4
  trade 827.14
  vacillate 627.8
changeable
  changed 139.9
  fickle 629.6
  inconstant 141.7
  interchangeable
    150.5
  irregular 18.3
  irresolute 627.9
  transient 111.7
  uncertain 514.15
  variable 141.6
  weak 160.17
change course 275.30
changed altered 139.9
  converted 145.19
change hands 817.4
changeless
  godlike 1013.20
  invariable 142.17
  permanent 140.7
changeling
  evil spirit 1016.12
  substitute 149.2
change of heart
  change 139.1
  change of mind 145.2
  penitence 873.4
change of life 126.7
change of mind
  about-face 628.1
  change of heart 145.2
  irresolution 627.1
change one's mind
  repent 873.7
  reverse oneself 628.6
  vacillate 627.8
channel
  n. bed 212.4
  conduit 396

informant 557.5
information theory
557.7
narrow place 205.3
outlet 303.9
passageway 657.4
radio 344.13
running water 395.1
seaway 275.10
trench 263.2
*v.* channelize 396.19
groove 263.3
pipe 271.13
**chant**
*n.* hymn 1032.3
repeat 103.5
song 462.13
*v.* sing 462.39
utter 594.26
**chaos** confusion 62.2
disorder 532.3
formlessness 247.1
lawlessness 740.2
noncohesion 51.1
outer space 375.3
violence 162.2
**chaotic**
confused 532.12
formless 247.4
lawless 740.6
muddled 62.16
vague 514.18
violent 162.17
**chaotically**
disorderly 62.19
lawlessly 740.7
nonuniformly 18.4
**chap** crack 201.2
man 420.5
person 417.3
**chaparral** 411.13
**chapel** church 1042.3
hall 192.4
**chaperon**
*n.* escort 73.5
guardian 699.7
maid 750.8
*v.* care for 699.19
escort 73.8
**chapfallen**
disappointed 541.5
distressed 866.22
glum 872.25
humiliated 906.13
**chaplain**
churchman 1038.9
clergyman 1038.2
**chaps** 265.5
**chapter**
book part 605.13
branch 788.10
church council 755.4
part of writing 55.2
topic 484.1
**char**
*n.* cleaning woman
681.14
*v.* burn 329.24
work 716.12
**character**
*n.* actor 612.2
characteristic 80.4

description 608.1
eccentric 474.3
function 656.3
gene 170.6
harmonics 463.12
honesty 974.1
kind 61.3
letter 581.1
man 420.5
nature 5.3
number 86.1
odd person 85.4
person 417.3
recommendation
968.4
repute 914.1
role 611.11
sign 568.2
status 7.5
symbol 581.2
temperament 525.3
*v.* describe 608.12
engrave 578.10
letter 581.6
represent 572.6
**character assassination**
defamation 971.2
scandal 558.8
smear campaign
744.14
**characteristic**
*n.* habit 642.4
nature 5.3
peculiarity 80.4
sign 568.2
*adj.* classificational
61.7
differentiative 16.9
peculiar 80.13
temperamental 525.7
typical 572.11
**characterization**
acting 611.9
description 608.1
distinction 80.8
impersonation 572.2
indication 568.1
representation 572.1
story element 608.9
**characterize**
describe 608.12
distinguish 80.10
indicate 568.17
represent 572.6
**characterizing** 16.9
**characterless**
formless 247.4
uninteresting 883.6
vacant 187.13
**charade** gesture 568.14
riddle 549.9
stage show 611.4
**charcoal**
art equipment 574.19
ashes 329.16
black 365.4
blacking 365.6
drawing 574.6
fuel 331.1
picture 574.14
**charge**
*n.* accusation 1005.1

arraignment 1004.3
attack 798.1
attribution 155.1
bill 840.1
burden 352.7
cathexis 690.41
commission 780.1
custody 761.5
dependent 764.6
duty 962.1
electric charge 342.5
expenses 843.3
explosive charge
801.10
fee 846.7
full measure 56.3
heraldic insignia
569.2
impediment 730.6
imposition 963.3
injunction 752.2
load 194.2
power 157.1
precept 751.1
price 846.1
protectorship 699.2
rocketry 281.8
supervision 747.2
task 656.2
the ministry 1037.9
thrill 857.2
*v.* accuse 1005.7
advise 754.6
attack 798.18
burden 352.13
command 752.9
commission 780.9
demand 846.14
electrify 342.23
fill 56.7
impose 963.4
prepare 720.9
radioactivate 327.9
receive credit 839.7
shoot 285.13
*interj.* attack! 798.32
**charge account** 839.2
**charge card** 839.3
**charged**
accused 1005.15
attributed 155.6
burdened 352.18
critical 129.10
electrified 342.31
exciting 857.28
fraught 56.12
radioactive 327.10
**charge in** 238.5
**charge off**
discount 847.2
forget 947.5
keep accounts 845.8
**charger** horse 414.10
war horse 800.32
**charily**
cautiously 895.13
economically 851.7
**charisma**
allurement 650.1
illustriousness 914.6
influence 172.1
power 157.1

**charismatic**
alluring 650.7
illustrious 914.19
influential 172.13
**charismatic movement**
1028.3
**charitable**
benevolent 938.15
giving 818.22
gratis 850.5
pitying 944.7
tolerant 526.11
**charity** accord 794.1
almsgiving 818.3
benevolence 938.4
donation 818.6
love 931.1
patronage 785.4
tolerance 526.4
virtue 980.5
**charity case** 838.4
**charivari** 453.3
**charlatan**
*n.* impostor 619.6
quack doctor 688.7
*adj.* quack 616.28
**Charley**
irregular 800.15
revolutionist 147.3
watchman 699.10
**charley horse** 424.2
**charm**
*n.* allurement 650.1
amulet 1036.5
beauty 900.1
bird group 74.6
influence 172.1
jewel 901.6
lovability 931.7
lure 650.2
pleasantness 863.2
sorcery 1035.1
spell 1036.1
superstition 502.3
*v.* delight 865.8
enamor 931.21
enchant 1036.8
engross 530.13
fascinate 650.6
persuade 648.23
**charmed**
dreamy 535.25
enamored 931.26
enchanted 1036.12
engrossed 530.18
pleased 865.12
**charmed circle** 788.6
**charmer**
beautiful person
900.8
bewitcher 1035.9
cunning person 735.6
deceiver 619.1
tempter 650.3
**charming**
alluring 650.7
bewitching 1036.11
influential 172.13
lovable 931.23
pleasant 863.7
**charnel house**
mortuary 410.9

tomb 410.16
**Charon** 1019.5
**chart**
  *n.* diagram 654.3
  list 88.2
  map 654.4
  outline 48.4
  representation 572.1
  *v.* organize 60.10
  plot 654.11
  represent 572.6
**chart a course**
  navigate 275.27
  pilot 275.14
**charter**
  *n.* exemption 762.8
  grant 777.5
  hire 780.5
  permission 777.1
  *v.* authorize 777.11
  commission 780.9
  hire 780.14
  rent out 780.15
**chartreuse** 371.4,6
**chary** cautious 895.9
  economical 851.6
**chase**
  *n.* groove 263.1
  horse race 796.13
  hunting 655.2
  pursuit 655.1
  woodland 411.11
  *v.* court 932.19
  drive out 310.14
  emboss 256.11
  follow 293.3
  hunt 655.9
  make haste 709.5
  pursue 655.8
  repulse 289.3
  sculpture 575.5
**chase after** 271.15
**chaser** act 611.8
  alcoholic drink 996.8
  pursuer 655.4
  sculptor 579.6
**chasm** crack 201.2
  depth 209.2
  opening 265.1
  pit 257.4
**chassis** bottom 212.2
  frame 245.4
  mounting 216.10
  radio receiver 344.3
**chaste** abstinent 992.10
  elegant 589.6
  perfect 677.6
  plain 902.6
  pure 980.8
  simple 45.6
  tasteful 897.8
  virtuous 988.4
**chasten**
  make plain 902.5
  moderate 163.6
  punish 1010.10
**chastened**
  restrained 163.11
  weak 765.15
**chastise** punish 1010.10
  reprove 969.17

**chastity**
  abstinence 992.2
  literary elegance
    589.1
  perfection 677.1
  purity 988
  virtue 980.3
**chat**
  *n.* chatter 596.3
  conversation 597.4
  *v.* chatter 596.5
  converse 597.10
**château** 191.8
**chatelaine**
  governor 749.5
  jewel 901.6
  mistress 749.2
**chattel** property 810.1
  slave 764.7
**chatter**
  *n.* idle talk 596.3
  rattle 455.3
  speech 594.1
  *v.* be cold 333.9
  bird sound 460.5
  expatiate 593.8
  rattle 455.6
  shake 324.11
  speak 594.20
  talk idly 596.5
**chatterbox**
  chatterer 596.4
  talker 594.18
**chatty**
  conversational 597.13
  intimate 922.20
  talkative 596.9
**chauffeur**
  *n.* driver 274.10
  male servant 750.4
  *v.* ride 273.32
**chauvinism**
  patriotism 941.2
  prejudice 527.4
  warlikeness 797.15
**chauvinist**
  intolerant person
    527.3
  militarist 800.5
  patriot 941.3
**chauvinist(ic)**
  militaristic 797.26
  prejudiced 527.12
  public-spirited 941.4
**cheap**
  disgraceful 915.11
  inexpensive 849.7
  inferior 680.9
  paltry 673.18
  stingy 852.9
  worthless 669.11
**cheapen** bargain 827.17
  corrupt 692.14
  depreciate 849.6
**cheat**
  *n.* deceiver 619.3
  fake 616.13
  fraud 618.8
  *v.* be dishonest 975.11
  deceive 618.17
**check**
  *n.* account of 87.6

bill 845.3
blemish 679.1
checkup 485.6
comparison 491.2
confinement 761.1
crack 201.2
curb 730.7
defeat 727.2
frustration 730.3
gambling 515.14
hindrance 730.1
impairment 692.8
label 568.13
making certain 513.8
mark 568.5
measure 490.2
negotiable instru-
  ment 835.11
opening 265.1
plaid 374.4
restraint 760.1
reverse 729.3
slowing 270.4
speech sound 594.13
stop 144.2
tag 835.12
  *v.* agree 26.6
  audit 87.14
  blemish 679.4
  break 49.12
  cleave 201.4
  compare 491.5
  confine 761.12
  defeat 727.11
  delay 132.8
  examine 485.23
  fend off 799.10
  hinder 730.10
  injure 692.15
  make certain 513.12
  mark 568.19
  monitor 344.26
  restrain 760.7
  slow 270.9
  stop 144.11
  variegate 374.7
**checkbook** 835.11
**checker**
  be changed 139.5
  variegate 374.7
**checkerboard**
  check 374.4
  plaything 878.16
**checkered**
  changeable 141.6
  plaid 374.14
**checkers** 878.34
**check in** arrive 300.6
  die 408.20
  record 570.16
**checking account**
  account 839.2
  funds 835.14
**checklist**
  directory 748.10
  itemization 88.1
  list 88.6
**checkmate**
  *n.* defeat 727.2
  end 144.2
  frustration 730.3
  *v.* defeat 727.11

stop 144.11
thwart 730.15
**check out** audit 87.14
  be qualified 720.15
  die 408.20
  examine 485.23
  leave 301.14
  make certain 513.12
**cheek** buttocks 241.5
  insolence 913.3
  rashness 894.1
  side 242.1
**cheeky** defiant 793.7
  impudent 913.9
**cheep** 460.5
**cheer**
  *n.* applause 968.2
  cheerfulness 870.1
  conviviality 922.3
  cry 459.1
  food 308.1
  happiness 865.2
  hurrah 876.2
  *v.* applaud 968.10
  assent 521.8
  comfort 887.6
  cry 459.6
  encourage 893.16
  give hope 888.10
  gladden 870.7
  refresh 695.2
  rejoice 876.6
  urge on 648.16
**cheerful**
  cheering 870.16
  cheery 870.11
  happy 865.13
  homelike 191.33
  optimistic 888.12
  pleasant 863.6
**cheerfully**
  cheerily 870.17
  hopefully 888.14
  pleasantly 863.11
**cheerfulness**
  auspiciousness 544.9
  good cheer 870
  happiness 865.2
  optimism 888.3
  pleasantness 863.4
**cheering**
  comforting 887.13
  gladdening 870.16
  promising 888.13
  refreshing 695.3
**cheerless**
  hopeless 889.12
  pleasureless 866.20
  unhappy 872.21
  unpleasant 864.20
**cheer up** 870.9
**cheery** see **cheerful**
**cheese** 308.47,53
**cheeseparing**
  *n.* economizing 851.2
  parsimony 852.1
  *adj.* economical 851.6
  meager 102.5
  parsimonious 852.7
**cheesy** bad 675.8
  base 915.12
  inferior 680.9

paltry 673.18
cheetah 414.27,58
chef cook 330.2
  master 749.1
chef d'œuvre
  masterpiece 733.10
  pattern of perfection
    677.4
  product 168.1
  work of art 574.11
chemical
  *n.* chemistry 379.1,11
  inorganic matter
    382.3
  *adj.* chemistry 379.7
chemical apparatus
  379.13
chemical element
  chemical 379.1,10
  element 376.2
chemist
  drugstore 687.36
  pharmacist 687.35
  store 832.4
chemistry 379.9
cherish care for 699.19
  foster 785.16
  harbor 813.7
  hold dear 931.19
  remember 537.13
cheroot 434.4
cherry bomb 453.5
cherub angel 1015.1
  child 125.3
  endearment 932.5
che sarà sarà 640.11
chess 878.34
chest breast 256.6
  depository 836.12
  storage place 660.6
chestnut
  *n.* horse 414.13
  old joke 881.9
  platitude 517.3
  *adj.* reddish-brown
    367.4
  redheaded 368.10
chevalier gallant 936.9
  knight 918.5
  rider 274.8
chevron angle 251.2
  crookedness 219.8
  heraldic insignia
    569.2
  military insignia
    569.5
chew
  *n.* bite 307.2
  chewing tobacco
    434.7
  *v.* eat 307.25
  pulp 390.5
  reprove 969.19
  use tobacco 434.14
chewing
  *n.* eating 307.1
  reproof 969.6
  tobacco chewing
    434.10
  *adj.* masticatory
    307.30
  tobacco 434.15

chewing gum
  chicle gum 389.6
  elastic substance
    358.3
chew out 969.19
chew the fat 597.9
chewy 359.4
chi 221.4
chiaroscuro
  lighting 335.19
  picture 574.14
chic
  *n.* smartness 644.3
  *adj.* dressed up 231.45
  smart 644.13
chicanery
  dishonesty 975.2
  sophistry 483.5
  stratagem 735.3
  trick 618.6
  trickery 618.4
chichi ornate 901.12
  showy 904.19
  ultrafashionable
    644.14
chick bird 414.33
  endearment 932.5
  girl 125.6
  poultry 414.34
  woman 421.6
  young chicken 125.8
chicken
  *n.* coward 892.5
  effeminate male
    421.10
  food 308.22
  homosexual 419.16
  military insignia
    569.5
  poultry 414.34,67
  weakling 160.6
  *v.* be a coward 892.8
  *adj.* cowardly 892.10
  effeminate 421.14
  weak 160.12
chicken feed
  fodder 308.4
  trifles 673.4
chicle 389.6
chide 969.17
chief
  *n.* heraldic insignia
    569.2
  leader 749.3
  master 749.1
  potentate 749.7
  principal 672.10
  superior 36.4
  supervisor 748.2
  *adj.* directing 747.12
  first 68.17
  front 240.10
  governing 741.18
  leading 292.3
  main 36.14
  most important
    672.23
  preceding 64.4
  top 211.10
chiefly generally 79.17
  mainly 36.17
  normally 84.9

on the whole 54.14*
  principally 68.18
chieftain 749.7
chieftaincy
  mastership 739.7
  region 181.1
chigger 414.40
chignon
  false hair 230.13
  hair 230.7
chilblain cold 333.2
  environmental dis-
    ease 686.31
  sore 686.35
child descendant 171.3
  innocent person
    984.4
  product 168.1
  unsophisticate 736.3
  youngster 125.3
childbearing 167.7
childhood origin 68.4
  youth 124.2
childish
  childlike 124.11
  senile 469.23
  simple-minded
    469.24
childishness
  childlikeness 124.4
  senility 469.10
  simple-mindedness
    469.11
  unwiseness 470.2
childless 166.4
childlike artless 736.5
  childish 124.11
  innocent 984.6
  senile 469.23
  simple-minded
    469.24
  trusting 501.22
child prodigy 733.12
children family 11.5
  posterity 171.1
  young people 125.2
child's play 673.5
chill
  *n.* cold 333.1
  cold sensation 333.2
  deterrent 652.2
  disease symptom
    686.8
  enmity 929.1
  indifference 636.1
  unfeeling 856.1
  unsociability 923.2
  *v.* be cold 333.9
  disincline 652.4
  make cold 333.10
  refrigerate 334.10
  *adj.* cool 333.12
  unfeeling 856.9
  unfriendly 929.9
chiller cooler 334.3
  motion picture
    611.16
chilling
  *n.* cold sensation
    333.2
  refrigeration 334.1

  *adj.* frightening
    891.36
  refrigerative 334.12
chilly aloof 912.12
  cold 333.15
  cool 333.12
  reticent 613.10
  unfeeling 856.9
  unfriendly 929.9
  unsociable 923.6
chime
  *n.* bell 454.4
  carillon 465.21
  music 462.3
  percussion instrument
    465.18
  repetitiousness 103.4
  ringing 454.3
  *v.* agree 26.6
  harmonize 462.36
  ring 454.8
  say 594.23
  sound similar 20.9
chime in 238.6
chimera hope 888.5
  illusion 519.1
  mosaic 44.8
  thing imagined 535.5
chimeric(al)
  illusory 519.9
  imaginary 535.22
  tenuous 4.6
chiming
  *n.* music 462.3
  ringing 454.3
  *adj.* harmonious
    462.50
  repetitious 103.15
  ringing 454.12
  similar sounding
    20.17
chimney deposit 383.7
  fireplace 329.11
  ravine 201.2
  smoke passage 396.18
chimpanzee 414.28,59
chin
  *n.* front 240.6
  *v.* converse 597.9
  speak 594.21
china
  *n.* brittleness 360.2
  ceramic ware 576.2,8
  *adj.* ceramic 576.7
chine crest 207.6
  ridge 256.3
chink
  *n.* crack 201.2
  faint sound 452.3
  groove 263.1
  ringing 454.3
  vulnerable point
    697.4
  *v.* faint sound 452.15
  open 265.12
  ring 454.8
  stop 266.7
chinoiserie 901.2
chinook 403.7
chintzy meager 102.5
  slovenly 62.15
  tasteless 898.10

**chip**
n. break 49.4
flake 227.3
gambling 515.14
impairment 692.8
lightness 353.2
piece 55.3
small amount 35.3
v. break 49.12
injure 692.15
**chip in** give 818.14
interrupt 238.6
participate 815.5
pay 841.18
**chip off the old block**
copy 24.3
descendant 171.3
likeness 20.3
**chip on one's shoulder**
challenge 793.2
warlikeness 797.15
**chipper**
cheerful 870.13
healthy 685.7
lively 707.17
**chippy** 989.14
**chips** money 835.2
sailor 276.6
**chiropodist** 688.8
**chiropractic**
n. healing art 688.2
adj. medical 688.18
**chiropractor** 688.5
**chirp**
n. insect sound 458.5
v. be cheerful 870.6
bird sound 460.5
rejoice 876.5
sing 462.39
stridulate 458.7
utter 594.26
**chisel**
n. sculpting tool 575.4
v. cheat 618.17
engrave 578.10
form 246.7
groove 263.3
process 167.11
sculpture 575.5
**chiseler** 619.3
**chisel in** 238.5
**chiseling**
n. engraving 578.2
adj. deceitful 618.20
**chit** child 125.3
debt 840.1
letter 604.2
little thing 196.4
**chitchat**
conversation 597.5
gossip 558.7
**chivalrous**
courageous 893.17
gallant 936.15
magnanimous 979.6
noble 918.10
**chivalry** courage 893.1
gallantry 936.2
magnanimity 979.2
nobility 918.2
warcraft 797.10
**chivy** annoy 866.13

pursue 655.8
**chlorinate**
add gas 401.8
react chemically
379.6
sanitize 681.24
**chloroform**
n. anesthetic 687.57
v. kill 409.13
render insensible
423.4
**chock**
n. curb 730.7
v. fill 56.7
obstruct 730.12
**chock-full** 56.11
**chocolate**
n. candy 308.54
adj. brown 367.3
**choice**
n. free choice 762.6
judgment 494.1
loophole 632.4
selection 637
the best 674.8
will 621.1
adj. best 674.18
tasteful 897.8
**choir** chorus 464.16
church part 1042.9
keyboard 465.20
**choirboy** 464.15
**choirmaster**
choral director
464.18
leader 748.6
**choke**
n. suffocation 409.7
violent death 408.6
v. be hot 328.22
close 266.6
destroy 693.15
die 408.24
extinguish 332.7
obstruct 730.12
overload 663.15
silence 451.8
stop 266.7
strangle 409.19
**chokedamp**
miasma 676.4
vapor 401.1
**choke on** 867.4
**choking**
n. destruction 693.6
extinguishing 332.2
obstruction 266.3
suffocation 409.7
violent death 408.6
adj. hindering 730.17
imperfectly spoken
595.12
**choler** bitterness 952.3
ill humor 951.1
**cholera** 686.12
**choleric**
n. personality type
690.15
adj. ill-humored
951.23
resentful 952.24
**cholesterol** 309.7

**chomp**
n. bite 307.2
v. chew 307.25
**choo-choo** 272.13
**choose** desire 634.14
select 637.13
will 621.2
**choosing**
n. choice 637.1
adj. selective 637.23
**choosy** fastidious 896.9
selective 637.23
**chop**
n. cheek 242.1
grain 308.4
hit 283.4
meat 308.19
rough surface 261.2
wave 395.14
v. be changed 139.5
notch 262.4
sever 49.11
**chop down** fell 318.5
raze 693.19
**chopfallen** see
**chapfallen**
**chop logic**
argue 482.16
differentiate 16.6
quibble 483.9
**chopper**
helicopter 280.5
motorcycle 272.8
**choppy**
discontinuous 72.4
irregular 138.3
jolting 324.20
nonuniform 18.3
rough 261.6
**chops** 265.5
**choral** 462.51
**chorale** choir 464.16
hymn 1032.3
sacred music 462.16
**chord**
n. harmonics 463.17
music 465.23
straight line 250.2
sympathy 855.5
v. harmonize 462.36
perform music 462.40
put in tune 462.37
**chore**
n. difficult thing
731.2
task 656.2
v. serve 750.13
work 716.12
**chorea**
nervous disorder
686.23
shaking 324.2
**choreographer** 611.27
**choreographic** 879.6
**choreography**
dancing 879.1
representation 572.1
**chorister**
choirmaster 464.18
choral singer 464.15
**chorography**
location 184.7

map 654.4
mensuration 490.9
**chortle**
n. laughter 876.4
v. laugh 876.8
**chorus**
n. agreement 26.1
choir 464.16
choral music 462.18
music division 462.24
poetic division
609.11
repeat 103.5
sequel 67.1
troupe 612.11
unanimity 521.5
v. imitate 22.5
say 594.23
sing 462.39
**chorus girl**
choral singer 464.15
dancer 879.3
entertainer 612.1
**chosen**
n. elect 637.12
the best 674.8
adj. selected 637.26
superior 36.12
**chow** 308.2
**chowder** soup 308.10
stew 308.11
**chrismal**
baptism 1040.7
church furnishing
1042.10
church vessel 1042.11
unction 1040.6
**Christ**
functions of 1013.17
God the Son 1013.12
**christen** begin 68.11
name 583.11
perform rites 1040.20
**Christendom**
Christianity 1020.6
the believing 1028.5
**christened** 583.14
**christening**
baptism 1040.7
naming 583.2
**Christian**
n. believer 1028.4
good person 985.3
religionist 1020.16,34
adj. honest 974.13
kind 938.13
orthodox 1024.7
pious 1028.8
**Christian**
**denominations**
1020.33
**Christianity**
Christianism
1020.6,32
piety 1028.2
**Christian name** 583.4
**Christian Science**
1020.13,33
**Christian Science**
**practitioner**
faith healer 688.12
religionist 1020.23

circumnavigate
  go around 321.4
  sail 275.13
circumscribe
  bound 234.4
  constrict 198.7
  limit 235.8
  qualify 507.3
  restrain 760.9
circumscription
  boundary 235.3
  bounds 235.1
  contraction 198.1
  demarcation 234
  enclosure 236.1
  exclusion 77.1
  qualification 507.1
  restriction 760.3
circumspect
  careful 533.10
  cautious 895.8
  judicious 467.19
  slow 270.10
circumstance
  component 58.2
  condition 8
  event 151.2
  fact 1.3
  pomp 904.6
  state 7.1
circumstances
  affairs 151.4
  assets 810.8
  environment 233.1
  situation 8.2
circumstantial
  conditional 8.7
  evidential 505.17
  happening 151.9
  unessential 6.4
circumstantiality
  meticulousness 533.3
  particularity 8.4
circumstantiate
  confirm 505.12
  itemize 8.6
circumvent
  deceive 618.13
  evade 631.7
  go around 321.4
  outwit 735.11
  thwart 730.15
circumvention
  avoidance 631.1
  deception 618.1
  outwitting 735.5
circus arena 802.1
  circle 253.2
  city district 183.9
  show 611.15
  theater 611.1
cirque 257.8
cirrhosis
  alcoholism 996.3
  liver disease 686.21
cirrose cloudy 404.7
  hairy 230.24
  threadlike 206.7
cirrus cloud 404.1
  curl 254.2
  filament 206.1
cist 410.16

cistern 398.1
citadel 799.6
citation
  accusation 1005.2
  attribution 155.2
  honor 916.4
  reference 505.6
  summons 752.7
cite accuse 1005.7
  call attention to
    530.10
  honor 916.8
  name 505.14
  particularize 8.6
  summon 752.12
cither 465.3
citified 183.10
citizen
  free person 762.11
  national 190.4
  noncombatant 803.5
citizenry people 417.2
  population 190.1
  the public 919.2
citizens band 344.13,29
citizenship
  nationality 189.2
  public spirit 941.1
citizenship papers 189.3
cittern 465.3
city
  n. districts of 183.6
  region 180.5
  town 183.1
  adj. urban 183.10
city dweller 190.6
city father
  legislator 746.3
  public official 749.17
city hall
  government building
    742.12
  political party 744.24
  town hall 183.5
city manager 749.17
city planner 579.10
city slicker
  sophisticate 733.16
  townsman 190.6
city-state 181.1
civic
  governmental 741.17
  political 744.43
  public 417.13
  public-spirited 941.4
  urban 183.10
civics 744.2
civil courteous 936.14
  decorous 897.10
  governmental 741.17
  lay 1039.3
  public 417.13
  sociable 922.18
civil ceremony 933.4
civil code 998.5
civilian lawyer 1003.4
  noncombatant 803.5
civility amenities 936.7
  courtesy 936.1
  cultivation 691.3
  decorousness 897.3
  etiquette 646.3

polite act 936.6
  sociability 922.1
  social convention
    645.1
civilization
  improvement 691.3
  society 642.3
civilize humanize 417.9
  make better 691.9
  teach 562.11
civilized
  improved 691.13
  learned 475.21
  tasteful 897.9
civil rights
  liberties 762.2
  rights 958.5
civil servant 749.16
civvies 231.8
clabber
  n. curd 354.7
  semiliquid 389.5
  v. make viscid 389.10
  thicken 354.10
clack
  n. chatter 596.3
  noisemaker 453.5
  rattle 455.3
  snap 456.2
  v. bird sound 460.5
  chatter 596.5
  rattle 455.6
  snap 456.7
clacker 453.5
clad 231.44
claim
  n. demand 753.1
  estate 810.4
  extortion 305.6
  false claim 649.2
  legal statement
    1004.7
  possession 808.1
  privilege 958.3
  v. demand 753.4
  extort 305.15
  lay claim to 753.5
  possess 808.4
  pretext 649.3
  require 639.9
  take 822.13
claimant
  accuser 1005.5
  petitioner 774.7
clairvoyance
  divining 543.2
  extrasensory percep-
    tion 1034.8
  foreknowledge 542.3
  intuition 481.1
  understanding 475.3
clairvoyant
  n. occultist 1034.14
  adj. foreseeing 542.7
  intuitive 481.5
  psychic 1034.23
clam
  n. food 308.25
  invertebrate 415.5
  uncommunicative
    person 613.5
  v. fish 655.10

clambake
  electioneering 744.12
  picnic 307.6
clamber up 315.11
clammy sweaty 311.22
  viscous 389.12
clamor
  n. dissonance 461.2
  entreaty 774.2
  noise 453.3
  outcry 459.4
  v. be noisy 453.8
  complain 875.13
  vociferate 459.8
clamor for
  demand 753.4
  entreat 774.11
  require 639.9
  wish for 634.16
clamorous
  demanding 753.8
  excited 857.22
  noisy 453.12
  urgent 672.21
  vociferous 459.10
clamp
  n. contractor 198.6
  hold 813.2
  v. fasten 47.7
  squeeze 198.8
clamp down on
  domineer 741.16
  suppress 760.8
clam up be silent 451.6
  silence! 451.14
clan class 61.2
  clique 788.6
  community 788.2
  kind 61.3
  race 11.4
clandestine 614.12
clang
  n. animal sound 460.1
  harsh sound 458.3
  ringing 454.3
  v. ring 454.8
  sound harshly 458.9
clank
  n. harsh sound 458.3
  ringing 454.3
  v. ring 454.8
  sound harshly 458.9
clannish
  cliquish 788.18
  contemptuous 966.8
  exclusive 896.13
  racial 11.7
clansman 11.2
clap
  n. applause 968.2
  explosive noise 456.1
  noise 453.3
  venereal disease
    686.16
  v. applaud 968.10
  close 266.6
  hit 283.13
  make explosive noise
    456.6
  put violently 184.12

**clapboard**
covering material 228.43
wood 378.3
**clapper** bell 454.4
noisemaker 453.5
**clappers** 465.18
**clapping** 968.2
**claptrap**
humbug 616.14
nonsense 547.2
specious argument 483.3
**claque** 968.8
**claqueur**
applauder 968.8
playgoer 611.32
**clarification**
explanation 552.4
facilitation 732.4
refinement 681.4
**clarify** explain 552.10
make clear 548.6
refine 681.22
simplify 45.5
**clarinet**
organ stop 465.22
wood wind 465.9
**clarion**
n. brass wind 465.8
call to arms 797.12
organ stop 465.22
v. blare 453.9
play music 462.43
**clarity** facility 732.1
intelligibility 548.2
literary elegance 589.1
transparency 339.1
visibility 444.2
**clash**
n. disaccord 795.1
dissonance 461.2
explosive noise 456.1
fight 796.4
harsh sound 458.3
hostility 929.3
impact 283.3
v. be dissonant 461.3
be inharmonious 795.8
collide 283.12
conflict 362.14
contend 796.14
counteract 178.6
differ 16.5
disagree 27.5
make explosive noise 456.6
oppose 15.4
sound harshly 458.9
**clashing**
clashingly colored 362.20
contrary 15.6
counteractive 178.8
disaccordant 795.15
disagreeing 27.6
hostile 929.10
jarring 461.5
opposing 790.8

**clasp**
n. embrace 932.2
hold 813.2
v. cohere 50.6
embrace 932.16
fasten 47.8
hold 813.6
seize 822.14
stay near 200.12
**class**
n. biology 61.5
category 61.2
community 788.2
goodness 674.1
laity 1039.1
nomenclature 583.1
rank 29.2
school 788.5
stock 11.4
students 566.11
v. analyze 48.8
categorize 61.6
judge 494.9
**classic** book 605.1
classical music 462.7
literature 602.12
pattern of perfection 677.4
work of art 574.11
**classic(al)**
antiquated 123.13
finished 677.9
model 25.8
outright 34.12
polished 589.6
simple 902.6
tasteful 897.8
written 602.24
**classicist**
antiquarian 123.5
elegant writer 589.4
scholar 476.3
**classification**
analysis 48.3
categorization 61
nomenclature 583.1
**classified**
arranged 60.14
catalogued 61.8
secret 614.11
**classify** analyze 48.8
arrange 60.11
categorize 61.6
keep secret 614.7
**classmate**
companion 928.3
partner 787.2
student 566.4
**classroom**
n. schoolroom 567.16
adj. scholastic 567.18
**classy** chic 644.13
ostentatious 904.18
**clatter**
n. chatter 596.3
noise 453.3
rattle 455.3
v. chatter 596.5
gossip 558.12
rattle 455.6
**clause**
book part 605.13

condition 507.2
legislative clause 742.17
part of writing 55.2
phrase 585.1
**clavichord** 465.13
**claw** injure 692.15
seize 822.14
torture 866.18
**clawed** footed 212.9
grasping 813.9
tortured 866.25
**claws** control 741.2
governance 739.5
grasping organs 813.4
**clay**
n. body 376.3
ceramic material 576.3
corpse 408.16
land 385.1
mankind 417.1
mud 389.8
pipe 434.6
softness 357.4
adj. ceramic 576.7
**clayey** earthy 385.7
soft 357.12
**clean**
v. cleanse 681.18
adj. chaste 988.4
honest 974.13
innocent 984.7
skillful 733.20
thorough 56.10
trim 248.5
unsoiled 681.25
adv. absolutely 56.15
cleanly 681.29
**clean-cut**
clearly visible 444.7
intelligible 548.10
shapely 248.5
**cleaner**
cleaning agent 681.17
janitor 681.14
**cleaning**
n. cleansing 681.2
devices 681.32
adj. cleansing 681.28
**cleanliness**
chastity 988.1
cleanness 681.1
innocence 984.1
**clean out** clean 681.18
eject 310.21
**cleanse** clean 681.18
purge 886.6
sanctify 1026.5
**cleanser** 681.17,30
**clean-shaven** 232.17
**cleansing**
n. cleaning 681.2
release 886.2
adj. atoning 1012.7
cleaning 681.28
relieving 886.9
**clean slate**
innocence 984.1
revolution 147.1
void 187.3
**clean sweep** 147.1

**clean up** arrange 60.12
clean 681.18
complete 722.6
profit 811.11
**clear**
v. acquit 1007.4
be high 207.16
disentangle 732.8
eject 310.21
eliminate 77.5
extricate 763.7
fly 278.47
jump 319.5
manage 724.11
pay in full 841.13
profit 811.11
refine 681.22
unblock 265.13
vindicate 1006.9
adj. audible 450.16
certain 513.13
clearly visible 444.7
easy 732.12
free 762.20
innocent 984.6
intelligible 548.10
lucid 335.31
manifest 555.8
open 265.18
polished 589.6
prosperous 728.13
rid of 762.30
simple 45.7
thorough 56.10
transparent 339.4
unfastened 49.22
unhampered 762.25
unindebted 841.23
unqualified 508.2
vacant 187.13
adv. astray 199.19
**clearance**
acquittal 1007.1
authorization 777.3
aviation 278.44
distance 199.1
elimination 77.2
evacuation 310.6
interval 201.1
latitude 762.4
pass 777.7
payment 841.1
space 179.4
spare 179.3
vindication 1006.1
**clear away**
dissipate 75.5
eject 310.21
eliminate 77.5
**clear-cut**
clearly visible 444.7
intelligible 548.10
**clearing**
acquittal 1007.1
disentanglement 732.5
evacuation 310.6
extrication 763.3
field 413.9
opening 265.1
space 179.4
vindication 1006.1

unwieldy 731.18
**clunk** 452.3
**cluster**
  *n.* bunch 74.7
  conglomeration 50.5
  solid 354.6
  throng 74.4
  *v.* assemble 74.18
  cohere 50.6
  come together 74.16
  thicken 354.10
**clutch**
  *n.* amount 28.2
  bird young 171.2
  crisis 129.4
  hold 813.2
  mechanism 348.7
  predicament 731.4
  urgency 672.4
  *v.* hold 813.6
  seize 822.14
**clutches** control 741.2
  governance 739.5
  grasping organs 813.4
**clutter**
  *n.* jumble 62.3
  large number 101.3
  radar interference
    346.12
  *v.* be numerous 101.5
  disarrange 63.2
**C-note** 835.7
**coach**
  *n.* athlete 878.20
  preparer 720.5
  railway car 272.14
  trainer 565.7
  tutor 565.6
  *v.* advise 754.5
  haul 271.12
  tutor 562.12
**coach-and-four** 272.5
**coached**
  accomplished 733.24
  prepared 720.16
**coachman** driver 274.9
  male servant 750.4
**coact** concur 177.2
  cooperate 786.3
  interact 13.8
**coadjutant** 786.5
**coadjutor**
  assistant 787.6
  associate 787.1
  clergyman 1038.9
**coagulate**
  *n.* coagulation 354.7
  *v.* cohere 50.6
  make viscid 389.10
  thicken 354.10
**coal**
  *n.* ashes 329.16
  black 365.4
  fire 328.16
  fuel 331.1,10
  *v.* burn 329.24
  fuel 331.8
  provision 659.9
**coalesce** combine 52.3
  cooperate 786.3
  mix 44.11
  unify 14.5

**coalition**
  affiliation 786.2
  association 788.1
  combination 52.1
  political front 744.33
**coarse** bitter 429.6
  carnal 987.6
  coarse-textured 351.6
  crude 898.11
  discourteous 937.6
  infelicitous 590.2
  inferior 680.9
  raucous 458.15
  rough 261.6
  thick 204.8
  undeveloped 721.12
  vulgar 990.8
**coarsen** corrupt 692.14
  give texture 351.4
  roughen 261.4
  sensualize 987.4
  vulgarize 898.9
**coarseness**
  carnality 987.2
  coarse texture 351.2
  crudeness 898.2
  discourtesy 937.1
  inferiority 680.3
  literary inelegance
    590.1
  raucousness 458.2
  thickness 204.2
  undevelopment 721.4
  vulgarity 990.3
**coast**
  *n.* border 235.4
  shore 385.2
  side 242.1
  slide 316.4
  *v.* be still 268.7
  do nothing 706.2
  glide 273.34
  go easily 732.9
  navigate 275.13
  sail 275.39
  slide 316.9
  take it easy 708.14
**coastal**
  bordering 235.11
  seashore 385.9
**coast guard**
  guard 699.9
  navy 800.26
  rescuers 702.2
**coastguardsman** 276.4
**coat**
  *n.* clothing 231.13,51
  coating 228.12
  cover 228.2
  hair 230.2
  layer 227.2
  paint 362.8
  pelt 229.1
  *v.* clothe 231.39
  color 362.13
  cover 228.24
**coating**
  *n.* coat 228.12
  coloring 362.12
  covering 228.1
  layer 227.2
  paint 362.8

  *adj.* covering 228.34
**coat of arms** 569.2
**coauthor**
  *n.* author 602.15
  collaborator 787.4
  *v.* write 602.21
**coax** importune 774.12
  lure 650.4
  urge 648.14
**coaxial** 226.14
**coaxial cable** 560.17
**cob** horse 414.18
  plant part 411.27
**cobalt** 689.9
**cobbler** mender 694.10
  shoemaker 231.37
**cobblestone**
  *n.* pavement 657.7
  *v.* cover 228.22
**cobweb** filament 206.1
  lightness 353.2
  snare 618.12
  weakness 160.7
**cocaine** 687.9,52
**coccus** 686.39
**cochlear** 254.8
**cock**
  *n.* male animal 420.8
  pile 74.10
  poultry 414.34
  stopper 266.4
  valve 396.10
  weather vane 403.17
  *v.* prepare 720.9
  pull back 295.5
  shoot 285.13
**cock-a-doodle-doo**
  460.5
**cockamamie** 470.10
**cock-and-bull story**
  616.11
**cockatrice**
  heraldic insignia
    569.2
  traitor 619.10
**cockeyed** askew 219.14
  defective eyes 440.12
  disorderly 62.13
  distorted 249.10
  drunk 996.31
  foolish 470.8
**cockle** 264.6
**cocklebur** 50.4
**cockles of the heart**
  inner nature 5.4
  seat of affections
    855.2
**cockney** 919.11
**Cockney**
  common man 919.7
  dialect 580.7
**cockpit** 802.1
**cockroach** 414.40,74
**cocksure** 513.21
**cocktail**
  alcoholic drink
    996.8,42
  cloud 404.1
**cocktail lounge** 996.19
**cocky** conceited 909.11
  defiant 793.7
  impudent 913.9

**coconspirator**
  accomplice 787.3
  schemer 654.8
**cocoon** 125.10
**coction** 329.2
**COD** 841.25
**coda** addition 41.2
  adjunct 41.1
  end 70.1
  music division 462.24
  sequel 67.1
**coddle** cook 330.4
  foster 785.16
  indulge 759.6
  make love 932.14
**coddled** cooked 330.6
  indulged 759.9
**code**
  *n.* arrangement 60.4
  cryptography 614.6
  ethics 957.1
  law code 998.5
  precepts 751.2
  rule 84.4
  telegraphy 560.2
  unintelligibility 549.7
  *v.* encode 614.10
**codeine** 687.12,54
**codex**
  manuscript 602.11
  rare book 605.3
**codicil** addition 41.2
  bequest 818.10
  sequel 67.1
**codify** classify 61.6
  legalize 998.9
  organize 60.10
  standardize 84.6
**co-ed** 566.5
**coeducational** 562.19
**coefficient** 786.5
**coequal**
  *n.* equal 30.4
  *adj.* equivalent 30.8
  identical 14.8
  reciprocal 13.13
  symmetric 248.4
**coerce** compel 756.7
  domineer 741.16
**coercion** 756.3
**coercive** 756.11
**coeternal**
  perpetual 112.7
  simultaneous 118.4
**coeval**
  *n.* contemporary
    118.2
  *adj.* innate 5.7
  simultaneous 118.4
**coexistence**
  foreign policy 744.5
  simultaneity 118.1
**coexistent**
  agreeing 26.9
  simultaneous 118.4
**coextend** parallel 218.4
  synchronize 118.3
**coextensive**
  identical 14.8
  parallel 218.6
**coffee break**
  interim 109.1

opponent 791.1

**combat fatigue**
combat neurosis
690.19
shock 686.24

**combative**
argumentative 482.19
attacking 798.30
quarrelsome 795.17
warlike 797.25

**combination**
affiliation 786.2
a preparation 720.3
assembly 74.1
association 788.1
composition 58.1
compound 44.5
concurrence 177.1
fusion 14.2
joining 47.1
mixture 44.1
relationship 9.1
union 52
unity 89.1

**combine**
n. association 788.1
business 788.9
union 52.1
v. accompany 73.7
amalgamate 52.3
assemble 74.18
compose 58.3
concur 177.2
cooperate 786.3
join 47.5
mix 44.11
unify 14.5

**combined**
accompanying 73.9
assembled 74.21
associated 788.16
concurrent 177.4
cooperating 786.5
mixed 44.15
united 52.5

**combining**
concurrent 177.4
unifying 89.12
uniting 52.7

**combo** compound 44.5
orchestra 464.12
union 52.1

**combustible**
n. fuel 331.1
adj. hot-tempered
951.25
inflammable 329.28

**combustion**
burning 329.5
fire 328.13

**come** appear 446.8
approach 296.3
arrive 300.6
be in the future
121.6
chance 156.11
emerge 303.12
occur 151.5
sex 419.25

**come about**
be changed 139.5
change course 275.30

come true 516.11
occur 151.5
rally 691.8
result 154.5
turn around 295.9

**come across**
deliver 818.13
find 488.3
meet 200.11
pay 841.16
project 555.7

**come again**
be repeated 103.11
recur 137.5
repeat 103.7
revisit 186.9

**come alive** awake 713.4
revive 407.8
understand 548.8

**come along**
be discovered 488.9
chance 156.11
fare 7.6
get better 691.7
manage 724.11
occur 151.6
progress 294.2
prosper 728.7

**come and go**
alternate 323.13
recur 137.5

**come apart**
become disordered
62.8
become nervous
859.7
be damaged 692.26
be excited 857.15
be separated 49.8
disintegrate 53.3
weaken 160.9

**come around**
acquiesce 775.3
agree 521.10
be changed 139.5
menstruate 311.18
recover 694.20
recur 137.5

**come at** arrive at 300.7
attack 798.15

**comeback** answer 486.1
countermeasure
178.5
gibe 967.2
recovery 694.8
retaliation 955.1

**come back**
answer 486.4
recover 694.20
recur 537.15
turn back 295.8

**come back at**
answer 486.4
react 284.5
retaliate 955.4

**come between**
intrude 238.5
sow dissension 795.14

**come by** acquire 811.8
inherit 819.7
receive 819.6

**come clean** 556.7

**comedian** actor 612.9
dramatist 611.27
humorist 881.12

**comedown**
descent 316.1
deterioration 692.3
disappointment
541.1
disparagement 971.1
failure 725.3
humiliation 906.2
humorousness 880.3
reverse 729.3

**come down**
descend 316.5
fall on evil days
729.11
fly 278.52
occur 151.5

**come down on**
attack 798.15
light on 316.10
punish 1010.11
reprove 969.18

**comedy** drama 611.6
humor 881.1
symbols of 611.7

**come forth**
appear 446.8
assert 555.6
be born 167.16
begin 68.13
be made public
559.16
emerge 303.12
find vent 632.10
occur 151.6

**come forward**
appear 446.8
approach 296.3
be ostentatious
904.12
volunteer 773.9

**come-hither** 650.7

**come-hither look**
flirtation 932.8
gaze 439.5

**come in** arrive 300.6
be received 819.8
enter 302.7
fly 278.52
lust 419.22

**come into**
acquire 811.8
inherit 819.7
join 788.14

**comeliness**
beauty 900.3
literary elegance
589.1

**comely**
beautiful 900.17
shapely 248.5
well-chosen 589.7

**come of** 154.5

**come of age** 126.9

**come off**
come apart 49.8
discontinue 668.4
occur 151.5
succeed 724.6

**come on**
approach 296.3
be imminent 152.2
be in the future
121.6
fare 7.6
find 488.3
follow 65.2
get better 691.7
make good 724.9
manage 724.11
occur 151.6
progress 294.2
prosper 728.7

**come-on** 650.2

**come out** act 611.34
appear 446.8
be born 68.13
be discovered 488.9
begin 68.9
be made public
559.16
be printed 603.18
be revealed 556.8
emerge 303.12
fare 7.6
find vent 632.10
result 154.5

**comer** incomer 302.4
modern 122.4
successful person
724.5

**come round**
acquiesce 775.3
be changed 139.5
change one's mind
628.6
make peace 804.10
rally 691.8
recover 694.20
recur 137.5

**comestibles** 308.1

**comet** 375.4

**come through**
accomplish 722.5
be understood 548.5
carry out 705.9
fare 7.6
make good 724.9
pay 841.16
save oneself 698.2
win through 724.12

**come to**
acquiesce 775.3
arrive 300.6
attend 186.8
cost 846.15
equal 30.5
extend to 199.6
recover 694.20
revive 407.8
total 54.8

**come together**
assemble 74.16
be joined 47.11
combine 52.3
converge 298.2
copulate 419.23
form 59.5
league 52.4
make peace 804.10

**come to light**
  appear 446.8
  be discovered 488.9
  be revealed 556.8
**come to mind**
  be remembered
    537.16
  occur to 478.18
**come to nothing**
  be destroyed 693.23
  be lost 812.6
  be unproductive
    166.3
  fail 725.12
  miscarry 314.3
  neutralize 178.7
**come to pass**
  come true 516.11
  occur 151.5
**come to terms**
  agree 521.10
  make peace 804.10
  strike a bargain
    827.18
  surrender 765.8
**come true**
  come about 516.11
  occur 151.5
**come up against**
  contend with 796.16
  find 488.3
  meet 200.11
**come upon**
  arrive at 300.7
  be unexpected 540.6
  find 488.3
  meet 200.11
**comeuppance**
  deserts 960.3
  reprisal 955.2
**come what may**
  necessarily 639.16
  perseveringly 625.9
  resolutely 624.20
  without fail 513.26
**comfit** 308.39
**comfort**
  *n.* aid 785.1
  condolence 946.1
  consolation 887.4
  contentment 868.1
  cover 228.10
  ease 887
  pleasure 865.1
  prosperity 728.1
  rest 711.1
  *v.* abet 785.14
  aid 785.11
  console 946.2
  reassure 887.6
**comfortable**
  comfy 887.11
  contented 868.7
  homelike 191.33
  pleased 865.12
  prosperous 728.12
  restful 711.10
  wealthy 837.13
**comfortably** 887.14
**comforter**
  consoler 887.5
  cover 228.10

**comforting**
  condolent 946.3
  consoling 887.13
**comfort station**
  rest room 192.26
  toilet 311.10
**comic**
  *n.* cartoon 574.17
  comedian 612.9
  humorist 881.12
  *adj.* comical 880.5
  theatrical 611.40
**comical** 880.5
**comic book**
  booklet 605.9
  cartoon 574.17
**coming**
  *n.* advancing 296.1
  advent 121.5
  appearance 446.1
  arrival 300.1
  imminence 152.1
  *adj.* approaching
    296.4
  arriving 300.9
  due 960.7
  emerging 303.18
  eventual 151.11
  future 121.8
  imminent 152.3
  successful 724.13
**coming and going** 323.5
**coming out**
  inauguration 68.5
  party 922.14
**comma** pause 144.4
  punctuation mark
    586.18
**command**
  *n.* commandment 752
  computer 349.19
  control 741.2
  direction 747.1
  governance 739.5
  precept 751.1
  skill 733.1
  supremacy 36.3
  understanding 475.3
  view 444.3
  will 621.1
  *v.* direct 747.8
  dominate 207.16
  govern 741.12
  know well 475.13
  order 752.9
  possess 808.4
  will 621.2
**commandant**
  commissioned officer
    749.18
  governor 749.5
  jailer 761.10
**commandeer**
  appropriate 822.20
  draft 780.16
**commander**
  commissioned officer
    749.18
  governor 749.5
  naval officer 749.20
  ship's officer 276.7
  superior 36.4

**commanding**
  authoritative 739.15
  directing 747.12
  governing 741.18
  imperative 752.14
**commandment**
  command 752.1
  precept 751.2
**command of language**
  diction 588.2
  eloquence 600.1
**commandos** 800.14
**command post** 226.6
**comme ci comme ça**
    680.7
**commemorate** 877.2
**commemoration**
  anniversary 137.4
  celebration 877.1
  memento 537.7
**commemorative**
  celebrative 877.3
  memorial 537.27
**commence** 68.7
**commencement**
  beginning 68.1
  ceremony 646.4
  source 153.5
**commend**
  approve 968.11
  commit 818.16
**commendable**
  good 674.12
  praiseworthy 968.20
**commendation**
  approval 968.3
  commitment 818.2
**commendatory** 968.16
**commensal**
  cooperating 786.5
  eating 307.29
  symbiotic 13.15
**commensurate**
  agreeing 26.9
  comparable 491.8
  equal 30.7
  satisfactory 868.11
  sufficient 661.6
**comment**
  *n.* commentary 606.2
  communication
    594.1
  criticism 494.2
  explanatory remark
    552.5
  remark 594.4
  *v.* remark 594.25
**commentary**
  addition 41.2
  comment 552.5
  treatise 606.2
**commentator**
  broadcaster 344.23
  critic 494.7
  expositor 606.4
  interpreter 552.7
**comment upon**
  discuss 597.12
  explain 552.11
  judge 494.14
  write upon 606.5

**commerce**
  business 656.1
  communication
    554.1
  copulation 419.8
  social intercourse
    922.4
  trade 827
**commercial**
  *n.* advertisement
    559.6
  announcement
    344.20
  radio broadcast
    344.18
  *adj.* business 827.21
  vocational 656.15
**commingle** 44.11
**commiserate**
  console 946.2
  pity 944.3
**commissar**
  autocrat 749.14
  delegate 781.2
  public official 749.17
**commissary**
  delegate 781.2
  hoard 660.1
  provider 659.6
  provisions 308.5
  store 832.6
**commission**
  *n.* commissioning 780
  delegates 781.13
  dividend 816.5
  injunction 752.2
  legislature 742.1
  meeting 74.2
  payment 841.7
  performance 705.2
  precept 751.1
  receipts 844.1
  task 656.2
  *v.* authorize 780.9
  command 752.9
  delegate 149.7
  repair 694.14
**commissioner**
  delegate 781.2
  peace officer 699.15
  public official 749.17
**commit**
  commission 780.9
  consign 818.16
  dedicate 816.11
  do 705.6
  imprison 761.17
  obligate 962.12
  promise 770.5
**commitment**
  cause 153.10
  commission 780.1
  consignment 818.2
  dedication 816.4
  duty 962.1
  friendship 927.7
  imprisonment 761.4
  promise 770.2
  resolution 624.1
  undertaking 715.1
  unselfishness 979.1
  zeal 635.2

commit suicide 409.22
committed
friendly 927.20
obliged 962.16
promised 770.8
resolute 624.11
unselfish 979.5
zealous 635.10
committee
council 755.2
delegates 781.13
meeting 74.2
committeeman
member 788.11
political worker 746.12
commodious
comfortable 887.11
spacious 179.9
useful 665.18
commodity 831.2
commodore 749.20
common
n. estate 810.4
green 411.7
park 878.14
adj. communal 815.9
cooperating 786.5
frequent 135.4
inferior 680.9
in plain style 591.3
lowborn 919.11
mediocre 680.8
medium 32.3
mutual 13.14
paltry 673.18
prevalent 79.12
prosaic 610.5
public 417.13
secondary 37.6
simple 902.6
trite 883.9
usual 84.8
vernacular 580.18
vulgar 898.14
well-known 475.27
commoner
average man 919.7
proletarian 919.1
student 566.7
common knowledge
made public 559.17
publicity 559.4
common law law 998.4
tradition 123.2
commonly
frequently 135.6
generally 79.17
inferiorly 680.12
mutually 13.17
normally 84.9
plainly 902.10
tritely 883.11
common man
a nobody 673.7
commoner 919.7
generality 79.3
people 417.2
commonness
customariness 642.7
frequency 135.1
inferiority 680.3

mediocrity 680.2
plainness 902.1
prevalence 79.2
prosaism 610.2
triteness 883.3
usualness 84.2
vulgarity 898.5
common people 919.1
commonplace
n. platitude 517.3
truism 79.8
adj. banal 883.9
in plain style 591.3
lowborn 919.11
mediocre 680.8
prosaic 610.5
simple 902.6
trite 79.16
usual 84.8
vulgar 898.14
well-known 475.27
commons
common people 919.1
dining room 192.11
park 878.14
rations 308.6
common sense
intelligence 467.6
reasonableness 482.9
commonweal
country 181.1
welfare 938.5
commonwealth
community 788.2
country 181.1
government 741.4
people 417.2
population 190.1
commotion
agitation 324.1
bustle 707.4
disturbance 62.4
excitement 857.3
noise 453.3
violence 162.2
communal
associational 788.17
common 815.9
cooperating 786.5
mutual 13.14
public 417.13
commune
community 788.2
district 180.5
commune with
communicate 554.6
converse 597.9
communicable
contagious 686.58
giveable 818.23
impartable 554.11
poisonous 684.7
transferable 271.17
communicant
believer 1028.4
informant 557.5
layman 1039.2
worshiper 1032.9
communicate
administer rites 1040.18

be in touch 554.6
be joined 47.11
converse 597.9
give 818.12
impart 554.7
inform 557.8
say 594.23
transfer 271.9
communicate with
converse 597.9
correspond 604.11
get in touch with 554.8
communication
conversation 597.1
giving 818.1
information 557.1
joining 47.1
letter 604.2
message 558.4
passageway 657.4
social intercourse 922.4
speech 554
transference 271.1
communications
electronic communications 554.5
radio 344.1
telecommunication 560
the press 605.23
communicative
conversational 597.13
informative 557.17
sociable 922.18
talkative 554.10
verbose 596.9
communion
accord 794.1
communication 554.1
conversation 597.1
correlation 13.1
participation 815.2
prayer 1032.4
religion 1020.3
school 788.5
social intercourse 922.4
Communion
Eucharist 1040.8
Mass 1040.10
communiqué
announcement 559.2
information 557.1
message 558.4
communism
Bolshevism 745.5
cooperation 786.1
participation 815.2
principle of government 741.8
Communist
Bolshevist 745.13
revolutionist 147.3
communist(ic)
communal 815.9
cooperating 786.5
Communist(ic)
Marxist 745.21
revolutionary 147.6

Communist Party
Communism 745.5
political party 744.24
community
accord 794.1
company 73.2
cooperation 786.1
correlation 13.1
ethnic group 418.1
participation 815.2
people 417.2
population 190.1
religion 1020.3
similarity 20.1
social intercourse 922.4
society 788.2
community center 183.5
communize
appropriate 822.20
communalize 815.7
politicize 745.16
commutation
compensation 33.1
interchange 150.1
substitution 149.1
travel 273.1
commute
interchange 150.4
substitute 149.4
travel 273.17
commuter 274.1
compact
n. case 193.14
contract 771
make-up 900.11
understanding 26.2
v. bargain 771.6
contract 198.7
densify 354.9
adj. close 266.12
concise 592.6
contracted 198.12
crowded 74.22
dense 354.12
joint 47.12
miniature 196.12
short 203.8
companion
accompanier 73.4
associate 787.1
copy 572.3
escort 73.5
fellow 928.3
knight 918.5
maid 750.8
parallel 20.3
ship part 277.26
stairs 315.3
companionable 922.18
companionship
company 73.2
fellowship 927.2
sociability 922.6
company actors 612.11
association 73.2
companion 928.3
firm 788.9
group 74.3
guest 925.6
military unit 800.19

sociability 922.6
team 788.7
workplace 719.1
**comparable**
analogous 20.11
approximate 9.8
comparative 491.8
relative 9.7
**comparative**
comparing 491.8
relative 9.7
**comparatively**
comparably 491.10
relatively 9.12
to a degree 35.10
**compare**
be comparable 491.7
liken 491.4
resemble 20.7
**comparison**
likening 491
similarity 20.1
substitute 149.2
**compartment**
chamber 192.2
ship 277.27
**compartmentalize**
49.18
**compass**
*n.* boundary 235.3
bounds 235.1
degree 29.1
distance 199.1
environment 233.1
gauge 490.20
guide 748.9
harmonics 463.6
range 179.2
*v.* accomplish 722.4
enclose 236.5
go around 321.4
succeed with 724.10
surround 233.6
**compassion**
kindness 938.1
leniency 759.1
pity 944.1
**compassionate**
kind 938.13
lenient 759.7
pitying 944.7
**compatibility**
accord 794.1
agreement 26.1
pleasantness 863.1
sociability 922.1
**compatible**
agreeing 26.9
in accord 794.3
pleasant 863.6
sociable 922.18
**compatriot**
associate 787.1
fellow citizen 190.5
**compel**
domineer 741.16
force 756.4
impel 283.10
motivate 648.12
necessitate 639.8
obsess 473.24

**compelling**
commanding 752.14
compulsory 756.9
motivating 648.25
obsessive 473.34
urgent 672.21
**compendious**
abridged 607.6
comprehensive 76.7
concise 592.6
short 203.8
**compendium** 607.1
**compensate**
atone 1012.4
equalize 30.6
interchange 150.4
make compensation
33.4
make restitution
823.5
pay 841.10
remedy 694.13
retaliate 955.5
**compensating**
contrary 15.6
offsetting 33.6
paying 841.21
**compensation**
atonement 1012.1
defense mechanism
690.30
penalty 1009.1
recompense 33
remuneration 841.3
reparation 694.6
reprisal 955.2
restitution 823.2
salary 841.4
**compensatory**
atoning 1012.7
offsetting 33.6
paying 841.21
restitutive 823.7
retaliatory 955.8
**compete**
contend against
790.4
contest 796.19
**competence**
ability 157.2
authority 739.1
preparedness 720.4
skill 733.1
sufficiency 661.1
**competent** able 157.14
authoritative 739.15
capable 733.22
fitted 720.17
legal 998.10
sufficient 661.6
**competently**
ably 157.16
skillfully 733.29
sufficiently 661.8
**competition**
opposition 790.2
rivalry 796.2
**competitive**
competing 796.24
opposing 790.8
**competitor**
athlete 878.20

combatant 800.1
opponent 791.2
**compilation**
book 605.4
collection 74.11
**compile** 74.18
**complacence** 868.2
**complacent**
contented 868.10
vain 909.8
**complain**
accuse 1005.7
be sick 686.43
groan 875.13
object 522.5
offer resistance 792.3
**complainant**
accuser 1005.5
malcontent 869.3
**complainer**
lamenter 875.7
malcontent 869.3
**complaining**
*n.* complaint 875.4
*adj.* discontented
869.5
plaintive 875.16
resistant 792.5
**complaint**
accusation 1005.1
disapproval 969.1
disease 686.1
grievance 875.4
legal statement
1004.7
objection 522.2
resistance 792.1
**complaisant**
conformable 82.5
considerate 938.16
courteous 936.14
indulgent 759.8
pleasant 863.6
soft 357.8
submissive 765.12
**complement**
*n.* adjunct 41.1
all 54.3
full measure 56.3
group 74.3
likeness 20.3
sailor 276.6
syntax 586.2
team 788.7
*v.* correlate 13.9
**complementary**
completing 56.13
reciprocal 13.13
**complete**
*v.* develop 148.6
end 70.7
execute 771.10
finish 722.6
fulfill 56.6
include 76.3
make perfect 677.5
perform 705.8
*adj.* accomplished
722.12
comprehensive 76.7
ended 70.8
intact 677.7

thorough 34.12
undivided 54.11
unqualified 508.2
whole 56.9
**completed** 722.11
**completely**
extremely 34.22
fully 8.13
perfectly 677.10
totally 56.14
**complete works** 605.4
**completion**
completing 722.2
execution 771.5
fulfillment 56.4
performance 705.2
result 154.2
**complex**
*n.* culture 642.3
obsession 473.13
perplex 46.2
psychological com-
plex 690.29
whole 54.1
*adj.* complicated 46.4
difficult 731.16
hard to understand
549.14
mixed 44.15
**complexion** color 362.1
looks 446.4
mode 7.4
nature 5.3
personality tendency
690.14
**complexity**
abstruseness 549.2
difficulty 731.1
intricacy 46
**compliance**
assent 521.1
conformity 82.1
consent 775.1
indulgence 759.2
obedience 766.1
observance 768.1
resignation 861.2
submission 765.1
willingness 622.1
**compliant**
agreeing 521.13
conformable 82.5
consenting 775.4
indulgent 759.8
obedient 766.3
observant 768.4
pliant 357.9
resigned 861.10
submissive 765.12
usable 665.22
willing 622.5
**complicate** add 40.4
increase 38.5
involve 46.3
make unintelligible
549.12
**complicated**
complex 46.4
hard to understand
549.14
**complication**
abstruseness 549.2

come with child
169.11
create 167.13
imagine 535.14
know 475.12
originate 153.11
phrase 588.4
suppose 499.10
think 478.8
understand 548.7
vivify 407.9
**conceived**
invented 167.23
known 475.26
**concentrate**
*n.* extract 305.8
*v.* contract 198.7
converge 298.2
densify 354.9
extract 305.16
focus 226.10
increase 38.5
pay attention 530.8
think 478.10
**concentrated**
attentive 530.15
central 226.11
contracted 198.12
dense 354.12
**concentration**
attention 530.1
centralization 226.8
contraction 198.1
convergence 298.1
densification 354.3
engrossment 530.3
extract 305.8
extraction 305.7
firmness 624.2
industry 707.6
intensification 38.2
perseverance 625.1
thoughtfulness 478.3
**concentration camp**
camp 191.29
killing site 409.12
prison 761.8
**concentric** 226.14
**concept** belief 501.6
idea 479.1
visualization 535.6
**conception** belief 501.6
creation 167.5
creative thought
535.2
idea 479.1
intellect 466.1
intelligence 467.1
plan 654.1
pregnancy 169.4
source 153.5
thought 478.1
understanding 475.3
visualization 535.6
**conceptual**
cognitive 478.21
ideational 479.9
imaginative 535.18
intelligent 467.12
mental 466.8
**conceptualize**
imagine 535.14

know 475.12
think 478.8
**concern**
*n.* affair 151.3
anxiety 890.1
business 656.1
carefulness 533.1
company 788.9
considerateness 938.3
importance 672.1
interest 530.2
relevance 9.4
study 475.10
sympathy 855.5
topic 484.1
workplace 719.1
*v.* involve 176.2
make attentive
530.12
relate to 9.5
trouble 731.12
upset 890.3
**concerned**
anxious 890.6
interested 530.16
involved 176.3
**concerning** 9.13
**concert**
*n.* agreement 26.1
concurrence 177.1
cooperation 786.1
music 462.3
music performance
462.34
unanimity 521.5
*v.* cooperate 786.3
plan 654.9
*adj.* music 462.52
**concert artist** 464.1
**concerted**
concurrent 177.4
cooperating 786.5
**concert hall** hall 192.4
theater 611.18
**concertmaster** 464.19
**concerto** 462.7
**concession**
acknowledgment
521.3
compromise 807.1
confession 556.3
discount 847.1
giving 818.1
grant 777.5
market 832.1
qualification 507.1
**concierge** 699.12
**conciliar** 755.5
**conciliate** 804.7
**conciliatory**
forgiving 947.6
pacificatory 804.12
unbelligerent 803.10
**concise** brief 592.6
short 203.8
taciturn 613.9
**conclave**
church council 755.4
conference 597.6
meeting 74.2
political convention
744.8

**conclude** arrange 771.9
complete 722.6
end 70.5
judge 494.10
resolve 624.7
suppose 499.10
**conclusion**
affirmation 523.1
aftermath 117.2
belief 501.6
compacting 771.4
completion 722.2
end 70.1
judgment 494.4
result 154.2
sequel 67.1
**conclusive**
certain 513.13
completory 722.9
convincing 501.26
evidential 505.17
final 70.10
mandatory 752.13
unqualified 508.2
**concoct**
construct 167.10
fabricate 616.18
imagine 535.14
invent 167.13
mix 44.11
plot 654.10
prepare 720.7
**concoction**
a preparation 720.3
compound 44.5
creation 167.5
fabrication 616.10
product 168.1
**concomitant**
*n.* adjunct 41.1
attendant 73.3
contemporary 118.2
*adj.* accompanying
73.9
concurrent 177.4
simultaneous 118.4
**concord** accord 794.1
agreement 26.1
cooperation 786.1
harmonics 463.17
music 462.3
order 59.1
treaty 771.2
unanimity 521.5
**concordance**
accord 794.1
agreement 26.1
concurrence 177.1
cooperation 786.1
music 462.3
reference book 605.6
unanimity 521.5
**concordant**
agreeing 26.9
concurrent 177.4
conformist 82.6
cooperating 786.5
in accord 794.3
music 462.50
pacific 803.9
unanimous 521.15

**concourse**
assembly 74.2
concurrence 177.1
convergence 298.1
flow 395.4
gathering 74.1
joining 47.1
**concrete**
*n.* building material
378.2
conglomeration 50.5
covering material
228.43
hardness 356.6
pavement 657.7
solid 354.6
*v.* cover 228.22
plaster 228.25
solidify 356.8
thicken 354.10
*adj.* dense 354.12
hard 356.10
particular 80.12
substantial 3.6
**concubine**
mistress 989.17
slave 764.7
wife 933.9
**concupiscence**
desire 634.1
lasciviousness 989.5
sexual desire 419.5
**concur** agree 521.9
collaborate 177.2
cooperate 786.3
match 26.6
synchronize 118.3
**concurrence**
accompaniment 73.1
assembly 74.1
assent 521.1
collaboration 177
convergence 298.1
cooperation 786.1
interaction 13.3
joining 47.1
parallelism 218.1
simultaneity 118.1
unanimity 521.5
**concurrent**
accompanying 73.9
collaborative 177.4
converging 298.3
cooperating 786.5
joint 47.12
parallel 218.6
simultaneous 118.4
unanimous 521.15
**concurrently**
concertedly 177.5
cooperatively 786.6
jointly 47.18
simultaneously 118.6
unanimously 521.17
**concussion**
impact 283.3
impairment 692.8
shock 162.8
**condemn**
censure 969.13
damn 1008.3
destroy 693.10

reactionary 745.17
right-wing 243.4
unprogressive 140.8
**Conservative** 744.27
**conservatory**
arbor 191.13
nursery 413.11
school 567.9
storage place 660.6
**conserve**
*n.* sweets 308.39
*v.* care for 699.19
preserve 701.7
reserve 660.12
**consider**
allow for 507.5
be considerate 938.10
believe 501.11
care 533.6
discuss 597.12
judge 494.8
reflect 478.12
suppose 499.10
think of 478.16
**considerable**
authoritative 739.15
important 672.16
large 195.16
numerous 101.6
powerful 34.6
**considerably** 34.15
**considerate**
careful 533.10
courteous 936.14
judicious 467.19
thoughtful 938.16
**consideration**
argument 482.5
attention 530.1
belief 501.6
carefulness 533.1
contemplation 478.2
discussion 597.7
esteem 914.3
gratuity 818.5
importance 672.1
judgment 494.5
judiciousness 467.7
motive 648.1
offset 33.2
recompense 841.3
respect 964.1
thoughtfulness 938.3
**considered**
intentional 653.9
logical 482.21
**considering** 155.9
**consign**
commission 780.9
commit 818.16
imprison 761.17
send 271.14
transfer 271.9
transfer property
817.3
**consignee** agent 781.3
recipient 819.3
**consignment**
commission 780.1
freight 271.7
giving 818.2

property transfer
817.1
remand 761.4
**consistency**
agreement 26.1
conformity 82.1
continuity 50.2
density 354.1
intelligibility 548.2
symmetry 248.1
tenacity 50.3
uniformity 17.1
**consistent**
agreeing 26.9
consecutive 50.11
faithful 974.20
intelligible 548.10
uniform 17.5
valid 516.13
**consistent with** 82.9
**consist of** 58.3
**consolation**
comfort 887.4
condolence 946.1
**consolation prize** 916.2
**console**
*n.* automation 349.15
keyboard 465.20
radio 344.7
radio receiver 344.3
*v.* comfort 887.6
condole with 946.2
**consolidate**
combine 52.3
contract 198.7
cooperate 786.3
densify 354.9
intensify 38.5
**consolidated**
combined 52.5
contracted 198.12
dense 354.12
**consolidation**
affiliation 786.2
cohesion 50.1
combination 52.1
contraction 198.1
densification 354.3
intensification 38.2
**consommé** 308.10
**consonance**
agreement 26.1
music 462.3
rhyme 609.10
uniformity 17.1
**consonant**
*n.* speech sound
594.13
*adj.* agreeing 26.9
music 462.50
phonetic 594.31
uniform 17.5
**consort**
accompanier 73.4
agreement 26.1
associate 787.1
companion 928.3
music 462.3
spouse 933.7
**consortium**
association 788.9
compact 771.1

understanding 26.2
**consort with**
accompany 73.7
be sociable 922.16
**conspectus**
abridgment 203.3
synopsis 607.1
**conspicuous**
clearly visible 444.7
manifest 555.12
notable 672.18
prominent 914.17
striking 34.10
**conspicuous
consumption** 854.1
**conspicuously**
exceptionally 34.20
famously 914.21
importantly 672.24
manifestly 555.16
visibly 444.8
**conspiracy**
chicanery 618.4
combination 52.1
concurrence 177.1
intrigue 654.6
stratagem 735.3
**conspirator**
schemer 654.8
traitor 619.10
**conspire** concur 177.2
cooperate 786.3
join 52.4
plot 654.10
**constable** 699.15
**constabulary**
jurisdiction 1000.4
police 699.17
**constancy**
continuity 71.1
durability 110.1
fidelity 974.7
firmness 624.2
frequency 135.2
friendship 927.7
monotony 17.2
permanence 140.1
perpetuity 112.1
perseverance 625.1
regularity 137.1
stability 142.1
uniformity 17.1
**constant**
*n.* atomic 326.26
*adj.* dyed 362.17
enduring 110.10
exact 516.16
faithful 974.20
firm 624.12
friendly 927.20
habitual 642.16
monotonous 71.8
observant 768.4
permanent 140.7
perpetual 112.7
persevering 625.7
regular 137.6
unbroken 135.5
unchangeable 142.17
uniform 17.5
**constantly** always 17.8
faithfully 974.25

perpetually 112.10
regularly 137.9
steadily 135.7
unceasingly 71.10
**constellation**
famous persons 914.9
fate 640.2
stars 375.5,28
**consternation** 891.1
**constipated** 266.11
**constipation**
disease symptom
686.8
indigestion 686.28
obstruction 266.3
**constituency**
electorate 744.22
membership 788.12
population 190.1
sphere of influence
172.4
**constituent**
*n.* component 58.2
ingredient 194.1
material 376.2
*adj.* component 58.5
essential 5.8
selective 637.23
**constitute**
compose 58.3
create 167.12
legalize 998.8
legislate 742.18
**constitution**
arrangement 60.1
composition 58.1
law 998.6
legislation 742.13
nature 5.3
production 167.4
structure 245.1
temperament 525.3
**constitutional**
*n.* exercise 716.6
walk 273.12
*adj.* governmental
741.17
healthful 683.5
innate 5.7
legal 998.10
temperamental 525.7
**constrain** compel 756.4
confine 761.12
moderate 163.6
necessitate 639.8
restrain 760.7
**constrained**
modest 908.11
restrained 760.13
reticent 613.10
tempered 163.11
**constraint**
compulsion 756.1
confinement 761.1
modesty 908.3
prudence 163.1
restraint 760.1
reticence 613.3
self-control 624.5
temperance 992.1
urge 648.6
**constrict** close 266.6

contract 198.7
narrow 205.11
obstruct 730.12
**constricted**
closed 266.9
contracted 198.12
narrow 205.14
narrow-minded 527.10
**constriction**
contraction 198.1
hindrance 730.1
narrowing 205.2
**construct**
*n.* building 245.2
*v.* compose 58.3
create 167.10
structure 245.8
**construction**
building 245.2
composition 58.1
interpretation 552.1
manufacture 167.3
meaning 545.3
phrase 585.1
structure 245.1
word 582.4
**constructive**
creative 167.19
helpful 785.21
interpretative 552.14
**construe**
interpret 552.9
render 552.12
**consul** 781.6
**consulate** house 191.6
mastership 739.7
office 719.8
**consult** 597.11
**consultant**
advisor 754.3
expert 733.11
**consultation**
advice 754.1
conference 597.6
**consume** burn 329.25
deplete 812.5
destroy 693.10
deteriorate 692.22
disintegrate 53.3
eat 307.20
shrink 198.9
use 665.13
use up 666.2
waste 854.4
wear away 39.6
**consumed**
burned 329.30
lost 812.7
reduced 39.10
shrunk 198.13
used up 666.4
wasted 854.9
**consumer** buyer 828.5
eater 307.14
user 665.9
**consumerism** 828.1
**consuming**
destructive 693.26
engrossing 530.20
unpleasant 864.23

**consummate**
*v.* accomplish 722.4
top 211.9
*adj.* complete 722.12
outright 34.12
perfect 677.9
thorough 56.10
top 211.10
**consummation**
accomplishment 722.1
completion 56.4
culmination 677.3
end 70.1
result 154.2
**consumption**
destruction 693.1
deterioration 692.4
eating 307.1
erosion 39.3
loss 812.2
shrinking 198.3
tuberculosis 686.15
use 665.1
using up 666
**consumptive**
*n.* sick person 686.40
*adj.* contractive 198.11
destructive 693.26
diseased 686.57
**contact**
*n.* communication 554.1
go-between 781.4
nearness 200.5
touch 425.1
*v.* be heard 448.13
come in contact 200.10
communicate with 554.8
**contact lens** 443.2
**contagious**
communicable 554.11
infectious 686.58
poisonous 684.7
transferable 271.17
**contain** close 266.6
enclose 236.5
entail 76.4
include 76.3
internalize 225.6
limit 234.5
restrain 760.7
total 54.8
**contained in** 58.4
**container**
enclosure 236.3
receptacle 193
**containment**
foreign policy 744.5
surrounding 233.5
**contaminate**
adulterate 44.13
corrupt 692.14
defile 682.17
infect 686.48
radioactivate 327.9
**contaminated**
diseased 686.56

morally corrupt 981.14
radioactive 327.10
unclean 682.20
unhealthful 684.5
**contemn** disdain 966.3
reject 638.2
**contemplate**
consider 478.12
expect 539.5
foresee 542.5
intend 653.7
look upon 478.17
scrutinize 439.15
study 564.12
think of 478.16
**contemplation**
consideration 478.2
engrossment 530.3
expectation 539.1
foresight 542.1
inaction 706.1
prayer 1032.4
quiescence 268.1
scrutiny 439.6
study 564.3
**contemporaneous**
present 120.2
simultaneous 118.4
**contemporary**
*n.* simultaneity 118.2
*adj.* modern 122.13
present 120.2
simultaneous 118.4
**contempt**
defiance 793.1
deprecation 969.2
disdain 966
impudence 913.2
indignity 965.2
rejection 638.1
**contemptible**
bad 675.9
base 915.12
offensive 864.18
paltry 673.18
**contemptuous**
arrogant 912.13
condemnatory 969.23
defiant 793.7
disdainful 966.8
disparaging 971.13
impudent 913.9
rejecting 638.4
**contend** affirm 523.4
argue 482.16
contest 796.14
contrapose 239.4
dispute 796.22
insist 753.7
oppose 790.4
struggle 716.11
**contender**
combatant 800.1
competitor 791.2
**contend for**
defend 1006.10
strive for 796.21
try for 714.8
**contend with**
fight with 796.18
offer resistance 792.3

treat 665.12
**content** capacity 195.2
components 194.1
**content**
*n.* contentment 868.1
pleasure 865.1
*v.* satisfy 868.4
*adj.* agreeing 521.13
consenting 775.4
pleased 865.12
satisfied 868.7
willing 622.5
**contention**
argumentation 482.4
contraposition 239.1
disaccord 795.1
hostility 929.3
opposition 790.1
quarrel 795.5
strife 796
**contentious**
aggravating 885.5
argumentative 482.19
quarrelsome 951.26
warlike 797.25
**contents** book 605.12
components 58.2
list 88.2
what is contained 194
**conterminous**
adjacent 200.16
simultaneous 118.4
**contest**
*n.* contention 796.1
game 878.9
match 796.3
*v.* argue 482.16
challenge 503.6
contend 796.14
contend against 790.4
contradict 790.6
deny 524.4
dispute 796.22
**contestant**
combatant 800.1
competitor 791.2
player 878.19
**context**
circumstance 8.2
environment 233.1
**contiguity**
juxtaposition 200.3
relationship 9.1
**contiguous** 200.16
**continence**
abstinence 992.2
celibacy 934.1
chastity 988.3
limitation 234.2
moderation 163.1
**continent**
*n.* mainland 386
region 180.6
*adj.* abstinent 992.10
chaste 988.6
**continental**
*n.* mainlander 386.3
*adj.* mainland 386.6
**contingency**
an uncertainty 514.8

govern 741.13
influence 172.8
moderate 163.6
possess authority
 739.13
restrain 760.7
**controller**
accountant 845.7
automation 349.14
financial officer
 836.11
supervisor 748.2
**controlling**
authoritative 739.15
directing 747.12
governing 741.18
most important
 672.23
**control mechanism**
 349.34
**control oneself**
calm oneself 858.7
restrain oneself 992.6
**controversial**
argumentative 482.19
contentious 951.26
uncertain 514.16
**controversy**
argumentation 482.4
contention 796.1
disagreement 27.1
quarrel 795.5
**controvert**
contradict 790.6
deny 524.4
discuss 597.12
oppose 15.4
refute 506.5
**contumacious**
refractory 767.10
ungovernable 626.12
**contumelious**
contemptuous 966.8
cursing 972.8
disdainful 912.13
disparaging 971.13
insolent 913.8
insulting 965.6
**contumely**
berating 969.7
contempt 966.1
curse 972.2
indignity 965.2
insolence 913.1
**contusion** 692.9
**conundrum** 549.9
**convalescence** 694.8
**convalescent** 694.23
**convalescent home**
 689.27
**convection** 271.1
**convene**
assemble 74.17
summon 752.12
**convenience**
benefit 665.4
comfortableness
 887.2
expedience 670.1
facility 785.9
leisure 710.1
machinery 348.4

rest room 311.10
timeliness 129.1
wieldiness 732.2
**conveniences**
comfort 887.3
equipment 659.4
**convenient**
comfortable 887.11
expedient 670.5
handy 665.19
nearby 200.15
timely 129.9
wieldy 732.14
**convent** 1042.6
**convention**
church council 755.4
compact 771.1
conference 597.6
custom 642.1
etiquette 646.3
fashion 644.1
meeting 74.2
political convention
 744.8
precept 751.2
social convention
 645.1
treaty 771.2
**conventional**
average 680.8
ceremonious 646.8
conformist 82.6
contractual 771.11
customary 642.15
decorous 645.5
orthodox 1024.7
traditional 123.12
usual 84.8
**conventual**
claustral 1042.16
monastic 1037.14
**converge**
be joined 47.11
come together 298.2
focus 226.10
gather 74.16
near 200.7
**conversant**
skilled 733.24
used to 642.18
versed in 475.19
**conversation**
communication
 554.1
interlocution 597
social intercourse
 922.4
speech 594.1
**conversational**
colloquial 597.13
communicational
 554.9
talkative 596.9
vernacular 580.18
**conversationalist**
converser 597.8
talker 594.18
**conversation piece** 85.5
**converse**
*n.* communication
 554.1
conversation 597.1

sociability 922.4
*v.* communicate 554.6
speak 594.20
talk together 597.9
**converse**
*n.* inverse 220.4
opposite 15.2
opposite side 239.3
*adj.* opposite 239.5
perverse 15.6
**conversion**
change 139.1
manufacture 167.3
mental block 538.3
misuse 667.1
proselytization 145.6
redemption 1026.4
reform 691.5
theft 824.1
transformation 145
**convert**
*n.* apostate 628.5
believer 1028.4
disciple 566.2
proselyte 145.7
*v.* change 145.11
convince 501.18
invert 220.5
misuse 667.4
process 167.11
remake 139.6
sanctify 1026.6
sell stocks 833.24
**converted**
changed 145.19
improved 691.13
pious 1028.10
reformed 139.9
sanctified 1026.9
sublimated 538.9
**convertible**
equivalent 30.8
interchangeable
 150.5
liquid 835.31
transformable 145.18
**convex** bowed 252.10
protuberant 256.12
rotund 255.8
**convexity**
curvature 252.1
mark 568.7
protuberance 256
sphericity 255.1
**convey** channel 396.19
communicate 554.7
say 594.23
transfer property
 817.3
transport 271.11
**conveyance**
impartation 554.2
property transfer
 817.1
theft 824.1
transportation 271.3
vehicle 272.1
**conveyer** 271.5
**convict**
*n.* criminal 986.10
prisoner 761.11

*v.* bring in a verdict
 1004.19
condemn 1008.3
convince 501.18
**conviction**
condemnation 1008.1
hope 888.1
strong belief 501.5
sureness 513.5
**convince**
cause to believe
 501.18
persuade 648.23
proselytize 145.16
**convinced**
believing 501.21
sure 513.21
**convincing**
believable 501.26
evidential 505.17
**convivial** festive 878.30
jovial 922.19
**convocation**
assembly 74.2
ceremony 646.4
church council 755.4
summons 752.5
**convolution**
brain 466.7
complexity 46.1
curvature 252.1
grandiloquence 601.1
twisting 254
**convoy**
*n.* escort 73.5
guard 699.14
*v.* escort 73.8
sail 275.46
**convulse** agitate 324.10
amuse 878.23
discompose 63.4
pain 424.7
torture 866.18
**convulsion**
disarrangement 63.1
disease symptom
 686.8
emotional outburst
 857.8
fit 952.8
frenzy 473.7
laughter 876.4
revolution 147.1
ruin 693.3
seizure 686.5
spasm 324.6
upheaval 162.5
**coo** bird sound 460.5
murmur 452.10
utter 594.26
**cook**
*n.* chef 330.2
maid 750.8
*v.* be hot 328.22
heat 329.17
prepare food 330.4
ruin 693.11
spoil 692.13
tamper with 616.17
**cooker** heater 329.10
types of 330.10
**cookery** cooking 330.1

heater 329.10
kitchen 330.3
cookie 308.42
cooking cookery 330
　heating 329.1
　styles of 330.9
cookout 307.6
cook up create 167.13
　fabricate 616.18
　improvise 630.8
　plot 654.10
　prearrange 641.3
cool
　n. cold 333.1
　composure 858.2
　moderation 163.1
　stability 142.1
　unastonishment
　　921.1
　v. calm 163.7
　disincline 652.4
　pacify 804.7
　refrigerate 334.10
　restrain 760.7
　adj. aloof 912.12
　calm 268.12
　cold 333.12
　coloring 362.15
　composed 858.12
　equable 163.13
　excellent 674.13
　feeling cold 333.15
　indifferent 636.6
　insolent 913.8
　reticent 613.10
　sensible 467.18
　stable 142.12
　unastonished 921.3
　unfeeling 856.9
　unfriendly 929.9
　unsociable 923.6
coolant 334.7
cooler chiller 334.3
　prison 761.9
coolie 271.5
cool it
　calm oneself 858.7
　stop 144.15
　take it easy 732.11
cool off
　calm oneself 858.7
　order 59.4
　restrain 760.7
cool one's heels
　await 539.8
　do nothing 706.2
　wait 132.14
coon's age 110.4
coop
　n. chicken house
　　191.22
　enclosure 236.3
　place of confinement
　　761.7
　prison 761.9
　v. confine 761.12
　enclose 236.5
co-op 832.1
cooperate agree 26.6
　be willing 622.3
　collaborate 786.3
　concur 177.2

interact 13.8
reciprocate 150.4
share 815.6
cooperation
　agreement 26.1
　collaboration 786
　concurrence 177.1
　interaction 13.3
　participation 815.2
　reciprocity 150.1
　sociability 922.6
cooperative
　n. association 788.1
　market 832.1
　adj. agreeing 26.9
　coacting 786.5
　communal 815.9
　concurrent 177.4
　helpful 785.22
　willing 622.5
co-opt 637.13
coordinate
　n. likeness 20.3
　v. equalize 30.6
　make agree 26.7
　organize 60.10
　symmetrize 248.3
　adj. concurrent 177.4
　equivalent 30.8
　symmetric 248.4
coordinated 733.20
coordinates
　bounds 235.1
　measurement 490.6
coordination
　adjustment 26.4
　automation 349.7
　equalization 30.2
　organization 60.2
　skill 733.1
　symmetrization 248.2
cop
　n. cone 255.5
　policeman 699.16
　v. steal 824.13
cop a plea
　confess 556.7
　get off 632.7
cope compete 796.19
　cover 228.19
　make shift 670.4
　survive 659.12
cope with
　behave toward 737.6
　contend with 796.18
　perform 705.8
　treat 665.12
copious
　abundant 101.8
　diffuse 593.11
　numerous 34.8
　plentiful 661.7
　productive 165.9
　voluminous 195.17
cop out
　compromise 807.2
　get off 632.7
　remain neutral 806.5
　seclude oneself 924.6
cop-out
　compromise 807.1
　excuse 1006.4

neutrality 806.1
copper
　n. currency metals
　　835.20
　policeman 699.16
　US money 835.7
　adj. metal 383.17
　reddish-brown 367.4
copse bunch 74.7
　grove 411.12
　thicket 411.13
copulate
　come together 74.16
　have sex 419.23
　join 47.5
　make love 932.13
　procreate 169.8
copy
　n. diagram 654.3
　edition 605.2
　image 572.3
　imitation 22.3
　music 462.28
　news 558.3
　picture 574.12
　printer's copy 603.4
　representation 24
　reproduction 169.1
　substitute 149.2
　the same 14.3
　written matter 602.10
　v. art 574.20
　borrow 821.4
　duplicate 91.3
　imitate 22.5
　impersonate 572.9
　remake 169.7
　repeat 103.7
　replicate 14.6
　reproduce 24.8
　resemble 20.7
　write 602.19
copyboy
　attendant 750.5
　errand boy 561.4
copycat 22.4
copyhold 810.5
copying machine
　603.25
copyist artist 579.1
　imitator 22.4
　writer 602.13
copyreader
　journalist 605.22
　proofreader 603.13
copyright
　n. restriction 234.3
　right 958.4
　safeguard 699.3
　v. limit 234.5
　preserve 701.7
　protect 699.18
copywriter
　author 602.15
　publicist 559.9
coquetry
　flirtation 932.8
　trifling 673.8
coquette flirt 932.10
　sweetheart 931.10
　tempter 650.3

coquettish
　alluring 650.7
　amatory 932.21
　fickle 629.6
Cora
　agriculture divinity
　　413.4
　deity of nether world
　　1019.5
　goddess 1014.5
coral reef island 386.2
　point of land 256.8
　shoal 210.2
cord string 206.2,9
　wood 378.3
cordage capacity 195.2
　ropework 206.3
cordial
　n. refresher 695.1
　tonic 687.8
　types of 996.41
　adj. fervent 855.23
　genial 927.15
　good-natured 938.14
　hospitable 925.11
　informal 647.3
　pleasing 863.6
　refreshing 695.3
cordon
　n. award 916.5
　guard 699.9
　obstacle 730.4
　quarantine 761.2
　v. enclose 236.5
　quarantine 761.13
　segregate 77.6
cordon bleu
　award 916.5
　expert 733.11
corduroy
　n. fabric 378.11
　rough surface 261.2
　adj. grooved 263.4
core
　n. center 226.2
　city district 183.6
　content 194.5
　essence 5.2
　important point
　　672.6
　interior 225.2
　middle 69.1
　summary 607.2
　adj. middle 69.4
cork
　n. bark 229.2
　float 277.11
　lightness 353.2
　stopper 266.4
　v. blacken 365.7
　cap 228.21
　confine 761.12
　retain 813.5
　stop 266.7
　suppress 760.8
corkscrew
　n. curl 254.2
　extractor 305.9
　opener 265.11
　v. twist 254.4
　adj. spiral 254.8

**corn**
n. fodder 308.4
  grain 411.5,46
  old joke 881.9
  platitude 517.3
  swelling 256.4
  tumor 686.36
v. preserve 701.8
**corn belt** 182.1
**corncob** pipe 434.6
  plant part 411.27
**corncrib** 660.7
**corneous** 356.10
**corner**
n. angle 251.2
  deviation 291.1
  hiding place 615.4
  impasse 731.5
  monopoly 808.3
  nook 192.3
  recess 257.7
  stock manipulation
    833.20
v. buy up 828.7
  monopolize 808.6
  place in difficulty
    731.15
  stock market 833.26
  turn 321.5
**cornered** angular 251.6
  at an impasse 731.23
  in danger 697.13
**cornerstone**
  foundation 216.7
  important point
    672.6
**cornet** brass wind 465.8
  cone 255.5
  organ stop 465.22
**corn-fed** 195.18
**cornice** 211.5,17
**cornify** 356.7
**cornucopia**
  horn of plenty 661.3
  source of supply
    660.4
  store 660.1
**corny** 883.9
**corollary** adjunct 41.1
  attendant 73.3
  conclusion 494.4
  result 154.1
**corona**
  chandelier 336.6
  cigar 434.4
  circle 253.2
  flower part 411.26
  light 335.14
  sun 375.13
**coronary**
n. cardiovascular dis-
  ease 686.17
adj. circular 253.11
  heart 225.10
**coronation**
  accession to power
    739.12
  installation 780.3
**coroner**
  death examiner
    408.18
  doctor 688.6

**coronet** circle 253.2
  heraldic insignia
    569.2
  jewel 901.6
  royal insignia 569.3
**corporal**
n. church furnishing
    1042.10
  noncommissioned of-
    ficer 749.19
adj. bodily 376.9
**corporal punishment**
    1010.4
**corporate**
  associated 788.16
  joined 52.6
  joint 47.12
**corporation**
  company 788.9
  workplace 719.1
**corporeal** 376.9
**corps** association 788.1
  group 74.3
  military subdivision
    800.19
  military unit 800.20
**corpse**
  dead body 408.16
  thin person 205.8
**corpulent** stout 195.18
  thick 204.8
**corpus** all 54.3
  body 376.3
  collection 74.11
  knowledge 475.1
  money 835.15
**Corpus Christi** 1040.15
**corpus delicti**
  corpse 408.16
  evidence 505.2
**corral** acquire 811.8
  assemble 74.18
  drive animals 416.8
  enclose 236.5
**correct**
v. conform 82.3
  disillusion 520.2
  punish 1010.10
  remedy 694.13
  reprove 969.17
  revise 691.12
adj. accurate 516.15
  conventional 645.5
  grammatical 586.17
  mannerly 936.16
  meticulous 533.12
  orthodox 1024.7
  suitable 958.8
  well-chosen 589.7
**correction**
  measurement 490.1
  punishment 1010.1
  repair 694.6
  reproof 969.5
  revision 691.4
**corrective**
n. remedy 687.1
adj. emendatory
    691.16
  punishing 1010.25
  remedial 687.39

**correlate**
n. counterpart 13.4
  likeness 20.3
v. interrelate 13.6
  relate 9.6
**correlated**
  correlative 13.10
  related 9.9
**correlation**
  comparison 491.1
  reciprocation 13
  relationship 9.2
**correlative**
  accompanying 73.9
  comparable 491.8
  correlated 13.10
  relative 9.7
  similar 20.13
**correspond** agree 26.6
  coincide 14.4
  communicate with
    554.8
  concur 177.2
  conform 82.3
  equal 30.5
  make parallel 218.5
  reciprocate 13.9
  relate to 9.5
  resemble 20.7
  write to 604.11
**correspondence**
  accord 794.1
  agreement 26.1
  communication
    554.1
  concurrence 177.1
  conformity 82.1
  correlation 13.1
  equality 30.1
  identity 14.1
  letter writing 604
  mail 604.5
  record 570.1
  similarity 20.1
  symmetry 248.1
  uniformity 17.1
**correspondent**
n. accused 1005.6
  correlate 13.4
  journalist 605.22
  letter writer 604.9
  likeness 20.3
adj. agreeing 26.9
  analogous 20.11
  equivalent 30.8
  identical 14.8
  reciprocal 13.13
  uniform 17.5
**corresponding**
  agreeing 26.9
  analogous 20.11
  conformist 82.6
  equivalent 30.8
  identical 14.8
  in accord 794.3
  reciprocal 13.13
**corridor**
  aviation 278.42
  district 180.1
  entrance 302.5
  hall 192.18
  passageway 657.4

**corrigible**
  improvable 691.17
  manageable 765.14
  remediable 694.25
**corroborate** 505.12
**corrode** decrease 39.6
  disintegrate 53.3
  eat away 692.24
  etch 578.11
**corrosion** decay 692.6
  decrease 39.3
  disintegration 53.1
**corrosive**
n. caustic 329.15
adj. acrimonious
    939.21
  corrupting 692.45
  disintegrative 53.5
  harmful 675.12
  ill-humored 951.17
  strong 600.11
**corrugated**
  grooved 263.4
  irregular 261.6
  rough 261.7
  wrinkled 264.8
**corrugation**
  groove 263.1
  rough surface 261.2
  wrinkle 264.3
**corrupt**
v. adulterate 44.13
  bribe 651.3
  debase 692.14
  decay 692.25
  defile 682.17
  demoralize 981.10
  indoctrinate 145.15
  misteach 563.3
  work evil 675.6
adj. bribable 651.4
  corrupted 981.14
  decayed 692.41
  dishonest 975.16
  erroneous 518.16
**corruptible**
  bribable 651.4
  mutable 111.7
  venal 975.23
**corrupting**
  corrosive 692.45
  harmful 675.12
**corruption**
  adulteration 44.3
  bribery 651.1
  colloquialism 582.6
  decay 692.6
  deterioration 692.2
  distortion 249.2
  evil 675.3
  filth 682.7
  improbity 975.1
  indoctrination 145.5
  mispronunciation
    595.5
  misteaching 563.1
  solecism 587.2
  turpitude 981.5
  wordplay 881.8
**corsage** flowers 411.23
  waist 231.15
**corsair** 825.7

corset supporter 216.2
  undergarment
    231.23,58
cortege
  attendance 73.6
  funeral 410.5
  procession 71.3
cortex armor 799.3
  exterior 224.2
  rind 229.2
  shell 228.15
cosm(o)– 375.1
cosmetic 900.20
cosmetics
  make-up 900.11
  sundries 831.6
cosmic(al) large 34.7
  universal 375.24
cosmology
  astronomy 375.18
  philosophy 500.1
cosmonaut 282.8
cosmopolitan
  *n.* citizen of the world
    190.4
  sophisticate 733.16
  *adj.* broad-minded
    526.8
  chic 644.13
  public 417.13
  traveled 273.39
  universal 79.14
  worldly-wise 733.26
cosmos 375.1
cossack 800.11
cosset foster 785.16
  indulge 759.6
  make love 932.14
cost
  *n.* expenses 843.3
  loss 812.1
  price 846.1
  *v.* plan expenditures
    843.5
  sell for 846.15
costly 848.11
cost of living
  economics 827.8
  expense 843.3
costume
  *n.* character dress
    231.9
  clothing 231.1
  suit 231.6
  theater 611.22
  *v.* outfit 231.40
costume designer
  designer 579.9
  theater man 611.28
costume party 922.11
cot bed 216.33
  cottage 191.9
coterie clique 788.6
  group 74.3
coterminous
  adjacent 200.16
  identical 14.8
  simultaneous 118.4
cottage
  bookbinding 605.16
  cabin 191.9
cottager 190.7

cotton fabric 378.11
  fiber 206.8
  medical dressing
    687.33
cotton belt 182.1
cottontail 414.29,58
cotton to
  be friends 927.9
  fall in love 931.20
  get along with 794.2
cottony 357.15
couch
  *n.* lair 191.26
  sofa 216.19,32
  *v.* be low 208.5
  depress 318.4
  lie down 318.11
  lurk 615.9
  phrase 588.4
  rest 711.6
couch, the 690.8
couchant low 208.7
  recumbent 214.8
cough
  *n.* breathing 403.18
  *v.* exhale 403.24
cough medicine 687.16
cough up 841.16
council
  advisory body 755
  association 788.1
  cabinet 742.8
  conference 597.6
  directorate 748.11
  meeting 74.2
  tribunal 1001.1
councilman
  legislator 746.3
  public official 749.17
counsel
  *n.* advice 754.1
  advisor 754.3
  bar 1003.5
  consideration 478.2
  intention 653.1
  lawyer 1003.1
  *v.* advise 754.5
  confer 597.11
counseling 690.5
counselor advisor 754.3
  lawyer 1003.1
count
  *n.* account of 87.6
  accusation 1005.1
  amount 28.2
  election returns
    744.21
  nobleman 918.4
  numeration 87.5
  particular 8.3
  sum 86.5
  *v.* be important
    672.11
  be judged 494.15
  have influence 172.10
  include in 76.3
  judge 494.8
  music 462.45
  number 87.10
  quantify 28.4
countenance
  *n.* approval 968.1

authorization 777.3
  composure 858.2
  face 240.4
  looks 446.4
  patronage 785.4
  *v.* abet 785.14
  accept 861.6
  approve 968.9
  encourage 648.21
  permit 777.10
counter
  *n.* gambling 515.14
  money 835.12
  opposite 15.2
  printing 603.6
  radiation 327.13
  radioactivity 327.6
  rear 241.7
  retaliation 955.1
  showcase 832.10
  table 216.15,29
  *v.* clash 15.4
  counteract 178.6
  defend 1006.10
  deny 524.4
  disagree 27.5
  fend off 799.10
  oppose 790.3
  retaliate 955.4
  thwart 730.15
  *adj.* adverse 729.13
  contrary 15.6
  dissimilar 21.4
  opposing 790.8
  reversed 295.12
  *adv.* in opposition
    790.9
  opposite 239.6
counteract clash 15.4
  contrapose 239.4
  counter 178.6
  offset 33.5
  oppose 790.3
  thwart 730.15
counteraction
  compensation 33.1
  counterworking 178
  opposition 790.1
  resistance 792.1
counterattack
  attack 798.1
  countermeasure
    178.5
counterbalance
  *n.* counterforce 178.4
  offset 33.2
  opposite 15.2
  weight 352.4
  *v.* equalize 30.6
  neutralize 178.7
  offset 33.5
  oppose 15.4
  stabilize 142.7
  weigh 352.10
counterclaim
  *n.* counterdemand
    33.3
  counterstatement
    486.2
  *v.* rebut 486.5
counterclockwise
  *adj.* left 244.4

*adv.* backwards 295.13
  leftward 290.26
  round 322.16
counter-culture 522.1
counterespionage 485.9
counterfeit
  *n.* copy 24.1
  counterfeit money
    835.10
  fake 616.13
  substitute 149.2
  *v.* affect 903.12
  coin 835.28
  fabricate 616.18
  fake 616.21
  imitate 22.5
  resemble 20.7
  *adj.* imitation 22.8
  similar 20.10
  substitute 149.8
  ungenuine 616.26
counterfeiter
  coiner 835.25
  deceiver 619.1
  imitator 22.4
counterfeiting
  coining 835.24
  imitation 22.1
counterforce 178.4
counterintelligence
  intelligence service
    781.12
  spying 485.9
counterirritant
  counteractant 178.3
  drug 687.32
countermand
  *n.* repeal 779.1
  *v.* repeal 779.2
  thwart 730.15
countermeasure 178.5
countermine
  *n.* entrenchment
    799.5
  *v.* plot 654.10
countermotion 295.4
countermove 670.2
counterorder 779.1
counterpane 228.10
counterpart
  correlate 13.4
  duplicate 24.3
  equal 30.4
  likeness 20.3
counterpoint
  meter 609.9
  music 462.20
  opposite 15.2
counterpose
  compare 491.4
  counteract 178.6
  oppose 15.4
counterproductive
  harmful 675.12
  hindering 730.17
  ineffective 158.15
counterrevolution
  countermeasure
    178.5
  revolution 147.1

**countersign**
n. identification 568.11
password 568.12
signature 583.10
v. promise 770.4
ratify 521.12
**counterspy** 781.9
**counterstatement**
justification 1006.2
rebuttal 486.2
**counterstroke**
countermeasure 178.5
retaliation 955.1
**counter to**
counteractively 178.10
in disagreement with 27.10
opposed to 790.10
**countervail**
be opposite 15.4
counteract 178.6
equalize 30.6
offset 33.5
oppose 790.3
**countervallation** 236.13
**counterweight**
counterforce 178.4
offset 33.2
scenery 611.25
stabilizer 142.20
**counterword**
ambiguous expression 550.2
portmanteau word 582.12
**countess** 918.6
**counting**
n. numeration 87.1
adj. inclusive 76.6
**countinghouse** 832.1
**countless** infinite 104.3
innumerable 101.10
much 34.8
**count on**
be hopeful 888.7
believe in 501.16
expect 539.6
plan on 653.6
**count one's chickens before they are hatched**
be optimistic 888.9
be rash 894.5
be wrong 518.11
mishandle 734.14
**count out** 77.4
**countrified** 182.7
**country**
n. jury 1002.7
nation 181
region 180.1
adj. rustic 182.6
**country, the**
agricultural region 182
land 385.1
**country bumpkin** 919.9
**country club** 788.3
**country cousin** 11.3

**country gentleman** 809.2
**countryman**
fellow citizen 190.5
peasant 919.8
**country music** 462.10
**countryside** 182.1
**county** country 181.1
district 180.5
**county seat** 183.4
**coup** act 705.3
expedient 670.2
instant 113.3
seizure 822.2
stratagem 735.3
**coup de grâce**
deathblow 409.10
end-all 70.4
ruin 693.2
**coup d'état**
revolt 767.4
revolution 147.1
seizure 822.2
**couple**
n. set 20.5
two 90.2
v. ally 52.4
come together 74.16
copulate 419.23
get married 933.16
join 47.5
join in marriage 933.15
pair 90.5
relate 9.6
**coupled**
accompanying 73.9
joined 47.13
leagued 52.6
married 933.22
paired 90.8
related 9.9
**couplet**
poetic division 609.11
two 90.2
**coupling** joining 47.1
joint 47.4
**coupon**
certificate 834.5
token 835.12
**courage** bravery 893
pluck 624.3
sureness 513.5
**courageous**
brave 893.17
plucky 624.14
**courier** guide 748.7
messenger 561.1
**course**
n. arena 802.1
aviation 278.43
career 267.2
channel 396.1
circuit 137.3
continuity 71.2
direction 290.1
dish 308.7
flow 395.4
journey 273.5
layer 227.1
manner 657.1

policy 654.5
process 164.2
progression 294.1
racecourse 878.12
route 657.2
serving 307.10
study 562.8
track 568.8
travel 273.1
trend 174.2
voyage 275.6
v. flow 395.16
hunt 655.9
travel 273.17
traverse 273.19
**course of action** 670.2
**courser** horse 414.10
hunter 655.5
speed 269.6
war horse 800.32
**court**
n. attendance 73.6
council 755.1
courthouse 1001.9
courtship 932.6
enclosure 236.3,12
influential persons 172.6
judiciary 1000.2
legislature 742.1
palace 191.8
playground 878.12
road 657.6
tribunal 1001.2
v. befriend 927.11
curry favor 907.8
solicit 774.14
woo 932.19
**courteous** polite 936.14
respectful 964.8
sociable 922.18
**courtesan** 989.15
**courtesy**
good behavior 737.2
good deed 938.7
polite act 936.6
politeness 936
respect 964.1
sociability 922.1
**courthouse**
court 1001.9
government building 742.12
town hall 183.5
**courtier** flatterer 970.4
follower 293.2
sycophant 907.3
**courting**
courtship 932.6
solicitation 774.5
**courtliness**
chivalry 936.2
etiquette 646.3
pride 905.2
**courtly**
dignified 905.12
flattering 970.8
gallant 936.15
**court-martial**
military court 1001.7
trial 1004.5
**courtroom** 1001.9

**courtship** 932.6
**courtyard** 236.3,12
**cousin** 11.3
**couturier**
designer 579.9
dressmaker 231.35
**cove** arch 252.4
arm of the sea 399.1
cave 257.5
man 420.5
nook 192.3
person 417.3
recess 257.7
**coven** 1035.8
**covenant**
n. compact 771.1
v. agree 521.10
contract 771.6
**cover**
n. blanket 228.10
bookbinding 605.15
concealment 615.2
covering 228.2
dish 308.7
flight 278.11
floor 212.3
hiding place 615.4
lid 228.5
pretext 649.1
protection 699.1
service 307.11
serving 307.10
shade 338.1
shelter 700.3
types of 228.38
v. be pregnant 169.12
bet 515.20
close 266.6
color 362.13
compensate 33.4
conceal 615.6
copulate 419.23
extend 179.7
include 76.3
join 47.5
overrun 313.5
protect 699.18
put on 228.19
shade 338.5
spell 108.5
stop 266.7
traverse 273.19
**cover charge** fee 846.7
service 307.11
**cover girl** 900.8
**covering**
n. coloring 362.12
concealment 615.1
cover 228.2
coverage 228
exterior 224.2
layer 227.2
pregnancy 169.5
adj. coating 228.34
concealing 615.15
inclusive 76.6
protecting 699.23
shading 338.6
**covering material**
building material 378.2
types of 228.43

lever 287.4
malcontent 869.3
odd person 85.4
pillory 1011.3
*v.* angle 251.5
reel in 287.9
rotate 322.9
*adj.* eccentric 474.4
**cranky**
antagonistic 178.8
capricious 629.5
disagreeing 27.6
discontented 869.5
eccentric 474.4
irascible 951.19
**cranny** crack 201.2
groove 263.1
hiding place 615.4
nook 192.3
**crap**
*n.* defecation 311.2
feces 311.4
humbug 616.14
nonsense 547.3
throw of dice 515.10
*v.* defecate 311.13
**crape** 875.6
**crap out** 725.9
**crappy** bad 675.8
fecal 311.20
filthy 682.23
**craps** deuce 90.3
dice 515.9
game of chance 515.8
throw of dice 515.10
**crash**
*n.* addiction 642.9
aviation 278.20
decrease 39.2
defeat 727.1
descent 316.1
destruction 693.4
explosive noise 456.1
failure 725.3
impact 283.3
insolvency 842.3
misfortune 729.2
stock market 833.5
*v.* aviation 278.53
bang 456.6
billow 395.22
collide 283.12
descend 316.5
fail 725.11
go bankrupt 842.7
intrude 238.5
shatter 49.13
sleep 712.18
thunder 453.6
**crash landing**
aviation 278.20
landing 278.18
**crass** outright 34.12
stupid 469.15
thick 204.8
vulgar 898.11
**crate**
*n.* automobile 272.9
storage place 660.6
*v.* package 236.9
put in 184.14
wrap 228.20

**crater** basin 257.2
blemish 679.1
pit 209.2
**crave** desire 634.18
entreat 774.11
request 774.9
**craven** 892.12
**craving**
*n.* addiction 642.9
coveting 634.6
*adj.* coveting 634.24
**craw** 193.3
**crawl**
*n.* creeping 273.9
slowness 270.2
swimming 275.11
*v.* be low 208.5
be servile 907.6
creep 273.25
feel creepy 426.7
go slow 270.6
lie 214.5
linger 110.7
**crawling**
*n.* creeping 273.9
radio reception
344.21
*adj.* creeping 273.38
crowded 74.22
obsequious 907.13
permeated 186.15
recumbent 214.8
reptile 414.51
slow 270.10
teeming 101.9
**crawl with**
abound 661.5
be numerous 101.5
infest 313.6
pervade 186.7
**crayon**
art equipment 574.19
picture 574.14
**craze**
*n.* blemish 679.1
caprice 629.1
enthusiasm 635.3
excitement 857.7
fad 644.5
impairment 692.8
mania 473.12
stripe 374.5
*v.* blemish 679.4
injure 692.15
madden 473.23
**crazy** absurd 470.10
distorted 249.10
foolish 470.8
insane 473.25
mentally deficient
469.22
variegated 374.9
**crazy about**
enthusiastic about
635.12
fond of 931.28
**crazy idea**
absurd idea 479.7
caprice 629.1
**creak**
*n.* shrill sound 458.4
stridulation 458.5

*v.* sound shrill 458.8
stridulate 458.7
**cream**
*n.* cleaning agent
681.17
milk 308.47
ointment 380.3
semiliquid 389.5
superiors 36.5
the best 674.8
*v.* foam 405.5
make viscid 389.10
overwhelm 727.8
*adj.* whitish 364.8
yellow 370.4
**cream of the crop** 674.8
**creamy**
semiliquid 389.11
soft-colored 362.21
whitish 364.8
yellow 370.4
**crease**
*n.* fold 264.1
wrinkle 264.3
*v.* engrave 578.10
fold 264.5
wrinkle 264.6
**create** begin 68.10
cause 153.11
form 246.7
imagine 535.14
make 167.10
originate 23.4
**creation**
beginning 68.1
divine function
1013.16
forming 246.5
origination 167.5
product 168.1
production 167.3
structure 245.1
universe 375.1
work of art 574.11
**creative**
beginning 68.15
godlike 1013.20
imaginative 535.18
original 23.5
originative 167.19
productive 165.9
**creativity** genius 467.8
inventiveness 535.3
originality 23.1
**creator** artist 579.1
doer 718.1
originator 153.4
producer 167.8
**creature** animal 414.2
associate 787.8
entity 3.3
figurehead 749.4
inferior 37.2
instrument 658.3
organism 406.2
person 417.3
product 168.1
retainer 750.1
sycophant 907.3
**creature comfort**
comfort 887.3
food 308.1

pleasure 865.1
**credence** altar 1042.12
belief 501.1
**credential**
certificate 570.6
recommendation
968.4
**credentials** 568.11
**credibility**
believability 501.8
veracity 974.3
**credibility gap**
insincerity 975.3
unbelievability 503.3
untruthfulness 616.8
**credible**
believable 501.24
logical 482.20
**credit**
*n.* account entry 845.5
attribution 155.1
belief 501.1
believability 501.8
difference 42.8
due 960.2
esteem 914.3
financial credit 839
influence 172.1
receipts 844.1
thanks 949.2
token of esteem
916.1
*v.* attribute to 155.4
believe 501.10
keep accounts 845.8
place to one's credit
839.5
thank 949.4
**creditable**
honest 974.13
praiseworthy 968.20
reputable 914.15
**credit card** 839.3
**credited**
accredited 839.8
attributed 155.6
believed 501.23
**creditor** 839.4
**credit rating**
credit 839.1
financial condition
836.5
**credit union**
association 788.1
credit 839.1
lending institution
820.4
**credo** creed 1023.2
religion 1020.1
system of belief
501.3
**Credo** 1040.10
**credulous**
easy of belief 502.8
fooled 470.8
trusting 501.22
**creed** affirmation 523.1
doctrine 1023.2
policy 654.5
religion 1020.1
system of belief
501.3

**creedbound**
 narrow-minded
  527.10
 orthodox 1024.8
**creek**
 arm of the sea 399.1
 running water 395.1
**creep**
 *n.* creeping 273.9
 obnoxious person
  986.6
 slowness 270.2
 *v.* be servile 907.6
 crawl 273.25
 feel creepy 426.7
 go slow 270.6
 linger 110.7
 lurk 615.9
**creeper** 411.4
**creep in** enter 302.7
 intrude 238.5
 join 788.14
**creeping**
 *n.* crawling 273.9
 radio reception
  344.21
 slowness 270.1
 *adj.* crawling 273.38
 permeated 186.15
 reptile 414.51
 slow 270.10
**creeps** chill 333.2
 gooseflesh 426.4
 trepidation 891.5
**creep up on** 540.6
**creep with**
 abound 661.5
 be numerous 101.5
 infest 313.6
 pervade 186.7
**creepy** bad 675.8
 crawly 426.11
 spooky 891.39
**cremate** burn 329.25
 the dead 410.20
**cremation**
 burning 329.5
 of the dead 410.2
**crenellate** fortify 799.9
 notch 262.4
**crêpe** 308.44
**crepuscule** dusk 134.3
 foredawn 133.4
**crescendo**
 *n.* expansion 197.1
 increase 38.1
 loudness 453.1
 music 462.25
 *v.* become larger
  197.5
 din 453.6
 increase 38.6
 make larger 197.4
 *adv.* music 462.54
**crescent**
 *n.* city district 183.9
 curve 252.5
 heraldic insignia
  569.2
 moon 375.11
 road 657.6
 semicircle 253.8

*adj.* crescent-shaped
  252.11
 growing 197.12
 waxing 38.8
**crest**
 *n.* feather 230.16
 heraldic insignia
  569.2
 notching 262.2
 peak 207.8
 summit 211.2
 top part 211.4
 wave 323.4
 *v.* top 211.9
**crestfallen**
 disappointed 541.5
 glum 872.25
 humiliated 906.13
**cretin** 471.8
**cretinism**
 gland disease 686.19
 mental deficiency
  469.9
**crevasse** pit 209.2
 ravine 201.2
**crevice** 201.2
**crew** aviation 279.4
 clique 788.6
 group 74.3
 staff 750.11
 team 788.7
**crib**
 *n.* abode 191.1
 bed 216.33
 brothel 989.9
 compartment 192.2
 gambling house
  515.15
 garner 660.7
 hut 191.10
 interpretation 552.3
 storage place 660.6
 *v.* cheat 618.17
 confine 761.12
 enclose 236.6
 imitate 22.5
 plagiarize 824.18
 steal 824.13
**crick**
 *n.* pain 424.2
 stridulation 458.5
 *v.* chirp 458.7
**cricket**
 animal 414.39,74
 fairness 976.3
 noisemaker 453.5
**crier** 561.3
**crime** illegality 999.4
 sin 982.2
 wrongdoing 982.1
**criminal**
 *n.* dishonest person
  975.10
 evildoer 943.1
 felon 986.10
 *adj.* dishonest 975.16
 evil 981.16
 guilty 983.3
 illegal 999.6
 improper 959.3
 sinful 982.6
**criminology** 998.7

**crimp**
 *n.* abductor 825.10
 fold 264.1
 hair 230.5
 sharper 619.4
 trench 263.2
 wrinkle 264.3
 *v.* abduct 824.19
 curl 254.5
 fold 264.5
 groove 263.3
 notch 262.4
 thwart 730.16
 wrinkle 264.6
 *adj.* pulverable 361.13
**crimson**
 *v.* become excited
  857.17
 become red 368.5
 blush 908.8
 make red 368.4
 *adj.* red 368.6
**cringe** be servile 907.6
 bow down before
  765.10
 cower 892.9
 flinch 891.21
 retract 297.3
 stoop 318.8
 wince 284.7
**cringle** hole 265.4
 sail part 277.14
**crinkle**
 *n.* convolution 254.1
 wrinkle 264.3
 *v.* roughen 261.5
 rustle 452.12
 twist 254.4
 wrinkle 264.6
**cripple**
 *n.* defective 686.42
 *v.* disable 158.9
 hamper 730.11
 impair 692.17
 weaken 160.10
**crippled**
 disabled 158.16
 injured 692.32
**crisis**
 business cycle 827.9
 critical point 129.4
 danger 697.1
 financial crisis 836.7
 important point
  672.6
 urgency 672.4
**crisp**
 *v.* curl 254.5
 fold 264.5
 *adj.* aphoristic 517.6
 brittle 360.4
 cold 333.14
 concise 592.6
 curly 254.9
 intelligible 548.10
 pulverable 361.13
 refreshing 695.3
**crisscross**
 *n.* cross 221.4
 *v.* cross 221.6
 *adj.* crossed 221.8
 *adv.* crosswise 221.13

**criterion** measure 490.2
 model 25.1
 rule 84.4
 test 489.2
**critic** author 602.15
 commentator 606.4
 connoisseur 897.7
 faultfinder 969.9
 interpreter 552.7
 judge 494.7
 specialist 81.3
**critical**
 commentative 606.6
 crucial 129.10
 dangerous 697.9
 difficult 731.16
 discriminating 492.7
 explanatory 552.15
 fastidious 896.9
 faultfinding 969.24
 judgmental 494.16
 meticulous 533.12
 precarious 697.12
 urgent 672.21
**critical point**
 crisis 129.4
 important point
  672.6
**criticism**
 commentary 606.2
 disapproval 969.4
 interpretation 552.8
 judgment 494.2
**criticize**
 disapprove 969.14
 judge 494.14
 write upon 606.5
**critique**
 commentary 606.2
 criticism 494.2
 iteration 103.2
**critter** animal 414.2
 cattle 414.6
 horse 414.10
 person 3.3
**croak**
 *n.* harsh sound 458.3
 speech defect 595.1
 *v.* bird sound 460.5
 complain 875.13
 die 408.20
 forebode 544.11
 kill 409.14
 sound harshly 458.9
 speak poorly 595.7
**crocheting** 223.6
**crock**
 ceramic ware 576.2
 inferior horse 414.14
**crockery** 576.2
**crocodile tears** 616.6
**croft** farm 413.8
 tract 180.4
**croissant** 308.31
**crone** 127.3
**Cronus** god 1014.5
 Time 105.2
**crony** associate 787.1
 companion 928.3
**crook**
 *n.* angle 251.2
 bend 219.3

cheat 619.3
clerical insignia 569.4
criminal 986.10
crosier 1041.3
curve 252.2
deviation 291.1
emblem of authority 739.9
evildoer 943.1
fireplace 329.12
staff 217.2
supporter 216.2
thief 825.1
*v.* angle 251.5
curve 252.6
deflect 291.5
distort 249.5
oblique 219.9
**crooked** angular 251.6
askew 219.14
curved 252.8
dishonest 975.16
distorted 249.10
falsehearted 616.31
zigzag 219.20
**croon** 462.39
**crooner** 464.13
**crop**
*n.* abdomen 193.3
breast 256.6
bunch 74.7
hair 230.4
harvest 413.15
plants 411.2
produce 168.2
whip 1011.1
yield 811.5
*v.* cut off 42.10
eat 307.26
farm 413.16
harvest 413.19
shorten 203.6
**crop out** appear 446.8
be visible 444.5
**cropped** 203.9
**cropper**
agriculturist 413.5
failure 725.3
tumble 316.3
**crop up** begin 68.13
occur 151.6
**crosier** cane 217.2
clerical insignia 569.4
emblem of authority 739.9
staff 1041.3
**cross**
*n.* adversity 729.1
affliction 866.8
cane 217.2
heraldic insignia 569.2
hybrid 44.9
impediment 730.6
insignia 569.1
instrument of execution 1011.5
memorial 570.12
sacred article 1040.11
signature 583.10
staff 1041.3
X 221.4

*v.* bless 1032.13
contradict 790.6
counteract 178.6
deny 524.4
disappoint 541.2
hybridize 44.14
intersect 221.6
oppose 790.3
pass 313.8
sail 275.13
thwart 730.15
*adj.* angry 952.26
crossed 221.8
crosswise 221.9
cruciform 221.10
disagreeing 27.6
hybrid 44.16
irascible 951.19
opposing 790.8
*adv.* crosswise 221.13
in opposition 790.9
**crossbar** 221.5
**crossbones** cross 221.4
death symbol 408.3
**crossbow** 801.17
**crossbreed**
*n.* hybrid 44.9
mixed race 418.4
*v.* breed 169.8
hybridize 44.14
**cross-check**
collate 491.5
make certain 513.12
**crosscurrent**
counterforce 178.4
flow 395.4
opposition 790.1
wind 403.1
**cross-examination**
grilling 485.12
trial 1004.5
**cross-eye**
defective vision 440.5
eye disease 686.13
**cross fire** gunfire 798.9
interchange 150.1
**cross-grained**
*adj.* coarse-textured 351.6
irascible 951.19
perverse 626.11
rough 261.6
*adv.* crosswise 221.13
roughly 261.12
**crosshatch**
engrave 578.10
sketch 574.20
**cross-hatching**
engraving 578.2
line 568.6
network 221.3
**crossing**
convergence 298.1
crossway 221.2
denial 524.2
intersection 221
miscegenation 44.4
opposition 790.1
travel 273.1
voyage 275.6
**cross off** 42.12
**cross one's mind** 478.18

**cross out** delete 42.12
obliterate 693.16
**crosspatch**
ill-humored person 951.11
misfit 27.4
**crosspiece** 221.5
**cross-purposes**
contrariety 15.1
disagreement 795.2
opposition 790.2
**cross-question**
*n.* question 485.10
*v.* grill 485.21
**cross reference** 505.6
**crossroad** 221.2
**crossroads**
turning point 129.4
village 183.2
**cross section**
crossing 221.1
part 55.1
representative 572.5
**crosswalk** 221.2
**crosswise**
*adj.* hindering 730.17
oblique 219.19
transverse 221.9
unwieldy 731.18
*adv.* across 221.13
transversely 219.24
**crotch** 299.4
**crotchet** angle 251.2
caprice 629.1
eccentricity 474.2
harmonics 463.14
**crotchety**
capricious 629.5
counteractive 178.8
eccentric 474.4
**crouch**
*n.* stoop 318.3
*v.* be low 208.5
be servile 907.6
bow down 765.10
cower 892.9
stoop 318.8
**croup** buttocks 241.4
respiratory disease 686.14
**crow**
*n.* black 365.4
laughter 876.4
lever 287.4
speech defect 595.1
*v.* bird sound 460.5
gloat 910.9
laugh 876.8
show a bold front 793.5
utter 594.26
**crowbar**
*n.* extractor 305.9
lever 287.4
*v.* pry 287.8
**crowd**
*n.* clique 788.6
group 74.3
the people 919.3
throng 74.4
viol 465.6
*v.* be numerous 101.5

come together 74.16
densify 354.9
fill 56.7
hasten 709.4
make haste 709.5
make one's way 294.4
obstruct 730.12
overload 663.15
shove 283.11
**crowded** dense 354.12
hurried 709.11
narrow 205.14
overfull 663.20
packed 74.22
teeming 101.9
**crowd in** enter 302.7
intrude 238.5
thrust in 304.7
**crowing**
*n.* gloating 910.4
*adj.* gloating 910.12
**crown**
*n.* book size 605.14
British money 835.8
capital 211.5
chandelier 336.6
circle 253.2
coin 835.4
completion 56.5
finishing touch 722.3
head 211.6
heraldic insignia 569.2
jewel 901.6,13
royal insignia 569.3
summit 211.2
tooth 258.5
top part 211.4
trophy 916.3
*v.* cap 228.21
complete 722.6
glorify 914.13
honor 916.8
install 780.11
make perfect 677.5
top 211.9
**Crown, the**
sovereignty 739.8
the government 741.3
**crowned** 211.12
**crowned head** 749.7
**crowning** chief 36.14
completory 722.9
ending 70.9
topping 211.11
**crowning touch** 70.4
**crow's-feet** 264.3
**crow's nest** 439.8
**crozier** see **crosier**
**crucial** causal 153.15
critical 129.10
urgent 672.21
**crucible**
chemical apparatus 379.13
converter 145.10
mixer 44.10
test 489.2
**crucified** pained 424.9
tortured 866.25
**crucifix** cross 221.4

sacred article 1040.11
**crucifixion**
capital punishment
1010.7
pain 424.6
torment 866.7
**crucify** execute 1010.19
pain 424.7
torture 866.18
work evil 675.6
**crude**
*n.* petroleum 380.4
raw material 721.5
*adj.* discourteous
937.6
garish 362.19
infelicitous 590.2
offensive 864.18
ostentatious 904.20
undeveloped 721.12
unprepared 721.10
vulgar 898.11
**crude oil** 380.4
**crudity**
undevelopment 721.4
vulgarity 898.2
**cruel** murderous 409.24
painful 424.10
pitiless 945.3
ruthless 939.24
**cruelly** brutally 939.33
distressingly 34.21
pitilessly 945.4
**cruelty**
brutal act 939.12
pitilessness 945.1
ruthlessness 939.11
**cruet** bottle 193.12
church vessel 1042.11
sacred article 1040.11
**cruise**
*n.* voyage 275.6
*v.* fly 278.45
sail 275.13
travel 273.20
**cruiser** boat 277.21
motorboat 277.4
naval vessel 277.24
police car 272.10
traveler 274.1
**cruising** aviation 278.1
water travel 275.1
**cruller** 308.43
**crumb**
*n.* minute thing 196.7
piece 55.3
powder 361.5
small amount 35.3
*v.* pulverize 361.9
sprinkle 75.6
**crumble**
become pulverized
361.10
be destroyed 693.22
decay 692.25
decrease 39.6
disintegrate 53.3
pulverize 361.9
weaken 160.9
**crumbling**
*n.* disintegration 53.1
pulverization 361.4

*adj.* deteriorating
692.46
old 123.14
weak 160.15
**crumbly** brittle 360.4
frail 160.14
pulverable 361.13
**crummy** bad 675.8
base 915.12
paltry 673.18
**crumpet** 308.31
**crumple**
*n.* wrinkle 264.3
*v.* distort 249.5
roughen 261.5
wrinkle 264.6
**crumpled**
distorted 249.10
rough 261.7
wrinkled 264.8
**crunch**
*n.* concussion 162.8
critical point 129.4
harsh sound 458.3
impact 283.3
predicament 731.4
urgency 672.4
*v.* collide 283.12
shatter 49.13
sound harshly 458.10
**crunched** 249.10
**crupper** buttocks 241.4
harness 659.5
**crusade** cause 153.10
military campaign
797.7
**crusade for** 968.13
**crush**
*n.* full measure 56.3
liking 634.2
love 931.4
loved one 931.13
pulp 390.2
squeezing 198.2
throng 74.4
*v.* conquer 727.10
humiliate 906.5
make grieve 872.19
make nervous 859.9
pulp 390.5
pulverize 361.9
refute 506.5
shatter 49.13
squeeze 198.8
subdue 764.9
suppress 760.8
**crushed**
conquered 727.16
disappointed 541.5
heartbroken 872.29
humiliated 906.13
powdery 361.11
subdued 764.15
suppressed 760.14
unnerved 859.13
wretched 866.26
**crusher** disproof 506.3
end-all 70.4
pulverizer 361.7
**crushing**
humiliating 906.14
laborious 716.18

mortifying 864.21
troublesome 731.17
**crust**
*n.* bread 308.28
exterior 224.2
incrustation 228.14
insolence 913.3
land 385.1
*v.* incrust 228.27
**crustacean** 414.54
**crusty** gruff 937.7
hardened 356.13
impudent 913.9
irascible 951.19
**crutch** fork 299.4
staff 217.2
supporter 216.2
**crux** cross 221.4
difficulty 731.7
dilemma 731.6
important point
672.6
puzzle 549.8
**cry**
*n.* animal sound 460.1
call 459
cheer 876.2
entreaty 774.2
lament 875.3
phrase 582.9
publicity 559.4
rumor 558.6
weeping 875.2
*v.* animal sound 460.2
call 459.6
cheer 876.6
cry aloud 459.9
proclaim 559.13
wail 875.11
weep 875.10
**crybaby** 160.6
**cry for** demand 753.4
entreat 774.11
require 639.9
wish for 634.16
**cry havoc** alarm 704.3
warn 703.5
**crying**
*n.* weeping 875.2
*adj.* animal sound
460.6
demanding 753.8
urgent 672.21
vociferous 459.10
weeping 875.17
**cryo–** 333.14
**cryogenics** cold 333.1
physics 325.1
refrigeration 334.1
**crypt** cavity 257.2
church part 1042.9
compartment 192.2
tomb 410.16
**cryptic**
inexplicable 549.17
latent 546.5
secret 614.11
**crypto** 619.11
**cryptography**
cryptoanalysis 614.6
interpretation 552.8
writing 602.1

**cryptologist** 552.7
**crystal**
*n.* amphetamine 687.9
precious stone 384.6
snow 333.8
*adj.* stony 384.11
transparent 339.4
**crystal ball**
divining 543.2
the future 121.1
**crystal-clear**
clearly visible 444.7
intelligible 548.10
manifest 555.8
transparent 339.4
**crystal gazer** 543.4
**crystalline**
crystal 384.11
intelligible 548.10
transparent 339.4
**crystallize** form 59.5
petrify 384.9
solidify 356.8
**crystallized** 356.13
**crystallography**
geology 384.8
minerology 383.10
physics 325.1
**cry wolf** 704.3
**cub** boy 125.5
young animal 125.8
**cubbyhole**
hiding place 615.4
nook 192.3
small place 196.3
**cube** dice 96.3
triplicate 94.2
**cubed** 251.9
**cubehead** 642.10
**cubes** 515.9
**cubic(al)** angular 251.9
spatial 179.8
**cubicle** bedroom 192.7
nook 192.3
**cub reporter** 605.22
**cuckold** 989.22
**cuckoldry**
adultery 989.7
love affair 931.6
**cuckoo**
*n.* imitator 22.4
songbird 464.23
*v.* bird sound 460.5
*adj.* insane 473.26
**cud** bite 307.2
chewing tobacco
434.7
**cuddle**
be loving 932.15
snuggle 887.10
**cuddly** 931.23
**cudgel** hit 283.17
punish 1010.14
**cue** clue 568.9
hair 230.7
hint 557.4
mood 525.4
playbook 611.26
plaything 878.16
reminder 537.6
role 611.11
tail 241.6

tip 557.3
**cuff**
   *n.* punishment 1010.3
   restraint 760.4
   slap 283.7
   *v.* punish 1010.13
   slap 283.16
**cuisine** cooking 330.1
   food 308.1
   kitchen 330.3
**cul-de-sac**
   dead end 266.3
   impasse 731.5
   road 657.6
**culinary** 330.5
**culinary art** 330.1
**cull** exclude 42.10
   procure 811.10
   select 637.14
   separate 77.6
**culling** 60.3
**culminate**
   complete 722.6
   make perfect 677.5
   top 211.9
**culminating**
   completory 722.9
   ending 70.9
   topping 211.11
**culmination**
   acme of perfection
      677.3
   completion 56.4
   end 70.1
   finishing 722.2
   result 154.2
   summit 211.2
**culpability** 983.1
**culpable**
   blameworthy 969.26
   guilty 983.3
**culprit** 986.9
**cult** religion 1020.2
   ritualism 1040.1
   system of belief
      501.3
   worship 1032.1
**cultism** piety 1028.1
   religion 1020.2
   ritualism 1040.1
   worship 1032.1
**cultist**
   *n.* religionist 1020.14
   *adj.* pious 1028.8
**cultivate**
   befriend 927.11
   foster 785.16
   improve 691.10
   process 167.11
   sensitize 422.9
   till 413.17
   train 562.14
**cultivated**
   improved 691.13
   learned 475.21
   tasteful 897.9
   well-bred 936.17
**cultivation**
   agriculture 413.1
   good breeding 936.4
   good taste 897.1
   manufacture 167.3

refinement 691.3
   tilling 413.13
   training 562.3
**cultural** 562.19
**Cultural Revolution**
   744.6
**culture**
   *n.* agriculture 413.1
   cultivation 691.3
   good breeding 936.4
   good taste 897.1
   people 418.1
   scholarship 475.5
   society 642.3
   Stone Age 123.24
   tilling 413.13
   *v.* raise animals 416.6
   till 413.17
**cultured**
   improved 691.13
   learned 475.21
   tasteful 897.9
   well-bred 936.17
**culvert** 396.2
**cumbersome**
   bulky 195.19
   clumsy 734.20
   hampering 730.18
   ponderous 352.17
   unwieldy 731.18
**cumbrous** bulky 195.19
   hampering 730.18
   ponderous 352.17
   stilted 590.3
**cum laude** 916.11
**cumulate**
   assemble 74.18
   store up 660.11
**cumulation**
   acquisition 811.2
   assemblage 74.9
   store 660.1
**cumulative**
   accumulative 74.23
   additive 40.8
   evidential 505.17
**cumulus** 404.1
**cuneate** 251.8
**cuneiform**
   *n.* character 581.2
   *adj.* wedge-shaped
      251.8
**cunning**
   *n.* craftiness 735
   deceit 618.3
   falseheartedness
      616.4
   shrewdness 467.3
   skill 733.1
   *adj.* crafty 735.12
   deceitful 618.20
   falsehearted 616.31
   pretty 900.18
   shrewd 467.15
   skillful 733.20
   well-devised 733.28
**cup**
   *n.* basin 257.2
   fate 640.2
   memorial 570.12
   trophy 916.3
   types of 193.10

*v.* be concave 257.12
   ladle 271.16
   make concave 257.13
   treat 689.33
**cupboard**
   storage place 660.6
   types of 193.19
**cupid** 931.9
**Cupid** god 1014.5
   love god 931.8
**cupidity** 634.8
**cupola** arch 252.4
   tower 207.11
**cupped** 257.16
**cupping**
   bloodletting 689.26
   extraction 305.3
**cur** bad person 986.7
   mongrel 414.24
**curable** 694.25
**curacy**
   church office 1037.5
   the ministry 1037.9
**curate**
   clergyman 1038.2
   dignitary 1038.9
**curative**
   remedial 687.39
   restorative 694.22
**curator**
   bookman 605.21
   financial officer
      836.11
   guardian 699.6
   manager 748.4
**curb**
   *n.* border 235.6
   harness 659.5
   hindrance 730.7
   pavement 657.7
   restraint 760.1
   stock exchange 833.7
   *v.* hinder 730.10
   restrain 760.7
   slow 270.9
**curbed** 760.13
**curbstone** border 235.6
   pavement 657.7
**curd** coagulation 354.7
   food 308.11
   semiliquid 389.5
**curdle**
   make viscid 389.10
   thicken 354.10
**curdled**
   thickened 354.14
   viscous 389.12
**cure**
   *n.* commission 780.1
   medical aid 689.15
   protectorship 699.2
   remedy 687.1
   restoration 694.7
   the ministry 1037.9
   *v.* break of 643.2
   dry 393.6
   preserve 701.8
   remedy 687.38
   restore to health
      694.15
   tan 720.6
   treat 689.30

**curé** clergyman 1038.2
   priest 1038.5
**cure-all** 687.3
**curfew** 134.5
**curing** preserving 701.2
   restoration 694.7
**curio** odd thing 85.5
   trifle 673.5
**curiosity** desire 634.1
   inquisitiveness 528
   interest 530.2
   marvel 920.2
   odd thing 85.5
**curious** careful 533.10
   inquiring 485.35
   inquisitive 528.5
   interested 530.16
   odd 85.11
**curiously** 85.19
**curl**
   *n.* coil 254.2
   curve 252.2
   hair 230.5
   *v.* coil 254.5
   curve 252.6
**curled** 254.9
**curlicue** 254.2
**curling iron** 254.3
**curl up** rest 711.6
   snuggle 887.10
**curly** 254.9
**currency**
   fashionableness 644.2
   money 835.1
   prevalence 79.2
   publicity 559.4
   usualness 84.2
**current**
   *n.* course 267.2
   direction 290.1
   electricity 342.2
   electron flow 343.6
   flow 395.4
   trend 174.2
   wind 403.1
   *adj.* customary 642.15
   existent 1.13
   fashionable 644.11
   happening 151.9
   made public 559.17
   present 120.2
   prevalent 79.12
   rumored 558.15
   usual 84.8
   well-known 475.27
**curricular** 562.20
**curriculum** 562.8
**curried** cooked 330.6
   pungent 433.7
**curry**
   *n.* stew 308.11
   *v.* comb 681.21
   cook 330.4
   tend animals 416.7
**curry favor** 907.8
**curse**
   *n.* adversity 729.1
   affliction 866.8
   bad influence 675.4
   bane 676.1
   malediction 972
   oath 972.4

**cutlery**
edge tools 348.2
tableware 348.3
**cutlet** 308.19
**cut loose**
be disorderly 62.10
escape 632.6
extricate 763.7
let oneself go 762.18
make merry 878.26
run amok 162.14
sail 275.48
**cutoff** boundary 235.3
shortcut 203.5
stop 144.2
**cut off**
*v.* dispossess 822.23
excise 42.10
exclude 77.4
interrupt 144.10
kill 409.13
put an end to 693.12
separate 49.9
sever 49.11
take from 822.21
*adj.* deprived of 812.8
**cut out**
*v.* destroy 693.14
discontinue 668.4
eliminate 77.5
excise 42.10
extract 305.10
plan 654.9
run off 301.13
separate 49.9
substitute for 149.5
*adj.* prearranged 641.5
**cut out for** 733.27
**cut-rate** 849.9
**cut short**
*v.* put an end to
693.12
shorten 203.6
silence 451.8
stop 144.11
*adj.* incomplete 57.5
shortened 203.9
**cutter** cutlery 348.2
garmentmaker 231.33
separator 49.7
shortener 203.4
tooth 258.5
**cut the mustard**
be able 157.11
manage 724.11
**cutthroat**
*n.* evildoer 943.3
killer 409.11
*adj.* competitive
796.24
extortionate 848.12
murderous 409.24
**cutting**
*n.* abbreviation 592.4
adulteration 44.3
apportionment 816.1
excerpts 607.4
harvest 413.15
morphology 582.3
piece 55.3
plant 411.3
reduction 42.2

separation 49.2
syntax 586.2
*adj.* acrimonious
161.13
caustic 939.21
cold 333.14
eloquent 600.11
penetrating 857.29
pungent 433.6
sharp 258.10
solvent 391.8
violent 162.15
**cutting remark** 967.2
**cutup** humorist 881.12
mischief-maker 738.3
player 878.19
**cut up**
*v.* apportion 816.6
be disorderly 62.11
divide 49.18
find fault 969.15
make grieve 872.19
misbehave 738.4
pain 866.17
play 878.25
*adj.* heartbroken
872.29
wretched 866.26
**cwm**
mountain hollow
257.8
ravine 201.2
**cyanosis** blueness 372.1
disease symptom
686.8
**Cybele** 1014.5
**cybernation**
automation 349.1
control 349.3
**cybernetic** 349.27
**cybernetics**
automation 349.2
biology 406.17
**cyborg** 349.12
**cycads** 412.6
**cyclamates** 431.2
**cycle**
*n.* age 107.4
atomics 326.7
circle 253.2
circuit 321.2
continuity 71.2
electric current 342.2
radio frequency
344.12
round 137.3
types of 272.29
wheel 272.8
*v.* go around 321.4
recur 137.5
ride 273.32
**cyclic(al)**
atomic 326.18
circular 253.11
continuous 71.8
periodic 137.7
recurrent 103.13
**cycling** 273.6
**cyclone**
emotional outburst
857.8
storm 162.4

weather 402.5
whirlwind 403.14
**cyclonic**
meteorology 402.13
rotary 322.15
stormy 403.26
**Cyclopean** huge 195.20
strong 159.15
**cyclopedia** lore 475.9
reference book 605.6
**cyclorama**
picture 574.12
scenery 611.25
spectacle 446.7
**cygnet** 414.33
**cylinder** 255.4
**cylindric(al)** 255.11
**cymbal**
doughnut 308.43
percussion instrument
465.18
**cynic** disparager 971.6
misanthrope 940.2
pessimist 889.7
**cynical** critical 969.24
misanthropic 940.3
pessimistic 889.16
sarcastic 967.13
**cynicism**
misanthropy 940.1
pessimism 889.6
sarcasm 967.5
**cynosure**
attractor 288.2
center of attraction
226.4
famous person 914.9
guiding star 748.8
ideal 25.4
**cyst** swelling 256.4
tumor 686.36
**cystic** 193.4
**cystic fibrosis** 686.11
**cytology** 406.17
**cytoplasm** 406.4
**czar** autocrat 749.14
ruler 749.8
**czarina** 749.11

**D**

**DA** 1003.4
**dab**
*n.* blemish 679.3
small amount 35.2
tap 283.6
*v.* coat 228.24
color 362.13
smooth 260.5
tap 283.15
**dabble**
half-know 477.11
moisten 392.12
spatter 682.18
trifle 673.13
waste time 708.12
**dabbler**
dilettante 476.6
ignoramus 477.8
trifler 673.9
**dacha** 191.6
**dactyl** 609.9

**dad**
antiquated person
123.8
father 170.9
**daddy** 170.9
**daddy longlegs** 414.36
**dado**
*n.* base 216.8
bottom 212.2
groove 263.1
*v.* groove 263.3
**daedal** complex 46.4
skillful 733.20
variegated 374.9
**daemon** genius 467.8
guardian angel
1014.22
spirit 1014.15
**daffiness**
foolishness 470.1
insanity 473.2
**daffy** foolish 470.8
insane 473.26
**daft** foolish 470.8
insane 473.25
**daftness** 473.1
**dagger**
*n.* cross 221.4
cutlery 348.2,13
types of 801.22
*v.* stab 798.25
**dago** 181.7
**daguerreotype**
*n.* photograph 577.4
*v.* photograph 577.14
**daily**
*n.* newspaper 605.11
periodical 605.10
*adj.* regularly 137.8
*adv.* constantly 135.7
periodically 137.10
**daily bread** food 308.1
support 785.3
**daily double** 515.4
**daintily** prettily 900.22
weakly 160.22
**daintiness**
cleanness 681.1
fastidiousness 896.3
fine texture 351.3
frailty 160.2
good taste 897.1
lightness 353.1
prettiness 900.5
smallness 35.1
**dainty**
*n.* delicacy 308.8
*adj.* clean 681.25
delicate 35.7
edible 307.31
elegant 897.9
fastidious 896.11
frail 160.14
light 353.11
pretty 900.18
smooth 351.8
tasty 428.8
**dairy** larder 660.8
plant 719.3
store 832.5
**dairy cows** 414.6
**dairy farmer** 416.2

**dairy-farming** 416.1
**dairy products** 308.47
**dais** platform 216.13
  seat of authority
  739.10
**daisy** 674.7
**Dalai Lama**
  Buddhist priest
  1038.15
  ruler 749.8
**dale** 257.9
**dalliance**
  flirtation 932.8
  lovemaking 932.1
  slowness 270.3
  trifling 673.8
  waiting 132.3
**dally** dawdle 270.8
  fritter away 854.5
  make love 932.13
  trifle 673.13
  wait 132.12
  waste time 708.13
**dallying**
  *n.* idling 708.4
  slowness 270.3
  trifling 673.8
  waiting 132.3
  *adj.* dawdling 270.11
  dilatory 132.17
**dam**
  *n.* barrier 730.5
  body of water 398.1
  mother 170.10
  *v.* hinder 730.10
  stop 144.11
  stop up 266.7
**damage**
  *n.* disadvantage 671.2
  harm 675.3
  impairment 692.1
  loss 812.1
  price 846.1
  *v.* hurt 675.6
  impair 692.11
**damaged**
  impaired 692.29
  imperfect 678.4
**damages**
  penalty 1009.3
  recompense 841.3
**damaging**
  corrupting 692.45
  harmful 675.12
**dame**
  form of address 421.8
  girl 125.6
  instructress 565.2
  matron 421.5
  mistress 749.2
  noblewoman 918.6
  old woman 127.3
  woman 421.6
**damn**
  trifle 673.5
  censure 969.13
  condemn 1008.3
  curse 972.5
  destroy 693.10
  send to hell 1019.6
  vilify 972.7
  *adj.* cursed 972.9

*interj.* curse 972.11
**damnable** cursed 972.9
  evil 981.16
  terrible 675.10
**damnation**
  condemnation 1008.1
  curse 972.1
  destruction 693.1
  disapproval 969.3
**damnatory**
  censorious 969.23
  condemnatory 1008.5
  cursing 972.8
**damned** cursed 972.9
  irreligious 1031.18
**damned, the** 1016.1
**damning** 505.17
**damn it!** 972.11
**damp**
  *n.* deterrent 652.2
  killjoy 872.14
  moisture 392.1
  silencer 451.4
  vapor 401.1
  *v.* cushion 163.8
  disincline 652.4
  extinguish 332.7
  hinder 730.10
  make sad 872.18
  moderate 163.6
  moisten 392.12
  muffle 451.9
  reduce 39.7
  stabilize 17.4
  suppress 760.8
  weaken 160.10
  *adj.* moist 392.15
**dampen** cushion 163.8
  disincline 652.4
  hinder 730.10
  make sad 872.18
  moderate 163.6
  moisten 392.12
  muffle 451.9
  reduce 39.7
  weaken 160.10
**damper** curb 730.7
  deterrent 652.2
  fireplace 329.12
  killjoy 872.14
  silencer 451.4
**dampness** 392.1
**damsel** 125.6
**dance**
  *n.* ball 879.2
  dancing 879.1,7
  flicker 335.8
  flutter 324.4
  get-together 74.2
  music 462.9
  steps 879.8
  *v.* be cheerful 870.6
  dancing 879.5
  flicker 335.25
  flutter 324.12
  play 878.25
  rejoice 876.5
  *adj.* dancing 879.6
**dance hall**
  amusement 878.11
  ballroom 879.4
  hall 192.4

**dancer** danseur 879.3
  entertainer 612.1
**dancing**
  *n.* light 335.8
  terpsichore 879
  *adj.* dance 879.6
  flickering 335.36
  fluttering 324.18
  happy 865.13
**dander** 952.6
**dandified**
  foppish 903.17
  ultrafashionable
  644.14
**dandruff** filth 682.7
  flake 227.3
**dandy**
  *n.* fashionable 644.7
  fop 903.9
  good thing 674.7
  *adj.* excellent 674.13
  foppish 903.17
**danger** peril 697
  uncertainty 514.6
**dangerous**
  perilous 697.9
  unreliable 514.19
**dangerous drug** 687.5
**dangerously** 697.17
**danger sign** 703.3
**dangle**
  attach oneself to
  907.10
  flaunt 904.17
  flourish 555.5
  hang 215.6
  oscillate 323.10
**dangling**
  *n.* pendency 215.1
  *adj.* loose 51.5
  pendent 215.9
  swinging 323.17
**Danish pastry**
  bun 308.31
  pastry 308.40
**dank** 392.15
**dankness** 392.2
**dapper** 644.13
**dapple**
  *n.* mark 568.5
  spottiness 374.3
  *v.* gray 366.3
  mark 568.19
  variegate 374.7
  *adj.* gray 366.4
  variegated 374.12
**dappled gray** 366.4
  mixed 44.15
  variegated 374.12
**dapple-gray**
  *n.* horse 414.13
  *adj.* gray 366.4
**dare**
  *n.* challenge 793.2
  *v.* be insolent 913.6
  confront 240.8
  defy 793.3
  defy danger 697.7
  have courage 893.10
  presume 961.6
  try 714.7

**daredevil**
  *n.* reckless person
  894.4
  *adj.* foolhardy 894.9
**daresay** believe 501.11
  suppose 499.10
  think probable 511.5
**daring**
  *n.* courage 893.6
  defiance 793.1
  display 904.4
  recklessness 894.3
  *adj.* audacious 893.21
  defiant 793.7
  foolhardy 894.9
  showy 904.19
**daringly**
  courageously 893.22
  foolhardily 894.12
  showily 904.26
**dark**
  *n.* lightlessness 337.1
  obscurity 549.3
  unenlightenment
  477.4
  *adj.* black 365.8
  blind 441.9
  cloudy 404.7
  complexion 365.10
  dark-colored 365.9
  dishonest 975.16
  evil 981.16
  gloomy 872.24
  ignorant 477.16
  indistinct 445.6
  lightless 337.13
  obscure 549.15
  ominous 544.17
  opaque 341.3
  secret 614.11
  secretive 614.15
  sullen 951.24
**dark age** 477.4
**Dark Ages** 107.5
**dark cloud**
  heavenly body 375.7
  omen 544.6
**darken**
  become excited
  857.17
  blacken 365.7
  blemish 679.6
  blind 441.7
  cloud 404.6
  grow dark 337.12
  make sad 872.18
  obscure 337.9
  opaque 341.2
**darkened**
  blinded 441.10
  stained 679.10
**darkening**
  blackening 365.5
  concealment 615.1
  dimming 337.6
**dark horse**
  political candidate
  746.9
  small chance 156.9
  unknown quantity
  477.7
**darkish** blackish 365.9

**deaden** cushion 163.8
desensitize 423.4
dull 337.10
make unfeeling 856.8
moderate 163.6
muffle 451.9
relieve 886.5
weaken 160.10
**dead end**
impasse 731.5
obstruction 266.3
**dead-end** 266.9
**deadening**
*n.* moderation 163.2
relief 886.1
weakening 160.5
*adj.* anesthetic 687.47
moderating 163.14
numbing 423.9
relieving 886.9
**deadeye** hole 265.4
shooter 285.9
**deadfall** 618.11
**dead giveaway** 556.2
**deadhead**
freeloader 850.3
playgoer 611.32
**dead heat**
contemporary 118.2
equality 30.3
**dead language** 580.2
**dead letter** letter 604.3
meaninglessness
547.1
**deadline**
boundary 235.3
crucial moment
129.5
**deadlock**
*n.* end 144.2
impasse 731.5
stalemate 30.3
standstill 268.3
*v.* prevent 730.13
stop 144.11
**deadly**
*adj.* deathly 408.29
destructive 693.26
fatal 409.23
harmful 675.12
poisonous 684.7
remarkable 34.11
*adv.* death 408.37
terribly 34.21
**dead march** dirge 875.5
funeral 410.5
music 462.11
slowness 270.2
**deadness**
insensibility 423.1
insipidness 430.1
lusterlessness 337.5
muffled tone 452.2
uninterestingness
883.1
**dead of night**
darkness 337.1
midnight 134.6
silence 451.1
**deadpan**
*adj.* inexpressive
549.20

*adv.* unfeelingly
856.14
**dead pan**
unexpressiveness
549.5
unfeeling 856.1
**dead reckoning**
navigation 275.2
position 184.3
**dead ringer**
image 572.3
the same 14.3
**dead set on** 624.16
**dead shot**
expert 733.11
shooter 285.9
**dead stop**
standstill 268.3
stop 144.2
**dead-tired** 717.8
**dead to**
insensible 856.10
unaware 477.13
**dead to the world**
absorbed 532.11
asleep 712.22
inattentive 531.7
unconscious 423.8
**deadweight**
burden 352.7
impediment 730.6
weight 352.1
**deadwood**
branch 411.18
refuse 669.4
**deaf**
hard of hearing 449.6
inattentive 531.7
narrow-minded
527.10
unpersuadable 626.13
**deaf-and-dumb**
**alphabet**
gesture 568.14
manual alphabet
449.3
**deafen** din 453.6
muffle 451.9
stun 449.5
**deafening**
intense 159.20
loud 453.10
**deaf-mute**
*n.* mute 451.3
the deaf 449.2
*adj.* deaf 449.6
**deafness**
hardness of hearing
449
incognizance 477.3
unpersuadableness
626.5
**deaf to**
insensible 856.10
refusing 776.6
unaware 477.13
**deal**
*n.* amount 28.2
bargain 827.5
compact 771.1
compromise 807.1
intrigue 172.3

much 34.4
portion 816.5
slab 227.2
transaction 827.4
undertaking 715.1
wood 378.3
*v.* apportion 816.8
distribute 60.9
give 818.12
hit 283.13
trade 827.14
**dealer** merchant 830.2
racketeer 826.4
stockbroker 833.10
**deal in** 827.15
**dealing**
commerce 827.1
communication
554.1
trading 827.2
**dealings** acts 705.3
affairs 151.4
commerce 827.1
communication
554.1
relationship 9.1
**deal out**
apportion 816.8
disperse 75.4
distribute 60.9
give 818.12
**deal with**
accomplish 722.4
behave toward 737.6
communicate 554.6
discourse upon 606.5
discuss 597.12
operate 164.5
perform 705.8
punish 1010.10
relate to 9.5
trade with 827.16
treat 665.12
**dean** chief 749.3
clergyman 1038.9
educator 565.9
executive 748.3
senior 127.5
superior 36.4
**deanery**
church office 1037.5
house 191.6
mastership 739.7
parsonage 1042.7
**dear**
*n.* endearment 932.5
loved one 931.13
*adj.* beloved 931.22
expensive 848.11
valuable 848.10
*adv.* at great cost
848.13
**dearth** scarcity 662.3
unproductiveness
166.1
**death** dying 408
end 70.1
ruin 693.2
symbols of 408.3
transience 111.1
**deathbed**
*n.* dying 408.9

*adj.* last-minute
132.18
**deathblow**
death stroke 409.10
defeat 727.1
early death 408.5
end-all 70.4
ruin 693.2
**death-dealing** 409.23
**death-defying** 894.9
**death grip** 813.2
**deathless**
immortal 112.9
indestructible 142.18
**deathly**
*adj.* deathlike 408.29
fatal 409.23
*adv.* death 408.37
terribly 34.21
**death rate** 408.13
**death rattle** 408.9
**death sentence** 1008.1
**death song** dirge 875.5
swan song 408.10
**death struggle**
dying 408.9
fight 796.6
**Death Valley** 166.2
**deathwatch**
dying 408.9
funeral rites 410.4
**death wish** 872.3
**deb** beginner 68.2
fashionable 644.7
**debacle** defeat 727.1
descent 316.1
disaster 693.4
revolution 147.1
**debar** exclude 77.4
obstruct 730.12
prevent 730.10
prohibit 778.3
**debarkation** 300.2
**debase** adulterate 44.13
corrupt 692.14
demote 783.3
depress 318.4
disgrace 915.8
disparage 971.8
humiliate 906.5
lower 208.6
misuse 667.4
**debased**
depressed 318.12
disreputed 915.12
low 208.7
morally corrupt
981.14
**debatable** 514.16
**debate**
*n.* contention 796.1
discussion 597.7
legislative procedure
742.14
speech 599.2
*v.* be irresolute 627.7
consider 478.12
declaim 599.10
discuss 597.12
**debater** arguer 482.12
public speaker 599.4

**debauch**
n. intemperance 993.2
revel 878.6
spree 996.5
v. be intemperate
993.6
be unchaste 989.19
corrupt 692.14
go on a spree 996.27
make merry 878.26
seduce 989.20
**debauched**
intemperate 993.8
morally corrupt
981.14
unchaste 989.25
**debauchery**
intemperance 993.2
profligacy 989.3
**debenture** bond 834.4
contract 771.3
negotiable instru-
ment 835.11
**debilitate** disable 158.9
fatigue 717.4
sicken 686.47
weaken 160.10
**debilitated** aged 126.18
fatigued 717.6
languid 708.19
unhealthy 686.50
unnerved 158.19
weak 160.12
**debility** fatigue 717.1
old age 126.5
unhealthiness 686.2
weakness 160.1
**debit**
n. account entry 845.5
expenditure 843.1
loss 812.1
v. keep accounts
845.8
**debonair** 870.12
**debouch** appear 446.9
eject 310.24
emerge 303.12
escape 632.10
**debrief** aviation 278.57
disband 75.8
**debris** deposit 271.8
grain 361.6
refuse 43.1
rubbish 669.5
**debt** borrowing 821.1
indebtedness 840
**debtee** 839.4
**debtor** borrower 840.4
borrowing 821.1
**debt service** 841.1
**debug** 487.2
**debunk** 520.2
**debunker** 971.6
**debut**
inauguration 68.5
party 922.14
theatrical perfor-
mance 611.13
**debutant** beginner 68.2
novice 566.9
**debutante** 644.7
**deca–** 99.22

**decade** period 107.2
ten 99.6
**decadence**
deterioration 692.3
turpitude 981.5
**decadent**
deteriorating 692.46
morally corrupt
981.14
**decal** adherent 50.4
graphic art 578.5
**decalogue** 957.1
**decamp**
break camp 301.15
flee 631.10
leave 301.10
**decant** eject 310.24
extract 305.12
transfer 271.16
**decapitate** 1010.19
**decathlon** 878.9
**decay**
n. decomposition
692.6
disintegration 53.1
dissociation 53.2
filth 682.7
rotting 692.7
v. decompose 692.25
disintegrate 53.3
**decease**
n. death 408.1
end 70.1
v. die 408.19
**deceased** dead 408.30
past 119.7
**deceased, the** 408.16
**deceit**
deceitfulness 618.3
stratagem 735.3
**deceitful**
cunning 735.12
dishonest 975.18
falsehearted 616.31
fraudulent 618.20
**deceive**
be dishonest 975.11
lie 616.19
live by one's wits
735.9
outwit 735.11
seduce 989.20
trick 618.13
**deceived** 477.14
**deceiver** affecter 903.7
criminal 986.10
deluder 619
dishonest person
975.10
evildoer 943.1
seducer 989.12
**deceiving** 618.19
**deceleration**
decrease 39.2
restraint 760.1
slowing 270.4
**decencies**
etiquette 646.3
propriety 958.2
**decency**
expedience 670.1
good taste 897.3

**honesty** 974.1
indulgence 759.2
propriety 958.2
seemliness 988.2
social convention
645.1
**decent**
conventional 645.5
decorous 897.10
expedient 670.5
honest 974.13
indulgent 759.8
kind 938.13
modest 988.5
right 958.8
sufficient 661.6
tolerable 674.19
**decently**
expediently 670.8
honestly 974.21
tastefully 897.11
tolerably 674.23
**decentralize** 75.7
**deception**
concealment 615.1
deceit 618
fakery 616.3
hoax 618.7
illusion 519.1
**deceptive**
deceiving 618.19
erroneous 518.16
illusory 519.9
specious 483.10
**decibel** 450.7
**decide** cause 153.13
determine 494.11
induce 648.22
influence 172.8
make sure 513.11
resolve 624.7
will 621.2
**decide against** 778.5
**decide between** 637.14
**decided** asserting 523.7
emphatic 672.20
ended 70.8
made sure 513.20
outright 34.12
resolute 624.11
sure 513.21
unqualified 508.2
**decidedly**
assertingly 523.9
certainly 513.23
positively 34.19
resolutely 624.17
**decide upon** 637.16
**deciduous**
arboreal 411.36
descending 316.11
plant 411.41
transient 111.7
**decimal**
numerical 86.8,9
ten 99.22
**decimal system** 86.2
**decimate**
destroy 693.10
murder 409.17
**decipher**
explain 552.10

solve 487.2
**decipherable**
legible 548.11
solvable 487.3
**decision** choice 637.1
judgment 494.5
legal decision 1004.9
resolution 624.1
will 621.1
**decision-making** 747.3
**decisive** causal 153.14
certain 513.13
convincing 501.26
crucial 129.10
evidential 505.17
mandatory 752.13
prompt 131.9
resolute 624.11
unqualified 508.2
**decisive moment** 129.5
**deck**
n. bundle 74.8
drug dose 687.6
floor 212.3
layer 227.1
playing cards 878.17
types of 277.28
v. clothe 231.38
hit 283.13
knock down 318.5
ornament 901.8
overpower 727.7
**deckhand** 276.6
**deckle edge** 262.2
**declaim** orate 599.10
overact 611.36
proclaim 559.13
speak 594.20
**declamatory**
elocutionary 599.12
grandiloquent 601.8
**declaration**
acknowledgment
521.3
affirmation 523.1
announcement 559.2
decree 752.4
legal statement
1004.7
profession of belief
501.7
remark 594.4
testimony 505.3
**declaration of war**
797.11
**declarative**
asserting 523.7
publicational 559.18
**declare** affirm 523.4
announce 559.12
decree 752.9
express belief 501.12
state 594.24
**declared**
affirmed 523.8
made public 559.17
**declare war** 797.19
**déclassé** 926.4
**declension**
decrease 39.2
descent 316.1
deterioration 692.3

morphology 582.3
refusal 776.1
**declination**
coordinates 490.6
descent 316.1
deterioration 692.3
deviation 291.1
obliquity 219.1
refusal 776.1
rejection 638.1
**decline**
*n.* cheapening 849.4
declivity 219.5
decrease 39.2
deterioration 692.3
end 70.3
fall 316.2
senility 469.10
shortcoming 314.1
stock prices 834.9
*v.* age 126.10
cheapen 849.6
decrease 39.6
degenerate 729.11
deteriorate 692.20
fail 686.45
fall short 314.2
grammaticize 586.16
incline 219.10
recede 297.2
refuse 776.3
reject 638.2
sink 316.6
weaken 160.9
**declining**
*n.* refusal 776.1
rejection 638.1
*adj.* aging 126.17
decreasing 39.11
descending 316.11
deteriorating 692.46
languishing 160.21
receding 297.5
sloping downward
219.16
**declivitous**
descending 316.11
sloping downward
219.16
**declivity** 219.5
**decoction**
a preparation 720.3
extract 305.8
extraction 305.7
heating 329.2
infusion 44.2
solution 391.3
**decode** 487.2
**decoding**
explanation 552.4
information theory
557.7
interpretation 552.3
solution 487.1
**décolleté**
*n.* nudity 232.3
*adj.* unclad 232.13
**decoloration** 363.3
**decommission** 804.11
**decomposable**
biodegradable 692.48
disintegrable 53.5

**decompose**
decay 692.25
disintegrate 53.3
**decomposed** 692.41
**decomposing** 53.5
**decomposition**
decay 692.6
disintegration 53.1
rotting 692.7
**deconcentrate** 75.7
**decongestant** 687.32
**decontaminate**
acquit 1007.4
sanitize 681.24
**decontamination**
mitigation 1006.5
radiation 327.1
sanitation 681.3
**decor**
ornamentation 901.1
stage scenery 611.25
**decorate** add 40.4
beautify 900.14
honor 916.8
make grandiloquent
601.7
ornament 901.8
**decorated**
high-flown 601.11
ornamented 901.11
**decoration** arts 574.1
award 916.5
beautification 900.10
extra 41.4
insignia 569.1
ornamentation 901.1
**decorative**
beautifying 900.20
ornamental 901.10
**decorator** 579.11
**decorous**
ceremonious 646.8
conventional 645.5
decent 988.5
right 958.8
solemn 871.3
tasteful 897.10
**decorum** decency 988.2
etiquette 646.3
good taste 897.3
propriety 958.2
social convention
645.1
**decoy**
*n.* fake buyer 828.6
lure 650.2
shill 619.5
trap 618.11
*v.* lure 650.4
trap 618.18
**decrease**
*n.* contraction 198.1
lessening 39
loss 812.2
reduction 42.2
*v.* contract 198.7
diminish 39.6
graduate 29.4
quantify 28.4
reduce 39.7
subtract 42.9
waste 812.5

**decree**
*n.* judgment 494.5
law 998.3
order 752.4
predetermination
640.1
*v.* command 752.9
legalize 998.8
legislate 742.18
pass judgment 494.13
will 621.2
**decrement**
decrease 39.1
deduction 42.7
depletion 39.3
loss 812.2
reduction 42.2
**decrepit** aged 126.18
dilapidated 692.35
senile 469.23
weak 160.15
**decrescendo**
*n.* decrease 39.2
faintness of sound
452.1
music 462.25
*adj.* decreasing 39.11
faint-sounding 452.16
*adv.* decreasingly
39.12
music 462.54
**decretory**
commanding 752.14
mandatory 752.13
**decry** censure 969.13
disparage 971.8
**dedicate** devote 816.11
sanctify 1026.5
**dedicated**
friendly 927.20
resolute 624.11
sanctified 1026.8
unselfish 979.5
zealous 635.10
**dedication**
book 605.12
devotion 816.4
duty 962.1
friendship 927.7
resolution 624.1
sanctification 1026.3
unselfishness 979.1
zeal 635.2
**deduce**
conclude 494.10
elicit 305.14
reason 482.15
suppose 499.10
**deduct** discount 847.2
reduce 39.7
subtract 42.9
**deductible**
*n.* insurance 699.4
*adj.* tax-free 846.18
**deduction**
conclusion 494.4
decrease 39.1
decrement 42.7
discount 847.1
logic 482.3
reasoning 482.1
relationship 9.1

subtraction 42.1
**deductive**
dialectic(al) 482.22
subtractive 42.13
**deed**
*n.* act 705.3
contract 771.3
courageous act 893.7
*v.* transfer property
817.3
**deedholder** 809.2
**deem** believe 501.11
judge 494.8
suppose 499.10
**de-emphasize**
make light of 673.11
minimize 39.9
soften 163.6
**de-energize** 158.9
**deep**
*n.* pit 209.2
*adj.* broad 204.6
colored 362.16
cunning 735.12
deep-felt 855.26
deep-toned 454.10
extensive 179.9
great 34.6
interior 225.7
learned 475.21
profound 209.10
recondite 549.16
wise 467.17
*adv.* beyond one's
depth 209.16
**deep, the** ocean 397.1
ocean depths 209.4
**deep-dyed**
confirmed 642.21
dyed 362.17
established 142.13
thorough 56.10
**deepen** aggravate 885.2
broaden 204.4
increase 38.5
lower 209.8
**deepening**
aggravation 885.1
increase 38.2
lowering 209.7
**deep freeze** 334.5
**deep-freeze** 334.11
**deep-rooted**
confirmed 642.21
deep 209.10
established 142.13
**deep-sea**
aquatic 275.58
deep-water 209.14
oceanic 397.8
**deep-seated**
confirmed 642.21
deep 209.10
established 142.13
intrinsic 5.6
**deep six** discard 668.3
funeral 410.5
tomb 410.16
**deep-six** 668.7
**deep sleep** 712.5
**deep thought**
engrossment 530.3

thoughtfulness 478.3
**deer** 414.5,58
**de-escalation** 318.1
**deface** blemish 679.4
  deform 249.7
  disfigure 899.5
**de facto** 1.15,16
**defalcation**
  deficiency 57.2
  misuse 667.1
  shortcoming 314.1
**defamation** 971.2
**defamatory** 971.13
**defame** malign 971.9
  stigmatize 915.9
**default**
  *n.* absence 187.4
  debt 840.2
  neglect 534.1
  nonobservance 769.1
  nonpayment 842.1
  shortcoming 314.1
  *v.* be absent 187.7
  lose 812.4
  neglect 534.6
  not pay 842.6
**defeat**
  *n.* disappointment
    541.1
  failure 725.1
  frustration 730.3
  vanquishment 727
  *v.* beat 36.7
  disappoint 541.2
  refute 506.5
  ruin 693.11
  thwart 730.15
  triumph over 726.6
  vanquish 727.6
**defeated**
  disappointed 541.5
  vanquished 727.14
**defeating**
  frustrating 730.20
  victorious 726.8
**defeatist**
  *n.* pessimist 889.7
  *adj.* pessimistic 889.16
**defecate** eject 310.21
  excrete 311.13
**defect**
  *n.* blemish 679.1
  deficiency 57.2
  disease 686.1
  fault 678.2
  *v.* apostatize 628.8
  desert 633.6
  renegade 145.13
**defection**
  apostasy 628.2
  change 139.1
  conversion 145.3
  desertion 633.2
  fault 678.2
  nonpayment 842.1
**defective**
  *n.* cripple 686.42
  simpleton 471.8
  *adj.* blemished 679.8
  faulty 518.16
  imperfect 678.4
  incomplete 57.4

insufficient 662.9
**defector** apostate 145.8
  turncoat 628.5
**defend** guard 799.8
  justify 1006.10
  protect 699.18
**defendant**
  accused 1005.6
  litigant 1004.11
  oppositionist 791.3
**defender**
  champion 799.7
  justifier 1006.8
  protector 699.5
  supporter 787.9
**defense**
  argumentation 482.4
  barrier 730.5
  countermeasure
    178.5
  counterstatement
    486.2
  guard 799
  justification 1006.2
  legal plea 1004.6
  protection 699.1
**defense counsel** 1003.4
**defenseless**
  forlorn 924.11
  helpless 158.18
  unprotected 697.14
**defense mechanism**
  avoidance 631.1
  defense 799.1
  defense reaction
    690.30
  mental block 538.3
**defensible**
  defendable 799.15
  just 976.8
  justifiable 1006.14
**defensive**
  defending 799.11
  protecting 699.23
**defer** 132.9
**deference**
  courtesy 936.1
  duty 962.1
  respect 964.1
  submission 765.1
**deferential**
  courteous 936.14
  dutiful 962.13
  respectful 964.8
  submissive 765.16
**deferment** 132.4
**defer to** obey 766.2
  respect 964.4
  submit to 765.9
**defiance**
  declaration of war
    797.11
  defying 793
  refractoriness 767.2
  resistance 792.1
  ungovernability 626.4
**defiant** defying 793.7
  refractory 767.10
  ungovernable 626.12
**deficiency** fault 678.2
  imperfection 678.1
  incompleteness 57.1

inferiority 37.3
  lack 57.2
  want 662.4
**deficiency disease**
    686.1,10
**deficient**
  imperfect 678.4
  incomplete 57.4
  inferior 37.7
  insufficient 662.9
  short of 314.5
  slipshod 534.12
**deficit** debt 840.2
  deficiency 57.2
  difference 42.8
  shortcoming 314.1
  want 662.4
**deficit spending** 843.1
**defile**
  *n.* narrow place 205.3
  passageway 657.4
  ravine 201.2
  *v.* corrupt 692.14
  demoralize 981.10
  dirty 682.17
  march 273.29
  misuse 667.4
  parade 71.7
  seduce 989.20
  stigmatize 915.9
  vilify 971.10
  work evil 675.6
**define**
  characterize 80.10
  circumscribe 234.4
  interpret 552.9
  mark 568.19
  name 583.11
  stabilize 142.9
**defined**
  circumscribed 234.6
  clearly visible 444.7
  intelligible 548.10
  particular 80.12
**defining**
  classificational 61.7
  limiting 234.9
**definite** audible 450.16
  certain 513.13
  circumscribed 234.6
  clearly visible 444.7
  intelligible 548.10
  particular 80.12
  resolute 624.11
  unqualified 508.2
**definitely**
  certainly 513.23
  exactly 516.20
  intelligibly 548.12
  particularly 80.15
  visibly 444.8
**definition**
  characterization 80.8
  circumscription 234.1
  intelligibility 548.2
  interpretation 552.1
  meaning 545.3
  naming 583.2
  television reception
    345.5
  visibility 444.2
**definitive** final 70.10

limiting 234.9
  outright 34.12
  unqualified 508.2
**deflagration**
  burning 329.5
  flash 328.14
**deflate** cheapen 849.6
  collapse 198.10
  disprove 506.4
  humiliate 906.4
  reduce 39.7
  render powerless
    158.11
**deflated**
  disproved 506.7
  flat 198.14
  reduced 39.10
**deflation**
  cheapening 849.4
  contraction 198.4
  decrease 39.1
  failure 725.3
  humiliation 906.2
**deflationary** 198.11
**deflect** curve 252.6
  dissuade 652.1
  divert 291.5
  oblique 219.9
  prevent 730.14
**deflection** angle 251.2
  curve 252.3
  deviation 291.2
  obliquity 219.1
  radar interference
    346.12
**deflower**
  corrupt 692.14
  possess sexually
    822.15
  seduce 989.20
**defluxion**
  descent 316.1
  flow 395.4
  outflow 303.4
**defocus** 445.4
**defoliant** 676.3
**defoliate** 49.14
**deform** blemish 679.4
  change 139.6
  distort 247.3
  misshape 249.7
**deformed**
  abnormal 85.13
  blemished 679.8
  malformed 249.12
  ugly 899.8
**deformity**
  blemish 679.1
  cripple 686.42
  disease 686.1
  malformation 249.3
  oddity 85.3
  ugliness 899.2
**defraud** cheat 618.17
  steal 824.13
**defrauder** 619.3
**defray** 841.18
**defrayment** 841.1
**defrock** depose 783.4
  disgrace 915.8
  dismiss 310.19
**defrost** 329.21

**deft** 733.20
**deftly** 733.29
**deftness** 733.1
**defunct** dead 408.30
  ended 70.8
  no more 2.10
  past 119.7
**defuse** 804.7
**defy**
  *n.* challenge 793.2
  *v.* challenge 793.3
  confront 240.8
  disobey 767.6
  have courage 893.10
  make war on 797.19
  not observe 769.4
  resist 792.2
  thwart 730.15
**dégagé** careless 534.11
  informal 647.3
  nonchalant 858.15
**degauss** 342.24
**degenerate**
  *n.* bad person 986.5
  *v.* be changed 139.5
  become disordered
    62.8
  corrupt 692.14
  defect 145.13
  deteriorate 729.11
  get worse 692.19
  go wrong 981.9
  *adj.* apostate 145.20
  changed 139.9
  deteriorating 692.46
  morally corrupt
    981.14
**degeneration**
  automation 349.6
  change 139.1
  deterioration 692.3
  turpitude 981.5
**degradable**
  decomposable 692.48
  disintegrable 53.5
**degradation**
  banishment 310.4
  baseness 915.3
  decay 692.6
  demotion 783.1
  depression 318.1
  deterioration 692.3
  dishonesty 975.2
  disintegration 53.1
  infamy 915.4
  turpitude 981.5
**degrade** corrupt 692.14
  demote 783.3
  disgrace 915.8
  dismiss 310.19
  disparage 971.8
  humiliate 906.5
**degrading**
  *n.* demotion 783.1
  *adj.* disgraceful 915.11
  insulting 965.6
**egree** academic 917.9
  compass 290.3
  grade 29
  harmonics 463.20
  measure 490.2
  music 462.29

order 59.2
title 917.6
**dehumanized** 939.24
**dehumidifier** 393.4
**dehumidify** 393.6
**dehydrate** dry 393.6
  preserve 701.8
**dehydrated** 393.9
**dehydration**
  drying 393.3
  preserving 701.2
**dehydrator** 393.4
**deice** 329.21
**deification**
  exaltation 317.1
  glorification 914.8
  idolization 1033.2
  praise 968.5
  respect 964.1
**deify** exalt 317.6
  glorify 914.13
  idolatrize 1033.5
  praise 968.12
  respect 964.4
**deign**
  condescend 906.7
  consent 775.2
**deism** 1020.5
**deist** 1020.15
**deity** see god
**deject** 872.18
**dejected**
  depressed 872.22
  sullen 951.24
**dejection**
  defecation 311.2
  emotional symptom
    690.23
  excrement 311.3
  sadness 872.3
  sullenness 951.8
**de jure** 998.12
**delay**
  *n.* hindrance 730.1
  slowing 270.4
  stoppage 132.2
  *v.* dawdle 270.8
  do nothing 706.2
  hinder 730.10
  postpone 132.9
  put aside 668.6
  retard 132.8
  slow 270.9
  wait 132.12
**delayed** late 132.16
  retarded 270.12
**delaying**
  dawdling 270.11
  dilatory 132.17
**dele** 693.16
**delectable**
  pleasant 863.9
  tasty 428.8
**delegate**
  *n.* deputy 781.2
  *v.* commission 780.9
  commit 818.16
  deputize 149.7
**delegation**
  accession to power
    739.12
  commission 780.1

commitment 818.2
delegates 781.13
substitution 149.1
**delete** cancel 70.7
  erase 42.12
  obliterate 693.16
  separate 49.9
**deleted** absent 187.10
  canceled 70.8
**deleterious**
  disadvantageous
    671.6
  harmful 675.12
**deletion** erasure 42.5
  obliteration 693.7
**deli** 832.5
**deliberate**
  *v.* be irresolute 627.7
  confer 597.11
  consider 478.12
  discuss 597.12
  think over 478.13
  *adj.* cautious 895.8
  intentional 653.9
  leisurely 710.6
  slow 270.10
**deliberately**
  intentionally 653.11
  slowly 270.13
  tardily 132.20
**deliberateness**
  caution 895.1
  intentionality 653.3
  leisureliness 710.2
  slowness 270.1
**deliberation**
  caution 895.1
  consideration 478.2
  discussion 597.7
  intentionality 653.3
  legislative procedure
    742.14
  leisureliness 710.2
  slowness 270.1
**delicacy**
  breakability 360.1
  considerateness 938.3
  decency 988.2
  difference 16.2
  discrimination 492.1
  emotional capacity
    855.4
  fastidiousness 896.3
  fine texture 351.3
  food 308.8
  frailty 160.2
  good taste 897.1
  lightness 353.1
  meticulousness 533.3
  precariousness 697.2
  prettiness 900.5
  sensitivity 422.3
  smallness 35.1
  softness 357.1
  subtlety 516.3
  tender feeling 855.6
  thinness 205.4
  unhealthiness 686.2
**delicate**
  considerate 938.16
  dainty 35.7
  decent 988.5

difficult 731.16
discriminating 492.7
emotionable 855.21
exact 516.16
fastidious 896.11
fragile 360.4
frail 160.14
light 353.11
meticulous 533.12
precarious 697.12
pretty 900.18
sensitive 422.14
smooth 351.8
soft 357.8
soft-colored 362.21
tasteful 897.9
tasty 428.8
thin 205.16
**delicate health** 686.2
**delicate issue** 795.7
**delicately**
  prettily 900.22
  softly 357.17
  weakly 160.22
**delicatessen** 832.5
**delicious** edible 307.31
  excellent 674.13
  pleasant 863.9
  tasty 428.8
**delight**
  *n.* affinity 174.1
  happiness 865.2
  *v.* amuse 878.23
  be pleased 865.9
  give pleasure 865.8
  gloat 910.9
  rejoice 876.5
**delighted**
  amused 878.28
  pleased 865.12
**delightful**
  amusing 878.29
  pleasant 863.7
  tasty 428.8
**delightfully** 863.12
**delight in** enjoy 865.10
  savor 428.5
**Delilah** 989.15
**delimit**
  circumscribe 234.4
  mark 568.19
**delimitation**
  boundary 235.3
  circumscription 234.1
**delineate**
  describe 608.12
  outline 235.9
  picture 574.20
  plan 654.12
  represent 572.6
**delineation**
  description 608.1
  diagram 654.3
  drawing 574.6
  line 568.6
  outline 235.2
  picture 574.14
  representation 572.1
**delineator**
  drawer 579.3
  limner 579.2

**delinquency**
immorality 981.1
nonobservance 769.1
nonpayment 842.1
shortcoming 314.1
sin 982.2
wrong 959.1
**delinquent**
*n.* bad person 986.9
defaulter 842.5
evildoer 943.1
*adj.* defaulting 842.10
wrong 959.3
**deliquescent**
decreasing 39.11
liquefied 391.6
**delirious**
excited 857.23
fervent 855.23
feverish 686.54
insane 473.31
overzealous 635.13
**deliriously**
frenziedly 857.33
madly 473.35
**delirium**
excitement 857.7
fever 686.6
thing imagined 535.5
thought disturbance
690.24
unsaneness 473.8
**delirium tremens**
alcoholism 996.3
hallucination 519.7
insanity 473.9
**deliver** give 818.13
liberate 763.4
release 886.6
rescue 702.3
say 594.23
transfer 271.9
transfer property
817.3
**deliverance**
escape 632.1
giving 818.1
judgment 494.5
liberation 763.1
property transfer
817.1
release 886.2
rescue 702.1
**deliverer**
preserver 701.4
savior 942.2
**delivery**
articulation 594.6
birth 167.7
escape 632.1
giving 818.1
liberation 763.1
property transfer
817.1
rescue 702.1
transference 271.1
**dell** ravine 201.2
valley 257.9
**delocalize** 271.10
**delouse** purify 681.18
sanitize 681.24
**delta** fan 299.4

plain 387.1
point of land 256.8
**deltoid** angular 251.8
diverging 299.8
spread 197.11
triangular 93.3
tripartite 95.4
**deludable** 502.9
**delude** 618.13
**deluded** 473.25
**deluder** 619.1
**deluge**
*n.* inundation 395.6
overabundance 663.2
rainstorm 394.2
throng 74.4
violent flow 395.5
wetting 392.6
*v.* drench 392.14
overflow 395.17
oversupply 663.14
submerge 320.7
**delusion**
deception 618.1
error 518.1
fakery 616.3
illusion 519.1
thought disturbance
690.24
**delusion of grandeur**
690.24
**delusive**
deceptive 618.19
erroneous 518.16
illusory 519.9
**deluxe** 904.21
**delve** excavate 257.15
search 485.30
till 413.17
**delve into** 485.22
**demagnetize** 342.24
**demagogue**
*n.* instigator 648.11
public speaker 599.4
*v.* declaim 599.10
**demagoguery** 599.1
**demand**
*n.* claim 753
extortion 305.6
fee 846.7
imposition 963.1
need 639.2
question 485.10
request 774.1
right 958.3
sale 829.1
*v.* call for 753.4
charge 846.14
extort 305.15
impose 963.4
inquire 485.19
oblige 756.5
prescribe 752.10
request 774.9
require 639.9
summon 752.12
**demand draft** 835.11
**demanding**
difficult 731.16
exacting 753.8
insistent 774.18
meticulous 533.12

strict 757.6
**demarcate**
characterize 80.10
circumscribe 234.4
discriminate 492.5
mark 568.19
**demarcation**
circumscription 234.1
differentiation 16.4
discrimination 492.3
exclusion 77.1
**demasculinize**
feminize 421.12
unman 158.12
**dematerialize**
disappear 447.2
disembody 4.4
immaterialize 377.6
spiritualize 1034.20
**demean** 906.5
**demeaning**
disgraceful 915.11
inferior 37.6
**demeanor**
behavior 737.1
looks 446.4
**demented** 473.25
**dementia** 473.1
**dementia praecox** 473.4
**Demerol** 687.12,54
**demesne** farm 413.8
real estate 810.7
region 180.2
sphere of work 656.4
**Demeter**
agriculture divinity
413.4
fertility goddess
165.5
goddess 1014.5
**demi–** half 92.5
hybrid 44.16
**demigod**
brave person 893.8
god 1014.3
good person 985.5
**demilitarization** 804.6
**demimonde** 989.15
**demise** death 408.1
property transfer
817.1
**demised** 408.30
**demission** 784.1
**demobilization**
demilitarization
804.6
disbandment 75.3
release 763.2
**demobilize**
demilitarize 804.11
disband 75.8
discharge 763.5
**democracy**
government 741.4
participation 815.2
**Democrat** 744.27
**democratic** 741.17
**Democratic Party**
744.24
**demography** 417.7
**demolish**
destroy 693.17

disassemble 49.15
refute 506.5
shatter 49.13
**demolition**
demolishment 693.5
refutation 506.2
**demon** devil 1016.7
enthusiast 635.5
evil spirit 1016.1
monster 943.6
spirit 1014.15
violent person 162.9
**Demon, the** 1016.3
**demoniac** 473.15
**demoniac(al)**
cruel 939.24
damnable 675.10
diabolic 1016.18
excited 857.23
wicked 981.13
**demonism**
idolatry 1033.1
Satanism 1016.15
sorcery 1035.2
**demonist** 1016.16
**demonize**
bewitch 1036.9
devilize 1016.17
**demonstrable**
certain 513.15
manifestable 555.13
provable 505.20
**demonstrate**
check 87.14
cite 505.14
evidence 505.9
explain 552.10
flaunt 904.17
manifest 555.5
object 522.5
prove 505.11
represent 572.8
teach 562.11
**demonstration**
citation 505.6
display 904.4
example 25.2
explanation 552.4
proof 505.4
protest 522.2
reasoning 482.1
representation 572.1
showing 555.2
**demonstrative**
communicative
554.10
emotional 855.19
evidential 505.18
explanatory 552.15
indicative 568.23
loving 931.25
manifestative 555.9
**demonstrator**
explainer 552.7
picket 699.13
**demoralize**
corrupt 981.10
intimidate 891.28
make nervous 859.9
**demos** 919.2
**demote** degrade 783.3
dismiss 310.19

**demotion**
degrading 783
depression 318.1
deterioration 692.3
ejection 310.4
**demulcent**
*n.* healing ointment 687.11
ointment 380.3
*adj.* palliative 163.16
relieving 886.9
remedial 687.40
softening 357.16
**demur**
*n.* objection 522.2
resistance 792.1
unwillingness 623.2
*v.* be irresolute 627.7
be unwilling 623.4
object 522.5
**demure** prudish 903.19
shy 908.12
solemn 871.3
**demurrer**
dissenter 522.3
justification 1006.2
legal plea 1004.6
objection 522.2
**demythologize** 552.10
**den**
disapproved place 191.28
hiding place 615.4
lair 191.26
office 719.8
place of vice 981.7
retreat 700.5
sanctum 192.8
**denature**
adulterate 44.13
change 139.6
corrupt 692.14
**deniable** 514.16
**denial** disavowal 524.2
justification 1006.2
opposition 790.1
privation 812.1
prohibition 778.1
recantation 628.3
refusal 776.1
refutation 506.2
rejection 638.1
temperance 992.1
unbelief 503.1
**denied** disproved 506.7
rejected 638.3
**denied to** 510.9
**denigrate**
blacken 365.7
deprecate 969.12
vilify 971.10
**denizen**
*n.* inhabitant 190.2
*v.* inhabit 188.9
**den of iniquity**
brothel 989.9
place of vice 981.7
**denomination**
Christian 1020.33
indication 568.1
kind 61.3
name 583.3

naming 583.2
religion 1020.3
school 788.5
specification 80.6
**denominational**
partisan 788.19
religions 1020.25
**denotative**
indicative 568.23
meaningful 545.10
**denote**
designate 568.18
indicate 568.17
mean 545.8
signify 505.9
**denouement** end 70.1
result 154.2
solution 487.1
story element 608.9
**denounce**
accuse 1005.7
censure 969.13
condemn 1008.3
threaten 973.1
**dense** compact 354.12
crowded 74.22
growing rank 411.40
hard 356.10
stupid 469.15
substantial 3.7
thick 204.8
**densify** 354.9
**density**
compactness 354
hardness 356.1
stupidity 469.3
substantiality 3.1
**dent**
*n.* indentation 257.6
mark 568.7
tooth 258.5
*v.* indent 257.14
**dental** medical 688.18
phonetic 594.31
toothlike 258.16
**dental bridge** 258.6
**dentate** grasping 813.9
notched 262.5
**dented** 257.17
**denti–** dental 688.18
tooth 258.5
**denticle** 258.5
**dentifrice**
cleaning agent 681.17
toothpaste 687.22
**dentist** 688.10
**dentistry** 688.4,19
**denture** 258.6
**denudant** 232.18
**denude** despoil 822.24
divest 232.5
tear apart 49.14
**denuded**
deprived of 812.8
divested 232.12
**denunciate**
accuse 1005.7
censure 969.13
condemn 1008.3
**denunciation**
accusation 1005.1
condemnation 1008.1

curse 972.1
disapproval 969.3
threat 973.1
**deny** contradict 790.6
disbelieve 503.5
disclaim 524.4
prohibit 778.3
recant 628.9
refuse 776.4
refute 506.5
reject 638.2
**deodorant**
*n.* deodorizer 438.3
*adj.* deodorizing 438.6
**deodorize**
falsify 616.16
stop odor 438.4
**depart**
absent oneself 187.8
die 408.19
digress 593.9
disappear 447.2
exit 303.11
flee 631.10
leave 301.6
separate 49.9
**departed** absent 187.10
dead 408.30
left 301.20
past 119.7
**departed, the** 408.16
**departed spirit** 1017.1
**depart from**
abandon 633.5
deviate 291.3
differ 16.5
**department** area 180.1
jurisdiction 1000.4
region 180.2
sphere of work 656.4
**department store** 832.1
**departure**
absence 187.4
death 408.1
deviation 291.1
difference 16.1
digression 593.4
disappearance 447.1
egress 303.1
leaving 301
**depend**
be contingent 507.6
be uncertain 514.11
hang 215.6
**dependable** sure 513.17
trustworthy 974.19
unhazardous 698.5
**dependence**
addiction 642.9
belief 501.1
pendency 215.1
relationship 9.2
subjection 764.3
supporter 787.9
trust 888.1
**dependent**
*n.* follower 293.2
hanger-on 907.5
retainer 750.1
subject 764.6
*adj.* contingent 507.9
habituated 642.19

pendent 215.9
subordinate 764.13
trusting 501.22
uncertain 514.17
**dependent on**
contingent 507.9
habituated 642.19
liable to 175.5
resulting from 154.8
**depend on**
be contingent 507.6
believe in 501.16
be subject to 764.12
result from 154.6
trust 501.17
**depersonalization** 690.27
**depict** act 611.35
describe 608.12
picture 574.20
represent 572.6
**depiction**
description 608.1
representation 572.1
**depilation** 232.4
**depilatory** 232.4
**deplane** 300.8
**deplete** consume 666.2
eject 310.21
waste 812.5
**depletion**
consumption 666.1
decrease 39.3
evacuation 310.6
loss 812.2
reduction 42.2
**depletion allowance** 818.8
**deplorable** bad 675.9
disgraceful 915.11
regrettable 873.10
unpleasant 864.20
**deplore** lament 875.8
regret 873.6
**deploy** allocate 184.10
arrange evidence 505.13
diverge 299.5
order 59.4
prepare 720.6
spread 197.6
**deployment**
arrangement 60.1
battle array 797.6
divergence 299.1
expansion 197.1
order 59.1
placement 184.5
**deplume** demote 783.3
despoil 822.24
disgrace 915.8
dismiss 310.19
**deponent** 505.7
**depopulate**
eject 310.16
murder 409.17
**deport** eject 310.17
eliminate 77.5
emigrate 303.16
transfer 271.9
**deportment** 737.1
**deposal** dismissal 310.5

ousting 783.2
resignation 784.1
unseating 185.2
**depose** affirm 523.5
dislodge 185.6
dismiss 310.19
remove from office 783.4
testify 505.10
**deposit**
*n.* mineral deposit 383.7
payment 841.1
placement 184.5
pledge 772.3
precipitation 354.5
residue 43.2
sediment 271.8
*v.* lay eggs 169.9
pledge 772.10
precipitate 354.11
put 184.13
secrete 615.7
store 660.10
**depositary**
financial officer 836.11
trustee 809.5
**deposition**
affirmation 523.2
certificate 570.6
deposal 783.2
legal statement 1004.7
placement 184.5
residue 43.2
statement of belief 501.4
testimony 505.3
**depository**
storage place 660.6
treasury 836.12
**depot** 660.6
**depravation**
deterioration 692.3
turpitude 981.5
**deprave** corrupt 692.14
work evil 675.6
**depraved** base 915.12
morally corrupt 981.14
**depravity**
baseness 915.3
turpitude 981.5
**deprecate**
attach little importance to 673.11
disapprove 969.12
underestimate 498.2
**deprecatory**
condemnatory 969.23
disparaging 971.13
modest 908.10
**depreciate**
attach little importance to 673.11
cheapen 849.6
deprecate 969.12
discount 847.2
disparage 971.8
reduce 39.7
subtract 42.9

underestimate 498.2
waste 812.5
**depreciation**
cheapening 849.4
decrease 39.1
deprecation 969.2
deterioration 692.3
discount 847.1
disparagement 971.1
loss 812.2
reduction 42.2
underestimation 498.1
**depredate**
destroy 693.10
plunder 824.16
**depredation**
destruction 693.1
plundering 824.5
**depress** debase 208.6
deepen 209.8
indent 257.14
lowering 318.4
make sad 872.18
reduce 39.7
**depressant** 687.12,54
**depressed**
dejected 872.22
indented 257.17
lowered 318.12
lowness 208.7
pleasureless 866.20
unfortunate 729.14
**depressed area** 838.3
**depressing**
discouraging 872.30
unpleasant 864.20
**depression**
business cycle 827.9
concavity 257.1
decrease 39.1
deepening 209.7
despair 866.6
distressfulness 864.5
emotional symptom 690.23
hard times 729.6
lowering 318
lowness 208.1
notch 262.1
pit 257.2
sadness 872.3
**deprivation**
absence 187.1
deposal 783.2
disassembly 49.6
divestment 822.6
ejection 310.4
loss 812.1
nonexistence 2.1
poverty 838.2
refusal 776.1
want 662.4
**deprive** dismiss 310.19
take from 822.21
**deprived**
bereaved 408.35
poor 838.8
**deprived of**
bereft 812.8
wanting 662.13
**depth** deepness 209

harmonics 463.4
interiority 225.1
pit 209.2
sagacity 467.5
size 195.1
thickness 204.2
**depth indicator** 209.17
**depthless**
insignificant 35.6
shallow 210.5
**depth sounding** 209.5
**deputation**
accession to power 739.12
commission 780.1
delegates 781.13
substitution 149.1
**deputize**
commission 780.9
delegate 149.7
empower 157.10
get an agent 781.14
**deputy** agent 781
assignee 780.8
assistant 787.6
lawyer 1003.1
manager 748.1
mediator 805.3
peace officer 699.15
substitute 149.2
**derange** disarrange 63.2
madden 473.23
sicken 686.47
**deranged**
disorderly 62.13
insane 473.25
**derangement**
abnormality 85.1
disarrangement 63.1
disorder 62.1
insanity 473.1
**derby** contest 796.3
race 796.12
**Derby** 796.13
**dereism**
defense mechanism 690.30
fantasy 535.7
illusion 519.1
**derelict**
*n.* abandoned thing 633.4
bad person 986.2
bum 708.9
outcast 926.4
*adj.* abandoned 633.8
dilapidated 692.35
negligent 534.10
outcast 926.10
unfaithful 975.20
**dereliction**
desertion 633.2
infidelity 975.5
neglect 534.1
nonobservance 769.1
sin 982.2
**deride**
be insolent 913.6
disdain 966.3
flout 793.4
ridicule 967.8

**de rigueur**
conventional 645.5
obligatory 962.15
**derisive**
condemnatory 969.23
defiant 793.7
disparaging 971.13
disrespectful 965.5
impudent 913.9
ridiculing 967.12
**derivable** 482.23
**derivation**
ancestry 170.4
borrowing 821.2
conclusion 494.4
etymology 582.16
linguistics 580.12
morphology 582.3
receiving 819.1
result 154.1
source 153.5
word 582.2
**derivative**
attributed 155.6
lexical 582.20
resulting 154.7
unproductive 166.5
**derive** acquire 811.8
conclude 494.10
elicit 305.14
receive 819.6
**derive from**
borrow 821.4
receive 819.6
result from 154.6
trace to 155.5
**derm(a)-** 229.1
**dermal** 229.6
**dermatitis**
deficiency disease 686.10
skin disease 686.33
**dermis** skin 229.1
skin layer 229.4
**dernier cri**
the latest thing 122.2
the rage 644.4
**derogation**
deterioration 692.3
disparagement 971.1
reduction 42.2
**derogative** 971.13
**derogatory**
disparaging 971.13
disreputable 915.10
**derrick** lifter 317.3
tower 207.11
**derrière** 241.4
**derring-do** 893.6
**dervish** ascetic 991.2
clergyman 1038.13
Muslim 1020.22
**descant**
*n.* melody 462.4
musical part 462.22
musical piece 462.5
overture 462.26
treatise 606.1
*v.* discourse upon 606.5
expatiate 593.7
sing 462.39

**descend**
  be disgraced 915.7
  change hands 817.4
  condescend 906.7
  fly 278.52
  go down 316.5
  gravitate 352.15
  incline 219.10
  move 267.5
**descendant**
  offspring 171.3
  posterity 171.1
  sequel 117.2
  successor 67.4
**descending**
  falling 316.11
  flowing 267.8
  sloping downward
    219.16
**descend upon**
  attack 798.15
  light on 316.10
**descent** ancestry 170.4
  continuity 71.2
  course 267.2
  declivity 219.5
  depression 318.1
  deterioration 692.3
  fall 316
  humiliation 906.2
  posterity 171.1
  reverse 729.3
  rocketry 281.9
  sequence 65.1
**describe**
  characterize 80.10
  interpret 552.9
  portray 608.12
**description**
  characterization 80.8
  interpretation 552.1
  kind 61.3
  portrayal 608
**descriptive**
  depictive 608.15
  interpretative 552.14
  linguistic 580.17
**descry** detect 488.5
  see 439.12
  understand 548.8
**desecrate**
  corrupt 692.14
  misuse 667.4
  profane 1030.4
**desecration**
  misuse 667.1
  sacrilege 1030.2
  wrong 959.2
**desensitize**
  make unfeeling 856.7
  render insensible
    423.4
**desert**
  n. plain 387.1
  space 179.4
  wasteland 166.2
  adj. barren 166.4
  dry 393.7
**desert**
  n. goodness 674.1
  reprisal 955.2
  v. abandon 633.6

**apostatize** 628.8
  be dishonest 975.12
  defect 145.13
  flee 631.10
**deserted**
  abandoned 633.8
  disused 668.10
  forlorn 924.11
  neglected 534.14
  vacant 187.14
**deserter** apostate 145.8
  desertion 633.2
  impious person
    1030.3
  turncoat 628.5
**desertion**
  abandonment 633.2
  apostasy 628.2
  defection 145.3
  flight 631.4
  forlornness 924.4
  impiety 1030.1
**deserts** due 960.3
  punishment 1010.1
  reprisal 955.2
**deserve** 960.5
**deserved** just 976.8
  warranted 960.9
**deserving** due 960.10
  praiseworthy 968.20
**desex** 158.12
**déshabillé** 231.20
**desiccate**
  deteriorate 692.21
  dry 393.6
  preserve 701.8
**desideratum**
  intention 653.1
  requirement 639.2
  thing desired 634.11
**design**
  n. arts 574.1
  composition 574.10
  diagram 654.3
  harmonics 463.11
  intention 653.1
  meaning 545.2
  motif 901.7
  picture 574.14
  plan 654.1
  story element 608.9
  stratagem 735.3
  trick 618.6
  work of art 574.11
  v. create 167.13
  intend 653.4
  picture 574.20
  plan 654.9
**designate**
  appoint 780.10
  indicate 568.18
  name 583.11
  nominate 637.19
  specify 80.11
**designation**
  appointment 780.2
  indication 568.1
  kind 61.3
  name 583.3
  naming 583.2
  nomination 637.8
  specification 80.6

**designed**
  intentional 653.9
  planned 654.13
**designer** planner 654.7
  producer 167.8
  stylist 579.9
**designing**
  n. arts 574.1
  adj. cunning 735.12
  scheming 654.14
**desirable**
  advisable 670.5
  likable 634.30
  pleasant 863.6
  suitable 637.24
  welcome 925.12
**desire**
  n. hope 888.1
  intention 653.1
  love 931.1
  request 774.1
  sexual desire 419.5
  thing desired 634.11
  will 621.1
  wish 634
  v. be eager 635.7
  be hopeful 888.7
  intend 653.4
  lust 419.22
  request 774.9
  will 621.1
  wish 634.14
**desirous**
  amorous 931.24
  eager 635.9
  wanting 634.21
**desirous of**
  anxious for 634.22
  envious 954.4
**desist**
  v. cease 144.6
  discontinue 668.4
  give up 633.7
  interj. cease! 144.14
**desk**
  church part 1042.13
  table 216.15
  workplace 719.1
**desolate**
  v. cause unpleasant-
    ness 864.12
  depopulate 310.16
  destroy 693.10
  make grieve 872.19
  adj. barren 166.4
  disconsolate 872.28
  forlorn 924.11
  wretched 866.26
**desolated**
  heartbroken 872.29
  ruined 693.28
**desolating**
  destructive 693.26
  unpleasant 864.23
**desolation** agony 864.4
  depopulation 310.3
  despair 866.6
  destruction 693.1
  forlornness 924.4
  sorrowfulness 872.12
  wasteland 166.2

**despair**
  n. desperation 889.2
  sadness 872.3
  wretchedness 866.6
  v. be despondent
    872.16
  be hopeless 889.10
**despatch, despatched**
  see dispatch etc.
**desperado**
  criminal 986.10
  killer 409.11
  ruffian 943.3
**desperate**
  hopeless 889.12
  in trouble 731.24
  mad 473.30
  reckless 894.8
**desperately**
  hopelessly 889.17
  recklessly 894.11
  violently 34.23
**desperation** 889.2
**despicable** bad 675.9
  contemptible 915.12
  offensive 864.18
  paltry 673.18
**despise** disdain 966.3
  reject 638.2
  scorn 793.4
**despised** disliked 867.9
  rejected 638.3
**despite**
  n. contempt 966.1
  defiance 793.1
  disrespect 965.2
  spite 939.6
  prep. regardless of
    33.9
**despiteful**
  hateful 930.8
  hostile 929.10
  spiteful 939.19
**despoil** degrade 692.14
  destroy 693.10
  plunder 824.16
  seduce 989.20
  strip clean 822.24
  work evil 675.6
**despoliation**
  destruction 693.1
  evil 675.3
  plundering 824.5
**despond**
  be hopeless 889.10
  despair 872.16
**despondency**
  despair 889.2
  sadness 872.3
**despondent**
  despairing 872.22
  hopeless 889.12
**despot** 749.14
**despotic**
  governmental 741.17
  imperious 739.16
**despotism**
  absolutism 741.9
  tyranny 741.10
**dessert** course 307.10
  delicacy 308.8

**devastate**
depopulate 310.16
destroy 693.10
**devastating**
destructive 693.26
gorgeous 900.19
**devastation**
depopulation 310.3
destruction 693.1
**develop**
become larger 197.5
create 167.13
disclose 556.4
evolve 148.5
expatiate 593.7
get better 691.7
grow 197.7
improve 691.10
increase 38.6
make larger 197.4
make perfect 677.5
manifest 555.5
mature 126.9
process photos
577.15
result 154.5
train 562.14
**developed**
complete 56.9
finished 677.9
grown 197.12
improved 691.13
mature 126.13
**developer**
planner 654.7
processing solution
577.13
**developing** 148.8
**develop into** 145.17
**development**
evolution 148.1
expatiation 593.6
genesis 169.6
growth 197.3
improvement 691.2
increase 38.1
maturation 126.6
music 462.24
result 154.1
story element 608.9
training 562.3
**developmental** 593.15
**deviant**
n. nonconformist 83.3
pervert 419.18
adj. changed 139.9
devious 291.7
eccentric 474.4
erroneous 518.16
nonconforming 83.5
oblique 219.13
sexual 419.32
wrong 959.3
**deviate**
n. pervert 419.18
v. be changed 139.5
be unorthodox
1025.8
deflect 291.5
depart from 291.3
detour 321.6
differ from 16.5

**digress** 593.9
err 518.9
oblique 219.9
**deviating**
circuitous 321.7
devious 291.7
different 16.7
nonuniform 18.3
**deviation**
abnormality 85.1
change 139.1
circuitousness 321.1
detour 321.3
difference 16.1
digression 593.4
distortion 249.1
divergence 299.1
eccentricity 474.1
inaccuracy 518.2
inconstancy 18.1
indirect course 291
nonconformity 83.1
obliquity 219.1
**device** audio 344.29
automatic 349.29
character 581.1
cleaning 681.32
electrical 342.36
electronic 343.20
expedient 670.2
figure of speech
551.1
heraldic insignia
569.2
instrument 658.3
instrumentality 658.2
means 658.1
motto 517.4
photosensitive 343.22
plan 654.1
pretext 649.1
sign 568.2
signature 583.10
story element 608.9
stratagem 735.3
tactic 735.4
tool 348.1
trick 618.6
**devil**
n. bad person 986.2
dust storm 403.13
enemy 929.6
evildoer 943.3
evil spirit 1016.7
mischief-maker 738.3
monster 943.6
printer 603.12
rascal 986.3
reckless person 894.4
violent person 162.9
v. annoy 866.13
cook 330.4
**Devil, the** 1016.2,3
**devil dog**
combatant 800.27
marine 276.4
**devilish** cruel 939.24
diabolic 1016.18
hellish 1019.8
mischievous 738.6
terrible 675.10
wicked 981.13

**devil-may-care**
nonchalant 858.15
reckless 894.8
unconcerned 636.7
**devilment**
annoyance 866.2
malice 939.5
mischief 738.2
**devilry** malice 939.5
mischief 738.2
Satanism 1016.15
wickedness 981.4
**Devil's Island** 761.8
**devil to pay, the**
penalty 1009.1
predicament 731.4
**devil worship**
idolatry 1033.1
Satanism 1016.15
**devious**
circuitous 321.7
complex 46.4
deviant 291.7
dishonest 975.16
oblique 219.13
shrewd 467.15
**devise**
n. bequest 818.10
v. bequeath 818.18
create 167.10
originate 167.13
plan 654.9
**devising** creation 167.5
manufacture 167.3
**devitalize**
sicken 686.47
unman 158.12
weaken 160.10
**devitalized**
unmanned 158.19
weakened 160.18
**devoid** nonexistent 2.7
vacant 187.13
wanting 662.13
**devolve**
change hands 817.4
commission 780.9
**devote**
busy oneself 656.10
dedicate 816.11
destine 640.7
sanctify 1026.5
spend 665.13
**devoted** destined 640.9
engrossed 530.17
faithful 974.20
friendly 927.20
loving 931.25
obedient 766.3
observant 768.4
pious 1028.8
resolute 624.11
sanctified 1026.8
unselfish 979.5
zealous 635.10
**devotee** believer 1028.4
desirer 634.12
fanatic 473.17
votary 635.6
**devote oneself to**
attend to 530.5
be determined 624.8

busy oneself with
656.11
espouse 968.13
practice 705.7
undertake 715.3
**devotion**
dedication 816.4
duty 962.1
fidelity 974.7
friendship 927.7
love 931.1
piety 1028.1
resolution 624.1
sanctification 1026.3
unselfishness 979.1
worship 1032.1
zeal 635.2
**devotions**
prayer 1032.4
worship 1032.8
**devour**
be credulous 502.6
destroy 693.10
eat 307.20
enjoy 865.10
gluttonize 994.4
ingest 306.11
**devouring**
n. eating 307.1
adj. greedy 634.27
**devout**
believing 501.21
observant 768.4
pious 1028.8
worshipful 1032.15
zealous 635.10
**dew**
n. dewdrops 392.4
v. moisten 392.12
**dewy** immature 124.10
moist 392.15
new 122.7
**dewy-eyed** 535.24
**Dexedrine** 687.9,52
**dexter**
adj. right 243.4
adv. rightward 243.7
**dexterity**
intelligence 467.2
rightness 243.2
skill 733.1
**dexterous**
intelligent 467.14
right-handed 243.5
skillful 733.20
**dextral** 243.4
**dextro–** 243.4
**dextrous**
right-handed 243.5
skillful 733.20
**dharma** 5.3
**dhoti** 231.19
**diabetes** 686.19
**diabetic** 686.57
**diabolic(al)**
cruel 939.24
devilish 1016.18
terrible 675.10
wicked 981.13
**diabolism**
Satanism 1016.15
sorcery 1035.2

**diabolize**
bewitch 1036.9
demonize 1016.17
**diacritical** 16.9
**diacritical mark**
586.15,19
**diadem** circle 253.2
jewel 901.6
royal insignia 569.3
**diaeresis** meter 609.9
separation 49.5
**diagnose**
interpret 552.9
treat 689.30
**diagnosis**
interpretation 552.1
judgment 494.5
medical diagnosis
689.13
**diagnostic**
differentiative 16.9
indicative 568.23
interpretative 552.14
**diagonal**
n. line 568.6
oblique 219.7
straight line 250.2
adj. transverse 219.19
**diagram**
n. outline 48.4
picture 574.14
plan 654.3
representation 572.1
v. plot 654.11
portray 574.20
represent 572.6
**diagrammatic** 654.15
**dial** measure 490.11
telephone 560.18
**dialect**
n. diction 588.1
idiom 580.7
language 580.1
adj. linguistic 580.20
**dialectic**
discussion 597.7
logic 482.2
**dialectic(al)**
argumentative 482.19
logic 482.22
**dialectical materialism**
communism 745.5
materialism 376.5
**dialectics** 482.2
**dialogue**
conversation 597.3
discussion 597.7
stage show 611.4
**dialysis** 53.2
**dialyze** 53.4
**diameter** bisector 92.3
middle 69.1
size 195.1
straight line 250.2
thickness 204.3
**diametric(al)** 15.7
**diamond**
gem stone 384.13
good person 985.1
good thing 674.5
hardness 356.6
playground 878.12

playing cards 878.17
**diamond in the rough**
good person 985.1
raw material 721.5
unshaped 247.2
**Diana** goddess 1014.5
moon goddess 375.12
**diapason**
harmony 462.3
interval 463.20
organ stop 465.22
range 179.2
register 463.6
tuning fork 465.25
**diaper** 231.19
**diaphanous**
lucid 335.31
thin 205.16
transparent 339.4
**diaphony** 461.1
**diaphragm**
abdomen 193.3
contraceptive 687.23
loudspeaker 450.8
middle 69.1
partition 237.5
**diarist** author 602.15
chronicler 608.11
chronologist 114.10
**diarrhea**
defecation 311.2
disease symptom
686.8
indigestion 686.28
**diary**
autobiography 608.4
chronicle 114.9
periodical 605.10
record book 570.11
**diaspora** 75.3
**diastole**
distension 197.2
pulse 137.3
**diathermic** 328.31
**diathermy** 689.6
**diathesis** heredity 170.6
nature 5.3
tendency 174.1
trait of character
525.3
**diatonic scale** 463.6
**diatribe** berating 969.7
speech 599.2
**dibble** fish 655.10
plant 413.18
**dice**
n. die 515.9
v. cube 96.3
**diced** 251.9
**dicey** chance 156.15
hazardous 697.10
uncertain 514.15
**dichotomy**
bisection 92.1
duality 90.1
separation 49.2
**dichromatic**
coloring 362.15
variegated 374.9
**dick** detective 781.11
policeman 699.16
**dicker** 827.17

**dickering** 827.3
**dicotyledon**
plant 411.3
seed plants 412.6
**dictate**
n. axiom 517.2
command 752.1
law 998.3
maxim 517.1
precept 751.1
v. command 752.9
dominate 741.15
necessitate 639.8
oblige 756.5
prescribe 752.10
**dictator** 749.14
**dictatorial**
arrogant 912.11
governmental 741.17
imperious 739.16
**dictatorship**
absolutism 741.9
directorship 747.4
government 741.4
mastership 739.7
**diction** phrase 585.2
speech 588
**dictionary**
lexicon 605.7
word list 88.4
**dictum**
affirmation 523.1
axiom 517.2
decree 752.4
judgment 494.5
maxim 517.1
precept 751.2
remark 594.4
**didactic** advisory 754.8
educational 562.19
poetic 609.17
prescriptive 751.4
**didactics** 562.1
**diddle** cheat 618.17
copulate 419.23
dally 708.13
deceive 618.13
waste time 708.12
**diddle away** 854.5
**die**
n. base 216.8
dice 515.9
engraving tool 578.9
model 25.6
v. be destroyed 693.23
burn out 332.8
cease to exist 2.5
decease 408.19
decline 692.20
disappear 447.2
end 70.6
fail 725.15
pass 119.6
**die away**
burn out 332.8
cease to exist 2.5
decrease 39.6
disappear 447.2
end 70.6
recede 297.2
**die down** 268.8

**diehard**
conservative 140.4
obstinate person
626.6
oppositionist 791.3
rightist 745.9
**die hard**
be determined 624.8
be obstinate 626.7
persevere 625.6
stand fast 792.4
**die-hard**
conservative 140.8
right-wing 745.17
**die is cast, the** 639.20
**dielectric**
n. electric conduction
342.13
adj. nonconducting
342.33
**die out**
become extinct
408.26
burn out 332.8
cease to exist 2.5
disappear 447.2
**dieresis** see diaeresis
**diesel fuel** 380.4
**diet**
n. council 755.1
legislature 742.1
meeting 74.2
nutrition 309.11
v. eat 307.18
go on a diet 309.17
slenderize 205.13
**dietary** 309.21
**dietetic** dietary 309.21
eating 307.29
**dietetics** diet 309.11
dietotherapeutics
309.14
**dieting** diet 309.11
eating 307.1
**dietitian**
hospital staff 688.14
nutritionist 309.13
**differ**
be inharmonious
795.8
disagree 27.5
dissent 522.4
diversify 18.2
not resemble 21.2
quarrel 795.11
vary 16.5
**difference**
abnormality 85.1
change 139.1
disaccord 795.2
disagreement 27.1
dissent 522.1
dissimilarity 21.1
heraldic insignia
569.2
inequality 31.1
nonuniformity 18.1
product 86.5
remainder 42.8
unlikeness 16
**different**
abnormal 85.9

differing 16.7
dissimilar 21.4
distinct 80.12
eccentric 474.4
new 122.11
nonuniform 18.3
**differential**
n. characteristic 80.4
difference 16.2
gear 348.6
adj. classificational
61.7
differentiative 16.9
discriminating 492.7
numerical 86.8
**differentiate**
characterize 80.10
discriminate 492.5
distinguish 16.6
diversify 18.2
graduate 29.4
signify 568.17
**differentiation**
characterization 80.8
differencing 16.4
discrimination 492.3
inconstancy 18.1
indication 568.1
mathematics 87.4
particularity 80.1
**differently**
dissimilarly 21.7
diversely 16.10
**different story** 16.3
**differing** different 16.7
disaccordant 795.15
disagreeing 27.6
dissenting 522.6
unwilling 623.5
**difficult** adverse 729.13
fastidious 896.10
hard 731.16
hard to understand
549.14
perverse 626.11
**difficulties**
adversity 729.1
poverty 838.1
**difficulty**
abstruseness 549.2
adversity 729.1
annoyance 866.2
disagreement 795.2
handicap 730.6
obstacle 730.4
trouble 731
**diffidence** demur 623.2
doubt 503.2
fearfulness 891.3
irresolution 627.3
modesty 908.2
**diffident**
demurring 623.7
fearful 891.31
irresolute 627.11
modest 908.10
**diffraction**
deflection 291.2
dispersion 75.1
wave phenomenon
323.4

**diffuse**
v. deflect 291.5
disperse 75.4
loosen 51.3
pervade 186.7
publish 559.10
radiate 299.6
shatter 49.13
spread 271.9
adj. copious 593.11
deviant 291.8
dispersed 75.9
extensive 79.13
plentiful 661.7
**dig**
n. gibe 967.2
hit 283.4
pit 257.4
push 283.2
v. deepen 209.8
drudge 716.14
emotionally respond
855.12
excavate 257.15
harvest 413.19
search 485.30
study 564.12
thrust 283.11
till 413.17
understand 548.7
**digest**
n. abridgment 607.1
inventory 60.4
law code 998.5
v. absorb 306.13
assimilate 309.16
classify 61.6
consider 478.12
consume 666.2
endure 861.7
learn 564.7
legalize 998.9
think over 478.13
understand 548.7
**digestible** 309.19
**digestion**
consumption 666.1
learning 564.2
nutrition 309.8
pulping 390.3
sorption 306.6
**digestive juice** 312.2
**diggings** mine 383.6
pit 257.4
quarters 191.3
**dig in** fortify 799.9
remain firm 624.9
**dig into** 485.22
**digit** finger 425.5
foot 212.5
number 86.1
**digital** grasping 813.9
numerical 86.8
**dignified**
eloquent 600.14
stately 905.12
**dignify** formalize 646.5
honor 914.12
**dignitary** 672.8
**dignity**
eloquence 600.6
formality 646.1

literary elegance
589.1
notability 672.2
personage 672.8
prestige 914.4
pride 905.2
**digress** detour 321.6
deviate 291.3
wander 593.9
**digression**
circuitousness 321.1
departure 593.4
detour 321.3
deviation 291.1
obliquity 219.1
**digressive**
circuitous 321.7
devious 291.7
discursive 593.13
oblique 219.13
**digs** 191.3
**dig up** assemble 74.18
be curious 528.3
find 488.4
procure 811.10
unearth 305.10
**dike**
n. barrier 730.5
body of water 398.1
crack 201.2
deposit 383.7
fortification 799.4
road 657.6
trench 263.2
v. excavate 257.15
groove 263.3
**dilapidated**
disintegrated 53.5
old 123.14
ramshackle 692.35
slovenly 62.15
unsteady 160.16
**dilapidation**
decay 692.6
disintegration 53.1
impairment 692.1
**dilate**
become larger 197.5
bulge 256.10
expatiate 593.7
make larger 197.4
**dilation**
distension 197.2
exaggeration 617.1
expatiation 593.6
swelling 256.4
**dilatory**
dawdling 270.11
delaying 132.17
indolent 708.18
reluctant 623.6
**dilemma** choice 637.3
perplexity 514.3
predicament 731.6
syllogism 482.6
**dilettante**
connoisseur 897.7
devotee 635.6
half scholar 476.6
ignoramus 477.8
specialist 81.3
trifler 673.9

**diligence**
attention 530.1
industry 707.6
painstakingness 533.2
perseverance 625.1
studiousness 564.4
**diligent**
attentive 530.15
industrious 707.22
painstaking 533.11
persevering 625.7
studious 564.17
**diligently**
carefully 533.15
industriously 707.27
perseveringly 625.8
**dilly** 674.7
**dillydally** dally 708.13
dawdle 270.8
wait 132.12
**diluent** 391.4
**dilute** adulterate 44.13
dissipate 75.5
rarefy 355.3
reduce 39.8
thin 205.12
weaken 160.11
**diluted** insipid 430.2
thin 205.16
watery 355.4
weakened 160.19
**diluvium** deposit 43.2
sediment 271.8
**dim**
v. be dark 337.12
blind 441.7
darken 337.9
decolor 363.5
lose distinctness
445.4
adj. colorless 363.7
darkish 337.15
dim-sighted 440.13
faint-sounding 452.16
indistinct 445.6
obscure 549.15
stupid 469.16
**dime** 835.7
**dime a dozen**
cheap 849.8
paltry 673.18
plentiful 661.7
**dimension** size 195.1
space 179.1
**dime store** 832.1
**dime-store** 849.8
**diminish** decrease 39.6
deteriorate 692.21
extenuate 1006.12
humiliate 906.5
moderate 163.6
narrow 205.11
qualify 507.3
recede 297.2
reduce 39.7
relieve 886.5
subtract 42.9
**diminishing**
decreasing 39.11
moderating 163.14
receding 297.5

**diminution**
  decrease 39.1
  depression 318.1
  moderation 163.2
  reduction 42.2
  relief 886.1
**diminutive**
  *n.* little thing 196.4
  nickname 583.7
  *adj.* miniature 196.12
  nominal 583.15
**dimness**
  colorlessness 363.2
  darkishness 337.4
  faintness of sound
    452.1
  indistinctness 445.2
  opaqueness 341.1
  stupidity 469.3
**dimple**
  *n.* indentation 257.6
  *v.* indent 257.14
**dim recollection** 538.1
**dim-sighted**
  blind 441.9
  dim 440.13
  undiscerning 469.14
**dim view** 969.1
**dimwit** 471.3
**dim-witted** 469.16
**din**
  *n.* noise 453.3
  *v.* noise 453.6
  repeat 103.10
**dine** eat 307.19
  feed 307.16
**diner** dinner 307.6
  eater 307.14
  railway car 272.14
  restaurant 307.15
**ding**
  *n.* ringing 454.3
  *v.* repeat 103.10
  ring 454.8
**dingbat** 471.2
**dingdong**
  *n.* fool 471.2
  regularity 17.2
  repetitiousness 103.4
  ringing 454.3
  *v.* ring 454.8
  *adj.* repetitious 103.15
**dingy** colorless 363.7
  dark 365.11
  dirty 682.22
  gray 366.4
**dining**
  *n.* eating 307.1
  *adj.* eating 307.29
**dining room**
  restaurant 307.15
  room 192.11
**dinky** little 196.10
  tidy 59.8
  unimportant 673.15
**dinner** meal 307.6
  party 922.11
**dinner dress** 231.11
**dinnerware** 831.4
**dinosaur**
  large animal 195.14
  reptile 414.30,60

  types of 123.26
**dint**
  *n.* hit 283.4
  indentation 257.6
  mark 568.7
  power 157.1
  *v.* indent 257.14
**diocese** district 180.5
  see 1037.8
**Dionysus**
  agriculture divinity
    413.4
  fertility god 165.5
  god 1014.5
  intoxication 996.2
  patron of drama
    611.31
**diorama** picture 574.13
  spectacle 446.7
**dip**
  *n.* bath 681.9
  candle 336.2
  declivity 219.5
  immersion 320.2
  pickpocket 825.2
  pit 257.2
  reduction 42.2
  *v.* color 362.13
  drench 392.14
  fly 278.49
  immerse 320.7
  incline 219.10
  ladle 271.16
  perform rites 1040.20
  signal 568.22
**diphtheria** 686.12
**diphthong** 594.13
**dip into** browse 564.13
  examine cursorily
    485.25
**diploma**
  certificate 570.6
  grant 777.5
**diplomacy**
  foreign policy 744.5
  Machiavellianism
    735.2
  skill 733.1
**diplomat** envoy 781.6
  expert 733.11
  Machiavellian 735.8
**diplomatic**
  ambassadorial 781.16
  cunning 735.12
  political 744.43
  skillful 733.20
**diplomatic corps** 781.7
**diplomatic immunity**
  762.8
**dipping**
  *n.* immersion 320.2
  *adj.* sloping downward
    219.16
**dipsomania**
  addiction 642.9
  alcoholism 996.3
  psychosis 473.3,36
**dipsomaniac**
  addict 642.10
  alcoholic 996.10
**diptych** picture 574.12
  record book 570.11

**dire** bad 675.9
  disastrous 729.15
  horrid 864.19
  ominous 544.17
  terrible 891.38
  unfortunate 729.14
**direct**
  *v.* address 604.14
  advise 754.5
  call attention to
    530.10
  command 752.9
  give directions 290.7
  govern 741.12
  influence 172.8
  manage 747.8
  music 462.46
  operate 164.5
  pilot 275.14
  point 290.6
  teach 562.11
  *adj.* artless 736.5
  candid 974.17
  continuous 71.8
  elegant 589.6
  exact 516.16
  in plain style 591.3
  intelligible 548.10
  lineal 170.14
  straight 250.6
  straightforward
    290.13
  unaffected 902.7
  *adv.* straight 290.24
**direct current** 342.2
**directed** 290.14
**directing**
  directive 747.12
  governing 741.19
**direction**
  address 604.10
  advice 754.1
  bearing 290
  directive 752.3
  drama production
    611.14
  government 741.1
  instructions 562.6
  management 747
  motivation 648.2
  operation 164.1
  pointer 568.4
  precept 751.1
  teaching 562.1
  trend 174.2
**directional** 290.14
**direction finder**
  aviation instrument
    278.61
  compass 748.9
  radar 346.4
**directive**
  *n.* direction 752.3
  *adj.* advisory 754.8
  aimed 290.14
  commanding 752.14
  managing 747.12
  motivating 648.25
**direct line**
  ancestry 170.4
  straight line 250.2

**directly**
  candidly 974.23
  exactly 516.20
  promptly 131.15
  soon 131.16
  straight 250.7
  unaffectedly 902.11
  unswervingly 290.24
**directness**
  artlessness 736.1
  candor 974.4
  intelligibility 548.2
  literary elegance
    589.1
  plain speech 591.1
  straightness 250.1
  unaffectedness 902.2
**director**
  businessman 830.1
  governor 749.5
  manager 748
  music 464.17
  theater man 611.28
**directorate**
  directors 748.11
  directorship 747.4
  the rulers 749.15
**directorship**
  directorate 747.4
  mastership 739.7
  supremacy 36.3
**directory** council 755.1
  directorate 748.11
  guidebook 748.10
  information 557.1
  reference book 605.6
  register 570.9
**dire necessity** 639.4
**dirge**
  *n.* funeral rites 410.4
  funeral song 875.5
  Mass 1040.9
  poem 609.6
  song 462.13
  *v.* lament 875.8
**dirigible** 280.11,18
**dirt** grime 682.6
  land 385.1
  obscenity 990.4
  scandal 558.8
**dirt cheap** 849.8
**dirt-free** 681.25
**dirtied** 682.21
**dirty**
  *v.* blemish 679.6
  dirty up 682.15
  *adj.* bad 675.8
  base 915.12
  cloudy 404.7
  cursing 972.8
  dingy 365.11
  evil 981.15
  lascivious 989.29
  muddy 389.14
  obscene 990.9
  stormy 403.26
  unclean 682.22
**dirty language** 972.3
**dirty look**
  disapproval 969.8
  resentment 952.2
**dirty old man** 989.11

dirty politics 744.14
dirty trick
  dishonesty 975.6
  trick 618.6
dirty word 972.4
dirty work
  dishonesty 975.6
  drudgery 716.4
Dis
  deity of nether world
    1019.5
  god 1014.5
disability disease 686.1
  inability 158.2
  penalty 1009.2
disable cripple 692.17
  incapacitate 158.9
  sicken 686.47
disabled
  crippled 692.32
  incapacitated 158.16
  weakened 160.18
disabuse 520.2
disabused 520.5
disaccord
  *n.* difference 16.1
  disagreement 27.1
  dissent 522.1
  enmity 929.2
  nonconformity 83.1
  opposition 790.2
  unharmoniousness
    795
  *v.* be inharmonious
    795.8
  differ 16.5
  disagree 27.5
disaccordant
  different 16.7
  disagreeing 27.6
  opposing 790.8
  unfriendly 929.9
  unharmonious 795.15
disaccustom 643.2
disaccustomed 643.4
disadvantage
  *n.* impediment 730.6
  inexpedience 671.2
  penalty 1009.2
  trouble 731.3
  *v.* harm 675.6
  inconvenience 671.4
disadvantaged
  indigent 838.8
  inferior 37.6
disadvantaged, the
  the poor 838.3
  the underprivileged
    919.6
disadvantageous
  harmful 675.12
  inexpedient 671.6
disaffected
  alienated 929.11
  averse 867.8
  unfaithful 975.20
disaffection
  dislike 867.1
  falling-out 795.4
  infidelity 975.5
disaffinity
  bad feeling 855.7

disaccord 795.1
dislike 867.1
enmity 929.1
repulsion 289.1
disaffirm 524.4
disaffirmation 524.2
disagree
  be inharmonious
    795.8
  conflict 16.5
  differ 27.5
  dissent 522.4
  not be good for
    684.4
  reject 776.3
disagreeable
  disagreeing 27.6
  irascible 951.19
  unkind 939.14
  unpleasant 864.17
  unsavory 429.5
disagreeableness
  unkindness 939.1
  unpleasantness 864.1
disagreeing
  clashing 27.6
  different 16.7
  disaccordant 795.15
  dissenting 522.6
  unwilling 623.5
disagreement
  contrariety 15.1
  difference 16.1
  disaccord 795.2
  disapproval 969.1
  discord 27
  dissent 522.1
  nonconformity 83.1
  refusal 776.1
  unwillingness 623.1
disallow deny 524.4
  disapprove 969.10
  not pay 842.6
  prohibit 778.3
  refuse 776.3
disappear
  absent oneself 187.8
  be destroyed 693.23
  be invisible 445.3
  be transient 111.6
  cease to exist 2.5
  hide oneself 615.8
  leave 301.8
  pass 119.6
  vanish 447.2
disappearance
  absence 187.4
  disappearing 447
  flight 631.4
  invisibility 445.1
disappoint
  defeat expectation
    541.2
  disillusion 520.2
  dissatisfy 869.4
  make hopeless 889.11
disappointed
  disapproving 969.22
  discontented 869.5
  disillusioned 520.5
  let down 541.5

disappointing
  not up to expectation
    541.6
  unsatisfactory 869.6
disappointment
  dashed hopes 541
  disapproval 969.1
  discontent 869.1
  disillusionment 520.1
  hopelessness 889.5
disapproval
  disapprobation 969
  dislike 867.1
  disparagement 971.1
  dissent 522.1
  rejection 638.1
  resentment 952.1
disapprove
  disfavor 969.10
  reject 638.2
  stigmatize 915.9
disapproved 638.3
disapprove of
  disapprove 969.10
  dislike 867.3
  disparage 971.8
  grimace 867.5
disarm
  demilitarize 804.11
  render powerless
    158.11
disarmament 804.6
disarming 936.18
disarrange
  agitate 324.10
  derange 63.2
  discontinue 72.3
  dislocate 185.5
  disorder 62.9
disarranged
  confused 63.5
  dislocated 185.9
  disorderly 62.13
disarrangement
  derangement 63
  dislocation 185.1
  disorder 62.1
disarray
  *n.* disorder 62.1
  *v.* disarrange 63.2
  undress 232.7
disarticulate
  disjoint 49.16
  dislocate 185.5
  separate 49.9
disarticulated
  separated 49.21
  unordered 62.12
disassemble
  demolish 693.17
  take apart 49.15
disassembly
  demolition 693.5
  dismantlement 49.6
disassociation
  separation 49.1
  unrelatedness 10.1
disaster fatality 409.8
  misfortune 729.2
  ruin 693.4
  upheaval 162.5

disastrous
  calamitous 729.15
  convulsive 162.22
  destructive 693.26
disavow deny 524.4
  recant 628.9
disavowal denial 524.2
  recantation 628.3
disband
  demilitarize 804.11
  disperse 75.8
  part company 49.19
disbandment
  demilitarization
    804.6
  dispersion 75.3
disbar depose 783.4
  dismiss 310.19
disbarment
  deposal 783.2
  ejection 310.4
disbelief
  nonreligiousness
    1031.5
  unbelief 503.1
  uncertainty 514.2
disbelieve
  be incredulous 504.3
  be irreligious 1031.14
  unbelieve 503.5
disbelieving
  atheistic 1031.19
  unbelieving 503.8
disburden
  disembarrass 732.8
  lighten 353.6
  relieve 886.7
  take from 822.21
  unload 310.22
disbursal
  apportionment 816.2
  expenditure 843.1
  payment 841.1
disburse
  apportion 816.8
  spend 843.5
disc record 570.10
  sound recording
    450.12
discard
  *n.* abandoned thing
    633.4
  disuse 668.3
  elimination 77.2
  rejection 638.1
  *v.* abandon 633.5
  eject 310.13
  reject 638.2
  throw away 668.7
discarded
  abandoned 633.8
  disproved 506.7
  disused 668.11
  rejected 638.3
discarnate
  ghostly 1017.8
  immaterial 377.7
discern detect 488.5
  know 475.12
  see 439.12
  understand 548.8

**discernible**
discoverable 488.10
knowable 475.25
manifest 555.8
visible 444.6
**discerning**
discriminating 492.8
sagacious 467.16
**discernment**
discrimination 492.2
sagacity 467.4
vision 439.1
**discharge**
n. accomplishment 722.1
acquittal 1007.1
detonation 456.3
dismissal 310.5
dispatch 705.2
ejection 310.1
electric discharge 342.6
emergence 303.2
eruption 310.7
excrement 311.3
excretion 311.1
execution 771.5
exemption 762.8
explosion 162.7
outflow 303.4
payment 841.1
performance 768.1
pus 388.3
receipt 844.2
release 763.2
relief 886.2
shot 285.5
v. accomplish 722.4
acquit 1007.4
blast 456.8
carry out 768.3
disband 75.8
dismiss 310.19
eject 310.13
erupt 162.12
excrete 311.12
execute 771.10
exempt 762.14
expel 310.24
explode 162.13
exude 303.15
free 886.6
pay in full 841.13
perform 705.8
release 763.5
shoot 285.13
unload 310.22
**discharged**
accomplished 722.10
paid 841.22
**discharge tube** 343.11,16
**disciple** believer 1028.4
convert 145.7
follower 293.2
man 787.8
religious founder 1022.2
student 566.2
**disciples** 788.5
**disciplinarian** 749.14

**disciplinary**
educational 562.19
punishing 1010.25
scientific 475.28
**discipline**
n. government 741.1
limitation 234.2
orderliness 59.3
punishment 1010.1
science 475.10
self-control 624.5
sphere of work 656.4
strictness 757.1
study 562.8
training 562.3
v. be strict 757.4
conform 82.3
govern 741.12
limit 234.5
punish 1010.10
train 562.14
**disciplined**
limited 234.7
patient 861.9
**disclaim** deny 524.4
recant 628.9
refuse 776.3
reject 638.2
**disclaimer** denial 524.2
recantation 628.3
refusal 776.1
**disclose** indicate 568.17
inform 557.8
manifest 555.5
reveal 556.4
say 594.23
testify 505.10
unclose 265.13
uncover 488.4
**disclosed**
manifest 555.10
open 265.18
revealed 556.9
visible 444.6
**disclosive**
manifestative 555.9
revealing 556.10
**disclosure**
appearance 446.1
discovery 488.1
impartation 554.2
indication 568.1
manifestation 555.1
revelation 556
testimony 505.3
**discolor** blemish 679.6
decolor 363.5
mark 568.19
**discoloration**
decoloration 363.3
mark 568.5
stain 679.2
**discolored**
blemished 679.10
colorless 363.7
**discombobulate**
confuse 532.7
excite 857.13
**discomfit**
confuse 532.7
defeat 727.9
dismay 891.27

embarrass 866.15
thwart 730.15
**discomfited**
defeated 727.14
disorderly 62.13
distressed 866.22
**discomfiture**
confusion 532.3
defeat 727.2
disappointment 541.1
disorder 62.1
frustration 730.3
mortification 866.4
**discomfort**
n. distressfulness 864.5
pain 424.1
unpleasure 866.1
v. cause unpleasantness 864.14
distress 866.16
**discommode**
inconvenience 671.4
trouble 731.12
**discompose**
agitate 324.10
annoy 866.13
bewilder 514.12
confuse 532.7
disarrange 63.4
disorder 62.9
embarrass 866.15
excite 857.13
give no pleasure 866.12
**discomposed**
agitated 324.16
bewildered 514.23
confused 532.12
disorderly 62.13
distressed 866.22
excited 857.21
**discomposure**
agitation 324.1
confusion 532.3
disarrangement 63.1
disorder 62.1
mortification 866.4
perplexity 514.3
unpleasure 866.1
**disconcert**
bewilder 514.12
confuse 532.7
dismay 891.27
embarrass 866.15
excite 857.13
mortify 864.13
thwart 730.15
**disconcerted**
bewildered 514.23
confused 532.12
disorderly 62.13
distressed 866.22
**disconcerting**
bewildering 514.25
frightening 891.36
frustrating 730.20
mortifying 864.21
**disconnect** 49.9
**disconnected**
discontinuous 72.4

incoherent 51.4
irregular 138.3
separated 49.21
unrelated 10.5
**disconnection**
discontinuity 72.1
psychology 690.27
separation 49.1
unrelatedness 10.1
**disconsolate**
hopeless 889.12
inconsolable 872.28
wretched 866.26
**disconsonant** 461.4
**discontent**
n. disapproval 969.1
dissatisfaction 869
ill humor 951.1
resentment 952.1
unhappiness 872.2
unpleasure 866.1
v. dissatisfy 869.4
give no pleasure 866.12
**discontented**
disapproving 969.22
dissatisfied 869.5
ill-humored 951.17
unhappy 872.21
**discontinuance**
cessation 144.1
disuse 668.2
interruption 72.1
**discontinue**
break the habit 643.3
cease 144.6
cease to use 668.4
interrupt 72.3
swear off 992.8
**discontinued**
discontinuous 72.4
disused 668.10
**discontinuity**
change 139.1
dislocation 185.1
gap 57.2
interruption 72
interval 201.1
irregularity 138.1
separation 49.1
**discontinuous**
disconnected 51.4
interrupted 72.4
irregular 138.3
separate 49.20
unordered 62.12
**discord** disaccord 795.1
disagreement 27.1
dissonance 461
noise 453.3
raucousness 458.2
**discordant**
clashingly colored 362.20
contrary 15.6
different 16.7
disaccordant 795.15
disagreeing 27.6
dissonant 461.4
**discothèque** 878.11
**discount**
n. price reduction 847

humiliation 906.2
iniquity 981.3
wrong 959.2
v. dishonor 915.8
disparage 971.8
humiliate 906.4
**disgraced** 915.13
**disgraceful** evil 981.16
shameful 915.11
wrong 959.3
**disgruntle** 869.4
**disgruntled**
disapproving 969.22
discontented 869.5
**disguise**
n. camouflage 618.10
concealment 615.2
costume 231.9
dissimilarity 21.1
fakery 616.3
v. conceal 615.6
falsify 616.16
make dissimilar 21.3
misrepresent 573.3
outfit 231.40
**disguised**
camouflaged 615.13
clothed 231.44
unseen 445.5
**disgust**
n. dislike 867.2
v. cause dislike 867.6
offend 864.11
repel 429.4
**disgusted** hating 930.7
pleasureless 866.20
sick of 664.6
**disgusting** bad 675.9
base 915.12
filthy 682.23
offensive 864.18
**dish**
n. food 308.7,58
receptacle 193.6
serving 307.10
v. be concave 257.12
ladle 271.16
make concave 257.13
ruin 693.11
thwart 730.15
**dishabille** 231.20,57
**disharmonious**
disaccordant 795.15
disagreeing 27.6
dissonant 461.4
**disharmony**
disaccord 795.1
disagreement 27.1
disorder 62.1
dissonance 461.1
**dishearten**
daunt 891.26
dissatisfy 869.4
make sad 872.18
prevent 730.14
**disheartened** 872.22
**disheartening**
depressing 872.30
frightening 891.36
unsatisfactory 869.6
**dishevel**
disarrange 63.2

disorder 62.9
**disheveled** 62.14
**dishonest**
dishonorable 975.16
falsehearted 616.31
insincere 616.32
untruthful 616.34
**dishonesty**
falseheartedness 616.4
fraud 618.8
improbity 975.1
untruthfulness 616.8
**dishonor**
n. disrepute 915.1
disrespect 965.1
improbity 975.1
nonpayment 842.1
v. desecrate 1030.4
disgrace 915.8
not pay 842.6
offend 965.4
**dishonorable**
dishonest 975.16
disreputable 915.10
**dishonorable discharge** 310.5
**dish out** give 818.12
ladle 271.16
**dishpan** 681.12
**dish the dirt** 558.12
**dishwasher**
washer 681.15
washing equipment 681.12,32
**dishwater**
dirtiness 682.9
refuse 669.4
weakness 160.7
**disillusion**
n. disapproval 969.1
disenchantment 520.1
v. disappoint 541.2
disenchant 520.2
**disillusioned**
disappointed 541.5
disapproving 969.22
disenchanted 520.5
**disillusionment**
disappointment 541.1
disapproval 969.1
disenchantment 520
**disincarnate**
dematerialize 377.6
spiritualize 1034.20
**disincarnation**
dematerialization 377.5
occultism 1034.19
**disinclination**
dislike 867.1
unwillingness 623.1
**disincline** 652.4
**disinclined**
averse 867.8
unwilling 623.5
**disinfect** 681.24
**disinfectant**
n. antiseptic 687.21,59
poison 676.3

adj. antiseptic 687.43
**disinfected** 681.27
**disinfection** 681.3
**disingenuous**
dishonest 975.18
insincere 616.32
specious 483.10
**disinherit** 822.23
**disinheritance** 822.7
**disintegrate**
become disordered 62.8
be damaged 692.26
be destroyed 693.22
come apart 49.8
crumble 361.10
decay 692.25
decompose 53.3
demolish 693.17
disband 75.8
pulverize 361.9
show fragility 360.3
strike dead 409.18
weaken 160.9
**disintegrating**
decomposing 53.5
deteriorating 692.46
weak 160.15
**disintegration**
decay 692.6
decomposition 53
destruction 693.1
disbandment 75.3
disorder 62.1
disruption 49.3
frailty 160.2
pulverization 361.4
**disinter** exhume 305.11
find 488.4
**disinterest**
n. apathy 856.4
impartiality 976.4
incurious 529.1
unconcern 636.2
unselfishness 979.1
v. disincline 652.4
**disinterested**
apathetic 856.13
impartial 976.10
incurious 529.3
unconcerned 636.7
unprejudiced 526.12
unselfish 979.5
**disinvolve**
disembarrass 732.8
extricate 763.7
simplify 45.5
**disjoin** change 16.6
discontinue 72.3
disintegrate 53.3
loosen 51.3
separate 49.9
**disjoint**
come apart 49.16
dislocate 185.5
separate 49.9
**disjointed**
dislocated 185.9
separated 49.21
**disjunct**
separated 49.21
unordered 62.12

unrelated 10.5
**disjunction**
differentiation 16.4
discontinuity 72.1
disintegration 53.1
disorder 62.1
elimination 77.2
noncohesion 51.1
relationship 9.1
separation 49.1
unrelatedness 10.1
**disjunctive**
n. part of speech 586.3
adj. alternative 637.22
discontinuous 72.4
disintegrative 53.5
separating 49.25
**disk** circle 253.2
layer 227.2
rotator 322.4
**disk jockey** 344.23
**dislike**
n. distaste 867
hate 930.1
unpleasure 866.1
v. hate 930.6
not care for 867.3
**disliked** 867.9
**dislocate**
disarrange 63.2
displace 185.5
unhinge 49.16
**dislocated**
disorderly 62.13
displaced 185.9
separated 49.21
**dislocation**
disarrangement 63.1
displacement 185
separation 49.1
**dislodge** displace 185.6
evict 310.15
extricate 763.7
remove 271.10
**disloyal**
apostate 628.11
unfaithful 975.20
**disloyalty**
apostasy 628.2
infidelity 975.5
**dismal** funereal 410.22
gloomy 872.24
gray 366.4
hopeless 889.12
pessimistic 889.16
uninteresting 883.6
unpleasant 864.20
**dismantle**
demolish 693.17
disassemble 49.15
undress 232.7
**dismay**
n. fear 891.1
v. bewilder 514.12
disconcert 891.27
distress 864.14
**dismayed**
bewildered 514.23
cowardly 892.10
frightened 891.33

**dismaying**
  bewildering 514.25
  frightening 891.36
  unpleasant 864.20
**dismember**
  tear apart 49.14
  torture 1010.18
**dismembered** 49.23
**dismiss** acquit 1007.4
  depose 783.4
  disband 75.8
  discharge 310.19
  disregard 531.4
  refute 506.5
  reject 638.2
  release 763.5
  send away 310.18
  send packing 289.3
  slight 966.6
**dismissal**
  acquittal 1007.1
  deposal 783.2
  disbandment 75.3
  discharge 310.5
  rejection 638.1
  release 763.2
  repulse 289.2
**dismissed**
  disproved 506.7
  rejected 638.3
**dismount**
  descend 316.7
  disassemble 49.15
  unseat 185.6
**disobedience**
  insubordination 767
  lawlessness 740.1
  refusal 776.1
  unwillingness 623.1
**disobedient**
  insubordinate 767.8
  lawless 740.5
  refusing 776.6
  unwilling 623.5
**disobey** 767.6
**disoblige**
  inconvenience 671.4
  offend 965.4
**disobliging** 939.16
**disorder**
  *n.* agitation 324.1
  confusion 532.3
  disarrangement 63.1
  disease 686.1
  disorderliness 62
  dissolution 51.1
  formlessness 247.1
  lawlessness 740.2
  misbehavior 738.1
  nonuniformity 18.1
  vagueness 514.4
  *v.* confuse 62.9
  deform 247.3
  disarrange 63.2
  sicken 686.47
**disordered**
  confused 532.12
  disarranged 63.5
  disorderly 62.13
  neurotic 690.45
  unordered 62.12
  vague 514.18

**disorderly**
  formless 247.4
  in disorder 62.13
  lawless 740.6
  misbehaving 738.5
  nonuniform 18.3
  violent 162.18
**disorderly conduct**
  738.1
**disorganization**
  confusion 532.3
  decay 692.6
  destruction 693.1
  disarrangement 63.1
  disbandment 75.3
  disintegration 53.1
  disorder 62.1
  lawlessness 740.2
**disorganize**
  confuse 532.7
  disarrange 63.2
  disband 75.8
  disintegrate 53.3
  disorder 62.9
**disorganized**
  confused 532.12
  disorderly 62.13
  lawless 740.6
**disorient** 532.7
**disorientation**
  confusion 532.3
  direction 290.5
  insanity 473.1
  thought disturbance
  690.24
**disoriented**
  bewildered 514.23
  insane 473.25
**disown** deny 524.4
  dispossess 822.23
  recant 628.9
  reject 638.2
**disowned**
  outcast 926.10
  rejected 638.3
**disownment**
  denial 524.2
  dispossession 822.7
  recantation 628.3
  rejection 638.1
**disparage**
  deprecate 969.12
  depreciate 971.8
  disdain 966.3
  disrespect 965.3
  reduce 42.9
  stigmatize 915.9
  underestimate 498.2
**disparagement**
  contempt 966.1
  deprecation 969.2
  depreciation 971
  disrespect 965.1
  reduction 42.2
  stigma 915.6
  underestimation
  498.1
**disparager** 971.6
**disparaging**
  condemnatory 969.23
  derogatory 971.13
  disrespectful 965.5

**disparate** different 16.7
  dissimilar 21.4
  unequal 31.4
**disparity**
  difference 16.1
  disagreement 27.1
  dissent 522.1
  dissimilarity 21.1
  inequality 31.1
  misunderstanding
  795.2
**dispassion** apathy 856.4
  impartiality 976.4
  inexcitability 858.1
  moderation 163.1
  unconcern 636.2
  unfeeling 856.1
**dispassionate**
  impartial 976.10
  inexcitable 858.10
  moderate 163.13
  unconcerned 636.7
  unfeeling 856.9
  unprejudiced 526.12
**dispassionately**
  inexcitably 858.16
  justly 976.11
  moderately 163.17
  unconcernedly
  636.10
  unfeelingly 856.14
**dispatch**
  *n.* accomplishment
  722.1
  information 557.1
  killing 409.1
  letter 604.2
  message 558.4
  performance 705.2
  promptness 131.3
  quickness 707.3
  speed 269.1
  *v.* accomplish 722.4
  eat 307.20
  hasten 709.4
  kill 409.13
  mail 604.13
  perform 705.8
  send 271.14
**dispatched** 722.10
**dispatcher** 274.13
**dispel** disappear 447.2
  dissipate 75.5
  do away with 310.20
  part company 49.19
**dispensable**
  apportionable 816.12
  justifiable 1006.14
  superfluous 663.17
  unimportant 673.15
**dispensary**
  drugstore 687.36
  hospital room 192.25
**dispensation**
  administration 747.3
  apportionment 816.2
  dispersion 75.1
  divine function
  1013.16
  government 741.1
  permission 777.1
  privilege 958.4

**relinquishment** 814.1
**dispense**
  apportion 816.8
  disperse 75.4
  give 818.12
  permit 777.9
  vend 829.9
**dispense with**
  exempt 762.14
  not use 668.5
  relinquish 814.3
**dispersal**
  disbandment 75.3
  dislocation 51.1
  disruption 49.3
  scattering 75.1
**disperse**
  apportion 816.8
  deflect 291.5
  disappear 447.2
  disband 75.8
  loosen 51.3
  part company 49.19
  radiate 299.6
  scatter 75.4
  shatter 49.13
  spread 197.6
**dispersed**
  deflected 291.8
  scattered 75.9
  separated 49.21
  unordered 62.12
**dispersion**
  apportionment 816.2
  deflection 291.2
  disappearance 447.1
  disbandment 75.3
  dislocation 51.1
  expansion 197.1
  radiating 299.2
  scattering 75
**dispirit** 872.18
**dispirited** bored 884.10
  dejected 872.22
**dispiriting** 872.30
**displace**
  come after 117.3
  depose 783.4
  dislocate 185.5
  dismiss 310.19
  remove 271.10
  substitute for 149.5
**displaced** 185.9
**displaced person**
  alien 78.3
  exile 185.4
  fugitive 631.5
  migrant 274.5
  outcast 926.4
**displacement**
  defense mechanism
  690.30
  deposal 783.2
  depth 209.6
  dislocation 185.1
  removal 271.2
  substitution 149.1
  transformation 139.2
**display**
  *n.* appearances 446.2
  false front 240.1
  manifestation 555.2

publication 559.1
radar signal 346.11
show 904.4
spectacle 446.7
type style 603.23
*v.* evidence 505.9
flaunt 904.17
indicate 568.17
make public 559.11
manifest 555.5
**displease**
be unpleasant 864.10
dissatisfy 869.4
**displeased** averse 867.8
disapproving 969.22
discontented 869.5
**displeasing**
unlikable 867.7
unpleasant 864.17
unsatisfactory 869.6
unsavory 429.5
**displeasure**
disapproval 969.1
discontent 866.1
dislike 867.1
resentment 952.1
unhappiness 872.2
unpleasantness 864.1
**disport** 878.25
**disposable** 666.5
**disposal**
administration 747.3
apportionment 816.2
arrangement 60.1
discard 668.3
elimination 77.2
order 59.1
property transfer 817.1
relinquishment 814.1
**dispose** allocate 184.10
apportion 816.8
distribute 60.9
govern 172.8
incline 290.8
induce 648.22
influence 172.7
order 59.4
tend 174.3
**disposed**
arranged 60.14
inclined to 174.6
minded 525.8
willing 622.5
**dispose of**
accomplish 722.4
complete 70.7
discard 668.7
eat 307.20
eliminate 77.5
give away 818.21
kill 409.13
perform 705.8
put an end to 693.12
refute 506.5
relinquish 814.3
**disposition**
administration 747.3
apportionment 816.2
arrangement 60.1
battle array 797.6
control 739.5

elimination 77.2
government 741.1
nature 5.3
order 59.1
placement 184.5
plan 654.1
property transfer 817.1
relinquishment 814.1
temperament 525.3
tendency 174.1
will 621.1
**dispossess** evict 310.15
take from 822.23
**dispossession**
deprivation 822.7
eviction 310.2
loss 812.1
**disproof** denial 524.2
disproving 506
**disproportion**
disorder 62.1
distortion 249.1
inconsistency 27.2
inequality 31.1
**disproportionate**
disagreeing 27.6
exaggerated 617.4
inconsistent 27.8
unequal 31.4
unordered 62.12
**disprove** deny 524.4
invalidate 506.4
**disproved** 506.7
**disputable** 514.16
**disputant**
arguer 482.12
combatant 800.1
oppositionist 791.3
**disputatious**
argumentative 482.19
contentious 951.26
quarrelsome 795.17
resistant 792.5
**dispute**
*n.* argumentation 482.4
contention 796.1
quarrel 795.5
questioning 485.11
resistance 792.1
*v.* argue 482.16
be doubtful 503.6
deny 524.4
fight over 796.22
object 522.5
offer resistance 792.3
quarrel 795.11
**disputed**
contradicted 506.7
doubted 503.12
**disqualification**
inability 158.2
unpreparedness 721.1
**disqualified**
disabled 158.16
unfit 721.9
**disqualify**
invalidate 158.10
make impossible 510.6

**disquiet**
*n.* agitation 324.1
anxiety 890.1
excitement 857.4
trepidation 891.5
unpleasure 866.1
*v.* agitate 324.10
distress 866.16
excite 857.13
frighten 891.23
give no pleasure 866.12
trouble 890.3
**disquieted**
agitated 324.16
anxious 890.6
distressed 866.22
excited 857.21
frightened 891.33
**disquieting**
exciting 857.28
frightening 891.36
worrisome 890.9
**disregard**
*n.* defiance 793.1
forgiveness 947.1
inattention 531.1
neglect 534.1
nonobservance 769.1
rejection 638.1
snub 966.2
unconcern 636.2
*v.* be broad-minded 526.7
be inattentive 531.2
condone 947.4
disobey 767.6
endure 861.7
flout 793.4
neglect 534.6
not observe 769.3
reject 638.2
relax conditions 507.5
slight 966.6
**disregarded**
forgiven 947.7
neglected 534.14
**disregardful**
careless 534.11
defiant 793.7
inattentive 531.6
inconsiderate 939.16
nonobservant 769.5
unconcerned 636.7
**disrepair**
impairment 692.1
uselessness 669.1
**disreputable** 915.10
**disreputable person** 986.1
**disrepute** 915
**disrespect**
*n.* disapproval 969.1
irreverence 965
*v.* not respect 965.3
**disrespectful**
discourteous 937.4
impudent 913.9
irreverent 965.5
**disrobe** 232.7
**disrobed** 232.13

**disrobing** 232.2
**disrupt** shatter 49.13
upset 730.15
**disruption**
destruction 693.1
disorder 62.1
dissolution 49.3
falling-out 795.4
lawlessness 740.2
misbehavior 738.1
**disruptive**
disintegrative 53.5
misbehaving 738.5
**dissatisfaction**
disappointment 541.1
disapproval 969.1
discontent 869.1
dissent 522.1
resentment 952.1
unpleasure 866.1
**dissatisfied**
disappointed 541.5
disapproving 969.22
discontented 869.5
**dissatisfy**
disappoint 541.2
discontent 869.4
**dissect** analyze 48.6
separate 49.17
**dissection** analysis 48.1
separation 49.5
**dissemblance**
fakery 616.3
unlikeness 21.1
**disseminate**
communicate 554.7
disperse 75.4
plant 413.18
publish 559.10
transfer 271.9
**disseminated**
dispersed 75.9
made public 559.17
**dissemination**
dispersion 75.1
planting 413.14
publication 559.1
transference 271.1
**dissension**
disaccord 795.3
disagreement 27.1
dissent 522.1
opposition 790.2
**dissent**
*n.* complaint 875.4
difference 16.1
disaccord 795.3
disagreement 27.1
disapproval 969.1
nonagreement 522
nonconformity 83.1
opposition 792.1
refusal 776.1
religion 1020.9
resistance 178.1
unwillingness 623.1
*v.* conflict 27.5
disagree 522.4
disapprove 969.10
diversify 18.2
not conform 83.4

offer resistance 792.3
refuse 776.3
**dissenter**
  nonconformist 83.3
  Protestant 1020.19
  protester 522.3
**dissenting**
  disapproving 969.22
  dissident 522.6
  nonconforming 83.5
  resistant 792.5
**dissertation** 606.1
**disservice**
  bad deed 939.13
  injustice 977.4
**dissidence**
  disagreement 27.1
  dissension 795.3
  dissent 522.1
**dissident**
  *n.* dissenter 522.3
  oppositionist 791.3
  *adj.* counteractive
    178.8
  disaccordant 795.15
  disagreeing 27.6
  dissenting 522.6
  nonconforming 83.5
**dissimilar**
  different 16.7
  incomparable 491.9
  unlike 21.4
**dissimilarity**
  difference 16.1
  unlikeness 21
**dissipate**
  be intemperate 993.6
  be lost 812.6
  be unchaste 989.19
  disappear 447.2
  dispel 75.5
  squander 854.3
  waste 812.5
**dissipated**
  dispersed 75.9
  intemperate 993.8
  lost 812.7
  reduced 39.10
  unchaste 989.25
  used up 666.4
  wasted 854.9
**dissipation**
  decrease 39.3
  disappearance 447.1
  dispersion 75.1
  intemperance 993.2
  loss 812.2
  prodigality 854.1
  profligacy 989.3
**dissociate**
  disintegrate 53.4
  separate 49.9
**dissociation**
  defense mechanism
    690.30
  disintegration 53.2
  fission 326.8
  mental dissociation
    690.27
  unrelatedness 10.1
**dissolute**
  intemperate 993.8

morally corrupt
  981.14
  unchaste 989.25
**dissolution** death 408.1
  decay 692.6
  decrease 39.3
  destruction 693.1
  disappearance 447.1
  disbandment 75.3
  disintegration 53.1
  disorder 51.1
  disruption 49.3
  liquefaction 391.1
**dissolvable**
  liquefiable 391.9
  separable 49.26
**dissolve**
  cease to exist 2.5
  destroy 693.10
  disappear 447.2
  disband 75.8
  disintegrate 53.3
  dissipate 75.5
  liquefy 391.5
**dissolving**
  liquefying 391.7
  vanishing 447.3
**dissolving agent** 391.4
**dissonance**
  difference 16.1
  disagreement 27.1
  discord 461.1
**dissonant**
  different 16.7
  disagreeing 27.6
  discordant 461.4
**dissuade** 652.3
**dissuasion** 652
**dissuasive** 652.5
**distaff side**
  female line 170.4
  female sex 421.3
  kinsmen 11.2
**distance**
  *n.* length 202.1
  location 184.2
  remoteness 199
  reticence 613.3
  setting 233.2
  unsociability 923.2
  *v.* surpass 36.10
**distant** aloof 912.12
  faint-sounding 452.16
  farfetched 10.7
  incurious 529.3
  remote 199.8
  reticent 613.10
  unsociable 923.6
**distaste**
  disapproval 969.1
  dislike 867.1
  unwillingness 623.1
**distasteful**
  unlikable 867.7
  unpleasant 864.17
  unsavory 429.5
**distemper**
  animal disease 686.38
  disease 686.1
  paint 362.8
**distend**
  become larger 197.5

be elastic 358.4
bulge 256.10
make larger 197.4
**distended**
  bulging 256.14
  corpulent 195.18
  dilated 197.13
  overfull 663.20
**distension**
  expansion 197.2
  overextension 663.7
  stretching 358.2
  swelling 256.4
**distill** boil 329.20
  extract 305.16
  flow out 303.14
  make liquor 996.29
  refine 681.22
  simplify 45.4
  trickle 395.18
  vaporize 401.8
**distillate** content 194.5
  extract 305.8
  result 154.1
**distillation**
  burning 329.5
  content 194.5
  extract 305.8
  extraction 305.7
  outflow 303.5
  product 168.1
  refinement 681.4
  simplification 45.2
  trickle 395.7
  vaporization 401.5
**distilled** 45.7
**distiller** 996.18
**distillery** liquor 996.20
  plant 719.3
**distinct** audible 450.16
  clearly visible 444.7
  different 16.7
  intelligible 548.10
  manifest 555.8
  particular 80.12
  separate 49.20
**distinction**
  characterization 80.8
  difference 16.1
  differentiation 16.4
  discrimination 492.3
  eminence 34.2
  literary elegance
    589.1
  nobility 918.1
  notability 672.2
  nuance 16.2
  repute 914.5
  token of esteem
    916.1
**distinctive**
  audible 450.16
  characteristic 80.13
  classificational 61.7
  differentiative 16.9
  discriminating 492.7
  typical 572.11
**distinctly**
  audibly 450.18
  certainly 513.23
  intelligibly 548.12
  manifestly 555.14

particularly 80.15
visibly 444.8
**distinguish**
  characterize 80.10
  detect 488.5
  differentiate 16.6
  discriminate 492.5
  honor 914.12
  recognize 537.12
  see 439.12
**distinguishable** 475.25
**distinguished**
  characteristic 80.13
  different 16.7
  eminent 34.9
  famous 914.16
  honored 916.9
  notable 672.18
  particular 80.12
  superior 36.12
**distinguishing**
  differentiative 16.9
  discriminating 492.7
  typical 572.11
**distort** blemish 679.4
  contort 249.5
  corrupt 692.14
  deflect 291.5
  deform 247.3
  falsify 616.16
  misinterpret 553.2
  misrepresent 573.3
  prejudice 527.9
  reason speciously
    483.8
**distorted**
  blemished 679.8
  contorted 249.10
  deviant 291.8
  erroneous 518.16
  falsified 616.26
  misinterpreted 553.3
**distortion**
  audio distortion
    450.13
  blemish 679.1
  contortion 249
  deflection 291.2
  error 518.1
  falsification 616.9
  misinterpretation
    553.1
  misrepresentation
    573.1
  parody 573.2
  sophistry 483.1
**distract**
  discompose 63.4
  disincline 652.4
  divert 532.6
  madden 473.23
**distracted**
  bewildered 514.23
  distraught 532.10
  excited 857.23
  inattentive 531.6
**distraction**
  confusion 532
  inattention 531.1
  insanity 473.1
**distraught**
  bewildered 514.23

distracted 532.10
insane 473.25
**distress**
*n.* affliction 866.8
anxiety 890.1
appropriation 822.5
discomfort 866.5
grief 864.5
mortification 866.4
pain 424.1
penalty 1009.3
poverty 838.1
*v.* afflict 866.16
cause unpleasantness
864.14
hurt 424.7
trouble 731.12
work evil 675.6
worry 890.3
**distressed**
afflicted 866.22
pained 424.9
poor 838.7
troubled 731.19
**distressing**
harmful 675.12
painful 424.10
unpleasant 864.20
worrisome 890.9
**distressingly**
sadly 34.21
unpleasantly 864.28
**distribute**
apportion 816.8
deliver 818.13
disperse 75.4
dispose 60.9
publish 559.10
**distributed**
dispersed 75.9
made public 559.17
**distribution**
apportionment 816.2
arrangement 60.1
dispersion 75.1
**distributive**
dispersive 75.11
proportionate 816.13
**distributor**
intermediary 237.4
merchant 830.2
**district**
*n.* area 180.1
location 184.1
region 180.5
*v.* apportion 49.18
**district attorney** 1003.4
**distrust**
*n.* doubt 503.2
jealousy 953.2
suspicion 895.2
*v.* be doubtful 503.6
be jealous 953.3
**distrustful**
doubtful 503.9
jealous 953.4
suspicious 895.9
**disturb** agitate 324.10
annoy 866.13
bewilder 514.12
confuse 532.7
discompose 63.4

disorder 62.9
distress 866.16
excite 857.13
mortify 864.13
trouble 731.12
upset 890.3
**disturbance**
agitation 324.1
anxiety 890.1
commotion 62.4
confusion 532.3
disarrangement 63.1
disorder 62.1
excitement 857.3
mortification 866.4
perplexity 514.3
violence 162.2
**disturbed**
agitated 324.16
annoyed 866.21
anxious 890.6
bewildered 514.23
confused 532.12
disorderly 62.13
distressed 866.22
excited 857.21
neurotic 690.45
psychotic 473.27
**disturbing**
annoying 864.22
bewildering 514.25
exciting 857.28
mortifying 864.21
worrisome 890.9
**disunion**
disagreement 27.1
falling-out 795.4
separation 49.1
**disunite** separate 49.9
sow dissension 795.14
**disunited**
alienated 929.11
separated 49.21
**disuse**
*n.* abandonment
633.1
antiquation 123.3
disusage 668
*v.* discontinue 668.4
**disused**
abandoned 633.8
obsolete 123.15
out of use 668.10
**disvalue** 969.12
**ditch**
*n.* barrier 730.5
channel 396.1
crack 201.2
entrenchment 799.5
trench 263.2
*v.* crash land 278.52
cut 201.4
discard 668.7
evade 631.7
groove 263.3
**ditchwater** 682.9
**ditheism** 1020.5
**ditheistic** 1020.24
**dither**
*n.* cold sensation
333.2
disquiet 857.4

excitement 857.5
nervousness 859.2
shake 324.3
*v.* be cold 333.9
be unintelligent
469.12
be unsure 514.10
blabber 596.5
vacillate 627.8
**ditto**
*n.* copy 24.3
equal 30.4
repeat 103.5
the same 14.3
*v.* agree with 521.9
copy 24.8
duplicate 91.3
equal 30.5
imitate 22.5
repeat 103.7
reproduce 14.6
*adv.* again 103.17
identically 14.9
**ditty** 462.13
**diuretic**
*n.* cleaning agent
681.17
remedy 687.17
*adj.* cleansing 681.28
therapeutic 687.48
**diurnal** 137.8
**diva** lead 612.6
vocalist 464.13
**divagate**
be inattentive 531.3
deviate 291.3
muse 532.9
oblique 219.9
travel 273.22
wander 291.4
**divan** council 755.1
government 742.8
**divaricate**
*v.* deviate 291.3
differ 16.5
diverge 299.5
diversify 18.2
fork 299.7
open 265.12
*adj.* diverging 299.8
nonuniform 18.3
**dive**
*n.* air maneuver
278.13
brothel 989.9
cheapening 849.4
decrease 39.2
disapproved place
191.28
plunge 320.1
saloon 996.19
submergence 275.8
tumble 316.3
*v.* cheapen 849.6
decrease 39.6
deepen 209.8
fly 278.50
plunge 320.6
sail 275.47
swim 275.56
**dive into** begin 68.7
rush into 709.7

set to work 716.15
**diver** plunger 320.4
swimmer 275.12
**diverge**
be changed 139.5
deflect 291.5
deviate 291.3
differ 16.5
disperse 75.4
divaricate 299.5
diversify 18.2
fall out 795.10
oblique 219.9
part company 49.19
**divergence**
abnormality 85.1
change 139.1
deviation 291.1
difference 16.1
disagreement 27.1
dispersion 75.1
dissimilarity 21.1
distance 199.1
divergency 299
eccentricity 474.1
falling-out 795.4
inconstancy 18.1
obliquity 219.1
**divergent**
abnormal 85.9
changed 139.9
different 16.7
disagreeing 27.6
dissimilar 21.4
diverging 299.8
eccentric 474.4
nonuniform 18.3
oblique 219.13
separate 49.20
**divers** different 16.7
diversified 19.4
several 101.7
**diverse** different 16.7
dissimilar 21.4
varied 19.4
**diversification**
change 139.1
differentiation 16.4
multiformity 19.1
nonuniformity 18.1
**diversified**
different 16.7
nonuniform 18.3
varied 19.4
**diversify**
be changed 139.5
change 139.6
differentiate 16.6
multiformity 19.2
vary 18.2
**diversion**
amusement 878.1
attack 798.1
change 139.1
deviation 291.1
distraction 532.1
military tactics 797.9
misuse 667.1
**diversity** change 139.1
difference 16.1
disagreement 27.1
dissent 522.1

documentation
  confirmation 505.5
  evidence 505.1
  record 570.1
documented
  evidential 505.17
  recorded 570.18
dodder age 126.10
  be weak 160.8
doddering aged 126.18
  senile 469.23
  unsteady 160.16
dodge
  n. equivocation 483.4
  evasive action 631.1
  expedient 670.2
  fraud 618.8
  retreat 284.3
  stratagem 735.3
  trick 618.6
  v. avoid 631.8
  equivocate 483.9
  live by one's wits
    735.9
  neglect 534.8
  prevaricate 613.7
  pull back 284.7
  shirk 631.9
  snub 966.7
dodger
  corn bread 308.29
  cunning person 735.6
  deceiver 619.1
  neglecter 534.5
  safety equipment
    699.3
dodging
  equivocation 483.5
  prevarication 613.4
  shirking 631.2
dodo 123.8
doe
  female animal 421.9
  goat 414.8
  hoofed animal 414.5
  rabbit 414.29
doer
  man of action 707.8
  worker 718
doff detach 49.10
  take off 232.6
dog
  n. bad person 986.7
  breeds of 414.72
  canine 414.22
  foot 212.5
  inferior horse 414.14
  male animal 420.8
  ugly thing 899.4
  v. annoy 866.13
  follow 293.3
  hunt 655.9
  make anxious 890.4
  obstruct 730.12
  pursue 655.8
dog days
  hot weather 328.7
  summer 128.3
dog-eared eared 448.16
  folded 264.7
  worn 692.33
dog-eat-dog 945.3

dogface 800.9
dogged obstinate 626.8
  persevering 625.7
  tormented 866.24
  worried 890.7
doggedly
  obstinately 626.14
  perseveringly 625.8
doggerel
  n. poetry 609.5
  adj. burlesque 967.14
  infelicitous 590.2
dogging
  annoyance 866.2
  following 293.1
  pursuit 655.1
doggy 414.45
doghouse
  kennel 191.21
  small place 196.3
dogie
  abandoned thing
    633.4
  animal 414.6
  waif 274.3
  young cow 125.8
dog in the manger
  hinderer 730.9
  selfish person 978.3
dog-in-the-manger 869.5
dogleg angle 251.2
  crookedness 219.8
  deviation 291.1
dogma a belief 501.2
  creed 1023.2
dogmatic
  believing 501.21
  certain 513.22
  doctrinal 501.27
  obstinate 626.8
  orthodox 1024.8
  prejudiced 527.12
  unpersuadable 626.13
dogmatics 1023.1
dogmatism
  obstinacy 626.1
  orthodoxy 1024.5
  unpersuadableness
    626.5
dogmatist
  doctrinaire 513.7
  intolerant person
    527.5
  obstinate person
    626.6
  orthodox 1024.6
dogmatize 513.10
do-gooder 938.8
dog's life, a 729.1
dog tag 568.11
dog-tired 717.8
dogtrot
  n. slowness 270.2
  speed 269.3
  v. go slow 270.6
dogwatch 108.3
dohickey 376.4
do in cheat 618.17
  defeat 727.6
  fatigue 717.4
  kill 409.14

ruin 693.11
doing
  n. act 705.3
  action 705.1
  affair 151.3
  behavior 737.1
  production 167.1
  adj. happening 151.9
doings activity 707.1
  acts 705.3
  affairs 151.4
  behavior 737.1
dojigger 376.4
do justice to
  be just 976.6
  do one's duty 962.10
  eat 307.22
  justify 1006.9
  observe 768.2
dolce 462.54
doldrums calm 268.5
  sadness 872.6
  wind zone 403.10
dole
  n. apportionment
    816.2
  donation 818.6
  part 55.1
  pittance 662.5
  portion 816.5
  small amount 35.2
  subsidy 818.8
  v. apportion 816.8
  give 818.12
doleful pitiful 944.8
  sorrowful 872.26
dolefully 872.36
dolittle 708.8
doll endearment 932.5
  figure 572.4
  girl 125.6
  good person 985.2
  little thing 196.5
  toy 878.16
  woman 421.6
dollar
  British money 835.8
  foreign money 835.9
  US money 835.7
dollhouse
  plaything 878.16
  small place 196.3
doll-like 124.12
dollop 55.3
doll up beautify 900.14
  dress up 231.41
  ornament 901.8
dolly figure 572.4
  narcotic 687.12
dolmen
  memorial 570.12
  tomb 410.16
dolor distress 866.5
  pain 424.1
dolorous
  sorrowful 872.26
  unpleasant 864.20
dolphin
  animal 414.35,64
  mammal 415.8
dolt bungler 734.8
  dunce 471.3

doltish 469.15
domain class 61.4
  country 181.1
  real estate 810.7
  region 180.2
  science 475.10
  sphere of work 656.4
dome
  n. arch 252.4
  head 211.6
  tower 207.11
  v. cover 228.21
  curve 252.6
domestic
  n. servant 750.2
  adj. home 191.32
  recluse 924.9
domesticate
  accustom 642.11
  settle 184.16
  tame 764.11
domesticated
  subdued 764.15
  tame 191.34
  weak 765.15
domesticity 191.2
domestic science 330.1
domicile
  n. abode 191.1
  v. house 188.10
  inhabit 188.7
dominance
  ascendancy 739.6
  influence 172.1
dominant
  n. key 463.15
  note 463.14
  adj. authoritative
    739.15
  chief 36.14
  governing 741.18
  influential 172.14
  most important
    672.23
  prevalent 79.12
  victorious 726.8
dominate
  be high 207.16
  govern 741.15
  have influence over
    172.11
  possess authority
    739.13
  prevail 79.10
  subject 764.8
domination
  ascendancy 739.6
  control 741.2
  despotism 741.10
  influence 172.1
  subjection 764.1
  view 444.3
domineer 741.16
domineering
  n. arrogance 912.1
  authoritativeness
    739.3
  despotism 741.10
  adj. arrogant 912.9
  imperious 739.16
**Dominican** 1038.18

**dominion**
 ascendancy 739.6
 control 741.2
 country 181.1
 governance 739.5
 ownership 808.2
 precedence 64.1
 region 180.2
 supremacy 36.3
**don**
 *n.* form of address
  420.7
 teacher 565.1
 *v.* put on 231.42
**Donar**
 Norse deity 1014.6
 thunder god 456.5
**donate**
 contribute 818.14
 give 818.12
 provide 659.7
**donation** gift 818.6
 giving 818.1
**done**
 *adj.* completed 722.11
 cooked 330.7
 ended 70.8
 exhausted 717.8
 produced 167.20
 worn-out 692.38
 *phr.* so be it 521.19
**donee** 819.4
**done for** dead 408.30
 defeated 727.14
 dying 408.33
 no more 2.10
 ruined 693.28
 terminated 70.8
**done with**
 disused 668.10
 ended 70.8
 finished 722.11
**dong** 454.8
**Don Juan** beau 931.12
 deceiver 619.1
 tempter 650.3
 unchaste person
  989.10
**donkey** ass 414.20,58
 dolt 471.3
 obstinate person
  626.6
**donna**
 form of address 421.8
 woman 421.5
**donnish**
 book-learned 475.22
 pedagogical 565.12
 studious 564.17
**donnybrook**
 commotion 62.4
 free-for-all 796.5
 noise 453.3
 quarrel 795.5
**donor** giver 818.11
 provider 659.6
**do nothing** idle 708.11
 not change 140.6
 not stir 706.2
**do-nothing**
 *n.* idler 708.8
 *adj.* indolent 708.18

 passive 706.6
**Don Quixote**
 knight 918.5
 visionary 535.13
**don't** 778.1
**don't make waves** 82.10
**doodad** 376.4
**doodle**
 *n.* fool 471.1
 picture 574.14
 *v.* dally 708.13
 picture 574.20
 play music 462.43
 scribble 602.20
 waste time 708.12
**doodlebug**
 dowsing 543.3
 rocket bomb 281.4
**doom**
 *n.* condemnation
  1008.1
 death 408.1
 end 70.1
 fate 640.2
 judgment 494.5
 ruin 693.2
 the future 121.3
 *v.* condemn 1008.3
 destine 640.7
 pass judgment 494.13
 send to hell 1019.6
 work evil 675.6
**doomed** destined 640.9
 hopeless 889.13
**doomful**
 destructive 693.26
 ominous 544.17
 unfortunate 729.14
**doomsday** 121.3
**do one's duty**
 do what is expected
  962.10
 eat 307.22
**do one's thing**
 act 705.4
 specialize 81.4
**door** entrance 302.6
 opening 265.7
 outlet 303.9
**doorbell** 454.4
**doorjamb**
 entrance 302.6
 post 217.4
**doorkeeper**
 gatekeeper 699.12
 holy orders 1038.4
**doorman** 699.12
**doormat** mat 228.9
 weakling 160.6
**doorpost**
 entrance 302.6
 post 217.4
**doorstop** 730.7
**doorway**
 entrance 302.6
 opening 265.7
**do over** convert 145.11
 repeat 103.7
 reproduce 169.7
**dope**
 *n.* contraband 826.3
 depressant 423.3

 film 577.10
 fuel 331.1
 narcotic 687.5
 stupid 471.3
 *v.* calculate 87.11
 medicate 689.31
 predict 543.9
 put to sleep 712.20
 render insensible
  423.4
 solve 487.2
**dope, the**
 information 557.1
 the facts 1.4
**doped** sleepy 712.21
 unconscious 423.8
**dope fiend** 642.10
**dopey** dazed 532.14
 inert 268.14
 languid 708.19
 stupid 469.16
**Doppelgänger**
 specter 1017.3
 the same 14.3
**do right by** 938.9
**dorm** 191.16
**dormancy**
 inactivity 708.1
 inertness 268.4
 latency 546.1
 passivity 706.1
**dormant** asleep 712.22
 do-nothing 706.6
 inert 268.14
 languid 708.19
 latent 546.5
**dormer** 265.8
**dormitory**
 abode 191.16
 bedroom 192.7
**dorsal** back 241.10
 phonetic 594.31
**dorsi–** 241.3
**dosage** 963.2
**dose**
 *n.* amount 28.2
 medicine 687.6
 portion 55.5
 venereal disease
  686.16
 *v.* impose 963.6
 medicate 689.31
**doss**
 *n.* bed 216.19
 housing 188.3
 sleep 712.2
 *v.* snooze 712.14
**dossier** 570.5
**dot**
 *n.* endowment 818.9
 mark 568.5
 music 463.12
 point 196.7
 small amount 35.2
 spottiness 374.3
 *v.* mark 568.19
 sprinkle 75.6
 variegate 374.7
**dotage** credulity 502.1
 old age 126.5
 senility 469.10
**dotard** old man 127.2

 senile 471.9
**dote** be insane 473.19
 be unintelligent
  469.12
**dote on** 931.18
**do the trick**
 accomplish 722.4
 be expedient 670.3
 be of use 665.17
 succeed with 724.10
**do time**
 be imprisoned 761.18
 spend time 108.5
**doting** aging 126.17
 credulous 502.8
 foolish 470.8
 senile 469.23
**dotted** spotted 374.13
 sprinkled 75.10
**dotty** eccentric 474.4
 insane 473.26
 spotted 374.13
**double**
 *n.* copy 24.3
 fold 264.1
 image 572.3
 specter 1017.3
 substitute 149.2
 the same 14.3
 turn 291.1
 *v.* copy 24.8
 duplicate 91.3
 evade 631.7
 fold 264.5
 increase 38.5
 middle 69.3
 repeat 103.7
 substitute for 149.5
 turn back 295.8
 *adj.* dishonest 975.21
 duplicate 91.4
 falsehearted 616.31
 two 90.6
**double agent**
 secret agent 781.9
 traitor 619.10
**double-check**
 make certain 513.12
 verify 87.14
**double cross** 975.8
**double-cross**
 betray 975.14
 deceive 618.13
**doubled** folded 264.7
 repeated 103.12
**double-dealer**
 criminal 986.10
 deceiver 619.1
 traitor 619.10
**double-dealing**
 *n.* dishonesty 975.6
 falseheartedness
  616.4
 *adj.* dishonest 975.21
 falsehearted 616.31
**double-decker** 272.12
**double Dutch** 549.7
**double-edged**
 acrimonious 161.13
 sharp 258.10
**double entendre**
 ambiguity 550.1

equivocation 550.2
joke 881.6
**double-header** 878.9
**double meaning** 550.1
**double-or-nothing** 515.4
**double personality**
  dissociation 690.27
  pathological type
    690.16
  psychosis 473.4
**double-quick**
  *n.* hastening 709.3
  march 273.15
  *adj.* fast 269.19
  hurried 709.11
  *adv.* fast 269.21
**doubles** 878.9
**doublet** two 90.2
  word 582.2
**double take**
  delay 132.2
  sequel 67.1
**double-talk** 547.2
**doublethink** 90.1
**double time**
  gratuity 818.5
  hastening 709.3
  march 273.15
**double-time**
  *v.* make haste 709.5
  *adj.* hurried 709.11
**doubleton** 90.3
**double vision** 440.1
**doubling** duality 90.1
  duplication 91.1
  fold 264.1
  lining 194.3
  repetition 103.1
**doubloon** 835.4
**doubt**
  *n.* agnosticism 1031.6
  apprehension 891.4
  jealousy 953.2
  skepticism 503.2
  uncertainty 514.2
  *v.* be irreligious
    1031.14
  be jealous 953.3
  be skeptical 503.6
  be uncertain 514.9
**doubted** 503.12
**doubter**
  agnostic 1031.12
  doubting Thomas
    503.4
**doubtful**
  agnostic 1031.20
  dishonest 975.16
  improbable 512.3
  skeptical 503.9
  unbelievable 503.10
  uncertain 514.16
  unsafe 697.11
**doubting**
  skeptical 503.9
  uncertain 514.15
**doubting Thomas**
  agnostic 1031.12
  doubter 503.4
**doubtless**
  *adj.* believing 501.21
  certain 513.16

*adv.* certainly 513.25
  probably 511.8
**doubtlessly**
  certainly 513.25
  probably 511.8
**douche**
  *n.* bath 681.8
  sprinkler 392.8
  washing 681.5
  *v.* moisten 392.12
  soak 392.13
  wash 681.19
**dough** money 835.2
  semiliquid 389.5
  softness 357.4
**doughboy** 800.7
**doughnut** 308.43
**doughy** pasty 390.6
  soft 357.12
  viscous 389.12
**dour** firm 757.7
  strict 757.6
  sullen 951.24
  unkind 939.22
  unyielding 626.9
**douse** extinguish 332.7
  immerse 320.7
  take off 232.6
**dousing**
  extinguishing 332.2
  immersion 320.2
**dove** bird 414.33,66
  innocent person
    984.4
  pacifist 803.6
  unsophisticate 736.3
**dovelike** avian 414.52
  innocent 984.6
  weak 765.15
**dovetail**
  *n.* joint 47.4
  *v.* agree 26.6
  fasten 47.8
  interact 13.8
**dovetailed** 13.12
**dovetailing** 26.10
**dowager** mistress 749.2
  old woman 127.3
  widow 935.4
  woman 421.5
**dowdy** 692.34
**dower**
  *n.* endowment 818.9
  talent 733.4
  *v.* endow 818.17
**do without**
  abstain 992.7
  not use 668.5
  relinquish 814.3
**Dow-Jones Industrial**
  **Average** 833.1
**down**
  *n.* beard 230.8
  descent 316.1
  feather 230.19
  fine texture 351.3
  hill 207.5
  lightness 353.2
  plain 387.1
  reverse 729.3
  softness 357.4
  *v.* bring down 318.5

descend 316.5
  eat 307.20
  endure 861.7
  *adj.* defeated 727.14
  dejected 872.22
  depressing 872.30
  descending 316.11
  laid up 686.55
  lower 208.8
  recorded 570.18
  sick 686.52
  *adv.* downward 316.13
  in cash 841.25
**down-and-out**
  destitute 838.9
  ruined 693.28
**down at the heel**
  indigent 838.8
  shabby 692.34
  slovenly 62.15
**downbeat**
  *n.* beat 137.3
  music 463.26
  *adj.* pessimistic 889.16
**downcast**
  dejected 872.22
  depressed 318.12
  downturned 316.12
**downdraft** 403.1
**downer** adversity 729.1
  dejection 872.3
  difficulty 866.2
  sedative 687.12
**downfall** defeat 727.1
  descent 316.1
  failure 725.3
  rainstorm 394.2
  ruin 693.3
**downgrade**
  *n.* declivity 219.5
  descent 316.1
  *v.* demote 783.3
  reduce 39.7
  *adj.* sloping downward
    219.16
  *adv.* down 316.13
  slantingly 219.23
**downhearted** 872.22
**downhill**
  *n.* declivity 219.5
  *adj.* descending
    316.11
  sloping downward
    219.16
  *adv.* down 316.13
  slantingly 219.23
**down home** 188.16
**down in the mouth**
  872.22
**down pat** 475.26
**downpour**
  descent 316.1
  flow 395.4
  rainstorm 394.2
**downright**
  *adj.* absolute 34.12
  candid 974.17
  thorough 56.10
  unqualified 508.2
  vertical 213.11
  *adv.* down 316.13
  extremely 34.22

unconditionally
  508.3
**Down's syndrome**
  genetic disease
    686.11
  mental deficiency
    469.9
**down the drain**
  no more 2.10
  wasted 854.9
**downtime**
  interim 109.1
  respite 711.2
**down-to-earth** 536.6
**downtown**
  *n.* city district 183.6
  *adj.* urban 183.10
**downtrodden** 764.16
**downturn**
  business cycle 827.9
  decrease 39.2
  descent 316.1
  deterioration 692.3
**down under** 180.6
**downward**
  *adj.* descending
    316.11
  flowing 267.8
  *adv.* down 316.13
**downward trend**
  descent 316.1
  deterioration 692.3
**downwind**
  leeward 242.9
  navigation 275.68
**downy** feathery 230.27
  fine 351.8
  light 353.10
  smooth 260.9
  soft 357.14
**dowry**
  endowment 818.9
  talent 733.4
**doxology** hymn 1032.3
  sacred music 462.16
**doxy** 989.17
**doyen** chief 749.3
  dean 127.5
**doze**
  *n.* sleep 712.2
  *v.* sleep 712.13
**dozen** 99.7
**doze off** 712.16
**DP** alien 78.3
  displaced person
    185.4
  fugitive 631.5
  migrant 274.5
  outcast 926.4
**drab** brown 367.3
  lackluster 337.17
  monotonous 17.6
**drabness** grayness 366.1
  lusterlessness 337.5
**Draconian** 939.24
**Dracula** 891.9
**draft**
  *n.* abridgment 607.1
  demand 753.1
  diagram 654.3
  displacement 209.6
  dose 687.6

drink 307.4
enlistment 780.6
intoxication 996.6
music 462.28
negotiable instru-
  ment 835.11
picture 574.14
pull 286.2
pulling 286.1
recruits 800.17
wind 403.1
written matter 602.10
*v.* enlist 780.16
extract 305.12
outline 654.12
picture 574.20
write 602.19
*adj.* pulling 286.6
**draft animal** 271.6
**draftee** 800.17
**drafting** drawing 574.6
enlistment 780.6
extraction 305.3
**draftsman** 579.3
**drafty** 403.25
**drag**
*n.* annoyance 866.2
attraction 288.1
aviation 278.36
boring person 884.4
burden 352.7
friction 350.5
gait 273.14
hindrance 730.7
influence 172.2
pull 286.2
slowing 270.4
tobacco smoking
  434.10
*v.* attract 288.4
dawdle 270.8
delay 132.8
follow 293.4
go slow 270.6
linger 110.7
pull 286.4
smooth 260.5
trail 215.6
use tobacco 434.14
walk 273.27
**dragged out**
lengthened 202.9
protracted 110.11
**draggle** befoul 682.19
pull 286.4
trail 215.6
**draggled** slovenly 62.15
soiled 682.21
**drag in** impose on 10.4
interpose 237.6
**dragnet** search 485.14
seizure 822.2
snare 618.12
**dragon**
ill-humored person
  951.11
monster 85.20
reptile 414.60
violent person 162.9
**drag on**
be tedious 884.5
continue 143.3

linger 110.7
persist 17.3
**dragoon**
*n.* cavalryman 800.11
*v.* coerce 756.7
intimidate 891.28
**drag out** elicit 305.14
expatiate 593.8
go slow 270.6
lengthen 202.7
postpone 132.9
protract 110.9
**drain**
*n.* channel 396.5
consumption 666.1
demand 753.1
depletion 812.2
filth receptacle
  682.12
outflow 303.4
*v.* consume 666.2
decolor 363.5
deplete 812.5
despoil 822.24
disable 158.9
drain off 822.13
dry 393.6
eject 310.21
emerge 303.13
exploit 665.16
extract 305.12
subtract 42.9
take from 822.21
**drainage** drying 393.3
evacuation 310.6
extraction 305.3
outflow 303.4
**drained** barren 166.4
bleached 363.8
exhausted 717.8
unhealthy 686.50
used up 666.4
weakened 160.18
**draining**
*n.* evacuation 310.6
exhaustion 717.2
extraction 305.3
*adj.* demanding 753.8
deteriorating 692.46
fatiguing 717.11
weakening 160.20
**drake**
male animal 420.8
poultry 414.34
**dram** dose 55.5
drink 307.4
intoxication 996.6
small amount 35.2
unit of weight 352.23
**drama**
representation 572.1
stage show 611.4
theater 611.1
**dramatic** poetic 609.17
show business 611.38
theatrical 904.24
vocal 462.51
**dramatics** display 904.4
theatrics 611.2
**dramatist**
author 602.15
playwright 611.27

**dramatize** affect 903.12
indicate 555.5
play up 672.15
theatricalize 611.33
**dramaturgic(al)** 611.38
**drape**
*n.* cover 228.2
hanging 215.4,13
shade 338.1
*v.* clothe 231.38
hang 215.6
**draper** clothier 231.32
merchant 830.3
**drapery** clothing 231.1
cover 228.2
fabric 378.5
ornamentation
  901.13
pendant 215.13
shade 338.1
**drastic** 162.15
**draught, draughtsman,
  draughty see draft**
  etc.
**draw**
*n.* attendance 186.4
attraction 288.1
equality 30.3
pull 286.2
ravine 201.2
tie 118.2
*v.* acquire 811.8
attract 288.4
constrict 198.7
describe 608.12
equal 30.5
extract 305.12
influence 172.9
lengthen 202.7
lure 650.4
picture 574.20
pull 286.4
receive 819.6
remove 305.10
represent 572.6
use tobacco 434.14
**draw and quarter**
tear apart 49.14
torture 1010.18
**drawback**
disadvantage 671.2
discount 847.1
fault 678.2
obstacle 730.4
**draw back**
flinch 891.21
pull back 284.7
retract 297.3
retreat 295.6
**drawbridge**
bridge 657.10
fortification 799.4
**drawer** sketcher 579.3
storage place 660.6
**draw in** constrict 198.7
involve 176.2
lure 650.4
narrow 205.11
reel in 287.9
retract 297.3
take in 306.12

**drawing**
*n.* art 574.6
diagram 654.3
extraction 305.1
graphic arts 578.1
lottery 515.11
picture 574.14
pulling 286.1
representation 572.1
suction 305.3
*adj.* attraction 288.5
pulling 286.6
**drawing card** 650.2
**drawing room**
parlor 192.5
railway car 272.14
society 644.6
train room 192.10
**drawl**
*n.* regional accent
  594.9
slowness 270.1
*v.* speak poorly 595.7
utter 594.26
**draw lots** 515.18
**drawn equal** 30.7
lengthened 202.9
tired-looking 717.7
**draw near**
approach 296.3
be imminent 152.2
be in the future
  121.6
near 200.7
**drawn-out**
lengthened 202.9
protracted 110.11
**draw on**
be imminent 152.2
be in the future
  121.6
induce 153.12
influence 172.9
lure 650.4
occur 151.6
seduce 931.21
**draw out** elicit 305.14
expatiate 593.8
extract 305.10
lengthen 202.7
protract 110.9
**draw the line**
be unwilling 623.3
discriminate 492.5
express prejudice
  527.8
limit 234.5
**draw up** form 59.5
raise 317.8
stop 144.7
write 602.19
**dray** 272.2
**drayage** charge 846.8
pulling 286.1
transportation 271.3
**dread**
*n.* anxiety 890.1
expectancy 539.3
fear 891.1
unpleasure 866.1
*v.* expect 539.5
fear 891.18

*adj.* terrible 891.38
**dreadful**
 *n.* fictional form
  608.8
 *adj.* awe-inspiring
  964.12
 bad 675.9
 horrid 864.19
 remarkable 34.11
 terrible 891.38
 ugly 899.11
**dreadfully** badly 675.14
 frightfully 891.42
 hideously 899.13
 terribly 34.21
 unpleasantly 864.27
**dream**
 *n.* abstractedness
  532.2
 beautiful person
  900.8
 desire 634.9
 good thing 674.7
 hallucination 519.7
 hope 888.5
 illusion 519.1
 imagination 535.9
 *v.* imagine 535.17
 muse 532.9
 suppose 499.10
**dream analysis** 690.8
**dreamer** 535.13
**dream girl** 931.14
**dreaming**
 *n.* abstractedness
  532.2
 imagination 535.8
 *adj.* abstracted 532.11
 dreamy 535.25
**dreamland**
 illusion 519.1
 paradise 535.11
 sleep 712.2
**dream up** create 167.13
 imagine 535.14
**dreamworld** 519.1
**dreamy**
 abstracted 532.11
 dreamful 535.25
 illusory 519.9
 sleepy 712.21
 tranquilizing 163.15
**dreary** gloomy 872.24
 gray 366.4
 ominous 544.17
 tedious 884.8
 uninteresting 883.6
 unpleasant 864.20
**dredge**
 *n.* excavator 257.10
 *v.* dig up 305.10
 excavate 257.15
 infuse 44.12
 raise 317.8
 sprinkle 75.6
**dredge up**
 assemble 74.18
 dig up 305.10
 raise 317.8
**dregs**
 bad people 986.12
 rabble 919.5

refuse 669.4
 residue 43.2
**drench**
 *n.* drink 307.4
 intoxication 996.6
 soaking 392.7
 *v.* overload 663.15
 soak 392.13
 tend animals 416.7
**drenched**
 intoxicated 996.30
 overfull 663.20
 soaked 392.17
**drenching**
 *n.* soaking 392.7
 *adj.* wetting 392.18
**dress**
 *n.* clothing 231.1,55
 gown 231.16
 insignia 569.1
 suit 231.6
 *v.* clothe 231.38
 equip 659.8
 fertilize 165.8
 groom 681.20
 oil 380.8
 ornament 901.8
 prepare 720.6
 rub 350.8
 smooth 260.5
 till 413.17
 treat 689.30
**dress circle** 611.20
**dress down**
 punish 1010.15
 reprove 969.18
**dressed to kill** 644.13
**dressing**
 agriculture 413.13
 clothing 231.1
 fertilizer 165.4
 medical dressing
  687.33
 polishing 350.2
 reproof 969.6
 stuffing 308.27
**dressing room**
 closet 192.15
 stage 611.21
**dressmaker** 231.35
**dressmaking** 231.31
**dress rehearsal** 611.14
**dress suit** 231.11,48
**dress up** dress 231.41
 falsify 616.16
 ornament 901.8
**dribble**
 *n.* leakage 303.5
 saliva 312.3
 small amount 35.2
 trickle 395.7
 *v.* leak 303.14
 salivate 312.6
 trickle 395.18
**dribble away**
 deplete 812.5
 deteriorate 692.22
 fritter away 854.5
**driblet** 35.2
**dried** 393.9
**dried-up** barren 166.4
 deteriorated 692.37

dried 393.9
 shrunk 198.13
**drier**
 art equipment 574.19
 desiccator 393.4
 paint 362.8
**drift**
 *n.* aviation 278.37
 course 267.2
 deposit 271.8
 deviation 291.1
 direction 290.1
 flock 74.5
 flow 395.4
 meaning 545.1
 pile 74.10
 radio reception
  344.21
 trend 174.2
 *v.* do nothing 706.2
 drift off course
  275.29
 float 275.54
 fly 278.45
 pile 74.19
 stray 291.4
 take it easy 708.14
 wander 273.22
**drift along** 294.3
**drift away** 297.2
**drifter**
 bad person 986.2
 fisher 655.6
 wanderer 274.2
**drifting** flowing 267.8
 wandering 273.36
**drill**
 *n.* exercise 716.6
 point 258.3
 rule 642.5
 study 564.3
 training 562.3
 types of 348.18
 *v.* deepen 209.8
 excavate 257.15
 plant 413.18
 puncture 265.16
 study 564.12
 train 562.14
**drillmaster** 565.7
**drink**
 *n.* alcoholic drink
  996.8
 beverage 308.48
 dram 996.6
 fluid 388.2
 liquor 996.12
 mixed 996.42
 ocean 397.1
 potation 307.4
 types of 308.49
 *v.* ingest 306.11
 quaff 307.27
 sorb 306.13
 tipple 996.23
**drinkable** 307.32
**drink in**
 attend to 530.5
 drink 307.27
 learn 564.7
 sorb 306.13
**drinking vessel** 193.10

**drink to** drink 307.27
 toast 996.28
**drink up** be dry 393.5
 drink 307.27
 imbibe 996.23
 sorb 306.13
**drip**
 *n.* boring person 884.4
 leakage 303.5
 trickle 395.7
 *v.* be damp 392.11
 leak 303.14
 trickle 395.18
**dripping wet** 392.17
**drive**
 *n.* acceleration 269.4
 aggressiveness 707.7
 attack 798.1
 cause 153.10
 desire 634.1
 eloquence 600.3
 flock 74.5
 haste 709.1
 impulse 283.1
 instinct 630.1
 machinery 348.4
 military campaign
  797.7
 power 157.1
 pushing 285.1
 ride 273.7
 road 657.6
 urge 648.6
 vim 161.2
 *v.* attack 798.17
 compel 756.4
 drift off course
  275.29
 drive animals 416.8
 excavate 257.15
 fish 655.10
 fly 278.46
 hunt 655.9
 hustle 707.13
 impel 283.10
 obsess 473.24
 operate 164.5
 push 285.10
 ride 273.32
 set in motion 267.6
 steer 747.9
 task 716.16
 thrust 283.11
**drive a bargain** 827.17
**drive away**
 dissipate 75.5
 repulse 289.3
**drive back**
 fend off 799.10
 repulse 289.3
**drive crazy** 473.23
**drive in** 304.7
**drive-in**
 restaurant 307.15
 theater 611.19
**drivel**
 *n.* nonsense 547.2
 saliva 312.3
 *v.* be insane 473.19
 be unintelligent
  469.12
 salivate 312.6

talk nonsense 547.5
**drive mad** 473.23
**drive on** hasten 709.4
  hustle 707.13
  impel 283.10
  make one's way 294.4
  urge on 648.16
**drive out** 310.14
**driver** coachman 274.9
  male servant 750.4
  motorist 274.10
  operator 164.4
  propeller 285.7
  tyrant 749.14
**driver's seat** 739.10
**drive up the wall**
  866.13
**driveway** 657.6
**driving**
  *n.* operation 164.1
  riding 273.6
  *adj.* aggressive 707.23
  attacking 798.29
  compelling 756.9
  eloquent 600.11
  impelling 283.20
  motivating 648.25
  moving 267.7
  obsessive 473.34
  propulsive 285.15
  rainy 394.10
**driving force**
  impulse 283.1
  pushing 285.1
**drizzle**
  *n.* rain 394.1
  *v.* rain 394.9
**drizzling** 394.10
**droit** 958.3
**droll** humorous 880.4
  witty 881.15
**drome** 278.22
**dromedary**
  beast of burden
  271.6
  hoofed animal 414.5
**drone**
  *n.* bagpipe 465.10
  bee 414.38
  continuity 71.2
  mumbling 595.4
  music 462.22
  nonworker 708.10
  regularity 17.2
  repetitiousness 103.4
  slow person 270.5
  voice 463.5
  *v.* hum 452.13
  persist 17.3
  speak poorly 595.9
**roning**
  *n.* hum 452.7
  mumbling 595.4
  *adj.* humming 452.20
  sounding 450.15
**ool**
  *.* nonsense 547.2
  saliva 312.3
  *.* be insane 473.19
  be unintelligent
  469.12
  salivate 312.6

talk nonsense 547.5
**droop**
  *n.* fall 316.2
  gait 273.14
  hang 215.2
  *v.* be despondent
  872.16
  deteriorate 692.21
  fail 686.45
  get tired 717.5
  hang 215.6
  sink 316.6
  weaken 160.9
**drooping**
  dejected 872.22
  descending 316.11
  deteriorating 692.46
  fatigued 717.6
  hanging 215.10
  languishing 160.21
  loose 51.5
  weak 160.12
**droopy** dejected 872.22
  fatigued 717.6
  hanging 215.10
  languid 708.19
  weak 160.12
**drop**
  *n.* advantage 36.2
  declivity 219.5
  decrease 39.2
  descent 316.1
  deterioration 692.3
  drink 996.6
  gallows 1011.5
  leakage 303.5
  mailbox 604.7
  medicine 687.4
  minute quantity
  196.7
  pause 144.3
  plunge 320.1
  scenery 611.25
  sphere 255.3
  trickle 395.7
  *v.* become exhausted
  717.5
  break the habit 643.3
  decrease 39.6
  descend 316.5
  discontinue 668.4
  faint 423.5
  fell 318.5
  flow out 303.14
  give birth 167.15
  give up 633.7
  gravitate 352.15
  incline 219.10
  let fall 318.7
  lose 812.4
  plunge 320.6
  relinquish 814.3
  reproduce 169.9
  shoot 285.13
  strike dead 409.18
  take off 232.6
  trickle 395.18
  weaken 160.9
**drop by** 922.17
**drop cloth** 228.9
**drop dead** 408.22
**drop in** enter 302.7

visit 922.17
**drop in on** 540.7
**drop in the bucket**
  pittance 662.5
  small amount 35.5
  trifle 673.5
**drop it** cease 144.6
  no matter 673.22
  stop! 144.15
**droplet** drop 255.3
  minute quantity
  196.7
**drop off** decrease 39.6
  descend 316.5
  die 408.20
  go to sleep 712.16
**dropout** 83.3
**drop out**
  abandon 633.5
  dissent 522.4
  not conform 83.4
**droppings** 311.4
**dropsy**
  disease symptom
  686.8
  distension 197.2
**drop the subject** 531.4
**dross** ashes 329.16
  residue 43.2
**drought** dryness 393.1
  thirst 634.7
  want 662.4
**drove**
  *n.* flock 74.5
  *v.* drive animals 416.8
**drover** guider 748.7
  herder 416.3
**drown**
  come to grief 729.10
  die 408.24
  drench 392.14
  submerge 320.7
  suffocate 409.19
  suppress 760.8
**drowned** dead 408.32
  flooded 395.25
  soaked 392.17
  underwater 209.13
**drown out** 453.7
**drowse**
  *n.* sleep 712.2
  *v.* sleep 712.13
**drowsiness**
  languor 708.6
  sleepiness 712.1
**drowsy** sleepy 712.21
  tranquilizing 163.15
**drub**
  *n.* hit 283.4
  stamp 283.9
  *v.* defeat 727.6
  pound 283.14
  punish 1010.14
  stamp 283.19
**drudge**
  *n.* grub 718.3
  servant 750.2
  *v.* be busy 707.10
  persevere 625.3
  serve 750.13
  work hard 716.14
**drudgery** 716.4

**drug**
  *n.* commodity 831.2
  depressant 423.3
  medicine 687.4–32
  types of 687.52–65
  *v.* make unfeeling
  856.8
  medicate 689.31
  put to sleep 712.20
  render insensible
  423.4
**drug addict** 642.10
**drug addiction** 642.9
**drug culture** 642.9
**drugged** languid 708.19
  sleepy 712.21
  unconscious 423.8
  unfeeling 856.9
**druggist** 687.35
**drug pusher** 826.4
**drugstore**
  pharmacy 687.36
  store 832.4
**drugstore cowboy** 442.1
**drug user** addict 642.10
  pathological type
  690.16
**Druid** idolater 1033.4
  pagan priest 1038.16
  predictor 543.4
**drum**
  *n.* cylinder 255.4
  instrument 465.19
  staccato sound 455.1
  *v.* bird sound 460.5
  make staccato sounds
  455.4
  music 462.45
  pulsate 323.12
  rain 394.9
  repeat 103.10
**drumbeat** 455.1
**drumbeating** 559.5
**drum major** 464.17
**drummer**
  percussionist 464.10
  traveling salesman
  830.5
**drumming**
  *n.* hit 283.4
  pulsation 323.3
  staccato sound 455.1
  *adj.* rainy 394.10
  staccato 455.7
**drum out** depose 783.4
  dismiss 310.19
  drive out 310.14
**drumstick** drum 465.19
  fowl part 308.23
  leg 273.16
**drunk**
  *n.* drunkard 996.10
  spree 996.5
  *adj.* fervent 855.23
  intoxicated 996.30
**drunkard** addict 642.10
  bad person 986.2
  drinker 996.10
**drunken** dizzy 532.15
  drinking 996.34
  intoxicated 996.30

**dummy**
  *n.* a nobody 673.7
  deputy 781.1
  dolt 471.3
  fake 616.13
  figure 572.4
  figurehead 749.4
  imitation 22.3
  man 787.8
  model 25.5
  mute 451.3
  nonentity 4.2
  pawn 658.3
  playing cards 878.17
  substitute 149.2
  typesetting 603.2
  *adj.* substitute 149.8
  ungenuine 616.26
**dummy up** 451.6
**dump**
  *n.* armory 801.2
  disapproved place 191.28
  filth receptacle 682.12
  filthy place 682.11
  gibe 967.2
  hoard 660.1
  hovel 191.12
  humiliation 906.2
  indignity 965.2
  refuse heap 682.10
  storage place 660.6
  trash pile 669.6
  *v.* discard 668.7
  humiliate 906.5
  relinquish 814.3
  sell 829.8
  sell stocks 833.24
  unload 310.22
**dumpling** 308.33
**dump on** disdain 966.3
  humiliate 906.5
  offend 965.4
  ridicule 967.9
**dumps**
  ill humor 951.10
  sadness 872.6
**dumpy**
  corpulent 195.18
  dwarf 196.13
  stubby 203.10
**dun**
  *n.* bill 845.3
  creditor 839.4
  horse 414.13
  *v.* bill 845.11
  importune 774.12
  *adj.* brown 367.3
**Dun and Bradstreet**
  rating credit 839.1
  financial condition 836.5
**dunce** dolt 471.3
  ignoramus 477.8
**dunderhead** 471.4
**dune** hill 207.5
**pile** 74.10
**dung** excretion 311.4
  fertilizer 165.4
**dungarees** 231.56
**dungeon** 761.8

**dunghill** 682.10
**dunk** drench 392.14
  immerse 320.7
**dunking**
  immersion 320.2
  soaking 392.7
**dunning**
  *n.* importuning 774.3
  *adj.* importunate 774.18
**duo** part music 462.17
  two 90.2
**duodecimal system** 86.2
**duodenal**
  intestinal 225.10
  twelve 99.24
**duodenum** 225.4
**duologue**
  conversation 597.3
  stage show 611.4
**dupable** 502.9
**dupe**
  *n.* agent 781.3
  copy 24.3
  credulous person 502.4
  gullible person 620
  instrument 658.3
  laughingstock 967.7
  sycophant 907.3
  unsophisticate 736.3
  *v.* copy 24.8
  deceive 618.13
  duplicate 91.3
  gull 470.7
**duplex**
  *n.* apartment house 191.15
  *adj.* double 91.4
  two 90.6
**duplicate**
  *n.* copy 24.3
  doubling 91.1
  image 572.3
  the same 14.3
  *v.* copy 24.8
  double 91.3
  repeat 103.7
  replicate 14.6
  reproduce 169.7
  *adj.* analogous 20.11
  double 91.4
  identical 14.7
**duplicated**
  repeated 103.12
  twin 90.6
**duplication** copy 24.3
  doubling 91
  duality 90.1
  imitation 22.3
  remaking 169.1
  repetition 103.1
  reproduction 24.2
  superfluity 663.4
**duplicity** deceit 618.3
  dishonesty 975.6
  duality 90.1
  falseheartedness 616.4
**durability**
  endurance 110
  permanence 140.1

  perpetuity 112.1
  substantiality 3.1
  toughness 359.1
**durable**
  enduring 110.10
  permanent 140.7
  substantial 3.7
  tough 359.4
**durables** 831.4
**duration**
  durability 110.1
  permanence 140.1
  term 107.3
  time 105.1
**duress** coercion 756.3
  imprisonment 761.3
  necessity 639.1
  power 157.1
**during** 105.14
**dusk**
  *n.* darkishness 337.4
  daylight 335.10
  evening 134.3
  *v.* be dark 337.12
  *adj.* dark 365.9
  darkish 337.15
  evening 134.8
**dusky** dark 365.9
  darkish 337.15
  evening 134.8
**dust**
  *n.* corpse 408.16
  dirt 682.6
  dryness 393.2
  land 385.1
  lightness 353.2
  powder 361.5
  refuse 669.4
  rubbish 669.5
  *v.* clean 681.18
  dirty 682.15
  sprinkle 75.6
**dustbin** 669.7
**dust bowl**
  the country 182.1
  wasteland 166.2
**dustheap** 669.6
**dust storm** 403.13
**dusty** dirty 682.22
  dry 393.7
  gray 366.4
  old 123.14
  powdery 361.11
  tedious 884.8
  uninteresting 883.6
  wayworn 273.40
**Dutch uncle** 754.3
**duteous** dutiful 962.13
  obedient 766.3
  observant 768.4
**dutiful** duteous 962.13
  obedient 766.3
  observant 768.4
  pious 1028.8
  respectful 964.8
**dutifully**
  duteously 962.18
  obediently 766.6
**duty** charge 963.3
  demand 753.1
  function 665.5
  job 656.3

  military service 797.13
  obligation 962
  respect 964.1
  rite 1040.3
  tariff 846.11
  task 656.2
  tax 846.10
  worship 1032.8
**duty-bound** 962.16
**dwarf**
  *n.* fairy 1014.18
  midget 196.6
  small amount 35.2
  *v.* minimize 39.9
  *adj.* little 196.13
**dwarfed**
  deformed 249.12
  meager 662.10
  undersized 196.13
**dwell** continue 110.6
  inhabit 188.7
**dweller** 190.2
**dwell in**
  be present 186.6
  exist in 1.11
**dwelling**
  *n.* abode 191.1
  habitation 188.1
  *adj.* resident 188.13
**dwell on**
  emphasize 672.13
  harbor revenge 956.5
  harp upon 884.7
  protract 110.9
  remember 537.13
  repeat 103.9
**dwindle** decrease 39.6
  disappear 447.2
  fail 686.45
  quiet 268.8
  recede 297.2
**dwindling**
  *n.* decrease 39.2
  *adj.* decreasing 39.11
  deteriorating 692.46
  quiescent 268.12
  receding 297.5
**dyad** 90.2
**dybbuk**
  evil spirit 1016.7
  specter 1017.1
**dye**
  *n.* coloring matter 362.8
  types of 362.22
  *v.* color 362.13
  infuse 44.12
**dyed** 362.16
**dyed-in-the-wool**
  confirmed 642.21
  dyed 362.17
  established 142.13
  thorough 56.10
**dying**
  *n.* death 408.1
  decrease 39.1
  deterioration 692.3
  extinguishing 332.2
  terminal case 408.15
  *adj.* expiring 408.33
  receding 297.5

**Easter** 1040.15
**easterly**
  *n.* wind 403.9
  *adj.* eastern 290.15
  *adv.* east 290.18
**Easterner** 190.11
**easy**
  *adj.* at ease 887.12
  cheap 849.7
  comfortable 887.11
  contented 868.7
  eloquent 600.9
  facile 732.12
  good-natured 938.14
  gullible 502.9
  indolent 708.18
  informal 647.3
  lax 758.4
  leisurely 710.6
  lenient 759.7
  light 353.11
  loose 51.5
  nonchalant 858.15
  pleased 865.12
  polished 589.6
  prosperous 728.12
  slow 270.10
  soft 357.8
  unchaste 989.26
  *adv.* cautiously 895.12
  *interj.* caution 895.14
**easy come, easy go**
  854.8
**easygoing**
  careless 534.11
  contented 868.7
  dilatory 132.17
  free 762.20
  informal 647.3
  lax 758.4
  lenient 759.7
  nonchalant 858.15
  unconcerned 636.7
**easy going** 732.1
**easy mark** 620.1
**Easy Street** 728.1
**eat** consume 666.2
  corrode 692.24
  endure 861.7
  etch 578.11
  feed 307.18
  ingest 306.11
**eat away** erode 692.24
  subtract 42.9
**eat crow**
  humble oneself 906.6
  recant 628.9
  submit 765.11
**eat, drink, and be merry**
  carouse 993.6
  go on a spree 996.27
  make merry 878.27
  make no provision
    721.7
**eating**
  *n.* feeding 307
  ingestion 306.4
  *adj.* feeding 307.29
**eat one's heart out**
  872.17
**eat one's words** 628.9
**eats** 308.2

**eat up**
  be credulous 502.6
  consume 666.2
  eat 307.20
  enjoy 865.10
  feast 307.22
**eau de Cologne** 436.3
**eaves** 228.6
**eavesdrop** 448.11
**eavesdropper**
  curious person 528.2
  listener 448.5
**eavesdropping** 448.2
**ebb**
  *n.* decrease 39.2
  deterioration 692.3
  standstill 268.3
  tide 395.13
  *v.* decline 692.20
  decrease 39.6
  flow 395.16
  move 267.5
  quiet 268.8
  recede 297.2
**ebb and flow**
  *n.* alternation 323.5
  tide 395.13
  *v.* alternate 323.13
  billow 395.22
  fluctuate 141.5
**ebb tide** low tide 208.2
  tide 395.13
**ebony**
  *n.* black 365.4
  blackness 365.1
  tree 411.50
  wood 378.9
  *adj.* black 365.8
  dark 337.13
**ebullient** bubbly 405.6
  excited 857.18
  hot 328.25
  lively 707.17
**ebullition**
  agitation 324.1
  bubbling 405.3
  excitement 857.3
  heating 329.2
  violence 162.2
**eccentric**
  *n.* erratic 474.3
  odd person 85.4
  *adj.* abnormal 85.9
  erratic 474.4
  humorous 880.4
  inconstant 141.7
  irregular 138.3
  odd 85.11
  off-center 185.12
**eccentricity**
  abnormality 85.1
  foolishness 470.1
  humorousness 880.1
  idiosyncrasy 474
  inconstancy 141.2
  irregularity 138.1
  trait of character
    525.3
**ecclesiastic** 1038.2
**ecclesiastic(al)**
  churchly 1042.15
  ministerial 1037.13

**ecclesiastical insignia**
  569.4
**echelon**
  battle array 797.6
  flight formation
    278.12
  rank 29.2
**echo**
  *n.* answer 486.1
  imitator 22.4
  keyboard 465.20
  music 462.23
  radar signal 346.11
  reaction 284.1
  recurrence 103.1
  reflection 24.7
  repeat 91.2
  reverberation 454.2
  sympathy 855.5
  *v.* agree with 521.9
  answer 486.4
  emotionally respond
    855.12
  imitate 22.5
  radar 346.16
  recur 103.11
  repeat 103.7
  reverberate 454.7
**echo chamber** 454.5
**echoic** answering 486.6
  imitative 22.9
  lexical 582.20
  repetitious 103.14
  representational
    572.10
  reverberating 454.11
**echoing**
  answering 486.6
  repetitious 103.14
  reverberating 454.11
**echo sounding** 209.5
**éclair** 308.40
**eclampsia** seizure 686.5
  spasm 324.6
**eclamptic** 324.19
**éclat** applause 968.2
  brilliancy 904.4
  publicity 559.4
  repute 914.1
**eclectic(al)**
  combined 52.5
  mixed 44.15
  philosophy 500.9
  selective 637.23
**eclipse**
  *n.* covering 228.1
  disappearance 447.1
  occultation 337.8
  *v.* blind 441.7
  conceal 615.6
  cover 228.19
  darken 337.9
  overshadow 36.8
**ecliptic**
  astronomy 375.16
  circle 253.3
**eco-** economic 827.22
  environment 233.1
  habitat 191.5
**ecological**
  ecotopic 13.15
  environmental 233.9

**ecology** biology 406.17
  ecosystem 13.5
  environment 233.4
  zoology 415.1
**economic(al)**
  cheap 849.7
  economics 827.22
  thrifty 851.6
**economically**
  shortly 203.12
  thriftily 851.7
**economics**
  economic science
    827.10
  finance 836.1
**economist**
  economic expert
    827.11
  finance 836.8
  thrifty person 851.3
**economize** 851.4
**economizer** 851.3
**economizing**
  *n.* economization
    851.2
  *adj.* economical 851.6
**economy**
  *n.* economic system
    827.7
  parsimony 852.1
  thrift 851
  *adj.* cheap 849.7
**ecosphere**
  atmosphere 402.2
  biosphere 407.6
  organic matter 406.1
**ecosystem** ecology 13.5
  environment 233.4
**ecru** brown 367.3
  yellow 370.4
**ecstasy**
  amorousness 931.3
  excitement 857.7
  fervor 855.10
  happiness 865.2
  trance 1036.3
**ecstatic** excited 857.23
  overjoyed 865.14
  rapt 532.11
**ectomorph** 690.15
**–ectomy** 689.23
**ectoplasm** cell 406.4
  occultism 1034.7
**ectoplasmic** 1017.7
**ecumenic(al)**
  broad-minded 526.8
  cooperating 786.5
  universal 79.14
**ecumenism**
  broad-mindedness
    526.1
  combination 52.1
  cooperation 786.1
**eczema**
  allergic disorder
    686.32
  skin disease 686.33
**eddy**
  *n.* backflow 395.12
  excitement 857.3
  rotation 322.2
  *v.* surge 395.21

whirl 322.11
**edema**
 disease symptom
  686.8
 distension 197.2
 increase 38.1
 swelling 256.4
**Eden** 535.11
**edentate** 259.4
**edge**
 *n.* acrimony 161.4
 advantage 36.2
 beginning 68.1
 border 235.4
 cutting edge 258.2
 pungency 433.1
 sharpness 258.1
 straight line 250.2
 summit 211.2
 *v.* border 235.10
 go sideways 242.5
 sharpen 258.9
 side 242.4
**edge in** enter 302.7
 interpose 237.6
 intrude 238.5
**edge tool** cutlery 348.2
 sharp edge 258.2
 types of 348.13
**edgewise** 242.8
**edgy** excitable 857.26
 impatient 862.6
 nervous 859.10
**edible**
 *n.* food 308.1
 *adj.* eatable 307.31
**edict**
 announcement 559.2
 decree 752.4
 law 998.3
**edification**
 learning 475.4
 teaching 562.1
**edifice** dwelling 191.6
 structure 245.2
**edificial**
 constructional 167.18
 structural 245.9
**edify**
 make better 691.9
 teach 562.11
**edifying** 562.19
**edit**
 comment upon
  552.11
 delete 42.12
 revise 691.12
 rewrite 602.19
**edition** issue 605.2
 music 462.28
 rendition 552.2
**editor** bookman 605.21
 commentator 606.4
 critic 494.7
 interpreter 552.7
 journalist 605.22
**editorial**
 *n.* commentary 606.2
 *adj.* explanatory
  552.15
 journalistic 605.26
**editorialize** 602.21

**educable** 564.18
**educate**
 make better 691.9
 teach 562.11
**educated**
 improved 691.13
 informed 475.18
 learned 475.21
 taught 564.16
**education**
 cultivation 691.3
 knowledge 475.4
 learning 564.1
 teaching 562.1
**educational**
 informative 557.17
 instructive 562.19
**educational institution**
  567.1
**educator** 565.1
**educe** 305.14
**edulcorate**
 refine 681.22
 sweeten 431.3
**eerie** awesome 920.11
 creepy 891.39
 deathly 408.29
 supernatural 85.15
 weird 1017.9
**eeriness**
 deathliness 408.12
 frighteningness 891.2
 ghostliness 1017.4
 supernaturalism 85.7
**efface** 693.16
**effaced** 538.8
**effect**
 *n.* aspect 446.3
 end 70.1
 influence 172.1
 intention 653.1
 meaning 545.1
 power 157.1
 product 168.1
 result 154
 sequel 117.2
 *v.* accomplish 722.4
 cause 153.11
 create 167.12
 do 705.6
 execute 771.10
 induce 153.12
**effected** 722.10
**effective** able 157.14
 effectual 665.20
 eloquent 600.11
 influential 172.13
 operative 164.9
 powerful 157.12
 practical 670.6
**effectively** ably 157.16
 eloquently 600.15
 powerfully 157.15
 usefully 665.25
**effectiveness**
 eloquence 600.3
 power 157.1
 supremacy 36.3
 utility 665.3
**effects**
 merchandise 831.1
 property 810.1

**effectual** able 157.14
 causal 153.14
 influential 172.13
 operative 164.9
 practical 670.6
 true 516.12
 useful 665.20
**effectuate**
 accomplish 722.4
 cause 153.11
 create 167.12
 do 705.6
 execute 771.10
 produce 167.9
**effeminate**
 bisexual 419.32
 frail 160.14
 womanish 421.14
**effeminize**
 feminize 421.12
 unman 158.12
**effervesce**
 be enthusiastic 635.8
 bubble 405.4
 sibilate 457.2
**effervescence**
 bubbling 405.3
 excitement 857.3
 liveliness 707.2
 sibilation 457.1
**effervescent**
 bubbly 405.6
 excited 857.18
 lively 707.17
 sibilant 457.3
**effete**
 deteriorating 692.46
 ineffective 158.15
 uninteresting 883.6
 used up 666.4
 weak 160.12
 weakened 160.18
 worn-out 692.38
**efficacious** able 157.14
 effectual 665.20
 influential 172.13
 operative 164.9
**efficiency** ability 157.2
 skill 733.1
 utility 665.3
**efficient** able 157.14
 competent 733.22
 effectual 665.20
 operative 164.9
 practical 670.6
**efficiently** ably 157.16
 skillfully 733.29
 usefully 665.25
**effigy** 572.3
**effluent**
 *n.* excrement 311.3
 tributary 395.3
 *adj.* outgoing 303.19
**effluvium**
 miasma 676.4
 occultism 1034.7
 odor 435.1
 vapor 401.1
**efflux** 303.4
**effort** act 705.3
 attempt 714.2
 endeavor 714.1

**exertion** 716.1
 expedient 670.2
 undertaking 715.1
**effortless** 732.12
**effortlessly** 732.15
**effrontery** 913.1
**effuse**
 *v.* emerge 303.12
 excrete 311.12
 exude 303.15
 *adj.* plentiful 661.7
**effusive** diffuse 593.11
 outgoing 303.19
 talkative 596.9
 unrestrained 554.10
**e.g.** 505.24
**egest** excrete 311.12
 vomit 310.25
**egg** embryo 406.15
 food 308.26
 ovum 406.12
 source 153.7
**eggbeater**
 agitator 324.9
 helicopter 280.5
 mixer 44.10
**egg cell** 406.12
**egghead**
 intellectual 476.1
 snob 912.7
**egglike** 406.25
**egg on** 648.16
**eggshell**
 *n.* brittleness 360.2
 egg 406.15
 *adj.* soft-colored
  362.21
 whitish 364.8,11
**egg white**
 albumen 406.15
 semiliquid 389.5
**ego** egotism 909.3
 intellect 466.4
 psyche 690.35
 self 80.5
**egocentric**
 *n.* egotist 909.5
 *adj.* egotistic 909.10
**egotism**
 selfishness 978.1
 vanity 909.3
**egotist**
 selfish person 978.3
 vain person 909.5
**egotistic(al)**
 selfish 978.5
 vain 909.10
**ego trip** ego 909.1
 self-seeking 978.1
**ego-trip**
 self-serving 978.4
 vanity 909.6
**egregious** bad 675.9
 excessive 663.16
 outright 34.12
 remarkable 34.10
 thorough 56.10
**egress**
 *n.* channel 396.1
 departure 301.1
 emergence 303
 evacuation 310.6

exit 303.9
*v.* exit 303.11
**Egyptian deities**
  1014.10
**eiderdown**
  down 230.19
  quilt 228.10
  softness 357.4
**eidetic** 537.23
**eidolon** aspect 446.3
  phantom 519.4
  specter 1017.1
  thing imagined 535.5
**eight** number 99.4
  team 788.7
**eighth**
  *n.* harmonics 463.9
  *adj.* eight 99.20
**eighty-eight** 465.20
**eighty-six** 668.7
**Einstein theory** 179.6
**either**
  *n.* any 79.5
  *adj.* both 90.7
  one 89.7
  *adv.* similarly 20.18
**ejaculate** climax 419.25
  eject 310.24
  exclaim 459.7
**ejaculation**
  ejection 310.7
  exclamation 459.2
  excretion 311.1
**ejaculatory**
  exclamatory 459.11
  lustful 419.29
**eject** eliminate 77.5
  erupt 162.12
  expel 310.13
  separate 49.9
  shoot 285.13
**ejection**
  emergence 303.3
  exclusion 77.2
  excrement 311.3
  excretion 311.1
  expulsion 310
  shot 285.5
**ejection seat**
  escape 632.3
  life preserver 701.5
**ejector** 310.11
**eke out** complete 56.6
  survive 659.12
  railway 657.8
  train 272.13
**elaborate**
  create 167.10
  develop 148.6
  expatiate 593.7
  improve 691.10
  make grandiloquent
  601.7
  *adj.* complex 46.4
  elegant 589.9
  grandiose 904.21
  ornate 901.12
  painstaking 533.11
**elaborateness**
  grandeur 904.5
  ornateness 901.2

**elaboration**
  development 148.1
  expatiation 593.6
  improvement 691.2
  manufacture 167.3
  ornamentation 901.1
  reiteration 103.2
**élan** animation 161.3
  eagerness 635.1
  gaiety 870.4
**elapse** be over 119.6
  pass 105.5
**elapsed** 119.7
**elastic**
  *n.* elastic substance
  358.3
  *adj.* expansive 197.9
  pliant 357.9
  recuperative 694.23
  resilient 358.7
**elasticity** muscle 159.2
  pliancy 357.2
  resilience 358
**elasticize** 358.6
**elate** cheer 870.8
  make proud 905.6
**elated** cheerful 870.11
  gloating 910.12
  overjoyed 865.14
  proud 905.10
  rejoicing 876.9
**elation**
  emotional symptom
  690.23
  gloating 910.4
  happiness 865.2
  rejoicing 876.1
**elbow**
  *n.* angle 251.2
  arm 287.5
  joint 47.4
  *v.* angle 251.5
  intrude 238.5
  thrust 283.11
**elbow grease** 716.1
**elbowroom**
  latitude 762.4
  spare 179.3
**elder**
  *n.* ancestors 170.7
  antiquated person
  123.8
  churchman 1038.10
  master 749.1
  Mormon priest
  1038.11
  old man 127.2
  personage 672.8
  public official 749.17
  senior 127.5
  wise man 468.1
  *adj.* prior 116.4
  senior 123.19
**elderly** aged 126.16
  antique 123.10
**elder statesman**
  expert 733.11
  statesman 746.2
  wise man 468.1
**eldest**
  *n.* first-born 127.5
  *adj.* oldest 123.19

**elect**
  *n.* chosen 637.12
  nobility 918.2
  the best 674.8
  *v.* appoint 637.20
  choose 637.13
  support politically
  744.41
  *adj.* best 674.18
  chosen 637.26
  particular 896.13
**elected** 637.26
**election**
  accession to power
  739.12
  appointment 637.9
  choice 637.1
  consecration 1037.10
  determinism 640.4
  political election
  744.15
**election district** 744.16
**electioneer**
  *n.* campaigner 746.10
  *v.* campaign 744.40
**elective**
  *n.* study 562.8
  *adj.* discretionary
  622.7
  optional 637.22
  selective 637.23
**elector**
  constituency 744.22
  selector 637.7
  voter 744.23
**electoral** 637.23
**electorate**
  district 180.5
  electors 744.22
  selector 637.7
**electric**
  streetcar 272.15
  train 272.13
**electric(al)**
  electricity 342.27
  exciting 857.28
**electrical engineer**
  342.20,34
**electrical parts and
  devices** 342.36
**electrical science**
  342.34
**electric car** 272.15
**electric chair** 1011.5
**electric current**
  electricity 342.2
  electron flow 343.6
**electric eye** 343.12,20
**electric field** 342.3
**electrician**
  electrotechnician
  342.19
  stage technician
  611.29
**electricity**
  electron movement
  342
  illuminant 335.20
  speed 269.6
  telegraphy 560.2
**electric meter** 342.38

**electric power**
  electricity 342.17
  power 157.4
**electric unit** 342.35
**electric wire** 342.39
**electrified**
  charged 342.31
  electricity 342.27
  startled 540.13
**electrify** energize 161.9
  excite 857.13
  make electric 342.23
  startle 540.8
**electrifying**
  electricity 342.27
  sudden 113.5
  surprising 540.11
**electro–**
  electricity 342.1
  electronics 343.1
**electrocute** 1010.19
**electrocution** 1010.7
**electrodynamics** 347.3
**electrolysis**
  electricity 342.22
  reaction 379.5
  surgical treatment
  689.21
**electrolytic**
  disintegrative 53.6
  electric 342.29
**electrolyze**
  disintegrate 53.4
  electrify 342.25
  react chemically
  379.6
**electromagnetic** 342.28
**electromagnetic field**
  electric field 342.3
  magnetism 342.9
**electromagnetism** 342.7
**electromagnetize**
  342.24
**electromotive force**
  342.11
**electron** atomics 326.6
  littleness 196.8
  negatron 343.3
**electron emission**
  electronics 343.5
  radiation 327.3
**electronic** 343.15
**electronic brain** 349.16
**electronic circuit**
  electronics 343.8
  radio circuit 344.9
**electronic device**
  343.20
**electronic meter** 343.21
**electronics**
  communications
  560.3
  physics 325.1
  radionics 343
**electronics engineer**
  343.14
**electron theory** 343.2
**electron tube**
  component 343.19
  special 343.18
  tube 343.11
  types of 343.16

electroplate
electrolyze 342.25
plate 228.26
electroplated 228.32
electroplating
electrolysis 342.22
plating 228.13
electroshock therapy
690.7
electrostatic
electricity 342.27
static 347.8
electrostatics 347.2
electrotherapy 689.6
electrotype
*n.* printing surface
603.8
*v.* make plates 603.15
eleemosynary
benevolent 938.15
giving 818.22
gratis 850.5
elegance
affectation 903.5
beauty 900.1
chic 644.3
decency 988.2
eloquence 600.2
etiquette 646.3
good breeding 936.4
good taste 897.1
grandeur 904.5
literary elegance 589
ornateness 901.2
parsimony 852.1
elegant affected 903.18
beautiful 900.16
chic 644.13
decent 988.5
eloquent 600.9
excellent 674.12
grandiose 904.21
ornate 901.12
polished 589.6
tasteful 897.9
elegiac(al)
dirgelike 875.18
poetic 609.17
elegist 609.13
elegize lament 875.8
poetize 609.15
elegy dirge 875.5
poem 609.6
element cause 153.1
chemical 379.1,10
component 58.2
environment 233.4
heater 329.10
mathematical 86.9
matter 376.2
particular 8.3
radioactive 327.12
elemental
*n.* spirit 1014.16
*adj.* basic 212.8
beginning 68.15
causal 153.15
chemical 379.7
essential 5.8
meteorology 402.13
elementary basic 212.8
beginning 68.15

causal 153.15
chemical 379.7
component 58.5
essential 5.8
simple 45.6
elementary education
education 562.10
elementary instruc-
tion 562.5
elementary metal
383.21
elementary particle
atomics 326.6
element 376.2
elementary school
567.5
elements basics 68.6
contents 194.1
elementary instruc-
tion 562.5
Eucharist 1040.8
weather 402.4
elephant animal 414.4
beast of burden
271.6
large animal 195.14
mammal 414.58;
415.8
elephantine
bulky 195.19
elephantlike 414.50
huge 195.20
stilted 590.3
uninteresting 883.6
elevate cheer 870.8
erect 213.9
glorify 914.13
heighten 207.18
make better 691.9
promote 782.2
raise 317.5
elevated
*n.* railway 657.8
train 272.13
*adj.* drunk 996.31
eloquent 600.14
eminent 914.18
grandiloquent 601.8
high 207.19
increased 38.7
magnanimous 979.6
majestic 34.9
proud 905.11
raised 317.9
elevation
ascension 315.1
diagram 654.3
eloquence 600.6
erection 213.4
glorification 914.8
height 207.1
increase 38.1
magnanimity 979.2
promotion 782.1
raising 317
repute 914.5
steep 207.2
elevator garner 660.7
lift 317.4
eleven number 99.7
team 788.7
eleventh 99.23

eleventh hour
crucial moment
129.5
curfew 134.5
lateness 132.1
eleventh-hour 132.18
elf bad child 125.4
dwarf 196.6
evil spirit 1016.8
fairy 1014.18
mischief-maker 738.3
elfdom 85.7
elfin dwarf 196.13
fairy 1014.27
elfish devilish 1016.19
fairy 1014.27
mischievous 738.6
elicit evoke 305.14
induce 153.12
prompt 648.13
elide eliminate 77.5
shorten 203.6
eligibility
inclusion 76.1
qualification 637.11
eligible
*n.* eligibility 637.11
*adj.* qualified 637.24
eliminate
destroy 693.14
discard 668.7
eject 310.21
eradicate 42.10
exclude 77.5
excrete 311.12
murder 409.16
shake off 310.20
elimination
destruction 693.6
discard 668.3
evacuation 310.6
excision 42.3
excretion 311.1
homicide 409.2
riddance 77.2
elision
abbreviation 592.4
shortening 203.3
elite
*n.* chosen 637.12
clique 788.6
nobility 918.2
society 644.6
superiors 36.5
the best 674.8
*adj.* best 674.18
high society 644.16
elite corps 800.14
elitist
*n.* snob 912.7
*adj.* arrogant 912.11
learned 475.23
elixir content 194.5
essence 5.2
extract 305.8
medicine 687.4
panacea 687.3
elk 414.5,58
ell angle 251.2
wing 41.3
ellipse curve 252.2
oval 253.6

ellipsis
abbreviation 592.4
shortening 203.3
ellipsoid 255.2
ellipsoid(al)
curved 252.13
globular 255.9
elliptic(al)
concise 592.6
curved 252.13
long 202.10
shortened 203.9
elocution
public speaking 599.1
speech 594.1
elocutionist
rhetorician 599.8
speaker 599.7
elongate 202.7
elongated
lengthened 202.9
long 202.10
elope 631.10
elopement flight 631.4
marriage 933.4
eloquence
articulateness 594.5
public speaking 599.1
rhetoric 600
eloquent
declamatory 599.12
silver-tongued 600.8
speaking 594.32
else
*adj.* other 16.8
*adv.* additionally
40.11
otherwise 16.11
elsewhere
*adj.* abstracted 532.11
*adv.* away 187.17
elucidate
explain 552.10
make clear 548.6
elucidation 552.4
elucidative 552.15
elude evade 631.7
outwit 735.11
thwart 730.15
elusion
avoidance 631.1
circumvention 735.5
elusive 631.15
Elysian
heavenly 1018.13
pleasant 863.8
Elysian fields 1018.10
emaciate
deteriorate 692.22
shrink 198.9
thin 205.12
emaciated
deteriorated 692.37
shrunk 198.13
thin 205.20
emanate
come after 117.3
emerge 303.12
radiate 299.6
result 154.6
**emanating** 303.18

**emanation**
emergence 303.2
light 335.1
occultism 1034.7
odor 435.1
radiating 299.2
**emancipate** 763.4
**emancipated**
free 762.20
liberated 763.10
**emancipation** 763.1
**emancipator** 942.2
**emasculate**
castrate 42.11
cripple 692.17
feminize 421.12
unman 158.12
**emasculated**
castrated 158.19
injured 692.32
unsexual 419.31
**emasculation**
castration 42.4
impotence 158.5
**embalm**
perpetuate 112.5
prepare for burial
410.21
preserve 701.8
scent 436.8
**embalmer** 410.8
**embalming**
embalmment 410.3
preserving 701.2
**embankment**
barrier 730.5
buttress 216.4
harbor 700.6
pile 74.10
railway 657.8
shore 385.2
**embargo**
*n.* exclusion 77.1
prohibition 778.1
*v.* exclude 77.4
prohibit 778.3
**embark**
get under way 275.19
go aboard 301.16
send 271.14
**embarkation**
departure 301.3
inauguration 68.5
water travel 275.5
**embark upon**
begin 68.9
undertake 715.3
**embarrass**
bewilder 514.12
cause trouble for
731.14
chagrin 866.15
confuse 532.7
hamper 730.11
humiliate 906.4
involve 176.2
mortify 864.13
**embarrassed**
bewildered 514.23
blushing 908.13
confused 532.12
distressed 866.22

humiliated 906.13
inconvenienced
731.19
indebted 840.8
poor 838.7
**embarrassing**
bewildering 514.25
humiliating 906.14
mortifying 864.21
**embarrassment**
confusion 532.3
discomfiture 866.4
humiliation 906.2
impediment 730.6
involvement 176.1
mortification 864.6
perplexity 514.3
poverty 838.1
predicament 731.4
shyness 908.4
**embassy**
commission 780.1
diplomats 781.7
house 191.6
message 558.4
office 719.8
**embattle** 799.9
**embattled**
at war 797.27
fortified 799.12
**embed** impress 142.9
inset 304.5
internalize 225.6
**embellish** falsify 616.16
improve 691.10
make grandiloquent
601.7
ornament 901.8
**embellished**
falsified 616.26
high-flown 601.11
improved 691.13
ornamented 901.11
**embellishment**
flowery language
601.4
improvement 691.2
music 463.18
ornamentation 901.1
superfluity 663.4
**ember** coal 328.16
residue 43.2
**Ember days** 1040.15
**embezzle** misuse 667.4
steal 824.1
**embezzlement**
misuse 667.1
theft 824.1
**embitter**
antagonize 929.7
impair 692.11
make grieve 872.19
make ill-humored
951.16
provoke 952.22
worsen 885.2
**embittered**
damaged 692.29
ill-humored 951.23
resentful 952.24
worsened 885.4
**emblazon** color 362.13

flaunt 904.17
ornament 901.8
praise 968.12
**emblem** example 25.2
insignia 569.1
symbol 568.3
**embodied**
bodied 376.10
composed of 58.4
**embodiment**
combination 52.1
composition 58.1
impersonation 572.2
incarnation 3.4
inclusion 76.1
manifestation 555.1
materiality 376.1
materialization 376.7
representative 572.5
whole 54.1
**embody** combine 52.3
compose 58.3
incarnate 3.5
include 76.3
manifest 555.5
materialize 376.8
represent 572.8
**embolden** abet 785.14
encourage 893.16
**embolism** 266.3
**emboss** 256.11
**embossed**
infixed 142.13
in relief 256.17
sculptured 575.7
**embossment**
mark 568.7
protuberance 256.2
relief 575.3
**embrace**
*n.* greeting 925.4
hold 813.2
hug 932.2
joint 47.4
welcome 925.2
*v.* adopt 637.15
cohere 50.6
converge 47.11
harbor 813.7
hold 813.6
hug 932.16
include 76.3
join 47.5
seize 822.14
surround 233.6
welcome 925.9
wrap 228.20
**embracing**
inclusive 76.6
surrounding 233.8
**embrocate**
medicate 689.31
oil 380.8
**embroider**
falsify 616.16
make grandiloquent
601.7
ornament 901.8
sew 223.5
**embroidered**
falsified 616.26
high-flown 601.11

**embroidery**
flowery language
601.4
needlework 223.6
ornamentation
901.1,13
**embroil** 63.4
**embroilment**
agitation 324.1
commotion 62.4
excitement 857.3
fight 796.4
quarrel 795.5
violence 162.2
**embryo** source 153.7
zygote 406.14
**embryology** 406.17
**embryonic**
beginning 68.15
causal 153.15
germinal 406.24
incomplete 57.4
infinitesimal 196.14
undeveloped 721.12
**embue** 648.20
**emcee**
broadcaster 344.23
manager 748.4
master of ceremonies
878.22
theater man 611.28
**emend**
make better 691.9
remedy 694.13
revise 691.12
**emerald**
*n.* gem stone 384.13
*adj.* green 371.4,6
**emerge** appear 446.8
come out 303.12
find vent 632.10
result from 154.6
**emergence**
appearance 446.1
egress 303.2
escape 632.1
**emergency** crisis 129.4
danger 697.1
hospital room 192.25
urgency 672.4
**emergent**
crucial 129.10
emerging 303.18
future 121.8
**emeritus**
*n.* academic rank
565.4
*adj.* retired 784.3
**emery** abrasive 260.14
sharpener 258.19
**emetic**
*n.* cleaning agent
681.17
unsavoriness 429.3
vomitive 687.18
*adj.* cleansing 681.28
vomitive 687.49
**emigrant** migrant 274.5
newcomer 78.4
outgoer 303.10
**emigrate**
emerge 303.16

leave 301.18
migrate 273.21
**emigration** egress 303.7
migration 273.4
**eminence**
authority 739.4
height 207.1
influence 172.1
loftiness 34.2
notability 672.2
protuberance 256.2
repute 914.5
steep 207.2
**eminent**
authoritative 739.15
exalted 914.18
high 207.19
important 672.18
prominent 34.9
protruding 256.13
superior 36.12
**eminent domain**
appropriation 822.5
ascendancy 739.6
**eminently**
exceptionally 34.20
illustriously 914.21
importantly 672.24
superlatively 36.16
**emir**
Muslim ruler 749.10
prince 918.7
title 917.3
**emissary** delegate 781.2
diplomat 781.6
messenger 561.1
**emission** ejection 310.7
emergence 303.2
excretion 311.1
**emit** eject 310.23
excrete 311.12
exude 303.15
issue 559.14
say 594.23
send out 401.8
**emollient**
n. healing ointment
687.11
ointment 380.3
adj. lubricant 380.10
relieving 886.9
remedial 687.40
softening 357.16
**emote** act 611.34
emotionalize 855.15
**emotion**
excitement 857.1
feeling 855.3
mental attitude 525.1
**emotional**
excitable 857.26
temperamental 525.7
visceral 855.19
**emotionalism**
emotionality 855.9
emotional symptom
690.23
excitability 857.9
**emotionalize**
act 611.34
emote 855.15

**emotionally**
feelingly 855.27
temperamentally
525.9
**emotions** 855.1
**emotive**
affecting 855.24
emotional 855.19
hysterical 855.20
**empanel** see **impanel**
**empathetic**
in accord 794.3
sensitive 422.14
**empathize**
emotionally respond
855.12
get along 794.2
**empathy** accord 794.1
sensitivity 422.3
sympathy 855.5
**emperor** 749.7
**emphasis**
importance 672.1
meter 609.9
music 463.25
speech accent 594.11
**emphasize** 672.13
**emphatic**
asserting 523.7
eloquent 600.13
emphasized 672.20
**emphatically**
assertingly 523.9
exceptionally 34.20
**emphysema** 686.14
**empire** authority 739.5
country 181.1
government 741.1
sovereignty 739.8
**empirical**
experimental 489.11
philosophy 500.9
**empiricism** ethics 957.2
experiment 489.1
materialism 376.5
**emplacement**
location 184.1
placement 184.5
platform 216.13
**emplane** 301.16
**employ**
n. business 656.1
service 750.12
use 665.1
v. exert 716.8
hire 780.13
occupy 656.10
practice 705.7
spend 665.13
use 665.10
**employable**
instrumental 658.6
useful 665.18
**employed** busy 707.21
hired 780.19
used 665.23
**employee**
hireling 750.3
subordinate 764.5
working person 718.2
**employees** 750.11
**employer** master 749.1

user 665.9
**employment**
action 705.1
business 656.1
hiring 780.4
position 656.5
service 750.12
use 665.1
utilization 665.8
work 716.4
**emporium**
market 832.1
marketplace 832.2
**empower**
authorize 777.11
commission 780.9
enable 157.10
**empowered**
authoritative 739.15
authorized 777.17
**empress** 749.11
**emptiness**
appetite 634.7
futility 669.2
insincerity 616.5
meaninglessness
547.1
nonexistence 2.1
space 179.1
stupidity 469.6
triviality 673.3
uninterestingness
883.1
unpleasure 866.1
vacancy 187.2
**empty**
v. drain 305.12
eject 310.21
emerge 303.13
adj. baseless 483.13
hungry 634.25
ignorant 477.12
ineffective 158.15
inexpressive 549.20
insincere 616.32
meaningless 547.6
specious 483.10
stupid 469.19
thoughtless 480.4
trivial 673.16
uninteresting 883.6
vacant 187.13
vain 669.13
**empty-handed** 662.12
**empty-headed**
ignorant 477.12
scatterbrained 532.16
stupid 469.19
thoughtless 480.4
**emptying**
draining 305.3
evacuation 310.6
**empty of**
void of 187.18
wanting 662.13
**empty pocket** 838.2
**emulate**
be as good as 674.11
compete 796.19
follow 22.7
**emulsifier**
emulsion 389.7

mixer 44.10
**emulsify**
make viscid 389.10
mix 44.11
**emulsion** film 577.10
semiliquid 389.7
**enable**
authorize 777.11
empower 157.10
make possible 509.5
prepare 720.8
**enact** accomplish 722.4
act 611.35
execute 705.8
indicate 555.5
legalize 998.8
legislate 742.18
represent 572.9
**enactment**
display 555.2
impersonation 572.2
law 998.3
legislation 742.13
performance 705.2
**enamel**
n. coating 228.12
v. coat 228.24
color 362.13
adj. ceramic 576.7
**enameling** 362.12
**enamor** 931.21
**enamored**
charmed 931.26
fond of 931.28
**en bloc** 54.13
**encamp** 188.11
**encampment**
camp 191.29
camping 188.4
military camp 802.3
**encapsulate** 228.20
**encase** enclose 236.6
package 236.9
wrap 228.20
**encephalic** 211.14
**encephalitis** 686.9
**enchant**
bewitch 1036.8
delight 865.8
engross 530.13
fascinate 650.6
**enchanted**
astonished 920.9
bewitched 1036.12
dreamy 535.25
enamored 931.26
engrossed 530.18
overjoyed 865.14
supernatural 85.16
**enchanter**
bewitcher 1035.9
deceiver 619.1
tempter 650.3
**enchanting**
alluring 650.7
bewitching 1036.11
engrossing 530.20
influential 172.1
pleasant 863.7
**enchantment**
allurement 650.1
amorousness 931.3

bad influence 675.4
bewitchment 1036.2
happiness 865.2
influence 172.1
pleasantness 863.2
sorcery 1035.1
supernaturalism 85.8
**enchantress**
beautiful person
900.8
bewitcher 1035.9
tempter 650.3
**enchased** 578.12
**encipher** 614.10
**encircle** besiege 798.19
enclose 236.5
go around 321.4
include 76.3
surround 233.7
**encircled**
circumscribed 234.6
surrounded 233.11
**encirclement**
military tactics 797.9
siege 798.5
surrounding 233.5
**encircling**
inclusive 76.6
surrounding 233.8
**enclave**
enclosure 236.3,12
tract 180.4
**enclose**
circumscribe 234.4
confine 761.12
immure 236.5
include 76.3
internalize 225.6
limit 235.8
surround 233.6
**enclosed**
confined 761.19
immured 236.10
surrounded 233.10
**enclosing**
confining 236.11
environing 233.8
inclusive 76.6
**enclosure**
confinement 236
contents 194.6
fortification 799.4
pen 236.3
prison 761.7
surrounding 233.5
types of 236.12
**ncoding** 557.7
**ncompass**
besiege 798.19
circle 253.10
combine 52.3
enclose 236.5
extend 179.7
go around 321.4
include 76.3
join 47.5
surround 233.6
**compassed**
included 76.5
surrounded 233.10
**core**
**.** applause 968.2

repeat 91.2
repeat performance
103.6
*adv.* duplication 91.7
repetition 103.17
*interj.* again! 103.18
approval 968.22
**encounter**
*n.* contest 796.3
impact 283.3
meeting 200.4
*v.* approach 296.3
collide 283.12
confront 240.8
contend with 796.16
experience 151.8
find 488.3
meet 200.11
oppose 790.5
**encounter therapy**
690.5
**encourage** abet 785.14
advise 754.6
cheer 870.7
comfort 887.6
further 785.17
hearten 893.16
motivate 648.21
**encouragement**
comfort 887.4
heartening 893.9
incentive 648.7
patronage 785.4
urging 648.5
**encouraging**
cheering 870.16
comforting 887.13
promising 888.13
provocative 648.27
**encroach** intrude 238.5
overstep 313.9
take liberties 961.7
usurp 961.8
**encroachment**
intrusion 238.1
overstepping 313.3
usurpation 961.3
**encrust** 228.27
**encumber** add 40.4
burden 352.13
hamper 730.11
**encumbered**
burdened 352.18
indebted 840.8
**encumbrance**
affliction 866.8
burden 352.7
dependent 764.6
impediment 730.6
**encyclical**
announcement 559.2
letter 604.3
**encyclopedia**
lore 475.9
reference book 605.6
**encyclopedic**
comprehensive 76.7
learned 475.21
**end**
*n.* athlete 878.20
boundary 235.3
completion 722.2

death 408.1
extremity 56.5
fate 640.2
objective 653.2
piece 55.3
portion 816.5
remainder 43.1
result 154.2
ruin 693.2
solution 487.1
stop 144.2
termination 70
*v.* be destroyed 693.23
cease 144.6
complete 722.6
destroy 693.12
kill 409.13
result 154.5
terminate 70.5
**end-all** 70.4
**endanger** 697.6
**endangered** 697.13
**endear** 931.21
**endearment**
lovemaking 932.4
lure 650.2
**endeavor**
*n.* act 705.3
attempt 714.2
effort 714
exertion 716.1
*v.* exert oneself 716.9
strive 714.4
try to 714.7
undertake 715.3
**ended**
completed 722.11
terminated 70.8
**endemic**
*n.* disease 686.1
*adj.* contagious 686.58
native 189.5
**ending**
*n.* completion 722.2
death 408.1
halt 144.2
termination 70.1
*adj.* closing 70.9
**endless**
continuous 71.8
infinite 104.3
innumerable 101.10
perpetual 112.7
wordy 593.12
**endlessly**
continuously 71.10
infinitely 104.4
perpetually 112.10
tediously 884.12
**endocrine**
*n.* secretion 312.2,9
*adj.* glandular 312.8
**endocrinology** 312.4
**endomorph** 690.15
**endomorphic** 195.18
**endorse** abet 785.14
approve 968.9
consent 775.2
guarantee 772.9
ratify 521.12
support politically
744.41

**endorsement**
approval 968.1
consent 775.1
ratification 521.4
signature 583.10
**endorser** assenter 521.7
supporter 787.9
**endow**
empower 157.10
give to 818.17
provide 659.7
**endowed**
dowered 818.26
possessing 808.9
provided 659.13
talented 733.27
**endowment**
dower 818.9
empowerment 157.8
giving 818.1
heredity 170.6
provision 659.1
support 785.3
talent 733.4
**endpaper** 605.12
**end result** result 154.2
solution 487.1
**endue** clothe 231.38
empower 157.10
**endurable** 868.13
**endurance**
continuance 143.1
durability 110.1
patience 861.1
permanence 140.1
perseverance 625.1
strength 159.1
**endure**
afford to pay 843.7
be patient 861.5
be tough 359.3
condone 947.4
continue 143.3
elapse 105.5
exist 1.9
experience 151.8
last 110.6
permit 777.10
persevere 625.2
remain 140.5
resist 792.2
stay alive 407.10
**enduring**
durable 110.10
patient 861.9
permanent 140.7
persevering 625.7
remembered 537.23
substantial 3.7
**endways**
*adj.* adjacent 200.16
*adv.* lengthwise
202.12
vertically 213.13
**enema**
cleaning agent 681.17
clyster 687.19
sprinkler 392.8
washing 681.5
**enemy**
*n.* foe 929.6
opponent 791.1

information 557.1
learning 475.4
lighting 335.19
teaching 562.1
**enlist** engage 780.16
induce 648.22
install 304.4
join 788.14
volunteer 108.5
**enlisted man** 800.8
**enlistment**
engagement 780.6
inducement 648.3
installation 306.2
recording 570.15
term 108.4
**enliven** amuse 878.23
cheer 870.7
energize 161.9
inspire 648.20
refresh 695.2
stimulate 857.12
**enlivened** 407.11
**en masse**
together 73.11
wholly 54.13
**enmesh** catch 822.17
cause trouble for
731.14
hamper 730.11
involve 176.2
trap 618.18
**enmity**
contention 796.1
disaccord 795.1
dislike 867.2
hate 930.2
opposition 790.2
unfriendliness 929
**ennoble** glorify 914.13
promote 782.2
**ennui** boredom 884.3
languor 708.6
unpleasure 866.1
**enormity**
baseness 915.3
crime 982.2
greatness 34.1
hugeness 195.7
indignity 965.2
**enormous** bad 675.9
excessive 663.16
huge 195.20
large 34.7
**enormously** 34.16
**enough**
*n.* sufficiency 661.1
*adj.* sufficient 661.6
*adv.* satisfactorily
868.15
sufficiently 661.8
*interj.* cease! 144.14
**nplane** 301.16
**nquire, enquirer,
enquiry** see **inquire**
etc.
**nrage** excite 857.11
infuriate 952.23
make hot 329.18
**nraged** 952.29
**n rapport**
agreeing 26.9

congenial 9.7
in harmony 794.3
pleasant 863.6
**enrapture** delight 865.8
enamor 931.21
fascinate 650.6
**enraptured**
astonished 920.9
enamored 931.26
excited 857.23
overjoyed 865.14
**enravish** delight 865.8
fascinate 650.6
**enravished**
astonished 920.9
overjoyed 865.14
**enrich** fertilize 165.8
make better 691.9
make grandiloquent
601.7
ornament 901.8
vitaminize 309.18
wealth 837.8
**enrichment**
fertilization 165.3
improvement 691.1
vitaminization 309.12
**enrobe** 231.38
**enroll** engage 780.16
install 304.4
join 788.14
list 88.8
record 570.16
**enrollment**
enlistment 780.6
installation 306.2
listing 88.7
recording 570.15
**en route**
on the move 273.41
on the way 271.19
**en route to**
forward 294.8
toward 290.28
**ensconce** conceal 615.6
settle 184.16
**ensemble**
*n.* choir 464.16
compound 44.5
orchestra 464.12
troupe 612.11
*adv.* together 73.11
**enshrine** enclose 236.5
exalt 317.6
glorify 914.13
inter 410.19
sanctify 1026.5
**enshroud** clothe 231.38
conceal 615.6
wrap 228.20
**ensign** flag 569.6
insignia 569.1
naval officer 749.20
**ensilage** 308.4
**enslave** conquer 822.19
domineer 741.16
subject 764.8
**ensnare** catch 822.17
lure 650.4
trap 618.18
**ensnarl** hamper 730.11
trap 618.18

**ensue** come after 117.3
come next 65.2
result 154.5
**ensuing** resulting 154.7
subsequent 117.4
succeeding 65.4
**ensure** guarantee 772.9
make sure 513.11
protect 699.18
**entail**
*n.* inheritance 819.2
*v.* imply 546.4
indicate 568.17
involve 76.4
will 818.18
**entailed** 752.13
**entangle** catch 822.17
cause trouble for
731.14
complicate 46.3
confuse 532.7
hamper 730.11
involve 176.2
trap 618.18
**entanglement**
complexity 46.1
deception 618.1
fortification 799.4
involvement 176.1
love affair 931.6
**entente** treaty 771.2
understanding 26.2
**enter** appear 446.8
begin 68.9
go in 302.7
insert 304.3
join 788.14
keep accounts 845.8
list 88.8
record 570.16
**entered** listed 88.9
recorded 570.18
**enteric** 225.10
**entering**
*n.* recording 570.15
*adj.* arriving 300.9
incoming 302.12
**enter into**
compose 58.3
participate 815.5
**enteritis** 686.9
**enterology** 225.5
**enterprise** act 705.3
business 656.1
company 788.9
courage 893.6
courageous act 893.7
initiative 707.7
plan 654.1
undertaking 715.1
vim 161.2
**enterprising**
daring 893.21
energetic 161.12
up-and-coming
707.23
venturesome 715.8
**entertain** amuse 878.23
entertain guests
925.8
harbor 813.7

take under consider-
ation 478.14
**entertainer** 612
**entertaining** 878.29
**entertainment**
amusement 878.1
party 922.11
pleasure 865.1
refreshment 307.5
theatrical perfor-
mance 611.13
**enter upon** begin 68.9
set to work 716.15
undertake 715.3
**enthrall** delight 865.8
engross 530.13
fascinate 650.6
subject 764.8
**enthralled**
astonished 920.9
engrossed 530.18
subjugated 764.14
**enthralling**
alluring 650.7
engrossing 530.20
pleasant 863.7
**enthrone** glorify 914.13
install 780.11
**enthuse** 635.8
**enthused** 635.11
**enthusiasm**
animation 161.3
eagerness 635.3
eloquence 600.5
interest 530.2
mania 473.12
willingness 622.1
**enthusiast**
fanatic 473.17
man of action 707.8
visionary 535.13
zealot 635.5
**enthusiastic**
eager 635.11
eloquent 600.13
energetic 161.12
fervent 855.23
interested 530.16
willing 622.5
**entice** 650.4
**enticement** 650.1
**enticing** 650.7
**entire** complete 56.9
sound 677.7
unqualified 508.2
whole 54.9
**entirely**
completely 56.14
perfectly 677.10
solely 89.14
wholly 54.13
**entirety**
completeness 56.1
whole 54.1
**entitle**
authorize 777.11
name 583.11
**entitled**
authorized 777.17
due 960.10
warranted 960.9
**entity** existence 1.1

match 30.5
parallel 218.4
*adj.* equalized 30.7
identical 14.8
interchangeable
150.5
parallel 218.6
proportionate 816.13
symmetric 248.4
uniform 17.5
**equality** identity 14.1
parity 30
symmetry 248.1
**equalize** balance 30.6
level 214.6
make agree 26.7
make uniform 17.4
smooth 260.5
symmetrize 248.3
**equalizer** 70.4
**equalizing**
*n.* equalization 30.2
*adj.* interchangeable
150.5
**equally**
accordingly 8.11
correspondingly
30.11
identically 14.9
justly 976.11
**equal to** able 157.14
competent 733.22
prepared for 720.18
satisfactory 868.11
sufficient 661.6
**equanimity**
composure 858.3
uniformity 17.1
**equate** associate 9.6
equalize 30.6
make parallel 218.5
**equation** equality 30.1
equalization 30.2
mathematics 86.9;
87.4
**equator**
astronomy 375.16
bisector 92.3
circle 253.3
hot place 328.11
latitude 180.3
middle 69.1
**equatorial** middle 69.4
warm 328.24
**equerry**
animal handler 416.2
male servant 750.4
**equestrian**
*n.* rider 274.8
*adj.* ungulate 414.49
**equidistance**
middle 69.2
parallelism 218.1
**equidistant**
middle 69.4
parallel 218.6
**equilateral**
equisized 30.10
symmetric 248.4
**equilibrium**
correlation 13.1
equality 30.1

equanimity 858.3
literary elegance
589.2
stability 142.1
symmetry 248.1
uniformity 17.1
**equine**
*n.* horse 414.10
*adj.* ungulate 414.49
**equinox**
astronomy 375.16
season 128.7
**equip** furnish 659.8
outfit 231.40
prepare 720.8
**equipage**
equipment 659.4
rig 272.5
**equipment**
electronic testing
343.23
fitting 720.2
matériel 659.4
photographic 577.19
preparation 720.1
printing 603.26
provision 659.1
ship 277.34
talent 733.4
**equipoise** equality 30.1
offset 33.2
**equipped**
prepared 720.16
provided 659.13
**equispaced**
equisized 30.10
parallel 218.6
**equitable** just 976.8
unprejudiced 526.12
**equity** equality 30.1
estate 810.4
justice 976.1
law 998.4
law code 998.5
stock 834.2
**equivalence**
agreement 26.1
comparability 491.3
correlation 13.1
equality 30.1
identity 14.1
**equivalent**
*n.* equal 30.4
likeness 20.3
offset 33.2
substitute 149.2
the same 14.3
*adj.* agreeing 26.9
analogous 20.11
identical 14.8
interchangeable
150.5
reciprocal 13.13
substitute 149.8
tantamount 30.8
**equivocal**
ambiguous 550.3
mixed 44.15
prevaricating 613.11
self-contradictory
15.8
uncertain 514.15

untruthful 616.34
**equivocate**
dodge 631.8
lie 616.19
prevaricate 613.7
quibble 483.9
vacillate 627.8
**equivocation**
ambiguous expression
550.2
avoidance 631.1
contrariety 15.3
falsification 616.9
prevarication 613.4
quibbling 483.5
sophistry 483.1
vacillation 627.2
**era** 107.5
**eradicate** annihilate 2.6
destroy 693.14
eliminate 77.5
excise 42.10
uproot 305.10
**eradicative**
exterminative 693.27
extractive 305.17
**erase** abrade 350.7
delete 42.12
kill 409.14
obliterate 693.16
**erased** 538.8
**eraser** 693.9
**erasure** abrasion 350.2
deletion 42.5
disappearance 447.1
obliteration 693.7
**Erato** Muse 535.2
music patron 464.22
poetry 609.12
**ere** 116.6
**Erebus** darkness 337.1
deity of nether world
1019.5
**erect**
*v.* create 167.10
raise 213.9
uplift 317.5
*adj.* honest 974.13
proud 905.8
raised 317.9
vertical 213.11
**erection**
elevation 317.1
erecting 213.4
house 191.6
manufacture 167.3
structure 245.2
**erg** 161.6
**ergo** 155.7
**eristic(al)**
argumentative 482.19
quarrelsome 795.17
**ermine** fur 229.8
heraldic insignia
569.2
royal insignia 569.3
**erode** abrade 350.7
consume 666.2
decrease 39.6
disappear 447.2
disintegrate 53.3
eat away 692.24

subtract 42.9
waste 812.5
wear 692.23
**eroded**
corroded 692.44
reduced 39.10
used up 666.4
wasted 812.7
weatherworn 692.36
**erogenous** 419.26
**Eros** god 1014.5
love 931.1
love god 931.8
**erosion** abrasion 350.2
consumption 666.1
decrease 39.3
disintegration 53.1
loss 812.2
subtraction 42.1
wear 692.5
**erotic** amorous 931.24
lascivious 989.29
sexual 419.26
**erotica** 602.12
**eroticism**
lasciviousness 989.5
sexual desire 419.5
**err**
be unorthodox
1025.8
be wrong 518.9
fail 725.13
go wrong 981.9
misjudge 496.2
sin 982.5
stray 291.4
**errancy** error 518.1
fallibility 514.7
**errand**
commission 780.1
task 656.2
**errand boy**
attendant 750.5
office boy 561.4
**errant** deviant 291.7
erroneous 518.16
uncertain 514.21
wandering 273.36
**errantry**
deviation 291.1
magnanimity 979.2
wandering 273.3
**errata** 605.12
**erratic**
*n.* eccentric 474.3
*adj.* abnormal 85.9
deviant 291.7
eccentric 474.4
inconstant 141.7
irregular 138.3
uncertain 514.15
uneven 18.3
unordered 62.12
**erratum** 518.3
**erroneous** false 616.25
imperfect 678.4
inaccurate 518.16
ungrammatical 587.4
unorthodox 1025.9
**error** bungle 734.5
computer 349.19
erroneousness 518

failure 725.4
heresy 1025.2
iniquity 981.3
misdeed 982.2
misinterpretation
553.1
misjudgment 496.1
mistake 518.3
**ersatz**
*n.* substitute 149.2
*adj.* imitation 22.8
similar 20.10
substitute 149.8
ungenuine 616.26
**erstwhile** 119.10
**eruct** belch 310.26
eject 310.24
erupt 162.12
**erudite** 475.21
**erudition**
learning 564.1
sagacity 467.5
scholarship 475.5
**erupt** appear 446.9
become sick 686.44
begin 68.13
burst forth 162.12
eject 310.24
emerge 303.12
find vent 632.10
**eruption** anger 952.9
ejection 310.7
emotional outburst
857.8
outburst 162.6
skin eruption 686.34
**eruptive**
excitable 857.26
volcanic 162.23
**erythrocyte** 388.4
**escalate** 317.5
**escalation** 317.1
**escalator** 317.4
**escallop, escalloped** see
scallop etc.
**escapade** 878.6
**escape**
*n.* avoidance 631.1
defense mechanism
690.30
departure 301.1
escaping 632
outlet 303.9
*v.* absent oneself
187.8
evade 631.7
flee 632.6
free oneself from
763.8
**escape artist** 632.5
**escape hatch**
conditior. 507.2
escape 632.3
loophole 632.4
secret passage 615.5
**escape notice**
be invisible 445.3
be latent 546.3
escape attention
531.5

**escapism**
defense mechanism
690.30
escape 632.1
**escapist** escapee 632.5
pathological type
690.16
visionary 535.13
**escarpment**
fortification 799.4
precipice 213.3
**eschatology**
doomsday 121.3
fate 70.1
theology 1023.1
**eschew** 992.7
**escort**
*n.* conductor 73.5
guard 699.14
*v.* conduct 73.8
**escrow** 772.2
**escutcheon** 569.2
**esophagus** 396.15
**esoteric**
confidential 614.14
individual 80.12
intrinsic 5.6
latent 546.5
occult 1034.22
recondite 549.16
secret 614.11
supernatural 85.15
**esoterica**
abstruseness 549.2
secrets 614.5
**esoterics** 1034.1
**ESP**
communication
554.1
extrasensory percep-
tion 1034.8
**especial** 80.12
**especially** chiefly 36.17
particularly 80.15
**Esperanto** 580.24
**espial** discovery 488.1
observation 439.2
spying 485.9
**espionage**
observation 439.2
spying 485.9
**esplanade**
horizontal 214.3
path 657.3
**espousal**
adoption 637.4
betrothal 770.3
wedding 933.4
**espouse** adopt 637.15
campaign for 968.13
defend 1006.10
get married 933.16
**esprit** accord 794.1
cooperation 786.1
gaiety 870.4
intellect 466.1
intelligence 467.2
soul 855.2
wit 881.1
**esprit de corps**
accord 794.1
cooperation 786.1

fellowship 927.2
partisanism 788.13
**espy** detect 488.5
see 439.12
**esquire** beau 931.12
escort 73.5
nobleman 918.4
**essay**
*n.* attempt 714.2
test 489.2
treatise 606.1
written matter 602.10
*v.* attempt 714.5
experiment 489.8
**essayist** author 602.15
discourser 606.3
**essence** content 194.5
existence 1.1
extract 305.8
important point
672.6
major part 54.6
meaning 545.1
odor 435.1
perfume 436.2
product 168.1
substance 5.2
summary 607.2
topic 484.1
**essential**
*n.* essence 5.2
fact 1.4
important point
672.6
requirement 639.2
*adj.* basic 212.8
fundamental 5.8
quintessential 305.18
requisite 639.13
simple 45.6
vital 672.22
**essentially**
extremely 34.22
fundamentally 5.10
on the whole 54.14
substantially 3.8
**establish**
accustom 642.11
begin 68.11
create 167.12
fix 184.15
ingrain 142.9
legalize 998.8
make sure 513.11
originate 153.11
prove 505.11
publicize 559.15
**established**
confirmed 642.21
customary 642.15
entrenched 142.13
located 184.17
made sure 513.20
proved 505.21
traditional 123.12
true 516.12
**establishment**
beginning 68.1
building 245.2
fixedness 142.2
foundation 184.6
hierarchy 61.4

making certain 513.8
organization 788.8
production 167.4
proof 505.4
store 832.1
superiors 36.5
workplace 719.1
**Establishment, the**
important persons
672.8
influential persons
172.6
the government
741.3
the rulers 749.15
**estate** class 61.2
house and grounds
191.7
people 417.2
property 810.4
state 7.1
**esteem**
*n.* approval 968.1
honor 914.3
influence 172.1
notability 672.2
respect 964.1
*v.* approve 968.9
believe 501.11
cherish 931.19
judge 494.8
rate highly 672.12
respect 964.4
**esteemed**
beloved 931.22
notable 672.18
reputable 914.15
respected 964.11
**ester** glyceryl 380.14
oil 380.1
**esthete, esthetic** see
aesthete etc.
**estimable**
calculable 87.16
good 674.12
honest 974.13
influential 172.13
measurable 490.15
notable 672.18
praiseworthy 968.20
reputable 914.15
venerable 964.12
**estimate**
*n.* belief 501.6
judgment 494.3
measurement 490.1
*v.* believe 501.11
calculate 87.11
judge 494.9
measure 490.11
**estimation** belief 501.6
calculation 87.3
esteem 914.3
judgment 494.3
measurement 490.1
respect 964.1
valuation 846.4
**estop** 730.14
**estrange**
antagonize 929.7
separate 49.9
sow dissension 795.1

estranged
 alienated 929.11
 separated 49.21
estrogen 312.10
estrous 419.30
estruate 419.22
estrus 419.6
estuarine alluvial 385.8
 aquatic 275.58
 estuary 399.2
estuary
 arm of the sea 399.1
 outlet 303.9
et al. and others 40.14
 more 100.10
etc. 40.14
et cetera
 and so forth 40.14
 more 100.10
etch affect 855.18
 engrave 578.11
 fix in the mind
  537.18
 imprint 142.9
etched 142.13
etching arts 574.1
 engraving 578.2
 engraving process
  578.3
 print 578.6
eternal godlike 1013.20
 infinite 104.3
 perpetual 112.7
eternally forever 104.4
 perpetually 112.10
eternity
 divine attribute
  1013.15
 forever 112.2
 Heaven 1018.1
 infinity 104.1
 long time 110.4
 perpetuity 112.1
 timelessness 106.1
ethane 331.1
ether air 402.1
 anesthetic 687.57
 coolant 334.7
 heavens 375.2
 height 207.2
 lightness 353.2
 vapor 4.3
ethereal airy 402.12
 ghostly 1017.7
 heavenly 1018.13
 high 207.19
 imaginary 535.22
 immaterial 377.7
 light 353.10
 tenuous 355.4
 thin 205.16
 unsubstantial 4.6
 vaporous 401.9
etherealize rarefy 355.3
 spiritualize 1034.20
 weaken 4.4
etherize gas 401.8
 render insensible
  423.4
ethical dutiful 962.13
 honest 974.13
 moral 957.6

ethics duty 962.1
 philosophy 500.1,11
 principles 957
ethnic 11.7
ethnic group
 party 788.4
 people 418.1
ethnocentric
 clannish 788.18
 exclusive 77.8
ethnology 417.7
ethos belief 501.6
 culture 642.3
 ethics 957.1
 ideology 479.8
 nature 5.3
 pervading attitudes
  525.5
ethyl 380.4
etiology
 attribution 155.1
 cause 153.1
etiquette custom 642.1
 good behavior 737.2
 social code 646.3
 social convention
  645.1
étude music 462.5
 treatise 606.1
etymologic(al) 582.20
etymology
 derivation 582.16
 linguistics 580.12
Eucharist rite 1040.8
 sacrament 1040.5
eucharistic(al) 1040.22
euchre 618.17
eugenics genetics 170.6
 improvement 691.1
eulogize 968.12
eulogy dirge 875.5
 funeral rites 410.4
 honor 916.4
 praise 968.5
 speech 599.2
eunuch 158.6
eupeptic
 cheerful 870.11
 contented 868.7
 healthy 685.7
 pleased 865.12
euphemism
 affectation 903.5
 preciosity 589.3
euphemistic 903.18
euphemize 613.7
euphonious
 balanced 589.8
 melodious 462.49
euphony
 literary elegance
  589.2
 music 462.3
euphoria
 contentment 868.1
 emotional symptom
  690.23
 pleasure 865.1
euphoric
 cheerful 870.11
 contented 868.7
 pleased 865.12

euphuism
 affectation 903.5
 florid style 551.1
 preciosity 589.3
Eurasian 44.9
eureka! 488.11
Europe
 continent 386.1
 region 180.6
eurythmics
 physical education
  562.9
 symmetry 248.1
Euterpe Muse 535.2
 music patron 464.22
 poetry 609.12
euthanasia death 408.7
 killing 409.1
evacuate
 abandon 633.5
 defecate 311.13
 eject 310.21
 emit 310.23
 leave 301.8
evacuation
 abandonment 633.1
 defecation 311.2
 departure 301.1
 voidance 310.6
evacuee fugitive 631.5
 migrant 274.5
evade avoid 631.7
 be dishonest 975.11
 equivocate 483.9
 escape 632.6
 outwit 735.11
 prevaricate 613.7
 pull back 284.7
 remain neutral 806.5
evaluate analyze 48.8
 judge 494.9
 measure 490.11
 price 846.13
evaluation analysis 48.3
 judgment 494.3
 measurement 490.1
 pricing 846.4
evanescent
 infinitesimal 196.14
 transient 111.7
 vanishing 447.3
evangel
 good news 558.2
 herald 561.2
evangelic(al)
 hyperorthodox
  1024.8
 orthodox 1024.7
 scriptural 1021.10
evangelist
 clergyman 1038.7
 converter 145.9
 herald 561.2
 religious founder
  1022.2
 worshiper 1032.9
evangelistic
 ministerial 1037.13
 scriptural 1021.10
evaporate
 be transient 111.6
 cease to exist 2.5

disappear 447.2
dissipate 75.5
dry 393.6
preserve 701.8
vaporize 401.8
evaporated 393.9
evaporation
 disappearance 447.1
 dispersion 75.1
 drying 393.3
 loss 812.2
 preserving 701.2
 vaporization 401.5
evaporative
 drying 393.10
 volatile 401.10
evasion
 avoidance 631.1
 circumvention 735.5
 equivocation 483.5
 escape 632.1
 neutrality 806.1
 prevarication 613.4
 retreat 284.3
 secrecy 614.1
evasive
 dishonest 975.16
 elusive 631.15
 equivocating 483.14
 prevaricating 613.11
 secretive 614.15
eve 134.2
even
 v. calm 163.7
 equal 30.5
 equalize 30.6
 level 214.6
 make uniform 17.4
 smooth 260.5
 symmetrize 248.3
 adj. equal 30.7
 exact 516.16
 flat 214.7
 interchangeable
  150.5
 just 976.8
 moderate 163.13
 neutral 806.7
 numerical 86.8
 parallel 218.6
 periodic 137.7
 smooth 260.9
 straight 250.6
 symmetric 248.4
 uniform 17.5
 adv. exactly 516.20
 indeed 36.17
 interchangeably
  150.6
 notwithstanding 33.8
evenhanded just 976.8
 unprejudiced 526.12
evening
 equalization 30.2
 symmetrization 248.2
evening
 n. nightfall 134.2
 adj. vesper 134.8
evening dress 231.11
evenly equally 30.11
 horizontally 214.9
 justly 976.11

moderately 163.17
smoothly 260.12
uniformly 17.7
**evenness** equality 30.1
horizontalness 214.1
moderation 163.1
regularity 137.1
smoothness 260.1
symmetry 248.1
uniformity 17.1
**evensong**
*n.* evening 134.2
worship 1032.8
*adj.* vesper 134.8
**event** circumstance 8.1
eventuality 151
game 878.9
occurrence 151.2
result 154.1
**even-tempered**
inexcitable 858.10
moderate 163.13
**eventful** 151.10
**eventide** 134.2
**eventual**
coming 151.11
final 70.10
future 121.8
**eventuality**
circumstance 8.1
event 151.1
futurity 121.4
likelihood 175.1
possibility 509.1
result 154.1
the future 121.1
**eventually** finally 70.11
in time 121.11
ultimately 151.12
**ever**
by any possibility
509.10
constantly 135.7
forever 112.12
**Everest** 207.7
**everglade** 400.1
**evergreen**
*n.* plant 411.3
tree 411.10
*adj.* arboreal 411.36
enduring 110.10
new 122.7
perennial 112.8
plant 411.41
**everlasting**
godlike 1013.20
immortal 112.9
perpetual 112.7
tedious 884.8
**evermore** 112.12
**ever so** greatly 34.15
indeed 36.17
**everted** 220.7
**every** 79.15
**everybody** all 79.4
people 417.2
**everyday**
customary 642.15
frequent 135.4
simple 902.6
usual 84.8
vernacular 580.18

**Everyman**
common man 919.7
generality 79.3
people 417.2
**everyone** all 79.4
people 417.2
**every other**
alternately 137.11
periodic 137.7
**everything** 54.3
**everywhere**
generally 79.18
in every direction
290.27
in every place 179.11
omnipresent 186.13
scatteringly 75.12
to everywhere 179.12
universally 375.27
**evict** dispossess 822.23
oust 310.15
**eviction**
dispossession 822.7
ejection 310.2
**evidence**
*n.* clue 568.9
information 557.1
legal argument
1004.8
manifestation 555.1
manifestness 555.3
proof 505
visibility 444.2
*v.* demonstrate 505.9
manifest 555.5
**evident**
clearly visible 444.7
manifest 555.8
visible 444.6
**evidential**
factual 505.17
indicative 568.23
manifestative 555.9
**evidently**
manifestly 555.14
visibly 444.8
**evil**
*n.* bane 676.1
gods of 1016.6
immorality 981.1
iniquity 981.3
injury 675.3
misdeed 982.2
trouble 731.3
*adj.* bad 675.7
corrupt 981.16
ominous 544.17
wrong 959.3
**evildoing**
*n.* wrongdoing 982.1
*adj.* sinful 982.6
**evil eye**
bad influence 675.4
curse 972.1
glare 439.5
malevolence 939.4
spell 1036.1
**evil-looking**
evil-fashioned 675.11
ugly 899.7
**evil-minded** evil 981.15
evil-fashioned 675.11

**evil nature** 981.1
**evilness** badness 675.1
wickedness 981.4
**evil spirit**
bad spirit 1016.7
deities 1014.15
demons 1016
**evince** evidence 505.9
manifest 555.5
**eviscerate**
disembowel 305.13
weaken 160.10
**evisceration**
disembowelment
305.4
weakening 160.5
**evocation**
description 608.1
elicitation 305.5
exorcism 1035.4
summons 752.5
**evocative**
extractive 305.17
recollective 537.22
**evoke** conjure 1035.11
describe 608.12
elicit 305.14
induce 153.12
prompt 648.13
remember 537.10
resemble 20.7
summon 752.12
**evolution**
gradual change 148
improvement 691.2
mathematics 87.4
**evolutionary** 148.8
**evolve** become 145.17
create 167.10
develop 148.5
expatiate 593.7
improve 691.10
originate 167.13
unravel 305.10
**evolving**
*n.* gradual change
148.1
*adj.* evolutionary
148.8
**evulsion** 305.1
**ewe**
female animal 421.9
sheep 414.7
**ex** excluding 77.9
from 303.22
**exacerbate**
antagonize 929.7
impair 692.11
increase 38.5
make ill-humored
951.16
provoke 866.14
worsen 885.2
**exacerbation**
excitation 857.10
increase 38.2
irritation 866.3
worsening 885.1
**exact**
*v.* charge 846.14
demand 753.4
extort 305.15

impose 963.4
oblige 756.5
require 639.9
wrest from 822.22
*adj.* detailed 8.9
discriminating 492.7
meticulous 533.12
precise 516.16
punctilious 646.10
**exacting**
demanding 753.8
difficult 731.16
extractive 305.17
fastidious 896.9
meticulous 533.12
overpriced 848.12
strict 757.6
**exaction** demand 753.1
extortion 305.6
fee 846.7
imposition 963.1
**exactly**
*adv.* meticulously
533.16
precisely 516.20
punctually 131.14
specifically 80.15
squarely 290.25
*interj.* yes 521.18
**exactness**
accuracy 516.3
meticulousness 533.3
**exaggerate**
increase 38.5
lie 616.19
misrepresent 573.3
overdo 663.10
overestimate 497.2
overrun 313.4
overstate 617.3
**exaggerated**
excessive 663.16
hyperbolic(al) 617.4
overestimated 497.3
**exaggeration**
excess 663.1
falsification 616.9
increase 38.2
lie 616.11
misrepresentation
573.1
overestimation 497.1
overrunning 313.1
overstatement 617
style 588.2
**exalt** cheer 870.8
elevate 317.6
glorify 914.13
increase 38.4
praise 968.12
promote 782.2
respect 964.4
sanctify 1026.5
worship 1032.11
**exaltation**
elevation 317.1
glorification 914.8
happiness 865.2
height 207.1
magnanimity 979.2
praise 968.5
promotion 782.1

repute 914.5
sanctification 1026.3
worship 1032.2
**exalted** cheerful 870.11
eminent 34.9
high 207.19
magnanimous 979.6
noble 918.10
overjoyed 865.14
prominent 914.18
raised 317.9
**exam** 485.2
**examination**
discussion 597.7
inspection 485.3
medical diagnosis
689.13
questioning 485.11
scrutiny 439.6
test 485.2
treatise 606.1
trial 1004.5
**examine** discuss 597.12
inspect 485.23
interrogate 485.20
scrutinize 439.15
study 564.12
**examiner** analyst 48.5
inquirer 485.15
tester 485.16
**examining** 485.36
**example**
*n.* citation 505.6
model 25.2
representative 572.5
taste 427.4
warning 703.1
*v.* cite 505.14
**exasperate**
annoy 866.13
provoke 952.22
trouble 864.15
**exasperated**
aggravated 885.4
annoyed 866.21
provoked 952.25
**exasperating**
aggravating 885.5
annoying 864.22
**exasperation**
aggravation 885.1
annoyance 866.2
excitation 857.10
incitement 648.4
resentment 952.1
unpleasantness 864.7
**Excalibur** 801.4
**excavate** deepen 209.8
dig 257.15
dig up 305.10
find 488.4
**excavation**
deepening 209.7
digging 257.11
discovery 488.1
extraction 305.1
hole 201.2
pit 257.4
**exceed** excel 36.6
loom 34.5
overdo 663.9
overrun 313.4

**exceedingly**
superlatively 36.16
very 34.18
**excel**
be expert at 733.17
surpass 36.6
**excellence**
goodness 674.1
good taste 897.1
nobility 914.5
superiority 36.1
**excellent**
*adj.* eminent 914.18
good 674.12
skillful 733.20
superior 36.12
tasteful 897.8
*interj.* approval
968.22
**except**
*v.* exclude 42.10
exempt 762.14
reject 638.2
*prep.* excluding 77.9
less 42.14
*conj.* unless 507.16
**excepted**
exempt 762.29
rejected 638.3
**excepting**
*prep.* excluding 77.9
less 42.14
*conj.* unless 507.16
**exception**
disapproval 969.4
exclusion 77.1
exemption 762.8
justification 1006.2
marvel 920.2
objection 522.2
odd thing 85.5
qualification 507.1
rejection 638.1
stipulation 753.2
**exceptional**
eccentric 474.4
exclusive 77.8
extraordinary 85.14
important 672.18
particular 80.12
remarkable 34.10
wonderful 920.10
**exceptionally**
extraordinarily 85.18
unusually 34.20
wonderfully 920.14
**excerpt**
*n.* extract 607.3
*v.* select 637.14
**excess**
*n.* exaggeration 617.1
excessiveness 663
exorbitance 848.4
intemperance 993.1
overrunning 313.1
surplus 43.4
undueness 961.1
*adj.* superfluous
663.17
**excessive**
exaggerated 617.4
inordinate 663.16

intemperate 993.7
overpriced 848.12
undue 961.10
violent 162.15
**excessively**
distressingly 34.21
exorbitantly 848.16
inordinately 663.22
intemperately 993.10
**excessiveness**
excess 663.1
exorbitance 848.4
fanaticism 473.11
intemperance 993.1
**exchange**
*n.* banter 882.1
communication
554.1
conversation 597.1
interchange 150.1
property transfer
817.1
retaliation 955.1
stock exchange 833.7
substitute 149.2
substitution 149.1
telephone number
560.12
trade 827.2
*v.* interchange 150.4
substitute 149.4
trade 827.14
transfer property
817.3
**exchequer**
depository 836.12
funds 835.14
storage place 660.6
**excise**
*n.* tax 846.11
*v.* cut out 42.10
extract 305.10
sever 49.11
**excision**
extraction 305.1
removal 42.3
separation 49.2
surgical operation
689.22
**excitable**
emotional 857.26
irascible 951.19
nervous 859.10
**excite** agitate 324.10
impassion 857.11
incite 648.17
interest 530.12
make hot 329.18
sensitize 422.9
**excited** agitated 324.16
fervent 855.23
impassioned 857.18
impatient 862.6
interested 530.16
**excitement**
agitation 324.1
emotion 857
excitation 857.10
fervor 855.10
heat 328.2
impatience 862.1
incitement 648.4

**exciting** alluring 650.7
desirable 634.30
eloquent 600.13
interesting 530.19
provocative 648.27
thrilling 857.28
**exclaim**
give an exclamation
459.7
remark 594.25
utter 594.26
**exclamation**
ejaculation 459.2
remark 594.4
**exclamatory** 459.11
**exclude** bar 77.4
disapprove 969.10
eject 310.13
except 42.10
expel 310.17
prevent 730.14
prohibit 778.3
reject 638.2
**excluded** barred 77.7
impossible 510.7
rejected 638.3
**excluding**
*adj.* exclusive 77.8
*prep.* barring 77.9
less 42.14
**exclusion** barring 77
disapproval 969.1
ejection 310.4
excision 42.3
prohibition 778.1
rejection 638.1
**exclusive**
*n.* news 558.3
*adj.* contemptuous
966.8
excluding 77.8
limiting 234.9
one 89.7
particular 896.13
prohibitive 778.6
unsociable 923.6
**exclusively**
simply 45.11
solely 89.14
**exclusiveness**
contempt 966.1
narrowness 77.3
particularity 896.5
partisanism 788.13
unsociability 923.3
**exclusive of**
excluding 77.9
less 42.14
**excogitate** 478.11
**excommunicate**
condemn 1008.3
curse 972.5
depose 783.4
eject 310.17
**excoriate**
criticize severely
969.21
peel 232.8
**excrement**
excretion 311.3
filth 682.7
**excremental** 311.20

**excrete**
discharge 311.12
exude 303.15
secrete 312.5
**excretion**
bodily discharge 311
evacuation 310.6
outflow 303.6
secretion 312.1
**excretory**
excretive 311.19
exudative 303.20
secretory 312.7
**excruciating**
painful 424.10
sensitive 422.15
unpleasant 864.23
**excruciatingly**
terribly 34.21
unpleasantly 864.28
**exculpate**
acquit 1007.4
forgive 947.3
justify 1006.9
**exculpation**
acquittal 1007.1
justification 1006.1
pardon 947.2
**excursion**
circuitousness 321.1
detour 321.3
deviation 291.1
digression 593.4
journey 273.5
obliquity 219.1
sight-seeing 442.4
**excursive**
circuitous 321.7
deviant 291.7
discursive 593.13
oblique 219.13
**excusable** 1006.14
**excuse**
n. acquittal 1007.1
alibi 1006.4
apology 1012.2
pardon 947.2
pretext 649.1
reason 153.2
v. acquit 1007.4
exempt 762.14
forgive 947.3
justify 1006.11
**excused** exempt 762.29
forgiven 947.7
**execrable** base 915.12
cursed 972.9
evil 981.16
infernal 675.10
offensive 864.18
**execrate** berate 969.20
curse 972.6
damn 972.5
hate 930.5
**execration**
berating 969.7
curse 972.1
hate 930.1
hated thing 930.3
**execute**
accomplish 722.4
kill 409.13

observe 768.3
perform 705.8
perform music 462.40
produce 167.9
put to death 1010.19
transact 771.10
**executed**
accomplished 722.10
produced 167.20
**execution**
accomplishment
722.1
appropriation 822.5
capital punishment
1010.7
instruments of 1011.5
killing 409.1
music 462.31
observance 768.1
operation 164.1
performance 705.2
production 167.1
transaction 771.5
**executive**
n. directorate 748.11
executive officer
748.3
governor 749.5
adj. administrative
747.14
governing 741.19
**executive officer**
assistant 787.6
commissioned officer
749.18
deputy 781.1
executive 748.3
**executive session** 614.2
**executor** doer 718.1
producer 167.8
**exegesis**
comment 552.5
explanation 552.4
**exemplar**
good person 985.4
idea 479.2
pattern of perfection
677.4
representative 25.2
**exemplary** model 25.8
perfect 677.9
praiseworthy 968.20
typical 572.11
warning 703.7
**exemplification**
citation 505.6
example 25.2
explanation 552.4
representation 572.1
**exemplify** cite 505.14
explain 552.10
represent 572.8
set an example 25.7
**exempt**
v. acquit 1007.4
free 762.14
adj. immune 762.29
**exemption**
freedom 762.8
immunity 1007.2
pardon 947.2
qualification 507.1

**exercise**
n. action 705.1
ceremony 646.4
exertion 716.6
lesson 562.7
music 462.5
operation 164.1
study 564.3
task 656.2
training 562.3
use 665.1
v. annoy 866.13
engross 530.13
exert 716.8
practice 705.7
train 562.14
use 665.10
**exert** exercise 716.8
use 665.10
**exertion** effort 716
endeavor 714.1
use 665.1
**exert oneself**
put forth one's
strength 716.9
struggle 714.4
try hard 714.11
**exfoliate** break 49.12
flake 227.5
scale 232.11
**exhale** breathe 403.24
give off 401.8
let out 310.23
smell 435.6
**exhaust**
n. aviation 278.39
miasma 676.4
outflow 303.4
outlet 303.9
rocketry 281.8
v. breathe 403.24
consume 666.2
drain 822.24
eject 310.24
empty 303.13
extract 305.12
fatigue 717.4
let out 310.23
oppress 864.16
overtax 663.10
purge 310.21
unman 158.12
waste 854.4
weaken 160.10
**exhausted** barren 166.4
impaired 692.38
tired 717.8
unhealthy 686.50
used up 666.4
weakened 160.18
**exhausting**
fatiguing 717.11
unpleasant 864.24
weakening 160.20
**exhaustion**
consumption 666.1
decrease 39.3
evacuation 310.6
fatigue 717.2
sickness 686.7
unhealthiness 686.2
waste 812.2

weakening 160.5
**exhaustive**
complete 722.12
great 34.6
thorough 56.10
whole 54.9
**exhibit**
n. display 555.2
evidence 505.1
spectacle 446.7
theatrical perfor-
mance 611.13
v. display 505.9
flaunt 904.17
manifest 555.5
**exhibition**
display 555.2
ostentation 904.4
spectacle 446.7
theatrical perfor-
mance 611.13
**exhibitionism**
display 904.4
divestment 232.1
immodesty 990.2
sexual preference
419.12
**exhibitionist**
sex deviant 419.17
show-off 904.11
**exhilarate**
amuse 878.23
cheer 870.7
energize 161.9
inspire 648.20
refresh 695.2
stimulate 857.12
**exhilarated**
cheerful 870.11
excited 857.18
pleased 865.12
refreshed 695.4
**exhilarating**
cheering 870.16
energizing 161.14
exciting 857.28
inspiring 648.26
refreshing 695.3
**exhilaration**
energizing 161.7
excitement 857.1
good humor 870.2
happiness 865.2
inspiration 648.9
refreshment 695.1
stimulation 857.10
**exhort** advise 754.6
urge 648.14
**exhortation**
advice 754.1
call to arms 797.12
inducement 648.3
speech 599.2
**exhume** disinter 305.11
find 488.4
**exigency** crisis 129.4
insistence 753.3
pressure 648.6
urgency 672.4
urgent need 639.4
**exigent** critical 129.10
demanding 753.8

meticulous 533.12
necessary 639.12
strict 757.6
urgent 672.21
**exiguity** fewness 102.1
insignificance 35.1
littleness 196.1
meagerness 662.2
thinness 205.4
**exiguous** little 196.10
meager 662.10
sparse 102.5
**exile**
*n.* alien 78.3
displaced person
185.4
ejection 310.4
elimination 77.2
emigration 303.7
migrant 274.5
outcast 926.4
*v.* eject 310.17
eliminate 77.5
emigrate 303.16
**exiled** displaced 185.10
excluded 77.7
**exist** be 1.8
be present 186.6
consist in 1.11
endure 110.6
live 407.7
**existence** being 1
life 407.1
presence 186.1
something 3.3
**existent** existing 1.13
living 407.11
present 120.2
**existential** 500.9
**existentialism** 1.7
**existing** existent 1.13
present 120.2
**exit**
*n.* channel 396.1
death 408.1
departure 301.1
egress 303.1
flight 631.4
outlet 303.9
passageway 657.4
*v.* absent oneself
187.8
depart 301.6
disappear 447.2
find vent 632.10
go out 303.11
:xodus act 611.8
departure 301.1
egress 303.1
:x officio 739.15
·xonerate
acquit 1007.4
forgive 947.3
xoneration
acquittal 1007.1
pardon 947.2
·xorbitance
exaggeration 617.1
excess 663.1
overcharge 848.4
·xorbitant
demanding 753.8

exaggerated 617.4
excessive 663.16
overpriced 848.12
violent 162.15
**exorcise** 1035.12
**exorcism**
conjuration 1035.4
spell 1036.1
**exorcist**
holy orders 1038.4
sorcerer 1035.7
**exotic** alluring 650.7
colorful 362.18
distant 199.8
foreign 78.5
unrelated 10.5
**expand** broaden 204.4
develop 148.6
expatiate 593.7
generalize 79.9
grow 197.5
increase 38.4
make larger 197.4
rarefy 355.3
spread 197.6
**expanded**
extended 197.10
increased 38.7
**expanding**
expatiating 593.15
increasing 38.8
**expanse** breadth 204.1
greatness 34.1
size 195.1
space 179.1
**expansion**
business cycle 827.9
development 148.1
dispersion 75.1
exaggeration 617.1
expatiation 593.6
growth 197
increase 38.1
size 195.1
space 179.1
**expansive** broad 204.6
extensive 197.9
spacious 179.9
talkative 596.9
unreserved 554.10
voluminous 195.17
**expatiate** 593.7
**expatiating** 593.15
**expatriate**
*n.* migrant 274.5
outcast 926.4
*v.* deport 77.5
eject 310.17
emigrate 303.16
leave 301.18
migrate 273.21
**expect** anticipate 539.5
be hopeful 888.7
believe 501.11
foresee 121.6
suppose 499.10
**expectancy** 539.1
**expectant**
anticipant 539.11
hopeful 888.11
**expectation**
anticipation 539

dueness 960.1
hope 888.1
probability 511.1
the future 121.1
unastonishment
921.1
**expected**
anticipated 539.13
unastonished 921.3
**expecting**
anticipant 539.11
pregnant 169.18
unastonished 921.3
**expectorant** 687.32
**expectorate** 312.6
**expedience** fitness 670
goodness 674.1
timeliness 129.1
**expedient**
*n.* instrumentality
658.2
machinations 735.4
means 670.2
recourse 700.2
stratagem 735.3
*adj.* fitting 670.5
good 674.12
timely 129.9
useful 665.18
**expedite**
facilitate 732.6
further 785.17
hasten 709.4
send 271.14
**expedition**
facilitation 732.4
furtherance 785.5
journey 273.5
military campaign
797.7
promptness 131.3
quest 715.2
quickness 707.3
speed 269.1
**expeditious**
active 707.18
fast 269.19
hasty 709.9
prompt 131.9
**expeditiously**
fast 269.21
hastily 709.12
promptly 131.15
with alacrity 707.26
**expel** banish 310.17
breathe 403.24
depose 783.4
disgorge 310.24
dismiss 310.19
eject 310.13
eliminate 77.5
separate 49.9
transfer 271.9
**expelled** 77.7
**expend** consume 666.2
pay out 841.14
spend 843.5
use 665.13
waste 854.4
**expendable**
consumable 666.5
replaceable 149.10

superfluous 663.17
**expended** lost 812.7
paid 841.22
**expenditure**
accounts 845.1
consumption 666.1
loss 812.2
price 846.1
spending 843
**expense** costs 843.3
loss 812.1
price 846.1
**expensive** 848.11
**experience**
*n.* emotion 855.3
event 151.2
knowledge 475.1
practical knowledge
733.9
sensation 422.1
*v.* emotions 855.11
have 151.8
sense 422.8
**experienced**
accustomed 642.17
practiced 733.26
**experiment**
*n.* attempt 714.2
experimentation 489
*v.* experimentalize
489.8
try 714.9
**experimental**
endeavoring 714.14
test 489.11
**experimentation** 489.1
**expert**
*n.* adept 733.11
advisor 754.3
connoisseur 897.7
scientist 475.11
specialist 81.3
*adj.* adept 733.25
finished 677.9
skillful 733.20
specialized 81.5
versed in 475.19
**expertise**
aesthetic taste 897.5
knowledge 475.1
profound knowledge
475.6
skill 733.1
**expertly** 733.29
**expiate** atone 1012.4
compensate 33.4
**expiation**
atonement 1012.1
compensation 33.1
**expiration**
breathing 403.18
death 408.1
end 70.1
**expire**
be destroyed 693.23
breathe 403.24
cease to exist 2.5
die 408.19
elapse 105.5
emit 310.23
end 70.6
**expired** no more 2.10

past 119.7
**explain**
explicate 552.10
facilitate 732.6
justify 1006.9
lecture 562.17
make clear 548.6
solve 487.2
**explanation**
example 25.2
interpretation 552.4
justification 1006.1
meaning 545.3
reason 153.2
solution 487.1
theorization 499.1
theory 499.2
**explanatory** 552.15
**expletive**
*n.* curse 972.4
exclamation 459.2
redundancy 103.3
superfluity 663.4
*adj.* superfluous
663.17
**explicable**
attributable 155.6
interpretable 552.17
solvable 487.3
**explicate**
expatiate 593.7
explain 552.10
make clear 548.6
**explicit** candid 974.17
intelligible 548.10
manifest 555.8
unqualified 508.2
**explode**
become angry 952.19
blast 456.8
blow up 162.13
come to nothing
725.12
disprove 506.4
fuel 331.8
get excited 857.15
**exploded**
disproved 506.7
not believed 503.12
**exploit**
*n.* act 705.3
courageous act 893.7
*v.* overcharge 848.7
take advantage of
665.15
use 665.16
**exploitable**
gullible 502.9
usable 665.22
**exploitation**
overcharge 848.5
utilization 665.8
**exploration**
adventure 715.2
reconnaissance 485.8
search 485.14
**exploratory**
examining 485.36
preceding 66.4
**explore**
investigate 485.22
search 485.30

**explorer** precursor 66.1
traveler 274.1
**explosion**
detonation 456.3
discharge 162.7
disproof 506.1
emotional outburst
857.8
increase 38.2
outburst 952.9
**explosive**
*n.* ammunition 801.9
speech sound 594.13
*adj.* banging 456.11
dangerous 697.9
excitable 857.26
hot-tempered 951.25
violent 162.23
**exponent** deputy 781.1
example 25.2
explainer 552.7
representative 572.5
supporter 787.9
**exponential** 86.8
**export**
*n.* sending abroad
303.8
transference 271.1
*v.* send 271.14
send abroad 303.17
transfer 271.9
**expose** disclose 556.4
disillusionize 520.2
disprove 506.4
divest 232.5
endanger 697.6
stigmatize 915.9
unclose 265.13
uncover 488.4
**exposé** disclosure 556.1
disproof 506.1
**exposed** airy 402.12
disproved 506.7
divested 232.12
manifest 555.10
open 265.18
unprotected 697.15
visible 444.6
vulnerable 175.5
wind-blown 403.27
**exposition**
disclosure 556.1
display 555.2
explanation 552.4
fair 832.2
lesson 562.7
music division 462.24
spectacle 446.7
treatise 606.1
**expositive**
descriptive 608.15
dissertational 606.6
explanatory 552.15
**expositor**
commentator 606.4
discourser 606.3
explainer 552.7
lecturer 599.5
**ex post facto**
back 119.12
subsequently 117.6

**expostulate**
advise 754.6
dissuade 652.3
object 522.5
**exposure**
appearance 446.1
disclosure 556.1
discovery 488.1
display 555.2
disproof 506.1
divestment 232.1
film exposure 577.9
liability 175.2
position 184.3
publicity 559.4
unprotectedness
697.3
visibility 444.1
**expound**
explain 552.10
lecture 562.17
**express**
*n.* carrier 271.5
mail 604.5
message 558.4
messenger 561.1
train 272.13
*v.* affirm 523.4
describe 608.12
evidence 505.9
extract 305.16
indicate 568.17
manifest 555.5
phrase 588.4
say 594.23
send 271.14
*adj.* exact 516.16
fast 269.19
intelligible 548.10
manifest 555.8
particular 80.12
unqualified 508.2
*adv.* posthaste 709.13
**expressed** 588.5
**expression**
diction 588.1
distillation 305.7
eloquence 600.1
extraction 305.1
indication 568.1
manifestation 555.1
maxim 517.1
music 462.31
phrase 585.1
remark 594.4
word 582.1
**expressionism** 573.1
**expressionless**
inexpressive 549.20
reticent 613.10
**expressive**
descriptive 608.15
eloquent 600.10
indicative 568.23
manifestative 555.9
meaningful 545.10
**expressly** exactly 516.20
intelligibly 548.14
manifestly 555.14
particularly 80.15
**expressway** 657.6

**expropriate**
appropriate 822.20
dispossess 822.23
**expulsion**
deposal 783.2
disgorgement 310.7
ejection 310.1
elimination 77.2
transference 271.1
**expulsive** 310.28
**expunge** cancel 70.7
delete 42.12
obliterate 693.16
**expunged** 70.8
**expurgate** clean 681.18
delete 42.12
**expurgated** 681.26
**exquisite**
affected 903.18
beautiful 900.16
chic 644.13
fastidious 896.11
meticulous 533.12
pleasant 863.7
sensitive 422.15
superb 674.17
tasty 428.8
**exquisitely**
beautifully 900.21
fashionably 644.18
intensely 34.20
meticulously 533.16
pleasantly 863.12
superbly 674.22
**extant** existent 1.13
present 120.2
**extemporaneous**
impromptu 630.12
unprepared 721.8
**extemporize**
be unprepared 721.6
improvise 630.8
**extend** be distant 199.5
be elastic 358.4
be long 202.6
broaden 204.4
cover 228.30
endure 110.6
expatiate 593.8
generalize 79.9
give 818.12
grow 197.5
increase 38.4
lengthen 202.7
make larger 197.4
offer 773.4
postpone 132.9
protract 110.9
reach 179.7
spread 197.6
straighten 250.5
stretch to 199.6
sustain 143.4
**extended**
expanded 197.10
extensive 179.9
increased 38.7
lengthened 202.9
meaningful 545.10
protracted 110.11
wordy 593.12
**extension** addition 41.

extraction 305.1
freeing 763.3
rescue 702.1
**extrinsic** exterior 224.6
external 6.3
extraneous 78.5
formal 646.7
irrelevant 10.6
**extrinsicality**
exteriority 224.1
externality 6
extraneousness 78.1
formality 646.1
**extroversion**
communicativeness
554.3
personality tendency
690.14
**extrovert** 690.15
**extroverted**
communicative
554.10
extrovert 690.47
**extrude** create 167.10
eject 310.13
emerge 303.12
protrude 256.9
**extrusion**
ejection 310.1
emergence 303.2
excretion 311.1
protuberance 256.2
**exuberance**
diffuseness 593.1
gaiety 870.4
happiness 865.2
plenty 661.2
productiveness 165.1
**exuberant**
diffuse 593.11
fervent 855.23
gay 870.14
plants 411.40
plentiful 661.7
productive 165.9
thriving 728.13
**exude** be damp 392.11
emit 303.15
excrete 311.12
sweat 311.16
**exult** be proud 905.5
gloat 910.9
rejoice 876.5
**exultant**
gloating 910.12
overjoyed 865.14
rejoicing 876.9
**exultation**
gloating 910.4
rejoicing 876.1
**exurb** 183.1
**eye**
*n.* belief 501.6
circlet 253.5
detective 781.11
diseases of 686.13
hole 265.4
look 439.3
mental outlook 525.2
protection 699.1
supervision 747.2
vision 439.1

visual organ 439.9
*v.* be a spectator
442.5
flirt 932.18
look at 439.14
scrutinize 439.15
stare 439.16
**eyeball**
*n.* eye 439.9
*v.* look at 439.14
*adj.* visual 439.21
**eyeball to eyeball**
confronting 239.6
contrary 15.6
facing 239.5
fronting 240.11
in opposition 790.9
**eye for an eye, an**
interchange 150.1
retaliation 955.3
**eyeful**
beautiful thing 900.7
look 439.3
**eyeglass** lens 443.1
spectacles 443.2
**eyelet** circlet 253.5
hole 265.4
**eye-opener**
alcoholic drink 996.8
surprise 540.2
**eye-opening**
astonishing 920.12
disclosive 556.10
**eye patch** 441.5
**eyeshade** 338.2
**eyesight**
field of view 444.3
vision 439.1
**eyesore** blemish 679.3
ugly thing 899.4
**eyestrain** 717.1
**eyewash** flattery 970.1
healing ointment
687.11
humbug 616.14
ointment 380.3
**eyewitness**
*n.* spectator 442.1
witness 505.7
*adj.* evidential 505.17

**F**

**fab** 674.13
**Fabian**
*n.* reformer 691.6
socialist 745.14
*adj.* reformational
691.16
socialist 745.22
**fable**
fabrication 616.10
fiction 608.7
story element 608.9
**fabled** 914.16
**fabric** building 245.2
cloth 378.5
content 194.5
frame 245.4
house 191.6
structure 245.1
substance 3.2

types of 378.11
weaving 222.1
**fabricate** compose 58.3
create 167.13
imagine 535.14
manufacture 167.10
trump up 616.18
**fabricated**
invented 167.23
made 167.22
trumped-up 616.29
**fabrication**
composition 58.1
creation 167.5
falsehood 616.10
manufacture 167.3
structure 245.1
**fabulous**
excessive 663.16
extraordinary 85.14
fabricated 616.29
fictional 608.17
fictitious 535.21
mythical 1014.25
remarkable 34.10
wonderful 920.10
**façade**
affectation 903.1
appearances 446.2
exterior 224.2
face 240.1
fakery 616.3
pretext 649.1
**face**
*n.* countenance 240.4
exterior 224.2
fakery 616.3
front 240.1
insolence 913.3
looks 446.4
nationalism 797.16
precipice 213.3
prestige 914.4
pride 905.1
type part 603.6
type style 603.6
worth 846.3
*v.* be imminent 152.2
color 362.13
confront 240.8
contrapose 239.4
cover 228.23
defy 793.3
expect 539.5
front on 240.9
line 194.7
oppose 790.5
stand up to 893.11
**face about** 295.10
**face down**
offer resistance 792.3
outbrave 893.12
**face guard** 799.17
**face-lift**
*n.* renovation 694.4
*v.* renovate 694.17
**face-lifting**
plastic surgery 689.25
renovation 694.4
**face-saving** 914.2
**facet** aspect 446.3
exterior 224.2

front 240.1
particular 8.3
**facetious** 881.15
**facetiousness** 881.2
**face to face**
adjacent 200.16
opposite 239.6
overtly 555.15
**face up to**
defy danger 697.7
offer resistance 792.3
stand up to 893.11
**face value**
stock price 834.9
worth 846.3
**facia** 240.1
**facial**
beautification 900.10
massage 350.3
**facies** 240.4
**facile** docile 765.13
easy 732.12
eloquent 600.9
pliant 357.9
teachable 564.18
**facilitate**
be instrumental
658.5
ease 732.6
further 785.17
**facilities**
accommodations
659.3
equipment 659.4
**facility** ability 157.2
aid 785.9
ease 732
eloquence 600.2
equipment 659.4
machinery 348.4
pliancy 357.2
skill 733.1
submissiveness 765.3
teachability 564.5
workplace 719.1
**facing**
*n.* coating 228.12
lining 194.3
*adj.* fronting 240.11
opposite 239.5
*adv.* frontward 240.13
*prep.* opposite 239.7
**facsimile**
communications
560.15
copy 24.3
imitation 22.3
the same 14.3
**fact** actuality 1.3
event 151.2
evidence 505.1
particular 8.3
truth 516.1
**fact-finding** 485.36
**faction**
disagreement 27.1
dissension 795.3
group 74.3
partisanism 788.13
political party 744.2
religion 1020.3
side 788.4

**factious**
  factional 795.17
  rebellious 767.11
**factor**
  *n.* agent 781.3
    cause 153.1
    component 58.2
    gene 170.6
    manager 748.4
    particular 8.3
  *v.* analyze 48.8
**factory** 719.3
**factory town** 719.2
**factotum** 750.9
**facts** evidence 505.1
  information 557.1
  knowledge 475.1
  particulars 1.4
**factual** certain 513.15
  evidential 505.17
  real 1.15
  true 516.12
**faculty** ability 157.2
  authority 739.1
  educators 565.10
  intellect 466.2
  privilege 958.3
  talent 733.4
**fad** caprice 629.1
  craze 644.5
  momentary triumph
    724.3
**faddish**
  fashionable 644.15
  fickle 629.6
**faddist**
  enthusiast 635.5
  fad 644.5
**fade** age 126.10
  become old 123.9
  bet 515.20
  be transient 111.6
  cease to exist 2.5
  decline 692.20
  decolor 363.5
  deteriorate 692.21
  disappear 447.2
  fail 686.45
  lose color 363.6
  pull back 284.7
  recede 297.2
  wèaken 160.9
**fade** insipid 430.2
  trite 883.9
  uninteresting 883.6
**faded** colorless 363.7
  weatherworn 692.36
**fade in** 446.8
**fade-in** 344.16
**fade out**
  cease to exist 2.5
  disappear 447.2
  lose color 363.6
**fade-out** decrease 39.1
  disappearance 447.1
  radio broadcasting
    344.16
  radio reception
    344.21
**fading**
  *n.* decoloration 363.3
  deterioration 692.3

disappearance 447.1
  radio reception
    344.21
  *adj.* aging 126.17
    deteriorating 692.46
    languishing 160.21
    receding 297.5
    transient 111.7
    vanishing 447.3
**faerie** fairyfolk 1014.17
  paradise 535.11
  supernaturalism 85.7
**faery** 1014.27
**fag**
  *n.* cigarette 434.5
    drudge 718.3
    drudgery 716.4
    homosexual 419.16
  *v.* drudge 716.14
    fatigue 717.4
    task 716.16
**fag end** extremity 70.2
  remainder 43.1
**fagged** exhausted 717.8
  fatigued 717.6
**faggot** 419.16
**fagot** bundle 74.8
  firewood 331.3
**Fahrenheit** 328.30
**Fahrenheit scale** 328.19
**fail** age 126.10
  be a flop 611.33
  be dishonest 975.12
  be inferior 37.4
  be insufficient 662.8
  be unsuccessful 725.8
  decline 692.20
  fail in health 686.45
  fail someone 725.16
  fall short 314.2
  go bankrupt 842.7
  neglect 534.6
  not accomplish 723.2
  weaken 160.9
**failed** insolvent 842.11
  unsuccessful 725.17
**failing**
  *n.* deterioration 692.3
    fault 678.2
    vice 981.2
  *adj.* deteriorating
    692.46
    incomplete 57.4
    insufficient 662.9
    languishing 160.21
    unhealthy 686.50
    unsuccessful 725.17
**fail-safe** 698.5
**failure** an error 518.3
  defeat 727.1
  deterioration 692.3
  disappointment
    541.1
  fault 678.2
  ineffectiveness 158.3
  inferiority 37.3
  insolvency 842.3
  insolvent 842.4
  neglect 534.1
  nonaccomplishment
    723.1
  nonobservance 769.1

nonsuccess 725
  shortcoming 314.1
  sin 982.2
  stage show 611.4
  unsuccessful person
    725.7
  vice 981.2
**failure of memory**
  538.2
**fain** desirous 634.22
  willing 622.5
**faint**
  *n.* unconsciousness
    423.2
  *v.* get tired 717.5
    swoon 423.5
    weaken 160.9
  *adj.* colorless 363.7
    faint-sounding 452.16
    fatigued 717.6
    indistinct 445.6
    irresolute 627.12
    sick 686.52
    weak 160.12
**faint heart** 892.4
**fainthearted**
  cowardly 892.10
  irresolute 627.12
**faint praise** 971.1
**fair**
  *n.* festival 878.4
    marketplace 832.2
  *adj.* appropriate 960.8
    auspicious 544.18
    beautiful 900.17
    clean 681.25
    courteous 936.14
    good 674.12
    honest 974.13
    just 976.8
    legible 548.11
    light 363.9
    mediocre 680.7
    pleasant 863.6
    probable 511.6
    prosperous 728.13
    rainless 393.8
    sunny 863.10
    tolerable 674.19
    unprejudiced 526.12
    whitish 364.8
  *adv.* justly 976.11
    pleasantly 863.11
**fair game**
  laughingstock 967.7
  opportunity 129.2
**fairly** justly 976.11
  legibly 548.13
  mediocrely 680.11
  moderately 35.10
  to a degree 29.7
  tolerably 674.23
**fairness** beauty 900.3
  colorlessness 363.2
  goodness 674.1
  honesty 974.1
  justice 976.3
  unprejudicedness
    526.5
  whiteness 364.1
**fair play** 976.3
**fair sex** 421.3

**fair shake** equality 30.3
  even chance 156.7
  fairness 976.3
**fair-spoken**
  flattering 970.8
  suave 936.18
**fair to middling**
  680.7,11
**fair trade**
  commerce 827.1
  price controls 846.6
**fair-trade** 846.13
**fairway** green 411.7
  playground 878.12
  runway 278.23
  seaway 275.10
**fair weather**
  good times 728.4
  hot weather 328.7
  pleasantness 863.4
  weather 402.4
**fair-weather friend**
  619.8
**fairy**
  *n.* homosexual 419.16
    lightness 353.2
    sprite 1014.18
  *adj.* elfin 1014.27
**fairyfolk** 1014.17
**fairy godmother**
  giver 818.11
  guardian angel
    1014.22
**fairyland**
  fairyfolk 1014.17
  paradise 535.11
**fairylike** 1014.27
**fairy tale** fictioh 608.7
  lie 616.11
**fait accompli**
  accomplishment
    722.1
  act 705.3
  reality 1.2
**faith** belief 501.1
  cause 153.10
  fidelity 974.7
  hope 888.1
  obedience 766.1
  orthodoxy 1024.2
  piety 1028.1
  promise 770.1
  religion 1020.1
  school 788.5
  sureness 513.5
  system of belief
    501.3
  virtue 980.5
  zeal 635.2
**faithful**
  believing 501.21
  descriptive 608.15
  exact 516.16
  friendly 927.20
  lifelike 20.16
  loving 931.25
  loyal 974.20
  obedient 766.3
  observant 768.4
  orthodox 1024.7
  persevering 625.7
  pious 1028.8

reliable 513.17
zealous 635.10
**faithfully**
descriptively 608.19
exactly 516.20
loyally 974.25
obediently 766.6
perseveringly 625.8
**faithful servant** 907.3
**faith healer** 688.12
**faith healing** 689.3
**faithless**
apostate 628.11
falsehearted 616.31
nonreligious 1031.19
unbelieving 503.8
unfaithful 975.20
**faithworthy**
reliable 513.17
trustworthy 974.19
**fake**
*n.* affecter 903.7
copy 24.1
hoax 618.7
impostor 619.6
sham 616.13
substitute 149.2
*v.* affect 903.12
fabricate 616.18
imitate 22.5
improvise 630.8
sham 616.21
tamper with 616.17
*adj.* assumed 903.16
imitation 22.8
similar 20.10
spurious 616.26
substitute 149.8
**fake out** fool 618.14
overshadow 36.8
**fakery** falseness 616.3
imitation 22.1
**fake up** 534.9
**fakir** ascetic 991.2
clergyman 1038.13
**falcate** 252.11
**falconry** 655.2
**falderal** see folderol
**fall**
*n.* autumn 128.4
backsliding 696.2
declivity 219.5
decrease 39.2
defeat 727.1
descent 316.1
deterioration 692.3
failure 725.3
false hair 230.13
hang 215.2
original sin 982.4
plunge 320.1
rain 394.1
ruin 693.3
tumble 316.3
waterfall 395.11
*v.* be defeated 727.12
be destroyed 693.22
cheapen 849.6
decline 692.20
decrease 39.6
descend 316.5
die 408.19

fail 725.11
go wrong 981.9
hang 215.6
incline 219.10
occur 151.5
plunge 320.6
rain 394.9
relapse 696.4
tumble 316.8
**fallacious**
deceptive 618.19
erroneous 518.16
false 616.25
illogical 483.11
illusory 519.9
sophistical 483.10
unorthodox 1025.9
**fallacy** deception 618.1
error 518.1
falseness 616.1
heresy 1025.2
sophistry 483.1
specious argument
483.3
**fall away**
apostatize 628.8
decline 692.20
decrease 39.6
fall short 314.2
incline 219.10
**fallback** recoil 284.3
retreat 295.2
**fall back**
be behind 241.8
get worse 692.19
pull back 284.7
relapse 696.4
retreat 295.6
**fall behind**
be behind 241.8
follow 293.4
regress 295.5
**fall by the wayside**
314.3
**fallen** carnal 987.6
cooked 330.8
dead 408.30
defeated 727.14
depressed 318.12
impious 1030.6
prostitute 989.28
reduced 39.10
ruined 693.28
unrighteous 981.12
**fallen angel** 986.5
**fall flat**
be uninteresting
883.4
fail 725.11
fall short 314.3
tumble 316.8
**fall for**
be credulous 502.6
fall in love 931.20
**fall from grace**
backsliding 696.2
impiety 1030.1
original sin 982.4
relapse 696.4
**fall guy** dupe 620.1
loser 727.5
scapegoat 149.3

**fallible** imperfect 678.4
uncertain 514.21
**fall in**
break down 692.27
collapse 198.10
fail 725.11
form 59.5
line up 71.6
**falling**
descending 316.11
deteriorating 692.46
pendent 215.9
sloping downward
219.16
**falling-out** 795.4
**falling sickness**
epilepsy 686.5
nervous disorder
686.23
seizure 324.6
**falling star** 375.15
**fall into**
become 145.17
incur 175.4
undertake 715.3
**fall into place** 59.5
**fall in with**
acquiesce 775.3
agree with 521.9
comply 82.3
conform 82.4
converge 298.2
find 488.3
get along with 794.2
incur 175.4
**fall off**
apostatize 628.8
come apart 49.8
decline 692.20
decrease 39.6
descend 316.5
incline 219.10
**fall on one's knees**
apologize 1012.5
beg for mercy 944.6
be servile 907.6
bow 964.6
bow down before
765.10
entreat 774.11
thank 949.4
**fallout** atomics 326.16
powder 361.5
radiation 327.1
**fall out** quarrel 795.10
result 154.5
**fallout shelter**
atomic explosion
326.16
shelter 700.3
**fallow**
*n.* farm 413.8
*v.* till 413.17
*adj.* barren 166.4
colorless 363.7
idle 708.17
unprepared 721.14
yellow 370.4
**falls** 395.11
**fall short**
be disappointing
541.3

be imperfect 678.3
be incomplete 57.3
be inferior 37.4
be insufficient 662.8
come short 314.2
fail 725.11
**fall through** fail 725.11
fall short 314.3
**fall to** begin 68.7
eat 307.18
set to work 716.15
undertake 715.3
**fall to pieces**
be damaged 692.26
be destroyed 693.22
be separated 49.8
crumble 361.10
decay 692.25
disintegrate 53.3
show fragility 360.3
**fall upon**
arrive at 300.7
attack 798.15
be unexpected 540.6
light on 316.10
meet 200.11
**false** deceitful 618.20
deceptive 618.19
erroneous 518.16
falsehearted 616.31
illegitimate 999.7
illusory 519.9
sanctimonious 1029.5
unfaithful 975.20
untrue 616.25
**false alarm** alarm 704.2
unsuccessful person
725.7
**false front**
affectation 903.1
disguise 618.10
display 904.4
fakery 616.3
front 240.1
**falsehearted**
deceitful 618.20
dishonest 975.18
false 616.31
treacherous 975.21
**falsehood**
falseness 616.1
lie 616.11
untruthfulness 616.8
**falsely**
deceptively 618.21
erroneously 518.20
untruly 616.35
**false modesty** 903.6
**false move** 518.4
**false name** 583.8
**falseness** deceit 618.3
deception 618.1
error 518.1
falseheartedness
616.4
falsehood 616
illusoriness 519.2
infidelity 975.5
sanctimony 1029.1
**false pretense** 616.3
**false reasoning** 483.1

**false show**
  affectation 903.1
  fakery 616.3
  illusoriness 519.2
**false step** 518.4
**falsetto**
  *n.* high voice 458.6
  speech defect 595.1
  voice 463.5
  *adj.* high 458.13
  vocal 462.51
**false witness**
  accusation 1005.4
  liar 619.9
**falsies** 231.24
**falsification**
  falsifying 616.9
  misrepresentation
    573.1
**falsified** 616.26
**falsify**
  be dishonest 975.11
  lie 616.19
  misrepresent 573.3
  misstate 616.16
**falsity** error 518.1
  fakery 616.3
  falseness 616.1
  infidelity 975.5
  lie 616.11
**falter**
  *n.* demur 623.2
  flounder 324.8
  irresolution 627.3
  shake 324.3
  voice 463.19
  *v.* be a coward 892.8
  be irresolute 627.7
  be unsure 514.10
  dawdle 270.8
  demur 623.4
  despair 889.10
  flounder 324.15
  shake 324.11
  stammer 595.8
**faltering** hesitant 623.7
  irresolute 627.11
  slow 270.10
  stammering 595.13
**fame** eminence 34.2
  notability 672.2
  publicity 559.4
  repute 914.1
**familiar**
  *n.* friend 928.1
  guardian angel
    1014.22
  *adj.* customary 642.15
  friendly 927.18
  informal 647.3
  insolent 913.8
  intimate 922.20
  trite 883.9
  usual 84.8
  vernacular 580.18
  well-known 475.27
**familiarity**
  friendship 927.5
  informality 647.1
  knowledge 475.1
  presumption 961.2
  sociability 922.1

**familiarize**
  accustom 642.11
  inform 557.8
**familiar with**
  used to 642.18
  versed in 475.19
**family**
  *n.* ancestry 170.4
  biology 61.5
  community 788.2
  kinsmen 11.2
  nomenclature 583.1
  people 11.5
  posterity 171.1
  race 11.4
  *adj.* lineal 170.14
  racial 11.7
**family planning** 166.1
**family tree** 170.5
**famine**
  unproductiveness
    166.1
  want 662.4
**famished**
  hungry 634.25
  ill-provided 662.12
**famous** eminent 34.9
  excellent 674.12
  reputable 914.16
**famously**
  excellently 674.21
  exceptionally 34.20
  notably 914.21
**fan**
  *n.* attender 186.5
  blower 403.21
  commender 968.8
  cooler 334.3
  devotee 635.6
  fanatic 473.17
  follower 293.2
  fork 299.4
  propeller 285.7
  specialist 81.3
  supporter 787.9
  ventilator 402.10
  *v.* air 402.11
  excite 857.11
  fail 725.9
  incite 648.17
  spread 197.6
**fanatic** believer 1028.4
  enthusiast 635.5
  infatuate 473.17
  intolerant person
    527.5
  lunatic 473.15
  obstinate person
    626.6
  odd person 85.4
**fanatic(al)** fiery 162.21
  narrow-minded
    527.10
  obstinate 626.8
  overeager 635.13
  overzealous 473.32
  zealous 1028.11
**fanaticism**
  narrow-mindedness
    527.1
  obstinacy 626.1
  overeagerness 635.4

  overzealousness
    473.11
  violence 162.2
  zeal 1028.3
**fancied**
  fabricated 616.29
  imaginary 535.19
**fancied up** 231.45
**fanciful**
  capricious 629.5
  ideational 479.9
  imaginary 535.20
  incredible 85.12
  tenuous 4.6
  unreal 2.8
**fancy**
  *n.* caprice 629.1
  desire 634.1
  idea 479.1
  illusion 519.3
  imagination 535.1
  impulse 630.1
  inclination 634.3
  love 931.1
  preference 637.5
  thing imagined 535.5
  will 621.1
  *v.* believe 501.11
  desire 634.14
  imagine 535.14
  love 931.18
  suppose 499.10
  *adj.* excessive 663.16
  expensive 848.11
  grandiose 904.21
  high-flown 601.11
  ornate 901.12
  ostentatious 904.18
  overpriced 848.12
  skillful 733.20
**fancy dress** 231.10
**fancy man** 989.18
**fancy talk** 910.2
**fancy that!** 920.22
**fancywork** 223.1
**fanfare**
  bookbinding 605.16
  celebration 877.1
  trumpet sound 453.4
**fanfaronade**
  bluster 911.1
  boasting 910.1
  celebration 877.1
  display 904.4
**fang**
  grasping organ 813.4
  pointed projection
    258.4
  poison injector 676.5
  tooth 258.5
**fanged** grasping 813.9
  toothed 258.16
**fan-jet** 278.32
**Fannie Mae** 834.4
**fanny** 241.5
**fan out** disperse 75.4
  diverge 299.5
  spread 197.6
**fan-shaped**
  diverging 299.8
  spread 197.11
  triangular 93.3

**fantail** rear 241.7
  tail 241.6
**fantasia** 462.6
**fantasize**
  fabricate 616.18
  imagine 535.14
**fantastic(al)**
  capricious 629.5
  fabricated 616.29
  fanciful 535.20
  foolish 470.10
  illusory 519.9
  incredible 85.12
  remarkable 34.10
  wonderful 920.10
**fantasy**
  *n.* abstractedness
    532.2
  caprice 629.1
  defense mechanism
    690.30
  desire 634.1
  fiction 608.7
  imagination 535.1
  phantom 519.4
  supernaturalism 85.8
  thing imagined 535.5
  *v.* dream 535.17
  muse 532.9
**fan the flame**
  burn 329.22
  excite 857.11
  incite 648.17
  sow dissension 795.14
**far**
  *adj.* distant 199.8
  *adv.* by far 34.17
  far off 199.15
**far and away**
  by far 34.17
  superlatively 36.16
**far and wide**
  abroad 199.16
  by far 34.17
  extensively 179.10
**faraway**
  abstracted 532.11
  distant 199.8
**farce** comedy 611.6
  humor 881.1
  ridicule 967.6
  stuffing 308.27
  trifle 673.5
**farcer** comedian 612.9
  dramatist 611.27
**farcical**
  burlesque 967.14
  comic 880.5
  theatrical 611.40
**far cry** difference 16.1
  distance 199.2
**fare**
  *n.* fee 846.7
  food 308.1
  traveler 274.1
  *v.* be in a state 7.6
  eat 307.18
  go 273.17
  result 154.5
  travel 273.20
**farewell**
  *n.* departure 301.4

Time 105.2
**fathom**
  investigate 485.22
  know 475.12
  measure 490.11
  measure depth 209.9
  solve 487.2
  understand 548.7
**fathomable**
  intelligible 548.9
  measurable 490.15
**fathomless** 209.11
**fatigue**
  *n.* disease symptom
    686.8
  languor 708.6
  tiredness 717
  weakening 160.5
  weakness 160.1
  work 716.4
  *v.* be tedious 884.5
  get tired 717.5
  tire 717.4
**fatigued** tired 717.6
  weakened 160.18
  worn-out 692.38
**fatigues** 231.1
**fatiguing** boring 884.9
  weakening 160.20
  wearying 717.11
**fat of the land**
  plenty 661.2
  prosperity 728.1
**fatso** 195.12
**fatten** feed 307.17
  fertilize 165.8
  increase 38.4
  make better 691.9
  make grow 197.8
  raise animals 416.6
  thicken 204.5
  thrive 728.8
**fatten on** eat 307.26
  sponge 907.11
**fatty**
  *n.* corpulent person
    195.12
  *adj.* oily 380.9
**fatuity**
  foolishness 470.1
  futility 669.2
  ineffectiveness 158.3
  thoughtlessness 480.1
**fatuous** foolish 470.8
  ineffective 158.15
  tenuous 4.6
  thoughtless 480.4
  trivial 673.16
  vain 669.13
**faucet** stopper 266.4
  valve 396.10
**fault** an error 518.3
  blemish 679.1
  crack 201.2
  defect 678.2
  fallacy 518.1
  misdeed 982.2
  vice 981.2
**faultfinding**
  *n.* complaint 875.4
  disapproval 969.4
  *adj.* critical 969.24

discontented 869.5
  plaintive 875.16
**faultless**
  accurate 516.15
  innocent 984.6
  perfect 677.6
**faulty** blemished 679.8
  erroneous 518.16
  guilty 983.3
  illogical 483.11
  imperfect 678.4
  ungrammatical 587.4
**faun** 1014.21
**fauna** 414.1
**faux pas** 518.5
**favor**
  *n.* approval 968.1
  courtesy 936.6
  esteem 914.3
  face 240.4
  gift 818.7
  good deed 938.7
  good terms 927.3
  inclination 634.3
  influence 172.2
  letter 604.2
  looks 446.4
  memento 537.7
  patronage 785.4
  pity 944.1
  preference 637.5
  prestige 172.1
  privilege 958.4
  respect 964.1
  superiority 36.1
  *v.* abet 785.14
  aid 785.11
  approve 968.9
  be kind 938.9
  desire 634.14
  discriminate 977.8
  do good 674.10
  further 785.17
  indulge 759.6
  make better 691.9
  oblige 785.19
  prefer 637.17
  resemble 20.7
  respect 964.4
**favorable**
  approving 968.17
  auspicious 544.18
  consenting 775.4
  expedient 670.5
  friendly 927.14
  good 674.12
  helpful 785.22
  promising 888.13
  timely 129.9
  willing 622.5
**favorably**
  advantageously 36.19
  amicably 927.21
  auspiciously 544.21
  consentingly 775.5
  helpfully 785.24
  kindly 938.18
  willingly 622.9
**favored**
  approved 968.19
  exempt 762.29
  fortunate 728.14

preferable 637.25
**favoring**
  approving 968.17
  auspicious 544.18
  instrumental 658.6
  preferential 637.25
  similar 20.10
**favorite**
  *n.* darling 931.15
  race horse 414.17
  *adj.* approved 968.19
  beloved 931.22
**favorite son** 746.9
**favoritism**
  injustice 977.3
  partiality 527.3
**favors of office** 744.36
**favor with**
  endow 818.17
  supply 818.15
**fawn**
  *n.* hoofed animal
    414.5
  young deer 125.8
  *v.* be servile 907.6
  give birth 167.15
  *adj.* brown 367.3
**fawning**
  *n.* flattery 970.1
  obsequiousness 907.2
  *adj.* flattering 970.8
  obsequious 907.13
**fawn upon**
  curry favor 907.8
  flatter 970.5
**fay** 1014.18
**faze** 891.26
**FBI** detectives 781.10
  police force 699.17
  US agency 742.11
**fealty** duty 962.1
  fidelity 974.7
  obedience 766.1
**fear**
  *n.* anxiety 890.1
  cowardice 892.1
  fright 891
  irresolution 627.4
  nervousness 859.1
  *v.* be afraid 891.18
  be irresolute 627.7
**fearful** afraid 891.31
  anxious 890.6
  cowardly 892.10
  frightening 891.36
  nervous 859.10
  remarkable 34.11
**fear-inspiring**
  frightening 891.36
  threatening 973.3
**fearless** 893.19
**fearsome** fearful 891.31
  frightening 891.36
**fear-stricken** 891.30
**feasibility**
  expedience 670.1
  possibility 509.2
  wieldiness 732.2
**feasible**
  expedient 670.5
  possible 509.7
  practical 670.6

wieldy 732.14
**feast**
  *n.* banquet 307.9
  festival 878.4
  food 308.1
  holiday 711.4
  holy day 1040.14
  treat 865.3
  *v.* eat 307.22
  gratify 865.6
  make merry 878.27
**feat**
  courageous act 893.7
  deed 705.3
  masterpiece 733.10
**feather**
  *n.* kind 61.3
  lightness 353.2
  plumage 230.18
  quill 230.16
  softness 357.4
  trifle 673.5
  *v.* fledge 230.21
  fly 278.49
  line 194.7
  ornament 901.9
  row 275.53
**feather bed** 357.4
**featherbedding** 663.4
**featherbrain** 471.7
**featherbrained**
  scatterbrained 532.16
  superficial 469.20
**feathered**
  ornamented 901.11
  plumaged 230.28
**featheredge** lip 235.4
  sharp edge 258.2
**feather in one's cap**
  trophy 916.3
  victory 726.1
**feathers** clothing 231.1
  plumage 230.18
**featherweight**
  *n.* boxing weight
    352.3
  little thing 196.4
  pugilist 800.2
  *adj.* lightweight
    353.12
  uninfluential 173.3
**feathery** light 353.10
  plumy 230.27
  soft 357.14
**featly**
  *adj.* agile 733.21
  *adv.* nimbly 733.29
**feature**
  *n.* aspect 446.3
  characteristic 80.4
  commodity 831.2
  component 58.2
  looks 446.4
  motion picture
    611.16
  salient point 672.7
  special 81.2
  treatise 606.1
  *v.* give a show 611.33
  give prominence
    672.14
  specialize 81.4

*adj.* specialized 81.5
**featureless**
  continuous 71.8
  formless 247.4
  general 79.11
  vacant 187.13
**features** face 240.4
  form 246.3
  looks 446.4
  outline 235.2
**febrile** excited 857.20
  fervent 855.23
  feverish 686.54
  overzealous 635.13
**fecal**
  excremental 311.20
  filthy 682.23
  malodorous 437.5
**feces** excretion 311.4
  residue 43.2
**feckless**
  improvident 721.15
  ineffective 158.15
  useless 669.9
**feculence** feces 311.4
  filthiness 682.2
**fecund** diffuse 593.11
  imaginative 535.18
  productive 165.9
**fecundate** enrich 165.8
  fertilize 169.10
**fed** agent 781.3
  detective 781.10
  peace officer 699.15
**federal**
*n.* peace officer
  699.15
*adj.* combining 52.7
  governmental 741.17
**Federal** agent 781.3
  detective 781.10
**federalese**
  jargon 580.10
  official jargon 744.37
**federalism** 741.8
**federalist(ic)** 741.17
**federalize** 52.4
**federate**
  cooperate 786.3
  join 52.4
**federated** 52.6
**federation**
  affiliation 786.2
  association 788.1
  combination 52.1
  government 741.4
**fed-up** bored 884.10
  satiated 664.6
**fee**
*n.* dues 846.7
  estate 810.5
  gratuity 818.5
  stipend 841.5
*v.* pay 841.10
**feeble** aged 126.18
  faint-sounding 452.16
  illogical 483.12
  impotent 158.13
  indistinct 445.6
  irresolute 627.12
  mentally deficient
  469.21

  unhealthy 686.50
  weak 160.12
**feebleminded**
  irresolute 627.12
  mentally deficient
  469.21
**feed**
*n.* food 308.4
  meal 307.5
*v.* burn 329.22
  dine 307.16
  eat 307.18
  encourage 648.21
  foster 785.16
  fuel 331.8
  gratify 865.6
  provision 659.9
  raise animals 416.6
  tend animals 416.7
**feedback**
  audio distortion
  450.13
  automation 349.6
**feeder** actor 612.2
  eater 307.14
  railway 657.8
  role 611.11
  tributary 395.3
**feed on** eat 307.26
  sponge 907.11
**feel**
*n.* discrimination
  492.1
  grope 485.5
  knack 733.6
  milieu 233.3
  texture 351.1
  touch 425.1
*v.* appear to be 446.10
  emotions 855.11
  experience 151.8
  intuit 481.4
  sense 422.8
  suppose 499.10
  touch 425.6
**feel around** 485.31
**feeler** offer 773.1
  question 485.10
  tactile organ 425.4
  testing device 489.4
  whisker 230.10
**feel for** grope 485.31
  pity 944.3
**feeling**
*n.* automation 349.21
  belief 501.6
  discrimination 492.1
  emotion 855.3
  fingering 425.2
  hunch 481.3
  mental attitude 525.1
  milieu 233.3
  pity 944.1
  sensation 422.1
  touch 425.1
*adj.* emotional 855.19
  examining 485.36
  intuitive 481.5
**feeling for** 174.1
**feeling out** 489.2
**feelings** 855

**feel one's way**
  be blind 441.8
  be careful 533.7
  be cautious 895.5
  grope 485.31
  progress 294.4
  try 714.9
**feel out** 489.9
**fee position** 808.1
**fee simple** estate 810.5
  possession 808.1
**feet of clay** 160.4
**feign** affect 903.12
  fake 616.21
**feigned**
  assumed 903.16
  falsified 616.26
**feint** fakery 616.3
  military tactics 797.9
  pretext 649.1
  stratagem 735.3
  thrust 798.3
  trick 618.6
**feisty** 951.19
**felicitate** 948.2
**felicitation** 948.1
**felicitous** apt 26.10
  decorous 897.10
  eloquent 600.8
  expedient 670.5
  pleasant 863.6
  timely 129.9
  well-chosen 589.7
**felicity** aptitude 733.5
  decorousness 897.3
  eloquence 600.1
  fitness 26.5
  happiness 865.2
  literary elegance
  589.1
  luckiness 728.2
  prosperity 728.1
**feline**
*n.* animal 414.3
  cat 414.26
*adj.* cunning 735.12
  felid 414.46
  furtive 614.12
**fell**
*n.* hill 207.5
  pelt 229.1
  plain 387.1
*v.* conquer 727.10
  drop 318.5
  lay 214.6
  raze 693.19
  shoot 285.13
  strike dead 409.18
*adj.* cruel 939.24
  terrible 891.38
**felled** 727.16
**fellow**
*n.* accompanier 73.4
  associate 787.1
  beau 931.12
  boy 125.5
  comrade 928.3
  equivalent 30.4
  friend 928.1
  image 572.3
  likeness 20.3
  man 420.5

  member 788.11
  person 417.3
  teacher 565.1
*adj.* accompanying
  73.9
  cooperating 786.5
**fellow feeling**
  accord 794.1
  cooperation 786.1
  good terms 927.3
  kindness 938.1
  sympathy 855.5
**fellowman** 928.1
**fellowship** accord 794.1
  affiliation 786.2
  association 922.6
  award 916.7
  camaraderie 922.2
  company 73.2
  cooperation 786.1
  friendship 927.2
  instructorship 565.11
  religion 1020.3
  social intercourse
  922.4
  society 788.3
  subsidy 818.8
**fellow traveler**
  Communist 745.13
  escort 73.5
  subversive 619.11
**felon** criminal 986.10
  evildoer 943.1
  sore 686.35
**felonious**
  dishonest 975.16
  illegal 999.6
  sinful 982.6
**felony** crime 999.4
  misdeed 982.2
**felt** 378.5,11
**female**
*n.* female being 421.4
*adj.* feminine 421.13
**female organs** 419.10
**female sex** 421.3
**feminine**
*n.* gender 586.10
*adj.* female 421.13
**femininity**
  female sex 421.3
  femineity 421
  sex 419.1
**feminism**
  effeminacy 421.2
  women's rights 958.6
**feminist** 958.7
**femme fatale**
  seductress 989.15
  temptress 650.3
**fence**
*n.* barrier 730.5
  boundary 236.4
  fortification 799.4
  middle course 806.3
  moderatism 745.2
  receiver 826.6
  types of 236.13
*v.* contend 796.14
  deal illicitly 826.7
  dodge 631.8
  enclose 236.7

equivocate 483.9
fortify 799.9
protect 699.18
**fence in** confine 761.12
enclose 236.5
**fence off** 237.8
**fence-sitter**
irresolute person
627.5
neutral 806.4
**fencing**
equivocation 483.5
prevarication 613.4
swordplay 796.8
**fend** prevent 730.14
protect 699.18
ward off 799.10
**fender** fireplace 329.11
partition 237.5
safety equipment
699.3
**fend for oneself** 762.19
**fend off**
prevent 730.14
repulse 289.3
ward off 799.10
**fenestra** 265.1
**fenestrated** 265.20
**feral** cruel 939.24
excited 857.23
fatal 409.23
funereal 410.22
savage 162.20
**ferment**
*n.* agitation 324.1
alterant 139.4
anger 952.7
bubbling 405.3
bustle 707.4
excitement 857.3
leavening 353.4
reaction 379.5
types of 353.18
violence 162.2
*v.* agitate 324.10
bubble 405.4
incite 648.17
leaven 353.7
react chemically
379.6
seethe 162.11
sour 432.4
**fermentation**
agitation 324.1
bubbling 405.3
excitement 857.3
leavening 353.4
reaction 379.5
souring 432.3
**fern** botany 412.5
plant 411.4,43
**ferocious** cruel 939.24
excited 857.23
savage 162.20
warlike 797.25
**ferociously**
cruelly 939.33
savagely 162.26
**ferocity** cruelty 939.11
warlikeness 797.15
**ferret** sharp eye 439.11
wild animal 414.28

**ferret-eyed** 439.22
**ferret out** find 488.4
search out 485.33
**ferric** 383.17
**ferry**
*n.* boat 277.21
passageway 657.4
*v.* fly 278.45
haul 271.12
**ferryman** 276.5
**fertile**
imaginative 535.18
plentiful 661.7
productive 165.9
**fertility**
diffuseness 593.1
inventiveness 535.3
plenty 661.2
productiveness 165.1
**fertility god**
agriculture divinity
413.4
forest god 1014.21
names of 165.5
**fertilization**
enrichment 165.3
impregnation 169.3
**fertilize** enrich 165.8
impregnate 169.10
till 413.17
**fertilizer** 165.4
**fervent**
eloquent 600.13
excited 857.20
industrious 707.22
passionate 855.23
zealous 635.10
**fervently**
eloquently 600.15
excitedly 857.32
industriously 707.27
passionately 855.28
zealously 635.15
**fervid** craving 634.24
excited 857.20
fervent 855.23
zealous 635.10
**fervidly**
excitedly 857.32
fervently 855.28
zealously 635.15
**fervor** eloquence 600.5
heat 328.2
industry 707.6
love 931.1
passion 855.10
zeal 635.2
**festal** merry 878.30
vacational 711.10
**festal board** 307.9
**fester**
*n.* sore 686.35
*v.* decay 692.25
hurt 424.7
suppurate 311.15
**festering**
*n.* corruption 692.2
pain 424.4
pus 311.6
sore 686.35
*adj.* decayed 692.41
sore 424.11

suppurative 311.21
**festival** 878.4
**festival day** 711.4
**festive** convivial 922.19
merry 878.30
**festive occasion** 878.4
**festivity**
celebration 877.1
conviviality 922.3
festival 878.4
meeting 74.2
merrymaking 878.3
party 922.11
rejoicing 876.1
treat 865.3
**festoon** curve 252.2
flowers 411.23
ornamentation
901.3,13
**festooned**
high-flown 601.11
ornamented 901.11
**fetal** beginning 68.15
embryonic 406.24
**fetch**
*n.* specter 1017.3
stratagem 735.3
trick 618.6
*v.* accomplish 722.4
arrive 300.6
attract 650.5
bring 271.15
conclude 494.10
cost 846.15
hit 283.13
sail for 275.35
travel 273.17
**fetching** alluring 650.7
pleasant 863.7
**fetch up** arrive 300.6
sail 275.33
stop 144.7
train 562.14
**fete** festival 878.4
meeting 74.2
**fete day** 711.4
**fetid** bad 675.9
filthy 682.23
malodorous 437.5
offensive 864.18
unsavory 429.7
**fetish** charm 1036.5
idol 1033.3
**fetishism**
idolatry 1033.1
sexual preference
419.12
sorcery 1035.1
**fetlock** foot 212.5
hair 230.6
**fetter**
*n.* curb 730.7
restraint 760.4
*v.* bind 47.10
hamper 730.11
restrain 760.10
**fettle**
*n.* condition 7.3
*v.* groom 681.20
**fetus** 406.14
**feud**
*n.* animosity 929.4

estate 810.5
possession 808.1
quarrel 795.5
revenge 956.1
*v.* contend 796.14
quarrel 795.11
**feudal**
imperious 739.16
real 810.10
subject 764.13
**feudalism**
principle of govern-
ment 741.8
subjection 764.1
**feudal system** 741.4
**fever** agitation 324.1
disease symptom
686.8
fever of excitement
857.6
frenzy 473.7
heat 328.1
sickness 686.6
**feverish**
agitated 324.16
excited 857.20
fervent 855.23
fevered 686.54
hasty 709.9
hot 328.25
overzealous 635.13
**few** least 37.8
not many 102.4
small 35.6
**few, a**
indefinite number
101.2
plurality 100.1
small number 102.2
**fewer** 102.6
**fey** eccentric 474.4
otherworldly 85.15
**fiancé** 931.16
**fiasco**
disappointment
541.1
failure 725.6
**fiat**
authorization 777.3
decree 752.4
**fib**
*n.* lie 616.11
*v.* lie 616.19
**fibbing** 616.8
**fiber** filament 206.1
flesh 406.1
nature 5.3
types of 206.8
**fibrillation**
disease symptom
686.8
irregularity 138.1
**fibrous**
threadlike 206.7
tough 359.4
**fickle** flighty 629.6
inconstant 141.7
irresolute 627.9
transient 111.7
uncertain 514.15
unfaithful 975.20

grasping organ 813.4
*v.* accuse 1005.7
condemn to death
409.20
designate 568.18
touch 425.6
**fingerboard**
keyboard 465.20
viol 465.6
**finger bowl** 681.12
**fingering**
indication 568.1
music 462.31
touching 425.2
**fingernails** 813.4
**finger painting**
painting 574.5
picture 574.15
**fingerprint** 568.7
**fini** 70.8
**finicky**
attentive 530.15
detailed 8.9
fastidious 896.10
meticulous 533.12
**finis** 70.1
**finish**
*n.* boundary 235.3
completion 722.2
end 70.1
literary elegance
589.1
perfection 677.1
polish 260.2
skill 733.8
symmetry 248.1
texture 351.1
*v.* complete 722.6
consume 666.2
dispose of 693.12
end 70.7
improve 691.10
kill 409.14
polish 260.7
refute 506.5
resolve 70.5
**finished**
accomplished 733.24
completed 722.11
dead 408.30
elegant 589.6
ended 70.8
past 119.7
perfected 677.9
polished 260.10
ruined 693.28
symmetric 248.4
used up 666.4
**finisher** disproof 506.3
end-all 70.4
finishing touch 722.3
garmentmaker 231.33
**finishing**
*n.* completion 722.2
consumption 666.1
*adj.* completory 722.9
ending 70.9
**finishing touch**
end-all 70.4
final touch 722.3
**finite** human 417.10
limited 234.7

numerical 86.8
**finitude** 111.1
**fink**
*n.* informer 557.6
strikebreaker 789.6
*v.* break a strike
789.10
inform on 557.12
**fiord** see fjord
**fire**
*n.* element 376.2
eloquence 600.5
fervor 855.10
fever 686.6
fever of excitement
857.6
gunfire 798.9
heat 328.13
inspiration 648.9
light source 336.1
pain 424.3
vim 161.2
zeal 635.2
*v.* become angry
952.17
begin 68.7
cook 330.4
dismiss 310.19
dry 393.6
energize 161.9
excite 857.11
explode 162.13
fire upon 798.22
heat 329.17
hurl at 798.28
ignite 329.22
incite 648.17
inspire 648.20
kindle 648.18
make ceramics 576.6
rocket 281.13
shoot 285.13
throw 285.11
*interj.* attack! 798.32
**fire and brimstone**
1019.2
**firearm** 801.5
**fireball** fuel 331.1
lightning 335.17
meteor 375.15
**fire bell** alarm 704.1
bell 454.4
**firebox** 329.10
**firebrand** coal 328.16
instigator 648.11
lighter 331.4
violent person 162.9
**firebrick**
building material
378.2
ceramic ware 576.2
**fire brigade** 332.4
**firebug** 329.8
**firecracker**
fireworks 328.33
noisemaker 453.5
**fired** cooked 330.6
excited 857.18
inspired 648.31
**firedamp** miasma 676.4
vapor 401.1

**fire-eater**
fire fighter 332.4
ill-humored person
951.11
reckless person 894.4
violent person 162.9
**fire escape**
escape 632.3
stairs 315.3
**fire extinguisher** 332.3
**fire fighter** 332.4
**fire fighting** 332.2
**firefly** glimmer 335.7
light 336.5
**fireguard**
fireplace 329.11
watchman 699.10
**fire hydrant**
extinguisher 332.3
hydrant 396.12
**fire iron** 329.12
**fireman**
fire fighter 332.4
sailor 276.6
trainman 274.13
**fireplace** hearth 329.11
home 191.4
**fireplug**
extinguisher 332.3
hydrant 396.12
**firepower** gunfire 798.9
troops 157.9
**fireproof**
*v.* flameproof 332.6
strengthen 159.12
*adj.* flameproof
332.10
resistant 159.18
**fireproofing** 332.5
**fireside**
fireplace 329.11
home 191.4
**fire tactics** 797.9
**firetrap** 618.11
**firewater** 996.13
**firewood**
kindling 331.3
wood 378.3
**fireworks** fire 328.17
gunfire 798.9
types of 328.33
**fire worship**
idolatry 1033.1
incendiarism 329.7
**firing** deposal 783.2
dismissal 310.5
fuel 331.1
gunfire 798.9
ignition 329.4
incitement 648.4
inspiration 648.9
throwing 285.3
**firing line** 802.2
**firm**
*n.* company 788.9
workplace 719.1
*v.* harden 356.7
stabilize 142.7
*adj.* close 266.12
crowded 74.22
dense 354.12
faithful 974.20

fastened 47.14
immovable 142.15
orthodox 1024.7
permanent 140.7
reliable 513.17
resolute 624.12
rigid 356.11
sound 159.16
stable 142.12
strict 757.7
substantial 3.7
unhazardous 698.5
unyielding 626.9
**firmament** 375.2
**firm hand** 757.3
**firmly** densely 354.15
faithfully 974.25
resolutely 624.17
securely 47.19
strictly 757.9
strongly 159.21
unyieldingly 626.15
**firm price** 773.3
**first**
*n.* beginning 68.3
*adj.* chief 36.14
foremost 68.17
front 240.10
leading 292.3
preceding 64.4
prior 116.4
*adv.* in front 240.12
initially 68.18
preferably 637.28
**first aid** 689.15
**first-born**
*n.* oldest 127.5
*adj.* oldest 123.19
**first-class**
first-rate 674.15
superlative 36.13
**first draft** trial 489.2
written matter 602.10
**first edition**
original 23.3
rare book 605.3
**firsthand**
evidential 505.17
new 122.7
original 23.5
**first impression** 68.3
**first lady** 749.2
**first light** 133.4
**first move** 68.3
**first name** 583.4
**first off** 68.18
**first place** 36.3
**first prize** award 916.2
supremacy 36.3
**first-rate**
excellent 674.15
superlative 36.13
**first refusal** 828.2
**first step** 68.3
**first string** 788.7
**first thing** 68.18
**firth** 399.1
**fiscal** 835.30
**fish**
*n.* animal 414.35,65
dupe 620.1
food 308.24

torpedo 281.16
US money 835.7
*v.* angle 655.10
**fisherman** fisher 655.6
  sailor 276.1
**fish for** seek 485.29
  solicit 774.14
**fish fry** 307.6
**fishhook** 618.12
**fishing**
  *n.* angling 655.3
  *adj.* pursuing 655.11
  searching 485.37
**fishmonger** 830.3
**fish out of water**
  misfit 27.4
  nonconformist 83.3
**fishpond**
  body of water 398.1
  habitat 191.24
**fish story**
  boasting 910.2
  lie 616.11
**fishwife**
  ill-humored person
    951.12
  merchant 830.3
**fishy** deceptive 618.19
  dishonest 975.16
  fishlike 414.53
  inexpressive 549.20
**fissile** atomics 326.20
  brittle 360.4
  separable 49.26
**fission**
  *n.* disintegration 53.2
  nuclear fission 326.8
  separation 49.2
  *v.* atomics 326.17
  bisect 92.4
  disintegrate 53.3
  shatter 49.13
**fissionable**
  atomics 326.20
  separable 49.26
**fissure**
  *n.* brain 466.7
  break 49.4
  crack 201.2
  discontinuity 72.2
  *v.* be damaged 692.26
  break 49.12
  open 265.12
  sever 49.11
**ist** handwriting 602.3
  pointer 568.4
**isticuffs** 796.9
**it**
  *n.* anger 952.8
  bustle 707.4
  emotional outburst
    857.8
  frenzy 473.7
  outbreak 162.5
  preparation 720.2
  seizure 686.5
  spasm 324.6
  spell 108.1
  *.* be expedient 670.3
  change 139.6
  conform 82.3
  equalize 30.6

equip 659.8
have place 184.8
make agree 26.7
outfit 231.40
prepare 720.8
suit 26.8
train 562.14
*adj.* apt 26.10
  competent 733.22
  due 960.8
  eligible 637.24
  expedient 670.5
  fitted 720.17
  healthy 685.7
  just 976.8
  right 958.8
  sufficient 661.6
  timely 129.9
  well-chosen 589.7
**fitful**
  discontinuous 72.4
  inconstant 141.7
  irregular 138.3
  jerky 324.19
  unordered 62.12
**fitfully**
  discontinuously 72.5
  haphazardly 62.18
  irregularly 138.4
  shakily 324.23
**fit in** conform 82.4
  have place 184.8
  implant 304.8
**fitness** ability 157.2
  decorousness 897.3
  eligibility 637.11
  expedience 670.1
  health 685.1
  preparedness 720.4
  propriety 958.2
  suitability 26.5
  timeliness 129.1
**fits and starts**
  irregularity 138.1
  shaking 324.2
**fitted** apt 26.10
  competent 733.22
  eligible 637.24
  prepared 720.17
  provided 659.13
**fitting**
  *n.* change 139.1
  equipment 659.4
  preparation 720.2
  *adj.* apt 26.10
  decorous 897.10
  expedient 670.5
  right 958.8
  timely 129.9
  useful 665.18
  well-chosen 589.7
**fit to be tied** 952.29
**five** number 99
  team 788.7
**five-and-ten**
  *n.* market 832.1
  *adj.* cheap 849.8
**five-percenter**
  influence user 744.30
  influential person
    172.6

**fix**
  *n.* drug dose 687.6
  narcotic injection
    689.18
  navigation 275.2
  perplexity 514.3
  position 184.3
  state 7.1
  *v.* accustom 642.11
  arrange 771.9
  bribe 651.3
  castrate 42.11
  circumscribe 234.4
  decide 494.11
  defeat 727.6
  direct 290.6
  dispose 60.9
  establish 184.15
  fasten 47.7
  form 246.7
  kill 409.14
  make agree 26.7
  make sure 513.11
  organize 60.10
  place 184.10
  prearrange 641.3
  prepare 720.6
  prove 505.11
  puncture 265.16
  punish 1010.11
  quantify 28.4
  repair 694.14
  resolve 624.7
  retaliate 955.7
  ruin 693.11
  specify 80.11
  stabilize 142.9
  touch up 691.11
**fixable** bribable 651.4
  remediable 694.25
**fixated** 473.33
**fixation**
  hindrance 730.1
  motionlessness 268.2
  obsession 473.13
  psychological fixation
    690.28
  settlement 184.6
  stabilization 142.2
**fixative**
  art equipment 574.19
  perfume 436.2
  stabilizer 142.20
**fixed** arranged 60.14
  circumscribed 234.6
  conditional 507.8
  confirmed 642.21
  defeated 727.14
  engrossed 530.18
  fastened 47.14
  firm 624.12
  in order 59.7
  located 184.17
  made sure 513.20
  motionless 268.13
  particular 80.12
  permanent 140.7
  prearranged 641.5
  proved 505.21
  stabilized 142.14
  stuck 142.16
  traditional 123.12

unqualified 508.2
**fixer**
  influence user 744.30
  mender 694.10
  processing solution
    577.13
**fixings** 58.2
**fixity**
  motionlessness 268.2
  stabilization 142.2
**fix on**
  attribute to 155.4
  decide upon 637.16
  direct 290.6
  pay attention 530.8
**fixture** adjunct 41.1
  equipment 659.4
  hard goods 831.4
  machinery 348.4
  stabilization 142.2
**fix up** arrange 60.12
  make ready 720.6
  make up 720.7
  ornament 901.8
  reconcile 804.8
  repair 694.14
**fizz**
  *n.* bubbling 405.3
  sibilation 457.1
  *v.* bubble 405.4
  sibilate 457.2
**fizzle**
  *n.* bubbling 405.3
  disappointment
    541.1
  failure 725.2
  sibilation 457.1
  *v.* be disappointing
    541.3
  bubble 405.4
  burn out 332.8
  come to nothing
    725.12
  sibilate 457.2
**fizzle out**
  be disappointing
    541.3
  be unproductive
    166.3
  burn out 332.8
  come to nothing
    725.12
  fall through 314.3
  weaken 160.9
**fizzling** 457.3
**fizzy** 405.6
**fjord** 399.1
**flabbergast** 920.6
**flabbergasted** 920.9
**flabby** flaccid 357.10
  impotent 158.13
  pulpy 390.6
  weak 160.12
**flaccid** flabby 357.10
  weak 160.12
**flack** gunfire 798.9
  promotion 559.5
  publicist 559.9
**flag**
  *n.* banner 569.6
  building material
    378.2

gaseousness 401.3
grandiloquence 601.1
**flatulent**
  bombastic 601.9
  distended 197.13
  ejective 310.28
  pompous 904.22
**flatware**
  hard goods 831.4
  tableware 348.3
**flaunt** display 904.17
  indicate 555.5
  wave 323.11
**flaunting**
  *n.* display 904.4
  waving 323.2
  *adj.* garish 362.19
  gaudy 904.20
  grandiloquent 601.8
  showy 904.19
**flautist** 464.4
**flavor**
  *n.* characteristic 80.4
  flavoring 428.3
  odor 435.1
  taste 427.1
  *v.* infuse 44.12
  savor 428.7
**flavored** 427.9
**flavorful** flavored 427.9
  flavorsome 428.9
**flavoring** 428.3
**flavorless** 430.2
**flavorsome**
  flavorful 428.9
  pleasant 863.9
**flaw**
  *n.* blemish 679.1
  crack 201.2
  error 518.1
  fault 678.2
  gust 403.6
  vice 981.2
  *v.* blemish 679.4
**flawed** blemished 679.8
  erroneous 518.16
  illegal 999.6
  illogical 483.11
**flawless**
  accurate 516.15
  perfect 677.6
**flay**
  criticize severely
    969.21
  despoil 822.24
  peel 232.8
  tear apart 49.14
**flea** animal 414.40,74
  jumper 319.4
**fleabag** 191.16
**flea-bitten** 374.13
**flea in one's ear**
  piece of advice 754.2
  warning 703.1
**flea market**
  marketplace 832.2
  sale 829.3
**fleck**
  *n.* blemish 679.3
  hair 230.6
  mark 568.5
  minute thing 196.7

small amount 35.2
spottiness 374.3
*v.* mark 568.19
variegate 374.7
**flection**
  angularity 251.1
  curve 252.3
  deflection 291.2
  fold 264.1
**fledge** feather 230.21
  mature 126.9
**fledgling**
  *n.* animal 414.33
  beginner 68.2
  boy 125.5
  modern 122.4
  novice 566.9
  young bird 125.8
  youngster 125.1
  *adj.* new 122.7
  undeveloped 721.11
**flee** cease to exist 2.5
  disappear 447.2
  escape 632.6
  fly 631.10
  run off 301.13
**fleece**
  *n.* hair 230.2
  head of hair 230.4
  hide 229.1,8
  softness 357.4
  white 364.2
  *v.* cheat 618.17
  despoil 822.24
  divest 232.5
  overcharge 848.7
  plunder 824.16
**fleeced** 838.8
**fleecy** soft 357.14
  woolly 230.24
**fleer**
  *n.* gibe 967.2
  ridicule 967.4
  *v.* make fun of 881.13
  offend 965.4
  ridicule 967.9
**fleet**
  *n.* group 74.3
  navy 800.26
  ships 277.10
  *v.* be transient 111.6
  speed 269.8
  *adj.* agile 733.21
  fast 269.19
  transient 111.8
**fleeting** transient 111.7
  vanishing 447.3
**flesh** body 376.3
  kinsmen 11.2
  mankind 417.1
  materiality 376.1
  meat 308.12
  organic matter 406.1
  sensuality 987.2
  sexuality 419.2
  skin 229.1
**flesh and blood**
  kinsmen 11.2
  materiality 376.1
**flesh-eater** 307.14
**flesh-eating** 307.29
**fleshly** human 417.10

lascivious 989.29
materialistic 376.9
sensual 987.6
sexual 419.26
unrighteous 981.12
unsacred 1027.3
**fleshpots**
  disapproved place
    191.28
  place of vice 981.7
  prosperity 728.1
**fleshy** corpulent 195.18
  pulpy 390.6
**fleur-de-lis**
  heraldic insignia
    569.2
  insignia 569.1
**flex**
  *n.* bend 252.3
  *v.* bend 252.6
**flexed** 291.8
**flexibility**
  changeableness 141.1
  conformity 82.1
  pliancy 357.2
  resilience 358.1
  submissiveness 765.3
  unstrictness 758.2
  versatility 733.3
  wieldiness 732.2
**flexible**
  changeable 141.6
  conformable 82.5
  docile 765.13
  folded 264.7
  pliant 357.9
  resilient 358.7
  unstrict 758.5
  versatile 733.23
  wieldy 732.14
**flexion** see **flection**
**flex one's muscles**
    720.13
**flexuous**
  crooked 219.20
  pliant 357.9
  winding 254.6
**flexure**
  angularity 251.1
  curve 252.3
  deflection 291.2
  fold 264.1
**flibbertigibbet** 471.7
**flick**
  *n.* blemish 679.3
  faint sound 452.3
  jerk 286.3
  mark 568.5
  motion picture
    611.16
  tap 283.6
  touch 425.1
  *v.* flutter 324.12
  jerk 286.5
  tap 283.15
  touch 425.6
**flicker**
  *n.* fire 328.13
  flutter 324.4
  light 335.8
  motion picture
    611.16

*v.* be hot 328.22
  flutter 324.12
  glimmer 335.25
**flickering**
  burning 328.27
  fluttering 324.18
  glittering 335.36
  inconstant 141.7
  irregular 138.3
  transient 111.8
**flier** advertising 559.8
  aviator 279.1
  circus artist 612.3
  gamble 515.1
  speeder 269.5
  stock speculation
    833.19
  train 272.13
**flight** air force 800.28
  arrows 801.16
  aviation 278.1
  birds 74.6
  course 267.2
  defense mechanism
    690.30
  departure 301.1
  escape 632.1
  large number 101.3
  migration 273.4
  music 463.18
  rocketry 281.9
  running away 631.4
  speed 269.1
  trip 278.9
**flight attendant** 279.4
**flight of fancy**
  idealization 535.7
  imagination 535.1
**flight path**
  aviation 278.25
  route 657.2
**flight plan** 278.3
**flight test** 489.3
**flighty** fickle 629.6
  inconstant 141.7
  insane 473.25
  superficial 469.20
  volatile 532.17
**flimflam**
  *n.* caprice 629.1
  deception 618.1
  fraud 618.8
  humbug 616.14
  lie 616.11
  *v.* cheat 618.17
**flimflam man** 619.3
**flimsy** flaccid 357.10
  fragile 360.4
  frail 160.14
  illogical 483.12
  shaky 4.7
  tenuous 355.4
  thin 205.16
  trivial 673.16
**flinch**
  *n.* retreat 284.3
  *v.* be startled 540.5
  demur 623.4
  pull back 284.7
  retract 297.3
  shrink 891.21

ornament 901.9
play 878.25
walk 273.27
**flounder**
*n.* tumble 324.8
*v.* be uncertain 514.9
bungle 734.11
fluctuate 141.5
have difficulty 731.10
sail 275.55
trip 316.8
tumble 324.15
wallow 322.13
**flour**
*n.* powder 361.5
white 364.2
*v.* pulverize 361.9
sprinkle 75.6
**flourish**
*n.* display 904.4
extra 41.4
figure of speech
551.1
flowery language
601.4
improvisation 462.27
music 463.18
ornamentation 901.1
waving 323.2
*v.* be famous 914.10
be healthy 685.5
boast 910.6
flaunt 904.17
grow 197.7
have energy 161.10
indicate 555.5
make grandiloquent
601.7
reach perfection
722.8
thrive 728.8
vegetate 411.31
wave 323.11
**flourishing**
*n.* waving 323.2
*adj.* growing 197.12
luxuriant 411.40
productive 165.9
thriving 728.13
**flout**
*n.* gibe 967.2
indignity 965.2
*v.* defy 793.4
disobey 767.6
not observe 769.4
offend 965.4
ridicule 967.9
**flow**
*n.* aviation 278.38
course 267.2
eloquence 600.2
excretion 311.1
glide 273.8
liquidity 388.1
literary elegance
589.1
plenty 661.2
stream 395.4
tide 395.13
*v.* abound 661.5
elapse 105.5
enter 302.9

flow out 303.13
glide 273.34
go easily 732.9
hang 215.6
move 267.5
result from 154.6
stream 395.16
travel 273.17
**flower**
*n.* blossom 411.22,44
essence 5.2
figure of speech
551.1
parts of 411.26
the best 674.8
*v.* be in flower 411.32
evolve 148.5
mature 126.9
ornament 901.9
thrive 728.8
**flower bed** 413.10
**flower child** 83.3
**flowered** floral 411.35
ornamented 901.11
**flowering**
*n.* blossoming 411.24
development 148.1
*adj.* floral 411.35
growing 197.12
thriving 728.13
young 124.9
**flowerlike** 900.16
**flower power**
benevolence 938.4
power 157.1
**flowers**
compilation 605.4
excerpts 607.4
menstruation 311.9
**flowery** figurative 551.3
floral 411.35
fragrant 436.9
high-flown 601.11
ornate 901.12
**flowing** cursive 602.22
eloquent 600.9
fluid 388.6
harmonious 589.8
pendent 215.9
running 267.8
streaming 395.24
**flown** 632.11
**flowoff** 303.4
**flow on** drench 392.14
elapse 105.5
progress 294.3
**flu**
infectious disease
686.12
respiratory disease
686.14
**flub**
*n.* botch 734.5
*v.* botch 734.12
**fluctuate**
be capricious 629.4
intermit 138.2
oscillate 323.10
vacillate 627.8
vary 141.5
**fluctuating**
inconstant 141.7

irregular 138.3
oscillating 323.15
vacillating 627.10
**fluctuation**
irregularity 138.1
oscillation 323.1
stock prices 834.9
vacillation 627.2
variation 141.3
**flue** down 230.19
fireplace 329.11
lightness 353.2
smoke passage 396.18
softness 357.4
**fluency**
diffuseness 593.1
eloquence 600.2
flow 395.4
liquidity 388.1
literary elegance
589.1
talkativeness 596.1
**fluent** eloquent 600.9
flowing 267.8
harmonious 589.8
liquid 388.6
streaming 395.24
talkative 596.9
**fluently**
eloquently 600.15
talkatively 596.11
**fluff**
*n.* bungle 734.5
down 230.19
error in speech 518.7
fine texture 351.3
lightness 353.2
softness 357.4
*v.* blunder 518.15
make pliant 357.6
**fluffy** downy 230.27
light 353.10
smooth 351.8
soft 357.14
superficial 469.20
**fluid**
*n.* gas 401.2
liquid 388.2
vapor 401.1
*adj.* changeable 141.6
liquid 388.6
**fluidity**
changeableness 141.1
gaseousness 401.3
liquidity 388.1
**fluidize** liquefy 391.5
put into a gas 401.8
**fluke**
chance event 156.6
invertebrates 415.5
stroke of luck 728.3
**fluky** 156.15
**flume** outlet 303.9
ravine 201.2
watercourse 396.2
**flummery** 547.2
**flummox**
bewilder 514.12
confuse 532.7
fail 725.9
thwart 730.15

**flump**
*n.* faint sound 452.3
*v.* sink 316.6
**flunk**
*n.* fiasco 725.6
*v.* fail 725.8
fail someone 725.16
**flunky** follower 293.2
inferior 37.2
man 787.8
retainer 750.1
servant 750.6
sycophant 907.3
working person 718.2
**fluoresce** 335.26
**fluorescence** 335.13
**fluorescent** 335.38
**fluoroscopy**
radiation physics
327.7
radiotherapy 689.8
**flurry**
*n.* agitation 324.1
bluster 911.1
bustle 707.4
confusion 532.3
excitement 857.3
gust 403.6
haste 709.1
rain 394.1
snow 333.8
speed 269.1
stock prices 834.9
*v.* agitate 324.10
confuse 532.7
excite 857.13
**flush**
*n.* blushing 908.5
fever 686.6
health 685.1
heat 328.12
jet 395.9
playing cards 878.17
reddening 368.3
shine 335.2
thrill 857.2
warmth 362.2
washing 681.5
*v.* become excited
857.17
become red 368.5
be hot 328.22
blush 908.8
cheer 870.8
flow 395.16
hunt 655.9
level 214.6
make proud 905.6
show resentment
952.14
soak 392.13
thrill 857.14
wash 681.19
*adj.* flat 214.7
full 56.11
healthy 685.11
plentiful 661.7
red-complexioned
368.9
robust 685.10
wealthy 837.13

middle 69.3
**folded** 264.7
**folder** advertising 559.8
 bookholder 605.20
 booklet 605.9
**folderol**
 music division 462.24
 nonsense 547.2
 ornamentation 901.3
 trifle 673.5
**folding money** 835.6
**foliage** 411.16
**foliate** 87.10
**foliated** layered 227.6
 leaved 411.38
**foliation** foliage 411.16
 numeration 87.1
 stratification 227.4
**folie** 473.1
**folio** book 605.1
 bookholder 605.20
 book part 605.12
 book size 605.14
 part of writing 55.2
**folk**
 *n.* people 417.2
 population 190.1
 race 11.4
 *adj.* traditional 123.12
**folk hero** 914.9
**folklore**
 mythology 1014.24
 superstition 502.3
 tradition 123.2
**folk music** 462.10
**folks** family 11.5
 kinsmen 11.2
**folksiness** 647.1
**folk singer** 464.14
**folksy** 647.3
**folktale** fiction 608.7
 tradition 123.2
**folkway** behavior 737.1
 culture 642.3
 custom 642.1
**follicle** cavity 257.2
 seed vessel 411.28
**follow**
 attach oneself to
  907.10
 be behind 241.8
 be inferior 37.4
 be proved 505.11
 cohere 50.7
 comply 768.2
 conform 82.3
 court 932.19
 emulate 22.7
 make parallel 218.5
 practice 705.7
 pursue 655.8
 resemble 20.7
 result 154.5
 seek 485.29
 specialize 81.4
 succeed 65.2
 take advice 754.7
 trace 485.34
 trail 293.3
 understand 548.7
 watch 439.14

**follow close upon**
 200.12
**follower**
 adherant 788.5
 attendant 73.6
 believer 1028.4
 devotee 635.6
 disciple 566.2
 hanger-on 907.5
 inferior 37.2
 lover 931.11
 man 787.8
 pursuer 655.4
 retainer 750.1
 successor 293.2
**following**
 *n.* attendance 73.6
 follower 293.2
 imitation 22.1
 posteriority 117.1
 pursuit 655.1
 sequence 65.1
 surveillance 485.9
 trailing 293
 *adj.* deducible 482.23
 later 117.4
 pursuing 655.11
 resulting 154.7
 similar 20.10
 succeeding 65.4
 trailing 293.5
**follow in the footsteps**
 of emulate 22.7
 follow 293.3
**follow suit** 22.7
**follow-through** 67.1
**follow up**
 be thorough 56.8
 come after 117.3
 persevere 625.5
 pursue 655.8
 trace 485.34
**follow-up**
 case history 689.11
 pursuit 655.1
 sequel 67.1
**folly** foolish act 470.4
 foolishness 470.1
**foment**
 *n.* agitation 324.1
 *v.* excite 857.11
 heat 329.17
 incite 648.17
 relieve 886.5
**fomentation**
 excitation 857.10
 incitement 648.4
 violence 162.2
**fond** credulous 502.8
 foolish 470.8
 hopeful 888.11
 loving 931.25
**fondle** cherish 813.7
 foster 785.16
 make love 932.14
 touch 425.8
**fondling**
 favorite 931.15
 lovemaking 932.1
**fondness**
 credulity 502.1
 liking 634.2

love 931.1
 tender feeling 855.6
**fond of**
 desirous of 634.22
 enamored of 931.28
**font** baptism 1040.7
 church vessel 1042.11
 jet 395.9
 origin 153.6
 printing 603.6
 source of supply
  660.4
**food** 308
**food for thought** 478.7
**food value** 309.1
**foofaraw**
 commotion 62.4
 dither 857.5
 ornamentation 901.3
 violence 162.2
**fool**
 *n.* buffoon 612.10
 dupe 620.1
 ignoramus 477.8
 laughingstock 967.7
 ninny 471
 *v.* be foolish 470.6
 deceive 618.14
 trifle 673.13
 *adj.* foolish 470.8
**foolable**
 befoolable 470.11
 gullible 502.9
**fool around**
 be foolish 470.6
 play 878.25
 trifle 673.13
**fool around with**
 meddle 238.7
 try out 489.8
**fool away** 854.5
**foolery**
 clownishness 881.5
 foolishness 470.1
 gibe 967.2
**foolhardy**
 daring 893.21
 harebrained 894.9
**foolheaded** 470.8
**fooling**
 *n.* banter 882.1
 clownishness 881.5
 deception 618.1
 ridicule 967.1
 teasing 882.2
 trifling 673.8
 *adj.* bantering 882.5
 ridiculing 967.12
**foolish**
 mischievous 738.6
 nonsensical 547.7
 preposterous 470.10
 silly 470.8
 trivial 673.16
 unintelligent 469.13
**foolishness**
 flightiness 532.5
 folly 470
 mischief 738.2
 stupidity 469.1
 thoughtlessness 480.1
 triviality 673.3

**fool notion**
 absurd idea 479.7
 caprice 629.1
**foolproof**
 resistant 159.18
 wieldy 732.14
**fool's paradise**
 hope 888.5
 illusion 519.1
**foot**
 *n.* anatomy 212.5
 bottom 212.2
 meter 609.9
 sail part 277.14
 *v.* dance 879.5
 float 275.54
 sail 275.21
 speed 269.8
 step 273.26
 walk 273.27
**footage** 202.1
**foot-candle** 335.21
**foot-dragging**
 *n.* hindrance 730.1
 slowness 270.1
 unwillingness 623.1
 *adj.* dilatory 132.17
 slow 270.10
**footfall** 273.13
**foothills** 207.5
**foothold** hold 813.2
 purchase 287.2
 support 216.5
**footing** bottom 212.2
 calculation 87.3
 fee 841.5
 foundation 216.6
 hold 813.2
 mental outlook 525.2
 purchase 287.2
 rank 29.2
 sphere of influence
  172.4
 state 7.1
 station 184.2
 support 216.5
 walking 273.10
**footlights** 611.23
**footloose and fancy-free**
 free 762.20
 wandering 273.36
**footman** 750.6
**footnote**
 comment 552.5
 record 570.4
**footprint** 568.7
**footrest** step 315.5
 support 216.5
**footslog** march 273.29
 walk 273.27
**foot soldier**
 infantryman 800.9
 pedestrian 274.6
**footsore** 717.6
**footstep** mark 568.7
 stair 315.5
 step 273.13
**footstone**
 foundation 216.7
 memorial 570.12
**foot the bill** 841.18
**footwear** 231.27

footwork 273.10
foozle
n. an error 518.6
bungle 734.5
fiasco 725.6
v. blunder 518.15
fail 725.13
fop dandy 903.9
fashionable 644.7
foppery
affectation 903.4
smartness 644.3
foppish
dandified 903.17
ultrafashionable
644.14
for
prep. in favor of
968.21
in preparation for
720.24
instead of 149.12
intending 653.12
on behalf of 785.26
conj. because 155.10
forage
n. food 308.4
search 485.14
v. feed 307.16
plunder 824.16
provision 659.9
search 485.30
for all practical
purposes
approximately 200.23
virtually 54.14
foray
n. plundering 824.5
raid 798.4
v. plunder 824.16
raid 798.20
forbear abstain 992.7
be patient 861.4
have pity 944.4
not do 706.3
not use 668.5
forbearance
avoidance 631.1
discontinuance 668.2
forgiveness 947.1
leniency 759.1
patience 861.1
pity 944.1
temperance 992.1
tolerance 526.4
forbearing
forgiving 947.6
lenient 759.7
patient 861.9
tolerant 526.11
forbid prevent 730.14
prohibit 778.3
forbidden 778.7
forbidden fruit
allurement 650.1
knowledge 475.8
prohibition 778.1
thing desired 634.11
forbidding
offensive 864.18
preventing 730.19
prohibitive 778.6

reticent 613.10
ugly 899.11
force
n. compulsion 756.2
effect 154.3
eloquence 600.3
energy 161.1
enterprise 707.7
influence 172.1
meaning 545.1
power 157.1
quantity 28.1
staff 750.11
strength 159.1
units 352.23
validity 516.4
violence 162.1
waterfall 395.11
v. compel 756.4
impose 963.6
motivate 648.12
seduce 989.20
thrust 283.11
thrust in 304.7
till 413.17
forced farfetched 10.7
involuntary 639.14
laborious 716.18
stilted 590.3
unwilling 623.5
forced march
hastening 709.3
walk 273.12
force-feed 307.17
force from 822.22
forceful
eloquent 600.11
emphatic 672.20
energetic 161.12
enterprising 707.23
powerful 157.12
strong 159.13
forcefully
eloquently 600.15
energetically 161.15
powerfully 157.15
strongly 159.21
forceless
impotent 158.13
uninfluential 173.3
force majeure
inevitability 639.7
power 157.1
forcemeat 308.12
stuffing 308.27
force of habit 642.4
force out 310.14
forceps 305.9
forces army 800.22
work force 157.9
forces of nature 402.4
force to the wall
corner 731.15
drive to ruin 693.25
force upon
impose 963.6
thrust upon 818.20
urge upon 773.8
forcible
coercive 756.11
eloquent 600.11
emphatic 672.20

energetic 161.12
powerful 157.12
strong 159.13
ford
n. passageway 657.4
shoal 210.2
v. pass 313.8
fore
n. front 240.1
adj. former 119.10
front 240.10
prior 116.4
fore and aft aft 275.69
from beginning to
end 56.18
forearm
n. arm 287.5
v. prepare for 720.11
take precautions
895.6
forearmed 539.11
forebears
ancestors 170.7
precursor 66.1
forebode
forewarn 703.6
portend 544.11
predict 543.9
threaten 973.2
foreboding
n. anxiety 890.1
apprehension 891.4
emotion 855.3
foreknowledge 542.3
forewarning 703.2
hunch 481.3
prediction 543.1
presentiment 544.2
threat 973.1
adj. anxious 890.6
forewarning 703.8
ominous 544.17
predictive 543.12
threatening 973.3
forecast
n. automation 349.7
foresight 542.1
prediction 543.1
v. plan 654.9
predict 543.9
adj. predicted 543.14
forecasting
meteorology 402.6
prediction 543.1
foreclose
dispossess 822.23
prevent 730.14
foreclosure
dispossession 822.7
obstruction 730.2
foredawn 133.4
foredestiny 640.1
foredoomed
destined 640.9
hopeless 889.13
forefathers 170.7
forefront front 240.1
vanguard 240.2
foreglimpse
n. foresight 542.1
v. anticipate 131.6
foresee 542.5

foreglimpsed 543.14
foregoing
aforegoing 119.11
leading 292.3
preceding 64.5
prior 116.4
foregone conclusion
640.1
foreground front 240.1
nearness 200.1
forehand early 131.7
front 240.10
forehanded
cautious 895.10
early 131.7
economical 851.6
foreseeing 542.7
forehead 240.5
foreign alien 78.5
external 224.8
extrinsic 6.3
unrelated 10.5
foreign affairs 744.5
foreign body 78.2
foreigner 78.3
foreign office 781.7
foreign policy 744.5
foreign service 781.7
foreknow 542.6
foreknowable 543.13
foreknowledge
foresight 542.3
predetermination
640.1
understanding 475.3
foreknown 543.14
forelock 230.6
foreman juror 1002.8
supervisor 748.2
forementioned 64.5
foremost
adj. chief 36.14
first 68.17
front 240.10
leading 292.3
most important
672.23
preceding 64.4
adv. before 292.4
in front 240.12
forenamed 64.5
forenoon 133.1
forensic
declamatory 599.12
legal 998.11
forensic medicine
jurisprudence 998.7
medicine 688.1
forensics 599.1
foreordained 640.8
forepaw 212.5
forerun
anticipate 131.6
be prior 116.3
go before 66.3
presage 544.14
forerunner
antecedent 116.2
harbinger 544.5
leader 748.6
messenger 561.2
precursor 66.1

preparer 720.5
**foresee**
anticipate 131.6
expect 539.5
foreknow 542.5
predict 543.9
project 121.6
**foreseeable**
foreseen 542.8
predictable 543.13
probable 511.6
**foreseeing**
cautious 895.10
foreknowing 542.7
predictive 543.11
sagacious 467.16
**foreseen**
expected 539.13
foreseeable 542.8
predicted 543.14
**foreshadow**
n. omen 544.3
v. portend 544.10
represent 572.8
**foreshadowed** 544.15
**foreshorten** 203.6
**foreshow** 544.10
**foreshown**
augured 544.15
predicted 543.14
**foresight**
clairvoyance 1034.8
earliness 131.1
plan 654.1
precaution 895.3
prediction 543.1
prevision 542
sagacity 467.4
the future 121.1
**foresighted**
cautious 895.10
early 131.7
foreknowing 542.7
sagacious 467.16
**forest**
n. hinterland 182.2
woodland 411.11
v. plant 413.18
adj. woodland 411.37
**forestall**
anticipate 131.6
deceive 618.13
expect 539.6
monopolize 808.6
prevent 730.14
**forestalling**
n. avoidance 631.1
obstruction 730.2
adj. expectant 539.11
preventing 730.19
**forestation** 413.3
**forested** 411.37
**forester**
arboriculturist 413.7
backwoodsman
190.10
**forest god**
agriculture divinity
413.4
sylvan deity 1014.21
**forest ranger**
forester 413.7

guardian 699.6
preserver 701.4
**forestry**
arboriculture 413.3
woodland 411.11
**foretaste**
n. appetizer 308.9
foreknowledge 542.4
v. anticipate 131.6
foresee 542.5
**foretell** predict 543.9
project 121.6
**forethought**
carefulness 533.1
foresight 542.2
intentionality 653.3
plan 654.1
precaution 895.3
**forethoughted**
cautious 895.10
foreseeing 542.7
sagacious 467.16
**foretoken**
n. omen 544.3
v. augur 544.12
predict 543.10
**foretold** 543.14
**forever**
n. an eternity 112.2
infinity 104.1
adv. eternally 112.12
infinitely 104.4
**forever and a day**
for a long time
110.14
forever 112.12
**forewarn**
forebode 544.11
warn 703.6
**forewarned** 539.11
**forewarning**
n. omen 544.4
warning 703.2
adj. foreboding 703.8
predictive 543.11
premonitory 544.16
**foreword** book 605.12
front 240.1
prelude 66.2
**for example**
for instance 505.24
incidentally 129.13
**for fear that** 175.6
**forfeit**
n. loss 812.1
penalty 1009.3
pledge 772.3
v. lose 812.4
**forfeited** 812.7
**forfeiture** loss 812.1
penalty 1009.3
**for fun** in fun 878.33
in jest 881.19
**forgather** 74.16
**forge**
n. metalworks 719.5
v. coin 835.28
fabricate 616.18
form 246.7
imitate 22.5
**forge ahead**
hustle 707.13

lead 240.7
make one's way 294.4
**forged imitation** 22.8
invented 616.29
made 167.22
**forger** coiner 835.25
deceiver 619.1
imitator 22.4
smith 718.7
**forgery** coining 835.24
copy 24.1
counterfeit 835.10
fabrication 616.10
fake 616.13
imitation 22.1
**forget** disregard 531.4
forgive and forget
947.5
not remember 538.5
**forgetful**
careless 534.11
inconsiderate 939.16
memoryless 538.9
**forgetfulness**
carelessness 534.2
inconsiderateness
939.3
obliviousness 538
**forget it**
by no means 524.10
disregard 531.4
no matter 673.22
**forgettable** 538.10
**forgivable** 1006.14
**forgive** acquit 1007.4
efface from the mem-
ory 538.6
have pity 944.4
pardon 947.3
**forgive and forget**
forget 947.5
make peace 804.10
**forgiven** 947.7
**forgiveness**
acquittal 1007.1
forgetfulness 538.1
forgivingness 947
pity 944.1
**forgiving** lenient 759.7
sparing 947.6
**forgo** abandon 633.7
avoid 992.7
not do 706.3
not use 668.5
relinquish 814.3
**forgone**
predetermined 640.8
relinquished 814.5
**for good** forever 112.12
to retain 813.11
**forgotten**
forgiven 947.7
past 119.7
unremembered 538.8
unthanked 950.5
**for instance** 505.24
**fork**
n. angle 251.2
bough 411.18
prong 299.4
tableware 348.3
tributary 395.3

v. angle 251.5
bisect 92.4
diverge 299.7
throw 285.11
transfer 271.16
**forked** angular 251.6
divergent 299.10
halved 92.6
**for keeps**
forever 112.12
to retain 813.11
**for kicks** 878.33
**fork out** give 818.12
pay out 841.14
spend 843.5
**fork over**
deliver 818.13
pay 841.16
**for laughs** 878.33
**forlorn**
abandoned 924.11
disconsolate 872.28
hopeless 889.12
**for love** 850.5
**form**
n. apparition 446.5
arrangement 60.1
aspect 446.3
body 376.3
condition 7.3
custom 642.5
document 570.5
formality 646.1
formula 751.3
grammar 246.6
harmonics 463.11
human form 246.4
idealism 377.3
illusion 519.4
kind 61.3
lair 191.26
law 998.3
mode 7.4
model 25.6
motif 901.7
precept 751.2
rite 1040.3
rule 84.4
shape 246
social convention
645.1
specter 1017.1
structure 245.1
students 566.11
way 657.1
v. be formed 246.8
compose 58.3
create 167.10
establish 167.12
order 59.4
shape 246.7
take order 59.5
train 562.14
**formal**
n. ceremony 646.4
formal clothes 231.11
adj. conventional
645.5
formative 246.9
gallant 936.15
grammatical 586.17
in a state 7.7

nominal 583.15
orderly 59.6
pompous 904.22
ritualistic 1040.22
serious 871.3
stilted 590.3
structural 245.9
stylized 646.7
**formaldehyde** 701.3
**formalist**
conformist 82.2
hypocrite 1029.3
mind-changer 628.4
pedant 476.5
ritualist 1040.2
**formalistic**
affected 903.18
conformist 82.6
formal 646.7
**formalities**
amenities 936.7
etiquette 646.3
**formality**
affectation 903.5
ceremony 646
law 998.3
pomp 904.6
rite 1040.3
ritual 646.4
rule 84.4
social convention
645.1
solemnity 871.1
**formalize**
execute 771.8
form 246.7
ritualize 646.5
standardize 84.6
**format** form 246.1
structure 245.1
**formation**
arrangement 60.1
composition 58.1
establishment 167.4
flight formation
278.12
form 246.1
forming 246.5
manufacture 167.3
order 59.1
structure 245.1
word 582.4
**formational**
formative 246.9
organizational 60.15
productional 167.17
**formative**
*n.* morphology 582.3
*adj.* beginning 68.15
causal 153.14
component 58.5
creative 167.19
formal 246.9
pliant 357.9
**former** older 123.19
past 119.10
preceding 64.5
prior 116.4
**formidable**
difficult 731.16
remarkable 34.10
terrible 891.38

weighty 672.19
**formless** abnormal 85.9
diffuse 593.11
shapeless 247.4
unordered 62.12
**formula** axiom 517.2
law 998.3
mathematics 86.9
precept 751.2
prescription 751.3
rite 1040.3
rule 84.4
**formulary**
*n.* formulas 751.3
law 998.3
rite 1040.3
rule 84.4
*adj.* formal 646.7
prescriptive 751.4
ritualistic 1040.22
**formulate**
create 167.10
legalize 998.8
phrase 588.4
say 594.23
write 602.21
**formulation**
arrangement 60.1
diction 588.1
manufacture 167.3
**fornicate**
be unchaste 989.19
copulate 419.23
**fornication**
adultery 989.7
copulation 419.8
**for nothing** 850.5,6
**for real** positively 34.19
real 1.15
**forsake** abandon 633.5
be dishonest 975.12
**forsaken**
abandoned 633.8
deserted 187.14
forlorn 924.11
outcast 926.10
unloved 867.10
**for sale** 829.16
**for show** 903.20
**forsooth**
certainly 513.23
truly 516.17
**forswear**
abandon 633.7
deny 524.4
recant 628.9
reject 638.2
relinquish 814.3
swear off 992.8
**forsworn**
deceitful 975.18
rejected 638.3
relinquished 814.5
untruthful 616.34
**fort** 799.6
**forte**
*n.* music 462.25
specialty 81.1
talent 733.4
*adj.* loud 453.10
*adv.* loudly 453.13
music 462.54

**forth** away 301.21
forward 294.8
out 303.21
**forthcoming**
*n.* appearance 446.1
approach 296.1
egress 303.1
imminence 152.1
*adj.* approaching
296.4
emerging 303.18
future 121.8
imminent 152.3
in preparation 720.22
**for the most part**
chiefly 36.17
generally 79.17
normally 84.9
on the whole 54.14
**for the record** 649.6
**for the time being**
now 120.3
temporarily 111.9
till then 109.5
**forthright**
*adj.* candid 974.17
*adv.* directly 290.24
**forthwith**
at once 113.8
promptly 131.15
**fortification**
confirmation 505.5
defense 799.4
strengthening 159.5
vitaminization 309.12
**fortified** 799.12
**fortify** add to 40.5
adulterate 44.13
confirm 505.12
defend 799.9
refresh 695.2
strengthen 159.11
vitaminize 309.18
**fortissimo**
*n.* music 462.25
*adj.* loud 453.10
*adv.* loudly 453.13
music 462.54
**fortitude** courage 893.4
patience 861.1
strength 159.1
virtue 980.5
will power 624.4
**Fort Knox** 836.12
**fortnight** fourteen 99.7
period 107.2
**fortnightly**
*n.* periodical 605.10
*adj.* regularly 137.8
**fortress** 799.6
**fortuitous** accessory 6.4
chance 156.15
**fortuity**
chance event 156.6
luck 156.1
**fortunate**
*n.* lucky person 728.6
*adj.* auspicious 544.18
lucky 728.14
successful 724.13
timely 129.9

**fortunately**
auspiciously 544.21
luckily 728.16
**fortune**
biography 608.4
chance 156.1
fate 640.2
gamble 515.1
prosperity 728.2
wealth 837.1
**fortune hunter** 978.3
**fortune's child** 728.6
**fortune-tell** 543.9
**fortune-teller** 543.4
**forty-niner** miner 383.9
traveler 274.1
**forty winks** 712.3
**forum** arena 802.1
city district 183.8
discussion 597.7
meeting 74.2
panel 755.3
tribunal 1001.1
**forward**
*v.* advance 294.5
be expedient 670.3
be instrumental
658.5
cause 153.13
deliver 818.13
encourage 785.17
hasten 709.4
impel 283.10
make better 691.9
push 285.10
send 271.14
*adj.* eager 635.9
foolhardy 894.9
front 240.10
immodest 990.6
insolent 913.8
meddlesome 238.9
premature 131.8
progressive 294.6
strong-willed 624.15
willing 622.5
*adv.* frontward 240.13
onward 294.8
**forward-looking**
modern 122.13
progressive 294.6
**forward motion**
course 267.2
progression 294.1
**forward pass** 285.4
**fosse**
entrenchment 799.5
trench 263.2
**fossil**
antiquated person
123.8
antiquity 123.6
remainder 43.1
**fossilize**
become old 123.9
harden 356.7
**fossilized** aged 126.18
antiquated 123.13
hardened 356.13
**foster**
*v.* advance 294.5
aid 785.16

care for 699.19
encourage 648.21
harbor 813.7
make better 691.9
motivate 648.12
nourish 307.17
train 562.14
*adj.* related 11.6
**fosterage** 785.4
**foster child** 171.3
**foster home** 700.4
**foster mother** 170.10
**fou**
*n.* lunatic 473.15
*adj.* intoxicated
996.30
**foul**
*n.* unfairness 977.2
*v.* catch 822.17
collide 283.12
defile 682.17
misuse 667.4
stop 266.7
*adj.* bad 675.9
base 915.12
blocked 266.11
cursing 972.8
decayed 692.41
evil 981.16
filthy 682.23
malodorous 437.5
obscene 990.9
offensive 864.18
stagnant 268.14
stormy 403.26
ugly 899.11
unfair 977.10
unhealthful 684.5
unsavory 429.7
**fouled** blocked 266.11
soiled 682.21
**foul language** 972.3
**foul matter** 682.7
**foul-mouthed** 990.9
**foul play**
chicanery 618.4
dishonesty 975.6
homicide 409.2
unfairness 977.2
**foul-tasting** 429.5
**foul-tongued** 990.9
**foul up** blunder 518.15
bungle 734.12
complicate 46.3
confuse 63.3
spoil 692.13
thwart 730.16
**foul-up** an error 518.6
bungler 734.9
confusion 62.2
**foul weather** 162.4
**found** begin 68.11
create 167.12
establish 142.9
fix 184.15
form 246.7
heat 329.24
originate 153.11
sculpture 575.5
**oundation** base 216.6
beginning 68.1
bottom 212.2

endowment 818.9
establishment 184.6
justification 1006.6
make-up 900.11
organization 788.8
premise 482.7
preparation 720.1
production 167.4
stability 142.6
**foundation garment**
corset 231.23
supporter 216.2
**founded on**
evidential 505.17
supported 216.24
**founder**
*n.* producer 167.8
*v.* capsize 275.44
break down 692.27
come to grief 729.10
fail 725.10
go lame 686.46
scuttle 320.8
sink 316.6
**foundered** 731.25
**foundering** 316.11
**foundling**
abandoned person
633.4
find 811.6
**foundry** 719.5
**found wanting**
imperfect 678.4
insufficient 662.9
**fountain**
*n.* ascent 315.1
jet 395.9
source 153.6
source of supply
660.4
*v.* shoot up 315.9
**fountainhead**
headwaters 395.2
source 153.6
**fountain of youth** 112.3
**four** 96
**four-eyed** 443.10
**four-flush** 616.21
**four-flusher** 619.6
**fourfold** 97.3
**Four Hundred, the**
nobility 918.2
society 644.6
**four-letter word** 972.4
**fourscore** 99.7
**foursome** four 96.1
game 878.9
**foursquare** four 96.4
honest 974.14
quadrangular 251.9
**fourth**
*n.* harmonics 463.20
one-fourth 98.2
*adj.* quarter 98.5
**fourth-class** 680.9
**fourth dimension** 179.6
**fourth estate**
news 558.1
the press 605.23
**four-wheeler** 272.4
**fowl**
*n.* bird 414.33

food 308.22
parts of 308.23
poultry 414.34
*v.* hunt 655.9
**fox** animal 414.25
cunning person 735.6
**fox fire** fire 328.13
phosphorescence
335.13
**foxhole**
entrenchment 799.5
hiding place 615.4
shelter 700.3
tunnel 257.5
**fox-trot** dance 879.5
run 269.10
**foxy** blemished 679.10
canine 414.45
cunning 735.12
reddish-brown 367.4
shrewd 467.15
**foyer** home 191.4
lobby 192.19
**fracas** commotion 62.4
free-for-all 796.5
noise 453.3
quarrel 795.5
**fraction** number 86.3
part 55.1
ratio 86.6
**fractionate** 401.8
**fractious**
irascible 951.19
opposing 790.8
refractory 767.10
resistant 792.5
ungovernable 626.12
unwilling 623.5
**fracture**
*n.* break 49.4
crack 201.2
impairment 692.8
*v.* amuse 878.23
be damaged 692.26
break 49.12
cleave 201.4
injure 692.15
**fragile** brittle 360.4
frail 160.14
transient 111.7
**fragility**
breakability 360.1
frailty 160.2
unhealthiness 686.2
**fragment**
*n.* excerpts 607.4
piece 55.3
small amount 35.2
*v.* demolish 693.17
pulverize 361.9
shatter 49.13
**fragmentary** 55.7
**fragrance** odor 435.1
perfume 436
**fragrant** aromatic 436.9
odorous 435.9
**fraidy-cat** 892.5
**frail** fragile 360.4
human 417.10
irresolute 627.12
thin 205.16
transient 111.7

unhealthy 686.50
unrighteous 981.12
weak 160.14
**frailty**
breakability 360.1
fault 678.2
humanness 417.5
irresolution 627.4
thinness 205.4
unhealthiness 686.2
vice 981.2
weakness 160.2
**frame**
*n.* accusation 1005.4
body 376.3
bottom 212.2
casing 245.4
film 577.10
form 246.1
human form 246.4
lip 235.4
mood 525.4
mounting 216.10
nature 5.3
skeleton 245.5
structure 245.1
*v.* accuse 1005.12
border 235.10
construct 167.10
create 167.13
form 246.7
phrase 588.4
plan 654.9
plot 654.10
prearrange 641.3
**frame of mind** 525.4
**frame of reference**
525.2
**frame-up**
accusation 1005.4
fake 616.13
intrigue 654.6
prearrangement
641.1
**framework** frame 245.4
frame of reference
525.2
outline 235.2
**franc** 835.9
**franchise**
*n.* exemption 762.8
grant 777.5
right 958.4
suffrage 744.17
voice 637.6
*v.* authorize 777.11
**Franciscan**
ascetic 991.2
religious 1038.18
**frangible** brittle 360.4
frail 160.14
**frank**
*n.* mail 604.5
postage 604.6
sausage 308.21
*adj.* artless 736.5
candid 974.17
communicative
554.10
in plain style 591.3
talkative 596.9
vulgar 990.8

**freeze out**
drive out 310.14
exclude 77.4
**freezer** 334.5
**freeze to** cohere 50.6
hold 813.6
**freezing**
*n.* preserving 701.2
refrigeration 334.1
*adj.* cold 333.14
refrigerative 334.12
**freezing point**
cold 333.1
temperature 328.3
**freight**
*n.* burden 352.7
cargo 194.2
charge 846.8
duty 963.3
impediment 730.6
shipment 271.7
train 272.13
transportation 271.3
*v.* burden 352.13
fill 56.7
put 184.14
send 271.14
transport 271.11
**freighted**
burdened 352.18
loaded 56.12
**freighter** carrier 271.5
ship 277.22
train 272.13
**French horn** 465.8
**French leave**
absence 187.4
flight 631.4
**frenetic** mad 473.30
overactive 707.24
overzealous 635.13
**frenzied** excited 857.23
mad 473.30
overactive 707.24
overzealous 635.13
violent 162.17
**frenzy**
*n.* confusion 532.3
excitement 857.7
insanity 473.7
overzealousness 635.4
seizure 686.5
violence 162.2
*v.* enrage 952.23
excite 857.11
madden 473.23
**Freon** 334.7
**frequence**
attendance 186.4
commonness 135.1
**frequency**
oftenness 135
oscillation 323.1
radio frequency
344.12
tone 450.2
wave 323.4
**frequency band**
frequency 323.1
radio 344.13
wave 323.4
**frequency curve** 511.2

**frequent**
*v.* attend 186.10
*adj.* habitual 642.16
prevalent 135.4
recurrent 103.13
**frequenter**
attender 186.5
guest 925.6
**frequenting** 186.4
**frequently**
commonly 135.6
habitually 642.23
repeatedly 103.16
**fresco**
*n.* coloring 362.12
picture 574.12
*v.* color 362.13
**fresh**
*n.* running water
395.1
violent flow 395.5
*adj.* additional 40.10
clean 681.25
cool 333.12
healthy 685.11
impudent 913.9
inexperienced 734.17
new 122.7
original 23.5
present 120.2
refreshing 695.3
remembered 537.23
renewed 122.8
undamaged 677.8
unused 668.12
windy 403.25
**freshen** air 402.11
blow 403.22
clean 681.18
refresh 695.2
refrigerate 334.10
touch up 691.11
**freshman** beginner 68.2
novice 566.9
student 566.6
**fresh start**
beginning 68.1
resumption 143.2
**fret**
*n.* ache 424.5
anger 952.7
dither 857.5
heraldic insignia
569.2
irritation 866.3
network 221.3
*v.* abrade 350.7
agitate 324.10
be angry 952.15
be ill-humored
951.14
be impatient 862.4
complain 875.13
feel anxious 890.5
grieve 872.17
hurt 424.7
impair 692.15
irritate 866.14
make anxious 890.4
nag 969.16
provoke 952.22
wear 692.23

**fretful** active 707.20
ill-humored 951.21
impatient 862.6
plaintive 875.16
**fretfulness**
impatience 862.1
petulance 951.5
**fretted** worried 890.7
woven 222.7
**fretting**
*n.* abrasion 350.2
impatience 862.1
worry 890.2
*adj.* abrasive 350.10
impatient 862.6
irritating 424.13
troublesome 890.9
**fretwork** 221.3
**Frey**
agriculture divinity
413.4
fertility god 165.5
Norse deity 1014.6
**Freya**
beautiful woman
900.9
love goddess 931.8
Norse deity 1014.6
**friable** brittle 360.4
pulverable 361.13
**friar** 1038.17
**friarhood** 1037.4
**friary** 1042.6
**fribble**
*n.* dandy 903.9
ornament 901.4
trifle 673.5
trifler 673.9
*v.* fritter away 854.5
trifle 673.13
waste time 708.12
*adj.* trivial 673.16
**fricassee**
*n.* stew 308.11
*v.* cook 330.4
**friction**
*n.* counteraction
178.1
disaccord 795.1
hostility 929.3
opposition 790.2
rubbing 350
touching 425.2
*adj.* frictional 350.9
**frictionless**
in accord 794.3
smooth-running
732.13
**fridge** 334.4
**fried** cooked 330.6
drunk 996.31
**friend** 928
**friend at court**
influential person
172.6
lawyer 1003.1
supporter 787.9
**friendless** alone 89.8
forlorn 924.11
helpless 158.18

**friendly**
*adj.* acquainted
927.16
amicable 927.14
comfortable 887.11
helpful 785.22
homelike 191.33
hospitable 925.11
sociable 922.18
*adv.* amicably 927.21
**friendship** 927
**frier** see fryer
**frieze**
architecture 211.17
ornamentation
901.14
**Frigg**
marriage goddess
933.14
Norse deity 1014.6
**fright** fear 891.1
ugly thing 899.4
**frighten** alarm 704.3
scare 891.23
startle 540.8
**frightened**
afraid 891.33
alarmed 704.4
nervous 859.10
**frightening**
*n.* intimidation 891.6
*adj.* frightful 891.36
**frighten off**
dissuade 652.3
scare away 891.29
**frightful**
frightening 891.36
remarkable 34.11
ugly 899.11
**frightfully**
fearfully 891.42
hideously 899.13
terribly 34.21
**frigid** cold 333.14
reticent 613.10
unfeeling 856.9
unsexual 419.31
unsociable 923.6
**Frigid Zones**
cold place 333.4
zone 180.3
**frill**
*n.* edging 235.7
extra 41.4
flowery language
601.4
fold 264.1
ornamentation 901.3
superfluity 663.4
*v.* fold 264.5
**frilly** ornate 901.12
showy 904.19
**fringe**
*n.* border 235.4
edging 235.7
exterior 224.2
hair 230.6
*v.* border 235.10
*adj.* peripheral 224.6
**fringe benefit** 841.6
**fringed** 235.12

defeat 727.2
disappointment
  541.1
neutralization 178.2
psychological stress
  690.21
thwarting 730.3
**fry**
  *n.* dish 308.7
  fish young 171.2
  minnow 414.35
  *v.* be hot 328.22
  cook 330.4
**fryer** food 308.22
  poultry 414.34
  young chicken 125.8
**fubsy** 195.18
**fud** 123.8
**fuddle**
  *n.* confusion 532.3
  intoxication 996.1
  *v.* confuse 532.7
  make drunk 996.22
  perplex 514.13
**fuddled** drunk 996.31
  foolish 470.8
  muddled 532.13
  perplexed 514.24
**fuddy-duddy**
  *n.* antiquated person
  123.8
  dotard 471.9
  fastidious person
  896.7
  *adj.* old 123.17
**fudge**
  *n.* candy 308.54
  nonsense 547.2
  *v.* cheat 618.17
  do carelessly 534.8
  fabricate 616.18
  falsify 616.16
  interpose 237.6
**fuel**
  *n.* firing 331
  rocketry 281.8
  *v.* provision 659.9
  stoke 331.8
**fuel oil** 380.11
**fugacious** 111.7
**fugacity** 111.1
**fugitive**
  *n.* criminal 986.10
  escapee 632.5
  fleer 631.5
  *adj.* escaped 632.11
  runaway 631.16
  transient 111.7
  vanishing 447.3
  wandering 273.36
**fugleman** leader 748.6
  model 25.1
  precursor 66.1
  superior 36.4
**fugue** amnesia 538.2
  music 462.19
  trance state 690.26
**führer** autocrat 749.14
  leader 748.6
**fulcrum** axis 322.5
  leverage 287.3
  supporter 216.2

**fulfill** accomplish 722.4
  act on 705.9
  complete 56.6
  execute 771.10
  observe 768.2
  suffice 661.4
**fulfillment**
  accomplishment
  722.1
  adjustment 690.34
  completion 56.4
  contentment 868.1
  execution 771.5
  observance 768.1
**fuliginous** 365.11
**full**
  *n.* completeness 56.2
  *adj.* blocked 266.11
  broad 204.6
  colored 362.16
  complete 56.9
  corpulent 195.18
  crowded 74.22
  detailed 8.9
  great 34.6
  intoxicated 996.30
  loud 453.10
  perfect 677.7
  plentiful 661.7
  replete 56.11
  resonant 454.9
  satiated 664.6
  thick 204.8
  unrestricted 762.26
  *adv.* squarely 290.25
**fullback** 878.20
**full blast** 157.1
**full-blooded**
  red-complexioned
  368.9
  strong 159.13
  wellborn 918.11
**full bloom**
  flowering 411.24
  maturity 126.2
**full-blown**
  full-size 195.22
  mature 126.13
**full-bodied**
  flavorful 428.9
  thick 204.8
**full circle** circuit 321.2
  rotation 322.1
**full consent** 762.6
**full dress** 231.11
**full feather** 231.10
**full fig** 231.1,10
**full-fledged**
  complete 56.9
  full-size 195.22
  grown 197.12
  mature 126.13
**full-grown**
  complete 56.9
  full-size 195.22
  grown 197.12
  mature 126.13
  ripe 722.13
**full house**
  full measure 56.3
  playing cards 878.17
**full measure** fill 56.3

plenty 661.2
**full nelson** 813.3
**fullness** breadth 204.1
  completeness 56.2
  continuity 71.1
  greatness 34.1
  loudness 453.1
  perfection 677.2
  plenty 661.2
  resonance 454.1
  satiety 664.1
  wholeness 54.5
**full of beans**
  frisky 870.14
  healthy 685.7
**full-scale**
  complete 56.9
  full-size 195.22
**full scope** 762.4
**full-sized** 195.22
**full speed ahead**
  at full speed 269.24
  command 275.77
**full stop**
  standstill 268.3
  stop 144.2
**full swing** 762.4
**full tilt** 707.25
**full time** 108.3
**fully** completely 56.14
  in full 8.13
  perfectly 677.10
  plentifully 661.9
**fulminate** blast 456.8
  explode 162.13
  fuel 331.8
**fulminate against**
  berate 969.20
  censure 969.13
  curse 972.5
**fulsome** bad 675.9
  base 915.12
  flattering 970.8
  grandiloquent 601.8
  malodorous 437.5
  obscene 990.9
  offensive 864.18
  suave 936.18
  uncritical 968.18
  unsavory 429.7
**fumble**
  *n.* bungle 734.5
  *v.* bungle 734.11
  confuse 63.3
  grope 485.31
**fumbled** 734.21
**fumbling**
  *n.* bungling 734.4
  *adj.* clumsy 734.20
**fume**
  *n.* agitation 324.1
  anger 952.7
  excitement 857.3
  odor 435.1
  smoke 329.16
  vapor 401.1
  violence 162.2
  *v.* be angry 952.15
  decolor 363.5
  exhale 310.23
  give off 401.8
  preserve 701.8

  seethe 162.11
  smoke 328.23
**fumigant**
  antiseptic 687.21
  deodorant 438.3
  poison 676.3
**fumigate** gas 401.8
  sanitize 681.24
  scent 436.8
  stop odor 438.4
**fumigation**
  deodorizing 438.2
  sanitation 681.3
  vaporization 401.5
**fuming** burning 328.27
  infuriated 952.29
  vaporous 401.9
**fun**
  *n.* amusement 878.2
  joke 881.6
  merriment 870.5
  pleasure 865.1
  *v.* joke 881.13
  *adj.* amusing 878.29
**function**
  *n.* action 705.1
  business 656.1
  ceremony 646.4
  intention 653.1
  rite 1040.3
  role 656.3
  syntax 586.2
  use 665.5
  *v.* act 705.4
  do duty 656.13
  operate 164.7
**functional**
  acting 705.10
  grammatical 586.17
  managerial 164.12
  occupational 656.16
  operating 164.11
  operative 164.9
  psychological 690.43
  useful 665.18
**functionalism**
  architecture 574.4
  utilitarianism 665.6
**functionary**
  agent 781.3
  official 749.16
  operator 164.4
**functioning**
  *n.* action 705.1
  operation 164.1
  *adj.* acting 705.10
  operating 164.11
**fund**
  *n.* capital 835.15
  collection 74.11
  money 835.14
  supply 660.2
  *v.* finance 836.15
  pay 841.18
  provide 659.7
  subsidize 818.19
  support 785.12
**fundament**
  bottom 212.1
  foundation 216.6
**fundamental**
  *n.* essence 5.2

foundation 216.6
important point
672.6
tone 450.2
*adj.* basic 212.8
beginning 68.15
causal 153.15
essential 5.8
simple 45.6
vital 672.22
**fundamentalism**
orthodoxy 1024.5
strictness 757.2
**fundamentalist**
*n.* orthodox 1024.4
*adj.* orthodox 1024.8
strict 757.7
**fundamentally**
essentially 5.10
extremely 34.22
**funding** 836.2
**funds** assets 810.8
means 658.1
money 835.14
**funebrial**
funereal 410.22
gloomy 872.24
**funeral**
*n.* burial 410.5
procession 71.3
*adj.* funereal 410.22
**funeral car** 410.10
**funeral director** 410.8
**funeral march**
dirge 875.5
music 462.11
slowness 270.2
**funeral parlor**
funeral establishment
410.9
workplace 719.1
**funereal** blackish 365.9
dark 337.14
funeral 410.22
gloomy 872.24
**fun-fair** 878.11
**fungicide** killer 409.3
poison 676.3
**fungous** 411.34
**fungus** blight 676.2
germ 686.39
plant 411.3,4; 412.3
tumor 686.36
types of 411.45
**funicular**
*n.* cableway 657.9
train 272.13
*adj.* threadlike 206.7
**funk**
*n.* coward 892.5
fear 891.1
*v.* be a coward 892.8
be afraid 891.19
flinch 891.21
frighten 891.23
**funky**
malodorous 437.5
melancholy 872.23
panicky 892.10
**fun-loving** 865.15
**funnel**
*n.* cone 255.5

convergence 298.1
smoke passage 396.18
tube 396.6
*v.* channel 396.19
converge 298.2
pipe 271.13
**funnel-shaped**
concave 257.16
conical 255.12
**funnies** 574.17
**funny** eccentric 474.4
humorous 880.4
odd 85.11
witty 881.15
**funny bone** 881.11
**funny feeling** 481.3
**funnyman**
comedian 612.9
humorist 881.12
**fur** coating 228.12
down 230.19
hair 230.2
heraldic insignia
569.2
pelt 229.1
types of 229.8
**furbelow** 235.7
**furbish** ornament 901.8
polish 260.7
renovate 694.17
rub 350.8
touch up 691.11
**furbished** 260.10
**furcate**
*v.* angle 251.5
fork 299.7
*adj.* angular 251.6
forked 299.10
**furfuraceous**
flaky 227.7
powdery 361.11
**Furies, the**
avenger 956.3
evil spirits 1016.11
rage 952.10
**furious** excited 857.23
hasty 709.9
infuriated 952.29
mad 473.30
overzealous 635.13
passionate 857.27
reckless 894.8
sharp 162.15
violent 162.17
**furiously** angrily 952.30
frenziedly 857.33
hastily 709.12
intensely 162.24
recklessly 894.11
severely 34.23
violently 162.25
**furl** roll 322.10
sail 275.50
**furlough**
*n.* absence 187.4
unemployment 708.3
vacation 711.3
*v.* dismiss 310.19
**furnace** atomics 326.13
heater 329.10,33
hot place 328.11
kiln 576.5

metalworks 719.5
**furnish** bear 167.14
equip 659.8
give 818.15
prepare 720.8
provide 659.7
**furnishing** fitting 720.2
provision 659.1
**furnishings**
equipment 659.4
merchandise 831.5
wardrobe 231.2
**furniture**
equipment 659.4
merchandise 831.5
typesetting 603.2,26
**furor** excitement 857.7
fervor 855.10
frenzy 473.7
insanity 473.1
mania 473.12
rage 952.10
violence 162.2
**furred** 230.24
**furrier** clothier 231.32
merchant 830.3
tailor 231.34
**furrow**
*n.* crack 201.2
groove 263
indentation 257.6
wrinkle 264.3
*v.* cut 201.4
engrave 578.10
excavate 257.15
groove 263.3
wrinkle 264.6
**furrowed**
engraved 578.12
grooved 263.4
wrinkled 264.8
**furry** cutaneous 229.6
downy 230.27
hairy 230.24
soft 357.14
**further**
*v.* advance 294.5
aid 785.17
*adj.* additional 40.10
more distant 199.10
renewed 122.8
*adv.* additionally
40.11
**furtherance** aid 785.5
development 148.1
improvement 691.1
progression 294.1
**furthermore** 40.11
**furthermost** 199.12
**furthest** extreme 34.13
farthest 199.12
**furtive** covert 614.12
deceitful 618.20
in hiding 615.14
**furtiveness** deceit 618.3
stealth 614.4
**furuncle** sore 686.35
swelling 256.4
**fury** excitement 857.7
fervor 855.10
frenzy 473.7

ill-humored person
951.11
ill-humored woman
951.12
overzealousness 635.4
rage 952.10
violence 162.2
violent person 162.9
witch 943.7
**fuse**
*n.* detonator 331.7,11
safety equipment
699.3
*v.* combine 52.3
come together 74.16
cooperate 786.3
liquefy 391.5
melt 329.21
mix 44.11
stick together 50.9
unify 14.5
**fused** combined 52.5
molten 329.31
**fusee** match 331.5
torch 336.3
**fusi–** 205.16
**fusible**
liquefiable 391.9
molten 329.31
**fusillade**
*n.* capital punishment
1010.7
detonation 456.3
gunfire 798.10
hit 283.4
shot 285.5
*v.* fire upon 798.22
**fusion** affiliation 786.2
alloy 383.4
combination 52.1
heating 329.3
identification 14.2
liquefaction 391.1
mixture 44.1
nuclear fusion 326.9
unity 89.1
**fuss**
*n.* agitation 324.1
bluster 911.1
bustle 707.4
commotion 62.4
dither 857.5
fastidious person
896.7
ornamentation 901.3
quarrel 795.5
violence 162.2
*v.* be fastidious 896.8
be impatient 862.4
bustle 707.12
complain 875.13
confuse 532.7
excite 857.13
feel anxious 890.5
nag 969.16
**fusspot** 896.7
**fussy** bustling 707.20
detailed 8.9
fastidious 896.10
meticulous 533.12
ornate 901.12
restless 857.25

**fust** become old 123.9
  stagnate 268.9
**fustian**
  *n.* bombast 601.2
  nonsense 547.2
  *adj.* bombastic 601.9
**fustigate**
  criticize severely
    969.21
  punish 1010.14
**fusty** malodorous 437.5
  old 123.14
  spoiled 692.43
  trite 883.9
**futile** foolish 470.8
  hopeless 889.13
  ineffective 158.15
  inexpedient 671.5
  trivial 673.16
  unsuccessful 725.17
  vain 669.13
**futility** failure 725.1
  ineffectiveness 158.3
  inexpedience 671.1
  meaninglessness
    547.1
  no hope 889.1
  triviality 673.3
  uselessness 669.2
**future**
  *n.* fate 640.2
  fiancée 931.16
  tense 586.12
  time to come 121
  *adj.* forthcoming
    121.8
  imminent 152.3
**futures** 834.11
**futuristic** 121.8
**futurity**
  eventuality 121.4
  forthcoming 152.1
  time to come 121.1
**fuzee** see **fusee**
**fuzz**
  *n.* down 230.19
  fine texture 351.3
  lightness 353.2
  policeman 699.16
  *v.* make uncertain
    514.14
**fuzzy** downy 230.27
  formless 247.4
  hairy 230.24
  indistinct 445.6
  obscure 549.15
  smooth 351.8
  vague 514.18

## G

**G** gravity 352.5
  thousand 99.10
  US money 835.7
**gab**
  *n.* chatter 596.3
  mouth 265.5
  speech 594.1
  *v.* chatter 596.5
  speak 594.20
**gabble**
  *n.* chatter 596.3

imperfect speech
  595.4
  nonsense 547.2
  *v.* bird sound 460.5
  chatter 596.5
  speak poorly 595.9
  talk nonsense 547.5
**gabby** 596.9
**Gabriel** angel 1015.4
  herald 561.2
**gad**
  *n.* goad 648.8
  wanderer 274.2
  *v.* wander 273.22
**gadabout** 274.2
**gad about** 273.22
**gadfly** goad 648.8
  motivator 648.10
**gadget** object 376.4
  tool 348.1
**Gaea**
  agriculture divinity
    413.4
  Earth 375.10
  goddess 1014.5
**gaff** 459.4
**gaffe** 518.5
**gaffer** old man 127.2
  supervisor 748.2
**gag**
  *n.* acting 611.9
  joke 881.6
  restraint 760.4
  silencer 451.4
  *v.* render powerless
    158.11
  sicken at 867.4
  silence 451.8
  suppress 760.8
  vomit 310.25
**gaga**
  enthusiastic about
    635.12
  foolish 470.8
  insane 473.26
  scatterbrained 532.16
**gage** challenge 793.2
  marihuana 687.13
  pledge 772.2
**gaggle**
  *n.* geese 74.6
  *v.* bird sound 460.5
**gag on** 503.5
**gaiety**
  cheerfulness 870.4
  colorfulness 362.4
  conviviality 922.3
  festivity 878.3
  happiness 865.2
  ornamentation 901.3
  showiness 904.3
**gain**
  *n.* automation 349.11
  electric gain 342.16
  good 674.4
  increase 38.1
  profit 811.3
  *v.* acquire 811.8
  arrive 300.6
  get better 691.7
  increase 38.6
  incur 175.4

overtake 269.17
  persuade 648.23
  receive 819.6
  win 726.4
**gainer** 320.1
**gainful**
  productive 811.15
  useful 665.21
**gains** profits 811.3
  receipts 844.1
  winnings 38.3
**gainsay**
  contradict 790.6
  deny 524.4
**gain the day** 726.4
**gain upon**
  approach 296.3
  overtake 269.17
**gain weight** 197.8
**gait** pace 273.14
  rate 267.4
**gal** 125.6
**gala**
  *n.* festival 878.4
  *adj.* festive 878.30
**galactic** celestial 375.25
  large 34.7
  universal 79.14
**galacto–** galaxy 375.6
  milk 388.3
**galaxy**
  famous persons 914.9
  island universe 375.6
  throng 74.4
**gale** breeze 403.5
  emotional outburst
    857.8
  windstorm 403.12
**gall**
  *n.* affliction 866.8
  bile 312.2
  bitterness 429.2
  ill humor 951.1
  impairment 692.8
  insolence 913.3
  irritation 866.3
  knob 256.3
  rancor 939.7
  rashness 894.1
  resentment 952.3
  *v.* abrade 350.7
  distress 424.7
  injure 692.15
  irritate 866.14
**gallant**
  *n.* beau 931.12
  brave person 893.8
  cavalier 936.9
  dandy 903.9
  unchaste person
    989.10
  *adj.* chivalrous 936.15
  courageous 893.17
  showy 904.19
  unchaste 989.25
**gallantry** chivalry 936.2
  courage 893.1
  courtship 932.6
  profligacy 989.3
**galled** annoyed 866.21
  sore 424.11
**galleon** 277.23

**gallery** art 574.18
  audience 448.6
  auditorium 192.4
  balcony 192.22
  corridor 192.18
  entrenchment 799.5
  layer 227.1
  museum 660.9
  observation post
    439.8
  passageway 657.4
  platform 216.13
  porch 192.21
  showroom 192.24
  theater part 611.20
**galley** kitchen 330.3
  sailboat 277.3,21
  trial print 603.5,26
  vessels 277.25
**galley slave**
  boatman 276.5
  drudge 718.3
  slave 764.7
**galling** abrasive 350.10
  annoying 864.22
  irritating 424.13
**gallivant** flirt 932.18
  wander 273.22
**gallop**
  *n.* gait 273.14
  speed 269.3
  *v.* ride 273.33
  run 269.10
**galloping** 269.19
**gallows**
  capital punishment
    1010.7
  instrument of execu-
    tion 1011.5
**gallstone** 686.21
**galoot** 471.2
**galore**
  *adj.* plentiful 661.7
  *adv.* greatly 34.15
**galvanic**
  electricity 342.27
  exciting 857.28
  provocative 648.27
**galvanize**
  electrify 342.23
  electrolyze 342.25
  energize 161.9
  motivate 648.12
  plate 228.26
  stimulate 857.12
**galvanized** 228.32
**gam**
  *n.* chat 597.4
  leg 273.16
  whales 74.5
  *v.* chat 597.10
**gambit** attempt 714.2
  beginning 68.3
  stratagem 735.3
  trick 618.6
**gamble**
  *n.* an uncertainty
    514.8
  probability 156.1
  risk 515
  *v.* be liable 175.3
  bet 515.20

endanger 697.6
game 515.18
risk 156.12
take chances 697.7
**gamble away** 854.3
**gamble on**
be certain 513.9
believe in 501.16
gamble 515.19
**gambler** 515.17
**gambling** gaming 515.7
illicit business 826.1
**gambling house**
gaming house 515.15
resort 191.27
**gambol**
*n.* frolic 878.5
jump 319.2
*v.* be cheerful 870.6
jump 319.6
play 878.25
rejoice 876.5
**gambrel** 273.16
**game**
*n.* animal life 414.1
cards 878.35
contest 796.3
fun 878.2
influence 172.3
laughingstock 967.7
meat 308.12
objective 653.2
plan 654.1
quarry 655.7
sport 878.9
stratagem 735.3
vocation 656.6
word list 878.34
*v.* gamble 515.18
*adj.* bold 893.18
crippled 692.32
plucky 624.14
willing 622.5
**gamecock**
brave person 893.8
combatant 800.1
**gamely**
courageously 893.22
pluckily 624.18
**game plan** 654.2
**games** contest 796.3
tournament 878.10
**gamesman** 746.6
**gamesmanship**
competition 796.2
cunning 735.1
**gamesome** frisky 870.14
playful 878.31
**gamete** 406.10
**game theory** 511.2
**game warden**
guardian 699.6
preserver 701.4
**gamic** gametic 406.22
sexual 419.26
**gamin** bad child 125.4
waif 274.3
**gamma globulin** 687.27
**gamma ray**
radiation 327.3
ray 335.5

**gammon**
*n.* bacon 308.16
humbug 616.14
nonsense 547.2
*v.* deceive 618.13
fake 616.21
**gamut** continuity 71.2
harmonics 463.6
range 179.2
**gamy** bold 893.18
malodorous 437.5
pungent 433.8
tainted 692.42
**gander**
male animal 420.8
poultry 414.34
**gang**
*n.* association 788.1
elk 74.5
group 74.3
staff 750.11
*v.* join 52.4
move 273.17
**gang around** 74.16
**gangland** 986.11
**gangling** lean 205.17
tall 207.21
**ganglion** nerve 422.6
nerve center 226.5
**gangplank**
bridge 657.10
entrance 302.5
**gangrene**
*n.* disease 686.37
filth 682.7
rotting 692.7
*v.* decay 692.25
**gangrened**
decayed 692.41
diseased 686.56
**gangster** bandit 825.4
criminal 986.10
evildoer 943.1
**gang up on** 798.15
**gangway**
*n.* bridge 657.10
entrance 302.5
*interj.* open up!
265.24
**ganja** 687.13,53
**gantlet** see gauntlet
**gaol** see jail
**gap**
*n.* break 49.4
crack 201.2
deficiency 57.2
discontinuity 72.2
opening 265.1
valley 257.9
*v.* cleave 201.4
gape 265.17
**gape**
*n.* crack 201.2
gaping 265.2
gaze 439.5
opening 265.1
*v.* be a spectator
442.5
be curious 528.3
gaze 439.16
wonder 920.5
yawn 265.17

**gaping**
*n.* yawning 265.2
*adj.* abysmal 209.11
astonished 920.9
cleft 201.7
expectant 539.11
yawning 265.19
**garage**
repair shop 719.6
room 192.27
**garb**
*n.* clothing 231.1
looks 446.4
*v.* clothe 231.38
**garbage** offal 682.9
refuse 669.4
**garbage can** 669.7
**garbage dump**
filth receptacle
682.12
refuse heap 682.10
**garble**
*n.* unintelligibility
549.7
*v.* confuse 63.3
distort 249.6
falsify 616.16
make unintelligible
549.12
misinterpret 553.2
misrepresent 573.3
**garbled**
distorted 249.11
falsified 616.26
hard to understand
549.14
incomplete 57.5
meaningless 547.6
misinterpreted 553.3
unauthentic 518.19
**garçon** boy 125.5
male servant 750.4
**garden**
*n.* agriculture 413.10
compilation 605.4
*v.* farm 413.16
*adj.* horticultural
411.35
mediocre 680.8
simple 902.6
**gardener**
horticulturalist 413.6
male servant 750.4
**gardening**
flower gardening
411.22
horticulture 413.2
**Garden of Eden** 535.11
**garden variety**
mediocrity 680.2
the ordinary 84.3
**garden-variety**
mediocre 680.8
simple 902.6
**Gargantuan**
huge 195.20
large 34.7
**gargle**
*n.* dentifrice 687.22
drink 996.6
*v.* tipple 996.23
wash 681.19

**gargoyle** conduit 396.8
ugly thing 899.4
**garish** bright 335.32
gaudy 904.20
grandiloquent 601.8
lurid 362.19
**garland**
*n.* circle 253.2
compilation 605.4
flowers 411.23
heraldic insignia
569.2
poetry 609.7
trophy 916.3
*v.* ornament 901.9
**garment** clerical 1041.5
clothing 231.1
parts of 231.66
raiment 231.3
**garmentmaker**
garmentworker
231.33
sewer 223.2
**garner**
*n.* granary 660.7
*v.* store up 660.11
**garnered** 660.14
**garnish**
*n.* ornamentation
901.1
*v.* appropriate 822.20
ornament 901.8
**garnished** 901.11
**garnishee** 822.20
**garnishment**
appropriation 822.5
ornamentation 901.1
summons 752.7
**garret** 192.16
**garrison**
*n.* guard 699.9
military unit 800.19
stronghold 799.6
*v.* fortify 799.9
**garrison state**
militarization 797.14
military government
741.4
**garrote**
*n.* capital punishment
1010.7
suffocation 409.7
*v.* execute 1010.19
strangle 409.19
**garrulous** 596.9
**gas**
*n.* belch 310.9
boasting 910.2
chatter 596.3
fart 310.10
fuel 331.1
great success 724.3
illuminant 335.20
nonsense 547.3
petroleum 380.4
types of 401.11
vapor 401.2
*v.* attack 798.17
chatter 596.5
provision 659.9
talk nonsense 547.5
**gasbag** aircraft 280.11

braggart 910.5
chatterer 596.4
**gas chamber**
capital punishment
1010.7
instrument of execu-
tion 1011.5
killing site 409.12
**gasconade**
bluster 911.3
boast 910.6
**gaseous** rarefied 355.4
tenuous 4.6
vaporous 401.9
**gash**
*n.* crack 201.2
groove 263.1
impairment 692.8
mark 568.5
notch 262.1
refuse 669.4
*v.* cleave 201.4
groove 263.3
injure 692.15
mark 568.19
notch 262.4
sever 49.11
**gasify** 401.8
**gas jet** 329.10
**gasket** hole 265.4
wadding 266.5
**gaslike** 401.9
**gaslit** 335.39
**gas main** 396.7
**gas meter** 401.7
**gasoline** fuel 331.1
illuminant 335.20
petroleum 380.4
**gasp**
*n.* breathing 403.18
*v.* become exhausted
717.5
be hot 328.22
breathe 403.24
utter 594.26
**gasser**
great success 724.3
stage show 611.4
**gas station** 832.7
**gassy** boastful 910.11
bombastic 601.9
distended 197.13
pompous 904.22
talkative 596.9
vaporous 401.9
**gastric**
abdominal 193.5
visceral 225.10
**gastric juice**
digestion 309.8
secretion 312.2
**gastritis**
gastrointestinal dis-
ease 686.27
inflammation 686.9
**gastro–** 193.3
**gastronome** 307.14
**gastronomic(al)** 307.29
**gastronomy**
aesthetic taste 897.5
eating 307.13
gluttony 994.2

**gat** gun 801.5
opening 265.1
**gate** barrier 730.5
conduit 396.4
entrance 302.6
floodgate 396.11
metal casting 383.5
receipts 844.1
valve 396.10
**gate, the** 310.5
**gâteau** 308.41
**gate-crasher** guest 925.6
intruder 238.3
newcomer 78.4
**gatehouse** 191.10
**gatekeeper** 699.12
**gatepost**
entrance 302.6
post 217.4
**gateway** 302.6
**gather**
*n.* fold 264.1
*v.* assemble 74.18
be imminent 152.2
blow up 403.22
come together 74.16
conclude 494.10
fold 264.5
grow 197.7
harvest 413.19
join 47.5
pick up 317.8
procure 811.10
suppose 499.10
**gather around**
come together 74.16
form 59.5
**gathered**
assembled 74.21
folded 264.7
joined 47.13
produced 167.22
stored 660.14
**gathering**
accumulation 74.9
acquisition 811.2
assembly 74.1
bookbinding 605.15
congregation 74.2
harvest 413.15
joining 47.1
part of writing 55.2
removal to heaven
1018.12
social gathering
922.10
sore 686.35
**gathering clouds**
danger 697.1
darkening 337.6
omen 544.6
warning sign 703.3
**gator** 414.30
**gauche** clumsy 734.20
ignorant 477.12
**gaucherie** 734.5
**gaucho** herder 416.3
rider 274.8
**gaudiness**
appearances 446.2
garishness 362.5
grandiloquence 601.1

paltriness 673.2
showiness 904.3
vulgarity 898.2
**gaudy** garish 362.19
grandiloquent 601.8
paltry 673.18
tawdry 904.20
vulgar 898.11
**gauge**
*n.* measure 490.2
measuring device
490.4
size 195.1
types of 490.20
*v.* analyze 48.8
judge 494.9
measure 490.11
size 195.15
**gauged** 490.14
**gauging** analysis 48.3
judgment 494.3
measurement 490.1
**gaunt** barren 166.4
lean 205.17
**gauntlet**
challenge 793.2
gloves 231.63
punishment 1010.2
**gaup** 439.16
**gauss** 342.9
**Gautama Buddha**
1022.4
**gauze** fog 404.2
medical dressing
687.33
**gauzy** smooth 351.8
thin 205.16
transparent 339.4
**gavel** 739.9
**gawk**
*n.* awkward person
734.8
oaf 471.5
*v.* be curious 528.3
gaze 439.16
wonder 920.5
**gawky** clumsy 734.20
lean 205.17
**gay** cheerful 870.14
colorful 362.18
convivial 922.19
festive 878.30
happy 865.13
homosexual 419.32
intoxicated 996.30
showy 904.19
unchaste 989.25
**gay deceiver**
deceiver 619.1
unchaste person
989.10
**gay dog** 989.10
**gaze**
*n.* stare 439.5
*v.* look at 439.14
see 439.16
wonder 920.5
**gazebo**
observation post
439.8
summerhouse 191.13

**gazelle**
hoofed animal
414.5,58
jumper 319.4
speed 269.6
**gazette**
newspaper 605.11
official document
570.8
periodical 605.10
**gazetteer**
dictionary 605.7
glossary 88.4
journalist 605.22
reference book 605.6
**gazpacho** 308.10
**Ge** see **Gaea**
**gear**
*n.* belongings 810.3
clothing 231.1
cordage 206.3
equipment 659.4
mechanism 348.6
rigging 277.12
workings 348.5
*v.* equip 659.8
**geared** 26.10
**gear to** conform 82.3
make agree 26.7
**gee!** 920.21
**geezer** 127.2
**Geiger counter**
photosensitive device
343.22
radiation counter
327.13
**geisha** dancer 879.3
entertainer 612.1
**Geist** 467.8
**gel**
*n.* semiliquid 389.5
*v.* thicken 354.10
**gelatin**
semiliquid 389.5
sweets 308.39
theater lighting
611.23
**gelatinous** 389.12
**geld** castrate 42.11
feminize 421.12
**gelded** castrated 158.19
sterile 166.4
**gelding** castration 42.4
horse 414.10
impotent 158.6
**gelid** cold 333.14
frozen 334.14
**gelignite** 801.9
**gelt** 835.2
**gem**
*n.* bun 308.31
good person 985.1
good thing 674.5
jewel 901.6
precious stone
384.6,13
*v.* ornament 901.9
**Gemara** 1021.5
**geminate**
*v.* duplicate 91.3
*adj.* double 91.4

**Gemini**
spacecraft 282.14
twins 90.4
**gem stone** 384.6,13
**gendarme**
French police 699.15
policeman 699.16
**gender**
grammatical form 586.10
sex 419.1
**gene** cell 406.9
genetics 170.6
**genealogical** 170.14
**genealogy**
pedigree 170.5
register 570.9
**general**
*n.* commissioned officer 749.18
*adj.* communal 815.9
governing 741.18
nonspecific 79.11
normal 84.7
public 417.13
undiscriminating 493.5
vague 514.18
vulgar 898.14
**generality** average 32.1
major part 54.6
ordinary 79.3
universality 79
usualness 84.2
vagueness 514.4
**generalization**
abstraction 79.8
generality 79.1
logic 482.3
**generalize**
reason 482.15
universalize 79.9
**generally**
approximately 200.23
in general 79.17
normally 84.9
on the average 32.5
vaguely 514.27
**general practice** 688.16
**general public**
citizenry 417.2
population 190.1
the people 919.2
**generalship**
directorship 747.4
warcraft 797.10
**general store** 832.1
**generate** cause 153.11
generate electricity 342.23
originate 167.13
procreate 169.8
**generation** age 107.4
birth 169.6
lifetime 110.5
procreation 169.2
production 167.5
**generative**
causal 153.15
creative 167.19
genetic 169.16

**generator**
auto part 272.25
creator 153.4
electrical device 342.36
electronic tube 343.18
engine 348.26
producer 167.8
system component 349.33
**generic** 79.11
**generosity**
benevolence 938.4
hospitality 925.1
liberality 853.1
magnanimity 979.2
plenty 661.2
**generous**
benevolent 938.15
copious 34.8
forgiving 947.6
giving 818.22
hospitable 925.11
indulgent 759.8
liberal 853.4
magnanimous 979.6
plentiful 661.7
productive 165.9
tolerant 526.11
voluminous 195.17
**generously**
abundantly 34.20
liberally 853.5
magnanimously 979.8
plentifully 661.9
**genesis** birth 169.6
development 148.3
origin 68.4
production 167.7
source 153.5
**genetic** causal 153.15
developing 148.8
generative 169.16
genic 406.20
hereditary 170.15
innate 5.7
racial 11.7
**genetic disease** 686.1,10
**genetics** biology 406.17
heredity 170.6
**genial** cheerful 870.11
cordial 927.15
genetic 169.16
good-natured 938.14
hospitable 925.11
pleasant 863.6
sociable 922.18
warm 328.24
**geniality**
cheerfulness 870.1
cordiality 927.6
good nature 938.2
hospitality 925.1
pleasantness 863.1
sociability 922.1
**genie** 1016.7
**genital** genetic 169.16
sexual 419.27
**genitals** 419.10
**genitor** 170.9
**genius** ability 157.2

creativity 467.8
evil spirit 1016.7
expert 733.13
first-rater 674.6
guardian angel 1014.22
imagination 535.2
inspiration 648.9
intelligence 467.2
nature 5.3
scholar 476.3
spirit 1014.15
superior 36.4
talent 733.4
talented person 733.12
**genocide** carnage 409.5
crime 982.2
killer 409.3
**genotype** biology 61.5
gene 406.9
type 25.1
**genre**
artistic style 574.9
form 246.1
kind 61.3
**gens** community 788.2
race 11.4
**genteel** chic 644.13
decorous 897.10
noble 918.10
well-bred 936.17
**gentile**
*n.* non-Jew 1025.6
unbeliever 1031.11
*adj.* racial 11.7
unorthodox 1025.10
**gentilhomme** 974.8
**gentility**
decorousness 897.3
good breeding 936.4
nobility 918.1
**gentle**
*v.* accustom 642.11
calm 163.7
domesticate 764.11
drive animals 416.7
soften 357.6
*adj.* faint-sounding 452.16
good-natured 938.14
lenient 759.7
light 353.11
moderate 163.10
noble 918.10
pitying 944.7
slow 270.10
soft 357.8
weak 765.15
well-bred 936.17
**gentlefolk** 918.3
**gentleman**
good person 985.1
honest person 974.8
male 420.4
male servant 750.4
nobleman 918.4
**gentlemanly**
masculine 420.11
noble 918.10
well-bred 936.17

**gentlemen's agreement**
compact 771.1
promise 770.2
**gentleness**
compassionateness 944.2
faintness of sound 452.1
good breeding 936.4
good nature 938.2
leniency 759.1
lightness 353.1
meekness 765.5
moderation 163.1
softness 357.1
tender feeling 855.6
**gentlewoman**
maid 750.8
noblewoman 918.6
woman 421.5
**gently** faintly 452.21
meekly 765.19
slowly 270.13
softly 357.17
**gentry**
aristocracy 918.3
folks 417.2
**genuflect**
bow down 765.10
curtsy 964.6
kneel 318.9
**genuflection**
crouch 318.3
obeisance 964.2
**genuine**
authentic 516.14
candid 974.17
honest 974.14
natural 736.6
real 1.15
**genuinely**
artlessly 736.7
authentically 516.18
candidly 974.23
really 1.16
**genus** biology 61.5
kind 61.3
nomenclature 583.1
**geo-** 385.1
**geodetic(al)**
geography 385.10
locational 184.18
measuring 490.13
**geodetics**
geography 385.4
geology 385.4
mensuration 490.9
**geographer** 385.5
**geographic(al)**
geography 385.10
locational 184.18
regional 180.8
**geography**
Earth 375.10
geographics 385.4
location 184.7
**geologic(al)** 385.10
**geological time periods** 107.10
**geologist**
geographer 385.5
minerologist 383.12

wardrobe 231.2
**get up** awake 713.4
create 167.10
dress up 231.41
get out of bed 713.6
prepare 720.7
rise 213.8
study up 564.14
**get-up-and-go**
enterprise 707.7
vim 161.2
**get well** recover 694.20
recuperate 685.6
**get with it**
set to work 716.15
take action 705.5
**gewgaw**
ornament 901.4
toy 878.16
trifle 673.5
**geyser**
hot spring 328.10
jet 395.9
**ghastly** colorless 363.7
deathly 408.29
terrible 891.38
ugly 899.11
**ghetto** 183.6
**ghetto-dwellers**
the poor 838.3
the underprivileged 919.6
**ghettoize** 77.6
**ghost**
*n.* author 602.15
frightener 891.9
specter 1017.1
substitute 149.2
television reception 345.5
*v.* float 275.54
substitute for 149.5
write 602.21
**ghostly** deathly 408.29
immaterial 377.7
spectral 1017.7
**ghost story**
fiction 608.7
lie 616.11
**ghostwrite**
substitute for 149.5
write 602.21
**ghoul** evil spirit 1016.7
frightener 891.9
monster 943.6
thief 825.1
**ghoulish** curious 528.5
devilish 1016.18
infernal 675.10
terrible 891.38
**GI** 800.7
**giant**
*n.* large person 195.13
names of 195.26
strong man 159.6
tall person 207.12
*adj.* huge 195.20
tall 207.21
**giant step** 199.2
**gibber**
*n.* chatter 596.3

imperfect speech 595.4
nonsense 547.2
*v.* be incomprehensible 549.10
chatter 596.5
speak poorly 595.9
talk nonsense 547.5
**gibbering**
*n.* imperfect speech 595.4
*adj.* chattering 596.10
**gibberish** jargon 580.9
nonsense 547.2
unintelligibility 549.7
**gibbous** bowed 252.10
convex 256.12
humpbacked 249.13
**gibe**
*n.* indignity 965.2
ridicule 967.2
witticism 881.7
*v.* make fun of 881.13
offend 965.4
ridicule 967.9
**giblets** fowl part 308.23
meat 308.20
viscera 225.4
**Gibraltar** 159.7
**giddy** delirious 473.31
dizzy 532.15
inconstant 141.7
intoxicated 996.30
scatterbrained 532.16
**gift**
*n.* aptitude 733.5
costless thing 850.1
intelligence 467.2
present 818.4
talent 733.4
*v.* contribute 818.14
give 818.12
**gifted**
intelligent 467.14
talented 733.27
**gifted child** 733.12
**gift of gab**
eloquence 600.1
talkativeness 596.1
**giftware** 831.6
**gig**
*n.* job 656.5
*v.* fish 655.10
**gigantic**
excessive 663.16
huge 195.20
large 34.7
strong 159.15
tall 207.21
**giggle**
*n.* laughter 876.4
*v.* laugh 876.8
**gigolo** beau 931.12
procurer 989.18
**GI Joe** 800.7
**gild** coat 228.24
color 362.13
falsify 616.16
make grandiloquent 601.7
make pleasant 863.5
yellow 370.3

**gilded** false 616.27
yellow 370.4
**gild the lily**
do superfluously 663.12
make pleasant 863.5
**gill** breathing 403.19
lady love 931.14
running water 395.1
valley 257.9
**gilt**
*n.* fakery 616.3
money 835.2
ornamentation 901.3
swine 414.9
*adj.* metal 383.17
yellow 370.4
**gilt-edged** 674.17
**gimcrack**
ornament 901.4
tool 348.1
toy 878.16
trifle 673.5
**gimmick**
expedient 670.2
object 376.4
story element 608.9
stratagem 735.3
tool 348.1
trick 618.6
**gin**
*n.* liquor 996.40
trap 618.11
*v.* make threads 206.6
separate 77.6
trap 618.18
**ginger** pungency 433.2
vim 161.2
**gingerbread**
cake 308.41
ornamentation 901.3
superfluity 663.4
**gingerly** 895.8
**gingivitis** 686.9
**gin mill** 996.19
**giraffe** 414.5
**gird** bind 47.9
encircle 233.7
strengthen 159.11
**girdle**
*n.* band 253.3
corset 231.23
strip 206.4
supporter 216.2
*v.* bind 47.9
circle 253.10
encircle 233.7
go around 321.4
**girl** child 125.6
lady love 931.14
maid 750.8
woman 421.5
**girl Friday** 750.3
**girl friend**
companion 928.3
lady love 931.14
**girlhood**
childhood 124.2
young people 125.2
**girlish** childish 124.11
feminine 421.13
thin 205.16

**girl next door** 79.3
**girl-watcher** 442.1
**girth**
*n.* band 253.3
fastener 47.20
harness 659.5
saddle 216.18
size 195.1
*v.* bind 47.9
**GI's** 311.2
**gist** content 194.5
essence 5.2
important point 672.6
major part 54.6
meaning 545.1
summary 607.2
topic 484.1
**give**
*n.* elasticity 358.1
pliancy 357.2
*v.* attribute 155.3
be elastic 358.5
be pliant 357.7
communicate 554.7
give for free 850.4
impose 963.6
present 818.12
provide 659.7
say 594.23
transfer property 817.3
**give a hand** aid 785.11
applaud 968.10
**give a lift** aid 785.11
cheer 870.7
help up 317.7
**give-and-take**
*n.* banter 882.1
compromise 807.1
conversation 597.1
interchange 150.1
justice 976.1
offset 33.2
retaliation 955.1
trade 827.2
*adj.* reciprocal 150.5
**giveaway**
*n.* divulgence 556.2
stage show 611.4
*adj.* cheap 849.9
**give away**
be damaged 692.26
discard 668.7
dispose of 818.21
divulge 556.6
join in marriage 933.15
relinquish 814.3
**give back**
replace 694.11
restore 823.4
**give birth**
bear young 167.15
vivify 407.9
**give birth to**
engender 68.14
originate 153.11
**give ground**
retreat 295.6
yield 765.7
**give in** be inferior 37.5

talkative 596.9
**glibness**
eloquence 600.1
suavity 936.5
talkativeness 596.1
**glib tongue** 735.6
**glide**
*n.* air maneuver 278.13
coast 273.8
slide 316.4
speech sound 594.13
*v.* coast 273.34
elapse 105.5
float 275.54
fly 278.45
go easily 732.9
slide 316.9
*adj.* phonetic 594.31
**glider** 280.12
**glim** 336.1
**glimmer**
*n.* hint 557.4
light 335.7
*v.* glitter 335.24
**glimmering**
*n.* hint 557.4
light 335.7
slight knowledge 477.6
*adj.* glittering 335.35
**glimpse**
*n.* glance 439.4
slight knowledge 477.6
*v.* glance 439.18
see 439.12
**glint**
*n.* light 335.6
shine 335.2
*v.* give light 335.23
glance 439.18
**glissade**
*n.* slide 316.4
*v.* glide 273.34
slide 316.9
**glissando**
music style 462.31
slide 316.4
**glisten**
*n.* light 335.7
*v.* glitter 335.24
**glistening** 335.35
**glitter**
*n.* light 335.7
showiness 904.3
*v.* be famous 914.10
be ostentatious 904.13
glimmer 335.24
**glittering**
glimmering 335.35
showy 904.19
**gloaming**
darkishness 337.4
dusk 134.3
**gloat** boast 910.9
gaze 439.16
**gloating**
*n.* boasting 910.4
*adj.* boasting 910.12
**gloat over** boast 910.9

enjoy 865.10
**global** complete 56.9
comprehensive 76.7
spherical 255.9
universal 79.14
unqualified 508.2
**globalize** 79.9
**globate** 255.9
**globe**
*n.* Earth 375.10
lamp shade 338.3
map 654.4
sphere 255.2
*v.* ball 255.7
**globe-trot** 273.20
**globe-trotter** 274.1
**globular** 255.9
**globule** ball 255.2
bubble 405.1
**globulin** 388.4
**glockenspiel** 465.18
**glom on to**
acquire 811.9
seize 822.14
**gloom**
*n.* darkness 337.2
gloominess 872.7
shadow 337.3
*v.* be dark 337.12
be ill-humored 951.15
darken 337.9
**gloominess**
darkness 337.2
gloom 872.7
pessimism 889.6
**gloomy** cloudy 404.7
dark 337.14
dismal 872.24
ominous 544.17
pessimistic 889.16
**glop** semiliquid 389.5
slime 682.8
**gloppy** 682.23
**Gloria** hymn 1032.3
Mass 1040.10
**glorification**
ennoblement 914.8
praise 968.5
sanctification 1026.3
worship 1032.2
**glorified**
eminent 914.18
heavenly 1018.13
saintly 1015.6
**glorify** ennoble 914.13
praise 968.12
sanctify 1026.5
worship 1032.11
**glorious** eminent 34.9
godlike 1013.20
gorgeous 900.19
grandiose 904.21
illustrious 914.19
intoxicated 996.30
superb 674.17
**glory**
*n.* brightness 335.4
divine attribute 1013.15
eminence 34.2
grandeur 904.5

halo 253.2
Heaven 1018.1
illustriousness 914.6
light 335.14
notability 672.2
praise 968.5
repute 914.1
token of esteem 916.1
worship 1032.2
*v.* gloat 910.9
rejoice 876.5
**glory in** 905.5
**gloss**
*n.* commentary 606.2
dictionary 605.7
extenuation 1006.5
fakery 616.3
footnote 552.5
interpretation 552.3
misrendering 553.1
polish 260.2
pretext 649.1
shallowness 210.1
shine 335.2
*v.* coat 228.24
color 362.13
comment upon 552.11
falsify 616.16
misinterpret 553.2
polish 260.7
*adj.* paint finish 362.21
**glossal** lingual 427.10
phonetic 594.31
**glossary**
dictionary 605.7
interpretation 552.3
list 88.4
**glossematics**
grammar 586.1
linguistics 580.12
**glossography** 582.15
**gloss over**
conceal 615.6
extenuate 1006.12
falsify 616.16
neglect 534.6
**glossy**
*n.* photoprint 577.5
*adj.* shiny 335.33
sleek 260.10
**glottal**
*n.* speech sound 594.13
*adj.* phonetic 594.31
**glottis** 594.19
**glove** challenge 793.2
handwear 231.63
**glow**
*n.* animation 161.3
beauty 900.1
eloquence 600.5
foredawn 133.4
health 685.1
heat 328.12
reddening 368.3
shine 335.2
warmth 362.2
*v.* be cheerful 870.6
become red 368.5

be excited 857.16
be famous 914.10
be healthy 685.5
be hot 328.22
flush 857.17
give light 335.23
look beautiful 900.15
**glower**
*n.* glare 439.5
resentment 952.2
scowl 951.9
*v.* be ill-humored 951.15
glare 439.17
show resentment 952.14
**glowering** 951.24
**glowing** burning 328.27
cheerful 870.11
coloring 362.15
eloquent 600.13
enthusiastic 635.11
excited 857.20
fervent 855.23
gorgeous 900.19
happy 865.13
luminous 335.30
red 368.6
red-complexioned 368.9
**glowworm** firefly 336.5
light 335.7
**glue**
*n.* adherent 50.4,13
semiliquid 389.5
*v.* join 47.5
stick together 50.9
**glued** 47.14
**gluey** adhesive 50.12
dense 354.12
viscous 389.12
**glum** morose 872.25
sullen 951.24
**glut**
*n.* overfullness 663.3
satiety 664.1
*v.* be tedious 884.5
eat 307.23
gluttonize 994.4
overload 663.15
satiate 664.4
**gluteal** 241.10
**gluten** 389.5
**glutinous**
adhesive 50.12
gluey 389.12
**glutted** overfull 663.20
satiated 664.6
**glutton** eater 307.14
gourmand 994.3
wolverine 414.28,58
**gluttonous**
eating 307.29
excessive 663.16
greedy 994.6
intemperate 993.7
**gluttony** eating 307.1
excess 663.1
greed 994
hoggishness 634.8
intemperance 993.1
sin 982.3

glyceride 309.7
glycerin 380.2
glyceryl ester 380.14
glyph 575.3
glyphic
  engraved 578.12
  sculptured 575.7
glyptic engraving 578.2
  sculpture 575.1
G-man
  detective 781.10
  peace officer 699.15
gnarl
  *n.* distortion 249.1
  knob 256.3
  *v.* animal sound 460.4
  distort 249.5
  roughen 261.4
  show resentment
    952.14
gnarled rough 261.8
  studded 256.16
gnash
  *n.* bite 307.2
  *v.* chew 307.25
gnash one's teeth
  lament 875.9
  show resentment
    952.14
gnat 196.7
gnaw abrade 350.7
  chew 307.25
  eat away 692.24
  hurt 424.7
gnawing
  *n.* ache 424.5
  pain 424.2
  *adj.* abrasive 350.10
  painful 424.10
gneiss 384.1,12
gnome dwarf 196.6
  fairy 1014.18
  maxim 517.1
  spirit 1014.16
gnomic
  aphoristic 517.6
  concise 592.6
gnu 414.5,58
go
  *n.* act 705.3
  attempt 714.2
  contest 796.3
  enterprise 707.7
  game 878.9
  spell 108.1
  success 724.1
  turn 108.2
  *v.* bear 290.8
  become 1.12
  be destroyed 693.23
  be distant 199.5
  cease to exist 2.5
  depart 301.6
  die 408.19
  disappear 447.2
  extend 179.7
  have place 184.8
  move 267.5
  operate 164.7
  pass 273.17
  progress 294.2
  recede 297.2

succeed 724.6
take action 705.5
tend 174.3
travel 273.18
*adj.* favorable 164.9
go about
  be made public
    559.16
  change course 275.30
  go around 321.4
  turn around 295.9
  undertake 715.3
  wander 273.22
go about one's business
  656.10
goad
  *n.* spur 648.8
  *v.* drive animals 416.8
  impel 283.10
  thrust 283.11
  urge 648.15
go after
  come after 117.3
  fetch 271.15
  follow 293.3
  pursue 655.8
  succeed 65.2
go against
  counteract 178.6
  oppose 790.3
go ahead begin 68.7
  get better 691.7
  hustle 707.13
  precede 64.2
  progress 294.2
go-ahead
  *n.* enterprise 707.7
  permission 777.1
  progression 294.1
  ratification 521.4
  *adj.* enterprising
    707.23
  progressive 294.6
goal destination 300.5
  end 70.1
  motive 648.1
  objective 653.2
  score 724.4
goalie 699.9
go all out
  be thorough 56.8
  do one's best 714.12
  exert oneself 716.9
  go all lengths 722.7
  go fast 269.13
  hustle 707.13
  let oneself go 762.18
  persevere 625.5
go along
  be in a state 7.6
  continue 143.3
  depart 301.6
  progress 294.2
  travel 273.17
go along with
  accompany 73.7
  acknowledge 521.11
  agree with 521.9
  be willing 622.3
  concur 177.3
  consent 775.2
  join with 786.4

submit to 765.6
goaltender 699.9
go around circle 321.4
  detour 321.6
  move 267.5
  rotate 322.9
  suffice 661.4
  surround 233.6
  turn 321.5
go around in circles
  be uncertain 514.9
  go around 321.4
go astray
  be unorthodox
    1025.8
  digress 593.9
  err 518.9
  fail 725.14
  go wrong 981.9
  miss 314.4
  stray 291.4
goat animal 414.8,58
  inferior horse 414.14
  jumper 319.4
  laughingstock 967.7
  scapegoat 149.3
  unchaste person
    989.11
go at attack 798.15
  travel 273.18
  undertake 715.3
goatee 230.8
goatherd guider 748.7
  herder 416.3
goatish
  lascivious 989.29
  lustful 419.29
  ungulate 414.49
go away
  *v.* depart 301.6
  disappear 447.2
  diverge 299.5
  recede 297.2
  *interj.* begone! 310.29
gob accumulation 74.9
  amount 28.2
  ball 255.2
  bite 307.2
  lump 195.10
  mouth 265.5
  piece 55.3
  sailor 276.4
go back back up 241.8
  be repeated 103.11
  remember 537.10
  retreat 295.6
  revert 146.5
  turn back 295.8
go back on
  abandon 633.5
  be dishonest 975.12
go back over
  re-examine 485.26
  remember 537.10
go back to
  resume 143.6
  revert to 146.6
  revisit 186.9
gobbet ball 255.2
  piece 55.3
  small amount 35.2

gobble
  bird sound 460.5
  consume 666.2
  destroy 693.10
  eat 307.21
  gluttonize 994.4
  ingest 306.11
gobbledygook
  bombast 601.2
  jargon 580.9
  nonsense 547.2
  official jargon 744.37
  unintelligibility 549.7
gobbler
  male animal 420.8
  turkey 414.34
gobbling
  gluttonous 994.6
  greedy 634.27
go before
  anticipate 131.6
  forerun 116.3
  lead 292.2
  pioneer 66.3
  precede 64.2
go-between
  instrument 658.3
  interagent 781.4
  interpreter 552.7
  liaison 237.4
  mediator 805.3
  messenger 561.1
go beyond
  exceed 663.9
  overrun 313.4
goblet 193.10
goblin evil spirit 1016.9
  fairy 1014.18
gobs 34.4
gocart 272.6,24,30
god agriculture 413.4
  commerce 827.12
  deity 1014
  discord 795.1
  earth 375.10
  evil 1016.6
  Fates 640.3
  fertility 165.5
  forest 1014.21
  good person 985.5
  household 191.30
  justice 976.5
  lightning 335.17
  love 931.8
  marriage 933.14
  moon 375.12
  Muses 535.2
  nether world 1019.5
  poetry Muses 609.12
  rain 394.6
  sea 397.4
  sun 375.14
  thunder 456.5
  war 797.17
  water 1014.20
  wind 403.3
God 1013
godawful 675.8
godchild 772.7
goddamn 972.9
goddess see god
goddess-like 900.17

godfather 772.6
God-fearing 1028.9
God forbid
  by no means 524.9
  disapproval 969.28
  worship 1032.17
godforsaken
  deserted 187.14
  forlorn 924.11
  out-of-the-way 199.9
Godhead 1013.10
godhood 1013.1
godless
  irreligious 1031.18
  ungodly 1031.17
godlike divine 1013.19
  eminent 34.9
  mythological 1014.26
  pious 1028.9
godliness deity 1013.1
  piety 1028.2
  sanctity 1026.1
  virtue 980.1
godly divine 1013.19
  pious 1028.9
  virtuous 980.7
go down
  be believed 501.20
  be defeated 727.12
  capsize 275.44
  decline 692.20
  descend 316.5
  fail 725.10
  sink 320.8
  submerge 316.6
God's country 181.2
godsend boon 811.7
  good thing 674.5
godson 772.7
Godspeed
  n. departure 301.4
  interj. farewell! 301.23
God's will 640.2
God the Father 1013.11
God the Holy Ghost
  1013.14
God the Son 1013.12
God willing 509.11
go easy caution 895.14
  take it easy 732.11
go easy on 944.4
goer outgoer 303.10
  speeder 269.5
  traveler 274.1
go far 724.9
gofer 750.5
goffer
  n. trench 263.2
  v. groove 263.3
go fly a kite 238.10
go for abet 785.14
  aim at 653.4
  attack 798.15
  be credulous 502.6
  fetch 271.15
  head for 290.10
  love 931.18
  represent 572.7
go for broke
  be determined 624.8
  be reckless 894.6
  do one's best 714.12

go all lengths 722.7
  persevere 625.5
go free get off 632.7
  go scot free 763.9
go-getter 707.8
goggle
  n. gaze 439.5
  v. bulge 256.10
  gaze 439.16
  squint 440.9
  adj. bulging 256.15
goggled bulging 256.15
  spectacled 443.10
goggle eyes
  defective eyes 440.6
  eye 439.9
goggles eyeshade 338.2
  safety equipment
  699.3
  spectacles 443.2
go-go energetic 161.12
  unreserved 762.23
  up-to-date 475.17
go in for adopt 637.15
  practice 705.7
  specialize 81.4
  study 564.15
  undertake 715.3
going
  n. death 408.1
  departure 301.1
  disappearance 447.1
  journeying 273.1
  motion 267.1
  adj. dying 408.33
  flowing 267.8
  operating 164.11
  traveling 273.35
going on
  happening 151.9
  in preparation 720.22
  in progress 294.7
  operating 164.11
goings-on activity 707.1
  affairs 151.4
  behavior 737.1
going strong
  thriving 728.13
  unweakened 159.19
go into begin 68.9
  compose 58.3
  develop 148.6
  discourse upon 606.5
  discuss 597.12
  enter 302.7
  investigate 485.22
  join 788.14
  participate 815.5
  undertake 715.3
go in with 786.4
go it alone 762.19
goiter 686.10
gold
  n. currency metals
  835.20
  metal 383.21
  money 835.1
  wealth 837.1
  yellowness 370.1
  adj. metal 383.17
  yellow 370.4

goldbrick
  n. fraud 618.9
  idler 708.8
  neglecter 534.5
  shirker 631.3
  slow person 270.5
  v. leave undone 534.7
  shirk 631.9
gold digger flirt 932.10
  miner 383.9
gold dust 383.3
golden
  auspicious 544.18
  melodious 462.49
  metal 383.17
  precious 848.10
  superb 674.17
  yellow 370.4
golden age 728.4
golden calf 1033.3
golden rule
  axiom 517.2
  ethics 957.2
  precept 751.2
golden touch, the 837.4
golden years, the 126.5
gold fever 383.8
gold-filled 383.17
gold mine mine 383.6
  rich source 837.3
  source of supply
  660.4
gold piece 835.4
gold rush 383.8
gold star 916.5
golem 471.8
Goliath giant 195.26
  strong man 159.6
Gomorrah 981.7
gonadal 312.8
gonads 419.10
go native 189.4
gondolier 276.5
gone absent 187.10
  dead 408.30
  departed 301.20
  exhausted 717.8
  hopeless 889.15
  lost 812.7
  no more 2.10
  past 119.7
  used up 666.4
  vanished 447.4
  weak 160.12
gone by ago 119.15
  obsolete 123.15
  past 119.7
gone on
  enthusiastic about
  635.12
  fond of 931.28
goner 889.8
gone to seed
  growing rank 411.40
  old 123.14
  out of practice
  734.18
gong
  n. bell 454.4
  percussion instrument
  465.18
  v. ring 454.8

Gongorism 589.3
gonif 825.1
gonorrhea 686.16
goo semiliquid 389.5
  sentimentality 855.8
goober 308.38
good
  n. welfare 674.4
  adj. auspicious 544.18
  authentic 516.14
  excellent 674.12
  expedient 670.5
  godlike 1013.20
  healthful 683.5
  honest 974.13
  just 976.8
  kind 938.13
  pious 1028.9
  pleasant 863.6
  right 958.8
  skillful 733.20
  solvent 836.17
  sufficient 661.6
  tasty 428.8
  valid 516.13
  virtuous 980.7
  adv. kindly 938.18
  interj. approval
  968.22
  yes 521.18
Good Book, the 1021.2
good-bye
  n. departure 301.4
  interj. farewell! 301.23
good chance
  gambling odds 515.6
  good opportunity
  129.3
  likelihood 156.8
  possibility 509.1
  probability 511.1
good deal 34.4
good deed 938.7
good enough
  adj. acceptable 868.12
  sufficient 661.6
  tolerable 674.19
  interj. approval
  968.22
  yes 521.18
good example 985.4
good fellow
  companion 928.4
  good person 985.1
good folk, the 1014.17
good for
  healthful 683.5
  helpful 785.21
  priced 846.16
  solvent 836.17
  useful 665.18
good form
  etiquette 646.3
  social convention
  645.1
good-for-nothing
  n. bad person 986.2
  bum 708.9
  adj. indolent 708.18
  worthless 669.11
good for you! 968.22
Good Friday 1040.15

good graces 927.3
good guy 985.2
good heavens! 920.21
good humor
  good nature 938.2
  good spirits 870.2
good-humored 938.14
good life, the 728.1
good-looking 900.17
good looks 900.4
good luck chance 156.1
  prosperity 728.2
goodly beautiful 900.17
  good 674.12
  large 195.16
  pleasant 863.6
good manners
  courtesy 936.3
  etiquette 646.3
  good behavior 737.2
good morning! 925.15
good name
  custom 827.6
  reputability 914.2
good-natured 938.14
goodness
  n. excellence 674
  healthfulness 683.1
  honesty 974.1
  kindness 938.1
  piety 1028.2
  pleasantness 863.1
  propriety 958.2
  savoriness 428.1
  virtue 980.1
  interj. wonder 920.21
good night! 301.24
good old days 119.2
good person
  benefactor 942.1
  gentleman 985
goods fabric 378.5
  freight 271.7
  merchandise 831.1
  property 810.1
goods, the ability 157.2
  genuine object 516.6
  information 557.1
  talent 733.4
good Samaritan 942.1
good shape
  good looks 900.4
  healthiness 685.2
  orderliness 59.3
good show! 948.4
good side of, the 927.3
good-size(d) 195.16
good sport 727.5
good taste
  literary elegance
    589.1
  savoriness 428.1
  taste 897.1
good terms 927.3
good time fun 878.2
  good opportunity
    129.3
good times 728.4
good turn 938.7
good vibrations 794.1
goodwill
  benevolence 938.4

custom 827.6
good terms 927.3
  patronage 785.4
  willingness 622.1
good word
  commendation 968.3
  news 558.2
good works 938.6
goody
  n. delicacy 308.8
  wife 933.9
  adj. sanctimonious
    1029.5
  interj. pleasure 865.17
goody-goody
  n. effeminate male
    421.10
  prude 903.11
  adj. affected 903.18
  hypocritic(al) 616.33
  sanctimonious 1029.5
gooey
  sentimental 855.22
  viscous 389.12
goof
  n. an error 518.6
  bungler 734.9
  fool 471.2
  v. blunder 518.15
  bungle 734.12
  fail 725.13
goofball bungler 734.9
  sedative 687.12
go off blast 456.8
  decline 692.20
  depart 301.6
  diverge 299.5
  explode 162.13
  occur 151.5
  succeed 724.6
  turn aside 291.6
go off half-cocked
  anticipate 131.6
  be unprepared 721.6
  prejudge 495.2
  rush into 709.7
  talk out of turn 130.5
go off on a tangent
  angle 251.5
  digress 593.9
goof off dawdle 270.8
  idle 708.11
  leave undone 534.7
  shirk 631.9
goof-off idler 708.8
  neglecter 534.5
  slow person 270.5
goofy foolish 470.8
  insane 473.26
googol
  large number 86.4
  number 99.13
goo-goo eyes 932.8
gook race 418.3
  semiliquid 389.5
goon combatant 800.1
  evildoer 943.4
  man 787.8
  strike enforcer 789.5
  violent person 162.9
go on be angry 952.15
  be disorderly 62.11

behave 737.4
  be in a state 7.6
  chatter 596.5
  continue 143.3
  depart 301.6
  elapse 105.5
  endure 110.6
  linger 110.7
  manage 724.11
  persevere 625.2
  persist 143.5
  progress 294.2
  rage 162.10
go on and on
  be infinite 104.2
  last forever 112.6
  linger 110.7
go one better
  excel 36.6
  outwit 735.11
goop 389.5
goose food 308.22
  poultry 414.34,66
  silly 471.6
goose bumps
  chill 333.2
  rough surface 261.2
  sensation 426.4
  trepidation 891.5
goose egg 2.2
goose grass 258.7
goose step 273.15
goose-step 273.29
goosy avian 414.52
  fearful 891.31
  sensitive 422.14
go out be distant 199.5
  burn out 332.8
  die 408.19
  end 70.6
  exit 303.11
  extend 179.7
  obsolesce 668.9
  strike 789.9
go out for
  practice 705.7
  undertake 715.3
go over
  apostatize 628.8
  examine 485.23
  grill 485.21
  rehearse a play
    611.37
  repeat 103.8
  study 564.12
  succeed 724.6
  traverse 273.19
go over big
  please 865.5
  succeed 724.6
go overboard
  go over the side
    275.45
  overdo 663.10
go over like a lead
    balloon
  be uninteresting
    883.4
  fail 725.9
GOP 744.24
go places 724.9
go public 834.12

Gordian knot
  complex 46.2
  dilemma 731.6
gore
  n. blood 388.4
  killing 409.1
  v. attack 798.26
  pierce 265.16
gorge
  n. gullet 396.15
  obstruction 266.3
  ravine 201.2
  v. eat 307.23
  gluttonize 994.4
  overload 663.15
  satiate 664.4
gorged overfull 663.20
  satiated 664.6
gorgeous
  beautiful 900.19
  colorful 362.18
  gaudy 904.20
Gorgon 1035.9
gorilla
  combatant 800.1
  evildoer 943.4
  killer 409.11
  primate 414.59
  strong man 159.6
  violent person 162.9
gormand 994.3
gormandize 994.4
gory blood red 368.7
  bloodstained 679.11
  murderous 409.24
Goshen 535.11
gosling
  hopeless case 889.8
  poultry 414.34
  young goose 125.8
go slow idle 270.6
  make one's way 294.4
  take one's leisure
    710.4
gospel
  n. good news 558.2
  sacred music 462.16
  system of belief
    501.3
  the truth 516.2
  adj. scriptural 1021.10
Gospel
  n. Mass 1040.10
  New Testament
    1021.4
  adj. scriptural 1021.10
gossamer
  n. filament 206.1
  lightness 353.2
  weakness 160.7
  adj. smooth 351.8
  thin 205.16
  transparent 339.4
gossamery frail 160.14
  light 353.10
  smooth 351.8
  tenuous 4.6
  threadlike 206.7
  transparent 339.4
gossip
  n. chatter 596.3
  companion 928.3

curious person 528.2
newsmonger 558.9
talebearing 558.7
*v.* chat 597.10
prattle 596.5
tattle 558.12
**go straight**
be straight 250.4
go directly 290.11
reform 691.9
**Goth** 898.7
**go the limit**
be thorough 56.8
do one's best 714.12
go all lengths 722.7
overindulge 993.5
persevere 625.5
**Gothic**
antiquated 123.13
fanciful 535.20
uncouth 898.12
unlearned 477.14
**go through**
carry out 705.9
chill 333.10
enter 302.8
experience 151.8
rehearse a play
611.37
repeat 103.8
search 485.30
spend 843.5
squander 854.3
**go through the motions**
616.21
**go to** attend 186.8
extend to 199.6
visit 273.24
**go to any length** 625.5
**go to bed** rest 711.6
retire 712.17
**go to extremes**
exaggerate 617.3
overdo 663.10
**go together** 26.6
**go to great lengths**
be careful 533.7
make every effort
714.13
**go to hell**
be damned 1019.7
go to ruin 693.24
**go to it** 716.15
**go too far**
be rash 894.5
overdo 663.10
overstep 313.9
**go to one's head**
addle the wits 473.22
be vain 909.7
dizzy 532.8
make drunk 996.21
**go to pieces**
become nervous
859.7
be destroyed 693.22
decay 692.25
disintegrate 49.8
weaken 160.9
**go to pot** be lost 812.6
fall on evil days
729.11

go bankrupt 842.7
go to ruin 693.24
**go to the dogs**
fall on evil days
729.11
go bankrupt 842.7
go to ruin 693.24
**go to town**
hustle 707.14
succeed 724.6
**gouge**
*n.* groove 263.1
indentation 257.6
*v.* blind 441.7
cheat 618.17
cut out 305.10
excavate 257.15
groove 263.3
overcharge 848.7
puncture 265.16
**gouging** 848.12
**goulash** 308.11
**go under**
be defeated 727.12
fail 725.10
go bankrupt 842.7
go to ruin 693.24
**go up** ascend 315.8
go bankrupt 842.7
go to ruin 693.24
increase 38.6
**go up in smoke**
be lost 812.6
be transient 111.6
burn 329.25
collapse 314.3
come to nothing
725.12
disappear 447.2
**gourmand**
connoisseur 897.7
eater 307.14
glutton 994.3
sensualist 987.3
**gourmet**
connoisseur 897.7
eater 307.14
sensualist 987.3
**gout**
inflammation 686.9
metabolic disease
686.20
**goût** savor 428.2
taste 427.1
**govern** direct 747.8
influence 172.8
possess authority
739.13
regulate 741.12
restrain 760.7
**governable** 765.14
**governess**
guardian 699.7
instructress 565.2
matron 749.2
**governing**
authoritative 739.15
controlling 741.18
directing 747.12
**government**
authorities 741.3
direction 747.1

district 180.5
governance 739.5
political science
744.2
protectorship 699.2
rule 741
**governmental**
governing 741.17
political 744.43
**governor**
automation 349.14
director 748.1
father 170.9
guardian 699.6
jailer 761.10
regional governor
749.13
ruler 749.5
safety equipment
699.3
**go with**
accompany 73.7
agree 26.6
assent 521.9
coact 177.3
stay near 200.12
**go without saying**
be certain 513.9
be manifest 555.7
**gown**
*n.* dress 231.16
ecclesiastical 1041.2
garment 231.3
*v.* clothe 231.39
**go wrong**
be disappointing
541.3
be unorthodox
1025.8
do wrong 981.9
err 518.9
fail 725.14
get out of order
692.28
go to ruin 693.24
**goy** 1025.6
**GP** 688.6
**grab**
*n.* a theft 824.10
seizure 822.2
*v.* acquire 811.9
capture 822.18
engross 530.13
impress 478.19
seize 822.14
snatch 635.7
**grab bag** 515.11
**grabble** grope 485.31
harvest 413.19
**grabby**
acquisitive 811.14
greedy 634.27
rapacious 822.26
**grace**
*n.* amenities 936.7
beauty 900.1
benevolence 938.4
conscience 957.5
eloquence 600.2
gift 818.7
good deed 938.7
good taste 897.1

literary elegance
589.1
music 463.18
pardon 947.2
pity 944.1
pleasantness 863.2
prayer 1032.4
reprieve 1007.3
sanctification 1026.3
skill 733.1
thanks 949.2
virtue 674.1
*v.* beautify 900.14
honor 914.12
ornament 901.8
**graceful** agile 733.21
beautiful 900.16
courteous 936.14
eloquent 600.9
polished 589.6
skillful 733.20
tasteful 897.9
**gracefully**
courteously 936.19
tastefully 897.11
**graceless** clumsy 734.20
infelicitous 590.2
irreclaimable 981.18
irreligious 1031.18
ugly 899.9
**gracelessly** 734.24
**grace period** 842.2
**Graces, the** 900.9
**grace with** 818.17
**¡gracias!** 949.6
**gracile** beautiful 900.16
polished 589.6
tasteful 897.9
thin 205.16
**gracious**
*adj.* courteous 936.14
hospitable 925.11
indulgent 759.8
informal 647.3
kind 938.13
liberal 853.4
pleasant 863.6
tasteful 897.9
*interj.* wonder 920.21
**gracious living** 728.1
**graciously**
courteously 936.19
good-naturedly
938.19
liberally 853.5
pleasingly 863.11
**gradation**
continuity 71.2
degree 29.3
grouping 60.3
order 59.2
phonetics 594.14
**grade**
*n.* category 61.2
degree 29.1
incline 219.4
students 566.11
*v.* classify 61.6
differentiate 29.4
incline 219.10
level 214.6
order 59.4

size 195.15
smooth 260.5
sort 60.11
**graded** arranged 60.14
classified 61.8
**gradient** incline 219.4
rising 213.5
**grading**
classification 61.1
degree 29.3
**gradual**
gradational 29.5
slow 270.10
**gradually**
by degrees 29.6
slowly 270.14
**graduate**
*n.* expert 733.11
graduated student
566.8
*v.* get better 691.7
grade 29.4
measure 490.11
promote 782.2
size 195.15
succeed 724.6
*adj.* scholastic 562.20
studentlike 566.12
**graduated** 29.5
**graduate school** 567.7
**graduation**
ceremony 646.4
gradation 29.3
promotion 782.1
**graffito** 581.5
**graft**
*n.* booty 824.11
bribery 651.1
fraud 618.8
insertion 304.1
political corruption
744.34
spoils of office
744.35
theft 824.1
*v.* fasten 47.7
insert 304.6
**grafter**
corrupt politician
746.5
thief 825.1
**grafting** 304.1
**grain**
*n.* food 308.4
granule 361.6
grass 411.5,46
kind 61.3
minute thing 196.7
nature 5.3
seed 411.29
small amount 35.2
texture 351.1
trait of character
525.3
*v.* color 362.13
crumble 361.10
give texture 351.4
pulverize 361.9
**raininess**
coarse texture 351.2
granularity 361.2

**grainy**
coarse-textured 351.6
granular 361.12
rough 261.6
**grammar** basics 68.6
diction 588.1
linguistics 580.12
syntax 586
textbook 605.8
**grammarian** 580.13
**grammar school**
elementary school
567.5
secondary school
567.6
**grammatic(al)**
correct 586.17
linguistic 580.17
**grammatical error** 518.7
**Gramophone** 450.11
**granary** 660.7
**grand**
*n.* piano 465.13
thousand 99.10
US money 835.7
*adj.* dignified 905.12
eloquent 600.14
eminent 914.18
excellent 674.12
grandiose 904.21
important 672.16
large 195.16
powerful 34.6
**grandchild** 171.3
**grande dame** 903.10
**grandee** 918.4
**grandeur**
eloquence 600.6
greatness 34.1
magnificence 904.5
pride 905.2
repute 914.5
sizableness 195.6
**grandfather**
ancestor 170.11
old man 127.2
**grandiloquence**
exaggeration 617.1
long word 582.10
magniloquence 601
pompousness 904.7
style 588.2
**grandiloquent**
exaggerated 617.4
ostentatious 601.8
pompous 904.22
**grandiose** grand 904.21
grandiloquent 601.8
**grandly**
dignifiedly 905.14
grandiosely 904.28
importantly 672.24
**grand mal** 686.5
**grandmother**
ancestor 170.12
old woman 127.3
**grandparent** 170.8
**Grand Prix** 796.12
**grand slam** score 724.4
victory 726.1
**grandson** 171.3

**grandstand**
*n.* observation post
439.8
*v.* be ostentatious
904.16
**grand theft** 824.2
**grand tour**
astronautics 282.1
journey 273.5
**grange** farm 413.8
ranch 191.7
**granite** hardness 356.6
rock 384.1,12
**granny**
antiquated person
123.8
fastidious person
896.7
grandmother 170.12
old woman 127.3
**grant**
*n.* charter 777.5
concession 507.1
giving 818.1
right 958.4
subsidy 818.8
*v.* acknowledge 521.11
concede 507.5
confess 556.7
consent 775.2
give 818.12
permit 777.9
suppose 499.10
**granted**
acknowledged 521.14
given 818.24
supposed 499.14
**granting**
*n.* giving 818.1
*conj.* admitting
507.13
**grantor** 818.11
**granular**
coarse-textured 351.6
grainy 361.12
infinitesimal 196.14
**granularity**
coarse texture 351.2
graininess 361.2
**granulate**
crumble 361.10
give texture 351.4
heal 694.21
pulverize 361.9
roughen 261.4
solidify 356.8
**granulated**
coarse-textured 351.6
granular 361.12
hardened 356.13
rough 261.6
**granule** grain 361.6
small amount 35.2
**grapeshot** 801.13
**grapevine**
grapevine telegraph
558.10
informant 557.5
rumor 558.6
vine 411.4
**graph**
*n.* character 581.1

diagram 654.3
outline 48.4
picture 574.14
*v.* plot 654.11
**graphemic** letter 581.8
linguistic 580.17
**graphic**
descriptive 608.15
eloquent 600.10
pictorial 574.22
representational
572.10
written 602.22
**graphically**
descriptively 608.19
eloquently 600.15
**graphic arts** arts 574.1
graphics 578
printing 603.1
**graphite** 380.2
**grapho–** 602.1
**graphologist** 602.14
**graphology** 602.3
**grapple**
*n.* hold 813.2,12
*v.* contend 796.14
fasten 47.7
hold 813.6
seize 822.14
**grapple with**
contend with 796.18
fight 796.14
oppose 790.4
**grasp**
*n.* control 741.2
handle 216.11
hold 813.2
understanding 475.3
*v.* hold 813.6
hug 50.6
know 475.12
seize 822.14
understand 548.7
**grasping**
*n.* greed 634.8
*adj.* acquisitive 811.14
demanding 753.8
greedy 634.27
rapacious 822.26
retentive 813.8
selfish 978.5
**grass**
*n.* grassland 411.8
marihuana 687.13
plant 411.5,46
*v.* feed 307.16
**grasshopper**
*n.* animal 414.39,74
jumper 319.4
*adj.* improvident
721.15
**grassland** farm 413.8
grass 411.8
land 385.1
plain 387.1
the country 182.1
**grass roots** root 153.5
the country 182.1
**grass widow** 935.2
**grassy** green 371.4
verdant 411.39

greenbacks 835.6
Green Berets 800.14
green book 570.8
greenery 411.1
greengrocer 830.3
greengrocery 832.5
greenhorn
  beginner 68.2
  dupe 620.1
  ignoramus 477.8
  newcomer 78.4
  student 566.9
  unskillful person
    734.7
greenhouse
  arbor 191.13
  nursery 413.11
green light light 336.4
  permission 777.1
  ratification 521.4
  signal 568.15
greenness color 371
  gullibility 502.2
  ignorance 477.1
  immaturity 124.3
  inexperience 734.2
  newness 122.1
  sourness 432.1
  undevelopment 721.4
greenroom
  reception room
    192.20
  stage 611.21
greens plants 411.1
  vegetables 308.35
green thumb 413.12
greeny beginner 68.2
  dupe 620.1
  ignoramus 477.8
greet address 594.27
  hail 925.10
  weep 875.10
greeting remark 594.4
  salutation 925.4
greetings
  n. regards 936.8
  salutations 925.3
  interj. salutations!
    925.15
gregarious
  sociable 922.18
  talkative 596.9
gremlin
  evil spirit 1016.8
  fairy 1014.18
grenade 801.14
grenadier
  infantryman 800.9
  tall person 207.12
grey see gray
greyhound 269.6
grid
  n. fireplace 329.12
  network 221.3
  stage 611.21
  television reception
    345.5
  v. net 221.7
griddle
  a. grill 329.12
  v. cook 330.4
griddlecake 308.44

gridiron
  fireplace 329.12
  network 221.3
  playground 878.12
  stage 611.21
grief despair 866.6
  distress 864.5
  misfortune 729.2
  pain 866.5
  regret 873.1
  sorrow 872.10
grief-stricken 872.26
grievance
  affliction 866.8
  bane 676.1
  complaint 875.4
  evil 675.3
  injustice 977.4
  objection 522.2
grieve distress 864.14
  excite pity 944.5
  lament 875.8
  make grieve 872.19
  offend 952.20
  pain 866.17
  sorrow 872.17
grieved pained 866.23
  sorrowful 872.26
griever lamenter 875.7
  mourner 410.7
grieving
  n. lamentation 875.1
  adj. lamenting 875.15
grievous bad 675.9
  disastrous 729.15
  pitiful 944.8
  sorrowful 872.26
  unpleasant 864.20
grievously
  disastrously 729.18
  distressingly 34.21
  sorrowfully 872.36
  unpleasantly 864.28
grill
  n. fireplace 329.12
  food 308.7
  restaurant 307.15
  v. cook 330.4
  interrogate 485.21
  torture 1010.18
grille network 221.3
  window 265.8
grilling
  n. cooking 330.1
  interrogation 485.12
  adj. hot 328.25
grim bad 675.8
  dire 864.19
  gloomy 872.24
  hopeless 889.12
  pleasureless 866.20
  solemn 871.3
  strict 757.6
  sullen 951.24
  terrifying 891.38
  ugly 899.7
  unhappy 872.21
  unkind 939.22
  unyielding 626.9
grimace
  n. scowl 951.9
  twitch 324.3

wry face 249.4
  v. be ill-humored
    951.15
  dislike 867.5
  make a face 249.8
  overact 611.36
  suffer pain 424.8
grimalkin cat 414.26
  witch 943.7
grime
  n. dirt 682.6
  v. dirty 682.15
grimly sadly 872.31
  solemnly 871.4
  strictly 757.8
  sullenly 951.30
  unkindly 939.31
  unpleasantly 864.27
  unyieldingly 626.15
Grim Reaper 408.3
grimy dingy 365.11
  dirty 682.22
grin
  n. smile 876.3
  v. smile 876.7
grin and bear it
  accept 861.6
  be cheerful 870.10
  submit 765.6
grind
  n. bookworm 476.4
  drudge 718.3
  drudgery 716.4
  harsh sound 458.3
  routine 642.6
  student 566.10
  study 564.3
  v. abrade 350.7
  chew 307.25
  domineer 741.16
  drudge 716.14
  file 260.8
  hurt 424.7
  pulverize 361.9
  sharpen 258.9
  shatter 49.13
  sound harshly 458.10
  study 564.12
grinder
  pulverizer 361.7
  sandwich 308.32
  tooth 258.5
grinding
  n. abrasion 350.2
  pulverization 361.4
  study 564.3
  adj. abrasive 350.10
  irritating 424.13
  laboring 716.17
  sounding harsh
    458.16
  tyrannical 739.16
  unpleasant 864.24
gringo 78.3
grinning
  n. ridicule 967.1
  smile 876.3
  adj. ridiculing 967.12
grip
  n. bite 161.4
  control 741.2
  governance 739.5

handle 216.11
  hold 813.2
  skill 733.1
  spasm 324.6
  understanding 475.3
  v. engross 530.13
  hold 813.6
  obsess 473.24
  seize 822.14
gripe
  n. ache 424.5
  complaint 875.4
  control 741.2
  hold 813.2
  indigence 838.2
  indigestion 686.28
  v. annoy 866.13
  complain 875.13
  hold 813.6
  hurt 424.7
  seize 822.14
gripman 274.12
grippe
  infectious disease
    686.12
  respiratory disease
    686.14
gripped
  engrossed 530.18
  obsessed 473.33
gripping
  engrossing 530.20
  obsessive 473.34
  retentive 813.8
gripping instrument
    813.12
grisly deathly 408.29
  terrible 891.38
  ugly 899.11
grist 660.2
gristle 359.2
grit
  n. courage 893.5
  grain 361.6
  pluck 624.3
  powder 361.5
  v. irritate 866.14
gritty bold 893.18
  coarse-textured 351.6
  granular 361.12
  plucky 624.14
  stony 384.11
grizzle
  n. gray hair 230.3
  horse 414.13
  v. gray 366.3
  whiten 364.5
  adj. gray 366.4
grizzled gray 366.4
  white 364.7
grizzly gray 366.4
  white 364.7
groan
  n. complaint 875.4
  harsh sound 458.3
  lament 875.3
  v. complain 875.13
  sound harshly 458.9
  wail 875.11
  wind sound 403.23
groaning board 307.9

**groat**
British money 835.8
powder 361.5
small amount 35.2
**grocer** 830.3
**groceries**
merchandise 831.7
provisions 308.5
**grocery** 832.5
**grog** 996.12,40
**groggy** dazed 532.14
inert 268.14
unsteady 160.16
**grogshop** 996.19
**groin** barrier 730.5
breakwater 216.4
fork 299.4
harbor 700.6
**grommet** circlet 253.5
hole 265.4
**groom**
*n.* animal handler
416.2
newlywed 933.6
*v.* arrange 60.12
preen 681.20
tend animals 416.7
train 562.14
**groomed** 720.16
**groomer** 565.7
**grooming** 562.3
**groove**
*n.* crack 201.2
furrow 263.1
path 657.3
printing 603.6
routine 642.6
*v.* cut 201.4
engrave 578.10
excavate 257.15
furrow 263.3
**grooved**
engraved 578.12
furrowed 263.4
**groove on** 865.10
**groovy**
*adj.* excellent 674.13
knowing 475.17
*interj.* pleasure 865.17
**grope**
*n.* feel 485.5
*v.* be uncertain 514.9
feel for 485.31
**grope in the dark**
be blind 441.8
be ignorant 477.10
feel for 485.31
**groping**
examining 485.36
ignorant 477.12
**gross**
*n.* gain 811.3
receipts 844.1
twelve dozen 99.8
*v.* profit 811.11
yield 844.4
*adj.* bad 675.9
base 915.12
carnal 987.6
coarse-textured 351.6
corpulent 195.18
growing rank 411.40

indecent 990.8
infelicitous 590.2
offensive 864.18
outright 34.12
stupid 469.15
thick 204.8
vulgar 898.11
whole 54.9
**gross income**
earnings 841.4
receipts 844.1
**grossly** badly 675.14
basely 915.17
exorbitantly 848.16
vulgarly 898.16
**gross national product**
827.7
**grotesque**
*n.* work of art 574.11
*adj.* abnormal 85.13
deformed 249.12
fanciful 535.20
foolish 470.10
ugly 899.8
**grotesquely** 85.19
**grotto** 257.5
**grouch**
*n.* ill-humored person
951.11
killjoy 730.9
malcontent 869.3
*v.* be ill-humored
951.14
complain 875.13
**grouchy** crabby 951.22
discontented 869.5
**ground**
*n.* arena 802.1
art equipment 574.19
bed 212.4
bottom 212.3
cause 153.1
enclosure 236.3
foundation 216.6
horizontal 214.3
justification 1006.6
land 385.1
motive 648.1
ocean depths 209.4
paint 362.8
premise 482.7
region 180.1
setting 233.2
station 184.2
*v.* electricity 342.26
entrench 142.9
establish 184.15
knock down 318.5
shipwreck 275.42
teach 562.11
*adj.* bottom 212.7
powdery 361.11
**groundbreaker** 66.1
**ground down** 764.16
**grounded**
aground 142.16
in difficulty 731.25
**grounded on**
evidential 505.17
supported 216.24
**ground floor**
earliness 131.1

story 192.23
**groundhog**
excavator 257.10
wild animal
414.28,58
**groundless**
baseless 483.13
unproved 506.8
unsubstantial 4.8
**groundling**
audience 448.6
person 417.3
playgoer 611.32
vulgar person 898.6
**grounds** cause 153.1
condition 507.2
evidence 505.1
foundation 216.6
green 411.7
justification 1006.6
real estate 810.7
residue 43.2
**groundsel** 216.9
**ground swell**
political movement
744.33
wave 395.14
**groundwork**
foundation 216.6
preparation 720.1
**group**
*n.* amount 28.2
art 574.23
association 788.1
bunch 74.7
class 61.2
clique 788.6
company 74.3
orchestra 464.12
religion 1020.3
set 20.5
*v.* analyze 48.8
arrange 60.11
assemble 74.18
classify 61.6
size 195.15
**grouped** arranged 60.14
classified 61.8
**groupie** 635.6
**grouping** analysis 48.3
arrangement 60.3
artistry 574.10
association 788.1
bunch 74.7
classification 61.1
company 74.3
division 61.2
**group therapy** 690.5
**grouse**
*n.* complaint 875.4
food 308.22
*v.* complain 875.13
**grousing**
*n.* complaint 875.4
*adj.* discontented
869.5
**grout** 228.25
**grove** bunch 74.7
valley 257.9
woodlet 411.12
**grovel** be low 208.5
be servile 907.6

be unchaste 989.19
bow down before
765.10
creep 273.25
crouch 318.8
lie 214.5
wallow 322.13
**groveler** 907.3
**groveling**
*n.* obsequiousness
907.2
*adj.* obsequious
907.13
recumbent 214.8
**grow** become 1.12
become higher
207.17
develop 197.7
evolve 148.5
farm 413.16
flower 411.31
increase 38.6
mature 126.9
process 167.11
raise animals 416.6
**grower**
agriculturist 413.5
producer 167.8
**grow from** 154.6
**growing**
*n.* manufacture 167.3
raising 413.12
*adj.* flourishing 197.12
immature 124.10
increasing 38.8
**grow into** 145.17
**growl**
*n.* harsh sound 458.3
reverberation 454.2
rumble 456.4
*v.* animal sound 460.4
complain 875.13
rumble 456.9
show resentment
952.14
sound harshly 458.9
utter 594.26
wind sound 403.23
**grown** adult 126.12
full-grown 197.12
manufactured 167.22
produced 167.20
**grownup** 127.1
**grown-up** adult 126.12
grown 197.12
**grow old** age 126.10
antiquate 123.9
**growth**
business cycle 827.9
conversion 145.1
development 197.3
disease symptom
686.8
increase 38.1
planting 411.2
progress 148.1
tumor 686.36
vegetation 411.30
**grow together**
be joined 47.11
cohere 50.6
**grow up** ascend 315.8

become higher
207.17
grow 197.7
mature 126.9
reach perfection
722.8
**grub**
*n.* drudge 718.3
food 308.2
young insect 125.10
*v.* drudge 716.14
excavate 257.15
procure 811.10
**grubby** dirty 682.22
infested 313.11
slovenly 62.15
**grubstake**
*n.* financing 836.2
*v.* finance 836.15
**grub up** dig up 305.10
procure 811.10
search out 485.33
**grudge**
*n.* spite 929.5
*v.* be parsimonious
852.5
be unwilling 623.3
envy 954.3
refuse 776.4
**grudging** envious 954.4
niggardly 852.8
reluctant 623.6
**grudgingly** 623.9
**gruel** cereal 308.34
semiliquid 389.5
thinness 205.7
weakness 160.7
**grueling**
fatiguing 717.11
laborious 716.18
punishing 1010.25
troublesome 731.17
weakening 160.20
**gruesome**
deathly 408.29
frightening 891.38
ugly 899.11
**gruff** brusque 937.7
grouchy 951.22
raucous 458.15
**grum** glum 872.25
sullen 951.24
**rumble**
*n.* harsh sound 458.3
reverberation 454.2
rumble 456.4
*v.* animal sound 460.4
complain 875.13
rumble 456.9
sound harshly 458.9
**rumbler** 869.3
**rumbling**
*n.* complaint 875.4
reverberation 454.2
*dj.* discontented
869.5
grouchy 951.22
**ume** blood 388.4
coagulation 354.7
**umpiness** 951.6
**umpy** 951.22
**ungy** 682.22

**grunt**
*n.* animal sound 460.1
infantryman 800.9
*v.* animal sound 460.3
complain 875.13
utter 594.26
**G-string**
clothing 231.19
supporter 216.2
**G suit** gravity 352.5
space suit 282.11
**guarantee**
*n.* guarantor 772.6
oath 523.3
promise 770.1
security 772.1
*v.* affirm 523.5
promise 770.4
protect 699.18
secure 772.9
**guaranteed**
assured 513.20
certified 772.11
promised 770.8
unhazardous 698.5
**guaranteed annual
income**
subsidy 818.8
welfare program
745.7
**guarantor**
endorser 521.7
warrantor 772.6
**guaranty**
*n.* guarantor 772.6
security 772.1
*v.* secure 772.9
**guard**
*n.* athlete 878.20
bodyguards 699.14
defender 799.7
defense 799.1
escort 73.5
guarder 699.9
household troops
800.31
jailer 761.10
protection 699.1
safeguard 699.3
trainman 274.13
vigilance 533.4
*v.* defend 799.8
escort 73.8
preserve 701.7
protect 699.18
restrain 760.7
**guard against**
defend 799.8
take precautions
895.6
**guarded** cautious 895.8
protected 699.21
restrained 760.13
reticent 613.10
suspicious 504.4
vigilant 533.13
**guardedly** 895.12
**guardhouse** 761.8
**guardian**
*n.* familiar spirit
1014.22
jailer 761.10

manager 748.4
protector 699.6
*adj.* protecting 699.23
**guardian angel**
familiar spirit
1014.22
protector 699.6
**guardianship**
directorship 747.4
protectorship 699.2
storage 660.5
usage 665.2
vigilance 533.4
**guarding**
*n.* custody 761.5
*adj.* defensive 799.11
protecting 699.23
**guardrail** 699.3
**gubernatorial** 741.17
**gudgeon** axis 322.5
dupe 620.1
**guerrilla** 800.15
**guess**
*n.* an uncertainty
514.8
unverified supposi-
tion 499.4
*v.* believe 501.11
conjecture 499.11
judge 494.9
predict 543.9
solve 487.2
**guesser** 499.8
**guessing** 514.23
**guesswork**
prediction 543.1
supposition 499.3
**guest** 925.6
**guest house** 191.16
**guff** chatter 596.3
nonsense 547.3
**guffaw**
*n.* laughter 876.4
*v.* laugh 876.8
**guidance** advice 754.1
direction 747.1
patronage 785.4
protectorship 699.2
teaching 562.1
**guide**
*n.* advisor 754.3
director 748.7
guardian angel
1014.22
hole 265.4
interpreter 552.7
pointer 568.4
precursor 66.1
specter 1017.1
teacher 565.1
trough 396.3
*v.* advise 754.5
direct 747.9
escort 73.8
go before 66.3
influence 172.8
lead 292.2
pilot 275.14
teach 562.11
**guidebook**
directory 748.10
handbook 605.5

information 557.1
**guideline** plan 654.1
precept 751.2
rule 84.4
**guidepost** 568.4
**guiding** 747.12
**guiding light** 648.1
**guiding principle**
main idea 479.4
policy 654.5
precept 751.2
**guiding star**
guide 748.8
motive 648.1
**guild** 788.3
**guile** cunning 735.1
deceit 618.3
**guileful** cunning 735.12
deceitful 618.20
shrewd 467.15
**guilefully**
cunningly 735.13
deceitfully 618.22
**guileless** artless 736.5
honest 974.18
trusting 501.22
**guilelessly**
artlessly 736.7
trustworthily 974.24
**guillotine**
*n.* capital punishment
1010.7
cloture 144.5
instrument of execu-
tion 1011.5
*v.* execute 1010.19
**guilt** 983
**guiltily** 983.5
**guiltless** innocent 984.6
virtuous 980.8
**guiltlessly** 984.9
**guilty** 983.3
**guinea**
British money 835.8
coin 835.4
**guinea pig**
experimentee 489.7
wild animal 414.28
**guise** aspect 446.3
behavior 737.1
clothing 231.1
cover 228.2
looks 446.4
mode 7.4
pretext 649.1
way 657.1
**guitar** 465.4
**gulch** ravine 201.2
watercourse 396.2
**gulf**
arm of the sea 399.1
concavity 257.4
gap 201.2
opening 265.1
pit 209.2
whirlpool 395.12
**gull**
*n.* dupe 620.1
*v.* cheat 618.17
deceive 618.13
dupe 470.7
**gullet** abdomen 193.3

orderly 59.6
usual 84.8
**habitually**
  frequently 135.6
  regularly 642.23
  usually 84.9
**habituate** 642.11
**habituated** 642.19
**habituating** 642.20
**habituation**
  accustoming 642.8
  addiction 642.9
**habitué** attender 186.5
  guest 925.6
**hachure** line 568.6
  map 654.4
  network 221.3
**hacienda** farm 413.8
  ranch 191.7
**hack**
  *n.* breathing 403.18
  cab 272.12
  coachman 274.9
  driver 274.10
  drudge 718.3
  hack writer 602.16
  horse 414.16
  inferior horse 414.14
  mark 568.5
  notch 262.1
  petty politician 746.4
  *v.* exhale 403.24
  ride 273.33
  sever 49.11
**hack it** be able 157.11
  manage 724.11
  stand the test 489.10
  suffice 661.4
**hackle**
  *n.* feather 230.16
  plumage 230.18
  *v.* comb 681.21
**hackneyed** dull 883.9
  habitual 642.16
  trite 79.16
  well-known 475.27
**Hades**
  deity of nether world
    1019.5
  god 1014.5
  hell 1019.3
  nether world 1019.1
**hag** evildoer 943.7
  old woman 127.3
  ugly person 899.4
  witch 1035.8
**haggard** colorless 363.7
  deathly 408.29
  excited 857.23
  fanatical 473.32
  thin 205.20
  tired-looking 717.7
**haggle**
  *n.* negotiation 827.3
  *v.* bargain 827.17
**haggling** 827.3
**hagiography**
  biography 608.4
  theology 1023.1
**ha-ha**
  *n.* laughter 876.4
  trench 263.2

*v.* laugh 876.8
**haiku** 609.6
**hail**
  *n.* greeting 925.4
  ice 333.6
  large number 101.3
  *v.* address 594.27
  applaud 968.10
  assent 521.8
  cry 459.6
  greet 925.10
  signal 568.22
  storm 333.11
  *interj.* approval
    968.23
  attention! 530.23
  greetings! 925.15
**hail-fellow-well-met**
  922.19
**Hail Mary** 1032.4
**hair** filament 206.1
  fur 230.2
  narrowness 205.1
  short distance 200.2
  small amount 35.2
  trifle 673.5
  weakness 160.7
**hairbreadth**
  narrowness 205.1
  short distance 200.2
**haircut** boy's 230.31
  hairdo 230.15
**hairdo** hairstyle 230.15
  women's 230.30
**hairdresser** 900.12
**hairiness**
  difficulty 731.1
  furriness 230
**hairless** 232.17
**hairlike**
  threadlike 206.7
  trichoid 230.23
**hairline** difference 16.2
  line 568.6
**hairpiece** 230.14
**hairpin**
  *n.* crookedness 219.8
  deviation 291.1
  *adj.* crooked 219.20
**hair-raising** 891.37
**hair remover** 232.4
**hair shirt** 1012.3
**hairsplitting**
  *n.* disapproval 969.4
  overdiscrimination
    492.3
  overparticularity
    896.4
  quibbling 483.5
  *adj.* critical 969.24
  overparticular 896.12
  quibbling 483.14
**hairstyle** 230.15
**hair-trigger** 269.19
**hairy** bad 675.8
  difficult 731.16
  hirsute 230.24
  rough 261.9
  threadlike 206.7
**hajj** 273.5
**halcyon** calm 268.12
  pacific 803.9

pleasant 863.10
  prosperous 728.13
**hale**
  *v.* pull 286.4
  *adj.* healthy 685.10
  strong 159.13
**half**
  *n.* bisection 92.2
  middle 69.2
  portion 816.5
  *adj.* part 92.5
  proportionate 816.13
**half-and-half**
  *n.* half 92.2
  milk 308.47
  *adj.* equal 30.7
  mixed 44.15
  neutral 806.7
  proportionate 816.13
  *adv.* in half 92.8
  midway 69.5
  proportionately
    816.14
**half-assed**
  half-learned 477.15
  slipshod 534.12
  unskillful 734.15
**halfback** 878.20
**half-baked**
  half-learned 477.15
  mentally deficient
    469.22
  premature 131.8
  undeveloped 721.11
**half-breed**
  *n.* hybrid 44.9
  *adj.* hybrid 44.16
**half-cocked**
  half-learned 477.15
  premature 131.8
  undeveloped 721.11
**halfhearted**
  indifferent 636.6
  weak 160.17
**half-life** 327.1,14
**half-moon**
  crescent 252.5
  moon 375.11
**half-pint** 196.10
**half time** interim 109.1
  shift 108.3
**halftone**
  color system 362.7
  harmonics 463.20
**halftone engraving**
  603.1
**half-truth** 616.11
**halfway**
  *adj.* half 92.5
  middle 69.4
  *adv.* midway 69.5
**halfway house**
  asylum 700.4
  middle 69.2
**halfway mark** 92.3
**half-wit** 471.8
**half-witted** 469.22
**halitosis** 437.1
**hall** arena 802.1
  corridor 192.18
  entrance 302.5
  house 191.6

room 192.4
  school 567.15
  theater 611.18
**hallelujah**
  *n.* cheer 876.2
  hymn 1032.3
  *interj.* worship
    1032.16
**hallmark**
  *n.* characteristic 80.4
  label 568.13
  sign 568.2
  *v.* label 568.20
**hall-of-famer** 733.14
**hallow** celebrate 877.2
  sanctify 1026.5
**hallowed**
  godlike 1013.20
  sanctified 1026.8
  traditional 123.12
**hallucinate** 519.8
**hallucination**
  deception 618.1
  illusion 519.7
  thing imagined 535.5
  thought disturbance
    690.24
**hallucinatory**
  deceptive 618.19
  psychedelic 519.10
**hallucinogen** 687.13,53
**hallucinogenic**
  hallucinatory 519.10
  psychochemical
    687.46
**hallway** 192.18
**halo** circle 253.2
  illustriousness 914.6
  light 335.14
**halt**
  *n.* delay 132.2
  impasse 731.5
  prevention 730.2
  respite 711.2
  standstill 268.3
  stop 144.2
  *v.* arrest 144.11
  be weak 160.8
  dawdle 270.8
  discontinue 144.6
  prevent 730.13
  quiet 268.8
  stammer 595.8
  stop 144.7
  walk 273.27
  *adj.* crippled 692.32
  *interj.* cease! 144.14
**halter**
  *n.* harness 659.5
  noose 1011.5
  restraint 760.4
  *v.* bind 47.10
**halting** crippled 692.32
  irregular 138.3
  slow 270.10
  stammering 595.13
  stilted 590.3
**haltingly**
  irregularly 138.4
  slowly 270.13
**halve** bisect 92.4
  sever 49.11

share 815.6
**halved** 92.6
**halving** bisection 92.1
  duality 90.1
**ham**
  *n.* acting 611.9
  actor 612.5
  leg 273.16
  pork 308.16
  radioman 344.24
  village 183.2
  *v.* emotionalize
    855.15
  overact 611.36
  *adj.* theatrical 611.38
**hamburger** beef 308.13
  sandwich 308.32
  steak 308.18
**hamlet** district 180.5
  village 183.2
**hammer**
  *n.* auditory organ
    448.7
  types of 348.19
  *v.* drudge 716.14
  pound 283.14
  repeat 103.10
  terrorize 162.10
**hammer and sickle**
  569.1
**hammer and tongs**
  laboriously 716.19
  resolutely 624.17
**hammer away at**
  drudge 716.14
  persevere 625.3
  repeat 103.9
  think hard 478.9
**hammerlock** 813.3
**hammer out**
  do carelessly 534.9
  form 246.7
**hammy**
  emotionalistic 855.20
  theatrical 611.38
**hamper**
  *n.* impediment 730.6
  restraint 760.4
  *v.* burden 352.13
  hinder 730.11
  package 236.9
  restrain 760.10
**hampered**
  burdened 352.18
  restrained 760.16
**hampering**
  *n.* hindrance 730.1
  *adj.* impeding 730.18
**hamstring**
  cripple 692.17
  disable 158.9
  hamper 730.11
  render powerless
    158.11
**hand**
  *n.* act 705.3
  applause 968.2
  assist 785.2
  control 741.2
  governance 739.5
  grasping organs 813.4
  handwriting 602.3

limb 55.4
  person 417.3
  playing cards 878.17
  pointer 568.4
  protectorship 699.2
  sailor 276.6
  side 242.1
  signature 583.10
  working person 718.2
  *v.* deliver 818.13
  transfer property
    817.3
**handbag** 836.14
**handbill** 559.8
**handbook**
  directory 748.10
  manual 605.5
  wager 515.3
**handcart** 272.3,28
**hand-clasp** 925.4
**handcuff**
  *n.* restraint 760.4
  *v.* render powerless
    158.11
  restrain 760.10
**hand down**
  bequeath 818.18
  transfer property
    817.3
**handed down** 123.12
**handful**
  difficult thing 731.2
  few 102.2
  small amount 35.2
**hand grenade** 801.14
**handicap**
  *n.* burden 352.7
  disadvantage 671.2
  disease 686.1
  horse race 796.13
  impediment 730.6
  penalty 1009.2
  *v.* burden 352.13
  hamper 730.11
  penalize 1009.4
**handicapped** 692.32
**handicapped, the**
  686.42
**handicraft** craft 574.3
  manufacture 167.3
  vocation 656.6
**handily**
  skillfully 733.29
  usefully 665.25
**hand in** 818.13
**hand in hand**
  amicably 927.21
  concurrently 177.5
  cooperatively 786.6
  sociably 922.21
  together 73.10
**hand-in-hand**
  friendly 927.18
  joined 47.13
  near 200.14
**handiwork** act 705.3
  manufacture 167.3
  product 168.1
  work 716.4
**handkerchief** 231.25
**handle**
  *n.* grip 216.11,27

name 583.3
  pretext 649.1
  projection 256.3
  title 917.1
  *v.* behave toward
    737.6
  deal with 665.12
  direct 747.8
  discourse upon 606.5
  discuss 597.12
  drive animals 416.7
  operate 164.5
  perform 705.8
  pilot 275.14
  sell 827.15
  touch 425.6
  use 665.10
**handler** operator 164.4
  trainer 565.7
**handle with kid gloves**
  be careful 533.7
  be lenient 759.5
**handling**
  direction 747.1
  operation 164.1
  performance 705.2
  touching 425.2
  treatment 665.2
  utilization 665.8
**handmade** 167.22
**handmaid**
  instrument 658.3
  maid 750.8
**hand-me-down**
  *n.* clothing 231.5
  *adj.* old 123.18
**hand on**
  bequeath 818.18
  communicate 554.7
  transfer 271.9
  transfer property
    817.3
**hand organ** 465.16
**handout**
  advertising 559.8
  donation 818.6
  information 557.1
  press release 559.3
**hand out**
  deliver 818.13
  give 818.12
**hand over**
  deliver 818.13
  give up 633.7
  pay over 841.15
  transfer 271.9
  transfer property
    817.3
**hand over fist**
  fast 269.21
  hastily 709.12
**handpick** 637.14
**handpicked**
  best 674.18
  chosen 637.26
**hands** control 741.2
  forces 157.9
  governance 739.5
**hands down** 732.15
**handshake**
  *n.* greeting 925.4
  *v.* curry favor 907.8

**hands-off policy** 631.1
**handsome**
  beautiful 900.16
  liberal 853.4
  magnanimous 979.6
**handsomely**
  beautifully 900.21
  liberally 853.5
  magnanimously 979.8
**handsomeness** 900.1
**hand-to-mouth** 721.15
**hand-to-mouth**
  existence 838.2
**handwear** 231.63
**handwriting** 602.3
**handwriting expert**
  602.14
**handwriting on the wall**
  fate 640.2
  omen 544.4
  warning sign 703.3
**handy**
  convenient 665.19
  miniature 196.12
  nearby 200.15
  skillful 733.20
  useful 658.6
  wieldy 732.14
**handy man** 733.11
**hang**
  *n.* declivity 219.5
  droop 215.2
  knack 733.6
  *v.* be contingent 507.6
  be uncertain 514.11
  dangle 215.6
  execute 1010.20
  hover 315.10
  procrastinate 132.11
  suspend 215.8
**hang about**
  attach oneself to
    907.10
  stay near 200.12
**hangar** aviation 278.24
  garage 192.27
  repair shop 719.6
**hang around**
  frequent 186.10
  idle 708.11
  wait 132.12
**hang around with**
  accompany 73.7
  be sociable 922.16
**hang back**
  be irresolute 627.7
  demur 623.4
  follow 293.4
  procrastinate 132.11
  pull back 284.7
**hangdog**
  humiliated 906.13
  servile 907.13
**hanger** caption 484.2
  pendant 215.4
  suspender 215.5,14
  woodland 411.11
**hanger-on**
  adherent 907.5
  follower 293.2
  lackey 787.8

political henchman
746.8
retainer 750.1
**hang fire**
be unproductive
166.3
do nothing 706.2
postpone 132.9
procrastinate 132.11
stagnate 268.9
stop 144.7
**hang in**
be patient 861.5
have courage 893.15
not weaken 159.9
persevere 625.4
persist 143.5
remain firm 624.9
**hang in effigy** 915.9
**hanging**
*n.* capital punishment
1010.7
cover 228.2
declivity 219.5
pendant 215.4,13
pendency 215.1
scenery 611.25
*adj.* downcast 316.12
loose 51.5
pendent 215.9
**hang in the balance**
514.11
**hangman** 1010.8
**hang off** 623.4
**hang on**
attribute to 155.4
be contingent 507.6
be uncertain 514.11
cohere 50.6
depend on 154.6
hold 813.6
keep alive 407.10
persevere 625.4
**hangout** 191.27
**hang out**
be discovered 488.9
be manifest 555.7
be visible 444.5
frequent 186.10
inhabit 188.7
overhang 215.7
**hangover**
intoxication 996.1
posteriority 117.1
**hang over**
be imminent 152.2
cover 228.30
project 215.7
**hang over one's head**
152.2
**hang together**
agree 26.6
be joined 47.11
cohere 50.6
cooperate 786.3
**hang up**
come to nothing
725.12
postpone 132.9
suspend 215.8
telephone 560.18
**hang-up** delay 132.2

obsession 473.13
obstacle 730.4
**hank** 206.1
**hanker after** 634.18
**hankering**
*n.* yearning 634.5
*adj.* wistful 634.23
**hanky-panky**
juggling 618.5
love affair 931.6
**Hanukkah** 1040.16
**hap**
*n.* chance 156.1
chance event 156.6
event 151.2
*v.* chance 156.11
occur 151.5
**haphazard**
*n.* random 156.4
*adj.* purposeless
156.16
slipshod 534.12
unordered 62.12
unprepared 721.8
**haphazardly**
carelessly 534.18
discontinuously 72.5
purposelessly 156.20
unsystematically
62.18
**hapless** 729.14
**happen** chance 156.11
occur 151.5
**happening**
*n.* event 151.2
fortuity 156.6
stage show 611.4
*adj.* occurring 151.9
**happenstance**
chance 156.1
chance event 156.6
event 151.2
nonessential 6.2
**happen upon** 488.3
**happily**
cheerfully 870.17
gladly 865.16
**happiness**
cheerfulness 870.1
contentment 868.1
decorousness 897.3
gladness 865.2
prosperity 728.1
**happy** apt 26.10
auspicious 544.18
cheerful 870.11
contented 868.7
decorous 897.10
expedient 670.5
glad 865.13
intoxicated 996.30
timely 129.9
well-chosen 589.7
**happy-go-lucky** 721.15
**happy hour** 711.2
**happy medium**
mean 32.1
middle course 806.3
moderation 163.1
**hara-kiri** 409.6
**harangue**
*n.* lesson 562.7

speech 599.2
*v.* declaim 599.10
lecture 562.17
**harass** besiege 798.19
fatigue 717.4
harm 675.6
intimidate 891.28
make anxious 890.4
persecute 667.6
torment 866.13
trouble 731.12
vex 864.15
**harassed**
tormented 866.24
troubled 731.19
worried 890.7
**harassing**
annoying 864.22
troublesome 890.9
**harassment**
annoyance 866.2
persecution 667.3
vexatiousness 864.7
worry 890.2
**harbinger**
*n.* herald 561.2
omen 544.5
precursor 66.1
*v.* presage 544.14
**harbor**
*n.* arm of the sea
399.1
destination 300.5
haven 700.6
refuge 700.1
*v.* house 188.10
protect 699.18
retain 813.7
**hard**
*adj.* addictive 642.20
adverse 729.13
alcoholic 996.36
bitter 429.6
callous 856.12
difficult 731.16
hard to understand
549.14
heartless 939.23
impenitent 874.5
industrious 707.22
inelastic 626.9
obdurate 626.10
painful 424.10
phonetic 594.31
pitiless 945.3
rigid 356.10
severe 939.22
solid 354.12
strict 757.7
strong 159.13
substantial 3.7
tough 359.4
wicked 981.17
*adv.* laboriously
716.19
near 200.20
**hard and fast**
aground 275.73
mandatory 752.13
prescriptive 751.4
**hardcase**
adversity 729.1

poor person 838.4
unlucky person 729.7
**hard-core**
fanatic 162.21
unyielding 626.9
**hard-earned**
difficult 731.16
laborious 716.18
**harden**
accustom 642.11
make tough 359.3
make unfeeling 856.6
petrify 384.9
solidify 356.7
strengthen 159.11
**hardened**
accustomed 642.17
callous 856.12
heartless 939.23
impenitent 874.5
solidified 356.13
toughened 359.6
wicked 981.17
**hardening**
*n.* habituation 642.8
immobility 140.1
solidification 354.3
strengthening 159.5
toughening 356.5
*adj.* toughening
356.14
**hardening of the
arteries** 686.17
**harden one's heart**
be unregretful 874.3
make unfeeling 856.6
refuse 776.3
show no mercy 945.2
**hard feelings**
animosity 929.4
bitterness 952.3
feelings 855.7
**hardfisted** 852.9
**hard-fought**
difficult 731.16
laborious 716.18
**hard goods** 831.4
**hard hat**
conservative 745.9
safety equipment
699.3
superpatriot 941.3
**hardheaded**
obstinate 626.8
practical 536.6
ungullible 504.5
**hardhearted**
callous 856.12
heartless 939.23
wicked 981.17
**hardiness**
courage 893.4
robustness 685.3
strength 159.1
toughness 359.1
**hard job**
difficult thing 731.2
hard work 716.5
**hard labor**
hard work 716.5
punishment 1010.2
**hard life** 729.1

**hardly**
infrequently 136.4
narrowly 205.22
rarely 85.17
scarcely 35.9
strictly 757.9
with difficulty 731.26
**hardness**
abstruseness 549.2
callousness 856.3
difficulty 731.1
firmness 159.3
heartlessness 939.10
impenitence 874.2
obduracy 981.6
pitilessness 945.1
rigidity 356
severity 939.9
solidity 354.1
strictness 757.2
toughness 359.1
**hardnose**
obstinate person
626.6
violent person 162.9
**hard-nosed** 626.10
**hard-of-hearing** 449.6
**hard pressed**
hurried 709.11
in trouble 731.24
**hard rock** 462.9
**hardship**
adversity 729.1
poverty 838.1
**hard stuff** drug 687.5
heroin 687.12
**hardtack** 308.30
**hard times** 729.6
**hard up**
in trouble 731.24
poor 838.7
**hardware**
computer 349.16
hard goods 831.4
**hardworking**
industrious 707.22
struggling 716.17
**hardy**
courageous 893.17
enduring 110.10
plant 411.41
robust 685.10
strong 159.13
tough 359.4
**hare**
mammal 414.58;
415.8
rabbit 414.29
speed 269.6
**harebrain** 471.7
**harebrained**
capricious 629.5
foolhardy 894.9
scatterbrained 532.16
**harelip** 249.3
**harem** 933.11
**hark**
v. hearken to 530.7
listen 448.11
*interj.* attention!
530.22
listen! 448.17

**hark back**
remember 537.10
revert to 146.6
turn back 146.5
**harlequin**
*n.* buffoon 612.10
check 374.4
variegation 374.6
*adj.* variegated 374.9
**harlot**
*n.* prostitute 989.16
*adj.* prostitute 989.28
**harlotry** 989.8
**harm**
*n.* bane 676.1
disadvantage 671.2
evil 675.3
impairment 692.1
*v.* impair 692.11
inconvenience 671.4
work evil 675.6
**harmed** 692.29
**harmful** adverse 729.13
disadvantageous
671.6
hurtful 675.12
malicious 939.18
unhealthful 684.5
**harmfully**
hurtfully 675.15
malevolently 939.28
**harmfulness**
hurtfulness 675.5
malice 939.5
unhealthfulness 684.1
**harmless**
hurtless 674.20
undamaged 677.8
unhazardous 698.5
**harmlessness**
hurtlessness 674.9
safety 698.1
**harmonic**
*n.* overtone 463.16
tone 450.2
*adj.* music 462.50
oscillating 323.15
**harmonica** 465.11
**harmonics**
harmony 463
music 462.3
**harmonious**
agreeing 26.9
balanced 589.8
coacting 177.4
coloring 362.15
conformist 82.6
cooperating 786.5
friendly 927.14
likeminded 794.3
music 462.50
orderly 59.6
pleasant 863.6
symmetric 248.4
**harmoniously**
cooperatively 786.6
in step 26.11
uniformly 59.9
**harmonium** 465.15
**harmonization**
coordination 26.4
orchestration 463.2

organization 60.2
score 462.5
symmetrization 248.2
**harmonize** agree 26.6
arrange 60.10
assonate 462.36
coact 177.2
compose 462.47
conform 82.3
cooperate 786.3
empathize 794.2
make agree 26.7
make uniform 17.4
order 59.4
reconcile 804.8
symmetrize 248.3
**harmony**
agreement 26.1
conformity 82.1
cooperation 786.1
friendship 927.3
harmonics 463.1
heaven 1018.6
literary elegance
589.2
music 462.3
order 59.1
peace 803.1
rapport 794.1
reference book 605.6
symmetry 248.1
unanimity 521.5
**harness**
*n.* armor 799.3
equipment 659.5
parachute 280.13
wardrobe 231.2
*v.* bind 47.10
drive animals 416.7
**harp** instrument 465.3
mouth organ 465.11
**harpist** 464.5
**harp on** dwell on 884.7
emphasize 672.13
repeat 103.9
**harpoon** 822.17
**harpooning** 655.3
**harpsichord** 465.13
**harpy**
monster 85.20; 943.6
predator 822.12
**harridan**
ugly person 899.4
unchaste woman
989.14
**harried**
tormented 866.24
worried 890.7
**harrow**
*n.* pointed projection
258.4
*v.* pain 424.7
smooth 260.5
till 413.17
torture 866.18
**harrowed** pained 424.9
tortured 866.25
**harrowing**
painful 424.10
unpleasant 864.23
**harry** annoy 866.13
attack 798.15

besiege 798.19
make anxious 890.4
persecute 667.6
**harsh**
acrimonious 161.13
bitter 429.6
clashing 461.5
clashingly colored
362.20
dissonant 461.4
gruff 937.7
imperfectly spoken
595.12
infelicitous 590.2
painful 424.10
pitiless 945.3
pungent 433.6
raucous 458.15
rough 261.7
strict 757.6
unkind 939.22
unpleasant 864.24
**harshly** gruffly 937.9
pitilessly 945.4
strictly 757.8
unkindly 939.31
**harshness**
acrimony 161.4
dissonance 461.2
gruffness 937.3
literary inelegance
590.1
offensiveness 864.2
pitilessness 945.1
pungency 433.1
raucousness 458.2
roughness 261.1
speech defect 595.1
strictness 757.1
unkindness 939.9
violence 162.1
**harum-scarum**
boisterous 162.19
in disorder 62.17
reckless 894.8
**harvest**
*n.* autumn 128.4
harvesting 413.15
produce 168.2
result 154.1
yield 811.5
*v.* acquire 811.8
produce 167.11
reap 413.19
**harvesting**
producing 167.3
reaping 413.15
**has-been**
*n.* antiquated person
123.8
*adj.* old-fashioned
123.16
past 119.7
**hash**
*n.* bungle 734.5
cannabis 687.13
fiasco 725.6
hodgepodge 44.6
jumble 62.3
meat 308.12,58
*v.* mix 44.11
**hashish** 687.13,53

indistinctness 445.2
vagueness 514.4
**hazy** dim 445.6
foggy 404.9
formless 247.4
muddled 532.13
obscure 549.15
vague 514.18
**H-blast** 326.16
**H-bomb** 801.15,30
**he** male 420.4
self 80.5
**head**
*n.* abridgment 607.1
book 605.12
brain 466.6
capital 211.5
caption 484.2
class 61.2
coin 240.1
drug user 642.10
foam 405.2
front 240.1
hair 230.4
headwaters 395.2
inflorescence 411.25
intellect 466.1
intelligent being 467.9
pate 211.6
person 417.3
point of land 256.8
portrait 574.16
pressure 283.2
rest room 311.10
sail part 277.14
source 153.5
superior 36.4
supervisor 748.2
topic 484.1
top part 211.4
water 392.3
*v.* bear 290.8
begin 68.10
caption 484.3
direct 747.8
front 240.7
govern 741.12
gravitate 352.15
head for 290.10
lead 292.2
precede 64.2
tend 174.3
top 211.9
*adj.* directing 747.12
first 68.17
front 240.10
governing 741.18
top 211.10
**headache** ache 424.5
annoyance 866.2
boring person 884.4
nervous disorder 686.23
trouble 731.3
**head count** list 88.6
numeration 87.5
**headdress**
clothing 231.25
hairdo 230.15
**headed for** 290.28
**header** plunge 320.1

tumble 316.3
**headfirst**
precipitously 709.15
recklessly 894.11
**headgear**
clothing 231.25
harness 659.5
**head-hunter** 409.11
**heading**
*n.* aviation 278.43
caption 484.2
class 61.2
direction 290.1
front 240.1
leading 292.1
topic 484.1
top part 211.4
*adj.* leading 292.3
topping 211.11
**headland** 256.8
**headless** topless 211.13
unintelligent 469.13
**headline**
*n.* caption 484.2
*v.* caption 484.3
give prominence 672.14
star 611.33
**headliner** 612.6
**headlong**
*adj.* fast 269.19
impulsive 630.9
precipitate 709.10
reckless 894.8
steep 219.18
sudden 113.5
*adv.* impulsively 630.13
precipitously 709.15
recklessly 894.11
**headman**
public official 749.17
supervisor 748.2
**headmaster** 565.9
**headmost**
*adj.* chief 36.14
front 240.10
leading 292.3
preceding 64.4
top 211.10
*adv.* before 292.4
in front 240.12
**head off** 291.6
**head of state** 749.6
**head over heels**
inversely 220.8
precipitously 709.15
recklessly 894.11
reversed 220.7
round 322.16
**head over heels in**
engrossed 530.17
involved in 176.4
**headphone**
loudspeaker 450.8
radiophone 560.5
**headpiece**
clothing 231.25
head 211.6
intellect 466.1
top part 211.4

**headquarters**
center 226.6
office 719.8
**headroom** 179.3
**headset**
loudspeaker 450.8
radiophone 560.5
**headshrinker** 690.13
**headsman** 1010.8
**heads or tails** 515.2
**head start**
advantage 36.2
earliness 131.1
**headstone**
cornerstone 216.7
memorial 570.12
**headstrong**
lawless 740.5
obstinate 626.8
**head up** begin 68.10
caption 484.3
direct 747.8
lead 240.7
precede 64.2
**headwater**
headstream 395.2
source 153.6
**headway**
improvement 691.1
progression 294.1
water travel 275.9
**head wind**
aviation 278.41
counterforce 178.4
nautical 403.11
opposition 790.1
wind 403.1
**headwork** study 564.3
thought 478.1
**heady** exciting 857.28
foamy 405.7
intoxicating 996.35
lawless 740.5
**heal** close up 694.21
restore to health 694.15
treat 689.30
**healer**
faith healer 688.12
therapist 688.5
**healing**
*n.* faith healing 689.3
restoration 694.7
*adj.* remedial 687.39
**health** normality 84.1
well-being 685
**health food** food 308.1
types of 309.26
**healthful** fit 685.7
salubrious 683.5
**healthiness**
goodness 674.1
salubrity 683.1
soundness 685.2
**health resort**
gathering place 191.27
spa 689.29
**healthy** good 674.12
healthful 685.7
large 195.16
salubrious 683.5

**heap**
*n.* amount 28.2
automobile 272.9
much 34.4
pile 74.10
store 660.1
throng 74.4
*v.* be generous 853.3
give 818.12
pile 74.19
put 184.14
store up 660.11
**hear**
*v.* be informed 557.14
catch 448.12
hearken to 530.7
judge 494.12
listen 448.11
sense 422.8
try 1004.17
*interj.* hark! 448.17
**hear a different drummer**
disagree 27.5
not conform 83.4
**hearer** listener 448.5
recipient 819.3
**hearing**
*n.* audition 448.2
earshot 448.4
examination 485.2
investigation 485.4
sense 422.5
sense of hearing 448
trial 1004.5
tryout 489.3
*adj.* auditory 448.14
**hearing aid** 448.8
**hearken**
*v.* listen 448.11
*interj.* hark! 448.17
**hearken to** hark 530.7
obey 766.2
**hearsay**
*n.* evidence 505.2
rumor 558.6
*adj.* evidential 505.17
**hearse** 410.10
**heart**
amphetamine 687.9
center 226.2
content 194.5
courage 893.5
diseases of 686.17
essence 5.2
fervor 855.10
important point 672.6
inner nature 5.4
interior 225.2
love 931.1
meat 308.20
middle 69.1
mood 525.4
psyche 466.4
seat of affections 855.2
seat of life 407.3
viscera 225.4
**heartache** despair 866
sadness 872.9

hedonist 987.3
hedonistic
  philosophy 500.9
  pleasure-loving
    865.15
  sensual 987.5
heebie-jeebies
  delirium tremens
    473.10
  nervousness 859.2
heed
  *n.* attention 530.1
  caution 895.1
  concern 533.1
  observance 768.1
  *v.* attend 530.6
  care 533.6
  listen 448.11
  obey 766.2
  observe 768.2
heedful
  attentive 530.15
  careful 533.10
  cautious 895.8
  considerate 938.16
heeding hearing 448.1
  observance 768.1
heedless careless 534.11
  forgetful 538.9
  improvident 721.15
  impulsive 630.10
  inattentive 531.6
  inconsiderate 939.16
  incurious 529.3
  unconcerned 636.7
heedlessly
  carelessly 534.18
  inconsiderately
    939.27
  on impulse 630.14
  recklessly 894.11
  unconcernedly
    636.10
heel
  *n.* bad person 986.6
  foot 212.5
  rear 241.1
  stern 241.7
  *v.* deviate 291.3
  equip 659.8
  follow 293.3
  sail 275.43
  turn around 295.9
heeler hanger-on 907.5
  partisan 744.27
  political henchman
    746.8
heft
  *n.* weight 352.1
  *v.* elevate 317.5
  weigh 352.10
hefty corpulent 195.18
  heavy 352.16
  laborious 716.18
  strong 159.13
  troublesome 731.17
hegira departure 301.1
  flight 631.4
heifer calf 414.6
  female animal 421.9
  girl 125.6
height altitude 207

culmination 677.3
degree 29.1
elevation 207.2
exaltation 317.1
harmonics 463.4
size 195.1
summit 211.2
supremacy 36.3
heighten
  elevate 207.18
  exalt 317.5
  increase 38.5
  intensify 885.2
heightened
  aggravated 885.4
  increased 38.7
heightening
  aggravation 885.1
  exaggeration 617.1
  increase 38.2
heinous bad 675.9
  base 915.12
  evil 981.16
  offensive 864.18
heir descendant 117.2
  heritor 819.5
  posterity 171.1
  successor 67.4
  survivor 43.3
heir apparent
  prince 918.7
  successor 819.5
heiress
  descendant 171.3
  recipient 819.5
heirloom 819.2
heist
  *n.* a theft 824.10
  stickup 824.3
  *v.* elevate 317.5
  rob 824.14
Hekate 375.12
held engrossed 530.18
  fixed 142.16
  obsessed 473.33
  possessed 808.8
  reserved 660.15
  supported 216.24
  unused 668.12
held up 132.16
Helen of Troy 900.9
helical circuitous 321.7
  spiral 254.8
helicopter 280.5,15
Helios god 1014.5
  sun god 375.14
heliport airport 278.22
  platform 216.13
helix 254.2
hell bedlam 62.5
  depths 209.3
  gambling house
    515.15
  hot place 328.11
  nether world 1019
  place of confinement
    761.7
  torment 866.7
hell-bent
  determined 624.16
  fast 269.21
hellcat evildoer 943.3

reckless person 894.4
violent person 162.9
witch 943.7
hellhole 981.7
hellion evildoer 943.4
  evil spirit 1016.7
  violent person 162.9
hellish atrocious 675.10
  cruel 939.24
  devilish 1016.18
  infernal 1019.8
  violent 162.17
  wicked 981.13
hello
  *n.* greeting 925.4
  *interj.* attention!
    530.23
  greetings! 925.15
  wonder 920.20
hell-raiser
  evildoer 943.3
  violent person 162.9
hell's kitchen 183.6
hell to pay 731.4
helm
  *n.* control 741.2
  management 747.5
  seat of authority
    739.10
  types of 277.33
  *v.* pilot 275.14
helmet
  heraldic insignia
    569.2
  safety equipment
    699.3
helmsman
  boatman 276.8
  pilot 748.7
helot slave 764.7
  sycophant 907.3
help
  *n.* aid 785.1
  assistant 787.6
  benefactor 942.1
  remedy 687.1
  servant 750.2
  serving 307.10
  staff 750.11
  subsidy 818.8
  *v.* aid 785.11
  do a favor 938.12
  do good 674.10
  facilitate 732.6
  prevent 730.14
  serve 750.13
  subsidize 818.19
helper assistant 785.7
  benefactor 942.1
  second 787.6
  subordinate 764.5
helpful
  beneficial 674.12
  considerate 938.16
  instrumental 658.6
  serving 785.21
  useful 665.18
helping
  *n.* food 307.10
  portion 816.5
  *adj.* assisting 785.20
  serving 750.14

helping hand
  assist 785.2
  benefactor 942.1
helpless
  defenseless 158.18
  drunk 996.33
  forlorn 924.11
  unprotected 697.14
helpmate
  assistant 787.6
  wife 933.9
helter-skelter
  *n.* commotion 62.4
  haste 709.1
  jumble 62.3
  *adj.* confused 62.16
  *adv.* carelessly 534.18
  hastily 709.12
  in disorder 62.17
  nonuniformly 18.4
  recklessly 894.11
hem
  *n.* border 235.4
  edging 235.7
  *v.* border 235.10
  enclose 236.7
  restrain 760.9
  stammer 595.8
hem– 388.4
he-man 420.6
hem and haw
  be irresolute 627.7
  dodge 631.8
  prevaricate 613.7
  stammer 595.8
hem in confine 761.12
  enclose 236.5
  restrain 760.9
hemisphere half 92.2
  region 180.2
hemispheric(al) 255.9
hemlock
  capital punishment
    1010.7
  poisonous plant
    676.7
hemmed in
  enclosed 236.10
  restrained 760.15
hemoglobin
  blood 388.4
  protein 309.23
hemophilia
  blood disease 686.18
  genetic disease
    686.11
hemorrhage
  *n.* bleeding 311.8
  disease symptom
    686.8
  *v.* bleed 311.17
hemorrhaging 311.23
hemorrhoid
  cardiovascular diseas
    686.17
  sore 686.35
hemp
  marihuana 687.13,5
  noose 1011.5
hen
  female animal 421.9
  poultry 414.34

woman 421.6
**hence** away 301.21
  therefore 155.7
**henceforth** 121.10
**henchman**
  follower 293.2
  hanger-on 907.5
  lackey 787.8
  political henchman
  746.8
**henna** 367.4,7
**henpeck**
  domineer 741.16
  nag 969.16
**henpecked**
  downtrodden 764.16
  obedient 766.5
**hep** 475.16,17
**hepatitis**
  infectious disease
  686.12
  inflammation 686.9
  liver disease 686.21
**Hephaestus** god 1014.5
  smith 718.7
**hept(a)–** 99.19
**her** female 421.4
  self 80.5
**Hera** goddess 1014.5
  marriage goddess
  933.14
**herald**
  *n.* delegate 781.2
  harbinger 544.5
  heraldic official
  749.21
  messenger 561.2
  precursor 66.1
  spokesman 781.5
  *v.* forerun 116.3
  introduce 66.3
  presage 544.14
  proclaim 559.13
**heraldry** insignia 569.1
  pomp 904.6
**herb** medicine 687.4
  plant 411.4,47
**herbaceous** 411.33
**herbarium** 413.10
**herbicide** killer 409.3
  poison 676.3
**herbivore** animal 414.3
  vegetarian 307.14
**herbivorous** 307.29
**Herculean**
  difficult 731.16
  huge 195.20
  laborious 716.18
  strong 159.15
**Hercules** giant 195.26
  strong man 159.6
  supporter 216.3
**herd**
  *n.* flock 74.5
  guider 904.6
  *v.* direct 747.9
  drive animals 416.8
**herder** 416.3
**herdsman** guider 748.7
  herder 416.3
**herd together**
  be sociable 922.16

come together 74.16
  confederate 73.7
**here**
  in this place 184.22
  now 120.3
  present 186.16
**hereafter** future 121.8
  in future 121.10
**hereafter, the**
  heaven 1018.3
  the future 121.2
**here and there**
  discontinuously 72.5
  in places 184.24
  scatteringly 75.12
  sparsely 102.8
**hereby** 658.7
**hereditary**
  genetic 406.20
  innate 5.7
  patrimonial 170.15
**heredity** gene 406.9
  heritage 170.6
**heresy** error 518.1
  inconsistency 27.2
  nonconformity 83.2
  unbelief 503.1
  unorthodoxy 1025.2
**heretic**
  misbeliever 1025.5
  nonconformist 83.3
**heretical**
  disagreeing 27.9
  erroneous 518.16
  nonconformist 83.6
  unbelieving 503.8
  unorthodox 1025.9
**heretofore**
  formerly 119.13
  previously 116.6
  until now 120.4
**herewith**
  by means of 658.7
  together 73.10
**heritage** heredity 170.6
  inheritance 819.2
**hermaphrodite**
  *n.* intersex 419.19
  *adj.* intersexual 419.33
**Hermes** god 1014.5
  god of trade 827.12
  messenger 561.1
**hermetic(al)**
  resistant 159.18
  sealed 266.12
  secret 614.11
**hermit** ascetic 991.2
  odd person 85.4
  recluse 924.5
  religious 1038.17
**hermitage** 700.5
**hero**
  brave person 893.8
  famous person 914.9
  god 1014.3
  good person 985.5
  ideal 25.4
  lead 612.6
  role 611.11
  victor 726.2
**heroic**
  courageous 893.17

eminent 34.9
  huge 195.20
  legendary 123.12
  magnanimous 979.6
  poetic 609.17
  vocal 462.51
**heroically**
  courageously 893.22
  pluckily 624.18
**heroics** boasting 910.1
  rashness 894.1
**heroin** 687.12,54
**heroine**
  brave person 893.8
  famous person 914.9
  goddess 1014.3
  good person 985.5
  lead 612.6
  role 611.11
**heroism** courage 893.1
  eminence 34.2
  magnanimity 979.2
**hero worship**
  idolatry 1033.1
  love 931.1
  praise 968.5
  respect 964.1
**hero-worship**
  praise 968.12
  respect 964.4
**herpes**
  infectious disease
  686.12
  skin disease 686.33
**herpetology** 415.1
**hesitant** cautious 895.8
  irresolute 627.11
  uncertain 514.15
  unwilling 623.7
**hesitate**
  be irresolute 627.7
  be unsure 514.10
  demur 623.4
  pause 144.9
  procrastinate 132.11
  stammer 595.8
**hesitating**
  irresolute 627.11
  stammering 595.13
  uncertain 514.15
  unwilling 623.7
**hesitation**
  caution 895.1
  demur 623.2
  irresolution 627.3
  pause 144.3
  procrastination 132.5
  stammering 595.3
  uncertainty 514.1
**heter(o)–** different 16.7
  dissimilar 21.4
  multiform 19.3
  nonuniform 18.3
**heterodox**
  disagreeing 27.9
  erroneous 518.16
  nonconformist 83.6
  unorthodox 1025.9
**heterogeneous**
  different 16.7
  diversified 19.4
  mixed 44.15

**heteronomous** 741.17
**heterosexual**
  *n.* straight 419.15
  *adj.* sexual 419.26
**heuristic**
  experimental 489.11
  investigating 485.36
**hew** fell 318.5
  form 246.7
  sever 49.11
**hex**
  *n.* bad influence 675.4
  curse 972.1
  spell 1036.1
  witch 1035.8
  *v.* bewitch 1036.9
  bring bad luck 729.12
  curse 972.5
  harm 675.6
**hexa–** 99.18
**hey!** attention! 530.23
  greetings! 925.15
  wonder 920.20
**heyday** 728.4
**H hour**
  attack time 798.14
  crucial moment
  129.5
**hiatus**
  discontinuity 72.2
  gap 57.2
  interval 201.1
  opening 265.1
**hibernal** cold 333.14
  winter 128.8
**hibernate**
  be idle 708.15
  be latent 546.3
  sleep 712.15
  stagnate 706.2
**hibernation**
  inactivity 708.1
  sleep 712.2
**hiccup**
  *n.* belch 310.9
  breathing 403.18
  *v.* belch 310.26
  inhale spasmodically
  403.24
**hick**
  *n.* bungler 734.9
  oaf 471.5
  rustic 919.9
  unsophisticate 736.3
  *adj.* countrified 182.7
**hickey** blemish 679.1
  object 376.4
**hick town** 183.3
**hidden**
  concealed 615.11
  latent 546.5
  recondite 549.16
  secluded 924.8
  secret 614.11
  unseen 445.5
**hide**
  *n.* pelt 229.1,8
  *v.* conceal 615.6
  defeat 727.6
  disappear 447.2
  hide oneself 615.8
  punish 1010.15

store up 660.11
**hideaway**
hiding place 615.4
retreat 700.5
**hidebound**
narrow-minded
527.10
orthodox 1024.8
prudish 903.19
strict 757.7
**hideous**
offensive 864.19
terrible 891.38
ugly 899.11
**hideously** uglily 899.13
unpleasantly 864.27
**hideout**
hiding place 615.4
retreat 700.5
**hiding**
*n.* concealment 615.1
covering 228.1
defeat 727.1
hiding place 615.4
punishment 1010.5
*adj.* concealing 615.15
**hiding place**
concealment 615.4
retreat 700.5
**hie** go to 273.24
hasten 709.4
rush 269.9
travel 273.17
urge on 648.16
**hiemal** cold 333.14
winter 128.8
**hierarchic(al)**
classified 61.8
gradational 29.5
ministerial 1037.16
**hierarchy**
class structure 61.4
government 741.4
mastership 739.7
order 59.2
priesthood 1037.7
rank 29.2
the rulers 749.15
**hieroglyphic**
character 581.2
representation 572.1
**hi-fi**
*n.* sound reproduction
system 450.11
*adj.* audible 450.16
**higgledy-piggledy**
confused 62.16
in disorder 62.17
nonuniformly 18.4
**high**
*n.* excitement 857.1
gear 348.6
intoxication 996.1
secondary school
567.6
stock price 834.9
stupor 712.6
weather 402.5
*adj.* cheerful 870.11
drunk 996.31
eminent 34.9
excessive 663.16

excited 857.18
expensive 848.11
famous 914.18
high-pitched 458.13
lofty 207.19
magnanimous 979.6
malodorous 437.5
noble 918.10
overjoyed 865.14
phonetic 594.31
proud 905.11
pungent 433.8
raised 317.9
tainted 692.42
unsavory 429.7
*adv.* aloft 207.26
intemperately 993.10
**high and dry**
aground 142.16
dry 393.7
in difficulty 731.25
in safety 698.6
**high and mighty**
arrogant 912.11
eminent 914.18
**highball**
*n.* alcoholic drink
996.8,42
*v.* speed 269.8
**highborn** 918.11
**highbrow**
*n.* intellectual 476.1
snob 912.7
*adj.* learned 475.23
**high camp**
comedy 611.6
vulgarity 898.1
**High Church** 1020.10
**High-Church** 1040.22
**high-class** 674.14
**higher** loftier 207.24
superior 36.12
**higher-up** superior 36.4
the rulers 749.15
**highest**
*n.* supremacy 36.3
*adj.* godlike 1013.20
high 207.24
most important
672.23
superlative 36.13
top 211.10
**highfalutin**
arrogant 912.9
boastful 910.11
grandiloquent 601.8
ostentatious 904.18
proud 905.11
**high-fidelity** 450.16
**high-fidelity system**
450.11
**high finance** 836.1
**high-flown**
arrogant 912.9
boastful 910.11
exaggerated 617.4
foolish 470.10
grandiloquent 601.8
ostentatious 904.18
proud 905.11
**high-flying**
ambitious 634.28

grandiloquent 601.8
ostentatious 904.18
**high-grade** 674.14
**high-handed** 739.16
**high-handedly**
by force 157.17
imperiously 739.19
**high-hat**
*v.* snub 966.5
*adj.* snobbish 912.14
**High Holy Days**
1040.16
**high horse** 912.1
**high jinks** 878.4
**highlands**
the country 182.1
upland 207.3
**high life** nobility 918.2
society 644.6
**highlight**
*n.* contrast 335.19
light 335.1
salient point 672.7
*v.* emphasize 672.13
flaunt 555.5
illuminate 335.28
indicate 568.17
**high liver**
gourmet 307.14
intemperate person
993.3
**high living** 993.2
**highly** 34.15
**high-minded**
honest 974.13
magnanimous 979.6
proud 905.11
**high-muck-a-muck**
672.9
**Highness** 917.2
**high noon** noon 133.5
summit 211.2
**high on the hog**
intemperately 993.10
prosperous 728.12
**high-pitched**
high 207.19
strident 458.13
**high-powered**
important 672.16
powerful 157.12
**high-priced** 848.11
**high-principled** 974.13
**highroad** facility 732.1
road 657.6
**high school** 567.6
**high seas** 397.1
**high sign** signal 568.15
warning sign 703.3
**high society**
nobility 918.2
society 644.6
**high-society** 644.16
**high-sounding**
grandiloquent 601.8
high-pitched 458.13
**high-speed** 269.20
**high-spirited**
excitable 857.26
mischievous 738.6
**high spirits**
good humor 870.2

happiness 865.2
mischief 738.2
**high-strung**
excitable 857.26
irascible 951.20
nervous 859.10
**hightail** depart 301.13
run 269.10
**high-test** 380.4
**high tide** fullness 56.2
high water 207.13
tide 395.13
**high time** fun 878.2
good opportunity
129.3
lateness 132.1
**high-water mark**
boundary 235.3
measurement 490.7
**highway** 657.6
**highwayman** 825.5
**highway robbery**
overcharge 848.5
theft 824.3
**hijack** coerce 756.7
rob 824.14
**hijacker** 825.5
**hijacking** 824.3
**hike**
*n.* increase 38.1
walk 273.12
*v.* elevate 317.5
increase 38.4
make larger 197.4
march 273.29
**hiker** 274.6
**hiking** expansion 197.1
walking 273.10
**hilarious** festive 878.30
humorous 880.4
merry 870.15
**hilarity**
humorousness 880.1
laughter 876.4
merriment 870.5
**hill**
*n.* bulge 256.3
down 207.5
pile 74.10
*v.* pile 74.19
**hillbilly**
backwoodsman
190.10
rustic 919.9
**hillock** 207.5
**hillocky** 256.14
**hill of beans** 673.5
**hilltop** 207.8
**hilly** 207.23
**him** male 420.4
self 80.5
**hind**
*n.* female animal
421.9
hoofed animal 414.5
peasant 919.8
*adj.* rear 241.9
**hind end**
buttocks 241.4
rear 241.1
**hinder** delay 132.8
fend off 799.10

obstruct 730.10
restrain 760.7
**hindmost** 241.9
**hindquarter** 241.3
**hindrance** delay 132.2
obstruction 730
restraint 760.1
**hindsight** 537.4
**Hindu deities** 1014.8
**hinge**
n. axis 322.5
joint 47.4
turning point 129.4
v. be contingent 507.6
depend on 154.6
fasten 47.8
**hint**
n. admixture 44.7
clue 568.9
implication 546.2
indication 568.1
intimation 557.4
reminder 537.6
small amount 35.4
taste 427.3
vague supposition
499.5
warning 703.1
v. augur 544.12
imply 546.4
indicate 568.17
intimate 557.10
promise 544.13
**hinterland**
back country 182.2
inland 225.3
region 180.1
setting 233.2
**hip**
n. buttock 241.4
joint 47.4
side 242.1
adj. fashionable
644.11
knowing 475.17
**hipped on**
enthusiastic about
635.12
fond of 931.28
**hippie**
n. nonconformist 83.3
adj. nonconformist
83.6
**hippo**
corpulent person
195.12
large animal 195.14
pachyderm 414.4
**Hippocrates** 688.15
**hippodrome** 802.1
**hippopotamus**
large animal 195.14
pachyderm 414.4,58
**hippy** 195.18
**hire**
n. earnings 841.4
fee 846.7
rental 780.5
v. employ 780.13
lease 780.14
rent out 780.15
**hired** employed 780.19

paid 841.22
**hired applauder** 611.32
**hired help** 750.11
**hired killer** 800.16
**hireling**
employee 750.3
mercenary 800.16
**hire purchase**
borrowing 821.1
payment 841.1
purchase 828.1
**hirsute** feathery 230.27
hairy 230.24
rough 261.9
**his nibs** 672.9
**hiss**
n. boo 967.3
sibilation 457.1
speech defect 595.1
v. animal sound 460.4
boo 967.10
bubble 405.4
sibilate 457.2
utter 594.26
**hissing**
n. audio distortion
450.13
boo 967.3
ridicule 967.1
sibilation 457.1
adj. ridiculing 967.12
sibilant 457.3
**histology** 245.7
**historian**
chronicler 608.11
recorder 571.2
**historical**
certain 513.15
descriptive 608.18
real 1.15
true 516.12
**historically**
formerly 119.13
truly 516.17
**historical records** 570.2
**historicity** reality 1.2
truth 516.1
**history** chronicle 608.4
record 570.1
the past 119.1
**histrionic**
affected 903.15
emotionalistic 855.20
ostentatious 904.24
theatrical 611.38
**histrionics**
display 904.4
dramatics 611.2
emotionalism 855.9
**hit**
n. blow 283.4
disapproval 969.4
drug dose 687.6
great success 724.3
narcotic injection
689.18
popular music 462.8
score 724.4
stage show 611.4
v. affect emotionally
855.17
agree 26.6

arrive 300.6
attack 798.15
beg 774.15
collide 283.12
contact 200.10
criticize 969.14
discover 488.2
impress 478.19
kill 409.14
lash out 798.16
shoot 285.13
strike 283.13
travel 273.18
**hit a nerve** 284.8
**hit back at** 955.4
**hit below the belt**
n. unfairness 977.2
v. be unjust 977.6
**hit bottom** 692.20
**hitch**
n. difficulty 731.7
gait 273.14
jerk 286.3
obstacle 730.4
pain 424.2
term 108.4
v. drive animals 416.7
fasten 47.8
hitchhike 273.30
jerk 286.5
join in marriage
933.15
walk 273.27
**hitchhike** 273.30
**hitchhiker** 274.6
**hither** 184.22
**hitherto**
formerly 119.13
previously 116.6
**hit it**
score a success 724.8
solve 487.2
**hit it off**
be friends 927.9
get along with 794.2
**hit man** 409.11
**hit-or-miss**
experimental 489.11
random 62.12
slipshod 534.12
uncertain 514.18
**hit or miss**
carelessly 534.18
experimentally
489.13
haphazardly 62.18
**hit the ceiling**
become angry 952.19
get excited 857.15
**hit the hay** 712.18
**hit the high spots**
abridge 607.5
browse 564.13
examine cursorily
485.25
neglect 534.8
scratch the surface
210.4
**hit the nail on the head**
be right 516.9
solve 487.2

**hit the road**
depart 301.9
wander 273.22
**hit the sack** 712.18
**hit the spot** 865.5
**hit up** beg 774.15
borrow 821.3
**hit upon**
arrive at 300.7
find 488.3
light on 316.10
**hive**
n. apiary 191.25
bees 74.6
large number 101.3
workplace 719.2
v. come together
74.16
settle 184.16
**hives**
allergic disorder
686.32
skin disease 686.33
skin eruption 686.34
**hoagy** 308.32
**hoar**
n. frost 333.7
adj. aged 126.16
white 364.7
**hoard**
n. gain 811.3
store 660.1
v. store up 660.11
**hoarding** poster 559.7
stinginess 852.3
**hoarfrost** 333.7
**hoarse**
imperfectly spoken
595.12
raucous 458.15
**hoary** aged 126.16
frosty 333.16
gray-haired 366.5
traditional 123.12
venerable 123.10
white 364.7
**hoax**
n. deception 618.7
fake 616.13
v. deceive 618.13
**hoaxer** 619.1
**hob** evil spirit 1016.9
fairy 1014.18
fireplace 329.11
shelf 216.14
**hobble**
n. gait 273.14
predicament 731.4
slowness 270.2
v. cripple 692.17
go slow 270.6
hamper 730.11
render powerless
158.11
restrain 760.10
walk 273.27
**hobby** 656.7
**hobbyhorse**
avocation 656.7
plaything 878.16
**hobbyist** 635.5

**hobgoblin**
  evil spirit 1016.9
  frightener 891.9
**hobnob with**
  be friends 927.9
  be sociable 922.16
**hobo** bad person 986.2
  beggar 774.8
  bum 708.9
  odd person 85.4
  vagabond 274.3
**hobo jungle** 191.29
**Hobson's choice**
  certainty 513.1
  choice 637.3
  choicelessness 639.6
**hock**
  *n.* leg 273.16
  pledge 772.2
  *v.* pledge 772.10
**hocking** 821.1
**hock shop** 820.4
**hocus-pocus**
  juggling 618.5
  nonsense 547.2
  occultism 1034.1
  spell 1036.4
  trick 618.6
**hodgepodge**
  conglomeration 44.6
  jumble 62.3
  miscellany 74.13
**Hodgkin's disease**
  686.18
**hoe** 413.17
**hoecake** 308.29
**hog**
  *n.* filthy person
  682.13
  glutton 994.3
  selfish person 978.3
  swine 414.9
  *v.* appropriate 822.19
  monopolize 808.6
**hogan** 191.11
**hogback** 207.6
**hog for, a** 634.27
**hogger** 274.12
**hoggish** filthy 682.24
  gluttonous 994.6
  greedy 634.27
  monopolistic 808.11
  ungulate 414.49
**hog-tie**
  render powerless
  158.11
  restrain 760.10
**hog-tied** 158.16
**hog wallow**
  marsh 400.1
  mud puddle 389.9
**hogwash**
  humbug 616.14
  nonsense 547.3
  refuse 669.4
**hog-wild** 857.23
**ho-ho**
  *n.* laughter 876.4
  *v.* laugh 876.8
**ho-hum** 883.6
**ho, hum!** 884.14
**hoi polloi** inferior 37.2

  masses 919.3
  the people 919.2
**hoist**
  *n.* lifter 317.3
  raise 317.2
  *v.* elevate 317.5
**hoity-toity**
  *n.* arrogance 912.1
  *adj.* arrogant 912.9
**hoke** acting 611.9
  humbug 616.14
**hoke up**
  fabricate 616.18
  imitate 22.5
**hokey** 22.8
**hokum** acting 611.9
  humbug 616.14
  nonsense 547.3
**hold**
  *n.* cellar 192.17
  compartment 192.2
  control 741.2
  custody 761.5
  grasp 813.2
  handle 216.11
  harmonics 463.12
  influence 172.1
  possession 808.1
  purchase 287.2
  seizure 822.2
  storage place 660.6
  stronghold 799.6
  support 216.5
  *v.* affirm 523.4
  believe 501.11
  be true 516.7
  cease 144.6
  cohere 50.6
  confine 761.12
  endure 110.6
  engross 530.13
  exist 1.8
  extend 179.7
  harbor 813.7
  include 76.3
  judge 494.8
  not do 706.3
  obsess 473.24
  possess 808.4
  remain 140.5
  restrain 760.7
  retain 813.6
  stabilize 142.7
  store up 660.11
  suffice 661.4
  support 216.21
  sustain 143.4
  *interj.* cease! 144.14
**hold a candle to** 491.7
**hold against** 1005.8
**holdback** curb 730.7
  hindrance 730.1
**hold back**
  abstain 992.7
  be stingy 852.6
  be temperate 992.6
  delay 132.8
  hinder 730.10
  not use 668.5
  refuse 776.4
  reserve 660.12
  restrain 760.7

  slow 270.9
**hold by** 768.2
**hold cheap** 966.3
**hold dear** 931.19
**hold down**
  keep subject 764.8
  suppress 760.8
**holder** container 193.1
  light 336.11
  possessor 809.1
  recipient 819.3
**hold everything**
  cease! 144.14
  wait 132.12
**hold fast** cohere 50.8
  hold 813.6
  persevere 625.4
  remain firm 624.9
  restrain 760.7
  stand fast 142.11
**hold forth**
  declaim 599.10
  lecture 562.17
  monologize 598.3
  offer 773.4
**hold good**
  be proved 505.11
  be reasonable 482.17
  be true 516.7
**hold in contempt**
  be insolent 913.6
  deprecate 969.12
  disdain 966.3
  disparage 971.8
**holding**
  *n.* estate 810.4
  possession 808.1
  retention 813.1
  shares 834.3
  *adj.* engrossing 530.20
  obsessive 473.34
  possessing 808.9
  retentive 813.8
  supporting 216.23
**holding company**
  company 788.9
  trust 833.16
**holdings**
  collection 74.11
  property 810.1
  resources 660.2
  shares 834.3
**hold it!** 144.14
**hold off** demur 623.4
  fend off 799.10
  not use 668.5
  postpone 132.9
  procrastinate 132.11
  repulse 289.3
**hold office**
  function 108.5
  hold a post 744.42
  work 656.14
**hold on**
  *v.* cohere 50.6
  continue 143.3
  direct 290.6
  endure 110.6
  hold 813.6
  persevere 625.4
  speculate in stocks
  833.23

  wait 132.12
  *interj.* cease! 144.14
**hold one's breath**
  await 539.8
  be still 268.7
  wait 132.12
  wonder 920.5
**hold one's ground**
  be obstinate 626.7
  remain firm 624.9
  resist 792.4
  retain 813.5
  stand fast 142.11
**hold one's tongue**
  be silent 451.5
  be uncommunicative
  613.6
  beware 895.7
  keep secret 614.7
**holdout** 789.4
**hold out**
  be obstinate 626.7
  endure 110.6
  not weaken 159.9
  offer 773.4
  persevere 625.4
  refuse 776.3
  remain firm 624.9
  remain stable 142.11
  resist 792.2
  stand fast 792.4
  strike 789.9
**hold out on**
  be stingy 852.6
  keep secret 614.7
**holdover**
  officeholder 746.11
  remainder 43.1
**hold over** 132.9
**hold together**
  agree 26.6
  be joined 47.11
  be true 516.7
  cohere 50.6
  cooperate 786.3
**hold true** 516.7
**holdup**
  automation 349.11
  delay 132.2
  hindrance 730.1
  overcharge 848.5
  slowing 270.4
  theft 824.3
**hold up** aid 785.12
  be true 516.7
  buoy up 353.8
  delay 132.8
  elevate 317.5
  flaunt 904.17
  hinder 730.10
  not weaken 159.9
  overcharge 848.7
  persevere 625.4
  postpone 132.9
  resist 792.2
  restrain 760.7
  rob 824.14
  slow 270.9
  stand fast 142.11
  stand the test 489.1
  support 216.21
**holdup man** 825.5

**hold water**
be proved 505.11
be reasonable 482.17
be true 516.7
**hold with**
approve 968.9
assent 521.8
consent 775.2
**hold your horses** 132.12
**hole**
*n.* aviation 278.41
cave 257.5
cavity 257.2
cellar 192.17
crack 201.2
disapproved place 191.28
fault 678.2
filthy place 682.11
hiding place 615.4
hovel 191.12
impasse 731.5
lair 191.26
location 184.1
opening 265.1
pit 209.2
place of vice 981.7
room 192.2
score 724.4
small place 196.3
*v.* puncture 265.16
**hole in one** 724.4
**hole in the wall**
nook 192.3
small place 196.3
**hole up** 615.8
**holey**
perforated 265.20
shabby 692.34
**holiday**
*n.* absence 187.4
celebration 877.1
day off 711.4
interim 109.1
pause 144.3
vacation 711.3
word list 137.12
*v.* vacation 711.9
*adj.* vacational 711.10
**holier-than-thou**
hypocritic(al) 616.33
sanctimonious 1029.5
**holiness**
divine attribute 1013.15
piety 1028.2
sanctity 1026.1
**holism** 54.5
**holistic** 54.9
**holler**
*n.* complaint 875.4
cry 459.1
*v.* complain 875.13
cry 459.6
object 522.5
**hollow**
*n.* cavity 257.2
compartment 192.2
opening 265.1
pit 209.2
*v.* be concave 257.12
make concave 257.13

*adj.* concave 257.16
deep-pitched 454.10
insincere 616.32
specious 483.10
stupid 469.19
uninteresting 883.6
vacant 187.13
vain 669.13
**hollow-eyed**
tired-looking 717.7
wasted 205.20
**hollow man**
affecter 903.7
nonentity 4.2
**hollow mockery** 616.5
**hollow ware**
hard goods 831.4
tableware 348.3
**holocaust**
carnage 409.5
destruction 693.1
sacrifice 1032.7
torment 866.7
**hologram** 577.5
**holograph**
document 570.5
original 23.3
written matter 602.10
**holographic(al)** 602.22
**holus-bolus** 894.11
**holy** godlike 1013.20
pious 1028.9
sacred 1026.7
**Holy Bible** 1021.2
**Holy Communion** 1040.8
**holy day** holiday 711.4
religious 1040.14
**Holy Father**
God 1013.11
pope 1038.9
**Holy Ghost**
functions of 1013.18
God the Holy Ghost 1013.14
**Holy Grail** 1040.11
**holy mackerel!** 920.19
**holy man** 985.6
**holy of holies**
retreat 700.5
sanctuary 1042.5
study 192.8
the sacred 1026.2
**holy orders**
consecration 1037.10
major orders 1038.4
sacrament 1040.5
the ministry 1037.1
**holy place** 1042.4
**Holy Sacrament, the** 1040.8
**holy smoke!** 920.19
**Holy Spirit, the** 1013.14
**holystone**
*n.* cleaning agent 681.17,32
*v.* wash 681.19
**holy terror**
bad child 125.4
evildoer 943.4
frightener 891.9

violent person 162.9
**Holy Trinity** 1013.10
**holy war**
military campaign 797.7
war 797.3
**homage** duty 962.1
fidelity 974.7
obedience 766.1
praise 968.5
respect 964.1
reverence 964.2
submission 765.1
worship 1032.1
**hombre** 420.4
**home**
*n.* abode 191.4
asylum 700.4
grave 121.2
habitat 191.5
infirmary 689.27
native land 181.2
*adj.* household 191.32
**homebody** 924.5
**home brew** 996.17
**homecoming** 300.3
**home economics**
cooking 330.1
domestic management 747.6
**home free** 698.6
**home furnishings** 831.5
**homeground** 181.2
**homegrown** 189.5
**home guard** 800.23
**home in on**
pinpoint 184.10
use radar 346.17
**homeland** 181.2
**homeless** alone 89.8
destitute 838.9
displaced 185.10
forlorn 924.11
**homelike**
comfortable 887.11
habitable 188.15
homey 191.33
**homely**
comfortable 887.11
common 919.11
homelike 191.33
humble 906.9
informal 647.3
in plain style 591.3
simple 902.6
stark 45.6
ugly 899.6
vulgar 898.14
**homemade** 167.22
**homemaker** 749.2
**homemaking**
domestic management 747.6
housekeeping 191.2
**homeostasis** 142.1
**homer**
message carrier 561.6
score 724.4
**Homeric** huge 195.20
poetic 609.17
**home rule**
government 741.4

independence 762.5
**home run** 724.4
**homesick** 634.23
**homesickness** 634.5
**homespun**
in plain style 591.3
made 167.22
natural 736.6
ordinary 902.6
rough 261.6
simple 45.6
vulgar 898.14
**homestead** farm 413.8
home 191.4
house and grounds 191.7
**homesteader**
settler 190.9
tenant 809.4
**homestretch** 70.3
**home towner** 190.5
**homeward**
*adj.* arriving 300.9
*adv.* toward 290.26
**homeward bound**
arriving 300.9
under way 275.63
**homework** lesson 562.7
task 656.2
**homey**
comfortable 887.11
homelike 191.33
informal 647.3
**homicidal** 409.24
**homicide** killer 409.11
killing 409.3
manslaughter 409.2
**homily** lecture 599.3
lesson 562.7
treatise 606.1
**homing pigeon**
bearer 271.5
message carrier 561.6
**hominid**
mankind 417.1
prehistoric man 123.7
**hominy grits** 308.34
**hommage** 968.5
**homme** 420.4
**homo**
homosexual 419.16
mankind 417.1
person 417.3
**homo–** identical 14.8
similar 20.10
uniform 17.5
**homoerotic** 419.32
**homogeneity**
identity 14.1
simplicity 45.1
uniformity 17.1
**homogeneous**
similar 20.10
simple 45.6
uniform 17.5
**homogenize**
make uniform 17.4
mix 44.11
**homogenizer** 44.10
**homologous**
approximate 9.8
reciprocal 13.13

homology 9.1
homonym
  the same 14.3
  word 582.1
Homo sapiens 417.1
homosexual
  *n.* homosexualist
  419.16
  *adj.* sexual 419.32
homosexuality 419.12
homunculus 196.6
honcho 672.10
hone 258.9
honest genuine 516.14
  unaffected 902.7
  upright 974.13
  virtuous 980.7
honestly
  genuinely 516.18
  uprightly 974.21
honest man
  good person 985.1
  honest person 974.8
honest-to-God
  genuine 516.14
  real 1.15
honesty
  authenticity 516.5
  probity 974.1
honey
  *n.* confection 308.39
  endearment 932.5
  good thing 674.7
  sweetener 431.2
  sweetheart 931.10
  *v.* flatter 970.6
  sweeten 431.3
honeycomb
  *n.* honey 431.2
  indentation 257.6
  porousness 265.9
  *v.* overthrow 693.20
  pervade 186.7
  puncture 265.16
  undermine 692.18
honeycombed
  holey 265.20
  indented 257.17
  permeated 186.15
honeyed
  flattering 970.8
  melodious 462.49
  pleasant 863.6
  sweet 431.4
honeymoon
  *n.* marriage 933.4
  *v.* go on a honeymoon
  933.17
honk
  *n.* loud sound 453.4
  *v.* bird sound 460.5
  blare 453.9
honky 418.3
honky-tonk 996.19
honor
  *n.* attribution 155.1
  chastity 988.1
  esteem 914.3
  examination 485.2
  honesty 974.1
  notability 672.2
  praise 968.5

real estate 810.7
  respect 964.1
  title 917.1
  token of esteem 916
  *v.* celebrate 877.2
  do honor 916.8
  esteem 914.12
  execute 771.10
  pay in full 841.13
  respect 964.4
  worship 1032.10
honorable
  honest 974.13
  honorary 916.10
  reputable 914.15
  venerable 964.12
honorable mention
  commendation 968.3
  honor 916.4
honorably
  honestly 974.21
  reputably 914.20
honorarium
  gratuity 818.5
  recompense 841.3
honorary 916.10
honored
  distinguished 916.9
  famous 914.16
  reputable 914.15
  respected 964.11
honorific
  *n.* name 583.3
  title 917.1
  *adj.* honorary 916.10
  nominal 583.15
  respectful 964.8
  titular 917.7
honor roll 88.6
hooch 996.13,17
hood
  *n.* bad person 986.6
  combatant 800.1
  cover 228.2
  hoodlum 943.4
  mischief-maker 738.3
  violent person 162.9
  *v.* clothe 231.39
  cover 228.19
  top 228.21
hooded clothed 231.44
  covered 228.31
hoodlum bandit 825.4
  combatant 800.1
  evildoer 943.4
  mischief-maker 738.3
  violent person 162.9
hoodoo
  *n.* bad influence 675.4
  charm 1036.5
  sorcery 1035.1
  *v.* bewitch 1036.9
  bring bad luck 729.12
hoodwink
  blindfold 441.7
  deceive 618.16
hoodwinked
  blinded 441.10
  mistaught 477.14
hooey humbug 616.14
  nonsense 547.3

hoof
  *n.* foot 212.5
  *v.* dance 879.5
  walk 273.26
hoof-and-mouth disease
  686.38
hoofbeat 273.13
hoofed footed 212.9
  ungulate 414.49
hoofer dancer 879.3
  entertainer 612.1
  pedestrian 274.6
hoofing dancing 879.1
  walking 273.10
hook
  *n.* anchor 277.16
  angle 251.2
  boxing 283.5
  curve 252.2
  grasping organs 813.4
  hanger 215.14
  lure 650.2
  point of land 256.8
  snare 618.12
  *v.* angle 251.5
  catch 822.17
  curve 252.6
  fasten 47.8
  persuade 648.23
  steal 824.13
  trap 618.18
hookah 434.6
hook-and-ladder 332.3
hooked angular 251.6
  curved 252.8
  habituated 642.19
  involved in 176.4
hooker
  prostitute 989.16
  ship 277.1,23
hook, line, and sinker
  54.13
hookup
  affiliation 786.2
  combination 52.1
  joining 47.1
  radio 344.8
hook up bind 47.10
  cooperate 786.3
  join 52.4
hookworm 686.12
hooky 187.4
hooligan
  bad person 986.6
  combatant 800.1
  hoodlum 943.4
  mischief-maker 738.3
  vulgar person 898.6
hoop 253.3
hoopla festivity 878.3
  publicity 559.4
  rejoicing 876.1
hooray
  *n.* cheer 876.2
  *v.* cheer 876.6
hoosegow 761.9
hoot
  *n.* boo 967.3
  cry 459.1
  trifle 673.5
  *v.* bird sound 460.5
  boo 967.10

cry 459.6
hootenanny
  music festival 462.33
  object 376.4
hop
  *n.* dance 879.2
  flight 278.9
  leap 319.1
  opium 687.12
  step 273.13
  *v.* dance 879.5
  fly 278.45
  leap 319.5
  run 269.10
  walk 273.27
hope
  *n.* belief 501.1
  expectation 539.2
  hopefulness 888
  possibility 509.1
  refuge 700.2
  thing desired 634.11
  virtue 980.5
  wish 634.1
  *v.* anticipate 121.6
  be hopeful 888.7
  expect 539.5
  wish for 634.16
hoped-for
  desired 634.29
  expected 539.13
  future 121.8
hopeful
  *n.* desirer 634.12
  optimist 888.6
  political candidate
  746.9
  youngster 125.1
  *adj.* cheerful 870.11
  expectant 539.11
  optimistic 888.11
  probable 511.6
hopefully
  cheerfully 870.17
  expectantly 539.15
  hopingly 888.14
  in the future 121.9
hopeless
  apathetic 856.13
  dying 408.33
  impossible 510.7
  unhopeful 889.12
hopeless case 889.8
hopelessly 889.17
hopelessness
  apathy 856.4
  impossibility 510.1
  no chance 156.10
  no hope 889
  sadness 872.3
hophead 642.10
hoping desirous 634.21
  hopeful 888.11
hopoff aviation 278.8
  departure 301.3
hop off 278.47
hopped-up
  excited 857.18
  impatient 862.6
hopper animal 414.39
  jumper 319.4
hop to it hurry 709.6

set to work 716.15
**horde**
*n.* the people 919.3
throng 74.4
*v.* come together
74.16
**horehound** 687.16
**horizon** distance 199.3
sky line 214.4
view 444.3
vision 439.1
**horizontal**
*n.* plane 214.3
*adj.* level 214.7
straight 250.6
**hormonal** 312.8
**hormone** drug 687.32
kinds of 312.10
secretion 312.2
**hormonology** 312.4
**horn**
*n.* alarm 704.1
brass wind 465.8
loudspeaker 450.8
noisemaker 453.5
saddle 216.18
wind instrument
465.7
*v.* attack 798.26
**hornbook** basics 68.6
elementary instruc-
tion 562.5
textbook 605.8
**horned**
horn-shaped 252.11
pointed 258.11
**hornet** 414.38
**hornet's nest**
hive 191.25
trouble 731.3
**hornify** 356.7
**horn in** 238.5
**horn of plenty** 661.3
**hornswaggle** 618.13
**horny** hard 356.10
lascivious 989.29
lustful 419.29
pointed 258.11
**horologic(al)** 114.15
**horology** 114.1
**horoscope** 375.20
**horrendous**
horrid 864.19
terrible 891.38
**horrible** bad 675.9
horrid 864.19
remarkable 34.11
terrible 891.38
ugly 899.11
**horribly** badly 675.14
frightfully 891.42
hideously 899.13
terribly 34.21
unpleasantly 864.27
**horrid** bad 675.9
horrible 864.19
terrible 891.38
ugly 899.11
**horridly** badly 675.14
frightfully 891.42
hideously 899.13
unpleasantly 864.27

**horrified** 891.34
**horrify** offend 864.11
terrify 891.25
**horrifying**
horrid 864.19
terrible 891.38
**horripilate**
be cold 333.9
frighten 891.23
roughen 261.4
**horripilation**
cold sensation 333.2
rough surface 261.2
trepidation 891.5
**horror** dislike 867.2
fear 891.1
frightener 891.9
torment 866.7
**horror-stricken** 891.34
**hors de combat**
defeated 727.14
out of action 158.17
**hors d'oeuvre** 308.9
**horse** animal 414.10
beast of burden 271.6
famous 414.19
breeds of 414.68
exercise device 716.7
heroin 687.12
mammal 414.58;
415.8
strength 159.7
trestle 216.16,30
**horse around**
be disorderly 62.11
be foolish 470.6
misbehave 738.4
play 878.25
trifle 673.13
**horseback**
*n.* ridge 207.6
*adv.* astride 216.25
on horseback 273.43
**horse blanket** 228.11
**horse doctor**
quack doctor 688.7
veterinary 688.11
**horsehair** hair 230.2
music 465.23
**horse latitudes**
calm 268.5
regions 180.3
wind zone 403.10
**horselaugh** 876.4
**horseless** 349.26
**horseman** 274.8
**horsemanship**
animal husbandry
416.1
riding 273.6
skill 733.1
**horse of a different
color** 16.3
**horse opera**
fiction 608.7
motion picture
611.16
**horseplay**
clownishness 881.5
misbehavior 738.1
**horsepower** 157.4

**horse racing**
game of chance 515.8
racing 796.11
**horse sense** 467.6
**horseshoe** 252.5
**horse trader**
cunning person 735.6
sharper 619.4
**horse trading** 827.2
**horsewhip**
*n.* whip 1011.1
*v.* punish 1010.14
**horsy** 414.49
**hortatory**
advisory 754.8
lecturing 562.19
persuasive 648.29
**horticultural**
agriculture 413.21
garden 411.35
**horticulture**
agriculture 413.2
flower gardening
411.22
**hosanna**
*n.* cheer 876.2
hymn 1032.3
*interj.* worship
1032.16
**hose**
*n.* hosiery 231.28
tube 396.6
*v.* moisten 392.12
**hosiery** hose 231.28
types of 231.61
**hospice** asylum 700.4
inn 191.16
**hospitable**
comforting 887.13
cordial 927.15
gracious 925.11
liberal 853.4
receptive 306.16
sociable 922.18
**hospital** 689.27
**hospitality**
comfortableness
887.2
cordiality 927.6
graciousness 925
housing 188.3
liberality 853.1
receptivity 306.9
sociability 922.1
**hospitalization** 689.15
**hospitalize** 686.47
**hospital room** 192.25
**host**
*n.* army 800.22
flock 74.5
large number 101.3
mine host 925.5
throng 74.4
*v.* entertain 925.8
**Host** Eucharist 1040.8
sacred article 1040.11
**hostage** 772.2
**hostel** 191.16
**hostess** attendant 750.5
aviation 279.4
host 925.5
waiter 750.7

**hostile** adverse 729.13
antagonistic 929.10
belligerent 797.25
contrary 15.6
counteractive 178.8
disagreeing 27.6
displeased 867.8
opposing 790.8
**hostilities** 797.1
**hostility**
antagonism 929.3
bad feeling 855.7
contention 796.1
contraposition 239.1
contrariety 15.1
dislike 867.2
opposition 790.2
warlikeness 797.15
**hostler** 416.2
**hot** angry 952.27
charged 342.31
detecting 488.10
enthusiastic about
635.12
excellent 674.13
excited 857.20
fervent 855.23
feverish 686.54
fiery 162.21
fugitive 631.16
heated 328.25
hot-tempered 951.25
in heat 419.30
lascivious 989.29
lustful 419.29
music 463.29
near 200.14
pungent 433.7
radioactive 327.10
red 368.6
stolen 824.22
warmed 329.29
zealous 635.10
**hot air** boasting 910.2
bombast 601.2
chatter 596.3
heat 328.9
nonsense 547.3
**hotbed**
birthplace 153.8
fertility 165.6
nursery 413.11
**hot blood**
hot temper 951.3
sexual desire 419.5
**hot-blooded**
lustful 419.29
warm-blooded 328.29
zealous 635.10
**hotbox** 322.6
**hot cake** 308.44
**hot dog**
*n.* sandwich 308.32
sausage 308.21
show-off 904.11
*v.* be ostentatious
904.16
*interj.* pleasure 865.17
**hotel** 191.16
**hotfoot**
*v.* hurry 709.6
run 269.10

*adv.* hastily 709.12
**hothead**
ill-humored person
951.11
violent person 162.9
**hotheaded**
fanatic 162.21
hot-tempered 951.25
passionate 857.27
reckless 894.8
**hothouse** 413.11
**hotly** excitedly 857.32
violently 34.23
**hot number** 419.4
**hot off the press** 122.10
**hot pants** 419.5
**hot seat**
capital punishment
1010.7
electric chair 1011.5
**hotshot** 904.11
**hot spring**
hot water 328.10
spa 689.29
**hot temper** 951.3
**hot-tempered** 951.25
**hot up** aggravate 885.2
heat 329.17
increase 38.5
**hot water** heat 328.10
predicament 731.4
**hot wave** 328.7
**hound**
*n.* bad person 986.7
dog 414.72
enthusiast 635.5
*v.* annoy 866.13
chase 655.8
follow 293.3
hunt 655.9
make anxious 890.4
persecute 667.6
urge on 648.16
**hounded**
tormented 866.24
worried 890.7
**hour** interval 107.1
period 107.2
time of day 114.2
**hourglass** 198.1
**houri**
beautiful woman
900.9
seductress 989.15
**hourly**
*adj.* regularly 137.8
*adv.* constantly 135.7
periodically 137.10
**house**
*n.* abode 191.6
ancestry 170.4
astrology 375.20
audience 448.6
building 245.2
clan 11.4
cloister 1042.6
company 788.9
family 11.5
market 832.1
ship room 192.9
theater 611.18
workplace 719.1

*v.* domicile 188.10
enclose 236.5
**houseboy** 750.4
**housebreak**
accustom 642.11
domesticate 764.11
train 562.14
**housebreaker** 825.3
**housebroken**
domesticated 191.34
subdued 764.15
weak 765.15
**housed** covered 228.31
domiciled 188.14
**household**
*n.* family 11.5
home 191.4
*adj.* home 191.32
simple 902.6
usual 84.8
well-known 475.27
**householder**
freeholder 190.7
proprietor 809.2
**household gods** 191.30;
1014.22
**household words** 591.1
**housekeep** 191.31
**housekeeper**
majordomo 750.10
manager 748.4
**housekeeping**
domesticity 191.2
domestic manage-
ment 747.6
**housemother** 749.2
**house of cards**
danger 697.1
fragility 360.2
weakness 160.7
**house of ill repute**
989.9
**house organ** 605.10
**housetop** 228.6
**house trailer**
mobile home 191.18
vehicle 272.18
**housewares** 831.4
**housewarming**
meeting 74.2
party 922.11
**housewife** 749.2
**housing**
*n.* aviation 278.24
cover 228.2,38
domiciliation 188.3
horsecloth 228.11
lodgings 191.3
radio receiver 344.3
*adj.* constructional
167.18
**hovel**
filthy place 682.11
house 191.12
**hover**
be imminent 152.2
be irresolute 627.7
fly 278.45
levitate 353.9
soar 315.10
stay near 200.12

**hovercraft**
aircraft 280.7
vehicle 272.21
**hovering** 278.59
**how** 657.11
**how about that!** 920.22
**how are you?** 925.15
**how come** 155.8
**how-do-you-do**
greeting 925.4
predicament 731.4
**howdy!** 925.16
**however**
anyhow 657.12
notwithstanding 33.8
**howl**
*n.* animal sound 460.1
complaint 875.4
cry 459.1
lament 875.3
noise 453.3
objection 522.2
shrill sound 458.4
*v.* animal sound 460.2
complain 875.13
cry 459.6
groan 875.11
object 522.5
sound shrill 458.8
wind sound 403.23
**howler** an error 518.6
joke 881.6
**howling**
*n.* animal sound 460.1
audio distortion
450.13
lamentation 875.1
*adj.* animal sound
460.6
excited 857.23
plaintive 875.16
remarkable 34.11
shrill 458.14
**how should I know?**
477.19
**hoyden** girl 125.6
mannish female
420.9
**HQ** 226.6
**hub** axle 322.5
center 226.2
convergence 298.1
fireplace 329.11
**hubbub** agitation 324.1
argumentation 482.4
bustle 707.4
commotion 62.4
noise 453.3
outcry 459.4
violence 162.2
**hubris** arrogance 912.2
insolence 913.1
presumption 961.2
rashness 894.1
sureness 513.5
**huckster**
*n.* publicist 559.9
vendor 830.6
*v.* bargain 827.17
vend 829.9
**huckstering**
exaggeration 617.1

selling 829.2
**huddle**
*n.* conference 597.6
*v.* come together
74.16
stay near 200.12
**hue**
*n.* color quality 362.6
nature 5.3
shade 362.1
*v.* color 362.13
**hue and cry**
alarm 704.1
noise 453.3
outcry 459.4
publicity 559.4
pursuit 655.1
**huff**
*n.* anger 952.7
*v.* blow 403.22
breathe 403.24
intimidate 891.28
make larger 197.4
provoke 952.22
**huffy** irascible 951.19
provoked 952.25
**hug**
*n.* embrace 932.2
greeting 925.4
hold 813.2
welcome 925.2
*v.* cohere 50.6
embrace 932.16
harbor 813.7
hold 813.6
seize 822.14
stay near 200.12
welcome 925.9
**huge** immense 195.20
large 34.7
**hugeness** greatness 34.1
vastness 195.7
**hugger-mugger**
*n.* secrecy 614.1
*v.* hush up 614.8
*adj.* confused 62.16
covert 614.12
*adv.* in disorder 62.17
**hugging** 932.1
**hulk** body 376.3
large thing 195.11
ship 277.1
wreck 692.10
**hulking** bulky 195.19
clumsy 734.20
unwieldy 731.18
**hull**
*n.* husk 228.16
seed vessel 411.28
ship 277.1
*v.* husk 232.9
**hullabaloo** bustle 707.4
noise 453.3
outcry 459.4
**hum**
*n.* audio distortion
450.13
continuity 71.2
droning 452.7
vocal music 462.12
*v.* persist 17.3
sing 462.39

sound 452.13
stammer 595.8
**human**
  *n.* person 417.3
  *adj.* kind 938.13
  mankind 417.10
  pitying 944.7
**humane** kind 938.13
  lenient 759.7
  pitying 944.7
**human factor** 80.1
**human interest** 855.9
**humanism**
  freethinking 1031.7
  mankind 417.8
  scholarship 475.5
**humanist**
  freethinker 1031.13
  scholar 476.3
**humanitarian**
  *n.* philanthropist 938.8
  *adj.* benevolent 938.15
**humanitarianism** 938.4
**humanities** 562.8
**humanity**
  humanness 417.5
  kindness 938.1
  leniency 759.1
  mankind 417.1
  pity 944.1
**humanize** 417.9
**human nature**
  humanness 417.5
  mankind 417.1
**humanoid**
  *n.* prehistoric man 123.7
  *adj.* manlike 417.11
  primitive 123.11
**human race** 417.1
**human rights**
  liberties 762.2
  rights 958.5
**humble**
  *v.* conquer 727.10
  demote 783.3
  humiliate 906.4
  subdue 764.9
  *adj.* common 919.11
  inferior 37.6
  lowly 906.9
  modest 908.9
  penitent 873.9
  resigned 861.10
  unselfish 979.5
  weak 765.15
**humbled**
  conquered 727.16
  humiliated 906.13
  lowered 906.12
  penitent 873.9
  subdued 764.15
**humbly** meekly 906.15
  modestly 908.14
  penitently 873.12
**humbug**
  *n.* fakery 616.3
  falsehood 616.14
  hoax 618.7
  impostor 619.6

nonsense 547.2
quackery 616.7
  *v.* deceive 618.13
**humdinger** 674.7
**humdrum**
  *n.* boring person 884.4
  repetitiousness 103.4
  tedium 884.1
  *adj.* monotonous 17.6
  prosaic 610.5
  repetitious 103.15
  tedious 884.8
**humid** moist 392.15
  sultry 328.28
**humidify** 392.12
**humidity**
  dampness 392.2
  sultriness 328.6
**humidor** cigar 434.4
  humidity instrument 392.10
**humiliate**
  disgrace 915.8
  humble 906.4
  mortify 864.13
  offend 965.4
  subdue 764.9
**humiliated**
  humbled 906.13
  subdued 764.15
**humiliating**
  disgraceful 915.11
  humbling 906.14
  insulting 965.6
  mortifying 864.21
**humiliation**
  disgrace 915.5
  humbleness 906.2
  indignity 965.2
  mortification 864.6
  snub 966.2
  subdual 764.4
**humility**
  humbleness 906
  inferiority 37.1
  meekness 765.5
  modesty 908.1
  resignation 861.2
  unselfishness 979.1
**humming**
  *n.* hum 452.7
  vocal music 462.12
  *adj.* droning 452.20
**hummock** 207.5
**humor**
  *n.* blood 388.4
  body fluid 388.3
  caprice 629.1
  moisture 392.1
  mood 525.4
  nature 5.3
  personality tendency 690.14
  wit 881.1
  *v.* indulge 759.6
**humoral**
  endocrine 312.8
  fluid 388.7
**humoresque** 462.6
**humoring** 759.3
**humorist** author 602.15
  wit 881.12

**humorless** 872.21
**humorous**
  amusing 878.29
  funny 880.4
  witty 881.15
**humorously**
  amusingly 880.6
  wittily 881.18
**hump**
  *n.* bulge 256.3
  mountain 207.7
  *v.* curve 252.6
  exert oneself 716.9
  hurry 709.6
  hustle 707.14
  rush 269.9
**humpbacked**
  bowed 252.10
  deformed 249.13
**humped** bowed 252.10
  convex 256.12
  humpbacked 249.13
**hun** 693.8
**Hun** 800.7
**hunch**
  *n.* bulge 256.3
  intuition 481.3
  presentiment 544.1
  unverified supposition 499.4
  *v.* crouch 318.8
  curve 252.6
**hunchback** 249.3
**hunchbacked** 249.13
**hunched** 252.10
**hundred district** 180.5
  number 99.8
**hung** 215.9
**hunger**
  *n.* appetite 634.7
  craving 634.6
  eating 307.1
  *v.* crave 634.18
  desire 634.19
  eat 307.18
**hungering**
  craving 634.24
  hungry 634.25
**hungry** craving 634.24
  ravenous 634.25
**hung up**
  distressed 866.22
  late 132.16
  obsessed 473.33
**hunk**
  accumulation 74.9
  amount 28.2
  lump 195.10
  piece 55.3
**hunky-dory** 674.13
**hunt**
  *n.* gunning 655.2
  search 485.14
  *v.* drive out 310.14
  go hunting 655.9
  persecute 667.6
  pursue 655.8
  search 485.30
  seek 485.29
**hunt down**
  discover 488.2
  hunt 655.9

trace 485.34
**hunter** horse 414.16
  huntsman 655.5
  pursuer 655.4
  seeker 485.17
  shooter 285.9
  sporting dog 414.23
**hunting**
  *n.* automation 349.21
  gunning 655.2
  pursuit 655.1
  search 485.14
  *adj.* pursuing 655.11
**hurdle**
  *n.* jump 319.1
  obstacle 730.4
  *v.* jump 319.5
**hurdles, the** 319.3
**hurdy-gurdy** 465.16
**hurdy-gurdy man** 464.9
**hurl**
  *n.* throw 285.4
  *v.* attack 798.28
  put violently 184.12
  throw 285.11
**hurl a brickbat** 965.4
**hurly-burly**
  agitation 324.1
  excitement 857.3
**hurrah**
  *n.* cheer 876.2
  cry 459.1
  *v.* cheer 876.6
  *interj.* approval 968.22
**hurricane**
  emotional outburst 857.8
  storm 162.4
  windstorm 403.12
**hurried** hasty 709.9
  reckless 894.8
  rushed 709.11
**hurry**
  *n.* excitement 857.3
  haste 709.1
  speed 269.1
  *v.* accelerate 709.4
  bustle 707.12
  hasten off 301.11
  make haste 709.5
  rush 269.9
  urge on 648.16
**hurry-scurry**
  *n.* excitement 857.3
  haste 709.1
  *v.* make haste 709.5
  *adv.* hastily 709.12
  recklessly 894.11
**hurry up**
  *v.* accelerate 269.14
  hasten 709.4
  speed 709.5
  *interj.* make haste! 709.16
**hurt**
  *n.* disadvantage 671.2
  distress 866.5
  evil 675.3
  impairment 692.1
  injury 692.8
  pain 424.1

*v.* ache 424.8
collide 283.12
distress 866.17
impair 692.11
injure 692.15
offend 952.20
pain 424.7
suffer 866.19
work evil 675.6
*adj.* damaged 692.29
distressed 866.23
pained 424.9
**hurtful** harmful 675.12
painful 424.10
**hurting**
*n.* impairment 692.1
pain 424.1
*adj.* afflicted 424.9
painful 424.10
**hurtle** collide 283.12
rush 269.9
throw 285.11
thrust 283.11
**husband**
*n.* married man 933.8
master 749.1
*v.* economize 851.4
reserve 660.12
**husbandly**
*adj.* loving 931.25
matrimonial 933.19
*adv.* economically
851.7
**husbandry**
agriculture 413.1
domestic manage-
ment 747.6
economy 851.1
management 747.1
**hush**
*n.* sibilation 457.1
silence 451.1
*v.* calm 163.7
fall silent 451.7
sibilate 457.2
silence 451.8
suppress 614.8
*interj.* silence! 451.14
**hushed**
quiescent 268.12
restrained 163.11
silent 451.10
**hush-hush** 614.11
**hush money**
bribe 651.2
fee 841.5
**husk**
*n.* hull 228.16
refuse 669.4
remainder 43.1
seed vessel 411.28
*v.* hull 232.9
**husking bee** 922.13
**husky**
*n.* beast of burden
271.6
*adj.* raucous 458.15
strong 159.13
**hussar** 800.11
**hussy**
impudent person
913.5

unchaste woman
989.14
**hustle**
*n.* dance 879.7
enterprise 707.7
haste 709.1
push 283.2
*v.* be active 707.13
make haste 709.5
shake 324.11
speed 709.4
thrust 283.11
work hard 716.13
**hustler**
man of action 707.8
prostitute 989.16
speeder 269.5
**hut** 191.10
**hutch**
*n.* hut 191.10
storage place 660.6
*v.* store 660.10
**huzzah**
*n.* cheer 876.2
*v.* cheer 876.6
**Hyades**
nymphs 1014.19
star cluster 375.8
**hyaline**
*n.* heavens 375.2
*adj.* glass 339.5
**hybrid**
*n.* crossbreed 44.9
hybrid word 582.11
*adj.* mongrel 44.16
**hybridize** 44.14
**hydrant**
extinguisher 332.3
fire hydrant 396.12
**hydrate** 379.6
**hydrated** 392.16
**hydration** 379.5
**hydraulic**
hydromechanical
347.11
water 392.16
**hydraulics** fluid 388.2
hydromechanics
347.4
**hydro–**
hydrogen 401.11
water 392.3
**hydrodynamics**
dynamics 347.3
hydromechanics
347.4
**hydroelectric** 342.27
**hydrogenate**
add gas 401.8
react chemically
379.6
**hydrogen bomb**
801.15,30
**hydrologic** 347.11
**hydrology** 347.4
**hydrolysis** 53.2
**hydrolytic**
disintegrative 53.6
electrolytic 342.29
**hydrolyze** 53.4
**hydromechanic(al)**
347.11

**hydromechanics**
hydraulics 347.4
mechanics 347.1
**hydrometer**
flowmeter 388.5
instrument 354.8
**hydrometric(al)** 347.11
**hydrophobia**
animal disease 686.38
infectious disease
686.12
phobia 891.12
rabies 473.6
**hydroplane**
*n.* aircraft 280.8
*v.* fly 278.45
**hydroponics**
agriculture 413.1
botany 412.1
**hydrosphere**
ocean 397.1
water 392.3
**hydrostatics**
aeronautics 278.2
hydromechanics
347.4
statics 347.2
**hydrous** 392.16
**hyena**
bad person 986.7
coyote 414.25,58
savage 943.5
**hygiene**
healthfulness 683.2
sanitation 681.3
**hygienic(al)**
healthful 683.5
sanitary 681.27
**hygienist** 683.3
**hygrology** 392.9
**hygrometer**
humidity instrument
392.10
weather instrument
402.8
**hygroscopic** 392.19
**hymen**
membrane 229.3
wedding song 933.4
**Hymen** god 1014.5
marriage god 933.14
**hymn**
*n.* paean 1032.3
sacred music 462.16
thanks 949.2
*v.* sing 462.39
worship 1032.11
**hymnal**
*n.* music 462.28
*adj.* vocal 462.51
**hymnist** 464.20
**hype**
*n.* addict 642.10
commendation 968.3
*v.* commend 968.11
**hyped** 642.19
**hyper–** excessive 663.16
external 224.6
fanatical 473.32
high 207.19
large 195.16
**hyperactive** 707.24

**hyperbola** 252.2
**hyperbole**
exaggeration 617.1
excess 663.1
misrepresentation
573.1
**hyperborean**
cold 333.14
northern 290.15
out-of-the-way 199.9
**hypercritical**
critical 969.24
overparticular 896.12
**Hyperion**
beautiful man 900.9
god 1014.5
sun god 375.14
**hyperkinesis** 707.9
**hyperkinetic** 707.24
**hypersensitive**
irascible 951.20
overparticular 896.12
sensitive 422.14
**hypersensitivity**
ill humor 951.4
overparticularity
896.4
sensitivity 422.3
**hypertension**
cardiovascular disease
686.17
disease symptom
686.8
**hypertensive** 686.57
**hypertrophy**
*n.* excess 663.1
oversize 195.5
*v.* overgrow 197.7
**hyphenate**
*n.* naturalized citizen
190.4
*v.* punctuate 586.16
**hypnosis**
hypnotic sleep 712.7
psychotherapy 690.5
suggestion therapy
690.6
trance 1036.3
**hypnotic**
*n.* sedative 687.12
sleep-inducer 712.10
*adj.* alluring 650.7
engrossing 530.20
mesmeric 712.24
sedative 687.45
sleep-inducing 712.23
**hypnotism**
hypnotherapy 690.5
mesmerism 712.8
suggestion therapy
690.6
**hypnotist** 712.9
**hypnotize**
cast a spell 1036.7
engross 530.13
fascinate 650.6
have influence over
172.11
put to sleep 712.20
**hypnotized**
astonished 920.9
enchanted 1036.12

**idiosyncratic(al)**
characteristic 80.13
differentiative 16.9
eccentric 474.4
indicative 568.23
personal 417.12
**idiot** lunatic 473.15
pathological type
690.16
simpleton 471.8
**idiot box** 345.11
**idiotic** foolish 470.8
mentally deficient
469.22
**idle**
*v.* do nothing 706.2
fritter away 854.5
go slow 270.6
loaf 708.11
stagnate 268.9
trifle 673.13
*adj.* baseless 483.13
do-nothing 706.6
inactive 708.17
leisure 710.5
motionless 268.13
slow 270.10
trivial 673.16
vain 669.13
**idleness**
inactivity 708.2
passivity 706.1
slowness 270.1
triviality 673.3
**idler** loafer 708.8
neglecter 534.5
vagrant 274.3
**idle rich** 708.10
**idle talk** chatter 596.3
gossip 558.7
**idol**
famous person 914.9
favorite 931.15
god 1014.2
good person 985.5
graven image 1033.3
likeness 572.3
**idolater** devotee 635.6
idol worshiper 1033.4
pagan 1025.7
venerator 1032.9
**idolatrize** 1033.5
**idolatrous**
idol worshiping
1033.7
pagan 1025.11
reverent 964.9
uncritical 968.18
**idolatry** flattery 970.3
idol worship 1033
love 931.1
paganism 1025.4
praise 968.5
respect 964.1
word list 1033.8
**idolistic** 1033.7
**idolization**
deification 1033.2
love 931.1
respect 964.1
word list 1033.8
**idolize** cherish 931.19

flatter 970.7
idolatrize 1033.5
praise 968.12
respect 964.4
worship 1032.10
**idol worship** 1033.1
**idyll** 609.6
**idyllic** pacific 803.9
poetic 609.17
**i.e.** 552.18
**if**
in the event that
151.13
provided that 507.14
supposing that
499.19
**iffy** chance 156.15
uncertain 514.16
**if necessary** 639.17
**igloo** arch 252.4
house 191.11
snow 333.8
**igneous** 328.26
**ignis fatuus** fire 328.13
illusion 519.1
phosphorescence
335.13
**ignite**
become angry 952.18
set fire to 329.22
**ignited** 328.27
**ignition** fire 328.13
kindling 329.4
rocketry 281.9
**ignobility** infamy 915.4
offensiveness 864.2
vulgarity 898.5
**ignoble**
disreputable 915.10
offensive 864.18
vulgar 898.15
**ignominious**
disreputable 915.10
wrong 959.3
**ignominy** infamy 915.4
wrong 959.2
**ignoramus** fool 471.1
know-nothing 477.8
novice 566.9
**ignorance**
inexperience 734.2
stupidity 469.1
unaccustomedness
643.1
unknowingness 477
**ignorant**
inexperienced 734.17
unaccustomed 643.4
unintelligent 469.13
unknowing 477.12
**ignore**
be broad-minded
526.7
condone 947.4
disobey 767.6
disregard 531.2
endure 861.7
exclude 77.4
extenuate 1006.12
neglect 534.6
reject 638.2
slight 966.6

**ignored**
neglected 534.14
rejected 638.3
unthanked 950.5
**ileac** 225.10
**ileum** 225.4
**ilk** kind 61.3
nature 5.3
**ill**
*n.* evil 675.3
*adj.* bad 675.7
ominous 544.17
sick 686.52
unkind 939.14
*adv.* badly 675.13
disadvantageously
671.9
unkindly 939.25
**ill-advised** see ill-
considered
**ill at ease** 866.22
**ill-behaved** 937.5
**ill-bred**
discourteous 937.6
uncouth 898.12
**ill-conceived** 675.11
**ill-considered**
botched 734.21
impulsive 630.11
inexpedient 671.5
premature 131.8
untimely 130.7
unwise 470.9
**illegal** prohibited 778.7
unjust 977.9
unlawful 999.6
wrong 959.3
**illegality** crime 999.4
injustice 977.1
unlawfulness 999
wrong 959.1
**illegible** 549.19
**illegitimate**
*n.* bastard 171.5
*adj.* illegal 999.6
spurious 999.7
ungenuine 616.26
**ill-equipped**
ill-provided 662.12
unfit 721.9
**ill-fated** 544.17
**ill-favored**
evil-fashioned 675.11
ugly 899.7
**ill-founded** 483.13
**ill-gotten**
dishonest 975.16
evil-fashioned 675.11
**ill-gotten gains** 824.11
**ill health** 686.2
**ill humor**
bad temper 951
contentiousness
482.13
discontent 869.1
**ill-humored**
argumentative 482.19
bad-tempered 951.18
**illiberal**
*n.* intolerant person
527.5

*adj.* narrow-minded
527.10
selfish 978.6
stingy 852.9
**illicit** illegal 999.6
prohibited 778.7
unchaste 989.27
**illicit business**
fraud 618.8
illegality 999.1
illegitimate business
826
**illiteracy** 477.5
**illiterate**
*n.* ignoramus 477.8
*adj.* unlearned 477.14
**ill nature**
ill humor 951.1
malevolence 939.4
**ill-natured**
ill-humored 951.18
malevolent 939.17
**illness** 686.1
**ill off**
ill-provided 662.12
poor 838.7
unfortunate 729.14
**illogic** 483.2
**illogical**
erroneous 518.16
unreasonable 483.11
**ill repute** 915.1
**ill-suited**
inappropriate 27.7
inexpedient 671.5
**ill-timed**
inappropriate 27.7
inexpedient 671.5
untimely 130.7
**illuminant**
*n.* light 335.20
light source 336.1
*adj.* luminous 335.30
**illuminate** color 362.13
explain 552.10
indicate 555.5
light up 335.28
ornament 901.9
**illuminated**
drunk 996.31
lit up 335.39
**illuminating**
educational 562.19
explanatory 552.15
lighting 335.40
**illumination**
applying color 362.11
explanation 552.4
learning 475.4
lighting 335.19
ornamentation 901.1
painting 574.5
picture 574.12
radiation 335.1
teaching 562.1
**ill-use**
*n.* mistreatment 667.2
use 665.1
*v.* mistreat 667.5
use badly 665.16
**illusion**
bewitchment 1036.2

immigrant
  incomer 302.4
  migrant 274.5
  naturalized citizen
    190.4
  newcomer 78.4
  settler 190.9
immigrate enter 302.11
  migrate 273.21
immigration
  influx 302.3
  migration 273.4
imminence
  approach 296.1
  expectation 539.1
  impendence 152
  the future 121.1
  threat 973.1
imminent
  approaching 296.4
  expected 539.13
  future 121.8
  impending 152.3
  threatening 973.3
immobile
  do-nothing 706.6
  motionless 268.13
  permanent 140.7
  stationary 142.15
immobility
  dormancy 706.1
  immovability 142.3
  inactivity 708.1
  motionlessness 268.2
  permanence 140.1
immobilize 142.7
immoderate
  excessive 663.16
  intemperate 993.7
  overpriced 848.12
  unrestrained 762.23
  violent 162.15
immodest
  conceited 909.11
  shameless 990.6
immodesty
  conceit 909.4
  shamelessness 990.2
immolate kill 409.13
  offer sacrifice
    1032.14
immolation
  killing 409.1
  oblation 1032.7
immoral
  dishonest 975.16
  vice-laden 981.11
immorality 981.1
immortal
  n. famous person
    914.9
  god 1014.2
  adj. eminent 914.18
  everlasting 112.9
  godlike 1013.20
  indestructible 142.18
  peerless 36.15
immortality
  eternal life 112.3
  indestructibility
    142.5
  life 407.1

posthumous fame
    914.7
immortalize
  glorify 914.13
  perpetuate 112.5
immortalized 914.18
immovable firm 624.12
  rigid 356.12
  stationary 142.15
  unfeeling 856.9
  unyielding 626.9
immune
  exempt 762.29
  resistant 685.12
  safe 698.4
immunity
  exemption 1007.2
  freedom 762.8
  immunology 689.17
  pardon 947.2
  resistance 685.4
  right 958.4
  safety 698.1
immunization
  immunity 685.4
  medical treatment
    689.17
immunize 689.34
immunized 698.4
immunology 689.17
immure confine 761.12
  enclose 236.6
  imprison 761.14
immured
  enclosed 236.10
  jailed 761.21
immutable
  enduring 110.10
  godlike 1013.20
  permanent 140.7
  persevering 625.7
  rigid 356.12
  unchangeable 142.17
  uniform 17.5
  unyielding 626.9
imp bad child 125.4
  branch 55.4
  evil spirit 1016.8
  fairy 1014.18
  mischief-maker 738.3
impact
  n. collision 283.3
  concussion 162.8
  effect 154.3
  meaning 545.1
  rocketry 281.9
  v. impress 142.9
  thrust in 304.7
impair damage 692.11
  subtract 42.9
  work evil 675.6
impaired
  damaged 692.29
  imperfect 678.4
impairment
  damage 692
  disadvantage 671.2
  imperfection 678.1
  reduction 42.2
impale
  puncture 265.16
  punish 1010.18

stab 798.25
  torture 866.18
impalpable
  immaterial 377.7
  infinitesimal 196.14
  powdery 361.11
  unsubstantial 4.5
impanel
  enroll a jury 1004.15
  list 88.8
  record 570.16
impanelment
  jury selection 1004.4
  recording 570.15
impart
  communicate 554.7
  disclose 556.4
  give 818.12
  say 594.23
  transfer 271.9
impartable
  communicable
    554.11
  giveable 818.23
  transferable 271.17
impartial just 976.10
  neutral 806.7
  unprejudiced 526.12
impartiality
  justice 976.4
  moderation 163.1
  neutrality 806.1
  unprejudicedness
    526.5
impassable 266.13
impasse corner 731.5
  dead end 266.3
impassion excite 857.11
  incite 648.17
impassioned
  amorous 931.24
  eloquent 600.13
  excited 857.18
  fervent 855.23
  zealous 635.10
impassive calm 268.12
  incurious 529.3
  inexcitable 858.10
  inexpressive 549.20
  reticent 613.10
  unfeeling 856.9
impatience
  eagerness 635.1
  impulsiveness 630.2
  restlessness 862
impatient eager 635.9
  impulsive 630.9
  restless 862.6
impatiently
  eagerly 635.14
  restlessly 862.8
impeach accuse 1005.7
  arraign 1004.14
  censure 969.13
impeachable
  blameworthy 969.26
  guilty 983.3
impeached 1005.15
impeachment
  accusation 1005.1
  arraignment 1004.3
  deposal 783.2

disapproval 969.3
impeccable
  innocent 984.7
  perfect 677.6
impecunious 838.7
impedance 342.12
impede delay 132.8
  hamper 730.11
  hinder 730.10
  slow 270.9
impediment
  burden 730.6
  hindrance 730.1
  obstruction 266.3
impedimenta
  belongings 810.3
  equipment 659.4
  freight 271.7
  hindrances 730.6
impeding 730.18
impel compel 756.4
  motivate 648.12
  obsess 473.24
  push 285.10
  set in motion 267.6
  thrust 283.10
impelled 648.30
impelling
  driving 283.20
  motivating 648.25
  moving 267.7
  obsessive 473.34
impend
  be imminent 152.2
  expect 539.10
  overhang 215.7
impending
  imminent 152.3
  overhanging 215.11
impenetrable
  dense 354.12
  growing rank 411.40
  impervious 266.13
  impregnable 159.17
  inaccessible 510.9
  unintelligible 549.13
impenitent 874.5
imperative
  n. command 752.1
  duty 962.1
  mood 586.11
  precept 751.2
  urgent need 639.4
  adj. authoritative
    739.15
  binding 962.15
  commanding 752.14
  compelling 756.9
  eloquent 600.11
  imperious 739.16
  mandatory 752.13
  necessary 639.12
  obligatory 756.10
  urgent 672.21
imperatively
  authoritatively
    739.18
  commandingly
    752.15
  compulsively 756.12
imperceptible
  infinitesimal 196.14

take liberties 961.7
**imposing**
corpulent 195.18
dignified 905.12
grandiose 904.21
weighty 672.19
**imposition**
demand 753.1
fraud 618.8
impediment 730.6
infliction 963
injustice 977.4
intrusion 238.1
presumption 961.2
tax 846.10
typesetting 603.2
**impossibility**
inconceivability 510
no chance 156.10
no hope 889.1
**impossible**
*adj.* fantastic 85.12
hopeless 889.14
not possible 510.7
numerical 86.8
unacceptable 869.7
*interj.* refusal 776.7
**impost** demand 753.1
tax 846.10
**impostor** fake 616.13
imitator 22.4
ringer 619.6
**imposture** fakery 616.3
fraud 618.8
imitation 22.1
quackery 616.7
**impotence**
futility 669.2
lack of influence
173.1
powerlessness 158
sexuality 419.2
unproductiveness
166.1
unstrictness 758.1
weakness 160.1
**impotent**
*n.* weakling 158.6
*adj.* powerless 158.13
sterile 166.4
uninfluential 173.3
unsexual 419.31
unstrict 758.4
useless 669.9
weak 160.12
**impound**
appropriate 822.20
confine 761.12
enclose 236.5
**impoverish**
bankrupt 842.8
consume 666.2
despoil 822.24
pauperize 838.6
**impoverished**
ill-provided 662.12
indigent 838.8
meager 662.10
used up 666.4
**impractical**
theoretical 499.13
unfeasible 510.8

unwieldy 731.18
visionary 535.24
**impracticality**
idealization 535.7
impossibility 510.2
unwieldiness 731.8
**imprecation**
curse 972.1
entreaty 774.2
**imprecatory** 972.8
**imprecise**
imperfect 678.4
inaccurate 518.17
ungrammatical 587.4
unstrict 758.4
vague 514.18
**impregnable**
impenetrable 159.17
indestructible 142.18
**impregnate**
fertilize 165.8
indoctrinate 562.13
infuse 44.12
inseminate 169.10
soak 392.13
**impregnated** 169.17
**impregnation**
fertilization 165.3
imbuement 44.2
indoctrination 562.2
insemination 169.3
soaking 392.7
**impresario**
manager 748.1
theater man 611.28
**impress**
*n.* characteristic 80.4
copy 24.5
effect 154.3
indentation 257.6
mark 568.7
print 578.6
printing 603.3
*v.* abduct 824.19
affect emotionally
855.17
appropriate 822.20
avail oneself of
665.14
enlist 780.16
fix in the mind
537.18
grab the thoughts
478.19
impact 142.9
indent 257.14
indoctrinate 562.13
mark 568.19
print 603.14
**impressed**
affected 855.25
engraved 578.12
infixed 142.13
**impression**
aspect 446.3
belief 501.6
characteristic 80.4
concavity 257.1
copy 24.5
description 608.1
edition 605.2
effect 154.3

emotion 855.3
form 246.1
hunch 481.3
idea 479.1
imitation 22.1
indentation 257.6
indoctrination 562.2
mark 568.7
print 578.6
printing 603.3
vague supposition
499.5
**impressionability**
emotional capacity
855.4
influenceability 172.5
physical sensibility
422.2
pliancy 357.2
teachability 564.5
**impressionable**
emotionable 855.21
influenceable 172.15
pliant 357.9
receptive 422.13
teachable 564.18
**impressive**
convincing 501.26
eloquent 600.11
exciting 857.28
grandiose 904.21
receptive 422.13
**impressively**
eloquently 600.15
exceptionally 34.20
grandiosely 904.28
**impressment**
abduction 824.8
appropriation 822.5
enlistment 780.6
**imprimatur**
permit 777.6
ratification 521.4
**imprint**
*n.* book 605.12
effect 154.3
indentation 257.6
label 568.13
mark 568.7
print 578.6
printing 603.3
*v.* fix in the mind
537.18
imbed 142.9
indent 257.14
mark 568.19
print 603.14
**imprinted**
engraved 578.12
infixed 142.13
**imprison** enclose 236.5
incarcerate 761.14
**imprisoned**
enclosed 236.10
jailed 761.21
**imprisonment**
enclosure 236.1
jailing 761.3
punishment 1010.2
**improbability**
inexpectation 540.1
odd thing 85.5

small chance 156.9
unlikelihood 512
**improbable**
farfetched 10.7
unexpected 540.10
unlikely 512.3
**improbity**
dishonesty 975
falseheartedness
616.4
**impromptu**
*n.* improvisation 630.5
music 462.27
*adj.* extemporaneous
630.12
unprepared 721.8
*adv.* extemporane-
ously 630.15
**improper** bad 675.7
evil 981.16
inappropriate 27.7
indecent 990.5
inexpedient 671.5
infelicitous 590.2
misbehaving 738.5
undue 961.10
ungrammatical 587.4
untimely 130.7
vulgar 898.10
wrong 959.3
**improperly**
unduly 34.21
vulgarly 898.16
wrongly 959.4
**impropriety**
indecency 990.1
injustice 977.1
literary inelegance
590.1
misbehavior 738.1
offense 982.2
undueness 961.1
unfitness 27.3
untimeliness 130.1
vulgarity 898.1
word 582.6
wrong 959.1
**improvable**
ameliorable 691.17
remediable 694.25
**improve**
be changed 139.5
change 139.6
excel 36.6
get better 691.7
make better 691.9
make perfect 677.5
recuperate 694.19
take advantage of
665.15
train 562.14
**improved**
bettered 691.13
changed 139.9
**improvement**
betterment 691
change 139.1
reformation 145.2
restoration 694.1
training 562.3
**improvidence**
rashness 894.1

thriftlessness 721.2
**improvident** rash 894.7
  thriftless 721.15
**improvisation**
  creation 167.5
  expedient 670.2
  extemporization
    630.5
  music 462.27
  unpreparedness 721.1
**improvisational** 670.7
**improvisational drama**
    611.4
**improvise**
  be unprepared 721.6
  create 167.13
  extemporize 630.8
**improvised**
  extemporaneous
    630.12
  makeshift 670.7
  unprepared 721.8
**imprudence**
  foolish act 470.4
  indiscrimination
    493.1
  rashness 894.1
  unwiseness 470.2
**imprudent** rash 894.7
  undiscriminating
    493.5
  unwise 470.9
**impudence**
  defiance 793.1
  disrespect 965.1
  impertinence 913.2
  rashness 894.1
**impudent**
  defiant 793.7
  disrespectful 965.5
  impertinent 913.9
  rash 894.7
**impugn** censure 969.13
  deny 524.4
  incriminate 1005.10
**impugned**
  accused 1005.15
  disproved 506.7
**impulse**
  impulsiveness 630
  instinct 481.2
  involuntariness 639.5
  power 157.4
  prematurity 131.2
  thrust 283
  urge 648.6
**impulsive**
  impelling 283.20
  impetuous 630.9
  inconstant 18.3
  instinctive 481.6
  involuntary 639.14
  mercurial 141.7
  motivating 648.25
  precipitate 709.10
  premature 131.8
  sudden 113.5
  transient 111.7
**impulsively**
  impetuously 630.13
  nonuniformly 18.4
  precipitously 709.15

prematurely 131.13
  suddenly 113.9
**impulsiveness**
  hastiness 709.2
  impetuousness 630.2
  inconstancy 141.2
  prematurity 131.2
**impunity** 1007.2
**impure** imperfect 678.4
  infelicitous 590.2
  obscene 990.9
  unchaste 989.23
  unclean 682.20
  unrighteous 981.12
**impurity**
  foreign body 78.2
  immorality 981.1
  imperfection 678.1
  literary inelegance
    590.1
  unchastity 989.1
  uncleanness 682.1
**imputable**
  attributable 155.6
  blameworthy 969.26
**imputation**
  accusation 1005.1
  attribution 155.1
  disapproval 969.4
  disparagement 971.4
  stigma 915.6
**impute** accuse 1005.7
  attribute 155.3
**in**
  *n.* access 306.3
    entrance 302.5
    good terms 927.3
  *adj.* entering 302.12
    friendly 927.17
    modern 122.13
  *adv.* inside 225.12
    inward 302.13
  *prep.* into 302.14
    located 184.26
    within 225.15
**in a bad way**
  in danger 697.13
  sick 686.52
  worn-out 692.38
**inability**
  incapability 158.2
  unskillfulness 734.1
**in a bind**
  in a predicament
    731.20
  late 132.16
**inaccessible**
  out-of-the-way 199.9
  reticent 613.10
  unaccessible 510.9
  unsociable 923.6
**inaccordant**
  different 16.7
  disagreeing 27.6
**inaccuracy**
  imperfection 678.1
  incorrectness 518.2
  misrepresentation
    573.1
  unmeticulousness
    534.4
  vagueness 514.4

**inaccurate**
  imperfect 678.4
  incorrect 518.17
  unmeticulous 534.13
  vague 514.18
**inaction**
  inactiveness 708.1
  motionlessness 268.2
  passiveness 706
**in action** acting 705.10
  operating 164.11
**inactivate** 158.9
**inactive**
  do-nothing 706.6
  idle 708.16
  inert 268.14
  leisurely 710.6
**inactivity**
  inactiveness 708
  leisureliness 710.2
  motionlessness 268.2
  passivity 706.1
  rest 711.1
**inadequacy** fault 678.2
  imperfection 678.1
  inability 158.2
  incompleteness 57.1
  inequality 31.1
  inferiority 37.3
  insufficiency 662.1
  shortcoming 314.1
  unsatisfactoriness
    869.2
  unskillfulness 734.1
**inadequate**
  imperfect 678.4
  incompetent 734.19
  incomplete 57.4
  ineffective 158.15
  inferior 37.7
  insufficient 662.9
  short of 314.5
  unequal 31.4
  unsatisfactory 869.6
**inadequately**
  imperfectly 678.5
  incompletely 57.6
  insufficiently 662.14
  unsatisfactorily
    869.9
  unskillfully 734.23
**inadmissible**
  exclusive 77.8
  inappropriate 27.7
  irrelevant 10.6
  unacceptable 869.7
**in advance**
  before 292.4
  early 131.11
  in front 240.12
  on loan 820.7
  prior to 116.7
**inadvertence**
  an error 518.4
  inattention 531.1
  neglect 534.1
**inadvertent**
  impulsive 630.10
  inattentive 531.6
  negligent 534.10
  unpremeditated
    630.11

**inadvertently**
  negligently 534.17
  unpremeditatedly
    630.14
**inadvisable**
  inexpedient 671.5
  unwise 470.9
**inalienable**
  inseparable 47.15
  intrinsic 5.6
  unimpartable 813.10
**in all conscience**
  candidly 974.23
  in justice 976.12
  positively 34.19
  reasonably 482.24
  rightly 958.9
**in all respects**
  exactly 516.20
  throughout 56.17
  wholly 54.13
**inalterable** 625.7
**in a manner of speaking**
  figuratively 551.4
  so to speak 20.19
  to a degree 35.10
**inamorata** 931.14
**inamorato** 931.12
**inane** foolish 470.8
  ignorant 477.12
  ineffective 158.15
  insipid 430.2
  meaningless 547.6
  stupid 469.19
  thoughtless 480.4
  trivial 673.16
  uninteresting 883.6
  vacant 187.13
  vain 669.13
**inanimate**
  *n.* gender 586.10
  *adj.* dead 408.30
    inanimated 382.5
    languid 708.19
**inanity**
  foolishness 470.1
  futility 669.2
  ignorant 477.1
  ineffectiveness 158.3
  insipidness 430.1
  meaninglessness
    547.1
  stupidity 469.6
  thoughtlessness 480.1
  triviality 673.3
  uninterestingness
    883.1
  void 187.3
**in a nutshell**
  concisely 592.8
  in summary 607.7
  on a small scale
    196.16
**in any case**
  anyhow 657.12
  in the event that
    151.13
  notwithstanding 33.8
**inappetence**
  apathy 856.4
  undesirousness 636.3

injure 692.15
notch 262.4
open 265.12
record 570.16
sever 49.11
**incised**
engraved 578.12
grooved 263.4
notched 262.5
**incision** crack 201.2
engraving 578.2
groove 263.1
impairment 692.8
notch 262.1
**incisive**
acrimonious 161.13
caustic 939.21
eloquent 600.11
energetic 161.12
sagacious 467.16
**incisor** 258.5
**incite** advise 754.6
excite 857.11
impel 283.10
instigate 648.17
**incitement**
excitation 857.10
impulse 283.1
incentive 648.7
inducement 648.4
**incitive** 648.28
**incivility**
discourtesy 937.1
uncouthness 898.3
**inclemency** cold 333.1
pitilessness 945.1
unkindness 939.9
violence 162.1
**inclement** cold 333.14
pitiless 945.3
unkind 939.22
**inclination**
aptitude 733.5
descent 316.1
desire 634.3
direction 290.1
injustice 977.3
obeisance 964.2
obliquity 219.2
preference 637.5
prejudice 527.3
slope 219.4
tendency 174.1
trait of character
525.3
will 621.1
**incline**
*n.* slope 219.4
stairs 315.3
*v.* bear 290.8
be willing 622.3
gravitate 352.15
induce 648.22
influence 172.7
lean 219.10
prefer 637.17
take an attitude
525.6
tend 174.3
**inclined**
desirous of 634.22
minded 525.8

motivated 648.30
oblique 219.15
prone to 174.6
tending to 174.5
willing 622.5
**inclining**
oblique 219.15
tending 174.4
**in clover**
in comfort 887.15
pleased 865.12
prosperous 728.12
**include** combine 52.3
comprise 76.3
enclose 236.5
internalize 225.6
join 47.5
**included**
comprised 76.5
involved 176.3
**including**
*adj.* composed of 58.4
containing 76.6
*prep.* with 40.12
**inclusion**
affiliation 786.2
combination 52.1
comprisal 76
enclosure 236.1
involvement 176.1
surrounding 233.5
**inclusive**
containing 76.6
joint 47.12
whole 54.9
**inclusive of**
composed of 58.4
with 40.12
**incognito**
*n.* anonymity 584.1
disguise 618.10
masquerader 619.7
privacy 614.2
*adj.* anonymous 584.3
disguised 615.13
private 614.13
**incognizance** 477.3
**incognizant** 477.13
**incoherent**
delirious 473.31
discontinuous 72.4
inconsistent 27.8
separate 49.20
uncohesive 51.4
unintelligible 549.13
vague 514.18
**in cold blood**
heartlessly 939.32
intentionally 653.11
unfeelingly 856.14
**incombustible** 332.9
**income** entrance 302.1
gain 811.3
receipts 844.1
remuneration 841.4
**income tax** 846.11
**incoming**
*n.* entrance 302.1
*adj.* arriving 300.9
entering 302.12
**incommensurable**
dissimilar 21.6

incomparable 491.9
inconsistent 27.8
unrelated 10.5
**incommensurate**
dissimilar 21.6
inconsistent 27.8
unsatisfactory 869.6
**incommodious**
inconvenient 671.7
narrow 205.14
**incommunicable**
indescribable 920.13
unimpartable 813.10
**incommunicado** 615.11
**incommutable** 142.17
**incomparable**
dissimilar 21.6
incommensurable
491.9
peerless 36.15
unrelated 10.5
**incomparably**
peerlessly 36.18
superlatively 36.16
**incompatibility**
difference 16.1
disaccord 795.1
enmity 929.1
inconsistency 27.2
unsociability 923.1
**incompatible**
different 16.7
disagreeing 27.6
inconsistent 27.8
unfriendly 929.9
unsociable 923.5
**incompetence**
inability 158.2
inferiority 37.3
insufficiency 662.1
unpreparedness 721.1
unskillfulness 734.1
**incompetent**
*n.* impotent 158.6
unskillful person
734.7
*adj.* incapable 734.19
inferior 37.7
insufficient 662.9
unable 158.14
unfit 721.9
**incomplete**
deficient 57.4
imperfect 678.4
insufficient 662.9
partial 55.7
**incompletely**
imperfectly 678.5
insufficiently 662.14
partially 57.6
somewhat 35.10
**incompleteness**
deficiency 57
discontinuity 72.1
imperfection 678.1
want 662.4
**incomprehensible**
fantastic 85.12
infinite 104.3
unintelligible 549.13
wonderful 920.10

**incomprehension**
incognizance 477.3
unperceptiveness
469.2
**incompressible** 354.12
**inconceivable**
fantastic 85.12
impossible 510.7
unbelievable 503.10
wonderful 920.10
**inconclusive**
illogical 483.11
unproved 506.8
unsubstantial 483.12
**in condition**
healthy 685.7
in order 59.7
state of being 7.8
**incongruity**
difference 16.1
humorousness 880.1
illogicalness 483.2
inconsistency 27.2
inexpedience 671.1
nonconformity 83.1
**incongruous**
clashingly colored
362.20
different 16.7
humorous 880.4
illogical 483.11
inconsistent 27.8
inexpedient 671.5
**inconsequence**
unimportance 673.1
unrelatedness 10.1
**inconsequent**
illogical 483.11
inconsistent 27.8
irrelevant 10.6
**inconsequential**
illogical 483.11
insignificant 35.6
unimportant 673.15
**inconsiderable**
insignificant 35.6
unimportant 673.15
**inconsiderate**
careless 534.11
discourteous 937.6
impulsive 630.10
unthoughtful 939.16
unwise 470.9
**inconsistency**
contrariety 15.1
difference 16.1
illogicalness 483.2
incongruity 27.2
inconstancy 141.2
noncohesion 51.1
nonconformity 83.1
nonuniformity 18.1
**inconsistent**
contrary 15.6
different 16.7
illogical 483.11
incoherent 51.4
incongruous 27.8
inconstant 141.2
nonuniform 18.3
**inconsolable** 872.28

**inconsonant**
different 16.7
inconsistent 27.8
**inconspicuous** 445.6
**inconstancy**
fickleness 629.3
infidelity 975.5
instability 141.2
irregularity 138.1
irresolution 627.1
nonuniformity 18.1
**inconstant**
changeable 141.7
fickle 629.6
irregular 138.3
nonobservant 769.5
nonuniform 18.3
transient 111.7
unfaithful 975.20
**incontestable**
certain 513.15
invincible 159.17
**incontinence**
excess 663.1
greed 634.8
intemperance 993.1
prodigality 854.1
unchastity 989.2
unrestraint 762.3
**incontinent**
excessive 663.16
intemperate 993.7
prodigal 854.8
unchaste 989.24
unrestrained 762.23
**incontrovertible**
certain 513.15
evidential 505.17
**inconvenience**
*n.* disadvantage 671.3
impediment 730.6
imposition 963.1
inexpedience 671.1
trouble 731.3
untimeliness 130.1
unwieldiness 731.8
*v.* discommode 671.4
take liberties 961.7
trouble 731.12
**inconvenient**
disadvantageous
671.7
untimely 130.7
unwieldy 731.18
**inconvertible**
unchangeable 142.17
unpayable 842.13
**inconvincible** 504.4
**incorporate**
combine 52.3
compose 58.3
embody 376.8
include 76.3
**incorporated**
associated 788.16
combined 52.5
embodied 376.10
joined 47.13
**incorporation**
affiliation 786.2
combination 52.1
composition 58.1

embodiment 376.7
inclusion 76.1
**incorporative** 52.7
**incorporeal**
*n.* immateriality
377.2
specter 1017.1
*adj.* ghostly 1017.7
immaterial 377.7
unsubstantial 4.5
**incorporeality**
immateriality 377.1
rarity 355.1
unsubstantiality 4.1
**incorrect**
inaccurate 518.17
infelicitous 590.2
ungrammatical 587.4
wrong 959.3
**incorrectly**
inaccurately 518.21
wrongly 959.4
**incorrigible**
confirmed 642.21
hopeless 889.15
irreclaimable 981.18
ungovernable 626.12
**incorrupt**
innocent 984.6
virtuous 980.9
**incorruptible**
immortal 112.9
indestructible 142.18
trustworthy 974.19
**incrassate**
*v.* fatten 204.5
make viscid 389.10
thicken 354.10
*adj.* distended 197.13
thickened 354.14
**increase**
*n.* addition 40.1
adjunct 41.1
aggravation 885.1
ascent 315.1
expansion 197.1
gain 38
multiplication 100.4
winnings 38.3
*v.* add to 40.5
advance 38.6
aggravate 885.2
amplify 38.4
become larger 197.5
develop 197.7
graduate 29.4
make larger 197.4
multiply 100.6
quantify 28.4
**increased**
aggravated 885.4
expanded 197.10
extended 38.7
multiple 100.8
**increasing** 38.8
**increasingly** 38.9
**incredible**
fantastic 85.12
foolish 470.10
improbable 512.3
remarkable 34.10
unbelievable 503.10

wonderful 920.10
**incredibly**
remarkably 34.20
unusually 85.17
wonderfully 920.14
**incredulity**
agnosticism 1031.6
unbelief 503.1
ungullibility 504
**incredulous**
skeptical 1031.20
unbelieving 503.8
ungullible 504.4
**increment** adjunct 41.1
increase 38.1
**incremental** 38.8
**incriminate** 1005.10
**incriminating** 1005.14
**incrimination** 1005.2
**incrustation**
covering 228.1
crust 228.14
**incrusted** 356.13
**incubate** 169.12
**incubation** 169.5
**incubator** 153.8
**incubus** burden 352.7
dream 535.9
evil spirit 1016.7
frightener 891.9
**inculcate**
fix in the mind
537.18
indoctrinate 562.13
**inculcated** 642.21
**inculcation** 562.2
**inculpable** 984.8
**inculpate** 1005.10
**inculpated**
accused 1005.15
guilty 983.3
**inculpatory** 1005.14
**incumbency**
burden 352.7
position 656.5
responsibility 962.2
the ministry 1037.9
**incumbent**
*n.* clergyman 1038.8
officeholder 746.11
resident 190.2
tenant 809.4
*adj.* covering 228.35
obligatory 962.14
overhanging 215.11
ponderous 352.17
**incumber, incumbered,
incumbrance** see
encumber etc.
**incur** 175.4
**incurable**
*n.* sick person 686.40
*adj.* hopeless 889.15
**incuriosity**
inattention 531.1
unconcern 636.2
uninquisitiveness 529
**incurious**
inattentive 531.6
unconcerned 636.7
uninquisitive 529.3

**incursion**
intrusion 238.1
overstepping 313.3
raid 798.4
**incursionary** 798.29
**incurve**
*n.* throw 285.4
*v.* be concave 257.12
curve 252.6
**incurved**
concave 257.16
curved 252.7
**indebted** in debt 840.8
insolvent 836.18
**indebtedness** 840.1
**indebted to**
grateful 949.5
obliged 962.16
**indecency**
eroticism 419.5
indelicacy 990
unchastity 989.1
vulgarity 898.1
**indecent**
indelicate 990.5
unchaste 989.23
vulgar 898.10
**indecipherable** 549.19
**indecision**
irresolution 627.1
uncertainty 514.1
**indecisive**
formless 247.4
inconstant 141.7
irresolute 627.9
uncertain 514.15
unproved 506.8
vague 514.18
weak 160.17
**indecisiveness**
formlessness 247.1
frailty 160.2
irresolution 627.1
uncertainty 514.1
vagueness 514.4
**indecorous**
indecent 990.5
infelicitous 590.2
vulgar 898.10
wrong 959.3
**indecorum**
indecency 990.1
vulgarity 898.1
wrong 959.1
**indeed**
*adv.* above all 36.17
certainly 513.23
positively 34.19
truly 516.17
*interj.* wonder 920.19
yes 521.18
**indefatigable**
continuing 143.7
industrious 707.22
persevering 625.7
**indefeasible**
inevitable 639.15
unchangeable 142.17
unimpartable 813.10
**indefensible**
unacceptable 869.7
unjust 977.12

**indefinable**
indescribable 920.13
inexplicable 549.18
vague 514.18
**indefinite**
formless 247.4
general 79.11
indistinct 445.6
uncertain 514.18
**indefinitely**
extremely 34.22
vaguely 514.27
**indeliberate** 630.11
**indelible**
deep-felt 855.26
dyed 362.17
indestructible 142.18
unforgettable 537.26
**indelicacy**
indecency 990.1
vulgarity 898.1
**indelicate**
indecent 990.5
vulgar 898.10
**indemnification**
atonement 1012.1
compensation 33.1
recompense 841.3
restitution 823.2
**indemnify**
compensate 33.4
make restitution
823.5
pay 841.10
retaliate 955.5
**indemnity**
atonement 1012.1
compensation 33.1
exemption 1007.2
pardon 947.2
recompense 841.3
security 772.1
**indemonstrable** 514.15
**indent**
n. appropriation 822.4
contract 771.3
demand 753.1
indentation 257.6
mark 568.7
request 774.1
summons 752.5
v. appropriate 822.19
demand 753.4
dent 257.14
depress 318.4
notch 262.4
request 774.9
summon 752.12
**indentation** dent 257.6
excavation 257.11
mark 568.7
notch 262.1
texture 351.1
**indented**
dented 257.17
notched 262.5
**indenture**
n. binding over 780.7
bond 834.4
contract 771.3
indentation 257.6
v. article 780.17

indentured 780.20
**indentured servant**
764.7
**independence**
freedom 762.5
nationhood 181.6
neutrality 806.1
nonpartisanism
744.26
pride 905.1
rallying theme 797.16
self-control 624.5
self-help 785.6
unrelatedness 10.1
voluntariness 622.2
wealth 837.1
**independent**
n. free lance 762.12
neutral 806.4
nonpartisan 744.28
adj. free 762.21
neutral 806.7
nonpartisan 744.45
proud 905.8
self-helpful 785.23
strong-willed 624.15
unrelated 10.5
voluntary 622.7
wealthy 837.13
**independently**
freely 762.32
proudly 905.13
voluntarily 622.10
**indescribable**
extraordinary 85.14
ineffable 920.13
**indestructible**
perpetual 112.7
undestroyable 142.18
**in detail**
at length 593.16
fully 8.13
meticulously 533.16
particularly 80.15
piece by piece 55.9
**indeterminate**
chance 156.15
formless 247.4
general 79.11
obscure 549.15
uncertain 514.18
**index**
n. arrangement 60.4
bibliography 605.19
book part 605.12
characteristic 80.4
contents 194.1
directory 748.10
figure 87.7
finger 425.5
hint 557.4
list 88.2
map 654.4
pointer 568.4
prohibition 778.1
reference book 605.6
sign 568.2
v. classify 61.6
list 88.8
record 570.16
**indexed** classified 61.8
listed 88.9

recorded 570.18
**Indian ocean** 397.3
peoples 418.3
**Indianapolis 500** 796.12
**Indian file** 71.2
**Indian house** 191.11
**Indian reservation**
701.6
**Indian summer** 128.5
**indicate** augur 544.12
evidence 505.9
hint 557.10
mean 545.8
show 555.5
signify 568.17
specify 80.11
**indicated**
augured 544.15
implied 546.7
requisite 639.13
**indicating** 568.23
**indication**
evidence 505.1
hint 557.4
manifestation 555.1
omen 544.3
sign 568
**indicative**
n. mood 586.11
adj. evidential 505.17
manifestative 555.9
meaningful 545.10
premonitory 544.16
significative 568.23
suggestive 546.6
**indicator**
automatic 349.37
depth 209.17
judge 1002.1
sign 568.2
**indict** accuse 1005.7
arraign 1004.14
censure 969.13
**indictable**
blameworthy 969.26
guilty 983.3
**indicted** 1005.15
**indictment**
accusation 1005.1
arraignment 1004.3
disapproval 969.3
**indifference**
apathy 856.4
carelessness 534.2
emotional symptom
690.23
inattention 531.1
incurious 529.1
inertia 268.4
languor 708.6
mediocrity 680.1
neutrality 806.2
nonchalance 858.5
nonreligiousness
1031.1
unconcern 636
unimportance 673.1
unprejudicedness
526.5
unstrictness 758.1
**indifferent**
apathetic 856.13

careless 534.11
inattentive 531.6
incurious 529.3
insipid 430.2
mediocre 680.7
neutral 806.7
nonchalant 858.15
nonreligious 1031.15
reluctant 623.6
unconcerned 636.6
unprejudiced 526.12
unstrict 758.4
**indifferently**
apathetically 856.15
equally 30.11
mediocrely 680.11
unconcernedly 636.9
**indigence** 838.2
**indigenous** innate 5.7
native 189.5
**indigent**
n. poor person 838.4
adj. poverty-stricken
838.8
**indigestible** 684.6
**indigestion**
disease symptom
686.8
dyspepsia 686.28
**indignant** angry 952.26
disapproving 969.22
**indignation**
disapproval 969.1
resentment 952.4
**indignity** affront 965.2
disparagement 971.1
**indirect**
circuitous 321.7
circumlocutory
593.14
collateral 151.11
deceitful 618.20
deviant 291.7
dishonest 975.16
oblique 219.13
**indirection**
circuitousness 321.1
circumlocution 593.5
deceit 618.3
deviation 291.1
improbity 975.1
obliquity 219.1
**indirectly**
by agent 781.17
circuitously 321.9
deceitfully 618.22
obliquely 219.21
**indiscernible**
infinitesimal 196.14
invisible 445.5
without distinction
493.6
**indiscreet**
indecent 990.5
rash 894.7
undiscriminating
493.5
unwise 470.9
**indiscretion**
an error 518.5
divulgence 556.2
foolish act 470.4

indecency 990.1
indiscrimination
493.1
misdeed 982.2
rashness 894.1
unwiseness 470.2
**indiscriminate**
extensive 79.13
mixed 44.15
purposeless 156.16
undiscriminating
493.5
unordered 62.12
**indiscrimination**
choicelessness 639.6
indiscriminateness
493
unconcern 636.2
**indispensable**
n. requirement 639.2
adj. requisite 639.13
vital 672.22
**indispose**
disincline 652.4
sicken 686.47
**indisposed** sick 686.52
unwilling 623.5
**indisposition**
disease 686.1
unwillingness 623.1
**indisputable**
certain 513.15
evidential 505.17
manifest 555.8
unqualified 508.2
**indistinct**
faint-sounding 452.16
imperfectly spoken
595.12
obscure 549.15
uncertain 514.18
unclear 445.6
without distinction
493.6
**indistinctly**
unintelligibly 549.22
vaguely 514.27
**indistinguishable**
identical 14.7
indistinct 445.6
without distinction
493.6
**indite** create 167.10
write 602.21
**individual**
n. organism 406.2
person 417.3
something 3.3
unit 89.4
adj. indicative 568.23
one 89.7
particular 80.12
personal 417.12
**individualism**
capitalism 745.8
characteristic 80.4
egotism 909.3
independence 762.5
individuality 80.1
selfishness 978.1
trait of character
525.3

**individualist**
capitalist 745.15
egotist 909.5
independent 762.12
misfit 27.4
selfish person 978.3
**individualistic**
capitalist 745.23
independent 762.21
nonconformist 27.9
particular 80.12
selfish 978.5
**individuality**
particularity 80.1
unity 89.1
**individualize**
differentiate 16.6
particularize 80.9
**individually**
personally 80.16
singly 89.13
**indivisible**
inseparable 47.15
nondivisible 354.13
one 89.7
simple 45.6
**indocile**
insubordinate 767.9
ungovernable 626.12
unwilling 623.5
**indocility**
disobedience 767.1
ungovernability 626.4
unwillingness 623.1
**indoctrinate**
brainwash 145.15
inculcate 562.13
propagandize 563.4
**indoctrinated** 189.6
**indoctrination**
brainwashing 145.5
inculcation 562.2
misteaching 563.2
**indolence**
inaction 706.1
inertia 268.4
laziness 708.5
slowness 270.1
vegetation 1.6
**indolent**
n. lazy person 708.7
adj. lazy 708.18
slow 270.10
**indomitable**
invincible 159.17
persevering 625.7
ungovernable 626.12
**indoor**
adj. interior 225.7
adv. inside 225.14
**indorse, indorsement**
see **endorse** etc.
**Indra**
Hindu deity 1014.8
thunder god 456.5
**indraft** influx 302.2
wind 403.1
**indubitable**
certain 513.15
manifest 555.8
**indubitably**
certainly 513.25

positively 34.19
probably 511.8
**induce** advise 754.6
cause 153.12
conclude 494.10
elicit 305.14
influence 172.7
persuade 648.22
**inducement**
allurement 650.1
gratuity 818.5
incentive 648.7
persuasion 648.3
**induct** begin 68.11
enlist 780.16
insert 304.4
install 780.11
**inductee** novice 566.9
recruit 800.17
**inductile** 356.12
**induction**
admission 306.2
basics 68.6
conclusion 494.4
consecration 1037.10
electrostatic induc-
tion 342.14
enlistment 780.6
inauguration 68.5
installation 780.3
logic 482.3
reasoning 482.1
**inductive** 482.22
**inductive reasoning**
logic 482.3
reasoning 482.1
**in due course**
in time 121.11
opportunely 129.12
soon 131.16
**indulge**
be intemperate 993.4
enjoy 865.10
give 818.15
humor 759.6
permit 777.10
**indulged**
forgiven 947.7
pampered 759.9
**indulgence**
considerateness 938.3
forgiveness 947.1
intemperance 993.1
leniency 759.3
patience 861.1
privilege 958.4
sufferance 777.2
tolerance 526.4
**indulgent**
considerate 938.16
intemperate 993.7
lenient 759.8
nonrestrictive 762.24
patient 861.9
permissive 777.14
tolerant 526.11
**indulge oneself**
be intemperate 993.4
be lawless 740.4
be selfish 978.4
**indurate**
v. harden 356.7

make unfeeling 856.6
adj. hardened 356.13
**indurated**
callous 856.12
hardened 356.13
wicked 981.17
**induration** 856.3
**industrial**
commercial 827.21
occupational 656.16
productional 167.17
**industrialist**
businessman 830.1
producer 167.8
**industrialization**
commercialization
827.13
production 167.2
**industrialize**
make businesslike
827.19
produce 167.9
**industrial park** 719.3
**industrials** 834.2
**industrial school**
prison 761.8
reform school 567.14
vocational school
567.8
**industrious**
active 707.22
painstaking 533.11
persevering 625.7
**industriously**
actively 707.27
carefully 533.15
laboriously 716.19
perseveringly 625.8
**industry**
commerce 827.1
company 788.9
industriousness 707.6
painstakingness 533.2
perseverance 625.1
work 716.4
**indwell**
be present 186.6
inhere 5.5
**indwelling**
n. intrinsicality 5.1
adj. intrinsic 5.6
present 186.12
**inebriant**
n. liquor 996.12
adj. intoxicating
996.35
**inebriate**
n. drunkard 996.10
v. make drunk 996.21
adj. intoxicated
996.30
**inebriation** 996.1
**inedible** 429.8
**ineducable** 469.15
**ineffable**
extraordinary 85.14
indescribable 920.13
sacred 1026.7
**ineffective**
incompetent 734.19
ineffectual 158.15
unable 158.14

**influenza**
  infectious disease
   686.12
  respiratory disease
   686.14
**influx** inflow 302.2
  intrusion 238.1
**info** 557.1
**in force** existent 1.13
  in use 665.24
  operating 164.11
  powerful 157.12
**inform** divulge 556.6
  inspire 648.20
  report 558.11
  teach 562.11
  tell 557.8
**informal** casual 231.46
  nonconformist 83.6
  slovenly 62.15
  unceremonious 647.3
  vernacular 580.18
**informality** 647
**informally** 647.4
**informant**
  examinee 485.18
  informer 557.5
  witness 505.7
**information**
  accusation 1005.1
  arraignment 1004.3
  communication
   554.1
  computer 349.19
  data 1.4
  facts 557
  knowledge 475.1
  news 558.1
  teaching 562.1
**information theory**
  automation 349.2
  communication
   554.5
  communication the-
   ory 557.7
  telecommunication
   560.1
**informative**
  educational 562.19
  enlightening 557.17
**informed**
  apprised 557.16
  enlightened 475.18
  prepared 720.16
**informed of**
  apprised 557.16
  cognizant of 475.16
**informer**
  accuser 1005.5
  betrayer 557.6
  source 557.5
  traitor 619.10
  witness 505.7
**inform on**
  accuse 1005.7
  betray 975.14
  divulge 556.6
  inform against 557.12
**fra** 208.10
**fraction**
  disobedience 767.1
  lawbreaking 999.3

**overstepping** 313.3
  violation 769.2
  wrong 959.1
**infrangible** firm 159.16
  indivisible 354.13
  unbreakable 359.5
**infrequency**
  fewness 102.1
  rarity 136
**infrequent** rare 136.2
  sparse 102.5
**infrequently**
  at intervals 72.5
  scarcely 102.8
  seldom 136.4
**infringe** borrow 821.4
  break the law 999.5
  encroach 313.9
  intrude 238.5
  usurp 961.8
  violate 769.4
**infringement**
  borrowing 821.2
  disobedience 767.1
  impairment 692.1
  intrusion 238.1
  lawbreaking 999.3
  overstepping 313.3
  usurpation 961.3
  violation 769.2
**in front** ahead 240.12
  before 292.4
**in front of** 239.7
**in full** at length 593.16
  completely 56.14
  fully 8.13
**in full swing**
  actively 707.25
  astir 707.19
  thriving 728.13
  unweakened 159.19
**in full view** 444.6
**in fun**
  for amusement
   878.33
  in sport 881.19
  mischievously 738.7
**infundibular**
  conical 255.12
  funnel-shaped 257.16
**infuriate**
  antagonize 929.7
  enrage 952.23
  excite 857.11
**infuriated** 952.29
**infuse** extract 305.16
  imbue 44.12
  indoctrinate 562.13
  insert 304.3
  inspire 648.20
  liquefy 391.5
  soak 392.13
**infusion**
  admixture 44.7
  baptism 1040.7
  distillation 305.8
  extraction 305.7
  imbuement 44.2
  indoctrination 562.2
  insertion 304.1
  inspiration 648.9
  soaking 392.7

**solution** 391.3
**in gear** 13.12
**in general** 79.17
**ingenious**
  cunning 735.12
  imaginative 535.18
  skillful 733.20
**ingenue** actor 612.2
  role 611.11
  unsophisticate 736.3
**ingenuity**
  inventiveness 535.3
  skill 733.1
**ingenuous** artless 736.5
  candid 974.17
  gullible 502.9
  immature 124.10
**ingest** consume 666.2
  eat 307.20
  learn 564.7
  take in 306.11
**ingesta** 308.1
**ingestion**
  consumption 666.1
  digestion 309.8
  eating 307.1
  learning 564.2
  taking in 306.4
**ingle** fire 328.13
  fireplace 329.11
  home 191.4
**inglorious**
  disreputable 915.10
  humble 906.9
  unrenowned 915.14
**ingoing**
  *n.* entrance 302.1
  *adj.* entering 302.12
  introverted 690.46
**ingot**
  currency metals
   835.20
  metal casting 383.5
**ingrain** color 362.13
  implant 142.9
**ingrained**
  deep-rooted 642.21
  dyed 362.17
  infixed 142.13
  intrinsic 5.6
**ingrate** 950.2
**ingratiate oneself**
  be servile 907.9
  gain influence 172.12
  influence 172.7
**ingratiating**
  obsequious 907.13
  suave 936.18
**ingratitude** 950
**ingredient**
  component 58.2
  content 194.1
**ingress** channel 396.1
  entrance 302
  inlet 302.5
**ingroup** clique 788.6
  group 74.3
  influential persons
   172.6
  the rulers 749.15
**ingrown** 142.13
**inhabit** exist in 1.11

**occupy** 188.7
  populate 188.9
  settle 184.16
**inhabitable** 188.15
**inhabitant**
  population 190.1
  resident 190.2
**inhabited** 188.12
**inhalant** 687.4
**inhalation**
  breathing 403.18
  taking in 306.5
  wind 403.1
**inhalator**
  breathing 403.18
  respirator 689.37
**inhale** breathe 403.24
  draw in 306.12
  smell 435.8
  use tobacco 434.14
**in hand**
  *adj.* happening 151.9
  operating 164.11
  orderly 59.6
  possessed 808.8
  restrained 163.11
  undertaken 715.7
  unused 668.12
  *adv.* in preparation
   720.22
  in production 167.25
  under control 741.20
**inharmonious**
  different 16.7
  disaccordant 795.15
  disagreeing 27.6
  off-color 362.20
  sounds 461.4
**in harmony**
  agreeing 26.9
  concurrently 177.5
  in accord 794.3
  in conformity with
   82.9
  jointly 47.18
**in heat** 419.30
**inhere** be present 186.6
  exist in 1.11
  indwell 5.5
**inherence**
  intrinsicality 5.1
  presence 186.1
**inherent**
  instinctive 481.6
  intrinsic 5.6
  present 186.12
**inherit**
  come into 819.7
  succeed 65.2
**inheritable**
  heritable 170.16
  transferable 817.5
**inheritance**
  bequest 818.10
  heredity 170.6
  heritage 819.2
**inherited**
  hereditary 170.15
  innate 5.7
**inheritor**
  descendant 171.1
  heir 819.5

nonfulfillment 769.1
**inobservant**
  inattentive 531.6
  nonobservant 769.5
**inoculate**
  immunize 689.34
  indoctrinate 562.13
  insert 304.3
  inspire 648.20
**inoculation**
  indoctrination 562.2
  insertion 304.1
  vaccination 689.18
**inoffensive**
  harmless 674.20
  pardonable 1006.14
**inoperable**
  hopeless 889.15
  impracticable 510.8
  unusable 669.14
**in operation**
  in use 665.24
  operating 164.11
**inoperative**
  in disrepair 692.39
  ineffective 158.15
  unusable 669.14
**inopportune**
  inexpedient 671.5
  untimely 130.7
**in opposition**
  adverse 729.13
  counteractively
    178.10
  dissenting 522.6
  in confrontation
    790.9
**in opposition to**
  facing 239.7
  in disagreement with
    27.10
  opposed to 790.10
**in order**
  in condition 7.8
  in turn 59.10
  orderly 59.7
**in order to**
  in preparation for
    720.24
  intending 653.12
**inordinance** 663.1
**inordinate**
  exaggerated 617.4
  excessive 663.16
  fanatical 473.32
  intemperate 993.7
  overpriced 848.12
**inordinately**
  excessively 663.22
  exorbitantly 848.16
  greatly 34.21
  intemperately 993.10
**inorganic**
  mineral 383.15
  unorganic 382.4
**inorganic matter** 382
**inornate** 902.9
**in particular** fully 8.13
  particularly 80.15
**in passing**
  hastily 709.12
  incidentally 129.13

on the way 271.19
**inpatient**
  resident 190.2
  sick person 686.40
**in person**
  personally 80.16
  presence 186.17
**in place** 184.19
**in place of** 149.12
**in plain sight**
  overtly 555.15
  visible 444.6
**inpouring** 302.12
**in power**
  in authority 739.21
  powerful 157.12
**in practice**
  in use 665.24
  operating 164.11
**in process**
  in preparation 720.22
  operating 164.11
  undertaken 715.7
**in production**
  in preparation 720.22
  under construction
    167.25
**in progress**
  going on 294.7
  in preparation 720.22
  undertaken 715.7
**in public**
  overtly 555.15
  publicly 559.19
**input** 302.1
**input data** 349.19
**inquest** autopsy 408.18
  inquiry 485.1
  jury 1002.7
  trial 1004.5
**in question**
  at issue 485.38
  pending 514.17
  uncertain 514.16
**inquietude**
  agitation 324.1
  anxiety 890.1
  excitement 857.4
  trepidation 891.5
  unpleasure 866.1
**inquire** ask 485.19
  be curious 528.3
**inquire for** 485.29
**inquire into**
  discourse upon 606.5
  take under consider-
    ation 478.14
**inquirer** asker 485.15
  curious person 528.2
  student 566.1
**inquiring**
  *n.* inquiry 485.1
  questioning 485.11
  *adj.* curious 528.5
  questioning 485.35
**inquiring mind**
  curiosity 528.1
  inquiry 485.1
**inquiry** canvass 485.13
  inquiring 485
  investigation 485.4
  question 485.10

trial 1004.5
**inquisition**
  grilling 485.12
  inquiry 485.1
  trial 1004.5
  tribunal 1001.1
**inquisitive**
  curious 528.5
  meddlesome 238.9
**inquisitor**
  curious person 528.2
  inquirer 485.15
**inquisitorial** 485.35
**in re** 9.13
**in reality** really 1.16
  truly 516.17
**in relation to** 9.13
**in reserve** aside 660.17
  imminent 152.3
  in readiness 720.21
**in return**
  in answer 486.7
  in compensation 33.7
  in retaliation 955.9
  interchangeably
    150.6
**inroad**
  impairment 692.1
  intrusion 238.1
  overstepping 313.3
  raid 798.4
**inrush**
  *n.* influx 302.2
  wind 403.1
  *v.* enter 302.9
**ins**
  officeholders 746.11
  the rulers 749.15
**insalubrious** 684.5
**insalubrity** 684.1
**ins and outs**
  circumstance 8.2
  vicissitudes 156.5
**insane** foolish 470.8
  mad 473.25
  overzealous 635.13
**insane asylum** 473.14
**insanely** 473.35
**insanity**
  foolishness 470.1
  insaneness 473
  mental deficiency
    469.9
  mental disorder
    690.17
**insatiable**
  gluttonous 994.6
  greedy 634.27
**inscribe** engrave 578.10
  fix in the mind
    537.18
  imprint 142.9
  letter 581.6
  record 570.16
  write 602.19
**inscribed**
  engraved 578.12
  recorded 570.18
  written 602.22
**inscription**
  book 605.12
  engraving 578.2

epitaph 410.18
  lettering 581.5
  memorial 570.12
  motto 517.4
  recording 570.15
  writing 602.1
**inscriptional** 570.19
**inscrutable** 549.13
**in season** 128.8
**insect** bad person 986.7
  bug 414.36,74
  invertebrate 415.5
**insecticide** killer 409.3
  poison 676.3
**insectivore** 414.3; 415.8
**insectivorous** 307.29
**insectlike** 414.55
**insecure**
  unreliable 514.19
  unsafe 697.11
  unsure 514.22
**insecurity**
  precariousness 697.2
  unreliability 514.6
**inseminate**
  fertilize 169.10
  plant 413.18
**inseminated** 169.17
**insemination**
  fertilization 169.3
  planting 413.14
**insensate**
  inanimate 382.5
  insensible 423.6
  unintelligent 469.13
  unwise 470.9
  violent 162.17
**insensibility**
  emotional symptom
    690.23
  inanimateness 382.2
  incognizance 477.3
  indiscrimination
    493.1
  insensitivity 423
  obliviousness 856.2
  unperceptiveness
    469.2
**insensible**
  imperceptible 445.5
  inanimate 382.5
  inattentive 531.7
  oblivious 856.10
  unaware 477.13
  undiscerning 469.14
  unfeeling 423.6
**insensitive**
  callous 856.12
  discourteous 937.6
  heartless 939.23
  insensible 423.6
  undiscriminating
    493.5
**insensitivity**
  callousness 856.3
  discourtesy 937.1
  heartlessness 939.10
  indiscrimination
    493.1
  insensibility 423.1
**insentient**
  inanimate 382.5

part 55.1
payment 841.1
**installment plan**
borrowing 821.1
credit 839.1
payment 841.1
**instance**
*n.* citation 505.6
example 25.2
particular 8.3
proposal 773.2
urging 648.5
*v.* cite 505.14
particularize 8.6
**instant**
*n.* moment 113.3
period 107.1
short time 111.3
*adj.* demanding 753.8
immediate 709.9
imminent 152.3
momentary 113.4
present 120.2
prompt 131.9
urgent 672.21
**instantaneous**
brief 203.8
immediate 113.4
prompt 131.9
**instantaneously**
instantly 113.6
quickly 269.23
**instantly** hastily 709.12
immediately 113.6
promptly 131.15
**instate**
inaugurate 780.11
install 304.4
**instead** 149.11
**instead of** 149.12
**instep** 212.5
**in step** agreeing 26.11
conformist 82.6
synchronous 118.5
**in step with** 82.9
**instigate** incite 648.17
induce 153.12
**instigation** 648.4
**instigative** 648.28
**instigator**
inciter 648.11
originator 153.4
producer 167.8
**instill**
fix in the mind
537.18
indoctrinate 562.13
infuse 44.12
**instilled** 642.21
**instillment**
indoctrination 562.2
infusion 44.2
**instinct** impulse 630.1
involuntariness 639.5
proclivity 481.2
sensitivity 174.1
talent 733.4
**instinctive**
animal 414.43
innate 5.7
involuntary 639.14
natural 481.6

**instinctively**
intuitively 481.7
involuntarily 639.18
**institute**
*n.* organization 788.8
school 567.1
*v.* establish 167.12
inaugurate 68.11
originate 153.11
**institution**
beginning 68.1
consecration 1037.10
establishment 167.4
law 998.3
organization 788.8
rite 1040.3
workplace 719.1
**institutional** 567.18
**institutionalize** 761.17
**institutor** 167.8
**in store**
*adj.* destined 640.9
imminent 152.3
possessed 808.8
*adv.* in readiness
720.21
in stock 660.16
**instruct** advise 754.5
command 752.9
inform 557.8
teach 562.11
**instructable** 564.18
**instructed** 475.18
**instruction**
advice 754.1
directive 752.3
information 557.1
learning 475.4
lesson 562.7
precept 751.1
teaching 562.1
**instructional** 562.19
**instructions**
computer 349.19
directions 562.6
**instructive**
advisory 754.8
commanding 752.14
educational 562.19
informative 557.17
prescriptive 751.4
**instructor**
academic rank 565.4
advisor 754.3
pilot 279.1
preparer 720.5
teacher 565.1
**instructorship** 565.11
**instructress** 565.2
**instrument**
*n.* agent 781.3
aviation 278.61
color 362.24
document 570.5
gripping 813.12
implement 658.3
measuring device
490.4
medical 689.36
music 465
optical 443.11
pointed 258.18

recording 571.3
sycophant 907.3
tool 348.1
weighing 352.22
*v.* music 462.47
tool 348.10
**instrumental**
helping 785.20
implemental 658.6
music 462.52
**instrumentalist**
*n.* musician 464.3
*adj.* philosophy 500.9
**instrumentality** 658.2
**instrumentation**
measurement 490.1
music 463.2
rocketry 281.1
tooling 348.8
**insubordinate**
*n.* rebel 767.5
*adj.* disobedient 767.9
lawless 740.5
**insubordination**
disobedience 767.1
lawlessness 740.1
**insubstantial**
illogical 483.12
immaterial 377.7
tenuous 355.4
thin 205.16
transient 111.7
unreliable 514.19
unsubstantial 4.5
**insubstantiality**
intangibility 4.1
tenuousness 355.1
thinness 205.4
unreliability 514.6
**in succession**
consecutively 71.11
in order 59.10
**insufferable** 864.25
**insufferably** 864.30
**insufficiency**
inability 158.2
inadequacy 662
inequality 31.1
inferiority 37.3
meagerness 35.1
shortcoming 314.1
unsatisfactoriness
869.2
**insufficient**
inadequate 662.9
inferior 37.7
short of 314.5
unequal 31.4
unsatisfactory 869.6
**insufficient funds** 842.3
**insufficiently**
inadequately 662.14
unsatisfactorily
869.9
**insular**
*n.* islander 386.4
*adj.* alone 89.8
exclusive 77.8
island 386.7
narrow-minded
527.10
region 180.9

secluded 924.7
separate 49.20
unrelated 10.5
**insularity**
exclusiveness 77.3
island 386.2
narrow-mindedness
527.1
**insulate**
electricity 342.26
island 386.5
segregate 77.6
strengthen 159.12
**insulated** 386.7
**insulating** 342.33
**insulation**
exclusiveness 77.3
safety equipment
699.3
**insulator** 342.13,36
**insulin** 312.10
**insult**
*n.* contempt 966.1
indignity 965.2
*v.* disdain 966.3
offend 965.4
**insulting**
audacious 913.8
insolent 965.6
**insuperable**
impracticable 510.8
impregnable 159.17
**insupportable** 864.25
**insuppressible** 626.12
**insurance**
precaution 895.3
protection 699.4
security 772.1
**insurance company**
699.4
**insurance policy**
contract 771.3
insurance 699.4
**insure**
make sure 513.11
protect 699.18
secure 772.9
**insured**
guaranteed 772.11
safe 698.4
**insurer** endorser 521.7
guarantor 772.6
**insurgence** 767.4
**insurgent**
*n.* rebel 767.5
*adj.* rebellious 767.11
**insurmountable** 510.8
**insurrection** 767.4
**insurrectionary**
rebellious 767.11
revolutionary 147.5
**insusceptible** 856.9
**in suspense**
expectant 539.12
inert 268.14
perplexed 514.24
uncertainly 514.26
undecided 514.17
**intact** chaste 988.6
complete 56.9
flawless 677.7
immature 124.10

new 122.7
preserved 701.11
safe 698.4
unaltered 140.7
unpierced 266.10
whole 54.10
**intaglio**
engraving process
578.3
engraving tool 578.9
model 25.6
relief 575.3
**intake** entrance 302.1
inlet 302.5
receipts 844.1
**intangibility**
immateriality 377.1
infinitesimalness
196.2
unsubstantiality 4.1
**intangible**
immaterial 377.7
infinitesimal 196.14
unsubstantial 4.5
**intangibles** 810.8
**integer** entity 89.4
number 86.3
whole 54.1
**integral**
component 58.5
numerical 86.8
one 89.7
sound 677.7
unitary 89.10
whole 54.9
**integrate** combine 52.3
equalize 30.6
form a whole 54.7
mix 44.11
symmetrize 248.3
unify 89.5
**integrated**
combined 52.5
joined 47.13
unitary 89.10
whole 54.9
**integration**
affiliation 786.2
combination 52.1
coordination 26.4
equalization 30.2
mathematics 87.4
mixture 44.1
symmetrization 248.2
unity 89.1
whole 54.1
**integrity**
completeness 56.1
honesty 974.1
individuality 80.1
simplicity 45.1
soundness 677.2
unity 89.1
whole 54.1
**integument**
cover 228.3
exterior 224.2
skin 229.1
**intellect**
intellectual 476.1
intelligence 467.1

**intelligent being**
467.9
mind 466
wise man 468.1
**intellectual**
*n.* intellectualist 476
scientist 475.11
wise man 468.1
*adj.* intelligent 467.12
learned 475.23
mental 466.8
temperamental 525.7
**intellectuality**
intelligence 467.1
scholarship 475.5
**intellectualize**
reason 482.15
think 478.8
**intelligence**
information 557.1
. intellect 466.1
intelligence service
781.12
intelligent being
467.9
knowledge 475.1
mental capacity 467
news 558.1
spirit 1014.15
spying 485.9
teachability 564.5
understanding 475.3
**intelligence agent** 781.9
**intelligence quotient**
intelligence 467.1
psychological test
690.11
**intelligence service**
781.12
**intelligence test** 690.11
**intelligence testing**
690.10
**intelligence work** 485.9
**intelligent**
intellectual 467.12
knowing 475.15
mental 466.8
teachable 564.18
**intelligently**
knowingly 475.29
understandingly
467.20
**intelligentsia** 476.2
**intelligibility**
comprehensibility
548
facility 732.1
meaningfulness 545.5
**intelligible**
comprehensible
548.9
meaningful 545.10
**intemperance**
excess 663.1
gluttony 994.1
indulgence 993
intoxication 996.2
prodigality 854.1
unchastity 989.2
unrestraint 762.3
**intemperate**
excessive 663.16

gluttonous 994.6
indulgent 993.7
prodigal 854.8
unchaste 989.24
unrestrained 762.23
violent 162.15
**intemperately**
excessively 663.22
immoderately 993.10
**intend** aim to 653.5
mean 545.9
plan 654.9
purpose 653.4
**intended**
*n.* fiancée 931.16
*adj.* betrothed 770.8
intentional 653.9
meant 545.11
**intense** acute 422.15
attentive 530.15
colorful 362.18
energetic 161.12
fervent 855.23
great 34.6
penetrating 159.20
violent 162.15
zealous 635.10
**intensely** acutely 34.20
energetically 161.15
fervently 855.28
strongly 159.21
zealously 635.15
**intensification**
aggravation 885.1
increase 38.2
**intensified**
aggravated 885.4
increased 38.7
**intensify**
aggravate 885.2
increase 38.6
strengthen 38.5
**intensity**
colorfulness 362.4
energy 161.1
greatness 34.1
light unit 335.21
loudness 453.1
violence 162.1
zeal 635.2
**intensive** 56.10
**intensive care** 192.25
**intent**
*n.* aim 653.1
meaning 545.2
*adj.* attentive 530.15
determined upon
624.16
engrossed 530.17
zealous 635.10
**intention**
meaning 545.2
motive 648.1
plan 654.1
purpose 653
will 621.1
**intentional** 653.9
**intentionally** 653.11
**intently**
attentively 530.21
zealously 635.15

**intentness**
attention 530.1
engrossment 530.3
zeal 635.2
**inter** 410.19
**interact** 13.8
**interacting**
communicational
554.9
interworking 13.12
**interaction**
communication
554.1
interworking 13.3
**inter alia** 40.11
**interassociation**
connection 47.2
interrelation 13.2
**interbreed** 44.14
**interbreeding** 44.4
**intercede** 805.6
**intercept** hinder 730.10
listen 448.11
**interception** 346.9
**intercession**
mediation 805.1
prayer 1032.4
**intercessional**
Christlike 1013.19
mediatory 805.8
**intercessor**
lawyer 1003.1
mediator 805.3
**interchange**
*n.* communication
554.1
exchange 150
interaction 13.3
passageway 657.4
retaliation 955.1
trade 827.2
transference 271.1
*v.* communicate 554.6
exchange 150.4
get along 794.2
interact 13.8
trade 827.14
**interchangeable**
exchangeable 150.5
indistinctive 493.6
transferable 271.17
**interchanged** 150.5
**intercollegiate** 567.18
**intercom**
communications
560.6
sound reproduction
system 450.11
**intercommunicate**
be joined 47.11
communicate 554.6
**intercommunication**
communication
554.1
interaction 13.3
joining 47.1
social intercourse
922.4
**intercommunicational**
554.9
**interconnect**
interjoin 47.6

**interplanetary travel**
282.1
**interplay**
*n.* communication
554.1
interaction 13.3
interchange 150.1
*v.* interact 13.8
**Interpol**
international organi-
zation 743.5
police force 699.17
**interpolate** 237.6
**interpolation**
addition 41.2
insertion 304.1
interjection 237.2
mathematics 87.4
music 462.27
**interpose**
interject 237.6
intrude 238.5
mediate 805.6
**interposition**
interlocation 237
intrusion 238.1
mediation 805.1
**interpret**
diagnose 552.9
perform music 462.40
solve 487.2
**interpretable**
construable 552.17
meaningful 545.10
**interpretation**
explanation 552
meaning 545.3
solution 487.1
**interpretative** 552.14
**interpreter**
explainer 552.7
musician 464.1
**interrelate**
interconnect 13.7
relate 9.6
**interrelated**
interconnected 13.11
related 9.9
**interrelation**
interconnection 13.2
relationship 9.2
**interrogate**
be curious 528.3
communicate with
554.8
question 485.20
**interrogation**
examination 485.11
question 485.10
**interrogative** 485.10
**interrogator** 485.15
**interrogatory**
communicational
554.9
inquiring 485.35
**interrupt**
discontinue 72.3
hinder 730.10
intrude 238.6
suspend 144.10
talk out of turn 130.5
**interrupted** 72.4

**interruption**
discontinuity 72.2
hindrance 730.1
interim 109.1
interval 201.1
intrusion 238.1
pause 144.3
untimeliness 130.1
**interruptive**
hindering 730.17
intrusive 238.8
**intersect** agree 26.6
converge 298.2
cross 221.6
**intersected** 221.8
**intersection**
agreement 26.1
crossing 221.1
crossroad 221.2
passageway 657.4
**interseptum** 237.5
**intersexuality** 419.14
**interspace**
*n.* interval 201.1
*v.* space 201.3
**interspaced** 201.6
**intersperse** 237.7
**interspersion** 237.3
**interstellar** 375.25
**interstice** 201.1
**interstitial** 201.5
**intertwine**
interact 13.8
mix 44.11
weave 222.6
**intertwined**
webbed 221.12
woven 222.7
**intertwining**
*n.* interaction 13.3
weaving 222.1
*adj.* weaving 222.8
**interurban**
*n.* train 272.13
*adj.* urban 183.10
**interval** degree 29.1
discontinuity 72.2
gap 57.2
harmonics 463.20
interim 109.1
opening 265.1
pause 144.3
period 107.1
space 201
**intervene**
hinder 730.10
interpose 237.6
intrude 238.5
mediate 805.6
pause 109.3
**intervening**
intermediate 237.10
mediatory 805.8
**intervention**
interposition 237.1
intrusion 238.1
mediation 805.1
**interview**
*n.* appointment 922.8
audition 448.2
conference 597.6
*v.* interrogate 485.20

**interviewer**
inquirer 485.15
journalist 605.22
**interweave**
interact 13.8
mix 44.11
weave 222.6
**interweaving**
*n.* interaction 13.3
weaving 222.1
*adj.* weaving 222.8
**interwork** 13.8
**interworking**
*n.* interaction 13.3
*adj.* interacting 13.12
**interwoven**
webbed 221.12
woven 222.7
**intestate** 818.25
**intestinal** 225.10
**intestinal fortitude**
courage 893.5
strength 159.1
**intestine** duct 396.13
meat 308.20
vitals 225.4
**in the act**
about to 121.13
red-handed 983.4
**in the air** aloft 207.26
rumored 558.15
**in the bag**
made sure 513.20
prearranged 641.5
**in the black** 811.16
**in the blood** 5.7
**in the cards**
destined 640.9
imminent 152.3
probable 511.6
**in the clear** free 762.20
innocent 984.6
in safety 698.6
legible 548.11
**in the dark**
at night 337.19
ignorant 477.16
secretly 614.17
**in the driver's seat**
in authority 739.21
influential 172.14
**in the know**
apprised 557.16
cognizant of 475.16
**in the long run**
eventually 151.12
generally 79.17
in time 121.11
on the average 32.5
on the whole 54.14
**in the neighborhood of**
about 200.26
around 233.12
near 200.14
**in the pink**
healthy 685.7
in order 59.7
**in the red**
at a loss 812.9
destitute 838.9
indebted 840.8
**in the swim** 644.11

**in the wind**
against the wind
275.65
happening 151.9
imminent 152.3
**in the works**
in preparation 720.22
in production 167.25
operating 164.11
planned 654.13
undertaken 715.7
**intimacy**
copulation 419.8
friendship 927.5
knowledge 475.1
relationship 9.1
sociability 922.1
**intimate**
*n.* friend 928.1
*v.* hint 557.10
imply 546.4
*adj.* familiar 922.20
friendly 927.18
homelike 191.33
individual 80.12
interior 225.7
joined 47.13
near 200.14
private 614.13
versed in 475.19
**intimated** 546.7
**intimately**
amicably 927.21
internally 225.11
**intimation**
admixture 44.7
clue 568.9
hint 557.4
hunch 481.3
implication 546.2
small amount 35.4
vague supposition
499.5
**in time** music 463.30
periodically 137.10
soon enough 131.12
synchronous 118.5
ultimately 121.11
**intimidate**
bluster 911.3
coerce 756.7
dissuade 652.3
domineer 741.16
frighten 891.28
threaten 973.2
**intimidated**
cowardly 892.10
terrified 891.34
**intimidating**
dissuasive 652.5
threatening 973.3
**intimidation**
bluster 911.1
coercion 756.3
dissuasion 652.1
frightening 891.6
threat 973.1
**into**
*adj.* knowing 475.17
*prep.* entering 302.14
in 225.15

**intolerable**
  insufferable 864.25
  outright 34.12
  unacceptable 869.7
  unlikable 867.7
**intolerably**
  insufferably 864.30
  unduly 34.21
  unsatisfactorily
    869.9
**intolerance**
  narrow-mindedness
    527.2
  nonendurance 862.2
  obstinacy 626.1
**intolerant**
  narrow-minded
    527.11
  obstinate 626.8
  unforbearing 862.7
**intonate** inflect 594.29
  sing 462.39
**intonation**
  accent 463.25
  harmonization 463.2
  inflection 594.7
  music 462.31
  tone 450.2
  vocal music 462.12
**intone** 462.39
**intoxicate** dizzy 532.8
  make drunk 996.21
  thrill 857.14
**intoxicated**
  drunk 996.30
  excited 857.23
  fervent 855.23
**intoxicating**
  exciting 857.28
  inebriating 996.35
**intoxication**
  excitement 857.7
  happiness 865.2
  inebriation 996
  poisoning 686.30
**intractability**
  disobedience 767.1
  rigidity 356.3
  ungovernability 626.4
**intractable**
  insubordinate 767.9
  rigid 356.12
  ungovernable 626.12
**intramural**
  internal 225.9
  scholastic 567.18
**intransient** 110.10
**intransigence** 626.2
**intransigent**
  *n.* obstinate person
    626.6
  oppositionist 791.3
  *adj.* unyielding 626.9
**intransitive**
  *n.* verb 586.4
  *adj.* grammatical
    586.17
**intransmutable** 142.17
**intraterritorial** 225.9
**intravenous** 689.19
**intrepid** 893.17
**intrepidly** 893.22

**intricacy**
  abstruseness 549.2
  complexity 46.1
  difficulty 731.1
**intricate**
  bewildering 514.25
  complex 46.4
  difficult 731.16
  hard to understand
    549.14
  mixed 44.15
**intrigue**
  *n.* dishonesty 975.3
  influence 172.3
  love affair 931.6
  plot 654.6
  stratagem 735.3
  *v.* fascinate 650.6
  maneuver 735.10
  plot 654.10
**intriguing**
  alluring 650.7
  pleasant 863.7
  scheming 654.14
**intrinsic**
  characteristic 80.13
  inherent 5.6
  interior 225.7
**intrinsically**
  characteristically
    80.17
  inherently 5.9
  internally 225.11
**introduce**
  acquaint 927.13
  begin 68.11
  bring in 306.14
  change 139.8
  go before 66.3
  insert 304.3
  interpose 237.6
  preface 64.3
  preinstruct 562.15
  propose 773.5
**introducer**
  originator 167.8
  transformer 139.4
**introduction**
  acquaintance 927.4
  act 611.8
  book 605.12
  bringing in 306.7
  elementary instruc-
    tion 562.5
  entrance 302.1
  inauguration 68.5
  innovation 139.3
  insertion 304.1
  interjection 237.2
  legislative procedure
    742.14
  music 462.26
  prelude 66.2
**introductory**
  beginning 68.15
  educational 562.19
  initiatory 306.18
**introit** 462.16
**Introit** hymn 1032.3
  Mass 1040.10
**intromission**
  admission 306.2

  insertion 304.1
**intromit** insert 304.3
  receive 306.10
**introspect** 478.12
**introspection** 478.6
**introspective**
  preoccupied 478.22
  thoughtful 478.21
**introversion**
  interiority 225.1
  inversion 220.1
  personality tendency
    690.14
  reticence 613.3
**introvert**
  *n.* personality type
    690.15
  *v.* invert 220.5
**introverted**
  inner-directed 690.46
  reticent 613.10
  reversed 220.7
**intrude** enter 302.7
  interlope 238.5
  interpose 237.6
  overstep 313.9
  talk out of turn 130.5
**intruder**
  foreign body 78.2
  incomer 302.4
  interloper 238.3
  newcomer 78.4
**intrusion**
  entrance 302.1
  extraneousness 78.1
  interloping 238
  interposition 237.1
  overstepping 313.3
  untimeliness 130.1
**intrusive**
  entering 302.12
  extraneous 78.5
  interfering 238.8
  overactive 707.24
  untimely 130.7
**intuit** foreknow 542.6
  sense 481.4
**intuition**
  clairvoyance 1034.8
  hunch 481.3
  intuitiveness 481
**intuitive**
  foreseeing 542.7
  intuitional 481.5
  premonitory 544.16
**intuitively** 481.7
**intumescence**
  distension 197.2
  swelling 256.4
  tumor 686.36
**in tune**
  harmonious 462.50
  in accord 794.3
**in turn**
  alternately 137.11
  consecutively 71.11
  in order 59.10
  reciprocally 150.6
**inundate**
  drench 392.14
  engulf 395.17
  make grieve 872.19

  oversupply 663.14
  overwhelm 693.21
  raid 798.20
  run over 313.7
  submerge 320.7
**inundated**
  flooded 395.25
  heartbroken 872.29
  soaked 392.17
  underwater 209.13
**inundation**
  overabundance 663.2
  overflow 395.6
  overrunning 313.1
  submergence 320.2
  wetting 392.6
**in unison**
  concurrently 177.5
  cooperatively 786.6
  harmonious 462.50
  in step 26.11
  jointly 47.18
  simultaneously 118.6
  unanimously 521.17
**inure** accustom 642.11
  make unfeeling 856.6
**inured**
  accustomed 642.17
  callous 856.12
  wicked 981.17
**invade** encroach 313.9
  intrude 238.5
  overrun 313.6
  raid 798.20
  usurp 961.8
**invader**
  assailant 798.13
  intruder 238.3
**invading** 798.29
**in vain** amiss 314.7
  unsuccessfully 725.18
**invalid**
  *n.* impotent 158.6
  recluse 924.5
  sick person 686.40
  *v.* sicken 686.47
  *adj.* bad 675.7
  illogical 483.11
  ineffective 158.15
  repealed 779.3
  unhealthy 686.50
**invalidate**
  abolish 693.13
  disprove 506.4
  disqualify 158.10
  nullify 178.7
  repeal 779.2
**invalidated**
  disabled 158.16
  disproved 506.7
**invalidation**
  disproof 506.1
  nullification 178.2
  repeal 779.1
**invaluable** 848.10
**invariable**
  tedious 884.8
  unchangeable 142.17
  uniform 17.5
**invariably**
  always 112.11
  permanently 140.9

**irresponsible**
exempt 762.29
inconstant 141.7
lawless 740.5
untrustworthy 975.19
**irretrievable**
hopeless 889.15
lost 812.7
unchangeable 142.17
**irretrievably**
absolutely 56.15
hopelessly 889.18
**irreverence**
disrespect 965.1
impiety 1030.1
**irreverent**
disrespectful 965.5
impious 1030.6
**irreversible**
confirmed 642.21
direct 290.13
hopeless 889.15
unchangeable 142.17
**irreversibly** 889.18
**irrevocable**
hopeless 889.15
inevitable 639.15
mandatory 752.13
unchangeable 142.17
**irrevocably**
absolutely 56.15
hopelessly 889.18
inevitable 639.19
**irrigate** dilute 160.11
moisten 392.12
wash 681.19
**irrigation**
washing 681.5
wetting 392.6
**irrigational** 392.18
**irritability**
dissension 795.3
excitability 857.9
irascibility 951.2
sensitivity 422.3
**irritable**
excitable 857.26
irascible 951.19
nervous 859.10
quarrelsome 795.17
sensitive 422.14
**irritant** 866.3
**irritate** aggravate 885.2
annoy 866.14
hurt 424.7
impair 692.11
make nervous 859.8
provoke 952.22
sow dissension 795.14
**irritated**
aggravated 885.4
annoyed 866.21
damaged 692.29
provoked 952.25
sore 424.11
**irritating**
aggravating 885.5
annoying 864.22
painful 424.13
pungent 433.6
**irritation**
adversity 729.1

aggravation 885.1
annoyance 866.3
excitation 857.10
incitement 648.4
pain 424.4
resentment 952.1
**irrupt** appear 446.9
begin 68.13
encroach 313.9
enter 302.7
intrude 238.5
**irruption**
emotional outburst
857.8
intrusion 238.1
raid 798.4
**irruptive**
attacking 798.29
entering 302.12
**Isaiah** 1022.1
**Ishmael** 926.4
**Ishtar** 1014.11
**Isis**
Egyptian deity
1014.10
fertility goddess
165.5
**Islam** 1020.12
**Islamic** 1020.30
**island**
n. airport 278.22
isle 386.2
adj. insular 386.7
**islander** 386.4
**island-hop** 386.5
**island universe** 375.6
**isle** 386.2
**ism** religion 1020.2
school 788.5
system of belief
501.3
**–ism** a belief 501.2
mannerism 903.2
process 164.2
state 7.1
**iso–** equal 30.7
identical 14.8
uniform 17.5
**isobar** isotope 326.5,21
weather 402.5
**isolate**
electricity 342.26
exclude 42.10
island 386.5
quarantine 761.13
segregate 77.6
separate 49.9
**isolated** alone 89.8
insular 386.7
private 614.13
quarantined 761.20
quiescent 268.12
secluded 924.7
separated 49.21
unrelated 10.5
**isolation**
aloneness 89.2
defense mechanism
690.30
exclusiveness 77.3
hospital room 192.25
privacy 614.2

quarantine 761.2
seclusion 924.1
separation 49.1
**isolationism**
foreign policy 744.5
noninterference
762.9
seclusion 924.1
**isolationist**
independent 762.12
recluse 924.5
**isomer** chemical 379.1
isotope 326.5
**isometric**
equisized 30.10
meteorology 402.13
**isometrics** 716.6
**isotherm** 402.5
**isothermal** 328.30
**isotope** 326.5
**Israelite**
n. Jew 1020.20
adj. Jewish 1020.29
**issue**
n. cause 153.10
edition 605.2
emergence 303.2
escape 632.1
family 11.5
important point
672.6
political platform
744.7
posterity 171.1
product 168.1
publication 559.1
question 485.10
result 154.1
securities issue 834.6
solution 487.1
topic 484.1
v. appear 446.8
apportion 816.8
begin 68.13
be made public
559.16
bring out 559.14
come after 117.3
disperse 75.4
emerge 303.12
find vent 632.10
flow 395.16
give 818.12
issue securities 834.12
monetize 835.26
print 603.14
result 154.5
start out 301.7
**issue forth**
appear 446.8
be born 167.16
begin 68.13
emerge 303.12
find vent 632.10
start out 301.7
**issueless** 166.4
**issue price** 834.9
**issuing** 303.18
**issuing company** 833.15
**isthmus**
constriction 198.1
narrow place 205.3

**it** genuine object 516.6
self 80.5
**italic**
n. type 603.6,23
adj. written 602.22
**italicize** 672.13
**italicized**
emphasized 672.20
written 602.22
**itch**
n. craving 634.6
sensation 426.3
sexual desire 419.5
skin disease 686.33
v. tingle 426.5
twitch 324.13
**itch for** lust 419.22
wish for 634.16
**itching**
n. craving 634.6
disease symptom
686.8
sensation 426.3
adj. craving 634.24
desirous of 634.22
itchy 426.10
lustful 419.29
**itching palm** 634.8
**itch to**
be impatient 862.4
want to 634.15
**itchy** curious 528.5
itching 426.10
sensitive 422.14
**item**
n. account entry 845.5
citation 505.6
commodity 831.2
component 58.2
individual 89.4
part 55.1
particular 8.3
record 570.4
adv. additionally
40.11
**itemization**
analysis 48.2
cataloging 88.7
circumstantiation 8.5
description 608.1
list 88.1
particularization 80.7
**itemize** analyze 48.7
circumstantiate 8.6
cite 505.14
list 88.8
particularize 80.9
summarize 87.12
**itemized** 88.9
**items** contents 194.1
list 88.1
**iterate** 103.8
**iterated** 103.12
**iteration**
duplication 91.1
reiteration 103.2
**iterative** 103.14
**itinerancy** 273.3
**itinerant**
n. wanderer 274.2
adj. traveling 273.35

**itinerary**
  directory 748.10
  route 657.2
**–itis**
  inflammation 686.9
  tendency 174.1
**itself** 80.5
**itsy-bitsy** 196.11
**IUD** 687.23
**ivied halls** 567.7
**ivories** dice 515.9
  keyboard 465.20
  teeth 258.6
**ivory**
  *n.* smooth surface
    260.3
  white 364.2,11
  *adj.* whitish 364.8
**ivory-carving** 575.1
**ivory tower** 700.5
**ivy**
  *n.* vine 411.4,51
  *adj.* green 371.4
**izzard** 70.1

**J**

**jab**
  *n.* gibe 967.2
  hit 283.4
  push 283.2
  thrust 798.3
  *v.* hit 283.13
  ridicule 967.9
  thrust 283.11
**jabber**
  *n.* chatter 596.3
  imperfect speech
    595.4
  nonsense 547.2
  *v.* chatter 596.5
  speak poorly 595.9
  talk nonsense 547.5
**jabberer** 596.4
**jack ass** 414.20
  flag 569.6
  lifter 317.3
  money 835.2
  playing card 878.17
  post 216.8
  sailor 276.1
**jackal** coyote 414.25,58
  man 787.8
  sycophant 907.3
**jackass** ass 414.20,58
  fool 471.1
**jacket**
  *n.* bookbinding
    605.15
  clothing 231.13
  hull 228.16
  pelt 229.1
  types of 231.51
  wrapper 228.18
  *v.* clothe 231.39
**jack-in-the-box** 878.16
**jackknife** dive 320.1
  edge tool 348.13
**jack-of-all-trades** 733.11
**jackpot** award 916.2
  stakes 515.5

**jackrabbit**
  hare 414.29,58
  jumper 319.4
**jacks** 878.16,34
**jack up** increase 38.4
  reprove 969.19
**Jacobin** radical 745.12
  revolutionist 147.3
**jactitation**
  boasting 910.1
  shaking 324.2
**jade**
  *n.* gem stone 384.13
  green color 371.6
  inferior horse 414.14
  unchaste woman
    989.14
  *v.* be tedious 884.5
  fatigue 717.4
  get tired 717.5
  satiate 664.4
**jaded** bored 884.10
  fatigued 717.6
  languid 708.19
  satiated 664.6
  worn-out 692.38
**jag**
  *n.* notch 262.1
  pointed projection
    258.4
  spree 996.5
  *v.* notch 262.4
**Jaganmati** 1014.8
**jagged** angular 251.6
  discontinuous 72.4
  nonuniform 18.3
  notched 262.5
  rough 261.7
**jaguar**
  animal 414.27,58
  variegation 374.6
**jail**
  *n.* prison 761.8
  *v.* enclose 236.5
  imprison 761.14
**jailbird** criminal 986.10
  prisoner 761.11
**jailbreak** 632.1
**jailed** enclosed 236.10
  imprisoned 761.21
**jailer** guard 699.9
  penology 1010.9
  warder 761.10
**jailing**
  imprisonment 761.3
  punishment 1010.2
**jalopy** 272.9
**jam**
  *n.* barrier 730.5
  delay 132.2
  Indian ruler 749.9
  large number 101.3
  obstruction 266.3
  perplexity 514.3
  predicament 731.4
  semiliquid 389.5
  state 7.1
  sweets 308.39
  throng 74.4
  *v.* become fixed
    142.10
  be numerous 101.5

**densify** 354.9
**drown out** 453.7
**fasten** 47.8
**fill** 56.7
**infix** 142.9
**obstruct** 730.12
**overload** 663.15
**stop** 266.7
**thrust** 283.11
  use radar 346.15
**jamb** leg 273.16
  post 217.4
**jamboree** 878.4
**jam in** enter 302.7
  thrust in 304.7
**jammed**
  blocked 266.11
  dense 354.12
  fastened 47.14
  fixed 142.16
  late 132.16
  overfull 663.20
  teeming 101.9
**jamming** 346.13
**jam-packed**
  crowded 74.22
  dense 354.12
  full 56.11
  overfull 663.20
  teeming 101.9
**jam session** 462.33
**jam through** 742.18
**Jane** 421.6
**Jane Doe** 583.8
**jangle**
  *n.* conflict 795.1
  dissonance 461.2
  harsh sound 458.3
  noise 453.3
  ringing 454.3
  *v.* be dissonant 461.3
  clash 795.8
  disagree 27.5
  ring 454.8
  sound harshly 458.9
**jangle the nerves**
  make nervous 859.8
  sound harshly 458.11
**jangling** clashing 461.5
  disagreeing 27.6
  sounding harsh
    458.16
**janitor** cleaner 681.14
  doorkeeper 699.12
  guardian 699.6
**Janus** 90.1
**Janus-like** 91.4
**Japanese deities**
  1014.14
**japanning** 362.12
**jape**
  *n.* banter 882.1
  gibe 967.2
  joke 881.6
  *v.* banter 882.4
  joke 881.13
  ridicule 967.9
**jar**
  *n.* bottle 193.12
  conflict 795.1
  dissonance 461.2
  harsh sound 458.3

**shake** 324.3
**surprise** 540.3
  *v.* be dissonant 461.3
  clash 795.8
  disagree 27.5
  excite 857.13
  make nervous 859.8
  package 236.9
  preserve 701.9
  shake 324.11
  sound harshly 458.9
  startle 540.8
**jargon**
  *n.* argot 580.9
  lingua franca 580.11
  nonsense 547.2
  unintelligibility 549.7
  *v.* speak 580.16
**jarring** clashing 461.5
  disagreeing 27.6
  exciting 857.28
  jolting 324.20
  nerve-wracking
    859.14
  sounding harsh
    458.16
  surprising 540.11
**jaundice**
  *n.* disease symptom
    686.8
  jealousy 953.1
  liver disease 686.21
  partiality 527.3
  yellow skin 370.2
  *v.* prejudice 527.9
  yellow 370.3
**jaundiced**
  ill-humored 951.23
  jealous 953.4
  prejudiced 527.12
  yellow-complexioned
    370.6
**jaundiced eye**
  jealousy 953.1
  partiality 527.3
**jaunt**
  *n.* journey 273.5
  walk 273.12
  *v.* travel 273.20
  wander 273.22
**jaunty** chic 644.13
  lighthearted 870.12
  showy 904.19
**javelin** 801.23
**jaw**
  *n.* mouth 265.5
  *v.* berate 969.20
  chatter 596.5
  speak 594.21
**jawboning** 648.3
**jawbreaker**
  long word 582.10
  pompous word 601.3
**jawbreaking**
  difficult 731.16
  polysyllabic 601.10
**jawing** 969.7
**jaws**
  grasping organs 813.4
  mouth 265.5
**jaywalk** 273.26
**jaywalker** 274.6

**jobber**
  intermediary 237.4
  merchant 830.2
  stockbroker 833.10
  working person 718.2
**jobbing**
  Machiavellianism
    735.2
  selling 829.2
  stockbroking 833.18
  trade 827.2
**jobholder** 718.2
**jobless** 708.17
**job lot** 831.1
**jock** athlete 878.20
  common soldier
    800.7
  he-man 420.6
  supporter 216.2
**jockey**
  n. rider 274.8
  saddle 216.18
  speeder 269.5
  v. compete 796.19
  maneuver 735.10
**jocose** 881.15
**jocular** merry 870.15
  witty 881.15
**jocularity**
  merriment 870.5
  wittiness 881.2
**jog**
  n. gait 273.14
  jerk 286.3
  knob 256.3
  notch 262.1
  push 283.2
  shake 324.3
  slowness 270.2
  v. jerk 286.5
  shake 324.11
  thrust 283.11
  walk 273.27
**joggling** 324.20
**jog on** continue 143.3
  plod 270.7
  progress 294.3
  walk 273.26
**jog the memory** 537.20
**jog trot** routine 642.6
  slowness 270.2
  speed 269.3
**jog-trot**
  repetitious 103.15
  tedious 884.8
**john** rest room 311.10
  toilet 311.11
**John Bull**
  England 181.5
  the government
    741.3
**John Doe** alias 583.8
  people 417.2
**John Hancock**
  ratification 521.4
  signature 583.10
**johnny** man 420.5
  person 417.3
  rest room 311.10
  toilet 311.11
**johnnycake** 308.29
**johnny-come-lately** 78.4

**Johnny on the spot**
  attentive 530.15
  prompt 131.9
**John Q. Public**
  common man 79.3
  everyone 417.2
  the people 919.2
**Johnsonian** 601.8
**joie de vivre**
  animation 161.3
  pleasure 865.1
**join** add 40.4
  assemble 74.18
  become a member
    788.14
  be near 200.9
  be sociable 922.16
  cohere 50.7
  combine 52.3
  compose 58.3
  concur 177.2
  connect 71.4
  cooperate 786.3
  enlist 780.16
  gather 47.5
  join in marriage
    933.15
  join together 52.4
  juxtapose 200.13
  meet 47.11
  participate 815.5
  side with 786.4
  unify 14.5
**join battle**
  contend against
    790.4
  fight 796.17
**joined**
  accompanying 73.9
  adjacent 200.16
  assembled 74.21
  coherent 50.11
  combined 52.5
  continuous 71.8
  joint 47.12
  related 9.9
  united 47.13
**joiner** member 788.11
  sociable person
    922.15
**join forces** 52.4
**joining**
  n. addition 40.1
  junction 47
  meeting 200.4
  union 47.4
  adj. connecting 47.16
**joint**
  n. brothel 989.9
  crack 201.2
  disapproved place
    191.28
  gambling house
    515.15
  juncture 47.4
  marihuana 687.13
  meat 308.12
  part 55.4
  place of vice 981.7
  v. fasten 47.8
  adj. accompanying
    73.9

  assembled 74.21
  combined 52.5
  communal 815.9
  concurrent 177.4
  cooperating 786.5
  joined 47.12
  mutual 13.14
**joint control** 815.1
**joint effort** 786.1
**jointly**
  collectively 73.11
  concurrently 177.5
  cooperatively 786.6
  mutually 13.17
  together 47.18
**joint operation**
  cooperation 786.1
  military operation
    797.8
**joint ownership** 815.1
**jointure**
  endowment 818.9
  joining 47.1
**joke**
  n. banter 882.1
  jest 881.6
  laughingstock 967.7
  trifle 673.5
  v. banter 882.4
  jest 881.13
**joker** condition 507.2
  deceiver 619.1
  difficulty 731.7
  humorist 881.12
  legislative clause
    742.17
  man 420.5
  mischief-maker 738.3
  obstacle 730.4
  person 417.3
  playing card 878.17
  surprise 540.2
  trick 618.6
**joking**
  n. banter 882.2
  wittiness 881.2
  adj. witty 881.15
**jollies** marines 800.27
  thrill 857.2
**jollity**
  conviviality 922.3
  festivity 878.3
  merriment 870.5
**jolly**
  n. marine 276.4
  v. banter 882.4
  flatter 970.6
  make merry 878.26
  adj. convivial 922.19
  festive 878.30
  intoxicated 996.30
  merry 870.15
**jollying**
  n. banter 882.2
  adj. bantering 882.5
**Jolly Roger** 569.6
**jolt**
  n. drink 996.6
  push 283.2
  shake 324.3
  surprise 540.3
  v. excite 857.13

  shake 324.11
  startle 540.8
  thrust 283.11
  walk 273.27
**jolting** bumpy 324.20
  exciting 857.28
  surprising 540.11
**Jonah**
  bad influence 675.4
  prophet 1022.1
**jongleur** poet 609.13
  singer 464.14
**joshing**
  n. banter 882.2
  ridicule 967.1
  wittiness 881.2
  adj. bantering 882.5
  ridiculing 967.12
  witty 881.15
**joss** 1033.3
**joss stick** 436.4
**jostle**
  n. push 283.2
  shake 324.3
  v. be dissonant 461.3
  be inharmonious
    795.8
  contend 796.14
  disagree 27.5
  shake 324.11
  thrust 283.11
**jot**
  n. mark 568.5
  minute thing 196.7
  small amount 35.2
  v. record 570.16
**jotting** 570.4
**jounce** 324.11
**journal**
  account book 845.4
  autobiography 608.4
  axle 322.6
  chronicle 114.9
  periodical 605.10
  record book 570.11
**journalese**
  n. jargon 580.10
  adj. journalistic
    605.26
**journalism** news 558.1
  the press 605.23
  writing 602.2
**journalist** 605.22
**journalistic** 605.26
**journey**
  n. travel 273.2
  trip 273.5
  v. travel 273.20
**journeyer** 274.1
**journeying**
  n. travel 273.1
  adj. traveling 273.35
**journeyman**
  artisan 718.6
  expert 733.11
  producer 167.8
**journey's end** 300.5
**joust**
  n. contest 796.3
  v. contend 796.14
**Jove** 1014.5
**jovial** convivial 922.19

festive 878.30
merry 870.15
**joviality**
conviviality 922.3
festivity 878.3
merriment 870.5
**jowl** cheek 242.1
jaws 265.5
**joy**
*n.* happiness 865.2
merriment 870.5
*v.* be pleased 865.9
gloat 910.9
rejoice 876.5
**joyful** cheering 870.16
festive 878.30
happy 865.13
merry 870.15
**joyfully**
cheerfully 870.17
happily 865.16
**joyfulness**
happiness 865.2
merriment 870.5
**joyless**
pleasureless 866.20
unhappy 872.21
unpleasant 864.20
**joylessly** 872.32
**joylessness**
distressfulness 864.5
unhappiness 872.2
unpleasure 866.1
**joyous, joyously** see
joyful etc.
**joyride**
*n.* ride 273.7
*v.* ride 273.32
**JP** 1002.1
**Jr.** 124.15
**jubilant**
gloating 910.12
overjoyed 865.14
rejoicing 876.9
**jubilate** celebrate 877.2
gloat 910.9
rejoice 876.5
**jubilation**
festivity 865.3
gloating 910.4
rejoicing 876.1
**jubilee**
anniversary 137.4
celebration 877.1
rejoicing 876.1
**Judaical** 1020.29
**Judaism** 1020.11,32
**Judas** criminal 986.10
traitor 619.10
**Judas-like** 975.22
**judge**
*n.* adjudicator 494.6
arbitrator 805.4
connoisseur 897.7
magistrate 1002
*v.* administer justice
1000.5
believe 501.11
exercise judgment
494.8
mediate 805.6
try 1004.17

**judgeship** 1000.3
**judgment**
adjudication 494
belief 501.6
condemnation 1008.1
discrimination 492.2
judiciary 1000.2
legal decision 1004.9
punishment 1010.1
sagaciousness 467.7
**judgmental**
condemnatory 969.23
judicial 494.16
**Judgment Day** 121.3
**judicature** court 1001.2
judgment 494.1
judiciary 1000.2
tribunal 1001.1
**judicial**
intelligent 467.19
judiciary 494.16
jurisdictional 1000.6
legal 998.10
tribunal 1001.10
**judicial process**
judiciary 1000.2
lawsuit 1004.1
**judiciary**
*n.* jurisdiction 1000.2
tribunal 1001.1
*adj.* judicial 494.16
jurisdictional 1000.6
tribunal 1001.10
**judicious**
cautious 895.8
discriminating 492.8
intelligent 467.19
judicial 494.16
moderate 163.10
**judiciously**
cautiously 895.12
intelligently 467.20
moderately 163.17
**judiciousness**
caution 895.1
discrimination 492.1
moderation 163.1
sagaciousness 467.7
**judo** 796.10
**jug** bottle 193.12
ceramic ware 576.2
prison 761.9
**Juggernaut** idol 1033.3
Vishnu 1014.9
**juggle** deceive 618.13
tamper with 616.17
**juggler** cheat 619.3
circus artist 612.3
trickster 619.2
**juggling** 618.5
**jughead** dolt 471.4
inferior horse 414.14
**jugular** 396.22
**juice**
electric current 342.2
fluid 388.2
**juiceless** 393.7
**juiciness**
immaturity 124.3
liquidity 388.1
pleasantness 863.3
**juicy** fluid 388.6

immature 124.10
interesting 530.19
pleasant 863.9
tasty 428.8
**jujitsu** 796.10
**jukebox** 450.11
**juke joint** 878.11
**jumble**
*n.* cake 308.41
confusion 532.3
hodgepodge 44.6
scramble 62.3
unintelligibility 549.7
*v.* be undiscriminating
493.3
confuse 63.3
deform 247.3
disorder 62.9
make unintelligible
549.12
mix 44.11
**jumbled** chaotic 62.16
confused 532.12
hard to understand
549.14
mixed 44.15
**jumbo**
*n.* large animal 195.14
large thing 195.11
*adj.* huge 195.20
**Jumbo** 414.4
**jump**
*n.* advantage 36.2
ascent 315.1
flight 278.9
increase 38.1
interval 201.1
leap 319.1
step 273.13
*v.* attack 798.15
be eager about 635.7
be frightened 891.20
be startled 540.5
contend 796.15
escape 632.6
flee 631.10
leap 319.5
leave undone 534.7
parachute 278.56
seize on 822.16
shake 324.11
walk 273.27
**jump bail** 631.10
**jumper** athlete 878.20
clothing 231.30
diver 320.4
leaper 319.4
**jump in** enter 302.7
get in 315.12
**jumping**
*n.* leaping 319.3
*adj.* leaping 319.7
**jumping-off place**
end 70.2
one-horse town 183.3
remote region 199.4
**jump on**
reprove 969.18
suppress 760.8
**jumps** 859.2
**jump ship** 187.9

**jump the gun**
anticipate 131.6
be impatient 862.4
prejudge 495.2
**jump to a conclusion**
495.2
**jump up** ascend 315.9
increase 38.4
rise 213.8
**jumpy** active 707.20
agitated 324.16
fearful 891.31
jerky 324.19
jittery 859.11
**junction** addition 40.1
assembly 74.1
cohesion 50.1
combination 52.1
composition 58.1
concurrence 177.1
joining 47.1
juxtaposition 200.3
passageway 657.4
railway 657.8
relationship 9.1
**juncture**
circumstance 8.1
joint 47.4
pause 144.4
period 107.1
speech 594.10
**jungle** complex 46.2
woodland 411.11
**junior**
*n.* inferior 37.2
student 566.6
subordinate 764.5
youngster 125.1
*adj.* inferior 37.6
succeeding 117.4
younger 124.15
**junior college** 567.7
**junior high school**
567.6
**junk**
*n.* abandoned thing
633.4
drugs 687.5
fake 616.13
heroin 687.12
rubbish 669.5
sailing vessel 277.23
*v.* discard 668.8
eject 310.13
*adj.* worthless 669.11
**junket** journey 273.5
pudding 308.45
**junkie** 642.10
**junking** 668.3
**junkman** 830.10
**junkyard** 669.6
**Juno** goddess 1014.5
marriage goddess
933.14
**Junoesque** 900.17
**junta** clique 788.6
combination 52.1
council 755.1
group 74.3
**Jupiter** god 1014.5
planet 375.9
**Jupiter Fidius** 976.5

Jupiter Fulgur 335.17
Jupiter Fulminator
  335.17
Jupiter Pluvius 394.6
juridic(al)
  judicial 494.16
  jurisdictional 1000.6
  legal 998.10
jurisdiction
  commission 780.1
  control 741.2
  governance 739.5
  legal authority 1000
  legality 998.1
  protectorship 699.2
  region 180.2
  supervision 747.2
  supremacy 36.3
jurisdictional 1000.6
jurisprudence 998.7
jurist 1003.2
juror 1002.8
jury 1002.7
jury box 1001.9
juryman 1002.8
jury-rig
  *n.* expedient 670.2
    improvisation 630.5
  *v.* do carelessly 534.9
    improvise 630.8
jury-rigged
  extemporaneous
    630.12
  makeshift 670.7
jury selection 1004.4
jus 998.3
just
  *adj.* accurate 516.15
    due 960.8
    fair 976.8
    godlike 1013.20
    honest 974.13
    legal 998.10
    reasonable 482.20
    unprejudiced 526.12
    valid 516.13
    virtuous 980.7
    well-chosen 589.7
  *adv.* exactly 516.20
    simply 45.11
    very 34.18
just about close 200.26
  nearly 200.22
just around the corner
  handy 665.19
  imminent 152.3
  in the future 121.9
  near 200.20
just deserts
  deserts 960.3
  reprisal 955.2
juste-milieu mean 32.1
  moderation 163.1
justice dueness 960.1
  equality 30.1
  honesty 974.1
  judge 1002.1
  judgment 494.6
  judiciary 1000.2
  justness 976
  legality 998.1

personifications
  976.5
  virtue 980.5
justiceship 1000.3
justifably 976.11
justifiable just 976.8
  logical 482.20
  permissible 777.15
  vindicable 1006.14
justification
  justice 976.1
  sanctification 1026.3
  typesetting 603.2
  vindication 1006
justified just 976.8
  sanctified 1026.9
  warranted 960.9
justifier 1006.8
justify acquit 1007.4
  typeset 603.16
  vindicate 1006.9
justifying 1006.13
just in case 151.13
justly 976.11
just right
  *adj.* accurate 516.15
    apt 26.10
    perfect 677.6
  *adv.* accurately 516.19
    in step 26.11
    perfectly 677.10
jut cover 228.30
  overhang 215.7
  protrude 256.9
jutting
  *n.* overhanging 215.3
  *adj.* overhanging
    215.11
    protruding 256.13
jutty breakwater 216.4
  harbor 700.6
juvenescent 124.9
juvenile
  *n.* actor 612.2
    book 605.1
    youngster 125.1
  *adj.* undeveloped
    721.11
    young 124.9
juvenile delinquent
  125.4
juvenility 124.1
juxtapose
  assemble 74.18
  bring near 200.13
juxtaposed 200.16
juxtaposition
  addition 40.1
  apposition 200.3
  assembly 74.1
juxtapositional 200.16

**K**

Kaiser 749.8
kaleidoscopic
  changeable 141.6
  formless 247.4
  variegated 374.9
Kali 1014.8
kama 1034.18

**Kama**
  Hindu deity 1014.8
  love god 931.8
kamikaze aircraft 280.9
  aviator 279.3
kangaroo jumper 319.4
  mammal 414.58;
    415.8
kangaroo court 1001.3
kaolin 576.3
kapok 357.4
kaput ended 70.8
  no more 2.10
  ruined 693.28
karate 796.10
karroo 166.2
kava 687.13
kayo see **KO**
kazoo 465.11
keck sicken at 867.4
  vomit 310.25
kedge anchor 275.15
  sail 275.48
keel
  *n.* bottom 212.2
    ship 277.1,26
  *v.* capsize 275.44
    incline 219.10
keelhaul 1010.18
keelhauling 1010.2
keel over
  capsize 275.44
  faint 423.5
  overturn 220.6
keen
  *n.* dirge 875.5
    lament 875.3
    shrill sound 458.4
  *v.* lament 875.8
    sigh 452.14
    sound shrill 458.8
    utter 594.26
  *adj.* acrimonious
    161.13
    alert 533.14
    caustic 939.21
    cold 333.14
    deep-felt 855.26
    eager 635.9
    energetic 161.12
    excellent 674.13
    exciting 857.29
    fervent 855.23
    intelligent 467.14
    pungent 433.6
    sensitive 422.15
    sharp 258.10
    shrill 458.14
    violent 162.15
    witty 881.15
keen about
  enthusiastic 635.11
  fond of 931.28
  interested 530.16
keenly
  caustically 939.30
  eagerly 635.14
  energetically 161.15
  fervently 855.28
keenness
  acrimony 161.4
  alertness 533.5

causticity 939.8
cold 333.1
eagerness 635.1
intelligence 467.2
pungency 433.1
sharpness 258.1
wittiness 881.2
keen on
  desirous of 634.22
  enthusiastic 635.11
  interested 530.16
keep
  *n.* accommodations
    659.3
    custody 761.5
    food 308.3
    prison 761.8
    stronghold 799.6
    support 785.3
  *v.* administer rites
    1040.18
    celebrate 877.2
    confine 761.12
    endure 110.6
    harbor 813.7
    obey 766.2
    observe 768.2
    preserve 701.7
    protect 699.18
    provide for 659.7
    raise animals 416.6
    remember 537.13
    reserve 660.12
    restrain 760.7
    retain 813.5
    stabilize 142.7
    store up 660.11
    support 785.12
    sustain 143.4
keep alive
  keep body and soul
    together 407.10
  perpetuate 112.5
  preserve 701.7
  sustain 143.4
keep an eye on
  care for 699.19
  keep informed
    557.15
  supervise 747.10
  watch 439.14
keep a stiff upper lip
  be cheerful 870.10
  have courage 893.15
  keep cool 858.9
keep a straight face
  871.2
keep at it
  be industrious 707.15
  persevere 625.2
  persist 143.5
keep back delay 132.8
  hinder 730.10
  keep secret 614.7
  not use 668.5
  reserve 660.12
  restrain 760.7
  slow 270.9
keep books 845.8
keep down
  domineer 741.16
  keep subject 764.8

young goat 125.8
young person 125.2
*v.* banter 882.4
fool 618.14
joke 881.13
**kid along** 970.6
**kid around** joke 881.13
trifle 673.13
**kidder** banterer 882.3
deceiver 619.1
**kidding**
*n.* banter 882.1
deception 618.1
jesting 882.2
*adj.* bantering 882.5
ridiculing 967.12
**kidnap** abduct 824.19
seize 822.14
**kidnapper** 825.10
**kidnapping**
abduction 824.8
seizure 822.2
**kidney**
diseases of 686.22
kind 61.3
meat 308.20
temperament 525.3
vitals 225.4
**kidney-shaped** 252.16
**kill**
*n.* quarry 655.7
running water 395.1
slaughter 409.1
*v.* amuse 878.23
delete 42.12
end 70.7
hush up 614.8
legislate 742.18
put an end to 693.12
slay 409.13
suppress 760.8
turn off 144.12
veto 778.5
**kill-crazy** 162.20
**killer** evildoer 943.3
slayer 409.11
violent person 162.9
**killer-diller** 674.7
**killing**
*n.* gain 811.3
great success 724.3
slaying 409
violence 162.3
violent death 408.6
*adj.* fatal 409.23
fatiguing 717.11
gorgeous 900.19
laborious 716.18
**killjoy** hinderer 730.9
pessimist 889.7
spoilsport 872.14
**kill oneself** 409.22
**kill time**
amuse oneself 878.24
spend time 105.6
waste time 708.12
**kiln**
*n.* oven 576.5
*v.* dry 393.6
**kilo** thousand 99.10
unit of weight 352.23

**kilocycle**
radio frequency
344.12
thousand 99.10
**kilometer**
linear measure 490.17
thousand 99.10
**kilowatt-hour**
electric unit 342.35
unit of energy 161.6
**kin** class 61.2
kind 61.3
kinsmen 11.2
**kind**
*n.* nature 5.3
race 11.4
sort 61.3
*adj.* benevolent
938.13
forgiving 947.6
friendly 927.14
good 674.12
helpful 785.22
indulgent 759.8
**kindergarten** 567.4
**kindergartner** 566.4
**kindhearted** 938.13
**kindle**
become angry 952.18
energize 161.9
excite 857.11
ignite 329.22
incite 648.18
make hot 329.18
**kindled** 328.27
**kindling**
*n.* firewood 331.3
ignition 329.4
*adj.* inflammatory
329.27
**kindly**
*adj.* benevolent
938.13
helpful 785.22
indulgent 759.8
*adv.* benevolently
938.18
fervently 855.28
pleasantly 863.11
**kindness**
benevolence 938
forgiveness 947.1
friendship 927.1
good deed 938.7
goodness 674.1
indulgence 759.2
pity 944.1
**kind of**
so to speak 20.19
to a degree 29.7
**kindred**
*n.* blood relationship
11.1
kinsmen 11.2
*adj.* akin 11.6
related 9.10
**kindred soul** 20.3
**kine** 414.6
**kinematograph**
photography 577.11
projector 577.12
theater 611.19

**kinescope**
cinematography
577.8
picture tube 345.18
**kinesic** 568.24
**kinesis** 267.1
**kinetic(al)**
dynamic 347.9
energetic 161.12
**kinetic energy** 161.1
**kinetics**
aeronautics 278.2
dynamics 347.3
motion 267.1
**kinfolk** 11.2
**king** businessman 830.1
chessman 878.18
chief 672.10
playing card 878.17
potentate 749.7
prince 918.7
**kingdom**
biological classifica-
tion 406.3
categorization 61.5
class 61.4
country 181.1
nomenclature 583.1
**kingdom come**
Heaven 1018.1
paradise 535.11
**kingfish** 749.3
**kingly** dignified 905.12
noble 918.10
sovereign 739.17
**kingmaker**
influential person
172.6
political intriguer
746.6
**kingpin** 749.3
**King's English, the**
580.4
**kingship**
noble rank 918.9
sovereignty 739.8
supremacy 36.3
**king-size** large 34.7
oversize 195.23
**king's ransom** 837.2
**kink**
*n.* caprice 629.1
curl 254.2
deformity 679.1
eccentricity 474.2
imperfection 678.2
pain 424.2
*v.* blemish 679.4
curl 254.5
**kinked**
blemished 679.8
curly 254.9
**kinky** capricious 629.5
curly 254.9
eccentric 474.4
unconventional 83.6
**kinship** accord 794.1
blood ties 11.1
relationship 9.3
similarity 20.2
**kinsmen** 11.2
**kiosk** hut 191.10

store 832.3
summerhouse 191.13
**kipper**
*n.* food 308.24
salmon 414.35
*v.* preserve 701.8
**kirk** 1042.1
**kishkes** abdomen 193.3
viscera 225.4
**kismet** 640.2
**kiss**
*n.* contact 200.5
greeting 925.4
lovemaking 932.3
touch 425.1
*v.* graze 200.10
greet 925.10
make love 932.17
touch lightly 425.7
**kissable** 931.23
**kiss and make up**
804.10
**kisser** face 240.4
mouth 265.5
**kiss good-bye**
lose 812.4
relinquish 814.3
**kit** equipment 659.4
kitten 414.26
set 74.12
viol 465.6
young cat 125.8
**kitchen**
*n.* cookroom 330.3
restaurant 307.15
room 192.14
*adj.* cooking 330.5
**kitchen cabinet**
council 755.1
legislature 742.8
**kitchen police** 800.19
**kite**
*n.* aircraft 280.1
counterfeit 835.10
types of 280.14
*v.* soar 315.10
**kited check** 842.3
**kith and kin** 11.2
**kitsch** literature 602.12
vulgarity 898.1
work of art 574.11
**kitten**
*n.* cat 414.26
child 125.3
young animal 125.8
*v.* give birth 167.15
**kittenish** feline 414.46
feminine 421.13
infantile 124.12
**kitty** funds 835.14
kitten 414.26
stakes 515.5
**kittycorner**
*adj.* diagonal 219.19
*adv.* diagonally 219.25
**Klaxon** alarm 704.1
noisemaker 453.5
**kleptomania** 824.12
**klieg light** 611.23
**klutz**
awkward person
734.8

fool 471.2
**klutzy** 469.15
**knack** ornament 901.4
 talent 733.6
**knave**
 mischief-maker 738.3
 playing card 878.17
 rascal 986.3
**knavery**
 dishonesty 975.2
 iniquity 981.3
 stratagem 735.3
**knavish**
 dishonest 975.17
 evil 981.16
 mischievous 738.6
**knead** form 246.7
 make pliant 357.6
 mix 44.11
 rub 350.6
 touch 425.8
**knee**
 *n.* angle 251.2
 joint 47.4
 leg 273.16
 *v.* kick 283.18
**knee-deep** deep 209.10
 shallow 210.5
**knee-high** little 196.10
 low 208.7
**kneel** bend 318.9
 be servile 907.6
 bow 964.6
**kneel to**
 bow down before
 765.10
 entreat 774.11
**knell**
 *n.* death 408.1
 death bell 410.6
 dirge 875.5
 ringing 454.3
 *v.* lament 875.8
 ring 454.8
**knickknack**
 ornament 901.4
 sundry 831.6
 toy 878.16
 trifle 673.5
**knife**
 *n.* cutlery 348.2
 tableware 348.3
 types of 801.21
 *v.* be dishonest 975.13
 stab 798.25
**knife-edged** 258.10
**knifing** 798.11
**knight**
 *n.* cavalier 918.5
 chessman 878.18
 combatant 800.1
 gallant 936.9
 rider 274.8
 *v.* promote 782.2
**knight-errantry** 979.2
**knighthood**
 chivalry 797.10
 noble rank 918.9
**knightly**
 courageous 893.17
 gallant 936.15
 magnanimous 979.6

noble 918.10
**knit** be joined 47.11
 contract 198.7
 fasten 47.7
 heal 694.21
 weave 222.6
 wrinkle 264.6
**knitted**
 constricted 198.12
 wrinkled 264.8
**knitting**
 constriction 198.1
 needlework 223.6
 weaving 222.1
**knob**
 *n.* ball 255.2
 bulge 256.3
 hill 207.5
 *v.* roughen 261.4
**knobbed**
 studded 256.16
 textured 351.7
**knobby** hilly 207.23
 rough 261.8
 studded 256.16
**knock**
 *n.* disapproval 969.4
 explosive noise 456.1
 hit 283.4
 *v.* collide 283.12
 criticize 969.14
 hit 283.13
 make explosive noise
 456.6
 pound 283.14
**knock about**
 mistreat 667.5
 wander 273.22
**knock around**
 discuss 597.12
 wander 273.22
**knock dead**
 amuse 878.23
 delight 865.8
 look beautiful 900.15
**knock down**
 auction 829.11
 disparage 971.8
 hit 283.13
 lower 318.5
 make nervous 859.9
 make sad 872.18
 raze 693.19
**knock-down-and-drag-out**
 *n.* free-for-all 796.5
 quarrel 795.6
 *adj.* boisterous 162.19
**knocker**
 disparager 971.6
 teat 256.6
**knock it off**
 cease 144.6
 stop! 144.15
**knock-kneed** 249.12
**knockoff** 22.3
**knock off**
 accomplish 722.4
 cut off 42.10
 die 408.20
 do carelessly 534.9
 improvise 630.8

stop work 144.8
 take a rest 711.8
 write 602.21
**knock on wood**
 be superstitious 502.7
 hope 888.8
**knockout**
 beautiful person
 900.8
 end-all 70.4
 good thing 674.7
 unconsciousness
 423.2
 victory 726.1
**knock out**
 delight 865.8
 do carelessly 534.9
 end 70.7
 fatigue 717.4
 form 246.7
 hit 283.13
 render insensible
 423.4
 render powerless
 158.11
 ruin 693.11
 write 602.21
**knockout drops**
 alcoholic drink 996.8
 barbiturate 687.12
 depressant 423.3
**knock over** raze 693.19
 rob 824.14
**knockwurst** 308.21
**knoll** hill 207.5
 peak 207.8
**knot**
 *n.* aviation 278.40
 ball 255.2
 bunch 74.7
 complex 46.2
 connection 47.3
 dilemma 731.6
 distortion 249.1
 hair 230.7
 knob 256.3
 puzzle 549.8
 solid 354.6
 speed 269.1
 types of 47.21
 *v.* clump 354.10
 complicate 46.3
 distort 249.5
 equal 30.5
 join 47.5
 wrinkle 264.6
**knothole** 265.4
**knotted**
 assembled 74.21
 complex 46.4
 difficult 731.16
 equal 30.7
 joined 47.13
 related 9.9
 rough 261.8
 studded 256.16
 wrinkled 264.8
**knotty** difficult 731.16
 hard to understand
 549.14
 rough 261.8
 studded 256.16

**know**
 be apprised 557.14
 be certain 513.9
 be friends 927.9
 experience 151.8
 have knowledge
 475.12
 recognize 537.12
 understand 548.7
**know, the** 557.1
**know all the answers**
 be expert 733.18
 know well 475.13
**know backwards and**
 **forwards**
 be expert 733.18
 know well 475.13
**know-how**
 knowledge 475.1
 skill 733.1
**knowing**
 cunning 735.12
 intelligent 467.12
 intentional 653.9
 knowledgeable
 475.15
 shrewd 467.15
 wise 467.17
 worldly-wise 733.26
**knowingly**
 consciously 475.29
 cunningly 735.13
 intelligently 467.20
 intentionally 653.11
**know inside out** 475.13
**know it all** 909.6
**know-it-all**
 *n.* egotist 909.5
 *adj.* conceited 909.11
**knowledge**
 familiarity 475
 information 557.1
 intelligence 467.1
 learning 564.1
**knowledgeable**
 knowing 475.15
 specialized 81.5
**known** 475.26
**known as** 583.14
**know no bounds**
 overdo 663.10
 overstep 313.9
 superabound 663.8
**know nothing** 477.9
**know-nothing**
 *n.* ignoramus 477.8
 *adj.* ignorant 477.12
 prejudiced 527.12
**know well**
 be informed 557.14
 be skillful 475.13
 master 564.9
**know what's what**
 be expert 733.18
 be intelligent 467.10
 discriminate 492.6
 know well 475.13
**knub** 351.1
**knuckle** joint 47.4
 meat 308.17
**knuckle down**
 exert oneself 716.9

submit 765.6
**knuckle down to**
  set to work 716.15
  undertake 715.3
**knucklehead** 471.4
**knuckleheaded** 469.17
**knuckles** 801.20
**knuckle under** 765.6
**knurl**
  *n.* knob 256.3
  *v.* notch 262.4
**knurled** rough 261.8
  studded 256.16
**KO**
  *n.* end-all 70.4
  unconsciousness
    423.2
  victory 726.1
  *v.* end 70.7
  render insensible
    423.4
  ruin 693.11
**kook** eccentric 474.3
  lunatic 473.15
  odd person 85.4
**kooky** eccentric 474.4
  foolish 470.8
  insane 473.26
  odd 85.11
**Koran** 1021.6
**Kore**
  agriculture divinity
    413.4
  deity of nether world
    1019.5
  goddess 1014.5
**kosher** clean 681.25
  conformist 82.6
  edible 307.31
  legal 998.10
  right 958.8
**kowtow**
  *n.* crouch 318.3
  obeisance 964.2
  *v.* bend 318.9
  be servile 907.6
  bow 964.6
  bow down before
    765.10
**Kraut** cabbage 308.35
  common soldier
    800.70
  German 181.7
**Krishna** 1014.9
**kudos** honor 916.4
  praise 968.5
  prestige 914.4
  repute 914.1
**kung-fu** 796.10
**kvetch** 869.3
**Kyrie Eleison**
  Mass 1040.10
  prayer 1032.4

**L**

**L** angle 251.2
  fifty 99.7
  railway 657.8
  stage 611.21
  wing 41.3
**lab** laboratory 489.5

workplace 719.7
**label**
  *n.* class 61.2
  heraldic insignia
    569.2
  kind 61.3
  name 583.3
  tag 568.13
  *v.* name 583.11
  tag 568.20
**labial**
  *n.* speech sound
    594.13
  *adj.* bordered 235.13
  phonetic 594.31
**labor**
  *n.* birth 167.7
  occupation 656.1
  task 656.2
  work 716.4
  *v.* be busy 707.10
  develop 148.6
  drudge 716.12
  endeavor 714.4
  flounder 324.15
  give birth 167.15
  repeat 103.9
  work 656.12
**laboratory**
  hospital room 192.25
  research laboratory
    489.5
  workplace 719.7
**labor camp** 761.8
**labored**
  laborious 716.18
  ornate 901.12
  repetitious 103.15
  stilted 590.3
**laborer**
  common person
    919.1
  working person 718.2
**labor in vain**
  *n.* labor lost 669.3
  *v.* fail 725.8
  go on a wild-goose
    chase 669.8
**laborious**
  difficult 731.16
  industrious 707.22
  toilsome 716.18
**laboriously**
  arduously 716.19
  industriously 707.27
  with difficulty 731.26
**labor of love**
  costless thing 850.1
  good deed 938.7
**labor organizer** 789.3
**labor-saving** 851.6
**labor-saving device**
  348.4
**labor under**
  be sick 686.43
  experience 151.8
**labor union** 789
**labor unionist** 789.3
**labyrinth** 46.2
**labyrinthine**
  complex 46.4
  curved 252.7

distorted 249.10
grandiloquent 601.8
wandering 291.7
winding 254.6
**lace**
  *n.* fabric 378.5
  network 221.3
  types of 378.12
  *v.* adulterate 44.13
  bind 47.9
  punish 1010.14
  weave 222.6
**laced** netlike 221.11
  woven 222.7
**lacerate** hurt 424.7
  injure 692.15
  tear apart 49.14
  torture 866.18
**lacerated**
  damaged 692.29
  notched 262.5
  pained 424.9
  severed 49.23
  tortured 866.25
**laceration**
  impairment 692.8
  slashing 49.2
  torment 866.7
**lachrymal**
  secretory 312.7
  tearful 875.17
  tearlike 388.7
**lachrymose**
  secretory 312.7
  tearful 875.17
**lacing**
  adulteration 44.3
  cord 206.9
  fastener 47.20
  network 221.3
  punishment 1010.4
  weaving 222.1
**lack**
  *n.* absence 187.1
  deficiency 57.2
  imperfection 678.1
  indigence 838.2
  want 662.4
  *v.* be incomplete 57.3
  be insufficient 662.8
  be poor 838.5
  fall short 314.2
  want 662.7
**lackadaisical**
  dilatory 132.17
  languid 708.19
  nonchalant 858.15
  unconcerned 636.7
**lackey** follower 787.8
  inferior 750.1
  servant 750.6
  sycophant 907.3
**lacking** absent 187.10
  deprived of 812.8
  imperfect 678.4
  incomplete 57.4
  insufficient 662.9
  nonexistent 2.7
  short of 314.5
  wanting 662.13
**lackluster**
  *n.* colorlessness 363.1

lusterlessness 337.5
mediocrity 680.1
*adj.* colorless 363.7
  lusterless 337.17
  mediocre 680.7
**lackwitted** 469.13
**laconic** concise 592.6
  taciturn 613.9
**lacquer**
  *n.* coating 228.12
  *v.* coat 228.24
  varnish 362.13
**lacquered** 260.10
**lactate** nurse 307.17
  secrete 312.5
**lactation**
  liquidity 388.1
  milk 388.3
  secretion 312.1
**lacteal** milky 388.8
  secretory 312.7
**lactic** 388.8
**lacuna**
  discontinuity 72.2
  gap 57.2
  hole 257.2
  interval 201.1
  opening 265.1
**lacustrian** 398.2
**lacustrine** 398.5
**lacy** netlike 221.11
  thin 205.16
**lad** boy 125.5
  man 420.5
**ladder** 315.4
**lade** burden 352.13
  fill 56.7
  put 184.14
**laden** burdened 352.18
  fraught 56.12
**la-di-da** 903.15
**ladies' man**
  beau 931.12
  dandy 903.9
  philanderer 932.11
**ladies' room** 311.10
**lading** burden 352.7
  freight 271.7
  full measure 56.3
  load 194.2
  placement 184.5
**ladino** 44.9
**ladle**
  *n.* types of 193.11
  *v.* transfer 271.16
**lady**
  form of address 421.8
  good person 985.1
  honest person 974.8
  lady love 931.14
  noblewoman 918.6
  wife 933.9
  woman 421.5
**Lady** 917.2
**lady bountiful** 818.11
**lady-killer** beau 931.12
  dandy 903.9
  philanderer 932.11
  unchaste person
    989.10
**ladylike**
  feminine 421.13

lap 395.8
adj. covering 228.35
water sound 452.19
lapse
n. an error 518.4
conversion 145.1
decrease 39.2
deterioration 692.3
end 70.3
fall 316.2
impiety 1030.1
misdeed 982.2
neglect 534.1
pause 144.3
regression 295.1
relapse 696.1
reversion 146.1
v. be wrong 518.9
decline 692.20
elapse 105.5
end 70.6
go wrong 981.9
neglect 534.6
pass 119.6
regress 295.5
relapse 696.4
revert 146.4
sink 316.6
lapsed carnal 987.6
impious 1030.6
past 119.7
unrighteous 981.12
lapse of memory 538.1
lapse of time 105.4
lap up
be credulous 502.6
drink 307.28
tipple 996.23
larboard 244.1
larcenous 824.20
larceny 824.2
lard
n. fat 380.13
pork 308.16
v. make better 691.9
oil 380.8
larder pantry 660.8
provisions 308.5
store 660.1
lares and penates
household gods
191.30
spirits 1014.22
large immense 34.7
liberal 853.4
sizable 195.16
largehearted
benevolent 938.15
liberal 853.4
magnanimous 979.6
argely
comprehensively
56.14
greatly 34.15
on a large scale
195.25
arge-minded 526.8
argeness greatness 34.1
liberality 853.1
sizableness 195.6
size 195.1

large-scale
extensive 79.13
large 195.16
largess gratuity 818.5
liberality 853.1
largo
n. musical passage
462.25
tempo 463.24
adv. music 462.55
lariat 618.12
lark
n. ascent 315.7
revel 878.6
songbird 464.23
v. make merry 878.26
larrup pound 283.14
punish 1010.15
larva bug 414.36
embryo 406.14
specter 1017.1
young insect 125.10
larval 406.24
laryngitis
inflammation 686.9
respiratory disease
686.14
larynx 594.19
lascivious
amorous 931.24
desirous 634.21
lecherous 989.29
sexual 419.29
lash
n. blow 283.7
goad 648.8
hair 230.12
whip 1011.1
v. anchor 275.15
bind 47.9
criticize severely
969.21
drive animals 416.8
goad 648.15
punish 1010.14
restrain 760.10
lashing
connection 47.3
punishment 1010.4
lash out at 798.16
lass girl 125.6
lady love 931.14
woman 421.5
lassitude fatigue 717.1
languor 708.6
weakness 160.1
lasso
n. loop 253.2
snare 618.12
v. catch 822.17
last
n. end 70.1
model 25.6
v. elapse 105.5
endure 110.6
live 407.10
live on 1.9
persevere 625.2
remain 140.5
adj. completory 722.9
departing 301.19
eventual 151.11

final 70.10
foregoing 119.11
newest 122.14
adv. finally 70.11
lasting durable 110.10
permanent 140.7
persevering 625.7
protracted 110.11
remembered 537.23
substantial 3.7
temporal 105.7
tough 359.4
unchangeable 142.17
last minute 132.1
last-minute hasty 709.9
late 132.18
last name 583.5
last resort
last expedient 670.2
refuge 700.2
last rites
funeral rites 410.4
unction 1040.6
last straw cause 153.3
limit of patience
862.3
Last Supper 1040.8
last word
culmination 677.3
dying word 67.1
end 70.1
final proposal 773.3
last word, the
novelty 122.2
the rage 644.4
latch close 266.6
fasten 47.8
late
adj. anachronous
115.3
belated 132.16
dead 408.30
delayed 270.12
former 119.10
recent 122.12
untimely 130.7
adv. behind 132.19
late bloomer 132.6
latecomer 132.6
late lamented
n. corpse 408.16
adj. dead 408.30
lately 122.16
latency
dormancy 268.4
latent meaningfulness
546.1
lateness
anachronism 115.1
newness 122.1
posteriority 117.1
tardiness 132
untimeliness 130.1
latent
concealed 615.11
dormant 268.14
secret 614.11
underlying 546.5
unseen 445.5
later
adj. future 121.8
late 132.18

recent 122.12
subsequent 117.4
adv. in the future
121.9
subsequently 117.6
lateral
n. speech sound
594.13
throw 285.4
v. go sideways 242.5
adj. phonetic 594.31
side 242.6
sided 242.7
latest newest 122.14
present 120.2
latest thing, the
novelty 122.2
the rage 644.4
lath
n. strip 206.4
thinness 205.7
wood 378.3
v. cover 228.23
lathe converter 145.10
tool 348.12
lather
n. dither 857.5
foam 405.2
impatience 862.1
sweat 311.7
v. defeat 727.6
foam 405.5
punish 1010.15
wash 681.19
latitude breadth 204.1
broad-mindedness
526.1
coordinates 490.6
freedom 762.4
map 654.4
spare 179.3
zone 180.3
latitudinarian
n. broad-minded per-
son 526.6
freethinker 1031.13
independent 762.12
adj. broad-minded
526.9
freethinking 1031.21
nonrestrictive 762.24
latrine
rest room 311.10
toilet 311.11
latter foregoing 119.11
recent 122.12
lattice
n. atom 326.7
frame 245.4
network 221.3
reactor 326.13
window 265.8
v. net 221.7
laud
n. hymn 1032.3
praise 968.5
worship 1032.2
v. praise 968.12
worship 1032.11
laudable good 674.12
praiseworthy 968.20
laudanum 687.12,54

laudatory 968.16
lauded 34.9
laugh
  n. joke 881.6
  laughter 876.4
  v. be cheerful 870.6
  be pleased 865.9
  chuckle 876.8
laughable
  foolish 470.10
  humorous 880.4
laugh at flout 793.4
  ridicule 967.8
laughing
  n. laughter 876.4
  adj. cheerful 870.11
  happy 865.13
laughingstock 967.7
laugh it up
  amuse oneself 878.24
  laugh 876.8
laugh off 531.4
laughs 878.2
laughter laughing 876.4
  merriment 870.5
launch
  n. motorboat 277.4,21
  rocketry 281.9
  v. inaugurate 68.11
  propose 773.5
  rocket 281.13
  start 285.14
  throw 285.11
launcher 801.19,27
launching 68.5
launching pad
  platform 216.13
  rocketry 281.10
launch into
  set to work 716.15
  undertake 715.3
launder 681.19
laundress 681.15
laundry
  laundering 681.6
  washery 681.11
laureate
  n. champion 733.14
  poet 609.13
  superior 36.4
  adj. honored 916.9
laurels 916.3
lava ashes 329.16
  rock 384.1,12
lavatory
  bathing place 681.10
  rest room 311.10
  room 192.26
  washing equipment
  681.12
lave soak 392.13
  wash 681.19
lavender 373.3,4
lavish
  v. give 818.12
  squander 854.3
  adj. liberal 853.4
  plentiful 661.7
  prodigal 854.8
  superabundant
  663.19
  teeming 101.9

lavishly liberally 853.5
  plentifully 661.9
  superabundantly
  663.24
lavishness
  grandeur 904.5
  overabundance 663.2
  plenty 661.2
  prodigality 854.1
lavish upon
  be generous 853.3
  give 818.15
lavish with 663.14
law
  n. axiom 517.2
  decree 752.4
  jurisprudence 998.7
  precept 751.2
  prohibition 778.1
  rule 84.4
  statute 998.3
  v. sue 1004.12
law, the 699.16
law-abiding
  honest 974.13
  obedient 766.3
law and order 803.2
lawbreaker
  criminal 986.10
  evildoer 943.1
lawbreaking
  disobedience 767.1
  illegality 999.3
  wrongdoing 982.1
law enforcement agency
  699.17
law enforcement agent
  699.15
lawful authentic 516.14
  just 976.8
  legal 998.10
  permissible 777.15
  valid 516.13
lawfully legally 998.12
  permissibly 777.19
lawfulness justice 976.1
  legality 998.1
  permissibility 777.8
lawgiver 746.3
lawless anarchic 740.5
  disobedient 767.8
  illegal 999.6
lawlessly 740.7
lawlessness anarchy 740
  disobedience 767.1
  illegality 999.1
  presumption 961.2
lawmaker 746.3
lawmaking
  n. legislation 742.13
  adj. legislative 742.19
lawn 411.7
law of averages 156.1
lawsuit
  accusation 1005.1
  legal action 1004
lawyer 1003
lax dilatory 132.17
  flaccid 357.10
  gentle 759.7
  inaccurate 518.17
  indolent 708.18

loose 51.5
  negligent 534.10
  nonrestrictive 762.24
  permissive 777.14
  phonetic 594.31
  unchaste 989.26
  unrestrained 762.23
  unstrict 758.4
  vague 514.18
laxative 687.17,62
laxity flaccidity 357.3
  inaccuracy 518.2
  looseness 51.2
  neglect 534.1
  nonobservance 769.1
  unchastity 989.4
  unstrictness 758.1
  vagueness 514.4
laxness
  dilatoriness 132.5
  flaccidity 357.3
  leniency 759.1
  looseness 51.2
  neglect 534.1
  unrestraint 762.3
  unstrictness 758
lay
  n. direction 290.1
  melody 462.4
  position 184.3
  song 462.13
  v. bet 515.20
  copulate 419.23
  exorcise 1035.12
  impose 963.4
  level 214.6
  lie 214.5
  moderate 163.6
  pacify 804.7
  place 184.11
  put 184.13
  relieve 886.5
  reproduce 169.9
  sail 275.48
  smooth 260.5
  adj. nonordained
  1039.3
lay aside
  disregard 531.4
  postpone 132.9
  put away 668.6
  remove 271.10
  segregate 77.6
lay away
  put away 668.6
  store 660.10
lay before
  confront 240.8
  propose 773.5
lay by be idle 708.15
  postpone 132.9
  prepare 720.11
  put away 668.6
  reserve 660.12
  water travel 275.17
lay down affirm 523.4
  bet 515.20
  give up 633.7
  layer 227.5
  level 214.6
  pay over 841.15
  postulate 499.12

prescribe 752.10
  put 184.13
  sail 275.43
  store 660.10
lay down the law
  command 752.11
  direct 747.8
  dogmatize 513.10
  dominate 741.15
layer
  n. atmospheric layer
  402.3
  stratum 227
  v. laminate 227.5
layered 227.6
layette 231.30
lay figure
  art equipment 574.19
  figure 572.4
  figurehead 749.4
  model 25.5
  nonentity 4.2
lay hands on
  acquire 811.9
  attack 798.15
  bless 1032.13
  minister 1040.19
  seize 822.14
lay in sail for 275.35
  store 660.10
laying on of hands
  benediction 1032.5
  rite 1040.4
lay into attack 798.15
  contend 796.15
lay it on thick
  be bombastic 601.6
  boast 910.7
  coat 228.24
  dramatize 903.12
  exaggerate 617.3
  flatter 970.6
  overdo 663.11
lay low
  bring down 318.5
  level 214.6
  strike dead 409.18
  weaken 160.10
layman
  nonprofessional
  718.5
  secular 1039.2
layoff dismissal 310.5
  pause 144.3
  unemployment 708.3
lay off
  v. be idle 708.15
  cease 144.6
  chart 654.11
  circumscribe 234.4
  dismiss 310.19
  measure off 490.12
  stop work 144.8
  take a rest 711.8
  interj. stop! 144.15
lay of the land, the 7.2
lay on administer 963.6
  coat 228.24
  contend 796.15
  cover 228.19
  impose 963.4
  punish 1010.14

learning
  intellectual acquire-
    ment 564
  knowledge 475.4
learn the ropes 564.9
lease
  n. estate 810.5
  hire 780.5
  possession 808.1
  v. hire out 780.15
  rent 780.14
leased 780.19
leasehold
  n. estate 810.5
  possession 808.1
  adj. real 810.11
leaseholder 809.4
lease-lend lend 820.5
  rent out 780.15
leash
  n. restraint 760.4
  trio 93.1
  v. bind 47.9
  restrain 760.10
least
  n. minority 102.3
  adj. humble 906.9
  minority 102.7
  smallest 37.8
  adv. less 37.9
leather
  n. skin 229.1,9
  toughness 359.2
  v. punish 1010.15
  adj. leathern 229.7
leatherneck
  marine 800.27
  mariner 276.4
leathery leather 229.7
  tough 359.4
leave
  n. absence 187.4
  departure 301.4
  permission 777.1
  vacation 711.3
  v. abandon 633.5
  bequeath 818.18
  depart 301.6
  die 408.28
  leave remaining 43.6
  leave undone 534.7
  permit 777.9
  plants 411.31
  resign 784.2
  separate 49.9
leave alone
  be permissive 777.12
  do nothing 706.4
  not change 140.6
  not interfere 762.16
leave behind
  abandon 633.5
  die 408.28
  leave remaining 43.6
  overtake 269.17
  surpass 36.10
leaved foliated 411.38
  green 371.4
leaven
  n. leavening 353.4,18
  transformer 139.4
  v. fill 186.7

infuse 44.12
qualify 507.3
raise 353.7
leavening
  n. fermentation 353.4
  adj. raising 353.16
leave no stone unturned
  be thorough 56.8
  make every effort
    714.13
  persevere 625.5
  ransack 485.32
  take precautions
    895.6
leave of absence
  absence 187.4
  vacation 711.3
leave off
  v. break the habit
    643.3
  cease 144.6
  discontinue 668.4
  give up 633.7
  interj. cease! 144.14
leave one cold
  be uninteresting
    883.4
  bore 884.6
leave out 77.4
leave-taking 301.4
leave undone 723.2
leave well enough alone
  see let well enough
    alone
leave word
  communicate 554.7
  inform 557.8
leaving
  abandonment 633.1
  absence 187.4
  departure 301.1
leaving out
  excluding 77.9
  less 42.14
leavings refuse 669.4
  remainder 43.1
lecher
  bad person 986.5
  philanderer 932.11
  unchaste person
    989.11
lecherous 989.29
lechery
  lasciviousness 989.5
  lovemaking 932.9
lectern
  church part 1042.13
  desk 216.15
lector
  churchman 1038.10
  holy orders 1038.4
  lecturer 565.8
lecture
  n. lesson 562.7
  reproof 969.5
  speech 599.3
  v. discourse 562.17
  reprove 969.17
  speak 599.11
lecturer
  academic rank 565.4
  churchman 1038.10

speaker 599.5
teacher 565.8
lecturing
  n. public speaking
    599.1
  adj. educational
    562.19
ledge
  hidden danger 697.5
  horizontal 214.3
  layer 227.1
  lip 235.4
  shelf 216.14
ledger
  account book 845.4
  list 88.5
  record book 570.11
lee
  n. protection 699.1
  side 242.2
  adj. side 242.6
leech
  n. adherent 50.4
  bloodsucker 414.41
  doctor 688.6
  extortionist 822.12
  invertebrate 415.5
  parasite 907.4
  sail part 277.14
  v. bleed 689.33
leeching 689.26
leer
  n. look 439.3
  ridicule 967.4
  signal 568.15
  v. scrutinize 439.15
  signal 568.22
leering
  n. ridicule 967.1
  adj. ridiculing 967.12
leery cautious 895.9
  doubtful 503.9
  suspicious 504.4
lees refuse 669.4
  residue 43.2
leeward
  n. lee side 242.2
  adj. side 242.6
  adv. downwind 242.9
  sailing 275.68
  toward 290.26
leeway aviation 278.37
  distance 199.1
  interval 201.1
  latitude 762.4
  spare 179.3
  water travel 275.9
left
  n. left side 244.1
  liberalism 745.3
  liberals 745.11
  adj. abandoned 633.8
  departed 301.20
  left-hand 244.4
  remaining 43.7
  adv. to the left 244.6
left-handed
  clumsy 734.20
  insulting 965.6
  oblique 219.13
  sinistromanual 244.5

left-handed compliment
  965.2
left-hander 244.3
leftist
  n. liberal 745.11
  adj. liberal 745.19
left out 77.7
leftover
  n. remainder 43.1
  surplus 663.5
  adj. remaining 43.7
  surplus 663.18
leftward
  counterclockwise
    290.26
  to the left 244.6
left wing
  left side 244.1
  liberalism 745.3
left-wing left 244.4
  liberal 745.19
left-winger
  left side 244.1
  liberal 745.11
lefty 244.3
leg
  n. assist 785.2
  electric circuit 342.4
  fowl part 308.23
  limb 273.16
  part 55.4
  support 217.6
  voyage 275.6
  v. walk 273.26
legacy bequest 818.10
  inheritance 819.2
  result 154.1
legal just 976.8
  legitimate 998.10
  permissible 777.15
  recorded 570.18
  valid 516.13
legal age 126.2
legal counselor 1003.1
legalistic formal 646.7
  legal 998.11
legality justice 976.1
  legitimacy 998
  permissibility 777.8
legalization 998.2
legalize
  authorize 777.11
  legitimize 998.8
legally
  legitimately 998.12
  permissibly 777.19
legal system 1000.2
legal tender 835.1
legate delegate 781.2
  diplomat 781.6
legatee 819.4
legation
  commission 780.1
  diplomats 781.7
  office 719.8
legato
  n. musical passage
    462.25
  music style 462.31
  adv. music 462.54
legend biography 608.
  caption 484.2

fiction 608.7
map 654.4
mythology 1014.24
posthumous fame
914.7
tradition 123.2
**legendary**
extraordinary 85.14
fabricated 616.29
famous 914.16
fictional 608.17
historical 608.18
imaginary 535.21
mythical 1014.25
traditional 123.12
**legerdemain** 618.5
**legging** 231.62
**leggy** 207.21
**legibility** 548.3
**legible** 548.11
**legibly** 548.13
**legion** army 800.22
large number 101.3
military unit 800.19
throng 74.4
**legionary** 800.6
**legislate** legalize 998.8
make laws 742.18
**legislation** law 998.3
lawmaking 742.13
legalization 998.2
**legislative**
congressional 742.19
legal 998.10
**legislator**
lawmaker 746.3
public official 749.17
**legislature**
council 755.1
legislation 742.13
legislative body 742
**legit**
*n.* theater 611.1
*adj.* legal 998.10
**legitimacy**
genuineness 516.5
justifiability 1006.7
legality 998.1
permissibility 777.8
right 739.1
**legitimate**
authentic 516.14
justifiable 1006.14
legal 998.10
logical 482.20
permissible 777.15
theatrical 611.38
valid 516.13
**legitimately**
genuinely 516.18
legally 998.12
permissibly 777.19
**g man** 605.22
**gume plant** 411.4
seed vessel 411.28
**work**
investigation 485.4
**walking** 273.10
411.23
**sure**
ease 710
*dj.* idle 708.17

leisured 710.5
**leisure class** 708.10
**leisured idle** 708.17
leisure 710.5
**leisurely**
*adj.* slow 270.10
unhurried 710.6
*adv.* slowly 270.13
tardily 132.20
**leitmotiv** 462.30
**lemon**
*n.* failure 725.2
sour thing 432.2
*adj.* yellow 370.4
**lend**
deal in money 835.27
loan 820.5
**lend a hand** 785.11
**lender** 820.3
**lending loaning** 820
money market 835.16
**lend-lease**
*n.* lease 780.5
lending 820.1
*v.* lend 820.5
rent out 780.15
**length** distance 199.1
longness 202
size 195.1
**lengthen**
continue 143.4
increase 38.4
prolong 202.7
protract 110.9
**lengthened**
prolonged 202.9
protracted 110.11
**lengthening**
*n.* continuance 143.1
prolongation 202.5
protraction 110.2
*adj.* increasing 38.8
**lengthwise**
along 202.12
horizontally 214.9
**lengthy long** 202.8
tall 207.21
wordy 593.12
**leniency**
considerateness 938.3
indulgence 759
moderation 163.2
patience 861.1
pity 944.1
softness 357.1
tolerance 526.4
unstrictness 758.1
**lenient**
considerate 938.16
indulgent 759.7
patient 861.9
permissive 777.14
pitying 944.7
tolerant 526.11
unstrict 758.4
**lenitive**
*n.* alleviator 163.3
ointment 380.3
palliative 687.10
*adj.* lubricant 380.10
palliative 163.16
qualifying 507.7

relieving 886.9
remedial 687.40
**lens** eye 439.9
glass 443
**lent** 820.6
**Lent** fast 995.3
holy day 1040.15
**Lenten**
abstinent 992.10
fasting 995.5
meager 662.10
**lento** 462.55
**leonine** 414.46
**leopard**
animal 414.27,58
variegation 374.6
**leper** 926.4
**leprechaun** 1014.18
**leprosy**
infectious disease
686.12
skin disease 686.33
**leprous** 686.57
**lesbian**
*n.* homosexual 419.16
mannish female
420.9
*adj.* bisexual 419.32
**lesbianism** 419.12
**lese majesty** 975.7
**lesion** distress 866.5
impairment 692.8
sore 686.35
**less**
*adj.* fewer 102.6
inferior 37.6
reduced 39.10
*adv.* decreasingly
39.12
least 37.9
*prep.* lacking 662.17
without 42.14
**lessee** renter 190.8
tenant 809.4
**lessen** decrease 39.6
mitigate 1006.12
moderate 163.6
reduce 39.7
relieve 886.5
subtract 42.9
**lessening**
*n.* decrease 39.1
moderation 163.2
reduction 42.2
relief 886.1
*adj.* decreasing 39.11
moderating 163.14
**lesser** inferior 37.6
reduced 39.10
**lesson** reproof 969.5
teaching 562.7
warning 703.1
**lest** 175.6
**let**
*n.* hindrance 730.1
hire 780.5
*v.* extract 305.12
hire out 780.15
permit 777.9
rent 780.14
suppose 499.10
*adj.* employed 780.19

**let alone**
*v.* abstain 992.7
avoid 631.6
do nothing 706.4
leave undone 534.7
not change 140.6
not interfere 762.16
not use 668.5
*prep.* excluding 77.9
in addition 40.12
**let be** do nothing 706.4
leave undone 534.7
not change 140.6
not interfere 762.16
suppose 499.10
**letdown**
disappointment
541.1
humiliation 906.2
moderation 163.2
slowing 270.4
**let down**
*v.* betray 975.14
deceive 618.13
depress 318.4
desert 633.6
disappoint 541.2
get worse 692.19
humiliate 906.4
moderate 163.9
relax 711.7
slow 270.9
*adj.* disappointed
541.5
**let drop** divulge 556.6
let fall 318.7
remark 594.25
**let fly** shoot 285.13
throw 285.11
**let fly at** hurl at 798.28
lash out at 798.16
**let go** acquit 1007.4
discharge 75.8
discontinue 668.4
dismiss 310.19
do nothing 706.5
exempt 762.14
leave undone 534.7
let oneself go 762.18
loosen 51.3
make merry 878.26
neglect 534.6
release 763.5
relinquish 814.4
**lethal** fatal 409.23
harmful 675.12
**lethality**
deadliness 409.9
harmfulness 675.5
**lethargic**
apathetic 856.13
languid 708.19
sleepy 712.21
**lethargy** apathy 856.4
emotional symptom
690.23
languor 708.6
sleepiness 712.1
stupidity 469.3
stupor 712.6
**let in** receive 306.10
welcome 925.7

**liberalism**
  broad-mindedness 526.2
  libertarianism 762.10
  noninterference 762.9
  progressivism 745.3
**liberality**
  broad-mindedness 526.2
  generosity 853
  giving 818.1
  gratuity 818.5
  hospitality 925.1
  magnanimity 979.2
  plenty 661.2
**liberalize** 762.13
**liberally**
  generously 853.5
  magnanimously 979.8
  plentifully 661.9
**liberate** detach 49.10
  disembarrass 732.8
  emancipate 763.4
  release 762.13
  rescue 702.3
**liberated** freed 763.10
  loose 762.20
**liberation** escape 632.1
  freeing 763
  liberalism 762.10
  rescue 702.1
  theft 824.1
**liberator** 942.2
**libertarian**
  *n.* broad-minded person 526.6
  independent 762.12
  *adj.* broad-minded 526.9
  liberal 762.24
**libertine**
  *n.* independent 762.12
  philanderer 932.11
  unchaste person 989.10
  *adj.* liberal 762.24
**libertinism**
  liberalism 762.10
  profligacy 989.3
**liberty**
  exemption 762.8
  freedom 762.1
  grant 777.5
  opportunity 129.2
  permission 777.1
  presumption 961.2
  right 958.4
  vacation 711.3
**libidinal**
  appetitive 634.21
  instinctive 481.6
  sexual 419.26
**libidinous**
  appetitive 634.21
  lascivious 989.29
  lustful 419.29
**libido** desire 634.1
  instinct 481.2
  love 931.1
  psyche 690.35

  sexuality 419.2
**librarian**
  bookman 605.21
  manager 748.4
  recorder 571.1
**library** archive 701.6
  bookroom 605.17
  collection 74.11
  edition 605.2
  room 192.6
  storage place 660.6
**libration** 323.1
**librettist**
  composer 464.20
  dramatist 611.27
  poet 609.13
**libretto** music 462.28
  playbook 611.26
**license**
  *n.* authority 780.1
  confusion 62.2
  exemption 762.8
  freedom 762.1
  lawlessness 740.1
  permission 777.1
  permit 777.6
  presumption 961.2
  profligacy 989.3
  right 958.4
  *v.* authorize 777.11
  charter 780.9
**licensed**
  authorized 777.17
  exempt 762.29
**licentious**
  intemperate 993.8
  lawless 740.5
  presumptuous 961.11
  unchaste 989.25
  unrestrained 762.23
**lichen** plant 411.4
  skin disease 686.33
**licit** legal 998.10
  permissible 777.15
**lick**
  *n.* attempt 714.2
  hit 283.4
  music 462.27
  rate 267.4
  small amount 35.4
  taste 427.2
  touch 425.1
  work 716.4
  *v.* best 36.7
  defeat 727.6
  drink 307.28
  lap 425.9
  perplex 514.13
  punish 1010.15
**licked** defeated 727.14
  perplexed 514.24
**lickerish**
  desirous 634.21
  lascivious 989.29
  lustful 419.29
**lickety-split** 269.21
**licking** defeat 727.1
  eating 307.1
  punishment 1010.5
**lid** clothing 231.25
  cover 228.5
  eyelid 439.9

  stopper 266.4
**lido** 385.2
**lie**
  *n.* direction 290.1
  falsehood 616.11
  position 184.3
  *v.* be dishonest 975.11
  be located 184.9
  be present 186.6
  extend 179.7
  falsify 616.19
  lie down 214.5
  ride at anchor 275.16
**lied** 462.13
**lie detector** 690.10
**lie down** couch 318.11
  lie 214.5
  rest 711.6
**lief** 622.9
**liege**
  *n.* master 749.1
  retainer 750.1
  subject 764.7
  *adj.* subject 764.13
**lie in** be located 184.9
  exist in 1.11
  give birth 167.15
  sail for 275.35
**lie in state** 410.21
**lie in wait**
  ambush 615.10
  await 539.8
  lurk 615.9
**lie low** be latent 546.3
  be low 208.5
  beware 895.7
  hide oneself 615.8
**lien** mortgage 772.4
  security 772.5
**lie on**
  be contingent 507.6
  be heavy upon 352.11
  oppress 729.8
  rest on 216.22
**lieu** location 184.1
  place 184.4
**lieutenant**
  assistant 787.6
  commissioned officer 749.18
  deputy 781.1
  naval officer 749.20
  peace officer 699.15
**life** a being 3.3
  affairs 151.4
  animation 161.3
  biography 608.4
  eagerness 635.1
  energizer 161.5
  existence 1.1
  gaiety 870.4
  lifetime 110.5
  liveliness 707.2
  living 407
  person 417.3
**life after death** 121.2
**life-and-death** 672.22
**lifeblood** blood 388.4
  seat of life 407.3
**lifeboat** escape 632.3
  life preserver 701.5

  rescue device 702.2
**life cycle** 407.3
**life force** 407.3
**life-giving**
  animating 407.12
  reproductive 169.15
**lifeguard**
  guardian 699.6
  rescuer 702.2
**life jacket** 701.5
**lifeless** dead 408.30
  inanimate 382.5
  inert 268.14
  lackluster 337.17
  languid 708.19
  uninteresting 883.6
**lifelike**
  authentic 516.14
  descriptive 608.15
  true to life 20.16
**lifeline** escape 632.3
  life preserver 701.5
  safety equipment 699.3
**lifelong** 110.13
**life of Riley, the** 728.1
**life of the party**
  energizer 161.5
  humorist 881.12
  mischief-maker 738.3
  sociable person 922.15
**life-or-death** 672.22
**life preserver**
  float 277.11
  life jacket 701.5
  safety equipment 699.3
**life principle**
  life force 407.3
  theosophy 1034.18
  vital principle 466.5
**lifer** 761.11
**lifesaver**
  guardian 699.6
  preserver 701.4
  rescuer 702.2
**lifesaving** 702.1
**life savings** 835.14
**life science** 406.17
**life-sized** 195.22
**life story** 608.4
**life-style** 737.1
**lifetime**
  *n.* duration 110.5
  life 407.1
  *adj.* lifelong 110.13
**lifework** cause 153.10
  vocation 656.6
**lift**
  *n.* assist 785.2
  a theft 824.10
  atmosphere 402.2
  aviation 278.35
  elevator 317.4
  heavens 375.2
  height 207.2
  improvement 691.1
  lifter 317.3
  raise 317.2
  ride 273.7
  thrill 857.2

wave 395.14
*v.* billow 395.22
cheer 870.8
elevate 317.5
make better 691.9
pay in full 841.13
steal 824.13
transport 271.11
lifter erector 317.3
fireplace 329.12
thief 825.1
lift-off 281.9
ligament cord 206.2
tendon 245.6
ligature
harmonics 463.12
ligament 206.2
printing 603.6
light
*n.* aspect 446.3
dawn 133.3
divine attribute
1013.15
explanation 552.4
glass 339.2
igniter 331.4
illumination 335
information 557.1
light source 336.1,8
light unit 335.21
mental outlook 525.2
ray 323.4
signal 336.9
speed 269.6
window 265.8
*v.* descend 316.7
grow bright 335.27
ignite 329.22
illuminate 335.28
land 278.52
strike a light 335.29
*adj.* agile 733.21
airy 402.12
cheerful 870.12
clear 335.31
colorless 363.9
easy 732.12
fickle 629.6
frail 160.14
phonetic 594.31
shallow 210.5
soft-colored 362.21
superficial 469.20
theatrical 611.40
thin 205.16
trivial 673.16
unchaste 989.26
unheavy 353.10
whitish 364.8
light bulb 336.1,8
lighted 335.39
lighten
disburden 353.6
grow bright 335.27
illuminate 335.28
moderate 163.6
relieve 886.7
lightened
bleached 363.8
illuminated 335.39
lightening
*n.* decoloration 363.3

disburdening 353.3
moderation 163.2
relief 886.3
*adj.* disburdening
353.15
illuminating 335.40
lighter 331.4
lightface 603.20
light-fingered 824.20
light fingers 824.12
light-footed
agile 733.21
fast 269.19
lightheaded
delirious 473.31
dizzy 532.15
lightheadedness 532.4
light heart 870.3
lighthearted 870.12
light holder 336.11
lighthouse alarm 704.1
marker 568.10
observation post
439.8
tower 207.11
lighting
*n.* ignition 329.4
illumination 335.19
*adj.* illuminating
335.40
inflammatory 329.27
light into attack 798.15
contend 796.15
punish 1010.12
set to work 716.15
lightless 337.13
lightly
capriciously 629.7
cheerfully 870.17
easily 732.15
negligently 534.17
scarcely 35.9
unimportantly 673.20
light meter
film exposure 577.9
light measure 335.21
lightness agility 733.2
cheerfulness 870.3
colorlessness 363.2
color quality 362.6
fickleness 629.3
frailty 160.2
lack of weight 353
luminousness 335.3
superficiality 469.7
thinness 205.4
triviality 673.3
unchastity 989.4
whiteness 364.1
lightning light 335.17
speed 269.6
lightning bug 336.5
lightning gods 335.17
lightning rod 699.3
light opera 462.35
light out 301.11
lightproof 266.12
lights belief 501.6
lungs 403.19
theater lighting
611.23

light show
flickering 335.8
iridescence 374.2
show 611.15
spectacle 446.7
lightsome
cheerful 870.12
clear 335.31
light source
illuminant 335.20
luminary 336
light touch 425.1
light up cheer up 870.9
excite 857.11
ignite 329.22
illuminate 335.28
light upon
alight on 316.10
arrive at 300.7
find 488.3
meet 200.11
lightweight
*n.* a nobody 673.7
boxing weight 352.3
dolt 471.3
inferior 37.2
little thing 196.4
pugilist 800.2
weakling 160.6
*adj.* frail 160.14
light 353.12
uninfluential 173.3
light-year
distance 199.1
outer space 375.3
lignitic 331.9
likable desirable 634.30
lovable 931.23
pleasant 863.6
tasty 428.8
like
*n.* equivalent 30.4
love 931.1
similarity 20.3
*v.* desire 634.14
enjoy 865.10
love 931.18
savor 428.5
*adj.* approximate 9.8
equal 30.7
identical 14.7
similar 20.10
*adv.* in the same way
as 657.11
similarly 20.18
like clockwork
continually 17.8
easily 732.15
methodically 59.9
regularly 137.9
smoothly 260.12
likelihood
expectation 539.4
good chance 156.8
liability 175.1
possibility 509.1
probability 511.1
likely
*adj.* apt 26.10
beautiful 900.17
expedient 670.5
minded 525.8

possible 509.6
probable 511.6
*adv.* probably 511.8
likely story 1006.4
likely to
inclined to 174.6
liable to 175.5
like mad fast 269.22
intensely 34.23
recklessly 894.11
violently 162.24
like-minded
agreeing 26.9
in accord 794.3
unanimous 521.15
liken 491.4
likeness analogue 20.3
aspect 446.3
copy 24.1
equality 30.1
image 572.3
picture 574.12
similarity 20.1
likewise
additionally 40.11
identically 14.9
similarly 20.18
liking fondness 634.2
love 931.1
tendency 174.1
will 621.1
Lilliputian
*n.* dwarf 196.6
*adj.* dwarf 196.13
lilt
*n.* meter 609.9
rhythm 463.22
song 462.13
*v.* be cheerful 870.6
rejoice 876.5
sing 462.39
utter 594.26
lily-livered 892.10
limb border 235.4
bough 411.18
leg 273.16
lever 287.4
part 55.4
limber pliant 357.9
weak 160.12
limber up
make pliant 357.6
prepare oneself
720.13
limbo hell 1019.1
place of confinemen
761.7
lime
*n.* snare 618.12
sour thing 432.2
*v.* hamper 730.11
trap 618.18
limelight
publicity 559.4
theater lighting
611.23
limen boundary 235
physical sensibility
422.2
limerick 609.6
limey Briton 181.7
sailor 276.1

**limit**
n. boundary 235.3
capacity 195.2
completion 56.5
end 70.2
limitation 234.2
summit 211.2
v. bound 235.8
narrow 205.11
qualify 507.3
restrain 760.9
restrict 234.5
specialize 81.4
**limit, the** 862.3
**limitation**
boundary 235.3
estate 810.4
narrowness 205.1
qualification 507.1
restraint 760.3
restriction 234.2
**limited**
n. train 272.13
adj. little 196.10
local 180.9
meager 662.10
moderate 163.11
narrow 205.14
qualified 507.10
restrained 760.15
restricted 234.7
specialized 81.5
**limiting**
bordering 235.11
enclosing 236.11
final 70.10
qualifying 507.7
restraining 760.12
restricting 234.9
**limitless**
godlike 1013.20
greedy 634.27
infinite 104.3
unrestricted 762.26
**limits** 235.1
**mn** describe 608.12
draw 574.20
outline 235.9
represent 572.6
**mner** 579.2
**mp**
n. gait 273.14
slowness 270.2
v. be weak 160.8
go slow 270.6
walk 273.27
adj. drooping 215.10
flaccid 357.10
weak 160.12
**mpet** adherent 50.4
food 308.25
invertebrate 415.5
**mpid**
intelligible 548.10
polished 589.6
transparent 339.4
**mping**
crippled 692.32
slow 270.10
**ne**
ancestry 170.4
artistry 574.10

battlefield 802.2
boundary 235.3
communications
560.17
conformity 82.1
cord 206.2
direction 290.1
engraving 578.2
fleet 277.10
kind 61.3
ledger line 462.29
length 202.4
letter 604.2
mark 568.6
melody 462.4
merchandise 831.1
music 462.22
poetic division
609.11
policy 654.5
political policy 744.4
posterity 117.2
procession 71.3
railway 657.8
route 657.2
row 71.2
sequence 65.1
specialty 81.1
species 11.4
story element 608.9
technique 657.1
track 568.8
trend 174.2
vanguard 240.2
vocation 656.6
v. align 71.5
arrange 60.9
border 235.10
engrave 578.10
fill 194.7
mark 568.19
outline 654.12
**lineage** ancestry 170.4
continuity 71.2
heirs 117.2
posterity 171.1
race 11.4
sequence 65.1
**lineal** consecutive 71.9
family 170.14
racial 11.7
straight 250.6
subsequent 117.4
**lineaments**
aspect 446.3
characteristic 80.4
exterior 224.2
face 240.4
form 246.3
looks 446.4
outline 235.2
**linear** consecutive 71.9
straight 250.6
**linebacker** 878.20
**lined up** 218.6
**lineman** athlete 878.20
electrician 342.19
telephone man
560.10
trainman 274.13
**linen** bedding 228.10
clothing 231.1

dry goods 831.3
underclothes 231.22
waist 231.15
**liner** lining 194.3
ship 277.5,22
**lines** artistic style 574.9
camp 191.29
harness 659.5
looks 446.4
outline 235.2
playbook 611.26
procedure 657.1
role 611.11
**lineup** list 88.6
order 59.1
plan 654.1
schedule 641.2
**line up** align 71.5
arrange 60.9
make parallel 218.5
order 59.4
queue 71.6
schedule 641.4
**linger** continue 143.3
dally 708.13
dawdle 270.8
follow 293.4
persist 110.7
wait 132.12
**lingerer** idler 708.8
slow person 270.5
**lingerie** 231.22
**lingering**
n. idling 708.4
protraction 110.2
slowness 270.3
waiting 132.3
adj. dawdling 270.11
procrastinating
132.17
protracted 110.11
reverberating 454.11
**lingo** jargon 580.9
language 580.1
**lingua franca** 580.11
**lingual**
linguistic 580.17
phonetic 594.31
spoken 594.30
tonguelike 427.10
**linguist**
linguistic scientist
580.13
polyglot 580.14
**linguistic**
communicational
554.9
philological 580.17
spoken 594.30
**linguistics** 580.12
**liniment** 687.11
**lining**
bookbinding 605.15
engraving 578.2
filling 194.3
**link**
n. intermediary 237.4
joint 47.4
part 55.4
relationship 9.1
torch 336.3
v. connect 71.4

couple 74.16
join 47.5
relate 9.6
**linkage** joining 47.1
relationship 9.1
**linked** continuous 71.8
joined 47.13
related 9.9
**Linotype** 603.2,21
**lint** down 230.19
medical dressing
687.33
powder 361.5
**lintel** 302.6
**lion** animal 414.27,58
brave person 893.8
heraldic insignia
569.2
idol 914.9
personage 672.8
strength 159.7
**lionhearted** 893.17
**lionize** glorify 914.13
praise 968.12
sight-see 442.6
**lion's share**
majority 100.2
major part 54.6
portion 816.5
**lion tamer** 612.3
**lip**
n. border 235.4
insolence 913.4
knob 256.3
wind instrument
465.7
v. be insolent 913.7
play music 462.43
say 594.23
**lipid** fat 309.7,23
oil 380.1,13
**lipped** 235.13
**lip reader** 449.2
**lip reading** 449.3
**lips** labia 419.10
mouth 265.5
vocal organ 594.19
**lip service**
hypocrisy 616.6
sanctimony 1029.2
**lipstick**
n. make-up 900.11
v. make red 368.4
**liquefaction**
liquidity 388.1
liquidization 391
**liquefied** 391.6
**liquefy** 391.5
**liquefying** 391.7
**liqueur** 996.41
**liquid**
n. drink 308.48
fluid 388.2
speech sound 594.13
adj. convertible
835.31
fluid 388.6
phonetic 594.31
watery 392.16
**liquid assets**
assets 810.8
ready money 835.18

livestock 414.1
live through
  endure 110.6
  persevere 625.4
  win through 724.12
live up to 768.2
live wire
  electric charge 342.5
  man of action 707.8
live with
  be broad-minded
    526.7
  persevere 625.4
  submit 765.6
livid angry 952.26
  black and blue
    365.12
  blue 372.3
  colorless 363.7
  deathly 408.29
  gray 366.4
  purple 373.3
living
  n. habitation 188.1
  life 407.1
  support 785.3
  the ministry 1037.9
  adj. alive 407.11
  burning 328.27
  energetic 161.12
  existent 1.13
  lifelike 20.16
  organic 406.19
  resident 188.13
living being
  animal 414.2
  organism 406.2
living quarters
  housing 188.3
  lodgings 191.3
living room 192.5
lizard 414.30,60
llano grassland 411.8
  plain 387.1
load
  n. affliction 866.8
  aviation 278.30
  burden 352.7
  contents 194.2
  explosive charge
    801.10
  freight 271.7
  full measure 56.3
  impediment 730.6
  much 34.3
  tax 963.2
  v. burden 352.13
  fill 56.7
  oppress 729.8
  prepare 720.9
  put 184.14
  shoot 285.13
  stuff 194.7
  tamper with 616.17
loaded
  burdened 352.18
  critical 129.10
  drunk 996.31
  fraught 56.12
  prepared 720.16
  wealthy 837.13
loader 276.9

loading burden 352.7
  imposition 963.1
  placement 184.5
loaf
  n. Eucharist 1040.8
  lump 195.10
  v. idle 708.11
loafer beggar 774.8
  idler 708.8
  vagabond 274.3
  vagrant 274.3
loafing 708.4
loamy earthy 385.7
  soft 357.12
loan
  n. lending 820.2
  v. lend 820.5
loaned 820.6
loaner 820.3
loaning 820.1
loan shark 820.3
loan-shark 820.5
loan-sharking
  illicit business 826.1
  lending 820.1
  overcharge 848.5
loath 623.6
loathe dislike 867.3
  hate 930.5
loathing
  n. dislike 867.2
  hate 930.1
  adj. hating 930.7
loathsome bad 675.9
  offensive 864.18
  ugly 899.11
lob elevate 317.5
  throw 285.11
lobar 215.12
lobby
  n. foyer 192.19
  influential persons
    172.6
  legislative lobby
    744.32
  v. influence 172.9
  legislate 742.18
  urge 648.14
lobbying
  inducement 648.3
  influence 172.3
  political influence
    744.29
lobbyist
  influential person
    172.6
  lobby 744.32
lobe brain 466.7
  ear 448.7
  part 55.4
  pendant 215.4
lobo 414.25
lobotomy 689.24
lobster
  invertebrates 415.5
  seafood 308.25
local
  n. branch 788.10
  labor union 789.1
  native 190.3
  railway car 272.14
  saloon 996.19

  train 272.13
  adj. dialect 580.20
  regional 180.9
local color 608.9
locale arena 802.1
  location 184.1
  setting 233.2
localism dialect 580.7
  political policy 744.4
  word 582.6
locality habitat 191.5
  location 184.1
localize locate 184.10
  restrain 760.9
localized 180.9
local yokel 190.3
locate discover 488.2
  settle 184.16
  situate 184.10
located 184.17
locating
  discovery 488.1
  placement 184.5
location
  discovery 488.1
  farm 413.8
  place 184
  placement 184.5
  position 7.1
locational
  positional 184.18
  regional 180.8
loch bay 399.1
  body of water 398.1
Loch Ness monster
  animal 414.35
  monster 85.20
lock
  n. floodgate 396.11
  hair 230.5
  restraint 760.5
  standstill 268.3
  wrestling hold 813.3
  v. agree 26.6
  close 266.6
  fasten 47.8
  obstruct 730.12
locker
  depository 836.12
  refrigerator 334.6
  storage place 660.6
locket 901.6
lock in imprison 761.14
  retain 813.5
lockjaw seizure 686.5
  tetanus 686.12
lockout exclusion 77.1
  refusing work 789.7
  stop 144.2
lock out close 266.6
  exclude 77.4
  refuse work 789.9
lock, stock, and barrel
  throughout 56.17
  wholly 54.13
lockup
  confinement 761.1
  prison 761.8
lock up close 266.6
  imprison 761.14
  secrete 615.7
loco 473.25

locomotion
  mobility 267.3
  travel 273.1
locomotive
  mechanical 347.7
  self-propelled 349.26
  vehicular 272.22
  walking 273.35
locus 184.1
locust 414.39,74
locution diction 588.1
  language 580.1
  phrase 585.1
  utterance 594.3
  word 582.1
lode deposit 383.7
  rich source 837.3
  source of supply
    660.4
lodestar
  center of attraction
    226.4
  guiding star 748.8
  magnet 288.3
  motive 648.1
  North Star 375.4
lodestone
  magnet 288.3
  thing desired 634.11
lodge
  n. association 788.10
  cottage 191.9
  house 191.6
  lair 191.26
  v. accommodate
    659.10
  become fixed 142.10
  establish 142.9
  house 188.10
  inhabit 188.7
  put 184.13
  store 660.10
lodged 188.14
lodger roomer 190.8
  tenant 809.4
lodging
  n. abode 191.1
  habitation 188.1
  housing 188.3
  quarters 191.3
  adj. resident 188.13
loess deposit 43.2
  geology 271.8
loft attic 192.16
  room 192.6
  workplace 719.1
loftily
  arrogantly 912.15
  dignifiedly 905.14
  grandiloquently
    601.12
  ostentatiously 904.25
lofty arrogant 912.9
  eloquent 600.14
  eminent 34.9
  famous 914.18
  grandiloquent 601.8
  high 207.19
  impartial 976.10
  magnanimous 979.6
  ostentatious 904.18
  proud 905.11

raised 317.9
**log**
  *n.* account book 845.4
  chronicle 114.9
  firewood 331.3
  record book 570.11
  speed meter 269.7
  wood 378.3
  *v.* keep accounts
    845.8
  record 570.16
  sail 275.48
**logarithmic** 86.8
**log cabin** 191.9
**loge** 611.20
**logged** 570.18
**logger** 413.7
**loggia** 192.18
**logging** forestry 413.3
  recording 570.15
**logic** philosophy 500.1
  reasonableness 482.9
  reasoning 482.2
**logical**
  reasonable 482.20
  valid 516.13
  wise 467.18
**logic-chopping**
  *n.* quibbling 483.5
  *adj.* quibbling 483.14
**logician** 482.11
**logistics**
  military operations
    797.8
  provision 659.1
**logjam** barrier 730.5
  delay 132.2
**logogram**
  character 581.2
  representation 572.1
  symbol 568.3
  wordplay 881.8
**logomachy**
  argumentation 482.4
  contention 796.1
  quarrel 795.5
**logorrhea**
  diffuseness 593.1
  logomania 596.2
  wordiness 593.2
**logotype** label 568.13
  printing 603.6
  symbol 568.3
**logroller**
  influence user 744.30
  political intriguer
    746.6
**logrolling**
  exchange 150.2
  legislative procedure
    742.14
  political influence
    744.29
**logy** 268.14
**loin** back 241.3
  meat 308.17
**loincloth** 231.19
**loins** 153.7
**loiter** dally 708.13
  dawdle 270.8
  follow 293.4
  idle 708.11

trifle 673.13
  wait 132.12
**loiterer** idler 708.8
  slow person 270.5
**loitering**
  *n.* idling 708.4
  slowness 270.3
  trifling 673.8
  *adj.* dawdling 270.11
  procrastinating
    132.17
**Loki**
  deity of nether world
    1019.5
  god of evil 1016.6
  Norse deity 1014.6
**loll** idle 708.11
  lie 214.5
  rest 711.6
**lollapaloosa** 674.7
**lolling**
  *n.* idling 708.4
  *adj.* recumbent 214.8
**lollygag** dally 708.13
  dawdle 270.8
  make love 932.13
**lollygagging**
  *n.* lovemaking 932.1
  slowness 270.3
  *adj.* dawdling 270.11
**lone** alone 89.8
  one 89.7
  sole 89.9
  solitary 924.10
**loneliness**
  aloneness 89.2
  solitude 924.3
**lonely** alone 89.8
  solitary 924.10
**loner** odd person 85.4
  selfish person 978.3
  solitary person 924.5
**lonesome** alone 89.8
  solitary 924.10
**lonesomeness**
  aloneness 89.2
  solitude 924.3
**lone wolf**
  odd person 85.4
  selfish person 978.3
**long**
  *n.* long time 110.4
  speculator 833.13
  *v.* want to 634.15
  wish for 634.16
  *adj.* lengthy 202.8
  protracted 110.11
  tall 207.21
  wordy 593.12
  *adv.* for a long time
    110.14
**long ago**
  *n.* old times 119.2
  *adv.* for a long time
    110.14
  long since 119.16
**longanimity**
  forgiveness 947.1
  patience 861.1
**long distance**
  telephone call 560.13

telephone operator
  560.9
**long-distance** 199.8
**long-established**
  confirmed 642.21
  established 142.13
  traditional 123.12
**longevity**
  durability 110.1
  life 407.1
  old age 126.5
  robustness 685.3
**long face** scowl 951.9
  solemnity 871.1
**long-faced** glum 872.25
  sad 872.20
  serious 871.3
**longhair** 123.8
**longhand**
  *n.* writing style 602.4
  *adj.* written 602.22
**long haul** 199.2
**longing**
  *n.* yearning 634.5
  *adj.* wistful 634.23
**longingly** 634.31
**longitude**
  astronomy 375.16
  coordinates 490.6
  length 202.1
  map 654.4
  zone 180.3
**long-lasting** 110.10
**long-lived**
  enduring 110.10
  tenacious of life
    407.11
**long range** 199.2
**long-range** 199.8
**longshoreman** 276.9
**long shot**
  chance event 156.6
  cinematography
    577.8
  gambling odds 515.6
  small chance 156.9
**longsighted**
  foreseeing 542.7
  poor-sighted 440.11
  sagacious 467.16
**long since**
  for a long time
    110.14
  long ago 119.16
  since 119.17
**long-standing**
  enduring 110.10
  traditional 123.12
**long-suffering**
  *n.* forgiveness 947.1
  patience 861.1
  tolerance 526.4
  *adj.* forgiving 947.6
  patient 861.9
  tolerant 526.11
**long suit** specialty 81.1
  talent 733.4
**long-term** 110.10
**long time** length 202.1
  long while 110.4
**long way** 199.2

**long-winded**
  protracted 110.11
  talkative 596.9
  tedious 884.8
  wordy 593.12
**long word**
  hard word 582.10
  pompous word 601.3
**loo** 311.10
**looby**
  awkward person
    734.8
  dolt 471.3
  rustic 919.9
  vulgar person 898.6
**look**
  *n.* aspect 446.3
  hint 557.4
  sight 439.3
  small amount 35.4
  *v.* appear to be 446.10
  gaze 439.16
  heed 530.6
  peer 439.13
  seek 485.29
  *interj.* attention!
    530.22
**look after**
  conserve 699.19
  serve 750.13
  tend 533.9
  watch 439.14
**look ahead** 542.5
**look-alikes** 20.5
**look alive**
  be vigilant 533.8
  pay attention 530.8
  make haste! 709.16
**look around** 485.30
**look at** examine 485.23
  take a look at 439.14
  take an attitude
    525.6
  watch 442.5
**look back** 537.10
**look down one's nose**
  be arrogant 912.8
  be fastidious 896.8
  grimace 867.5
  look askance 439.19
  snub 966.5
**look down upon**
  be high 207.16
  disdain 966.3
**looked-for**
  expected 539.13
  future 121.8
**looker**
  beautiful person
    900.8
  recipient 819.3
  spectator 442.1
**look for** expect 539.6
  hope 121.6
  seek 485.29
  solicit 774.14
**look for trouble** 795.1
**look forward to**
  expect 539.6
  foresee 542.5
  hope 121.6
**look in** enter 302.7

visit 922.17
**looking glass** 443.5
**looking up**
  improving 691.15
  promising 888.13
**look into** 485.22
**look like**
  appear to be 446.10
  resemble 20.7
**look on**
  be a spectator 442.5
  look at 439.14
  see 439.12
  witness 186.8
**lookout** business 656.1
  observation 439.2
  observation post
    439.8
  view 446.6
  vigilance 533.4
  warner 703.4
  watchman 699.10
**look out**
  v. be vigilant 533.8
  beware 895.7
  pay attention 530.8
  interj. caution 895.14
**look over**
  examine 485.23
  front on 240.9
  scrutinize 439.15
**looks** 446.4
**look the other way**
  be blind 441.8
  be broad-minded
    526.7
  disregard 531.2
**look through** 485.30
**look-through** 485.3
**look to** attend to 530.5
  avail oneself of
    665.14
  expect 539.6
  protect 699.19
  tend 174.3
**look up**
  get better 691.7
  seek 485.29
**look up to** 964.4
**loom**
  n. forthcoming 152.1
  weaver 222.5
  v. appear 446.8
  ascend 315.8
  be imminent 152.2
  be in the future
    121.6
  exceed 34.5
  weave 222.6
**looming**
  n. mirage 519.6
  adj. imminent 152.3
**loom large**
  be visible 444.4
  stand out 34.5
**loon** dolt 471.3
  lunatic 473.15
  **loony** foolish 470.8
  insane 473.26
  **loonybin** 473.14

**loop**
  n. air maneuver
    278.16
  circle 253.2
  circuit 321.2
  electric circuit 342.4
  hole 265.4
  tab 256.3
  v. curve 252.6
  encircle 233.7
  fly 278.49
  weave 222.6
**loophole**
  fortification 799.4
  hole 265.4
  observation post
    439.8
  outlet 303.9
  way out 632.4
**loose**
  v. detach 49.10
  disjoin 51.3
  facilitate 732.6
  free 763.6
  relax 163.9
  adj. adrift 275.61
  discursive 593.13
  drooping 215.10
  escaped 632.11
  flaccid 357.10
  free 762.20
  illogical 483.11
  inaccurate 518.17
  informal 647.3
  negligent 534.10
  slack 51.5
  slovenly 62.15
  unchaste 989.26
  unfastened 49.22
  ungrammatical 587.4
  unrestrained 762.23
  unstrict 758.4
  vague 514.18
**loose ends**
  nonaccomplishment
    723.1
  slipshodness 534.3
**loosen** detach 49.10
  free 763.6
  make pliant 357.6
  relax 163.9
  slacken 51.3
**looseness**
  flaccidity 357.3
  inaccuracy 518.2
  informality 647.1
  neglect 534.1
  slackness 51.2
  slovenliness 62.6
  unchastity 989.4
  unstrictness 758.1
  vagueness 514.4
**loosening**
  n. moderation 163.2
  unstrictness 758.1
  adj. softening 357.16
**loosen up**
  amuse 878.23
  amuse oneself 878.24
**loose woman** 989.14
**loosing** 763.2

**loot**
  n. booty 824.11
  v. plunder 824.16
  seize 822.14
  wreck 162.10
**looter** 825.6
**looting**
  n. plundering 824.5
  rapacity 822.9
  violence 162.3
  adj. plunderous
    824.21
**lop**
  v. cut off 42.10
  hang 215.6
  adj. drooping 215.10
**lope**
  n. speed 269.3
  v. ride 273.33
  run 269.10
**lopped** 57.5
**loppy** 215.10
**lopsided**
  asymmetric 249.10
  unbalanced 31.5
**loquacious** 596.9
**loquacity** 596.1
**loran** aviation 278.6
  direction finder 748.9
  navigation 275.2
  radar 346.3
**lord** master 749.1
  nobleman 918.4
  proprietor 809.2
**Lord God** 1013.2
  title 917.2
**lord it over** 741.16
**lordliness**
  arrogance 912.3
  authoritativeness
    739.3
  pride 905.2
**lordly** arrogant 912.11
  dignified 905.12
  imperious 739.16
**lordship**
  mastership 739.7
  noble rank 918.9
  ownership 808.2
  supremacy 36.3
**Lordship** 917.2
**lore**
  body of knowledge
    475.9
  mythology 1014.24
  superstition 502.3
  tradition 123.2
**Lorelei** 650.3
**lorgnette** 443.2
**lorry** 272.11
**lose** be defeated 727.12
  fail 725.8
  mislay 812.4
  not remember 538.5
  waste 854.4
**lose face**
  be disgraced 915.7
  be inferior 37.5
**lose ground** lag 314.2
  regress 295.5
  slow 270.9

**lose heart**
  be despondent
    872.16
  despair 889.10
**lose one's head** 470.6
**loser** defeatee 727.5
  unlucky person 729.7
  unsuccessful person
    725.7
**lose sight of**
  neglect 534.6
  not remember 538.5
**lose weight** 205.13
**loss** decrease 39.3
  disadvantage 671.2
  impairment 692.1
  losings 812.3
  privation 812
**loss of memory** 538.2
**loss of speech** 595.6
**lost** abstracted 532.11
  bewildered 514.23
  forgotten 538.8
  gone 812.7
  hopeless 889.15
  irreclaimable 981.18
  irreligious 1031.18
  unwon 727.13
  vanished 447.4
  wasted 854.9
**lost in** 530.17
**lost in thought**
  absorbed in thought
    478.22
  abstracted 532.11
**lost soul**
  bad person 986.5
  evil spirit 1016.1
**lot**
  n. amount 28.2
  amount of stock
    834.3
  bunch 74.7
  chance 156.1
  fate 640.2
  kind 61.3
  large number 101.3
  much 34.4
  plenty 661.2
  portion 816.5
  product 168.4
  real estate 810.7
  state 7.1
  tract 180.4
  v. allot 816.9
  gamble 515.18
**lot, a** 34.15
**lot, the** 54.3
**Lothario** beau 931.12
  unchaste person
    989.10
**lotion**
  cleaning agent 681.17
  healing ointment
    687.11
  ointment 380.3
  toilet water 436.3
**lottery** 515.11
**lotus-eater** idler 708.8
  visionary 535.13
**loud**
  adj. demanding 753.8

garish 362.19
gaudy 904.20
intense 159.20
noisy 453.10
vulgar 898.11
*adv.* loudly 453.13
**loud and clear** 548.10
**loudly** aloud 453.13
demandingly 753.10
strongly 159.21
**loudmouthed**
loud-voiced 453.11
vociferous 459.10
**loudness** din 453
garishness 362.5
showiness 904.3
sound 450.1
vulgarity 898.2
**loudspeaker** 450.8
**lounge**
*n.* reception room
192.20
*v.* idle 708.11
lie 214.5
rest 711.6
**lounger** 708.8
**lounging**
*n.* idling 708.4
recumbency 214.2
*adj.* recumbent 214.8
**lour, louring** see **lower**
etc.
**louse** animal 414.40
bad person 986.6
**louse up**
blunder 518.15
bungle 734.12
complicate 46.3
spoil 692.13
thwart 730.16
**lousy** bad 675.9
infested 313.11
**lout**
awkward person
734.8
oaf 471.5
rustic 919.9
unsophisticate 736.3
vulgar person 898.6
**loutish** boorish 898.13
clumsy 734.20
countrified 182.7
discourteous 937.6
**louver** 396.17
**lovable**
desirable 634.30
likable 931.23
**love**
*n.* accord 794.1
affection 931
beloved 931.13
benevolence 938.4
endearment 932.5
friendship 927.1
gods of 931.8
liking 634.2
regards 936.8
sexuality 419.2
virtue 980.5
*v.* be fond of 931.18
desire 634.14
enjoy 865.10

have deep feelings
855.14
savor 428.5
**love affair** 931.6
**love child** 171.5
**loved** 931.22
**loveless**
undesirous 636.8
unloved 867.10
**love letter**
billet-doux 932.12
letter 604.3
**loveliness** beauty 900.1
lovability 931.7
pleasantness 863.2
**lovelock** 230.5
**lovelorn** loving 931.25
unloved 867.10
**lovely** beautiful 900.16
lovable 931.23
pleasant 863.7
**lovemaking**
copulation 419.8
love 931.1
petting 932
sexuality 419.2
**love nest** cottage 191.9
rendezvous 922.9
**love potion** 419.7
**lover** admirer 931.11
desirer 634.12
endearment 932.5
friend 928.1
supporter 787.9
**lovesick** 931.25
**love song** 462.13
**love story** 608.7
**loving**
affectionate 931.25
considerate 533.10
godlike 1013.20
kind 938.13
**lovingly**
considerately 533.15
fondly 931.29
**low**
*n.* business cycle 827.9
gear 348.6
stock price 834.9
weather 402.5
*v.* animal sound 460.2
*adj.* cheap 849.7
common 919.11
deep 454.10
dejected 872.22
disappointed 969.22
disreputable 915.12
dying 408.33
evil 981.16
faint-sounding 452.16
humble 906.9
indecent 990.8
infelicitous 590.2
inferior 37.6
lowered 318.12
phonetic 594.31
short 203.8
small 35.6
unelevated 208.7
vulgar 898.15
*adv.* faintly 452.21

near the ground
208.9
**lowborn** 919.11
**lowbrow**
*n.* ignoramus 477.8
*adj.* unlearned 477.14
**Low Church** 1020.10
**low class** 680.4
**low-class** 680.9
**low-down** 915.12
**lowdown, the** 557.2
**lower**
*n.* darkness 337.2
scowl 951.9
*v.* be dark 337.12
be ill-humored
951.15
be imminent 152.2
forebode 544.11
show resentment
952.14
threaten 973.2
**lower**
*v.* cheapen 849.6
debase 208.6
deepen 209.8
demote 783.3
excavate 257.15
humiliate 906.5
make sad 872.18
raze 318.4
reduce 39.7
sink 316.6
*adj.* down 208.8
inferior 37.6
reduced 39.10
**lower case** 603.6
**lower-case** literal 581.8
typographical 603.20
**lower class**
common people
919.1
inferior 37.2
**lowered**
depressed 318.12
humble 906.12
reduced 39.10
**lower house**
legislature 742.1
lower chamber 742.4
**lowering**
cheapening 849.4
decrease 39.1
deepening 209.7
downthrow 318.1
fall 316.2
**lowering**
*n.* darkness 337.2
*adj.* dark 337.14
imminent 152.3
ominous 544.17
overhanging 215.11
sullen 951.24
threatening 973.3
**lowest bottom** 212.7
cheap 849.9
humble 906.9
least 37.8
undermost 208.8
**low grade** 680.4
**low-grade** 680.9
**lowing** 460.6

**lowland** 182.6
**lowlands** lowland 208.3
plain 387.1
the country 182.1
**lowlife** 986.2
**lowly** common 919.11
humble 906.9
inferior 37.6
unappreciated 867.9
**lowness** disrepute 915.3
faintness of sound
452.1
prostration 208
resonance 454.1
sadness 872.3
shortness 203.1
vulgarity 898.5
**low opinion** 969.1
**low-pitched** 454.10
**low price** 849.2
**low-priced** 849.7
**low priority** 673.1
**low-priority** 673.14
**low profile** 445.2
**low-profile** 445.6
**low-spirited**
dejected 872.22
uninteresting 883.6
**low spirits** 872.3
**low-test** 680.9
**low tide**
low water 208.2
tide 395.13
**low voice** 452.4
**low-voiced** 452.16
**lox** coolant 334.7
rocketry 281.8
**loyal** faithful 974.20
firm 624.12
obedient 766.3
observant 768.4
persevering 625.7
zealous 635.10
**loyalist** 744.27
**loyal opposition**
opponents 791.1
political party 744.24
**loyalty** duty 962.1
fidelity 974.7
firmness 624.2
obedience 766.1
perseverance 625.1
zeal 635.2
**lozenge**
heraldic insignia
569.2
pill 687.7
**LSD** 687.13,53
**lubber**
awkward person
734.8
idler 708.8
oaf 471.5
sailor 276.2
**lubricant**
*n.* lubricator 380.2
*adj.* lubricating 380.
**lubricate**
facilitate 732.6
oil 380.8
smooth 260.5

**lubricating**
n. lubrication 380.6
adj. lubricant 380.10
**lubrication** 380.6
**lubricious**
lascivious 989.29
slippery 260.11
**lubritorium** 380.7
**lucid**
intelligible 548.10
light 335.31
polished 589.6
sane 472.4
translucent 340.5
transparent 339.4
**lucidity**
clairvoyance 1034.8
intelligibility 548.2
lightness 335.3
literary elegance
589.1
sanity 472.1
translucence 340.2
transparency 339.1
**Lucifer**
morning star 375.4
Satan 1016.3
**luck** chance 156.1
gamble 515.1
prosperity 728.2
uncertainty 514.1
**Luck** 156.2
**luckily**
auspiciously 544.21
fortunately 728.16
**luckless** 729.14
**lucky** auspicious 544.18
fortunate 728.14
timely 129.9
**lucky piece** 1036.5
**lucrative** gainful 811.15
paying 841.21
**lucre** gain 811.3
money 835.1
wealth 837.1
**lucubration**
consideration 478.2
study 564.3
treatise 606.1
written matter 602.10
**ludicrous**
foolish 470.10
humorous 880.4
**lug**
n. ear 448.7
pull 286.2
v. pull 286.4
transport 271.11
**luggage**
belongings 810.3
freight 271.7
types of 193.17
**lugubrious** 872.26
**lukewarm**
indifferent 636.6
nonreligious 1031.15
warm 328.24
**lull**
, calm 268.5
discontinuity 72.2
inactivity 708.1
interim 109.1

pause 144.3
respite 711.2
silence 451.1
v. calm 163.7
put to sleep 712.20
quiet 268.8
relieve 886.5
**lullaby**
cradlesong 462.15
sleep-inducer 712.10
**lulling**
n. moderation 163.2
relief 886.1
adj. tranquilizing
163.15
**lulu** 674.7
**lumbago**
disease symptom
686.8
inflammation 686.9
**lumbar** 241.10
**lumber**
n. impediments 730.6
rubbish 669.5
wood 378.3
v. flounder 734.11
hamper 730.11
plod 270.7
walk 273.27
**lumbering**
n. forestry 413.3
walking 273.10
adj. bulky 195.19
clumsy 734.20
slow 270.10
stilted 590.3
**lumberjack** 413.7
**lumberyard** 660.6
**lumen** 335.21
**luminary**
n. famous person
914.9
first-rater 674.6
light source 336.1
principal 672.10
adj. light 335.41
**luminesce** 335.26
**luminescence** 335.13
**luminescent** 335.38
**luminous**
glowing 335.30
godlike 1013.20
illuminated 335.39
intelligible 548.10
**lummox** bungler 734.9
oaf 471.5
**lump**
n. accumulation 74.9
bulge 256.3
bungler 734.9
clump 195.10
corpulent person
195.12
mark 568.7
piece 55.3
solid 354.6
swelling 256.4
v. be patient 861.5
thicken 354.10
**lumpen** base 915.12
countrified 182.7
formless 247.4

idle 708.17
slovenly 62.15
**lumpen proletariat**
common people
919.1
nonworkers 708.10
**lumpish** boorish 898.13
bulky 195.19
clumsy 734.20
countrified 182.7
languid 708.19
ponderous 352.17
stupid 469.15
thickened 354.14
**lump sum** 835.13
**lump together**
assemble 74.18
combine 52.3
join 47.5
**lumpy** bulky 195.19
rough 261.8
thickened 354.14
**Luna** 375.12
**lunacy**
foolishness 470.1
insanity 473.1
**lunar** celestial 375.25
moon-shaped 252.11
**lunar module** 282.2
**lunatic**
n. fool 471.1
madman 473.15
adj. insane 473.25
**lunatic fringe**
extremists 745.12
fanatic 473.17
**lunch**
n. meal 307.6
v. eat 307.19
**lunch counter** 307.15
**luncheon** 307.6
**lunchroom** 307.15
**lung** breathing 403.19
vitals 225.4
**lunge**
n. thrust 798.3
v. thrust at 798.16
walk 273.27
**lunkhead** 471.4
**lupine** canine 414.45
rapacious 822.26
**lurch**
n. bend 219.3
flounder 324.8
gait 273.14
swing 323.6
v. flounder 324.15
oscillate 323.10
sail 275.55
tumble 316.8
walk 273.27
**lurching** irregular 138.3
swinging 323.17
**lure**
n. allurement 650.2
attractor 288.2
incentive 648.7
snare 618.12
v. attract 288.4
entice 650.4
induce 648.22
trap 618.18

**lurid** brown 367.3
colorless 363.7
deathly 408.29
garish 362.19
gaudy 904.20
grandiloquent 601.8
obscene 990.9
red 368.6
sensational 857.30
**lurk** be latent 546.3
couch 615.9
**lurking**
imminent 152.3
in hiding 615.14
latent 546.5
**luscious**
oversweet 431.5
pleasant 863.9
tasty 428.8
**lush**
n. drunkard 996.11
v. drink 996.24
adj. growing rank
411.40
ornate 601.11
productive 165.9
tasty 428.8
**lust** greed 634.8
lasciviousness 989.5
sexual desire 419.5
sin 982.3
will 621.1
**lust after** crave 634.18
desire 634.14
lust 419.22
**luster**
n. beauty 900.6
chandelier 336.6
illustriousness 914.6
period 107.2
polish 260.2
shine 335.2
v. give light 335.23
polish 260.7
**lusterless**
colorless 363.7
lackluster 337.17
**lustful** desirous 634.21
lascivious 989.29
prurient 419.29
**lustily**
energetically 161.15
loudly 453.13
strongly 159.21
**lustral** atoning 1012.7
cleansing 681.28
**lustrous**
illustrious 914.19
luminous 335.30
shiny 335.33
**lusty** corpulent 195.18
energetic 161.12
robust 685.10
strong 159.13
**lute** 465.4
**Lutheran** 1020.27,35
**lux** 335.21
**luxate** disjoint 49.16
dislocate 185.5
**luxuriant** florid 601.11
growing rank 411.40
ornate 901.12

plentiful 661.7
productive 165.9
**luxuriate**
superabound 663.8
vegetate 411.31
**luxuriate in**
be intemperate 993.4
enjoy 865.10
**luxurious**
comfortable 887.11
expensive 848.11
grandiose 904.21
ornate 901.12
pleasant 863.7
sensual 987.5
wealthy 837.13
**luxury** grandeur 904.5
pleasantness 863.2
pleasure 865.1
prosperity 728.1
sensuality 987.1
superfluity 663.4
**lyceum** hall 192.4
secondary school
567.6
**lye** cleanser 681.30
disinfectant 687.59
**lying**
*n.* lowness 208.1
recumbency 214.2
untruthfulness 616.8
*adj.* recumbent 214.8
untruthful 616.34
**lying-in** 167.7
**lymph** 388.3
**lymphatic**
*n.* duct 396.13
*adj.* fluid 388.7
languid 708.19
secretory 312.7
**lymphocyte** 388.4
**lynch** hang 1010.20
kill 409.13
**lynching**
capital punishment
1010.7
killing 409.1
**lynch law** 740.2
**lynx** animal 414.27,58
keen eye 439.11
**lyre** 465.3
**lyric** 609.6
**lyric(al)** choral 462.51
melodious 462.49
poetic 609.17
**lyricist**
composer 464.20
poet 609.13
**lyric theater** 462.35
**lysis** 693.1
**Lysol** 687.59

**M**

**ma** 170.10
**ma'am** 421.8
**Mab** 1014.18
**macabre**
deathly 408.29
terrible 891.38
weird 1017.9
**macadam** 657.7

**macaroni** dandy 903.9
food 308.33
**mace** club 801.26
emblem of authority
739.9
insignia 569.1
**macerate** pulp 390.5
soak 392.13
torture 866.18
waste away 198.9
**Mach** 269.2
**Machiavellian**
*n.* cunning person
735.8
deceiver 619.1
political intriguer
746.6
schemer 654.8
*adj.* cunning 735.12
falsehearted 616.31
scheming 654.14
**machinate**
maneuver 735.10
plot 654.10
**machination**
chicanery 618.4
intrigue 654.6
stratagem 735.4
**machinator**
cunning person 735.7
political intriguer
746.6
schemer 654.8
traitor 619.10
**machine**
*n.* association 788.1
automobile 272.9
converter 145.10
copying 603.25
machinery 348.4,21
political party 744.24
typesetting 603.21
writing 602.31
*v.* process 167.11
tool 348.10
**machine-made** 167.22
**machinery**
enginery 348.4
equipment 659.4
instrumentality 658.2
mechanism 348.5
types of 348.21
**machine shop** 719.3
**machinist**
mechanic 348.9
stage technician
611.29
**machismo** 420.2
**macho** 420.12
**macrobiotic** 110.10
**macrocosm** 375.1
**maculate**
blemished 679.9
spotted 374.13
unchaste 989.23
**mad**
*n.* anger 952.5
*v.* madden 473.23
*adj.* angry 952.26
excited 857.23
foolish 470.8
frenzied 473.30

insane 473.25
reckless 894.8
violent 162.17
**mad about**
enthusiastic about
635.12
fond of 931.28
**madam**
form of address 421.8
mistress 749.2
procurer 989.18
**madame**
form of address 421.8
title 917.4
**madcap**
*n.* humorist 881.12
reckless person 894.4
violent person 162.9
*adj.* fanatic 162.21
foolhardy 894.9
**madden**
antagonize 929.7
dement 473.23
enrage 952.23
excite 857.11
**maddening** 857.28
**mad dog** evildoer 943.3
violent person 162.9
**made**
man-made 167.22
produced 167.20
successful 724.13
**mademoiselle**
form of address 421.8
girl 125.6
**made of** 58.4
**made-up**
fabricated 616.29
invented 167.23
**mad for** 634.22
**madhouse** 473.14
**madly**
frenziedly 857.33
furiously 34.23
insanely 473.35
recklessly 894.11
turbulently 162.25
violently 162.24
**madman** 473.15
**madness**
excitement 857.7
foolishness 470.1
infectious disease
686.12
insanity 473.1
**Madonna** 1015.5
**madrigal**
choral music 462.18
poem 609.6
**maelstrom**
agitation 324.1
bustle 707.4
swirl 322.2
whirlpool 395.12
**maestro** musician 464.1
teacher 565.1
**Mae West** 701.5
**maffick**
be disorderly 62.11
be noisy 453.8
celebrate 877.2

**Mafia**
illicit business 826.1
the underworld
986.11
**Mafioso**
racketeer 826.4
violent person 162.9
**magazine** armory 801.2
periodical 605.10
storage place 660.6
**magenta** 373.3,4
**maggot** bug 414.36
caprice 629.1
eccentricity 474.2
thing imagined 535.5
white 364.2
young insect 125.10
**maggoty**
capricious 629.5
eccentric 474.4
fanciful 535.20
filthy 682.23
spoiled 692.43
unsavory 429.7
**Magi** 468.5
**magic** charisma 914.6
illusoriness 519.2
sorcery 1035.1
**magic(al)**
illustrious 914.19
sorcerous 1035.14
supernatural 85.16
**magically** 34.20
**magic carpet** 1036.6
**magician**
entertainer 612.1
expert 733.13
illusionist 519.2
sorcerer 1035.6
trickster 619.2
**magic lantern** 577.12
**magic wand** 1036.6
**magisterial**
arrogant 912.11
authoritative 513.18
chief 36.14
dignified 905.12
imperious 739.16
jurisdictional 1000.6
skillful 733.20
**magistracy**
district 180.5
judgeship 1000.3
mastership 739.7
**magistrate**
arbitrator 805.4
executive 748.3
judge 1002.1
public official 749.1
**Magna Charta** 762.2
**magna cum laude**
916.11
**magnanimity**
ambition 634.10
eminence 34.2
forgiveness 947.1
generosity 979.2
liberality 853.1
tolerance 526.4
**magnanimous**
eminent 34.9
forgiving 947.6

generous 979.6
liberal 853.4
tolerant 526.11
**magnanimously**
generously 979.8
magnificently 34.20
**magnate**
businessman 830.1
nobleman 918.4
personage 672.8
**magnesia**
antacid 687.63
laxative 687.62
**magnet** attractor 288.3
center of attraction
226.4
thing desired 634.11
**magnetic**
attracting 288.5
engrossing 530.20
influential 172.13
magnetism 342.28
**magnetic field**
electric field 342.3
magnetism 342.9
**magnetic force** 342.9
**magnetic pole** 342.8
**magnetic tape**
computer 349.18
record 570.10
**magnetism**
allurement 650.1
attraction 288.1
desirability 634.13
influence 172.1
magnetic attraction
342.7
**magnetize** attract 288.4
influence 172.9
make magnetic
342.24
mesmerize 712.20
**magnification**
exaggeration 617.1
expansion 197.1
glorification 914.8
increase 38.2
intensification 885.1
praise 968.5
worship 1032.2
**magnificence**
grandeur 904.5
superexcellence 674.2
**magnificent**
eminent 34.9
grandiose 904.21
superb 674.17
**magnificently**
grandiosely 904.28
splendidly 34.20
superbly 674.22
**magnified**
aggravated 885.4
eminent 914.18
exaggerated 617.4
increased 38.7
**magnifier** 443.1
**magnify**
aggravate 885.2
exaggerate 617.3
glorify 914.13
increase 38.5

make larger 197.4
praise 968.12
worship 1032.11
**magnifying glass** 443.1
**magnitude**
astronomy 375.8
greatness 34.1
quantity 28.1
size 195.1
**magpie** bird 414.66
chatterer 596.4
collector 74.15
hodgepodge 44.6
**magus** 1035.6
**maharaja** 749.9
**maharani**
princess 918.8
sovereign queen
749.11
**mahatma** expert 733.13
good person 985.6
occultist 1034.11
wise man 468.1
**maid** girl 125.6
maidservant 750.8
spinster 934.4
**maiden**
n. girl 125.6
instrument of execu-
tion 1011.5
spinster 934.4
adj. childish 124.11
first 68.17
new 122.7
unmarried 934.7
**maidenhead**
celibacy 934.1
chastity 988.3
childhood 124.2
hymen 229.3
**maiden lady** 934.4
**maidenly** chaste 988.6
childish 124.11
feminine 421.13
new 122.7
unmarried 934.7
**maiden name** 583.5
**maiden speech** 68.5
**maid of honor** 933.5
**mail**
n. armor 799.3
carriers of 561.6
covering 228.15
plumage 230.18
post 604.5
v. post 604.13
send 271.14
**mailbox** 604.7
**mail carrier** 561.5
**mail coach**
mail carrier 561.6
stagecoach 272.12
**mailed fist, the** 756.3
**mailing list** 604.5
**maillot** 231.29
**mailman** 561.5
**mail-order house** 832.1
**maim** cripple 692.17
disable 158.9
injure 692.15
tear apart 49.14

**maiming**
impairment 692.1
impotence 158.5
**main**
n. conduit 396.7
continent 386.1
ocean 397.1
adj. chief 36.14
first 68.17
great 34.6
most important
672.23
**main drag** 657.6
**main idea** 479.4
**mainland**
n. continent 386.1
adj. continental 386.6
**mainlander** 386.3
**main line** 657.8
**mainlining**
drug dose 687.6
narcotic injection
689.18
**mainly** chiefly 36.17
generally 79.17
normally 84.9
on the whole 54.14
principally 68.18
**main office**
headquarters 226.6
office 719.8
**main point**
important point
672.6
summary 607.2
topic 484.1
**mainspring**
motive 648.1
source 153.6
**mainstay**
n. supporter 216.2
upholder 787.9
v. support 216.21
**mainstream** 174.2
**maintain** affirm 523.4
aid 785.12
believe 501.11
defend 1006.10
endure 110.6
insist 753.7
pay for 841.19
preserve 701.7
provide for 659.7
retain 813.5
support 216.21
sustain 143.4
**maintenance**
conservation 140.2
continuance 143.1
durability 110.1
payment 841.8
preservation 701.1
retention 813.1
support 216.1
sustenance 785.3
**maintenance man**
694.10
**maître d'hôtel**
majordomo 750.10
manager 748.4
waiter 750.7

**majestic**
dignified 905.12
eloquent 600.14
eminent 34.9
godlike 1013.20
grandiose 904.21
sovereign 739.17
**majesty**
divine attribute
1013.15
eloquence 600.6
eminence 34.2
grandeur 904.5
potentate 749.7
pride 905.2
sovereignty 739.8
**Majesty** 917.2
**major**
n. adult 127.1
commissioned officer
749.18
harmonics 463.15
study 562.8
adj. important 672.16
senior 123.19
superior 36.12
**majordomo**
manager 748.4
servant 750.10
**major in** specialize 81.4
study for 564.15
**majority**
n. major part 54.6
maturity 126.2
most 100.2
superiority 36.1
adj. most 100.9
**majority leader** 746.3
**major-league** 672.16
**make**
n. composition 58.1
form 246.1
kind 61.3
making 168.4
receipts 844.1
structure 245.1
temperament 525.3
yield 811.5
v. accomplish 722.4
acquire 811.8
act 705.4
arrive 300.6
cause 153.11
compel 756.4
compose 58.3
convert 145.11
create 167.10
do 705.6
execute 771.10
flow 395.16
make up 720.7
perform 705.8
sail for 275.35
travel 273.18
**make a deal**
compromise 807.2
contract 771.6
purchase 828.7
strike a bargain
827.18
**make advances**
approach 773.7

befriend 927.11
communicate with
554.8
influence 172.9
**make a face** 249.8
**make a federal case**
be thorough 56.8
overemphasize
672.13
**make a killing**
profit 811.11
score a success 724.8
speculate in stocks
833.23
win 726.4
**make a living** 659.11
**make allowance for**
allow for 507.5
condone 947.4
extenuate 1006.12
**make amends**
atone 1012.4
compensate 33.4
make restitution
823.5
repay 841.11
retaliate 955.5
**make a mountain out
of a molehill**
exaggerate 617.3
overemphasize
672.13
**make an example of**
1010.10
**make an impression**
affect emotionally
855.17
be heard 448.13
be remembered
537.14
impress 478.19
**make a point of**
contend for 796.21
make contingent
507.4
resolve 624.7
**make a scene** 855.15
**make a show of**
affect 903.12
be ostentatious
904.13
fake 616.21
indicate 555.5
**make believe** 616.21
**make-believe**
*n.* fantasy 535.5
*adj.* imaginative
535.21
ungenuine 616.26
**make clear**
explain 552.10
facilitate 732.6
make it clear 548.6
manifest 555.5
**make do** create 167.13
manage 670.4
substitute 149.4
**make ends meet**
economize 851.4
support oneself
659.12

**make fun of**
joke 881.13
ridicule 967.8
**make good**
atone 1012.4
be honest 974.9
be prosperous 728.9
compensate 33.4
complete 56.6
grow rich 837.9
make restitution
823.5
meet an obligation
962.11
observe 768.2
prove 505.11
remedy 694.13
repay 841.11
succeed 724.9
**make haste**
hasten 709.5
make it quick! 709.16
rush 269.9
**make hay while the sun
shines**
be industrious 707.16
improve the occasion
129.8
**make headway**
get better 691.7
make good 724.9
progress 294.2
prosper 728.7
sail 275.21
**make it** arrive 300.6
be able 157.11
make good 724.9
manage 724.11
**make known**
communicate 554.7
divulge 556.5
make public 559.11
**make light of**
attach little impor-
tance to 673.11
disregard 531.2
take it easy 732.11
underestimate 498.2
**make love**
copulate 419.23
pet 932.13
procreate 169.8
**make merry**
celebrate 877.2
revel 878.26
**make money**
grow rich 837.9
profit 811.11
**make no bones about**
not hesitate 624.10
speak plainly 591.2
**make nothing of**
attach little impor-
tance to 673.11
not understand
549.11
underestimate 498.2
**make one's mark**
be famous 914.10
be ostentatious
904.13
be prosperous 728.9

make good 724.9
**make one's way**
go to 273.24
make better 691.9
make good 724.9
support oneself
659.12
work one's way 294.4
**make out**
copulate 419.23
detect 488.5
execute 771.10
fare 7.6
know 475.12
make love 932.13
make shift 670.4
manage 724.11
persist 143.5
prove 505.11
recognize 537.12
record 570.16
see 439.12
solve 487.2
survive 659.12
understand 548.8
write 602.19
**make-out artist** 932.11
**make over**
convert 145.11
reproduce 169.7
transfer 271.9
transfer property
817.3
**make peace**
cease hostilities 804.9
mediate 805.7
**make plain**
explain 552.10
manifest 555.5
**make possible**
enable 509.5
permit 777.9
**make public** 559.11
**maker** artist 579.1
creator 153.4
doer 718.1
poet 609.13
producer 167.8
types of 718.12
**make sense**
be intelligible 548.4
be reasonable 482.17
**makeshift**
*n.* expedient 670.2
improvisation 630.5
substitute 149.2
*adj.* expedient 670.7
extemporaneous
630.12
imperfect 678.4
substitute 149.8
unprepared 721.8
**make the best of it**
accept 861.6
be optimistic 888.9
submit 765.6
**make the grade**
be able 157.11
manage 724.11
suffice 661.4
**make the most of**
accept 861.6

take advantage of
665.15
**make the scene**
go to 273.24
participate 815.5
succeed 724.9
**makeup** book 605.12
composition 58.1
cosmetics 900.11
disguise 21.1
form 246.1
nature 5.3
structure 245.1
temperament 525.3
theatrical makeup
611.22
**make up** arrange 771.9
assemble 74.18
complete 56.6
compose 58.3
create 167.13
devise 167.10
fabricate 616.18
improvise 630.8
make peace 804.10
prepare 720.7
typeset 603.16
**make up one's mind**
convince oneself
501.19
decide 494.11
determine upon
637.16
persuade oneself
648.24
resolve 624.7
**make up to**
befriend 927.11
communicate with
554.8
curry favor 907.8
head for 290.10
influence 172.9
repay 841.11
**make waves** 83.4
**make way**
make room 265.14
open up! 265.24
sail 275.21
**making** earning 811.1
make 168.4
manufacture 167.3
structure 245.1
**makings** capacity 733.4
components 58.2
gain 811.3
**mal–** abnormal 85.9
bad 675.7
inappropriate 27.7
insufficient 662.9
**maladjusted**
inappropriate 27.7
incapable 734.19
**maladjustment**
mental disorder
690.17
unfitness 27.3
unskillfulness 734.1
**maladroit**
clumsy 734.20
inferior 37.7
**malady** 686.1

**malaise** agitation 324.1
　anxiety 890.1
　disease 686.1
　pain 424.1
　sadness 872.3
　unpleasure 866.1
**malapropism**
　error in speech 518.7
　figure of speech
　　551.5
　solecism 587.2
　wordplay 881.8
**malapropos**
　inappropriate 27.7
　inexpedient 671.5
　untimely 130.7
**malaria**
　infectious disease
　　686.12
　miasma 676.4
　vapor 401.1
**malarial** 686.57
**malarial fever** 686.12
**malarkey** 547.3
**malcontent**
　*n.* faultfinder 869.3
　hinderer 730.9
　lamenter 875.7
　rebel 767.5
　*adj.* discontented
　　869.5
**mal de mer** 686.29
**male**
　*n.* male being 420.4
　*adj.* masculine 420.11
**male chauvinism** 527.4
**male chauvinist** 527.5
**malediction** 972.1
**maledictory** 972.8
**malefactor**
　bad person 986.9
　evildoer 943.1
**maleness**
　masculinity 420.1
　sex 419.1
**male organs** 419.10
**male sex** 420.3
**malevolence**
　badness 675.1
　enmity 929.3
　hate 930.1
　ill will 939.4
**malevolent** bad 675.7
　harmful 675.12
　hostile 929.10
　ill-disposed 939.17
**malevolently**
　harmfully 675.15
　maliciously 939.28
**malfeasance**
　misdeed 982.2
　mismanagement
　　734.6
　misuse 667.1
　wrongdoing 982.1
**malformation**
　deformity 249.3
　oddity 85.3
**malformed**
　abnormal 85.13
　deformed 249.12
　ugly 899.8

**malice** enmity 929.3
　hate 930.1
　maliciousness 939.5
**malicious**
　hostile 929.10
　malevolent 939.18
**maliciously** 939.28
**malign**
　*v.* defame 971.9
　*adj.* fatal 409.23
　harmful 675.12
　malicious 939.18
　poisonous 684.7
　savage 162.20
**malignancy**
　deadliness 409.9
　harmfulness 675.5
　malice 939.5
　poisonousness 684.3
**malignant**
　cancerous 686.57
　fatal 409.23
　harmful 675.12
　hostile 929.10
　malicious 939.18
　poisonous 684.7
　savage 162.20
**malignant growth**
　686.36
**malignantly**
　harmfully 675.15
　malevolently 939.28
**malinger**
　leave undone 534.7
　shirk 631.9
**malingerer**
　impostor 619.6
　neglecter 534.5
　shirker 631.3
**malingering**
　*n.* shirking 631.2
　*adj.* evasive 631.15
**mall** 657.3
**malleable**
　changeable 141.6
　conformable 82.5
　docile 765.13
　influenceable 172.15
　pliant 357.9
　teachable 564.18
　wieldy 732.14
**mallet** hammer 348.19
　sculpting tool 575.4
**malnutrition**
　deficiency disease
　　686.10
　dietary deficiency
　　662.6
**malocchio**
　bad influence 675.4
　curse 972.1
　evil eye 1036.1
　glare 439.5
　ill will 939.4
**malodorous** fetid 437.5
　filthy 682.23
　odorous 435.9
　offensive 864.18
**malpractice**
　mismanagement
　　734.6
　misuse 667.1

　wrongdoing 982.1
**maltreat** mistreat 667.5
　work evil 675.6
**maltreatment** 667.2
**mama** 170.10
**mama's boy**
　effeminate male
　　421.10
　spoiled child 759.4
　weakling 160.6
**mammal**
　animal 414.3,58
　vertebrates 415.7
**mammalian**
　mammary 256.18
　vertebrate 414.44
**mammary** 256.18
**mammary gland** 256.6
**mammon** money 835.1
　wealth 837.1
**mammoth**
　*n.* large animal 195.14
　pachyderm 414.4,58
　prehistoric animal
　　123.26
　*adj.* huge 195.20
　large 34.7
**mammy** mother 170.10
　nurse 699.8
**man**
　*n.* adult 127.1
　beau 931.12
　brave person 893.8
　chessman 878.18
　follower 907.5
　henchman 787.8
　husband 933.8
　male 420.4
　male servant 750.4
　male sex 420.3
　mammals 415.8
　mankind 417.1
　person 417.3
　prehistoric 123.25
　primate 414.59
　*v.* equip 659.8
　fortify 799.9
　*interj.* pleasure 865.17
**Man, the** 418.3
**mana**
　animistic spirit
　　1014.12
　power 157.1
**man-about-town**
　dandy 903.9
　fashionable 644.7
　sociable person
　　922.15
　sophisticate 733.16
**manacle**
　*n.* restraint 760.4
　*v.* render powerless
　　158.11
　restrain 760.10
**manacled** 760.16
**manage**
　accomplish 722.4
　come through 7.6
　contrive 724.11
　deal with 665.12
　direct 747.8
　drive animals 416.7

　economize 851.4
　govern 741.12
　handle 705.8
　make shift 670.4
　operate 164.5
　persist 143.5
　pilot 275.14
　survive 659.12
　use 665.10
**manageability**
　governability 765.4
　wieldiness 732.2
　workability 164.3
**manageable**
　cheap 849.7
　governable 765.14
　wieldy 732.14
　workable 164.10
**management**
　direction 747.1
　directorate 748.11
　economy 851.1
　executives 748.3
　government 741.1
　operation 164.1
　performance 705.2
　protectorship 699.2
　supremacy 36.3
　the rulers 749.15
　treatment 665.2
　utilization 665.8
**manager**
　businessman 830.1
　director 748.1
　governor 749.5
**managerial**
　directing 747.12
　operational 164.12
**managership** 747.4
**managing**
　directing 747.12
　governing 741.19
**mañana**
　*n.* the future 121.1
　*adv.* in the future
　　121.9
**man and wife** 933.10
**manchild** 125.5
**mandarin**
　intellectual 476.1
　official 749.16
　snob 912.7
　wise man 468.1
**mandate**
　*n.* commission 780.1
　injunction 752.2
　legal order 752.6
　possession 808.1
　referendum 742.16
　territory 181.1
　*v.* command 752.9
**mandated** 752.13
**mandatory**
　binding 962.15
　commanded 752.13
　necessary 639.12
　obligatory 756.10
　prescriptive 751.4
**mandibles**
　grasping organs 813.4
　jaws 265.5
**mandolin** 465.4

mandrake 712.10
mane hair 230.2
  head of hair 230.4
man-eater
  cannibal 307.14
  killer 409.11
  savage 943.5
  shark 414.35
man-eating 307.29
manège
  horse training 416.1
  riding 273.6
  school 567.12
maneuver
  *n.* act 705.3
  expedient 670.2
  military operations
    797.8
  stratagem 735.3
  *v.* fly 278.49
  manage 747.8
  manipulate 735.10
  operate 164.5
  plot 654.10
  sail 275.46
  take action 705.5
maneuverability
  wieldiness 732.2
  workability 164.3
maneuverable
  wieldy 732.14
  workable 164.10
maneuvering
  intrigue 654.6
  machinations 735.4
man Friday
  retainer 750.3
  right-hand man 787.7
manfully
  laboriously 716.19
  pluckily 624.18
mange 686.38
manger 192.2
mangle smooth 260.6
  tear apart 49.14
mangled
  damaged 692.29
  incomplete 57.5
  severed 49.23
manhandle
  mistreat 667.5
  remove 271.10
  transport 271.11
man-hater hater 930.4
  misanthrope 940.2
man-hating 940.3
manhole 265.4
manhood
  courage 893.1
  male sex 420.3
  masculinity 420.1
  maturity 126.2
man-hour 107.2
mania craving 634.6
  craze 473.12
  emotional symptom
    690.23
  insanity 473.1
  overzealousness 635.4
  types of 473.36
maniac 473.15

maniac(al)
  excited 857.23
  mad 473.30
manic excited 857.18
  insane 473.25
manic-depressive
  *n.* psychotic 473.16
  *adj.* psychotic 473.27
manic-depressive
  psychosis
  mania 473.12
  melancholia 473.5
  mental disorder
    690.17
manic state 857.1
manicure
  *n.* beautification
    900.10
  *v.* groom 681.20
manicurist 900.12
manifest
  *n.* account 845.3
  list 88.5
  *v.* appear 556.8
  demonstrate 555.5
  disclose 556.4
  evidence 505.9
  expose 265.13
  flaunt 904.17
  indicate 568.17
  *adj.* obvious 555.8
  visible 444.6
manifestation
  appearance 446.1
  disclosure 556.1
  display 555
  evidence 505.1
  exhibition 904.4
  indication 568.1
  visibility 444.1
manifested 555.13
manifesting 555.9
manifestly
  obviously 555.14
  positively 34.19
  really 1.16
  visibly 444.8
manifesto
  affirmation 523.1
  announcement 559.2
  statement of belief
    501.4
manifold
  multiform 19.3
  multiple 100.8
man in the street
  a nobody 673.7
  average person 79.3
  common man 919.7
  people 417.2
manipulate
  exploit 665.16
  fly 278.46
  manage 747.8
  maneuver 735.10
  operate 164.5
  tamper with 616.17
  touch 425.6
  use 665.10
manipulated 616.30
manipulation
  automation 349.7

intrigue 654.6
machination 735.4
management 747.1
masturbation 419.9
operation 164.1
stock manipulation
  833.20
touching 425.2
utilization 665.8
manipulator
  cunning person 735.7
  influential person
    172.6
  operator 164.4
mankind
  humankind 417
  male sex 420.3
manlike
  anthropoid 417.11
  masculine 420.11
manliness
  courage 893.1
  masculinity 420.1
manly
  courageous 893.17
  honest 974.13
  masculine 420.11
man-made
  made 167.22
  ungenuine 616.26
manna delicacy 308.8
  gift 818.7
  godsend 811.7
  support 785.3
mannequin
  figure 572.4
  model 25.5
manner aspect 446.3
  behavior 737.1
  custom 642.1
  exteriority 224.1
  kind 61.3
  mode 7.4
  specialty 81.1
  style 588.2
  way 657.1
mannered
  affected 903.15
  behaved 737.7
  elegant 589.9
  figurative 551.3
mannerism
  affectation 903.1
  characteristic 80.4
  eccentricity 474.2
  habit 903.2
  preciosity 589.3
  style 588.2
mannerist
  pretender 903.7
  stylist 588.3
mannerly
  *adj.* well-mannered
    936.16
  *adv.* courteously
    936.19
manner of speaking
  diction 588.2
  expression 585.1
  figure of speech
    551.1
  voice quality 594.8

manners
  behavior 737.1
  custom 642.1
  etiquette 646.3
  mannerliness 936.3
mannish
  bisexual 419.32
  mannified 420.13
  masculine 420.11
man of action 707.8
man of the world
  fashionable 644.7
  sophisticate 733.16
man-of-war 277.6
manor 810.7
manor house 191.6
manorial
  property 810.10
  residential 191.32
manpower 157.4
manqué 725.17
manse house 191.6
  parsonage 1042.7
mansion abode 191.8
  astrology 375.20
manslaughter 409.2
mantel 216.14
mantilla 231.26
mantle
  *n.* brain 466.7
  cover 228.2,38
  emblem of authority
    739.9
  insignia 569.1
  vestment 1041.2
  *v.* become excited
    857.17
  become red 368.5
  blush 908.8
  clothe 231.39
  cover 228.19
  foam 405.5
  show resentment
    952.14
mantled
  clothed 231.44
  covered 228.31
mantra 1032.3
manual
  handbook 605.5
  keyboard 465.20
  ritualistic manual
    1040.12
  textbook 605.8
manual art 574.3
manual labor 716.4
manufacture
  *n.* preparation 720.1
  product 168.1
  production 167.3
  structure 245.1
  *v.* create 167.10
  fabricate 616.18
manufactured
  fabricated 616.29
  made 167.22
manufacturer 167.8
manufacturing
  *n.* production 167.3
  *adj.* productional
    167.17
manure excretion 311.

fertilizer 165.4
manure pile 682.10
manuscript
n. handwriting 602.3
printer's copy 603.4
rare book 605.3
written matter 602.10
adj. written 602.22
many
n. large number 101.3
adj. different 16.7
diversified 19.4
frequent 135.4
much 34.8
numerous 101.6
plentiful 661.7
many-sided
changeable 141.6
mixed 44.15
sided 242.7
versatile 733.23
Maoism
Communism 745.5
revolutionism 147.2
Maoist
n. Communist 745.13
revolutionist 147.3
adj. Communist
745.21
revolutionary 147.6
map
n. chart 654.4
face 240.4
representation 572.1
v. plot 654.11
represent 572.6
use radar 346.17
map maker 654.4
mapped 490.14
mar be ugly 899.5
blemish 679.4
bungle 734.11
deform 249.7
impair 692.12
maraca 465.18
marathon
n. race 796.12
therapy 690.5
adj. protracted 110.11
maraud 824.16
marauder 825.6
marauding
n. plundering 824.5
adj. plunderous
824.21
marble
n. hardness 356.6
plaything 878.16
sculpture 575.2
smooth surface 260.3
variegation 374.6
v. variegate 374.7
adj. hard 356.10
white 364.7
marbled striped 374.15
variegated 374.12
marbleize 374.7
marbleized 374.15
marblelike hard 356.10
stone 384.10
marcel
n. hairdo 230.15

v. style the hair
230.22
march
n. boundary 235.3
frontier 235.5
military step 273.15
music 462.11
progression 294.1
protest 522.2
region 180.2
walk 273.12
v. border 235.10
exit 303.11
march off 301.6
march with 200.12
progress 294.3
protest 522.5
walk 273.29
march against 798.17
marcher 274.6
marching 273.10
Mardi Gras
festival 878.4
holy day 1040.15
mare
female animal 421.9
horse 414.10
plain 387.1
margarine 308.47
margin
n. border 235.4
difference 16.2
distance 199.1
interval 201.1
latitude 762.4
pledge 772.3
spare 179.3
stock margin 834.10
surplus 663.5
v. border 235.10
marginal
bordering 235.11
unimportant 673.14
marginalia
addition 41.2
record 570.4
marginally 235.15
marijuana 687.13,53
marijuana smoker
642.10
marimba 465.18
marina 700.6
marinate 701.8
marination
infusion 44.2
preserving 701.2
marine
n. navy 800.26
sailor 276.4
adj. nautical 275.57
oceanic 397.8
marine animal
414.35,63
marine biology 397.6
mariner seaman 276
traveler 274.1
marines
elite troops 800.14
sea soldiers 800.27
marionette doll 878.16
figure 572.4
marital 933.19

maritime
nautical 275.57
oceanic 397.8
mark
n. blemish 679.3
boundary 235.3
characteristic 80.4
customer 828.4
diacritical 586.19
effect 154.3
evidence 505.1
grade 29.1
harmonics 463.12
importance 672.1
indicator 568.10
kind 61.3
marking 568.5
objective 653.2
punctuation 586.18
reference 586.20
repute 914.5
sign 568.2
signature 583.10
v. blemish 679.6
celebrate 877.2
characterize 80.10
destine 640.7
differentiate 16.6
engrave 578.10
evidence 505.9
heed 530.6
indicate 568.17
judge 494.9
letter 581.6
make a mark 568.19
punctuate 586.16
specify 80.11
markdown 849.4
mark down
cheapen 849.6
record 570.16
marked
characteristic 80.13
destined 640.9
engraved 578.12
famous 914.16
notable 672.18
remarkable 34.10
superior 36.12
markedly
characteristically
80.17
conspicuously 555.16
exceptionally 34.20
importantly 672.24
visibly 444.8
marker aviation 278.19
indicator 568.10
memorial 570.12
recorder 571.1
market
n. city district 183.8
clientele 828.3
commerce 827.1
marketplace 832.2
mart 832
sale 829.1
v. deal in 827.15
sell 829.8
shop 828.8
adj. sales 829.13
market, the 833.1

marketable 829.14
market index 833.1
marketing
n. commerce 827.1
purchase 828.1
selling 829.2
adj. sales 829.13
marketplace
arena 802.1
city district 183.8
mart 832.2
market research 829.2
market value
stock price 834.9
worth 846.3
marking
characteristic 80.4
engraving 578.2
insignia 569.1
mark 568.5
mark off allot 816.9
characterize 80.10
circumscribe 234.4
differentiate 16.6
mark 568.19
measure off 490.12
plot 654.11
marksman
expert 733.11
infantryman 800.9
shooter 285.9
marksmanship 733.1
mark time await 539.8
be still 268.7
stay 132.12
time 114.11
marmalade 308.39
maroon
v. abandon 633.5
adj. red 368.6
marooned
abandoned 633.8
in difficulty 731.25
marquee poster 559.7
theater lighting
611.23
marquis 918.4
marred
blemished 679.8
damaged 692.30
deformed 249.12
ugly 899.6
marriage
combination 52.1
joining 47.1
matrimony 933
sexuality 419.2
wedding 933.4
marriageable
adult 126.12
nubile 933.21
marriage broker 933.13
marriage deities 933.14
marriage license 777.6
marriage vow 770.3
married joined 52.6
matrimonial 933.19
wedded 933.22
marrow center 226.2
content 194.5
essence 5.2
meat 308.20

marry ally 52.4
get married 933.16
join 47.5
wed 933.15
Mars god 1014.5
planet 375.9
war god 797.17
marsh
filthy place 682.12
marshland 400
marshal
n. commissioned offi-
cer 749.18
master of ceremonies
878.22
peace officer 699.15
v. arrange evidence
505.13
distribute 60.9
escort 73.8
join 47.5
order 59.4
prepare 720.6
marshy moist 392.15
swampy 400.3
marsupial
n. animal 414.3
adj. vascular 193.4
vertebrate 414.44
mart city district 183.8
market 832.1
marketplace 832.2
martial 797.25
martial arts 796.10
martial law law 998.4
militarization 797.14
military government
741.4
martinet 749.14
martyr
n. saint 1015.1
sufferer 866.11
v. kill 409.13
torment 424.7
torture 866.18
martyrdom
killing 409.1
pain 424.6
punishment 1010.2
torment 866.7
martyred dead 408.30
pained 424.9
saintly 1015.6
marvel
n. phenomenon 920.2
wonder 920.1
v. wonder 920.5
marvelous
extraordinary 85.14
remarkable 34.10
superb 674.17
wonderful 920.10
marvelously
exceptionally 34.20
extraordinarily 85.18
superbly 674.22
wonderfully 920.14
Marxism
Communism 745.5
materialism 376.5
socialism 745.6

Marxist
n. Communist 745.13
materialist 376.6
revolutionist 147.3
socialist 745.14
adj. Communist
745.21
materialist 376.11
revolutionary 147.6
mascara 900.11
mascot 1036.5
masculine
n. gender 586.10
male 420.4
adj. male 420.11
masculinity
masculineness 420
sex 419.1
mash
n. fodder 308.4
hodgepodge 44.6
love 931.4
meal 307.6
pulp 390.2
v. pulp 390.5
pulverize 361.9
soften 357.6
masher dandy 903.9
philanderer 932.11
pulper 390.4
pulverizer 361.7
mashing 361.4
mask
n. cover 228.2
dance 879.2
disguise 618.10
party 922.11
pretext 649.1
safety equipment
699.3
sculpture 575.3
v. conceal 615.6
cover 228.19
falsify 616.16
masked covered 228.31
disguised 615.13
masochism 419.12
masochist 419.17
mason 579.6
masonry 378.2
masque dance 879.2
masquerade 618.10
party 922.11
stage show 611.4
masquerade
n. costume 231.9
dance 879.2
disguise 618.10
fakery 616.3
impersonation 572.2
party 922.11
v. hide oneself 615.8
impersonate 572.9
outfit 231.40
pose as 616.22
masquerader 619.7
mass
n. abundance 34.3
accumulation 74.9
conglomeration 50.5
gravity 352.5
large number 101.3

lump 195.10
major part 54.6
plurality 100.2
quantity 28.1
sacred music 462.16
size 195.1
solid 354.6
store 660.1
substantiality 3.1
thickness 204.2
throng 74.4
units 352.23
v. assemble 74.18
cohere 50.6
come together 74.16
join 47.5
put 184.14
adj. gravitational
352.20
Mass parts of 1040.10
rite 1040.9
worship 1032.8
massacre
n. carnage 409.5
violence 162.3
v. murder 409.17
massage
n. rubbing 350.3
v. make pliant 357.6
rub 350.6
touch 425.8
treat 689.30
masses inferiors 37.2
the people 919.3
masseur 350.4
massing cohesion 50.1
joining 47.1
massive bulky 195.19
dense 354.12
heavy 352.16
large 34.7
ponderous 352.17
substantial 3.7
thick 204.8
mass murder 409.5
mass-produced 167.20
mass production 167.2
mass spectrography
326.1
mast spar 277.13
supporter 216.2
tower 207.11
types of 277.29
mastectomy 689.23
master
n. artisan 718.6
artist 579.1
boy 125.5
captain 276.7
chief 749.3
educator 565.9
expert 733.13
governor 749.5
judge 1002.4
lord 749
producer 167.8
proprietor 809.2
superior 36.4
teacher 565.1
title 917.6
victor 726.2
wise man 468.1

work of art 574.11
v. conquer 727.10
dominate 741.15
learn 564.9
subdue 764.9
understand 548.7
adj. chief 36.14
governing 741.18
most important
672.23
Master
form of address 420.7
title 917.3
masterful
arrogant 912.11
finished 677.9
imperious 739.16
skillful 733.20
masterfully
imperiously 739.19
skillfully 733.29
mastermind
n. expert 733.13
scholar 476.3
wise man 468.1
v. direct 747.8
master of ceremonies
broadcaster 344.23
manager 748.4
theater man 611.28
toastmaster 878.22
masterpiece
masterwork 733.10
pattern of perfection
677.4
product 168.1
work of art 574.11
mastership
control 741.2
directorship 747.4
mastery 739.7
skill 733.1
supremacy 36.3
mastery conquest 727.1
control 741.2
influence 172.1
mastership 739.7
preparedness 720.4
skill 733.1
supremacy 36.3
understanding 475.3
victory 726.1
masthead 568.13
masticate chew 307.25
pulp 390.5
mastodon
large animal 195.14
pachyderm 414.4
masturbate 419.24
masturbation 419.9
mat
n. arena 802.1
bedding 216.20
hair 230.4
lusterlessness 337.5
partition 237.5
rug 228.9
v. dull 337.10
weave 222.6
adj. colorless 363.7
lackluster 337.17

**matador**
bullfighter 800.4
killer 409.11
**match**
n. contest 796.3
equivalent 30.4
game 878.9
igniter 331.5
image 572.3
light source 336.1
marriage 933.1
two 90.2
v. agree 26.6
assemble 74.18
be comparable 491.7
coincide 14.4
compare 491.4
contrast 239.4
equal 30.5
give in kind 955.6
join in marriage
933.15
make parallel 218.5
pair 90.5
parallel 218.4
resemble 20.7
size 195.15
synchronize 118.3
**matched** coupled 90.8
joined 47.13
married 933.22
twin 90.6
**matching**
n. comparison 491.1
contest 796.3
adj. analogous 20.11
coloring 362.15
**matchless** best 674.18
peerless 36.15
**matchmaker** 933.13
**mate**
n. accompanier 73.4
companion 928.3
equivalent 30.4
image 572.3
likeness 20.3
partner 787.2
ship's officer 276.7
spouse 933.7
v. copulate 419.23
get married 933.16
pair 90.5
**mated** coupled 90.8
joined 47.13
married 933.22
**material**
n. content 194.5
covering 228.43
fabric 378.5,11
lore 475.9
matter 376.2
resources 378
store 660.1
substance 3.2
writing 602.30
adj. carnal 987.6
corporeal 376.9
essential 5.8
evidential 505.17
important 672.16
relevant 9.11
substantial 3.6

vital 672.22
worldly 1031.16
**materialism**
carnality 987.2
nonreligiousness
1031.2
philosophy 500.3
physicism 376.5
**materialist**
atomist 376.6
irreligionist 1031.10
**materialistic**
businesslike 656.15
carnal 987.6
materialist 376.11
philosophy 500.9
worldly 1031.16
**materiality**
existence 1.1
importance 672.1
materialness 376
matter 376.2
relevance 9.4
substantiality 3.1
**materialization**
appearance 446.1
corporealization
376.7
embodiment 3.4
event 151.1
manifestation 555.1
occultism 1034.6
production 167.4
specter 1017.1
**materialize**
appear 446.8
be discovered 488.9
be formed 246.8
corporealize 376.8
create 167.12
embody 3.5
indicate 555.5
manifest oneself
555.6
occur 151.6
**matériel**
equipment 659.4
materials 378.1
store 660.1
**maternal** loving 931.25
motherly 170.13
**maternity**
blood relationship
11.1
motherhood 170.3
**mathematical**
exact 516.16
numerical 87.17
**mathematical elements**
86.9
**mathematician** 87.9
**mathematics**
numeration 87.2
types of 87.18
**matinee** 922.10
**matinee idol**
actor 612.2
favorite 931.15
**mating** 419.8
**mating call** 460.1
**matins** morning 133.1
worship 1032.8

**matri–** 170.13
**matriarch**
antiquated person
123.8
mistress 749.2
mother 170.10
**matriarchal** 741.17
**matriarchy** 741.5
**matricide** 409.3
**matriculate** 570.16
**matriculation** 570.15
**matrilineage** 11.1
**matrimonial** 933.19
**matrimonial bureau**
933.13
**matrimony**
marriage 933.1
sacrament 1040.5
**matrix** deposit 383.7
form 246.1
model 25.6
womb 153.9
**matron** mistress 749.2
wife 933.9
woman 421.5
**matronly**
feminine 421.13
middle-aged 126.14
**matte** 577.5
**matted** complex 46.4
disorderly 62.14
hairy 230.24
**matter**
n. affair 151.3
body fluid 388.3
business 656.1
content 194.5
material 376.2
motive 648.1
particular 8.3
printer's copy 603.4
pus 311.6
quantity 28.1
substance 3.2
topic 484.1
trouble 731.3
written matter 602.10
v. be important
672.11
fester 311.15
**matter of course** 642.5
**matter of fact**
event 151.2
fact 1.3
prosaicness 883.2
**matter-of-fact**
dull 883.8
in plain style 591.3
practical 536.6
prosaic 610.5
simple 902.6
**mattress** 216.20
**maturation** aging 126.6
completion 722.2
development 148.1
growth 197.3
improvement 691.2
**mature**
v. complete 56.6
create 167.10
debt 840.7
develop 167.13

evolve 148.5
grow 197.7
grow up 126.9
improve 691.10
make perfect 677.5
ripen 722.8
adj. adult 126.12
complete 56.9
developed 126.13
due 840.10
experienced 733.26
finished 677.9
grown 197.12
prepared 720.16
ripe 722.13
**matured** complete 56.9
experienced 733.26
finished 677.9
ripe 722.13
**maturing** 148.8
**maturity**
adulthood 126.2
completion 722.2
debt 840.1
preparedness 720.4
**matzo** bread 308.28
ritualistic article
1040.11
**maudlin** foolish 470.8
intoxicated 996.30
sentimental 855.22
**maul** bruise 692.16
injure 692.15
mistreat 667.5
pound 283.14
terrorize 162.10
**mauled** 866.23
**mausoleum**
memorial 570.12
tomb 410.16
**mauve** 373.3,4
**maven** 897.7
**maverick**
n. cattle 414.6
nonconformist 83.3
obstinate person
626.6
odd person 85.4
rebel 767.5
adj. nonconformist
83.6
**mavis** 464.23
**maw** abdomen 193.3
mouth 265.5
**mawkish**
oversweet 431.5
sentimental 855.22
unsavory 429.7
**maxi–** 195.16
**maxilli–** 265.5
**maxim** a belief 501.2
aphorism 517
precept 751.2
rule 84.4
**maximal**
plentiful 661.7
superlative 36.13
top 211.10
**maximize** 38.4
**maximum**
n. completion 56.5
plenty 661.2

summit 211.2
supremacy 36.3
*adj.* great 34.6
superlative 36.13
top 211.10
may be able 157.11
be allowed 777.13
maybe 509.9
Mayday 704.1
mayhem 692.1
mayor 749.17
mayoralty
magistracy 1000.3
mastership 739.7
Mazda 1013.6
maze
*n.* bewilderment 532.3
complex 46.2
confusion 532.3
*v.* confuse 532.7
perplex 514.13
mazy complex 46.4
curved 252.7
flowing 395.24
inconstant 141.7
wandering 291.7
winding 254.6
MC broadcaster 344.23
manager 748.4
master of ceremonies
878.22
theater man 611.28
McCarthyism 667.3
McCoy, the 516.6
MD 688.6
me 80.5
mea culpa
apology 1012.2
penitence 873.4
meadow
grassland 411.8
marsh 400.1
meadowy 411.39
meager dwarf 196.13
lean 205.17
narrow 205.14
scanty 662.10
small 35.6
sparse 102.5
meal grain 308.4
powder 361.5
rations 308.6
repast 307.5
meal ticket 836.9
mealy colorless 363.7
powdery 361.11
mealymouth
hypocrite 619.8
sycophant 907.3
mealymouthed
flattering 970.8
hypocritic(al) 616.33
insincere 616.32
obsequious 907.13
sanctimonious 1029.5
mean
*n.* median 32
middle 69.1
middle course 806.3
*v.* augur 544.12
imply 546.4
indicate 568.17

intend 653.4
show 555.5
signify 545.8
*adj.* average 32.3
base 915.12
common 919.11
difficult 731.16
excellent 674.13
humble 906.9
inferior 37.7
intervening 237.10
irascible 951.19
malicious 939.18
meager 662.10
middle 69.4
narrow-minded
527.10
niggardly 852.8
paltry 673.18
poor 680.9
selfish 978.6
servile 907.12
vulgar 898.15
mean business 624.8
meander
*n.* complex 46.2
convolution 254.1
curve 252.3
*v.* stray 291.4
twist 254.4
wander 273.22
meandering
*n.* circuitousness 321.1
convolution 254.1
discursiveness 593.3
*adj.* circuitous 321.7
complex 46.4
curved 252.7
deviating 291.7
flowing 395.24
wandering 273.36
winding 254.6
meanie 986.6
meaning
implication 546.2
indication 568.1
intention 653.1
interpretation 552.1
ominousness 544.7
purport 545
meaningful
eloquent 600.10
indicative 568.23
premonitory 544.16
significant 545.10
meaningfully
eloquently 600.15
significantly 545.13
meaningfulness
eloquence 600.1
suggestiveness 545.5
meaningless
uncommunicative
613.8
unmeaning 547.6
unordered 62.12
useless 669.9
meaninglessly 547.8
meanly basely 915.17
inferiorly 680.12
malevolently 939.28
stingily 852.11

meanness
baseness 915.3
humility 906.1
inferiority 37.3
irascibility 951.2
malice 939.5
meagerness 662.2
mediocrity 680.3
narrow-mindedness
527.1
niggardliness 852.2
paltriness 673.2
selfishness 978.2
servility 907.1
smallness 35.1
vulgarity 898.5
means assets 810.8
expedient 670.2
funds 835.14
manner 657.1
resources 660.2
tool 348.1
ways 658
means to an end
expedient 670.2
means 658.1
meant implied 545.11
indicated 546.7
intentional 653.9
meantime
*n.* meanwhile 109.2
*adv.* meanwhile 109.5
meanwhile
*n.* meantime 109.2
*adv.* meantime 109.5
time 105.10
measles 686.12
measly base 915.12
diseased 686.57
petty 673.17
measurable
calculable 87.16
mensurable 490.15
measure
*n.* act 705.3
amount 28.2
area 490.18
capacity 195.2
degree 29.1
expedient 670.2
gauge 490.2
law 998.3
length 202.1
literary elegance
589.2
measuring device
490.4
melody 462.4
mensuration 490.1
meter 609.9
metrics 609.8
music notation
463.12
poetic division
609.11
portion 816.5
precaution 895.3
quantity 28.1
rhythm 463.22
sign 568.2
size 195.1
space 179.1

step 164.2
tempo 462.24
volume 490.19
word list 490.17
*v.* calculate 87.11
compare 491.4
fit 26.7
gauge 490.11
judge 494.9
number 87.10
quantify 28.4
size 195.15
traverse 273.19
measured
gauged 490.14
harmonious 589.8
metrical 609.18
music 463.28
periodic 137.7
quantitative 28.5
temperate 992.9
uniform 17.5
measure for measure
compensation 33.1
interchange 150.1
justice 976.1
retaliation 955.3
measurement
judgment 494.3
mensuration 490
numeration 87.1
quantity 28.1
size 195.1
measure off 490.12
measure out
apportion 816.8
measure off 490.12
measure up to
be comparable 491.7
equal 30.5
qualify 720.15
measuring
*n.* measurement 490.1
*adj.* metric 490.13
meat content 194.5
copulation 419.8
essence 5.2
flesh 308.12
food 308.1
genitals 419.10
important point
672.6
major part 54.6
meal 307.5
nut 308.38
sex object 419.4
summary 607.2
sustenance 785.3
topic 484.1
meat-eater 307.14
meat-eating 307.29
meathead 471.4
meathooks 813.4
meaty
corpulent 195.18
meaningful 545.10
mechanic
aircraftsman 279.6
artisan 718.6
mechanician 348.9
mender 694.10

**mechanical**
  involuntary 639.14
  machinelike 348.11
  mechanistic 347.7
  uniform 17.5
**mechanics** art 733.7
  physics 325.1
  theoretical mechanics
    347
**mechanism** art 733.7
  control 349.34
  instrument 658.3
  instrumentality 658.2
  machinery 348.4
  materialism 376.5
  works 348.5
**mechanistic**
  materialist 376.11
  mechanical 347.7
  philosophy 500.9
**mechanize** 348.10
**mechanized** 348.11
**medal** award 916.6
  insignia 569.1
  relief 575.3
**medalist** 733.14
**medallion** medal 916.6
  relief 575.3
**meddle** advise 754.5
  hinder 730.10
  pry 528.4
  tamper with 238.7
**meddler** advisor 754.3
  busybody 238.4
**meddlesome**
  meddling 238.9
  prying 528.6
**meddling**
  n. intrusiveness 238.2
  adj. meddlesome
    238.9
**media**
  communications
    554.5
  telecommunications
    560.1
**medial**
  intervening 237.10
  medium 32.3
  middle 69.4
**median**
  n. mean 32.1
  middle 69.1
  adj. intervening
    237.10
  medium 32.3
  middle 69.4
**mediary** 237.4
**mediate**
  be instrumental
    658.5
  intercede 805.6
  reconcile 804.8
**mediating**
  instrumental 658.6
  intercessory 805.8
**mediation**
  instrumentality 658.2
  intercession 805
  pacification 804.1
**mediator** deputy 781.4
  instrument 658.3

intermediary 237.4
  intermediator 805.3
**mediatory**
  Christlike 1013.19
  intercessory 805.8
**medic** 688.5
**Medicaid**
  medicine 688.1
  welfare program
    745.7
**medical** 688.18
**medical examiner**
  death examiner
    408.18
  doctor 688.6
**medical instrument**
  689.36
**medical practice** 688.16
**Medicare**
  medicine 688.1
  welfare program
    745.7
**medicate** 689.31
**medication**
  medical aid 689.15
  medicine 687.4
  therapy 689.1
**medicinal** 687.39
**medicine**
  branches of 688.19
  healing art 688
  liquor 996.13
  remedy 687.4
  therapy 689.1
**medicine man**
  quack doctor 688.7
  sorcerer 1035.7
**medico** 688.6
**medieval** 123.13
**medievalist** 123.5
**mediocre**
  imperfect 678.4
  inferior 37.7
  medium 32.3
  middle 69.4
  moderate 680.7
  unskillful 734.15
**mediocrity**
  a nobody 673.7
  average 32.1
  imperfection 678.1
  inferiority 37.3
  mediocreness 680
  second-rater 680.5
  unskillfulness 734.1
  unskillful person
    734.7
**meditate**
  consider 478.12
  intend 653.7
  ponder over 478.13
**meditation**
  consideration 478.2
  engrossment 530.3
  inaction 706.1
  prayer 1032.4
**meditative**
  abstracted 532.11
  do-nothing 706.6
  engrossed 530.17
  thoughtful 478.21

**medium**
  n. art equipment
    574.19
  book size 605.14
  doer 718.1
  environment 233.4
  go-between 781.4
  instrument 658.3
  intermediary 237.4
  matter 194.5
  mean 32.1
  mediator 805.3
  middle course 806.3
  paint 362.8
  psychic 1034.13
  substance 3.2
  theater lighting
    611.23
  adj. average 32.3
  cooked 330.7
  intervening 237.10
  mediocre 680.7
  middle 69.4
**medium of exchange**
  835.1
**medley**
  n. hodgepodge 44.6
  miscellany 74.13
  music 462.6
  adj. coloring 362.15
  mixed 44.15
  variegated 374.9
**Medusa**
  bewitcher 1035.9
  monster 85.20
**meed** portion 816.5
  recompense 841.3
**meek** humble 906.10
  modest 908.9
  resigned 861.10
  submissive 765.15
**meekly** humbly 906.15
  modestly 908.14
  resignedly 861.12
  submissively 765.19
**meerschaum** 434.6
**meet**
  n. assembly 74.2
  contest 796.3
  game 878.9
  tournament 878.10
  v. agree with 521.9
  assemble 74.17
  be joined 47.11
  collide 283.12
  come together 74.16
  compete 796.19
  conform 82.3
  confront 240.8
  converge 298.2
  encounter 200.11
  experience 151.8
  observe 768.2
  oppose 790.5
  stand up to 893.11
  suffice 661.4
  adj. conventional
    645.5
  decorous 897.10
  expedient 670.5
  just 976.8
  timely 129.9

**meet halfway**
  compromise 807.2
  mediate 805.6
**meet head-on**
  contrapose 239.4
  counteract 178.6
  face up to 893.11
  meet 200.11
  offer resistance 792.3
**meeting**
  n. assembly 74.2
  conference 597.6
  contest 796.3
  convergence 298.1
  encounter 200.4
  impact 283.3
  joining 47.1
  rendezvous 922.9
  worship 1032.8
  adj. assembled 74.21
  concurrent 177.4
  converging 298.3
  in contact 200.17
  joining 47.16
**meetinghouse**
  church 1042.1
  hall 192.4
**meeting of minds**
  agreement 26.3
  unanimity 521.5
**meet the eye**
  appear 446.8
  attract attention
    530.11
  be visible 444.4
**meg(a)–** great 34.7
  large 195.16
  million 99.31
**megacycles** 344.12
**megaphone** 448.8
**melancholia**
  despair 866.6
  emotional symptom
    690.23
  mental disorder
    690.17
  psychosis 473.5
  sadness 872.5
**melancholic**
  n. personality type
    690.15
  sad person 872.13
  adj. bored 884.10
  sad 872.23
**melancholy**
  n. boredom 884.3
  despair 866.6
  sadness 872.5
  sullenness 951.8
  thoughtfulness 478.3
  adj. bored 884.10
  sad 872.23
  sullen 951.24
**mélange** 44.6
**melanic** 365.10
**melanism** 365.1
**meld**
  n. combination 52.1
  v. combine 52.3
**melding** 52.1
**melee** commotion 62.4
  free-for-all 796.5

**meliorate**
be changed 139.5
change 139.6
get better 691.7
make better 691.9
**mellifluous**
melodious 462.49
pleasant 863.6
sweet 431.4
**mellow**
v. evolve 148.5
mature 126.9
reach perfection
722.8
soften 357.6
adj. intoxicated
996.30
mature 126.13
melodious 462.49
pleasant 863.6
resonant 454.9
ripe 722.13
soft 357.8
soft-colored 362.21
**mellowing**
maturation 126.6
softening 357.5
**mellowness**
pleasantness 863.1
resonance 454.1
softness 357.1
**melodeon** 465.15
**melodic** 462.49
**melodics** 463.1
**melodious** 462.49
**melodist**
composer 464.20
vocalist 464.13
**melodrama**
emotionalism 855.9
stage show 611.4
**melodramatic**
emotionalistic 855.20
sensational 857.30
theatrical 611.38
**melodramatics**
dramatics 611.2
emotionalism 855.9
**melody** tune 462.4
tunefulness 462.2
**melt** affect 855.16
be transient 111.6
disappear 447.2
excite pity 944.5
have pity 944.4
heat 329.21
liquefy 391.5
**meltable**
liquefiable 391.9
molten 329.31
**melt away**
cease to exist 2.5
decrease 39.6
disappear 447.2
**melt down**
extract 305.16
liquefy 391.5
melt 329.21
**melted** liquefied 391.6
molten 329.31
penitent 873.9

**melting**
n. disappearance
447.1
heating 329.3
liquefaction 391.1
adj. liquefying 391.7
loving 931.25
pitying 944.7
vanishing 447.3
**melting pot**
converter 145.10
mixer 44.10
United States 181.3
**member**
belonger 788.11
part 55.4
**membership**
inclusion 76.1
members 788.12
sociability 922.6
**membrane** layer 227.2
skin 229.3
**membranous** 227.6
**memento**
memorial 570.12
remembrance 537.7
**memo** 570.4
**memoir**
biography 608.4
memorandum 570.4
remembering 537.4
treatise 606.1
**memorabilia**
archives 570.2
history 608.4
matters of impor-
tance 672.5
memento 537.7
**memorable**
notable 672.18
rememberable 537.25
**memorandum**
record 570.4
reminder 537.6
**memorial**
n. biography 608.4
memento 537.7
memorandum 570.4
monument 570.12
record 570.1
adj. celebrative 877.3
commemorative
537.27
**memorialize**
celebrate 877.2
petition 774.10
**memorize**
commit to memory
537.17
learn 564.8
**memory**
celebration 877.1
computer 349.17
engram 690.36
posthumous fame
914.7
remembrance 537
retrospection 119.4
**men** male sex 420.3
people 417.2
troops 157.9
working force 750.11

**menace**
n. danger 697.1
threat 973.1
v. be imminent 152.2
forebode 544.11
threaten 973.2
work evil 675.6
**menacing**
dangerous 697.9
imminent 152.3
ominous 544.17
threatening 973.3
**ménage**
domestic manage-
ment 747.6
family 11.5
home 191.4
**menagerie**
collection 74.11
zoo 191.19
**mend**
n. improvement 691.1
v. get better 691.7
make better 691.9
recover health 685.6
repair 694.14
**mendable** 694.25
**mendacious** 616.34
**mendacity** lie 616.11
untruthfulness 616.8
**Mendel's law** 170.6
**mender** 694.10
**mendicancy**
beggary 774.6
indigence 838.2
**mendicant**
n. ascetic 991.2
beggar 774.8
nonworker 708.10
religious 1038.17
adj. ascetic 991.3
begging 774.16
indigent 838.8
**mending**
n. improvement 691.1
repair 694.6
adj. improving 691.15
**menfolk** 420.3
**menial**
n. servant 750.2
working person 718.2
adj. servile 907.12
serving 750.14
**meningitis**
infectious disease
686.12
inflammation 686.9
**meniscus**
crescent 252.5
lens 443.1
**menopause** 126.7
**menorah** 1040.11
**mensch** 985.1
**menses** 311.9
**menstrual**
bleeding 311.24
momentary 137.8
**menstruate** 311.18
**menstruation** 311.9
**mensuration**
measurement 490.1
metrology 490.9

**menswear** 231.1
**mental**
cognitive 478.21
insane 473.25
intellectual 466.8
temperamental 525.7
**mental block**
memory obstruction
538.3
thought disturbance
690.24
**mental case** 473.16
**mental deficiency**
insanity 473.1
mental retardation
469.9
**mental health**
health 685.1
sanity 472.1
**mental hospital**
hospital 689.27
insane asylum 473.14
**mental illness**
insanity 473.1
mental disorder
690.17
**mentality**
intellect 466.1
intelligence 467.1
intelligent being
467.9
**mentally** 525.9
**mentally ill** 473.27
**mentally retarded**
469.22
**mental picture** 535.6
**mental telepathy**
1034.9
**mention**
n. honor 916.4
information 557.1
remark 594.4
v. call attention to
530.10
inform 557.8
remark 594.25
specify 80.11
**mentor** advisor 754.3
preparer 720.5
teacher 565.1
wise man 468.1
**menu**
bill of fare 307.12
list 88.5
schedule 641.2
**meow** 460.2
**Mephistopheles** 1016.5
**mercantile** 827.21
**mercantilism** 827.12
**mercantilistic** 827.21
**mercenary**
n. hireling 750.3
soldier 800.16
adj. corruptible
975.23
employed 780.19
greedy 634.27
**merchandise**
n. commodities 831
provision 659.2
v. deal in 827.15
sell 829.8

supernaturalism
1034.3
**metastasis**
inversion 220.3
transference 271.1
transformation 139.2
**mete** apportion 816.8
give 818.12
measure 490.11
**meteor**
heavenly body 375.15
space hazard 282.10
**meteoric**
celestial 375.25
flashing 335.34
transient 111.8
**meteorologic(al)** 402.13
**meteorologist**
aviation 279.4
weather scientist
402.7
**meteorology**
aeronautics 278.2
weather science 402.6
**meter**
*n.* electric 342.38
electronic 343.21
measurer 490.10
measuring device
490.4
metrics 609.8
music 463.22
periodicity 137.2
poetry 609.9
*v.* measure 490.11
**metered** 490.14
**methadone** 687.12
**methane** 331.1
**Methedrine** 687.9,52
**method** art 733.7
behavior 737.1
means 658.1
orderliness 59.3
plan 654.1
way 657.1
**methodical**
orderly 59.6
punctilious 646.10
regular 137.6
uniform 17.5
**methodically**
invariably 17.8
regularly 137.9
systematically 59.9
**methodized**
arranged 60.14
planned 654.13
**methodologist** 82.2
**methodology**
behavior 737.1
orderliness 59.3
plan 654.1
way 657.1
**Methuselah**
antiquated person
123.8
old man 127.2
**meticulous**
accurate 516.15
attentive 530.15
careful 533.12
conscientious 974.15

detailed 8.9
fastidious 896.9
observant 768.4
punctilious 646.10
strict 757.6
**meticulousness**
accuracy 516.3
carefulness 533.3
conscientiousness
974.2
fastidiousness 896.1
strictness 757.1
**métier** specialty 81.1
talent 733.4
vocation 656.6
**metric(al)**
measuring 490.13
music 463.28
prosodical 609.18
**metrically** 609.20
**metrics** music 463.22
prosody 609.8
speech accent 594.11
**metric system** 490.1
**métro** railway 657.8
train 272.13
**metronome**
music 465.25
oscillator 323.9
**metronomic(al)**
chronologic(al)
114.15
periodic 137.7
**metropolis**
center 226.7
city 183.1
district 180.5
**metropolitan** 183.10
**mettle** animation 161.3
courage 893.5
pluck 624.3
temperament 525.3
**mettlesome**
bold 893.18
energetic 161.12
excitable 857.26
plucky 624.14
**mew**
*n.* lair 191.26
retreat 700.5
*v.* animal sound 460.2
confine 761.12
enclose 236.5
**mewl** 460.2
**mews** barn 191.20
street 657.6
**mezzanine** 192.23
**mezzo** 69.4
**mezzo-soprano**
*n.* high voice 458.6
vocalist 464.13
*adj.* high 458.13
**miasma** poison 676.4
stench 437.1
vapor 401.1
**miasmic**
malodorous 437.5
offensive 864.18
poisonous 684.7
vaporous 401.9
**Mick** 181.7

**Mickey Finn**
alcoholic drink 996.8
barbiturate 687.12
depressant 423.3
**Mickey Mouse**
inferior 680.9
simple 732.12
**micr(o)–**
infinitesimal 196.14
microscopy 443.6
million 99.31
**microbe** germ 686.39
minute thing 196.7
organism 406.2
**microbial** 196.15
**microbiology** 406.17
**microcosm** 196.5
**microcosmic(al)** 196.14
**microdot** 570.10
**microfiche**
computer 349.18
copy 24.4
record 570.10
**microfilm**
*n.* computer 349.18
film 577.10
record 570.10
*v.* copy 24.8
photograph 577.14
**microorganic** 196.15
**microorganism**
germ 686.39
minute thing 196.7
organism 406.2
types of 196.18
**microphone**
amplifier 450.9,19
radio transmitter
344.4
**microscope** 443.13
**microscopic**
exact 516.16
infinitesimal 196.14
optical 443.9
**microscopy**
optics 443.6
types of 196.17
**microtome** 49.7
**microwave** 344.11
**micturition** 311.5
**mid**
*adj.* middle 69.4
phonetic 594.31
*prep.* among 44.18
between 237.12
**Midas** 837.7
**Midas touch** 837.4
**midday**
*n.* noon 133.5
*adj.* noon 133.7
**midden**
dunghill 682.10
trash pile 669.6
**middle**
*n.* center 226.2
mean 32.1
midst 69
voice 586.14
*v.* bisect 69.3
centralize 226.9
*adj.* central 226.11
intervening 237.10

medial 69.4
mediatory 805.8
**middle age** 126.4
**middle-aged** 126.14
**Middle Ages** 107.5
**Middle America** 680.5
**Middle American** 82.2
**middlebrow** 477.8
**middle class**
common people
919.1
mediocrity 680.5
**middle-class**
bourgeois 919.12
mediocre 680.8
**Middle East** 180.6
**middle ground**
mean 32.1
middle course 806.3
**middleman** agent 781.4
intermediary 237.4
mediator 805.3
merchant 830.2
**middlemost**
central 226.11
middle 69.4
**middle of the road**
mean 32.1
middle course 806.3
moderatism 745.2
**middle-of-the-road**
medium 32.3
moderate 745.18
**middle-of-the-roader**
moderate 163.4
politics 745.10
**middle school** 567.6
**middleweight**
boxing weight 352.3
pugilist 800.2
**Middle West** 180.7
**middling** average 32.3
mediocre 680.7
middle 69.4
**middy** 276.4
**midge** dwarf 196.6
minute thing 196.7
**midget**
*n.* dwarf 196.6
*adj.* dwarf 196.13
**midland**
*n.* inland 225.3
*adj.* inland 225.8
middle 69.4
**midmost**
*n.* middle 69.1
*adj.* central 226.11
middle 69.4
**midnight**
*n.* night 134.6
*adj.* black 365.8
nocturnal 134.9
**midriff** abdomen 193.3
middle 69.1
partition 237.5
**midsection** 237.5
**midshipman**
sailor 276.4
student 566.6
**midst**
*n.* middle 69.1
*prep.* among 44.18

between 237.12
**midterm** 485.2
**midtown**
  *n.* city district 183.6
  *adj.* urban 183.10
**mid-Victorian**
  *n.* antiquated person
    123.8
  prude 903.11
  *adj.* antiquated
    123.13
  prudish 903.19
**midway**
  *n.* middle 69.2
  *adj.* middle 69.4
  neutral 806.7
  *adv.* halfway 69.5
  mediumly 32.4
**midwife** healer 688.5
  means 658.3
**mien** behavior 737.1
  exteriority 224.1
  looks 446.4
**miff**
  *n.* anger 952.7
  *v.* annoy 866.13
  provoke 952.22
**miffed** annoyed 866.21
  provoked 952.25
**might**
  authoritativeness
    739.2
  greatness 34.1
  power 157.1
  strength 159.1
**might and main**
  exertion 716.1
  power 157.1
**might be** 509.4
**mightily**
  authoritatively
    739.18
  powerfully 157.15
  strongly 159.21
  very 34.18
**mighty**
  *adj.* authoritative
    739.15
  considerable 34.6
  eminent 914.18
  huge 195.20
  powerful 157.12
  strong 159.13
  *adv.* very 34.18
**migraine** ache 424.5
  nervous disorder
    686.23
**migrant** bird 414.33
  migrator 274.5
  working person 718.2
**migrant worker**
  farm hand 413.5
  traveler 274.5
  working person 718.2
**migrate** 273.21
**migration**
  transference 271.1
  travel 273.4
**migratory** 273.36
**mikado** 749.8
**mike** 450.9
**milady** title 917.2

woman 421.5
**milch** 388.8
**milcher** 414.6
**mild**
  good-natured 938.14
  insipid 430.2
  lenient 759.7
  moderate 163.10
  pleasant 863.10
  soft 357.8
  warm 328.24
  weak 765.15
**mildew**
  *n.* blight 676.2
  decay 692.6
  fetidness 437.2
  *v.* decay 692.25
**mildewed**
  malodorous 437.5
  old 123.14
  spoiled 692.43
**mildly** meekly 765.19
  moderately 35.10
**mildness**
  good nature 938.2
  insipidness 430.1
  leniency 759.1
  meekness 765.5
  moderation 163.1
**mileage** distance 199.1
  fee 841.5
  length 202.1
**milepost** mark 568.10
  pointer 568.4
  post 217.4
**miles per hour** 269.1
**milestone**
  important point
    672.6
  mark 568.10
**milieu** arena 802.1
  atmosphere 233.3
  environment 233.1
  neighborhood 180.1
**militancy** activity 707.1
  warlikeness 797.15
**militant**
  *n.* combatant 800.1
  man of action 707.8
  *adj.* active 707.17
  warlike 797.25
**militarism**
  foreign policy 744.5
  military government
    741.4
  warlikeness 797.15
**militarist** 800.5
**militaristic** 797.26
**militarization** 797.14
**militarize** 797.24
**military**
  *n.* army 800.22
  *adj.* warlike 797.25
**military court** 1001.7
**military insignia** 569.5
**military operations**
  strategy 797.8
  warfare 797.1
**military police** 699.17
**military school** 567.13
**military science** 797.10
**militate** 164.7

**militate against**
  contend against
    790.4
  counteract 178.6
**militia** 800.23
**milk**
  *n.* body fluid 388.3
  fluid 388.2
  food 308.47
  white 364.2
  *v.* deprive 822.21
  despoil 822.24
  exploit 665.16
  extract 305.12
  overact 611.36
  tend animals 416.7
  *adj.* milky 388.8
**milk and honey** 728.1
**milker** 414.6
**milkiness**
  liquidity 388.1
  whiteness 364.1
**milking** 305.3
**milk run** 278.11
**milksop** coward 892.5
  effeminate male
    421.10
  fool 471.1
  weakling 160.6
**milky** fluid 388.8
  weak 160.17
  white 364.7
**Milky Way** 375.6
**mill**
  *n.* plant 719.3
  pulverizer 361.7
  types of 348.23
  US money 835.7
  *v.* assemble 74.16
  move around 322.12
  notch 262.4
  process 167.11
  pulverize 361.9
  tool 348.10
**milled** made 167.22
  powdery 361.11
**millenarian**
  *n.* optimist 888.6
  *adj.* optimistic 888.12
**millennial**
  idealized 535.23
  thousand 99.30
**millennium**
  good times 728.4
  paradise 535.11
  period 107.2
  thousand 99.10
**millet** 308.34
**milli-** 99.30
**milliner** hatter 231.36
  store 832.4
**millinery**
  clothing 231.25
  garment making
    231.31
**milling** 167.3
**million**
  *n.* immense number
    101.4
  number 99.11
  *adj.* numerous 101.6
**millionaire** 837.6

**millstone** burden 352.7
  pulverizer 361.7
**millstone around one's**
  **neck**
  affliction 866.8
  impediment 730.6
**millstream** 395.1
**mill town** 719.2
**milord** 917.2
**Milquetoast**
  coward 892.5
  irresolute person
    627.5
  weakling 160.6
**mime**
  *n.* actor 612.2
  comedy 611.6
  imitator 22.4
  *v.* act 611.34
  gesture 568.21
  imitate 22.6
  impersonate 572.9
**mimeograph**
  *n.* printing 603.1
  *v.* copy 24.8
  print 603.14
**mimer** actor 612.2
  imitator 22.4
**mimetic** imitative 22.9
  representational
    572.10
**mimic**
  *n.* actor 612.2
  imitator 22.4
  *v.* imitate 22.6
  impersonate 572.9
  resemble 20.7
  *adj.* imitative 22.9
**mimicry** acting 611.9
  imitation 22.2
  impersonation 572.2
**miming** acting 611.9
  impersonation 572.2
**minaret** 207.11
**minatory** 973.3
**mince**
  *n.* gait 273.14
  meat 308.12
  *v.* affect 903.14
  extenuate 1006.12
  grind 49.13
  speak poorly 595.7
  walk 273.27
**mincing** 903.18
**mind**
  *n.* belief 501.6
  desire 634.1
  intellect 466.1
  intention 653.1
  memory 537.1
  mood 525.4
  psyche 690.35
  spirit 466.4
  theosophy 1034.18
  trait of character
    525.3
  will 621.1
  *v.* be unwilling 623.3
  beware 895.7
  care for 699.19
  heed 530.6
  obey 766.2

remember 537.10
resent 952.13
tend 533.6
**mind-altering drug**
687.13
**mind-blowing**
exciting 857.28
hallucinatory 519.10
**mind-boggler** 549.8
**mind-boggling** 920.12
**minded** disposed 525.8
inclined to 174.6
motivated 648.30
willing 622.5
**mind-expanding**
hallucinatory 519.10
psychochemical
687.46
**mind-expanding drug**
687.13
**mindful**
attentive 530.15
cautious 895.8
cognizant of 475.16
considerate 938.16
knowledgeable
475.15
observant 768.4
remembering 537.24
suggestive 537.22
vigilant 533.10
**mindfully**
attentively 530.21
cautiously 895.12
considerately 938.21
watchfully 533.15
**mindless** animal 414.43
careless 534.11
inconsiderate 939.16
incurious 529.3
purposeless 156.16
unaware 477.13
unconcerned 636.7
unintelligent 469.13
unwise 470.9
violent 162.17
**mindlessly**
unconcernedly
636.10
violently 162.25
**mindlessness**
foolishness 470.1
incognizance 477.3
stupidity 469.1
unconcern 636.2
violence 162.1
**mind one's own**
**business**
be incurious 529.2
not interfere 762.16
**mind one's P's and Q's**
be careful 533.7
be courteous 936.11
behave oneself 737.5
**mind reader** 1034.15
**mind reading** 1034.9
**mind's eye**
imagination 535.1
memory 537.1
**mind your own business**
238.10

**mine**
*n.* entrenchment
799.5
minerology 383.6
pit 257.4
rich source 837.3
source 153.6
source of supply
660.4
trap 618.11
weapons 801.31
*v.* blow up 693.18
deprive 822.21
excavate 257.15
extract 305.10
fortify 799.9
mining 383.14
plant a mine 798.24
process 167.11
tunnel 209.8
undermine 692.18
**mined** 167.22
**miner** excavator 257.10
mineworker 383.9
**mineral**
*n.* inorganic substance
383.1,19
ore 383.2
*adj.* inanimate 382.4
inorganic 383.15
**mineral kingdom**
class 61.4
inorganic matter
382.1
ore 383.1
**mineralogical** 383.18
**mineralogist**
geologist 385.5
mineral science
383.12
**mineralogy**
geology 385.4
mineral science
383.10
**mineral oil** 380.1,11
**mineral spring** 689.29
**miner's lung** 686.14
**Minerva**
goddess 1014.5
war goddess 797.17
**mineworker** 383.9
**mingle**
be sociable 922.16
mix 44.11
**mingled** 44.15
**mingling** 44.1
**mingy** niggardly 852.8
selfish 978.6
**mini** miniature 196.5
small fry 196.4
**mini–** 196.12
**miniature**
*n.* image 572.3
little thing 196.5
picture 574.12
portrait 574.16
*adj.* diminutive
196.12
small 35.6
**miniaturization** 39.1
**miniaturize** 196.9

**miniaturized**
miniature 196.12
reduced 39.10
**minibike** 272.8,29
**minim**
minute quantity
196.7
note 463.14
rest 463.21
small amount 35.2
**minimal** least 37.8
miniature 196.12
sufficient 661.6
**minimally** scarcely 35.9
sufficiently 661.8
**minimization**
belittling 39.5
underestimation
498.1
**minimize** belittle 39.9
disparage 971.8
make light of 673.11
underestimate 498.2
**minimized** 39.10
**minimum**
*n.* small amount 35.2
sufficiency 661.1
*adj.* least 37.8
sufficient 661.6
**minimum wage** 841.4
**mining**
excavation 257.11
extraction 305.1
manufacture 167.3
mines 383.8
tunneling 209.7
**mining engineer** 383.12
**minion** favorite 931.15
follower 787.8
pawn 658.3
retainer 750.1
sycophant 907.3
**minister**
*n.* clergyman 1038.2
delegate 781.2
diplomat 781.6
public official 749.17
*v.* officiate 1040.19
**ministerial**
administrative 747.14
diplomatic 781.16
ecclesiastical 1037.13
governing 741.19
helping 785.20
instrumental 658.6
**ministering**
helping 785.20
instrumental 658.6
serving 750.14
**minister of state** 749.17
**minister to**
be instrumental
658.5
help 785.18
protect 699.19
serve 750.13
treat 689.30
**ministration** aid 785.1
service 750.12
**ministry** aid 785.1
cabinet 742.8
clergy 1038.1

jurisdiction 1000.4
pastorate 1037
protectorship 699.2
service 750.12
the rulers 749.15
**minor**
*n.* harmonics 463.15
study 562.8
youngster 125.1
*adj.* immature 124.10
inferior 37.6
unimportant 673.15
**minority**
*n.* few 102.3
immaturity 124.3
inferiority 37.1
wardship 158.2
*adj.* least 102.7
**minority group**
minority 102.3
party 788.4
**minority interests**
744.31
**minority leader** 746.3
**minority opinion** 522.1
**minor key** 463.15
**minor matter** 673.6
**Minos**
deity of nether world
1019.5
god of justice 976.5
judge 1002.6
**minstrel**
music drama 462.35
musician 464.1
poet 609.13
singer 464.14
**minstrel show**
music drama 462.35
stage show 611.4
**mint**
*n.* model 25.6
much 34.4
plant 719.3
wealth 837.2
*v.* coin 835.28
create 167.13
form 246.7
innovate 122.5
*adj.* new 122.9
undamaged 677.8
unused 668.12
**mintage** coining 835.24
creation 167.5
money 835.1
product 168.1
**mint condition**
healthiness 685.2
newness 122.1
**minted** 167.23
**minus**
*n.* deduction 42.7
subtraction 42.6
*adj.* deprived of 812.8
electric 342.32
nonexistent 2.7
short of 314.5
*prep.* excluding 42.14
lacking 662.17
**minuscule** literal 581.8
miniature 196.12

**minute**
  *n.* account entry 845.5
     instant 113.3
     period 107.2
     stage 107.1
     time of day 114.2
  *v.* keep accounts
     845.8
     record 570.16
  *adj.* detailed 8.9
     meticulous 533.12
     particular 80.12
     tiny 196.11
     unimportant 673.15
**minutely** fully 8.13
     meticulously 533.16
     particularly 80.15
     scarcely 35.9
**minutemen** 800.23
**minutes** record 570.4
     reports 570.7
**minutiae**
     minute things 196.7
     particular 8.3
     small amount 35.2
     trivia 673.4
**minx** bad child 125.4
     impudent person
     913.5
     mischief-maker 738.3
     woman 421.6
**miracle** marvel 920.2
     stage show 611.4
     supernaturalism 85.8
**miracle play** 611.4
**miracle-worker** 1035.5
**miraculous**
     supernatural 85.16
     wonderful 920.10
**miraculously** 920.14
**mirage**
     apparition 446.5
     deception 618.1
     disappointment
     541.1
     illusion 519.6
**mire**
  *n.* filthy place 682.12
     marsh 400.1
     mud 389.8
     slime 682.8
  *v.* bog down 400.2
     dirty 682.15
**mirror**
  *n.* glass 443.5
     good person 985.4
     ideal 25.4
     model 25.1
     prototype 677.4
  *v.* imitate 22.5
     represent 572.8
     resemble 20.7
**mirror image, the** 15.2
**mirroring** image 572.3
     imitation 22.1
**mirth**
     amusement 878.1
     merriment 870.5
**mirthful** 870.15
**miry** dirty 682.22
     marshy 400.3
     muddy 389.14

**misadventure** 729.2
**misalliance**
     marriage 933.1
     misconnection 10.2
     unfitness 27.3
**misanthrope**
     hater 930.4
     man-hater 940.2
**misanthropic** 940.3
**misanthropy**
     antisociality 940
     hate 930.1
**misapplication**
     error 518.1
     misconnection 10.2
     misinterpretation
     553.1
     misuse 667.1
     sophistry 483.1
**misapply** err 518.12
     misinterpret 553.2
     misuse 667.4
     reason speciously
     483.8
**misapprehend**
     err 518.13
     misinterpret 553.2
**misapprehension**
     an error 518.3
     misinterpretation
     553.1
**misappropriate** 667.4
**misappropriation** 667.1
**misbegotten**
     abnormal 85.13
     bastard 999.7
     deformed 249.12
     ugly 899.8
**misbehave** 738.4
**misbehavior** 738
**misbelief** heresy 1025.2
     illusion 519.1
**misbelieve**
     be unorthodox
     1025.8
     disbelieve 503.5
**misbeliever** 1025.5
**miscalculate** err 518.9
     misjudge 496.2
**miscalculation**
     an error 518.3
     misjudgment 496.1
**miscarriage**
     an error 518.3
     failure 725.5
**miscarriage of justice**
     977.4
**miscarry** fail 725.14
     fall short 314.4
**miscegenate**
     get married 933.16
     hybridize 44.14
**miscegenation**
     crossbreeding 44.4
     marriage 933.1
**miscellaneous** 44.15
**miscellany**
     assemblage 74.13
     compilation 605.4
     hodgepodge 44.6
     selections 607.4
**mischance** 729.2

**mischief**
     disaccord 795.1
     disadvantage 671.2
     evil 675.3
     impairment 692.1
     misbehavior 738.2
     mischief-maker 738.3
**mischief-maker**
     instigator 648.11
     prankster 738.3
     troublemaker 943.2
**mischievous**
     devilish 1016.19
     harmful 675.12
     roguish 738.6
**misconceive** err 518.13
     misinterpret 553.2
**misconception**
     an error 518.3
     illusion 519.1
     misinterpretation
     553.1
**misconduct**
  *n.* misbehavior 738.1
     mismanagement
     734.6
     misuse 667.1
     wrongdoing 982.1
  *v.* err 518.12
     mismanage 734.13
**misconstruction**
     distortion 249.2
     error 518.1
     falsification 616.9
     misinterpretation
     553.1
     misjudgment 496.1
     solecism 587.2
**misconstrue**
     distort 249.6
     misinterpret 553.2
     misjudge 496.2
**misconstrued** 553.3
**miscreant** 986.5
**miscue**
  *n.* an error 518.4
     bungle 734.5
  *v.* bungle 734.11
     err 518.13
**misdate**
  *n.* anachronism 115.1
  *v.* mistime 115.2
**misdated** 115.3
**misdating** 115.1
**misdeed** 982.2
**misdemeanor**
     crime 999.4
     misbehavior 738.1
     misdeed 982.2
     wrongdoing 982.1
**misdirect** distort 249.6
     mislead 618.15
     mismanage 734.13
     misteach 563.3
**misdirected**
     botched 734.21
     mistaught 563.5
**misdirection**
     deception 618.2
     distortion 249.2
     mismanagement
     734.6

     misteaching 563.1
**mise-en-scène**
     drama production
     611.14
     setting 233.2
     stage setting 611.24
**miser** collector 74.15
     niggard 852.4
**miserable**
     adverse 729.13
     base 915.12
     paltry 673.18
     unhappy 872.21
     wretched 866.26
**miserably** basely 915.17
     distressingly 34.21
**Miserere** 1032.3
**miserly** few 102.5
     greedy 634.27
     meager 662.10
     stingy 852.9
**misery** despair 866.6
     pain 424.1
     sorrow 872.10
     unhappiness 872.2
**misfeasance** error 518.1
     misdeed 982.2
     mismanagement
     734.6
     misuse 667.1
     wrongdoing 982.1
**misfire**
  *n.* failure 725.5
  *v.* come to nothing
     725.12
     miss 314.4
**misfit** intruder 78.2
     naysayer 27.4
     nonconformist 83.3
**misfortune** 729.2
**misgiving**
  *n.* anxiety 890.1
     apprehension 891.4
     doubt 503.2
     foreboding 544.2
  *adj.* anxious 890.6
     fearful 891.32
**misgovern** 734.13
**misguidance**
     deception 618.2
     mismanagement
     734.6
     misteaching 563.1
**misguide**
     mislead 618.15
     mismanage 734.13
     misteach 563.3
**misguided**
     botched 734.21
     mistaught 563.5
     unwise 470.9
**mishandle**
     mismanage 734.13
     mistreat 667.5
     misuse 667.4
**mishandling**
     mismanagement
     734.6
     misuse 667.1
**mishap** 729.2
**mishmash**
     hodgepodge 44.6

jumble 62.3
**misidentify** 518.13
**misinform**
mislead 618.15
misteach 563.3
**misinformation**
deception 618.2
misteaching 563.1
**misinformed**
mistaught 563.5
unlearned 477.14
**misinterpret**
distort 249.6
err 518.13
misjudge 496.2
misunderstand 553.2
**misinterpretation**
distortion 249.2
error 518.1
misjudgment 496.1
misunderstanding 553
**misjudge**
miscalculate 496.2
misinterpret 553.2
**misjudgment**
an error 518.3
error 518.1
misinterpretation 553.1
poor judgment 496
**mislaid** 185.11
**mislay** lose 812.4
misplace 185.7
**mislaying** 185.3
**mislead** deceive 618.15
lie 616.19
misteach 563.3
seduce 989.20
**misleading**
*n.* deception 618.2
misteaching 563.1
*adj.* deceptive 618.19
illusory 519.9
misteaching 563.6
**misled** 563.5
**mismanage** err 518.12
mishandle 734.13
misuse 667.4
**mismanaged** 734.21
**mismanagement**
mishandling 734.6
misuse 667.1
**mismatch**
*n.* unfitness 27.3
*v.* disagree 27.5
**mismatched**
inappropriate 27.7
unequal 31.4
**misname** 583.12
**misnomer**
*n.* wrong name 583.9
*v.* misname 583.12
**misogynist**
celibate 934.2
hater 930.4
woman-hater 940.2
**misogyny**
celibacy 934.1
hate 930.1
**misplace** lose 812.4
mislay 185.7

**misplaced**
disorderly 62.13
inappropriate 27.7
mislaid 185.11
out of line 83.7
**misplay**
*n.* an error 518.3
*v.* err 518.12
**misprint**
*n.* an error 518.3
*v.* err 518.12
**misprize** disdain 966.3
underestimate 498.2
**misprized** 867.9
**mispronounce** 595.11
**mispronounced** 595.12
**mispronunciation**
error in speech 518.7
speech defect 595.5
**misquote** err 518.12
falsify 616.16
misinterpret 553.2
misrepresent 573.3
**misquoted**
distorted 249.11
unauthentic 518.19
**misread**
*v.* err 518.12
misinterpret 553.2
*adj.* misinterpreted 553.3
**misreading**
misinterpretation 553.1
misjudgment 496.1
**misremember** 538.5
**misrender** distort 249.6
misinterpret 553.2
**misrendering** 553.1
**misrepresent**
belie 573.3
distort 249.6
falsify 616.16
**misrepresentation**
distortion 249.2
false representation 573
falsification 616.9
**misrepresented** 249.11
**misrule**
*n.* confusion 62.2
lawlessness 740.2
mismanagement 734.6
*v.* mismanage 734.13
**miss**
*n.* an error 518.3
failure 725.4
girl 125.6
*v.* be imperfect 678.3
be inattentive 531.2
fail 725.13
fall short 314.4
leave undone 534.7
lose 812.4
want 662.7
**Miss** 421.8
**missal** 1040.12
**Miss America** 900.8
**missed** 534.14
**misshape** 249.7

**misshapen**
abnormal 85.13
deformed 249.12
ugly 899.8
unordered 62.12
**missile**
*n.* names of 281.15
projectile 285.6
rocket 281.3,14
weapon 801.12
*adj.* projectile 285.16
**missilery** arms 801.1
ballistics 801.3
rocketry 281.1
**missing** absent 187.10
incomplete 57.4
nonexistent 2.7
vanished 447.4
wanting 662.13
**missing link** gap 57.2
prehistoric man 123.7
**mission**
*n.* church 1042.1
commission 780.1
delegates 781.13
duty 962.1
flight 278.11
military operation 797.8
task 656.2
undertaking 715.2
vocation 656.6
*v.* commission 780.9
**missionary**
converter 145.9
evangelist 1038.7
**missive** 604.2
**misspeak** err 518.14
mispronounce 595.11
**misspell** 518.12
**misspend** 854.6
**misspent** 854.9
**misstate** falsify 616.16
misrepresent 573.3
**misstated** 518.19
**misstatement**
an error 518.3
falsification 616.9
misrepresentation 573.1
**misstep** 518.4
**miss the boat**
be late 132.7
miscarry 314.4
miss an opportunity 130.6
**miss the mark**
fail 725.13
fall short 678.3
miss 314.4
**mist**
*n.* confusion 532.3
fog 404.2
obscurity 549.3
rain 394.1
spirit 4.3
*v.* cloud 404.6
confuse 532.7
lose distinctness 445.4
**mistake**
*n.* an error 518.3

bungle 734.5
failure 725.4
*v.* err 518.13
misinterpret 553.2
**mistaken**
in error 518.18
misinterpreted 553.3
**mistaught**
misinstructed 563.5
unlearned 477.14
**misteach**
misinstruct 563.3
misrepresent 573.3
**misteaching**
*n.* misinstruction 563
misrepresentation 573.1
*adj.* misinstructive 563.6
**Mister**
form of address 420.7
title 917.3
**mistime** ill-time 130.4
misdate 115.2
**mistimed**
anachronous 115.3
untimely 130.7
**mistiming** 115.1
**mistral** 403.9
**mistreat** ill-use 667.5
work evil 675.6
**mistreatment** 667.2
**mistress**
instructress 565.2
kept woman 989.17
lady love 931.14
matron 749.2
proprietor 809.2
**Mistress**
form of address 421.8
title 917.4
**mistrial** 1004.5
**mistrust**
*n.* caution 895.2
doubt 503.2
jealousy 953.2
*v.* be doubtful 503.6
be jealous 953.3
**mistrustful**
cautious 895.9
doubtful 503.9
**misty** foggy 404.9
formless 247.4
indistinct 445.6
insubstantial 205.16
muddled 532.13
obscure 549.15
rainy 394.10
**misunderstand**
err 518.13
misinterpret 553.2
**misunderstanding**
an error 518.3
disagreement 795.2
misinterpretation 553.1
**misunderstood**
disliked 867.9
misinterpreted 553.3
**misusage** abuse 667.1
error in speech 518.7
solecism 587.2

**misuse**
  *n.* an error 518.3
  corruption 692.2
  distortion 249.2
  misapplication 667
  use 665.1
  *v.* corrupt 692.14
  distort 249.6
  err 518.12
  exploit 665.16
  misemploy 667.4
**mite** animal 414.40
  British money 835.8
  bug 414.36
  child 125.3
  minute quantity
    196.7
  minute thing 196.7
  pittance 662.5
  small amount 35.2
**miter**
  *n.* clerical insignia
    569.4
  joint 47.4
  *v.* fasten 47.8
**Mithras** 1014.5
**mitigate**
  be changed 139.5
  change 139.6
  extenuate 1006.12
  moderate 163.6
  qualify 507.3
  reduce 39.8
  relax 163.9
  relieve 886.5
  weaken 160.10
**mitigating**
  moderating 163.14
  qualifying 507.7
  relieving 886.9
**mitigation**
  change 139.1
  decrease 39.1
  extenuation 1006.5
  moderation 163.2
  pity 944.1
  relief 886.1
  weakening 160.5
**mitigator** 163.3
**mitosis** 406.16
**mitzvah**
  good deed 938.7
  precept 751.2
**mix**
  *n.* hodgepodge 44.6
  predicament 731.4
  *v.* be sociable 922.16
  be undiscriminating
    493.3
  blend 44.11
  combine 52.3
  compose 58.3
  concoct 720.7
**mixable** 44.17
**mixed** combined 52.5
  imperfect 678.4
  mingled 44.15
**mixed bag** 44.6
**mixed-blood** 44.9
**mixed marriage** 933.1
**mixed-up** complex 46.4
  confused 532.12

**disordered** 62.16
**mixer** blender 44.10
  dance 879.2
  radio 344.7
  radioman 344.24
  sociable person
    922.15
**mixing** blending 44.1
  radio broadcasting
    344.16
  televising 345.3
**mixture**
  a preparation 720.3
  blending 44
  combination 52.2
  composition 58.1
  compound 44.5
  medicine 687.4
  miscellany 74.13
  organ stop 465.22
  solution 391.3
  variety 16.1
**mix up**
  complicate 46.3
  confuse 532.7
  disarrange 63.3
  scramble 44.11
**mix-up** 62.2
**mnemonic**
  *n.* memory training
    537.9
  *adj.* recollective
    537.22
**moan**
  *n.* lament 875.3
  *v.* lament 875.8
  sigh 452.14
  wail 875.11
  wind sound 403.23
**moaning**
  *n.* lamentation 875.1
  sigh 452.8
  *adj.* lamenting 875.15
**moat** barrier 730.5
  entrenchment 799.5
  gap 201.2
  trench 263.2
**mob** association 788.1
  clique 788.6
  group 74.3
  large number 101.3
  throng 74.4
**mob, the**
  the people 919.3
  the underworld
    986.11
**mobile**
  *n.* sculpture 575.2
  work of art 574.11
  *adj.* changeable 141.6
  moving 267.7
**mobile home**
  abode 191.18
  trailer 272.18
**mobile unit** 345.7
**mobility**
  changeableness 141.1
  motivity 267.3
**mobilization**
  assembly 74.1
  call to arms 797.12
  enlistment 780.6

**militarization** 797.14
  motion 267.1
  preparation 720.1
**mobilize**
  assemble 74.18
  call to arms 797.23
  enlist 780.16
  join 47.5
  militarize 797.24
  prepare 720.6
  set in motion 267.6
**mobilized** 720.16
**Möbius strip** 71.2
**mob rule**
  government 741.4
  lawlessness 740.2
**mobster** bandit 825.4
  criminal 986.10
  evildoer 943.1
**mock**
  *n.* fake 616.13
  gibe 967.2
  indignity 965.2
  *v.* adopt 821.4
  deceive 618.13
  imitate 22.6
  joke 881.13
  offend 965.4
  ridicule 967.9
  *adj.* imitation 22.8
  similar 20.10
  substitute 149.8
  ungenuine 616.26
**mocker** 22.4
**mockery**
  burlesque 967.6
  imitation 22.2
  indignity 965.2
  insincerity 616.5
  laughingstock 967.7
  ridicule 967.1
  trifle 673.5
**mock-heroic**
  comic 880.5
  poetic 609.17
**mocking**
  *n.* imitation 821.2
  *adj.* ridiculing 967.12
**mockingbird**
  imitator 22.4
  songbird 464.23
**mock-up** imitation 22.3
  model 25.5
**mod**
  fashionable 644.11
  modern 122.13
**modal** 7.7
**modality** form 246.1
  state 7.1
**mode** fashion 644.1
  form 246.1
  grammar 586.11
  harmonics 463.10
  manner 7.4
  state 7.1
  style 588.2
  syllogism 482.6
  way 657.1
**model**
  *n.* beautiful person
    900.8
  duplicate 24.3

**figure** 572.4
  form 246.1
  good person 985.4
  harmonics 463.11
  idea 479.2
  image 572.3
  imitation 22.3
  measure 490.2
  original 23.2
  pattern 25
  *v.* emulate 22.7
  form 246.7
  sculpture 575.5
  *adj.* exemplary 25.8
  perfect 677.9
  praiseworthy 968.20
**modeled** 575.7
**modeler** 579.6
**modeling**
  forming 246.5
  sculpture 575.1
**moderate**
  *n.* moderation 745.10
  politics 163.4
  *v.* limit 234.5
  mediate 805.6
  qualify 507.3
  restrain 163.6
  slow 270.9
  *adj.* centrist 745.18
  cheap 849.7
  lenient 759.7
  mediocre 680.7
  medium 32.3
  mild 163.10
  neutral 806.7
  sedate 858.14
  slow 270.10
  temperate 992.9
  tolerable 674.19
**moderately**
  cheaply 849.10
  in moderation 163.17
  mediocrely 680.11
  slowly 270.13
  temperately 992.12
  to a degree 35.10
  tolerably 674.23
**moderation**
  limitation 234.2
  middle course 806.3
  restraint 163
  sedateness 858.4
  temperance 992.1
**moderator**
  arbitrator 805.4
  judge 1002.1
  mitigator 163.3
**modern**
  *n.* modern man 122.4
  *adj.* fashionable
    644.11
  new 122.13
  present 120.2
**modern dance** 879.1
**modernist**
  modern 122.4
  poet 609.13
**modernization** 122.3
**modernize** 122.6
**modernized** 122.13
**modest** cheap 849.7

decent 988.5
humble 906.9
inferior 37.6
mediocre 680.7
meek 908.9
reticent 613.10
unselfish 979.5
unwilling 623.7
**modestly**
humbly 906.15
mediocrely 680.11
meekly 908.14
to a degree 35.10
**modesty** decency 988.2
demur 623.2
humility 906.1
mediocrity 680.1
reticence 613.3
unostentatiousness
908
unselfishness 979.1
**modicum** piece 55.3
portion 816.5
small amount 35.2
**modifiable**
changeable 141.6
convertible 145.18
**modification**
change 139.1
diversification 16.4
qualification 507.1
speech sound 594.13
**modified**
changed 139.9
qualified 507.10
**modifier** syntax 586.2
transformer 139.4
**modify** change 139.6
diversify 16.6
qualify 507.3
**modifying** 507.7
**modish**
dressed up 231.45
modern 122.13
stylish 644.12
**modiste** 231.35
**modulate**
be changed 139.5
change 139.6
inflect 594.29
moderate 163.6
qualify 507.3
**modulation**
change 139.1
harmonization 463.2
intonation 594.7
moderation 163.2
radio 344.14
**modulator** 163.3
**module** individual 89.4
spacecraft 282.2
**modus operandi** 657.1
**modus vivendi**
truce 804.5
way of life 737.1
**mogul** personage 672.8
snow 333.8
**moiety**
community 788.2
half 92.2
middle 69.2
piece 55.3

portion 816.5
**moil**
n. agitation 324.1
work 716.4
v. drudge 716.14
seethe 322.12
**moiré**
n. variegation 374.6
adj. iridescent 374.10
**moist** 392.15
**moisten** 392.12
**moistening**
n. wetting 392.6
adj. wetting 392.18
**moisture** dampness 392
liquidity 388.1
rain 394.1
**moistureproof** 393.11
**molar**
n. tooth 258.5
adj. dental 258.16
**molasses** adherent 50.4
semiliquid 389.5
sweetening 431.2
**mold**
n. blight 676.2
characteristic 80.4
copy 24.6
decay 692.6
form 246.1
fungus 412.3
germ 686.39
kind 61.3
land 385.1
model 25.6
nature 5.3
plant 411.4,45
structure 245.1
temperament 525.3
v. conform 82.3
create 167.10
decay 692.25
form 246.7
imagine 535.14
make ceramics 576.6
sculpture 575.5
**moldable** docile 765.13
pliant 357.9
teachable 564.18
**molded** made 167.22
sculptured 575.7
**molder**
n. sculptor 579.6
v. become old 123.9
decay 692.25
disintegrate 53.3
quiet 268.8
**moldering**
dilapidated 53.5
old 123.14
quiescent 268.12
spoiled 692.43
**molding** copy 24.6
forming 246.5
manufacture 167.3
sculpture 575.1
structure 245.1
**moldy**
malodorous 437.5
old 123.14
spoiled 692.43
**mole** barrier 730.5

blemish 679.1
blind 441.4
breakwater 216.4
bulge 256.3
harbor 700.6
mark 568.5
tumor 686.36
**molecular** 196.14
**molecular weight**
chemistry 379.4
system of weight
352.8
**molecule** atomics 326.7
chemical 379.1
matter 376.2
particle 196.8
small amount 35.2
**molehill** hill 207.5
pile 74.10
trifle 673.5
**molest** annoy 866.13
harm 675.6
mistreat 667.5
persecute 667.6
**mollify** calm 163.7
pacify 804.7
relieve 886.5
soften 357.6
**mollifying**
pacificatory 804.12
softening 357.16
tranquilizing 163.15
**mollycoddle**
n. effeminate male
421.10
spoiled child 759.4
weakling 160.6
v. indulge 759.6
**Moloch** 1014.11
**molt** 232.10
**molten** liquefied 391.6
melted 329.31
**mom** 170.10
**moment**
authority 739.4
importance 672.1
impulse 283.1
influence 172.1
instant 113.3
period 107.2
short time 111.3
stage 107.1
**momentarily**
instantly 113.6
shortly 111.10
**momentary**
instantaneous 113.4
regular 137.8
transient 111.7
**moment of truth**
crucial moment
129.5
period 107.1
**momentous**
authoritative 739.15
eventful 151.10
important 672.16
influential 172.13
**momentum** 283.1
**monad** element 376.2
one 89.3
particle 196.8

person 3.3
**monarch** 749.7
**monarchic(al)**
governmental 741.17
sovereign 739.17
**monarchism**
political conservatism
745.1
principle of govern-
ment 741.8
**monarchist** 745.9
**monarchy**
absolutism 741.9
government 741.4
**monasterial**
claustral 1042.16
monastic 1037.14
**monastery** 1042.6
**monastic**
n. celibate 934.2
religious 1038.17
adj. celibate 934.6
claustral 1042.16
monkish 1037.14
**monasticism**
asceticism 991.1
celibacy 934.1
monkhood 1037.4
**monaural** system 450.11
**monde** 644.6
**monetary** 835.30
**money** funds 835.14
legal tender 835
wealth 837.1
**moneybags**
rich man 837.6
wealth 837.1
**money changer**
banker 836.10
broker 830.9
**moneyed** 837.13
**money-hungry** 634.27
**moneylender**
banker 836.10
lender 820.3
**money-mad** 634.27
**moneymaking**
n. acquisition 811.1
adj. businesslike
656.15
gainful 811.15
paying 841.21
**moneyman** 836.8
**money market** 835.16
**money order** 835.11
**money-raising** 821.1
**money-saving** 851.6
**money's worth**
bargain 849.3
worth 846.3
**monger** 830.2
**mongolism**
genetic disease
686.11
mental deficiency
469.9
**mongoloid** 469.22
**mongoloid idiot** 471.8
**mongrel**
n. bad person 986.7
cur 414.24
hybrid 44.9

*adj.* hybrid 44.16
**mongrelization** 44.4
**mongrelize** 44.14
**moniker** 583.3
**monition** advice 754.1
  dissuasion 652.1
  summons 752.7
  tip 557.3
  warning 703.1
**monitor**
  *n.* advisor 754.3
  informant 557.5
  radioman 344.24
  student 566.1
  supervisor 748.2
  teacher 565.5
  television technician 345.13
  warner 703.4
  *v.* observe 485.23
  radio 344.26
**monitoring**
  televising 345.3
  vigilance 533.4
**monitory**
  advisory 754.8
  dissuasive 652.5
  informative 557.17
  premonitory 544.16
  warning 703.7
**monk** celibate 934.2
  ferret 414.28
  monkey 414.28
  religious 1038.17
**monkey**
  *n.* anger 952.6
  ape 414.28
  British money 835.8
  dupe 620.1
  imitator 22.4
  laughingstock 967.7
  mammal 415.8
  *v.* trifle 673.13
**monkey business** 618.5
**monkeying** 673.8
**monkeyshines**
  clownishness 881.5
  prank 881.10
**monkey with** 238.7
**monkhood** 1037.4
**monkish** celibate 934.6
  monastic 1037.14
**mono** 450.11
**monochromatic** 362.15
**monochrome**
  *n.* color system 362.7
  painting 574.5
  *adj.* coloring 362.15
  pictorial 574.22
**monocle** 443.2
**monocotyledon** 411.3
**monocratic**
  authoritative 739.15
  governmental 741.17
  imperious 739.16
**monody** dirge 875.5
  monophony 462.21
  unison 462.3
  poem 609.6
**monogamist** 933.12
**monogamous** 933.20
**monogamy** 933.2

**monogram**
  character 581.1
  identification 568.11
  signature 583.10
**monograph** 606.1
**monolith** breccia 384.1
  memorial 570.12
**monolithic** simple 45.6
  stony 384.11
  uniform 17.5
**monologist** actor 612.2
  soliloquist 598.2
**monologue**
  regularity 17.2
  soliloquy 598.1
  stage show 611.4
**monomania**
  engrossment 530.3
  obsession 473.13
**monomaniac** 473.17
**mononucleosis** 686.12
**monopolist**
  restrictionist 760.6
  selfish person 978.3
**monopolistic** 808.11
**monopolize**
  appropriate 822.19
  buy up 828.7
  engross 530.13
  possess 808.6
  stock market 833.26
**monopoly**
  exclusive possession 808.3
  restraint of trade 760.1
  stock manipulation 833.20
**monorail** railway 657.8
  train 272.13
**monosyllable** 582.1
**monotheism** 1020.5
**monotheist** 1020.15
**monotheistic** 1020.24
**monotone**
  *n.* continuity 71.2
  regularity 17.2
  repetitiousness 103.4
  tone 450.2
  *adj.* repetitious 103.15
  sounding 450.15
**monotonous**
  continuous 71.8
  repetitious 103.15
  same 17.6
  tedious 884.8
**monotonously**
  continuously 71.10
  tediously 884.12
  uniformly 17.7
**monotony**
  continuity 71.1
  regularity 17.2
  repetitiousness 103.4
  tedium 884.1
  tone 450.2
**monsieur** 420.7
**Monsignor** 917.5
**monsoon**
  wet weather 394.4
  wind 403.1

**monster**
  *n.* fiend 943.6
  frightener 891.9
  large animal 195.14
  monstrosity 85.6
  mythical 85.20
  ugly thing 899.4
  violent person 162.9
  *adj.* huge 195.20
  large 34.7
**monstrosity**
  abnormality 85.1
  deformity 249.3
  hugeness 195.7
  monster 85.6
  oddity 85.3
  ugly thing 899.4
**monstrous**
  abnormal 85.13
  bad 675.9
  base 915.12
  deformed 249.12
  evil 981.16
  excessive 663.16
  foolish 470.10
  huge 195.20
  large 34.7
  ugly 899.8
**monstrously**
  basely 915.17
  oddly 85.19
**montage**
  photograph 577.3
  picture 574.12
**month** 107.2
**monthlies** 311.9
**monthlong** 110.12
**monthly**
  *n.* periodical 605.10
  *adj.* regularly 137.8
**monument** figure 572.4
  gravestone 410.17
  marker 568.10
  memorial 570.12
  tower 207.11
**monumental**
  high 207.19
  huge 195.20
  large 34.7
  sculptural 575.6
**monumentalize** 112.5
**moo** 460.2
**mooch** beg 774.15
  idle 708.11
  wander 273.22
**moocher** beggar 774.8
  guest 925.6
  nonworker 708.10
**mooching**
  *n.* beggary 774.6
  *adj.* begging 774.16
**mood**
  grammatical form 586.11
  humor 525.4
  story element 608.9
  syllogism 482.6
**moodiness**
  capriciousness 629.2
  glumness 872.8
  inconstancy 141.2
  sullenness 951.8

**moody** capricious 629.5
  glum 872.25
  inconstant 141.7
  sullen 951.24
**moolah** 835.2
**moon**
  *n.* changeableness 141.4
  goddesses 375.12
  light source 336.1
  month 107.2
  satellite 375.11
  *v.* idle 708.11
  muse 532.9
**moonbeam** 335.11
**moonfaced** 195.18
**mooning**
  *n.* abstractedness 532.2
  *adj.* abstracted 532.11
**moonless** 337.13
**moonlight**
  *n.* moonshine 335.11
  *v.* make liquor 996.29
  work 656.12
**moonlighting** 656.5
**moonlit** 335.39
**moon-shaped** 252.11
**moonshine**
  *n.* bootleg liquor 996.17,40
  humbug 616.14
  moonlight 335.11
  nonsense 547.3
  specious argument 483.3
  *v.* deal illicitly 826.7
  make liquor 996.29
**moonshiner**
  liquor maker 996.18
  racketeer 826.4
**moon-struck** 473.25
**moor**
  *n.* highland 207.3
  hill 207.5
  marsh 400.1
  plain 387.1
  the country 182.1
  *v.* anchor 275.15
  arrive 300.8
  fasten 47.7
  restrain 760.10
  settle 184.16
  stabilize 142.8
**moored** 142.16
**mooring** anchor 277.16
  arrival 300.2
  harbor 700.6
  settlement 184.6
**moot**
  *v.* argue 482.16
  propose 773.5
  *adj.* doubted 503.12
  theoretical 499.13
  uncertain 514.16
**moot point** 485.10
**mop**
  *n.* hair 230.4
  *v.* grimace 249.8
  wash 681.19
**mope**
  *n.* idler 708.8

Mother of God 1015.5
mother-of-pearl
  *n.* iridescence 335.18
  variegation 374.6
  *adj.* iridescent 374.10
  soft-colored 362.21
mother's milk 388.3
mother superior
  mistress 749.2
  nun 1038.19
mother tongue 580.3
motif edging 235.7
  music 462.30
  ornamental motif
    901.7,13
  story element 608.9
  topic 484.1
motile 267.7
motility 267.3
motion
  *n.* act 164.2
  activity 707.1
  gesture 568.14
  legislative motion
    742.17
  mechanism 348.5
  movement 267
  proposal 773.2
  travel 273.1
  trend 174.2
  *v.* gesture 568.21
motionless
  do-nothing 706.6
  inactive 708.16
  unmoving 268.13
motion picture
  cinema 611.16
  cinematography
    577.8
motion sickness
  environmental dis-
    ease 686.31
  nausea 686.29
motivate impel 283.10
  induce 153.12
  set in motion 267.6
  stimulate 648.12
motivated
  moved 648.30
  teachable 564.18
motivating 648.25
motivating force 161.5
motivation
  inducement 648.2
  motion 267.1
  teachability 564.5
motivational
  motivating 648.25
  moving 267.7
motive
  *n.* intention 653.1
  motivation 648
  music 462.30
  topic 484.1
  *adj.* impelling 283.20
  motivating 648.25
  moving 267.7
  propulsive 285.15
motive power
  energizer 161.5
  impulse 283.1
  machinery 348.4

mobility 267.3
  pushing 285.1
motivity 267.3
motley
  *n.* buffoon 612.10
  comedy 611.7
  costume 231.9
  *v.* polychrome 374.7
  *adj.* coloring 362.15
  dappled 374.12
  different 16.7
  mixed 44.15
  nonuniform 18.3
  variegated 374.9
motor
  *n.* aircraft 280.17
  automobile 272.9
  converter 145.10
  machinery 348.4,26
  *v.* ride 273.32
  *adj.* moving 267.7
motorbike 272.8,29
motorboat
  *n.* powerboat 277.4
  *v.* sail 275.13
motorcade 71.3
motorcar 272.9
motorcycle
  *n.* vehicle 272.8,29
  *v.* ride 273.32
motorcycling 273.6
motorcyclist 274.11
motor-driven 348.11
motoring 273.6
motor inn 191.17
motorist 274.10
motorize 348.10
motor launch 277.4
motorman 274.12
motor oil 380.4
motor vehicle 272.9
mottle
  *n.* mark 568.5
  spottiness 374.3
  *v.* mark 568.19
  variegate 374.7
mottled 374.12
motto caption 484.2
  heraldic insignia
    569.2
  maxim 517.1
  slogan 517.4
moue grimace 249.4
  scowl 951.9
mould, moulder,
    mouldering, mouldy
    see mold etc.
mound
  *n.* barrier 730.5
  fortification 799.4
  hill 207.5
  memorial 570.12
  pile 74.10
  *v.* pile 74.19
mount
  *n.* ascent 315.1
  equine 414.10
  horse 414.16
  mountain 207.7
  mounting 216.10
  *v.* ascend 315.8

become higher
  207.17
  be high 207.15
  bestride 315.12
  climb 315.11
  copulate 419.23
  dramatize 611.33
  fly 278.48
  increase 38.6
  lift up 317.7
  move 267.5
  ride 273.33
mountain bulge 256.3
  hill 207.7
  much 34.3
mountain climber
  315.6
mountain dew 996.17
mountaineer
  backwoodsman
    190.10
  climber 315.6
  traveler 274.1
mountain lion 414.27
mountain man 190.10
mountainous
  hilly 207.23
  huge 195.20
  large 34.7
mountaintop
  peak 207.8
  summit 211.2
mountebank
  entertainer 612.1
  impostor 619.6
mountebankery 616.7
mounted 273.43
mounted policeman
  policeman 699.15
  rider 274.8
Mounties 699.17
mounting
  *n.* ascent 315.1
  drama production
    611.14
  increase 38.1
  motion 267.2
  support 216.10
  *adj.* ascending 315.14
  high 207.19
  moving 267.8
Mount Olympus
  1018.10
mount up to
  cost 846.15
  total 54.8
mourn
  cause unpleasantness
    864.14
  grieve 872.17
  lament 875.8
mourner griever 410.7
  lamenter 875.7
mournful
  funereal 410.22
  pitiable 864.20
  plaintive 875.16
  sorrowful 872.26
mournfulness
  distressfulness 864.5
  sorrowfulness 872.11

mourning
  *n.* lamentation 875.1
  mourning garment
    875.6
  *adj.* lamenting 875.15
mouse bruise 692.9
  coward 892.5
  little thing 196.4
  shy person 908.6
mouse-colored 366.4
mouser 414.26
mousetrap
  rocketry 281.10
  trap 618.11
mousse foam 405.2
  pudding 308.45
  sweets 308.39
mousy cowardly 892.10
  fearful 891.31
  gray 366.4
  rodent 414.48
  shy 908.12
  silent 451.10
mouth
  *n.* arm of the sea
    399.1
  eater 307.14
  opening 265.5
  *v.* be hypocritical
    616.23
  chew 307.25
  declaim 599.10
  grimace 249.8
  lick 425.9
  speak 594.20
  speak imperfectly
    595.9
mouthful bite 307.2
  full measure 56.3
  pompous word 601.3
mouthing
  hypocrisy 616.6
  imperfect speech
    595.4
mouthlike 265.23
mouth organ 465.11
mouthpiece
  criminal 1003.4
  informant 557.5
  lawyer 1003.1
  mediator 805.3
  spokesman 781.5
  telephone 560.4
  wind instrument
    465.7
mouthwash
  cleaning agent 681.17
  dentifrice 687.22
mouth-watering
  alluring 650.7
  appetizing 428.10
  desirable 634.30
mouthy 601.9
movable
  changeable 141.6
  influenceable 172.15
  transferable 271.17
movable feast 711.4
movables 810.2
move
  *n.* act 705.3
  attempt 714.2

expedient 670.2
motion 267.1
stratagem 735.3
*v.* act 705.4
advise 754.6
affect 855.16
behave 737.4
budge 267.5
change residence
  184.16
excite 857.11
excite pity 944.5
impel 283.10
influence 172.7
motivate 648.12
progress 294.2
propose 773.5
push 285.10
remove 271.10
sell 829.8
set in motion 267.6
travel 273.17
**move away**
  depart 301.6
  recede 297.2
**move back** 295.6
**moved affected** 855.25
  excited 857.18
  motivated 648.30
**move in** 172.12
**move into** 715.3
**movement**
  activity 707.1
  art 574.23
  artistic style 574.9
  cause 153.10
  defecation 311.2
  displacement 271.2
  feces 311.4
  gesture 568.14
  group 74.3
  mechanism 348.5
  meter 609.9
  military operation
    797.8
  motion 267.1
  music division 462.24
  political front 744.33
  rhythm 463.22
  story element 608.9
  travel 273.1
  trend 174.2
**movements**
  action 705.1
  behavior 737.1
  mechanism 348.5
**move out** 301.6
**mover** doer 718.1
  motivator 648.10
  originator 153.4
  producer 167.8
  wanderer 274.2
**movie**
  *n.* motion picture
    611.16
  *adj.* theatrical 611.38
**moviegoer** 611.32
**movie house** 611.19
**movie star** 612.4
**movies, the** 611.17
**moving**
  *n.* displacement 271.2

motion 267.1
motivation 648.2
travel 273.1
*adj.* affecting 855.24
  eloquent 600.14
  exciting 857.28
  impelling 283.20
  mobile 267.7
  motivating 648.25
  pitiful 944.8
  progressive 294.6
  saddening 864.20
  traveling 273.35
**moving picture** 611.16
**moving spirit**
  inspiration 648.9
  motivator 648.10
**moving staircase** 317.4
**mow**
  *n.* garner 660.7
  grimace 249.4
  pile 74.10
  scowl 951.9
  *v.* grimace 249.8
  harvest 413.19
  shorten 203.6
  smooth 260.5
**mow down** fell 318.5
  raze 693.19
**mowed** 203.9
**moxie** liveliness 707.2
  pluck 624.3
  power 157.1
**MP** legislator 746.3
  peace officer 699.15
  police force 699.17
**Mr.** 420.7
**Mrs.** 421.8
**Mrs. Grundy**
  conformist 82.2
  conventionalist 645.3
  social convention
    645.1
**Ms.** 421.8
**MS**
  nervous disorder
    686.23
  written matter 602.10
**much**
  *n.* abundance 34.3
  sufficiency 661.2
  *adj.* many 34.8
  plentiful 661.7
  *adv.* greatly 34.15
**much ado about
  nothing**
  overreaction 617.2
  triviality 673.3
**mucilage**
  adherent 50.4,13
  lubricant 380.2
  semiliquid 389.5
**mucilaginous** 389.12
**muck**
  *n.* fertilizer 165.4
  filth 682.7
  mud 389.8
  slime 682.8
  *v.* dirty 682.15
**muck around** 673.13
**mucked up**
  confused 62.16

mixed up 46.4
spoiled 692.31
**muckrake** 971.10
**muckraker** critic 494.7
  disparager 971.6
**muckraking**
  defamation 971.2
  smear campaign
    744.14
**muck up**
  blunder 518.15
  complicate 46.3
  confuse 63.3
  dirty 682.15
  spoil 692.13
**muck-up** 518.6
**mucky** filthy 682.23
  muddy 389.14
**mucous** 389.13
**mucous membrane**
  229.3
**mucus** body fluid 388.3
  filth 682.7
  lubricant 380.2
  secretion 312.2
  semiliquid 389.5
**mud** dirt 682.6
  marsh 400.1
  slush 389.8
**muddle**
  *n.* confusion 532.3
  disorder 62.2
  fiasco 725.6
  *v.* be undiscriminating
    493.3
  bungle 734.11
  complicate 46.3
  disorder 62.9
  fluster 532.7
  make uncertain
    514.14
  obscure 247.3
  perplex 514.13
  scramble 63.3
**muddled**
  befuddled 532.13
  disordered 62.16
  intoxicated 996.30
  perplexed 514.24
  stupid 469.18
**muddlehead** 471.4
**muddleheaded**
  befuddled 532.13
  stupid 469.18
**muddle through**
  manage 724.11
  move forward 294.4
**muddy**
  *v.* dirty 682.15
  make uncertain
    514.14
  *adj.* colorless 363.7
  dingy 365.11
  dirty 682.22
  marshy 400.3
  mucky 389.14
  obscure 549.15
**mud flat** 400.1
**mudhole**
  mud puddle 389.9
  pit 257.3
**mudlark** 274.3

mudpack 900.11
**mud puddle** 389.9
**mudslinger** 971.6
**mudslinging**
  defamation 971.2
  smear campaign
    744.14
**muff**
  *n.* bungle 734.5
  bungler 734.9
  *v.* bungle 734.11
**muffed** 734.21
**muffin** 308.31
**muffle**
  *n.* nose 256.7
  silencer 451.4
  *v.* cover 228.19
  hush up 614.8
  mute 451.9
  silence 451.8
**muffled**
  covered 228.31
  latent 546.5
  muted 452.17
**muffled tone** 452.2
**muffler**
  auto part 272.25
  neckwear 231.64
  silencer 451.4
**muffle up** 231.38
**mufti**
  clergyman 1038.13
  clothing 231.8
  judge 1002.3
**mug**
  *n.* cup 193.10
  dupe 620.1
  evildoer 943.4
  face 240.4
  laughingstock 967.7
  mouth 265.5
  photograph 577.3
  *v.* attack 798.15
  grimace 249.8
  overact 611.36
  photograph 577.14
  rob 824.14
  terrorize 162.10
**mugger**
  assailant 798.13
  evildoer 943.4
  robber 825.5
  student 566.10
  violent person 162.9
**mugginess**
  dampness 392.2
  sultriness 328.6
**mugging** attack 798.1
  theft 824.3
**muggy** moist 392.15
  sultry 328.28
**mug shot** 577.3
**mugwump**
  apostate 628.5
  independent 762.12
  irresolute person
    627.5
  neutral 806.4
  nonpartisan 744.28
  procrastination 132
**mugwumpery**
  irresolution 627.1

neutrality 806.1
nonpartisanism
  744.26
**Muhammad** 1022.4
**Muhammadan**
  *n.* Muslim 1020.22
  *adj.* Muslim 1020.30
**Muhammadanism**
  1020.12
**mulatto**
  crossbreed 44.9
  mixed race 418.4
**mulch** 413.17
**mulct**
  *n.* penalty 1009.3
  *v.* cheat 618.17
  penalize 1009.5
**mule**
  beast of burden
  271.6
  hybrid 44.9
  obstinate person
  626.6
  spinner 206.5
  sumpter mule 414.21
**mulish** obstinate 626.8
  ungulate 414.49
**null** heat 329.17
  sweeten 431.3
**nullion** 217.4
**null** over 478.13
**multicolor** 374.1
**multicolored** 374.9
**multifaceted** 44.15
**multifarious**
  complex 46.4
  different 16.7
  multiform 19.3
  numerous 101.6
**multifold**
  multiform 19.3
  multiple 100.8
  numerous 101.6
**multiform** 19.3
**multiformity** 19
**multilateral**
  angular 251.11
  sided 242.7
**multilingual** 580.14
**multimillionaire** 837.6
**multinational** 44.15
**multiparous** 169.15
**multipartite** 49.20
**multiphase** 19.3
**multiple**
  multiplication
  100.4
  *adj.* multiform 19.3
  numerous 101.6
  plural 100.8
**multiple sclerosis**
  686.23
**multiplication**
  increase 38.1
  mathematics 87.4
  multiplying 100.4
  procreation 169.2
  proliferation 165.2
**multiplication table**
  100.4
**multiplicity**
  multiformity 19.1

numerousness 101.1
**multiplied**
  increased 38.7
  plural 100.8
**multiplier** 100.4
**multiply**
  be numerous 101.5
  be productive 165.7
  calculate 87.11
  increase 38.6
  procreate 169.8
  proliferate 100.6
**multiplying**
  *n.* multiplication
  100.4
  *adj.* increasing 38.8
**multiracial** 44.15
**multitude**
  abundance 34.3
  large number 101.3
  populace 919.3
  throng 74.4
**multitudinous**
  much 34.8
  numerous 101.6
**mum** mute 451.12
  taciturn 613.9
**mumble**
  *n.* murmur 452.4
  muttering 595.4
  *v.* chew 307.25
  murmur 452.10
  speak poorly 595.9
  utter 594.26
**mumbling**
  *n.* imperfect speech
  595.4
  murmur 452.4
  *adj.* murmuring
  452.18
**mumbo jumbo**
  charm 1036.5
  evil spirit 1016.10
  jargon 580.9
  juggling 618.5
  nonsense 547.2
  obscurity 549.3
  occultism 1034.1
  spell 1036.4
**mummer** actor 612.2
  entertainer 612.1
  masquerader 619.7
**mummery** acting 611.9
  ceremony 646.4
  disguise 618.10
  hypocrisy 616.6
  sanctimony 1029.1
**mummification**
  corpse 408.16
  drying 393.3
  embalmment 410.3
  preserving 701.2
**mummified** 393.9
**mummify** dry 393.6
  prepare for burial
  410.21
  preserve 701.8
**mummy** corpse 408.16
  dryness 393.2
  mother 170.10
**mumps**
  ill humor 951.10

infectious disease
  686.12
  sadness 872.6
**munch**
  *n.* bite 307.2
  *v.* chew 307.25
**munching** 307.1
**mundane** prosaic 610.5
  unimaginative 536.5
  unsacred 1027.3
  worldly 1031.16
**municipal** 183.10
**municipal building**
  183.5
**municipality** city 183.1
  jurisdiction 1000.4
**munificence** 853.1
**munificent** 853.4
**munition** 659.8
**munitions** arms 801.1
  equipment 659.4
  store 660.1
**mural**
  *n.* picture 574.12
  *adj.* partitioned
  237.11
**murder**
  *n.* homicide 409.2
  *v.* bungle 734.11
  commit murder
  409.16
**murdered** 734.21
**murderer** 409.11
**murderous** cruel 939.24
  savage 162.20
  slaughterous 409.24
**murk**
  *n.* darkishness 337.4
  obscurity 549.3
  *v.* blacken 365.7
  darken 337.9
**murky** darkish 337.15
  dingy 365.11
  discolored 679.10
  obscure 549.15
**murmur**
  *n.* lament 875.3
  undertone 452.4
  *v.* complain 875.13
  mutter 452.10
  speak imperfectly
  595.9
  utter 594.26
  wind sound 403.23
**murmured** 452.16
**murmurer** 869.3
**murmuring**
  *n.* complaint 875.4
  imperfect speech
  595.4
  undertone 452.4
  *adj.* discontented
  869.5
  whispering 452.18
**muscle**
  *n.* exertion 716.1
  strength 159.2
  voluntary 159.22
  *v.* exert strength
  159.10
**muscle-bound**
  rigid 757.7

strong 159.14
**muscle in** 238.5
**muscle man**
  evildoer 943.4
  strong man 159.6
**muscular** 159.14
**muscular dystrophy**
  686.11
**muscularity** 159.2
**musculature** 159.2
**muse**
  *n.* abstractedness
  532.2
  inspiration 535.2
  *v.* consider 478.12
  daydream 532.9
  remark 594.25
**Muse** genius 467.8
  music patrons 464.22
  names of 535.2
  poetic source 609.12
**museum**
  collection 74.11
  gallery 660.9
  preserve 701.6
**museum piece**
  odd thing 85.5
  work of art 574.11
**mush** cereal 308.34
  face 240.4
  mouth 265.5
  pulp 390.2
  sentimentality 855.8
  walk 273.12
**mushiness**
  pulpiness 390.1
  sentimentality 855.8
**mushroom**
  *n.* botany 412.3
  fungus 411.4,45
  *v.* balloon 255.7
  grow 197.7
  *adj.* upstart 919.13
**mushroom cloud**
  atomics 326.16
  cloud 404.1
**mushy** pulpy 390.6
  sentimental 855.22
  weak 160.17
**music** harmonics 463.1
  melody 462
  patrons 464.22
  score 462.28
**musical**
  *n.* comedy 611.6
  music drama 462.35
  *adj.* musically inclined
  462.48
  tuneful 462.49
**musical comedy**
  comedy 611.6
  music drama 462.35
**musicale** 462.33
**musical instrument** 465
**musicality**
  harmonics 463.1
  melody 462.2
  musical talent 462.32
**music box** 465.17
**music director** 464.17
**music festival** 462.33
**music hall** hall 192.4

fictional 608.17
imaginary 535.21
mythological 1014.25
**mythical monsters**
85.20
**mythicize** 608.13
**mythmaker**
imaginer 535.12
narrator 608.10
**mythological**
fictional 608.17
fictitious 535.21
mythical 1014.25
traditional 123.12
**mythology**
fiction 608.7
folklore 1014.24
tradition 123.2
**mythomania** 616.8
**mythos** fiction 608.7
story element 608.9

**N**

**nab** arrest 761.16
capture 822.18
**nabbing** 822.2
**nabob** personage 672.8
regional governor
749.13
rich man 837.6
**nacre**
iridescence 335.18
variegation 374.6
**nacreous**
iridescent 335.37
soft-colored 362.21
variegated 374.10
**nada** 2.2
**nadir** bottom 212.2
lowest point 208.4
**nag**
*n.* horse 414.10
inferior horse 414.14
tormentor 866.10
*v.* annoy 866.13
find fault 969.16
importune 774.12
remind 537.20
urge 648.14
**nagging**
*n.* disapproval 969.4
importuning 774.3
*adj.* critical 969.24
ill-humored 951.21
importunate 774.18
unforgettable 537.26
**naiad** 1014.20
**naif** dupe 620.1
unsophisticate 736.3
**nail**
*n.* grasping organs
813.7
hardness 356.6
strength 159.7
catch 822.17
fasten 47.8
recognize 537.12
seize 822.14
**nail down**
make sure 513.11
prove 505.11

stabilize 142.7
**naïve** artless 736.5
foolable 470.11
gullible 502.9
ignorant 477.12
immature 124.10
trusting 501.22
**naïveté**
artlessness 736.1
gullibility 502.2
**naked** manifest 555.10
nude 232.14
open 265.18
simple 45.7
unadorned 902.8
unprotected 697.15
visible 444.6
**naked eye** eye 439.9
view 444.3
**namby-pamby**
*n.* sentimentality
855.8
weakling 160.6
*adj.* affected 903.18
frail 160.14
mediocre 680.7
sentimental 855.22
**name**
*n.* appellation 583.3
idol 914.9
personage 672.8
repute 914.1
*v.* appoint 780.10
cite 505.14
denominate 583.11
indicate 568.18
nominate 637.19
specify 80.11
*adj.* important 672.16
**name-calling** 971.2
**named**
aforementioned 64.5
called 583.14
chosen 637.26
**name day** 137.4
**name-dropper**
snob 912.7
upstart 919.10
**nameless**
anonymous 584.3
unrenowned 915.14
**namely**
nominally 80.18
to explain 552.18
**name of the game**
672.6
**namesake** 583.3
**naming**
*n.* appointment 780.2
calling 583.2
indication 568.1
nomination 637.8
*adj.* indicative 568.23
**nanny**
female animal 421.9
goat 414.8
nurse 699.8
**nap**
*n.* sleep 712.3
texture 351.1
*v.* sleep 712.13
**napery** dry goods 831.3

fabric 378.5
**nappies** 231.19
**napping**
abstracted 532.11
inattentive 531.8
sleepy 712.21
unaware 477.13
**nappy** downy 230.27
intoxicated 996.30
textured 351.7
**narc**
*n.* detective 781.10
informer 557.6
policeman 699.15
*v.* inform on 557.12
**narcissism**
selfishness 978.1
sexual preference
419.12
vanity 909.1
**narcissist** egotist 909.5
selfish person 978.3
sex deviant 419.17
**narcissistic**
egotistic 909.10
selfish 978.5
vain 909.8
**Narcissus**
beautiful man 900.9
egotist 909.5
**narcohypnosis**
hypnosis 712.7
hypnotherapy 690.5
stupor 712.6
**narcolepsy** 712.6
**narcosis**
insensibility 423.1
stupor 712.6
**narcotic**
*n.* depressant 423.3
opiate 687.12
*adj.* deadening 423.9
sedative 687.45
sleep-inducing 712.23
**narcotics addict** 642.10
**narcotics agent** 781.10
**narcotics pusher** 826.4
**narcotics traffic** 826.1
**narcotize**
put to sleep 712.20
render insensible
423.4
**narcotized**
sleepy 712.21
unconscious 423.8
**nares** nose 256.7
nostrils 435.5
**narrate** 608.13
**narration**
description 608.2
story 608.6
**narrative**
*n.* description 608.2
story 608.6
*adj.* descriptive 608.16
poetic 609.17
**narrator** 608.10
**narrow**
*v.* constrict 198.7
limit 234.5
qualify 507.3
restrain 760.9

simplify 45.4
specialize 81.4
taper 205.11
*adj.* exclusive 77.8
limited 234.7
meager 662.10
meticulous 533.12
narrow-minded
527.10
phonetic 594.31
poor 838.7
prudish 903.19
thin 205.14
**narrow down** 184.10
**narrow escape** 632.2
**narrow-gauge**(d)
narrow 205.14
narrow-minded
527.10
**narrowing**
*n.* contraction 198.1
exclusion 77.1
simplification 45.2
tapering 205.2
*adj.* restraining 760.12
**narrowly** 205.22
**narrow margin** 16.2
**narrow-minded** 527.10
**narrow-mindedness** 527
**narrows**
arm of the sea 399.1
strait 205.3
**narrow the gap**
approach 296.3
converge 298.2
**nasal**
*n.* speech sound
594.13
*adj.* breathing 403.29
imperfectly spoken
595.12
phonetic 594.31
**nasalization** 595.1
**nasalize** 595.10
**nasalized** 594.31
**nascency** birth 167.7
origin 68.4
**nascent** 68.15
**nasi–** 256.7
**nasty** bad 675.9
discourteous 937.6
filthy 682.23
malicious 939.18
obscene 990.9
offensive 864.18
unsavory 429.7
**nasty crack** 881.7
**nasty look** 969.8
**natal** beginning 68.15
native 189.5
**natal day** 137.4
**nation**
community 417.2
country 181.1
people 418.1
population 190.1
race 11.4
**national**
*n.* citizen 190.4
*adj.* public 417.13
racial 11.7
universal 79.14

**national anthem**
rallying device 797.16
song 462.13
**national assembly** 742.1
**national debt** 840.1
**national emergency**
797.14
**National Guard** 800.23
**nationalism**
foreign policy 744.5
nationhood 181.6
patriotism 941.2
**nationalist** 941.3
**nationalistic** 941.4
**nationality**
country 181.1
nationhood 181.6
nativeness 189.1
patriotism 941.2
people 417.2
race 418.1
**nationalization**
appropriation 822.5
communization
815.3
naturalization 189.3
socialism 745.6
**nationalize**
appropriate 822.20
communize 815.7
politicize 745.16
**national park** 701.6
**native**
*n.* inhabitant 190.3
*adj.* indigenous 189.5
innate 5.7
natural 736.6
plain 902.7
undeveloped 721.13
**native environment**
191.5
**native land** 181.2
**native language** 580.3
**nativeness** 189
**native tongue** 580.3
**nativity**
astrology 375.20
birth 167.7
nativeness 189.1
origin 68.4
**NATO**
international organi-
zation 743.5
treaty 771.2
**natter**
*n.* chatter 596.3
*v.* chatter 596.5
**nattily** 644.18
**natty** 644.13
**natural**
*n.* hairdo 230.15
harmonics 463.14
odd person 85.4
simpleton 471.8
sure success 724.2
talented person
733.12
throw of dice 515.10
*adj.* artless 736.6
authentic 516.14
informal 647.3
innate 5.7

instinctive 481.6
in the raw 721.13
lifelike 20.16
normal 84.7
plain 902.7
plainspoken 591.3
simple 589.6
typical 572.11
**natural gas** 331.1
**naturalism**
authenticity 516.5
materialism 376.5
naturalness 736.2
normality 84.1
**naturalist**
biologist 406.18
materialist 376.6
**naturalistic**
authentic 516.14
descriptive 608.15
materialist 376.11
normal 84.7
philosophy 500.9
typical 572.11
**naturalization**
conversion 145.1
habituation 642.8
naturalized citizen-
ship 189.3
**naturalize**
accustom 642.11
convert 145.11
grant citizenship
189.4
**naturalized**
accustomed 642.17
adopted 189.6
converted 145.19
**naturalized citizen**
190.4
**natural law** 84.4
**naturally**
*adv.* artlessly 736.7
consequently 154.9
genuinely 516.18
informally 647.4
in plain words 591.4
intrinsically 5.9
normally 84.9
unaffectedly 902.11
*interj.* yes 521.18
**naturalness**
artlessness 736.2
authenticity 516.5
informality 647.1
literary elegance
589.1
normality 84.1
original condition
721.3
plainness 902.2
plain speech 591.1
**natural right**
liberty 762.2
privilege 958.3
**natural science**
physics 325.1
science 475.10
**natural selection** 148.3
**natural state** 721.3
**natural world** 376.2
**nature** artlessness 736.2

character 5.3
characteristic 80.4
kind 61.3
matter 376.2
original condition
721.3
temperament 525.3
universe 375.1
**Nature** 1013.9
**naturist** 232.3
**naturistic** naked 232.14
normal 84.7
**naught**
insignificance 673.6
nothing 2.2
**naughty**
disobedient 767.8
evil 981.16
misbehaving 738.5
**naughty word** 972.4
**nausea**
disease symptom
686.8
dislike 867.2
queasiness 686.29
unpleasure 866.1
vomiting 310.8
**nauseant**
cleaning agent 681.17
emetic 687.18
unsavoriness 429.3
**nauseate** disgust 429.4
offend 864.11
**nauseated**
disgusted 866.20
sick 686.53
**nauseating**
filthy 682.23
offensive 864.18
unsavory 429.7
**nauseous**
nauseated 686.53
offended 866.20
unsavory 429.7
**nautical** marine 275.57
oceanic 397.8
**naval** 275.57
**naval academy** 567.13
**naval cadet** 276.4
**naval officer**
military officer
749.20
officer 276.7
**naval vessel** 277.6,24
**navar** aviation 278.6
radar 346.2
**nave** axle 322.5
center 226.2
church part 1042.9
**navel** 226.2
**navigable** 275.59
**navigate** fly 278.45
locate 184.10
pilot 275.14
sail 275.13
**navigation**
aviation 278.6
direction 290.1
location 184.7
water travel 275.1
**navigational**
locational 184.18

nautical 275.57
**navigator**
aviation 279.4
deckhand 276.6
mariner 276.1
pilot 748.7
ship's officer 276.7
**navvy** excavator 257.10
working person 718.2
**navy**
chewing tobacco
434.7
fleet 277.10
naval forces 800.26
**navy man** sailor 276.4
serviceman 800.6
**nay**
*n.* negation 524.1
refusal 776.1
side of controversy
482.14
vote 637.6
*interj.* no 524.8
**naysayer** misfit 27.4
oppositionist 791.3
**naysaying** 524.1
**Nazarene** 1020.16
**Nazism** 741.8
**NB** 530.22
**NCO** 749.19
**Neanderthal**
*n.* barbarian 898.7
*adj.* uncouth 898.12
**neap**
*n.* low tide 208.2
tide 395.13
*adj.* low 208.7
**near**
*v.* approach 296.3
be imminent 152.2
be in the future
121.6
come near 200.7
resemble 20.7
*adj.* approaching
296.4
approximate 9.8
close 200.14
friendly 927.18
imminent 152.3
left 244.4
narrow 205.14
similar 20.14
stingy 852.9
*adv.* nearby 200.20
nearly 200.22
*prep.* at 184.26
close to 200.24
**nearby**
*adj.* handy 200.15
*adv.* beside 242.10
near 200.20
**Near East** 180.6
**nearer** 200.18
**nearest** 200.19
**nearing**
*n.* approach 296.1
*adj.* approaching
296.4
close 200.14
future 121.8
imminent 152.3

**negotiable instrument**
  credit instrument
    839.3
  negotiable paper
    835.11
**negotiables** 834.1
**negotiate**
  bargain 827.17
  contract 771.7
  discuss 597.11
  jump 319.5
  manage 724.11
  mediate 805.6
  transfer property
    817.3
**negotiation**
  commerce 827.3
  conference 597.6
  transaction 827.4
**negotiator**
  go-between 781.4
  labor unionist 789.3
  mediator 805.3
**Negro** 418.3
**Negro spiritual** 462.16
**neigh** 460.2
**neighbor**
  *n.* friend 928.1
  near 200.6
  *v.* adjoin 200.9
  be near 200.13
  *adj.* adjacent 200.16
**neighborhood**
  district 180.1
  environment 233.1
  nearness 200.1
**neighboring**
  adjacent 200.16
  surrounding 233.8
**neighborliness**
  friendship 927.1
  hospitality 925.1
**neighborly**
  friendly 927.14
  helpful 785.22
  hospitable 925.11
**neither** 524.7
**Nembutal** 687.12
**nemesis** bane 676.1
  justice 976.1
  punishment 1010.1
**Nemesis** avenger 956.3
  goddess of evil
    1016.6
  goddess of justice
    976.5
  rage 952.10
**neo–** abnormal 85.9
  beginning 68.15
  imitation 22.8
  new 122.7
**neolith** 123.6
**neolithic** 123.20
**neologism**
  innovation 139.3
  modern 122.4
  word 582.8
**neonatal** 124.12
**neophyte** beginner 68.2
  believer 1028.4
  convert 145.7
  student 566.9

**neoplasm** 686.36
**nepenthe** 538.1
**nephew** 11.3
**nephology**
  cloud study 404.4
  meteorology 402.6
**nephritis**
  inflammation 686.9
  kidney disease 686.22
**nephrosis** 686.22
**ne plus ultra**
  climax 56.5
  perfection 677.3
  summit 211.2
  supremacy 36.3
**nepotism**
  injustice 977.3
  spoils of office
    744.35
**Neptune** god 1014.5
  planet 375.9
  sailor 276.1
  sea god 397.4
  water god 1014.20
**nerval** 422.12
**nerve**
  *n.* courage 893.5
  insolence 913.3
  neuron 422.6
  self-assertion 624.6
  stability 142.1
  *v.* encourage 893.16
  strengthen 159.11
**nerve center**
  ganglion 226.5
  inner nature 5.4
**nerveless**
  unmanned 158.19
  unnervous 860.2
  weak 160.12
**nerve-racking** 859.14
**nerves** 859.1
**nervous**
  agitated 324.16
  anxious 890.6
  eloquent 600.11
  excitable 857.26
  fearful 891.31
  high-strung 859.10
  neural 422.12
  sensitive 422.14
**nervous breakdown**
  mental disorder
    690.17
  nervousness 859.4
  sickness 686.7
**nervous disorder**
  mental disorder
    690.17
  neuropathy 686.23
**nervousness**
  agitation 324.1
  anxiety 890.1
  eloquence 600.3
  excitability 857.9
  sensitivity 422.3
  trepidation 891.5
  uneasiness 859
**nervous prostration**
  exhaustion 717.2
  nervousness 859.4
  sickness 686.7

**nervous system** 422.6
**nervous tension**
  anxiety 890.1
  tension 859.3
**nervous wreck**
  tension 859.5
  wreck 692.10
**nervy** agitated 324.16
  bold 893.18
  impudent 913.9
  nervous 859.10
  strong 159.13
**nescience** 477.1
**nest**
  *n.* abode 191.1
  animal abode 191.25
  animal young 171.2
  birthplace 153.8
  large number 101.3
  *v.* inhabit 188.7
  settle 184.16
**nest egg** funds 835.14
  reserve 660.3
**nester** 190.9
**nesting**
  *n.* habitation 188.1
  *adj.* avian 414.52
**nestle** cuddle 932.15
  protect 699.18
  put to bed 712.19
  snuggle 887.10
**nestling**
  *n.* beginner 68.2
  bird 414.33
  lovemaking 932.1
  young bird 125.8
  *adj.* new 122.7
**nestor** 754.3
**Nestor** old man 127.2
  wise man 468.2
**net**
  *n.* difference 42.8
  gain 811.3
  network 221.3
  porousness 265.9
  price 846.2
  produce 168.2
  radio 344.8
  receipts 844.1
  snare 618.12
  weight 352.1
  *v.* acquire 811.8
  arrest 761.15
  catch 822.17
  fish 655.10
  hamper 730.11
  profit 811.11
  trap 618.18
  weave 222.6
  web 221.7
  yield 844.4
  *adj.* remaining 43.7
**nether** 208.8
**nethermost** 212.7
**nether world**
  deities 1019.5
  depths 209.3
  hell 1019.1
**net income**
  earnings 841.4
  receipts 844.1
**netted** 221.11

**netting** arrest 761.6
  network 221.3
**nettle**
  *n.* thorn 258.7
  *v.* annoy 866.13
  incite 648.17
  provoke 952.22
**nettled**
  annoyed 866.21
  provoked 952.25
**network** radio 344.8
  webwork 221.3
**net worth** assets 810.8
  worth 846.3
**neur(o)–** 422.6
**neural** 422.12
**neuralgia** 686.23
**neuritis**
  inflammation 686.9
  nervous disorder
    686.23
**neurological**
  medical 688.18
  neural 422.12
**neurologist**
  neurology 422.7
  physician 688.8
**neuron** 422.6
**neurosis**
  mental disorder
    690.17
  nervousness 859.4
  psychoneurosis
    690.19
  psychosis 473.3
**neurotic**
  *n.* pathological type
    690.16
  *adj.* psychoneurotic
    690.45
  psychotic 473.27
**neuter**
  *n.* gender 586.10
  neutral 806.4
  *adj.* do-nothing 706.6
  indifferent 636.6
  neutral 806.7
  unsexual 419.31
**neutral**
  *n.* gear 348.6
  independent 762.12
  moderate 163.4
  nonpartisan 744.28
  uncommitted person
    806.4
  *adj.* colorless 363.7
  do-nothing 706.6
  impartial 976.10
  indefinite 79.11
  independent 762.21
  indifferent 636.6
  nonpartisan 744.45
  uncommitted 806.7
  unprejudiced 526.1
  unsexual 419.31
  weak 160.17
**neutral ground** 806.3
**neutrality**
  avoidance 631.1
  impartiality 976.4
  inaction 706.1
  indifference 636.1

prowling 273.9
*adj.* noctambulant
273.37
**nihilism** anarchy 740.2
pessimism 889.6
radicalism 745.4
thought disturbance
690.24
**nihilist** anarchist 740.3
destroyer 693.8
pessimist 889.7
radical 745.12
savage 943.5
**nihilistic**
anarchistic 740.6
destructive 693.26
pessimistic 889.16
radical 745.20
**Nike** 1014.5
**nil** 2.2
**nimble** agile 733.21
alert 533.14
fast 269.19
intelligent 467.14
quick 707.18
**nimble-fingered** 733.21
**nimble-footed**
agile 733.21
fast 269.19
**nimbleness**
agility 733.2
alertness 533.5
intelligence 467.2
quickness 707.3
**nimble-witted**
intelligent 467.14
witty 881.15
**nimbly** skillfully 733.29
with alacrity 707.26
**nimbus** cloud 404.1
illustriousness 914.6
light 335.14
**Nimrod** hunter 655.5
shooter 285.9
**nincompoop** 471.3
**nine** number 99.5
team 788.7
**nine days' wonder**
marvel 920.2
momentary triumph
724.3
transient 111.5
**ninny** 471.3
**nip**
*n.* bite 307.2
cold 333.1
dose 55.5
drink 307.4
hold 813.2
liquor 996.6
pain 424.2
pinch 198.2
pungency 433.2
small amount 35.3
*v.* be pungent 433.5
chill 333.10
converge 298.2
cut off 42.10
freeze 334.11
hasten off 301.11
hold 813.6
hurt 424.7

pinch 198.8
put an end to 693.12
seize 822.14
shorten 203.6
speed 269.8
steal 824.13
tipple 996.23
**nip and tuck** 30.7
**nip in the bud**
kill 409.13
prevent 730.13
put an end to 693.12
**nipped**
constricted 198.12
shortened 203.9
**nipper** child 125.3
grasping organ 813.4
**nipple** teat 256.6
tube 396.6
**nippled** 256.18
**nippy** cold 333.14
pungent 433.7
**nirvana**
forgetfulness 538.1
heaven 1018.9
quiescence 268.1
thoughtfreeness
480.1
unconsciousness
423.2
undesirousness 636.3
**nirvanic**
desireless 636.8
thoughtfree 480.4
unconscious 423.8
**nit** animal 414.40
disapproval 969.4
**nitpick**
find fault 969.15
quibble 483.9
**nitpicker**
fastidious person
896.6
faultfinder 969.9
quibbler 483.7
**nit-picking**
disapproval 969.4
quibbling 483.5
**nitrate**
*n.* fertilizer 165.4
*v.* react chemically
379.6
**nitration** 379.5
**nitrogen**
fertilizer 165.4
gas 401.11
**nitroglycerin** 801.9
**nitty-gritty, the** fact 1.3
fundamental 5.2
**nitwit** 471.3
**nitwitted** 469.17
**nix**
*n.* negation 524.1
nothing 2.2
refusal 776.1
water god 1014.20
*interj.* no 524.10
**no**
*n.* negation 524.1
refusal 776.1
side of controversy
482.14

vote 637.6
*adv.* not at all 2.11
*interj.* nay 524.8
refusal 776.7
**no-account**
uninfluential 173.3
worthless 669.11
**nobby** chic 644.13
excellent 674.13
**nobility**
aristocracy 918.2
eloquence 600.6
eminence 34.2
grandeur 904.5
high birth 918
honesty 974.1
importance 914.5
magnanimity 979.2
mastership 739.7
pride 905.2
superiors 36.5
**noble**
*n.* nobleman 918.4
*adj.* aristocratic
918.10
dignified 905.12
eloquent 600.14
eminent 34.9
excellent 674.12
grandiose 904.21
honest 974.13
magnanimous 979.6
notable 672.18
reputable 914.15
unchangeable 142.17
**nobleman** 918.4
**noble-minded** 979.6
**noblesse oblige** 936.2
**noblewoman** 918.6
**nobly**
dignifiedly 905.14
grandiosely 904.28
honestly 974.21
magnanimously 979.8
magnificently 34.20
reputably 914.20
**nobody** nonentity 4.2
no one 187.6
unimportant person
673.7
**nobody's fool**
intelligent 467.14
ungullible 504.5
**no chance**
chance 156.10
gambling odds 515.6
impossibility 510.1
**no choice** choice 637.3
choicelessness 639.6
**noct(o)-** 134.4
**noctambulation** 273.11
**nocturnal** 134.9
**nocturne** 462.5
**nod**
*n.* affirmative expres-
sion 521.2
approval 968.1
bow 318.3
greeting 925.4
hint 557.4
obeisance 964.2
ratification 521.4

signal 568.15
stupor 712.6
summons 752.5
*v.* assent 521.8
bow 964.6
consent 775.2
go to sleep 712.16
greet 925.10
hang 215.6
neglect 534.6
signal 568.22
**nodding**
abstracted 532.11
drooping 215.10
inattentive 531.8
sleepy 712.21
**noddle** brain 466.6
head 211.6
**node** dilemma 731.6
protuberance 256.5
solid 354.6
wave 323.4
**no-deposit** 666.5
**no doubt**
certainly 513.25
probably 511.8
**nodular** rough 261.8
studded 256.16
**nodule** 256.5
**nodus** 731.6
**noël** 462.13
**no end** greatly 34.15
indeed 36.17
innumerably 101.12
plentifully 661.9
**no end to**
infinite 104.3
innumerable 101.10
long 202.8
**noetic** cognitive 478.21
intelligent 467.12
mental 466.8
**noggin** brain 466.6
head 211.6
**no go**
*n.* failure 725.1
*adj.* hopeless 889.14
useless 669.9
**no-good**
*n.* bad person 986.2
*adj.* worthless 669.11
**nohow**
*adv.* anyhow 657.12
noway 35.11
*interj.* by no means
524.9
**no ifs, ands, or buts**
certainly 513.23
really 1.16
unconditionally
508.3
**noise**
*n.* computer 349.19
dissonance 461.2
information theory
557.7
loud noise 453.3
meaninglessness
547.1
pandemonium 62.5
radio reception
344.21

nonmetallic 383.16
nonmilitant 803.10
no-no curse 972.4
  prohibition 778.1
nonobjective 527.12
nonobservance
  inattention 531.1
  nonconformity 83.1
  nonfulfillment 769
  nonreligiousness
    1031.1
  refusal 776.1
nonobservant
  nonconforming 83.5
  nonreligious 1031.15
  unfaithful 769.5
nonoccupancy 187.2
nonoccurrence
  absence 187.1
  nonexistence 2.1
nonopposing 765.12
nonopposition 765.1
nonordained 1039.3
nonpareil
  good person 985.4
  superior 36.4
  the best 674.8
nonparticipation 706.1
nonpartisan
  *n.* independent
    762.12
  neutral 806.4
  politics 744.28
  *adj.* independent
    762.21
  neutral 806.7
  political 744.45
nonpartisanism
  independence 744.26
  neutrality 806.1
nonpaying 842.10
nonpayment 842
nonperformance
  neglect 534.1
  nonaccomplishment
    723.1
  nonobservance 769.1
nonperishable 142.18
nonpermanent 111.7
nonphysical 377.7
nonplus
  *n.* dilemma 731.6
  perplexity 514.3
  *v.* perplex 514.13
  refute 506.5
  thwart 730.15
nonplussed
  at an impasse 731.22
  perplexed 514.24
nonpoetic 610.4
nonpoisonous 674.20
nonpolluted 681.25
nonporous 354.12
nonproductive 166.4
nonprofessional
  *n.* amateur 718.5
  *adj.* avocational
    656.17
nonrecognition
  incognizance 477.3
  ingratitude 950.1
nonreligious lay 1039.3

unreligious 1031.15
nonrepresentationalism
  573.1
nonresident 187.11
nonresistance
  foreign policy 744.5
  inaction 706.1
  resignation 861.2
  submission 765.1
nonresistive soft 357.8
  submissive 765.12
nonrestrictive
  permissive 534.10
  unrestrictive 762.24
nonreturnable 142.17
nonsectarian
  undenominational
    1020.26
  universal 79.14
nonsense
  foolishness 470.3
  meaninglessness
    547.2
nonsense talk 596.3
nonsense verse 609.5
nonsensical
  foolish 470.10
  meaningless 547.7
non sequitur
  discontinuity 72.1
  specious argument
    483.3
nonsked 278.1
nonspecific
  general 79.11
  vague 514.18
nonspiritual
  carnal 987.6
  materialistic 376.9
nonstop
  continuous 71.8
  perpetual 112.7
nonsubjective 6.3
nontaxable 846.18
nontoxic 674.20
nonuniform
  changeable 141.6
  discontinuous 72.4
  dissimilar 21.4
  irregular 138.3
  uneven 18.3
  unordered 62.12
nonuniformity
  changeableness 141.1
  discontinuity 72.1
  disorder 62.1
  dissimilarity 21.1
  inequality 31.1
  irregularity 138.1
  multiformity 19.1
  roughness 261.1
  unevenness 18
nonunion 49.1
nonunion shop 789.2
nonuple 99.21
nonuse 668.1
nonviable 408.33
nonviolence
  inaction 706.1
  moderation 163.1
  peaceableness 803.4

nonviolent
  moderate 163.10
  unbelligerent 803.10
nonvirulent 674.20
nonworker 708.10
noodle brain 466.6
  food 308.33
  head 211.6
nook corner 251.2
  cubby 192.3
  hiding place 615.4
  recess 257.7
noon
  *n.* meridian 211.2
  midday 133.5
  *adj.* noonday 133.7
no one 187.6
noose
  *n.* instrument of exe-
    cution 1011.5
  loop 253.2
  snare 618.12
  *v.* catch 822.17
  hang 1010.20
  loop 222.6
  trap 618.18
noosphere
  atmosphere 402.2
  biosphere 407.6
  organic matter 406.1
  idea 479.2
nope 524.10
nor 524.7
nor'east 290.20
nor'easter 403.9
norm average 32.1
  convention 751.2
  ethics 957.1
  pervading attitude
    525.5
  rule 84.4
  standard 490.2
normal
  *n.* average 32.1
  college 567.7
  straight line 250.2
  vertical 213.2
  *adj.* average 32.3
  common 79.12
  customary 642.15
  natural 84.7
  orderly 59.6
  ordinary 680.8
  orthogonal 251.7
  right 958.8
  sane 472.4
  typical 572.11
normality
  mediocrity 680.2
  prevalence 79.2
  propriety 958.2
  sanity 472.1
  usualness 84
normalize
  make uniform 17.4
  order 59.4
  organize 60.10
  standardize 84.6
normally
  customarily 642.22
  generally 79.17
  naturally 84.9

normal school 567.7
normative right 958.8
  usual 84.8
Norse deities 1014.6
north
  *n.* direction 290.3
  region 180.7
  *adj.* northern 290.15
  *adv.* northward 290.16
northeast
  *n.* direction 290.3
  region 180.7
  *adj.* northeastern
    290.15
  *adv.* northeastward
    290.20
Northener 190.11
norther 403.9
northerly
  *adj.* northern 290.15
  *adv.* north 290.16
northern 290.15
northern lights 335.16
north pole 342.8
North Pole
  cold place 333.4
  opposites 239.2
  remote region 199.4
North Star
  guiding star 748.8
  star 375.4
northward
  *n.* north 290.3
  *adv.* north 290.16
northwest
  *n.* direction 290.3
  region 180.7
  *adj.* northwestern
    290.15
  *adv.* northwestward
    290.21
northwesterly
  *adj.* northwestern
    290.15
  *adv.* northwest 290.21
north wind 403.9
nor'wester 403.9
no say 173.1
nose
  *n.* nozzle 396.9
  olfactory organ 435.5
  person 417.3
  protuberance 256.7
  prow 240.3
  *v.* meddle 238.7
  nuzzle 425.8
  pry 528.4
  smell 435.8
  trace 485.34
nose around
  be curious 528.3
  search 485.30
nosebleed 311.8
nose count list 88.6
  numeration 87.5
nose dive
  air maneuver 278.13
  cheapening 849.4
  dive 320.1
  failure 725.3
nose-dive
  cheapen 849.6

dive 320.6
fly 278.50
**nosegay** bundle 74.8
  flowers 411.23
  fragrance 436.1
**nose ring** jewel 901.6
  ring 253.3
**nose-tickling** 433.6
**nosh**
  *n.* light meal 307.7
  *v.* eat 307.24
**no-show** 187.5
**nostalgia**
  sentimentality 855.8
  wistfulness 634.4
  yearning 634.5
**nostalgic**
  sentimental 855.22
  wistful 634.23
**nostril**
  air passage 396.17
  nose 256.7
  olfactory organ 435.5
**no strings attached**
  508.3
**nostrum** 687.2
**no sweat** 732.15
**nosy**
  meddlesome 238.9
  prying 528.6
  searching 485.37
**not** 524.8
**nota bene** 530.22
**notability**
  celebrity 914.9
  eminence 34.2
  importance 672.2
  personage 672.8
  repute 914.5
**not a bit** none 2.3
  not at all 35.11
**notable**
  *n.* celebrity 914.9
  personage 672.8
  *adj.* conspicuous
    555.12
  famous 914.16
  important 672.18
  memorable 537.25
  remarkable 34.10
**notably**
  conspicuously 555.16
  exceptionally 34.20
  famously 914.21
  importantly 672.24
**not accept**
  be incredulous 504.3
  deny 524.4
  not permit 778.4
**not admit** deny 524.4
  disbelieve 503.5
**not allow** 778.4
**not all there**
  insane 473.25
  mentally deficient
    469.22
**notarize** 521.12
**notarized** 521.14
**notarized statement**
**notary certificate** 570.6
**notary deposition** 523.2
**notary endorser** 521.7

recorder 571.1
**not at all**
  by no means! 524.9
  never 106.4
  none 2.11
  noway 35.11
**notate** 572.6
**notation**
  account entry 845.5
  comment 552.5
  harmonics 463.12
  mathematics 87.4
  music 462.28
  number 86.1
  record 570.4
  representation 572.1
**not bad** 674.19
**not believe** 503.5
**not budge**
  be obstinate 626.7
  do nothing 706.2
  stand fast 142.11
**not buy**
  disbelieve 503.5
  refuse 776.3
**not care**
  be incurious 529.2
  not mind 636.4
**not care for**
  dislike 867.3
  neglect 534.6
**not care to** 623.3
**not catching** 813.10
**notch**
  *n.* crack 201.2
  degree 29.1
  indentation 257.6
  mark 568.5
  nick 262
  *v.* indent 257.14
  mark 568.19
  nick 262.4
**notched**
  indented 257.17
  nicked 262.5
**notching** 262.2
**not comparable**
  dissimilar 21.6
  inferior 37.7
**not compare**
  be inferior 37.4
  not resemble 21.2
**not concern** 10.3
**not count** 673.10
**not counting** 42.14
**not cricket**
  not done 83.6
  unfair 977.10
**not done**
  unconventional 83.6
  undercooked 330.8
  wrong 959.3
**note**
  *n.* account entry 845.5
  addition 41.2
  animal sound 460.1
  certificate 570.6
  cognizance 475.2
  comment 552.5
  importance 672.1
  interval 463.20
  letter 604.2

melody 462.4
mood 525.4
musical scale 463.14
negotiable instru-
  ment 835.11
observation 439.2
paper money 835.5
record 570.4
regard 530.1
remark 594.4
repute 914.5
securities 834.1
sign 568.2
tone 463.4
treatise 606.1
undertone 233.3
*v.* heed 530.6
indicate 568.17
keep accounts 845.8
record 570.16
remark 594.25
**not easy**
  difficult 731.16
  troublesome 729.13
**notebook** book 605.1
  record book 570.11
**noted** 914.16
**not enough** 662.9
**noteworthy**
  extraordinary 85.14
  notable 672.18
  particular 80.12
  remarkable 34.10
**not guilty** 984.6
**not have a chance**
  be impossible 510.4
  not stand a chance
    156.14
**not hesitate**
  be willing 622.3
  remain firm 624.10
**nothing**
  a nobody 673.7
  insignificancy 673.6
  nil 2.2
  thing of naught 4.2
  void 187.3
**nothing doing**
  by no means 524.10
  disapproval 969.28
  refusal 776.7
**nothing like** 21.5
**nothingness**
  nonexistence 2.1
  space 179.1
  unconsciousness
    423.2
  void 187.3
**nothing of the kind**
  different thing 16.3
  dissimilar 21.5
  no! 524.8
**nothing special** 680.5
**not hold up** 518.8
**notice**
  *n.* advertisement
    559.6
  announcement 559.2
  attention 530.1
  cognizance 475.2
  commentary 606.2
  criticism 494.2

demand 753.1
information 557.1
legal order 752.6
observation 439.2
press release 559.3
warning 703.1
*v.* detect 488.5
heed 530.6
see 439.12
**noticeable**
  appreciable 490.15
  conspicuous 555.12
  manifest 555.8
  remarkable 34.10
  visible 444.6
**noticeably**
  appreciably 490.16
  conspicuously 555.16
  manifestly 555.14
  positively 34.19
  visibly 444.8
**notification**
  announcement 559.2
  impartation 554.2
  information 557.1
  legal order 752.6
  warning 703.1
**notify** herald 544.14
  inform 557.8
  warn 703.5
**not in keeping with**
  27.10
**not in the habit of**
  643.4
**not in the mood** 623.5
**notion** belief 501.6
  caprice 629.1
  idea 479.1
  impulse 630.1
  vague supposition
    499.5
**notional**
  capricious 629.5
  fanciful 535.20
  ideational 479.9
  imaginary 535.19
  imaginative 535.18
  theoretical 499.13
**notions** 831.6
**not know** 477.11
**not kosher**
  dishonest 975.16
  unconventional 83.6
**not likely**
  improbability 512.4
  refusal 776.7
**not listen**
  be inattentive 531.2
  disobey 767.6
**not make sense** 549.10
**not matter**
  be indifferent to
    636.5
  be unimportant
    673.10
**not mind**
  disobey 767.6
  not care 636.4
**notoriety**
  conspicuousness
    555.4
  disreputability 915.2

publicity 559.4
repute 914.1
**notorious**
acclaimed 914.16
bad 675.9
conspicuous 555.12
dishonest 975.17
disreputable 915.10
immodest 990.6
well-known 475.27
**not permit** 778.4
**not remember** 538.5
**not resemble** 21.2
**not right**
erroneous 518.16
insane 473.25
**not stand for**
not permit 778.4
not tolerate 969.11
**not surprised** 539.11
**not swallow**
be incredulous 504.3
disbelieve 503.5
**not there** 532.11
**not to be believed**
503.10
**not to be had**
inaccessible 510.9
scarce 662.11
**not tolerate**
disapprove 969.11
not permit 778.4
**not to mention** 40.12
**not touch**
abstain 992.7
avoid 631.6
not use 668.5
**not true**
erroneous 518.16
false 616.25
**not understand** 549.11
**not wash** 518.8
**not with it** 477.13
**notwithstanding** 33.8
**not work**
be ineffective 158.7
fail 725.8
**nought** see **naught**
**noun** 586.5
**nourish**
encourage 648.21
feed 307.17
foster 785.16
sustain 309.15
**nourishing**
gastronomical 307.29
nutritious 309.19
**nourishment**
food 308.3
nutrition 309.1
support 785.3
**nous** God 1013.8
intellect 466.1
intelligence 467.2
**nouveau riche**
modern 122.4
upstart 919.10
vulgar person 898.6
**nouveau-riche** 919.13
**nova** 375.8
**novel**
*n.* book 605.1

fictional form 608.8
*adj.* new 122.11
original 23.5
**novelist** author 602.15
narrator 608.10
**novelties** 831.6
**novelty** fad 644.5
innovation 122.2
newness 122.1
originality 23.1
**novena** nine 99.5
worship 1032.8
**novice** beginner 68.2
nun 1038.19
tyro 566.9
**novocaine** 687.57
**now**
*n.* the present 120.1
*adj.* modern 122.13
*adv.* at once 113.8
at present 120.3
recently 122.16
*interj.* make haste!
709.16
**now and then** 136.5
**noway**
by no means 524.9
nowise 35.11
**no way** despair 889.2
no! 524.10
**nowhere**
*n.* remote region
199.4
*adv.* in no place
187.16
**nowise** 35.11
**now or never** 129.12
**noxious** harmful 675.12
malicious 939.18
malodorous 437.5
offensive 864.18
poisonous 684.7
unhealthful 684.5
unsavory 429.7
**nozzle** conduit 396.9
nose 256.7
sprinkler 392.8
**nth degree** 56.5
**nuance** difference 16.2
discrimination 492.3
implication 546.2
shading 29.1
**nub** bulge 256.3
center 226.2
content 194.5
essence 5.2
important point
672.6
texture 351.1
**nubbin** bulge 256.3
little thing 196.4
**nubby** studded 256.16
textured 351.7
**nubile**
adolescent 124.13
adult 126.12
marriageable 933.21
**nucle(o)-**
atomics 326.6
cell nucleus 406.7
center 226.2
**nuclear** atomic 326.19

cellular 406.23
central 226.12
middle 69.4
**nuclear chemistry** 326.1
**nuclear energy** 326.15
**nuclear fission** 326.8
**nuclear fusion** 326.9
**nuclear physicist** 326.3
**nuclear physics**
atomics 326.1
physics 325.1
**nuclear power**
atomic energy 326.15
power 157.4
**nuclear reactor** 326.13
**nuclear weapons** 801.1
**nucleus** atomics 326.6
cell nucleus 406.7
center 226.2
essence 5.2
middle 69.1
source 153.7
**nude**
*n.* nudity 232.3
work of art 574.11
*adj.* naked 232.14
unadorned 902.8
**nudge**
*n.* hint 557.4
push 283.2
signal 568.15
touch 200.5
*v.* goad 648.15
graze 200.10
push 283.11
remind 537.20
set in motion 267.6
signal 568.22
**nudie** 611.16
**nudist**
*n.* nudity 232.3
*adj.* naked 232.14
**nudity** nakedness 232.3
plainness 902.3
**nudzh**
*n.* tormentor 866.10
*v.* annoy 866.13
**nugatory**
ineffective 158.15
trivial 673.16
worthless 669.11
**nugget**
currency metals
835.20
lump 195.10
**nuisance**
annoyance 866.2
boring person 884.4
**nuisance value** 730.1
**null** devoid 187.13
insignificant 547.6
nonexistent 2.7
**null and void**
repealed 779.3
without content
187.13
**nullification**
denial 524.2
destruction 693.6
neutralization 178.2
political policy 744.4
repeal 779.1

**nullify** cancel 693.13
debts 842.9
deny 524.4
neutralize 178.7
repeal 779.2
**nullity**
insignificancy 673.6
meaninglessness
547.1
nonexistence 2.1
thing of naught 4.2
**numb**
*v.* chill 333.10
make unfeeling 856.8
relieve 886.5
render insensible
423.4
*adj.* apathetic 856.13
inactive 708.19
insensible 423.6
**number**
*n.* act 611.8
amount 28.2
edition 605.2
grammatical form
586.8
indefinite number
101.2
kind 61.3
large 99.10–13;
101.3,4
music 463.22
numeral 86
part of writing 55.2
sum 86.5
vocation 656.6
*v.* analyze 48.7
numerate 87.10
quantify 28.4
total 54.8
**number among** 76.3
**numbering**
*n.* counting 87.1
*adj.* inclusive 76.6
**numberless** 101.10
**number one** 80.5
**numbers** lottery 515.8
many 101.3
mathematics 87.2
meter 609.9
metrics 609.8
quantity 28.1
**numbers runner** 515.16
**numbing**
*n.* relief 886.1
*adj.* anesthetic 687.47
cold 333.14
deadening 423.9
relieving 886.9
**numbness** apathy 856.
insensibility 423.1
**numerable**
calculable 87.16
measurable 490.15
**numeral** 86.1
**numerate** 87.10
**numeration** 87
**numerative**
enumerative 87.15
measuring 490.13
numerical 86.8

**numeric(al)**
  arithmetical 86.8
  mathematical 87.17
**numerous** many 101.6
  much 34.8
  plentiful 661.7
  plural 100.7
**numinous**
  awesome 920.11
  godlike 1013.20
  illustrious 914.19
  sacred 1026.7
  sorcerous 1035.14
  supernatural 85.15
  unintelligible 549.13
**numismatic** 835.30
**numismatics** 835.22
**numskull** 471.4
**nun** celibate 934.2
  religious 1038.19
**nuncio** diplomat 781.6
  messenger 561.1
**nunnery** 1042.6
**nuptial**
  matrimonial 933.19
  sexual 419.26
**nuptials** 933.4
**nurse**
  *n.* healer 688.13
  nursemaid 699.8
  *v.* care for 699.19
  cherish 813.7
  foster 785.16
  nourish 307.17
  train 562.14
  treat 689.30
**nursemaid** maid 750.8
  nurse 699.8
**nursery** bedroom 192.7
  birthplace 153.8
  hospital room 192.25
  plantation 413.11
  preschool 567.4
**nurseryman** 413.6
**nursery rhyme** 609.6
**nursery school** 567.4
**nursing home**
  asylum 700.4
  infirmary 689.27
**nurture**
  *n.* food 308.3
  support 785.3
  training 562.3
  *v.* care for 699.19
  cherish 813.7
  encourage 648.21
  foster 785.16
  make better 691.9
  nourish 307.17
  raise animals 416.6
  train 562.14
**nut**
  *n.* eccentric 474.3
  enthusiast 635.5
  fanatic 473.17
  food 308.38,52
  lunatic 473.15
  odd person 85.4
  plant seed 411.29
  specialist 81.3
  *v.* harvest 413.19
**nuthouse** 473.14

**nutrient**
  *n.* nutriment 309.3
  *adj.* nutritious 309.19
**nutriment** food 308.3
  nutrient 309.3
**nutrition**
  cooking 330.1
  eating 307.1
  nourishment 309
**nutritionist** 309.13
**nutritious**
  gastronomical 307.29
  nourishing 309.19
**nutritive value** 309.1
**nuts** 473.26
**nuts about**
  enthusiastic about
    635.12
  fond of 931.28
**nutshell**
  *n.* small amount 35.2
  *v.* abridge 607.5
**nutty** eccentric 474.4
  flavorful 428.9
  foolish 470.8
  insane 473.26
**nuzzle** cuddle 932.15
  touch 425.8
**nylon** fabric 378.11
  fiber 206.8
**nymph** bug 414.36
  fairy 1014.19
  larva 406.14
  young insect 125.10
**nymphet** girl 125.6
  nymph 1014.19
  unchaste woman
    989.14
**nymphomania**
  eroticism 419.5
  lasciviousness 989.5
**nymphomaniac**
  sex deviant 419.17
  unchaste woman
    989.14

## O

**O!** 920.20
**oaf**
  awkward person
    734.8
  lout 471.5
  unsophisticate 736.3
**oafish** clumsy 734.20
  stupid 469.15
**oak** hardness 356.6
  strength 159.7
  tree 411.50
  wood 378.9
**oak leaf** 569.5
**oar** boatman 276.5
  paddle 277.15
**oarsman** 276.5
**oath** affirmation 523.3
  curse 972.4
  promise 770.1
**oatmeal** 308.34
**oats** fodder 308.4
  grain 411.46
**obdurate**
  callous 981.17

  hard 356.10
  heartless 939.23
  impenitent 874.5
  insensible 423.6
  obstinate 626.10
  strict 757.7
**obedience**
  compliance 766
  conformity 82.1
  resignation 861.2
  submission 765.1
**obedient**
  compliant 766.3
  conformable 82.5
  dutiful 962.13
  resigned 861.10
  submissive 765.12
**obediently**
  compliantly 766.6
  conformably 82.7
  submissively 765.17
**obeisance** bow 318.3
  homage 964.2
  obsequiousness 907.2
  submission 765.1
**obeisant**
  deferential 765.16
  obsequious 907.13
  respectful 964.10
**obelisk**
  memorial 570.12
  tower 207.11
**Oberon** 1014.18
**obese** 195.18
**obesity** 195.8
**obey** accept 861.6
  mind 766.2
  submit 765.6
**obfuscate**
  confuse 247.3
  darken 337.9
  make unintelligible
    549.12
  misteach 563.3
  obscure 615.6
**obituary**
  *n.* biography 608.4
  death notice 408.14
  memorial 570.12
  *adj.* epitaphic 410.22
  recorded 570.19
**object** entity 3.3
  meaning 545.2
  objective 653.2
  syntax 586.2
  thing 376.4
**object** disagree 27.5
  disapprove 969.10
  offer resistance 792.3
  protest 522.5
**objectify**
  externalize 224.5
  visualize 535.15
**objecting**
  protesting 522.7
  resistant 792.5
**objection**
  defense 1006.2
  demur 623.2
  disapproval 969.1
  obstacle 730.4
  protest 522.2

  resistance 792.1
**objectionable**
  offensive 864.18
  unacceptable 869.7
  unpraiseworthy
    969.25
**objective**
  *n.* intention 653.2
  lens 443.1
  will 621.1
  *adj.* extrinsic 6.3
  unfeeling 856.9
  unprejudiced 526.12
**objectivity**
  extrinsicality 6.1
  unfeeling 856.1
  unprejudicedness
    526.5
**object lesson**
  example 25.2
  lesson 562.7
  warning 703.1
**objector**
  dissenter 522.3
  oppositionist 791.3
**objet d'art** 574.11
**oblation** gift 818.4
  offering 1032.7
**obligate** oblige 962.12
  promise 770.5
**obligated** liable 840.9
  obliged 962.16
  promised 770.8
**obligation**
  compulsion 756.1
  condition 507.2
  debt 840.1
  duty 962.1
  good deed 938.7
  gratitude 949.1
  liability 175.1
  necessity 639.1
  promise 770.2
  undertaking 715.1
**obligatory**
  binding 962.15
  compulsory 756.10
  mandatory 752.13
  necessary 639.12
**oblige** be kind 938.9
  compel 756.5
  favor 785.19
  indulge 759.6
  necessitate 639.8
  obligate 962.12
**obliged** grateful 949.5
  obligated 962.16
**obliging**
  considerate 938.16
  courteous 936.14
  indulgent 759.8
**oblique**
  *n.* diagonal 219.7
  *v.* deviate 219.9
  *adj.* circuitous 321.7
  circumlocutory
    593.14
  slanting 219.13
  transverse 221.9
**obliterate** debts 842.9
  expunge 693.16
  forget 538.6

**obliteration**
  debts 842.2
  erasure 693.7
  forgetfulness 538.1
**oblivion**
  forgetfulness 538.1
  inconsiderateness
    534.2
  insensibility 856.2
  thoughtfreeness
    480.1
  unconsciousness
    423.2
**oblivious**
  abstracted 532.11
  asleep 712.22
  forgetful 538.9
  inattentive 531.7
  insensible 856.10
  thoughtfree 480.4
  unconscious 423.8
  unmindful 534.11
**oblong** long 202.10
  quadrangular 251.9
**obloquy** criticism 969.4
  curse 972.2
  infamy 915.4
**obnoxious** bad 675.9
  base 915.12
  offensive 864.18
**oboe** organ stop 465.22
  wood wind 465.9
**oboist** 464.4
**obscene** cursing 972.8
  lewd 990.9
  offensive 864.18
  salacious 989.29
  vulgar 898.11
**obscenity** cursing 972.3
  expletive 972.4
  lasciviousness 989.5
  lewdness 990.4
  offensiveness 864.2
  vulgarity 898.2
**obscure**
  v. blind 441.7
  blur 247.3
  cloud 404.6
  conceal 615.6
  cover 228.19
  darken 337.9
  equivocate 483.9
  make uncertain
    514.14
  make unintelligible
    549.12
  misteach 563.3
  opaque 341.2
  adj. concealed 615.11
  dark 337.13
  hard to understand
    549.14
  indistinct 247.4
  opaque 341.3
  shadowy 445.6
  unintelligible 549.15
  unrenowned 915.14
  vague 514.18
**obscured**
  blinded 441.10
  concealed 615.11
  covered 228.31

  dark 337.13
  hard to understand
    549.14
  latent 546.5
**obscurity**
  a nobody 673.7
  darkness 337.1
  formlessness 247.1
  indistinctness 445.2
  opaqueness 341.1
  unintelligibility 549.3
  vagueness 514.4
**obsequies** 410.4
**obsequious**
  deferential 765.16
  flattering 970.8
  obeisant 964.10
  servile 907.13
**observable**
  manifest 555.8
  visible 444.6
**observance**
  attention 530.1
  celebration 877.1
  ceremony 646.4
  conformity 82.1
  custom 642.1
  execution 771.5
  keeping 768
  obedience 766.1
  observation 439.2
  piety 1028.1
  rite 1040.3
  vigilance 533.4
**observant**
  attentive 530.15
  dutiful 962.13
  regardful 768.4
  vigilant 533.13
**observation**
  attention 530.1
  idea 479.1
  keeping 768.1
  opinion 501.6
  remark 594.4
  surveillance 485.9
  viewing 439.2
**observatory**
  astronomy 375.17
  observation post
    439.8
**observe**
  abide by 771.10
  administer rites
    1040.18
  celebrate 877.2
  conform 82.3
  examine 485.23
  formalize 646.5
  heed 530.6
  keep 768.2
  obey 766.2
  remark 594.25
  see 439.12
  watch 439.14
**observer** aviator 279.3
  examiner 485.16
  spectator 442.1
**obsess**
  be in one's mind
    537.14
  bewitch 1036.9

  cause unpleasantness
    864.16
  demonize 1016.17
  engross 530.13
  haunt 1017.6
  possess 473.24
**obsessed**
  affected 855.25
  bewitched 1036.13
  engrossed 530.17
  haunted 1017.10
  possessed 473.33
  remembering 537.24
**obsession**
  bewitchment 1036.2
  emotional symptom
    690.23
  engrossment 530.3
  fixation 473.13
  spirit control 1017.5
**obsessive**
  compelling 473.34
  engrossing 530.20
  unforgettable 537.26
**obsolesce**
  become old 123.9
  fall into disuse 668.9
**obsolescence** 668.1
**obsolete** disused 668.10
  out of action 158.17
  passé 123.15
  past 119.7
**obstacle**
  hindrance 730.4
  obstruction 266.3
**obstetric(al)** 688.18
**obstetrician** 688.8
**obstinacy**
  opposition 790.2
  perseverance 625.1
  refractoriness 767.2
  resistance 792.1
  resolution 624.1
  strength 159.1
  strictness 757.2
  stubbornness 626
  tenacity 50.3
  uninfluenceability
    173.2
  unwillingness 623.1
**obstinate**
  disobedient 767.8
  opposing 790.8
  persevering 625.7
  persistent 50.12
  resolute 624.11
  strict 757.7
  strong 159.13
  stubborn 626.8
  uninfluenceable
    173.4
**obstreperous**
  noisy 453.12
  refractory 767.10
  ungovernable 626.12
  violent 162.18
  vociferous 459.10
**obstruct** delay 132.8
  fend off 799.10
  hinder 730.12
  slow 270.9
  stop 266.7

**obstructed**
  clogged 266.11
  delayed 132.16
**obstruction** clog 266.3
  delay 132.2
  hindrance 730.1
  obstacle 730.4
  slowing 270.4
**obstructionist**
  hinderer 730.8
  oppositionist 791.3
**obstructive**
  hindering 730.17
  resistant 792.5
**obtain** acquire 811.8
  elicit 305.14
  exist 1.8
  fetch 271.15
  induce 153.12
  prevail 79.10
  receive 819.6
**obtainable**
  accessible 509.8
  attainable 811.13
**obtrude** eject 310.13
  intrude 238.5
  thrust upon 818.20
**obtrusive**
  conceited 909.11
  conspicuous 555.12
  gaudy 904.20
  insolent 913.8
  interfering 238.8
**obtuse** blunt 259.3
  insensitive 423.6
  stupid 469.16
  unfeeling 856.9
**obverse**
  n. counterpart 20.3
  front 240.1
  opposite 15.2
  opposite side 239.3
  adj. contrary 15.6
  opposite 239.5
**obviate** 730.14
**obviation** 730.2
**obvious**
  clearly visible 444.7
  manifest 555.8
**obviously**
  manifestly 555.14
  positively 34.19
  really 1.16
  visibly 444.8
**ocarina** 465.9
**occasion**
  n. cause 153.1
  circumstance 8.1
  event 151.2
  opportunity 129.2
  requirement 639.2
  v. cause 153.11
**occasional**
  causal 153.14
  circumstantial 8.7
  happening 151.9
  incidental 129.11
  infrequent 136.3
**occasionally**
  discontinuously 72.5
  sometimes 136.5
**Occident** 180.6

**occidental** 290.15
**occipital** 241.10
**occlude** close 266.6
  obstruct 730.12
**occlusion** closure 266.1
  hindrance 730.1
  stoppage 686.5
**occlusive**
  hindering 730.17
  phonetic 594.31
**occult**
  *v.* conceal 615.6
  cover 228.19
  darken 337.9
  *adj.* abtruse 549.16
  concealed 615.11
  latent 546.5
  mystical 1034.22
  otherworldly 377.7
  secret 614.11
  supernatural 85.15
**occult, the**
  immateriality 377.1
  mysticism 1034
  secrets 614.5
  supernaturalism 85.7
**occultation**
  concealment 615.1
  covering 228.1
  disappearance 447.1
  eclipse 337.8
**occultism**
  immateriality 377.1
  mysticism 1034
**occultist** 1034.11
**occupancy**
  habitation 188.1
  possession 808.1
**occupant**
  inhabitant 190.2
  tenant 809.4
**occupation**
  action 705.1
  business 656.1
  conquest 822.4
  habitation 188.1
  operation 164.1
  possession 808.1
  vocation 656.6
**occupational** 656.16
**occupational disease**
  686.1,31
**occupational therapy**
  psychotherapy 690.5
  therapy 689.2
**occupied**
  absorbed in thought
  478.22
  busy 707.21
  engrossed 530.17
  inhabited 188.12
**occupy**
  appropriate 822.19
  busy 656.10
  engross 530.13
  include 76.3
  inhabit 188.7
  pervade 186.7
  possess 808.4
  preoccupy 478.20
**occur** be present 186.6
  exist 1.8

  happen 151.5
  occur to 478.18
**occurrence**
  appearance 446.1
  circumstance 8.1
  event 151.2
  existence 1.1
  presence 186.1
**ocean** much 34.3
  sea 397
**ocean depths**
  ocean 397.1
  the deep 209.4
**oceanic** marine 397.8
  nautical 275.57
**ocean liner** 277.5
**oceanographer**
  measurer 490.10
  scientist 397.7
**oceanography**
  depth measurement
  209.5
  mensuration 490.9
  thalassography 397.6
**Oceanus** sea god 397.4
  water god 1014.20
**ocelot**
  animal 414.27,58
  variegation 374.6
**ocherous** orange 369.2
  yellow 370.4
**Ockham's razor** 852.1
**o'clock** 114.16
**oct(a)–** 99.20
**octagonal**
  angular 251.10
  eight 99.20
**octane** 331.1
**octave** eight 99.4
  harmonics 463.9
  interval 463.20
  organ stop 465.22
  poetic division
  609.11
**octet** eight 99.4
  electron 343.3
  group 786.1
  part music 462.17
  poetic division
  609.11
**octogenarian**
  eighty 99.7
  old man 127.2
**octopus** 414.63; 415.5
**octoroon** 44.9
**octuple** 99.20
**ocular**
  *n.* lens 443.1
  *adj.* visual 439.21
**oculist** healer 688.5
  ophthalmologist
  443.7
  physician 688.8
**OD**
  *n.* commissioned offi-
  cer 749.18
  sailor 276.1
  ship's officer 276.7
  *v.* be killed 409.22
  die 408.24
  take ill 686.44

**odalisque**
  seductress 989.15
  slave 764.7
**odd** dissimilar 21.4
  eccentric 474.4
  insane 473.25
  numerical 86.8
  occasional 136.3
  queer 85.11
  remaining 43.7
  sole 89.9
  unequal 31.4
**oddball**
  *n.* eccentric 474.3
  intruder 78.2
  misfit 27.4
  odd person 85.4
  *adj.* eccentric 474.4
  odd 85.11
**oddity**
  eccentricity 474.1
  odd person 85.4
  odd thing 85.5
  queerness 85.3
**odd job** 656.2
**odds** advantage 36.2
  difference 16.1
  disagreement 795.2
  even chance 156.7
  gambling odds 515.6
  inequality 31.1
  probability 511.1
**odds and ends**
  hodgepodge 44.6
  miscellany 74.13
  refuse 43.1
  sundries 831.6
**ode** 609.6
**Odin**
  Norse deity 1014.6
  war god 797.17
**odious** bad 675.9
  base 915.12
  filthy 682.23
  offensive 864.18
  unlikable 867.7
**odium** hate 930.1
  infamy 915.4
**odor** characteristic 80.4
  fragrance 436.1
  smell 435
**odorize** perfume 436.8
  scent 435.7
**odorizer** 436.6
**odorless** 438.5
**odorous** fragrant 436.9
  malodorous 437.5
  odoriferous 435.9
**odyssey** 273.2
**Oedipus complex**
  690.29
**œuvre**
  compilation 605.4
  product 168.1
**of** 9.13
**of age** adult 126.12
  marriageable 933.21
**of consequence** 672.17
**of course**
  certainly 513.23
  consequently 154.9
  yes! 521.18

**off**
  *v.* kill 409.14
  *adj.* delirious 473.31
  dissimilar 21.4
  dissonant 461.4
  erroneous 518.16
  idle 708.17
  imperfect 678.4
  inferior 680.10
  insane 473.25
  occasional 136.3
  odd 85.11
  right side 243.4
  tainted 692.42
  *adv.* at a distance
  199.14
  away 301.21
  oceanward 397.11
  *prep.* less 42.14
**offal** filth 682.9
  refuse 669.4
**off and on**
  alternately 137.11
  changeably 141.8
  irregularly 138.4
  to and fro 323.21
**off-balance**
  off-center 185.12
  unequal 31.5
**off-base**
  improper 959.3
  inappropriate 130.7
  misbehaving 738.5
**offbeat**
  *n.* music 463.26
  *adj.* dissimilar 21.4
  nonconformist 83.6
  unusual 85.10
**off-center** 185.12
**off chance**
  possibility 509.1
  small chance 156.9
**off-color**
  colored 362.20
  indecent 990.7
  sick 686.52
  wrong 959.3
**off duty** idle 708.17
  on one's own time
  711.12
**offend** affront 965.4
  anger 952.20
  be ugly 899.5
  be unpleasant 864.11
  sin 982.5
**offender** 986.9
**offense** attack 798.1
  crime 999.4
  indignity 965.2
  misdeed 982.2
  provocation 952.11
  resentment 952.2
  violation 769.2
**offensive**
  *n.* attack 798.1
  *adj.* attacking 798.30
  bad 675.9
  discourteous 937.6
  insulting 965.6
  malodorous 437.5
  obscene 990.9
  ugly 899.11

unpleasant 864.18
unsavory 429.7
vulgar 898.10
warlike 797.25
**offer**
*n.* attempt 714.2
giving 818.1
proposal 773
*v.* adduce evidence
505.13
attempt 714.5
bid 828.9
give 818.12
proffer 773.4
put to choice 637.21
**offered** 622.7
**offering**
donation 818.6
gift 818.4
oblation 1032.7
proposal 773.1
**offertory**
donation 818.6
hymn 1032.3
sacred music 462.16
sacrifice 1032.7
**off-guard**
inattentive 531.8
negligent 534.10
**offhand**
*adj.* careless 534.11
extemporaneous
630.12
informal 647.3
nonchalant 858.15
*adv.* carelessly 534.18
extemporaneously
630.15
informally 647.4
**office** aid 785.1
ceremony 646.4
commission 780.1
function 665.5
good deed 938.7
jurisdiction 1000.4
occupation 656.3
position 656.5
rite 1040.3
room 192.6
tip 557.3
workplace 719.8
worship 1032.8
**office boy**
attendant 750.5
errand boy 561.4
**officeholder**
official 749.16
politician 746.11
**officer**
commissioned officer
749.18
executive 748.3
official 749.16
on ships 276.7
policeman 699.15
**official**
*n.* agent 781.3
executive 748.3
officer 749.16
*adj.* authentic 513.18
authorized 739.15
governing 741.19

governmental 741.17
occupational 656.16
prescriptive 751.4
recorded 570.18
**officialdom** 749.15
**officialese**
jargon 580.10
official jargon 744.37
**officiate**
administer 747.11
do duty 656.13
judge 494.12
minister 1040.19
**officious** 238.9
**offing** distance 199.3
the future 121.1
**offish** aloof 912.12
reticent 613.10
unsociable 923.6
**off-key** 461.4
**off limits** limited 234.8
prohibited 778.7
**offscourings** offal 682.9
rabble 919.5
refuse 43.1
waste 669.4
**off season** 128.1
**offset**
*n.* automation 349.21
collateral descendant
171.4
counterbalance 33.2
neutralizer 178.3
offprint 603.3
opposite 15.2
printing 603.1
*v.* counteract 33.5
cushion 163.8
neutralize 178.7
oppose 15.4
**offsetting**
*n.* compensation 33.1
neutralization 178.2
*adj.* compensating
33.6
neutralizing 178.9
**offshoot** adjunct 41.1
affiliate 788.10
branch 55.4
by-product 168.3
collateral descendant
171.4
fork 299.4
party 788.4
plants 411.18
religion 1020.3
result 154.1
**offshore** 397.11
**offspring** child 125.3
descendant 171.3
family 11.5
posterity 171.1
product 168.1
result 154.1
sequel 117.2
**off the beaten track**
85.10
**off the cuff** 630.12,15
**off the record** 614.14,20
**off the wall**
insane 473.26
odd 85.11

**off-year** 130.2
**often** frequently 135.6
repeatedly 103.16
**ogle**
*n.* flirtation 932.8
gaze 439.5
*v.* be a spectator
442.5
flirt 932.18
gaze 439.16
scrutinize 439.15
**ogre** frightener 891.9
monster 85.20; 943.6
**oh!** 920.20
**ohm** 342.12,35
**oil**
*n.* animal 380.13
fat 380
flattery 970.1
fuel 331.1
healing ointment
687.11
illuminant 335.20
mineral 380.11
picture 574.15
vegetable 380.12
*v.* facilitate 732.6
flatter 970.6
fuel 331.8
grease 380.8
medicate 689.31
provision 659.9
smooth 260.5
**oiling** 380.6
**oily** flattering 970.8
greasy 380.9
hypocritic(al) 616.33
slippery 260.11
suave 936.18
**ointment** balm 380.3
healing ointment
687.11
money 835.2
unction 1040.6
**OK**
*n.* approval 968.1
consent 775.1
permission 777.1
ratification 521.4
*v.* approve 968.9
consent 775.2
permit 777.9
ratify 521.12
*adj.* acceptable 868.12
accurate 516.15
excellent 674.13
tolerable 674.19
*interj.* yes 521.18
**old** adult 126.12
aged 126.16
age-old 123.10
disused 668.10
experienced 733.26
former 119.10
**old country, the**
native land 181.2
Old World 180.6
**old days** 119.2
**older**
*n.* old man 127.2
senior 127.5
*adj.* elder 123.19

prior 116.4
**oldest**
*n.* first-born 127.5
*adj.* eldest 123.19
**Old Faithful** 328.10
**old-fashioned**
conservative 140.8
disused 668.10
gallant 936.15
old 123.16
**old fogy**
conservative 140.4
dotard 471.9
old person 123.8
**old-fogy** 123.17
**old hand** 733.15
**old hat**
old-fashioned 123.16
trite 883.9
**old lady**
girl friend 931.14
old woman 127.3
wife 933.9
**old-line**
conservative 140.8
established 142.13
politics 745.17
**old maid**
fastidious person
896.7
prude 903.11
spinster 934.4
**old man**
antiquated person
123.8
boy friend 931.12
elder 127.2
father 170.9
grandfather 170.11
husband 933.8
**Old Man, the**
commander 276.7
commissioned officer
749.18
**old master** artist 579.1
work of art 574.11
**oldness** ancientness 123
elderliness 126.5
**old pro**
professional 718.4
veteran 733.15
**old salt** sailor 276.3
veteran 733.15
**old saw** 517.3
**old school** 140.4
**old story**
old times 119.2
platitude 517.3
**Old Testament** 1021.3
**old-timer**
antiquated person
123.8
old man 127.2
veteran 733.15
**old times** 119.2
**old wives' tale** 502.3
**old woman**
antiquated person
123.8
effeminate male
421.10

fastidious person
896.7
grandmother 170.12
old lady 127.3
wife 933.9
**old-world**
antiquated 123.13
gallant 936.15
¡ole! 968.22
oleo 308.47
olfactories 435.5
olfactory 435.12
olio hodgepodge 44.6
stew 308.11
olive 371.4
olive branch 804.2
ology 475.10
Olympiad 878.10
Olympian aloof 912.12
detached 856.13
heavenly 1018.13
high 207.19
impartial 976.10
reticent 613.10
unsociable 923.6
Olympic gods 1014.5
Olympics contest 796.3
tournament 878.10
Olympus
heaven 1018.10
mountain 207.7
om! 1032.16
ombudsman
judge 1002.4
mediator 805.3
omega 70.1
omelet 308.26
omen
*n.* portent 544.3
prediction 543.1
warning sign 703.3
*v.* portend 544.10
ominous
harmful 675.12
inauspicious 729.14
portentous 544.17
predictive 543.12
threatening 973.3
omission an error 518.4
deficiency 57.2
deletion 42.5
exclusion 77.1
insufficiency 662.4
mismanagement
734.6
neglect 534.1
nonaccomplishment
723.1
nonobservance 769.1
sin 982.2
mit delete 42.12
exclude 77.4
leave undone 534.7
mitting 77.9
mni– multiform 19.3
universal 79.14
unqualified 508.2
nnibus
. bus 272.12
compilation 605.4
*dj.* comprehensive
76.7

thorough 56.10
whole 54.9
omnifarious 19.3
omnipotence
almightiness 157.3
divine attribute
1013.15
omnipotent
almighty 157.13
godlike 1013.20
omnipresence
all-presence 186.2
completeness 56.1
divine attribute
1013.15
omnipresent
all-present 186.13
godlike 1013.20
pervasive 56.10
omniscience
divine attribute
1013.15
profound knowledge
475.6
omniscient
godlike 1013.20
knowing 475.15
omnivorous
eating 307.29
gluttonous 994.6
greedy 634.27
on
*adj.* happening 151.9
*adv.* after which 117.7
astride 216.25
forward 294.8
*prep.* against 200.25
at 184.26
atop 211.16
by means of 658.7
covering 228.37
in relation to 9.13
toward 290.28
on account 839.10
on account of
because of 155.9
for 785.26
on and off 141.8
on and on
constantly 135.7
continuously 71.10
increasingly 38.9
on a par 30.7
on approval
at choice 637.27
on trial 489.14
on behalf of for 785.26
instead of 149.12
on board
aboard 275.62
here 184.22
present 186.12
on call handy 665.19
in cash 841.25
on demand 753.11
once
*adj.* former 119.10
*adv.* one time 136.6
past 119.14
singly 89.13
whenever 105.12
once in a while 136.5

once upon a time
119.14
oncoming
*n.* approach 296.1
beginning 68.1
*adj.* approaching
296.4
progressive 294.6
on condition 507.12
on demand
at demand 753.11
in cash 841.25
on duty 707.21
one
*n.* only 89.3
person 417.3
*adj.* combined 52.5
godlike 1013.20
identical 14.7
married 933.22
quantifier 28.5
single 89.7
whole 54.9
one and all
*n.* everybody 79.4
the entirety 54.3
*adj.* every 79.15
*adv.* completely 56.14
unanimously 521.17
one and only one 89.3
sole 89.9
one-armed bandit
515.12
one by one
respectively 80.19
separately 49.28
singly 89.13
on edge
impatient 862.6
in suspense 539.12
nervous 859.10
one-horse little 196.10
petty 673.17
one-horse town 183.3
one mind 521.5
on end
continuously 71.10
vertically 213.13
oneness accord 794.1
agreement 26.1
identity 14.1
individuality 80.1
simplicity 45.1
unity 89.1
whole 54.1
one-night stand 611.12
one-piece 89.11
onerous
hampering 730.18
laborious 716.18
ponderous 352.17
troublesome 731.17
unpleasant 864.24
one's best effort 714.3
regards 936.8
oneself 80.5
one-sided
asymmetric 249.10
prejudiced 527.12
sided 242.7
unipartite 89.11
unjust 977.11

onetime 119.10
one time 136.6
one-track mind 473.13
one-two 283.5
one-upmanship
competition 796.2
cunning 735.1
superiority 36.1
one-way 290.13
ongoing
*n.* course 267.2
progression 294.1
*adj.* happening 151.9
improving 691.15
operating 164.11
progressive 294.6
on guard
cautious 895.8
defensively 799.16
vigilant 533.13
on hand handy 665.19
in store 660.16
possessed 808.8
present 186.12
on high aloft 207.26
celestially 1018.14
on ice
made sure 513.20
prearranged 641.5
on loan 820.7
onlooker
neighbor 200.6
spectator 442.1
only
*adj.* sole 89.9
*adv.* simply 45.11
solely 89.14
to a degree 35.10
onomatopoeia
echoic word 582.17
imitation 22.1
onomatopoeic
imitative 22.9
lexical 582.20
representational
572.10
on one's knees
*adj.* deferential 765.16
humble 906.12
obeisant 964.10
obsequious 907.13
supplicatory 774.16
worshipful 1032.15
*adv.* humbly 906.15
obsequiously 907.15
on one's last legs
aged 126.18
dying 408.33
exhausted 717.8
worn-out 692.38
on one's mind 478.24
on one's own
at will 621.5
independently 762.32
singlehandedly 89.13
on one's toes 533.14
on paper
theoretically 499.16
written 602.22
on purpose 653.11
on record 570.18
onrush course 267.2

flow 395.4
on schedule 539.14
onset attack 798.1
  beginning 68.1
  printing 603.1
onshore 385.11
onslaught attack 798.1
  berating 969.7
  impact 283.3
  violence 162.3
onstage 611.41
on stream 720.22
on tap 665.19
on tenterhooks
  anxious 890.6
  in suspense 539.12
  perplexed 514.24
on the ball alert 533.14
  attentive 530.15
  clear-witted 467.13
on the beam
  knowing 475.17
  sideways 242.8
  straight 250.7
on the blink 692.39
on the block 829.17
on the brink
  about to 121.13
  at the limit 235.15
  near 200.24
on the cuff 839.10
on the double
  fast 269.21
  hurried 709.11
  make haste! 709.16
on the fence
  neutral 806.7
  nonpartisan 744.45
on the fritz
  disorderly 62.13
  in disrepair 692.39
on the go busy 707.21
  in motion 267.9
  traveling 273.41
on the house
  as a gift 818.27
  gratis 850.5
on the job alert 533.14
  attentive 530.15
  busy 707.21
on the level 974.14
on the lookout 533.13
on the lookout for
  after 655.12
  expectant 539.11
  searching 485.37
on the make
  ambitious 634.28
  out for 714.15
on the mend 691.15
on the move
  busy 707.21
  in motion 267.9
  on the go 273.41
on the nose 290.14
on the other hand
  contrarily 15.9
  notwithstanding 33.8
  otherwise 16.11
  sideways 242.8
on the quiet 614.18

on the right track
  488.10
on the rocks
  aground 275.73
  in difficulty 731.25
  insolvent 842.11
on the run busy 707.21
  hastily 709.12
  in motion 267.9
  traveling 273.41
on the shelf 668.10
on the side
  additionally 40.11
  beside 242.10
on the spot
  adj. hasty 709.9
  in a predicament
    731.20
  in danger 697.13
  adv. here 184.22
  instantly 113.6
  now 120.3
  promptly 131.15
on the take 651.4
on the verge
  about to 121.13
  at the limit 235.15
  near 200.24
on the wagon 992.10
on the wane
  decreasing 39.11
  on the decline 692.47
on the way
  en route 271.19
  in preparation 720.22
on the whole
  generally 79.17
  in the long run 54.14
  judgment 494.17
  on the average 32.5
on time 131.14
on to 475.16
ontogeny 148.3
ontology
  philosophy 500.1,11
  philosophy of being
    1.7
on trial
  in litigation 1004.21
  under examination
    489.14
on trust
  believingly 501.28
  on credit 839.10
onus burden 963.3
  burden of proof
    505.4
  duty 962.1
  guilt 983.1
  impediment 730.6
  stigma 915.6
onward
  adj. progressive 294.6
  adv. forward 294.8
  frontward 240.13
oodles 34.4
ooze
  n. mud 389.8
  outflow 303.6
  slime 682.8
  v. be damp 392.11
  exude 303.15

opacity obscurity 549.3
  opaqueness 341.1
  stupidity 469.3
opalescence
  iridescence 335.18
  play of color 374.2
opalescent
  iridescent 335.37
  rainbowlike 374.10
  soft-colored 362.21
opaque
  v. darken 341.2
  adj. intransparent
    341.3
  obscure 549.15
  stupid 469.15
op. cit. 505.25
open
  v. begin 68.12
  cleave 201.4
  disclose 556.4
  give a show 611.33
  spread 197.6
  unclose 265.12
  adj. accessible 509.8
  artless 736.5
  candid 974.17
  champaign 387.3
  communicative
    554.10
  disconnected 51.4
  free-spoken 762.22
  honest 974.14
  hospitable 925.11
  influenceable 172.15
  in plain style 591.3
  leisure 710.5
  liberal 853.4
  made public 559.17
  manifest 555.10
  open-minded 526.10
  phonetic 594.31
  receptive 306.16
  spread 197.11
  uncertain 514.17
  unclosed 265.18
  unprotected 697.15
  unrestricted 762.26
  vacant 187.14
  visible 444.6
open, the 224.3
open-air airy 402.12
  outdoor 224.7
open and aboveboard
  974.14
open-and-shut
  evident 555.8
  guaranteed 513.20
open-and-shut case
  513.2
open arms entree 306.3
  welcome 925.2
open classroom school
  567.2
open door entree 306.3
  foreign policy 744.5
  hospitality 925.1
opener beginning 68.5
  key 265.11
open-eyed
  astonished 920.9
  attentive 530.15

curious 528.5
  vigilant 533.13
open fire begin 68.12
  fire upon 798.22
open forum
  arena 802.1
  discussion 597.7
  forum 755.3
openhanded
  liberal 853.4
  magnanimous 979.6
openhearted
  artless 736.5
  candid 974.17
  hospitable 925.11
  liberal 853.4
opening aperture 265
  appearance 446.1
  beginning 68.1
  crack 201.2
  display 555.2
  entrance 302.5
  entree 306.3
  opportunity 129.2
  outlet 303.9
  passageway 657.4
  position 656.5
  vacancy 187.2
opening move 68.3
openly artlessly 736.7
  candidly 974.23
  externally 224.9
  overtly 555.15
  publicly 559.19
  unashamedly 34.21
open market
  marketplace 832.2
  stock market 833.1
open mind 526.3
open-minded
  broad-minded 526.10
  influenceable 172.15
  liberal 762.24
openmouthed
  astonished 920.9
  attentive 530.15
  curious 528.5
  gaping 265.19
  vociferous 459.10
openness
  accessibility 509.3
  artlessness 736.1
  candor 974.4
  communicativeness
    554.3
  embracement 76.1
  influenceability 172.5
  liability 175.2
  manifestness 555.3
  open-mindedness
    526.3
  plain speech 591.1
  receptivity 306.9
  talkativeness 596.1
  unprotectedness
    697.3
open question 514.8
open road, the 273.3
open sesame
  influence 172.6
  key 265.11
  open up! 265.24

**overburden**
burden 352.13
oppress 729.8
overload 663.15
**overburdened**
burdened 352.18
overloaded 663.20
**overcareful** 895.11
**overcast**
*n.* aviation 278.41
cloudiness 404.3
darkening 337.6
*v.* cloud 404.6
darken 337.9
*adj.* cloudy 404.7
dark 337.14
**overcautious** 895.11
**overcharge**
*n.* exorbitance 848.5
overfullness 663.3
psychology 690.41
*v.* exaggerate 617.3
make grandiloquent
601.7
overload 663.15
overprice 848.7
**overclouded** 404.7
**overcoat**
clothing 231.13
types of 231.53
**overcome**
*v.* defeat 727.7
excel 36.6
triumph over 726.6
unnerve 859.9
*adj.* defeated 727.14
drunk 996.33
heartbroken 872.29
overwrought 857.24
unnerved 859.13
**overcompensation**
690.30
**overconfidence**
rashness 894.1
sureness 513.5
**overconfident**
rash 894.7
sure 513.21
**overconscientious**
conscientious 974.15
overparticular 896.12
**overcooked** 330.7
**overcount** 497.2
**overcritical**
critical 969.24
overparticular 896.12
**overcrossing**
bridge 657.10
crossing 221.2
**overdeveloped**
excessive 663.16
overgrown 197.12
oversize 195.23
**overdo**
exaggerate 617.3
go too far 663.10
overindulge 993.5
**overdone**
affected 903.15
cooked 330.7
exaggerated 617.4
excessive 663.21

grandiloquent 601.8
**overdose**
*n.* drug dose 687.6
overabundance 663.2
satiety 664.3
*v.* oversupply 663.14
satiate 664.4
take sick 686.44
**overdraft** debt 840.2
insolvency 842.3
**overdraw**
exaggerate 617.3
misrepresent 573.3
overextend 663.13
overspend 854.7
**overdrawn**
exaggerated 617.4
overdone 663.21
**overdress** 231.41
**overdrive**
*n.* gear 348.6
*v.* overtax 663.10
overwork 716.16
**overdue**
expected 539.13
late 132.16
unpunctual 115.3
**overeager**
overzealous 635.13
reckless 894.8
**overeat** 994.5
**overelaborate**
elegant 589.9
grandiloquent 601.8
ornate 901.12
**overemotional** 855.20
**overemphasis**
exaggeration 617.1
overdoing 663.6
**overemphasize**
emphasize 672.13
overdo 663.10
**overenthusiastic**
fanatical 473.32
overzealous 635.13
reckless 894.8
**overestimate**
*n.* overestimation
497.1
*v.* exaggerate 617.3
flatter 970.7
overreckon 497.2
**overestimated**
exaggerated 617.4
overrated 497.3
**overexcited** 857.24
**overexercise** 663.10
**overexert**
exert oneself 716.10
overtax 663.10
**overexpand** 663.13
**overexpansion** 663.7
**overextend**
exert oneself 716.10
overdraw 663.13
**overextension**
exertion 716.2
overactivity 707.9
overdrawing 663.7
**overexuberant** 663.19
**overfed** overfull 663.20
overgorged 994.7

overweight 195.23
satiated 664.6
**overfill** fill 56.7
overload 663.15
satiate 664.4
**overflow**
*n.* abundance 593.1
overfullness 663.3
plenty 661.2
spillage 395.6
*v.* abound 661.5
flow over 395.17
superabound 663.8
**overflowing** much 34.8
overfull 663.20
plentiful 661.7
profuse 593.11
teeming 101.9
**overfull** full 56.11
overloaded 663.20
satiated 664.6
**overgarment**
clothing 231.12
types of 231.50
**overgrow**
grow larger 197.7
grow rank 411.31
overrun 313.5
spread 197.6
superabound 663.8
**overgrown**
excessive 663.16
growing rank 411.40
large 34.7
overdeveloped 197.12
overrun 313.10
oversize 195.23
**overgrowth**
excess 663.1
overrunning 313.1
oversize 195.5
**overhang**
*n.* projection 215.3
*v.* be imminent 152.2
cover 228.30
project 215.7
**overhanging**
*n.* projection 215.3
*adj.* imminent 152.3
projecting 215.11
**overhaul**
*n.* examination 485.3
repair 694.6
*v.* check 87.14
examine 485.23
overtake 269.17
repair 694.14
take account of 845.9
**overhead**
*n.* expenses 843.3
roof 228.6
*adv.* over 207.26
**overhear**
be informed 557.14
hear 448.12
**overheated**
heated 329.29
hot 328.25
**overindulge**
be intemperate 993.5
overdo 663.10
overeat 994.5

**overindulgent**
indulgent 759.8
intemperate 993.7
unstrict 758.4
**overjoyed** 865.14
**overkill**
atomic attack 798.1
exaggeration 617.1
**overland** 385.11
**overlap**
*n.* agreement 26.1
cover 228.4
superfluity 663.4
*v.* agree 26.6
cover 228.30
**overlapping**
*n.* cover 228.4
*adj.* covering 228.35
**overlarge**
exaggerated 617.4
excessive 663.16
oversize 195.23
**overlay**
*n.* cover 228.4
*v.* cover 228.19
make grandiloquent
601.7
**overlie** 228.30
**overload**
*n.* burden 352.7
overfullness 663.3
*v.* burden 352.13
make grandiloquent
601.7
oppress 729.8
overfill 663.15
**overloaded**
burdened 352.18
high-flown 601.11
overfull 663.20
**overlong** 110.11
**overlook**
*n.* observation post
439.8
*v.* accept 861.6
be broad-minded
526.7
be high 207.16
bewitch 1036.9
condone 947.4
disregard 531.2
examine 485.23
front on 240.9
neglect 534.6
permit 777.10
slight 966.6
supervise 747.10
**overlooked**
forgiven 947.7
neglected 534.14
**overlord** master 749.1
potentate 749.7
**overly** 663.22
**overlying** 228.35
**overmaster**
domineer 741.16
overcome 727.7
subdue 764.9
**overmatched** 727.14
**overmodest** 903.19
**overmuch**
*n.* excess 663.1

*adj.* excessive 663.16
superabundant
663.19
*adv.* excessively
663.22
**overnice**
affected 903.18
elegant 589.9
overparticular 896.12
**overnight** 134.11
**over one's head**
deep 209.16
hard to understand
549.14
**overparticular** 896.12
**overpass**
*n.* bridge 657.10
crossing 221.2
overrunning 313.1
passageway 657.4
*v.* exceed 663.9
excel 36.6
outdistance 36.10
overrun 313.4
traverse 273.19
**overpay** 848.8
**overplay** outdo 36.9
overdo 663.10
**overplayed** 611.38
**overplus** excess 43.4
surplus 663.5
**overpopulation** 663.2
**overpower**
be strong 159.8
drown out 453.7
overcome 727.7
**overpowered**
defeated 727.14
overexcited 857.24
**overpowering**
exciting 857.28
invincible 159.17
overwhelming 727.17
**overprice** 848.7
**overpriced** 848.12
**overprint** 603.14
**overrate** 497.2
**overrated** 497.3
**overreach**
deceive 618.13
exaggerate 617.3
exceed 663.9
outwit 735.11
overrun 313.4
**overreact**
exaggerate 617.3
overdo 663.10
overestimate 497.2
**overrefined**
affected 903.18
elegant 589.9
overparticular 896.12
sensitive 422.14
specious 483.10
**overreligious**
fanatical 473.32
zealous 1028.11
**override**
conquer 727.10
cover 228.30
domineer 741.16
outdo 36.9

repeal 779.2
trample 313.7
**overriding** 672.23
**overripe** aged 126.15
unsavory 429.7
**overrule** repeal 779.2
rule 741.14
**overruling** chief 36.14
imperious 739.16
most important
672.23
**overrun**
*n.* overgoing 313.1
surplus 663.5
*v.* conquer 822.19
exceed 663.9
grow over 411.31
infest 313.6
overflow 395.17
overgo 313.4
pervade 186.7
run over 313.7
spread 197.6
superabound 663.8
typeset 603.16
*adj.* growing rank
411.40
overspread 313.10
**overrunning**
infestation 313.2
overflow 395.6
overgoing 313
permeation 186.3
**overseas**
*adj.* absent 187.11
distant 199.11
*adv.* across the sea
397.12
abroad 78.6
**oversee** 747.10
**overseer** 748.2
**oversell**
exaggerate 617.3
oversupply 663.14
**oversensitive**
irascible 951.20
overparticular 896.12
sensitive 422.14
**overset**
*n.* inversion 220.2
surplus 663.5
*v.* capsize 275.44
overcome 727.7
overthrow 693.20
overturn 220.6
**oversexed** 419.26
**overshadow**
be high 207.16
cloud 404.6
darken 337.9
eclipse 36.8
shade 338.5
**overshoot** exceed 663.9
fly 278.52
overrun 313.4
**oversight**
an error 518.4
government 741.1
neglect 534.1
nonobservance 769.1
protectorship 699.2
supervision 747.2

**oversimplification**
oversimplicity 45.3
undevelopment 721.4
**oversimplified** 45.10
**oversize**
*n.* outsize 195.5
*adj.* outsize 195.23
**oversleep** be late 132.7
miss an opportunity
130.6
sleep 712.13
**oversold** 617.4
**overspend**
overpay 848.8
overtax 663.10
spend more than one
has 854.7
**overspread**
*v.* cover 228.19
disperse 75.4
infest 313.6
overrun 313.5
pervade 186.7
superabound 663.8
*adj.* overrun 313.10
**overstate**
exaggerate 617.3
falsify 616.16
misrepresent 573.3
overestimate 497.2
**overstated** 617.4
**overstay** 132.15
**overstep** exceed 663.9
overrun 313.4
take liberties 961.7
transgress 313.9
**overstrain**
exert oneself 716.10
fatigue 717.4
overextend 663.13
overtax 663.10
**overstretch** 663.13
**overstuffed** full 56.11
overfull 663.20
satiated 664.6
upholstered 228.33
**oversubtle** 483.10
**oversupply**
*n.* overabundance
663.2
surplus 663.5
*v.* overprovide 663.14
**oversweet** 431.5
**overt** 555.10
**overt act** 705.3
**overtake**
come after 117.3
make drunk 996.22
outstrip 269.17
**overtax** burden 352.13
exert oneself 716.10
overcharge 848.7
overdo 663.10
overwork 716.16
**over-the-counter market**
833.7
**over the hill** 126.15
**overthrow**
*n.* change 139.1
defeat 727.1
deposal 783.2
downthrow 318.2

inversion 220.2
refutation 506.2
revolution 147.1
ruin 693.3
upheaval 162.5
*v.* change 139.6
depose 783.4
destroy 693.20
overcome 727.7
overturn 220.6
refute 506.5
revolt 767.7
revolutionize 147.4
**overthrown**
defeated 727.14
disproved 506.7
ruined 693.28
**overtime** 108.3
**overtire** 717.4
**overtired** 717.9
**overtly** 555.15
**overtone**
harmonics 463.16
implication 546.2
meaning 545.1
milieu 233.3
tone 450.2
**overture** music 462.26
offer 773.1
prelude 66.2
**overturn**
*n.* defeat 727.1
downthrow 318.2
inversion 220.2
revolution 147.1
ruin 693.3
*v.* capsize 275.44
defeat 727.7
invert 220.6
overthrow 693.20
refute 506.5
revolutionize 147.4
**overvalue** 497.2
**overview**
abridgment 607.1
scrutiny 439.6
**overweening**
confident 513.21
excessive 663.16
insolent 913.8
presumptuous 912.10
rash 894.7
vain 909.6
**overweight**
*n.* overfullness 663.3
oversize 195.5
weight 352.1
*v.* burden 352.13
outweigh 352.14
overload 663.15
*adj.* corpulent 195.18
heavy 352.16
oversize 195.23
**overwhelm**
astonish 920.6
defeat 727.8
destroy 693.21
drown out 453.7
overflow 395.17
overpower 159.8
oversupply 663.14
raid 798.20

refute 506.5
sadden 872.19
subdue 764.9
submerge 320.7
**overwhelmed**
astonished 920.9
defeated 727.14
flooded 395.25
heartbroken 872.29
overwrought 857.24
**overwhelming**
astonishing 920.12
evidential 505.17
exciting 857.28
invincible 159.17
overpowering 727.17
**overwork**
*n.* overdoing 663.6
*v.* drive 716.16
overtax 663.10
work hard 716.13
**overworked**
ornate 901.12
trite 79.16
**overwrought**
exaggerated 617.4
grandiloquent 601.8
ornate 901.12
overdone 663.21
overexcited 857.24
**overzealous**
fanatical 473.32
obstinate 626.8
overeager 635.13
reckless 894.8
zealous 1028.11
**ovine** 414.49
**oviparous** 406.25
**ovoid**
*n.* oval 253.6
*adj.* egg-shaped 253.12
globular 255.9
**ovule** egg 406.15
gamete 406.12
oval 253.6
**ovum** egg 406.12
source 153.7
**owe** 840.5
**owed** due 960.7
unpaid 840.10
**owing**
attributable 155.6
due 960.7
payable 840.10
**owing to**
because of 155.9
resulting from 154.8
**owl** bird 414.33,66
omen 544.6
**owlish** 564.17
**own**
*v.* acknowledge 521.11
confess 556.7
possess 808.5
*adj.* possessed 808.8
**own accord** 762.7
**owner** 809.2
**ownership** 808.2
**own free will** 762.7
**owning**
*n.* confession 556.3
possession 808.1

*adj.* possessing 808.9
**own up** 556.7
**ox**
awkward person
734.8
beast of burden
271.6
bull 414.6
strength 159.7
**oxcart** 272.3,23
**oxidation**
burning 329.5
decay 692.6
reaction 379.5
**oxidize** corrode 692.24
heat 329.24
react chemically
379.6
**oxygen** 401.11
**oxygenate**
add gas 401.8
air 402.11
**oxygen tent**
breathing 403.18
respirator 689.37
**oxymoron**
contrariety 15.3
dilemma 731.6
impossibility 510.1
inconsistency 27.2
**oyez!** attention! 530.22
hark! 448.17
**oyster** food 308.25
fowl part 308.23
**ozone** 402.1

**P**

**pa** 170.9
**PA** 450.11
**pabulum** 308.3
**pace**
*n.* gait 273.14
rate 267.4
step 273.13
*v.* lead 292.2
measure 490.11
proceed 273.26
ride 273.33
row 275.53
walk 273.27
**pacer** 414.18
**pacesetter** 748.6
**pachyderm** 414.4
**pacific** calm 268.12
conciliatory 804.12
meek 765.15
peaceful 803.9
unbelligerent 803.10
**pacification**
moderation 163.2
peacemaking 804
truce 804.5
**pacifier**
alleviator 163.3
peacemaker 805.5
sedative 687.12
**pacifism** inaction 706.1
moderation 163.1
peaceableness 803.4
**pacifist** 803.6

**pacifistic**
moderate 163.10
unbelligerent 803.10
**pacify** calm 163.7
conciliate 804.7
quiet 268.8
regularize 59.4
**pacifying**
pacificatory 804.12
tranquilizing 163.15
**pack**
*n.* amount 28.2
bundle 74.8
film 577.10
flock 74.5
freight 271.7
group 74.3
impediment 730.6
large number 101.3
much 34.4
parachute 280.13
playing cards 878.17
set 74.12
*v.* be numerous 101.5
bundle 74.20
fill 56.7
impress 142.9
obstruct 730.12
overload 663.15
package 236.9
prearrange 641.3
put 184.14
stop 266.7
stuff 194.7
tamper with 616.17
transport 271.11
wrap 228.20
**package**
*n.* all 54.3
bundle 74.8
combination 52.1
container 236.2
*v.* assemble 74.20
enclose 236.9
wrap 228.20
**packaged**
assembled 74.21
wrapped 228.31
**package deal** all 54.3
combination 52.1
transaction 827.4
**package tour** 273.5
**packaging** 236.2
**pack animal** 271.6
**pack away** put 184.14
store 660.10
**packed** blocked 266.11
crowded 74.22
dense 354.12
full 56.11
jammed 142.16
overfull 663.20
prearranged 641.5
tampered with
616.30
teeming 101.9
**packet** bundle 74.8
ship 277.1,22
**packet boat** 561.6
**pack in** enter 302.7
thrust in 304.7
**packing** carrying 271.3

contents 194.3
packaging 236.2
placement 184.5
wadding 266.5
**packing house** 719.3
**pack off** dismiss 310.18
send away 289.3
**pack of troubles** 866.8
**pack rat** 74.15
**pact** 771.1
**pad**
*n.* abode 191.1
bedding 216.20
buffer 237.5
faint sound 452.3
foot 212.5
horse 414.18
mark 568.7
record book 570.11
safety equipment
699.3
*v.* creep 273.25
cushion 886.5
drag out 593.8
faint sound 452.15
fill 56.7
line 194.7
repeat 103.8
walk 273.26
**padded** 593.12
**padded cell** 473.14
**padding** contents 194.3
creeping 273.9
extra 41.4
redundancy 103.3
safety equipment
699.3
softening 357.5
superfluity 663.4
wadding 266.5
**paddle**
*n.* agitator 324.9
gait 273.14
instrument of punish-
ment 1011.2
oar 277.15
*v.* churn 324.10
moisten 392.12
punish 1010.15
row 275.53
walk 273.27
**paddle wheel** 285.7
**paddling** 1010.5
**paddy** 413.9
**paddy wagon** 272.10
**padlock**
*n.* restraint 760.5
*v.* close 266.6
**padre**
clergyman 1038.2
priest 1038.5
**padrone** 749.1
**paean** hymn 1032.3
praise 968.5
rejoicing 876.2
sacred music 462.16
thanks 949.2
**paella** 308.11
**paesano** 190.5
**pagan**
*n.* heathen 1025.7
irreligious 1031.11

*adj.* heathen 1025.11
  idolatrous 1033.7
  irreligious 1031.19
  unlearned 477.14
**paganism**
  heathenism 1025.4
  idolatry 1033.1
  unenlightenment
    477.4
**page**
  *n.* attendant 750.5
  book 605.12
  paper 378.6
  part of writing 55.2
  *v.* number 87.10
  summon 752.12
**pageant** display 904.4
  spectacle 446.7
  stage show 611.4
**pageantry** display 904.4
  spectacle 446.7
**paginate** 87.10
**pagination** 87.1
**pagoda** temple 1042.2
  tower 207.11
**paid** discharged 841.22
  employed 780.19
**pain**
  *n.* disease symptom
    686.8
  distress 866.5
  punishment 1010.1
  suffering 424
  unpleasantness 864.5
  *v.* discomfort 864.14
  grieve 866.17
  hurt 424.7
**pained** grieved 866.23
  hurt 424.9
**painful** hurtful 424.10
  laborious 716.18
  troublesome 731.17
  unpleasant 864.20
**painfully** terribly 34.21
  unpleasantly 864.28
  with difficulty 731.26
**pain in the neck**
  annoyance 866.2
  boring person 884.4
**pain-killer**
  depressant 423.3
  sedative 687.12
**painless** 732.12
**pains** exertion 716.1
  painstakingness 533.2
**painstaking**
  *n.* painstakingness
    533.2
  *adj.* diligent 533.11
**painstakingly** 533.15
**paint**
  *n.* art equipment
    574.19
  coating 228.12
  coloring matter 362.8
  horse 414.13
  make-up 900.11
  types of 362.23
  *v.* color 362.13
  describe 608.12
  embellish 901.8
  ornament 901.9

picture 574.20
  represent 572.6
**paintbrush** 574.19
**painter** artist 579.4
  cougar 414.27,58
  names of 579.13
**painting** art 574.5
  coloring 362.12
  graphic arts 578.1
  picture 574.15
**paint the town red**
  go on a spree 996.27
  make merry 878.26
**pair**
  *n.* deuce 90.3
  number 86.3
  playing cards 878.17
  rig 272.5
  set 20.5
  two 90.2
  *v.* assemble 74.18
  combine 52.4
  couple 90.5
  join 47.5
**paired**
  accompanying 73.9
  combined 52.6
  coupled 90.8
  joined 47.13
  married 933.22
**pairing** duality 90.1
  joining 47.1
**pair off** average 32.2
  couple 90.5
  get married 933.16
  join 52.4
**paisano** 190.5
**pajamas** 231.21,56
**pal**
  *n.* companion 928.3
  *v.* be sociable 922.16
**palace** 191.8
**paladin**
  brave person 893.8
  defender 799.7
**palaestra** arena 802.1
  gymnasium 567.11
  sports 878.8
**palatable** edible 307.31
  tasty 428.8
**palatal**
  *n.* speech sound
    594.13
  *adj.* phonetic 594.31
**palate**
  discrimination 492.1
  organ of taste 427.5
  taste 427.1
  vocal organ 594.19
**palatial**
  grandiose 904.21
  mansional 191.32
**palaver**
  *n.* chatter 596.3
  conference 597.6
  conversation 597.3
  flattery 970.1
  nonsense 547.2
  speech 594.1
  *v.* chatter 596.5
  confer 597.11
  flatter 970.5

**palazzo** 191.8
**pale**
  *n.* bounds 235.1
  enclosure 236.3
  heraldic insignia
    569.2
  region 180.2
  stake 217.6
  tract 180.4
  *v.* be afraid 891.19
  become excited
    857.17
  decolor 363.5
  enclose 236.7
  lose color 363.6
  lose distinctness
    445.4
  *adj.* colorless 363.7
  deathly 408.29
  indistinct 445.6
  soft-colored 362.21
  unhealthy 686.50
  uninteresting 883.6
  whitish 364.8
**paleface** 418.3
**paleness**
  colorlessness 363.2
  deathliness 408.12
  indistinctness 445.2
  uninterestingness
    883.1
  whiteness 364.1
**paleo-** old 123.10
  past 119.7
**paleography**
  alphabet 581.3
  handwriting 602.3
  interpretation 552.8
  linguistics 580.12
**paleolith** 123.6
**paleolithic** 123.20
**paleontology** 406.17
**palette** 574.19
**palindrome**
  inversion 220.3
  wordplay 881.8
**palinode** poem 609.6
  recantation 628.3
**palisade**
  *n.* fortification 799.4
  precipice 213.3
  stake 217.6
  *v.* enclose 236.7
  fortify 799.9
**pall**
  *n.* cover 228.2,38
  graveclothes 410.14
  secrecy 614.3
  *v.* be tedious 884.5
  satiate 664.4
**palladium** 699.3
**pallbearer** 410.7
**pallet** 216.20,33
**palliate**
  extenuate 1006.12
  moderate 163.6
  qualify 507.3
  relieve 886.5
**palliative**
  *n.* alleviator 163.3
  extenuation 1006.5
  remedy 687.10

*adj.* alleviative 163.16
  justifying 1006.13
  qualifying 507.7
  relieving 886.9
  remedial 687.40
**pallid** colorless 363.7
  terrified 891.34
  uninteresting 883.6
**pallor**
  colorlessness 363.2
  complexion 362.1
  deathliness 408.12
  uninterestingness
    883.1
**palm**
  *n.* grasping organ
    813.4
  supremacy 36.3
  trophy 916.3
  *v.* steal 824.13
  take 822.13
  touch 425.6
**palmate** 299.8
**palmistry** 543.2,15
**palm off on** 963.7
**palm oil** 818.5
**Palm Sunday** 1040.15
**palmy** 728.13
**palooka** 800.2
**palp** 425.4
**palpable**
  manifest 555.8
  substantial 3.6
  touchable 425.11
  weighable 352.19
**palpate** 425.6
**palpitant**
  pulsating 323.18
  staccato 455.7
**palpitate**
  be excited 857.16
  flutter 324.12
  make staccato sounds
    455.4
  pulsate 323.12
**palpitating** 323.18
**palpitation**
  cardiovascular disease
    686.17
  excitement 857.4
  flutter 324.4
  pulsation 323.3
  staccato sound 455.1
  trepidation 891.5
**palsied** aged 126.18
  diseased 686.57
  shaking 324.17
**palsy**
  nervous disorder
    686.23
  paralysis 686.25
  shaking 324.2
**palsy-walsy** 927.19
**palter** equivocate 483.9
  prevaricate 613.7
**paltry** base 915.12
  inferior 680.9
  meager 662.10
  selfish 978.6
  trifling 673.18
**paludal** 400.3
**pampas** grassland 411.8

plain 387.1
pamper foster 785.16
  indulge 759.6
pampered 759.9
pampering 759.3
pamphlet 605.9
pan
  *n.* face 240.4
  types of 193.9
  *v.* cook 330.4
  criticize 969.14
  mine 383.14
  photograph 577.14
  ridicule 967.8
Pan fertility god 165.5
  forest god 1014.21
panacea 687.3
panache feather 230.16
  flamboyance 904.3
pancake
  *n.* griddlecake 308.44
  *v.* fly 278.52
panchromatic 577.17
pancreas 309.8
pancreatic 312.8
pandect
  abridgment 607.1
  law code 998.5
  treatise 606.1
pandemic
  *n.* epidemic 686.4
  *adj.* contagious 686.58
  prevalent 79.12
pandemonium
  bedlam 62.5
  noise 453.3
  violence 162.2
Pandemonium
  dystopia 535.11
  hell 1019.1
pander
  *n.* procurer 989.18
  *v.* be unchaste 989.21
pandering 989.8
pander to
  cater to 907.7
  help 785.18
  serve 750.13
pandit 565.1
Pandora's box 731.3
pandowdy 308.40
pane glass 339.2
  layer 227.2
  window 265.8
panegyric
  *n.* praise 968.5
  *adj.* approbatory
    968.16
panel
  *n.* forum 755.3
  jury 1002.7
  layer 227.2
  litigant 1004.11
  meeting 74.2
  partition 237.5
  *v.* impanel a jury
    1004.15
  partition 237.8
paneling
  types of 378.10
  wood 378.3
panelist 599.4

panel show 611.4
pang distress 866.5
  pain 424.2
pangs of conscience
  873.2
panhandle 774.15
panhandler
  beggar 774.8
  nonworker 708.10
panhandling 774.6
panic
  *n.* fear 891.1
  financial crisis 833.22
  funny story 881.6
  nervousness 859.1
  *v.* be frightened
    891.20
  defeat 727.9
  frighten 891.24
panicked
  defeated 727.14
  panicky 891.35
panicky
  cowardly 892.10
  nervous 859.10
  panic-prone 891.35
panning
  *n.* ridicule 967.1
  *adj.* ridiculing 967.12
panoply armor 799.3
  throng 74.4
panorama
  picture 574.12
  spectacle 446.7
  view 446.6
panoramic 76.7
pan out 154.5
panpipe 465.9
pan shot 577.8
pansy
  homosexual 419.16
  weakling 160.6
pant
  *n.* breathing 403.18
  *v.* become exhausted
    717.5
  be excited 857.16
  be hot 328.22
  breathe 403.24
  pulsate 323.12
  utter 594.26
  wish for 634.16
pantaloon
  clothing 231.18,56
  old man 127.2
Pantaloon 612.10
pantheism
  heresy 1025.2
  philosophy 500.4
  religion 1020.5
pantheistic
  philosophy 500.9
  religious 1020.24
  unorthodox 1025.9
pantheon
  temple 1042.2
  the gods 1014.1
panther 414.27,58
panting
  *n.* breathlessness
    717.3
  excitement 857.4

*adj.* breathing 403.29
  breathless 717.10
  eager 635.9
  precipitate 709.10
pantomime
  *n.* actor 612.2
  gesture 568.14
  impersonation 572.2
  stage show 611.4
  *v.* act 611.34
  gesture 568.21
  impersonate 572.9
pantry 660.8
pants
  clothing 231.18,58
  types of 231.56
pantywaist
  effeminate male
    421.10
  weakling 160.6
pap diet 309.11
  father 170.9
  food 308.3
  nipple 256.6
  semiliquid 389.5
papa father 170.9
  pope 1038.9
papacy
  mastership 739.7
  pontificate 1037.6
papal 1037.15
papalism 1020.7
paper
  *n.* document 570.5
  freeloader 850.3
  free pass 850.2
  material 378.6
  negotiable instru-
    ment 835.11
  newspaper 605.11
  thinness 205.7
  treatise 606.1
  types of 378.13
  white 364.2
  written matter 602.10
  *v.* cover 228.23
paperback 605.1
paper profits 811.3
papers archives 570.2
  citizenship 189.3
  document 570.5
paper tiger 903.7
paperweight 352.6
papery
  deteriorated 692.37
  frail 160.14
  thin 205.16
papilla 256.6
papillary 256.18
papilloma 256.3
papist
  *n.* Catholic 1020.18
  *adj.* Catholic 1020.28
  papal 1037.15
papoose 125.7
pappy
  *n.* father 170.9
  *adj.* insipid 430.2
papule 686.35
papyrus 602.11
par
  *n.* average 32.1

equality 30.1
  stock price 834.9
  *adj.* equal 30.7
parable 608.7
parabola 252.2
parabolic(al)
  curved 252.13
  fictional 608.17
parachute
  *n.* aviation 280.13
  life preserver 701.5
  *v.* bail out 278.56
  descend 316.5
  dive 320.6
parachute jump
  dive 320.1
  parachute 280.13
parachutist 279.8
parade
  *n.* display 904.4
  path 657.3
  procession 71.3
  spectacle 446.7
  walk 273.12
  *v.* file 71.7
  flaunt 904.17
  indicate 555.5
  march 273.29
  walk 273.28
parade ground 802.1
paradiddle 455.1
paradigm model 25.1
  morphology 582.3
paradisal
  heavenly 1018.13
  idealized 535.23
paradise garden 413.10
  happiness 865.2
  park 878.14
  preserve 701.6
  theater part 611.20
  utopia 535.11
Paradise
  Heaven 1018.1
  the future 121.2
paradisiac(al)
  heavenly 1018.13
  pleasant 863.8
paradox
  contrariety 15.3
  dilemma 731.6
  impossibility 510.1
  inconsistency 27.2
paradoxical
  impossible 510.7
  inconsistent 27.8
  self-contradictory
    15.8
paraffin fuel 331.1
  illuminant 335.20
  petroleum 380.4,11
paragon
  beautiful person
    900.8
  good person 985.4
  ideal 25.4
  pattern of perfection
    677.4
  superior 36.4
  the best 674.8
paragraph
  *n.* book part 605.13

part of writing 55.2
phrase 585.1
treatise 606.1
*v.* phrase 588.4
**parallel**
*n.* entrenchment 799.5
equal 30.4
latitude 180.3
likeness 20.3
map 654.4
parallel line 218.2
*v.* agree 26.6
be comparable 491.7
be parallel 218.4
compare 491.4
equal 30.5
relate 9.6
resemble 20.7
*adj.* accompanying 73.9
analogous 20.11
comparable 491.8
equidistant 218.6
related 9.9
**parallel bars** 716.7
**paralleling**
analogous 20.11
parallel 218.6
**parallelism**
accompaniment 73.1
agreement 26.1
comparison 491.1
equality 30.1
equidistance 218
similarity 20.1
symmetry 248.1
**parallelograph** 218.3
**paralogism**
specious argument 483.3
syllogism 482.6
**paralysis**
disease symptom 686.8
inaction 706.1
paralyzation 686.25
**paralytic**
*n.* cripple 686.42
*adj.* diseased 686.57
do-nothing 706.6
**paralyze** astonish 920.6
deaden 856.8
render powerless 158.11
stupefy 423.4
terrify 891.25
**paralyzed**
disabled 158.16
do-nothing 706.6
drunk 996.33
terrified 891.34
**paralyzing** 891.37
**paramedic**
hospital staff 688.14
parachutist 279.8
**parameter**
bounds 235.1
condition 507.2
measure 490.2
**paramount**
*n.* chief 672.10

master 749.1
potentate 749.7
*adj.* best 674.18
chief 36.14
dominant 741.18
principal 672.23
top 211.10
**paramountcy**
importance 672.1
superexcellence 674.2
supremacy 36.3
**paramour** lover 931.11
mistress 989.17
**paranoia**
dissociation 690.27
mental disorder 690.17
psychosis 473.4
**paranoid**
*n.* psychotic 473.16
*adj.* psychotic 473.27
**paranymph**
assistant 787.6
deputy 781.1
supporter 787.9
wedding attendant 933.5
**parapet** barrier 730.5
fortification 799.4
**paraphernalia**
belongings 810.2
equipment 659.4
**paraphilia** 419.12
**paraphrase**
*n.* imitation 22.3
interpretation 552.3
*v.* rephrase 552.13
**paraplegia** 686.25
**paraplegic** 686.42
**paraprofessional**
aide 787.6
teacher 565.5
**parapsychology**
psychics 1034.4
psychology 690.1
**parasite** animal 414.40
attendant 73.6
bloodsucker 414.41
follower 293.2
nonworker 708.10
plant 411.4
sycophant 907.4
**parasitic**
commensal 13.15
indolent 708.18
obsequious 907.13
rapacious 822.26
symbiotic 177.4
**parasitism**
commensality 13.5
obsequiousness 907.2
symbiosis 177.1
**parasol** shade 338.1,8
umbrella 228.7
**paratrooper** 279.8
**paratroops** army 800.22
elite troops 800.14
**parboiled** 330.6
**Parcae** 640.3
**parcel**
*n.* amount 28.2
bundle 74.8

part 55.1
real estate 810.7
several 101.2
*v.* bundle 74.20
divide 49.18
package 236.9
quantify 28.4
share 816.6
**parceled** 816.12
**parceling** 816.1
**parcel of land**
field 413.9
tract 180.4
**parcel out**
apportion 816.8
distribute 60.9
divide 49.18
**parcel post** 604.5
**parch** be hot 328.22
burn 329.24
dry 393.6
shrink 198.9
**parched** burned 329.30
dried 393.9
shrunk 198.13
thirsty 634.26
**parchment**
brittleness 360.2
document 570.5
dryness 393.2
manuscript 602.11,29
written matter 602.10
**pardner**
companion 928.3
partner 787.2
**pardon**
*n.* acquittal 1007.1
excuse 947.2
pity 944.1
*v.* acquit 1007.4
forgive 947.3
have pity 944.4
**pardonable** 1006.14
**pardoned** 947.7
**pare** cheapen 849.6
cut off 42.10
peel 232.8
reduce 39.7
sever 49.11
**paregoric**
narcotic 687.12
sedative 687.12
**parent**
*n.* originator 153.4
progenitor 170.8
*adj.* ancestral 170.13
**parentage** 170.1
**parental**
ancestral 170.13
loving 931.25
protecting 699.23
**parenthesis**
discontinuity 72.1
interjection 237.2
inversion 220.3
**parenthesize**
bracket 236.8
punctuate 586.16
**parenthetic(al)**
discontinuous 72.4
incidental 129.11
interjectional 237.9

irrelevant 10.6
**paresis** paralysis 686.25
venereal disease 686.16
**par excellence** 36.16
**parfait** 308.46
**parfum** 436.2
**parget** color 362.13
plaster 228.25
**pariah** odd person 85.4
outcast 926.4
recluse 924.5
**parietal**
enclosing 236.11
partitioned 237.11
**pari-mutuel**
gambling 515.4
pari-mutuel machine 515.13
**paring** flake 227.3
piece 55.3
refuse 669.4
remnant 43.1
**parish** diocese 1037.8
district 180.5
laity 1039.1
**parishioner** 1039.2
**parity** equality 30.1
similarity 20.1
stock price 834.9
**park**
*n.* armory 801.2
commons 878.14
enclosure 236.3
grassland 411.8
green 411.7
preserve 701.6
woodland 411.11
*v.* place 184.11
settle 184.16
**Parkinson's disease** 686.23
**parkway** 657.6
**parlance** diction 588.1
language 580.1
**parlay**
*n.* wager 515.3
*v.* bet 515.20
increase 38.4
**parley**
*n.* advice 754.1
conference 597.6
peace offer 804.2
*v.* confer 597.11
**parliament** 742.1
**parliamentarianism** 741.8
**parliamentary**
governmental 741.17
legislative 742.19
**parlor**
living room 192.5
workplace 719.1
**parlor car**
railway car 272.14
train room 192.10
**parlous** 697.9
**parochial**
exclusive 77.8
local 180.9
narrow-minded 527.10

parochialism
  exclusiveness 77.3
  narrow-mindedness
    527.1
parochial school 567.10
parody
  *n.* humor 881.1
  imitation 22.3
  misrepresentation
    573.2
  paraphrase 22.1
  ridicule 967.6
  *v.* misrepresent 573.3
  ridicule 967.11
parol
  *n.* word of mouth
    594.3
  *adj.* speech 594.30
parole
  *n.* language 580.1
  promise 770.1
  release 763.2
  speech 594.1
  utterance 594.3
  *v.* release 763.5
parolee 761.11
paroxysm anger 952.8
  emotional outburst
    857.8
  fit 162.5
  frenzy 473.7
  pain 424.2
  seizure 686.5
  spasm 324.6
parquet check 374.4
  floor 212.3
  theater part 611.20
parricide 409.3
parrot
  *n.* conformist 82.2
  imitator 22.4
  *v.* imitate 22.6
  memorize 537.17
  repeat 103.7
parrotlike 103.14
parrotry 22.2
parry dodge 631.8
  equivocate 483.9
  fend off 799.10
  prevaricate 613.7
  refute 506.5
parrying
  equivocation 483.5
  prevarication 613.4
parse analyze 48.7
  grammaticize 586.16
parsimonious
  economical 851.6
  meager 662.10
  niggardly 852.7
parsimony
  economy 851.1
  meagerness 662.2
  niggardliness 852
parsing analysis 48.2
  grammar 586.1
parson 1038.2
parsonage house 191.6
  pastorage 1042.7
part
  *n.* allotment 816.5
  amount 28.2

book part 605.13
component 58.2
contents 194.1
district 180.1
estate 810.4
function 656.3
length 202.3
music division 462.24
music score 462.28
portion 55
role 611.11
situation 7.5
voice part 462.22
*v.* apportion 816.6
die 408.19
disband 75.8
divorce 935.5
interspace 201.3
open 265.12
part company 49.19
separate 49.9
*adj.* half 92.5
incomplete 57.4
partial 55.7
*adv.* partly 55.8
to a degree 35.10
partake eat 307.18
  participate 815.5
  take 822.13
partaking
  *n.* participation 815.1
  sociability 922.6
  *adj.* participating
    815.8
part and parcel 58.2
part company
  disband 75.8
  fall out 795.10
  separate 49.19
parted 201.6
parterre
  horizontal 214.3
  theater part 611.20
parthenogenesis 169.6
Parthian shot
  gibe 967.2
  remark 594.4
  sequel 67.1
partial
  *n.* tone 450.2
  *adj.* half 92.5
  imperfect 678.4
  incomplete 57.4
  part 55.7
  partisan 788.19
  prejudiced 527.12
  unjust 977.11
partiality
  inclination 634.3
  one-sidedness 977.3
  partisanism 788.13
  preference 637.5
  prejudice 527.3
partially
  imperfectly 678.5
  incompletely 57.6
  partly 55.8
  to a degree 35.10
  unjustly 977.13
partial to
  desirous of 634.22
  fond of 931.28

partible 49.26
participant
  *n.* participator 815.4
  *adj.* participating
    815.8
participate 815.5
participating 815.8
participation
  inclusion 76.1
  partaking 815
  sociability 922.6
participator 815.4
participial 586.17
participle 586.3
particle
  minute thing 196.7
  part of speech 586.3
  piece 55.3
  small amount 35.2
  subatomic 326.24
parti-color
  *n.* variegation 374.1
  *adj.* variegated 374.9
particular
  *n.* citation 505.6
  event 151.2
  instance 8.3
  part 55.1
  the facts 1.4
  the specific 80.3
  *adj.* classificational
    61.7
  detailed 8.9
  fastidious 896.9
  meticulous 533.12
  proportionate 816.13
  selective 637.23
  special 80.12
particularity
  characteristic 80.4
  circumstantiality 8.4
  fastidiousness 896.1
  individuality 80
  meticulousness 533.3
  unity 89.1
particularization
  circumstantiation 8.5
  description 608.1
  differentiation 16.4
  logic 482.3
  specialization 80.7
particularize
  be accurate 516.10
  circumstantiate 8.6
  cite 505.14
  differentiate 16.6
  expatiate 593.7
  specialize 80.9
particularly
  chiefly 36.17
  exceptionally 34.20
  fastidiously 896.14
  fully 8.13
  singly 89.13
  specially 80.15
parting
  *n.* death 408.1
  departure 301.1
  disbandment 75.3
  good-by 301.4
  separation 49.1
  *adj.* departing 301.19

separating 49.25
parting shot gibe 967.2
  sequel 67.1
partisan
  *n.* follower 293.2
  friend 928.1
  guerrilla 800.15
  party member 744.27
  supporter 787.9
  *adj.* factional 788.19
  factious 795.17
  party 744.44
  prejudiced 527.12
  unjust 977.11
partisanism
  cliquism 788.13
  injustice 977.3
  partisanship 744.25
  politics 744.1
  religion 1020.4
partisan politics 744.1
partition
  *n.* apportionment
    816.1
  divider 92.3
  dividing wall 237.5
  separation 49.1
  *v.* apportion 816.6
  compartmentalize
    49.18
  divide 237.8
partitioned
  separate 49.20
  walled 237.11
partly
  *adj.* half 92.5
  *adv.* partially 55.8
  to a degree 35.10
part music 462.17
partner
  *n.* accompanier 73.4
  associate 787.2
  companion 928.3
  participator 815.4
  spouse 933.7
  *v.* assemble 74.18
  cooperate 786.3
  join 52.4
partner in crime 787.3
partnership
  affiliation 786.2
  association 788.1
  companionship 73.2
  company 788.9
  participation 815.1
part of speech 586.3
parts airplane 280.16
  airship 280.19
  auto 272.25
  computer 349.32
  contents 194.1
  district 180.1
  electrical 342.36
  engine 348.27
  garment 231.66
  radar 346.20
  radio receiver 344.30
  radio transmitter
    344.31
  ship 277.26
  talent 733.4

master 749.1
play backer 611.31
protector 699.5
provider 659.6
supporter 787.9
**patronage**
clientele 828.3
custom 827.6
fosterage 785.4
political patronage
744.36
protectorship 699.2
recommendation
968.4
**patronize**
be arrogant 912.8
finance 836.15
sponsor 785.15
trade with 827.16
**patronizing**
*n.* arrogance 912.1
*adj.* arrogant 912.9
snobbish 912.14
**patroon** 749.1
**patsy**
credulous person
502.4
dupe 620.1
scapegoat 149.3
**patter**
*n.* acting 611.9
faint sound 452.3
jargon 580.9
rain 394.1
sales talk 829.5
staccato sound 455.1
*v.* act 611.34
chatter 596.5
faint sound 452.15
gab 594.20
make staccato sounds
455.4
pound 283.14
rain 394.9
speak 580.16
**pattern** behavior 737.1
diagram 654.3
form 246.1
gestalt 690.39
good person 985.4
habit 642.4
harmonics 463.11
idea 479.2
measure 490.2
model 25.1
motif 901.7
original 23.2
structure 245.1
**paucity** fewness 102.1
scarcity 662.3
**paul** 1022.2
**paunch** 193.3
**paunchy** 195.18
**pauper** 838.4
**pauperism** 838.2
**pauperize** 838.6
**pauperized**
ill-provided 662.12
indigent 838.8
**pause**
*v.* delay 132.2
demur 623.2

discontinuity 72.2
harmonics 463.12
interim 109.1
juncture 144.4
music 463.21
respite 711.2
rest 144.3
speech 594.10
*v.* be irresolute 627.7
demur 623.4
hesitate 144.9
recess 109.3
take a rest 711.8
**pave** 228.22
**paved** 228.31
**pavement**
bottom 212.3
building material
378.2
flooring 228.9,43
foundation 216.6
road 657.7
**pave the way**
facilitate 732.6
prepare the way
720.12
**pavilion** 191.10
**paw**
*n.* foot 212.5
grasping organ 813.4
*v.* touch 425.6
**pawky** cautious 895.8
cunning 735.12
fastidious 896.10
shrewd 467.15
**pawn**
*n.* chessman 878.18
inferior 37.2
instrument 658.3
pledge 772.2
*v.* borrow 821.3
pledge 772.10
**pawnbroker**
broker 830.9
lender 820.3
lending institution
820.4
**pawned** 772.12
**pawnshop** 820.4
**paw print** 568.7
**pax** peace 803.1
rite 1040.4
sacred article 1040.11
**pax vobiscum!**
farewell! 301.23
peace! 803.11
**pay**
*n.* punishment 1010.1
remuneration 841.4
*v.* be of use 665.17
be profitable 811.12
do 705.6
experience 151.8
finance 836.15
overpay 848.8
punish 1010.11
recompense 841.10
retaliate 955.5
spend 843.5
yield 844.4
**payable** due 960.7
owed 840.10

**pay as you go**
*v.* pay 841.17
*adv.* in cash 841.25
**pay attention**
attend to 530.5
care 533.6
court 932.19
pay heed 530.8
**pay back**
compensate 33.4
interchange 150.4
make restitution
823.5
repay 841.11
retaliate 955.5
**pay dirt** 383.7
**payee** 819.3
**payer** 841.9
**paying**
*n.* payment 841.1
*adj.* gainful 811.15
remunerative 841.21
**paying guest**
lodger 190.8
tenant 809.4
**payload**
aviation 278.30
freight 271.7
load 194.2
rocketry 281.3
warhead 801.10
**paymaster**
financial officer
836.11
payer 841.9
**payment**
expenditure 843.1
incentive 648.7
pay 841
punishment 1010.1
remuneration 841.4
**pay no attention to**
be inattentive 531.2
disobey 767.6
slight 966.6
**payoff** bribe 651.2
end 70.1
payment 841.1
result 154.2
**pay off**
be of use 665.17
be profitable 811.12
bribe 651.3
drift off course
275.29
pay in full 841.13
retaliate 955.5
sail 275.23
yield 844.4
**payola** 651.2
**pay one's respects to**
936.12
**pay out**
apportion 816.8
pay 841.14
punish 1010.11
settle with 841.12
spend 843.5
**payroll** 841.4
**pay the piper**
be punished 1010.23
pay 841.18

**PBX** 560.8
**PDQ** 131.15
**pea** 411.4
**peabrain** 471.4
**pea-brained** 469.13
**peace**
*n.* accord 794.1
agreement 26.1
comfortableness
887.2
order 59.1
peacefulness 803
quiescence 268.1
silence 451.1
truce 804.5
*interj.* peace be with
you! 803.11
silence! 451.14
**peaceable** calm 268.12
friendly 927.14
moderate 163.10
pacific 803.9
unbelligerent 803.10
weak 765.15
**peace and quiet** 803.2
**peace be with you!**
farewell! 301.23
peace! 803.11
**peaceful** calm 268.12
comfortable 887.11
composed 858.12
homelike 191.33
in accord 794.3
moderate 163.10
pacific 803.9
**peacefully**
comfortably 887.14
quietly 268.18
**peacefulness**
comfortableness
887.2
composure 858.2
peace 803.2
quiescence 268.1
**peace lover** 803.6
**peace-loving** 803.10
**peacemaker**
make-peace 805.5
pacifier 163.3
pacifist 803.6
**peacemongering** 804.1
**peace offering**
atonement 1012.1
gift 818.4
pacification 804.2
sacrifice 1032.7
**peace officer** 699.15
**peace of mind**
composure 858.2
contentment 868.1
peace of heart 803.3
**peace pipe** 804.2
**peacetime**
*n.* peace 803.1
*adj.* pacific 803.9
**peach**
*n.* beautiful person
900.8
good thing 674.7
*v.* divulge 556.6
inform on 557.12
*adj.* orange 369.2

peach fuzz beard 230.8
fine texture 351.3
peachy downy 230.27
excellent 674.13
peacock
n. bird 414.33
male animal 420.8
strutter 904.10
variegation 374.6
v. pose 903.13
strut 904.15
peacocky
conceited 909.11
strutting 904.23
peak
n. business cycle 827.9
completion 56.5
culmination 677.3
mountain 207.8
pointed projection 258.4
speech sound 594.13
summit 211.2
wave 395.14
v. billow 395.22
fail 686.45
top 211.9
peaked thin 205.20
topped 211.12
unhealthy 686.50
peal
n. boom 456.4
loud sound 453.4
ringing 454.3
v. blare 453.9
boom 456.9
din 453.6
ring 454.8
pealing
n. ringing 454.3
adj. loud 453.10
ringing 454.12
thundering 456.12
peanut 308.38,52
peanut gallery
observation post 439.8
theater part 611.20
peanuts 673.4
pearl
n. drop 255.3
good person 985.1
good thing 674.5
white 364.2,11
adj. gray 366.4
whitish 364.8
pearliness
iridescence 335.18
variegation 374.2
whiteness 364.1
pearly gray 366.4
iridescent 335.37
soft-colored 362.21
variegated 374.10
whitish 364.8
peasant
agriculturist 413.5
countryman 919.8
vulgar person 898.6
peasantry 919.1
peashooter 801.5
peas in a pod 20.5

pea soup 404.2
peat 331.1,10
pebble
n. pebblestone 384.4
small amount 35.2
v. cover 228.22
pebbly granular 361.12
stony 384.11
peccadillo 982.2
peccant bad 675.7
decayed 692.41
diseased 686.56
erroneous 518.16
evil 981.16
guilty 983.3
unhealthful 684.5
peck
n. abundance 34.3
much 34.4
tap 283.6
v. eat 307.24
nag 969.16
tap 283.15
pecking order 61.4
pectoral 256.18
peculate 667.4
peculiar
characteristic 80.13
classificational 61.7
differentiative 16.9
eccentric 474.4
indicative 568.23
odd 85.11
other 16.8
personal 417.12
peculiarity
characteristic 80.4
eccentricity 474.1
habit 642.4
mannerism 903.2
oddity 85.3
sign 568.2
style 588.2
peculiarize 80.9
peculiarly
characteristically 80.17
chiefly 36.17
exceptionally 34.20
oddly 85.19
pecuniary 835.30
pedagogical
educational 562.20
teacherish 565.12
pedagogue 565.1
pedagogy 562.1
pedal
n. lever 287.4
music 465.20
v. push 285.10
ride 273.32
adj. footed 212.9
pedant
bombastic person 601.5
bookish person 476.5
conformist 82.2
pedantic
affected 903.18
book-learned 475.22
conformist 82.6
formal 646.7

grandiloquent 601.8
pedagogical 565.12
studious 564.17
pedantry
affectation 903.5
formalism 646.2
scholarship 475.5
peddle 829.9
peddler 830.6
peddling 829.2
pedestal 216.8
pedestrian
n. walker 274.6
adj. prosaic 610.5
traveling 273.35
uninteresting 883.6
unskillful 734.15
pediatric 688.18
pediatrician 688.8
pedicel base 216.8
plant stem 411.19
pedigree
genealogy 170.5
register 570.9
pee
n. urine 311.5
v. urinate 311.14
peek
n. glance 439.4
v. look 439.13
pry 528.4
peekaboo 339.4
peel
n. hull 228.16
layer 227.2
rind 229.2
stronghold 799.6
v. cut off 42.10
pare 232.8
tear apart 49.14
peeled 232.14
peel off
come apart 49.8
fly 278.46
peep
n. glance 439.4
v. bird sound 460.5
look 439.13
pry 528.4
reconnoiter 485.27
peepers eye 439.9
spectacles 443.2
peephole hole 265.4
observation post 439.8
Peeping Tom 528.2
peer
n. equal 30.4
nobleman 918.4
v. be curious 528.3
examine 485.23
investigate 485.22
look 439.13
peerage 918.2
peerless best 674.18
matchless 36.15
perfect 677.6
peeve
n. complaint 875.4
grudge 929.5
hated thing 930.3
v. annoy 866.13

provoke 952.22
peeved annoyed 866.21
provoked 952.25
peevish
discontented 869.5
ill-humored 951.21
plaintive 875.16
peewee
n. child 125.3
dwarf 196.6
little thing 196.4
adj. tiny 196.11
peg
n. degree 29.1
drink 307.4
knob 256.3
stake 217.6
stopper 266.4
swig 996.6
throw 285.4
tooth 258.5
v. drudge 716.14
fasten 47.8
peg away 707.15
persevere 625.3
plod 270.7
recognize 537.12
restrain 760.10
throw 285.11
walk 273.27
pejorative 971.13
pelagic nautical 275.57
oceanic 397.8
pelf gain 811.3
money 835.1
wealth 837.1
pellagra 686.10
pellet
n. ball 255.2
shot 801.13
types of 255.14
v. attack 798.27
pellicle coating 228.12
layer 227.2
membrane 229.3
pell-mell
n. commotion 62.4
excitement 857.3
adv. hastily 709.12
pellucid
intelligible 548.10
lucid 335.31
polished 589.6
translucent 340.5
transparent 339.4
pelt
n. hair 230.2
hit 283.4
skin 229.1
types of 229.8
v. attack 798.27
pound 283.14
rain 394.9
shoot 285.13
throw 285.11
pen
n. composition 602.2
enclosure 236.3
farm 413.8
place of confinement 761.7
prison 761.8

writer 602.13
writing 602.1,30
*v.* confine 761.12
enclose 236.5
write 602.19
**penal** 1010.25
**penal code** 998.5
**penal colony** 761.8
**penalize**
bring in a verdict
1004.19
condemn 1008.3
handicap 1009.4
punish 1010.10
**penalty** discount 847.1
impediment 730.6
legal decision 1004.9
penalization 1009
punishment 1010.1
**penance**
atonement 1012.3
penalty 1009.1
penitence 873.4
sacrament 1040.5
**pen-and-ink**
picture 574.14
writing 602.1
**penates**
household gods
191.30
spirits 1014.22
**pence** 835.8
**penchant**
inclination 634.3
tendency 174.1
**pencil**
*n.* art equipment
574.19
artistic style 574.9
ray 335.5
*v.* mark 568.19
picture 574.20
write 602.19
**penciled** 602.22
**pencil pushing** 602.1
**pencraft**
handwriting 602.3
writing 602.2
**pend**
be uncertain 514.11
hang 215.6
**pendant** adjunct 41.1
hanger 215.4
likeness 20.3
types of 215.13
**pendency** 215
**pendent** hanging 215.9
uncertain 514.17
**pending**
*adj.* overhanging
215.11
pendent 215.9
uncertain 514.17
*prep.* during 105.14
**pendulous**
oscillating 323.15
pendent 215.9
**pendulum**
continuity 71.2
oscillator 323.9
**penetrable**
accessible 509.8

intelligible 548.9
permeable 265.22
vulnerable 697.16
**penetrate** affect 855.16
be remembered
537.14
be understood 548.5
chill 333.10
enter 302.8
infuse 44.12
insert 304.3
perforate 265.16
pervade 186.7
see through 488.8
understand 548.8
**penetrating**
acrimonious 161.13
caustic 939.21
cold 333.14
deep-felt 855.26
eloquent 600.11
exciting 857.29
intense 159.20
pungent 433.6
sagacious 467.16
shrill 458.14
strong-smelling
435.10
**penetration**
discrimination 492.2
entrance 302.1
infusion 44.2
insertion 304.1
perforation 265.3
permeation 186.3
sagacity 467.4
**penicillin** 687.60
**peninsula**
continent 386.1
point of land 256.8
**peninsular** 256.19
**penis** 419.10
**penitence**
apology 1012.2
penance 1012.3
repentance 873.4
**penitent**
*n.* confessor 873.5
*adj.* repentant 873.9
**penitential**
atoning 1012.7
compensating 33.6
repentant 873.9
**penitentiary**
clergyman 1038.9
priest 1038.5
prison 761.8
**penmanship** 602.3
**pen name** 583.8
**pennant** 569.6
**pennate**
feathered 230.28
fluffy 230.27
**penned**
enclosed 236.10
written 602.22
**penniless** 838.9
**penny**
British money 835.8
US money 835.7
**penny-a-liner** 602.16

**penny-pinching**
*n.* stinginess 852.3
*adj.* stingy 852.9
**penny-wise and pound-**
**foolish**
parsimonious 852.7
prodigal 854.8
**pennyworth**
bargain 849.3
worth 846.3
**penology** 1010.1
**pen pal** 604.9
**penscript**
handwriting 602.3
written matter 602.10
**pension** inn 191.16
subsidy 818.8
**pensioned** 784.3
**pensioner**
beneficiary 819.4
dependent 764.6
hireling 750.3
student 566.7
**pension off**
cause to resign 784.2
depose 783.4
discard 668.8
dismiss 310.19
subsidize 818.19
**pensive**
abstracted 532.11
melancholy 872.23
thoughtful 478.21
**pensively** sadly 872.34
thoughtfully 478.23
**pensiveness**
dreaminess 535.8
melancholy 872.5
thoughtfulness 478.3
**penstock**
floodgate 396.11
trough 396.3
**pent(a)–** 99.17
**pentagonal** 251.10
**Pentagonese** 580.10
**pentane** 331.1
**Pentecost**
holy day 1040.15
Jewish holiday
1040.16
**penthouse**
apartment 191.14
house 191.6
roof 228.6
**pent-up**
confined 761.19
enclosed 236.10
restrained 760.13
**penumbra** 337.3
**penurious** 852.8
**penury** 838.2
**pen yan** 687.12
**peon** peasant 919.8
retainer 750.1
slave 764.7
sycophant 907.3
**peonage** service 750.12
servility 907.1
subjection 764.1
**people**
*n.* family 11.5
folk 11.4

kinsmen 11.2
laity 1039.1
persons 417.2
population 190.1
race 418
the populace 919.2
*v.* populate 188.9
settle 184.16
**peopled** 188.12
**peopling**
population 188.2
settlement 184.6
**pep** eloquence 600.4
liveliness 707.2
vim 161.2
**pepless** 708.19
**pepper**
*n.* condiments 308.55
vim 161.2
*v.* fire upon 798.22
flavor 428.7
mark 568.19
shoot 285.13
sprinkle 75.6
variegate 374.7
**pepper-and-salt** 374.12
**peppered** holey 265.20
spotted 374.13
sprinkled 75.10
**peppery**
hot-tempered 951.25
pungent 433.7
**pep pill** 687.9
**peppy** eloquent 600.12
energetic 161.12
lively 707.17
**pep rally** 648.4
**pepsin** 309.9,25
**pep talk**
incitement 648.4
speech 599.2
**peptic** 309.20
**peptic ulcer** 686.27
**peptide** 309.6,23
**pep up** 161.9
**per** by means of 658.7
for each 80.20
in conformity with
82.9
**perambulate**
promenade 273.28
traverse 273.19
walk 273.26
**perambulator** 272.6
**per annum** 80.19
**per capita** each 80.19
proportionate 816.13
**perceivable**
manifest 555.8
visible 444.6
**perceive** detect 488.5
feel emotion 855.11
know 475.12
see 439.12
sense 422.8
understand 548.8
**perceived** 475.26
**percent** 86.6
**percentage**
benefit 665.4
discount 847.1
estate 810.4

expedience 670.1
gain 811.3
incentive 648.7
part 55.1
portion 816.5
ratio 86.6
**perceptible**
knowable 475.25
manifest 555.8
measurable 490.15
visible 444.6
**perceptibly**
manifestly 555.14
measurably 490.16
visibly 444.8
**perception**
cognizance 475.2
discrimination 492.2
idea 479.1
sagacity 467.4
sensation 422.1
vision 439.1
**perceptive**
discriminating 492.8
knowing 475.15
sagacious 467.16
sensible 422.13
**perch**
*n.* birdhouse 191.23
support 216.5
*v.* descend 316.7
inhabit 188.7
rest on 216.22
settle 184.16
sit 268.10
**perchance**
by chance 156.19
possibly 509.9
**percipient**
knowing 475.15
sagacious 467.16
**percolate**
be damp 392.11
be learned 564.7
exude 303.15
filter in 302.10
liquefy 391.5
operate 164.7
refine 681.22
soak 392.13
sorb 306.13
trickle 395.18
**percolation**
entrance 302.1
liquefaction 391.1
outflow 303.6
refinement 681.4
seepage 306.6
soaking 392.7
trickle 395.2
**percolator** 681.13
**percussion**
concussion 162.8
impact 283.3
percussion instrument
465.18
**percussionist** 464.10
**percussive**
*n.* percussion instru-
ment 465.18
*adj.* crashing 283.21
**per diem** 80.19

**perdition**
destruction 693.1
hell 1019.1
loss 812.1
**perdurable**
enduring 110.10
perpetual 112.7
**perdure** 110.6
**peregrinate**
travel 273.20
traverse 273.19
wander 273.22
**peregrine**
*n.* wanderer 274.2
*adj.* walking 273.35
**peremptory**
commanding 752.14
dogmatic 513.22
imperious 739.16
mandatory 752.13
obligatory 962.15
unqualified 508.2
**perennial**
*n.* plant 411.3
*adj.* abiding 110.10
constant 135.5
continuous 71.8
enduring 110.10
evergreen 112.8
plant 411.41
**perennially**
constantly 135.7
continuously 71.10
perpetually 112.10
**perfect**
*n.* tense 586.12
*v.* complete 722.6
develop 677.5
end 70.7
excel 36.6
improve 691.10
*adj.* accurate 516.15
complete 722.12
faultless 677.6
outright 34.12
thorough 56.10
unqualified 508.2
unrestricted 762.26
**perfected** ended 70.8
finished 677.9
improved 691.13
**perfection**
accomplishment
722.2
accuracy 516.3
completion 56.4
culmination 677.3
faultlessness 677
good looks 900.4
improvement 691.2
**perfectionist**
*n.* conformist 82.2
fastidious person
896.6
optimist 888.6
*adj.* fastidious 896.9
optimistic 888.12
**perfectly**
absolutely 56.15
accurately 516.19
extremely 34.22
faultlessly 677.10

**perfect pitch** 462.32
**perfervid**
fanatical 473.32
overzealous 635.13
zealous 635.10
**perfidious**
dishonest 975.21
falsehearted 616.31
**perfidy** 975.6
**perforate** 265.16
**perforated** 265.20
**perforation** 265.3
**perform**
accomplish 722.4
act 611.34
do duty 656.13
execute 705.8
indicate 555.5
observe 768.3
operate 164.7
perform music 462.40
produce 167.9
represent 572.9
**performable**
possible 509.7
workable 164.10
**performance**
accomplishment
722.1
acting 611.9
action 705.2
ceremony 646.4
deed 705.3
display 555.2
impersonation 572.2
music 462.31
music program
462.34
observance 768.1
operation 164.1
production 167.1
theatrical perfor-
mance 611.13
**performer**
affecter 903.7
doer 718.1
entertainer 612.1
musician 464.1
**performing**
*n.* acting 611.9
impersonation 572.2
operation 164.1
*adj.* acting 705.10
**perfume**
*n.* fragrance 436.1
scent 436.2
*v.* gas 401.8
odorize 435.7
scent 436.8
**perfumed** 436.9
**perfumer**
fragrance 436.5
merchant 830.3
scent article 436.6
**perfunctory**
careless 534.11
indifferent 636.6
reluctant 623.6
unconcerned 636.7
unwilling 623.5
**perfuse** insert 304.3
transfer 271.9

treat 689.33
**perfusion**
insertion 304.1
transference 271.1
transfusion 689.20
**pergola** corridor 192.18
summerhouse 191.13
**perhaps**
*n.* unverified supposi-
tion 499.4
*adv.* possibly 509.9
**perigee**
astronomy 375.16
nearness 200.3
spacecraft 282.2
**peril**
*n.* danger 697.1
uncertainty 514.6
*v.* endanger 697.6
**perilous**
dangerous 697.9
unreliable 514.19
**perilously** 697.17
**perimeter**
bounds 235.1
environment 233.1
**period**
astronomy 375.16
degree 29.1
duration 105.1
end 70.1
geological 107.10
menstruation 311.9
meter 609.9
music division 462.24
pause 144.4
phrase 585.1
season 128.1
time 107
wave 323.4
**periodic(al)**
continuous 71.8
cyclic 137.7
journalistic 605.26
oscillating 323.15
recurrent 103.13
**periodical**
publication 559.1
serial 605.10
**periodically** 137.10
**periodicity**
continuity 71.2
oscillation 323.1
recurrence 137.2
season 128.1
**periodontic** 688.18
**periodontics** 688.4
**period style** 901.7
**peripatetic**
*n.* pedestrian 274.6
wanderer 274.2
*adj.* traveling 273.35
**peripatetics** 273.2
**peripheral**
exterior 224.6
outlinear 235.14
surrounding 233.8
**periphery**
bounds 235.1
environment 233.1
exterior 224.2
**periscope** 320.5

perish
become old 123.9
be destroyed 693.23
cease to exist 2.5
die 408.19
disappear 447.2
perishable
mortal 408.34
transient 111.7
perished 2.10
perish the thought!
969.28
peritoneum 229.3
peritonitis
gastrointestinal dis-
ease 686.27
inflammation 686.9
perjured
dishonest 975.18
untruthful 616.34
perjure oneself
be dishonest 975.12
swear falsely 616.20
perjurer 619.9
perjury
dishonesty 975.3
falsification 616.9
perks booty 824.11
extra pay 841.6
gain 811.3
gratuity 818.5
perk up cheer up 870.9
elevate 317.5
energize 161.9
get better 691.7
recuperate 694.19
refresh 695.2
perky conceited 909.11
lighthearted 870.12
lively 707.17
permanence
changelessness 140
durability 110.1
perpetuity 112.1
perseverance 625.1
stability 142.4
permanent
n. hairdo 230.15
adj. changeless 140.7
enduring 110.10
godlike 1013.20
perpetual 112.7
persevering 625.7
stable 142.17
permanently
perpetually 112.10
steadfastly 140.9
permeable
exudative 303.20
pervious 265.22
permeate infuse 44.12
pervade 186.7
soak 392.13
permeated
saturated 186.15
soaked 392.17
permeation
infusion 44.2
pervasion 186.3
soaking 392.7
permissible 777.15

permission
allowance 777
consent 775.1
exemption 762.8
ratification 521.4
permissive
n. mood 586.11
adj. consenting 775.4
indulgent 759.8
lax 758.4
negligent 534.10
nonrestrictive 762.24
permitting 777.14
permissiveness
indulgence 759.3
neglect 534.1
sufferance 777.2
tolerance 526.4
unrestraint 762.3
unstrictness 758.1
permit
n. license 777.6
v. allow 777.9
consent 775.2
make possible 509.5
ratify 521.12
permitted
allowed 777.16
exempt 762.29
permutable
changeable 141.6
interchangeable
150.5
permutation
interchange 150.1
transformation 139.2
pernicious fatal 409.23
harmful 675.12
pernickety 896.10
perorate
declaim 599.10
end 70.5
expatiate 593.8
peroration end 70.1
sequel 67.1
speech 599.2
peroxide
n. bleach 363.10
v. decolor 363.5
perpend 478.12
perpendicular
n. straight line 250.2
vertical 213.2
adj. orthogonal 251.7
plumb 213.12
perpetrate 705.6
perpetration 705.2
perpetual
constant 135.5
enduring 110.10
everlasting 112.7
godlike 1013.20
infinite 104.3
permanent 140.7
perpetually
constantly 135.7
everlastingly 112.10
permanently 140.9
perpetuate
preserve 112.5
sustain 143.4

perpetuation
continuance 143.1
preservation 112.4
perpetuity
constancy 135.2
durability 110.1
eternity 112
infinity 104.1
length 202.1
perplex astonish 920.6
be incomprehensible
549.10
bewilder 514.13
complicate 46.3
confuse 532.7
make doubt 503.7
thwart 730.15
trouble 731.12
perplexed
at an impasse 731.22
bewildered 514.24
complex 46.4
confused 532.12
hard to understand
549.14
perplexing
bewildering 514.25
inexplicable 549.17
perplexity
bewilderment 514.3
complexity 46.1
confusion 532.3
dilemma 731.6
obscurity 549.3
puzzle 549.8
perquisite
belonging 810.2
booty 824.11
extra pay 841.6
gain 811.3
gratuity 818.5
per se essentially 5.10
singly 89.13
persecute annoy 866.13
make anxious 890.4
oppress 667.6
work evil 675.6
persecuted
tormented 866.24
worried 890.7
persecution
annoyance 866.2
mistreatment 667.3
torment 866.7
persecutor 866.10
Persephone
agriculture divinity
413.4
deity of nether world
1019.5
goddess 1014.5
perseverance
continuance 143.1
obstinacy 626.1
patience 861.1
persistence 625
resolution 624.1
persevere
be obstinate 626.7
be patient 861.5
continue 143.5
persist 625.2

succeed 724.12
persevering
obstinate 626.8
patient 861.9
persistent 625.7
resolute 624.11
persiflage banter 882.1
witticism 881.7
persist cohere 50.6
continue 143.5
endure 110.6
insist 753.7
keep alive 407.10
live on 1.9
persevere 625.2
prevail 17.3
remain 140.5
retain 813.5
persistence
continuance 143.1
durability 110.1
insistence 753.3
permanence 140.1
perseverance 625.1
resolution 624.1
tenacity 50.3
uniformity 17.1
persistent
adhesive 50.12
continuing 143.7
demanding 753.8
habitual 642.16
long-lasting 110.10
permanent 140.7
persevering 625.7
resolute 624.11
reverberating 454.11
unforgettable 537.26
uniform 17.5
persistently
for a long time
110.14
habitually 642.23
perseveringly 625.8
resolutely 624.17
persnickety 896.10
person body 376.3
entity 3.3
grammatical form
586.7
human 417.3
individual 89.4
physique 246.4
role 611.11
persona individual 89.4
person 3.3
psyche 690.35
personable
beautiful 900.17
influential 172.13
personage chief 749.3
famous person 914.9
important person
672.8
person 417.3
role 611.11
persona grata 985.1
personal
individual 417.12
particular 80.12
private 614.13

**peter out**
become exhausted 717.5
be consumed 666.3
be disappointing 541.3
be unproductive 166.3
cease to exist 2.5
fall through 314.3
weaken 160.9
**petite** 196.10
**petit four** 308.41
**petition**
*n.* prayer 1032.4
request 774.1
*v.* pray 1032.12
request 774.10
**petitionary** 774.16
**petitioner**
accuser 1005.5
supplicant 774.7
worshiper 1032.9
**petit mal** 686.5
**pet name** 583.7
**pet peeve**
complaint 875.4
grudge 929.5
hated thing 930.3
**petrification**
antiquity 123.6
hardening 356.5
petrifaction 384.7
**petrified**
antiquated 123.13
hardened 356.13
mineral 383.15
stone 384.10
terrified 891.34
**petrified forest** 123.6
**petrify** astonish 920.6
harden 356.7
lithify 384.9
mineralize 383.13
terrify 891.25
**petrifying**
hardening 356.14
terrifying 891.37
**petrol**
illuminant 335.20
petroleum 380.4
**petroleum**
illuminant 335.20
oil 380.4,11
**petrology**
geology 384.8
minerology 383.10
**petticoat**
*n.* undergarment 231.58
*adj.* feminine 421.13
**pettifog** argue 482.16
find fault 969.15
**pettifogger**
faultfinder 969.9
lawyer 1003.3
quibbler 483.7
sharper 619.4
**pettifoggery**
chicanery 618.4
sophistry 483.5

**pettiness**
baseness 915.3
inferiority 37.3
narrow-mindedness 527.1
selfishness 978.2
smallness 35.1
unimportance 673.1
**petting**
lovemaking 932.1
touching 425.2
**pettish** 951.21
**petty** base 915.12
inferior 37.7
insignificant 35.6
narrow-minded 527.10
quibbling 483.14
selfish 978.6
trivial 673.17
**petty cash** 835.19
**petty officer** 749.20
**petulance**
capriciousness 629.2
complaint 875.4
discontent 869.1
ill humor 951.5
**petulant**
capricious 629.5
discontented 869.5
ill-humored 951.21
plaintive 875.16
**pew**
church seat 1042.14
compartment 192.2
**pewter** 383.17
**peyote** 687.13,53
**pfc.** 800.8
**Phaëthon** deity 1014.5
sun god 375.14
**phalanx** group 74.3
military unit 800.19
**phallic** 419.27
**phallic symbol** 690.37
**phallus** 419.10
**phantasm**
deception 618.1
phantom 519.4
specter 1017.1
thing imagined 535.5
**phantasmagoria**
phantom 519.4
spectacle 446.7
**phantasmagoric** 519.9
**phantasmal**
ghostly 1017.7
illusory 519.9
imaginary 535.22
**phantasy** see **fantasy**
**phantom**
*n.* apparition 446.5
frightener 891.9
illusion 519.4
specter 1017.1
spirit 4.3
thing imagined 535.5
*adj.* ghostly 1017.7
illusory 519.9
immaterial 377.7
**phantomlike**
ghostly 1017.7
tenuous 4.6

**pharaoh**
autocrat 749.14
ruler 749.8
**pharisaic(al)**
hypocritic(al) 616.33
sanctimonious 1029.5
**pharisee** deceiver 619.8
hypocrite 1029.3
**pharmaceutic(al)** 687.50
**pharmaceutics** 687.34
**pharmacist** 687.35
**pharmacological** 687.50
**pharmacologist** 687.35
**pharmacology**
biology 406.17
pharmacy 687.34
**pharmacopoeia** 687.37
**pharmacy**
drugstore 687.36
hospital room 192.25
pharmacology 687.34
store types 832.4
**pharos** mark 568.10
observation post 439.8
**pharyngeal**
*n.* speech sound 594.13
*adj.* phonetic 594.31
**pharynx** gullet 396.15
vocal organ 594.19
**phase** 446.3
**phatic** 547.6
**phenobarbital** 687.12,54
**phenomenal**
eventful 151.10
extraordinary 85.14
wonderful 920.10
**phenomenology** 500.1
**phenomenon**
apparition 446.5
event 151.2
marvel 920.2
**phew!**
unpleasantness 864.31
wonder 920.20
**Philadelphia lawyer**
arguer 482.12
cunning person 735.6
lawyer 1003.3
**philander**
be unchaste 989.19
flirt 932.18
**philanderer**
beau 931.12
unchaste person 989.10
woman chaser 932.11
**philandering** 932.9
**philanthropic**
benevolent 938.15
giving 818.22
**philanthropist**
altruist 938.8
giver 818.11
**philanthropy**
benevolence 938.4
charity 818.3
**philharmonic** 462.48

**Philharmonic** 464.12
**philippic**
berating 969.7
speech 599.2
**Philistine**
*n.* conformist 82.2
vulgar person 898.6
*adj.* callous 856.12
unlearned 477.14
vulgar 898.14
worldly 1031.16
**philological** 580.17
**philologist**
linguist 580.13
scholar 476.3
**philology** 580.12
**philosopher**
names of 500.13
reasoner 482.11
scholar 476.3
thinker 500.6
types of 500.12
wise man 468.1
**philosophical**
composed 858.12
patient 861.9
sensible 467.18
thinking 500.8
**philosophize**
practice philosophy 500.7
reason 482.15
**philosophy**
composure 858.2
ideology 479.8
physics 325.1
reasoning 482.1
schools of 500.11
thought 560
**phlebitis** 686.9
**phlebotomy**
bloodletting 689.26
extraction 305.3
**phlegm** apathy 856.4
body fluid 388.3
languor 708.6
**phlegmatic**
*n.* personality type 690.15
*adj.* apathetic 856.13
incurious 529.3
inert 268.14
languid 708.19
**phobia**
fear 891.1,10–17
hated thing 930.3
neurosis 690.19
**phobic** 690.45
**Phoebe** five 99.1
moon goddess 375.12
**Phoebus** god 1014.5
sun god 375.14
**phon** 450.7
**phonate** 594.23
**phone**
*n.* sound 450.1
speech 594.13
telephone 560.4
types of 448.18
*v.* telephone 560.18
**phone book**
directory 748.10

**pick and choose**
  be discriminating
    492.4
  be fastidious 896.8
  choose 637.13
**picked** best 674.18
  chosen 637.26
**picker** farm hand 413.5
  string musician 464.5
**picket**
  *n.* demonstrator
    699.13
  guard 699.9
  stake 217.6
  strike enforcer 789.5
  watchman 699.10
  *v.* enclose 236.7
  object 522.5
  restrain 760.10
  strike 789.9
  torture 1010.18
**picketing** protest 522.2
  punishment 1010.2
**pickings** booty 824.11
  gain 811.3
**pickle**
  *n.* perplexity 514.3
  predicament 731.4
  sour thing 432.2
  state 7.1
  *v.* make drunk 996.22
  preserve 701.8
**pickled** drunk 996.31
  salty 433.9
  sour 432.5
**pickling** 701.2
**pick-me-up** drink 996.7
  refresher 695.1
  tonic 687.8
**pick off** 285.13
**pick one's brains**
  interrogate 485.20
  plagiarize 824.18
**pick out**
  call attention to
    530.10
  designate 568.18
  discriminate 492.5
  eliminate 77.5
  exclude 42.10
  extract 305.10
  see 439.12
  select 637.14
  separate 77.6
  specify 80.11
**pickpocket** 825.2
**pick to pieces**
  demolish 693.17
  find fault 969.15
  tear apart 49.14
**pickup**
  acceleration 269.4
  drink 996.7
  friend 928.1
  improvement 691.1
  increase 38.2
  radio 344.17
  ride 273.7
  sound reproduction
    system 450.11
  television camera
    345.10

unchaste woman
  989.14
**pick up** arrest 761.15
  capture 822.18
  cheer 870.7
  detect 488.5
  fetch 271.15
  get better 691.7
  procure 811.10
  raise 317.8
  recuperate 694.19
  refresh 695.2
  stimulate 857.12
  use radar 346.17
**Pickwickian** 547.7
**picky** 896.9
**picnic**
  *n.* easy thing 732.3
  festival 878.4
  fun 878.2
  meal 307.6
  victory 726.1
  *v.* eat 307.19
**picot** 262.4
**pictogram**
  character 581.2
  representation 572.1
  symbol 568.3
**pictograph** 581.2
**pictographic**
  literal 581.8
  representational
    572.10
**pictorial**
  *n.* periodical 605.10
  *adj.* pictural 574.22
  representational
    572.10
**picture**
  *n.* art work 574.12
  beautiful thing 900.7
  copy 24.1
  description 608.1
  image 572.3
  likeness 20.3
  motion picture
    611.16
  photograph 577.3
  radar signal 346.11
  sign 568.2
  television reception
    345.5
  visualization 535.6
  *v.* describe 608.12
  portray 574.20
  represent 572.6
  visualize 535.15
**picture, the** plan 654.1
  the facts 1.4
**picture gallery** 660.9
**picture show** 611.16
**picturesque**
  ornate 901.12
  pictorial 574.22
**pictures, the** 611.17
**picture tube** 345.18
**picturing** 535.6
**picturization**
  painting 574.5
  representation 572.1
**piddle**
  *n.* urine 311.5

  *v.* dally 708.13
  trifle 673.13
  urinate 311.14
  waste time 708.12
**piddling** little 196.10
  petty 673.17
  sparse 102.5
**pidgin** 580.11
**pie** easy thing 732.3
  foreign money 835.9
  pastry 308.40
**piebald**
  *n.* horse 414.13
  *adj.* variegated 374.12
**piece** chessman 878.18
  coin 835.4
  distance 199.1
  girl 125.6
  gun 801.5
  length 202.3
  music 462.5
  news 558.3
  particle 55.3
  portion 816.5
  role 611.11
  sample 25.3
  sex object 419.4
  stage show 611.4
  treatise 606.1
  work of art 574.11
  written matter 602.10
**pièce de résistance**
  dish 308.7
  the best 674.8
**piecemeal**
  piece by piece 55.9
  separately 49.28
**piece of cake** 732.3
**piece of one's mind**
  969.6
**piece together**
  compose 58.3
  create 167.10
  join 47.5
**pied** 374.12
**pied-à-terre** 191.9
**pie-eyed** 996.31
**pie in the sky** 535.23
**pier** buttress 216.4
  harbor 700.6
  pillar 217.5
  post 216.8
**pierce** affect 855.16
  chill 333.10
  enter 302.8
  hurt 424.7
  injure 692.15
  pain 866.17
  perforate 265.16
  stab 798.25
  understand 548.8
**piercing**
  *n.* attacking 798.11
  perforation 265.3
  *adj.* acrimonious
    161.13
  caustic 939.21
  cold 333.14
  deep-felt 855.26
  eloquent 600.11
  exciting 857.29
  intense 159.20

  loud 453.10
  painful 424.10
  pungent 433.6
  sagacious 467.16
  shrill 458.14
  violent 162.15
**pier glass** 443.5
**Pierian** 609.17
**pietistic**
  believing 501.21
  religious 1028.8
  sanctimonious 1029.5
**piety** devoutness 1028
  sanctimony 1029.1
**piffle**
  *n.* nonsense 547.3
  *v.* talk nonsense 547.5
**piffling** 673.17
**pig** bad person 986.7
  filthy person 682.13
  glutton 994.3
  intolerant person
    527.5
  mammal 414.58;
    415.8
  metal casting
    383.5,22
  motorcycle 272.8
  policeman 699.16
  pork 308.16
  slob 62.7
  swine 414.9,58
**pigboat** 277.9
**pigeon**
  *n.* bird 414.33,66
  dupe 620.1
  food 308.22
  *v.* cheat 618.17
  deceive 618.13
**pigeon-breasted** 256.18
**pigeonhearted** 892.10
**pigeonhole**
  *n.* class 61.2
  file 88.3
  hole 265.4
  small place 196.3
  *v.* classify 61.6
  legislate 742.18
  list 88.8
  postpone 132.9
  put away 668.6
**pigeonholed**
  classified 61.8
  neglected 534.14
**pigeonholing** 61.1
**pigeon-toed** 249.12
**pig-farming** 416.1
**piggish** filthy 682.24
  gluttonous 994.6
  greedy 634.27
  ungulate 414.49
**piggy bank** 836.12
**pigheaded** 626.8
**pig in a poke**
  an uncertainty 514.8
  bargain 827.5
  matter of chance
    515.2
**piglet** swine 414.9
  young pig 125.8

**pigment**
n. art equipment 574.19
black 365.14
blue 372.4
brown 367.6
coloring matter 362.8
gray 366.6
green 371.6
orange 369.3
pink 368.13
purple 373.4
red 368.12
reddish brown 367.7
white 364.11
yellow 370.7
v. color 362.13
**pigmentation** 362.11
**pigsty**
filthy place 682.11
hovel 191.12
**pigtail**
chewing tobacco 434.7
hair 230.7,30
tail 241.6
**pike** peak 207.8
road 657.6
**piker** gambler 515.17
vagabond 274.3
**pilaster** pillar 217.5
post 216.8
tower 207.11
**pile**
n. atomics 326.13
building 245.2
cardiovascular disease 686.17
down 230.19
hair 230.2
heap 74.10
leaf 411.17
much 34.4
plant beard 230.9
post 216.8
sore 686.35
stake 217.6
store 660.1
texture 351.1
wealth 837.2
v. heap 74.19
pile in 315.12
put 184.14
**pile drive** 283.11
**pile house** 398.3
**pile it on**
be bombastic 601.6
exaggerate 617.3
overdo 663.11
**pile out** 713.6
**pileup** 729.2
**pile up** heap 74.19
shipwreck 275.42
store up 660.11
**pilfer** misuse 667.4
steal 824.13
**pilfering** misuse 667.1
theft 824.1
**pilgrim**
religious 1038.17
traveler 274.1

**pilgrimage**
n. journey 273.5
quest 715.2
v. travel 273.20
**pill** bad person 986.6
boring person 884.4
medicine 687.7
**pill, the** 687.23
**pillage**
n. plundering 824.5
v. plunder 824.16
seize 822.14
wreck 162.10
**pillaging**
n. plundering 824.5
rapacity 822.9
violence 162.3
adj. plunderous 824.21
**pillar** base 216.8
column 217.5
cylinder 255.4
memorial 570.12
protector 699.5
stability 142.6
tower 207.11
**pillar of society**
good person 985.3
personage 672.8
**pillbox** 799.6
**pillhead** 642.10
**pillory**
n. restraint 760.4
stocks 1011.3
v. disgrace 915.8
punish 1010.10
ridicule 967.8
stigmatize 915.9
**pillow**
n. bedding 216.20
softness 357.4
v. support 216.21
**pillowcase** 228.10
**pilose** 230.24
**pilot**
n. aviator 279.1
boatman 276.8
guide 748.7
operator 164.4
safety equipment 699.3
v. direct 747.9
fly 278.46
operate 164.5
steer 275.14
adj. experimental 489.11
**pilotage** aviation 278.1
direction 747.1
fee 846.7
navigation 275.2
pilotship 275.4
position 184.3
**pilot balloon** 489.4
**pilot light** 329.10
**pilot model**
model 25.5
original 23.2
**pilot program** 489.3
**pilotship**
airmanship 278.3
helmsmanship 275.4

**pilpul** 482.4
**pily** 351.7
**pimp**
n. bad person 986.5
procurer 989.18
v. be unchaste 989.21
**pimping** 989.8
**pimple**
n. blemish 679.1
mark 568.7
sore 686.35
swelling 256.4
v. roughen 261.4
**pimply**
blemished 679.8
rough 261.6
**pin**
n. axle 322.5
insignia 569.1
jewel 901.6
legs 273.16
stopper 266.4
trifle 673.5
v. fasten 47.8
**pinafore** 231.17,55
**pinball** 515.8
**pinball machine** 515.12
**pince-nez** 443.2
**pincers**
contractor 198.6
extractor 305.9
grasping organs 813.4
**pinch**
n. arrest 761.6
a theft 824.10
crisis 129.4
danger 697.1
difficulty 731.7
indigence 838.2
pain 424.2
predicament 731.4
small amount 35.2
small place 196.3
squeezing 198.2
urge 648.6
urgency 672.4
v. arrest 761.16
be parsimonious 852.5
converge 298.2
hurt 424.7
sail 275.25
squeeze 198.8
steal 824.13
adj. substitute 149.8
**pinch bar** 287.4
**pinchbeck**
n. fake 616.13
ornamentation 901.3
adj. ungenuine 616.26
**pinched**
constricted 198.12
in trouble 731.24
poor 838.7
thin 205.20
**pinch-hit**
represent 781.14
substitute for 149.5
**pinch hitter**
deputy 781.1
substitute 149.2

**pinching**
n. parsimony 852.1
theft 824.1
adj. cold 333.14
stingy 852.9
**pinch pennies** 852.5
**pinchpenny** 852.8
**pindling** 196.10
**pin down**
localize 184.10
restrain 760.10
specify 80.11
stabilize 142.7
**pine** deteriorate 692.21
fail 686.45
grieve 872.17
weaken 160.9
wish for 634.16
**pine barrens** 411.11
**pine cone** cone 255.5
inflorescence 411.25
**pinfeather** 230.16
**pinhead** dolt 471.4
point 196.7
top part 211.4
**pinhole** 265.4
**pining**
n. sorrow 872.10
yearning 634.5
adj. dejected 872.22
deteriorating 692.46
languishing 160.21
wistful 634.23
**pinion**
n. feather 230.16
wing 55.4
v. restrain 760.10
**pinioned** 230.28
**pink**
n. acme of perfection 677.3
colors 368.13
pinkness 368.2
radical 745.12
v. notch 262.4
puncture 265.16
adj. healthy 685.11
pinkish 368.8
radical 745.20
**pink elephants** 473.10
**pink eye** 686.13
**pinkie** 425.5
**pinko** 745.12
**pink slip** 310.5
**pin money** 835.19
**pinnacle**
completion 56.5
culmination 677.3
peak 207.8
summit 211.2
tower 207.11
**pinnate** 230.27
**pin on** accuse 1005.7
attribute to 155.4
**pinpoint**
n. location 184.1
point 196.7
v. attribute to 155.4
locate 184.10
use radar 346.17
adj. exact 516.16

**pinpointing**
placement 184.5
radar operation 346.8
**pinprick**
shallowness 210.1
trifle 673.5
**pins and needles**
anxiety 890.1
insensibility 423.1
sensation 426.1
**pintle** 322.5
**pinto**
*n.* horse 414.13
*adj.* variegated 374.12
**pint-sized** 196.10
**pinup**
beautiful person 900.8
photograph 577.3
**pinwheel** 878.16
**piny**
*n.* backwoodsman 190.10
*adj.* arboreal 411.36
**pioneer**
*n.* military engineer 800.13
precursor 66.1
settler 190.9
traveler 274.1
vanguard 240.2
*v.* begin 68.10
change 139.8
go before 66.3
lead 240.7
**pious** believing 501.21
religious 1028.8
sanctimonious 1029.5
**piousness**
devoutness 1028.1
sanctimony 1029.1
**pip**
*n.* animal disease 686.38
good thing 674.7
military insignia 569.5
radar signal 346.11
seed 411.29
*v.* bird sound 460.5
**pip, the** 686.1
**pipe**
*n.* cylinder 255.4
shrill sound 458.4
tobacco pipe 434.6
tube 396.6
wind instrument 465.7
woodwind 465.9
*v.* bird sound 460.5
blare 453.9
channel 271.13
convey 396.19
play music 462.43
sing 462.39
sound shrill 458.8
utter 594.26
wind sound 403.23
**pe down**
fall silent 451.7
silence! 451.14

**pipe dream**
abstractedness 532.2
dream 535.9
hope 888.5
illusion 519.1
**pipe-dream**
dream 535.17
muse 532.9
**pipelike** 396.20
**pipeline**
*n.* inside information 557.2
news channel 558.10
tube 396.6
*v.* channel 271.13
**piper** 464.4
**pipe roll** 570.1
**pipes** bagpipe 465.10
boatswain 276.7
**pipette**
*n.* extractor 305.9
tube 396.6
*v.* extract 305.12
**pipe up**
blow up 403.22
speak up 594.22
start music 462.38
vociferate 459.8
**piping**
*n.* tube 396.6
*adj.* pacific 803.9
prosperous 728.13
shrill 458.14
**pippin** 674.7
**pip-squeak**
a nobody 673.7
dwarf 196.6
**piquant** alluring 650.7
appetizing 428.10
eloquent 600.12
exciting 857.28
interesting 530.19
provocative 648.27
pungent 433.6
**pique**
*n.* anger 952.7
resentment 952.2
*v.* annoy 866.13
incite 648.17
interest 530.12
provoke 952.22
rouse 648.19
stimulate 857.12
**piqued** annoyed 866.21
interested 530.16
provoked 952.25
**piracy**
buccaneering 824.6
plagiarism 824.7
**pirate**
*n.* corsair 825.7
plagiarist 825.9
sailor 276.1
*v.* borrow 821.4
buccaneer 824.17
plagiarize 824.18
**piratelike** 824.20
**pirating** 821.2
**pirouette**
*n.* rotation 322.2
*v.* rotate 322.9

**piscatory**
fishlike 414.53
pursuing 655.11
**pisci–** 414.35
**pismire** 414.37
**piss**
*n.* urine 311.5
*v.* urinate 311.14
**piss and vinegar**
gaiety 870.4
liveliness 707.2
vim 161.2
**piss away** 854.5
**pissed** angry 952.26
drunk 996.31
**pissed-off** 952.26
**pistil** 411.26
**pistol**
*n.* gun 801.5
*v.* shoot 285.13
strike dead 409.18
**pistol-whip** 1010.14
**piston** 285.7
**pit**
*n.* arena 802.1
audience 448.6
blemish 679.1
cavity 257.2
deep 209.2
exchange 833.7
indentation 257.6
mine 383.6
plant seed 411.29
stage 611.21
texture 351.1
theater part 611.20
tomb 410.16
well 275.4
*v.* indent 257.14
**pit against**
contrapose 239.4
sow dissension 795.14
**pitapat**
*n.* excitement 857.4
faint sound 452.3
flutter 324.4
palpitation 323.3
staccato sound 455.1
*adj.* pulsating 323.18
**pitch**
*n.* aviation 278.34
black 365.4
degree 29.1
flounder 324.8
harmonics 463.4
inclination 219.2
incline 219.4
intonation 594.7
plunge 320.1
sales talk 829.5
speech 599.2
summit 211.2
throw 285.4
tone 450.2
*v.* camp 188.11
descend 316.5
erect 213.9
establish 184.15
incline 219.10
lurch 316.8
oscillate 323.10
plunge 320.6

**sail** 275.55
throw 285.11
tumble 324.15
**pitch-black** black 365.8
dark 337.13
**pitch camp** 188.11
**pitched**
inclining 219.15
phonetic 594.31
**pitcher** 285.8
**pitch in** begin 68.7
eat 307.18
set to work 716.15
**pitching**
*n.* throwing 285.3
*adj.* swinging 323.17
**pitch into**
attack 798.15
contend 796.15
set to work 716.15
undertake 715.3
**pitchman**
publicist 559.9
sharper 619.4
solicitor 830.7
**pitch pipe** 465.25
**pitchy** black 365.8
dark 337.13
resinous 381.3
**piteous** pitiful 944.8
unpleasant 864.20
**pitfall**
hidden danger 697.5
trap 618.11
**pith** center 226.2
content 194.5
courage 893.5
essence 5.2
important point 672.6
meaning 545.1
pluck 624.3
pulp 390.2
summary 607.2
**pithy** aphoristic 517.6
concise 592.6
meaningful 545.10
pulpy 390.6
soft 357.11
**pitiful** bad 675.9
disgraceful 915.11
paltry 673.18
pitiable 944.8
**pitiless** savage 162.20
unmerciful 945.3
**pitilessness**
heartlessness 939.10
unmercifulness 945
violence 162.1
**pits, the** 675.2
**pittance**
donation 818.6
insufficiency 662.5
small amount 35.2
**pitted** indented 257.17
rough 261.6
textured 351.7
**pitter-patter**
*n.* excitement 857.4
faint sound 452.3
flutter 324.4
palpitation 323.3

future 121.8
intentional 653.9
prearranged 641.5
prepared 720.16
**planner** designer 654.7
producer 167.8
**planning**
organization 60.2
prearrangement
641.1
preparation 720.1
scheme 654.1
**plan on** expect 539.9
figure on 653.6
**plant**
*n.* equipment 659.4
shill 619.5
vegetable 411.3
vegetation 411
workplace 719.3
*v.* establish 184.15
implant 413.18
infix 142.9
populate 188.9
secrete 615.7
tamper with 616.17
**plantar** 212.9
**plantation** farm 413.8
peopling 188.2
settlement 184.6
vegetation 411.2
**plant-eater** 307.14
**planted** 184.17
**planter**
agriculturist 413.5
farm hand 413.5
settler 190.9
**planting** plants 411.2
sowing 413.14
**plant life** 411.1
**plantlike** 411.33
**plaque** 570.12
**plash**
*n.* body of water
398.1
lap 395.8
rainstorm 394.2
sprinkle 392.5
*v.* lap 395.19
make a liquid sound
452.11
**plashy** muddy 389.14
watery 392.16
**plasma** 388.4
**plasmic**
metabolic 246.10
protoplasmic 406.20
**plaster**
*n.* adherent 50.4
building material
378.2
medical dressing
687.33
pulp 390.2
types of 228.44
*v.* cover 228.25
make drunk 996.22
smooth 260.5
treat 689.30
**plastered** 996.31
**plastic**
*n.* resin 381.1

synthetic 378.7
types of 378.14
*adj.* changeable 141.6
conformable 82.5
conformist 82.6
docile 765.13
formative 246.9
influenceable 172.15
mediocre 680.8
plasmatic 246.10
pliant 357.9
teachable 564.18
**Plasticine** 575.4
**plasticity**
changeableness 141.1
pliancy 357.2
submissiveness 765.3
teachability 564.5
**plastic person** 82.2
**plastic surgery**
operation 689.25
surgery 688.3
**plat**
*n.* field 413.9
pleat 264.2
real estate 810.7
tract 180.4
*v.* fold 264.5
**plate**
*n.* covering 228.13
engraving 578.7
false teeth 258.6
label 568.13
layer 227.2
meat 308.17
photography 577.10
printing surface 603.8
serving 307.10
shell 228.15
*v.* cover 228.26
**plateau** degree 29.1
interim 109.1
plain 387.1
tableland 207.4
**plated** 228.32
**platen** 603.9,26
**platform**
*n.* arena 802.1
horizontal 214.3
mark 568.10
policy 654.5
political platform
744.7
stage 216.13
*v.* make a speech
599.9
**plating** coating 228.13
layer 227.2
**platinum blond** 362.9
**platinum-blond** 364.9
**platitude** cliché 517.3
truism 79.8
**platitudinous**
aphoristic 517.6
banal 883.9
trite 79.16
well-known 475.27
**Platonic** chaste 988.6
idealist 377.8
philosophy 500.10
**Platonic love**
chastity 988.3

love 931.1
**platoon** group 74.3
military unit 800.19
team 788.7
**platter** 570.10
**platypus** 414.58; 415.8
**plaudit** 968.2
**plausibility**
believability 501.8
probability 511.3
reasonableness 482.9
superficial soundness
483.1
**plausible**
believable 501.24
false 616.27
logical 482.20
possible 509.6
probable 511.7
specious 483.10
**play**
*n.* action 705.1
computer 349.19
frolic 878.5
fun 878.2
gambling 515.7
game 878.9
joke 881.6
latitude 762.4
light 335.8
risk 515.1
space 179.3
stage show 611.4
wager 515.3
written matter 602.10
*v.* act 611.34
affect 903.12
be operative 164.7
bet 515.20
fake 616.21
flicker 335.25
gamble 515.18
jet 395.20
operate 164.5
perform action 705.4
perform music 462.40
represent 572.9
sport 878.25
trifle 673.13
use 665.10
**playa** plain 387.1
shore 385.2
**playacting** acting 611.9
fakery 616.3
**playactor** actor 612.2
affecter 903.7
deceiver 619.1
**play around** flirt 932.18
trifle 673.13
**play around with**
consider 478.12
try out 489.8
**play ball** 786.3
**playbill** 641.2
**playbook** book 605.1
script 611.26
**playboy** player 878.19
sociable person
922.15
**playbroker** 611.30
**play by ear**
be unprepared 721.6

improvise 630.8
perform music 462.40
**play by the rules** 974.9
**play down**
de-emphasize 673.11
minimize 39.9
moderate 163.6
**play dumb**
be silent 451.5
keep secret 614.7
**played out**
exhausted 717.8
weakened 160.18
worn-out 692.38
**player** actor 612.2
athlete 878.20
competitor 791.2
frolicker 878.19
gambler 515.17
musician 464.1
**play favorites** 977.8
**playful** frisky 870.14
mischievous 738.6
prankish 881.17
sportive 878.31
**playfulness** gaiety 870.4
mischief 738.2
wittiness 881.4
**play games** 735.10
**play God** 961.8
**playgoer** 611.32
**playground** 878.12
**play havoc with**
bungle 734.11
impair 692.12
work evil 675.6
**play hooky** 187.9
**playhouse**
small place 196.3
theater 611.18
**playing**
*n.* acting 611.9
gambling 515.7
impersonation 572.2
trifling 673.8
*adj.* flickering 335.36
**playing cards** 878.17
**playing field** 878.12
**playmate**
companion 928.3
mistress 989.17
partner 787.2
**play-off** 878.9
**play on** exploit 665.16
impose 963.7
**play on words**
*n.* wordplay 881.8
*v.* joke 881.13
**play out** 717.5
**playroom**
playground 878.12
recreation room
192.12
**play safe**
keep safe 698.3
take precautions
895.6
**play the game**
be fair 976.7
behave oneself 737.5
conform 82.4

observe the proprie-
ties 645.4
**play the market** 833.23
**plaything** dupe 620.1
  instrument 658.3
  toy 878.16
**play up** 672.15
**play up to**
  befriend 927.11
  curry favor 907.8
  flatter 970.6
**play with fire**
  be reckless 894.6
  defy danger 697.7
  mishandle 734.14
**playwright** 611.27
**plaza** city district 183.8
  marketplace 832.2
**plea** argument 482.5
  entreaty 774.2
  justification 1006.2
  legal plea 1004.6
**pleach** 222.6
**plead**
  adduce evidence
    505.13
  argue 482.16
  argue one's case
    1004.18
  entreat 774.11
  urge 648.14
**pleader** deputy 781.1
  justifier 1006.8
  lawyer 1003.1
  motivator 648.10
**plead guilty**
  confess 556.7
  repent 873.7
**pleading**
  n. argument 482.5
  justification 1006.2
  lawyers 1003.5
  legal plea 1004.6
  adj. imploring 774.17
**pleasance** park 878.14
  pleasantness 863.1
**pleasant**
  cheerful 870.11
  friendly 927.14
  good 674.12
  melodious 462.49
  pleasing 863.6
  rainless 393.8
**pleasantly**
  amicably 927.21
  cheerfully 870.17
  pleasingly 863.11
**pleasantness**
  cheerfulness 870.1
  goodness 674.1
  pleasingness 863
**pleasantry** banter 882.1
  humor 881.1
  jocularity 881.2
  pleasantness 863.1
  witticism 881.7
**please**
  v. give pleasure 865.5
  indulge 759.6
  prefer 637.17
  interj. if you please
    774.20

**pleased**
  contented 868.7
  delighted 865.12
**pleasing**
  n. indulgence 759.3
  adj. beautiful 900.17
  desirable 634.30
  eloquent 600.9
  pleasant 863.6
  tasteful 897.8
  tasty 428.8
  welcome 925.12
**pleasurable** 863.6
**pleasure**
  amusement 878.1
  command 752.1
  desire 634.1
  enjoyment 865
  option 637.2
  pleasantness 863.1
  will 621.1
**pleasureless**
  joyless 866.20
  unhappy 872.21
**pleasure-loving**
  n. pleasure principle
    865.4
  adj. pleasure-seeking
    865.15
**pleasure principle**
  desire 634.1
  pleasure-loving 865.4
  psyche 690.35
  sensuality 987.1
**pleasure-seeker**
  player 878.19
  sensualist 987.3
**pleasure-seeking**
  n. sensuality 987.1
  adj. pleasure-loving
    865.15
  sensual 987.5
**pleat**
  n. fold 264.2
  trench 263.2
  v. fold 264.5
  groove 263.3
**pleated** folded 264.7
  grooved 263.4
**plebe** 566.6
**plebeian**
  n. common man
    919.7
  adj. common 919.11
  vulgar 898.14
**plebiscite**
  referendum 742.16
  vote 637.6
**pledge**
  n. debt 840.1
  drink 996.9
  member 788.11
  oath 523.3
  promise 770.1
  security 772.2
  v. contribute 818.14
  drink 307.27
  give security 772.10
  obligate 962.12
  promise 770.4
  toast 996.28
**pledged** affirmed 523.8

chargeable 840.9
  obliged 962.16
  promised 770.8
  staked 772.12
**pledget** 687.33
**pleiad** 914.9
**Pleiades**
  nymphs 1014.19
  star cluster 375.8
**plenary** full 56.11
  great 34.6
  unrestricted 762.26
**plenipotentiary**
  n. diplomat 781.6
  adj. diplomatic 781.16
  omnipotent 157.13
**plenitude**
  continuity 71.1
  fullness 56.2
  greatness 34.1
  intactness 677.2
  plenty 661.2
  quantity 34.3
  store 660.1
**plentiful**
  abundant 101.8
  much 34.8
  plenty 661.7
  productive 165.9
  superabundant
    663.19
**plenty**
  n. numerousness
    101.1
  overabundance 663.2
  plenitude 661.2
  quantity 34.3
  store 660.1
  adj. plentiful 661.7
  sufficient 661.6
  adv. greatly 34.15
**plenum** continuity 71.2
  matter 376.2
  meeting 74.2
  universe 375.1
**plethora** fullness 56.2
  overabundance 663.2
  overfullness 663.3
**pleura** 229.3
**pleurisy** 686.14
**pleuriform** 221.11
**plexus** ganglion 422.6
  network 221.3
**pliability**
  irresolution 627.4
  pliancy 357.2
  submissiveness 765.3
  teachability 564.5
  wieldiness 732.2
  willingness 622.1
**pliable** docile 765.13
  folded 264.7
  influenceable 172.15
  irresolute 627.12
  pliant 357.9
  teachable 564.18
  usable 665.22
  wieldy 732.14
**pliant**
  conformable 82.5
  docile 765.13
  influenceable 172.15

pliable 357.9
  unstrict 758.5
  wieldy 732.14
  willing 622.5
**plicate**
  v. fold 264.5
  adj. folded 264.7
**pliers** 305.9
**plight**
  n. adversity 729.1
  danger 697.1
  perplexity 514.3
  predicament 731.4
  promise 770.1
  state 7.1
  v. affiance 770.6
  promise 770.4
**plighted** 770.8
**plinth** 216.8
**plod**
  n. slowness 270.2
  v. drudge 716.14
  go slowly 270.7
  persevere 625.3
  walk 273.27
**plodder** drudge 718.3
  slow person 270.5
**plodding**
  n. perseverance 625.1
  adj. laboring 716.17
  persevering 625.7
  uninteresting 883.6
**plop**
  v. bubble 405.4
  plunge 320.6
  put violently 184.12
  sink 316.6
  adv. squarely 290.25
  suddenly 113.9
**plot**
  n. diagram 654.3
  field 413.9
  intrigue 654.6
  real estate 810.7
  story element 608.9
  stratagem 735.3
  tract 180.4
  v. foresee 121.6
  maneuver 735.10
  map 654.11
  prearrange 641.3
  premeditate 653.8
  scheme 654.10
**plotted** future 121.8
  measured 490.14
  planned 654.13
  prearranged 641.5
**plotter** schemer 654.8
  traitor 619.10
**plotting**
  n. intrigue 654.6
  prearrangement
    641.1
  adj. scheming 654.14
**plow**
  n. farm machine
    348.22
  v. fly 278.49
  groove 263.3
  till 413.17
**plowland** 413.8
**plowman** 413.5

**ploy** influence 172.3
  revel 878.6
  stratagem 735.3
  trick 618.6
**pluck**
  *n.* courage 893.5
  jerk 286.3
  spunk 624.3
  *v.* despoil 822.24
  divest 232.5
  extract 305.10
  fail someone 725.16
  harvest 413.19
  jerk 286.5
  procure 811.10
  strum 462.41
**plucky** bold 893.18
  resolute 624.14
**plug**
  *n.* commendation
    968.3
  hydrant 396.12
  inferior horse 414.14
  publicity 559.4
  radio 344.20
  snare 618.12
  stopper 266.4
  *v.* commend 968.11
  drudge 716.14
  persevere 625.3
  plod 270.7
  publicize 559.15
  shoot 285.13
  stop 266.7
**plug away**
  be industrious 707.15
  drudge 716.14
  persevere 625.3
**plugged** 266.11
**plugging**
  *n.* perseverance 625.1
  *adj.* laboring 716.17
  persevering 625.7
**plug in** 342.23
**lug-ugly**
  combatant 800.1
  evildoer 943.4
**lum**
  British money 835.8
  dividend 834.7
  good thing 674.5
  political patronage
    744.36
  purple color 373.4
  thing desired 634.11
**lumage** 230.18
**lumb**
  *n.* plumb line 213.6
  vertical 213.2
  weight 352.6
  *v.* close 266.6
  fathom 209.9
  investigate 485.22
  make vertical 213.10
  measure 490.11
  solve 487.2
  understand 548.8
  *dj.* perpendicular
    213.12
  thorough 56.10
  *dv.* absolutely 56.15
  exactly 516.20

perpendicularly
  213.14
  squarely 290.25
**plumbing** 659.4
**plume**
  *n.* feather 230.16
  *v.* groom 681.20
  ornament 901.9
**plumed**
  feathered 230.28
  ornamented 901.11
  topped 211.12
**plummet**
  *n.* cheapening 849.4
  plumb 213.6
  weight 352.6
  *v.* cheapen 849.6
  decrease 39.6
  descend 316.5
  plunge 320.6
**plummeting**
  *n.* cheapening 849.4
  descent 316.1
  *adj.* descending
    316.11
**plump**
  *n.* faint sound 452.3
  *v.* fatten 197.8
  make pliant 357.6
  plunge 320.6
  put violently 184.12
  sink 316.6
  vote 637.18
  *adj.* corpulent 195.18
  *adv.* squarely 290.25
  suddenly 113.9
**plump for** 785.14
**plumpness** 195.8
**plumy** 230.27
**plunder**
  *n.* booty 824.11
  pillaging 824.5
  *v.* pillage 824.16
**plunderer** 825.6
**plundering**
  *n.* pillaging 824.5
  *adj.* looting 824.21
**plunderous** 824.21
**plunge**
  *n.* cheapening 849.4
  decrease 39.2
  dive 320
  flounder 324.8
  gamble 515.1
  investment 836.3
  speed 269.3
  stock speculation
    833.19
  swimming pool
    878.13
  tumble 316.3
  *v.* bet 515.20
  cheapen 849.6
  decrease 39.6
  descend 316.5
  dive 320.6
  gravitate 352.15
  invest 836.16
  make haste 709.5
  move 267.5
  rush into 709.7
  sail 275.55

speculate in stocks
  833.23
  tumble 324.15
**plunge into** begin 68.7
  be willing 622.3
  rush into 709.7
  set to work 716.15
  stab 798.25
  study 564.12
  thrust in 304.7
  undertake 715.3
**plunger** diver 320.4
  gambler 515.17
  stock speculator
    833.11
**plunging**
  *n.* course 267.2
  diving 320.3
  *adj.* abysmal 209.11
  descending 316.11
  flowing 267.8
  perpendicular 213.12
  steep 219.18
**plunk**
  *n.* faint sound 452.3
  hit 283.4
  *v.* faint sound 452.15
  hit 283.13
  plunge 320.6
  put violently 184.12
  strum 462.41
  *adv.* squarely 290.25
  suddenly 113.9
**plunk down** 841.16
**plural**
  *n.* number 586.8
  plurality 100.1
  *adj.* more than one
    100.7
**pluralism** mixture 44.1
  nonuniformity 18.1
  philosophy 500.5
  plurality 100.1
  principle of govern-
    ment 741.8
**pluralistic**
  governmental 741.17
  mixed 44.15
  nonuniform 18.3
  plural 100.7
**plurality**
  large number 101.3
  majority 100.2
  major part 54.6
  pluralness 100
**plus**
  *n.* addition 40.2
  surplus 663.5
  *v.* add 40.4
  *adj.* additional 40.10
  electric 342.32
  *adv.* additionally
    40.11
  *prep.* with 40.12
**plush**
  *n.* softness 357.4
  *adj.* grandiose 904.21
  soft 357.15
**Pluto**
  deity of nether world
    1019.5
  god 1014.5

planet 375.9
**plutocracy** 837.5
**plutocrat** 837.6
**pluvial** 394.10
**ply**
  *n.* fold 264.1
  layer 227.2
  *v.* change course
    275.30
  exert 716.8
  fold 264.5
  importune 774.12
  sail 275.25
  seafare 275.13
  touch 425.6
  traverse 273.19
  urge upon 773.8
  use 665.10
**ply one's trade**
  trade 827.14
  work 656.12
**plywood** layer 227.2
  wood 378.3,10
**PM** afternoon 134.1
  modulation 344.14
**pneuma**
  life force 407.3
  psyche 466.4
**pneumatic** airy 402.12
  beautiful 900.17
  bulging 256.14
  gas 401.9
  mechanical 347.10
**pneumatics**
  aeronautics 278.2
  gas 401.2
  mechanics 347.5
  meteorology 402.6
**pneumonia**
  infectious disease
    686.12
  respiratory disease
    686.14
**PO** 604.8
**poach** cook 330.4
  steal 824.13
**poacher** 825.1
**poaching**
  cooking 330.1
  theft 824.1
**pock**
  *n.* blemish 679.1
  indentation 257.6
  sore 686.35
  swelling 256.4
  texture 351.1
  *v.* indent 257.14
**pocked**
  indented 257.17
  spotted 374.13
**pocket**
  *n.* aviation 278.41
  container 193.2
  funds 835.14
  pit 257.2
  purse 836.14
  *v.* enclose 236.5
  endure 861.7
  legislate 742.18
  put in 184.14
  take 822.13
  *adj.* miniature 196.12

**pocketbook**
  purse 836.14
  record book 570.11
**pocket money** 835.19
**pockmark**
  *n.* blemish 679.1
  indentation 257.6
  *v.* indent 257.14
**pockmarked**
  indented 257.17
  spotted 374.13
**pocky** rough 261.6
  spotted 374.13
  syphilitic 686.57
**pod**
  *n.* hull 228.16
  seals 74.5
  seed vessel 411.28
  *v.* husk 232.9
**PO'd** 952.26
**podgy** corpulent 195.18
  stubby 203.10
**podiatrist** 688.8
**podium** 216.13
**poem**
  beautiful thing 900.7
  verse 609.6
  written matter 602.10
**poesy** bad poetry 609.3
  poetic inspiration
    609.12
  poetic works 609.7
  verse 609.1
**poet** author 602.15
  imaginer 535.12
  versifier 609.13
**poetaster** 609.14
**poetic(al)** lyric 609.17
  visionary 535.24
**poetic justice**
  justice 976.1
  poetics 609.2
**poetic license** 609.2
**poetics** 609.2
**poetize** 609.15
**poetry** grace 600.2
  Muses 609.12
  verse 609
**pogrom** 409.5
**poignancy**
  acrimony 161.4
  distressfulness 864.5
  eloquence 600.4
  incisiveness 600.3
  pungency 433.1
**poignant**
  acrimonious 161.13
  deep-felt 855.26
  eloquent 600.12
  incisive 600.11
  painful 424.10
  pungent 433.6
  sensitive 422.15
  unpleasant 864.20
**point**
  *n.* acrimony 161.4
  angle 251.2
  benefit 665.4
  cutlery 348.2
  degree 29.1
  direction 290.1
  engraving tool 578.9

extremity 70.2
important point
  672.6
intention 653.1
item 89.4
joke 881.6
location 184.1
mark 568.5
meaning 545.1
minute quantity
  196.7
particular 8.3
pause 144.4
peak 207.8
point of land 256.8
printing 603.6
punctuation
  586.15,18
scout 66.1
sculpting tool 575.4
small amount 35.2
summit 211.2
time 107.1
tip 258.3
topic 484.1
types of 258.18
vanguard 240.2
*v.* bear 290.8
direct 290.6
gravitate 352.15
mark 568.19
punctuate 586.16
sharpen 258.9
tend 174.3
**point at**
  call attention to
    530.10
  designate 568.18
  direct 290.6
  ridicule 967.8
**point-blank**
  exactly 516.20
  in plain words 591.4
  squarely 290.25
**pointed** angular 251.6
  aphoristic 517.6
  concise 592.6
  emphatic 672.20
  meaningful 545.10
  sharp 258.11
  witty 881.15
**pointedly**
  concisely 592.7
  exceptionally 34.20
  intentionally 653.11
**pointer** guide 748.7
  information 557.3
  sign 568.4
**pointless** blunt 259.3
  uninteresting 883.6
  useless 669.9
**pointlessly** dully 883.10
  uselessly 669.15
**pointlessness**
  futility 669.2
  uninterestingness
    883.1
**point of departure**
  301.5
**point of view**
  belief 501.6
  mental outlook 525.2

viewpoint 439.7
**point out**
  call attention to
    530.10
  direct to 290.7
  specify 80.11
  symbolize 568.18
**point to**
  attribute to 155.4
  augur 544.12
  call attention to
    530.10
  designate 568.18
  direct 290.6
  evidence 505.9
  tend 174.3
**point up** 672.13
**poise**
  *n.* behavior 737.1
  equality 30.1
  equanimity 858.3
  gesture 568.14
  sureness 513.5
  *v.* equalize 30.6
  hover 315.10
**poised** balanced 30.9
  composed 858.13
  sure 513.21
**poison**
  *n.* bad liquor 996.14
  evil 675.3
  killer 409.11
  toxicity 684.3
  types of 676.6
  venom 676.3
  *v.* corrupt 692.14
  kill 409.13
  make toxic 686.49
  radioactivate 327.9
  work evil 675.6
**poisoned**
  diseased 686.56
  radioactive 327.10
**poisoner** 409.11
**poisoning**
  corruption 692.2
  execution 1010.7
  intoxication 686.30
  killing 409.1
**poisonous**
  harmful 675.12
  toxic(al) 684.7
  unsavory 429.7
**poisonous plant** 676.7
**poison pen** 971.5
**poke**
  *n.* container 193.2
  hit 283.4
  purse 836.14
  push 283.2
  signal 568.15
  *v.* dally 708.13
  goad 648.15
  go slow 270.6
  hit 283.13
  lash out at 798.16
  search 485.30
  signal 568.22
  thrust 283.11
  touch 425.6
**poke around**
  grope 485.31

search 485.30
**poker** 329.12
**poker face**
  unexpressiveness
    549.5
  unfeeling 856.1
**poker-faced** 549.20
**pokey** 761.9
**poking**
  searching 485.37
  slow 270.10
**poky** base 915.12
  little 196.10
  petty 673.17
  slovenly 62.15
  slow 270.10
  uninteresting 883.6
**pol** 746.1
**polar** final 70.10
  magnetic 342.28
  opposite 239.5
**Polaris**
  guiding star 748.8
  North Star 375.4
**polarity**
  contraposition 239.1
  contrariety 15.1
  duality 90.1
  electric polarity 342.8
  symmetry 248.1
**polarization**
  contraposition 239.1
  disagreement 795.2
  electric polarity 342.8
  repulsion 289.1
**polarize** 239.4
**polarized** 239.5
**polarizing** 795.17
**pole**
  *n.* axis 322.5
  beam 217.3
  electric polarity 342.8
  end 70.2
  flagpole 217.1
  mast 277.13
  oar 277.15
  opposite 239.2
  post 216.8
  remote region 199.4
  shaft 217.1
  summit 211.2
  tower 207.11
  wood 378.3
  *v.* push 285.10
**polecat**
  bad person 986.7
  skunk 414.28
  stinker 437.3
**polemic** arguer 482.12
  argumentation 482.4
  conflict 796.1
  quarrel 795.5
**polemic(al)**
  argumentative 482.1
  contentious 951.26
  quarrelsome 795.17
**polemicist** 482.12
**poles apart**
  different 16.7
  opposite 239.6

**polestar**
center of attraction
226.4
guiding star 748.8
magnet 288.3
North Star 375.4
**pole vault** 319.1
**police**
*n.* police force 699.17
*v.* clean 60.12
keep watch 699.20
protect 699.18
**police car** 272.10
**policed** 699.21
**policeman** 699.15
**police state** 741.4
**police whistle**
alarm 704.1
signal 568.15
**policy** contract 771.3
game of chance 515.8
insurance 699.4
judiciousness 467.7
plan 654.5
political policy 744.4
**polio**
infectious disease
686.12
paralysis 686.25
**polis** city 183.1
city-state 181.1
**polish**
*n.* cultivation 691.3
gloss 260.2
good breeding 936.4
good taste 897.1
literary elegance
589.1
smoother 260.4
types of 260.14
*v.* improve 691.10
rub 350.8
shine 260.7
touch up 691.11
**polished**
complete 722.12
elegant 589.6
improved 691.13
perfected 677.9
shiny 335.33
sleek 260.10
tasteful 897.9
well-bred 936.17
**polish off**
accomplish 722.4
end 70.7
kill 409.14
**polite** 936.14
**politely** 936.19
**politeness**
courtesy 936.1
etiquette 646.3
**politic** cautious 895.8
cunning 735.12
expedient 670.5
judicious 467.19
political 744.43
skillful 733.20
**political**
governmental 741.17
politic 744.43

**political party**
faction 788.4
party 744.24
**political science** 744.2
**politician**
expert 733.11
Machiavellian 735.8
politico 746
**politicize**
democratize 745.16
politick 744.38
**politicking** 744.12
**politics**
Machiavellianism
735.2
political affairs 744
political science
744.2
**polity** country 181.1
government 741.1
judiciousness 467.7
people 417.2
policy 654.5
political policy 744.4
politics 744.1
**polka dot** mark 568.5
spottiness 374.3
**polka-dot** 374.13
**poll**
*n.* canvass 485.13
election returns
744.21
head 211.6
list 88.6
polling place 744.20
tax 846.11
vote 637.6
*v.* canvass 485.28
count votes 637.18
number 87.10
record 570.16
shorten 203.6
**pollen** 406.11
**pollinate** 169.10
**pollination** 169.3
**polliwog**
amphibian 414.32
sailor 276.2
young frog 125.8
**pollster** 485.15
**pollute**
adulterate 44.13
contaminate 682.17
corrupt 692.14
make drunk 996.22
misuse 667.4
work evil 675.6
**polluted** drunk 996.31
morally corrupt
981.14
unclean 682.20
unhealthful 684.5
**pollution**
adulteration 44.3
contamination 682.4
corruption 692.2
evil 675.3
misuse 667.1
unhealthfulness 684.1
**Pollyanna** 888.6
**poltergeist**
evil spirit 1016.8

**occultism** 1034.6
specter 1017.1
**poltroon**
*n.* coward 892.6
*adj.* dastardly 892.12
**poly–** abnormal 85.9
multiform 19.3
numerous 101.6
**polyandry** 933.2
**polychromatic**
coloring 362.15
variegated 374.9
**polychrome**
*n.* variegation 374.1
*adj.* pictorial 574.22
variegated 374.9
**polygamist** 933.12
**polygamy** 933.2
**polyglot** linguist 580.14
reference book 605.6
**polygraph** 690.10
**polyhedral**
angular 251.11
sided 242.7
**Polyhymnia**
Muse 535.2
music patron 464.22
poetry 609.12
**polymer**
chemical 379.1
synthetic 378.7
**polymerization** 379.5
**polymerize** 379.6
**polymorphic** 19.3
**polynomial** 100.8
**polyp**
gastrointestinal dis-
ease 686.27
sore 686.35
**polyphonic** 462.53
**polyphonic prose**
poetry 609.4
prose 610.1
**polyphony** 462.20
**polysyllabic** 601.10
**polysyllable**
long word 582.10
word 582.1
**polytechnic** 567.8
**polytheism** 1020.5
**polytheist** 1020.15
**polytheistic** 1020.24
**pomade**
*n.* ointment 380.3
*v.* oil 380.8
**pomander** 436.6
**pommel**
*n.* saddle 216.18
*v.* pound 283.14
punish 1010.14
**pomp** formality 646.1
ostentation 904.6
procession 71.3
spectacle 446.7
**pomposity**
formality 646.1
grandiloquence 601.1
self-importance 904.7
sureness 513.5
**pompous**
ceremonious 646.8
confident 513.21

grandiloquent 601.8
self-important 904.22
stilted 590.3
**pond** 398.1
**ponder**
be irresolute 627.7
consider 478.12
think over 478.13
**ponderable**
substantial 3.6
weighable 352.19
**ponderous**
bulky 195.19
clumsy 734.20
heavy 352.16
stilted 590.3
uninteresting 883.6
unwieldy 731.18
**ponderousness**
bulkiness 195.9
clumsiness 734.3
literary inelegance
590.1
uninterestingness
883.1
unwieldiness 731.8
weight 352.1
**pone** 308.29
**pontiff** 1038.9
**pontifical**
dogmatic 513.22
papal 1037.15
pompous 904.22
**pontificate**
*n.* mastership 739.7
papacy 1037.6
*v.* be bombastic 601.6
be ostentatious
904.14
dogmatize 513.10
**pontoon** 277.11
**pony**
British money 835.8
horse 414.11
interpretation 552.3
little thing 196.4
race horse 414.17
**ponytail** 230.5,30
**pooch** 414.22
**pooh-pooh**
ridicule 967.9
slight 966.6
**pool** association 788.9
body of water 398.1
funds 835.14
stakes 515.5
stock market 833.17
swimming pool
878.13
**pooling**
centralization 226.8
cooperation 786.1
**poolroom**
gambling house
515.15
playground 878.12
**pooped**
exhausted 717.8
languid 708.19
weak 160.12
worn-out 692.38

poop out
  become exhausted
    717.5
  come to nothing
    725.12
  fall through 314.3
  fatigue 717.4
  weaken 160.9
poor base 915.12
  humble 906.9
  illogical 483.12
  ill-provided 662.12
  indigent 838.7
  inferior 680.9
  meager 662.10
  paltry 673.18
  sparse 102.5
  thin 205.20
  unfavorable 969.22
  unskillful 734.15
  weak 160.15
poor, the
  the needy 838.3
  the underprivileged
    919.6
poor devil
  bad person 986.2
  poor person 838.4
  sufferer 866.11
poorhouse 700.4
poorly basely 915.17
  inferiorly 680.12
  meagerly 662.15
  unskillfully 734.23
poor taste 898.1
poor timing 130.2
pop
  n. antiquated person
    123.8
  detonation 456.3
  drink 308.48
  faint sound 452.3
  father 170.9
  popular music 462.8
  vulgarity 898.1
  v. blast 456.8
  bulge 256.10
  faint sound 452.15
  adj. popular 898.14
  adv. suddenly 113.9
pop culture 898.1
pope 1038.9
popery 1020.7
popeyed
  astonished 920.9
  bulging 256.15
  defective eyes 440.12
popeyes eye 439.9
  defective eyes 440.6
pop in enter 302.7
  insert 304.3
popish
  Catholic 1020.28
  papal 1037.15
pop off 408.20
popover 308.31
popping 456.11
poppycock 547.3
populace people 417.2
  population 190.1
popular
  approved 968.19

beloved 931.22
  common 898.14
  customary 642.15
  desired 634.29
  famous 914.16
  fashionable 644.11
  lay 1039.3
  prevalent 79.12
  public 815.9
  usual 84.8
popular front 744.33
popularity
  applause 968.2
  fashionableness 644.2
  love 931.1
  repute 914.1
popularize
  explain 552.10
  make clear 548.6
  vulgarize 898.9
popular music 462.8
popular prices 849.2
populate people 188.9
  settle 184.16
populated 188.12
population
  inhabitants 190
  people 417.2
  peopling 188.2
  settlement 184.6
  stars 375.8
populous
  crowded 74.22
  inhabited 188.12
  teeming 101.9
pop up appear 446.9
  arrive 300.6
  ascend 315.9
  be unexpected 540.6
  chance 156.11
  occur 151.6
porcelain
  n. ceramic ware
    576.2,8
  adj. ceramic 576.7
porch
  church part 1042.9
  entrance 302.6
  veranda 192.21
porcine 414.49
porcupine 414.28,58
pore duct 396.13
  opening 265.1
  outlet 303.9
pore over
  examine 485.23
  scrutinize 439.15
  study 564.12
pork meat 308.16
  political patronage
    744.36
pork barrel
  booty 824.11
  depository 836.12
  political patronage
    744.36
  swapping 150.2
porker 414.9
pornographic 990.9
pornography film 990.4
  literature 602.12
  obscenity 990.4

porosity 265.9
porous
  exudative 303.20
  holey 265.21
porpoise 414.35,64
porridge cereal 308.34
  pulp 390.2
  semiliquid 389.5
port
  n. airport 278.22
  behavior 737.1
  demeanor 446.4
  destination 300.5
  harbor 700.6
  left side 244.1
  outlet 303.9
  refuge 700.1
  window 265.8
  adj. left 244.4
  adv. leftward 244.6
portability 271.4
portable 271.17
portage fee 846.7
  transportation 271.3
portal entrance 302.6
  foyer 192.19
portend
  forebode 544.11
  forewarn 703.6
  predict 543.10
portent
  forewarning 703.2
  omen 544.3
  ominousness 544.7
portentous
  extraordinary 85.14
  forewarning 703.8
  ominous 544.17
  weighty 672.19
porter carrier 271.5
  doorkeeper 699.12
  trainman 274.13
portfolio
  bookholder 605.20
  emblem of authority
    739.9
  securities 834.1
porthole hole 265.4
  window 265.8
portico
  colonnade 217.5
  foyer 192.19
  passageway 657.4
portion
  n. amount 28.2
  dose 55.5
  drink 307.4
  drug dose 687.6
  endowment 818.9
  fate 640.2
  length 202.3
  part 55.1
  serving 307.10
  share 816.5
  v. apportion 816.6
  dole out 816.8
  segment 49.18
portioning 816.1
portly 195.18
portmanteau word
  ambiguous expression
    550.2

counter word 582.12
  hybrid word 582.11
portrait copy 24.1
  description 608.1
  image 572.3
  photograph 577.3
  picture 574.16
portraitist 579.4
portraiture
  description 608.1
  painting 574.5
  portrait 574.16
  representation 572.1
portray act 611.35
  describe 608.12
  picture 574.20
  represent 572.6
portrayal acting 611.9
  description 608.1
  impersonation 572.2
  portrait 574.16
  representation 572.1
portraying 572.10
pose
  n. affectation 903.3
  behavior 737.1
  fakery 616.3
  gesture 568.14
  v. postulate 499.12
  posture 903.13
  propose 773.5
  put 184.11
pose as
  impersonate 572.9
  pretend to be 616.22
Poseidon god 1014.5
  sailor 276.1
  sea god 397.4
  water god 1014.20
poser dilemma 731.6
  hypocrite 1029.3
  impostor 619.6
  posturer 903.8
  puzzle 549.8
poseur imitator 22.4
  impostor 619.6
  posturer 903.8
posh chic 644.13
  grandiose 904.21
posing
  affectation 903.3
  fakery 616.3
  impersonation 572.2
posit postulate 499.12
  put 184.11
position
  n. affirmation 523.1
  attitude 525.1
  belief 501.6
  class 61.2
  function 656.3
  job 656.5
  location 184.1
  orientation 184.3
  outlook 525.2
  political policy 744.4
  premise 482.7
  prestige 914.4
  rank 29.2
  remark 594.4
  role 7.5
  state 7.1

*v.* locate 184.10
**positioned** 184.17
**positioning** 184.5
**position paper**
  affirmation 523.1
  announcement 559.2
  policy 654.5
  statement of belief
    501.4
**positive**
  *n.* copy 24.5
    photoprint 577.5
  *adj.* agreeing 26.9
    asserting 523.7
    believing 501.21
    certain 513.13
    convinced 513.21
    dogmatic 513.22
    electric 342.32
    emphatic 672.20
    helpful 785.21
    numerical 86.8
    outright 34.12
    real 1.15
    unpersuadable 626.13
    unqualified 508.2
**positively**
  *adv.* assertingly 523.9
    certainly 513.23
    decidedly 34.19
    exactly 516.20
    really 1.16
  *interj.* yes 521.18
**positive pole** 342.8
**positivism**
  dogmatism 513.6
  materialism 376.5
  practicalness 536.2
**positivist**
  dogmatist 513.7
  obstinate person
    626.6
  realist 536.3
**positivistic**
  dogmatic 513.22
  materialist 376.11
  philosophy 500.9
  practical 536.6
**posse** group 74.3
  military unit 800.19
  police force 699.17
  search 485.14
**possess** bewitch 1036.9
  demonize 1016.17
  haunt 1017.6
  have 808.4
  know 475.12
  obsess 473.24
  take 822.13
**possessed**
  bewitched 1036.13
  excited 857.23
  haunted 1017.10
  insane 473.28
  obsessed 473.33
  overjoyed 865.14
  owned 808.8
**possession**
  bewitchment 1036.2
  equanimity 858.3
  insanity 473.1
  material wealth 837.1

obsession 473.13
  owning 808
  property 810.1
  self-control 624.5
  spirit control 1017.5
  taking 822.1
  territory 181.1
**possessive**
  proprietary 808.10
  selfish 978.5
**possessor** 809
**possibility**
  conceivability 509
  good chance 156.8
  latency 546.1
  liability 175.1
**possible**
  conceivable 509.6
  latent 546.5
  numerical 86.8
**possibly** 509.9
**possum** 414.28,58
**post**
  *n.* branch 788.10
    column 216.8
    mail 604.5
    market 832.1
    messenger 561.1
    pillar 217.5
    position 656.5
    shaft 217.4
    station 184.2
    stronghold 799.6
    wood 378.3
  *v.* commission 780.9
    inform 557.9
    keep accounts 845.8
    list 88.8
    mail 604.13
    make haste 709.5
    pay 841.16
    place 184.11
    pledge 772.10
    publicize 559.15
    record 570.16
    rush 269.9
    send 271.14
**postage** 604.6
**postal** 604.15
**postcard** 604.4
**postdate**
  *n.* date 114.4
    posteriority 117.1
  *v.* date 114.13
    mistime 115.2
**postdated** 115.3
**postdiluvian** 117.5
**posted**
  informed 475.18
  located 184.17
  pledged 772.12
  recorded 570.18
**poster**
  mail carrier 561.6
  sign 559.7
**posterior**
  *n.* buttocks 241.4
    rear 241.1
  *adj.* following 65.4
    rear 241.9
    subsequent 117.4

**posteriority**
  sequence 65.1
  subsequence 117
  the future 121.1
**posterity** kinsmen 11.2
  progeny 171
  sequel 117.2
  successor 67.4
**postern**
  *n.* back 241.1
    entrance 302.6
  *adj.* rear 241.9
**postgraduate**
  *n.* graduated student
    566.8
  *adj.* scholastic 562.20
    studentlike 566.12
**posthaste** fast 269.21
  hastily 709.13
**posthumous**
  afterdeath 117.5
  postmortem 408.36
**posting**
  appointment 780.2
  placement 184.5
  recording 570.15
**postman** 561.5
**postmark** 604.6
**postmeridian** 134.7
**postmortem**
  *n.* autopsy 408.18
  *v.* examine 485.23
  *adj.* after death
    408.36
**post office** 604.8
**postpaid** 841.22
**postpone** delay 132.9
  put away 668.6
**postponement** 132.4
**postprandial**
  after-dinner 117.5
  eating 307.29
**postscript**
  addition 41.2
  sequel 67.1
**postulant** novice 566.9
  nun 1038.19
  petitioner 774.7
**postulate**
  *n.* axiom 517.2
    fact 1.3
    preliminary 66.2
    premise 482.7
    principle 5.2
    supposition 499.3
  *v.* predicate 499.12
    propose 773.5
**posture**
  *n.* behavior 737.1
    belief 501.6
    fakery 616.3
    gesture 568.14
    looks 446.4
    mental attitude 525.1
    state 7.1
  *v.* pose 903.13
**posturer** 903.8
**posturing** 903.3
**postwar** 117.5
**posy** bouquet 411.23
  bundle 74.8
  compliment 968.6

flower 411.22
**pot**
  *n.* abdomen 193.3
    batch 34.4
    ceramic ware 576.2
    cooker 330.10
    marihuana 687.13
    stakes 515.5
    trophy 916.3
    types of 193.8
    wealth 837.2
  *v.* make ceramics
    576.6
    package 236.9
    plant 413.18
    preserve 701.9
    shoot 285.13
**potable**
  *n.* drink 308.48
    liquor 996.12
  *adj.* drinkable 307.32
**potage** 308.10
**potation**
  beverage 308.48
  drink 307.4
  drinking 307.3
  liquor 996.12
  snort 996.6
  spree 996.5
**potato** 308.35
**pot-au-feu** 308.10
**potbellied**
  bulging 256.14
  corpulent 195.18
**potbelly**
  abdomen 193.3
  corpulent person
    195.12
**potboiler** 602.16
**potency**
  authoritativeness
    739.2
  energy 161.1
  influence 172.1
  power 157.1
  sexuality 419.2
  strength 159.1
  virility 420.2
**potent**
  authoritative 739.15
  influential 172.13
  powerful 157.12
  sexual 419.26
  strong 159.13
  virile 420.12
**potentate** 749.7
**potential**
  *n.* capacity 733.4
    mood 586.11
    possibility 509.1
    voltage 342.11
  *adj.* latent 546.5
    possible 509.6
**potentiality**
  latency 546.1
  possibility 509.1
  power 157.1
**pothead** 642.10
**pother**
  *n.* bustle 707.4
    commotion 62.4
    disorder 532.3

dither 857.5
perplexity 514.3
*v.* annoy 866.13
confuse 532.7
disconcert 514.12
trouble 731.12
**pothole** 257.3
**potholed** 261.6
**potion** dose 687.6
drink 996.6
**potluck**
haphazard 156.4
matter of chance
515.2
**potpourri**
hodgepodge 44.6
music 462.6
scent article 436.6
**potshot**
*n.* matter of chance
515.2
shot 285.5
*v.* shoot 285.13
**potted** 996.31
**potter**
*n.* ceramist 579.7
*v.* fritter away 854.5
trifle 673.13
waste time 708.12
**potter's field** 410.15
**pottery** ceramics 576.1
ceramic ware 576.2
plant 719.3
**potty**
*n.* toilet 311.11
*adj.* insane 473.26
**pouch** 256.10
**pouched** 256.15
**poultice**
*n.* medical dressing
687.33
pulp 390.2
*v.* relieve 886.5
treat 689.30
**poultry** 414.34
**pounce**
*n.* grasping organ
813.4
leap 319.1
plunge 320.1
swoop 316.1
*v.* descend 316.5
jump 319.5
plunge 320.6
**pounce upon**
attack 798.15
be unexpected 540.6
jump 319.5
plunge 320.6
seize on 822.16
surprise 540.7
**pound**
*n.* British money
835.8
foreign money 835.9
hit 283.4
kennel 191.21
place of confinement
761.7
staccato sound 455.1
unit of weight 352.23
*v.* ache 424.8

attack 798.15
beat 283.14
bruise 692.16
confine 761.12
make staccato sounds
455.4
music 462.45
pulverize 361.9
repeat 103.10
sail 275.55
thrust in 304.7
**poundage**
capacity 195.2
charge 846.8
weight 352.1
**pound away**
drudge 716.14
persevere 625.3
**pound-foolish** 854.8
**pounding**
*n.* pulverization 361.4
staccato sound 455.1
*adj.* staccato 455.7
**pour**
*n.* rainstorm 394.2
violent flow 395.5
*v.* abound 661.5
eject 310.24
flow 395.16
give 818.12
gush 303.13
rain 394.9
transfer 271.16
**pour forth**
chatter 596.5
eject 310.24
say 594.23
**pouring** flowing 395.24
rainy 394.10
**pour it on**
hustle 707.14
speed 269.8
work hard 716.13
**pout**
*n.* grimace 249.4
scowl 951.9
*v.* be ill-humored
951.15
bulge 256.10
grimace 249.8
**poverty** poorness 838
scarcity 662.3
**poverty-stricken** 838.8
**POW** 761.11
**powder**
*n.* dust 361.5
explosive 801.9
make-up 900.11
medicine 687.4
*v.* crumble 361.10
leave 301.10
pulverize 361.9
sprinkle 75.6
**powdered**
powdery 361.11
sprinkled 75.10
**powderiness** 361
**powdery** 361.11
**power**
*n.* authoritativeness
739.2
control 741.2

country 181.1
eloquence 600.3
energy 161.1
governance 739.5
greatness 34.1
impulse 283.1
influence 172.1
means 658.1
personage 672.8
potency 157
prerogative 739.1
privilege 958.3
strength 159.1
supremacy 36.3
talent 733.4
will power 624.4
*v.* impel 283.10
**powered** 348.11
**power elite**
important persons
672.8
superiors 36.5
the rulers 749.15
**powerful**
authoritative 739.15
eloquent 600.11
great 34.6
influential 172.13
potent 157.12
strong 159.13
**powerfully**
authoritatively
739.18
eloquently 600.15
potently 157.15
strongly 159.21
very 34.18
**powerhouse**
man of action 707.8
power station 342.18
strong man 159.6
**powerless**
impotent 158.13
uninfluential 173.3
weak 160.12
**power of attorney**
commission 780.1
substitution 149.1
**power plant**
aviation 278.33
machinery 348.4
plant 719.3
powerhouse 342.18
**power reactor** 326.13
**powers that be, the**
influential persons
172.6
officeholders 746.11
the government
741.3
the rulers 749.15
**power structure**
hierarchy 61.4
power 157.1
rank 29.2
superiors 36.5
the rulers 749.15
**powwow**
*n.* conference 597.6
political convention
744.8
*v.* confer 597.11

**pox** 686.16
**practicability**
possibility 509.2
utility 665.3
workability 164.3
**practicable**
expedient 670.6
possible 509.7
workable 164.10
**practical**
businesslike 656.15
expedient 670.6
operative 164.9
possible 509.7
realistic 536.6
sensible 467.18
ungullible 504.5
usable 665.22
useful 665.18
wieldy 732.14
workable 164.10
**practicality**
intelligence 467.6
possibility 509.2
realism 536.2
utility 665.3
wieldiness 732.2
**practical joke** 881.10
**practical joker**
deceiver 619.1
mischief-maker 738.3
**practically**
approximately 200.23
expediently 670.8
usefully 665.25
**practice**
*n.* action 705.1
behavior 737.1
custom 642.1
exercise 716.6
experience 733.9
habit 642.4
mathematics 87.4
observance 768.1
operation 164.1
rite 1040.3
study 564.3
training 562.3
tryout 489.3
vocation 656.6
way 657.1
*v.* act 705.4
busy oneself with
656.11
exercise 705.7
experiment 489.8
observe 768.3
operate 164.5
rehearse 611.37
repeat 103.8
study 564.12
train 562.14
use 665.10
**practiced**
accomplished 733.24
experienced 733.26
**practicing**
acting 705.10
observant 768.4
**practitioner** 718.1
**praetor** 1002.2

**pragmatic(al)**
  expedient 670.6
  philosophy 500.9
  practical 536.6
  sensible 467.18
  useful 665.18
**pragmatism**
  experiment 489.1
  functionalism 665.6
  materialism 376.5
  practicalness 536.2
**pragmatist** 536.3
**prairie** grassland 411.8
  horizontal 214.3
  plain 387.1
  space 179.4
  the country 182.1
**praise**
  n. approval 968.5
  flattery 970.1
  honor 916.4
  thanks 949.2
  worship 1032.2
  v. flatter 970.5
  honor 916.8
  laud 968.12
  worship 1032.11
**praiseworthy** 968.20
**pram** 272.6
**prana**
  life principle 466.5
  soul 407.3
  theosophy 1034.18
**prance**
  n. gait 273.14
  jump 319.2
  v. dance 879.5
  jump 319.6
  ride 273.33
  strut 904.15
  walk 273.27
**prancing**
  n. leaping 319.3
  adj. leaping 319.7
**prandial** 307.29
**prank**
  n. trick 881.10
  v. dress up 231.41
  ornament 901.8
**prankish**
  mischievous 738.6
  waggish 881.17
**prankster**
  humorist 881.12
  mischief-maker 738.3
**prate**
  n. chatter 596.3
  nonsense 547.2
  v. chatter 596.5
  talk nonsense 547.5
**pratfall** an error 518.6
  failure 725.3
  tumble 316.3
**prattle**
  n. chatter 596.3
  nonsense 547.2
  speech 594.1
  v. blabber 596.5
  chat 597.10
  talk nonsense 547.5
**prattler** 596.4
**prawn** 308.25

**praxis** action 705.1
  behavior 737.1
  custom 642.1
  habit 642.4
**pray**
  v. entreat 774.11
  petition 774.10
  supplicate 1032.12
  interj. please 774.20
**prayer** entreaty 774.2
  supplication 1032.4
  worship 1032.8
**prayer book**
  book 605.1
  ritualistic manual
    1040.12
**prayerful**
  petitionary 774.16
  pious 1028.8
  worshipful 1032.15
**preach** advise 754.6
  discourse 562.17
  lecture 599.11
**preacher**
  expounder 599.5
  lecturer 565.8
  minister 1038.3
**preaching**
  inducement 648.3
  lecture 599.3
**preachy** 754.8
**preamble**
  n. prelude 66.2
  v. preface 64.3
**prearrange** plan 654.9
  precontrive 641.3
  prepare 720.6
**prearranged**
  precontrived 641.5
  prepared 720.16
**prearrangement**
  plan 654.1
  preordering 641
  preparation 720.1
**precarious**
  dangerous 697.12
  unreliable 514.19
**precative**
  imploring 774.17
  petitionary 774.16
  worshipful 1032.15
**precaution**
  n. forethought 895.3
  v. forewarn 703.6
**precautionary**
  cautious 895.10
  forewarning 703.8
**precautious** 895.10
**precede** antecede 64.2
  begin 68.10
  be prior 116.3
  go before 66.3
  lead 292.2
  outrank 36.11
**precedence**
  antecedence 64
  authority 739.4
  importance 672.1
  leading 292.1
  priority 116.1
  rank 29.2
  superiority 36.1

**precedent**
  antecedent 116.2
  judgment 494.5
  model 25.1
  precursor 66.1
**preceding**
  n. antecedence 64.1
  leading 292.1
  adj. antecedent 64.4
  foregoing 119.11
  leading 292.3
  preliminary 66.4
  prior 116.4
**precept** a belief 501.2
  directive 752.3
  legal order 752.6
  maxim 517.1
  rule 751
**preceptive**
  commanding 752.14
  educational 562.19
  prescriptive 751.4
**precinct** arena 802.1
  district 180.5
  election district
    744.16
  nearness 200.1
  region 180.2
**precincts**
  environment 233.1
  neighborhood 180.1
**preciosity**
  affectation 903.5
  formalism 646.2
  pretentiousness 589.3
**precious**
  n. endearment 932.5
  adj. affected 903.18
  beloved 931.22
  elegant 589.9
  outright 34.12
  punctilious 646.10
  valuable 848.10
**precious stone**
  gem 384.6
  jewel 901.6
**precipice** cliff 213.3
  peak 207.8
**precipitant**
  hasty 709.10
  reckless 894.8
  sudden 113.5
**precipitate**
  n. deposit 43.2
  result 154.1
  sedimentation 354.5
  v. deposit 354.11
  descend 316.5
  fell 318.5
  gravitate 352.15
  hasten 709.4
  rain 394.9
  adj. fast 269.19
  hasty 709.10
  impulsive 630.9
  premature 131.8
  reckless 894.8
  sudden 113.5
  unprepared 721.8
**precipitation**
  deposit 354.5
  downcast 318.2

  hastiness 709.2
  impulsiveness 630.2
  prematurity 131.2
  rain 394.1
  recklessness 894.2
  sediment 43.2
  speed 269.1
**precipitous**
  hasty 709.10
  perpendicular 213.12
  reckless 894.8
  steep 219.18
  sudden 113.5
**précis**
  abridgment 607.1
  summary 203.3
**precise**
  v. be accurate 516.10
  particularize 80.9
  adj. detailed 8.9
  discriminating 492.7
  exact 516.16
  fastidious 896.9
  meticulous 533.12
  particular 80.12
  punctilious 646.10
**precisely**
  adv. exactly 516.20
  meticulously 533.16
  particularly 80.15
  punctually 131.14
  squarely 290.25
  thus 8.10
  interj. yes 521.18
**precisian**
  n. conformist 82.2
  fastidious person
    896.6
  pedant 476.5
  adj. affected 903.18
  punctilious 646.10
**precision**
  accuracy 516.3
  fastidiousness 896.1
  meticulousness 533.3
  specification 80.6
**precisionist** 476.5
**preclude** exclude 77.4
  prevent 730.14
  prohibit 778.3
**precluding** 77.9
**preclusive**
  exclusive 77.8
  preventing 730.19
  prohibitive 778.6
**precocious** 131.8
**precognition**
  foreknowledge 542.3
  intuition 481.1
  understanding 475.3
**precognitive**
  foreseeing 542.7
  intuitive 481.5
**preconceive** 495.2
**preconceived** 495.3
**preconception**
  partiality 527.3
  prejudgment 495.1
**preconscious**
  n. psyche 690.35
  adj. subconscious
    690.48

**prelapsarian**
  innocent 984.6
  prior 116.5
**prelate** 1038.9
**preliminary**
  *n.* inauguration 68.5
  prelude 66.2
  preparation 720.1
  *adj.* preceding 64.4
  precursory 66.4
  prefatory 68.16
**prelude**
  *n.* music 462.26
  preamble 66.2
  precedence 64.1
  *v.* preface 64.3
**preludial**
  preceding 64.4
  preliminary 68.16
**premarital** 989.27
**premarital relations**
  989.7
**premature**
  too early 131.8
  untimely 130.7
**prematurely** 131.13
**prematurity**
  earliness 131.2
  untimeliness 130.1
**premeditate**
  calculate 653.8
  prearrange 641.3
**premeditated**
  prearranged 641.5
  predeliberated 653.10
**premeditation**
  forethought 542.2
  intentionality 653.3
  prearrangement
    641.1
**premier**
  *n.* ruler 749.6
  *adj.* first 68.17
  most important
    672.23
**premiere**
  *n.* theatrical perfor-
    mance 611.13
  *v.* give a show 611.33
**premise**
  *n.* antecedent 116.2
  basis for belief 505.1
  logic 482.7
  prelude 66.2
  supposition 499.3
  *v.* preface 64.3
**premises** 180.1
**premium**
  *n.* debt 840.3
  discount 847.1
  extra 41.4
  extra pay 841.6
  gratuity 818.5
  *adj.* expensive 848.11
**premonition**
  clairvoyance 1034.8
  forewarning 703.2
  hunch 481.3
  presentiment 544.1
**premonitory**
  augural 544.16
  forewarning 703.8

**predictive** 543.12
**prenatal** 68.15
**preoccupation**
  abstractedness 532.2
  appropriation 822.4
  emotional symptom
    690.23
  engrossment 530.3
  obsession 473.13
  perseverance 625.1
  possession 808.1
  thoughtfulness 478.3
**preoccupied**
  absorbed in thought
    478.22
  abstracted 532.11
  engrossed 530.17
  inattentive 531.7
  obsessed 473.33
  persevering 625.7
**preoccupy**
  absorb the thought
    478.20
  appropriate 822.19
  engross 530.13
  obsess 473.24
**preordain** 640.6
**preordained** 640.8
**prep**
  *n.* preparation 720.1
  *v.* prepare 720.6
**prepaid** 841.22
**preparation**
  foresight 542.1
  harmonization 463.2
  making ready 720
  manufacture 167.3
  medicine 687.4
  provision 659.1
  training 562.3
**preparatory**
  preceding 64.4
  preparative 720.20
**preparatory school**
  567.6
**prepare**
  arrange for 720.11
  cook 330.4
  create 167.10
  equip 659.8
  get ready to 720.10
  make ready 720.6
  provide 659.7
  take precautions
    895.6
  train 562.14
  write 602.21
**prepared**
  accomplished 733.24
  expectant 539.11
  foreseeing 542.7
  provided 659.13
  ready 720.16
**preparedness**
  carefulness 533.1
  foreign policy 744.5
  readiness 720.4
**preparer** 720.5
**preponderance**
  ascendancy 739.6
  influence 172.1
  majority 100.2

  superiority 36.1
**preponderant**
  chief 36.14
  dominant 741.18
  influential 172.14
**preponderate**
  dominate 741.15
  excel 36.6
**preposition** 586.3
**prepositional**
  *n.* case 586.9
  *adj.* grammatical
    586.17
**prepossess**
  appropriate 822.19
  prejudice 527.9
**prepossessed**
  biased 527.12
  obsessed 473.33
**prepossessing**
  alluring 650.7
  pleasant 863.7
**prepossession**
  appropriation 822.4
  obsession 473.13
  possession 808.1
  preference 637.5
  prejudgment 495.1
  prejudice 527.3
**preposterous**
  fanciful 535.20
  foolish 470.10
  impossible 510.7
  overpriced 848.12
  unbelievable 503.10
  undue 961.9
**prepotency**
  ascendancy 739.6
  power 157.1
  superiority 36.1
**prepotent**
  dominant 741.18
  influential 172.14
  powerful 157.12
**preprandial** 307.29
**prepublication** 542.1
**prerequisite**
  *n.* condition 507.2
  preparation 720.1
  requirement 639.2
  *adj.* preparatory
    720.20
  requisite 639.13
**prerogative**
  authority 739.1
  privilege 958.3
  superiority 36.1
**presage**
  *n.* foreknowledge
    542.3
  prediction 543.1
  presentiment 544.1
  *v.* portend 544.10
  predict 543.9
**presaged**
  augured 544.15
  predicted 543.14
**presbytery**
  church council 755.4
  church office 1037.5
  church part 1042.9
  clergy 1038.1

  parsonage 1042.7
**preschool**
  *n.* school 567.4
  *adj.* scholastic 567.18
**preschooler**
  infant 125.7
  pupil 566.4
**prescience**
  foreknowledge 542.3
  predetermination
    640.1
**prescribe** advise 754.5
  direct 747.8
  impose on 963.6
  legalize 998.8
  order 752.10
  remedy 687.38
**prescribed**
  customary 642.15
  limited 234.7
  preceptive 751.4
**prescript**
  directive 752.3
  law 998.3
  maxim 517.1
  precept 751.1
**prescription**
  custom 642.1
  directive 752.3
  formula 751.3
  law 998.3
  limitation 234.2
  possession 808.1
  precept 751.1
  privilege 958.3
  remedy 687.1
  rule 84.4
**prescriptive**
  commanding 752.14
  customary 642.15
  exclusive 77.8
  instructive 751.4
  mandatory 752.13
  traditional 123.12
  usual 84.8
**presence**
  apparition 446.5
  behavior 737.1
  existence 1.1
  ghost 1017.1
  hereness 186
  looks 446.4
  phantom 519.4
**present**
  *n.* gift 818.4
  now 120
  tense 586.12
  time 105.1
  *v.* acquaint 927.13
  adduce evidence
    505.13
  confront 240.8
  direct 290.6
  dramatize 611.33
  give 818.12
  give for free 850.4
  manifest 555.5
  offer 773.4
  phrase 588.4
  put to choice 637.21
  say 594.23
  supply 659.7

*adj.* at hand 186.12
existent 1.13
immediate 120.2
**presentable**
beautiful 900.17
giveable 818.23
tolerable 674.19
**presentation**
appearance 446.1
consecration 1037.10
display 555.2
gift 818.4
giving 818.1
information 557.1
introduction 927.4
offer 773.1
party 922.14
spectacle 446.7
theatrical perfor-
mance 611.13
**present-day**
modern 122.13
present 120.2
**presentiment**
emotion 855.3
foreboding 544
foreknowledge 542.3
forewarning 703.2
hunch 481.3
prediction 543.1
**presently** 131.16
**presentment**
arraignment 1004.3
display 555.2
giving 818.1
representation 572.1
theatrical perfor-
mance 611.13
**preservation**
conservation 701
divine function
1013.16
maintenance 140.2
perpetuation 112.4
protection 699.1
retention 813.1
storage 660.5
**preservative**
*n.* preservative me-
dium 701.3
*adj.* conservative
140.8
preservatory 701.10
**preserve**
*n.* refuge 700.1
reserve 701.6
sweets 308.39
*v.* care for 699.19
conserve 701.7
cure 701.8
perpetuate 112.5
reserve 660.12
retain 813.5
sustain 143.4
**preserved** kept 701.11
reserved 660.15
**preserver** 701.4
**preshrunk** 198.13
**preside**
administer justice
1000.5
entertain 925.8

govern 741.12
officiate 747.11
**presidency**
directorship 747.4
mastership 739.7
supremacy 36.3
**president**
educator 565.9
executive 748.3
head of state 749.6
**presiding** 747.14
**press**
*n.* enlistment 780.6
extractor 305.9
impulse 648.6
informant 557.5
printing 603.9,24
printing office 603.11
squeezing 198.2
throng 74.4
thrust 283.2
urgency 672.4
*v.* appropriate 822.20
be heavy upon
352.11
coax 648.14
compel 756.6
densify 354.9
embrace 932.16
enlist 780.16
hasten 709.4
importune 774.12
insist 753.7
smooth 260.6
squeeze 198.8
strain 716.10
thrust 283.11
urge upon 773.8
**press, the** news 558.1
public press 605.23
**press agent** agent 781.3
publicist 559.9
**press charges** 1005.7
**pressed** 709.11
**pressing**
*n.* extraction 305.7
importuning 774.3
urging 648.5
*adj.* compelling 756.9
demanding 753.8
motivating 648.25
urgent 672.21
**press notice** 559.4
**press on** elapse 105.5
hustle 707.13
make haste 709.5
make one's way 294.4
**press release** 559.3
**pressure**
*n.* adversity 729.1
authority 739.4
aviation 278.31
burden 352.7
coercion 756.3
drive 648.6
entreaty 774.3
influence 172.1
insistence 753.3
necessity 639.4
squeezing 198.2
tension 859.3
thrust 283.2

touching 425.2
urgency 672.4
urging 648.5
*v.* compel 756.6
importune 774.12
urge 648.14
**pressure group**
influential persons
172.6
interest group 744.31
party 788.4
**prestidigitation**
illusoriness 519.2
juggling 618.5
**prestidigitator**
entertainer 612.1
trickster 619.2
**prestige**
authority 739.4
influence 172.1
notability 672.2
repute 914.4
respect 964.1
superiority 36.1
**prestigious**
authoritative 739.15
influential 172.13
notable 672.18
reputable 914.15
respected 964.11
**presto**
*n.* music 462.25
tempo 463.24
*adj.* instantaneous
113.4
*adv.* music 462.56
**presumable**
probable 511.6
supposable 499.15
**presumably**
probably 511.8
supposedly 499.17
**presume**
be hopeful 888.7
be insolent 913.6
believe 501.11
entail 76.4
expect 539.5
imply 546.4
judge 494.8
prejudge 495.2
suppose 499.10
take the liberty 961.6
think probable 511.5
**presumed**
expected 539.13
implied 546.7
prejudged 495.3
supposed 499.14
**presume upon**
exploit 665.16
impose 963.7
take liberties 961.7
**presumption**
arrogance 912.2
belief 501.6
entailment 76.2
hope 888.1
implication 546.2
insolence 913.1
meddling 238.2
prejudgment 495.1

probability 511.1
recklessness 894.3
supposition 499.3
undueness 961.2
**presumptive**
evidential 505.17
probable 511.6
supposed 499.14
**presumptuous**
arrogant 912.10
foolhardy 894.9
insolent 913.8
meddlesome 238.9
undue 961.11
**presuppose** entail 76.4
imply 546.4
prejudge 495.2
suppose 499.10
**presupposed**
implied 546.7
prejudged 495.3
**presupposition**
implication 546.2
prejudgment 495.1
prelude 66.2
premise 482.7
supposition 499.3
**pre-teens** 124.2
**pretend** affect 903.12
fake 616.21
lay claim to 753.5
presume 961.6
pretext 649.3
try to 714.7
usurp 961.8
**pretended**
assumed 903.16
falsified 616.26
pretexted 649.5
**pretender**
affecter 903.7
impostor 619.6
usurper 961.4
**pretending** 616.3
**pretense**
affectation 903.1
fakery 616.3
ostentation 904.1
pretext 649.1
privilege 958.3
reason 153.2
**pretension**
affectation 903.1
fakery 616.3
grandiloquence 601.1
ostentation 904.1
pretext 649.1
privilege 958.3
**pretentious**
affected 903.15
boastful 910.11
elegant 589.9
grandiloquent 601.8
ostentatious 904.18
**preternatural** 85.15
**preternaturalism**
otherworldliness 85.7
supernaturalism
1034.2
**pretext**
*n.* excuse 649
fakery 616.3

paint 362.8
preinstruction 562.4
**primitive**
*n.* native 190.3
prehistoric man 123.7
word 582.2
*adj.* basic 212.8
beginning 68.15
causal 153.15
essential 5.8
former 119.10
native 189.5
old 123.11
uncouth 898.12
**primness**
affectation 903.6
formality 646.1
**primogenitors** 170.7
**primogeniture**
inheritance 819.2
oldness 123.1
seniority 126.3
**primordial**
causal 153.15
primitive 123.11
**primp** dress up 231.41
ornament 901.8
**primrose** pink 368.8
yellow 370.4
**primrose path** 657.2
**prince**
good person 985.1
nobleman 918.7
potentate 749.7
**princely**
dignified 905.12
grandiose 904.21
liberal 853.4
magnanimous 979.6
noble 918.10
sovereign 739.17
**princess**
noblewoman 918.8
sovereign queen
749.11
**principal**
*n.* capital 835.15
chief 672.10
educator 565.9
lead 612.6
master 749.3
organ stop 465.22
superior 36.4
*adj.* chief 36.14
first 68.17
most important
672.23
**principality**
angel 1015.1
country 181.1
district 180.5
leadership 739.7
predominancy 739.6
**principle** a belief 501.2
axiom 517.2
cause 153.1
commitment 153.10
essence 5.2
foundation 216.6
motive 648.1
precept 751.2
rule 84.4

**principled** 974.13
**principles** basics 68.6
ethics 957.1
honesty 974.1
policy 654.5
**print**
*n.* copy 24.5
effect 154.3
engraving 578.6
imprint 603.3
indentation 257.6
mark 568.7
photography 577.5
photoprint 24.5
picture 574.12
type 603.6
*v.* engrave 578.10
imbed 142.9
mark 568.19
process photos
577.15
publish 603.14
represent 572.6
**printed**
engraved 578.12
in print 603.19
written 602.22
**printed circuit**
electric circuit 342.4
electronic circuit
343.8
**printed matter**
printing 603.10
written matter 602.10
**printer**
bookman 605.21
press 603.11
pressman 603.12
writer 602.18
**printer's devil**
attendant 750.5
printer 603.12
**printing** edition 605.2
graphic arts 578.1
publication 559.1
representation 572.1
typography 603
writing style 602.4
**printing equipment**
603.26
**printing press**
printing 603.9
types of 603.24
**printmaking**
graphic arts 578.1
printing 603.1
**printout**
computer 349.18
written matter 602.10
**prior** former 119.10
leading 292.3
preceding 64.4
previous 116.4
**priority**
anteriority 240.1
authority 739.4
importance 672.1
leading 292.1
precedence 64.1
previousness 116
superiority 36.1
**prism** 443.1

**prismatic**
angular 251.11
coloring 362.15
variegated 374.9
**prison** 761.8
**prisonbreak** 632.1
**prisoner**
accused 1005.6
convict 761.11
**prison guard** 761.10
**prison term** 108.4
**prissy** 421.14
**pristine** causal 153.15
innocent 984.6
natural 721.13
new 122.7
primitive 123.11
undamaged 677.8
unused 668.12
**prittle-prattle**
*n.* chatter 596.3
*v.* chat 597.10
**privacy** aloneness 89.2
retreat 700.5
seclusion 924.1
secrecy 614.2
**private**
*n.* enlisted man 800.8
*adj.* confidential
614.13
individual 80.12
inner 5.6
personal 417.12
secluded 924.8
**privateer**
*n.* pirate 825.7
sailor 276.1
*v.* pirate 824.17
**privateering** 824.6
**private eye** 781.11
**privately**
personally 80.16
secretly 614.19
**private parts** 419.10
**privation**
divestment 822.6
indigence 838.2
loss 812.1
**privilege**
*n.* exemption 762.8
right 958.4
superiority 36.1
*v.* authorize 777.11
**privileged**
authorized 777.17
confidential 614.14
exempt 762.29
**privy**
*n.* outhouse 311.10
*adj.* cognizant of
475.16
furtive 614.12
private 614.13
secluded 924.8
**privy council**
cabinet 742.8
council 755.1
**prize**
*n.* award 916.2
booty 824.11
good thing 674.5
leverage 287.1

memorial 570.12
pry 287.4
the best 674.8
thing desired 634.11
*v.* cherish 931.19
judge 494.9
measure 490.11
price 846.13
pry 287.8
rate highly 672.12
respect 964.4
*adj.* best 674.18
**prized** beloved 931.22
priced 846.16
respected 964.11
**prizefight** 796.9
**prizefighter** 800.2
**prizewinner** 733.14
**PR man** 559.9
**pro**
*n.* affirmative 482.14
argument 482.5
expert 733.11
professional 718.4
*adj.* approving 968.17
occupational 656.16
*prep.* in favor of
968.21
**pro and con** 482.19
**probability**
chance 156.1
expectation 539.1
good chance 156.8
liability 175.1
likelihood 511
possibility 509.1
prediction 543.1
tendency 174.1
the future 121.1
**probable**
expected 539.13
future 121.8
likely 511.6
possible 509.6
predictable 543.13
**probably**
in the future 121.9
likely 511.8
**probate**
*n.* bequest 818.10
*v.* confirm 505.12
**probation** 489.2
**probationary**
experimental 489.11
on probation 566.13
**probationer**
beginner 68.2
novice 566.9
nurse 688.13
**probe**
*n.* investigation 485.4
nurse 688.13
rocket 281.6
search 485.14
spacecraft 282.6,14
testing device 489.4
*v.* investigate 485.22
measure 490.11
sound out 489.9
**probing**
*n.* deepening 209.7
questioning 485.11

affirmed 523.8
pretexted 649.5
**profession**
acknowledgment
521.3
affirmation 523.1
false claim 649.2
profession of belief
501.7
testimony 505.3
vocation 656.6
**professional**
*n.* expert 733.11
worker 718.4
*adj.* accomplished
733.24
occupational 656.16
scholastic 562.20
skillful 733.20
**professionalism** 656.8
**professor**
academic rank 565.4
expert 733.11
teacher 565.1
**professorial**
pedagogical 565.12
studious 564.17
**professorship** 565.11
**proffer**
*n.* offer 773.1
*v.* give 818.12
offer 773.4
**proffered** 622.7
**proficiency**
ability 157.2
preparedness 720.4
profound knowledge
475.6
skill 733.1
**proficient** able 157.14
expert 677.9
skillful 733.20
suited 720.17
**profile**
*n.* biography 608.4
contour 246.2
description 608.1
diagram 654.3
outline 235.2
portrait 574.16
side 242.1
*v.* outline 235.9
**profit**
*n.* benefit 665.4
expedience 670.1
gain 811.3
good 674.4
incentive 648.7
receipts 844.1
*v.* be expedient 670.3
be of use 665.17
do good 674.10
make money 811.11
**profitable**
expedient 670.5
gainful 811.15
good 674.12
helpful 785.21
paying 841.21
useful 665.21

**profit by**
improve the occasion
129.8
take advantage of
665.15
**profiteer**
*n.* predator 822.12
*v.* overcharge 848.7
**profiteering** 848.5
**profitless** 669.12
**profit sharing** 815.2
**profligacy**
dissoluteness 989.3
prodigality 854.1
turpitude 981.5
**profligate**
*n.* bad person 986.5
unchaste person
989.10
*adj.* morally corrupt
981.14
prodigal 854.8
unchaste 989.25
**profound** deep 209.10
deep-felt 855.26
huge 195.20
learned 475.21
outright 34.12
recondite 549.16
wise 467.17
**profundity**
abstruseness 549.2
depth 209.1
sagacity 467.5
sizableness 195.6
**profuse** diffuse 593.11
exaggerated 617.4
liberal 853.4
plentiful 661.7
prodigal 854.8
teeming 101.9
**profusely**
abundantly 34.20
liberally 853.5
numerously 101.12
plentifully 661.9
**profusion**
diffuseness 593.1
numerousness 101.1
plenty 661.2
prodigality 854.1
quantity 34.3
**progenitor**
ancestor 170.7
parent 170.8
**progeny** 171.1
**prognosis**
judgment 494.5
medical prognosis
689.14
prediction 543.1
**prognostic**
predictive 543.11
premonitory 544.16
**prognosticate**
predict 543.9
risk 156.12
**prognosticator** 543.4
**program**
*n.* announcement
559.2
list 88.6

music performance
462.34
plan 654.1
political platform
744.7
political program
744.6
schedule 641.2
undertaking 715.1
*v.* automate 349.23
indoctrinate 562.13
list 88.8
plan 654.9
schedule 641.4
**program director**
344.23
**programmer**
broadcaster 344.23
computer 349.22
**progress**
*n.* advance 294.1
continuance 143.1
conversion 145.1
course 267.2
development 148.1
improvement 691.1
journey 273.5
rate 267.4
travel 273.1
water travel 275.9
*v.* advance 294.2
evolve 148.5
get better 691.7
make good 724.9
move 267.5
prosper 728.7
travel 273.17
**progressing**
developing 148.8
improving 691.15
progressive 294.6
traveling 273.35
**progression**
advance 294
continuation 143.1
continuity 71.2
development 148.1
improvement 691.1
numbers 86.7
sequence 65.1
**progressive**
*n.* liberal 745.11
reformer 691.6
*adj.* consecutive 71.9
flowing 267.8
gradational 29.5
improving 691.15
liberal 745.19
modern 122.13
progressing 294.6
**progressivism**
liberalism 745.3
reform 691.5
**prohibit** exclude 77.4
forbid 778.3
make impossible
510.6
prevent 730.14
restrain 760.7
**prohibited**
excluded 77.7
forbidden 778.7

impossible 510.7
**prohibition**
exclusion 77.1
forbidding 778
obstruction 730.2
restraint 760.1
temperance 992.3
**prohibitive**
exclusive 77.8
overpriced 848.12
preventing 730.19
prohibiting 778.6
**project**
*n.* intention 653.1
plan 654.2
task 656.2
the future 121.1
undertaking 715.1
*v.* come across 555.7
extrapolate 224.5
foresee 121.6
intend 653.4
overhang 215.7
plan 654.9
protrude 256.9
represent 572.8
rocket 281.13
show 577.16
throw 285.12
**projected** future 121.8
intentional 653.9
planned 654.13
**projectile**
*n.* trajectile 285.6
weapon 801.12
*adj.* trajectile 285.16
**projecting**
overhanging 215.11
protruding 256.13
**projection** acting 611.9
defense mechanism
690.30
diagram 654.3
display 555.2
extrapolate 224.4
map 654.4
overhanging 215.3
plan 654.2
pointed projection
258.4
protuberance 256.2
representation 572.1
throwing 285.3
**projector**
motion-picture
577.12
planner 654.7
rocketry 281.10
weapon 801.19
**proletarian**
*n.* common man
919.7
working person 718.2
*adj.* middle-class
919.12
**proletariat** 919.1
**proliferate**
abound 661.5
be productive 165.7
increase 38.6
multiply 100.6
procreate 169.8

**proliferation**
increase 38.1
multiplication 100.4
procreation 169.2
productiveness 165.2
**prolific** diffuse 593.11
imaginative 535.18
productive 165.9
teeming 101.9
**prolix**
superfluous 663.17
talkative 596.9
tedious 884.8
wordy 593.12
**prolixity**
superfluity 663.4
talkativeness 596.1
tediousness 884.2
wordiness 593.2
**prologue** act 611.8
prelude 66.2
**prolong** lengthen 202.7
postpone 132.9
protract 110.9
sustain 143.4
**prolongation**
continuance 143.1
lengthening 202.5
postponement 132.4
protraction 110.2
sequence 65.1
**prolonged**
lengthened 202.9
protracted 110.11
**prom** dance 879.2
gathering 74.2
music performance
462.34
**promenade**
*n.* dance 879.2
path 657.3
procession 71.3
walk 273.12
*v.* parade 71.7
walk 273.28
**prominence**
authority 739.4
conspicuousness
555.4
eminence 34.2
height 207.1
notability 672.2
protuberance 256.2
repute 914.5
visibility 444.2
**prominent**
authoritative 739.15
clearly visible 444.7
conspicuous 555.12
eminent 34.9
high 207.19
notable 672.18
outstanding 914.17
protruding 256.13
**prominently**
conspicuously 555.16
exceptionally 34.20
famously 914.21
importantly 672.24
superlatively 36.16
visibly 444.8

**promiscuity**
disorder 62.1
indiscrimination
493.1
unchastity 989.4
**promiscuous**
mixed 44.15
purposeless 156.16
slipshod 534.12
unchaste 989.26
undiscriminating
493.5
unordered 62.12
**promise**
*n.* compact 771.1
hope 888.1
omen 544.3
pledge 770
prediction 543.1
*v.* be probable 511.4
contract 771.6
foretoken 544.13
give hope 888.10
pledge 770.4
**promised**
augured 544.15
contracted 771.12
expected 539.13
pledged 770.8
**promised land**
Heaven 1018.1
paradise 535.11
**promising**
auspicious 544.18
hopeful 888.13
probable 511.6
**promissory** 770.7
**promissory note**
contract 771.3
negotiable instru-
ment 835.11
**promontory** 256.8
**promote** advance 294.5
be expedient 670.3
be instrumental
658.5
commend 968.11
further 785.17
hasten 782.2
make better 691.9
motivate 648.12
publicize 559.15
**promoter**
commender 968.8
planner 654.7
publicist 559.9
supporter 787.9
**promotion**
commendation 968.3
furtherance 785.5
improvement 691.1
preferment 782
progression 294.1
publicity 559.5
selling 829.2
**prompt**
*n.* hint 557.4
reminder 537.6
*v.* advise 754.6
hint 557.10
induce 648.22
influence 172.7

motivate 648.13
remind 537.20
*adj.* alert 533.14
consenting 775.4
eager 635.9
fast 269.19
hasty 709.9
punctual 131.9
swift 707.18
willing 622.5
**prompter**
motivator 648.10
reminder 537.6
theater man 611.28
**prompting**
motivation 648.2
reminder 537.6
**promptly**
eagerly 635.14
fast 269.21
hastily 709.12
willingly 622.8
with alacrity 707.26
without delay 131.15
**promptness**
alacrity 707.3
alertness 533.5
consent 775.1
eagerness 635.1
hastiness 709.2
punctuality 131.3
speed 269.1
willingness 622.1
**promulgate**
command 752.9
execute 771.10
proclaim 559.13
publish 559.10
**prone**
deferential 765.16
inclined 174.6
liable 175.5
low 208.7
minded 525.8
recumbent 214.8
willing 622.5
**prong** fork 299.4
tributary 395.3
**pronged** forked 299.10
pointed 258.11
**pronoun** 586.5
**pronounce**
affirm 523.4
announce 559.12
command 752.9
pass judgment 494.13
say 594.23
**pronounced**
affirmed 523.8
clearly visible 444.7
conspicuous 555.12
outright 34.12
voiced 594.30
**pronouncement**
affirmation 523.1
announcement 559.2
decree 752.4
judgment 494.5
remark 594.4
**pronto** at once 113.8
promptly 131.15
quickly 269.23

**pronunciation** 594.6
**proof**
*n.* confirmation 505.5
copy 24.5
engraving 578.8
evidence 505.1
information 557.1
manifestation 555.1
proving 505.4
reasoning 482.1
test 489.2
trial print 603.5
*v.* insulate 159.12
print 603.14
*adj.* resistant 159.18
**proofread** 603.17
**prop**
*n.* propeller 285.7
stage property 611.22
supporter 216.2
*v.* bolster 785.12
strengthen 159.11
support 216.21
**propaganda** 563.2
**propagandize** 563.4
**propagate** disperse 75.4
procreate 169.8
publish 559.10
**propagation**
dispersion 75.1
procreation 169.2
publication 559.1
**propagative** 169.15
**propane** 331.1
**propel** impel 283.10
motivate 648.12
push 285.10
set in motion 267.6
**propellant**
*n.* fuel 331.1
propeller 285.7
rocketry 281.8
*adj.* moving 267.7
propulsive 285.15
**propeller** 285.7
**propelling**
*n.* pushing 285.1
*adj.* moving 267.7
propulsive 285.15
**propensity**
aptitude 733.5
inclination 634.3
tendency 174.1
trait of character
525.3
**proper** accurate 516.15
characteristic 80.13
conventional 645.5
decent 988.5
decorous 897.10
due 960.8
expedient 670.5
just 976.8
orthodox 1024.7
outright 34.12
right 958.8
suitable 82.9
useful 665.18
well-chosen 589.7
**properly**
accurately 516.19
conventionally 645.6

expediently 670.8
justly 976.11
rightly 958.9
tastefully 897.11
**proper thing**
custom 642.1
fairness 976.3
fashion 644.1
moral rightness 958.1
**propertied**
possessing 808.9
proprietary 810.9
**property**
characteristic 80.4
holdings 810
indication 568.2
nature 5.3
possession 808.1
real estate 810.7
resources 660.2
stage property 611.22
wealth 837.1
**prophecy**
prediction 543.1
revelation 1021.9
the future 121.1
**prophesied**
future 121.8
predicted 543.14
**prophesy foresee** 121.6
predict 543.9
**prophet**
predictor 543.4
religious leader 1022
visionary 535.13
**prophetic**
predictive 543.11
scriptural 1021.10
**prophet of doom**
pessimist 889.7
predictor 543.4
warner 703.4
**Prophets, the** 1021.3
**prophylactic**
*n.* contraceptive
687.23
counteractant 178.3
preventive 687.20
safeguard 699.3
*adj.* hindering 730.19
preventive 687.42
protecting 699.23
sanitary 681.27
**prophylaxis**
hygiene 683.2
medical treatment
689.16
**propinquity**
blood relationship
11.1
nearness 200.1
relationship 9.1
**propitiate atone** 1012.4
pacify 804.7
worship 1032.14
**propitiation**
atonement 1012.1
pacification 804.1
worship 1032.6
**propitiatory**
atoning 1012.7
Christlike 1013.19

pacificatory 804.12
**propitious**
auspicious 544.18
promising 888.13
timely 129.9
well-disposed 785.22
**proponent** 1006.8
**proportion**
*n.* comparability
491.3
comparison 491.1
degree 29.1
equality 30.1
literary elegance
589.2
mathematics 87.4
order 59.1
portion 816.5
ratio 86.6
size 195.1
space 179.1
symmetry 248.1
*v.* equalize 30.6
make agree 26.7
prorate 816.7
size 195.15
symmetrize 248.3
**proportional**
relative 9.7
respective 816.13
spatial 179.8
**proportional
representation**
vote 637.6
voting 744.18
**proportionate**
agreeing 26.9
equal 30.7
relative 9.7
respective 816.13
satisfactory 868.11
sufficient 661.6
**proportionately**
equally 30.11
in proportion 816.14
relatively 9.12
**proposal advice** 754.1
courtship 932.7
intention 653.1
nomination 637.8
offer 773.2
project 654.2
**propose advise** 754.5
court 932.20
intend 653.4
nominate 637.19
offer 773.5
postulate 499.12
**proposed** 653.9
**proposition**
*n.* assertion 523.1
axiom 517.2
premise 482.7
project 654.2
proposal 773.2
supposition 499.3
undertaking 715.1
*v.* make advances
773.7
propose 773.5
**propound**
postulate 499.12

propose 773.5
**propped** 216.24
**proprietary**
*n.* medicine 687.4
ownership 808.2
proprietor 809.2
*adj.* possessive 808.10
propertied 810.9
**proprieties**
conventions 645.2
etiquette 646.3
**proprietor** 809.2
**propriety**
decency 988.2
decorousness 897.3
decorum 958.2
expedience 670.1
fitness 26.5
justice 976.1
literary elegance
589.1
normality 84.1
rightness 958.2
social convention
645.1
timeliness 129.1
**propulsion**
aviation 278.33
impulse 283.1
power 157.4
pushing 285.1
**propulsive** 285.15
**pro rata priced** 846.16
proportionate 816.13
respectively 816.14
**prorate charge** 846.14
proportion 816.7
**prosaic**
businesslike 656.15
dull 883.8
in plain style 591.3
simple 902.6
unimaginative 536.5
unpoetic 610.5
**prosaicism**
dullness 883.2
platitude 517.3
unimaginativeness
536.1
unpoeticalness 610.2
**proscenium front** 240.1
stage 611.21
**proscribe**
condemn 1008.3
eject 310.17
ostracize 926.6
prohibit 778.3
**proscribed** 234.7
**proscription**
condemnation 1008.1
curse 972.1
limitation 234.2
ostracism 926.3
prohibition 778.1
**proscriptive**
condemnatory 1008.5
prohibitive 778.6
**prose**
*n.* plainness 883.2
platitude 517.3
writing 610

*v.* be uninteresting
883.5
write prose 610.3
*adj.* in prose 610.4
plain 883.8
**prosecute**
execute 771.10
practice 705.7
pursue 655.8
sue 1004.12
**prosecution**
accusation 1005.1
execution 771.5
lawsuit 1004.1
pursuit 655.1
**prosecutor**
accuser 1005.5
lawyer 1003.4
**proselyte**
apostate 628.5
believer 1028.4
convert 145.7
disciple 566.2
**proselytize** 145.16
**proselytizer** 145.9
**prosodic(al)** 609.18
**prosody metrics** 609.8
music 463.22
speech accent 594.11
**prospect**
*n.* customer 828.4
expectation 539.1
foresight 542.1
hope 888.1
look 439.3
possibility 509.1
probability 511.1
sight 446.6
the future 121.1
view 444.3
*v.* mine 383.14
**prospecting** 383.8
**prospective**
expected 539.13
future 121.8
**prospector** 383.9
**prospectus**
intention 653.1
prediction 543.1
project 654.2
schedule 641.2
**prosper succeed** 724.6
thrive 728.7
**prosperity**
business cycle 827.9
good times 728.4
prosperousness 728
success 724.1
wealth 837.1
**prosperous**
auspicious 544.18
successful 724.13
thriving 728.12
wealthy 837.13
**prosthetics** 688.3
**prostitute**
*n.* harlot 989.16
*v.* be unchaste 989.21
corrupt 692.14
misuse 667.4
*adj.* whorish 989.28

narrow-mindedness
527.1
rusticity 182.3
**proving ground**
rocketry 281.7
testing area 489.5
**provision**
*n.* condition 507.2
food 308.1
foresight 542.1
giving 818.1
precaution 895.3
preparation 720.1
stipulation 753.2
store 660.1
supplying 659
support 785.3
*v.* feed 307.16
provender 659.9
**provisional**
cautious 895.10
circumstantial 8.7
conditional 507.8
experimental 489.11
interim 109.4
makeshift 670.7
preparatory 720.20
substitute 149.8
unreliable 514.19
**proviso** condition 507.2
legislative clause
742.17
stipulation 753.2
**provisory**
conditional 507.8
interim 109.4
**provocateur** 648.11
**provocation**
affront 952.11
aggravation 885.1
cause 153.3
excitation 857.10
incentive 648.7
incitement 648.4
irritation 866.3
vexatiousness 864.7
**provocative**
aggravating 885.5
alluring 650.7
appetizing 428.10
desirable 634.30
exciting 857.28
interesting 530.19
prompting 648.27
**provoke**
aggravate 885.2
annoy 866.13
antagonize 929.7
be insolent 913.7
contrive 153.12
incense 952.22
incite 648.17
interest 530.12
irritate 866.14
prompt 648.13
sow dissension 795.14
stimulate 857.12
vex 864.15
**provoked**
aggravated 885.4
annoyed 866.21
nettled 952.25

**provoking**
annoying 864.22
eloquent 600.13
exciting 857.28
interesting 530.19
provocative 648.27
**provost** educator 565.9
executive 748.3
**prow** 240.3
**prowess** courage 893.1
skill 733.1
**prowl**
*n.* stealth 614.4
*v.* creep 273.25
lurk 615.9
wander 273.22
**prowl car** 272.10
**prowler** 825.1
**proximate**
approaching 296.4
following 65.4
near 200.14
relative 9.8
**proximity**
nearness 200.1
relationship 9.1
**proxy**
*n.* ballot 744.19
commission 780.1
deputy 781.1
substitute 149.2
vote 637.6
voter 744.23
*adj.* substitute 149.8
**prude** 903.11
**prudence**
caution 895.1
economy 851.1
expedience 670.1
foresight 542.1
judiciousness 467.7
moderation 163.1
vigilance 533.4
virtue 980.5
**prudent** cautious 895.8
economical 851.6
foreseeing 542.7
judicious 467.19
moderate 163.10
vigilant 533.13
**prudish**
fastidious 896.9
priggish 903.19
**prune** cut off 42.10
sever 49.11
shorten 203.6
thin out 413.17
**pruned** concise 592.6
shortened 203.9
**prurience** craving 634.6
curiosity 528.1
lasciviousness 989.5
sexual desire 419.5
**prurient** craving 634.24
curious 528.5
lascivious 989.29
lustful 419.29
**pry**
*n.* curious person
528.2
lever 287.4
leverage 287.1

meddler 238.4
*v.* be inquisitive 528.4
investigate 485.22
lever 287.8
look 439.13
meddle 238.7
search 485.30
**prying**
inquisitive 528.6
meddlesome 238.9
searching 485.37
**pry loose from** 822.22
**pry open** 265.15
**pry out** grill 485.21
search out 485.33
**PS** 67.1
**psalm**
*n.* hymn 1032.3
sacred music 462.16
*v.* sing 462.39
**psalmbook** book 605.1
psalter 1040.13
**Psalms, the** 1040.13
**psalter** book 605.1
psalmbook 1040.13
**pseudo** imitation 22.8
ungenuine 616.26
**pseudo–** abnormal 85.9
fictitious 535.21
illusory 519.9
similar 20.10
substitute 149.8
unsubstantial 4.5
**pseudonym** 583.8
**psoriasis** 686.33
**psst!** 448.17
**psych** discompose 63.4
solve 487.2
**psych(o)–** mind 466.1
psychology 690.1
spirit 1017.1
**psyche** intellect 466.1
psychology 690.35
spirit 466.4
**psychedelic**
*n.* hallucinogen
687.13
*adj.* hallucinatory
519.10
**psychochemical**
687.46
**psyched up** 720.16
**psychiatric**
psychological 690.43
psychotherapeutic
690.44
**psychiatrist**
physician 688.8
psychologist 690.12
psychotherapist
690.13
**psychiatry** 690.3
**psychic** predictor 543.4
spiritualist 1034.13
**psychic(al)**
ghostly 1017.7
immaterial 377.7
mental 466.8
spiritual 1034.23
supernatural 85.15
**psychic(al) phenomena**
1034.6

**psychics**
immateriality 377.1
occultism 1034.4
**psycho**
*n.* psychotic 473.16
*adj.* insane 473.25
**psychoanalysis**
psychology 690.2
psychotherapy 690.8
**psychoanalyst** 690.13
**psychoanalytic(al)**
690.44
**psychoanalyze** 690.42
**psychodrama**
catharsis 690.32
psychotherapy 690.5
stage show 611.4
**psychokinesia** 473.7
**psychokinesis** 1034.6
**psychologic(al)**
mental 466.8
psychiatric 690.43
**psychological block**
defense mechanism
690.31
thought disturbance
690.24
**psychological moment**
crucial moment
129.5
period 107.1
**psychological test**
690.11
**psychological warfare**
cold war 797.5
demoralization 891.6
psychology 690.1
warfare 797.4
**psychologist** 690.12
**psychologize** 690.42
**psychology**
mental attitude 525.1
science of man 417.7
science of mind 690
**psychometrics**
mensuration 490.9
psychology 690.1
**psychometry** 690.10
**psychoneurosis** 690.19
**psychoneurotic**
*n.* pathological type
690.16
*adj.* neurotic 690.45
**psychopath**
pathological type
690.16
psychotic 473.16
**psychopathic**
insane 473.27
psychological 690.43
**psychopathy**
personality disorder
690.18
psychosis 473.3
**psychosis** insanity 473.3
mental disorder
690.17
**psychosomatic** 690.43
**psychotherapist** 690.13
**psychotherapy**
psychology 690.5
therapy 689.1

psychotic
  *n.* lunatic 473.16
  pathological type
    690.16
  *adj.* insane 473.27
  psychological 690.43
psych out solve 487.2
  unnerve 859.9
ptisan 687.4
ptomaine poisoning
  686.30
pub inn 191.16
  saloon 996.19
puberty 124.6
pubescent
  adolescent 124.13
  hairy 230.24
  smooth 351.8
  soft 357.14
public
  *n.* clientele 828.3
  follower 293.2
  inn 191.16
  people 417.2
  populace 919.2
  population 190.1
  saloon 996.19
  *adj.* communal 815.9
  external 224.6
  general 417.13
  popular 898.14
  published 559.17
  well-known 475.27
public-address system
  450.11
publican
  bartender 996.18
  taxer 846.12
public assistance
  subsidy 818.8
  welfare program
    745.7
publication book 605.1
  dispersion 75.1
  impartation 554.2
  information 557.1
  manifestation 555.1
  printing 603.1
  promulgation 559
public defender 1003.4
public enemy
  criminal 986.10
  enemy 929.6
  evildoer 943.1
public health 683.2
public house
  inn 191.16
  saloon 996.19
public image
  affectation 903.1
  appearances 446.2
publicist
  commentator 606.4
  journalist 605.22
  lawyer 1003.4
  publicizer 559.9
publicity
  exposure 559.4
  information 557.1
  repute 914.1
publicize 559.15
publicizing 559.5

public knowledge 559.4
publicly
  in public 559.19
  overtly 555.15
public opinion
  belief 501.6
  political influence
    744.29
public relations 559.4
public relations man
  559.9
public school
  school 567.2
  secondary school
    567.6
public servant
  officeholder 746.11
  official 749.16
public speaker
  orator 599.6
  speechmaker 599.4
public speaking 599
public spirit 941
public-spirited 941.4
public trough
  booty 824.11
  depository 836.12
  spoils of office
    744.35
public utility 788.9
publish disperse 75.4
  divulge 556.5
  print 603.14
  promulgate 559.10
published 559.17
publisher
  bookman 605.21
  informant 557.5
publishing
  printing 603.1
  promulgation 559.1
  the press 605.23
publishing house 603.11
puce 368.6
puck bad child 125.4
  evil spirit 1016.8
  mischief-maker 738.3
Puck 1016.8
pucker
  *n.* anxiety 890.1
  confusion 532.3
  dither 857.5
  wrinkle 264.3
  *v.* constrict 198.7
  wrinkle 264.6
puckered
  constricted 198.12
  wrinkled 264.8
puckering 198.1
puckish
  devilish 1016.19
  mischievous 738.6
pudding food 308.45
  pulp 390.2
  semiliquid 389.5
  softness 357.4
puddinghead
  dolt 471.4
  ignoramus 477.8
puddle
  body of water 398.1
  mud puddle 389.9

pudency
  blushing 908.5
  decency 988.2
pudenda 419.10
pudgy
  corpulent 195.18
  stubby 203.10
puerile childish 124.11
  simple-minded
    469.24
puerility
  childishness 124.4
  simple-mindedness
    469.11
  unwiseness 470.2
puff
  *n.* breathing 403.18
  commendation 968.3
  distension 197.2
  foam 405.2
  make-up 900.11
  pastry 308.40
  publicity 559.4
  softness 357.4
  tobacco smoking
    434.10
  wind 403.4
  *v.* become exhausted
    717.5
  blow 403.22
  boast 910.6
  breathe 403.24
  exaggerate 617.3
  exhale 310.23
  make larger 197.4
  praise 968.12
  promote 968.11
  publicize 559.15
  use tobacco 434.14
puffball 411.4
puffed up
  conceited 909.11
  distended 197.13
  exaggerated 617.4
  overestimated 497.3
  proud 905.10
puffing
  breathing 403.29
  breathless 717.10
puff up
  become larger 197.5
  be vain 909.7
  make larger 197.4
  praise 968.12
puffy corpulent 195.18
  distended 197.13
  windy 403.25
pug
  *n.* foot 212.5
  mark 568.7
  pugilist 800.2
  *adj.* stubby 203.10
pugilism 796.9
pugilist athlete 878.20
  fighter 800.2
pugnacious
  quarrelsome 795.17
  warlike 797.25
pug-nosed 249.12
puissant
  authoritative 739.15
  powerful 157.12

  strong 159.13
puke
  *n.* vomit 310.8
  *v.* sicken at 867.4
  vomit 310.25
puky filthy 682.23
  nauseated 686.53
pulchritude 900.1
pule
  animal sound 460.2
  whine 875.12
puling
  animal sound 460.6
  plaintive 875.16
Pulitzer Prize 916.2
pull
  *n.* attraction 288.1
  draw 286.2
  drink 307.4
  exertion 716.2
  heaving 286.1
  influence 172.2
  power 157.1
  swig 996.6
  trial print 603.5
  *v.* attract 288.4
  deflect 291.5
  draw 286.4
  drink 307.27
  exert oneself 716.10
  extract 305.10
  lengthen 202.7
  print 603.14
  restrain 760.7
  row 275.53
  use tobacco 434.14
pull a fast one
  deceive 618.13
  outwit 735.11
pullback
  reduction 39.4
  retreat 284.3
  withdrawal 295.2
pull back demur 623.4
  dodge 631.8
  draw back 284.7
  hesitate 627.7
  regress 295.5
  retract 297.3
  retreat 295.6
  separate 49.9
pull down
  acquire 811.8
  be paid 841.20
  bring down 318.5
  depress 318.4
  raze 693.19
  receive 819.6
pullet poultry 414.34
  young chicken 125.8
pull in arrest 761.16
  arrive 300.6
  reel in 287.9
  restrain 760.7
  retract 297.3
pulling
  *n.* drinking 307.3
  extraction 305.1
  traction 286
  *adj.* attracting 288.5
  drawing 286.6

**push down**
depress 318.4
fly 278.49
**pushed** 709.11
**pusher** aircraft 280.2
racketeer 826.4
**push forward**
further 785.17
make one's way 294.4
**push in** enter 302.7
intrude 238.5
thrust in 304.7
**pushing**
enterprising 707.23
meddlesome 238.9
propulsive 285.15
**push on**
accelerate 709.4
make haste 709.5
make one's way 294.4
**pushover** dupe 620.1
easy thing 732.3
thing of naught 4.2
victory 726.1
weakling 160.6
**push upon**
thrust upon 818.20
urge upon 773.8
**pushy**
enterprising 707.23
insolent 913.8
meddlesome 238.9
self-assertive 624.15
**pusillanimity** 892.3
**pusillanimous** 892.12
**puss** cat 414.26
face 240.4
**pussycat**
beautiful person
900.8
cat 414.26
good person 985.2
**pussyfoot**
be cautious 895.5
creep 273.25
dodge 631.8
equivocate 483.9
lurk 615.9
**pussyfooting**
*n.* creeping 273.9
equivocation 483.5
political doubletalk
744.37
*adj.* equivocating
483.14
**pustule** blemish 679.1
sore 686.35
swelling 256.4
**put**
*n.* dolt 471.3
stock option 833.21
throw 285.4
*v.* affirm 523.4
attribute 155.3
impose 963.4
invest 836.16
phrase 588.4
place 184.11
throw 285.11
*adj.* phrased 588.5
**put about**
change course 275.30

**publish** 559.10
turn around 295.9
**put across**
bring about 722.5
impose 963.7
make clear 548.6
succeed with 724.10
**put aside**
disregard 531.4
postpone 132.9
put away 668.6
remove 271.10
reserve 660.12
segregate 77.6
**putative**
attributed 155.6
supposed 499.14
**put away**
accomplish 722.4
divorce 935.5
eat 307.20
kill 409.13
lay away 668.6
secrete 615.7
store 660.10
**put back**
change course 275.30
fend off 799.10
impair 692.11
repulse 289.3
restore 694.11
return 823.4
turn back 295.8
**put before**
confront 240.8
propose 773.5
**put down**
attribute 155.4
conquer 727.10
deprecate 969.12
destroy 693.15
disdain 966.3
disparage 971.8
humiliate 906.5
impose 963.4
kill 409.13
offend 965.4
pay over 841.15
put 184.13
record 570.16
ridicule 967.9
show up 36.8
suppress 760.8
**put-down** gibe 967.2
humiliation 906.2
indignity 965.2
**put forth** exert 716.8
flaunt 904.17
germinate 411.31
issue 559.14
propose 773.5
say 594.23
start out 301.7
**put in** arrive 300.8
enter 302.7
establish 184.15
insert 304.3
install 780.11
internalize 225.6
interrupt 238.6
plant 413.18
sail for 275.35

use 665.13
**put it to**
confront 240.8
propose 773.5
**put off** avoid 631.13
disincline 652.4
dodge 631.8
postpone 132.9
put to sea 275.19
repel 864.11
sail away from 275.36
take off 232.6
**put-off** 649.1
**put on**
accelerate 269.14
affect 903.12
apply 963.6
be ostentatious
904.14
cover 228.19
don 231.42
dramatize 611.33
fake 616.21
gull 470.7
impose 963.7
inflict on 963.4
intrude 238.5
lift up 317.7
tease 882.4
**put-on**
*n.* affectation 903.1
fake 616.13
gibe 967.2
*adj.* assumed 903.16
falsified 616.26
**put oneself out**
be unselfish 979.3
endeavor 714.10
exert oneself 716.9
**put one's foot down**
be resolute 624.9
insist 753.7
lay down the law
752.11
not permit 778.4
refuse 776.3
stand fast 142.11
**put out**
bewilder 514.12
confuse 532.7
destroy 693.15
dismay 891.27
dissatisfy 869.4
eject 310.13
embarrass 866.15
evict 310.15
exert 716.8
extinguish 332.7
humiliate 906.4
inconvenience 671.4
issue 559.14
make public 559.11
print 603.14
spend 843.5
trouble 731.12
**put-out**
bewildered 514.23
confused 532.12
distressed 866.22
provoked 952.25
**put over**
bring about 722.5

impose 963.7
make clear 548.6
manage 724.11
succeed with 724.10
**putrefaction** 692.7
**putrefactive** 692.40
**putrefied** 692.41
**putrefy** 692.25
**putrid** bad 675.8
decayed 692.41
filthy 682.23
malodorous 437.5
**put right**
direct to 290.7
remedy 694.13
**putsch** 767.4
**put something over**
618.13
**put straight**
disillusion 520.2
remedy 694.13
straighten 250.5
**putter** trifle 673.13
waste time 708.12
**putterer** idler 708.8
trifler 673.9
**puttering** 673.8
**put through**
bring about 722.5
carry out 705.9
channel 396.19
execute 771.10
legislate 742.18
manage 724.11
succeed with 724.10
**put together**
assemble 74.18
combine 52.3
compose 58.3
connect 47.5
create 167.10
make up 720.7
**put to rights**
arrange 60.8
remedy 694.13
**put up**
accommodate 659.1(
create 167.10
establish 184.15
house 188.10
increase 38.4
nominate 637.19
offer 773.4
pay over 841.15
pledge 772.10
preserve 701.9
put up for sale
829.10
store up 660.11
suspend 215.8
**put-up**
fabricated 616.29
pledged 772.12
prearranged 641.5
**put-up job**
accusation 1005.4
fake 616.13
prearrangement
641.1
**put upon** apply 963.◼
impose 963.7
inflict on 963.4

pit 257.4
source of supply
660.4
*v.* dig up 305.10
excavate 257.15
mine 383.14
**quart** 490.19
**quarter**
*n.* area 180.1
direction 290.1
fourth 98.2
heraldic insignia
569.2
part 55.1
period 107.2
pity 944.1
side 242.1
US money 835.7
*v.* divide by four 98.3
house 188.10
settle 184.16
*adj.* fourth 98.5
**quarterback**
*n.* athlete 878.20
*v.* direct 747.8
**quartered**
housed 188.14
quadrisected 98.4
severed 49.23
**quartering**
heraldic insignia
569.2
housing 188.3
quadrisection 98.1
**quarterly**
*n.* periodical 605.10
*adj.* momentary 137.8
**quartermaster**
officer 276.7
provider 659.6
**quartern** 98.2
**quarter note** 463.14
**quarters** 191.3
**quartet**
cooperation 786.1
four 96.1
orchestra 464.12
part music 462.17
**quartile** 96.4
**quarto**
book size 605.14
fourth 98.2
**quasar** 375.8
**quash** destroy 693.15
hush up 614.8
suppress 760.8
**quasi**
*adj.* imitation 22.8
nominal 583.15
similar 20.14
ungenuine 616.26
*adv.* imitatively 22.11
supposedly 499.17
**quaternary**
*n.* four 96.1
*adj.* four 96.4
**quatrain** 609.11
**quaver**
*n.* excitement 857.4
harmonics 463.14
music 463.19
shake 324.3

speech defect 595.1
*v.* be excited 857.16
shake 324.11
sing 462.39
speak poorly 595.7
tremble 891.22
**quavering**
*n.* excitement 857.4
shaking 324.2
*adj.* imperfectly spo-
ken 595.12
shaking 324.17
**quay** 700.6
**queasy**
fastidious 896.10
nauseated 686.53
**queen** bee 414.38
chessman 878.18
homosexual 419.16
playing card 878.17
princess 918.8
sovereign 749.11
termite 414.37
the best 674.8
**queenly**
dignified 905.12
noble 918.10
sovereign 739.17
**queenship**
noble rank 918.9
sovereignty 739.8
**queer**
*n.* counterfeit 835.10
homosexual 419.16
*v.* disable 158.9
spoil 692.13
thwart 730.16
*adj.* eccentric 474.4
homosexual 419.32
insane 473.25
odd 85.11
ungenuine 616.26
**queer duck** 85.4
**queered** 692.31
**quell** calm 163.7
conquer 727.10
destroy 693.15
subdue 764.9
suppress 760.8
**quelled**
conquered 727.16
restrained 163.11
subdued 764.15
suppressed 760.14
**quench** destroy 693.15
disincline 652.4
extinguish 332.7
gratify 865.6
suppress 760.8
**querulous**
discontented 869.5
ill-humored 951.21
plaintive 875.16
**query**
*n.* question 485.10
*v.* be curious 528.3
be doubtful 503.6
inquire 485.19
interrogate 485.20
**que será será** 640.11
**quest**
*n.* pursuit 655.1

search 485.14
undertaking 715.2
*v.* pursue 655.8
seek 485.29
**question**
*n.* an uncertainty
514.8
doubt 503.2
legislative motion
742.17
puzzle 549.8
query 485.10
remark 594.4
topic 484.1
*v.* be curious 528.3
be doubtful 503.6
be uncertain 514.9
communicate with
554.8
inquire 485.19
interrogate 485.20
**questionable**
deceptive 618.19
dishonest 975.16
doubtful 503.10
improbable 512.3
uncertain 514.16
**questioner**
curious person 528.2
inquirer 485.15
**questioning**
*n.* interrogation
485.11
*adj.* communicational
554.9
doubtful 503.9
inquiring 485.35
**question mark**
puzzle 549.8
question 485.10
**questionnaire**
*n.* canvass 485.13
list 88.6
*v.* canvass 485.28
**queue**
*n.* hair 230.7
row 71.2
sequel 67.2
tail 241.6
*v.* line up 71.6
**quibble**
*n.* cavil 483.4
disapproval 969.4
*v.* argue 482.16
cavil 483.9
find fault 969.15
**quibbler** caviler 483.7
faultfinder 969.9
**quibbling**
*n.* caviling 483.5
disapproval 969.4
*adj.* caviling 483.14
critical 969.24
**quiche** 308.40
**quick**
*n.* inner nature 5.4
sensitive area 422.4
*adj.* alert 533.14
eager 635.9
fast 269.19
hasty 709.9
hot-tempered 951.25

impulsive 630.9
intelligent 467.14
lively 707.18
living 407.11
prompt 131.9
skillful 733.20
sudden 113.5
teachable 564.18
transient 111.8
willing 622.5
*adv.* fast 269.21
**quicken**
accelerate 269.14
come to life 407.8
energize 161.9
facilitate 732.6
further 785.17
hasten 709.4
refresh 695.2
sensitize 422.9
stimulate 857.12
vivify 407.9
**quickening**
*n.* acceleration 269.4
energizing 161.7
facilitation 732.4
hastening 709.3
vivification 407.5
*adj.* energizing 161.14
life-giving 407.12
**quickly** eagerly 635.14
hastily 709.12
impulsively 630.13
promptly 131.15
shortly 111.10
swiftly 269.21
with alacrity 707.26
**quickness** alacrity 707.3
alertness 533.5
eagerness 635.1
hastiness 709.2
impulsiveness 630.2
intelligence 467.2
promptness 131.3
skill 733.1
speed 269.1
teachability 564.5
**quicksand** danger 697.1
marsh 400.1
pitfall 697.5
predicament 731.4
**quicksilver**
*n.* changeableness
141.4
speed 269.6
*adj.* fickle 629.6
lively 707.17
metal 383.17
**quickstep** 273.15
**quick-tempered** 951.25
**quick-witted**
intelligent 467.14
witty 881.15
**quid** bite 307.2
British money 835.8
chewing tobacco
434.7
essence 5.2
**quiddity** essence 5.2
quibble 483.4
**quid pro quo**
interaction 13.3

*adj.* prejudiced 527.12
**rack**
*n.* gait 273.14
gear 348.6
instrument of torture
1011.4
meat 308.17
pain 424.6
punishment 1010.2
slowness 270.2
storage place 660.6
strain 716.2
torment 866.7
*v.* pain 424.7
punish 1010.18
strain 716.10
torture 866.18
walk 273.27
**racked** affected 855.25
pained 424.9
tortured 866.25
**racket** commotion 62.4
elastic object 358.3
fraud 618.8
illicit business 826.1
noise 453.3
pandemonium 62.5
plaything 878.16
rattle 455.3
stratagem 735.3
violence 162.2
vocation 656.6
**racketeer** bandit 825.4
criminal 986.10
evildoer 943.1
extortionist 822.12
illicit businessman
826.4
**rackets, the**
illicit business 826.1
the underworld
986.11
**racking** painful 424.10
unpleasant 864.23
**rack one's brains**
think hard 478.9
try to recall 537.21
**rack rent** fee 846.9
high price 848.3
**racon** aviation 278.19
radar beacon 346.7
**raconteur** 608.10
**racy** eloquent 600.12
indecent 990.7
interesting 530.19
pungent 433.7
**radar** aviation 278.6,61
electronics 343.1,20
navigation 275.2
radio detection and
ranging 346
types of 346.18
**radar antenna** 346.22
**radarman** 346.14
**radar parts** 346.20
**radar reflector** 346.23
**radarscope** 346.21
**raddle**
*n.* network 221.3
*v.* weave 222.6
**raddled** drunk 996.31
woven 222.7

**radial** converging 298.3
radiating 299.9
**radiance** beauty 900.6
brightness 335.4
cheerfulness 870.1
divergence 299.2
illustriousness 914.6
light 335.1
**radiant**
*n.* axis 322.5
meteor 375.15
*adj.* cheerful 870.11
godlike 1013.20
gorgeous 900.19
happy 865.13
illustrious 914.19
luminous 335.30
**radiant energy**
light 335.1
radiation 327.1
**radiate**
broadcast 344.25
diverge 299.6
give light 335.23
spread 75.4
use radar 346.15
**radiating**
converging 298.3
diverging 299.9
**radiation**
dispersion 75.1
divergence 299.2
glow 335.1
lighting 335.19
radioactivity 327
ray 335.5
space hazard 282.10
**radiation counters and
chambers** 327.13
**radiation physics**
physics 325.1
radiology 327.7
**radiation sickness**
686.31
**radiator** heater 329.32
radioactive substance
327.5
radio transmitter
344.4
**radical**
*n.* atomics 326.7
character 581.2
chemical 379.1
extremist 745.12
foundation 216.6
left winger 244.1
morphology 582.3
reformer 691.6
root 153.5
valent 326.23
*adj.* basic 212.8
causal 153.15
essential 5.8
extreme 745.20
left-wing 244.4
numerical 86.8
reformational 691.16
revolutionary 147.5
thorough 56.10
utmost 34.13
**radicalism** excess 663.1
extremism 745.4

reform 691.5
**radically** 34.22
**radical right** 745.9
**radio**
*n.* communications
560.3
electronics 343.1,20
informant 557.5
news medium 558.1
radio communication
344
radio receiver 344.3
types of 344.29
*v.* broadcast 344.25
communicate 560.19
*adj.* telecommunica-
tional 560.20
wireless 344.28
**radioactivate** 327.9
**radioactive** 327.10
**radioactive element**
327.12
**radioactive particle**
327.4
**radioactive unit** 327.14
**radioactivity** 327.1
**radio aerial** 344.32
**radio antenna** 344.32
**radiobroadcast** 344.18
**radiobroadcasting**
344.16
**radio control**
automation 349.2
remote control 349.4
**radioelement**
radioactive substance
327.5
radiotherapeutic sub-
stance 689.9
word list 327.12
**radiogram**
diagnostic picture
689.10
photograph 577.6
telegram 560.14
**radiolocator** 346.19
**radiologist**
atomic scientist 326.3
physician 688.8
radiation physicist
327.8
**radiology**
atomics 326.1
radiation physics
327.7
radiotherapy 689.8
**radioman** 344.24
**radion** 327.4
**radionics**
electronics 343.1
physics 325.1
**radio operator**
radioman 344.24
sailor 276.6
**radiophone** 560.5
**radio program** 344.18
**radiorays** light 335.5
radiation 327.3
**radio receiver**
parts 344.30
radio 344.3
**radioscope** 327.6

**radiosensitive** 327.11
**radio show** 611.4
**radio signal** 344.10
**radio station**
space station 282.5
transmitting station
344.6
**radio technician**
electrician 342.19
radioman 344.24
**radiotelegraphy**
communications
560.3
radio 344.1
**radiotherapist** 688.14
**radiotherapy**
radiation physics
327.7
radiotherapeutics
689.7
**radio transmission**
344.16
**radio transmitter**
parts 344.31
transmitter 344.4
**radio tube** 343.11
**radio wave**
electric wave 344.11
wave 323.4
**radium** caustic 329.15
radioelement 327.12
radiotherapeutic sub-
stance 689.9
**radius** circle 253.2
convergence 298.1
radiating 299.2
range 179.2
size 195.1
straight line 250.2
thickness 204.3
**radix** plant root 411.20
source 153.5
**RAF** 800.29
**raff** rabble 919.5
rubbish 669.5
**raffish** 898.13
**raffle**
*n.* lottery 515.11
*v.* gamble 515.18
**Raffles** 825.11
**raft**
*n.* float 277.11
much 34.4
*v.* haul 271.12
**rafter** 217.7
**rag**
*n.* apparel 231.1
fabric 378.5
garment 231.3
music 462.9
newspaper 605.11
old clothing 231.5
refuse 669.4
remnant 43.1
sail 277.14
scenery 611.25
tempo 463.24
*v.* banter 882.4
berate 969.20
music 462.44
ridicule 967.8
**raga** 463.10

**ragamuffin** 274.3
**rage**
  *n.* excitement 857.7
  fad 644.5
  fit 952.8
  frenzy 473.7
  mania 473.12
  passion 952.10
  the latest thing 644.4
  violence 162.2
  *v.* be angry 952.15
  be excited 857.15
  be insane 473.19
  blow 403.22
  bluster 911.3
  storm 162.10
**ragged**
  nonuniform 18.3
  raucous 458.15
  rough 261.7
  severed 49.23
  shabby 692.34
  slovenly 62.15
  tormented 866.24
**raggedy** shabby 692.34
  slovenly 62.15
**raging** blustering 911.4
  excited 857.23
  infuriated 952.29
  mad 473.30
  stormy 403.26
  violent 162.17
**ragman**
  junk dealer 830.10
  vagrant 274.3
**ragout** 308.11
**rag out** clothe 231.38
  dress up 231.41
**ragpicker** 274.3
**ragtag** 919.4
**ragtime**
  *n.* music 462.9
  tempo 463.24
  *adj.* music 463.29
**rah** 876.2
**aid**
  *n.* attack 798.4
  plundering 824.5
  stock manipulation 833.20
  *v.* attack 798.20
  plunder 824.16
**aider** assailant 798.13
  plunderer 825.6
**ail**
  *n.* fence 236.4
  railway 657.8
  thinness 205.7
  *v.* confine 761.12
  enclose 236.7
**il at** berate 969.20
  ridicule 967.9
**iling**
  *.* fence 236.4,13
  *adj.* ridiculing 967.12
**illery** banter 882.1
  ridicule 967.1
**ilroad**
  *.* railway 657.8
  hasten 709.4
  legislate 742.18
**lroader** 274.13

**railroad man** 274.13
**railway** 657.8
**railway car** 272.14
**railway express** 271.3
**raiment**
  *n.* clothing 231.1
  garment 231.3
  *v.* clothe 231.38
**rain**
  *n.* gods 394.6
  rainfall 394
  television reception 345.5
  water 392.3
  *v.* abound 661.5
  descend 316.5
  drench 392.14
  give 818.12
  precipitate 394.9
**rainbow**
  *n.* barbiturate 687.12
  iridescence 335.18
  light 335.14
  omen 544.6
  variegation 374.6
  *adj.* coloring 362.15
**rainbowlike**
  iridescent 335.37
  variegated 374.10
**raindrop** drop 255.3
  rain 394.1
**rainfall** moisture 392.1
  rain 394.1
**rain forest** 411.11
**rain gauge** 394.7
**rainmaker**
  aviator 279.1
  cloud seeder 394.5
**rainmaking** 394.5
**rain or shine**
  come what may 624.20
  perseveringly 625.9
  without fail 513.26
**rainstorm**
  downpour 394.2
  storm 162.4
**rainy** moist 392.15
  showery 394.10
  stormy 403.26
**rainy day**
  hard times 729.6
  wet weather 394.4
**raise**
  *n.* height 207.2
  increase 38.1
  promotion 782.1
  *v.* assemble 74.18
  begin 68.11
  communicate with 554.8
  conjure 1035.11
  create 167.10
  elevate 317.5
  emboss 256.11
  enlist 780.16
  erect 213.9
  farm 413.16
  glorify 914.13
  grow 167.11
  increase 38.4
  leaven 353.7

**make better** 691.9
**make larger** 197.4
**promote** 782.2
**raise animals** 416.6
**rouse** 648.19
**say** 594.23
**train** 562.14
**raised** expanded 197.10
  grown 167.22
  increased 38.7
  in relief 256.17
  lifted 317.9
  produced 167.20
**raise hell**
  be angry 952.15
  be disorderly 62.11
  be noisy 453.8
  cause trouble 731.13
  confuse 532.7
  make merry 878.26
**raiser**
  agriculturist 413.5
  producer 167.8
**raising**
  *n.* elevation 317.1
  erection 213.4
  expansion 197.1
  growing 413.12
  manufacture 167.3
  training 562.3
  *adj.* leavening 353.16
**raison d'être**
  cause 153.10
  objective 653.2
**raja** 749.9
**rake**
  *n.* inclination 219.2
  pointed projection 258.4
  thinness 205.7
  unchaste person 989.10
  *v.* be unchaste 989.19
  comb 681.21
  fire upon 798.22
  incline 219.10
  ransack 485.32
  till 413.17
**rake-off** gain 811.3
  payment 841.7
  portion 816.5
**rakish** jaunty 904.19
  unchaste 989.25
**rally**
  *n.* call to arms 797.12
  contest 796.3
  electioneering 744.12
  meeting 74.2
  protest 522.2
  recovery 694.8
  stock prices 834.9
  tournament 878.10
  *v.* aid 785.11
  arrange evidence 505.13
  assemble 74.18
  banter 882.4
  call to arms 797.23
  come together 74.16
  dispose 60.9
  improve 691.8
  incite 648.17

  object 522.5
  recover 694.20
  recuperate 694.19
  ridicule 967.9
**rallying cry**
  call to arms 797.12
  cry 459.1
  signal 568.16
**rally round** form 59.5
  join with 786.4
**ram**
  *n.* male animal 420.8
  sheep 414.7
  *v.* sail 275.41
  thrust 283.11
**Rama** 1014.9
**Ramadan** fast 995.3
  holy day 1040.17
**ramate** 411.38
**ramble**
  *n.* amble 273.12
  wandering 273.3
  *v.* be insane 473.19
  chatter 596.5
  digress 593.9
  travel 273.22
  wander 291.4
**rambler** 274.2
**rambling**
  *n.* deviation 291.1
  discursiveness 593.3
  wandering 273.3
  *adj.* delirious 473.31
  discursive 593.13
  distracted 532.10
  inconstant 141.7
  irregular 138.3
  unintelligible 549.13
  traveling 273.36
  wandering 291.7
**rambunctious** 162.19
**ram down one's throat**
  compel 756.6
  thrust upon 818.20
**ramification**
  bisection 92.1
  branching 299.3
  complexity 46.1
  fork 299.4
  limb 411.18
  offshoot 55.4
**ramify** bisect 92.4
  branch 299.7
  complicate 46.3
  increase 38.5
  spread 197.6
**ram in** fill 56.7
  thrust in 304.7
**ramjet** 280.3,17
**ramous**
  branched 299.10
  leafy 411.38
**ramp**
  *n.* fraud 618.8
  incline 219.4
  stairs 315.3
  *v.* ascend 315.11
  be excited 857.15
  cheat 618.17
  jump 319.6
  rage 162.10
  rise 213.8

**rampage**
n. commotion 62.4
v. rage 162.10
**rampageous** 162.19
**rampant**
ascending 315.14
lawless 740.5
plentiful 661.7
prevalent 79.12
raised 317.9
unrestrained 762.23
vertical 213.11
violent 162.18
**rampart** barrier 730.5
buttress 216.4
fortification 799.4
**ramrodlike** 356.11
**ramshackle**
dilapidated 692.35
unsteady 160.16
**rana** 749.9
**ranch**
n. farm 413.8
house and grounds
191.7
v. farm 413.16
raise animals 416.6
**rancher**
agriculturist 413.5
animal raiser 416.2
**rancid**
malodorous 437.5
tainted 692.42
unsavory 429.7
**rancor** animosity 929.4
bitterness 952.3
revengefulness 956.2
virulence 939.7
**rancorous**
hostile 929.10
resentful 952.24
revengeful 956.6
virulent 939.20
**R and D** 489.1
**random**
n. haphazard 156.4
adj. purposeless
156.16
uncertain 514.18
unordered 62.12
**randomness**
disorder 62.1
purposelessness 156.3
uncertainty 514.1
**random sample**
part 55.1
probability 156.1
testing sample 489.4
**random shot**
haphazard 156.4
matter of chance
515.2
**randy** lascivious 989.29
lustful 419.29
**range**
n. arena 802.1
aviation 278.10
degree 29.1
direction 290.1
distance 199.1
earshot 448.4
grassland 411.8

habitat 191.5
harmonics 463.6
latitude 762.4
mountains 207.9
row 71.2
scope 179.2
size 195.1
view 444.3
vision 439.1
v. align 71.5
be distant 199.5
classify 61.6
dispose 60.9
extend 179.7
size 195.15
traverse 273.19
wander 273.22
**ranged** arranged 60.14
embattled 797.27
**ranger**
elite troops 800.14
forester 413.7
guardian 699.6
preserver 701.4
**rangy** 207.21
**rani** princess 918.8
sovereign queen
749.11
**rank**
n. authority 739.4
class 61.2
military unit 800.19
nobility 918.1
order 59.2
organ stop 465.22
prestige 914.4
row 71.2
standing 29.2
state 7.1
syntax 586.2
v. align 71.5
arrange 60.11
be judged 494.15
classify 61.6
judge 494.9
order 59.4
precede 64.2
size 195.15
take precedence
36.11
adj. bad 675.9
base 915.12
evil 981.16
filthy 682.23
growing lush 411.40
malodorous 437.5
outright 34.12
pungent 433.8
rough 261.6
tainted 692.42
unsavory 429.7
vulgar 990.8
**rank and file**
army 800.22
common people
919.1
**ranked** arranged 60.14
classified 61.8
**ranking**
n. classification 61.1
grouping 60.3
judgment 494.3

adj. authoritative
739.15
chief 36.14
most important
672.23
**rankle**
be remembered
537.14
decay 692.25
fester 311.15
hurt 424.7
provoke 952.22
**rankled**
remembering 537.24
resentful 952.24
**ransack** plunder 824.16
rummage 485.32
**ransom**
n. recovery 823.3
rescue 702.1
v. recover 823.6
redeem 694.12
rescue 702.3
**rant**
n. bluster 911.1
bombast 601.2
nonsense 547.2
v. be angry 952.15
be excited 857.15
be insane 473.19
bluster 911.3
declaim 599.10
overact 611.36
rage 162.10
**ranter** blusterer 911.2
hypocrite 1029.3
public speaker 599.4
**ranting**
n. delirium 473.8
adj. blustering 911.4
delirious 473.31
excited 857.23
infuriated 952.29
mad 473.30
**rap**
n. condemnation
1008.1
disapproval 969.4
discussion 597.7
explosive noise 456.1
faint sound 452.3
hit 283.4
tap 283.6
trifle 673.5
v. criticize 969.14
discuss 597.12
faint sound 452.15
make explosive noise
456.6
pound 283.14
tap 283.15
**rapacious**
gluttonous 994.6
grasping 822.26
greedy 634.27
**rapacity** gluttony 994.1
greed 634.8
predacity 822.9
**rape**
n. debauchment 989.6
plundering 824.5

sexual possession
822.3
violence 162.3
v. possess sexually
822.15
seduce 989.20
terrorize 162.10
**rapid**
n. rapids 395.10
adj. constant 135.5
fast 269.19
steep 219.18
**rapidity**
constancy 135.2
promptness 131.3
speed 269.1
**rapidly**
constantly 135.7
swiftly 269.21
**rapids** descent 316.1
eruption 162.6
running water 395.10
**rapist**
debaucher 989.12
sex deviant 419.17
violent person 162.9
**rapping**
n. conversation 597.1
speech 594.1
adj. banging 456.11
**rapport** accord 794.1
agreement 26.1
good terms 927.3
pleasantness 863.1
relationship 9.1
**rapprochement**
accord 794.1
reconciliation 804.3
**rapscallion**
mischief-maker 738.3
rascal 986.3
**rap session** 597.7
**rapt**
absorbed in thought
478.22
abstracted 532.11
engrossed 530.18
overjoyed 865.14
persevering 625.7
**raptorial** grasping 813.9
rapacious 822.26
**rapture**
amorousness 931.3
excitement 857.7
happiness 865.2
trance 1036.3
**rapturous** 865.14
**rare** airy 355.4
cooked 330.8
few 102.5
infrequent 136.2
notable 672.18
other 16.8
scarce 662.11
superior 36.12
thin 205.16
uncooked 721.10
unusual 85.10
wonderful 920.10
**rarefied** dainty 35.7
diluted 160.19
ethereal 355.4

tenuous 4.6
thin 205.16
**rarefy** attenuate 355.3
dematerialize 4.4
dilute 160.11
make larger 197.4
thin 205.12
**rarely**
infrequently 136.4
scarcely 662.16
sparsely 102.8
unusually 85.17
**raring to** 635.9
**rarity** fewness 102.1
infrequency 136.1
marvel 920.2
odd thing 85.5
scarcity 662.3
thinness 205.4
unsubstantiality 355
unusualness 85.2
**rascal**
mischief-maker 738.3
scoundrel 986.3
**rascally** 975.17
**rash**
*n.* disease symptom
686.8
skin eruption 686.34
*adj.* brash 894.7
impulsive 630.9
precipitate 709.10
**rasher** portion 55.3
slice 227.2
**rashness** brashness 894
hastiness 709.2
impulsiveness 630.2
**rasp**
*n.* harsh sound 458.3
*v.* abrade 350.7
hurt 424.7
irritate 866.14
sound harshly 458.10
**raspberry** 967.3
**rasping**
*n.* abrasion 350.2
powder 361.5
refuse 669.4
*adj.* abrasive 350.10
irritating 424.13
sounding harsh
458.16
**Rasputin** 172.6
**raspy** 458.16
**rat**
*n.* bad person 986.6
false hair 230.13
mammal 414.58
strikebreaker 789.6
traitor 619.10
*v.* break a strike
789.10
desert 633.6
divulge 556.6
inform on 557.12
**ratable**
*n.* taxation 846.10
*adj.* chargeable 846.17
**rat-a-tat**
pulsation 323.3
staccato sound 455.1
**ratchet** 258.4

**rate**
*n.* debt 840.3
gait 267.4
price 846.1
rank 29.2
ratio 86.6
tax 846.11
worth 846.3
*v.* be judged 494.15
berate 969.20
classify 61.6
deserve 960.5
judge 494.9
measure 490.11
precede 64.2
price 846.13
quantify 28.4
reprove 969.17
**rated** classified 61.8
priced 846.16
**rather**
*v.* prefer 637.17
*adv.* contrarily 15.9
instead 149.11
notwithstanding 33.8
preferably 637.28
to a degree 29.7
tolerably 674.23
*interj.* exactly! 516.23
yes! 521.18
**rathskeller** 996.19
**ratification**
authorization 777.3
confirmation 505.5
consent 775.1
endorsement 521.4
**ratified** chosen 637.26
endorsed 521.14
**ratify** adopt 637.15
authorize 777.11
confirm 505.12
consent 775.2
endorse 521.12
**rating** berating 969.7
classification 61.1
credit 839.1
grade 61.2
judgment 494.3
measurement 490.1
rank 29.2
reproof 969.5
valuation 846.4
**ratio**
comparability 491.3
degree 29.1
intellect 466.1
proportion 86.6
**ratiocination**
reasoning 482.1
thought 478.1
**ration**
*n.* amount 28.2
portion 816.5
*v.* apportion 816.8
budget 816.10
**rational**
intelligent 467.12
logical 482.20
mental 466.8
numerical 86.8
practical 536.6
reasoning 482.18

sane 472.4
sensible 467.18
**rationale**
explanation 552.4
reason 153.2
**rationalism**
reasoning 482.1
theology 1023.1
**rationalist** 482.11
**rationalistic**
explanatory 552.15
philosophy 500.9
**rationality**
comprehension 467.1
intellect 466.1
practicalness 536.2
reasoning 482.1
sanity 472.1
sense 482.9
soundness 467.6
**rationalization**
defense mechanism
690.30
justification 1006.1
organization 60.2
plan 654.1
reasoning 482.1
sophistry 483.1
**rationalize**
deduce 482.15
explain 552.10
justify 1006.9
organize 60.10
plan 654.9
reason speciously
483.8
**rationally**
intelligently 467.20
reasonably 482.24
**rationing**
apportionment 816.1
restraint 760.1
**rations** food 308.6
store 660.1
**rat race** busyness 707.5
drudgery 716.4
futility 669.2
whirlpool 322.2
**rat's nest** complex 46.2
jumble 62.3
**rattail** hair 230.7
tail 241.6
**rattan** bamboo 378.4
instrument of punish-
ment 1011.2
**rattle**
*n.* chatterer 596.4
clatter 455.3
noise 453.3
noisemaker 453.5
percussion instrument
465.18
*v.* chatter 596.5
clatter 455.6
confuse 532.7
excite 857.13
joggle 283.11
talk nonsense 547.5
weaken 160.10
**rattlebrain** 471.7
**rattlebrained**
scatterbrained 532.16

stupid 469.19
**rattletrap** 692.10
**rattrap** 618.11
**ratty** infested 313.11
rodent 414.48
shabby 692.34
**raucous**
dissonant 461.4
harsh 458.15
**raunchy** 990.9
**ravage**
*n.* debauchment 989.6
destruction 693.1
overrunning 313.2
plundering 824.5
*v.* corrupt 692.14
destroy 693.10
overrun 313.6
plunder 824.16
seduce 989.20
**ravaged**
dilapidated 53.5
infested 313.11
ruined 693.28
spoiled 692.43
tired-looking 717.7
**ravager**
debaucher 989.12
plunderer 825.6
**ravages of time**
disintegration 53.1
time 105.3
wear 692.5
**rave** be angry 952.15
be enthusiastic 635.8
be excited 857.15
be insane 473.19
berate 969.20
bluster 911.3
rage 162.10
**ravel**
*n.* complex 46.2
*v.* complicate 46.3
simplify 45.5
solve 487.2
**raveled** 46.4
**raven**
*n.* black 365.4
omen 544.6
*adj.* black 365.8
**raven** gluttonize 994.4
hunger 634.19
plunder 824.16
**ravenous**
gluttonous 994.6
greedy 634.27
hungry 634.25
rapacious 822.26
**ravine** crack 201.2
valley 257.9
**raving**
*n.* delirium 473.8
*adj.* blustering 911.4
delirious 473.31
excited 857.23
gorgeous 900.19
infuriated 952.29
mad 473.30
violent 162.17
**ravioli** 308.33
**ravish** corrupt 692.14
delight 865.8

plunder 824.16
possess sexually
  822.15
seduce 989.20
**ravished** excited 857.23
  overjoyed 865.14
**ravisher**
debaucher 989.12
plunderer 825.6
**ravishing** alluring 650.7
exciting 857.28
gorgeous 900.19
pleasant 863.7
**ravishment**
debauchment 989.6
excitement 857.7
happiness 865.2
plundering 824.5
sexual possession
  822.3
**raw**
*n.* sensitive area 422.4
*adj.* cold 333.14
garish 362.19
ignorant 477.12
immature 124.10
indecent 990.8
inexperienced 734.17
naked 232.14
new 122.7
obscene 972.8
sore 424.11
undeveloped 721.11
unprepared 721.10
vulgar 898.11
wind-blown 403.27
**raw, the** 232.3
**rawboned** 205.17
**raw deal**
bad luck 729.5
injustice 977.4
**rawhide**
*n.* leather 229.1
whip 1011.1
*v.* punish 1010.14
**raw material**
crude 721.5
resources 378.1
**raw nerve**
provocation 952.11
sensitive area 422.4
**raw recruit**
beginner 68.2
novice 566.9
recruit 800.17
**ray**
*n.* light 335.5
radiation 299.2
vertebrate 415.7
wave 323.4
*v.* radiate 299.6
**rayless** blind 441.9
dark 337.13
**ray of sunshine**
optimist 888.6
sunbeam 335.10
**raze** abrade 350.7
bring down 318.5
demolish 693.19
lay 214.6
obliterate 693.16
**razorback** 414.9

**razor-edged** 258.10
**razz**
*n.* boo 967.3
*v.* banter 882.4
ridicule 967.8
**razzing**
*n.* banter 882.2
ridicule 967.1
*adj.* ridiculing 967.12
**RDF**
direction finder 748.9
radiolocator 346.4,19
**re** 9.13
**reach**
*n.* bay 399.1
degree 29.1
distance 199.1
earshot 448.4
length 202.1
range 179.2
size 195.1
*v.* arrive 300.6
be heard 448.13
bribe 651.3
come upon 300.7
communicate with
  554.8
deliver 818.13
equal 30.5
excite pity 944.5
extend 179.7
extend to 199.6
sail for 275.35
suffice 661.4
travel 273.18
**reachable** 509.8
**reach out**
be distant 199.5
be long 202.6
extend 179.7
**react** answer 486.4
be affected 855.12
respond 284.5
**reactance** 342.12
**reaction** answer 486.1
aviation 278.33
belief 501.6
counteraction 178.1
effect 154.3
emotion 855.3
mental disorder
  690.17
political conservatism
  745.1
regression 295.1
resistance 792.1
response 284
**reactionary**
*n.* conservative 745.9
malcontent 869.3
old liner 123.8
recalcitrant 284.4
right-winger 243.1
*adj.* conservative
  745.17
counteractive 178.8
reactive 284.9
regressive 295.11
reversionary 146.7
right-wing 243.4
**reactionism** 745.1

**reactivate**
energize 161.11
militarize 797.24
restore 694.11
**reactive** 284.9
**reactor** 326.13
**read** declaim 599.10
interpret 552.9
proofread 603.17
sound out 489.9
study 564.12
study to be 564.15
understand 548.7
**readable**
intelligible 548.9
interesting 530.19
legible 548.11
meaningful 545.10
**read between the lines**
  552.9
**reader**
academic rank 565.4
advertisement 559.6
churchman 1038.10
computer 349.18
elocutionist 599.7
holy orders 1038.4
journalist 605.22
lecturer 599.5
lens 443.1
proofreader 603.13
teacher 565.8
textbook 605.8
**readership** 565.11
**readily** eagerly 635.14
easily 732.15
willingly 622.8
with alacrity 707.26
**readiness**
alertness 533.5
consent 775.1
cunning 735.1
eagerness 635.1
earliness 131.1
foresight 542.1
preparedness 720.4
promptness 131.3
quickness 707.3
skill 733.1
teachability 564.5
tendency 174.1
willingness 622.1
**reading**
interpretation 552.1
measure 490.2
radar signal 346.11
rendition 552.2
scholarship 475.5
speech 599.2
study 564.3
**reading glass** 443.1
**reading matter**
literature 602.10
printed matter
  603.10
**reading, writing, and
arithmetic** 562.5
**readjustment**
adjustment 690.34
rehabilitation 145.4
**readout**
computer 349.18

measure 490.2
**read the riot act**
lay down the law
  752.11
reprove 969.17
**ready**
*v.* prepare 720.6
repair 694.14
train 562.14
*adj.* alert 533.14
consenting 775.4
cunning 735.12
eager 635.9
expectant 539.11
foreseeing 542.7
handy 665.19
inclined to 174.6
prepared 720.16
prompt 131.9
quick 707.18
skillful 733.20
teachable 564.18
willing 622.5
**ready-made**
made 167.22
ready-formed 720.19
tailored 231.47
**ready-mades** 231.4
**ready-to-wear**
*n.* clothing 231.4
*adj.* manufactured
  167.22
ready-made 720.19
tailored 231.47
**reagent** 379.1
**real**
*n.* number 86.3
*adj.* actual 1.15
authentic 516.14
certain 513.15
land 810.10
numerical 86.8
substantial 3.6
true 516.12
*adv.* very 34.18
**real estate** land 385.1
property 810.7
tract 180.4
**realign** change 139.6
make parallel 218.5
rearrange 60.13
**realignment**
change 139.1
rearrangement 60.7
**realism**
authenticity 516.5
materialism 376.5
normality 84.1
practicalness 536.2
**realist**
*n.* materialist 376.6
pragmatist 536.3
*adj.* materialist
  376.11
philosophy 500.9
practical 536.6
**realistic**
authentic 516.14
businesslike 656.15
descriptive 608.15
lifelike 20.16
materialist 376.11

rejection 638.1
relinquishment 814.1
repeal 779.1
withdrawal 628.3
**recap**
*n.* abridgment 203.3
iteration 103.2
summary 607.2
*v.* re-cover 228.29
repair 694.14
shorten 203.6
summarize 87.12
**recapitulate**
repeat 103.8
shorten 203.6
summarize 87.12
**recapitulation**
abridgment 203.3
iteration 103.2
numeration 87.5
summary 607.2
**recapture**
*n.* recovery 823.3
*v.* recover 823.6
remember 537.10
**recede** regress 295.5
retreat 297.2
**receding**
*n.* recession 297.1
*adj.* retreating 297.5
**receipt**
*n.* acknowledgment
844.2
acquisition 819.1
answer 486.1
formula 751.3
income 844.1
reception 306.1
remedy 687.1
*v.* get income 844.3
**receipts** accounts 845.1
gain 811.3
income 844
**receivable** due 840.10
receptive 306.16
**receivables** 844.1
**receive** admit 306.10
assent 521.8
believe 501.10
get 819.6
get income 844.3
include 76.3
take 822.13
use radar 346.17
welcome 925.7
**received**
accepted 819.10
acknowledged 521.14
approved 968.19
believed 501.23
conventional 645.5
customary 642.15
official 513.18
orthodox 1024.7
traditional 123.12
**receiver** believer 1028.4
container 193.1
fence 826.6
financial officer
836.11
radio receiver
344.3,29

recipient 819.3
telegraphy 560.2
telephone 560.4
**receiver part**
radio 344.30
television 345.17
**receivership** 842.3
**receiving**
*n.* receival 819
reception 306.1
*adj.* getting 819.9
**recension**
revision 691.4
written matter 602.10
**recent** former 119.10
late 122.12
**recently**
formerly 119.13
now 122.16
**receptacle**
biological 193.18
container 193.1
flower part 411.26
types of 193.6
**reception**
acquisition 822.1
belief 501.1
entrance 302.1
inclusion 76.1
meeting 74.2
radio reception
344.21
receiving 819.1
social gathering
922.10
taking in 306
welcome 925.2
**receptionist**
doorkeeper 699.12
host 925.5
**receptive**
admissive 306.16
emotionable 855.21
hospitable 925.11
influenceable 172.15
open-minded 526.10
pliant 357.9
receiving 819.9
sensible 422.13
sensory 422.11
teachable 564.18
willing 622.5
**recess**
*n.* hiding place 615.4
interim 109.1
interior 225.2
niche 257.7
nook 192.3
pause 144.3
respite 711.2
retreat 700.5
seclusion 924.1
*v.* indent 257.14
let up 144.9
pause 109.3
postpone 132.9
take a rest 711.8
**recession**
business cycle 827.9
hard times 729.6
niche 257.7
regression 295.1

retreat 297
surrender 765.2
**recessive**
recessional 297.4
regressive 295.11
reversionary 146.7
**recessive character**
170.6
**recharge**
energize 161.11
revive 694.16
**recherché** chic 644.13
unusual 85.10
**recidivate** regress 295.5
relapse 696.4
revert 146.4
**recidivism**
apostasy 628.2
backsliding 696.2
immorality 981.1
impiety 1030.1
regression 295.1
reversion 146.1
**recidivist**
*n.* apostate 628.5
backslider 696.3
bad person 986.5
impious person
1030.3
repeater 146.3
*adj.* impious 1030.6
reversionary 146.7
unrighteous 981.12
**recipe** formula 751.3
remedy 687.1
**recipient**
*n.* receiver 819.3
*adj.* receiving 819.9
welcoming 306.16
**reciprocal**
*n.* likeness 20.3
*adj.* alternate 323.19
communal 815.9
complementary 13.13
cooperating 786.5
mutual 150.5
numerical 86.8
periodic 137.7
retaliatory 955.8
**reciprocate**
alternate 323.13
cooperate 786.3
correspond 13.9
get along 794.2
interchange 150.4
retaliate 955.4
**reciprocation**
alternation 323.5
correlation 13.1
interchange 150.1
retaliation 955.1
**reciprocity**
accord 794.1
cooperation 786.1
correlation 13.1
interchange 150.1
**recital** iteration 103.2
lesson 562.7
music performance
462.34
narrative 608.2
speech 599.2

**recitation** lesson 562.7
speech 599.2
**recitative** 462.14
**recite** declaim 599.10
memorize 537.17
narrate 608.13
repeat 103.8
state 594.24
summarize 87.12
**reciter** actor 612.2
elocutionist 599.7
narrator 608.10
**reckless** careless 534.11
fast 269.19
impulsive 630.9
rash 894.8
unconcerned 636.7
unwise 470.9
**recklessly**
carelessly 534.18
impulsively 630.13
rashly 894.11
unconcernedly
636.10
**recklessness**
carelessness 534.2
impulsiveness 630.2
rashness 894.2
unconcern 636.2
unwiseness 470.2
**reckon** believe 501.11
calculate 87.11
judge 494.9
suppose 499.10
**reckonable** 87.16
**reckoning**
account 845.2
bill 845.3
calculation 87.3
count 87.6
fee 841.5
judgment 494.3
numeration 87.5
sum 86.5
**reckon on**
believe in 501.16
expect 539.6
plan on 653.6
**reckon with**
include 76.3
settle with 841.12
take cognizance of
530.9
**reclaim** aid 785.11
recover 823.6
redeem 694.12
reform 145.12
rehabilitate 145.14
**reclaimable** 694.25
**reclamation**
atonement 1012.1
recovery 823.3
reformation 145.2
rehabilitation 145.4
restoration 694.2
reversion 146.1
**recline** lean on 216.22
lie down 318.11
repose 214.5
rest 711.6
**reclining**
*n.* lowness 208.1

recumbency 214.2
*adj.* recumbent 214.8
**recluse**
*n.* eccentric 474.3
shut-in 924.5
*adj.* sequestered 924.9
**recognition**
acknowledgment
521.3
cognizance 475.2
commendation 968.3
discovery 488.1
due 960.2
reidentification 537.5
repute 914.1
story element 608.9
thanks 949.2
**recognizable**
knowable 475.25
visible 444.6
**recognizance**
contract 771.3
pledge 772.2
promise 770.2
**recognize**
acknowledge 521.11
detect 488.5
know 475.12
reidentify 537.12
see 439.12
thank 949.4
**recognized**
acknowledged 521.14
conventional 645.5
known 475.26
received 819.10
traditional 123.12
**recoil**
*n.* demur 623.2
effect 154.3
reaction 178.1
rebound 284.2
retaliation 955.1
retreat 284.3
*v.* demur 623.4
dodge 631.8
flinch 891.21
pull back 284.7
rebound 284.6
shudder at 867.5
**recollect** 537.10
**recollected**
remembered 537.23
reminiscent 119.8
unexcited 858.13
**recollection**
memory 537.1
remembering 537.4
retrospection 119.4
**recommence** 143.6
**recommend**
*n.* recommendation
968.4
*v.* advise 754.5
commend 968.11
propose 773.5
urge 648.14
**recommendable** 670.5
**recommendation**
advice 754.1
testimonial 968.4
**recommended** 968.19

**recompense**
*n.* atonement 1012.1
compensation 33.1
remuneration 841.3
reparation 694.6
reprisal 955.2
restitution 823.2
*v.* atone 1012.4
compensate 33.4
make restitution
823.5
pay 841.10
remedy 694.13
retaliate 955.5
**reconcilable** 26.9
**reconcile** accept 861.6
conciliate 804.8
conform 82.3
make agree 26.7
**reconciled**
contented 868.7
resigned 861.10
**reconciliation**
adjustment 26.4
conciliation 804.3
conformity 82.1
contentment 868.1
**reconciliatory** 804.12
**recondite**
abstruse 549.16
concealed 615.11
**recondition**
rehabilitate 145.14
renovate 694.17
repair 694.14
**reconnaissance**
flight 278.11
reconnoitering 485.8
**reconnoiter**
look 439.14
scout out 485.27
traverse 273.19
**reconnoitering** 485.8
**reconsider**
re-examine 485.26
think over 478.15
**reconsideration**
afterthought 478.5
remembering 537.4
**reconstitute**
rearrange 60.13
remake 169.7
restore 694.11
**reconstruct**
change 139.6
remake 169.7
restore 694.18
**reconstruction**
remaking 694.5
reproduction 169.1
**reconstructive** 169.14
**record**
*n.* chronicle 114.9
description 608.4
register 570
reports 570.7
sound recording
450.12
supremacy 36.3
*v.* chronicle 608.14
register 570.16
tape 570.16

write 602.19
**record book**
account book 845.4
reference book 605.6
**record changer** 450.11
**recorder**
accountant 845.7
clerk 570.13
computer 349.18
judge 1002.4
registrar 571
telegraph 560.24
wood wind 465.9
**record holder** 733.14
**recording**
*n.* copy 24.4
documentation 570.1
registry 570.15
sound recording
450.12
*adj.* recordative
570.17
**recording instrument**
571.3
**recording secretary**
602.13
**record keeping**
automation 349.7
recording 570.15
**record player** 450.11
**recount**
*n.* election returns
744.21
numeration 87.5
*v.* narrate 608.13
repeat 103.8
summarize 87.12
**recounting**
iteration 103.2
narrative 608.2
numeration 87.5
**recoup**
*n.* recovery 823.3
*v.* recover 823.6
redeem 694.12
repay 841.11
**recourse**
instrumentality 658.2
means 658.1
refuge 700.2
**recover** rally 691.8
recover health 685.6
redeem 694.12
regain 823.6
rescue 702.3
survive 694.20
**recovery**
business cycle 827.9
improvement 691.1
rally 694.8
reformation 694.2
rescue 702.1
retrieval 823.3
**recreant**
*n.* bad person 986.5
coward 892.6
impious person
1030.3
turncoat 628.5
*adj.* apostate 628.11
dastardly 892.12
dishonest 975.17

impious 1030.6
unfaithful 975.20
**re-create** change 139.6
rebuild 694.18
remake 169.7
**recreation**
amusement 878.1
refreshment 695.1
**re-creation**
change 139.1
reconstruction 694.5
reproduction 169.1
**recreational** 878.29
**recriminate** 1005.11
**recrimination** 1005.3
**recriminatory** 1005.13
**rec room** 192.12
**recrudescence**
relapse 696.1
renewal 145.2
revival 694.3
**recrudescent**
relapsing 696.5
renascent 694.24
**recruit**
*n.* beginner 68.2
conscript 800.17
newcomer 78.4
novice 566.9
*v.* add to 40.5
call to arms 797.23
employ 780.13
enlist 780.16
provide 659.7
recuperate 694.19
restore 694.11
revive 694.16
**recruitment**
call to arms 797.12
enlistment 780.6
**rectal** 225.10
**rectangle** 96.1
**rectangular** long 202.10
quadrangular 251.9
right-angled 251.7
**rectifiable** 694.25
**rectification**
compensation 33.1
correction 691.4
repair 694.6
**rectify**
compensate 33.4
conform 82.3
make agree 26.7
refine 681.22
remedy 694.13
revise 691.12
straighten 250.5
**rectilinear** 250.6
**rectitude**
honesty 974.1
virtue 980.1
**recto** book 605.12
right side 243.1
**rector**
clergyman 1038.2
director 748.1
educator 565.9
patriarch 1038.9
**rectory** house 191.6
parsonage 1042.7
the ministry 1037.9

rectum 225.4
recumbency
  lowness 208.1
  proneness 214.2
recumbent
  inclining 219.15
  low 208.7
  reclining 214.8
recuperate
  get better 694.19
  rally 691.8
  recover 823.6
  recover health 685.6
recuperation
  recovery 694.8
  retrieval 823.3
recuperative 694.23
recur be frequent 135.3
  be remembered
   537.15
  be repeated 103.11
  occur periodically
   137.5
recurrence
  continuity 71.2
  periodicity 137.2
  relapse 696.1
  repetition 103.1
recurrent
  continuous 71.8
  frequent 135.4
  habitual 642.16
  periodic 137.7
  repeating 103.13
  unforgettable 537.26
recusant
  disobedient 767.8
  dissenting 522.6
  nonconforming 83.5
recycle 694.12
red
  n. barbiturate 687.12
  colors 368.12
  radical 745.12
  redness 368.1
  revolutionist 147.3
  adj. blushing 908.13
  radical 745.20
  reddish 368.6
  sore 424.11
  uncooked 721.10
Red
  n. Communist 745.13
  revolutionist 147.3
  adj. Communist
   745.21
redact 691.12
red-baiting
  persecution 667.3
  prejudice 527.4
red blood cell 388.4
red-blooded
  bold 893.18
  strong 159.13
Red Book
  official document
   570.8
  register 570.9
redcap carrier 271.5
  trainman 274.13
red cent trifle 673.5
  US money 835.7

redcoat 800.7
red-complexioned 368.9
redden
  become excited
   857.17
  become red 368.5
  blush 908.8
  make red 368.4
  show resentment
   952.14
red devil 687.12
reddish brown colors
  367.7
redecorate 901.8
redeem aid 785.11
  atone 1012.4
  convert 145.12
  pay 841.18
  reclaim 694.12
  recover 823.6
  rescue 702.3
  sanctify 1026.6
  settle 841.13
  substitute 149.4
redeemable due 960.7
  payable 840.10
  remediable 694.25
  rescuable 702.4
redeemed
  converted 145.19
  forgiven 947.7
  liberated 763.10
  pious 1028.10
  saintly 1015.6
  sanctified 1026.9
redeemer 942.2
redeeming
  atoning 1012.7
  restitutive 823.7
redemption
  atonement 1012.1
  conversion 145.2
  pardon 947.2
  recovery 823.3
  reformation 694.2
  rescue 702.1
  salvation 1026.4
redemptive
  atoning 1012.7
  Christlike 1013.19
  restitutive 823.7
red-faced
  humiliated 906.13
  red-complexioned
   368.9
red flag signal 568.15
  warning sign 703.3
red-green blindness
  441.3
red-handed
  in the act 983.4
  murderous 409.24
redhead 362.9
redheaded 368.10
red herring
  food 308.24
  stratagem 735.3
red-hot excited 857.20
  fervent 855.23
  fiery 162.21
  hot 328.25
  zealous 635.10

red-letter day 711.4
red light light 336.4
  signal 568.15
  warning sign 703.3
red-light district
  brothel 989.9
  city district 183.6
red man 418.3
redneck 190.10
redness
  dim-sightedness 440.2
  heat 328.12
  reddishness 368
redo ornament 901.8
  remake 169.7
  repeat 103.7
redolence
  fragrance 436.1
  odor 435.1
redolent fragrant 436.9
  odorous 435.9
  recollective 537.22
redouble
  duplicate 91.3
  increase 38.5
  repeat 103.7
redoubt 799.4
redoubtable 891.38
redound to
  cause 153.13
  tend 174.3
redress
  n. atonement 1012.1
  compensation 33.1
  recompense 841.3
  reparation 694.6
  restitution 823.2
  v. atone 1012.4
  make restitution
   823.5
  remedy 694.13
  repay 841.11
  retaliate 955.5
redskin 418.3
red tape delay 132.2
  officialism 741.11
  routine 642.6
reduce analyze 48.6
  cheapen 849.6
  conquer 727.10
  contract 198.7
  convert to 145.11
  decrease 39.7
  demote 783.3
  depress 318.4
  dilute 160.11
  discount 847.2
  humiliate 906.5
  impoverish 838.6
  moderate 163.6
  qualify 507.3
  quantify 28.4
  react chemically
   379.6
  relieve 886.5
  shorten 203.6
  sicken 686.47
  simplify 45.4
  slenderize 205.13
  subdue 764.9
  subtract 42.9
  weaken 160.10

reduced cheap 849.9
  conquered 727.16
  decreased 39.10
  depressed 318.12
  diluted 160.19
  humble 906.12
  poor 838.7
  subdued 764.15
  unhealthy 686.50
reducing
  n. slenderizing 205.9
  adj. moderating
   163.14
  slenderizing 205.21
reduction
  cheapening 849.4
  contraction 198.1
  conversion 145.1
  decrease 39.1
  demotion 783.1
  depression 318.1
  diminution 42.2
  discount 847.1
  mathematics 87.4
  moderation 163.2
  reaction 379.5
  relief 886.1
  shortening 203.3
  subdual 764.4
  weakening 160.5
reductive
  decreasing 39.11
  oversimplified 45.10
  subtractive 42.13
  undeveloped 721.12
redundancy
  diffuseness 593.1
  excess 43.4
  information theory
   557.7
  overabundance 663.2
  superfluity 663.4
  tautology 103.3
redundant
  diffuse 593.11
  repetitious 103.14
  superfluous 663.17
red-up 60.6
red, white, and blue
  569.6
reed arrow 801.16
  grass 411.5,46
  plant stem 411.19
  tube 396.6
  weakness 160.7
  wind instrument
   465.7
  wood wind 465.9
reed stop 465.22
reeducate
  rehabilitate 145.14
  teach 562.11
reef
  n. hidden danger
   697.5
  island 386.2
  point of land 256.8
  shoal 210.2
  v. sail 275.50
  slow 270.9
  take precautions
   895.6

**reefer**
marihuana 687.13
railway car 272.14
refrigerator 334.4
**reefy** 210.6
**reek**
*n.* smoke 329.16
stench 437.1
vapor 401.1
*v.* exhale 310.23
exude 303.15
give off 401.8
smell 435.6
smoke 328.23
stink 437.4
**reeking**
*n.* stench 437.1
*adj.* burning 328.27
intense 159.20
malodorous 437.5
strong-smelling
435.10
vaporous 401.9
**reel**
*n.* flounder 324.8
rotation 322.2,17
swing 323.6
windlass 287.7
*v.* be drunk 996.26
eddy 395.21
flounder 324.15
oscillate 323.10
pull back 284.7
sail 275.55
whirl 322.11
wind in 287.9
**reeling**
*n.* rotation 322.1
*adj.* intoxicated
996.30
rotating 322.14
swinging 323.17
**reenact** 694.11
**reentry**
regression 295.1
return 300.3
spacecraft 282.2
**reestablish**
remake 169.7
restore 694.11
**reeve**
peace officer 699.15
public official 749.17
**re-examine**
recheck 485.26
think over 478.15
**refection** food 308.3
invigoration 695.1
refreshment 307.5
**refectory** 192.11
**refer** see **refer to**
**referable**
attributable 155.6
relative 9.7
**referee**
*n.* arbitrator 805.4
judge 1002.1
umpire 494.6
*v.* judge 494.12
mediate 805.6
**reference**
*n.* aspect 446.3

attribution 155.2
citation 505.6
meaning 545.1
punctuation 586.15
recommendation
968.4
relevance 9.4
*v.* cite 505.15
**reference book**
book 605.6
directory 748.10
**reference mark**
punctuation 586.15
types of 586.20
**referendum**
election 744.15
political referendum
742.16
vote 637.6
**referent** 545.1
**referential**
figurative 551.3
meaningful 545.10
suggestive 546.6
**refer to**
attribute to 155.4
avail oneself of
665.14
call attention to
530.10
cite 505.15
confer with 597.11
designate 568.18
mean 545.8
relate to 9.5
remark 594.25
**refill** complete 56.6
restore 694.11
**refine** extract 305.16
finish 691.10
make better 691.9
melt 329.21
process 167.11
purify 681.22
sensitize 422.9
simplify 45.4
subtract 42.9
**refined**
discriminating 492.7
exact 516.16
fastidious 896.11
improved 691.13
meticulous 533.12
perfected 677.9
polished 589.6
produced 167.22
purified 681.26
sensitive 422.14
smooth 351.8
tasteful 897.9
well-bred 936.17
**refinement**
accuracy 516.3
cultivation 691.3
difference 16.2
discrimination 492.1
extract 305.8
fastidiousness 896.3
fine texture 351.3
good breeding 936.4
good taste 897.1
improvement 691.2

literary elegance
589.1
meticulousness 533.3
purification 681.4
simplification 45.2
subtraction 42.1
**refinery** plant 719.3
refining place 681.13
**reflect** consider 478.12
curve 252.6
imitate 22.5
radar 346.16
remark 594.25
remember 537.10
represent 572.8
think over 478.13
**reflection**
consideration 478.2
curve 252.3
disapproval 969.4
disparagement 971.4
idea 479.1
image 572.3
judiciousness 467.7
light 335.9
radar signal 346.11
reaction 284.1
reflex 24.7
remark 594.4
remembering 537.4
stigma 915.6
**reflective**
judicious 467.19
thoughtful 478.21
**reflector**
astronomy 375.17
mirror 443.5
radar 346.23
**reflect upon** 969.13
**reflex**
*n.* conditioning
690.33
effect 154.3
impulse 630.1
reaction 284.1
reflection 24.7
*v.* curve 252.6
*adj.* involuntary
639.14
reactive 284.9
reversed 295.12
unpremeditated
630.11
**reflex action**
involuntariness 639.5
reaction 284.1
**reflexive**
*n.* voice 586.14
*adj.* involuntary
639.14
reactive 284.9
unpremeditated
630.11
**refluent** flowing 267.8
reflex 284.9
**reflux** course 267.2
eddy 395.12
reaction 284.1
regression 295.1
tide 395.13
**reform**
*n.* change 139.1

improvement 691.5
renewal 145.2
*v.* change 139.6
change one's ways
145.12
make better 691.9
purify 681.18
repent 873.7
restore 694.11
sanctify 1026.6
**re-form**
reconstruct 694.18
remake 169.7
reshape 145.12
**reformation**
change 139.1
improvement 691.5
penitence 873.4
redemption 1026.4
regeneration 145.2
restoration 694.1
**reformatory**
prison 761.8
reform school 567.14
**reformed**
changed 139.9
converted 145.19
improved 691.13
purified 681.26
**reformer**
politician 746.1
reformist 691.6
**reform school**
prison 761.8
school 567.14
**refound** 169.7
**refract** 291.5
**refraction**
deflection 291.2
radar interference
346.12
**refractive** 291.8
**refractor** 375.17
**refractory**
ceramic 576.7
disobedient 767.10
nonconforming 83.5
opposing 790.8
resistant 792.5
ungovernable 626.12
unwilling 623.5
**refrain**
*n.* melody 462.4
music division 462.24
poetic division
609.11
repeat 103.5
sequel 67.1
*v.* abstain 992.7
cease 144.6
not do 706.3
not use 668.5
**refraining**
abstinence 992.2
avoidance 631.1
**refresh** air 402.11
amuse 878.23
freshen 695.2
refrigerate 334.10
renovate 694.17
revive 694.16
strengthen 159.11

**regularity**
constancy 135.2
monotony 17.2
normality 84.1
order 59.1
recurrence 137
smoothness 260.1
symmetry 248.1
**regularize**
make uniform 17.4
normalize 84.6
order 59.4
organize 60.10
symmetrize 248.3
**regularly**
constantly 135.7
habitually 642.23
methodically 59.9
normally 84.9
smoothly 260.12
systematically 137.9
uniformly 17.8
**regulate** direct 747.8
govern 741.12
influence 172.8
legalize 998.8
make agree 26.7
make uniform 17.4
order 59.4
organize 60.10
qualify 507.3
**regulation**
*n.* adjustment 26.4
directive 752.3
government 741.1
law 998.3
management 747.1
organization 60.2
precept 751.2
rule 84.4
*adj.* customary 642.15
prescriptive 751.4
usual 84.8
**regulator** 349.14
**regulatory**
directing 747.12
governing 741.18
**regurgitate** flow 395.16
repeat 103.7
vomit 310.25
**regurgitation**
eddy 395.12
repetition 103.1
vomiting 310.8
**rehabilitate**
justify 1006.9
recondition 145.14
restore 694.11
**rehabilitation**
adjustment 690.34
justification 1006.1
reconditioning 145.4
restoration 694.1
reversion 146.1
**rehabilitative** 1006.13
**rehash**
*n.* iteration 103.2
*v.* paraphrase 552.13
repeat 103.8
**rehearsal**
drama production
611.14

iteration 103.2
narrative 608.2
numeration 87.5
training 562.3
tryout 489.3
**rehearse** narrate 608.13
rehearse a play
611.37
repeat 103.8
report 558.11
summarize 87.12
train 562.14
**reification** 3.4
**reify** 3.5
**reign**
*n.* authority 739.5
government 741.1
influence 172.1
prevalence 79.2
*v.* prevail 79.10
rule 741.14
**reigning**
governing 741.18
prevalent 79.12
**reimburse**
make restitution
823.5
repay 841.11
**reimbursement**
payment 841.2
restitution 823.2
**rein**
*n.* restraint 760.1
*v.* restrain 760.7
slow 270.9
**reincarnate**
embody 376.8
repeat 103.7
**reincarnation**
embodiment 376.7
repetition 103.1
transformation 139.2
**reindeer**
beast of burden
271.6
hoofed animal
414.5,58
**reinforce** aid 785.12
add to 40.5
confirm 505.12
increase 38.5
stiffen 356.9
strengthen 159.11
support 216.21
**reinforced**
hardened 356.13
increased 38.7
**reinforcement**
addition 40.1
adjunct 41.1
aid 785.8
conditioning 690.33
confirmation 505.5
increase 38.2
provision 659.1
strengthening 159.5
supporter 216.2
wave phenomenon
323.4
**reins** harness 659.5
management 747.5
restraint 760.4

**reinstate** justify 1006.9
restore 694.11
**reinstatement**
justification 1006.1
restoration 694.1
reversion 146.1
**reinstitute**
remake 169.7
restore 694.11
**reissue**
*n.* iteration 103.2
printing 603.3
reproduction 169.1
*v.* monetize 835.26
print 603.14
remake 169.7
repeat 103.8
**reiterate**
*v.* repeat 103.8
*adj.* repeated 103.12
**reiteration**
diffuseness 593.1
duplication 91.1
platitude 517.3
repetition 103.2
**reiterative**
diffuse 593.11
repetitious 103.14
**reject**
*n.* abandoned thing
633.4
discard 668.3
*v.* be incredulous
504.3
contradict 790.6
disapprove 969.10
disbelieve 503.5
discard 668.7
eject 310.13
exclude 77.4
prohibit 778.3
refuse 776.3
repudiate 638.2
vomit 310.25
**rejected**
discarded 668.11
disproved 506.7
outcast 926.10
repudiated 638.3
unloved 867.10
**rejection**
disapproval 969.1
discard 668.3
dissent 522.1
ejection 310.1
exclusion 77.1
opposition 790.1
prohibition 778.1
refusal 776.1
repudiation 638
unbelief 503.1
**rejoice** cheer 870.7
enjoy 865.10
jubilate 876.5
**rejoicing**
*n.* celebration 877.1
jubilation 876
*adj.* jubilant 876.9
merry 870.15
**rejoin** answer 486.4
rebut 486.5
**rejoinder** answer 486.1

counterstatement
486.2
**rejuvenate**
make young 124.8
revive 694.16
**rejuvenation** 694.3
**rekindle** burn 329.22
revive 694.16
**relapse**
*n.* falling back 696
regression 295.1
reversion 146.1
*v.* get worse 692.19
regress 295.5
return to 696.4
revert 146.4
**relate** associate 9.6
communicate with
554.8
compare 491.4
narrate 608.13
refer to 9.5
report 558.11
state 594.24
suit 26.8
summarize 87.12
**related** connected 9.9
germane 9.10
kindred 11.6
**relation**
blood relationship
11.1
comparison 491.1
connection 9
involvement 176.1
meaning 545.1
narrative 608.2
role 7.5
**relations** affairs 151.4
copulation 419.8
kinsmen 11.2
relationship 9.1
**relationship**
blood relationship
11.1
connection 9.1
**relative**
*n.* kinsman 11.2
*adj.* comparative
491.8
relational 9.7
**relatively**
comparatively 491.10
relevantly 9.12
to a degree 35.10
**relativity**
correlation 13.1
relationship 9.2
space 179.6
**relator** 608.10
**relax**
amuse oneself 878.24
be comfortable 887.8
be pliant 357.7
calm oneself 858.7
entertain 878.23
loosen 51.3
make pliant 357.6
moderate 163.9
relent 944.4
rest 711.7
slow 270.9

waive 507.5
**relaxation**
  amusement 878.1
  decrease 39.1
  looseness 51.2
  moderation 163.2
  rest 711.1
  softening 357.5
  unstrictness 758.1
  weakening 160.5
**relaxed** at ease 887.12
  flaccid 357.10
  informal 647.3
  leisurely 710.6
  loose 51.5
  negligent 534.10
  slow 270.10
  thoughtless 480.4
  unnervous 860.2
  unstrict 758.4
**relaxing**
  comfortable 887.11
  moderating 163.14
  softening 357.16
**relay**
  *n.* computer part
    349.32
  electrical part 342.36
  race 796.12
  shift 108.3
  *v.* transfer 271.9
**relay station**
  radio station 344.6
  television relay 345.9
**release**
  *n.* acquittal 1007.1
  death 408.1
  disbandment 75.3
  escape 632.1
  exemption 762.8
  information 557.1
  liberation 763.2
  message 558.4
  permission 777.1
  press release 559.3
  receipt 844.2
  relief 886.2
  relinquishment 814.1
  rescue 702.1
  *v.* acquit 1007.4
  detach 49.10
  disband 75.8
  dismiss 310.19
  exempt 762.14
  extricate 763.7
  free 763.5
  permit 777.9
  relieve 886.6
  relinquish 814.4
  rescue 702.3
**released** dead 408.30
  exempt 762.29
  free 762.20
  liberated 763.10
  relinquished 814.5
**relegate** commit 818.16
  eject 310.17
  exclude 77.4
**relent**
  be moderate 163.5
  be pliant 357.7
  have pity 944.4

submit 765.6
**relentless**
  industrious 707.22
  inevitable 639.15
  persevering 625.7
  pitiless 945.3
  resolute 624.11
  strict 757.7
  unyielding 626.9
**relentlessness**
  industry 707.6
  inevitability 639.7
  perseverance 625.1
  pitilessness 945.1
  resolution 624.1
  strictness 757.2
  unyieldingness 626.2
**relevance** fitness 26.5
  meaning 545.1
  pertinence 9.4
**relevant** apt 26.10
  pertinent 9.11
**reliability**
  believability 501.8
  certainty 513.4
  stability 142.1
  trustworthiness
    974.6
**reliable**
  believable 501.24
  evidential 505.17
  stable 142.12
  sure 513.17
  trustworthy 974.19
  unhazardous 698.5
**reliance** belief 501.1
  expectation 539.1
  hope 888.1
  mainstay 787.9
  support 216.1
**relic**
  antiquated person
    123.8
  antiquity 123.6
  memento 537.7
  record 570.1
  sacred article 1040.11
**relics** corpse 408.16
  remainder 43.1
**relict** survivor 43.3
  widow 935.4
**relief** aid 785.1
  consolation 887.4
  easement 886
  embossment 575.3
  interim 109.1
  lightening 353.3
  outline 235.2
  pity 944.1
  protuberance 256.2
  reinforcements 785.8
  remedy 687.1
  sculpture 575.1
  subsidy 818.8
  substitute 149.2
  turn 108.2
  welfare program
    745.7
**relieve** aid 785.11
  comfort 887.6
  diversify 18.2
  ease 886.5

lighten 353.6
  spell 108.5
  substitute for 149.5
  take from 822.21
**religion** faith 1020
  piety 1028.1
  system of belief
    501.3
  theology 1023.1
  word list 1020.32
**religionist**
  believer 1020.14
  pietist 1029.3
  word list 1020.34
  zealot 1028.4
**religious**
  *n.* clergyman 1038.17
  *adj.* conscientious
    974.15
  exact 516.16
  meticulous 533.12
  pious 1028.8
  sacred 1026.7
  theistic 1020.24
  theological 1023.4
**relinquish**
  abandon 144.6
  cease to use 668.4
  give up 633.7
  release 814.3
  resign 784.2
  surrender 765.8
**relinquished**
  disused 668.10
  released 814.5
**relinquishment**
  abandonment 633.3
  cessation 144.1
  discontinuance 668.2
  release 814
  resignation 784.1
  surrender 765.2
**reliquary**
  church vessel 1042.11
  memorial 570.12
  shrine 1042.4
  tomb 410.16
**relish**
  *n.* appetite 634.7
  fervor 855.10
  flavoring 428.3
  liking 634.2
  pleasure 865.1
  pungency 433.2
  savor 428.2
  taste 427.1
  *v.* eat 307.18
  enjoy 865.10
  savor 428.5
**reliving** 119.4
**relocate**
  change residence
    184.16
  move 271.10
**relocation** 271.2
**reluct**
  contend against
    790.4
  offer resistance 792.3
  revolt 767.7
**reluctance**
  electricity 342.12

resistance 792.1
  slowness 270.1
  unwillingness 623.1
**reluctant**
  grudging 623.6
  resistant 792.5
  slow 270.10
**reluctantly**
  grudgingly 623.9
  slowly 270.13
**rely on**
  be hopeful 888.7
  believe in 501.16
  rest on 216.22
  trust 501.17
**remain** be left 43.5
  be present 186.6
  be still 268.7
  continue 143.3
  endure 110.6
  inhabit 188.7
  persist 140.5
**remainder**
  difference 42.8
  estate 810.5
  part 55.1
  posteriority 117.1
  residue 43
  surplus 663.5
**remaining**
  continuing 143.7
  enduring 110.10
  permanent 140.7
  resident 188.13
  surplus 663.18
  surviving 43.7
**remains** antiquity 123.6
  corpse 408.16
  record 570.1
  residue 43.1
**remake** change 139.6
  reconstruct 694.18
  reproduce 169.7
**remaking** change 139.1
  reconstruction 694.5
  reproduction 169.1
**remand**
  *n.* commitment 761.4
  restitution 823.1
  *v.* commit 818.16
  imprison 761.17
  restore 823.4
**remark**
  *n.* attention 530.1
  commentary 606.2
  interjection 237.2
  statement 594.4
  *v.* comment 594.25
  heed 530.6
  write upon 606.5
**remarkable**
  extraordinary 85.14
  notable 672.18
  outstanding 34.10
  wonderful 920.10
**remarkably**
  exceptionally 34.20
  extraordinarily 85.18
  importantly 672.24
  wonderfully 920.14
**remedial**
  curative 687.39

helpful 785.21
relieving 886.9
restorative 694.22
**remedy**
*n.* aid 785.1
counteractant 178.3
cure 687
relief 886.1
repair 694.6
restoration 694.7
*v.* aid 785.11
cure 687.38
rectify 694.13
restore to health
694.15
treat 689.30
**remember** recall 537.10
remind 537.20
**rememberable**
memorable 537.25
notable 672.18
**remembered**
recollected 537.23
reminiscent 119.8
**remembrance**
celebration 877.1
memento 537.7
memorial 570.12
memory 537.1
posthumous fame
914.7
regards 936.8
reminder 537.6
reminiscence 537.4
retrospection 119.4
**remind** 537.20
**reminder**
memorandum 570.4
remembrance 537.6
**remindful** 537.22
**reminisce** 537.11
**reminiscence**
remembering 537.4
retrospection 119.4
**reminiscent**
recollective 537.22
retrospective 119.8
**remiss** dilatory 132.17
indolent 708.18
negligent 534.10
unstrict 758.4
**remissible** 1006.14
**remission**
acquittal 1007.1
decrease 39.2
moderation 163.2
pardon 947.2
pause 144.3
reduction 42.2
**remit** acquit 1007.4
be moderate 163.5
commit 818.16
exempt 762.14
forgive 947.3
imprison 761.17
pay 841.10
reduce 39.8
relax 163.9
restore 823.4
send 271.14
**emittance** 841.1
**emitted** forgiven 947.7

paid 841.22
**remittent** 686.6
**remnant** 43.1
**remodel**
reconstruct 694.18
re-form 145.12
**remodeling** 694.5
**remonstrance**
advice 754.1
dissuasion 652.1
objection 522.2
resistance 792.1
**remonstrate**
advise 754.6
dissuade 652.3
object 522.5
offer resistance 792.3
**remonstrative**
advisory 754.8
protesting 522.7
**remorse** 873.1
**remorseful** 873.8
**remorseless**
pitiless 945.3
unregretful 874.4
**remote** aloof 912.12
distant 199.8
farfetched 10.7
reticent 613.10
secluded 924.7
selfish 978.5
unsociable 923.6
**remote control** 349.4
**remote-control** 349.28
**removable** 271.17
**removal**
departure 301.1
deposal 783.2
discard 668.3
dislocation 185.1
dismissal 310.5
displacement 271.2
divestment 232.1
ejection 310.1
elimination 77.2
evacuation 310.6
extraction 305.1
homicide 409.2
release 886.2
separation 49.1
subtraction 42.1
surgical operation
689.22
**remove**
*n.* degree 29.1
*v.* depose 783.4
detach 49.10
discard 668.7
dismiss 310.19
divest 232.5
eject 310.13
eliminate 77.5
eradicate 693.14
evacuate 310.21
extract 305.10
interspace 201.3
leave 301.8
move 271.10
murder 409.16
release 886.6
subtract 42.9
take off 232.6

**removed** alone 89.8
distant 199.8
interspaced 201.6
reticent 613.10
secluded 924.7
separated 49.21
unrelated 10.5
unsociable 923.6
**remunerate** pay 841.10
remedy 694.13
**remuneration**
recompense 841.3
salary 841.4
**remunerative**
gainful 811.15
paying 841.21
useful 665.21
**renaissance** 694.3
**renascence**
rebirth 169.1
renewal 145.2
revival 694.3
**renascent**
renewed 694.24
reproductive 169.14
**rencontre**
contest 796.3
meeting 200.4
**rend** demolish 693.17
extract from 305.15
injure 692.15
sever 49.11
wrest 822.22
**render**
communicate 554.7
convert 145.11
deliver 818.13
describe 608.12
do 705.6
execute 771.10
extract 305.16
give 818.12
interpret 552.12
melt 329.21
pay 841.10
perform music 462.40
relinquish 814.3
represent 572.6
**rendering**
description 608.1
extraction 305.7
interpretation 552.2
music 462.31
representation 572.1
**rendezvous**
*n.* meeting 74.2
tryst 922.9
*v.* come together
74.16
**rendition**
description 608.1
extraction 305.7
interpretation 552.2
music 462.31
representation 572.1
restitution 823.1
**renegade**
*n.* apostate 145.8
impious person
1030.3
turncoat 628.5
*v.* defect 145.13

*adj.* apostate 145.20
impious 1030.6
traitorous 628.11
**renege** abandon 633.5
defect 145.13
recant 628.9
repeal 779.2
**renew** change 139.6
innovate 122.5
reform 145.12
refresh 695.2
renovate 694.17
repeat 103.7
resume 143.6
revive 694.16
stimulate 857.12
**renewal** change 139.1
reformation 145.2
refreshment 695.1
relapse 696.1
renovation 694.4
repetition 103.1
resumption 143.2
revival 694.3
**renewed** changed 139.9
converted 145.19
new 122.8
refreshed 695.4
renascent 694.24
sanctified 1026.9
**renitency**
hardness 356.2
perverseness 178.1
resistance 792.1
unwillingness 623.1
**renitent**
counteractive 178.8
reluctant 623.6
resistant 792.5
rigid 356.11
**rennet** 308.45
**renounce** cease 144.6
deny 524.4
discontinue 668.4
give up 633.7
recant 628.9
reject 638.2
relinquish 814.3
surrender 765.8
swear off 992.8
**renounced**
disused 668.10
rejected 638.3
relinquished 814.5
**renovate** recover 823.6
renew 122.5
reproduce 169.7
restore 694.17
touch up 691.11
**renovation**
renewal 694.4
reproduction 169.1
**renown** eminence 34.2
notability 672.2
repute 914.1
**renowned**
eminent 34.9
famous 914.16
**rent**
*n.* break 49.4
crack 201.2
hire 780.5

impairment 692.8
rent money 846.9
*v.* charter 780.15
cleave 201.4
hire 780.14
open 265.12
*adj.* cleft 201.7
damaged 692.29
severed 49.23
**rental** hire 780.5
rent money 846.9
**rent control** 846.6
**rented** 780.19
**renter** lodger 190.8
tenant 809.4
**renunciation**
abandonment 633.3
apostasy 145.3
cessation 144.1
denial 524.2
discontinuance 668.2
recantation 628.3
relinquishment 814.1
surrender 765.2
temperance 992.1
**renunciative**
denying 524.5
rejecting 638.4
repudative 628.12
**reoccurrence**
periodicity 137.2
repetition 103.1
**reorder** 60.13
**reorganization**
rearrangement 60.7
reproduction 169.1
**reorganize**
rearrange 60.13
remake 169.7
**repair**
*n.* condition 7.3
reparation 694.6
*v.* atone 1012.4
mend 694.14
touch up 691.11
**repairman** 694.10
**repair shop** 719.6
**repair to** 273.24
**reparable** 694.25
**reparation**
atonement 1012.1
compensation 33.1
recompense 841.3
repair 694.6
restitution 823.2
**reparative**
atoning 1012.7
compensating 33.6
paying 841.21
restitutive 823.7
restorative 694.22
retaliatory 955.8
**repartee** answer 486.1
witticism 881.7
**repast** 307.5
**repatriate**
rehabilitate 145.14
restore 823.4
**repay**
be profitable 811.12
compensate 33.4

make restitution
823.5
pay 841.11
retaliate 955.5
**repayment**
compensation 33.1
payment 841.2
restitution 823.2
**repeal**
*n.* revocation 779
*v.* abolish 693.13
revoke 779.2
**repeat**
*n.* encore 91.2
repetition 103.5
replay 103.6
*v.* duplicate 91.3
imitate 22.5
memorize 537.17
publish 559.10
recur 137.5
redo 103.7
reproduce 169.7
resound 103.11
**repeated**
constant 135.5
iterated 103.12
**repeatedly**
frequently 135.6
often 103.16
**repeater** gun 801.5
returnee 146.3
voter 744.23
**repel**
cause dislike 867.6
disgust 429.4
disincline 652.4
fend off 799.10
offend 864.11
prevent 730.14
rebuff 776.5
reject 638.2
repulse 289.3
resist 792.2
**repellent**
offensive 864.18
repulsive 289.4
resistant 792.5
**repelling**
*n.* repulsion 289.1
*adj.* repulsive 289.4
ugly 899.11
**repent** 873.7
**repentance**
penance 1012.3
penitence 873.4
**repentant**
atoning 1012.7
penitent 873.9
**repercussion**
concussion 162.8
effect 154.3
music 462.31
reaction 178.1
recoil 284.2
**repercussive**
recoiling 284.10
reverberating 454.11
**repertory** list 88.1
numeration 87.5
storage place 660.6
store 660.1

theater 611.10
**repertory company**
612.11
**repetition**
constancy 135.2
continuance 143.1
copy 24.3
duplication 91.1
imitation 22.1
recurrence 103
regularity 137.1
reproduction 169.1
**repetitious** 103.14
**repetitive**
continuous 71.8
diffuse 593.11
habitual 642.16
monotonous 17.6
repetitious 103.14
**rephrase** 552.13
**repine** lament 875.8
regret 873.6
**replace**
come after 117.3
dismiss 310.19
restore 694.11
substitute for 149.5
**replaceable**
consumable 666.5
substitutable 149.10
**replacement**
exchange 149.1
restoration 694.1
substitute 149.2
successor 67.4
**replacing** 149.12
**replay** 103.6
**replenish**
complete 56.6
provide 659.7
restore 694.11
**replete** full 56.11
plentiful 661.7
satiated 664.6
**repletion** fullness 56.2
overfullness 663.3
plenty 661.2
satiety 664.1
**replevin**
*n.* pledge 772.2
recovery 823.3
*v.* appropriate 822.20
recover 823.6
**replica** copy 24.3
imitation 22.3
the same 14.3
**replicate** copy 24.8
duplicate 91.3
reproduce 14.6
**replication**
answer 486.1
copy 24.3
counterstatement
486.2
duplication 91.1
gene 170.6
**reply**
*n.* answer 486.1
communication
554.1
justification 1006.2
letter 604.2

reaction 284.1
retaliation 955.1
*v.* answer 486.4
communicate with
554.8
correspond 604.12
defend 1006.10
react 284.5
**report**
*n.* account 608.3
announcement 559.2
commentary 606.2
criticism 494.2
explosion 162.7
explosive noise 456
harmonics 463.14
hymn 1032.3
information 557.1
publicity 559.4
record 570.7
repute 914.1
rumor 558.6
*v.* announce 559.12
communicate 554.7
inform 557.8
narrate 608.13
pass judgment 494.13
present oneself
186.11
relate 558.11
reproach 1005.7
**reportage** 558.1
**reported**
made public 559.17
rumored 558.15
**reporter**
informant 557.5
journalist 605.22
newsmonger 558.9
spokesman 781.5
**repose**
*n.* leisure 710.1
moderation 163.1
recumbency 214.2
rest 711.1
sleep 712.2
stillness 268.1
*v.* be located 184.9
be still 268.7
exist in 1.11
lie 214.5
put 184.13
take rest 711.6
trust 501.17
**reposeful**
comfortable 887.11
moderate 163.13
quiescent 268.12
**reposing** dead 408.30
quiescent 268.12
recumbent 214.8
**reposit** put 184.13
store 660.10
**repository** friend 928.1
storage place 660.6
treasury 836.12
**repossess** 823.6
**repossession**
dispossession 822.7
recovery 823.3
**repoussé**
*n.* relief 575.3

*adj.* in relief 256.17
  sculptured 575.7
**reprehend**
  censure 969.13
  reprove 969.17
**reprehensible**
  bad 675.9
  blameworthy 969.26
  evil 981.16
  guilty 983.3
**reprehension**
  disapproval 969.3
  reproof 969.5
**represent** act 6l̄t.35
  be a deputy 781.14
  delineate 572.6
  describe 608.12
  manifest 555.5
  mediate 805.6
  substitute for 149.5
  visualize 535.15
**representation**
  acting 611.9
  copy 24.1
  delineation 572
  description 608.1
  display 555.2
  fakery 616.3
  idea 479.1
  imitation 22.3
  lawyers 1003.5
  picture 574.12
  representative 572.5
  reproduction 24.3
  sign 568.2
  spectacle 446.7
  substitution 149.1
  vote 637.6
**representative**
  *n.* deputy 781.1
  example 25.2
  legislator 746.3
  model 25.1
  representation 572.5
  sign 568.2
  substitute 149.2
  *adj.* deputy 781.15
  descriptive 608.15
  indicative 568.23
  model 25.8
  representational
    572.10
**repress** blunt 259.2
  control feelings 858.8
  domineer 741.16
  hinder 730.10
  hush up 614.8
  prohibit 778.3
  retain 813.5
  suppress 760.8
**epressed**
  forgetful 538.9
  restrained 760.14
  reticent 613.10
**epression**
  defense mechanism
    690.31
  hindrance 730.1
  keeping secret 614.3
  mental block 538.3
  prohibition 778.1
  retention 813.1

reticence 613.3
  suppression 760.2
**repressive**
  hindering 730.17
  prohibitive 778.6
  restraining 760.11
  tyrannical 739.16
**reprieve**
  *n.* absolution 947.2
  delay 132.2
  pardon 1007.3
  pity 944.1
  release 886.2
  *v.* have pity 944.4
  pardon 1007.5
  release 886.6
**reprimand**
  *n.* reproof 969.5
  stigma 915.6
  *v.* reprove 969.17
  stigmatize 915.9
**reprint**
  *n.* copy 24.5
  iteration 103.2
  printing 603.3
  *v.* print 603.14
  remake 169.7
  repeat 103.8
**reprisal** requital 955.2
  revenge 956.1
**reprise** 103.6
**reproach**
  *n.* accusation 1005.1
  disgrace 915.5
  reproof 969.5
  stigma 915.6
  *v.* accuse 1005.7
  censure 969.13
  disgrace 915.8
**reproachful** 969.23
**reprobate**
  *n.* bad person 986.5
  *v.* censure 969.13
  *adj.* dishonest 975.17
  evil 981.16
  irreligious 1031.18
  morally corrupt
    981.14
  unsacred 1027.3
**reproduce**
  be productive 165.7
  copy 24.8
  duplicate 91.3
  grow 197.7
  remake 169.7
  repeat 103.7
  replicate 14.6
**reproduction** copy 24.3
  duplication 91.1
  facsimile 24.2
  growth 197.3
  imitation 22.3
  picture 574.12
  productiveness 165.2
  remaking 169
  repetition 103.1
**reproductive**
  procreative 169.15
  re-creative 169.14
**reproof** 969.5
**reprove** 969.17

**reptile**
  *n.* animal 414.30,60
  bad person 986.7
  vertebrate 414.3;
    415.7
  *adj.* creeping 273.38
  reptilian 414.51
**reptilian**
  *n.* reptile 414.30
  *adj.* base 915.12
  reptile 414.51
**republic** country 181.1
  government 741.4
**republican** 741.17
**Republican** 744.27
**Republican Party**
  744.24
**repudiate** deny 524.4
  exclude 77.4
  not pay 842.6
  recant 628.9
  refuse 776.3
  reject 638.2
**repudiation**
  denial 524.2
  dissent 522.1
  exclusion 77.1
  nonpayment 842.1
  recantation 628.3
  refusal 776.1
  rejection 638.1
**repudiative**
  abjuratory 628.12
  denying 524.5
  unbelieving 503.8
**repugnance**
  contrariety 15.1
  counteraction 178.1
  disagreement 27.1
  dislike 867.2
  hate 930.1
  hostility 929.3
  offensiveness 864.2
  opposition 790.2
  unsavoriness 429.3
  unwillingness 623.1
**repugnant**
  contrary 15.6
  counteractive 178.8
  denying 524.5
  disagreeing 27.6
  hostile 929.10
  offensive 864.18
  opposing 790.8
  ugly 899.11
**repulse**
  *n.* defeat 727.2
  rebuff 289.2
  recoil 284.2
  refusal 776.2
  rejection 638.1
  resistance 792.1
  snub 966.2
  *v.* fend off 799.10
  refuse 776.5
  reject 638.2
  repel 289.3
  resist 792.2
  snub 966.5
**repulsion** dislike 867.2
  repelling 289
  resistance 792.1

**repulsive** bad 675.9
  filthy 682.23
  malodorous 437.5
  offensive 864.18
  repellent 289.4
  ugly 899.11
**reputable**
  esteemed 914.15
  honest 974.13
  influential 172.13
  notable 672.18
**reputation**
  notability 672.2
  repute 914.1
**repute**
  *n.* custom 827.6
  influence 172.1
  notability 672.2
  reputation 914
  *v.* suppose 499.10
**request**
  *n.* petition 774
  proposal 773.2
  *v.* petition 774.9
**requiem** dirge 875.5
  funeral rites 410.4
  Mass 1040.9
  sacred music 462.16
**require** charge 846.14
  demand 753.4
  dictate 756.5
  entail 76.4
  necessitate 639.9
  obligate 962.12
  prescribe 752.10
  want 662.7
**required**
  imperative 756.10
  mandatory 752.13
  obligatory 962.15
  requisite 639.13
**requirement**
  demand 753.1
  necessity 639.2
**requisite**
  *n.* condition 507.2
  requirement 639.2
  *adj.* needful 639.13
**requisition**
  *n.* appropriation 822.4
  demand 753.1
  request 774.1
  requirement 639.2
  summons 752.5
  *v.* appropriate 822.19
  demand 753.4
  request 774.9
  summon 752.12
**requital**
  recompense 841.3
  reprisal 955.2
  restitution 823.2
**requite**
  interchange 150.4
  make restitution
    823.5
  remedy 694.13
  repay 841.11
  retaliate 955.5
**rerun** 344.18
**rescind** delete 42.12
  repeal 779.2

observe 768.2
regard 964.4
relate to 9.5
**respectable**
honest 974.13
mediocre 680.7
reputable 914.15
tolerable 674.19
**respectable citizen**
985.3
**respected**
esteemed 964.11
reputable 914.15
**respectful**
approbatory 968.16
courteous 936.14
dutiful 962.13
regardful 964.8
**respecting** 9.13
**respective**
mutual 13.14
particular 80.12
proportionate 816.13
**respectively** each 80.19
mutually 13.17
proportionately
816.14
**respects**
compliments 936.8
regards 964.3
**respiration** 403.18
**respirator** 689.37
**respire** breathe 403.24
live 407.7
**respite**
n. delay 132.2
interim 109.1
pardon 1007.3
pause 144.3
release 886.2
rest 711.2
v. pardon 1007.5
**resplendence**
beauty 900.6
brightness 335.4
grandeur 904.5
illustriousness 914.6
**resplendent**
bright 335.32
gorgeous 900.19
illustrious 914.19
**respond** answer 486.4
defend 1006.10
emotionally respond
855.12
interchange 150.4
react 284.5
sense 422.8
**respondent**
n. accused 1005.6
answerer 486.3
adj. answering 486.6
reactive 284.9
**respond to** agree 26.6
behave toward 737.6
communicate with
554.8
get along with 794.2
reciprocate 13.9
**esponse** answer 486.1
communication
554.1

effect 154.3
emotion 855.3
hymn 1032.3
justification 1006.2
music 462.23
reaction 284.1
refrain 462.24
sensation 422.1
sympathy 855.5
**responsibility**
attribution 155.1
commission 780.1
duty 962.2
operation 164.1
supervision 747.2
trustworthiness
974.6
**responsible**
answerable 962.17
chargeable 840.9
liable to 175.5
trustworthy 974.19
**responsive**
answering 486.6
communicational
554.9
emotionable 855.21
influenceable 172.15
pliant 357.9
reactive 284.9
resilient 358.7
sensitive 422.14
willing 622.5
**rest**
n. death 408.1
fulcrum 287.3
leisure 710.1
music 463.21
pause 144.3
quiescence 268.1
remainder 43.1
repose 711
respite 711.2
silence 451.1
step 315.5
supporter 216.2
v. be contingent 507.6
be located 184.9
be still 268.7
calm 163.7
do nothing 706.2
exist in 1.11
pause 144.9
plead 1004.18
put 184.13
remain 43.5
ride at anchor 275.16
take it easy 711.6
**rest assured**
be certain 513.9
be hopeful 888.7
believe 501.14
**restate**
paraphrase 552.13
repeat 103.8
**restaurant**
dining room 192.11
eating house 307.15
**rest easy**
be content 868.5
persuade oneself
648.24

**restful**
comfortable 887.11
pacific 803.9
quiescent 268.12
tranquilizing 163.15
vacational 711.10
**rest home** asylum 700.4
infirmary 689.27
**resting place** end 70.1
supporter 216.2
tomb 410.16
**restitution**
atonement 1012.1
compensation 33.1
payment 841.2
recompense 841.3
restoration 694.1
return 823
reversion 146.1
**restitutive**
atoning 1012.7
compensatory 823.7
restorative 694.22
retaliatory 955.8
**restive**
discontented 869.5
impatient 862.6
obstinate 626.8
refractory 767.10
reluctant 623.6
restless 857.25
ungovernable 626.12
**restless** active 707.20
agitated 324.16
discontented 869.5
fidgety 857.25
impatient 862.6
inconstant 141.7
wakeful 713.7
**restlessness**
activeness 707.4
agitation 324.1
discontent 869.1
excitement 857.4
impatience 862.1
inconstancy 141.2
motion 267.1
wakefulness 713.1
**rest on**
be contingent 507.6
be heavy upon
352.11
believe in 501.16
stand on 216.22
**restoration**
improvement 691.1
justification 1006.1
recovery 823.3
reproduction 169.1
reestablishment 694
restitution 823.1
reversion 146.1
vitaminization 309.12
**restorative**
n. energizer 161.5
remedy 687.1
tonic 687.8
adj. compensatory
823.7
remedial 687.39
reparative 694.22
reproductive 169.14

tonic 687.44
**restore** aid 785.11
justify 1006.9
make restitution
823.4
put back 694.11
recover 823.6
reproduce 169.7
vitaminize 309.18
**restrain** bind 760.10
compel 756.4
confine 761.12
constrain 760.7
hinder 730.10
limit 234.5
moderate 163.6
purify 902.5
qualify 507.3
**restrained**
constrained 760.13
enclosed 236.10
modest 908.11
polished 589.6
reticent 613.10
subdued 163.11
tasteful 897.8
temperate 992.9
**restraining**
compelling 756.9
constraining 760.11
**restrain oneself**
be temperate 992.6
calm oneself 858.7
control 760.7
**restraint**
compulsion 756.1
confinement 761.1
constraint 760
defense mechanism
690.31
equanimity 858.3
good taste 897.4
hindrance 730.1
literary elegance
589.1
moderation 163.1
modesty 908.3
reticence 613.3
self-control 624.5
shackle 760.4
subjection 764.1
temperance 992.1
**restraint of trade**
commerce 827.1
constraint 760.1
**restrict** allot 816.9
confine 761.12
limit 234.5
narrow 205.11
qualify 507.3
restrain 760.9
specialize 81.4
**restricted**
bounded 234.7
confined 761.19
limited 234.8
narrow 205.14
qualified 507.10
restrained 760.15
secret 614.11
specialized 81.5

**restriction**
confinement 761.1
exclusion 77.1
hindrance 730.1
limitation 234.2
narrowness 205.1
qualification 507.1
restraint 760.3
**restrictive**
exclusive 77.8
hindering 730.17
limiting 234.9
qualifying 507.7
restraining 760.12
**rest room**
bathing place 681.10
lavatory 311.10
room 192.26
**restructure**
change 139.6
rearrange 60.13
remake 169.7
**result**
*n.* effect 154.1
product 168.1
solution 487.1
*v.* be the effect of 154.6
come after 117.3
ensue 154.5
happen 151.7
**resultant**
*n.* effect 154.1
*adj.* ensuing 154.7
happening 151.9
**resume**
be repeated 103.11
recommence 143.6
recover 823.6
repeat 103.8
**résumé**
biography 608.4
iteration 103.2
summary 607.2
**resumption**
recommencement 143.2
recovery 823.3
repetition 103.1
**resurgence** 694.3
**resurgent**
renascent 694.24
reproductive 169.14
**resurrect** remake 169.7
revive 694.16
**resurrection**
rebirth 169.1
removal to heaven 1018.12
revival 694.3
**resuscitate** aid 785.11
restore 694.16
revive 407.8
stimulate 857.12
**retable** altar 1042.12
shelf 216.14
**retail**
*n.* sale 829.1
*v.* deal in 827.15
disperse 75.4
publish 559.10
repeat 103.8

sell 829.8
*adj.* commercial 827.21
sales 829.13
**retailer** merchant 830.2
provider 659.6
**retailing**
*n.* provision 659.1
selling 829.2
trade 827.2
*adj.* sales 829.13
**retail store** 832.1
**retain** engage 780.13
keep 813.5
remember 537.13
reserve 660.12
stabilize 142.7
sustain 143.4
**retained**
remembered 537.23
reserved 660.15
**retainer** dependent 750
fee 841.5
hanger-on 907.5
**retaining wall** 216.4
**retake**
*n.* cinematography 577.8
recovery 823.3
*v.* recover 823.6
**retaliate**
compensate 33.4
interchange 150.4
retort 955.4
revenge 956.4
**retaliation**
compensation 33.1
interchange 150.1
reciprocation 955
revenge 956.1
**retaliatory**
compensating 33.6
interchangeable 150.5
retributive 955.8
revengeful 956.6
**retard** delay 132.8
hinder 730.10
restrain 760.7
slow 270.9
**retardant** 792.5
**retardation** delay 132.2
hindrance 730.1
mental deficiency 469.9
restraint 760.1
slowing 270.4
**retarded** late 132.16
mentally deficient 469.22
restrained 760.13
slowed down 270.12
**retardee** 132.6
**retch** sicken at 867.4
vomit 310.25
**retell** narrate 608.13
repeat 103.8
**retention** keeping 813
memory 537.3
refusal 776.1
tenacity 50.3
**retentive** keeping 813.8

recollective 537.22
**rethink**
reconsider 478.15
re-examine 485.26
**reticence** 613.3
**reticent** 613.10
**reticle** 221.3
**reticular** 221.11
**retina** 439.9
**retinue**
attendance 73.6
staff 750.11
**retire**
be concave 257.12
be modest 908.7
be uncommunicative 613.6
be unsociable 923.4
depose 783.4
discard 668.8
dismiss 310.19
go to bed 712.17
leave 301.8
pay in full 841.13
recede 297.2
resign 784.2
retreat 295.6
seclude oneself 924.6
**retired** disused 668.10
leisured 710.5
private 614.13
secluded 924.7
superannuated 784.3
**retirement**
departure 301.1
deposal 783.2
dismissal 310.5
disuse 668.1
leisure 710.1
payment 841.1
privacy 614.2
recession 297.1
resignation 784.1
reticence 613.3
retreat 295.2
seclusion 924.1
**retiring** hollow 257.16
modest 908.11
receding 297.5
reticent 613.10
**retort**
*n.* answer 486.1
converter 145.10
countermeasure 178.5
recrimination 1005.3
retaliation 955.1
vaporizer 401.6
witticism 881.7
*v.* answer 486.4
retaliate 955.4
**retouch**
tamper with 616.17
touch up 691.11
**retrace**
re-examine 485.26
remember 537.10
**retract** deny 524.4
pull back 297.3
recant 628.9
relinquish 814.3
repeal 779.2

**retractile** 297.6
**retraction** denial 524.2
recantation 628.3
recession 297.1
reduction 42.2
relinquishment 814.1
repeal 779.1
**retread**
*n.* renovation 694.4
tire 253.4
*v.* repair 694.14
**retreat**
*n.* asylum 700.4
decrease 39.2
departure 301.1
fallback 295.2
hiding place 615.4
recession 297.1
recoil 284.3
refuge 700.5
sanctum 192.8
seclusion 924.1
summerhouse 191.13
surrender 765.2
*v.* be concave 257.12
be irresolute 627.7
fall back 295.6
incline 219.10
leave 301.8
pull back 284.7
recede 297.2
**retreating**
hollow 257.16
receding 297.5
**retrench**
economize 851.5
reduce 39.7
restrain 760.7
shorten 203.6
subtract 42.9
**retrenchment**
cutback 39.4
economizing 851.2
reduction 42.2
restraint 760.1
shortening 203.3
**retribution**
punishment 1010.1
recompense 841.3
reprisal 955.2
restitution 823.2
**retributive**
paying 841.21
punishing 1010.25
restitutive 823.7
retaliatory 955.8
**retrievable** 694.25
**retrieval** recovery 823.3
reformation 694.2
rescue 702.1
**retrieve** fetch 271.15
recover 823.6
redeem 694.12
rescue 702.3
**retroaction**
reaction 284.1
regression 295.1
**retroactive** back 119.12
reactive 284.9
regressive 295.11
**retrocede** recede 297.2
regress 295.5

reviewer author 602.15
  commentator 606.4
  critic 494.7
revile berate 969.20
  curse 972.7
  ridicule 967.9
  vilify 971.10
revilement
  berating 969.7
  curse 972.2
  defamation 971.2
revise
  *n.* improvement 691.4
  trial print 603.5
  *v.* emend 691.12
  re-examine 485.26.
  remake 169.7
  rewrite 602.19
revision
  improvement 691.4
  re-examination 485.7
  reproduction 169.1
revisional
  emendatory 691.16
  reproductive 169.14
revisionism
  communism 745.5
  nonconformity 83.2
  reform 691.5
revisionist
  *n.* Communist 745.13
  reformer 691.6
  *adj.* Communist
  745.21
  reformational 691.16
revisit 186.9
revival change 139.1
  energizing 161.7
  improvement 691.1
  piety 1028.3
  rebirth 169.1
  recovery 823.3
  reformation 145.2
  refreshment 695.1
  remembrance 119.4
  restoration 694.3
  worship 1032.8
revivalist
  evangelist 1038.7
  worshiper 1032.9
revive aid 785.11
  be changed 139.5
  change 139.6
  cheer up 870.9
  come to life 407.8
  rally 694.20
  recover 823.6
  refresh 695.2
  remake 169.7
  remember 537.10
  repeat 103.7
  restore 694.16
  stimulate 857.12
  touch up 691.11
revived changed 139.9
  refreshed 695.4
  reminiscent 119.8
  renascent 694.24
reviving 687.44
revocation denial 524.2
  recantation 628.3
  repeal 779.1

revoke abolish 693.13
  deny 524.4
  recant 628.9
  repeal 779.2
revolt
  *n.* counteraction
  178.1
  rebellion 767.4
  resistance 792.1
  revolution 147.1
  strike 789.7
  *v.* offend 864.11
  offer resistance 792.3
  rebel 767.7
  revolutionize 147.4
  shudder at 867.5
  strike 789.9
revolted 866.20
revolting
  offensive 864.18
  ugly 899.11
revolution
  change 139.1
  circuit 321.2
  disruption 49.3
  inversion 220.2
  lawlessness 740.2
  radical change 147
  reform 691.5
  revolt 767.4
  rotation 322.1
  round 137.3
revolutionary
  *n.* radical 745.12
  rebel 767.5
  reformer 691.6
  revolutionist 147.3
  violent person 162.9
  *adj.* changed 139.9
  counteractive 178.8
  original 23.5
  radical 745.20
  rebellious 767.11
  reformational 691.16
  revolutionist 147.5
  violent 162.18
revolutionist
  *n.* lawless person
  740.3
  radical 745.12
  rebel 767.5
  revolutionary 147.3
  *adj.* radical 745.20
  revolutionary 147.6
revolutionize
  change 139.8
  originate 23.4
  overthrow 147.4
  revolt 767.7
revolutions per minute
  322.3
revolve
  go around 321.4
  invert 220.5
  recur 137.5
  rotate 322.9
  think over 478.13
revolver 801.5,27
revolve upon 507.6
revs 322.3
revue 611.4

revulsion
  inversion 220.1
  reaction 284.1
  reversion 146.1
  revolution 147.1
revulsive reactive 284.9
  revolutionary 147.5
reward
  *n.* award 916.2
  death 408.1
  incentive 648.7
  recompense 841.3
  reprisal 955.2
  *v.* pay 841.10
  retaliate 955.5
rewarding
  gratifying 863.6
  paying 841.21
  valuable 665.21
reword
  paraphrase 552.13
  repeat 103.8
rework 691.12
rewrite
  *n.* revision 691.4
  *v.* revise 691.12
  write 602.19
rewrite man 605.22
reynard
  cunning person 735.6
  fox 414.25
RF 344.12
RF amplifier 344.10,30
RFD 604.5
Rhadamanthus
  deity of nether world
  1019.5
  god of justice 976.5
  judge 1002.6
rhapsodic(al)
  overjoyed 865.14
  poetic 609.17
rhapsodist
  enthusiast 635.5
  poet 609.13
  singer 464.14
  visionary 535.13
rhapsodize
  be enthusiastic 635.8
  idealize 535.16
rhapsody 462.7
rhetoric diction 588.1
  eloquence 600.1
  grandiloquence 601.1
  public speaking 599.1
  style 588.2
rhetorical
  declamatory 599.12
  grandiloquent 601.8
rhetorical question
  485.10
rhetorician
  bombastic person
  601.5
  orator 599.6
  stylist 588.3
  teacher of rhetoric
  599.8
rheum
  body fluid 388.3
  disease symptom
  686.8

  respiratory disease
  686.14
  secretion 312.2
rheumatic
  *n.* sick person 686.40
  *adj.* diseased 686.57
rheumatic fever 686.12
rheumatism 686.9
rheumy fluid 388.7
  secretory 312.7
Rh factor
  antibody 687.27
  blood 388.4
rhinestone 901.6
rhinoceros 414.4; 415.8
rhinoplasty 689.25
rhizome 411.20
rhomboid
  *n.* obliquity 219.7
  *adj.* quadrangular
  251.9
rhubarb
  argumentation 482.4
  food 308.35,50
  noise 453.3
  quarrel 795.6
rhyme
  *n.* poem 609.6
  poetry 609.1
  repetitiousness 103.4
  similar sound 20.6
  types of 609.10
  *v.* poetize 609.16
  sound similar 20.9
rhyming
  assonant 609.19
  repetitious 103.15
  similar sounding
  20.17
rhythm
  literary elegance
  589.2
  meter 609.9
  music 463.22
  periodicity 137.2
  pulsation 323.3
  speech accent 594.11
rhythm-and-blues 462.9
rhythmic(al)
  metrical 609.18
  music 463.28
  periodic 137.7
  pulsating 323.18
rhythmics 463.1
rialto city district 183.8
  marketplace 832.2
rib
  *n.* meat 308.17
  ridge 256.3
  wife 933.9
  *v.* banter 882.4
ribald
  *n.* vulgar person 898.6
  *adj.* obscene 990.9
  risqué 972.8
  vulgar 898.11
ribaldry cursing 972.3
  obscenity 990.4
  vulgarity 898.2
ribbed 263.4
ribber 882.3
ribbing 882.2

**ribbon**
n. award 916.5
memorial 570.12
ray 335.5
strip 206.4
v. ornament 901.9
**riboflavin** 309.4
**rice paddy** 413.9
**rich** colorful 362.18
expensive 848.11
flavorful 428.9
humorous 880.4
interesting 530.19
melodious 462.49
oily 380.9
ornate 901.12
oversweet 431.5
plentiful 661.7
precious 848.10
productive 165.9
resonant 454.9
wealthy 837.13
**rich, the** 837.5
**riches** 837.1
**rich man**
capitalist 745.15
wealthy man 837.6
**rick**
n. pile 74.10
storage place 660.6
store 660.1
v. pile 74.19
**rickets** 686.10
**rickety** aged 126.18
deformed 249.12
diseased 686.57
loose 51.5
unfastened 49.22
unsteady 160.16
**rickrack** 262.2
**ricksha** 272.3
**ricochet**
n. recoil 284.2
v. recoil 284.6
**rictus** grimace 249.4
shake 324.3
**rid** see get rid of
**riddance**
elimination 77.2
escape 632.1
relinquishment 814.1
**riddle**
n. enigma 549.9
network 221.3
perplexity 514.3
porousness 265.9
refining equipment
681.13
sieve 60.5
the unknown 477.7
v. be incomprehensi-
ble 549.10
mark 568.19
puncture 265.16
separate 77.6
shoot 285.13
sift 60.11
solve 487.2
strike dead 409.18
**riddled** 265.20
**ride**
n. drive 273.7

v. annoy 866.13
banter 882.4
drive 273.32
float 275.54
rest on 216.22
ride at anchor 275.16
ridicule 967.8
sail 275.40
**ride out**
keep safe 698.2
sail 275.40
stand fast 142.11
**rider** addition 41.2
equestrian 274.8
horse 414.16
legislative clause
742.17
**ride roughshod over**
domineer 741.16
run over 313.7
**ride to hounds** 655.9
**ridge**
n. back 241.3
bulge 256.3
head 211.6
hill 207.6
summit 211.2
wrinkle 264.3
v. emboss 256.11
wrinkle 264.6
**ridicule**
n. banter 882.1
contempt 966.1
deprecation 969.2
derision 967
disrespect 965.1
impudence 913.2
v. be insolent 913.6
deprecate 969.12
deride 967.8
disdain 966.3
disrespect 965.3
make fun of 881.13
**ridiculing**
condemnatory 969.23
derisive 967.12
disparaging 971.13
disrespectful 965.5
**ridiculous**
foolish 470.10
humorous 880.4
impossible 510.7
unbelievable 503.10
**riding** district 180.5
driving 273.6
**rife** plentiful 661.7
prevalent 79.12
rumored 558.15
teeming 101.9
**riff** music 462.27
rapids 395.10
**riffle**
n. rapids 395.10
wave 395.14
v. shuffle 63.3
**riffraff** offal 682.9
rabble 919.5
rubbish 669.5
**rifle**
n. gun 801.5,27
infantryman 800.9
soldier 800.6

v. groove 263.3
plunder 824.16
ransack 485.32
**rifleman**
infantryman 800.9
shooter 285.9
soldier 800.6
**rift**
n. blemish 679.1
break 49.4
crack 201.2
falling-out 795.4
fault 678.2
v. open 265.12
adj. cleft 201.7
**rig**
n. carriage 272.5
costume 231.9
equipment 659.4
ropework 277.12
ruler 749.8
suit 231.6
wardrobe 231.2
v. equip 659.8
outfit 231.40
plot 654.10
prearrange 641.3
tamper with 616.17
**rigamarole** 547.2
**rigged** decked 277.17
prearranged 641.5
provided 659.13
tampered with
616.30
**rigged out** 231.44
**rigging** cordage 206.3
equipment 659.4
intrigue 654.6
ropework 277.12
stock manipulation
833.20
supporter 216.2
types of 277.31
**right**
n. accuracy 516.3
authority 739.1
conservatives 745.9
due 960.2
estate 810.4
justice 976.1
justification 1006.6
liberty 762.2
moral rightness 958
privilege 958.3
right side 243.1
stock option 833.21
v. arrange 60.8
make agree 26.7
remedy 694.13
adj. accurate 516.15
apt 26.10
conventional 645.5
decorous 897.10
expedient 670.5
honest 974.13
just 976.8
orthodox 1024.7
proper 958.8
right-hand 243.4
sane 472.4
straight 250.6
adv. absolutely 56.15

directly 290.24
exactly 516.20
excellently 674.21
rightly 958.9
squarely 290.25
to the right 243.7
very 34.18
interj. exactly 516.23
sailing 275.76
yes 521.18
**right-about-face**
n. about-face 295.3
change of mind 628.1
v. turn around 295.10
**right and left**
all round 233.13
extensively 179.10
sideways 242.8
**right-angled**
orthogonal 251.7
perpendicular 213.12
**right away**
at once 113.8
promptly 131.15
**righteous**
honest 974.13
pious 1028.9
right 958.8
virtuous 980.7
**righteous, the** 1028.5
**righteousness**
honesty 974.1
piety 1028.2
propriety 958.2
virtue 980.1
**rightful**
authentic 516.14
due 960.8
just 976.8
legal 998.10
right 958.8
**rightfully** duly 960.11
justly 976.11
rightly 958.9
**right hand**
right-hand man 787.7
right side 243.1
**right-hand** 243.4
**right-handed** 243.5
**right-hand man**
retainer 750.3
right hand 787.7
subordinate 764.5
**rightist**
conservative 745.9
diehard 140.4
**rightly**
accurately 516.19
expediently 670.8
justly 976.11
rightfully 958.9
**right mind** 472.1
**right-minded**
honest 974.13
virtuous 980.7
**rightness** 516.3
**right-of-way** road 657.6
superiority 36.1
**right on!**
congratulations 948.4
exactly 516.23
that's it 26.13

**Right Reverend, the**
  *n.* clergyman 1038.2
  *adj.* title 917.8
**right side** 243
**right side of, the** 927.3
**right sort** 985.1
**right thing, the**
  fairness 976.3
  moral rightness 958.1
  propriety 645.2
**rightward**
  clockwise 290.26
  to the right 243.7
**right wing**
  rightists 745.9
  right side 243.1
**right-wing**
  conservative 745.17
  diehard 140.8
  right 243.4
**right-winger**
  conservative 140.4
  rightist 745.9
  right side 243.1
**rigid** exact 516.16
  firm 159.16
  formal 646.9
  inflexible 142.15
  meticulous 533.12
  permanent 140.7
  stiff 356.11
  strict 757.7
  unyielding 626.9
**rigidity** accuracy 516.3
  firmness 624.2
  hardness 356.2
  immobility 142.3
  immutability 140.1
  strictness 757.2
  unyieldingness 626.2
**rigidly** exactly 516.20
  formally 646.12
  permanently 140.9
  strictly 757.9
  unyieldingly 626.15
**rigmarole** 547.2
**rigor** accuracy 516.3
  acrimony 161.4
  adversity 729.1
  asceticism 991.1
  cold 333.1
  difficulty 731.1
  hardness 356.2
  meticulousness 533.3
  strictness 757.2
  violence 162.1
**rigorous**
  acrimonious 161.13
  adverse 729.13
  cold 333.14
  difficult 731.16
  exact 516.16
  meticulous 533.12
  strict 757.7
  unyielding 626.9
  violent 162.15
**rigorously**
  exactly 516.20
  meticulously 533.16
  strictly 757.9
  unyieldingly 626.15
  violently 162.24

**rile** agitate 324.10
  annoy 866.13
  provoke 952.22
**riled** angry 952.26
  annoyed 866.21
**rim**
  *n.* border 235.4
  circle 253.4
  *v.* border 235.10
**rime** crack 201.2
  frost 333.7
**rimed** 333.16
**rimose** 201.7
**rimple**
  *n.* wrinkle 264.3
  *v.* wrinkle 264.6
**rind** exterior 224.2
  hull 228.16
  peel 229.2
  shallowness 210.1
  skin 229.1
**ring**
  *n.* arena 802.1
  association 788.1
  atomics 326.7
  band 253.3
  boxing 796.9
  circle 253.2
  clerical insignia 569.4
  clique 788.6
  handle 256.3
  insignia 569.1
  jewel 901.6
  light 335.14
  ringing 454.3
  telephone call 560.13
  *v.* din 453.6
  encircle 233.7
  telephone 560.18
  tintinnabulate 454.8
**ring a bell** 284.8
**ringed**
  circumscribed 234.6
  encircled 233.11
**ringer** impostor 619.6
  substitute 149.2
**ring in** arrive 300.6
  begin 68.11
  record time 114.12
  substitute 149.4
**ringing**
  *n.* tintinnabulation 454.3
  *adj.* loud 453.10
  pealing 454.12
**ringleader**
  instigator 648.11
  leader 748.6
  political leader 746.7
**ringlet** circlet 253.5
  curl 254.2
  hair 230.5
**ringmaster**
  circus artist 612.3
  showman 611.28
**rings** 716.7
**ringside** 439.8
**ringworm**
  infectious disease 686.12
  skin disease 686.33
**rink** 878.12

**rinse**
  *n.* cleaning agent 681.17
  washing 681.5
  *v.* soak 392.13
  wash 681.19
**rinsing** refuse 669.4
  washing 681.5
  wetting 392.6
**riot**
  *n.* commotion 62.4
  free-for-all 796.5
  funny story 881.6
  great success 724.3
  plenty 661.2
  revolt 767.4
  violence 162.3
  *v.* be disorderly 62.10
  contend 796.14
  revolt 767.7
  vegetate 411.31
  wreck 162.10
**rioter** combatant 800.1
  rebel 767.5
**rioting** 162.3
**riot of color**
  colorfulness 362.4
  variegation 374.1
**riotous**
  growing rank 411.40
  intemperate 993.8
  plentiful 661.7
  rebellious 767.11
  superabundant 663.19
  unrestrained 762.23
  violent 162.18
**rip**
  *n.* break 49.4
  impairment 692.8
  tide 395.13
  unchaste person 989.10
  *v.* injure 692.15
  open 265.12
  speed 269.8
  tear apart 49.14
  torture 866.18
  wrest 822.22
**RIP** 410.24
**riparian** 385.9
**ripe** complete 56.9
  experienced 733.26
  finished 677.9
  fully developed 722.13
  marriageable 933.21
  mature 126.13
  prepared 720.16
  timely 129.9
**ripen** become 145.17
  evolve 148.5
  fester 311.15
  improve 691.10
  make perfect 677.5
  mature 126.9
  reach perfection 722.8
**ripened**
  experienced 733.26
  finished 677.9
**rip off** 824.14

**rip-off** fraud 618.7
  phony 616.13
  theft 824.10
**riposte**
  *n.* answer 486.1
  justification 1006.2
  witticism 881.7
  *v.* answer 486.4
  defend 1006.10
  react 284.5
**rip out** 305.10
**ripping**
  *n.* separation 49.2
  wresting 305.6
  *adj.* excellent 674.13
**ripple**
  *n.* rapids 395.10
  rough surface 261.2
  splash 452.5
  wave 395.14
  wrinkle 264.3
  *v.* agitate 324.10
  make a liquid sound 452.11
  wrinkle 264.6
**rippled** 264.8
**ripply** 261.6
**rip-roaring** noisy 453.12
  violent 162.17
**riptide** 395.13
**rise**
  *n.* acclivity 219.6
  appearance 446.1
  ascent 315.1
  development 148.1
  height 207.2
  improvement 691.1
  increase 38.1
  promotion 782.1
  reaction 284.1
  rising 213.5
  source 153.5
  wave 395.14
  *v.* appear 446.8
  ascend 315.8
  begin 68.13
  be high 207.15
  billow 395.22
  din 453.6
  elevate 317.5
  get up 713.6
  incline 219.10
  increase 38.6
  levitate 353.9
  make good 724.9
  move 267.5
  result from 154.6
  revive 407.8
  revolt 767.7
  stand up 213.8
**rise above** accept 861.6
  be high 207.16
  exceed 34.5
  triumph over 726.6
**riser** 315.5
**risibility** laughter 876.4
  wit 881.11
**risible** humorous 880.4
  merry 870.15
**rising**
  *n.* acclivity 219.6
  appearance 446.1

rocking
  swinging 323.17
  tranquilizing 163.15
rocking chair 323.9
rocking horse 878.16
Rock of Gibraltar 142.6
rock the boat 83.4
rocky hard 356.10
  rough 261.7
  sick 686.52
  stony·384.11
  unsafe 697.11
  unsteady 160.16
rococo
  n. ornateness 901.2
  adj. abnormal 85.13
  fanciful 535.20
  ornate 901.12
rod atomics 326.13
  emblem of authority
    739.9
  gun 801.5
  instrument of punish-
    ment 1011.2
  royal insignia 569.3
  shaft 217.1
rod and reel 655.3
rodent
  n. animal 414.3; 415.8
  adj. rodential 414.48
rodeo assembly 74.1
  show 611.15
rodlike 356.11
rodomontade
  bluster 911.1
  boasting 910.1
  bombast 601.2
  nonsense 547.2
roe egg 406.15
  female animal 421.9
  food 308.24
  hoofed animal
    414.5,58
roebuck 414.5,58
roentgenograph
  diagnostic picture
    689.10
  photograph 577.6
roentgenotherapy 689.7
Roentgen ray 327.3
Roger 521.18
Roget's 605.7
rogue
  inferior horse 414.14
  mischief-maker 738.3
  rascal 986.3
roguery
  dishonesty 975.2
  mischief 738.2
rogues' gallery 577.3
roguish
  dishonest 975.17
  mischievous 738.6
  prankish 881.17
roil
  n. agitation 324.1
  opaqueness 341.1
  v. agitate 324.10
  annoy 866.13
  be disorderly 62.10
  provoke 952.22
  seethe 322.12

roiled annoyed 866.21
  opaque 341.3
roily disorderly 62.13
  opaque 341.3
roister
  be disorderly 62.10
  bluster 911.3
  make merry 878.26
roisterous
  blustering 911.4
  boisterous 162.19
role capacity 7.5
  function 665.5
  occupation 656.3
  part 611.11
role-player 619.1
roll
  n. air maneuver
    278.14
  boom 456.4
  bun 308.31
  bundle 74.8
  curl 254.2
  cylinder 255.4
  document 570.5
  film 577.10
  flounder 324.8
  gait 273.14
  length 202.3
  list 88.6
  money 835.17
  record 570.1
  rotation 322.1
  staccato sound 455.1
  swing 323.6
  throw of dice 515.10
  wave 395.14
  v. billow 395.22
  bird sound 460.5
  boom 456.9
  flounder 324.15
  fly 278.49
  go easily 732.9
  level 214.6
  make staccato sounds
    455.4
  oscillate 323.10
  progress 294.2
  push 285.10
  reverberate 454.7
  sail 275.55
  smooth 260.6
  travel 273.17
  trundle 322.10
  walk 273.27
  wallow 322.13
roll around 137.5
rollback discount 847.1
  reduction 39.4
  regression 295.1
roll back reduce 39.7
  retrench 851.5
roll call
  legislative procedure
    742.14
  list 88.6
roller cylinder 255.4
  medical dressing
    687.33
  pulverizer 361.7
  rotator 322.4,17
  smoother 260.4,13

wave 395.14
roller coaster 878.15
roller-skate 273.34
roller skates 272.20
rollick
  n. frolic 878.5
  v. bluster 911.3
  play 878.25
  rejoice 876.5
rollicking
  blustering 911.4
  boisterous 162.19
  frisky 870.14
roll in arrive 300.6
  be intemperate 993.4
rolling
  n. air maneuver
    278.13
  progression 294.1
  rotation 322.1
  television reception
    345.5
  adj. hilly 207.23
  resonant 454.9
  rotating 322.14
  swinging 323.17
  thundering 456.12
  wavy 254.10
rolling stock 272.13
rolling stone
  changeableness 141.4
  rotator 322.4
  wanderer 274.2
roll on elapse 105.5
  progress 294.3
  travel 273.17
roll out get up 713.6
  indicate 555.5
roll up bundle 74.20
  roll 322.10
  squeeze 198.8
roly-poly
  n. corpulent person
    195.12
  adj. corpulent 195.18
roman
  fictional form 608.8
  type 603.6,23
Roman candle
  fireworks 328.33
  signal 568.15
Roman Catholic
  n. Catholic
    1020.18,35
  adj. Catholic 1020.28
Roman Catholicism
  1020.7,33
romance
  n. fabrication 616.10
  fiction 608.7
  idealization 535.7
  love affair 931.6
  music 462.6
  thing imagined 535.5
  v. idealize 535.16
  narrate 608.13
romancer
  narrator 608.10
  visionary 535.13
Roman deities 1014.5
Roman-nosed 252.8
Roman numerals 86.2

romantic
  n. visionary 535.13
  adj. fictional 608.17
  loving 931.25
  sentimental 855.22
  visionary 535.24
romanticism
  amorousness 931.3
  idealization 535.7
  sentimentality 855.8
romanticize 535.16
romanticized
  fictional 608.17
  visionary 535.24
Romany 274.4
Rome 1020.7
Romeo 931.12
Romeo and Juliet
  931.17
romp
  n. frolic 878.5
  girl 125.6
  mannish female
    420.9
  v. be cheerful 870.6
  jump 319.6
  play 878.25
  rejoice 876.5
rompers 231.30,56
rondeau music 462.19
  poem 609.6
  round 253.9
rondelle 253.2
rondo music 462.19
  round 253.9
rood cross 221.4
  sacred article 1040.11
roof
  n. abode 191.1
  home 191.4
  house 191.6
  housetop 228.6
  top 211.1
  types of 228.39
  v. cover 228.21
roofed 228.31
roofing
  building material
    378.2
  roof 228.6,43
rooftop roof 228.6
  top 211.1
rook
  n. chessman 878.18
  v. cheat 618.17
rookery
  birthplace 153.8
  filthy place 682.11
rookie beginner 68.2
  newcomer 78.4
  novice 566.9
  recruit 800.17
room
  n. capacity 195.2
  chamber 192
  interval 201.1
  latitude 762.4
  lodgings 191.3
  opportunity 129.2
  spare 179.3
  v. house 188.10
  inhabit 188.7

roomer lodger 190.8
  tenant 809.4
roomette
  railway car 272.14
  train room 192.10
rooming house 191.16
roommate
  companion 928.3
  partner 787.2
room-temperature
  328.24
roomy airy 402.12
  broad 204.6
  comfortable 887.11
  spacious 179.9
roorback report 558.6
  smear campaign
  744.14
roost
  n. birdhouse 191.23
  lodgings 191.3
  v. inhabit 188.7
  settle 184.16
  sit 268.10
rooster
  male animal 420.8
  poultry 414.34
root
  n. morphology 582.3
  plant root 411.20
  source 153.5
  word 582.2
  v. applaud 968.10
  base on 212.6
  become fixed 142.10
  establish 142.9
  search 485.30
  urge on 648.16
  vegetate 411.31
rooted
  confirmed 642.21
  established 142.13
  traditional 123.12
rooter
  commender 968.8
  devotee 635.6
rootlike 411.33
root out destroy 693.14
  eliminate 42.10
  eradicate 77.5
  extract 305.10
  search out 485.33
  uproot 185.6
rope
  n. capital punishment
  1010.7
  cigar 434.4
  cord 206.2,9
  latitude 762.4
  noose 1011.5
  types of 277.31
  v. bind 47.9
  catch 822.17
  lure 650.4
  restrain 760.10
rope off
  circumscribe 234.4
  quarantine 761.13
ropes 172.3
ropewalker 878.21
ropeway 657.9

ropework
  cordage 206.3
  rigging 277.12
ropy threadlike 206.7
  tough 359.4
  viscous 389.12
Rorschach test 690.11
rosary prayer 1032.4
  sacred article 1040.11
rose
  n. conduit 396.9
  emblem 569.1
  heraldic insignia
  569.2
  pinkness 368.2,13
  adj. pink 368.8
rose-colored
  optimistic 888.12
  pink 368.8
rose oil 436.2
rosette 308.40
rose water 436.3
rosé wine 996.16
Rosh Hashanah 1040.16
rosin
  n. resin 381.1
  v. resin 381.2
rosiny 381.3
roster list 88.6
  record 570.1
  schedule 641.2
rostrum beak 256.7
  church part 1042.13
  front 240.3
  platform 216.13
rosy cheerful 870.11
  healthy 685.11
  optimistic 888.12
  pink 368.8
  prosperous 728.13
  red-complexioned
  368.9
rosy-cheeked
  healthy 685.11
  red-complexioned
  368.9
rot
  n. animal disease
  686.38
  blight 676.2
  filth 682.7
  nonsense 547.3
  putrefaction 692.7
  v. decay 692.25
rota list 88.6
  record 570.1
Rota 1001.6
rotary
  n. crossing 221.2
  adj. circuitous 321.7
  flowing 267.8
  periodic 137.7
  rotational 322.15
rotary press 603.9,24
rotate fly 278.47
  invert 220.5
  move 267.5
  recur 137.5
  revolve 322.9
rotation aviation 278.8
  continuity 71.2
  revolution 322

round 137.3
  sequence 65.1
rotator rotor 322.4
  types of 322.17
rote 537.4
rotgut 996.14
Rothschild 837.7
rotogravure 603.1
rotor propeller 285.7
  rotator 322.4,17
rotor plane 280.5,15
rotten bad 675.9
  decayed 692.41
  dishonest 975.16
  filthy 682.23
  horrid 864.19
  malodorous 437.5
  morally corrupt
  981.14
  unsavory 429.7
  weak 160.15
rotten egg 437.3
rotter 986.8
rotting decayed 692.41
  putrefactive 692.40
rotund convex 256.12
  corpulent 195.18
  round 255.8
rotunda 192.1
roué 989.10
rouge
  n. makeup 900.11
  redness 368.1
  v. make red 368.4
rough
  n. combatant 800.1
  diagram 654.3
  evildoer 943.3
  rough surface 261.2
  vulgar person 898.6
  v. coarsen 261.4
  mistreat 667.5
  adj. acrimonious
  161.13
  bitter 429.6
  boisterous 162.19
  coarse-textured 351.6
  difficult 731.16
  gruff 937.7
  irregular 138.3
  jolting 324.20
  nonuniform 18.3
  pungent 433.6
  raucous 458.15
  undeveloped 721.12
  unkind 939.22
  unsmooth 261.6
  violent 162.15
  vulgar 898.11
  adv. unsmoothly
  261.11
rough-and-ready
  uncouth 898.12
  unprepared 721.8
rough-and-tumble
  n. commotion 62.4
  adj. boisterous 162.19
roughcast
  v. do carelessly 534.9
  form 246.7
  plaster 228.25

adj. undeveloped
  721.12
  unsmooth 261.6
rough diamond
  good person 985.1
  raw material 721.5
rough draft
  picture 574.14
  trial 489.2
rough edges 723.1
roughen agitate 324.10
  coarsen 261.4
  give texture 351.4
roughhew
  do carelessly 534.9
  form 246.7
roughhewn
  undeveloped 721.12
  unsmooth 261.6
roughhouse
  n. commotion 62.4
  misbehavior 738.1
  v. be disorderly 62.11
  misbehave 738.4
rough it 188.11
roughly
  approximately 200.23
  generally 79.17
  irregularly 138.4
  unkindly 939.31
  unsmoothly 261.11
  vulgarly 898.16
roughneck
  n. evildoer 943.4
  vulgar person 898.6
  adj. boorish 898.13
roughness
  acrimony 161.4
  aviation 278.41
  coarse texture 351.2
  gruffness 937.3
  irregularity 138.1
  literary inelegance
  590.1
  pungency 433.1
  raucousness 458.2
  undevelopment 721.4
  unkindness 939.9
  unsmoothness 261
  violence 162.1
  vulgarity 898.2
rough out
  do carelessly 534.9
  form 246.7
  outline 654.12
rough sketch 489.2
rouleau bundle 74.8
  coin 835.4
  cylinder 255.4
roulette 515.8
roulette wheel 515.12
round
  n. canon 253.9
  circle 253.2
  circuit 321.2
  continuity 71.2
  degree 29.1
  drinks 996.6
  meat 308.17
  music 462.19
  playing cards 878.17
  region 180.2

revolution 137.3
rotation 322.2
route 657.2
routine 642.6
spell 108.2
sphere of work 656.4
step 315.5
*v.* circle 253.10
curve 252.6
go around 321.4
make round 255.6
rotate 322.9
turn 321.5
turn around 295.9
*adj.* candid 974.17
circuitous 321.7
circular 253.11
full 56.11
polished 589.6
rotund 255.8
unqualified 508.2
*adv.* around 322.16
in the vicinity 233.12
**roundabout**
*n.* amusement device
878.15
detour 321.3
rotator 322.4
*adj.* circuitous 321.7
devious 46.4
diffuse 593.14
peripheral 224.6
surrounding 233.8
winding 254.6
**round about**
*adv.* circuitously 321.9
in every direction
290.27
in the vicinity 233.12
round 322.16
*prep.* through 290.29
throughout 184.27
**round and round**
alternately 137.11
changeably 141.8
round 322.16
to and fro 323.21
windingly 254.11
**rounded** blunt 259.3
bulging 256.14
circular 253.11
phonetic 594.31
rotund 255.8
**roundel** circle 253.2
poem 609.6
**roundelay**
music 462.19
poem 609.6
**rounder**
intemperate person
993.3
unchaste person
989.10
vagabond 274.3
**roundhouse**
boxing 283.5
garage 192.27
repair shop 719.6
**roundly**
approximately 200.23
candidly 974.23
completely 56.14

**roundness** candor 974.4
circularity 253.1
sphericity 255.1
**round off** 722.6
**round out** bulge 256.10
complete 722.6
fill out 56.6
make round 255.6
**round robin** 604.3
**round-shouldered**
249.12
**roundsman**
peace officer 699.15
watchman 699.10
**round table** 755.3
**round-the-clock** 71.8,10
**round trip** circuit 321.2
journey 273.5
**roundup** 74.1
**round up**
assemble 74.18
drive animals 416.8
procure 811.10
**roundworm** 414.75;
415.5
**rouse** awake 713.4
awaken 713.5
elicit 305.14
energize 161.9
excite 857.11
incite 648.19
**rousing**
*n.* awakening 713.2
*adj.* energizing 161.14
provocative 648.27
refreshing 695.3
remarkable 34.11
**roustabout** sailor 276.6
stevedore 276.9
working person 718.2
**rout**
*n.* agitation 324.1
attendance 73.6
defeat 727.2
large number 101.3
rabble 919.4
throng 74.4
*v.* defeat 727.9
drive out 310.14
**route** 657.2
**routine**
*n.* act 611.8
continuity 71.2
habit 642.6
order 59.1
way 657.1
*adj.* frequent 135.4
habitual 642.16
medium 32.3
orderly 59.6
ordinary 79.12
**routinely**
frequently 135.6
generally 79.17
habitually 642.23
uniformly 17.7
**routinize** order 59.4
organize 60.10
**rove**
*n.* wandering 273.3
*v.* travel 273.22
wander 291.4

**rover** pirate 825.7
wanderer 274.2
**roving**
*n.* discursiveness 593.3
wandering 273.3
*adj.* discursive 593.13
inconstant 141.7
traveling 273.36
wandering 291.7
**row**
*n.* file 71.2
road 657.6
*v.* align 71.5
paddle 275.53
push 285.10
sail 275.13
**row**
*n.* agitation 324.1
commotion 62.4
free-for-all 796.5
noise 453.3
quarrel 795.6
violence 162.2
*v.* be noisy 453.8
quarrel 795.12
**rowdy**
*n.* combatant 800.1
evildoer 943.3
mischief-maker 738.3
vulgar person 898.6
*adj.* boisterous 162.19
boorish 898.13
misbehaving 738.5
noisy 453.12
**rowing** 275.1
**royal**
*n.* book size 605.14
potentate 749.7
*adj.* dignified 905.12
excellent 674.12
sovereign 739.17
**royal insignia**
insignia 569.3
royalty 739.8
**royalism**
political conservatism
745.1
principle of govern-
ment 741.8
**royalist** 745.9
**royalty**
aristocracy 918.1
nobility 918.2
payment 841.7
potentate 749.7
receipt 844.1
sovereignty 739.8
**rpm** revolutions 322.3
speed 269.1
**RSVP** 604.16
**rub**
*n.* bone of contention
795.7
contact 200.5
crisis 129.4
difficulty 731.7
disaccord 795.1
friction 350.1
obstacle 730.4
touch 425.1
*v.* abrade 350.7
affect 572.6

dry 393.6
frictionize 350.6
graze 200.10
hurt 424.7
polish 260.7
touch 425.8
treat 689.30
**rubber**
*n.* contraceptive
687.23
elastic substance
358.3
eradicator 693.9
playing cards 878.17
pliancy 357.4
types of 358.9
*adj.* rubbery 358.8
**rubber band** 358.3
**rubber check** 835.10
**rubberize** 358.6
**rubberneck**
*n.* curious person
528.2
sight-seer 442.3
traveler 274.1
*v.* be curious 528.3
sight-see 442.6
travel 273.20
*adj.* spectating 442.7
**rubber stamp**
*n.* ratification 521.4
*v.* ratify 521.12
**rubbery**
changeable 141.6
elastic 358.8
flaccid 357.10
weak 160.12
**rubbing**
*n.* copy 24.4
friction 350.1
image 572.3
reproduction 24.2
touching 425.2
*adj.* frictional 350.9
in contact 200.17
**rubbish**
abandoned thing
633.4
junk 669.5
nonsense 547.2
rabble 919.5
refuse 43.1
trifles 673.4
**rubbishy**
nonsensical 547.7
paltry 673.18
**rubble** rock 384.1
rubbish 669.5
**rubdown** 350.3
**rub down**
frictionize 350.6
tend animals 416.7
**rube**
*n.* bungler 734.9
oaf 471.5
rustic 919.9
unsophisticate 736.
*adj.* countrified 182
**rubella** 686.12
**rubicund** red 368.6
red-complexioned
368.9

direction 290.1
flight 278.9
flow 395.4
freedom 762.1
generality 79.3
impairment 692.8
journey 273.5
lair 191.26
length 202.3
make 168.4
migration 273.4
music 463.18
path 657.3
playing engagement
611.12
prevalence 79.2
race 796.12
route 657.2
routine 642.6
running water 395.1
sequence 71.2
speed 269.3
trend 174.2
voyage 275.6
*v.* be operative 164.7
direct 747.8
elapse 105.5
endure 110.6
extend 179.7
fester 311.15
flee 631.10
float 275.54
flow 395.16
hunt 655.9
incur 175.4
injure 692.15
liquefy 391.5
make haste 709.5
melt 329.21
migrate 273.21
move 267.5
navigate 275.13
nominate 637.19
operate 164.5
pilot 275.14
print 603.14
raise animals 416.6
run for office 744.39
sail 275.22
smuggle 826.8
sprint 269.10
steer 747.9
thrust 283.11
travel 273.17
**runabout** 274.2
**run across** find 488.3
meet 200.11
**run after**
befriend 927.11
curry favor 907.2
fetch 271.15
pursue 655.8
**run against**
*n.* attack 798.1
*v.* counteract 178.6
oppose 790.3
thrust 283.11
**run aground**
come to grief 729.10
shipwreck 275.42
**run along**
go away! 310.29

run off 301.13
**run amok**
be disorderly 62.10
be insane 473.19
go berserk 162.14
**run around** 932.18
**runaround, the**
avoidance 631.1
circumvention 735.5
**run at**
*n.* attack 798.1
*v.* charge 798.18
**runaway**
*n.* fugitive 631.5
*adj.* escaped 632.11
fugitive 631.16
**run away** flee 631.10
run off 301.13
**run back** 295.6
**rundle** rotator 322.4
running water 395.1
step 315.5
**rundown**
airmanship 278.3
summary 607.2
**run down**
become exhausted
717.5
decline 692.20
discover 488.2
disparage 971.8
fail 686.45
quiet 268.8
run over 313.7
sail 275.41
trace 485.34
**run-down**
dilapidated 692.35
fatigued 717.6
unhealthy 686.50
weakened 160.18
worn-out 692.38
**run dry** 666.3
**rune** character 581.2
sorcery 1035.1
**run for** head for 290.10
sail for 275.35
**run foul of**
collide 283.12
contend with 796.16
meet 200.11
sail 275.41
**rung** degree 29.1
step 315.5
**runic** 609.17
**run in** arrest 761.16
capture 822.18
interpose 237.6
sail 275.41
thrust in 304.7
visit 922.17
**run-in**
*n.* quarrel 795.6
*adj.* broken-in 642.17
**run into**
become 145.17
collide 283.12
cost 846.15
find 488.3
meet 200.11
sail 275.41
total 54.8

**runnel**
running water 395.1
watercourse 396.2
**runner** branch 411.18
conduit 396.4
messenger 561.1
operator 164.4
part 55.4
sled part 272.19
smuggler 826.5
speeder 269.5
**runner-up** 726.2
**running**
*n.* candidacy 744.10
direction 747.1
heating 329.3
liquefaction 391.1
motion 267.1
operation 164.1
pus 311.6
*adj.* continuous 71.8
cursive 602.22
fast 269.19
flowing 267.8
operating 164.11
pouring 395.24
present 120.2
prevalent 79.12
*adv.* consecutively
71.11
**running head**
caption 484.2
label 568.13
**running mate** 746.9
**running start**
advantage 36.2
beginning 68.1
earliness 131.1
**runny** exudative 303.20
fluid 388.6
**runoff** election 744.15
game 878.9
outflow 303.4
**run off** flee 631.10
print 603.14
run away 301.13
**run off with**
abduct 824.19
steal 824.13
**run of the mill** 79.3
**run-of-the-mill** 680.8
**run on** chatter 596.5
connect 71.4
continue 143.3
elapse 105.5
endure 110.6
progress 294.3
**run out**
*v.* become exhausted
717.5
be consumed 666.3
be destroyed 693.23
desert 633.6
drive out 310.14
elapse 105.5
emerge 303.13
end 70.6
exit 303.11
expatiate 593.8
find vent 632.10
*adj.* obsolete 123.15
past 119.7

**run out of steam** 725.15
**run over** abound 661.5
browse 564.13
examine 485.23
number 87.10
overflow 395.17
repeat 103.8
think over 478.13
trample 313.7
**run ragged** 717.6
**run rings around** 36.9
**run riot**
be disorderly 62.10
carouse 993.6
overrun 313.5
revolt 767.7
run amok 162.14
superabound 663.8
**runs** 311.2
**run scared** 892.8
**runt** a nobody 673.7
dwarf 196.6
little thing 196.4
**run the gauntlet** 893.11
**run through**
browse 564.13
persist 17.3
pervade 186.7
puncture 265.16
rehearse a play
611.37
spend 843.5
squander 854.3
stab 798.25
**run-through**
drama production
611.14
examination 485.3
summary 607.2
**run true to form** 17.3
**runty** dwarf 196.13
low 208.7
**runway** airstrip 278.23
path 657.3
**run wild**
be disorderly 62.10
let oneself go 762.18
run amok 162.14
**rupture**
*n.* break 49.4
crack 201.2
falling-out 795.4
impairment 692.8
*v.* be damaged 692.26
break 49.12
cleave 201.4
injure 692.15
open 265.15
**ruptured** broken 49.24
damaged 692.29
**rural**
agricultural 413.20
natural 736.6
rustic 182.6
**ruralize** 182.5
**ruse** stratagem 735.3
trick 618.6
**rush**
*n.* attack 798.1
course 267.2
demand 753.1
eruption 162.6

**sameness** identity 14.1
  regularity 17.2
  similarity 20.1
  tedium 884.1
**samiel**
  dust storm 403.13
  hot wind 403.7
**samisen** 465.4
**sample**
  *n.* part 55.1
  specimen 25.3
  taste 427.4
  testing sample 489.4
  *v.* canvass 485.28
  taste 427.7
  try out 489.8
  *adj.* typical 572.11
**Samson**
  brave person 893.8
  strong man 159.6
**samurai** 918.3
**sanatorium** 689.27
**sanctified**
  eminent 914.18
  hallowed 1026.8
  pietistic 1029.5
  redeemed 1028.10
**sanctify** glorify 914.13
  hallow 1026.5
**sanctimonious**
  hypocritic(al) 616.33
  pietistic 1029.5
  prudish 903.19
  zealous 1028.11
**sanctimony**
  affectation 903.6
  hypocrisy 616.6
  pietism 1029
  zeal 1028.3
**sanction**
  *n.* approval 968.1
  authorization 777.3
  consent 775.1
  legalization 998.2
  ratification 521.4
  *v.* approve 968.9
  authorize 777.11
  consent 775.2
  legalize 998.8
  ratify 521.12
**sanctioned**
  authorized 777.17
  legal 998.10
**sanctity** piety 1028.2
  sacredness 1026
**sanctuary**
  hiding place 615.4
  holy of holies 1042.5
  preserve 701.6
  refuge 700.1
**sanctum** retreat 700.5
  room 192.8
  sanctuary 1042.5
**sanctus** 1040.10
**sand**
  , grain 361.6
  stone 384.2
  grind 260.8
  rub 350.8
  sandalwood 436.4
  sandbag
  weight 352.6

*v.* hit 283.17
  weigh down 352.12
**sandbank**
  hidden danger 697.5
  island 386.2
  shoal 210.2
**sandbar**
  hidden danger 697.5
  island 386.2
  sand 384.2
  shoal 210.2
**sandblast** abrade 350.8
  grind 260.8
**sand dune** hill 207.5
  sand 384.2
**sander** 260.13
**sandhog** 257.10
**sanding** 350.2
**sandpaper**
  *n.* rough surface 261.2
  *v.* grind 260.8
  rub 350.8
**sandstone** 384.1,12
**sandstorm** 403.13
**sandwich**
  *n.* food 308.32
  *v.* interpose 237.6
**sandwich board** 559.7
**sandy** dry 393.7
  granular 361.12
  stony 384.11
  yellow 370.4
**sane** intelligent 467.12
  logical 482.20
  mentally sound 472.4
  practical 536.6
  sensible 467.18
**Sanforized** 198.13
**sangfroid**
  composure 858.2
  stability 142.1
**sanguinary**
  bloodstained 679.11
  cruel 939.24
  murderous 409.24
  savage 162.20
  warlike 797.25
**sanguine**
  *n.* personality type
    690.15
  *adj.* blood red 368.7
  cheerful 870.11
  expectant 539.11
  hopeful 888.11
  red-complexioned
    368.9
**sanitary** clean 681.27
  healthful 683.5
**sanitation**
  cleansing 681.3
  hygiene 683.2
**sanitize** 681.24
**sanity**
  intelligence 467.1
  sensibleness 467.6
  saneness 472
**sannyasi** ascetic 991.2
  Hindu priest 1038.14
**sans** 662.17
**sans-culotte**
  radical 745.12
  revolutionist 147.3

**sans serif** 603.6,23
**sans souci** 868.7
**Santa Claus**
  giver 818.11
  Saint Nicholas
    1014.23
**sap**
  *n.* content 194.5
  dupe 620.1
  entrenchment 799.5
  essence 5.2
  fluid 388.2
  fool 471.2
  *v.* attenuate 4.4
  excavate 257.15
  impair 692.18
  undermine 693.20
  weaken 160.10
**sapid** flavored 427.9
  tasty 428.8
**sapient**
  *n.* wise man 468.1
  *adj.* wise 467.17
**sapless** dry 393.7
  insipid 430.2
  weak 160.12
**sapling** sprout 125.9
  tree 411.10
  youngster 125.1
**saponaceous** 380.9
**saporific** 427.9
**sapped** 160.18
**sapper**
  excavator 257.10
  military engineer
    800.13
**sapphic** bisexual 419.32
  poetic 609.17
**sapphire**
  *n.* gem stone 384.13
  *adj.* blue 372.3
**sapphism** 419.12
**sappy** fluid 388.6
  foolish 470.8
  immature 124.10
  sentimental 855.22
**saprolite** 384.1
**saprophyte** 411.4
**saprophytic**
  putrefactive 692.40
  symbiotic 177.4
**sarcasm** humor 881.1
  irony 967.5
**sarcastic** 967.13
**sarcoma** 686.36
**sarcophagus** 410.11
**sardonic** 967.13
**sarge** 749.19
**sartorial** 231.47
**Sartrian** 500.10
**sash** 245.4
**sashay** depart 301.6
  travel 273.17
  walk 273.27
**sass**
  *n.* insolence 913.4
  *v.* be insolent 913.7
**sassy** 913.9
**Satan**
  deity of nether world
    1019.5
  liar 619.9

  the Devil 1016.3
**satanic** cruel 939.24
  diabolic 1016.18
  terrible 675.10
  wicked 981.13
**Satanism**
  diabolism 1016.15
  sorcery 1035.2
**Satanist** 1016.16
**sate** gratify 865.6
  satiate 664.4
**sated** languid 708.19
  satiated 664.6
**satellite**
  attendance 73.6
  country 181.1
  follower 293.2
  hanger-on 907.5
  list 282.14
  man 787.8
  moon 375.11
  spacecraft 282.6,14
**satiate** be tedious 884.5
  fill 56.7
  gratify 865.6
  overload 663.15
  sate 664.4
**satiated** bored 884.10
  full 56.11
  overfull 663.20
  sated 664.6
**satin**
  *n.* fine texture 351.3
  smooth surface 260.3
  softness 357.4
  *adj.* smooth 351.8
**satiny** sleek 260.10
  smooth 351.8
  soft 357.15
**satire**
  disparagement 971.5
  humor 881.1
  poem 609.6
  poetry 609.4
  ridicule 967.6
  sarcasm 967.5
**satiric(al)**
  burlesque 967.14
  sarcastic 967.13
**satirist** humorist 881.12
  lampooner 971.7
  poet 609.13
**satirize**
  lampoon 971.12
  ridicule 967.11
**satisfaction**
  atonement 1012.1
  compensation 33.1
  contentment 868.1
  duel 796.7
  observance 768.1
  payment 841.1
  pleasure 865.1
  recompense 841.3
  reparation 694.6
  restitution 823.2
  satiety 664.1
  sufficiency 661.1
**satisfactional** 1012.7
**satisfactory**
  convincing 501.26
  satisfying 868.11

sufficient 661.6
tolerable 674.19
**satisfied**
believing 501.21
contented 868.7
pleased 865.12
satiated 664.6
**satisfy** atone 1012.4
content 868.4
convince 501.18
feed 307.16
gratify 865.6
indulge 759.6
make sure 513.11
observe 768.2
pay in full 841.13
reward 841.10
satiate 664.4
suffice 661.4
**satisfying**
convincing 501.26
paying 841.21
pleasant 863.6
satiating 664.7
satisfactory 868.11
**satori** intuition 481.1
quiescence 268.1
**saturate** fill 56.7
infuse 44.12
overload 663.15
satiate 664.4
soak 392.13
**saturated** full 56.11
overfull 663.20
permeated 186.15
satiated 664.6
soaked 392.17
**saturation**
color intensity 362.4
color purity 362.6
fullness 56.2
infusion 44.2
overfullness 663.3
satiety 664.1
soaking 392.7
**saturation point**
fullness 56.2
radiation 327.1
satiety 664.1
**Saturday night special**
801.5
**saturnalia** 993.2
**saturnalian** 993.9
**saturnine** 872.24
**satyr**
forest god 1014.21
sex deviant 419.17
unchaste person
989.11
**sauce**
*n.* admixture 44.7
cold 308.56
hodgepodge 44.6
hot 308.57
insolence 913.4
liquor 996.13
pulp 390.2
*v.* be insolent 913.7
flavor 428.7
**saucer** 253.2
**saucer-shaped**
concave 257.16

curved 252.13
**saucy** defiant 793.7
impudent 913.9
**sault** rapids 395.10
waterfall 395.11
**sauna** bath 681.8
bathing place 681.10
**saunter**
*n.* gait 273.14
slowness 270.2
walk 273.12
*v.* go slow 270.6
walk 273.27
wander 273.22
**sausage** 308.21
**sauté** 330.4
**sautéed** 330.6
**savage**
*n.* barbarian 898.7
brute 943.5
violent person 162.9
*v.* injure 692.15
mistreat 667.5
terrorize 162.10
torture 866.18
work evil 675.6
*adj.* cruel 939.24
fatal 409.23
fierce 162.20
infuriated 952.29
uncouth 898.12
warlike 797.25
**savagery** cruelty 939.11
uncouthness 898.3
unenlightenment
477.4
violence 162.1
**savanna** grassland 411.8
plain 387.1
**savant** expert 733.11
scholar 476.3
scientist 475.11
specialist 81.3
wise man 468.1
**savate** 796.9
**save**
*v.* aid 785.11
economize 851.4
keep safe 698.3
not use 668.5
preserve 701.7
prevent 730.14
rescue 702.3
reserve 660.12
retain 813.5
sanctify 1026.6
store up 660.11
*prep.* excluding 77.9
less 42.14
*conj.* unless 507.16
**saved** pious 1028.10
preserved 701.11
reserved 660.15
saintly 1015.6
sanctified 1026.9
unused 668.12
**save face** 905.7
**save one's breath**
be silent 451.5
be uncommunicative
613.6
**saver** preserver 701.4

thrifty person 851.3
**saving**
*n.* economizing 851.2
preservation 701.1
rescue 702.1
*adj.* economical 851.6
preservative 701.10
*prep.* excluding 77.9
in deference to
964.13
**saving clause**
condition 507.2
legislative clause
742.17
loophole 632.4
**savings** funds 835.14
reserve 660.3
**savings and loan
association**
bank 836.13
lending institution
820.4
**savior** preserver 701.4
redeemer 942.2
rescuer 702.2
**Savior** 1013.12
**Savitar**
Hindu deity 1014.8
sun god 375.14
**savoir-faire**
mannerliness 936.3
skill 733.1
**savor**
*n.* characteristic 80.4
fervor 855.10
odor 435.1
relish 428.2
taste 427.1
*v.* eat 307.18
enjoy 865.10
flavor 428.7
relish 428.5
taste 427.7
**savorless** 430.2
**savory**
*n.* delicacy 308.8
*adj.* edible 307.31
flavored 427.9
fragrant 436.9
pleasant 863.9
tasty 428.8
**savvy**
*n.* intelligence 467.2
skill 733.1
understanding 475.3
*v.* know 475.12
understand 548.7
**saw**
*n.* maxim 517.1
notching 262.2
types of 348.14
*v.* fiddle 462.42
sever 49.11
**sawbones** doctor 688.6
surgeon 688.9
**sawbuck** trestle 216.16
US money 835.7
**sawdust** powder 361.5
refuse 43.1
**sawhorse** 216.16
**sawmill** 719.3

**saw-toothed**
angular 251.6
notched 262.5
rough 261.7
**saxhorn** 465.8
**saxophone** 465.9
**say**
*n.* affirmation 523.1
authority 739.1
free choice 762.6
influence 172.1
remark 594.4
speech 599.2
supremacy 36.3
turn 108.2
vote 637.6
*v.* affirm 523.4
answer 486.4
speak up 594.22
suppose 499.10
utter 594.23
*adv.* approximately
200.23
**saying**
affirmation 523.1
maxim 517.1
remark 594.4
**sayonara!** 301.23
**say-so** affirmation 523.1
authority 739.1
command 752.1
free choice 762.6
**say the word**
command 752.9
permit 777.9
**sc.**
by interpretation
552.18
namely 80.18
**scab**
*n.* blemish 679.1
crust 228.14
sore 686.35
strikebreaker 789.6
*v.* blemish 679.4
break a strike 789.10
crust 228.27
heal 694.21
**scabby** base 915.12
blemished 679.8
filthy 682.23
flaky 227.7
**scabies**
animal disease 686.3
skin disease 686.33
**scabrous** flaky 227.7
indecent 990.7
**scads** much 34.4
plenty 661.2
**scaffold**
instrument of execu-
tion 1011.5
support 216.12
**scag** 687.12
**scalawag**
inferior horse 414.14
rascal 986.3
**scald**
*n.* burn 329.6
impairment 692.8
*v.* be hot 328.22
injure 692.15

**scalded** 692.29
**scalding** 328.25
**scale**
  *n.* break 49.4
    coating 228.12
    continuity 71.2
    crust 228.14
    degree 29.1
    flake 227.3
    harmonics 463.6
    ladder 315.4
    map 654.4
    measure 490.2,20
    range 179.2
    size 195.1
    step 315.5
    types of 352.22
  *v.* ascend 315.11
    break 49.12
    flake 232.11
    layer 227.5
    raid 798.20
**scale down**
  make small 196.9
  reduce 39.7
**scaling** disruption 49.3
  raid 798.4
**scallop**
  *n.* food 308.25
    notching 262.2
    shell 228.42
  *v.* cook 330.4
    notch 262.4
    twist 254.4
**scalloped** cooked 330.6
  notched 262.5
**scalp** peel 232.8
  speculate in stocks
    833.23
**scalper** salesman 830.4
  stock speculator
    833.11
**scaly** flaky 227.7
  powdery 361.11
**scam**
  *n.* swindle 618.8
  *v.* swindle 618.17
**scamp**
  *n.* mischief-maker
    738.3
    rascal 986.3
  *v.* be parsimonious
    852.5
    neglect 534.8
**scamper**
  *n.* haste 709.1
    speed 269.3
  *v.* hurry away 301.11
    make haste 709.5
    rush 269.9
**scamping**
  negligent 534.10
  parsimonious 852.7
**scampish**
  dishonest 975.17
  mischievous 738.6
**scan**
  examination 485.3
  view 444.3
  analyze 48.7
  browse 564.13
  examine 485.23

**poetize** 609.16
  skim over 485.25
  use radar 346.17
**scandal** disgrace 915.5
  gossip 558.8
  iniquity 981.3
  slander 971.3
  wrong 959.2
**scandalous** bad 675.9
  disgraceful 915.11
  disparaging 971.13
  evil 981.16
  wrong 959.3
**scanning**
  *n.* data processing
    349.20
    metrics 609.8
    radar operation 346.8
    televising 345.3
  *adj.* metrical 609.18
**scansion** analysis 48.2
  metrics 609.8
**scant**
  *v.* be parsimonious
    852.5
    limit 234.5
  *adj.* incomplete 57.4
    meager 662.10
    narrow 205.14
    sparse 102.5
    wanting 662.13
**scantiness**
  fewness 102.1
  insignificance 35.1
  littleness 196.1
  meagerness 662.2
  scarcity 662.3
**scantling** 195.1
**scanty** incomplete 57.4
  meager 662.10
  narrow 205.14
  scarce 662.11
  sparse 102.5
**scape** picture 574.13
  shaft 217.1
  view 446.6
**scapegoat**
  sacrifice 1032.7
  substitute 149.3
**scapegrace**
  bad person 986.5
  mischief-maker 738.3
**scar**
  *n.* blemish 679.1
    mark 568.5
    precipice 213.3
  *v.* blemish 679.4
    mark 568.19
**scarab** 1036.5
**scarce**
  insufficient 662.11
  rare 136.2
  sparse 102.5
**scarcely** hardly 35.9
  infrequently 136.4
  insufficiently 662.16
  sparsely 102.8
  to a degree 29.7
**scarcity** fewness 102.1
  rarity 136.1
  sparsity 662.3

**scare**
  *n.* fear 891.1
  *v.* frighten 891.23
    scare away 891.29
**scarecrow** figure 572.4
  frightener 891.9
  ugly thing 899.4
**scared** 891.30
**scared stiff** 891.34
**scaredy-cat** 892.5
**scarehead** 484.2
**scare off** 652.3
**scarer** 891.9
**scare up** 811.10
**scarf**
  *n.* joint 47.4
    neckwear 231.64
  *v.* fasten 47.8
**scarify** blemish 679.4
  criticize severely
    969.21
  mark 568.19
  notch 262.4
  torture 866.18
**scariness** 891.2
**scarlet**
  prostitute 989.28
  red 368.6
**scarlet fever** 686.12
**scarlet woman** 989.16
**scarp**
  fortification 799.4
  incline 219.4
  precipice 213.3
**scarred** 679.8
**scary** fearful 891.31
  frightening 891.36
**scat**
  *n.* nonsense 547.3
    vocal music 462.12
  *interj.* go away!
    310.29
**scathe**
  *n.* impairment 692.1
  *v.* criticize severely
    969.21
    work evil 675.6
**scathing**
  acrimonious 161.13
  caustic 939.21
**scatological**
  fecal 311.20
  jargonish 580.19
  obscene 972.8
**scatology** cursing 972.3
  jargon 580.9
**scat singing** 462.12
**scatter**
  *n.* deflection 291.2
  *v.* defeat 727.9
    deflect 291.5
    disarrange 63.2
    disband 75.8
    disperse 75.4
    loosen 51.3
    part company 49.19
    radiate 299.6
    shatter 49.13
    squander 854.3
**scatterbrain** 471.7
**scatterbrained**
  giddy 532.16

**inconstant** 141.7
  stupid 469.19
**scattered**
  confused 62.16
  defeated 727.14
  deviant 291.8
  dispersed 75.9
  few 102.5
  separated 49.21
**scattering**
  *n.* dispersion 75.1
    disruption 49.3
    few 102.2
    noncohesion 51.1
    radiating 299.2
  *adj.* dispersive 75.11
**scavenge** 681.18
**scavenger** animal 414.3
  sweeper 681.16
**scenario**
  playbook 611.26
  project 654.2
**scenario writer**
  author 602.15
  dramatist 611.27
**scend**
  *n.* wave 395.14
  *v.* billow 395.22
    sail 275.55
**scene** act 611.8
  arena 802.1
  outburst 952.9
  picture 574.13
  setting 233.2
  stage scenery 611.25
  view 446.6
**scenery** arena 802.1
  stage scenery 611.25
  view 446.6
**scenic** 611.38
**scent**
  *n.* clue 568.9
    fragrance 436.1
    hint 557.4
    odor 435.1
    perfume 436.2
    sense of smell 435.4
    track 568.8
  *v.* detect 488.6
    odorize 435.7
    perfume 436.8
    smell 435.8
**scented** 436.9
**scepter**
  emblem of authority
    739.9
  royal insignia 569.3
**schedule**
  *n.* list 88.1
    plan 654.1
    program 641.2
  *v.* allot 816.9
    budget 843.5
    list 88.8
    plan 654.9
    slate 641.4
**scheduled** listed 88.9
  planned 654.13
  slated 641.4
**schema** outline 48.4
  plan 654.1
  representation 572.1

**schematic**
analytical 48.9
diagrammatic 654.15
**scheme**
*n.* influence 172.3
intrigue 654.6
outline 48.4
plan 654.1
story element 608.9
stratagem 735.3
trick 618.6
*v.* maneuver 735.10
plot 654.10
prearrange 641.3
premeditate 653.8
**schemer**
cunning person 735.7
plotter 654.8
traitor 619.10
**scheming**
*n.* intrigue 654.6
prearrangement
641.1
*adj.* calculating 654.14
cunning 735.12
deceitful 618.20
dishonest 975.18
**scherzo** 462.25
**schism** desertion 633.2
falling-out 795.4
religion 1020.3
**schismatic**
apostate 628.5
dissenter 522.3
religionist 1020.17
**schismatic(al)**
dissenting 522.6
religions 1020.25
repudative 628.12
**schist** 384.1
**schizoid**
*n.* pathological type
690.16
personality type
690.15
psychotic 473.16
*adj.* psychotic 473.27
**schizophrenia**
dissociation 690.27
mental disorder
690.17
psychosis 473.4
**schizophrenic**
*n.* psychotic 473.16
*adj.* psychotic 473.27
**schlemiel** fool 471.2
unlucky person 729.7
**schlep**
*n.* slob 62.7
wearisome trip
273.12
*v.* plod 270.7
**schlock**
*n.* inferior article
680.6
*adj.* bad 675.9
**schlump** 62.7
**schmaltzy** 855.22
**schmuck** 471.1
**schnapps** 996.12,40
**schnorrer** 774.8
**schnozzle** 256.7

**scholar**
learned man 476.3
scientist 475.11
specialist 81.3
student 566.1
wise man 468.1
**scholarly**
educational 562.20
learned 475.21
scientific 475.28
studious 564.17
**scholarship**
award 916.7
erudition 475.5
studiousness 564.4
subsidy 818.8
**scholastic**
*n.* scholar 476.3
theologian 1023.3
*adj.* bookish 475.22
educational 562.20
institutional 567.18
learned 475.21
philosophy 500.9
studious 564.17
**scholiast**
commentator 606.4
critic 494.7
interpreter 552.7
**scholium**
comment 552.5
record 570.4
**school**
*n.* art 574.23
artistic style 574.9
educational institu-
tion 567
fish 74.5
order 788.5
religion 1020.3
system of belief
501.3
*v.* teach 562.11
*adj.* scholastic 567.18
**school board** 567.17
**schoolbook** 605.8
**schoolboy** boy 125.5
pupil 566.4
**schooled** 475.18
**schoolhouse** 567.15
**schooling** 562.1
**schoolman**
academician 565.3
scholar 476.3
theologian 1023.3
**schoolmarm** 565.2
**schoolmaster** 565.1
**schoolmate**
companion 928.3
partner 787.2
student 566.4
**school of thought** 500.1
**schoolroom** 567.16
**schoolteacher** 565.1
**sciatic** 241.10
**sciatica** 686.23
**science** art 733.7
electrical 342.34
knowledge 475.10
**science fiction** 608.7
**scientific** exact 516.16
practical 536.6

technical 475.28
**scientism** 536.2
**scientist** 475.11
**sci-fi** 608.7
**scilicet**
by interpretation
552.18
namely 80.18
**scintilla** light 335.7
small amount 35.4
spark 328.15
**scintillate**
be intelligent 467.11
glitter 335.24
joke 881.13
**scintillating**
burning 328.27
glittering 335.35
intelligent 467.14
witty 881.15
**scintillation** light 335.7
spark 328.15
television reception
345.5
witticism 881.7
**sciolism** 477.6
**scion** branch 55.4
descendant 171.3
offshoot 411.18
sprout 125.9
**scissile** brittle 360.4
fissionable 326.20
separable 49.26
**scission** 49.2
**scissor** 49.11
**scissure** 201.2
**sclerosis** atrophy 686.8
cardiovascular disease
686.17
hardening 356.5
**scoff**
*n.* gibe 967.2
indignity 965.2
*v.* be irreligious
1031.14
ridicule 967.9
**scoff at** disobey 767.6
flout 793.4
make fun of 881.13
offend 965.4
**scoffing**
*n.* agnosticism 1031.6
ridicule 967.1
*adj.* condemnatory
969.23
ridiculing 967.12
**scofflaw** 986.10
**scold**
*n.* faultfinder 969.9
ill-humored woman
951.12
*v.* bird sound 460.5
reprove 969.17
**scolding**
complaint 875.4
reproof 969.5
**sconce** brain 466.6
fortification 799.4
head 211.6
light holder 336.11
penalty 1009.3
**scone** 308.31

**scoop**
*n.* news 558.3
piece 55.3
pit 257.2
*v.* excavate 257.15
transfer 271.16
**scoop, the**
information 557.1
the facts 1.4
**scoot** 269.9
**scope** degree 29.1
latitude 762.4
legality 998.1
meaning 545.1
opportunity 129.2
optical instrument
443.3
range 179.2
size 195.1
types of 443.12
view 444.3
vision 439.1
**scorch**
*n.* burn 329.6
impairment 692.8
*v.* be hot 328.22
blemish 679.6
burn 329.24
criticize severely
969.21
dry 393.6
injure 692.15
speed 269.8
**scorched**
burned 329.30
damaged 692.29
dried 393.9
**scorcher** hot day 328.8
speeder 269.5
**scorching**
*n.* burning 329.5
*adj.* caustic 939.21
fiery 162.21
hot 328.25
**score**
*n.* account 845.2
bill 845.3
debt 840.1
engraving 578.2
groove 263.1
line 568.6
mark 568.5
motive 648.1
music piece 462.5
notation 572.1
notch 262.1
playbook 611.26
price 846.1
success 724.4
sum 86.5
the facts 1.4
twenty 99.7
written music 462.2
*v.* acquire 811.8
calculate 87.11
compose 462.47
engrave 578.10
groove 263.3
list 88.8
mark 568.19
notch 262.4
score a success 724

**scoreboard** 570.10
**scored** grooved 263.4
  notched 262.5
**scorer** composer 464.20
  recorder 571.1
**scores** 101.3
**scoria** ashes 329.16
  residue 43.2
  rock 384.1
**scorn**
  *n.* contempt 966.1
  *v.* be fastidious 896.8
  disdain 966.3
  flout 793.4
**scorned** 638.3
**scornful**
  contemptuous 966.8
  rejecting 638.4
**scorpion** 414.36
**scot** fee 846.7
  payment 841.5
**scotch**
  *n.* curb 730.7
  mark 568.5
  notch 262.1
  *v.* hinder 730.10
  injure 692.15
  mark 568.19
  notch 262.4
  thwart 730.15
**Scotch** 851.6
**scot-free**
  escaped 632.11
  free 762.20
**Scotland Yard** 699.17
**scoundrel**
  dishonest person
    975.10
  rascal 986.3
**scour** abrade 350.7
  polish 260.7
  ransack 485.32
  rush 269.9
  scour out 310.21
  traverse 273.19
  wash 681.19
**scourge**
  *n.* bane 676.1
  epidemic 686.4
  punishment 1010.1
  whip 1011.1
  *v.* punish 1010.14
**scouring** abrasion 350.2
  refuse 669.4
  remainder 43.1
  washing 681.5
**scout**
  *n.* precursor 66.1
  secret agent 781.9
  vanguard 240.2
  watchman 699.10
  *v.* flout 793.4
  look 439.14
  reconnoiter 485.27
  reject 638.2
  ridicule 967.9
  search out 485.33
  spurn 966.4
  traverse 273.19
**scouting**
  reconnaissance 485.8
  rejection 638.1

**scowl**
  *n.* disapproval 969.8
  frown 951.9
  resentment 952.2
  *v.* be ill-humored
    951.15
  show resentment
    952.14
**scrabble**
  *n.* creeping 273.9
  scribbling 602.7
  *v.* creep 273.25
  excavate 257.15
  grope 485.31
  scribble 602.20
**scrag**
  *n.* scrawny horse
    414.15
  *v.* end 70.7
  hang 1010.20
**scraggly** rough 261.7
  slovenly 62.15
**scraggy** dwarf 196.13
  lean 205.17
  rough 261.7
**scram**
  *v.* depart 301.9
  flee 631.11
  *interj.* go away!
    310.30
**scramble**
  *n.* bustle 707.4
  commotion 62.4
  creeping 273.9
  fight 796.4
  flight 278.11
  haste 709.1
  hodgepodge 44.6
  jumble 62.3
  unintelligibility 549.7
  *v.* confuse 63.3
  contend 796.14
  creep 273.25
  hustle 707.13
  make haste 709.5
  make unintelligible
    549.12
  mix 44.11
  rush 269.9
**scrambled**
  hard to understand
    549.14
  meaningless 547.6
  mixed 44.15
**scramble for** 822.16
**scramble up** 315.11
**scrap**
  *n.* minute thing 196.7
  piece 55.3
  quarrel 795.6
  refuse 669.4
  remainder 43.1
  rubbish 669.5
  small amount 35.3
  *v.* discard 668.8
  end 70.5
  quarrel 795.12
**scrapbook**
  compilation 605.4
  record book 570.11
**scrape**
  *n.* abrasion 350.2

  harsh sound 458.3
  impairment 692.8
  obeisance 964.2
  perplexity 514.3
  predicament 731.4
  *v.* abrade 350.7
  bow 964.6
  economize 851.4
  engrave 578.10
  excavate 257.15
  fiddle 462.42
  graze 200.10
  injure 692.15
  sound harshly 458.10
  touch lightly 425.7
**scrape along**
  manage 724.11
  survive 659.12
**scrape through** 632.8
**scrape together**
  assemble 74.18
  procure 811.10
**scrap iron** 669.4
**scrapper**
  combatant 800.1
  oppositionist 791.3
**scrapple** 308.12
**scrappy**
  contentious 951.26
  discontinuous 72.4
  incomplete 57.4
  irregular 138.3
  warlike 797.25
**scratch**
  *n.* abrasion 350.2
  blemish 679.1
  engraving 578.2
  fodder 308.4
  groove 263.1
  harsh sound 458.3
  impairment 692.8
  mark 568.5
  misrepresentation
    573.2
  scribbling 602.7
  shallowness 210.1
  *v.* end 70.5
  engrave 578.10
  excavate 257.15
  groove 263.3
  injure 692.15
  mark 568.19
  misrepresent 573.4
  obliterate 693.16
  picture 574.20
  scribble 602.20
  sound harshly 458.10
  tingle 426.5
  work hard 716.13
**scratched**
  grooved 263.4
  scribbled 602.23
**scratch pad** 570.11
**scratch test** 689.17
**scratch the surface**
  half-know 477.11
  touch upon 210.4
**scratchy**
  irritating 424.13
  scribbled 602.23
  sounding harsh
    458.16

**scrawl**
  *n.* illegibility 549.4
  scribbling 602.7
  *v.* scribble 602.20
**scrawly** 602.23
**scrawny** lean 205.17
  meager 662.10
**screak**
  *n.* shrill sound 458.4
  *v.* animal sound 460.2
  sound shrill 458.8
**scream**
  *n.* cry 459.1
  funny story 881.6
  lament 875.3
  shrill sound 458.4
  *v.* animal sound 460.2
  cry 459.6
  sound shrill 458.8
  utter 594.26
  wail 875.11
  wind sound 403.23
**screamer** an error 518.6
  caption 484.2
**screaming** garish 362.19
  gaudy 904.20
  humorous 880.4
  vociferous 459.10
**screaming meemies, the**
  473.10
**scree** breccia 384.1
  deposit 271.8
**screech**
  *n.* cry 459.1
  shrill sound 458.4
  *v.* animal sound 460.2
  cry 459.6
  sound shrill 458.8
  utter 594.26
  wind sound 403.23
**screen**
  *n.* arranger 60.5
  concealment 615.2
  cover 228.2,38
  network 221.3
  porousness 265.9
  pretext 649.1
  refining equipment
    681.13
  safeguard 699.3
  scenery 611.25
  shade 338.1,8
  television receiver
    345.11,17
  *v.* arrange 60.11
  conceal 615.6
  cover 228.19
  defend 799.8
  discriminate 492.5
  project 577.16
  protect 699.18
  refine 681.22
  separate 77.6
  shade 338.5
**screen, the** 611.17
**screened**
  covered 228.31
  protected 699.21
  shaded 338.7
**screenwriter** 611.27
**screw**
  *n.* curl 254.2

distortion 249.1
instrument of torture 1011.4
jailer 761.10
propeller 285.7
*v.* be parsimonious 852.5
cheat 618.17
copulate 419.23
demand 753.4
distort 249.5
fasten 47.8
overcharge 848.7
rotate 322.9
twist 254.4
wrest from 822.22
**screw around** 673.13
**screwball**
*n.* eccentric 474.3
lunatic 473.15
odd person 85.4
throw 285.4
*adj.* eccentric 474.4
insane 473.26
**screw up**
blunder 518.15
bungle 734.12
complicate 46.3
confuse 63.3
fasten 47.7
spoil 692.13
stiffen 356.9
**screw-up** an error 518.6
confusion 62.2
**screwy** eccentric 474.4
foolish 470.8
insane 473.26
**scribble**
*n.* illegibility 549.4
misrepresentation 573.2
scribbling 602.7
*v.* misrepresent 573.4
write 602.20
**scribbler**
hack writer 602.16
penman 602.13
**scribbly** 602.23
**scribe**
*n.* author 602.15
clergyman 1038.12
recorder 571.1
writer 602.13
*v.* write 602.19
**scrim** 611.25
**scrimmage** fight 796.4
free-for-all 796.5
**scrimp**
be parsimonious 852.5
economize 851.4
**scrimping**
*n.* economizing 851.2
parsimony 852.1
*adj.* economical 851.6
meager 102.5
parsimonious 852.7
**scrimshaw** 575.1
**scrip** currency 835.1
document 570.5
paper money 835.5
token 835.12

written matter 602.10
**script** document 570.5
handwriting 602.3
playbook 611.26
representation 572.1
type 603.6,23
writing system 581.3
written matter 602.10
**scriptural**
Biblical 1021.10
orthodox 1024.7
written 602.22
**scripture** 1021
**Scripture** 1021.2
**scriptwriter**
author 602.15
dramatist 611.27
**scrivener**
recorder 571.1
writer 602.13
**scroll**
*n.* curl 254.2
document 570.5
list 88.6
manuscript 602.11
rare book 605.3
record 570.1
viol 465.6
written matter 602.10,29
*v.* write 602.19
**scrolled** 254.8
**scrooge** 852.4
**scrotal** 419.27
**scrotum** 419.10
**scrounge** beg 774.15
steal 824.13
**scrounger** beggar 774.8
thief 825.1
**scrounging**
*n.* beggary 774.6
theft 824.1
*adj.* begging 774.16
indolent 708.18
**scrub**
*n.* abrasion 350.2
a nobody 673.7
brushwood 411.14
shrubbery 411.9
washing 681.5
woodland 411.11
*v.* abrade 350.7
stop 144.6
wash 681.19
**scrubby** base 915.12
bushy 411.36
dwarf 196.13
paltry 673.18
vulgar 898.15
wooded 411.37
**scrubland** 411.11
**scruffy** base 915.12
dirty 682.22
paltry 673.18
shabby 692.34
**scrumptious**
excellent 674.13
tasty 428.8
**scrunch**
*n.* harsh sound 458.3
*v.* pulverize 361.9
sound harshly 458.10

**scruple**
*n.* compunction 873.2
conscientiousness 974.2
demur 623.2
doubt 503.2
objection 522.2
small amount 35.2
*v.* be doubtful 503.6
be irresolute 627.7
demur 623.4
object 522.5
**scrupulous**
careful 533.12
conscientious 974.15
doubtful 503.9
dutiful 962.13
fastidious 896.9
observant 768.4
punctilious 646.10
stickling 623.7
**scrutable** 548.9
**scrutinize**
examine 485.23
make a close study of 485.24
pay attention 530.8
survey 439.15
**scrutiny**
close attention 530.4
examination 485.3
overview 439.6
**scuba**
breathing apparatus 403.18
diving equipment 320.5
**scuba diver** 320.4
**scud**
*n.* cloud 404.1
foam 405.2
gust 403.6
rainstorm 394.2
speed 269.3
*v.* float 275.54
rush 269.9
**scuff**
*n.* abrasion 350.2
impairment 692.8
*v.* abrade 350.7
injure 692.15
walk 273.27
**scuffle**
*n.* fight 796.4
struggle 716.3
*v.* contend 796.14
struggle 716.11
walk 273.27
**scull**
*n.* oar 277.15
*v.* row 275.53
sail 275.13
**sculler** 276.5
**scullery** 330.3
**scullery maid**
maid 750.8
washer 681.15
**scullion** servant 750.2
washer 681.15
**sculpt** form 246.7
sculpture 575.5
**sculptor** artist 579.6

names of 579.14
sculpture 575.1
**sculptural** 575.6
**sculpture**
*n.* arts 574.1
figure 572.4
forming 246.5
modeling 575
sculptured piece 575.2
*v.* engrave 578.10
form 246.7
model 575.5
**sculptured**
engraved 578.12
sculpted 575.7
**scum**
*n.* coating 228.12
foam 405.2
layer 227.2
offal 682.9
rabble 919.5
refuse 669.4
residue 43.2
slime 682.8
sperm 406.11
*v.* cover 228.19
foam 405.5
**scummy** base 915.12
filmy 227.6
filthy 682.23
paltry 673.18
**scum of the earth**
bad people 986.12
offal 682.9
rabble 919.5
**scupper** 396.5
**scurf** filth 682.7
flake 227.3
offal 682.9
**scurfy** filthy 682.23
flaky 227.7
powdery 361.11
**scurrilous** cursing 972.8
disparaging 971.13
insulting 965.6
obscene 990.9
**scurry**
*n.* haste 709.1
speed 269.3
*v.* make haste 709.5
rush 269.9
**scurvy**
*n.* deficiency disease 686.10
*adj.* bad 675.9
base 915.12
paltry 673.18
vulgar 898.15
**scutcheon** 569.2
**scute** 228.15
**scuttle**
*n.* entrance 302.6
gait 273.14
haste 709.1
speed 269.3
*v.* bankrupt 842.8
be a coward 892.8
capsize 275.44
make haste 709.5
ruin 693.11
rush 269.9

**seepage**
infiltration 302.1
outflow 303.6
sorption 306.6
trickle 395.7
**seep in** filter in 302.10
learn 564.7
sorb 306.13
**seer** predictor 543.4
spectator 442.1
visionary 535.13
wise man 468.1
**see red** 952.17
**seesaw**
*n.* alternation 323.5
amusement device 878.15
interaction 13.3
oscillator 323.9
*v.* alternate 323.13
fluctuate 141.5
*adj.* alternate 323.19
*adv.* reciprocally 13.16
to and fro 323.21
**seethe**
be agitated 324.15
be angry 952.15
be excited 857.15
be hot 328.22
boil 329.20
bubble 405.4
fume 162.11
mill 322.12
soak 392.13
swarm 74.16
**see the light**
appear 446.8
be made public 559.16
come to life 407.8
understand 548.8
**seething**
*n.* agitation 324.1
heating 329.2
soaking 392.7
*adj.* angry 952.27
excited 857.20
hot 328.25
**see through**
penetrate 488.8
understand 548.8
**see to** attend to 530.5
care for 699.19
operate 164.5
seek 485.29
**segment**
*n.* part 55.1
portion 816.5
religion 1020.3
straight line 250.2
*v.* analyze 48.6
apportion 49.18
**segmental**
analytical 48.9
partial 55.7
**segmentation**
analysis 48.1
separation 49.1
**segregate**
. differentiate 16.6
discriminate 492.5
exclude 77.6

quarantine 761.13
separate 49.9
*adj.* unrelated 10.5
**segregated**
quarantined 761.20
secluded 924.7
separated 49.21
**segregation**
differentiation 16.4
discrimination 492.3
exclusiveness 77.3
prejudice 527.4
quarantine 761.2
seclusion 924.1
**seigneur** master 749.1
nobleman 918.4
**seismic** 162.22
**seismograph** 323.8
**seismology** 323.7
**seize** arrest 761.15
fasten upon 822.16
perceive 475.12
take 822.14
take command 739.14
understand 548.7
usurp 961.8
**seized with** 855.25
**seize the day**
make no provision 721.7
squander 854.3
use the occasion 129.8
**seizure**
accession to power 739.12
arrest 761.6
attack of illness 686.5
disease symptom 686.8
emotional outburst 857.8
frenzy 473.7
haul 822.10
hold 813.2
pain 424.2
spasm 324.6
taking 822.2
usurpation 961.3
**seldom**
infrequently 136.4
rarely 85.17
**select**
*n.* the best 674.8
*v.* appoint 780.10
choose 637.14
designate 568.18
discriminate 492.5
specify 80.11
*adj.* best 674.18
chosen 637.26
exclusive 77.8
particular 896.13
**selection**
appointment 780.2
choice 637.1
excerpt 607.3
grouping 60.3
indication 568.1
specification 80.6

**selective**
choosing 637.23
discriminating 492.7
exclusive 77.8
fastidious 896.9
particular 896.13
**selective service**
enlistment 780.6
military service 797.13
**selectman** 749.17
**Selene** 375.12
**self** ego 80.5
psyche 690.35
soul 466.4
**self–** alone 89.8
automatic 349.25
independent 762.21
individual 80.12
intrinsic 5.6
**self-abasement**
humiliation 906.2
unselfishness 979.1
**self-absorption**
selfishness 978.1
unfeeling 856.1
**self-abuse** 419.9
**self-acting**
automated 349.25
voluntary 622.7
**self-adjusting** 349.25
**self-admiration**
selfishness 978.1
vanity 909.1
**self-analysis** 873.3
**self-appointed**
meddlesome 238.9
presumptuous 912.10
**self-assertive** 624.15
**self-assured**
composed 858.13
sure 513.21
**self-centered**
egotistic 909.10
selfish 978.5
**self-command**
equanimity 858.3
self-control 624.5
**self-complacent**
complacent 868.10
vain 909.8
**self-confidence**
equanimity 858.3
pride 905.1
sureness 513.5
**self-confident**
composed 858.13
proud 905.8
sure 513.21
**self-congratulatory** 909.8
**self-conscious** 908.12
**self-contained**
independent 762.21
selfish 978.5
unsociable 923.5
**self-content**
*n.* complacence 868.2
vanity 909.1
*adj.* complacent 868.10
vain 909.8

**self-contradiction**
contrariety 15.3
error 518.1
impossibility 510.1
inconsistency 27.2
**self-contradictory**
erroneous 518.16
illogical 483.11
impossible 510.7
inconsistent 27.8
paradoxical 15.8
**self-control**
equanimity 858.3
moderation 163.1
patience 861.1
restraint 760.1
self-command 624.5
sobriety 992.1
**self-controlled**
automated 349.25
composed 858.13
patient 861.9
strong-willed 624.15
**self-deception**
deception 618.1
illusion 519.1
**self-defense** 799.1
**self-denial**
asceticism 991.1
moderation 163.1
self-control 624.5
sobriety 992.1
unselfishness 979.1
**self-denying**
ascetic 991.3
unselfish 979.5
**self-deprecating**
humble 906.11
modest 908.10
**self-destruction** 409.6
**self-destructive**
destructive 693.26
murderous 409.24
**self-determination**
automation 349.1
government 741.4
independence 762.5
nationhood 181.6
rallying theme 797.16
voluntariness 622.2
**self-determined**
independent 762.21
voluntary 622.7
**self-discipline**
self-control 624.5
temperance 992.1
**self-disciplined** 624.15
**self-doubt** doubt 503.2
modesty 908.2
**self-doubting**
humble 906.11
modest 908.10
**self-educated** 475.24
**self-effacing**
modest 908.10
unselfish 979.5
**self-esteem** pride 905.1
selfishness 978.1
vanity 909.1
**self-esteeming**
proud 905.8
selfish 978.5

vain 909.8
**self-evident**
certain 513.15
manifest 555.8
**self-explanatory** 555.8
**self-governing**
automated 349.25
governmental 741.17
independent 762.21
**self-government**
automation 349.1
government 741.4
independence 762.5
nationhood 181.6
self-control 624.5
**self-gratification** 865.1
**self-hatred** 873.3
**self-help** 785.6
**self-identity**
identity 14.1
individuality 80.1
**self-immolation**
burning 329.5
sacrifice 1032.7
suicide 409.6
unselfishness 979.1
**self-importance**
importance 672.1
pompousness 904.7
sureness 513.5
vanity 909.1
**self-important**
important 672.16
pompous 904.22
sure 513.21
vain 909.8
**self-improvement** 785.6
**self-indulgence**
intemperance 993.1
pleasure 865.1
selfishness 978.1
**self-indulgent**
intemperate 993.7
selfish 978.5
**self-interest**
egotism 909.3
selfishness 978.1
**selfish** egotistic 909.10
self-seeking 978.5
**selfishly** 978.7
**selfishness**
egotism 909.3
self-serving 978
**self-knowledge** 475.1
**selfless**
impartial 976.10
unselfish 979.5
**selflessness**
impartiality 976.4
unselfishness 979.1
**selfness** identity 14.1
individuality 80.1
**self-pity** 944.1
**self-pitying** 944.9
**self-possessed**
composed 858.13
strong-willed 624.15
**self-possession**
equanimity 858.3
self-control 624.5
**self-preservation** 799.1

**self-propelled**
automatic 349.26
propelled 285.17
**self-protection** 799.1
**self-regulating** 349.25
**self-reliance**
independence 762.5
pride 905.1
sureness 513.5
**self-reliant**
independent 762.21
proud 905.8
sure 513.21
**self-respect** pride 905.1
vanity 909.1
**self-respecting**
proud 905.8
vain 909.8
**self-restrained**
composed 858.13
strong-willed 624.15
**self-restraint**
equanimity 858.3
moderation 163.1
self-control 624.5
sobriety 992.1
**self-revealing** 554.10
**self-righteous** 1029.5
**self-righteousness**
1029.1
**self-sacrificing** 979.5
**selfsame**
*n.* the same 14.3
*adj.* identical 14.7
**self-satisfaction**
complacence 868.2
vanity 909.1
**self-satisfied**
complacent 868.10
vain 909.8
**self-seeker** 978.3
**self-seeking**
*n.* selfishness 978.1
*adj.* selfish 978.5
**self-server** 978.3
**self-service** 307.11
**self-serving**
*n.* selfishness 978.1
*adj.* selfish 978.5
**self-styled**
nominal 583.15
ungenuine 616.26
**self-sufficient**
independent 762.21
proud 905.8
selfish 978.5
unsociable 923.5
vain 909.8
**self-sustaining** 785.23
**self-taught**
learned 475.24
taught 564.16
**self-willed**
disobedient 767.8
lawless 740.5
obstinate 626.8
**self-winding** 349.25
**sell** bring in 829.12
convince 501.18
deal in 827.15
persuade 648.23
provision 659.9

publicize 559.15
sell stocks 833.24
transfer property
817.3
vend 829.8
**seller** 830.4
**seller's market**
commerce 827.1
high prices 848.3
insufficiency 662.1
prosperity 728.5
sale 829.1
**sell for cost** 846.15
realize 829.12
**selling**
*n.* inducement 648.3
merchandising 829.2
supplying 659.1
*adj.* sales 829.13
**sellout** betrayal 975.8
selling 829.2
**sell out** betray 975.14
desert 633.6
inform on 557.12
sell 829.8
sell stocks 833.24
**sell short** sell 829.8
sell stocks 833.24
underestimate 498.2
**selvage** border 235.4
edging 235.7
**semantic**
indicative 568.23
linguistic 580.17
meaning 545.12
**semantics**
linguistics 580.12
meaning 545.7
word study 582.15
**semaphore** 568.15
**semblance** copy 24.1
fakery 616.3
form 446.3
illusoriness 519.2
image 572.3
pretext 649.1
similarity 20.1
**semen** secretion 312.2
sperm 406.11
**semester** 107.2
**semi** 272.11
**semi–** half 92.5
imitation 22.8
incomplete 57.4
medium 32.3
partial 55.7
similar 20.10
**semiannual** 137.8
**semiautomatic**
*n.* robot 349.12
*adj.* automated
349.25
**semicircle** curve 252.5
half 92.2
half circle 253.8
**semicircular** 252.11
**semicolon** 144.4
**semiconductor** 342.13
**semiconscious** 423.8
**semidark** 337.15
**semigloss** 362.21

**semiliquid**
*n.* fluid 388.2
semifluid 389.5
*adj.* semifluid 389.11
**semiliquidity** 389
**semimonthly** 137.8
**seminal** causal 153.15
fertilizing 165.11
genital 419.27
imaginative 535.18
productive 165.9
reproductive 169.15
secretory 312.7
spermatic 406.22
**seminar**
discussion 597.7
study 562.8
**seminarian** 566.5
**seminary**
religious school
567.10
school 567.1
secondary school
567.6
**semiprecious stone**
384.6
**semiretired** 710.5
**semiskilled** 734.16
**Semitic deities** 1014.11
**semitransparent** 340.4
**semiweekly** 137.8
**semiyearly** 137.8
**Senate** 742.3
**senator** 746.3
**senatorial** 742.19
**send** broadcast 344.25
communicate 554.7
delight 865.8
dispatch 271.14
mail 604.13
remove 271.10
start 285.14
surge 395.22
use radar 346.15
**send away**
dismiss 310.18
dispatch 271.14
eject 310.17
repulse 289.3
**send for** 752.12
**send forth**
dispatch 271.14
eject 310.24
issue 559.14
start 285.14
**send off** begin 68.7
dismiss 310.18
dispatch 271.14
repulse 289.3
start 285.14
**send-off** beginning 68.
departure 301.4
**send out**
commission 780.9
eject 310.24
emit 401.8
**senile**
*n.* dotard 471.9
*adj.* aged 126.18
feeble-minded 469.2
old 123.17
**senility** dotage 469.10

elderliness 126.5
oldness 123.1
psychosis 473.3
weakness 160.3
**senior**
*n.* chief 749.3
elder 127.5
student 566.6
superior 36.4
*adj.* authoritative
739.15
elder 123.19
prior 116.4
**senior citizen** 127.2
**seniority**
authority 739.4
eldership 126.3
oldness 123.1
superiority 36.1
**señor** 420.7
**señora** 421.8
**señorita** 421.8
**sensation** brain 466.6
emotion 855.3
great success 724.3
marvel 920.2
sense 422
thrill 857.2
**sensational**
eloquent 600.11
emotionalistic 855.20
exciting 857.30
gaudy 904.20
grandiose 601.8
superb 674.17
wonderful 920.10
**sensationalism**
dramatics 611.2
emotionalism 855.9
exaggeration 617.1
grandiloquence 601.1
showiness 904.3
**sense**
*n.* discrimination
492.1
emotion 855.3
intelligence 467.1
meaning 545.1
milieu 233.3
rationality 467.6
reasonableness 482.9
sensation 422.1
*v.* detect 488.5
feel 855.11
intuit 481.4
perceive 422.8
understand 548.7
**senseless** foolish 470.8
illogical 483.11
imprudent 470.9
inanimate 382.5
insane 473.25
meaningless 547.6
unconscious 423.8
unintelligent 469.13
unordered 62.12
**sense of humor** 881.11
**senses** five senses 422.5
sanity 472.1
wits 466.2
**sensibility**
cognizance 475.2

discrimination 492.1
emotional capacity
855.4
pliancy 357.2
sagacity 467.4
sentience 422.2
**sensible** aware 475.15
cheap 849.7
cognizant of 475.16
emotionable 855.21
grateful 949.5
intelligent 467.12
logical 482.20
perceptible 422.13
practical 536.6
reasonable 467.18
sane 472.4
substantial 3.6
weighable 352.19
**sensing** 481.5
**sensitive**
discriminating 492.7
emotionable 855.21
excitable 857.26
fastidious 896.9
pliant 357.9
responsive 422.14
sensory 422.11
sore 424.11
touchy 951.20
**sensitivity**
discrimination 492.1
emotional capacity
855.4
excitability 857.9
fastidiousness 896.1
sensitiveness 422.3
touchiness 951.4
**sensitivity to** 174.1
**sensitivity training**
690.5
**sensitize** 422.9
**sensory** 422.11
**sensual** carnal 987.5
lascivious 989.29
sexual 419.26
**sensualist** 987.3
**sensuality** carnality 987
lasciviousness 989.5
sexuality 419.2
**sensuous** pleasant 863.7
sensory 422.11
**sentence**
*n.* condemnation
1008.1
judgment 494.5
legal decision 1004.9
maxim 517.1
part of writing 55.2
phrase 585.1
remark 594.4
*v.* condemn 1008.3
pass judgment 494.13
**sententious**
advisory 754.8
aphoristic 517.6
concise 592.6
grandiloquent 601.8
meaningful 545.10
**sentience**
physical sensibility
422.2

wakefulness 713.1
**sentient** 422.13
**sentiment**
attitude 525.1
belief 501.6
emotion 855.3
feeling 855.1
idea 479.1
love 931.1
sentimentality 855.8
**sentimental**
foolish 470.8
loving 931.25
mawkish 855.22
**sentimentality**
amorousness 931.3
mawkishness 855.8
**sentimentalize** 855.15
**sentry** warner 703.4
watchman 699.10
**sentry box** 191.10
**separable** 49.26
**separate**
*v.* analyze 48.6
arrange 60.11
bound 235.8
differentiate 16.6
disband 75.8
discriminate 492.5
dissent 522.4
dissolve marriage
935.5
diverge 299.5
divide 49.9
fall out 795.10
interspace 201.3
open 265.12
part company 49.19
partition 237.8
quarantine 761.13
refine 681.22
segregate 77.6
sow dissension 795.14
*adj.* alone 89.8
different 16.7
distinct 49.20
secluded 924.7
unrelated 10.5
**separated**
alienated 929.11
alone 89.8
different 16.7
disjoined 49.21
distant 199.8
interspaced 201.6
quarantined 761.20
secluded 924.7
unmarried 935.7
unrelated 10.5
**separately**
particularly 80.15
severally 49.28
singly 89.13
**separateness**
aloneness 89.2
difference 16.1
noncohesion 51.1
unrelatedness 10.1
**separation** analysis 48.1
differentiation 16.4
disbandment 75.3
discrimination 492.3

disjunction 49
dissolution of mar-
riage 935.1
distance 199.1
divergence 299.1
exclusiveness 77.3
falling-out 795.4
partition 237.5
quarantine 761.2
seclusion 924.1
sifting 681.4
**separatism** 49.1
**separatist**
*n.* apostate 628.5
dissenter 522.3
*adj.* repudative 628.12
**separative**
differentiative 16.9
disintegrative 53.5
exclusive 77.8
separating 49.25
**sepia** 367.3
**sepsis** 686.30
**sept** ancestry 170.4
class 61.2
race 11.4
**septal** 237.11
**septet**
cooperation 786.1
part music 462.17
poetic division
609.11
seven 99.3
**septic** diseased 686.56
putrefactive 692.40
unhealthful 684.5
**septicemia** 686.30
**septic tank** 682.12
**septuagenarian**
old man 127.2
seventy 99.7
**septum** 237.5
**sepulcher** 410.16
**sepulchral** deep 454.10
funereal 410.22
**sequel** aftermath 117.2
continuation 67
following 293.1
result 154.1
**sequence**
coherence 50.2
continuity 71.2
following 293.1
order 59.2
posteriority 117.1
result 154.1
series 65
**sequential**
coherent 50.11
consecutive 71.9
deducible 482.23
resulting 154.7
succeeding 65.4
**sequester**
appropriate 822.20
separate 49.9
**sequestered**
concealed 615.11
private 614.13
quiescent 268.12
recluse 924.9
separated 49.21

sequitur 67.1
seraglio 933.11
seraphic angelic 1015.6
  lovable 931.23
  pious 1028.9
  virtuous 980.7
seraphim angels 1015.1
  celestial beings
    1015.3
sere
  deteriorated 692.37
  dried 393.9
  worn 692.33
serenade
  *n.* courtship 932.6
  song 462.13
  *v.* court 932.19
  sing 462.39
serendipity
  chance 156.1
  discovery 488.1
serene clear 335.31
  composed 858.12
  moderate 163.13
  pacific 803.9
serenity
  composure 858.2
  moderation 163.1
  peace 803.2
  quiescence 268.1
serf retainer 750.1
  slave 764.7
  sycophant 907.3
serfdom service 750.12
  servility 907.1
  subjection 764.1
sergeant
  noncommissioned of-
    ficer 749.19
  peace officer 699.15
serial
  *n.* book 605.1
  installment 605.13
  periodical 605.10
  radio broadcast
    344.18
  stage show 611.4
  *adj.* coherent 50.11
  consecutive 71.9
  journalistic 605.26
  periodic 137.7
series biology 61.5
  circuit 137.3
  continuity 71.2
  edition 605.2
  following 293.1
  numbers 86.7
  sequence 65.1
  set 74.12
serigraphy 578.5
serious dangerous 697.9
  eloquent 600.14
  great 34.6
  resolute 624.11
  sedate 858.14
  solemn 871.3
  thoughtful 478.21
  weighty 672.19
  zealous 635.10
seriously
  positively 34.19
  resolutely 624.17

solemnly 871.4
zealously 635.15
seriousness
  importance 672.3
  resolution 624.1
  sedateness 858.4
  solemnity 871.1
  zeal 635.2
sermon lecture 599.3
  lesson 562.7
  reproof 969.5
sermonize
  expound 562.17
  lecture 599.11
sermonizer
  lecturer 599.5
  preacher 1038.3
serous fluid 388.7
  secretory 312.7
serpent
  bad person 986.7
  brass wind 465.8
  snake 414.31
  traitor 619.10
serpentine
  convoluted 254.7
  cunning 735.12
  curved 252.7
  flowing 395.24
  reptile 414.51
  wandering 291.7
  winding 254.6
serrate
  *v.* notch 262.4
  *adj.* angular 251.6
  notched 262.5
  rough 261.7
serration 262.2
serried continuous 71.8
  crowded 74.22
  dense 354.12
serum antitoxin 687.27
  blood 388.4
  body fluid 388.3
  transfusion 689.20
servant assistant 787.6
  hanger-on 907.5
  instrument 658.3
  retainer 750
  slave 764.7
  subordinate 764.5
  working person 718.2
serve
  *n.* throw 285.4
  *v.* act 705.4
  be expedient 670.3
  be inferior 37.4
  be instrumental
    658.5
  be of use 665.17
  copulate 419.23
  do duty 656.13
  do good 674.10
  give 818.12
  help 785.18
  soldier 797.22
  suffice 661.4
  suit 26.8
  summon 752.12
  tend 174.3
  throw 285.11
  work for 750.13

serve as 572.7
serve one right
  be just 976.6
  get one's deserts
    960.6
  punish 1010.10
  retaliate 955.5
serve time
  be imprisoned 761.18
  spend time 108.5
service
  *n.* agency 658.2
  aid 785.1
  benefit 665.4
  business 656.1
  ceremony 646.4
  employment 750.12
  food 307.11
  good deed 938.7
  liturgy 1040.3
  military service
    797.13
  military unit 800.21
  obedience 766.1
  portion 307.10
  position 656.5
  rigging 277.12
  subservience 764.2
  task 656.2
  throw 285.4
  worship 1032.8
  *v.* copulate 419.23
  repair 694.14
serviceable
  helpful 785.21
  instrumental 658.6
  useful 665.18
serviceman
  military man 800.6
  repairman 694.10
service station 832.7
servile
  deferential 765.16
  downtrodden 764.16
  inferior 37.6
  serving 750.14
  slavish 907.12
  submissive 765.12
  subservient 764.13
servility inferiority 37.1
  obedience 766.1
  obeisance 964.2
  slavishness 907
  subjection 764.1
  submissiveness 765.3
serving
  *n.* food 307.10
  rigging 277.12
  *adj.* acting 705.10
  attending 750.14
  helping 785.20
serving girl 750.8
servitude service 750.12
  subjection 764.1
servomechanism
  automation 349.13
  mechanism 348.5
  types of 349.30
sesquicentennial
  anniversary 137.4
  one-hundred-fifty
    99.8

sesquipedalian
  *n.* long word 582.10
  *adj.* high-flown 601.10
  long 202.8
  stilted 590.3
session
  church council 755.4
  conference 597.6
  meeting 74.2
  period 107.2
set
  *n.* all 54.3
  assemblage 74.12
  class 61.2
  clique 788.6
  cohesion 50.1
  company 74.3
  course 267.2
  direction 290.1
  edition 605.2
  flow 395.4
  form 246.1
  group 20.5
  position 184.3
  radio receiver 344.3
  setting 611.24
  sprout 125.9
  trait of character
    525.3
  trend 174.2
  *v.* adjust 26.7
  aim 290.8
  allot 816.9
  brood 169.12
  cohere 50.6
  designate 80.11
  direct 290.6
  establish 184.15
  fasten 47.7
  flow 395.16
  form 246.7
  heal 694.21
  impose 963.4
  incline 174.3
  place 184.11
  plant 413.18
  prepare 720.9
  prescribe 752.10
  set to music 462.47
  sharpen 258.9
  sink 316.6
  sit 268.10
  solidify 356.8
  stabilize 142.9
  thicken 354.10
  typeset 603.16
  *adj.* circumscribed
    234.6
  customary 642.15
  established 142.13
  fastened 47.14
  firm 624.12
  fixed 142.14
  hardened 356.13
  inveterate 642.21
  located 184.17
  made sure 513.20
  obstinate 626.8
  planned 654.13
  prepared 720.16
  sharp 258.10
  trite 883.9

**Set**
Egyptian deity
1014.10
god of evil 1016.6
**seta** bristle 261.3
hair 230.2
**set about** begin 68.7
set to work 716.15
undertake 715.3
**set above** 637.17
**set against**
antagonize 929.7
provoke 795.14
**set an example** 25.7
**set apart** allot 816.9
characterize 80.10
commit 816.11
differentiate 16.6
discriminate 492.5
exclude 42.10
interspace 201.3
partition 237.8
reserve 660.12
sanctify 1026.5
segregate 77.6
separate 49.9
**set aside** allot 816.9
disregard 531.4
exclude 42.10
postpone 132.9
put away 668.6
remove 271.10
repeal 779.2
reserve 660.12
segregate 77.6
separate 49.9
waive 507.5
**setback** defeat 727.2
disappointment
541.1
hindrance 730.1
regression 295.1
relapse 696.1
reverse 729.3
slowing 270.4
**set back** hinder 730.10
recess 257.14
restrain 760.7
slow 270.9
**set before**
confront 240.8
offer 637.21
prefer 637.17
propose 773.5
**set down** affirm 523.4
attribute 155.4
humiliate 906.5
put 184.13
record 570.16
reprove 969.17
**set forth** attest 505.9
describe 608.12
manifest 555.5
postulate 499.12
propose 773.5
say 594.23
start out 301.7
**set in** begin 68.7
gather 403.22
implant 142.9
indent 257.14
insert 304.3

**set in motion**
impel 283.10
motivate 648.12
move 267.6
start 285.14
**setoff**
counterbalance 33.2
discount 847.1
opposite 15.2
outset 301.2
printing 603.3
**set off** allot 816.9
beautify 900.14
border 235.10
compare 491.4
counteract 33.5
differentiate 16.6
discriminate 492.5
explode 162.13
head for 290.10
kindle 648.18
measure off 490.12
oppose 15.4
ornament 901.8
start out 301.7
**set on**
v. attack 798.15
base on 212.6
incite 648.17
sow dissension 795.14
adj. desirous of
634.22
determined upon
624.16
**set out** begin 68.7
dispose 60.9
head for 290.10
ornament 901.8
phrase 588.4
plot 654.11
start out 301.7
**set right** adjust 26.7
compensate 33.4
direct to 290.7
disillusion 520.2
remedy 694.13
teach 562.11
**set sail** begin 68.7
hoist sail 275.20
**set straight**
direct to 290.7
disillusion 520.2
reform 145.12
remedy 694.13
reprove 969.17
straighten 250.5
**setting**
n. arena 802.1
background 233.2
hardening 356.5
motif 901.7
mounting 216.10
orchestration 463.2
planting 413.14
scenery 611.24
thickening 354.4
typesetting 603.2
adj. descending
316.11
**settle** arrange 771.9
compromise 807.2
conform 82.3

decide 494.11
defeat 727.6
descend 316.7
fly down 278.50
gravitate 352.15
kill 409.14
light on 316.10
locate 184.16
make sure 513.11
mediate 805.7
organize 60.10
pay in full 841.13
populate 188.9
prove 505.11
punish 1010.11
reconcile 804.8
refute 506.5
resolve 624.7
ruin 693.11
sink 316.6
stabilize 142.9
transfer property
817.3
**settled**
contracted 771.12
defeated 727.14
ended 70.8
established 142.13
firm 624.12
fixed 142.14
inhabited 188.12
inveterate 642.21
located 184.17
made sure 513.20
paid 841.22
proved 505.21
**settle down**
be moderate 163.5
fly 278.52
locate 184.16
mature 126.9
sink 316.6
**settle for** 868.5
**settle in** 188.9
**settlement**
arrangement 771.4
community 788.2
compromise 807.1
endowment 818.9
establishment 184.6
estate 810.4
payment 841.1
peopling 188.2
proof 505.4
property transfer
817.1
reconciliation 804.4
territory 181.1
**settler** arrival 302.4
assigner 818.11
disproof 506.3
end-all 70.4
greenhorn 78.4
inhabitant 190.9
**settle upon**
attribute to 155.4
decide upon 637.16
endow 818.17
**settle with**
arrange 771.9
pay 841.12
punish 1010.10

retaliate 955.7
**set to** begin 68.7
fasten 47.7
quarrel 795.11
set to work 716.15
undertake 715.3
**set-to** controversy 482.4
quarrel 795.6
**setup** composition 58.1
easy thing 732.3
order 59.1
plan 654.1
prearrangement
641.1
structure 245.1
**set up** aid 785.11
begin 68.11
conceive 153.11
contrive 654.9
create 167.10
elevate 317.5
erect 213.9
establish 184.15
finance 836.15
glorify 914.13
install 167.12
order 59.4
pay for 841.19
prearrange 641.3
provoke 952.22
refresh 695.2
remedy 694.13
**set upon** 798.15
**seven-league boots**
1036.6
**seventh**
n. harmonics 463.20
adj. seven 99.19
**seventh heaven**
happiness 865.2
heaven 1018.5
summit 211.2
**sever** differentiate 16.6
discriminate 492.5
separate 49.11
**several**
n. indefinite number
101.2
plurality 100.1
adj. different 16.7
diversified 19.4
many 101.7
particular 80.12
proportionate 816.13
**severally** each 80.19
proportionately
816.14
separately 49.28
singly 89.13
variously 19.5
**severance**
differentiation 16.4
elimination 77.2
separation 49.2
**severe**
acrimonious 161.13
cold 333.14
difficult 731.16
exact 516.16
gruff 937.7
painful 424.10
plain 902.9

free oneself from
763.8
**shaker** 324.9
**shakes**
delirium tremens
473.10
excitement 857.4
nervousness 859.2
shaking 324.2
**shake up** agitate 324.10
awaken 713.5
censure 969.13
excite 857.13
fluff 357.6
rearrange 60.13
weaken 160.10
**shake-up**
makeshift 670.2
rearrangement 60.7
**shaking**
*n.* agitation 324.2
excitement 857.4
waving 323.2
*adj.* imperfectly spoken 595.12
jittery 859.11
vibrating 324.17
**shaky** aged 126.18
cold 333.15
fearful 891.31
flimsy 4.7
imperfectly spoken
595.12
jittery 859.11
loose 51.5
shaking 324.17
unfastened 49.22
unreliable 514.19
unsafe 697.11
unsteady 160.16
**shallow**
*n.* shoal 210.2
*v.* become shallow
210.3
*adj.* half-learned
477.15
negligible 35.6
not deep 210.5
superficial 469.20
trivial 673.16
**shallowness**
depthlessness 210
exteriority 224.1
inattention 531.1
slight knowledge
477.6
superficiality 469.7
triviality 673.3
**sham**
*n.* affectation 903.1
display 904.4
fake 616.13
hoax 618.7
impostor 619.6
pretense 616.3
pretext 649.1
*v.* affect 903.12
fake 616.21
*adj.* assumed 903.16
imitation 22.8
ungenuine 616.26
**shaman** 1035.7

**shamble**
*n.* gait 273.14
slowness 270.2
*v.* walk 273.27
**shambles**
battlefield 802.2
butchery 409.4
destruction 693.1
killing site 409.12
**shame**
*n.* decency 988.2
disgrace 915.5
humiliation 906.2
iniquity 981.3
regret 873.1
wrong 959.2
*v.* disgrace 915.8
humiliate 906.4
**shamed**
humiliated 906.13
in disrepute 915.13
**shamefaced**
humiliated 906.13
regretful 873.8
shy 908.12
**shameful** bad 675.9
disgraceful 915.11
evil 981.16
regretful 873.8
wrong 959.3
**shameless**
brazen 913.10
dishonest 975.16
gaudy 904.20
immodest 990.6
unregretful 874.4
wicked 981.17
wrong 959.3
**shampoo**
*n.* cleaning agent
681.17
washing 681.5
*v.* wash 681.19
**shamrock**
insignia 569.1
three 93.1
**shanghai** abduct 824.19
coerce 756.7
seize 822.14
**Shangri-la** 535.11
**shank** leg 273.16
meat 308.17
printing 603.6
shaft 217.6
**shanty** 191.10
**shapable** 357.9
**shape**
*n.* aspect 446.3
characteristic 80.4
condition 7.3
form 246.1
human form 246.4
illusion 519.4
image 446.5
kind 61.3
mode 7.4
specter 1017.1
structure 245.1
*v.* be formed 246.8
conform 82.3
create 167.10
fashion 246.7

imagine 535.14
make ceramics 576.6
plan 654.9
**shaped** made 167.22
planned 654.13
**shapeless**
abnormal 85.9
formless 247.4
inconstant 141.7
obscure 549.15
ugly 899.8
unordered 62.12
vague 514.18
**shapely**
beautiful 900.17
well-shaped 248.5
**shape up**
be formed 246.8
be in a state 7.6
get better 691.7
order 59.5
**shard**
*n.* piece 55.3
refuse 669.4
*v.* pulverize 361.9
show fragility 360.3
**share**
*n.* allotment 816.5
amount of stock
834.3
part 55.1
*v.* apportion 816.6
communicate 554.7
emotionally respond
855.12
participate 815.6
**sharecrop** 413.16
**sharecropper** 413.5
**sharecropping**
agriculture 413.1
participation 815.2
**shareholder**
participator 815.4
stockholder 833.14
**sharing**
*n.* accord 794.1
apportionment 816.1
impartation 554.2
participation 815.1
sociability 922.6
sympathy 855.5
*adj.* participating
815.8
**shark** expert 733.11
fish 414.35,65
predator 822.12
savage 943.5
sharper 619.4
vertebrates 415.7
**sharp**
*n.* expert 733.11
gambler 515.17
harmonics 463.14
sharper 619.4
*adj.* acrimonious
161.13
alert 533.14
angular 251.6
bitter 429.6
caustic 939.21
chic 644.13
cold 333.14

cunning 735.12
deceitful 618.20
deep-felt 855.26
dissonant 461.4
gruff 937.7
intelligent 467.14
keen 258.10
painful 424.10
penetrating 857.29
pungent 433.6
quick 707.18
sensitive 422.15
shrill 458.14
steep 219.18
strong-smelling
435.10
unpleasant 864.20
violent 162.15
witty 881.15
*adv.* punctually
131.14
suddenly 113.9
**sharp ear** 448.3
**sharpen**
aggravate 885.2
edge 258.9
increase 38.5
sensitize 422.9
stimulate 857.12
tool 348.10
**sharpener** cutlery 348.2
types of 258.19
**sharper** deceiver 619.4
gambler 515.17
**sharp eye**
keen eye 439.10
vigilance 533.4
**sharp-eyed**
clear-sighted 439.22
vigilant 533.13
**sharpness**
acrimony 161.4
alertness 533.5
bitterness 864.5
causticity 939.8
chic 644.3
cold 333.1
cunning 735.1
dissonance 461.1
gruffness 937.3
intelligence 467.2
keenness 258
pungency 433.1
quickness 707.3
stridence 458.1
unpleasant taste
429.2
violence 162.1
wittiness 881.2
**sharp-nosed** 435.13
**sharpshooter**
infantryman 800.9
shooter 285.9
**sharp-sighted** 439.22
**shatter** break 360.3
demolish 693.17
madden 473.23
splinter 49.13
**shattered** broken 49.24
damaged 692.29
**shatterproof**
resistant 159.18

unbreakable 359.5
**shave** cheapen 849.6
 cheat 618.17
 cut off 42.10
 deal in money 835.27
 graze 200.10
 shorten 203.6
 smooth 260.5
 subtract 42.9
**shaved** 203.9
**shaven** 232.17
**shaving** flake 227.3
 hairlessness 232.4
 piece 55.3
 refuse 669.4
 remainder 43.1
 thinness 205.7
**shay** 272.4
**she** female 421.4
 self 80.5
**sheaf** 74.8
**shear** cut off 42.10
 despoil 822.24
 divest 232.5
 shorten 203.6
**sheared** 203.9
**sheath** case 228.17
 skin 229.1
**sheathe** clothe 231.38
 cover 228.23
 wrap 228.20
**sheathed** 228.31
**sheathing**
 *n.* covering 228.1
 sheath 228.17
 wood 378.3
 *adj.* covering 228.34
**shed**
 *n.* aviation 278.24
 hut 191.10
 *v.* cast 232.10
**shedding** 232.2
**sheen** 335.2
**sheep** animal 414.7
 breeds of 414.70
 conformist 82.2
 imitator 22.4
 laity 1039.1
**sheepish**
 blushing 908.13
 penitent 873.9
 ungulate 414.49
**sheepishly**
 guiltily 983.5
 penitently 873.12
 shyly 908.15
**sheepskin** 570.6
**sheer**
 *n.* bend 219.3
 deviation 291.1
 *v.* change course 275.30
 deviate 291.3
 veer 219.9
 *adj.* perpendicular 213.12
 stark 35.8
 steep 219.18
 thorough 56.10
 transparent 339.4
 unadulterated 45.7
 *adv.* absolutely 56.15

perpendicularly 213.14
**sheer off** dodge 631.8
 pull back 284.7
 turn aside 291.6
**sheet** bedding 228.10
 layer 227.2
 newspaper 605.11
 page 55.2
 paper 378.6
 white 364.2
**sheeting** sheet 228.10
 wood 378.3
**sheet metal** 383.5
**sheik** 931.12
**sheikh**
 clergyman 1038.13
 prince 918.7
 ruler 749.8
**shelf** layer 227.1
 ledge 216.14
 shoal 210.2
 storage place 660.6
**shell**
 *n.* armor 799.3
 atomics 326.4
 auditory organ 448.7
 cartridge 801.11
 cavity 257.2
 crust 228.14
 exterior 224.2
 frame 245.4
 hull 228.16
 shield 228.15
 shot 801.13
 stage 611.21
 types of 228.42
 *v.* fire upon 798.22
 husk 232.9
**shellac**
 overwhelm 727.8
 varnish 362.13
**shellacking**
 utter defeat 727.3
 varnishing 362.12
**shellfire** 798.9
**shellfish** 308.25
**shell game** fraud 618.9
 game of chance 515.8
**shell out** give 818.12
 pay out 841.14
 spend 843.5
**shell shock**
 combat neurosis 690.19
 shock 686.24
**shelter**
 *n.* cover 228.2
 lodgings 191.3
 protection 699.1
 refuge 700.3
 *v.* house 188.10
 protect 699.18
**sheltered**
 protected 699.21
 quiescent 268.12
**sheltering** 699.23
**shelve** incline 219.10
 postpone 132.9
 put away 668.6
**shelved** 534.14

**shenanigans**
 clownishness 881.5
 prank 881.10
**shepherd**
 *n.* clergyman 1038.2
 escort 73.5
 guardian 699.6
 guider 748.7
 herder 416.3
 *v.* care for 699.19
 direct 747.9
 drive animals 416.8
 escort 73.8
**sherbet** 308.46
**sheriff** 699.15
**Sherlock Holmes** 781.10
**Shetland pony** 414.11,68
**shibboleth**
 password 568.12
 phrase 582.9
**shield**
 *n.* armor 799.3
 cover 228.2
 heraldic insignia 569.2
 safeguard 699.3
 shell 228.15
 *v.* cover 228.19
 defend 799.8
 protect 699.18
**shielded**
 covered 228.31
 protected 699.21
**shielding**
 covering 228.34
 defensive 799.11
 protecting 699.23
**shift**
 *n.* change 139.1
 clothing 231.15
 conversion 145.1
 deviation 291.1
 device 670.2
 dislocation 185.1
 displacement 271.2
 period 108.3
 stratagem 735.3
 trick 618.6
 *v.* be changed 139.5
 be dishonest 975.11
 change course 275.30
 convert 145.11
 deviate 291.3
 dodge 631.8
 equivocate 483.9
 fluctuate 141.5
 live by one's wits 735.9
 move 267.5
 remove 271.10
 vacillate 627.8
**shift for oneself** 762.19
**shifting**
 *n.* deviation 291.1
 equivocation 483.5
 fluctuation 141.3
 *adj.* devious 291.7
 inconstant 141.7
 unreliable 514.19
 wandering 273.36

**shiftless**
 improvident 721.15
 indolent 708.18
**shiftlessness**
 improvidence 721.2
 indolence 708.5
**shifty** cunning 735.12
 deceitful 618.20
 dishonest 975.16
 evasive 631.15
 furtive 614.12
 inconstant 141.7
 secretive 614.15
 treacherous 975.21
 unreliable 514.19
**shill**
 *n.* decoy 619.5
 fake buyer 828.6
 *v.* bid 828.9
**shillelagh** 217.2
**shilling**
 British money 835.8
 foreign money 835.9
**shilly-shally**
 be irresolute 627.7
 dawdle 270.8
 fluctuate 627.8
**shilly-shallying**
 *n.* fluctuation 627.2
 irresolution 627.3
 slowness 270.3
 *adj.* dawdling 270.11
 fluctuating 627.10
 irresolute 627.11
**shimmer**
 *n.* light 335.7
 *v.* glitter 335.24
**shimmering**
 *n.* light 335.7
 *adj.* glittering 335.35
**shimmy** 879.5
**shin**
 *n.* leg 273.16
 *v.* ascend 315.11
**shindig** dance 879.2
 meeting 74.2
 party 922.11
**shindy**
 commotion 62.4
 dance 879.2
 noise 453.3
 party 922.11
 quarrel 795.6
**shine**
 *n.* bootleg liquor 996.17
 daylight 335.10
 light 335.2
 liking 931.1
 polish 260.2
 *v.* be eloquent 600.7
 be expert at 733.17
 be famous 914.10
 be ostentatious 904.13
 give light 335.23
 look beautiful 900.15
 polish 260.7
 rub 350.8
 touch up 691.11
**shiner** 692.9

**shine up to**
  befriend 927.11
  curry favor 907.8
**shingle**
  *n.* detritus 361.6
  gravel 384.3
  roof covering
    228.6,43
  seashore 385.2
  wood 378.3
  *v.* cover 228.23
  overlap 228.30
  style the hair 230.22
**shingled**
  covering 228.35
  granular 361.12
  stony 384.11
**shingles** herpes 686.12
  nervous disorder
    686.23
  skin disease 686.33
**shining**
  gorgeous 900.19
  illustrious 914.19
  luminous 335.30
  shiny 335.33
**shining example**
  good person 985.4
  ideal 25.4
**shinny** 315.11
**shiny** clean 681.25
  luminous 335.30
  shining 335.33
  sleek 260.10
**ship**
  *n.* aircraft 280.1
  boat 277
  dirigible 280.11
  parts of 277.26
  types of 277.22
  *v.* haul 271.12
  put 184.14
  send 271.14
**shipmate**
  companion 928.3
  partner 787.2
**shipment** freight 271.7
  transportation 271.3
**shipper** 271.5
**shipping** ships 277.10
  transportation 271.3
**ship route** 275.10
**shipshape** tidy 59.8
  trim 277.20
**ship's log** 570.11
**shipwreck**
  *n.* misfortune 729.2
  wreck 693.4
  *v.* destroy 693.10
  run aground 275.42
**shipwrecked** 731.25
**shipyard** harbor 700.6
  plant 719.3
**shire** 180.5
**shirk** dodge 631.9
  leave undone 534.7
**shirker**
  goldbricker 631.3
  neglecter 534.5
**shirr** cook 330.4
  wrinkle 264.6
**shirt** 231.15,54

**shit**
  *n.* bad person 986.6
  defecation 311.2
  feces 311.4
  heroin 687.12
  nonsense 547.3
  trifle 673.5
  *v.* defecate 311.13
**shitty** bad 675.8
  fecal 311.20
  filthy 682.23
**Shiva God** 1013.4
  Hindu deity 1014.8
**shiver**
  *n.* cold sensation
    333.2
  excitement 857.4
  nervousness 859.2
  piece 55.3
  sensation 426.4
  shake 324.3
  small amount 35.3
  thrill 857.2
  trepidation 891.5
  *v.* be cold 333.9
  be excited 857.16
  shake 324.11
  shatter 49.13
  tremble 891.22
**shivering**
  *n.* cold sensation
    333.2
  shaking 324.2
  *adj.* cold 333.15
  jittery 859.11
  shaking 324.17
**shivery** brittle 360.4
  cold 333.15
  fearful 891.31
  jittery 859.11
  shaking 324.17
**shoal**
  *n.* fish 74.5
  hidden danger 697.5
  large number 101.3
  shallow 210.2
  *adj.* shallow 210.5
**shock**
  *n.* bunch 74.7
  concussion 162.8
  disease symptom
    686.8
  distress 866.5
  electric discharge
    342.6
  head of hair 230.4
  impact 283.3
  jolt 324.3
  misfortune 729.2
  stupor 712.6
  surprise 540.3
  traumatism 686.24
  *v.* electrify 342.23
  excite 857.13
  jolt 324.11
  offend 864.11
  startle 540.8
  terrify 891.25
**shock absorber** 163.3
**shocked** 540.13
**shocker** fiction 608.7
  surprise 540.2

**shocking** bad 675.9
  disgraceful 915.11
  horrid 864.19
  outright 34.12
  sudden 113.5
  surprising 540.11
  terrible 891.38
**shock tactics**
  attack 798.1
  warfare 797.9
**shock therapy**
  psychotherapy 690.7
  therapy 689.2
**shock troops** 800.14
**shod** 231.44
**shoddy**
  *n.* fake 616.13
  rubbish 669.5
  *adj.* bad 675.9
  base 915.12
  cheap 849.7
  paltry 673.18
  shabby 692.34
  slovenly 62.15
  ungenuine 616.26
  worthless 669.11
**shoe**
  *n.* types of 231.27,60
  *v.* clothe 231.39
**shoemaker** 231.37
**shoestring** 835.17
**shofar** 1040.11
**shogun** 749.8
**shoo**
  do away with 310.20
  go away! 310.29
**shoo-in**
  sure success 724.2
  victor 726.2
**shook** confused 532.12
  startled 540.13
**shook-up** jittery 859.11
  weak 160.12
**shoot**
  *n.* branch 411.18
  deposit 383.7
  descendant 171.4
  hunt 273.5
  rapids 395.10
  rocketry 281.9
  sprout 125.9
  trough 396.3
  twinge 424.2
  weaving 222.3
  *v.* discharge 285.13
  execute 1010.19
  explode 162.13
  fire upon 798.22
  hunt 655.9
  immunize 689.34
  photograph 577.14
  radiate 335.23
  rocket 281.13
  row 275.53
  rush 269.9
  skim 275.54
  sprout 411.31
  strike dead 409.18
  twinge 424.8
**shoot ahead**
  hustle 707.13
  outdistance 36.10

  pass 313.8
  spurt 269.16
**shoot down** end 70.7
  ruin 693.11
  shoot 285.13
  strike dead 409.18
**shooting**
  *n.* capital punishment
    1010.7
  gunfire 798.9
  hunting 655.2
  killing 409.1
  pain 424.2
  throwing 285.3
  *adj.* painful 424.10
**shooting star**
  meteor 375.15
  omen 544.6
**shoot-out** 798.9
**shoot up** ascend 315.9
  become higher
    207.17
  grow 197.7
  increase 38.6
  protrude 256.9
  sprout 411.31
**shop**
  *n.* market 832.1
  office 719.8
  workplace 719.1
  *v.* market 828.8
**shopkeeper**
  common person
    919.1
  merchant 830.2
**shoplift** 824.13
**shoplifter** 825.1
**shopper** 828.5
**shopping** 828.1
**shopping center**
  center 226.7
  city district 183.6
  marketplace 832.2
**shoptalk** 580.10
**shopworn** 692.33
**shoran** aviation 278.6
  direction finder 748.9
  navigation 275.2
  radar 346.3
**shore**
  *n.* border 235.4
  coast 385.2
  side 242.1
  *v.* buttress 785.12
  support 216.21
  *adj.* aquatic 275.58
  seashore 385.9
**shore up** bolster 785.12
  stiffen 356.9
  strengthen 159.11
  support 216.21
**shorn**
  deprived of 812.8
  reduced 39.10
**short**
  *n.* electric circuit
    342.4
  motion picture
    611.16
  speculator 833.12
  *v.* electricity 342.23
  *adj.* brief 203.8

brisk 111.8
concise 592.6
deficient 314.5
gruff 937.7
imperfect 678.4
incomplete 57.4
insignificant 35.6
little 196.10
low 208.7
needing 662.13
poor 838.7
taciturn 613.9
*adv.* abruptly 203.13
**shortage**
deficiency 57.2
imperfection 678.1
need 662.4
shortcoming 314.1
**shortbread** 308.42
**shortchange** 618.17
**short circuit** 342.4
**short-circuit** 342.23
**shortcoming**
falling short 314
fault 678.2
imperfection 678.1
inequality 31.1
want 662.4
**shortcut** route 657.2
shortest way 203.5
straight line 250.2
**shorten** abridge 607.5
be concise 592.5
condense 203.6
contract 198.7
miniaturize 196.9
reduce 39.7
subtract 42.9
**shortened**
abbreviated 203.9
concise 592.6
**shorter** 39.10
**shortest** 37.8
**shortfall**
shortcoming 314.1
want 662.4
**shorthand**
*n.* character 581.2
stenography 602.8
*adj.* stenographic
602.27
written 602.22
**shorthanded** 662.12
**short-lived** 111.7
**shortly** briefly 203.12
concisely 592.7
fleetingly 111.10
gruffly 937.9
soon 131.16
**short of** below 37.9
deficient 314.5
needing 662.13
**short shrift**
pitilessness 945.1
rebuff 776.2
**shortsighted**
narrow-minded
527.10
poor-sighted 440.11
undiscerning 469.14
unwise 470.9
**shortstop** 878.20

short story 608.8
**short-tempered** 951.25
**short-term** 111.8
**shortwave**
*n.* radio wave 344.11
*adj.* radio 344.28
**shot**
*n.* attempt 714.2
bullet 801.13
cinematography
577.8
detonation 456.3
discharge 285.5
dose 687.6
drink 996.6
fee 846.7
flash 269.6
guess 499.4
injection 689.18
photograph 577.3
portion 55.5
rocketry 281.9
shooter 285.9
throw of dice 515.10
wager 515.3
*adj.* ended 70.8
spoiled 692.31
unnerved 859.13
variegated 374.9
**shotgun** 801.5
**shot-put** 285.4
**shot through**
holey 265.20
permeated 186.15
variegated 374.9
**should** must 639.10
ought to 962.3
**shoulder**
*n.* bulwark 216.4
joint 47.4
meat 308.17
printing 603.6
ridge 256.3
shelf 216.14
supporter 216.2
*v.* support 216.21
thrust 283.11
**shout**
*n.* cheer 876.2
laughter 876.4
yell 459.1
*v.* be manifest 555.7
cheer 876.6
laugh 876.4
proclaim 559.13
yell 459.6
**shout down** 453.7
**shouting** 459.10
**shove**
*n.* pushing 285.1
thrust 283.2
*v.* deal illicitly 826.7
move 267.6
push 285.10
thrust 283.11
**shovel**
*n.* types of 348.15
*v.* excavate 257.15
transfer 271.16
**shove off** depart 301.9
die 408.20
put to sea 275.19

sail away from 275.36
**shoving**
*n.* pushing 285.1
*adj.* propulsive 285.15
**show**
*n.* affectation 903.1
appearances 446.2
display 904.4
exhibition 555.2
fakery 616.3
illusoriness 519.2
indication 568.1
marketplace 832.2
pretext 649.1
spectacle 446.7
stage show 611.4
theatrical perfor-
mance 611.13
*v.* appear 446.8
be visible 444.4
direct to 290.7
disclose 556.4
evidence 505.9
explain 552.10
indicate 568.17
manifest 555.5
project 577.16
prove 505.11
teach 562.11
**showboat**
show-off 904.11
theater 611.18
**show business**
amusement 878.11
theater 611
**showcase**
counter 832.10
glass 339.2
**showdown** 15.1
**shower**
*n.* bath 681.8
party 922.11
plenty 661.2
rain 394.1
spray 392.5
sprinkler 392.8
washing equipment
681.12
*v.* abound 661.5
bathe 681.19
give 818.12
rain 394.9
**show girl** 612.1
**showing**
*n.* appearance 446.1
display 555.2
indication 568.1
*adj.* disclosive 556.10
exposed 232.12
manifestative 555.9
visible 444.6
**showing-off** 904.4
**showman** 611.28
**showmanship** 611.3
**shown**
manifested 555.13
proved 505.21
**shown up** 506.7
**show off** 904.16
**show-off** 904.11
**showroom**
display room 192.24

salesroom 832.9
**show through**
be revealed 444.4
be transparent 339.3
**show up** appear 446.8
arrive 300.6
attend 186.8
be discovered 488.9
be visible 444.4
disclose 556.4
disillusionize 520.2
disprove 506.4
occur 151.6
overshadow 36.8
**showy** flaunting 904.19
grandiloquent 601.8
**shrapnel** 801.13
**shred**
*n.* piece 55.3
small amount 35.3
strip 206.4
*v.* make threads 206.6
pulverize 361.9
tear apart 49.14
**shredded**
powdery 361.11
severed 49.23
**shrew**
ill-humored woman
951.12
mammal 415.8,58
**shrewd** cunning 735.12
intelligent 467.15
knowing 475.15
**shrewdness**
cunning 735.1
intelligence 467.3
**shrewish**
ill-humored 951.21
quarrelsome 795.17
ungovernable 626.12
**shriek**
*n.* cry 459.1
laughter 876.4
loud sound 453.4
shrill sound 458.4
*v.* blare 453.9
cry 459.6
laugh 876.8
screech 458.8
utter 594.26
wail 875.11
wind sound 403.23
**shrieking** garish 362.19
shrill 458.14
**shrift** confession 556.3
pardon 947.2
**shrill**
*n.* shrill sound 458.4
*adj.* dissonant 461.4
piercing 458.14
**shrimp**
*n.* a nobody 673.7
dwarf 196.6
invertebrates 415.5
little thing 196.4
seafood 308.25
*v.* fish 655.10
**shrine**
holy place 1042.4
memorial 570.12
tomb 410.16

**shrink**
n. psychotherapist 690.13
v. be modest 908.7
decrease 39.6
demur 623.4
deteriorate 692.21
dodge 631.8
flinch 891.21
pull back 284.7
recede 297.2
retract 297.3
shrivel 198.9
waste 812.5
wince 424.8
**shrinkage** decrease 39.3
loss 812.2
reduction 42.2
shrinking 198.3
**shrink from** 867.5
**shrinking**
n. contraction 198.3
demur 623.2
adj. fearful 891.31
modest 908.11
receding 297.5
reticent 613.10
stickling 623.7
**shrinking violet** 908.6
**shrive** acquit 1007.4
administer rites 1040.21
forgive 947.3
**shrivel** age 126.10
deteriorate 692.21
dry 393.6
shrink 198.9
**shriveled** aged 126.18
deteriorated 692.37
dried 393.9
dwarf 196.13
emaciated 205.20
shrunk 198.13
**shroud**
n. cover 228.2
graveclothes 410.14
supporter 216.2
v. clothe 231.38
conceal 615.6
protect 699.18
wrap 228.20
**shrouded** 228.31
**Shrove Tuesday** 1040.15
**shrub** 411.9,49
**shrubbery**
garden 413.10
shrub 411.9
**shrug**
n. gesture 568.14
v. accept 861.6
gesture 568.21
**shrug off** dismiss 531.4
not care 636.4
underestimate 498.2
**shrunken**
depleted 812.7
deteriorated 692.37
reduced 39.10
shrunk 198.13
stunted 196.13
**htick** 611.8

**shuck**
n. hull 228.16
v. husk 232.9
**shudder**
n. excitement 857.4
quiver 324.3
thrill 857.2
v. be cold 333.9
quiver 324.11
**shudder at**
dislike 867.5
hate 930.5
**shuddering**
n. dislike 867.2
shaking 324.2
adj. shaking 324.17
**shuffle**
n. confusion 532.3
gait 273.14
prevarication 613.4
quibble 483.4
slowness 270.2
v. confuse 63.3
dance 879.5
equivocate 483.9
fluctuate 141.5
mix 44.11
walk 273.27
**shuffled**
confused 532.12
disorderly 62.13
**shuffling**
n. disarrangement 63.1
equivocation 483.5
fluctuation 141.3
adj. dilatory 132.17
equivocating 483.14
inconstant 141.7
slow 270.10
**shul** 1042.2
**shun** abstain 992.7
avoid 631.6
snub 966.7
**shunning** 631.1
**shunt** push 285.10
remove 271.10
turn aside 291.6
**shunted** 534.14
**shush**
n. sibilation 457.1
v. hush up 614.8
sibilate 457.2
silence 451.8
interj. silence! 451.14
**shut**
v. close 266.6
turn off 144.12
adj. closed 266.9
**shutdown**
cessation 144.1
closure 266.1
**shut down**
close up 266.8
go bankrupt 842.7
silence 451.8
stop work 144.8
suppress 760.8
turn off 144.12
**shut-eye** 712.2
**shut in** confine 761.12
enclose 236.5

**shut-in**
n. recluse 924.5
sick person 686.40
adj. confined 761.19
enclosed 236.10
recluse 924.9
**shut off**
v. obstruct 730.12
separate 49.9
turn off 144.12
adj. secluded 924.7
separated 49.21
**shutout** 727.3
**shut out**
v. bar 778.3
exclude 77.4
obstruct 730.12
overwhelm 727.8
adj. defeated 727.15
excluded 77.7
**shutter** close up 266.8
shade 338.5
**shutting** 266.1
**shuttle**
n. air travel 278.10
loom 222.5
oscillator 323.9
train 272.13
v. alternate 323.13
**shut up**
v. be silent 451.5
close 266.6
close shop 266.8
confine 761.12
enclose 236.5
refute 506.5
adj. recluse 924.9
interj. silence! 451.14
**shy**
v. be frightened 891.20
be startled 540.5
dodge 631.8
equivocate 483.9
falter 627.7
flinch 284.7
hurl at 798.28
scruple 623.4
throw 285.11
turn aside 291.6
withdraw 297.3
adj. cautious 895.9
doubtful 503.9
fearful 891.31
incomplete 57.4
stickling 623.7
timid 908.12
wanting 662.13
**shylocking**
lending 820.1
overcharge 848.5
**shyness** demur 623.2
fearfulness 891.3
timidity 908.4
**shyster**
cunning person 735.6
lawyer 1003.3
rascal 986.3
sharper 619.4
**sí** 521.18
**Siamese twins** 90.4

**sib**
n. kinsmen 11.2
adj. related 11.6
**Siberia**
cold place 333.4
remote region 199.4
**sibilant** 457.3
**sibilate** hiss 457.2
utter 594.26
**sibilation** sibilance 457
speech defect 595.1
**sibling**
n. kinsmen 11.2
adj. related 11.6
**sibyl** 543.6
**sic** 516.19
**sick**
disconsolate 872.28
ill 686.52
insane 473.25
weary 884.10
**sick bay** 689.27
**sicken** afflict 686.47
contract 686.44
get worse 692.19
offend 864.11
**sicken at** 867.4
**sickening**
offensive 864.18
unsavory 429.7
**sick humor** 881.1
**sickle** 252.5
**sick leave** 187.4
**sickle-cell anemia**
blood disease 686.18
genetic disease 686.11
**sickly** colorless 363.7
unhealthy 686.50
**sick mind** 473.1
**sickness** disease 686.1
insanity 473.1
**sick of** bored 884.10
satiated 664.6
**sick person** 686.40
**sickroom** 689.27
**sic on** incite 648.17
sow dissension 795.14
**siddur** 1040.12
**side**
n. ancestry 170.4
arrogance 912.1
aspect 446.3
bluster 911.1
boasting 910.1
border 235.4
conceit 909.4
faction 788.4
flank 242
incline 219.4
ostentation 904.2
role 611.11
script 611.26
side of controversy 482.14
straight line 250.2
viewpoint 525.2
v. border 235.10
flank 242.4
set aside 271.10
turn aside 291.6
adj. indirect 219.13

put to silence 451.8
refute 506.5
render powerless
 158.11
strike dead 409.18
suppress 760.8
*interj.* hush! 451.14
**silencer** 451.4
**silent** still 451.10
 taciturn 613.9
 unexpressed 546.9
**silent film** 611.16
**silent majority**
 mediocrity 680.5
 party 788.4
**silhouette**
 *n.* form 246.2
 outline 235.2
 picture 574.14
 portrait 574.16
 reflection 24.7
 shadow 337.3
 *v.* outline 235.9
**silicic** 383.15
**silicone** 380.2
**silicosis** 686.14
**silk** fabric 378.5,11
 fine texture 351.3
 lawyer 1003.4
 smooth surface 260.3
 softness 357.4
**silken** sleek 260.10
 soft 357.15
**silk-screen printing**
 graphic art 578.5
 printing 603.1
**silk-stocking**
 *n.* nobleman 918.4
 *adj.* elite 644.16
**silky** sleek 260.10
 smooth 351.8
 soft 357.15
 threadlike 206.7
**sill** foundation 216.6
 threshold 216.9
**silly**
 *n.* a fool 471.6
 *adj.* dazed 532.14
 foolish 470.8
 nonsensical 547.7
 trivial 673.16
**silo** granary 660.7
 rocketry 281.10
**silt** deposit 271.8
 dregs 43.2
**silvan** see **sylvan**
**silver**
 *n.* chemical element
 379.10
 currency metals
 835.20
 lightness 364.1
 money 835.1
 tableware 348.3
 whiteness 364.2
 *v.* gray 366.3
 whiten 364.5
 *adj.* eloquent 600.8
 gray 366.4
 metal 383.17
 white 364.7
**silvering** 364.3

**silver lining** 888.3
**silver plate**
 flatware 348.3
 plating 228.13
**silver-plate** 228.26
**silver-plated**
 metal 383.17
 plated 228.32
**silver-tongued**
 eloquent 600.8
 melodious 462.49
**silverware**
 hard goods 831.4
 tableware 348.3
**silvery** gray 366.4
 melodious 462.49
 metal 383.17
 white 364.7
**silviculture**
 forestry 413.3
 woodland 411.11
**similar**
 approximate 9.8
 comparable 491.8
 like 20.10
**similarity**
 comparability 491.3
 likeness 20
 relationship 9.1
**similarize**
 approximate 20.8
 make agree 26.7
**similarly**
 additionally 40.11
 correspondingly
 20.18
 thus 8.10
**simile**
 comparison 491.1
 figure of speech
 551.5
 similarity 20.1
**similitude**
 comparison 491.1
 copy 24.1
 image 572.3
 likeness 20.3
 similarity 20.1
**simmer**
 be angry 952.15
 be hot 328.22
 boil 329.20
 bubble 405.4
 cook 330.4
 seethe 162.11
**simmer down** 858.7
**Simon Legree** 749.14
**simon-pure**
 genuine 516.14
 hypocritical 616.33
 simple 45.6
**simpatico** 927.14
**simper**
 *n.* smile 876.3
 *v.* affect 903.14
 smile 876.7
**simpering** 903.18
**simple** artless 736.5
 easy 732.12
 genuine 516.14
 gullible 502.9
 homelike 191.33

humble 906.9
 ignorant 477.12
 informal 647.3
 intelligible 548.10
 mentally deficient
 469.22
 mere 35.8
 ordinary 902.6
 plain 45.6
 plain-speaking 591.3
 single 89.7
 soft-colored 362.21
 tasteful 897.8
 unaffected 589.6
**simpleminded**
 artless 736.5
 mentally deficient
 469.22
**simpleton** 471.8
**simplicity**
 artlessness 736.1
 facility 732.1
 good taste 897.4
 gullibility 502.2
 ignorance 477.1
 informality 647.1
 intelligibility 548.2
 literary elegance
 589.1
 mental deficiency
 469.9
 paring down 39.1
 plainness 902.1
 plain speech 591.1
 rusticity 182.3
 unity 89.1
 unmixedness 45
**simplification**
 disentanglement 45.2
 explanation 552.4
 facilitation 732.4
**simplified** 45.9
**simplify** clarify 548.6
 explain 552.10
 facilitate 732.6
 make plain 902.5
 pare 39.7
 streamline 45.4
**simplistic**
 oversimplified 45.10
 undeveloped 721.12
**simply** artlessly 736.7
 easily 732.15
 informally 647.4
 in plain words 591.4
 intelligibly 548.12
 plainly 902.10
 purely 45.11
 solely 89.14
 tastefully 897.11
 to a degree 35.10
**simulacrum**
 aspect 446.3
 copy 24.1
 fake 616.13
 illusoriness 519.2
 image 572.3
 likeness 20.3
 representation 616.3
**simulate** affect 903.12
 assume 821.4
 fake 616.21

imitate 22.5
 resemble 20.7
**simulated**
 assumed 903.16
 falsified 616.26
 similar 20.10
**simulation**
 assumption 821.2
 fakery 616.3
 imitation 22.1
 similarity 20.1
**simultaneity**
 accompaniment 73.1
 concurrence 177.1
 instantaneousness
 113.1
 simultaneousness 118
**simultaneous**
 accompanying 73.9
 concurrent 118.4
**simultaneously**
 at once 113.8
 at the same time
 105.9
 concurrently 118.6
**sin**
 *n.* error 518.1
 iniquity 981.3
 misconduct 982.1
 wrong 982.2
 *v.* do wrong 981.8
 transgress 982.5
**since**
 *adv.* ago 119.15
 subsequently 117.6
 until now 119.17
 *conj.* because 155.10
**sincere** artless 736.5
 candid 974.17
 genuine 516.14
 resolute 624.11
 zealous 635.10
**sincerity**
 artlessness 736.1
 authenticity 516.5
 candor 974.4
 resolution 624.1
 zeal 635.2
**sinecure** 732.3
**sine qua non**
 condition 507.2
 important point
 672.6
**sinew** eloquence 600.3
 muscle 159.2
 power 157.1
**sine wave** 323.5
**sinewy** eloquent 600.11
 strong 159.14
 tough 359.4
**sinful** bad 675.7
 evil 981.16
 iniquitous 982.6
 ungodly 1031.17
 wrong 959.3
**sing**
 *n.* music festival
 462.33
 *v.* be cheerful 870.6
 be pleased 865.9
 bird sound 460.5
 divulge 556.6

**six of one and half a
dozen of the other**
choicelessness 639.6
equality 30.3
identical 14.8
indistinctive 493.6
**six-shooter** gun 801.5
weapon 801.27
**sixth**
*n.* fraction 99.14
harmonics 463.20
*adj.* six 99.18
**sixth sense**
clairvoyance 1034.8
intuition 481.1
sense 422.5
**sizable**
considerable 195.16
large 34.7
**size**
*n.* largeness 195
semiliquid 389.5
book size 605.14
*v.* adjust 195.15
arrange 60.11
examine 485.23
measure 490.11
**size up** examine 485.23
measure 490.11
scrutinize 439.15
**sizzle** *n.* hissing 457.1
*v.* be angry 952.15
hiss 457.2
speed 269.8
**sizzler** hot day 328.8
percussion instrument
465.18
speeder 269.5
**sizzling**
*n.* sibilation 457.1
snap 456.2
*adj.* angry 952.27
sibilant 457.3
**skate**
*n.* ice skates 272.20
vertebrate 415.7
*v.* glide 273.34
**skateboard**
*n.* skates 272.20
*v.* glide 273.34
**skating** 273.8
**skedaddle**
*v.* be a coward 892.8
be frightened 891.20
flee 631.10
leave 301.10
rush 269.9
*interj.* go away!
310.30
**skein** filament 206.1
geese 74.6
**skeletal** lean 205.17
skeleton 245.10
wasted 205.20
**skeleton**
*n.* abridgment 607.1
bones 245.5
corpse 408.16
diagram 654.3
frame 245.4
outline 235.2
support 216.10

thinness 205.7
thin person 205.8
wreck 692.10
*adj.* skeletal 245.10
**skeptic** 1031.12
**skeptical**
agnostic 1031.20
doubtful 503.9
incredulous 504.4
uncertain 514.15
**skepticism**
agnosticism 1031.6
doubt 503.2
incredulity 504.1
**sketch**
*n.* abridgment 607.1
act 611.8
description 608.1
diagram 654.3
essay 606.1
picture 574.14
stage show 611.4
*v.* abridge 607.5
act 611.34
describe 608.12
outline 654.12
picture 574.20
plot 654.11
**sketchbook**
art equipment 574.19
book 605.1
**sketching** 574.6
**sketchy**
imperfect 678.4
incomplete 57.4
**skew**
*n.* bend 219.3
deviation 291.1
*v.* deflect 291.5
diverge 219.9
go sideways 242.5
squint 440.9
unbalance 31.3
*adj.* askew 219.14
deviant 291.8
unequal 31.4
**skewed** askew 219.14
deviant 291.8
unequal 31.4
**skewer** fasten 47.8
puncture 265.16
**ski**
*n.* vehicle 272.20
*v.* glide 273.34
**skid**
*n.* slide 316.4
*v.* fly 278.49
glide 273.34
go sideways 242.5
slide 316.9
**skid row** 183.6
**skiing** 273.8
**ski lift** 657.9
**skill** art 733.7
memory 537.1
skillfulness 733
superiority 36.1
**skilled**
accomplished 733.24
proficient in 733.25
**skillful** expert 733.20
good 674.12

**skill-less** 734.15
**skim** browse 564.13
examine cursorily
485.25
float 275.54
glide 273.34
graze 200.10
neglect 534.8
scratch the surface
210.4
slide 316.9
speed 269.8
touch lightly 425.7
**skimp**
be parsimonious
852.5
economize 851.4
neglect 534.8
**skimping**
*n.* economizing 851.2
parsimony 852.1
*adj.* economical 851.6
meager 102.5
negligent 534.10
parsimonious 852.7
**skimpy** meager 662.10
sparse 102.5
**skin**
*n.* coating 228.12
contraceptive 687.23
dermis 229
diseases of 686.33
exterior 224.2
hull 228.16
layer 227.2
peel 229.2
shallowness 210.1
US money 835.7
*v.* abrade 350.7
best 36.7
defeat 727.6
despoil 822.24
injure 692.15
overcharge 848.7
peel 232.8
tear apart 49.14
**skin-deep**
cutaneous 229.6
insignificant 35.6
shallow 210.5
**skin diving** 320.3
**skin flick**
obscenity 990.4
pornographic film
611.16
**skinflint** 852.4
**skinful**
full measure 56.3
satiety 664.1
**skin game** 618.9
**skinned** 727.14
**skinny** cutaneous 229.6
lean 205.17
**skinny-dip** 275.56
**skin-popping**
drug dose 687.6
narcotic injection
689.18
**skip**
*n.* leap 319.1
step 273.13
*v.* be absent 187.9

be cheerful 870.6
dance 879.5
escape 632.6
flee 631.10
jump 319.6
leap 319.5
leave 301.10
omit 534.7
play 878.25
rejoice 876.5
walk 273.27
**skip it** 673.22
**skip over**
examine cursorily
485.25
neglect 534.8
**skipper**
*n.* captain 276.7
naval officer 749.20
*v.* direct 747.8
**skirmish**
*n.* fight 796.4
*v.* contend 796.14
**skirt**
*n.* border 235.4
dress 231.16
girl 125.6
outskirts 235.1
types of 231.55
woman 421.6
*v.* avoid 631.7
border 235.10
flank 242.4
go around 321.4
graze 200.10
**skit** act 611.8
stage show 611.4
**skittish**
excitable 857.26
fearful 891.31
fickle 629.6
frisky 870.14
sensitive 422.14
shy 908.12
**Skivvies** 231.22,58
**skoal!** 996.37
**skulduggery** 618.4
**skulk**
*n.* foxes 74.5
shirker 631.3
*v.* cower 892.9
lurk 615.9
shirk 631.9
**skulk away** 631.12
**skulking**
cowering 892.13
in hiding 615.14
sneaking 614.12
**skull** cranium 211.7
death symbol 408.3
**skull and crossbones**
death symbol 408.3
insignia 569.1
warning sign 703.3
**skull session** 562.7
**skunk**
*n.* bad person 986.7
stinker 437.3
wild animal 414.28
*v.* overwhelm 727.8
**sky** heavens 375.2
height 207.2

**sleepiness**
  drowsiness 712
  fatigue 717.1
  languor 708.6
**sleeping** asleep 712.22
  dead 408.30
  inattentive 531.8
  inert 268.14
  latent 546.5
**sleeping bag** 216.20
**sleeping pill**
  depressant 423.3
  sedative 687.12
**sleeping sickness**
  infectious disease
    686.12
  stupor 712.6
**sleep it off**
  recuperate 694.19
  sober up 997.2
**sleepless** alert 533.14
  industrious 707.22
  persevering 625.7
  vigilant 533.13
  wakeful 713.7
**sleeplessness**
  alertness 533.5
  wakefulness 713.1
**sleep on**
  postpone 132.9
  take under consider-
    ation 478.14
**sleepwalk** 273.31
**sleepwalker**
  nightwalker 274.7
  sleeper 712.12
**sleepwalking**
  nightwalking 273.11
  sleep 712.2
  trance state 690.26
**sleep with** 419.23
**sleepy** drowsy 712.21
  languid 708.19
**sleepyhead**
  sleeper 712.12
  slow person 270.5
**sleet**
  *n.* ice 333.5
  *v.* storm 333.11
**sleety** 333.14
**leigh**
  *n.* sled 272.19
  *v.* glide 273.34
**leigh bell** 454.4
**leight** chicanery 618.4
  stratagem 735.3
  trick 618.6
**leight of hand**
  illusoriness 519.2
  juggling 618.5
  trick 618.6
**ender**
  beautiful 900.17
  meager 662.10
  narrow 205.14
  thin 205.16
  trivial 673.16
**enderize** 205.13
**enderizing**
  *1.* reducing 205.9
  *adj.* reducing 205.21
**euth** 781.10

**sleuthing** 485.4
**slew** bunch 74.7
  much 34.4
**slice**
  *n.* layer 227.2
  piece 55.3
  portion 816.5
  slash 49.4
  *v.* apportion 816.6
  sever 49.11
**slice of life** 608.1
**slick**
  *v.* oil 380.8
  polish 260.7
  *adj.* cunning 735.12
  glib 600.8
  oily 380.9
  shrewd 467.15
  skillful 733.20
  sleek 260.10
  slippery 260.11
  tidy 59.8
  *adv.* cunningly 735.13
**slicked up** 231.45
**slicker** sharper 619.4
  smoother 260.4
  sophisticate 733.16
**slide**
  *n.* escape 632.3
  glide 273.8
  photograph 577.3
  slip 316.4
  smooth surface 260.3
  transparency 577.5
  wind instrument
    465.7
  *v.* decline 692.20
  elapse 105.5
  glide 273.34
  go easily 732.9
  slip 316.9
**slide back** 696.4
**slide projector** 577.12
**slide trombone** 465.8
**sliding**
  *n.* gliding 273.8
  *adj.* deteriorating
    692.46
**sliding scale** 841.4
**slight**
  *n.* neglect 534.1
  nonobservance 769.1
  snub 966.2
  *v.* disparage 971.8
  disregard 531.2
  flout 793.4
  ignore 966.6
  neglect 534.8
  *adj.* frail 160.14
  little 196.10
  meager 662.10
  shallow 210.5
  tenuous 355.4
  thin 205.16
  trivial 673.16
**slighted** 534.14
**slightest** 37.8
**slightly**
  meagerly 662.15
  on a small scale
    196.16
  scarcely 35.9

  to a degree 29.7
**slim**
  *n.* thin person 205.8
  *adj.* meager 662.10
  sparse 102.5
  thin 205.16
**slim down** 205.13
**slime** filth 682.7
  mud 389.8
  slop 682.8
**slimming** 205.21
**slim pickings** 662.2
**slimy** filthy 682.23
  flattering 970.8
  viscous 389.12
**sling**
  *n.* medical dressing
    687.33
  throw 285.4
  weapon 801.18
  *v.* hurl 798.28
  suspend 215.8
  throw 285.11
**slingshot** 801.18
**slink** cower 892.9
  creep 273.25
  lurk 615.9
  twist 254.4
  walk 273.27
**slink off** 631.12
**slinky** cowering 892.13
  furtive 614.12
  thin 205.16
**slip**
  *n.* anchorage 277.16
  an error 518.4
  aviation 278.25
  bungle 734.5
  ceramic material
    576.3
  evasive action 631.1
  failure 725.4
  girl 125.6
  harbor 700.6
  little thing 196.4
  misdeed 982.2
  mud 389.8
  pillowcase 228.10
  record 570.10
  scion 411.18
  slide 316.4
  sprout 125.9
  strip 206.4
  thinness 205.7
  trial print 603.5
  youngster 125.1
  *v.* bungle 734.11
  decline 692.20
  degenerate 729.11
  drift 275.54
  elapse 105.5
  err 518.9
  fail 725.13
  give 818.12
  glide 273.34
  lapse 981.9
  sink 725.10
  slide 316.9
**slip, the** 735.5
**slip away**
  absent oneself 187.8
  avoid 631.12

  escape 632.9
**slip back**
  get worse 692.19
  regress 295.5
  relapse 696.4
  revert 146.4
**slip in** enter 302.7
  insert 304.3
  intrude 238.5
**slip into** 231.42
**slip of the tongue** 518.4
**slip out of**
  absent oneself 187.8
  avoid 631.12
  shirk 631.9
  slip away 632.9
  take off 232.6
**slippage**
  deterioration 692.3
  slide 316.4
**slippery**
  cunning 735.12
  deceitful 618.20
  dishonest 975.16
  evasive 631.15
  oily 380.9
  precarious 697.12
  slick 260.11
  treacherous 975.21
  unreliable 514.19
**slipping**
  deteriorating 692.46
  dying 408.33
  out of practice
    734.18
**slipshod** careless 62.15
  slovenly 534.12
  ungrammatical 587.4
  unstrict 758.4
**slipup** error 518.4
  failure 725.4
**slip up** err 518.9
  fail 725.13
**slit**
  *n.* break 49.4
  crack 201.2
  groove 263.1
  *v.* cleave 201.4
  groove 263.3
  injure 692.15
  open 265.12
  sever 49.11
  *adj.* cleft 201.7
  damaged 692.29
  grooved 263.4
  severed 49.23
**slither**
  *n.* gait 273.14
  glide 273.8
  slide 316.4
  *v.* glide 273.34
  slide 316.9
  walk 273.27
**slithering**
  *n.* gliding 273.8
  *adj.* reptile 414.51
**slithery** slippery 260.11
  viscous 389.12
**sliver** intrusion 78.2
  piece 55.3
  small amount 35.3
**slob** bungler 734.9

disorderly person
62.7
ice 333.5
mud 389.8
slime 682.8
**slobber**
*n.* flattery 970.2
saliva 312.3
*v.* be insane 473.19
be unintelligent
469.12
moisten 392.12
salivate 312.6
**slobber over**
emotionalize 855.15
flatter 970.5
**sloe** 365.8
**slog** drudge 716.14
hit 283.13
persevere 625.3
walk 273.27
**slogan**
call to arms 797.12
motto 517.4
phrase 582.9
**slop**
*n.* muck 389.8
mud puddle 389.9
offal 682.9
refuse 669.4
sentimentality 855.8
slime 682.8
*v.* moisten 392.12
overflow 395.17
**slope**
*n.* grade 219.4
inclination 219.2
*v.* incline 219.10
**sloping** 219.15
**sloppy** clumsy 734.20
filthy 682.23
loose 51.5
muddy 389.14
sentimental 855.22
slipshod 534.12
slovenly 62.15
unstrict 758.4
watery 392.16
**slops** clothes 231.5
fodder 308.4
offal 682.9
refuse 669.4
**slosh**
*n.* lapping 395.8
mud 389.8
slime 682.8
snow 333.8
splash 392.5
*v.* make a liquid sound
452.11
moisten 392.12
overflow 395.17
splash 395.19
**sloshy** filthy 682.23
muddy 389.14
**slot**
*n.* crack 201.2
opening 265.1
syntax 586.2
*v.* cut 201.4
**sloth** apathy 856.4
bear pack 74.5

despair 889.2
indolence 708.5
languor 708.6
mammal 415.8,58
sin 982.3
slowness 270.1
torpor 1.6
unconcern 636.2
**slothful**
indolent 708.18
slow 270.10
**slot machine**
gambling device
515.12
vending machine
832.8
**slotted** 265.20
**slouch**
*n.* awkward person
734.8
gait 273.14
idler 708.8
slowness 270.2
*v.* droop 316.6
idle 708.11
walk 273.27
**slough**
*n.* castoff skin 229.5
gangrene 686.37
marsh 400.1
morass 731.4
mud puddle 389.9
offal 682.9
putrefaction 692.7
*v.* discard 668.7
shed 232.10
**slovenly** dirty 682.22
disorderly 62.15
slipshod 534.12
ungrammatical 587.4
**slow**
*v.* slow down 270.9
*adj.* indolent 708.18
infrequent 136.2
languid 708.19
late 132.16
leisurely 710.6
lingering 132.17
not fast 270.10
reluctant 623.6
stupid 469.16
uninteresting 883.6
*adv.* late 132.19
slowly 270.13
tardily 132.20
**slowdown**
business cycle 827.9
decrease 39.2
delay 132.2
economizing 851.2
slowing 270.4
strike 789.7
**slow down** delay 132.8
moderate 163.6
prevent 730.13
relax 711.7
retard 760.7
retrench 851.5
slow up 270.9
strike 789.9
**slowing down**
restraint 760.1

slowing 270.4
**slowly** dully 883.10
gradually 29.6
slow 270.13
tardily 132.20
**slow motion** 270.2
**slowness** delay 132.2
gait 273.14
indolence 708.5
infrequency 136.1
languor 708.6
leisureliness 710.2
procrastination 132.5
slow motion 270
stupidity 469.3
uninterestingness
883.1
unwillingness 623.1
**slowpoke** 270.5
**slow starter** 132.6
**slow time**
march 273.15
time 114.3
**slow up** 270.9
**slow-up** delay 132.2
slowing 270.4
**slow-witted** 469.16
**sludge** ice 333.5
mud 389.8
slime 682.8
**sludgy** filthy 682.23
muddy 389.14
**sluff** see **slough**
**slug**
*n.* bullet 801.13
dose 55.5
hit 283.4
idler 708.8
invertebrate 415.5
printing 603.7
slow person 270.5
token 835.12
typesetting 603.2
*v.* hit 283.13
**slugabed**
lazy person 708.7
sleeper 712.12
**sluggard** idler 708.8
slow person 270.5
**sluggish**
apathetic 856.13
dilatory 132.17
inert 268.14
languid 708.19
meandering 395.24
slow 270.10
stupid 469.16
**sluice**
*n.* channel 396.5
floodgate 396.11
outlet 303.9
stream bed 396.2
*v.* drench 392.14
flow out 303.13
wash 681.19
**slum** city district 183.6
filthy place 682.11
**slumber**
*n.* rest 268.1
sleep 712.2
*v.* sleep 712.13
stagnate 268.9

**slumberer** 712.12
**slumbering**
asleep 712.22
inert 268.14
**slumberland** 712.2
**slumlord** 809.3
**slummy**
dilapidated 692.35
squalid 682.25
**slump**
*n.* business cycle 827.9
decrease 39.2
depreciation 849.4
deterioration 692.3
droop 316.2
hard times 729.6
shortcoming 314.1
stock market 833.5
*v.* decline 692.20
devaluate 849.6
droop 316.6
lag 314.2
**slur**
*n.* disparagement
971.4
harmonics 463.12
music style 462.31
stigma 915.6
*v.* blemish 679.6
defame 971.9
examine cursorily
485.25
neglect 534.8
stigmatize 915.9
**slur over**
examine cursorily
485.25
extenuate 1006.12
neglect 534.8
obscure 615.6
**slurp**
*n.* drink 307.4
ingestion 306.4
*v.* drink 307.28
inhale 306.12
**slurp up** 306.13
**slush**
garrulousness 596.1
mud 389.8
sentimentality 855.8
slime 682.8
snow 333.8
**slush fund** 744.35
**slushy** filthy 682.23
muddy 389.14
sleety 333.14
**slut** dog 414.22
female animal 421.9
filthy person 682.13
neglecter 534.5
slob 62.7
unchaste woman
989.14
**sluttish** slipshod 534.1?
slovenly 62.15
**sly** cunning 735.12
furtive 614.12
shrewd 467.15
**smack**
*n.* characteristic 80.4
explosive noise 456.?
heroin 687.12

hint 44.7
hit 283.4
kiss 932.3
punishment 1010.3
slap 283.7
small amount 35.4
taste 427.1
*v.* collide 283.12
hit 283.13
kiss 932.17
make explosive noise
456.6
punish 1010.13
slap 283.16
taste 427.7
*adv.* squarely 290.25
suddenly 113.9
**smacking**
energetic 161.12
lively 707.17
**smack of** resemble 20.7
savor of 428.6
**small**
*adj.* base 915.12
humble 906.9
inferior 37.7
insignificant 35.6
little 196.10
meager 662.10
narrow-minded
527.10
selfish 978.6
thin 205.16
unimportant 673.15
*adv.* on a small scale
196.16
**small chance**
doubtfulness 512.1
gambling odds 515.6
unlikelihood 156.9
**small change**
petty cash 835.19
trifles 673.4
**smaller** fewer 102.6
reduced 39.10
**smallest** 37.8
**small fry**
little thing 196.4
nobodies 673.7
young people 125.2
**small hours**
foredawn 133.4
lateness 132.1
**small-minded** 527.10
**smallness**
baseness 915.3
humility 906.1
inferiority 37.3
littleness 196.1
meagerness 662.2
narrow-mindedness
527.1
selfishness 978.2
small amount 35
sparsity 102.1
unimportance 673.1
**small potatoes**
a nobody 673.7
mediocrity 680.5
**smallpox** 686.12
**small print** 507.2
**small talk** 597.5

**small-time** 673.17
**smarm** 970.2
**smarmy** 970.8
**smart**
*n.* pain 424.3
*v.* feel acutely 855.16
resent 952.12
suffer pain 424.8
*adj.* alert 533.14
elegant 644.13
fashionable 644.11
impudent 913.9
intelligent 467.14
quick 707.18
ridiculing 967.12
tidy 59.8
witty 881.15
**smart aleck**
egotist 909.5
impudent person
913.5
**smart-alecky**
conceited 909.11
impudent 913.9
ridiculing 967.12
**smart ass**
impudent person
913.5
wiseacre 468.6
**smart-ass**
impudent 913.9
ridiculing 967.12
**smarten up** 901.8
**smarts** intellect 466.1
intelligence 467.2
**smart set** 644.6
**smarty** 913.5
**smash**
*n.* concussion 162.8
defeat 727.1
destruction 693.4
failure 725.3
great success 724.3
hit 283.4
impact 283.3
pulp 390.2
stock market 833.5
wreck 729.2
*v.* collide 283.12
conquer 727.10
demolish 693.17
level 693.19
mash 357.6
pulp 390.2
pulverize 361.9
shatter 49.13
suppress 760.8
surge 395.22
**smashed**
conquered 727.16
damaged 692.29
drunk 996.31
suppressed 760.14
**smashing**
*n.* bookbinding
605.15
demolition 693.5
impact 283.3
pulverization 361.4
suppression 760.2
*adj.* concussive 283.21
excellent 674.13

**smashup**
destruction 693.4
impact 283.3
wreck 729.2
**smattering**
dabbling 673.8
slight knowledge
477.6
small amount 35.4
**smear**
*n.* blemish 679.3
defamation 971.2
soil 682.5
stigma 915.6
*v.* blemish 679.6
coat 228.24
color 362.13
daub 380.8
overwhelm 727.8
soil 682.16
stigmatize 915.9
vilify 971.10
**smell**
*n.* odor 435.1
sense 422.5
smelling 435.4
trace 35.4
*v.* be aromatic 435.6
detect 488.6
scent 435.8
sense 422.8
stink 437.4
trace 485.34
**smell bad** 437.4
**smell good** 436.7
**smelly**
malodorous 437.5
odorous 435.9
**smelt** melt 329.21
process 167.11
**smelter** 719.5
**smelting** burning 329.5
manufacture 167.3
**smidgen** 35.2
**smile**
*n.* greeting 925.4
grin 876.3
*v.* be cheerful 870.6
be pleased 865.9
grin 876.7
**smile upon** 785.14
**smiling**
*n.* grin 876.3
*adj.* cheerful 870.11
happy 865.13
**smirch**
*n.* blemish 679.3
smear 682.5
smudging 365.5
stigma 915.6
*v.* blemish 679.6
smudge 365.7
soil 682.16
vilify 971.10
**smirched**
blemished 679.10
dingy 365.11
soiled 682.21
unchaste 989.23
**smirk**
*n.* ridicule 967.4
smile 876.3

*v.* simper 903.14
smile 876.7
**smirking** happy 865.13
ridiculing 967.12
**smite** hit 283.13
impress 855.17
punish 1010.14
**smith** artisan 718.7
producer 167.8
types of 718.10
**smithereen** piece 55.3
small amount 35.3
**smithy** 719.5
**smitten**
enamored 931.26
fond of 931.28
**smock** 231.17
**smog** 404.2
**smoke**
*n.* black 365.4
fume 329.16
spirit 4.3
tobacco 434.3
tobacco smoking
434.10
transient 111.5
vapor 401.1
*v.* be angry 952.15
blacken 365.7
cloud 404.6
dirty 682.15
dry 393.6
emit 310.23
evaporate 401.8
fume 328.23
preserve 701.8
stain 679.6
use tobacco 434.14
**smoke out** 310.14
**smoker** party 922.11
railway car 272.14
smoking room 434.13
tobacco user 434.11
**smoke screen**
disguise 618.10
pretext 649.1
**smokestack** 396.18
**smoking**
*n.* preserving 701.2
tobacco smoking
434.10
vaporization 401.5
*adj.* burning 328.27
smoky 401.9
tobacco 434.15
**smoky** dingy 365.11
dirty 682.22
gray 366.4
smoking 401.9
stained 679.10
**smolder**
be angry 952.15
be excited 857.15
be hot 328.22
be latent 546.3
stagnate 268.9
**smoldering**
angry 952.27
burning 328.27
inert 268.14
**smooch**
*n.* kiss 932.3

*v.* kiss 932.17
make love 932.13
**smooth**
*v.* appease 804.7
calm 163.7
facilitate 732.6
flatten 260.5
give texture 351.4
level 214.6
make uniform 17.4
rub 350.8
straighten 250.5
*adj.* calm 268.12
continuous 71.8
cunning 735.12
easy 732.12
eloquent 600.8
fine 351.8
flat 260.9
flattering 970.8
fluent 600.9
hairless 232.17
harmonious 589.8
horizontal 214.7
slick 380.9
straight 250.6
suave 936.18
talkative 596.9
uniform 17.5
**smoother** polish 260.4
types of 260.13
**smoothly**
cunningly 735.13
easily 732.15
eloquently 600.15
evenly 260.12
quietly 268.18
**smooth-running** 732.13
**smooth sailing** 732.1
**smooth talker** 735.6
**smooth the way**
facilitate 732.6
make possible 509.5
make probable 511.4
oil 380.8
**smooth-tongued**
eloquent 600.8
flattering 970.8
suave 936.18
**smorgasbord**
appetizer 308.9
restaurant 307.15
**smother** be hot 328.22
control feelings 858.8
destroy 693.15
die 408.24
extinguish 332.7
hush up 614.8
restrain 163.6
strangle 409.19
suppress 760.8
wrap 228.20
**smothered**
muffled 452.17
secret 614.11
suppressed 760.14
**smudge**
*n.* blackening 365.5
fume 401.1
smoke 329.16
soil 682.5
stain 679.3

stigma 915.6
*v.* blacken 365.7
smoke 328.23
soil 682.16
**smudged** 682.21
**smudgy** dingy 365.11
dirty 682.22
**smug** chic 644.13
complacent 868.10
prudish 903.19
suave 936.18
vain 909.8
**smuggle** 826.8
**smuggler** 826.5
**smuggling** 826.2
**smugness**
affectation 903.6
contentment 868.2
suavity 936.5
vanity 909.1
**smut**
*n.* ashes 329.16
black 365.4
blemish 679.3
blight 676.2
darkening 365.5
dirt 682.6
filth 682.7
fungus 411.4,45
obscenity 990.4
powder 361.5
residue 43.2
soil 682.5
*v.* blacken 365.7
soil 682.16
**smutty** dingy 365.11
dirty 682.22
obscene 990.9
spoiled 692.43
**snack**
*n.* light meal 307.7
piece 55.3
*v.* eat 307.24
**snack bar** 307.15
**snafu**
*n.* complex 46.2
mix-up 62.2
*v.* confuse 63.3
spoil 692.13
thwart 730.16
*adj.* confused 62.16
**snag**
*n.* difficulty 731.7
fault 678.2
hidden danger 697.5
obstacle 730.4
pointed projection
258.4
tooth 258.5
*v.* catch 822.17
**snaggled** rough 261.7
toothed 258.16
**snail** food 308.25
invertebrate 415.5
slow person 270.5
**snail's pace** 270.2
**snake**
*n.* bad person 986.7
serpent 414.31
traitor 619.10
types of 414.61
*v.* creep 273.25

jerk 286.5
pull 286.4
twist 254.4
wander 291.4
**snake eyes** 90.3
**snake in the grass**
evil 675.3
hidden danger 697.5
traitor 619.10
**snake oil** 687.2
**snake pit** 46.2
**snaky**
convolutional 254.6
cunning 735.12
reptile 414.51
wandering 291.7
winding 254.7
**snap**
*n.* bite 307.2
cold weather 333.3
crack 456.2
easy thing 732.3
elasticity 358.1
photograph 577.3
pungency 433.2
tap 283.6
trifle 673.5
vim 161.2
*v.* animal sound 460.4
be damaged 692.26
break 49.12
close 266.6
crack 456.7
fasten 47.8
hit 283.13
photograph 577.14
show resentment
952.14
tap 283.15
throw 285.11
utter 594.26
*adj.* hasty 709.9
impulsive 630.11
unprepared 721.8
**snap at** be angry 952.16
seize on 822.16
**snap back** react 284.5
recoil 284.6
**snap judgment** 630.4
**snap out of it**
cheer up 870.9
recover 694.20
**snapper** 453.5
**snapping**
*n.* snap 456.2
*adj.* cracking 456.10
**snappish** 951.19
**snappy** cold 333.14
energetic 161.12
fast 269.19
lively 707.17
pungent 433.7
**snapshot** 577.3
**snap up** energize 161.9
seize 822.14
**snare**
*n.* drum 465.19
lure 650.2
trap 618.12
*v.* catch 822.17
steal 824.13
trap 618.18

**snarl**
*n.* complex 46.2
grimace 249.4
harsh sound 458.3
quarrel 795.5
*v.* animal sound 460.4
complicate 46.3
hamper 730.11
show resentment
952.14
sound harshly 458.9
trap 618.18
utter 594.26
wind sound 403.23
**snarled complex** 46.4
disorderly 62.14
**snarled up** 692.31
**snarl up**
complicate 46.3
confuse 63.3
mess up 692.13
**snatch**
*n.* jerk 286.3
piece 55.3
seizure 822.2
*v.* abduct 824.19
force from 822.22
jerk 286.5
jump at 635.7
seize 822.14
steal 824.13
**snazzy** chic 644.13
flashy 904.19
**sneak**
*n.* coward 892.6
rascal 986.3
*v.* cower 892.9
creep 273.25
lurk 615.9
smuggle 826.8
**sneak in** intrude 238.5
join 788.14
**sneaking**
*n.* creeping 273.9
*adj.* cowering 892.13
furtive 614.12
in hiding 615.14
**sneak off** 631.12
**sneak out** 187.8
**sneak preview** 611.16
**sneaky** cowering 892.13
cunning 735.12
deceitful 618.20
furtive 614.12
**sneer**
*n.* ridicule 967.4
snub 966.2
*v.* disdain 966.3
ridicule 967.9
**sneering**
contemptuous 966.8
ridiculing 967.12
**sneeze**
*n.* breathing 403.18
sibilation 457.1
*v.* exhale 403.24
sibilate 457.2
**sneeze at** disdain 966.
disregard 531.4
**snicker**
*n.* laughter 876.4
ridicule 967.4

*v.* laugh 876.8
**snicker at** 967.8
**sniff**
 *n.* breathing 403.18
 inhalation 306.5
 sibilation 457.1
 snub 966.2
 *v.* detect 488.6
 inhale 306.12
 sibilate 457.2
 smell 435.8
 snort 403.24
**sniffle**
 *n.* breathing 403.18
 inhalation 306.5
 sibilation 457.1
 *v.* inhale 306.12
 sibilate 457.2
 snort 403.24
**sniffles, the** 686.14
**sniff out** detect 488.6
 trace 485.34
**sniffy** breathing 403.29
 contemptuous 966.8
 snobbish 912.14
**snifter** 996.6
**snigger**
 *n.* laughter 876.4
 ridicule 967.4
 *v.* laugh 876.8
**sniggle**
 *n.* snare 618.12
 *v.* catch 822.17
 trap 618.18
**snip**
 *n.* minute thing 196.7
 piece 55.3
 runt 196.4
 sailor 276.6
 small amount 35.3
 *v.* sever 49.11
**snipe** criticize 969.14
 fire upon 798.22
 shoot 285.13
**sniper**
 infantryman 800.9
 shooter 285.9
**snippet**
 little thing 196.4
 minute thing 196.7
 piece 55.3
 small amount 35.3
**nippy** gruff 937.7
 snobbish 912.14
**nitch**
 *n.* informer 557.6
 *v.* inform on 557.12
 steal 824.13
**nivel**
 be hypocritical
  616.23
 be sanctimonious
  1029.4
 weep 875.10
**niveler** 1029.3
**niveling**
 *n.* weeping 875.2
 *adj.* obsequious
  907.13
 sanctimonious 1029.5
 weeping 875.17
**ob** 912.7

**snobbery**
 particularity 896.5
 priggishness 912.6
**snobbish**
 contemptuous 966.8
 exclusive 77.8
 particular 896.13
 priggish 912.14
**snoop**
 *n.* curious person
  528.2
 listener 448.5
 meddler 238.4
 *v.* meddle 238.7
 pry 528.4
**snoopy**
 meddlesome 238.9
 prying 528.6
**snoot** 256.7
**snootful**
 full measure 56.3
 satiety 664.1
**snooty**
 contemptuous 966.8
 snobbish 912.14
**snooze**
 *n.* nap 712.3
 *v.* get some shut-eye
  712.14
**snore**
 *n.* breathing 403.18
 harsh sound 458.3
 sibilation 457.1
 *v.* breathe 403.24
 sibilate 457.2
 sleep 712.13
 sound harshly 458.9
**snoring**
 *n.* breathing 403.18
 *adj.* breathing 403.29
 sibilant 457.3
**snorkel**
 diving equipment
  320.5
 extinguisher 332.3
 tube 396.6
**snort**
 *n.* drink 307.4
 intoxication 996.6
 laughter 876.4
 ridicule 967.4
 sibilation 457.1
 snub 966.2
 *v.* animal sound 460.3
 disdain 966.3
 inhale 403.24
 laugh 876.8
 sibilate 457.2
 utter 594.26
**snot** body fluid 388.3
 filth 682.7
**snotty**
 contemptuous 966.8
 mucous 389.13
 snobbish 912.14
**snout** conduit 396.9
 nose 256.7
**snow**
 *n.* cocaine 687.9
 ice 333.8
 television reception
  345.5

**white** 364.2
 *v.* deceive 618.13
 give 818.12
 storm 333.11
**snowball**
 *n.* accumulation 74.9
 snow 333.8
 *v.* ball 255.7
 become larger 197.5
 increase 38.6
**snowbank** 333.8
**snowbird** 642.10
**snow-blind** 441.10
**snowbound**
 frozen 333.18
 restrained 760.15
**snowcapped** 333.17
**snowdrift** pile 74.10
 snow 333.8
**snowed-in** 333.18
**snowfall** 333.8
**snowflake** 333.8
**snow job**
 persuasion 648.3
 subterfuge 618.1
**snowman** figure 572.4
 snow 333.8
**snowmobile** 272.19
**snowshoes** 272.20
**snowstorm** snow 333.8
 storm 162.4
 television reception
  345.5
**snow under**
 overwhelm 727.8
 snow 333.11
**snowy** chaste 988.4
 snowlike 333.17
 white 364.7
**snub**
 *n.* rebuff 966.2
 repulse 289.2
 *v.* hinder 730.10
 ostracize 310.17
 rebuff 966.5
 refuse 776.5
 restrain 760.7
 send away 289.3
 shorten 203.6
 *adj.* shortened 203.9
**snub-nosed**
 deformed 249.12
 stubby 203.10
**snuff**
 *n.* breathing 403.18
 inhalation 306.5
 sibilation 457.1
 tobacco 434.8
 *v.* extinguish 332.7
 inhale 306.12
 sibilate 457.2
 smell 435.8
 snort 403.24
**snuffbox** 434.8
**snuffle**
 *n.* breathing 403.18
 inhalation 306.5
 sanctimony 1029.1
 sibilation 457.1
 *v.* be hypocritical
  616.23

 be sanctimonious
  1029.4
 inhale 306.12
 nasalize 595.10
 sibilate 457.2
 smell 435.8
 snort 403.24
**snuff out**
 destroy 693.15
 extinguish 332.7
**snuffy**
 breathing 403.29
 dirty 682.22
 tobacco 434.15
**snug**
 *v.* make comfortable
  887.9
 *adj.* close 266.12
 comfortable 887.11
 homelike 191.33
 safe 698.7
 seaworthy 277.18
 taciturn 613.9
 tidy 59.8
 unsociable 923.5
**snuggery** cottage 191.9
 nook 192.3
**snuggle** cuddle 932.15
 nestle 887.10
**so**
 *adj.* similar 20.12
 *adv.* accurately 516.19
 equally 30.11
 greatly 34.15
 in this way 657.11
 similarly 20.18
 thus 8.10
 very 34.18
 *conj.* intending 653.12
 provided 507.15
**soak**
 *n.* drenching 392.7
 drunkard 996.11
 *v.* drench 392.13
 extract 305.16
 hit 283.13
 overcharge 848.7
 overload 663.15
 tipple 996.23
**soaked**
 drenched 392.17
 drunk 996.31
 full 56.11
 overfull 663.20
**soaker** drunkard 996.10
 rainstorm 394.2
**soak in**
 be learned 564.7
 be understood 548.5
 filter in 302.10
 sorb 306.13
**soaking**
 *n.* drenching 392.7
 extraction 305.7
 infusion 44.2
 *adj.* absorbent 306.17
 soaked 392.17
 wetting 392.18
**soak up** drink 307.28
 dry 393.6
 learn 564.7
 sorb 306.13

sponge up 393.5
so-and-so 584.2
soap
  n. cleaning agent
    681.17
  flattery 970.1
  television show 611.4
  types of 681.31
  v. flatter 970.6
  wash 681.19
soapbox 216.13
soap opera
  radio broadcast
    344.18
  sentimentality 855.8
  stage show 611.4
soapy flattering 970.8
  foamy 405.7
  oily 380.9
  suave 936.18
soar be high 207.15
  exceed 34.5
  fly 278.45
  move 267.5
  take off 315.10
soaring
  n. ascent 315.1
  aviation 278.1
  course 267.2
  adj. eminent 34.9
  flowing 267.8
  high 207.19
sob
  n. lament 875.3
  v. sigh 452.14
  speak poorly 595.9
  utter 594.26
  weep 875.10
  wind sound 403.23
SOB 986.6
sobbing
  n. sigh 452.8
  weeping 875.2
  adj. weeping 875.17
so be it 521.19
sober dark 365.9
  dignified 905.12
  gray 366.4
  in plain style 591.3
  moderate 163.10
  sedate 858.14
  sensible 467.18
  soft-colored 362.21
  solemn 871.3
  temperate 992.9
  thoughtful 478.21
  unintoxicated 997.3
  weighty 672.19
soberly
  dignifiedly 905.14
  moderately 163.17
  sedately 858.17
  solemnly 871.4
sober up
  become unintoxi-
    cated 997.2
  come to one's senses
    472.2
  moderate 163.6
sobriety
  blackness 365.2
  moderation 163.1

pride 905.2
  sanity 472.1
  sedateness 858.4
  sensibleness 467.6
  solemnity 871.1
  temperance 992.1
  unintoxicatedness
    997
sobriquet 583.7
sob sister 605.22
sob story 855.8
so-called
  nominal 583.15
  pretexted 649.5
  ungenuine 616.26
soccer 878.8,34
sociability
  communicativeness
    554.3
  friendship 927.1
  good behavior 737.2
  gregariousness 922
  informality 647.1
  talkativeness 596.1
sociable
  associational 788.17
  communicative
    554.10
  friendly 927.14
  informal 647.3
  social 922.18
  talkative 596.9
social
  n. social gathering
    922.10
  adj. amiable 922.18
  associational 788.17
  communal 815.9
  public 417.13
social call 922.7
social class
  community 788.2
  social grouping 922.5
social climber 919.10
social climbing 634.10
social-climbing 634.28
social convention
  custom 642.1
  social usage 645
social director 878.22
social grace
  etiquette 646.3
  sociability 922.1
social intercourse
  communication
    554.1
  sociability 922.4
socialism
  collective ownership
    745.6
  participation 815.2
  principle of govern-
    ment 741.8
socialist 745.14
socialist(ic)
  communal 815.9
  socialist 745.22
Socialist Party 744.24
socialite 644.7
socialize
  appropriate 822.20
  communize 815.7

make better 691.9
  politicize 745.16
socialized medicine
  medicine 688.1
  welfare program
    745.7
social outcast 926.4
social pressure 744.29
Social Register 570.9
social science
  behavior 737.1
  science 475.10
social security
  insurance 699.4
  welfare program
    745.7
social service 938.5
social set 922.5
social work 938.5
social worker 938.8
society
  n. association 788.1
  community 788.2
  company 73.2
  culture 642.3
  ethnic group 418.1
  fellowship 788.3
  laity 1039.1
  mankind 417.2
  people of fashion
    644.6
  population 190.1
  religion 1020.3
  sociability 922.6
  adj. associational
    788.17
socio-economic 827.22
sociologist 417.7
sociology 417.7
sock
  n. comedy 611.7
  costume 231.9
  hit 283.4
  hosiery 231.28,61
  v. clothe 231.39
  hit 283.13
sockdolager
  disproof 506.3
  end-all 70.4
socket 257.2
Socrates 468.2
Socratic 500.10
sod land 385.1
  turf 411.6
soda drink 308.48,49
  extinguisher 332.3
soda jerk 750.7
sodden
  v. soak 392.13
  adj. cooked 330.8
  intoxicated 996.30
  soaked 392.17
Sodom 981.7
sodomist 419.17
sodomy 419.9
sofa couch 216.19
  types of 216.32
so far thus far 235.16
  to a degree 35.10
  until now 120.4
soft
  comfortable 887.11

cowardly 892.10
  easy 732.12
  effeminate 421.14
  faint-sounding 452.16
  gullible 502.9
  impotent 158.13
  lenient 759.7
  light 353.11
  loving 931.25
  mentally deficient
    469.21
  moderate 163.10
  muddy 389.14
  not hard 357.8
  out of practice
    734.18
  pacific 803.9
  phonetic 594.31
  pitying 944.7
  pulpy 390.6
  sentimental 855.22
  soft-colored 362.21
  tender 855.21
  unintoxicating 997.4
  unstrict 758.4
  weak 160.12
soft-cover 605.1
soft drink 308.48
soften affect 855.16
  cushion 163.8
  excite pity 944.5
  extenuate 1006.12
  feminize 421.12
  lose distinctness
    445.4
  mash 357.6
  moderate 163.6
  muffle 451.9
  qualify 507.3
  relieve 886.5
softened
  muffled 452.17
  not hard 357.8
  penitent 873.9
  qualified 507.10
  restrained 163.11
  soft-colored 362.21
softening
  n. extenuation 1006.5
  making soft 357.5
  moderation 163.2
  relief 886.1
  weakening 160.5
  adj. making soft
    357.16
  moderating 163.14
  qualifying 507.7
  relieving 886.9
soften up
  besiege 798.19
  flatter 970.6
  influence 172.7
  make soft 357.6
  weaken 160.10
soft goods 831.3
softhearted
  emotionable 855.21
  kind 938.13
  pitying 944.7
softly faintly 452.21
  gently 357.17

**softness**
  comfortableness
    887.2
  cowardice 892.1
  faintness of sound
    452.1
  gullibility 502.2
  impotence 158.1
  leniency 759.1
  lightness 353.1
  looseness 758.1
  mental deficiency
    469.8
  nonresistiveness 357
  pulpiness 390.1
  soft color 362.3
  tender feeling 855.6
  texture 351.3
  weakness 160.1
**soft-pedal**
  extenuate 1006.12
  muffle 451.9
  silence 451.8
**soft sell** 829.2
**soft soap** flattery 970.1
  hypocrisy 616.6
  inducement 648.3
  suavity 936.5
**soft-soap**
  be hypocritical
    616.23
  flatter 970.6
  urge 648.14
**soft-spoken**
  speaking 594.32
  suave 936.18
**soft spot**
  sensitive area 422.4
  tendency 174.1
  vulnerable point
    697.4
**softwood**
  *n.* wood 378.3
  *adj.* arboreal 411.36
**ofty** 160.6
**oggy** 392.17
**oigné** chic 644.13
  dressed up 231.45
  stylish 644.12
**oil**
  *n.* dirtiness 682.5
  land 385.1
  region 180.1
  types of 385.13
  *v.* blemish 679.6
  corrupt 981.10
  dirty 682.16
  seduce 989.20
  stigmatize 915.9
  vilify 971.10
**iled**
  blemished 679.10
  sullied 682.21
  unchaste 989.23
**il science** 385.4
**ily** 385.7
**iree** meeting 74.2
  social gathering
    922.10
**ourn**
  *.* stay 188.5
  stay 188.8

**sojourner**
  resident 190.2
  transient 111.4
**Sol** 375.14
**solace**
  *n.* amusement 878.1
  comfort 887.4
  *v.* amuse 878.23
  comfort 887.6
**solar** 375.25
**solarium** parlor 192.5
  porch 192.21
**solar plexus** 422.6
**solar rays** 335.5
**solar system** 375.9
**solder** heat 329.24
  join 47.5
  sculpture 575.5
  stick together 50.9
**soldier**
  *n.* shirker 631.3
  termite 414.37
  warrior 800.6
  *v.* bear arms 797.22
  shirk 631.9
**soldier of fortune**
    800.16
**soldiery** 800.22
**sold on**
  believing 501.21
  pleased 865.12
**sole**
  *n.* bottom 212.2
  foot 212.5
  *adj.* one 89.7
  unique 89.9
  unmarried 934.7
**solecism** an error 518.5
  missaying 518.7
  specious argument
    483.3
  ungrammaticism
    587.2
**solely** exclusively 89.14
  simply 45.11
**solemn**
  celebrative 877.3
  ceremonious 646.8
  dignified 905.12
  eloquent 600.14
  gloomy 872.24
  pious 1028.8
  pompous 904.22
  reverent 964.9
  sedate 858.14
  sober 871.3
  uninteresting 883.6
  weighty 672.19
  worshipful 1032.15
**solemnity**
  ceremony 646.4
  eloquence 600.6
  formality 646.1
  gloom 872.7
  importance 672.3
  liturgy 1040.3
  pomp 904.6
  pride 905.2
  sedateness 858.4
  somberness 871
  uninterestingness
    883.1

**solemnize**
  administer rites
    1040.18
  celebrate 877.2
  formalize 646.5
**solemnly**
  dignifiedly 905.14
  formally 646.11
  sadly 872.31
  soberly 871.4
**solenoid** 288.3
**sol-fa**
  *n.* harmonics 463.7
  vocal music 462.12
  *v.* sing 462.39
**solicit**
  make advances 773.7
  request 774.14
**solicitation**
  canvass 774.5
  inducement 648.3
  political campaign
    744.13
  prostitution 989.8
**soliciting** 989.8
**solicitor**
  canvasser 830.7
  lawyer 1003.1
  petitioner 774.7
**solicitous** anxious 890.6
  careful 533.10
  considerate 938.16
  courteous 936.14
**solicitude**
  anxiety 890.1
  carefulness 533.1
  caution 895.1
  considerateness 938.3
  courtesy 936.1
**solid**
  *n.* solid body 354.6
  *adj.* complete 56.9
  crowded 74.22
  dense 354.12
  excellent 674.13
  firm 159.16
  hard 356.10
  permanent 140.7
  reliable 513.17
  solvent 836.17
  stable 142.12
  sturdy 3.7
  substantial 3.6
  unanimous 521.15
  undivided 89.7
  valid 516.13
**solidarity** accord 794.1
  completeness 56.1
  cooperation 786.1
  unity 89.1
**solid fuel** 281.8
**solidification**
  cohesion 50.1
  combination 52.1
  contraction 198.1
  densification 354.3
  hardening 356.5
  unity 89.1
**solidified**
  contracted 198.12
  hardened 356.13
**solidify** cohere 50.6

  combine 52.3
  contract 198.7
  densify 354.9
  embody 3.5
  set 356.8
**solidity**
  completeness 56.1
  density 354.1
  firmness 159.3
  hardness 356.1
  immobility 142.3
  permanence 140.1
  reliability 513.4
  solvency 836.6
  stability 142.1
  substantiality 3.1
  unity 89.1
  validity 516.4
**solid-state device**
    343.13
**solidus** 219.7
**soliloquist** 598.2
**soliloquize** 598.3
**soliloquy** 598
**solitary**
  *n.* odd person 85.4
  recluse 924.5
  *adj.* alone 924.10
  one 89.7
  withdrawn 89.8
**solitary confinement**
    761.8
**solitude**
  aloneness 924.3
  privacy 89.2
**solo**
  *n.* flight 278.9
  keyboard 465.20
  melody 462.4
  monologue 598.1
  music 462.14
  *v.* fly 278.46
  *adj.* alone 89.8
**soloist** 464.1
**Solomon** judge 1002.6
  wise man 468.2
**solon** legislator 746.3
  statesman 746.2
**so long!** 301.23
**solstice** 128.7
**solubility** 391.2
**soluble**
  liquefiable 391.9
  solvable 487.3
**solution** answer 487
  expedient 670.2
  explanation 552.4
  harmonization 463.2
  liquefaction 391.1
  mixture 391.3
**solvable** 487.3
**solve** explain 552.10
  liquefy 391.5
  resolve 487.2
**solvency** 836.6
**solvent**
  *n.* cleaning agent
    681.17
  dissolvent 391.4
  thinning agent
    205.10
  types of 391.10

make grieve 872.19
**sorrowful**
  grieving 872.26
  plaintive 875.16
  unpleasant 864.20
**sorry** disgraceful 915.11
  paltry 673.18
  regretful 873.8
  unhappy 872.21
  vulgar 898.15
**sorry lot** 986.5
**sorry plight** 731.4
**sort**
  *n.* kind 61.3
  nature 5.3
  *v.* analyze 48.8
  arrange 60.11
  classify 61.6
  discriminate 492.5
  size 195.15
**sorted** arranged 60.14
  classified 61.8
**sortie** attack 798.1
  flight 278.11
**sorting** analysis 48.3
  classification 61.1
  data processing
    349.20
  grouping 60.3
**sort of**
  so to speak 20.19
  to a degree 29.7
**sort out** analyze 48.8
  arrange 60.11
  discriminate 492.5
  make sure 513.11
  separate 77.6
  simplify 45.5
  solve 487.2
  think about 478.11
**SOS** 704.1
**so-so**
  *adj.* mediocre 680.7
  *adv.* mediocrely
    680.11
**sot** 996.10
**so to speak**
  figuratively 551.4
  in a manner of speak-
    ing 20.19
**sottish** drinking 996.34
  stupid 469.15
**sotto voce**
  in an undertone
    452.22
  music 462.54
  secretly 614.17
**sou**
  foreign money 835.9
  trifle 673.5
**soubrette** actor 612.2
  maid 750.8
  role 611.11
**sou'easter** 403.9
**soufflé**
  *n.* eggs 308.26
  foam 405.2
  *adj.* bubbly 405.6
  light 353.10
**soul** being 3.3
  content 194.5
  creativity 467.8

essence 5.2
fervor 855.10
individual 89.4
inner nature 5.4
interior 225.2
life force 407.3
mortal 417.3
particularity 80.1
psyche 466.4
seat of affections
  855.2
theosophy 1034.18
**soulful** 855.19
**soulless**
  inanimate 382.5
  unfeeling 856.9
**soul mate** likeness 20.3
  lover 931.17
**soul-searching** 873.3
**soul-stirring** 857.28
**sound**
  *n.* arm of the sea
    399.1
  earshot 448.4
  sonance 450
  testing device 489.4
  *v.* appear to be 446.10
  blare 453.9
  dive 320.6
  fathom 209.9
  feel out 489.9
  investigate 485.22
  make a noise 450.14
  measure 490.11
  play music 462.43
  reverberate 454.7
  ring 454.8
  say 594.23
  *adj.* firm 159.16
  good 674.12
  healthy 685.9
  intact 677.7
  logical 482.20
  orthodox 1024.7
  practical 536.6
  *v.* publish 559.10
  *adj.* reliable 513.17
  sane 472.4
  sensible 467.18
  solvent 836.17
  stable 142.12
  substantial 3.7
  unhazardous 698.5
  valid 516.13
**sound barrier**
  aviation 278.40
  sonics 450.6
  speed 269.2
**sounded**
  sonorous 450.15
  speech 594.30
**sound effects** 344.18
**sounder**
  telegraphy 560.2
  testing device 489.4
**sounding**
  *n.* depth measurement
    209.5
  sonation 450.4
  *adj.* reverberating
    454.11
  ringing 454.12

sonorous 450.15
**sounding board** 454.5
**sounding out** 489.2
**soundless** deep 209.11
  silent 451.10
**sound like**
  appear to be 446.10
  resemble 20.7
**soundness**
  firmness 159.3
  goodness 674.1
  healthiness 685.2
  intelligence 467.6
  orthodoxy 1024.1
  perfectness 677.2
  reasonableness 482.9
  reliability 513.4
  sanity 472.1
  solvency 836.6
  stability 142.1
  substantiality 3.1
  validity 516.4
**sound out** 489.9
**soundproof**
  *v.* proof 159.12
  *adj.* resistant 159.18
**soundproofing** 451.4
**sound sleep** 712.5
**sound track** 577.10
**sound truck** 450.11
**sound wave**
  sound 450.1
  wave 323.4
**soup** aviation 278.41
  food 308.10
  processing solution
    577.13
  semiliquid 389.5
  thinness 205.7
**soup-and-fish** 231.11
**soupçon**
  admixture 44.7
  small amount 35.4
**soup up** 38.5
**sour**
  *n.* sour thing 432.2
  tartness 432.1
  taste 427.1
  *v.* acidify 432.4
  aggravate 885.2
  make ill-humored
    951.16
  *adj.* bitter 429.6
  dissonant 461.4
  ill-humored 951.23
  pungent 433.6
  tainted 692.42
  tart 432.5
  unpleasant 864.17
**source**
  headwaters 395.2
  informant 557.5
  motive 648.1
  origin 153.5
  source of supply
    660.4
**source book** 605.6
**sourdough** miner 383.9
  sour thing 432.2
**soured** acerbic 432.5
  aggravated 885.4
  disappointed 541.5

ill-humored 951.23
  tainted 692.42
**sour grapes**
  disparagement 971.1
  sour thing 432.2
**souring**
  acidification 432.3
  aggravation 885.1
**sourness**
  animosity 929.4
  discontent 869.1
  dissonance 461.1
  ill humor 951.1
  pungency 433.1
  tartness 432
  unpleasant taste
    429.2
**sour note** 461.1
**sourpuss** hinderer 730.9
  sad person 872.13
**sousaphone** 465.8
**souse**
  *n.* drunkard 996.11
  immersion 320.2
  soaking 392.7
  *v.* drink 996.24
  immerse 320.7
  make drunk 996.22
  soak 392.13
**soused** drunk 996.31
  soaked 392.17
**south**
  *n.* direction 290.3
  region 180.7
  *adj.* southern 290.15
  *adv.* southward 290.17
**southeast**
  *n.* direction 290.3
  region 180.7
  *adj.* southeastern
    290.15
  *adv.* southeastward
    290.22
**southerly** 290.15
**southern** 290.15
**Southerner** 190.11
**southpaw**
  *n.* left-hander 244.3
  *adj.* left-handed 244.5
**south pole** 342.8
**South Pole**
  cold place 333.4
  opposites 239.2
  remote region 199.4
**southward**
  *n.* south 290.3
  *adv.* south 290.17
**southwest**
  *n.* direction 290.3
  region 180.7
  *adj.* southwestern
    290.15
  *adv.* southwestward
    290.23
**souvenir**
  memento 537.7
  memory 537.1
**sou'wester** 403.9
**sovereign**
  *n.* coin 835.4
  potentate 749.7
  *adj.* chief 36.14

shakily 324.23
**spastic**
*n.* sick person 686.40
*adj.* convulsive 162.22
irregular 138.3
jerky 324.19
**spat**
*n.* fish young 171.2
quarrel 795.5
*v.* quarrel 795.11
**spate** eruption 162.6
flow 395.4
much 34.4
overabundance 663.2
plenty 661.2
quantity 34.3
rainstorm 394.2
throng 74.4
violent flow 395.5
**spatial** 179.8
**spatter**
*n.* blemish 679.3
sprinkle 392.5
staccato sound 455.1
*v.* blemish 679.5
dirty 682.18
moisten 392.12
rain 394.9
sprinkle 75.6
**spattered**
blemished 679.9
sprinkled 75.10
**spattering**
*n.* sprinkling 75.1
wetting 392.6
*adj.* staccato 455.7
**spatula**
art equipment 574.19
sculpting tool 575.4
**spawn**
*n.* egg 406.15
fish young 171.2
*v.* create 167.13
reproduce 169.9
**spay** 42.11
**speak** address 594.27
affirm 523.4
communicate 554.6
converse 597.9
indicate 568.22
inform 557.8
make a speech 599.9
remark 594.25
signal 275.52
sound 450.14
talk 594.20
use language 580.16
**speakeasy** 996.19
**speaker**
loudspeaker 450.8
manager 748.5
speechmaker 599.4
spokesman 781.5
talker 594.18
**speak for**
defend 1006.10
represent 781.14
**speak for itself**
be intelligible 548.4
be manifest 555.7
evidence 505.9

**speaking**
*n.* communication 554.1
public speaking 599.1
speech 594.1
utterance 594.3
*adj.* lifelike 20.16
talking 594.32
**speaking of**
incidentally 129.13
in relation to 9.13
**speak out** affirm 523.4
be honest 974.12
manifest oneself 555.6
speak up 594.22
stand up to 893.11
**speak to** address 594.27
reprove 969.18
**speak up** affirm 523.4
manifest oneself 555.6
speak out 594.22
stand up to 893.11
**speak up for** 1006.10
**speak well of** 968.11
**spear**
*n.* branch 411.18
leaf 411.17
plant stem 411.19
types of 801.23
*v.* catch 822.17
puncture 265.16
stab 798.25
**spearhead**
*n.* vanguard 240.2
*v.* lead 292.2
**spearlike** 258.14
**spear side** kinsmen 11.2
male line 170.4
**special**
*n.* commodity 831.2
feature 81.2
newspaper 605.11
train 272.13
*adj.* classificational 61.7
detailed 8.9
notable 672.18
other 16.8
particular 80.12
**special case**
particularity 80.2
qualification 507.1
**special delivery** 604.5
**Special Forces** 800.14
**special interests**
influential persons 172.6
pressure group 744.31
**specialist**
*n.* authority 81.3
physician 688.8
stockbroker 833.10
*adj.* specialized 81.5
**speciality**
particularity 80.2
pursuit 81.1
talent 733.4
**specialization**
differentiation 16.4
particularization 80.7

strong point 81.1
vocation 656.6
**specialize**
differentiate 16.6
feature 81.4
limit 234.5
particularize 80.9
specify 80.11
**specialized** 81.5
**specialize in**
practice 705.7
specialize 81.4
study to be 564.15
**special school** 567.2
**special treatment**
furtherance 785.5
qualification 507.1
**specialty**
characteristic 80.4
component 58.2
contract 771.3
particularity 80.2
pursuit 81
science 475.10
study 562.8
vocation 656.6
**specialty shop** 832.4
**specie** coin 835.4
money 835.1
**species** biology 61.5
kind 61.3
nomenclature 583.1
race 11.4
**specific**
*n.* characteristic 80.3
remedy 687.1
*adj.* circumscribed 234.6
classificational 61.7
detailed 8.9
particular 80.12
**specifically** fully 8.13
particularly 80.15
**specification**
circumscription 234.1
condition 507.2
description 608.1
designation 80.6
indication 568.1
particularization 8.5
qualification 507.1
**specific gravity**
density 354.1
gravity 352.5
**specifics** 1.4
**specified** 507.8
**specify**
call attention to 530.10
circumscribe 234.4
indicate 568.18
itemize 8.6
name 583.11
stipulate 80.11
**specimen**
representative 572.5
sample 25.3
taste 427.4
**specious** false 616.27
hollow 483.10
illusory 519.9
pretexted 649.5

**speciousness**
appearances 446.2
fakery 616.3
rationalization 483.1
**specious reasoning**
rationality 482.1
sophistry 483.1
**speck**
*n.* blemish 679.3
impurity 78.2
mark 568.5
minute thing 196.7
small amount 35.2
spottiness 374.3
*v.* blemish 679.5
mark 568.19
sprinkle 75.6
variegate 374.7
**speckled**
blemished 679.9
spotted 374.13
sprinkled 75.10
**specs** 443.2
**spectacle** display 904.4
marvel 920.2
sight 446.7
stage show 611.4
**spectacled** 443.10
**spectacles** 443.2
**spectacular**
astonishing 920.12
dramatic 611.38
gaudy 904.20
theatrical 904.24
**spectator**
attender 186.5
audience 448.6
observer 442
playgoer 611.32
recipient 819.3
witness 505.7
**specter**
frightener 891.9
ghost 1017
illusion 519.4
spirit 1014.15
**spectral**
coloring 362.15
ghostly 1017.7
illusory 519.9
variegated 374.9
**spectrograph**
astronomy 375.17
photograph 577.7
**spectrometer** 443.15
**spectrometry**
color 362.10
optics 443.6
**spectroscope**
astronomy 375.17
types of 443.12,15
**spectroscopy**
astronomy 375.19
color 362.10
optics 443.6
**spectrum**
color system 362.7
continuity 71.2
illusion 519.5
radio frequency 344.12
range 179.2

variegation 374.6
speculate
  consider 478.12
  gamble 515.18
  invest 836.16
  predict 543.9
  speculate in stocks
    833.23
  theorize 499.9
speculation
  consideration 478.2
  gambling 515.7
  investment 836.3
  prediction 543.1
  risk 515.1
  stock speculation
    833.19
  theorization 499.1
  unverified supposi-
    tion 499.4
speculative
  gambling 515.21
  hazardous 697.10
  theoretical 499.13
  thoughtful 478.21
  uncertain 514.16
speculator
  gambler 515.17
  philosopher 500.6
  stock speculator
    833.11
  theorist 499.7
speech
  n. address 599.2
  communication
    554.1
  conversation 597.3
  diction 588.1
  figures of 551.5
  language 580.1
  talking 594
  adj. communicational
    554.9
  linguistic 594.30
speech defect
  mental symptom
    690.25
  speech impediment
    595
speechify 599.9
speechless mute 451.12
  taciturn 613.9
speechmaker 599.4
speech organ 594.19
speed
  n. amphetamine 687.9
  aviation 278.40
  hastiness 709.2
  velocity 269.1
  v. facilitate 732.6
  further 785.17
  go fast 269.8
  hasten 709.4
  urge on 648.16
speedboat 277.4
speed demon 269.5
speeder driver 274.10
  racer 269.5
speed freak 642.10
speedily hastily 709.12
  promptly 131.15
  swiftly 269.21

speediness
  promptness 131.3
  quickness 707.3
  swiftness 269.1
speed of sound
  aviation 278.40
  sonics 450.6
  swiftness 269.2
speedometer 269.7
speedup
  acceleration 269.4
  increase 38.2
speed up
  accelerate 269.14
  hasten 709.4
speedway 657.6
Speedwriting 602.8
speedy fast 269.19
  hasty 709.9
  lively 707.18
  prompt 131.9
  sudden 113.5
  transient 111.8
spell
  n. bad influence 675.4
  bout 137.3
  charm 1036
  period 107.1
  respite 711.2
  shift 108
  sorcery 1035.1
  superstition 502.3
  term 107.3
  turn 108.2
  v. augur 544.12
  bewitch 1036.7
  fascinate 650.6
  mean 545.8
  orthographize 581.7
  substitute for 149.5
  take turns 108.5
spellbind
  be eloquent 600.7
  cast a spell 1036.7
  engross 530.13
  fascinate 650.6
spellbinder
  bewitcher 1035.9
  orator 599.6
spellbinding
  n. sorcery 1035.1
  adj. alluring 650.7
  bewitching 1036.11
  eloquent 600.8
  engrossing 530.20
spellbound
  astonished 920.9
  dreamy 535.25
  enchanted 1036.12
  engrossed 530.18
spelldown 581.4
speller 605.8
spelling 581.4
spell out develop 148.6
  explain 552.10
  itemize 8.6
  make clear 548.6
  particularize 80.9
  spell 581.7
Spencerian writing
  602.4
spend consume 666.2

disburse 843.5
experience 151.8
occupy 656.10
use 665.13
waste 854.4
spender
  expender 843.4
  prodigal 854.2
spending money 835.19
spendthrift
  n. prodigal 854.2
  adj. prodigal 854.8
spent exhausted 717.8
  paid 841.22
  used up 666.4
  wasted 854.9
  weakened 160.18
  worn-out 692.38
sperm copulation 419.8
  secretion 312.2
  spermatozoa 406.11
spermatic
  gametic 406.22
  genital 419.27
  reproductive 169.15
  secretory 312.7
spermatozoa 406.11
spermatozoon
  source 153.7
  sperm 406.11
spermicide 687.23
spew
  n. eruption 162.6
  jet 395.9
  vomit 310.8
  v. eject 310.24
  erupt 162.12
  flow out 303.13
  jet 395.20
  spit 312.6
  vomit 310.25
sphere arena 802.1
  ball 255.2
  occupation 656.4
  rank 29.2
  region 180.2
  science 475.10
  space 179.1
  star 375.4
sphere of influence
  foreign policy 744.5
  orbit 172.4
spherical
  globular 255.9
  spatial 179.8
sphericity 255
sphincter 253.2
sphinxlike 549.17
spic 181.7
spiccato
  n. harmonics 463.14
  music passage 462.25
  music style 462.31
  adv. music 462.54
spice
  n. admixture 44.7
  flavoring 428.3
  fragrance 436.1
  pungency 433.2
  types of 308.55
  v. flavor 428.7
spiceless 430.2

spick and span 681.26
spicule 258.7,18
spicy fragrant 436.9
  interesting 530.19
  pungent 433.7
  risqué 990.7
spider bug 414.36
  invertebrates 415.5
  spinner 206.5
spider web 206.1
spidery lean 205.17
  unsteady 160.16
spiel
  n. sales talk 829.5
  v. declaim 599.10
  publicize 559.15
  speak 594.21
spieler publicist 559.9
  public speaker 599.4
  sharper 619.4
  showman 611.28
  solicitor 830.7
spiff up 231.41
spiffy chic 644.13
  excellent 674.13
spigot stopper 266.4
  valve 396.10
spike
  n. inflorescence
    411.25
  plant part 411.27
  rig 272.5
  stopper 266.4
  thorn 258.7
  v. adulterate 44.13
  disable 158.9
  puncture 265.16
  stab 798.25
  thwart 730.15
spiked 258.11
spile
  n. stake 217.6
  stopper 266.4
  v. stop 266.7
spill
  n. inversion 220.2
  lighter 331.4
  overflow 395.6
  stopper 266.4
  strip 206.4
  tumble 316.3
  v. confess 556.7
  divulge 556.6
  overflow 395.17
  waste 854.4
spill over
  overflow 395.17
  superabound 663.8
spill-over 395.6
spill the beans 556.6
spillway 396.2
spin
  n. air maneuver
    278.15
  ride 273.7
  rotation 322.1
  whirl 322.2
  v. air crash 278.53
  air maneuver 278.49
  eddy 395.21
  fish 655.10
  make threads 206.6

move 267.5
rotate 322.9
turn around 295.9
whirl 322.11
spinal cord 422.6
spinal meningitis 686.9
spindle 322.5,17
spindleshanks 205.8
spindle-shaped 258.14
spindle side
female line 170.4
kinsmen 11.2
spindly lean 205.17
unsteady 160.16
spindrift foam 405.2
sprinkle 392.5
spine
protuberance 256.3
ridge 207.6
supporter 216.2
thorn 258.7,18
spine-chilling 857.30
spined 258.11
spineless
inconstant 141.7
irresolute 627.12
weak 160.12
spinet 465.13
spinner snare 618.12
thread maker 206.5
spinning
n. rotation 322.1
adj. rotating 322.14
spinning wheel 206.5
spin out
expatiate 593.8
lengthen 202.7
protract 110.9
spinster
single woman 934.4
spinner 206.5
spinsterhood 934.1
spinsterly 934.7
spiny difficult 731.16
pointed 258.11
spiracle
air passage 396.17
hole 265.4
outlet 303.9
spiral
n. air maneuver
278.13
circuitousness 321.1
curl 254.2
galaxy 375.6
v. ascend 315.8
fly 278.49
go around 321.4
soar 315.10
adj. circuitous 321.7
curled 254.8
piraling
n. circuitousness 321.1
adj. ascending 315.14
overpriced 848.12
pire
n. leaf 411.17
plant stem 411.19
pointed projection
258.4
summit 211.2
tower 207.11

v. ascend 315.8
be high 207.15
soar 315.10
spirit
n. animation 161.3
content 194.5
courage 893.5
deity 1014.15
eagerness 635.1
eloquence 600.4
enterprise 707.7
essence 5.2
extract 305.8
fervor 855.10
gaiety 870.4
genius 467.8
inner nature 5.4
life force 407.3
liveliness 707.2
meaning 545.1
milieu 233.3
mood 525.4
nature 5.3
occultism 1034.5
pluck 624.3
psyche 466.4
seat of affections
855.2
shadow 4.3
specter 1017.1
theosophy 1034.18
zeal 635.2
v. abduct 824.19
inspire 648.20
spirited bold 893.18
eager 635.9
eloquent 600.12
energetic 161.12
gay 870.14
lively 707.17
zealous 635.10
spiritless
apathetic 856.13
dejected 872.22
uncourageous 892.11
unfeeling 856.9
uninteresting 883.6
spirits alcohol 996.40
gaiety 870.4
liquor 996.12
mood 525.4
spiritual
n. sacred music
462.16
adj. ghostly 1017.7
immaterial 377.7
mental 466.8
pious 1028.9
psychic 1034.23
sacred 1026.7
supernatural 85.15
temperamental 525.7
spiritualism
idealism 377.3
occultism 1034.5
spiritualist
idealist 377.4
psychic 1034.13
spiritualistic
idealist 377.8
psychic 1034.23

spirituality
heaven 1018.6
immateriality 377.1
piety 1028.2
spiritualize
attenuate 4.4
dematerialize 377.6
etherealize 1034.20
refine 681.22
spiritual leader 1038.5
spiritually 525.9
spirituous
alcoholic 996.36
tenuous 4.6
spirit world 377.1
spirochete 686.39
spit
n. fireplace 329.12
jet 395.9
point of land 256.8
saliva 312.3
sibilation 457.1
v. animal sound 460.4
expectorate 312.6
jet 395.20
puncture 265.16
rain 394.9
show resentment
952.14
sibilate 457.2
snap 456.7
stab 798.25
spitball 285.4
spite grudge 929.5
hate 930.1
hostility 929.3
spitefulness 939.6
spiteful hostile 929.10
irascible 951.19
malevolent 939.19
spitfire
ill-humored woman
951.12
violent person 162.9
spitting distance 200.2
spitting image
likeness 572.3
the same 14.3
spittle 312.3
spit upon 966.4
splash
n. blemish 679.3
display 904.4
lap 395.8
mark 568.5
ripple 452.5
spottiness 374.3
sprinkle 392.5
v. be ostentatious
904.13
blemish 679.5
dramatize 672.15
lap 395.19
make a liquid sound
452.11
moisten 392.12
spatter 682.18
splash-down 282.2
splashing
n. wetting 392.6
adj. water sound
452.19

splashy muddy 389.14
showy 904.19
watery 392.16
splat
n. explosive noise
456.1
wood 378.3
v. make explosive
noise 456.6
splatter
n. blemish 679.3
rain 394.1
sprinkle 392.5
v. blemish 679.5
make staccato sounds
455.4
moisten 392.12
spatter 682.18
sprinkle 75.6
splattered
blemished 679.9
sprinkled 75.10
splay
n. dispersion 75.1
expansion 197.1
v. disperse 75.4
diverge 299.5
spread 197.6
adj. spread 197.11
splayfoot
n. deformity 249.3
foot 212.5
adj. deformed 249.12
spleen bitterness 952.3
boredom 884.3
ill humor 951.1
unpleasure 866.1
vitals 225.4
spleeny 951.19
splendid bright 335.32
excellent 674.12
gorgeous 900.19
grandiose 904.21
illustrious 914.19
superb 674.17
splendidly
excellently 674.21
gorgeously 900.23
grandiosely 904.28
magnificently 34.20
splendiferous
grandiose 904.21
superb 674.17
splendor beauty 900.6
brightness 335.4
grandeur 904.5
illustriousness 914.6
splendorous
bright 335.32
gorgeous 900.19
illustrious 914.19
splenetic bored 884.10
glandular 312.8
irascible 951.19
resentful 952.24
splice
n. bond 47.1
connection 47.3,20
v. bind 47.9
join 47.5
join in marriage
933.15

weave 222.6
**spliced** joined 47.13
related 9.9
**splint**
*n.* medical dressing
687.33
*v.* treat 689.30
**splinter**
*n.* break 49.4
intruder 78.2
party 788.4
piece 55.3
small amount 35.3
thinness 205.7
*v.* shatter 49.13
**splinter group** 788.4
**split**
*n.* blemish 679.1
break 49.4
crack 201.2
falling-out 795.4
opening 265.1
stock 834.2
*v.* apportion 816.6
be damaged 692.26
bisect 92.4
blemish 679.4
break 49.12
cleave 201.4
demolish 693.17
disintegrate 53.3
fall out 795.10
flee 631.11
incise 265.12
laugh 876.6
leave 301.10
open 265.15
section 49.18
separate 49.9
sever 49.11
*adj.* blemished 679.8
cleft 201.7
damaged 692.29
halved 92.6
severed 49.23
**split hairs**
differentiate 16.6
discriminate 492.5
quibble 483.9
**split-level** 191.6
**split personality**
dissociation 690.27
pathological type
690.16
psychosis 473.4
**split second** 113.3
**split the difference**
average 32.2
compromise 807.2
share 815.6
**splitting**
*n.* apportionment
816.1
disintegration 53.2
separation 49.2
*adj.* violent 162.15
**split up**
apportion 816.6
disband 75.8
divide 49.18
divorce 935.5
part company 49.19

**split-up** 75.3
**splotch**
*n.* blemish 679.3
mark 568.5
spottiness 374.3
*v.* blemish 679.5
mark 568.19
spatter 682.18
variegate 374.7
**splotchy**
blemished 679.9
spotted 374.13
**splurge**
*n.* display 904.4
*v.* be ostentatious
904.13
spend 843.5
**splutter**
*n.* bluster 911.1
flutter 324.4
sibilation 457.1
staccato sound 455.1
*v.* bluster 911.3
flutter 324.12
make staccato sounds
455.4
sibilate 457.2
speak poorly 595.9
**spoil**
*n.* booty 824.11
*v.* be ugly 899.5
bungle 734.11
decay 692.25
impair 692.12
indulge 759.6
plunder 824.16
thwart 730.15
**spoilage** decay 692.6
rotting 692.7
**spoiled** botched 734.21
damaged 692.30
decayed 692.41
indulged 759.9
ruined 693.28
ugly 899.6
unsavory 429.7
**spoiled brat** 125.4
**spoil for** 634.16
**spoils of office**
booty 824.11
graft 744.35
**spoilsport**
hinderer 730.9
killjoy 872.14
**spoils system** 744.35
**spoke**
convergence 298.1
curb 730.7
radiating 299.2
rung 315.5
**spoken** speech 594.30
vernacular 580.18
**spoken language** 580.5
**spoken word, the** 594.3
**spokesman**
deputy 781.5
informant 557.5
mediator 805.3
public speaker 599.4
**spoliate** 824.16
**spoliation**
destruction 693.1

loss 812.1
plundering 824.5
**sponge**
*n.* absorbent 306.6
animal 414.35
bath 681.8,32
drunkard 996.11
eradicator 693.9
lightness 353.2
medical dressing
687.33
parasite 907.4
porousness 265.9
pulp 390.2
washing 681.5
*v.* be a parasite 907.11
dry 393.6
get for free 850.4
moisten 392.12
obliterate 693.16
sorb 306.13
wash 681.19
**sponger**
nonworker 708.10
parasite 907.4
**sponge up** be dry 393.5
drink 307.28
**sponging**
*n.* obsequiousness
907.2
sorption 306.6
washing 681.5
*adj.* indolent 708.18
parasitic 907.13
**spongy**
absorbent 306.17
porous 265.21
pulpy 390.6
soft 357.11
**sponsor**
*n.* financer 836.9
guarantor 772.6
supporter 787.9
*v.* be responsible
962.9
finance 836.15
patronize 785.15
secure 772.9
**sponsorship**
financing 836.2
guarantorship 772.8
patronage 785.4
**spontaneity**
unpremeditation
630.4
voluntariness 622.2
**spontaneous**
automated 349.25
instinctive 481.6
unpremeditated
630.11
voluntary 622.7
**spontaneously**
instinctively 481.7
voluntarily 622.10
**spoof**
*n.* hoax 618.7
*v.* fool 618.14
**spoofing** 618.1
**spook**
*n.* specter 1017.1
*v.* discompose 63.4

frighten 891.23
haunt 1017.6
**spooked** afraid 891.30
haunted 1017.10
**spooky** creepy 891.39
haunted 1017.10
weird 1017.9
**spoon**
*n.* tableware 348.3
*v.* apportion 816.8
ladle 271.16
make love 932.13
**spoonerism**
error in speech 518.7
word 582.4
wordplay 881.8
**spoon-feed** 785.16
**spoonlike** 257.16
**spoor** clue 568.9
hint 557.4
odor 435.1
track 568.8
**sporadic**
contagious 686.58
dispersed 75.9
inconstant 18.3
irregular 138.3
unordered 62.12
**sporadically**
disjointedly 49.27
haphazardly 62.18
irregularly 138.4
nonuniformly 18.4
scatteringly 75.12
**spore** germ 686.39
organic matter
406.13
**sport**
*n.* athlete 878.20
athletics 878.8
banter 882.1
dandy 903.9
fun 878.2
gambler 515.17
game 878.9
hunting 655.2
joke 881.6
loser 727.5
misfit 27.4
toy 878.16
transformation 139.2
word list 878.34
*v.* flaunt 904.17
gamble 515.18
hunt 655.9
play 878.25
wear 231.43
**sporting**
*n.* gambling 515.7
hunting 655.2
*adj.* athletic 878.32
fair 976.9
**sporting chance**
gambling 515.2
good chance 156.8
**sportive** frisky 870.14
mischievous 738.6
playful 878.31
prankish 881.17
**sportscast**
*n.* radio broadcast
344.18

suppress 760.8
**squelcher** 506.3
**squelchy** muddy 389.14
  pulpy 390.6
  soft 357.13
**squib** detonator 331.7
  disparagement 971.5
  humor 881.1
  ridicule 967.6
**squint**
  *n.* defective vision
    440.5
  obliquity 219.1
  *v.* look askance 439.19
  squinch 440.9
**squinting** askew 219.14
  poor-sighted 440.11
**squire**
  *n.* attendant 750.5
  beau 931.12
  escort 73.5
  nobleman 918.4
  proprietor 809.2
  *v.* court 932.19
  escort 73.8
**squirm**
  *n.* wiggle 324.7
  *v.* be excited 857.16
  be impatient 862.4
  wiggle 324.14
**squirm out of**
  excuse 1006.11
  slip away 632.9
**squirmy**
  impatient 862.6
  wiggly 324.21
**squirrel away**
  prepare 720.11
  store up 660.11
**squirrel cage**
  routine 642.6
  tedium 884.1
**squirt**
  *n.* a nobody 673.7
  ejection 310.7
  jet 395.9
  *v.* eject 310.24
  jet 395.20
**squish**
  *n.* sibilation 457.1
  *v.* shatter 49.13
  sibilate 457.2
**squishy** muddy 389.14
  pulpy 390.6
  soft 357.13
**Sr.**
  *n.* form of address
    420.7
  senior 127.5
  *adj.* senior 123.19
**SRO** full 56.11
  present 186.19
**SS** 800.14
**SST** 280.3
**stab**
  *n.* attempt 714.2
  impairment 692.8
  pain 424.2
  thrust 798.3
  unverified supposi-
    tion 499.4
  *v.* aggrieve 866.17

attack 798.25
  injure 692.15
  pain 424.7
  puncture 265.16
**stabbing**
  *n.* attacking 798.11
  *adj.* acrimonious
    161.13
  caustic 939.21
  exciting 857.29
  painful 424.10
**stabile** sculpture 575.2
  work of art 574.11
**stability**
  aviation 278.29
  continuity 71.1
  durability 110.1
  firmness 142
  moderation 163.1
  permanence 140.1
  perpetuity 112.1
  perseverance 625.1
  reliability 513.4
  strength 159.3
  substantiality 3.1
  uniformity 17.1
**stabilization** 142.2
**stabilize** calm 163.7
  immobilize 142.7
  make uniform 17.4
**stabilizer**
  moderator 163.3
  types of 142.20
**stable**
  *n.* barn 191.20
  filthy place 682.11
  group 74.3
  race horses 414.17
  *v.* enclose 236.5
  house 188.10
  *adj.* continuing 110.10
  faithful 974.20
  firm 159.16
  incessant 71.8
  permanent 140.7
  persevering 625.7
  reliable 513.17
  restrained 163.11
  sturdy 3.7
  substantial 142.12
  unhazardous 698.5
  uniform 17.5
**stableman** 416.2
**staccato**
  *n.* frequency 135.2
  harmonics 463.14
  music passage 462.25
  music style 462.31
  pulsation 323.3
  staccato sound 455
  *adj.* constant 135.5
  drumming 455.7
  pulsating 323.18
  *adv.* music 462.54
**stack**
  *n.* bookholder 605.20
  hoard 660.1
  library 192.6
  much 34.4
  pile 74.10
  smoke passage 396.18
  storage place 660.6

*v.* pile 74.19
  put 184.14
  tamper with 616.17
**stacked**
  assembled 74.21
  beautiful 900.17
  prearranged 641.5
**stacked deck** 641.1
**stack the cards**
  cheat 618.17
  prearrange 641.3
**stack up**
  *n.* landing 278.18
  *v.* be comparable
    491.7
  equal 30.5
  pile 74.19
  resemble 20.7
  turn out 7.6
**stadium** arena 802.1
  hall 192.4
**staff**
  *n.* council 755.1
  emblem of authority
    739.9
  insignia 569.1
  music 462.29
  pastoral staff 1041.3
  personnel 750.11
  post 216.8
  stick 217.2
  supporter 216.2
  *v.* equip 659.8
**staff of life** 308.28
**stag**
  hoofed animal 414.5
  jumper 319.4
  male animal 420.8
  party 922.11
  stock speculator
    833.11
**stage**
  *n.* arena 802.1
  layer 227.1
  period 107.1
  platform 216.13
  playing area 611.21
  rank 29.2
  setting 233.2
  stagecoach 272.12
  support 216.12
  *v.* dramatize 611.33
**stage, the** 611.1
**stagecoach** 272.12
**stagecraft** 611.3
**stage fright**
  fearfulness 891.3
  nervousness 859.1
  shyness 908.4
**stagehand** 611.29
**stage manager** 611.28
**stage name** 583.8
**stage presence** 611.9
**stage show** show 611.4
  spectacle 446.7
**stagestruck** 611.38
**stage whisper** 452.4
**stag film** 990.4
**stagger**
  *n.* aviation 278.25
  flounder 324.8
  gait 273.14

irregularity 138.1
  *v.* astonish 920.6
  be drunk 996.26
  be irresolute 627.6
  excite 857.13
  flounder 324.15
  fluctuate 141.5
  frighten 891.23
  make doubt 503.7
  startle 540.8
  tumble 316.8
  walk 273.16
  zigzag 219.12
**staggered**
  astonished 920.9
  crooked 219.20
  startled 540.13
**staggering**
  *n.* walking 273.10
  *adj.* astonishing
    920.12
  irregular 138.3
  slow 270.10
  surprising 540.11
**stagnant**
  do-nothing 706.6
  inert 268.14
  languid 708.19
**stagnate**
  do nothing 706.2
  merely exist 1.10
  vegetate 268.9
**stagy** affected 903.15
  ostentatious 904.24
  theatrical 611.38
**staid** sedate 858.14
  solemn 871.3
  unimaginative 536.5
**stain**
  *n.* blemish 679.3
  coloring matter
    362.8,23
  mark 568.5
  soil 682.5
  stigma 915.6
  *v.* blemish 679.6
  color 362.13
  mark 568.19
  soil 682.16
  stigmatize 915.9
**stained**
  blemished 679.10
  colored 362.16
  soiled 682.21
**staining**
  applying color 362.11
  coloring 362.12
**stainless** chaste 988.4
  clean 681.25
  honest 974.13
  innocent 984.7
  perfect 677.6
**stair** degree 29.1
  step 315.5
**stairway** 315.3
**stake**
  *n.* district 180.5
  estate 810.4
  financing 836.2
  horse race 796.13
  instrument of execu-
    tion 1011.5

jackpot 515.5
pledge 772.3
portion 816.5
shaft 217.6
wager 515.3
*v.* bet 515.20
finance 836.15
pledge 772.10
**stakeout** 485.9
**stake out**
circumscribe 234.4
reconnoiter 485.27
**staker** financer 836.9
race horse 414.17
**stale** insipid 430.2
old 123.14
tainted 692.42
trite 883.9
**stalemate**
*n.* end 144.2
equality 30.3
impasse 731.5
*v.* stop 144.11
**stalk**
*n.* base 216.8
gait 273.14
journey 273.5
plant stem 411.19
search 485.14
shaft 217.1
*v.* hunt 655.9
lurk 615.9
strut 904.15
trace 485.34
walk 273.27
**stalking** hunting 655.2
pursuit 655.1
search 485.14
stealth 614.4
**stalking-horse**
concealment 615.3
horse 414.16
political candidate
746.9
pretext 649.1
**stall**
*n.* air maneuver
278.13
barn 191.20
church seat 1042.14
compartment 192.2
hut 191.10
procrastination 132.5
store 832.3
theater part 611.20
*v.* aviation 278.54
fail 725.15
prevent 730.13
procrastinate 132.11
stick 144.7
stop 144.11
**stallion** horse 414.10
male animal 420.8
**stalwart**
*n.* brave person 893.8
partisan 744.27
strong man 159.6
supporter 787.9
*adj.* corpulent 195.18
courageous 893.17
robust 685.10
strong 159.13

**stamen** 411.26
**stamina** courage 893.5
perseverance 625.1
pluck 624.3
strength 159.1
toughness 359.1
**stammer**
*n.* stammering 595.3
*v.* be embarrassed
908.8
look guilty 983.2
stutter 595.8
**stammering**
*n.* redundancy 103.3
shyness 908.4
stuttering 595.3
*adj.* shy 908.12
stuttering 595.13
**stamp**
*n.* characteristic 80.4
copy 24.6
die 25.6
engraving tool 578.9
form 246.1
hit 283.9
kind 61.3
label 568.13
mark 568.7
postage 604.6
printing 603.3
quality 5.3
ratification 521.4
sign 568.2
temperament 525.3
type 603.6
*v.* etch 142.9
fix in the mind
537.18
form 246.7
hit 283.19
impress upon 855.18
indent 257.14
label 568.20
mark 568.19
print 603.14
walk 273.27
**stamped**
engraved 578.12
ratified 521.14
**stampede**
*n.* fear 891.1
*v.* be frightened
891.20
defeat 727.9
rush 709.4
send scuttling 891.24
**stamping**
bookbinding 605.15
coining 835.24
**stamping ground**
resort 191.27
sphere of influence
172.4
**stamp out**
annihilate 2.6
destroy 693.15
eliminate 42.10
extinguish 332.7
**stance**
affirmation 523.1
belief 501.6
gesture 568.14

looks 446.4
mental attitude 525.1
support 216.5
**stanch** stop 266.7
suppress 760.8
**stanchion** post 217.4
support 216.8
**stand**
*n.* affirmation 523.1
base 216.8
growth 411.2
impasse 731.5
mental outlook 525.2
playing engagement
611.12
quiescence 268.3
resistance 792.1
station 184.2
stop 144.2
store 832.3
support 216.5,26
table 216.15
*v.* afford to pay 843.7
be located 184.9
be patient 861.5
be present 186.6
be still 268.7
endure 110.6
exist 1.8
face up to 792.3
idle 708.11
pay for 841.19
remain 140.5
resist 792.2
run for office 744.39
settle 184.16
stand erect 213.7
suffice 661.4
**stand a chance**
be likely 175.3
be possible 509.4
have a chance 156.13
**stand aloof**
abstain 992.7
avoid 631.6
be uncommunicative
613.6
be unsociable 923.4
do nothing 706.4
keep away 199.7
refuse 776.3
separate 49.9
snub 966.7
**stand apart** differ 16.5
separate 49.9
stand alone 89.6
**standard**
*n.* base 216.8
degree 29.1
ethics 957.1
flag 569.6
good person 985.4
measure 490.2
model 25.1
post 217.4
precept 751.2
rule 84.4
test 489.2
*adj.* authoritative
513.18
customary 642.15
indistinctive 493.6

interchangeable
150.5
medium 32.3
model 25.8
orthodox 1024.7
prescriptive 751.4
routine 79.12
usual 84.8
**standard-bearer**
pacemaker 748.6
political leader 746.7
**standard deviation**
inaccuracy 518.2
statistics 511.2
**standardize**
make uniform 17.4
normalize 84.6
order 59.4
systematize 60.10
**standard of living** 827.8
**standard operating**
procedure 642.5
**stand aside** resign 784.2
separate 49.9
**stand back** 295.6
**stand behind**
back 785.13
sponsor 772.9
**standby** actor 612.7
supporter 787.9
**stand by** adjoin 200.9
back 785.13
be prepared 720.14
defend 799.8
sailing 275.75
stay near 200.12
**stand down**
abandon 633.5
resign 784.2
**stand-down**
pause 144.3
truce 804.5
**stand fast**
be firm 142.11
be still 268.7
hold out 624.9
resist 792.4
**stand for** affirm 523.4
be patient 861.5
designate 568.18
indicate 568.17
mean 545.8
permit 777.10
sail for 275.35
**stand-in** actor 612.7
deputy 781.1
substitute 149.2
**stand in for**
represent 781.14
substitute for 149.5
**standing**
*n.* candidacy 744.10
durability 110.1
permanence 140.1
prestige 914.4
rank 29.2
state 7.1
station 184.2
support 216.5
*adj.* inert 268.14
**standing order**
custom 642.5

law 998.3
rule 84.4
**standing room only**
full 56.11
present 186.19
**stand in the way**
obstruct 730.12
thwart 730.15
**standoff** end 144.2
equality 30.3
even chance 156.7
**stand off**
keep away 199.7
recede 297.2
sail away from 275.36
**standoffish**
aloof 912.12
reticent 613.10
unsociable 923.6
**stand on** affirm 523.4
be contingent 507.6
be the duty of 962.5
insist 753.7
rest on 216.22
**stand on ceremony**
646.6
**stand out**
be apparent 555.7
be important 672.11
be obstinate 626.7
be visible 444.4
exceed 34.5
protrude 256.9
**stand over**
govern 741.12
postpone 132.9
supervise 747.10
**standpat**
n. rightist 745.9
adj. conservative
745.17
diehard 140.8
do-nothing 706.6
unyielding 142.15
**stand pat**
be conservative 140.6
be obstinate 626.7
bet 515.20
stand fast 142.11
**standpipe** tower 207.11
tube 396.6
**standpoint**
mental outlook 525.2
station 184.2
viewpoint 439.7
**standstill** impasse 731.5
quiescence 268.3
stop 144.2
**stand still**
be conservative 140.6
repose 268.7
**stand together**
agree 26.6
cooperate 786.3
join 52.4
**stand to lose** 175.3
**stand up** be erect 213.7
be true 516.7
not weaken 159.9
persevere 625.4
rear 315.8
resist 792.2

rise 213.8
stand the test 489.10
straighten 250.5
suffice 661.4
**stand-up comic** 612.9
**stand up for**
defend 1006.10
sponsor 772.9
**stand up to**
face up to 893.11
meet an obligation
962.11
offer resistance 792.3
**Stanford-Binet test**
690.11
**stanza**
music division 462.24
poetic division
609.11
**stapes** 448.7
**staphylococcus** 686.39
**staple**
n. commodity 831.2
marketplace 832.2
materials 378.1
merchandise 831.1
source of supply
660.4
v. fasten 47.8
adj. fixed 142.14
**star**
n. award 916.5
expert 733.13
famous person 914.9
first-rater 674.6
heavenly body
375.4,8
lead 612.6
light source 336.1
military insignia
569.5
principal 672.10
successful person
724.5
superior 36.4
v. act 611.34
be important 672.11
emphasize 672.13
give a show 611.33
give prominence
672.14
take precedence
36.11
adj. chief 36.14
**starboard**
n. right side 243.1
v. change course
275.31
adj. right 243.4
adv. rightward 243.7
interj. sailing 275.76
**starch**
nutrient 309.5,22
semiliquid 389.5
vim 161.2
**starched** formal 646.9
rigid 356.11
**starchy** rigid 356.11
viscous 389.12
**star-crossed** 729.14
**stare**
n. gaze 439.5

v. be curious 528.3
gaze 439.16
wonder 920.5
**stare down** defy 793.3
gaze 439.16
outbrave 893.12
**starets**
antiquated person
123.8
good person 985.6
master 749.1
teacher 565.1
wise man 468.1
**starfish** 415.5
**stargaze** 532.9
**stargazer**
astrologer 375.23
astronomer 375.22
**stargazing**
n. abstractedness
532.2
astrology 375.20
astronomy 375.19
adj. abstracted 532.11
**staring**
astonished 920.9
clearly visible 444.7
conspicuous 555.12
**stark**
adj. bare 45.6
mere 35.8
outright 34.12
plain 902.9
unaffected 591.3
adv. absolutely 56.15
**stark-naked** 232.14
**stark-raving mad** 473.30
**starless** 337.13
**starlight** 335.12
**starlike**
luminous 335.30
star-shaped 258.17
**starlit** 335.39
**starred** 672.20
**starry** celestial 375.25
luminous 335.30
**starry-eyed**
enthusiastic about
635.12
happy 865.13
visionary 535.24
**stars** 640.2
**Stars and Stripes** 569.6
**star-spangled**
celestial 375.25
illuminated 335.39
**start**
n. advantage 36.2
beginning 68.1
boundary 235.3
jerk 286.3
outset 301.2
point of departure
301.5
surprise 540.3
v. be damaged 692.26
be frightened 891.20
begin 68.7
be surprised 540.5
come apart 49.8
depart 301.7
hunt 655.9

jump 319.5
launch 285.14
propose 773.5
pull back 284.7
set to work 716.15
**starter** 414.17
**starting point**
beginning 68.1
boundary 235.3
point of departure
301.5
**startle** alarm 704.3
astonish 920.6
be surprised 540.5
frighten 891.23
jump 891.20
surprise 540.8
**startled** alarmed 704.4
frightened 891.33
shocked 540.13
**startling**
astonishing 920.12
frightening 891.36
sudden 113.5
surprising 540.11
**start up** appear 446.9
ascend 315.9
begin 68.8
found 68.11
jump 319.5
launch 285.14
protrude 256.9
**starvation**
n. fasting 995.1
violent death 408.6
want 662.4
adj. meager 662.10
**starvation diet** 995.2
**starve**
be parsimonious
852.5
be poor 838.5
die 408.24
hunger 634.19
kill 409.13
**starved** hungry 634.25
ill-provided 662.12
wasted 205.20
**starveling** 838.4
**stash**
n. hiding place 615.4
v. secrete 615.7
store 660.10
**stasis** immobility 140.1
inaction 706.1
stagnation 268.4
**stat**
n. copy 24.5
v. copy 24.8
**state**
n. condition 7
country 181.1
district 180.5
grandeur 904.5
people 417.2
pomp 904.6
v. affirm 523.4
declare 594.24
express belief 501.12
phrase 588.4
publish 559.12
specify 80.11

*adj.* public 417.13
**stated** affirmed 523.8
circumscribed 234.6
conditional 507.8
fixed 142.14
made public 559.17
made sure 513.20
**statehood** 181.6
**statehouse** 742.12
**stateless person**
displaced person
185.4
fugitive 631.5
migrant 274.5
**stately**
ceremonious 646.8
dignified 905.12
eloquent 600.14
grandiose 904.21
**statement**
account 608.3
affirmation 523.1
announcement 559.2
bill 845.3
information 557.1
legal statement
1004.7
list 88.5
music division 462.24
numeration 87.5
premise 482.7
record 570.7
remark 594.4
testimony 505.3
**state of affairs**
concerns 151.4
situation 7.2
**state of mind** 525.4
**state of war** 797.1
**stateroom**
ship room 192.9
train room 192.10
**States, the** 181.3
**stateside** 181.3
**statesman**
expert 733.11
politician 746.2
**statesmanlike**
governmental 744.43
political 746.13
skillful 733.20
**statesmanship** 744.3
**static**
*n.* audio distortion
450.13
pandemonium 62.5
radio reception
344.21
*adj.* do-nothing 706.6
electricity 342.27
inert 268.14
mechanical 347.8
permanent 140.7
quiescent 268.13
sedentary 708.16
**static electricity** 342.1
**statics** forces 157.7
mechanics 347.2
physics 325.1
**station**
*n.* class 61.2
farm 413.8

position 656.5
prestige 914.4
rank 29.2
state 7.1
status 184.2
*v.* place 184.11
**stationary**
do-nothing 706.6
immovable 142.15
inactive 708.16
motionless 268.13
permanent 140.7
**station break** 344.19
**stationery** paper 378.6
types of 602.29
**station identification**
344.19
**stationmaster** 274.13
**statistical** 87.15
**statistician**
calculator 87.8
mathematician 87.9
**statistics** figures 87.7
mathematical proba-
bility 511.2
**statuary**
*n.* figure 572.4
sculptor 579.6
sculpture 575.1
*adj.* sculptural 575.6
**statue** figure 572.4
sculpture 575.2
work of art 574.11
**statuelike**
motionless 268.13
sculptural 575.6
**statuesque**
beautiful 900.17
dignified 905.12
sculptural 575.6
tall 207.21
**stature** authority 739.4
height 207.1
prestige 914.4
**status** class 61.2
prestige 914.4
rank 29.2
role 7.5
state 7.1
station 184.2
**status quo**
circumstance 8.2
situation 7.2
**status seeker** 919.10
**status-seeking** 634.10
**statute** law 998.3
prohibition 778.1
**statutory** legal 998.10
prescriptive 751.4
**staunch** close 266.12
faithful 974.20
firm 624.12
friendly 927.20
orthodox 1024.8
reliable 513.17
solid 159.16
**staunchly**
faithfully 974.25
resolutely 624.17
strongly 159.21
**stave** music 462.29

poetic division
609.11
staff 217.2
step 315.5
supporter 216.2
wood 378.3
**stave off**
fend off 799.10
postpone 132.9
prevent 730.14
**stay**
*n.* corset 231.23
curb 730.7
delay 132.2
exemption 1007.2
obstruction 730.2
pause 144.3
respite 711.2
sojourn 188.5
stop 144.2
supporter 216.2
*v.* be still 268.7
cease 144.6
cohere 50.6
continue 143.3
delay 132.8
endure 110.6
inhabit 188.7
obstruct 266.7
postpone 132.9
prevent 730.13
remain 140.5
settle at 184.16
slow 270.9
sojourn 188.8
stop 144.11
stay for 539.8
support 216.21
wait 132.12
**stay-at-home**
*n.* recluse 924.5
*adj.* recluse 924.9
untraveled 268.15
**staying power**
continuance 143.1
perseverance 625.1
strength 159.1
**stay in line**
conform 82.4
obey 766.2
**stay put** be still 268.7
cohere 50.6
stand fast 142.11
**stay up** 132.12
**stay up for** 539.8
**stead** location 184.1
place 184.4
**steadfast**
enduring 110.10
faithful 974.20
firm 624.12
friendly 927.20
permanent 140.7
persevering 625.7
reliable 513.17
stable 142.12
uniform 17.5
**steadily**
constantly 135.7
faithfully 974.25
inexcitably 858.16
moderately 163.17

perpetually 112.10
regularly 137.9
resolutely 624.17
uniformly 17.8
**steady**
*n.* sweetheart 931.10
*v.* calm 163.7
stabilize 142.7
*adj.* continuing 143.7
endless 71.8
faithful 974.20
firm 624.12
inexcitable 858.10
orderly 59.6
periodic 137.7
persevering 625.7
regular 135.5
reliable 513.17
stable 142.12
substantial 3.7
unhazardous 698.5
uniform 17.5
uninterrupted 112.7
unnervous 860.2
*interj.* caution 895.14
sailing 275.76
**steady state**
automation 349.9
continuity 71.1
stability 142.1
**steady state theory**
375.18
**steak** 308.18
**steal**
*n.* a theft 824.10
bargain 849.3
*v.* borrow 821.4
creep 273.25
lurk 615.9
take 822.13
thieve 824.13
**steal away** 631.12
**stealing**
*n.* booty 824.11
creeping 273.9
theft 824.1
*adj.* lurking 615.14
**steal one's thunder**
730.15
**stealth** cunning 735.1
secrecy 614.4
**steal the show** 611.34
**stealthy**
cunning 735.12
furtive 614.12
in hiding 615.14
**steam**
*n.* heat 328.10
power 157.1
vapor 401.1
water 392.3
*v.* be hot 328.22
cook 330.4
exhale 310.23
give off 401.8
heat 329.17
sail 275.13
**steam bath** 328.11
**steamboat**
*n.* steamer 277.2
*v.* sail 275.13

**steamed up**
  enthusiastic about
    635.12
  excited 857.18
**steamer** food 308.25
  steamboat 277.2,22
**steaming**
  *n.* vaporization 401.5
  water travel 275.1
  *adj.* excited 857.20
  fervent 855.23
  vaporous 401.9
**steam pipe**
  heater 329.10
  tube 396.6
**steam propulsion** 285.2
**steamroller**
  *n.* force 756.2
  pulverizer 361.7
  *v.* coerce 756.7
  level 214.6
  overwhelm 727.8
  raze 693.19
  *adj.* coercive 756.11
**steam room** 681.10
**steamship** 277.2
**steam shovel** 257.10
**steam up** excite 857.11
  prepare 720.9
**steamy** excited 857.20
  fervent 855.23
  lustful 419.29
  vaporous 401.9
**steed** 414.10
**steel**
  *n.* cutlery 348.2
  hardness 356.6
  stock type 834.2
  strength 159.7
  sword 801.4
  *v.* harden 356.7
  make unfeeling 856.6
  strengthen 159.11
  *adj.* metal 383.17
**steel band** 464.12
**steeled** callous 856.12
  hardened 356.13
**steel mill** 719.5
**steel oneself**
  be determined 624.8
  be unregretful 874.3
  get up nerve 893.13
**steelworks**
  foundry 719.5
  metalworks 719.4
**steely** callous 856.12
  firm 624.12
  gray 366.4
  hard 356.10
  metal 383.17
  strong 159.13
  unyielding 626.9
**steep**
  *n.* height 207.2
  precipice 213.3
  *v.* extract 305.16
  infuse 44.12
  soak 392.13
  *adj.* difficult 731.16
  excessive 663.16
  expensive 848.11
  high 207.19

perpendicular 213.12
  precipitous 219.18
**steeple**
  pointed projection
    258.4
  tower 207.11
**steeplechase**
  horse race 796.13
  jump 319.1
  leaping 319.3
**steeplechaser**
  race horse 414.17
  rider 274.8
**steer**
  *n.* bull 414.6
  male animal 420.8
  tip 557.3
  *v.* bear 290.8
  direct to 290.7
  drive 747.9
  head for 290.10
  operate 164.5
  pilot 275.14
**steer clear of**
  avoid 631.6
  be inhospitable 926.5
  keep away 199.7
  snub 966.7
  turn aside 291.6
**steering**
  automation 349.7
  direction 290.1
  operation 164.1
  pilotage 747.1
**steering committee**
  748.11
**steersman**
  boatman 276.8
  operator 164.4
  pilot 748.7
**Steinway** 465.13
**stela** 570.12
**stellar** celestial 375.25
  chief 36.14
  theatrical 611.38
**stem**
  *n.* ancestry 170.4
  base 216.8
  bow 240.3
  fork 299.4
  leg 273.16
  morphology 582.3
  plant stem 411.19
  printing 603.6
  race 11.4
  root 153.5
  shaft 217.1
  tube 396.6
  *v.* branch 299.7
  confront 240.8
  contest 790.4
  progress 294.2
  result from 154.6
  stop 144.11
**stemware** 339.2
**stench**
  *n.* odor 435.1
  stink 437
  *v.* stop 266.7
**stencil**
  *n.* graphic art 578.5
  picture 574.12

printing 603.1
  *v.* picture 574.20
**stenographer**
  recorder 571.1
  shorthandwriter
    602.17
**stenography** 602.8
**stentorian**
  loud-voiced 453.11
  resounding 453.10
**step**
  *n.* act 705.3
  attempt 714.2
  dance 879.8
  degree 29.1
  expedient 670.2
  gait 273.14
  harmonics 463.20
  layer 227.1
  mark 568.7
  process 164.2
  rate 267.4
  short distance 200.2
  stair 315.5
  tread 273.13
  *v.* measure 490.11
  run 269.10
  step over 313.8
  walk 273.26
**step aside** dodge 631.8
  resign 784.2
  separate 49.9
  turn away 291.6
**step backward** 671.2
**step by step**
  by degrees 29.6
  consecutively 71.11
  in order 59.10
**stepchild**
  descendant 171.3
  relative by marriage
    12.3
**step down**
  electricity 342.23
  reduce 39.7
**step forward**
  progress 294.2
  volunteer 773.9
**step in** enter 302.7
  mediate 805.6
**stepladder** 315.4
**step lively**
  hustle 707.13
  ’ make haste! 709.16
  run 269.10
**stepmother**
  parent 170.10
  relative by marriage
    12.3
**step on it**
  accelerate 269.14
  hurry 709.6
  make haste! 709.17
  rush 269.9
**step out**
  make merry 878.26
  take off 232.6
**steppe** grassland 411.8
  horizontal 214.3
  plain 387.1
  prairie 182.1
  space 179.4

**stepper** horse 414.18
  speeder 269.5
**stepping-stone**
  bridge 657.10
  opportunity 129.2
  stair 315.3
  step 315.5
**steps** precaution 895.3
  stairs 315.3
**step stool** 315.5
**step up**
  accelerate 269.14
  approach 296.3
  electricity 342.23
  increase 38.5
**step-up**
  acceleration 269.4
  increase 38.2
**stereo** 450.11
**stereopticon** 577.12
**stereoscopic**
  optical 443.9
  spatial 179.8
**stereoscopy** 443.6
**stereotype**
  *n.* habit 642.4
  printing surface 603.8
  *v.* fix 142.9
  make plates 603.15
  make uniform 17.4
**stereotyped** dull 883.9
  habitual 642.16
  indistinctive 493.6
  routine 79.12
  trite 79.16
**stereotypy** 603.1
**sterile** fruitless 669.12
  ineffective 158.15
  sanitary 681.27
  uninteresting 883.6
  unproductive 166.4
**sterility** cleanness 681.1
  uninterestingness
    883.1
  unproductiveness
    166.1
**sterilization** 681.3
**sterilize**
  emasculate 158.12
  sanitize 681.24
**sterling**
  *n.* money 835.1
  *adj.* genuine 516.14
  honest 974.13
  monetary 835.30
  superb 674.17
**stern**
  *n.* buttocks 241.5
  rear 241.1
  tail end 241.7
  *adj.* strict 757.6
  unkind 939.22
  unyielding 626.9
**sternway** course 267.2
  regression 295.1
  water travel 275.9
**steroid** 309.7
**stertor**
  breathing 403.18
  sibilation 457.1
**stertorous**
  breathing 403.29

**strafe**
  *n.* bombardment
    798.7
  *v.* fire upon 798.22
**straggle** follow 293.4
  stray 291.4
  stretch 202.6
  walk 273.27
  wander 273.22
**straggling**
  dispersed 75.9
  stretched 202.9
  unordered 62.12
  wandering 273.36
**straight**
  *n.* direct 250.2
  heterosexual 419.15
  playing cards 878.17
  *adj.* accurate 516.15
  candid 974.17
  conformist 82.6
  continuous 71.8
  direct 290.13
  honest 974.14
  sexual 419.26
  simple 45.7
  thorough 56.10
  trustworthy 974.19
  undeviating 250.6
  unqualified 508.2
  virtuous 980.7
  *adv.* accurately 516.19
  directly 290.24
  exactly 516.20
  squarely 290.25
  unswervingly 250.7
**straight and narrow, the**
  980.1
**straightaway**
  *n.* straight line 250.2
  *adj.* direct 290.13
  *adv.* at once 113.8
  promptly 131.15
**straightedge** 250.3
**straighten out**
  arrange 771.9
  make better 691.9
  mediate 805.7
  rectify 250.5
  reprove 969.17
**straight face**
  solemnity 871.1
  unexpressiveness
    549.5
  unfeeling 856.1
**straight-faced** 871.3
**straightforward**
  *adj.* candid 974.17
  direct 290.13
  easy 732.12
  elegant 589.6
  in plain style 591.3
  intelligible 548.10
  simple 45.8
  unaffected 902.7
  *adv.* directly 290.24
**traightjacket** 760.4
**traightlaced** 757.7
**traight man** 612.2
**traightness** 250
**traight-out**
  candid 974.17

unqualified 508.2
**straight shooter** 974.8
**straight-shooting** 974.14
**strain**
  *n.* ancestry 170.4
  anxiety 890.1
  class 61.2
  endeavor 714.1
  enmity 929.1
  exertion 716.2
  fatigue 717.1
  kind 61.3
  lengthening 202.5
  melody 462.4
  music division 462.24
  overdoing 663.6
  overextension 663.7
  people 418.1
  poetic division
    609.11
  pull 286.2
  race 11.4
  stretching 358.2
  style 588.2
  tension 859.3
  trait of character
    525.3
  *v.* be irresolute 627.7
  demur 623.4
  distort 249.6
  endeavor 714.4
  exude 303.15
  falsify 616.16
  injure 692.15
  lengthen 202.7
  overextend 663.13
  refine 681.22
  tax oneself 716.10
  try for 714.8
**strained** anxious 890.6
  distorted 249.11
  farfetched 10.7
  laborious 716.18
  lengthened 202.9
  tense 859.12
  unfriendly 929.9
**strainer**
  porousness 265.9
  refining equipment
    681.13
**straining**
  *n.* distortion 249.2
  exertion 716.2
  falsification 616.9
  filtering 303.6
  overextension 663.7
  purification 681.4
  *adj.* fatiguing 717.11
  irresolute 627.11
  laboring 716.17
**strait**
  *n.* arm of the sea
    399.1
  crisis 129.4
  danger 697.1
  narrow place 205.3
  predicament 731.4
  *adj.* limited 234.7
  narrow 205.14
**straiten** enclose 236.6
  limit 234.5
  narrow 205.11

restrain 760.7
**straitened**
  in trouble 731.24
  limited 234.7
  meager 662.10
  poor 838.7
**straitjacket**
  *n.* restraint 760.4
  *v.* restrain 760.10
**straitlaced**
  narrow-minded
    527.10
  orthodox 1024.8
  prudish 903.19
  strict 757.7
**straits**
  arm of the sea 399.1
  poverty 838.1
  predicament 731.4
**strand**
  *n.* filament 206.1
  shore 385.2
  *v.* shipwreck 275.42
**stranded**
  aground 142.16
  in difficulty 731.25
**strange** eccentric 474.4
  extraneous 78.5
  insane 473.25
  new 122.11
  odd 85.11
  unknown 477.17
  unrelated 10.5
  wonderful 920.10
**strangeness**
  atomics 326.6
  eccentricity 474.1
  insanity 473.1
  newness 122.1
  oddity 85.3
**stranger** alien 78.3
  foreigner 77.3
**strangle** choke 409.19
  close 266.6
  constrict 198.7
  destroy 693.15
  die 408.24
  execute 1010.19
  obstruct 730.12
  render powerless
    158.11
  suppress 760.8
**strangled**
  constricted 198.12
  hoarse 458.15
  imperfectly spoken
    595.12
**stranglehold**
  hindrance 730.1
  restraint 760.4
  wrestling hold 813.3
**strangler**
  executioner 1010.8
  killer 409.11
**strangling**
  *n.* capital punishment
    1010.7
  suffocation 409.7
  suppression 760.2
  violent death 408.6
  *adj.* hindering 730.17

**strangulated**
  choked 266.9
  constricted 198.12
**strangulation**
  capital punishment
    1010.7
  constriction 198.1
  destruction 693.6
  obstruction 266.3
  suffocation 409.7
  violent death 408.6
**strap**
  *n.* stock option 833.21
  strip 206.4
  whip 1011.1
  *v.* bandage 689.30
  bind 47.9
  punish 1010.14
  restrain 760.10
  sharpen 258.9
**straphanger** 274.1
**strapless** 232.13
**strap oil** 1010.6
**strapped** broke 838.10
  poor 838.7
  restrained 760.16
**strapping**
  *n.* punishment 1010.4
  *adj.* corpulent 195.18
  strong 159.13
**stratagem** artifice 735.3
  expedient 670.2
  intrigue 654.6
  pretext 649.1
  trick 618.6
**strategic**
  cunning 735.12
  planned 654.13
**strategist**
  cunning person 735.7
  planner 654.7
  political intriguer
    746.6
**strategy** plan 654.1
  scheme 735.3
  warfare 797.9
**strati–** 227.1
**stratification**
  classification 61.1
  layering 227.4
**stratified** classified 61.8
  layered 227.6
**stratify** 227.5
**stratosphere**
  atmospheric layer
    402.3
  aviation 278.41
  height 207.2
**stratum**
  atmospheric layer
    402.3
  class 61.2
  layer 227.1
**stratus** 404.1
**straw**
  *n.* fodder 308.4
  lightness 353.2
  plant stem 411.19
  refuse 43.1
  trifle 673.5
  tube 396.6
  *adj.* yellow 370.4

**sublease**
n. hire 780.5
possession 808.1
v. hire out 780.15
rent 780.14
**sublet**
v. hire out 780.15
rent 780.14
adj. employed 780.19
**sublimate**
n. deposit 43.2
v. control feelings
858.8
refine 681.22
vaporize 401.8
**sublimated** 538.9
**sublimation**
defense mechanism
690.30
mental block 538.3
refinement 681.4
vaporization 401.5
**sublime**
v. refine 681.22
vaporize 401.8
adj. eloquent 600.14
eminent 914.18
exalted 34.9
gorgeous 900.19
lofty 207.19
magnanimous 979.6
pleasant 863.8
raised 317.9
**subliminal**
instinctive 481.6
subconscious 690.48
**sublittoral** 397.5
**submarine**
n. diving equipment
320.5
warship 277.9,24
adj. underwater
209.13
**submerge** dive 275.47
drench 392.14
immerse 320.7
sink 316.6
**submerged**
depressed 318.12
latent 546.5
soaked 392.17
underwater 209.13
unseen 445.5
**submerged in**
engrossed 530.17
involved in 176.4
**submergence**
decline 316.2
depth 209.6
immersion 320.2
sinking 318.1
water travel 275.8
**submerging** 316.11
**submersible** 320.9
**submersion**
depth 209.6
engrossment 530.3
immersion 320.2
inundation 395.6
wetting 392.6
**submission**
compliance 765

consent 775.1
obedience 766.1
obeisance 964.2
offer 773.1
resignation 861.2
**submissive**
assenting 521.13
compliant 765.12
conformable 82.5
consenting 775.4
downtrodden 764.16
humble 906.10
obedient 766.3
obeisant 964.10
pliant 357.9
resigned 861.10
servile 907.12
**submit** accept 861.6
acquiesce 775.3
advise 754.5
affirm 523.4
be pliant 357.7
nominate 637.19
obey 766.2
offer 773.4
propose 773.5
put 184.11
yield 765.6
**submittal** 765.1
**subnormal**
abnormal 85.9
mentally deficient
469.22
**suborder** biology 61.5
class 61.2
**subordinate**
n. inferior 37.2
retainer 750.1
subject 764.5
v. arrange 60.11
subject 764.8
adj. inferior 37.6
subject 764.13
**subordinate to** 764.17
**subordination**
gradation 59.2
grouping 60.3
inferiority 37.1
subservience 764.2
**suborn** 651.3
**subornation** 651.1
**subplot** 608.9
**subpoena**
n. legal action 1004.2
summons 752.7
v. litigate 1004.13
summon 752.12
**sub rosa** 614.17
**subscribe** abet 785.14
belong 788.15
give 818.14
**subscriber**
assenter 521.7
giver 818.11
**subscribe to**
assent 521.8
ratify 521.12
secure 772.9
**subscript** 67.1
**subscription**
donation 818.6
giving 818.1

ratification 521.4
signature 583.10
**subsequence** 117.1
**subsequent** after 117.4
following 65.4
**subsequently** 117.6
**subsequent to** 117.8
**subserve**
be inferior 37.4
be instrumental
658.5
cause 153.13
**subservience**
inferiority 37.1
servility 907.1
subjection 764.2
submissiveness 765.3
**subservient**
deferential 765.16
helping 785.20
inferior 37.6
instrumental 658.6
servile 907.12
subject 764.13
submissive 765.12
**subside** decline 692.20
decrease 39.6
ebb 267.5
quiet 268.8
settle 352.15
sink 316.6
**subsidence**
decline 316.2
decrease 39.2
landslide 316.4
standstill 268.3
**subsidiary**
n. nonessential 6.2
adj. endowed 818.26
helping 785.20
unessential 6.4
**subsiding**
decreasing 39.11
descending 316.11
deteriorating 692.46
quiescent 268.12
**subsidize** endow 818.19
pay for 841.19
provide 659.7
sponsor 836.15
support 216.21
sustain 785.12
**subsidy** grant 818.8
maintenance 785.3
payment 841.8
provision 659.1
sponsoring 836.2
support 216.1
**subsist** abide 140.5
endure 110.6
exist 1.8
live 407.7
remain 43.5
survive 659.12
**subsistence**
n. accommodations
659.3
existence 1.1
support 785.3
adj. meager 662.10
**subsistent** 1.13
**subsoil** 385.1

**subsonic** 450.17
**subsonics** 450.6
**substance body** 3.1
content 194.5
essence 5.2
funds 835.14
grounds 1006.6
important point
672.6
major part 54.6
material 378.1
matter 376.2
meaning 545.1
quantity 28.1
stuff 3.2
summary 607.2
topic 484.1
wealth 837.1
**substandard**
inferior 680.10
vernacular 580.18
**substandard language**
580.6
**substantial**
authoritative 739.15
dense 354.12
essential 5.8
important 672.16
influential 172.13
large 195.16
material 376.9
meaningful 545.10
real 1.15
reliable 513.17
solvent 836.17
stable 142.12
substantive 3.6
sufficient 661.6
valid 516.13
**substantiality**
existence 1.1
materiality 376.1
plenty 661.2
reliability 513.4
stability 142.1
substantialness 3
validity 516.4
**substantially**
essentially 3.8
fundamentally 5.10
on the whole 54.14
sufficiently 661.8
**substantiate**
confirm 505.12
materialize 376.8
particularize 8.6
test 489.8
**substantiated**
proved 505.21
true 516.12
**substantiating** 505.19
**substantiation**
assurance 513.8
confirmation 505.5
embodiment 3.4
materialization 376.?
**substantive**
n. part of speech
586.5
adj. essential 5.8
grammatical 586.17
substantial 3.6

woo 932.19
suet 308.13
suffer be patient 861.5
    be punished 1010.22
    be sick 686.43
    experience 151.8
    feel pain 424.8
    hurt 866.19
    permit 777.10
sufferable 868.13
sufferance
    patience 861.1
    permission 777.2
sufferer
    sick person 686.40
    victim 866.11
suffering
    n. distress 866.5
    pain 424.1
    adj. pained 424.9
    tolerant 777.14
suffice
    be of use 665.17
    be satisfactory 868.6
    do 661.4
sufficiency
    ability 157.2
    adequacy 661
    satisfactoriness 868.3
    tolerableness 674.3
sufficient
    enough 661.6
    satisfactory 868.11
    tolerable 674.19
    valid 516.13
suffix
    n. addition 41.2
    morphology 582.3
    sequel 67.1
    v. add 40.4
    place after 65.3
suffocate be hot 328.22
    destroy 693.15
    die 408.24
    obstruct 730.12
    strangle 409.19
    suppress 760.8
suffocating
    n. suppression 760.2
    adj. airless 268.16
    strong-smelling 435.10
    sultry 328.28
suffocation
    destruction 693.6
    smothering 409.7
    violent death 408.6
suffrage
    franchise 744.17
    participation 815.1
    vote 637.6
suffragette
    suffrage 744.17
    women's rightist 958.7
suffuse imbue 44.12
    pervade 186.7
suffusion flush 908.5
    infusion 44.2
    permeation 186.3
suffusive 186.14

sugar
    n. endearment 932.5
    money 835.2
    nutrient 309.5
    sweetening 431.2
    v. sweeten 431.3
sugarcoat 431.3
sugar daddy
    beau 931.12
    patron 818.11
sugar off 431.3
sugary 431.4
suggest advise 754.5
    evidence 505.9
    hint 557.10
    imply 546.4
    indicate 568.17
    mean 545.8
    promise 544.13
    propose 773.5
    remind 537.20
    resemble 20.7
suggested 546.7
suggestible 172.15
suggestion advice 754.1
    clue 568.9
    disparagement 971.4
    hint 557.4
    implication 546.2
    indication 568.1
    influence 172.1
    proposal 773.2
    small amount 35.4
    tinge 44.7
    vague supposition 499.5
suggestive
    allusive 546.6
    eloquent 600.10
    evidential 505.17
    indicative 568.23
    meaningful 545.10
    recollective 537.22
    risqué 990.7
suggestive of 20.10
suicidal
    dejected 872.22
    destructive 693.26
    murderous 409.24
    wretched 866.26
suicide killer 409.3
    self-murder 409.6
sui generis
    peerless 36.15
    unique 16.8
    unusual 85.10
suit
    n. accusation 1005.1
    courtship 932.6
    entreaty 774.2
    lawsuit 1004.1
    prayer 1032.4
    set 74.12
    solicitation 774.5
    suit of clothes 231.6
    types of 231.48
    v. adjust 720.8
    conform 82.3
    fit 26.8
    outfit 231.40
suitability
    eligibility 637.11

expedience 670.1
    fitness 26.5
    propriety 958.2
    readiness 720.4
    tastefulness 897.3
    timeliness 129.1
suitable apt 26.10
    decorous 897.10
    eligible 637.24
    expedient 670.5
    right 958.8
    sufficient 661.6
    timely 129.9
suitable for 82.9
suite apartment 191.14
    music 462.9
    retinue 73.6
    set 74.12
suited apt 26.10
    competent 733.22
    fitted 720.17
suit oneself 762.19
suitor accuser 1005.5
    aspirant 634.12
    litigant 1004.11
    lover 931.11
    petitioner 774.7
sukkah 1040.11
Sukkoth 1040.16
sulfa drug
    types of 687.61
    wonder drug 687.29
sulfonate 379.6
sulfuric 383.15
sulfurous hellish 1019.8
    malodorous 437.5
    mineral 383.15
sulk 951.14
sulks ill humor 951.10
    sadness 872.6
    unwillingness 623.1
sullen glum 872.25
    obstinate 626.8
    perverse 626.11
    sulky 951.24
    unsociable 923.5
    unwilling 623.5
sullied soiled 682.21
    unchaste 989.23
sully defile 682.17
    demoralize 981.10
    seduce 989.20
    soil 682.16
    stigmatize 915.9
    vilify 971.10
sulphuric, sulphurous
    see sulfuric etc.
sultan 749.10
sultanate country 181.1
    sovereignty 739.8
sultry obscene 990.9
    stifling 328.28
sum
    n. addition 40.2
    amount 28.2
    extent 28.1
    meaning 545.1
    number 86.5
    summary 607.2
    sum of money 835.13
    total 54.2
    v. add 40.6

calculate 87.12
summa cum laude 916.11
summarily
    concisely 592.7
    shortly 203.12
    swiftly 131.15
summarize
    abridge 607.5
    review 103.8
    shorten 203.6
    sum up 87.12
summary
    n. abridgment 203.3
    iteration 103.2
    numeration 87.5
    résumé 607.2
    adj. concise 592.6
    expeditious 131.9
    short 203.8
summation
    abridgment 203.3
    addition 40.2
    legal argument 1004.8
    numeration 87.5
    recapitulation 607.2
    sum 86.5
summer
    n. hot weather 328.7
    season 128.3
    v. spend time 105.6
    adj. summery 128.8
summerhouse
    arbor 191.13
    nursery 413.11
summer school 567.2
summer stock 611.1
summertime 128.3
summery green 371.4
    summer 128.8
    warm 328.24
summing up
    iteration 103.2
    legal argument 1004.8
    numeration 87.5
summit
    completion 56.5
    conference 597.6
    culmination 677.3
    peak 207.8
    top 211.2
summon
    assemble 74.17
    attract 650.5
    call for 752.12
    conjure 1035.11
    enlist 780.16
    evoke 305.14
    invite 774.13
summons
    n. bidding 752.5
    call 568.16
    enlistment 780.6
    invitation 774.4
    legal action 1004.2
    subpoena 752.7
    v. litigate 1004.13
    summon 752.12
summon up
    elicit 305.14

excite 857.11
prompt 648.13
remember 537.10
summon 752.12
visualize 535.15
sumo 796.10
sump
  body of water 398.1
  channel 396.5
  filth receptacle
    682.12
  marsh 400.1
sumpter
  beast of burden
    271.6
  horse 414.16
  mule 414.21
sumptuary 835.30
sumptuous
  expensive 848.11
  grandiose 904.21
sum up calculate 87.12
  repeat 103.8
  shorten 203.6
sun
  *n.* gods 375.14
  heavenly body 375.13
  light source 336.1
  period 107.2
  year 107.2
  *v.* bask 329.19
  dry 393.6
sunbaked 393.9
sunbath 689.5
sunbathe 329.19
sunbeam 335.10
Sunbelt 180.7
sunburn
  *n.* burn 329.6
  *v.* brown 367.2
sunburned
  burned 329.30
  red-complexioned
    368.9
  reddish-brown 367.4
sundae 308.46
sunday
  *n.* day of rest 711.5
  holy day 1040.14
  *v.* vacation 711.9
sunday best 231.10
sunday driver 274.10
sunday painter 673.9
sunday school 567.10
sunder
  demolish 693.17
  sever 49.11
sundered 201.7
sundown 134.2
sundowner
  alcoholic drink 996.8
  bad person 986.2
  vagabond 274.3
sundries
  miscellany 74.13
  notions 831.6
sundry diversified 19.4
  several 101.7
sunglasses
  eyeshade 338.2
  spectacles 443.2
sunk depressed 318.12

hollow 257.16
spoiled 692.31
sunken
  depressed 318.12
  hollow 257.16
  underwater 209.13
sunless 337.13
sunlight 335.10
sunlit 335.39
sunny cheerful 870.11
  luminous 335.30
  optimistic 888.12
  pleasant 863.10
  warm 328.24
sunny side 863.4
sunrise dawn 133.3
  east 290.3
sunroom 192.5
sunscreen 338.4
sunset evening 134.2
  west 290.3
sunshade shade 338.1
  umbrella 228.7
sunshine
  daylight 335.10
  good times 728.4
  happiness 865.2
sunshiny
  luminous 335.30
  warm 328.24
sunspot 375.13
sunstroke
  environmental dis-
    ease 686.31
  heatstroke 686.26
suntan 367.2
sunup 133.3
sun worship 1033.1
sun worshiper 1033.4
sup
  *n.* guzzle 996.6
  sip 307.4
  small amount 35.4
  taste 427.2
  *v.* dine 307.19
  drink 307.27
  taste 427.7
  tipple 996.23
super
  *n.* actor 612.7
  book size 605.14
  superintendent 748.2
  *adj.* superb 674.17
  superior 36.12
superable 509.7
superabound
  overabound 663.8
  overrun 313.4
superabundance
  diffuseness 593.1
  excess 663.2
  plenty 661.2
  productiveness 165.1
  quantity 34.3
superabundant
  diffuse 593.11
  excessive 663.19
  much 34.8
  plentiful 661.7
  productive 165.9
  teeming 101.9

superannuate
  become old 123.9
  depose 783.4
  discard 668.8
  dismiss 310.19
  obsolesce 668.9
  resign 784.2
superannuated
  antiquated 123.13
  disused 668.10
  retired 784.3
superb eminent 34.9
  excellent 674.17
  grandiose 904.21
superbly
  exquisitely 674.22
  grandiosely 904.28
  skillfully 733.29
supercharged
  loaded 56.12
  overfull 663.20
supercilious
  contemptuous 966.8
  disdainful 912.13
supercooled
  cold 333.14
  cooled 334.13
superego
  conscience 957.5
  psyche 690.35
  self 80.5
supereminent
  chief 36.14
  eminent 914.18
  superb 674.17
supererogatory 663.17
superficial
  apparent 446.11
  exterior 224.6
  formal 646.7
  frivolous 469.20
  half-learned 477.15
  hasty 709.9
  insignificant 35.6
  shallow 210.5
  surface 179.8
  trivial 673.16
  uninteresting 883.6
superficiality
  appearances 446.2
  exteriority 224.1
  frivolousness 469.7
  inattention 531.1
  shallowness 210.1
  slight knowledge
    477.6
  triviality 673.3
  uninterestingness
    883.1
superficially
  apparently 446.12
  externally 224.9
  hastily 709.12
  unimportantly 673.20
  vapidly 883.10
superfine
  grandiose 904.21
  superb 674.17
superfluity
  diffuseness 593.1
  excess 43.4
  extravagance 663.4

ornamentation 901.3
profusion 34.3
superfluous
  excessive 663.17
  remaining 43.7
  unessential 6.4
  useless 669.9
supergovernment 741.7
superheat
  *n.* heat 328.1
  *v.* heat 329.17
superheated 329.29
superhighway 657.6
superhuman
  divine 1013.19
  supernatural 85.15
superimpose 228.19
superimposed 228.35
superincumbent
  covering 228.35
  overhanging 215.11
  ponderous 352.17
superintend 747.10
superintendence
  directorship 747.4
  supervision 747.2
superintendent
  *n.* peace officer
    699.15
  supervisor 748.2
  *adj.* supervising
    747.13
superior
  *n.* chief 749.3
  head 36.4
  *adj.* arrogant 912.9
  authoritative 739.15
  excellent 674.14
  greater 36.12
  higher 207.24
  important 672.16
  remarkable 34.10
superiority
  abnormality 85.1
  ascendancy 739.6
  goodness 674.1
  importance 672.1
  overpassing 313.1
  power 157.1
  precedence 64.1
  preeminence 36
superlative
  *n.* exaggeration 617.1
  the best 674.8
  *adj.* consummate
    34.12
  exaggerated 617.4
  lofty 207.19
  supreme 36.13
Superman 159.6
supermarket
  market 832.1
  store 832.5
supernal
  heavenly 1018.13
  high 207.19
supernatant 353.13
supernatural
  divine 1013.19
  ghostly 1017.7
  immaterial 377.7
  occult 1034.22

suppose 499.10
adj. disputed 503.12
doubtful 503.10
uncertain 514.16
**suspecting**
cautious 895.9
doubtful 503.9
incredulous 504.4
**suspend** depose 783.4
dismiss 310.19
hang 215.8
interrupt 144.10
postpone 132.9
release 886.6
repeal 779.2
**suspended**
discontinuous 72.4
hanging 215.9
latent 268.14
unused 668.12
**suspended animation**
708.1
**suspender** hanger 215.5
types of 215.14
**suspense**
abeyance 268.4
anxiety 890.1
expectancy 539.3
pendency 215.1
uncertainty 514.1
**suspenseful**
anxious 890.6
exciting 857.28
uncertain 514.17
**suspension**
cessation 668.2
delay 132.2
deposal 783.2
dismissal 310.5
elimination 77.2
hanging 215.1
harmonization 463.2
inactivity 708.1
interruption 72.2
pause 144.3
release 886.2
repeal 779.1
respite 711.2
**suspicion** caution 895.2
doubt 503.2
hint 557.4
hunch 481.3
incredulity 504.1
jealousy 953.2
small amount 35.4
trace 44.7
vague supposition
499.5
**suspicious**
cautious 895.9
dishonest 975.16
doubtful 503.9
incredulous 504.4
jealous 953.4
unbelievable 503.10
uncertain 514.16
**suspire** 403.24
**sustain** bear 216.21
be patient 861.5
buoy up 353.8
confirm 505.12
defend 1006.10

endure 110.6
experience 151.8
feed 307.16
foster 785.16
nourish 309.15
preserve 701.7
protract 143.4
strengthen 159.11
support 785.12
**sustained**
constant 135.5
continuing 143.7
permanent 140.7
supported 216.24
**sustainer**
radio broadcast
344.18
supporter 787.9
upholder 216.2
**sustaining**
n. support 216.1
adj. supporting 216.23
**sustenance**
continuance 143.1
food 308.1
morsel 308.3
support 785.3
upkeep 216.1
**susurration**
imperfect speech
595.4
murmur 452.4
**sutler** 659.6
**sutra** 517.1
**suttee** burning 329.5
sacrifice 1032.7
suicide 409.6
**suture** filament 206.1
joint 47.4
sewing 223.1
**svelte** 205.16
**Svengali**
hypnotist 712.9
influential person
172.6
**swab** wash 681.19
wipe 393.6
**swabbie** 276.4
**swaddle** bind 47.9
clothe 231.38
wrap 228.20
**swag**
n. booty 824.11
fall 316.2
sway 219.2
swing 323.6
v. curve 252.6
hang 215.6
incline 219.10
lurch 323.10
sink 316.6
adj. drooping 215.10
**swagger**
n. bluster 911.1
boasting 910.1
gait 273.14
ostentation 904.8
v. bluster 911.3
boast 910.6
strut 904.15
walk 273.27

**swaggerer**
blusterer 911.2
impudent person
913.5
strutter 904.10
**swaggering**
blustering 911.4
brazen 913.10
strutting 904.23
**swagger stick** 217.2
**swagman**
bad person 986.2
fence 826.6
vagabond 274.3
**swain** beau 931.12
escort 73.5
**swallow**
n. bite 307.2
ingestion 306.4
speed 269.6
v. be credulous 502.6
believe 501.10
consume 666.2
eat 307.20
endure 861.7
ingest 306.11
recant 628.9
submit 765.6
**swallowing** 306.4
**swallow up**
consume 666.2
destroy 693.10
**swamp**
n. filthy place 682.12
marsh 400.1
predicament 731.4
v. drench 392.14
overflow 395.17
oversupply 663.14
overwhelm 693.21
**swamped**
flooded 395.25
in difficulty 731.25
soaked 392.17
**swampy** marshy 400.3
moist 392.15
**swan** bird 414.33,66
white 364.2
**swan dive** 320.1
**swank**
n. ostentation 904.2
swagger 904.8
v. be ostentatious
904.14
strut 904.15
adj. chic 644.13
grandiose 904.21
**swanky** chic 644.13
grandiose 904.21
**swansdown**
down 230.19
softness 357.4
**swan song**
death song 408.10
end 70.1
farewell performance
462.33
sequel 67.1
theatrical perfor-
mance 611.13
**swap**
n. bargain 827.5

exchange 150.2
explosive noise 456.1
v. interchange 150.4
make explosive noise
456.6
trade 827.14
**swapping**
exchange 150.2
trade 827.2
**sward** 411.6
**swarm**
n. flock 74.6
large number 101.3
migration 273.4
overrunning 313.2
v. come together
74.16
migrate 273.21
overrun 313.6
superabound 663.8
**swarming**
n. migration 273.4
overrunning 313.2
adj. crowded 74.22
permeated 186.15
productive 165.9
superabundant
663.19
teeming 101.9
**swarm with**
abound 661.5
be numerous 101.5
infest 313.6
pervade 186.7
**swarthiness**
blackness 365.2
darkness 337.1
**swarthy** 365.9
**swash**
n. lap 395.8
ostentation 904.8
sprinkle 392.5
strutter 904.10
watercourse 396.2
v. lap 395.19
moisten 392.12
splash 452.11
strut 904.15
**swashbuckler**
blusterer 911.2
combatant 800.1
strutter 904.10
**swashbuckling**
blustering 911.4
strutting 904.23
**swastika** charm 1036.
cross 221.4
insignia 569.1
**swat**
n. hit 283.4
v. hit 283.13
**swatch** 25.3
**swath** 71.2
**swathe** bind 47.9
clothe 231.38
wrap 228.20
**sway**
n. authority 739.5
flounder 324.8
government 741.1
inclination 219.2
influence 172.1

supremacy 36.3
swing 323.6
*v.* collapse 692.27
diverge 219.9
flounder 324.15
fluctuate 141.5
incline 219.10
influence 172.7
persuade 648.23
pitch 275.55
prejudice 527.9
prompt 648.22
rule 741.14
swing 323.10
**swayable** 172.15
**swayback** 249.3
**swaybacked** 249.12
**swayed**
prejudiced 527.12
unjust 977.11
**swaying**
influential 172.14
swinging 323.17
**swear** affirm 523.5
blaspheme 1030.5
curse 972.6
express belief 501.12
promise 770.4
swear in 523.6
testify 505.10
**swear by** 501.16
**swear in**
call to witness
1004.16
place under oath
523.6
**swearing** cursing 972.3
deposition 523.2
**swear off**
break the habit 643.3
relinquish 814.3
renounce 992.8
**swear to** affirm 523.5
ratify 521.12
**wearword** 972.4
**weat**
*n.* body fluid 388.3
bustle 707.4
confusion 532.3
impatience 862.1
nervousness 859.2
perspiration 311.7
trepidation 891.5
work 716.4
*v.* await 539.8
be damp 392.11
be hot 328.22
be impatient 862.4
condense 395.18
perspire 311.16
strain 714.4
work 716.16
work hard 716.13
**eat bath** bath 681.8
heat therapy 689.5
**eat blood**
endeavor 714.4
exert oneself 716.10
**eater** 231.52
**eating**
. trickle 395.7
*dj.* hot 328.25

laboring 716.17
sweaty 311.22
**sweat it** 716.11
**sweat it out**
await 539.8
be impatient 862.4
not weaken 159.9
wait 132.13
**sweat over** 478.9
**sweatshop** 719.1
**sweaty** hot 328.25
perspiring 311.22
**sweep**
*n.* curve 252.3
deviation 291.1
glide 273.8
horse race 796.13
lottery 515.11
oar 277.15
range 179.2
sweeper 681.16
view 446.6
vision 439.1
*v.* clean 681.23
curve 252.6
glide 273.34
go easily 732.9
overwhelm 395.17
plunder 824.16
push 285.10
reach 179.7
speed 269.8
touch lightly 425.7
traverse 273.19
use radar 346.17
**sweep away** 693.14
**sweeper** 681.16
**sweeping**
*n.* gliding 273.8
*adj.* comprehensive
76.7
extensive 79.13
revolutionary 147.5
thorough 56.10
vague 514.18
**sweepings** refuse 669.4
remainder 43.1
**sweeping statement**
79.8
**sweep out** clean 681.18
eject 310.21
sweep 681.23
**sweepstakes**
award 916.2
gambling 515.4
game of chance 515.8
horse race 796.13
lottery 515.11
**sweet**
*n.* confection 308.39
endearment 932.5
sweetness 431.1
taste 427.1
*adj.* clean 681.25
fragrant 436.9
good-natured 938.14
harmonious 589.8
lovable 931.23
melodious 462.49
pleasant 863.6
soft-colored 362.21
sweetish 431.4

**sweetbread**
meat 308.20
veal 308.14
**sweeten** clean 681.18
dulcify 431.3
make pleasant 863.5
**sweetener**
gratuity 818.5
incentive 648.7
sweetening 431.2
**sweetening**
incentive 648.7
types of 431.2
**sweetheart**
endearment 932.5
good thing 674.7
lover 931.10
**sweetie**
endearment 932.5
sweetheart 931.10
**sweetly** 938.19
**sweetmeat** 308.39
**sweetness and light**
855.8
**sweet nothings**
endearment 932.4
flattery 970.1
**sweet on** 931.28
**sweet potato** 465.9
**sweet shop** 832.4
**sweet sixteen** 124.14
**sweet-smelling** 436.9
**sweet talk**
endearment 932.4
flattery 970.1
glibness 936.5
hypocrisy 616.6
inducement 648.3
**sweet-talk**
be hypocritical
616.23
make love 932.13
urge 648.14
**sweet tooth** 634.7
**swell**
*n.* dandy 903.9
distension 197.2
harmonics 463.12
hill 207.5
keyboard 465.20
loudness 453.1
nobleman 918.4
swelling 256.4
wave 395.14
*v.* be excited 857.16
be ostentatious
904.14
be vain 909.7
billow 395.22
bulge 256.10
din 453.6
expand 197.5
increase 38.6
inflate 197.4
overextend 663.13
*adj.* chic 644.13
excellent 674.13
grandiose 904.21
*interj.* approval
968.22
**swelled-headed** 909.11
**swellhead** 909.5

**swelling**
*n.* distension 197.2
increase 38.1
loudness 453.1
lump 256.4
overextension 663.7
sore 686.35
*adj.* bombastic 601.9
bulging 256.14
increasing 38.8
**swelter**
*n.* sultriness 328.6
sweat 311.7
*v.* be hot 328.22
sweat 311.16
**swelterer** 328.8
**sweltering** 328.25
**swept** 395.25
**swept-back** 241.12
**swept up** 530.17
**swerve**
*n.* angle 251.2
bend 219.3
deviation 291.1
*v.* be changed 139.5
change course 275.30
deviate 291.3
diverge 219.9
dodge 631.8
pull back 284.7
veer 251.5
**swerving**
*n.* deviation 291.1
*adj.* devious 291.7
**swift** fast 269.19
hasty 709.9
lively 707.18
prompt 131.9
sudden 113.5
transient 111.8
**swiftly** hastily 709.12
promptly 131.15
rapidly 269.21
transiently 111.10
with alacrity 707.26
**swiftness**
hastiness 709.2
promptness 131.3
quickness 707.3
speed 269.1
transience 111.2
**swig**
*n.* drink 307.4
snort 996.6
*v.* booze 996.24
drink 307.27
**swill**
*n.* drink 307.4
fodder 308.4
mud 389.8
offal 682.9
refuse 669.4
snort 996.6
*v.* booze 996.24
drink 307.27
ingest 306.11
**swim**
*n.* fashion 644.1
swimming 275.11
*v.* bathe 775.56
**swim fins** 320.5
**swimmer** 275.12

**swimming**
n. aquatics 275.11
dizziness 532.4
sports 878.8
adj. aquatic 275.58
dizzy 532.15
**swimmingly**
easily 732.15
prosperously 728.15
successfully 724.14
**swimming pool** 878.13
**swim suit** 231.29
**swindle**
n. fake 616.13
fraud 618.8
theft 824.1
v. cheat 618.17
overcharge 848.7
steal 824.13
**swindler** cheat 619.3
criminal 986.10
cunning person 735.6
thief 825.1
**swindle sheet** 843.3
**swine** bad person 986.7
breeds of 414.71
filthy person 682.13
pig 414.9
sensualist 987.3
slob 62.7
**swineherd** 416.3
**swing**
n. action 705.1
amusement device
878.15
blow 283.4
boxing 283.5
flounder 324.8
gait 273.14
hang 215.2
meter 609.9
music 462.9
oscillator 323.9
rhythm 463.22
room 179.3
scope 762.4
stock prices 834.9
sway 323.6
thrust 798.3
trend 174.2
v. alternate 323.13
be hanged 1010.21
be promiscuous
989.19
flounder 324.15
fluctuate 141.5
hang 215.6
lash out at 798.16
manage 724.11
music 462.44
sail 275.55
sway 323.10
swivel 322.9
tend toward 174.3
turn around 295.9
walk 273.27
wave 323.11
adj. music 462.52
**swing district** 744.16
**swinger**
libertine 989.10
nonconformist 83.3

socialite 644.7
**swinging**
n. deviation 291.1
promiscuity 989.4
sway 323.6
swiveling 322.1
adj. pendent 215.9
swaying 323.17
**swing shift** 108.3
**swing vote** 744.28
**swinish** carnal 987.6
filthy 682.24
gluttonous 994.6
greedy 634.27
intemperate 993.7
ungulate 414.49
**swipe**
n. disapproval 969.4
gibe 967.2
hit 283.4
v. hit 283.13
ridicule 967.9
steal 824.13
**swirl**
n. agitation 324.1
bustle 707.4
curl 254.2
eddy 395.12
excitement 857.3
rotation 322.2
v. agitate 324.10
eddy 395.21
twist 254.4
whirl 322.11
**swirling**
n. excitement 857.3
rotation 322.1
adj. rotating 322.14
**swish**
n. sibilation 457.1
v. rustle 452.12
sibilate 457.2
splash 452.11
**swishing** 452.19
**switch**
n. branch 55.4
change 139.1
conversion 145.1
exchange 150.2
false hair 230.13
rod 1011.2
story element 608.9
substitution 149.1
surprise 540.2
twig 411.18
v. apostatize 628.8
convert 145.11
interchange 150.4
punish 1010.14
substitute 149.4
trade 827.14
transfer 271.9
turn aside 291.6
**switchback**
crookedness 219.8
railway 657.8
**switchboard**
lightboard 611.21
telephone 560.8
**switch off**
electricity 342.23
turn off 144.12

**switch on** 342.23
**switch-over** 145.1
**swivel**
n. axis 322.5
v. rotate 322.9
turn around 295.9
**swivet** confusion 532.3
dither 857.5
**swollen** boastful 910.11
bombastic 601.9
bulging 256.15
corpulent 195.18
distended 197.13
full 56.11
increased 38.7
overfull 663.20
pompous 904.22
proud 905.10
**swoon**
n. stupor 712.6
unconsciousness
423.2
v. faint 423.5
**swoop**
n. descent 316.1
plunge 320.1
v. descend 316.5
plunge 320.6
**swoop down upon**
attack 798.15
seize on 822.16
**sword blade** 801.4
combatant 800.1
cutlery 348.2,13
types of 801.24
**swordlike** 258.15
**sword of Damocles**
precariousness 697.2
threat 973.1
**swordplay** 796.8
**sword side**
kinsmen 11.2
male line 170.4
male sex 420.3
**swordsman** 800.1
**sword swallower** 612.3
**sworn** affirmed 523.8
promised 770.8
**sworn off** 992.10
**sworn statement**
certificate 570.6
deposition 523.2
testimony 505.3
**sworn to**
affirmed 523.8
ratified 521.14
**swot**
n. drudge 718.3
v. memorize 537.17
study 564.12
**swotting** 564.3
**sybarite** 987.3
**sybaritic** 987.5
**sycophancy**
flattery 970.1
obsequiousness 907.2
**sycophant** cajoler 970.4
flatterer 907.3
lackey 787.8
**sycophantic**
flattering 970.8
obsequious 907.13

**syllabary**
alphabet 581.3
representation 572.1
**syllabic**
n. character 581.1
adj. phonetic 594.31
**syllabify** 581.7
**syllable**
n. poetic division
609.11
speech sound 594.13
word 582.1
v. spell 581.7
**syllabus** 607.1
**syllogism** logic 482.6
reasoning 482.3
**sylph** fairy 1014.18
spirit 1014.16
**sylphlike** fairy 1014.27
thin 205.16
**sylvan**
backwoods 182.8
forest 411.37
**sylvan deity** 1014.21
**symbiosis**
coaction 177.1
cooperation 786.1
ecology 13.5
joining 47.1
**symbiotic** agreeing 26.9
coacting 177.4
cooperating 786.5
ecological 13.15
**symbol** character 581.1
harmonics 463.12
insignia 569.1
number 86.1
psychological symbol
690.37
representation 572.1
sign 568.3
substitute 149.2
type 25.2
unit of meaning
545.6
**symbolic(al)**
implicative 546.10
indicative 568.23
meaningful 545.10
semantic 545.12
**symbolism**
designation 568.3
implication 546.2
occultism 1034.1
psychological symbol
690.37
ritualism 1040.1
**symbolize**
designate 568.18
mean 545.8
metaphorize 551.2
represent 572.6
**symbolizing** 572.10
**symmetric(al)**
balanced 248.4
equal 30.9
harmonious 589.8
orderly 59.6
**symmetrize**
balance 248.3
make uniform 17.4

**taboo**
*n.* exclusion 77.1
 prohibition 778.1
*v.* exclude 77.4
 prohibit 778.3
*adj.* jargonish 580.19
 prohibited 778.7
**tabular** classified 61.8
 flat 214.7
**tabula rasa**
 clean sweep 147.1
 ignorant 477.1
 thoughtlessness 480.1
 void 187.3
**tabulate** classify 61.6
 list 88.8
 record 570.16
**tabulated** 88.9
**tabulation**
 classification 61.1
 listing 88.7
 recording 570.15
**tachometer** 269.7
**tachycardia**
 cardiovascular disease
 686.17
 disease symptom
 686.8
**tacit** implicit 546.8
 wordless 451.11
**taciturn** concise 592.6
 untalkative 613.9
**tack**
*n.* cordage 206.3
 deviation 291.1
 direction 290.2
 harness 659.5
 way 657.1
*v.* be changed 139.5
 change course 275.30
 deviate 291.3
 fasten 47.8
**tackle**
*n.* athlete 878.20
 belongings 810.3
 cordage 206.3
 equipment 659.4
 harness 659.5
 hoist 317.3
 purchase 287.6
 rigging 277.12
 types of 287.10
*v.* attempt 714.6
 pursue 705.7
 reel in 287.9
 set to work 716.15
 undertake 715.3
**tack on** 40.4
**tacky** adhesive 50.12
 frail 160.14
 inferior 680.9
 moist 392.15
 shabby 692.34
 slovenly 62.15
 viscous 389.12
**tact**
 considerateness 938.3
 courtesy 936.1
 discrimination 492.1
 sensitivity 422.3
 skill 733.1

**tactful**
 considerate 938.16
 courteous 936.14
 discriminating 492.7
 sensitive 422.14
 skillful 733.20
**tactic** expedient 670.2
 stratagem 735.3
**tactical** cunning 735.12
 planned 654.13
**tactician**
 cunning person 735.7
 planner 654.7
**tactics** behavior 737.1
 machinations 735.4
 plan 654.1
 warfare 797.9
**tactile** tactual 425.10
 tangible 425.11
**tactless** careless 534.11
 discourteous 937.6
 undiscriminating
 493.5
**tad** 125.3
**tadpole**
 amphibian 414.32
 young frog 125.8
**tag**
*n.* extremity 70.2
 label 568.13
 name 583.3
 sequel 67.1
 small amount 35.3
 token 835.12
 trailer 67.2
*v.* add 40.4
 allot 816.9
 follow 293.3
 label 568.20
 name 583.11
**tag along** 293.3
**tag line** 517.4
**t'ai chi chu'an** 796.10
**tail**
*n.* addition 41.2
 back 241.1
 book part 605.12
 buttocks 241.5
 cauda 241.6
 extremity 70.2
 follower 293.2
 hair 230.7
 limb 55.4
 rear 241.1
 sequel 67.2
*v.* follow 293.3
 trail 485.34
*adj.* caudal 241.11
 final 70.10
 rear 241.9
**tailgate** follow 293.3
 stay near 200.12
**tailing** following 293.1
 surveillance 485.9
**tailor**
*n.* garmentmaker
 231.34
 sewer 223.2
*v.* adapt 26.7
 form 246.7
 sew 223.4
**tailored** apt 26.10

 custom-made 231.47
**tailoring** 231.31
**tailpiece** adjunct 41.1
 music division 462.24
 rear 241.1
 sequel 67.2
 tail 241.6
**tails**
 formal clothes
 231.11,51
 opposite side 239.3
**tailspin**
 air maneuver 278.15
 failure 725.3
**tail wind**
 aviation 278.41
 nautical 403.11
 wind 403.1
**taint**
*n.* blemish 679.3
 fault 678.2
 infection 686.3
 peculiarity 80.4
 stigma 915.6
 tinge 44.7
*v.* blemish 679.6
 corrupt 692.14
 defile 682.17
 infect 686.48
 stigmatize 915.9
 work evil 675.6
**tainted**
 blemished 679.10
 diseased 686.56
 morally corrupt
 981.14
 soiled 682.21
 spoiled 692.42
 unchaste 989.23
 unhealthful 684.5
**take**
*n.* booty 824.11
 catch 822.10
 cinematography
 577.8
 gain 811.3
 receipts 844.1
*v.* acquire 811.8
 become sick 686.44
 believe 501.11
 borrow 821.4
 burn 329.23
 catch 822.17
 condone 947.4
 eat 307.18
 endure 861.7
 entail 76.4
 interpret 552.9
 possess sexually
 822.15
 receive 819.6
 steal 824.13
 submit to 765.6
 succeed 724.6
 suppose 499.10
 take possession
 822.13
 transport 271.11
 understand 548.7
**take aback**
 dismay 891.27
 startle 540.8

**take a crack at**
 attempt 714.6
 lash out at 798.16
**take action** 705.5
**take advantage of**
 exploit 665.16
 impose 963.7
 improve the occasion
 129.8
 use 665.15
**take after** emulate 22.7
 resemble 20.7
**take apart**
 demolish 693.17
 disassemble 49.15
 tear apart 49.14
**take a powder**
 flee 631.11
 leave 301.10
**take aside**
 talk to 594.27
 tell confidentially
 614.9
**take a stand** 555.6
**take away**
 remove 271.10
 subtract 42.9
 take from 822.21
**take back**
 apologize 1012.5
 deny 524.4
 recant 628.9
 recover 823.6
 restore 823.4
**take by storm**
 raid 798.20
 seize 822.14
 win easily 726.5
**take by surprise** 540.7
**take care**
*v.* be careful 533.7
 beware 895.7
 pay attention 530.8
*interj.* caution 895.14
**take care of**
 accomplish 722.4
 bribe 651.3
 care for 699.19
 kill 409.14
 look after 533.9
 operate 164.5
 perform 705.8
 please oneself 978.4
 punish 1010.11
 serve 750.13
 supervise 747.10
**take chances**
 gamble 515.19
 risk 697.7
**take charge**
 be able 157.11
 take command
 739.14
**take-charge** 161.12
**take cover**
 hide oneself 615.8
 take refuge 700.7
**take down**
 bring down 318.5
 depress 318.4
 disassemble 49.15
 eat 307.20

humiliate 906.5
raze 693.19
record 570.16
reprove 969.17
**take effect** 164.7
**take exception**
  disapprove 969.10
  dissent 522.4
  find fault 969.15
**take five** pause 109.3
  take a rest 711.8
**take for** believe 501.11
  suppose 499.10
**take for granted**
  believe 501.10
  be unastonished
    921.2
  expect 539.5
  imply 546.4
  neglect 534.6
  suppose 499.10
**take from** reduce 39.7
  subtract 42.9
  take away from
    822.21
**take heart**
  be comforted 887.7
  cheer up 870.9
  hope 888.8
  take courage 893.14
**take-home pay**
  earnings 841.4
  economics 827.8
**take in** accept 925.7
  attend 186.8
  be a spectator 442.5
  capture 822.18
  deceive 618.13
  eat 307.20
  encompass 47.5
  entail 76.4
  enter 302.7
  extend 179.7
  gain 819.6
  hear 448.12
  include 76.3
  learn 564.7
  receive 306.10
  see 439.12
  shorten 203.6
  sorb 306.13
  understand 548.7
**take into account**
  allow for 507.5
  include 76.3
  take cognizance of
    530.9
**take issue with**
  deny 524.4
  dispute 796.22
  dissent 522.4
  oppose 790.3
  take it believe 501.11
  endure 861.8
  hold 661.4
  not weaken 159.9
  submit 765.6
  suppose 499.10
**take it easy**
  be cautious 895.5
  calm oneself 858.7
  go easy 732.11

idle 708.14
rest 711.6
*interj.* caution 895.14
**take it or leave it**
  be indifferent 636.5
  have no choice
    639.11
**take liberties**
  be insolent 913.6
  disrespect 965.3
  presume on 961.7
**take notice** heed 530.6
  take cognizance of
    530.9
**taken unawares**
  surprised 540.12
  unprepared 721.8
**taken with**
  compared to 491.11
  fond of 931.28
  pleased 865.12
**takeoff** ascent 315.1
  aviation 278.8
  beginning 68.1
  departure 301.3
  imitation 22.1
  outset 301.2
  point of departure
    301.5
  ridicule 967.6
**take off** ascend 315.10
  begin 68.7
  detach 49.10
  discount 847.2
  excise 42.10
  fly 278.47
  get better 691.7
  imitate 22.6
  impersonate 572.9
  kill 409.13
  leave 301.10
  put an end to 693.12
  remove 232.6
**take off for** 290.10
**take off on**
  imitate 22.6
  ridicule 967.11
**take on** adopt 821.4
  assume 819.6
  attempt 714.6
  be angry 952.15
  complain 875.13
  contend against
    790.4
  employ 780.13
  engage in 705.7
  fight with 796.17
  fret 890.5
  grieve 872.17
  set to work 716.15
  undertake 715.3
**take one's time**
  dally 708.13
  idle 708.11
  linger 270.8
**take one's leisure**
  710.4
  wait 132.12
**take out** escort 73.8
  exclude 42.10
  extract 305.10
**takeover** 822.4

**take over** acquire 811.9
  adopt 821.4
  appropriate 822.19
  assume 819.6
  take command
    739.14
  usurp 961.8
**take pains**
  be careful 533.7
  endeavor 714.10
**take place** 151.5
**taker** recipient 819.3
  seizer 822.11
**take shape** form 59.5
  shape up 246.8
**take sides** argue 482.16
  back 785.13
  side with 786.4
**take steps**
  take action 705.5
  take precautions
    895.6
**take stock** check 87.14
  take account of 845.9
**take the blame** 962.9
**take the bull by the**
  **horns**
  attempt 714.5
  be determined 624.8
  face up to 893.11
**take the opportunity**
  129.7
  undertake 715.3
**take the cake** best 36.7
  win 726.4
**take the consequences**
  1010.23
**take the edge off**
  blunt 259.2
  moderate 163.6
  pacify 804.7
  weaken 160.10
**take the law into one's**
  **own hands**
  break the law 999.5
  defy authority 740.4
  have one's will 621.3
  not observe 769.4
**take the liberty** 961.6
**take the rap**
  be punished 1010.23
  be responsible 962.9
  substitute 149.6
**take time**
  spend time 105.6
  wait 132.12
**take to** desire 634.14
  engage in 705.7
  fall in love 931.20
  get used to 642.13
  turn to 665.14
**take to task**
  accuse 1005.7
  punish 1010.10
  reprove 969.17
**take turns** 108.5
**take up** acquire 811.9
  adopt 637.15
  appropriate 822.19
  begin 68.9
  collect 74.18
  deal with 606.5

discuss 597.12
engage in 656.11
engross 530.13
espouse 968.13
glean 811.10
include 76.3
patronize 785.15
pay in full 841.13
pursue 705.7
raise 317.8
sorb 306.13
undertake 715.3
**take upon oneself**
  be responsible 962.9
  presume 961.6
  undertake 715.3
**take up with**
  bear with 861.5
  befriend 927.10
  be sociable 922.16
  confer 597.11
**take with a grain of salt**
  allow for 507.5
  be doubtful 503.6
**taking**
  *n.* borrowing 821.2
  getting 819.1
  sexual possession
    822.3
  taking possession 822
  *adj.* alluring 650.7
  catching 822.25
  contagious 686.58
  desirable 634.30
  pleasant 863.7
**taking away** loss 812.1
  subtraction 42.1
  taking 822.1
**taking in**
  learning 564.2
  reception 306.1
  seizure 822.2
**taking over**
  accession to power
    739.12
  appropriation 822.4
**taking place** 151.9
**talcum powder** 900.11
**tale** gossip 558.7
  lie 616.11
  reckoning 86.5
  story 608.6
**talebearer**
  informer 557.6
  newsmonger 558.9
**talebearing**
  *n.* gossip 558.7
  *adj.* gossipy 558.14
**talent** ability 157.2
  artistry 574.8
  genius 467.8
  intelligence 467.2
  skill 733.4
**talented person**
  733.12
**talented** gifted 733.27
  intelligent 467.14
**taleteller**
  narrator 608.10
  newsmonger 558.9
**talisman** 1036.5

**talk**
n. address 599.2
conversation 597.3
diction 588.1
gossip 558.7
language 580.1
lesson 562.7
rumor 558.6
speech 594.1
v. chatter 596.5
communicate 554.6
discuss 597.12
divulge 556.6
gossip 558.12
make a speech 599.9
patter 594.20
speak 580.16
**talkathon**
legislative procedure 742.14
speech 599.2
**talkative**
communicative 554.10
disclosive 556.10
loquacious 596.9
speaking 594.32
wordy 593.12
**talk back** answer 486.4
be insolent 913.7
**talk big**
be bombastic 601.6
boast 910.7
exaggerate 617.3
**talk dirty** 972.6
**talk down** land 278.52
outtalk 596.7
**talked-about**
famous 914.16
rumored 558.15
well-known 475.27
**talkee-talkee**
chatter 596.3
lingua franca 580.11
ungrammaticalness 587.1
**talker**
conversationalist 597.8
speaker 594.18
speechmaker 599.4
**talkie** 611.16
**talking**
n. communication 554.1
speech 594.1
adj. speaking 594.32
**talking point** 482.5
**talking-to** 969.6
**talk into** 648.23
**talk nonsense**
chatter 596.5
twaddle 547.5
**talk of the town**
repute 914.1
rumor 558.6
**talk out of** 652.3
**talk over** confer 597.11
convince 501.18
discuss 597.12
persuade 648.23
**talk show** 611.4

**talk to** address 594.27
reprove 969.18
**talk turkey** 591.2
**talk with** 597.9
**talky** 596.9
**tall** boastful 910.11
grandiloquent 601.8
high 207.21
large 195.16
long 202.8
unbelievable 503.10
**tall order** 731.2
**tallow** 380.1
**tallowy** 380.9
**tall ship** 277.3
**tall story**
boasting 910.2
lie 616.11
**tally**
n. account 845.2
agreement 26.1
count of 87.6
label 568.13
likeness 20.3
list 88.1
reports 570.7
sum 86.5
v. add 40.6
agree 26.6
calculate 87.11
coincide 14.4
conform 82.3
list 88.8
number 87.10
**tallyho**
n. hunting cry 459.3
interj. hunting cry 655.13
**tallying** 87.1
**tally sheet** 88.1
**Talmud**
scripture 1021.5
tradition 123.2
**Talmudic** 1021.11
**taloned** footed 212.9
grasping 813.9
**talons** authority 739.5
control 741.2
grasping organs 813.4
**tambourine** 465.19
**tame**
v. accustom 642.11
domesticate 764.11
drive animals 416.7
moderate 163.6
adj. domesticated 191.34
dull 268.14
moderate 163.10
weak 765.15
**tamed**
domesticated 191.34
subdued 764.15
weak 765.15
**tamer** 416.2
**taming**
habituation 642.8
subdual 764.4
**Tammany Hall**
political party 744.24
politics 744.1
**tamp** pack in 304.7

**stamp** 257.14
thrust 283.11
**tamper with**
adulterate 44.13
bribe 651.3
falsify 616.17
meddle 238.7
**tampon**
medical dressing 687.33
wadding 266.5
**tan**
v. brown 367.2
cure 720.6
punish 1010.15
adj. brown 367.3
**tandem**
n. rig 272.5
adv. behind 241.13
**tang** characteristic 80.4
poison injector 676.5
pungency 433.2
taste 427.1
**tangent** borderer 200.6
convergence 298.1
straight line 250.2
**tangential**
converging 298.3
in contact 200.17
**tangibility**
manifestness 555.3
substantiality 3.1
touchableness 425.3
**tangible**
n. asset 810.8
substance 3.2
adj. manifest 555.8
substantial 3.6
touchable 425.11
**tangle**
n. complex 46.2
v. catch 822.17
complicate 46.3
contend 796.18
hamper 730.11
involve 176.2
trap 618.18
**tangled** 46.4
**tangy** 433.7
**tank**
n. body of water 398.1
railway car 272.14
storage place 660.6
v. package 236.9
**tank car** 272.14
**tanked** 996.31
**tanker** ship 277.22,24
tank corpsman 800.12
**tank town** 183.3
**tanned** 367.3
**tannery** 719.3
**tanning** 1010.5
**tantalize** attract 650.5
disappoint 541.2
interest 530.12
seduce 931.21
**tantalizing**
alluring 650.7
appetizing 428.10
desirable 634.30

disappointing 541.6
exciting 857.28
interesting 530.19
pleasant 863.7
**tantamount**
equivalent 30.8
reciprocal 13.13
**tantrum** 952.8
**Taoist** 1020.31
**tap**
n. explosive noise 456.1
faint sound 452.3
faucet 266.4
hole 265.4
outlet 303.9
plant root 411.20
rap 283.6
touch 425.1
tube 396.6
valve 396.10
v. extract 305.12
faint sound 452.15
keep time 462.45
listen 448.11
make explosive noise 456.6
open 265.12
pipe 271.13
puncture 265.16
rap 283.15
take from 822.21
touch 425.6
**tap dancer** 879.3
**tap dancing** 879.1
**tape**
n. medical dressing 687.33
record 570.10
sound recording 450.12
strip 206.4
v. fasten 47.5
record 570.16
**tape deck** 450.11
**tape measure** 206.4
**tape memory**
computer 349.17
memory 537.1
**taper**
n. candle 336.2
lighter 331.4
light source 336.1
narrowing 205.2
wick 336.7
v. converge 298.2
narrow 205.11
sharpen 258.9
**tape recorder** 450.11
**tapered**
cone-shaped 205.15
pointed 258.11
**tapering**
n. narrowing 205.2
adj. pointed 258.11
tapered 205.15
**tapestry** 574.12
**tapeworm**
appetite 634.7
invertebrate 415.5
worm 414.42,75

outright 34.12
painstaking 533.11
**thoroughbred**
*n.* horse 414.68
nobleman 918.4
*adj.* wellborn 918.11
**thoroughfare** 657.6
**thoroughly**
carefully 533.15
completely 56.14
perfectly 677.10
**thoroughness**
caution 895.1
completeness 56.1
painstakingness 533.2
**those** 80.14
**though** 33.8
**thought**
*n.* admixture 44.7
advice 754.1
attention 530.1
belief 501.6
cogitation 478
considerateness 938.3
expectation 539.1
idea 479.1
inmost thoughts
478.4
remark 594.4
small amount 35.4
speed comparisons
269.6
*adj.* cognitive 478.21
**thoughtful**
careful 533.10
cogitative 478.21
considerate 938.16
courteous 936.14
judicious 467.19
serious 871.3
**thoughtfulness**
carefulness 533.1
considerateness 938.3
contemplativeness
478.3
courtesy 936.1
judiciousness 467.7
solemnity 871.1
**thoughtless**
careless 534.11
foolish 470.8
impulsive 630.10
inattentive 531.6
inconsiderate 939.16
scatterbrained 532.16
shiftless 721.15
unskillful 734.15
unwise 470.9
vacuous 480.4
**thoughtlessness**
carelessness 534.2
flightiness 532.5
foolishness 470.1
impulsiveness 630.3
inattention 531.1
inconsiderateness
939.3
shiftlessness 721.2
unskillfulness 734.1
unwiseness 470.2
vacuity 480
**thought-out** 482.21

**thought-provoking**
530.19
**thought transference**
1034.9
**thousand**
*n.* immense number
101.4
number 99.10
*adj.* numerous 101.6
**thrall** slave 764.7
subjection 764.1
**thrash** defeat 727.6
pound 283.14
punish 1010.14
separate 77.6
**thrash about**
be uncertain 514.9
toss and turn 324.15
**thrashing** defeat 727.1
punishment 1010.4
**thrash out** analyze 48.8
argue 482.16
**thrash over** 103.9
**thread**
*n.* filament 206.1
row 71.2
types of 206.8
weakness comparisons
160.7
*v.* connect 71.4
**threadbare** trite 883.9
worn 692.33
**threadlike** stringy 206.7
thin 205.16
**threads** 231.1
**threat** danger 697.1
menace 973
warning 703.1
**threaten**
be imminent 152.2
be in the future
121.6
forebode 544.11
intimidate 891.28
menace 973.2
warn 703.5
work evil 675.6
**threatened**
augured 544.15
in danger 697.13
**threatening**
dangerous 697.9
imminent 152.3
menacing 973.3
ominous 544.17
**three**
*n.* number 93
*adj.* triple 93.3
**3-D**
*n.* motion picture
611.16
photography 577.1
*adj.* optical 443.9
photographic 577.17
spatial 179.8
**three-dimensional**
optical 443.9
photographic 577.17
spatial 179.8
thick 204.8
tripartite 95.4

**threefold**
*adj.* triple 94.3
*adv.* triply 94.5
**three R's** 562.5
**threesome** game 878.9
trio 93.1
**thresh** pound 283.14
separate 77.6
**threshold**
boundary 235.3
entrance 302.6
foyer 192.19
sill 216.9
**thresh over** 103.9
**thrice** 94.5
**thrift** 851.1
**thriftiness** 851.1
**thriftless** 721.15
**thrift shop** 832.4
**thrifty** 851.6
**thrill**
*n.* excitement 857.2
pain 424.2
sensation 426.1
*v.* be excited 857.16
delight 865.8
excite 857.14
suffer pain 424.8
tingle 426.5
**thrilled** excited 857.18
pleased 865.12
**thriller** fiction 608.7
motion picture
611.16
**thrilling**
exciting 857.28
pleasant 863.7
**thrive** grow 197.7
have energy 161.10
prosper 728.8
**thriving**
growing 197.12
productive 165.9
prospering 728.13
**throat** gullet 396.15
narrow place 205.3
**throaty** hoarse 458.15
imperfectly spoken
595.12
phonetic 594.31
**throb**
*n.* excitement 857.4
flutter 324.4
music 463.26
pulsation 323.3
staccato sound 455.1
*v.* be excited 857.16
flutter 324.12
make staccato sounds
455.4
pain 424.8
pulsate 323.12
resonate 454.6
**throbbing**
*n.* excitement 857.4
pulsation 323.3
staccato sound 455.1
*adj.* aching 424.12
music 463.28
pulsating 323.18
resonant 454.9
staccato 455.7

**throes**
compunction 873.2
distress 866.5
pain 424.2
seizure 686.5
spasm 324.6
**thrombosis**
cardiovascular disease
686.17
seizure 686.5
**throne**
*n.* royal seat 739.11
toilet 311.11
*v.* glorify 914.13
install 780.11
**throne room** 192.20
**throng**
*n.* large number 101.3
multitude 74.4
*v.* be numerous 101.5
come together 74.16
**throttle**
render powerless
158.11
seize 822.14
silence 451.8
slow 270.9
strangle 409.19
suppress 760.8
**throttling**
suffocation 409.7
suppression 760.2
**through**
*adj.* ended 70.8
finished 722.11
*adv.* breadthwise
204.9
*prep.* by means of
658.7
during 105.14
over 184.27
via 290.29
**through and through**
thorough 56.10
throughout 56.17
**throughout**
*adv.* all over 56.17
scatteringly 75.12
*prep.* during 105.14
over 184.27
**throw**
*n.* dice roll 515.10
fling 285.4
*v.* discompose 63.4
fling 285.11
give birth 167.15
hurl at 798.28
knock down 318.5
make ceramics 576.6
perplex 514.13
put violently 184.12
**throwaway**
*n.* advertising 559.8
discard 668.3
*adj.* disposable 666.5
**throw away**
discard 668.7
do away with 310.20
eject 310.13
reject 638.2
squander 854.3
underplay 611.36

**throwback**
adversity 729.3
regression 295.1
relapse 696.1
reversion 146.2
**throw down**
knock down 318.5
overthrow 693.20
raze 693.19
**thrower** 285.8
**throw in** insert 304.3
interpose 237.6
**throw in with**
cooperate 786.4
join 52.4
**throw off**
break the habit 643.3
do away with 310.20
do carelessly 534.9
free oneself from
763.8
improvise 630.8
let out 310.23
say 594.23
separate 49.9
shed 232.10
take off 232.6
unseat 185.6
**throw out**
discard 668.7
eject 310.24
oust 310.13
reject 638.2
separate 49.9
**throw over**
abandon 633.5
discard 668.7
eliminate 77.5
subvert 693.20
**throw stick**
spear-thrower 801.18
weapon 801.12
**throw together**
do carelessly 534.9
improvise 630.8
mix 44.11
**throw up**
abandon 633.7
elevate 317.5
relinquish 814.3
vomit 310.25
**thrum**
*n.* staccato sound
455.1
*v.* hum 452.13
make staccato sounds
455.4
music 462.45
strum 462.41
**thrumming**
*n.* hum 452.7
*adj.* humming 452.20
staccato 455.7
**thrush**
infectious disease
686.12
songbird 464.23
**thrust**
*n.* acceleration 269.4
attack 798.3
aviation 278.32
drive 285.1

impulse 283.1
major part 54.6
power 157.4
push 283.2
rocketry 281.8
vim 161.2
*v.* attack 798.17
impel 283.10
propel 285.10
put violently 184.12
shove 283.11
**thrust aside** 531.4
**thrust back** 289.3
**thrust down** 318.4
**thrust in** drive in 304.7
enter 302.7
interpose 237.6
intrude 238.5
**thrust out** eject 310.13
extend 179.7
ostracize 310.17
**thrust upon**
force upon 818.20
urge upon 773.8
**thruway** 657.6
**thud**
*n.* faint sound 452.3
*v.* faint sound 452.15
**thug** bandit 825.4
combatant 800.1
criminal 986.10
evildoer 943.3
killer 409.11
man 787.8
**thumb**
*n.* finger 425.5
*v.* hitchhike 273.30
touch 425.6
**thumbnail sketch** 607.1
**thumb one's nose at**
disdain 966.3
flout 793.4
**thumbprint** 568.7
**thumbscrew** 1011.4
**thumbs-down**
disapproval 969.1
refusal 776.1
**thumbs-up** 521.2
**thumb through**
browse 564.13
examine cursorily
485.25
**thump**
*n.* faint sound 452.3
hit 283.4
*v.* hit 283.13
make staccato sounds
455.4
music 462.45
pound 283.14
punish 1010.14
thud 452.15
**thumper** 195.11
**thumping**
*n.* staccato sound
455.1
*adj.* huge 195.21
remarkable 34.11
staccato 455.7
**thunder**
*n.* gods 456.5
noise 453.3

rainstorm 394.3
reverberation 454.2
rumbling 456.5
*v.* boom 456.9
din 453.6
proclaim 559.13
utter 594.26
**thunderbolt**
lightning 335.17
speed 269.6
surprise 540.2
**thundercloud**
cloud 404.1
omen 544.6
warning sign 703.3
**thundering**
*n.* curse 972.1
reverberation 454.2
rumbling 456.5
*adj.* huge 195.21
intense 159.20
reverberating 454.11
rumbling 456.12
**thunderous**
loud 453.10
rumbling 456.12
**thunderstorm**
rainstorm 394.3
storm 162.4
thunder 456.5
**thunderstruck** 920.9
**thus**
for instance 505.24
hence 155.7
in this way 657.11
similarly 20.18
so 8.10
**thus far** so far 235.16
to a degree 35.10
until now 120.4
**thwack**
*n.* explosive noise
456.1
hit 283.4
*v.* hit 283.13
make explosive noise
456.6
**thwart**
*v.* defeat 727.11
disappoint 541.2
frustrate 730.15
neutralize 178.7
*adj.* across 221.9
deviate 219.19
*adv.* crosswise 221.13
**thwarted** 541.5
**thwarting**
circumvention 735.5
frustration 730.3
neutralization 178.2
**thyroidal** 312.8
**tiara**
clerical insignia 569.4
jewel 901.6
royal insignia 569.3
**tic**
emotional symptom
690.23
nervousness 859.1
obsession 473.13
twitch 324.3

**tick**
*n.* animal 414.41
bug 414.36
clicking 455.2
faint sound 452.3
financial credit 839.1
instant 113.3
mark 568.5
*v.* click 455.5
faint sound 452.15
mark 568.19
operate 164.7
pulsate 323.12
**ticked off** 952.26
**ticker** clock 114.6
heart 225.4
stock exchange 833.7
telegraphy 560.2,23
**ticker tape**
record 570.10
stock exchange 833.7
tape 206.4
**ticket**
*n.* ballot 744.19
certificate 570.6
dismissal 310.5
label 568.13
permission 777.1
token 835.12
*v.* label 568.20
**ticking**
*n.* clicking 455.2
*adj.* staccato 455.7
**tickle**
*n.* sensation 426.2
*v.* amuse 878.23
attract 650.5
delight 865.8
incite 648.17
interest 530.12
tap 283.15
thrill 857.14
titillate 426.6
**tickled** amused 878.28
interested 530.16
pleased 865.12
**tickler** 537.6
**tickling**
*n.* sensation 426.2
*adj.* alluring 650.7
interesting 530.19
titillative 426.9
**ticklish** difficult 731.1
irascible 951.20
precarious 697.12
sensitive 422.14
titillative 426.9
unreliable 514.19
**ticklish spot** 731.4
**tick off**
make angry 952.21
mark 568.19
**ticktock**
*n.* clicking 455.2
*v.* click 455.5
pulsate 323.12
**tidal** aquatic 275.58
flowing 395.24
**tidal wave**
election returns
744.21
oscillation 323.4

swell 395.14
upheaval 162.5
**tidbit** delicacy 308.8
scandalous rumor
558.8
**fiddly** dizzy 532.15
intoxicated 996.30
**tide** flow 395.4
ocean 397.1
tidal current 395.13
time 105.1
**tide gate**
floodgate 396.11
tideway 395.13
**tidemark** 490.7
**tide over** endure 110.6
keep safe 698.2
**tidewater**
*n.* shore 385.2
tide 395.13
*adj.* estuary 399.2
**tidings** 558.1
**tidy**
*v.* arrange 60.12
clean 681.18
*adj.* cleaned 681.26
large 195.16
tolerable 674.19
trim 59.8
**tidy sum**
large number 101.3
much 34.4
wealth 837.2
**tie**
*n.* equality 30.3
fidelity 974.7
harmonics 463.12
insignia 569.1
intermediary 237.4
joining 47.1
neckwear 231.64
relationship 9.1
security 772.1
simultaneity 118.2
*v.* bind 47.9
compel 756.4
equal 30.5
join 47.5
obligate 962.12
relate 9.6
restrain 760.10
secure 142.8
**~ed** equal 30.7
fixed 142.16
joined 47.13
obliged 962.16
related 9.9
restrained 760.16
**~d up** busy 707.21
indebted 840.8
involved in 176.4
restrained 760.16
**~ in** cooperate 786.3
**~join** 52.4
**~relate to** 9.5
**~in** affiliation 786.2
**~joining** 47.1
**~elationship** 9.1
**~ale** 829.1
**~r** layer 227.1
**~ow** 71.2
**up** anchor 275.15

arrive 300.8
bind 47.9
bundle 74.20
cooperate 786.3
monopolize 808.6
restrain 760.10
**tie-up** affiliation 786.2
combination 52.1
delay 132.2
splice 47.1
strike 789.7
**tiff**
*n.* anger 952.7
quarrel 795.5
*v.* quarrel 795.11
**tiger** animal 414.27,58
brave person 893.8
savage 943.5
stakes 515.5
violent person 162.9
**tight**
*adj.* close 266.12
coherent 50.11
concise 592.6
drunk 996.31
fastened 47.14
lengthened 202.9
meager 102.5
narrow 205.14
resistant 159.18
rigid 356.11
shipshape 277.20
stingy 852.9
tidy 59.8
*adv.* securely 47.19
**tighten** fasten 47.7
lengthen 202.7
reel in 287.9
restrain 760.9
squeeze 198.8
stiffen 356.9
**tightening**
*n.* deepening 38.2
squeezing 198.2
*adj.* increasing 38.8
**tightfisted** 852.9
**tight-lipped** 613.9
**tight money** 835.16
**tightness**
exclusiveness 77.3
meagerness 102.1
narrowness 205.1
stiffness 356.2
stinginess 852.3
tenacity 50.3
**tight rein** 757.3
**tightrope walker**
circus artist 612.3
gymnast 878.21
**tights** 231.9,56,61
**tight spot**
predicament 731.4
small place 196.3
**tight squeeze**
closeness 205.1
narrow escape 632.2
poverty 838.1
predicament 731.4
small place 196.3
**tightwad** 852.4
**tigress**
female animal 421.9

ill-humored woman
951.12
violent person 162.9
witch 943.7
**tile**
*n.* building material
378.2
ceramic ware 576.2
pavement 657.7
*v.* cover 228.23
**tiling**
building material
378.2
ceramic ware 576.2
flooring 228.9
**till**
*n.* booty 824.11
depository 836.12
*v.* cultivate 413.17
*prep.* until 105.15
**tiller** agriculturist 413.5
management 747.5
**tilling** 413.13
**tilt**
*n.* contest 796.3
inclination 219.2
*v.* charge 798.18
contend 796.14
contend with 796.18
incline 219.10
throw 285.11
tumble 316.8
**tilt at windmills** 669.8
**tilting** 219.15
**timbal** 465.19
**timbale** 308.40
**timber** beam 217.3
spar 277.13
tree 411.10
wood 378.3
woodland 411.11
**timbered** 411.37
**timberland** 411.11
**timbre**
manner of speaking
594.8
tonality 450.3
**timbrel** 465.19
**Timbuktu** 199.4
**time**
*n.* date 114.4
duration 105
generation 107.4
geological 107.10
leisure 710.1
music 463.24
opportunity 129.2
period 107.1
shift 108.3
tenure 108.4
term 107.3
time of day 114.2
turn 108.2
*v.* measure time
114.11
synchronize 118.3
**Time** 105.2
**time and a half** 818.5
**time and motion study**
efficiency engineering
747.7

time measurement
114.9
**time bomb** 801.14,30
**timecard** 114.9
**time flies** 105.17
**time-honored**
customary 642.15
traditional 123.12
venerable 964.12
**time immemorial**
*n.* antiquity 119.3
*adv.* for a long time
110.14
**timekeeper**
chronologist 114.10
chronometer 114.6
recorder 571.1
**timekeeping**
*n.* chronology 114.1
*adj.* chronologic(al)
114.15
**time lag** delay 132.2
period 107.1
**timeless** dateless 106.3
godlike 1013.20
old 123.10
perpetual 112.7
**timelessness**
datelessness 106
perpetuity 112.1
**timeliness**
expedience 670.1
seasonableness 129
**timely** expedient 670.5
opportune 129.9
**time off**
*n.* interim 109.1
vacation 711.3
*v.* take turns 108.5
**time out**
*n.* interim 109.1
respite 711.2
*v.* leave 301.14
record time 114.12
**timepiece**
chronometer 114.6
types of 114.17
**timer**
chronologist 114.10
chronometer 114.6
control mechanism
349.34
**times, the** affairs 151.4
the present 120.1
**time-saving** 851.6
**timeserver**
flatterer 907.3
selfish person 978.3
temporizer 628.4
traitor 619.10
**time sheet** 114.9
**time signature** 463.12
**time study**
efficiency engineering
747.7
time chart 114.9
**timetable** 114.9
**timeworn** aged 126.18
old 123.14
shabby 692.33
trite 883.9
**time zone** 114.3

timid cowardly 892.10
  fearful 891.31
  irresolute 627.11
  shy 908.12
timidity
  cowardice 892.1
  fearfulness 891.3
  shyness 908.4
timing adjustment 26.4
  chronology 114.1
  music 463.24
  skill 733.1
  synchronism 26.1
timorous
  cowardly 892.10
  fearful 891.31
  shy 908.12
timpani 465.19
tin
  *v.* package 236.9
  preserve 701.9
  *adj.* metal 383.17
  ungenuine 616.26
tincture
  *n.* admixture 44.7
  coloring matter 362.8
  heraldic insignia
    569.2
  hue 362.1
  small amount 35.4
  *v.* color 362.13
  infuse 44.12
tinder 331.6
tin ear 448.3
tined 258.11
tinge
  *n.* admixture 44.7
  color 362.1
  implication 546.2
  small amount 35.4
  taste 427.3
  *v.* color 362.13
  influence 172.7
  infuse 44.12
tinged 362.16
tingle
  *n.* pain 424.3
  ringing 454.3
  sensation 426
  thrill 857.2
  *v.* be excited 857.16
  prickle 426.5
  ring 454.8
  suffer pain 424.8
tingling
  *n.* pain 424.3
  ringing 454.3
  sensation 426.1
  thrill 857.2
  *adj.* excited 857.18
  prickly 426.8
  ringing 454.12
  sore 424.11
tinhorn
  *n.* gambler 515.17
  mediocrity 680.5
  *adj.* petty 673.17
tinker
  *n.* mender 694.10
  *v.* repair 694.14
  trifle 673.13
tinkering 673.8

tinker's damn, a 673.5
tinkle
  *n.* faint sound 452.3
  ringing 454.3
  *v.* faint sound 452.15
  ring 454.8
tinkling
  *n.* ringing 454.3
  *adj.* ringing 454.12
tinny inferior 680.9
  metal 383.17
  sound 458.15
Tin Pan Alley 464.2
tinsel
  *n.* fake 616.13
  light 335.7
  ornamentation 901.3
  *v.* glitter 335.24
  ornament 901.9
  *adj.* false 616.27
  ungenuine 616.26
tinselly 335.35
tint
  *n.* admixture 44.7
  color quality 362.6
  engraving 578.2
  shade 362.1
  *v.* color 362.13
  picture 574.20
tinted 362.16
tinting 362.11
tintinnabulary 454.12
tintype
  *n.* photograph 577.4
  *adj.* photographic
    577.17
tiny insignificant 35.6
  little 196.11
tip
  *n.* extra pay 841.6
  extremity 70.2
  gratuity 818.5
  inclination 219.2
  information 557.3
  piece of advice 754.2
  point 258.3
  summit 211.2
  surplus 663.5
  touch 283.6
  vocal organ 594.19
  *v.* cap 228.21
  incline 219.10
  inform 557.11
  overturn 220.6
  sail 275.43
  top 211.9
  touch 283.15
  warn 703.5
tip off inform 557.11
  warn 703.5
tip-off clue 568.9
  information 557.3
  warning 703.1
tipped inclining 219.15
  topped 211.12
tipping 219.15
tipple drink 307.27
  guzzle 996.23
tipster gambler 515.17
  informant 557.5
  predictor 543.5
tipsy inclining 219.15

intoxicated 996.30
tip the scales 352.10
tiptoe
  *n.* creeping 273.9
  *v.* be cautious 895.5
  creep 273.25
  lurk 615.9
  *adj.* creeping 273.38
  *adv.* on tiptoe 207.26
tip-top
  *n.* summit 211.2
  *adj.* first-rate 674.15
  superlative 36.13
  uppermost 211.10
tirade berating 969.7
  lament 875.3
  outpour 593.1
  speech 599.2
tire
  *n.* kinds of 253.4
  *v.* be tedious 884.5
  cause unpleasantness
    864.16
  clothe 231.38
  get tired 717.5
  make tired 717.4
tired bored 884.10
  clothed 231.44
  exhausted 717.8
  fatigued 717.6
  worn-out 692.38
tired of bored 884.10
  satiated 664.6
tireless
  industrious 707.22
  persevering 625.7
tiresome
  annoying 864.22
  boring 884.9
  fatiguing 717.11
  prosaic 610.5
tiring boring 884.9
  fatiguing 717.11
tisane 687.4
tissue fabric 378.5
  flesh 406.1
  network 221.3
  structure 245.1
  weaving 222.1
tit little thing 196.4
  teat 256.6
titan 195.13
Titan strong man 159.6
  sun god 375.14
Titania 1014.18
titanic great 34.7
  huge 195.20
tit for tat
  interaction 13.3
  offset 33.2
  reciprocity 150.1
  retaliation 955.3
  substitution 149.1
tithe
  *n.* donation 818.6
  tax 846.10
  tenth 99.14
  *v.* charge 846.14
  *adj.* ten 99.22
Titian red 368.6
  reddish-brown 367.4
  redheaded 368.10

titillate amuse 878.23
  attract 650.5
  delight 865.8
  interest 530.12
  thrill 857.14
  tickle 426.6
titillating
  alluring 650.7
  amusing 878.29
  interesting 530.19
titivate dress up 231.41
  falsify 616.16
  ornament 901.8
title
  *n.* book part 605.12
  caption 484.2
  class 61.2
  estate 810.4
  honorific 917
  name 583.3
  possession 808.1
  privilege 958.3
  publication 605.1
  *v.* caption 484.3
  name 583.11
titled named 583.14
  noble 918.10
titleholder 809.2
title page book 605.12
  caption 484.2
  label 568.13
titrate 48.6
titration 48.1
titter
  *n.* laughter 876.4
  *v.* laugh 876.8
tittle mark 568.5
  minute thing 196.7
  punctuation 586.15
  small amount 35.2
tittle-tattle
  *n.* gossip 558.7
  jabber 596.3
  small talk 597.5
  *v.* chat 597.10
  gossip 558.12
  jabber 596.5
titular honorific 917.7
  nominal 583.15
tizzy confusion 532.3
  dither 855.5
TLC carefulness 533.1
  support 785.3
TM 690.5
T-man 781.10
TNT 801.9
to as far as 199.20
  intending 653.12
  into 302.14
  toward 290.28
  until 105.15
toad
  amphibian 414.32,62
  sycophant 907.3
to a degree
  relatively 9.12
  somewhat 29.7
  to a certain extent
    35.10
toadstool 411.4,45
toady
  *n.* sycophant 907.3

*v.* be servile 907.6
**toadying**
  *n.* obsequiousness
    907.2
  *adj.* obsequious
    907.13
**to a fault** 663.23
**to and fro**
  alternately 137.11
  back and forth
    323.21
  changeably 141.8
  reciprocally 13.16
**to-and-fro**
  *n.* alternation 323.5
  *adj.* alternate 323.19
**toast**
  *n.* bread 308.28
  celebration 877.1
  drinking 996.37
  fine lady 903.10
  pledge 996.9
  *v.* be hot 328.22
  cook 330.4
  drink 307.27
  drink to 996.28
  *adj.* brown 367.3
**toastmaster** 878.22
**toasty** 328.24
**to a T** exactly 516.22
  to completion 722.14
  to perfection 677.11
**tobacco**
  *n.* smoke 434
  *adj.* tobaccoy 434.15
**tobacconist**
  merchant 830.3
  snuffman 434.12
  store 832.4
**to be expected**
  as expected 539.14
  imminently 152.4
  normally 84.9
**to blame**
  censurable 969.26
  guilty 983.3
  responsible 962.17
**tobogganing** 273.8
**to come**
  approaching 296.4
  future 121.8
  imminent 152.3
  scheduled 641.6
**ocsin** 704.1
**TO'd** 952.26
**o date** 120.4
**oday**
  *n.* the present 120.1
  *adv.* now 120.3
**oddle**
  *n.* gait 273.14
  *v.* go slow 270.6
  walk 273.27
**ddle along**
  depart 301.6
  go slow 270.6
**ddler** 125.7
**ddling**
  *z.* walking 273.10
  *adj.* slow 270.10
**-do** agitation 324.1
  bustle 707.4

commotion 62.4
excitement 857.3
**toe** bottom 212.2
  foot 212.5
**toehold** grip 813.2
  purchase 287.2
  support 216.5
  wrestling hold 813.3
**toe the mark**
  conform 82.4
  obey 766.2
**to extremes**
  in excess 663.23
  intemperately 993.10
**toft** enclosure 236.3,12
  farm 413.8
  home 191.4
  ranch 191.7
  real estate 810.7
**tog** 231.38
**together**
  *adj.* composed 858.13
  in accord 794.3
  sane 472.4
  *adv.* collectively 73.11
  concurrently 177.5
  continuously 71.10
  cooperatively 786.6
  jointly 47.18
  simultaneously 118.6
  unanimously 521.17
**together with**
  among 44.18
  in addition to 40.12
  in agreement with
    26.12
  in association with
    73.12
**toggle**
  *n.* joint 47.4,20
  *v.* fasten 47.8
**togs** clothing 231.1
  garment 231.3
**toil**
  *n.* snare 618.12
  work 716.4
  *v.* drudge 716.14
  entrap 730.11
  work 656.12
**toiler**
  common person
    919.1
  working person 718.2
**toilet** latrine 311.10
  rest room 192.26
  stool 311.11
**toiletries** 831.6
**toilette** 231.1
**toilet water** 436.3
**toiling** 716.17
**toilsome**
  difficult 731.16
  fatiguing 717.11
  laborious 716.18
**token**
  *n.* characteristic 80.4
  currency 835.12
  evidence 505.1
  label 568.13
  memento 537.7
  omen 544.3
  password 568.12

record 570.1
substitute 149.2
symbol 568.3
unit of meaning
    545.6
*v.* augur 544.12
show 555.5
*adj.* cheap 849.7
substitute 149.8
**tokenism** 616.6
**token payment** 772.2
**tolerable**
  adequate 674.19
  bearable 868.13
  mediocre 680.7
**tolerably** fairly 674.23
  mediocrely 680.11
  satisfactorily 868.15
  to a degree 35.10
**tolerance**
  addiction 642.9
  broad-mindedness
    526.4
  forgiveness 947.1
  inaccuracy 518.2
  inclusion 76.1
  latitude 762.4
  leniency 759.1
  liberalism 762.10
  patience 861.1
  sufferance 777.2
**tolerant**
  broad-minded 526.11
  considerate 938.16
  forgiving 947.6
  lenient 759.7
  liberal 762.24
  patient 861.9
  permissive 777.14
**tolerate**
  be broad-minded
    526.7
  be lenient 759.5
  be patient 861.5
  permit 777.10
**toll**
  *n.* fee 846.7
  ringing 454.3
  tax 846.10
  *v.* ring 454.8
**tollbooth** hut 191.10
  prison 761.8
**tollgate** 302.6
**tolling**
  *n.* death bell 410.6
  ringing 454.3
  *adj.* ringing 454.12
**tom** cat 414.26
  male cat 420.8
  male turkey 420.8
  turkey 414.34
**tomato** food 308.35,50
  girl 125.6
  woman 421.6
**tomb** memorial 570.12
  sepulcher 410.16
**tomblike** 410.22
**tomboy** girl 125.6
  mannish female
    420.9
**tomboyish** 420.13
**tombstone** 570.12

**tomcat** cat 414.26
  male animal 420.8
**Tom, Dick, and Harry**
  common man 79.3
  nobodies 673.7
  the people 919.2
**tome** 605.1
**tomfool** 471.1
**tomfoolery** 881.5
**Tommy** 800.7
**tomorrow**
  *n.* the future 121.1
  *adv.* in the future
    121.9
**Tom Thumb** 196.6
**tomtit** 196.4
**tom-tom** drum 465.19
  staccato sound 455.1
**tonal harmonics** 463.27
  phonetic 594.31
  sounding 450.15
**tonality**
  harmonics 463.4
  key 463.15
  lighting 335.19
  melody 462.2
  sound frequency
    463.3
  timbre 450.3
**tone**
  *n.* artistry 574.10
  behavior 737.1
  color quality 362.6
  harmonics 463.4
  interval 463.20
  intonation 594.7
  manner of speaking
    594.8
  melody 462.2
  milieu 233.3
  mode 7.4
  mood 525.4
  muscle 159.2
  nature 5.3
  note 463.14
  pitch 450.2
  resilience 358.1
  shade 362.1
  story element 608.9
  trend 174.2
  way 657.1
  *v.* color 362.13
  influence 172.7
**tone-deaf** 449.6
**tone down**
  decolor 363.5
  dull 337.10
  moderate 163.6
  muffle 451.9
  put in tune 462.37
  soften 357.6
**toneless** colorless 363.7
  droning 450.15
**tone of voice** 594.8
**tone up** furbish 691.11
  put in tune 462.37
**tongue**
  *n.* bell 454.4
  language 580.1
  meat 308.20
  organ of taste 427.5
  palate 427.1

point of land 256.8
shaft 217.1
utterance 594.3
vocal organ 594.19
*v.* lick 425.9
play music 462.43
**tongue in cheek**
*n.* insincerity 616.5
*adj.* insincere 616.32
**tongue-lash** 969.20
**tongue-lashing** 969.7
**tonguelike** 427.10
**tongue-tied**
mute 451.12
taciturn 613.9
**tonic**
*n.* drink 308.48
energizer 161.5
harmonics 463.15
medicine 687.8
refresher 695.1
*adj.* energizing 161.14
harmonics 463.27
healthful 683.5
phonetic 594.31
refreshing 695.3
stimulating 687.44
**tonight** 120.3
**tonnage** capacity 195.2
charge 846.8
ships 277.10
weight 352.1
**tons** 34.3
**tonsilitis**
inflammation 686.9
respiratory disease
686.14
**tonsillectomy** 689.23
**tonsure** 232.4
**tonsured** 232.17
**tontine** 515.11
**tonus** 358.1
**tony** 904.18
**too** additionally 40.11
excessively 663.22
**too bad**
disgraceful 915.11
wretched 675.9
**tool**
*n.* agent 781.3
edge 348.13
gripping 813.12
instrument 348
means 658.3
sycophant 907.3
types of 348.12
*v.* engrave 578.10
mechanize 348.10
**tooled** 578.12
**tooling** engraving 578.2
instrumentation
348.8
**too little** 662.9
**too much**
*n.* excess 663.1
intemperance 993.1
*adj.* excessive 663.16
extreme 34.13
insufferable 864.25
intemperate 993.7
*adv.* excessively
663.22

**too much for**
beyond one 158.20
impracticable 510.8
**to order** 752.16
**too soon**
premature 131.8,13
untimely 130.7
**toot**
*n.* loud sound 453.4
revel 878.6
spree 996.5
*v.* blare 453.9
play music 462.43
**tooth**
*n.* anatomy 258.5
pointed projection
258.4
roughness 261.1
taste 427.1
*v.* give texture 351.4
notch 262.4
**toothache** 424.5
**tooth and nail**
laboriously 716.19
resolutely 624.17
savagely 162.26
**toothed** dental 258.16
grasping 813.9
notched 262.5
pointed 258.11
**toothless** 259.4
**toothlike** 258.16
**toothpaste**
cleaning agent 681.17
dentifrice 687.22
**toothsome**
desirable 634.30
tasty 428.8
**tootle**
*n.* loud sound 453.4
*v.* blare 453.9
play music 462.43
**too-too** 663.22
**tootsy** 212.5
**top**
*n.* completion 56.5
cover 228.5
culmination 677.3
exterior 224.2
plaything 878.16
roof 228.6
rotator 322.4,17
summit 211.2
tent 228.8
upper side 211
*v.* be high 207.16
cap 211.9
cover 228.21
excel 36.6
*adj.* expensive 848.11
highest 211.10
superlative 36.13
**top, the**
important persons
672.8
the rulers 749.15
**top brass**
directorate 748.11
important persons
672.8
officer 749.18
the rulers 749.15

**topcoat** 231.13
**top dog** chief 749.3
paramount 672.10
superior 36.4
victor 726.2
**top-drawer** 674.15
**tope**
*n.* grove 411.12
memorial 570.12
shrine 1042.4
tomb 410.16
tower 207.11
*v.* drink 996.23
**topflight** chief 36.14
first-rate 674.15
**top-heavy**
corpulent 195.18
unbalanced 31.5
**topic** question 485.10
story element 608.9
subject 484
**topical** local 180.9
present 120.2
thematic 484.4
**to pieces** 49.29
**topknot** feather 230.16
hair 230.7
top part 211.4
**topless** bare 232.16
headless 211.13
high 207.19
unclad 232.13
**toplofty** arrogant 912.9
contemptuous 966.8
high 207.19
**topmost** highest 211.10
most important
672.23
superlative 36.13
**top-notch**
first-rate 674.15
superlative 36.13
**top off** complete 56.6
crest 211.9
fill 56.7
fuel 331.8
perfect 722.6
provision 659.9
**topographer**
mapper 654.4
measurer 490.10
**topographic**(al)
locational 184.18
measuring 490.13
regional 180.8
**topography**
location 184.7
map 654.4
mensuration 490.9
**topped** 211.12
**topping**
*n.* architectural 211.17
icing 211.3
*adj.* crowning 211.11
first-rate 674.15
high 207.19
superior 36.12
**topping-off**
completion 56.4
rounding-out 722.2
**topple**
be destroyed 693.22

collapse 692.27
knock down 318.5
overturn 220.6
tumble 316.8
**top priority** 64.1
**tops** 674.15
**tops, the** 674.8
**top secret** 614.11
**top sergeant** 749.19
**top shape** 685.2
**topside**
*n.* top 211.1
*adv.* on board 275.62
on top 211.15
**topsoil** land 385.1
layer 227.1
**topsy-turvy**
*adj.* confused 62.16
reversed 220.7
*adv.* contrarily 15.9
inversely 220.8
**tor** mountain 207.7
peak 207.8
**Torah**
Old Testament
1021.3
ritualistic book
1040.12
**torch**
*n.* blowtorch 329.14
flare 336.3,8
lighter 331.4
light source 336.1
*v.* fish 655.10
set fire to 329.22
**torchbearer** 748.6
**torch singer** 464.13
**torch song** 462.13
**toreador** 800.4
**torment**
*n.* agony 864.4
bane 676.1
pain 424.6
pest 866.10
punishment 1010.2
torture 866.7
worry 890.2
*v.* annoy 866.13
cause unpleasantness
864.12
make anxious 890.4
make grieve 872.19
pain 424.7
persecute 667.6
torture 866.18
trouble 731.12
work evil 675.6
**tormented**
pained 424.9
plagued 866.24
worried 890.7
**tormenting**
annoying 864.22
painful 424.10
troublesome 890.9
unpleasant 864.23
**tormentor** pest 866.10
scenery 611.25
**torn** affected 855.25
alienated 929.11
damaged 692.29
severed 49.23

shabby 692.34
**tornado**
emotional outburst
857.8
storm 162.4
whirlwind 403.14
**torpedo**
*n.* evildoer 943.4
killer 409.11
missile 281.3
types of 281.16
weapon 801.12
*v.* attack 798.22
ruin 693.11
shoot 285.13
**torpid** apathetic 856.13
changeless 140.7
inert 268.14
languid 708.19
**torpor** apathy 856.4
immobility 140.1
inertia 268.4
languor 708.6
vegetation 1.6
**torque** aviation 278.31
necklace 901.6
**torrent** eruption 162.6
speed 269.6
violent flow 395.5
**torrid** 328.25
**Torrid Zone**
hot place 328.11
zone 180.3
**torsion** aviation 278.31
convolution 254.1
deflection 291.2
distortion 249.1
**torsional**
distortive 249.9
winding 254.6
**torso** 376.3
**tort** crime 999.4
misdeed 982.2
**torte** 308.41
**tortilla** 308.29
**tortoise**
reptile 414.30,60
slow person 270.5
**tortoise shell** 374.6
**tortoise-shell** 374.10
**tortuous** curved 252.7
distorted 249.10
grandiloquent 601.8
winding 254.6
**torture**
*n.* agony 864.4
instruments of 1011.4
pain 424.6
punishment 1010.2
torment 866.7
*v.* cause unpleasant-
ness 864.12
distort 249.6
hurt 424.7
misinterpret 553.2
punish 1010.18
torment 866.18
work evil 675.6
**tortured**
affected 855.25
distorted 249.11
narrowed 866.25

pained 424.9
**torturing**
distortion 249.2
misinterpretation
553.1
**torturous**
painful 424.10
unpleasant 864.23
**Tory** partisan 744.27
rightist 745.9
**to smithereens** 49.29
**to spare** remaining 43.7
superfluous 663.17
unused 668.12
**toss**
*n.* even chance 156.7
flounder 324.8
gamble 515.2
throw 285.4
*v.* be excited 857.16
billow 395.22
flounder 324.15
gamble 515.18
hurl at 798.28
oscillate 323.10
put violently 184.12
sail 275.55
search 485.32
throw 285.11
**toss and turn**
be excited 857.16
stay awake 713.3
tumble 324.15
**toss off**
do carelessly 534.9
drink 996.23
eating 307.27
improvise 630.8
**toss out** discard 310.13
do carelessly 534.9
improvise 630.8
**toss-up**
an uncertainty 514.8
even chance 156.7
gamble 515.2
**tot** child 125.3
drink 307.4
**total**
*n.* addition 40.2
score 86.5
sum 54.2
*v.* add 40.6
amount to 54.8
calculate 87.12
demolish 693.17
*adj.* complete 56.9
comprehensive 76.7
cumulative 74.23
great 34.6
outright 34.12
sound 677.7
thorough 56.10
universal 79.14
unqualified 508.2
whole 54.9
**totalitarian**
authoritative 739.15
governmental 741.17
**totality**
completeness 56.1
everyone 79.4
fullness 54.5

universe 375.1
whole 54.1
**total loss**
deprivation 812.1
destruction 693.4
failure 725.2
**totally**
completely 56.14
extremely 34.22
perfectly 677.10
solely 89.14
wholly 54.13
**total recall** 537.3
**tote**
*n.* totalizer 515.13
*v.* add 40.6
transport 271.11
**totem**
community 788.2
guardian angel
1014.22
race 11.4
symbol 568.3
**tote up** add 40.6
calculate 87.12
total 54.8
**to the fore** 240.12
**to the good**
gainfully 811.16
helpfully 785.24
to one's credit 839.9
**to the hilt**
completely 56.14
throughout 56.17
**to the letter** 516.20
**to the point** apt 26.10
concise 592.6
in plain words 591.4
relevant 9.11
**to the tune of**
as much as 28.7
at a price 846.19
**totter**
*n.* flounder 324.8
gait 273.14
*v.* age 126.10
be weak 160.8
collapse 692.27
flounder 324.15
fluctuate 141.5
go slow 270.6
tumble 316.8
vacillate 627.8
walk 273.27
**tottering**
*n.* fluctuation 141.3
oscillation 323.5
walking 273.10
*adj.* aged 126.18
on the decline 692.47
slow 270.10
tumbledown 316.11
unsteady 160.16
**tottery** aged 126.18
dilapidated 692.35
unsafe 697.11
unsteady 160.16
**touch**
*n.* admixture 44.7
communication
554.1
contact 200.5

feel 425
implication 546.2
knack 733.6
motif 901.7
music 462.31
sense 422.5
signal 568.15
small amount 35.4
tap 283.6
*v.* affect 855.16
beg 774.15
borrow 821.3
contact 200.10
equal 30.5
excite pity 944.5
feel 425.6
relate to 9.5
sense 422.8
signal 568.22
tap 283.15
**touch and go**
an uncertainty 514.8
even chance 156.7
gamble 515.2
**touch-and-go**
ticklish 697.12
uncertain 514.15
**touch a nerve** 422.10
**touch bottom**
be despondent
872.16
decline 692.20
fall on evil days
729.11
**touchdown**
landing 278.18
score 724.4
**touched**
affected 855.25
insane 473.25
penitent 873.9
**touching**
*n.* borrowing 821.1
contact 200.5
feeling 425.2
*adj.* affecting 855.24
in contact 200.17
pitiful 944.8
poignant 864.20
*prep.* in relation to
9.13
**touch off**
explode 162.13
ignite 329.22
kindle 648.18
**touchstone**
measure 490.2
test 489.2
**touch up** 691.11
**touch upon**
call attention to
530.10
discourse upon 606.5
examine cursorily
485.25
graze 425.7
neglect 534.8
relate to 9.5
scratch the surface
210.4
**touchy**
excitable 857.26

**travel**
n. journeying 273
journeys 273.2
pace 267.4
progression 294.1
transference 271.1
v. journey 273.17
move 267.5
progress 294.2
traverse 273.19
**traveled** 273.39
**traveler** goer 274
traveling salesman
830.5
**traveler's check** 835.11
**traveling**
n. journeying 273.1
adj. journeying 273.35
moving 267.7
**traveling salesman**
830.5
**travelogue** 599.3
**travel-worn** 273.40
**traverse**
n. crosspiece 221.5
v. contradict 790.6
cross 221.6
oppose 790.3
sail 275.13
travel over 273.19
adj. crosswise 221.9
adv. crosswise 221.13
**travesty**
n. exaggeration 617.1
humor 881.1
imitation 22.3
misrepresentation
573.2
ridicule 967.6
v. exaggerate 617.3
misrepresent 573.3
ridicule 967.11
**trawl**
n. snare 618.12
v. fish 655.10
pull 286.4
**trawling** 655.3
**treacherous**
deceitful 618.20
dishonest 975.21
falsehearted 616.31
unreliable 514.19
unsafe 697.11
**treachery**
dishonesty 975.6
falseheartedness
616.4
unreliability 514.6
**treacle**
semiliquid 389.5
sweetening 431.2
**tread**
n. degree 29.1
footstep 273.13
gait 273.14
rate 267.4
stair 315.5
v. stamp 283.19
walk 273.26
**treadle**
n. lever 287.4
v. push 285.10

**treadmill**
drudgery 716.4
pillory 1011.3
regularity 17.2
routine 642.6
tedium 884.1
**tread upon**
domineer 741.16
trample 313.7
**tread water**
be still 268.7
swim 275.56
**treason** apostasy 145.3
betrayal 628.2
dishonesty 975.7
**treasonable**
apostate 145.20
rebellious 767.11
renegade 628.11
traitorous 975.22
**treasure**
n. collection 74.11
funds 835.14
good thing 674.5
store 660.1
wealth 837.1
v. cherish 931.19
harbor 813.7
rate highly 672.12
remember 537.13
store up 660.11
**treasured**
beloved 931.22
stored 660.14
**treasure-house**
depository 836.12
storage place 660.6
**treasurer**
executive 748.3
financial officer
836.11
payer 841.9
**treasure trove**
discovery 488.1
find 811.6
**treasury**
depository 836.12
hoard 660.1
ready money 835.18
storage place 660.6
**treasury note**
paper money 835.5
securities 834.1
**treat**
n. delicacy 308.8
payment 841.8
refreshment 307.5
regalement 865.3
v. behave toward
737.6
care for 689.30
deal with 665.12
discourse upon 606.5
discuss 597.12
operate on 164.6
pay for 841.19
practice medicine
688.17
prepare 720.6
remedy 687.38
**treatise** 606

**treatment**
artistry 574.10
discussion 597.7
medical aid 689.15
preparation 720.1
therapy 689.1
treatise 606.1
usage 665.2
**treat with**
mediate 805.6
negotiate 771.7
**treaty** 771.2
**treble**
n. high voice 458.6
melody 462.4
singing part 462.22
voice 463.5
v. triplicate 94.2
adj. high 458.13
triple 94.3
vocal 462.51
**treble clef** 463.13
**tree**
n. gallows 1011.5
genealogy 170.5
mast 277.13
timber 411.10
types of 411.50
v. corner 731.15
**treed** 731.23
**tree farming** 413.3
**treelike**
arboreal 411.36
branched 299.10
**trefoil** 93.1
**trek**
n. journey 273.5
migration 273.4
v. migrate 273.21
travel 273.20
**trellis** 221.3
**tremble**
n. excitement 857.4
music 463.19
nervousness 859.2
shake 324.3
v. be afraid 891.22
be cold 333.9
be excited 857.16
be nervous 859.6
be weak 160.8
shake 324.11
**trembling**
n. excitement 857.4
shaking 324.2
adj. fearful 891.31
jittery 859.11
shaking 324.17
**tremendous**
huge 195.20
large 34.7
superb 674.17
terrible 891.38
**tremendously**
frightfully 891.42
superbly 674.22
vastly 34.16
**tremolo** music 463.19
organ stop 465.22
**tremor**
excitement 857.4
music 463.19

shake 324.3
speech defect 595.1
thrill 857.2
**tremulous**
fearful 891.31
imperfectly spoken
595.12
jittery 859.11
shaking 324.17
**trench**
n. channel 396.1
crack 201.2
ditch 799.5
ocean depths 209.4
shelter 700.3
trough 263.2
valley 257.9
v. channel 396.19
cut 201.4
excavate 257.15
groove 263.3
intrude 238.5
**trenchant**
acrimonious 161.13
caustic 939.21
eloquent 600.11
energetic 161.12
pungent 433.6
sagacious 467.16
**trencherman**
eater 307.14
glutton 994.3
**trench foot** 686.31
**trench mouth** 686.12
**trend**
n. course 267.2
direction 290.1
drift 174.2
fashion 644.1
flow 395.4
v. bear 290.8
deviate 291.3
flow 395.16
tend 174.3
**trend-setter** 644.7
**trendy** 644.11
**trepidation**
agitation 324.1
excitement 857.4
fear 891.5
nervousness 859.1
**trespass**
n. intrusion 238.1
lawbreaking 999.3
misdeed 982.2
overstepping 313.3
usurpation 961.3
violation 769.2
v. break the law 999.5
intrude 238.5
not observe 769.4
overstep 313.9
sin 982.5
usurp 961.8
**trespasser** 238.3
**trespassing**
intrusion 238.1
lawbreaking 999.3
usurpation 961.3
**tress** 230.5
**trestle** horse 216.16
railway 657.8

**triable** 999.6
**triad** harmonics 463.17
  three 93.1
**triage** 60.3
**trial**
  *n.* adversity 729.1
  annoyance 866.2
  attempt 714.2
  contest 796.3
  examination 485.2
  experiment 489.1
  legal action 1004.5
  number 586.8
  preparation 720.1
  test 489.2
  tribulation 866.9
  *adj.* experimental
    489.11
  tentative 714.14
  three 93.3
**trial and error**
  attempt 714.2
  experiment 489.1
**trial balloon**
  question 485.10
  testing device 489.4
**trial run** 489.3
**triangle** bell 454.4
  geometry 251.13
  love affair 931.6
  percussion instrument
    465.18
  pillory 1011.3
  straightedge 250.3
  three 93.1
**triangular** triform 93.3
  trilateral 251.8
  tripartite 95.4
**triangulate**
  measure 490.11
  pinpoint 184.10
**triangulation**
  measurement 490.1
  radar operation 346.8
**tribal** 11.7
**tribe** biology 61.5
  group 74.3
  kind 61.3
  race 11.4
**tribesman** 11.2
**tribulation**
  adversity 729.1
  trial 866.9
**tribunal**
  *n.* council 755.1
  court 1001
  platform 216.13
  *adj.* judicial 1001.10
**tribune** judge 1002.2
  platform 216.13
**tributary**
  *n.* feeder 395.3
  *adj.* subject 764.13
**tribute**
  attribution 155.2
  celebration 877.1
  demand 753.1
  fee 841.5
  gift 818.4
  honor 916.4
  praise 968.5
  tax 846.10

**trice** 113.3
**trich(o)–** 230.2
**trichotomy** 95.1
**trick**
  *n.* characteristic 80.4
  deception 618.6
  eccentricity 474.2
  expedient 670.2
  habit 642.4
  illusion 519.1
  intrigue 654.6
  knack 733.6
  mannerism 903.2
  playing cards 878.17
  prank 881.10
  pretext 649.1
  shift 108.3
  stratagem 735.3
  style 588.2
  *v.* deceive 618.13
  fool 618.14
  live by one's wits
    735.9
  play a practical joke
    881.14
**trickery**
  chicanery 618.4
  juggling 618.5
  ornamentation 901.3
  stratagem 735.3
  wittiness 881.4
**trickle**
  *n.* few 102.2
  flow 395.7
  leakage 303.5
  *v.* dribble 395.18
  leak out 303.14
**trickle away** 692.22
**trick out**
  dress up 231.41
  falsify 616.16
  make grandiloquent
    601.7
  ornament 901.8
**trickster**
  cunning person 735.6
  deceiver 619.2
**tricky** cunning 735.12
  deceitful 618.20
  difficult 731.16
  dishonest 975.16
  misleading 618.19
  treacherous 975.21
  waggish 881.17
**tricolor**
  *n.* flag 569.6
  *adj.* variegated 374.9
**tricycle** 272.8,29
**trident**
  *n.* fork 299.4
  three 93.1
  *adj.* tripartite 95.4
**tried and true**
  experienced 733.26
  friendly 927.20
  tested 489.13
  traditional 123.12
  trustworthy 974.19
**triennial**
  *n.* anniversary 137.4
  plant 411.3
  *adj.* periodic 137.8

**trifle**
  *n.* bagatelle 673.5
  pastry 308.40
  pudding 308.45
  small amount 35.5
  thing of naught 4.2
  trivia 673.4
  *v.* be foolish 470.6
  fritter away 854.5
  leave undone 534.7
  make love 932.13
  treat lightly 673.13
  waste time 708.12
**trifler** dallier 673.9
  dilettante 476.6
  idler 708.8
  neglecter 534.5
**trifle with**
  disrespect 965.3
  do carelessly 534.9
**trifling**
  *n.* dallying 673.8
  idling 708.4
  *adj.* insignificant 35.6
  quibbling 483.14
  trivial 673.16
**triform** 93.3
**trifurcate**
  forked 299.10
  tripartite 95.4
**trig** chic 644.13
  shipshape 277.20
  tidy 59.8
**trigger** kindle 648.18
  use radar 346.17
**trigger-happy**
  jumpy 891.31
  warlike 797.25
**trigger man**
  evildoer 943.4
  killer 409.11
**trigonometry**
  angle measurement
    251.3
  mathematics 87.18
**trig up** 60.12
**trike** 272.8
**trilateral** sided 242.7
  triangular 251.8
  tripartite 95.4
**trilingual** 580.14
**trill**
  *n.* music 463.19
  *v.* bird sound 460.5
  flow out 303.14
  make a liquid sound
    452.11
  sing 462.39
**trilogy** 93.1
**trim**
  *n.* clothing 231.1
  condition 7.3
  ornamentation 901.1
  preparedness 720.4
  *v.* border 235.10
  change one's mind
    628.7
  cheapen 849.6
  cut the hair 230.22
  defeat 727.6
  fasten 47.7
  ornament 901.8

**prepare** 720.6
  punish 1010.15
  reel in 287.9
  remain neutral 806.5
  reprove 969.18
  sail 275.49
  shorten 203.6
  straighten up 60.12
  *adj.* chic 644.13
  polished 589.6
  ready 277.19
  shapely 248.5
  shipshape 277.20
  tidy 59.8
**trimester** period 107.2
  three 93.1
**trimmed**
  bordered 235.12
  defeated 727.14
  ornamented 901.11
  rigged 277.17
  shortened 203.9
**trimming**
  *n.* bookbinding
    605.15
  defeat 727.1
  edging 235.7
  extra 41.4
  ornamentation 901.1
  *adj.* mind-changing
    628.10
**trinity** three 93.1
  threeness 93.2
**Trinity** 1013.10
**trinket** ornament 901.4
  toy 878.16
  trifle 673.5
**trinomial** 583.17
**trio** cooperation 786.1
  music arrangement
    462.5
  orchestra 464.12
  part music 462.17
  three 93.1
**trip**
  *n.* an error 518.4
  bungle 734.5
  flight 278.9
  flock 74.5
  illusion 519.1
  journey 273.5
  misdeed 982.2
  thing imagined 535.5
  tumble 316.3
  *v.* bungle 734.11
  dance 879.5
  err 518.9
  fantasy 535.17
  go wrong 981.9
  jump 319.6
  knock down 318.5
  overcome 727.7
  play 878.25
  run 269.10
  trap 618.18
  tumble 316.8
  walk 273.27
**tripartite** 95.4
**tripe** intestines 225.4
  meat 308.20
  nonsense 547.3

**triple**
v. increase 38.5
  triplicate 94.2
adj. three 93.3
  triplicate 94.3
**triplet**
  harmonics 463.14
  music 463.24
  poetic division
    609.11
  three 93.1
**triplex** three 93.3
  triple 94.3
**triplicate**
n. copy 24.3
  triplication 94.1
v. copy 24.8
  triple 94.2
adj. triple 94.3
**tripper**
  drug user 642.10
  traveler 274.1
**tripping**
n. hallucination 519.7
adj. eloquent 600.9
  harmonious 589.8
**triptych** picture 574.12
  record book 570.11
  three 93.1
**trisect** 95.3
**trisection** 95
**triste** 872.24
**trite** banal 883.9
  commonplace 79.16
  habitual 642.16
  trivial 673.16
  well-known 475.27
**Triton** sea god 397.4
  water god 1014.20
**triumph**
n. celebration 877.1
  gloating 910.4
  great success 724.3
  rejoicing 876.1
  victory 726.1
v. best 36.7
  be victorious 726.3
  defeat 727.6
  gloat 910.9
  prevail over 726.6
  win through 724.12
**triumphant**
  gloating 910.12
  successful 724.13
  victorious 726.8
**trivet** fireplace 329.12
  three 93.1
**trivia**
  small amount 35.2
  trifles 673.4
**trivial** inferior 37.7
  insignificant 35.6
  quibbling 483.14
  shallow 210.5
  trifling 673.16
  worthless 669.11
**triviality**
  foolishness 470.1
  futility 669.2
  inferiority 37.3
  shallowness 210.1
  smallness 35.1

**trifle** 673.5
  unimportantness
    673.3
**troche** 687.7
**trochee** 609.9
**troglodyte**
  caveman 123.7
  vulgar person 898.7
**troika**
  cooperation 786.1
  trio 93.1
**troll**
n. monster 85.20
  music 462.19
v. fish 655.10
  propel 285.10
  pull 286.4
  roll 322.10
  sing 462.39
**troller** 655.6
**trolley**
  handcar 272.16,23
  streetcar 272.15
**trollop**
  bad person 986.5
  slob 62.7
  unchaste woman
    989.14
**trombone**
  brass wind 465.8
  organ stop 465.22
**trombonist** 464.4
**troop** flock 74.5
  group 74.3
  military unit 800.19
**trooper**
  cavalryman 800.11
  mounted police
    699.15
  state police 699.17
  war-horse 800.32
**troops** army 800.22
  forces 157.9
**trophy**
  good thing 674.5
  memento 537.7
  memorial 570.12
  prize 916.3
  thing desired 634.11
**tropical** 328.24
**tropics**
  hot place 328.11
  zone 180.3
**tropism** 174.1
**tropological**
  figurative 551.3
  interpretative 552.14
**troposphere**
  atmospheric layer
    402.3
  aviation 278.41
**trot**
n. crib 552.3
  gait 273.14
  old woman 127.3
  repetitiousness 103.4
  speed 269.3
v. ride 273.33
  run 269.10
**troth**
n. betrothal 770.3
  fidelity 974.7

**promise** 770.1
v. affiance 770.6
  promise 770.4
**trot out** 555.5
**trots** defecation 311.2
  indigestion 686.28
**trotter** foot 212.5
  horse 414.18
  legs 273.16
  pork 308.16
**troubadour**
  poet 609.13
  singer 464.14
  wanderer 274.2
**trouble**
n. adversity 729.1
  affliction 866.8
  annoyance 866.2
  anxiety 890.1
  commotion 62.4
  difficulty 731.3
  exertion 716.1
  impediment 730.6
  imposition 963.1
  inconvenience 671.3
v. agitate 324.10
  beset 731.12
  bother 890.3
  discompose 63.4
  distress 866.16
  excite 857.13
  inconvenience 671.4
  take liberties 961.7
  vex 864.15
**troubled**
  agitated 324.16
  annoyed 866.21
  anxious 890.6
  distressed 866.22
  excited 857.21
  in difficulty 731.19
**troublemaker**
  instigator 648.11
  mischief-maker 943.2
**troubleshooter** 694.10
**troubleshooting** 694.6
**troublesome**
  adverse 729.13
  annoying 864.22
  difficult 731.17
  hindering 730.17
  inconvenient 671.7
  laborious 716.18
  worrisome 890.9
**troubling**
  annoying 864.22
  exciting 857.28
**troublous**
  adverse 729.13
  agitated 324.16
  violent 162.17
**trough**
n. aviation 278.41
  basin 257.2
  channel 396.1
  gutter 396.3
  peak 395.14
  trench 263.2
  valley 257.9
  wave 323.4
v. excavate 257.15
  groove 263.3

**trounce** best 36.7
  criticize severely
    969.21
  defeat 727.6
  punish 1010.14
**trouncing** defeat 727.1
  punishment 1010.4
**troupe**
n. actors 612.11
  group 74.3
v. act 611.34
**trouper** 612.2
**trousers** 231.18
**trousseau** 231.2
**trove** discovery 488.1
  find 811.6
**trowel** 348.16
**troy weight** 352.8
**truancy** absence 187.4
  shirking 631.2
**truant**
n. absentee 187.5
  bad person 986.2
  shirker 631.3
adj. absent 187.12
**truce** armistice 804.5
  pause 144.3
**truck**
n. commerce 827.1
  communication
    554.1
  groceries 831.7
  railway car 272.14
  rubbish 669.5
  types of 272.26
  vehicle 272.11
v. haul 271.12
  trade 827.14
**truckage** 271.3
**trucker** carrier 271.5
  truck driver 274.10
**truck farm** 413.8
**truck farming** 413.1
**truckler** 907.3
**truckle to**
  be servile 907.7
  bow down before
    765.10
**truckling**
n. obsequiousness
    907.2
adj. obsequious
    907.13
**truckload** 194.2
**truckman**
  coachman 274.9
  truck driver 274.10
**truculence**
  cruelty 939.11
  gruffness 937.3
  warlikeness 797.15
**truculent** cruel 939.24
  gruff 937.7
  warlike 797.25
**trudge**
n. slowness 270.2
  walk 273.12
v. plod 270.7
  walk 273.27
**trudging**
n. walking 273.10
adj. slow 270.10

true
v. make agree 26.7
adj. certain 513.13
faithful 974.20
firm 624.12
friendly 927.20
observant 768.4
orthodox 1024.7
real 1.15
straight 250.6
trustworthy 974.19
unerroneous 516.12
veracious 974.16
true believer
orthodox 1024.4
truster 501.9
true blue fidelity 974.7
honest person 974.8
true-blue
faithful 974.20
orthodox 1024.7
traditional 123.12
true course
aviation 278.43
direction 290.2
true faith 1024.2
true grit 624.3
truelove
faithful love 931.1
loved one 931.13
true to form
characteristic 80.13
typical 572.11
true to life
authentic 516.14
descriptive 608.15
lifelike 20.16
true to type 572.11
truism axiom 517.2
generalization 79.8
truly
adv. certainly 513.23
in fact 516.17
in reality 1.16
positively 34.19
truthfully 974.22
interj. yes 521.18
trump
n. good person 985.2
last expedient 670.2
playing cards 878.17
v. excel 36.6
trumped-up 616.29
trumpery
nonsense 547.2
ornamentation 901.3
trifles 673.4
trumpet
n. brass wind 465.8
loud sound 453.4
organ stop 465.22
v. blare 453.9
flaunt 904.17
play music 462.43
praise 968.12
proclaim 559.13
utter 594.26
trumpeter 464.4
trump up 616.18
truncate cut off 42.10
deform 249.7
shorten 203.6

truncated
concise 592.6
deformed 249.12
incomplete 57.5
trundle push 285.10
roll 322.10
trunk base 216.8
body 376.3
communications
560.17
cylinder 255.4
nose 256.7
plant stem 411.19
railway 657.8
trunk line
communications
560.17
railway 657.8
trunks 231.29,56
truss
n. bundle 74.8
v. bind 47.9
bundle 74.20
render powerless
158.11
trust
n. association 788.9
belief 501.1
\ commission 780.1
confidence 888.1
estate 810.4
financial credit 839.1
investment company
833.16
sureness 513.5
v. accept 501.10
be hopeful 888.7
believe in 501.15
confide in 501.17
delegate 818.16
give credit 839.6
trust company 836.13
trusted 501.23
trustee fiduciary 809.5
financial officer
836.11
recipient 819.3
trusteeship 780.1
truster believer 501.9
zealot 1028.4
trusting artless 736.5
credulous 502.8
trustful 501.22
trusting soul
credulous person
502.4
dupe 620.1
trustworthy
believable 501.24
dependable 974.19
reliable 513.17
unhazardous 698.5
trusty
n. honest person
974.8
prisoner 761.11
adj. believable 501.24
reliable 513.17
trusting 501.22
trustworthy 974.19
truth axiom 517.2
certainty 513.1

reality 1.2
unfalseness 516
veracity 974.3
truthful
unerroneous 516.12
veracious 974.16
truthless false 616.25
untruthful 616.34
try
n. attempt 714.2
test 489.2
v. attempt 714.5
burden 729.8
judge 494.12
refine 681.22
strive for 714.8
test 489.8
try a case 1004.17
trying adverse 729.13
experimental 489.11
fatiguing 717.11
testing 485.36
troublesome 731.17
weakening 160.20
tryout audition 448.2
preparation 720.1
rehearsal 489.3
theatrical perfor-
mance 611.13
try out
experiment 489.8
give a show 611.33
prepare 720.6
tryst 922.9
tsar see czar
T square
instrument 213.6
straightedge 250.3
tsunami
tidal wave 162.5
wave 395.14
tsures 866.8
tub
n. automobile 272.9
basin 193.7
bath 681.8
corpulent person
195.12
ship 277.1
washing equipment
681.12
v. wash 681.19
tuba 465.8
tubby corpulent 195.18
stubby 203.10
tube
n. camera 345.19
cylinder 255.4
electron tube
343.11,16
photoelectric 343.17
picture 345.18
pipe 396.6
railway 657.8
special electronic
343.18
train 272.13
v. channel 271.13
tuber 411.20
tubercle bulge 256.3
plant root 411.20
sore 686.35

tubercular
diseased 686.57
nodular 256.16
tuberculin test 689.17
tuberculosis
disease 686.12
epidemic disease
686.4
respiratory disease
686.15
tuberosity
bulging 256.1
protuberance 256.2
tuberous
herbaceous 411.33
nodular 256.16
tubing 396.6
tub-thumper 599.4
tubular
cylindrical 255.11
pipelike 396.20
tuck
n. fold 264.1
v. fold 264.5
tucked 264.7
tucker
n. apron 231.17,64
food 308.1
rations 308.6
v. fatigue 717.4
tuckered out 717.8
tuck in eat 307.20
insert 304.3
make comfortable
887.9
put to bed 712.19
tuft beard 230.8
clump 74.7
feather 230.16
growth 411.2
hair 230.6
tufted
feathered 230.29
verdant 411.39
tug
n. attraction 288.1
exertion 716.2
harness 659.5
pull 286.2
v. attract 288.4
exert oneself 716.10
pull 286.4
tug-of-war fight 796.4
pulling 286.1
tuition 562.1
tuitional 562.19
tumble
n. collapse 725.3
fall 316.3
flounder 324.8
jumble 62.3
v. be defeated 727.12
be destroyed 693.22
be excited 857.16
be undiscriminating
493.3
confuse 63.3
fall 316.8
find 488.3
flounder 324.15
knock down 318.5
roll about 322.13

sail 275.55
**tumbledown**
  descending 316.11
  dilapidated 692.35
  unsteady 160.16
**tumbler**
  circus artist 612.3
  gymnast 878.21
**tumbling** 878.8
**tumescence**
  distension 197.2
  increase 38.1
  swelling 256.4
**tumid** bombastic 601.9
  bulging 256.15
  distended 197.13
  pompous 904.22
**tummy** 193.3
**tumor**
  disease symptom
    686.8
  growth 686.36
  swelling 256.4
**tumorous**
  bulging 256.15
  diseased 686.57
**tumult** agitation 324.1
  bustle 707.4
  commotion 62.4
  excitement 857.3
  noise 453.3
  violence 162.2
**tumultuous**
  blustering 911.4
  excited 857.22
  noisy 453.12
  violent 162.17
**tundra**
  cold place 333.4
  plain 387.1
**tune**
  n. harmonics 463.4
  melody 462.2
  music 462.3
  song 462.4
  v. harmonize 462.36
  make agree 26.7
  prepare 720.8
  put in tune 462.37
  regulate 60.10
**tuned** 462.50
**tune down**
  moderate 163.6
  radio 344.27
  reduce 39.7
  soften 357.6
**tuneful** 462.49
**tune in** radio 344.27
  use radar 346.17
**tuneless** 461.4
**tuning fork** 465.25
**tunnel**
  n. burrow 257.5
  channel 396.1
  entrenchment 799.5
  lair 191.26
  passageway 657.4
  . deepen 209.8
  excavate 257.15
**tunneling** 209.7
**tunnel vision** 440.1

**tuppence**
  British money 835.8
  trifle 673.5
**turbid** disorderly 62.13
  muddy 389.14
  opaque 341.3
**turbidity**
  agitation 324.1
  muddiness 389.4
  opaqueness 341.1
**turbine** 285.7
**turbojet** 280.3,15
**turboprop** 280.2
**turbulence**
  agitation 324.1
  air flow 278.38
  atmospheric condi-
    tion 278.41
  disorder 62.1
  excitement 857.3
  roughness 261.1
  violence 162.2
**turbulent** active 707.20
  agitated 324.16
  disorderly 62.13
  excited 857.22
  noisy 453.12
  rebellious 767.11
  stormy 403.26
  violent 162.17
**turd** bad person 986.6
  feces 311.4
**turf** fuel 331.1
  racecourse 878.12
  sod 411.6
  territory 172.4
**turflike** 411.39
**turgid** bombastic 601.9
  bulging 256.15
  distended 197.13
  pompous 904.22
  stilted 590.3
**turistas** 311.2
**turkey** failure 725.2
  food 308.22
  poultry 414.34
**Turkish** 434.2
**Turkish bath** 681.8
**turmoil** agitation 324.1,
  commotion 62.4
  excitement 857.3
  jumble 62.3
  lawlessness 740.2
  violence 162.2
**turn**
  n. act 705.3
  aptitude 733.5
  bend 219.3
  cast 7.4
  change 139.1
  circuit 321.2
  crisis 129.4
  curve 252.3
  deviation 291.1
  distortion 249.1
  form 246.1
  good deed 938.7
  inclination 634.3
  journey 273.5
  looks 446.4
  music 463.18

recurring action
  137.3
  reversion 146.1
  rotation 322.2
  shift 108.3
  show business 611.8
  spell 108.2
  stock speculation
    833.19
  surprise 540.3
  tendency 174.1
  trait of character
    525.3
  transaction 827.4
  walk 273.12
  v. bear 290.8
  be changed 139.5
  blunt 259.2
  change course 275.30
  curve 252.6
  deflect 291.5
  deviate 291.3
  direct 290.6
  distort 249.5
  fluctuate 141.5
  go around 321.5
  oblique 219.9
  recur 137.5
  rotate 322.9
  tend 174.3
  turn around 295.9
  turn back 146.5
  twist 254.4
**turnabout**
  about-face 295.3
  change 139.1
  change of mind 628.1
  reversion 146.1
  turncoat 628.5
**turn about**
  v. about face 295.9
  invert 220.5
  turn back 146.5
  adv. alternately
    137.11
  consecutively 71.11
  reciprocally 150.6
**turn a deaf ear to**
  disregard 531.2
  refuse 776.3
  show no mercy 945.2
**turn against**
  betray 975.15
  defect 145.13
**turnaround**
  about-face 295.3
  change of mind 628.1
**turn around**
  about face 295.9
  invert 220.5
  turn back 146.5
  rotate 322.9
**turn aside**
  be changed 139.5
  deflect 291.6
  deviate 291.3
  digress 593.9
  disincline 652.4
  fend off 799.10
  prevent 730.14
  pull back 284.7
**turn away** deflect 291.6

  disincline 652.4
  dismiss 310.18
  reject 638.2
**turn away from**
  avoid 631.6
  disregard 531.4
  look away 439.20
  snub 966.5
**turn back**
  be repeated 103.11
  change back 146.5
  change course 275.30
  convert 145.11
  deflect 291.6
  repulse 289.3
  retreat 295.8
**turncoat**
  n. convert 145.8
  defector 628.5
  traitor 619.10
  adj. traitorous 975.22
**turndown** 776.1
**turn down** invert 220.5
  refuse 776.3
**turned around**
  backwards 220.8
  bewildered 514.23
  dizzy 532.15
  reversed 295.12
**turned-off**
  disapproving 969.22
  uninterested 636.7
**turned-on**
  enthusiastic about
    635.12
  excited 857.18
  interested 530.16
**turned-up** curved 252.9
  stubby 203.10
  upturned 315.15
**turn in** betray 975.14
  go to bed 712.18
  invert 220.5
**turning**
  n. circuitousness 321.1
  convolution 254.1
  curve 252.3
  deviation 291.1
  rotation 322.1
  adj. devious 291.7
  rotating 322.14
  winding 254.6
**turning point**
  crisis 129.4
  important point
    672.6
**turn inside out**
  invert 220.5
  ransack 485.32
**turn into**
  be changed 139.5
  become 1.12
  be converted into
    145.17
  convert 145.11
  translate 552.12
**turnkey** 761.10
**turn loose** 763.5
**turn off**
  discharge 310.19
  disincline 652.4
  dismiss 310.18

eccentricity 474.2
extra 41.4
hair 230.7
partiality 527.3
story element 608.9
tendency 174.1
trait of character
525.3
*v.* corrupt 692.14
deflect 291.5
deform 679.4
distort 249.5
falsify 616.16
misrepresent 573.3
oblique 219.9
prejudice 527.9
rotate 322.9
torture 424.7
wander 291.4
weave 222.6
wind 254.4
**twist around one's little
finger**
dominate 741.15
have influence over
172.11
have subject 764.10
**twisted**
blemished 679.8
complex 46.4
distorted 249.10
eccentric 474.4
falsified 616.26
pained 424.9
perverted 249.11
prejudiced 527.12
**twister**
doughnut 308.43
whirlwind 403.14
**twisting**
*n.* convolution 254.1
misinterpretation
553.1
misrepresentation
573.1
weaving 222.1
*adj.* wandering 291.7
winding 254.6
**twist one's arm**
compel 756.6
persuade 648.23
urge 648.14
**twisty** crooked 219.20
winding 254.6
**twit**
*n.* banter 882.1
gibe 967.2
*v.* banter 882.4
bird sound 460.5
reproach 1005.7
ridicule 967.9
sing 462.39
**witch**
*n.* instant 113.3
jerk 286.3
pain 424.2
shake 324.3
*v.* be excited 857.16
fidget 324.13
jerk 286.5
suffer pain 424.8

**twitching**
*n.* emotional symptom
690.23
jerking 324.5
nervousness 859.1
*adj.* jerky 324.19
**twitchy** jerky 324.19
jittery 859.11
**twitter**
*n.* agitation 324.1
banterer 882.3
dither 857.5
excitement 857.4
shake 324.3
*v.* be excited 857.16
bird sound 460.5
shake 324.11
sing 462.39
**twitting**
*n.* banter 882.2
ridicule 967.1
*adj.* bantering 882.5
ridiculing 967.12
**'twixt** 237.12
**two**
*n.* pair 90.2
*adj.* double 90.6
**two-bit** 673.17
**two bits** fourth 98.2
US money 835.7
**two-by-four**
*n.* wood 378.3
*adj.* little 196.10
petty 673.17
**two-dimensional** 179.8
**two-faced**
deceitful 618.20
dishonest 975.21
double 91.4
falsehearted 616.31
**twofer** 850.2
**two-fisted** 420.12
**twofold**
*adj.* double 91.4
*adv.* doubly 91.5
**two-handed** 733.23
**twopenny** 673.18
**two-ply** double 91.4
layered 227.6
**two shakes**
instant 113.3
short time 111.3
**two-sided** bilateral 91.4
bipartite 90.6
sided 242.7
**twosome** game 878.9
pair 90.2
**two-step** 879.5
**two-time**
be false 616.24
betray 975.14
deceive 618.13
**two-time loser** 146.3
**two-timer** cheat 619.3
criminal 986.10
**two-way** 13.14
**two-wheeler** 272.3
**tycoon**
businessman 830.1
personage 672.8
ruler 749.8

**tympanum**
auditory organ 448.7
drum 465.19
eardrum 229.3
**type**
*n.* example 25.2
form 246.1
kind 61.3
measure 490.2
model 25.1
nature 5.3
odd person 85.4
omen 544.3
preference 637.5
print 603.6
representative 572.5
specialty 81.1
symbol 568.3
temperament 525.3
unit of meaning
545.6
*v.* classify 61.6
write 602.19
**typeface** 603.6,23
**typescript**
printer's copy 603.4
written matter 602.10
**typeset** 603.19
**typesetter** 603.12
**typesetting machine**
typesetting 603.2
types of 603.21
**type size** 603.22
**type style** 603.23
**typewriter** 602.31
**typewriting** 602.1
**typewritten** 602.22
**typhoid fever** 686.12
**Typhoid Mary** 686.41
**typhoon** storm 162.4
whirlwind 403.14
windstorm 403.12
**typhus** 686.12
**typical**
classificational 61.7
indicative 568.23
model 25.8
normal 84.7
representational
572.11
**typify** augur 544.12
symbolize 568.18
**typifying** 572.10
**typing** 602.1
**typist** 602.18
**typo** 518.3
**typographer** 603.12
**typographic(al)** 603.20
**typographical error**
518.3
**typography** 603.1
**typology** 61.1
**Tyr** Norse deity 1014.6
war god 797.17
**tyrannical** 739.16
**tyrannize**
domineer 741.16
subdue 764.9
**tyrannized** 764.16
**tyranny**
absolutism 741.9
despotism 741.10

force 756.2
government 741.4
subjection 764.1
**tyrant** 749.14
**tyro** beginner 68.2
novice 566.9

        **U**

**ubiquitous**
godlike 1013.20
omnipresent 186.13
pervasive 56.10
recurrent 103.13
**ubiquity**
completeness 56.1
divine attribute
1013.15
omnipresence 186.2
**U-boat** 277.9
**udder** 256.6
**UFO** 282.3
**ugh!** 864.31
**uglify** 899.5
**ugliness**
irascibility 951.2
raucousness 458.2
unpleasantness 864.1
unsightliness 899
**ugly** irascible 951.19
threatening 697.9
unpleasant 864.17
unsightly 899.6
**ugly customer**
evildoer 943.4
ill-humored person
951.11
violent person 162.9
**UHF** 344.12
**ukase**
announcement 559.2
decree 752.4
**ukulele** 465.4
**ulcer**
gastrointestinal dis-
ease 686.27
sore 686.35
**ulcerated**
decayed 692.41
diseased 686.56
**ulterior**
additional 40.10
extraneous 78.5
farther 199.10
secret 614.11
**ultimate**
*n.* culmination 677.3
*adj.* completory 722.9
eventual 151.11
farthest 199.12
final 70.10
future 121.8
irrevocable 752.13
top 211.10
**ultimately**
eventually 151.12
finally 70.11
in time 121.11
**ultimatum**
condition 507.2
demand 753.1
final proposal 773.3

**unawares**
ignorantly 477.18
innocently 984.9
suddenly 113.9
unexpectedly 540.14
**unawed**
unastonished 921.3
undaunted 893.20
**unbalance**
*n.* inequality 31.1
insanity 473.1
*v.* madden 473.23
upset 31.3
**unbalanced**
eccentric 185.12
ill-balanced 31.5
insane 473.25
unjust 977.9
**unbearable**
insufferable 864.25
outright 34.12
**unbeatable**
invincible 159.17
peerless 36.15
**unbeaten**
untrodden 122.7
unused 668.12
victorious 726.9
**unbeautiful** 899.6
**unbecoming**
disgraceful 915.11
inappropriate 27.7
indecent 990.5
vulgar 898.10
**unbefitting**
inappropriate 27.7
inexpedient 671.5
untimely 130.7
**unbeknown** 477.17
**unbelief** disbelief 503
nonreligiousness
1031.5
unorthodoxy 1025.3
**unbelievable**
fantastic 85.12
incredible 503.10
**unbeliever**
atheist 1031.11
doubter 503.4
gentile 1025.6
impious person
1030.3
**unbelieving**
atheistic 1031.19
disbelieving 503.8
unorthodox 1025.10
**unbend** be pliant 357.7
ease up 163.9
relax 711.7
straighten 250.5
**unbending** firm 624.12
rigid 356.12
straight 250.6
strict 757.7
unyielding 626.9
**unbent** 250.6
**unbiased**
impartial 976.10
unprejudiced 526.12
**unbidden**
unwanted 867.11
unwelcome 926.9

voluntary 622.7
**unbigoted**
broad-minded 526.8
liberal 762.24
**unbind** detach 49.10
loose 763.6
**unblemished**
chaste 988.4
clean 681.25
honest 974.13
innocent 984.7
perfect 677.6
**unblenching**
undaunted 893.20
unnervous 860.2
**unblessed**
unfortunate 729.14
unsacred 1027.3
**unblinking** alert 533.14
undaunted 893.20
unnervous 860.2
**unblock**
facilitate 732.6
open 265.13
**unbolt** detach 49.10
loose 763.6
**unborn** 2.9
**unbosoming** 556.3
**unbothered** 868.8
**unbound** free 762.27
liberated 763.10
unfastened 49.22
unrestricted 762.26
**unbounded**
godlike 1013.20
infinite 104.3
unrestricted 762.26
**unbowed** straight 250.6
victorious 726.9
**unbreakable**
nonbreakable 359.5
solid 159.16
**unbridled**
excessive 663.16
intemperate 993.7
lawless 740.5
unchaste 989.25
unrestrained 762.23
violent 162.18
**unbroken**
constant 135.5
continuous 71.8
direct 290.13
smooth 260.9
straight 250.6
undamaged 677.8
uniform 17.5
untamed 762.28
**unbuckle** detach 49.10
loose 763.6
**unburden** lighten 353.6
relieve 886.7
unload 310.22
**unburdened** 762.25
**unbusinesslike** 734.16
**unbutton** 49.10
**uncalculated** 630.11
**uncalculating**
honest 974.18
impulsive 630.10
**uncalled-for**
impudent 913.9

needless 669.10
superfluous 663.17
unwanted 867.11
voluntary 622.7
**uncandid**
dishonest 975.18
insincere 616.32
**uncanny**
awesome 920.11
creepy 891.39
deathly 408.29
weird 1017.9
**uncared-for**
neglected 534.14
unappreciated 867.9
**uncaused** 156.15
**unceasing**
constant 135.5
continuous 71.8
perpetual 112.7
persistent 143.7
**uncelebrated** 915.14
**unceremonious** 647.3
**uncertain**
ambiguous 550.3
doubtful 503.9
inconstant 141.7
irregular 138.3
irresolute 627.9
speculative 515.21
unsafe 697.11
unsure 514.15
vague 445.6
**uncertainty**
ambiguity 550.1
chance 156.1
doubt 503.2
expectancy 539.3
gamble 515.1
inconstancy 141.2
irregularity 138.1
irresolution 627.1
unsafeness 697.2
unsureness 514
vagueness 445.2
**uncertified**
unauthoritative
514.20
unproved 506.8
**unchain** detach 49.10
loose 763.6
**unchained** 762.27
**unchallengeable** 5.6
**unchallenged**
certain 513.16
unanimous 521.15
**unchangeable**
invariable 142.17
permanent 140.7
uniform 17.5
unyielding 626.9
**unchanging**
constant 135.5
godlike 1013.20
invariable 142.17
permanent 140.7
uniform 17.5
**unchaperoned** 534.14
**uncharacterized** 79.11
**uncharitable**
narrow-minded
527.10

unbenevolent 939.15
**uncharted** 477.17
**unchary** 894.7
**unchaste** obscene 990.9
sensual 987.5
unrighteous 981.12
unvirtuous 989.23
**unchastity**
immorality 981.1
indecency 990.1
lechery 932.9
sensuality 987.1
unvirtuousness 989
**unchecked**
candid 974.17
lawless 740.5
permanent 140.7
unauthoritative
514.20
unrestrained 762.23
**uncheerful**
pessimistic 889.16
unhappy 872.21
**unchivalrous** 978.6
**unchristian**
cruel 939.24
unbelieving 1031.19
ungodly 1031.17
unorthodox 1025.10
**uncirculated** 122.9
**uncircumscribed**
infinite 104.3
unqualified 508.2
unrestricted 762.26
**uncivil**
discourteous 937.4
uncouth 898.12
**uncivilized**
cruel 939.24
savage 162.20
uncouth 898.12
**unclad** 232.13
**unclasp** detach 49.10
relinquish 814.4
**unclassified**
disclosed 555.10
unknown 477.17
unordered 62.12
**uncle** 11.3
**unclean** bad 675.9
dirty 682.20
obscene 990.9
unchaste 989.23
unrighteous 981.12
**unclear**
faint-sounding 452.16
formless 247.4
illegible 549.19
indistinct 445.6
obscure 549.15
vague 514.18
**unclench** 265.13
**Uncle Sam**
the government
741.3
United States 181.5
**unclever** 734.15
**unclog**
clean out 310.21
facilitate 732.6
open 265.13
**unclogged** open 265.18

misrepresent 573.3
**understated** 897.8
**understatement**
good taste 897.4
misrepresentation
573.1
**understood**
known 475.26
supposed 499.14
tacit 546.8
traditional 123.12
**understructure**
foundation 216.6
structure 245.3
**understudy**
*n.* actor 612.7
deputy 781.1
substitute 149.2
*v.* represent 781.14
substitute for 149.5
**undertake** agree 771.6
attempt 714.5
engage in 705.7
promise 770.5
set about 715.3
set to work 716.15
**undertaken**
assumed 715.7
contracted 771.12
**undertaker** 410.8
**undertaking** act 705.3
attempt 714.2
business 656.1
commitment 770.2
enterprise 715
pledge 772.2
**under-the-counter**
covert 614.12
illegal 999.6
**under the impression**
501.21
**under the influence**
996.30
**under the sun**
everywhere 179.11
existent 1.13
on the earth 385.12
**under-the-table**
covert 614.12
illegal 999.6
**undertone**
implication 546.2
meaning 545.1
milieu 233.3
murmur 452.4
**undertow** flow 395.4
hidden danger 697.5
**undervalue** 498.2
**underwater** 209.13
**under way**
at sea 275.63
happening 151.9
in motion 267.9
in preparation 720.22
undertaken 715.7
**underwear** 231.22
**underweight**
*n.* leanness 205.5
weight 352.1
*adj.* lean 205.17
lightweight 353.12

**underworld**
depths 209.3
hell 1019.1
organized crime
986.11
**under wraps**
concealed 615.11
secret 614.11
**underwrite**
promise 770.4
protect 699.18
ratify 521.12
secure 772.9
**underwriter**
endorser 521.7
guarantor 772.6
insurance man 699.4
**undeserved**
undue 961.9
unjust 977.9
**undesignated** 584.3
**undesigned**
unintentional 156.17
unpremeditated
630.11
**undesigning**
honest 974.18
natural 736.6
**undesirable**
*n.* bad person 986.1
outcast 926.4
*adj.* inexpedient 671.5
unacceptable 869.7
unpleasant 864.17
unwelcome 926.9
**undesired** 867.11
**undesirous** 636.8
**undestroyed**
permanent 140.7
undamaged 677.8
**undetached**
prejudiced 527.12
unjust 977.11
**undetected** 615.12
**undetermined**
chance 156.15
irresolute 627.9
uncertain 514.18
undecided 514.17
unproved 506.8
**undeveloped**
immature 124.10
imperfect 678.4
incomplete 57.4
inexperienced 734.17
new 122.7
unfinished 721.12
**undeviating**
direct 290.13
exact 516.16
straight 250.6
unchangeable 142.17
uniform 17.5
**undevised** 721.8
**undies** 231.22
**undifferentiated**
continuous 71.8
general 79.11
indistinctive 493.6
simple 45.6
uniform 17.5
**undigested** 721.11

**undignified**
inelegant 590.2
vulgar 898.10
**undiluted** 45.7
**undiminished**
complete 56.9
unabated 34.14
unweakened 159.19
whole 54.11
**undine** spirit 1014.16
water god 1014.20
**undiplomatic** 534.11
**undirected**
purposeless 156.16
unordered 62.12
wandering 291.7
**undiscerning**
blind 441.9
unperceptive 469.14
unwise 470.9
**undisciplined**
disobedient 767.8
intemperate 993.7
lawless 740.5
unrestrained 141.7
**undisclosable** 614.11
**undisclosed**
secret 614.11
unknown 477.17
unrevealed 615.12
**undiscoverable**
inaccessible 510.9
unknown 477.17
**undiscovered**
unknown 477.17
unrevealed 615.12
**undiscriminating**
indiscriminate 493.5
unconcerned 636.7
**undisguised**
genuine 516.14
honest 974.18
unobscured 555.11
visible 444.6
**undismayed** 893.20
**undisputed**
believed 501.23
unquestioned 513.16
**undissembling**
honest 974.18
natural 736.6
**undistinguished**
humble 906.9
undifferentiated
493.6
unrenowned 915.14
**undistorted**
genuine 516.14
straight 250.6
**undisturbed**
calm 268.12
unexcited 858.11
untroubled 868.8
**undivided** joined 47.13
one 89.7
whole 54.11
**undo** defeat 727.6
demolish 693.17
destroy 693.13
detach 49.10
make nervous 859.9
negate 178.7

open 265.13
ruin 693.11
solve 487.2
take off 232.6
**undoing** defeat 727.1
destruction 693.1
disassembly 49.6
neutralization 178.2
**undone**
defeated 727.14
heartbroken 872.29
hopeless 889.15
neglected 534.14
ruined 693.28
terrified 891.34
unaccomplished
723.3
unfastened 49.22
unnerved 859.13
**undoubted**
believed 501.23
certain 513.16
true 516.12
**undoubtedly**
certainly 513.25
truly 516.17
**undoubting**
believing 501.21
credulous 502.8
sure 513.21
unqualified 508.2
**undreamed-of**
unthought-of 480.5
unusual 85.10
**undress**
*n.* dishabille 231.20
plainness 902.3
*v.* unclothe 232.7
**undressed**
unadorned 902.8
unclad 232.13
**undressing** 232.2
**undrinkable** 429.8
**undue** excessive 663.16
overpriced 848.12
undeserved 961.9
unjust 977.9
wrong 959.3
**undulant** curved 252.7
periodic 137.7
rolling 254.10
waving 323.16
**undulate** billow 395.22
fly 278.49
recur 137.5
wave 323.11
**undulating**
rolling 254.10
waving 323.16
**unduly**
excessively 663.22
exorbitantly 848.16
improperly 34.21
**unduplicated** 23.6
**undurable** 111.7
**undutiful**
disobedient 767.8
impious 1030.6
nonreligious 1031.1
**undying**
continuing 143.7
immortal 112.9

indestructible 142.18
uneager 636.8
unearned 961.9
unearth dig up 305.10
 find 488.4
unearthly
 deathly 408.29
 heavenly 1018.13
 immaterial 377.7
 odd 85.11
 pious 1028.9
 preposterous 503.10
 supernatural 85.15
 weird 1017.9
uneasiness
 anxiety 890.1
 discontent 869.1
 impatience 862.1
 nervousness 859.1
 trepidation 891.5
 unpleasure 866.1
uneasy agitated 324.16
 anxious 890.6
 discontented 869.5
 distressed 866.22
 impatient 862.6
 nervous 859.10
 pleasureless 866.20
 restless 857.25
uneatable 429.8
uneconomical 721.15
uneducated
 unlearned 477.14
 vernacular 580.18
unelaborate 902.9
unelevated 208.7
unembarrassed
 immodest 990.6
 unhampered 762.25
unembellished
 natural 736.6
 prosaic 610.5
 unadorned 902.8
unembodied 377.7
unemotional 856.9
unemployable
 idle 708.17
 unserviceable 669.14
unemployed
 idle 708.17
 motionless 268.13
 unused 668.12
unemployed, the
 708.10
unemployment
 idleness 708.2
 inoccupation 708.3
unencumbered 762.25
unending
 continuous 71.8
 perpetual 112.7
unendowed
 unable 158.14
 unskilled 734.16
unendurable 864.25
unenhanced 35.8
unenjoyable
 uninteresting 883.7
 unpleasant 864.17
unenlightened
 blind 441.9
 ignorant 477.12

unenterprising
 cautious 895.8
 indolent 708.18
unentertaining 883.7
unenthralled 762.28
unenthusiastic
 reluctant 623.6
 undesirous 636.8
unentitled 961.9
unenvied 965.7
unequal different 16.7
 disparate 31.4
 irregular 138.3
 nonuniform 18.3
 unjust 977.9
unequaled 36.15
unequipped
 incompetent 734.19
 unfit 721.9
unequitable 977.9
unequivocal
 candid 974.17
 clear 548.10
 outright 34.12
 positive 513.13
 unqualified 508.2
 unrestricted 762.26
unerring exact 516.16
 infallible 513.19
 virtuous 980.9
unescorted 89.8
unessential
 n. accessory 6.2
 adj. accessory 6.4
 incidental 8.7
 irrelevant 10.6
 needless 669.10
 superfluous 663.17
 unimportant 673.15
unestablished
 uncertain 514.17
 unproved 506.8
 unsettled 185.10
unethical 975.16
uneuphonious 590.2
uneven
 imperfect 678.4
 irregular 138.3
 nonuniform 18.3
 rough 261.6
 unequal 31.4
 unjust 977.9
unevenly
 irregularly 138.4
 nonuniformly 18.4
 roughly 261.11
 unequally 31.6
 unjustly 977.13
unevenness
 imperfection 678.1
 inequality 31.1
 irregularity 138.1
 nonuniformity 18.1
 roughness 261.1
uneventful
 tedious 884.8
 uninteresting 883.7
unexacting
 undiscriminating
  493.5
 unmeticulous 534.13
 unstrict 758.5

unexaggerated 516.14
unexamined 534.16
unexampled 85.14
unexcelled 36.15
unexceptionable
 acceptable 868.12
 believable 501.24
 praiseworthy 968.20
 unimpeachable 984.8
 unobjectionable
  674.19
unexceptional
 mediocre 680.8
 normal 84.7
unexcited 858.11
unexciting 883.7
unexecuted 723.3
unexempt from 962.17
unexercised 668.12
unexhausted
 refreshed 695.5
 unweakened 159.19
unexpected
 chance 156.15
 sudden 113.5
 unanticipated 540.10
 unimaginable 85.12
 unusual 85.10
unexpectedness
 not anticipated 540.1
 suddenness 113.2
unexplainable 549.18
unexplained
 unknown 477.17
 unrevealed 615.12
unexplored
 unexamined 534.16
 unknown 477.17
 unrevealed 615.12
unexposed
 unknown 477.17
 unrevealed 615.12
unexpressed
 tacit 451.11
 unspoken 546.9
unexpurgated
 complete 56.9
 whole 54.12
unextended 377.7
unextinguished
 burning 328.27
 unmitigated 162.16
unfacile 734.15
unfactual
 erroneous 518.16
 inaccurate 518.17
unfaded
 undamaged 677.8
 unweakened 159.19
unfading dyed 362.17
 enduring 110.10
 immortal 112.9
 permanent 140.7
unfailing
 faithful 974.20
 permanent 140.7
 persevering 625.7
 reliable 513.17
unfair 977.10
unfairness 977.2
unfaithful
 disloyal 975.20

nonobservant 769.5
unfaithfulness
 infidelity 975.5
 love affair 931.6
unfaltering
 confident 513.21
 persevering 625.7
 unhesitating 624.13
 unnervous 860.2
unfamiliar
 ignorant 477.12
 new 122.11
 unknown 477.17
 unusual 85.10
unfamiliarity
 inexperience 734.2
 newness 122.1
 unaccustomedness
  643.1
 unknown 477.1
unfamiliar with
 inexperienced 734.17
 unaccustomed 643.4
unfanciful
 genuine 516.14
 unimaginative 536.5
unfashionable
 old-fashioned 123.16
 unconventional 83.6
unfasten 49.10
unfastened 49.22
unfathomable
 deep 209.11
 infinite 104.3
 unintelligible 549.13
unfathomed
 deep 209.11
 unknown 477.17
unfavorable
 adverse 729.13
 disadvantageous
  671.6
 disapproving 969.22
 ominous 544.17
 opposing 790.8
 untimely 130.7
unfavorably
 adversely 729.16
 disapprovingly 969.27
 inauspiciously 544.20
unfearful 893.19
unfeasible 510.8
unfed fasting 995.5
 ill-provided 662.12
unfeeling
 n. emotionlessness
  856
 heartlessness 939.10
 insensibility 423.1
 adj. heartless 939.23
 inanimate 382.5
 insensible 423.6
 pitiless 945.3
 unemotional 856.9
unfeigning
 genuine 516.14
 honest 974.18
 natural 736.6
 unaffected 902.7
unfelt 423.6
unfeminine
 ill-bred 937.6

mannish 420.13
**unfetter** detach 49.10
  loose 763.6
**unfettered** 762.27
**unfilled** hungry 634.25
  vacant 187.14
**unfinish** 721.4
**unfinished**
  imperfect 678.4
  unaccomplished
    723.3
  undeveloped 721.12
  unskilled 734.16
**unfit**
  inappropriate 27.7
  incompetent 734.19
  inexpedient 671.5
  unable 158.14
  unqualified 721.9
  unserviceable 669.14
  untimely 130.7
  wrong 959.3
**unfixed**
  inconstant 141.7
  uncertain 514.17
  undetermined 506.8
  unfastened 49.22
**unflagging**
  industrious 707.22
  persevering 625.7
  unweakened 159.19
**unflappable**
  firm 624.12
  inexcitable 858.10
  stable 142.12
**unflattering**
  genuine 516.14
  honest 974.18
**unflavored** 430.2
**unflawed** 677.6
**unfledged**
  immature 124.10
  inexperienced 734.17
  new 122.7
  undeveloped 721.11
**unflinching**
  persevering 625.7
  stable 142.12
  undaunted 893.20
  unhesitating 624.13
  unnervous 860.2
**unfold** amplify 593.7
  develop 148.7
  disclose 556.4
  explain 552.10
  manifest 555.5
  open 265.13
  result 154.5
  spread 197.6
**unfolding**
  *n.* appearance 446.1
  development 148.2
  disclosure 556.1
  display 555.2
  expansion 593.6
  flowering 411.24
  *adj.* developing 148.8
**unforced**
  *adj.* free 762.23
  voluntary 622.7
  *adv.* at will 621.5

**unforeseeable**
  chance 156.15
  uncertain 514.15
  unexpected 540.10
**unforeseen**
  chance 156.15
  sudden 113.5
  unexpected 540.10
**unforgettable**
  notable 672.18
  remembered 537.26
**unforgivable**
  improper 981.16
  unpardonable 977.12
**unforgiving** 945.3
**unforgotten** 537.23
**unformed**
  immature 124.10
  undeveloped 721.12
  unshaped 247.5
**unfortified** simple 45.7
  unprotected 697.14
**unfortunate**
  *n.* unlucky person
    729.7
  *adj.* inexpedient 671.5
  ominous 544.17
  unlucky 729.14
  unsuccessful 725.17
  untimely 130.7
**unfortunately**
  inauspiciously 544.20
  inexpediently 671.8
  inopportunely 130.8
  unluckily 729.17
**unfounded**
  baseless 483.13
  false 616.25
  illusory 519.9
  unauthentic 518.19
  unproved 506.8
**unfree** 764.14
**unfreeze** 329.21
**unfrequented** 924.7
**unfriendliness**
  enmity 929.1
  inhospitality 926.1
  unsociability 923.1
  warlikeness 797.15
**unfriendly** averse 867.8
  belligerent 797.25
  inhospitable 926.7
  inimical 929.9
  opposing 790.8
  unsociable 923.5
**unfrock** depose 783.4
  disgrace 915.8
  dismiss 310.19
**unfrozen** 328.24
**unfruitful** 166.4
**unfulfilled**
  discontented 869.5
  unaccomplished
    723.3
  unsatisfied 866.20
**unfulfilling** 869.6
**unfurl** develop 148.7
  disclose 556.4
**unfurnished** 721.9
**unfussy** plain 902.9
  unmeticulous 534.13
**ungag** 763.6

**ungagged** 762.27
**ungainly** clumsy 734.20
  ugly 899.9
**ungallant**
  discourteous 937.4
  uncourageous 892.11
**ungenerous**
  narrow-minded
    527.10
  selfish 978.6
  stingy 852.9
  unbenevolent 939.15
**ungentlemanly** 937.6
**ungenuine** 616.26
**ungettable** 510.9
**ungiving** rigid 356.12
  unyielding 626.9
**unglorified** 915.14
**unglue** detach 49.10
  loosen 51.3
**unglued** 859.13
**ungodliness**
  immorality 981.1
  nonreligiousness
    1031.3
**ungodly** devilish 675.10
  irreligious 1031.17
  preposterous 503.10
  unvirtuous 981.12
**ungovernable** 626.12
**ungoverned** free 762.28
  lawless 740.5
  unrestrained 762.23
**ungraceful**
  clumsy 734.20
  infelicitous 590.2
  ugly 899.9
**ungracious**
  discourteous 937.4
  inhospitable 926.7
  unkind 939.14
**ungraded** 62.12
**ungrammatic(al)** 587.4
**ungrammaticalness** 587
**ungrateful** 950.4
**ungratified**
  discontented 869.5
  unsatisfied 866.20
**ungratifying** 869.6
**ungrounded**
  baseless 483.13
  unsubstantial 4.8
**ungrudging**
  consenting 775.4
  liberal 853.4
  willing 622.6
**unguarded** artless 736.5
  candid 974.17
  impulsive 630.10
  inattentive 531.8
  negligent 534.10
  unintentional 156.17
  unprotected 697.14
**unguent**
  *n.* healing ointment
    687.11
  ointment 380.3
  *adj.* oily 380.9
**unguessed** 540.10
**ungulate**
  *n.* animal 414.3
  *adj.* footed 212.9

hoofed 414.49
**unhabitable** 926.8
**unhallowed** 1027.3
**unhampered**
  communicative
    554.10
  unimpeded 762.25
  unrestricted 508.2
**unhand** release 763.5
  relinquish 814.4
**unhandicapped** 762.25
**unhandsome** 899.6
**unhandy** clumsy 734.20
  inconvenient 671.7
  untimely 130.7
  unwieldy 731.18
**unhappiness**
  disapproval 969.1
  discontent 869.1
  sadness 872.2
  unpleasure 866.1
**unhappy**
  disapproving 969.22
  discontented 869.5
  inexpedient 671.5
  pleasureless 866.20
  uncheerful 872.21
  unfortunate 729.14
  untimely 130.7
**unhappy about** 873.8
**unharmed** safe 698.4
  undamaged 677.8
**unharness** 763.6
**unharnessing** 763.2
**unhasty** 710.6
**unhatched** 721.8
**unhazardous** 698.5
**unhealthful** 684.5
**unhealthy** sickly 686.50
  unhealthful 684.5
  unsafe 697.11
  unwholesome 686.51
**unhearable** 451.10
**unheard-of** new 122.11
  unknown 477.17
  unrenowned 915.14
  unusual 85.10
  wondrous 920.10
**unhearing** deaf 449.6
  unaware 477.13
**unheated** 333.13
**unheeded** 534.15
**unheedful**
  careless 534.11
  inattentive 531.6
  inconsiderate 939.16
**unhelpful**
  inconsiderate 939.16
  useless 669.14
**unheralded** 540.10
**unheroic** 892.11
**unhesitating**
  confident 513.21
  unfaltering 624.13
  unqualified 508.2
**unhidden** open 265.18
  unobscured 555.11
  visible 444.6
**unhinge**
  dislocate 185.5
  madden 473.23
  separate 49.16

in accord 794.3
integrated 89.10
joined 47.13
United Kingdom 181.4
United Nations
international organization 743
supranational government 741.7
United States
country 181.3
regions of 180.7
uniting
n. addition 40.1
adj. combining 52.7
concurrent 177.4
converging 298.3
unifying 89.12
unit pricing 846.4
unity accord 794.1
completeness 56.1
divine attribute 1013.15
identity 14.1
indivisibility 354.2
oneness 89
simplicity 45.1
totality 54.1
uniformity 17.1
wholeness 54.5
universal
n. idea 479.2
idealism 377.3
adj. comprehensive 76.7
cosmic 375.24
global 79.14
infinite 104.3
pervasive 56.10
total 54.9
usual 84.8
universality
completeness 56.1
generality 79.1
infinity 104.1
wholeness 54.5
universalize 79.9
universally
everywhere 179.11
generally 79.18
universe cosmos 375
frame of reference 525.2
university
n. college 567.7
adj. scholastic 567.18
univocal certain 513.13
intelligible 548.10
unipartite 89.11
unjaundiced 526.12
unjoined
discontinuous 72.4
separate 49.20
unordered 62.12
unjust 977.9
unjustifiable 977.12
unjustified 961.9
unkempt rough 261.6
slovenly 62.15
uncouth 898.12
unkind 939.14
unkindly 939.14,25

unkindness 939
unknowable
unintelligible 549.13
unknown 477.17
unknowing
ignorant 477.12
unaware 477.13
unknowingly
ignorantly 477.18
innocently 984.9
unknown
anonymous 584.3
concealed 615.11
not known 477.17
unrenowned 915.14
unknown, the
the future 121.2
the unknowable 477.7
unlabored
natural 589.6
undeveloped 721.12
unlace 49.10
unladylike 937.6
unlamented 867.9
unlatch detach 49.10
loose 763.6
open 265.13
unlawful illegal 999.6
prohibited 778.7
wrong 959.3
unlawfulness
illegality 999.1
impropriety 977.1
wrong 959.1
unlax 711.7
unlearn 538.6
unlearned
inerudite 477.14
instinctive 481.6
unleash detach 49.10
free 763.6
loosen 51.3
unless
prep. excluding 77.9
conj. excepting 507.16
unlettered 477.14
unlicensed 778.7
unlicked
immature 124.10
uncouth 898.12
undeveloped 721.12
unformed 247.5
unlikable
distasteful 867.7
hateful 930.8
unpleasant 864.17
unsavory 429.5
unlike different 16.7
dissimilar 21.4
incomparable 491.9
unlikelihood
improbability 512.1
small chance 156.9
unlikely 512.3
unlimited
godlike 1013.20
infinite 104.3
intemperate 993.7
omnipotent 157.13
unqualified 508.2
unrestricted 762.26

unlit 337.13
unliterary
unlearned 477.14
vernacular 580.18
unlivable 926.8
unload lighten 353.6
relieve 886.7
sell 829.8
sell stocks 833.24
unpack 310.22
unloading
evacuation 310.6
lightening 353.3
relief 886.3
unlock detach 49.10
explain 552.10
loose 763.6
open 265.13
solve 487.2
unlooked-for
chance 156.15
sudden 113.5
unexpected 540.10
unloosen detach 49.10
free 763.6
unloosing 763.2
unlovable 867.7
unloved 867.10
unlovely 899.6
unloving
unfeeling 856.9
unkind 939.14
unloyal
nonobservant 769.5
unfaithful 975.20
unluckily
inauspiciously 544.20
unfortunately 729.17
unlucky
ominous 544.17
unfortunate 729.14
untimely 130.7
unlucky day fate 640.2
wrong time 130.2
unmade uncreated 2.9
unprepared 721.8
unmake 693.17
unmaking 693.5
unman
domineer 741.16
frighten 891.23
make nervous 859.9
subdue 764.9
unnerve 158.12
weaken 160.10
unmanageability
clumsiness 734.3
ungovernability 626.4
unwieldiness 731.8
unmanageable
ungovernable 626.12
unwieldy 731.18
unmanly
cowardly 892.10
effeminate 421.14
unmanned
cowardly 892.10
devitalized 158.19
terrified 891.34
unnerved 859.13
untended 187.14
unmannerly 937.5

unmarked
undamaged 677.8
unheeded 534.15
unmarketable 829.15
unmarred 677.8
unmarried
n. celibate 934.2
adj. unwedded 934.7
unmask 556.4
unmasking 556.1
unmatched best 674.18
dissimilar 21.4
peerless 36.15
unmatured
inexperienced 734.17
premature 131.8
unmeant 156.17
unmeasured
infinite 104.3
innumerable 101.10
intemperate 993.7
unrestrained 762.23
unrestricted 762.26
unmelodious 461.4
unmelted cold 333.13
impenitent 874.5
unmentionable
base 915.12
indescribable 920.13
unmentionables 231.22
unmentioned 546.9
unmerciful
heartless 939.23
pitiless 945.3
unmerited undue 961.9
unjust 977.9
unmethodical
haphazard 62.12
irregular 138.3
unmilitary 803.10
unmindful
careless 534.11
forgetful 538.9
inattentive 531.6
inconsiderate 939.16
incurious 529.3
unaware 477.13
unconcerned 636.7
ungrateful 950.4
unmingled 45.7
unmistakable
certain 513.13
clearly visible 444.7
intelligible 548.10
manifest 555.8
unqualified 508.2
unmistaken 516.12
unmitigated
changed 139.9
outright 34.12
thorough 56.10
undiminished 34.14
unqualified 508.2
unsoftened 162.16
unmixed pure 677.6
simple 45.7
unmolested 698.4
unmoor 275.18
unmoored 275.61
unmotivated 156.16
unmourned 867.9

**unproficient** 734.15
**unprofitable**
  disadvantageous
  671.6
  fruitless 669.12
**unprofitably**
  at a loss 812.9
  disadvantageously
  671.9
**unprofound**
  shallow 210.5
  superficial 469.20
**unprogressive**
  conservative 140.8
  right-wing 745.17
**unprohibitive** 777.14
**unpromising**
  ominous 544.17
  unlikely 512.3
**unprompted**
  unintentional 156.17
  voluntary 622.7
**unpronounced**
  silent 451.10
  unexpressed 546.9
**unpropitious**
  ominous 544.17
  opposing 790.8
  untimely 130.7
**unprosperous**
  poor 838.7
  unfortunate 729.14
**unprotected**
  defenseless 697.14
  helpless 158.18
**unprovable**
  uncertain 514.15
  undemonstrable
  506.9
**unproved**
  erroneous 518.16
  illogical 483.12
  not proved 506.8
  unauthoritative
  514.20
**unprovided**
  ill-provided 662.12
  unfit 721.9
**unprovidential** 729.14
**unprovincial** 526.8
**unpublishable** 614.14
**unpublished** 546.9
**unqualified**
  absolute 56.10
  complete 677.7
  genuine 516.14
  inappropriate 27.7
  incompetent 734.19
  insufficient 662.9
  outright 34.12
  unable 158.14
  unconditional 508.2
  unfit 721.9
  unrestricted 762.26
**unquelled** free 762.28
  unmitigated 162.16
  victorious 726.9
**unquenchable**
  greedy 634.27
  inextinguishable
  142.18

**unquestionable**
  believable 501.24
  certain 513.15
  intrinsic 5.6
  true 516.12
**unquestioned**
  believed 501.23
  certain 513.16
**unquestioning** 508.2
**unquiet** active 707.20
  agitated 324.16
  impatient 862.6
  pleasureless 866.20
  restless 857.25
**unquotable** 614.14
**unravel**
  come apart 49.8
  disentangle 305.10
  explain 552.10
  extricate 763.7
  simplify 45.5
  solve 487.2
**unraveling**
  extrication 763.3
  solution 487.1
**unreachable** 510.9
**unread** 477.14
**unreadable** 549.19
**unready** careless 534.11
  inattentive 531.8
  inexpectant 540.9
  late 132.16
  unprepared 721.8
  untimely 130.7
**unreal** illusory 519.9
  imaginary 535.19
  nonexistent 2.8
  tenuous 4.6
  ungenuine 616.26
**unrealistic** unreal 2.8
  visionary 535.24
**unreality**
  idealization 535.7
  illusoriness 519.2
  nonexistence 2.1
  unsubstantiality 4.1
**unrealizable** 510.8
**unrealized**
  unaccomplished
  723.3
  unseen 445.5
**unreason** 470.2
**unreasonable**
  capricious 629.5
  excessive 663.16
  fanatical 473.32
  illogical 483.11
  overpriced 848.12
  unjust 977.12
  unwise 470.9
**unreasonableness**
  excess 663.1
  exorbitance 848.4
  illogicalness 483.2
  unwiseness 470.2
**unreasoning**
  emotionalistic 855.20
  impulsive 630.10
  thoughtless 480.4
  unintelligent 469.13
**unrecalled** 538.8

**unreceptive**
  inhospitable 926.7
  uninfluenceable
  173.4
**unrecognizable** 445.6
**unrecognized** 950.5
**unrecollected** 538.8
**unrecorded** 546.9
**unredeemable** 981.18
**unreduced**
  undiminished 34.14
  whole 54.11
**unreel** 148.7
**unrefined**
  coarse-textured 351.6
  countrified 182.7
  discourteous 937.6
  infelicitous 590.2
  rough 261.6
  undeveloped 721.12
  unlearned 477.14
  vulgar 898.12
**unreflecting**
  impulsive 630.10
  unwise 470.9
**unrefreshed** 717.6
**unrefutable**
  certain 513.15
  proved 505.22
**unrefuted**
  proved 505.22
  true 516.12
**unregarded**
  neglected 534.14
  unheeded 534.15
  unrespected 965.7
**unregenerate**
  irreclaimable 981.18
  irreligious 1031.18
  obstinate 626.8
  unsacred 1027.3
**unregretful** 874.4
**unregretted**
  disliked 867.9
  unrepented 874.6
**unrehearsed** 630.12
**unreined** lawless 740.5
  unrestrained 762.23
**unrelated** 10.5
**unrelaxed** rigid 356.11
  tense 859.12
**unrelenting**
  drawn out 593.12
  persevering 625.7
  strict 757.7
  unyielding 626.9
**unreliability**
  fickleness 629.3
  inconstancy 141.2
  unbelievability 503.3
  uncertainty 514.6
  unsafeness 697.2
  untrustworthiness
  975.4
**unreliable** fickle 629.6
  inconstant 141.7
  unauthentic 518.19
  uncertain 514.19
  unsafe 697.11
  untrustworthy 975.19
**unrelieved**
  continuous 71.8

  featureless 187.13
  monotonous 17.6
  outright 34.12
**unremarkable** 680.8
**unremitting**
  constant 135.5
  industrious 707.22
  perpetual 112.7
  persevering 625.7
  sustained 143.7
  unchangeable 142.17
  uninterrupted 71.8
**unremorseful**
  pitiless 945.3
  unregretful 874.4
**unremunerated** 842.12
**unremunerative** 669.12
**unrenowned** 915.14
**unrepeatable** 990.9
**unrepeated** 89.9
**unrepentant** 874.5
**unrepressed**
  communicative
  554.10
  unrestrained 762.23
**unreproachful** 968.18
**unrequested** 622.7
**unrequired**
  needless 669.10
  voluntary 622.7
**unrequited**
  unpaid 842.12
  unthanked 950.5
**unresemblance** 21.1
**unresembling** 21.4
**unresentful** 947.6
**unreserve** candor 974.4
  communicativeness
  554.3
  unrestraint 762.3
**unreserved**
  artless 736.5
  candid 974.17
  communicative
  554.10
  thorough 56.10
  unqualified 508.2
  unrestrained 762.23
**unresolved** 627.9
**unrespectable** 915.10
**unresponsive**
  heartless 939.23
  unfeeling 856.9
  uninfluenceable
  173.4
**unrest** agitation 324.1
  excitement 857.4
  motion 267.1
**unrestful** 857.25
**unrestrained**
  candid 974.17
  communicative
  554.10
  excessive 663.16
  fervent 855.23
  free 762.23
  intemperate 993.7
  lawless 740.5
  unchaste 989.24
  unstrict 758.4
  wavering 141.7

**nrestraint**
candor 974.4
communicativeness
554.3
freedom 762.3
intemperance 993.1
lawlessness 740.1
unchastity 989.2
unstrictness 758.1
**nrestricted**
communicative
554.10
open 265.18
thorough 56.10
undiminished 34.14
unlimited 762.26
unqualified 508.2
**nreticent** 554.10
**nreturnable** 142.17
**nrevealed**
secret 614.11
undisclosed 615.12
unknown 477.17
**nrewarded**
unpaid 842.12
unthanked 950.5
**nrewarding**
disadvantageous
671.6
fruitless 669.12
**nrhythmical** 138.3
**nriddle** 487.2
**nrighteous**
ungodly 1031.17
unvirtuous 981.12
wrong 959.3
**nrightful** 977.9
**nripe** ignorant 477.12
immature 124.10
inexperienced 734.17
premature 131.8
sour 432.5
undeveloped 721.11
untimely 130.7
**nrivaled** 36.15
**nrobed** 232.13
**nroll** develop 148.7
disclose 556.4
open 265.13
**nromantic**
genuine 516.14
practical 536.6
prosaic 610.5
unimaginative 536.5
**nruffled** calm 268.12
smooth 260.9
unaffected 856.11
unexcited 858.11
uniform 17.5
**nruliness**
lawlessness 740.2
refractoriness 767.2
ungovernability 626.4
unrestraint 762.3
violence 162.3
**nruly** lawless 740.6
refractory 767.10
ungovernable 626.12
unrestrained 762.23
violent 162.18
**nsacred** 1027.3
**nsaddle** depose 783.4

unseat 185.6
**unsafe** 697.11
**unsaid** tacit 451.11
unexpressed 546.9
**unsaintly**
ungodly 1031.17
unvirtuous 981.12
**unsalable** 829.15
**unsalutary** 684.5
**unsalvageable** 889.15
**unsanctified** 1027.3
**unsanctioned** 778.7
**unsanctity** 1027
**unsanitary** 684.5
**unsated** 634.27
**unsatisfactory**
disappointing 541.6
inadequate 869.6
insufficient 662.9
**unsatisfied**
discontented 869.5
greedy 634.27
lustful 419.29
pleasureless 866.20
**unsatisfying**
insufficient 662.9
unsatisfactory 869.6
**unsavory**
dishonest 975.16
disreputable 915.10
insipid 430.2
unpalatable 429.5
unpleasant 864.17
**unsay** 628.9
**unsaying** 628.3
**unscarred** 677.8
**unscathed** safe 698.4
undamaged 677.8
**unscented** 438.5
**unscholarly** 477.14
**unschooled**
unlearned 477.14
unskilled 734.16
**unscientific** 483.11
**unscramble**
simplify 45.5
solve 487.2
untangle 732.8
**unscratched** 677.8
**unscrew** 49.10
**unscrubbed** 682.20
**unscrupulous**
dishonest 975.16
unmeticulous 534.13
**unsearched** 534.16
**unseasonable**
inappropriate 27.7
inexpedient 671.5
mistimed 115.3
untimely 130.7
**unseasoned**
immature 124.10
inexperienced 734.17
unaccustomed 643.4
undeveloped 721.11
**unseat** depose 783.4
dislocate 49.16
dislodge 185.6
**unsecurable** 510.9
**unseeing** blind 441.9
unaware 477.13
unwise 470.9

**unseemly**
*adj.* inappropriate
27.7
indecent 990.5
inexpedient 671.5
infelicitous 590.2
vulgar 898.10
wrong 959.3
*adv.* vulgarly 898.16
**unseen** invisible 445.5
unheeded 534.15
unrevealed 615.12
**unselective** 493.5
**unselfconfident**
modest 908.10
unsure 514.22
**unselfish**
impartial 976.10
liberal 853.4
selfless 979.5
**unselfishness**
impartiality 976.4
liberality 853.1
selflessness 979
**unsentimental** 536.6
**unserviceable** 669.14
**unsettle** confuse 532.7
disturb 62.9
excite 857.13
upset 63.4
**unsettled** active 707.20
changeable 141.7
confused 532.12
disorderly 62.13
displaced 185.10
excited 857.21
insane 473.25
irregular 138.3
irresolute 627.9
restless 857.25
uncertain 514.17
unproved 506.8
**unsettling** 857.28
**unsex** 42.11
**unsexed**
castrated 158.19
unsexual 419.31
**unsexual** 419.31
**unshackle** 763.6
**unshackled** free 762.27
liberated 763.10
**unshaded** 555.11
**unshakable** 142.12
**unshaken** calm 860.2
firm 624.12
unweakened 159.19
**unshaped** 247.5
**unshapely** 899.8
**unsharpened** 259.3
**unshaven** 230.25
**unsheathe**
disclose 556.4
divest 232.5
open 265.13
**unsheltered** 697.14
**unshorn** hairy 230.24
whole 54.11
**unshrinking** calm 860.2
communicative
554.10
undaunted 893.20
unhesitating 624.13

willing 622.6
**unsightly**
slovenly 62.15
ugly 899.6
**unskilled**
inexperienced 734.17
unaccomplished
734.16
**unskillful** bad 675.7
inexpert 734.15
inferior 37.7
**unslakeable** 634.27
**unsmiling**
solemn 871.3
unhappy 872.21
**unsmooth** 261.6
**unsnarl**
disentangle 732.8
extricate 763.7
put in order 60.8
simplify 45.5
straighten 250.5
**unsociable**
misanthropic 940.3
uncommunicative
613.8
unfriendly 929.9
ungregarious 923.5
**unsocial** 923.5
**unsoftened**
impenitent 874.5
unmitigated 162.16
**unsoiled** chaste 988.4
clean 681.25
innocent 984.7
**unsold** 829.15
**unsoldierly** 892.11
**unsolicited**
neglected 534.14
voluntary 622.7
**unsolicitous**
careless 534.11
discourteous 937.6
unconcerned 636.7
**unsolvable**
complex 46.5
inexplicable 549.18
**unsolved** 615.12
**unsophisticate** 736.3
**unsophisticated**
artless 736.5
gullible 502.9
simple 45.7
unadorned 902.8
**unsophistication**
artlessness 736.1
gullibility 502.2
plainness 902.3
simplicity 45.1
**unsorrowful** 874.4
**unsorted** 62.12
**unsought** 622.7
**unsound** flimsy 4.7
illogical 483.12
imperfect 678.4
insane 473.25
insolvent 836.18
unhealthy 686.50
unorthodox 1025.9
unreliable 514.19
unsafe 697.11
unwholesome 686.51

unwise 470.9
weak 160.15
**unsparing**
industrious 707.22
liberal 853.4
strict 757.6
unkind 939.22
**unspeakable** evil 981.16
extraordinary 85.14
horrendous 864.19
indescribable 920.13
ineffable 1026.7
insulting 965.6
**unspecified**
anonymous 584.3
general 79.11
vague 514.18
**unspectacular** 680.8
**unspent** 668.12
**unspiritual**
carnal 987.6
materialistic 376.9
worldly 1031.16
**unspoiled** natural 736.6
outright 34.12
preserved 701.11
undamaged 677.8
**unspoken** secret 614.11
tacit 451.11
unexpressed 546.9
**unsportsmanlike** 977.10
**unspotted** chaste 988.4
clean 681.25
honest 974.13
innocent 984.7
perfect 677.6
**unstable**
changeable 141.7
transient 111.7
unbalanced 31.5
unreliable 514.19
unsafe 697.11
wavering 18.3
weak 160.15
**unstaffed** 187.14
**unstained** chaste 988.4
clean 681.25
honest 974.13
**unsteadfast**
inconstant 141.7
unfaithful 975.20
unreliable 514.19
**unsteady**
changeable 141.7
fluttering 324.18
inconstant 18.3
irregular 138.3
shaky 160.16
unbalanced 31.5
unreliable 514.19
unsafe 697.11
**unstick** detach 49.10
loosen 51.3
**unstinting** 853.4
**unstirred**
unaffected 856.11
unexcited 858.11
**unstop** 265.13
**unstoppable** 639.15
**unstopped**
constant 135.5
continuous 71.8

open 265.18
**unstrained** 860.2
**unstrap** detach 49.10
loose 763.6
**unstressed** 594.31
**unstruck** 856.11
**unstrung**
terrified 891.34
unnerved 859.13
weak 160.12
**unstuck** 49.22
**unstudied**
informal 647.3
unexamined 534.16
unpremeditated 630.11
unprepared 721.8
vernacular 580.18
**unsturdy** 160.15
**unsubject**
exempt 762.29
free 762.28
**unsubmissive**
insubordinate 767.9
nonconforming 83.5
resistant 792.5
ungovernable 626.12
**unsubstantial**
frail 160.14
illogical 483.12
illusory 519.9
immaterial 377.7
intangible 4.5
tenuous 355.4
unreal 2.8
unreliable 514.19
weak 160.15
**unsubstantiated** 506.8
**unsubtle** 493.5
**unsuccessful** 725.17
**unsuccessfulness** 725.1
**unsuitability**
inexpedience 671.1
insufficiency 662.1
unfitness 27.3
unpreparedness 721.1
unsatisfactoriness 869.2
untimeliness 130.1
uselessness 669.1
vulgarity 898.1
wrong 959.1
**unsuitable**
inappropriate 27.7
inexpedient 671.5
unacceptable 869.7
unserviceable 669.14
untimely 130.7
vulgar 898.10
wrong 959.3
**unsuited**
inappropriate 27.7
unfit 721.9
**unsullied** chaste 988.4
clean 681.25
honest 974.13
innocent 984.7
natural 721.13
**unsung** disliked 867.9
unexpressed 546.9
unrenowned 915.14
**unsupplied** 662.12

**unsupportable**
baseless 483.13
unprovable 506.9
**unsupported**
alone 89.8
baseless 483.13
unproved 506.8
**unsuppressed**
communicative 554.10
unrestrained 762.23
**unsure** ignorant 477.12
uncertain 514.15
unconfident 514.22
unreliable 514.19
unsafe 697.11
untrustworthy 975.19
**unsurpassed**
best 674.18
peerless 36.15
**unsurprised**
expectant 539.11
unastonished 921.3
**unsusceptible**
unchangeable 142.17
unfeeling 856.9
uninfluenceable 173.4
**unsuspected**
believed 501.23
unknown 477.17
**unsuspecting**
credulous 502.8
inexpectant 540.9
trusting 501.22
unaware 477.13
unprotected 697.14
**unsuspicious**
artless 736.5
credulous 502.8
trusting 501.22
**unsustainable**
baseless 483.13
unprovable 506.9
**unsustained**
baseless 483.13
illogical 483.12
unproved 506.8
**unswayable** 173.4
**unswayed**
impartial 976.10
uninfluenced 173.5
unprejudiced 526.12
**unsweet** 432.5
**unswept** 682.20
**unswerving**
direct 290.13
firm 624.12
persevering 625.7
straight 250.6
**unsymmetric(al)**
distorted 249.10
nonuniform 62.12
**unsympathetic**
pitiless 945.3
unfeeling 856.9
unkind 939.14
**unsystematic**
haphazard 62.12
irregular 138.3
nonuniform 18.3

**untactful**
inconsiderate 534.11
undiscriminating 493.5
**untainted** chaste 988.4
clean 681.25
innocent 984.7
perfect 677.6
unspoiled 701.11
**untaken** 187.14
**untalented**
unable 158.14
unintelligent 469.13
unskilled 734.16
**untalkative** 613.9
**untalked-of** 546.9
**untamable** 626.12
**untamed** free 762.28
savage 162.20
uncouth 898.12
**untangle**
extricate 763.7
simplify 45.5
solve 487.2
**untangling**
extrication 763.3
solution 487.1
**untapped** 668.12
**untarnished**
chaste 988.4
clean 681.25
honest 974.13
**untaught**
unlearned 477.14
unskilled 734.16
**unteachable** 469.15
**untempered** 162.16
**untenable**
baseless 483.13
helpless 158.18
unacceptable 869.7
**untenanted** 187.14
**untended**
neglected 534.14
unstaffed 187.14
**untested** 506.8
**untether** 763.6
**unthankful** 950.4
**unthinkable**
impossible 510.7
unbelievable 503.10
**unthinking**
careless 534.11
impulsive 630.10
inconsiderate 939.16
involuntary 639.14
thoughtless 480.4
unintelligent 469.13
unintentional 156.17
unwise 470.9
**unthoughtful**
impulsive 630.10
inconsiderate 939.16
unwise 470.9
**unthought-of**
undreamed-of 480.5
unheeded 534.15
unintentional 156.17
unusual 85.10
**untidy** dirty 682.22
slipshod 534.12
slovenly 62.15

untie detach 49.10
loose 763.6
untied adrift 275.61
free 762.27
liberated 763.10
unfastened 49.22
until 105.15
untilled fallow 721.14
unproductive 166.4
untimely
inappropriate 27.7
inexpedient 671.5
late 132.16
premature 131.8
unseasonable 130.7
untimid 893.19
untired 695.5
untiring
persevering 625.7
tough 359.4
untold infinite 104.3
innumerable 101.10
secret 614.11
uncertain 514.17
unexpressed 546.9
untouchable
n. outcast 926.4
adj. out-of-the-way
199.9
prohibited 778.7
sacred 1026.7
unfeeling 856.9
untouched
impenitent 874.5
natural 721.13
new 122.7
safe 698.4
unaffected 856.11
undamaged 677.8
unknown 477.17
unused 668.12
untoward
adverse 729.13
bad 675.7
ominous 544.17
untimely 130.7
untrained
unaccustomed 643.4
unskilled 734.16
untraveled 268.15
untreated 721.12
untried
inexperienced 734.17
new 122.7
unproved 506.8
untrimmed
honest 974.18
unadorned 902.8
untrodden new 122.7
unpierced 266.10
unused 668.12
untroubled
pacific 803.9
still 268.12
unbothered 868.8
unexcited 858.11
untrue
erroneous 518.16
false 616.25
nonobservant 769.5
unfaithful 975.20
untrusting 503.9

untrustworthy
dishonest 975.19
unreliable 514.19
unsafe 697.11
untruth error 518.1
falseness 616.1
lie 616.11
untruthful
dishonest 616.34
insincere 975.18
untutored
unlearned 477.14
unskilled 734.16
untwist simplify 45.5
solve 487.2
unusable 669.14
unused new 122.7
not used 668.12
remaining 43.7
surplus 663.18
unaccustomed 643.4
unused to
inexperienced 734.17
unaccustomed 643.4
unusual new 122.11
rare 136.2
uncommon 85.10
unusually
exceptionally 34.20
uncommonly 85.17
unutterable
indescribable 920.13
ineffable 1026.7
secret 614.11
unuttered
secret 614.11
silent 451.10
tacit 451.11
unexpressed 546.9
unvalued
unappreciated 867.9
underestimated 498.3
unvarnished
genuine 516.14
honest 974.18
in plain style 591.3
natural 736.6
unadorned 902.8
unvarying
constant 135.5
permanent 140.7
tedious 884.8
unchangeable 142.17
uniform 17.5
unveil disclose 556.4
expose 232.5
unclose 265.13
unveiling
disclosure 556.1
display 555.2
inauguration 68.5
unventilated
airless 268.16
closed 266.9
unverified
unauthoritative
514.20
unproved 506.8
unversed
ignorant 477.12
inexperienced 734.17

unvirtuous
unchaste 989.23
unrighteous 981.12
unvoiced silent 451.10
unexpressed 546.9
unwanted
undesired 867.11
unwelcome 926.9
unwarned
inexpectant 540.9
unprotected 697.14
unwarrantable
illegal 999.6
unjust 977.12
unwarranted
baseless 483.13
illegal 999.6
overpriced 848.12
unauthoritative
514.20
undue 961.9
unwary artless 736.5
inattentive 531.8
negligent 534.10
rash 894.7
unwashed 682.20
unwatched
neglected 534.14
unprotected 697.14
unwatchful
inattentive 531.8
negligent 534.10
unwavering
persevering 625.7
stable 142.12
sure 513.21
unnervous 860.2
unweakened 159.19
unwearied
industrious 707.22
persevering 625.7
refreshed 695.5
unweave simplify 45.5
solve 487.2
unwed 934.7
unweeded 411.40
unwelcome
disliked 867.11
unpleasant 864.17
unwanted 926.9
unwell 686.52
unwholesome
diseased 686.51
unhealthful 684.5
unwieldy bulky 195.19
clumsy 734.20
inconvenient 671.7
ponderous 352.17
stilted 590.3
unmanageable 731.18
unwilling
disinclined 623.5
involuntary 639.14
refusing 776.6
unwind
calm oneself 858.7
develop 148.7
relax 711.7
simplify 45.5
unwise
inexpedient 671.5
injudicious 470.9

unintelligent 469.13
unwished 867.11
unwitting
involuntary 639.14
unaware 477.13
unintentional 156.17
unwomanly 420.13
unwonted
unaccustomed 643.4
unusual 85.10
unworkable
impracticable 510.8
unserviceable 669.14
unworldly
heavenly 1018.13
immaterial 377.7
pious 1028.9
supernatural 85.15
unworried 868.8
unworthy
n. bad person 986.1
adj. evil 981.16
undue 961.9
unimportant 673.19
unwrap disclose 556.4
open 265.13
take off 232.6
unwrinkled 260.9
unwritten
speech 594.30
traditional 123.12
unexpressed 546.9
unyielding firm 624.12
immovable 142.15
inevitable 639.15
invincible 159.17
obstinate 626.9
pitiless 945.3
resistant 792.5
rigid 356.12
strict 757.7
substantial 3.7
uninfluenceable
173.4
up
n. increase 38.1
v. ascend 315.8
elevate 317.5
increase 38.4
make larger 197.4
promote 782.2
adj. awake 713.8
adv. aloft 207.26
upward 315.16
vertically 213.13
prep. toward 290.28
up-and-coming 707.23
up and down
alternately 137.11
perpendicularly
213.14
to and fro 323.21
up-and-down
alternate 323.19
perpendicular 213.12
up-and-up 974.14
upbeat
n. improvement 691.1
music 463.26
pulse 137.3
adj. optimistic 888.12
upbraid 969.17

increase 38.1
**uptight**
conventional 82.6
tense 859.12
**up to able** 157.14
competent 733.22
prepared for 720.18
scheming 654.14
sufficient 661.6
until 105.15
**up-to-date**
fashionable 644.11
informed 475.18
modern 122.13
present 120.2
**up to one's ears in**
busy 707.21
involved in 176.4
**up-to-the-minute**
fashionable 644.11
modern 122.13
present 120.2
**uptown**
*n.* city district 183.6
*adj.* urban 183.10
*adv.* up 315.16
**uptrend**
improvement 691.1
increase 38.1
upturn 315.2
**upturn**
*n.* business cycle 827.9
increase 38.1
inversion 220.2
uptrend 315.2
*v.* overturn 220.6
slope up 315.13
**upturned** 315.15
**upward**
*adj.* ascending 315.14
flowing 267.8
*adv.* aloft 207.26
up 315.16
**upwards of**
about 200.26
several 101.7
**upwind** ascend 315.8
fly 278.52
**upwind**
water travel 275.68
windward 242.9
**uranium** 327.12
**uranium 235** 326.5
**uranology** 375.19
**urban** 183.10
**urbane**
courteous 936.14
decorous 897.10
sociable 922.18
**urbanite** 190.6
**urban renewal**
housing 188.3
renovation 694.4
**urchin** bad child 125.4
waif 274.3
**urge**
*n.* desire 634.1
impulse 630.1
motivation 648.6
*v.* advise 754.6
egg on 648.16
hasten 709.4

incite 648.14
insist 753.7
pressure 774.12
**urgency**
dire necessity 639.4
entreaty 774.3
importance 672.4
insistence 753.3
motivation 648.6
precedence 64.1
**urgent**
*adj.* demanding 753.8
eloquent 600.13
hasty 709.9
important 672.21
motivating 648.25
necessary 639.12
pressing 774.18
*interj.* make haste!
709.16
**urgently** 753.10
**urge upon** 773.8
**urinal** rest room 311.10
toilet 311.11
**urinalysis** 689.13
**urinary** 311.20
**urinate** 311.14
**urine** body fluid 388.3
excretion 311.5
**urn** ceramic ware 576.2
funeral urn 410.12
**ursine** 414.47
**urtext** 25.1
**USA** 181.3
**usable** 665.22
**usage**
acceptation 545.4
custom 642.1
diction 588.1
employment 665.1
habit 642.4
language 580.1
phrase 585.1
treatment 665.2
word 582.1
**use**
*n.* benefit 665.4
custom 642.1
employment 665
estate 810.4
function 665.5
habit 642.4
utility 665.3
wear 692.5
*v.* behave toward
737.6
deal with 665.12
employ 665.10
exert 716.8
exploit 665.16
practice 705.7
**used** employed 665.23
lost 812.7
old 123.18
wasted 854.9
**used to**
accustomed 642.17
familiar with 642.18
habituated 642.19
**used up**
consumed 666.4
exhausted 717.8

lost 812.7
weakened 160.18
worn-out 692.38
**useful**
employable 665.18
expedient 670.5
good 674.12
helpful 785.21
instrumental 658.6
**usefulness**
expedience 670.1
goodness 674.1
helpfulness 785.10
utility 665.3
**useless**
disadvantageous
671.6
ineffective 158.15
pointless 669.9
unsuccessful 725.17
**uselessness**
failure 725.1
ineffectiveness 158.3
inexpedience 671.1
inutility 669
**user** addict 642.10
employer 665.9
legal right of use
665.7
**use up** consume 666.2
fatigue 717.4
spend 665.13
waste 854.4
**usher**
*n.* attendant 750.5
doorkeeper 699.12
escort 73.5
theater man 611.28
wedding attendant
933.5
*v.* escort 73.8
**usher in**
announce 116.3
begin 68.11
pioneer 66.3
precede 64.2
**usual** customary 642.15
frequent 135.4
mediocre 680.8
medium 32.3
ordinary 79.12
regular 84.8
routine 59.6
typical 572.11
**usual, the** 84.3
**usually**
customarily 642.22
frequently 135.6
generally 79.17
normally 84.9
**usurer** 820.3
**usurious** 848.12
**usurp**
appropriate 822.19
assume 961.8
encroach 313.9
take command
739.14
**usurpation**
accession to power
739.12
appropriation 822.4

overstepping 313.3
seizure 961.3
**usurper** arrogator 961.4
tyrant 749.14
**usury**
illicit business 826.1
interest 840.3
lending 820.1
overcharge 848.5
**utensil** container 193.1
equipment 659.4
tool 348.1
**uterine** genital 419.27
related 11.6
**uterus** sex organ 419.10
womb 153.9
**utilitarian**
businesslike 656.15
philosophy 500.9
useful 665.18
**utility**
*n.* company 788.9
helpfulness 785.10
machinery 348.4
usefulness 665.3
*adj.* substitute 149.8
**utilization** 665.8
**utilize** employ 665.10
use materials 378.8
**utmost**
*n.* completion 56.5
summit 211.2
*adj.* extreme 34.13
superlative 36.13
**utopia**
good times 728.4
hope 888.5
paradise 535.11
**utopian**
*n.* optimist 888.6
reformer 691.6
visionary 535.13
*adj.* idealized 535.23
optimistic 888.12
reformational 691.16
**utter**
*v.* disperse 75.4
divulge 556.5
monetize 835.26
pass counterfeit
money 835.28
say 594.23
*adj.* outright 34.12
sound 677.7
thorough 56.10
unqualified 508.2
**utterance**
affirmation 523.1
articulation 594.6
phrase 585.1
remark 594.4
speaking 594.3
word 582.1
**uttered** 594.30
**utterly**
completely 56.16
extremely 34.22
**U-turn**
about-face 295.3

steam 328.10
thing imagined 535.5
*v.* be bombastic 601.6
bluster 911.3
boast 910.6
exhale 310.23
talk nonsense 547.5
**vaporization** 401.5
**vaporize** destroy 693.10
evaporate 401.8
strike dead 409.18
**vaporizer** 401.6
**vaporous**
fanciful 535.22
gaseous 401.9
rare 355.4
tenuous 4.6
**vapor trail**
aviation 278.39
track 568.8
**vaquero** herder 416.3
rider 274.8
**variability**
changeability 141.2
inconstancy 18.1
irregularity 138.1
**variable**
changeable 141.6
inconstant 141.7
irregular 138.3
uncertain 514.15
uneven 18.3
**variably**
changeably 141.8
irregularly 138.4
**variance**
difference 16.1
disagreement 795.2
disparity 27.1
dissatisfaction 522.1
**variant** different 16.7
disagreeing 27.6
**variation** change 139.1
deviation 291.1
difference 16.1
discrimination 16.4
fluctuation 141.3
inconstancy 141.2
multiformity 19.1
music arrangement
462.5
music division 462.24
unevenness 18.1
**varied** different 16.7
diversified 19.4
mixed 44.15
**variegate** diversify 18.2
polychrome 374.7
**variegated**
different 16.7
many-colored 374.9
nonuniform 18.3
rainbow 362.15
**variegation**
comparisons 374.6
difference 16.1
multicolor 374
multiformity 19.1
nonuniformity 18.1
**variety** biology 61.5
change 139.1
difference 16.1

inconstancy 141.2
kind 61.3
miscellany 74.13
multiformity 19.1
nonuniformity 18.1
plurality 100.1
sect 1020.3
theater 611.1
**variety store** 832.1
**variform** 18.3
**various** different 16.7
diversified 19.4
nonuniform 18.3
plural 100.7
several 101.7
**varmint**
bad person 986.7
creature 414.2
vermin 414.3
**varnish**
*n.* art equipment
574.19
coating 228.12
extenuation 1006.5
fakery 616.3
pretext 649.1
*v.* color 362.13
conceal 615.6
distort 249.6
extenuate 1006.12
falsify 616.16
make grandiloquent
601.7
polish 260.7
**varsity** college 567.7
team 788.7
**vary** alternate 141.5
be changed 139.5
change 139.6
deviate 291.3
differ 16.5
differentiate 16.6
disagree 27.5
diversify 19.2
intermit 138.2
make dissimilar 21.3
vacillate 627.8
variegate 18.2
**varying** different 16.7
inconstant 18.3
**vas** 396.13
**vascular** tubular 396.21
vesicular 193.4
**vase** 576.2
**vasectomy** 689.23
**vassal**
*n.* feudatory 750.1
subject 764.7
*adj.* subject 764.13
**vassalage** 764.1
**vast** extensive 179.9
huge 195.20
large 34.7
**vastly**
extensively 179.10
immensely 34.16
**vastness** greatness 34.1
hugeness 195.7
**vat** 660.6
**Vatican**
church house 1042.8
papacy 1037.6

**vaudeville**
stage show 611,4
theater 611.1
**vaudevillian**
*n.* entertainer 612.1
*adj.* theatrical 611.38
**vault**
*n.* arch 252.4
ascent 315.1
compartment 192.2
depository 836.12
heavens 375.2
jump 319.1
storage place 660.6
tomb 410.16
*v.* ascend 315.9
curve 252.6
leap 319.5
**vaulted** 252.10
**vaulter** 319.4
**vaulting** arch 252.4
curvature 252.1
leaping 319.3
**vaunt**
*n.* boasting 910.1
display 904.4
*v.* boast 910.6
flaunt 904.17
**Vayu**
Hindu deity 1014.8
wind god 403.3
**VD** 686.16
**veal** 308.14
**vector** aviation 278.43
carrier 686.41
direction 290.2
infection 686.3
straight line 250.2
**Vedas, the** 1021.7
**veer**
*n.* angle 251.2
bend 219.3
deviation 291.1
*v.* angle 251.5
be changed 139.5
change course 275.30
deflect 219.9
deviate 291.3
sidle 242.5
turn around 295.9
turn aside 291.6
**veering** devious 291.7
irregular 138.3
**vegetable**
*n.* food 308.35,50
plant 411.3
*adj.* do-nothing 706.6
herbaceous 411.33
inert 708.19
**vegetable kingdom**
class 61.4
plants 411.1
**vegetable oil** oil 380.1
types of 380.12
**vegetarian**
*n.* abstainer 992.4
herbivore 307.14
*adj.* abstinent 992.10
eating 307.29
herbaceous 411.33
**vegetarianism**
abstinence 992.2

diet 309.11
herbivorism 307.1
**vegetate**
do nothing 706.2
grow 411.31
mature 197.7
merely exist 1.10
stagnate 268.9
**vegetation**
existence 1.6
growth 411.30
inaction 706.1
maturation 197.3
plants 411.1
stagnation 268.4
**vehemence**
acrimony 161.4
eloquence 600.5
fervor 855.10
industry 707.6
power 157.1
rage 952.10
violence 162.1
zeal 635.2
**vehement**
acrimonious 161.13
eloquent 600.13
industrious 707.22
passionate 857.27
violent 162.15
zealous 635.10
**vehicle** conveyance 272
instrument 658.3
paint 362.8
photography 577.10
stage show 611.4
**vehicular** 272.22
**veil**
*n.* clothing 231.26
concealment 615.2
cover 228.2,38
pretext 649.1
secrecy 614.3
shade 338.1,8
*v.* conceal 615.6
cover 228.19
keep secret 614.7
shade 338.5
**veiled** covered 228.31
latent 546.5
shaded 338.7
vague 514.18
**vein**
*n.* artery 396.14
deposit 383.7
mood 525.4
nature 5.3
source of supply
660.4
style 588.2
thinness 205.7
*v.* variegate 374.7
**veinous** 396.21
**veld** grassland 411.8
plain 387.1
the country 182.1
**velocity** gait 273.14
motion 267.1
speed 269
**velvet** comfort 887.1
easy thing 732.3
fine texture 351.3

prosperity 728.1
smooth surface 260.3
softness 357.4
velvety downy 230.27
sleek 260.10
smooth 351.8
soft 357.15
venal bribable 651.4
corruptible 975.23
greedy 634.27
venality 975.9
vend 829.9
vendetta
animosity 929.4
quarrel 795.5
revenge 956.1
vending 829.2
vending machine 832.8
vendor peddler 830.6
vending machine
832.8
veneer
n. coating 228.12,43
layer 227.2
shallowness 210.1
v. cover 228.23
venerable aged 126.16
dignified 905.12
old 123.10
reputable 914.15
reverend 964.12
sacred 1026.7
traditional 123.12
venerate respect 964.4
worship 1032.10
veneration piety 1028.1
respect 964.1
worship 1032.1
venerative pious 1028.8
reverent 964.9
worshipful 1032.15
venereal
aphrodisiac 419.28
sexual 419.26
venereal disease
infectious disease
686.12
social disease 686.16
venery
copulation 419.8
hunting 655.2
profligacy 989.3
quarry 655.7
vengeance 956.1
vengeful 956.6
venial 1006.14
venire
jury selection 1004.4
panel 1002.7
writ 752.7
venison 308.12
venom animosity 929.4
evil 675.3
poison 676.3
rancor 939.7
unhealthfulness 684.3
violence 162.1
venomous
harmful 675.12
hostile 929.10
poisonous 684.7
rancorous 939.20

violent 162.15
venous, 396.21
vent
n. air passage 396.17
emergence 303.2
escape 632.1
hole 265.4
outlet 303.9
parachute 280.13
v. divulge 556.5
eject 310.21
ventilate air 402.11
discuss 597.12
divulge 556.5
make public 559.11
refrigerate 334.10
stop odor 438.4
ventilation airing 402.9
deodorizing 438.2
discussion 597.7
publication 559.1
ventilator
aerator 402.10
air passage 396.17
cooler 334.3
fan 403.21
ventral 193.5
ventriloquism 594.16
ventriloquist 594.16
venture
n. gamble 515.1
investment 836.3
stock speculation
833.19
undertaking 715.1
v. attempt 714.5
gamble 515.19
have courage 893.10
invest 836.16
speculate in stocks
833.23
take the liberty 961.6
undertake 715.3
ventured 715.7
venturesome
daring 893.21
dynamic 707.23
enterprising 715.8
experimental 714.14
hazardous 697.10
venue 184.2
Venus
beautiful woman
900.9
deity 1014.5
love goddess 931.8
planet 375.9
star 375.4
veracious true 516.12
upright 974.16
veracity honesty 974.3
truth 516.1
veranda 192.21
verb 586.4
verbal authentic 516.14
communicational
554.9
grammatical 586.17
semantic 545.12
speech 594.30
vocabular 582.19
verbalize 594.23

verbatim
adj. authentic 516.14
adv. exactly 516.20
verbiage diction 588.1
vocabulary 582.14
wordiness 593.2
verbose
superfluous 663.17
talkative 596.9
wordy 593.12
verbosity
superfluity 663.4
talkativeness 596.1
wordiness 593.2
verboten 778.7
verdant green 371.4
plants 411.39
verdict judgment 494.5
legal decision 1004.9
verdigris
n. patina 371.2,6
v. turn green 371.3
verdure
greenness 371.1
plants 411.1
verge
n. border 235.4
bound 235.1
insignia 569.1
v. adjoin 200.9
bear 290.8
border 235.10
tend 174.3
verging on 200.24
verifiable
certain 513.15
provable 505.20
verification
assurance 513.8
collation 491.2
proof 505.5
test 489.2
verified proved 505.21
tried 489.12
true 516.12
verify check 87.14
collate 491.5
confirm 505.12
prove 513.12
test 489.8
verily positively 34.19
truly 516.17
verisimilar
authentic 516.14
probable 511.6
veritable honest 974.14
real 1.15
thorough 56.10
true 516.12
verity honesty 974.3
truth 516.1
vermicide killer 409.3
poison 676.3
worm medicine
687.24
vermiform
serpentine 254.7
wormlike 414.56
vermilion
v. make red 368.4
adj. red 368.6
vermin animal 414.3,40

bad person 986.7
rabble 919.5
verminous
insectile 414.55
rodent 414.48
vernacular
n. informal language
580.5
jargon 580.9
living language 580.2
mother tongue 580.3
plain speech 591.1
substandard language
580.6
adj. colloquial 580.18
local 180.9
native 189.5
usual 84.8
vulgar 898.14
vernal green 371.4
immature 124.10
new 122.7
spring 128.8
vernal equinox
astronomy 375.16
season 128.7
versatile
ambidextrous 733.23
fickle 629.6
handy 665.19
versatility
ambidexterity 733.3
inconstancy 18.1
verse
n. book part 605.13
maxim 517.1
music division 462.24
part of writing 55.2
poem 609.6
poetic division
609.11
poetry 609.1
prelude 66.2
v. inform 557.8
poetize 609.15
versed in
informed in 475.19
skilled in 733.25
versification
metrics 609.8
poetics 609.2
versifier 609.14
versify 609.15
version imitation 22.3
music 462.28
religion 1020.3
rendition 552.2
written matter 602.10
verso book 605.12
left side 244.1
versus direction 290.28
opposed to 790.10
opposite 239.7
vertebrate
n. animal 414.3
adj. chordate 414.44
vertex angle 251.2
summit 211.2
vertical
n. upright 213.2
adj. steep 219.18
straight 250.6

top 211.10
upright 213.11
**vertigo**
disease symptom
686.8
dizziness 532.4
**verve** eagerness 635.1
eloquence 600.4
fervor 855.10
gaiety 870.4
liveliness 707.2
lively imagination
535.4
vim 161.2
**very** exceedingly 34.18
to a degree 29.7
**vesicle** blemish 679.1
blister 256.3
bubble 405.1
**vesicular**
blistering 405.6
tubular 396.21
vascular 193.4
**vesper**
*n.* evening 134.2
worship 1032.8
*adj.* evening 134.8
**vessel** container 193.1
drinking 193.10
duct 396.13
naval 277.24
sailing 277.23
ship 277.1
**vest**
*n.* waistcoat 231.14,58
*v.* belong to 808.7
endow 818.17
establish 184.15
**Vesta** deity 1014.5
household goddess
191.30
**vestal**
*n.* virgin 934.4
*adj.* chaste 988.6
**vested** clothed 231.44
established 142.13
**vested interest**
estate 810.4
pressure group 744.31
privilege 958.3
**vestibule**
auditory organ 448.7
entrance 302.5
foyer 192.19
**vestige** admixture 44.7
antiquity 123.6
clue 568.9
mark 568.7
record 570.1
remainder 43.1
**estment**
canonical 1041.1
clothing 231.1
cover 228.2
garment 231.3
**est-pocket** 196.12
**estry**
church council 755.4
church part 1042.9
**et**
*n.* soldier 800.18
veteran 733.15

veterinary 688.11
*v.* examine 485.24
scrutinize 439.15
study 564.12
**vetch** 411.4,44
**veteran**
*n.* expert 733.15
old man 127.2
soldier 800.18
*adj.* experienced
733.26
**veterinarian** 688.11
**veto**
*n.* legislative veto
742.15
prohibition 778.2
*v.* legislate 742.18
put one's veto upon
778.5
**vetoed** 778.7
**vex** bother 866.13
irk 864.15
make anxious 890.4
provoke 952.22
trouble 731.12
**vexation**
annoyance 866.2
anxiety 890.1
bane 676.1
evil 675.3
resentment 952.1
**vexatious**
annoying 864.22
troublesome 731.17
**vexed** annoyed 866.21
provoked 952.25
troubled 731.19
worried 890.7
**vexing** 864.22
**VHF** 344.12
**via** 290.29
**viability**
activation 161.8
life 407.1
possibility 509.2
satisfactoriness 868.3
workability 164.3
**viable**
acceptable 868.12
capable of living
407.11
energizing 161.14
of importance 672.17
possible 509.7
workable 164.10
**viaduct** bridge 657.10
crossing 221.2
**viands** 308.1
**vibes**
percussion instrument
465.18
sympathy 855.5
**vibrancy**
oscillation 323.1
resonance 454.1
**vibrant**
energetic 161.12
resonant 454.9
**vibraphone** 465.18
**vibrate**
be frequent 135.3
oscillate 323.10

resonate 454.6
shake 324.11
**vibrating**
constant 135.5
oscillating 323.15
resonant 454.9
shaking 324.17
**vibration**
frequency 135.2
oscillation 323.1
shaking 324.2
sympathy 855.5
**vibrato** music 463.19
organ stop 465.22
**vibrator** agitator 324.9
massage 350.3
oscillator 323.9
**vicar** clergyman 1038.9
deputy 781.1
substitute 149.2
**vicarage** house 191.6
parsonage 1042.7
the ministry 1037.9
**vicarious** 149.8
**vice**
*n.* deputy 781.1
misbehavior 738.1
moral badness 981
weakness 981.2
wrongdoing 982.1
*prep.* replacing 149.12
**vice-president**
deputy 781.8
executive 748.3
substitute 149.2
**viceroy** deputy 781.8
regional governor
749.13
**vice versa**
contrarily 15.9
inversely 220.8
reciprocally 13.16
**vichyssoise** 308.10
**vicinity**
environment 233.1
nearness 200.1
neighborhood 180.1
**vicious** bad 675.7
cruel 939.24
harmful 675.12
immoral 981.11
savage 162.20
wicked 981.16
**vicious circle**
circle 253.2
futility 669.2
sophistry 483.1
vicissitudes 156.5
**vicissitude**
adversity 729.1
chance 156.5
fluctuation 141.3
**victim** dupe 620.1
laughingstock 967.7
loser 727.5
quarry 655.7
sufferer 866.11
unfortunate 729.7
**victimization**
deception 618.1
persecution 667.3
**victimize** cheat 618.17

outwit 735.11
overcharge 848.7
persecute 667.6
**victor**
successful person
724.5
winner 726.2
**Victorian**
*n.* prude 903.11
*adj.* antiquated
123.13
prudish 903.19
**victorious** 726.8
**victory** success 724.1
triumph 726
**Victrola** 450.11
**victuals** 308.1
**video**
*n.* television 345.1
*adj.* televisional
345.16
**videocast** 559.10
**videotape**
*n.* record 570.10
television broadcast
345.2
*v.* record 570.16
**vie**
be as good as 674.11
be comparable 491.7
compete 796.19
contend against
790.4
contend for 796.21
**view**
*n.* aspect 446.3
belief 501.6
intention 653.1
judgment 494.3
look 439.3
mental outlook 525.2
picture 574.13
scene 446.6
scope 444.3
*v.* contemplate 478.17
heed 530.6
see 439.12
take an attitude
525.6
watch 439.14
**viewer** audience 819.3
spectator 442.1
televiewer 345.12
**viewfinder** 443.4
**viewing** 439.2
**viewpoint** aspect 446.3
mental outlook 525.2
standpoint 439.7
station 184.2
**vigil** wakefulness 713.1
wariness 533.4
worship 1032.8
**vigilance** 533.4
**vigilant**
prepared 720.16
protecting 699.23
wary 533.13
**vigilantes** 699.17
**vignette**
description 608.1
fictional form 608.8
picture 574.14

print 578.6
**vigor** eloquence 600.3
energy 161.1
gaiety 870.4
robustness 685.3
strength 159.1
vitality 157.1
**vigorous**
eloquent 600.11
energetic 161.12
fervent 855.23
powerful 157.12
robust 685.10
strong 159.13
thriving 728.13
tough 359.4
**viking** pirate 825.7
sailor 276.1
**vile** bad 675.9
base 915.12
cursing 972.8
dishonest 975.17
evil 981.16
filthy 682.23
malodorous 437.5
obscene 990.9
offensive 864.18
paltry 673.18
unsavory 429.7
vulgar 898.15
**vilification**
berating 969.7
curse 972.2
defamation 971.2
**vilify** berate 969.20
blaspheme 1030.5
curse 972.7
revile 971.10
stigmatize 915.9
**vilifying**
condemnatory 969.23
disparaging 971.13
**villa** 191.8
**village**
*n.* district 180.5
hamlet 183.2
*adj.* urban 183.10
**villager** 190.6
**villain** actor 612.2
evildoer 943.1
rascal 986.3
role 611.11
**villainous** bad 675.9
dishonest 975.17
evil 981.16
**villainy**
dishonesty 975.2
iniquity 981.3
**villein** 764.7
**villenage**
possession 808.1
subjection 764.1
**villous** 230.24
**vim** gaiety 870.4
liveliness 707.2
power 157.1
verve 161.2
**vincible** 697.16
**vindicate** acquit 1007.4
justify 1006.9
**vindication**
acquittal 1007.1

justification 1006.1
**vindicative** 1006.13
**vindicator**
avenger 956.3
defender 799.7
justifier 1006.8
**vindictive** 956.6
**vine** plant 411.4
types of 411.51
**vinegar**
preservative 701.3
sour thing 432.2
**vinegarish**
ill-humored 951.23
sour 432.5
**vineyard** 413.10
**viniculture** 413.2
**vintage** 811.5
**vintner**
liquor dealer 996.18
merchant 830.3
**viol** 465.5
**viola** organ stop 465.22
viol 465.6
**violate**
break the law 999.5
corrupt 692.14
disobey 767.6
misuse 667.4
not observe 769.4
possess sexually
822.15
seduce 989.20
terrorize 162.10
work evil 675.6
**violation**
abomination 959.2
crime 999.4
disobedience 767.1
infraction 769.2
mistreatment 667.2
misuse 667.1
seduction 989.6
sexual possession
822.3
violence 162.3
wrong 959.1
**violator** 989.12
**violence**
acrimony 161.4
coercion 756.3
cruelty 939.11
excitability 857.9
mistreatment 667.2
rage 952.10
vehemence 162
**violent**
*n.* violent person
162.9
*adj.* acrimonious
161.13
coercive 756.11
excited 857.23
mad 473.30
passionate 857.27
vehement 162.15
**violently**
frenziedly 857.33
furiously 34.23
vehemently 162.24
**violet** 373.3
**violin** 465.6

**violinist** 464.5
**VIP**
influential person
172.6
notable 672.8
superior 36.5
**viper** bad person 986.7
snake 414.31,61
**virago**
ill-humored woman
951.12
mannish female
420.9
violent person 162.9
witch 943.7
**virgin**
*n.* girl 125.6
spinster 934.4
*adj.* chaste 988.6
childless 166.4
country 182.8
natural 721.13
new 122.7
undamaged 677.8
unknown 477.17
unmarried 934.7
**virginal** chaste 988.6
immature 124.10
natural 721.13
new 122.7
unmarried 934.7
**virginity** chastity 988.3
newness 122.1
original condition
721.3
unwed state 934.1
**Virgin Mary, the**
1015.5
**virgule** diagonal 219.7
line 568.6
**virile** 420.12
**virility**
masculinity 420.2
maturity 126.2
power 157.1
**virtu**
aesthetic taste 897.5
artistry 574.8
work of art 574.11
**virtual** 546.5
**virtually**
almost entirely 54.14
potentially 546.11
**virtue** chastity 988.1
courage 893.1
ethics 957.3
grace 674.1
honesty 974.1
moral goodness 980
power 157.1
**virtuosity**
aesthetic taste 897.5
musicianship 462.32
skill 733.1
superiority 36.1
**virtuoso**
*n.* connoisseur 897.7
expert 733.13
first-rater 674.6
musician 464.1
superior 36.4
*adj.* musical 462.48

skillful 733.20
**virtuous** chaste 988.4
good 674.12
honest 974.13
moral 980.7
**virulence**
animosity 929.4
bitterness 952.3
deadliness 409.9
harmfulness 675.5
poisonousness 684.3
power 157.1
rancor 939.7
rigor 161.4
violence 162.1
**virulent** fatal 409.23
harmful 675.12
hostile 929.10
poisonous 684.7
rancorous 939.20
resentful 952.24
rigorous 161.13
violent 162.15
**virus** germ 686.39
infection 686.3
organism 406.2
poison 676.3
**visa** certificate 570.6
pass 777.7
ratification 521.4
signature 583.10
**visage** face 240.4
looks 446.4
**vis-à-vis**
against 200.25
contrary to 239.6
opposite 15.10
versus 790.10
**viscera**
seat of affections
855.2
vitals 225.4
**visceral**
emotional 855.19
internal 225.10
**viscid** adhesive 50.12
dense 354.12
semiliquid 389.12
tough 359.4
**viscosity** solidity 354.1
tenacity 50.3
thickness 389.2
**viscount** 918.4
**viscous**
semiliquid 389.12
solid 354.12
thick 204.8
**vise** 198.6
**viselike** 813.8
**Vishnu** God 1013.4
Hindu deity 1014.8
incarnations of
1014.9
**visibility**
aviation 278.41
manifestness 555.3
visibleness 444
**visible** apparent 446.11
discernible 444.6
manifest 555.8
ocular 439.21
**visibly** by sight 439.23

*adj.* voluntary 622.7
**voluptuous**
 pleasant 863.7
 sensual 987.5
 sexual 419.26
**volute**
 *n.* curl 254.2
 *adj.* spiral 254.8
**vomit**
 *n.* emetic 687.18
 vomiting 310.8
 *v.* disgorge 310.25
 erupt 162.12
 flow out 303.13
 jet 395.20
 sicken at 867.4
**vomiting**
 disease symptom
 686.8
 disgorgement 310.8
 nausea 686.29
**vomitory**
 *n.* outlet 303.9
 *adj.* ejective 310.28
 emetic 687.49
**vomity** bad 675.8
 filthy 682.23
 unsavory 429.7
**voodoo**
 *n.* bad influence 675.4
 charm 1036.5
 sorcery 1035.1
 witch doctor 1035.7
 *v.* bewitch 1036.9
 *adj.* sorcerous 1035.14
**voodooism** 1035.1
**voracious**
 gluttonous 994.6
 greedy 634.27
 hungry 634.25
**voracity** gluttony 994.1
 greed 634.8
**vortex** aviation 278.39
 bustle 707.4
 curl 254.2
 excitement 857.3
 rotation 322.2
 whirlpool 395.12
**vortical** flowing 395.24
 rotary 322.15
**votary** believer 1028.4
 desirer 634.12
 devotee 635.6
 follower 293.2
 man 787.8
 supporter 787.9
 worshiper 1032.9
**vote**
 *n.* approval 968.1
 choice 637.6
 legislative procedure
 742.14
 politics 744.18
 suffrage 744.17
 *v.* cast one's vote
 637.18
 participate 815.5
 support politically
 744.41
**vote in** 637.20
**voter** elector 744.23
 selector 637.7

**voting** choice 637.6
 going to the polls
 744.18
 participation 815.1
**voting age** 126.2
**votive** 770.7
**votive candle** 1040.11
**votive offering**
 donation 818.6
 sacrifice 1032.7
**vouch**
 *n.* affirmation 523.1
 *v.* affirm 523.5
 promise 770.4
 testify 505.10
**vouched for** 523.8
**voucher**
 certificate 570.6
 negotiable instru-
 ment 835.11
 receipt 844.2
 recommendation
 968.4
 witness 505.7
**vouchsafe**
 condescend 906.7
 give 818.12
 permit 777.9
**vow**
 *n.* oath 523.3
 promise 770.1
 *v.* affirm 523.5
 express belief 501.12
 promise 770.4
**vowel**
 *n.* speech sound
 594.13
 *adj.* phonetic 594.31
**vox populi** belief 501.6
 unanimity 521.5
**voyage**
 *n.* journey 273.5
 water travel 275.6
 *v.* pass over 273.19
 sail 275.13
 travel 273.20
**voyager** 274.1
**voyeur**
 curious person 528.2
 sex deviant 419.17
**voyeurism**
 curiosity 528.1
 sexual preference
 419.12
**VP** 748.3
**vs.** against 790.10
 opposite 239.7
**V-shaped** angular 251.6
 forked 299.10
**Vulcan** god 1014.5
 smith 718.7
**vulcanize** heat 329.24
 make elastic 358.6
**vulgar** common 919.11
 discourteous 937.6
 gaudy 904.20
 indecent 898.10
 inelegant 590.2
 inferior 37.6
 uncouth 990.8
**vulgarian** 898.6

**vulgarism**
 literary inelegance
 590.1
 tastelessness 898.1
 word 582.6
**vulgarity**
 discourtesy 937.1
 indecency 898
 inferiority 37.3
 literary inelegance
 590.1
 uncouthness 990.3
**vulgarize** coarsen 898.9
 corrupt 692.14
 make clear 548.6
**vulgar language**
 cursing 972.3
 jargon 580.9
**vulgate** 580.6
**Vulgate** 1021.2
**vulnerability**
 fragility 360.1
 liability 175.2
 pregnability 697.4
 unpreparedness 721.1
**vulnerable** fragile 360.4
 helpless 158.18
 liable to 175.5
 pregnable 697.16
**vulpine** canine 414.45
 cunning 735.12
**vulture** 822.12
**vulturous** 822.26
**vulva** 419.10
**vulval** 419.27
**V-weapon** 281.4
**vying**
 *n.* competition 796.2
 opposition 790.2
 *adj.* competitive
 796.24

## W

**wacky** eccentric 474.4
 foolish 470.8
 insane 473.26
**wad**
 *n.* accumulation 74.9
 lump 195.10
 money 835.17
 much 34.4
 wealth 837.2
 *v.* fill 56.7
 line 194.7
 squeeze 198.8
**wadding**
 contents 194.3
 stopping 266.5
**waddle**
 *n.* gait 273.14
 slowness 270.2
 *v.* go slow 270.6
 walk 273.27
**wade** 275.56
**wade into**
 attack 798.15
 set to work 716.15
**wade through**
 drudge 716.14
 study 564.12
**wadi** ravine 201.2

 running water 395.1
 valley 257.9
 watercourse 396.2
**wading** 275.11
**wafer** cracker 308.30
 Eucharist 1040.8
 layer 227.2
 thinness 205.7
**waffle**
 *n.* pancake 308.44
 *v.* chatter 596.5
 equivocate 613.7
 talk nonsense 547.5
**waft**
 *n.* transportation
 271.3
 wind 403.4
 *v.* be buoyed up 353.8
 blow 403.22
 transport 271.11
**wag**
 *n.* humorist 881.12
 mischief-maker 738.3
 swing 323.6
 wiggle 324.7
 *v.* oscillate 323.10
 wave 323.11
 wiggle 324.14
**wage**
 *n.* remuneration 841.4
 *v.* practice 705.7
**wage earner** 718.2
**wager**
 *n.* an uncertainty
 514.8
 bet 515.3
 *v.* bet 515.20
 gamble 515.19
**wage war** battle 797.18
 contend 796.14
**waggery** mischief 738.2
 wittiness 881.4
**waggish**
 mischievous 738.6
 playful 878.31
 prankish 881.17
**waggle**
 *n.* swing 323.6
 wiggle 324.7
 *v.* oscillate 323.10
 wiggle 324.14
**wagon**
 *n.* police car 272.10
 vehicle 272.2
 *v.* haul 271.12
**wagoner** carrier 271.5
 coachman 274.9
**waif**
 abandoned thing
 633.4
 vagabond 274.3
**wail**
 *n.* lament 875.3
 shrill sound 458.4
 *v.* animal sound 460.2
 cry 875.11
 sigh 452.14
 sound shrill 458.8
 utter 594.26
 wind sound 403.23
**wailing**
 *n.* lamentation 875.1

*adj.* capricious 629.5
  inconstant 141.7
  reckless 894.8
  unchaste 989.26
  unrestrained 762.23
  unrighteous 981.12
**war**
*n.* armed conflict
  797.1
  contention 796.1
  gods 797.17
  military campaign
  797.7
  military science
  797.10
  word list 797.29
*v.* battle 797.18
  contend 796.14
**warble**
  bird sound 460.5
  sing 462.39
  utter 594.26
**warbler** bird 414.33,66
  songbird 464.23
  vocalist 464.13
**warbling** 462.12
**war cry**
  battle cry 797.12
  challenge 793.2
  signal 568.16
  whoop 459.1
**ward** custody 761.5
  defense 799.1
  dependent 764.6
  election district
  744.16
  hospital room 192.25
  infirmary 689.27
  protectorship 699.2
  stronghold 799.6
  territorial division
  180.5
**warden**
  doorkeeper 699.12
  executive 748.3
  guardian 699.6
  jailer 761.10
  public official 749.17
**warder** guard 699.9
  guardian 699.6
  jailer 761.10
**ward heeler**
  follower 293.2
  hanger-on 907.5
  partisan 744.27
  political henchman
  746.8
**ward off** dodge 631.8
  fend off 799.10
  prevent 730.14
  repulse 289.3
**wardrobe** closet 192.15
  furnishings 231.2
**wardship**
  dependence 764.3
  inability 158.2
  protectorship 699.2
**ware** commodity 831.2
  merchandise 831.1
**warehouse**
*n.* market 832.1
  storage place 660.6

*v.* store 660.10
**warfare** combat 797
  contention 796.1
**war game** 797.8
**warhead**
  explosive charge
  801.10
  rocketry 281.3
**war-horse**
  charger 800.32
  horse 414.10
  old woman 127.3
  politician 746.1
  soldier 800.18
  veteran 733.15
**warlike**
  contending 796.23
  militant 797.25
**warlock** 1035.5
**warlord** 749.14
**warm**
*v.* energize 161.9
  excite 857.11
  heat 329.17
  make red 368.4
*adj.* coloring 362.15
  comfortable 887.11
  cordial 927.15
  detecting 488.10
  eloquent 600.13
  excited 857.20
  fervent 855.23
  hospitable 925.11
  hot 328.24
  kind 938.13
  near 200.14
  red 368.6
  wealthy 837.13
  zealous 635.10
**warm-blooded** 328.29
**warmed-over**
  heated 329.29
  repeated 103.12
  trite 883.9
**warmer** 329.10
**warmhearted**
  cordial 927.15
  emotionable 855.21
  hospitable 925.11
  kind 938.13
  pitying 944.7
**warming**
*n.* heating 329.1
*adj.* heating 329.26
**warmly**
  amicably 927.21
  eloquently 600.15
  excitedly 857.32
  fervently 855.28
  kindly 938.18
**warmonger** 800.5
**warmongering**
*n.* warlikeness 797.15
*adj.* militaristic 797.26
**warm spring**
  hot water 328.10
  spa 689.29
**warmth**
  animation 161.3
  cordiality 927.6
  eloquence 600.5
  fervor 855.10

glow 362.2
  heat 328.1
  hospitality 925.1
  kindness 938.1
  zeal 635.2
**warm up** begin 68.8
  heat 329.17
  prepare oneself
  720.13
  prime 720.9
  revive 694.16
**warm-up** 720.1
**warn** advise 754.6
  alarm 704.3
  caution 703.5
  demand 753.4
  dissuade 652.3
  forebode 544.11
  threaten 973.2
**warning**
*n.* advice 754.1
  caution 703
  demand 753.1
  dissuasion 652.1
  omen 544.4
  threat 973.1
  tip 557.3
*adj.* advisory 754.8
  cautioning 703.7
  premonitory 544.16
**war of nerves**
  cold war 797.5
  demoralization 891.6
**warp**
*n.* bend 219.3
  blemish 679.1
  deviation 291.1
  distortion 249.1
  tendency 174.1
  trait of character
  525.3
  weaving 222.3
*v.* be changed 139.5
  blemish 679.4
  corrupt 692.14
  deflect 291.5
  distort 249.5
  falsify 616.16
  misrepresent 573.3
  prejudice 527.9
  sail 275.48
  tend 174.3
**war paint** 900.11
**warp and woof**
  structure 245.1
  weaving 222.1
**warpath** 797.15
**warped**
  blemished 679.8
  distorted 249.10
  falsified 616.26
  morally corrupt
  981.14
  prejudiced 527.12
  unjust 977.11
**warplane** 280.9,15
**warrant**
*n.* authorization 777.3
  certificate 570.6
  commission 780.1
  instrument 834.1
  justification 1006.6

legal order 752.6
  legal summons
  1004.2
  negotiable instru-
  ment 835.11
  oath 523.3
  permit 777.6
  ratification 521.4
  receipt 844.2
  right 958.4
  security 772.1
*v.* acknowledge 521.11
  affirm 523.5
  authorize 777.11
  commission 780.9
  express belief 501.12
  justify 1006.9
  promise 770.4
  prove 505.12
  ratify 521.12
  secure 772.9
  testify 505.10
**warrantable** fair 976.8
  justifiable 1006.14
  permissible 777.15
**warranted**
  acknowledged 521.14
  affirmed 523.8
  authorized 777.17
  fair 976.8
  guaranteed 772.11
  justified 960.9
  made sure 513.20
  promised 770.8
**warrantee** 772.7
**warrant officer**
  naval officer 749.20
  noncommissioned of-
  ficer 749.19
**warrantor** 772.6
**warranty**
  authorization 777.3
  certificate 570.6
  promise 770.1
  security 772.1
**warren** fertility 165.6
  filthy place 682.11
  tunnel 257.5
**warring**
*n.* warfare 797.1
*adj.* clashing 461.5
  contending 796.23
  warlike 797.25
**warrior** 800.6
**warship** 277.6,24
**wart** blemish 679.1
  bulge 256.3
  dwarf 196.6
  little thing 196.4
  tumor 686.36
**wartime** 797.1
**wary** cautious 895.9
  cunning 735.12
  doubtful 503.9
  incredulous 504.4
  vigilant 533.13
**wash**
*n.* ablution 681.5
  aviation 278.39
  cleaning agent 681.17
  color 362.8
  laundering 681.6

disappear 447.2
disintegrate 53.3
end 70.6
subtract 42.9
waste 812.5
weaken 160.9
**wear down**
deteriorate 692.23
fatigue 717.4
influence 172.7
persuade 648.23
**weariness**
boredom 884.3
fatigue 717.1
languor 708.6
weakness 160.1
**wearing apparel** 231.1
**wearisome**
annoying 864.22
boring 884.9
fatiguing 717.11
gloomy 872.24
laborious 716.18
**wear off**
deteriorate 692.23
end 70.6
**wear on**
be tedious 884.5
fatigue 717.4
linger 110.7
**wear out**
cause unpleasantness
864.16
deteriorate 692.23
fatigue 717.4
**wear thin**
be uninteresting
883.4
weaken 160.9
**wear well**
be healthy 685.5
endure 110.6
**weary**
v. be tedious 884.5
cause unpleasantness
864.16
get tired 717.5
make tired 717.4
adj. bored 884.10
fatigued 717.6
gloomy 872.24
languid 708.19
**wearying** boring 884.9
fatiguing 717.11
unpleasant 864.24
**weasel**
n. sharp-eye 439.11
sled 272.19
wild animal
414.28,58
v. prevaricate 613.7
pull back 284.7
**weasel word**
ambiguous expression
550.2
prevarication 613.4
**weather**
n. climate 402.4
windward side 242.3
v. keep safe 698.2
ride out 275.40
sail 275.24

stand fast 142.11
wear 692.23
win through 724.12
adj. windward 242.6
**weather balloon** 402.8
**weather-beaten** 692.36
**weatherboard**
n. windward side
242.3
wood 378.3
v. cover 228.23
**weather bureau** 402.7
**weathercock**
changeableness 141.4
mind-changer 628.4
testing device 489.4
wind instrument
403.17
**weather eye**
seamanship 275.3
sharp eye 439.10
vigilance 533.4
**weatherglass** 402.8
**weathering** 692.5
**weatherman** 402.7
**weather map**
map 654.4
meteorology 402.5
**weatherproof**
v. proof 159.12
adj. resistant 159.18
**weather report** 402.7
**weather the storm**
keep safe 698.2
recover 694.20
sail 275.40
stand fast 142.11
win through 724.12
**weather vane**
changeableness 141.4
testing device 489.4
weather instrument
402.8
wind instrument
403.17
**weatherworn** 692.36
**weave**
n. fabric 378.5
interlacing 222.1
network 221.3
structure 245.1
texture 351.1
v. interlace 222.6
**weaver** interlacer 222.4
loom 222.5
**weaving**
n. interlacing 222
network 221.3
adj. twining 222.8
**weazen** dry 393.6
shrink 198.9
**weazened** dried 393.9
shrunk 198.13
**web**
n. fabric 378.5
filament 206.1
network 221.3
printing press 603.9
structure 245.1
weaving 222.1
v. net 221.7
weave 222.6

**webbed** 221.12
**web-footed** 221.12
**Webster's** 605.7
**wed** combine 52.4
get married 933.16
join in marriage
933.15
relate 9.6
**wedded**
conjugal 933.19
joined 47.13
married 933.22
paired 52.6
related 9.9
**wedding**
combination 52.1
marriage 933.4
**wedge**
n. character 581.2
v. fasten 47.8
impress 142.9
pry 287.8
**wedged** fastened 47.14
fixed 142.16
**wedge in** enter 302.7
interpose 237.6
thrust in 304.7
**wedge-shaped**
tapered 205.15
triangular 251.8
**wedlock** 933.1
**wee** 196.11
**weed**
n. intruder 78.2
marihuana 687.13
plant 411.3
refuse 669.4
types of 411.52
v. subtract 42.9
till 413.17
**weed killer** 676.3
**weed out**
eliminate 77.5
extract 305.10
till 413.17
**weeds**
mourning garment
875.6
widowhood 935.3
**weedy**
growing rank 411.40
herbaceous 411.33
**week** period 107.2
seven 99.3
**weekend**
n. vacation 711.3
v. spend time 105.6
vacation 711.9
**weekly**
n. newspaper 605.11
periodical 605.10
adj. regularly 137.8
**weenie** 308.21
**weep**
n. outflow 303.6
v. be damp 392.11
excrete 311.12
exude 303.15
fester 311.15
flow out 303.14
hang 215.6
lament 875.8

rain 394.9
secrete 312.5
sob 875.10
trickle 395.18
**weep for** console 946.2
pity 944.3
**weeping**
n. outflow 303.6
secretion 312.1
sobbing 875.2
adj. pendent 215.9
soaked 392.17
tearful 875.17
**weepy**
exudative 303.20
tearful 875.17
**weevil** 414.40,74
**weevily** insectile 414.55
spoiled 692.43
unsavory 429.7
**weft** fabric 378.5
network 221.3
weaving 222.3
**weigh** analyze 48.8
be important 672.11
compare 491.4
consider 478.12
have influence 172.10
heft 352.10
measure 490.11
**weigh anchor**
detach 49.10
embark 301.16
up-anchor 275.18
**weigh down**
hamper 730.11
oppress 729.8
weight 352.12
**weighed down**
burdened 352.18
sad 872.20
**weigh-in** 352.9
**weighing** 48.3
**weighing instrument**
352.22
**weight**
n. affliction 866.8
authority 739.4
charge 963.3
exercise device 716.7
formality 646.1
heaviness 352
heavy object 352.6
impediment 730.6
importance 672.1
influence 172.1
power 157.1
units 352.23
validity 516.4
v. burden 352.12
fill 56.7
heft 352.10
impose 963.4
**weighted down**
encumbered 352.18
sad 872.20
**weightless** light 353.10
unsubstantial 4.5
**weightlessness**
lightness 353.1
space hazard 282.10
**weightlifter** 878.21

weight-watch 205.13
weighty
  authoritative 739.15
  eloquent 600.14
  evidential 505.17
  heavy 352.16
  important 672.19
  influential 172.13
  large 34.7
  solemn 871.3
  unpleasant 864.24
  valid 516.13
weigh upon
  be heavy upon
    352.11
  burden 352.13
  cause unpleasantness
    864.16
  make sad 872.18
  oppress 729.8
weir barrier 730.5
  floodgate 396.11
  outlet 303.9
weird
  n. fate 640.2
  spell 1036.1
  adj. awesome 920.11
  creepy 891.39
  deathly 408.29
  eerie 1017.9
  foolish 470.10
  odd 85.11
  sorcerous 1035.14
weirdo eccentric 474.3
  lunatic 473.15
Weird Sisters
  Fates 640.3
  witches 1035.8
welcome
  n. arrival 300.4
  assent 521.1
  hospitality 925.2
  liberality 853.1
  reception 306.1
  v. assent 521.8
  greet 925.9
  incur 175.4
  adj. desirable 925.12
  pleasant 863.6
  interj. greetings!
    925.14
welcoming
  hospitable 925.11
  receptive 306.16
weld
  n. joint 47.4
  v. heat 329.24
  join 47.5
  sculpture 575.5
  stick together 50.9
welder
  blowtorch 329.14
  types of 348.24
welfare
  n. charity 938.5
  good 674.4
  prosperity 728.1
  subsidy 818.8
  welfare program
    745.7
  adj. benevolent
    938.15

welfare state
  government 741.4
  social service 938.5
  welfarism 745.7
welkin
  atmosphere 402.2
  heavens 375.2
well
  n. body of water
    398.1
  depth 209.2
  fountainhead 153.6
  pit 257.4
  source of supply
    660.4
  v. flow out 303.13
  jet 395.20
  overflow 395.17
  adj. healthy 685.8
  adv. ably 157.16
  excellently 674.21
  kindly 938.18
  skillfully 733.29
  successfully 724.14
  interj. wonder 920.22
well-advised 467.19
well-balanced
  composed 858.13
  sensible 467.18
  stable 142.12
  symmetric 248.4
well-behaved 936.16
well-being
  comfort 887.1
  contentment 868.1
  good 674.4
  health 685.1
  pleasure 865.1
  prosperity 728.1
wellborn 918.11
well-bred
  genteel 936.17
  wellborn 918.11
well-built
  beautiful 900.17
  made 167.22
  strong 159.14
  substantial 3.7
well-coordinated 733.20
well-defined
  clearly visible 444.7
  intelligible 548.10
well-disposed
  approving 968.17
  friendly 927.14
  helpful 785.22
  well-meaning 938.17
  willing 622.5
well done!
  approval 968.22
  congratulations 948.4
well-done cooked 330.7
  skillful 733.20
well-dressed
  chic 644.13
  dressed up 231.45
well-earned 960.9
well-equipped 659.14
well-fed 195.18
well-fixed 837.13
well-groomed
  chic 644.13

tidy 59.8
well-grounded
  established 142.13
  logical 482.20
  reliable 513.17
  substantial 3.7
  valid 516.13
  well-informed 475.20
well-informed 475.20
well-kept
  preserved 701.11
  tidy 59.8
well-known
  famous 914.16
  trite 883.9
well-understood
  475.27
well-laid 733.28
well-liked 931.22
well-made
  beautiful 900.17
  made 167.22
  shapely 248.5
  substantial 3.7
well-mannered
  ceremonious 646.8
  mannerly 936.16
well-meaning
  friendly 927.14
  helpful 785.22
  well-intentioned
    938.17
well-off 837.13
well-oiled 732.13
well-planned 733.28
well-provided
  plentiful 661.7
  well-supplied 659.14
well-put 589.7
well-read
  versed in 475.19
  well-informed 475.20
well-regulated 59.6
well-set
  established 142.13
  strong 159.14
  symmetric 248.4
well-spent 665.21
well-spoken
  articulate 594.32
  eloquent 600.8
  mannerly 936.16
wellspring
  fountainhead 153.6
  source of supply
    660.4
well-thought-of
  approved 968.19
  reputable 914.15
  venerated 964.11
well-timed
  expedient 670.5
  timely 129.9
well-to-do 837.13
well-versed
  informed 475.18
  skilled in 733.25
  well-informed 475.20
well-wisher
  friend 928.1
  supporter 787.9

well-worn
  damaged 692.33
  habitual 642.16
  trite 883.9
welsh not pay 842.6
  shirk 631.9
welsher defaulter 842.5
  shirker 631.3
welt
  n. blemish 679.1
  edging 235.7
  ridge 256.3
  sore 686.35
  v. punish 1010.15
welter
  n. flounder 324.8
  jumble 62.3
  v. crouch 318.8
  flounder 324.15
  sail 275.55
  wallow 322.13
welterweight
  boxing weight 352.3
  pugilist 800.2
wen blemish 679.1
  swelling 256.4
  tumor 686.36
wench girl 125.6
  hussy 989.14
  maid 750.8
  woman 421.6
wenching 989.3
werewolf
  demon 1016.13
  frightener 891.9
  monster 943.6
weskit 231.14
west
  n. direction 290.3
  v. turn west 290.9
  adj. western 290.15
  adv. westward 290.19
West Occident 180.6
  region 180.7
westerly
  n. wind 403.9
  adj. western 290.15
western 290.15
Western fiction 608.7
  motion picture
    611.16
West Point 567.13
westward
  n. west 290.3
  adv. west 290.19
wet
  n. drink 996.6
  moisture 392.1
  rain 394.1
  wet weather 394.4
  v. moisten 392.12
  urinate 311.14
  adj. foolish 470.8
  moist 392.15
wetback
  Mexican 181.7
  migrant 274.5
wet blanket
  boring person 884.4
  deterrent 652.2
  extinguisher 332.3
  hinderer 730.9

killjoy 872.14
wetlands 210.2
wet nurse 699.8
wet-nurse foster 785.16
  suckle 307.17
wet suit
  bathing suit 231.29
  diving equipment
    320.5
whack
  n. attempt 714.2
  explosive noise 456.1
  hit 283.4
  punishment 1010.3
  turn 108.2
  v. hit 283.13
  make explosive noise
    456.6
  punish 1010.13
whack down 318.5
whacked 717.8
whacking huge 195.21
  remarkable 34.11
whacky see wacky
whale
  n. animal 414.35;
    415.8
  large animal 195.14
  large thing 195.11
  v. beat 1010.14
  fish 655.10
  punish 1010.15
whaler fisher 655.6
  sailor 276.1
whaling
  n. fishing 655.3
  punishment 1010.5
  adj. huge 195.21
wham
  n. explosive noise
    456.1
  v. hit 283.13
  make explosive noise
    456.6
whammy
  n. bad influence 675.4
  charm 1036.5
  curse 972.1
  evil eye 1036.1
  glare 439.5
  malevolence 939.4
  v. bring bad luck
    729.12
wharf 700.6
what
  n. whatever 79.6
  interj. wonder 920.19
whatever
  n. anything 79.6
  adv. of any kind 61.9
what for 155.8
what-for
  punishment 1010.1
  reproof 969.6
  reason 153.2
what's-his-name 584.2
what's what fact 1.3
  the truth 516.2
heal 686.35
heat fodder 308.4
  grain 411.46
hee! 865.17

wheedle cajole 774.12
  flatter 970.5
  urge 648.14
wheedling
  n. cajolement 774.3
  flattery 970.1
  inducement 648.3
  adj. cajoling 774.18
  flattering 970.8
  persuasive 648.29
wheel
  n. circle 253.2
  important person
    672.9
  instrument of torture
    1011.4
  management 747.5
  potter's wheel 576.4
  propeller 285.7
  rotation 322.2
  rotator 322.4
  round 137.3
  types of 322.18
  vehicle 272.8
  v. change one's mind
    628.6
  go around 321.4
  recur 137.5
  ride 273.32
  rotate 322.9
  turn around 295.9
  whirl 322.11
wheel chair 272.7
wheeler-dealer
  influential person
    172.6
  man of action 707.8
  political intriguer
    746.6
wheelhorse
  horse 414.16
  partisan 744.27
  politician 746.1
wheeling and dealing
  827.2
wheelman 276.8
wheel of fortune
  Chance 156.2
  changeableness 141.4
  fate 640.2
  gambling device
    515.12
wheels
  automobile 272.9
  mechanism 348.5
wheels within wheels
  complex 46.2
  mechanism 348.5
wheelworks 348.5
wheeze
  n. breathing 403.18
  joke 881.6
  sibilation 457.1
  v. become exhausted
    717.5
  breathe 403.24
  sibilate 457.2
wheezing
  breathing 403.29
  breathless 717.10
  sibilant 457.3
whelk food 308.25

sore 686.35
whelm destroy 693.21
  drench 392.14
  overflow 395.17
  oversupply 663.14
  overwhelm 727.8
  submerge 320.7
whelp
  n. bad person 986.7
  boy 125.5
  dog 414.22
  young dog 125.8
  v. give birth 167.15
whelped 167.21
when although 33.8
  at which time 105.8
  while 105.16
whence away 301.21
  hence 155.7
whenever
  anytime 105.12
  when 105.8
where 184.20
whereabouts
  n. location 184.1
  adv. where 184.20
whereas
  n. condition 507.2
  conj. because 155.10
  when 105.16
wherefore
  after which 117.7
  hence 155.7
  judgment 494.17
  why 155.8
wherefore, the 153.2
where it's at
  situation 7.2
  the truth 516.2
wheresoever 184.21
whereupon
  after which 117.7
  when 105.8
wherever 184.21
wherewithal
  funds 835.14
  means 658.1
  money 835.1
whet
  n. appetizer 308.9
  incentive 648.7
  v. incite 648.17
  increase 38.5
  sensitize 422.9
  sharpen 258.9
  stimulate 857.12
whet the appetite
  taste good 428.4
  tempt 650.5
whey fluid 388.2
  food 308.47
whichever 79.6
which see 505.25
whiff
  n. clue 568.9
  odor 435.1
  wind 403.4
  v. blow 403.22
  smell 435.8
  strike out 725.9
whiffet a nobody 673.7
  wind 403.4

Whig 744.27
while
  n. meantime 109.2
  period 107.1
  time 105.1
  conj. when 105.16
while away
  fritter away 854.5
  use 665.13
while away the time
  amuse oneself 878.24
  spend time 105.6
  waste time 708.12
whim caprice 629.1
  eccentricity 474.2
  thing imagined 535.5
whimper
  n. lament 875.3
  v. weep 875.10
  whine 875.12
whimpering
  n. weeping 875.2
  adj. plaintive 875.16
  weeping 875.17
whimsical
  capricious 629.5
  eccentric 474.4
  erratic 141.7
  fanciful 535.20
  humorous 880.4
  uncertain 514.15
  witty 881.15
whimsy caprice 629.1
  eccentricity 474.1
  thing imagined 535.5
whim-wham
  caprice 629.1
  ornament 901.4
  toy 878.16
  trifle 673.5
whine
  n. lament 875.3
  shrill sound 458.4
  v. animal sound 460.2
  sigh 452.14
  sound shrill 458.8
  utter 594.26
  whimper 875.12
whiner 869.3
whining
  n. complaint 875.4
  sigh 452.8
  adj. animal sound
    460.6
  plaintive 875.16
  shrill 458.14
whinny 460.2
whip
  n. amusement ride
    878.15
  blow 283.7
  driver 274.9
  goad 648.8
  lash 1011
  legislator 746.3
  v. agitate 324.10
  defeat 727.6
  drive animals 416.8
  foam 405.5
  goad 648.15
  hasten 709.4
  make viscid 389.10

pound 283.14
punish 1010.14
slap 283.16
**whip hand**
advantage 36.2
ascendancy 739.6
influence 172.1
**whiplash goad** 648.8
whip 1011.1
**whip off** 301.11
**whipped bubbly** 405.6
defeated 727.14
**whippersnapper**
a nobody 673.7
bad child 125.4
impudent person
913.5
**whipping defeat** 727.1
punishment 1010.4
rigging 277.12
**whipping boy** 149.3
**whipping post** 1011.3
**whipsaw** 833.25
**whip up agitate** 324.10
dash off 630.8
excite 857.11
incite 648.17
seize 822.14
**whir**
*n.* rotation 322.1
*v.* hum 452.13
**whirl**
*n.* backflow 395.12
bustle 707.4
curl 254.2
excitement 857.3
revel 878.7
ride 273.7
rotation 322.2
*v.* eddy 395.21
move 267.5
spin 322.11
turn around 295.9
twist 254.4
**whirligig**
amusement device
878.15
changeableness 141.4
rotator 322.4
**whirling**
*n.* rotation 322.1
*adj.* rotating 322.14
**whirlpool**
*n.* backflow 395.12
vortex 322.2
*v.* whirl 322.11
**whirlpool bath**
bath 681.8
hydrotherapy 689.4
massage 350.3
**whirlwind**
emotional outburst
857.8
vortex 322.2
wind 403.14
**whirly** 322.15
**whirlybird** 280.5
**whirring**
*n.* hum 452.7
*adj.* humming 452.20
**whish**
*n.* sibilation 457.1

*v.* rustle 452.12
sibilate 457.2
**whisk**
*n.* agitator 324.9
tap 283.6
*v.* agitate 324.10
foam 405.5
speed 269.8
sweep 681.23
tap 283.15
transport 271.11
**whiskered** 230.25
**whiskers** 230.8
**whiskey** 996.40
**whisper**
*n.* hint 557.4
imperfect speech
595.4
murmur 452.4
rumor 558.6
tip 557.3
touch 425.1
*v.* inform 557.11
rumor 559.10
say 594.23
speak faintly 452.10
speak imperfectly
595.9
tell confidentially
614.9
utter 594.26
wind sound 403.23
**whispering**
*n.* imperfect speech
595.4
murmur 452.4
*adj.* murmuring
452.18
**whispering campaign**
disparagement 971.4
scandal 558.8
smear campaign
744.14
**whistle**
*n.* alarm 704.1
audio distortion
450.13
loud sound 453.4
noisemaker 453.5
shrill sound 458.4
sibilation 457.1
signal 568.16
wood wind 465.9
*v.* be cheerful 870.6
bird sound 460.5
blare 453.9
boo at 967.10
play music 462.43
rejoice 876.5
sibilate 457.2
sing 462.39
sound shrill 458.8
wind sound 403.23
**whistle-blower** 557.6
**whistle for** 774.9
**whistle-stop**
*n.* one-horse town
183.3
*v.* electioneer 744.40
**whistling**
*n.* sibilation 457.1
*adj.* shrill 458.14

**whit** 35.2
**white**
*n.* albumen 406.15
colors 364.11
race 418.3
whiteness 364.1
*v.* whiten 364.5
whitewash 364.6
*adj.* aged 126.16
blank 187.13
chaste 988.4
clean 681.25
color 364.7
colorless 363.7
comparisons 364.2
innocent 984.7
**whitecaps** 395.14
**white-collar worker**
718.2
**white corpuscle** 388.4
**white elephant**
burden 730.6
gift 818.4
**white feather**
coward 892.5
cowardice 892.4
**white flag**
peace offer 804.2
signal 568.15
**white goods**
dry goods 831.3
hard goods 831.4
**Whitehall** 741.3
**white-hot fiery** 162.21
hot 328.25
zealous 635.10
**White House** 191.6
**white hunter** 655.5
**white lie** 616.11
**white lightning** 996.17
**white man** 418.3
**whiten**
become excited
857.17
blanch 364.5
clean 681.18
decolor 363.5
lose color 363.6
**whitening**
albification 364.3
decoloration 363.3
whitewash 364.4
**white paper**
announcement 559.2
information 557.1
official document
570.8
**white slave** 989.16
**white slaver** 989.18
**white slavery** 826.1
**whitewash**
*n.* excusing 1006.5
utter defeat 727.3
whitening 364.4
*v.* acquit 1007.4
color 362.13
conceal 615.6
falsify 616.16
gloss over 1006.12
overwhelm 727.8
whiten 364.6

**whitewashing**
coloring 362.12
excusing 1006.5
utter defeat 727.3
whitening 364.3
**white water** 405.2
**whitey** 418.3
**whither** 184.20
**Whitsuntide** 1040.15
**whittle**
*n.* cutlery 348.2
*v.* sever 49.11
**whittler** 579.6
**whittling** 575.1
**whiz**
*n.* expert 733.13
good thing 674.7
sibilation 457.1
*v.* hum 452.13
sibilate 457.2
speed 269.8
**who cares?** 636.11
**whodunit** 608.7
**whoever** 79.7
**whole**
*n.* all 79.4
comprehensiveness
76.1
contents 194.1
quantity 28.1
sum 86.5
totality 54
*adj.* complete 56.9
comprehensive 76.7
healthy 685.9
one 89.7
sound 677.7
total 54.9
unqualified 508.2
**wholehearted** 624.11
**whole hog** 54.4
**whole-hog** 56.10
**wholeness**
completeness 56.1
goodness 674.1
individuality 80.1
intactness 677.2
totality 54.5
unity 89.1
**whole picture** 8.2
**wholesale**
*n.* sale 829.1
*v.* deal in 827.15
sell 829.8
*adj.* commercial
827.21
extensive 79.13
plentiful 661.7
sales 829.13
thorough 56.10
undiscriminating
493.5
*adv.* cheaply 849.10
**wholesale house** 832.1
**wholesaler**
intermediary 237.4
merchant 830.2
**wholesaling**
selling 829.2
trade 827.2
**wholesome**
healthful 683.5

**willful**
disobedient 767.8
intentional 653.9
lawless 740.5
obstinate 626.8
voluntary 622.7
**willies** 859.2
**willing**
consenting 775.4
game 622.5
obedient 766.3
teachable 564.18
venturesome 714.14
volitional 621.4
**willingness**
consent 775.1
gameness 622
obedience 766.1
teachability 564.5
tendency 174.1
**will-o'-the-wisp**
deception 618.1
fire 328.13
illusion 519.1
phosphorescence 335.13
**willowy** pliant 357.9
thin 205.16
**will power**
resolution 624.4
will 621.1
**willy-nilly**
haphazardly 72.5
in disorder 62.17
necessarily 639.16
**wilt** be tired 717.5
deteriorate 692.21
fail 686.45
make tired 717.4
sweat 311.16
weaken 160.9
**wilted**
deteriorated 692.37
sweaty 311.22
**wily** cunning 735.12
deceitful 618.20
shrewd 467.15
**win**
*n.* victory 726.1
*v.* acquire 811.8
best 36.7
be victorious 726.4
persuade 648.23
**wince**
*n.* retreat 284.3
*v.* demur 623.4
flinch 891.21
pull back 284.7
retract 297.3
suffer pain 424.8
**winch** 287.7
**wind**
*n.* air current 403
belch 310.9
breathing 403.18
fart 310.10
gods 403.3
nonsense 547.3
speed 269.6
wind instrument 465.7
*v.* air 402.11

blare 453.9
fatigue 717.4
play music 462.43
**wind**
change course 275.30
convolve 254.4
curve 252.6
prepare 720.9
rotate 322.9
trap 618.18
wander 291.4
**wind around one's little finger**
have influence over 172.11
have subject 764.10
**windbag** braggart 910.5
chatterer 596.4
**windblown** 403.27
**windburn** 329.6
**wind direction** 403.16
**winded** 717.10
**windfall** find 811.6
good thing 674.5
**wind gauge** 269.7
**wind in** 287.9
**winding**
*n.* convolution 254.1
*adj.* convolutional 254.6
wandering 291.7
**wind instrument** 465.7
**windjammer**
braggart 910.5
chatterer 596.4
sailboat 277.3
sailor 276.1
**windlass** capstan 287.7
lifter 317.3
**windless** 268.16
**window** opening 265.8
radar countermeasure 346.13
**window dresser** 579.11
**window dressing**
fakery 616.3
false front 240.1
ornamentation 901.1
**windowed** 265.20
**windowpane**
glass 339.2
window 265.8
**window-shop** 828.8
**window-shopping** 828.1
**windpipe** 396.16
**windproof** 266.12
**windshield** 699.3
**wind sock**
aviation 278.19
wind instrument 403.17
**windstorm** storm 162.4
wind 403.12
**windswept** 403.27
**wind tunnel** 396.17
**windup**
completion 722.2
end 70.1
**wind up**
complete 722.6
end 70.5
prepare 720.9

**windward**
*n.* side 242.3
*adj.* side 242.6
*adv.* side 242.9
toward 290.26
upwind 275.68
**windy** airy 355.4
blowy 403.25
boastful 910.11
bombastic 601.9
distended 197.13
talkative 596.9
tenuous 4.6
trivial 673.16
wordy 593.12
**wine**
*n.* alcoholic beverage 996.16
types of 996.39
*adj.* red 368.6
**wine and dine** 307.16
**wine cellar**
cellar 192.17
storage place 660.6
**wine merchant**
liquor dealer 996.18
merchant 830.3
**winery** plant 719.3
winemaking 996.20
**wine shop** 996.19
**wine steward** 750.7
**wing**
*n.* affiliate 788.10
air force 800.28
annex 41.3
appendage 55.4
fowl part 308.23
group 74.3
military unit 800.19
party 788.4
protectorship 699.2
scenery 611.25
*v.* cripple 692.17
disable 158.9
fly 278.45
transport 271.11
**wingding** 878.6
**winged** 269.19
**wing it** depart 301.6
improvise 630.8
**wings**
military insignia 569.5
stage 611.21
**wink**
*n.* glance 439.4
hint 557.4
instant 113.3
nap 712.3
signal 568.15
*v.* blink 440.10
signal 568.22
**wink at** be blind 441.8
be broad-minded 526.7
condone 947.4
consent 775.2
disregard 531.2
permit 777.10
**winner**
good thing 674.5
man of action 707.8

successful person 724.5
sure success 724.2
victor 726.2
**winning**
*n.* acquisition 811.1
victory 726.1
*adj.* alluring 650.7
desirable 634.30
lovable 931.23
persuasive 172.13
pleasant 863.7
victorious 726.8
**winnings** gains 38.3
profits 811.3
**winning streak** 726.1
**winnow**
*n.* refining equipment 681.13
*v.* air 402.11
analyze 48.8
discriminate 492.5
refine 681.22
select 637.14
separate 77.6
**wino** 996.11
**win out** succeed 724.12
win 726.4
**win over**
convert 145.16
convince 501.18
persuade 648.23
**winsome** alluring 650.7
cheerful 870.11
lovable 931.23
pleasant 863.7
**winter**
*n.* cold weather 333.3
season 128.6
*v.* spend time 105.6
*adj.* wintry 128.8
**wintry** cold 333.14
winter 128.8
**wipe**
*n.* disappearance 447.1
*v.* clean 681.18
dry 393.6
**wipe out** annihilate 2.6
clean 681.18
debts 842.9
destroy 693.14
eliminate 42.10
end 70.7
kill 409.14
obliterate 693.16
**wire**
*n.* cord 206.2
electric 342.39
telegram 560.14
*v.* bind 47.9
communicate 560.19
**wiredrawn**
smooth 351.8
thin 205.16
**wireless**
*n.* communications 560.3
radio 344.1
radiophone 560.5
radio receiver 344.3
*v.* broadcast 344.25

*adj.* radio 344.28
telecommunicational
560.20
**wireman**
electrician 342.19
telegraph 560.16
**Wirephoto**
communications
560.15
photograph 577.3
**wire-puller**
cunning person 735.7
influence user 744.30
influential person
172.6
political intriguer
746.6
schemer 654.8
**wire-pulling**
influence 172.3
intrigue 654.6
machination 735.4
political influence
744.29
**wire service**
news medium 558.1
telegraphy 560.2
**wiretap**
*n.* spying 485.9
*v.* listen 448.11
**wiry** strong 159.14
threadlike 206.7
tough 359.4
**wisdom**
expedience 670.1
maxim 517.1
sagacity 467.5
understanding 475.3
**wise**
*n.* aspect 446.3
way 657.1
*adj.* expedient 670.5
knowing 475.15
learned 475.21
sage 467.17
ungullible 504.5
**wiseacre** 468.6
**vise-ass**
*n.* impudent person
913.5
*adj.* impudent 913.9
**visecrack**
*n.* witticism 881.7
*v.* joke 881.13
**visecracker** 881.12
**vise guy**
impudent person
913.5
wiseacre 468.6
**isely** 467.20
**ise man**
intellectual 476.1
intelligent being
467.9
sage 468
**ise to** 475.16
**ise up** inform 557.8
see through 488.8
**ish**
*t.* desire 634.1
request 774.1
thing desired 634.11

will 621.1
*v.* desire 634.14
request 774.9
want to 634.15
will 621.2
**wishbone fork** 299.4
fowl part 308.23
**wish-bringer** 1036.6
**wished-for** 634.29
**wish for** 634.16
**wish-fulfilling** 535.24
**wish fulfillment**
defense mechanism
690.30
desire 634.1
idealization 535.7
**wishful thinker** 535.13
**wishful thinking**
credulity 502.1
deception 618.1
defense mechanism
690.30
idealization 535.7
wistfulness 634.4
**wishing** 634.21
**wishing well** 1036.6
**wish well** 938.11
**wishy-washy**
inconstant 141.7
insipid 430.2
mediocre 680.7
weak 160.17
**wisp** bunch 74.7
little thing 196.4
phosphorescence
335.13
**wispy** frail 160.14
thin 205.16
**wistful**
melancholy 872.23
regretful 873.8
thoughtful 478.21
wishful 634.23
**wit** cunning 735.1
humor 881
humorist 881.12
intelligence 467.1
skill 733.1
**witch**
*n.* hag 943.7
ill-humored woman
951.12
old woman 127.3
sorceress 1035.8
ugly thing 899.4
violent person 162.9
*v.* enchant 1036.9
fascinate 650.6
**witchcraft** 1035.1
**witch doctor** 1035.7
**witchery**
allurement 650.1
enchantment 1036.2
pleasantness 863.2
sorcery 1035.1
supernaturalism 85.7
**witch-hunt**
investigation 485.4
persecution 667.3
**witching**
*n.* dowsing 543.3
*adj.* alluring 650.7

enchanting 1036.11
pleasant 863.7
**with** among 44.18
by means of 658.7
in agreement with
26.12
in company with
73.12
in cooperation with
786.8
in spite of 33.9
near 184.26
plus 40.12
**with a grain of salt**
conditionally 507.11
doubtingly 503.13
**with a vengeance**
extremely 34.22
powerfully 157.15
utterly 56.16
violently 162.24
**with bated breath**
expectantly 539.15
fearfully 891.40
humbly 906.15
in an undertone
452.22
in suspense 539.12
secretly 614.17
**with child** 169.18
**withdraw**
back out 633.5
be secluded 89.6
dissent 522.4
extract 305.10
leave 301.8
pull back 297.3
recant 628.9
recede 297.2
repeal 779.2
resign from 784.2
retreat 295.6
separate 49.9
subtract 42.9
**withdrawal**
abandonment 633.1
aloneness 89.2
defense mechanism
690.30
departure 301.1
dissent 522.1
elimination 77.2
emotional symptom
690.23
extraction 305.1
incurious 529.1
recantation 628.3
recession 297.1
repeal 779.1
resignation 784.1
reticence 613.3
retreat 295.2
seclusion 924.1
separation 49.1
unfeeling 856.1
**withdrawn** alone 89.8
apathetic 856.13
incurious 529.3
private 614.13
reticent 613.10
secluded 924.7
unsociable 923.6

**wither** age 126.10
deteriorate 692.21
dry 393.6
shrink 198.9
weaken 686.45
**withered** aged 126.18
deteriorated 692.37
dried 393.9
shrunk 198.13
thin 205.20
**withering**
*n.* deterioration 692.4
drying 393.3
shrinking 198.3
*adj.* caustic 939.21
contemptuous 966.8
destructive 693.26
deteriorating 692.46
**withhold** abstain 992.7
be stingy 852.6
keep secret 614.7
refuse 776.4
reserve 660.12
restrain 760.7
**within**
*adv.* in 225.12
*prep.* in 225.15
**within bounds**
moderately 163.17
reasonably 482.24
temperately 992.12
**within reach**
accessible 509.8
near 200.20
present 186.12
**with it** in step 26.11
knowing 475.17
**with one's eyes open**
*adj.* disillusioned
520.5
vigilant 533.13
*adv.* intentionally
653.11
sleeplessly 713.9
**with open arms**
amicably 927.21
eagerly 635.14
hospitably 925.13
willingly 622.8
**without**
*adv.* externally 224.9
*prep.* excluding 77.9
lacking 662.17
minus 42.14
void of 187.18
**without delay**
at once 113.8
promptly 131.15
**without doubt**
believingly 501.28
certainly 513.25
positively 34.19
**without exception**
*adj.* comprehensive
76.7
unqualified 508.2
*adv.* always 112.11
regularly 17.8
universally 79.18
**without fail** 513.26
**without foundation**
flimsy 4.8

**work**
*n.* act 705.3
action 705.1
barrier 730.5
book 605.1
business 656.1
fortification 799.4
function 665.5
labor 716.4
music 462.5
operation 164.1
product 168.1
stage show 611.4
task 656.2
undertaking 715.1
vocation 656.6
work of art 574.11
written matter 602.10
*v.* accomplish 722.4
act 705.4
be busy 707.10
be expedient 670.3
bubble 405.4
busy oneself 656.12
cause 153.11
form 246.7
function 164.7
influence 172.7
labor 716.12
mix 44.11
operate 164.5
overwork 716.16
produce 167.9
react chemically
  379.6
solve 487.2
suffice 661.4
till 413.17
use 665.10
**workable**
operable 164.10
possible 509.7
practical 670.6
solvable 487.3
**workaday**
businesslike 656.15
prosaic 902.6
**work against** 178.6
**work at**
have a job 656.12
practice 705.7
**workbench**
bench 216.15
workplace 719.1
**workbook**
record book 570.11
textbook 605.8
**work clothes** 231.1
**worked up**
angry 952.26
excited 857.18
**worker** bee 414.38
doer 718.1
hireling 750.3
termite 414.37
types of 718.13
working person 718.2
**work evil** 675.6
**work for**
have a job 656.12
help 785.18
serve 750.13

**work force** 157.9
**work hard** 716.13
**workhorse**
drudge 718.3
horse 414.16
**workhouse**
asylum 700.4
workplace 719.1
**work in** enter 302.7
interpose 237.6
intrude 238.5
**working**
*n.* action 705.1
agriculture 413.13
operation 164.1
reaction 379.5
solution 487.1
utilization 665.8
*adj.* acting 705.10
businesslike 656.15
busy 707.21
laboring 716.17
leavening 353.16
operating 164.11
**working class** 919.1
**working-class** 919.12
**workingman** 718.2
**workings** action 705.1
mechanism 348.5
mine 383.6
operation 164.1
pit 257.4
**workman** 718.2
**workmanlike**
adequate 674.19
skillful 733.20
**workmanship**
manufacture 167.3
skill 733.1
**work of art** 574.11
**work on** exploit 665.16
impose 963.7
influence 172.9
nag at 774.12
operate on 164.6
urge 648.14
**work oneself up** 857.15
**workout** exercise 716.6
rehearsal 489.3
**work out**
accomplish 722.4
arrange 771.9
calculate 87.11
carry out 705.9
develop 148.6
expand 593.7
plan 654.9
result 154.5
solve 487.2
**workplace** 719
**workroom** studio 192.6
workplace 719.1
**works** acts 705.3
benevolences 938.6
inside parts 225.4
mechanism 348.5
plant 719.4
**works, the** 54.4
**workshop** 719.1
**work stoppage**
stop 144.2
strike 789.7

**work toward** 174.3
**work up** agitate 324.10
excite 857.11
incite 648.17
plan 654.9
provoke 952.22
**work-up** 689.13
**work well**
run smoothly 732.9
succeed 724.6
**work wonders** 724.6
**world** Earth 375.10
much 34.3
people 417.2
regions of 180.6
universe 375.1
**worldly**
materialistic 376.9
nonreligious 1031.16
practical 536.6
sophisticated 733.26
unsacred 1027.3
**worldly-wise** 733.26
**worlds apart** 16.7
**world-shaking** 672.16
**world view**
ideology 479.8
pervading attitudes
  525.5
system of belief
  501.3
**world-weary**
bored 884.10
dejected 872.22
**world-wide** 79.14
**worm**
*n.* animal 414.42,75
bad person 986.7
blight 676.2
*v.* creep 273.25
go slow 270.6
twist 254.4
**worm-eaten** 692.43
**worm in**
interpose 237.6
intrude 238.5
**worm out of**
elicit 305.14
excuse 1006.11
interrogate 485.20
slip away 632.9
**wormwood** 429.2
**wormy** filthy 682.23
infested 313.11
spoiled 692.43
wormlike 414.56
**worn** damaged 692.33
dilapidated 53.5
eroded 39.10
fatigued 717.6
secondhand 123.18
timeworn 123.14
tired-looking 717.7
trite 883.9
weakened 160.18
**worn away** lost 812.7
used up 666.4
**worn-out**
disused 668.10
exhausted 717.8
impaired 692.38
used up 666.4

**weakened** 160.18
**worried**
tormented 866.24
troubled 731.19
vexed 890.7
**worrisome**
annoying 864.22
troublesome 890.9
**worry**
*n.* annoyance 866.2
anxiety 890.2
trouble 731.3
*v.* annoy 866.13
feel anxious 890.5
make anxious 890.4
trouble 731.12
vex 864.15
**worrying**
*n.* worry 890.2
*adj.* annoying 864.22
troublesome 890.9
**worrywart** 889.7
**worse** aggravated 885.4
changed 139.9
damaged 692.29
**worsen** aggravate 885.2
be changed 139.5
change 139.6
deteriorate 692.19
get worse 885.3
impair 692.11
**worsened**
aggravated 885.4
damaged 692.29
**worsening**
*n.* aggravation 885.1
change 139.1
*adj.* deteriorating
  692.46
**worship**
*n.* love 931.1
piety 1028.1
prayer 1032
respect 964.1
*v.* adore 1032.10
cherish 931.19
respect 964.4
**worshiper**
devotee 635.6
supplicant 1032.9
**worshipful**
idolizing 964.9
pious 1028.8
reputable 914.15
reverent 1032.15
traditional 123.12
venerable 964.12
**worshiping**
*n.* prayer 1032.1
*adj.* admiring 964.9
reverent 1032.15
**worst**
*v.* defeat 727.6
get the better of 36.7
*adj.* bad 675.9
**worsted** 727.14
**wort** 411.4
**worth**
*n.* benefit 665.4
esteem 914.3
expensiveness 848.2
goodness 674.1

importance 672.1
value 846.3
*adj.* possessing 808.9
priced 846.16
**worthless** bad 675.9
disadvantageous
671.6
paltry 673.18
unimportant 673.19
useless 669.11
**worthwhile**
expedient 670.5
gainful 811.15
useful 665.21
**worthy**
*n.* famous person
914.9
good person 985.1
personage 672.8
*adj.* competent 733.22
dignified 905.12
eligible 637.24
honest 974.13
praiseworthy 968.20
reputable 914.15
valuable 848.10
warranted 960.9
**worthy of** 960.10
**Wotan**
Norse deity 1014.6
war god 797.17
**would-be**
nominal 583.15
presumptuous 912.10
**wound**
*n.* distress 866.5
impairment 692.8
sore 686.35
*v.* damage 675.6
grieve 866.17
hurt 424.7
injure 692.15
offend 952.20
**wounded**
aggrieved 866.23
pained 424.9
**wound up**
completed 722.11
ended 70.8
past 119.7
**woven** interlaced 222.7
webbed 221.12
**wow**
*n.* audio distortion
450.13
funny story 881.6
great success 724.3
*v.* amuse 878.23
delight 865.8
*interj.* pleasure 865.17
wonder 920.20
**wrack**
*n.* destruction 693.1
plant 411.4,42
wreck 693.4
*v.* destroy 693.10
**wrack and ruin** 693.1
**wracked** 855.25
**wrack up** 693.17
**wraith** double 1017.3
phantom 519.4
specter 1017.1

**wrangle**
*n.* quarrel 795.5
*v.* argue 482.16
dispute 796.22
drive animals 416.8
quarrel 795.11
**wrangler** arguer 482.12
combatant 800.1
herder 416.3
oppositionist 791.3
student 566.7
**wrangling**
*n.* argumentation
482.4
contention 796.1
*adj.* quarrelsome
795.17
**wrap**
*n.* clothing 231.20
wrapper 228.18
*v.* bind 47.9
bundle 74.20
clothe 231.38
cover 228.20
enclose 236.5
surround 233.6
**wrapped**
covered 228.31
surrounded 233.10
**wrapped up**
assembled 74.21
completed 722.11
**wrapped up in**
engrossed 530.17
fond of 931.28
involved in 176.4
**wrapper** binder 228.18
bookbinding 605.15
clothing 231.20
**wrapping**
*n.* covering 228.1
wrapper 228.18
*adj.* covering 228.34
surrounding 233.8
**wraps**
concealment 615.2
secrecy 614.3
**wrap up** bind 47.9
bundle 74.20
clothe 231.38
complete 722.6
package 228.20
**wrath** anger 952.5
sin 982.3
**wrathful** 952.26
**wreak** effect 705.6
inflict 963.5
**wreak havoc**
destroy 693.10
do harm 675.6
**wreath** circle 253.2
flowers 411.23
heraldic insignia
569.2
trophy 916.3
weaving 222.2
**wreathe** encircle 233.7
ornament 901.9
weave 222.6
**wreathed**
ornamented 901.11
surrounded 233.10

**woven** 222.7
**wreck**
*n.* automobile 272.9
destruction 693.1
disaster 693.4
misfortune 729.2
nervous wreck 859.5
ruins 692.10
*v.* demolish 693.17
destroy 693.10
disable 158.9
impair 692.12
rage 162.10
shipwreck 275.42
**wreckage** 693.5
**wrecked**
damaged 692.30
in difficulty 731.25
ruined 693.28
**wrecker**
destroyer 693.8
plunderer 825.6
savage 943.5
**wrench**
*n.* distortion 249.1
distress 866.5
impairment 692.8
jerk 286.3
pain 424.2
types of 348.20
wresting 305.6
*v.* distort 249.5
exact from 305.15
injure 692.15
jerk 286.5
misinterpret 553.2
misrepresent 573.3
wrest 822.22
**wrest**
*n.* distortion 249.1
extraction 305.6
*v.* distort 249.5
extort 305.15
extract 305.10
seize 822.22
**wresting** 305.6
**wrestle**
*n.* struggle 716.3
*v.* contend 796.14
struggle 716.11
**wrestler** athlete 878.20
fighter 800.3
**wrestling** 796.10
**wretch**
bad person 986.2
sufferer 866.11
**wretched**
adverse 729.13
bad 675.9
base 915.12
miserable 866.26
paltry 673.18
squalid 682.25
unhappy 872.21
unpleasant 864.20
**wriggle**
*n.* wiggle 324.7
*v.* be excited 857.16
wiggle 324.14
**wriggler** 125.10
**wriggly** 324.21
**wright** artisan 718.6

producer 167.8
types of 718.11
**wring**
*n.* distortion 249.1
wresting 305.6
*v.* cause pain 424.7
distort 249.5
extract 305.16
torture 866.18
twist 254.4
wrest 822.22
**wringer** 305.9
**wringing** 305.6
**wrinkle**
*n.* corrugation 264.3
extra 41.4
fad 644.5
groove 263.1
*v.* age 126.10
corrugate 264.6
groove 263.3
pucker 198.7
roughen 261.5
**wrinkled** aged 126.16
constricted 198.12
corrugated 264.8
deteriorated 692.37
grooved 263.4
rough 261.7
**wrist** arm 287.5
joint 47.4
**wristband**
bracelet 253.3
jewel 901.6
**writ** document 570.5
legal action 1004.2
legal order 752.6
**write** author 602.21
correspond 604.11
create 167.10
describe 608.12
music 462.47
pen 602.19
record 570.16
represent 572.6
**write-in** 637.6
**write off** debts 842.9
discount 847.2
forget 947.5
repeal 779.2
**write-off** debts 842.2
discount 847.1
repeal 779.1
**write out**
draw up 602.19
record 570.16
spell 581.7
**writer** author 602.15
correspondent 604.9
discourser 606.3
penner 602.13
**writer's cramp**
nervous disorder
686.23
occupational disease
686.31
writing 602.2
**write up**
comment upon 606
publicize 559.15
record 570.16
report 558.11

**write-up**
commentary 606.2
publicity 559.4
**writhe**
be excited 857.16
distort 249.5
suffer 866.19
suffer pain 424.8
wiggle 324.14
**writhing** 324.21
**writing**
authorship 602.2
book 605.1
character 581.1
document 570.5
representation 572.1
written language 602
written matter 602.10
**writing expert** 602.14
**writing machine** 602.31
**writing material** 602.30
**writing system**
script 581.3
word list 581.9
writing 602.9
**written** destined 640.9
in writing 602.22
**written down** 570.18
**wrong**
n. crime 999.4
error 518.1
evil 675.3
grievance 977.4
impropriety 959
iniquity 981.3
injustice 977.1
misdeed 982.2
v. be unjust 977.7
harm 675.6
adj. bad 675.7
erroneous 518.16
evil 981.16
improper 959.3
inappropriate 671.5
mistaken 518.18
sinful 982.6
unjust 977.9
untimely 130.7
adv. badly 675.13
erroneously 518.20
improperly 959.4
**wrongdoer**
bad person 986.9
evildoer 943.1
**wrongdoing**
crime 999.4
misbehavior 738.1
mismanagement
734.6
sin 982
vice 981.1
**wrongful** illegal 999.6
unjust 977.9
wrong 959.3
**wrongheaded**
perverse 626.11
stupid 469.15
**wrong impression**
delusion 519.1
misjudgment 496.1
wrong move 518.4
wrong side 244.1

**wrong time** 130.2
**wrong'un**
bad person 986.5
trick 618.6
**wrong-way** 295.12
**wroth** 952.26
**wrought** 722.10
**wrought-up**
angry 952.26
excited 857.18
**wrung** pained 424.9
tortured 866.25
**wry** 219.14
**wryneck**
deformity 249.3
inflammation 686.9

## X

x 477.7
X cross 221.4
signature 583.10
ten 99.6
**Xanadu** 535.10
**xenophobia**
exclusiveness 77.3
hate 930.1
phobia 891.10
prejudice 527.4
**xerography**
printing 603.1
reproduction 24.2
**Xerox**
n. copy 24.5
photograph 577.5
v. copy 24.8
photograph 577.14
**X ray**
diagnostic picture
689.10
hospital room 192.25
photograph 577.6
radiation 327.3
ray 335.5
**X-ray** irradiate 689.32
photograph 577.14
**xylography** 578.3
**xylophone** 465.18

## Y

**yacht**
n. sailing vessel 277.23
v. sail 275.13
**yachting** 275.1
**yachtsman** 276.5
**yak**
n. cattle 414.6
chatter 596.3
v. chatter 596.5
speak 594.21
**yammer**
n. cry 459.1
shrill sound 458.4
v. cry 459.6
sound shrill 458.8
whine 875.12
**yammering** 459.10
**yank**
n. jerk 286.3
v. jerk 286.5
**Yankee** dialect 580.7

Northerner 190.11
revolutionist 147.3
**yap**
n. cry 459.1
mouth 265.5
v. animal sound 460.2
complain 875.13
cry 459.6
nag at 969.16
speak 594.21
utter 594.26
**yapping**
n. complaint 875.4
adj. vociferous 459.10
**yard**
n. enclosure 236.3,12
thousand 99.10
US money 835.7
workplace 719.3
v. enclose 236.5
**yardage** 202.1
**yard goods** 831.3
**yardman** 274.13
**yardstick** 490.2,20
**yarn** cord 206.2,8
joke 881.6
lie 616.11
story 608.6
**yaw**
n. aviation 278.28
deviation 291.1
v. change course
275.30
drift off course
275.29
fly 278.49
sail 275.55
**yawn**
n. gaping 265.2
opening 265.1
v. gape 265.17
**yawning**
n. gaping 265.2
sleepiness 712.1
adj. abysmal 209.11
gaping 265.19
sleepy 712.21
**yawp**
n. cry 459.1
lament 875.3
v. animal sound 460.2
cry 459.6
utter 594.26
wail 875.11
**yaws** 686.12
**yea**
n. affirmative expres-
sion 521.2
approval 968.1
vote 637.6
adv. indeed 36.17
**year** 107.2
**yearbook**
periodical 605.10
record book 570.11
reports 570.7
**yearling** calf 414.6
infant 125.7
**yearlong** 110.12
**yearly** 137.8
**yearn for** 634.16

**yearning**
n. love 931.1
yen 634.5
adj. wistful 634.23
**years** age 126.1
long time 110.4
**yeast** 139.4
**yeasty** excited 857.18
foamy 405.7
leavening 353.16
light 353.10
**yecchy** bad 675.8
filthy 682.23
**yeeuck!**
contempt 966.10
unpleasantness
864.31
**yegg** 825.3
**yell**
n. cheer 876.2
cry 459.1
v. cheer 876.6
cry 459.6
utter 594.26
wail 875.11
**yell at** 969.20
**yelling** 459.10
**yellow**
n. barbiturate 687.12
colors 370.7
yellowness 370.1
yolk 406.15
v. turn yellow 370.3
adj. cowardly 892.10
jealous 953.4
sensational 857.30
yellowish 370.4
**yellow fever** 686.12
**yellow-haired** 370.5
**yellow jacket**
barbiturate 687.12
wasp 414.38,74
**yellow journalism** 855.9
**Yellow Pages** 748.10
**yellow race** race 418.2
yellow skin 370.2
**yellow skin** 370.2
**yellow streak** 892.4
**yelp**
n. cry 459.1
v. animal sound 460.2
complain 875.13
cry 459.6
utter 594.26
**yelping** 459.10
**yen**
foreign money 835.9
yearning 634.5
**yen for** 634.16
**yenta**
curious person 528.2
meddler 238.4
newsmonger 558.9
**yeoman**
agriculturist 413.5
attendant 750.5
bodyguard 699.14
retainer 750.1
sailor 276.6
**yeoman's service** 785.1

# ABBREVIATIONS USED
# IN THIS BOOK

| | | | |
|---|---|---|---|
| adj(s) | . . . . | adjective(s) | masc . . . . masculine |
| adv(s) | . . . . | adverb(s) | Mass . . . . Massachusetts |
| aero . | . . . . | aeronautics | math . . . . mathematics |
| anat . | . . . . | anatomy | Md . . . . Maryland |
| anon | . . . . | anonymous | med . . . . . medicine, medical |
| Arab | . . . | Arabic | mil . . . . . military |
| archit | . . . | architecture | min . . . . . mining |
| Ariz . | . . . | Arizona | mus . . . . music |
| astron | . . . | astronomy | myth . . . . mythology |
| Austral | . . . | Australian | n . . . . . noun(s) |
| biol . | . . . | biology | N . . . . . North, Northern |
| bot . | . . . | botany | naut . . . . nautical |
| Brit . | . . . | British | NC . . . . North Carolina |
| Cal . | . . . | California | Norw . . . . Norwegian |
| Can . | . . . | Canadian | Pg . . . . . Portuguese |
| chem | . . . | chemistry | phr(s) . . . . phrase(s) |
| Chin | . . . | Chinese | phys . . . . physics |
| conj(s) | . . . | conjunction(s) | pl . . . . . plural |
| Dan . | . . . | Danish | Pol . . . . . Polish |
| derog | . . . | derogatory | prep(s) . . . . preposition(s) |
| dial . | . . . | dialectal | RI . . . . . Rhode Island |
| Du . | . . . | Dutch | Rom . . . . Roman |
| . | . . . | East, Eastern | RR . . . . . railroading |
| eccl . | . . . | ecclesiastical | Russ . . . . Russian |
| Eng . | . . . | England, English | S . . . . . South, Southern |
| etc. . | . . . | et cetera | Scot . . . . Scottish |
| fem . | . . . | feminine | sing . . . . singular |
| Fla . | . . . | Florida | Skt . . . . Sanskrit |
| Fr . | . . . | French | Sp . . . . Spanish |
| geol . | . . . | geology | Sp Amer . . . . Spanish American |
| Ger . | . . . | German | Swah . . . . Swahili |
| Gk . | . . . | Greek | Swed . . . . Swedish |
| gram | . . . | grammar | Tenn . . . . Tennessee |
| Heb . | . . . | Hebrew | Turk . . . . Turkish |
| her . | . . . | heraldry | US . . . . . United States |
| Hind . | . . . | Hindustani | USSR . . . . Union of Soviet |
| Hung | . . . | Hungarian | Socialist Republics |
| interj(s) | . . . | interjection(s) | v . . . . . verb(s) |
| . | . . . | Irish | Va . . . . . Virginia |
| Ital . | . . . | Italian | Vt . . . . . Vermont |
| Jap . | . . . | Japanese | W . . . . . West, Western |
| . | . . . | Kentucky | Yid . . . . Yiddish |
| . | . . . | Latin | zool . . . . zoology |
| . | . . . | Louisiana | |